Flat Horses
of 2003

Flat Horses

of 2003

Edited by Graham Dench
and Nick Pulford

Cover photographs: Alamshar by Edward Whitaker,
Dalakhani by Panoramic.

Other photographs: Edward Whitaker, Martin Lynch,
Gerry and Mark Cranham, Caroline Norris, Frank Sorge,
Enzo De Nardin, Dan Abraham, Bill Selwyn, Ed Byrne,
Bancroft Photography, Matthew Webb, George Selwyn, APRH,
Scoop/Dyga, horsephotos.com, EPA, Getty Images, AP, PA,
Action Images, Reuters.

Programming and data by Brett Campbell.

Special thanks for their invaluable assistance to Mark Bowers,
James Crispe, Steve Dennis, John Kettle, Nigel Jones and
Victor Jones.

Published in 2003 by Raceform Ltd,
Compton, Newbury, Berkshire RG20 6NL.
Raceform Ltd is a wholly-owned subsidiary of Trinity Mirror plc.

A catalogue record for this book is available from the British Library.

ISBN 1-904317-44-8

Designed by Robin Gibson.
Printed by William Clowes, Suffolk.

Flat Horses

of 2003

Contents

Foreword

by Brough Scott

I T WAS a season to remember. All year we looked forward, now there is relish in looking back, not just across the calendar but around the continents too.

For the pleasure in girding up the Racing Post and Raceform resources in this volume is to put to use, and into perspective, the great waves of information that wash through our systems every hour of every day. The jokes about yesterday's newspapers being today's fish and chip wrapping will always apply to daily publications. But here, in quick time, are reviews of the top 100 performers who interest us worldwide as well as ratings for all those who ran in these islands during the 2003 turf season. Here is something to last.

Having committed myself to writing about Falbrav and Dalakhani I had to remember how marvellously transitory a year can be. How much was still undecided when both horses limbered up in separate races at Longchamp in April. Back then you might have guessed Dalakhani's route through to the Arc, but not one punter in ten thousand would have charted Falbrav's glorious journey through eight consecutive Group 1 races to Santa Anita and the Breeders' Cup.

Back then few would have guessed that Godolphin would, by their unique standards, have a European 'annus miserabilis'. Few would have foreseen that Ballydoyle would have to battle back from a dismal start. And while all race fans welcomed the announcement that Hawk Wing and High Chaparral would run as four-year-olds, many pragmatists looked at recent history and wondered at the wisdom of it.

Not the least of the season's satisfactions was that, while Hawk Wing limped out soon after his astonishing Newbury reappearance, High Chaparral overcame early injury to produce two of the most stirring runs this watcher has ever seen. Throughout his career High Chaparral was all too often damned with faint praise; how good it is now to look back at what was involved in that extraordinary record of ten victories and two Arc de Triomphe thirds in the 12 races since he was beaten a short head on his debut at Punchestown back in 2001.

The extent to which the older horses can glow in the memory was never better demonstrated than by Persian Punch. When the old hero slugged home more than five lengths behind Mr Dinos in his seventh consecutive Henry II Stakes at Sandown in May, who would have thought that by the season's end he could, at ten years old, have come good again in the Goodwood Cup and would bring the house down with that immortal effort in the Jockey Club Cup at Newmarket on Champions Day?

But the real delight of looking back at a Flat racing season is mixing assessments of youthful promise with acknowledgements of proven glory. The thought that by this time next year we will all know the respective merits of One Cool Cat, American Post, Grey Swallow, Snow Ridge, Three Valleys and Milk It Mick, and that they will be radically different than they were at the start of proceedings, is both a challenge and a reality check. It is also something that sends the fingers picking through these pages to remind ourselves of the 2003 status quo.

We are thrilled to bring this to you. Please enjoy.

Introduction

by Graham Dench

FLAT HORSES OF 2003 combines extensive features by the Racing Post's top writers on the season's top 100 horses with an introduction to more than 60 juvenile 'young pretenders' to top honours next year. In addition, there is an A to Z directory of every horse who ran in Britain, complete with their definitive Racing Post Ratings.

The aim is to provide not only a very good 'read', but also a valuable betting tool and a comprehensive reference.

The section to which everyone will turn first is the top 100, in which writers including Alastair Down, Paul Haigh, Tom O'Ryan, Brough Scott and James Willoughby offer forthright, stimulating and often controversial opinions on all of the top horses.

Each piece is complemented by a detailed race record, plus extensive breeding details presented in a style that will be familiar to readers of the Racing Post's bloodstock pages, with expert insight from Tony Morris and Janet Hickman.

The final make-up of the top 100 horses may not satisfy everyone, but it's probably fair to say that 100 different people would have come up with as many different lists. The vast majority of horses picked themselves, however, and only a fraction are likely to be considered contentious.

For the record, here's how we went about making our selections. To begin with, we included every horse who won a Group 1 race in Britain, France or Ireland in 2003 – that's more than half of the list taken care of for starters.

A European bias is inevitable, but we also included the Triple Crown winners from the United States, Funny Cide and Empire Maker – great horses and great stories – and other top US-based horses who are of particular interest to British readers, such as the brilliant former John Gosden-trained dirt horse Mineshaft and the Breeders' Cup Turf dead-heater Johar.

Finally, we endeavoured to bring you 'the best of the rest'. This is where it became more difficult, but with one eye firmly on achievement and the other looking out for potential, we hope we have come up with a selection that will please all but a tiny minority.

The young pretenders section comprises the most highly rated two-year-olds who did not quite make it into the top 100, plus less exposed horses of genuine potential, many of whom feature in ante-post lists for the 2004 Classics. These are the sort of horses who will feature among the top 100 in another 12 months.

In the directory section can be found Racing Post Ratings for every horse who ran in Britain during the turf season. They are the work of Paul Curtis and Simon Turner, who crowned another superb season for the paper's handicapping team by topping the 53-runner Coral/Racing Post 2003 naps table for the Flat. They stand the closest scrutiny. Indeed, they are the best in the business.

Racing Post Ratings are also included for the top horses from around the world in an international classification that takes account of the best races in Europe, North America, Australia, Hong Kong, Japan and the UAE. They make fascinating reading.

Our records cover all racing up to the end of the 2003 British turf season (November 8).

The top 100 horses
of 2003

Figure in bold by each horse's name is its definitive Racing Post Rating

Pedigree assessments by Tony Morris (TM) and Janet Hickman (JH)

Acclamation

4yo bay colt   **119**

Royal Applause - Princess Athena (Ahonoora)
Owner Dulford Cavaliers
Trainer L G Cottrell
Breeder Tedwood Bloodstock Ltd And Partners

Career: **15** starts | won **6** | second **3** | third **4** | **£335,353** win and place

By Mark Blackman

THERE can be few finer advertisements for syndicate ownership than Acclamation. Just ask John Boswell, a long-time supporter of the colt's trainer Gerald Cottrell and spokesman for the Dulford Cavaliers, in whose colours the son of Royal Applause raced.

Six wins – including victories in the valuable St Leger Yearling Stakes as a two-year-old and the Group 2 Diadem Stakes at Ascot in September 2003 – would have been more than enough to convince him that the 33,000 guineas price tag as a yearling was money well spent. Throw in frame finishes in another Diadem Stakes, the Temple Stakes, the King's Stand, the Nunthorpe and the Prix de l'Abbaye, and Acclamation's career, which spanned three seasons of ultra-consistent sprinting, represents nothing short of a major triumph for the small guy.

If Acclamation's victory in the Diadem – a first Group success for 78-year-old Cottrell – was well deserved, his third to Crystal Castle in the race 12 months earlier was a testament to the Devon trainer's fine touch. It was the colt's seasonal debut, and his first start for more than a year because of continual problems with mucus in his lungs. Given a clear run with him, his connections insisted, there was much more to come at four.

After a reappearance third to Airwave in Sandown's Temple Stakes, Acclamation headed for Royal Ascot in June, for the Group 2 King's Stand Stakes run on fast ground over five furlongs. Sent off at 16-1 in a field of 20, he missed the beat at the start but travelled nicely in midfield as the Australian raider Choisir cut out a fierce pace on the stands' rail. Pat Eddery, partnering Acclamation for the first time, asked him for his effort two furlongs out, but the gaps were closing in front of him as he approached the furlong pole. When he finally saw daylight, he picked up strongly, but Choisir was not to be caught and held Acclamation by a diminishing length.

Acclamation (Frankie Dettori) wins Ascot's Group 2 Diadem Stakes in September

Considering the traffic problems, Acclamation would have had strong claims to reverse the form in the Golden Jubilee Stakes four days later, but Cottrell, after much deliberation, decided not to ask him to run again so soon. Choisir duly completed a famous Royal Ascot double.

The following month saw Acclamation run the only below-par race of his life as he trailed in 11th in the July Cup. His very wide draw looked a reasonable excuse, but he was also found to be suffering from an infection soon after the race.

His confidence restored by a victory in a minor six-furlong event at Doncaster – in which he did well to dead-heat with Chookie Heiton after meeting trouble in running – Acclamation dropped back to the minimum trip for the Nunthorpe at York, where July Cup winner Oasis Dream started a red-hot favourite. A stumble at the start did not help Acclamation's cause, but again he came home like a horse in need of a sixth furlong to finish just under four lengths third to John Gosden's colt. "I'm delighted, but why do we have to run into the best sprinter there has been for years?" mused Cottrell's wife, Peggy.

After winning a Listed contest at Goodwood, Acclamation lined up as a 9-1 chance for the 14-runner Diadem. The fast ground and the stiff, uphill Ascot straight played to Acclamation's strengths and he responded with a typically game effort. Handy throughout from his ideal draw in stall two, there was to be no repeat of the traffic problems

2003   Race record

4th Prix de l'Abbaye de Longchamp - Majestic Barriere (Group 1) (Longchamp, October 5) 2yo+ 5f Holding **116** (TS 107) 19 ran. *Tracked leaders, every chance well over 1f out, lost 2nd well inside final furlong, beaten 1½l by Patavellian*

1st Millennium & Copthorne Hotels Diadem Stakes (Group 2) (Ascot, September 27) 3yo+ 6f Good to firm **118** (TS 102) 14 ran. *Chased leaders, led inside final furlong, driven out, beat Polar Way by ¾l*

1st Starlit Stakes (Listed) (Goodwood, September 13) 3yo+ 6f Good to firm **114** (TS 90) 5 ran.*Tracked leaders, ridden to lead approaching final furlong, headed just inside final furlong, soon narrow lead again, driven out and edged right close home, beat Torosay Spring by hd*

3rd Victor Chandler Nunthorpe Stakes (Group 1) (York, August 21) 2yo+ 5f Good to firm **114** (TS 103) 8 ran. *Stumbled start, chased leaders, driven over 2f out, stayed on same pace, beaten 3¾l by Oasis Dream*

1st Dead-heat Unison Trade Union Positively Public Conditions Stakes (Doncaster, August 2) 3yo+ 6f Good **113** (TS 88) 8 ran. *Tracked leaders, headway well over 1f out, ridden to chase leader inside final furlong, driven and got up on line, dead-heated with Chookie Heiton*

11th Darley July Cup (Group 1) (Newmarket (July), July 10) 3yo+ 6f Good to firm **100** (TS 86) 16 ran. *Held up, headway under pressure over 2f out, weakened final furlong, beaten 9¼l by Oasis Dream*

2nd King's Stand Stakes (Group 2) (Ascot, June 17) 3yo+ 5f Good to firm **119** (TS 103) 20 ran. *Slowly into stride, held up off the pace in midfield, effort 2f out, not clear run 1f out, ran on strongly last 150yds, never going to catch winner, beaten 1l by Choisir*

3rd Tripleprint Temple Stakes (Group 2) (Sandown, May 26) 3yo+ 5f Good to firm **106** (TS 100) 7 ran. *Tracked leaders, ridden and effort 2f out, challenged just over 1f out, one pace inside final furlong, beaten 3¼l by Airwave*

2002

3rd Bentinck Stakes (Listed) (Newmarket, October 18) 3yo+ 6f Good **112** (TS 73) 14 ran
● **3rd** Brunswick Diadem Stakes (Group 2) (Ascot, September 28) 3yo+ 6f Good to firm **111** (TS 96) 11 ran

Other notable runs

2001 1st £200000 St Leger Yearling Stakes (Doncaster, September 12) 2yo 6f Good to firm **104** (TS 75) 22 ran ● **1st** Cantor Sport Spread Betting Novice Stakes (Newbury, August 5) 2yo 5f Good to firm **93** (TS 67) 8 ran ● **1st** EBF Maiden Stakes (Sandown, June 15) 2yo 5f Good to firm **91** (TS 65) 10 ran

that had ended his chance of winning the King's Stand over the same course three months earlier, and after Frankie Dettori had taken him to the front just inside the furlong pole he ran out a game and decisive three-quarter-length winner from Polar Way, with the pace-setting Lochridge a neck back in third.

Fears that a drop back to the flying five in the Prix de l'Abbaye at Longchamp would find Acclamation out at the highest level proved well founded. He finished strongly but could never challenge the progressive Patavellian, coming home a creditable fourth. Considering that the drop in trip and easier ground counted heavily against him, it was an admirable effort.

Acclamation was sold after the Diadem to Rathbarry Stud in Ireland,

Acclamation

bay colt, 26-4-1999

Royal Applause b 1993	Waajib	Try My Best	Northern Dancer / Sex Appeal
		Coryana	Sassafras / Rosolini
	Flying Melody	Auction Ring	Bold Bidder / Hooplah
		Whispering Star	Sound Track / Peggy West
Princess Athena b 1985	Ahonoora	Lorenzaccio	Klairon / Phoenissa
		Helen Nichols	Martial / Quaker Girl
	Shopping Wise	Floribunda	Princely Gift / Astrentia
		Sea Melody	Tudor Minstrel / Cowes

Bred by Tedwood Bloodstock Ltd and Partners. 33,000gns Doncaster St Leger yearling

Sire Royal Applause

Won 9 of 15 starts, inc. Coventry S.-Gr3, Gimcrack S.-Gr2, Middle Park S.-Gr1, Duke of York S.-Gr2, Cork and Orrery S.-Gr2, Haydock Sprint Cup-Gr1. Half-brother to 2yo Gr1 winners In Command and Lyric Fantasy. Stands at Royal Studs, 2003 fee £10,000. Oldest progeny 4. Sire of: Acclamation (Gr2), Mister Cosmi (Gr2), Nevisian Lad (Gr2), Majestic Missile (Gr3), Peak To Creek (Gr3).

Dam Princess Athena

Won 3 of 14 starts, inc. Queen Mary S.-Gr3. Biggest win at two, but compiled fair list of places in Group 3 and Listed sprints after 2yo season. Best at 5f. Dam of: Instinction (1991 f by Never So Bold; unraced), Saxon Bay (1992 g by Cadeaux Genereux; unplaced), Waypoint (1993 f by Cadeaux Genereux; useful winner, dam of Gr2 2yo winner Never A Doubt), Defiance (1995 g by Warning; placed), Ocean Reef (1996 f by Lugana Beach; winner), Kissing Time (1997 f by Lugana Beach; winner), Acclamation (1999 c by Royal Applause; Gr2 winner, Gr1-placed), 2001 c by Efisio, 2002 f by Efisio (120,000gns Doncaster St Leger yearling).

Pedigree assessment

Bred for speed, displayed plenty of it, and will be an influence for precocious speed at stud. Even so, he trained on well, as did both his sire and dam, and it is not difficult to see Acclamation siring tough sprinters from his new home, Rathbarry Stud. *JH*

where he is to stand his first season as a stallion for a fee to be decided. He leaves his connections with many fantastic memories and it will be most interesting to see how his Efisio half-sister, sold in the same Doncaster sale-ring as he was for a record 120,000 guineas in September, fares in 2004 under the guidance of Barry Hills. Victory in the valuable race attached to that sale at the St Leger meeting would represent a remarkable family double.

Airwave

3yo bay filly   123

Air Express (Ire) - Kangra Valley (Indian Ridge)

Owner Henry Candy & Partners

Trainer H Candy

Breeder R T And Mrs Watson

Career: **11** starts | won **4** | second **2** | third **2** | **£289,307** win and place

By Lee Mottershead

FOR Airwave, it was the season that got away. A season when the Henry Candy-trained filly managed to win just one race yet regularly did enough to suggest that much more was deserved. Yet, for all the disappointments, Airwave was still responsible for one of the most enduring memories of the 2003 campaign.

It happened just over a furlong out in the Tripleprint Temple Stakes. This was Airwave's seasonal reappearance, the first run of a three-year-old career that promised so much, her juvenile campaign having ended with the surprise defeat of Russian Rhythm in the Cheveley Park Stakes. That was a victory that stamped Airwave as an exceptional sprinting prospect, the daughter of Air Express providing Chris Rutter with the biggest and last success of his career as she outspeeded the unbeaten Russian Rhythm and inflicted upon her a one-and-a-half-length defeat.

From Candy, there was never any serious consideration of the 1,000 Guineas, not even a tentative crack at a spring Classic trial. Wisely resisting the temptation of trying to stretch a sprinter into a Classic miler, Candy knew that Airwave was a speedster pure and simple, describing her as faster than his 2002 Nunthorpe hero, Kyllachy.

She proved him right at Sandown, but only after defying unfavourable late omens. Desperately weak both in the ring and on the betting exchanges, Airwave was required to carry a Group 1 penalty against six classy rivals while no longer enjoying the physical advantage she had held over juvenile contemporaries. Then there was the start, or for Airwave, the lack of it. Never one of the quickest out of the gate, she was by some way the slowest, giving away five lengths and immediately finding herself detached from the field, almost invariably an irredeemable error over five furlongs.

In the subsequent seconds, she was simply devastating. Allowed time to recover by her new partner, Dane O'Neill, she suddenly scythed through

Airwave (Dane O'Neill) sprints to glory in the Temple Stakes at Sandown. She would not win again

the field from halfway until she was on the heels of the leader, Repertory, approaching the furlong marker. It was then that Airwave and O'Neill posted one of the year's defining moments, O'Neill having enough confidence to take a pull and rein back his mount, an almost unthinkable move in a high-class sprint. When he did press the button, Airwave surged clear up the punishing Sandown hill, scorching past the post three lengths clear of Repertory. The mantle of 2003 champion sprinter was seemingly there for the taking.

She did not take it. The first sign that things were not going to be so straightforward came at Royal Ascot. Straight after the Temple, Candy said that he would sidestep the Group 2 King's Stand Stakes in favour of the Group 1 six-furlong Golden Jubilee Stakes. Bookmakers were convinced of Airwave's sprinting supremacy and offered odds-on ante-post quotes. Eventually sent off the 11-8 favourite, Airwave was again slowly away – though not nearly as badly as at Sandown – and again moved through the race like a dream, tanking along as Australia's Choisir, winner of the King's Stand four days earlier, blazed a trail. Going after

2003   Race record

11th Prix de l'Abbaye de Longchamp - Majestic Barriere (Group 1) (Longchamp, October 5) 2yo+ 5f Holding **95** (TS 83) 19 ran. *Mid-division on rails when not clear run just over 2f out, trying to improve when hampered inside final furlong, beaten 7½l by Patavellian*

6th Millennium & Copthorne Hotels Diadem Stakes (Group 2) (Ascot, September 27) 3yo+ 6f Good to firm **113** (TS 94) 14 ran. *Held up in rear, not clear run 2f out, switched right and good headway entering final furlong, not reach leaders, beaten 2¼l by Acclamation*

3rd Stanley Leisure Sprint Cup (Group 1) (Haydock, September 6) 3yo+ 6f Good to soft **114** (TS 95) 10 ran. *Tracked leaders going well, ridden 1f out, stayed on same pace close home, beaten 2l by Somnus*

3rd Darley July Cup (Group 1) (Newmarket (July), July 10) 3yo+ 6f Good to firm **120** (TS 103) 16 ran. *Held up, headway and not clear run over 1f out, ran on, beaten 1¾l by Oasis Dream*

2nd Golden Jubilee Stakes (Group 1) (Ascot, June 21) 3yo+ 6f Firm **121** (TS 93) 17 ran. *Slowly into stride, soon recovered, headway to track leaders going well from 3f out, quickened to chase winner final furlong, kept on but no impression, beaten ½l by Choisir*

1st Tripleprint Temple Stakes (Group 2) (Sandown, May 26) 3yo+ 5f Good to firm **123** (TS 108) 7 ran. *Started slowly and lost 5l, detached in last pair until rapid progress from 2f out, led going easily just inside final furlong, pushed clear, impressive, beat Repertory by 3l*

2002

1st Betfair Cheveley Park Stakes (Group 1) (Newmarket, October 4) 2yo 6f Firm **114** (TS 63) 6 ran ● **1st** Faucets First For Faucets Firth of Clyde Stakes (Listed) (Ayr, September 21) 2yo 6f Good **100** (TS 56) 10 ran ● **4th** £200000 St Leger Yearling Stakes (Doncaster, September 11) 2yo 6f Good **96** (TS 64) 21 ran ● **1st** EBF Rainbows Children's Hospice Median Auction Maiden Fillies' Stakes (Leicester, July 31) 2yo 6f Soft **82** (TS 43) 8 ran ● **2nd** EBF Median Auction Maiden Fillies' Stakes (Kempton, July 17) 2yo 6f Good to firm **82** (TS 51) 15 ran

Choisir over a furlong out, Airwave was asked to take him and could not, falling to a half-length defeat.

In many ways, it was the same story in the Darley July Cup. With Kieren Fallon replacing the suspended O'Neill, Airwave travelled like a winner waiting to happen, only for the winning not to happen. Admittedly not enjoying the clearest passage, Airwave engaged top gear too late and finished an almost identical distance behind Choisir. The only difference this time was that the foreign raider found Oasis Dream his superior.

For Airwave, the second half of the season was not as productive as the first. Forced to miss a Nunthorpe Stakes rematch with Oasis Dream due to an infection, she returned at Haydock in the Stanley Leisure Sprint Cup with Candy extremely pessimistic, reckoning his stable star would get weary after a rushed preparation. Candy was right, but there was plenty to like about the run, as Airwave oozed class for most of the race before emptying on the heavy ground and taking third behind Somnus.

That was as good as it got. On her final two starts the hold-up performer encountered the inevitable problem a hold-up performer faces – traffic. She found plenty of it in Ascot's Diadem Stakes and then again in the Prix de l'Abbaye, in which she was sent off favourite according to British industry prices but was never travelling as smoothly as she can.

Airwave   *bay filly, 12-2-2000*

		Topsider	Northern Dancer
			Drumtop
	Salse		
		Carnival Princess	Prince John
Air Express			Carnival Queen
b 1994			
		Caucasus	Nijinsky
			Quill
	Ibtisamm		
		Lorgnette	High Hat
			Mlle Lorette

		Ahonoora	Lorenzaccio
			Helen Nichols
	Indian Ridge		
		Hillbrow	Swing Easy
Kangra Valley			Golden City
ch 1991			
		Tina's Pet	Mummy's Pet
			Merry Weather
	Thorner Lane		
		Spinner	Blue Cashmere
			Penny Pincher

Bred by Richard and Tessa Watson. 12,000gns Doncaster St Leger yearling

Sire Air Express

Won 4 of 15 starts, inc. Premio Parioli-Gr2, Mehl-Mulhens-Rennen-Gr2, Queen Elizabeth II S.-Gr1, also 3rd Dewhurst S.-Gr1. By top-class 7f to 1m performer out of 1m winner who is very closely related to Canadian Gr3 winner Au Printemps (dam of Gr1 winners Greenwood Lake, Success Express). Stood at National Stud, died 2001. Oldest progeny 3. Sire of: Airwave (Cheveley Park S.-Gr1), Bonaire (Gr3).

Dam Kangra Valley

Won 1 of 6 starts. Both parents sprinters, from family of fast Clantime. Dam of: Danakim (1997 g by Emarati; winner), Beverley Macca (1998 f by Piccolo; winner), Kangarilla Road (1999 g by Magic Ring; winner), Airwave (2000 f by Air Express; Gr1 winner), Soundwave (2001 f by Prince Sabo; unraced), 2002 c by Royal Applause (160,000gns Tattersalls Houghton yearling). Covered in 2003 by Dansili.

Pedigree assessment

Speed is her forte and she thus follows the pattern of her family, though she is by far the most classy performer to emerge from it in recent generations. When she goes to stud, that speed and precocity will be her hallmark, and she thus is likely to suit stallions who themselves were best at up to a mile or who tend to impart a fair amount of speed. Her pedigree, which is either free of, or has a light dose of, the most common influences, gives plentiful mating opportunities for her. *JH*

This was not a bad season for Airwave, but a frustrating one. With a further three Group 1 placings in the bag, her paddocks value is already huge, yet she will be around in 2004. Lady Luck will inevitably have something to say in how she fares, but the feeling abides that Airwave will be hard done by if she retires without another Group 1 prize to her credit.

Alamshar (Ire)

3yo bay colt	**133**

Key Of Luck (USA) - Alaiyda (USA) (Shahrastani (USA))
Owner H H Aga Khan
Trainer John M Oxx
Breeder His Highness The Aga Khan's Studs

Career: **9** starts | won **5** | second **1** | third **1** | **£1,210,715** win and place

By Alastair Down

THERE is a grammatical term for a contradiction in terms – an oxymoron. The 2003 Flat season was further proof of something you can't contradict. John Oxx – 'e no moron.

Just three seasons after masterminding the classic campaign of dual Derby and Arc de Triomphe winner Sinndar, Oxx was back, around daffodil time, with Alamshar, another colt with pretensions to filling the Sinndar mould.

Back in 2000, Sinndar kind of sneaked in from left field on punters as a possible answer to the Derby. After nearly every triallist's copybook had been blotted, or at least smudged, you could still back him at as long as 16-1 at the end of the last serious week of mock exams that is York's splendid May meeting.

But while the betting public remain strangely impervious to Oxx's talent and his remarkable strike-rate in Britain, something King George day was to prove, the bookmakers have long learned their lesson and, as Alamshar's early three-year-old career began to mirror that of Sinndar, they kept him very much on the right side.

Anyone with half a brain will have long realised that the training profession is not short of show ponies – people whose ego, reputation or ambition are all too swiftly brought in as substitutes for performance, professionalism and talent.

Quietly spoken and a painstaking thinker about his work, Oxx is the antithesis of the saloon bar trainer. He succeeded his father at the family's ever expanding yard on the edge of The Curragh, just a quiet amble from the gallops, and while it is a place of modern methods, it is greatly enhanced by human roots unmatched in any yard in Europe. Head man Tony Shanahan has worked there over 40 years, travelling man Paschal Corrigan 35, assistant Jimmy O'Neill over 27, and senior lad Jack O'Shea is a 40-year man.

**Alamshar (Johnny Murtagh) storms clear of Sulamani for
a memorable win in the King George at Ascot**

And all the combined experience of Oxx, his team and even the expertise
of a French chiropractor, who racked up many an air mile over the summer,
were required as Alamshar was anything but an easy horse to train.

Throughout the season Alamshar was plagued by a slight lameness
which only became a problem when he did his most serious pieces of
work. Given that Oxx would not ask him proper questions until late in
his preparation for a particular race, this led to several eve-of-race scares
with the horse, which is when the chiropractor would jet in from France.

Oxx said: "Basically it was a weakness in his back, part muscular
and part skeletal." One thing is for sure, the period of waiting for the
problems to manifest themselves added greatly to the strain – though
you never got a clue to that from Oxx's apparently unruffled demeanour.
He would have made a devastatingly effective Cold War spy.

Early in the season, Oxx told the Aga Khan's racing manager, Pat
Downes: "We will send him down the Sinndar route until he tells us we
have no right to be doing so." He kicked off on April 13 in the Ballysax
Stakes but went down by half a length to the enterprisingly ridden Aidan
O'Brien pacemaker Balestrini, the general consensus being that he was
the moral winner.

On May 11, after suffering a pre-race scare, he had a much harder
race than desirable when Johnny Murtagh drove him home by a head
from The Great Gatsby in Leopardstown's ever-informative Derrinstown

2003 — Race record

6th Emirates Airline Champion Stakes (Group 1) (Newmarket, October 18) 3yo+ 10f Good to firm **113** (TS 85) 12 ran. *Slowly into stride, soon with leader, led over 5f out, ridden over 3f out, headed over 2f out, weakening when not much room over 1f out, beaten 6¾l by Rakti*

4th Ireland The Food Island Champion Stakes (Group 1) (Leopardstown, September 6) 3yo+ 10f Good to firm **123** (TS 111) 7 ran. *Tracked leaders in 3rd, improved into 2nd under 3f out, 3rd and ridden 2f out, 4th and no impression final furlong, kept on, beaten 2l by High Chaparral*

1st King George VI And Queen Elizabeth Diamond Stakes (Group 1) (Ascot, July 26) 3yo+ 12f Good **133** (TS 98) 12 ran. *Soon tracked leader, led well over 2f out and kicked clear, in no danger from over 1f out, ridden out, impressive, beat Sulamani by 3½l*

1st Budweiser Irish Derby (Group 1) (Curragh, June 29) 3yo 12f Good **128** (TS 112) 9 ran. *Moderate 5th, 4th and progress halfway, 2nd and ridden to challenge over 2f out, slight advantage from over 1f out, stayed on well under pressure, beat Dalakhani by ½l*

3rd Vodafone Derby (Group 1) (Epsom, June 7) 3yo 12f Good **121** (TS 103) 20 ran. *Raced in midfield, 9th straight, ridden 3f out, progress under pressure 2f out, closed on leaders 1f out, stayed on same pace final furlong, beaten 1l by Kris Kin*

1st Derrinstown Stud Derby Trial Stakes (Group 2) (Leopardstown, May 11) 3yo 10f Good to yielding **109** (TS 101) 6 ran. *Settled 3rd, pushed along 3f out, headway early straight, ridden to lead under 1f out, kept on under pressure, all out, beat The Great Gatsby by hd*

2nd PW McGrath Memorial Ballysax Stakes (Group 3) (Leopardstown, April 13) 3yo 10f Good to firm **115** (TS 93) 5 ran. *Held up in moderate 4th, headway entering straight, 2nd over 1f out, ran on strongly, nearest at finish, beaten ½l by Balestrini*

2002

1st Juddmonte Beresford Stakes (Group 3) (Curragh, October 13) 2yo 1m Good to yielding **110** (TS 44) 10 ran ● **1st** Harvest Festival EBF Maiden (Listowel, September 26) 2yo 1m Firm **83** 7 ran

Stud Derby Trial over ten furlongs.

Taken as a pair the two races did little to add to Alamshar's lustre, the general view being that, while being a worthy Derby candidate, he perhaps lacked the spark of brilliance to win at Epsom. That view was to be borne out on the big day itself, but high summer was eventually to prove that he was a colt cut from very special cloth indeed.

It cannot have helped that Alamshar was wrong in his back again two days before the Derby and in the race itself Murtagh was always just a length and a half or so off 'position A'. Any doubts about his stamina were laid to rest as he closed them down to the line, but by that time Kieren Fallon had burgled the race on Kris Krin. One left Epsom that evening with the nagging feeling that this was a race Alamshar could easily have won – that in some way we hadn't seen all he had to offer.

Oxx, phlegmatic as ever, said: "I was as happy as you could be in defeat, but disappointed he didn't ping round with a bit more zip to him." The opportunity for Alamshar to prove himself incontrovertibly top-class came 22 days later in the Irish Derby at The Curragh. It was an event enhanced beyond measure by one of the most sporting decisions in recent racing history when the Aga Khan gave the go-ahead to Alain de Royer-Dupré and Oxx to pitch his two ace middle-distance colts Dalakhani and Alamshar

**Alamshar and Johnny Murtagh claim their first Group 1
of the season as they beat Dalakhani in the Irish Derby**

in against each other. The crucial phase of the race came when Christophe
Soumillon committed Dalakhani to reel in the pacemaker up the Curragh
straight, for Murtagh just delayed his bid for a few strides, knowing full
well that Alamshar was a fighter and that Dalakhani was now exposed
as a target. The main protagonists had it to themselves in the final furlong
but to the undisguised delight of the home crowd Alamshar, with the
grey horse to aim at, always had the upper hand.

Alamshar had indeed been sent down the Sinndar route and, despite
missing out on the big prize at Epsom, had rewarded Oxx and his team
with a second Irish Derby in three years. But whereas Sinndar had been
rested with the Arc in mind after his nine-length win at The Curragh –
Oxx still insists he was not quite himself that day! – Alamshar was
immediately carded for the King George and Queen Elizabeth Diamond
Stakes at Ascot.

He was as low as 5-2 for the midsummer crown a few days before the
race, but fears over fast ground and bullish noises from rival camps led
him to go for what our Cockney friends would call a 'ball of chalk' in
the market. On the day of the race he was utterly friendless and drifted

out to a ludicrous starting price of 13-2. But if he was chronically uneasy in the market he was on awesomely good terms with himself throughout the race. Murtagh kept him handy and he showed that hallmark
of a real good colt in travelling supremely well throughout. Asked to go
and win his race from the home turn, Alamshar's response was nothing short of a joy to behold and he proceeded to put a good field to the
sword, trouncing Sulamani by an unequivocal three and a half lengths.

If closing defeats over ten furlongs in both the Irish Champion and
its Newmarket equivalent took some shine off Alamshar's season, that
shouldn't blind the critics to the fact that he was the second-best middle-
distance colt of his generation. The only contemporary you could put
above him in the pecking order is Dalakhani, and when they met in the
Irish Derby on The Curragh, Alamshar was comprehensively the superior.

What is more, the Irish Champion has claims to being the classiest
race of the entire year, with Alamshar beaten a neck, a head and a length
and a half by High Chaparral, Falbrav and Islington, all of whom went
on to cover themselves with glory in the Breeders' Cup.

Oxx says: "He did nothing wrong that day and if he hadn't been eased
a touch would only have been beaten a length. Perhaps the thing about
that afternoon was that it was the first hint that, despite me saying all
summer that he needed fast ground, he really didn't like good to firm
ground, as he just hung right a little.

"My heart wasn't really in running him at Newmarket. But we couldn't
go to Canada for veterinary reasons following his sale to Japan and the
Japanese were keen to run. But again he was leaning to the right as if
not enjoying the ground.

"Looking back and being absolutely super-critical you could say that
he lacked a little bit of Sinndar's toughness. Sinndar, and indeed Ridgewood
Pearl, would gallop through the fires of hell without batting an eyelid,
but having said that Alamshar was a cracking colt on his day and wouldn't
be too far behind. But you have to concede that the colt rated above
him, Dalakhani, won the French Derby on firm and the Arc impressively
on heavy and that takes some doing."

There was a regrettable postscript to Alamshar's season with the
anouncement that Murtagh would be replaced as Oxx's stable jockey
for the 2004 season by Mick Kinane, who is to be superseded at Ballydoyle
by Jamie Spencer. Racing being a gossip factory, it was whispered that
Murtagh had succumbed to the problems that haunted him of old, but
nothing could have been further from the truth. He has always struggled
with his weight and a fall at Royal Ascot meant that for some weeks he
could not pursue his weight-control regime as usual.

Oxx is very attached to Murtagh and the pair's loyalty to each other
is a byword. He said: "Johnny and I have had a great association and
been through some hoops together. He is very much the sort of man
you want to have around. But people simply don't understand the strains

Alamshar

bay colt, 18-4-2000

Key Of Luck br 1991	Chief's Crown	Danzig	**Northern Dancer** Pas de Nom
		Six Crowns	Secretariat Chris Evert
	Balbonella	Gay Mecene	Vaguely Noble Gay Missile
		Bamieres	Riverman Bergamasque
Alaiyda ch 1991	Shahrastani	Nijinsky	**Northern Dancer** Flaming Page
		Shademah	Thatch Shamim
	Aliysa	Darshaan	Shirley Heights Delsy
		Alannya	Relko Nucciolina

Bred by HH Aga Khan's Studs in Ireland.

Sire **Key Of Luck**

Won 6 of 17 races, inc. Prix d'Arenberg-Gr3, Dubai Duty Free S. Compact, well-made sort. Speedy and precocious juvenile who overcame injuries to develop high-class form on dirt and sand over 10f. Half-brother to Anabaa. Sire of: Alamshar (Irish Derby-Gr1, King George VI & Queen Elizabeth S.-Gr1), Miss Emma (Gr3).

Dam **Alaiyda**

Ran only at 3 years, won 1 of 5 races. Just a useful handicapper, won a 10f maiden, stayed 2m. Dam of: Albaiyda (1996 f by Brief Truce; unraced), Alaya (1997 f by Ela-Mana-Mou; winner), Alaynia (1998 f by Hamas; placed on Flat and in a bumper), Alaipour (1999 g by Kahyasi; placed 4th only start), Alamshar (2000 c by Key Of Luck; Classic winner), 2001 f by Desert Sun.

Pedigree assessment

In light of what he achieved on his next two outings, it seems a mystery how Alamshar failed to win the Derby. A small, neat colt, he seemed the sort who would cope with Epsom's idiosyncratic contours better than most, but on the day he was unable to deliver. He trounced the pair who beat him later, and his King George performance ranked among the best seen in Britain at a mile and a half in recent years. He was not the same force at ten furlongs, as his efforts at Leopardstown and Newmarket indicated. He will be at stud in Japan in 2004. *TM*

involved in getting up each day with four or five pounds to shed. You only have to look at him to see how tough it must be – he is built more like a jump jockey than a Flat one and I can see him resuming around the 9st 2lb mark and gradually working his way down. One thing's for sure, there will be plenty of very good rides for him. He is a great big-race jockey and everyone knows it."

American Post

2yo brown colt **115**

Bering - Wells Fargo (Sadler's Wells (USA))

Owner K Abdullah

Trainer Mme C Head-Maarek

Breeder Juddmonte Farms

Career: **4** starts	won **3**	second **1**	third **0**	**£292,987** win and place

By Lee Mottershead

HE'S NAUGHTY, but ever so nice – and anyway, you can get away with being a bit naughty when you're as good as American Post. Although he may have appeared on the unruly side at times, he's no worse than "playful" according to trainer Criquette Head-Maarek, and "he would never do anything wrong". She's sure of that.

She's also sure that American Post is one special racehorse. On that particular subject, few would disagree. In two Group 1 races, American Post showed himself to be a juvenile of outstanding ability, a colt blessed with instant acceleration, and capable of producing that acceleration on both the deepest and fastest of ground. He also showed himself to be a little on the temperamental side.

You could forgive any horse for getting excited at Longchamp on Arc day. American Post got very excited. In the preliminaries for the Prix Jean Luc Lagardere, the son of Bering was more than a tad difficult. First reluctant to step foot on the racecourse, he then became fractious at the start, rearing up repeatedly before consenting to enter the stalls. It was soon all forgiven.

Before his appearance in the Longchamp showpiece, American Post had made little impact outside French racing circles. Beaten a short head on his debut over Deauville's six furlongs, he went one better when winning over an extra furlong at Longchamp in mid-September. He looked good, but the earth was far from on fire. It soon would be.

The 2003 Prix Jean Luc Lagardere did not seem a great renewal of France's premier two-year-old prize. Formerly run as the Grand Criterium and staged for the first time in memory of the late France-Galop supremo, it would be contested by just six juveniles, three of whom represented Aidan O'Brien, but none appearing to come from his first division. Additionally, it would be run on almost unraceable holding ground. American Post went through it like the proverbial knife through butter.

**American Post (Christophe Soumillon) lands the Group 1
Racing Post Trophy at Doncaster in October**

In a steadily run affair, he sat ready to pounce just behind leader Charming Prince until asked to win his race by Richard Hughes two furlongs out. As scintillating as Rock Of Gibraltar two years before, American Post displayed the rare ability to quicken instantly and brilliantly in the muddiest of conditions, immediately putting unbridgeable daylight between himself and his rivals. He may not have beaten much, but he beat them senseless, taking his bow four lengths clear of Charming Prince.

We did not expect to see American Post at Doncaster, but Doncaster is where he went. Running American Post in the Racing Post Trophy presented owner Khalid Abdullah with a perfect opportunity to seal his first British owners' championship. It also presented American Post with his first competitive experience of fast ground.

As had been the case with the Lagardere, the 2003 Racing Post Trophy attracted a small and not obviously vintage field. Every punter at Doncaster

1st Racing Post Trophy (Group 1) (Doncaster, October 25) 2yo 1m Good to firm **114** (TS 56) 4 ran. *Tracked leader, led over 1f out, ridden out, beat Fantastic View by 1³/₄l*

1st Prix Jean Luc Lagardere (Grand Criterium) (Group 1) (Longchamp, October 5) 2yo 7f Holding **117** (TS 62) 6 ran. *Unruly start, tracked leaders disputing 3rd, smooth progress to lead over 1¹/₂f out, driven clear, easily, beat Charming Prince by 4l*

1st Prix du Casino Barriere de Royan (Longchamp, September 14) 2yo 7f Good to soft **96** (TS 54) 9 ran. *Raced in 4th to straight, quickened to lead 1f out, soon in command, pushed out, beat Dealer Choice by 2l*

2nd Prix du Pre d'Auge (Unraced Colts & Geldings) (Deauville, July 31) 2yo 6f Soft **101** 6 ran. *Disputed lead, took definite advantage inside final furlong, caught last strides, beaten shd by Ximb*

seemed to want to be with American Post. Despite the presence of the much-vaunted Magritte – representing Aidan O'Brien, successful with Brian Boru and High Chaparral in the previous two seasons – and impressive Group 3 winner Fantastic View, the French raider was sent off a red-hot 5-6 favourite.

Far better behaved than in Paris, American Post's dominance was not reflected in his one-and-three-quarter-length defeat of Fantastic View. Always cruising under Christophe Soumillon with leader Magritte nicely in his sights, he quickened decisively just over a furlong from home. He edged right – Soumillon put it down to his being "a bit babyish" – but moved clear, not appearing to love the quick conditions but still winning without being asked for maximum effort.

It was the first French victory in the Group 1 contest for 29 years, the previous Gallic success having come with Green Dancer, sent to Doncaster by Head-Maarek's father, Alec Head. For the winning trainer, American Post's triumph was an emotional affair, made all the more so by a call to her mobile phone from Head senior, at home in Normandy, as she unsaddled American Post and spoke to the press in the winner's enclosure.

If American Post makes the expected progress from two to three, there could be more tears of joy for Head-Maarek in the future. Although prominent in the 2,000 Guineas betting, Abdullah is reportedly favouring a crack at the French equivalent, possibly mindful that in Three Valleys he already boasts a serious challenger for the Newmarket Classic. Perhaps even more intriguingly, American Post went into winter quarters as ante-post favourite for the Vodafone Derby. As a son of Bering out of a half-sister to St Leger second High And Low, the Blue Riband distance should suit ideally. Yet life is not always that simple.

Few horses with his natural pace truly stay 12 furlongs, while his head carriage at Doncaster hardly suggested a horse crying out to run down Tattenham Hill on fast ground.

Regardless of where his stamina snaps, American Post seems sure to take high rank among the three-year-olds of 2004. Naughty or not.

American Post   *brown colt, 3-2-2001*

Bering ch 1983	Arctic Tern	Sea-Bird	Dan Cupid / Sicalade
		Bubbling Beauty	Hasty Road / Almahmoud
	Beaune	Lyphard	**Northern Dancer** / Goofed
		Barbra	Le Fabuleux / Biobelle
Wells Fargo b 1996	Sadler's Wells	**Northern Dancer**	Nearctic / Natalma
		Fairy Bridge	Bold Reason / Special
	Cruising Height	Shirley Heights	Mill Reef / Hardiemma
		Nomadic Pleasure	Habitat / Petite Marmite

Bred by Juddmonte Farms in England

Sire **Bering**

Won 5 of 7 races, inc. Prix Noailles-Gr2, Prix Hocquart-Gr2, Prix du Jockey-Club-Gr1, Prix Niel-Gr3. Also 2nd (to Dancing Brave) in Prix de l'Arc de Triomphe-Gr1. Handsome, striking individual. Top-notch middle-distance performer, effective on any ground, with an outstanding turn of foot. Chipped a bone in a knee on final start. Sire of: Beau Sultan (Gr3), Peter Davies (Racing Post Trophy-Gr1), Serrant (Gr2), Steamer Duck (Gran Criterium-Gr1), Break Bread (Gr3), Special Price (Gr2), Signe Divin (Gr2), Matiara (Poule d'Essai des Pouliches-Gr1), Ramona H.-Gr1), Pennekamp (Prix de la Salamandre-Gr1, Dewhurst S.-Gr1, 2,000 Guineas-Gr1), Salmon Ladder (Gr3), Vertical Speed (Gr2), Glorosia (Fillies' Mile-Gr1), Miss Berbere (Gr2), Moiava (Gr2), Neptune's Bride (Gr3), Stella Berine (Gr3), Urban Ocean (Gr3), Three Points (Gr3), Art Contemporain (Gr3), Ing Ing (Gr3), Lady Catherine (Gr3), American Post (Prix Jean-Luc Lagardere-Gr1, Racing Post Trophy-Gr1).

Dam **Wells Fargo**

Unraced. Half-sister to Yorkshire Oaks and St Leger runner-up High And Low. Dam of American Post (2001 c by Bering; dual Gr1 winner), her only foal.

Pedigree assessment

American Post registered two important end-of-season wins that so impressed one bookmaker that he was quoted at no more than 6-1 for the Derby. That offer was perhaps understandable in light of the colt's pedigree background; his sire was an outstanding 12f performer and his dam, though unraced, was by a staying influence and half-sister to a St Leger runner-up. There are factors aplenty for stamina in his make-up. However, particularly at Doncaster, American Post looked much more a miler than a middle-distance performer and it is noticeable in Bering's record that a number of his progeny seemingly bred to stay proved much more effective at shorter trips. He still lacks a top-level winner beyond nine furlongs. Chances are that his next shot at Classic glory will come in the Poule d'Essai des Poulains. *TM*

Ange Gabriel (Fr)

5yo grey horse   **123**

Kaldounevees (Fr) - Mount Gable (Head For Heights)

Owner Mme Henri Devin

Trainer E Libaud

Breeder Mme Henri Devin

Career: **20** starts | won **12** | second **3** | third **2** | £1,402,185 win and place

By Lee Mottershead

IT WOULD be one of the great injustices of the 2003 Flat season were Ange Gabriel to be remembered for, or judged on, his tame display in the Prix de l'Arc de Triomphe. The horse who trailed in more than 16 lengths behind Dalakhani at Longchamp was a shadow of the real Ange Gabriel. The real Ange Gabriel was a genuine Group 1 performer, one of the middle-distance stars of the campaign.

Ange Gabriel's connections may well look back on what happened in 2003 with a sense of regret, kicking themselves for taking a decision which may have denied the son of Kaldounevees a fair crack at a European championship victory. At the end of 2002, on the back of a sparkling success in Hong Kong, trainer Eric Libaud and owner Antonia Devin singled out the King George VI and Queen Elizabeth Diamond Stakes as the race they most wanted to win with Ange Gabriel. They changed their minds. Instead of running at Ascot – in what was admittedly a high-class renewal of the King George – they set their stall out for the Arc and found themselves racing on atrocious ground, on which Ange Gabriel was never happy and never competitive.

The plan to go to Ascot had been announced in the moments following the then-four-year-old Ange Gabriel's victory in the Hong Kong Vase. Successful earlier that season in the Grand Prix de Saint-Cloud before missing the Arc due to a setback, Ange Gabriel confirmed himself a top-class performer at Sha Tin, coming home in front of fellow French raider Aquarelliste with America's Falcon Flight filling the same third position he had earlier managed behind High Chaparral in the Breeders' Cup Turf.

Despite the huge value and increasing prestige associated with the Hong Kong International Races, they take place at a time when most eyes in Europe are focused on jumpers, a factor which possibly contributed to Ange Gabriel not receiving the billing he almost certainly merited when

Ange Gabriel (Thierry Jarnet) lands a second consecutive win in the Group 1 Grand Prix de Saint-Cloud in June

next seen out in the Dubai Sheema Classic.

British bookmakers were convinced the race would be dominated by the unlucky Arc second Sulamani, running for the first time in Godolphin's colours. In the sense that Sulamani won, the bookmakers were right, but in the sense that Ange Gabriel might be swept aside, they were wrong.

Ange Gabriel's Hong Kong success represents the grey's single best performance, but what he achieved in Dubai comes close. Of all the races at the World Cup fixture, the Sheema Classic has, in recent years, increased most in profile. The 2003 renewal featured, as well as Sulamani and Ange Gabriel, two of the latter's Sha Tin victims in Ekraar and Polish Summer, Hong Kong Cup third Dano-Mast and new Godolphin recruits Highest and Califet. No matter. The Sheema Classic of 2003 turned into a two-horse race.

While Sulamani stalked his rivals from the rear, regular rider Thierry Jarnet maintained a prominent position on Ange Gabriel, sitting in third until grabbing leader Celtic Silence well over a furlong out. It was at this point that Ange Gabriel displayed the quality that marked him down as a seriously smart racehorse, unleashing an instant change of gear which appeared likely to settle proceedings there and then. That, though, did not take into account the dazzling acceleration of Sulamani. Yet, although Sulamani took over inside the final half-furlong, Frankie Dettori's mount was unable to achieve clear water, his opponent cutting back into his advantage close home.

Revenge would be Ange Gabriel's three months later when, on the back of a smooth triumph in the Group 2 Grand Prix de Chantilly, he emulated

2003   Race record

9th Prix de l'Arc de Triomphe Lucien Barriere (Group 1) (Longchamp, October 5) 3yo+ 12f Holding **108** (TS 92) 13 ran. *Mid-division, 9th straight, beaten 2f out, beaten 16½l by Dalakhani*

1st Prix Foy Gray d'Albion Barriere (Group 2) (Longchamp, September 14) 4yo+ 12f Good to soft **120** (TS 81) 4 ran. *Led over 1½f out, tracked leader until led again 2f out, pushed along, comfortably, beat Martaline by 2½l*

1st Grand Prix de Saint-Cloud (Group 1) (Saint-Cloud, June 29) 3yo+ 12f Good **121** (TS 106) 10 ran. *Raced in 3rd, went 2nd halfway, led inside final furlong, ridden out, beat Polish Summer by 1½l*

1st Grand Prix de Chantilly (Group 2) (Chantilly, June 8) 4yo+ 12f Good **122** (TS 110) 7 ran. *Held up disputing last, 5th halfway, pushed along and smooth headway over 1½f out to close up, led over 1f out, ran on well final furlong, beat Martaline by 1½l*

2nd Dubai Sheema Classic (Group 1) (Nad Al Sheba, March 29) 4yo+ 12f Good **123** (TS 120) 16 ran. *Always close up, 3rd straight, led well over 1f out, hard ridden and headed 100yds out, kept on one pace, beaten ¾l by Sulamani*

2002

1st Hong Kong Vase (Group 1) (Sha Tin, December 15) 3yo+ 12f Good to firm **124** 14 ran ● **1st** Prix du Conseil de Paris (Group 2) (Longchamp, October 20) 3yo+ 12f Soft **117** (TS 57) 6 ran ● **1st** Grand Prix de Saint-Cloud (Group 1) (Saint-Cloud, June 30) 3yo+ 12f Good **119** (TS 112) 6 ran ● **2nd** Dead-heat Grand Prix de Chantilly (Group 2) (Chantilly, June 9) 4yo+ 12f Good **118** (TS 102) 11 ran ● **3rd** Prix Jean de Chaudenay - Grand Prix du Printemps (Group 2) (Saint-Cloud, May 20) 4yo+ 12f Good to soft **112** (TS 85) 5 ran ● **2nd** Prix d'Hedouville (Group 3) (Longchamp, April 18) 4yo+ 12f Good **114** (TS 84) 11 ran ● **1st** Prix Lord Seymour (Listed) (Longchamp, March 31) 4yo+ 12f Soft **109** 5 ran

Other notable runs

2001 1st Prix de Reux (Listed) (Deauville, August 7) 3yo+ 12½f Very soft (TS 44) 10 ran ● **1st** Prix Marot (Saint-Cloud, June 13) 3yo 10½f Good 10 ran ● **1st** Prix de la Chezine (Nantes, May 5) 3yo 12f Heavy 7 ran ● **1st** Prix Jeanne de Laval (Angers, April 1) 3yo 11½f Holding 7 ran ● **1st** Prix France Galop (Maiden) (Argentan, March 4) 3yo 9½f Soft 12 ran

Helissio by securing back-to-back victories in the Grand Prix de Saint-Cloud. This, though, was a race in which Sulamani completely failed to fire, a messy race in which Godolphin pacemaker Millstreet dictated a leisurely gallop, resulting almost inevitably in a sprint down the short Saint-Cloud straight. Again ridden close to the lead by Jarnet, Ange Gabriel quickened handsomely when sent about his business, coming home clear and unruffled, his nearest pursuer Polish Summer occupying the same bridesmaid's berth he had 12 months earlier.

With the King George swerved in favour of the typical French summer break, Ange Gabriel returned to cruise home in a very ordinary Prix Foy before sinking in the Longchamp mud on Arc day. Assessing him is tricky. On no single piece of form could he be described as outstanding. Yet, on his favoured fast ground, and most certainly in Hong Kong and Dubai, he showed himself in possession of abundant class and more than deserving of his status as a triple Group 1 winner.

Ange Gabriel

grey horse, 2-3-1998

Kaldounevees gr 1991	Kaldoun	Caro	Fortino / Chambord
		Katana	Le Haar / Embellie
	Safaroa	Satingo	Petingo / Saquebute
		Traverse Afar	Prince John / Giftbearer
Mount Gable b 1986	Head For Heights	Shirley Heights	Mill Reef / Hardiemma
		Vivante	Bold Lad / Focal
	Cupids Hill	Sallust	Pall Mall / Bandarilla
		Sweet Jewel	Will Somers / Diamond Deuce

Bred by Mme Henri Devin in France

Sire Kaldounevees

Won 3 of 14 races, inc. Prix Edmond Blanc-Gr3, Prix du Chemin de Fer du Nord-Gr3. Also 2nd in Bayerisches Zuchtrennen-Gr1, Man o'War S.-Gr1, 4th in Arlington Million-Gr1. Smart performer from 8-11f, and would probably have stayed further. Tough and consistent, effective on any ground bar very soft. Broke blood vessel on final start. Sire of: Terre A Terre (Prix de l'Opera-Gr1, Dubai Duty Free-Gr1), Ange Gabriel (Grand Prix de Saint-Cloud-Gr1 (twice), Hong Kong Vase-Gr1).

Dam Mount Gable

Won 2 of 26 races. Modest handicapper, useful in her class. Lacked pace, but effective up to 15f and showed quite consistent form over three seasons, except on very soft ground. Dam of: Mount Eagle (1994 c by Pampabird; placed in France), Montbraye (1995 c by Tel Quel; unplaced in France), Dubayotte (1997 g by Turgeon; placed in France), Ange Gabriel (1998 c by Kaldounevees; triple Gr1 winner), Angello (2001 c by Kaldounevees; unraced to date).

Pedigree assessment

Ange Gabriel is most effective when the ground is good or faster, so he is not the ideal type for racing in France. But he struck lucky in the comparatively kind summer of 2003 after a successful overseas tour that had yielded him a win in the Hong Kong Vase in December and a second in the Dubai Sheema Classic in March. He had conditions that he appreciated at Chantilly, Saint-Cloud and Longchamp, notching a hat-trick of victories that showed him to better advantage than ever. He was entitled to bid for the Arc after that, but then his luck ran out and he was never able to use himself on the sticky ground that compromised so many chances that weekend. He will be back to confirm that he is a top-rank performer in 2004, and when conditions suit he will again be a threat to all. *TM*

Attraction

2yo bay filly   **117**

Efisio - Flirtation (Pursuit Of Love)
Owner Duke Of Roxburghe
Trainer M Johnston
Breeder Floors Farming

Career: **5** starts | won **5** | second **0** | third **0** | **£101,450** win and place

By Richard Austen

"EVEN if we get her through her problem and get her to the Guineas, there will still be the big variable of does she or does she not stay a mile. My biggest regret is not having had an opportunity to run her in a Group 1 race over six furlongs, something we knew she could do."

Mark Johnston's reflections in October sum up the position at the end of Attraction's two-year-old season. She never ran in a Group 1 event, but there is no doubt whatsoever that she had the ability to win one.

The best performances by a two-year-old filly in 2003 came not in the Cheveley Park, the Moyglare Stud Stakes, the Fillies' Mile, the Morny, Marcel Boussac, Lowther or any of the events that might normally produce the champion two-year-old filly, they came in the Queen Mary Stakes and Cherry Hinton Stakes, both won in devastating fashion by Attraction.

The facts of Attraction's racecourse appearances, spanning ten weeks and five races, take some enumerating but the essence is easy to summarise – she was far too good for whichever horse lined up against her. Connections were not confident that she would make a winning debut, in a median auction contest at Nottingham, but she did so easily. She quickly added a novice stakes at Thirsk and the Listed Hilary Needler Trophy at Beverley, the latter in particularly good style, before going to Royal Ascot.

She and the David Loder-trained Catstar dominated the betting for the Queen Mary, at 13-8 and 7-2 respectively, and they dominated the Group 3 race too. In Attraction's absence, Catstar would have been a highly impressive five-length winner from the subsequent Cheveley Park runner-up Majestic Desert. Yet Attraction beat her comprehensively by three lengths, after making virtually every yard.

Catstar was not seen again but Sheikh Mohammed, her owner, fielded three other fillies against the 4-7 favourite Attraction in the Group 2

Attraction (Kevin Darley) romps to her fifth victory in the Cherry Hinton at Newmarket in July

Chippenham Lodge Stud Cherry Hinton Stakes at the Newmarket July meeting. He again had to settle for second. Attraction had a 3lb penalty, and scrimmaging at the stalls meant an enforced change of tactics. In addition there was the question of whether such an outstandingly speedy filly would stay six furlongs. Yet once a gap appeared on the rails in the penultimate furlong Attraction surged ahead to put five lengths between herself and course-and-distance Listed winner Pearl Grey. It was a magnificent performance, and another that was well in advance of the form typically shown by Group-winning fillies in the summer.

Showing that Attraction could be held up and stayed six furlongs opened up, as her trainer put it, "numerous" big-race targets. Sadly, she could not bid for any of them. The outstanding juvenile filly of 2003 was not seen out after July 8.

Precautionary x-rays taken on both front limbs prior to the Prix Morny showed bony changes in her knees, which gave Johnston cause for

Race record

1st Chippenham Lodge Stud Cherry Hinton Stakes (Group 2) (Newmarket (July), July 8) 2yo 6f Good **117** (TS 88) 8 ran. *Hampered start, soon chasing leaders, led over 1f out, soon clear, beat Pearl Grey by 5l*

1st Queen Mary Stakes (Group 3) (Ascot, June 18) 2yo 5f Good to firm **110** (TS 91) 14 ran. *Made all, ridden and pressed 1f out, ran on strongly final furlong, beat Catstar by 3l*

1st Hilary Needler Trophy (Listed) (Beverley, June 4) 2yo 5f Good to firm **101** (TS 74) 9 ran. *Soon tracking leaders, led over 2f out, driven well clear 1f out, eased towards finish, beat Tolzey by 2½l*

1st EBF Carlton Miniott Novice Fillies' Stakes (Thirsk, May 17) 2yo 5f Good **80** (TS 67) 6 ran. *Edgy at start, with leader, shaken up to lead over 1f out, kept on well, beat Mirasol Princess by 2l*

1st Harby Novice Median Auction Stakes (Nottingham, April 29) 2yo 5f Good **86** (TS 41) 9 ran. *With leader, led over 1f out, ran on well, beat Avid Spell by 5l*

concern, but when she missed that race it was on account of suffering an overreach while swimming. Then, in late September, she cracked a pedal bone and had to miss the Cheveley Park. At the time she was 10-1 clear favourite for the 1,000 Guineas.

Attraction is a remarkable filly, all the more remarkable when one considers that she was put into training with Johnston only after her owner-breeder, the Duke of Roxburghe, had decided against sending her to the sales because of the unconventional conformation of her front legs. "She's got offset knees and she toes in," said Johnston.

The racing layman might not spot the finer points of her front legs but not so many would miss her action, a wide-reaching, splayed style of galloping that brought back memories to some of one recent eccentric at a vastly lower level, Bronze Runner, a horse who nonetheless was still running at the age of 12. "Attraction's very wide in front," said Johnston. "There's no doubt it's fairly abnormal, but I've trained worse, much worse."

Elaborating, Johnston added: "Attraction is the most magnificent creature side on, with a fantastic body on her and fantastic hind legs – very, very powerful. So she has front-limb faults. It's amazing how you go to the sales and everybody can tell you whether it's offset, or it toes in or it toes out, or it's got splints or it's back at the knee, and a lot of the time they forget to tell you whether it's a nice horse or not. I think people lose sight of the fact that Attraction is a magnificent-looking filly. She has faults from the knee down, on her front legs only, but conformation does not start at the knee."

Attraction's fractured pedal bone is unrelated to her conformation, but the ongoing problems with her knees are related. Her future as a Classic candidate is clearly in the balance, although a Guineas preparation is planned if she makes a full recovery. What is not in the balance is her status as the year's top two-year-old filly. She is head and shoulders above the rest of her own sex and Johnston says that she is the best two-year-old of either sex he has trained.

Attraction   *bay filly, 19-2-2001*

		Forli	Aristophanes
			Trevisa
		Formidable	
		Native Partner	Raise A Native
	Efisio		Dinner Partner
	b 1982		
		High Top	Derring-do
			Camenae
		Eldoret	
		Bamburi	Ragusa
			Kilifi
		Groom Dancer	Blushing Groom
			Featherhill
		Pursuit Of Love	
		Dance Quest	Green Dancer
	Flirtation		Polyponder
	b 1994		
		Sun Prince	Princely Gift
			Costa Sola
		Eastern Shore	
		Land Ho	Primera
			Lucasland

Bred by Floors Farming in Britain

Sire Efisio

Won 8 of 26 races, inc. Horris Hill S.-Gr3, Challenge S.-Gr3, Premio Emilio Turati-Gr1, Premio Chiusura-Gr2. Half-brother to Gr1 winner Mountain Bear and to dam of Gr1 winner Timboroa. Stands at Highclere Stud, 2003 fee £9,000. Oldest progeny 14. Sire of: Casteddu (Gr3), Pips Pride (Phoenix S.-Gr1), Young Ern (Gr3), Hever Golf Rose (Prix de l'Abbaye-Gr1), Tomba (Prix de la Foret-Gr1), Uruk (Gr3), Heads Will Roll (Gr3), Guys And Dolls (Gr3), Pearly Shells (Prix Vermeille-Gr1), Le Vie dei Colori (Premio Vittorio di Capua-Gr1), Attraction (Gr2).

Dam Flirtation

Unraced at 2, unplaced sole start at 3. By top-class sprinter out of half-sister to very useful middle-distance filly Carmita (by Caerleon). Dam of: Aunty Mary (1999 f by Common Grounds; winner), Attraction (2001 f by Efisio; Gr2 winner), 2002 c by Inchinor.

Pedigree assessment

Attraction descends from the very fast Lucasland and has plenty of fast stallions in her pedigree, hence her speed. However, Efisio tends to get tough and progressive performers, and if she returns to the racecourse there is every reason to believe Attraction can continue to show high-class form, probably at up to 7f. *JH*

Bago (Fr)
2yo bay or brown colt   **118+**

Nashwan (USA) - Moonlight's Box (USA) (Nureyev (USA))
Owner Niarchos Family
Trainer J E Pease
Breeder Niarchos Family

Career: **4** starts | won **4** | second **0** | third **0** | **£129,123** win and place

By James Willoughby

ANYTHING is possible for Bago. In this regard, the budding French superstar sets his connections a poser. Have they enough confidence in his stamina to focus on the French Derby? Or should they go for Guineas glory first?

All these are nice problems for the Niarchos family and their advisers. They were precipitated by Bago's hugely impressive performance in the Group 1 Criterium International at Saint-Cloud in November. The Criterium International, over a mile, is becoming a very influential two-year-old race. Dalakhani won it in 2002, while the previous renewal fell to Act One. Jonathan Pease, who handled the abbreviated career of the latter, now has a similar talent to nurture in Bago.

At Saint-Cloud, Bago was 2-5 favourite to beat six rivals, including his pacemaker Alnitak. The ex-claiming horse Joursanvault was second favourite at a shade under 3-1, but anyone who saw him swept aside by Bago in the Prix des Aigles at Longchamp in September would not have been in a hurry to take those odds. Acropolis promised to pose Bago more of a threat. The sole representative of a multiple Aidan O'Brien entry, he had looked uneasy on deep ground in the Prix Jean Luc Lagardere on Arc day and was said to be much better than that form suggested.

In the event it was the Mick Channon-trained Top Seed who gave Bago most to think about, but it was not much of a contest. Bago hardly flexed a muscle while powering to the front over a furlong out, striding six lengths clear as if ground conditions were very firm, not very soft.

The Criterium was hardly the strongest two-year-old race run in Europe, but it is churlish to decry the winner. It was said of Dalakhani that his early form had an incestuous look to it, but horses with big reputations tend to scare away worthy opponents in their formative days. On looks, movement and acceleration, Bago appears to be one from the top drawer.

Pease compares Bago favourably with Act One, saying: "I think he was

**Bago (Thierry Gillet) romps home in the Group 1
Criterium International at Saint-Cloud in November**

a better two-year-old than Act One. He has always needed a mile and
I hope he will stay further."

Thierry Gillet, who has ridden Bago to all his successes, was also very
impressed. "We were cruising throughout and I let him do it himself. I
never had to use my whip and this colt has never been extended. I think
he will stay further and he certainly feels like a top-class colt."

Both trainer and jockey touched on the question of stamina. Though
Bago shapes as though he will stay middle distances well, his pedigree
does not necessarily give the corresponding impression. Bago is by Nashwan out of the unraced Moonlight's Box, who should have appreciated
a mile on pedigree, for she is a daughter of Nureyev and Coup de Genie.

The Prix Morny and Salamandre winner Coup de Genie was third to
Las Meninas in the 1994 1,000 Guineas. She has five foals of racing
age, three of whom were top-class juveniles like herself, including the
latest Prix Marcel Boussac winner Denebola. Coup de Genie is clearly
passing on a lot of her speed.

Nashwan gets few sprinters, but plenty of his progeny are effective
around a mile. Among his best runners, the dual King George winner

2003   Race record

1st Criterium International (Group 1) (Saint-Cloud, November 1) 2yo 1m Very soft **118** (TS 90) 7 ran. *Held up and behind in 6th, closed up over 3f out, 6th and brought very wide entering straight, led over 1½f out, pushed clear, very easily, beat Top Seed by 6l*

1st Prix des Chenes (Group 3) (Longchamp, September 20) 2yo 1m Good **111** (TS 54) 7 ran. *Broke best, settled disputing 4th, 5th straight, pulled out over 1f out, ridden and quickened to lead over 100yds out, ran on well, beat Valixir by 1½l*

1st Prix des Aigles (Longchamp, September 2) 2yo 1m Soft **96** 7 ran. *Raced in 3rd behind steady pace, outpaced 2f out, ran on strongly final furlong to lead 100yds out, beat Joursanvault by 2l*

1st Prix de Bourguebus (Unraced Colts & Geldings) (Deauville, August 5) 2yo 1m Good to soft 11 ran. *Always close up, disputed lead 2f out until led 1f out, pushed clear, easily, beat Marnix by 2l*

Swain, Juddmonte International Stakes heroine One So Wonderful and the top-class US turf distaffer Wandesta were all suited by middle distances, but the likes of Myself and Didina showed smart form over seven furlongs. Judging the distance potential of Nashwan's runners is best achieved with due heed to the female family. And by this measure, Bago seems likely to prove best at up to a mile and a quarter.

Before the Criterium International, Bago was unbeaten in three starts. He opened his account in a newcomers' event at Deauville in August and won twice the following month. The opposition was no better than Listed class for the Prix des Aigles, which served as the ideal graduation race for Bago. Much more was needed in the Group 3 Prix des Chenes back at Longchamp but, powering away to beat Valixir by a length and a half, Bago earned a triple-figure Racing Post Rating.

The latter contest was the closest Bago came to encountering top of the ground; judging by the times, it was genuinely good going that day. The prospect of faster conditions, if connections have it in mind to travel to Newmarket, Epsom or The Curragh with Bago next season, might be a quandary. "We won't be making any decisions about the colt's future until the spring," the Niarchos family's racing manager, Alan Cooper, reported. "He is already in the Epsom Derby and the Irish Classics and will be put in all the top races when they close."

Bago's next appearance is awaited with huge anticipation, wherever it proves to be. The Poule d'Essai des Poulains over a mile at Longchamp might even be too sharp for him, if the ground comes up fast. Moreover, he would be likely to face American Post. Newmarket seems a bigger gamble, however, with One Cool Cat, Grey Swallow and the rest in opposition. If Bago's stamina was assured, the Prix Lupin/Prix du Jockey-Club is the traditional route for French middle-distance horses. If he does not get a mile and a half, however, the chance for Classic glory will have passed.

On decisions like these rests the fate of a potential champion.

Bago

bay/brown colt, 3-2-2001

	Red God	Nasrullah
		Spring Run
Blushing Groom		
	Runaway Bride	Wild Risk
		Aimee
Nashwan		
ch 1986		
	Bustino	Busted
		Ship Yard
Height Of Fashion		
	Highclere	Queen's Hussar
		Highlight
	Northern Dancer	Nearctic
		Natalma
Nureyev		
	Special	Forli
		Thong
Moonlight's Box		
b 1996		
	Mr Prospector	Raise A Native
		Gold Digger
Coup de Genie		
	Coup de Folie	Halo
		Raise The Standard

Bred by Niarchos Family in France

Sire Nashwan

Won 6 of 7 races, inc. 2,000 Guineas-Gr1, Derby-Gr1, Eclipse S.-Gr1, King George VI & Queen Elizabeth S.-Gr1. Big, rangy individual and a superb mover. A tip-top performer from 8-12f, much the most impressive of his generation. Died in July 2002. Sire of: Wandesta (Santa Ana H.-Gr1, Santa Barbara H.-Gr1, Matriarch S.-Gr1), Aqaarid (Fillies' Mile-Gr1), Didina (Gr2), Myself (Gr3), Silent Warrior (Gr3), Swain (Coronation Cup-Gr1, King George VI & Queen Elizabeth S.-Gr1 (twice)), Bint Salsabil (Gr3), Bint Shadayid (Gr3), One So Wonderful (York International S.-Gr1), Elhayq (Gr2), Haami (Gr3), Rabah (Gr3), Special Nash (Gr2), Mistle Song (Gr3), Nadia (Prix Saint-Alary-Gr1), Najah (Gr2), With Reason (Gr3), Bago (Criterium International-Gr1).

Dam Moonlight's Box

Unraced, but is a half-sister to Gr1 winner Denebola and Gr3 winners Snake Mountain and Loving Kindness, her dam's only other racing-age produce. Dam of Bago (2001 c by Nashwan; unbeaten Gr1 winner).

Pedigree assessment

Several of the 2003 crop of two-year-olds did nothing wrong. None of them did everything more convincingly right than Bago, who more than lived up to the hype that had developed around him over his first three races by winning the fourth in devastating style. Remarkably, he is only the second son of Nashwan to win a juvenile Pattern event, and the second – after Swain – to have won more than once in Pattern company, but the wait for a second superstar might now be over. There is every reason to believe that Bago will train on, and the recent record of his connections on the distaff side of his pedigree allows confidence in his merit. How far he will stay is a moot point, given that Nashwan's progeny have a stamina index in excess of ten furlongs, while the family is more noted for its speed than its staying power. It seems likely that the family will hold sway. *TM*

Big Bad Bob (Ire)

3yo brown colt   **121**

Bob Back (USA) - Fantasy Girl (Ire) (Marju (Ire))
Owner Windflower Overseas Holdings Inc
Trainer J L Dunlop
Breeder Windflower Overseas Holdings Inc

Career: **12** starts | won **7** | second **2** | third **0** | **£95,814** win and place

By John Hopkins

THREE wins from six starts, including a success in Group company, might have all the appearances of a creditable 2003 campaign, but Big Bad Bob arguably did not reach the heights expected of him and his season ended in a heavy defeat in Germany.

The free-going son of Bob Back began the season on the fringes of the Derby picture after winning his last four starts at two, culminating in an impressive victory in the Listed Autumn Stakes at Ascot, in which he had made all in typical fashion to defeat the useful Rainwashed Gold by three and a half lengths. That race had been won by such luminaries as Nayef, Daliapour, Dr Fong and Nashwan, and connections added Big Bad Bob to the Derby entry at the first supplementary stage on April 10 at a cost of £9,000, although the Italian Derby remained a likely alternative.

The race chosen to determine the route Big Bad Bob would take was the extended ten-furlong Dee Stakes at Chester – a logical target, given that he had won twice at the track as a two-year-old. In the event, only three others turned out, with his main rival appearing to be Barry Hills's recent Lingfield maiden winner Private Charter. Sent off the 4-9 favourite, Big Bad Bob was ridden by Kieren Fallon in preference to Sir Michael Stoute's challenger, the unconsidered 20-1 shot Kris Kin. The first sign that all was not going to plan came after just two furlongs, when Big Bad Bob, leading as usual, jinked on the road crossing the track. Fallon would have had a greater shock when Kris Kin, ridden by Fergal Lynch, came sailing past inside the final furlong; Big Bad Bob was swamped for speed and was beaten two lengths into second. Fallon reported that his mount had not travelled as well as he had hoped, and Derby ambitions were shelved.

After an absence of more than a month, Big Bad Bob returned to attempt a mile and a half for the first time in Royal Ascot's Group 2

Big Bad Bob (Pat Eddery) makes all to land the Listed Prix Ridgway at Deauville in August

King Edward VII Stakes, his stock having risen considerably in the meantime when Kris Kin landed a massive gamble under Fallon in the Derby. Sent off 11-4 second favourite, he was pressed for the lead by Delsarte and set far too strong a pace before folding tamely when headed two out, eventually finishing last of the eight runners, more than 18 lengths behind the winner, High Accolade. Worryingly, paddock watchers reported that he had not coped with the preliminaries and was not developing physically.

It is to the credit of John Dunlop's team that Big Bad Bob's career was quickly turned around. A minor five-runner conditions event over an extended ten furlongs at Haydock in mid-July was the launch-pad and, after enjoying an uncontested lead, Big Bad Bob drew right away from Lundy's Lane to win by 11 lengths. The bare form indicated this was a colt up to winning in Group company and any suggestion that it had been a 'soft' success was dispelled when the runner-up won a conditions event at Kempton next time from Royal Lodge winner Al Jadeed

2003   Race record

11th Ernst & Young Euro-Cup (Group 2) (Frankfurt, September 21) 3yo+ 10f Soft **50** 11 ran. *Set strong pace, headed 2f out, weakened quickly, beaten 36l by Fruhlingssturm*

1st Furstenberg-Rennen (Group 3) (Baden-Baden, August 31) 3yo 10f Good **121** 7 ran. *Made all, went 5l clear 2f out, eased closing stages, beat Senex by ¾l*

1st Prix Ridgway (Listed) (Deauville, August 10) 3yo 10f Good to soft **112** (TS 102) 7 ran. *Made all, pushed out, ran on strongly, beat Bailador by 2l*

1st GAP Personnel Conditions Stakes (Haydock, July 19) 3yo 10½f Good to firm **122** (TS 82) 5 ran. *Raced keenly, soon led, drew clear 3f out, ran on well, beat Lundy's Lane by 11l*

8th King Edward VII Stakes (Group 2) (Ascot, June 20) 3yo 12f Good to firm **88** (TS 58) 8 ran. *Raced freely, led at fast pace, headed over 2f out, soon weakened, eased final furlong, beaten 18½l by High Accolade*

2nd Philip Leverhulme Dee Stakes (Group 3) (Chester, May 8) 3yo 10½f Good to firm **115** (TS 82) 4 ran. *Soon led, jinked on road crossing after 2f, gradually increased pace from over 3f out, headed inside final furlong, not pace of winner, beaten 2l by Kris Kin*

2002

1st Tom McGee Autumn Stakes (Listed) (Ascot, October 12) 2yo 1m Good to firm **111** (TS 81) 6 ran ● **1st** Renault Master Vans Conditions Stakes (Chester, September 25) 2yo 7½f Good to firm **96** (TS 63) 5 ran ● **1st** Rippleffect Novice Stakes (Chester, August 29) 2yo 7½f Good **101** (TS 62) 7 ran ● **1st** nitex.co.uk Median Auction Maiden Stakes (Newcastle, August 16) 2yo 7f Good **91** (TS 40) 11 ran ● **2nd** EBF Median Auction Maiden Stakes (Folkestone, July 29) 2yo 7f Good to firm **83** (TS 35) 11 ran ● **7th** Mercedes-Benz of Newbury EBF Maiden Stakes (Newbury, July 4) 2yo 7f Good to firm **71** (TS 28) 13 ran

and a couple of older horses.

With ten furlongs established as his trip, Big Bad Bob completed a straightforward victory in the Listed Prix Ridgway at Deauville in August, beating Bailador by two lengths on significantly softer ground than when successful previously, and later that month he was on his travels again, this time to Germany.

Odds-on for the Group 3 Furstenberg-Rennen at Baden-Baden, he again made all and was five lengths clear two out before Pat Eddery allowed him to coast to victory by three-quarters of a length from Senex. Again the form looked strong – the runner-up had previously finished second to Policy Maker, later a promoted winner of the Group 2 Grand Prix de Deauville – and it confirmed Big Bad Bob among the second tier of middle-distance three-year-olds. Dunlop reported that the colt had "learned to be more amenable", but that he "needs it good or faster".

Big Bad Bob returned to Germany for what turned out to be his last race of the season in the Group 2 Ernst & Young Euro-Cup at Frankfurt on soft ground in September. The good work of the previous months seemed to come undone; he went off too fast and was beaten two out, finishing last of 11, some 36 lengths behind the winner, Fruhlingssturm, whom he had beaten into fifth on his previous start.

Jockey John Egan had to dismount shortly after the line with the colt exhausted on what was an extremely warm day. Fortunately, he was

Big Bad Bob

brown colt, 30-3-2000

Bob Back br 1981	Roberto	Hail To Reason	Turn-to Nothirdchance
		Bramalea	Nashua Rarelea
	Toter Back	Carry Back	Saggy Joppy
		Romantic Miss	Beauchef Roman Zephyr
Fantasy Girl br 1994	Marju	Last Tycoon	Try My Best Mill Princess
		Flame Of Tara	Artaius Welsh Flame
	Persian Fantasy	Persian Bold	Bold Lad (Ire) Relkarunner
		Gay Fantasy	Troy Miss Upward

Bred by Windflower Overseas Holdings Inc in Ireland

Sire **Bob Back**

Won 5 of 21 starts, inc. Premio Tevere-Gr2, Premio Presidente della Repubblica-Gr1, Prince of Wales's S.-Gr2), also 2nd Derby Italiano-Gr1, Man o'War S.-Gr1. Form over 12f but best over 10f. By Derby winner and influential middle-distance stallion out of triple US Graded winner. Stands at Ballylinch Stud as a dual-purpose sire, 2003 fee €6,500. Oldest progeny 14. Sire on Flat of: Bob's Return (St Leger-Gr1), Inner City (Gr3), Wren (Gr3), Big Bad Bob (Gr3).

Dam **Fantasy Girl**

Unplaced in 9 starts. By top-class miler out of fair 12f winner who was Listed-placed over 2m. Dam of: Demosthenes (1999 c by Lycius; unplaced), Big Bad Bob (2000 c by Bob Back; Gr3 winner), 2001 c by Sri Pekan, 2002 f by Charnwood Forest.

Pedigree assessment

Given that his sire has done best on the Flat with middle-distance performers and that his dam comes from a good, quite stout family, Big Bad Bob should stay 12f on pedigree. However, Bob Back was best over 10f and Marju over 1m, and it is possible the free-running Big Bad Bob takes more after them in distance terms. There is every encouragement on pedigree that he will continue to do well at four. *JH*

reported to be none the worse for the experience afterwards.

Big Bad Bob's requirements are straightforward. Although he is bred to stay further, he is ideally suited by ten furlongs and his best form is on a good or fast surface when allowed an uncontested lead – aside from his maiden victory, his six other wins have come in fields of seven or fewer. He reportedly stays in training and looks sure to clock up the miles in Europe again.

Black Sam Bellamy (Ire)
4yo bay colt   **123**

Sadler's Wells (USA) - Urban Sea (USA) (Miswaki (USA))
Owner Michael Tabor
Trainer A P O'Brien
Breeder Sunderland Holdings Ltd And Orpendale

Career: **18** starts | won **4** | second **2** | third **3** | **£444,206** win and place

By Alan Sweetman

GALILEO'S full-brother Black Sam Bellamy provided early vindication of John Magnier's decision to keep him in training as a four-year-old with an emphatic victory in the Tattersalls Gold Cup at The Curragh in May. Although this looked the weakest renewal of the ten-furlong contest since it obtained Group 1 status in 1999, his performance in beating British challenger Highdown by eight lengths proved all the more reassuring on account of the fact that the race came less than a month after he had trailed in last of nine finishers behind Fair Mix in the Prix Ganay at Longchamp.

The manner of his victory confirmed the definite preference for soft going that had been evident in his form at two and three, but it was not until October, when he contested the Prix de l'Arc de Triomphe in a supporting role for stablemate High Chaparral for the second year in succession, that he again had ground conditions to suit.

Undoubtedly the most curious aspect of Black Sam Bellamy's 18-race career, spanning three seasons, is the fact that he competed in Ireland on just three occasions and that he maintained an unbeaten record on home territory. His first two outings, in the autumn of his juvenile season, were in maidens at Newmarket, before he formed part of a major assault by Ballydoyle on the Criterium de Saint-Cloud in November. The outcome was one of several triumphs for the stable in the juvenile category during the 2001 season, with Black Sam Bellamy completing a one-two-three behind Ballingarry and Castle Gandolfo.

The following April the Sadler's Wells colt gave a workmanlike performance to land the odds in a mile-and-a-quarter maiden at The Curragh, and that was to be his single appearance in Ireland as a three-year-old. Following a promoted second in the Group 2 Prix Hocquart at Longchamp, he was sent back to France to contest the Prix du Jockey-Club and emerged with a respectable fifth place behind Sulamani, just

**Black Sam Bellamy (Mick Kinane) runs away with the
Group 1 Tattersalls Gold Cup at The Curragh in May**

in front of his stablemates Castle Gandolfo and Diaghilev. Next on his
agenda was Royal Ascot, where he was stepped up in distance to contest
the Queen's Vase. Sent off favourite, he never looked happy on the fast
ground and was soundly beaten in fifth behind Mamool. Having missed
a scheduled engagement in the St Leger, it was three and a half months
before he appeared again as High Chaparral's Arc pacemaker. A long-
prominent showing set him up perfectly for the Gran Premio del Jockey
Club at San Siro two weeks later and, with the ground in his favour
and Mick Kinane at his strongest, he prevailed narrowly from the Yorkshire
Oaks runner-up Guadalupe to secure his first Group 1 victory.

On his initial venture as a four-year-old, Black Sam Bellamy impressed
as a well-matured sort in making all to beat useful dual-purpose performer
Holy Orders in a ten-furlong Listed race at Leopardstown. Thereafter,
he was campaigned exclusively at Group 1 level and his Tattersalls Gold
Cup victory marked his third and final appearance in Ireland.

He earned respect in defeat behind Warrsan and Highest in the
Coronation Cup but did not have the resources of stamina to be competitive
over the extended distance of the Gold Cup at Royal Ascot. It was back
to ten furlongs for his next outing in Germany. After trying to make all
at a strong pace he weakened into fifth place in a contest in which his

2003   Race record

4th Gran Premio Del Jockey Club (Group 1) (San Siro, October 19) 3yo+ 12f Good **102** 5 ran. *Set good pace until headed 3f out, weakened, beaten 13l by Ekraar*

6th Prix de l'Arc de Triomphe Lucien Barriere (Group 1) (Longchamp, October 5) 3yo+ 12f Holding **117** (TS 104) 13 ran. *Tracked leader, led halfway to over 3f out, 2nd straight, weakened well over 1f out, beaten 10½l by Dalakhani*

2nd Grosser Bugatti Preis (Grosser Preis von Baden) (Group 1) (Baden-Baden, September 7) 3yo+ 12f Good **123** 8 ran. *Led after 2f, headed 1f out, kept on under strong pressure, beaten ½l by Mamool*

5th Grosser Dallmayr-Preis (Bayerisches Zuchtrennen) (Group 1) (Munich, August 3) 3yo+ 10f Good **110** 7 ran. *Soon led, set strong pace until headed 2f out, no extra, beaten 4¾l by Ransom O'War*

8th Gold Cup (Group 1) (Ascot, June 19) 4yo+ 2m4f Good to firm **112** (TS 55) 12 ran. *Chased leader 11f, stayed in 3rd, ridden 3f out, weakened over 1f out, beaten 11l by Mr Dinos*

3rd Vodafone Coronation Cup (Group 1) (Epsom, June 6) 4yo+ 12f Good **122** (TS 98) 9 ran. *Pressed leader, led 3f out, soon ridden and pressed, joined well over 1f out, narrowly headed inside final furlong, kept on well, beaten ½l by Warrsan*

1st Tattersalls Gold Cup (Group 1) (Curragh, May 25) 4yo+ 10½f Yielding to soft **123** (TS 92) 8 ran. *Close up in 2nd, ridden entering straight, soon led, clear 2f out, stayed on strongly, impressive, beat Highdown by 8l*

9th Prix Ganay (Group 1) (Longchamp, April 27) 4yo+ 10½f Very soft **98** (TS 84) 9 ran. *Soon led, pushed along entering straight, headed 2f out, ridden and soon weakened, beaten 13½l by Fair Mix*

1st Alleged Stakes (Listed) (Leopardstown, March 29) 4yo+ 10f Good **116** (TS 87) 8 ran. *Made all, ridden and quickened clear from 2f out, easily, beat Holy Orders by 2½l*

2002

1st Gran Premio del Jockey Club e Coppa d'Oro (Group 1) (San Siro, October 20) 3yo+ 12f Soft **118** 8 ran ● **10th** Prix de l'Arc de Triomphe - Lucien Barriere (Group 1) (Longchamp, October 6) 3yo+ 12f Good **114** (TS 100) 16 ran ● **5th** Queen's Vase (Group 3) (Ascot, June 21) 3yo 2m Good to firm **99** (TS 57) 14 ran ● **5th** Prix du Jockey-Club (Group 1) (Chantilly, June 2) 3yo 12f Good **111** (TS 89) 15 ran ● **2nd** Prix Hocquart (Group 2) (Longchamp, May 8) 3yo 12f Good **111** (TS 92) 7 ran ● **1st** Hotel Keadeen Maiden (Curragh, April 7) 3yo 10f Good to yielding **95** 18 ran

Other notable runs

2001 3rd Criterium de Saint-Cloud (Group 1) (Saint-Cloud, November 13) 2yo 10f Heavy **110** 10 ran

Tattersalls Gold Cup victim Highdown finished second. Second place behind Mamool in the Grosser Bugatti Preis was a fairer reflection of a level of ability which he confirmed by finishing sixth in the Arc.

A year earlier the Longchamp showpiece had provided the launch pad for his Milan triumph and O'Brien was hoping for a repetition of history in the Gran Premio del Jockey Club, but his bid produced a tame fourth place as the much-travelled Ekraar brought the curtain down on his career with a first Group 1 victory. It may have been one race too many for a horse who had been in action from the outset of the season.

He has been retired to stud in Germany and will stand at Gestut Fahrhof.

Black Sam Bellamy   *bay colt, 21-4-1999*

			Nearco
		Nearctic	Lady Angela
	Northern Dancer		
		Natalma	Native Dancer
Sadler's Wells			Almahmoud
b 1981			
		Bold Reason	Hail To Reason
			Lalun
	Fairy Bridge		
		Special	Forli
			Thong
			Raise A Native
		Mr Prospector	Gold Digger
	Miswaki		
		Hopespringseternal	Buckpasser
Urban Sea			Rose Bower
ch 1989			
		Lombard	Agio
			Promised Lady
	Allegretta		
		Anatevka	Espresso
			Almyra

Bred by Sunderland Holdings Ltd and Orpendale in Ireland

Sire Sadler's Wells

Won 6 of 11 races, inc. Beresford S.-Gr3, Irish Derby Trial-Gr2, Irish 2,000 Guineas-Gr1, Eclipse S.-Gr1, Phoenix Champion S.-Gr1. Also 2nd in Prix du Jockey-Club-Gr1, King George VI & Queen Elizabeth S.-Gr1. Impeccably bred top-class performer from 8-12f, handsome, tough and consistent. Sire of Gr1 winners: Braashee, French Glory, In The Wings, Old Vic, Prince Of Dance, Scenic, Salsabil, Opera House, Saddlers' Hall, El Prado, Johann Quatz, Masad, Barathea, Fatherland, Fort Wood, Intrepidity, Carnegie, King's Theatre, Northern Spur, Moonshell, Muncie, Poliglote, Chief Contender, Dance Design, Luna Wells, Cloudings, Ebadiyla, Entrepreneur, In Command, Kayf Tara, Dream Well, Greek Dance, King Of Kings, Leggera, Commander Collins, Daliapour, Montjeu, Saffron Walden, Aristotle, Beat Hollow, Subtle Power, Galileo, Imagine, Milan, Perfect Soul, Sequoyah, Ballingarry, Black Sam Bellamy, Gossamer, High Chaparral, Islington, Quarter Moon, Sholokhov, Alberto Giacometti, Brian Boru, Refuse To Bend, Yesterday.

Dam Urban Sea

Won 8 races from 2 to 5, inc. Prix Exbury-Gr3, Prix Gontaut-Biron-Gr3, Prix de l'Arc de Triomphe-Gr1, Prix d'Harcourt-Gr2, also placed Prix Vermeille-Gr1, Canadian International S.-Gr1, Prix Ganay-Gr1. Tough, effective 10-12f. Very closely related to 2,000 Guineas winner King's Best and half-sister to dam of Prix du Jockey-Club winner Anabaa Blue. Dam of: Urban Ocean (1996 c by Bering; Gr3 winner), Melikah (1997 f by Lammtarra; Listed winner, Gr1-placed), Galileo (1998 c by Sadler's Wells; Classic winner), Black Sam Bellamy (1999 c by Sadler's Wells; Gr1 winner), Atticus (2000 c by Sadler's Wells; unraced), All Too Beautiful (2001 f by Sadler's Wells; unraced), My Typhoon (2002 f by Giant's Causeway).

Pedigree assessment

Not nearly as good as his brother Galileo, but still had the class to collect an Irish Group 1 win over ten furlongs. He should prove popular at Gestut Fahrhof – where his fee is €7,500 for 2004 – and the fact that he comes from a German family will be no hindrance. Will undoubtedly sire mainly middle-distance progeny. *TM*

Bollin Eric

4yo bay colt   **124**

Shaamit (Ire) - Bollin Zola (Alzao (USA))
Owner Sir Neil Westbrook
Trainer T D Easterby
Breeder Sir Neil And Lady Westbrook

Career: **18** starts | won **4** | second **4** | third **5** | **£506,293** win and place

By Tom O'Ryan

T TAKES more than just ability. If a horse's achievements were further measured by toughness and consistency, then Bollin Eric would surely be entitled to take even higher rank on the scoresheet. As the four-year-old prepares to take up stallion duties at the National Stud, his impressive CV is hallmarked by a glowing testament to his durability. In 18 races, he finished out of the first four only once, and that in no less an acid test than the Prix de l'Arc de Triomphe.

His 2002 St Leger triumph made him only the second winner of an English Classic in 25 years to be trained in the North, but that Group 1 success meant that it was never going to be easy for him in 2003. Looking bigger, stronger and more mature than he had done as a three-year-old, he made his reappearance in the old John Porter Stakes at Newbury. Beaten just over three lengths into fourth by Warrsan, he produced a performance that more than satisfied his trainer Tim Easterby, who confessed that, so well had Bollin Eric done over the winter, "he looked more like a show-horse than a racehorse" when he stripped him of his paddock sheet beforehand.

The Group 2 Yorkshire Cup, closer to home, was chosen as his next outing. Once again saddled with his Group 1-winning penalty, he was sent off the 2-1 favourite and his supporters were sitting pretty early in the home straight as Kevin Darley gave him the office to go and he quickly asserted his superiority. However, after producing a striking, but brief, injection of pace, Bollin Eric drifted to his left and began to make heavy weather of his task. Headed by old foe Warrsan more than a furlong out, the two of them were then overhauled by Mamool, fourth to Bollin Eric in the St Leger, who went on to win by half a length, with the local hope finishing rather tamely back in third.

'Grandstand jockeys' seemed to adopt the view that Darley had gone for home too soon, but such criticism, made as always in hindsight,

**Bollin Eric (Kevin Darley) wins the Group 3 Lonsdale
Stakes at York in August**

should perhaps have been balanced by the fact that Bollin Eric's regular
rider was entitled to believe that his St Leger-winning partner would
stay on strongly. The overriding impression was that the colt still had not
quite come to himself. It did not take long, though, before he did.

Faced with the decision of where to go next, and over what distance,
Easterby decided to forgo the step up to two and a half miles in the Ascot
Gold Cup and revert to the 12 furlongs of the Hardwicke Stakes. Given
a more patient ride, Bollin Eric, once more carrying his 5lb penalty, ran
a blinder, striking the front approaching the final furlong, only to be
nailed late on by Indian Creek, who took the spoils by a neck, with the
remainder of the field three lengths and more in arrears.

On the face of it, Bollin Eric proved slightly disappointing on his next
start in the Princess of Wales's Stakes at Newmarket, finishing fourth
to Millenary, beaten four lengths, but Easterby subsequently discovered
that the colt was slightly lame after losing a shoe during the race. The
King George VI and Queen Elizabeth Diamond Stakes was targeted as
Bollin Eric's next assignment, his first Group 1 assault since the St Leger.
He acquitted himself handsomely, finishing fourth, beaten a total of six
lengths, and, most notably, chasing home three Derby winners in
Alamshar, Sulamani and Kris Kin.

Stepped up to two miles for the first (and only) time, in the Group 3
Lonsdale Stakes at York the following month, Bollin Eric comfortably
accounted for Cover Up, Zindabad and Persian Punch. The scene was

2003   Race record

8th Prix de l'Arc de Triomphe Lucien Barriere (Group 1) (Longchamp, October 5) 3yo+ 12f
Holding **112** (TS 98) 13 ran. *Rear early, headway halfway, 4th straight, weakened well over 1f
out, beaten 13½l by Dalakhani*

4th Irish Field St Leger (Group 1) (Curragh, September 13) 3yo+ 1m6f Good to firm **120** (TS
34) 6 ran. *Held up in rear, progress into 4th after halfway, kept on under pressure from 2f out,
beaten 2l by Vinnie Roe*

1st Weatherbys Insurance Lonsdale Stakes (Group 3) (York, August 19) 3yo+ 2m Good to
firm **123** (TS 79) 6 ran. *Held up, effort over 3f out, stayed on to lead over 1f out, ran on well,
beat Cover Up by 2l*

4th King George VI And Queen Elizabeth Diamond Stakes (Group 1) (Ascot, July 26) 3yo+
12f Good **124** (TS 98) 12 ran. *Took keen hold early, held up behind leaders, ridden over 3f out,
unable to quicken over 2f out, stayed on same pace from over 1f out, beaten 6l by Alamshar*

4th Princess of Wales's UAE Equestrian And Racing Federation Stakes (Group 2) (Newmarket
(July), July 8) 3yo+ 12f Good **121** (TS 100) 6 ran. *Chased leaders, ridden and every chance over
1f out, no extra inside final furlong, beaten 4l by Millenary*

2nd Hardwicke Stakes (Group 2) (Ascot, June 21) 4yo+ 12f Firm **124** (TS 116) 9 ran. *Took
keen hold, held up in 5th, effort over 2f out, progress to lead over 1f out, driven final furlong,
headed last 75yds, ran on but just held, beaten nk by Indian Creek*

3rd Emirates Airline Yorkshire Cup (Group 2) (York, May 15) 4yo+ 1m6f Good to firm **121**
(TS 101) 8 ran. *Tracked leaders, quickened to lead over 3f out, edged left over 2f out, headed
over 1f out, weakened and eased well inside final furlong, beaten 4½l by Mamool*

4th Dubai Irish Village Stakes (Registered As The John Porter Stakes) (Group 3) (Newbury,
April 12) 4yo+ 12f Good to firm **118** (TS 88) 9 ran. *Reared in stalls, behind, headway over 3f
out, chased winner over 2f out, no impression, one pace final furlong, beaten 3¼l by Warrsan*

2002

1st Rothmans Royals St Leger (Group 1) (Doncaster, September 14) 3yo 1m6½f Good to firm
122 (TS 99) 8 ran ● **3rd** Great Voltigeur Stakes (Group 2) (York, August 20) 3yo 12f Good
117 (TS 95) 6 ran ● **3rd** Manchester Evening News July Trophy Stakes (Listed) (Haydock, July
14) 3yo 12f Good to firm **108** (TS 48) 3 ran ● **2nd** King Edward VII Stakes (Group 2) (Ascot,
June 21) 3yo 12f Good to firm **110** (TS 85) 7 ran ● **2nd** Convergent Dante Stakes (Group 2)
(York, May 15) 3yo 10½f Good to firm **116** (TS 81) 9 ran ● **3rd** Feilden Stakes (Listed)
(Newmarket, April 18) 3yo 9f Good to firm **108** (TS 80) 10 ran

Other notable runs

2001 1st Ralph Raper Memorial Prince of Wales Cup (Nursery) (Doncaster, September 13) 2yo
1m Good **95** (TS 64) 18 ran ● **1st** EBF Beverley Lions Median Auction Maiden Stakes
(Beverley, August 26) 2yo 8½f Good to firm **82** 12 ran

set for him to bid to become the first horse to complete the English-
Irish St Leger double. Little, though, went right for him at The Curragh.
Held up in a moderately run race, he was caught flat-footed when the
tempo suddenly increased half a mile from home. As Vinnie Roe
battled to a historic third Leger win ahead of Gamut and Great Voltigeur
winner Powerscourt, Bollin Eric, staying on strongly again at the end,
was beaten just two lengths into fourth place.

Bollin Eric again finished behind Vinnie Roe in the Arc, but the pair
were unplaced in the Longchamp showpiece, both comfortably beaten

Bollin Eric   *bay colt, 18-2-1999*

		Busted	Crepello
			Sans le Sou
	Mtoto		
		Amazer	Mincio
			Alzara
Shaamit			
b 1993			
		Habitat	Sir Gaylord
			Little Hut
	Shomoose		
		Epithet	Mill Reef
			Namecaller
		Lyphard	Northern Dancer
			Goofed
	Alzao		
		Lady Rebecca	Sir Ivor
			Pocahontas
Bollin Zola			
b 1986			
		Ballad Rock	Bold Lad
			True Rocket
	Sauntry		
		Crestia	Prince Tenderfoot
			Indian Maid

Bred by Sir Neil and Lady Westbrook in England

Sire Shaamit

Won 2 of 6 races, inc. Derby S.-Gr1. Also 3rd in King George VI & Queen Elizabeth S.-Gr1. Leggy, somewhat unprepossessing individual, but a high-class 12f performer with a good turn of foot, effective on good and faster ground. Died 2001. Sire of: Bollin Eric (St Leger S.-Gr1, Lonsdale S.-Gr3).

Dam Bollin Zola

Won 2 of 10 races. Lengthy sort. Useful handicapper at 3 years, probably best at 7f, effective on any ground. Dam of: Bollin Mary (1991 f by Chilibang; placed, died at 3), Bollin Sophie (1992 f by Efisio; unplaced), Bollin Joanne (1993 f by Damister; Gr3 winner), Bollin Terry (1994 c by Terimon; winner), Bollin Ann (1995 f by Anshan; winner), Bollin Roland (1996 c by Reprimand; unplaced), Bollin Rock (1997 g by Rock City; unplaced), Bollin Eric (1999 c by Shaamit; Classic winner).

Pedigree assessment

The 2002 St Leger winner showed admirable consistency almost throughout his four-year-old career, failing to run to form only in the Arc, where he encountered soft ground for the first time in his life. In the course of the season he defied critics who felt he lacked the pace to prove a potent factor over 12 furlongs, notably as runner-up in the Hardwicke Stakes and fourth in the King George, and those who reckoned his free-running style would inhibit him at two miles were contradicted by his Lonsdale Stakes victory at York. He was a thoroughly likeable racehorse. Now he must seek to become a favourite with breeders, having returned to his birthplace, the National Stud. *TM*

in holding ground in a race won so memorably by the classy Dalakhani.

Bollin Eric will be memorable for other reasons, not least in the North, and particularly to Easterby and Darley in providing each of them with their first English Classic triumphs. Owned and bred by Sir Neil and Lady Westbrook, loyal patrons of the Easterby family through three generations, 'Eric' did them proud. Nobody could have asked for more.

Brian Boru

3yo bay colt **125**

Sadler's Wells (USA) - Eva Luna (USA) (Alleged (USA))

Owner Mrs John Magnier

Trainer A P O'Brien

Breeder Juddmonte Farms

Career: **9** starts | won **3** | second **2** | third **2** | **£511,039** win and place

By Alan Sweetman

THE summer of 2002 marked one of the most difficult periods experienced by Aidan O'Brien since his installation at Ballydoyle. The stable housed a dual Derby hero in High Chaparral and an evolving legend in Rock Of Gibraltar, but for the first time since the start of O'Brien's tenure, many of the two-year-olds fell victim to a coughing epidemic. It was a tribute to the steely resilience that lies beneath the trainer's youthful exterior that he managed to overcome the crisis well before the end of the campaign. The horse who did most to rescue the situation was Brian Boru, a Sadler's Wells colt out of the American-bred Eva Luna, an Alleged mare with the same name as the Irish-bred filly who won the 1994 Phoenix Stakes for Jim Bolger.

Brian Boru's dam won the Park Hill Stakes over a mile and six, so there was quiet satisfaction at Ballydoyle when he recovered from a slow break to win a maiden over seven furlongs first time out at The Curragh in June 2002. Soon afterwards, the coughing outbreak began to take hold and more than three months elapsed before Brian Boru returned to The Curragh as the selected of four runners for O'Brien in the Beresford Stakes, a race won by his sire in 1983 and by the stable in six successive years from 1996. Made favourite to continue that sequence, Brian Boru hit the front a furlong out but failed to resist a powerful challenge from the John Oxx-trained Alamshar.

Against the background of his layoff, it was a satisfactory effort, auguring well for his chance in the Racing Post Trophy just under two weeks later. With the team now well on the way back to full health, Powerscourt and The Great Gatsby also lined up in the Doncaster event won by High Chaparral the previous year. It was not the strongest renewal, and conditions were testing, but Brian Boru showed a good attitude and hinted forcibly at reserves of stamina in wearing down Powerscourt.

Brian Boru's three-year-old campaign started on a respectable note

Brian Boru (Jamie Spencer) gets the better of High Accolade in the Seabiscuit St Leger at Doncaster

in the Derrinstown Stud Derby Trial at Leopardstown in May. Burdened with a Group 1 penalty, it was never going to be an easy task and third place behind Alamshar and The Great Gatsby was sufficient to confirm the long-held conviction of connections that he was their leading hope for the Vodafone Derby.

However, Epsom provided the nadir of Brian Boru's season. He began to lose contact over two furlongs out, just when it might have been expected that his stamina would kick into action, and dropped away tamely. Three weeks later in the Budweiser Irish Derby at The Curragh, Mick Kinane rejected him in favour of Epsom runner-up The Great Gatsby, with Jamie Spencer taking over. In securing fourth place, Brian Boru turned around that aspect of the Epsom form, but with the race dominated by Alamshar and Dalakhani, his reputation was now in decline.

After an absence of nearly two months, the rehabilitation process got underway with a fine second behind Powerscourt in the Great Voltigeur Stakes at York. O'Brien now faced a dilemma concerning St Leger options. He could attempt to win two Group 1s on the same day by sending one of the York principals to The Curragh and the other to Doncaster, or send both to Doncaster on the basis that the final British Classic, for

2003   Race record

3rd Pattison Canadian International (Grade 1) (Woodbine, October 19) 3yo+ 12f Yielding **117** 10 ran. *Raced in last, closed up approaching straight, 8th on wide outside straight, ridden 1½f out, stayed on to line, beaten 1l by Phoenix Reach*

1st Seabiscuit St Leger Stakes (Group 1) (Doncaster, September 13) 3yo 1m6½f Good **125** (TS 97) 12 ran. *Held up and behind, smooth headway over 3f out, led approaching final furlong, hard ridden and edged left, kept on well, beat High Accolade by 1¼l*

2nd Daily Telegraph Great Voltigeur Stakes (Group 2) (York, August 19) 3yo 12f Good to firm **121** (TS 92) 9 ran. *Held up, good headway over 2f out, led just inside final furlong, headed and no extra towards finish, beaten nk by Powerscourt*

4th Budweiser Irish Derby (Group 1) (Curragh, June 29) 3yo 12f Good **117** (TS 99) 9 ran. *Towards rear, progress early straight, moderate 4th and kept on from 1½f out, beaten 6½l by Alamshar*

16th Vodafone Derby (Group 1) (Epsom, June 7) 3yo 12f Good **92** (TS 63) 20 ran. *Tracked leaders, close 6th on inner straight, soon ridden, weakened well over 2f out, beaten 21l by Kris Kin*

3rd Derrinstown Stud Derby Trial Stakes (Group 2) (Leopardstown, May 11) 3yo 10f Good to yielding **109** (TS 101) 6 ran. *Held up, 5th into straight, 4th over 1f out, kept on under pressure, beaten 2¾l by Alamshar*

2002

1st Racing Post Trophy (Group 1) (Doncaster, October 26) 2yo 1m Soft **114** (TS 56) 9 ran ● **2nd** Juddmonte Beresford Stakes (Group 3) (Curragh, October 13) 2yo 1m Good to yielding **110** (TS 44) 10 ran ● **1st** EBF Flemings Garage Maiden (Curragh, June 28) 2yo 7f Good **90** (TS 64) 12 ran

all its current reputation as a faded glory, might still be considered more prestigious than its all-aged Irish equivalent. In the end, only Brian Boru was dispatched to Doncaster, where he was installed as 5-4 favourite in a field of 12, befitting his status as the only Group 1 winner in the line-up. With Kinane staying at home to partner Powerscourt at The Curragh, Spencer again took the ride, and rose to the challenge in magnificent fashion. Two months later he replaced Kinane as stable jockey at Ballydoyle.

Switching off his mount at the rear, he began to wind him up from around three furlongs out and got to the front a furlong from home. Although Brian Boru's resolution had been called into question in some quarters, he maintained his effort under strong pressure to see off the challenge of High Accolade, the only Group 2 winner in the race.

If Spencer won plaudits for his tactical awareness at Doncaster, such was not the case in the Canadian International at Woodbine the following month, the consensus being that he overdid the waiting tactics in a race won by the St Leger third, Phoenix Reach.

However, the essential objective of Brian Boru's season had been accomplished in securing the Classic victory that must have appeared a fading dream for O'Brien on the evening after the Vodafone Derby. He stays in training at four in a bid to consolidate a restored reputation.

Brian Boru

bay colt, 16-3-2000

		Nearctic	Nearco
			Lady Angela
	Northern Dancer		
		Natalma	Native Dancer
Sadler's Wells			Almahmoud
b 1981			
		Bold Reason	Hail To Reason
			Lalun
	Fairy Bridge		
		Special	Forli
			Thong
		Hoist The Flag	Tom Rolfe
			Wavy Navy
	Alleged		
		Princess Pout	Prince John
Eva Luna			Determined Lady
b 1992			
		Star Appeal	Appiani
			Sterna
	Media Luna		
		Sounion	Vimy
			Esquire Girl

Bred by Juddmonte Farms in England

Sire Sadler's Wells

Won 6 of 11 races, inc. Beresford S.-Gr3, Irish Derby Trial-Gr2, Irish 2,000 Guineas-Gr1, Eclipse S.-Gr1, Phoenix Champion S.-Gr1. Also 2nd in Prix du Jockey-Club-Gr1, King George VI & Queen Elizabeth S.-Gr1. Impeccably bred top-class performer from 8-12f, handsome, tough and consistent. Sire of Gr1 winners: Braashee, French Glory, In The Wings, Old Vic, Prince Of Dance, Scenic, Salsabil, Opera House, Saddlers' Hall, El Prado, Johann Quatz, Masad, Barathea, Fatherland, Fort Wood, Intrepidity, Carnegie, King's Theatre, Northern Spur, Moonshell, Muncie, Poliglote, Chief Contender, Dance Design, Luna Wells, Cloudings, Ebadiyla, Entrepreneur, In Command, Kayf Tara, Dream Well, Greek Dance, King Of Kings, Leggera, Commander Collins, Daliapour, Montjeu, Saffron Walden, Aristotle, Beat Hollow, Subtle Power, Galileo, Imagine, Milan, Perfect Soul, Sequoyah, Ballingarry, Black Sam Bellamy, Gossamer, High Chaparral, Islington, Quarter Moon, Sholokhov, Alberto Giacometti, Brian Boru, Refuse To Bend, Yesterday.

Dam Eva Luna

Unraced until 4 years, won 4 of 9 races, inc. Park Hill S.-Gr3. Tall, sparely-made sort. Smart stayer, consistent, effective on good to firm and soft ground, stayed 2m well. Dam of Moon Search (1999 f by Rainbow Quest; Group 2 winner in France), Brian Boru (2000 c by Sadler's Wells; Classic winner), Soviet Moon (2001 f by Sadler's Wells; unraced to date).

Pedigree assessment

Only two started at shorter odds than Brian Boru in the Derby; only four finished behind him. Of the two excuses offered for him at the time – failure to act on the course, and failure to act on the ground – the second was soon proved invalid, as at The Curragh and at York he encountered similar underfoot conditions and coped well enough. His Voltigeur effort was striking enough to make him a warm favourite for the St Leger and he collected that Classic with aplomb. As his pedigree predicted, staying is his game and at 12 furlongs in the best company it seems likely that he will continue to be found wanting. He could well come into his own as a Cup horse. *TM*

Bright Sky (Ire)

4yo chestnut filly **120**

Wolfhound (USA) - Bright Moon (USA) (Alysheba (USA))
Owner Ecurie Wildenstein
Trainer E Lellouche
Breeder Dayton Investments Ltd

Career: **16** starts | won **6** | second **4** | third **3** | **£436,745** win and place

By Robert Carter

WAS Bright Sky as good in 2003 as she had been in 2002, when she won the Prix de Diane and Prix de l'Opera? Certainly – even though her sole success was in a Group 2 and she was beaten when a hot favourite to win another Opera.

Connections had thought of her as a candidate for the Arc – a race in which the Wildenstein stable has an excellent record with older fillies, and an even better one all round – ever since her success in the Prix de l'Opera on Arc day 2002. However, the Opera was the race she ended up contesting again, plans having been changed only eight days before. It seemed a sensible decision considering Bright Sky had run poorly behind Falbrav when trying 11 furlongs in the 2002 Japan Cup. That view was confirmed by her disappointing effort when she finally attempted a mile and a half in the Breeders' Cup Turf. Unfortunately the change of plan did not return the expected dividend in the Opera.

Bright Sky took on Falbrav again when she made her seasonal debut in the Group 1 Prix d'Ispahan, run in heavy rain at Longchamp in mid-May. She had the help of Poussin as pacemaker but, though always well in touch, Dominique Boeuf allowed all except Execute to race in front of her. Falbrav was handier and got through on the rail to lead more than one furlong out while Bright Sky was challenging on the outside. He was holding her throughout the final furlong but Bright Sky ran on well without being given a hard race and was beaten only one and a half lengths.

She did not reappear until the Group 2 Prix d'Astarte on the opening Sunday of the main Deauville meeting in August. That straight mile contest was also the race chosen to bring back Six Perfections after her difficulties in both the English and Irish 1,000 Guineas, and she started favourite at 5-4, with Bright Sky third in the betting at 49-10. Bright Sky raced well in touch from her rail draw while Six Perfections was running very

Bright Sky (Dominique Boeuf, nearside) just beats Six Perfections in the Prix d'Astarte at Deauville in August

freely on the outside. When Six Perfections joined the leaders a furlong and a half out Bright Sky, who had moved off the rail, was being pushed along close behind them. Six Perfections hit the front below the distance but, while Thierry Thulliez pushed her out all the way, Boeuf was winding up a strong challenge. He hit Bright Sky three times inside the final furlong and she came outside the favourite to head her 80 yards from home and then hold her, pushed out from that point, by a neck.

The Prix d'Astarte was a race Bright Sky's connections wanted to win more. Perhaps not surprisingly, they did not take on Six Perfections again in the Prix Jacques le Marois over course and distance two weeks later, a prize which the Niarchos family have loved to win ever since they began to sponsor it under the Haras de Fresnay-le-Buffard banner in 1986. Six Perfections was their eighth winner of the race since that date.

Bright Sky waited for the Group 1 Prix du Moulin at Longchamp, over a right-handed mile on the first Sunday of September, for which she started favourite. She settled in fourth behind Lohengrin, Nebraska Tornado and Refuse To Bend as far as the straight but was caught flat-footed when Nebraska Tornado quickened to challenge one and a half furlongs out. She ran on to be beaten half a length and one length by Nebraska Tornado and Lohengrin and was never touched with the whip.

After that, she looked a good thing for the Prix de l'Opera and started a hot favourite. Boeuf eased her off the rails to avoid the weakening pacemakers approaching the straight and moved her up to third. Bright

2003   Race record

6th John Deere Breeders' Cup Turf (Grade 1) (Santa Anita, October 25) 3yo+ 12f Firm **115** 9 ran. *Disputed 6th, ridden and disputing 4th straight, soon beaten, beaten 8¼l by Johar and High Chaparral*

3rd Prix de l'Opera - Casino Barriere d'Enghien (Group 1) (Longchamp, October 5) 3yo+ 10f Holding **115** (TS 91) 11 ran. *Raced in 6th on inside, shaken up and headway to go 3rd straight, pushed along over 2f out, led 1½f out, ran on until headed close home, beaten ½l by Zee Zee Top*

3rd Netjets Prix du Moulin de Longchamp (Group 1) (Longchamp, September 7) 3yo+ 1m Good to soft **117** (TS 91) 14 ran. *Disputed 3rd, 4th straight, outpaced over 1f out, ran on inside final furlong, nearest at finish, beaten 1½l by Nebraska Tornado*

1st Prix d'Astarte (Group 2) (Deauville, August 3) 3yo+ 1m Good to soft **117** (TS 104) 12 ran. *Mid-division on rail, disputing 5th halfway, pushed along 1½f out, quickened and headway to challenge approaching final furlong, ridden to lead close home, beat Six Perfections by nk*

2nd Prix d'Ispahan (Group 1) (Longchamp, May 18) 4yo+ 9f Soft **120** (TS 107) 8 ran. *Held up towards rear in 7th, disputed 5th on outside straight, progress and quickened to challenge 2f out, went 2nd over 1f out, ran on to line, beaten 1½l by Falbrav*

2002

13th Japan Cup (Grade 1) (Nakayama, November 24) 3yo+ 11f Firm **102** 16 ran ● **1st** Prix de l'Opera - Casino Barriere d'Enghien les Bains (Group 1) (Longchamp, October 6) 3yo+ 10f Good **123** (TS 99) 12 ran ● **3rd** Prix Vermeille Hermitage Barriere de la Baule (Group 1) (Longchamp, September 15) 3yo 12f Good to firm **113** (TS 100) 11 ran ● **1st** Prix de Diane Hermes (Group 1) (Chantilly, June 9) 3yo 10½f Good **117** (TS 99) 15 ran ● **2nd** Prix Saint-Alary (Group 1) (Longchamp, May 19) 3yo 10f Good (TS 88) 12 ran ● **2nd** Prix Vanteaux (Group 3) (Longchamp, April 28) 3yo 9f Good (TS 79) 8 ran ● **2nd** Prix Finlande (Listed) (Longchamp, April 7) 3yo 9f Good to firm (TS 69) 7 ran

Other notable runs

1st Prix Belle Sicambre (Maisons-Laffitte, November 12) 2yo 9f Heavy 8 ran ● **1st** Prix de la Faisanderie (Longchamp, October 21) 2yo 9f Heavy 7 ran ● **1st** Prix Deauville Aime Le Cheval (Maiden Fillies) (Clairefontaine, July 22) 2yo 7f Soft 15 ran

Sky went second early in the straight and hit the front one and a half furlongs out. But she could not draw away and was caught by Zee Zee Top and Yesterday, both of whom came with flying runs on the wide outside, four or five strides from home. They beat her by a head and a neck, while Trumbaka rallied on the rail to be only a head further back.

Bright Sky followed up with a poor run at Santa Anita, but that was only her fifth race of the year and the Wildensteins were keen to give her one more chance in Hong Kong. They brought back Aquarelliste, her immediate predecessor as winner of the Prix de Diane, as a five-year-old and sent her to stud only after she had won the Group 3 Prix Exbury and run ninth to Moon Ballad in the Dubai World Cup. Both the late Daniel Wildenstein and his sons, Alec and Guy, have been keen to see their fillies race beyond the age of three. The Wildensteins' Allez France and All Along both won the Arc at four and Bright Sky, though she will not emulate them, may still have more to give.

Bright Sky

chestnut filly, 8-5-1999

			Nearctic
		Northern Dancer	Natalma
	Nureyev		
		Special	Forli
Wolfhound			Thong
ch 1989			Tom Fool
		Buckpasser	Busanda
	Lassie Dear		
		Gay Missile	Sir Gaylord
			Missy Baba
			Raise A Native
		Alydar	Sweet Tooth
	Alysheba		
		Bel Sheba	Lt Stevens
Bright Moon			Belthazar
ch 1990			Nijinsky
		Ile de Bourbon	Roseliere
	Bonshamile		
		Narration	Sham
			Diary

Bred by Dayton Investments Ltd in Ireland

Sire **Wolfhound**

Won 6 of 16 races, inc. Diadem S.-Gr3, Prix de la Foret-Gr1, Haydock Park Sprint Cup-Gr1. Smallish, strong, good-bodied type, effective on any ground and up to 7f. Fluent mover, and an honest, consistent performer who could set the pace or come from behind. Sire of: Bright Sky (Prix de Diane-Gr1, Prix de l'Opera-Gr1).

Dam **Bright Moon**

Won 5 of 13 races, inc. Prix Minerve-Gr3, Prix de Pomone-Gr2, Grand Prix d'Evry-Gr2, Prix de Pomone-Gr2. Also 3rd in Prix Vermeille-Gr1, 4th in Grand Prix de Saint-Cloud-Gr1, 5th in Prix de l'Arc de Triomphe-Gr1. Lengthy, strong sort, effective on any ground. Never ran at less than 10.5f, lacked acceleration to be a tip-top performer at 12f, but always competitive, granted a strong pace. Wore blinkers, but extremely game and consistent. Dam of: Bright Stone (1996 g by Bigstone; winner), Buffalo Dance (1997 f by Sadler's Wells; unplaced), Big Shot (1998 g by Lure; placed), Bright Sky (1999 f by Wolfhound; Classic winner), Blue Icon (2000 f by Peintre Celebre; winner), Boukhara (2001 f by Rainbow Quest; unraced to date).

Pedigree assessment

The great breeders obtain successful results from sires who fail for others, and the Wildensteins, pere et fils, have long been celebrated in that regard. Bright Sky represents a case in point as the only product of any distinction in Europe by Wolfhound, who was banished to South Africa with a dire reputation to live down. In 2003 she could not emulate her achievements of the previous year, when she twice scored at Group 1 level, but that should not be taken to indicate that her form fell away. She beat Six Perfections in the Group 2 Prix d'Astarte, ran right up to her best when third in the Prix du Moulin, and her only sub-par performance came against proven superiors in the Breeders' Cup Turf. It will be fascinating to see how Alec Wildenstein chooses to mate her. *TM*

Carnival Dancer
5yo bay horse   **122**

Sadler's Wells (USA) - Red Carnival (USA) (Mr Prospector (USA))
Owner Cheveley Park Stud
Trainer Mrs A J Perrett
Breeder Cheveley Park Stud Ltd

Career: **17** starts | won **5** | second **3** | third **1** | **£229,475** win and place

By Seb Vance

THERE cannot be many more daunting challenges for a trainer than being charged with improving a former Sir Michael Stoute inmate. If the Newmarket genius can't get to the bottom of a horse, then who can? Well, in this case, it was Amanda Perrett, who welcomed Carnival Dancer to her Sussex yard as a five-year-old for the 2003 season.

A Group 3 winner at three, he had been only lightly raced in 2002 but had given another glimpse of what he might be capable of with his fourth to Storming Home in the Champion Stakes at Newmarket. In 2003 he enjoyed a full season and eclipsed all his previous efforts, having much his most successful campaign and signing off by finding only one too good in the Champion Stakes. Even taking into account that he may have improved with age, Perrett must take the lion's share of the credit, as the horse's owners, Cheveley Park Stud, quite rightly recognised.

Reflecting on Carnival Dancer's season, the stud's managing director, Chris Richardson, said: "We've always said he has a lot of ability and the change of scenery has really worked this year. I couldn't compliment Amanda and Mark Perrett and their team enough for what they've achieved with him."

It is a shame that Perrett does not have the chance to add to those achievements, as instead Carnival Dancer embarks on a new career at his owners' stud. A ten-furlong Group 1 contest could well have been within his compass had he stayed in training, for he had multiple Group 1 winners Russian Rhythm, Alamshar, Nayef and Vespone all well beaten in the Champion, where only Rakti, who arrived fresh at Newmarket after just two previous runs in 2003, proved his superior.

A 33-1 chance and ridden for the first time by Darryll Holland, who was on a high following his Dewhurst win on fellow 'spare' Milk It Mick earlier in the day, Carnival Dancer was held up as usual and was still travelling smoothly entering the final two furlongs, looking booked for

Carnival Dancer (Olivier Peslier) wins La Coupe at Longchamp, the first of two Group 3 wins in France

a place at worst. However, he was hampered approaching the final furlong and in no time at all Rakti had flown. It would be fanciful to say Carnival Dancer was an unlucky loser, but nevertheless he ran a blinder.

Interestingly, this personal best came on ground that was officially good to firm, which had hitherto been regarded as unsuitable. But as High Chaparral confirmed in the Breeders' Cup Turf, not all Sadler's Wells' progeny appreciate juice and it is a shame this preconception was not shattered earlier. Who knows what Carnival Dancer might have achieved had he been given more opportunities on a similar surface?

Carnival Dancer won three races for Perrett, although the year had started inauspiciously in the Gordon Richards Stakes at Sandown, where Pat Eddery took over the reins for the first time and adopted more positive tactics. Carnival Dancer hit the front fully three furlongs from home but faded to finish fifth of eight behind Indian Creek, whom he later had behind him in third place in the Champion.

A return to more restrained tactics in a conditions race at Newmarket did the trick next time and this time Eddery was at his best, staying cool when apparently hemmed in on the stands' rails approaching the two-furlong marker. He gradually angled Carnival Dancer to the outside to obtain a run and and then seized his moment when the gap came.

A highly respectable third to the mighty Falbrav in the Prix d'Ispahan was followed by two wins at Group 3 level back in France on good to soft, sandwiched between which was a close second in another Group 3,

2003   Race record

2nd Emirates Airline Champion Stakes (Group 1) (Newmarket, October 18) 3yo+ 10f Good to firm **122** (TS 100) 12 ran. *Held up, headway and hampered over 1f out, ridden to chase winner inside final furlong, stayed on, beaten 2l by Rakti*

11th Prix Dollar - Fouquet's Barriere (Group 2) (Longchamp, October 4) 3yo+ 9½f Holding **92** (TS 51) 14 ran. *Held up, 11th straight, never a factor, beaten 15l by Weightless*

1st Prix Gontaut-Biron (Group 3) (Deauville, August 16) 4yo+ 10f Good to soft **120** (TS 91) 8 ran. *Raced in 4th, shaken up approaching straight, pushed along and headway in centre 2f out, ridden over 1f out and ran on to lead 150yds out, ran on well, beat Without Connexion by ½l*

2nd Meld Stakes (Group 3) (Leopardstown, July 26) 3yo+ 10f Good to firm **122** (TS 81) 5 ran. *Held up in touch, 4th and ridden 2f out, 2nd and challenged inside final furlong, kept on well under pressure, just failed, beaten hd by Mingun*

1st La Coupe (Group 3) (Longchamp, June 19) 4yo+ 10f Good to soft **111** (TS 90) 9 ran. *In touch, disputing 3rd straight, shaken up over 1½f out and not clear run, headway in centre from 1f out to lead close home, pushed out, beat Naheef by ½l*

3rd Prix d'Ispahan (Group 1) (Longchamp, May 18) 4yo+ 9f Soft **117** (TS 104) 8 ran. *In touch in 6th, 7th on inside straight, pushed along 2f out, ridden and ran on from over 1f out to take 3rd final 100yds, beaten 4½l by Falbrav*

1st The Curragh 'Home of The Irish Classics' Conditions Stakes (Newmarket, May 3) 4yo+ 10f Good **107** (TS 69) 10 ran. *Held up in touch, switched right over 1f out, ridden to lead inside final furlong, ran on strongly, beat Sensible by 1¾l*

5th Bet attheraces 0800 083 83 83 Gordon Richards Stakes (Group 3) (Sandown, April 26) 4yo+ 10f Good **105** (TS 86) 8 ran. *Tracked leader 7f out, led over 3f out, shaken up and headed 2f out, gradually faded, beaten 5½l by Indian Creek*

2002

13th Premio Roma-SIS (Group 1) (Capannelle, November 17) 3yo+ 10f Good to soft **55** 14 ran ● **4th** Emirates Airline Champion Stakes (Group 1) (Newmarket, October 19) 3yo+ 10f Good **117** (TS 94) 11 ran ● **5th** TFMCyntergy Ltd Winter Hill Stakes (Group 3) (Windsor, August 24) 3yo+ 10f Good to firm **87** (TS 67) 5 ran ● **4th** Gala Bingo Berkshire Stakes (Listed) (Windsor, May 26) 4yo+ 11½f Soft **103** 6 ran

Other notable runs

2001 1st Sodexho Prestige Scottish Classic (Group 3) (Ayr, July 16) 3yo+ 10f Good to soft **118** (TS 62) 6 ran ● **1st** Michael Sobell Maiden Stakes (York, June 16) 3yo 1m Good to soft **89** (TS 64) 6 ran **2000 4th** Lawdirect Conditions Stakes (Newmarket, October 27) 2yo 1m Soft **84** (TS 59) 10 ran

this time in Ireland. His first win came in La Coupe at Longchamp, where he beat Naheef by half a length after Olivier Peslier had left it late. Peslier was back in the saddle again for the Prix Gontaut-Biron at Deauville, where he settled Carnival Dancer in fourth before bringing the 6-5 favourite up the centre of the track to lead inside the final furlong and beat Without Connexion by half a length.

His last appearance in France came in the Prix Dollar at Longchamp on the Saturday of Arc weekend. The holding ground was meant to suit, but, like the majority of British challengers, he failed to cope with it anything like so well as the locals. He ran a stinker, but it was the only blip in an otherwise creditable campaign.

Carnival Dancer

bay horse, 22-1-1998

		Nearctic	Nearco
	Northern Dancer		Lady Angela
		Natalma	**Native Dancer**
Sadler's Wells			Almahmoud
b 1981		Bold Reason	Hail To Reason
	Fairy Bridge		Lalun
		Special	Forli
			Thong
		Raise A Native	**Native Dancer**
	Mr Prospector		Raise You
		Gold Digger	Nashua
Red Carnival			Sequence
b 1992		Seattle Slew	Bold Reasoning
	Seaside Attraction		My Charmer
		Kamar	Key To The Mint
			Square Angel

Bred by Cheveley Park Stud in Britain

Sire Sadler's Wells

Won 6 of 11 races, inc. Beresford S.-Gr3, Irish Derby Trial-Gr2, Irish 2,000 Guineas-Gr1, Eclipse S.-Gr1, Phoenix Champion S.-Gr1. Also 2nd in Prix du Jockey-Club-Gr1, King George VI & Queen Elizabeth S.-Gr1. Impeccably bred top-class performer from 8-12f, handsome, tough and consistent. Sire of Gr1 winners: Braashee, French Glory, In The Wings, Old Vic, Prince Of Dance, Scenic, Salsabil, Opera House, Saddlers' Hall, El Prado, Johann Quatz, Masad, Barathea, Fatherland, Fort Wood, Intrepidity, Carnegie, King's Theatre, Northern Spur, Moonshell, Muncie, Poliglote, Chief Contender, Dance Design, Luna Wells, Cloudings, Ebadiyla, Entrepreneur, In Command, Kayf Tara, Dream Well, Greek Dance, King Of Kings, Leggera, Commander Collins, Daliapour, Montjeu, Saffron Walden, Aristotle, Beat Hollow, Subtle Power, Galileo, Imagine, Milan, Perfect Soul, Sequoyah, Ballingarry, Black Sam Bellamy, Gossamer, High Chaparral, Islington, Quarter Moon, Sholokhov, Alberto Giacometti, Brian Boru, Refuse To Bend, Yesterday.

Dam Red Carnival

Won 2 of 7 races, inc. Cherry Hinton S.-Gr2, also placed in Nell Gwyn S.-Gr3 and Challenge S.-Gr2. Superbly bred, sister to US champion 2yo filly Golden Attraction and very closely related to Gr1 winner Cape Town (by Seeking The Gold) out of Gr1 Kentucky Oaks winner. Dam of: Carnival Dancer (1998 c by Sadler's Wells; Gr3 winner, Gr1-placed), Funfair (1999 g by Singspiel; Listed winner), Desert Lord (2000 c by Green Desert; winner).

Pedigree assessment

Below the highest class, which is reflected in his starting fee of £4,000 at Cheveley Park Stud. But he possesses an outstanding pedigree; his sire also has established pair Barathea and In The Wings in Europe, while his dam is from a family that has done superbly both in the US and in Europe. Speed on his dam's side will prevent him from being a one-dimensional influence for stamina. His chance at stud may well depend on the quality of mares he receives from Cheveley Park itself; given good opportunities, he could do well. *JH*

Carry On Katie (USA)

2yo brown filly **109**

Fasliyev (USA) - Dinka Raja (USA) (Woodman (USA))
Owner Mohammed Rashid
Trainer J Noseda
Breeder Swordlestown Stud

Career: **3** starts | won **3** | **£153,308** win and place

By James Willoughby

GODOLPHIN mean business in 2004. The annual transfer of horses owned by the Maktoums and their associates from other stables is the strongest yet. Carry On Katie is an obvious standout among the draft of last season's juveniles, having completed an unbeaten season for trainer Jeremy Noseda in the Group 1 Cheveley Park Stakes at Newmarket. The Fasliyev filly had made her debut in the famous black-and-white livery of Lucayan Stud at Ascot in July where, starting 7-4 favourite in a five-runner maiden, she was wildly impressive in beating Three Secrets by 12 lengths.

She was obviously of Pattern-race potential, so one can therefore only wonder how much Dubai businessman Mohammed Rashid stumped up to secure her purchase. His resolve would have been stiffened by the advice of Sheikh Mohammed, who was reportedly very taken by Carry On Katie's performance.

Carry On Katie went at least some way to defraying her price tag in the Group 2 Peugeot Lowther Stakes at York in August. Conditions were significantly faster and the opposition markedly tougher than at Ascot. She made light of both.

Noseda had warned that Carry On Katie might not be experienced enough for the Lowther. It looked as if he would be proved correct when she went down to post a bundle of nerves. Her talent still shone through. Frankie Dettori wisely allowed her to stride on in front against the stands rail. She travelled powerfully, gradually winding up the pressure on her eight opponents, before subduing them finally with an extra surge of energy below the distance.

In the aftermath of her two-length defeat of Badminton, there were plenty who wanted to focus more on her temperament than the quality of her performance. In addition to her antics on the way to post, she had tended to drift markedly left in the closing stages. Plenty of horses

Carry On Katie (Frankie Dettori) holds off Majestic Desert to land the Cheveley Park at Newmarket in October

do the same at York, however, the pull-up area being a sharp dog-leg in that direction.

Flighty she may be, ungenuine she is not. Carry On Katie once more looked a handful in the preliminaries for the Cheveley Park, but this time she was taken to post steadily some 15 minutes before the off. She came back altogether more focused. Dettori again allowed Carry On Katie to get on with it. This time, however, she was taken on and headed by the speedy China Eyes. It seemed as if she had been forced to go a step too quickly when Majestic Desert came flying at her in the Dip, but she managed to lengthen her stride and hold on by a short head.

While Carry On Katie deserved huge credit for her success in the context of the run of the race, her performance was removed from the stalk-and-pounce style of a potential 1,000 Guineas winner. Her free-going tendencies look to have become ingrained and the obvious conclusion is that she races like a sprinter. Her former trainer does not concur. "I think she has a good chance of getting a mile," Noseda said after the Cheveley Park. "She's relaxing more and growing up more. It will be a test, but I'd be more than hopeful. She has as good a chance as anything in next year's Guineas."

Simon Crisford, Godolphin's racing manager, appears to take a more

2003   Race record

1st Sky Bet Cheveley Park Stakes (Group 1) (Newmarket, October 2) 2yo 6f Good to firm **109** (TS 52) 10 ran. *Led over 4f out, ridden over 1f out, ran on, beat Majestic Desert by shd*

1st Peugeot Lowther Stakes (Group 2) (York, August 21) 2yo 6f Good to firm **106** (TS 70) 9 ran. *Very free going to post, made all, hung left and edged towards centre after 1f, shaken up over 1f out, ran on well, beat Badminton by 2l*

1st Merchant Maiden Stakes (Ascot, July 25) 2yo 6f Good **106** (TS 53) 5 ran. *Dwelt, took keen hold and led after 1f, set moderate pace and ran green, pushed clear inside final 2f, easily, beat Three Secrets by 12l*

conservative stance. "It depends what trip she wants," he said. "We've still got the Guineas very much in mind, if her owner Mohammed Rashid decides to point her there."

Carry On Katie's pedigree is reasonably encouraging about her prospects of getting a mile. Though her sire Fasliyev was a brilliant two-year-old over six furlongs, he never got the chance to try longer distances due to injury. He was bred to stay a mile, however, being a son of Nureyev from the family of two Classic-placed colts in the US.

Fasliyev has made a remarkable start at stud which precipitated a quantum leap in his covering fee at Coolmore, from €20,000 to €75,000. Only Sadler's Wells, among the Tipperary stud's other stallions, is more expensive. Fasliyev equalled the record of 34 individual winners in his first season when daughter Ouimonamour won at Maisons-Laffitte in November. The haul included seven stakes winners, four of whom collected European Group races. In addition to Carry On Katie, Much Faster won the Group 2 Prix Robert Papin and Group 3 Prix du Bois, Russian Valour the Group 3 Norfolk Stakes and Kings Point the Group 3 Superlative Stakes.

Carry On Katie's dam is a sister to an ordinary ten-furlong winner out of a half-sister to two top-class winners over the same trip, Grise Mine and Kostroma. There is also middle-distance blood further back.

In addition to Carry On Katie, Godolphin have taken charge of another smart filly in Cairns, an easy winner of the Rockfel Stakes for Mick Channon. At the end of the turf season Carry On Katie was priced at around 10-1 for the Guineas and Cairns a few points longer. In the colts' division, Bayeux, Byron and Kheleyf join the Dubai stable from David Loder, while Duke Of Venice and Leicester Square will both move from Mark Johnston. Sheikh Mohammed's dream of winning the Kentucky Derby with a horse trained in Dubai will rest with Ruler's Court and Tizdubai, both Grade 2 winners in California for Eoin Harty.

Carry On Katie is likely to play a significant part in this impressive team. She seems too highly strung to last out a mile in the Guineas but should still prove an asset to Godolphin. The danger is, however, that her delicate psychological balance may be disturbed by the attempt to stretch her out in distance.

Carry On Katie   *brown filly, 14-1-2001*

		Northern Dancer	Nearctic
	Nureyev		Natalma
		Special	Forli
Fasliyev			Thong
b 1997		Mr Prospector	Raise A Native
	Mr P's Princess		Gold Digger
		Anne Campbell	Never Bend
			Repercussion
		Mr Prospector	Raise A Native
	Woodman		Gold Digger
		Playmate	Buckpasser
Dinka Raja			Intriguing
b/br 1995		Sadler's Wells	Northern Dancer
	Miss Profile		Fairy Bridge
		Katie May	Busted
			Cawston's Pride

Bred by Swordlestown Stud in Kentucky. €100,000 Deauville August yearling

Sire Fasliyev

Unbeaten in 5 races, all at 2 years, inc. Coventry S.-Gr3, Phoenix S.-Gr1, Prix Morny-Gr1. Strong, early-maturing sort, who showed precocious talent before early retirement owing to a fractured pastern. Sire of: Carry On Katie (Cheveley Park S.-Gr1), Kings Point (Gr3), Much Faster (Gr2), Russian Valour (Gr3).

Dam Dinka Raja

Won 1 of 2 races. Late-developing, delicate type and modest performer judged on limited available evidence. Ran only at a mile, but looked capable of staying further. Dam of: Geebeekay (2000 c by Peintre Celebre; unplaced); Carry On Katie (2001 f by Fasliyev; Gr1 winner).

Pedigree assessment

Carry On Katie was a major contributor to the fine first season enjoyed by her much-hyped sire, emulating him as an unbeaten two-year-old, and her transfer to Godolphin was confirmed at the end of October. She will be wintering in Dubai, where she will continue the growing-up process that seemed to be underway when she displayed a more settled character in the Cheveley Park Stakes. There is no knowing yet whether Fasliyev's stock will train on, but Carry On Katie has the physical scope to develop and she should again be effective as a three-year-old. However, with speedy elements dominating in her pedigree background, she seems a dubious proposition for the Rowley Mile and she may always be a sprinter. *TM*

Casual Look (USA)

3yo bay filly **114**

Red Ransom (USA) - Style Setter (USA) (Manila (USA))
Owner W S Farish
Trainer A M Balding
Breeder W S Farish

Career: **11** starts | won **2** | second **2** | third **3** | **£363,587** win and place

By Rodney Masters

THAT will do for starters. A fourth place in the Grand National, a third in the St Leger, a win in the Canadian International at Woodbine, all topped off by an emotion-charged triumph in the Vodafone Oaks, and more than 50 other winners.

In the unlikely event of him taking an hour or two off, Andrew Balding can reflect on a job well done during his first year in charge at Kingsclere's Park House Stables. When he took over the main seat from father Ian at the start of 2003, no doubt he would have settled for that wide variety of achievement.

A debut-season Classic winner at Epsom was not unique, and those to have launched off under that same momentous rocket include Roger Charlton. Quest For Fame's enduring claim to fame was the thrust he gave his trainer's career by winning the 1990 Derby, and Casual Look, who ended the season in the US under the care of Neil Howard, may be best remembered for doing the same for Balding.

A decent juvenile, and a running-on sixth to Russian Rhythm in the 1,000 Guineas, Casual Look arrived at Epsom with reliable form, despite having just one win from half a dozen outings, in a Bath maiden, which she had taken by eight lengths. All in all, a solid case for the Oaks could be made for her within the form book, and that was not lost on punters. A welter of each-way money shrank her odds from 14-1 to 10-1.

With little more than three furlongs to run, a place dividend seemed the most her supporters could expect as, taking a wide path down the middle of the course, she was under a full drive from Martin Dwyer. Summitville, leading the field, appeared to be holding her advantage, possibly extending it. Then, after looking likely to drop back, Casual Look's stamina kicked in and she tenaciously whittled down the leader to seize command in the final 100 yards. Yesterday came late, but too late, and the Balding filly held on by a neck.

Casual Look (Martin Dwyer) just holds Yesterday to land the Oaks at Epsom in June

What happened next provided one of the classic moments of BBC sports coverage in 2003. The camera cut to Clare Balding for a live interview with her brother. No question, just the trickle of tears. The pair were too choked with emotion to speak. Clare, never previously caught short in this way, turned the microphone to her father. Again, the silence was as audible as it was crippling. Not a word was said, but words weren't necessary. It made such refreshing entertainment for millions of viewers because it was so different from the traditional string of clichés.

Then it was on to The Curragh for the Irish Oaks, where Casual Look would seek to become the tenth filly to complete the double. After all the fuss at Epsom as to how unlucky the runner-up had been, it was always going to be a case of Yesterday once more.

So much so that Aidan O'Brien's filly was sent off 11-8 favourite, with Casual Look drifting out to a worryingly generous 7-1. Neither won, but Casual Look, who finished third to Vintage Tipple and L'Ancresse, stretched her advantage to two lengths over the fourth-placed Yesterday. It was the fourth time she had beaten the Irish 1,000 Guineas winner.

Casual Look had chased leader L'Ancresse hard throughout and had nothing in reserve to counter the charge from Vintage Tipple. That tough experience may well have been responsible for her lifeless performance in the following month's Yorkshire Oaks, where the normally consistent

2003   Race record

3rd Queen Elizabeth II Challenge Cup (Grade 1) (Keeneland, October 11) 3yo 9f Firm **107** 10 ran. *Held up in rear, headway well over 2f out, 6th straight, ran on well final furlong, nearest at finish, beaten ¾l by Film Maker*

8th Prix Vermeille Fouquet's Barriere (Group 1) (Longchamp, September 14) 3yo 12f Good to soft **104** (TS 86) 11 ran. *Soon disputing 2nd, headway to lead 4f out, 3 lengths clear approaching straight, ridden 2f out, headed approaching final furlong, no extra, beaten 9¾l by Mezzo Soprano*

7th Aston Upthorpe Yorkshire Oaks (Group 1) (York, August 20) 3yo+ 12f Good to firm **105** (TS 84) 8 ran. *Held up, effort over 4f out, never on terms, beaten 8½l by Islington*

3rd Darley Irish Oaks (Group 1) (Curragh, July 13) 3yo 12f Good **113** (TS 96) 11 ran. *Tracked leader in moderate 2nd, ridden approaching straight, closer in 2nd from under 2f out, no extra inside final furlong, beaten 1¾l by Vintage Tipple*

1st Vodafone Oaks (Group 1) (Epsom, June 6) 3yo 12f Good **114** (TS 75) 15 ran. *Tracked leaders, close 5th straight, ridden and effort on outer over 2f out, driven to challenge 1f out, led last 100yds, just held on, beat Yesterday by nk*

6th Sagitta 1,000 Guineas (Group 1) (Newmarket, May 4) 3yo 1m Good to firm **107** (TS 86) 19 ran. *Chased leaders, not clear run and lost place 2f out, ran on inside final furlong, beaten 4¾l by Russian Rhythm*

2002

2nd Owen Brown Rockfel Stakes (Group 2) (Newmarket, October 19) 2yo 7f Good **106** (TS 64) 11 ran ● **2nd** Meon Valley Stud Fillies' Mile (Group 1) (Ascot, September 28) 2yo 1m Good to firm **106** (TS 72) 10 ran ● **1st** Terry Knight Racegoers Club Maiden Stakes (Bath, September 16) 2yo 1m Firm **82** (TS 55) 5 ran ● **4th** EBF Douglas Maiden Fillies' Stakes (Div I) (Salisbury, August 29) 2yo 7f Good to firm **76** (TS 35) 13 ran ● **3rd** Woodcote Stud Maiden Fillies' Stakes (Ascot, July 12) 2yo 6f Good **71** (TS 38) 8 ran

filly beat home just one of the eight runners, never threatening to take a hand. Dwyer reported that at no stage was she travelling.

Casual Look's swansong in Europe, the Prix Vermeille, raised obvious cause for concern that she was on the decline, because her sequence of match wins against Yesterday came to an end. The latter was beaten a head by Mezzo Soprano, with Casual Look eighth.

Dwyer tracked Yesterday's pacemaker, Butterfly Blue, but the latter folded sooner than anticipated and Casual Look was left three lengths clear into the straight. That is not her preferred method of operation and it was not surprising that she folded quite tamely once headed.

Although she made her US debut in Keeneland's Queen Elizabeth II Challenge Cup in October with Balding's name alongside her own, by then Casual Look was in the care of Howard, who trains all of owner Will Farish's American string. Ridden by Robbie Albarado, she finished fast to claim third, beaten only three-quarters of a length by Film Maker.

It was a highly satisfactory American debut from a filly who will not go down among the best Oaks winners of the past decade, but will long be remembered for the part she played in fast-tracking the career of her trainer.

Casual Look

bay filly, 10-5-2000

Red Ransom b 1987	Roberto	Hail To Reason	Turn-to Nothirdchance
		Bramalea	Nashua Rarelea
	Arabia	Damascus	Sword Dancer Kerala
		Christmas Wind	Nearctic Bally Free
Style Setter ch 1990	Manila	Lyphard	Northern Dancer Goofed
		Dona Ysidra	Le Fabuleux Matriarch
	Charleston Rag	General Assembly	Secretariat Exclusive Dancer
		Music Ville	Charlottesville Meadow Music

Bred by William S Farish in Kentucky

Sire Red Ransom

Won 2 of 3 races up to 6f. Speedy and precocious, had tall reputation, and was bred to stay at least a mile, but career cut short by injury. Sire of: Bail Out Becky (Del Mar Oaks-Gr1), Petrouchka (Gr3), Sri Pekan (Gr2), Upper Noosh (Gr3), Trail City (Gr2), Wandering Star (Gr2), Intikhab (Gr2), Rojo Dinero (Gr3), Comic Strip (Gr3), Stay Sound (Gr3), Crystal Symphony (Gr3), Perfect Sting (Garden City H.-Gr1, Queen Elizabeth II Challenge Cup S.-Gr1, Breeders' Cup Filly & Mare Turf-Gr1), Pico Teneriffe (Gr3), China Visit (Gr2), Ekraar (Gran Premio del Jockey Club-Gr1), Shining Hour (Gr3), Slew The Red (Gr3), New Economy (Gr2), Mr Mellon (Gr2), Van Rouge (Gr3), Cassis (Gr3), Casual Look (Oaks S.-Gr1), Fairly Ransom (Gr2), Ransom O'War (Bayerisches Zuchtrennen-Gr1).

Dam Style Setter

Won 3 of 15 races. Useful miler, placed in minor stakes race, equally effective on dirt and turf. Dam of: Racket Club (1995 g by Alysheba; minor winner on turf and dirt), Shabby Chic (1996 f by Red Ransom; Listed winner, Gr3-placed in France, Gr1-placed in US), Set The Mood (1997 f by Dixie Brass; unraced), unnamed (1998 c by Smart Strike; unraced), American Style (1999 c by Quiet American; smart winner, Gr2-placed), Casual Look (2000 f by Red Ransom; Classic winner), Saville Row (2001 c by Gone West; Listed-placed winner in France).

Pedigree assessment

We did not see vintage versions of the Epsom Classics in 2003. Like Kris Kin, Casual Look showed progressive form up to and including the first weekend in June, but she could not rise above that standard, and at both York and Longchamp she fell some way below it. She showed encouraging signs of a resurgence on her last outing for Andrew Balding in the Queen Elizabeth II Challenge Cup at Keeneland, but a month or so later it was announced that she had been retired and would be covered by Mineshaft. *TM*

Choisir (Aus)

4yo chestnut colt **128**

Danehill Dancer (Ire) - Great Selection (Aus) (Lunchtime (Zim))				
Owner T W Wallace & Partners				
Trainer Paul Perry				
Breeder R M Daisley				

Career: **23** starts	won **7**	second **5**	third **6**	**£889,182** win and place

By Paul Haigh

THERE was a certain amount of good-humoured amusement when it was announced that the Australian sprinter Choisir was coming to Britain to run at Royal Ascot. Even without taking into consideration that he was a southern-hemisphere three-year-old who would be running as a four-year-old and therefore be asked to concede what many think an unfair amount of weight to his near contemporaries, the geographical problems in his path seemed insurmountable. The tilt was reckoned admirably sporting, but essentially quixotic.

There was even more amusement when paddock watchers examined the new arrival in the parade ring before the King's Stand Stakes on the meeting's opening Tuesday. "Hefty", "common-looking" and "tank-like" were three of the adjectives applied. "Looks more like a two-mile chaser," remarked one judge with a perhaps understandably condescending smile. In comparison with some of his more elegant rivals, Choisir did indeed have the rather lumpen look about him of a horse who was probably "going to have trouble getting out of his own way". All of which helps to explain why punters made the – in retrospect – quite astonishing mistake of letting him go off at 25-1.

It would be incorrect to say that all present realised this mistake as soon as the gates opened. In fact, after Johnny Murtagh had bounced 'the tank' out from his middle draw and quickly established a couple of lengths' lead, the acknowledgement that the big chestnut could indeed run a bit really encouraged nothing much more than idle curiosity about the point in the race at which he would inevitably fold. It was only at about the furlong pole that realisation dawned. Choisir wasn't going to do any such thing. In fact, he was in the process of running his rivals into the ground.

The roars of admiration as he cracked Acclamation and the rest were tinged to some extent with disbelief. But to the credit of the Ascot crowd

Choisir (Johnny Murtagh) crowns his spell in Britain with victory in the Group 1 Golden Jubilee at Royal Ascot

there was nothing half-hearted about the reception Choisir, now hastily redesignated "this great bull of a horse", received as he came into the winner's enclosure. Even the racing ignoramuses who attend the meeting primarily for social reasons and the opportunity to suck up champagne were aware of the magnitude of what they had witnessed, what an improbable feat had been achieved.

Maybe nobody actually went wandering round muttering: "This changes everything". But there was certainly an instant recognition of two startling new realities: (a) that there is now nowhere on earth that a horse cannot challenge for a major prize if he really is good enough and (b) that it's not just human Australians we have to worry about in sporting events any more: now it's their bloody horses too.

The other aspect of the revelatory performance that deserves a mention was the way that everyone took to Choisir's own humans; how much they enjoyed owner-trainer Paul Perry's quiet, non-triumphalist satisfaction and the euphoria of Lyle Weaver, the colt's 67-year-old strapper (the Aussie name for a stable lad, and one we might consider as we struggle to find a more respectful term for those who do racing's toughest job).

None of this, however, quite prepared the British racing public for the announcement that, not satisfied with the smash-and-grab raid on the

2003   Race record

2nd Darley July Cup (Group 1) (Newmarket (July), July 10) 3yo+ 6f Good to firm **126** (TS 112) 16 ran. *Led over 4f, unable to quicken near finish, beaten 1½l by Oasis Dream*

1st Golden Jubilee Stakes (Group 1) (Ascot, June 21) 3yo+ 6f Firm **125** (TS 105) 17 ran. *Raced in centre of course and made virtually all, edged gradually to stands' side over 2f out, ridden and ran on strongly final furlong, beat Airwave by ½l*

1st King's Stand Stakes (Group 2) (Ascot, June 17) 3yo+ 5f Good to firm **128** (TS 112) 20 ran. *Made all and soon crossed to nearside rail, drew clear from 2f out, 3l up inside final furlong, pushed out, beat Acclamation by 1l*

6th Rosemount Estate Newmarket Handicap (Group 1) (Flemington, March 8) 3yo+ 6f Good **104** 21 ran. *Prominent throughout, outpaced final 1½f, honest effort, beaten 3¾l by Belle Du Jour*

7th Futurity Stakes (Group 1) (Caulfield, March 1) 4yo+ 7f Good **102** 12 ran. *Led until headed soon after leaving final bend, stayed on one pace straight, beaten 6¼l by Yell*

3rd Oakleigh Plate (Handicap) (Group 1) (Caulfield, February 22) 3yo+ 5½f Good to soft **123** 14 ran. *Missed break and 12th early, improved to 8th turning for home, stayed on strongly straight (not suited by wet track), beaten ½l by River Dove*

1st TEAC Lightning Stakes (Group 1) (Flemington, February 9) 3yo+ 5f Good **123** 9 ran. *(Field split in two down straight track) Made all inside group, beat Spinning Hill by ¾l*

2002

1st Emirates Classic (Group 2) (Flemington, November 7) 3yo+ 6f Good 9 ran ● **3rd** L'Oreal (Flemington, November 2) 6f Good 8 ran ● **3rd** Carlton Draught Caulfield Guineas (Group 1) (Caulfield, October 12) 3yo 1m Good 16 ran ● **3rd** Stan Fox (Randwick, September 28) 7f Good 10 ran ● **4th** Heritage (Rosehill, September 21) 6f Good 9 ran ● **4th** Rom Consul (Randwick, September 7) 6f Good 8 ran ● **5th** Up & Coming (Warwick Farm, August 24) 6f Good 8 ran ● **3rd** Moet & Chandon Champagne Stakes (Group 1) (Randwick, April 13) 2yo 1m Good 6 ran ● **2nd** Lindemans Wines Sires Produce Stakes (Group 1) (Randwick, April 1) 2yo 7f Good 11 ran ● **3rd** AAMI Golden Slipper (Group 1) (Rosehill, March 23) 2yo 6f Good 15 ran ● **2nd** Pago Pago (Rosehill, March 16) 6f Good 7 ran ● **1st** Skyline Stakes (Group 3) (Canterbury, March 2) 2yo 6f Good 5 ran ● **1st** Inglis Stakes (Warwick Farm, January 19) 2yo 6f Good 9 ran ● **2nd** 2yo (Canterbury, January 12) 2yo 5½f Good 12 ran

Group 2 King's Stand, Choisir was going to turn out for the meeting's even more prestigious sprint, the Golden Jubilee Stakes, over an extra furlong on the Saturday. Up a level to Group 1, he was to meet, among others, the filly Airwave, who had created such a powerful impression in coming from last after missing the break to win the Temple Stakes on the bridle.

The mere idea of running twice at the Royal meeting put Choisir's connections in conflict not only with received wisdom but with the RSPCA which, by coincidence, picked that very week to launch an argument that it was somehow cruel to ask any horse to race more than once a week. Nobody told Choisir. As things turned out, if there was any cruelty involved, it was only towards those who wound up having to race against him.

Once again the Australian horse broke with such speed and enthusiasm that most of his rivals were a couple of lengths down before they'd gone

50 yards. However, on this occasion, Murtagh steered a central course from a middle draw, edging only gradually over to the supposedly favoured stands rail as the race progressed.

It was a decision that made no noticeable difference to the outcome. Airwave was again rather slow into stride – though nowhere near as slow as she had been at Sandown – but quickly moved up to the heels of those following the leader, apparently going better than anything. She quickened to get within a length or so of Choisir a furlong out, and that was as far as her progress went. It may have been that 'the bull' just didn't stop, or that the filly just didn't see out the sixth furlong. But in the last 100 yards she was always being held as Choisir, Murtagh, the Perry family and Weaver went on to record what may well have been the most extraordinary double in the meeting's history.

How good a performance was it? Well, the fact that this time, in spite of Tuesday's feat, Choisir went off at 13-2 gives a fair indication of the strength of the opposition. Far behind him were most of the best sprinters Britain could muster. As well as Airwave, the field included the previous year's July Cup and Prix de l'Abbaye winner, Continent, and subsequent Challenge Stakes winner, Just James. In fourth place was the previous season's Guineas fourth, Zipping, who at the time was probably the best sprinter trained in France. And behind too was the filly Belle du Jour, now in the care of Dermot Weld, who had once recorded a victory over Choisir back home in Australia. Only the American challenger, Morluc, who had twice in successive Hong Kong Sprints run to within a head of Falvelon, the Australian whose exploits had encouraged the Perrys to think their horse might be world class, had a valid excuse, as he went lame and trailed in last.

According to Weaver: "The reception he got was better than for a Melbourne Cup. The crowd really know their horses and appreciate a good one. Ascot topped it all off. That was the highlight of my career and I can go home now and say I've been there and I've done that. Even walking back to the dope box the crowd was cheering him. It was unreal."

But that was not the end of the story, because now the British were finally convinced the question that needed an answer was whether 'The Winged Bull', as he was now described, was going to stay on at his temporary quarters at Geoff Wragg's yard and complete the sweep of races that would lead to his coronation as European champion sprinter. The July Cup at Newmarket was the obvious target if he wasn't going home, followed by the Nunthorpe over the five furlongs at York that would probably suit him even better than Ascot's.

For some time the question hung in the air, with Perry proving himself as astute a businessman as he is a trainer as he pondered the best way to maximise his horse's new-found status. "He will not run in the July Cup unless he's sold," was the original line. "But he's definitely for sale." Meanwhile, Airwave was announced to have been in season at the time of the Golden Jubilee, with her connections eager for a rematch if Choisir's chose to take her on again.

Then we were given to understand that Choisir was definitely going home, before a final decision that he'd go for the July Cup after all. At what point a deal had been decided in principle over his ownership is not known, but he was going to run at Newmarket in the same colours as at Ascot.

For the fairy story to have had a perfect ending it would have been necessary for Choisir to have seen off the opposition on the July course with exactly the same panache he'd shown at the Royal meeting. But that was not quite the way it was going to be. Once again Murtagh bounced him out fast – from a plum draw this time – and once again Choisir, sent off favourite for the first time by a converted punting public, established his usual early lead.

But John Gosden had had time to sharpen up Oasis Dream since his third place in the King's Stand, his first outing of the season, and Choisir was never quite able to shake loose. A couple of furlongs out it was clear the Gosden colt was going at least as well as the leader, and with relatively little effort he drew alongside, and then away. Choisir kept on well for second, thereby confirming his previous supremacy over Airwave, and there was certainly no disgrace in his having succumbed to a colt who was immediately hailed as the best British sprinter in years. But there was a hint of anti-climax nevertheless.

Choisir's fans, of which there were now as many as for any visiting horse in memory, began to persuade themselves that the problem was that final furlong, and that over the easy five at York their hero might be able to make the score with the July Cup winner 2-1 in his favour. But that hypothesis was never tested as news emerged that a sale had been agreed with Coolmore and that Choisir was to retire to stud.

The purchasers, shrewd as ever, had seen his potential as a stallion who could sire highly marketable progeny to both southern and northern hemisphere times. But not even they, surely, would have paid the figure of £10 million that was initially bandied about. According to Byron Rogers, nominations manager of Arrowfield Stud in New South Wales: "We were the underbidders at A$9 million." Coolmore are thought to have paid around A$12 million (just under £5 million), which still makes Choisir a valuable sire by sprinting standards.

So does his success open the floodgates to Australian sprinters who want to come and plunder British races, as many British as well as Australian pundits now believe? Possibly, since two, Yell and Spinning Hill, were rated his superiors back home. But how many will actually want to for British prize-money now that Choisir has proved it can be achieved?

What Choisir did, perhaps, was provide Europe with a lesson in how to sprint – straight from the gate and running hard for as long as possible.

Choisir   *chestnut colt, 18-9-1999*

	Danehill	Danzig	Northern Dancer / Pas de Nom
Danehill Dancer b 1993		Razyana	His Majesty / Spring Adieu
	Mira Adonde	Sharpen Up	Atan / Rocchetta
		Lettre d'Amour	Caro / Lianga
Great Selection b 1980	Lunchtime	Silly Season	Tom Fool / Double Deal
		Great Occasion	Hornbeam / Golden Wedding
	Pensive Mood	Biscay	Star Kingdom / Magic Symbol
		Staid	Minor Portion / Straightlaced

Bred by RM Daisley in New South Wales. A$55,000 Inglis Classic yearling

Sire **Danehill Dancer**

Won 4 of 11 races, inc. Phoenix S.-Gr1, National S.-Gr1, Greenham S.-Gr3. Also 2nd in Dewhurst S.-Gr1. Strong, well-made, lengthy sort. Smart performer with a good turn of foot, equally effective at 6f and 7f. Sire in Europe of: Lady Dominatrix (Gr3), Where Or When (Queen Elizabeth II S.-Gr1), Ziria (Gr3), Barbajuan (Gr3), Venturi (Gr3). Also sire of 4 southern hemisphere crops, inc. Jar Jar Binks (Gr3), Choisir (Lightning S.-Gr1, Golden Jubilee S.-Gr1), Private Steer (Stradbroke H.-Gr1).

Dam **Great Selection**

Won 1 of 11 races. Sydney-based sprinter, briefly useful at 2 years, failed to train on. Dam of: Supermarket (1995 f by Zephyr Zip; won 8 races), Great Chic (1996 f by Prince Of Birds; unplaced), Danny Dancer (1998 g by Danehill Dancer; won 3 races), Choisir (1999 c by Danehill Dancer; Gr1 winner).

Pedigree assessment

The bold initiative by Choisir's Australian connections to campaign him in England paid off handsomely, and he enlivened the summer sprinting scene with a scintillating Royal Ascot double. Unfortunately, that enterprise was not matched by his Irish purchasers, who opted to retire him after his defeat by Oasis Dream at Newmarket, where his form was certainly on a par with his previous runs in Britain. He might well have enlivened the autumn as well. A burly brute of a horse, he will be based at Castlehyde Stud in 2004 at a fee of €15,000, while, thanks to his high-profile exploits, his sire has had his fee increased by 50 per cent at Coolmore, to €45,000. *TM*

It's a style that works around the world, though not so often here, where horses are invariably asked to settle even in five-furlong contests. Perhaps what he did couldn't have been done in any but the driest summer since records began. But his great distinction is that he came, he did it, and, whatever happens in future, he'll always remain the first.

Clodovil (Ire)

3yo grey colt **117**

Danehill (USA) - Clodora (Fr) (Linamix (Fr))
Owner Lagardere Family
Trainer A Fabre
Breeder M Lagardere

Career: **8 starts** | won **5** | second **0** | third **0** | **£186,249** win and place

By Robert Carter

JEAN-LUC LAGARDERE, the breeder of Clodovil, died on March 14, 2003, at the age of 75, only two months before that colt stretched his unbeaten record to five in the Gainsborough Poule d'Essai des Poulains. The 2002 season had been Lagardere's worst for ten years, with only 21 wins and just one Pattern-race success, that of Bernimixa in the Group 2 Prix de Pomone. Yet within weeks of his death, both Clodovil and Fair Mix, two seemingly quite ordinary individuals, rose to Group 1 stardom. Fair Mix had been let go 18 months earlier, but Clodovil carried Lagardere's colours, now representing his family.

Lagardere, who had been President of France-Galop – the ruling body of French racing – since 1995, bought his first horse in 1966 and his first stud farm, the Haras du Val-Henry, the following year. He added the Haras d'Ouilly, once the property of Francois Dupre, in 1981 and also adopted the Dupre colours, of grey jacket, pink cap. Lagardere's name did not appear among winning owners until 1975 but he had built a successful stable before that, competing in his wife's name. Resless Kara gave him his first Group 1 success in the 1988 Prix de Diane and Linamix his second in the 1990 Poule d'Essai des Poulains.

Both were homebreds and Lagardere topped the breeders' list on the first of seven occasions thanks to the success of Linamix in 1990. That unfashionably bred grey, who came from the last crop sired by the 1984 Prix du Moulin winner Mendez before his export to Japan, was retired to Val-Henry and remained at the heart of his owner's success. His first 21 Group winners were all homebreds, including Fragrant Mix and Sagamix, whose victories in the Grand Prix de Saint-Cloud and Prix de l'Arc de Triomphe in 1998 propelled Lagardere to the top of the owners' list for the first and only time. However, the Juddmonte Farms-bred Martaline spoiled the sequence when he won the Group 3 Prix d'Hedouville in April.

Clodovil (Christophe Soumillon) tastes Classic success in the Poule d'Essai des Poulains at Longchamp in May

Clodovil, who is out of a Group 2-winning daughter of Linamix, entered the Poule d'Essai as the winner of two midsummer juvenile races and two recent contests. That was good enough to earn favouritism in a field of ten that included three trained by Aidan O'Brien and three from England. Clodovil was keen to get on with it, but Christophe Soumillon restrained him in a close fifth place on the rail as far as the straight. His first attempt at progress was foiled but he found a gap inside the final two furlongs between the leader, Krataios, and Sign Of The Wolf, in spite of Thierry Jarnet's efforts on the latter to keep him in. Clodovil led a furlong and a half from home and was driven out to score by a length and a half from the O'Brien-trained Catcher In The Rye, who came with a strong run after being last into the straight.

Andre Fabre, who trained the son of Danehill, said: "He's a midget who had the guts to squeeze through the gap." Danehill died just two days after the Poulains and Fabre said: "He was the best stallion in the world. He was successful in Europe, Australia and America. His progeny were speedy and genuine and he sired winners over all distances and of both sexes."

It was the Australians who discovered that the speedy Danehill could sire Derby winners, but it was the French who put the finishing touch to that aspect of his career when his son Westerner won the Prix du

2003   Race record

5th Netjets Prix du Moulin de Longchamp (Group 1) (Longchamp, September 7) 3yo+ 1m
Good to soft **115** (TS 80) 14 ran. *Always well in touch, 5th straight, kept on steadily, beaten 4½l by Nebraska Tornado*

8th Prix du Haras de Fresnay-Le Buffard-Jacques le Marois (Group 1) (Deauville, August 17) 3yo+ 1m Good to soft **94** (TS 58) 12 ran. *Held up in rear towards inside, last halfway, ridden over 1½f out, never a threat, beaten 15l by Six Perfections*

5th St James's Palace Stakes (Group 1) (Ascot, June 17) 3yo 1m Good to firm **112** (TS 95) 11 ran. *Chased leaders, ridden to press leaders when not much room inside final 2f, edged left over 1f out, soon one pace, edged right inside final furlong, beaten 4½l by Zafeen*

1st Gainsborough Poule d'Essai des Poulains (Group 1) (Longchamp, May 11) 3yo 1m Good to soft **117** (TS 95) 10 ran. *First to show, restrained in touch, 6th straight on inside, found gap well over 1f out, led approaching final furlong, driven out, beat Catcher In The Rye by 1l*

1st Prix de Fontainebleau (Group 3) (Longchamp, April 20) 3yo 1m Good to soft **106** (TS 53) 6 ran. *Held up in last, went 5th entering straight, headway on outside from 1f out to lead close home, beat Shuttle Diplomacy by nk*

1st Prix Machado (Longchamp, April 6) 3yo 1m Good to soft 4 ran. *Made all, set steady pace until quickening over 2f out, comfortably, beat Marshall by 2l*

2002

1st Prix Fast Fox (Saint-Cloud, July 2) 2yo 6f Good to soft 8 ran ● **1st** Prix Marigot (Unraced Colts & Geldings) (Saint-Cloud, June 5) 2yo 4½f Very soft 6 ran

Cadran and Prix Royal-Oak in October.

Clodovil won his first two races at Saint-Cloud. His small size made him an obvious sort to exploit as a two-year-old and he would have moved on to the Group 3 Prix de Cabourg if injury had not intervened. Instead, he was out of action for nine months until early April 2003, when he beat the subsequent Prix de Guiche winner Marshall by two lengths in a minor race over a mile at Longchamp.

That race was run on the *moyenne piste*, but he switched to the more sweeping turns of the *grande piste* for the Group 3 Prix de Fontainebleau, over the same mile as the Poule d'Essai des Poulains, two weeks later. Clodovil was squeezed out at the start and dropped to last while his stable companion Shuttle Diplomacy took them along, but he came up the outside and ran on well to lead four or five strides from home. Less than half a length covered the first five, but as is often the case in these tight French finishes, the right horse had won.

His Poulains victory obliged Clodovil to take on the best, but his limitations were exposed when he was only fifth to Zafeen in the St James's Palace Stakes, a well-beaten eighth behind Six Perfections in the Prix Jacques le Marois and fifth again behind Nebraska Tornado in the Prix du Moulin. He was beaten a little under five lengths at Ascot and Longchamp and, while both were creditable performances in their own right, he retired to stud without another win. He was bought towards the end of the year by Rathasker Stud, County Kildare, where he will stand for €12,000.

Clodovil

grey colt, 9-4-2000

Danehill b 1986	Danzig	Northern Dancer	Nearctic **Natalma**
		Pas de Nom	Admiral's Voyage Petitioner
	Razyana	His Majesty	Ribot Flower Bowl
		Spring Adieu	Buckpasser **Natalma**
Clodora gr 1994	Linamix	Mendez	Bellypha Miss Carina
		Lunadix	Breton Lutine
	Cloche d'Or	Good Times	Great Nephew Never Angel
		Chrysicabana	Home Guard Copocabana

Bred by Jean-Luc Lagardere in Ireland

Sire Danehill

Won 4 of 9 races, inc. Cork and Orrery S.-Gr3, Haydock Park Sprint Cup-Gr1. Medium-sized, strong, good-bodied individual, markedly back at the knee. Died in May 2003. Sire, in northern hemisphere, of: Danish (Queen Elizabeth II Challenge Cup-Gr1), Kissing Cousin (Coronation S.-Gr1), Danehill Dancer (Phoenix S.-Gr1, National S.-Gr1), Tsukuba Symphony (NHK Mile Cup-Gr1), Desert King (National S.-Gr1, Irish 2,000 Guineas-Gr1, Irish Derby-Gr1), Fairy King Prawn (Yasuda Kinen-Gr1), Tiger Hill (Grosser Preis von Baden-Gr1, twice, Bayerisches Zuchtrennen-Gr1), Indian Danehill (Prix Ganay-Gr1), Wannabe Grand (Cheveley Park S.-Gr1), Aquarelliste (Prix de Diane-Gr1, Prix Vermeille-Gr1, Prix Ganay-Gr1), Banks Hill (Coronation S.-Gr1, Breeders' Cup Filly & Mare Turf-Gr1, Prix Jacques le Marois-Gr1), Mozart (July Cup-Gr1, Nunthorpe S.-Gr1), Regal Rose (Cheveley Park S.-Gr1), Dress To Thrill (Matriarch S.-Gr1), Landseer (Poule d'Essai des Poulains-Gr1), Rock Of Gibraltar (Grand Criterium-Gr1, Dewhurst S.-Gr1, 2,000 Guineas-Gr1, Irish 2,000 Guineas-Gr1, St James's Palace S.-Gr1, Sussex S.-Gr1, Prix du Moulin de Longchamp-Gr1), Spring Star (Gr2), Spartacus (Phoenix S.-Gr1, Gran Criterium-Gr1), Westerner (Prix du Cadran-Gr1, Prix Royal-Oak-Gr1), Clodovil (Poule d'Essai des Poulains-Gr1).

Dam Clodora

Ran only at 3 years, won 3 of 7 races, inc. Prix de l'Opera-Gr2. Showed progressive form in short career, effective on any ground, best at around 9f on fast surface. Dam of: Clodoronic (1999 c by Zafonic; unraced), Clodovil (2000 c by Danehill; Classic winner), Cloridja (2001 f by Indian Ridge; unraced to date).

Pedigree assessment

The Poule d'Essai des Poulains had a substandard look about it, with only the hitherto unbeaten Clodovil hinting he might be of genuine Classic calibre. He duly preserved his perfect record, but first impressions were subsequently confirmed; he never won again, and none of those behind him were to achieve much distinction. Perhaps the firm ground he encountered for the first time at Ascot compromised his effort and the performances that followed. If that was not the case, we must conclude that he was just lucky to face a weak Poulains field; it is impossible to rate him up to the level of a normal Classic winner. He has gone to stud at Rathasker, at a fee of €12,000. *TM*

Dai Jin

3yo bay colt   **121**

Peintre Celebre (USA) - Dawlah (Shirley Heights)
Owner W H Sport International
Trainer A Schutz
Breeder Gestut Schlenderhan

Career: **8** starts | won **4** | second **2** | third **1** | **£402,839** win and place

By Robert Carter

TWENTY-NINE German-trained horses have taken their chance in the Arc, starting with Oleander, who was fifth in 1928 and third the following year. The only winner was the 119-1 chance Star Appeal, who sliced his way through a large field in 1975, but there have been other good efforts, including a close fifth from Nebos in 1980, a fourth from Lando on unsuitable ground in 1995, and third places from Borgia in 1997 and Tiger Hill in 1998.

Challenger number 29 was Dai Jin, the Deutsches Derby winner, who went to post for the 2003 edition as a live outsider on ground that was sure to bring his stamina into play. Dai Jin was well away, but lost a position in midfield after two furlongs and soon found himself at the back. He was last and being pushed along before halfway, about a dozen lengths off the lead, and although Olivier Peslier brought him to the outside at the top of the hill he was still near the back.

He received a reminder entering the straight, when less than two lengths behind Dalakhani, but could keep on at only the same pace and passed the post in seventh place, beaten around ten lengths. On the face of things it was a somewhat disappointing effort, but it was discovered that he had suffered a tendon injury during the race. The immediate reaction from connections was that it was serious and a few weeks later he was retired to stud.

Trainer Andreas Schutz, not for the first time, had launched the fleet in the BMW Deutsches Derby at Hamburg, with Dai Jin one of his five runners. Stable jockey Andrasch Starke chose the Preis der Diana (Oaks) winner, Next Gina, so Peslier, who had won the 1997 Derby on Borgia for Schutz's father, Bruno, and that year's Arc on Dai Jin's sire, Peintre Celebre, took the mount on the colt.

Dai Jin had won the second of two starts as a juvenile and, following two defeats in the spring, had regained the winning thread in the Group 2

Dai Jin (left, Olivier Peslier) runs on strongly to beat Ransom O'War in the Deutsches Derby at Hamburg

Oppenheim Union-Rennen over a mile and three furlongs at Cologne, his home track, three weeks before the Derby. In the Derby itself, he was outpaced early and had only six of his 19 rivals behind on the final turn. However, he had progressed to eighth straightening up and then worked his way steadily up the outside to catch stablemate Storm Trooper about 120 yards out. Ransom O'War, trained by Erika Mader, spoiled a clean sweep for Schutz by running on for second, a length and a quarter behind, but Schutz was third, fourth and fifth with Storm Trooper, Next Gina and Akihito. Cherub, his remaining runner, was tenth.

Schutz described Dai Jin as "a small horse and nothing special to look at, but with a real fighting heart" and announced that the Arc was the target. He ran just once in between, in the Group 1 Credit Suisse Private Banking-Pokal, over a mile and a half at Cologne, where

2003   Race record

7th Prix de l'Arc de Triomphe Lucien Barriere (Group 1) (Longchamp, October 5) 3yo+ 12f Holding **116** (TS 96) 13 ran. *Held up in rear, headway 4f out, 8th straight, soon beaten, beaten 10½l by Dalakhani*

1st Credit Suisse Private Banking-Pokal (Group 1) (Cologne, August 17) 3yo+ 12f Good **121** 5 ran. *Soon niggled along in last, reminder 4f out, ridden and headway on outside over 2f out, led 1½f out, edged right, ran on, beat Next Desert by 2½l*

1st BMW Deutsches Derby (Group 1) (Hamburg, July 6) 3yo 12f Soft **116** 20 ran. *Towards rear, niggled along halfway, 14th over 4f out, headway 3f out, 8th straight, strong run down outside to lead last 120yds, ran on well, beat Ransom O'War by 1¼l*

1st Oppenheim-Union-Rennen (Group 2) (Cologne, June 15) 3yo 11f Good 7 ran. *Held up, last straight, strong run on inner to lead well inside final furlong, driven out, beat North Lodge by nk*

2nd Jean Harzheim-Rennen (Listed) (Cologne, May 18) 3yo 11f Good 5 ran. *Led until headed and no extra close home, beaten hd by Darlan*

2nd Preis der Dreijahrigen (Listed) (Dusseldorf, April 27) 3yo 8½f Soft 9 ran. *Held up towards rear, stayed on well final 2f, not reach winner, beaten 3l by Glad Hunter*

2002

1st Grosser Preis der Dortmunder Stadtwerke (Restricted Listed) (Dortmund, September 28) 2yo 7f Good 15 ran ● **3rd** Restricted Listed (Dusseldorf, September 15) 2yo 1m Good 6 ran

Peslier was soon at work as his mount lost touch with the other four runners. Dai Jin was still last into the straight but was now finding his feet. He took over from his stable companion, the 2002 Deutsches Derby winner Next Desert, ridden by Starke, 300 yards from home and, though edging right, ran on to beat him by two and a half lengths. The Coronation Cup winner, Warrsan, who had made a lot of the running, was two lengths further back in third.

Dai Jin was the 11th Deutsches Derby winner to be bought at Baden-Baden's yearling sale. Yearling auctions are not particularly significant in Germany, and at one time the one-day sale at Baden-Baden had the field to itself. The yearlings were submitted mainly by the big owner-breeders, but while each stud would select a yearling for sale it was rarely clear if this was a horse of which they were proud or one they would prefer to be rid of. The popularity of the sale has gradually increased, however, as has the number catalogued, that figure reaching 264 in 2003. Out of a mare who won a Doncaster maiden in 1995, when trained by Tom Jones, Dai Jin was the only lot offered by Gestut Schlenderhan and was bought for DM95,000 (then about £30,900) on behalf of WH International, a sports and entertainment management firm based in Trier, near the border with Luxembourg. The company takes its name from the initials of its founder, Werner Heinz, and its main source of sporting business is motor racing, including representing Grand Prix driver Nick Heidfeld.

Dai Jin will start his stud career at Gestut Zoppenbroich for a fee of €7,500 in 2004.

Dai Jin

bay colt, 4-2-2000

		Northern Dancer	Nearctic
	Nureyev		Natalma
Peintre Celebre		Special	Forli
ch 1994			Thong
		Alydar	Raise A Native
	Peinture Bleue		Sweet Tooth
		Petroleuse	Habitat
			Plencia
		Mill Reef	Never Bend
	Shirley Heights		Milan Mill
		Hardiemma	Hardicanute
Dawlah			Grand Cross
b 1992		Seattle Slew	Bold Reasoning
			My Charmer
	Urjwan	White Star Line	**Northern Dancer**
			Fast Line

Bred by Gestut Schlenderhan in England. DM95,000 Baden-Baden yearling

Sire **Peintre Celebre**

Won 5 of 7 races, inc. Prix Greffulhe-Gr2, Prix du Jockey-Club-Gr1, Grand Prix de Paris-Gr1, Prix de l'Arc de Triomphe-Gr1. Quite well-made, medium-sized individual, tip-top performer at 10-12f, with exceptional acceleration. Sire of: Dai Jin (Deutsches Derby-Gr1, Aral Pokal-Gr1), Super Celebre (Gr2), Vallee Enchantee (Gr2), Pearl Of Love (Gran Criterium-Gr1).

Dam **Dawlah**

Won 1 of 9 races. Lengthy sort, winner at 10f, seemed to stay 18f, just useful form. Dam of: unnamed (1997 c by Sadler's Wells; died young), Danika (1998 f by Fairy King; unraced), Dai Jin (2000 c by Peintre Celebre; Classic winner).

Pedigree assessment

Sold as a yearling at Baden-Baden for less than half what it cost to breed him, Dai Jin established himself as the best three-year-old from the first crop of Peintre Celebre. His bargain price no doubt reflected his ordinary looks and his total inability to use himself in his slower paces, but he belied those appearances when it came to running, displaying athletic merit of a high order when winning the Deutsches Derby and when beating the previous winner of that Classic, Next Desert, at Cologne. His form, strikingly progressive to that point, warranted a shot at the Arc, but the bid misfired and he finished seventh, carrying a tendon injury that unfortunately caused his retirement. The first son of Peintre Celebre to go to stud, Dai Jin will stand at Gestut Zoppenbroich at a fee of €7,500 in 2004. *TM*

Dalakhani (Ire)

3yo grey colt **134**

Darshaan - Daltawa (Ire) (Miswaki (USA))
Owner H H Aga Khan
Trainer A de Royer-Dupre
Breeder H H The Aga Khan's Studs

Career: **9** starts | won **8** | second **1** | third **0** | **£1,409,270** win and place

By Brough Scott

EAVING Longchamp there was a sense of wonderment with a little twist of regret. It had been one of those cold, clear autumn days too beautiful to last. In Dalakhani's Arc de Triomphe we had seen a brilliant young colt fulfil what seven generations of breeding had planned for him. But now the day and his track career were ending. There would be no more clues as to whether Dalakhani was great or just good.

The Aga Khan's policy of retiring his Classic winners is so long established that it would be churlish to moan too much, especially in a year when his studs gave us two such excellent colts as Alamshar and Dalakhani. Yet Dalakhani's dazzling talents beg a wider comparison than the Prix du Jockey-Club and the six other successes among his own age group. The Arc was the first and only time he took on the other generations. The need now is to get the feel of him as well as the form book.

We knew his potential. His successes in all three races as a two-year-old, climaxing in the Group 1 Criterium International at Saint-Cloud in heavy going, had left the normally imperturbable Alain de Royer-Dupré positively drooling with expectation. Dalakhani's early season was slated to take the standard route to the Prix du Jockey-Club, but the public were soon to realise that this was anything but a standard horse.

Dalakhani is not exactly small, standing 1.64m (16 hands) at the shoulder, but he is light and lithe. Throughout the year he regularly checked out at 445 kilos on the weighbridge – fascinatingly, almost 100 kilos (15st) lighter than Falbrav – and the impression you got both in repose and in action was of elegance and ease. He was a runner who moved with grace, an impression heightened by a peculiar white puff at the end of his otherwise grey tail that flicked in the wind as he galloped.

His two preliminary races passed smoothly enough; a half-length defeat of the unpronounceable Jipapibaquigrafo in the Greffuhle and then a length victory in the Lupin over the Wildenstein runner Super Celebre

Dalakhani (Christophe Soumillon) tops his season by winning the Prix de l'Arc de Triomphe at Longchamp

most remarked on by jockey Christophe Soumillon's boasts as to how much more his horse had in the tank. Purists get irritated at such flim-flam, but showmanship is no bad thing for a sport that still has something of a stuffed shirt image. Come the finish of the Prix du Jockey-Club, Soumillon was into a slightly juvenile taunting of Super Celebre, left arm outstretched in a signal to overtake, but much more interesting was what had gone before.

Because, for many of us, this was a first real look at this new star – and what a look it was. For Dalakhani in mid-event was one of the sweetest sights you will ever see on a racetrack. Soumillon rode him beautifully, his long body folded perfectly above his galloping partner, a full length of rein looped free to allow Dalakhani to reach out forward with his neck and forelegs as the stride skimmed him across the turf beneath.

You could see what de Royer-Dupré had meant when he said: "I have never had anything like him. His movement is so elastic, there is such a flow about him. He is a very special horse." That mid-race moment was exciting because it gives you the promise of the finish ahead. All season few delivered more impressively than Dalakhani when Soumillon let him stride up to the leader that day at Chantilly. The horse ran with his ears half back but there was no doubting his greyhound-type hunger for action as he coursed down the leaders, then easily held Super Celebre at bay.

Four weeks later race fans had an unexpected bonus. The Aga Khan

2003   Race record

1st Prix de l'Arc de Triomphe Lucien Barriere (Group 1) (Longchamp, October 5) 3yo+ 12f Holding **134** (TS 117) 13 ran. *Held up, headway well over 3f out, 6th straight, led 1f out, ridden out, beat Mubtaker by ³/₄l*

1st Prix Niel Casino Barriere d'Enghien (Group 2) (Longchamp, September 14) 3yo 12f Good to soft **124** (TS 91) 7 ran. *Held up in 6th, 5th straight, shaken up 2f out, ran on to lead over 1f out, ran on well and found more when pressed close home, beat Doyen by 1¹/₂l*

2nd Budweiser Irish Derby (Group 1) (Curragh, June 29) 3yo 12f Good **127** (TS 111) 9 ran. *Settled in 3rd, took closer order approaching straight, led travelling well over 2f out, soon ridden and strongly pressed, headed over 1f out, kept on well final furlong, beaten ¹/₂l by Alamshar*

1st Prix du Jockey-Club (Group 1) (Chantilly, June 1) 3yo 12f Good **124** (TS 103) 7 ran. *Raced in 4th, smooth headway to lead 2f out, pushed along and quickened 1f out, ran on well, beat Super Celebre by 2l*

1st Prix Lupin (Group 1) (Longchamp, May 11) 3yo 10¹/₂f Good to soft **119** (TS 99) 7 ran. *Raced in 3rd on inside, led 1¹/₂f out, shaken up over 1f out and ran on, pushed out, beat Super Celebre by 1l*

1st Prix Greffuhle (Group 2) (Longchamp, April 20) 3yo 10¹/₂f Good to soft **112** (TS 83) 5 ran. *Raced in 3rd, pushed along to lead approaching final furlong, ran on well, comfortably, beat Jipapibaquigrafo by ¹/₂l*

2002

1st Criterium International (Group 1) (Saint-Cloud, November 2) 2yo 1m Heavy **117** (TS 56) 5 ran ● **1st** Prix des Chenes (Group 3) (Longchamp, September 22) 2yo 1m Good to soft **112** (TS 82) 5 ran ● **1st** Prix du Pre d'Auge (Unraced Colts & Geldings) (Deauville, August 29) 2yo 7f Good to soft 8 ran

decided to let his French champion travel to The Curragh for the Irish Derby. It would pit him against Alamshar, his fellow graduate from the nearby Gilltown Stud nursery. There would be no fewer than six runners from Ballydoyle. Racegoers expected a Dalakhani treat, French 'turfistes' a coronation. It was not to be.

Soumillon erred. The 22-year-old Belgian is a rider of tremendous gifts and, normally, of great self-confidence. But in the opening few seconds of the Irish Derby he seemed to let nervousness get to him. Drawn over against the rail, he jumped quickly out of the stalls and took up a position behind the two hell-for-leather pacemakers. It was as if he was anxious to get clear of any dastardly Ballydoyle plot to enclose him. But he had the classiest horse – he could afford to play last. In those first few seconds he had thrown his best weapon away.

You could see how the race would unfold. High Country and Handel were never going to keep up the gallop beyond the final turn and Soumillon was bound to be stranded in front with a good two furlongs to go. He would be a sitting duck if something was good enough and tough enough to pick him off. Alamshar was.

In a perfect world, such strategic misfortunes should still not have sunk Dalakhani's chance. It was even possible to wonder just how enthusiastic he was about the closing struggle and cynics went so far as to say this was the result that would suit his owner best. But in view of Alamshar's blossoming prowess, and in view of Dalakhani's apparently unflinching resolve at the Arc in October, the best analysis of the Curragh debacle surely comes from the trainer. "He was ridden as a leader," said de Royer-Dupré in his shrugging, no-nonsense way, "and he is not a leader."

While Alamshar carried the green Aga Khan silks to King George triumph, Dalakhani took a Deauville holiday. Alamshar's subsequent lacklustre efforts in the Irish and English Champion Stakes were reminders of the strain of keeping a three-year-old on the go through the season. Deauville was a delight for Dalakhani, a sea-breeze escape from the oven that was Chantilly during an intense heatwave. He was never a giant, but when he returned to action he was certainly refreshed.

First up was the Prix Niel and once again the mid-race images of Dalakhani and Soumillon were a real delight. He always moved easily in the seven-runner field but then stretched with purpose to sprint home ahead of Doyen. The fractions show that after an opening seven furlongs in 1min 30sec the race ran 22.5 for the next quarter and then came home in three final furlongs of 12.0, 11.3, and 11.8. Royer-Dupre said the colt could be a lot sharper. Arc rivals took note.

Then the weather threatened to turn it into a mudbath. The Prix Niel penetrometer reading of 3.3 had moved down the scale by Arc day to 4.5 – officially holding. Despite his Group 1 win in similar going as a two-year-old, Dalakhani's connections were fearful that the testing conditions would compromise the flow of their colt's wondrous stride. Punters took the hint. High Chaparral, a close and honourable, if slightly ring-rusty, third in 2002, was made favourite, according to industry prices, on the strength of his tremendous Irish Champion Stakes battle with Falbrav and Islington. Punters got it wrong.

If Soumillon seemed to lack confidence at The Curragh, at Longchamp on Arc day he positively purred with it and his little partner purred back. Drawn on the wide outside, he broke smartly to feel the rhythm of the race, then eased Dalakhani back so that for a long way he had only one or two of his 12 rivals behind him. Yet horse and rider looked content, looked ready to gather in this field when they wanted.

With Diyapour as pacemaker for Dalakhani and with High Chaparral's stablemate Black Sam Bellamy also on the attack, the opening seven furlongs were taken in 1min 29.10sec, nine-tenths of a second quicker than the Prix Niel, run on much faster going. Up front, they would pay for it. Along the false straight, Soumillon and Dalakhani closed, ready to pounce. This is the stage in the Arc when the eye looks for dangers. Mick Kinane was already hard at work on High Chaparral along the rail, his colt lacking a bit of the zip of Leopardstown. Behind him Kris Kin was in worse trouble, ahead Black Sam Bellamy was coming to the end of his tether and it was the surprise packet Mubtaker who went

**Come on then . . . Soumillon taunts his rivals as he and
Dalakhani glide to victory in the Prix du Jockey-Club**

best of all. Soumillon went after him. But he had to work.

With ears set back in effort, Dalakhani hunted the leader down, got
ahead a furlong out and held on convincingly rather than spectacularly
to have three-quarters of a length to spare at the line, the final furlongs
being ground out in 12.6, 12.2 and 13.2. To beat Mubtaker by so small
a margin hardly seems championship class. But High Chaparral was
another five lengths adrift in third. All a horse can do is to beat those
in front of him. A final time of 2min 32.3sec showed the demands of
the ground compared to Peintre Celebre's record 2min 24.6sec in 1997
or even Dancing Brave's rocket-finish 2min 27.7sec in 1986, when he
clocked an incredible 11.2sec over both the last two furlongs.

After just nine races it was to be Dalakhani's last hurrah on the racetrack
and no horse ever left a better final impression.The demands of the
racecourse test temperament as well as physique. On Arc day Dalakhani
won honours in both departments.

He was certainly a very good horse. His strict achievements do not
quite rank him among the Mill Reefs and Nijinskys as he did not pitch
at a Classic over a mile. But he probably could have won the French
2,000 Guineas and he showed more natural speed than any Arc winner
since Dancing Brave. For two brief seasons there was certainly a touch
of greatness about him. Dalakhani was what breeding racehorses was
intended for. He had class in every line.

Dalakhani

grey colt, 16-2-2000

Darshaan br 1981	Shirley Heights	Mill Reef	Never Bend
			Milan Mill
		Hardiemma	Hardicanute
			Grand Cross
	Delsy	Abdos	Arbar
			Pretty Lady
		Kelty	Venture
			Marilla
Daltawa gr 1989	Miswaki	Mr Prospector	Raise A Native
			Gold Digger
		Hopespringseternal	Buckpasser
			Rose Bower
	Damana	Crystal Palace	Caro
			Hermieres
		Denia	Crepello
			Rose Ness

Bred by HH Aga Khan in Ireland

Sire Darshaan

Won 5 of 8 races, inc. Criterium de Saint-Cloud-Gr2, Prix Greffulhe-Gr2, Prix Hocquart-Gr2, Prix du Jockey Club-Gr1. Strong, workmanlike type. The best 12f 3yo in a very good crop, but disappointing after midsummer. Died May 2001. Sire of: Arzanni (Gr2), Game Plan (Gr2), Hellenic (Yorkshire Oaks-Gr1), Kotashaan (San Luis Rey S.-Gr1, San Juan Capistrano Invitational H.-Gr1, Eddie Read H.-Gr1, Oak Tree Invitational H.-Gr1, Breeders' Cup Turf-Gr1), Grand Plaisir (Gr2), Darnay (Gr2), Truly A Dream (Gr2), Key Change (Yorkshire Oaks-Gr1), Mark Of Esteem (2,000 Guineas-Gr1, Queen Elizabeth II S.-Gr1), Make No Mistake (Gr2), Mutamam (Gr2), Sayarshan (Gr2), Cerulean Sky (Prix Saint-Alary-Gr1), Josr Algarhoud (Gr2), Dilshaan (Racing Post Trophy-Gr1), Olden Times (Prix Jean Prat-Gr1), Sayedah (Gr2), Dalakhani (Criterium International-Gr1, Prix Lupin-Gr1, Prix du Jockey-Club-Gr1, Prix de l'Arc de Triomphe-Gr1), Mezzo Soprano (Prix Vermeille-Gr1), Necklace (Moyglare Stud S.-Gr1). Also got Aliysa, finished first in Oaks, disqualified.

Dam Daltawa

Won 2 of 4 races, inc. 1 Listed, also 2nd in Prix Penelope-Gr3. Unraced after April of second season. Smart form, promised to stay 12f. Dam of: Daylami (1994 c by Doyoun; winner of Poule d'Essai des Poulains-Gr1, Eclipse S.-Gr1, Man o'War S.-Gr1, Coronation Cup-Gr1, King George VI & Queen Elizabeth S.-Gr1, Irish Champion S.-Gr1, Breeders' Cup Turf-Gr1), Daymarti (1995 c by Caerleon; Listed winner, Gr1-placed), Daltabad (1997 c by Priolo; unraced), Daltaiyma (1998 f by Doyoun; winner), Dalakhani (2000 c by Darshaan; Classic winner), Dalataya (2001 f by Sadler's Wells; unraced to date).

Pedigree assessment

Like Sea-Bird, Brigadier Gerard and Alleged, Dalakhani suffered a single blot on his record – and it is arguable that his defeat in the Irish Derby owed more to riding tactics than to any deficiency of his. Of course, he never established himself in the same class as the aforementioned illustrious trio, but that also was hardly his fault. His last performance, in the Arc, showed him to greater advantage than ever before, and another season in training might have enabled him to enhance his reputation; his half-brother Daylami was pounds better as an older horse. Whatever, his was an exemplary career, and he departs for stud with a proud performance record and an exciting pedigree, totally free of Northern Dancer. He will be based at Gilltown at a fee of €45,000. *TM*

Denebola (USA)

2yo brown filly   **108**

Storm Cat (USA) - Coup de Genie (USA) (Mr Prospector (USA))

Owner Niarchos Family

Trainer P Bary

Breeder Flaxman Holdings Ltd

Career: **4** starts | won **2** | second **0** | third **1** | **£134,627** win and place

By Tom Segal

MATING the best with the best seldom works, and it must be at least 1,000-1 that one of Andre Agassi and Steffi Graf's offspring will go on to win Wimbledon. But you can bet your bottom dollar that the bookies would not have offered anywhere near those sort of odds about this Storm Cat-Coup de Genie filly winning the 1,000 Guineas after she was foaled in 2001.

They would have been right too, because after an impressive display in the Group 1 Prix Marcel Boussac on Arc day, Denebola went into winter quarters as one of the ante-post favourites for the Guineas, in which she would be trying to make amends for the unlucky defeat of her stablemate Six Perfections the previous year.

In contrast to the colts' version, the 1,000 Guineas is almost invariably won by one of the top juvenile fillies of the previous year, or at least one who had contested Group races. Not so long ago the trends spotters would have been drooling over a filly with Denebola's credentials, for in a six-year spell starting in 1988 the Guineas was won by French fillies Miesque, Ravinella and Hatoof, while two of the other three winners in the same period had won the Boussac.

Since then everything has changed, with the Rockfel and Cheveley Park Stakes taking over as the best trials, but with better luck Six Perfections would probably have revived the old trend, and if Pascal Bary opts to send Denebola over to Newmarket she will have a major chance of breaking the long losing run.

The debate over whether to stay at home for the Pouliches or go for the Guineas will no doubt rage in the Bary camp through the winter but, given the mess that races at the Rowley Mile course tend to get into in the spring these days, it would not be the greatest surprise if it were decided to keep Denebola at home.

French horses are trained to produce a brilliant turn of foot at the

**Denebola (Christophe Lemaire) impresses in the Group 1
Prix Marcel Boussac at Longchamp in October**

end of their races, which is why they have such a good record on America's
tight tracks, and for the most part are not really suited by the style of
racing in Britain or Ireland, where the emphasis is on grinding on as
fast as possible for as long as possible. Greats such as Suave Dancer
and Dalakhani were beaten for exactly that reason at The Curragh and
no French horse has won an English Classic since 1995.

Denebola looked particularly 'French' in the way she scythed through
the field at Longchamp and if she stays at home she will have several
advantages. Besides not having to go to the track at which her stablemate suffered so badly in 2003, she is already proven at Longchamp
and will more than likely have the soft ground that suits her so well.
Furthermore, Bary has suggested she is a bit tricky and so he may not
want to risk her in front of thousands at Newmarket when she can canter
down to the start in front of one man and his chien on her own doorstep.

2003   Race record

1st Prix Marcel Boussac Royal Barriere de Deauville (Group 1) (Longchamp, October 5) 2yo 1m Holding **108** (TS 74) 16 ran. *Held up towards rear to straight, looking for gap from over 2f out, got through 1½f out, led inside final furlong, driven out, beat Green Noon by sht-nk*

3rd Prix Morny Casinos Barriere (Group 1) (Deauville, August 31) 2yo 6f Soft **106** (TS 71) 8 ran. *Held up on rails, last to well over 1f out, ran on well inside final furlong, nearest at finish, beaten 2l by Whipper*

1st Prix de Cabourg (Group 3) (Deauville, August 2) 2yo 6f Good to soft **99** (TS 76) 8 ran. *Held up in 6th, switched towards inside 1½f out, squeezed through gap and headway over 1f out, ridden to lead 100yds out, ran on well, beat Bonaire by ½l*

4th Prix de Cleronde (Deauville, July 9) 2yo 5½f Good to soft **79** (TS 54) 7 ran. *Dwelt, joined leaders after 2f, every chance at distance, ran green when ridden, one pace last 150yds, beaten 2½l by Marching West*

British racing fans are inclined to regard the English Classics as the races to win, but Six Perfections did not win any Guineas, yet ended the season with a higher profile than any other three-year-old miler in the world, so Classic success certainly is not the be all and end all.

Having said that, it would be a shame if Denebola failed to turn up at Newmarket. She would bring added class to the proceedings, as there did not appear to be any great strength in depth in the British and Irish juvenile fillies of 2003.

In terms of form, her Boussac win was nothing sensational, but the manner of her victory undoubtedly was. Drawn on the outside in a field of 16, in which Moyglare Stud Stakes winner Necklace was a warm favourite at 7-4, Christophe Lemaire took his time but, from two furlongs out, there was only ever going to be one winner provided Denebola lasted home. The margin of victory over Green Noon was only narrow, but the two principals were nicely clear of the pack, which was headed by outsider Tulipe Royale. What's more, Denebola gave the strong impression that she took things easy when in front and afterwards Bary suggested she had a similar level of ability to Six Perfections.

Speed looked Denebola's principal asset in the Boussac, as it had done in her three previous races, two of which had been at Deauville, where she beat Bonaire in the Group 3 Prix de Cabourg before finishing a much-improved third behind Whipper in the Group 1 Prix Morny. Lemaire overdid the waiting tactics in the Morny, but Denebola still failed by only a short head to catch her previously unbeaten stablemate Much Faster for second place.

A mile will be her optimum trip and, on pedigree, faster ground should not be a problem, so Denebola has all the ingredients needed to make up into a top-class three-year-old. Whether it's a case of once bitten, twice shy for Bary, or of taking the bull by the horns and going for the Guineas, Denebola is a filly of considerable potential. It may be stretching things to suggest she is the next Six Perfections, but she looks sure to play a big part in the better fillies' mile races.

Denebola

brown filly, 6-4-2001

			Nearctic
		Northern Dancer	**Natalma**
	Storm Bird		
		South Ocean	New Providence
Storm Cat			Shining Sun
br 1983			Bold Ruler
		Secretariat	Somethingroyal
	Terlingua		
		Crimson Saint	Crimson Satan
			Bolero Rose
			Native Dancer
		Raise A Native	Raise You
	Mr Prospector		
		Gold Digger	Nashua
Coup de Genie			Sequence
b 1991			Hail To Reason
		Halo	Cosmah
	Coup de Folie		
		Raise The Standard	Hoist The Flag
			Natalma

Bred by Flaxman Holdings Ltd in Kentucky

Sire Storm Cat

Won 4 of 8 races, inc. Young America S.-Gr1, also 2nd (beaten a nose) in Breeders' Cup Juvenile-Gr1. Medium-sized, strongly made sort, who took more after his dam than his sire. Top-class, extremely game 2yo who had surgery for bone chips in off knee at end of season; never wholly sound thereafter. Sire of Gr1 winners: Harlan, November Snow, Desert Stormer, Missed The Storm, Mistle Cat, Sardula, Tabasco Cat, Hennessy, Aldiza, Sharp Cat, Catinca, Aljabr, Cat Thief, Forestry, Tactical Cat, Finder's Fee, Giant's Causeway, High Yield, Black Minnaloushe, Raging Fever, Sophisticat, Dessert, Hold That Tiger, Nebraska Tornado, Storm Flag Flying, Denebola, One Cool Cat.

Dam Coup de Genie

Won 4 of 9 races, inc. Prix de Cabourg-Gr3, Prix Morny-Gr1, Prix de la Salamandre-Gr1, also 3rd in 1,000 Guineas-Gr1, 4th in Breeders' Cup Juvenile Fillies-Gr1. Sparely-made sister to Machiavellian, high-class performer, effective up to a mile on both heavy and good to firm. Broke blood vessels in 2 races at 2 (ran on Lasix in US), suffered attack of pleurisy after second start at 3. Dam of: Moonlight's Box (1996 f by Nureyev; unraced; dam of Gr1 winner Bago), Snake Mountain (1998 c by AP Indy; Gr3 winner), Glia (1999 f by AP Indy; Listed winner, Gr2-placed), Loving Kindness (2000 f by Seattle Slew; Gr3 winner, Gr1-placed), Denebola (2001 f by Storm Cat; Gr1 winner).

Pedigree assessment

They do not come much better bred than this filly, whose pedigree is all class, and she certainly looked a class act in the Prix Marcel Boussac, showing a sharp turn of foot. As she got a mile comfortably at two, it is tempting to think that she might excel over longer trips at three, but her closest antecedents are all factors for speed rather than stamina and the likelihood is that she will be kept at the distance that has already been shown to suit her. She will have options either side of the Channel for her Guineas bid and will surely prove a factor whichever choice is made. *TM*

Domedriver (Ire)

5yo bay horse	**126**

Indian Ridge - Napoli (Baillamont (USA))
Owner Niarchos Family
Trainer P Bary
Breeder Niarchos Family

Career: 21 starts	won **6**	second **5**	third **3**	**£677,020** win and place

By Tom Segal

MICHAEL OWEN would be the first to admit that, in terms of natural ability, he's no Johan Cruyff or Diego Maradona. But what he does have is a knack of being in the right place at the right time, and that is half the battle in getting to the top of the tree.

Domedriver would not have been anywhere near as good a racehorse as Rock Of Gibraltar, but he was there to smash the ball into the back of the net at the Breeders' Cup of 2002 at Arlington when circumstances and a long hard season got the better of 'The Rock'.

That victory can never be taken away from Domedriver, but it did hang as a bit of a millstone round his neck as he went through 2003 without adding another victory to his CV before being packed off to Lanwades Stud following his seventh in the Prix du Moulin at Longchamp. So why did a horse who had appeared to have the world at his feet only a few months previously end his racing career under a bit of a cloud?

The most obvious reason is that, after winning in the States, he was simply overrated. As the 2003 Breeders' Cup showed once again, few American turf horses are up to the standard of the top Europeans, and so with Rock Of Gibraltar drawn out wide and asked to make up a lot of ground on the outside, Domedriver got a bit lucky. However, that is a massive oversimplification, because Domedriver travelled really strongly that day and showed a great turn of foot when asked to quicken, proving himself a horse to be reckoned with.

Consequently, there must have been other reasons to explain why Domedriver did not really fulfil his potential. Perhaps one was that he was never able to race under similar conditions to those he encountered at Arlington. In a way it was a shame he was French-based, because Domedriver's 15 minutes of fame came in a fast-run race round a bend, whereas slowly run races, often on straight tracks, are the norm in France.

Domedriver failed to fulfil the potential of 2002 and laboured in the shadow of stablemate Six Perfections

A more controversial but equally important reason for Domedriver's disappointing year was that Pascal Bary and the Niarchos family had an even better miler in the shape of Six Perfections, so their eye was slightly off the ball as far as Domedriver was concerned.

It was surely no coincidence that his best performance of the year came when a fast-finishing runner-up to his stablemate, the subsequent Breeders' Cup Mile winner, in the Prix Jacques le Marois at Deauville in August. That race was set up to suit Six Perfections, with Bary running a sprinter as a pacemaker to ensure a really strong pace, and it would not have taken a brain surgeon to work out afterwards that an out-and-out gallop was a necessity for Domedriver. Unfortunately, on his only subsequent start, in the Moulin, he got trapped in the rear in a slowly run race and was never going to make up the lost ground,

2003   Race record

7th Netjets Prix du Moulin de Longchamp (Group 1) (Longchamp, September 7) 3yo+ 1m Good to soft **112** (TS 82) 14 ran. *Held up, 12th straight, switched outside approaching final furlong, finished well, beaten 5¼l by Nebraska Tornado*

2nd Prix du Haras de Fresnay-le Buffard-Jacques le Marois (Group 1) (Deauville, August 17) 3yo+ 1m Good to soft **126** (TS 109) 12 ran. *Held up towards rear, 11th halfway, pushed along 1½f out and closed up, driven and went 2nd 150yds out, ridden and ran on close home, beaten snk by Six Perfections*

5th Prix Messidor (Group 3) (Deauville, July 13) 3yo+ 1m Good to soft **111** (TS 92) 10 ran. *Held up towards rear, 9th 2f out, headway well over 1f out, kept on but never reached challenging position, beaten 1l by Special Kaldoun*

4th Juddmonte Lockinge Stakes (Group 1) (Newbury, May 17) 4yo+ 1m Good **94** (TS 68) 6 ran. *Chased winner, ridden and weakened inside final 3f, hung right approaching final furlong, beaten 20l by Hawk Wing*

2nd Prix du Muguet (Group 2) (Saint-Cloud, May 1) 4yo+ 1m Good **124** (TS 96) 10 ran. *Held up disputing last, 4 lengths off leader entering straight, shaken up 2f out and headway to challenge in centre, every chance 1f out, no extra close home, beaten snk by Dandoun*

2002

1st Netjets Breeders' Cup Mile (Grade 1) (Arlington, October 26) 3yo+ 1m Yielding **125** 14 ran ● **1st** Prix Daniel Wildenstein (Prix du Rond-Point) Casino Barriere de la Rochelle (Group 2) (Longchamp, October 5) 3yo+ 1m Good to soft **115** (TS 96) 11 ran ● **2nd** Prix du Haras de Fresnay-le-Buffard-Jacques le Marois (Group 1) (Deauville, August 18) 3yo+ 1m Good to soft **123** (TS 109) 8 ran ● **2nd** Prix Messidor (Group 3) (Deauville, July 6) 3yo+ 1m Very soft **116** (TS 88) 10 ran ● **1st** Prix du Chemin de Fer du Nord (Group 3) (Chantilly, June 9) 4yo+ 1m Good **117** (TS 55) 11 ran ● **5th** Prix du Palais-Royal (Group 3) (Longchamp, May 30) 3yo+ 7f Soft **109** (TS 87) 7 ran

Other notable runs

2001 **5th** Prix du Rond-Point Casino Barriere de la Rochelle (Group 2) (Longchamp, October 6) 3yo+ 1m Very soft **107** (TS 78) 6 ran ● **3rd** Prix Quincey (Group 3) (Deauville, August 28) 3yo+ 1m Good (TS 50) 8 ran ● **1st** Prix de Tourgeville (Listed) (Deauville, August 9) 3yo 1m Very soft (TS 81) 8 ran ● **2nd** Prix de la Jonchere (Group 3) (Chantilly, June 18) 3yo 1m Good **106** 7 ran ● **3rd** Prix Djebel (Listed) (Longchamp, April 13) 3yo 7f Heavy (TS 64) 8 ran **2000** **1st** Prix Isonomy (Listed) (Maisons-Laffitte, October 27) 2yo 1m Very soft 4 ran ● **1st** Prix de la Maniguette (Chantilly, September 20) 2yo 1m Soft 12 ran

finishing just over five lengths behind Nebraska Tornado.

Possibly the Niarchos team had already secured a deal for Domedriver to stand at stud and so were not overly concerned with how he fared in the Moulin. Possibly, since the Moulin attracted its largest field in years, they assumed that the pace would be strong. Either way, this was surely a major opportunity missed.

Packed off to stud afterwards, Domedriver never got the chance to prove himself the star he had looked ready to become in the aftermath of the 2002 Breeders' Cup and, taking his career as a whole, he simply failed to win enough races to be considered an outstanding miler. However, he left the strong impression that he could have achieved a lot more than he did.

Domedriver   *bay horse, 15-3-1998*

		Lorenzaccio	Klairon / Phoenissa
	Ahonoora	Helen Nichols	Martial / Quaker Girl
Indian Ridge ch 1985	Hillbrow	Swing Easy	Delta Judge / Free Flowing
		Golden City	Skymaster / West Shaw
	Baillamont	Blushing Groom	Red God / Runaway Bride
Napoli b 1991		Lodeve	Shoemaker / Locust Time
	Bella Senora	Northern Dancer	Nearctic / Natalma
		Sex Appeal	Buckpasser / Best In Show

Bred by Niarchos Family in Ireland

Sire **Indian Ridge**

Won 5 of 11 races, inc. Jersey S.-Gr3, Duke of York S.-Gr3, King's Stand S.-Gr2. Lengthy, attractive sort, a hard puller, too impetuous to get a mile. Sire of: Fumo di Londra (Gr3), Island Magic (Gr3), Ridgewood Ben (Gr3), Blomberg (Gr3), Definite Article (National S.-Gr1), Ridgewood Pearl (Irish 1,000 Guineas-Gr1, Coronation S.-Gr1, Prix du Moulin de Longchamp-Gr1, Breeders' Cup Mile-Gr1), Tumbleweed Ridge (Gr3), Compton Place (July Cup-Gr1), Handsome Ridge (Gr2), Indian Rocket (Gr2), Bardonecchia (Gr3), Cassandra Go (Gr3), Namid (Prix de l'Abbaye de Longchamp-Gr1), St Clair Ridge (Gr3), Indian Mary (Gr3), Nicobar (Gr2), Domedriver (Breeders' Cup Mile-Gr1), High Pitched (Gr3), Indian Creek (Gr2), Munir (Gr3), Nayyir (Gr2), Sights On Gold (Gr3), Campsie Fells (Gr3), Indian Haven (Irish 2,000 Guineas-Gr1), Snow Ridge (Gr2).

Dam **Napoli**

Won 4 races in France at 3 and 4, including 3 Listed races over 9-10f, also 3rd Prix Minerve-Gr3. Sister to 10f Gr3 winner d'Arros out of sister to El Gran Senor and Try My Best. Dam of: Forest Rain (1997 f by Caerleon; winner), Domedriver (1998 c by Indian Ridge; Gr1 winner), Tau Ceti (1999 c by Hernando; Gr3 winner), Neutrina (2000 f by Hector Protector; unraced), Ledi (2001 c by Night Shift; placed), 2002 f by Machiavellian.

Pedigree assessment

Indian Ridge has done pretty well with his sire sons, considering most of them were conceived cheaply and just missed the top class. Domedriver carries strong credentials, both in terms of his racecourse record and his female family, and at Lanwades Stud he is in the right place to have a carefully managed career. He is likely to cover plenty of middle-distance mares and will get progeny who stay beyond a mile as a result. An interesting stallion prospect. *JH*

Doyen (Ire)

3yo bay colt **122**

Sadler's Wells (USA) - Moon Cactus (Kris)
Owner Sheikh Mohammed
Trainer A Fabre
Breeder Sheikh Mohammed

Career: **6** starts | won **3** | second **1** | third **0** | **£116,470** win and place

By Richard Austen

GODOLPHIN have a fine prospect for 2004 in the shape of Doyen. They make it their business, of course, to have a stable full of fine prospects. However, with this colt, a brother to the 1995 Oaks winner Moonshell, an early standard bearer for them, they surely have the richest material for the top races over a mile and a half.

Trained hitherto in France by André Fabre and unheard of at the start of his three-year-old campaign, Doyen ended it by making the frame in the Prix de l'Arc de Triomphe. On paper, he bears a resemblance to another three-year-old whom Fabre trained for Sheikh Mohammed in 1995, one that filled third place in the Arc, and that colt's name was Swain. It is asking an awful lot for Doyen to approach the level of achievement that Swain attained for Godolphin, but his progress so far has been unrelenting and he does not have to find much more to emerge as a colt in the top class.

Doyen's starting point was a modest one. Swain was unraced as a juvenile and punters at Maisons-Laffitte in October 2002 probably wished that Doyen had followed suit when they sent him off at evens in a 17-runner field and he managed only fifth, wandering markedly under pressure.

There were signs of greenness on his reappearance in a minor event over a mile and a half at Saint-Cloud in March as well, but on this occasion it came when Doyen was in the lead and he went on to justify favouritism in clear-cut style. Two months later, Doyen took his chance in smooth fashion in a Listed race at Lyon Parilly and now he was ready for Group races. Appearing in a four-runner renewal of the Group 3 Prix du Lys at Longchamp in June, and with Frankie Dettori taking the ride for the first time, Doyen was held up and impressed in the way he came through from the back to win by four lengths from subsequent Group 2 winner Policy Maker.

Doyen (Frankie Dettori) on his way to post for the Prix Niel, in which he finished second to Dalakhani

As far as races such as the Arc were concerned, these results seemed pretty immaterial, for just four days after Doyen had done battle at lowly Lyon Parilly, Dalakhani's pre-eminence among the middle-distance three-year-olds in France had become crystal clear in the Prix du Jockey-Club. Both colts were put away during July and August, Dalakhani having in the meantime lost his unbeaten record to Alamshar in the Irish Derby, and when they re-emerged in mid-September it was against each other in the Group 2 Prix Niel at Longchamp on the day of Arc trials.

In a race in which Doyen was only just shaded as second favourite by Kris Kin on the Pari-Mutuel behind Dalakhani, he split the two Derby heroes and ran another race full of promise. Held up in last in a field of seven, he quickened well in the straight and possibly got his head in front briefly before Dalakhani asserted in the final furlong and beat him a length and a half. The bookmakers were understandably impressed

4th Prix de l'Arc de Triomphe Lucien Barriere (Group 1) (Longchamp, October 5) 3yo+ 12f Holding **121** (TS 102) 13 ran.

Always in touch, 7th straight, switched left and headway from 2f out, one pace final furlong, beaten 7¼l by Dalakhani

2nd Prix Niel Casino Barriere d'Enghien (Group 2) (Longchamp, September 14) 3yo 12f Good to soft **122** (TS 88) 7 ran.

Held up in last, pushed along over 2f out, ran on strongly from over 1½f out, ridden and challenged final furlong, kept on gamely, beaten 1½l by Dalakhani

1st Prix du Lys (Group 3) (Longchamp, June 22) 3yo 12f Good to soft **122** (TS 54) 4 ran.

Raced in last, pushed along entering straight and good headway to lead inside final furlong, ran on strongly, pushed out, beat Policy Maker by 4l

1st Coupe des Trois Ans (Listed) (Lyon Parilly, May 28) 3yo 12f Soft 3 ran.

Close up in main group behind clear leader, led 1½f out, pushed out, easily, beat French Polo by 1½l

1st Prix Cadet Roussel (Saint-Cloud, March 29) 3yo 12f Good (TS 85) 9 ran.

Pressed leader until led 1½f out, ducked right over 1f out, ran on well, beat Loved'n Lost by 2½l

2002

5th Prix Hunyade (Unraced) (Maisons-Laffitte, October 2) 2yo 9f Good 17 ran

and cut the rangy Doyen to third favourite for the Arc, at odds as short as 7-2.

With Dalakhani not at his best in the Prix Niel and likely to come on markedly for the race, a lot more was required of Doyen to improve past him. As usual, Fabre's words were worth listening to, particularly so with his having already trained five Arc winners, more than any other trainer. "I hope he has improved enough to get his revenge on Dalakhani," said Fabre, "and I hope the pace of the race will be stronger than when he was beaten by him in the Prix Niel. Hopefully Frankie will have him a little handier this time. You can never be confident, but he has the right pedigree and we have fingers crossed. He is a nervous individual and hopefully his inexperience of such an occasion will not get the better of him."

Doyen did improve, but not by anything like enough to get near Dalakhani. The plan to have him closer to the pace than in the Prix Niel ran into traffic problems before the home turn and once more he was having to make up ground on Dalakhani in the straight, but Doyen's response once in the clear saw Mubtaker and High Chaparral get the better of him as well. He was beaten around seven lengths. It was the first time he had raced on soft ground since Lyon Parilly and Fabre reflected: "The ground probably didn't suit him, but it was the same for everybody. That's as good as he is for the moment."

That may have been the case, but it will be a disappointment if Doyen does not prove top class in 2004.

Doyen

bay colt, 22-4-2000

		Nearco
	Nearctic	Lady Angela
Northern Dancer		
	Natalma	Native Dancer
Sadler's Wells		Almahmoud
b 1981		Hail To Reason
	Bold Reason	Lalun
Fairy Bridge		
	Special	Forli
		Thong
		Atan
	Sharpen Up	Rocchetta
Kris		
	Doubly Sure	Reliance
Moon Cactus		Soft Angels
b 1987		Never Bend
	Mill Reef	Milan Mill
Lady Moon		
	Moonlight Night	Levmoss
		Lovely Light

Bred by Sheikh Mohammed in Ireland

Sire **Sadler's Wells**

Won 6 of 11 races, inc. Beresford S.-Gr3, Irish Derby Trial-Gr2, Irish 2,000 Guineas-Gr1, Eclipse S.-Gr1, Phoenix Champion S.-Gr1. Also 2nd in Prix du Jockey-Club-Gr1, King George VI & Queen Elizabeth S.-Gr1. Impeccably bred top-class performer from 8-12f, handsome, tough and consistent. Sire of Gr1 winners: Braashee, French Glory, In The Wings, Old Vic, Prince Of Dance, Scenic, Salsabil, Opera House, Saddlers' Hall, El Prado, Johann Quatz, Masad, Barathea, Fatherland, Fort Wood, Intrepidity, Carnegie, King's Theatre, Northern Spur, Moonshell, Muncie, Poliglote, Chief Contender, Dance Design, Luna Wells, Cloudings, Ebadiyla, Entrepreneur, In Command, Kayf Tara, Dream Well, Greek Dance, King Of Kings, Leggera, Commander Collins, Daliapour, Montjeu, Saffron Walden, Aristotle, Beat Hollow, Subtle Power, Galileo, Imagine, Milan, Perfect Soul, Sequoyah, Ballingarry, Black Sam Bellamy, Gossamer, High Chaparral, Islington, Quarter Moon, Sholokhov, Alberto Giacometti, Brian Boru, Refuse To Bend, Yesterday.

Dam **Moon Cactus**

Won 3 of 7 starts, inc. Prestige S.-Gr3, also 2nd Prix de Diane-Gr1, 3rd Nassau S.-Gr2. Effective 10f-12f. Sister to 8.5f Gr3 winner Shining Steel. Dam of: Moonshell (1992 f by Sadler's Wells; Classic winner), Moonfire (1993 f by Sadler's Wells; placed), Ocean Of Storms (1995 c by Arazi; Listed winner, Gr2-placed), Hatha Anna (1997 c by Sadler's Wells; AusGr2 winner), Shamaat Hayaaty (1998 f by Sadler's Wells; winner, Listed-placed), Avionic (1999 c by In The Wings; winner), Doyen (2000 c by Sadler's Wells; Gr3 winner), 2002 c by In The Wings, 2003 f by In The Wings.

Pedigree assessment

Progressing well, like so many offspring of Sadler's Wells. His pedigree is watertight as far as 12f is concerned and Doyen probably would have the scope to stay further, but Group 1 brackets over 12f or even 10f are likely to be the target for 2004. *JH*

Dubai Destination (USA)
4yo bay colt **126**

Kingmambo (USA) - Mysterial (USA) (Alleged (USA))
Owner Godolphin
Trainer Saeed Bin Suroor
Breeder Calumet Farm

Career: **8 starts** | won **4** | second **2** | third **0** | **£238,416** win and place

By James Willoughby

DUBAI DESTINATION ran clean away from his rivals in the Group 1 Queen Anne Stakes at Royal Ascot – and straight through the pain barrier in the process. It was a spectacular performance, but it came at a price.

Dubai Destination was set up for this peak effort by success in a Nottingham conditions event just two weeks earlier in June. It was his first start for over a year, but he looked really well and ran the same way. Picking up strongly for only routine encouragement, he subdued the useful miler Binary File by six lengths, suggesting he was a great deal better still.

Simon Crisford, racing manager to the colt's owners, Godolphin, expressed his satisfaction with the performance. "He's a class horse and, now that we have got him back, hopefully he'll stay sound," he said. The caveat to Crisford's effusion was a reference to Dubai Destination's chequered physical history. Following an inspiring juvenile campaign in which he defeated Rock Of Gibraltar in the Champagne Stakes at Doncaster in 2001, the Kingmambo colt was held up during the following winter with an injury to his hind leg.

Dubai Destination's Classic aspirations were seriously compromised by this infirmity. He did not make the track as a three-year-old until the Predominate Stakes at Goodwood in May and, though he ran well to finish second to Coshocton, the manner in which he came home over the 11 furlongs persuaded his connections to shelve plans to run him in the Derby. A further leg injury – this time to his off-fore – knocked Dubai Destination out of the St James's Palace Stakes and he duly missed the remainder of that campaign.

Given both the depth of his talent and the extent of his frailties, Dubai Destination was under close scrutiny for his comeback effort at Nottingham. All eyes were on the freedom of his movement and the cadence of his

**Dubai Destination (Frankie Dettori) storms home in the
Queen Anne at Royal Ascot**

stride. In the event, he showed no ill-effects, but the outing was hardly
demanding and the injury-plagued colt could afford to gallop well within
himself on the way to a bloodless triumph.

The Queen Anne proved to be a different matter. Though clearing away
from the field to win by four lengths from Tillerman, Dubai Destination
looked slightly awkward under pressure, giving three hefty flashes of
his tail as he strode up to the line. The aftermath of his victory was a
triumphant moment for the Godolphin operation. Crisford reaffirmed
their high regard for the colt, but he did not explain Dubai Destination's
apparent signs of distress.

There is no such thing as an easy race in Group 1 company – something Crisford is quick to point out himself – and the demanding effort
that Dubai Destination produced on good to firm going precipitated a
dramatic loss of form in his final two outings.

At Deauville in August, he travelled strongly for six furlongs in the

2003   Race record

8th Queen Elizabeth II Stakes (Sponsored By NetJets) (Group 1) (Ascot, September 27) 3yo+ 1m Good to firm **107** (TS 90) 8 ran. *Chased leaders, ridden 3f out, weakened rapidly over 2f out, beaten 9½l by Falbrav*

5th Prix du Haras de Fresnay-Le Buffard-Jacques le Marois (Group 1) (Deauville, August 17) 3yo+ 1m Good to soft **116** (TS 95) 12 ran. *Mid-division towards outside, pushed along to chase leaders over 1½f out, ran on but never in challenging position, beaten 4¾l by Six Perfections*

1st Queen Anne Stakes (Group 1) (Ascot, June 17) 4yo+ 1m Good to firm **126** (TS 106) 10 ran. *Settled towards rear, progress on outer 3f out, led 2f out, ridden clear over 1f out, flashed tail but ran on well final furlong, beat Tillerman by 4l*

1st Scottish Equitable/Jockeys Association Conditions Stakes (Nottingham, June 4) 3yo+ 1m Good to firm **117** (TS 86) 4 ran. *Always going well, led over 2f out, shaken up over 1f out, soon clear, easily, beat Binary File by 6l*

2002

2nd Letheby & Christopher Predominate Stakes (Listed) (Goodwood, May 21) 3yo 11f Good **118** (TS 55) 6 ran

Other notable runs

1st Rothmans Royals Champagne Stakes (Group 2) (Doncaster, September 14) 2yo 7f Good to soft **119** (TS 75) 8 ran ● **1st** Strutt & Parker Maiden Stakes (Newmarket (July), July 10) 2yo 7f Good to soft **98** (TS 60) 13 ran

Prix Jacques le Marois, but found little off the bridle and was beaten more than four lengths into fifth by Six Perfections. While the defeat was blamed on an easy surface, he once again looked uncomfortable when asked to stretch.

Worse was to follow in the Queen Elizabeth II Stakes back at Ascot in September. Though having the benefit of a six-week freshening, Dubai Destination barely got as far as the home turn before he showed signs of distress. "Something must have been wrong," said his jockey, Frankie Dettori.

The modern thoroughbred is arguably less sound than his ancestors in general terms. Why else do trainers fight shy of running their best horses on unwatered ground? Generations of breeding for speed and paying little heed to soundness may have had a detrimental effect, despite the advances made during the same period in veterinary science. Now, more than ever, a big run today can mean a poor one tomorrow.

Dubai Destination was retired after the ignominy of finishing last to Falbrav and will reportedly stand at Dalham Hall Stud at Newmarket. For all his undoubted ability, his racing career was blighted by his inability to sustain physical wellbeing. His Queen Anne victory was stunning, but a fragile racehorse whose career ends in disappointment is often regarded less fondly than a durable one of less talent.

It is not how fast they run, but how often they run fast.

Dubai Destination

bay colt, 10-2-1999

Kingmambo b 1990	Mr Prospector	Raise A Native	Native Dancer
			Raise You
		Gold Digger	Nashua
			Sequence
	Miesque	Nureyev	Northern Dancer
			Special
		Pasadoble	Prove Out
			Santa Quilla
Mysterial b 1994	Alleged	Hoist The Flag	Tom Rolfe
			Wavy Navy
		Princess Pout	Prince John
			Determined Lady
	Mysteries	Seattle Slew	Bold Reasoning
			My Charmer
		Phydilla	Lyphard
			Godzilla

Bred by Calumet Farm in Kentucky. $1,500,000 Keeneland July yearling

Sire Kingmambo

Won 5 of 13 races, inc. Poule d'Essai des Poulains-Gr1, St James's Palace S.-Gr1, Prix du Moulin de Longchamp-Gr1. Medium-sized, attractive individual. Among the best milers of his generation, game, consistent, with a good turn of foot. Sire of: American Boss (Gr2), El Condor Pasa (NHK Mile Cup-Gr1, Japan Cup-Gr1, Grand Prix de Saint-Cloud-Gr1), Mambo Twist (Gr3), Parade Ground (Gr2), Admire Mambo (Gr2), Lemon Drop Kid (Futurity S.-Gr1, Belmont S.-Gr1, Travers S.-Gr1, Whitney S.-Gr1, Woodward H.-Gr1), Monarch's Maze (Gr2), Bluemamba (Poule d'Essai des Pouliches-Gr1), King Cugat (Gr2), Kingsalsa (Gr3), King's Best (2,000 Guineas-Gr1), Parade Leader (Gr2), Penny's Gold (Gr3), King Fidelia (Gr3), Malhub (Golden Jubilee S.-Gr1), Okawango (Grand Criterium-Gr1), Voodoo Dancer (Garden City H.-Gr1), Dubai Destination (Queen Anne S.-Gr1), Walzerkonigin (Gr2), Governor Brown (Gr3), Russian Rhythm (1,000 Guineas-Gr1, Coronation S.-Gr1, Nassau S.-Gr1).

Dam Mysterial

Ran twice unplaced at 3 years, half-sister to dual Gr1-winning sprinter Agnes World and champion Japanese sprinter-miler Hishi Akebono. Dam of: Dubai Destination (1999 c by Kingmambo; Gr1 winner), Cino (2000 c by Dehere; unraced), Destination Dubai (2001 c by Kingmambo; placed 2nd twice, only races to date).

Pedigree assessment

Dubai Destination was apparently destined for the top when he comfortably lowered Rock Of Gibraltar's colours in the Champagne Stakes at two, but training troubles then intervened, and 21 months passed before that potential was realised. It was a performance worth waiting for, his dominant display in the Queen Anne Stakes providing one of the highlights of Royal Ascot, but it was all downhill again after that. There is a serious soundness issue with Kingmambo's stock, as he is able to get top-class athletes but also sires a high proportion who fail to reach the racecourse; as Dubai Destination is the product of an unsound mare, it is perhaps fortunate that he was able to show occasional flashes of brilliance. *TM*

Echoes In Eternity (Ire)

3yo bay filly   **112**

Spinning World (USA) - Magnificient Style (USA) (Silver Hawk (USA))
Owner Godolphin
Trainer Saeed Bin Suroor
Breeder Swettenham Stud

Career: **6** starts | won **3** | second **0** | third **1** | **£69,771** win and place

By David Dew

THERE appeared to be no stopping Godolphin's spending spree after the end of the 2002 Flat season, as they brandished their cheque-book in an attempt to secure a hatful of potential big-race winners. One they thought fitted the bill was the promising two-year-old filly Echoes In Eternity, a Newmarket maiden winner on her only start.

Trained at the time by John Gosden and racing in the colours of Robert Sangster, the daughter of Spinning World was sent off the stable's second string and looked particularly green both going to post and when stuck against the far rail at the halfway stage of the mile contest. However, a decisive move about two furlongs from home saw her switched to overcome the traffic and she powered up the hill to leave Discreet Brief and eight others trailing in her wake.

It was a performance that understandably raised eyebrows at the Godolphin camp, which had made two highly significant previous purchases from Sangster in the 1994 Oaks and Irish Derby heroine Balanchine and the 1998 1,000 Guineas winner Cape Verdi, and nobody was surprised when a deal was struck.

Echoes In Eternity wintered in Dubai and then took part in private trials during the spring. Speculation is invariably rife as to the merit of performances in such contests, but while there was nothing wrong with her staying-on third behind Gonfilia and subsequent Pretty Polly Stakes winner Hi Dubai, Godolphin's racing manager, Simon Crisford, felt that the new acquisition had plenty of ground to make up if she was to have any chance in either the 1,000 Guineas or the Oaks.

That assertion was to prove spot-on. Echoes In Eternity made her first start for her new connections in the Musidora Stakes at York in May. She was sent off a 2-1 favourite to emulate her dam, the 1996 winner Magnificient Style, but after racing wide and leading briefly three furlongs

Echoes In Eternity (Jamie Spencer) holds off Macadamia to take the Sun Chariot at Newmarket in October

out, she lost her place and folded tamely to finish a well-beaten last of eight behind Cassis.

Jamie Spencer, who had been handed the ride due to the suspension of Frankie Dettori, reported that the filly had slipped both when leaving the stalls and on the home turn and that she never felt quite right. Still, despite the excuses, there was an air of disappointment as Godolphin's tardy start to the season continued and they were still without a serious Classic hope.

Given a break of three months after York, during which time she was pin-fired because of an injury to her off-side hock, Echoes In Eternity returned to the track in August but continued to disappoint. When she followed a third place behind Hoh Buzzard in a weakish Listed race over ten furlongs at Salisbury by finishing a well-beaten eighth of nine behind Lady Bear in a better race of the same status at Sandown, admittedly on unsuitably softish ground, there must have been a temptation to

2003   Race record

1st Peugeot Sun Chariot Stakes (Group 2) (Newmarket, October 4) 3yo+ 1m Good to firm **112** (TS 88) 10 ran. *Led 2f, remained handy, led over 2f out, ridden out, beat Macadamia by nk*

1st Royal Bank of Scotland John Musker Fillies' Stakes (Listed) (Yarmouth, September 17) 3yo+ 10f Good to firm **104** (TS 84) 9 ran. *Soon tracking leader, led over 3f out, stayed on well, beat Silence Is Golden by 1¼l*

8th Sunley Atalanta Stakes (Listed) (Sandown, August 30) 3yo+ 1m Good to soft **78** (TS 41) 9 ran. *Tracked leaders, ridden and close up 2f out, soon weakened, beaten 10½l by Lady Bear*

3rd EBF Upavon Fillies' Stakes (Listed) (Salisbury, August 13) 3yo+ 10f Good to firm **97** (TS 57) 5 ran. *Chased winner after 2f, ridden to challenge from 3f out, still every chance over 1f out, weakened and lost 2nd inside final furlong, beaten 2l by Hoh Buzzard*

8th Tattersalls Musidora Stakes (Group 3) (York, May 13) 3yo 10½f Good to firm **78** (TS 43) 8 ran. *Raced wide, joined leader 7f out, led 3f out, soon headed, lost place over 1f out, eased inside final furlong, beaten 15½l by Cassis*

2002

1st Cliff Brants' Champagne Retirement EBF Maiden Fillies' Stakes (Newmarket, September 24) 2yo 1m Good to firm **93** (TS 77) 10 ran

draw stumps. However, there was little to lose by persevering and at last it paid off. With Godolphin starting to hit form, Echoes In Eternity was given another crack in Listed company over ten furlongs at Yarmouth in September and, with the ground riding good to firm, she seemingly had her ideal conditions.

Helped by the strong pace forced by Silence Is Golden, she finally earned some valuable black type by being taken wide of her rivals before joining at the head of affairs and quickening impressively clear to the line. She beat Silence Is Golden by a length and a quarter, with hot favourite Beneventa two lengths away in third. It was by some way her best run so far.

Three weeks later it got even better, when Echoes In Eternity returned to the scene of her impressive two-year-old debut to take the Group 2 Peugeot Sun Chariot Stakes, these days run over a mile. Always to the fore in a field of ten, in which every runner had won in Listed company at least, she took it up from Londonnetdotcom in the final two furlongs and was ridden out, after idling slightly in the closing stages, to score a cosy neck success over Macadamia. The runner-up had developed into a smart miler, following her Hunt Cup win at Royal Ascot with a length defeat of Waldmark in the Group 2 Falmouth Stakes at Newmarket, and this was smart form.

When at last she came good, Echoes In Eternity looked so promising that it has been decided to keep her in training as a four-year-old. There is talk of a crack at the Beverly D at Arlington, and if she maintained the rate of progress she was showing at the end of the season it would be no surprise to see her ending up in the Breeders' Cup Filly & Mare Turf. The best has yet to come.

Echoes In Eternity

bay filly 26-3-2000

		Northern Dancer	**Nearctic** Natalma
	Nureyev		
		Special	Forli Thong
Spinning World ch 1993			
		Riverman	Never Bend River Lady
	Imperfect Circle		
		Aviance	Northfields Minnie Hauk
		Roberto	Hail To Reason Bramalea
	Silver Hawk		
		Gris Vitesse	Amerigo Matchiche
Magnificient Style b 1993			
		Icecapade	**Nearctic** Shenanigans
	Mia Karina		
		Basin	Tom Rolfe Delta

Bred by Swettenham Stud in Ireland

Sire **Spinning World**

Won 8 races, inc. Prix Saint Roman-Gr3, Irish 2,000 Guineas-Gr1, Prix Jacques le Marois-Gr1, Prix du Muguet-Gr2, Prix Jacques le Marois-Gr1, Prix du Moulin-Gr1, Breeders' Cup Mile-Gr1. By outstanding sire out of Cheveley Park Stakes runner-up from excellent family. Stands at Coolmore Stud, 2004 fee €17,500. Oldest progeny 4. Sire of: King Of Happiness (Gr3), Quad's Melody (Gr3), Echoes In Eternity (Gr2), Spinola (Gr2)

Dam **Magnificient Style**

Won 2 of 4 races in Europe, inc. Musidora S.-Gr3. Later placed in US. Half-sister to Grade 1 winner Siberian Summer. Dam of: Stylelistick (1999 f by Storm Cat; US stakes winner, Gr3-placed), Echoes In Eternity (2000 f by Spinning World; Gr2 winner), Percussionist (2001 c by Sadler's Wells; placed), 2002 f by Sadler's Wells.

Pedigree assessment

By a miler out of a smart 10f winner, so no surprise she has won stakes events over both trips. That distance span gives her plentiful opportunities in Europe and North America next year to gain further stakes wins. Comes from a fine US family that has also done well in Europe and has obvious credentials as a broodmare prospect. *JH*

Ekraar (USA)

6yo bay horse   **121**

Red Ransom (USA) - Sacahuista (USA) (Raja Baba (USA))
Owner Hamdan Al Maktoum
Trainer M P Tregoning
Breeder Peter M Brant

Career: **25** starts | won **8** | second **3** | third **5** | £945,162 win and place

By Richard Austen

EKRAAR always did look a better class of pacemaker. When the six-year-old signed on for front-running duties on Nayef's behalf in the Prince of Wales's Stakes at Royal Ascot, only two of the ten-strong field had won more races – and this was not just because Ekraar had age on his side. He also had earnings of £798,198 and, although the vast majority of that was gathered in defeat, Ekraar was a high-class performer of long standing. This he reiterated in the Gran Premio del Jockey Club in October, his most important success and almost certainly the final start in a long and honourable career before going to stud.

Ekraar was trained by Marcus Tregoning as a two- and three-year-old when he won four races, three of them Group 3s, before embarking on two years' service with Godolphin. An injury to Nayef's workmate Mubtaker early in 2003 was a blow to Tregoning at the time but didn't look so calamitous later on, because Mubtaker returned revitalised in the autumn and Ekraar, as Tregoning related, "was the perfect horse to take over the same role. I asked Sheikh Hamdan if I could have him back – I knew they were coming to the end with him, they'd done what they could with him – and it was amazing he's ended on such a high note."

Godolphin got only one Listed victory out of Ekraar and struggled to get him back to form as a four-year-old, but they finally did so in December of that year when he came within an ace of winning the Hong Kong Vase. He ran creditably for the most part after that and, during his spell carrying the royal blue, ran in eight Group or Grade 1 events in five different countries. Earlier in his career, he had run in the Racing Post Trophy (finishing third) and Poule d'Essai des Poulains (fourth), but the level required to win a Group 1 always seemed just out of reach.

Back with Tregoning for 2003, the Dubai Sheema Classic at Nad Al

Ekraar (Richard Hills) finally breaks his Group 1 duck in the Gran Premio del Jockey Club at San Siro

Sheba in March was a fresh case in point. Ekraar, 25-1 with the British bookmakers, gave his running to take a valuable third prize in front of 13 others but was thoroughly eclipsed by Sulamani and Ange Gabriel. "He'll also be entered in all the top races," Tregoning nevertheless revealed in May, "in case we feel the need to slot in a pacemaker for Nayef."

After a workmanlike victory at 4-11 in a conditions stakes at Doncaster in June, Ekraar was asked to fulfil just such a duty at Royal Ascot. He fluffed his lines slightly with a slow start but still seemed to unsettle the front-running favourite Moon Ballad, an erstwhile Godolphin stablemate, after a couple of furlongs and when Ekraar weakened out of contention, Moon Ballad wasn't long in following him. Nayef won. Who says there isn't competition between the Maktoum brothers?

"He's had a little bit of a break and needed one," said Tregoning when Ekraar was next seen out in a Listed race at Newmarket in October. There were only four other runners to try to make the six-year-old's farewell to British racing a losing one, and none succeeded as Ekraar took over two out in a tactical race and held Compton Bolter by a length.

With five runners again in the Gran Premio del Jockey Club at Milan 16 days later, Ekraar was at the eleventh hour presented with clearly his best opportunity to grab a Group 1 victory. Black Sam Bellamy beat him into third in the same event in 2002, but the 2003 edition was run

2003   Race record

1st Gran Premio Del Jockey Club (Group 1) (San Siro, October 19) 3yo+ 12f Good **121** 5 ran. *Raced in 3rd, headway on outside to press leaders 3f out, led over 2f out, driven out, beat Maktub by 2l*

1st Fishpools Furnishings Godolphin Stakes (Listed) (Newmarket, October 3) 3yo+ 12f Good to firm **118** (TS 89) 5 ran. *Held up in touch, led 2f out, ridden out, beat Compton Bolter by 1l*

10th Prince of Wales's Stakes (Group 1) (Ascot, June 18) 4yo+ 10f Good to firm **92** (TS 74) 10 ran. *Slowly into stride, soon driven and pressed leader 7f out until over 4f out, soon beaten, beaten 19½l by Nayef*

1st Worthington's Conditions Stakes (Doncaster, June 7) 3yo+ 10½f Good **98** (TS 87) 6 ran. *Held up, headway on outer over 3f out, ridden over 1f out, stayed on to lead last 50yds, beat Leo's Luckyman by ½l*

3rd Dubai Sheema Classic (Group 1) (Nad Al Sheba, March 29) 4yo+ 12f Good **118** (TS 113) 16 ran. *Towards rear early, mid-division halfway, 7th straight, good headway over 2f out, one pace final furlong, beaten 4l by Sulamani*

2002

4th Hong Kong Vase (Group 1) (Sha Tin, December 15) 3yo+ 12f Good to firm **121** 14 ran ● **3rd** Gran Premio del Jockey Club e Coppa d'Oro (Group 1) (San Siro, October 20) 3yo+ 12f Soft **115** 8 ran ● **2nd** Premio Presidente della Repubblica SIS (Group 1) (Capannelle, May 12) 4yo+ 10f Good **121** 9 ran ● **5th** Dubai Sheema Classic (Group 1) (Nad Al Sheba, March 23) 4yo+ 12f Good **104** 15 ran

Other notable runs

2001 2nd Hong Kong Vase (Group 1) (Sha Tin, December 16) 3yo+ 12f Good to firm **123** 14 ran ● **1st** Amco Corporation Troy Stakes (Listed) (Doncaster, September 14) 3yo+ 12f Good to soft **116** (TS 102) 7 ran ● **3rd** Prix d'Ispahan (Group 1) (Longchamp, May 20) 4yo+ 9f Good **113** (TS 105) 5 ran **2000 1st** flutter.com Select Stakes (Group 3) (Goodwood, September 9) 3yo+ 10f Good **123** (TS 108) 5 ran ● **1st** Petros Rose of Lancaster Stakes (Group 3) (Haydock, August 12) 3yo+ 10½f Good **115** (TS 84) 9 ran ● **1st** Newbury Show 2000 Conditions Stakes (Newbury, July 16) 3yo+ 10f Good to firm **113** (TS 113) 7 ran **1999 3rd** Racing Post Trophy (Group 1) (Doncaster, October 23) 2yo 1m Soft **111** (TS 103) 9 ran ● **1st** Champagne Lanson Vintage Stakes (Group 3) (Goodwood, July 29) 2yo 7f Good to firm **114** (TS 103) 5 ran

on much faster ground and this time Black Sam Bellamy was reeled in without any problems. Warrsan was soon fighting a losing battle, which left the home side's Maktub as Ekraar's only danger. Once Ekraar forced his head in front, however, there was no passing him and he won by a couple of lengths.

First prize of £131,494 in Milan meant that Ekraar's career earnings fell short of the million by little more than £50,000. Game and durable, he was reportedly lazy on the gallops at home as a two-year-old and often wore blinkers or a visor afterwards, but not for any of his major victories, nor in any race in 2003 except the Prince of Wales's Stakes. Following his retirement to stud he will be missed by all associated with him. Richard Hills summed it up when he said: "This horse is a proper friend. He has done a job for us, both on and off the course."

Ekraar   *bay horse, 13-2-1997*

| | | Hail To Reason | Turn-to |
| | | | Nothirdchance |

		Roberto		
Red Ransom			Bramalea	Nashua
b 1987				Rarelea
			Damascus	Sword Dancer
	Arabia			Kerala
		Christmas Wind	Nearctic
			Bally Free

Structured pedigree:

Red Ransom (b 1987)
- Roberto
  - Hail To Reason — Turn-to / Nothirdchance
  - Bramalea — Nashua / Rarelea
- Arabia
  - Damascus — Sword Dancer / Kerala
  - Christmas Wind — Nearctic / Bally Free

Sacahuista (b 1984)
- Raja Baba
  - Bold Ruler — Nasrullah / Miss Disco
  - Missy Baba — My Babu / Uvira
- Nalees Flying Flag
  - Hoist The Flag — Tom Rolfe / Wavy Navy
  - Nalee — Nashua / Levee

Bred by Peter Brant in US. $200,000 Keeneland November foal

Sire **Red Ransom**

Won 2 of 3 races up to 6f. Speedy and precocious, had tall reputation, and was bred to stay at least a mile, but career cut short by injury. Sire of: Bail Out Becky (Del Mar Oaks-Gr1), Petrouchka (Gr3), Sri Pekan (Gr2), Upper Noosh (Gr3), Trail City (Gr2), Wandering Star (Gr2), Intikhab (Gr2), Rojo Dinero (Gr3), Comic Strip (Gr3), Stay Sound (Gr3), Crystal Symphony (Gr3), Perfect Sting (Garden City H.-Gr1, Queen Elizabeth II Challenge Cup S.-Gr1, Breeders' Cup Filly & Mare Turf-Gr1), Pico Teneriffe (Gr3), China Visit (Gr2), Ekraar (Gran Premio del Jockey Club-Gr1), Shining Hour (Gr3), Slew The Red (Gr3), New Economy (Gr2), Mr Mellon (Gr2), Van Rouge (Gr3), Cassis (Gr3), Casual Look (Oaks S.-Gr1), Fairly Ransom (Gr2), Ransom O'War (Bayerisches Zuchtrennen-Gr1).

Dam **Sacahuista**

Won 6 of 21 races, inc. Oak Leaf S.-Gr1, Adirondack S.-Gr2, Schuylerville S.-Gr3, Breeders' Cup Distaff-Gr1, Spinster S.-Gr1, also 2nd Hollywood Starlet S.-Gr1, Del Mar Futurity-Gr1, Arlington-Washington Lassie S.-Gr1, Hollywood Oaks-Gr1. Champion North American 3yo filly. Half-sister to Belmont runner-up Johns Treasure from good US family of Geri and Raging Fever. Dam of: Alyhuista (1990 c by Alydar; unraced), Hussonet (1991 c by Mr Prospector; winner, stakes-placed), Balenciaga (1992 f by Gulch; unplaced), Buck Strider (1993 c by Easy Goer; winner), Hishi Saturday (1994 c by AP Indy; winner), Ekraar (1997 c by Red Ransom; Gr1 winner), Dynamix (1998 c by AP Indy; winner), Spinning Wild (1999 c by Spinning World; placed), Dossier (2001 f by Storm Cat; unraced), 2002 c by Storm Cat.

Pedigree assessment

Possesses American pedigree that would have been consistent with a mile performer on dirt, but Ekraar has excelled over middle distances on turf. Red Ransom's sire Roberto is likely to have been influential there, and the family further back includes some top-class European performers. Bred to be fairly precocious – and did win a Group 3 event at two – but has proved durable. He will stand at stud in Italy in 2004 and is also due to shuttle to New Zealand for the southern hemisphere season. *JH*

Empire Maker (USA)

3yo brown colt **125**

Unbridled (USA) - Toussaud (USA) (El Gran Senor (USA))

Owner Juddmonte Farms

Trainer R J Frankel

Breeder Juddmonte Farms

| Career: **8** starts | won **4** | second **3** | third **1** | £1,244,097 win and place |

By James Willoughby

THE first suggestion of the foot problems which eventually led to Empire Maker's retirement came in the Florida Derby at Gulfstream Park in March. Though he was, on the face of it, wildly impressive, he refused to switch leads in the straight.

A racehorse is allowed to do pretty much its own thing in Europe, but the uniformity of US dirt tracks demands a more rigid approach to the mechanics of movement. Horses are taught to change to their near-fore lead to negotiate the tight, left-handed home bends, before transferring their weight to the opposite leg for the relatively short straights.

When a thoroughbred refuses to comply with these demands, there is often a deep-set malaise. The greenhorn can easily be forgiven, but a deeper explanation is required where a more seasoned individual is concerned.

Fears that Empire Maker was hurting were assuaged to a certain extent by his decisive defeat of Funny Cide in their final Kentucky Derby prep race, the Wood Memorial Stakes at Aqueduct in April. The Unbridled colt hacked along merrily for most of the way and did eventually consent to switch leads after prolonged coercion from his jockey, Jerry Bailey. It has to be noted, however, that he did not find a great deal off the bridle under the muddy conditions.

Success in these two influential prep races not surprisingly propelled Empire Maker into strong favouritism for the Kentucky Derby. Moreover, there were plenty of experienced observers who strongly believed that the 25-year wait for a Triple Crown successor to Affirmed was coming to an end. What they had failed to consider, however, was their hero's feet of clay.

Just days before the Derby, Empire Maker's trainer, Bobby Frankel, ran into problems. A bruised off-fore hoof had forced the postponement of several key workouts and all Frankel could do was to have his star

**Empire Maker (Jerry Bailey) rounds the fourth turn ahead
of Funny Cide on his way to victory in the Belmont Stakes**

colt walked around the track. Though no connection between the injury
and Empire Maker's gimping in Florida was ever admitted, a causal link
is not difficult to establish.

Empire Maker was a superior racehorse to Funny Cide, but he could
not prove it at Churchill Downs. It is true that being forced to race wide
compromised his chance, but his tendency to hang quite violently left
under pressure was the substantive cause of his defeat.

Had Empire Maker ended the first Saturday in May wearing a blanket
of roses rather than a poultice, then Frankel would have sent him to
collect the second Classic jewel, the Preakness Stakes at Pimlico. Instead,
he was rested up for the concluding leg of the Triple Crown at Belmont
in June.

The day of the Belmont perhaps marked the zenith of Empire Maker's
soundness, for he managed to change legs adroitly in the closing stages
and did not veer from a true line to anything like the extent of his previous
races. So powerfully did he travel on the shoulder of Triple Crown aspirant
Funny Cide that the result looked a formality from a long way out, though

2003   Race record

2nd Jim Dandy Stakes (Grade 2) (Dirt) (Saratoga, August 3) 3yo 9f Fast **118** 6 ran. *Outpaced early stages, improved from about 2f out, stayed on gamely closing stages, beaten nk by Strong Hope*

1st Belmont Stakes (Grade 1) (Dirt) (Belmont Park, June 7) 3yo 12f Sloppy **125** 6 ran. *Went 2nd pressing leader after 2f, led 3f out, ran on gamely when challenged 1f out, drawing away close home, beat Ten Most Wanted by ³/₄l*

2nd Kentucky Derby (Grade 1) (Dirt) (Churchill Downs, May 3) 3yo 10f Fast **120** 16 ran. *Raced in 8th on outside, headway over 3f out, pressing leaders in 3rd entering straight, edged left over 1f out, kept on to take 2nd close home, beaten 1³/₄l by Funny Cide*

1st Wood Memorial Stakes (Grade 1) (Dirt) (Aqueduct, April 12) 3yo 9f Muddy **124** 8 ran. *Raced wide, tracked leading pair until taking narrow lead inside final furlong, stayed on gamely, beat Funny Cide by ¹/₂l*

1st Florida Derby (Grade 1) (Dirt) (Gulfstream Park, March 15) 3yo 9f Fast **125** 7 ran. *Tracked leaders, improved into 2nd 2f out, driven out to win easily, beat Trust N Luck by 9³/₄l*

2nd Sham Stakes (Dirt) (Santa Anita, February 7) 3yo 9f Fast 7 ran. *In rear early, improved from over 2f out, stayed on, beaten 1l by Man Among Men*

2002

3rd Remsen Stakes (Grade 2) (Dirt) (Aqueduct, November 30) 9f Fast 8 ran ● **1st** Maiden (Dirt) (Belmont Park, October 20) 2yo 1m Fast 130 ran

Empire Maker had to be driven out to hold the late challenge of Ten Most Wanted, as his old rival faded to third.

Given the hometown support for Funny Cide's quest, it was only to be expected that Empire Maker was cast in the role of spoiler. But the vehemence of the New York crowd's reaction took many by surprise. As the victor walked back in front of the stands, he engendered such ill feeling in some quarters that he was greeted with a cascade of audible derision. Bailey was particularly indignant at this asperity, repeatedly pointing down to his mount as if affronted by the public's apathy towards a top-class racehorse in his pomp.

With his career back on the right footing, Empire Maker threatened to play a major role in the remainder of the season's marquee events. But a rare example of misjudgement from Bailey left him runner-up to Strong Hope in the Jim Dandy at Saratoga, then a cough prevented his participation in the Travers Stakes on the same track.

When Empire Maker sustained another injury to a hoof – this time his near-fore – Frankel had to cancel his preparation for the Jockey Club Gold Cup in September and his stable star was consigned to the breeding shed. With looks and pedigree to match his high-class form, the half-brother to Chester House should prove a valuable addition to the roster at Juddmonte Farms, Kentucky.

Interestingly, Empire Maker's covering fee of $100,000 places him on a par with another highly valued first-season sire, Mineshaft. It is a desperate pity for the sport that two such inspirational runners never got to compare talents on the track.

Empire Maker

brown colt, 27-4-2000

		Mr Prospector	Raise A Native / Gold Digger
	Fappiano		
		Killaloe	Dr Fager / Grand Splendor
Unbridled b 1987			
		Le Fabuleux	Wild Risk / Anguar
	Gana Facil		
		Charedi	**In Reality** / Magic
		Northern Dancer	Nearctic / Natalma
	El Gran Senor		
		Sex Appeal	Buckpasser / Best In Show
Toussaud b 1989			
		In Reality	Intentionally / My Dear Girl
	Image Of Reality		
		Edee's Image	Cornish Prince / Ortalan

Bred by Juddmonte Farms in Kentucky

Sire **Unbridled**

Won 8 of 24 races, inc. Florida Derby-Gr1, Kentucky Derby-G1, Breeders' Cup Classic-Gr1. Champion 3yo colt. Big, strong sort, ideally suited by 10f on dirt, but Gr1-placed only start on grass. Died October 2001. Sire of: Grindstone (Kentucky Derby-Gr1), Unbridled's Song (Breeders' Cup Juvenile-Gr1, Florida Derby-Gr1), Banshee Breeze (Coaching Club American Oaks-Gr1, Alabama S.-Gr1, Spinster S.-Gr1, Apple Blossom H.-Gr1, Go For Wand H.-Gr1), Manistique (Santa Margarita H.-Gr1, Vanity H.-Gr1, Santa Maria H.-Gr1), Anees (Breeders' Cup Juvenile-Gr1), Broken Vow (Gr2), Red Bullet (Preakness S.-Gr1), Unshaded (Travers S.-Gr1), Exogenous (Gazelle H.-Gr1, Beldame S.-Gr1), Surya (Gr2), Belterra (Gr1), Saarland (Gr2), Empire Maker (Florida Derby-Gr1, Wood Memorial S.-Gr1, Belmont S.-Gr1), Santa Catarina (Gr2), Halfbridled (Del Mar Debutante S.-Gr1, Oak Leaf S.-Gr2, Breeders' Cup Juvenile Fillies-Gr1).

Dam **Toussaud**

Won 7 of 15 races, inc. Criterion S.-Gr3, Wilshire H.-Gr2, Gamely H.-Gr1, American H.-Gr2. Also 4th in Breeders' Cup Mile-Gr1. Lengthy, powerful sort who showed progressive form throughout her career. Dam of: Chester House (1995 c by Mr Prospector; Gr1 winner), Honest Lady (1996 f by Seattle Slew; Gr1 winner), Decarchy (1997 c by Distant View; Gr2 winner), Civilisation (1998 c by Gone West; unplaced, lost an eye in accident, at stud in West Virginia), Chiselling (1999 c by Woodman; Gr1 winner), Empire Maker (2000 c by Unbridled; Classic winner).

Pedigree assessment

Empire Maker was supposed to become the hero of the Triple Crown. Instead – at least to New Yorkers – he became cast as its villain, reversing the Kentucky Derby form with Funny Cide in the Belmont, and restoring the order established in their earlier meeting in the Wood Memorial. The scoreline remained 2-1, because the promise of further meetings was never fulfilled, but that hardly seemed to matter when the season petered out for both. Beaten by the ordinary Strong Hope in the Jim Dandy Stakes, Empire Maker then kept finding excuses for absence and his retirement was announced before the Breeders' Cup came along; there can be little doubt that he was no longer sound. Immaculately bred and, according to Bobby Frankel, the best horse he has trained, Empire Maker is to stand for a fee of $100,000 at Juddmonte Farms in Kentucky. *TM*

Etoile Montante (USA)

3yo chestnut filly **118**

Miswaki (USA) - Willstar (USA) (Nureyev (USA))

Owner K Abdullah

Trainer Mme C Head-Maarek

Breeder Juddmonte Farms

Career: **9** starts	won **5**	second **2**	third **1**	**£175,993** win and place

---

By Graham Dench

CONNECTIONS of Etoile Montante were made to sweat before she eventually gained the Group win that had looked a mere formality for her at the end of her two-year-old campaign, but in the end it was well worth the wait. Group-race success came very late in the year, but it came at the highest level, the filly gaining deserved reward for her placings on all of her three previous ventures into Group 1 company by beating British-trained outsider Royal Millennium in the Prix de la Foret at Longchamp in October, one of the last prestigious prizes of the French season.

Etoile Montante's form at two suggested a very bright future indeed, with the Poule d'Essai des Pouliches the obvious early target and Royal Ascot's Coronation Stakes a possibility later on if all went well. She had looked good when winning a newcomers' race at Deauville and she had followed up with another ready success at Longchamp before finding only the brilliant Six Perfections too good for her after making the running in the Prix Marcel Boussac back on the latter track.

Even then, though beaten decisively by the winner, she finished fully five lengths and more clear of the remainder in a typically strong field, earning herself a mark of 116 on the International Classification, upsides Russian Rhythm and behind only Six Perfections and Airwave among the fillies.

The new season did not begin well for Etoile Montante when she was beaten into fourth place in her prep race, the Prix de la Grotte, also at Longchamp, yet in the absence of Six Perfections, who had been an unlucky second to Russian Rhythm in the 1,000 Guineas the previous weekend, she still looked very much the one to beat in the Pouliches which, while numerically up to scratch, looked nowhere near as strong as its Newmarket counterpart.

She started favourite but never really looked like beating front-

Etoile Montante (Olivier Peslier) takes the Prix de la Foret at Longchamp in October

running Maiden Tower and in the end was relegated to third when Musical Chimes swept past them both to lead close home and win by a length and a short neck.

A Listed-race win at Compiegne followed shortly after the Pouliches, but Etoile Montante was not seen to full advantage until she returned from a midsummer break. Her second to Porlezza over a distance short of her best in the six-and-a-half-furlong Prix Maurice de Gheest at Deauville represented a more than satisfactory return to action and a second Listed success in the Prix du Pin at Longchamp, back up to seven furlongs, was another step in the right direction. However, with opportunities drying up, it was the Foret, over seven once again, that really mattered.

In a race in which cross-Channel challengers outnumbered locals by six to four, Etoile Montante was sent off odds-on at 1-2, coupled with her owner Khalid Abdullah's 1,000 Guineas third Intercontinental, who also had an obvious chance.

Ridden by Oliver Peslier, who had already won two races that afternoon

2003   Race record

1st Prix de la Foret (Group 1) (Longchamp, October 12) 3yo+ 7f Very soft **118** (TS 98) 10 ran. *Raced in 5th, 3rd straight, pushed along in centre 1½f out, ridden to challenge 1f out, led 100yds out, ran on well, beat Royal Millennium by 1½l*

1st Prix du Pin (Listed) (Longchamp, September 20) 3yo+ 7f Good **111** (TS 83) 14 ran. *Disputed lead until led approaching final furlong, pushed clear, easily, beat Star Valley by 2l*

2nd Prix Maurice de Gheest (Group 1) (Deauville, August 10) 3yo+ 6½f Good to soft **113** (TS 43) 12 ran. *Always in touch, hard ridden well over 1f out, ran on well under pressure inside final furlong, took 2nd on line, beaten 1l by Porlezza*

1st Prix des Lilas (Listed) (Compiegne, May 26) 3yo 1m Very soft **103** 9 ran. *chased leader, led over 1f out, ran on well, beat State Of Art by ½l*

3rd Gainsborough Poule d'Essai des Pouliches (Group 1) (Longchamp, May 11) 3yo 1m Good to soft **112** (TS 96) 12 ran. *Prominent on rail, 3rd straight, short of room 2f out and switched outside, ridden 1½f out and went 2nd, ran on under pressure, not trouble leader, beaten 1¼l by Musical Chimes*

4th Prix de la Grotte (Group 3) (Longchamp, April 20) 3yo 1m Good to soft **104** 8 ran. *Led to just inside final furlong, one pace, beaten 1l by Maiden Tower*

2002

2nd Prix Marcel Boussac Criterium Pouliches-Royal Barriere de Deauville (Group 1) (Longchamp, October 6) 2yo 1m Good **114** (TS 74) 10 ran ● **1st** Prix du Casino Barriere de Royan (Longchamp, September 15) 2yo 1m Good to firm **93** 8 ran ● **1st** Prix de Noiremare (Deauville, August 31) 2yo 7f Good to soft 13 ran

and went on to land two more, she was given a great ride and produced late on the outside with her challenge.

Quickening well, considering the testing conditions, she came with a strong run to score by a length and a half and the same from Royal Millennium and Saratan, with Intercontinental back in fourth. Zinziberine's fifth place meant that only Royal Millennium prevented the French quartet from completing a clean sweep.

It was mission accomplished for trainer Criquette Head-Maarek, who had won with Dedication in 2002 and had also won the race on three previous occasions, notably in 1983 with Ma Biche, one of the very best fillies of her era and successful also in the Cheveley Park Stakes and the 1,000 Guineas.

In the immediate aftermath of the Foret, Head-Maarek said: "She's formidable and tough and won like a really good filly. She's always done everything asked of her. It's difficult to reproach her in any way and I'd love to keep her in training as a four-year-old."

The plan at the end of the season, however, was for Etoile Montante to run at Hollywood Park and then remain in the United States with Bobby Frankel, perhaps prompted by the fact that Six Perfections and Nebraska Tornado will stay in training in France. When the Miswaki filly is eventually retired to the paddocks, she will be a valuable addition to Juddmonte's broodmare band.

Etoile Montante   *chestnut filly, 3-2-2000*

		Raise A Native	Native Dancer
			Raise You
	Mr Prospector		
		Gold Digger	Nashua
			Sequence
Miswaki			
ch 1978			
		Buckpasser	Tom Fool
			Busanda
	Hopespringseternal		
		Rose Bower	Princequillo
			Lea Lane
		Northern Dancer	Nearctic
			Natalma
	Nureyev		
		Special	Forli
			Thong
Willstar			
ch 1993			
		Nijinsky	**Northern Dancer**
			Flaming Page
	Nijinsky Star		
		Chris Evert	Swoon's Son
			Miss Carmie

Bred by Juddmonte Farms in Kentucky

Sire Miswaki

Won 6 of 13 races, inc. Prix de la Salamandre-Gr1 at 2, 1 Listed race in US at 4. High-class 2yo in France, smart performer on dirt and grass, just below top level, at 3 in US. Small, well-made individual; effective up to 8f, but stock frequently stay further. Sire of: Le Belvedere (Gr2), Miscrown (Gr3), Papal Power (Hopeful S.-Gr1), Midyan (Gr3), Whakilyric (Gr3), Balawaki (Gr2), Miswaki Tern (Gr2), Waki River (Criterium de Saint-Cloud-Gr1), Aliocha (Gr3), Black Tie Affair (Philip H. Iselin H.-Gr1, Breeders' Cup Classic-Gr1), Exploding Prospect (Gr3), Mistaurian (Gr3), Now Listen (Gr3), Misil (Premio Parioli-Gr1, Premio Roma-Gr2, Gran Premio del Jockey Club-Gr1), Umatilla (Karrakatta Plate [Aus]-Gr1), Urban Sea (Prix de l'Arc de Triomphe-Gr1), Marvelous Crown (Japan Cup-Gr1), Grafin (Gr3), Porto Varas (Gr3), Allied Forces (Gr2), Diligence (Gr2), Kistena (Prix de l'Abbaye de Longchamp-Gr1), Abou Zouz (Gr2), Hurricane State (Gr3), Magellano (Gr3), Inexplicable (Gr3), Tertullian (Gr3), Rossini (Gr2), Tough Speed (Gr3), Panis (Gr3), Perfect Touch (Gr3), Etoile Montante (Prix de la Foret-Gr1).

Dam Willstar

Won 1 of 5 races. Slow to come to hand, showed quite progressive form in brief career, racing only at a mile and never on extremes of going. Dam of: Prima Centauri (1998 f by Distant View; unplaced), Starfan (1999 f by Lear Fan; Listed-placed winner), Etoile Montante (2000 f by Miswaki; Gr1 winner), Spacecraft (2001 f by Distant View; unraced to date).

Pedigree assessment

The Juddmonte production line delivered outstanding performers in Europe and America throughout 2003, with two sisters from its exceptional broodmare band contributing three of them. Viviana, the more distinguished racemare, was responsible for US Grade 1 winners Tates Creek and Sightseek, while Willstar had a celebrity of her own in Etoile Montante, a decisive winner of the Prix de la Foret. She is due to race in the States in 2004 and could well make her mark in top fillies' races on grass. When the time comes she will make an attractive mate for one of the firm's new stallions. *TM*

Fair Mix (Ire)

5yo grey horse   **121**

Linamix (Fr) - Fairlee Wild (USA) (Wild Again (USA))
Owner Ecurie Week-End
Trainer M Rolland
Breeder Snc Lagardere Elevage

Career: **14** starts | won **6** | second **1** | third **1** | **£149,011** win and place

By Robert Carter

MOST horses are quick to show their ability, but the career of Fair Mix was a measured climb up each step of the ladder over 18 months. It began when he was claimed after winning his second race and peaked with victory over Execute and Falbrav in the Prix Ganay.

It is hard to conceive of a Group 1 winner emerging from the claiming ranks in Britain, even allowing for the enhancements to the system made in 2003, but it is by no means uncommon in the United States or France. For the past few years, the French have staged a day of seven claimers at Saint-Cloud before the Arc on which each race is named after a successful claim, including Polytain (the 1992 Prix du Jockey-Club winner) and Cardmania (1993 Breeders' Cup Sprint). The name of Fair Mix will surely join them.

To start at the peak, Fair Mix was always being aimed at the Ganay and began 2003 at the earliest possible moment, finishing fifth to Aquarelliste in the Group 3 Prix Exbury and then being caught close home by Ana Marie in the Group 2 Prix d'Harcourt, over one and a quarter miles, at Longchamp.

The pair met again in the Ganay, over an extra half-furlong at Longchamp, where Ana Marie was favourite ahead of Falbrav, who was having his first run since his Japan Cup victory, and Fair Mix. The five-year-old broke best but was soon headed by Black Sam Bellamy, Chancellor and Valentino. He disputed third, between Valentino and Kaieteur, from halfway until Olivier Peslier sent him on inside the final two furlongs and, though soon chased by Falbrav, he kept on to score by two and a half lengths from Execute, who snatched second in the last strides. Peslier hit him left-handed ten times in a sustained drive, but Fair Mix did not flinch. Ana Marie never threatened before dead-heating for fifth with Valentino.

Fair Mix (Olivier Peslier) takes the Prix Ganay at Longchamp in April

Fair Mix made an inauspicious start to his career when eighth at Le Croise-Laroche late in his three-year-old season, owned at the time by his breeder, Jean-Luc Lagardere, and trained by André Fabre. However, it was a different story a few weeks later, when he reappeared in the Prix de Dourdan, a one-mile claimer run on holding ground at Saint-Cloud, where he was entered for Ff120,000.

This time he finished three lengths and upwards clear of 16 rivals and attracted numerous claims. Ecurie Week-End put in the highest bid at Ff265,555 (about £25,000) and the stable, which is run by a tipping publication, sent Fair Mix to Marcel Rolland, who had already tried to buy him privately.

Ecurie Week-End's only horse on the Flat, Fair Mix has done them proud. They had, however, already enjoyed big-race success in another field, with the American trotting mare, Moni Maker, winner of the Prix d'Amerique, the most important prize in the French version of the sport, at Vincennes in 1999.

Rolland won the Group 1 Prix du Cadran with Molesnes in 1994 but is best known for his handling of handicappers, both on the Flat and over hurdles. He had won a valuable hurdle prize each year from 1998 to 2000 with Kim, who was also owned by Week-End, and schooled Fair Mix regularly after taking charge of him before opting to keep him on the Flat.

2003 {Race record}

6th Prix du Conseil de Paris (Group 2) (Longchamp, October 19) 3yo+ 12f Good to soft (TS 102) 9 ran. *Raced in 2nd, 3rd and pushed along straight, ridden 2f out, stayed on at one pace but never dangerous, beaten 4¼l by Vallee Enchantee*

1st Prix Ganay (Group 1) (Longchamp, April 27) 4yo+ 10½f Very soft **121** (TS 110) 9 ran. *Raced in 4th, 3rd straight, pushed along over 2f out and quickened to lead 2f out, ridden approaching final furlong, ran on well, beat Execute by 2 1/2l*

2nd Prix d'Harcourt (Group 2) (Longchamp, March 30) 4yo+ 10f Good **117** (TS 100) 11 ran. *Prominent, 2nd straight, led over 1½f out, ridden 1f out, headed and no extra close home, beaten snk by Ana Marie*

5th Prix Exbury (Group 3) (Saint-Cloud, March 8) 4yo+ 10f Very soft **102** (TS 53) 7 ran. *Close up early, dropped towards rear 6f out, last straight, ridden and stayed on from over 1f out, beaten 7½l by Aquarelliste*

2002

8th Prix de l'Arc de Triomphe - Lucien Barriere (Group 1) (Longchamp, October 6) 3yo+ 12f Good **117** (TS 111) 16 ran ● **1st** La Coupe de Maisons-Laffitte (Group 3) (Maisons-Laffitte, September 17) 3yo+ 10f Good **114** (TS 84) 7 ran ● **3rd** Grand Prix de Deauville Lucien Barriere (Group 2) (Deauville, August 25) 3yo+ 12½f Good **113** (TS 73) 7 ran ● **1st** Prix de Reux (Listed) (Deauville, August 6) 3yo+ 12½f Very soft **100** (TS 66) 9 ran ● **7th** Grand Prix de Chantilly (Group 2) (Chantilly, June 9) 4yo+ 12f Good **113** (TS 96) 11 ran ● **1st** Prix Tierce Magazine/Association la Licorne (Handicap) (Longchamp, May 8) 4yo 10f Good 18 ran ● **1st** Prix de la Reine Marguerite (Handicap) (Longchamp, April 18) 4yo 10f Good 18 ran ● **Unplaced** Handicap de l'Ile de France (Handicap) (Saint-Cloud, March 16) 4yo 1m Holding 18 ran

Other runs

1st Prix de Dourdan (Claimer) (Saint-Cloud, December 1) 3yo 1m Heavy 17 ran ● **8th** Prix Miguel Clement (Le Croise-Laroche, November 8) 3yo 10½f Heavy 8 ran

Fair Mix won handicaps at Longchamp on his second and third appearances for his new connections, and on his fifth he added a Listed event at Deauville. He then ran third in the Group 2 Grand Prix de Deauville - after which Lagardere congratulated Rolland on his success with the horse - before winning the Group 3 La Coupe de Maisons-Laffitte. He ended the 2002 season by finishing eighth in the Arc.

An injury to Fair Mix's near-fore knee in the Ganay required surgery to remove a chip, but it was intended in any case that he would be put away for a second crack at the Arc. That race came and went without him, but he resurfaced two weeks after the Arc in the Prix du Conseil de Paris, over the same course and distance, and struggled home in sixth behind Vallee Enchantee.

To what extent his injury was to blame is hard to say, for while the form he showed that afternoon was some way below the level he had appeared to run to in the Ganay, one could say the same of all of his earlier efforts. Indeed, one could argue that he was flattered by the Ganay result as a whole, and not just by the taking of such a notable scalp as Falbrav's.

Fair Mix

grey horse, 26-4-1998

Linamix gr 1987	Mendez	Bellypha	Lyphard
			Belga
		Miss Carina	Caro
			Miss Pia
	Lunadix	Breton	Relko
			La Melba
		Lutine	Alcide
			Mona
Fairlee Wild b 1988	Wild Again	Icecapade	Nearctic
			Shenanigans
		Bushel-n-Peck	Khaled
			Dama
	Raise Me	Mr Prospector	Raise A Native
			Gold Digger
		Leave Me	Never Bend
			Raise The Levee

Bred by SNC Lagardere Elevage

Sire Linamix

Won 4 of 10 races, inc. Prix La Rochette-Gr3, Prix de Fontainebleau-Gr3, Poule d'Essai des Poulains-Gr1. Also 2nd in Grand Criterium-Gr1, Prix Jacques le Marois-Gr1, Prix du Moulin de Longchamp-Gr1, Champion S.-Gr1. Big, angular, round-actioned, free-running sort. Won only over a mile, but stayed 10f. Sire of: Diamond Mix (Gr2), Housamix (Gr2), Miss Satamixa (Prix Jacques le Marois-Gr1), Walk On Mix (Gr2), Manninamix (Gr3), Clodora (Gr2), Fragrant Mix (Grand Prix de Saint-Cloud-Gr1), Oa Baldixe (Gr3), Diamonixa (Gr3), Pinmix (Gr3), Sagamix (Prix de l'Arc de Triomphe-Gr1), Amilynx (Prix Royal-Oak-Gr1, twice), Artistique (Gr3), Sage et Jolie (Gr2), Slickly (Grand Prix de Paris-Gr1, Prix du Moulin de Longchamp-Gr1, Premio Vittorio di Capua-Gr1, twice), Goldamix (Criterium de Saint-Cloud-Gr1), Miraculous (Gr3), Diamilina (Gr2), Fair Mix (Prix Ganay-Gr1), Vahorimix (Poule d'Essai des Poulains-Gr1, Prix Jacques le Marois-Gr1), Bernimixa (Gr2), Martaline (Gr3), Diasilixa (Gr3), Visorama (Gr3).

Dam Fairlee Wild

Won 6 of 37 races. Just a useful sprinter-miler, who accumulated high earnings thanks to a lucrative State-bred scheme. Dam of: Fairly Grey (1995 f by Linamix; winner, twice Gr3-placed), Fairlee Mixa (1996 f by Linamix; winner), Fairly Fair (1997 f by Always Fair; unraced, died as 2yo), Fair Mix (1998 c by Linamix; Gr1 winner), Farlee Hill (1999 c by Danehill; winner).

Pedigree assessment

Bought out of a Saint-Cloud claimer as a three-year-old with a view to a career over jumps, Fair Mix never made it into that branch of the business. Instead he made dramatic improvement as a Flat performer and rounded off his 2002 campaign with an honest eighth place in the Arc, less than six lengths from the winner. In 2003 he needed a couple of races to get his act together, but in the Ganay he delivered a career-best performance that suggested he would prove a potent factor at the top level for the rest of the season. It was not to be. A knee chip was discovered, surgery was required, and nearly six months passed before Fair Mix came back, performing about 7lb below his Ganay level in the Prix du Conseil. That was still smart form, but it remains to be seen whether he can reach Group 1 calibre again. *TM*

Falbrav (Ire)

5yo bay horse **132**

Fairy King (USA) - Gift Of The Night (USA) (Slewpy (USA))

Owner Scuderia Rencati Srl

Trainer L M Cumani

Breeder Azienda Agricola Francesca

Career: **25** starts | won **12** | second **5** | third **5** | **£3,021,108** win and place

By Brough Scott

NOT JUST a champion but a warrior too – every month in 2003 from April to October Falbrav went into battle. Nine times in all, every start at Group 1 level and that ninth effort in the Breeders' Cup as good a performance as any. No other top European horse in recent times has had a campaign to match it. And his year continued. Back in Newmarket from Santa Anita, he was immediately being readied for a final target a month away in Hong Kong.

Falbrav did not always win – indeed, High Chaparral bested him both times they met. But even that titan could not stand comparison for versatility and endurance.

Third in the Ganay over ten and a half furlongs, victory in the Ispahan over nine, muddled defeat over ten in the Prince of Wales's, redemption over the same distance in the Eclipse, wide-running fifth in the King George over a mile and a half (or in view of the course steered, make that a mile and five), back to ten furlongs and total dominance at York, then total frustration over that trip at Leopardstown, down to a mile for a power-packed display at Ascot, before going so near and yet so far over a mile and a half behind the dead-heaters Johar and High Chaparral under the hot Californian sun.

It took us time to get used to Falbrav after his move to Newmarket in January. In all of 2003 he only once started favourite and that was not until the Queen Elizabeth II Stakes at Ascot, his eighth race of the year. He may have been Italian-owned and Cumani-trained, but their strategy was almost Australian in its approach. Find a big race, aim for it, run in it, then look for the next one; rest, aim and run again; and again and again and again. In our culture such no-frills campaigning is almost downgraded as desperation. It was not until Falbrav pulverised the Juddmonte field at York that we really began to realise what a monster had developed in our midst.

Falbrav (Kieren Fallon) lands the first of his four Group 1 wins in the Prix d'Ispahan at Longchamp in May

For the beauty of Falbrav is that what you see is what you get – 16.3 hands at the shoulder, 540 kilos on the weighbridge, a magnificent, aggressive, bull thoroughbred whose confident maturity as a five-year-old reminds us what we can miss when the Classic generation is hustled off to stud. This is an athlete without fear or frailty who does not suffer fools gladly. To see him in early November, glowering down, his bright bay coat still gleaming despite the strains of his Breeders' Cup exertions showing clearly across the ribs and loins, was to rejoice in the old maxim: that a racehorse is for racing.

By then his career record read 12 wins and some £3 million in prize-money from 25 starts in four seasons, and over three continents and six countries. Uniquely he has won Group 1 races at eight, nine, ten, 11 and 12 furlongs, seven Group 1 successes in all. The trail that began with a first-time-out victory in a one-mile two-year-old maiden at San Siro on September 3, 2000, is as long, honourable and eventful as that of any champion racehorse in recent memory.

That opening success was his only score in four runs as a two-year-old, while at three he won three from six starts but is best remembered for his second to Morshdi in the Italian Derby. It was at four that he began to register on the international front, Luciano d'Auria saddling him to beat Godolphin contenders in back-to-back Group 1s, the ten-

2003   Race record

3rd John Deere Breeders' Cup Turf (Grade 1) (Santa Anita, October 25) 3yo+ 12f Firm **128**
9 ran. *Disputed 4th, pushed along and went 2nd over 2f out, driven approaching straight, led over 1f out, headed final strides, beaten hd by Johar and High Chaparral*

1st Queen Elizabeth II Stakes (Sponsored By NetJets) (Group 1) (Ascot, September 27) 3yo+ 1m Good to firm **129** (TS 120) 8 ran. *Broke well, keen early, soon settled to track leader, driven to lead 1½f out, pushed clear inside final furlong, comfortably, beat Russian Rhythm by 2l*

2nd Ireland The Food Island Champion Stakes (Group 1) (Leopardstown, September 6) 3yo+ 10f Good to firm **126** (TS 121) 7 ran. *Held up, checked early, 5th 3½f out, 4th into straight, not clear run over 1f out, 2nd and switched to inner inside final furlong, ran on well, just failed, beaten nk by High Chaparral*

1st Juddmonte International Stakes (Group 1) (York, August 19) 3yo+ 10½f Good to firm **132** (TS 119) 8 ran. *Tracked leaders, effort over 3f out, quickened to lead over 2f out, kept on well, beat Magistretti by 2l*

5th King George VI And Queen Elizabeth Diamond Stakes (Group 1) (Ascot, July 26) 3yo+ 12f Good **120** (TS 92) 12 ran. *Raced alone against farside rail until joined main group in 4th 4f out, driven to chase winner 2f out to over 1f out, weakened, beaten 9l by Alamshar*

1st Coral-Eclipse Stakes (Group 1) (Sandown, July 5) 3yo+ 10f Good to firm **126** (TS 118) 15 ran. *Tracked leaders on inner, smooth progress to lead over 2f out, drew 2l clear and in command over 1f out, driven out final 150yds, beat Nayef by ¾l*

5th Prince of Wales's Stakes (Group 1) (Ascot, June 18) 4yo+ 10f Good to firm **114** (TS 98) 10 ran. *Bumped after 1f, headway on outside 3f out, staying on but not pace to reach leaders when not much room inside final furlong, beaten 7½l by Nayef*

1st Prix d'Ispahan (Group 1) (Longchamp, May 18) 4yo+ 9f Soft **126** (TS 113) 8 ran. *In touch in 5th on inside, disputed 5th straight, pushed along and headway on inside 2f out, led over 1 1/2f out, ridden and ran on well 1f out, driven out, beat Bright Sky by 1½l*

3rd Prix Ganay (Group 1) (Longchamp, April 27) 4yo+ 10½f Very soft **117** (TS 105) 9 ran. *Held up towards rear, 7th straight, pushed along and not quicken 2f out, ridden and ran on to go 2nd 1f out, lost 2nd final strides, beaten 2½l by Fair Mix*

2002

1st Japan Cup (Grade 1) (Nakayama, November 24) 3yo+ 11f Firm **121** 16 ran ● **9th** Prix de l'Arc de Triomphe - Lucien Barriere (Group 1) (Longchamp, October 6) 3yo+ 12f Good **117** (TS 111) 16 ran ● **3rd** Prix Foy Gray d'Albion Barriere (Group 2) (Longchamp, September 15) 3yo+ 12f Good to firm **117** (TS 77) 5 ran ● **1st** Gran Premio di Milano (Group 1) (San Siro, June 16) 3yo+ 12f Firm **119** 7 ran ● **1st** Premio Presidente della Repubblica SIS (Group 1) (Capannelle, May 12) 4yo+ 10f Good **123** 9 ran ● **1st** Premio Sannita (Capannelle, April 21) 4yo+ 9f Heavy 7 ran

Other notable runs

2001 1st Premio Conte Felice Scheibler (Capannelle, November 4) 3yo 10f Good 15 ran ● **3rd** Premio Giuseppe Ippolito Fassati (Restricted Listed) (San Siro, September 23) 3yo 11f Heavy 7 ran ● **1st** Premio Nico e Vittorio Castelini (San Siro, September 2) 3yo 11f Soft 7 ran ● **2nd** Derby Italiano - Yoga (Group 1) (Capannelle, May 27) 3yo 12f Good to firm **112** 19 ran ● **1st** Premio Palazzetto (San Siro, March 31) 3yo 10f Heavy 4 ran **2000 2nd** Premio Guido Berardelli (Group 2) (Capannelle, November 5) 2yo 9f Heavy 9 ran ● **1st** Premio Luvignano (Maiden) (San Siro, September 3) 2yo 1m Good 11 ran

A second Group 1 of the year as Darryll Holland takes over on Falbrav (left) to win the Eclipse at Sandown

furlong Premio Presidente della Repubblica and the 12-furlong Gran Premio di Milano, and he closed his season with that dramatic blitz finish in the Japan Cup at its temporary home in Nakayama. It had seemed a crowning triumph. Who would guess that the best was yet to come?

The decision during the winter by owner Luciano Salice to switch Falbrav to Newmarket presented Luca Cumani with one of the great challenges of his career. Luca had made his name handling top horses like Tolomeo and Barathea, but he needed another champion to complete the climb back from the doldrums to which his split with the Aga Khan had confined him in 1998. Falbrav was a triple Group 1 winner but his form would still need to improve to beat Europe's very best. Here was a training team on its mettle.

"I know the Italian system," says Cumani, son of a successful Milanese trainer. "It tends to be a bit less severe than the one I use at Newmarket so I was anxious not to overdo Falbrav early on. He is never impressive in his canters and although he worked well enough before his first run in the Ganay I felt he was a bit short of fitness. We were delighted with that run and even more when he returned to win the Ispahan impressively."

By now Cumani and his team were getting excited. "I think the horse was suited by going up these hills," says his groom Keith Ledington.

Falbrav (Darryll Holland) sprints clear of Magistretti to take the Juddmonte International at York in August

"He had a bit of a belly on him when he came but he really began to muscle up across his loins and quarters." Nottinghamshire-born Ledington, who did the same duties with Barathea and earlier had spells down the mines and with Securicor when his early racing dreams had come to nothing, is just the sort of quiet expert on whom men like Cumani depend. No surprise, then, that he will not get drawn into any recriminations about his horse's apparently lacklustre performance when only fifth behind Nayef, beaten seven and a half lengths, in the Prince of Wales's Stakes at Royal Ascot.

"It was just a bit of a non-event," says Ledington. "The jock [Mirco Demuro, who had ridden him as a two-year-old] didn't know Ascot, got a bit stuck on the outside and never really got going. But he accepted things and that was good for the horse." Without getting into silly chauvinism, a study of the video does suggest that the short-legged Demuro was unable to galvanise his massive partner in the way which Darryll Holland made a trademark in the three victories that followed.

The first of those wins came in the Eclipse, and Ledington and Cumani's Ascot analysis was confirmed when Falbrav quickened clear two furlongs out, decisively turning the tables on Nayef. Admittedly Falbrav had a

Falbrav (Darryll Holland) drops back to a mile to complete his quartet of Group 1s in the Queen Elizabeth II at Ascot

brilliant run round the inside rail all the way and Nayef was not done any favours by the Godolphin pacemaker early in the straight, but this was still a top-class performance by any standards.

It was also an ideal start to the Holland-Falbrav partnership which was then somewhat tarnished by a fairly nonsensical strategy in Alamshar's King George VI and Queen Elizabeth Stakes at Ascot. It's one thing to take the 'Willie Carson, under the trees' route on the outside for the Old Mile course, quite another to pursue it for a full mile and a half and to stay out wide round Swinley Bottom. The ground, if softer than the official 'good', still produced a 2min 33sec finishing time and Falbrav's fading to finish a nine-length fifth could be ascribed as much to his eccentric navigation as to lack of stamina or unsuitable going.

York was the ultimate in redemptions. Rarely do you get a horserace with the winner looking so dominant throughout. With no worries about the going, Holland tracked Nayef through and then put him ruthlessly to the sword when the two came to duel more than two furlongs from home. Magistretti ran on well to be second but this was the hailing of a champion. Falbrav and his jockey had made it look easy. Less than three weeks later at Leopardstown for the Irish Champion, they would be made to remember how difficult it could be.

The real truth about jockeys' tactics is not what they say publicly but what they think in private when they watch the video. Darryll Holland had his best-ever season in 2003 and his three victories on Falbrav in England will stay with him till he croaks. In particular the revelation of Falbrav's pure speed when returned to a mile for Ascot's Queen Elizabeth II Stakes, stalking the leader and then having far too many guns for the Classic winner Russian Rhythm and Tillerman. But it is the photo-finish defeats at Leopardstown and Santa Anita that Darryll will continue to play in his head. Why did he get trapped in the Irish Champion's mile and a quarter? Did he go too soon in the Breeders' Cup mile and a half? It will be the first question, not the second, that upsets his sleep.

The final stages at Leopardstown are much more complicated than they look on TV. In the space of three and a half furlongs the runners make a 180-degree turn at the same time as the ground dips and then rises again to the finish. Falbrav's one snag as a race ride was that he could waste energy pulling too hard in the early stages.

Holland still had his arms stretched to the sockets as Moon Ballad and Alamshar took over from the pacemaking France going to the final turn. Just ahead of him, Mick Kinane was taking High Chaparral to the outside, while Kieren Fallon began to work Islington up from the back. In far less time than it takes to read this sentence, Holland had to make up his mind whether to go inside after Alamshar and hope for a split, or go outside and be forced to swing four wide into the straight. He went for the inner. He didn't get the split. It will haunt him.

Everything went wrong from that moment. With three Group 1 winners up ahead of him and another, Islington, closing the door on the outside, he was the ultimate example of being all dressed up with nowhere to go. Even in the last 100 yards he was unlucky when High Chaparral rolled him towards the rail, but the stewards were surely right to rule that it was not that which cost him the race.

If Holland should criticise himself for the Leopardstown ride, he should snooze soundly over his Santa Anita efforts. Sure, he committed a doubtful stayer for the line only to be run down. But the season showed that Falbrav's biggest weapon was his match-winning kick two furlongs out. That was the key at Sandown, York and Ascot. Circumstances meant it never got played at Leopardstown. Now, running to that extra-tight Santa Anita turn, Holland correctly asked Falbrav to attack. Straight-ening up with only a furlong and a half to run he took a couple of lengths out of his field. In the final 100 yards, his fading stamina just failed to repel the dead-heaters' assault. No more need be said.

Falbrav's year gives huge credit to his connections and to himself. He was handsome, talented, tough, sound and almost uniquely versatile, as good at a mile as a mile and a quarter and not much worse over a mile and a half. He preferred fast ground but won on soft. "He was the best horse I have ever trained or ever will," says Cumani. For the rest of us, he will be remembered as one of the best we ever saw.

Falbrav   *bay horse, 28-2-1998*

		Nearctic	Nearco
			Lady Angela
		Northern Dancer	
		Natalma	Native Dancer
			Almahmoud
	Fairy King		
	b 1982	Bold Reason	Hail To Reason
			Lalun
		Fairy Bridge	
		Special	Forli
			Thong
		Seattle Slew	Bold Reasoning
			My Charmer
		Slewpy	
		Rare Bouquet	Prince John
			Forest Song
	Gift Of The Night		
	br 1990	Lithiot	Ribot
			Lithia
		Little Nana	
		Nenana Road	Kirkland Lake
			Sena

Bred by Azienda Agricola Francesca in Ireland

Sire **Fairy King**

Ran only once, last, fracturing sesamoid, in a Listed race at Phoenix Park as 3yo. Brother to Sadler's Wells. Retired from stud 1998, died 1999. Sire of: Pharoah's Delight (Phoenix S.-Gr1), Fairy Heights (Fillies' Mile-Gr1), Shinko King (Takamatsunomiya Hai-Gr1), Turtle Island (Phoenix S.-Gr1, Irish 2,000 Guineas-Gr1), Ya Malak (Nunthorpe S. [dead-heat]-Gr1), Prince Arthur (Premio Parioli-Gr1), Almushtarak (Gr2), Helissio (Prix Lupin-Gr1, Grand Prix de Saint-Cloud-Gr1, twice, Prix de l'Arc de Triomphe-Gr1, Prix Ganay-Gr1), Kool Kat Katie (Gr2), Revoque (Prix de la Salamandre-Gr1, Grand Criterium-Gr1), Pharatta (Gr2), Princely Heir (Phoenix S.-Gr1), Roi Gironde (Gr2), Second Empire (Grand Criterium-Gr1), Victory Note (Poule d'Essai des Poulains-Gr1), Fairy Queen (Gr2), Oath (Derby S.-Gr1), Royal Kingdom (Gr2), Xua (Gr2), Beckett (National S.-Gr1), Falbrav (Premio Presidente della Repubblica-Gr1, Gran Premio di Milano-Gr1, Japan Cup-Gr1, Prix d'Ispahan-Gr1, Eclipse S.-Gr1, York International S.-Gr1, Queen Elizabeth II S.-Gr1), King Of Tara (Gr2).

Dam **Gift Of The Night**

Won 1 of 6 races. Useful 2yo, effective up to a mile (2nd in Listed company) and on any going, but lacked an ideal racing temperament. Dam of: Fanofadiga (1995 f by Alzao; winner), Fiur (1996 c by Grand Lodge; winner), Fafinta (1997 f by Indian Ridge; winner), Falbrav (1998 c by Fairy King; multiple Gr1 winner).

Pedigree assessment

In 2002 Falbrav was the best horse trained in Italy. In 2003 he was the best horse trained in England, and between 8-10 furlongs on top of the ground probably the best anywhere in the world. He ran only in Group 1 company, distinguishing himself in France, Ireland and America as well as in his adopted home nation. Beyond his best trip he was also top-class, yielding only close home in the Breeders' Cup Turf. The second outstanding runner produced by Fairy King from a Slewpy mare, he now takes the place of the first, Helissio (who is to stand at the National Stud), at Shadai Farm on Hokkaido. With seven Group 1 victories on his CV, one of them in the 2002 Japan Cup, he has plenty to recommend himself to Japanese breeders. *TM*

Fidelite (Ire)

3yo chestnut filly **113**

In The Wings - Onereuse (Sanglamore (USA))
Owner Wertheimer Et Frere
Trainer Mme C Head-Maarek
Breeder Wertheimer Et Frere

Career: **8 starts** | won **2** | second **1** | third **1** | **£91,471** win and place

By Graham Dench

PRONOUNCED correctly by a native of her homeland, Fidelite's name has a charming ring to it. In the hands of the Australian whose Prix de Diane commentary was broadcast to viewers enjoying Attheraces' invaluable new Sunday service from France, it sounded almost ugly. "Fiddle Light", he called her, and she proceeded to run like the entirely different horse he made her sound. She ran abysmally.

It is a measure of how much Fidelite progressed in the spring that she should start such a hot favourite for the Diane, the French Oaks, little more than two months after getting off the mark. A narrow defeat of Liska in an ordinary fillies' race over ten furlongs at Longchamp at the end of March told us little more than that she had made the progress one would have hoped for through the winter, and fourth place behind Campsie Fells in a steadily run Group 3, the Prix Vanteaux, over a slightly shorter trip on the same course, was nothing to write home about either.

But if Fidelite's profile at that stage was unexceptional, that all changed at Longchamp once more in May when she lined up for the Group 1 Prix Saint-Alary, back up to ten furlongs again. Starting relatively unfancied at around 10-1 in a market dominated by her recent conqueror Campsie Fells and Godolphin's Pretty Polly Stakes winner Hi Dubai, she stepped up dramatically on all previous form and came with a long sweeping run at the end of a fast-run race to lead inside the final furlong and put daylight between herself and her rivals. Hi Dubai was beaten comprehensively by two lengths into second place, while the earlier form with Campsie Fells was turned around to the tune of nearly eight lengths.

The Saint-Alary was won by a succession of outstanding fillies back in the 1970s – fillies such as Pistol Packer, Dahlia, Comtesse de Loir, Nobiliary and Three Troikas, all of whom went on to make their mark at the highest level. However, standards have slipped and, although there

**Fidelite (Olivier Peslier) beats Hi Dubai in the Group 1
Prix Saint-Alary at Longchamp**

have been exceptions, such as the 1993 winner Intrepidity, who went
on to win the Oaks, it is these days seldom the strongest of races by
Group 1 standards.

Nevertheless, in a Prix de Diane line-up that included the French 1,000
Guineas winner Musical Chimes, Fidelite still looked a worthy favourite
and there was no shortage of optimism from Criquette Head-Maarek,
who was bidding for a third success in the race following those with
the outstanding fillies Harbour, another Saint-Alary winner, back in 1982
and Egyptband in 2000.

Head-Maarek reported that Fidelite had done everything asked of her
since the Saint-Alary, but when the race got under way she never gave
her supporters the slightest hope and trailed home a poor eighth of ten
behind Nebraska Tornado.

Regular rider Olivier Peslier reported that he could never follow the
pace and that she was not the same filly. Head-Maarek wondered if the

7th Prix du Conseil de Paris (Group 2) (Longchamp, October 19) 3yo+ 12f Good to soft (TS 80) 9 ran. *Raced in 4th, 6th and driven straight, unable to quicken, beaten 10½l by Vallee Enchantee*

3rd Prix Vermeille Fouquet's Barriere (Group 1) (Longchamp, September 14) 3yo 12f Good to soft **113** (TS 98) 11 ran. *Mid-division, 6th straight, ridden over 2f out, stayed on under pressure to take 3rd close home, beaten 3¼l by Mezzo Soprano*

8th Prix de Diane Hermes (Group 1) (Chantilly, June 8) 3yo 10½f Good **104** (TS 78) 10 ran. *Towards rear, disputing 6th towards outside straight, ridden over 2f out, no impression, beaten 5¾l by Nebraska Tornado*

1st Prix Saint-Alary (Group 1) (Longchamp, May 18) 3yo 10f Soft **113** (TS 76) 9 ran. *Held up in 8th, pushed along over 2f out, headway in centre over 1½f out, ridden approaching final furlong, led just inside final furlong, ran on well, beat Hi Dubai by 2l*

4th Prix Vanteaux (Group 3) (Longchamp, April 27) 3yo 9f Very soft **99** 6 ran. *Slowly into stride, held up in rear, went 5th straight, stayed on one pace, took 4th close home, beaten 3l by Campsie Fells*

1st Prix de Croissy (Longchamp, March 30) 3yo 10f Good **100** 6 ran. *Disputed 2nd on outside, led 50yds out, ridden out, beat Liska by nk*

2002

2nd Prix de Vulaines (Maisons-Laffitte, October 18) 2yo 9f Soft 9 ran ● **Unplaced** Prix Discrete (Unraced Fillies) (Saint-Cloud, September 9) 2yo 1m Good 19 ran

ground had been too quick, but offered no real excuse.

Fidelite salvaged much of her reputation when she returned from a traditional French break to finish third behind Mezzo Soprano and Yesterday in what looked a strong renewal of the Prix Vermeille, clearly appreciating the step up to a mile and a half. She came from off the pace in a fast-run race, just as she had done in the Saint-Alary, and got the best of a good battle for third, around three lengths behind the two principals.

However, a good performance was once again followed by a bad one when she failed to take advantage of what looked a golden opportunity in the Prix du Conseil de Paris, a mere Group 2, in which she was beaten more than ten lengths into seventh behind Vallee Enchantee. The winner was an old rival who on balance enjoyed the best of their clashes, but Fidelite had beaten her in the Vermeille and on that form ought to have been very much involved in the finish.

One often looks in vain for an explanation for a horse's lack of consistency and in Fidelite's case it is probably academic now, since there is little to be gained from keeping her in training. What one can say with a degree of certainty, however, is that she was very well suited by a strongly run race and waiting tactics. In that respect she takes after her sire, In The Wings, whom many will remember coming from well off the pace to land the 1990 Breeders' Cup Turf, having earlier that year landed Epsom's Coronation Cup impressively under the most confident of rides.

Fidelite

chestnut filly, 18-1-2000

		Northern Dancer	Nearctic / Natalma
	Sadler's Wells		
		Fairy Bridge	Bold Reason / Special
In The Wings b 1986			
		Shirley Heights	Mill Reef / Hardiemma
	High Hawk		
		Sunbittern	Sea Hawk / Pantoufle
		Sharpen Up	Atan / Rocchetta
	Sanglamore		
		Ballinderry	Irish River / Miss Manon
Onereuse b 1994			
		Top Ville	High Top / Sega Ville
	J'ai Deux Amours		
		Pollenka	Reliance / Polana

Bred by Wertheimer et Frere in Ireland

Sire **In The Wings**

Won 7 of 11 races, inc. Prix du Prince d'Orange-Gr3, Coronation Cup-Gr1, Grand Prix de Saint-Cloud-Gr1, Prix Foy-Gr3, Breeders' Cup Turf-Gr1. Also 2nd in Prix Ganay-Gr1, 4th in Prix de l'Arc de Triomphe-Gr1, 5th in King George VI & Queen Elizabeth S.-Gr1. Small, quite sturdily-built individual. Off the course for 13 months from August as 2yo because of a chipped knee. Best suited by 12f with some give in the ground. Sire of: Irish Wings (Gr3), Singspiel (Canadian International S.-Gr1, Japan Cup-Gr1, Dubai World Cup, Coronation Cup-Gr1, York International S.-Gr1), Winged Love (Irish Derby-Gr1), Annaba (Gr2), Apprehension (Gr3), Just In Fun (Gr3), Right Wing (Gr3), Boreas (Gr3), Central Park (Derby Italiano-Gr1, Premio Presidente della Repubblica-Gr1), Cloud Castle (Gr3), Thief Of Hearts (Gr3), Tillerman (Gr2), Air Marshall (Gr2), Davide Umbro (Gr2), Earlene (Gr2), Kutub (Bayerisches Zuchtrennen-Gr1, Gran Premio del Jockey Club-Gr1), Saldenschwinge (Gr3), Zanzibar (Oaks d'Italia-Gr1), Act One (Criterium International-Gr1, Prix Lupin-Gr1), Mamool (Grosser Preis von Baden-Gr1, Preis von Europa-Gr1), Mellow Park (Gr3), Savannah Bay (Gr3), Trumbaka (Gr3), Abunawwas (Gr3), Fidelite (Prix Saint-Alary-Gr1), New South Wales (Gr3), Soldier Hollow (Gr3), Weightless (Gr2).

Dam **Onereuse**

A non-winner, placed 2nd twice and 3rd once from 8 races. Half-sister to Irish Derby winner Winged Love (by In The Wings). Modest handicap-class performer, tried at a variety of distances. Dam of: Amour Multiple (1999 c by Poliglote; winner), Fidelite (2000 f by In The Wings; Gr1 winner), unnamed (2001 c by In The Wings).

Pedigree assessment

Three-year-old filly form at middle distances was not noted for its consistency in 2003 and Fidelite was one of a number whose campaign resembled the curate's egg. The Saint-Alary showed her in a promising light, but in the Diane she never looked like justifying heavy support. A bold run into third in the Vermeille, on ground probably faster than she cared for, then gave her an obvious favourite's chance for the Prix du Conseil, but in that Group 2 event she was thoroughly outpaced. The progeny of In The Wings frequently improve with age and experience, and if she is allowed the opportunity to redeem herself in 2004, she might yet establish herself in the top flight. *TM*

Funny Cide (USA)

3yo chestnut gelding   **125**

Distorted Humor (USA) - Belle's Good Cide (USA) (Slewacide (USA))
Owner Sackatoga Stable
Trainer B Tagg
Breeder WinStar Farm

Career: **11** starts | won **5** | second **2** | third **2** | **£1,320,277** win and place

by Nicholas Godfrey

MERICAN racing bathed in the 'Seabiscuit effect' in 2003 as the story of the broken-down horse revitalised by a broken-down trainer put bums on seats from New York to LA, with a stopover in London. First had come Laura Hillenbrand's award-winning book – a well-received romanticised history that became a surprise bestseller – and then came the movie, the homespun, feelgood hit of the summer. The film's makers were blessed with fairytale material in the story of a horse who triumphed against the odds and won the hearts of a down-trodden nation during the Great Depression of the 1930s. If they ladled on the schmaltz and played a little fast and loose with the odd factoid, then, hey, this is Hollywood, what are you gonna do?

It was not only on celluloid that a horse from the wrong side of the tracks entranced a nation, however: on the racecourse, in a story with uncanny resonances to Seabiscuit, the unfashionable gelding Funny Cide captured his place in the hearts of the US public with his own version of the American dream, equine-style.

There were many better performers than Funny Cide in 2003 in the States, but it was this New York-bred gelding who became known as the 'People's Horse'. He earned the sobriquet by winning the first two legs of the Triple Crown, an unexpected victory in the Kentucky Derby – the one horserace that really interests the rank-and-file Stateside – being followed by a startling win in the Preakness Stakes. Abject defeats later in the season tarnished his reputation among the cognoscenti, but by then his status as a Seabiscuit of the modern era was assured.

It was quite a tale. Funny Cide, a cheaply bought horse who had to be gelded before beginning his racing career, was owned by a syndicate of old high-school buddies who clubbed together in 1995 to buy their first horse at $5,000 a head. The Sackatoga syndicate – the name combines their home town, Sackets Harbor, in upstate New York, with Saratoga

Funny Cide (Jose Santos) powers to victory in the first leg of the Triple Crown, the Kentucky Derby

Springs, where managing partner Jackson Knowlton lives – was put together over a few beers at a party. The syndicate played up their status as relatively 'ordinary Joes' by travelling to the races in a yellow school bus. After some moderate successes, the syndicate had money in the bank in 2002 when they bought their ninth horse, the two-year-old Funny Cide, in a private deal for $75,000.

If the Sackatoga syndicate made for unlikely heroes, Funny Cide's 65-year-old trainer Barclay Tagg – a pessimistic, little-known veteran notorious for his saturnine outlook – was an even less obvious candidate. A Belmont-based former steeplechase jockey, Tagg had trained a couple of Grade 1 winners in his time – but, equally, he was once left with just a single horse when an owner deserted his stable on Christmas Day.

The third component of the improbable team behind Funny Cide was jockey Jose Santos, America's top-earning rider for four successive years in the late 1980s before a dramatic fall from grace. By 2001, having been bedevilled by injuries and other problems, Santos had dropped to 61st in the money rankings, attracting the cruellest of nicknames. Such was his lack of success that devotees of the New York circuit had dubbed him the 'Human Anchor'. High-profile victories on Lemon Drop Kid and

2003   Race record

9th Breeders' Cup Classic - Powered by Dodge (Grade 1) (Dirt) (Santa Anita, October 25) 3yo+ 10f Fast **101** 10 ran. *4th when hung right first turn, prominent until over 2f out, 7th and beaten straight, beaten 15l by Pleasantly Perfect*

3rd Haskell Invitational Handicap (Grade 1) (Dirt) (Monmouth Park, August 3) 3yo 9f Fast **106** 7 ran. *Close up in 5th to straight, soon one pace, beaten 9l by Peace Rules*

3rd Belmont Stakes (Grade 1) (Dirt) (Belmont Park, June 7) 3yo 12f Sloppy **118** 6 ran. *Led until headed 3f out, one pace, beaten 5l by Empire Maker*

1st Preakness Stakes (Grade 1) (Dirt) (Pimlico, May 17) 3yo 9½f Good **125** 10 ran. *Raced in 3rd until went 2nd 6f out, led just over 2f out, ridden clear, ran on strongly, beat Midway Road by 9¾l*

1st Kentucky Derby (Grade 1) (Dirt) (Churchill Downs, May 3) 3yo 10f Fast **123** 16 ran. *Tracked leaders in 3rd, disputed lead just under 2f out until led over 1f out, driven out, beat Empire Maker by 1¾l*

2nd Wood Memorial Stakes (Grade 1) (Dirt) (Aqueduct, April 12) 3yo 9f Muddy **123** 8 ran. *Bumped leaving stalls, soon tracking leader, strong effort inside final 2f, stayed on well, beaten ½l by Empire Maker*

2nd La Derby (Grade 2) (Dirt) (Fair Grounds, March 9) 3yo 8½f Fast **112** 10 ran. *Clear early, set pace, headed inside final 2f and dropped to 4th, rallied final furlong, beaten 1l by Peace Rules*

5th Holy Bull Stakes (Grade 3) (Dirt) (Gulfstream Park, January 18) 3yo 8½f Fast 13 ran. *Broke well, ran wide first bend, chased leading trio between 4f out and final furlong, tired closing stages, beaten 6¾l by Offlee Wild*

2002

1st Sleepy Hollow Stakes (Belmont Park, October 19) 2yo 1m Fast 6 ran ● **1st** Bongard Stakes (Belmont Park, September 29) 2yo 7f Fast 10 ran ● **1st** Maiden (Belmont Park, September 8) 2yo 6f Fast 12 ran

Volponi saw him back on the upswing. At the age of 42, he was looking to Funny Cide to complete the rehabilitation.

However, if those most closely associated with Funny Cide believed in the horse as they headed to Churchill Downs on the first Saturday in May, they were very much in the minority. Funny Cide had failed to win in all three starts at three and looked held by several of his Derby rivals, including the much-vaunted Empire Maker and his Bobby Frankel-trained stablemate Peace Rules. If Funny Cide was not considered a no-hoper, he was clearly an outsider, seventh choice in a field of 16 behind 5-2 favourite Empire Maker, rated by many as having the potential to become the first Triple Crown winner for 25 years. Empire Maker's price was inflated by his having been at the centre of a pre-race scare after a bruised foot interrupted his preparation.

A crowd of 148,530, the fifth-largest in Derby history, attended the 129th renewal of America's most famous horserace. They watched Funny Cide enjoy a dream journey in what was a clean race. Settled just behind the early pacesetters, he challenged the leader Peace Rules leaving the backstretch, the pair passing the two-furlong marker upsides. Just behind, seemingly waiting to pounce, was Empire Maker, who had travelled wide in midfield for much of the race. Empire Maker moved up threateningly on entering the stretch, but he simply could not go past the ultra-game Funny Cide, who seemed to pull away again as the post neared. The unexpected winner scored by one and three-quarter lengths, covering the ten furlongs in 2min 1.19sec.

Frankel appeared incredulous. "Who is that horse?" he was heard to ask someone standing next to him as battle was joined in the stretch. Soon, nobody would need to ask the identity of Funny Cide. If Frankel was shocked, then so were the experts: Funny Cide was the first New York-bred ever to win the race, and the first gelding for 74 years since Clyde van Dusen in 1929. "No joke – it's Funny Cide!" ran the punning headline of the local paper, the Louisville Courier-Journal, while a report in the Racing Post summed up the consensus view. "Funny Cide?" it asked. "Funny result."

Breeding snobs pointed to the winner's relatively plebeian antecedents, but his being a gelding mattered not a jot to Tagg. "I don't mind," he said. "I'm not into breeding; I train racehorses." Knowlton was in his element. "We're the American dream," he said. "It's like the lottery – a dollar and a dream. And guess what? We hit it."

Funny Cide had already done enough to earn a place in the public's affections, a hold that was only strengthened by a spurious accusation from Frank Carlson of the Miami Herald that Santos had been carrying an electronic device in his whip hand at Churchill Downs. The allegation was quickly discredited, but not without adding to Funny Cide's popularity.

Nobody, though, could touch him in the Preakness Stakes, the second leg of the Triple Crown that took place a fortnight after the Derby, at Pimlico. In the absence of Empire Maker, Funny Cide's chief rival on paper was Peace Rules, but it was no contest. While it might not have been the strongest field ever assembled, Funny Cide produced an astonishing performance. Having been sent up to challenge Peace Rules six furlongs out, he put that rival away after racing menacingly alongside for three furlongs, unleashing a powerful turn of foot straightening for home that shot him well clear. The resistance of Peace Rules was shattered; he trailed in fourth as Funny Cide, in a thoroughly dominating effort, drew clear to win by nine and three-quarter lengths from outsider Midway Road. In an emotionally charged gesture, Santos waited until his mount crossed the line to open his clenched fist wide, to show there was no electronic device or anything else contained within. Even if he had, he would not have needed it: Funny Cide was truly imperious at Pimlico. But, in Triple Crown terms, the job was only two-thirds done.

America in general went Funny Cide crazy after the Preakness romp. New York, where he was bred, was particularly susceptible. Funny Cide's name was everywhere in the week preceding the Belmont Stakes, the third and final leg of the Triple Crown: on front pages of nearly all the dailies, all over television and radio news bulletins, on badges bearing the legend 'New York loves Funny Cide', on top of taxis, where Belmont Park neatly moved in among the usual electronic adverts with the line 'East Side, West Side, we're all rooting for Funny Cide.'

There may have been six horses in the Belmont, but New York was a one-horse town. The foul weather that turned the Belmont Park track to a quagmire did not deter Funny Cide's legion of fans from descending on the racecourse to cheer on their hero. The official crowd figure was 101,864 – and most went home disappointed as Empire Maker spoiled the party. Although Funny Cide was sent off the even-money favourite, the betting market was the only place he held sway. Not for nothing is the mile-and-a-half Belmont regarded as America's test of champions – and the sense of anticlimax was palpable as Empire Maker comprehensively upstaged the horse who had gatecrashed his party at Churchill Downs. Funny Cide, finding the trip too far and unsuited by the soggy track, came home third, five lengths behind the winner.

The defeat did not seem to hurt Funny Cide's popularity – and the Sackatoga team wasted few opportunities to market their goldmine. The horse had his own website (www.funnycide.com) and a range of merchandise including T-shirts, baseball caps and a CD featuring the output of someone called Blue Hand Luke. Crowds ten deep turned out during Saratoga's summer meeting simply to see him walk around the parade ring on designated 'Funny Cide days'. On the track, however, his performances in the latter half of the year struggled to match anything like the levels of excitement he achieved in the spring. Reappearing two months after Belmont in the Haskell Invitational at Monmouth Park, he finished a disappointing third, nine lengths behind old rival Peace Rules.

The much-anticipated rematch with Empire Maker in Saratoga's Travers Stakes came to nothing as both horses missed the race and Empire Maker was retired before the Breeders' Cup Classic, in which Funny Cide was given the chance to restore his reputation and embellish his credentials for end-of-season divisional honours. By now, though, few serious players considered him to have any real chance. Funny Cide finished ninth of ten, the glories of his early-season achievements now distant memories.

Such dismal performances took much of the shine off his exploits in the first half of the season, as speed-figures guru Andy Beyer explained in the Washington Post, pointing out that Funny Cide had won the Derby "with the aid of a perfect ground-saving trip while adversity befell some of his main rivals" and dominated an "unusually weak field" in the Preakness. "Funny Cide is fast, versatile, gutsy and beloved, but he did not deserve a place in the pantheon of the sport's all-time greats."

However, the story of Funny Cide contains something that cannot be described in simple form figures, as Beyer himself was quick to acknow-ledge. "The excitement associated with the Belmont demonstrated how much the sport needs stars with whom fans can identify," he said, recalling a telecast that drew 24 million viewers, making it the highest-rated race

Funny Cide   *chestnut gelding, 20-4-2000*

Distorted Humor ch 1993	Forty Niner	Mr Prospector	Raise A Native / Gold Digger
		File	Tom Rolfe / Continue
	Danzig's Beauty	Danzig	Northern Dancer / Pas de Nom
		Sweetest Chant	Mr Leader / Gay Sonnet
Belle's Good Cide ch 1993	Slewacide	Seattle Slew	Bold Reasoning / My Charmer
		Evasive	Buckpasser / Summer Scandal
	Belle Of Killarney	Little Current	Sea-Bird / Luiana
		Cherished Moment	Graustark / Pumpkin Patch

Bred by WinStar Farm in New York. $22,000 Fasig-Tipton New York Preferred Sale yearling

Sire **Distorted Humor**

Won 8 of 23 races, inc. Salvator Mile-Gr3, Commonwealth Breeders' Cup S.-Gr2, Churchill Downs H.-Gr2, Ack Ack H.-Gr3. Neat, well-made sort who showed high-class form up to 9f in each of three seasons. Always Lasix user from midway in 3yo campaign. Sire of: Awesome Humor (Spinaway S.-Gr1), Funny Cide (Kentucky Derby-Gr1, Preakness S.-Gr1), Go Rockin' Robin (Gr2), Humorous Lady (Gr2).

Dam **Belle's Good Cide**

Won 2 of 26 races. Just a useful sprinter in modest company. Placed 3rd in one of only 2 starts on turf, no form on a muddy track. Dam of: Coincide (1999 c by Cozzene; winner), Funny Cide (2000 g by Distorted Humor; Classic winner), Rockcide (2001 f by Personal Flag; unraced to date).

Pedigree assessment

Funny Cide added a colourful chapter to the romance of the sport, but the dream of Triple Crown glory fell apart in the Belmont Stakes and the unfashionably bred chestnut's season with it. A fever and a high blood count were cited as his excuses for a dull effort in the Haskell, but his even more lacklustre showing in the Breeders' Cup Classic was a dire disappointment, given that his trainer re-routed him there, convinced of his return to form. With no stud career to come, Funny Cide has to be a racehorse or nothing; let's hope he can retrieve his reputation in 2004. Showed marked improvement to land his nation's premier Classic and evidently well suited by 10f. *TM*

for more than a decade. Even if he never wins another race, Funny Cide's place in history is assured. As the great D Wayne Lukas said, "Fifty years from now, we may be having a movie about Funny Cide."

After all, the story of his Kentucky Derby victory was no less compelling than that of Seabiscuit, and just as much of a fairytale. The American public did not need Hollywood to tell them that.

Gamut (Ire)

4yo bay colt **121**

Spectrum (Ire) - Greektown (Ela-Mana-Mou)

Owner Mrs G Smith

Trainer Sir Michael Stoute

Breeder Ballymacoll Stud Farm Ltd

Career: **9** starts | won **3** | second **3** | third **2** | **£89,031** win and place

By Daniel Hill

IN THE short term at least, Gamut is likely to go down in memory as the horse who forgot to read the script when widely expected to provide Pat Eddery with a fairytale finish to a magnificent career. But there is a lot more to Gamut than that and it was hardly his fault that he was sent off at such unrealistic odds to win a hot little Doncaster conditions race in which there was always a danger that he would find the distance of a mile and a half too short. His third behind Scott's View at 1-2 was well short of his best form, but it wasn't a disaster.

Gamut was understandably overshadowed in a stable that housed the Derby winner Kris Kin, the 1,000 Guineas winner Russian Rhythm and the Breeders' Cup Filly & Mare Turf winner Islington. But he showed steady improvement in 2003 and his second to Vinnie Roe in the Irish St Leger at The Curragh was undoubtedly a classy performance.

His season kicked off at a shower-hit Newbury in May in the ten-runner Aston Park Stakes over an extended 13 furlongs, a race the stable had won recently with both Election Day and Dark Shell. Judged on his form as a three-year-old the previous season – when his best run in three starts was his fourth behind Systematic in the Troy Stakes – he had excellent prospects of being involved in the finish, particularly since he was receiving 6lb from Persian Punch (notoriously rusty on his seasonal reappearance) and it had been over a year since second favourite Fight Your Corner had entered the winner's enclosure.

Gamut was sent off a well supported 6-4 favourite at Newbury and those who braved the rain to get to the betting ring were left smiling when he got the better of a bumping match with Swing Wing around half a mile out and won by three-quarters of a length from Fight Your Corner, with Swing Wing two and a half lengths away in third and Persian Punch a remote fourth. It was a performance that saw Gamut go down in plenty of notebooks as a horse to follow, as he looked just the sort

**Gamut (Kieren Fallon) wins at Newbury in May. He went
on to record his highest rating in the Irish St Leger**

his trainer traditionally has done well with.

It would have been no surprise to have seen Gamut stepped up in
trip again on his next start, but instead he was upped in class, for the
Group 2 Princess of Wales's Stakes over a mile and a half at
Newmarket's July meeting, where he ran well to finish third behind
Millenary and Bandari, beaten two and a half lengths by the winner.

Although unable to find a change of gear inside the final furlong he
left the impression at Newmarket that he could really make his presence
felt in Group company given softer ground and a longer trip, but the
opportunity to try a stiffer test of stamina was again denied him for the
time being. Not that it mattered.

Dropping back in distance marginally for a Class C conditions event
at Windsor in August and obliged to concede 7lb to the four-year-old
Millstreet, he got the better of a terrific duel which saw the pair pull
clear without either rider really going for his mount until inside the final
furlong. Only a head separated them at the line but Gamut, who
appreciated the well-watered track, always looked just the stronger.

Once again, Gamut ran as if a stiffer test of stamina would suit, so
the one and three-quarter miles of the Irish St Leger at The Curragh

3rd CIU Serlby Stakes (Listed) (Doncaster, November 8) 3yo+ 12f Good **111** (TS 86) 7 ran. *Tracked leaders, switched wide after 2f, driven along and went second over 3f out, kept on same pace, beaten 4½l by Scott's View*

2nd Irish Field St Leger (Group 1) (Curragh, September 13) 3yo+ 1m6f Good to firm **121** (TS 36) 6 ran. *Led, quickened entering straight, headed 1½f out, kept on well under pressure, beaten 1l by Vinnie Roe*

1st "2004 Royal Windsor Three Day Racing Festival" Conditions Stakes (Windsor, August 23) 3yo+ 11½f Good to firm **118** (TS 96) 5 ran. *Soon tracking leader, upsides from 3f out, ridden 2f out as pace quickened, stayed on under pressure to lead close home, beat Millstreet by hd*

3rd Princess of Wales's UAE Equestrian And Racing Federation Stakes (Group 2) (Newmarket (July), July 8) 3yo+ 12f Good **118** (TS 98) 6 ran. *Slowly into stride, held up, headway over 3f out, ridden and not clear run 1f out, stayed on same pace, beaten 2½l by Millenary*

1st skybet.com Stakes (Registered As The Aston Park Stakes) (Listed) (Newbury, May 17) 4yo+ 1m5½f Good **114** (TS 102) 10 ran. *In rear, headway on rails 5f out, tracking leaders when not much room edged right and hampered 4f out, led inside final 3f, kept on well final furlong, beat Fight Your Corner by ¾l*

2002

4th Amco Corporation Troy Stakes (Listed) (Doncaster, September 13) 3yo+ 12f Good to firm **111** (TS 82) 7 ran ● **2nd** '2003 Royal Windsor Three Day Racing Festival' Conditions Stakes (Windsor, August 24) 3yo+ 11½f Good to firm **109** (TS 72) 4 ran ● **1st** Peter Smith Memorial Maiden Stakes (Newbury, April 19) 3yo 11f Good to firm **96** (TS 73) 9 ran

looked right up his street. In a field of six that included Vinnie Roe, Bollin Eric and Powerscourt, Gamut ran a really game race from the front and went down by only a length to Vinnie Roe, who was completing a historic hat-trick of wins in the race. Powerscourt was a short head away in third. It was Gamut's best performance yet, and all the more admirable considering the ground was plenty fast enough for him.

Where now for Gamut? If Stoute's last two Aston Park winners, Dark Shell and Election Day, are a guide, Gamut might pursue a career over hurdling (Dark Shell ran six times for Nicky Henderson, winning once) or embark on a Cup campaign on the Flat (Election Day went on to finish third behind Celeric in the 1997 Ascot Gold Cup).

It is by no means impossible that Gamut will one day be tried over hurdles, for he was sold privately before his Doncaster race to Gay Smith. Smith and her husband Derrick are friends of Eddery and the 11-times champion jockey rode one of the strongest finishes of his career on their subsequent Triumph Hurdle winner Spectroscope when landing a massive gamble in a handicap at Goodwood in 2002. They also had the classy, but ill-fated, Coolnagorna with Jonjo O'Neill.

Gamut reportedly stays with Stoute, for now at least, and in the short term a Cup campaign would be more appropriate than hurdling. His pedigree suggests there is a fair chance he will stay well and his relaxed style of racing, even when dictating the pace as he did at The Curragh, will help.

Gamut

bay colt, 19-3-1999

Spectrum b 1992	Rainbow Quest	Blushing Groom	Red God Runaway Bride
		I Will Follow	Herbager Where You Lead
	River Dancer	Irish River	Riverman Irish Star
		Dancing Shadow	Dancer's Image Sunny Valley
Greektown ch 1985	Ela-Mana-Mou	Pitcairn	Petingo Border Bounty
		Rose Bertin	High Hat Wide Awake
	Edinburgh	Charlottown	Charlottesville Meld
		Queen's Castle	Sovereign Path Country House

Bred by Ballymacoll Stud Farm in Ireland

Sire Spectrum

Won 4 of 9 races, inc. Irish 2,000 Guineas-Gr1, Champion S.-Gr1. Rangy, good-looking, fine mover with good turn of foot. Stands at Coolmore, 2004 fee €15,000. Oldest progeny 5. Sire of: Golan (2,000 Guineas-Gr1, King George VI and Queen Elizabeth S.-Gr1), Dancing (Gr2), Just James (Gr2), Marionnaud (Gr3), Rum Charger (Gr3).

Dam Greektown

Dual winner at 3 in France over 10-12f, including in Listed company. Half-sister to top-class stayer Sought Out (by Rainbow Quest) and smart 10-12f filly Queen Helen (by Troy) out of smart 2yo and middle-distance filly Edinburgh. Dam of: Athens Belle (1990 f by Groom Dancer; Listed winner), Grecian Knight (1991 c by Groom Dancer; unraced), Multicoloured (1993 c by Rainbow Quest; Gr2 winner), Grecian Bride (1994 f by Groom Dancer; unraced), Greek Myth (1996 f by Sadler's Wells; unplaced), Town Girl (1997 f by Lammtarra; unplaced), Danse Grecque (1998 f by Sadler's Wells; unraced), Gamut (1999 c by Spectrum; Listed winner, Gr1-placed), Rainbow City (2000 f by Rainbow Quest; winner), Wedding Cake (2001 f by Groom Dancer; unraced).

Pedigree assessment

Product of a successful formula, for this is also the family of Spectrum's best son Golan. In addition, Spectrum's sire Rainbow Quest is responsible for close family members Multicoloured (who stayed 13f) and Sought Out, who stayed extreme distances. Sought Out's smart sons Cover Up and Researched also stay at least 12f. Gamut is proven over 14f and he has the pedigree to be effective over further. *JH*

Grey Swallow (Ire)

2yo grey colt   **119+**

Daylami (Ire) - Style Of Life (USA) (The Minstrel (Can))
Owner Mrs Rochelle Quinn
Trainer D K Weld
Breeder Mrs C L Weld

Career: **2** starts | won **2** | second **0** | third **0** | £38,282 win and place

By Alan Sweetman

IN 1964, a teenage Dermot Weld first imposed his presence on the Irish racing scene when riding Ticonderoga to win what was then known as the Player's Navy Cut Amateur Handicap at Galway. Thus, even before he succeeded his father Charlie at Rosewell House in 1972, the annual festival had begun to exercise a hold on his imagination, accentuated when the remarkable Spanner won the big amateur race in three of his first four years as a trainer and gave him a first Galway Hurdle victory into the bargain.

These days, Weld is recognised as one of racing's great adventurers, whose ability to exploit opportunities in every corner of the globe has brought international acclaim, and yet the Galway meeting remains one of his essential priorities.

From an early stage, Weld made a habit of targeting Galway's opening-night two-year-old maiden. He soon came to realise that, because of the demanding nature of the track, it was a big advantage for a two-year-old to travel to Galway with a run under its belt, and a regular pattern emerged which would have many of Ireland's most astute form students on the lookout months in advance for 'Dermot's Galway two-year-old'. Only sporadically has he broken his own rule by introducing a particularly forward juvenile at the meeting.

The emergence of Aidan O'Brien's powerful two-year-old squads has increased the competitive nature of Irish juvenile maidens and Galway has not been immune to the Ballydoyle phenomenon. Thus the statistics have begun to take on a slightly different appearance. Before 2003, Weld had won the race in question on 15 occasions, but the six most recent renewals had yielded but a single success.

In 2003, fate took a major hand in Weld's choice of horse for the Galway event. Early indications from the gallops on The Curragh were that a grey colt from the first crop of Daylami was the stable's best two-year-

Grey Swallow (Pat Smullen) runs away with the Group 3 Killavullan Stakes at Leopardstown in October

old. Named Grey Swallow, he was pencilled in for a debut run at The Curragh in June. On the morning of the race, Weld contacted the Registry Office of the Turf Club, asking for permission that Grey Swallow be loaded last into the stalls. His request was turned down. If Weld was frustrated by the negative response from the authorities, he was absolutely fuming after what eventually happened, for, in a bizarre incident, Grey Swallow, backed down to 1-2 favouritism in a field of nine, became wedged on the central partition of the stalls after a horse in the adjoining stall had tried to climb on top of him.

His resultant withdrawal forced a revision of plans, and once Weld was satisfied that the grey had suffered no lasting ill-effects from the misadventure he decided to send him to Galway without the benefit of a run. Here the opposition was headed by Rock Of Cashel, an own-brother to Rock Of Gibraltar.

The Ballydoyle colt had taken a while to get the hang of things when

2003   Race record

1st Killavullan Stakes (Group 3) (Leopardstown, October 27) 2yo 7f Good **119** (TS 81) 4 ran. *Tracked leaders in 3rd, improved to lead 1½f out, quickened clear, impressive, beat Newton by 8l*

1st GPT Access Equipment EBF Maiden (Galway, July 28) 2yo 7f Soft **100** 9 ran. *Tracked leaders in 4th, 3rd and challenged on outer entering straight, soon led and drew clear, impressive, beat Rock Of Cashel by 10l*

third on his debut at The Curragh (subsequently promoted to second), and the fact that Weld had saddled the fourth horse home in the race, Relaxed Gesture, gave him a handle on the form.

However, punters pinned their faith in the experience and pedigree of Rock Of Cashel and he was sent off the 4-5 favourite, with Grey Swallow an 11-8 chance. Neutrals expecting a hard-fought contest were sorely disappointed. Rock Of Cashel hung left all the way under Mick Kinane and Grey Swallow surged past on the outside turning for home and scampered clear to win by ten lengths. It was an impressive performance and Weld was quick to outline a number of Group 1 targets, including the National Stakes and the Dewhurst.

Those races came and went before Grey Swallow recorded another spectacular victory in the Group 3 Killavullan Stakes at Leopardstown in late October. He had only three opponents and it would be overly simplistic to adopt a collateral line of form through the Prix Jean Luc Lagardere and Racing Post Trophy winner American Post as a definitive guide to his ability.

However, the manner of his eight-length defeat of the Ballydoyle-trained Newton (previously beaten seven lengths in the Prix Jean Luc Lagardere), quickening clear in the last furlong and a half to leave his rivals for dead, was convincing enough to strengthen significantly his ante-post claims for the 2,000 Guineas, a race won in 2003 by the stable's Refuse To Bend.

Weld, who the previous weekend had endured a miserable Breeders' Cup, was full of praise for the colt and said: "Grey Swallow is a class act and did it very impressively. He does only what he has to, and that is a sign of a very good horse. Maybe he can repeat what I did this year and win the 2,000 Guineas."

Grey Swallow looks every bit as exciting a prospect as Refuse To Bend at the same stage and British bookmakers certainly seemed to think a Guineas double a strong possibility as they immediately slashed his ante-post odds to as short as 6-1 second favourite behind One Cool Cat. As for the colt's longer-term prospects, they will hinge upon how far he is going to stay.

Weld expects him to stay ten furlongs at least and his pedigree does not rule out further. However, he shows so much pace that it may be the outer limit.

Grey Swallow   *grey colt, 19-2-2001*

Daylami gr 1994	Doyoun	Mill Reef	Never Bend / Milan Mill
		Dumka	Kashmir / Faizebad
	Daltawa	Miswaki	Mr Prospector / Hopespringseternal
		Damana	Crystal Palace / Denia
Style Of Life b 1985	The Minstrel	Northern Dancer	Nearctic / Natalma
		Fleur	Victoria Park / Flaming Page
	Bubinka	Nashua	Nasrullah / Segula
		Stolen Date	Sadair / Stolen Hour

Bred by Mrs C L Weld in Ireland. 150,000gns Tattersalls Houghton yearling

Sire **Daylami**

Won 11 of 21 starts, inc. Prix de Fontainebleau-Gr3, Poule d'Essai des Poulains-Gr1, Tattersalls Gold Cup-Gr2, Eclipse S.-Gr1, Man O'War S.-Gr1, Coronation Cup-Gr1, King George VI and Queen Elizabeth S.-Gr1, Irish Champion S.-Gr1, Breeders' Cup Turf-Gr1. Effective 1m-12f. Tough, genuine. Very closely related to Dalakhani (Darshaan-Daltawa). Stands at Gilltown Stud, 2004 fee €20,000. Oldest progeny 2. Sire of: Grey Swallow (Gr3).

Dam **Style Of Life**

Won 2 of 8 starts. Fair form at up to 1m. Sister to Listed winner Seasonal Pickup (grand-dam of Sights On Gold). Dam of: Style For Life (1990 f by Law Society; winner, Listed-placed, dam of Gr1 winner Night Style), The Breadman (1991 g by Thatching; placed), Stylish Ways (1992 g by Thatching; winner, Gr3-placed), Yudrik (1994 g by Lahib; winner), Central Lobby (1995 c by Kenmare; winner, Gr3-placed), Rustic (1996 f by Grand Lodge; winner, Gr3-placed), 1999 Irish Style (f by Mujadil; winner), Grey Swallow (2001 c by Daylami; Gr3 winner), 2002 f by Sinndar.

Pedigree assessment

Daylami is an unknown quantity with his older progeny, but he is highly likely to get horses over the 1m to 12f range. Grey Swallow will have no trouble staying 1m and has a good chance of lasting 10f, but in terms of the Derby it might be worth bearing in mind that there is a fair amount of speed in Style Of Life's pedigree and that Daylami initially excelled at 1m. *JH*

Hawk Wing (USA)

4yo bay colt   **134**

Woodman (USA) - La Lorgnette (Can) (Val de l'Orne (Fr))
Owner Mrs John Magnier
Trainer A P O'Brien
Breeder Hill 'n' Dale Farms

Career: **12** starts | won **5** | second **5** | third **0** | **£1,056,740** win and place

By James Willoughby

HAWK WING ended his career as a mass of contradictions. His legacy is complicated, and a degree of deconstruction is required to establish it. For it is not so much the facts of his achievements that fascinate, but the issues wrapped tightly around them.

From the anticipation which surrounded his two-year-old debut at Tipperary to the bathos of his final start at Royal Ascot, Hawk Wing never failed to generate discussion and arouse interest. Whenever he looked through a bridle, the world was looking back.

The seminal moment of Hawk Wing's career was his extraordinary victory in the Juddmonte Lockinge Stakes at Newbury in May, his first start of 2003 and, as it turned out, the penultimate outing of his career. At the end of his three-year-old season, the argument against his wonder-horse status had seemingly been won. True to his duplicitous nature, however, he managed to start the dispute afresh.

Seven horses went behind the stalls for the first British Group 1 race of the season open to older horses. Only six consented to enter, however, the recalcitrance of Desert Deer causing a sea-change in the tactical balance of the contest. In stark contrast to the likes of Domedriver, Where Or When and Tillerman – Hawk Wing's main rivals – Desert Deer was the only source of early pace. So, when the six remaining contestants got underway, it was not clear what was going to happen. Hawk Wing's rider Mick Kinane had been planning to accept a lead and he showed no little enterprise in the revised circumstances by taking Hawk Wing to the front. In the process, he might have uncovered the key to his mercurial partner.

What followed was sensational. Allowed to flaunt his ground-consuming stride and terrific pace rather than being restrained, as had been the norm, Hawk Wing proceeded to force his opponents to the point of

**Hawk Wing (Mick Kinane) pulverises the field with an
extraordinary performance in the Lockinge at Newbury**

exhaustion. With three furlongs still to run, he was clear and still travelling
strongly. Carrying his head high, showing the whites of his eyes and
flicking his ears backwards and forwards, Hawk Wing looked to be running
on fear. Whatever, it was a powerful stimulus, and he came home 11
lengths to the good over Where Or When, with Olden Times another

2003   Race record

7th Queen Anne Stakes (Group 1) (Ascot, June 17) 4yo+ 1m Good to firm **101** (TS 75)
10 ran. *Soon in midfield, effort over 2f out, shaken up and found nil well over 1f out, weakened, finished lame, beaten 11l by Dubai Destination*

1st Juddmonte Lockinge Stakes (Group 1) (Newbury, May 17) 4yo+ 1m Good **134** (TS 128)
6 ran. *Made all, driven clear approaching final 2f, carried head high, edged right inside final furlong, unchallenged, beat Where Or When by 11l*

2002

7th Breeders' Cup Classic (Grade 1) (Dirt) (Arlington, October 26) 3yo+ 10f Fast **95** 12 ran
● **2nd** Queen Elizabeth II Stakes (Sponsored by NetJets) (Group 1) (Ascot, September 28)
3yo+ 1m Good to firm **119** (TS 86) 5 ran ● **2nd** Ireland The Food Island Champion Stakes
(Group 1) (Leopardstown, September 7) 3yo+ 10f Good **123** (TS 110) 7 ran ● **1st** Coral
Eurobet Eclipse Stakes (Group 1) (Sandown, July 6) 3yo+ 10f Good to soft **126** (TS 85) 5 ran
● **2nd** Vodafone Derby (Group 1) (Epsom, June 8) 3yo 12f Good to soft **127** (TS 102) 12 ran
● **2nd** Sagitta 2,000 Guineas (Group 1) (Newmarket, May 4) 3yo 1m Good to firm **125** (TS
103) 22 ran

Other notable runs

1st Aga Khan Studs National Stakes (Group 1) (Curragh, September 16) 2yo 7f Good to firm
117 (TS 94) 7 ran ● **1st** King Of Kings EBF Futurity Stakes (Group 2) (Curragh, August 25)
2yo 7f Good **115** (TS 83) 6 ran ● **1st** EBF Maiden (Tipperary, May 24) 2yo 7f Good to firm **88**
10 ran

eight lengths back in third.

For many, the Lockinge belatedly confirmed the promise of Hawk Wing's slingshot finish in the Sagitta 2,000 Guineas at Newmarket 12 months previously. Many observers who claimed he made up seven lengths on the winner from a poor position were deceived by the fact that he was much nearer the camera than Rock Of Gibraltar. In fact, sectional times revealed that the truth was half that margin, and it had to be remembered that the winner had gone off at a searing pace. Nevertheless, the fact that punters love unlucky losers more than hard-fought winners ensured that the Hawk Wing legend took fire.

The big, strong colt had ignited the flame at two, when successful in three of his four starts, culminating in the Group 1 Aga Khan Studs National Stakes at The Curragh in September. After the manner in which urban myths become attached to legends, Hawk Wing was credited with taking just 1min 20.90sec for his success. His correct time – which has been independently corroborated by sources outside the Racing Post – was a full second slower, a revision which should be officially ratified by the Irish Turf Club.

Hawk Wing came down to earth with a corresponding thud in the Vodafone Derby. It was a performance which first created the impression in many that he did not relish a battle. He cruised up to his stablemate High Chaparral two furlongs out, then his head came up under pressure as his reserves of stamina ebbed away.

On the form book, it was a great effort to run such a superb middle-distance horse close, but the overriding impression was that Hawk Wing had been forced through the pain barrier, and that he might not be keen to pass another horse under maximum pressure again. He never did.

Nevertheless, he was just too classy for a below-par Coral Eurobet Eclipse Stakes field in the Sandown mud, beating his pacemaker, Sholokhov, to land the second Group 1 of his career. Surprisingly, this hollow victory seemed to validate his reputation according to some, though to most it still left serious questions.

Hawk Wing ran another great race when beaten a short head by Grandera in the Ireland The Food Island Champion Stakes at Leopardstown. He took a long time to master Best Of The Bests in the straight, before the winner's withering run caught him cold.

At this time, Hawk Wing's form seemed to be levelling out at a Racing Post Rating in the mid to high 120s – a figure commensurate with a solid Group 1 horse who is vulnerable only to an outstanding rival. He ran below this form when beaten comfortably by Where Or When in the Queen Elizabeth II Stakes at Ascot, however.

Hawk Wing's tame response to pressure at Ascot was hard to forgive and marked the nadir of his reputation. Even his most ardent fans could not come up with an excuse. His trainer, Aidan O'Brien, bizarrely tried to blame the going in the immediate aftermath of his colt's defeat, before seemingly recanting. "Nobody died," he said.

A trip to Arlington for the Breeders' Cup Classic represented a final throw of the dice, but even medication could not restore his zest on his first, and only, attempt on dirt. He finished seventh of the 12 runners behind shock winner Volponi, but he was by no means the only horse to run badly in the ten-furlong race and the performance should not be held against him.

If Hawk Wing's detractors were in the ascendancy at the end of his three-year-old season, they were readily chastened by the Lockinge. Here, it appeared, was the redemption of a superstar, and the realisation of the ability which those associated with him always said he possessed. The problem for handicappers is detaching those endorsements from their consciousness in coming up with a rating for the Lockinge. The dichotomy is this: not many Group 1s are won by 11 lengths, but fewer still of these wide-margin winners were beaten in five of their previous six starts.

A modern approach to the interpretation of the Lockinge lies in the mechanics of pace. When any race is won by a wide margin, beaten horses tend to run way below form. This is especially true when a front-running winner exerts internal pressure on his rivals in the middle part of the race.

The defence for crediting Hawk Wing with a rating of historical resonance is the assertion that his rivals cannot all have run below form. Ironically, this is exactly what happens in races which evolve like the Lockinge. Even Where Or When, the runner-up, recorded a desperately slow split time for the final two furlongs.

It is fair to credit Hawk Wing with some improvement on his three-year-old form, but a figure in the high 130s is too much. The precise rating that Hawk Wing is awarded is of no practical importance, of course, but it leads to false conclusions which betray a misunderstanding of the nature of wide-margin wins.

Hawk Wing's defeat in the Group 1 Queen Anne Stakes at Royal Ascot was the final nail in the coffin of his reputation for many, irrespective of the diagnosis of a knee injury. While his abject display was a poor reflection on his reliability and, possibly, his temperament, it is of no account in colouring his Lockinge performance.

One wonders why the decision was taken to revert to waiting tactics at Ascot. Surely the Lockinge should have persuaded his connections that the key to Hawk Wing – if there was one – was to take him out of a competitive scenario. Perhaps they were guilty of consuming their own hype.

Whatever justification is advanced for an exalted rating of the Lockinge, Hawk Wing can never be described as a champion. According to the Oxford English Dictionary, a champion is "one who has defeated or surpassed all rivals in competition".

Such a description clearly needs to be modified when it comes to horseracing, for even a true champion like Dalakhani was beaten once – but a career record of five wins and seven defeats well and truly disqualifies Hawk Wing from such honourable classification in its semantic sense.

Hawk Wing now has a change of role within the Coolmore organisation, joining the line-up of stallions at the County Tipperary stud. Had he excelled in the Breeders' Cup Classic, Kentucky sister stud Ashford might have become his home, as it is to his sire, Woodman. But it is to an European audience that Hawk Wing has demonstrated his abilities and it is largely European breeders who will be patronising him at an advertised fee of €25,000 in 2004. He is a major face in an influx of several new stallions at Coolmore, but he is not the most expensive; that distinction lies with High Chaparral at €35,000.

It would be churlish not to recognise the huge talent that Hawk Wing possessed. And more creditable still was the manner in which his appearances stimulated debate about the sport on the track, rather than the countless side-issues by which racing is obsessionally and so poorly portrayed.

It is an important principle for the sport to heed that music tends to atrophy when it gets too far from the dance. Hawk Wing got us to raise our voices for the right reasons, even if we were rarely singing from the same hymn sheet.

Hawk Wing
bay colt, 15-3-1999

Woodman ch 1983	Mr Prospector	Raise A Native	Native Dancer / Raise You
		Gold Digger	Nashua / Sequence
	Playmate	Buckpasser	Tom Fool / Busanda
		Intriguing	Swaps / Glamour
La Lorgnette b 1982	Val de l'Orne	Val de Loir	Vieux Manoir / Vali
		Aglae	Armistice / Aglae Grace
	The Temptress	Nijinsky	Northern Dancer / Flaming Page
		La Sevillana	Court Harwell / Giraldilla

Bred by Hill 'n' Dale Farms in Kentucky.
$225,000 Keeneland November foal, $300,000 Fasig-Tipton Saratoga yearling

Sire Woodman

Won 3 of 5 races, inc. Anglesey S.-Gr3, Curragh Futurity S.-Gr3. Smallish, good-bodied sort, acted on firm and soft ground. Showed useful turn of foot, best form at 7-8f, but made no progress from 2 to 3 years and may not have been entirely genuine. Sire of Gr1 winners: Hansel, Hector Protector, Mahogany Hall, Gay Gallanta, Hishi Akebono, Timber Country, Bosra Sham, Hula Angel, Way Of Light, Ciro, Chiselling, Hawk Wing.

Dam La Lorgnette

Won 5 of 19 races, inc. Natalma S.-Gr3, Canadian Oaks, Queen's Plate. Rated 2nd best of her sex at 3 in Canada. High-class performer up to 10f, adept on dirt and turf. 2nd in only start at 12f. Dam of: Alexandrina (1987 f by Conquistador Cielo; minor stakes winner in Canada, dam of Canadian champion and Gr1 winner Thornfield), Elegant Wisdom (1988 f by Devil's Bag; placed), Halo My Darlin (1989 f by Halo; winner), Le Montrealais (1990 c by Gone West; winner), Polish Academy (1991 c by Polish Navy; unraced), La Andaluza (1992 f by Regal Classic; unraced), Dr Sardonica (1993 c by Rahy; winner, Gr3-placed), Chevalier (1996 c by Ascot Knight; placed), Dr Raymond (1998 c by Rahy; winner), Hawk Wing (1999 c by Woodman; Gr1 winner).

Pedigree assessment

It is axiomatic in racing that when you see a performance that looks too good to be true, it is because it is too good to be true. Handicappers, preferring their neat mathematics to vague horseman's lore, have trouble accepting the adage, and Hawk Wing's performance in the 2003 Lockinge Stakes had them staunchly defending their position over an outcome that others believed demanded a different interpretation. For most it was literally incredible that, this once in his life, the Woodman colt should perform at such an exalted level, but the arguments were futile, incapable of achieving consensus. What we know for certain is that Hawk Wing is an extremely handsome, gifted athlete who occasionally excelled and who only twice finished worse than second – when unsuited by dirt at the Breeders' Cup, and when coming back lame in his final outing at Ascot. He will be at Coolmore in 2004, covering at a fee of €25,000. *TM*

High Accolade
3yo bay colt   **123**

Mark Of Esteem (Ire) - Generous Lady (Generous (Ire))
Owner Lady Tennant
Trainer M P Tregoning
Breeder Deerfield Farm

Career: **13** starts | won **5** | second **3** | third **2** | **£289,773** win and place

By Lee Mottershead

HIGH ACCOLADE did not run in the Derby, but he would have won it if he had. Marcus Tregoning may only have been joking in the Royal Ascot winner's enclosure, but had he taken his place in the Epsom line-up, High Accolade would surely not have been disgraced. Although by no means the best British-trained middle-distance three-year-old in 2003, there were few better. More to the point, there were few tougher or more durable, or, for that matter, downright quirky.

Described by connections as "lazy", "idle" and "a bit of a character", the son of Mark Of Esteem on more than one occasion showed himself to be a complicated individual. He wore blinkers once, wore a visor once and, prior to finishing second in the St Leger, seemed more than a little reluctant to put his best hoof forward. Yet, although it was sometimes possible to call his attitude into question, his talent was never in doubt.

Nor, for that matter, would it have been accurate to say that High Accolade was unhelpful in a finish – quite the opposite, in fact. When push came to shove, he showed a thoroughly admirable attitude, his ungainly head carriage in no way reflective of a shirker.

We saw a lot of High Accolade. Trained as a juvenile by Richard Hannon, winning once in a four-race campaign that ended with defeat in a nursery, he was transferred to Tregoning by owner Lady Tennant. His three-year-old campaign began with success in a Bath conditions race, which prompted Tregoning to direct his charge at Goodwood's Predominate Stakes, the last recognised trial for the Vodafone Derby. His performance there was one that set a dilemma for connections.

There was a lot to like about the way High Accolade won. Punched along and seemingly still quite green through the early stages, Martin Dwyer's mount nevertheless picked up in grand fashion up the straight, coming from last to first and unleashing a potent turn of foot to breeze past Westmoreland Road and seize the contest. Derby quotes were issued

High Accolade (Martin Dwyer) on his way to victory in the King Edward VII at Royal Ascot

by bookmakers, but High Accolade was not in the race and, after careful consideration, he would not be supplemented.

Instead he was sent for the Ascot 'Derby', the King Edward VII Stakes. In scoring readily, he left all those associated with the horse wondering what might have been, an impressive turn of foot once again taking him to the front, again only after Dwyer had been forced to niggle sooner than he might have liked. Now, although Epsom may have gone by without him, High Accolade was a Group 2 winner and getting closer to the best around.

Next time at Newmarket he finished last while arguably running the best race of his life to that point. Meeting older horses for the first time, he finished sixth of six in the Princess of Wales's Stakes but, according to the form book, he might never have run better, with the 2002 St Leger winner Bollin Eric less than two lengths in front in fourth. The 2003 St Leger was now very definitely High Accolade's aim.

Two Leger trials came along before Doncaster. He ran well in one – beaten a short head by Phoenix Reach under a penalty when visored in the Gordon Stakes – and not so well in the other, trailing in more than nine lengths behind Powerscourt and Brian Boru when blinkered

2003   Race record

2nd Tote St Simon Stakes (Group 3) (Newbury, October 25) 3yo+ 12f Good to firm **123** (TS 86) 9 ran. *Tracked leader after 2f, led over 3f out, ridden over 2f out, headed over 1f out, kept on but not pace of winner inside final furlong, beaten 3l by Imperial Dancer*

1st Tommy's (The Baby Charity) Cumberland Lodge Stakes (Group 3) (Ascot, September 28) 3yo+ 12f Firm **122** (TS 49) 5 ran. *Made all, set steady pace until kicked on over 2f out, clear final furlong, pushed out, beat Compton Bolter by 3l*

2nd Seabiscuit St Leger Stakes (Group 1) (Doncaster, September 13) 3yo 1m6½f Good **122** (TS 94) 12 ran. *Held up, reminders halfway, ridden and headway over 3f out, led briefly over 1f out, edged left, kept on, held towards finish, beaten 1¼l by Brian Boru*

6th Daily Telegraph Great Voltigeur Stakes (Group 2) (York, August 19) 3yo 12f Good to firm **111** (TS 76) 9 ran. *Took keen hold early, lost place 7f out and soon pushed along, never happy after, kept on final 2f, beaten 9½l by Powerscourt*

2nd Peugeot Gordon Stakes (Group 3) (Goodwood, July 29) 3yo 12f Good **118** (TS 90) 10 ran. *Hampered in midfield after 3f, progress to chase leaders over 2f out, soon driven, pulled out over 1f out, ran on well final furlong, just failed, beaten shd by Phoenix Reach*

6th Princess of Wales's UAE Equestrian And Racing Federation Stakes (Group 2) (Newmarket (July), July 8) 3yo+ 12f Good **117** (TS 82) 6 ran. *Chased leaders, pushed along over 5f out, stayed on same pace final 2f, beaten 5½l by Millenary*

1st King Edward VII Stakes (Group 2) (Ascot, June 20) 3yo 12f Good to firm **115** (TS 95) 8 ran. *Settled off the pace in midfield, closed 4f out, ridden over 2f out, ran on to lead 1f out, driven clear final furlong, beat Delsarte by 2l*

1st Letheby & Christopher Predominate Stakes (Listed) (Goodwood, May 20) 3yo 11f Good **113** (TS 57) 7 ran. *Held up in last place, last and pushed along over 3f out, progress on outer over 2f out, led over 1f out and edged right, driven and stayed on well, beat Unigold by 1½l*

1st 25th June Is Ladies Evening Classified Stakes (Bath, May 6) 3yo (0-95) 10f Good to firm **95** (TS 49) 6 ran. *Held up, ridden 3f out, switched right 1f out, strong run to lead close home, beat Heisse by ¾l*

2002

3rd Sodexho Nursery (Ascot, September 29) 2yo 7f Good to firm **99** (TS 68) 11 ran ● **8th** Iveco Daily Solario Stakes (Group 3) (Sandown, August 31) 2yo 7f Good to firm **86** (TS 33) 11 ran ● **1st** Renault Trafic Van Maiden Stakes (Newbury, July 19) 2yo 7f Good to firm **86** (TS 50) 12 ran ● **3rd** Mercedes-Benz of Newbury EBF Maiden Stakes (Newbury, July 4) 2yo 7f Good to firm **79** (TS 35) 13 ran

in the Great Voltigeur Stakes.

In the Leger itself he was the first beaten, receiving reminders at halfway and doing a very good impression of a horse out of love with racing. Then he ignited, took an interest and took the lead over a furlong out, losing that lead to Brian Boru but losing little else, his reputation greatly enhanced as a St Leger runner-up.

Had Tregoning listened to his own first thoughts and retired High Accolade for the season, both he and the horse would have missed out. Running just 15 days after Doncaster, Dwyer executed new tactics, making every yard to win the Cumberland Lodge Stakes, beating smart performers Compton Bolter and Indian Creek with bags of authority. Subsequently unsuited by the false ground up Newbury's straight when second in the

High Accolade   *bay colt, 22-4-2000*

		Mark Of Esteem b 1993	Darshaan	Shirley Heights	Mill Reef

Pedigree table:

			Shirley Heights	Mill Reef
	Darshaan			Hardiemma
Mark Of Esteem b 1993		Delsy	Abdos
				Kelty
	Homage	Ajdal	**Northern Dancer**
				Native Partner
		Home Love	Vaguely Noble
				Homespun
	Generous	Caerleon	Nijinsky
				Foreseer
Generous Lady ch 1994		Doff The Derby	Master Derby
				Margarethen
	Northern Blossom	Snow Knight	Firestreak
				Snow Blossom
		Victorian Heiress	**Northern Dancer**
				Victoriana

Bred by Deerfield Farm in Britain. 60,000gns Tattersalls October yearling

Sire **Mark Of Esteem**

Won 4 of 7 races, inc. 2,000 Guineas-Gr1, Goodwood Mile-Gr2, Queen Elizabeth II S.-Gr1. Quite small, rather lightly built but quite attractive, athletic mover with sharp acceleration. Stands at Dalham Hall Stud, 2004 fee £12,000. Oldest progeny 5. Sire of: Ameerat (1,000 Guineas-Gr1), Redback (Gr3), Spring Oak (Gr3), High Accolade (Gr2).

Dam **Generous Lady**

Won 4 of 15 starts. Listed-placed over 1m4f. Half-sister to smart 1m4f+ performer Jape (by Alleged) out of a champion Canadian 3yo filly. Dam of: Summer Wine (1999 f by Desert King; winner), High Accolade (2000 c by Mark Of Esteem; Gr2 winner), Zangeal (2001 c by Selkirk; unraced), 2002 f by Mark Of Esteem.

Pedigree assessment

Undoubtedly receives his stamina from Generous Lady, but there is little in his pedigree to suggest he will be suited by extreme distances, and he should continue to be effective over 1m4f. *JH*

St Simon Stakes, he nevertheless ran his best race yet according to Racing Post Ratings, chasing home the improved Imperial Dancer.

Twice an Ascot winner, High Accolade is set to try to make that three times with the Hardwicke Stakes already earmarked as an early target in 2004. His form suggests he must progress further if he is to make his mark in the premier middle-distance Group 1 races. However, providing his wayward tendencies do not get the better of him, such improvement would hardly come as the biggest surprise in the world. He is a credit to all connected with him.

High Chaparral (Ire)

4yo bay colt   **128**

Sadler's Wells (USA) - Kasora (Ire) (Darshaan)
Owner Michael Tabor
Trainer A P O'Brien
Breeder S Coughlan

Career: **13** starts | won **10** | second **1** | third **2** | **£3,446,310** win and place

By Paul Haigh

THE prestige of the Derby took some heavy knocks in the 1990s. Its status has always depended on the plausibility, or otherwise, of the contention that its winner is the best three-year-old colt in the world; and in that grim decade – for Epsom anyway – few of its winners were able to sustain their own reputations, much less improve the reputation of the race.

The 2000s have so far been a lot kinder to the great race. First Sinndar went on to win the Arc. Then Sakhee, the colt who finished second to him, went on to take an Arc himself. But the colt who was probably to do more for the world's most famous Classic than any in the last 30 years was the 2002 winner High Chaparral.

Michael Tabor knew he had a serious racehorse very soon after the son of Sadler's Wells went into training at Ballydoyle. Whenever he was invited to discuss the pecking order at Aidan O'Brien's then imperious stable, High Chaparral's was the name he produced first, and last. He may have felt the confidence was justified when, after narrow defeat in a pipe-opener at Punchestown and a comfortable Tipperary maiden victory a week later, O'Brien sent High Chaparral to win his first Group 1, the Racing Post Trophy. That confidence only grew in the run-up to Epsom the following year.

As the Derby approached, however, there was some doubt as to whether High Chaparral or the physically magnificent Hawk Wing, an obviously unlucky loser of the 2,000 Guineas, was the stable's first string. When stable jockey Mick Kinane opted for Hawk Wing, it triggered a betting battle between two Ballydoyle factions as well as in the public at large – a battle in which High Chaparral's owner played his usual prominent part.

The memory of how High Chaparral and Johnny Murtagh took the lead early in the straight, met the challenge of the apparently cantering

High Chaparral (Mick Kinane) beats Falbrav in a highly controversial Irish Champion Stakes

Hawk Wing and then turned it back is still vivid. Afterwards, however, much of the talk was of how Hawk Wing had failed to stay. The winning margin of two lengths should not have left much room for doubt about the merit of the winner, particularly as the third, Moon Ballad, then a very decent horse at the height of his confidence and subsequently a five-length winner of the Dubai World Cup, was a full 12 lengths away in third.

But perhaps High Chaparral did not quite get the credit he deserved at the time – not even after following up with a comfortable victory lap in the Irish Derby, where he was followed home by stablemates Sholokhov and Ballingarry, the future Canadian International winner.

Illness then interrupted the colt's three-year-old career. A coughing epidemic swept through Ballydoyle and the dual Derby winner was one of the worst sufferers. O'Brien managed to get him back to something like match fitness in time for the Arc, but the Derby winner probably still was not the colt he had been in midsummer when going down at Longchamp to Marienbard and Sulamani. Whether he had quite returned to that peak in time for the Breeders' Cup Turf at Arlington is debatable, but perhaps he didn't have to be, as he demonstrated the gap that exists between top-class European and American turf form by mowing down With Anticipation and Falcon Flight to win by a length and a quarter.

Even the triumph in Chicago failed to see High Chaparral accorded

2003   Race record

1st Dead-heat John Deere Breeders' Cup Turf (Grade 1) (Santa Anita, October 25) 3yo+ 12f
Firm **128** 9 ran. *Disputing 4th, pushed along over 2f out, ridden and 3rd straight, quickened to
challenge 150yds out, headed post, dead-heated with Johar*

3rd Prix de l'Arc de Triomphe Lucien Barriere (Group 1) (Longchamp, October 5) 3yo+ 12f
Holding **124** (TS 113) 13 ran. *Always prominent, 3rd straight, hard ridden over 2f out, kept on
one pace, beaten 5¾l by Dalakhani*

1st Ireland The Food Island Champion Stakes (Group 1) (Leopardstown, September 6) 3yo+
10f Good to firm **127** (TS 121) 7 ran. *Tracked leaders in 4th, 3rd approaching straight, 2nd and
challenged 2f out, led 1f out, edged left, kept on well under pressure, all out, beat Falbrav by nk*

1st Royal Whip Stakes (Group 2) (Curragh, August 10) 3yo+ 10f Good to firm **121** (TS 70) 6
ran. *Settled 3rd, headway 2f out, led and hung right briefly over 1f out, stayed on well, beat
Imperial Dancer by ¾l*

2002

1st John Deere Breeders' Cup Turf (Grade 1) (Arlington, October 26) 3yo+ 12f Yielding **126** 8
ran ● **3rd** Prix de l'Arc de Triomphe - Lucien Barriere (Group 1) (Longchamp, October 6)
3yo+ 12f Good **124** (TS 112) 16 ran ● **1st** Budweiser Irish Derby (Group 1) (Curragh, June
30) 3yo Good to yielding **124** (TS 82) 9 ran ● **1st** Vodafone Derby (Group 1) (Epsom,
June 8) 3yo 12f Good to soft **130** (TS 106) 12 ran ● **1st** Derrinstown Stud Derby Trial Stakes
(Group 3) (Leopardstown, May 12) 3yo 10f Good to firm **119** (TS 99) 5 ran ● **1st** Ballysax
Stakes (Listed) (Leopardstown, April 14) 3yo 10f Good to firm **116** (TS 86) 7 ran

Other notable runs

2001 1st Racing Post Trophy (Group 1) (Doncaster, October 27) 2yo 1m Heavy **116** (TS 89) 6
ran ● **1st** Super Sunday Nenagh EBF Maiden (Tipperary, October 7) 2yo 7f Soft **93** 16 ran

quite the respect he deserved, though, as all the Breeders' Cup post-
mortems seemed to dwell on Rock Of Gibraltar's eye-catching failure in
the Mile rather than on his stablemate's (some thought) merely
workmanlike achievement in the Turf. At the end-of-season prize-giving
ceremonies it was the miler who got all the accolades. Most analysts
seemed willing, in spite of the valid excuse for that defeat, to judge High
Chaparral on his third place in the Arc.

Coolmore-Ballydoyle, an operation for which commercial considerations
are absolutely dominant, did not until recently believe in keeping successful
three-year-olds in training and they could hardly have been encouraged
by their first foray into this field with the injury-prone Milan. The fact
that, in spite of what he'd achieved, High Chaparral remained an underrated
horse, may have had something to do with their decision to allow him
to prove his worth again at four.

Sadly, in the spring of 2003 it looked as though they might have made
a rare commercial error as their champion jarred a shoulder, an injury
that kept him off the track until the second half of the season. While
many of the obvious targets were being run, including the King George,
High Chaparral languished in his box and it was not until August, in
the relatively modest Group 2 Royal Whip Stakes at The Curragh, that

he finally made his comeback.

O'Brien warned beforehand that the race was part of a preparation and that his horse was unlikely to be more than 75 per cent fit. But as it turned out 75 per cent was enough as High Chaparral had no serious difficulty in giving 7lb and a three-quarters of a length beating to Mick Channon's grand five-year-old Imperial Dancer, who came to the race in form. The victory was widely acclaimed as yet another demonstration of his trainer's enormous talent. It was a fair indication of the horse's ability, too.

The outing was expected to have brought High Chaparral on. But even so, as he approached his next and far more ambitious target, he was still being described as "no more than 90 per cent", with the Arc and the Breeders' Cup his obvious longer-term aims. There were plenty of other reasons for thinking he might not win the Irish Champion Stakes. One was the distance, which it was thought would be well short of his best. Another was the ground which, it was thought, would be too firm for him, particularly after his injury. The most important reason, though, was the quality of the opposition, which included the easy winner of the King George, Alamshar, and the brilliant Falbrav, who had already been described by his trainer, without provoking any great cries of dissent, as "the best ten-furlong horse in the world".

What was to prove the most controversial race of the season generated controversy even before it was run, as there were accusations that, by watering in order to guarantee High Chaparral's participation, the Curragh management was in fact favouring him over the recognised fast-ground horse Falbrav. Some even suggested the stable was guilty of blackmailing the course by threatening to withdraw him if the going was firm.

In fact, all O'Brien had said was that he wanted to be able to satisfy himself the ground was "safe". The course produced going that nobody felt inclined to complain about afterwards, and while there were plenty of complaints about the riding tactics employed, both by Mick Kinane and by Darryll Holland, there were none about the quality of the contest, with High Chaparral going to the front more than a furlong from home, then showing huge determination to hold Falbrav and the subsequent Breeders' Cup Filly & Mare Turf winner Islington by a neck and a head.

Just how unlucky the runner-up was will be debated for as many years as the race is remembered. But a couple of points need to be made about the winner's performance, too. He was not as fit as the second and he had the tactical (and finishing) speed for Kinane to be able to position him exactly where Holland least wanted to find him at every stage of the race.

After that magnificent effort it was widely assumed that High Chaparral would be able to improve both for the extra distance and for the softer going at Longchamp, and he was therefore sent off favourite, even over the French champion Dalakhani, to win the Arc. In the event he disappointed his supporters – not completely, because he was able to battle on for third place behind Dalakhani and Mubtaker – but at no stage was he travelling with the fluency that might have been expected of a likely winner.

Some thought he might be retired after that defeat. Happily his connections thought otherwise and he was sent instead to Santa Anita to attempt the unprecedented feat of successfully defending his title in the Breeders' Cup Turf. The result of this decision, and of the late decision to run Falbrav in the Turf rather than the Classic, was perhaps the greatest race in Breeders' Cup history, and one of the greatest in the history of the sport.

When Falbrav charged into the lead over a furlong out it looked certain that he would reverse the Leopardstown verdict High Chaparral held over him, even though it was well known that the mile and a half was beyond his optimum. But under a fierce drive from Kinane, whose last great triumph as Ballydoyle stable jockey this was to be (though we didn't know it then), High Chaparral gradually began to claw him back. He caught Falbrav a few strides from the line and then just held the flying finish of the Californian Johar to force a dead-heat.

It was a tremendous finale to a tremendous career. In 12 starts since his two-year-old bow, all but four of them at Group 1, High Chaparral won ten and suffered defeat only in successive Arcs. Some may think the suggestion that he was never as good running right-handed may have been no more than a convenient excuse for these defeats. But the fact remains that, after that initial outing, he was never beaten running left-handed and the visual evidence certainly seems to give weight to the argument, as on neither visit to Longchamp did he really show the determination that became his trademark.

That kind of determination is as rare as it is magnificent and it was never seen to better effect than in that epic at Santa Anita, a race that showed the 2002 Derby winner for what he was: an absolute pro, who acted on any going, never ran a bad race. Most significantly of all, perhaps – although Johar very nearly made it – never once allowed himself to be headed again in any race in which he had taken the lead.

There were all sorts of reasons for rejoicing that the decision to keep him in training had been more than justified. It helped provide us with a memorable season and at least one hugely memorable race. It should, unless there are pressing financial reasons to do otherwise, persuade the people behind him that keeping horses in training at four isn't such a bad idea after all.

The aspect that will most delight traditionalists, though, is that, by establishing himself as one of the greats on both sides of the Atlantic, High Chaparral performed a major PR job on the race in which he first began to build his mighty reputation. If there is no room for another statue at Epsom, they should pull something down and make room now.

High Chaparral

bay colt, 1-3-1999

Sadler's Wells b 1981	Northern Dancer	Nearctic	Nearco / Lady Angela
		Natalma	Native Dancer / Almahmoud
	Fairy Bridge	Bold Reason	Hail To Reason / Lalun
		Special	Forli / Thong
Kasora b 1993	Darshaan	Shirley Heights	Mill Reef / Hardiemma
		Delsy	Abdos / Kelty
	Kozana	Kris	Sharpen Up / Doubly Sure
		Koblenza	Hugh Lupus / Kalimara

Bred by Sean Coughlan in Ireland. 270,000gns Tattersalls Houghton yearling

Sire Sadler's Wells

Won 6 of 11 races, inc. Beresford S.-Gr3, Irish Derby Trial-Gr2, Irish 2,000 Guineas-Gr1, Eclipse S.-Gr1, Phoenix Champion S.-Gr1. Also 2nd in Prix du Jockey-Club-Gr1, King George VI & Queen Elizabeth S.-Gr1. Impeccably bred top-class performer from 8-12f, handsome, tough and consistent. Sire of Gr1 winners: Braashee, French Glory, In The Wings, Old Vic, Prince Of Dance, Scenic, Salsabil, Opera House, Saddlers' Hall, El Prado, Johann Quatz, Masad, Barathea, Fatherland, Fort Wood, Intrepidity, Carnegie, King's Theatre, Northern Spur, Moonshell, Muncie, Poliglote, Chief Contender, Dance Design, Luna Wells, Cloudings, Ebadiyla, Entrepreneur, In Command, Kayf Tara, Dream Well, Greek Dance, King Of Kings, Leggera, Commander Collins, Daliapour, Montjeu, Saffron Walden, Aristotle, Beat Hollow, Subtle Power, Galileo, Imagine, Milan, Perfect Soul, Sequoyah, Ballingarry, Black Sam Bellamy, Gossamer, High Chaparral, Islington, Quarter Moon, Sholokhov, Alberto Giacometti, Brian Boru, Refuse To Bend, Yesterday.

Dam Kasora

Unraced, out of a Gr2 winner who also ran 2nd in the Prix du Moulin and 3rd in the Prix de l'Arc de Triomphe. Dam of: Oriental Ben (1998 c by Ridgewood Ben; winner), High Chaparral (1999 c by Sadler's Wells; dual Classic winner), Mora Bai (2000 f by Indian Ridge; unraced), Treasure The Lady (2001 f by Indian Ridge; winner).

Pedigree assessment

High Chaparral has gone to stud at Coolmore, commanding a fee of €35,000. Nobody can say he deserves any less at the end of a splendid career that brought him Group 1 victories in each of his three racing seasons, and ten wins from 13 starts overall. He never finished worse than his third places in the Prix de l'Arc de Triomphe, and if his very best performances came at a mile and a half, he was almost equally effective over ten furlongs. As a runner he was the equal of his sire, and though it would seem a folly to predict that he will match Sadler's Wells's overall achievements at stud, he may well emulate him by getting a few sons better than himself. Discerning breeders will surely afford him the opportunity to do so. *TM*

Highest (Ire)

4yo bay colt **122**

Selkirk (USA) - Pearl Kite (USA) (Silver Hawk (USA))
Owner Godolphin
Trainer Saeed Bin Suroor
Breeder Saeed Manana

Career: **12** starts | won **3** | second **6** | third **1** | **£274,976** win and place

By Seb Vance

I T CAME as no surprise at all to see Godolphin snap up Highest at
the end of the 2002 season. As a three-year-old, who had started
that season a maiden and worked his way through handicaps to
finish it nearly a Classic winner, he fitted the bill perfectly for the Dubai
operation.

With the expected improvement from three to four, the 2002 St Leger
runner-up had all the makings of a high-class middle-distance performer,
as his former owners recognised. Following the sale, Tim Jones, speaking
for the Highclere Thoroughbred syndicate, said: "They [Godolphin] have
obviously had him on their shopping list for some time and who can
blame them, as he is the most lovely horse with all the right credentials
to go on and make up into a significant performer as a four-year-old."

Godolphin have enjoyed reasonable success with other horses bought
from Highclere, a prime example being Beekeeper, who finished third
in the 2002 Melbourne Cup. However, Highest's 2003 season never really
caught fire and was cut short by a niggling injury; he was not seen after
finishing fifth to Indian Creek in the Hardwicke Stakes at Royal Ascot
in June. However, in finishing second in a Group 1 showpiece, the son
of Selkirk did have time to match the achievements of the preceding
season and there is always 2004, as he stays in training.

The season started promisingly enough in Dubai, where he took the
Group 3 Dubai City of Gold Stakes over 12 furlongs on turf in March.
For a race so early in the year, there was a classy and competitive
12-strong field, including Narrative (winner of the corresponding race
12 months previously), Beekeeper, Fight Your Corner, Crimson Quest
(fourth in the 2002 Dubai World Cup) and Simeon, third in the French
Derby when trained by Mark Johnston. Highest, held up off the pace,
made smooth progress to quicken clear three out and win by three-quarters
of a length under Frankie Dettori. Things were looking good.

Highest (Frankie Dettori) on his way to the start for the Coronation Cup, in which he finished second to Warrsan

On the back of that, he was only an 8-1 chance for the Group 1 Dubai Sheema Classic, in which Dettori understandably switched allegiance to warm favourite Sulamani. In the saddle was Jamie Spencer, at the time a regular super-sub, not only for Godolphin, but also for racing's other superpower, Ballydoyle, later to retain him as stable jockey for 2004.

Highest's seventh of 16 in the £750,000-to-the-winner contest was a disappointing effort, especially as he finished around three and a half lengths behind Grand Ekinoks, the Turkish horse he had beaten into second on his previous start. Highest simply stayed on, looking as if the 12 furlongs was barely adequate.

Back on British soil, Highest came up against established older stayers in the Group 2 Jockey Club Stakes at Newmarket, such as Warrsan, Millenary and Boreas, as well as a contemporary in Bandari, who had always threatened to do big things without ever getting there.

Highest finished a well-beaten third in the 12-furlong contest to Warrsan but fared best of the trio who raced detached from the strong pace set by Bandari. His performance can to some extent be attributed to the patchy form of the Godolphin horses who, by and large, were not ready for the early season party and fell short of the standard usually expected

2003 — Race record

5th Hardwicke Stakes (Group 2) (Ascot, June 21) 4yo+ 12f Firm **111** (TS 101) 9 ran. *Held up in last trio, effort over 2f out, ridden and not quicken well over 1f out, one pace after, beaten 5¼l by Indian Creek*

2nd Vodafone Coronation Cup (Group 1) (Epsom, June 6) 4yo+ 12f Good **122** (TS 98) 9 ran. *Held up in midfield, progress and close 5th straight, pressed leader over 2f out, narrow lead inside final furlong, headed last 100yds, kept on, beaten ½l by Warrsan*

3rd Sagitta Jockey Club Stakes (Group 2) (Newmarket, May 2) 4yo+ 12f Good to soft **112** (TS 70) 6 ran. *Held up, headway 3f out, ridden over 1f out, weakened inside final furlong, beaten 5½l by Warrsan*

7th Dubai Sheema Classic (Group 1) (Nad Al Sheba, March 29) 4yo+ 12f Good **110** (TS 101) 16 ran. *Headway 4f out, ridden 2f out, one pace, beaten 9¾l by Sulamani*

1st Dubai City of Gold Stakes (Nad Al Sheba, March 8) 4yo+ 12f Firm **116** 12 ran. *In touch towards rear, steady headway from halfway, quickened well to lead final 1½f, pushed out, beat Grand Ekinoks by ¾l*

2002

2nd Rothmans Royals St Leger Stakes (Group 1) (Doncaster, September 14) 3yo 1m6½f Good to firm **120** (TS 96) 8 ran ● **2nd** Great Voltigeur Stakes (Group 2) (York, August 20) 3yo 12f Good **117** (TS 95) 6 ran ● **1st** Woodcote Stud Classified Stakes (Ascot, July 12) 3yo (0-95) 12f Good **99** (TS 36) 3 ran ● **2nd** King George V Stakes (0-105 handicap) (Ascot, June 20) 3yo 12f Good to firm **109** (TS 95) 19 ran ● **1st** Levy Board Maiden Stakes (Leicester, May 27) 3yo 12f Good to soft **87** 13 ran ● **2nd** Bryant Homes Maiden Stakes (Chester, May 7) 3yo 10½f Good to firm **96** (TS 80) 7 ran

Other runs

2001 2nd Federation of Bloodstock Agents Maiden Stakes (Div I) (Newmarket, October 19) 2yo 1m Good to soft **97** (TS 72) 20 ran

of them at the Newmarket Guineas meeting. For Sheikh Mohammed's team, it was a pattern that did not get much better as the season went on and, along with Ballydoyle, on the whole they suffered a below-par domestic campaign.

Highest was at his best in the Group 1 Coronation Cup, a race he might even have won had the heavens not opened, for he is a proven fast-ground performer. The five and a half lengths Warrsan had on him at Newmarket was reduced to half a length at Epsom, where Highest took the lead briefly inside the final furlong before being headed in the last 100 yards by Clive Brittain's game performer. He was clearly improving and this should have been the launch pad.

Much was expected for what turned out to be Highest's final outing of 2003, when he lined up as 5-2 favourite for the Group 2 Hardwicke Stakes. He was equipped with a visor for the first time, having veered slightly right in the heat of battle at Epsom, but it was a swansong to forget. Having been held up, he stayed on only steadily, never looking likely to justify the support. Possibly he should have been ridden closer to the pace, given his stamina, but that's being picky.

Highest was injured afterwards and was given a break in anticipation

Highest

bay colt, 28-4-1999

			Native Dancer
		Atan	Mixed Marriage
	Sharpen Up		
		Rocchetta	Rockefella
Selkirk			Chambiges
ch 1988			
		Nebbiolo	Yellow God
			Novara
	Annie Edge		
		Friendly Court	Be Friendly
			No Court
		Roberto	Hail To Reason
			Bramalea
	Silver Hawk		
		Gris Vitesse	Amerigo
Pearl Kite			Matchiche
b 1991			
		Storm Bird	Northern Dancer
			South Ocean
	Spur Wing		
		Equal Change	Arts And Letters
			Fairness

Bred by Saeed Manana in Ireland. 125,000gns Tattersalls October yearling

Sire **Selkirk**

Won 6 of 15 races, inc. Queen Elizabeth II S.-Gr1, Lockinge S.-Gr2, Goodwood Mile-Gr2, Challenge S.-Gr2. Big, powerful, long-striding individual, effective on any ground, very game, best at a mile, with excellent turn of foot. Sire of: Hidden Meadow (Gr3), Kirkwall (Gr2), Orford Ness (Gr3), Squeak (Beverly Hills H.-Gr1, Matriarch H.-Gr1), Border Arrow (Gr3), Country Garden (Gr2), Field Of Hope (Prix de la Foret-Gr1), Trans Island (Gr2), Sign Of Hope (Gr2), Valley Chapel (Gr3), Wince (1,000 Guineas-Gr1), Harbour Island (Gr3), Altieri (Gr2), Independence (Gr2), Highdown (Gr2), Leadership (Gran Premio di Milano-Gr1), Sulk (Prix Marcel Boussac-Gr1), Welsh Diva (Gr3), Favourable Terms (Gr2), Red Bloom (Fillies' Mile-Gr1).

Dam **Pearl Kite**

Won 1 of 7 starts, also 2nd Ribblesdale S.-Gr2, March S.-L, 3rd Doonside Cup-L. Effective from 12-14f. Very closely related to useful stayer Jaseur (by Lear Fan). Dam of: Pearl Barley (1996 f by Polish Precedent; winner), Shamaiel (1997 f by Lycius; Listed winner), Nayyir (1998 g by Indian Ridge; Gr2 winner), Highest (1999 c by Selkirk; Gr3 winner, Gr1-placed), College Fund Girl (2000 f by Kahyasi; winner), 2002 c by Desert King.

Pedigree assessment

Highest lacks that really big win which would reinforce his stallion credentials. On pedigree, there is little encouragement to step him up to extreme distances, for Selkirk very rarely gets good stayers and the dam is not from an ultra-stout family. *JH*

of a late-season return. However, hopes of returning to the fray were dashed when the problem returned. He will never reach the heights of Daylami, Fantastic Light or Sakhee, but he could yet figure in top-level 12- and 14-furlong races, and one day may even nick one. Possibly the Coronation Cup.

Ikhtyar (Ire)

3yo bay colt **125**

Unfuwain (USA) - Sabria (USA) (Miswaki (USA))
Owner Hamdan Al Maktoum
Trainer J H M Gosden
Breeder Rockwell Bloodstock

Career: **5** starts | won **2** | second **1** | third **1** | £36,071 win and place

By Richard Austen

THE Irish 2,000 Guineas, Scottish Derby, Meld Stakes, Rose of Lancaster, Prix Guillaume d'Ornano, Celebration Mile, Irish Champion Stakes and Queen Elizabeth II Stakes – all races in which Ikhtyar might have run but did not. Ikhtyar is well capable of winning a Group race, quite possibly a Group 1, but the wait goes on for him to prove it. The wait was long enough for him just to try.

The best weather forecast, it is said, is to ignore what the forecasters have to say and simply look for a repeat of what happened the day before. In the summer of 2003, that proved highly accurate and meant weeks on end without significant rainfall. Ikhtyar was one of those who spent far too long in his box as a consequence.

He had made his racecourse debut in a maiden at Newbury's Greenham meeting, where he impressed with his physique but looked very green in the preliminaries; drifting from 2-1 to 7-2, he finished third. The even-money winner Kalaman was immediately talked of as a Classic candidate, and so was Ikhtyar after bolting up at the second time of asking in a conditions stakes at Sandown 13 days later.

Both colts were given serious consideration for the Irish 2,000 Guineas, but they went head to head in the Listed Heron Stakes at Kempton instead. Ikhtyar took up the option amid protestations from John Gosden at the unfairness of the entry system for the Irish Classic (a supplementary being required once a second entry opportunity had passed in December) and possibly with a desire not to pitch him in at the deep end. Gosden would soon be praying for any opportunity to race on the sort of ground that prevailed that day on The Curragh. On good to firm at Kempton, Ikhtyar easily saw off five useful rivals but was himself comfortably outpointed for a second time by Kalaman.

Angus Gold, owner Sheikh Hamdan's racing manager, later observed that "after Kempton we know that he doesn't want fast ground". The

Ikhtyar (Richard Hills) wins the Gala Stakes at Sandown in July, the highlight of a frustratingly thin campaign

trouble was that every time Ikhtyar was mentioned with a Group-race target, fast ground was there to rule him out. The Meld Stakes at an evening meeting at Leopardstown in July got him out of his box, but not into the starting stalls when the forecasters got it wrong and the ground turned good to firm from good to yielding on the day of the race.

What made all this so frustrating was not the collateral form line with unlucky St James's Palace Stakes favourite Kalaman, but a performance that Ikhtyar produced himself, one that can be rated higher than anything that Kalaman has achieved.

The Gala Stakes over a mile and a quarter at Sandown at the start of July attracted a very strong field by Listed-race standards, including older horses Burning Sun, Naheef and Island House, but the 5-2 favourite Ikhtyar beat them all virtually out of sight and in a very good time. Six lengths was the official margin (from lightly raced stablemate Royal Stamp, then Naheef) after Ikhtyar had travelled smoothly and then unleashed

2003   Race record

9th Prix Dollar - Fouquet's Barriere (Group 2) (Longchamp, October 4) 3yo+ 9½f Holding **101** (TS 56) 14 ran. *Mid-division on inside, 7th straight, angled out over 2f out, effort when hampered and snatched up over 1f out, not pressed after, beaten 9¾l by Weightless*

1st Gala Stakes (Listed) (Sandown, July 4) 3yo+ 10f Good **125** (TS 98) 12 ran. *Held up in rear, steady progress on outer from 3f out, led and edged right over 1f out, shaken up and soon clear, impressive, beat Royal Stamp by 6l*

2nd Pacemaker Heron Stakes (Listed) (Kempton, May 24) 3yo 1m Good to firm **111** (TS 55) 7 ran. *Led until headed inside final 3f, led again inside final 2f, ridden and headed approaching final furlong, kept on well but not pace of winner, beaten 1½l by Kalaman*

1st Restaurants & Accommodation Tiptop Conditions Stakes (Sandown, April 25) 3yo 1m Good to firm **99** (TS 22) 5 ran. *Led after 1f, made rest, stretched clear from 3f out, unchallenged, beat Always Esteemed by 5l*

3rd Dubai International Airport Maiden Stakes (Newbury, April 12) 3yo 1m Good to firm **82** (TS 64) 14 ran. *Headway 3f out, chased leaders from 2f out, outpaced approaching final furlong, beaten 5¾l by Kalaman*

an impressive turn of foot at the two-furlong marker. His performance earned him a Racing Post Rating of 125 – a staggering figure for a Listed-race winner and the equal of Derby victor Kris Kin, who ran to only 123 at Epsom and achieved his best figure in the King George VI and Queen Elizabeth Diamond Stakes at Ascot.

After that, races of Group 3, Group 2 and Group 1 status all seemed realistic propositions – with the Irish Champion earning particular attention from his trainer – but the summer went by without Ikhtyar going anywhere.

The problem was not confined to Ikhtyar, of course. Dandoun, Nayyir, Tout Seul, Statue Of Liberty and Middlemarch all joined Ikhtyar as final declarations for the Queen Elizabeth II Stakes, only to be withdrawn because of the firm going. The weathermen had got it wrong again and, as a result, Ascot had not watered.

Miracle of miracles, however, there was give in the ground aplenty at Longchamp one week later and five of the six were finally given the green light. Tout Seul, Statue Of Liberty and Dandoun finished sixth, seventh and eighth in the Prix de la Rochelle, and Middlemarch was fifth in the Prix Dollar. Ikhtyar did worst of all, starting coupled 6-4 favourite for the Dollar but managing only ninth. It was an afternoon when only the locals seemed to handle the gluey conditions, and for Ikhtyar the long wait had resulted in a stunning anticlimax.

The scale of Ikhtyar's defeat at Longchamp is not explained solely by the interference he suffered in the straight, but memories are not so short that his superb performance at Sandown can be forgotten. Richard Hills insisted afterwards that he "still has a big future", and in all probability he has. It will be a surprise if he fails to win a Group race, and possibly a major one.

Ikhtyar

bay colt, 26-3-2000

		Nearctic	Nearco
	Northern Dancer		Lady Angela
		Natalma	Native Dancer
Unfuwain b 1985			Almahmoud
	Height Of Fashion	Bustino	Busted
			Ship Yard
		Highclere	Queen's Hussar
			Highlight
	Miswaki	Mr Prospector	Raise A Native
			Gold Digger
		Hopespringseternal	Buckpasser
Sabria b 1991			Rose Bower
	Flood	Riverman	Never Bend
			River Lady
		Hail Maggie	Hail To Reason
			Margarethen

Bred by Rockwell Bloodstock in Ireland.
65,000gns Tattersalls December Foal, Ir£380,000 Goffs Orby yearling

Sire **Unfuwain**

Won 6 of 10 starts, inc. Chester Vase-Gr3, Princess of Wales's S.-Gr2, John Porter S.-Gr3, Jockey Club S.-Gr2. Strong, rangy, good-bodied, roundish action, genuine and consistent. Outstanding pedigree, half-brother to Nashwan and Nayef. Stood at Nunnery Stud, died January 2002. Oldest progeny 13. Sire of: Bolas (Irish Oaks-Gr1), Alpha City (Gr3), Mamlakah (Gr3), Alhaarth (Dewhurst S.-Gr1), Gulland (Gr3), Zahrat Dubai (Nassau S.-Gr1), Lahan (1,000 Guineas-Gr1), Petrushka (Irish Oaks-Gr1, Yorkshire Oaks-Gr1, Prix de l'Opera-Gr1), Lailani (Irish Oaks-Gr1, Nassau S.-Gr1, Flower Bowl Invitational-Gr1, Dano-Mast (Gr2), Amiwain (Gr2), Ranin (Gr3), Fruhlingssturm (Gr2), Medici (Gr3).

Dam **Sabria**

Unraced half-sister to smart 2yo and middle-distance performer King Sound from family of Generous and Triptych. Dam of: Ghita (1996 f by Zilzal; winner), Sabreon (1997 f by Caerleon; winner), Landseer (1999 c by Danehill; Classic winner), Ikhtyar (2000 c by Unfuwain; Listed winner), Truman (2001 c by Entrepreneur; unplaced), 2002 c by Dansili, 2003 c by Danehill.

Pedigree assessment

Has fulfilled his pedigree by proving effective from a mile to ten furlongs. The aim now will be a major Pattern win and he certainly has sufficient class in his pedigree to do that, for he is from a family noted for outstanding performers, not just good ones. Interestingly, Unfuwain has sired just one Group 1-winning male, though Ikhtyar is certainly one of his best sons. *JH*

Imperial Dancer
5yo bay horse   **121**

Primo Dominie - Gorgeous Dancer (Ire) (Nordico (USA))
Owner Imperial Racing
Trainer M R Channon
Breeder Launceston Stud

Career: **50** starts | won **10** | second **4** | third **9** | **£310,017** win and place

By Richard Austen

AT 66-1, Imperial Dancer was the complete outsider of the field in the Champion Stakes. He didn't run like it. One and a half furlongs out, he was the only horse still on the bridle, but this was not as happy a state of affairs as it sounds. Boxed in, there was no chance to show what he could do off the bridle, only two of the other 11 runners had been beaten off and all but one of the remainder got in Imperial Dancer's way as Ted Durcan attempted to extricate him.

Houdini he was not, and after moving seven horses wide, Imperial Dancer ran on well but in time to take only fourth. It was a fine result, but not so good as he might have achieved with daylight at the right juncture. Six Group 1 winners still finished behind Imperial Dancer, including turf celebrities Russian Rhythm, Alamshar and Nayef. The one horse who did not impede him, though, was Rakti, who had already made the winning move, and Imperial Dancer surely would not have wiped out the eventual four and a quarter lengths deficit with him.

"I'm convinced we would have pushed the winner, but I'm not saying we would have won," reflected Imperial Dancer's trainer, Mick Channon. "People forget he gave 3lb to Black Minnaloushe and was beaten three-quarters of a length, and that horse went on to win a Guineas and St James's Palace Stakes."

That was true, but three years and almost countless good runs from Imperial Dancer had passed in the interim. There was no disputing his hardiness but, improved at four years and again at five, Imperial Dancer has emerged as a high-class performer. This is a horse who ran in March as a two-year-old, a tremendous credit to himself and his trainer.

When he reappeared in March as a five-year-old, Imperial Dancer had been an established Group-race performer for almost a year. Victory in the Rosebery at Kempton on April Fool's Day 2002 seemed to signal goodbye to handicaps and he added wins in a Listed race at Goodwood

Imperial Dancer (Ted Durcan) lands the Group 3 St Simon Stakes at Newbury in October

and Group 3s at Ayr and The Curragh. However, his first seven appearances in 2003 saw him struggle to produce much for his efforts in a variety of Group races in France, Britain and Ireland.

For the first time in 16 months, Channon tried Imperial Dancer in a handicap. A £29,000 event at Glorious Goodwood saw him run off a BHB handicap mark of 109, with Sam Hitchcott taking off 5lb. Imperial Dancer came from the clouds to lead on the post. Held up – often right out the back – before trying to produce a late burst, with his head held rather high, is Imperial Dancer's well-established style of running. It is not going to work every time – far from it – and in most of his six starts after Goodwood the old Imperial Dancer would have needed all the luck in the world to figure prominently, such was the quality of opposition.

He did not have to produce his peak form when emerging in front in the Listed Doonside Cup at Ayr in September, but he surely was not, for instance, going to run down High Chaparral in the Royal Whip at The Curragh. In receipt of 7lb, Imperial Dancer did, however, get to within three-quarters of a length of the dual Derby winner. The Champion Stakes made it clearer still that he should be seen in a new light and the Tote St Simon Stakes at Newbury one week after that made it blindingly obvious.

Unproven over a mile and a half, despite several previous attempts, Imperial Dancer not only surged almost from last to first in the space

2003 Race record

1st Tote St Simon Stakes (Group 3) (Newbury, October 25) 3yo+ 12f Good to firm **121** (TS 93) 9 ran. *Held up in rear, steady headway over 2f out to lead over 1f out, pushed clear final furlong, beat High Accolade by 3l*

4th Emirates Airline Champion Stakes (Group 1) (Newmarket, October 18) 3yo+ 10f Good to firm **118** (TS 95) 12 ran. *Held up, not clear run from over 2f out, switched right over 1f out, ran on, beaten 4¼l by Rakti*

6th Prix Dollar - Fouquet's Barriere (Group 2) (Longchamp, October 4) 3yo+ 9½f Holding **111** (TS 73) 14 ran. *Held up, 8th straight, stayed on at one pace under pressure final 2f, beaten 4l by Weightless*

1st Weatherbys stallionbook.co.uk Stakes (Listed) (Registered As The Doonside Cup) (Ayr, September 20) 3yo+ 11f Good **115** (TS 76) 7 ran. *Held up, headway 3f out, not much room from over 1f out until inside final furlong, stayed on well to lead close home, beat Island House by ½l*

3rd Prix Foy Gray d'Albion Barriere (Group 2) (Longchamp, September 14) 4yo+ 12f Good to soft **113** (TS 72) 4 ran. *Held up, last straight, never a factor, beaten 4½l by Ange Gabriel*

2nd Royal Whip Stakes (Group 2) (Curragh, August 10) 3yo+ 10f Good to firm **113** (TS 61) 6 ran. *Held up in 5th, ridden and kept on well from 1½f out, beaten ¾l by High Chaparral*

1st Littlewoods Bet Direct Summer Stakes (Handicap) (Goodwood, July 29) 4yo+ 10f Good **119** (TS 98) 15 ran. *Held up in rear, hampered on inner over 3f out, not clear run 2f out and switched left, 9th 1f out, storming run final furlong to lead on post, beat April Stock by hd*

5th Daily Record Scottish Derby (Group 2) (Ayr, July 21) 3yo+ 10f Good **113** (TS 79) 8 ran. *Held up in touch, effort over 2f out, ran on final furlong, beaten 1¾l by Princely Venture*

7th Tattersalls Gold Cup (Group 1) (Curragh, May 25) 4yo+ 10½f Yielding to soft **95** 8 ran. *Held up in rear, no impression straight, beaten 17l by Black Sam Bellamy*

5th betfair.com Ormonde Stakes (Group 3) (Chester, May 8) 4yo+ 1m5½f Good to firm **103** (TS 38) 7 ran. *Held up, headway over 4f out, every chance 3f out, soon ridden, weakened well over 1f out, beaten 13l by Asian Heights*

3rd Bet attheraces 0800 083 83 83 Gordon Richards Stakes (Group 3) (Sandown, April 26) 4yo+ 10f Good **114** (TS 96) 8 ran.*Tracked leaders, ridden and effort over 2f out, unable to quicken under pressure over 1f out, one pace after, beaten 2¼l by Indian Creek*

5th Dubai Irish Village Stakes (Registered As The John Porter Stakes) (Group 3) (Newbury, April 12) 4yo+ 12f Good to firm **111** (TS 81) 9 ran. *Held up in rear, some headway 3f out, soon one pace, ridden and stayed on again final furlong, beaten 5¼l by Warrsan*

7th Prix d'Harcourt (Group 2) (Longchamp, March 30) 4yo+ 10f Good **108** (TS 91) 11 ran. *Held up in rear, last straight, some late headway but never a factor, beaten 5l by Ana Marie*

4th Prix Exbury (Group 3) (Saint-Cloud, March 8) 4yo+ 10f Very soft **105** (TS 57) 7 ran. *Held up in last, headway to go 5th straight, ridden over 1f out, hard ridden to dispute distant 2nd 100yds out, no extra, beaten 5½l by Aquarelliste*

Other wins

2002 1st Meld Stakes (Group 3) (Curragh, July 27) 3yo+ 10f Good **118** (TS 98) 8 ran ● **1st** Sodexho Prestige Scottish Classic (Group 3) (Ayr, July 15) 3yo+ 10f Good **111** (TS 89) 4 ran ● **1st** Festival Stakes (Listed) (Goodwood, May 23) 4yo+ 10f Good **116** (TS 88) 7 ran ● **1st** Coral Eurobet Rosebery Stakes (0-105 handicap) (Kempton, April 1) 4yo+ 10f Good **106** (TS 84) 18 ran **2001 1st** Arran Conditions Stakes (Ayr, October 15) 3yo 1m Heavy **96** (TS 61) 8 ran ● **1st** Links of London Eglinton Nursery (York, August 22) 2yo 7f Good **99** (TS 100) 13 ran ● **1st** 'Catering By Amadeus Medium Rare' Maiden Stakes (Warwick, April 24) 2yo 5f Heavy **80** (TS 73) 4 ran

Imperial Dancer — *bay horse, 30-4-1998*

Primo Dominie b 1982	Dominion	Derring-do	Darius
			Sipsey Bridge
		Picture Palace	Princely Gift
			Palais Glide
	Swan Ann	My Swanee	Petition
			Grey Rhythm
		Anna Barry	Falls Of Clyde
			Anagram
Gorgeous Dancer b 1989	Nordico	Northern Dancer	Nearctic
			Natalma
		Kennelot	Gallant Man
			Queen Sucree
	Simply Gorgeous	Hello Gorgeous	Mr Prospector
			Bonny Jet
		Parthica	Parthia
			Violetta

Bred by Launceston Stud in Britain. 40,000gns Tattersalls October yearling

Sire **Primo Dominie**

Won 6 of 16 starts, inc. Coventry S.-Gr3, July S.-Gr3, Richmond S.-Gr2, King George S.-Gr3, also 3rd Middle Park S.-Gr1, 2nd King's Stand S.-Gr1, York Sprint Championship-Gr1. Showed best form as an older horse over 5f. Half-brother to Gr1-winning 2yo Swan Princess. Stood at Cheveley Park Stud, retired. Oldest progeny 15. Sire of: Dalnamein (Peruvian 1,000 Guineas-Gr1), Lara's Idea (Gr2), Arranvanna (Gr2), Millyant (Gr2), First Trump (Middle Park S.-Gr1), Bruttina (Gr3), Perryston View (Gr2), Tijiyr (Gr2), Primo Valentino (Middle Park S.-Gr1), Imperial Dancer (Gr3), Romantic Liason (Gr3).

Dam **Gorgeous Dancer**

Won 1 of 8 starts. Effective 10-14f. By stallion who tended to get sprinters and milers, out of unraced half-sister to Irish Oaks winner Give Thanks (dam of Alshakr, grand-dam of Harayir). Dam of: Lucayan Spring (1995 g by Ela-Mana-Mou; placed), Lafite (1996 f by Robellino; Listed winner), Imperial Dancer (1998 c by Primo Dominie; Gr3 winner), Perfect Storm (1999 c by Vettori; winner), Classical Dancer (2001 f by Dr Fong; placed), 2002 f by Diktat, 2003 c by Royal Applause.

Pedigree assessment

A very rare middle-distance horse for Primo Dominie (along with Tijiyr), but his toughness is far more common among the sire's progeny. The stamina has come from the dam, who is a descendant of the outstanding Moller mare Horama. *JH*

of 100 yards, he was also able to keep up the effort in a clear lead over the last two furlongs. A three-length verdict over the King Edward VII and Cumberland Lodge Stakes winner High Accolade was career-best form in Imperial Dancer's 50th race. "Our horses are for racing," said Channon, "and he is a proper horse."

Indian Creek

5yo brown horse   **119**

Indian Ridge - Blue Water (USA) (Bering)
Owner Seymour Cohn
Trainer D R C Elsworth
Breeder Mrs Rebecca Philipps

Career: **23** starts | won **6** | second **1** | third **6** | **£386,505** win and place

By Mark Blackman

FTER Indian Creek had finished fourth of 18 in a Windsor maiden on his debut in May 2001, the Racing Post analysis stated: "Slowly away, he made eye-catching progress and will improve with experience." That assessment was to prove half-right. After three campaigns in high-class company, he has learned next to nothing about breaking from the stalls, but is firmly established just below the top class.

Straightforwardness will never rank high in the list of Indian Creek's qualities. Invariably a sluggish starter, and prone to run lazily in the early stages, he has nevertheless now been placed three times in Group 1 company. His third behind Rakti in the Emirates Airline Champion Stakes at Newmarket in October 2003 followed a similar placing behind Nayef in the same race two years earlier, and a second to Grandera in the 2002 Prince of Wales's Stakes at Royal Ascot. All three placings were achieved in identical fashion – coming from a long way back after seeming to lose all chance at the start. If only he could jump off on terms with his rivals, he would be dangerous.

After a run on the all-weather in February, Indian Creek began his 2003 turf campaign just as he had 12 months earlier – with a Group 3 victory. His success in the Gordon Richards Stakes at Sandown in April was achieved in typical style, as he came from last place with a sustained run on the outside and bravely thrust his head in front of Bourgainville in the last 50 yards, winning by a neck. Afterwards, trainer David Elsworth declared: "He's a very difficult horse for the press to weigh up – and an even more difficult one for his trainer!"

Indian Creek returned to the Esher venue for the Group 3 Brigadier Gerard Stakes over the same ten furlongs a month later. Despite the presence of stablemates Island Sound and Rainbow End, the pace was moderate, and while he was able to produce his customary strong finish, it was not enough to peg back Sights On Gold. He finished third but

**Indian Creek (Richard Quinn, nearside) battles to master
Bollin Eric in the Hardwicke Stakes at Royal Ascot**

Elsworth had seen enough to try something new with him – a step up
to a mile and half for the Hardwicke Stakes at Royal Ascot.

Stamina doubts saw Indian Creek sent off at 14-1 in a field of nine.
The market was headed at 5-2 by Godolphin's Highest, from the 2002
Hardwicke winner Zindabad and St Leger first and third, Bollin Eric
and Bandari. Ground conditions were lightning-fast by the last day of
a meeting played out in baking sunshine.

As Zindabad burst from the stalls alongside leader Compton Bolter,
Indian Creek immediately found himself in last and Richard Quinn was
required to keep his mind on the job through the first half of the race.
Turning for home, Zindabad had most of his rivals struggling except
Bollin Eric, who ranged up to head him at the quarter-mile pole. But
at the same point Indian Creek was beginning to make relentless progress
on the wide outside and by the furlong marker he had passed all bar
Bollin Eric, who was running a blinder under his 5lb penalty. As the
pair drew three lengths clear of Zindabad, Quinn was able to urge his
mount into the lead inside the last 75 yards and gain the spoils by a
hard-fought neck.

The King George was nominated by Elsworth as the immediate target,
with an even more ambitious tilt at the Melbourne Cup also mooted.
In the event, he ran in neither. Rain on the day of the Ascot race forced
his withdrawal from that, while the attempt on Australia's favourite race

2003   Race record

3rd Emirates Airline Champion Stakes (Group 1) (Newmarket, October 18) 3yo+ 10f Good to firm **119** (TS 97) 12 ran. *Outpaced, headway over 2f out, ridden to chase winner over 1f out, stayed on same pace inside final furlong, beaten 3½l by Rakti*

3rd Tommy's (The Baby Charity) Cumberland Lodge Stakes (Group 3) (Ascot, September 28) 3yo+ 12f Firm **117** (TS 51) 5 ran. *Held up in touch, chased winner over 4f out, ridden and every chance over 2f out, soon unable to quicken, one pace over 1f out, beaten 3¼l by High Accolade*

3rd Coral September Stakes (Group 3) (Kempton, September 6) 3yo+ 12f Good **118** (TS 98) 5 ran. *Dwelt, raced in last, ridden 4f out, chased leading pair 2f out, soon outpaced and beaten, beaten 6½l by Mubtaker*

5th Juddmonte International Stakes (Group 1) (York, August 19) 3yo+ 10½f Good to firm **119** (TS 108) 8 ran. *Slowly into stride, behind and pushed along, headway on outside 3f out, never near leaders, beaten 5½l by Falbrav*

1st Hardwicke Stakes (Group 2) (Ascot, June 21) 4yo+ 12f Firm **119** (TS 111) 9 ran. *Slowly into stride, last and ran in snatches, taken to wide outside and ridden over 2f out, good progress over 1f out, ran on well to lead last 75yds, beat Bollin Eric by nk*

3rd betfair.com Brigadier Gerard Stakes (Group 3) (Sandown, May 27) 4yo+ 10f Good to firm **115** (TS 75) 8 ran. *Dwelt, held up in last, ridden over 2f out, no progress until ran on well final furlong, took 3rd last stride, beaten 2l by Sights On Gold*

1st Bet attheraces 0800 083 83 83 Gordon Richards Stakes (Group 3) (Sandown, April 26) 4yo+ 10f Good **115** (TS 97) 8 ran. *Settled in last, progress on outer from over 2f out, ridden to chase leader 1f out, sustained challenge to lead last 50yds, beat Bourgainville by nk*

4th Littlewoods Bet Direct Winter Derby Trial Conditions Stakes (Lingfield, AW, February 22) 4yo+ 10f Standard **105** (TS 64) 10 ran. *Mid-division, ridden 2f out, stayed on final furlong, never near to challenge, beaten 5¼l by Parasol*

2002

8th Hong Kong Cup (Group 1) (Sha Tin, December 15) 3yo+ 10f Good to firm 12 ran ● **6th** Emirates Airline Champion Stakes (Group 1) (Newmarket, October 19) 3yo+ 10f Good **113** (TS 91) 11 ran ● **4th** Juddmonte International Stakes (Group 1) (York, August 20) 3yo+ 10½f Good **118** (TS 105) 7 ran ● **5th** Coral Eurobet Eclipse Stakes (Group 1) (Sandown, July 6) 3yo+ 10f Good to soft **106** (TS 73) 5 ran ● **2nd** Prince of Wales's Stakes (Group 1) (Ascot, June 19) 4yo+ 10f Good to firm **119** (TS 109) 12 ran ● **6th** Tattersalls Gold Cup (Group 1) (Curragh, May 26) 4yo+ 10½f Soft **105** (TS 67) 8 ran ● **1st** Weatherbys Earl of Sefton Stakes (Group 3) (Newmarket, April 17) 4yo+ 9f Good to firm **117** (TS 99) 11 ran

Other notable runs

2001 3rd Dubai Champion Stakes (Group 1) (Newmarket, October 20) 3yo+ 10f Good to soft **115** (TS 80) 12 ran ● **1st** EBF Classified Stakes (Ascot, September 28) 3yo+ (0-95) 10f Good **99** (TS 81) 8 ran ● **1st** Adenstar Rated Stakes (0-95 handicap) (Goodwood, July 1) 3yo 10f Good to firm **98** (TS 77) 5 ran ● **1st** East Dean Maiden Stakes (Goodwood, June 15) 3yo 1m Good to firm **81** (TS 65) 7 ran

– in which Elsworth's grand stayer Persian Punch was twice placed – was abandoned in favour of another British campaign.

After three decent efforts in races that simply were not run to suit, Indian Creek headed to Newmarket's Champion Stakes, but as the gates opened he allowed all his rivals a two-stride start before he consented to join the party in a detached last. Skilfully worked into contention by

Indian Creek

brown horse, 22-2-1998

Indian Ridge ch 1985	Ahonoora	Lorenzaccio	Klairon / Phoenissa
		Helen Nichols	Martial / Quaker Girl
	Hillbrow	Swing Easy	Delta Judge / Free Flowing
		Golden City	Skymaster / West Shaw
Blue Water br 1992	Bering	Arctic Tern	Sea-Bird / Bubbling Beauty
		Beaune	Lyphard / Barbra
	Shining Water	Riverman	Never Bend / River Lady
		Radiance	Blakeney / Sybarite

Bred by Rebecca Philipps in Britain. 46,000gns Tattersalls October yearling

Sire **Indian Ridge**

Won 5 of 11 races, inc. Jersey S.-Gr3, Duke of York S.-Gr3, King's Stand S.-Gr2. Lengthy, attractive sort, a hard puller, too impetuous to get a mile. Sire of: Fumo di Londra (Gr3), Island Magic (Gr3), Ridgewood Ben (Gr3), Blomberg (Gr3), Definite Article (National S.-Gr1), Ridgewood Pearl (Irish 1,000 Guineas-Gr1, Coronation S.-Gr1, Prix du Moulin de Longchamp-Gr1, Breeders' Cup Mile-Gr1), Tumbleweed Ridge (Gr3), Compton Place (July Cup-Gr1), Handsome Ridge (Gr2), Indian Rocket (Gr2), Bardonecchia (Gr3), Cassandra Go (Gr3), Namid (Prix de l'Abbaye de Longchamp-Gr1), St Clair Ridge (Gr3), Indian Mary (Gr3), Nicobar (Gr2), Domedriver (Breeders' Cup Mile-Gr1), High Pitched (Gr3), Indian Creek (Gr2), Munir (Gr3), Nayyir (Gr2), Sights On Gold (Gr3), Campsie Fells (Gr3), Indian Haven (Irish 2,000 Guineas-Gr1), Snow Ridge (Gr2).

Dam **Blue Water**

Won 5 races in France at 3 and 4, inc. Prix des Tourelles-Listed, also 3rd Prix de Flore-Gr3. Effective over 10-12f. Sister to useful 8-10f French gelding Norton Sound. Dam of: Indian Creek (1998 c by Indian Ridge; Gr2 winner, Gr1-placed), Honorine (2000 f by Mark Of Esteem; winner), 2001 c by Barathea.

Pedigree assessment

It is Blue Water who has put the stamina in Indian Creek, though he has still slightly outlasted his pedigree by proving effective over 12f. Obviously has done enough to earn a place at stud in the future, and with Indian Ridge as his sire, Northern Dancer appearing just once in the fifth generation, Never Bend just once in the fourth and Mr Prospector absent, he could carve a useful niche for himself. He is the sort who might achieve his greatest popularity in continental Europe. *JH*

Dane O'Neill, he held every chance as he closed on the front rank with more than a furlong to run but was unable to live with Rakti from that point. He eventually surrendered second to Carnival Dancer as his exertions told, but this was the closest he had come to winning a Group 1, albeit in a race in which the market leaders all ran way below form.

Indian Haven

3yo chestnut colt   **118**

Indian Ridge - Madame Dubois (Legend Of France (USA))
Owner Peter Gleeson, Julian Smith, Loz Conway
Trainer P W D'Arcy
Breeder Cliveden Stud Ltd

Career: **9** starts | won **3** | second **0** | third **0** | **£170,666** win and place

By Richard Austen

"WON 1 race (6f) at 2 years, 2002 and £5,873 viz EBF Maiden Stakes, Yarmouth, and placed once." Tattersalls could not be accused of any outlandish claims that the Advertising Standards Authority might take exception to with its catalogue entry on lot 399 at the Horses In Training Sales in October 2002. And, for once, even the auctioneer underplayed the potential of the two-year-old colt in question. In the midst of all those exports to the Middle East and the USA, the recruits to hurdling and the sprinters on their way to Dandy Nicholls, there lurked a future Classic winner. Judged on that entry in the catalogue, he could have been just a fair handicapper in the making, but seven months later Indian Haven was the winner of the Irish 2,000 Guineas.

In 2001, the Mill Reef Stakes winner Firebreak appeared at the same sale and was bought for a record 525,000 guineas by Godolphin. Indian Haven fetched 95,000 guineas and made his way back to trainer Paul d'Arcy rather than to Dubai. He did experience a change of stables before his next race, but that was simply from one premises on the Hamilton Road in Newmarket to another, as a result of a breakdown in relations between d'Arcy and his landlord, one of the original syndicate that owned Indian Haven.

Indian Haven lacked Firebreak's results, but he would have had black type of his own had he not been hampered in the Gimcrack. He went on to finish fifth in the Champagne Stakes at Doncaster and well beaten in the Dewhurst, with his trainer later explaining: "Indian Haven had a problem and needed time off, but I was unable to give it to him through outside pressure."

Indian Haven's 2003 owners also own d'Arcy's new yard, Green Ridge Stables, and, just three weeks after the trainer had moved in, their investment in the yard and the trainer was rewarded with victory in the

Indian Haven (John Egan) powers home to land the Irish 2,000 Guineas at The Curragh in May

Victor Chandler European Free Handicap. Only six turned up in a weak renewal, but Indian Haven was undeniably impressive in the way he quickened up to score by two and a half lengths.

The infinitely greater return of a Classic triumph was not immediately forthcoming. In the post-mortems after both the Guineas at Newmarket, it was Six Perfections' misfortunes from stall one that grabbed the headlines, but Thierry Thulliez would have had an inkling of the unhappy experience that might be in store for him after watching what happened when Indian Haven set out from the same berth 24 hours earlier. If the stalls are in the centre of the course for the Guineas, there is a risk of an unsatisfactory race if the field splits into two; when they are on the stands side, the near certainty is that there will be bunching and interference. With the latter position adopted in 2003, with Indian Haven held up hitherto and John Egan again declining the option to race up with the pace, the result was that Indian Haven received a repeated and right royal buffeting. He had no chance to show what he was capable of.

2003	Race record

11th Emirates Airline Champion Stakes (Group 1) (Newmarket, October 18) 3yo+ 10f Good to firm **96** (TS 66) 12 ran. *Tracked leaders, weakening when not much room over 1f out, beaten 16½l by Rakti*

11th St James's Palace Stakes (Group 1) (Ascot, June 17) 3yo 1m Good to firm **65** (TS 35) 11 ran. *Chased leader, ridden and weakening when badly hampered 2f out, beaten 25l by Zafeen*

1st Entenmann's Irish 2,000 Guineas (Group 1) (Curragh, May 24) 3yo 1m Soft **118** (TS 92) 16 ran. *Held up in touch, 5th and ridden 2f out, led under 1 1/2f out, stayed on well, comfortably, beat France by 1l*

14th Sagitta 2,000 Guineas (Group 1) (Newmarket, May 3) 3yo 1m Good **99** (TS 90) 20 ran. *Held up in touch, hampered over 6f out, not clear run and hampered over 1f out, never able to challenge, beaten 8l by Refuse To Bend*

1st Victor Chandler European Free Handicap (Listed) (Newmarket, April 16) 3yo 7f Good to firm **108** (TS 84) 6 ran. *Held up in touch, pulled hard, ridden to lead and edged left inside final furlong, ran on well, beat Baron's Pit by 2½l*

2002

15th Darley Dewhurst Stakes (Group 1) (Newmarket, October 19) 2yo 7f Good **66** (TS 25) 16 ran ● **5th** Rothmans Royals Champagne Stakes (Group 2) (Doncaster, September 13) 2yo 7f Good to firm **101** (TS 39) 11 ran ● **6th** Scottish Equitable Gimcrack Stakes (Group 2) (York, August 21) 2yo 6f Good **95** (TS 57) 11 ran ● **1st** EBF Maiden Stakes (Yarmouth, July 3) 2yo 6f Good to firm **70** (TS 34) 6 ran

Asserting, as Egan did, that Indian Haven would definitely have won the Guineas, involved a degree of imagination, as 13 other horses finished in front of him. Four who did so (all of them less than three lengths behind the winner) were also present in a 16-runner line-up for the Entenmann's Irish 2,000 Guineas three weeks later.

Bookmakers and punters, however, latched on to Indian Haven and he started 8-1 at The Curragh compared to 20-1 at Newmarket, his owners having forked out again, this time €40,000, with the supplementary entry fee. Aidan O'Brien had taken four of the last six editions of the race and fielded five runners in a bid to make it five from seven, but the prize went to d'Arcy as Indian Haven, checked, but only for a moment, beat the O'Brien second string France by a length.

The form of this win looks modest now by Classic standards. Indian Haven looked as though he could improve on it but didn't get much of a chance. At 6-1, he was beaten before being badly hampered two furlongs out in the St James's Palace Stakes and was later found to have a foot abscess. He was reportedly working in good style just before the Queen Elizabeth II Stakes more than three months later but was not declared, and his performance at 33-1 in the Champion Stakes was not worth waiting for.

Indian Haven is a very doubtful stayer at a mile and a quarter anyway, but, an imposing colt, he should win more good races at around a mile. His best effort, at The Curragh, was on the softest ground he has encountered.

Indian Haven   *chestnut colt, 21-2-2000*

Indian Ridge ch 1985	Ahonoora	Lorenzaccio	Klairon Phoenissa
		Helen Nichols	Martial Quaker Girl
	Hillbrow	Swing Easy	Delta Judge Free Flowing
		Golden City	Skymaster West Shaw
Madame Dubois ch 1987	Legend Of France	Lyphard	Northern Dancer Goofed
		Lupe	Primera Alcoa
	Shadywood	Habitat	Sir Gaylord Little Hut
		Milly Moss	Crepello Bally's Mil

Bred by Cliveden Stud Ltd in England. 62,000gns Tattersalls October yearling;
retained 95,000gns Tattersalls 2002 Autumn Sales

Sire Indian Ridge

Won 5 of 11 races, inc. Jersey S.-Gr3, Duke of York S.-Gr3, King's Stand S.-Gr2. Lengthy, attractive sort, a hard puller, too impetuous to get a mile. Sire of: Fumo di Londra (Gr3), Island Magic (Gr3), Ridgewood Ben (Gr3), Blomberg (Gr3), Definite Article (National S.-Gr1), Ridgewood Pearl (Irish 1,000 Guineas-Gr1, Coronation S.-Gr1, Prix du Moulin de Longchamp-Gr1, Breeders' Cup Mile-Gr1), Tumbleweed Ridge (Gr3), Compton Place (July Cup-Gr1), Handsome Ridge (Gr2), Indian Rocket (Gr2), Bardonecchia (Gr3), Cassandra Go (Gr3), Namid (Prix de l'Abbaye de Longchamp-Gr1), St Clair Ridge (Gr3), Indian Mary (Gr3), Nicobar (Gr2), Domedriver (Breeders' Cup Mile-Gr1), High Pitched (Gr3), Indian Creek (Gr2), Munir (Gr3), Nayyir (Gr2), Sights On Gold (Gr3), Campsie Fells (Gr3), Indian Haven (Irish 2,000 Guineas-Gr1), Snow Ridge (Gr2).

Dam Madame Dubois

Won 5 of 8 races, inc. Park Hill S.-Gr2, Prix de Royallieu-Gr2. Big, lengthy, angular type, high-class performer who stayed 14f well. Half-sister to the dam of Daggers Drawn. Dam of: Richelieu (1992 g by Kris; winner), Place de l'Opera (1993 f by Sadler's Wells; Listed-placed winner; dam of Gr3 winner High Pitched), Blanche Dubois (1994 f by Nashwan; unraced; dam of smart winners Lady High Havens and Middlemarch), Nuance (1995 f by Rainbow Quest; placed), Galette (1996 f by Caerleon; winner), Paragon Of Virtue (1997 g by Cadeaux Genereux; winner), Count Dubois (1998 c by Zafonic; Gr1 winner), Indian Haven (2000 c by Indian Ridge; Classic winner), Massif Centrale (2001 c by Selkirk; unraced to date).

Pedigree assessment

Everything that could go wrong for Indian Haven in the 2,000 Guineas duly did go wrong, but the act of faith expressed by his supplementary entry for Ireland's counterpart Classic was rewarded with a comfortable victory on rain-softened ground that evidently suited him. Unfortunately, he encountered fast conditions on both his subsequent outings, coming back last – and lame – in the St James's Palace Stakes, then, after a long layoff, beating only the tailed-off Vespone in the Champion Stakes. Clearly a gifted miler when on song, and entitled to stay further, judging by the usual output of his high-class female line, he has his physical problems, reportedly stemming from a foot problem. If his trainer can find a solution, he may yet confirm his class at four. *TM*

Islington (Ire)

4yo bay filly **123**

Sadler's Wells (USA) - Hellenic (Darshaan)
Owner Exors of the late Lord Weinstock
Trainer Sir Michael Stoute
Breeder Ballymacoll Stud Farm Ltd

Career: **14** starts | won **6** | second **0** | third **4** | **£991,240** win and place

By Lee Mottershead

THE first time is always special; first kiss, first love, first British-trained winner at a California Breeders' Cup. Islington's place in Turf history is assured. She did what 31 horses had tried unsuccessfully to do before her. She succeeded where Dancing Brave had not. Her achievement was huge. In clinching the 2003 Breeders' Cup Filly & Mare Turf, Islington did far more than place a wonderful seal on a wonderful career. She restored British pride. At the previous five Breeders' Cups held in California, all 30 British challengers had been beaten, among them Dancing Brave, Sonic Lady, Barathea and Opera House. The heat, the humidity and the opposition had left them flagging. The record was embarrassing.

If numerical strength is a sign of confidence, then Britain's hopes for Santa Anita 2003 were not high. A mere four horses made the journey: Falbrav and Sulamani for the Turf, Oasis Dream for the Mile and Islington for the Filly & Mare Turf. The long wait was about to come to an end, but before Islington even got to Santa Anita a lot had happened.

That Islington even raced in 2003, never mind participated in the Breeders' Cup, was something of a surprise. She certainly did not need to. She had been a powerful force the previous season. Under the tutelage of Sir Michael Stoute, she had won the Musidora Stakes and the Vodafone Nassau Stakes before returning to York to run away with the Aston Upthorpe Yorkshire Oaks, taking the last two events – both Group 1s – by a combined total of nine lengths. Add to that an honourable two-length fifth in the Prix de l'Arc de Triomphe and a third in the Breeders' Cup Filly & Mare Turf at Arlington, and it was obvious she was already a seriously hot property.

Then there was her breeding. Hers was the most regal of pedigrees. Bred by her late owner Lord Weinstock, she was a daughter of Sadler's Wells, the outstanding sire of his generation, while her dam, Hellenic –

**Islington (Kieren Fallon) gets up to beat L'Ancresse in the
Breeders' Cup Filly & Mare Turf at Santa Anita in October**

herself by the mighty broodmare sire Darshaan – had shown herself to
be a dominant force both on the racecourse and as a mother. Successful
in the Yorkshire Oaks and only narrowly denied by Snurge in the St
Leger, her previous matings to Sadler's Wells had produced the classy
pair Greek Dance and Election Day. There was no doubt about it: the
connections of Islington had no need to race her at four. Her
performances and breeding already ensured she was worth a fortune
as a broodmare. They took the brave decision and kept her racing. They
may soon have regretted it.

Things went wrong in the spring, a foot problem leaving Islington
increasingly behind schedule. There were targets on the horizon, yet
she appeared unready to take them up. The Group 1 Tattersalls Gold
Cup came and went, then the Brigadier Gerard Stakes took place without
any sign of Islington.

Stoute could wait no longer. The Prince of Wales's Stakes would be
the centrepiece of Royal Ascot. There was Moon Ballad, the devastating

2003   Race record

1st Breeders' Cup Filly & Mare Turf (Grade 1) (Santa Anita, October 25) 3yo+ 10f Firm **122** 12 ran. *Disputed 4th, 3rd and pushed along straight, ridden and ran on to challenge 1f out, led 100yds out, driven out, beat L'Ancresse by nk*

3rd Ireland The Food Island Champion Stakes (Group 1) (Leopardstown, September 6) 3yo+ 10f Good to firm **123** (TS 118) 7 ran. *Held up in rear, progress 3f out, 5th into straight, 3rd and kept on well inside final furlong, beaten ½l by High Chaparral*

1st Aston Upthorpe Yorkshire Oaks (Group 1) (York, August 20) 3yo+ 12f Good to firm **118** (TS 111) 8 ran. *Tracked leaders, led over 2f out, stayed on well inside final furlong, beat Ocean Silk by 1l*

6th Coral-Eclipse Stakes (Group 1) (Sandown, July 5) 3yo+ 10f Good to firm **116** (TS 109) 15 ran. *Raced in midfield on inner, effort over 2f out, driven to chase leading pair over 1f out, faded last 150yds, beaten 3¼l by Falbrav*

3rd Prince of Wales's Stakes (Group 1) (Ascot, June 18) 4yo+ 10f Good to firm **118** (TS 103) 10 ran. *Tracked leaders, pushed along 3f out, driven and stayed on from 2f out, no impression when switched left 1f out, edged left and one pace inside final furlong, beaten 3½l by Nayef*

2002

3rd Breeders' Cup Filly & Mare Turf (Grade 1) (Arlington, October 26) 3yo+ 10f Yielding **115** 12 ran ● **5th** Prix de l'Arc de Triomphe - Lucien Barriere (Group 1) (Longchamp, October 6) 3yo+ 12f Good **119** (TS 108) 16 ran ● **1st** Aston Upthorpe Yorkshire Oaks (Group 1) (York, August 21) 3yo+ 12f Good **121** (TS 110) 11 ran ● **1st** Vodafone Nassau Stakes (Group 1) (Goodwood, August 3) 3yo+ 10f Good to firm **123** (TS 75) 10 ran ● **8th** Vodafone Oaks (Group 1) (Epsom, June 7) 3yo 12f Soft **94** (TS 54) 14 ran ● **1st** Tattersalls Musidora Stakes (Group 3) (York, May 14) 3yo 10½f Good to firm **111** (TS 76) 5 ran ● **1st** Sanctuary Group Maiden Fillies' Stakes (Newbury, April 19) 3yo 10f Good to firm **88** (TS 45) 16 ran

Other runs

3rd South Eastern Electrical Oh So Sharp Stakes (Listed) (Newmarket, October 6) 2yo 7f Good **99** (TS 71) 12 ran ● **6th** Q103 Maiden Fillies' Stakes (Newmarket (July), August 17) 2yo 7f Good **64** (TS 41) 10 ran

winner of the Dubai World Cup. There was Falbrav, hero of the previous year's Japan Cup and winner of the Prix d'Ispahan on just his second start since joining Luca Cumani. There was Nayef, the steady rock of the Group 1 arena and a proven force around Ascot. There was also Islington.

It had been a rushed preparation but, sooner or later, Islington had to race. Signs in the preliminaries were not auspicious. Uptight and sweaty, she went freely to post, both leaking and expending valuable energy reserves. The doubts were soon erased. At no stage did she look like winning but this was still an admirable effort. Running for the first time since her gallant third at Arlington, she stuck on gamely up the straight, taking third, beaten three and a half lengths by Nayef, but in front of Falbrav, Grandera and Moon Ballad. She had trained on.

Or maybe not. Although she achieved only a little less in the Coral-Eclipse Stakes, it was somehow disappointing. As Falbrav held off Nayef to land the spoils, Islington could finish only sixth. Once again, she was

**Islington lands her third Group 1 success under Kieren
Fallon as she takes her second Yorkshire Oaks**

unhappy in the minutes leading up to the race and this time was flat
in the race itself, becoming weary inside the final furlong. She had regressed
since Ascot and Stoute blamed Stoute, kicking himself for not listening
to his first thoughts and holding fire after the Prince of Wales's. He learned
his lesson.

Islington returned at York a different filly. Bidding to emulate Only
Royale by landing back-to-back wins in the Yorkshire Oaks, she was
sent off an 8-11 favourite, despite meeting opponents of the calibre of
Vodafone Oaks heroine Casual Look. Far less anxious than she had been
at Ascot and Sandown, and minus the cross noseband she wore for those
two defeats, she attacked midway up the straight, Kieren Fallon
sending her to the front well over two furlongs out, stamping Islington's
authority hard and early. It was a long last quarter-mile, the year-younger
Ocean Silk flashing down the outside as Islington idled.

To the eye, it was workmanlike, nowhere near as devastating as 2002,
but it was still a third Group 1 success, still Stoute's eighth Yorkshire
Oaks. Both he and Fallon were adamant that Islington was as good as
ever, the champion jockey arguing that he had never ridden in a stronger
Yorkshire Oaks. The fire in Islington once again burned bright.

She ran the race of her life in defeat. The field for the Irish Champion
Stakes was stunning, so that Islington was sent off a whopping 16-1.
Most punters dismissed her, preferring Irish Derby and King George

winner Alamshar, old rival Falbrav, the outstanding High Chaparral, Irish Oaks heroine Vintage Tipple and Moon Ballad. On this occasion, it would be Fallon, not Stoute, who had cause to point accusingly in the mirror.

At York he went too soon, at Leopardstown too late. Fifth into the straight, Islington remained behind four horses going into the final 300 yards. Then, with Alamshar beaten and High Chaparral and Falbrav scrapping furiously, Islington suddenly charged down the outside, unleashed by Fallon for an explosive burst. It was so nearly her race. While most bemoaned Falbrav's bad luck, few granted Islington the praise she deserved. She had been beaten just a neck and a head behind High Chaparral and Falbrav. It was her finest hour in Europe.

Nothing mattered now but the Breeders' Cup. Islington would not go to Santa Anita as an afterthought. This was what her season had been about, her date with destiny. Back among her own sex, she was sent off 29-10 favourite to win the Filly & Mare Turf. There was nothing of the calibre of High Chaparral or Falbrav to beat, but it would still be hard. If York was her ideal track, Santa Anita was the opposite, only seven furlongs in circumference and with a straight so short that if you blinked you missed it. At a more galloping track in Arlington, she had been outpaced, so could she really do better around Santa Anita?

Returning to the track where he rebuilt himself after a six-month suspension earlier in his career, Fallon rode the perfect race. Fast from the gate, he immediately pushed Islington into a forward position, taking her one horse off the fence approaching the clubhouse turn. Down the back, Bien Nicole made an early bid for glory, drawing ten lengths clear at halfway, the pack stringing out behind her. No need for panic. Sweeping around the final bend, Bien Nicole stopped, L'Ancresse grabbed the lead and then, on the crest of the final turn, Islington attacked, moving from sixth to second in a matter of strides.

The best horse in the race, perfectly poised and with history pulling her like a magnet, she raced for the wire. A furlong out, she was level with L'Ancresse, soon after she was in front, Fallon, strong but restrained, not required to dig into his deepest reserves. There were four cracks of the whip, no more. She was always going to win. History was hers, the winning margin a neck, her superiority far greater, Yesterday two and a half lengths back in third. The Americans beaten and the spell broken, Britain had her first California Breeders' Cup winner, and she was magnificent. The Filly & Mare Turf may not be the hardest of the Breeders' Cup races to win. Yet it was still there to be won and Islington won it. She could do no more.

A filly out of the very top drawer, she achieved the rare distinction of excelling at both three and four. Whatever she produces as a broodmare, she has already cemented her place in the racing annals. On a hot afternoon at Santa Anita, she became British racing's favourite girl.

Islington

bay filly, 12-2-1999

		Nearctic	Nearco
			Lady Angela
	Northern Dancer		
		Natalma	Native Dancer
Sadler's Wells			Almahmoud
b 1981			
		Bold Reason	Hail To Reason
			Lalun
	Fairy Bridge		
		Special	Forli
			Thong
		Shirley Heights	Mill Reef
			Hardiemma
	Darshaan		
		Delsy	Abdos
Hellenic			Kelty
b 1987			
		Homeric	Ragusa
			Darlene
	Grecian Sea		
		Sea Venture	Diatome
			Knighton House

Bred by Ballymacoll Stud in Ireland

Sire **Sadler's Wells**

Won 6 of 11 races, inc. Beresford S.-Gr3, Irish Derby Trial-Gr2, Irish 2,000 Guineas-Gr1, Eclipse S.-Gr1, Phoenix Champion S.-Gr1. Also 2nd in Prix du Jockey-Club-Gr1, King George VI & Queen Elizabeth S.-Gr1. Impeccably bred top-class performer from 8-12f, handsome, tough and consistent. Sire of Gr1 winners: Braashee, French Glory, In The Wings, Old Vic, Prince Of Dance, Scenic, Salsabil, Opera House, Saddlers' Hall, El Prado, Johann Quatz, Masad, Barathea, Fatherland, Fort Wood, Intrepidity, Carnegie, King's Theatre, Northern Spur, Moonshell, Muncie, Poliglote, Chief Contender, Dance Design, Luna Wells, Cloudings, Ebadiyla, Entrepreneur, In Command, Kayf Tara, Dream Well, Greek Dance, King Of Kings, Leggera, Commander Collins, Daliapour, Montjeu, Saffron Walden, Aristotle, Beat Hollow, Subtle Power, Galileo, Imagine, Milan, Perfect Soul, Sequoyah, Ballingarry, Black Sam Bellamy, Gossamer, High Chaparral, Islington, Quarter Moon, Sholokhov, Alberto Giacometti, Brian Boru, Refuse To Bend, Yesterday.

Dam **Hellenic**

Won 3 of 6 races, inc. Ribblesdale S.-Gr2, Yorkshire Oaks-Gr1. Also 2nd in St Leger-Gr1. Big, strong, plain sort, and a poor mover. Untested on ground faster than good. Dam of: Election Day (1992 c by Sadler's Wells; Listed winner, Gr1-placed), Desert Beauty (1994 f by Green Desert; winner, Listed-placed), Greek Dance (1995 c by Sadler's Wells; Gr1 winner), Greek Academy (1996 g by Royal Academy; unraced), Welsh Star (1997 c by Caerleon; unraced), Islington (1999 f by Sadler's Wells; multiple Gr1 winner), Olympienne (2000 f by Sadler's Wells; unraced), New Morning (2001 f by Sadler's Wells; placed 4th on debut, only run to date).

Pedigree assessment

Islington has never turned in less than an honest, high-class performance, and the rewards for her consistency have been huge, culminating in a thoroughly deserved triumph at the Breeders' Cup. Equally effective at ten furlongs and 12, and competitive with the best males, she represents the currently highly successful cross between Sadler's Wells and Darshaan, while stemming from a family that has served Ballymacoll Stud famously for four decades. It is a fact that not every top racemare becomes a successful broodmare, but it will be surprising if Islington fails to bring further credit to her family in that role, which she takes up in 2004. *TM*

Jardines Lookout (Ire)

6yo bay gelding **119**

Fourstars Allstar (USA) - Foolish Flight (Ire) (Fool's Holme (USA))

Owner Ambrose Turnbull Associates

Trainer A P Jarvis

Breeder Minch Bloodstock

Career: **27** starts	won **4**	second **4**	third **4**	£318,201 win and place

By Lee Mottershead

I T IS easier to like him knowing he got beat. Had he won, we would still have respected him, even admired him, but it would have been harder to like him. Yet because Jardines Lookout went down by the shortest of short heads to Persian Punch in the spine-tingling duel that was the Goodwood Cup, we can like him all the more.

It was a stupendous race, a battle to end all battles, two brave horses refusing to give an inch, scrapping as if their lives depended on it. For the majority watching at Goodwood and elsewhere, the right horse won. The right horse had also won two years earlier when Jardines Lookout was again edged out by Persian Punch in the Lonsdale Stakes. Jardines Lookout has never been the luckiest of horses.

His season, though, was not all about Goodwood. His 2003 campaign was planned around a second assault on the Melbourne Cup, the nation-stopping event in which he finished an honourable seventh in 2002. Flemington would be where his season ended. It began at York in May.

Unraced as a two-year-old and not always that consistent thereafter, Jardines Lookout had never before won on his seasonal reappearance. In fact, there had been only four wins in total. Disqualified after passing the post first in the Melrose Handicap at three, he repeatedly knocked on the door before landing a major prize in the 2002 Goodwood Cup.

A proper stayer, the one and three-quarter miles of the Yorkshire Cup was never going to be a sufficient test for Jardines Lookout. Fifth and third in the previous two runnings, this time he became outpaced as the pace quickened up the straight, eventually finishing sixth to Mamool. He would meet him again at a later date.

It was a rush for Alan Jarvis to get his stable star to the Gold Cup, post-York examinations revealing the six-year-old had pulled muscles in his back. Jardines Lookout did get to Royal Ascot and, not for the first time, provided fuel for those who doubted his commitment. Perfectly

**Jardines Lookout (Darryll Holland, nearside) goes down
by a short head to Persian Punch in the Goodwood Cup**

positioned just behind the leaders by first-time rider Darryll Holland,
Jardines Lookout seemed sure to run a big race as the field climbed
out of Swinley Bottom.

Then, inexplicably, he shuffled himself right back through the pack,
dropping down to ninth with last place looking a distinct possibility,
until he suddenly reignited himself, powering down the straight to claim
fourth, just a length behind runner-up Persian Punch. Not for the first
time, Jardines Lookout had run a strange race.

His commitment could not be doubted at Goodwood. If anything, he
was too fired up, as by taking the lead off Persian Punch with over two
furlongs still to run, he made the cardinal mistake of giving the old warrior
more than enough time to respond. Yet that day at Goodwood, Jardines
Lookout fought harder than he ever had, having another go at Persian
Punch after his rival had forced his way past 100 yards from the finish.
The winning post came just too soon. In another couple of strides, Jardines
Lookout would almost certainly have won. Nevertheless, it was his finest
hour. Learning his lesson, Holland brought Jardines Lookout wide of
Persian Punch when making his bid for fame in the Lonsdale Stakes.
It made no difference, the duo finishing one place behind Persian Punch
in fifth of the six runners.

2003   Race record

3rd Tooheys New Melbourne Cup (Group 1) (Handicap) (Flemington, November 4) 3yo+ 2m Good **119** 23 ran. *Towards rear early, headway around outside before halfway, 7th straight, outpaced and hard ridden in 9th over 1f out, finished well to take 3rd on line, beaten 4¼l by Makybe Diva*

5th Weatherbys Insurance Lonsdale Stakes (Group 3) (York, August 19) 3yo+ 2m Good to firm **113** (TS 69) 6 ran. *Chased leaders, brought wide over 4f out, soon outpaced, kept on final 2f, beaten 4l by Bollin Eric*

2nd Lady O Goodwood Cup (Group 2) (Goodwood, July 31) 3yo+ 2m Good **119** (TS 110) 9 ran. *Chased winner, pushed up to challenge from 6f out, driven to lead narrowly over 2f out, edged right over 1f out, headed last 100yds, rallied, just held, beaten shd by Persian Punch*

4th Gold Cup (Group 1) (Ascot, June 19) 4yo+ 2m4f Good to firm **116** (TS 63) 12 ran. *Chased leaders, ridden, not keen and lost place 4f out, rallied under pressure from 2f out, kept on well close home, beaten 7l by Mr Dinos*

6th Emirates Airline Yorkshire Cup (Group 2) (York, May 15) 4yo+ 1m6f Good to firm **110** (TS 86) 8 ran. *In rear-division, pushed along 1m out, outpaced final 3f, beaten 11½l by Mamool*

2002

7th Tooheys New Melbourne Cup (Handicap) (Group 1) (Flemington, November 5) 3yo+ 2m Good **114** 23 ran ● **4th** GNER Doncaster Cup (Group 3) (Doncaster, September 12) 3yo+ 2m2f Good to firm **113** (TS 88) 8 ran ● **6th** Weatherbys Insurance Lonsdale Stakes (Group 3) (York, August 20) 3yo+ 2m Good **113** (TS 89) 7 ran ● **1st** JPMorgan Private Bank Goodwood Cup (Group 2) (Goodwood, August 1) 3yo+ 2m Good to firm **119** (TS 108) 9 ran ● **9th** Gold Cup (Group 1) (Ascot, June 20) 4yo+ 2m4f Good to firm **109** (TS 12) 15 ran ● **3rd** Merewood Homes Yorkshire Cup (Group 2) (York, May 16) 4yo+ 1m6f Good to firm **115** (TS 44) 7 ran

Other notable runs

2001 2nd Weatherbys Insurance Lonsdale Stakes (Group 3) (York, August 21) 3yo+ 2m Good **117** (TS 87) 10 ran ● **3rd** Gold Cup (Group 1) (Ascot, June 21) 4yo+ 2m4f Good to firm **116** (TS 71) 12 ran **2000 1st** Auker Rhodes Conditions Stakes (Doncaster, November 3) 3yo+ 1m6½f Heavy **92** (TS 51) 10 ran ● **1st** Abu Dhabi Rated Stakes (0-100 handicap) (Newmarket, September 16) 3yo+ 1m6f Soft **111** (TS 97) 6 ran ● **1st** Odstock Maiden Stakes (Salisbury, July 15) 3yo+ 1m6f Good **94** (TS 71) 14 ran

It would be well over two months before we saw him again. The vibes before the Melbourne Cup were not good. Jardines Lookout shared top weight with Mamool, Jarvis expressed concern that his charge was a gallop short, and local punters dismissed him at 40-1. He did not run like a 40-1 shot. Struggling with what Holland described as "a six-furlong pace", he was unable to lay up with the early gallop, seemingly out with the washing until making some headway approaching the final turn.

Still only treading water early in the straight, he suddenly flew inside the final 100 yards, weaving through to claim third in a photo-finish. Carrying 10lb more than the winner Makybe Diva and 12lb more than runner-up She's Archie, Jardines Lookout emerged by some way the best horse in the race. He earned £139,770 for his efforts, a fitting reward for a mighty performance.

Jardines Lookout
bay gelding, 28-4-1997

			Nearctic
		Northern Dancer	Natalma
	Compliance		
		Sex Appeal	Buckpasser
Fourstars Allstar			Best In Show
b 1988			Noble Jay
		Bold Arian	Riverval
	Broadway Joan		
		Courtneys Doll	Wakefield Tower
			Rapport
		Noholme	Star Kingdom
			Oceana
	Fools Holme		
		Fancifool	Vaguely Noble
Foolish Flight			Foolish One
ch 1991			Herbager
		Sea Hawk	Sea Nymph
	Black Crow		
		Cafe Au Lait	Espresso
			Blue Sash

Bred by Minch Bloodstock in Ireland.
Ir8,600gns Goffs December foal, Ir20,000gns Goffs Challenge yearling

Sire **Fourstars Allstar**

Won 14 races, inc. Irish 2,000 Guineas-Gr1, Bernard Baruch H.-Gr2, twice, Elkhorn S.-Gr2, also 3rd Breeders' Cup Mile-Gr1. Best at around 1m. Brother to Gr2 winner Fourstardave and to dam of Gr2 winner Mystic Lady. Stands at Coolmore (NH). Oldest progeny 6. Sire of: Jardines Lookout (Gr2).

Dam **Foolish Flight**

Unplaced in 4 starts at 2. By South African-raced sire, out of mare from family of Compton Bolter, Insatiable, Seazun. Dam of: Campari (1995 f by Distinctly North; placed), unnamed (1996 c by Tirol), Jardines Lookout (1997 g by Fourstars Allstar; Gr2 winner, Gr1-placed), Light-Flight (1998 f by Brief Truce; winner), Turfcare Flight (2000 f by Mujadil; unplaced), 2001 f by Goldmark.

Pedigree assessment

By a very tough performer out of a mare from a family noted for its toughness. Jardines Lookout therefore lives up to his pedigree, though he stays better than virtually all his talented relatives. *JH*

Not surprisingly, a third tilt at the Melbourne Cup is the big aim for Jardines Lookout in 2004. A credit to his relatively small stable, he showed himself to be better than ever at six, forging a strong relationship with Holland and confirming himself among the world's staying elite. He may not have won a race in 2003, but no horse was more valiant in defeat.

Johar (USA)

4yo bay colt **128**

Gone West (USA) - Windsharp (USA) (Lear Fan (USA))
Owner The Thoroughbred Corporation
Trainer Richard E Mandella
Breeder The Thoroughbred Corporation

Career: **15** starts | won **6** | second **4** | third **2** | **£969,015** win and place

By James Willoughby

ICHARD MANDELLA had the sort of day that trainers dare not dream about at the 20th Breeders' Cup at Santa Anita. The Californian became the first to win four races at one meeting: the Juvenile Fillies' with Halfbridled, the Juvenile with Action This Day, the Classic with Pleasantly Perfect and the Turf with Johar.

The last-named success came via a dead-heat with High Chaparral, the first in Breeders' Cup history. In the process, Johar proved himself a turf performer of the highest standing, mixing it with both the defending champion and Falbrav in the tightest of finishes.

Johar had to come back from a serious injury to reach the summit of world turf racing. In January, he completed a hat-trick in the Grade 2 San Marcos Handicap over a mile and a quarter at Santa Anita, adding to his successes in the Grade 2 Oak Tree Derby at the same venue and the Grade 1 Hollywood Derby.

Soon after the San Marcos, Mandella discovered the colt had a stress fracture of his near shoulder, which necessitated a seven-month lay-off. "I always thought Johar was as good as any man's horse on the grass, but we had to stop with him," the trainer said.

Johar was reportedly short of peak fitness when returning to the track at Del Mar in August, when he ran on to finish about a length behind Sarafan over a mile and a sixteenth. Considering the trip was on the short side and he was checked early on, it was an encouraging return to duty.

The top-class Storming Home stood in Johar's way in the Grade 1 Clement L Hirsch Memorial Turf Championship back at Santa Anita at the end of September. After pondering his tactical options in a four-horse race devoid of front-runners, Mandella decided it was better for Johar's jockey, Alex Solis, to let him stride on, rather than finding his late finish compromised by lack of pace.

**Johar (Alex Solis, nearside) is driven up to dead-heat with
High Chaparral (centre) in the Breeders' Cup Turf**

The change of tactics did not suit Johar, who was easily picked off
by the latent power of Storming Home. Mandella was not discouraged,
however. "He had never been in front before, even in his work, and I
thought he ran a tremendous race," he said.

The Breeders' Cup Turf had a different tactical context, with the front-
runners Balto Star and The Tin Man bound to ensure a true-run race.
After a furlong, Johar could see them all, but the colt was moving evenly
and Solis was unhurried. As the pace intensified turning out of the back
straight, Johar had plenty to do, especially when Falbrav struck for home
on straightening up. Solis still did not panic, however, and Johar reached
out gamely in an unforgettable finish to snatch a deserved share of the
spoils.

In an echo of the Breeders' Cup Filly & Mare Turf, which had pitted
the strength of Kieren Fallon against a comparatively inanimate Edgar
Prado, there was a sharp contrast between the vigour of Mick Kinane
on High Chaparral and Solis on Johar. But to infer from this visual

2003   Race record

1st Dead-heat John Deere Breeders' Cup Turf (Grade 1) (Santa Anita, October 25) 3yo+ 12f Firm **128** 9 ran. *Held up in last, progress approaching straight, 6th towards outside straight, finished strongly to join leader post, dead-heated with High Chaparral*

2nd Clement L Hirsch Memorial Turf Championship (Grade 1) (Santa Anita, September 28) 3yo+ 10f Firm **121** 5 ran. *Led, hard ridden from distance, headed and unable to quicken well inside final furlong, beaten ½l by Storming Home*

3rd H F Brubaker Handicap (Del Mar, August 22) 3yo+ 8½f Firm **112** 3 ran. *Held up last of 3, effort 1f out, just missed 2nd, beaten 1¼l by Sarafan*

1st San Marcos Stakes (Grade 2) (Santa Anita, January 20) 4yo+ 10f Firm **119** 7 ran. *Held up in rear, headway 3f out, 5th and not clear run 2f out, ran on well final furlong to lead last strides, beat The Tin Man by hd*

2002

1st Hollywood Derby (Grade 1) (Hollywood Park, December 1) 3yo 9f Firm **121** 9 ran ● **1st** Oak Tree Derby (Grade 2) (Santa Anita, October 13) 3yo 9f Firm 8 ran ● **2nd** Del Mar Derby (Grade 2) (Del Mar, September 7) 3yo 9f Firm 9 ran ● **2nd** Oceanside Stakes (Del Mar, July 24) 3yo 1m Firm 6 ran ● **3rd** Cinema Grade 3 Handicap (Hollywood Park, June 30) 3yo 9f Firm 7 ran ● **2nd** Will Rogers Stakes (Grade 3) (Hollywood Park, June 1) 3yo 1m Firm 5 ran ● **4th** La Puente Stakes (Santa Anita, April 14) 3yo 1m Firm 8 ran ● **1st** Allowance race (Santa Anita, March 28) 3yo 1m Firm 7 ran ● **1st** Maiden (Santa Anita, February 24) 3yo 9f Firm 7 ran ● **6th** Maiden (Dirt) (Santa Anita, February 9) 3yo 1m Fast 10 ran ● **5th** Maiden (Dirt) (Santa Anita, January 21) 3yo 7f Fast 10 ran

impression a general disparity of effectiveness between jockeys on either side of the Atlantic would be a mistake.

US jockeys ride shorter and with their weight slightly more towards a horse's withers than most Europeans. Their style is most efficient in dirt races, in which a horse must be allowed to run freely and gather momentum. In turf events, it is necessary to restrain a horse through the first part of the race before releasing its energy in a furious finishing burst, the strength and dynamism of a jockey playing a significant part in the rate at which a horse picks up pace.

Provided European riders adjust to the tactical nuances of the US turf courses, in which experience plays a vital part, it is probable they hold something of an advantage in a driving finish. On dirt, however, US jockeys are more adept at getting horses to travel smoothly in the early part of a race and maintain their balance and effectiveness in the closing stages, when horses are considerably more tired than in races on firm turf.

The US jockeys who have made an impact in Britain, such as Steve Cauthen and Gary Stevens, have been most effective when riding from the front. Though it is generally assumed that this is due to superior judgement of pace, the truth is that in this position they are free to allow their mounts to dissipate their energy evenly and to build up momentum, just as if the race were on dirt rather than turf.

Solis, a 39-year-old native of Panama, is a tremendously effective rider who knows the California turf courses of Santa Anita, Hollywood Park

Johar   *bay colt, 28-2-1999*

		Raise A Native	Native Dancer / Raise You
	Mr Prospector		
Gone West br 1984		Gold Digger	Nashua / Sequence
	Secrettame	Secretariat	Bold Ruler / Somethingroyal
		Tamerett	Tim Tam / Mixed Marriage
	Lear Fan	Roberto	Hail To Reason / Bramalea
		Wac	Lt Stevens / Belthazar
Windsharp br 1991	Yes She's Sharp	Sharpen Up	Atan / Rocchetta
		Yes Sir	Sir Gaylord / Fun House

Bred by The Thoroughbred Corporation in US

Sire Gone West

Won 6 of 17 starts, inc. Dwyer S.-Gr1, Gotham S.-Gr2, Withers S.-Gr2, also 2nd Wood Memorial S.-Gr1. Effective 6-9f. Brother to Lion Cavern out of Gr3-winning half-sister to Known Fact. Stands at Mill Ridge Farm, 2003 fee $125,000. Oldest progeny 14. Sire of Gr1 winners: West By West (Nassau County H.), Link River (John A Morris H.), Zafonic (Prix Morny, Prix de la Salamandre, Dewhurst S., 2,000 Guineas), Lassigny (Canadian International S.), Da Hoss (Breeders' Cup Mile, twice), Grand Slam (Futurity S., Champagne S.), Commendable (Belmont S.), Came Home (Hopeful S., Santa Anita Derby, Pacific Classic), Johar (Hollywood Derby, Breeders' Cup Turf).

Dam Windsharp

Won 11 of 29 starts, inc. San Luis Rey S.-Gr1, San Luis Obispo H.-Gr2, Beverly Hills H.-Gr1, Santa Ana H.-Gr2), also 2nd Matriarch S.-Gr1, San Juan Capistrano Inv.-Gr1. Effective 9-12f on turf. Dam of: Johar (1999 c by Gone West; Gr1 winner), Dessert (2000 f by Storm Cat; Gr1 winner), Ancient Art (2001 c by Storm Cat; unraced). In foal to Gone West. Sold $6.1 million 2003 Keeneland November Sale.

Pedigree assessment

Joins Commendable and Lassigny as a top-level 12f winner among Gone West's progeny. The stamina comes from Windsharp, who progressed with age. There is an extensive US programme for turf horses effective around 10f and Johar is an obvious candidate to add to his Gr1 total. *JH*

and Del Mar intimately. Having ridden just one previous Breeders' Cup winner in 40 tries before 2003, he received the inaugural Bill Shoemaker award for his victories on Johar and Pleasantly Perfect, plus his second on Minister Eric in the Juvenile. It was some day for him, too.

Kaieteur (USA)

4yo bay colt   **121**

Marlin (USA) - Strong Embrace (USA) (Regal Embrace (Can))

Owner Mrs Susan McCarthy

Trainer B J Meehan

Breeder Nelson McMakin

Career: **14** starts | won **3** | second **4** | third **2** | £248,479 win and place

---

By John Hopkins

A LARGELY unheralded winner of a Group 1 in Germany as a three-year-old, Kaieteur was much more to the fore in 2003, showing himself an improved performer with two notable efforts in top-class company.

Interviewed in the spring, trainer Brian Meehan was bullish about Kaieteur's prospects, saying he was "much stronger". He also warned that the colt would not be fired up for his return in the Group 1 Prix Ganay at Longchamp in April, and the 30-1 shot did not perform with great promise, one-paced inside the final furlong and a seven-length eighth of nine behind Fair Mix.

It was another month and a half before Kaieteur returned to action (he was reported to have had "a small problem") in the Prince of Wales's Stakes at Royal Ascot. He was sent off an unconsidered 66-1 chance and again performed like a horse flattered by the Group 1 victory to his name; although he stayed on close home, he never threatened in a top-class field and was beaten 11 lengths into sixth behind Nayef.

Understandably, given that he appeared to have been found wanting against the best, Kaieteur started at 100-1 for the Coral-Eclipse at Sandown, which drew a competitive and larger-than-usual field of 15, including Nayef, Islington, Falbrav and Olden Times, all of whom had finished ahead of him at Ascot. On paper, his prospects appeared remote, but he thrived in a fast-run contest, staying on strongly to finish third, beaten two and a quarter lengths by Falbrav and reducing the gap from Ascot on runner-up Nayef to a length and a half.

In many ways, the Eclipse was unsatisfactory, since several runners encountered interference and less than eight lengths separated the first ten. Kaieteur, who enjoyed a clear run, was used to anchor the form; for the record, his Racing Post Rating of 121 was 5lb higher than his previous best. Further confusion stemmed from the fact that Kaieteur

Kaieteur stays in training and could be worth another chance over a mile and a half

produced this career-best on good-to-firm ground; he had previously seemed best suited by some cut and the ground in Munich when he scored his Group 1 success was soft.

However, any thoughts that his Eclipse effort might not be repeated were dispelled on his next start. Immediately after Sandown, Meehan nominated the Arlington Million as a race that would suit Kaieteur down to the ground, and so it proved. Kaieteur started 14-1 in a field including King George runner-up Sulamani, having his first run in the US, high-class German performer Paolini and Storming Home, the Champion Stakes winner by then unbeaten in two US starts. A big run from Kaieteur looked unlikely when he dropped to ninth three out in the ten-furlong event, but he rallied strongly under hard driving to launch a challenge inside the final furlong. In as dramatic a conclusion to a top-level event as you could find, Storming Home, who appeared set to run out a comfortable winner, veered sharply right with around 50 yards to run, causing serious interference to both Paolini and Kaieteur.

Remarkably, Storming Home passed the post in front, with Sulamani, who had been staying on widest of all and was unaffected by the mayhem, finishing second; Paolini and Kaieteur dead-heated for third. Storming Home was subsequently demoted to fourth and Sulamani promoted to

2003 Race record

7th Emirates Airline Champion Stakes (Group 1) (Newmarket, October 18) 3yo+ 10f Good to firm **113** (TS 90) 12 ran. *Held up, headway and hampered over 1f out, never troubled leaders, beaten 7l by Rakti*

3rd Tote Select Stakes (Group 3) (Goodwood, September 13) 3yo+ 10f Good to firm **113** (TS 91) 5 ran. *Chased leaders, led 3f out, ridden 2f out, headed just inside final furlong, stayed on well, beaten ½l by Leporello*

2nd Dead-heat Arlington Million XXI (Grade 1) (Arlington, August 16) 3yo+ 10f Good **120** 13 ran. *Disputed 6th, lost place over 3f out, 9th straight, stayed on well under pressure, disputing 3rd when hampered last strides, dead-heated for 3rd, placed dead-heat 2nd, beaten hd by Sulamani*

3rd Coral-Eclipse Stakes (Group 1) (Sandown, July 5) 3yo+ 10f Good to firm **121** (TS 113) 15 ran. *Raced in midfield, ridden 3f out, progress 2f out, stayed on from over 1f out, nearest finish, beaten 2¼l by Falbrav*

6th Prince of Wales's Stakes (Group 1) (Ascot, June 18) 4yo+ 10f Good to firm **107** (TS 91) 10 ran. *Behind, ridden and stayed on from over 2f out but never near leaders, beaten 11l by Nayef*

8th Prix Ganay (Group 1) (Longchamp, April 27) 4yo+ 10½f Very soft **108** (TS 96) 9 ran. *Raced in 5th, 4th and pushed along towards outside straight, ridden and closed up 2f out, one pace final furlong, beaten 7½l by Fair Mix*

2002

7th Emirates Airline Champion Stakes (Group 1) (Newmarket, October 19) 3yo+ 10f Good **111** (TS 83) 11 ran ● **1st** Grosser Dallmayr-Preis (Bayerisches Zuchtrennen) (Group 1) (Munich, August 4) 3yo+ 10f Soft **116** 8 ran ● **2nd** Prix Eugene Adam (Grand Prix de Maisons-Laffitte) (Group 2) (Maisons-Laffitte, July 14) 3yo 10f Very soft **112** (TS 94) 6 ran ● **4th** King Edward VII Stakes (Group 2) (Ascot, June 21) 3yo 12f Good to firm **108** (TS 82) 7 ran ● **2nd** Heathorns Classic Trial (Group 3) (Sandown, April 26) 3yo 10f Good to soft **106** (TS 76) 4 ran ● **1st** Blue Square Conditions Stakes (Kempton, March 30) 3yo 10f Good **93** (TS 66) 5 ran

Other runs

1st End of Season Median Auction Maiden Stakes (Div II) (Bath, October 25) 2yo 1m Good **83** 15 ran ● **2nd** Markham & District Miners Welfare Society Maiden Stakes (Newbury, September 22) 2yo 7f Good to firm **92** (TS 67) 18 ran

first; Paolini and Kaieteur were now joint-second.

Kaieteur was entered for the Irish Champion Stakes but was ruled out when Meehan decided it was "a bit soon after Arlington", adding that the colt had picked up a slight throat and chest infection. However, he was back in action soon after, when his sights were lowered to the Group 3 Select Stakes at Goodwood. Although he ran creditably against younger rivals, he found the progressive Leporello and Muqbil just too good in a finish of necks. A five-runner field was unlikely to bring out the best in Kaieteur, but Meehan felt his charge "didn't fire like he can" and that the race had indeed come too soon.

Kaieteur performed around 8lb below his Eclipse mark at Goodwood and it was a similar story on his next start, in the Champion Stakes,

Kaieteur   *bay colt, 25-3-1999*

		Nijinsky	**Northern Dancer** / Flaming Page
	Sword Dance		
		Rosa Mundi	Secretariat / Lisadell
Marlin b 1993			
		Damascus	Sword Dancer / Kerala
	Syrian Summer		
		Special Warmth	Lucky Mike / Piece Of Pie
		Vice Regent	**Northern Dancer** / Victoria Regina
	Regal Embrace		
		Close Embrace	Nentego / Hold Me Close
Strong Embrace b 1988			
		Bold LB	Bold Bidder / Pretty Fancy
	Topper B Bold		
		Break Point	Top Lea / Wembley Blue

Bred by Nelson McMakin. Unsold $36,000 Fasig-Tipton Kentucky July yearling

Sire Marlin

Won 9 of 26 races, inc. Secretariat S.-Gr1, Hollywood Derby-Gr1, San Luis Rey S.-Gr2, San Juan Capistrano H.-Gr1, Sunset H.-Gr2, Arlington Million-Gr1. Big, strong, lengthy sort. Turf specialist, most effective between 10-12f. Among the best US grass performers at 4, broke down in last start before intended Breeders' Cup Turf bid. Sire of: Kaieteur (Bayerisches Zuchtrennen-Gr1).

Dam Strong Embrace

Won 11 of 35 races, inc. minor stakes race at Finger Lakes. Placed 3rd in Listed sprint at 5 years. Tough sprinter, useful in her class, who raced exclusively on dirt. Dam of: Red Reef (1995 c by Red Ransom; useful dirt/turf performer, winner, Listed-placed), Happy Light (1996 c by Rahy; unplaced in Japan), Hannah's Baby (1998 c by Golden Gear; placed), Kaieteur (1999 c by Marlin; Gr1 winner), Gotcha Guv (2000 c by Marlin; unraced), Strong Cat (2001 c by Forest Wildcat; unraced to date).

Pedigree assessment

Unfashionably bred Kaieteur completed the season without a win to show for his efforts, but at least two of those efforts earned him plaudits for resolute efforts in top company. Unfortunately, consistency is not Kaieteur's strong suit, and in his races before and after those sterling midsummer displays he ran pounds below his best. A British Group 1 will probably always be beyond him, but he scored at that level in Munich at three and may yet achieve another on his travels. *TM*

although, in his defence, he was stopped more than a furlong out before running on to be beaten seven lengths by Rakti in second.

Kaieteur stays in training and is again likely to contest the top ten-furlong events. He appears to be versatile regarding the ground but ideally needs a true-run race. He seemed to stay a mile and a half when tried at three and may be worth another chance over that distance.

Kalaman (Ire)

3yo bay colt   **126**

Desert Prince (Ire) - Kalamba (Ire) (Green Dancer (USA))
Owner H H Aga Khan
Trainer Sir Michael Stoute
Breeder His Highness The Aga Khan's Studs

Career: **6** starts │ won **2** │ second **2** │ third **0** │ **£93,258** win and place

By Lee Mottershead

LIKE the camera, it's often said the form book never lies. Yet with Kalaman it certainly told a few porkies. Few horses carried taller reputations. A half-brother to Breeders' Cup Turf hero Kalanisi, Kalaman was bred to move a bit and he did, but, as fast as he moved, he could win no more than a Listed race at Kempton.

His tale, however, is not that simple. He is a mystery, an unexplained conundrum, a horse who in midsummer looked a Group 1 winner waiting to happen, only for the winning never to happen, his season tailing off with two performances which fell at least a stone below what he achieved when robbed at Royal Ascot.

At Kempton in May things were going very nicely. A promising fourth in a Leicester maiden the previous autumn, Kalaman had made a successful and highly pleasing seasonal reappearance when winning a Newbury maiden over a mile. Dipping his hooves into altogether classier waters for the first time, he was upped in grade for the Heron Stakes, the Sir Michael Stoute-trained colt sticking at a mile and up against a field which included Ikhtyar, behind Kalaman at Newbury but subsequently a runaway Sandown winner. Pointing his toe and grabbing the ground inside the final furlong, Kalaman powered clear under Christophe Soumillon, winning the race in much the same way Kalanisi had a few years earlier. So far, so good.

That Kalaman should then be pointed at the St James's Palace Stakes was no surprise. The regard in which he was held had already been confirmed by Stoute having earlier earmarked him for the Irish 2,000 Guineas, only rerouting to Kempton when rain hammered The Curragh. As ever, the St James's Palace was littered with names from the spring Classics, the race hosting four of the first seven in the 2,000 Guineas, the first, second and third from the Irish 2,000 Guineas, and the winners of both the French and German 2,000 Guineas. This was a good race,

Kalaman ((Johnny Murtagh) wins at Newbury in April – a promising start to a frustrating campaign

yet a race Kalaman should have won but did not.

Not that Johnny Murtagh did anything wrong. Rather, Lady Luck decided not to bestow her favours on Kalaman. Travelling as strongly as a 5-2 favourite should negotiating the bend into Ascot's short straight, Kalaman was poised and ready to strike, itching to be unleashed. It would not be his day. Just as Darryll Holland went for glory aboard Zafeen, Kalaman found himself with nowhere to go, trapped in a box while the race carried on without him. When he became free, the bird had flown, his splendid late surge taking him into a closing second but no better. It was one that got away.

Yet in defeat there is hope, and in Kalaman's defeat there was a lot about which to be hopeful. Over a mile he was clearly a Group 1 performer, but everything about his Ascot effort suggested that he would be even

2003   Race record

2nd Shadwell Stud Joel Stakes (Group 3) (Newmarket, October 3) 3yo+ 1m Good to firm **110** (TS 67) 4 ran. *Held up, headway over 1f out, ridden inside final furlong, stayed on same pace, beaten 1¼l by Splendid Era*

7th Juddmonte International Stakes (Group 1) (York, August 19) 3yo+ 10½f Good to firm **112** (TS 92) 8 ran. *Soon tracking leaders, effort over 3f out, every chance over 2f out, lost place over 1f out, beaten 9¼l by Falbrav*

2nd St James's Palace Stakes (Group 1) (Ascot, June 17) 3yo 1m Good to firm **126** (TS 106) 11 ran. *Behind, headway to track leaders over 2f out, going well when badly hampered inside final quarter mile, switched left and finished strongly, not recover, beaten 1l by Zafeen*

1st Pacemaker Heron Stakes (Listed) (Kempton, May 24) 3yo 1m Good to firm **117** (TS 60) 7 ran. *Slowly into stride, soon tracking leaders, shaken up and led approaching final furlong, quickened inside final furlong, comfortably, beat Ikhtyar by 1½l*

1st Dubai International Airport Maiden Stakes (Newbury, April 12) 3yo 1m Good to firm **95** (TS 81) 14 ran. *Slowly into stride, behind, steady headway from 3f out to lead inside final 2f, pushed along and readily held strong challenge inside final furlong, beat Act Of Duty by ¾l*

2002

4th EBF Reference Point Maiden Stakes (Div I) (Leicester, October 15) 2yo 7f Good to soft **78** (TS 19) 13 ran

better over further. Not surprisingly, then, he returned after a two-month break in York's extended ten-furlong Juddmonte International, Soumillon back on board, replacing the sidelined Murtagh.

The Kalaman who ran at York was not the Kalaman who appeared at Ascot. Off the bridle over three furlongs out, he was almost immediately a spent force, eventually beating only a pacemaker. It was an unfathomable performance, the Aga Khan's 15-8 favourite beaten far too early for lack of stamina to be offered as an excuse.

His chance for redemption came just over six weeks later in Newmarket's Group 3 Joel Stakes. Back over a mile, Kalaman was held up last of four by Soumillon as Michael Hills dictated an ordinary gallop on Splendid Era. When the leader quickened passing the Bushes, Kalaman was still last, forced to make up ground just as Splendid Era hit top gear. He did close, for a moment seeming likely to reel in the hare, but the effort of bridging the gap had taken its toll, Kalaman flattening out and coming in a length-and-a-quarter second. A great jockey who got even greater in 2003, 'Soumi' had not been seen at his most super.

We saw no more of Kalaman. A Listed success nothing like enough to cement his place at stud, he will be back in 2004, a riddle waiting to be solved. His critics will point to a record in decline and even suggest that the St James's Palace form looks a lot less solid than it did at the time. His supporters, though, may well have the last laugh. A horse with more physical scope than Kalanisi – who matured gloriously with age – and with a trainer who excels with older horses, Kalaman has a point to prove. Don't be surprised if he proves it.

Kalaman
bay colt, 22-5-2000

		Danzig	**Northern Dancer**
			Pas de Nom
	Green Desert		
		Foreign Courier	Sir Ivor
Desert Prince			Courtly Dee
b 1995			
		Bustino	Busted
			Ship Yard
	Flying Fairy		
		Fairy Footsteps	Mill Reef
			Glass Slipper
		Nijinsky	**Northern Dancer**
			Flaming Page
	Green Dancer		
		Green Valley	Val de Loir
Kalamba			Sly Pola
b 1991			
		Riverman	Never Bend
			River Lady
	Kareena		
		Kermiya	Vienna
			Embellie

Bred by the Aga Khan in Ireland

Sire Desert Prince

Won 5 of 11 races, inc. Irish 2,000 Guineas-Gr1, Prix du Moulin-Gr1, Queen Elizabeth II S.-Gr1, also 2nd St James's Palace S.-Gr1, 3rd Poule d'Essai des Poulains-Gr1. By top-class sprinter with very good record as sire of 2yos, sprinters and milers. Half-brother to 2yo Gr3 winner Ontario (by Storm Cat) out of daughter of 1,000 Guineas winner Fairy Footsteps. Stands at Irish National Stud, 2004 fee €35,000. Oldest progeny 3. Sire of: France (Gr3), Foss Way (Gr3), Mail The Desert (Moyglare Stud S.-Gr1).

Dam Kalamba

Placed sole start at 2, placed once from 4 starts at 3. Sister to 10f Listed winner Karaferya out of smart miler. Dam of: Kalanisi (1996 c by Doyoun; Gr1 winner), Kalimanta (1997 f by Lake Coniston; unplaced), Kalambara (1998 f by Bluebird; winner), Kalambari (1999 g by Kahyasi; winner), Kalaman (2000 c by Desert Prince; Listed winner, Gr1-placed), 2002 c by Daylami, 2003 f by Rainbow Quest.

Pedigree assessment

Has fulfilled his pedigree stamina-wise by excelling at a mile. His half-brother Kalanisi improved well with age and the best family members tend to excel after their 2yo season, so Kalaman may well progress further. *JH*

Kris Kin (USA)

3yo chestnut colt **125**

Kris S (USA) - Angel In My Heart (Fr) (Rainbow Quest (USA))
Owner Saeed Suhail
Trainer Sir Michael Stoute
Breeder Flaxman Holdings Ltd

Career: **7** starts | won **3** | second **0** | third **2** | **£991,378** win and place

By Nicholas Godfrey

NYONE can make a mistake. Although Sir Michael Stoute secured his seventh trainers' title in 2003, with hindsight he might reflect that it was perhaps not his finest hour when he deemed Kris Kin unworthy of the £1,100 it would have cost to keep him in the Vodafone Derby at the end of his two-year-old campaign.

On the other hand, Stoute will no doubt consider that it was one of the most satisfying pieces of humble pie he has ever asked himself to eat when he persuaded the colt's owner, Saeed Suhail, to re-enter the son of Kris S for Britain's premier Classic at the final supplementary stage. Although it cost the owner £90,000 – rather more than it would have done if Kris Kin had never left the race – the first prize he duly earned under Kieren Fallon in June was worth £852,600. He was the first supplementary entry to win the Derby.

Stoute, who described Kris Kin as "one of the laziest horses" he had trained, was by no means alone in being misled by a horse more indolent in his work than Homer Simpson, the very antithesis of a 'morning glory'. Appearances had been deceptive from an early age, it seems. As a yearling, he was not retained by his breeders, the Niarchos family, who sold him at the Keeneland September Sales in 2001, where he was knocked down for $275,000 to bloodstock agent Charlie Gordon-Watson on behalf of Suhail.

Fallon, too, rightly lauded after the Derby for a masterly ride, was fooled by Kris Kin prior to his seasonal debut in 2003. Having partnered him in a typically sluggish piece of work ahead of Chester's Dee Stakes, the champion rejected him in favour of odds-on favourite Big Bad Bob. Punters, clearly, had not expected too much either: Kris Kin was the 20-1 outsider of four in the Group 3 event.

Such an inflated starting price was unusual for a Freemason Lodge contender in such a small field, particularly one who had shown a

Kris Kin (Kieren Fallon) powers past The Great Gatsby to land the Derby – a first for a supplementary entry

degree of promise as a juvenile, when he landed a soft-ground back-end maiden over seven furlongs at Doncaster, picking up well from off the pace.

Indeed, it was touch and go whether Kris Kin would participate in the Dee Stakes at all on account of the fast ground – he was jarred up as a two-year-old – and he was left in only when the contest looked like cutting up to a match at the overnight stage. It proved a fortunate decision. With Fergal Lynch deputising for Fallon, Kris Kin was held up in a race not run at a breakneck gallop before producing a telling turn of foot to lead inside the final furlong, beating Big Bad Bob a couple of lengths, with subsequent Derby Italiano runner-up Private Charter a further three lengths back.

All in all, a decent effort from an inexperienced colt whose apparent greenness was betrayed when he jinked after the line, dislodging his rider. But while the result suggested he was very much on the upgrade, it was not immediately hailed as a possible prelude to Derby success.

Oath won the Dee Stakes before his Derby success; few considered Kris Kin likely to repeat the dose. "The King Edward VII Stakes at Royal Ascot looks an obvious target," suggested the Racing Post analysis.

Stoute, who deserves enormous credit for taking the plunge in the end, confirmed Kris Kin's Epsom participation – with Fallon on board

2003   Race record

11th Prix de l'Arc de Triomphe Lucien Barriere (Group 1) (Longchamp, October 5) 3yo+ 12f Holding **65** (TS 28) 13 ran. *Mid-division, ridden and 8th on inside when hampered over 3f out, not recover, 12th straight, eased, beaten 45l by Dalakhani*

3rd Prix Niel Casino Barriere d'Enghien (Group 2) (Longchamp, September 14) 3yo 12f Good to soft **118** (TS 83) 7 ran. *Raced in 3rd on rail, 4th and pushed along straight, ran on until no extra inside final furlong, beaten 4l by Dalakhani*

3rd King George VI And Queen Elizabeth Diamond Stakes (Group 1) (Ascot, July 26) 3yo+ 12f Good **125** (TS 87) 12 ran. *Towards rear, pushed along 5f out, driven and struggling 3f out, stayed on from 2f out to take 3rd inside final furlong, nearest finish, beaten 5½l by Alamshar*

1st Vodafone Derby (Group 1) (Epsom, June 7) 3yo 12f Good **123** (TS 105) 20 ran. *Pushed along to hold place in midfield after 4f, 8th straight, progress over 2f out, switched right over 1f out, driven and ran on to lead final 100yds, beat The Great Gatsby by 1l*

1st Philip Leverhulme Dee Stakes (Group 3) (Chester, May 8) 3yo 10½f Good to firm **119** (TS 86) 4 ran. *Hampered slightly start, held up in last place, headway over 1f out, soon switched right when not clear run, quickened to lead inside final furlong, ran on well, unseated rider after line, beat Big Bad Bob by 2l*

2002

1st Weatherbys Bank EBF October Maiden Stakes (Div I) (Doncaster, October 25) 2yo 7f Good to soft **82** (TS 42) 12 ran ● **15th** Unfuwain EBF Maiden Stakes (Newmarket, October 3) 2yo 7f Good to firm **58** (TS 13) 26 ran

for the first time in public – just days before the race. The 224th Vodafone Derby, run on good ground, featured a maximum field of 20, with the majority of pre-raceday attention focusing on three Irish-trained horses who vied for ante-post favouritism. They were headed by Dermot Weld's 2,000 Guineas winner Refuse To Bend, eventually sent off 11-4 favourite, Derrinstown Stud Derby Trial winner Alamshar, out to emulate 2000 winner Sinndar for John Oxx, and winter favourite Brian Boru. The last-named was looking to complete a historic hat-trick for his trainer Aidan O'Brien after Galileo and High Chaparral. Although his credentials had taken a knock when he was only third to Alamshar in his prep run, Brian Boru was still a 9-2 chance, only half a point longer than his Leopardstown conqueror.

Kris Kin, having only his fourth race and the second of his three-year-old career, was something of an unknown quantity. Yet on the day he was the only horse apart from the Irish trio quoted in single-figure odds after a massive off-course gamble saw him backed to 6-1 from a morning price of 14-1 as what became known as the 'Fallon factor' took hold.

Such public faith in the champion jockey mirrored that which used to be accorded Lester Piggott when the Derby came around. It is hardly surprising: the dominant rider of his era, Fallon was riding at the peak of his powers in 2003, when he landed his sixth jockeys' championship in seven years with his best-ever total – and this after a spell in a drying-out clinic over the winter had raised question marks over his future.

Fallon produced a peach on Kris Kin to land a hammer blow against the bookmakers. With Brian Boru's stablemate The Great Gatsby making the running, Kris Kin had come down Tattenham Corner in midfield on the rail, just off Refuse To Bend and Brian Boru. The Great Gatsby was given the most astute of rides by Pat Eddery in his final Derby, dictating the pace before being sent on three out.

The move did for his better-fancied stablemate Brian Boru, who fell away early in the straight, while Refuse To Bend, a non-stayer, was also toiling. Kris Kin edged between the pair, taking fourth with two furlongs to run before being pulled outside for a run. Although The Great Gatsby managed to keep everything else at bay, he could not repel Kris Kin's late bid for glory.

The horse who had crept into the Derby consciousness at a late stage got up in the last 100 yards to score by a decisive length from The Great Gatsby, who held off Alamshar, ridden to get the trip but never travelling particularly well, and the late-comer Norse Dancer.

According to Stoute, who was winning his third Derby to add to the victories of Shergar and Shahrastani, much of the credit was down to Fallon, whom he said had produced "one of the greatest rides you will ever see at Epsom". The bookmakers, stung, also pinpointed the rider. Ladbrokes' spokesman Mike Dillon said: "Fallon is God in the betting shops because he gives everything a ride, and this was a betting shop gamble. Fallon is their man."

However, if the layers had cause to remember the 2003 Derby for a long time, the handicappers were not overly impressed. On what he achieved at Epsom, Kris Kin could not be rated among the better recent Derby winners. Despite the ground not having ridden particularly fast, Kris Kin's winning time was barely a second outside Lammtarra's track record. However, a Racing Post Rating of 123 for the performance rated him no more than an average winner compared to the likes of High Chaparral (130), Galileo (127) and Sinndar (127), while BHB handicapper Nigel Gray, who raised Kris Kin's rating by 14lb to 122, put him 4lb lower than High Chaparral and Galileo and 3lb inferior to Sinndar.

Kris Kin was also generally considered inferior to Dalakhani, the French colt who had won the Prix du Jockey-Club in hugely impressive fashion the Sunday before the Epsom Classic. Irish bookmakers Paddy Power, for example, made Dalakhani 1-2 favourite in a head-to-head book with Kris Kin in the Budweiser Irish Derby.

In the event, the prices proved theoretical, since Kris Kin missed the Irish Classic owing to the prevailing fast ground. In Ireland, Dalakhani was beaten by Epsom third Alamshar, who went on to uphold the reputation of the Classic generation with a convincing victory on his next outing in the King George VI and Queen Elizabeth Diamond Stakes. Among those in his wake was Kris Kin, the Epsom tables having been comprehensively turned. Alamshar won by three and a half lengths from

Sulamani, himself two lengths clear of Kris Kin, who once again was doing all his best work at the end. He was never really able to get into the race, having been drawn wide and obliged to race deep. Nevertheless, he appeared to be struggling from a long way out before staying on into third from an unpromising position.

Third place in a classy field was still a fair effort – indeed, it rated marginally higher than Epsom – albeit one that seemed to confirm his low-to-middle ranking among recent Derby winners. In days gone by, the St Leger would have been a natural target for such a strong stayer, but the modern era's disaffection for the final Classic is such that it was never on the cards for Kris Kin, whose connections immediately started thinking in terms of the Arc after the King George.

It mattered little. Kris Kin was never again seen to advantage as his career ended in anticlimax. Although there seemed grounds to expect improvement after a respectable third place behind Dalakhani in the Prix Niel in September, his Arc performance was abject.

While connections had been keen to avoid fast ground with him, Kris Kin was always struggling in the holding conditions at Longchamp. As usual, he had been unable to lie up close enough to a decent pace and needed to be pushed even to get as close as mid-division before being chopped off on entering the straight – Fallon said he was "wiped out" by Frankie Dettori on Doyen. As Dalakhani was busy confirming his superstar status, Kris Kin was allowed to coast home before passing the post 11th of 13, 20 lengths adrift of the main body of the field. Only the two pacemakers finished behind him.

Although he would have been closer without the interference, Kris Kin would have done well to make the first five. It was a dismal showing and connections announced three days later that he was to be retired to Hamdan Al Maktoum's Derrinstown Stud at a fee of €8,000 (October 1 terms). To judge from the fee, it seems that, even in retirement from the track, Kris Kin will not be held in the greatest esteem.

Kris Kin left for stallion duties with a record of three wins from only seven career starts that featured a real mixed bag of performances. "We'll never know how good he was because he was so laid-back," said Fallon. "It's a shame we didn't see the best of him after the Derby – I thought the best was yet to come."

Kris Kin needed a strong gallop to bring his stamina into play, which meant the way the Derby was run played to his strengths. It would be impossible to rate him more highly than an ordinary winner of the Classic, and among recent victors he will be remembered alongside the likes of Benny The Dip and High-Rise rather than Sinndar and High Chaparral.

Then again, given that events conspired against him after his Epsom victory to preclude his enhancing his reputation, it is plausible that we have underestimated Kris Kin's abilities. After all, we would not be the first.

Kris Kin

chestnut colt, 5-3-2000

Kris S b 1977	Roberto	Hail To Reason	Turn-to Nothirdchance
		Bramalea	Nashua Rarelea
	Sharp Queen	Princequillo	Prince Rose Cosquilla
		Bridgework	Occupy Feale Bridge
Angel In My Heart ch 1992	Rainbow Quest	Blushing Groom	Red God Runaway Bride
		I Will Follow	Herbager Where You Lead
	Sweetly	Lyphard	Northern Dancer Goofed
		Sweet And Lovely	Tanerko Lilya

Bred by Flaxman Holdings Ltd in Kentucky. $275,000 Keeneland September yearling

Sire Kris S (USA)

Won 3 of 5 races, including a 9f restricted stakes in California at 3. A big, strong horse, not very sound. Died in 2002. Sire of: Evening Kris (Jerome H.-Gr1), Prized (Breeders' Cup Turf-Gr1, San Luis Rey S.-Gr1), Stocks Up (Hollywood Starlet S.-Gr1), Cheval Volant (Hollywood Starlet S.-Gr1, Las Virgenes S.-Gr1), Lyin To The Moon (Gr2), Hollywood Wildcat (Hollywood Oaks-Gr1, Breeders' Cup Distaff-Gr1, Gamely H.-Gr1), Kissin Kris (Haskell Invitational H.-Gr1), Brocco (Breeders' Cup Juvenile-Gr1, Santa Anita Derby-Gr1), You And I (Metropolitan H.-Gr1), Class Kris (Gr2), Arch (Super Derby-Gr1), Diamond On The Run (Gr2), Dr Fong (St James's Palace S.-Gr1), Midnight Line (Gr2), Soaring Softly (Flower Bowl Invitational H.-Gr1, Breeders' Cup Filly & Mare Turf-Gr1), Adonis (Gr2), Apple Of Kent (Gr2), Krisada (Gr2), Peshtigo (Gr3), Kudos (Oaklawn H.-Gr1), Kumari Continent (Gr2), Julie Jalouse (Gr2), Whitmore's Conn (Sword Dancer Invitational H.-Gr1), Kicken Kris (Secretariat S.-Gr1), Kris Kin (Derby S.-Gr1), Action This Day (Breeders' Cup Juvenile-Gr1), Lucky Story (Gr2).

Dam Angel In My Heart (Fr)

Won 3 of 15 races, notably Prix Psyche (Gr3) at 3 years, also placed in top filly races in France and US. High-class, consistent performer, effective on any ground, probably best at around 10f. Dam of: Venturer (1998 c by Gone West; winner), Mimalia (1999 f by Silver Hawk; placed), Kris Kin (2000 c by Kris S; Classic winner), Seyalateralligator (2001 c by Cherokee Run; $250,000 Keeneland yearling, unraced to date).

Pedigree assessment

Seemed a revelation on Derby Day, but did not progress, and autumn performances proved very disappointing. Given his sire's success with older horses in the States, perhaps he might have been granted the chance to redeem himself at four, but presumably his well-documented idleness at home allowed no confidence in a form recovery. Retired to Derrinstown Stud at a fee of €8,000, a remarkably low price for a Derby winner in his first season. His pedigree is not particularly fashionable, but it is different, with Northern Dancer in the further reaches, and his sire's other European Gr1 winner, Dr Fong, has started promisingly in England. Breeders will surely be tempted to take a punt at the price and give him the chance to make a name for himself at stud. *TM*

L'Ancresse (Ire)

3yo bay filly   **121**

Darshaan - Solo de Lune (Ire) (Law Society (USA))
Owner Michael Tabor
Trainer A P O'Brien
Breeder Britton House Stud Ltd

Career: **11** starts | won **2** | second **3** | third **0** | **£240,464** win and place

By Tony Smurthwaite

SHE was a pacemaker, she was thrust into four consecutive Classics, tried at the St Leger trip, then retired – such was the unlikely backdrop to a wonderful farewell from L'Ancresse when giving Islington a run right to the wire in the Filly & Mare Turf on Breeders' Cup day. It was clearly not at all meant to be, but for a late change of heart.

Her trainer Aidan O'Brien had signed off Michael Tabor's "tough and hardy" filly for a career in the Coolmore broodmare band after she had managed a win – her first for the trainer – in a moderate Listed contest in mid-October. There were but 13 days between that effort and a certain raceday at Santa Anita, so L'Ancresse must have whinnied something especially sweet in the ear of her trainer to have not only convinced him that she was ready for more, but on the other side of the northern hemisphere, on a track described as being like the inside of a barrel, and in temperatures stifling even by west coast standards.

It was true to the story of her season that she was regarded as secondary to her more feted stablemate, Yesterday, at Santa Anita. What was not in the script was that she would give Islington such a battle that there was only a neck in it at the line. Some said if Kieren Fallon had been on L'Ancresse and Edgar Prado on Islington rather than vice versa the order would have been reversed. Whatever, this was ten furlongs that altered perceptions of the runner-up, if not the already renowned winner.

O'Brien had treated L'Ancresse to an unforgiving programme – five Group 1s in a row after showing potential when second to Dimitrova in the Leopardstown 1,000 Guineas Trial in mid-April. This was L'Ancresse's debut for O'Brien after a transfer from Roger Charlton, for whom she finished fifth in the Rockfel Stakes shortly after Tabor bought her from her British breeder, Dick Fowlston.

The new owner might have questioned the wisdom of the deal when L'Ancresse took a shot at the 1,000 Guineas in Newmarket three weeks

L'Ancresse (Mick Kinane) scores a Listed success at The Curragh in October. It was her only win of the campaign

after Leopardstown. At 50-1, her finishing position of 15th behind Russian Rhythm on fast ground suggested here was a filly way out of her league. Accordingly, a water-carrier's role was settled upon when L'Ancresse set the pace for Yesterday in the Irish 1,000 Guineas at The Curragh. This time the going was soft and it may well have aided her bid. That she only succumbed in the final two furlongs and stayed on for fourth as her stablemate landed the win hinted at reserves of stamina.

So it was that within two weeks she was turned out again at Epsom for the Oaks, over half a mile further than she had run previously. The experiment was to prove worthless. L'Ancresse was hampered early in the race, became detached and was pulled up by Kevin Darley as Casual Look and Yesterday fought out the finish.

With no lasting damage done, O'Brien prepared L'Ancresse for the Irish Oaks. Again she was used to set up the pace for Yesterday, a warm favourite to turn the tables on Casual Look. Bursting out in front, L'Ancresse appeared to find a system with which she was content. Bowling along on good ground, she had daylight between her rivals when she met the

2003   Race record

2nd Breeders' Cup Filly & Mare Turf (Grade 1) (Santa Anita, October 25) 3yo+ 10f Firm **121**
12 ran. *Chased clear leader, steady headway to close up from halfway, driven to lead approaching
straight, ran on until headed and no extra 100yds out, beaten nk by Islington*

1st Rathbarry Stud's Barathea Finale Stakes (Listed) (Curragh, October 12) 3yo+ 12f Good to
yielding **114** (TS 92) 11 ran. *Made all and clear for much, reduced advantage and strongly
pressed from under 2f out, stayed on well under pressure inside final furlong, beat Scott's View
by 2½l*

4th ACMC Park Hill Stakes (Group 3) (Doncaster, September 10) 3yo+ 1m6½f Good **100** (TS
72) 8 ran. *Mid-division, effort over 3f out, kept on final furlong, beaten 9l by Discreet Brief*

5th Aston Upthorpe Yorkshire Oaks (Group 1) (York, August 20) 3yo+ 12f Good to firm **108**
(TS 88) 8 ran. *Led after 2f until 3f out, outpaced final 2f, beaten 6¼l by Islington*

2nd Darley Irish Oaks (Group 1) (Curragh, July 13) 3yo 12f Good **113** (TS 96) 11 ran. *Led and
clear throughout, still clear and ridden early straight, reduced advantage from under 2f out,
headed well inside final furlong, no extra close home, beaten 1½l by Vintage Tipple*

Pulled Up Vodafone Oaks (Group 1) (Epsom, June 6) 3yo 12f Good 15 ran. *In touch until
hampered after 3f, soon last and detached, tailed off and virtually pulled up in straight,
dismounted near finish, behind Casual Look*

4th Entenmann's Irish 1,000 Guineas (Group 1) (Curragh, May 25) 3yo 1m Soft **108** (TS 86) 8
ran. *Led, ridden over 2½f out, headed 2f out, 4th and no extra inside final furlong, beaten 3¼l by
Yesterday*

15th Sagitta 1,000 Guineas (Group 1) (Newmarket, May 4) 3yo 1m Good to firm **70** (TS 39)
19 ran. *Prominent, bumped over 2f out, soon weakened, beaten 21l by Russian Rhythm*

2nd Leopardstown 1,000 Guineas Trial Stakes (Listed) (Leopardstown, April 13) 3yo 7f Good
to firm **108** (TS 71) 10 ran. *Settled 4th, 3rd straight, 2nd 1f out, ran on strongly under pressure
close home, just failed, beaten hd by Dimitrova*

2002

5th Owen Brown Rockfel Stakes (Group 2) (Newmarket, October 19) 2yo 7f Good **96** (TS 52)
11 ran ● **1st** Dubai Duty Free Millennium Millionaire EBF Fillies' Conditions Stakes (Newbury,
September 20) 2yo 7f Good to firm **86** (TS 42) 7 ran

straight. Only a well-timed run from Frankie Dettori on 12-1 shot Vintage
Tipple did for L'Ancresse.

The effort delighted O'Brien. Six weeks later he promoted L'Ancresse
to lead role as his only runner in the Yorkshire Oaks. Back on fast ground,
L'Ancresse again raced off in front but this time was a spent force after
a mile and faded, one-paced, into fifth behind Islington. There was more
reason to be pessimistic after her next run, when only fourth in the Park
Hill Stakes, the fillies' St Leger. Held up, she failed to excel in what looked
an ordinary renewal. It was back to the front-running tactics a month
later and victory over 12 furlongs in the Listed Finale Stakes, with the
tough Scott's View in second.

That looked to be it. L'Ancresse had finished second in a Classic widely
regarded as below average, had been dropped appreciably in grade in
order to open her seasonal account in late autumn, and was ready to
slink off into likely ignominy.

Then came California.

L'Ancresse

bay filly, 13-1-2000

			Mill Reef	Never Bend
		Shirley Heights		Milan Mill
	Darshaan		Hardiemma	Hardicanute
	b 1981			Grand Cross
			Abdos	Arbar
		Delsy		Pretty Lady
			Kelty	Venture
				Marilla
			Alleged	Hoist The Flag
		Law Society		Princess Pout
	Solo de Lune		Bold Bikini	Boldnesian
	b 1990			Ran-tan
			Caerleon	Nijinsky
		Truly Special		Foreseer
			Arctique Royale	Royal And Regal
				Arctic Melody

Bred by Britton House Stud in Ireland

Sire **Darshaan**

Won 5 of 8 races, inc. Criterium de Saint-Cloud-Gr2, Prix Greffulhe-Gr2, Prix Hocquart-Gr2, Prix du Jockey Club-Gr1. Strong, workmanlike type. The best 12f 3yo in a very good crop, but disappointing after midsummer. Died May 2001. Sire of: Arzanni (Gr2), Game Plan (Gr2), Hellenic (Yorkshire Oaks-Gr1), Kotashaan (San Luis Rey S.-Gr1, San Juan Capistrano Invitational H.-Gr1, Eddie Read H.-Gr1, Oak Tree Invitational H.-Gr1, Breeders' Cup Turf S.-Gr1), Grand Plaisir (Gr2), Darnay (Gr2), Truly A Dream (Gr2), Key Change (Yorkshire Oaks-Gr1), Mark Of Esteem (2,000 Guineas-Gr1, Queen Elizabeth II S.-Gr1), Make No Mistake (Gr2), Mutamam (Gr2), Sayarshan (Gr2), Cerulean Sky (Prix Saint-Alary-Gr1), Josr Algarhoud (Gr2), Dilshaan (Racing Post Trophy-Gr1), Olden Times (Prix Jean Prat-Gr1), Sayedah (Gr2), Dalakhani (Criterium International-Gr1, Prix Lupin-Gr1, Prix du Jockey-Club-Gr1, Prix de l'Arc de Triomphe-Gr1), Mezzo Soprano (Prix Vermeille-Gr1), Necklace (Moyglare Stud S.-Gr1). Also got Aliysa, finished first in Oaks, disqualified.

Dam **Solo de Lune**

Won once over 11f at 3 in France, also 2nd German Listed event. Half-sister to 10f Gr2 winner Truly A Dream (by Darshaan; dam of Catcher In The Rye) and 15f Gr2 winner Wareed (by Sadler's Wells) out of an 11f Gr3 winner. Dam of: Diner de Lune (1995 f by Be My Guest; Listed winner), Cerulean Sky (1996 f by Darshaan; Gr1 winner), Bright Halo (1997 f by Bigstone; winner), Qaatef (1998 c by Darshaan; winner, Gr3-placed), Ho Hi The Moon (1999 f by Be My Guest; winner), L'Ancresse (2000 f by Darshaan; Listed winner, Gr1-placed), Bywayofthestars (2001 f by Danehill; unraced), 2002 f by Dubai Millennium.

Pedigree assessment

L'Ancresse, who has a watertight 12f pedigree, is a high-class daughter of a superb broodmare sire. Moreover, she is very closely related to a couple of high-class fillies now at stud and the family is packed with good broodmares. L'Ancresse is certain to be given every chance to further enhance the family record. *JH*

Leadership

4yo bay colt   126

Selkirk (USA) - Louella (USA) (El Gran Senor (USA))

Owner Godolphin

Trainer Saeed Bin Suroor

Breeder Mrs A Rothschild and London Thoroughbred Services

Career: **12** starts	won **5**	second **2**	third **2**	£237,811 win and place

By Mark Blackman

WHAT was one to make of Godolphin's purchase in late 2002 of two of owner Khalid Abdullah's most promising horses, Lateen Sails and Leadership? Neither operation can be accused of smoking behind the bike sheds during 'racing acumen' classes, so who would be proved shrewdest in 2003? And what of the quote from Henry Cecil, who, in Lateen Sails, had seen a potential Classic winner whisked away? "Although ownership is not a commercial venture for Mr Abdullah, every horse has its price and is therefore for sale," he said. "You have to be realistic."

While the sums involved remained undisclosed, the initial assessment has to be a points victory for Godolphin. Lateen Sails won a Listed race in Britain and a Group 3 in France, and looks a potential star of 2004, while Leadership made the transition from smart handicapper to Group 1 winner with a battling success in Italy.

Leadership's final start for former trainer Sir Michael Stoute had come in the Group 3 September Stakes at Kempton, where he was swamped close home by Asian Heights in a race run at a more moderate pace than ideal. He had previously been placed in the King George V Handicap at Royal Ascot and the John Smith's Cup at York, and had won a competitive handicap back on the Knavesmire.

Following his transfer to Godolphin, he was immediately flown out to Dubai, where he evidently enjoyed his long break in the sun. He did not race there and following his return to Britain it was not until the first day of June that he was deemed ready for a return to racecourse action.

That return came in the Listed Berkshire Stakes over an extended 11 furlongs at Windsor, for which he was sent off the 8-11 favourite in a field of five. Tracking the pace-setting Putra Sandhurst, Leadership travelled smoothly throughout the race before improving his position to lead with

**Leadership (Richard Hills) lands the Group 1 Gran Premio
di Milano at San Siro in June**

around three furlongs to run. Driven along at the head of affairs with
a quarter of a mile to go, he responded gamely and by the furlong pole
had asserted his authority on the contest. At the line, he had a length
and three-quarters to spare over Potemkin. What had looked a tight affair
on official BHB figures had been won by a progressive performer with
more to offer – trainer Saeed Bin Suroor insisted afterwards that Leadership
had "needed the race".

Connections were certain he needed fast ground to show his best form
and, with that in mind, they found him an attractive opening for his
return to Pattern company – the Group 1 Gran Premio di Milano, run
over a mile and a half on firm ground at San Siro. Fellow British raider
Warrsan, winner of the Coronation Cup at Epsom on his previous start,
was the 1-5 favourite, and Leadership was sent off a 4-1 chance, with
two home-trained hopes and two German raiders all going off at 8-1
and more in a field of six.

The British duo dominated from start to finish. Warrsan held the lead
for barely a furlong before Leadership headed him and settled into a

2003   Race record

12th King George VI And Queen Elizabeth Diamond Stakes (Group 1) (Ascot, July 26) 3yo+ 12f Good **82** (TS 42) 12 ran.
Tracked leaders, ridden 3f out, beaten over 2f out, weakened very rapidly over 1f out, beaten 34l by Alamshar

1st Gran Premio di Milano (Group 1) (San Siro, June 22) 3yo+ 12f Firm **126** 6 ran.
Led after 1f, quickened 3f out, 1½l clear 2f out, ridden approaching final furlong, ran on well to line, beat Warrsan by 1¾l

1st Gala Casinos Berkshire Stakes (Listed) (Windsor, June 1) 4yo+ 11½f Good to firm **115** (TS 83) 5 ran.
Tracked leaders, went 2nd over 6f out, led inside final 3f, driven 2f out, stayed on to go clear final furlong, readily, beat Potemkin by 1¾l

2002

2nd Milcars September Stakes (Group 3) (Kempton, September 7) 3yo+ 12f Good to firm **114** (TS 55) 6 ran ● **1st** Motability Supported By Royal SunAlliance Rated Stakes (0-105 handicap) (York, August 21) 3yo+ 10½f Good **112** (TS 97) 9 ran ● **3rd** 43rd John Smith's Cup (0-110 handicap) (York, July 13) 3yo+ 10½f Good **109** (TS 88) 20 ran ● **3rd** King George V Stakes (0-105 handicap) (Ascot, June 20) 3yo 12f Good to firm **110** (TS 96) 19 ran ● **1st** Golborne Rated Stakes (0-95 handicap) (Haydock, May 24) 3yo 10½f Good to soft **98** (TS 66) 10 ran ● **5th** kempton.co.uk Handicap (0-85) (Kempton, May 6) 3yo 9f Good **87** (TS 60) 19 ran

steady pace. With three furlongs to run, Richard Hills quickened the tempo, poaching a lead of a couple of lengths that his compatriot never looked like getting back. Leadership ran on strongly all the way to the line to gain his first Group success. Warrsan, who was reportedly affected by an allergic reaction to mosquitos at the start, finished nine lengths clear of the smart Italian colt Maktub in third.

Connections reiterated their belief that Leadership was at home on the very fast ground and nominated the King George VI and Queen Elizabeth Diamond Stakes at Ascot in July as his next aim. Despite his being the least renowned of Godolphin's three runners behind Sulamani and Grandera, the Dubai operation made it clear that he was there on merit, and that a good run was expected.

However, the elements conspired to deny him the chance to show what he could do against the best in Europe, for it rained on the day of the race, the ground became loose and Leadership trailed in an abject last of 12. Warrsan, equally at home on fast and easy ground, finished sixth.

Leadership failed to make the track again, but Godolphin's racing manager, Simon Crisford, denied that there was anything physically wrong with him after Ascot and confirmed that he remains in training, with high hopes held for him in 2004. A Racing Post Rating of 126 for his San Siro effort represents a high-class performance and he remains a most interesting prospect for further Group 1 success over a mile and a half when the ground rides genuinely fast.

Leadership   *bay colt, 24-2-1999*

Selkirk ch 1988	Sharpen Up	Atan	Native Dancer / Mixed Marriage
		Rocchetta	Rockefella / Chambiges
	Annie Edge	Nebbiolo	Yellow God / Novara
		Friendly Court	Be Friendly / No Court
Louella b 1994	El Gran Senor	Northern Dancer	Nearctic / Natalma
		Sex Appeal	Buckpasser / Best In Show
	Celtic Loot	Irish River	Riverman / Irish Star
		Witwatersrand	Mr Prospector / Sleek Belle

Bred by Mrs A Rothschild and London Thoroughbred Services in Britain.
Tattersalls December foal, Ir£350,000 Goffs Orby yearling

Sire Selkirk

Won 6 of 15 races, inc. Queen Elizabeth II S.-Gr1, Lockinge S.-Gr2, Goodwood Mile-Gr2, Challenge S.-Gr2. Big, powerful, long-striding individual, effective on any ground, very game, best at a mile, with excellent turn of foot. Sire of: Hidden Meadow (Gr3), Kirkwall (Gr2), Orford Ness (Gr3), Squeak (Beverly Hills H.-Gr1, Matriarch H.-Gr1), Border Arrow (Gr3), Country Garden (Gr2), Field Of Hope (Prix de la Foret-Gr1), Trans Island (Gr2), Sign Of Hope (Gr2), Valley Chapel (Gr3), Wince (1,000 Guineas-Gr1), Harbour Island (Gr3), Altieri (Gr2), Independence (Gr2), Highdown (Gr2), Leadership (Gran Premio di Milano-Gr1), Sulk (Prix Marcel Boussac-Gr1), Welsh Diva (Gr3), Favourable Terms (Gr2), Red Bloom (Fillies' Mile-Gr1).

Dam Louella

Placed at 3 in France. Sister to fair winners Don Bosio (7f) and Himself (10f). Dam of: Leadership (1999 c by Selkirk; Gr1 winner), Rita Skeater (2000 f by Hector Protector; non-winner), 2001 c by Groom Dancer.

Pedigree assessment

Gained his Group 1 win over 12f, having previously proved effective over 10f. His pedigree is more in keeping with a 10f performer, for Louella, though from the American family of Yorkshire Cup winner Churlish Charm and Irish Derby winner Sir Harry Lewis (both by strong stamina influences), is not that stoutly bred. Has progressed well with age, in common with many offspring of the miler Selkirk. *JH*

Leporello (Ire)

3yo bay colt   **119**

Danehill (USA) - Why So Silent (Mill Reef (USA))
Owner Mrs P W Harris
Trainer P W Harris
Breeder Pendley Farm

Career: **7** starts | won **6** | second **0** | third **1** | **£139,271** win and place

By Graham Dench

T WAS a shame that a minor injury robbed Leporello of the chance to prove himself at Group 1 level in Newmarket's Champion Stakes. Few horses had progressed as quickly through the summer and he had fully earned his place in the line-up by beating Muqbil and Kaieteur in Goodwood's Tote Select Stakes – a Group 3 race won in the late 1980s by both Dancing Brave and Mtoto as well as the subsequent Champion Stakes winner Legal Case, and more recently by Singspiel, Nayef and Moon Ballad. However, he suffered a bruising time in a rough race and the experience, as trainer Peter Harris feared at the time, had left its mark.

Leporello had travelled well and had yet to be asked for his effort when he was turned sideways and lost his back legs two furlongs from home as Muqbil, who was looking for a way out, pushed Priors Lodge on to him. Although he had the class to recover and get home in a finish of necks – providing jockey Ian Mongan with a first Group win in the process – it did not come as the greatest of surprises when, three weeks ahead of the Champion, Harris announced that the colt was finished for the season.

Leporello had evidently missed ten days' work after returning home from Goodwood very stiff, and since he had been kept pretty busy throughout the summer it was decided to call it a day and save him for a four-year-old campaign.

At the time of his last appearance Leporello was still hugely progressive and he would surely have acquitted himself well at Newmarket, especially as so many of the big names were below form on the day. The Select Stakes had been his sixth win from seven starts in a career that had begun unheralded barely four months earlier on a bread-and-butter card at Lingfield, and there was every indication that we had yet to see he best of him.

Leporello runs on strongly at Haydock in August to record the fourth of his six victories

He also to overcame problems in running when winning the Stan James Now Online Winter Hill Stakes at Windsor, also Group 3, three weeks before Goodwood, and had really impressed there in what developed into a tactical affair. He had nowhere to go approaching the furlong marker and still had a good couple of lengths to make up on Bourgainville when an opening presented itself. But Richard Quinn, who had ridden Leporello in all but one of his previous races, was well aware of what the colt was capable of and he quickened impressively to score by a neck, without recourse to the whip.

Although Leporello had won the Lingfield maiden in which he had made

2003   Race record

1st Tote Select Stakes (Group 3) (Goodwood, September 13) 3yo+ 10f Good to firm **117** (TS 87) 5 ran. *Took keen hold 3f, tracked leaders, headway on outside when bumped and lost action 2f out, driven to lead just inside final furlong, held on well, beat Muqbil by nk*

1st Stan James Now Online Winter Hill Stakes (Group 3) (Windsor, August 23) 3yo+ 10f Good to firm **119** (TS 86) 6 ran. *Held up in rear and took keen hold, headway 3f out, not clear run 2f out, quickened between horses over 1f out, strong run under hand driving, led last strides, beat Bourgainville by nk*

1st Tote Exacta Stakes (0-105 handicap) (Haydock, August 9) 3yo+ 10½f Good to firm **113** (TS 84) 13 ran. *Held up in midfield, headway 3f out, not clear run over 2f out, ran on strongly to lead well inside final furlong, beat Silence Is Golden by 1l*

1st Bonusprint Stakes (0-105 handicap) (Newmarket (July), July 9) 3yo 10f Good to firm **98** (TS 76) 15 ran. *Held up in touch, not clear run over 1f out, ridden to lead inside final furlong, hung left, ran on, beat Tiber by shd*

3rd EBF Classified Stakes (Newmarket (July), June 20) 3yo (0-90) 1m Good to firm **94** (TS 24) 3 ran. *Tracked leader, ridden and every chance over 1f out, unable to quicken inside final furlong, beaten 1¾l by Lago D'Orta*

1st IG Index Classified Stakes (Sandown, June 5) 3yo (0-80) 1m Good to firm **87** (TS 75) 9 ran. *Held up towards rear, progress over 2f out, shaken up to chase leader over 1f out, ridden to lead narrowly final 100yds, ran on well, beat Desert Opal by ½l*

1st Care Fund Maiden Stakes (Lingfield, May 17) 3yo 7f Good to soft **74** (TS 50) 18 ran. *Held up in rear of main group, steady progress from over 2f out, pushed into lead last 150yds, comfortably, beat Pequenita by 1¼l*

his debut and had followed up a couple of weeks later in a better-class conditions event at Sandown, it would have been easy to have dismissed him as just another horse after he was foiled in a classified stakes at Newmarket when bidding for his hat-trick. However, that defeat – he finished last of three, albeit beaten little more than a length behind Lago d'Orta – is easily explained, as they had gone no gallop and he had raced too freely. Indeed the more we saw of Leporello, the clearer it became that he is a confirmed hold-up horse who will always be best served by a strong pace.

Lack of a proper gallop was not a concern when he returned to Newmarket's July meeting for one of the summer's most fiercely contested handicaps, and he came from off the pace to short-head Tiber in a race which went on to produce plenty of winners. He repeated the dose against his elders in a similar contest at Haydock a month later, overcoming serious traffic problems to sweep to the front well inside the final furlong and beat Silence Is Golden, but that success effectively forced him out of all but the most valuable handicaps.

It is impossible to say how much further Leporello can progress, but both Harris and Quinn envisage him making a cracking four-year-old and one can see why. Races like the Eclipse and the Champion Stakes are likely to be on his agenda and, granted the fast ground and solid pace that shows his killer finishing burst to best advantage, a major prize could come his way.

Leporello

bay colt, 02-3-2000

			Nearctic
		Northern Dancer	**Natalma**
	Danzig		
		Pas de Nom	Admiral's Voyage
Danehill			Petitioner
b 1986			Ribot
		His Majesty	Flower Bowl
	Razyana		
		Spring Adieu	Buckpasser
			Natalma
		Never Bend	Nasrullah
			Lalun
	Mill Reef		
		Milan Mill	Princequillo
Why So Silent			Virginia Water
ch 1986			Klairon
		Luthier	Flute Enchantee
	Sing Softly		
		Melody Hour	Sing Sing
			Arvonia

Bred by Pendley Farm in Ireland

Sire **Danehill**

Won 4 of 9 races, inc. Cork and Orrery S.-Gr3, Haydock Park Sprint Cup-Gr1. Medium-sized, strong, good-bodied individual, markedly back at the knee. Died in May 2003. Sire, in northern hemisphere, of: Danish (Queen Elizabeth II Challenge Cup-Gr1), Kissing Cousin (Coronation S.-Gr1), Danehill Dancer (Phoenix S.-Gr1, National S.-Gr1), Tsukuba Symphony (NHK Mile Cup-Gr1), Desert King (National S.-Gr1, Irish 2,000 Guineas-Gr1, Irish Derby-Gr1), Fairy King Prawn (Yasuda Kinen-Gr1), Tiger Hill (Grosser Preis von Baden-Gr1, twice, Bayerisches Zuchtrennen-Gr1), Indian Danehill (Prix Ganay-Gr1), Wannabe Grand (Cheveley Park S.-Gr1), Aquarelliste (Prix de Diane-Gr1, Prix Vermeille-Gr1, Prix Ganay-Gr1), Banks Hill (Coronation S.-Gr1, Breeders' Cup Filly & Mare Turf-Gr1, Prix Jacques le Marois-Gr1), Mozart (July Cup-Gr1, Nunthorpe S.-Gr1), Regal Rose (Cheveley Park S.-Gr1), Dress To Thrill (Matriarch S.-Gr1), Landseer (Poule d'Essai des Poulains-Gr1), Rock Of Gibraltar (Grand Criterium-Gr1, Dewhurst S.-Gr1, 2,000 Guineas-Gr1, Irish 2,000 Guineas-Gr1, St James's Palace S.-Gr1, Sussex S.-Gr1, Prix du Moulin de Longchamp-Gr1), Spring Star (Gr2), Spartacus (Phoenix S.-Gr1, Gran Criterium-Gr1), Westerner (Prix du Cadran-Gr1, Prix Royal-Oak-Gr1), Clodovil (Poule d'Essai des Poulains-Gr1).

Dam **Why So Silent**

Unraced. By Derby winner and outstanding sire out of high-class 10-14f mare. Very closely related to smart stayer Top Cees and half-sister to 10f Listed/Gr 3 winner Supreme Sound. Dam of: Whispering Loch (1991 c by Lomond; unplaced), Poppy Carew (1992 f by Danehill; Listed winner, Gr2-placed), Pennyfair (1993 f by Fairy King; unraced), Calypso Grant (1994 f by Danehill; Listed winner), Oh Hebe (1995 f by Night Shift; winner, dam of Gr2 winner Devious Boy), Juno Marlowe (1996 f by Danehill; winner), Supreme Silence (1997 g by Bluebird; winner), Rose Peel (1998 f by Danehill; winner), Leporello (2000 c by Danehill; Gr3 winner), 2002 f by Grand Lodge.

Pedigree assessment

Leporello's four sisters recorded most of their best form between 7f and 10f, though Poppy Carew did win over 12f. So, although Danehill is capable of getting the occasional high-class 12f performer and Why So Silent is stoutly bred, it may be that Leporello remains a 10f specialist. Plenty of progressive horses close up in his pedigree, which is encouraging for 2004. *JH*

Lucky Story (USA)

2yo brown colt **117**

Kris S (USA) - Spring Flight (USA) (Miswaki (USA))

Owner Abdulla Buhaleeba

Trainer M Johnston

Breeder WinStar Farm

Career: **5 starts** | won **4** | second **0** | third **0** | £132,593 win and place

By James Willoughby

A good heart these days is hard to find. Rare courage in one so young carried Lucky Story to victory in the Champagne Stakes. He simply would not lie down, first during a prolonged tussle with Haafhd, then while turning back the flailing challenge of Auditorium by the length of his extended neck.

Mark Johnston's charismatic colt produced a memorable performance at Doncaster. It was also a very useful effort in terms of merit. There is no doubt now that Lucky Story is a serious contender for the 2,000 Guineas at Newmarket.

The first indication that Lucky Story might be one of the best juveniles of the season came at Pontefract in late June. Four winners were set against him in a field of seven for the Spindrifter Conditions Stakes over six furlongs. The result could not have been more emphatic.

Not only did the six-length winning margin over Mac The Knife suggest that Lucky Story could be something out of the top drawer; the manner in which he accomplished it was extraordinary. He still looked palpably green as he powered clear with terrific zest, deceptively seeming to gather momentum as he ran uphill. Good horses all have something distinctive about them and the signs with Lucky Story were unmistakable.

Lucky Story was seeing the racecourse for only the third time at Pontefract and, while it is something of a cliché that Johnston's horses improve with experience, his performance represented a huge leap forward.

On his debut at Ayr in May, he did not seem to have a clue what to do, though it was obvious that the outing would put an edge on him after he stayed on late in fourth behind Clifden. Defeat did not sully his tall home reputation, however, and some big bets were landed when Lucky Story returned to the west of Scotland track to defeat three rivals in his maiden. Starting at 4-11, he cleared away to win by five lengths.

For all the promise suggested by those two runs at Ayr, and impressive

Lucky Story (Darryll Holland, nearside) narrowly lands the Champagne Stakes at Doncaster in September

though his Pontefract win was, it was now time for the acid test. Lucky Story had to be launched into Pattern company to see if he was as good as reputed.

In the early days of his training career, Johnston engendered widespread confidence in his capabilities by sending horses south to win major prizes at Ascot and Goodwood. The latter course, in particular, is known to hold great fondness for him and he always compiles a strong team for the Glorious meeting in late July.

The timing was perfect for Lucky Story to make his Pattern-race bow in the Group 2 Veuve Clicquot Vintage Stakes at the Sussex track. Though facing no easy task on paper, he was sent off as 6-5 favourite, his trainer's tag of being "the best I've had since Mister Baileys" perhaps still resounding in the ears of some backers.

Again, Lucky Story looked an unusual combination of talent and inexperience. At one point he looked to be coming off the bridle straightening for home, but the top turn at Goodwood is reasonably sharp and it turned out that his difficulties were only navigational. The manner

2003   Race record

1st Champagne Stakes (Group 2) (Doncaster, September 12) 2yo 7f Good **117** (TS 65) 6 ran. *Made all, pushed along over 2f out, ridden and edged right over 1f out, edged left entering final furlong, hung right inside final furlong, driven and held on well, beat Auditorium by nk*

1st Veuve Clicquot Vintage Stakes (Group 2) (Goodwood, July 30) 2yo 7f Good to soft **112** (TS 81) 9 ran. *Tracked leaders, ridden to lead over 2f out, idled over 1f out, driven and stayed on strongly inside final furlong, beat The Mighty Tiger by 1¼l*

1st Spindrifter Conditions Stakes (Pontefract, June 30) 2yo 6f Good to soft **103** (TS 56) 7 ran. *Prominent, led over 2f out, stayed on strongly to go clear final furlong, beat Mac The Knife by 6l*

1st Lisa Mobs 30th Birthday Maiden Stakes (Ayr, June 20) 2yo 6f Good to firm **77** 4 ran. *Close up, led over 2f out, ridden and hung left over 1f out, kept on strongly, eased close home, beat Red Romeo by 5l*

4th EBF Ayr May Novice Stakes (Ayr, May 29) 2yo 6f Good to soft **70** 7 ran. *Soon niggled in touch, ridden halfway, no impression until stayed on final furlong, nearest finish, beaten 2½l by Clifden*

in which he forged clear soon after was very taking.

One of the most engaging aspects of that defeat of The Mighty Tiger was that he managed to record one of the juvenile time performances of the season, despite idling markedly in front. Horses usually beat the clock only when they are carried deep into the contest by the ideal pace set-up, in the same way that athletes benefit from pacemakers during world-record attempts. But – to extend the metaphor – Lucky Story had spent the last lap waving to the crowd.

The importance of Lucky Story's subsequent gutsy effort at Doncaster cannot be overstated in the light of his Goodwood display. It had to be a possibility that his playful streak could turn to something more sinister, but the way he went about his business in a slowly run race allayed any such fears. Incidentally, Lucky Story sweated considerably in the paddock that day. Rather than being a cause for concern, however, the tendency is considered typical of the best offspring of his sire, Kris S, and was evident also on occasions in Kris Kin.

Doncaster in September proved to be the last we saw of the imposing Lucky Story. It seemed a great shame that a poor workout forced his withdrawal from the Dewhurst Stakes.

Even without that chance to garner championship honours, Lucky Story has proved another great advertisement for his trainer's ability to free himself of the constraints of received wisdom when selecting suitable young stock. The brother to Dr Fong cost just $95,000 as a yearling at Keeneland, presumably because many viewed his conformation as being less than ideal.

The next – and most compelling – chapter of Lucky Story will centre on the Rowley Mile, where his comparison with 1994 2,000 Guineas winner Mister Baileys is likely to get the ultimate test. The step up to a mile can only suit him: One Cool Cat and his pals had better be ready for a fight.

Lucky Story   *brown colt, 01-2-2001*

		Hail To Reason	Turn-to
			Nothirdchance
	Roberto		
		Bramalea	Nashua
Kris S			Rarelea
br 1977			
		Princequillo	Prince Rose
			Cosquilla
	Sharp Queen		
		Bridgework	Occupy
			Feale Bridge

		Mr Prospector	Raise A Native
			Gold Digger
	Miswaki		
		Hopespringseternal	Buckpasser
Spring Flight			Rose Bower
b 1987			
		Coco La Terreur	Nearctic
			Ciboulette
	Coco La Investment		
		Great Investment	Saidam
			Modern

Bred by WinStar Farm in US. $95,000 Keeneland September yearling

Sire Kris S (USA)

Won 3 of 5 races, including a 9f restricted stakes in California at 3. A big, strong horse, not very sound. Died in 2002. Sire of: Evening Kris (Jerome H.-Gr1), Prized (Breeders' Cup Turf-Gr1, San Luis Rey S.-Gr1), Stocks Up (Hollywood Starlet S.-Gr1), Cheval Volant (Hollywood Starlet S.-Gr1, Las Virgenes S.-Gr1), Lyin To The Moon (Gr2), Hollywood Wildcat (Hollywood Oaks-Gr1, Breeders' Cup Distaff-Gr1, Gamely H.-Gr1), Kissin Kris (Haskell Invitational H.-Gr1), Brocco (Breeders' Cup Juvenile-Gr1, Santa Anita Derby-Gr1), You And I (Metropolitan H.-Gr1), Class Kris (Gr2), Arch (Super Derby-Gr1), Diamond On The Run (Gr2), Dr Fong (St James's Palace S.-Gr1), Midnight Line (Gr2), Soaring Softly (Flower Bowl Invitational H.-Gr1, Breeders' Cup Filly & Mare Turf-Gr1), Adonis (Gr2), Apple Of Kent (Gr2), Krisada (Gr2), Peshtigo (Gr3), Kudos (Oaklawn H.-Gr1), Kumari Continent (Gr2), Julie Jalouse (Gr2), Whitmore's Conn (Sword Dancer Invitational H.-Gr1), Kicken Kris (Secretariat S.-Gr1), Kris Kin (Derby S.-Gr1), Action This Day (Breeders' Cup Juvenile-Gr1), Lucky Story (Gr2).

Dam Spring Flight

Won 8 of 34 starts. Effective at up to 1m, mainly ran on dirt, did win on turf. Dam of: Stylized (1994 f by Sovereign Dancer; winner), Dr Fong (1995 c by Kris S; Gr1 winner), Crown Of Spring (1996 f by Chief's Crown; winner), Holy Belle (1997 f by Holy Bull; winner), Northward Bound (1998 c by Kris S; non-winner), Lucky Story (2001 c by Kris S; Gr2 winner), 2002 c by Lemon Drop Kid, 2003 c by Tiznow.

Pedigree assessment

Has shown more class than his brother Dr Fong at a similar stage of their careers. Dr Fong progressed well, Kris S tends to get progeny who progress well, and dam Spring Flight kept her form well, so the signs are encouraging that Lucky Story can confirm himself in the top class in 2004. A mile will be his trip. *JH*

Magistretti (USA)

3yo bay colt   **125**

Diesis - Ms Strike Zone (USA) (Deputy Minister (Can))
Owner M Tabor
Trainer N A Callaghan
Breeder Tri-County Farms

Career: **9** starts | won **3** | second **4** | third **0** | **£292,798** win and place

By Graham Dench

MAGISTRETTI will not go down among the very best winners of York's Dante Stakes, but the fact that he won the race at all is a measure of how much he had improved since ending his juvenile campaign effectively sacrificed as a pacemaker for the Aidan O'Brien-trained favourite Van Nistelrooy in the Royal Lodge Stakes at Ascot.

That improvement will have come as no surprise to anyone who saw the Diesis colt at two, for the moment he first set foot on a racecourse for his winning debut at Sandown he impressed as a grand physical specimen, and one who was sure to progress as he matured. Magistretti failed to win again after the Dante, but Group 1 second places behind Vespone at Longchamp and Falbrav back at York again suggest he never stopped improving and trainer Neville Callaghan's optimism that the colt will make the breakthrough at that level as a four-year-old looks well founded.

The Dante has a well-deserved reputation for being one of the key trials for Epsom, its roll of honour over the last 25 years featuring a host of horses who have gone on to distinguish themselves, among them Derby winners Shirley Heights, Shahrastani, Reference Point, Erhaab and Benny The Dip. However, the latest renewal, sponsored by the Tote, could not have worked out worse, since only one of the ten runners managed to win in the rest of the season.

That was hardly Magistretti's fault, however, and in a properly run race he did well to get up close home and beat the inexperienced front-runner Tuning Fork, who had made his racecourse debut only 11 days earlier, by half a length after being given plenty to do. Success at York followed a narrow defeat of Dunhill Star in another recognised trial, the bet365 Feilden Stakes at Newmarket, and earned Magistretti his place in the Vodafone Derby line-up, in which only six horses were preferred

Magistretti (Kevin Darley) strides out to take the Group 2 Dante Stakes at York in May

in the betting, but his backers there got no run. Kevin Darley, who had taken over from regular rider Kieren Fallon in the Dante, never had Magistretti in position and, having been last into the straight, the colt merely kept on through tired horses to finish a remote ninth of 20 behind Kris Kin.

Although Magistretti's Derby effort was a long way below his mile-and-a-quarter form, it would be a mistake to conclude that the trip was beyond him, or for that matter the track. Indeed connections are convinced that he will get a mile and a half and have earmarked Epsom's Coronation Cup as a likely early target in 2004. They will have drawn plenty of encouragement from the style in which Magistretti was going on at the finish of both the Grand Prix de Paris, in which Vespone beat him only a length and a half, and the Juddmonte International, for on both tracks

2003   Race record

2nd Juddmonte International Stakes (Group 1) (York, August 19) 3yo+ 10½f Good to firm **125** (TS 107) 8 ran. *In touch, pushed along over 4f out, stayed on well to take 2nd inside final furlong, beaten 2l by Falbrav*

2nd Juddmonte Grand Prix de Paris (Group 1) (Longchamp, June 22) 3yo 10f Good to soft **119** (TS 97) 11 ran. *Held up in rear, 9th but closing on outside straight, ridden and switched outside 1½f out, ran on well but too late to worry winner, beaten 1½l by Vespone*

9th Vodafone Derby (Group 1) (Epsom, June 7) 3yo 12f Good **104** (TS 79) 20 ran. *Well in rear, dropped to last straight, stayed on one pace final 2f, no danger, beaten 13l by Kris Kin*

1st Tote Dante Stakes (Group 2) (York, May 14) 3yo 10½f Good to firm **111** (TS 84) 10 ran. *In touch, headway and pushed along over 3f out, ridden and edged left 2f out, driven entering final furlong, stayed on well to lead near finish, beat Tuning Fork by ½l*

1st bet365 Feilden Stakes (Listed) (Newmarket, April 17) 3yo 9f Good to firm **108** (TS 81) 6 ran. *Held up, headway to chase clear leader halfway, led well over 2f out, all out, beat Dunhill Star by hd*

2002

5th Hackney Empire Royal Lodge Stakes (Group 2) (Ascot, September 28) 2yo 1m Good to firm **98** (TS 62) 9 ran ● **2nd** McKeever St Lawrence Conditions Stakes (Doncaster, September 11) 2yo 7f Good **95** (TS 48) 6 ran ● **2nd** Weatherbys Superlative Stakes (Listed) (Newmarket (July), July 11) 2yo 7f Good to soft **98** (TS 63) 7 ran ● **1st** Palletline Tenth Anniversary Maiden Stakes (Sandown, June 15) 2yo 7f Good **83** 4 ran

he shaped very much as if he would get further.

The Juddmonte, in which Fallon was back on board, represents easily Magistretti's best form to date. While flattered to get within two lengths of Falbrav, who left his rivals for dead approaching the two-furlong marker, Magistretti stayed on really well from off the pace to take second, nicely clear of the race's 2002 winner Nayef, the progressive Irish challenger Mingun and the Hardwicke winner Indian Creek.

Many would have found it impossible to resist temptation to press on and aim Magistretti at one of the big autumn middle-distance prizes. However, owner Michael Tabor, who numbers the top-class two-year-old Danehill Dancer and the Stewards' Cup gamble Danetime – not to mention Champion Hurdle second Royal Derbi - among many winners he had with Callaghan before his recent high-profile success with John Magnier and Aidan O'Brien, is a patient man and can afford to wait.

He did not resist when the trainer revealed immediately after the Juddmonte that he would like to put Magistretti away in order to give him plenty of time to develop. Callaghan is on record predicting as much as 5lb to 7lb more improvement, but that might be asking too much based on the Racing Post Rating of 125 he recorded in the Juddmonte, as that would take him past the likes of Sulamani and into the realms of Falbrav and Mubtaker. But just a pound or two's improvement would put a major prize within his grasp and he could probably win a Group 1 abroad without improving another ounce.

Magistretti
bay colt, 05-3-2000

		Atan	Native Dancer
			Mixed Marriage
	Sharpen Up		
		Rocchetta	Rockefella
Diesis			Chambiges
ch 1980			
		Reliance	Tantieme
			Relance
	Doubly Sure		
		Soft Angels	Crepello
			Sweet Angel
		Vice Regent	Northern Dancer
			Victoria Regina
	Deputy Minister		
		Mint Copy	Bunty's Flight
Ms Strike Zone			Shakney
b 1994			
		Mr Prospector	Raise A Native
			Gold Digger
	Bat Prospector		
		Batucada	Roman Line
			Whistle A Tune

Bred by Tri-County Farms in US. Ir£170,000 Goffs Orby yearling

Sire Diesis

Won 3 of 6 starts, inc. Middle Park S.-Gr1, Dewhurst S.-Gr1. Lengthy, light-framed. Brother to Kris. Stands at Mill Ridge Farm, Kentucky, 2003 fee $30,000. Oldest progeny 18. Sire of Gr1 winners: Diminuendo (Oaks S., Irish Oaks, Yorkshire Oaks), Elmaamul (Eclipse S., Phoenix Champion S.), Keen Hunter (Prix de l'Abbaye), Rootentootenwooten (Demoiselle S.), Knifebox (Premio Roma), Husband (Canadian International S.), Halling (Eclipse S., twice, York International, twice, Prix d'Ispahan), Storm Trooper (Hollywood Turf H.), Ramruma (Oaks S., Irish Oaks, Yorkshire Oaks), Love Divine (Oaks S.), Three Valleys (Middle Park S.).

Dam Ms Strike Zone

Won at 3 in US. By excellent North American sire out of winning sister to high-class 10-12f colt Damister. Dam of: Zonaki (1999 c by Miswaki; unplaced), Magistretti (2000 c by Diesis; Gr2 winner, Gr1-placed), Dream Out Loud (2001 f by Stravinsky; unraced), 2003 f by King Of Kings.

Pedigree assessment

In the mould of most of Diesis's other high-class males in that he excels at around 10f, and that is in keeping with the distaff side of his pedigree. Has already done enough to earn himself a fair stud place in due course and has every chance of improving his top-level stakes record. Diesis has a mixed record as a sire of sires, though Halling has done well and Elmaamul is capable of siring very smart performers. *JH*

Mamool (Ire)

4yo bay colt   **124**

In The Wings - Genovefa (USA) (Woodman (USA))
Owner Godolphin
Trainer Saeed Bin Suroor
Breeder Sheikh Mohammed

Career: **15** starts | won **6** | second **2** | third **1** | **£632,890** win and place

By Lee Mottershead

HE SUCCEEDED where we expected him to fail, and failed where we expected him to succeed. So goes the story of Mamool's season in 2003.

He did not begin the campaign as an obvious contender for top-flight middle-distance honours. Fifth in the German Derby and fourth in the St Leger on his final two outings in 2002, Mamool was no superstar at three. Yet at four, he supplemented a Yorkshire Cup success by landing back-to-back Group 1 victories over a mile and a half.

He did begin the campaign as an obvious contender for top-flight staying honours. Yet sent off favourite for the Gold Cup, he ran out of gas, finishing only fifth to Mr Dinos. Even worse, he became the first modern-day favourite to finish last in the Melbourne Cup. Talk about ups and downs.

It started with an up, and a big one. Having beaten Godolphin stablemate Pugin at Nad Al Sheba in February, Mamool went to the Emirates Airline Yorkshire Cup a fit horse and came home a very fast horse. The turn of foot he unleashed to cut down subsequent Coronation Cup hero Warrsan was as impressive as it was unexpected. Mamool's St Leger conqueror Bollin Eric, admittedly conceding 5lb, was soundly beaten in third.

The fact that Mamool could accelerate so decisively at the end of a strongly run mile and three-quarters inevitably cast doubts about whether he could be as effective over a stamina-sapping two and a half miles in the Gold Cup. His stamina was sapped. Mamool was at no point able to throw down a challenge to runaway winner Mr Dinos up the straight, coming home more than seven lengths behind the colt he had beaten in the previous year's Queen's Vase. Back to the drawing board.

There was not a great deal to be enthusiastic about in Mamool's next outing. Back after a two-month break in the Geoffrey Freer Stakes, the Mamool who reappeared at Newbury was not the Mamool who had won at York. Now his attitude was very much in question. He seemed

Mamool (Frankie Dettori) lands the Grosser Bugatti Preis at Baden-Baden, the first of two Group 1 wins in Germany

unenthusiastic under pressure, appearing to hang fire when asked to extend up the straight, shifting left for good measure.

Thus it was all the more surprising when he produced by some way the best performance of his life just three weeks later. Running over a mile and a half for the first time in over a year, he got the better of Black Sam Bellamy after a furious final-furlong tussle for the Grosser Bugatti Preis at Baden-Baden. There was no doubting his commitment this time and there was speculation about a possible crack at the Prix de l'Arc de Triomphe.

Twenty-one days on and he was at it again, notching another Group 1 German triumph, and this time a deal more comfortably, beating fellow British raider Albanova by one and a quarter lengths in Cologne's Preis von Europa. Mamool was riding an upward curve.

Like most of Godolphin's season, Mamool's assault on the Melbourne Cup ended in complete disappointment. The morning selection of flagship Australian newspaper The Age and the 11-2 favourite, Mamool appeared to hold the best credentials of any Godolphin contender for the Melbourne Cup. The operation had come close before, most notably with Give The

2003   Race record

23rd Tooheys New Melbourne Cup (Group 1) (Handicap) (Flemington, November 4) 3yo+ 2m Good **82** 23 ran. *Raced keenly in 3rd, 8th and weakening straight, eased, finished lame, beaten 35l by Makybe Diva*

1st Preis von Europa (Group 1) (Cologne, September 28) 3yo+ 12f Soft **118** 6 ran. *Led after 1½f, set steady pace, went to outside in back straight, headed at halfway, led 2f out, ridden out, beat Albanova by 1½l*

1st Grosser Bugatti Preis (Grosser Preis von Baden) (Group 1) (Baden-Baden, September 7) 3yo+ 12f Good **124** 8 ran. *Led 2f, settled in 4th, 3rd on outside straight, led 1f out, driven out, beat Black Sam Bellamy by ½l*

3rd Stan James Geoffrey Freer Stakes (Group 2) (Newbury, August 16) 3yo+ 1m5½f Good to firm **117** (TS 90) 5 ran. *Held up in rear, switched right to outside over 3f out and hung left under pressure, one pace and never dangerous, beaten 6½l by Mubtaker*

5th Gold Cup (Group 1) (Ascot, June 19) 4yo+ 2m4f Good to firm **116** (TS 60) 12 ran. *Held up in rear, good headway on inside 4f out, staying on but no impression when switched left 2f out, took 3rd over 1f out, kept on same pace, beaten 7½l by Mr Dinos*

1st Emirates Airline Yorkshire Cup (Group 2) (York, May 15) 4yo+ 1m6f Good to firm **122** (TS 105) 8 ran. *Held up in last, effort over 3f out, went 3rd 2f out, hard ridden and stayed on well to lead near finish, beat Warrsan by ½l*

1st Khas El Dhaheb (Nad Al Sheba, February 27) 4yo+ 1m6f Good 10 ran. *In touch towards rear, good headway straight, led 1½f out, soon clear, comfortably, beat Pugin by 1¼l*

2002

4th Rothmans Royals St Leger Stakes (Group 1) (Doncaster, September 14) 3yo 1m6½f Good to firm **116** (TS 89) 8 ran ● **5th** BMW Deutsches Derby (Group 1) (Hamburg, July 7) 3yo 12f Heavy **98** 17 ran ● **1st** Queen's Vase (Group 3) (Ascot, June 21) 3yo 2m Good to firm **108** (TS 65) 14 ran ● **4th** attheraces Sky Channel 418 Derby Trial Stakes (Group 3) (Lingfield, May 11) 3yo 11½f Good **98** (TS 46) 6 ran

Other notable runs

4th Gran Criterium (Group 1) (San Siro, October 21) 2yo 1m Heavy **101** 8 ran ● **1st** Uniq Foodservice Gold Cup EBF Maiden Stakes (Goodwood, September 26) 2yo 1m Good **91** 6 ran ● **2nd** Washington Singer Stakes (Listed) (Newbury, August 17) 2yo 7f Good to firm **98** (TS 68) 4 ran

Slip and Central Park, but in Mamool they looked to have the perfect raider, a 12-furlong Group 1 winner who stayed two miles.

Making the most of Mamool's handy draw, Frankie Dettori plotted him into an ideal early position, passing the post first time in a stalking third. However, when pressure was applied, Mamool folded – and quickly. Sheikh Mohammed had again failed in his dream to lift the Cup, his number one challenger last, 12 lengths behind the nearest horse in front of him. Dettori reported Mamool moved "awfully", not surprisingly considering that it transpired the colt had broken a right-hind fetlock.

It was a miserable end to a largely miserable season for Godolphin. Yet, despite the Melbourne misery, Mamool was one of Godolphin's success stories, a largely unheralded horse who was superbly placed to win two of the worst Group 1 races run all season.

Mamool

bay colt, 19-3-1999

			Nearctic
		Northern Dancer	Natalma
	Sadler's Wells		
		Fairy Bridge	Bold Reason
			Special
In The Wings			
b 1986			Mill Reef
		Shirley Heights	Hardiemma
	High Hawk		
		Sunbittern	Sea Hawk
			Pantoufle
			Raise A Native
		Mr Prospector	Gold Digger
	Woodman		
		Playmate	Buckpasser
			Intriguing
Genovefa			
b 1992		Far North	**Northern Dancer**
			Fleur
	Reigning Countess		
		Countess Fager	Dr Fager
			Compassionately

Bred by Sheikh Mohammed in Ireland

Sire In The Wings

Won 7 of 11 races, inc. Prix du Prince d'Orange-Gr3, Coronation Cup-Gr1, Grand Prix de Saint-Cloud-Gr1, Prix Foy-Gr3, Breeders' Cup Turf-Gr1. Also 2nd in Prix Ganay-Gr1, 4th in Prix de l'Arc de Triomphe-Gr1, 5th in King George VI & Queen Elizabeth S.-Gr1. Small, quite sturdily-built individual. Off the course for 13 months from August as 2yo because of a chipped knee. Best suited by 12f with some give in the ground. Sire of: Irish Wings (Gr3), Singspiel (Canadian International S.-Gr1, Japan Cup-Gr1, Dubai World Cup, Coronation Cup-Gr1, York International S.-Gr1), Winged Love (Irish Derby-Gr1), Annaba (Gr2), Apprehension (Gr3), Just In Fun (Gr3), Right Wing (Gr3), Boreas (Gr3), Central Park (Derby Italiano-Gr1, Premio Presidente della Repubblica-Gr1), Cloud Castle (Gr3), Thief Of Hearts (Gr3), Tillerman (Gr2), Air Marshall (Gr2), Davide Umbro (Gr2), Earlene (Gr2), Kutub (Bayerisches Zuchtrennen-Gr1, Preis von Europa-Gr1, Gran Premio del Jockey Club-Gr1), Saldenschwinge (Gr3), Zanzibar (Oaks d'Italia-Gr1), Act One (Criterium International-Gr1, Prix Lupin-Gr1), Mamool (Grosser Preis von Baden-Gr1, Preis von Europa-Gr1), Mellow Park (Gr3), Savannah Bay (Gr3), Trumbaka (Gr3), Abunawwas (Gr3), Fidelite (Prix Saint-Alary-Gr1), New South Wales (Gr3), Soldier Hollow (Gr3), Weightless (Gr2).

Dam Genovefa

Won 2 of 8 races, inc. Prix de Royaumont-Gr3. Also twice Gr2-placed. Well-made sort. Smart, consistent middle-distance/staying performer, effective on firmish and soft ground. Dam of: Ejlaal (1997 f by Caerleon; winner), Genova (1998 f by Darshaan; winner), Mamool (1999 c by In The Wings; dual Gr1 winner), Self Portrait (2000 f by Peintre Celebre; unraced), Serengeti Sky (2001 c by Southern Halo; unraced to date).

Pedigree assessment

It was Mamool's turn to spearhead the annual Godolphin challenge for the 2003 Melbourne Cup and he arrived at Flemington strongly fancied to claim the prize. His performance there was quite out of character; from a handy third place as the race began in earnest, he dropped right out to finish 23rd and last behind the English-bred auction reject Makybe Diva, having broken his near-hind fetlock. His future is uncertain, but what is certain is that, on his European form, Mamool was a much-improved horse in 2003 and a consistent one. *TM*

Mezzo Soprano (USA)

3yo bay filly **118**

Darshaan - Morn Of Song (USA) (Blushing Groom (Fr))
Owner Godolphin
Trainer Saeed Bin Suroor
Breeder Darley Stud Management

Career: **9** starts | won **4** | second **1** | third **2** | **£178,970** win and place

By Nicholas Godfrey

MEZZO SOPRANO, a lovely-looking filly from a prestigious family, started the season as Godolphin's chief hope of success in the fillies' Classics. She did not figure as any sort of factor in the 1,000 Guineas and never even contested the Oaks, but her learning curve arched ever upwards during the summer until a string of progressive efforts culminated in the sort of result that many had, by then, considered beyond her: success at the top level, in the Group 1 Prix Vermeille.

This immensely likeable filly became Godolphin's number one hope for high honours in the distaff division when comfortably scoring from five rivals in the UAE 1,000 Guineas on the sand at Nad Al Sheba, and she arrived in Newmarket before the Guineas at single figures in the betting for both fillies' Classics.

She was painfully short on experience, however. Besides her Dubai victory, the form of which was impossible to quantify, Mezzo Soprano had raced just once, hacking up from a big field of unraced fillies in testing conditions at Deauville as a juvenile for André Fabre.

Sent off a mere 7-1 shot for the Guineas, she barely showed, inexperience being cited as the primary cause for an uninspiring effort which saw her trail home among the backmarkers in 14th behind Russian Rhythm.

As a daughter of Darshaan out of a half-sister to Singspiel, Mezzo Soprano could have been expected to improve with maturity and, with sights lowered, she progressed over the summer, recording fair efforts in decent company. She was runner-up to Ocean Silk in the Listed Lupe Stakes before finishing third in a pair of Group races, the Ribblesdale Stakes at Royal Ascot and the Prix de Psyche at Deauville.

By now, Mezzo Soprano's preferred style of racing was firmly established. She habitually raced keenly, just off the pace, before being produced a couple of furlongs out and staying on with gusto, albeit without exhibiting any startling change of gear. In this fashion, she got back in the winning

Mezzo Soprano (Frankie Dettori, farside) beats Yesterday to take the Prix Vermeille at Longchamp

groove in Listed company in the Galtres Stakes at the Ebor meeting, holding off Thingmebob by a neck for her best effort to date.

Fair enough, but there was still nothing to suggest that she was about to achieve the sort of headline performance hoped for at the start of the year, as trainer Saeed Bin Suroor was forced to admit when he said: "We have given her a chance in the big races this year, but she is not good enough to win a Group 1." He must have been pleasantly surprised by her next outing, three and a half weeks later at Longchamp, when Mezzo Soprano belatedly became Godolphin's sole Group 1 winner from the Classic generation of 2003.

The Prix Vermeille, the only Group 1 contest on the Arc trials card three weeks before the main event at Longchamp, was no easy option. A cracking field of high-class middle-distance fillies featured seven Group winners, among them Classic winners Casual Look and Yesterday. In contrast, Mezzo Soprano boasted merely Listed-race success, but, racing on ground with a bit of give for the first time over a mile and a half, she was able to step up again on anything she had previously achieved.

With Yesterday's pacemaker, Butterfly Blue, setting a generous gallop, Mezzo Soprano disputed second with Casual Look behind the 'hare'. The pacemaker folded fully half a mile out, leaving Casual Look in front sooner than ideal. But while the Oaks winner was three lengths clear of Mezzo Soprano two furlongs out, she fell into a heap.

2003   Race record

10th Breeders' Cup Filly & Mare Turf (Grade 1) (Santa Anita, October 25) 3yo+ 10f Firm **110** 12 ran. *Mid-division, 6th and pushed along straight, one pace from over 1f out, beaten 7l by Islington*

1st Prix Vermeille Fouquet's Barriere (Group 1) (Longchamp, September 14) 3yo 12f Good to soft **118** (TS 104) 11 ran. *Led 1f then disputing 2nd, 2nd straight and pushed along, ridden to lead approaching final furlong, found more under pressure when strongly pressed final furlong, beat Yesterday by hd*

1st EBF Galtres Stakes (Listed) (York, August 21) 3yo+ 12f Good to firm **111** (TS 66) 10 ran. *Tracked leaders, stayed on to lead over 1f out, held on well, edged left inside final furlong, held on well, beat Thingmebob by nk*

3rd Prix de Psyche (Group 3) (Deauville, August 9) 3yo 10f Good to soft **107** (TS 85) 15 ran. *Led, effort and edged left 1½f out, soon ridden, headed just inside final furlong, lost 2nd 100yds out, kept on, beaten 2¼l by Commercante*

3rd Ribblesdale Stakes (Group 2) (Ascot, June 19) 3yo 12f Good to firm **106** (TS 76) 9 ran. *Tracked leader, challenged over 2f out, ridden to lead narrowly well over 1f out, headed and one pace final 150yds, beaten 2¼l by Spanish Sun*

2nd Caffreys Lupe Stakes (Listed) (Goodwood, May 21) 3yo 10f Good to firm **100** (TS 62) 8 ran. *Waited with in touch, ridden over 3f out, kept on but not quicken final furlong, beaten 1¼l by Ocean Silk*

14th Sagitta 1,000 Guineas (Group 1) (Newmarket, May 4) 3yo 1m Good to firm **72** (TS 41) 19 ran. *Prominent, ridden over 2f out, weakened over 1f out, beaten 20l by Russian Rhythm*

1st UAE 1,000 Guineas (Dirt) (Nad Al Sheba, March 13) 3yo 1m Fast 6 ran. *Always in touch, 4th straight, shaken up to lead 1½f out, soon clear, pushed out, beat Gonfilia by 3l*

2002

1st Prix de Grandouet (Unraced Fillies) (Deauville, August 10) 2yo 1m Very soft 16 ran

As Casual Look faded, Dettori pushed Mezzo Soprano on and, while her rider was quoted as saying she was inclined to "stop in front", he also said he thought she would "pull out more". She certainly did the latter, responding gamely as she was strongly pressed, and possibly headed for a stride or two, by Yesterday, who had made her move from the rear. Mezzo Soprano's tenacity won the day by a head in a thrilling battle, the principals having put daylight between themselves and the rest.

Despite good to soft ground, Mezzo Soprano had scored in the second-fastest time in the race's history. Unlike previous Vermeille winners such as Leggera, Volvoreta and Aquarelliste, however, she would not have the chance to contest the Arc itself. "This was her Arc," said Godolphin racing manager Simon Crisford.

A subsequent tilt at the Breeders' Cup Filly & Mare Turf was really an afterthought and ten furlongs around a tight oval failed to show the filly in her best light as she trailed home unsighted.

No matter. Having improved steadily from race to race, Mezzo Soprano amply demonstrated that, in a non-vintage year for middle-distance fillies, she had become one of the best. Her class, attitude and pedigree suggest tremendous potential as a broodmare.

Mezzo Soprano

bay filly, 1-3-2000

		Mill Reef	Never Bend
			Milan Mill
	Shirley Heights		
		Hardiemma	Hardicanute
			Grand Cross
Darshaan			
br 1981			Arbar
		Abdos	Pretty Lady
	Delsy		
		Kelty	Venture
			Marilla
		Red God	Nasrullah
			Spring Run
	Blushing Groom		
		Runaway Bride	Wild Risk
			Aimee
Morn Of Song			
b 1988		Halo	Hail To Reason
			Cosmah
	Glorious Song		
		Ballade	Herbager
			Miss Swapsco

Bred by Darley Stud Management in Kentucky

Sire Darshaan

Won 5 of 8 races, inc. Criterium de Saint-Cloud-Gr2, Prix Greffulhe-Gr2, Prix Hocquart-Gr2, Prix du Jockey Club-Gr1. Strong, workmanlike type. The best 12f 3yo in a very good crop, but disappointing after midsummer. Died May 2001. Sire of: Arzanni (Gr2), Game Plan (Gr2), Hellenic (Yorkshire Oaks-Gr1), Kotashaan (San Luis Rey S.-Gr1, San Juan Capistrano Invitational H.-Gr1, Eddie Read H.-Gr1, Oak Tree Invitational H.-Gr1, Breeders' Cup Turf-Gr1), Grand Plaisir (Gr2), Darnay (Gr2), Truly A Dream (Gr2), Key Change (Yorkshire Oaks-Gr1), Mark Of Esteem (2,000 Guineas-Gr1, Queen Elizabeth II S.-Gr1), Make No Mistake (Gr2), Mutamam (Gr2), Sayarshan (Gr2), Cerulean Sky (Prix Saint-Alary-Gr1), Josr Algarhoud (Gr2), Dilshaan (Racing Post Trophy-Gr1), Olden Times (Prix Jean Prat-Gr1), Sayedah (Gr2), Dalakhani (Criterium International-Gr1, Prix Lupin-Gr1, Prix du Jockey-Club-Gr1, Prix de l'Arc de Triomphe-Gr1), Mezzo Soprano (Prix Vermeille-Gr1), Necklace (Moyglare Stud S.-Gr1). Also got Aliysa, finished first in Oaks, disqualified.

Dam Morn Of Song

Won 3 of 7 races up to a mile, showing just modest form, but sister to Rahy (sire of Fantastic Light) and half-sister to Singspiel. Dam of: Dawn Chorus (1994 c by Danzig; died young), Murhkatel (1995 c by Theatrical; unplaced), Halwa Song (1996 f by Nureyev; unraced), unnamed (1998 f by Storm Cat; unraced), Musical (1999 f by In The Wings; placed), Mezzo Soprano (2000 f by Darshaan; Gr1 winner), unnamed (2001 c by Deputy Minister).

Pedigree assessment

Mezzo Soprano had no form at shorter distances to match her 12f efforts, so she always seemed to be on a fool's errand at the Breeders' Cup. It was a shame to see her finish on such a dull note after a game display in the Vermeille. She was presumably now joined the ever-expanding band of Darley broodmares and ought to prove a notable asset. Her family tends to produce as many bad runners as good, but when they are good they can be very good. *TM*

Milk It Mick

2yo bay colt **118**

Millkom - Lunar Music (Komaite (USA))
Owner Paul J Dixon
Trainer J A Osborne
Breeder Mrs Yvette Dixon

Career: **12** starts | won **5** | second **1** | third **2** | **£214,565** win and place

By Tony Smurthwaite

DOGGEDNESS is a virtue already resonant in the fledgling training career of Jamie Osborne, and in the case of Milk It Mick it is an attribute wonderfully transmitted to his horses.

Colts having their 12th run simply do not win the Darley Dewhurst Stakes, yet that is the paradoxical parable of Milk It Mick. He had lost a maiden, Listed events and races at Group 3 and Group 2 level, so as he cantered to post for the Dewhurst his odds of 33-1 made it clear punters felt it was a pattern that could only continue.

Tout Seul had been enough of a shocker 12 months earlier, making his seventh start and winning at 25-1 in a contest widely panned as non-vintage. How Milk It Mick's victory will be viewed with hindsight is to come, but the confused silence as he came wide and fast to trump Three Valleys told of one of the shocks of the season. Bookmakers were unmoved over Milk It Mick's 2,000 Guineas claims and handicappers were left to take a fresh look at the two-year-old pecking order.

This mattered little to Osborne, in tears afterwards and attracting the right type of headlines after his clashes with the authorities as a jockey over charges of race-fixing, and as a trainer when covertly filmed by the BBC charming prospective owners with tales of skulduggery. What better advert for his proper talents than Milk It Mick, an artisan on breeding and a yeoman turned nobleman in the workplace.

Milk It Mick's season started in April with a slow-starting fifth at Haydock, experience that was used to good effect three weeks later when he won at Beverley, aided by a high draw. Another three weeks passed, then along came win number two, again on fast ground but now over six furlongs, making virtually all at Windsor to give the impression that here, at least, was a formidable galloper.

Attributes of a more valuable hue than painted at Windsor surfaced 17 days later when Osborne donned morning suit and Milk It Mick put

Milk It Mick (Darryll Holland) gets up for a shock defeat of Three Valleys in the Dewhurst

up his best effort yet to be three lengths third to Pearl Of Love in the Chesham Stakes at Royal Ascot. A seventh furlong had brought forth further improvement in form, yet fairytale endings were still unimaginable.

Nonetheless, Osborne saw something in the Chesham that led to Milk It Mick's next three starts – runs five to seven – being back at six furlongs. That they began within eight days of the Chesham and happened inside a month epitomised the dogged qualities of their exponent.

A win in auction stakes company at Salisbury was followed by a fourth place to Nevisian Lad in the Group 2 July Stakes at Newmarket and fourth again to Venables in the Listed Rose Bowl Stakes at Newbury, where he was too keen and gave the impression that he would welcome time off. A whole month later he was back, returning to seven furlongs for the Listed Washington Singer Stakes, but was royally put in his place (third, to be exact) by Haafhd, the five-length winner.

Milk It Mick was out again just 15 days later in the Group 3 Solario Stakes at Sandown. This was his first experience of good-to-soft ground and he appeared to relish the conditions, beating all bar the adroitly ridden Barbajuan after being held up in a race that did not pan out in his favour.

Another 13 days on and no sign of respite. In fact it was back up to Group 2 for the Champagne Stakes at Doncaster, where slow early fractions appeared to catch him out. He took a keen hold once more and weakened into fifth, well behind the winner Lucky Story, albeit around three lengths

2003   Race record

1st Darley Dewhurst Stakes (Group 1) (Newmarket, October 18) 2yo 7f Good to firm **118** (TS 89) 12 ran. *Held up, headway over 1f out, ridden to lead inside final furlong, ran on, beat Three Valleys by hd*

1st Somerville Tattersall Stakes (Group 3) (Newmarket, October 2) 2yo 7f Good to firm **112** (TS 74) 8 ran. *Hampered start, held up, headway over 1f out, ran on under pressure to lead near finish, beat Bayeux by nk*

5th Champagne Stakes (Group 2) (Doncaster, September 12) 2yo 7f Good **99** (TS 46) 6 ran. *Took keen hold, held up in touch, headway over 2f out, ridden and weakened over 1f out, beaten 5½l by Lucky Story*

2nd Iveco Daily Solario Stakes (Group 3) (Sandown, August 30) 2yo 7f Good to soft **108** (TS 64) 8 ran. *Raced in midfield, effort over 2f out, driven to chase winner inside final furlong, kept on well but always held, beaten ½l by Barbajuan*

3rd Stan James Online Stakes (Registered As The Washington Singer Stakes) (Listed) (Newbury, August 15) 2yo 7f Good to firm **100** (TS 70) 8 ran. *In touch, pushed along over 3f out, kept on final 2f and stayed on inside final furlong, gaining on 2nd close home but no chance with winner, beaten 5½l by Haafhd*

4th Shadwell Stud Rose Bowl Stakes (Listed) (Newbury, July 18) 2yo 6f Good to firm **99** (TS 63) 6 ran. *Took keen hold, soon with leaders, strong challenge from 2f out, still every chance when hung right under pressure inside final furlong, one pace, beaten 1¼l by Venables*

4th TNT July Stakes (Group 2) (Newmarket (July), July 9) 2yo 6f Good to firm **102** (TS 46) 8 ran. *Soon pushed along in rear, ran on under pressure final furlong, not pace to challenge, beaten 2l by Nevisian Lad*

1st Taittinger Champagne Auction Stakes (Conditions Race) (Salisbury, June 26) 2yo 6f Firm **94** (TS 29) 8 ran. *Held up in touch on outside, smooth headway on bit from 2f out to lead 1f out, shaken up inside final furlong, soon clear, comfortably, beat Romancero by 1¼l*

3rd Chesham Stakes (Listed) (Ascot, June 18) 2yo 7f Good to firm **93** (TS 61) 13 ran. *Chased leaders, pushed along 3f out, progress over 1f out, driven to chase winner briefly entering final furlong, stayed on same pace, beaten 3l by Pearl Of Love*

1st Family Fun Novice Auction Stakes (Div I) (Windsor, June 1) 2yo 6f Good to firm **87** (TS 40) 12 ran. *Made virtually all, hard driven and stayed on well final 2f, beat Goblin by 1¼l*

1st Coachman Amara Median Auction Maiden Stakes (Beverley, May 10) 2yo 5f Good to firm **87** (TS 70) 15 ran. *Chased leaders, ridden along 2f out, chased winner over 1f out, stayed on under pressure to lead near finish, beat Harry Up by ¾l*

5th Sense Direct/Marian Brown Maiden Auction Stakes (Haydock, April 19) 2yo 5f Good to firm **68** (TS 51) 18 ran. *Slowly into stride and behind in centre, headway over 2f out, stayed on well final furlong, nearest finish, beaten 3¾l by Caldy Dancer*

behind third-placed Haafhd.

A trait was being crystallised in Milk It Mick's form and when he resurfaced 20 days later the strong pace was so to his liking in the Group 3 Somerville Tattersall Stakes that he won. Even so, post-race talk of a shot at the Dewhurst appeared over the top.

Osborne agreed, saying on the eve of the Dewhurst that "you'd have to be on something" to think his horse could win. All eyes were on the principals – Three Valleys, Haafhd and the highly regarded pair Duke Of Venice and Snow Ridge. When Three Valleys sprinted clear of the pack a furlong out the form book looked the winner. Yet he faltered, his acceleration flattened, and guess who was coming late, wide and fast?

Milk It Mick

bay colt, 25-3-2001

		Bold Lad	Bold Ruler
	Cyrano de Bergerac		Barn Pride
Millkom		Miss St Cyr	Brigadier Gerard
b 1991			Miss Paris
		Mummy's Game	Mummy's Pet
	Good Game		Final Game
		Bright Brook	Deep Diver
			Caronbrook
		Nureyev	Northern Dancer
	Komaite		Special
		Brown Berry	Mount Marcy
Lunar Music			Brown Baby
b 1994		Lucky Wednesday	Roi Soleil
	Lucky Candy		Pavlova
		Be My Sweet	Galivanter
			Sweet Councillor

Bred by Yvette Dixon in England. Bought in 14,000gns as Doncaster October yearling

Sire Millkom

Won 12 of 19 races, inc. Prix de Guiche-Gr3, Prix Jean Prat-Gr1, Grand Prix de Paris-Gr1, Prix du Prince d'Orange-Gr3, Man o'War S.-Gr1. High-class performer who stayed 12f and had good turn of foot. Started at stud in England, sent to France after poor support in third season. Sire of: Milk It Mick (Dewhurst S.-Gr1).

Dam Lunar Music

Won 3 of 33 races, all at 5f, inc. 2 sellers at 2, minor race at 4. Inconsistent, plating-class performer. Dam of: Discoed (2000 f by Distinctly North; unplaced), Milk It Mick (2001 c by Millkom; Gr1 winner), and a Mind Games yearling filly (100,000gns Doncaster October yearling in 2003), her only foals.

Pedigree assessment

It is possible that some of the Dewhurst contenders did not do themselves justice, but there was much to admire about the way Milk It Mick won. The French did not take his sire's provincial form seriously until he won and kept winning in Paris; this well-made, honest athlete just might be a chip off the old block. With his unconventional pedigree, which would normally be considered at best second-rate, it is hard to predict the limit of his stamina. Speed influences abound, but Millkom defied them by lasting 12f and it is perfectly possible that his son will do the same. He should certainly be able to get the Guineas mile by spring. *TM*

Milk It Mick beat Three Valleys by a head, with Haafhd a length and a quarter back in third. Osborne had a first Group 1 win and championed his charge for staying healthy throughout the campaign.

A shot at the 2,000 Guineas back on the Rowley Mile will no doubt be considered and, while improvement is the imponderable, there will be few tougher in the field. However he fares there, let's hope he has a happier second season than Tout Seul.

Millenary

6yo bay horse **121**

Rainbow Quest (USA) - Ballerina (Ire) (Dancing Brave (USA))
Owner L Neil Jones
Trainer J L Dunlop
Breeder Abergwaun Farms

Career: **24** starts | won **7** | second **6** | third **4** | **£632,931** win and place

By David Dew

MILLENARY is very much the elder statesman of John Dunlop's Arundel yard. He's been there, done it, and got all the memorabilia. He celebrated his biggest victory when staying on gamely to beat Air Marshall in the 2000 St Leger at Doncaster and still mixes it with the best, winning again at Pattern level in 2003.

However, Millenary did have his fair share of poor fortune, and what was a good campaign could have been a superb one if he had been dealt just a little more luck. Take his run in the Group 2 Prix Jean de Chaudenay at Saint-Cloud in May, for example. He always goes well in the early part of the season and, after his staying-on second to Warrsan in the Jockey Club Stakes at Newmarket on his reappearance, he was sent to France with a seemingly top-notch chance of adding another success to his CV. And he did, only for it to be taken away in the stewards' room after he was deemed to have impeded runner-up Loxias in the closing stages. What made it all the harder to take was that Millenary was the clear winner on merit, giving weight and putting in a particularly determined effort to pull out that little bit more after being headed.

There was talk of sending Millenary back to France in July for a crack at the Grand Prix de Saint-Cloud, but connections eventually swerved that clash with Ange Gabriel, Sulamani and company and went instead to Newmarket in search of his third win at the track, and his second in the Group 2 Princess of Wales's Stakes.

Following his foray in France, and the tendency to hang and lean that he had previously shown both at home and on the track, Millenary was fitted with blinkers and the headgear appeared to help. Millenary took the lead in the final furlong after being held up in last and was driven out to give Bandari a sound beating, with Gamut third and the 2002 St Leger winner Bollin Eric in fourth.

The King George at Ascot was the next port of call, but the blinkers

Millenary (Pat Eddery) wins his second Princess of Wales's Stakes at Newmarket in July

failed to do the trick again and he finished only eighth behind Alamshar. It was no great surprise, though, as he was 16-1 and had been soundly beaten on his previous two attempts in domestic Group 1 company since his St Leger win. In short, it was a performance that confirmed the view that he will always be found wanting in the highest class.

For Millenary's final two starts, connections tried something a little different. Off came the blinkers and he was taken to Deauville for the first time in his career to have a crack at the Group 2 Grand Prix de Deauville. However, despite the soft ground he is thought to enjoy, he hung once again and finished only fourth. The headgear was kept off again at Newmarket in October when he was sent for a crack at the Group 3 Jockey Club Cup, where he was trying two miles for the first time, and on faster ground than ideal. Dunlop said before the race that the trip would not be a problem, and he was right. However, once again Millenary's luck was out.

Having been sent past a seemingly labouring Persian Punch with more than two furlongs to go, he was there to be shot at, and the one stayer

2003   Race record

2nd Jockey Club Cup (Group 3) (Newmarket, October 18) 3yo+ 2m Good to firm **119** (TS 78) 6 ran. *Held up, headway 4f out, led over 2f out, ridden over 1f out, edged left and headed near finish, beaten shd by Persian Punch*

4th Grand Prix de Deauville Lucien Barriere (Group 2) (Deauville, August 31) 3yo+ 12½f Soft **112** (TS 30) 7 ran. *Led, raced alone on rails in back straight, headed approaching final furlong, one pace, beaten 4¾l by Polish Summer*

8th King George VI And Queen Elizabeth Diamond Stakes (Group 1) (Ascot, July 26) 3yo+ 12f Good **114** (TS 84) 12 ran. *Well in rear, ridden well over 3f out, no progress under pressure over 2f out, beaten 13l by Alamshar*

1st Princess of Wales's UAE Equestrian And Racing Federation Stakes (Group 2) (Newmarket (July), July 8) 3yo+ 12f Good **121** (TS 103) 6 ran. *Held up, headway to lead and edged right 1f out, driven out, beat Bandari by 1½l*

2nd Prix Jean de Chaudenay (Group 2) (Saint-Cloud, May 21) 4yo+ 12f Good to soft **121** (TS 103) 6 ran. *Led after 2f, hung right and leant on challenging rival from 1½f out, just held on, disqualified and placed 2nd*

2nd Sagitta Jockey Club Stakes (Group 2) (Newmarket, May 2) 4yo+ 12f Soft **121** (TS 81) 6 ran. *Always prominent, ridden to chase winner 2f out, edged left inside final furlong, stayed on, beaten 1½l by Warrsan*

2002

5th Gran Premio del Jockey Club e Coppa d'Oro (Group 1) (San Siro, October 20) 3yo+ 12f Soft **103** 8 ran ● **5th** Jefferson Smurfit Memorial Irish St Leger (Group 1) (Curragh, September 14) 3yo+ 1m6f Good to firm **106** (TS 79) 8 ran ● **3rd** Credit Suisse Private Banking Pokal (Group 1) (Cologne, August 11) 3yo+ 12f Soft **113** 7 ran ● **1st** Princess of Wales's UAE Equestrian And Racing Federation Stakes (Group 2) (Newmarket (July), July 9) 3yo+ 12f Good to soft **118** (TS 108) 7 ran ● **3rd** Hardwicke Stakes (Group 2) (Ascot, June 22) 4yo+ 12f Good to firm **119** (TS 89) 7 ran ● **2nd** Sagitta Jockey Club Stakes (Group 2) (Newmarket, May 3) 4yo+ 12f Good **120** (TS 76) 9 ran

Other notable runs

2001 2nd Jefferson Smurfit Memorial Irish St Leger (Group 1) (Curragh, September 15) 3yo+ 1m6f Good to firm **121** (TS 104) 8 ran ● **2nd** Stan James Geoffrey Freer Stakes (Group 2) (Newbury, August 18) 3yo+ 1m5½f Good to firm **121** (TS 105) 5 ran ● **3rd** Vodafone Coronation Cup (Group 1) (Epsom, June 8) 4yo+ 12f Good to firm **116** (TS 90) 6 ran ● **1st** Sagitta Jockey Club Stakes (Group 2) (Newmarket, May 4) 4yo+ 12f Good **121** (TS 91) 7 ran **2000 1st** Rothmans Royals St Leger (Group 1) (Doncaster, September 9) 3yo 1m6½f Good to firm **119** (TS 91) 11 ran ● **1st** Peugeot Gordon Stakes (Group 3) (Goodwood, August 1) 3yo 12f Good to firm **118** (TS 100) 10 ran ● **1st** Victor Chandler Chester Vase (Group 3) (Chester, May 9) 3yo 12½f Good **104** (TS 102) 8 ran ● **1st** Peter Smith Memorial Maiden Stakes (Newbury, April 14) 3yo 11f Soft **85** (TS 4) 6 ran

you don't want firing the bullets is Persian Punch. Had it been any other horse, Millenary would probably have ended his season on a high, but the David Elsworth-trained veteran finally regained the lead in the last stride or two and claimed his third win in the race.

Millenary has now proved himself effective from 12 to 16 furlongs, and especially so at Newmarket, where he has yet to finish out of the first two in six outings, all in Pattern company. Although he is unlikely

Millenary

bay horse, 21-4-1997

		Red God	Nasrullah
			Spring Run
	Blushing Groom		
		Runaway Bride	Wild Risk
			Aimee
Rainbow Quest b 1981			
		Herbager	Vandale
			Flagette
	I Will Follow		
		Where You Lead	Raise A Native
			Noblesse
		Lyphard	Northern Dancer
			Goofed
	Dancing Brave		
		Navajo Princess	Drone
			Olmec
Ballerina b 1991			
		Dancer's Image	Native Dancer
			Noors Image
	Dancing Shadow		
		Sunny Valley	Val de Loir
			Sunland

Bred by Abergwaun Farms

Sire Rainbow Quest

Won 6 of 14 races, inc. Great Voltigeur S.-Gr2, Coronation Cup-Gr1, Prix de l'Arc de Triomphe-Gr1. Also 2nd in Dewhurst S-Gr1, Irish Derby-Gr1, Eclipse S.-Gr1, 3rd in Prix du Jockey-Club-Gr1, King George VI & Queen Elizabeth S-Gr1, 4th in 2,000 Guineas-Gr1. Medium-sized, attractive, good mover, somewhat light and leggy in training. Top-class performer in each of 3 seasons, only once out of the frame, effective on any ground except heavy. Sire of Gr1 winners: Knight's Baroness, Quest For Fame, Saumarez, Sought Out, Armiger, Bright Generation, Raintrap, Urgent Request, Rainbow Dancer, Sakura Laurel, Sunshack, Spectrum, Fiji, Croco Rouge, Nedawi, Special Quest, Edabiya, Millenary.

Dam Ballerina

Won 1 of 5 races. Lengthy, quite attractive type, good mover. Seemed to stay 10f. Lightly raced, and only on good or faster surface. Dam of: Little Giant (1996 c by Caerleon; placed at 2 in Ireland), Millenary (1997 c by Rainbow Quest; Classic winner), Head In The Clouds (1998 f by Rainbow Quest; winner), Angel Of The Gwaun (1999 f by Sadler's Wells; unraced), Let The Lion Roar (2001 c by Sadler's Wells; winner).

Pedigree assessment

There is little or no demand for St Leger winners at stud these days, so they might as well race on until they cease to be competitive as racehorses. There was no sign that Millenary, the hero of 2000 on Town Moor, had lost his zest for the game as a six-year-old and it is a shame that breeders do not want his admirable attributes, though that is a bonus for racegoers. *TM*

to be risked when it's really firm, he is not so beholden to the ground as has sometimes been suggested.

He will now have to manage without regular jockey Pat Eddery, who has ridden him in all but a handful of races, but there is no other reason why he should not continue to hold his own in all but the very best company – granted just a bit more luck.

Mineshaft (USA)

4yo bay or brown colt **131**

A P Indy (USA) - Prospectors Delite (USA) (Mr Prospector (USA))

Owner W S Farish

Trainer N J Howard

Breeder W S Farish, James Elkins And W T Webber Jr

Career: **18** starts	won **10**	second **3**	third **1**	£**1,430,703** win and place

By James Willoughby

TO WATCH Mineshaft do his thing was less a reminder of the awe that thoroughbreds can engender than a complete revelation. These words are used carefully, for few have inspired the same depth of feeling in those who watch them run.

Define a brilliant racehorse as you choose. Perhaps by the unique combination of his famous triumphs; perhaps by the glowing tributes of his connections; perhaps by the memory of a single moment of his career. Mineshaft had glorious association with all these things, but mostly he represented something quite precious to those who believe in the merits of the sport.

If champion thoroughbreds had all to be kicked, bullied and driven to express their ability, where would that leave us? How could we delight at their achievements while they recoil in front of our eyes?

Mineshaft was the panacea to this unease; he was the nonpareil who did it all unreservedly from gate to wire and from race to race, not like an automaton processing a set of instructions, but as a free spirit exploring the extent of his athleticism joyfully and revelling in its implications.

On the midpoint of the far turn at Belmont in the Woodward Stakes in September, Mineshaft took off out of Robbie Albarado's hands. The jockey was waiting to pounce on the leader Hold That Tiger, but his mount picked up so suddenly and unexpectedly that Albarado never had a say in when they hit the front.

The onlooker knew that the surge was coming but still could only half-anticipate the force of it. And its impact was affirmed by a split time of 22.8 seconds for the relevant quarter-mile. Imagine: this is not far short of flat-out sprinting speed in a nine-furlong dirt race, which is a stern test of stamina on Belmont's deep, sandy track.

Having freed himself of the field's attentions, Mineshaft strutted his stuff during the final furlong, winning by over four lengths from a rallying

**Mineshaft (Robbie Albarado) lands the Woodward at
Belmont, where he later took the Jockey Club Gold Cup**

Hold That Tiger, who himself ran a fine race and pulled a long way clear
of the remainder.

So many times, circumstance as much as ability can be the mother
of impressive performances. Then emotion enters the equation, encouraging
the enthusiast deeper into his delusion until good becomes great. There
was nothing of this about Mineshaft's Woodward.

Jerry Brown, one of the best-known US speed handicappers, described
Mineshaft as "the fastest horse of all time". His bitter rival, Len Friedman,
would like to have disagreed if only his interpretation would allow. But
he used the word "sensational" when asked about Mineshaft's Woodward
win.

If speed figures don't convince you, maybe the influential US turf writer
Steve Haskin will. "Mineshaft's races became mere formalities. He had
them won so early, he made the last quarter-mile seem irrelevant, serving

2003   Race record

1st Jockey Club Gold Cup (Grade 1) (Dirt) (Belmont Park, September 27) 3yo+ 10f Fast **128** 5 ran. *Raced in 3rd, went 2nd 4f out, led 3f out, pushed clear over 1½f out, easily, beat Quest by 4¼l*

1st Woodward Stakes (Grade 1) (Dirt) (Belmont Park, September 6) 3yo+ 9f Fast **125** 5 ran. *Patiently ridden in 4th, smooth headway around outside 3f out, led on bit just under 2f out, shaken up and quickened clear 1f out, impressive, beat Hold That Tiger by 4¼l*

1st Suburban Handicap (Grade 1) (Dirt) (Belmont Park, July 5) 3yo+ 10f Fast **131** 8 ran. *Always in front rank, cruised into lead 2f out, ridden out, beat Volponi by 2¼l*

2nd Stephen Foster Handicap (Grade 1) (Dirt) (Churchill Downs, June 14) 3yo+ 9f Fast **131** 10 ran. *Bumped start, mid-division to halfway, good headway and led from over 2f out, headed 100yds out, beaten hd by Perfect Drift*

1st Pimlico Special Handicap (Grade 1) (4yo+) (Dirt) (Pimlico, May 16) 4yo+ 9½f Sloppy **126** 9 ran. *Stalked leaders to halfway, headway from over 2f out, challenged inside final 2f and led at distance, driven out, beat Western Pride by 3¾l*

1st Ben Ali Stakes (Grade 3) (Dirt) (Keeneland, April 25) 4yo+ 9f Fast 4 ran. *Checked slightly at start, chased leading pair, took up running inside final 2f, easily, beat American Style by 9l*

1st New Orleans Handicap (Grade 2) (Dirt) (Fair Grounds, March 2) 4yo+ 9f Fast 11 ran. *Broke well, settled behind leader, took up running over 2f out, driven out, beat Olmodavor by 3½l*

2nd Whirlaway Handicap (Grade 3) (Dirt) (Fair Grounds, February 9) 4yo+ 8½f Fast **104** 8 ran. *Mid-division until headway closing stages, stayed on well for second, beaten 2½l by Balto Star*

1st Diplomat Way Handicap (Dirt) (Fair Grounds, January 19) 4yo+ 8½f Fast 7 ran. *Prominent, led over 2f out, all out, beat Learned by nose*

2002

1st Claiming Allowance Race (Dirt) (Fair Grounds, December 20) 3yo+ 1m Fast 9 ran ● **1st** Allowance Race (Dirt) (Churchill Downs, November 27) 3yo+ 1m Fast 11 ran ● **2nd** CPL Industries Challenge Trophy (Conditions Stakes) (Doncaster, September 13) 3yo 1m Good to firm **92** (TS 81) 8 ran ● **6th** Sovereign Stakes (Listed) (Salisbury, August 15) 3yo+ 1m Good to firm **109** (TS 80) 9 ran ● **3rd** Prix Daphnis (Group 3) (Maisons-Laffitte, July 28) 3yo 9f Good **110** (TS 55) 9 ran ● **10th** Britannia Handicap (0-105) (Ascot, June 20) 3yo 1m Good to firm **100** (TS 72) 31 ran ● **4th** Davis Group Fairway Stakes (Listed) (Newmarket, June 1) 3yo 10f Good to firm **101** (TS 69) 5 ran ● **1st** Hastings Maiden Stakes (Newmarket, May 5) 3yo 1m Good to firm **102** (TS 80) 17 ran ● **4th** Dubai International Airport Maiden Stakes (Div II) (Newbury, April 20) 3yo 1m Good to firm **75** (TS 39) 14 ran

as nothing more than an opportunity for the fans to stand and cheer and pay tribute to an extraordinary athlete."

Both Brown and Friedman are leading proponents of the bounce theory, the contrarian philosophy of peaks and troughs, central to which is the tenet that horses are vulnerable to defeat in their next start following an extraordinary effort. Both men agreed that Mineshaft would pay the price for his exuberance when he next appeared in the Jockey Club Gold Cup at Belmont later in September.

And, to a certain extent, they were proved correct. Notwithstanding his four-length defeat of the allowance winner Quest, Mineshaft seemed to return to the ranks of the mortals on this occasion, which proved to be the final opportunity to see him on track. Again he took command turning for home, but this time Albarado had to reach for the whip and coerce, where previously he had only cajoled. Simply put, Mineshaft did not look himself.

Six days after the Gold Cup, Mineshaft was retired on account of a floating bone chip in his off-fore ankle. It was also discovered he had deterioration in a kneebone and a non-displaced chip in the near-fore ankle. All three injuries were minor but could have flared up nastily had he taken up his final challenge in the Breeders' Cup Classic on the sun-baked surface of Santa Anita.

Some wondered whether Mineshaft's physical problems were a convenient excuse to withdraw him from battle at the peak of his commercial value. It had already been announced that he would retire to stud at the end of the season, and a fee of $100,000 per mating had been fixed. When a modern-day stallion can earn $10m a year in the covering shed, even the $4m purse of the Breeders' Cup Classic is considered insufficient temptation to put reputation at risk.

Arguments against the premature retirement of leading thoroughbreds have been made many times before. In Mineshaft's case, the sense of frustration for racing fans was heightened because we never got to see him matched with horses such as Candy Ride, Congaree, Medaglia d'Oro or Empire Maker.

Racing in the US faces the increasing problem that top horses have so many options that they can easily hide instead of run. And that represents the antithesis of what the sport needs to stimulate attention. Unless a remedy to this can be found, the danger is that racing could provide an echo for the drain of interest from boxing, another sport where reputations are protected for the sake of financial gain.

Apart from Volponi, the previous season's shock Breeders' Cup Classic winner whom Mineshaft defeated easily in the Suburban Handicap in July, Perfect Drift was just about the only other top-class horse who dared to take on the imperious Mineshaft. The two conspired to produce the greatest race of the entire US campaign in the Stephen Foster Handicap at Churchill Downs in June.

Mineshaft was coming off his first Grade 1 victory in the Pimlico Special the previous month. Since leaving the care of John Gosden, for whom he had won a Newmarket maiden and been placed in Group 3 company the previous year, the four-year-old had thrived on dirt for his new trainer, Neil Howard. His only defeat had come on his first start on the surface after allowing the talented front-runner Balto Star an easy lead in the Whirlaway Handicap at Fair Grounds in February.

Notwithstanding the rate of Mineshaft's progression, the Stephen Foster was no easy task. For one thing, he was set a lofty task to concede 8lb to Perfect Drift, the previous season's Kentucky Derby third. Furthermore, he drew the outside stall in a field of ten. That he was defeated by only a head was a testament to both his ability and determination.

The result could have been different had not Albarado made the only big-race mistake of his association with Mineshaft. In a race run at a very strong pace, Albarado allowed Mineshaft to open a clear lead as early as the home turn, rather than sitting back and letting him find his way to the lead in a less exhausting fashion.

Having sailed past Perfect Drift and his wily jockey Pat Day, Mineshaft began to lose momentum halfway up the straight as his more evenly ridden rival unleashed his powerful finishing kick. Mineshaft was caught stone cold and, though he rallied tenaciously in the final strides, the post came just too soon.

The Stephen Foster was a stunning race to watch and a reminder that the true worth of a champion thoroughbred so often comes only in defeat. At the weights, Mineshaft put up probably the best handicap performance of the season, an opinion given much credence by Perfect Drift's later exploits.

Mineshaft went on to win the Grade 1 Suburban Handicap at Belmont in July in brilliant style, before being given a short pause which refreshed him for his spectacular performance in the Woodward. This was another good call from Howard, who did not put a foot wrong in his training of the elegant colt.

Mineshaft's career now passes from Howard's hands to those at Lane's End Farm, Kentucky. He seems certain to be highly successful as a stallion, as far as these things can be judged. His sire, AP Indy, is one of the premier middle-distance influences in the US, while his dam comes from one of Will Farish's best families. He also has looks on his side, being variously described as "beautiful", "striking" and "dazzling" by those who saw him in the flesh.

Mineshaft's legacy as a racehorse could be to encourage more international owners to blood their future dirt stars on the kinder training surfaces of Europe. When Howard first looked at Mineshaft on his arrival from Britain, he described him as being a "baked cake", inasmuch as he was already the finished article and bore no physical or mental scars.

There is a far higher attritional rate with young horses in the US because of the unforgiving nature of their dirt surfaces. Most horses are trained at the racetrack, so it is not practical to exercise them on turf, which must be saved for racing. Grade 1-winning dirt horses make it to the top through toughness as much as ability. In Europe, fewer prodigiously talented horses fall by the wayside, which helps to explain why Group 1 racing is generally more competitive than in the US, where small fields predominate for most of the best races.

While it is hard to believe that we will see another top US dirt horse benefit from a European upbringing with quite the spectacular effect of Mineshaft, it is by no means impossible that the great horse might just have started a trend.

Mineshaft

bay/brown colt, 15-2-1999

		Bold Reasoning	Boldnesian
	Seattle Slew		Reason To Earn
		My Charmer	Poker
AP Indy			Fair Charmer
b 1989		Secretariat	Bold Ruler
	Weekend Surprise		Somethingroyal
		Lassie Dear	Buckpasser
			Gay Missile

		Raise A Native	Native Dancer
	Mr Prospector		Raise You
		Gold Digger	Nashua
Prospectors Delite			Sequence
ch 1989		Hoist The Flag	Tom Rolfe
	Up The Flagpole		Wavy Navy
		The Garden Club	Herbager
			Fashion Verdict

Bred by William S Farish, James Elkins & W Temple Webber Jr in Kentucky

Sire AP Indy

A $2.9 million yearling, top price of 1990. Won 8 of 11 races, inc. Hollywood Futurity-Gr1, San Rafael S.-Gr2, Santa Anita Derby-Gr1, Peter Pan S.-Gr2, Belmont S.-Gr1, Breeders' Cup Classic-Gr1. Champion 3yo and Horse of the Year at 3. Raced without medication. Strong, well-made, 16hh. A tip-top performer at 10-12f, probably the best son of his sire, and half-brother to Preakness winner Summer Squall. Sire of: Accelerator (Gr3), A P Assay (Gr2), Pulpit (Gr2), Royal Indy (Gazelle H.-Gr1), Runup The Colors (Alabama S.-Gr1), Tomisue's Delight (Ruffian H.-Gr1, Personal Ensign H.-Gr1), Golden Missile (Pimlico Special H.-Gr1), Let (Gr2), Lu Ravi (Gr2), Old Trieste (Gr2), Stephen Got Even (Donn H.-Gr1), Symboli Indy (NHK Mile Cup-Gr1), Aptitude (Hollywood Gold Cup S.-Gr1, Jockey Club Gold Cup-Gr1), Secret Status (Kentucky Oaks-Gr1, Mother Goose S.-Gr1), A P Valentine (Champagne S.-Gr1), Jilbab (CCA Oaks-Gr1), Jump Start (Gr2), Mineshaft (Pimlico Special H.-Gr1, Suburban H.-Gr1, Woodward S.-Gr1, Jockey Club Gold Cup-Gr1), Passing Shot (Personal Ensign H.-Gr1), Tempera (Breeders' Cup Juvenile Fillies-Gr1), Indy Five Hundred (Garden City H.-Gr1), Yell (Gr2).

Dam Prospectors Delite

Won 6 of 9 races, inc. Fair Grounds Oaks-Gr3, Ashland S.-Gr1, Acorn S.-Gr1. Also 3rd in Kentucky Oaks. Rated 7th-best 3yo filly on Daily Racing Form Handicap, 4lb below champion November Snow. High-class performer at 8-9f. Half-sister to 3 other Graded winners. Dam of: Tomisue's Delight (1994 f by AP Indy; dual Gr1 winner), Delta Music (1995 f by Dixieland Band; stakes-winner, Gr3-placed), Monashee Mountain (1997 c by Danzig; dual Gr3 winner), Rock Slide (1998 c by AP Indy; stakes winner, Gr3-placed), Mineshaft (1999 c by AP Indy; triple Gr1 winner).

Pedigree assessment

When the question was posed after the Jockey Club Gold Cup as to what was the plan for Mineshaft, it was disappointing to get the response that that had been the plan. With Candy Ride already declared an absentee, it seemed he would only have to turn up to collect the Breeders' Cup Classic. With his impeccable pedigree background (for US racing) to complement his impressive performance record, he will not go short of patronage at Will Farish's Lane's End Farm, where he will take up stud duties in 2004 at a fee of $100,000. *TM*

Moon Ballad (Ire)

4yo chestnut colt   **123** a131

Singspiel (Ire) - Velvet Moon (Ire) (Shaadi (USA))

Owner Godolphin

Trainer Saeed Bin Suroor

Breeder Newgate Stud Co

Career: **14** starts | won **5** | second **3** | third **1** | **£2,758,807** win and place

By Richard Austen

I F A horse is going to show top-class form once, and once only, the world's most valuable race is not a bad event in which to do it. Moon Ballad reserved his career best for the Dubai World Cup and, in a race that lacked any established stars on sand, he won it with the sort of ease enjoyed by his stablemate Dubai Millennium three years earlier.

Though well short of the form achieved by Dubai Millennium, this was a top-class show, and one that Moon Ballad failed to repeat, on turf or sand. What followed in Europe and the United States was for the most part an abject failure, but a season that contains victory in the Dubai World Cup cannot really be called a disappointment, can it?

"For me, this is the most important raceday of the season," stated Frankie Dettori in the run-up to the race – just as well, given that there cannot be any doubt that Sheikh Mohammed, his boss, feels the same. The nearby adventures of George Bush and Tony Blair had not boosted the event's wider popularity, though, and only two runners for the first prize of over £2.3 million emerged from the United States, in the shape of recent Grade 1 Donn Handicap winner Harlan's Holiday and the outsider Blue Burner. Nayef, the sole British-trained challenger, had once again spent the winter in Dubai, but the high-class mare Aquarelliste made the journey from France. The previous year's 66-1 runner-up Sei Mei was back, while three others from Saudi Arabia included the Kevin McAuliffe-trained Grundlefoot. In addition to Nayef, the Maktoums fielded Grandera and Moon Ballad, both representing Godolphin, and the rank outsider State Shinto.

Progressive though he was as a three-year-old, when he won the Dante and Select Stakes and was runner-up to Nayef in the Champion Stakes as well as third to High Chaparral in the Derby, Moon Ballad had not matched Grandera's best form. He had, however, made the better impression when winning his Dubai World Cup warm-up. Dettori was

**Moon Ballad (Frankie Dettori) scores a stunning success
in the Dubai World Cup at Nad Al Sheba**

persuaded and, with 11-8 favourite Nayef and 5-1 shot Grandera failing
to match their turf form, he encountered no problems in having his
judgement vindicated. Harlan's Holiday did best of the chasers as Moon
Ballad made all to score by five lengths. "I got the same feeling as I had
when I rode Dubai Millennium," said the winning jockey, "because when
I turned for home I couldn't hear the other horses. All I could hear was
the crowd cheering."

For all the confidence in his camp, Moon Ballad's performance was
a revelation. One explanation was that he was suited by racing on dirt.
Another was proffered by Simon Crisford, Godolphin's racing manager,
when he explained that the horse had improved both mentally and
physically and that in 2002 "we were always thinking of looking to his
four-year-old campaign."

After the Dubai World Cup, none of the plans for Moon Ballad came
to fruition. Dominating a competitive field for the Prince of Wales's Stakes
at Royal Ascot proved completely beyond him, with connections later
stating that they had been too easy on him in the build-up. The winner,

2003   Race record

5th Jockey Club Gold Cup (Grade 1) (Dirt) (Belmont Park, September 27) 3yo+ 10f Fast **89** 5 ran. *Raced in 2nd, disputed lead briefly after 2f, relegated to 3rd 4f out, weakened over 2f out, beaten 23l by Mineshaft*

5th Ireland The Food Island Champion Stakes (Group 1) (Leopardstown, September 6) 3yo+ 10f Good to firm **123** (TS 118) 7 ran. *Settled in 2nd, led 3½f out, strongly pressed straight, headed 1f out, soon no extra, beaten 2¼l by High Chaparral*

5th Sussex Stakes (Group 1) (Goodwood, July 30) 3yo+ 1m Good to soft **116** (TS 93) 9 ran. *Tracked leaders, brought wide into straight, effort over 2f out, pressed leaders under pressure from over 1f out, not quicken last 150yds, beaten 1l by Reel Buddy*

9th Prince of Wales's Stakes (Group 1) (Ascot, June 18) 4yo+ 10f Good to firm **103** (TS 86) 10 ran. *Soon led, narrowly headed 3f out, ridden and weakened 2f out, beaten 13½l by Nayef*

1st Dubai World Cup (Group 1) (Dirt) (Nad Al Sheba, March 29) 4yo+ 10f Fast **131** (TS 110) 11 ran. *Made most, pushed clear over 2f out, ridden out, impressive, beat Harlan's Holiday by 5l*

1st Sheikh Maktoum bin Rashid al Maktoum Challenge (Round II) (Dirt) (Nad Al Sheba, February 13) 4yo+ 9f Fast 6 ran. *Made all, ridden clear 1½f out, comfortably, beat Go Underground by 6l*

2002

2nd Emirates Airline Champion Stakes (Group 1) (Newmarket, October 19) 3yo+ 10f Good **123** (TS 97) 11 ran ● **1st** Select Stakes (Group 3) (Goodwood, September 14) 3yo+ 10f Good **122** (TS 86) 6 ran ● **3rd** Vodafone Derby (Group 1) (Epsom, June 8) 3yo 12f Good to soft **109** (TS 78) 12 ran ● **1st** Convergent Dante Stakes (Group 2) (York, May 15) 3yo 10½f Good to firm **118** (TS 84) 9 ran ● **2nd** Pearl And Coutts Newmarket Stakes (Listed) (Newmarket, May 3) 3yo 10f Good **108** (TS 60) 7 ran ● **4th** UAE Derby (Group 2) (Dirt) (Nad Al Sheba, March 23) 3yo 10f Fast **109** 14 ran ● **1st** As Nasr Leisureland & Cyclone Cup (Dirt) (Nad Al Sheba, March 2) 3yo+ 9f Fast 6 ran

Nayef, had a pacemaker to try to deny Moon Ballad an easy lead. In the Sussex Stakes at Goodwood, the Godolphin team perplexingly did the job themselves by assigning front-running duties to Blatant; Moon Ballad never got his head in front and finished fifth. He performed a lot better in a red-hot line-up for the Irish Champion Stakes in September – with the Ballydoyle team taking their turn to field the pacemaker – but it was good enough once again only for fifth behind High Chaparral.

This run appeared to set Moon Ballad up nicely for a return to dirt in preparation for his long-term target, the Breeders' Cup Classic, but he was a poor last of five in the Jockey Club Gold Cup at Belmont Park. This inauspicious first encounter with the Americans on their own patch not surprisingly turned out to be his last, and the announcement came two weeks later that he and Grandera had been retired. They will stand at stud under Darley management in Japan.

Moon Ballad was suited by a mile and a quarter. His best turf efforts were on fast ground, but they were not in the same league as his Dubai World Cup triumph. He often had his tongue tied, but after his non-staying third in the 2002 Derby he was fitted with headgear only once, at Leopardstown. The various aids he wore may or may not have had some role in explaining away a spectacularly mixed season.

Moon Ballad   *chestnut colt, 4-3-1999*

		Sadler's Wells	**Northern Dancer** Fairy Bridge
	In The Wings		
		High Hawk	Shirley Heights Sunbittern
Singspiel b 1992			
		Halo	Hail To Reason Cosmah
	Glorious Song		
		Ballade	Herbager Miss Swapsco
		Danzig	**Northern Dancer** Pas de Nom
	Shaadi		
		Unfurled	Hoist The Flag Lemon Souffle
Velvet Moon b 1991			
		Relkino	Relko Pugnacity
	Park Special		
		Balilla	Balidar Fighting

Bred by Newgate Stud Company in Ireland. 350,000gns Tattersalls October yearling

Sire Singspiel

Won 9 of 20 races, inc. Gordon Richards S.-Gr3, Select S.-Gr3, Canadian International S.-Gr1, Japan Cup-Gr1, Coronation Cup-Gr1, Eclipse S.-Gr1, York International S.-Gr1. Also 2nd in Coronation Cup-Gr1 and Breeders' Cup Turf-Gr1, 4th in King George VI & Queen Elizabeth S-Gr1. Strong, medium-sized, quite attractive type. Tough, game and consistent performer, effective on any ground, top-class from 10-12f. Retired after having fractured off-fore cannonbone shortly before 1997 Breeders' Cup Turf. Sire of: Moon Ballad (Dubai World Cup-Gr1), Songlark (Gr3), Sweet Folly (Gr3), Via Milano (Gr3).

Dam Velvet Moon

Won 4 of 12 races, inc. Lowther S.-Gr2. Tall, quite attractive sort. Effective on good and fast ground, below form on soft. Tended to pull, had high head carriage, did not always appear resolute, but smart at her best, with useful turn of foot, and stayed 10f well. Dam of: unnamed (1996 c by Generous; died as a foal), Velvet Lady (1997 f by Nashwan; winner), Syria (1998 f by Halling; unraced), Moon Ballad (1999 c by Singspiel; Gr1 winner), Velouette (2000 f by Darshaan; unraced), Velvet Queen (2001 f by Singspiel; unraced to date).

Pedigree assessment

The form of the Dubai World Cup winner regularly seems to be overrated, or there is some other reason why horses apparently capable of great things on sand in March tend not to register that level of performance subsequently on other surfaces. Moon Ballad is the latest to have followed that pattern, seducing most observers into the belief that his five-length triumph at Nad Al Sheba represented significantly improved form, but failing to reach a place in four later efforts, and only in the Irish Champion Stakes attaining the standard he had achieved at Newmarket the previous year. His declared long-term objective, the Breeders' Cup Classic, went by without him, following his dismal display when last of five in Mineshaft's Jockey Club Gold Cup. He has departed for stud duty in Japan, where his sire scored one of his notable victories. *TM*

Mr Dinos (Ire)

4yo bay colt   **123**

Desert King (Ire) - Spear Dance (Gay Fandango (USA))
Owner C Shiacolas
Trainer P F I Cole
Breeder Mocklerstown House Stud

Career: **12** starts | won **6** | second **3** | third **1** | **£345,658** win and place

By Graham Dench

EMOTIONAL scenes in the winner's enclosure are hardly uncommon, but few can have expected to see the normally aloof and urbane Paul Cole with tears in his eyes when Mr Dinos returned after destroying his 11 rivals in the Gold Cup at Royal Ascot.

Cole, who had not been as emotional even when winning the Derby with Generous 12 years previously, had been struggling with unhealthy horses for weeks, around 70 per cent of his string having been hit with flu or summer colds, and he and his staff, notably long-serving groom Tom Pirie, had gone to enormous lengths to keep Mr Dinos isolated from infection, only to find an additional obstacle in the immediate run-up to the race, when the ground dried out so much that Mr Dinos might not even have run if owner Constantinos Shiacolas was not already committed to travelling over from Cyprus.

Those circumstances no doubt contributed to Cole's emotional state, but it was plainly the race itself that got to him above all, as he explained afterwards when he said: "If I had to name a race I wanted to win it would be the Gold Cup. For me the Gold Cup is Royal Ascot. I've never had a runner in the race before, and it's a race I've dreamed of winning. This is awesome for me. It's nearly as exciting as winning the Derby."

Mr Dinos was hugely impressive in the Gold Cup, given a typical no-nonsense ride by Kieren Fallon, who was booked when it became clear that Frankie Dettori, who had been on board for a classy defeat of Pole Star in Sandown's Henry II Stakes three weeks earlier, would be required for old rival Mamool.

Fallon had Mr Dinos perfectly poised throughout and after sending him past Persian Punch approaching the final turn he wasted no time in pressing home the advantage. Once Mr Dinos was in front nothing ever looked remotely like troubling him and he forged further and further clear before coasting home a six-length winner from Persian Punch, who

Mr Dinos (Kieren Fallon) coasts home alone in the Gold Cup at Royal Ascot in June

got the better of Pole Star, Jardines Lookout, Mamool and Savannah Bay in a good battle for the places.

It was an overwhelming display of superiority, one of the best perform-ances recorded over an extreme distance in years and an effort that marked down Mr Dinos as the one to beat in Cup races for the foreseeable future. Sadly, however, Cole's fears about the ground proved well founded. Within days it emerged that the colt was "a little sore" and would therefore be out of action until September, at least, when the Irish St Leger was mooted as a possible target. Unseasonably dry weather held up Mr Dinos' preparation, and the Irish St Leger went by without him. However, Longchamp's Prix du Cadran was nominated as an alternative target and, following a workout after racing at Newbury one afternoon, Cole expressed himself well satisfied with the colt's condition ahead of that race.

No horse had won both the Gold Cup and the Cadran in the same season since Sagaro in 1976, but Mr Dinos stood out on form and was heavily odds-on. Unfortunately, we did not see the real Mr Dinos that day. Nor for that matter did we see the real Persian Punch. In conditions more akin to Cheltenham in March – they were far more holding and

2003   Race record

6th Prix du Cadran - Casinos Barriere (Group 1) (Longchamp, October 5) 4yo+ 2m4f Holding **93** 10 ran. *Raced in 4th, pushed along over 5f out, ridden and under pressure approaching straight, 3rd straight but no impression, beaten 28l by Westerner*

1st Gold Cup (Group 1) (Ascot, June 19) 4yo+ 2m4f Good to firm **123** (TS 69) 12 ran. *Raced in 3rd until tracked leader 9f out, led over 3f out, forged clear from 2f out, easily, beat Persian Punch by 6l*

1st Bonusprint Henry II Stakes (Group 2) (Sandown, May 26) 4yo+ 2m½f Good to firm **121** (TS 92) 10 ran. *Tracked leading pair, effort to lead over 2f out, shaken up and in command over 1f out, pushed out, beat Pole Star by 2½l*

2002

1st Prix Royal-Oak (Group 1) (Longchamp, October 27) 3yo+ 1m7½f Heavy **115** (TS 14) 7 ran ● **5th** Rothmans Royals St Leger (Group 1) (Doncaster, September 14) 3yo 1m6½f Good to firm **110** (TS 79) 8 ran ● **1st** Prix Berteux - Etalon Marchand de Sable (Group 3) (Vichy, July 27) 3yo 1m7f Good **115** 5 ran ● **2nd** Foster's Lager Northumberland Plate (Handicap) (Newcastle, June 29) 3yo+ 2m Good to firm **112** (TS 62) 16 ran ● **2nd** Queen's Vase (Group 3) (Ascot, June 21) 3yo 2m Good to firm **107** (TS 64) 14 ran ● **1st** Betfair.com Conditions Stakes (York, May 14) 3yo 1m6f Good to firm **99** 4 ran ● **1st** Jockey Club 250th Anniversary Maiden Stakes (Newmarket, April 16) 3yo 12f Good to firm **89** (TS 62) 5 ran ● **3rd** Tom Collins Maiden Stakes (Kempton, April 1) 3yo 11f Good **84** 5 ran

Other runs

2001 **2nd** EBF Maiden Stakes (Ascot, July 27) 2yo 7f Good to firm **90** (TS 64) 6 ran

gluey than when Mr Dinos had won the Prix Royal-Oak (French St Leger) on the same course the previous October – the two Ascot principals were toiling a long way from home and trailed home streets behind the good French stayer Westerner.

No serious damage was done, but Cole resisted the temptation to bid for a repeat win in the Royal-Oak and put him away for 2004, with the Gold Cup very much the intended centrepiece of what is likely to be a fairly limited campaign once again if he is to avoid firm ground as much as possible.

The Gold Cup has had probably as high a proportion of multiple winners as any mixed-age Group 1, with Sagaro, Gildoran, Le Moss and Kayf Tara all multiple modern winners who won the race for the first time at Mr Dinos' age, and Sadeem, Drum Taps and Royal Rebel among later starters who achieved a similar feat in recent times. The chances of Mr Dinos following in their footsteps are excellent, for only Westerner, who may need the mud, can touch him on form and, so far, it is hard to identify an emerging threat among the three-year-olds of 2003.

The one worry is the ground. It is often said that horses who do not enjoy racing on firm ground will go on it once. Mr Dinos has won four times now on quickish ground, but the Gold Cup ground was the firmest he has encountered and it left its mark. What if the ground comes up just as firm again?

Mr Dinos

bay colt, 19-2-1999

		Northern Dancer
	Danzig	Pas de Nom
Danehill		
	Razyana	His Majesty
		Spring Adieu
Desert King		
b 1994		**Northern Dancer**
	Nureyev	Special
Sabaah		
	Dish Dash	Bustino
		Loose Cover
		Aristophanes
	Forli	Trevisa
Gay Fandango		
	Gay Violin	Sir Gaylord
		Blue Violin
Spear Dance		
b 1982		Rustam
	Double Jump	Fair Bid
Lancette		
	Persian Union	Persian Gulf
		Reconcile

Bred by Mocklerstown House Stud in Ireland.
IR£40,000gns Goffs Orby yearling; 42,000gns Tattersalls Breeze-Up 2yo

Sire Desert King

Won 5 of 12 races, inc. National S.-Gr1, Tetrarch S.-Gr3, Irish 2,000 Guineas-Gr1, Irish Derby-Gr1. Also placed 2nd in York International S.-Gr1, Irish Champion S-Gr1. Attractive, robust-looking individual, particularly impressive behind the saddle. Powerful galloper, with a rather round action, effective on firmish and softish ground. High-class performer from 8-12f. Sire of: Makybe Diva (Melbourne Cup-Gr1), Maranilla (Gr3), Mr Dinos (Prix Royal-Oak-Gr1, Gold Cup-Gr1).

Dam Spear Dance

Won 2 of 22 races. Just a useful handicapper on her day, best at 3 and in the mud. Dam of: Masai Warrior (1987 g by Petorius; winner), Lambada Girl (1988 f by Petorius; winner), Bahi (1989 c by Tate Gallery; Listed winner, Gr3-placed in Australia), Running Spear (1990 f by Commanche Run; unraced), Mountain Hop (1992 f by Tirol; unraced), Rainbow Java (1993 f by Fairy King; winner), Risk Material (1995 c by Danehill; Gr3 winner), Specifiedrisk (1996 f by Turtle Island; unraced), Lake Nyasa (1997 f by Lake Coniston; unplaced), Mr Dinos (1999 c by Desert King; dual Gr1 winner).

Pedigree assessment

Danehill (Cork and Orrery) and Gay Fandango (Jersey) collected Royal Ascot victories in dashes up the straight course. Their grandson Mr Dinos had to do a lap of the round course in addition to notch his. The staying elements transmitted in his parents' female lines are what is crucial to Mr Dinos, a natural stayer who added the 2003 Gold Cup to the previous year's Group 1 victory in the Prix Royal-Oak. He won it in great style, too, with one of the best performances in that race in recent years, but could not follow up in his only subsequent race, the Prix du Cadran, in which, like several of his rivals, he was undone by the gluey consistency of the Longchamp mud. In any other conditions he relishes extreme distances and it will take a good one to thwart his bid for a repeat Gold Cup win in 2004. *TM*

Mubtaker (USA)

6yo chestnut horse   **132**

Silver Hawk (USA) - Gazayil (USA) (Irish River (Fr))
Owner Hamdan Al Maktoum
Trainer M P Tregoning
Breeder Warren W Rosenthal

Career: **17** starts | won **8** | second **6** | third **3** | **£479,497** win and place

By Richard Austen

"AN EQUINE superstar", "truly exceptional" and "a genius" were among the descriptions applied to Dalakhani. So how, then, should we describe Mubtaker, the 33-1 shot who ran Dalakhani to three-quarters of a length when the French champion produced the best performance of his career in the Prix de l'Arc de Triomphe?

Mubtaker is three years older than Dalakhani and was first seen on a racecourse back in October 1999, but anyone thinking they knew everything about him was in for a surprise at Longchamp on October 5. Never before seen in a Group 1 race, not even in Italy or Germany and let alone a race like the Arc, Mubtaker came second in the most important race on the European calendar and ran on strongly to keep himself at Dalakhani's quarters. A superstar, truly exceptional, a genius? Well, Mubtaker is only just behind him.

Mubtaker was lightly raced for a horse that had run in each of the last five seasons; the Arc was his 17th race and Dalakhani's ninth. During those first 16 appearances Mubtaker compiled a record of eight wins, five seconds and three thirds, never therefore out of the placings.

Having run once to take second place at Deauville as a two-year-old for David Loder, he failed to make the grade in two private trials with Godolphin at Nad Al Sheba the following April and his official three-year-old career did not begin until late October, in the care now of Marcus Tregoning, when he hacked up in a maiden at Newbury. Third of four in a Listed race the following month, he plied his trade at that level almost exclusively in an eight-race four-year-old career, but three victories earned him his first crack at a Group race that November, only for him to disappoint when third of five at 8-13 in the St Simon Stakes, transferred from Newbury to Newmarket.

Disappointments are unheard of in the rest of Mubtaker's career on the racecourse – those came when that career was interrupted by injury

Mubtaker (Richard Hills) runs out an easy winner of the Geoffrey Freer at Newbury in August

– but the post-Arc comparison with a horse like Dalakhani, a very good Prix du Jockey-Club winner, was something undreamed of for nearly all of it. At the start of the 2002 turf season, for instance, Tregoning stated that Mubtaker "has improved with age and I see him filling the void left by the now-retired Albarahin".

Albarahin was another son of Silver Hawk noted for his consistency and tenacity over several seasons, but it was not until almost the last throw of the dice that he won his first and only Group race. There are other similarities in the way that both he and Mubtaker failed to cut it early on with Godolphin and had injuries, but the strong suspicion is that Tregoning also saw some comparison in terms of class. For all his admirable qualities, Albarahin was not by any stretch of the imagination a top-class performer.

Mubtaker's opportunities to win his first Group race during 2002 turned out to be extremely limited, initially because of an injury sustained while in training in Dubai early in the year. However, he did the job at the second time of asking that summer, when justifying favouritism in clear-cut fashion in the Geoffrey Freer Stakes at Newbury. "He's a wonderful horse for us and it was important for him to win a Group race, so job done," said his trainer.

2nd Prix de l'Arc de Triomphe Lucien Barriere (Group 1) (Longchamp, October 5) 3yo+ 12f
Holding **132** (TS 123) 13 ran. *Always prominent, went 2nd over 4f out, led over 3f out, headed
1f out, ran on same pace, beaten ¾l by Dalakhani*

1st Coral September Stakes (Group 3) (Kempton, September 6) 3yo+ 12f Good **129** (TS 111)
5 ran. *Led, narrowly headed over 1m, led again 4f out, shaken up over 2f out, galloped on
strongly and drew away from over 1f out, beat First Charter by 5l*

1st Stan James Geoffrey Freer Stakes (Group 2) (Newbury, August 16) 3yo+ 1m5½f Good to
firm **124** (TS 100) 5 ran. *Held up in touch, went 2nd 4f out, led over 3f out, clear over 2f out,
comfortably, beat Systematic by 3½l*

1st cantorindex.co.uk 'Instant Account Opening' Steventon Stakes (Listed) (Newbury, July 19)
3yo+ 10f Good to firm **118** (TS 100) 7 ran. *Tracked leaders, went 2nd over 5f out, led over 2f
out, ridden over 1f out, ran on gamely final furlong, beat Parasol by 1½l*

2002

1st Stan James Geoffrey Freer Stakes (Group 2) (Newbury, August 17) 3yo+ 1m5½f Good to
firm **123** (TS 87) 7 ran ● **2nd** Princess of Wales's UAE Equestrian And Racing Federation
Stakes (Group 2) (Newmarket (July), July 9) 3yo+ 12f Good to soft **118** (TS 108) 7 ran

Other notable runs

2001 3rd Levy Board St Simon Stakes (Group 3) (Newmarket, November 2) 3yo+ 12f Good
to soft **110** (TS 99) 5 ran ● **1st** Fishpools Furnishings Godolphin Stakes (Listed) (Newmarket,
October 5) 3yo+ 12f Good **121** (TS 106) 9 ran ● **2nd** Dubai Arc Trial (Listed) (Newbury,
September 22) 3yo+ 11f Good to firm **118** (TS 92) 5 ran ● **1st** Ladbrokes Fred Archer Stakes
(Listed) (Newmarket (July), June 30) 4yo+ 12f Good to firm **117** (TS 96) 7 ran ● **2nd**
Regional Newspaper Of The Year - Leicester Mercury Stakes (Listed) (Leicester, June 17) 4yo+
12f Good **117** (TS 97) 8 ran ● **1st** Badger Brewery Festival Stakes (Listed) (Goodwood, May
24) 4yo+ 10f Good to firm **111** (TS 58) 5 ran ● **3rd** Magnolia Stakes (Listed) (Kempton, April
16) 4yo+ 10f Soft **108** (TS 93) 9 ran **2000 3rd** CIU Serlby Stakes (Listed) (Doncaster,
November 4) 3yo+ 12f Heavy **98** (TS 69) 4 ran ● **1st** Vineyard At Stockcross Maiden Stakes
(Newbury, October 21) 3yo 10f Heavy **101** (TS 90) 12 ran **1999 2nd** Prix de Caen
(Deauville, October 20) 2yo 7f Good 5 ran

Much grander aspirations had to be put on hold. Mubtaker's blood
test failed to please before the Canadian International and, after falling
to the bout of coughing in his stable before the Breeders' Cup Turf, he
failed to bounce back in time for the Hong Kong Vase. The stop-start
nature of Mubtaker's career was no help in bringing the true extent of
his ability to the fore, but the fact that he was targeted at such races
indicated that he was now considered as a good deal more than a successor
to Albarahin.

The horse who really looms large in Mubtaker's career, though, is Nayef.
Albarahin's final race saw him perform pacemaking duties for Nayef in
the 2001 Champion Stakes and in the two seasons since, while Mubtaker
merited attention in his own right, he was just as likely to be mentioned
when Nayef was in action instead, in his role as Nayef's lead horse and
work companion.

When Nayef went back to Dubai in the winter of 2002-03, Mubtaker was there with him and in training once again for a race at the Dubai World Cup meeting. For the second time in a year, positive reports about the way Mubtaker was working preceded only a spell on the sidelines when he picked up an injury to a joint on his near-hind.

"He has done sterling service leading Nayef and is a very solid performer in his own right," was how Tregoning summed him up in his Stable Tour interview in the Racing Post early in the 2003 season. "I'm sure he can win another Group race."

When Mubtaker made it back to the track, it was a little later in July than in 2002 but it was immediately apparent that he was as good as ever. He had not raced over a trip as short as a mile and a quarter since May 2001 but, aided by a good pace, he was still able to see off a smart field in a Listed race at Newbury.

"Mubtaker adores fast ground and he's blessed with the talent to win at any distance from a mile to two miles," reported the winning trainer. At the upper end of that range, the Melbourne Cup made plenty of appeal to the winning connections, but when further celebration ensued after Mubtaker's second Geoffrey Freer four weeks later, a realisation that he was now likely to be handicapped out of Melbourne Cup contention came with it. That and the new hope that Mubtaker could give a good account in top mile-and-a-half races.

There were only five runners in the Geoffrey Freer, with Mubtaker at 4-6, and it is not hard to pick holes in the form, but third-placed Mamool was just about to register a Group 1 double in Germany and, more importantly, there was no mistaking the fact that, in beating Systematic by three and a half lengths, Mubtaker did so with ease. "I know I train him," said Tregoning, "but I was impressed."

Two years earlier, Albarahin went to the Longchamp Arc meeting and took advantage of a small field to register his Group success in the Prix Dollar. Mubtaker was now on course for the Arc itself but he still had time to add another victory in much calmer waters in another five-runner race for the Coral September Stakes at Kempton. In the form he showed earlier in the summer and with a record that was almost impossible to fault for reliability, Mubtaker stood out in the 12-furlong contest and was sent off at 8-13.

The following day's Group 1 Grosser Bugatti Preis over the same distance at Baden-Baden featured two of the horses he had beaten in the Geoffrey Freer and one of them, Mamool, won it. The prize-money in Germany was about 16 times the amount that Mubtaker was running for in the September Stakes. He would have had an excellent chance of taking it too judged on his Kempton display, in which he made most of the running and drew five lengths clear of March Stakes winner First Charter, to whom he was conceding 5lb, in the final furlong.

In the Arc, Mubtaker was sent off at 33-1 on the Pari-Mutuel, the British bookmakers having been more circumspect that morning and priced him up at odds ranging from 25-1 to 14-1. First Charter was running as a pacemaker. No six-year-old had ever won the race and Motrico's being a seven-year-old when he won it for the second time back in 1932 probably did not lend much encouragement either.

Only five six-year-olds – and no horse older than that – had ever been placed and the only one to have done so in the last 40 years was Ardross in 1982. Out of a field of 13 for the latest edition, only Doyen, Policy Maker and Mubtaker had not previously run in a Group 1 race. The form line through Mamool suggested that Mubtaker could have been a Group 1 winner as recently as four weeks previously, but Mubtaker's first venture at the top level was still in doubt until a couple of hours beforehand. The assumption, one held by his connections, was that the holding ground would be against him.

He had not raced on soft or heavy, though, since his two starts at three years and his reappearance at four, when he won his maiden and showed useful form in defeat in two Listed races. It is hard to put much of a gloss on 18th of 19 for the Tregoning-trained Dominica in the Prix de l'Abbaye, but it was after that race that the trainer gave the green light to Mubtaker's Arc challenge.

Early in the straight, Mubtaker confounded the odds and the doubts by quickening three lengths clear. From a wide draw, he had been ridden close to the lead by Richard Hills and had a start on the apparent principals once he set the race alight with his bid for home three furlongs out. But although only one horse emerged to try to chase him down, it was pretty quickly apparent that that horse would have his measure. Mubtaker relinquished the lead to Dalakhani a furlong out and, although he battled back with the utmost tenacity and the favourite could not put daylight between them, the decisive move had been made. "You know how fond we are of this horse after all the work he has done with Nayef and the Group races he's won," said an emotional Hills. "He's as brave as they come."

Nayef has been retired but Mubtaker is due to race on. Tregoning is accumulating a superb record with his older horses and it would be a surprise if Group 1 victory did not come Mubtaker's way, presuming that injury does not intervene. Reflecting on Mubtaker's role in Nayef's quadruple Group 1-winning career, Tregoning said: "He led him in a lot of his work, not just galloping but cantering – he was a vital part of our armour. I think Nayef needed a horse like him to carry him along and he was certainly well capable of doing that."

With Nayef probably ideally suited by a mile and a quarter, whereas Mubtaker, in Tregoning's view, would stay a mile and three-quarters "standing on his head", Nayef was the quicker horse in their home work, probably the longest of which was conducted over a mile. None of Nayef's racecourse performances, however, rates so highly as that put up by his lead horse Mubtaker in the Arc.

Mubtaker

chestnut horse, 31-2-1997

		Hail To Reason	Turn-to
			Nothirdchance
	Roberto		
		Bramalea	Nashua
Silver Hawk			Rarelea
b 1979			
		Amerigo	Nearco
			Sanlinea
	Gris Vitesse		
		Matchiche	Mat de Cocagne
			Chimere Fabuleuse
		Riverman	Never Bend
			River Lady
	Irish River		
		Irish Star	Klairon
			Botany Bay
Gazayil			
ch 1985		Far North	Northern Dancer
			Fleur
	Close Comfort		
		Caterina	Princely Gift
			Radiopye

Bred by Warren W Rosenthal in Kentucky

Sire Silver Hawk

Won 3 of 8 races, inc. Craven Stakes-Gr3. Also 2nd in Irish Derby-Gr1, 3rd in Derby-Gr1. Cracked a cannonbone in July at 3 and retired. Smallish, strong, well-made sort, high-class from a mile up, well suited by 12f. Sire of: Dansil (Gr2), Hawkster (Norfolk S.-Gr1, Secretariat S.-Gr1, Oak Tree Invitational S.-Gr1), Lady In Silver (Prix de Diane-Gr1), Silver Ending (Pegasus H.-Gr1), Magnificient Star (Yorkshire Oaks-Gr1), Red Bishop (San Juan Capistrano H.-Gr1), Silver Wisp (Gr2), Silver Wizard (Gr2), Zoonaqua (Oak Leaf S.-Gr1), Devil River Peek (Premio Vittorio di Capua-Gr1), Hawk Attack (Secretariat S.-Gr1), Memories Of Silver (Queen Elizabeth II Invitational Challenge Cup S.-Gr1, Beverly D S.-Gr1), Benny The Dip (Derby S.-Gr1), Albarahin (Gr2), Grass Wonder (Asahi Hai Sansai S.-Gr1, Takarazuka Kinen-Gr1, Arima Kinen-Gr1), Mutafaweq (St Leger S.-Gr1, Deutschland Preis-Gr1), Mubtaker (Gr2), Wonder Again (Garden City H.-Gr1), Almushahar (Gr2).

Dam Gazayil

Won 2 of 11 races, a Chepstow maiden at 2 and a minor race at Morphettville (Australia) at 4. Lengthy, sparely-made type who showed early promise, but made little physical progress, and showed only modest form. Dam of: Inspirasi (1991 f by Jackson Square; winner in Australia); Prime Ville (1993 f by Polish Patriot; winner in Australia), Cinnamon Sky (1994 g by Damister; winner in Australia), Crystal Downs (1996 f by Alleged; winner, Gr1-placed), Mubtaker (1997 c by Silver Hawk; dual Gr2 winner), El Giza (1998 c by Cozzene; unplaced), unnamed (1999 f by Thunder Gulch; unraced), Spirit Of Gold (2000 c by Silver Hawk; unplaced), Tree Chopper (2001 c by Woodman; winner).

Pedigree assessment

Mubtaker convinced any remaining doubters of his Group 1 quality with a tremendous effort in the Arc de Triomphe; it took a genuine star to beat him and he had several proven celebrities in arrears. He will be approaching the veteran stage in 2004, but he is still comparatively lightly raced, does not know how to turn in a dull effort and seems certain to make his presence felt again in top middle-distance company. He must be acknowledged as one of the best sons of his underrated sire and runs true to that half of his pedigree, travelling easily through his races, quickening up well and staying on gamely. A thoroughly admirable performer, and, considering his former physical problems, a notable tribute to his trainer's prowess. *TM*

Musical Chimes (USA)

3yo bay filly   **115**

In Excess - Note Musicale (Sadler's Wells (USA))

Owner Maktoum Al Maktoum

Trainer N Drysdale

Breeder Gainsborough Farm

Career: **10** starts | won **2** | second **1** | third **1** | **£241,210** win and place

By Robert Carter

FIRST-TIME blinkers are not the answer for every trainer's problem horse, nor are they a gift to the alert backer. They turned the late-running Musical Chimes into a wild horse in the early stages of the Breeders' Cup Filly & Mare Turf.

Musical Chimes did not start as quickly as some but was ridden along and soon forced her way among the leaders on the short downhill run to the main turf course. She was going fast and pulling where the turf crosses the dirt track and she jumped onto it. She was third as they hit the grass once more but objected to Gary Stevens' attempts at restraint and jumped again in front of the stands. Musical Chimes, who was also tried in a rubber bit, finally settled in fourth but was in trouble before reaching the far turn and was beaten when hampered by Tates Creek on the inside just over two furlongs out. It was a sorry end to an excellent season but, if she stays in training and never sees a pair of blinkers again, she could dominate the strong programme for fillies and mares in southern California in the spring.

A powerfully built filly, Musical Chimes had produced a strong finish in all her best efforts at three, starting with the Prix La Camargo at Saint-Cloud in late March. She had not been closer than fourth in three attempts as a juvenile and was given plenty of time to find her feet in this Listed mile contest before producing a good late run on the outside. She ended up about three lengths fourth behind Maiden Tower, Fidelio's Miracle and Welcome Millenium, then stepped down in class to open her account in the Prix Fould, a conditions event that was little more than a maiden, at Longchamp the following month.

It was a good choice, both to give her a taste of victory and to avoid the trio she had chased home at Saint-Cloud. They had met once more in the Group 3 Prix de la Grotte, half an hour before the Fould, when Maiden Tower again triumphed over Fidelio's Miracle and Welcome

Musical Chimes (Christophe Soumillon, centre) lands the Poule d'Essai des Pouliches at Longchamp in May

Millenium, scoring by half a length and a head with the future Group 1 winner, Etoile Montante, a neck further back.

Musical Chimes was ready for them when they met in the Gainsborough Poule d'Essai des Pouliches, sponsored by her owner, three weeks later. Christophe Soumillon settled her towards the rear, while Maiden Tower took them along, and she was ninth of the 12 into the straight. Soumillon had been looking for a gap between Londonnetdotcom and Fidelio's Miracle but, when Acago, who got there before him, was badly hampered, he switched to the rails. Musical Chimes responded well to his driving, producing a strong run to burst between Maiden Tower and Etoile Montante about 80 yards from home. She beat that pair by one length and a short neck, with Welcome Millenium one and a half lengths back in fourth. Her success completed a four-timer for her jockey, including a rare Group 1 hat-trick.

Musical Chimes did not win again after her Classic success and, in mid-season, opinions differed about her best trip. She finished a creditable third to Nebraska Tornado and Time Ahead in the Prix de Diane, racing in seventh as far as the straight and then staying on under pressure from two furlongs out. She reached third just inside the final furlong but never looked capable of worrying the first two, though beaten only

2003   Race record

11th Breeders' Cup Filly & Mare Turf (Grade 1) (Santa Anita, October 25) 3yo+ 10f Firm **83** 12 ran. *Raced in 3rd and pulled very hard, lost place over 2f out, 11th and beaten straight, beaten 22l by Islington*

2nd Yellow Ribbon Stakes (Grade 1) (Santa Anita, September 28) 3yo+ 10f Firm **115** 8 ran. *Held up in 7th, 6th straight, strong run on outside final furlong to take 2nd last strides, beaten ¾l by Tates Creek*

10th Prix d'Astarte (Group 2) (Deauville, August 3) 3yo+ 1m Good to soft **101** (TS 73) 12 ran. *Mid-division, pushed along over 1½f out, no impression, beaten 10½l by Bright Sky*

3rd Prix de Diane Hermes (Group 1) (Chantilly, June 8) 3yo 10½f Good **111** (TS 85) 10 ran. *Mid-division, disputing 6th straight, pushed along over 2f out, ridden and stayed on in centre from 1½f out, went 3rd approaching final furlong, kept on, beaten 1¾l by Nebraska Tornado*

1st Gainsborough Poule d'Essai des Pouliches (Group 1) (Longchamp, May 11) 3yo 1m Good to soft **115** (TS 99) 12 ran. *10th on rail straight, pushed along over 2f out, progress on inside over 1½f out, hard ridden over 1f out, ran on strongly to lead close home, beat Maiden Tower by 1l*

1st Prix Fould (Longchamp, April 20) 3yo 1m Good to soft 11 ran. *Led approaching final furlong, ran on well, comfortably, beat Wedding Night by 2l*

4th Prix la Camargo (Listed) (Saint-Cloud, March 25) 3yo 1m Good **99** (TS 67) 10 ran. *Not clear run approaching final furlong, stayed on well, beaten 3l by Maiden Tower*

2002

6th Prix Miesque (Group 3) (Maisons-Laffitte, November 5) 2yo 7f Holding **94** (TS 49) 9 ran
● **5th** (disq from 1st) Prix Cordova (Fillies) (Maisons-Laffitte, October 15) 2yo 7f Good 8 ran
● **4th** Prix Discrete (Unraced Fillies) (Saint-Cloud, September 9) 2yo 1m Good 19 ran

three-quarters of a length and a length. However, when put back to a mile in the Group 2 Prix d'Astarte on the opening Sunday of the Deauville meeting, she ran much worse, never being nearer than midfield and finishing tenth of 12 behind Bright Sky.

That ended her European career and her next race was the Grade 1 Yellow Ribbon Stakes, over the same one and a quarter miles as the Filly & Mare Turf, at Santa Anita on the last Sunday of September. Scorning the chance to use bute and lasix, unlike virtually every other European trainer, André Fabre sent her out in great shape. Musical Chimes was seventh of the eight runners for a long way and still only sixth coming into the straight, then unleashed a strong run in the final furlong which carried her into second in the last strides. She was still three-quarters of a length behind the odds-on Tates Creek at the line, however.

Stevens, who rode her for the first time that day, said: "She was just a little green. I had to take hold of her twice and it might have cost me the win." Musical Chimes joined the Hollywood Park-based Neil Drysdale, already trainer of her maternal uncle, Storming Home, after the Yellow Ribbon and trainer and jockey must have decided, on that evidence, that blinkers were the key to her future. She started second favourite for the Filly & Mare Turf, behind Islington and at marginally shorter odds than Tates Creek, but nothing went right for her.

Musical Chimes

bay filly, 29-4-2000

			Fortino
		Caro	Chambord
	Siberian Express		
		Indian Call	Warfare
In Excess			La Morlaye
b 1987			Sing Sing
		Saulingo	Saulisa
	Kantado		
		Vi	Vilmorin
			Dotterel
			Nearctic
		Northern Dancer	Natalma
	Sadler's Wells		
		Fairy Bridge	Bold Reason
Note Musicale			Special
b 1995			Raise A Native
		Mr Prospector	Gold Digger
	It's In The Air		
		A Wind Is Rising	Francis S
			Queen Nasra

Bred by Gainsborough Farm LLC in Kentucky

Sire In Excess

Won 11 of 25 races, inc. Volante H.-Gr3, San Gabriel H.-Gr3, San Fernando S.-Gr2, Metropolitan H.-Gr1, Suburban H.-Gr1, Whitney H.-Gr1, Woodward S.-Gr1. Smart juvenile sprinter at 2 in England, good on grass in US at 3, top-class there on dirt at 4, effective from 7-10f. Sire of: In Excessive Bull (Gr3), Indian Charlie (Santa Anita Derby-Gr1), Romanceishope (Gr2), Above Perfection (Gr3), Icecoldbeeratreds (Gr2), Excessivepleasure (Gr3), Musical Chimes (Poule d'Essai des Pouliches-Gr1).

Dam Note Musicale

Unraced but impeccably bred, out of a top-class US racemare. Dam of: Musical Chimes (2000 f by In Excess; Classic winner), Top Of The Bill (2001 c by Lear Fan; unraced to date).

Pedigree assessment

Another of the in-and-outers among the three-year-old filly division, Musical Chimes had her moment of glory in the Poule d'Essai des Pouliches, could not reproduce that form over the Diane's longer trip, then made no show when returned to a mile at Deauville. A change of environment was required and she showed an immediate benefit for her switch to California, chasing Tates Creek home in the Yellow Ribbon. Uncharacteristically, she refused to settle in the Breeders' Cup Filly & Mare Turf, squandering her chance before the turn for home. Before that lapse she seemed a natural to make her mark in America and she may yet do so, perhaps even on a dirt surface. *TM*

Nayef (USA)

5yo bay horse **129**

Gulch (USA) - Height Of Fashion (Fr) (Bustino)
Owner Hamdan Al Maktoum
Trainer M P Tregoning
Breeder Shadwell Farm Inc

Career: **20** starts | won **9** | second **2** | third **5** | **£2,359,840** win and place

By Rodney Masters

DURING a farewell season that was to peak in midsummer and end tamely, Nayef was to feature more than once in a tournament of team tactics with various combatants fielded by Godolphin. They were legitimately and intelligently played by his own camp at Royal Ascot, but an incident in the return bout a few weeks later in the Coral-Eclipse could have been construed as downright shabby sportsmanship when Jamie Spencer, on a Godolphin second string, was suspended for causing interference to Nayef. This unpalatable 'spoiler' incident led to Spencer, sensibly, issuing a public apology the following day.

But more of that unsavoury episode later. Nayef, who goes into retirement with loyal service medals pinned to his bridle, conjures rich and far-reaching memories, stretching back to when this most handsome of horses launched off amid a booming fanfare as a half-brother to Nashwan and Unfuwain in the Haynes, Hanson and Clark Conditions Stakes of 2000.

Shortly after that Newbury win, it was more than a shade of odds-on that he would be snared by the annual autumn sweep of the Godolphin net. Fortunately, they failed to hook him, for it must be doubtful whether Nayef would have reached the same level of achievement under the changed regime. Marcus Tregoning and his backroom team at Kingwood House understood this horse so well, the reason undoubtedly being that under the leadership of Dick Hern they had so much experience with the previous progeny of his dam, Height Of Fashion.

Sheikh Hamdan, to his credit, understood that, and he was also influenced by the fact that Nayef was the perfect platform to bolster Tregoning's career. Neither horse nor trainer was to let him down. While rarely breathtaking in victory because he was not blessed with the acceleration of some of his contemporaries, Nayef nevertheless rightly earned acclaim for the way he knuckled down to grind out his wins. It was so good to watch.

**Nayef (Richard Hills) wins the Group 1 Prince of Wales's
Stakes at Royal Ascot in June**

That method was to become his trademark over a career that spanned
four seasons and included four strikes at Group 1 level. Some onlookers,
mostly those fitted with the flittering attention span of a butterfly, have
suggested that he was something of an underachiever, but that theory
is shallow-rooted and can revolve only on the fact that he did not measure
up to some of his relatives by annexing a Classic or a King George.

True, Nayef had at various stages been winter favourite for the 2,000
Guineas and Derby, but it turned out that he played his best matches
in the second half of every year. Significantly, apart from his successes
in the Dubai Sheema Classic of 2002 and the Prince of Wales's Stakes
of 2003, he failed to register a win before the month of August.

Accordingly, perhaps we already had sufficient evidence on that score
by the start of his final season to take him on when he was sent off 11-8
favourite on his return to Nad Al Sheba for the Dubai World Cup. There
he met a fully pumped-up, eyes-bulging Moon Ballad. At no stage during
the race was Nayef threatening. He was to finish third, six lengths behind
the winner, and a length adrift of the USA's Harlan's Holiday.

Tregoning was of the opinion that Nayef, despite working with enthus-

2003   Race record

8th Emirates Airline Champion Stakes (Group 1) (Newmarket, October 18) 3yo+ 10f Good to firm **109** (TS 85) 12 ran. *Chased leaders, ridden and every chance 2f out, weakened over 1f out, beaten 9¼l by Rakti*

3rd Juddmonte International Stakes (Group 1) (York, August 19) 3yo+ 10½f Good to firm **122** (TS 111) 8 ran. *Chased leader, ridden to lead 3f out, soon headed, stayed on same pace, beaten 3¾l by Falbrav*

7th King George VI And Queen Elizabeth Diamond Stakes (Group 1) (Ascot, July 26) 3yo+ 12f Good **117** (TS 88) 12 ran. *Prominent, ridden 3f out, disputed 2nd briefly under pressure 2f out, soon weakened, beaten 11l by Alamshar*

2nd Coral-Eclipse Stakes (Group 1) (Sandown, July 5) 3yo+ 10f Good to firm **124** (TS 116) 15 ran. *Prominent, effort when bumped over 2f out, every chance soon after, chased winner, no impression until stayed on inside final furlong, always held, beaten ¾l by Falbrav*

1st Prince of Wales's Stakes (Group 1) (Ascot, June 18) 4yo+ 10f Good to firm **129** (TS 113) 10 ran. *In touch, headway to track leader 4f out, slight lead from 3f out, driven 2f out, clear over 1f out, pushed out final furlong, readily, beat Rakti by 2 1/2l*

3rd Dubai World Cup (Group 1) (Nad Al Sheba, March 29) 4yo+ 10f Fast **120** (TS 98) 11 ran. *Always in touch, 5th straight, 3rd and ridden 2f out, stayed on at one pace, beaten 6l by Moon Ballad*

2002

1st Juddmonte International Stakes (Group 1) (York, August 20) 3yo+ 10½f Good **125** (TS 112) 7 ran ● **2nd** King George VI And Queen Elizabeth Diamond Stakes (Group 1) (Ascot, July 27) 3yo+ 12f Good to firm **129** (TS 112) 9 ran ● **4th** Prince of Wales's Stakes (Group 1) (Ascot, June 19) 4yo+ 10f Good to firm **115** (TS 104) 12 ran ● **3rd** Tattersalls Gold Cup (Group 1) (Curragh, May 26) 4yo+ 10½f Soft **114** (TS 77) 8 ran ● **1st** Dubai Sheema Classic (Group 1) (Nad Al Sheba, March 23) 4yo+ 12f Good **121** 15 ran

Other notable runs

2001 1st Dubai Champion Stakes (Group 1) (Newmarket, October 20) 3yo+ 10f Good to soft **123** (TS 90) 12 ran ● **1st** Royal Court Theatre Cumberland Lodge Stakes (Group 3) (Ascot, September 30) 3yo+ 12f Soft **123** (TS 96) 7 ran ● **1st** Select Stakes (Group 3) (Goodwood, September 12) 3yo+ 10f Good to firm **122** (TS 81) 3 ran ● **1st** Petros Rose of Lancaster Stakes (Group 3) (Haydock, August 11) 3yo+ 10½f Good **117** (TS 82) 5 ran ● **3rd** Peugeot Gordon Stakes (Group 3) (Goodwood, July 31) 3yo 12f Good to firm **115** (TS 97) 11 ran ● **3rd** Macau Jockey Club Craven Stakes (Group 3) (Newmarket, April 19) 3yo 1m Soft **108** (TS 62) 8 ran **2000 1st** Tom McGee Autumn Stakes (Listed) (Ascot, October 7) 2yo 1m Heavy **116** 6 ran ● **1st** Haynes, Hanson And Clark Conditions Stakes (Newbury, September 15) 2yo 1m Good to firm **96** (TS 59) 7 ran

iasm on the sand during his preparation through the winter, was more potent on grass. Those words were to be remembered come high summer.

Then, revenge on Moon Ballad was to be executed in devastating style in a very different arena, with changed tactics, when the pair returned to the racecourse in the Prince of Wales's Stakes, which also included Islington, Falbrav and the 2002 winner, Grandera.

Moon Ballad had bossed throughout in Dubai and Tregoning was not going to let him do so again. That's where the team tactics came into play, with Nayef's stable companion Ekraar, ridden by Willie Supple and a subsequent Group 1 winner, nagging Moon Ballad for the lead.

Tregoning's Ascot game plan worked to prefection. Shortly after Moon Ballad had finally seen off the harrying Ekraar, Nayef ranged alongside, travelling like a winner. Moon Ballad attempted to kick again, but Nayef had his measure as they straightened for home and stretched away to record one of his more impressive wins, beating Rakti by two and a half lengths, with Islington back in third. The trainer, heartfelt in his praise of both winning rider Richard Hills and Supple, deserves a sizeable slice of the credit himself, too.

In agreement with Sheikh Hamdan, he had decided to take the patient route and target Royal Ascot rather than the earlier Coronation Cup, having come to the conclusion that horses who winter elsewhere can take time to reacclimatise. Tregoning had the uncanny gift of knowing just where he was with Nayef, particularly in the final two seasons. Much to his credit, he was willing to share that view and it became conspicuous how often his quoted predictions in the Racing Post's race previews came true.

He had been robustly confident about the outcome of Nayef's next appearance in the Eclipse, where the colt was the subject of some thumping wagers, driving his odds in from 5-2 to 6-4. Godolphin fielded the Dettori-ridden Grandera and Spencer's mount Narrative, who was 100-1.

The incident between Narrative and Nayef at a crucial stage shortly after straightening for home somewhat overshadowed Falbrav's fine win. Nayef was ideally positioned in the slipstream of his pacemaker, Izdiham, when Spencer and Narrative cut across to give the favourite a bump and then sit in front of him.

Meanwhile, Falbrav had gone for home, and although Nayef battled bravely to cut back the deficit, he was three-parts of a length down at the line. Taking into account the interference, and also Falbrav's excellent performances later in the year, this was a superb effort by Nayef. Whether he would he have won but for the carve-up is hard to say. One fact, however, was beyond doubt. It had been one of the toughest races of Nayef's career. Immediately afterwards, he looked totally exhausted. Sadly, he would never be the same again.

It is worth replaying the words of Spencer's apology 24 hours later. Suspended for five days, he denied that it was an attempt at sabotage and was at pains to stress that it had not been a plot by Godolphin.

He said: "I want to apologise to the connections of Nayef because I brushed him and it looked worse on TV. I was under no instructions from Godolphin or Sheikh Mohammed going into the race as a spoiler. I've let down the team of Godolphin by what has happened, resulting in bad press that nobody needs."

He added: "I'm disappointed that it's happened and that it's made everybody look a bit unsporting, which it was never meant to be. I'm disappointed I let Godolphin down. I was supposed to be there as a pacemaker to ensure there was a strong pace through the second half of the race that would suit Grandera. The horse was rolling about under pressure. It looks bad on TV but under no circumstances was I there as a spoiler for Nayef or any other horse in the race. There will definitely be no appeal. It's best left."

Evidence that Nayef had been bottomed by the Sandown experience came later the same month when he started 3-1 favourite for the King George VI and Queen Elizabeth Diamond Stakes. The previous year he had missed out narrowly against Golan, but it was clear before the turn that he was not going to get so close this time. He struggled home in seventh, one of the few times in his life he had finished out of the frame.

While Richard Hills was inclined to blame the tacky ground, pointing out that Nayef was not equipped with the action to cope with such conditions, there is a strong case for the theory that the King George had been left behind on the slopes of Esher.

Over the years a variety of interesting assumptions were to spin around Nayef, one of the more interesting, despite his decent record at Ascot, that he was more potent on a left-handed course.

True, one of his most exhilarating performances had come at York in the 2002 Juddmonte International when he had gained revenge on Golan for Ascot, tenaciously refusing to allow the latter by in one of the most thrilling encounters of that season.

A year on, it was back to Yorkshire to seek a repeat, and pitched in against him yet again was regular adversary Falbrav. It presented the ideal opportunity to put matters right with that arch-rival after the Eclipse, but, sadly, Nayef was again some way short of his best.

Although Izdiham played his role as pacemaker, passing the baton to his stable companion with three furlongs to run, Nayef was unable to trade punches with Falbrav, who went on to win by two lengths. Splitting him and the one-paced Nayef was the 115-rated Magistretti, clear second-best by a length and three-quarters. In the paddock at York, Nayef had looked rather short of his best.

In the previous season, he had failed to reappear after the Juddmonte success, having succumbed to the coughing that was prevalent at Kingwood House in that autumn, but Tregoning was anxious to see the colt off to stud at Shadwell with a win to his name. The obvious target was the Emirates Airline Champion Stakes, which Nayef had won two years previously. However, in the countdown to Newmarket, Tregoning once again more or less marked our card. He pointed out that the colt had been on the go since January, when he started his build-up to the Dubai World Cup, and said: "It's very difficult to go right from the beginning until right to the end as we are asking him to do."

Accordingly, it came as no surprise when Nayef drifted in the betting at Newmarket and ran flat, finishing eighth behind Rakti. Three weeks later he left Kingwood House for the final time.

Nayef

bay horse, 1-5-1998

		Raise A Native	Native Dancer
			Raise You
	Mr Prospector		
		Gold Digger	Nashua
Gulch			Sequence
b 1984			
		Rambunctious	Rasper
			Danae
	Jameela		
		Asbury Mary	Seven Corners
			Snow Flyer
		Busted	Crepello
			Sans le Sou
	Bustino		
		Ship Yard	Doutelle
Height Of Fashion			Paving Stone
b 1979			
		Queen's Hussar	March Past
			Jojo
	Highclere		
		Highlight	Borealis
			Hypericum

Bred by Shadwell Farm in Kentucky

Sire Gulch

Won 13 of 32 races, inc. Tremont S.-Gr3, Saratoga Special-Gr2, Hopeful S.-Gr1, Futurity S.-Gr1, Bay Shore S.-Gr3, Wood Memorial S.-Gr1, Metropolitan H.-Gr1, Potrero Grande H.-Gr3, Carter H.-Gr1, Metropolitan H.-Gr1, Breeders' Cup Sprint-Gr1. Also placed 12 times, inc. 3rd in Belmont S-Gr1. Attractive, medium-sized, well-balanced sort, with a quick action and an excellent turn of foot. Essentially a sprinter-miler, best on a fast surface. Barely got 9f, never competitive at longer distances. Untried on grass. Sire of notable winners: Great Navigator (Hopeful S.-Gr1), Wallenda (Super Derby-Gr1), Harayir (1,000 Guineas-Gr1), Thunder Gulch (Florida Derby-Gr1, Kentucky Derby-Gr1, Belmont S.-Gr1, Travers S.-Gr1), Torrential (Prix Jean Prat-Gr1), Esteemed Friend (Gr2), Panama Canal (Gr3), Swift Gulliver (Gr3), Nasty Storm (Gr2), Nayef (Champion S.-Gr1, York International S.-Gr1, Prince of Wales's S.-Gr1), Mariensky (Gr2), Scrimshaw (Gr2).

Dam Height Of Fashion

Won 5 of 7 races, inc. May Hill S.-Gr3, Fillies' Mile-Gr3, Princess of Wales's S.-Gr2. Big, rangy sort, impressive in action. Best on a galloping course, stayed 12f well and would have got further. Deteriorated in looks and racing character and wore blinkers last 3 starts. Untried on soft ground. Dam of: Alwasmi (1984 c by Northern Dancer; Gr3 winner), Unfuwain (1985 c by Northern Dancer; Gr2 winner), Nashwan (1986 c by Blushing Groom; dual Classic winner), Mukddaam (1987 c by Danzig; Listed winner, Gr2-placed), Manwah (1988 f by Lyphard; placed), Bashayer (1990 f by Mr Prospector; winner, Listed-placed), Wijdan (1991 f by Mr Prospector; Listed-placed, dam of Gr2 winner Oriental Fashion), Deyaajeer (1992 f by Dayjur; unplaced), Sarayir (1994 f by Mr Prospector; Listed winner), Burhan (1995 c by Riverman; unraced, died at 3), unnamed (1997 c by Riverman; died as yearling), Nayef (1998 c by Gulch; multiple Gr1 winner).

Pedigree assessment

Nayef has spent four years under the spotlight, initially bearing a burden of expectation as the last product of an illustrious mare, subsequently realising those aspirations in a thoroughly meritorious career. He never let the side down and proved a worthy successor to half-brothers Nashwan and Unfuwain. Now he starts all over again, retiring to Nunnery Stud with the responsibility of filling the void created by the deaths of that pair in 2002. There is no reason why he should fail to emulate them, and at the competitive fee of £15,000 he will get plenty of chances. *TM*

Nayyir

5yo chestnut gelding **123**

Indian Ridge - Pearl Kite (USA) (Silver Hawk (USA))
Owner Abdulla Al Khalifa
Trainer G A Butler
Breeder Saeed Manana

Career: **14** starts | won **6** | second **1** | third **1** | **£234,294** win and place

By Daniel Hill

RECUPERATION is best achieved in the sun, and it was with the sun on his back that Nayyir recovered from a life-threatening illness that struck him down in Hong Kong at the end of 2002. An assault on the Hong Kong Mile was abandoned after Nayyir picked up a severe case of diarrhoea, causing him to lose 42 kilos in weight. Plasma had to be flown out to Hong Kong and it was only thanks to vet Christopher Osborne and the careful attention of Nayyir's groom, Jenny Hedland, that Nayyir survived.

A period in the warmth of Dubai led to Nayyir recovering, in the words of trainer Gerard Butler, both "physically and mentally", and his career was back on track. In fact, given his problems, Nayyir had a very successful 2003 season, winning the Group 2 Lennox Stakes at Goodwood for the second year in succession and also going close to winning the Challenge Stakes at Newmarket for a second time.

Nayyir falls snugly into the category of seven-furlong specialist: he has run over the trip five times, won on four of those occasions and finished a half-length second on the other. However, connections were keen to give Nayyir another try over six furlongs in 2003, as he had not done himself justice when favourite for Haydock's Sprint Cup as a four-year-old. Having been pulled out on account of the fast ground when lined up to reappear in the Group 1 Golden Jubilee Stakes at Royal Ascot, he returned the following week in the six-furlong Group 3 Chipchase Stakes at Newcastle, but despite starting 11-4 favourite could finish only sixth of 12, outpaced over a furlong out.

However, a switch to his ideal distance in the Group 2 Lennox Stakes at Glorious Goodwood showed him in a much better light. Despite having won the race the previous year, Nayyir was allowed to go off at a generous 6-1 in a field of 13, the 4-1 joint-favourites being three-year-old Jersey Stakes runner-up Arakan and the previous year's Celebration Mile winner

Nayyir (Eddie Ahern) lands the Group 2 Lennox Stakes for the second year running at Goodwood in July

Tillerman, who had shown himself as good as ever when winning a Group 3 at Ascot on his previous start.

Punters at Goodwood must be prepared to be frustrated. The configuration of the track, with its undulations and downhill run into the home straight, means that jockeys are reluctant to go too fast, often resulting in bunching and lack of room in the straight. If your selection is held up and stuck behind a wall of horses with two furlongs to go, nine times out of ten you may as well tear up your betting slip.

In the Lennox Stakes, the doomsday scenario was realised for supporters of Arakan, whereas Nayyir, ridden by Eddie Ahern, found a smooth passage to victory. Having been held up, Nayyir made steady progress on the outer from over two furlongs out, leading more than a furlong from home and then just holding on from the unlucky Arakan, who suffered a nightmare passage but came fast and late to get within a head. It was a welcome change of luck for Nayyir and also for Butler, who had been out of form for several weeks.

If luck was on Nayyir's side at Goodwood, it deserted him on his final outing of the season at Newmarket. Bidding for a repeat victory in the Challenge Stakes and ridden by Jamie Spencer in the absence of the suspended Ahern, he was always travelling well in the rear but had to

2003   Race record

2nd Victor Chandler Challenge Stakes (Group 2) (Newmarket, October 18) 3yo+ 7f Good to firm **122** (TS 100) 11 ran. *Held up, raced keenly, headway and switched right inside final furlong, ran on well, beaten ½l by Just James*

8th Prix Maurice de Gheest (Group 1) (Deauville, August 10) 3yo+ 6½f Good to soft **103** (TS 36) 12 ran. *Held up towards rear, ridden and headway 2f out, stayed on one pace from over 1f out, beaten 5l by Porlezza*

1st Lennox Stakes (Group 2) (Goodwood, July 29) 3yo+ 7f Good **119** (TS 101) 13 ran. *Held up in rear, steady progress on outer from over 2f out, ridden to lead over 1f out, stayed on well, just held on, beat Arakan by hd*

6th Kronenbourg 1664 Chipchase Stakes (Group 3) (Newcastle, June 28) 3yo+ 6f Good to soft **105** (TS 78) 12 ran. *Prominent, ridden and outpaced over 1f out, no impression inside final furlong, beaten 5½l by Orientor*

2002

1st Victor Chandler Challenge Stakes (Group 2) (Newmarket, October 19) 3yo+ 7f Good **123** (TS 106) 17 ran ● **10th** Stanley Leisure Sprint Cup (Group 1) (Haydock, September 7) 3yo+ 6f Good to firm **102** (TS 63) 14 ran ● **3rd** Prix Maurice de Gheest (Group 1) (Deauville, August 11) 3yo+ 6½f Very soft **114** (TS 71) 9 ran ● **1st** Theo Fennell Lennox Stakes (Group 3) (Goodwood, August 2) 3yo+ 7f Good to firm **118** (TS 80) 9 ran ● **4th** Queen Anne Stakes (Group 2) (Ascot, June 18) 3yo+ 1m Good **114** (TS 96) 12 ran ● **1st** Vodafone Diomed Stakes (Group 3) (Epsom, June 8) 3yo+ 8½f Good to soft **116** (TS 98) 9 ran ● **1st** John Johnson 'Lifetime In Racing' Rated Stakes (0-95 handicap) (Beverley, May 21) 3yo+ 8½f Good **103** (TS 66) 9 ran ● **4th** attheraces.co.uk Rated Stakes (0-95 handicap) (Sandown, April 27) 4yo+ 1m Good to soft **96** (TS 74) 12 ran ● **6th** Littlewoods Bet Direct Daily Special Offers Classified Stakes (Lingfield, AW, March 25) 3yo+ (0-80) 10f Standard **69** (TS 55) 6 ran ● **1st** Call Bet Direct Free On 0800 329393 Maiden Stakes (Div II) (Lingfield, AW, March 6) 3yo+ 7f Standard **88** (TS 74) 11 ran

be switched to make his challenge, a manoeuvre that cost him the race. Nayyir picked up tremendously well inside the final furlong but the post came too soon and he was beaten half a length by the 16-1 shot Just James. In a few more strides he would have prevailed.

In between, Nayyir had disappointed behind Porlezza in the Group 1 Prix Maurice de Gheest, over six and a half furlongs at Deauville. The good to soft ground may have been against him there – his other below-par run of 2003 was on a similar surface at Newcastle – but Ahern blamed a slow start, while Butler said later: "He's not a good traveller any more and the race came too quickly after Goodwood. It was my fault, I shouldn't have run him."

Nayyir is one of the best seven-furlong horses in training – only Trade Fair recorded a better Racing Post Rating over the trip all year – and a diet of top races at that distance is likely to be on the agenda again in 2004. Before that, Nayyir is set for another winter in Dubai, where there are plans for him to run in the Godolphin Mile.

He will be six in 2004 but didn't make his racecourse debut until four. There will be no stud career for him as he is a gelding, so connections will persevere with him as long as he holds his form and enjoys his racing.

Nayyir

chestnut gelding, 7-4-1998

Indian Ridge ch 1985	Ahonoora	Lorenzaccio	Klairon / Phoenissa
		Helen Nichols	Martial / Quaker Girl
	Hillbrow	Swing Easy	Delta Judge / Free Flowing
		Golden City	Skymaster / West Shaw
Pearl Kite b 1991	Silver Hawk	Roberto	Hail To Reason / Bramalea
		Gris Vitesse	Amerigo / Matchiche
	Spur Wing	Storm Bird	Northern Dancer / South Ocean
		Equal Change	Arts And Letters / Fairness

Bred by Saeed Manana in Britain. 15,000gns Tattersalls October yearling, 57,000gns Tattersalls Breeze-up two-year-old

Sire **Indian Ridge**

Won 5 of 11 races, inc. Jersey S.-Gr3, Duke of York S.-Gr3, King's Stand S.-Gr2. Lengthy, attractive sort, a hard puller, too impetuous to get a mile. Sire of: Fumo di Londra (Gr3), Island Magic (Gr3), Ridgewood Ben (Gr3), Blomberg (Gr3), Definite Article (National S.-Gr1), Ridgewood Pearl (Irish 1,000 Guineas-Gr1, Coronation S.-Gr1, Prix du Moulin de Longchamp-Gr1, Breeders' Cup Mile-Gr1), Tumbleweed Ridge (Gr3), Compton Place (July Cup-Gr1), Handsome Ridge (Gr2), Indian Rocket (Gr2), Bardonecchia (Gr3), Cassandra Go (Gr3), Namid (Prix de l'Abbaye de Longchamp-Gr1), St Clair Ridge (Gr3), Indian Mary (Gr3), Nicobar (Gr2), Domedriver (Breeders' Cup Mile-Gr1), High Pitched (Gr3), Indian Creek (Gr2), Munir (Gr3), Nayyir (Gr2), Sights On Gold (Gr3), Campsie Fells (Gr3), Indian Haven (Irish 2,000 Guineas-Gr1), Snow Ridge (Gr2).

Dam **Pearl Kite**

Won 1 of 7 starts, also 2nd Ribblesdale S.-Gr2, March S.-L, 3rd Doonside Cup-L. Effective from 12-14f. Very closely related to useful stayer Jaseur (by Lear Fan). Dam of: Pearl Barley (1996 f by Polish Precedent; winner), Shamaiel (1997 f by Lycius; Listed winner), Nayyir (1998 g by Indian Ridge; Gr2 winner), Highest (1999 c by Selkirk; Gr3 winner, Gr1-placed), College Fund Girl (2000 f by Kahyasi; winner), 2002 c by Desert King.

Pedigree assessment

Far faster than his half-brother Highest, thanks to his sire Indian Ridge. This gelding is well established as primarily a seven-furlong specialist who can stretch his stamina to an easy mile. Tough, like many of his sire's offspring, and should continue to show smart form. *JH*

Nebraska Tornado (USA)

3yo brown filly   **120**

Storm Cat (USA) - Media Nox (Lycius (USA))

Owner K Abdullah

Trainer A Fabre

Breeder Juddmonte Farms Inc

Career: **5** starts | won **4** | second **0** | third **0** | **£315,662** win and place

By James Willoughby

THE synergy of horse and trainer is one of the enduring themes of the sport. Brilliant trainers need great horses to elevate their careers; great horses need the guidance of brilliant trainers to fulfil their potential.

So it is with Nebraska Tornado and André Fabre. The filly flattered her trainer when winning the Prix de Diane and Prix du Moulin in the manner of a prodigious talent. But she might not have reached anything like the same heights without Fabre's judgement and experience.

According to reports, it was a backward Nebraska Tornado who made her debut in a newcomers event at Saint-Cloud on May 5. As a juvenile, she had never convinced her trainer she was sufficiently forward for a race, though Fabre always held in her high regard.

After her decisive debut defeat of Precious Pearl – who went on to be Group-placed – it was clear that Nebraska Tornado was a Pattern-class filly. However, she was still too inexperienced to be sent straight for the Prix de Diane, so Fabre opted for the intermediate target of the Listed Prix Melisande at Longchamp on May 22.

Nebraska Tornado again won comfortably, this time looking as if Classic pretensions were indeed realistic. However, a mile and a quarter in the mud was bound to have taken something out of her and Fabre had a decision to make with Chantilly just 17 days away.

At this point, it was make or break for Nebraska Tornado. A heavy defeat could have set her back both mentally and physically, especially as she still had some developing to do in both areas. But Fabre seems to know instinctively when a gamble is worth taking with a promising horse, and he was once again gloriously vindicated.

Sent off third favourite in a field of ten in which the Prix Saint-Alary winner Fidelite and Fabre's Pouliches heroine Musical Chimes were preferred in the market, Nebraska Tornado proved reluctant to enter

Nebraska Tornado (Richard Hughes) wins her first Group 1 of the season in the Prix de Diane at Chantilly in June

the stalls but did everything right in the race itself. She settled well, close to an even pace, accelerated sharply on demand when her jockey Richard Hughes asked and soon had control of the race. A stubborn Time Ahead reduced the winning margin to three-quarters of a length at the line, but Nebraska Tornado was always going to hold on. Musical Chimes was a length away in third and favourite Fidelite a disappointing eighth.

Nebraska Tornado was given a break through midsummer, as is the norm with Fabre's best horses, and she did plenty of growing in that period. She was reportedly a much stronger horse when she reappeared in the Group 1 Prix Jacques le Marois at Deauville in August.

Fabre was not concerned about reverting from ten and a half furlongs to a mile with Nebraska Tornado, such was the speed she was showing at home. And it was not lack of pace that beat her but being drawn

2003   Race record

1st Netjets Prix du Moulin de Longchamp (Group 1) (Longchamp, September 7) 3yo+ 1m Good to soft **120** (TS 91) 14 ran. *Soon tracking leader, 2nd straight, ridden to lead 1f out, ran on well, beat Lohengrin by ½l*

6th Prix du Haras de Fresnay-Le Buffard-Jacques le Marois (Group 1) (Deauville, August 17) 3yo+ 1m Good to soft **109** (TS 81) 12 ran. *Prominent, disputing 3rd halfway, driven to lead 2f out until headed over 1f out, one pace, beaten 6¼l by Six Perfections*

1st Prix de Diane Hermes (Group 1) (Chantilly, June 8) 3yo 10½f Good **114** (TS 89) 10 ran. *Reluctant to load, raced in close 2nd, led 2f out, pushed along and quickened 2 lengths clear over 1½f out, ridden approaching final furlong, ran on well, beat Time Ahead by ¾l*

1st Prix Melisande (Listed) (Longchamp, May 22) 3yo 10f Very soft **97** (TS 56) 12 ran. *Raced in 2nd, headway to lead approaching final furlong, ran on strongly, beat La Sabana by 1½l*

1st Prix Hildegarde (Unraced Fillies) (Saint-Cloud, May 5) 3yo 1m Soft 12 ran. *Always prominent, led over 1f out, ran on strongly, beat Precious Pearl by 1½l*

away from the pace on a straight track at Deauville which often features a bias when the ground is soft. Nebraska Tornado travelled well to halfway, but it was all she could do to finish mid-division in a field of 12, around six lengths behind Six Perfections.

Redemption came at Longchamp in the Group 1 Prix du Moulin the following month, in which Hughes was again seen to good effect in the plate. Nebraska Tornado struck for home early off only a steady pace and held the high-class Japanese runner Lohengrin by half a length. The likes of Bright Sky, Soviet Song, Clodovil, Domedriver and Refuse To Bend were further back, though not all of them were ridden to best advantage.

The only negative aspect of Nebraska Tornado's performance came before the start. She was ridden round the paddock and had to be forced into the stalls, once again showing something of a wilful nature. Hopefully, this is merely the attitude of a prima donna, rather than the first signs of her becoming a jade.

Fabre was keen on sending Nebraska Tornado to the Breeders' Cup at Santa Anita, but her owner Khalid Abdullah had two strong US-trained candidates for the Filly & Mare Turf in Heat Haze and Tates Creek, and it was evidently decided that the Mile was the wrong race for her at that stage of her career. All being well, she will get her chance at Lone Star Park, Texas, in 2004.

The 58-year-old Fabre has done a typically wonderful job with a filly who could become a force on the world stage. But this is no more than we should expect. After all, he has been champion trainer in France every year since 1987; he has masterminded a record five Prix de l'Arc de Triomphe successes; as well as numerous achievements in France, he has won three Coronation Cups, two renewals of the 2,000 Guineas and three Breeders' Cup races, including the Classic on dirt with Arcangues. He truly deserves to be accorded a position among the greats of his profession.

Nebraska Tornado   *brown filly 19-1-2000*

			Nearctic
		Northern Dancer	Natalma
	Storm Bird		
		South Ocean	New Providence
			Shining Sun
Storm Cat			
br 1983			Bold Ruler
		Secretariat	Somethingroyal
	Terlingua		
		Crimson Saint	Crimson Satan
			Bolero Rose
			Raise A Native
		Mr Prospector	Gold Digger
	Lycius		
		Lypatia	Lyphard
			Hypatia
Media Nox			
ch 1993		Nijinsky	**Northern Dancer**
			Flaming Page
	Sky Love		
		Gangster Of Love	Round Table
			Woozem

Bred by Juddmonte Farms in Kentucky

Sire Storm Cat

Won 4 of 8 races, inc. Young America S.-Gr1, also 2nd (beaten a nose) in Breeders' Cup Juvenile-Gr1. Medium-sized, strongly made sort, who took more after his dam than his sire. Top-class, extremely game 2yo who had surgery for bone chips in off knee at end of season; never wholly sound thereafter. Sire of Gr1 winners: Harlan, November Snow, Desert Stormer, Missed The Storm, Mistle Cat, Sardula, Tabasco Cat, Hennessy, Aldiza, Sharp Cat, Catinca, Aljabr, Cat Thief, Forestry, Tactical Cat, Finder's Fee, Giant's Causeway, High Yield, Black Minnaloushe, Raging Fever, Sophisticat, Dessert, Hold That Tiger, Nebraska Tornado, Storm Flag Flying, Denebola, One Cool Cat.

Dam Media Nox

Won 5 of 8 races, inc. Prix du Bois-Gr3, Buena Vista H.-Gr2. Smart but delicate performer. Showed precocious speed, but later got a mile well. Used Lasix and Bute in California. Dam of: Burning Sun (1999 c by Danzig; Gr2 winner), Nebraska Tornado (2000 f by Storm Cat; Classic winner), Media Empire (2001 c by Danzig; unraced).

Pedigree assessment

A campaign of five races, well spaced out, after a blank first season suggests that Nebraska Tornado took after her dam and was not the most robust of individuals. But she did enough in those few outings to indicate that she represented better class than Media Nox, and in the second of her Group 1 wins, in open-age and mixed company, she turned in what looked like a first-class performance under a shrewd tactical ride. In light of the disappointing efforts by Heat Haze and Tates Creek for the Juddmonte concern in the Breeders' Cup Filly & Mare Turf, there was possibly some regret that she did not join the party at Santa Anita, as was originally intended. She stays in training and may yet get her chance at a Breeders' Cup. *TM*

Necklace

2yo bay filly   **109**

Darshaan - Spinning The Yarn (Barathea (Ire))
Owner M Tabor & Mrs John Magnier
Trainer A P O'Brien
Breeder Meon Valley Stud

Career: **4** starts | won **2** | second **1** | third **0** | **£141,493** win and place

By Alan Sweetman

VIEWED at its most fundamental level, it is self-evident that the function of the training operation supervised by Aidan O'Brien at Ballydoyle is to turn high-class colts into potential stallions for Coolmore and its associated studs. Fillies have never been central to the scheme of things at Ballydoyle, even in its previous incarnation under the incomparable Vincent O'Brien. And yet, just as his illustrious predecessor managed to win a good share of top-class races with a relatively small pool of fillies, so his successor has made fine use of his resources in the distaff area.

In 1997, when O'Brien burst onto the Classic scene, Classic Park won the Irish 1,000 Guineas and the following year Shahtoush became his first Oaks winner. In 2000 Sequoyah took the Moyglare Stud Stakes, Ireland's top race for juvenile fillies, and Quarter Moon followed suit in 2001, the same year that Imagine became his highest-achieving filly by capturing the Irish 1,000 Guineas and the Oaks. Quarter Moon's sister Yesterday was the principal standard-bearer for the Ballydoyle fillies in 2003, beating Six Perfections in the Irish 1,000 Guineas and finishing a luckless second in the Oaks.

Further Group 1 honours were achieved by the Darshaan filly Necklace, who became the stable's third Moyglare winner in four seasons. Necklace was an uneasy 3-1 favourite on her debut at The Curragh in July, her odds reflecting not only a growing awareness among punters that the Ballydoyle juveniles were more in need of an introductory outing than in previous seasons, but also pedigree-based worries that she might find the six-furlong trip a bit sharp.

A slow break did not help her cause, but she ended up second by three-quarters of a length to Soviet Belle, an apprentice-ridden outsider trained by O'Brien's one-time mentor Jim Bolger and a half-sister to that trainer's 1995 Moyglare winner Priory Belle.

Necklace (Mick Kinane) takes the Group 1 Moyglare Stud Stakes at The Curragh in August

By the time that Necklace next appeared, in the Robert H Griffin Debutante Stakes over an additional furlong at The Curragh in August, the market sent out much more encouraging signals. Even though she faced eight previous winners in the Group 3 contest, there was genuine confidence behind her and she was backed down to 7-4 favouritism. Produced from off the pace by Mick Kinane, she picked up well to win by a length from Caldy Dancer, a British-trained filly who had won her first two races but had already been shown to have limitations when raised in class.

A very disappointing performance on the part of another British raider, Lucky Pipit, gave the Debutante Stakes form a suspect complexion, but O'Brien was already looking ahead to the Moyglare Stud Stakes back at The Curragh three weeks later, and Necklace was nonetheless sent off favourite for a race in which it appeared that her most dangerous opponent was River Belle, unbeaten winner of the Princess Margaret Stakes at Ascot. Once again, the failure of a British filly to run to expectations greatly eased the task facing Necklace. With River Belle

2003   **Race record**

10th Prix Marcel Boussac Royal Barrière de Deauville (Group 1) (Longchamp, October 5) 2yo 1m Holding **90** (TS 46) 16 ran. *Held up in rear, last straight, ridden 2f out, no real progress, beaten 9¼l by Denebola*

1st Moyglare Stud Stakes (Group 1) (Curragh, August 31) 2yo 7f Good to firm **109** (TS 82) 11 ran. *Held up, 6th on inner 2½f out, 4th and ridden 1½f out, 3rd and challenged 1f out, stayed on well to lead 100yds out, beat Red Feather by 1l*

1st Robert H Griffin Debutante Stakes (Group 3) (Curragh, August 10) 2yo 7f Good to firm **104** (TS 60) 13 ran. *Held up, 9th halfway, 5th 2f out, led 1f out, stayed on well, beat Caldy Dancer by 1l*

2nd Kildare Architects EBF Maiden (Curragh, July 12) 2yo 6f Good to yielding **83** 12 ran. *Slowly away and in rear, improved on inner into 6th 3f out, switched out and driven along 1½f out, 4th 1f out, ridden and kept on inside final furlong, beaten ¾l by Soviet Belle*

making little impression in fifth, Kinane's mount merely had to reproduce her previous superiority over the Debutante third Red Feather in order to capture the Group 1 prize. Leading around 100 yards out, she scored by a length from Red Feather, with Clive Brittain's Menhoubah a short head away in third and Misty Heights almost upsides too.

A more demanding test awaited Necklace in the Fillies' Mile at Ascot, though this traditionally strong contest was already relatively weak in terms of previous Pattern-race form even before O'Brien decided to withdraw her, citing unsuitably fast ground. Following this abortive trip to Britain, O'Brien decided to re-route Necklace to Longchamp for the Prix Marcel Boussac, where she was to encounter ground that was in marked contrast to Ascot. O'Brien also sent Oh So Precious in a supporting role and not for the first time during the 2003 season the use of a pacemaker failed to produce the desired outcome for the Ballydoyle team, with Necklace unable to make any significant progress from the rear of the field after Oh So Precious had been responsible for a strong gallop. Necklace finished tenth of the 16 runners behind Denebola and O'Brien, who had not anticipated any problem with the holding ground, afterwards expressed the view that the Ascot trip might have had an adverse effect on her performance.

Despite her Marcel Boussac defeat Necklace ended the season the ante-post favourite for the Oaks, admittedly at odds of 16-1 and upwards in a market that is always difficult for bookmakers to price so far in advance. Even if one is prepared to overlook the French run, she still needs to improve significantly on the bare form of her two Group wins if she is to play as big a part in the Classics as her Ballydoyle predecessors, but reference to her pedigree provides grounds for optimism regarding her long-term future. Her dam, Spinning The Yarn, is a half-sister to Opera House and Kayf Tara, brothers who distinguished themselves over longer distances as older horses, as well as to Zee Zee Top, a Group 1 winner over ten furlongs in the Prix de l'Opera.

Necklace

bay filly, 24-2-2001

			Mill Reef	Never Bend
		Shirley Heights		Milan Mill
	Darshaan		Hardiemma	Hardicanute
	br 1981			Grand Cross
			Abdos	Arbar
		Delsy		Pretty Lady
			Kelty	Venture
				Marilla
			Sadler's Wells	Northern Dancer
		Barathea		Fairy Bridge
	Spinning The Yarn		Brocade	Habitat
	gr 1989			Canton Silk
			High Top	Derring-do
		Colorspin		Camenae
			Reprocolor	Jimmy Reppin
				Blue Queen

Bred by Meon Valley Stud in England. 600,000gns Tattersalls Houghton yearling

Sire Darshaan

Won 5 of 8 races, inc. Criterium de Saint-Cloud-Gr2, Prix Greffulhe-Gr2, Prix Hocquart-Gr2, Prix du Jockey Club-Gr1. Strong, workmanlike type. The best 12f 3yo in a very good crop, but disappointing after midsummer. Died May 2001. Sire of: Arzanni (Gr2), Game Plan (Gr2), Hellenic (Yorkshire Oaks-Gr1), Kotashaan (San Luis Rey S.-Gr1, San Juan Capistrano Invitational H.-Gr1, Eddie Read H.-Gr1, Oak Tree Invitational H.-Gr1, Breeders' Cup Turf-Gr1), Grand Plaisir (Gr2), Darnay (Gr2), Truly A Dream (Gr2), Key Change (Yorkshire Oaks-Gr1), Mark Of Esteem (2,000 Guineas-Gr1, Queen Elizabeth II S.-Gr1), Make No Mistake (Gr2), Mutamam (Gr2), Sayarshan (Gr2), Cerulean Sky (Prix Saint-Alary-Gr1), Josr Algarhoud (Gr2), Dilshaan (Racing Post Trophy-Gr1), Olden Times (Prix Jean Prat-Gr1), Sayedah (Gr2), Dalakhani (Criterium International-Gr1, Prix Lupin-Gr1, Prix du Jockey-Club-Gr1, Prix de l'Arc de Triomphe-Gr1), Mezzo Soprano (Prix Vermeille-Gr1), Necklace (Moyglare Stud S.-Gr1). Also got Aliysa, finished first in Oaks, disqualified.

Dam Spinning The Yarn

Ran only once as a 3yo, showing some promise, and was retired through injury. Half-sister to Gr1 winners Opera House, Kayf Tara and Zee Zee Top, from a family upgraded to the highest level in recent generations. Dam of: Necklace (2001 f by Darshaan; Gr1 winner).

Pedigree assessment

Necklace's purchase price as a yearling said all that needed to be said about her pedigree and physical attributes, and her first three efforts on the racecourse suggested that the huge outlay had been justified. Her comprehensive failure at the fourth time of asking need not mean that that view should be revised. Having opted not to chance her on Ascot's firm ground, her connections switched her to Longchamp, where she encountered softer terrain than ever before, and the Marcel Boussac was nearly over before she could find her stride. She was bred to be an Oaks filly and looked one in the making at The Curragh. Granted good ground or faster, she still can be, and she seems a better bet for that than for the Guineas, where speedier types make more appeal. *TM*

Norse Dancer (Ire)

3yo bay colt **119**

Halling (USA) - River Patrol (Rousillon (USA))

Owner J C Smith

Trainer D R C Elsworth

Breeder Ralph Ergnist and Bruno Faust

Career: **11** starts | won **2** | second **0** | third **2** | **£166,028** win and place

By David Dew

THE 2003 season was an unmitigated triumph for David Elsworth – a campaign in which he roughly doubled his average yearly haul of prize-money and one that saw him pass the £1m mark for the first time. Elsworth will forever be remembered for his association with Desert Orchid but, along with Persian Punch and Indian Creek, it was Norse Dancer who helped him to such a successful season.

Cheaply bought at 26,000 guineas, Norse Dancer failed to win as a three-year-old but proved himself a high-class performer in defeat, easily recouping more for his connections than his sire Halling's other main protagonists during the season – Chancellor, Dandoun, Parasol and Franklins Gardens.

Norse Dancer started his Classic season with wins in a Salisbury maiden and an Ascot novice stakes already under his belt from his juvenile campaign, but the balance of his form suggested that plenty of improvement was needed for him to have any chance of winning a Classic. That view was reflected in the betting market when he made his seasonal debut in the 2,000 Guineas at Newmarket as one of the rank outsiders at 100-1. Elsworth, however, warned before the race that "it wouldn't be the biggest turn-up in history if he was in the first four or even won," and it was he who was proved correct, as his colt was pushed, shoved and cajoled to finish third behind Refuse To Bend and Zafeen, worried out of the runner-up slot only close home.

Having come within a length of Classic glory, connections had to think long and hard over what came next. Among the possibilities were the Irish 2,000 Guineas, the Dante and the French Derby. However, after weighing up the options, owner Jeff Smith decided instead to fork out the £90,000 supplementary fee required to put him in the Derby at Epsom, in which he had never previously had a runner.

Richard Quinn, who had partnered Norse Dancer in four of his five

Norse Dancer endured a season of near-misses and disappointments, finishing placed in three Group 1 races

outings as a two-year-old, was reunited with the colt at Epsom after Philip Robinson had been in the saddle in the Guineas. However, his riding became the subject of heated debate after Norse Dancer had made up an enormous amount of ground from the back of the field to look sure to be involved in the finish until the effort of doing so much so quickly proved unsustainable and his effort flattened out. Kris Kin beat him around two and a half lengths into fourth.

Though Quinn earned a tidy percentage from Norse Dancer's effort, Smith did not even recoup his supplementary fee and looked furious. He said: "He's a very, very good horse, but he had an awful lot to do." Elsworth clearly shared the sentiment, but seemed a little more forgiving. He said: "He was left quite a lot to do. One's a little frustrated in a way – there's only one result and it's the only chance that he'd get. I'm disappointed with the result but delighted the horse has run so well."

Norse Dancer had been sitting plumb last swinging around Tattenham Corner but, as at Newmarket, he had not broken from the stalls particularly well and had been urged along in the early stages before settling down.

2003   Race record

7th Queen Elizabeth II Stakes (Sponsored By NetJets) (Group 1) (Ascot, September 27) 3yo+ 1m Good to firm **110** (TS 91) 8 ran. *Held up in rear, ridden and effort on outside from over 2f out, never a danger, beaten 8l by Falbrav*

6th Juddmonte International Stakes (Group 1) (York, August 19) 3yo+ 10½f Good to firm **115** (TS 96) 8 ran. *In rear, effort 4f out, hung left over 2f out, never near leaders, beaten 7½l by Falbrav*

3rd Sussex Stakes (Group 1) (Goodwood, July 30) 3yo+ 1m Good to soft **117** (TS 85) 9 ran. *Held up in last trio, progress over 2f out, ridden to lead narrowly over 1f out, found little in front, headed last 75yds, beaten nk by Reel Buddy*

12th Coral-Eclipse Stakes (Group 1) (Sandown, July 5) 3yo+ 10f Good to firm **95** (TS 73) 15 ran. *Soon in midfield, pushed along halfway, effort on outer under pressure 2f out, weakened over 1f out, beaten 17l by Falbrav*

4th Vodafone Derby (Group 1) (Epsom, June 7) 3yo 12f Good **119** (TS 100) 20 ran. *Raced in last until 19th and wide straight, rapid and sustained progress from 3f out, closed on leaders 1f out, no extra final 100yds, beaten 2½l by Kris Kin*

3rd Sagitta 2,000 Guineas (Group 1) (Newmarket, May 3) 3yo 1m Good **115** (TS 109) 20 ran. *Soon pushed along and prominent, ridden over 1f out, ran on, beaten 1l by Refuse To Bend*

2002

7th Racing Post Trophy (Group 1) (Doncaster, October 26) 2yo 1m Soft **89** (TS 18) 9 ran ● **4th** Hackney Empire Royal Lodge Stakes (Group 2) (Ascot, September 28) 2yo 1m Good to firm **102** (TS 67) 9 ran ● **4th** Champagne Victor Vintage Stakes (Group 3) (Goodwood, July 31) 2yo 7f Good to firm **102** (TS 63) 10 ran ● **1st** Alfred Franks & Bartlett Sunglasses Novice Stakes (Ascot, July 13) 2yo 7f Good **101** (TS 71) 9 ran ● **1st** Herbert And Gwen Blagrave Maiden Stakes (Salisbury, June 27) 2yo 7f Firm **86** (TS 29) 9 ran

Quinn picked up on that point, hitting back at the critics by saying: "The horse just wasn't travelling in the early part of the race and that's all there was to it. The course wasn't a problem, it's just the way he runs."

Whether or not Quinn's ride cost Norse Dancer the Derby remains open to debate, but the colt's performance there underlined in no uncertain terms that he had the ability to win a major prize. Unfortunately it was not forthcoming.

The Coral-Eclipse was an obvious next stop for Norse Dancer, who, Elsworth reckoned, had not had too gruelling a race in the Derby, but the colt's attempt to follow in the footsteps of his sire Halling, a dual Eclipse winner, went awry. Norse Dancer looked easily the pick of the three-year-olds but was never in the hunt and finished among the backmarkers.

The fitting of a visor helped to some extent in the Sussex Stakes at Goodwood but, after hitting the front over a furlong out, he gave way to Reel Buddy and Statue Of Liberty and was beaten a head and a short head. That was the closest he came to victory all season, as he subsequently failed to trouble anybody except his connections in either the Juddmonte International or Queen Elizabeth II Stakes, ridden in the former by

Norse Dancer   *bay colt, 03-4-2000*

Halling ch 1991	Diesis	Sharpen Up	Atan / Rocchetta
		Doubly Sure	Reliance / Soft Angels
	Dance Machine	Green Dancer	Nijinsky / Green Valley
		Never A Lady	Pontifex / Camogie
River Patrol b 1988	Rousillon	Riverman	Never Bend / River Lady
		Belle Dorine	Marshua's Dancer / Palsy Walsy
	Boathouse	Habitat	Sir Gaylord / Little Hut
		Ripeck	Ribot / Kyak

Bred by Ralph Ergnist and Bruno Faust in Ireland. 26,000gns Tattersalls December foal

Sire **Halling**

Won 12 of 18 races, inc. Cambridgeshire H., Eclipse S.-Gr1, twice, York International-Gr1, twice, Prix d'Ispahan-Gr1. Oldest progeny 5. Stood 2003 at Dalham Hall Stud, due to stand 2004 in Dubai. Sire of: Chancellor (Gr2), Dandoun (Gr2), Giovane Imperatore (Gr2), Fisich (Gr2), Franklins Gardens (Gr3).

Dam **River Patrol**

Won 1 of 8 starts in Britain. Half-sister to St Leger 3rd Dry Dock, to smart 7f-1m colt Showboat and to dam of Gr1-winning 2yo Mail The Desert. Sold 17,000gns carrying Norse Dancer at 1999 Tattersalls December Sale. Dam of: Regal Patrol (1994 g by Red Ransom, winner), Russillo (1995 c by Belmez, winner), Rouanne (1996 f by Unfuwain, winner), Riviera Ligure (1997 f by Hernando, non-winner), Norse Dancer (2000 c by Halling; Gr1-placed), River Blue (2001 f by Ashkalani, in training in Germany), Rosewater (2002 f by Winged Love).

Pedigree assessment

The enigmatic Norse Dancer has high-class form from 1m to 12f. He comes from a stout family, though use of speedy stallions has enabled some family members to show quite a lot of pace. That has happened with Norse Dancer, whose first two dams are by miler Rousillon and speed influence Habitat. But with both Halling and River Patrol appreciating 10f, Norse Dancer may ultimately follow suit. On pedigree, there is every encouragement that he will continue to show his class. *JH*

Robinson again and in the latter by Martin Dwyer.

Norse Dancer stays in training and if anyone can find the key to him it is Elsworth, whose instincts with such horses border on the uncanny. Quirky he may be, but this is a colt who is far too talented to go another season without winning a decent race.

Oasis Dream

3yo bay colt **131**

Green Desert (USA) - Hope (Ire) (Dancing Brave (USA))
Owner K Abdullah
Trainer J H M Gosden
Breeder Juddmonte Farms

Career: **9** starts | won **4** | second **2** | third 1 | **£433,737** win and place

By James Willoughby

O ASIS DREAM was so fast he nearly turned back time. His victory in the Victor Chandler Nunthorpe Stakes led to claims that he was the best sprinter in the world. What a shame he never got the chance to prove it.

The champion sprinter of 2003 established his claims for the title when winning the Darley July Cup at Newmarket. In his way was the Australian marvel Choisir, who had dominated two races at Royal Ascot. To beat him would take some performance, and that is exactly what Oasis Dream produced.

There was much conjecture during the July meeting about the nebulous effect of the draw. Though the advantage of racing against a rail is often responsible for the perception of a bias, the majority of trainers and jockeys were convinced that the ground on the far side of the course was faster than elsewhere.

That Oasis Dream had to break from stall 11 in the middle of the track was of great concern to John Gosden. The Manton trainer's pre-race statements generally contain a litany of references to the influence of the draw and he made no exception on this occasion.

Having the fastest horse is generally of far greater importance, however, and, if there was a disadvantage to be overcome, Oasis Dream's terrific early pace took care of it. He soon occupied a position on the shoulder of the trailblazing Choisir, only a couple of horse-widths off the rail.

Watching a brilliant sprinter in his pomp is a reminder of how much thoroughbreds love to run. Pumping his front legs, curling his knees and empowering the whole from his rippling quarters, Oasis Dream repeatedly punched a hole in the air. So relentless was his action and so steady his gaze that he looked to be lost in rhythm by halfway.

Choisir was not stopping, however, and Oasis Dream was required to focus intently during the final two furlongs. It flies in the face of reason

**Oasis Dream (Richard Hughes) lands the July Cup at
Newmarket, leaving Choisir in his wake**

to say he quickened, but he certainly found extra reserves to maintain
his momentum. It was enough to subdue the Australian star and carry
Oasis Dream to victory by a length and a half.

Paul Perry, the trainer of Choisir, was as gracious in defeat as he had
been ebullient in victory at Ascot – something that cannot be said of all
his compatriots involved in the sport. A fascinating adjunct of his soliloquy
about the winner was the point he made about the contrasting form
cycles of the two great sprinters. "The winner was a fresh horse, trained
for the race, while Choisir had already done his job and was on the way
down."

Three weeks earlier, a rusty Oasis Dream had been unable to cope
with a razor-sharp Choisir in the King's Stand Stakes at Royal Ascot.
Oasis Dream nevertheless shaped very well in third on his belated reappearance, having been too sleepy in his outlook during the spring to facilitate
a 2,000 Guineas preparation, which would have been futile anyway.

By general consensus, Oasis Dream would have no problem stepping
down to five furlongs for the Nunthorpe. After all, he had shown fine
pace in the July Cup and could have gone faster still during the early
stages had Richard Hughes encouraged him into a more hurried cadence.

2003   Race record

10th NetJets Breeders' Cup Mile (Grade 1) (Santa Anita, October 25) 3yo+ 1m Firm **106** 13 ran. *Broke well, pushed along to gain prominent position, 4th straight, driven over 1f out, hard ridden final furlong, unable to quicken, beaten 7¾l by Six Perfections*

2nd Stanley Leisure Sprint Cup (Group 1) (Haydock, September 6) 3yo+ 6f Good to soft **120** (TS 101) 10 ran. *With leader, led 2f out, soon ridden, headed inside final furlong, not quicken, beaten 1¼l by Somnus*

1st Victor Chandler Nunthorpe Stakes (Group 1) (York, August 21) 2yo+ 5f Good to firm **131** (TS 116) 8 ran. *Made all, quickened over 2f out, shaken up over 1f out, soon clear, impressive, beat The Tatling by 2½l*

1st Darley July Cup (Group 1) (Newmarket (July), July 10) 3yo+ 6f Good to firm **128** (TS 112) 16 ran. *Always prominent, chased leader over 2f out, led over 1f out, ridden out, beat Choisir by 1½l*

3rd King's Stand Stakes (Group 2) (Ascot, June 17) 3yo+ 5f Good to firm **118** (TS 96) 20 ran. *Prominent, ridden well over 1f out, soon chased winner, no impression and lost 2nd inside final furlong, beaten 2½l by Choisir*

2002

1st Shadwell Stud Middle Park Stakes (Group 1) (Newmarket, October 3) 2yo 6f Good to firm **121** (TS 91) 10 ran ● **1st** EBF Colwick Park Maiden Stakes (Nottingham, September 20) 2yo 6f Good to firm **91** (TS 28) 5 ran ● **2nd** EBF Alliance Capital Maiden Stakes (Sandown, August 30) 2yo 7f Good to firm **85** (TS 53) 11 ran ● **5th** EBF Sandown Maiden Stakes (Salisbury, August 14) 2yo 6f Good to firm **62** (TS 35) 12 ran

Oasis Dream was true to this impression at York. He took just a few yards to gather top pace, thereafter striding out with irresistible vigour. The race was over by halfway, but the show was only just beginning. Oasis Dream had fled the scene of the contest and was now in pursuit of a legend – Dayjur and his 1990 track record of 56.16 seconds.

This was one of the occasions when a clock on the screen would have elevated the moment for viewers, as it does on similar occasions in the US. It is commonplace there for track records, and even split times, to draw an audible gasp from spectators. Though racing on turf does not lend itself to the same ease of time comparison, it is still a test of how fast a horse can get from A to B. The opportunity to drag the sport in Britain forward and spark the minds of a technological generation continues to be spurned.

Oasis Dream stopped the clock at 56.20 seconds and missed Dayjur's mark by a nose. He was not flattered by the comparison, either, as the going was probably faster on the equivalent day 13 years before.

When a horse owns the capability to run times of this magnitude over five furlongs, it is rare that they are as effective on soft going as on fast. Heavy rain before the Haydock Park Sprint Cup in September therefore compromised Oasis Dream's chance. He seemed to be labouring from some way out before finishing a well-beaten second to Somnus, the winner coping much better with the conditions.

The Breeders' Cup was now on the horizon for Oasis Dream, but not

**Oasis Dream and Richard Hughes make it a Group 1
double with success in the Nunthorpe at York**

before a dalliance with the Prix de l'Abbaye at Longchamp which ended
with the deluge in Paris. Gosden then set about preparing his star for
his trip to Santa Anita without another race, choosing the Mile on turf
as his target, rather than the Sprint on dirt.

Gosden drew a parallel between Oasis Dream and the 1986 Breeders'
Cup Mile winner, Last Tycoon, who himself had been a leading sprinter
in Europe and won the same five-furlong Group 1 at York. The two were
inherently different in running style, however, the former being a fast-
twitch early pacer, the latter a strong finisher who was held up.

Stretching out a speedball like Oasis Dream necessitates taking him
out of his natural game and away from his defining characteristics. So
why did Gosden fight shy of taking up the challenge of beating the US
sprinters?

A belief has somehow developed that the Breeders' Cup races on dirt
represent a quixotic challenge for European horses. But the failure of
top-class sprinters like Double Schwartz, Green Desert, Lochsong, Stravinsky and Mozart was not down to the fast pace, kickback or the bend.
Instead, it was down to their preparation: either the inability to break
cleanly or the effects of a punishing season in which they had already

peaked. The examples of 1991 Breeders' Cup Sprint winner Sheikh Albadou and Dayjur, unlucky runner-up the previous season, show that success on dirt is not a romantically unattainable proposition, but a realistic target for a specially prepared horse who is still relatively fresh.

Oasis Dream might have been on a familiar surface in the Mile, but he was running over an unnatural trip. He had no problems with a wide draw, nor were the tight turns (which his trainer had colourfully described as akin to "running round the inside of a barrel") any hindrance to his chance. He was already struggling when catching a bump in the straight, fading to finish tenth of the 13 runners behind Six Perfections. As his trainer admitted, he just did not stay.

Though Oasis Dream was established as a sprinter long before Santa Anita, his pedigree contains a fair measure of stamina. His sire, Green Desert, is primarily an influence for speed, but gets milers when the female family contributes stamina. Oasis Dream's distaff side certainly qualifies on that score. His dam, Hope, who is a sister to the Irish Oaks winner Wemyss Bight, has already bred a Classic miler in the French 1,000 Guineas winner Zenda, as well as a Listed winner over the distance in Hopeful Light.

Pedigree was probably an influential factor in the decision to try Oasis Dream over seven furlongs on his second start as a two-year-old. On his debut he had stayed on well without being knocked about over six furlongs and he seemed to get the longer trip well enough when second to subsequent Listed winner Rimrod at Sandown.

Oasis Dream was beginning to show tremendous speed in his work at that time, however, and the reversion to six furlongs saw him win his next two starts, a maiden at Nottingham and the Group 1 Middle Park Stakes at Newmarket.

Such was the searing pace he displayed in the latter that he became the first juvenile to dip under 1min 10 sec for six furlongs on the Rowley Mile.

To a certain extent, sprinters are born and not bred. Few of the best have one-dimensional pedigrees, perhaps requiring that extra bit of inherent endurance to give them the edge in very fast-run, taxing races. There is evidence from biopsies carried out in the US that training can gradually have the effect of changing a horse's proportion of muscle fibres, and by extension its distance requirements as a racehorse. Gosden touched on this when he claimed to have changed Oasis Dream's training regimen before the Nunthorpe in order to sharpen him up for the drop down in distance.

Oasis Dream was an immense talent with a perfect big-race temperament. "He doesn't give a damn about anything," said Hughes. The Nunthorpe was one of the most impressive displays of raw pace ever and fully merited Oasis Dream being given the edge over Choisir as King of the Sprinters.

Oasis Dream — *bay colt, 30-3-2000*

Green Desert b 1983	Danzig	**Northern Dancer**	Nearctic Natalma
		Pas de Nom	Admiral's Voyage Petitioner
	Foreign Courier	Sir Ivor	Sir Gaylord Attica
		Courtly Dee	**Never Bend** Tulle
Hope b 1991	Dancing Brave	Lyphard	**Northern Dancer** Goofed
		Navajo Princess	Drone Olmec
	Bahamian	Mill Reef	**Never Bend** Milan Mill
		Sorbus	Busted Censorship

Bred by Juddmonte Farms in England

Sire Green Desert

Won 5 of 14 races, inc. July S.-Gr3, Flying Childers S.-Gr2, July Cup-Gr1, Haydock Park Sprint Cup-Gr2. Also 2nd in 2,000 Guineas-Gr1. Small, strong individual, and a grand mover. Tough, consistent performer, effective sprinting and at a mile. Sire of: Redden Burn (Gr2), Sheikh Albadou (Nunthorpe S.-Gr1, Breeders' Cup Sprint-Gr1, Haydock Park Sprint Cup-Gr1), Gabr (Gr2), Owington (July Cup-Gr1), Cape Cross (Lockinge S.-Gr1), Desert Prince (Irish 2,000 Guineas-Gr1, Prix du Moulin de Longchamp-Gr1, Queen Elizabeth II S.-Gr1), Greenlander (Gr2), Tamarisk (Haydock Park Sprint Cup-Gr1), White Heart (Charles Whittingham H.-Gr1, Churchill Downs Turf Classic S.-Gr1 (twice)), Bint Allayl (Gr2), Invincible Spirit (Haydock Park Sprint Cup-Gr1), Rose Gypsy (Poule d'Essai des Pouliches-Gr1), Oasis Dream (Middle Park S.-Gr1, July Cup-Gr1, Nunthorpe S.-Gr1), Byron (Gr2).

Dam Hope

Ran only once, unplaced over 10f at Chantilly as 3yo, but sister to Irish Oaks winner Wemyss Bight (dam of Beat Hollow). Lengthy type, who suffered severe arthritic condition, eventually leading to fusion of vertebrae. Dam of: Hopeful Light (1997 g by Warning; dual Listed winner), Harvest (1998 f by Zafonic; unraced), Zenda (1999 f by Zamindar; Classic winner), Oasis Dream (2000 c by Green Desert; triple Gr1 winner).

Pedigree assessment

Defeated by Somnus and the soft ground at Haydock, deprived of a run in the Abbaye because of the gluey conditions, then down the field at the Breeders' Cup, Oasis Dream suffered an anti-climactic end to a campaign that promised continued triumphs in the summer. Brilliant in the July Cup, he was dominant in the Nunthorpe, giving one of the best sprinting displays of recent years. But soggy going did not suit him, and a tearaway speedster over a straight course was always going to find it tough over Santa Anita's turning mile from an outside draw. The fastest son of his sire, whose Group 1 miler Cape Cross has made a promising start at stud, he will not lack demand as a stallion at Banstead Manor at a fee of £25,000 in 2004. *TM*

One Cool Cat (USA)

2yo bay colt   **121+**

Storm Cat (USA) - Tacha (USA) (Mr Prospector (USA))

Owner Mrs John Magnier

Trainer A P O'Brien

Breeder WinStar Farm

Career: **5** starts	won **4**	second **0**	third **0**	**£265,786** win and place

By James Willoughby

"**H**E doth nothing but talk of his horse." If Portia was unimpressed by a potential suitor's discourse in The Merchant of Venice, goodness knows what she would have made of Aidan O'Brien. "I think I'll knock a door in the bedroom to put him up for the winter"; "I've never come across such a blast of speed"; "the moves he makes just knock you dead"; "he has a mid-race surge that makes him very unusual"; "he goes from first to third and still has two more gears"; "he's a very serious and unusual horse in that he will make up five or six lengths in his work at home".

One Cool Cat was the subject of O'Brien's eulogies, but he could have left the talking to the horse. The Storm Cat colt annexed the two best juvenile races in Ireland – the Independent Waterford Wedgwood Phoenix Stakes and the Dunnes Stores National Stakes at The Curragh – and would have been a match for any two-year-old in Europe.

Winning Group 1 races at two can sometimes be the death knell for a horse's long-term prospects. A testament to this is the poor subsequent record of winners of the Phoenix Stakes. The fact that a horse is ahead of its contemporaries in August is almost proof that it will not be in the same position the following season. Some horses are so precocious that they burn up a great deal of mental energy while still immature. Moreover, there is also evidence that running hard at two can even cause physical harm. The manner in which One Cool Cat landed his first Group 1 win at The Curragh was the antidote to these fears.

Part of the champion's disposition in a racehorse is the tendency to do just enough. There is little point wasting energy on wide-margin wins. Superfluity creates the bigger impression, but competency lasts longer. Training plays its part. One Cool Cat was taught to stalk and pounce on the Ballydoyle gallops, an exercise which conditions a horse to comply with the instructions of its jockey. First it has to settle and race at an

One Cool Cat (Mick Kinane) lands his first Group 1 of the season in the Phoenix Stakes at The Curragh in August

even cadence, then it must accelerate until there are no more horses to pass.

One Cool Cat gave a masterclass of this discipline when winning the Phoenix Stakes. The early pace was very taxing and exuberance would have been costly, but One Cool Cat settled nicely and seemed always in control. Switched to the outside, he conjured a strong run to lead just inside the furlong marker, sustaining his momentum to the line with comfort.

The Phoenix was billed as a match between the winner and Three Valleys, but the disappointing effort of the latter rendered the contest less competitive. A length defeat of his stable companion Old Deuteronomy did not

2003   Race record

1st Dunnes Stores National Stakes (Group 1) (Curragh, September 14) 2yo 7f Good to firm **121** (TS 70) 8 ran. *Held up in rear, headway 2f out, 4th 1½f out, 3rd and challenged final furlong, led over 100yds out, stayed on well, beat Wathab by 1l*

1st Independent Waterford Wedgwood Phoenix Stakes (Group 1) (Curragh, August 10) 2yo 6f Good **117** (TS 92) 7 ran. *Held up in touch, 5th and switched to outer over 1½f out, quickened to lead under 1f out, ran on well, comfortably, beat Old Deuteronomy by 1l*

1st Dubai Duty Free Anglesey Stakes (Group 3) (Curragh, July 13) 2yo 6½f Good **112** (TS 54) 6 ran. *Held up in rear, switched to outer and smooth headway into 4th ½f out, led under 1f out, ridden out to assert final furlong, comfortably, beat Leicester Square by 1½l*

1st Leonard Sainer EBF Maiden Stakes (York, June 14) 2yo 6f Good to firm **90** (TS 43) 6 ran. *Held up, headway, hung left and led over 1f out, ran on strongly, beat Manntab by 3½l*

4th Mull Of Kintyre EBF Maiden (Curragh, April 27) 2yo 5f Good to yielding **77** (TS 39) 10 ran. *Tracked leaders in 6th, 5th and outpaced 1½f out, kept on inside final furlong, beaten 4½l by Steel Light*

convince everybody that they had witnessed a performance with the substance to match its style.

O'Brien was coy about the identity of One Cool Cat's next race, the Dewhurst Stakes being mentioned only as a possibility. The Newmarket Group 1 has never been uppermost in the Ballydoyle trainer's plans, however, and he decided to stay at home for the National Stakes, back at The Curragh in September.

In terms of its legacy, the National Stakes is just about the polar opposite of the Phoenix, three of the four most recent winners having been Refuse To Bend, Hawk Wing and Sinndar. One Cool Cat added his name to the list with a compelling display.

O'Brien's near-obsessional use of pacemakers has not always been to his advantage. It worked a treat on this occasion, however, the rabbit Haydn inducing Pearl Of Love to follow him at a suicidal pace while One Cool Cat loafed around in rear. Two furlongs out, Mick Kinane was full of confidence on One Cool Cat. He elected to keep cover, rather than switching to the outside, reasoning no doubt that he had plenty of horse underneath him and the gaps usually come in those circumstances.

One Cool Cat duly had to wait for a run, but he burst through an opening when it appeared inside the last, went at least a couple of lengths clear, then idled, allowing the strong-finishing Wathab to reduce the gap to a length. It was a deeply authoritative performance, both in terms of its visual impression and merit. Pearl Of Love, close behind Wathab in third, went on to win the Gran Criterium at San Siro the following month.

One Cool Cat's win precipitated a level of praise from his trainer that would have made the mighty Hawk Wing green with envy. What a different figure O'Brien cuts now to the laconic individual at the head of King Of Kings at Newmarket in 1998. The fiery 2,000 Guineas winner was typical of the type of juvenile he cultivated then. His young horses were quick

One Cool Cat and Mick Kinane complete a Group 1 double in the National Stakes at The Curragh

to make an impact, but not all made the improvement that is now the stable's hallmark.

On his first racecourse appearance in April, One Cool Cat was unrecognisable from the horse he had become by the end of the season. He went off a well-backed 11-8 favourite in a 10-runner maiden at The Curragh over five furlongs. Running green at halfway, he kept on willingly to finish fourth, around four and a half lengths behind the winner, Steel Light.

Rumours that One Cool Cat was the latest O'Brien runner to benefit considerably from an outing preceded him to York for his second start. It is a cliché, but this was a classic example of a horse being backed as if defeat were out of the question. The bookmakers took a defensive stance and asked for odds about One Cool Cat, but big bets still flew in and he went off 4-9. He made short work of a decent field.

O'Brien chose the Group 3 Dubai Duty Free Anglesey Stakes at The Curragh in July to further One Cool Cat's education. He was always hacking along behind a fair pace and accelerated sharply on demand to win by a length and a half from Leicester Square.

One Cool Cat's exploits described above not only reflect credit on his trainer but vindicate the decision to shell out $3.1 million for him as a yearling. It might seem easy purchasing champion racehorses when your resources are substantial, but Coolmore supremo John Magnier and his chief adviser Demi O'Byrne have a superb record at the sales by any token.

One Cool Cat is a son of the world's most expensive stallion Storm Cat, who stands at Overbrook Farm in Kentucky at a fee of $500,000. Coolmore's investment in Storm Cat has been huge, not just in yearlings but in annual breeding rights for their mares.

Coolmore are in the business of making stallions and plainly see Storm Cat as potentially a highly influential sire of sires. The best runner by the sire to have been trained by O'Brien is Giant's Causeway, whose first two-year-olds will race next season. The 'Iron Horse' stood at Coolmore for one season before being transferred to Ashford in Kentucky.

One Cool Cat is currently worth far in excess of his yearling purchase price, provided he is not a disappointment at three. His first target is the 2,000 Guineas at Newmarket for which O'Brien will send him without a preparatory race - a trend he has done much to further.

O'Brien has trained two winners of the first colts' Classic: King Of Kings in 1998 and Rock Of Gibraltar in 2002. That he has saddled no less than four beaten favourites might be disconcerting for those tempted to take a short price about One Cool Cat.

Closer inspection assuages these fears. Hawk Wing hardly let his trainer down when second in Rock Of Gibraltar's year, while Giant's Causeway occupied the same position in 2000 after contesting a furious early pace which left him a sitting duck for King's Best. Orpen, the beaten favourite in 1999, was a hugely doubtful stayer, while Hold That Tiger should have been contesting his Classic at Churchill Downs rather than Newmarket.

For all his towering promise, One Cool Cat went into the winter break an uneconomically short price for the 2,000 Guineas at around 2-1. The Dermot Weld-trained Grey Swallow is a genuine threat on the form book, while the Mark Johnston-trained pair of Pearl Of Love and Lucky Story both promise to improve with age. There is also the possibility that a lightly raced Godolphin runner could emerge in Dubai during the winter.

In addition to the threat posed by the opposition is that of the draw, which these days can influence all large-field races on the Rowley Mile. Ante-post backers should remember: there is more than one way to skin a cat.

One Cool Cat

bay colt, 26-3-2001

Storm Cat br 1983	Storm Bird	**Northern Dancer**	Nearctic Natalma
		South Ocean	New Providence Shining Sun
	Terlingua	Secretariat	Bold Ruler Somethingroyal
		Crimson Saint	Crimson Satan Bolero Rose
Tacha b/br 1992	Mr Prospector	Raise A Native	Native Dancer Raise You
		Gold Digger	Nashua Sequence
	Savannah Dancer	**Northern Dancer**	Nearctic Natalma
		Valoris	Tiziano Vali

Bred by WinStar Farm in Kentucky. $3.1 million Keeneland July yearling

Sire Storm Cat

Won 4 of 8 races, inc. Young America S.-Gr1, also 2nd (beaten a nose) in Breeders' Cup Juvenile-Gr1. Medium-sized, strongly made sort, who took more after his dam than his sire. Top-class, extremely game 2yo who had surgery for bone chips in off knee at end of season; never wholly sound thereafter. Sire of Gr1 winners: Harlan, November Snow, Desert Stormer, Missed The Storm, Mistle Cat, Sardula, Tabasco Cat, Hennessy, Aldiza, Sharp Cat, Catinca, Aljabr, Cat Thief, Forestry, Tactical Cat, Finder's Fee, Giant's Causeway, High Yield, Black Minnaloushe, Raging Fever, Sophisticat, Dessert, Hold That Tiger, Nebraska Tornado, Storm Flag Flying, Denebola, One Cool Cat.

Dam Tacha

Won 1 of 9 races. Just a useful miler, placed 2nd once from 2 outings on grass. Sister to Gr2 winner Sha Tha (dam of Gr2 winner State Shinto). Dam of: Dominique's Show (1999 f by Theatrical; unraced), Seattle Tac (2000 f by Seattle Slew; winner), One Cool Cat (2001 c by Storm Cat; Gr1 winner).

Pedigree assessment

Since John Magnier purchased a block of lifetime breeding rights in Storm Cat, a steady stream of major winners by the world's most highly priced sire has flowed out of Ballydoyle, with the $3.1 million colt One Cool Cat as the latest star. He was the most precocious and the most accomplished of the O'Brien juvenile string, and after his National Stakes victory (but before apparently consequential events elsewhere) he was named a short-priced favourite for the 2,000 Guineas. The first colts' Classic of 2004 may now prove more competitive than bookmakers imagined then, and it should be borne in mind that not since Giant's Causeway has a Ballydoyle Storm Cat product won Pattern races at both two and three years; the last few of note were essentially two-year-olds. This one, though, does have scope, and the Rowley Mile should be within his compass. *TM*

Patavellian (Ire)

5yo bay gelding **121**

Machiavellian (USA) - Alessia (Caerleon (USA))

Owner D J Deer

Trainer R Charlton

Breeder D J and Mrs Deer

Career: **19** starts | won **7** | second **1** | third **3** | **£202,701** win and place

By Lee Mottershead

THE transformation of Patavellian began on a nondescript afternoon at Chepstow in September 2002. It was completed on an anything but nondescript afternoon at Longchamp 13 months later. It was a transformation which even his trainer Roger Charlton could scarcely believe.

At the start of his three-year-old season, Patavellian and the Prix de l'Abbaye would have been chalk-and-cheese bedfellows. Midway through 2002, the one-time Willie Muir inmate was languishing in minor mile-and-a-quarter handicaps, freefalling in the ratings. Then Charlton opted to change tack, deciding that Patavellian should be dropped in trip, fitted with blinkers and allowed to run. In Chepstow's Abergavenny Autos Handicap he ran very quickly, making all to win the seven-furlong handicap off a lowly mark of 64. He ran very quickly twice more that season, bolting up in a classified stakes over the same course and distance before justifying favouritism in a Newmarket six-furlong handicap.

At the start of 2003, Patavellian was rated 82 and Charlton declared that the five-year-old could be a Wokingham contender. Ironically, that was the one race the horse failed to win during a season in which he went from good handicapper, to outstanding handicapper, to Group 1 hero.

Draw biases at Windsor can be pronounced. For the track's opening Monday evening meeting in late April they were very pronounced. Horses racing towards the far rail in sprints were greatly favoured. Six of the first seven home in the Tote Exacta Classified Stakes raced against that rail. The exception was Patavellian, who made most and forged nearly nine lengths clear of his closest pursuer on 'his' side of the track.

Patavellian immediately became an ante-post plunge for the Wokingham, a horse in which everybody seemed to have some sort of financial interest. Fingers, though, were to be burnt.

Patavellian (Steve Drowne) storms to Group 1 glory in the Prix de l'Abbaye at Longchamp

Looking back it is hard to believe that Patavellian did not win the Wokingham. Receiving weight from horses who would later be clearly his inferior, Patavellian raced off a mark of 90, a rating he would have improved upon by around two stone within less than four months. Refitted with the blinkers that had been left off at Windsor, the son of Machiavellian was never travelling as strongly as had become his custom, perhaps unwilling to let himself down on what even the official going description conceded to be firm ground. The Wokingham worked out better than any other major handicap run in 2003. The four horses who finished in front of Patavellian would all become Group 3 winners within the next three months. Patavellian would do even better.

First, though, came the Cups, Bunbury and Stewards'. Back over seven furlongs in the Bunbury, Patavellian was stunning. Ridden by Steve Drowne for the first time in over a year, Patavellian went off at five-furlong speed, creating a lead so large that good reason said he had to flounder and lose. Good reason was denied, Patavellian was not, albeit holding on by just a short head from Mine.

At Goodwood he won again, and won well. Fire Up The Band, regarded by many as a good thing, was thumped a long-looking three and a half lengths into second. Swamped by the press afterwards, it was put to

2003   Race record

1st Prix de l'Abbaye de Longchamp - Majestic Barriere (Group 1) (Longchamp, October 5)
2yo+ 5f Holding **121** (TS 111) 19 ran. *Always in touch, headway halfway, led well over 1f out, driven out, beat The Trader by 1l*

1st Vodafone Stewards' Cup (Handicap) (Goodwood, August 2) 3yo+ 6f Good **117** (TS 110) 29 ran. *Raced against farside rail, pressed leaders, led well over 2f out, easily drew clear over 1f out, impressive, beat Fire Up The Band by 3½l*

1st Ladbrokes Bunbury Cup (0-105 handicap) (Newmarket (July), July 10) 3yo+ 7f Good to firm **103** (TS 96) 20 ran. *Edged right start, made all, clear halfway, all out, beat Mine by shd*

5th Wokingham Stakes (0-110 handicap) (Ascot, June 21) 3yo+ 6f Firm **98** (TS 85) 29 ran. *Tracked farside leaders, ridden over 2f out, effort to dispute lead 1f out, one pace after, beaten 3l by Fayr Jag*

1st Tote Exacta Classified Stakes (Windsor, April 28) 3yo+ (0-80) 6f Good **92** (TS 84) 15 ran. *Led nearside group after 1f, ridden clear of remainder over 1f out, hung left but overall leader final furlong, ran on well, beat Material Witness by 1¾l*

2002

1st Links Handicap (0-85) (Newmarket, October 4) 3yo+ 6f Firm **91** (TS 70) 19 ran ● **1st** Daffodil Leisure Classified Stakes (Chepstow, September 23) 3yo+ (0-70) 7f Good to firm **101** (TS 78) 15 ran ● **1st** Renault Abergavenny Autos UK Handicap (0-65) (Chepstow, September 12) 3yo+ 7f Good **76** (TS 65) 18 ran ● **9th** arenaleisureplc.com Handicap (0-75) (Lingfield, AW, August 29) 3yo+ 10f Standard **53** (TS 23) 14 ran ● **7th** Tote Exacta Stakes (0-80 handicap) (Bath, July 8) 3yo+ 10f Good **55** (TS 38) 9 ran ● **12th** Pemberton Greenish Redfern Stakes (0-80 handicap) (Kempton, June 12) 3yo+ 9f Soft **53** (TS 31) 16 ran ● **3rd** Shooting Star Trust Handicap (0-80) (Sandown, June 4) 3yo+ 1m Good to firm **73** (TS 58) 18 ran ● **3rd** Tryon Handicap (0-80) (Salisbury, May 16) 3yo+ 7f Good **73** (TS 59) 19 ran

Charlton that Patavellian was obviously a Group performer. Charlton disagreed, arguing that his charge had won off just 95 and that a Listed race would be a big enough jump for his next assignment.

Events and Patavellian's owner, John Deer, forced Charlton to change his mind. Sidelined by injury after Goodwood, Patavellian was not fit for racing again until early October, when options were limited. Charlton wanted to go for a Group 3 at Newmarket, Deer wanted to go for the Abbaye. Deer won, and so did Patavellian.

Making his Group-race debut, running over five furlongs for the first time and on desperately heavy ground, Patavellian was being asked what Charlton considered an "impossible" question. Yet Patavellian responded instantly when a gap appeared over a furlong out and held on to lead home a British 1-2-3-4. The close proximity of runner-up The Trader in second cast doubts upon the form, yet third-placed The Tatling had earlier chased home Oasis Dream in the Nunthorpe while the fourth, Acclamation, had been successful in the Diadem Stakes eight days earlier.

What now for Patavellian? Life will not be easy. The Group 1 penalty he must shoulder in 2004 in all but the very best races will be no small burden. Yet his transformation in 2003 suggested that a new sprinting star may have landed on the scene.

Patavellian

bay gelding, 17-3-1998

			Native Dancer
		Raise A Native	Raise You
	Mr Prospector		
		Gold Digger	Nashua
Machiavellian			Sequence
br 1987			
		Halo	Hail To Reason
			Cosmah
	Coup de Folie		
		Raise The Standard	Hoist The Flag
			Natalma
		Nijinsky	Northern Dancer
			Flaming Page
	Caerleon		
		Foreseer	Round Table
			Regal Gleam
Alessia			
b 1992		Habitat	Sir Gaylord
			Little Hut
	Kiss		
		Miss Petard	Petingo
			Miss Upward

Bred by D J and Mrs Deer in Ireland

Sire Machiavellian

Won 4 of 7 races, inc. Prix Morny-Gr1, Prix de la Salamandre-Gr1. Also 2nd in 2,000 Guineas-Gr1. Medium-sized, quite attractive individual. Quick-actioned, with a useful turn of foot. Barely lasted a mile. Sire of: Kokuto Julian (Japan Gr3), Phantom Gold (Gr2), Sinyar (Gr3), Vettori (Poule d'Essai des Poulains-Gr1), Susu (Gr2), Titus Livius (Gr2), Whitewater Affair (Gr2), Invermark (Prix du Cadran-Gr1), Kahal (Gr2), Majorien (Gr2), Rebecca Sharp (Coronation S.-Gr1), Almutawakel (Prix Jean Prat-Gr1, Dubai World Cup-Gr1), Fictitious (Gr3), Horatia (Gr3), Best Of The Bests (Prix d'Ispahan-Gr1), Magic Mission (Gr3), Medicean (Lockinge S.-Gr1, Eclipse S.-Gr1), Morning Pride (Gr3), No Excuse Needed (Gr2), Patavellian (Prix de l'Abbaye de Longchamp-Gr1), Storming Home (Champion S.-Gr1, Charles Whittingham Memorial H.-Gr1, Clement L. Hirsch Memorial S.-Gr1), Street Cry (Dubai World Cup-Gr1), Medecis (Gr3), Evolving Tactics (Gr2).

Dam Alessia

Won 1 of 8 races. Sister to smart 12-14f filly Casey and half-sister to very useful stayer Crack out of daughter of Ribblesdale Stakes winner Miss Petard. Dam of: Patavellian (1998 g by Machiavellian; Gr1 winner), Alashaan (1999 f by Darshaan; placed), Avonbridge (2000 c by Averti; Listed winner, Gr1-placed), Avessia (2001 f by Averti; unplaced), 2002 c by Dr Fong.

Pedigree assessment

Judged on his pedigree it is no surprise he has run successfully over at least 7f, or even that he has been tried over 10f, as he ought not to be a sprinter. Bred on identical lines to useful 10f filly Delauncy (dam of smart 10f colt Delsarte). Interestingly, Patavellian's quite stoutly bred dam was dropped to 7f-1m after running unsuccessfully in Listed company at up to 12f, indicating that she showed speed. He should be placed profitably again in 2004. *JH*

Pearl Of Love (Ire)

2yo bay colt **115**

Peintre Celebre (USA) - Aunt Pearl (USA) (Seattle Slew (USA))

Owner M Doyle

Trainer M Johnston

Breeder Swettenham Stud

Career: **6** starts | won **4** | second **1** | third **1** | **£227,117** win and place

By Graham Dench

A CCORDING to the ante-post lists, Lucky Story is Mark John-ston's principal hope for the 2,000 Guineas. That may be the case, but do not underestimate his stablemate Pearl Of Love, who showed form of a similar level and also has the Guineas as his first major target.

Pearl Of Love has already met the Guineas favourite, One Cool Cat, and been beaten comprehensively into third, but while not even Johnston was inclined to offer excuses that day, there are grounds for thinking that he is a bit better than that bare form suggests. There will be no running away from a rematch.

It was impossible not to be impressed with One Cool Cat, who won the seven-furlong National Stakes at The Curragh easing up by a length, with his ears pricked, having had to wait for an opening. But the outsider Wathab, successful only twice in nine previous starts, also took Pearl Of Love's measure late on that day and there is a suggestion, at least, that Pearl Of Love had paid the price for racing prominently and getting involved too soon in a race which unfolded late, and in which the principals came from off the pace.

Johnston was visibly deflated after Pearl Of Love's defeat. He had clearly expected better from the colt, who had beaten Wathab more than four lengths into fourth when making short work of the Aidan O'Brien colts Tumblebrutus and The Mighty Tiger in the Group 2 Galileo Futurity Stakes over the same course and distance three weeks previously.

Darryll Holland, who rode Pearl Of Love in all but the first of his six races, was deeply impressed by Pearl Of Love in the Futurity, in which he made all and won by three and a half lengths. He was in no doubt that Pearl Of Love was "a proper 2,000 Guineas horse" and, in a reference that echoed Christophe Soumillon's about Dalakhani earlier in the summer, added that there was "a fifth gear" which he did not have to use.

**Pearl Of Love (Darryll Holland) rounds off the season
with victory in the Group 1 Gran Criterium at San Siro**

The Futurity was Pearl Of Love's third win, following a runaway success
in a Doncaster maiden that has a fine tradition as a source of classy
juveniles, and a smart defeat of Tycoon in Royal Ascot's Chesham Stakes,
where he made light of his winner's penalty and had the race in safe
keeping well over a furlong from home. He was his stable's third Chesham
winner in four years, following Helm Bank and Celtic Silence, and looked
very good value for the length and a half by which he scored.

The Queen Mary winner Attraction had looked the obvious stand-out
in Johnston's enviable Royal Ascot team, yet in the build-up to the meeting
the trainer had plumped for Pearl Of Love as his banker. After Pearl Of
Love had followed the filly's example, he said: "From the start this was
my one for the meeting. I know it's hard to say that, with Attraction
having rock-solid form, but I just think this is a magnificent, progressive
horse. I've got a gut feeling he's got it all – he's got the looks, he's got
a great temperament, he's got plenty of speed and he's got the pedigree."

2003   Race record

1st Gran Criterium (Group 1) (San Siro, October 19) 2yo 1m Good **115** 11 ran. *Headway on outside to lead after 3f, ridden over 2f out, ran on gamely, driven out, beat Spirit Of Desert by ½l*

3rd Dunnes Stores National Stakes (Group 1) (Curragh, September 14) 2yo 7f Good to firm **114** (TS 67) 8 ran. *Tracked leaders in 2nd, led 2½f out, strongly pressed over 1f out, headed over 100yds out, no extra close home, beaten 1¼l by One Cool Cat*

1st Galileo EBF Futurity Stakes (Group 2) (Curragh, August 23) 2yo 7f Good to firm **115** (TS 84) 8 ran. *Made all, quickened clear 1½f out, driven out inside final furlong, easily, beat Tumblebrutus by 3½l*

1st Chesham Stakes (Listed) (Ascot, June 18) 2yo 7f Good to firm **102** (TS 73) 13 ran. *Made virtually all, kicked clear over 1f out, unchallenged after, beat Tycoon by 1½l*

1st EBF Zetland Maiden Stakes (Doncaster, May 24) 2yo 6f Good **93** (TS 67) 11 ran. *Made most, quickened clear over 1f out, easily, beat New Mexican by 5l*

2nd Tote EBF Maiden Stakes (York, May 14) 2yo 6f Good to firm **87** (TS 51) 5 ran. *Tracked leader, headway to challenge 2f out, ridden to lead over 1f out, soon headed, rallied well final furlong, kept on, beaten ½l by Botanical*

Lucky Story and Pearl Of Love both figured among the five-day acceptors for the Dewhurst, but Pearl Of Love was always doubtful and when Lucky Story was scratched following a lacklustre gallop Johnston relied instead on the supplementary entry Duke Of Venice.

It is pure conjecture, but Pearl Of Love might have made a race of it in the Dewhurst, as the level of form he showed in his two races at The Curragh was only a length or so behind that recorded by Milk It Mick and Three Valleys. Instead he was aimed at the following afternoon's one-mile Gran Criterium at San Siro, a 'softer' Group 1 over a trip that promised to suit him better and a race Johnston had won with Lend A Hand in 1997.

Odds-on for a prize that last stayed at home back in 1995, the wide-drawn Pearl Of Love could not immediately adopt the front-running role that had served him so well for his three wins, but he was at the head of affairs towards the end of the back straight and in command from the home turn. He was always finding enough in the straight and beat the Italian-trained fourth favourite Spirit Of Desert by half a length, with the Solario winner Barbajuan close behind in third.

Johnston announced immediately that Pearl Of Love would not be seen again until Newmarket. His 1994 Guineas winner Mister Baileys went to Newmarket without a 'prep' race, and so did Bijou d'Inde, a close third in 1996, and Lend A Hand, second to King Of Kings in 1998, so there is unlikely to be any deviation from that plan. He said: "His next race will be the 2,000 Guineas. I've always felt that once you've won a Group 1 there's no reason to step back. There's very little money in the trial races and you are running against horses you've already beaten with nothing much to gain and plenty to lose."

How Pearl Of Love does as a three-year-old is going to depend upon

Pearl Of Love

bay colt, 22-1-2001

			Northern Dancer	Nearctic
		Nureyev		Natalma
			Special	Forli
	Peintre Celebre			Thong
	ch 1994		Alydar	**Raise A Native**
		Peinture Bleue		Sweet Tooth
			Petroleuse	Habitat
				Plencia
			Bold Reasoning	Boldnesian
		Seattle Slew		Reason To Earn
			My Charmer	Poker
	Aunt Pearl			Fair Charmer
	b 1989		Mr Prospector	**Raise A Native**
		Mr P's Girl		Gold Digger
			Native Street	Native Dancer
				Beaver Street

Bred by Swettenham Stud in Ireland. 100,000gns Tattersalls Houghton yearling

Sire **Peintre Celebre**

Won 5 of 7 races, inc. Prix Greffulhe-Gr2, Prix du Jockey-Club-Gr1, Grand Prix de Paris-Gr1, Prix de l'Arc de Triomphe-Gr1. Quite well-made, medium-sized individual, tip-top performer at 10-12f, with exceptional acceleration. Sire of: Dai Jin (Deutsches Derby-Gr1, Aral Pokal-Gr1), Super Celebre (Gr2), Vallee Enchantee (Gr2), Pearl Of Love (Gran Criterium-Gr1).

Dam **Aunt Pearl**

Won 2 races from 17 starts. Grand-daughter of Grade 1 winner Native Street, also grand-dam of Dowsing and Fire The Groom. Dam of: Social Charter (1995 c by Nureyev; Gr3 winner), Kalidasa (1996 f by Nureyev; winner, Gr3-placed), Halcyon Bird (1997 f by Storm Bird; unraced), Social Order (1998 g by Sadler's Wells; hurdle winner), Imperial Theatre (1999 c by Sadler's Wells; winner), Drama Club (2000 f by Sadler's Wells; placed), Pearl Of Love (2001 c by Peintre Celebre; Gr1 winner), 2002 c by Giant's Causeway.

Pedigree assessment

Peintre Celebre should ensure Pearl Of Love stays 10f, but Aunt Pearl may prevent him from lasting 12f. Progeny of Peintre Celebre tend to progress well from 2 to 3, which is encouraging for Pearl Of Love's prospects, especially as Aunt Pearl is not from a particularly precocious family. *JH*

the progress he makes over the winter and how far he stays. As Johnston points out, he was a professional from race two and more of a ready-made two-year-old than the bigger, rangier and greener Lucky Story. On the other hand, he has the pedigree more of a three-year-old than a two-year-old. As for the distance issue, he should still have the speed for a mile in May and has a middle-distance pedigree. Yet while Johnston thinks he "will stay well beyond a mile", there is no guaranteeing he will get the mile and a half of the Derby.

Persian Punch (Ire)

10yo chestnut gelding   **119**

Persian Heights - Rum Cay (USA) (Our Native (USA))

Owner J C Smith

Trainer D R C Elsworth

Breeder Adstock Manor Stud

| Career: **62** starts | won **20** | second **8** | third **11** | £1,008,785 win and place |

By Lee Mottershead

I T WAS his year. There were many better horses around, but none contributed more to the season. For Persian Punch, phenomenon is no longer too strong a word. It has all been said but it is all worth repeating. To hail Persian Punch as the most popular Flat racehorse in Britain is not sufficient. He has gone beyond the levels of popularity we normally associate with the money-dominated sport of Flat racing. In terms of looks, physique and public appeal, he is a jumper who does not jump, a racehorse who has grabbed the affections of racegoers to a far greater extent than any other in the sport's recent history.

It is not undeserved affection. His curriculum vitae may lack a Group 1 success, but to suggest that Persian Punch is merely a courageous old plodder would be grossly inaccurate. In 2003, under the wise guidance of David Elsworth, he once again confirmed himself one of the very best stayers of recent years, adding four more victories to his name, including three of the four major Cup races.

He is also the toughest. Persian Punch's public standing has been built on performances of the utmost bravery, performances which have seen him snatch victory from the jaws of defeat, performances which have left normally hardened observers unable to resist anthropomorphic tributes. On three occasions in 2003, Jeff Smith's gelding forged a short-head success. While his seven-length triumph in the Doncaster Cup was thrilling, it was also uncharacteristic.

His season began later than usual, a minor setback keeping him away until Newbury's Aston Park Stakes. Racing over an inadequate trip and carrying a 6lb penalty, he understandably struggled. Yet there was plenty of encouragement in his honourable fourth. This was a good start.

There was also plenty to admire in Persian Punch's next outing. On three occasions – in 1997, 1998 and 2000 – victory had been his in Sandown's Henry II Stakes. In 2003, he appeared in the race for the

Persian Punch (Martin Dwyer) strides out to land the Group 2 Doncaster Cup in runaway style

seventh consecutive year, and, for the seventh consecutive year, he appeared under a different jockey. Ray Cochrane, Walter Swinburn, Richard Quinn, Philip Robinson, Kieren Fallon and Jimmy Fortune had all pushed and shoved him over Sandown's stiff two miles, Cochrane, Swinburn and Robinson all finishing breathless but victorious. In 2003 it was the turn of Martin Dwyer.

Dwyer's first experience aboard Persian Punch had come in the previous season's Geoffrey Freer Stakes when he replaced Richard Hughes, who had been found guilty of going off too quickly on the gelding's previous start in the Goodwood Cup, Persian Punch trailing in a long last and prompting many to demand his retirement. Retired he was not, Dwyer coming in for the ride and immediately cementing a partnership that has now endured longer than any other in the horse's long career.

At Sandown, Persian Punch was unable to notch a fourth Henry II win, running creditably in fourth but not doing enough to suggest that a first Gold Cup success was about to come his way.

Royal Ascot has always proved a thorn in his heel. Third in the Queen's Vase at three, Persian Punch has returned every year since, on every occasion contesting the Gold Cup with connections hoping that one of Flat racing's most famous hoodoos could finally be broken. It never has

2003   Race record

1st Jockey Club Cup (Group 3) (Newmarket, October 18) 3yo+ 2m Good to firm **119** (TS 78) 6 ran. *Led and soon clear, pushed along over 6f out, ridden and headed over 2f out, rallied under pressure to lead near finish, beat Millenary by shd*

8th Prix du Cadran - Casinos Barriere (Group 1) (Longchamp, October 5) 4yo+ 2m4f Holding **73** 10 ran. *Led narrowly until headed after 5f, disputing lead halfway, driven 6f out, 5th and soon beaten straight, beaten 48l by Westerner*

1st GNER Doncaster Cup (Group 2) (Doncaster, September 11) 3yo+ 2m2f Good **119** (TS 96) 6 ran. *Made all, pushed clear halfway, ridden over 3f out and stayed on strongly, beat Dusky Warbler by 7l*

4th Weatherbys Insurance Lonsdale Stakes (Group 3) (York, August 19) 3yo+ 2m Good to firm **117** (TS 73) 6 ran. *Led, pushed along 10f out, headed over 2f out, outpaced approaching final furlong, beaten 3½l by Bollin Eric*

1st Lady O Goodwood Cup (Group 2) (Goodwood, July 31) 3yo+ 2m Good **119** (TS 110) 9 ran. *Led, pushed along halfway, driven over 4f out, headed over 2f out, rallied in typically gallant fashion to lead again last 100yds, just held on, beat Jardines Lookout by shd*

1st Addleshaw Goddard Stakes (Registered As The Esher Stakes) (Listed) (Sandown, July 5) 4yo+ 2m½f Good to firm **113** (TS 59) 5 ran. *Led, pushed along 5f out, ridden 3f out, headed 2f out, looked held 1f out, rallied most gamely final 100yds to lead final stride, beat Cover Up by shd*

2nd Gold Cup (Group 1) (Ascot, June 19) 4yo+ 2m4f Good to firm **117** (TS 65) 12 ran. *Led, pushed along after 1m, driven along again from 6f out, headed over 3f out, stayed on gamely to hold 2nd place final 2f, no chance with winner, beaten 6l by Mr Dinos*

4th Bonusprint Henry II Stakes (Group 2) (Sandown, May 26) 4yo+ 2m½f Good to firm **109** (TS 83) 10 ran. *Pressed leader, led 10f out, ridden and headed over 2f out, kept on same pace, beaten 5¾l by Mr Dinos*

4th skybet.com Stakes (Registered As The Aston Park Stakes) (Listed) (Newbury, May 17) 4yo+ 1m5½f Good **106** (TS 87) 10 ran. *Chased leaders, soon pushed along, went 2nd 7f out, led over 4f out, headed over 3f out, weakened final 2f, beaten 10½l by Gamut*

Other wins

2002 1st Jockey Club Cup (Group 3) (Newmarket, October 19) 3yo+ 2m Good **117** (TS 104) 8 ran ● **1st** Catisfield Hinton And Stud Conditions Stakes (Salisbury, September 5) 3yo+ 1m6f Good to firm **110** (TS 63) 5 ran **2001** 1st Weatherbys Insurance Lonsdale Stakes (Group 3) (York, August 21) 3yo+ 2m Good **122** (TS 92) 10 ran ● **1st** JPMorgan Private Bank Goodwood Cup (Group 2) (Goodwood, August 2) 3yo+ 2m Good **123** (TS 104) 12 ran **2000** 1st Jockey Club Cup (Group 3) (Newmarket, October 14) 3yo+ 2m Good to soft **124** (TS 122) 9 ran ● **1st** Prix Kergorlay Groupe Lucien Barriere (Group 2) (Deauville, August 20) 3yo+ 1m7f Good to soft **116** 7 ran ● **1st** Bonusprint Stakes (Registered As The Henry II Stakes) (Group 3) (Sandown, May 29) 4yo+ 2m½f Heavy **113** (TS 23) 7 ran **1999** 1st Dransfield Novelty Company Conditions Stakes (Doncaster, November 5) 3yo+ 1m6½f Soft **104** (TS 65) 5 ran ● **1st** Weatherbys Insurance Lonsdale Stakes (Group 3) (York, August 18) 3yo+ 2m Good to firm **115** (TS 67) 5 ran ● **1st** Bonusprint Henry II Stakes (Group 3) (Sandown, May 25) 4yo+ 2m½f Good **116** (TS 80) 11 ran ● **1st** Sagaro Stakes Group 3 (Newmarket, May 1) 4yo+ 2m Good to soft **118** (TS 72) 10 ran **1997** 1st Bonusprint Henry II Stakes (Sandown, May 26) 4yo+ 2m½f Good to firm **106** (TS 71) 7 ran ● **1st** Quantel Aston Park Stakes (Newbury, May 17) 4yo+ 1m5½f Soft **114** (TS 87) 6 ran **1996** 1st Bahrain Trophy (Listed) (Newmarket (July), July 11) 3yo 1m7f Good to firm **100** (TS 104) 6 ran ● **1st** Bishopstone Conditions Stakes (Salisbury, June 11) 3yo 1m6f Good **88** (TS 76) 5 ran ● **1st** Bowring Group Median Auction Maiden Stakes (Windsor, May 13) 3yo 10f Good to firm **76** (TS 68) 18 ran been. Soundly beaten when favourite in both 1997 and 1998, he was dismissed at 20-1 and 16-1 when similarly well beaten the following two years. Then, dispelling the notion that the Gold Cup was not for him, he ran one of the best races of his life in 2001, going down by just a head to Royal Rebel after a pulsating, head-bobbing duel. Twelve months later, it was disappointment but not disgrace as he came in sixth, around four lengths behind the returning hero Royal Rebel.

Thus, when Persian Punch lined up as one of 12 starters in the 2003 Gold Cup, hopes could not be high. Appearing to have plenty to find on form and with his unfortunate record at Ascot to boot, he was once again sent off at 20-1. Yet Elsworth had not lost faith, reasoning that his stable star represented wonderful value and that whatever beat him would win. On both counts Elsworth was right.

Persian Punch ran a screamer. Although six lengths inferior to Mr Dinos, one of the most impressive Gold Cup winners in years, he still acquitted himself with great credit, beating the remaining ten and showing his customary grit and determination to maintain his runner-up berth up the straight. That grit and determination would be seen again – and regularly – before the season's close.

Sandown was the start of something special. There was something inevitable about Persian Punch's success in the inaugural running of the Listed Esher Stakes. Kieren Fallon does not make many mistakes but at Sandown he made one. Having stalked the pace-setting Persian Punch, he sent Cover Up to the front two furlongs out, passing Persian Punch on the big man's inside, going a length up but giving his opponent plenty of time to respond. He responded. Climbing a hill that has witnessed some of the sport's best finishes, Persian Punch dragged back Cover Up stride by stride, inching into the leader's advantage with each deep breath. You knew he was going to get there. The head said he could not, but the heart knew he would and he did. We cherished it, thinking it perhaps the defining moment of the season, blissfully unaware that the box of delights would be opened again – and soon.

He had won the Goodwood Cup before, seeing off Double Honour under one-time regular rider Richard Quinn in 2001. The winning margin that day was one and a half lengths. It would be a lot less this time.

In many ways, it was a carbon copy of Sandown, Jardines Lookout on this occasion taking over the role of best supporting actor, Persian Punch once again the lead. Headed two furlongs out, Persian Punch again rallied heroically, getting to the front 100 yards from the line before resisting the final thrust from the gallant Jardines Lookout.

Goodwood ignited. Having roared him home, they ran from the stands, flocking as one to the winner's enclosure, hailing the conquering hero. Elsworth sported dark glasses lest the tears were made public, Smith came out with more superlatives and Dwyer looked for an oxygen mask.

The Lonsdale Stakes at York was not such a happy occasion. It was never going to be easy. At least two of Persian Punch's opponents, the previous year's St Leger winner Bollin Eric and Zindabad – good enough to finish third in a King George – were far speedier, yet Dwyer knew that to go too fast early would lead to Persian Punch emptying in the closing stages. In the end, Dwyer became overly cautious and found himself outpaced up the flat straight, fourth but far from disgraced.

We could not have predicted what happened at Doncaster. Never before had Persian Punch been so utterly and completely dominant, the strong early tempo he dictated ruthless in its efficiency, his main rivals all in submission before they turned into the straight. Persian Punch galloped up the long Doncaster straight alone, imperious and majestic. This was his moment, his equivalent of the Open golf champion's victorious Sunday stroll up the 18th fairway. At Doncaster he was brilliant.

At Longchamp he wasn't. There are few opportunities for stayers to land a Group 1 prize, the Prix du Cadran representing one of those. Unfortunately, on the first Sunday in October Paris's premier racecourse represented a swamp, in which Persian Punch sank. Headed a long way from home, he began to lose touch at the head of the false straight, eventually trailing home 48 lengths behind Westerner.

Yet, to see Persian Punch in the days after Longchamp, it would have been impossible to guess he had had a race. He bounced back from his French exertions with gusto, so much so that Elsworth reversed his original decision and pointed the gelding at the Jockey Club Cup, a race that had gone the horse's way 12 months earlier and in 2000.

This was as good as it gets, the highlight of the season and as satisfying an experience as the sport can provide. He had regularly won races in the gloriously theatrical manner in which he was to win the 2003 Jockey Club Cup, yet this was better. This was the best. Racing just 13 days after his Cadran slog and in search of a victory that would take his earnings past £1 million, he set off at his usual unrelenting rate of knots, coming under a Dwyer drive a full mile and a quarter from home. Two furlongs out, Millenary passed him on the bridle, then Kasthari on his outside, Tholjanah on his inside. He had gone from first to fourth in a matter of strides. He could not win. Then, though, he met the rising ground and rose to the occasion, a flick across the nose from the whip of Tholjanah's rider Richard Hills only igniting him more. He was roused, thousands of racegoers urging him forward, united like few racing audiences have been before or will be again. He passed the post as one with Millenary. Mercifully, the wait for the verdict was short, Channel 4 commentator Simon Holt remarking that "this place has erupted" when Persian Punch was declared the winner, again by a short head.

Dwyer paraded Persian Punch in front of the stands before a fanfare greeted his return to the winner's enclosure. Newmarket, a racecourse that rarely does sincere emotion, did sincere emotion. And we loved it.

It was the end to a remarkable season, to his season. At the ripe old

Persian Punch   *chestnut gelding, 13-4-1993*

		Bold Lad	Bold Ruler
	Persian Bold		Barn Pride
Persian Heights		Relkarunner	Relko
ch 1985			Running Blue
	Ready And Willing	Reliance	Tantieme
			Relance
		No Saint	Narrator
			Vellada
	Our Native	Exclusive Native	Raise A Native
			Exclusive
Rum Cay		Our Jackie	Crafty Admiral
ch 1985			Rakahanga
	Oraston	Morston	Ragusa
			Windmill Girl
		Orange Cap	Red God
			Hymette

Bred by Adstock Manor Stud in Ireland. 14,000gns Tattersalls October yearling

Sire Persian Heights

Won 4 of 10 races, inc. St James's Palace S.-Gr1. Also disqualified 'winner' of York International S.-Gr1, 2nd in Champion S-Gr1. Rangy, handsome horse, and a game, consistent performer with a sharp turn of foot. Died March 1993. Sire of: Persian Brave (Gr3), Persian Punch (Gr2 x 4, Gr3 x 9).

Dam Rum Cay

Ran 3 times at 4, winning a 2m bumper and a 14.6f maiden. Leggy, angular type. Dam of: Visual (1990 c by Rousillon; winner), Island Magic (1991 c by Indian Ridge; Gr3 winner), Persian Punch (1993 g by Persian Heights; multiple Pattern winner), Rum Baba (1994 g by Tirol; winner), Cobra Lady (1995 f by Indian Ridge; unplaced), Bahamas (1997 g by Barathea; winner), Red Bartsia (1998 f by Barathea; winner), Wadmaan (1999 c by Singspiel; placed), Bourbonella (2000 f by Rainbow Quest; unraced).

Pedigree assessment

At the age of ten, the nation's favourite horse took his tally of Pattern wins to 13, matching the record set by Brigadier Gerard and equalled subsequently by Ardross and Acatenango. His pedigree offers no clues as to his extraordinary talents; like America's John Henry in the 1980s and our own Brown Jack between the wars, he has performed far above the level that might have been predicted from his background and has maintained that standard way beyond a normal span. *TM*

age of ten, a horse whom many observers wanted retired a year earlier, enjoyed his best-ever campaign and reached heights of form comparable to those he attained in his youth.

Flat racing has seen nothing like it in years. He is a gentle giant yet with a positively ruthless will to win, his continued presence enriching the sport. He embodies everything that is great about the racehorse. There can be no greater compliment.

Phoenix Reach (Ire)

3yo bay colt   **120**

Alhaarth (Ire) - Carroll's Canyon (Ire) (Hatim (USA))

Owner Winterbeck Manor Stud

Trainer A M Balding

Breeder Miss Christine Kiernan

Career: **5** starts	won **3**	second **1**	third **1**	**£443,591** win and place

By Graham Dench

ONE would have thought it impossible for Andrew Balding to have bettered winning a Classic in his first season as the licence-holder at Kingsclere, yet in many ways the success of Phoenix Reach in the Canadian International at Woodbine was just as rewarding as Casual Look's famous victory at Epsom.

Financially it was certainly more lucrative, as the International's first prize of just under £360,000 beat the Oaks purse by almost £120,000. Then there was the satisfaction of winning such a prestigious prize on another continent. But, above all, it was the challenge.

Casual Look had been straightforward to train, inasmuch as training any animal as delicate and highly strung as a thoroughbred racehorse can be considered straightforward. Phoenix Reach had not. Indeed he had suffered such a serious injury on the gallops as a two-year-old that for many months it was odds against him making it to the racecourse again. Bad news for any horse, but all the more so for one who had been regarded all spring as possibly the best prospect in the yard and one who had gone a long way towards confirming as much against Norse Dancer on his debut at Salisbury.

Balding, who at the time was technically assisting his father, Ian, takes up the story: "It was a day or two before he was due to run in one of those good conditions races at Newbury and he was just having a nice blow when he pulled up on three legs at the top of the hill. When he was x-rayed it was discovered he'd split a pastern, and it was as bad a split pastern as you'll see. It had gone right up into the fetlock and needed a plate and three pins in it.

"He was stood in his box for months back at Kingsclere, and when we got him out again in the spring he was never one hundred per cent. There was a fair bit of reaction to the injury, so much so that he had to have another operation to remove the plate and pins. We never thought

Phoenix Reach (Martin Dwyer, right) holds on to land the Canadian International at Woodbine in October

he'd make it back to the racecourse, and that he did is all down to our vet, Simon Knapp."

Six weeks of swimming and walking helped Balding get some of the excess weight off Phoenix Reach following his enforced incarceration, and a brief but welcome wet spell allowed him to get three good gallops into him. The rest, thankfully, was relatively plain sailing. Making his belated reappearance in a maiden race at Newbury in July, Phoenix Reach overcame traffic problems to win impressively. By the end of the month he had established himself as a serious St Leger prospect by beating a host of fellow Doncaster entries in the Peugeot Gordon Stakes at Goodwood.

Phoenix Reach demonstrated levels of both class and guts that are rare in one so inexperienced at Goodwood, getting home by a short head and half a length from High Accolade and Hawk Flyer. Bookmakers were impressed and elevated all three to the head of the Leger betting.

Phoenix Reach improved again in the St Leger, as one would have expected, but circumstances conspired to deny him the opportunity to perform to his optimum there. He was short of room at a crucial stage

1st Pattison Canadian International (Grade 1) (Woodbine, October 19) 3yo+ 12f Yielding
118 10 ran. *Led, pulling hard early, headed halfway, close 5th straight, driven and ran on 1½f out, led 1f out, ridden out, ran on well, beat Macaw by ¾l*

3rd Seabiscuit St Leger (Group 1) (Doncaster, September 13) 3yo 1m6½f Good **120** (TS 91) 12 ran. *Tracked leaders, effort when short of room briefly over 2f out, soon ridden, kept on final furlong, beaten 2¾l by Brian Boru*

1st Peugeot Gordon Stakes (Group 3) (Goodwood, July 29) 3yo 12f Good **113** (TS 85) 10 ran. *Hampered in midfield after 3f, progress 3f out to lead 2f out, narrowly headed just over 1f out, rallied gamely to lead last 150yds, just held on, beat High Accolade by shd*

1st Stan James 08000 383384 Maiden Stakes (Newbury, July 3) 3yo 12f Good **88** (TS 69) 14 ran. *In rear, steady headway to track leaders and not clear run 2f out, hampered over 1f out, switched right and quickened to lead final 100yds, comfortably, beat Arresting by 1¼l*

2002

2nd Herbert And Gwen Blagrave Maiden Stakes (Salisbury, June 27) 2yo 7f Firm **86** (TS 29) 9 ran

and, in his trainer's view, raced on the worst of the ground, so did pretty well to finish third behind favourite Brian Boru and High Accolade, beaten under three lengths by the winner and doing best of those that had raced up with the pace.

The result of the Canadian International tended to support Balding's view that Phoenix Reach might have won the St Leger with better luck, since he had Brian Boru back in third. However, by general consensus Brian Boru was not ridden to best advantage at Woodbine and the visor with which Phoenix Reach was equipped for the first time – he is lazy at home and his sire Alhaarth had improved for the application of headgear – was another factor.

Judging from Phoenix Reach's behaviour in the preliminaries, the headgear might have sharpened him up too much, as he got himself into a bit of a state. But the ponies that lead horses to the start in Canada and the United States were possibly to blame, since Balding says Phoenix Reach has always been "very randy". In the race itself the colt was the ultimate professional and, given a terrific ride by Martin Dwyer, who was still on a high following his emotional win on Persian Punch the previous day, he won by three-quarters of a length from the vastly improved former Jim Goldie handicapper Macaw. Brian Boru was another head away.

The Coronation Cup is likely to be the first big target for Phoenix Reach in 2004, but anything is possible if all goes well there. While a mile and a half is arguably his optimum trip, he clearly stays further and yet possibly also has enough speed to be effective over shorter distances. Balding admits he could end up anywhere and he does not rule out aiming him at the huge prizes on offer in Australia in the autumn. He is quite a prospect.

Phoenix Reach

bay colt, 05-3-2000

Alhaarth b 1993	Unfuwain	Northern Dancer	Nearctic Natalma
		Height Of Fashion	Bustino Highclere
	Irish Valley	Irish River	Riverman Irish Star
		Green Valley	Val de Loir Sly Pola
Carroll's Canyon ch 1989	Hatim	Exclusive Native	Raise A Native Exclusive
		Sunday Purchase	TV Lark Dame Fritchie
	Tuna	Silver Shark	Buisson Ardent Palsaka
		Vimelette	Vimy Sea Parrot

Bred by Christine Kiernan in Ireland
Ir£16,000 Goffs November foal, 36,000gns Doncaster St Leger yearling

Sire Alhaarth

Won 8 of 17 races, inc Vintage S.-Gr3, Solario S.-Gr3, Champagne S.-Gr2, Dewhurst S.-Gr1, Prix du Rond Point-Gr2, Curragh International S.-Gr2, Prix Dollar-Gr2. Strong, well-proportioned, excellent mover. Stands at Derrinstown Stud, Ireland, 2004 fee €25,000. Oldest progeny 4, sire of: Bandari (Gr2), Dominica (Gr2), Maharib (Gr3), Misterah (Gr3), Phoenix Reach (Canadian International S.-Gr1).

Dam Carroll's Canyon

Unraced. By well-bred Gr1 winner but disappointing sire, half-sister to Arc winner Carroll House (by Lord Gayle). Dam of: The Director (1993 g by Prince Rupert; winner), Kilbride Lass (1994 f by Lahib; unraced), unnamed (1995 c by Indian Ridge; unraced), Capriolo (1996 g by Priolo; winner), Athlumney Pearl (1997 f by Lycius; unraced), Arenas (1999 c by Revoque, winner in Greece), Phoenix Reach (2000 c by Alhaarth; Gr1 winner), Royal Canyon (2001 f by Royal Applause; unplaced), 2002 f by Shinko Forest.

Pedigree assessment

His pedigree indicated he would appreciate at least 10f and should be effective over 12f, and he has fulfilled that. Alhaarth, though he gained his biggest win at two, was highly effective at four, while Carroll House progressed well with age. With that in mind, the lightly raced Phoenix Reach has every chance of making further progress in 2004. *JH*

Porlezza (Fr)

4yo chestnut filly **116**

Sicyos (USA) - Pupsi (Fr) (Matahawk)
Owner Mme E Hilger
Trainer Y De Nicolay
Breeder Paul Hilger

Career: **17** starts | won **5** | second **2** | third **1** | **£177,306** win and place

By Richard Austen

SUCCESSFULLY defending their top prizes has usually proved much too much for French-trained sprinters in recent years, but Porlezza did her bit to keep the flag flying in 2003 by winning the Prix Maurice de Gheest. It was the first time since 1997 that the French had managed to keep that Deauville Group 1 prize at home. They were fancied to do so in the latest running, but not with Porlezza.

At 16-1, Porlezza faced 11 rivals, headed by 22-10 favourite Zipping, who was back on home turf after his fourth places in the Golden Jubilee Stakes at Royal Ascot and the July Cup at Newmarket. Proven Group 1 sprinters were otherwise nowhere to be seen, but Criquette Head-Maarek's three-year-old filly Etoile Montante had been placed over a mile in both the Prix Marcel Boussac and Poule d'Essai des Pouliches.

Lucky Strike, trained in Holland, had a chance, having won the Prix de la Porte Maillot in June, but the five-strong raiding party from Britain looked more potent: Gerard Butler's Nayyir had to improve on what he showed to take third in the same race 12 months earlier but arrived on the back of a Group 2 success over seven furlongs at Goodwood, while Tante Rose had been third at Goodwood, Mail The Desert had won the previous year's Moyglare Stud Stakes, Listed winner Avonbridge was on the upgrade and Atavus was bidding to spring one of his surprises.

In contrast to most of her opponents, Porlezza was stepping up in trip. Hitherto she had usually been seen over five furlongs and indeed she was quick enough to have gone down by only two lengths, always in touch, over Goodwood's sharp five in a Group 3 12 months earlier.

The Maurice de Gheest showed that she was capable of a telling late burst over a furlong and a half further. Held up, Porlezza was last and looking for room one and a half furlongs out but a furlong later she had made up the five lengths required to put her nose in front. Etoile Montante was staying on again at the death and Avonbridge kept on well in the

Porlezza (Christophe Soumillon) lands the Group 1 Prix Maurice de Gheest at Deauville in August

front rank but Porlezza passed the post ahead by a length. One runner did not finish. Zipping staggered in rear and fell in sickening fashion at halfway, but miraculously he was able to walk back to the stables soon afterwards and was diagnosed as having broken a blood vessel.

Some might debate whether six and a half furlongs is a sprint distance, but Porlezza was undoubtedly one of the top French sprinters. In fact, it is not too hard to argue that she showed her best form over five furlongs on fast ground two months before the Maurice de Gheest. On that occasion, Porlezza was bidding for her second consecutive victory in the Prix du Gros-Chene.

The Group 2 at Chantilly had been the highlight of her three-year-old season, preceding her Goodwood fourth and a 12th of 17 in the Nunthorpe at York, but something of a higher order was required to repeat the dose in 2003. Zipping was there again, meeting Porlezza on the same terms as in the Maurice de Gheest, as was another familiar and serious sparring partner in Swedish Shave. Captain Rio and Lady Dominatrix were British challengers, joined by The Trader, 16-1 for this event but about to show on several occasions in 2003 that he was better than ever. The Gros-Chene was one of them but Porlezza led in the final furlong to beat The

2003   Race record

5th Prix de l'Abbaye de Longchamp - Majestic Barriere (Group 1) (Longchamp, October 5) 2yo+ 5f Holding **112** (TS 104) 19 ran. *Always in touch, headway 2f out, reached 3rd briefly inside final furlong, one pace, beaten 2l by Patavellian*

1st Prix Maurice de Gheest (Group 1) (Deauville, August 10) 3yo+ 6½f Good to soft **114** (TS 51) 12 ran. *Held up in rear, switched left well over 1f out, rapid headway approaching final furlong, led inside final furlong, driven out, beat Etoile Montante by 1l*

7th (disq from 5th) Prix de Ris-Orangis (Group 3) (Deauville, July 6) 3yo+ 6f Good to soft **104** (TS 96) 7 ran. *In touch, 3rd halfway, ridden and went 2nd inside final furlong, no extra close home, finished 5th, disqualified and placed last after jockey failed to weigh in*

1st Prix du Gros-Chene (Group 2) (Chantilly, June 1) 3yo+ 5f Good **116** (TS 98) 8 ran. *Always close up, ridden and quickened to lead inside final furlong, pushed out, beat The Trader by ¾l*

7th Prix de Saint-Georges (Group 3) (Longchamp, May 11) 3yo+ 5f Good to soft **89** (TS 75) 7 ran. *Unruly in stalls and unseated jockey, prominent in 3rd, disputing 2nd halfway, lost place from 1½f out, beaten 6¾l by Best Walking*

2002

7th Prix de l'Abbaye de Longchamp - Majestic Barriere (Group 1) (Longchamp, October 6) 2yo+ 5f Good **101** (TS 92) 20 ran ● **3rd** Prix du Petit Couvert (Group 3) (Longchamp, September 12) 3yo+ 5f Good **111** (TS 77) 8 ran ● **12th** Victor Chandler Nunthorpe Stakes (Group 1) (York, August 22) 2yo+ 5f Good to firm **101** (TS 79) 17 ran ● **4th** King George 200th Anniversary Stakes (Group 3) (Goodwood, August 1) 3yo+ 5f Good **111** (TS 94) 14 ran ● **1st** Prix du Gros-Chene (Group 2) (Chantilly, June 2) 3yo+ 5f Good **108** (TS 69) 7 ran ● **2nd** Prix de Saint-Georges (Group 3) (Longchamp, May 12) 3yo+ 5f Soft **106** (TS 72) 10 ran ● **7th** Prix Servanne (Listed) (Chantilly, April 23) 3yo+ 5½f Good (TS 54) 7 ran

Other wins

2001 1st Prix de la Vallee d'Auge (Listed) (Deauville, August 21) 2yo 5f Good to soft (TS 71) 5 ran ● **1st** Prix de la Verrerie (Unraced) (Chantilly, June 29) 2yo 6f Good 11 ran

Trader by three-quarters of a length, with Zipping third, later promoted to second.

The latest season brought Porlezza three defeats. On her reappearance, she misbehaved and injured herself in the stalls, reportedly for the second year running. She was a close fifth, disqualified when her jockey failed to weigh in, over six furlongs on good to soft ground in the Prix de Ris-Orangis at Deauville. The trip seemed an excuse at the time, but not after the Maurice de Gheest five weeks later. Conserving her for a last-to-first run may have helped her gain that win, which was reportedly the first Group 1 success by a Deauville trainer.

Yves de Nicolay, Porlezza's trainer, said after the Maurice de Gheest: "Now we've succeeded at this distance, who knows what she can do over a mile?" Porlezza's next start, however, was back at five for the Prix de l'Abbaye and she ran creditably to be the only non-British runner in the first eight, coming from the rear to be beaten about two lengths in fifth. The Maurice de Gheest was retained, but Kistena (1996) and Imperial Beauty (2001) are the only French winners of their premier sprint in the past 25 years.

Porlezza

chestnut filly, 07-2-1999

		Northern Dancer	Nearctic / Natalma
	Lyphard		
		Goofed	Court Martial / Barra
Sicyos ch 1981			
		Habitat	Sir Gaylord / Little Hut
	Sigy		
		Satu	Primera / Creation
		Sea Hawk	Herbager / Sea Nymph
	Matahawk		
		Carromata	St Paddy / Carrozza
Pupsi b 1985			
		Bolkonski	Balidar / Perennial
	Poitevine		
		Pola de Raggia	River Peace / Sly Pola

Bred by Paul Hilger in France

Sire Sicyos

Won 3 races, inc. Prix d'Arenberg-Gr3, Prix de Saint-Georges-Gr3, also 3rd Prix de l'Abbaye-Gr1. Best at 5f. By top-class miler and fine sire out of top-class sprinter. Stands at Haras du Petit Tellier, 2003 fee €2,000. Sire of: Bulington (Gr3), Mister Sicy (Gr3), Sicy d'Alsace (Del Mar Oaks-Gr1), Porlezza (Prix Maurice de Gheest-Gr1).

Dam Pupsi

Won 5 races in France at 4 and 5 at around 10f. By high-class stayer out of grand-daughter of top-class 2yo/sprinter Sly Pola. Dam of: Pingeli (1993 g by Dancing Spree; placed), Porto Ronco (1995 g by Dancing Spree; unplaced), Ponte Brolla (1997 f by Highest Honor; winner, Listed-placed), Porlezza (1999 f by Sicyos; Gr1 winner), Porza (2000 f by Septieme Ciel; placed), Pozzo (2001 c by Medaaly; non-winner).

Pedigree assessment

The sire was a sprinter and, with the exception of Matahawk, the dam has a speedy pedigree. Clearly in Porlezza's case, Matahawk's stamina counts for nothing. Not an obvious top-class performer on pedigree, but Sicyos has turned up with the occasional high-class horse in the past, and Porlezza is distantly related to some outstanding performers. *JH*

Powerscourt

3yo bay colt **121**

Sadler's Wells (USA) - Rainbow Lake (Rainbow Quest (USA))

Owner Mrs John Magnier

Trainer A P O'Brien

Breeder Juddmonte Farms

Career: **8** starts | won **3** | second **3** | third **1** | **£184,369** win and place

---

By Alan Sweetman

THE two Aidan O'Brien-trained colts who dominated the finish of a maiden at Naas in the first week of August 2002 went on to experience sharply contrasting fortunes. The winner, Macedonian King, was sacrificed as a pacemaker in Pattern races on his next three starts and disappeared from public view thereafter, while runner-up Powerscourt ended his juvenile season with a Group 1 placing to his credit and consolidated his reputation during a high-level three-year-old campaign.

Having obtained another runner-up spot on his second outing as a juvenile, behind Lateen Sails at Newmarket, Powerscourt was backed down to 1-3 favouritism at Punchestown in mid-October, when he made heavy weather of beating Latino Magic by a neck after veering badly to the left towards the finish. It required a stewards' inquiry to confirm the result and the form looked ordinary. This was deceptive since Latino Magic went on to put his young trainer Robbie Osborne on the map in 2003 by winning three handicaps and a Listed race.

O'Brien was sufficiently encouraged by Powerscourt's effort to allow him to take his chance in the Racing Post Trophy at Doncaster, a race in which he had supplied the winner in three of the five previous seasons. Here George Duffield sent him to the front two furlongs out before he was reeled in by stablemate Brian Boru, who thus confirmed his home reputation as a leading Derby candidate for 2003.

By the time of Powerscourt's reappearance in the Budweiser Irish Derby, Brian Boru had been a major disappointment at Epsom. Ballydoyle supplied six of the nine runners in the premier Irish Classic, but none of them was a match for the Aga Khan-owned pair Alamshar and Dalakhani. The 150-1 shot Roosevelt proved best, taking third place ahead of Brian Boru, with Powerscourt in sixth. Although somewhat inconclusive as a test of whether Powerscourt had trained on

Powerscourt (Mick Kinane, right) wins the Group 2 Great Voltigeur from stablemate Brian Boru at York in August

satisfactorily, it was enough to make him an odds-on favourite for a ten-furlong conditions event at Leopardstown in July. Renewing rivalry with Napper Tandy, who had finished two lengths behind him in the Irish Derby, he made all in convincing fashion.

Two years earlier, O'Brien had sent out Milan to become the first Irish-trained winner of York's Daily Telegraph Great Voltigeur Stakes since Alleged in 1977. This time he had two candidates for the race, Brian Boru and Powerscourt. Mick Kinane opted for Powerscourt, leaving Jamie Spencer on Brian Boru, who was having his first run since the Irish Derby. Kinane took the initiative by going to the front two furlongs out, at a stage when Spencer was beginning to produce Brian Boru from off the pace with a promising challenge. Brian Boru got to the front just inside the final furlong, before Powerscourt, possibly that bit sharper as a result of his interim outing, seized control again in the closing stages

2003   Race record

3rd Irish Field St Leger (Group 1) (Curragh, September 13) 3yo+ 1m6f Good to firm **121** (TS 25) 6 ran. *Close up in 2nd, driven along and outpaced entering straight, 3rd 2f out, stayed on well under pressure final furlong, beaten 1l by Vinnie Roe*

1st Daily Telegraph Great Voltigeur Stakes (Group 2) (York, August 19) 3yo 12f Good to firm **121** (TS 92) 9 ran. *Tracked leaders, ridden to lead over 2f out, headed just inside final furlong, rallied to regain lead close home, beat Brian Boru by nk*

1st Seapoint Race (Leopardstown, July 16) 3yo+ 10f Good **112** (TS 72) 5 ran. *Made all, ridden entering straight, strongly pressed 1½f out, kept on well to assert inside final furlong, beat Napper Tandy by 1½l*

6th Budweiser Irish Derby (Group 1) (Curragh, June 29) 3yo 12f Good **111** (TS 91) 9 ran. *Moderate 6th, ridden and no impression straight, beaten 10½l by Alamshar*

2002

2nd Racing Post Trophy (Group 1) (Doncaster, October 26) 2yo 1m Soft **111** (TS 52) 9 ran ● **1st** www.punchestown.com EBF Maiden (Punchestown, October 17) 2yo 7½f Soft **92** 17 ran ● **2nd** JRA London Office's 10th Anniversary Maiden Stakes (Newmarket, October 2) 2yo 1m Good to firm **102** (TS 74) 6 ran ● **2nd** Orpen EBF Maiden (Naas, August 5) 2yo 7f Yielding to soft **85** (TS 40) 16 ran

to land the Group 2 prize.

With Brian Boru now earmarked for the St Leger at Doncaster, O'Brien decided to keep Powerscourt on home territory in an attempt to break Vinnie Roe's grip on the all-aged Irish equivalent on the same afternoon. Apart from a spell in the late 1980s, when it was won in three successive years by a three-year-old filly, the Irish St Leger has been dominated by older horses over the past two decades. Vinnie Roe, who proved an exception to the rule in 2001, confirmed the overall trend with his victory the following year and was now attempting to become the first horse to win the race three times in a row.

The opposition to Powerscourt also included a pair of talented British four-year-olds, Bollin Eric and Gamut, and it was Gamut who raised the tempo early in the straight. When his move was quickly covered by Vinnie Roe, one might have expected Powerscourt, a ten-furlong winner only two months earlier, to produce an immediate change of pace. Crucially, his response was delayed and by the time he started to stay on inside the final furlong Vinnie Roe already had matters firmly under control, while Gamut maintained his effort well enough to hold on to second place by a short head. For the moment, the race essentially remains the preserve of the older horses.

Coolmore's welcome change of policy on keeping a number of high-class performers in training at four means that both Powerscourt and Brian Boru will continue at Ballydoyle in 2004. It will be interesting to see if Powerscourt has the requisite stamina for Cup races. If not, there should still be plenty of opportunities for him in Group races at a mile and a half to 14 furlongs.

Powerscourt

bay colt, 01-4-2000

Sadler's Wells b 1981	Northern Dancer	Nearctic	Nearco / Lady Angela
		Natalma	Native Dancer / Almahmoud
	Fairy Bridge	Bold Reason	Hail To Reason / Lalun
		Special	Forli / Thong
Rainbow Lake b 1990	Rainbow Quest	Blushing Groom	Red God / Runaway Bride
		I Will Follow	Herbager / Where You Lead
	Rockfest	Stage Door Johnny	Prince John / Peroxide Blonde
		Rock Garden	Roan Rocket / Nasira

Bred by Juddmonte Farms in Britain

Sire Sadler's Wells

Won 6 of 11 races, inc. Beresford S.-Gr3, Irish Derby Trial-Gr2, Irish 2,000 Guineas-Gr1, Eclipse S.-Gr1, Phoenix Champion S.-Gr1. Also 2nd in Prix du Jockey-Club-Gr1, King George VI & Queen Elizabeth S.-Gr1. Impeccably bred top-class performer from 8-12f, handsome, tough and consistent. Sire of Gr1 winners: Braashee, French Glory, In The Wings, Old Vic, Prince Of Dance, Scenic, Salsabil, Opera House, Saddlers' Hall, El Prado, Johann Quatz, Masad, Barathea, Fatherland, Fort Wood, Intrepidity, Carnegie, King's Theatre, Northern Spur, Moonshell, Muncie, Poliglote, Chief Contender, Dance Design, Luna Wells, Cloudings, Ebadiyla, Entrepreneur, In Command, Kayf Tara, Dream Well, Greek Dance, King Of Kings, Leggera, Commander Collins, Daliapour, Montjeu, Saffron Walden, Aristotle, Beat Hollow, Subtle Power, Galileo, Imagine, Milan, Perfect Soul, Sequoyah, Ballingarry, Black Sam Bellamy, Gossamer, High Chaparral, Islington, Quarter Moon, Sholokhov, Alberto Giacometti, Brian Boru, Refuse To Bend, Yesterday.

Dam Rainbow Lake

Won 3 of 6 starts inc. Lancashire Oaks-Gr3, Ballymacoll Stud S.-Listed. Daughter of a useful 8-12f filly. Dam of: Brimming (1995 c by Generous; winner), Barbican (1996 c by Caerleon; unplaced), Unaware (1997 g by Unfuwain; winner), Polish Lake (1998 f by Polish Precedent; unraced), Lake Of Dreams (1999 g by Polish Precedent; non-winner), Powerscourt (2000 c by Sadler's Wells; Gr2 winner, Gr1-placed), Kind (2001 f by Danehill; placed), 2002 f by Desert Prince, 2003 c by Zafonic. In foal to Sadler's Wells.

Pedigree assessment

Has already shown smart form over 14f, and has the pedigree to tackle longer distances. His sire gets a fair proportion of classy 12f+ performers, his half-brother Brimming showed useful form over 14f in a short career, and his dam stayed 12f well. Powerscourt's pedigree gives every encouragement that he will make further progress from 3 to 4. *JH*

Rakti

4yo bay colt **126**

Polish Precedent (USA) - Ragera (Ire) (Rainbow Quest (USA))

Owner Gary A Tanaka

Trainer M A Jarvis

Breeder Azienda Agricola Rosati Colareti

Career: **14** starts | won **8** | second **2** | third **1** | **£977,170** win and place

By Paul Haigh

T WILL go down as the year in which one Italian champion raised the prestige of racing in the country where he first made his mark to a level it has not reached since the days of the great Ribot. But Falbrav was not the only Italian champion to transfer to Britain and make a huge impact in the very highest class.

Until he went to Michael Jarvis at the beginning of the 2003 season, Rakti was known in Britain, if he was known at all, only as the Italian horse who wouldn't go in the stalls for the previous year's Champion Stakes. Back home – if you can call it that, because he is in fact British-bred, by Polish Precedent out of a Rainbow Quest mare – he was already a superstar, if a slightly fading one, as the vagaries of temperament that led him to disgrace himself at Newmarket had made him a difficult horse to train.

The idiosyncrasies had not yet developed in the early part of his career when, in the care of Bruno Grizzetti, he won six successive races at two and three – the fifth in this sequence, the Derby Italiano at the Capannelle, being by far the most significant, for it was in this race that, on ground softer than he really likes and over a trip that may be just beyond his best, he still had a length and a half to spare over the Aidan O'Brien-trained Ballingarry, subsequently third to High Chaparral in the Irish Derby and winner of the Canadian International at Woodbine. Following this victory, he was bought by Japanese-American financier Gary Tanaka, a man to whom frontiers are irrelevant, and put away until September to be prepared for the big autumn prizes.

Rakti won his comeback race all right, a Listed event that did nothing much for his reputation, before suffering defeat when he put in a disastrous performance on heavy ground in a conditions race at San Siro that he should have won easily. And from there his season ended very disappointingly, with the refusal to go into the stalls at Newmarket followed

Rakti (Philip Robinson) impresses in the Group 1 Champion Stakes at Newmarket in October

by third place at the Capanelle, again on heavy ground, and tenth of 14 in the Premio Roma, where the ground, officially good to soft, could hardly have been responsible for his dismal showing.

The obvious decline persuaded Tanaka that a change of scene was necessary. Rakti was moved to Jarvis and the process of repairing his evidently fragile confidence and enthusiasm was begun.

Jarvis's first job was to cure an aversion to the stalls that had surfaced even before the Champion Stakes debacle, and for achieving this every credit is due to Steve 'Yarmy' Dyble, Britain's very own horse whisperer, who established a relationship so close that, according to his new trainer, Rakti would prick his ears and look round expectantly if Dyble spoke within 50 yards of him. Rakti's new-found contentment was reflected on the racecourse, when, ridden now by Philip Robinson instead of Mirco Demuro, he returned to the Capannelle to land the Group 1 Premio Presidente della Repubblica by a neck from the French-trained Tigertail. Jarvis thought afterwards that "he'd tired a bit" in the last of the ten furlongs, although "that was only to be expected on his first run of the season".

The first sign for British fans of what he could do came next time out at Royal Ascot, where he was allowed to start at 50-1 by punters who clearly had little respect for Italian form. He finished second to Nayef, then at the very peak of his powers, in the Prince of Wales's Stakes, with an astonishing array of talent behind him that included (in finishing

2003 — Race record

1st Emirates Airline Champion Stakes (Group 1) (Newmarket, October 18) 3yo+ 10f Good to firm **126** (TS 104) 12 ran. *Tracked leaders, raced keenly, led 2f out, clear 1f out, driven out, beat Carnival Dancer by 2l*

2nd Prince of Wales's Stakes (Group 1) (Ascot, June 18) 4yo+ 10f Good to firm **123** (TS 108) 10 ran. *Took keen hold, chased leaders, ridden to chase winner 2f out, kept on but no impression, beaten 2½l by Nayef*

1st Premio Presidente della Repubblica (Group 1) (Capannelle, May 11) 4yo+ 10f Good **114** 8 ran. *Reluctant to load, dwelt, soon racing in 4th, 4th straight, headway over 3f out, led over 2f out, driven out, beat Tigertail by nk*

2002

10th Premio Roma-SIS (Group 1) (Capannelle, November 17) 3yo+ 10f Good to soft **74** 14 ran ● **3rd** Premio Conte Felice Scheibler (Capannelle, November 3) 3yo 10f Heavy 12 ran ● **6th** Premio M.se Giuseppe Ippolito Fassati (Conditions Race) (San Siro, September 22) 3yo 11f Heavy 6 ran ● **1st** Premio Villa Borghese (Listed) (Capannelle, September 8) 3yo 10f Good to soft 7 ran ● **1st** Derby Italiano (Group 1) (Capannelle, May 26) 3yo 12f Good to firm **116** 16 ran ● **1st** Premio Botticelli (Listed) (Capannelle, May 1) 3yo 10½f Good 10 ran ● **1st** Premio Barba Toni (Conditions Race) (Capannelle, March 10) 3yo 11f Heavy 8 ran

Other wins

2001 1st Premio Furigolo (Conditions Race) (Capannelle, November 25) 2yo 10f Soft 9 ran ● **1st** Premio Teatro Gozzoli (Maiden) (Pisa, November 2) 2yo 10f Good 7 ran

order) Islington, Olden Times, Falbrav, Kaieteur, Grandera, Paolini, Moon Ballad and Ekraar. One or two of those he beat that day may have failed to give their running – notably Falbrav, perhaps – but surely not all of them. It was now that most unbiased form students realised that here was a horse of unusual ability – particularly since Rakti had failed to settle early on and had run out of steam in the last few yards as a result.

Sadly, Rakti came out of that race with a cracked hind fetlock, an injury that put paid to his summer as he spent the next four weeks in his box. He was back in the autumn, however, appropriately enough in the very Champion Stakes in which he'd disgraced himself a year earlier. This time he made no mistake, travelling smoothly throughout, cruising to the front as soon as he was asked and drawing away to win by a couple of lengths.

Unquestionably several of those who had looked to be his most serious rivals had gone well over the top. Nayef, Alamshar and Russian Rhythm, for example, were only shadows of the horses they had been in midsummer. But there was no doubting the class of that performance. Afterwards Jarvis described Rakti, with characteristic distaste for hyperbole, as "pretty high up among the best I've trained". Robinson went even further: "My personal opinion is that he might be the best miler in the world. It's very rarely that you travel that well in a race like that. He's a very good horse – a machine."

Rakti

bay colt, 10-2-1999

Polish Precedent b 1986	Danzig	Northern Dancer	Nearctic Natalma
		Pas de Nom	Admiral's Voyage Petitioner
	Past Example	Buckpasser	Tom Fool Busanda
		Bold Example	Bold Lad Lady Be Good
Ragera b 1992	Rainbow Quest	Blushing Groom	Red God Runaway Bride
		I Will Follow	Herbager Where You Lead
	Smageta	High Top	Derring-do Camenae
		Christine	Crocket Denning Report

Bred by Azienda Agricola Rosati Colarieti in England

Sire Polish Precedent

Won 7 of 9 races, inc. Prix du Palais Royal-Gr3, Prix de la Jonchere-Gr3, Prix Messidor-Gr3, Prix Jacques le Marois-Gr1, Prix du Moulin de Longchamp-Gr1. Big, lengthy sort, top-class miler, inferior only to Zilzal at 3. Sire of: Red Route (Gr2), Pilsudski (Grosser Preis von Baden-Gr1, Breeders' Cup Turf-Gr1, Eclipse S.-Gr1, Irish Champion S.-Gr1, Champion S.-Gr1, Japan Cup-Gr1), Pure Grain (Irish Oaks-Gr1, Yorkshire Oaks-Gr1), Riyadian (Gr2), Predappio (Gr2), Social Harmony (Gr3), Noushkey (Gr3), Polish Summer (Gr2), Sobieski (Gr2), Rakti (Derby Italiano-Gr1, Premio Presidente della Repubblica-Gr1, Champion S.-Gr1).

Dam Ragera

Placed twice from 3 starts in Italy, modest performer on limited evidence available. Dam of: Riksha (1997 f by Zilzal; won 12 races in Italy), Rasana (1998 f by Royal Academy; unplaced in Italy and Ireland), Rakti (1999 c by Polish Precedent; Classic winner), Radha (2000 f by Bishop Of Cashel; unraced).

Pedigree assessment

Some of those behind him on Champions Day were surely over the top at the end of a long season, but we should not assume that Rakti's win was all about the shortcomings of others. Ten furlongs clearly suits him well, but he has the speed to figure at the top level over a mile, and his Derby Italiano victory in 2002 showed that a mile and a half was no problem. Like Falbrav in 2003, he could easily make his mark over a variety of distances in 2004, if his connections decided to campaign him that way. *TM*

Red Bloom

2yo bay filly **110**

Selkirk (USA) - Red Camellia (Polar Falcon (USA))
Owner Cheveley Park Stud
Trainer Sir Michael Stoute
Breeder Cheveley Park Stud Ltd

Career: **3** starts │ won **2** │ second **0** │ third **1** │ **£122,642** win and place

By Seb Vance

CHEVELEY PARK STUD must be wondering if Russian Rhythm's stunning achievements in 2003 can ever be matched by another filly of theirs. There is a long way to go before Red Bloom emulates Russian Rhythm's three Group 1 wins, but she has made a great start and, on the back of an impressive success in the Fillies' Mile at Ascot, went into winter quarters vying for 1,000 Guineas favouritism with Denebola. While it is fair to say that she owes her position at the head of the betting market in part to the absence of a genuine star among the juvenile fillies, she is a genuine Classic prospect.

Denebola, the Prix Marcel Boussac winner, could well be the pick of the Europeans, but she may stay at home for the French equivalent, given the nightmare her trainer, Pascal Bary, and her owners, the Niarchos family, experienced with Six Perfections in both the English and Irish 1,000 Guineas.

One can make cases for the two leading Godolphin acquisitions, but there are drawbacks with both; the Cheveley Park Stakes winner Carry On Katie may be too speedy to last the extra two furlongs, while the Rockfel Stakes victress Cairns needs to improve again quickly to win the 1,000 Guineas.

Red Bloom has plenty going for her, even though it was by no means a strong renewal of the Fillies' Mile after lightning-fast conditions prompted four defections from an intended field of 11. She accounted for some promising maiden winners and smashed the juvenile track record set around half an hour earlier by Snow Ridge in the Royal Lodge.

Following the withdrawal of Necklace, Sheikh Mohammed's purchase Punctilious was made 13-8 favourite on the strength of a couple of minor wins and a tall reputation. That filly made the running but Kieren Fallon sent Red Bloom in pursuit straightening for home and drove her into a decisive lead approaching the furlong marker. Despite idling a little,

Red Bloom (Kieren Fallon) stretches out to land the Group 1 Fillies' Mile at Ascot in September

she held on by a length and a quarter from Sundrop, who carried Sheikh Mohammed's second colours but collared Punctilious close home.

Compared to Sundrop, who was blocked by Punctilious and only found a clear passage once the winner had flown, Red Bloom enjoyed a dream run. However, it would be stretching things to suggest that Sundrop was unlucky and Fallon's post-race comment left nobody in doubt that he regarded his mount as the best filly on the day.

The champion jockey, winning the race for the first time, said: "She's killed them. She's going the right way and has a big future. She came there cruising, and no sooner has she hit the front than she's pricked her ears and pulled up with me. Otherwise she would have been even more impressive."

When Fallon talks so highly of a horse, it is worth taking note, and Sir Michael Stoute, who had last won the race with Untold in 1985, was also upbeat: "I thought she did it very well and she's an exciting prospect." The owners had been slightly concerned about the conditions, as Cheveley

2003   Race record

1st Meon Valley Stud Fillies' Mile (Group 1) (Ascot, September 27) 2yo 1m Good to firm **110** (TS 88) 7 ran. *Chased leaders, ridden and headway 3f out, chased leader 2f out, led approaching final furlong, edged right inside final furlong, driven out, beat Sundrop by 1¼l*

1st Hoofbeats Maiden Fillies' Stakes (Newmarket (July), August 16) 2yo 7f Good to firm **90** (TS 61) 12 ran. *Led, headed over 5f out, led over 4f out, ridden clear and edged right over 1f out, ran on, beat Silk Fan by 2l*

3rd EBF Gossamer Maiden Fillies' Stakes (Newbury, July 18) 2yo 6f Good to firm **80** (TS 37) 13 ran. *Soon chasing leaders, driven to challenge inside final 2f, edged left under pressure inside final furlong, one pace when edged right close home, beaten 1½l by Nataliya*

Park's managing director, Chris Richardson, revealed after the race, saying: "She's a filly we've always held in high regard and the form of her Newmarket race has been franked. I was a little concerned about the ground as she's a Selkirk filly, but we came here hoping for a big run. It was a track record and she could be very special."

Red Bloom's three outings as a juvenile were all on good to firm ground, the first of which was at Newbury in July, when she was fancied to oblige at the first time of asking. However, the 13-8 favourite found the six furlongs too short and showed her inexperience in finishing only third behind outsiders Nataliya and Kunda.

While at face value it looked a slightly disappointing debut, the first two were subsequently placed in Listed races and Red Bloom herself stepped up markedly on the form when upped to seven furlongs at Newmarket the following month. Ridden with confidence by Brett Doyle, the even-money shot led over four furlongs out and held a two-length advantage at the line over subsequent dual scorer Silk Fan. Spotlight, successful later in a Newmarket Listed event, was third.

Red Bloom has looked better each time she has been stepped up in trip, but whether the Oaks is within her range is highly questionable. Selkirk was a high-class miler, while her dam Red Camellia, who was out of a five-furlong sprinter, suffered an injury-blighted career and never raced beyond a mile. Red Camellia won her first three starts in fine style, including Goodwood's Group 3 Prestige Stakes, and went to the Fillies' Mile as the heavily backed second favourite, but edged left when she came under pressure, finishing a length and a half behind the winner, Reams Of Verse, in fourth place. A knee fracture was soon identified as the cause of her steering failure, and surgery followed. She came back nobly with a bold third in the Poule d'Essai des Pouliches, but her problem was not solved and she made only one more appearance.

On breeding, therefore, Red Bloom's best hope probably lies in the Guineas and it would be no surprise to see her follow Russian Rhythm's suit and head there without a prep race. She could well be the best of the home bunch, but beware the French if they turn up, especially Denebola and the Marcel Boussac runner-up, Green Noon.

Red Bloom
bay filly, 11-3-2001

		Atan	Native Dancer / Mixed Marriage
	Sharpen Up		
		Rocchetta	Rockefella / Chambiges
Selkirk ch 1988			
		Nebbiolo	Yellow God / Novara
	Annie Edge		
		Friendly Court	Be Friendly / No Court
		Nureyev	Northern Dancer / Special
	Polar Falcon		
		Marie d'Argonne	Jefferson / Mohair
Red Camellia b 1994			
		Mummy's Pet	Sing Sing / Money For Nothing
	Cerise Bouquet		
		Rosia Bay	High Top / Ouija

Bred by Cheveley Park Stud Ltd in England

Sire Selkirk

Won 6 of 15 races, inc. Queen Elizabeth II S.-Gr1, Lockinge S.-Gr2, Goodwood Mile-Gr2, Challenge S.-Gr2. Big, powerful, long-striding individual, effective on any ground, very game, best at a mile, with excellent turn of foot. Sire of: Hidden Meadow (Gr3), Kirkwall (Gr2), Orford Ness (Gr3), Squeak (Beverly Hills H.-Gr1, Matriarch H.-Gr1), Border Arrow (Gr3), Country Garden (Gr2), Field Of Hope (Prix de la Foret-Gr1), Sign Of Hope (Gr2), Trans Island (Gr2), Valley Chapel (Gr2), Wince (1,000 Guineas-Gr1), Harbour Island (Gr3), Altieri (Gr2), Independence (Gr2), Highdown (Gr2), Leadership (Gran Premio di Milano-Gr1), Sulk (Prix Marcel Boussac-Gr1), Welsh Diva (Gr3), Favourable Terms (Gr2), Red Bloom (Fillies' Mile-Gr1).

Dam Red Camellia

Won 3 of 6 races, inc. Prestige S.-Gr3. Also 3rd in Poule d'Essai des Pouliches-Gr1. Lengthy, quite well-made. High-class performer at 2, suffered knee fracture in Fillies' Mile, returned after surgery with excellent Classic effort, below form only subsequent outing. Dam of: Red Garland (2000 f by Selkirk; unraced), Red Bloom (2001 f by Selkirk; Gr1 winner).

Pedigree assessment

We would know more about Red Bloom if the Moyglare heroine Necklace had not been a late defector from the Fillies' Mile. But what we did learn from the Ascot race was that she was very progressive, could produce an impressive gear-change, and – at that time – was still novicey, idling once she had taken command. Necklace might have exposed that weakness, perhaps, but we can depend on Red Bloom being more professional at three. Her sire had had only two previous juvenile Pattern winners, and it is at three that his stock tend to blossom. There are stamina factors deep in the filly's dam-line, but it seems likely that a mile will always suit her best, and she must feature on any short-list for the 1,000 Guineas. *TM*

Reel Buddy (USA)

5yo chestnut horse **118**

Mr Greeley (USA) - Rosebud (Indian Ridge)

Owner Speedlith Group

Trainer R Hannon

Breeder Stronach Stables

Career: **34** starts | won **9** | second **4** | third **5** | **£426,878** win and place

By Nicholas Godfrey

REEL BUDDY, a classy enough performer though one with the odd quirk, was neither born great nor achieved greatness. However, when he recorded one of the biggest shocks of the year with an unexpected win in the Sussex Stakes, he certainly had greatness thrust upon him – even if much of the glory was reflected.

The five-year-old's surprise victory at Goodwood could be put down to a number of factors – most crucially the dead ground that blunted many of his main rivals, and the canniest of rides from his jockey. That this jockey was Pat Eddery means the race is likely to live long in the memory, however, since it provided the 11-times champion with an emotional Group 1 victory in the season he retired from the saddle after a career spanning five decades.

The epitome of professionalism, Dublin-born Eddery, who turned 51 in March, had long since imprinted an indelible mark on racing thanks to a remarkable career that started in the mid-1960s. Only Sir Gordon Richards has ridden more winners in Britain than Eddery, whose incredible big-race haul includes three Epsom Derbys – nine Derbys altogether if you include Ireland and France – four Arcs and two Breeders' Cup races.

Eddery had his first ride in 1967 at The Curragh and rode his first winner, Alvaro, at Epsom two years later after moving to Britain and joining Frenchie Nicholson's academy. Champion apprentice in 1971, he claimed his first fully fledged jockeys' title in 1974 as stable jockey to Peter Walwyn, for whom he won the following year's Derby on Grundy.

After seven years at Seven Barrows, he had become the most in-demand jockey in racing, the reward for which was a five-year stint with Vincent O'Brien followed by another seven as Khalid Abdullah's retained jockey. Such high-profile positions inevitably brought him into contact with many of the best horses of the time, among them Golden Fleece, El Gran Senor, Rainbow Quest, Pebbles, Bosra Sham and the peerless Dancing Brave.

Reel Buddy and Pat Eddery after their shock win in the Sussex Stakes: "a real choking moment," said the jockey

Reel Buddy, for all his talent and durability, is not fit to be mentioned in the same breath. But if the Richard Hannon-trained five-year-old was clearly no Dancing Brave, he earned a deserved place in the affections of both the rider and the wider public for ensuring Eddery's final season did not pass without his dining at the top table one last time.

Group 1 victories, once so plentiful, had become an increasingly rare treat for the rider in recent years, although shortly before announcing his decision to retire in June at Windsor, Eddery had come agonisingly close to a famous victory with a tremendous front-running effort in the Derby on The Great Gatsby.

Eddery cited a new ownership venture as the catalyst for his decision to quit the saddle. But while he reluctantly admitted he would never be able to overtake Richards' all-time mark of 4,870 victories in Britain, he identified his overriding remaining ambition in his final season as partnering just one more Group 1 winner.

With the best will in the world, Reel Buddy must have looked an unlikely accomplice in the rider's quest for a fitting send-off. The horse was in the middle of his fourth full season of racing, during which time his limitations had been exposed on intermittent forays in the highest grade.

Indeed, Reel Buddy's eight wins before the Sussex Stakes included

2003   Race record

14th Netjets Prix du Moulin de Longchamp (Group 1) (Longchamp, September 7) 3yo+ 1m Good to soft **105** (TS 71) 14 ran. *Held up in rear, rapid headway over 3f out to go 6th straight, weakened well over 1f out, beaten 9¾l by Nebraska Tornado*

1st Sussex Stakes (Group 1) (Goodwood, July 30) 3yo+ 1m Good to soft **118** (TS 93) 9 ran. *Held up in last, effort over 2f out, switched to inner and closed over 1f out, urged along and led last 75yds, all out, beat Statue Of Liberty by hd*

2nd Vodafone Diomed Stakes (Group 3) (Epsom, June 7) 3yo+ 8½f Good **114** (TS 88) 10 ran. *Dwelt, held up in detached last, went 9th straight, effort and plenty to do 2f out, cajoled along and ran on over 1f out, took 2nd last 100yds, beaten 1¼l by Gateman*

5th Juddmonte Lockinge Stakes (Group 1) (Newbury, May 17) 4yo+ 1m Good **93** (TS 66) 6 ran. *Raced alone stands' side, with winner 5f, beaten 21l by Hawk Wing*

3rd Bet attheraces Mile (Group 2) (Sandown, April 26) 4yo+ 1m Good **112** (TS 93) 9 ran. *Dwelt, held up in last pair and well off the pace, effort on inner when not clear run 2f out, switched left inside final furlong, ran on well last 150yds, beaten 2¾l by Desert Deer*

11th Cammidge Trophy (Listed) (Doncaster, March 22) 3yo+ 6f Good **92** (TS 83) 13 ran. *In mid-division, driven along halfway, soon well outpaced, beaten 9l by Red Carpet*

8th Doncaster Mile (Listed) (Doncaster, March 20) 4yo+ 1m Good **38** 8 ran. *Very slowly into stride, pulled hard, always behind, beaten 37l by Dandoun*

2002

16th Victor Chandler Challenge Stakes (Group 2) (Newmarket, October 19) 3yo+ 7f Good **76** (TS 52) 17 ran ● **3rd** Celebration Mile (Group 2) (Goodwood, August 24) 3yo+ 1m Good to firm **114** (TS 93) 7 ran ● **1st** Stan James Hungerford Stakes (Group 3) (Newbury, August 17) 3yo+ 7f Good to firm **115** (TS 86) 10 ran ● **3rd** Sussex Stakes (Group 1) (Goodwood, July 31) 3yo+ 1m Good to firm **117** (TS 102) 5 ran ● **10th** Darley July Cup (Group 1) (Newmarket (July), July 11) 3yo+ 6f Good to soft **95** (TS 62) 14 ran ● **6th** Duke of York Stakes (Group 3) (York, May 16) 3yo+ 6f Good to firm **106** (TS 87) 12 ran ● **1st** Merewood Homes Spring Trophy Stakes (Listed) (Haydock, May 4) 3yo+ 7f Good to soft **118** (TS 89) 7 ran ● **1st** NGK Spark Plugs Abernant Stakes (Listed) (Newmarket, April 16) 3yo+ 6f Good to firm **114** (TS 87) 9 ran ● **1st** Quail Conditions Stakes (Kempton, April 1) 3yo+ 6f Good **105** (TS 81) 8 ran

Other wins

2001 1st ABN Amro Stakes (0-110 handicap) (Goodwood, May 23) 3yo 7f Good to firm **112** (TS 94) 11 ran ● **1st** H & K Commissions (Bookmakers) Stakes (0-100 handicap) (Newmarket, May 4) 3yo 7f Good **107** (TS 90) 20 ran **2000 1st** Claro Conditions Stakes (Ripon, August 29) 2yo 5f Good **89** (TS 98) 9 ran ● **1st** Sunday Maiden Auction Stakes (Bath, August 20) 2yo 5f Good **93** (TS 93) 10 ran

only one at Group 3 level – the previous year's Hungerford Stakes – and a pair of Listed-race wins. Although he had excelled himself behind Rock Of Gibraltar in the previous year's Sussex Stakes, it required something of a leap of faith to imagine his winning in the highest grade.

Any thoughts of success were hardly encouraged by Reel Buddy's erratic form prior to the Sussex, for it had become evident that he needed things to drop just right to be seen to best effect. Habitually held up for a late turn of foot, he resented the whip and that old euphemism 'enigmatic' was often bandied about alongside his name.

Having said that, the 2003 Sussex Stakes was by no means the greatest race in the world – and the rain-sodden ground proved the most efficient of levellers. Under the circumstances, victory for Reel Buddy, though unlikely, was not inconceivable, especially when probable favourite Kalaman and the 2002 Queen Elizabeth II Stakes winner Where Or When were pulled out on the day of the race to leave a field of nine.

Of those, there were major doubts over the first three in the betting. Trade Fair, the unexposed favourite, was no certainty to relish the underfoot conditions and subsequently proved best at trips short of a mile, while the Dubai World Cup winner Moon Ballad clearly preferred faster ground and was being tried at a distance short of his best. Zafeen, third-best at 11-2, was a miler through and through – but he, too, had produced his worst effort in testing conditions.

Reel Buddy was still a 20-1 joint-seventh choice. Connections hardly exuded confidence, either, as Richard Hannon junior, doing the honours for his father, admitted after the race when he said the horse was running only at the insistence of owner Bill Jones of the Speedlith Group. "You couldn't fancy him, but he is the kind of horse that can pull one out of the bag sometimes," he said. "He really does accelerate."

Eddery, well aware of his trump card, played it to perfection to "burgle the race", to borrow a phrase from Alastair Down's report in the following day's Racing Post.

It was a muddling contest. Bizarrely, given Moon Ballad's preference for making all, Godolphin fielded a pacemaker in Blatant, who duelled with his counterpart for the Ballydoyle team, Spartacus, doing the honours for Statue Of Liberty. As the pacesetters dropped away, Zafeen got to the front two furlongs out, where Moon Ballad made his move, albeit under pressure. Trade Fair folded tamely a furlong out to finish sixth.

The first three came from farthest back. Norse Dancer led narrowly for a stride or two below the distance, where Statue Of Liberty, hard ridden and switched right, was running on strongly.

In a five-way photo, however, it was Reel Buddy and Eddery who gained a popular verdict in a thrilling finish that produced margins of a head, a short head and two necks. Having let his rivals play their hands, Eddery had waited and waited before switching from behind a wall of horses across to the rails, where a charmed run saw him prevail in the last 50 yards from Statue Of Liberty and Norse Dancer.

"There is no point in getting older if you don't get smarter in the process," reported Down. In the Sussex Stakes, nobody was smarter than Eddery, who, even in such a desperate finish, had kidded his mount home, not having been tempted to get stuck into a horse whose foibles he knew all too well.

"He's a funny old horse and you mustn't get at him," the rider said afterwards. "If you get at him he can stop on you and all you can do is squeeze him up. Turning for home I thought we had no chance because there was a lot of ground to make up, but the field started to come back to him and he enjoyed going through horses."

As Jon Lees reported in the next day's Racing Post: "Cries of 'Come on Grandad!' and 'There's life in the old dog yet!' rang out across Goodwood's winner's enclosure to mark a universally popular, yet increasingly rare, result," he wrote, while the paper's headline described it as a "fairytale". On Reel Buddy's return, a phalanx of his colleagues gathered outside the weighing room to congratulate Eddery. Not a man renowned for excessive displays of emotion, he seemed genuinely moved – he was later to describe it as a "real choking moment" – and many thought he would call it a day there and then.

The rider himself, though, typically for a man well known for giving his all whether it is a seller or a Classic, was already thinking of his next engagement. "I have still got to ride for Mr [John] Dunlop and I will ride until the end of the season," he said. "Riding a big win like that may get me on something good. I'm off to Leicester now. It's back to the grind."

The last few months of "grind" after the Sussex Stakes had the air of a farewell tour as Eddery demonstrated more than once that his powers were barely diminished, most notably in a Champions Day double that featured his first Cesarewitch victory on Landing Light. Three weeks later, on November Handicap day, more than 36 years after he had had his first ride at The Curragh in August 1967, Eddery's riding career in Britain ended, though the very next day came news that he was set to be awarded another Group 1, the Middle Park Stakes, following a positive dope test from Three Valleys.

He leaves the weighing room with more than 4,600 winners to his name in Britain, among them 14 Classics, 73 Royal Ascot winners, 28 centuries of winners, including a double ton in 1990, when he achieved his best score of 209. He also rode 11 Classic winners in Ireland, where he won the title in 1982 to go alongside his 11 in Britain, a tally that equalled Lester Piggott, whose career score of 4,493 winners was surpassed by Eddery in 2002.

When he rode his final winner – the 4,632nd of his career, or 4,633rd if Balmont is awarded the Middle Park – only Richards' mark remained beyond reach. "On statistics alone, his greatness is beyond question," commented racing's pre-eminent historian John Randall in the Racing Post in the week of the rider's retirement. "He has always been the ultimate professional," he added, with no hint of hyperbole.

Fittingly, Eddery was not alone in bowing out at the end of 2003. Reel Buddy, his old sparring partner, was also retired after just one more outing when he finished last in the Prix du Moulin. He is due to stand at Bearstone Stud in Shropshire in 2004.

Harsh though it sounds, Reel Buddy simply got lucky in that the Sussex Stakes played very much to his strengths in conditions that didn't suit

Reel Buddy

chestnut horse, 8-2-1998

		Mr Prospector	Raise A Native / Gold Digger
	Gone West		
		Secrettame	Secretariat / Tamerett
Mr Greeley ch 1992			
		Reviewer	Bold Ruler / Broadway
	Long Legend		
		Lianga	Dancer's Image / Leven Ones
		Ahonoora	Lorenzaccio / Helen Nichols
	Indian Ridge		
		Hillbrow	Swing Easy / Golden City
Rosebud b 1992			
		Song	Sing Sing / Intent
	Tiszta Sharok		
		Tin Tessa	Martinmas / Gala Tess

Bred by Stronach Stables in Kentucky
$16,000 Keeneland January yearling, 23,000gns Doncaster St Leger yearling

Sire **Mr Greeley**

Won 5 of 16 races, inc. Spectacular Bid S.-Gr3, Swale S.-Gr3, Lafayette S.-Gr3. Also placed 2nd in Breeders' Cup Sprint-Gr1. Regular Lasix user, but won a Gr3 without. Sire of: El Corredor (Cigar Mile H.-Gr1), Celtic Melody (Distaff H.-Gr1), Fan Club's Mister (Gr2), Reel Buddy (Sussex S.-Gr1), Miss Lodi (Gr3), Nonsuch Bay (Mother Goose S.-Gr1), Puck (Gr3), Whywhywhy (Futurity S.-Gr1). Also sire of Miss Kornikova (Oakleigh Plate-Gr1) from 1 crop conceived in Australia.

Dam **Rosebud**

Won 3 of 13 races. Quite modest sprinter-miler. Dam of: Reel Buddy (1998 c by Mr Greeley; Gr1 winner), Rosie Red Bear (1999 f by Explosive Red; unraced), Our Ramblin' Rose (2000 f by Demaloot Demashoot; unplaced).

Pedigree assessment

Mr Greeley was beaten no more than a neck in the 1995 Breeders' Cup Sprint, though the rest of his form suggested that he was not a Grade 1-calibre performer. Like father, like son. The 2003 Sussex Stakes was not up to its usual high standard and Reel Buddy stole a race that in normal conditions he would never have won. One of few sons of his sire to have competed in Britain, from an unfashionable distaff background, he will have something different to offer breeders. *TM*

his chief rivals. Nevertheless, in four seasons' racing, he repaid his yearling purchase price of 23,000 guineas many times over. It is seldom wise to ascribe human attributes to a horse but perhaps we may be allowed to suggest that he had a distinct sense of occasion as well, having picked the right day to record his sole success of his final campaign. Pat Eddery won't forget him in a hurry, that's for sure.

Refuse To Bend (Ire)

3yo bay colt **126**

Sadler's Wells (USA) - Market Slide (USA) (Gulch (USA))

Owner Moyglare Stud Farm

Trainer D K Weld

Breeder Moyglare Stud Farm Ltd

Career: **8** starts | won **5** | second **0** | third **0** | £361,905 win and place

By Paul Haigh

MOYGLARE, managed by septuagenarian Stan Cosgrove for billionaire nonagenarian Walter Haefner, is arguably Ireland's most respected stud. Haefner has kept it for over 40 years as a serious hobby, during which time it has produced a whole string of top-class performers – never two such close relations, however, who turned out quite so dissimilar in their racing styles as Media Puzzle and his half-brother Refuse To Bend.

In November 2002, Media Puzzle, trained like Haefner's other Irish horses by Dermot Weld, achieved what would once have been thought the impossible by winning the Melbourne Cup (Weld, of course, being the man who had already proved it wasn't impossible at all).

By something rather more than coincidence, Refuse To Bend, his Sadler's Wells half-brother, had just returned to winter quarters at the place of his birth, after an unbeaten two-year-old career that included victory over the hugely expensive Van Nistelrooy in the National Stakes. He was already being thought of as a Classic colt. Media Puzzle's Australian triumph confirmed his status as one of the hottest properties around.

When Refuse To Bend went back into training in the spring he did nothing to lower the high opinion generally held of him. In his comeback race he gave weight (a Group 1 penalty) and an efficient beating to other potential Classic contenders in the Leopardstown 2,000 Guineas Trial, shortly after which it was announced that his next target would be the 2,000 Guineas at Newmarket. Tales of spectacular work meant that he went to the Rowley Mile as 9-2 joint-second favourite in an open-looking contest.

In retrospect the 20-runner field for the Guineas was heavier on quantity than quality, with only runner-up Zafeen and unlucky-in-running Indian Haven doing much for the form in subsequent races. But nobody could argue with the way Refuse To Bend dealt with his rivals, charging into

Refuse To Bend (Pat Smullen) swoops to capture the 2,000 Guineas at Newmarket in May

the lead going into the Dip and striding home with his regular rider, Pat Smullen, already punching the air.

In view of his breeding, a widespread assumption grew that the Guineas winner could only improve when asked to compete over longer distances and there were more than a few who suggested that we might at last have found a three-year-old to deprive Nijinsky of his title of 'the last-ever winner of the Triple Crown'. Some even believed that he had got the really difficult leg out of the way.

News of his work in the weeks leading up to the Derby was not at all encouraging, though. Indeed, he failed so comprehensively to please Weld that there was talk he might be withdrawn; and if it weren't for the thought that 'there's only one Derby', it's quite likely he would have been.

Refuse To Bend did start favourite at Epsom, albeit an uneasy one. But even before they rounded Tattenham Corner it was clear his unbeaten record had no more than seconds to live. There was no response when Smullen began to drive him and he trailed home 13th behind Kris Kin.

Nobody, not even his great trainer, was quite sure what the problem was. Some thought he must have been sick; some that he'd hated the track; others that he'd simply failed to stay – although the fact that he'd

2003   Race record

11th NetJets Breeders' Cup Mile (Grade 1) (Santa Anita, October 25) 3yo+ 1m Firm **103** 13 ran. *Slowly into stride, 5th and ridden approaching straight, one pace final furlong, beaten 8¾l by Six Perfections*

11th Netjets Prix du Moulin de Longchamp (Group 1) (Longchamp, September 7) 3yo+ 1m Good to soft **109** (TS 70) 14 ran. *Pulled hard early, disputed 3rd, ridden and beaten over 1f out, beaten 8¼l by Nebraska Tornado*

1st Desmond Stakes (Group 3) (Leopardstown, August 17) 3yo+ 1m Good to firm **126** (TS 108) 7 ran. *Tracked leaders in 2nd, led early straight, quickened clear over 1f out, easily, beat Latino Magic by 3l*

13th Vodafone Derby (Group 1) (Epsom, June 7) 3yo 12f Good **99** (TS 72) 20 ran. *Tracked leading group, 7th straight, ridden and no progress 3f out, soon beaten, beaten 16l by Kris Kin*

1st Sagitta 2,000 Guineas (Group 1) (Newmarket, May 3) 3yo 1m Good **118** (TS 111) 20 ran. *Tracked leaders, ridden to lead inside final furlong, ran on, beat Zafeen by ¾l*

1st Leopardstown 2,000 Guineas Trial Stakes (Listed) (Leopardstown, April 13) 3yo 1m Good to firm **111** (TS 94) 8 ran. *Settled 3rd, headway entering straight, ridden to lead over 1½f out, kept on final furlong, beat Good Day Too by ½l*

2002

1st Aga Khan Studs National Stakes (Group 1) (Curragh, September 15) 2yo 7f Good to firm **113** (TS 49) 7 ran ● **1st** Bagenalstown EBF Maiden (Div I) (Gowran Park, August 14) 2yo 7f Good **87** 13 ran

been in trouble long before stamina should have been a factor suggested this explanation was simplistic at best.

Whatever the reason, he disappeared from view until home gallops suggested his wellbeing had returned. Improvement at home was reflected on the course when, once again giving away a penalty, he ran out the three-length winner of the Group 3 Desmond Stakes at Leopardstown on August 17, a performance that was his best by some way according to Racing Post Ratings. As a result he was pitched back in at the top level in the Prix du Moulin in September. But he proved a bitter disappointment, pulling early, then getting left behind in humiliating fashion as soon as the leaders quickened off a typically slow French pace.

Undeterred, or perhaps as a final fling, connections sent him to Santa Anita, in the hope that the faster ground and pace in the Breeders' Cup Mile would suit him better. But once again he performed abjectly, fading quickly in the straight to finish 11th of 13.

And that was that for a year that had promised so much. Perhaps, as those wise after the event were quick to suggest, he'd simply been overrated. Perhaps there was a physical or an attitude problem that may still be overcome.

A Classic is a Classic, however and, whatever the disappointments that followed, both for those at Moyglare and for Godolphin, who bought him in midsummer, his Guineas win can never be taken away. He will be back in training at four but, so far as 2003 was concerned, he remained no more than a hero who might have been.

Refuse To Bend

bay colt, 17-3-2000

		Nearctic	Nearco
	Northern Dancer		Lady Angela
Sadler's Wells		Natalma	Native Dancer
b 1981			Almahmoud
		Bold Reason	Hail To Reason
	Fairy Bridge		Lalun
		Special	Forli
			Thong
		Mr Prospector	Raise A Native
	Gulch		Gold Digger
		Jameela	Rambunctious
Market Slide			Asbury Mary
ch 1991		Grenfall	Graustark
	Grenzen		Primonetta
		My Poly	Cyclotron
			Polywich

Bred by Moyglare Stud Farm Ltd in Ireland

Sire **Sadler's Wells**

Won 6 of 11 races, inc. Beresford S.-Gr3, Irish Derby Trial-Gr2, Irish 2,000 Guineas-Gr1, Eclipse S.-Gr1, Phoenix Champion S.-Gr1. Also 2nd in Prix du Jockey-Club-Gr1, King George VI & Queen Elizabeth S.-Gr1. Impeccably bred top-class performer from 8-12f, handsome, tough and consistent. Sire of Gr1 winners: Braashee, French Glory, In The Wings, Old Vic, Prince Of Dance, Scenic, Salsabil, Opera House, Saddlers' Hall, El Prado, Johann Quatz, Masad, Barathea, Fatherland, Fort Wood, Intrepidity, Carnegie, King's Theatre, Northern Spur, Moonshell, Muncie, Poliglote, Chief Contender, Dance Design, Luna Wells, Cloudings, Ebadiya, Entrepreneur, In Command, Kayf Tara, Dream Well, Greek Dance, King Of Kings, Leggera, Commander Collins, Daliapour, Montjeu, Saffron Walden, Aristotle, Beat Hollow, Subtle Power, Galileo, Imagine, Milan, Perfect Soul, Sequoyah, Ballingarry, Black Sam Bellamy, Gossamer, High Chaparral, Islington, Quarter Moon, Sholokhov, Alberto Giacometti, Brian Boru, Refuse To Bend, Yesterday.

Dam **Market Slide**

Won 5 of 19 races. Lengthy sort, useful sprinter on turf and dirt, half-sister to Twilight Agenda. Dam of: Media Puzzle (1997 g by Theatrical; Gr1 winner), Ripple Of Pride (1999 f by Sadler's Wells; winner), Refuse To Bend (2000 c by Sadler's Wells; Classic winner), Genuine Charm (2001 f by Sadler's Wells; unraced to date).

Pedigree assessment

As half-brother to a Melbourne Cup winner, Refuse To Bend raised hopes that he might achieve Triple Crown fame after his smooth victory in the 2,000 Guineas, but it turned out that he conformed to the familiar Sadler's Wells pattern. When they have the speed to excel at a mile, they do not also have the stamina for 12 furlongs. After his Epsom debacle, he was kept to a mile for his remaining races, registering a career-best effort under his Group 1 penalty in the Desmond Stakes before slumping to ignominious defeats at Longchamp and Santa Anita. There were no obvious excuses for those failures and the Godolphin team, for whom he will race in 2004, need to restore him to form before he embarks on his stud career. *TM*

Russian Rhythm (USA)

3yo chestnut filly **123**

Kingmambo (USA) - Balistroika (USA) (Nijinsky (Can))

Owner Cheveley Park Stud

Trainer Sir Michael Stoute

Breeder Brushwood Stable

Career: **9** starts | won **6** | second **2** | third **0** | **£654,120** win and place

---

By James Willoughby

NO RACE could be more eagerly anticipated than a rematch between Russian Rhythm and Six Perfections. The two champion fillies are expected to stay in training and will hopefully renew rivalry in 2004.

The Sagitta 1,000 Guineas at Newmarket in May was the scene of their only meeting to date, but the result provided no conclusive evidence of their relative merits. While Kieren Fallon assuredly steered Sir Michael Stoute's filly through a gap to grab first run and eventually victory, Thierry Thulliez was panic-stricken on the French challenger and did her no justice whatsoever.

The vigour with which Six Perfections finished, after encountering serious trouble, reduced the winning margin to a length and a half. Moreover, it created the impression that the result could easily have been different. As later events confirmed, however, Russian Rhythm was never the sort to win by a wide margin and may well have had sufficient in reserve to meet a challenge if it had come.

Thulliez's misadventures naturally made for the main focus of press attention. As a result, Russian Rhythm did not receive the credit she deserved. Not only did she settle the contest with a definitive burst of speed, but she also showed no little determination in the heat of battle.

The possibility existed that Russian Rhythm had not been fully forward for her first race of the season. In the build-up to the Classic, her trainer reported that she was not working with the same flair of her juvenile days. There were even suggestions that she would not make the race.

The notion that there was more to come from Russian Rhythm was serenely vindicated in the Coronation Stakes at Royal Ascot. Set up for a peak effort by her Newmarket exertions, the Kingmambo filly turned in one of the time performances of the season. Track records do not always correspond with historically significant performances, especially

Russian Rhythm (Kieren Fallon) lands her first Group 1 success of the season, the 1,000 Guineas at Newmarket

when the ground is as fast as it was at Royal Ascot. Nevertheless, in covering the Old Mile in 1min 38.51sec, Russian Rhythm proved herself a terrific equine athlete.

The pivotal moment of the Coronation Stakes came on the home turn, when Russian Rhythm's pacemaker Fantasize ran wide under Gary Stevens and allowed her stablemate an unmolested run up the inside. While not specifically in contravention of the rules of racing, the manoeuvre represented a flagrant use of team tactics.

Again, Russian Rhythm accelerated so sharply that she was nearly a chestnut blur. And, once more, she gave the impression there was plenty in reserve. Though the runner-up Soviet Song initially made inroads into her advantage a furlong out, Russian Rhythm was full value for a length and a half by the end.

A compelling aspect of this performance was the speed with which Russian Rhythm covered the final furlong. Fast-run races usually result in slow-motion finishes but, in spite of this relationship, both the winner and runner-up recorded surprisingly good splits. The ability to

2003   Race record

5th Emirates Airline Champion Stakes (Group 1) (Newmarket, October 18) 3yo+ 10f Good to firm **111** (TS 83) 12 ran. *Tracked leaders, raced keenly, every chance 2f out, soon edged left, no extra final furlong, beaten 6¼l by Rakti*

2nd Queen Elizabeth II Stakes (Sponsored By NetJets) (Group 1) (Ascot, September 27) 3yo+ 1m Good to firm **121** (TS 107) 8 ran. *Took keen hold early, tracked leaders, ridden and headway over 2f out, chased winner 1f out, kept on gamely but no impression inside final furlong, beaten 2l by Falbrav*

1st Vodafone Nassau Stakes (Group 1) (Goodwood, August 2) 3yo+ 10f Good **121** (TS 99) 8 ran. *Took keen hold and soon in 3rd, not clear run over 3f out and lost place, renewed effort to chase leader over 1f out, driven to lead last 50yds, gamely, beat Ana Marie by nk*

1st Coronation Stakes (Group 1) (Ascot, June 20) 3yo 1m Good to firm **123** (TS 112) 9 ran. *Tracked leaders, quickened to lead approaching final 2f, driven out close home and ran on well, beat Soviet Song by 1½l*

1st Sagitta 1,000 Guineas (Group 1) (Newmarket, May 4) 3yo 1m Good to firm **118** (TS 100) 19 ran. *Held up in touch, switched right over 1f out, led inside final furlong, ridden out, beat Six Perfections by 1½l*

2002

2nd Betfair Cheveley Park Stakes (Group 1) (Newmarket, October 4) 2yo 6f Firm **109** (TS 57) 6 ran ● **1st** Peugeot Lowther Stakes (Group 2) (York, August 22) 2yo 6f Good to firm **114** (TS 89) 5 ran ● **1st** Princess Margaret Stakes (Group 3) (Ascot, July 27) 2yo 6f Good to firm **111** (TS 65) 6 ran ● **1st** Villas At Stonehaven Tobago EBF Maiden Fillies' Stakes (Newmarket (July), June 28) 2yo 6f Good to firm **90** (TS 57) 6 ran

accelerate off a fast pace is one of the hallmarks of a champion.

After proving her brilliance, Russian Rhythm was required to show heart to complete a Group 1 hat-trick in the Nassau Stakes at Goodwood. She took a strong hold on her first try at ten furlongs and was left in tight quarters when the pace quickened early in the straight. It did not look good for a stride or two, but Russian Rhythm picked up most gamely under strong pressure and collared the French challenger Ana Marie by a neck.

The effort to pull off this victory was considerable for Russian Rhythm and probably left its mark. She had looked rather laboured under pressure and for the first time had to be called on for maximum effort.

Stoute does not have a reputation for being a supreme trainer of fillies for nothing, however. He managed to freshen up Russian Rhythm to run second to Falbrav in the Queen Elizabeth II Stakes at Ascot in September, when she seemed to make light of reportedly being in season before the race. However, the Champion Stakes at Newmarket three weeks later proved a race too far and she faded into mid-division behind Rakti after taking a keen hold.

Some sought an alternative explanation for Russian Rhythm's defeat at Newmarket in the ten-furlong distance. According to this theory, she got the trip purely 'on class' at Goodwood, before being exposed in a deeper contest against males. This conveniently ignores that she was

More Group 1 glory as Sir Michael Stoute's star filly lands the Coronation Stakes at Royal Ascot from Soviet Song

ill at ease more than two furlongs from home in the Champion.

The likelihood of a rematch between Russian Rhythm and Six Perfections was increased when the European Pattern Committee announced a new programme for older fillies and mares, commencing in 2004. Five new Group 1 contests have been created, in order to encourage owners and breeders to prolong the careers of talented three-year-old fillies in Europe and discourage their migration to the US or retirement. The enhancements to races in Britain, France, Germany and Ireland are concentrated in the eight- to ten-furlong category and should provide an attractive programme for a filly like Russian Rhythm against runners of her own sex.

The most significant changes are a new Group 2 at Royal Ascot over a mile for older females and the upgrading of the Falmouth Stakes at the Newmarket July meeting to Group 1. It remains to be seen whether the penalty structure of the former would make it a desirable target for Russian Rhythm, but the latter almost certainly will be.

Whatever Russian Rhythm's success on the track as a four-year-old, there is little need for her to press her credentials as a broodmare. She is already priceless, being a triple Group 1-winning daughter of Kingmambo and from the family of the Cheveley Park winners Desirable and Park

And that makes it three: taking the Nassau Stakes at Goodwood by a neck from French raider Ana Marie

Appeal and the Irish Oaks winner Alydaress.

The purchase of Russian Rhythm for 440,000 guineas at the 2001 Houghton Sales was another example of the acumen of Cheveley Park Stud's managing director, Chris Richardson. The stud had been keen to buy a descendant of influential broodmare Balidaress, who produced the top-class fillies mentioned above as well as Russian Rhythm's unraced dam Balistroika.

Cheveley Park Stud, which is owned by David and Patricia Thompson, has flourished under the guidance of Richardson. Apart from Russian Rhythm, other fillies to gain black type in the red, white and blue livery in 2003 were Red Bloom, Danehurst, Chorist, Chic, Entrap, Fantasize, Humouresque and Irresistible. That is some record and strongly suggests the stud will continue on an upward curve.

Russian Rhythm looks sure to play a major part in that success herself, both on and off the track. Provided she carries her energy and enthusiasm for racing into a third campaign, there is no reason why she should not reassert herself at the highest level. Indeed, it is not out of the question that she could find some further improvement. The opportunity to watch her race again is one that should be cherished.

Russian Rhythm

chestnut filly, 12-2-2000

		Raise A Native	Native Dancer
	Mr Prospector		Raise You
Kingmambo		Gold Digger	Nashua
b 1990			Sequence
		Nureyev	**Northern Dancer**
	Miesque		Special
		Pasadoble	Prove Out
			Santa Quilla
		Northern Dancer	Nearctic
	Nijinsky		Natalma
		Flaming Page	Bull Page
Balistroika			Flaring Top
ch 1988		Balidar	Will Somers
	Balidaress		Violet Bank
		Innocence	Sea Hawk
			Novitiate

Bred by Brushwood Stable in Kentucky
$370,000 Keeneland November foal, 440,000gns Tattersalls Houghton yearling

Sire Kingmambo

Won 5 of 13 races, inc. Poule d'Essai des Poulains-Gr1, St James's Palace S.-Gr1, Prix du Moulin de Longchamp-Gr1. Medium-sized, attractive individual. Among the best milers of his generation, game, consistent, with a good turn of foot. Sire of: American Boss (Gr2), El Condor Pasa (NHK Mile Cup-Gr1, Japan Cup-Gr1, Grand Prix de Saint-Cloud-Gr1), Mambo Twist (Gr3), Parade Ground (Gr2), Admire Mambo (Gr2), Lemon Drop Kid (Futurity S.-Gr1, Belmont S.-Gr1, Travers S.-Gr1, Whitney S.-Gr1, Woodward H.-Gr1), Monarch's Maze (Gr2), Bluemamba (Poule d'Essai des Pouliches-Gr1), King Cugat (Gr2), Kingsalsa (Gr3), King's Best (2,000 Guineas-Gr1), Parade Leader (Gr2), Penny's Gold (Gr3), King Fidelia (Gr3), Malhub (Golden Jubilee S.-Gr1), Okawango (Grand Criterium-Gr1), Voodoo Dancer (Garden City H.-Gr1), Dubai Destination (Queen Anne S.-Gr1), Walzerkonigin (Gr2), Governor Brown (Gr3), Russian Rhythm (1,000 Guineas-Gr1, Coronation S.-Gr1, Nassau S.-Gr1).

Dam Balistroika

Unraced half-sister to Gr1 winners Desirable (also dam of Gr1 winner Shadayid), Park Appeal (also dam of Gr1 winner Cape Cross and grand-dam of Gr1 winner Diktat) and Alydaress. Dam of Lanseria (1993 f by Diesis; unraced), unnamed (1994 f by Diesis; died young), Alawal (1995 c by Miswaki; winner), Zenno Keima (1996 c by Gone West; winner), Ive Gota Bad Liver (1997 f by Mt Livermore; winner, Gr3-placed), Balade Russe (1999 f by Gone West; winner), Russian Rhythm (2000 f by Kingmambo; Classic winner), Marisa (2001 f by Swain; unraced to date).

Pedigree assessment

Russian Rhythm undoubtedly profited from the ill-luck suffered by Six Perfections in the 1,000 Guineas, but she scarcely needed to apologise for that. Hers was a first-class performance, and she went on to confirm her status as top home-based filly in the Coronation Stakes and Nassau Stakes, on the latter occasion facing older competition for the first time. Her merit in mixed company was established in the Queen Elizabeth II Stakes, when she improved again but found Falbrav in imperious form. Sadly, she did not give her running in the Champion Stakes, but she will hopefully be back in action in 2004. Racegoers would welcome her back if connections opted to postpone the start of her innings as an exciting broodmare prospect. *TM*

Six Perfections (Fr)

3yo black filly **123**

Celtic Swing - Yogya (USA) (Riverman (USA))

Owner Niarchos Family

Trainer P Bary

Breeder Niarchos Family

| Career: **10** starts | won **6** | second **4** | third **0** | £943,692 win and place |

By Richard Austen

J ERRY BAILEY, read on. Thierry Thulliez and Johnny Murtagh, please turn forward to the next chapter. Six Perfections' three-year-old season was also a tale of three jockeys, for while high-class performances from the filly herself are now almost taken for granted, the same could not be said of the men on board, two of whom found events conspiring badly against them. She had six races in 2003, but they will not go down in history as the Six Perfections.

When Six Perfections embarked on her three-year-old campaign, all seemed set fair. After all, she was the top two-year-old filly of 2002 and had all the credentials one would look for in a potential champion. The Prix Imprudence at Maisons-Laffitte, four weeks before the 1,000 Guineas, went the same way as Six Perfections' last three races as a two-year-old and resulted in an easy victory.

She lined up at Newmarket a 7-4 favourite – and that against 18 opponents in what looked a very strong renewal, even allowing for doubts over whether Russian Rhythm had yet come to hand. There was no doubt that Thulliez, her regular jockey, would adopt waiting tactics, to exploit her superb turn of foot, so as the previous day's 2,000 Guineas well illustrated, stall one wasn't without its pitfalls. Nobody said it would be easy. But did it have to be quite this difficult?

Approaching the final furlong, Thulliez and Six Perfections were still last of the 19, having run into the back of a weakening rival in one earlier attempt to find a way through, but most strikingly of all they were about to make their challenge on the wide outside, having been drawn against the stands' rail. Six Perfections went past 17 horses but, sensational effort as it was, catching Russian Rhythm was beyond her.

Russian Rhythm was drawn in stall two and racing against the rails three furlongs out, next to Six Perfections, before Kieren Fallon moved her forward through the gap that materialised when Thulliez embarked on his early manoeuvrings. The distance between the two fillies at the

Six Perfections (Jerry Bailey) lands a famous victory in the Breeders' Cup Mile at Santa Anita in October

line was a length and a half.

"She was the best filly, but second best in the race," observed a stunned Pascal Bary, the trainer of Six Perfections. "It was still a magnificent occasion," he added later. "The English love their racing and there was a wonderful ambience. Apart from the race, everything was perfect."

Clues that others shared Bary's view of the result came when the filly lined up in the smallest Irish 1,000 Guineas field since 1939 and started at 30-100, with Murtagh replacing Thulliez. "It's very simple – we want to have an Irish jockey in Ireland," said Alan Cooper, racing manager to the Niarchos family, owners of Six Perfections.

If anything, the Irish Guineas turned out to be even more of a farce for Six Perfections. There were eight runners instead of 19, but more than enough still to get in her way. "She was stuck on the rail and it was not a very good pace," reflected Bary after Six Perfections' new jockey had this time clung to his position and waited. "I knew it would be difficult, and *voila*."

"They didn't open up when I needed them to, but I still thought I'd

2003   Race record

1st NetJets Breeders' Cup Mile (Grade 1) (Santa Anita, October 25) 3yo+ 1m Firm **121** 13 ran. *Reluctant to load, mid-division, 9th straight, pushed along and headway over 1f out, driven and quickened to lead 150yds out, ran on well, driven out, beat Touch Of The Blues by ³/₄l*

1st Prix du Haras de Fresnay-Le Buffard-Jacques le Marois (Group 1) (Deauville, August 17) 3yo+ 1m Good to soft **123** (TS 100) 12 ran. *Held up in touch, 5th halfway, pushed along over 1¹/₂f out, ridden and led over 1f out, ran on well under pressure to line, beat Domedriver by snk*

2nd Prix d'Astarte (Group 2) (Deauville, August 3) 3yo+ 1m Good to soft **116** (TS 97) 12 ran. *Tracking leaders towards outside, disputing 3rd halfway, shaken up over 2f out, quickened to lead approaching final furlong, ran on until headed close home, beaten nk by Bright Sky*

2nd Entenmann's Irish 1,000 Guineas (Group 1) (Curragh, May 25) 3yo 1m Soft **117** (TS 96) 8 ran. *Held up, 4th and trapped on inner 2f out, clear run final furlong, just failed, beaten shd by Yesterday*

2nd Sagitta 1,000 Guineas (Group 1) (Newmarket, May 4) 3yo 1m Good to firm **115** (TS 95) 19 ran. *Held up, hampered over 2f out, switched right and headway over 1f out, ran on well, not reach winner, beaten 1¹/₂l by Russian Rhythm*

1st Prix Imprudence (Listed) (Maisons-Laffitte, April 7) 3yo 7f Good **106** (TS 36) 7 ran. *Always close up in centre, pulled hard early, hampered 1¹/₂f out, soon recovered, quickened to lead inside final furlong, not extended, beat Campsie Fells by 1¹/₂l*

2002

1st Prix Marcel Boussac Criterium Pouliches-Royal Barriere de Deauville (Group 1) (Longchamp, October 6) 2yo 1m Good **118** (TS 80) 10 ran ● **1st** Prix du Calvados (Group 3) (Deauville, August 23) 2yo 7f Good **109** (TS 65) 8 ran ● **1st** Prix Roland de Chambure (Listed) (Deauville, July 11) 2yo 7f Very soft **105** (TS 77) 7 ran ● **2nd** Prix des Jardins (Unraced Fillies) (Chantilly, June 17) 2yo 5¹/₂f Good to soft 13 ran

get there," reported Murtagh after Mick Kinane on Yesterday had first held him in and then got first run. "I wouldn't have done it any different." Yesterday, eighth at Newmarket, beat Six Perfections by a short head.

We all make mistakes, and at Newmarket on May 4 and The Curragh on May 25 it was the turn of Messrs Thulliez and Murtagh. "It is too much. Two Guineas gone – whoosh!" groaned Bary at The Curragh. "We will just have to try again." Trouble was, the mile Classics had finished. The Prix de Diane, over an extended mile and a quarter, was just a fortnight away and Six Perfections had earned a rest.

Six Perfections looked destined to be remembered as the filly who should have been a dual Guineas winner but wasn't. Bary was beginning to look like one of the world's most accomplished stoics. He had the horse but not the prize, a strange inversion of what happened in 1981 at the start of Bary's career when he trained only one horse, won a claimer and returned home afterwards with the prize but not the horse.

Some bookmakers offered odds about who would ride Six Perfections next and, just over two months later, they had to pay out on the favourite when the honour reverted to Thulliez in the Prix d'Astarte at Deauville. Favourite backers who persevered with Six Perfections herself, however, again had their fingers burned. Eclipsed at 6-5, it was possible to argue

It all comes right for Thierry Thulliez on Six Perfections (nearside) in the Jacques le Marois at Deauville in August

that on this occasion Six Perfections saw too much daylight – it must have come as a shock to her, after all – but this narrow defeat at the hands of top-class four-year-old Bright Sky could not be blamed on the sort of atrocious luck that afflicted her in both Guineas.

Immediately after the Newmarket contest, there seemed to be near unanimity in the conclusion that Six Perfections was the best horse on the day. A few months later, some were reconsidering, because while Six Perfections emerged from her break to notch another second place, Russian Rhythm had marched on victorious at Royal Ascot and Goodwood.

Six Perfections' camp appeared satisfied after the d'Astarte, however, perhaps because it was a warm-up for the Prix du Haras de Fresnay-le-Buffard Jacques le Marois, sponsored by the Niarchos stud. The late Stavros Niarchos and his family had won the race seven times, beginning with Miesque in 1987 and 1988.

A good field of 12 was assembled in Six Perfections' bid for win number eight, including Godolphin favourite Dubai Destination and Japanese challengers Lohengrin and Telegnosis; André Fabre fielded an eye-catching trio in Vahorimix, successful in the race in 2001 but infertile at stud, and two three-year-olds who had gone one better than Six Perfections in a Classic, the Prix de Diane winner Nebraska Tornado and Poule d'Essai des Poulains victor Clodovil.

Godolphin and the Niarchos family both fielded pacemakers and, with a good pace and room aplenty, Six Perfections emerged in front a furlong out. She had done so in the d'Astarte as well, a little earlier, and been beaten. The same scenario loomed large in the Jacques le Marois, too, and this time connections would have only themselves to blame if Six Perfections were eclipsed, because the threat came from the Niarchos-Bary second-string Domedriver. A short neck was the final margin between them and, miracle of miracles, Six Perfections passed the post in front.

Whether victory in the Jacques le Marois represented redemption for Six Perfections' season must be debatable from a British or Irish perspective. For winning jockey Thulliez, seemingly, it was not enough, because in the NetJets Breeders' Cup Mile at Santa Anita the "when in Rome" argument won out again and the ride went to Bailey.

The Niarchos family had another proud tradition to maintain in the Mile and Thulliez had done his bit 12 months earlier when guiding Domedriver home at Arlington, following their triumphs with Miesque (1987 and 1988) and Spinning World (1997). Bailey, though, had won more Breeders' Cup races (13) than any other jockey.

"I think that if you go to Chicago or Belmont, maybe you can use a French jockey," Bary explained. "Here, if you can get the best American jockey on an American track you must do it." Many argued, however, that the task was beyond any jockey when Six Perfections was drawn wide in stall 13. "It's not a good number," said her trainer.

When the Breeders' Cup had last visited Santa Anita, in 1993, there was chaos at the first turn in the Mile. If the field was bunched, Six Perfections could easily be forced wide. Trying to come from the back was most unlikely to be a viable option. One thing seemed for certain, though, 53-10 shot Six Perfections was never going to win the dash for a prominent pitch with those drawn inside her including front-runner Peace Rules and three further strong candidates for a leading early role.

Bailey was warned that Six Perfections would be fractious at the start, but was also told that she had "the ability to wait and to finish very, very fast." She duly played up before eventually consenting to enter the stalls riderless. The effectiveness of her turn of foot depended on Bailey getting her into a competitive position.

He did so, thanks to a frantic early pace that had the field strung out, with Bailey asking her to improve before the first turn and then racing in mid-division with only one horse inside her. With about four lengths to make up as they entered the short final straight, she angled out, squeezed through as Touch Of The Blues launched a challenge down the outside, and then outran him to win by three-quarters of a length.

The French maintained their superior record at the Breeders' Cup – it was their 13th win – and it was Bary's third success, following Miss Alleged (1991 Turf) and Domedriver. Six Perfections also upheld a family tradition because the magnificent Miesque is a half-sister to her dam. Six Perfections is not quite in Miesque's class, but her finishing kick is not too dissimilar.

Six Perfections

black filly, 24-2-2000

		Mr Prospector	Raise A Native Gold Digger
	Damister		
		Batucada	Roman Line Whistle A Tune
Celtic Swing br 1992			
		Welsh Pageant	Tudor Melody Picture Light
	Celtic Ring		
		Pencuik Jewel	Petingo Fotheringay
		Never Bend	Nasrullah Lalun
	Riverman		
		River Lady	Prince John Nile Lily
Yogya ch 1993			
		Prove Out	Graustark Equal Venture
	Pasadoble		
		Santa Quilla	Sanctus Neriad

Bred by Niarchos Family in France

Sire Celtic Swing

Won 5 of 7 races, inc. Racing Post Trophy-Gr1, Greenham S.-Gr3, Prix du Jockey-Club-Gr1. Also 2nd in 2,000 Guineas-Gr1. Champion European 2yo. Tall, angular type, with poor foreleg conformation. Top-class performer from 8-12f, effective on good to firm ground, outstanding on soft. Suffered knee ligament damage in Irish Derby, never ran again. Sire of: Six Perfections (Prix Marcel Boussac-Gr1, Prix Jacques le Marois-Gr1, Breeders' Cup Mile-Gr1).

Dam Yogya

Unraced half-sister to outstanding miler Miesque (dam of Gr1 winners Kingmambo and East Of The Moon). Dam of: Six Perfections (2000 f by Celtic Swing; multiple Gr1 winner).

Pedigree assessment

The cheers and applause that rang out for Six Perfections as she cantered to the post before the 1,000 Guineas turned out to be premature. That was not to be her coronation day, and nor was it at The Curragh three weeks later; wretched luck in running robbed her of both. But the filly who had threatened to dominate the distaff mile scene finally came good – so good that she was able to see off males as well – in the Prix Jacques le Marois and, to worldwide acclaim, in the Breeders' Cup Mile. Her sporting connections now want her to emulate her 'aunt' Miesque by doubling up in the latter event; if she stays sound, she will surely do Europe credit again at Lone Star Park. *TM*

She ended 2003 the equal of Russian Rhythm according to Racing Post Ratings and remains in training, with the Jacques le Marois and Breeders' Cup Mile her major targets. A rematch would be worth going a long way to see, but wherever she turns up high drama is on the cards, as her jockey grapples once again with the instruction "don't hit the front too soon".

Somnus

3yo bay gelding **123**

Pivotal - Midnight's Reward (Night Shift (USA))
Owner Legard Sidebottom & Sykes
Trainer T D Easterby
Breeder Lady Legard

Career: **13** starts | won **7** | second **1** | third **0** | **£424,940** win and place

By Tom O'Ryan

MOULDING sows' ears into silk purses has been the hallmark of the Easterby family for as long as most of us care to remember. The talent, honed to perfection under both codes by brothers Mick and Peter, has clearly not been lost on Tim Easterby, Peter's son, who, for the second time in four seasons, transformed a horse of humble beginnings into a star sprinter.

The sensational success of Somnus in the Stanley Leisure Sprint Cup at Haydock in September was the crowning glory of an unlikely hero, who had been led out unsold as a yearling at Doncaster Sales at 13,500 guineas – a modest figure in this day and age, but still almost double the amount Easterby had paid for Pipalong, winner of the corresponding Group 1 showpiece in 2000.

Pipalong's 7,000 guineas purchase price paled into insignificance beside her mighty deeds on the racecourse, which netted her around £500,000 before she was sold as a prospective broodmare for 600,000 guineas.

Somnus has likewise made a mockery of his initial public appearance in a sale ring. His exploits as a juvenile were nothing short of startling. In winning four of his five starts, he clinched hugely valuable sales races at Doncaster and Redcar, conquering such notables as Tout Seul and Airwave, the subsequent winners of the Dewhurst and Cheveley Park Stakes, and being awarded an International Classification rating of 118; a remarkable figure for a horse who had never run in a Group race.

However, 2003 did not begin well for Somnus. He ran disappointingly on his reappearance at Ascot at the end of April, but was off-colour for a short time afterwards. He went back to Ascot for the Royal meeting, making his debut in Pattern company and stepping up to seven furlongs for the first time in the Group 3 Jersey Stakes. After chasing the leaders, he faded when the chips were down, leaving some observers to deduce that he did not stay, some more to suggest he had not yet come to himself,

Somnus (Ted Durcan, nearside) lands the Group 1 Stanley Leisure Sprint Cup at Haydock in September

and others to conclude that he had not trained on.

If the jury were out, they did not need to deliberate for long. Somnus bounced back to winning form in a conditions race at Haydock over six furlongs and followed up in a Listed event over the same distance at Newbury. He was then desperately unlucky not to complete a hat-trick in the Shergar Cup Sprint at Ascot, meeting all sorts of traffic problems before finishing fast, in fourth place, behind Move It.

Sent off the 6-5 favourite to gain compensation in a Listed race at Newmarket next time, Somnus was once again denied, this time by his talented stablemate Fayr Jag, who took the honours by a neck. Though pleased to win the race, Easterby took the view that Somnus may have been inconvenienced by the dip in the course. Where to go next was the question, not least because the son of Pivotal, although effective on fast ground, is considered infinitely better on an easy surface.

Easterby took the brave decision to declare Somnus for the Sprint Cup and prayed that the rain came. It duly arrived on cue, turning previously quick ground good to soft and enabling the three-year-old

2003 — Race record

7th Prix de l'Abbaye de Longchamp - Majestic Barriere (Group 1) (Longchamp, October 5) 2yo+ 5f Holding **108** (TS 97) 19 ran. *Outpaced to halfway, headway well over 1f out, never nearer, beaten 4½l by Patavellian*

1st Stanley Leisure Sprint Cup (Group 1) (Haydock, September 6) 3yo+ 6f Good to soft **123** (TS 106) 10 ran. *Held up, headway when ridden and switched left over 1f out, led inside final furlong, ran on, beat Oasis Dream by 1¼l*

2nd Hopeful Stakes (Listed) (Newmarket (July), August 22) 3yo+ 6f Good to firm **98** (TS 71) 6 ran. *Held up, ridden and not much room over 1f out, ran on well inside final furlong, not reach winner, beaten nk by Fayr Jag*

4th Dubai Duty Free Shergar Cup Sprint (Ascot, August 9) 3yo 6f Good to firm **102** (TS 73) 9 ran. *Tracked leaders, not clear run well over 1f out until inside final furlong, ran on well near finish, not recover, beaten ¾l by Move It*

1st David Wilson Homes Stakes (Registered As The Hackwood Stakes) (Listed) (Newbury, July 19) 3yo+ 6f Good to firm **118** (TS 87) 14 ran. *In touch, hard driven from over 2f out, strong run under pressure final furlong, led close home, beat Ashdown Express by nk*

1st Thwaites Smooth Beer Conditions Stakes (Haydock, July 5) 3yo+ 6f Good **118** (TS 87) 11 ran. *Midfield, ridden over 2f out, headway over 1f out, led well inside final furlong, ran on well, beat Maltese Falcon by 2½l*

8th Jersey Stakes (Group 3) (Ascot, June 18) 3yo 7f Good to firm **85** (TS 63) 14 ran. *Chased leaders, ridden over 2f out, weakened approaching final furlong, beaten 11l by Membership*

5th Sodexho Pavilion Stakes (Listed) (Ascot, April 30) 3yo 6f Good **95** (TS 64) 9 ran. *Ridden halfway, no headway final 2f, beaten 6l by Striking Ambition*

2002

1st betabet Two-Year-Old Trophy (Redcar, October 5) 2yo 6f Firm **114** (TS 50) 18 ran ● **1st** £200000 St Leger Yearling Stakes (Doncaster, September 11) 2yo 6f Good **104** (TS 73) 21 ran ● **1st** Steve Nesbitt Challenge Trophy Nursery (Ripon, August 27) 2yo 6f Good **94** (TS 64) 13 ran ● **1st** John O'Brien Median Auction Maiden Stakes (York, July 13) 2yo 6f Good **77** (TS 33) 19 ran ● **5th** EBF Hoopers For Fashion Maiden Stakes (Ripon, June 20) 2yo 6f Good to firm **53** 6 ran

to register a length-and-a-quarter success over the hot favourite Oasis Dream, with Airwave, who had reportedly suffered a less-than-ideal preparation, three-parts of a length further back in third.

While justifiable excuses, because of the change of ground, were put forward for the defeat of July Cup and Nunthorpe winner Oasis Dream – a horse rated 9lb superior to Somnus – Easterby's gelding clearly relished the rain-soaked surface as he promoted himself to Group 1 winner in only his second attempt in Pattern company.

Opportunities for Somnus were scarce after Haydock and connections took the view that he was well worth supplementing for the Prix de l'Abbaye. Once again the ground came in his favour, but, tackling five furlongs for the first time, he was found wanting for early toe before staying on to be beaten around four lengths into seventh behind Patavellian.

Somnus will be denied a future career as a stallion, because he was gelded even before his career had started. Easterby, though, knows only too well that had the horse not been castrated, the chances are he would

Somnus
bay gelding, 27-4-2000

Pivotal ch 1993	Polar Falcon	Nureyev	**Northern Dancer** Special
		Marie d'Argonne	Jefferson Mohair
	Fearless Revival	Cozzene	Caro Ride The Trails
		Stufida	Bustino Zerbinetta
Midnight's Reward b 1986	Night Shift	**Northern Dancer**	Nearctic Natalma
		Ciboulette	Chop Chop Windy Answer
	Margaret's Ruby	Tesco Boy	Princely Gift Suncourt
		Pixie Jet	Polly's Jet Sailanna

Bred by Lady Legard in England. Bought in 13,500gns Doncaster St Leger Yearling Sales

Sire Pivotal

Won 4 of 6 races, inc. King's Stand S.-Gr2, Nunthorpe S.-Gr1. Powerfully-built, attractive sort, high-class sprinter on preferred fast ground seemingly best at 5f. Sire of: Golden Apples (Del Mar Oaks-Gr1, Beverly D S.-Gr1, Yellow Ribbon S.-Gr1), Kyllachy (Nunthorpe S.-Gr1), Low Pivot (Gr3), Needwood Blade (Gr3), Ratio (Gr3), Silvester Lady (Preis der Diana-Gr1), Captain Rio (Gr2), Chorist (Gr3), Megahertz (John C. Mabee H.-Gr1), Stolzing (Gr3), Humouresque (Gr3), Somnus (Haydock Park Sprint Cup-Gr1).

Dam Midnight's Reward

Won 1 of 8 races. Useful sprinter in modest company at 2, cracked bone and retired after two indifferent runs at 3. Dam of: Lettermore (1990 f by Elegant Air; winner in Belgium), Soca King (1992 c by Midyan; winner), Midnight Cookie (1993 c by Midyan; placed), Damaya (1994 f by Formidable; winner in France), Dayo (1996 g by Robellino; unplaced), Midnight's Dream (1997 c by Elmaamul; winner, stakes-placed in Poland), Pasithea (1998 f by Celtic Swing; winner), Forest Prize (1999 f by Charnwood Forest; winner), Somnus (2000 g by Pivotal; Gr1 winner).

Pedigree assessment

There was nothing in Somnus's pedigree to hint that he would develop Group 1 sprinting form, hence his rejection at the yearling sales. But his sire has become the surprise success in Britain's stallion ranks in recent years, with a marked facility to add class to families and to get stock who stay further than he did himself. Somnus has good form on fast ground at six furlongs, but it would be unwise to conclude that five furlongs is too short despite his defeat in the Prix de l'Abbaye. *TM*

never have scaled such great heights, so difficult was he to break as a yearling. The good news is that he will be displaying his sprinting prowess – and hopefully adding to his rags-to-riches tale – for some considerable time to come.

Soviet Song (Ire)

3yo bay filly   **118**

Marju (Ire) - Kalinka (Ire) (Soviet Star (USA))
Owner Elite Racing Club
Trainer J R Fanshawe
Breeder Elite Racing Club

Career: **7** starts	won **3**	second **1**	third **0**	**£228,689** win and place

By Seb Vance

A SEASON that promised so much for Soviet Song ultimately resulted in precious little. The James Fanshawe-trained filly had hovered around the front of the Classic betting through the winter and big things were expected for the Fillies' Mile heroine.

The anticipation of a possible Guineas win started bubbling in earnest following that Ascot success. It was a first Group 1 win for jockey Oscar Urbina and also for the owners, the Elite Racing Club, whose multitude of members invaded the unsaddling enclosure. While the talk of what she could do as a three-year-old was big, it was fully justified. She showed an electric turn of pace to win at Ascot and end the 2002 season unbeaten in three starts. On each occasion, Soviet Song beat only the top class – the speedy Airwave on her debut and the subsequent Oaks third Summitville at Newmarket, before trouncing Casual Look, later the Oaks winner, in the Fillies' Mile.

However, Soviet Song finished 2003 without adding to her Ascot success and had the misfortune to run into the brilliant Russian Rhythm on three occasions. Her four starts all came in Group 1 contests, and while she never disgraced herself – a second, two fourths and a fifth confirm that – she never quite looked like winning.

Soviet Song arrived at Newmarket for the 1,000 Guineas a well-fancied 4-1 shot, although the fast conditions were felt to be against her despite her having won twice on good to firm ground as a juvenile. In addition, and perhaps more importantly, Fanshawe's horses were suffering from flu. As it turned out, her fourth place, after she had loomed up as a serious challenger before flattening out in the closing stages, was a good effort. She was only four and a quarter lengths behind Russian Rhythm.

Both Fanshawe and Urbina, having only his second Classic ride and matching the fourth achieved on Mons in the 1996 St Leger, declared themselves satisfied, insisting there would be more to come when she

Soviet Song (Oscar Urbina) could not add to her three victories of 2002 but stays in training

was fully fit. Bookmakers agreed and initially priced her as low as 12-1 for the Oaks, although connections almost immediately ruled out the Epsom Classic, preferring instead to stick to a mile.

The Irish 1,000 Guineas was a no-go after Soviet Song scoped badly and her reappearance was postponed until the Coronation Stakes at Royal Ascot. Again, she was not at her peak for the rematch with Russian Rhythm and connections expressed concern that the race would come too soon for her. She may not have been match-fit, but Soviet Song got closer to her Newmarket conqueror this time round, with the deficit now only a length and a half, with Mail The Desert three lengths back in third.

While Soviet Song never looked like exacting revenge, the signs were encouraging. A thrilled Fanshawe said after the race: "The advantage we have with the autumn is that we know she goes on soft ground, so she has something up her sleeve."

After deciding against the Nassau Stakes and Celebration Mile, an opportunity arrived for Soviet Song, and it looked a good one. As Fanshawe had hoped, her next start was on good-to-soft ground and came in the Prix du Moulin at Longchamp, almost three months after the Coronation.

2003   Race record

5th Queen Elizabeth II Stakes (Sponsored By NetJets) (Group 1) (Ascot, September 27) 3yo+ 1m Good to firm **111** (TS 93) 8 ran. *Held up in rear, ridden and effort over 2f out, never going pace to reach leaders, beaten 6¼l by Falbrav*

4th Netjets Prix du Moulin de Longchamp (Group 1) (Longchamp, September 7) 3yo+ 1m Good to soft **114** (TS 81) 14 ran. *Held up, 11th straight on inside, good headway well over 1f out, kept on at one pace final furlong, beaten 3l by Nebraska Tornado*

2nd Coronation Stakes (Group 1) (Ascot, June 20) 3yo 1m Good to firm **118** (TS 107) 9 ran. *Held up in rear, headway on outside from 3f out, edged right inside final 2f, chased winner 1f out, kept on well but no impression close home, beaten 1½l by Russian Rhythm*

4th Sagitta 1,000 Guineas (Group 1) (Newmarket, May 4) 3yo 1m Good to firm **108** (TS 86) 19 ran. *Held up, headway over 2f out, every chance over 1f out, no extra inside final furlong, beaten 4¼l by Russian Rhythm*

2002

1st Meon Valley Stud Fillies' Mile (Group 1) (Ascot, September 28) 2yo 1m Good to firm **112** (TS 77) 10 ran ● **1st** Milcars Sweet Solera Stakes (Listed) (Newmarket (July), August 10) 2yo 7f Soft **111** (TS 50) 8 ran ● **1st** EBF Median Auction Maiden Fillies' Stakes (Kempton, July 17) 2yo 6f Good to firm **83** (TS 53) 15 ran

However, the race was a copybook French one and the British raiders were caught out. In a finish that was dominated by horses who had raced prominently, Soviet Song fared best of the cross-Channel raiding party, putting in her best work at the end of the mile contest and finishing three lengths behind Nebraska Tornado in fourth.

There would be no excuses over fitness for the Queen Elizabeth II Stakes at Ascot, run 20 days after the Longchamp event and at the meeting where she had destroyed a high-class field 12 months earlier. However, the main talking point leading up to the exciting renewal, which featured Russian Rhythm, Dubai Destination and Falbrav, was the jockey change. Urbina was kicked off the horse who made his name and Jamie Spencer, of whom Fanshawe was making increasing use, took over.

Reacting to the news, Urbina said: "I haven't done anything wrong on her – she hasn't been at her best all year. I know her and I know she is very well in herself now – and it is typical that I won't be on her." As it turned out, he didn't miss much. There were no excuses prior to the race, connections reporting her 100 per cent, and her fifth place behind Falbrav must go down as a disappointing effort. For the third time she was beaten by Russian Rhythm, by exactly the same distance as she had been in the Guineas. In her defence, the ground was lightning-fast and led to six defections from the scheduled line-up. Similar conditions ruled out a bid for the Champion Stakes.

Soviet Song stays in training and there will be improved opportunities for older fillies in 2004, so she may yet add another Group 1 success. A race like the Falmouth Stakes, due to be upgraded to Group 1 and won by stablemate Macadamia in 2003, would be ideal for her.

Soviet Song

bay filly, 18-2-2000

		Try My Best	**Northern Dancer** / Sex Appeal
	Last Tycoon	Mill Princess	Mill Reef / Irish Lass
Marju br 1988	Flame Of Tara	Artaius	Round Table / Stylish Pattern
		Welsh Flame	Welsh Pageant / Electric Flash
	Soviet Star	Nureyev	**Northern Dancer** / Special
		Veruschka	Venture / Marie d'Anjou
Kalinka b 1994	Tralthee	Tromos	Busted / Stilvi
		Swalthee	Sword Dancer / Amalthee

Bred by Elite Racing Club in Ireland

Sire Marju

Won 3 of 7 races, inc. Craven S.-Gr3, St James's Palace S.-Gr1, also 2nd Derby-Gr1. Effective 1m-12f. Half-brother to Salsabil out of high-class 1m-10f filly. Stands at Derrinstown Stud, 2004 fee €16,000. Oldest progeny 10. Sire of: My Emma (Yorkshire Oaks-Gr1, Prix Vermeille-Gr1), Indigenous (HK Gr2), Mahboob (Gr3), Della Scala (Gr3), Marine (Gr3), Miletrian (Gr2), Oriental Fashion (Gr2), Sapphire Ring (Gr2), Naheef (Gr3), Marbye (Gr3), Soviet Song (Fillies' Mile-Gr1), Stormont (Gr2).

Dam Kalinka

Won 1 of 10 Flat races, also unplaced in 2 hurdles. By top-class sprinter-miler out of smart 2yo and 10f filly who is a half-sister to grand-dam of Milwaukee Brew. Dam of: Baralinka (1999 f by Barathea; winner), Soviet Song (2000 f by Marju; Gr1 winner), Penzance (2001 c by Pennekamp; winner), 2002 f by Groom Dancer.

Pedigree assessment

Continued to show very smart form over 1m this year despite failing to win. Her pedigree is basically that of a miler but leaves open the possibility of stepping up to 10f. That should give her a broad range of options in 2004, especially with the Group 1 penalty discharged. *JH*

Storming Home

5yo bay horse   **124**

Machiavellian (USA) - Try To Catch Me (USA) (Shareef Dancer (USA))
Owner Maktoum Al Maktoum
Trainer N Drysdale
Breeder Gainsborough Stud Management Ltd

Career: **24** starts | won **8** | second **4** | third **3** | **£1,001,091** win and place

By James Willoughby

IT was a solid gold plot. The Comeback Kid with shot-up knees; the return to prominence in a million-dollar race; the perfect ride until an unexpected swerve; the horrific fall under flying hooves just yards from success. Gary Stevens would kill for a script like that as his acting career gathers momentum in the wake of his role as jockey George 'Iceman' Woolf in the movie Seabiscuit. Unfortunately for him, the events were for real and could easily have killed him.

Storming Home was the villain of the piece. A big, fine horse, he was shipped to Neil Drysdale in California at the end of 2002 with past performances for Barry Hills which included a victory in the Champion Stakes at Newmarket.

During his career in Europe, Storming Home showed the odd streak of wilfulness which encouraged his former trainer to try him in sheepskin cheekpieces on a couple of occasions, including in the Champion. With those aids not fashionable in the US, Drysdale used blinkers for his Stateside debut in the $400,000 Jim Murray Handicap over a mile and a half at Hollywood Park in May. Storming Home made an immediate impact, sweeping through from the rear to beat Denon by two lengths.

More followed in the Grade 1 Charles Whittingham Handicap, again at Hollywood. This time, Storming Home was forced to make his challenge five horses wide and got to the front only inside the final furlong. Stevens blamed his poor run round on the aggressive tactics of one or two of his rival jockeys, including Pat Valenzuela.

Given the extra energy required of Storming Home to overcome his travails, Drysdale decided to freshen the five-year-old for the Arlington Million on August 16. The two-month break certainly did the trick.

It should be appreciated at this point how important riding Storming Home in the Million was for Stevens. The jockey had stated that the five-year-old was one of the main reasons he resisted retirement following

Storming Home (Gary Stevens) takes the Clement L Hirsch Memorial Turf Championship at Santa Anita in September

the latest in a series of five knee operations conducted late in 2002.

For most of the way, Storming Home gave Stevens an armchair ride. The opening half-mile of 49 seconds on rain-soaked ground was an honest one and Storming Home was in a good tactical position towards the back of the 13 runners, some ten lengths off the lead, but Stevens was quick to take closer order, so that he was on the heels of the leaders and travelling well turning for home. Storming Home was then switched to the outside and accelerated sharply, reaching the front inside the final half furlong. Down the outside, Sulamani began to find his stride, but Storming Home looked sure to be saved by the wire.

What transpired was horrific. Storming Home ducked violently right just yards before the line and Stevens, who clung frantically to the reins, was hurled to the ground and struck by an onrushing rival. "I thought, I'm going to get disqualified and I'm going to get killed too," Stevens recalled. Fortunately, he was wrong on the more important count.

Having caused a chain reaction which hampered both dead-heaters for third, Kaieteur and Paolini, Storming Home's relegation to fourth was a formality under US rules and second-home Sulamani was awarded the race. Unlike in Britain and Ireland, it is deemed irrelevant in the US whether the interferer improved his position as a result of his actions. It is enough that he caused the interference on its own.

Apart from the ignominy of disqualification, the 40-year-old Stevens suffered a collapsed lung and broken vertebrae in his upper back.

2003   Race record

7th John Deere Breeders' Cup Turf (Grade 1) (Santa Anita, October 25) 3yo+ 12f Firm **113** 9 ran. *Disputing 6th, pushed along 2½f out, disputing 4th straight, one pace from over 1f out, beaten 9¼l by Johar and High Chaparral*

1st Clement L Hirsch Memorial Turf Championship (Grade 1) (Santa Anita, September 28) 3yo+ 10f Firm **122** 5 ran. *Held up in rear, headway over 2f out, 3rd on outside straight, ran on to lead well inside final furlong, ridden out, beat Johar by ½l*

4th (disq from 1st) Arlington Million XXI (Grade 1) (Arlington, August 16) 3yo+ 10f Good **120** 13 ran. *Held up, rapid headway halfway, 4th 3f out, led inside final furlong, ridden out, propped and went right last strides, fell just after line, finished 1st, disqualified and placed 4th*

1st Charles Whittingham Handicap (Grade 1) (Hollywood Park, June 14) 3yo+ 10f Firm **124** 6 ran. *Held up in 5th to straight, came wide, ran on to lead inside final furlong, ridden out, beat Mister Acpen by ¾l*

1st Jim Murray Memorial Handicap (Hollywood Park, May 10) 3yo+ 12f Firm **124** 8 ran. *Held up in rear, headway on outside over 3f out, went 2nd entering straight, led well over 1f out, ran on well, beat Denon by 2l*

2002

15th Japan Cup (Grade 1) (Nakayama, November 24) 3yo+ 11f Firm **102** 16 ran ● **1st** Emirates Airline Champion Stakes (Group 1) (Newmarket, October 19) 3yo+ 10f Good **124** (TS 103) 11 ran ● **1st** Fishpools Furnishings Godolphin Stakes (Listed) (Newmarket, October 4) 3yo+ 12f Firm **120** (TS 56) 4 ran ● **3rd** Amco Corporation Troy Stakes (Listed) (Doncaster, September 13) 3yo+ 12f Good to firm **111** (TS 91) 7 ran ● **6th** King George VI And Queen Elizabeth Diamond Stakes (Group 1) (Ascot, July 27) 3yo+ 12f Good to firm **114** (TS 93) 9 ran ● **2nd** Hardwicke Stakes (Group 2) (Ascot, June 22) 4yo+ 12f Good to firm **119** (TS 89) 7 ran ● **2nd** Vodafone Coronation Cup (Group 1) (Epsom, June 7) 4yo+ 12f Soft **119** (TS 79) 6 ran ● **3rd** Sagitta Jockey Club Stakes (Group 2) (Newmarket, May 3) 4yo+ 12f Good **121** (TS 76) 9 ran

Other wins

2001 1st King Edward VII Stakes (Group 2) (Ascot, June 22) 3yo 12f Good to firm **114** (TS 81) 12 ran ● **1st** Stanley Racing Blue Riband Trial Stakes (Conditions Race) (Epsom, April 25) 3yo 10f Soft **106** (TS 57) 5 ran **2000 1st** EBF Hugo & The Huguenotes Maiden Stakes (Newmarket (July), August 4) 2yo 7f Good **96** (TS 76) 10 ran

Amazingly, he made his comeback just 19 days later and was back into the swing of things well in time for the ride on Storming Home in his Breeders' Cup Turf prep race, the Grade 1 Clement L Hirsch Memorial Turf Championship at Santa Anita on September 28.

In a slowly run race, Storming Home picked off the eventual Turf dead-heater Johar easily. But he could not confirm the form on the big day. After tracking the leaders going well, Storming Home weakened quickly and returned well beaten. He was found to have injured a heel.

It was an unfortunate end to the racecourse career of the horse Stevens described in the build-up to the Breeders' Cup as "the most gifted turf horse I have ever ridden", but Storming Home's long-term future was already assured. It had been announced shortly before the race that he was to stand at Nunnery, Shadwell's stallion branch, in Norfolk in 2004.

Storming Home
bay horse, 14-2-1998

		Raise A Native	Native Dancer
			Raise You
	Mr Prospector		
		Gold Digger	Nashua
Machiavellian			Sequence
b 1987			
		Halo	Hail To Reason
			Cosmah
	Coup de Folie		
		Raise The Standard	Hoist The Flag
			Natalma
		Northern Dancer	Nearctic
			Natalma
	Shareef Dancer		
		Sweet Alliance	Sir Ivor
			Mrs Peterkin
Try To Catch Me			
b 1986			
		Mr Prospector	**Raise A Native**
			Gold Digger
	It's In The Air		
		A Wind Is Rising	Francis S
			Queen Nasra

Bred by Gainsborough Stud Management Ltd in England

Sire Machiavellian

Won 4 of 7 races, inc. Prix Morny-Gr1, Prix de la Salamandre-Gr1. Also 2nd in 2,000 Guineas-Gr1. Medium-sized, quite attractive individual. Quick-actioned, with a useful turn of foot. Barely lasted a mile. Sire of: Kokuto Julian (Japan Gr3), Phantom Gold (Gr2), Sinyar (Gr3), Vettori (Poule d'Essai des Poulains-Gr1), Susu (Gr2), Titus Livius (Gr2), Whitewater Affair (Gr2), Invermark (Prix du Cadran-Gr1), Kahal (Gr2), Majorien (Gr2), Rebecca Sharp (Coronation S.-Gr1), Almutawakel (Prix Jean Prat-Gr1, Dubai World Cup-Gr1), Fictitious (Gr3), Horatia (Gr3), Best Of The Bests (Prix d'Ispahan-Gr1), Magic Mission (Gr3), Medicean (Lockinge S.-Gr1, Eclipse S.-Gr1), Morning Pride (Gr3), No Excuse Needed (Gr2), Patavellian (Prix de l'Abbaye de Longchamp-Gr1), Storming Home (Champion S.-Gr1, Charles Whittingham Memorial H.-Gr1, Clement L. Hirsch Memorial S.-Gr1), Street Cry (Dubai World Cup-Gr1), Medecis (Gr3), Evolving Tactics (Gr2).

Dam Try To Catch Me

Won 1 of 8 races. Game and consistent handicap-class miler, never worse than 5th. Lacked a turn of foot. Dam of: Nawafell (1991 f by Kris; winner), Desert Frolic (1993 f by Persian Bold; winner), Sandrella (1995 f by Darshaan; unraced), Follow That Dream (1996 f by Darshaan; winner), Storming Home (1998 c by Machiavellian; multiple Gr1 winner), True Courage (1999 c by Machiavellian; placed), Storming Kate (2000 f by Lion Cavern; unraced to date), Try The Air (2001 f by Foxhound; unplaced).

Pedigree assessment

There always was an eccentric side to Storming Home, a fact he underlined again when contriving an original way of snatching defeat from the jaws of victory in the Arlington Million. Yards from home, the race in safe-keeping, he ducked right and impeded two of his challengers, and though he crossed the line in front (and just before parting company with his jockey), the stewards had no option but to take his number down. That spoiled the 100 per cent record compiled by the 2002 Champion Stakes winner since his arrival in the States, but it did not harm his reputation as the most proficient middle-distance grass horse over there. He seemed to have forfeited that when disappointing at the Breeders' Cup, but came back with a bruised heel as an excuse. He promptly returned to England to begin a stud career at Nunnery at a fee of £10,000. *TM*

Sulamani (Ire)

4yo bay colt **128**

Hernando (Fr) - Soul Dream (USA) (Alleged (USA))
Owner Godolphin
Trainer Saeed Bin Suroor
Breeder Niarchos Family

Career: **12** starts | won **7** | second **2** | third **0** | £2,293,916 win and place

By Nicholas Godfrey

LUDICROUS though it may seem to suggest it of a horse who claimed three top-level victories and finished second in one of the most prestigious races of the season, the overriding impression of Sulamani's season must be one of anticlimax. Close, but no cigar, as the saying goes. And when a horse is rumoured to have cost an eight-figure sum, connections have every right to hope for the cigar.

To be fair, Sulamani did his bit for Godolphin, who acquired him at the end of his three-year-old campaign from the Niarchos family, for whom he had won the Prix du Jockey-Club and finished an unlucky-looking runner-up in the Arc when trained in France by Pascal Bary. Indeed, he earned a prominent place in the Dubai team's short history when ending an excruciating wait for their 100th Group or Grade 1 win with the most bizarre of victories in the Arlington Million in August, when the antics of the errant Storming Home meant that the Godolphin colt, only fourth best on merit, claimed a lucrative first prize.

In doing so, he provided one of the few highpoints in a torrid year for Sheikh Mohammed's hand-picked team. Since its inception in 1994, Godolphin has established itself as the most international stable in the world, with bases on three continents. Their 100 Group/Grade 1 successes have featured races in 12 different countries: America, Britain, Canada, Dubai, France, Germany, Hong Kong, Ireland, Italy, Germany, Japan and Singapore.

Yet despite near-unalloyed success in its formative years, the wheel has turned in the last couple of seasons. David Loder's juvenile academy at Evry was abandoned after disappointing results; now the concept of a private trainer of two-year-olds in Europe has been curtailed altogether. Eoin Harty's West Coast base in America has produced a Breeders' Cup winner (Imperial Gesture in 2002), but 2003 proved a major disappointment when Godolphin did not have a runner in the Kentucky

**Sulamani (David Flores, left) takes the Arlington Million
as Storming Home unships Gary Stevens and is demoted**

Derby, the race Sheikh Mohammed covets above all others.

The 2003 campaign was undeniably one of Godolphin's least successful, in spite of a typically rousing start on home territory at Nad Al Sheba, where Moon Ballad routed his field in the Dubai World Cup and Sulamani landed the mile-and-a-half Sheema Classic in great style.

If only the season had ended in March: just seven more top-level successes had followed by the end of the British turf season. No mean tally in itself, but the figures papered over the cracks, since none of these wins came in any of the truly great races that represent Godolphin's *raison d'etre* and Mezzo Soprano's Prix Vermeille was the only one from a Classic crop that misfired once more.

A notable feature of Godolphin's history has been an uncanny knack of finding an absolute top-notcher among the older horses, like Swain, Daylami, Dubai Millennium, Sakhee and Fantastic Light. Sulamani was plainly expected to be next in line.

Unraced at two, he had thrived at three in 2002, when his style of racing was defined by a withering turn of foot. Regardless of the size of the outlay, it looked money well spent when the son of Hernando produced his customary finishing burst to mow down Ange Gabriel in the Dubai Sheema Classic on his first outing for his new owners.

Hometown advantage or not, Sulamani dispelled rumours that his

2003 {Race record}

5th John Deere Breeders' Cup Turf (Grade 1) (Santa Anita, October 25) 3yo+ 12f Firm **118** 9 ran. *Disputing 6th, bumped on turn leaving home straight, pushed along 2 1/2f out, 7th straight, one pace from over 1f out, beaten 6½l by Johar and High Chaparral*

1st Turf Classic Invitational Stakes (Grade 1) (Belmont Park, September 27) 3yo+ 12f Firm **122** 7 ran. *Held up last, switched out when clipped heels and stumbled over 2f out, soon recovered, strong run on outside to lead just inside final furlong, soon clear, easily, beat Deeliteful Irving by 2¾l*

1st Arlington Million XXI (Grade 1) (Arlington, August 16) 3yo+ 10f Good **120** 13 ran. *Held up towards rear, 10th straight, strong run on outside to take 2nd behind Storming Home on line, awarded race*

2nd King George VI And Queen Elizabeth Diamond Stakes (Group 1) (Ascot, July 26) 3yo+ 12f Good **128** (TS 103) 12 ran. *Settled towards rear, progress over 2f out, driven to chase winner over 1f out, edged right and no impression final furlong, beaten 3½l by Alamshar*

4th Grand Prix de Saint-Cloud (Group 1) (Saint-Cloud, June 29) 3yo+ 12f Good **113** (TS 98) 10 ran. *Held up disputing 5th, 7th straight on outside, ridden 2f out, never able to challenge, finished 5th, placed 4th, beaten 4l by Ange Gabriel*

1st Dubai Sheema Classic (Group 1) (Nad Al Sheba, March 29) 4yo+ 12f Good **126** (TS 122) 16 ran. *Held up towards rear, good headway on outside from over 2f out, ridden well over 1f out, led 100yds out, ran on well, beat Ange Gabriel by ¾l*

2002

2nd Prix de l'Arc de Triomphe - Lucien Barriere (Group 1) (Longchamp, October 6) 3yo+ 12f Good **126** (TS 113) 16 ran ● **1st** Prix Niel Casino Barriere-d'Enghien les Bains (Group 2) (Longchamp, September 15) 3yo 12f Good to firm **110** 3 ran ● **1st** Prix du Jockey-Club (Group 1) (Chantilly, June 2) 3yo 12f Good **124** (TS 105) 15 ran ● **1st** Prix de L'Avre (Chantilly, May 15) 3yo 12f Good to soft **107** (TS 75) 8 ran ● **1st** Prix Sanctus (Maisons-Laffitte, April 30) 3yo 12f Soft 7 ran ● **7th** Prix de Champerret (French-Bred Colts & Geldings) (Longchamp, April 7) 3yo 10f Good to firm (TS 62) 13 ran

change of stable had not been an immediate success with an impressive display in which he swept round the field from fully 12 lengths adrift turning for home, quickening on three separate occasions according to Frankie Dettori. It was a performance that suggested he would become a major player in all the key international races over a mile and a half: it was accorded a Racing Post Rating the equal of his Arc effort, his best to date.

As a result, when Leadership won the Gran Premio di Milano on June 22 to record Godolphin's 99th Group/Grade 1 win, those closest to him must have confidently been expecting Sulamani to complete the ton. What they may not have forecast is that it would take nearly two months.

Indeed, when Sulamani was sent off odds-on to do the job with a winning return to Europe in the Grand Prix de Saint-Cloud, a week after Leadership's Italian victory, his trainer suggested that it was "looking good for our 100th Group 1 winner".

It was an unusually bold statement and Saeed Bin Suroor will probably count to ten if ever he feels moved to repeat it in the future. Sulamani, looking in need of the outing, let the side down badly with a sluggish, laboured effort and could finish only fourth to old rival Ange Gabriel. Although there were plausible excuses – ever-changing legs suggested he was feeling the fast ground and he looked distinctly uncomfortable in trying to sprint off an ordinary gallop – it was not exactly the display connections wanted.

Furthermore, it cannot have done much to bolster confidence ahead of his next assignment, the King George VI and Queen Elizabeth Diamond Stakes, one of the showpiece races for which he had been purchased. In the event, despite Sulamani's producing what was arguably the best effort of his career in ratings terms, he was soundly beaten into second by Alamshar. Take the winner out and we would have been lauding an emphatic victor over a strong field, but, unfortunately for Godolphin, Alamshar was there – three and a half lengths in front at the line, having gained first run as Sulamani circled the field from way back.

Although Sulamani's change of gear appeared to be back, it was evident that he now seemed to need a little time to find top speed. When he did so at Ascot, Sulamani had little trouble putting daylight between himself and third-placed Kris Kin and, given the pre-race doubts and the 12lb he was giving the winner at weight-for-age terms, the performance augured well for the second half of the season.

Traditionalists would have been thinking strongly about another tilt at the Arc, but the remainder of Sulamani's campaign was geared instead towards the Breeders' Cup Turf. First stop, surprisingly, was Chicago, for the Arlington Million, a race in which European-based horses have thrived over the years and one in which, finally, Godolphin's frustrating wait for their 100th top-grade victory would be ended, albeit in extraordinary fashion after one of the season's most peculiar race finishes – and surely one of the most unaccountable for many a year.

Despite an interrupted preparation with a stone bruise and the ten-furlong trip's being short of his best, Sulamani was well fancied to win the Million, where his chief rival was the 2002 Champion Stakes winner, Storming Home, now rated the top US turf performer. A major worry, though, was Sulamani's hold-up style of racing, for Arlington's run-in is short even by US turf standards and follows a tight home bend.

Sulamani, settled in rear, had to go around the entire field after the home turn and lost still more ground when he drifted wide. Though he made inexorable progress in the straight, he would still have finished only fourth but for an aberration from Storming Home that brought to mind such notorious incidents as the Devon Loch debacle, Dayjur's jumped shadow and the 'stun gun' horse Ile de Chypre. Cruising to victory, Storming Home jinked violently right into Gary Stevens' whip 50 yards from the line, interfering with Kaieteur and Paolini in the process and allowing Sulamani to edge past the pair in the shadow of the post.

Stevens, who had performed miracles to stay on as long as he did, was dislodged after the line, where on the floor he was kicked by another runner. The stewards, correctly applying the Stateside version of the rules, had little option but to disqualify Storming Home. He may well have kept the race in Britain.

The beneficiary of all this was Sulamani. Godolphin may have got their hundred, but, as Paul Haigh noted in his Racing Post report, there was little doubt where the sympathies of the Chicago crowd lay. "It can hardly have felt like the triumph the Dubaians have been anticipating ever since Moon Ballad won the Dubai World Cup," wrote Haigh, "and it was received, extraordinarily and more than a little unfairly, not with admiring applause, but with something like outrage, and a sustained chorus of boos. If the truth is told, Sulamani, even though he ran magnificently over a distance clearly too short for him, will have to go down as one of the luckiest-ever winners of a major event."

There was no need for such good fortune next time out, when Sulamani trounced a weak-looking field in the $750,000 Turf Classic Invitational at Belmont in late September. The race looked the perfect prep for his ultimate target, the Breeders' Cup, as Godolphin's standard bearer made mincemeat of demonstrably inferior rivals. Having been all but on the floor when clipping heels at the top of the stretch, he cut through the field to run out the easy winner by two and three-quarter lengths from Deeliteful Irving. According to the Daily Racing Form, Sulamani had "more than lived up to the hype that surrounded him".

Although the form could not be rated particularly highly, the manner of the victory offered reason enough to consider that the wheels were back on the wagon ahead of the Breeders' Cup Turf, where it was not surprising to see Sulamani vying for favouritism alongside Falbrav and Storming Home. However, while the race produced one of the most exciting finishes in living memory, Sulamani was never a factor and finished fifth, well adrift of dead-heaters High Chaparral and Johar. It was an insipid effort, all the more disappointing considering how many of the European raiders covered themselves with glory at Santa Anita.

Sulamani had appeared to stumble during the race, but Frankie Dettori blamed instead the steady early fractions, which he said neutralised Sulamani's finishing kick. His remarks represented a tacit admission that, while his mount possesses undoubted class, he seems to need things to go his own way at the very highest level.

Stoutly bred – he is out of an Alleged mare – Sulamani needs all of a mile and a half, a strong gallop and preferably enough of a straight for his acceleration to come into play. He stays in training and ought to enjoy further top-grade success, but if another crack at the King George and the big US targets are on the agenda, it would be a major help if he could be persuaded to settle somewhat closer to the action.

Sulamani can look pretty special when it all comes together, like it did in Dubai, but he now has a little to prove. Still, three out of six ain't bad, and seven out of 12 overall, with more than $2m earned, is hardly

Sulamani
bay colt, 9-4-1999

Hernando b 1990	Niniski	Nijinsky	**Northern Dancer** Flaming Page
		Virginia Hills	**Tom Rolfe** Ridin' Easy
	Whakilyric	Miswaki	Mr Prospector Hopespringseternal
		Lyrism	Lyphard Pass A Glance
Soul Dream br 1990	Alleged	Hoist The Flag	**Tom Rolfe** Wavy Navy
		Princess Pout	Prince John Determined Lady
	Normia	Northfields	**Northern Dancer** Little Hut
		Mia Pola	Relko Polamia

Bred by the Niarchos Family in Ireland

Sire **Hernando**

Won 7 of 20 races, inc. Prix Lupin-Gr1, Prix du Jockey-Club-Gr1, Prix Niel-Gr2, Prix Gontaut-Biron-Gr3 (twice). Also 2nd in Irish Derby-Gr1, Prix de l'Arc de Triomphe-Gr1, Turf Classic-Gr1, 3rd and 4th in Japan Cup-Gr1. Strong, attractive, fluent mover, with an excellent turn of foot. Acted on any ground, equally effective at 10f and 12f. Tough, very genuine performer, competitive at the top level on three continents. Sire of: Holding Court (Prix du Jockey-Club-Gr1), Asian Heights (Gr3), Mr Combustible (Gr2), Sulamani (Prix du Jockey-Club-Gr1, Arlington Million-Gr1, Turf Classic Invitational S.-Gr1), Tau Ceti (Gr3), Hanami (Gr2), Just Wonder (Gr3).

Dam **Soul Dream**

Won 1 of 6 races. Leggy, plain, modest performer, stayed 12f. Dam of: Dream Well (1995 c by Sadler's Wells; dual Derby winner), Archipelago (1996 c by Caerleon; winner), Conundrum (1998 c by Caerleon; unraced), Sulamani (1999 c by Hernando; Classic winner), Awakened (2000 c by Sadler's Wells; unraced), Kyatikyo (2001 c by Machiavellian; unraced to date).

Pedigree assessment

The transfer fee for Sulamani when he joined Godolphin after his unlucky defeat in the 2002 Arc supposedly ran to eight figures, the largest sum ever given for an active racehorse to continue racing. If the money mattered to his purchaser, he could hardly yet be called a bargain, but he did add two Grade 1 wins to his CV – a lucky one in the Arlington Million and a soft one in a sub-standard Turf Classic at Belmont. His stud duties have been deferred for another year and he will be making further repayments, in various currencies, in 2004. *TM*

to be sniffed at. What's more, without him, Godolphin's cupboard would have looked pretty bare in 2003 and, whatever he achieves in the future, his role in landing that elusive 100th top-level victory probably made him seem like he was worth his weight in gold.

Which is probably not far off what they paid for him.

Super Celebre (Fr)

3yo bay colt   **121**

Peintre Celebre (USA) - Supergirl (USA) (Woodman (USA))

Owner Ecurie Wildenstein

Trainer E Lellouche

Breeder Jean-Pierre Dubois

Career: **5** starts | won **2** | second **2** | third **1** | **£231,174** win and place

By Robert Carter

IT WAS Super Celebre's misfortune to have to chase home Dalakhani in both the Prix Lupin and Prix du Jockey-Club. He was beaten by one length in the Lupin and by twice that margin at Chantilly, but he never gave up trying. He was then put away in typical French fashion for an autumn campaign. However, it was announced in early September that he had suffered a recurrence of a foot problem which had troubled him after the Lupin. That could have done him a favour, though. He could well have ended up in vain pursuit of Dalakhani in either the Prix Niel or the Arc, possibly both. At least he will not face that task when he returns in 2004.

Super Celebre had looked a useful prospect as a juvenile, running third of 15 to Sign Of The Wolf in a race for debutants at Saint-Cloud in September and winning the Prix Mieuxce by six lengths from On Your Way, at Maisons-Laffitte two months later. That nine-furlong contest was run on heavy ground, a fact which could prove important to his prospects in 2004.

The going was officially good or good to soft in each of his three races as a three-year-old but, in reality, it was on the fast side each time. All too often, the ground is watered to produce the desired effect when the going is tested in the morning, then dries up in the hours before racing. Elie Lellouche and his jockey, Dominique Boeuf, were both anxious to see Super Celebre perform on softer ground again but never had the chance.

The colt made his first appearance as a three-year-old in the Group 2 Prix Noailles, over 11 furlongs at Longchamp in early April. His juvenile form did not mean much, but Super Celebre had gone the right way over the winter and was a confidently supported 11-10 favourite. He started off third of the eight runners but kept losing places, though not his proximity to the leader, so that he was sixth into the straight. Boeuf

Super Celebre (Dominique Boeuf) lands the Group 2 Prix Noailles at Longchamp in April

launched his effort on the outside and Super Celebre quickened past his rivals to lead more than a furlong from home. He was soon pushed into a commanding lead and his jockey spent most of the final 100 yards patting him down the neck. He won by an easy two and a half lengths from Coroner, who grabbed second on the line from Jipapibaquigrafo, the Brazilian-owned colt who ran Dalakhani to half a length in the Prix Greffulhe 14 days later.

Dalakhani was the even-money favourite for the Lupin, with Super Celebre a 2-1 chance in a field of seven. Held up in sixth as far as the straight, while the favourite raced in third, Super Celebre took a little longer than his rival to pick up but ran on strongly on the outside from

2003   Race record

2nd Prix du Jockey-Club (Group 1) (Chantilly, June 1) 3yo 12f Good **121** (TS 99) 7 ran. *Raced in 5th, shaken up and closed up on leaders 2f out, driven over 1f out, kept on but not pace of winner, beaten 2l by Dalakhani*

2nd Prix Lupin (Group 1) (Longchamp, May 11) 3yo 10½f Good to soft **117** (TS 97) 7 ran. *Held up, 6th straight, shaken up and progress over 1½f out, ridden and quickened well over 1f out, kept on but unable to reach winner, beaten 1l by Dalakhani*

1st Prix Noailles (Group 2) (Longchamp, April 6) 3yo 11f Good to soft **115** (TS 90) 8 ran. *Held up in 5th, 6th straight, headway on outside to lead 1½f out, pushed clear, easily, beat Coroner by 2½l*

2002

1st Prix Mieuxce (Maisons-Laffitte, November 8) 2yo 9f Heavy (TS 64) 8 ran ● **3rd** Prix Prompt (Unraced Colts & Geldings) (Saint-Cloud, September 9) 2yo 1m Good 15 ran

one and a half furlongs out. He overtook the Aidan O'Brien-trained pair, Alberto Giacometti and Balestrini, but was making no impression on Dalakhani in the final half-furlong and Boeuf accepted defeat.

Dalakhani only needed to be pushed out to win, but Super Celebre's connections were nevertheless hopeful that the extra furlong and a half of the Prix du Jockey-Club would be in his favour. The two principals were drawn in adjoining stalls and Super Celebre received a slight brush from Dalakhani as they left the gates. Boeuf settled him in fifth, tracking the favourite, as far as the straight while first Diyapour and then Papineau – another promising colt who did not race after the Jockey-Club – took them along. When Christophe Soumillon switched Dalakhani to the outside with more than two furlongs to run and soon took over, Super Celebre tracked him but never had a chance of catching him. He closed the gap to around a length and a quarter, but then Dalakhani was ridden clear and Boeuf again did not give his mount a hard race in fruitless pursuit.

Super Celebre's sire, Peintre Celebre, who set a new course record when winning the 1997 Arc, remained in training as a four-year-old but suffered an injury two days before he was to make his reappearance in the Prix Ganay. His reputation was already made, but Super Celebre needs another season to prove himself. If the foot injury had ended his career, he would have retired the lightly raced winner of a weak Group 2. The fact that he was good enough to win many runnings of the Jockey-Club and arguably superior to the first two in the Derby, Kris Kin and The Great Gatsby, will be no help at all for his stud prospects unless he can get a big win on the board.

His lack of a Group 1 win will be an advantage in placing him to begin with in 2004 and, provided there is no recurrence of the foot problem, he will be a candidate for top honours in France. With Dalakhani retired to stud and Doyen switched to Godolphin, there would not be a better middle-distance four-year-old in the country. What's more, after just five runs we have probably yet to see the very best of him.

Super Celebre

bay colt, 16-2-2000

			Northern Dancer	Nearctic
				Natalma
		Nureyev		
			Special	Forli
				Thong
	Peintre Celebre			
	ch 1994		Alydar	Raise A Native
				Sweet Tooth
		Peinture Bleue		
			Petroleuse	Habitat
				Plencia
			Mr Prospector	Raise A Native
				Gold Digger
		Woodman		
			Playmate	Buckpasser
				Intriguing
	Supergirl			
	b 1994		Jim French	Graustark
				Dinner Partner
		Southern Seas		
			Schonbrunn	Pantheon
				Scheherezade

Bred by Jean-Pierre Dubois in France

Sire Peintre Celebre

Won 5 of 7 races, inc. Prix Greffulhe-Gr2, Prix du Jockey-Club-Gr1, Grand Prix de Paris-Gr1, Prix de l'Arc de Triomphe-Gr1. Quite well-made, medium-sized individual, tip-top performer at 10-12f, with exceptional acceleration. Sire of: Dai Jin (Deutsches Derby-Gr1, Aral Pokal-Gr1), Super Celebre (Gr2), Vallee Enchantee (Gr2), Pearl Of Love (Gran Criterium-Gr1).

Dam Supergirl

Unraced half-sister to top-class 8-10f performer Steinlen and to the dam of Irish Derby winner Zagreb. Dam of: Superman (1999 g by Bigstone; winner), Super Celebre (2000 c by Peintre Celebre; Gr2 winner, Gr1-placed), Super Lina (2001 f by Linamix; unraced to date).

Pedigree assessment

Super Celebre made a pleasing start to his second campaign with a smooth victory in the Prix Noailles that automatically established him as a legitimate Classic candidate. He underlined the point in the Lupin with another improved performance, quickening impressively to deliver a strong challenge that failed by only a length against Dalakhani. Many felt that he held a realistic chance of reversing the form in the Prix du Jockey-Club. He did improve again at Chantilly, but so – and to a greater degree – did his nemesis. It was then planned to rest him before an autumn campaign, but his holiday was extended by injury and he did not reappear. There will be no Dalakhani to contend with in 2004 and, if he comes back 100 per cent, he will surely prove a force in the top middle-distance events. *TM*

The Great Gatsby (Ire)

3yo bay colt **121**

Sadler's Wells (USA) - Ionian Sea (Slip Anchor)
Owner Mrs John Magnier
Trainer A P O'Brien
Breeder Orpendale

Career: **8** starts | won **1** | second **3** | third **0** | £385,578 win and place

By Richard Austen

"O'BRIEN on the brink of immortality," said the Racing Post's front page on Derby Day. No trainer had sent out three consecutive winners of the Blue Riband, but O'Brien had his chance. Indeed, he had four chances. Brian Boru was the shortest-priced of the quartet at 9-2 third favourite, followed by Alberto Giacometti, a drifting 12-1 chance, The Great Gatsby at 20-1 and Balestrini at 66-1, but the race brought a major revision in the pecking order: the Irish warrior king was vanquished by the sculptor of 'thin man' bronzes, who was himself seen off by an Italian author, and they all lost out to the classic American novel. The Great Gatsby led nearly all the way up the straight. But he was not quite good enough to give his trainer that place in history.

Speaking after the race, and unfortunately not before it, The Great Gatsby's jockey, Pat Eddery, reported: "Aidan said he was getting better – early in the year he was working with Alberto Giacometti and was getting beaten three lengths, but now he is beating him three. That was very encouraging."

In the race, The Great Gatsby's superiority over Alberto Giacometti grew to more than 14 lengths, but the margin that mattered most was the length by which he lost out to Kris Kin. Eddery did not risk any hard-luck stories on his final Derby attempt and had The Great Gatsby in the first two throughout: when they finally had the measure of Dutch Gold three furlongs out, the only other runner in close proximity was Balestrini; two furlongs out, The Great Gatsby was clear by two lengths, but entering the last half-furlong Kris Kin, Alamshar and Norse Dancer had all begun to close and The Great Gatsby could hold off only two of them.

'Mr Nobody from Nowhere': that was the description contemptuously applied to Jay Gatsby by his rival Tom Buchanan in F Scott Fitzgerald's

The Great Gatsby was an excellent second in the Derby, but that was as good as it got

1925 novel. It's stretching things a bit to describe an Aidan O'Brien-trained three-year-old as having come from nowhere, but when the latest season commenced and contenders from Ballydoyle took prominent places, as usual, in ante-post lists for the Classics, The Great Gatsby was among the 'others on request'. The O'Brien colts and their respective merits were the subject of as many whispers and rumours as Jay Gatsby, but The Great Gatsby didn't feature in any of them.

After landing the odds in his maiden, at the second attempt, The Great Gatsby had run in three Group races as a two-year-old and shown progressive form without threatening to win one. In the process, he was beaten by three stable companions – once each by Powerscourt and Alberto Giacometti and twice by Brian Boru. In a racecourse gallop in April, Brian Boru finished in front of him again and when they made their reappearances proper in the Derrinstown Stud Derby Trial, Brian Boru

2003 _____ Race record

5th Budweiser Irish Derby (Group 1) (Curragh, June 29) 3yo 12f Good **113** (TS 93) 9 ran. *Moderate 4th, 5th after halfway, ridden approaching straight, one pace, beaten 9½l by Alamshar*

2nd Vodafone Derby (Group 1) (Epsom, June 7) 3yo 12f Good **121** (TS 103) 20 ran. *Made most, definite advantage over 2f out, ridden 2l clear over 1f out, headed final 100yds, just held on for 2nd, beaten 1l by Kris Kin*

2nd Derrinstown Stud Derby Trial Stakes (Group 2) (Leopardstown, May 11) 3yo 10f Good to yielding **109** (TS 101) 6 ran. *Soon led, ridden and strongly pressed straight, headed under 1f out, rallied under pressure, just failed, beaten hd by Alamshar*

2002 _____

4th Criterium de Saint-Cloud (Group 1) (Saint-Cloud, November 9) 2yo 10f Heavy **99** 10 ran ● **4th** Racing Post Trophy (Group 1) (Doncaster, October 26) 2yo 1m Soft **102** (TS 38) 9 ran ● **6th** Juddmonte Beresford Stakes (Group 3) (Curragh, October 13) 2yo 1m Good to yielding **98** 10 ran ● **1st** Dawn Hi And Lo EBF Maiden (Galway, August 3) 2yo 8½f Good to yielding **78** 13 ran ● **2nd** Pride Of Tipperary EBF Maiden (Tipperary, July 21) 2yo 7f Good **80** 16 ran

was 11-4 and The Great Gatsby 9-1 in a six-runner race. It was The Great Gatsby who ran odds-on Alamshar to a head, putting up a bold show from the front, with Brian Boru (giving them 5lb) in third. The post-race coverage centred on Alamshar and Brian Boru.

Fitzgerald's Gatsby came close but could not realise his dream. His time in the sun was brief. For O'Brien's version, his time in the spotlight was almost up once the Derby had been run. In the Irish Derby three weeks later, 6-1 third favourite and heading an O'Brien squad of six, The Great Gatsby was beaten nine and a half lengths into fifth. Trying to come from the rear, he was beaten early in the straight. "He seemed to be fine beforehand but he had a hard race at Epsom," reflected his trainer. The Great Gatsby was not seen again and a report in late September revealed that he was about to be sold to 'overseas interests'.

When Aidan O'Brien set about rationalising his mass entry for the 2003 Derby and whittled the numbers down from seven to five and from five to four, the clue was there that he did not have an outstanding candidate. Held back by sickness as two-year-olds and usually in need of their first runs at three, the latest crop at Ballydoyle took some sorting and it is even easier to see why from an end-of-season perspective. Brian Boru and Powerscourt ended top of the pile but the occasional best efforts of The Great Gatsby, Roosevelt, Alberto Giacometti, Hold That Tiger, Catcher In The Rye and Mingun weren't far behind. None was a Galileo or High Chaparral.

The Great Gatsby is by Sadler's Wells out of a half-sister to notable Sadler's Wells colts in Oscar, runner-up in the 1997 Prix du Jockey-Club, and Blue Stag, runner-up in the 1990 Derby. "His parents were shiftless and unsuccessful farm people," is how the origins of Fitzgerald's Gatsby were described, but there was never much chance of humble origins for any colt carrying the colours of Sue Magnier.

The Great Gatsby

bay colt, 26-2-2000

Sadler's Wells b 1981	Northern Dancer	Nearctic	Nearco
			Lady Angela
		Natalma	Native Dancer
			Almahmoud
	Fairy Bridge	Bold Reason	Hail To Reason
			Lalun
		Special	Forli
			Thong
Ionian Sea b 1989	Slip Anchor	Shirley Heights	Mill Reef
			Hardiemma
		Sayonara	Birkhahn
			Suleika
	Snow Day	Reliance	Tantieme
			Relance
		Vindaria	Roi Dagobert
			Heavenly Body

Bred by Orpendale in Ireland

Sire **Sadler's Wells**

Won 6 of 11 races, inc. Beresford S.-Gr3, Irish Derby Trial-Gr2, Irish 2,000 Guineas-Gr1, Eclipse S.-Gr1, Phoenix Champion S.-Gr1. Also 2nd in Prix du Jockey-Club-Gr1, King George VI & Queen Elizabeth S.-Gr1. Impeccably bred top-class performer from 8-12f, handsome, tough and consistent. Sire of Gr1 winners: Braashee, French Glory, In The Wings, Old Vic, Prince Of Dance, Scenic, Salsabil, Opera House, Saddlers' Hall, El Prado, Johann Quatz, Masad, Barathea, Fatherland, Fort Wood, Intrepidity, Carnegie, King's Theatre, Northern Spur, Moonshell, Muncie, Poliglote, Chief Contender, Dance Design, Luna Wells, Cloudings, Ebadiyla, Entrepreneur, In Command, Kayf Tara, Dream Well, Greek Dance, King Of Kings, Leggera, Commander Collins, Daliapour, Montjeu, Saffron Walden, Aristotle, Beat Hollow, Subtle Power, Galileo, Imagine, Milan, Perfect Soul, Sequoyah, Ballingarry, Black Sam Bellamy, Gossamer, High Chaparral, Islington, Quarter Moon, Sholokhov, Alberto Giacometti, Brian Boru, Refuse To Bend, Yesterday.

Dam **Ionian Sea**

Won twice at 3 in France, including Prix Robert de Cholet-Listed. Effective over 12f. Half-sister to Derby 2nd Blue Stag and Prix du Jockey-Club 2nd Oscar (both by Sadler's Wells) out of a smart 12f filly. Dam of: Ithaca (1994 c by Groom Dancer; winner, Gr3-placed), Ionospere (1995 c by Green Desert; winner), Najano (1996 g by Selkirk; winner), Marigold (1998 f by Marju; winner), The Great Gatsby (2000 c by Sadler's Wells; winner, Classic-placed), Magritte (2001 c by Sadler's Wells; winner, Gr1-placed).

Pedigree assessment

Bred to stay at least 12f, and, on pedigree, is an obvious candidate to step up to long-distance races. His very close relative Oscar has been covering in Coolmore's NH division. *JH*

The Tatling (Ire)

6yo bay or brown gelding   **119**

Perugino (USA) - Aunty Eileen (Ahonoora)

Owner Dab Hand Racing

Trainer J M Bradley

Breeder Patrick J Power

Career: **46** starts | won **7** | second **10** | third **6** | **£263,012** win and place

By Richard Austen

COMPARING Group-class horses and his own not so long ago, Milton Bradley made them sound like different breeds. He had trained some spectacularly durable and prolific winners, but his string wasn't known for its quality. "Class horses are so different to ours," he said in 2001. "If I couldn't train some of them with a sheepdog and a bag of nuts, I'd give up." It would have been the end of a long and increasingly distinguished career. Bradley always had the utmost confidence that he could train a high-class horse, however, and now he knows it for certain, thanks to the 2003 exploits of The Tatling.

Royal Boxer, fourth in the 1980 Champion Hurdle at 300-1, and multiple scorers Mighty Marine, Grey Dolphin and Yangtse-Kiang were notable Bradley-trained horses in the days when he was predominantly a jumps trainer. During the 1980s he had 11 winners on the Flat.

Reinventing himself, though, as a trainer chiefly of sprint handicappers, his Flat totals rocketed to 33 for 1999, 47 in 2000 and 62 in 2001. Suddenly, Bradley was one of the most upwardly mobile trainers around. At the age of 66. Two years on, his career reached another level again.

Reflecting on those views about training high-class horses, Bradley's opinion has not altered radically: "It seemed so far away at that stage, something we only dreamt of, but if you can get them they're no harder to train than the run-of-the-mill handicapper – actually, they're easier. I'd like to have anybody's top-class horses and I'd like them to have a go with mine. I know who'd commit suicide first."

Bradley got his chance with The Tatling when he claimed him for £15,000 at Catterick in July 2002. That was The Tatling's only win in eight starts and roughly a year with Dandy Nicholls. Before that, The Tatling was trained by Michael Bell, with whom he lost his way after winning twice and being runner-up in the Cornwallis Stakes at two. He carries some "nuts and bolts" following a knee operation after his final start in 2001.

**The Tatling (Darryll Holland, farside) gets up to land the
Group 3 King George Stakes at Goodwood in July**

Bradley himself underwent a hip replacement in the summer of 2003,
hot on the heels of the resurgent Clive Brittain as a fine advert for the
operation. Bradley's second visit to a racecourse afterwards was to Glorious
Goodwood for the King George Stakes, in which The Tatling was his first
runner in a Group race. He started 11-4 favourite, the 12 months since
his Catterick claimer having yielded handicap wins at Sandown and York
in 2002, a close second in the Ayr Gold Cup, third in the 2003 Wokingham
at Royal Ascot and a Listed triumph at Sandown. The Tatling had travelled
easily thus far over five or six furlongs and it was the same story in the
Group 3 at Goodwood where, once the gaps came, he was also able to
quicken readily and score by a neck. "He's in the Nunthorpe and that's
the obvious race to go for," said his ecstatic trainer, "but it's more than
I could dream of."

The 9-1 joint-third favourite at York, Group 1 success proved beyond
The Tatling but it was the best performance over five furlongs in recent
years that beat him; racing in fourth, he went past Dominica and
Acclamation readily enough but the trail-blazing champion Oasis Dream
was well beyond recall and beat him by two and a half lengths. Six furlongs
on rain-softened ground in the Sprint Cup at Haydock proved too much,
but The Tatling remained consistent through the autumn when the

2003   Race record

4th Bentinck Stakes (Group 3) (Newmarket, October 17) 3yo+ 6f Good to firm **119** (TS 74) 14 ran. *Held up in touch, ridden and every chance inside final furlong, unable to quicken near finish, beaten 1l by Ashdown Express*

3rd Prix de l'Abbaye de Longchamp - Majestic Barriere (Group 1) (Longchamp, October 5) 2yo+ 5f Holding **117** (TS 107) 19 ran. *Mid-division, headway 2f out, kept on to take 3rd last strides, beaten 1¼l by Patavellian*

5th Millennium & Copthorne Hotels Diadem Stakes (Group 2) (Ascot, September 27) 3yo+ 6f Good to firm **112** (TS 95) 14 ran. *Towards rear, effort and not clear run well over 1f out, switched left, nearest finish, beaten 2l by Acclamation*

5th Dubai International Airport World Trophy (Group 3) (Newbury, September 20) 3yo+ 5f Good to firm **111** (TS 100) 9 ran. *Tracked leaders in centre of course, ridden and effort over 1f out, kept on same pace inside final furlong, beaten 2l by Ratio*

6th Stanley Leisure Sprint Cup (Group 1) (Haydock, September 6) 3yo+ 6f Good to soft **106** (TS 86) 10 ran. *In touch, ridden over 1f out, soon outpaced, beaten 5¾l by Somnus*

2nd Victor Chandler Nunthorpe Stakes (Group 1) (York, August 21) 2yo+ 5f Good to firm **119** (TS 108) 8 ran. *Tracked leaders, stayed on to go 2nd 1f out, no chance with winner, beaten 2½l by Oasis Dream*

1st King George Stakes (Group 3) (Goodwood, July 31) 3yo+ 5f Good **114** (TS 97) 9 ran. *Held up in last, smooth progress 2f out, closing when not clear run entering final furlong and switched right, ran on well to lead last 50yds, beat Dragon Flyer by nk*

3rd David Wilson Homes Stakes (Registered As The Hackwood Stakes) (Listed) (Newbury, July 19) 3yo+ 6f Good to firm **117** (TS 91) 14 ran. *Steadied start, held up in rear, steady headway from over 1f out, ran on well final furlong, not reach leaders, beaten 1½l by Somnus*

1st Porcelanosa Sprint Stakes (Listed) (Sandown, July 5) 3yo+ 5f Good **116** (TS 106) 13 ran. *Raced against farside rail and soon in midfield, progress over 1f out, effort to lead last 100yds, held on near finish, beat Bali Royal by hd*

6th Northern Rock Gosforth Park Cup (Rated Stakes) (0-105 handicap) (Newcastle, June 27) 3yo+ 5f Good to firm **98** (TS 78) 10 ran. *Missed break, headway on outside 2f out, no impression inside final furlong, beaten 5½l by Mornin Reserves*

3rd Wokingham Stakes (0-110 handicap) (Ascot, June 21) 3yo+ 6f Firm **114** (TS 102) 29 ran. *Slowly into stride, soon tracked nearside leaders, ridden to challenge and upsides 1f out, stayed on same pace final furlong, beaten 1½l by Fayr Jag*

4th Gala Casinos Handicap (0-105) (Windsor, May 31) 3yo+ 5f Good to firm **110** (TS 102) 18 ran. *Dwelt, held up towards rear, progress over 1f out, ridden to press leaders inside final furlong, kept on but always held, beaten 1¼l by Dubaian Gift*

2nd Langleys Solicitors Rated Stakes (0-105 handicap) (York, May 15) 4yo+ 6f Good to firm **110** (TS 101) 8 ran. *Held up, headway over 2f out, every chance over 1f out, switched right inside final furlong, not quicken, beaten ¾l by Border Subject*

2nd (disq from 1st) Curtis Medical Rated Stakes (0-110 handicap) (Newmarket, May 4) 4yo+ 6f Good to firm **113** (TS 105) 16 ran. *Started slowly, held up, switched right and headway over 1f out, edged left and led well inside final furlong, just held on, finished 1st, placed 2nd behind Capricho*

2nd Quail Conditions Stakes (Kempton, April 21) 3yo+ 6f Good to firm **103** (TS 66) 8 ran. *Held up stands' side, headway to join leader over 1f out, not quicken final furlong, beaten 1½l by Danger Over*

2002 wins

1st Coral Eurobet Sprint Trophy (0-105 handicap) (York, October 12) 3yo+ 6f Good to firm **107** (TS 90) 19 ran ● **1st** Sunshine Coach Rated Stakes (0-100 handicap) (Sandown, August 31) 3yo+ 5f Good to firm **96** (TS 81) 15 ran ● **1st** Leyburn Claiming Stakes (Catterick, July 24) 3yo+ 5f Good to firm **90** (TS 68) 16 ran

The Tatling

bay or brown gelding, 23-4-1997

Perugino br 1991	Danzig	Northern Dancer	Nearctic Natalma
		Pas de Nom	Admiral's Voyage Petitioner
	Fairy Bridge	Bold Reason	Hail To Reason Lalun
		Special	Forli Thong
Aunty Eileen b 1983	Ahonoora	Lorenzaccio	Klairon Phoenissa
		Helen Nichols	Martial Quaker Girl
	Safe Haven	Blakeney	Hethersett Windmill Girl
		Amazer	Mincio Alzara

Bred by Patrick Power in Ireland. Ir54,000gns Tattersalls (Ireland) September yearling, 11,000gns Tattersalls July 4yo

Sire **Perugino**

Won sole race, over 6f at 2. Superbly bred, by outstanding speed influence out of dam of Sadler's Wells, Tate Gallery and Fairy King. Formerly stood at Coolmore, exported to Germany. Oldest progeny 7. Sire of: Banyumanik (Gr3), Gino's Spirits (Gr3), The Tatling (Gr3), Next Gina (Preis der Diana-Gr1).

Dam **Aunty Eileen**

Unraced half-sister to high-class sprinter Lugana Beach out of half-sister to Mtoto. Dam of: unnamed (1988 c by Soughaan), Ambitious Venture (1989 c by Gorytus; winner), Moving Image (1990 f by Nordico; winner), Just Do It Joey (1991 f by Glenstal; winner), Astuti (1993 f by Waajib; winner), Daintree (1994 f by Tirol; winner), Amazing Dream (1996 f by Thatching; Listed winner, Gr3-placed), The Tatling (1997 g by Perugino; Gr3 winner, Gr1-placed), unnamed (1998 c by Dolphin Street), Moritat (2000 c by Night Shift; placed), 2002 c by Fasliyev.

Pedigree assessment

The Tatling comes from a fairly speedy family, despite the presence of Mtoto and Mutamam in it, and has inherited the pace that his 'uncle' Lugana Beach had. Perugino, by speed influence Danzig, has helped too. *JH*

highlight was his close third, from a wide draw on holding ground, in the Prix de l'Abbaye.

As for the trainer, the trip to Longchamp was Bradley's first abroad, a weekend away during which he saw the sights in an open-topped bus and returned with some hair-raising tales of driving the horsebox in Paris. There was no visit to the Moulin Rouge: "The owners went there, I think, but I didn't want to get my mind warped so I didn't go."

Three Valleys (USA)

2yo chestnut colt   **117**

Diesis - Skiable (Ire) (Niniski (USA))

Owner K Abdullah

Trainer R Charlton

Breeder Juddmonte Farms Inc

| Career: **5** starts | won **3** | second **1** | third **1** | **£219,716** win and place |

By James Willoughby

IN 1724, the King of Denmark summoned Christian Heinrich Heinecken to Copenhagen. Heinecken had a vast knowledge of the Bible, history and geography, and spoke Latin and French to an impressive degree. After falling ill, the German genius successfully predicted his own death the following year – at the tender age of five.

Not every precocious talent burns itself out so dramatically. Three Valleys, for instance, managed to sustain his early brilliance long enough to finish first past the post in the Middle Park Stakes at Newmarket in October. Whether he will be the same force when the 2,000 Guineas comes round in May 2004 is another matter.

His young life has not been without its setbacks. He was a beaten favourite in two Group 1 races and, after testing positive for the banned substance clenbuterol, is likely to be disqualified from the Middle Park, providing the second sample confirms the finding.

Notwithstanding his Middle Park run and concluding second place in the Dewhurst Stakes, Three Valleys put up easily his most impressive performance in the Coventry Stakes at Royal Ascot in June. Its merit was affirmed by the clock.

Three Valleys went off at 7-1 for the Coventry, in spite of both an effortless debut success at Nottingham and reports of his superlative workouts. He was an odds-on chance by the time the field reached halfway.

The early pace in the Royal Ascot opener was very strong. Not that you could tell by watching Three Valleys. A smooth and light-actioned mover, he was skipping along merrily just behind the pace, seemingly oblivious to the torrid early fractions. Taking it up before two out, he stretched eight lengths clear.

It is true that Racing Post Ratings have Three Valleys improving slightly later in the season, but that is mainly because the level of two-year-old ratings rise throughout the campaign. The clock is not so circumspect,

Three Valleys (Richard Hughes) takes the Group 1 Middle Park Stakes at Newmarket in October

however, and every leading time expert awarded Three Valleys an extremely high figure for his juvenile track-record display.

Running so hard on fast ground raised concerns that Three Valleys would recoil from his exertions at Royal Ascot. After all, he had edged markedly right in the closing stages when at full extent. It was a malaise of the lungs, rather than the legs, that led to his subsequent disappointment.

Three Valleys was supposedly in fine condition before the Phoenix Stakes at The Curragh in August. His clash with One Cool Cat was billed as a showdown between potential two-year-old champions. Three Valleys ran a lifeless race in third, however, and was found to have mucus in his lungs, so it was not a meaningful comparison of their respective merits.

Roger Charlton, the trainer of Three Valleys, duly confined his star colt to quarters in order to facilitate recovery in time for the major two-year-old races of the autumn. The infection was reportedly a little slow-moving, however, and some measure of expediency was required of Charlton in order to get Three Valleys ready for the Middle Park Stakes.

Perhaps the haste of his preparation manifested itself in a rather tepid finishing effort by Three Valleys, an impression confirmed both by the colt's jockey, Richard Hughes, and sectional times. It was the only minor

2nd Darley Dewhurst Stakes (Group 1) (Newmarket, October 18) 2yo 7f Good to firm **117** (TS 89) 12 ran. *Held up, headway over 2f out, led over 1f out, ridden and headed inside final furlong, ran on, beaten hd by Milk It Mick*

1st Shadwell Stud Middle Park Stakes (Group 1) (Newmarket, October 3) 2yo 6f Good to firm **117** (TS 87) 12 ran. *Chased leaders, led 2f out, edged left inside final furlong, ridden out, beat Balmont by ³/₄l*

3rd Independent Waterford Wedgwood Phoenix Stakes (Group 1) (Curragh, August 10) 2yo 6f Good **103** (TS 76) 7 ran. *Close up in 3rd, 2nd after halfway, led 1¹/₂f out, headed and no extra under 1f out, beaten 4l by One Cool Cat*

1st Coventry Stakes (Group 3) (Ascot, June 17) 2yo 6f Good to firm **115** (TS 90) 13 ran. *Tracked leaders, led going well 2f out, shaken up and edged right approaching final furlong, pushed clear inside final furlong, impressive, beat Botanical by 8l*

1st EBF Novice Stakes (Nottingham, May 16) 2yo 6f Good to soft **83** (TS 51) 6 ran. *Dwelt, soon tracking leaders going well, shaken up over 1f out, led last 150yds, smoothly, beat Grand Rich King by 2¹/₂l*

blemish on a strong performance, however, during which Three Valleys travelled conspicuously smoothly and accelerated sharply on demand to beat Balmont by three-quarters of a length.

More than a month elapsed before news emerged of Three Valleys' positive test for clenbuterol. Charlton said that the drug had been administered as a treatment for an ongoing mucus problem, but that dosage had ceased well before the six and a half days stipulated under Jockey Club rules as necessary to clear the colt's system before the Middle Park.

Just days before, a positive test was also announced on Amanda Perrett's Tillerman, runner-up in the Queen Anne Stakes at Royal Ascot, the presence of clenbuterol in his post-race sample again being responsible. Like Charlton, Perrett said she had adhered strictly to the guidelines for the timing of the drug's use.

Three Valleys scoped clear of his persistent lung problems before the Dewhurst Stakes, in which he was trying seven furlongs for the first time. The step up in trip ought to have been of little concern for the colt on pedigree, but his free-going style raised significant doubts.

Once again, Three Valleys hacked along for most of the way, looking sure to win running down into the Dip. He was surprisingly outkicked by Milk It Mick, however, the winner coming from further behind in a race run at only a fair pace to halfway. Using the winner as a reference, Three Valleys appeared to rally. It has to be noted, however, that several others closed down on him themselves. It is still possible that Three Valleys is a sprinter.

It is the clock that provides the most interesting gauge of Three Valleys' development, or lack of it to be more precise. Disregarding weight-for-age provision, the Racing Post's Topspeed time figures had Three Valleys failing to improve a pound between the Coventry and the Dewhurst. While ratings derived from race times can never define merit without evidence

Three Valleys

chestnut colt, 19-2-2001

Diesis ch 1980	Sharpen Up	Atan	Native Dancer / Mixed Marriage
		Rocchetta	Rockefella / Chambiges
	Doubly Sure	Reliance	Tantieme / Relance
		Soft Angels	Crepello / Sweet Angel
Skiable ch 1990	Niniski	Nijinsky	Northern Dancer / Flaming Page
		Virginia Hills	Tom Rolfe / Ridin' Easy
	Kerali	High Line	High Hat / Time Call
		Sookera	Roberto / Irule

Bred by Juddmonte Farms in US

Sire Diesis

Won 3 of 6 starts, inc. Middle Park S.-Gr1, Dewhurst S.-Gr1. Lengthy, light-framed. Brother to Kris. Stands at Mill Ridge Farm, Kentucky, 2003 fee $30,000. Oldest progeny 18. Sire of Gr1 winners: Diminuendo (Oaks S., Irish Oaks, Yorkshire Oaks), Elmaamul (Eclipse S., Phoenix Champion S.), Keen Hunter (Prix de l'Abbaye), Rootentootenwooten (Demoiselle S.), Knifebox (Premio Roma), Husband (Canadian International S.), Halling (Eclipse S., twice, York International, twice, Prix d'Ispahan), Storm Trooper (Hollywood Turf H.), Ramruma (Oaks S., Irish Oaks, Yorkshire Oaks), Love Divine (Oaks S.), Three Valleys (Middle Park S.).

Dam Skiable

Won 3 of her 4 races in France, later won over 1m and stakes placed over 9f on turf in US. Very closely related to Listed-winning Kahyasi fillies Arrive (over 15f) and Hasili (as a 2yo; dam of Banks Hill, Dansili, Heat Haze, Intercontinental). Dam of: Grail (1997 f by Quest For Fame; winner), Back Pass (1998 f by Quest For Fame; winner), Lahberhorn (1999 c by Affirmed; winner), Ski Jump (2000 c by El Prado; winner), Three Valleys (2001 c by Diesis; Gr1 winner), 2003 f by Miswaki.

Pedigree assessment

Three Valleys has shown more speed and precocity than his pedigree suggests he should have. None of his four siblings won at two and they struck at upwards of a mile. His dam also progressed with age and relished a mile, as did Hasili's quartet of top-class offspring. All this suggests Three Valleys should have no trouble with the Guineas trip and has every chance of training on. *JH*

of even pace, an underlying truth is suggested by this measure – Three Valleys' contemporaries were catching up with him.

However, it is important to recognise the fact that he was a cracking good two-year-old. His Coventry Stakes victory will remain untarnished in the memory, whatever happens next term.

Tillerman
7yo bay horse **121**

In The Wings - Autumn Tint (USA) (Roberto (USA))
Owner K Abdullah
Trainer Mrs A J Perrett
Breeder Juddmonte Farms

Career: **26** starts | won **7** | second **2** | third **5** | **£402,328** win and place

By David Dew

AMANDA PERRETT has been steadily raising her game for a few seasons now. The stable did well in terms of prize-money again in 2003 and the decision to keep Tillerman in training following his Group 2 win in the Celebration Mile at Goodwood helped owner Khalid Abdullah take his first Flat owners' title from Hamdan Al Maktoum.

Connections used a Leicester conditions race as a springboard to greater things in 2002 and the Midlands venue was also the starting point for Tillerman's latest campaign. He has often gone well after a break, and after being held up off the pace and produced late he squeezed between Gateman and Twilight Blues to just get the best of a tight finish to the Group 3 Tom Fruit Leicestershire Stakes, in which the first four home were covered by less than a length.

After a disappointing last of six behind Hawk Wing in the Lockinge Stakes at Newbury in May, he was sent to his beloved Ascot for a crack at the Queen Anne Stakes, a race boasting Group 1 status for the first time, and one in which Tillerman had finished an unlucky runner-up to No Excuse Needed in 2002. The pre-race hype concentrated on Hawk Wing, the impressive Lockinge winner, but the wheels came off the Aidan O'Brien bandwagon that day as Dubai Destination finally fulfilled his early promise with a smooth success. Tillerman, held up as ever, ran on well in the closing stages and took the runner-up spot for the second year running. It was an effort that was up there with his best, but months later it was revealed that he had tested positive for a banned substance that had been administered under veterinary advice to relieve a breathing problem. Disqualification appeared inevitable.

There is no doubt that Tillerman reserves his best efforts for Ascot and he returned there for a crack at the Group 3 Michael Page International Silver Trophy in July. Facing far inferior opposition to the Queen Anne, he was entitled to win and did so, coming with a trademark late run

Tillerman (Richard Hughes) wins the Group 3 Michael Page International Silver Trophy at Ascot in July

from last to first and getting the better of Beauchamp Pilot. It was a particularly sweet success for Richard Hughes, who days earlier had worn the same colours successfully on Oasis Dream in the July Cup and who opted to ride Tillerman instead of travelling to York for the winning ride on Far Lane in the John Smith's Cup.

Tillerman did not win again, but after a poor run behind Nayyir in the Group 2 Lennox Stakes at Goodwood, where he finished a "distressed" last of 13, he did manage to bounce back once again. Although the Celebration Mile market was dominated by the progressive three-year-old Arakan, to many it was a rematch between Tillerman and Where Or When, first and fourth 12 months previously, when the latter's trainer, Terry Mills, was incensed by the tactics Hughes employed on the winner. However, while Tillerman again just got the better of his old rival in third, they were eclipsed in another tactical race, which was dominated throughout by Priors Lodge and Passing Glance.

Back at Ascot again for the Queen Elizabeth II Stakes, Tillerman was beaten only by Falbrav and Russian Rhythm, running to a significantly higher level than he had when third 12 months previously.

If there was anything new to be learned about Tillerman in 2003 it was that nowadays he ideally needs further than seven furlongs. He has always been best on fast ground and when held up off the pace in a strongly run race – the faster the leaders go the better – and he can

2003 Race record

9th Victor Chandler Challenge Stakes (Group 2) (Newmarket, October 18) 3yo+ 7f Good to firm **105** (TS 82) 11 ran. *Held up, pulled hard, not clear run over 1f out, never troubled leaders, beaten 5l by Just James*

3rd Queen Elizabeth II Stakes (Sponsored By NetJets) (Group 1) (Ascot, September 27) 3yo+ 1m Good to firm **121** (TS 110) 8 ran. *Held up in rear, steady headway on rails from 2f out, ran on well final furlong but no impression on leaders, beaten 3¼l by Falbrav*

3rd Celebration Mile (Group 2) (Goodwood, August 23) 3yo+ 1m Good to firm **113** (TS 82) 6 ran. *Steadied start, took keen hold and held up in last, progress to chase leading pair 2f out, pulled out to challenge over 1f out, soon one pace, beaten 2¼l by Priors Lodge*

13th Lennox Stakes (Group 2) (Goodwood, July 29) 3yo+ 7f Good **42** (TS 11) 13 ran. *Dwelt, held up in rear, progress on inner when slightly hampered over 2f out, weakened and eased over 1f out, tailed off, beaten 29l by Nayyir*

1st Michael Page International Silver Trophy Stakes (Group 3) (Ascot, July 12) 4yo+ 1m Good to firm **121** (TS 98) 5 ran. *Restrained start and held up in last, progress 2f out, shaken up to lead last 150yds, in command after, beat Beauchamp Pilot by ¾l*

2nd Queen Anne Stakes (Group 1) (Ascot, June 17) 4yo+ 1m Good to firm **118** (TS 94) 10 ran. *Held up in last pair, smooth progress over 2f out, ridden to dispute 2nd over 1f out, hanging right but kept on well, no chance with winner, beaten 4l by Dubai Destination*

6th Juddmonte Lockinge Stakes (Group 1) (Newbury, May 17) 4yo+ 1m Good **84** (TS 55) 6 ran. *Held up in rear and no cover, shaken up over 3f out, no response, beaten 24l by Hawk Wing*

1st Tom Fruit Leicestershire Stakes (Group 3) (Leicester, April 26) 4yo+ 7f Good to firm **116** (TS 83) 6 ran. *Held up, headway and not much room over 1f out and inside final furlong, ran on to lead post, beat Gateman by shd*

2002

10th Hong Kong Mile (Group 1) (Sha Tin, December 15) 3yo+ 1m Good to firm **108** 12 ran ● **3rd** Queen Elizabeth II Stakes (Sponsored by NetJets) (Group 1) (Ascot, September 28) 3yo+ 1m Good to firm **112** (TS 81) 5 ran ● **1st** Celebration Mile (Group 2) (Goodwood, August 24) 3yo+ 1m Good to firm **115** (TS 93) 7 ran ● **15th** Tote International Stakes (Handicap) (Ascot, July 27) 3yo+ 7f Good to firm **95** (TS 73) 28 ran ● **6th** Antec International Criterion Stakes (Group 3) (Newmarket (July), June 29) 3yo+ 7f Good to firm **105** (TS 54) 6 ran ● **2nd** Queen Anne Stakes (Group 2) (Ascot, June 18) 3yo+ 1m Good **121** (TS 105) 12 ran ● **1st** Golden Jubilee Conditions Stakes (Leicester, June 4) 3yo+ 7f Good to firm **110** (TS 67) 10 ran

Other notable runs

2001 **3rd** Tote International Stakes (Handicap) (Ascot, July 28) 3yo+ 7f Good to firm **120** (TS 104) 28 ran ● **4th** Cork And Orrery Stakes (Group 2) (Ascot, June 21) 3yo+ 6f Good to firm **113** (TS 101) 21 ran **2000** **1st** Tote International Stakes (Handicap) (Ascot, July 29) 3yo+ 7f Good to firm **121** (TS 101) 24 ran **1999** **1st** EBF Further Flight Classified '90' Stakes (Newmarket (July), October 1) 3yo+ (0-90) 1m Good to soft **109** (TS 85) 8 ran ● **1st** Boddingtons Median Auction Maiden Stakes (Lingfield, August 24) 3yo 9f Good to firm **90** (TS 81) 7 ran

still produce a telling burst of speed when he has his conditions.

The likelihood of him gaining an elusive first Group 1 win becomes slimmer by the year, but he has done remarkably well for a late-starter who began his career beating nonentities in a nine-furlong maiden auction at Lingfield, and he will always be a favourite with Perrett and Hughes.

Tillerman

bay horse, 03-3-1996

			Nearctic
		Northern Dancer	Natalma
	Sadler's Wells		
		Fairy Bridge	Bold Reason
In The Wings			Special
b 1986			
		Shirley Heights	Mill Reef
			Hardiemma
	High Hawk		
		Sunbittern	Sea Hawk
			Pantoufle
			Turn-to
		Hail To Reason	Nothirdchance
	Roberto		
		Bramalea	Nashua
			Rarelea
Autumn Tint			
b 1985			Ribot
		Graustark	Flower Bowl
	Autumn Glory		
		Golden Trail	Hasty Road
			Sunny Vale

Bred by Juddmonte Farms in Britain

Sire In The Wings

Won 7 of 11 races, inc. Prix du Prince d'Orange-Gr3, Coronation Cup-Gr1, Grand Prix de Saint-Cloud-Gr1, Prix Foy-Gr3, Breeders' Cup Turf-Gr1. Also 2nd in Prix Ganay-Gr1, 4th in Prix de l'Arc de Triomphe-Gr1, 5th in King George VI & Queen Elizabeth S.-Gr1. Small, quite sturdily-built individual. Off the course for 13 months from August as 2yo because of a chipped knee. Best suited by 12f with some give in the ground. Sire of: Irish Wings (Gr3), Singspiel (Canadian International S.-Gr1, Japan Cup-Gr1, Dubai World Cup, Coronation Cup-Gr1, York International S.-Gr1), Winged Love (Irish Derby-Gr1), Annaba (Gr2), Apprehension (Gr3), Just In Fun (Gr3), Right Wing (Gr3), Boreas (Gr3), Central Park (Derby Italiano-Gr1), Premio Presidente della Repubblica-Gr1), Cloud Castle (Gr3), Thief Of Hearts (Gr3), Tillerman (Gr2), Air Marshall (Gr2), Davide Umbro (Gr2), Earlene (Gr2), Kutub (Bayerisches Zuchtrennen-Gr1, Preis von Europa-Gr1, Gran Premio del Jockey Club-Gr1), Saldenschwinge (Gr3), Zanzibar (Oaks d'Italia-Gr1), Act One (Criterium International-Gr1, Prix Lupin-Gr1), Mamool (Grosser Preis von Baden-Gr1, Preis von Europa-Gr1), Mellow Park (Gr3), Savannah Bay (Gr3), Trumbaka (Gr3), Abunawwas (Gr3), Fidelite (Prix Saint-Alary-Gr1), New South Wales (Gr3), Soldier Hollow (Gr3), Weightless (Gr2).

Dam Autumn Tint

Won once over 12f at 3 in France. Half-sister to French Group winners Glorify (12f) and Doree (5.5f at 2), and bred along very similar lines to top-class 8-10f filly Ryafan. Dam of: Minatina (1990 f by Ela-Mana-Mou; winner), From The Left (1991 c by Ela-Mana-Mou; unplaced), Autumn Wings (1992 f by In The Wings; placed), Kentucky Fall (1993 f by Lead On Time; winner), Welsh Autumn (1995 f by Tenby; Listed winner, Gr3-placed), Tillerman (1996 c by In The Wings; Gr2 winner, Gr1-placed). Sold 20,000gns 1996 Tattersalls December Sales, sent to Japan.

Pedigree assessment

Has long defied his pedigree by proving effective from 6f to 1m. A colt by In The Wings out of a middle-distance winner from the excellent US middle-distance family of Brian's Time, Dynaformer, Monarchos and Sunshine Forever would be expected to stay at least 10f, probably further. Having said that, family members can show a fair amount of pace when by speedier stallions. Tillerman almost certainly will get progeny who stay better than he does if given a well-deserved chance at stud. *JH*

Trade Fair

3yo bay colt **126**

Zafonic (USA) - Danefair (Danehill (USA))
Owner K Abdullah
Trainer R Charlton
Breeder Juddmonte Farms

Career: **8** starts | won **4** | second **0** | third **2** | **£106,866** win and place

By James Willoughby

THE jury is out on Trade Fair. Under consideration is a serious charge: that a colt as talented as any seen in 2003 did not always put it all in. Chief witness for the defence was Mr Roger Charlton of Beckhampton. Trade Fair's trainer sounded convincing when blaming the one-mile trip and softish ground for his colt's tame surrender in the Sussex Stakes at Goodwood in July. It was harder to believe his excuse for Trade Fair's flop in the Challenge Stakes at Newmarket in October, however.

The jury were shown a video of the Criterion Stakes at Newmarket in June, like the Challenge run over seven furlongs and on similar ground. On that occasion, Trade Fair was allowed most of his own way and crushed Just James by four lengths in a fast time. It was pointed out that the same Just James outbattled Trade Fair in the Challenge.

The counsel for the prosecution presented a lengthy deposition on the subject of the Challenge, the central plank of which was that Trade Fair was a long way below form, with no obvious excuse. He was not compromised by lack of room – unlike several of his rivals – and should have had the comfortable beating of Just James on Criterion Stakes form. Moreover, after being perfectly placed behind the leader on the stands rail, his effort petered out tamely.

Charlton contended that the Challenge was the conclusive evidence that Trade Fair is a sprinter. This could well prove correct, but the prosecution pointed to a couple of conflicting statements.

Before the Challenge, Charlton commented: "Trade Fair has improved mentally with every race and has become very relaxed now. He was almost idle in his last race at Newbury." After the race, however, the trainer appeared to execute a swift about-turn and said: "He probably wants to go faster and I imagine he'll have a sprinting campaign next year."

When these statements were read out in juxtaposition, the judge looked

Trade Fair (Richard Hughes) lands the Group 3 Criterion Stakes at Newmarket in June

over his half-moon spectacles and appeared unimpressed. He allowed the prosecution to proceed down another line of inquiry, emanating from an incident which occurred during Trade Fair's preparation for the 2,000 Guineas in the spring.

In what was expected to be a routine work session at Beckhampton, Trade Fair disappointed badly. On his return to the yard, it was found that the colt had broken blood vessels, just like his sire Zafonic had done in the 1993 Sussex Stakes, an ailment which forced the retirement of the brilliant 2,000 Guineas winner.

A veterinary expert called to the stand to expound on the subject of bleeding in racehorses was quick to point out that scientific research has found no congenital link between incidences of the condition referred to as Exercise Induced Pulmonary Haemmorhage (EIPH). It was acknowledged that this assertion seems to fly in the face of empirical evidence on the matter, but scientific fact is scientific fact.

While listening carefully to this diversion – and even looking decidedly interested at one point – the judge ruled it inadmissable that a causal link existed between Trade Fair's bleeding in the spring and his tame

5th Victor Chandler Challenge Stakes (Group 2) (Newmarket, October 18) 3yo+ 7f Good to firm **114** (TS 90) 11 ran. *Tracked leader, led over 2f out, headed and unable to quicken inside final furlong, beaten 1¾l by Just James*

1st Dubai Duty Free Cup (Listed) (Newbury, September 19) 3yo+ 7f Good to firm **124** (TS 83) 5 ran. *Made all, pushed along over 1f out, quickened clear final furlong, comfortably, beat Lago D'Orta by 3l*

6th Sussex Stakes (Group 1) (Goodwood, July 30) 3yo+ 1m Good to soft **104** (TS 67) 9 ran. *Held up in midfield, steady progress to join leaders 2f out, every chance 1f out, weakened rapidly, beaten 7l by Reel Buddy*

1st Betfair Criterion Stakes (Group 3) (Newmarket (July), June 28) 3yo+ 7f Good to firm **126** (TS 90) 11 ran. *Tracked leaders, led over 1f out, ridden clear, beat Just James by 4l*

1st Cheveley Park Stud King Charles II Stakes (Listed) (Newmarket, May 31) 3yo 7f Good to firm **115** (TS 69) 5 ran. *Made all, quickened over 2f out, comfortably, beat Membership by 2½l*

2002

3rd Darley Dewhurst Stakes (Group 1) (Newmarket, October 19) 2yo 7f Good **112** (TS 79) 16 ran ● **1st** Dubai Duty Free Golf World Cup Maiden Stakes (Newbury, September 21) 2yo 7f Good to firm **97** (TS 59) 12 ran ● **3rd** EBF Girton Maiden Stakes (Newmarket (July), August 23) 2yo 7f Good to firm **94** (TS 41) 16 ran

submission in the Challenge Stakes. After all, he pointed out, there was no veterinary evidence from Newmarket to support what amounts only to a hypothesis on the part of the prosecution. At this point, a number of experienced spectators in the public gallery began to whisper conspiratorially, one or two even getting up and leaving as if convinced they had heard enough.

Another interesting incident transpired later in the case. After the jury had reviewed videos of Trade Fair's other impressive performances during 2003, his win on his belated seasonal reappearance in the King Charles II Stakes at Newmarket in May and his success in a five-runner Listed race at Newbury in September, the judge had to caution the counsel for the prosecution on account of his pointed use of the adjective "bloodless" to describe the manner of Trade Fair's success in the latter event.

After this slur, the defence counsel asked the jury to balance the charge of dishonesty levelled against Trade Fair with his reputable family heritage. His mother, Danefair, was a high-class runner over middle distances in France while Prove and Erudite, two other relatives of Trade Fair, were upstanding racehorses proven in the very best Group-race circles.

This line of defence appeared to be a mistake. The prosecution countered that breeding of this stout nature suggested that Trade Fair should have no problems lasting out a mile and that it was another reason why his weak finishes at Goodwood and Newmarket were hard to forgive.

In what is expected to be a long-running case on Trade Fair's resolution, there are plenty more twists to come. Anyone interested in following the case should turn up at the relevant racecourses next season.

Trade Fair

bay colt, 12-1-2000

Zafonic b 1990	Gone West	Mr Prospector	Raise A Native Gold Digger
		Secrettame	Secretariat Tamerett
	Zaizafon	The Minstrel	**Northern Dancer** Fleur
		Mofida	Right Tack Wold Lass
Danefair b 1992	Danehill	Danzig	**Northern Dancer** Pas de Nom
		Razyana	His Majesty Spring Adieu
	Roupala	Vaguely Noble	Vienna Noble Lassie
		Cairn Rouge	Pitcairn Little Hills

Bred by Juddmonte Farms in England

Sire Zafonic

Won 5 of 7 races, inc. Prix Morny-Gr1, Prix de la Salamandre-Gr1, Dewhurst S.-Gr1, 2,000 Guineas-Gr1. Big, powerfully built, commanding individual, splendid mover. Bled when well beaten in Sussex S.-Gr1, final start. Sire of: Xaar (Prix de la Salamandre-Gr1, Dewhurst S.-Gr1), Alrassaam (Gr2), Kareymah (Gr3), Shenck (Gr2), Pacino (Gr2), Clearing (Gr3), Count Dubois (Gran Criterium-Gr1), Endless Summer (Gr2), Ozone Layer (Gr3), Dupont (Gr2), Ibn Al Haitham (Gr3), Maybe Forever (Gr3), Zee Zee Top (Prix de l'Opera-Gr1), Zipping (Gr2), Aynthia (Gr3), Trade Fair (Gr3), Zafeen (St James's Palace S.-Gr1).

Dam Danefair

Ran only at 3 years, won all 4 races, inc. Prix Minerve-Gr3. Smart 10-12f performer who cracked a pastern in her Gr3 win and had to be retired. Dam of: Zafair (1998 f by Zafonic; unplaced), Fieldfare (1999 f by Selkirk; placed 4th), Trade Fair (2000 c by Zafonic; Gr3 winner), Well Known (2001 f by Sadler's Wells; placed 2nd only outing to date).

Pedigree assessment

One of the few disappointing aspects to a generally triumphant season for Juddmonte Farms was the failure of Trade Fair to claim a Group 1 victory. A creditable third in the Dewhurst last year, he had to miss the Guineas because of a broken blood-vessel, but came back for impressive victories at Listed and Group 3 level at Newmarket, hinting that his breakthrough at the top was imminent. He had his chance at Goodwood, but the ground turned against him, and when his season ended with a dull effort in the Challenge Stakes, it seemed that perhaps his talents had been exaggerated. Transfer to the States, and help from Lasix, would seem an obvious option for him. If he stays at home, he may remain a dubious proposition in top company. *TM*

Vespone (Ire)

| 3yo chestnut colt | **123** |

Llandaff (USA) - Vanishing Prairie (USA) (Alysheba (USA))
Owner Godolphin
Trainer Saeed Bin Suroor
Breeder Gestut Sohrenhof

Career: **7** starts | won **4** | second **2** | third **0** | £277,158 win and place

By Tony Smurthwaite

RONALDO, Zidane and Figo all suffered the same trauma and came through it, and so Vespone must claw back his reputation after a high-value transfer was followed by an utterly dismal home debut.

His mid-season switch from Nicolas Clément in France to Saeed Bin Suroor in England raised all sorts of expectations for one whose previous two runs had yielded back-to-back wins in Group 1 races, the only currency that matters to his purchasers, Godolphin. Much like the Real Madrid galacticos, Vespone was a 'made man' when Sheikh Mohammed came calling, convincing front-running victories in the Prix Jean Prat and Grand Prix de Paris alerting the bloodstock world to a talent of considerable proportions.

What followed was rather more taxing to assess. Off the course for four months, he variously sparkled or failed to fire on Newmarket Heath depending on the source, and when finally asked to go about his public duties wandered home stone last of 12 behind Rakti in the Champion Stakes at Newmarket under a very nonplussed Frankie Dettori.

News management being what it is at Godolphin, the precise welfare of Vespone during his settling-in period might never be fully known, but his extended rest period coincided with a bleak summer for the stable. Despite reaching the landmark of 100 Group and Grade 1 wins worldwide in less than 10 years when Sulamani was awarded the Arlington Million, there were abject efforts leading to retirement for three of Godolphin's biggest stars; Moon Ballad, Grandera and Dubai Destination. Added to that there was barely a three-year-old worthy of the blue silks, 25-1 shot Graikos being their the only representative in the Derby.

On the back of such relative insipidness, Vespone has the mantle there awaiting his coronation, albeit with one key caveat. After his run at Newmarket, Godolphin racing manager Simon Crisford suggested a drop

Vespone (Christophe Lemaire) makes all the running to take the Grand Prix de Paris at Longchamp in June

in trip to a mile would be among Vespone's revised criteria, thereby ruling him out of the ten-furlong contests that increasingly seem to provide the benchmark for immortality.

Vespone's win in the Grand Prix de Paris, following a smooth win over the same distance in the Prix la Force, offered top-class form at ten furlongs, the trip required to win major pots such as the Dubai World Cup, Prince of Wales's Stakes, Coral-Eclipse, Juddmonte International and the Champion Stakes at Leopardstown and Newmarket respectively, not to mention the Breeders' Cup Classic and Hong Kong Cup.

Moreover, that Longchamp victory must have gone a long way to convincing Sheikh Mohammed to buy. Vespone was a warm order, the 17-10 favourite, and mimicked the uncomplicated tactics that proved successful in the Jean Prat, making all. The strategy proved so suited to Vespone and his rider Christophe Lemaire that the winner posted a time almost three seconds faster than the standard – equivalent to 15 lengths.

Though the opposition may not have compared to other Group 1 races run in France during the season, the performance of the winner was extremely eye-catching. Lemaire asked for acceleration with three furlongs to run and Vespone found it, galloping home a length and a half clear.

Magistretti, who ran on for second place under Christophe Soumillon, had won the Feilden Stakes and the Dante Stakes, then run ninth in the Derby at Epsom when making the most of a problematic position

2003   Race record

12th Emirates Airline Champion Stakes (Group 1) (Newmarket, October 18) 3yo+ 10f Good to firm **79** (TS 48) 12 ran. *Raced wide, with leaders, joined main group over 5f out, weakened 2f out, beaten 26l by Rakti*

1st Juddmonte Grand Prix de Paris (Group 1) (Longchamp, June 22) 3yo 10f Good to soft **123** (TS 100) 11 ran. *Made all, ran on well, beat Magistretti by 1½l*

1st Prix Jean Prat (Group 1) (Chantilly, June 1) 3yo 9f Good **119** (TS 100) 8 ran. *Made all, ridden out, ran on strongly, beat Prince Kirk by 3l*

1st Prix la Force (Group 3) (Saint-Cloud, May 5) 3yo 10f Soft **111** (TS 82) 5 ran. *Tracking leader when hampered after 3f, then began pulling, 3rd straight, led over 1½f out, driven clear, ran on well, beat Vadalix by 2l*

2nd Prix Djebel (Listed) (Maisons-Laffitte, April 7) 3yo 7f Good **102** (TS 75) 7 ran. *In touch on inside, outpaced approaching final furlong, rallied and finished well to take 2nd closing stages, beaten 1½l by Mister Charm*

1st Prix Flambeau (Saint-Cloud, March 20) 3yo 1m Good 8 ran. *Chased leaders, quickened to lead inside final furlong, driven out, beat Vocaliste by 2l*

2002

2nd Prix Antivari (Maisons-Laffitte, November 25) 2yo 7f Heavy 10 ran

towards the rear in the early stages. He went on to finish runner-up to Falbrav in the Juddmonte International while the third horse home, Look Honey, came out a month later and won the Prix Eugene Adam, a Group 2 race over ten furlongs. In fourth was Lateen Sails, running for Godolphin.

It was three weeks earlier that Vespone had first fired the imagination, in the Jean Prat. This was the first major event in which he had been asked to make all and he appeared to relish the role. On good going he ground down his rivals from the front, without doubt an eye-catching way to triumph, and ran on strongly to score by three lengths from Prince Kirk, who could not reproduce similar form again during the season.

Nonetheless, Vespone had clocked the first of two fast times that summer, shaving nearly two seconds off the standard over Chantilly's nine furlongs. Lemaire celebrated his first Group 1 win, a happy outcome after he had taken Vespone to the front on realising the dearth of pace. Afterwards, Clément said he had ordered Lemaire to follow similar instructions as "we knew already that the colt stayed". It was a pity that the performance came on the same card as Dalakhani's tour de force in the Prix du Jockey-Club, all the more so for a colt whose sire, Llandaff, stood for a stud fee of £80 in Switzerland and is now based in Poland.

It was also a pity that he was not seen in public more often. A chestnut colt not overblessed with size, he offered the compact silhouette of a sprinter rather than the angular frame of a stayer. Perhaps, looking at him, a mile may well be his forte at the highest level in 2004. In the opera La Serva Pardona the character of Vespone is a mute servant who successfully masquerades as a lofty governor in order to please his employer. Sheikh Mohammed would be happy with that.

Vespone

chestnut colt, 14-2-2000

Llandaff ch 1990	Lyphard	**Northern Dancer**	Nearctic Natalma
		Goofed	Court Martial Barra
	Dahlia	Vaguely Noble	Vienna Noble Lassie
		Charming Alibi	Honeys Alibi Adorada
Vanishing Prairie ch 1990	Alysheba	Alydar	Raise A Native Sweet Tooth
		Bel Sheba	Lt Stevens Belthazar
	Venise	Nureyev	**Northern Dancer** Special
		Virunga	Sodium Vale

Bred by Gestut Sohrenhof in Ireland. Ff450,000 Deauville August yearling

Sire **Llandaff**

Won 5 of 16 races, inc. Jersey Derby-Gr2, Lexington S.-Gr3. Smart grass-course performer up to 10f at 3 years, brother to Gr1 winner Dahar and half-brother to 3 other Gr1 winners. Stood in Switzerland, now based in Poland. Sire of: Vespone (Prix Jean Prat-Gr1, Grand Prix de Paris-Gr1).

Dam **Vanishing Prairie**

Ran only at 3 years, winning 2 of 5 races. Quite modest middle-distance performer, but from top-class family. Dam of: Verzasca (1995 f by Sadler's Wells; Listed-placed winner), La Sylphide (1996 f by Barathea; Gr3 winner), Vanishing Dancer (1997 g by Llandaff; winner), Verdi (1998 c by Llandaff; Listed-placed winner), World Trust (1999 c by Acatenango; unraced), Vespone (2000 c by Llandaff; dual Gr1 winner).

Pedigree assessment

Vespone's parents lacked nothing in the pedigree department, but it was nevertheless surprising that they should combine in the production of a dual Group 1 winner in France. Llandaff had shown some respectable form in the States at three, but attracted no interest from major studs and was obliged to take his chance in Switzerland; he did not even last there and was moved on to Poland within months of his consequential mating with Vanishing Prairie, a cast-off from the Wildenstein broodmare band. Vespone's rise to prominence alerted the predatory instincts of Godolphin, but he could hardly have made a less auspicious debut in his new colours when last in the Champion Stakes. That may indicate physical problems and his best form may now be history. *TM*

Vinnie Roe (Ire)

5yo brown horse   **122**

Definite Article - Kayu (Tap On Wood)
Owner Seamus Sheridan
Trainer D K Weld
Breeder Mrs Virginia Moeran

Career: **20** starts | won **11** | second **1** | third **2** | **£708,875** win and place

By Alan Sweetman

NO IRISH trainer possesses a greater sense of history than Dermot Weld, whose mould-breaking sorties to the corners of the globe have played a major part in enhancing Ireland's stature in the world of international racing. Weld sets great store by the accumulation of records and the attainment of milestones, and one can be reasonably sure that the occasion which gave him most satisfaction during 2003 was Vinnie Roe's third successive victory in the Irish St Leger.

During the 1990s Weld broke fresh ground when the remarkable Vintage Crop became the first to win the race twice since it was opened to older horses in 1983. That feat was equalled by both Oscar Schindler and Kayf Tara, stimulating Weld's ambition to find a horse who might ultimately go one better. In the autumn of 2001, the trainer faced a dilemma when contemplating whether to send the three-year-old Vinnie Roe for the St Leger at Doncaster or walk him down the road for Ireland's equivalent.

It was already becoming apparent that Vinnie Roe was a tougher than average customer. Winner of two of his three juvenile starts, including a nine-furlong Listed race at Leopardstown, he resumed at three in smart company, finishing around four lengths behind Galileo in both the Ballysax Stakes and the Derrinstown Stud Derby Trial.

Stepped up to a mile and a half, he took fourth behind Morshdi in the Derby Italiano, three and a half lengths adrift of another who was to progress to greater things in the fullness of time, runner-up Falbrav. Then, after finishing seventh behind Galileo in the Budweiser Irish Derby, he won Listed races over a mile and six at Leopardstown and The Curragh to bring the St Leger options into focus.

Aware that no three-year-old colt had won the Irish St Leger since David O'Brien sent out Shergar's offspring Authaal 15 years earlier, Weld admitted that he deliberated long before committing Vinnie Roe to a clash with opposition that included three older challengers from Britain with

**Vinnie Roe (Pat Smullen) wins his third consecutive Irish
St Leger at The Curragh in September**

a wealth of experience between them - Millenary, Marienbard and Persian
Punch.

On the afternoon that the Aidan O'Brien-trained Milan routed his
contemporaries at Doncaster, Vinnie Roe upheld the honour of the Classic
generation in beating Millenary by two lengths. Weld now revealed that
the main reason for running Vinnie Roe at The Curragh was to see how
he would cope against older horses, with a view to a possible challenge
for the Melbourne Cup, an aspiration subsequently postponed in favour
of the Prix Royal-Oak at Longchamp, where he confirmed his reputation
with a convincing win.

After kicking off his four-year-old career with another Listed success
at Leopardstown, Vinnie Roe was deprived of a sixth successive victory
only by a neck when losing out to Royal Rebel in the Ascot Gold Cup,
run on ground that was perhaps a bit faster than ideal for him. After
that it was plain sailing at Leopardstown in a prep run before a second
Irish St Leger was garnered with a characteristically professional display.

This time, the Melbourne Cup had headed Vinnie Roe's agenda from

2003   Race record

4th Prix Royal-Oak (Group 1) (Longchamp, October 26) 3yo+ 1m7½f Holding **115** (TS 66) 14 ran. *Held up in mid-division, progress on outside approaching straight, disputing 3rd straight, pressing leaders 2f out, 2nd and ridden 1½f out, one pace close home, beaten 4½l by Westerner*

5th Prix de l'Arc de Triomphe Lucien Barriere (Group 1) (Longchamp, October 5) 3yo+ 12f Holding **120** (TS 107) 13 ran. *Prominent, 5th straight, 3rd briefly over 2f out, soon one pace, beaten 8¾l by Dalakhani*

1st Irish Field St Leger (Group 1) (Curragh, September 13) 3yo+ 1m6f Good to firm **122** (TS 38) 6 ran. *Tracked leaders in 3rd, improved into close 2nd over 2f out, led 1½f out, stayed on well under pressure final furlong, beat Gamut by 1l*

1st Ballyroan Stakes (Listed) (Leopardstown, August 17) 3yo+ 12f Good to firm **107** (TS 59) 6 ran. *Settled 3rd, 4th 5f out, 5th and ridden early straight, improved into 2nd under 1f out, stayed on well to lead near finish, beat Carpanetto by hd*

2002

4th Tooheys New Melbourne Cup (Handicap) (Group 1) (Flemington, November 5) 3yo+ 2m Good **125** 23 ran ● **1st** Jefferson Smurfit Memorial Irish St Leger (Group 1) (Curragh, September 14) 3yo+ 1m6f Good to firm **121** (TS 102) 8 ran ● **1st** Ballyroan Stakes (Listed) (Leopardstown, August 18) 3yo+ 12f Good **118** (TS 98) 8 ran ● **2nd** Gold Cup (Group 1) (Ascot, June 20) 4yo+ 2m4f Good to firm **116** (TS 19) 15 ran ● **1st** Saval Beg Stakes (Listed) (Leopardstown, May 30) 3yo+ 1m6f Soft **116** 7 ran

Other wins

2001 **1st** Prix Royal-Oak (Group 1) (Longchamp, October 28) 3yo+ 1m7½f Heavy **116** (TS 91) 13 ran ● **1st** Jefferson Smurfit Memorial Irish St Leger (Group 1) (Curragh, September 15) 3yo+ 1m6f Good to firm **124** (TS 97) 8 ran ● **1st** Ballycullen Stakes (Listed) (Curragh, August 25) 3yo+ 1m6f Good **113** (TS 43) 8 ran ● **1st** www.ppg.ie Challenge Stakes (Listed) (Leopardstown, July 21) 3yo+ 1m6f Good **107** 6 ran **2000** **1st** EBF Eyrefield Stakes (Listed) (Leopardstown, November 12) 2yo 9f Soft **106** 19 ran ● **1st** Goffs Median Auction Maiden (Leopardstown, June 28) 2yo 7f Good to firm **86** 9 ran

the outset of the season and he travelled to Australia in company with the five-year-old Media Puzzle, who earned his place in the line-up for the continent's showpiece by winning the Geelong Cup. After hitting the front around three furlongs out, Vinnie Roe was headed by his stablemate at the two-pole but maintained his effort so gamely that it was only inside the final 50 yards or so that he weakened into fourth as his trainer captured the coveted trophy for the second time.

Weld waited until August before giving Vinnie Roe his first outing of 2003, producing him in fine shape for a mile-and-a-half Listed race at Leopardstown, where he had to overcome the drawback of a slowish pace on his way to a gritty victory over race-fit three-year-old Carpanetto. Nor was the gallop particularly strong when he gained his third consecutive Irish St Leger the following month, quickening past the four-year-old Gamut after the pair had stolen a decisive march on Powerscourt, whose Great Voltigeur victory over Brian Boru provided a line of form that embraced the St Leger at Doncaster.

The prime objective of the season accomplished, connections had nothing

Vinnie Roe   *brown horse, 06-4-1998*

		Ahonoora	Lorenzaccio
			Helen Nichols
	Indian Ridge		
		Hillbrow	Swing Easy
Definite Article			Golden City
b 1992			
		Moorestyle	Manacle
			Guiding Star
	Summer Fashion		
		My Candy	Lorenzaccio
			Candy Gift
		Sallust	Pall Mall
			Bandarilla
	Tap On Wood		
		Cat O'Mountaine	Ragusa
Kayu			Marie Elizabeth
ch 1985			
		English Prince	Petingo
			English Miss
	Ladytown		
		Supreme Lady	Grey Sovereign
			Ulupis Sister

Bred by Virginia Moeran in Ireland.
Ir48,000gns Goffs November foal, Ir£50,000 Goffs Orby yearling

Sire Definite Article

Won 5 of 11 starts, inc. National S.-Gr1, Tattersalls Gold Cup-Gr2, also 2nd Irish Derby-Gr1. Effective 10-12f. Half-brother to Dante Stakes winner Salford Express, but stayed better than pedigree indicates. Stands at Morristown Lattin Stud, 2003 fee €8,000. Oldest progeny 5. Sire of: Vinnie Roe (Irish St Leger-Gr1, three times, Prix Royal-Oak-Gr1), Grammarian (Gr2), Supreme Rabbit (HK Gr2).

Dam Kayu

Unraced. By top-class miler who is also broodmare sire of Ridgewood Pearl (by Indian Ridge), out of half-sister to Irish St Leger winner M-Lolshan, from family of Fairy Queen, Right Wing and Tashawak. Dam of: Rich Victim (1992 c by Lapierre; stakes winner in Hong Kong), Vincitore (1993 g by Petorius; winner), Acquaiura (1994 f by Astronef; winner), Khartoum (1996 g by Common Grounds; winner), Divine Prospect (1997 f by Namaqualand; winner), Vinnie Roe (1998 c by Definite Article; multiple Gr1 winner), 2002 f by Definite Article. Mare died 2003.

Pedigree assessment

His grand-dam is a half-sister to an Irish St Leger winner, but Vinnie Roe still stays better than his pedigree indicates he should. The Indian Ridge-Tap On Wood cross has worked extremely well, and Vinnie Roe is one of the best – and the stoutest – of its examples. An admirable horse who will make a popular dual-purpose sire in time. *JH*

to lose by running Vinnie Roe in the Arc, in which he finished a perfectly respectable fifth to Dalakhani. The season ended on an unexpectedly tame note when he was only fourth behind Westerner in his quest for a second win in the Royal-Oak, but he remains a thoroughly creditable Group 1 performer, blessed with a formidable blend of speed and stamina.

Vintage Tipple (Ire)

3yo bay filly   **116**

Entrepreneur - Overruled (Ire) (Last Tycoon)
Owner Patrick J O'Donovan
Trainer P Mullins
Breeder Sir Edmund Loder

Career: **6** starts | won **3** | second **1** | third **0** | **£175,033** win and place

---

By Alan Sweetman

VINTAGE TIPPLE supplied one of the outstanding moments of the Irish season with an Irish Oaks victory that would be hard to beat for the outpouring of emotion it precipitated. True to form, the man at the centre of it all, octogenarian trainer Paddy Mullins, wore a slighly bemused look in the winner's enclosure, apparently wondering what all the fuss was about.

Mullins was in his early 20s when starting off with his father, training jumpers, mostly hunter chasers, at Goresbridge in County Kilkenny. Taking over the licence in 1954, he operated in low-key fashion until his career started to blossom in the 1960s. A succession of high-class jumpers brought him to the fore and his status as one of the greats of the Irish turf was secured when the mare Dawn Run completed a historic Champion Hurdle and Cheltenham Gold Cup double in 1986.

However, in the trainer's own mind, the finest moment of his career had taken place more than a decade earlier when the filly Hurry Harriet turned over the mighty Allez France in the 1973 Champion Stakes. He may be a jumping man to the core, but he has always relished the fact that he sent out Nor at 66-1 and Lucky Drake at 100-1 to obtain fourth places in successive runnings of the Irish Sweeps Derby, and he betrayed an uncharacteristic degree of pride in Hurry Harriet, whose victories also included the Pretty Polly, the Ballymoss Stakes (now the Tattersalls Gold Cup) and the International Stakes.

It was thus that many of the more seasoned observers of the Irish scene sat up and took notice when Mullins, usually given to understatement rather than hyperbole, was heard to invoke comparisons with Hurry Harriet after Vintage Tipple had made a winning debut in a maiden over a mile at the 2002 Tralee Festival. Just over two weeks later, he sent her for a winners' race over seven furlongs at The Curragh and an impressive four-length defeat of Coco Palm, winning with the minimum

Vintage Tipple (Frankie Dettori) strides out to Classic glory in the Irish Oaks at The Curragh in July

of fuss despite a slowish start, was sufficient to endorse a strong home reputation.

Mullins chose the Athasi Stakes at The Curragh in late April for Vintage Tipple's first three-year-old outing and she was sent off second favourite, paddock observers noting that she looked rather less forward than the favourite, Walayef.

The race bore out this belief, but Vintage Tipple stayed on well enough in second to suggest a realistic chance of reversing the form in their scheduled rematch in the Irish 1,000 Guineas. As it turned out, only Walayef made the return trip to The Curragh the following month, when she picked up an injury that brought a promising career to a premature end. Vintage Tipple had suffered a setback and Mullins now faced a race against time if she was to get the Classic opportunity that he believed her talents deserved in the Irish Oaks.

After a luckless defeat in the Oaks at Epsom, the Irish 1,000 Guineas winner Yesterday headed the market for an Irish equivalent that appeared notably strong, thanks to the presence of the Epsom winner Casual Look,

2003   Race record

6th Rathbarry Stud's Barathea Finale Stakes (Listed) (Curragh, October 12) 3yo+ 12f Good to yielding **101** 11 ran. *Chased leaders, moderate 5th and ridden entering straight, 3rd and no impression under pressure from under 3f out, beaten 14½l by L'Ancresse*

7th Ireland The Food Island Champion Stakes (Group 1) (Leopardstown, September 6) 3yo+ 10f Good to firm **64** 7 ran. *Chased leaders, 5th halfway, ridden and weakened 4f out, trailing straight, beaten 33l by High Chaparral*

1st Darley Irish Oaks (Group 1) (Curragh, July 13) 3yo 12f Good **116** (TS 99) 11 ran. *Chased leaders, moderate 5th approaching straight, 4th and stayed on strongly under pressure from 2f out to lead well inside final furlong, beat L'Ancresse by 1½l*

2nd EBF Athasi Stakes (Group 3) (Curragh, April 27) 3yo+ 7f Good **101** (TS 73) 8 ran. *Tracked leaders on stands' side, 4th and ridden 1½f out, 2nd and kept on final furlong, beaten 2l by Walayef*

2002

1st Loder EBF Fillies Race (Curragh, September 14) 2yo 7f Good to firm **98** (TS 77) 6 ran

● **1st** EBF Fillies Maiden (for the O'Brien Cup) (Tralee, August 27) 2yo 1m Good **88** 16 ran

---

as well as the winner and runner-up from the Ribblesdale, Spanish Sun and Ocean Silk.

Mullins booked Frankie Dettori for Vintage Tipple and seldom can a jockey/trainer pairing have presented such a contrast as that between the extrovert showmanship of the loquacious Italian and the innate modesty of the taciturn Irishman. Local wits speculated on how riding instructions might be delivered and received, and nobody was particularly surprised to learn afterwards that there had been none. But for all his habitual flamboyance, Dettori chose the occasion to deliver a simple but deadly effective ride, holding Vintage Tipple in a perfect position throughout before producing her late to collar Yesterday's pace-setting stablemate L'Ancresse, who was later to prove a better filly than she was given credit for at the time. Vintage Tipple beat L'Ancresse by a length, with Casual Look third and Yesterday fourth.

The remainder of the season was to prove anticlimactic. Vintage Tipple hardly managed to raise a gallop when finishing a remote last in the Irish Champion Stakes and became very warm in the preliminaries when unplaced behind L'Ancresse at The Curragh on her final outing. However, in a sense, those two races merely serve to illustrate the magnitude of her Classic triumph. After the Irish Oaks, Dettori had described her as "very hot", and the Mullins team, in which the trainer's son Tom has played an increasingly influential role in recent seasons, walked a potentially lethal tightrope in order to produce her at the very peak of her form, neither undercooked nor boiling over, on the day that really mattered.

That was the day when an 84-year-old maestro finally took on the mantle of Classic-winning trainer, adding another chapter to one of the great legends of Irish sport.

Vintage Tipple

bay filly, 17-1-2000

		Northern Dancer	Nearctic / Natalma
	Sadler's Wells		
		Fairy Bridge	Bold Reason / Special
Entrepreneur b 1994			
		Exclusive Native	Raise A Native / Exclusive
	Exclusive Order		
		Bonavista	Dead Ahead / Ribotina
		Try My Best	**Northern Dancer** / Sex Appeal
	Last Tycoon		
		Mill Princess	Mill Reef / Irish Lass
Overruled b 1993			
		Bustino	Busted / Ship Yard
	Overcall		
		Melodramatic	Tudor Melody / Irish Flight

Bred by Sir Edmund Loder in Ireland. €16,500 Goffs February 2yo

Sire Entrepreneur

Won 3 of 6 races, inc. 2,000 Guineas-Gr1. Also 4th in Derby-Gr1. Attractive sort who ran only on good or faster ground, best form at a mile. Sire of: Princely Venture (Gr2), Vintage Tipple (Irish Oaks-Gr1).

Dam Overruled

Won 2 of 6 races up to 10f, but seemed to stay 14f. Leggy individual who showed early promise but failed to progress. Dam of: Spettro (1998 c by Spectrum; winner, Gr1-placed), Leinster House (1999 g by Grand Lodge; unraced), Vintage Tipple (2000 f by Entrepreneur; Classic winner), Vintage Fizz (2001 c by Ashkalani; unplaced only start to date).

Pedigree assessment

Vintage Tipple enjoyed one moment in the sun, scoring a comfortable Irish Oaks victory that seemed to place her among the very best of her age and sex over middle distances. But no confirmation of that form was forthcoming, and after an ambitious bid – and desperately disappointing effort – against more seasoned Group 1 celebrities in the Irish Champion Stakes, she sank to another dull defeat in Listed company. Nevertheless, her Classic win stands as a tribute to her popular veteran trainer, and for her breeder, whose family has enjoyed almost a century of success with descendants of the 1904 Filly Triple Crown winner Pretty Polly. Vintage Tipple is nine generations removed from Pretty Polly, all bred at Eyrefield Lodge Stud, close to The Curragh. *TM*

Voix du Nord (Fr)

2yo bay colt   **114**

Valanour (Ire) - Dame Edith (Fr) (Top Ville)

Owner Baron Thierry van Zuylen de Nyevelt

Trainer D Smaga

Breeder Baron Thierry van Zuylen de Nyevelt

Career: **6** starts | won **2** | second **3** | third **0** | **£95,007** win and place

By Robert Carter

MOST of the leading French two-year-olds were lightly raced, so it is a pleasure to find a colt who links many of them together. Voix du Nord did not show much in the way of brilliance himself but ran six times and never shirked a fight. Victory in the final Group 1 of the French season, the Criterium de Saint-Cloud, was a well-deserved consolation for much honest effort.

Voix du Nord made his debut in the Prix de Marolles, over seven furlongs on the round course, at Deauville in early July. Thierry Gillet was in the saddle that day but Dominique Boeuf, who rides for David Smaga when available, took the mount for the rest of the season. Gillet held up the son of Valanour towards the rear until beginning to close on the turn. Voix du Nord ran on creditably in the final furlong and a half but was still five lengths behind Diamond Green at the line.

Diamond Green had taken over early in the straight and was soon in complete command. He showed how good he could be with a ready success in the Group 3 Prix la Rochette, also over seven furlongs, at Longchamp in early September. He responded immediately when shaken up to score by a comfortable two and a half lengths from Charming Prince, who took second in the last strides. Charming Prince went on to finish four lengths second to American Post in the Prix Jean-Luc Lagardere (Grand Criterium), a race that Diamond Green would have contested but for the late change in the ground.

Voix du Nord followed his promising debut with a three-length success in the Prix d'Etreham, over an extra half-furlong of Deauville's round course, in early August. He was promoted to Listed company in the Criterium du Fonds Europeen de l'Elevage, still on Deauville's round course but again trying an extra half-furlong. He started favourite but proved no match for the John Gosden-trained Gwaihir. Voix du Nord was never far behind the front-running winner and delivered a promising challenge

Voix du Nord (Dominique Boeuf) wins the Criterium de Saint-Cloud at the end of a busy first season

early in the straight. However, Gwaihir was too strong in the final furlong and ran on to beat him by one and a half lengths. Gwaihir returned to France for the Group 3 Prix Thomas Bryon, at Saint-Cloud in mid-October, but stood no chance when the once-raced Apsis quickened past over a furlong out and was flattered to be beaten only three lengths.

Another upward step followed, in the Group 3 Prix des Chenes over one mile at Longchamp. Voix du Nord proved no match for the top two in the betting, Bago and Valixir, but ran his usual game race under a vigorous ride. Soon pushed along to hold a good position, he went second at halfway and joined the leader early in the straight. He had every chance, but first Valixir and then Bago coasted past and he lost third to Happy Crusader in the last strides. Bago beat Valixir by one and a half lengths with the other pair two lengths and a neck behind.

Voix du Nord then tried nine furlongs in the Group 3 Prix de Conde at Longchamp in mid-October. This was a difficult race to watch as attention was distracted by the leader, Akritas, a colt trained, like Happy Crusader, by Paul Cole. He started hanging away from the rails approaching

2003   **Race record**

1st Criterium de Saint-Cloud (Group 1) (Saint-Cloud, November 8) 2yo 10f Good to soft **114** (TS 103) 10 ran. *Raced in 5th, ridden and headway over 1f out, led 150yds out, driven out, beat Simplex by 1½l*

2nd Prix de Conde (Group 3) (Longchamp, October 19) 2yo 9f Good to soft **107** (TS 87) 6 ran. *Raced in 3rd, 3rd straight, disputed lead 2f out until led 1½f out, headed and no extra final 50yds, beaten ½l by Latice*

4th Prix des Chenes (Group 3) (Longchamp, September 20) 2yo 1m Good **99** (TS 66) 7 ran. *Soon tracking leader, 2nd straight, ridden and every chance 2f out, soon one pace, beaten 3¾l by Bago*

2nd Criterium du Fonds Europeen de l'Elevage (Listed) (Deauville, August 23) 2yo 1m Good to soft **99** (TS 37) 8 ran. *Raced in 2nd throughout, pressed winner 1½f out until no extra final 150yds, beaten 1½l by Gwaihir*

1st Prix d'Etreham (Deauville, August 9) 2yo 7½f Good to soft **90** 9 ran. *Raced in 2nd until led 2f out, quickened clear, easily, beat Lougo by 3l*

2nd Prix de Marolles (Unraced Colts & Geldings) (Deauville, July 6) 2yo 7f Good to soft 10 ran. *Held up in rear, headway over 2f out, stayed on strongly down outside to take 2nd close home, no chance with winner, beaten 5l by Diamond Green*

the straight but went wider still once in line for home until Davy Bonilla was obliged to pull him up. Meanwhile, Voix du Nord had put his nose in front and gradually built up a lead of more than one length.

It looked as if he might hang on but the once-raced Latice picked up strongly to catch him five or six strides from home. Latice won by half a length with Prospect Park and Day Or Night two lengths and a short head behind. Latice, who had made a winning debut at Fontainebleau in early September, was the first female to land the Conde since Shemaka in 1992. That filly went on to win the Prix de Diane and Latice's connections will be aiming as high.

Voix du Nord found his distance in the Criterium de Saint-Cloud. He was hampered by Happy Crusader in the early stages before settling in fifth as far as the straight. When Boeuf worked him to the outside coming off the turn, he had quite a bit of ground to make up but he responded well to strong driving to catch Simplex 150 yards out and beat him by one and a half lengths. Day Or Night, given a much less demanding ride, stayed on from the back to finish a further four lengths behind, with Happy Crusader only sixth.

Baron Thierry van Zuylen de Nyevelt, whose colours are carried by Voix du Nord, has been a successful owner-breeder for close on half a century. He owned the 1981 Grand Prix de Deauville winner Perrault and still had a half-share when that horse won the Arlington Million the following year. He had another Grade 1 victory in the United States in 1991 when the Smaga-trained Leariva followed her success in the Group 2 Prix d'Astarte at Deauville by winning the Budweiser International at Laurel Park.

The Baron, who has a London address, owns the Haras de Varaville

Voix du Nord — *bay colt, 27-2-2001*

Valanour br 1992	Lomond	Northern Dancer	Nearctic / Natalma
		My Charmer	Poker / Fair Charmer
	Vearia	Mill Reef	Never Bend / Milan Mill
		Val Divine	Val de Loir / Pola Bella
Dame Edith b 1995	Top Ville	High Top	Derring-do / Camenae
		Sega Ville	Charlottesville / La Sega
	Girl Of France	Legend Of France	Lyphard / Lupe
		Water Girl	Faraway Son / Warsaw

Bred by Baron Thierry van Zuylen de Nyevelt

Sire Valanour

Won 5 of 9 races, inc. Prix de Guiche-Gr3, Grand Prix de Paris-Gr1, Prix d'Harcourt-Gr2, Prix Ganay-Gr1. Effective over 10f. By 2,000 Guineas winner, half-brother to Prix de Diane winner Vereva out of useful half-sister to several high-class performers over 1m+ including Valiyar, Vayrann. Stands under French National Stud banner. Oldest progeny 5. Sire of: Voix du Nord (Criterium de Saint-Cloud-Gr1).

Dam Dame Edith

Unplaced in 3 races. Half-sister to 2yo 1m Gr3 winner Varxi and 12f Listed winner Snow Cap out of useful miler. Dam of: unnamed (2000 f by Exit To Nowhere), Voix du Nord (2001 c by Valanour; Gr1 winner), Captivance (2002 f by Kendor).

Pedigree assessment

From a stout family that is also represented by Westerner, and will have no problems staying 12f. The best offspring of his very well-bred sire. *JH*

in Normandy and became a vendor at Deauville for the first time in August, selling a colt by Ashkalani out of Leariva for €35,000 (£23,800) and a Kendor half-sister to Voix du Nord for €107,000 (£72,800). One of his greatest successes on the racecourse came in October 1998 when his homebred Lexa, trained by his daughter Cordelia, won the Group 2 Prix de Royallieu. One of his greatest disappointments came in September when State Of Art, who had recovered from an operation on a fractured cannon bone to win the Group 3 Prix de la Nonette, broke down in the Prix Vermeille. This time she did not survive.

But at least the Baron can nurse hopes of Classic success with his Criterium winner.

Warrsan (Ire)

5yo bay horse **124**

Caerleon (USA) - Lucayan Princess (High Line)

Owner Saeed Manana

Trainer C E Brittain

Breeder Saeed Manana

Career: **25** starts | won **6** | second **8** | third **2** | **£523,061** win and place

By Lee Mottershead

WITHIN the sprinting ranks, the jump from decent handicapper to top-flight Group performer is not unusual. The leap from one to the other is not impossibly huge and, with an improving animal, it is a gap which can be bridged. For those racing over middle distances it is harder, the pool of genuine Group horses being larger and competition stronger. It takes a seriously progressive performer to make the transition. Warrsan showed himself to be such a horse.

In the spring of 2002, Warrsan was hardly a languishing nonentity, yet he was still nothing like the horse who was to positively shine just 12 months later. In his first two starts as a four-year-old, he was beaten off a mark of 84, then a Goodwood success sent his handicap mark soaring to 100 and a subsequent five-length eighth to Royal Rebel in the Gold Cup at Royal Ascot forced him up to 111 and out of handicaps.

That the handicap route had been closed off was not going to be a problem. Although unsuccessful in a number of attempts at Group level in the second half of 2002, Warrsan showed himself to be a legitimate player, ending his second season on the track – he did not race at two – with fine seconds in the Cumberland Lodge and St Simon Stakes.

That Warrsan should have made further strides from four to five ought not to have been a surprise. Half-brothers Needle Gun and Luso both got better with age and Warrsan was evidently of the same vintage. Making his reappearance in the Dubai Irish Village Stakes, a race better known as the John Porter, Warrsan benefited from a change in tactics to score his first Group 1 triumph. Asked to run from the front for the first time, he set a sensible gallop, winding up the pace and seeing off all challenges up the straight, finally holding off the late thrust of Asian Heights. While there was clearly a lot to like about Warrsan's performance, not everyone was convinced. They were forgetting the Clive Brittain factor.

The previous seasons had not been altogether happy ones for Brittain,

**Warrsan (Philip Robinson, left) gets up to land the
Group 1 Coronation Cup at Epsom in June**

a troublesome left hip making his life as an active trainer increasingly
hard to maintain. Then he had his hip replaced and, as if by magic,
things changed. In the spring of 2003, Brittain's flow of winners, as well
as his own stride, improved dramatically and, in Warrsan, he had a horse
going places. The next place Warrsan went was Newmarket for the Group
2 Jockey Club Stakes, in which Saeed Manana's charge was sent off
joint-outsider at 12-1 for a six-runner contest which featured some of
the previous season's most progressive three-year-olds – Balakheri, Bandari
and Highest – as well as former St Leger winner and Newmarket specialist
Millenary.

Warrsan beat them all, utilising his fitness edge as he quickened into
the lead two furlongs out before posting a convincing one-and-a-half-
length defeat of Millenary. Upped to a mile and three-quarters in the
Yorkshire Cup, Warrsan ran even better, failing by only half a length to
give Mamool 4lb and finishing four lengths clear of Bollin Eric. Mamool
went on to become a Group 1 winner, but Warrsan got there first.

His finest hour came at Epsom. It may not have been the greatest
renewal of the Vodafone Coronation Cup, but Warrsan could do no more
than win, and win he did, displaying a fine attitude under regular rider
Philip Robinson to grab Highest well inside the final furlong before battling
home for a narrow success. Just 16 days later, he came within a length
and three-quarters of back-to-back Group 1 victories when chasing home

2003   Race record

3rd Gran Premio Del Jockey Club (Group 1) (San Siro, October 19) 3yo+ 12f Good **114** 5 ran. *Raced in 2nd until led narrowly 3f out, headed over 2f out, one pace, beaten 5l by Ekraar*

3rd Credit Suisse Private Banking-Pokal (Group 1) (Cologne, August 17) 3yo+ 12f Good **117** 5 ran. *Disputed lead until led after 1f, set good pace, ridden over 2½f out, edged left, headed 2f out, one pace, beaten 4½l by Dai Jin*

6th King George VI And Queen Elizabeth Diamond Stakes (Group 1) (Ascot, July 26) 3yo+ 12f Good **119** (TS 91) 12 ran. *Settled in rear, ridden and no progress over 4f out, kept on same pace on wide outside final 2f, beaten 9½l by Alamshar*

2nd Gran Premio di Milano (Group 1) (San Siro, June 22) 3yo+ 12f Firm **123** 6 ran. *Led 1f then 2nd, ridden to chase leader 2f out, kept on under pressure but always being held by winner, beaten 1¾l by Leadership*

1st Vodafone Coronation Cup (Group 1) (Epsom, June 6) 4yo+ 12f Good **123** (TS 99) 9 ran. *Tracked leaders, close 6th straight, not clear run over 2f out and switched right, hard ridden and ran on to lead last 100yds, kept on gamely, beat Highest by ½l*

2nd Emirates Airline Yorkshire Cup (Group 2) (York, May 15) 4yo+ 1m6f Good to firm **124** (TS 108) 8 ran. *Tracked leaders, effort over 3f out, stayed on to lead over 1f out, ran on well, headed near finish, beaten ½l by Mamool*

1st Sagitta Jockey Club Stakes (Group 2) (Newmarket, May 2) 4yo+ 12f Good to soft **120** (TS 81) 6 ran. *Chased leader, came centre and led over 2f out, ridden out, beat Millenary by 1½l*

1st Dubai Irish Village Stakes (Registered As The John Porter Stakes) (Group 3) (Newbury, April 12) 4yo+ 12f Good to firm **116** (TS 88) 9 ran. *Made all, pushed along from 3f out, quickened and stayed on final furlong, held on well, beat Asian Heights by shd*

2002

2nd Electricity Direct St Simon Stakes (Group 3) (Newbury, October 26) 3yo+ 12f Soft **117** (TS 88) 13 ran ● **2nd** Young Vic Theatre Cumberland Lodge Stakes (Group 3) (Ascot, September 29) 3yo+ 12f Good to firm **115** (TS 75) 5 ran ● **4th** Jefferson Smurfit Memorial Irish St Leger (Group 1) (Curragh, September 14) 3yo+ 1m6f Good to firm **117** (TS 97) 8 ran ● **2nd** Catisfield Hinton And Stud Conditions Stakes (Salisbury, September 5) 3yo+ 1m6f Good to firm **111** (TS 64) 5 ran ● **5th** Stan James Geoffrey Freer Stakes (Group 2) (Newbury, August 17) 3yo+ 1m5½f Good to firm **110** (TS 71) 7 ran ● **1st** Qualitair Holdings Conditions Stakes (Newmarket (July), July 19) 3yo+ 12f Good to firm **109** (TS 76) 4 ran ● **8th** Gold Cup (Group 1) (Ascot, June 20) 4yo+ 2m4f Good to firm **111** (TS 12) 15 ran ● **1st** Bonusprint Rated Stakes (0-100 handicap) (Goodwood, May 23) 4yo+ 1m6f Good **104** (TS 85) 11 ran ● **2nd** Grundon Stakes (Registered As The Aston Park Stakes) (Listed) (Newbury, May 18) 4yo+ 1m5½f Good to firm **102** (TS 69) 6 ran ● **2nd** March Handicap (0-100) (Newmarket, May 5) 4yo+ 12f Good to firm **98** (TS 49) 16 ran ● **7th** Babraham Handicap (0-95) (Newmarket, April 17) 4yo+ 12f Good to firm **93** (TS 68) 23 ran

Other notable runs

2001 **2nd** Tote Sporting Index Autumn Cup (0-100 handicap) (Newbury, September 22) 3yo+ 1m5½f Good to firm **89** (TS 43) 11 ran ● **1st** Jim Macdonald-Buchanan Handicap (0-85) (Sandown, July 26) 3yo 1m6f Good to firm **85** (TS 68) 10 ran

Leadership in the Gran Premio di Milano.

While the first half of the season had been hugely successful for Warrsan, it had also been busy, so it was therefore not entirely surprising that things did not work out quite as well in the following months. Having

Warrsan
bay horse, 28-2-1998

		Northern Dancer	Nearctic Natalma
	Nijinsky	Flaming Page	Bull Page Flaring Top
Caerleon b 1980	Foreseer	Round Table	Princequillo Knight's Daughter
		Regal Gleam	Hail To Reason Miz Carol
	High Line	High Hat	Hyperion Madonna
		Time Call	Chanteur Aleria
Lucayan Princess b 1983	Gay France	Sir Gaylord	Turn-to Somethingroyal
		Sweet And Lovely	Tanerko Lilya

Bred by Saeed Manana in Ireland

Sire Caerleon

Won 4 of 8 races, inc. Anglesey S.-Gr3, Prix du Jockey-Club-Gr1, Benson & Hedges Gold Cup-Gr1. Also 2nd in Irish Derby-Gr1. Good-looking, compact, top-class middle-distance performer. Died in February 1998. Sire of Gr1 winners: Caerwent, Welsh Guide, Kostroma, Atoll, Caerlina, Generous, In A Tiff, Only Royale, Biwa Heidi, Tenby, Moonax, Auriette, Fusaichi Concorde, Grape Tree Road, Lady Carla, Shake The Yoke, Cape Verdi, Innuendo, Mukhalif, Sunspangled, Marienbard, Preseli, Warrsan.

Dam Lucayan Princess

Won 2 of 4 races. inc. Sweet Solera S.-Listed. Leggy, light-framed, attractive sort, effective on any ground, stayed 12f well. Same family as Kris Kin. Dam of: Celia Brady (1988 f by Last Tycoon; winner), Lucca (1989 f by Sure Blade; unplaced), Needle Gun (1990 c by Sure Blade; Gr2 winner, Gr1-placed), Luana (1991 f by Shaadi; winner, Listed-placed), Luso (1992 c by Salse; multiple Gr1 winner), Lunda (1993 f by Soviet Star; unplaced), Cloud Castle (1995 f by In The Wings; Gr3 winner), Maskunah (1997 f by Sadler's Wells; unraced), Warrsan (1998 c by Caerleon; Gr1 winner), Mreef (1999 c by Sadler's Wells; unraced), Mantesera (2000 f by In The Wings; unraced to date).

Pedigree assessment

Like most of the staying types by Caerleon – Generous was the most notable exception – Warrsan cannot deliver instant acceleration on demand, but he is a game battler, true to a pedigree that assured him stamina in excess of speed. Weak and immature in his early days, he has repaid the patience of his trainer, who also developed the talents of his half-brothers Needle Gun and Luso, collecting four Group 1 wins with the latter, the last of them as a six-year-old. *TM*

been unsuited by the steady early gallop when sixth in the King George VI and Queen Elizabeth Diamond Stakes, he finished his season abroad, placed but not disgraced in two of Europe's less sexy Group 1 events.

A fast ground-loving, thoroughly genuine racehorse, Warrsan will be back in 2004 and further improvement cannot be ruled out.

Westerner

4yo bay colt **122**

Danehill (USA) - Walensee (Troy)
Owner Ecurie Wildenstein
Trainer E Lellouche
Breeder Dayton Investments Ltd

Career: **15** starts | won **4** | second **6** | third **1** | **£210,097** win and place

By Graham Dench

ANYONE can see that Westerner is a rattling good stayer. Indeed he's a match for any around on the form he showed in the autumn, when he slaughtered Mr Dinos and Persian Punch in the Prix du Cadran and then ran away with the Prix Royal-Oak. But if he travels over to England for a rematch in the Ascot Gold Cup there will be questions to answer. To begin with, he is highly unlikely to find the testing conditions that plainly suit him so well. Perhaps as significantly, he will be denied the use of an aid that may well have been crucial to the dramatic improvement he showed towards the end of the 2003 campaign.

Earplugs were possibly just as big a factor as the going in Westerner's improvement, and the Jockey Club's rules on their employment are much stricter than those in place in France. Were he to wear them at Ascot they would have to remain in place for the entire duration of the race. In France, where they are typically connected by short strings and are easily removable, jockeys are permitted to whip them out at the opportune moment, when a change of gear is required for a final effort. The sudden increased awareness can trigger the horse's natural flight mechanism.

Earplugs are in everyday use in the trotting world and Westerner's jockey Dominique Boeuf is keen on their use in racing on nervy types who find racing stressful and are inclined to run free without them. It is unlikely to have been pure coincidence that their application on Westerner coincided with the Danehill colt winning the last two of the three races in which they were used, especially as the same team also employed them successfully on stablemate Vallee Enchantee.

The difference when Westerner first wore them in the Prix Gladiateur at Longchamp in September was admittedly only limited, as he finished just a length closer to Darasim than he had done when chasing him home under broadly similar conditions in the Prix Kergorlay at Deauville three weeks earlier. But it was a different story another three

---

Westerner (Dominique Boeuf) lands the Prix du Cadran at Longchamp, with his earplugs clearly visible

weeks on in the Cadran, on Arc day, and again at the end of October in the Prix Royal-Oak, the French St Leger, though the stiffer tests of stamina he faced in those races were obviously factors too.

The Cadran's two and a half miles in gruelling conditions was right up Westerner's street and he was plainly going much the best of the principals, though still only fifth, when he was tightened up between Mr Dinos and Persian Punch approaching the finishing straight. It is not clear from video replays precisely where Boeuf elected to pull the plugs out, but they can be seen flailing about on either side of his head in the straight, when he made ground on the 2001 Cadran winner Germinis towards the centre of the track. He went to the front with around a furlong and a half to go and stormed five lengths clear.

Even tougher opposition faced Westerner in the Royal-Oak, where a field of 14 included the triple Irish St Leger winner Vinnie Roe, recently fifth in the Arc, yet he was every bit as impressive. Boeuf can be seen on video grabbing for the earplugs with just under two furlongs to go, whereupon Westerner took off and quickly went two or three lengths clear. Outsider Alcazar flew in the closing stages but was never going to get to him and was beaten two and a half lengths.

Westerner did not race at two and spent the vast majority of his first season racing at a mile, not surprisingly perhaps with sprinter Danehill as his sire and his tendency to race a bit keenly. He won just a minor

2003   Race record

1st Prix Royal-Oak (Group 1) (Longchamp, October 26) 3yo+ 1m7½f Holding **120** (TS 71) 14 ran. *In touch, disputing 4th halfway, disputing 3rd straight, headway to lead over 1½f out, quickened clear over 1f out, ran on strongly, ridden out, beat Alcazar by 2½l*

1st Prix du Cadran - Casinos Barriere (Group 1) (Longchamp, October 5) 4yo+ 2m4f Holding **122** 10 ran. *Raced in 6th, headway towards outside over 4f out, 4th and pushed along straight, ran on strongly in centre to lead 1½f out, ridden clear, beat Germinis by 5l*

2nd Prix Gladiateur Royal Thalasso Barriere (Group 3) (Longchamp, September 14) 4yo+ 1m7½f Good to soft **113** (TS 19) 9 ran. *In touch, 4th halfway, shaken up and headway 2f out to go 2nd, driven to chase leader 1½f out, kept on but never able to challenge winner, beaten 2l by Darasim*

2nd Prix Kergorlay (Group 2) (Deauville, August 24) 3yo+ 1m7f Good to soft **112** (TS 95) 9 ran. *Held up on inside tracking leaders, disputing 5th straight, pushed along and ran on over 1½f out, ridden and disputing 2nd final furlong, went 2nd on line, beaten 3l by Darasim*

2nd Prix Maurice de Nieuil (Group 2) (Maisons-Laffitte, July 19) 4yo+ 1m6f Good to soft **110** (TS 98) 7 ran. *Raced in 5th, driven 2f out, ran on under pressure to take 2nd final 100yds, beaten ¾l by Martaline*

5th Grand Prix de Chantilly (Group 2) (Chantilly, June 8) 4yo+ 12f Good **105** (TS 91) 7 ran. *Led, shaken up 2f out, headed 1½f out, kept on under pressure until weakened inside final furlong, beaten 6¼l by Ange Gabriel*

1st Prix de la Porte de Madrid (Listed) (Longchamp, May 8) 4yo+ 12f Soft **100** (TS 43) 8 ran. *Raced in 2nd until led over 5f out, drew steadily clear from over 1½f out, pushed out, beat Spray Gun by 2½l*

11th Prix Altipan (Listed) (Saint-Cloud, March 15) 4yo+ 1m Good to soft 13 ran. *Never a factor, beaten 7l by Gaelic Lord*

2002

3rd Prix Tantieme (Listed) (Saint-Cloud, November 19) 3yo+ 1m Heavy **95** (TS 55) 11 ran ● **8th** Prix Daniel Wildenstein (Prix du Rond-Point) Casino Barriere de la Rochelle (Group 2) (Longchamp, October 5) 3yo+ 1m Good to soft **105** (TS 81) 11 ran ● **2nd** Prix de Tourgeville (Listed) (Deauville, August 6) 3yo 1m Very soft **100** (TS 45) 8 ran ● **4th** Prix de la Jonchere (Group 3) (Chantilly, June 17) 3yo 1m Good to soft **102** (TS 59) 5 ran ● **2nd** Prix de Pontarme (Listed) (Chantilly, May 29) 3yo 1m Soft (TS 44) 5 ran ● **1st** Prix du Coeur Volant (Maisons-Laffitte, May 7) 3yo 1m Soft 8 ran ● **2nd** Prix de Champerret (French-Bred Colts & Geldings) (Longchamp, April 7) 3yo 10f Good to firm (TS 68) 13 ran

event at Maisons-Laffitte over that distance and was still racing at a mile when he made his reappearance at Saint-Cloud in March. However, something must have clicked then either with Boeuf, with trainer Elie Lellouche, or with Westerner himself, because from there onwards it was a mile and a half and more all of the way. Westerner won a Listed race over 12 furlongs at Longchamp in May and followed with a series of solid efforts in Group company.

Westerner stays in training and it will be fascinating to see if he can reproduce his form on faster ground and, just as importantly, without the aid of earplugs. He possibly will, for he is no mere slogger and has a telling turn of foot for a stayer. If he can, then Mr Dinos had better look to his laurels.

Westerner
bay colt, 17-5-1999

		Northern Dancer	Nearctic / Natalma
Danehill (b 1986)	Danzig		
		Pas de Nom	Admiral's Voyage / Petitioner
	Razyana	His Majesty	Ribot / Flower Bowl
		Spring Adieu	Buckpasser / Natalma
Walensee (b 1982)	Troy	Petingo	Petition / Alcazar
		La Milo	Hornbeam / Pin Prick
	Warsaw	Bon Mot	Worden / Djebel Idra
		War Path	Blue Prince / Alyxia

Bred by Dayton Investments in Britain

Sire Danehill

Won 4 of 9 races, inc. Cork and Orrery S.-Gr3, Haydock Park Sprint Cup-Gr1. Medium-sized, strong, good-bodied individual, markedly back at the knee. Died in May 2003. Sire, in northern hemisphere, of: Danish (Queen Elizabeth II Challenge Cup-Gr1), Kissing Cousin (Coronation S.-Gr1), Danehill Dancer (Phoenix S.-Gr1, National S.-Gr1), Tsukuba Symphony (NHK Mile Cup-Gr1), Desert King (National S.-Gr1, Irish 2,000 Guineas-Gr1, Irish Derby-Gr1), Fairy King Prawn (Yasuda Kinen-Gr1), Tiger Hill (Grosser Preis von Baden-Gr1, twice, Bayerisches Zuchtrennen-Gr1), Indian Danehill (Prix Ganay-Gr1), Wannabe Grand (Cheveley Park S.-Gr1), Aquarelliste (Prix de Diane-Gr1, Prix Vermeille-Gr1, Prix Ganay-Gr1), Banks Hill (Coronation S.-Gr1, Breeders' Cup Filly & Mare Turf-Gr1, Prix Jacques le Marois-Gr1), Mozart (July Cup-Gr1, Nunthorpe S.-Gr1), Regal Rose (Cheveley Park S.-Gr1), Dress To Thrill (Matriarch S.-Gr1), Landseer (Poule d'Essai des Poulains-Gr1), Rock Of Gibraltar (Grand Criterium-Gr1, Dewhurst S.-Gr1, 2,000 Guineas-Gr1, Irish 2,000 Guineas-Gr1, St James's Palace S.-Gr1, Sussex S.-Gr1, Prix du Moulin de Longchamp-Gr1), Spring Star (Gr2), Spartacus (Phoenix S.-Gr1, Gran Criterium-Gr1), Westerner (Prix du Cadran-Gr1, Prix Royal-Oak-Gr1), Clodovil (Poule d'Essai des Poulains-Gr1).

Dam Walensee

Won 3 of 9 races, inc. Prix Vermeille-Gr1. Very progressive at 3, stayed 12f, daughter of Listed-winning half-sister to top-class US filly Waya from family of Voix du Nord. Dam of: Waldensian (1988 c by Shareef Dancer; winner), War Arrow (1990 g by Top Ville; jumps winner), Wild Ride (1991 f by Niniski; non-winner), Wild Life (1993 f by Nashwan; unraced), World Cup (1994 c by Epervier Bleu; non-winner), Wagram (1995 f by Nashwan; unraced), War Game (1996 f by Caerleon; Gr2 winner), Watteau (1998 g by Loup Solitaire; winner), Westerner (1999 c by Danehill; Gr1 winner), Wildest Hope (2001 c by Wolfhound; unraced).

Pedigree assessment

In stamina terms, Westerner is most definitely his mother's son. Danehill gets few top-class middle-distance performers, let alone stayers. Having established himself as a highly progressive stayer, Westerner should excel again in 2004. *JH*

Whipper (USA)

2yo bay colt **115**

Miesque's Son (USA) - Myth To Reality (Fr) (Sadler's Wells (USA))

Owner R C Strauss

Trainer Robert Collet

Breeder Flaxman Holdings Ltd

Career: 7 starts	won 3	second 0	third 1	£184,324 win and place

By Richard Austen

WHIPPER, but not the whipper-in. At 258-10, the Robert Collet-trained two-year-old started as rank outsider for the Group 1 Prix Morny at Deauville in August – the next longest price in an eight-runner line-up was 91-10 – but he failed to follow the others home at the expected respectful distance.

If three runners from Ballydoyle had not been coupled in the betting, Whipper would have been at shorter odds than the pacemaker Haydn, but not the rest. Much Faster, Denebola and Carrizo Creek had already won a Group race – the unbeaten Much Faster had won two of them and one Listed – while Haskilclara was a Listed winner and Old Deuteronomy and Colossus had three second places between them in either Group 1 or Group 2 contests. Whipper's success had been in the French provinces and he had also been beaten there.

The Morny revealed his true colours. For much of the race, it looked as if Much Faster would land odds of 9-10 as she took over from Haydn two furlongs out, but Whipper was close behind her. Driven out by Sebastian Maillot to take the favourite's measure inside the final furlong, he went on to score by two lengths, with Denebola running on from the back for third and the Irish and British challengers left floundering.

Maillot was riding his first Group winner. The unlikely hero, though, was definitely Whipper, whose starting price was not the only set of figures that apparently spoke against him. After the Morny he carried the well-known colours of Robert Strauss, but for the five runs up to and including his Group 1 triumph he was owned by Elias Zaccour, having passed through the Keeneland sales ring two years earlier, as a foal, for $4,000. Compare that with the Ff520,000 paid for Much Faster, €200,000 for Haydn and the fortunes that would probably have been produced, had they been sent to auction, for Storm Cat's offspring Denebola and Old Deuteronomy.

**Whipper (Sebastian Maillot) scores a shock win in the
Group 1 Prix Morny at Deauville in August**

Whipper's victory in the provinces came earlier in August over five
and a half furlongs on soft ground at Chateaubriant, well and truly off
the beaten track for a Group 1 winner. This race did provide a line to
the British form book, however, because three-length runner-up
Raphoola had earlier won sellers at Chepstow and Lingfield.

Whipper took only 13 days to prove himself much better than the bare
result of that triumph at 1-2 suggested, by winning the Morny, but the
glaring signs were there much earlier that he was held in high regard.
When he made his debut in early July, it was in a Group 3 – in the Prix
du Bois at Deauville, in which Much Faster was the winner and Whipper
was fifth.

Whipper also met with defeat at Vichy, when third of 12 to the useful
filly Black Escort, and had been back to Deauville at the start of August

1st Criterium de Maisons-Laffitte (Group 2) (Maisons-Laffitte, October 31) 2yo 6f Holding **115** (TS 80) 10 ran. *Tracked leader in middle, led over 2f out, driven clear, well in command final furlong, beat Chineur by 2½l*

5th Shadwell Stud Middle Park Stakes (Group 1) (Newmarket, October 3) 2yo 6f Good to firm **111** (TS 80) 12 ran. *Held up, ran on inside final furlong, nearest finish, beaten 2l by Three Valleys*

1st Prix Morny Casinos Barriere (Group 1) (Deauville, August 31) 2yo 6f Soft **115** (TS 82) 8 ran. *Always in touch, tracking 2nd, driven to lead inside final furlong, ran on, beat Much Faster by 2l*

1st Prix de Longchamp (Chateaubriant, August 18) 2yo 5½f Soft 7 ran. *Held up in 4th, headway on outside from 2f out, led 1f out, ran on well, easily, beat Raphoola by 3l*

4th Prix de Cabourg (Group 3) (Deauville, August 2) 2yo 6f Good to soft **86** (TS 58) 8 ran. *Raced in 5th towards outside, stayed on at one pace from over 1f out, beaten 5¼l by Denebola*

3rd Prix des Reves d'Or (Vichy, July 20) 2yo 5f Good 12 ran. *Disputed lead until headed inside final furlong, one pace, beaten 2½l by Black Escort*

5th Prix du Bois (Group 3) (Deauville, July 5) 2yo 5f Soft **80** (TS 51) 8 ran. *Towards rear, headway to dispute 4th 1½f out until inside final furlong, one pace, promising, beaten 5½l by Much Faster*

to take fourth behind Denebola in the Group 3 Prix de Cabourg.

The spectacular reversal of form with Much Faster and Denebola in the Morny was in some quarters put down to testing ground following a downpour on the morning of the race. Whipper's connections, however, were happy to let him loose next on good to firm at Newmarket for the Middle Park Stakes. He was sent off at 16-1 but beaten only two lengths.

"It doesn't matter about the ground for him," said Collet. "If it's fast or soft, it's all the same." A suicidal early pace from the pacemakers led to some awkward decision-making for those jockeys in pursuit and Christophe Soumillon's efforts to secure cover for Whipper resulted in his trying to come from a long way back; disputing last place two furlongs out, he had nine horses in front of him at the furlong marker and finished fifth.

The Criterium de Maisons-Laffitte four weeks later gave Whipper another chance to show what he could do on holding ground over six furlongs and, unpenalised, he started 13-10 favourite and ran out a clear-cut winner, two and a half lengths and the same in front of Listed winner Chineur and his erstwhile conqueror Black Escort.

"You don't have many like him," said Collet, "and now Whipper will run in the Prix Djebel before going back to Newmarket for the 2,000 Guineas. He has stamina on the dam's side, so should get a mile, and Whipper has the class to win the Guineas."

His sire should ring a few bells – Miesque's Prospector would have been just about the only less inspiring name that connections could have come up with for him – and although Miesque's Son himself was best at six to seven furlongs, Whipper shapes as if he will be suited by the step up from six furlongs.

Whipper

bay colt, 13-3-2001

		Raise A Native	Native Dancer
	Mr Prospector		Raise You
Miesque's Son		Gold Digger	Nashua
br 1992			Sequence
	Miesque	Nureyev	**Northern Dancer**
			Special
		Pasadoble	Prove Out
			Santa Quilla
	Sadler's Wells	**Northern Dancer**	Nearctic
			Natalma
Myth To Reality		Fairy Bridge	Bold Reason
b 1986			Special
	Millieme	Mill Reef	Never Bend
			Milan Mill
		Hardiemma	Hardicanute
			Grand Cross

Bred by Flaxman Holdings in US. $4,000 Keeneland November foal

Sire Miesque's Son

Won 1 of 9 starts, inc. Prix de Ris-Orangis-Gr3, also 2nd in Prix Maurice de Gheest-Gr1, Prix de la Foret-Gr1. Late maturing, effective over 6-7f. Brother to Kingmambo, by outstanding US sire out of outstanding miler who is half-sister to dam of Six Perfections. Stood until 2003 in US, recently moved to Haras des Chartreux. Oldest progeny 5. Sire of: Miesque's Approval (Gr3), Whipper (Prix Morny-Gr1).

Dam Myth To Reality

Won 4 races at 3 in France including 3 Listed, 2nd Prix Minerve-Gr3. Effective over 12f. Sister to smart 12f+ performer Casamasa out of sister to Shirley Heights. Dam of: Sonofogy (1992 c by Ogygian; winner), Magic Spin (1993 f by Lord Avie; winner), Assos (1994 c by Alleged; Listed winner, Gr3-placed), Mambo Jambo (1995 f by Kingmambo; winner, dam of Gr1-placed Ocean Silk), Fireinthewind (1996 c by Alleged; winner), Indigo Myth (1997 c by Kingmambo; winner, stakes-placed), Meteorite Sun (1998 c by Miesque's Son; winner), Whipper (2001 c by Miesque's Son; Gr1 winner), Divine Proportions (2002 f by Kingmambo), 2003 f by Mt Livermore.

Pedigree assessment

Has done his winning over 6f but should have no problems with 1m. Has an outside chance of lasting 10f but 12f will be too far. Much encouragement on both sides of his pedigree that he will train on well and he is from a family that produces genuinely top-class performers. By far the best performer by his sire, who is not in the same league as his brother Kingmambo as a racehorse or stallion but who has a peerless pedigree. *JH*

Yesterday (Ire)

3yo bay filly   **118**

Sadler's Wells (USA) - Jude (Darshaan)

Owner Mrs John Magnier & Mrs Richard Henry

Trainer A P O'Brien

Breeder Premier Bloodstock

Career: **13** starts	won **3**	second **4**	third **2**	**£442,125** win and place

By Alan Sweetman

THE Sadler's Wells filly Yesterday began to establish herself as one of the leading Irish juvenile fillies of 2002 at a time when her full-sister and Ballydoyle stablemate Quarter Moon, a former winner of the Moyglare Stud Stakes, was consolidating her reputation. Although she failed to win at three, Quarter Moon upheld her status as an outstanding broodmare prospect with second places in three successive Classic attempts, in the Irish 1,000 Guineas, the Vodafone Oaks and the Irish Oaks.

After winning a maiden over seven furlongs at Tipperary in June on her second outing as a juvenile, Yesterday stepped up to Pattern company for the first time in the Group 3 Robert Griffin Debutante Stakes at The Curragh in August, finishing a satisfactory second to the Kevin Prendergast-trained Rainbows For All. Her next outing was in the Prix Marcel Boussac, won in brilliant fashion by Six Perfections, and her sixth place at Longchamp was just a touch disappointing in relation to two other Irish-trained fillies in the race, the third, Luminata, and fifth, Miss Helga.

That pair would ultimately prove to be much inferior to Yesterday, whose form took a turn for the better when she finished third behind Luvah Girl and Casual Look in the Group 2 Rockfel Stakes at Newmarket, and signed off her first season with a convincing four-length win from Eklim in a Listed race at Leopardstown. The distance was nine furlongs and, with his experience of handling Quarter Moon providing a template, O'Brien immediately nominated the Vodafone Oaks as her main objective.

Keen to provide Yesterday with more experience in Group 1 company, O'Brien started her off for the season in the 1,000 Guineas. She finished a respectable eighth behind Russian Rhythm, but when it came to the Irish equivalent at The Curragh there seemed little reason to believe that she could reverse form with Six Perfections, who had run into all sorts of trouble on her way to finishing second at Newmarket.

Yesterday (Mick Kinane, right) on her way to Group 1 success in the Irish 1,000 Guineas at The Curragh in May

Johnny Murtagh was enlisted by Pascal Bary to give the benefit of his local knowledge on Six Perfections, who was sent off 30-100 favourite, with Yesterday an 11-2 chance in a field of eight. What transpired was a tactical triumph for Mick Kinane on Yesterday who capitalised in ruthless but thoroughly legitimate fashion when Six Perfections became trapped on the rails at a crucial stage. Kinane maintained the agony for Murtagh for as long as possible before striking for home, and Yesterday knuckled down well to resist Six Perfections by a short head.

With a Classic victory secured over a trip that had generally been deemed inadequate, the omens looked favourable for Yesterday's bid to avenge Quarter Moon's defeat in the Vodafone Oaks. However, at Epsom it was her turn to adopt the unlucky loser's tag, her path repeatedly blocked as Kinane desperately searched for gaps from fully a quarter of a mile out. In the end, she lost out by a neck to Casual Look, who had finished a couple of places in front of her at Newmarket.

The following month the pair clashed again in the Irish Oaks, a race that looked stronger than many recent renewals. Whatever its ultimate merit in terms of form, the race provided a heart-warming triumph for octogenarian trainer Paddy Mullins with Vintage Tipple, who beat the Ballydoyle second-string L'Ancresse, with Casual Look taking third, and thus finishing in front of Yesterday, somewhat lacklustre in fourth on this occasion, for the fourth time in her career.

The final phase of Yesterday's career was marked by two near-misses

2003   Race record

3rd Breeders' Cup Filly & Mare Turf (Grade 1) (Santa Anita, October 25) 3yo+ 10f Firm **117** 12 ran. *Held up in 10th, progress approaching straight, 5th straight, ridden over 1f out, took 3rd final furlong, ran on, beaten 2¾l by Islington*

2nd Prix de l'Opera - Casino Barriere d'Enghien (Group 1) (Longchamp, October 5) 3yo+ 10f Holding **117** (TS 87) 11 ran. *Held up towards rear, last straight, pushed along 2f out, stayed on in centre 1 1/2f out, hard ridden to challenge final furlong, nearest at finish, beaten hd by Zee Zee Top*

2nd Prix Vermeille Fouquet's Barriere (Group 1) (Longchamp, September 14) 3yo 12f Good to soft **118** (TS 104) 11 ran. *Held up towards rear, pushed along over 3f out, 5th straight, ran on well from 2f out to press leaders, ridden and every chance final furlong, held close home, beaten hd by Mezzo Soprano*

4th Darley Irish Oaks (Group 1) (Curragh, July 13) 3yo 12f Good **110** (TS 92) 11 ran. *Held up in rear of mid-division, moderate 8th approaching straight, kept on under pressure from 2f out without reaching leaders, beaten 3¾l by Vintage Tipple*

2nd Vodafone Oaks (Group 1) (Epsom, June 6) 3yo 12f Good **116** (TS 75) 15 ran. *Held up in midfield, 9th straight, not clear run twice over 2f out, closed on leaders but nowhere to go 1f out, switched left, ran on well, unlucky, beaten nk by Casual Look*

1st Entenmann's Irish 1,000 Guineas (Group 1) (Curragh, May 25) 3yo 1m Soft **115** (TS 96) 8 ran. *Tracked leaders in 4th, 3rd 2f out, ridden to challenge over 1f out, led well inside final furlong, kept on under pressure, all out, beat Six Perfections by shd*

8th Sagitta 1,000 Guineas (Group 1) (Newmarket, May 4) 3yo 1m Good to firm **102** (TS 89) 19 ran. *Tracked leaders, ridden and every chance over 1f out, no extra final furlong, beaten 7l by Russian Rhythm*

2002

1st Eyrefield Stakes (Listed) (Leopardstown, November 10) 2yo 9f Heavy **108** (TS 73) 18 ran ● **3rd** Owen Brown Rockfel Stakes (Group 2) (Newmarket, October 19) 2yo 7f Good **102** (TS 59) 11 ran ● **6th** Prix Marcel Boussac Criterium Pouliches-Royal Barriere de Deauville (Group 1) (Longchamp, October 6) 2yo 1m Good **102** (TS 59) 10 ran ● **2nd** Robert Griffin Debutante Stakes (Group 3) (Curragh, August 11) 2yo 7f Soft **91** (TS 58) 9 ran ● **1st** Tipperary Town EBF Fillies Maiden (Tipperary, June 26) 2yo 7f Soft **86** 6 ran ● **8th** Swordlestown Stud Sprint Stakes (Listed) (Naas, June 3) 2yo 6f Soft **79** (TS 57) 11 ran

in Group 1 races in France and a contribution to a fine European effort at the Breeders' Cup meeting. Her performance in staying on from off the pace to finish a head second to Mezzo Soprano in the Prix Vermeille at Longchamp in September was noteworthy for the fact that she had six previous Group winners behind, and in losing out by the same margin to Zee Zee Top in the Prix de l'Opera, after a run that was by no means trouble-free, there was at least the consolation that she finished in front of dual Group 1 winner Bright Sky.

A fine third to Islington in the Breeders' Cup Filly & Mare Turf at Santa Anita was overshadowed by her stablemate L'Ancresse in taking the runner-up spot, but confirmed her status as one of the leading European fillies of her generation. With more luck she might well have won several Group 1s. On the other hand, if Six Perfections had not endured such a nightmare at The Curragh, she would not have won one at all.

Yesterday

bay filly, 27-2-2000

		Nearctic	Nearco
			Lady Angela
	Northern Dancer		
		Natalma	Native Dancer
Sadler's Wells			Almahmoud
b 1981			
		Bold Reason	Hail To Reason
			Lalun
	Fairy Bridge		
		Special	Forli
			Thong
		Shirley Heights	Mill Reef
			Hardiemma
	Darshaan		
		Delsy	Abdos
Jude			Kelty
b 1994			
		Crystal Palace	Caro
			Hermieres
	Alruccaba		
		Allara	Zeddaan
			Nucciolina

Bred by Premier Bloodstock in Ireland

Sire Sadler's Wells

Won 6 of 11 races, inc. Beresford S.-Gr3, Irish Derby Trial-Gr2, Irish 2,000 Guineas-Gr1, Eclipse S.-Gr1, Phoenix Champion S.-Gr1. Also 2nd in Prix du Jockey-Club-Gr1, King George VI & Queen Elizabeth S.-Gr1. Impeccably bred top-class performer from 8-12f, handsome, tough and consistent. Sire of Gr1 winners: Braashee, French Glory, In The Wings, Old Vic, Prince Of Dance, Scenic, Salsabil, Opera House, Saddlers' Hall, El Prado, Johann Quatz, Masad, Barathea, Fatherland, Fort Wood, Intrepidity, Carnegie, King's Theatre, Northern Spur, Moonshell, Muncie, Poliglote, Chief Contender, Dance Design, Luna Wells, Cloudings, Ebadiyla, Entrepreneur, In Command, Kayf Tara, Dream Well, Greek Dance, King Of Kings, Leggera, Commander Collins, Daliapour, Montjeu, Saffron Walden, Aristotle, Beat Hollow, Subtle Power, Galileo, Imagine, Milan, Perfect Soul, Sequoyah, Ballingarry, Black Sam Bellamy, Gossamer, High Chaparral, Islington, Quarter Moon, Sholokhov, Alberto Giacometti, Brian Boru, Refuse To Bend, Yesterday.

Dam Jude

Unplaced in 4 starts, sold 92,000gns Tattersalls December Sales. Sister to smart 2yo Alouette (dam of Albanova, Alborada) and Irish Oaks 3rd Arrikala, half-sister to Alleluia (Gr3) and Last Second (Gr2). Dam of: Quarter Moon (1999 f by Sadler's Wells; Gr1 winner), Yesterday (2000 f by Sadler's Wells; Classic winner), Because (2001 f by Sadler's Wells; unraced), 2002 c by Sadler's Wells, 2003 c by Sadler's Wells.

Pedigree assessment

Her temperament may have been different from her sister Quarter Moon, but the two fillies had similar racing careers; both were at least smart at 2, both stayed 12f but were effective over 1m and 10f. The family is best known for its performers around 10f, hence the touch of speed both fillies possessed. There are several high-class racemares being covered by top stallions very close up in Yesterday's pedigree, which helps to make her a priceless broodmare prospect. *JH*

Zafeen (Fr)

3yo bay colt　　　　　　　　　　　　　　　　　　123

Zafonic (USA) - Shy Lady (Fr) (Kaldoun (Fr))

Owner Godolphin

Trainer Saeed Bin Suroor

Breeder Gainsborough Stud Management Ltd

Career: **11** starts | won **3** | second **4** | third **0** | **£342,967** win and place

By Tom Segal

A NUMBER of components are needed to rise to the top in any profession. Ability is no doubt the major prerequisite, but the importance of luck should never be underestimated. With a fair roll of the dice, Zafeen could have been the premier three-year-old miler of his generation and enjoyed a far higher profile.

It seems very strange to categorise the St James's Palace Stakes winner as underrated, but that is almost certainly the case with Zafeen who, even in victory, was never given the credit he deserved, the gloss being taken off his Royal Ascot performance by the perceived ill fortune of the runner-up, Kalaman.

It was not Zafeen's fault that Kalaman did not have the speed to get himself out of a sticky situation. In contrast, Zafeen did everything right at Ascot, travelling with the natural exuberance and authority of a top-class racehorse on his favoured fast ground and quickening clear when asked. Yes, Kalaman was stopped in his run and charged home late on, but that was only after Zafeen had put the race firmly to bed in a matter of strides.

Maybe if Mick Channon's colt had come into the Ascot race with the reputation of Kalaman then the aftermath would have been different, but through no fault of his own Zafeen came into the race with three straight defeats by his name, and in Britain horses who lose, whatever the circumstances, are seldom held in the same regard as horses who win, whatever the company they keep.

Zafeen needed his comeback run when beaten in the Greenham at Newbury, but the 2,000 Guineas was a different matter, and that is the race which will go down as the big one that got away. The Rowley Mile at Newmarket has become a nightmare for the clerk of the course whenever there is a dry spring, because if the stalls are left in the middle of the track there is a huge advantage racing up the far side, as Mister Baileys

Zafeen (Darryll Holland) holds the unlucky-in-running Kalaman in the St James's Palace Stakes at Royal Ascot

and Rock Of Gibraltar have proved, while trouble in running is nigh on guaranteed if the stalls are left on the stands side. In fact, the two Newmarket Classics can be among the roughest races of the year, with all those drawn low fighting for a position and getting in each other's way, a situation which can allow a clear run up the outside for a horse drawn very high, like Golan and Refuse To Bend, the winners in 2001 and 2003 respectively.

From his single-figure draw Zafeen certainly was not the worst sufferer, but neither did he enjoy anything like a clear passage, being stopped in his run on three separate occasions. Refuse To Bend had flown by the time he got into the clear and he failed by three-quarters of a length

2003   Race record

4th Sussex Stakes (Group 1) (Goodwood, July 30) 3yo+ 1m Good to soft **117** (TS 85) 9 ran. *Tracked leaders, effort to lead just over 2f out, narrowly headed over 1f out, every chance well inside final furlong, no extra last 75yds, beaten ½l by Reel Buddy*

1st St James's Palace Stakes (Group 1) (Ascot, June 17) 3yo 1m Good to firm **123** (TS 109) 11 ran. *Tracked leaders, ridden to challenge when hung right just inside final 2f, led well over 1f out, driven out, beat Kalaman by 1l*

14th Entenmann's Irish 2,000 Guineas (Group 1) (Curragh, May 24) 3yo 1m Soft **96** 16 ran. *Prominent on farside, close 5th 3f out, weakened from 2f out, beaten 11l by Indian Haven*

2nd Sagitta 2,000 Guineas (Group 1) (Newmarket, May 3) 3yo 1m Good **116** (TS 109) 20 ran. *Tracked leaders, ridden over 1f, not clear run inside final furlong, ran on, beaten ¾l by Refuse To Bend*

2nd Lane's End Greenham Stakes (Group 3) (Newbury, April 12) 3yo 7f Good to firm **109** (TS 75) 8 ran. *Held up in touch, ridden 2f out, quickened to lead over 1f out, headed just inside final furlong, kept on but not pace of winner, beaten 1¼l by Muqbil*

2002

4th Darley Dewhurst Stakes (Group 1) (Newmarket, October 19) 2yo 7f Good **109** (TS 75) 16 ran ● **5th** Shadwell Stud Middle Park Stakes (Group 1) (Newmarket, October 3) 2yo 6f Good to firm **102** (TS 68) 10 ran ● **1st** Dubai Duty Free Mill Reef Stakes (Group 2) (Newbury, September 20) 2yo 6f Good to firm **112** (TS 54) 8 ran ● **2nd** Prix Morny Casinos Barriere (Group 1) (Deauville, August 25) 2yo 6f Good **114** (TS 85) 6 ran ● **1st** Phil Small Marquees Maiden Stakes (Salisbury, July 26) 2yo 6f Good to firm **79** (TS 29) 7 ran ● **2nd** EBF Netton Maiden Stakes (Salisbury, July 5) 2yo 6f Good **77** (TS 26) 11 ran

to peg him back.

Given Zafeen's style of racing and pedigree, the soft ground at The Curragh for the Irish 2,000 Guineas was never going to be his cup of tea. Those who say that a good horse will go on any ground are talking nonsense, and conditions that day were desperate. To add to Zafeen's problems, he got trapped on the wide outside while all the action was taking place on the stands rail.

The speed Zafeen showed at Royal Ascot was still in evidence on his only subsequent start in the Sussex Stakes at Glorious Goodwood, but the rain-softened ground did not play to his strengths. That said, it was more the way the race was run that led to his downfall because the three horses who filled the placings were last turning for home, indicating that the others had started their runs for home too early. Zafeen did best of them in fourth place, but it was another case of what might have been.

Godolphin bought Zafeen privately after Goodwood and, in terms of natural ability, they will have few better horses in 2004. Considering how well they do with their older horses it will be surprising if he does not make up for lost time and win one or more of the top mile races, and he shows so much speed that it would not be the greatest surprise if he was dropped back to six furlongs for a race like the July Cup, provided the ground was fast.

Zafeen

bay colt, 25-4-2000

Zafonic b 1990	Gone West	Mr Prospector	Raise A Native Gold Digger
		Secrettame	Secretariat Tamerett
	Zaizafon	The Minstrel	Northern Dancer Fleur
		Mofida	Right Tack Wold Lass
Shy Lady b 1994	Kaldoun	Caro	Fortino Chambord
		Katana	Le Haar Embellie
	Shy Danceuse	Groom Dancer	Blushing Groom Featherhill
		Shy Princess	Irish River Shy Dawn

Bred by Gainsborough Stud Management in France

Sire Zafonic

Won 5 of 7 races, inc. Prix Morny-Gr1, Prix de la Salamandre-Gr1, Dewhurst S.-Gr1, 2,000 Guineas-Gr1. Big, powerfully built, commanding individual, splendid mover. Bled when well beaten in Sussex S.-Gr1, final start. Sire of: Xaar (Prix de la Salamandre-Gr1, Dewhurst S.-Gr1), Alrassaam (Gr2), Kareymah (Gr3), Shenck (Gr2), Pacino (Gr2), Clearing (Gr3), Count Dubois (Gran Criterium-Gr1), Endless Summer (Gr2), Ozone Layer (Gr3), Dupont (Gr2), Ibn Al Haitham (Gr3), Maybe Forever (Gr3), Zee Zee Top (Prix de l'Opera-Gr1), Zipping (Gr2), Aynthia (Gr3), Trade Fair (Gr3), Zafeen (St James's Palace S.-Gr1).

Dam Shy Lady

Won 2 of 3 races at 2 in Germany, notably 6f Listed Oppenheim Rennen. Half-sister to 10f Listed winner Sweet Story out of half-sister to high-class sprinter Diffident. Dam of: Ya Hajar (1999 f by Lycius; Gr3 winner), Zafeen (2000 c by Zafonic; Gr1 winner), Lady Marshall (2001 f by Octagonal; non-winner), Min Asl Wafi (2002 f by Octagonal).

Pedigree assessment

Milers have predominated among Zafonic's best progeny, and Shy Lady brought to him the pedigree of a miler, hence Zafeen's ideal trip. Zafeen is from a tough family full of progressive horses, whereas the late Zafonic has tended to excel with his younger offspring. If Zafeen has inherited the family toughness, then he could well be close to the top of the mile rankings again next year. *JH*

Zee Zee Top

4yo bay filly **116**

Zafonic (USA) - Colorspin (Fr) (High Top)

Owner Helena Springfield Ltd

Trainer Sir Michael Stoute

Breeder Meon Valley Stud

Career: **7** starts │ won **3** │ second **1** │ third **2** │ **£157,717** win and place

By Mark Blackman

SIR MICHAEL STOUTE raced just three four-year-old fillies in 2003, so to win Group 1 races with two of the three must go down as an impressive strike-rate. But while Yorkshire Oaks and Breeders' Cup Filly & Mare Turf winner Islington had already scored twice at that level, Zee Zee Top's prospects of gaining top-grade success would have been altogether less obvious at the start of her campaign.

This product of Meon Valley Stud's long-standing broodmare Colorspin – also the dam of Opera House and Kayf Tara – did not see a racecourse until the October of her three-year-old season, when she won a Pontefract maiden and finished a promising second to Salim Toto in a Listed race at Newmarket. Two days short of the anniversary of her debut win, she thundered up the rain-sodden Longchamp straight on Arc day to narrowly defeat Yesterday – the winner of one Classic, and desperately unlucky in another – and hot favourite Bright Sky, also a Classic winner, in a thrilling renewal of the Prix de l'Opera.

Stablemates of Yesterday and Bright Sky helped to force a very strong pace at Longchamp, with the result that the first five home all came from well off the speed, and with varying degrees of luck in running. Turning into the straight, the eventual first and second were filling the last two positions, but it was Kieren Fallon who was first to find running room aboard Zee Zee Top, and that proved decisive. He conjured from her a tremendous surge in the final quarter-mile, passing virtually the whole field and mastering Bright Sky close home before holding the late flurry of Yesterday, who was never quite able to get to her after the winner had got first run.

Afterwards, connections of Zee Zee Top pointed to the rain-softened ground – which she was encountering for the first time since her Newmarket run the previous autumn – as the reason for her improvement. According to Racing Post Ratings, she improved around 8-10lb on the level of form

Zee Zee Top (Kieren Fallon, spots) just gets the better of Yesterday to win the Prix de l'Opera at Longchamp

at which she had seemingly reached a plateau in Group company, so it is reasonable to conclude that the underfoot conditions were an important factor.

Until her Opera win, Zee Zee Top had been campaigned in Pattern races on much faster ground in Britain and Ireland and, while she had posted form that clearly marked her down as smart, she had begun to look exposed as just below Group 1 class. An impressive Listed victory on her reappearance at York in May was followed in June by an unlucky run in the Group 2 Pretty Polly Stakes at The Curragh, where she struggled to find running room when it was needed a furlong and a half out but finished strongly to take second behind Hanami. She was subsequently placed behind the third home, Snippets, having been deemed to have caused interference when angling for her challenge.

Stoute saw enough there to convince him that his filly was ready for a step up to Group 1 company and she was pitched in against her

2003   Race record

1st Prix de l'Opera - Casino Barriere d'Enghien (Group 1) (Longchamp, October 5) 3yo+ 10f Holding **116** (TS 91) 11 ran. *Towards rear, 10th on rails straight, pushed along 2f out, driven and headway 1½f out, ran on strongly to lead close home, driven out, beat Yesterday by hd*

6th Aston Upthorpe Yorkshire Oaks (Group 1) (York, August 20) 3yo+ 12f Good to firm **108** (TS 98) 8 ran. *Tracked leaders, ridden and outpaced over 4f out, kept on final 2f, beaten 6½l by Islington*

3rd Vodafone Nassau Stakes (Group 1) (Goodwood, August 2) 3yo+ 10f Good **107** (TS 98) 8 ran. *Slowly into stride, recovered to lead after 2f, headed 3f out, hampered on inner over 2f out and soon outpaced, ran on again to take 3rd near finish, beaten 5¼l by Russian Rhythm*

3rd (disq from 2nd) Audi Pretty Polly Stakes (Group 2) (Curragh, June 28) 3yo+ 10f Good **105** (TS 89) 8 ran. *Tracked leaders on inner, 3rd early straight, not clear run when switched left 1½f out, every chance 1f out, kept on well, finished 2nd, placed 3rd behind Hanami*

1st tote.co.uk Middleton Stakes (Listed) (York, May 14) 4yo+ 10½f Good to firm **107** (TS 67) 6 ran. *Tracked leaders, lead over 5f out, ridden 2f out, kept on well final furlong, beat Chorist by 1l*

2002

2nd Lanwades Stud Severals Stakes (Listed) (Newmarket, October 17) 3yo+ 10f Good to soft **102** (TS 82) 15 ran ● **1st** Caroni Maiden Stakes (Pontefract, October 7) 3yo 1m Firm **72** (TS 29) 6 ran

stablemate Russian Rhythm, the 1,000 Guineas and Coronation Stakes winner, in the Nassau Stakes over ten furlongs at Glorious Goodwood. Slowly into her stride in a field of eight, she took up the running after a quarter of a mile but was swamped when the pace increased, though she showed great tenacity to battle back for third.

It was a run that suggested a step up to a mile and a half might be in her favour and she duly lined up next time in the Yorkshire Oaks – again as 'second string' to an illustrious stablemate, this time Islington. While seemingly disappointing in sixth, beaten over six lengths, her performance was arguably a career-best effort at the time and she did not appear to lack for stamina, keeping on well in the closing stages. Those stamina reserves undoubtedly served her well at Longchamp six weeks later.

Zee Zee Top's Racing Post Rating of 116 was the lowest awarded to a winner of the Prix de l'Opera since the race was elevated to Group 1 status in 2000, when Stoute was also successful, with Petrushka.

There is little doubt that, with Yesterday seemingly unlucky, Bright Sky running below her best and rank outsider Nashwan Rose beaten only around three lengths in seventh, this was not a performance to have the purists looking for somewhere to sit down and digest what they had just seen.

None of that will have concerned her connections, for whom another Group 1-winning descendant of Reprocolor, Colorspin's dam, is plenty enough cause for celebration. Zee Zee Top has been retired and returns to her owners' Meon Valley Stud, where she was bred.

Zee Zee Top

bay filly, 21-4-1999

Zafonic b 1990	Gone West	Mr Prospector	Raise A Native Gold Digger
		Secrettame	Secretariat Tamerett
	Zaizafon	The Minstrel	Northern Dancer Fleur
		Mofida	Right Tack Wold Lass
Colorspin b 1983	High Top	Derring-do	Darius Sipsey Bridge
		Camenae	Vimy Madrilene
	Reprocolor	Jimmy Reppin	Midsummer Night Sweet Molly
		Blue Queen	Majority Blue Hill Queen

Bred by Meon Valley Stud in Britain

Sire Zafonic

Won 5 of 7 races, inc. Prix Morny-Gr1, Prix de la Salamandre-Gr1, Dewhurst S.-Gr1, 2,000 Guineas-Gr1. Big, powerfully built, commanding individual, splendid mover. Bled when well beaten in Sussex S.-Gr1, final start. Sire of: Xaar (Prix de la Salamandre-Gr1, Dewhurst S.-Gr1), Alrassaam (Gr2), Kareymah (Gr3), Shenck (Gr2), Pacino (Gr2), Clearing (Gr3), Count Dubois (Gran Criterium-Gr1), Endless Summer (Gr2), Ozone Layer (Gr3), Dupont (Gr2), Ibn Al Haitham (Gr3), Maybe Forever (Gr3), Zee Zee Top (Prix de l'Opera-Gr1), Zipping (Gr2), Aynthia (Gr3), Trade Fair (Gr3), Zafeen (St James's Palace S.-Gr1).

Dam Colorspin

Won 3 of 7 races, inc. Irish Oaks-Gr1. Stayed 12f well, best on ground with give. By 2,000 Guineas winner whose legacy has been stamina, out of high-class 10f+ filly and influential broodmare. Dam of: Opera House (1988 c by Sadler's Wells; multiple Gr1 winner), Highland Dress (1989 c by Lomond; winner, Gr2-placed), Polanski (1991 c by Polish Precedent; placed), Stencil (1992 g by Nashwan; unplaced), Color Precedent (1993 f by Polish Precedent; unraced), Kayf Tara (1994 c by Sadler's Wells; multiple Gr1 winner), Spinning The Yarn (1996 f by Barathea; unplaced, dam of Gr1 winner Necklace), Mafnood (1997 c by Rainbow Quest; non-winner), Turn Of A Century (1998 f by Halling; winner), Zee Zee Top (1999 f by Zafonic; Gr1 winner), Feel Good Factor (2000 g by Singspiel; placed), 2001 c by Mark Of Esteem.

Pedigree assessment

A Group 1-winning half-sister to two Group 1 winners, plus the dam of another, out of an Irish Oaks winner equals an extremely valuable broodmare prospect. Zafonic injected a touch of extra pace into Zee Zee Top, who was quite late maturing in common with many of her relatives. With no Sadler's Wells (who links so well with the family), one cross of Northern Dancer and no Never Bend in her pedigree, Zee Zee Top will have plenty of top-class mating options. *JH*

The young pretenders

of 2003

Figure in bold by each horse's name is its definitive Racing Post Rating

Comments by Richard Austen (RA), Graham Dench (GD) and Simon Turner (ST)

Pedigree assessments by Tony Morris (TM) and Janet Hickman (JH)

Akimbo (USA)   94+

b c Kingmambo (USA) - All At Sea (USA) (Riverman (USA)) April 1
Owner K Abdullah **Trainer** H R A Cecil **Breeder** Juddmonte Farms
1 start: won **0**, second **1**, **£2,264** win and place

HENRY CECIL has endured a couple of lean years by his standards but has an exciting colt on his hands in the shape of Akimbo. All the rage at 8-11 on his debut in a warm seven-furlong maiden at Newbury in August, he found John Dunlop's exciting Mukafeh just too good, but showed more than enough in defeat to suggest he could have a big future.

Ridden up with the pace, Akimbo quickened clear of a strong field with Mukafeh, the pair having a good tussle. The official distances did not convey the superiority they had over the remainder of the field and Akimbo can safely be regarded as significantly better than the bare form,

Race record
2nd Stan James Online EBF Maiden Stakes (Newbury, August 16) 2yo 7f Good to firm **94** (TS 64) 11 ran.

Pedigree assessment
Sire Kingmambo (Mr Prospector) High-class 2yo, progressed into top-class miler at three, won three Group 1 races including Poulains and St James's Palace Stakes. Superbly bred, out of Miesque. Excellent US-based sire, has good record with 2yos but does best with older progeny at up to 1m (Dubai Destination, King's Best, Malhub, Russian Rhythm), occasionally gets a top-class 10f+ horse. **Dam All At Sea** Won over 1m at two and showed top-class form over 1m (won Prix du Moulin) to 12f (2nd Oaks) at three. Her six earlier foals include several useful performers at up to 1m, including miler Insinuate (by Mr Prospector). **Conclusion** All At Sea had more pace than her Oaks second indicates and is passing it on. Akimbo looks set to be a miler.

which is decent enough as it stands anyway, with the third, fifth and sixth all going on to win their maidens.

Not seen again as a juvenile, Akimbo is one of the most exciting maidens in training, and if he comes to hand early enough he could well head to the 2,000 Guineas. He was widely quoted in ante-post lists for the Guineas in the autumn and, even if that level of competition proves too hot, he should be a force at Listed level at least. *ST*

Always First   88+

b c Barathea (Ire) - Pink Cristal (Dilum (USA)) March 29
Owner Saeed Suhail **Trainer** Sir Michael Stoute **Breeder** D B Clark and A L and Mrs Penfold **1 start:** won **1**, **£7,255** win and place

THE future looks very bright for Always First, who could not have been more impressive in winning a strong seven-furlong conditions event at Sandown in August. The omens were not good for the first foal of Pink

Akimbo: one of the most exciting maidens in training

Cristal beforehand, as stable jockey Kieren Fallon was unable to ride and his odds drifted worryingly before the off. What's more, once the race was underway things seemed to be happening a bit too quickly, as he was first off the bridle and running green at halfway. However,

Race record
1st Pizza Hut UK Conditions Stakes (Sandown, August 13) 2yo 7f Good to firm **88** (TS 78) 6 ran.
Pedigree assessment
Sire Barathea (Sadler's Wells) Promising dual 7f winner at 2, later top-class miler, won Irish 2,000 Guineas and Breeders' Cup Mile, also respectable form over 6f and 12f. Good sire, does well with 2yos (Barathea Guest, Tobougg) and milers (Enrique). **Dam Pink Crista**l Unraced at 2, later showed useful form over 7-8f. Half-sister to smart 8-10f horse Crystal Hearted and to dam of high-class 2yos Crystal Music and Solar Crystal and high-class 10-12f filly State Crystal. This is her first foal. **Conclusion** Should stay 1m, has outside chance of staying 10f.

as he met the rising ground the complexion of the race changed dramatically and he picked up well to dispatch some solid markers with ease.

The form of the Sandown contest is very strong, with runner-up Mutahayya going on to win a conditions event at Chester before placing in Listed company and third-placed Gwaihir doing even better, collecting a Listed prize before finishing runner-up in the Group 3 Thomas Bryon at Saint-Cloud. Sir Michael Stoute and Saeed Suhail, who have won Classics with Kris Kin and King's Best in recent years, have another top-class prospect on their hands in Always First, who sits in the 'could be anything' drawer at this stage of his career. *ST*

American Post 117

See entry in the top 100 horses, page 28

Antonius Pius (USA) 104

b c Danzig (USA) - Catchascatchcan (Pursuit Of Love) April 23
Owner M Tabor & Mrs John Magnier **Trainer** A P O'Brien **Breeder** Dr T Ryan
3 starts: won **2**, second **0**, third **0**, **£58,818** win and place

ANTONIUS PIUS looked a potential star for Aidan O'Brien after winning his first two starts, but the jury is most definitely out as to which way the $1.5m colt will go.

The son of Danzig made a highly satisfactory winning debut in the first seven-furlong two-year-old maiden of the season at Gowran Park – an event O'Brien has farmed in recent years, succeeding with Group 1 winners Landseer and Spartacus among others. Racing prominently throughout, he dispatched his two rivals comfortably by six lengths.

Stepped back to six furlongs for his second start in the Group 2 Railway Stakes, Antonius Pius maintained his unbeaten record in good style, tracking the leaders before delivering a late winning challenge to

Race record
11th Darley Dewhurst Stakes (Group 1) (Newmarket, October 18) 2yo 7f Good to firm **102** (TS 92) 12 ran.
1st Anheuser Busch Railway Stakes (Group 2) (Curragh, June 29) 2yo 6f Good **104** (TS 97) 7 ran.
1st May EBF Maiden (Gowran Park, May 14) 2yo 7f Yielding to soft **84** 3 ran.

Pedigree assessment
Sire Danzig (Northern Dancer) Unbeaten winner of three minor races at 2 and 3 at up to 7f in US. Outstanding sire, excels with 2yos, sprinters and milers, only rarely gets high-class horses over 10f+. **Dam Catchascatchcan** Unraced at 2, progressed into high-class 12f filly at 3, won Yorkshire Oaks, unbeaten. By sprinter but from stout family. This is her first foal. **Conclusion** Given the dam's stamina, there is a chance Antonius Pius could be one of Danzig's middle-distance horses. Should stay 10f, just possible he may last 12f.

see off Andrew Balding's Spanish Ace. Everything looked bright at that stage, but Spanish Ace failed to advertise the form and when Antonius Pius reappeared after a break in the Dewhurst he was uneasy in the market and ultimately well held after running too free for his own good behind surprise winner Milk It Mick. It is far too soon to be writing him off, but he will have something to prove at three. *ST*

Apsis 104+

b c Barathea (Ire) - Apogee (Shirley Heights) March 12
Owner K Abdullah **Trainer** A Fabre **Breeder** Juddmonte Farms
2 starts: won **2**, **£30,844** win and place

"EASILY." That was the word the Racing Post's French reporter plumped for to sum up the manner in which Apsis won both his races. "Made all, easily" and "quickened to lead over 1f out, easily". Those are the shorthand descriptions of two performances that mark Apsis down as a horse to reckon with as a three-year-old.

It is a shame he did not take on Bago in the Criterium International at Saint-Cloud in November, and his bare form cannot rival what Bago accomplished in that Group 1, but the Prix Thomas Bryon over the same course and distance just over two weeks earlier suggested that Apsis might have been a serious adversary.

Apsis was 3-5 favourite for the Group 3 over a mile, the same odds

Race record
1st Prix Thomas Bryon (Group 3) (Saint-Cloud, October 14) 2yo 1m Good to soft 104 (TS 87) 6 ran.
1st Prix de Fontenoy (Longchamp, September 20) 2yo 1m Good 79 4 ran.

Pedigree assessment
Sire **Barathea** (Sadler's Wells) Useful 7f winner at two, progressed into top-class miler, won Irish 2,000 Guineas and Breeders' Cup Mile. Also showed useful form over 6f and 12f. Good record as a sire, especially with 2yos (Barathea Guest, Charming Prince, Tobougg) and older performers over 1m+ (Enrique, Shield). **Dam Apogee** Smart French 3yo, won 12f Group 3 event. Daughter of Oaks/Irish Oaks 2nd Bourbon Girl. Her five earlier foals include two middle-distance fillies in France by Sadler's Wells, namely high-class Dance Routine and useful Light Ballet. A stout family which has produced several good 12f horses by Sadler's Wells. Barathea is not such a strong stamina influence, but Apsis should be effective over 10f and has a good chance of staying further.

he held when seeing off three rivals in a newcomers' event over the same distance on good ground at Longchamp in September, with horses carrying the Wertheimer and Wildenstein colours forced into the minor placings as he made all. The Thomas Bryon field contained only two more runners, but second and third favourites Always King and Gwaihir had both won Listed races on their previous starts and the other three all brought form from Group or Listed races. Apsis was tucked in this time and was impressive again, going past the front-running Gwaihir before the final furlong and cruising home three lengths ahead, with the rest strung out.

Barathea was a miler, but he gets plenty of horses who stay further and the dam's side of the pedigree, jam-packed with good mile-and-a-half performers, suggests Apsis will be one of them. Perhaps he will reappear over middle distances. His owner, Khalid Abdullah, has a strong candidate for the Poule d'Essai des Poulains in American Post. *RA*

Attraction   117

See entry in the top 100 horses, page 36

Auditorium   112

b c Royal Applause - Degree (Warning) March 30
Owner Cheveley Park Stud **Trainer** Sir Michael Stoute **Breeder** Old Mill Stud and
S C Williams **5 starts:** won **2**, second **1**, third **0**, **£61,153** win and place

ONE would hardly have guessed that Auditorium was one of Sir Michael
Stoute's very best two-year-old colts when he finished only eighth of 12
on his debut at Newmarket in July, but that is undoubtedly the case.
Indeed, while yet to win in better than Listed grade, he is clearly a
Group winner waiting to happen and he would be just the sort for a
race like Royal Ascot's Jersey Stakes if he falls short in either class or
stamina in the Classic trials.

Auditorium may well have fooled Stoute himself, for the colt showed

Race record
4th Shadwell Stud Middle Park Stakes (Group 1) (Newmarket, October 3) 2yo 6f Good to firm **112** (TS 98) 12 ran.
2nd Champagne Stakes (Group 2) (Doncaster, September 12) 2yo 7f Good **112** (TS 83) 6 ran.
1st Ripon Champion Two Yrs Old Trophy (Listed) (Ripon, August 25) 2yo 6f Good to firm **105** (TS 78) 4 ran.
1st Jacobean Maiden Stakes (Pontefract, August 6) 2yo 6f Good to firm **80** (TS 68) 7 ran.
8th Invesco Perpetual Maiden Stakes (Newmarket (July), July 19) 2yo 6f Good to firm **68** 12 ran.

Pedigree assessment
Sire Royal Applause (Waajib) Top-class 2yo and sprinter, won six Group races, notably
Middle Park Stakes and Haydock Sprint Cup. Very good sprint sire, excels with 2yos (Majestic Missile,
Mister Cosmi, Nevisian Lad, Peak To Creek), also sire of Acclamation. **Dam Degree** Modest 1m
winner at 4. Dam of two earlier foals , notably high-class sprint 2yo Mister Cosmi (also by Royal
Applause), a 1m Listed winner at 3 in Germany. **Conclusion** Given the record of his sire and
brother, he is not guaranteed to improve on his record at 3. Should remain best at up to 7f.

so little at home that he was not given any big-race entries and had to
be supplemented for both Doncaster's Champagne Stakes and the
Middle Park at Newmarket after following up a maiden win at Pontefract
by easily taking the scalp of prolific winner and big earner Peak To Creek
in the Champion Two Yrs Old Trophy at Ripon.

In purely financial terms the supplementary entries were only a
qualified success. Yet Auditorium enhanced his reputation no end by
running the high-class Lucky Story to a neck over seven furlongs at

Auditorium: a Group winner waiting to happen

Doncaster and he did it no harm when fourth to Three Valleys, beaten only a length and a half, at Newmarket. At Doncaster he and the winner bumped one another in the last half-furlong or so but still left hot favourite Haafhd trailing two lengths behind in third. At Newmarket he was soon being pushed along by Kieren Fallon, who reported he was still immature, but responded to the champion's urgings and ran to a similar level of form in failing by only a neck to claim third from Holborn. *GD*

Azamour (Ire) 109+

b c Night Shift (USA) - Asmara (USA) (Lear Fan (USA)) March 8
Owner H H Aga Khan **Trainer** John M Oxx **Breeder** His Highness The Aga Khan's Studs **2** starts: won **2**, **£63,311** win and place

COMPARISONS with Alamshar were inevitable after Azamour had followed in his stablemate's footsteps by landing the Group 2 Juddmonte Beresford Stakes at The Curragh in October. But while Azamour also carried the Aga Khan's colours and was described by John Oxx as possibly the best in his promising team of two-year-olds, he is likely to have a very different programme as a three-year-old.

The Beresford was only Azamour's second race and followed an impressive debut defeat of Pulitser in a seven-furlong maiden on the same course, where his opponents were mainly fellow newcomers. His second outing represented a far tougher task for him, but the Derby quotes that were handed out after he had got the better of front-running Relaxed Gesture in determined fashion and scored by a neck were almost certainly premature. As Oxx pointed out, his pedigree suggests

Race record
1st Juddmonte Beresford Stakes (Group 2) (Curragh, October 12) 2yo 1m Good to yielding **109** (TS 66) 6 ran.

1st Pizza Stop EBF Maiden (Curragh, September 14) 2yo 7f Good to firm **98** (TS 59) 9 ran.

Pedigree assessment
Sire Night Shift (Northern Dancer) minor winner over 6f at three. Very effective sire, generally an influence for speed, has good record with 2yos, sprinters and milers (Baron's Pit, Deportivo, Eveningperformance, Lochangel, Nicolotte), occasionally gets top-class performers over further (Daryaba, In The Groove). **Dam Asmara** 7f 2yo winner, later won 10f Listed event and showed useful form over 7-10f. Half-sister to high-class 10-12f performer Astarabad (by Alleged). Her 3 earlier foals have won over 7f, 2 of them as 2yos. **Conclusion** Has already won over 1m but that should be the limit of his stamina on pedigree.

stamina limitations, and indeed he may prove best at around a mile.

Although Relaxed Gesture is much better than his subsequent defeat at Santa Anita suggests, the Beresford did not work out as well as the earlier maiden race did. Nevertheless, Azamour remains a smart prospect and is surely a colt we will hear plenty more of. The Irish 2,000 Guineas looks an obvious early target if connections choose to avoid One Cool Cat and company at Newmarket. *GD*

Bachelor Duke (USA) 114+

b c Miswaki (USA) - Gossamer (USA) (Seattle Slew (USA)) March 11
Owner Duke Of Devonshire **Trainer** J A R Toller **Breeder** Airlie Stud
3 starts: won **0**, second **0**, third **2**, **£18,969** win and place

BACHELOR DUKE'S next chance to get off the mark may come in the 2,000 Guineas. He has had three opportunities so far and failed to take them, but failure simply isn't an appropriate word to use for a horse who was touched off in the Group 3 Somerville Tattersall Stakes and beaten only about a length and a half in the Group 1 Dewhurst.

Those two pieces of smart form were crammed into a two-year-old campaign that lasted all of one month and one day. Commencing as second favourite in a seven-furlong maiden at Yarmouth on September 17, Bachelor Duke was green but ran on well to finish third of 15. On October 2 he was third again, but this time at 25-1 in the eight-runner Somerville Tattersall, when he came just two necks away from winning.

The result of that race was not widely thought to have much bearing when the winner, Milk It Mick, and Bachelor Duke returned to Newmarket for the Dewhurst, sent off at 33-1 and 25-1 respectively in the midst of all those well-touted colts from the major stables, but Milk It Mick won it and Bachelor Duke too earned a glowing report. Held up in rear, Bachelor Duke had to make his bid through the middle of the pack and, with whips flailing in front of him from the jockeys on his left and right, he

Race record
4th Darley Dewhurst Stakes (Group 1) (Newmarket, October 18) 2yo 7f Good to firm **114** (TS 104) 12 ran.
3rd Somerville Tattersall Stakes (Group 3) (Newmarket, October 2) 2yo 7f Good to firm **111** (TS 94) 8 ran.
3rd EBF Maiden Stakes (Yarmouth, September 17) 2yo 7f Good to firm **73** (TS 66) 15 ran.

Pedigree assessment
Sire Miswaki (Mr Prospector) Top-class French 2yo over 6-7f, later showed high-class form in US. Very good sire, does well with 2yos (Abou Zouz, Rossini) and with older horses at wide variety of distances (Kistena, Urban Sea). **Dam Gossamer** Won twice in US, half-sister to smart 2yo and miler Miss Tobacco. Her three earlier foals include Bachelor Duke's very close relative Translucid, useful over 10-12f. **Conclusion** Should be suited by 1m, only has outside chance of lasting 10f.

was hit over the head more than once. He looked to find his stride only in the last 100 yards and, while he was not making dramatic inroads, he stayed on well enough for fourth.

A €125,000 yearling purchase, Bachelor Duke will relish at least a mile and has the physique of a good three-year-old prospect. His trainer, James Toller, had a Classic horse in 2003 in the filly Hanami, who arguably ran her best race in the Guineas on her reappearance. Bachelor Duke could be significantly better. *RA*

Badminton   103

b f Zieten (USA) - Badawi (USA) (Diesis) February 23
Owner Sheikh Marwan Al Maktoum **Trainer** C E Brittain **Breeder** Darley
3 starts: won **1**, second **1**, third **1**, **£42,125** win and place

THIS filly is "the next Crimplene", according to her trainer Clive Brittain. The latter clause has sometimes seemed a weighty proviso, given that the veteran trainer has held a fair number of his charges in high regard, but the 2003 campaign was his best for several years and it is easy to see why he is so enthusiastic about Badminton. There is a very long way to go, but Badminton ended her two-year-old season having shown very similar form to Crimplene at the same stage four years earlier.

It is Crimplene's three-year-old achievements, of course, rather than what she did at two years, that would make her a fine horse to emulate. Also owned by Sheikh Marwan Al Maktoum, Crimplene improved dramatically in the first few months of the 2000 turf season and her campaign took her to seven different countries, with wins in both the German and Irish Guineas, the Coronation Stakes and the Nassau.

Crimplene ended her first season with third place in the Cheveley Park Stakes and Badminton filled the same position, following a debut success in a five-runner maiden at Doncaster in June and a second of nine to Carry On Katie in the Group 2 Lowther at York just under two months later. Badminton put in her best work late on at York, beaten two

Race record

3rd Sky Bet Cheveley Park Stakes (Group 1) (Newmarket, October 2) 2yo 6f Good to firm **103** (TS 61) 10 ran.

2nd Peugeot Lowther Stakes (Group 2) (York, August 21) 2yo 6f Good to firm **103** (TS 81) 9 ran.

1st bet365 call 08000 322 365 EBF Maiden Fillies' Stakes (Doncaster, June 28) 2yo 6f Good to firm **79** (TS 57) 5 ran.

Pedigree assessment

Sire Zieten (Danzig) Top-class 2yo, won Middle Park S, later high-class performer over 5-7f. Bred for speed, brother to top-class 2yo Blue Duster. Useful speed sire, does well with 2yos (Seazun, Torgau). **Dam Badawi** Unraced at 2, later useful 8-9f winner. Her 6 earlier foals include fair 6-7f 3yo winner Cala (by Desert Prince) and several winners around 1m. **Conclusion** Has good chance of staying 1m, but may prove most effective at slightly shorter.

lengths, and was staying on again when going down by fractionally less to the same winner in the Cheveley Park.

The step up to a mile, probably via one or more of the Classic trials, is one obvious move that could see Badminton make marked improvement. Raced only at six furlongs on good to firm ground, she has looked game so far and is worth considering among the Guineas outsiders. Whether she will be the next Crimplene remains to be seen, but one thing is for sure – there will not be another Clive Brittain. *RA*

Bago   118+

See entry in the top 100 horses, page 40

Balmont (USA)   115

b c Stravinsky (USA) - Aldebaran Light (USA) (Seattle Slew (USA)) March 11
Owner Sanford R Robertson **Trainer** J Noseda **Breeder** Sanford R Robertson
6 starts: won 3, second 2, third 0, £123,719 win and place

CONNECTIONS of Balmont, including retiring jockey Pat Eddery, received an unexpected bonus the day after the turf season ended when it emerged that Three Valleys had tested positive for clenbuterol after

Balmont: driven out by Pat Eddery in the Gimcrack

Race record

7th Darley Dewhurst Stakes (Group 1) (Newmarket, October 18) 2yo 7f Good to firm **111** (TS 102) 12 ran.

2nd Shadwell Stud Middle Park Stakes (Group 1) (Newmarket, October 3) 2yo 6f Good to firm **115** (TS 100) 12 ran.

1st Scottish Equitable Gimcrack Stakes (Group 2) (York, August 20) 2yo 6f Good to firm **113** (TS 99) 9 ran.

1st Stan James 08000 383 384 EBF Novice Stakes (Newmarket (July), July 25) 2yo 6f Good **73** (TS 39) 4 ran.

1st Donns Solicitors Maiden Stakes (Doncaster, July 10) 2yo 6f Good to firm **89** (TS 52) 10 ran.

2nd NGK Spark Plugs Maiden Stakes (Newmarket (July), June 20) 2yo 6f Good to firm **84** (TS 51) 7 ran.

Pedigree assessment

Sire Stravinsky (Nureyev) High-class 2yo over 6-7f, progressed into top-class sprinter at 3, won July Cup and Nunthorpe Stakes. Encouraging start this year with first 2yos, also sire of 6f Listed winner Venables. **Dam Aldebaran Light** Triple winner at 3 in US, half-sister to smart US sprinter Blazonry. Balmont is her first foal. **Conclusion** Not guaranteed to stay a mile, although sire is an unknown quantity with his older horses.

winning the Middle Park Stakes and faced virtually inevitable disqualification. Balmont will be the chief beneficiary when Three Valleys' case goes to Portman Square, for he had finished an excellent second in the Middle Park, albeit beaten fair and square by three-quarters of a length after having his chance. The circumstances might be far from ideal, but Group 1-winning status will not sit too uncomfortably on the colt's shoulders as he had already won another of the season's most prestigious juvenile prizes, when taking the Gimcrack Stakes at York.

The Gimcrack, in which Balmont settled nicely on the lead and kept pulling out more to hold Fokine gamely by a head, completed a hat-trick of front-running six-furlong wins. It was the first race in which he had been seriously tested – following a debut second at Newmarket he had won his maiden at Doncaster pretty much as he liked and been found even easier pickings when a 1-11 winner of a conditions race at Newmarket – and he answered every call in commendable fashion.

Balmont's season ended on a flat note in the Dewhurst, in which he finished only seventh behind Milk It Mick. His odds of 10-1 in a field of 12 looked a fair reflection of his chance and few expected him to win, but he was entitled to finish a few places closer. It might simply have been one run too many, but an alternative explanation emerged the following morning when he was found to be lame on his near fore. Eddery had told Jeremy Noseda that Balmont had not stretched out in the race when he came off the bridle and it transpired that he had popped an abscess in his heel, a matter of no long-term concern but a viable explanation for a below-par performance.

Balmont shapes as if he will get the mile of the 2,000 Guineas, but if he has serious Classic pretensions they probably lie abroad. Wherever he is campaigned, however, he ought to continue to acquit himself with credit. *GD*

Barbajuan (Ire) 112

b c Danehill Dancer (Ire) - Courtier (Saddlers' Hall (Ire)) January 29
Owner Team Havana **Trainer** N A Callaghan **Breeder** Liam Brennan
7 starts: won 3, second **0**, third **1**, **£82,232** win and place

THERE was understandably a temptation to conclude that Barbajuan was flattered by his seemingly much-improved defeat of Milk It Mick in the Solario Stakes at Sandown. The form of his earlier wins at Lingfield and Kempton and his fourth in the Coventry would not have come within 20lb of what he appeared to achieve, and the Solario was a tactical race in which Darryll Holland gave Barbajuan a canny front-running ride on unseasonably soft ground and came alone up the far rail in the straight, while some of those racing up the centre, the runner-up in particular, did not have the race run to suit them.

That notion was dispelled, however, when Barbajuan was stepped up to Group 1 company for the National Stakes at The Curragh and the Gran Criterium at San Siro. His Curragh fourth behind One Cool Cat in one of the most competitive juvenile races of the season more than confirmed his new-found status among the leading juvenile colts, while a San Siro third to fellow British challenger Pearl Of Love was arguably an even better effort.

It is hard to know what the future holds for Barbajuan, since he was

Race record

3rd Gran Criterium (Group 1) (San Siro, October 19) 2yo 1m Good **112** 11 ran.
4th Dunnes Stores National Stakes (Group 1) (Curragh, September 14) 2yo 7f Good to firm **109** (TS 83) 8 ran.
1st Iveco Daily Solario Stakes (Group 3) (Sandown, August 30) 2yo 7f Good to soft **109** (TS 89) 8 ran.
5th Weatherbys Superlative Stakes (Group 3) (Newmarket (July), July 10) 2yo 7f Good to firm **88** (TS 89) 9 ran.
4th Coventry Stakes (Group 3) (Ascot, June 17) 2yo 6f Good to firm **88** (TS 78) 13 ran.
1st Manor Conditions Stakes (Kempton, May 24) 2yo 6f Good to firm **87** (TS 67) 7 ran.
1st EBF Maiden Stakes (Lingfield, May 9) 2yo 5f Good **75** (TS 63) 7 ran.

Pedigree assessment

Sire Danehill Dancer (Danehill) Top-class 2yo, won Phoenix and National Stakes and 2nd Dewhurst. At 3, won 7f Greenham Stakes but later showed useful sprint form. Good sire of 2yos and older horses at up to 1m (Choisir, Lady Dominatrix, Venturi, Where Or When, Ziria). **Dam Courtier** Unraced, should have stayed beyond 1m, from family of high-class 10-12f filly Hawajiss and several good 2yos. **Conclusion** Should be effective at 1m and plenty of encouragement from sire and dam's family that he will train on.

clearly quite a precocious individual at two and his pedigree is not that of a colt who is likely to improve significantly as he steps up in distance. Indeed while the San Siro race, in which he finished closer to Pearl Of Love than he had done at The Curragh, suggests he gets a mile, one would not bet on him staying a great deal further. However, it is a good sign that he was still improving at the end of the season and the indications so far are that he is not unduly beholden to the ground, although it remains to be seen how effective he is on extremes. *GD*

Bayeux (USA)   111

b c Red Ransom (USA) - Elizabeth Bay (USA) (Mr Prospector (USA)) April 8
Owner Sheikh Mohammed **Trainer** D R Loder **Breeder** Darley
3 starts: won **1**, second **1**, third **0**, **£17,001** win and place

IT WOULD have been hard to enthuse about Bayeux after he had trailed home only eighth of nine behind Kings Point in the seven-furlong Superlative Stakes at Newmarket's July meeting. He started joint-favourite on the strength of a debut win from similarly promising types in heavy mist at Goodwood but was in trouble with more than a furlong to go and was beaten more than 11 lengths.

However, a breathing problem was suggested at the time as an explanation – it was possibly significant that it was the only occasion he has been fitted with a tongue tie – and it was a very different Bayeux who returned to the track for the Somerville Tattersall Stakes over the same distance on Newmarket's Rowley course in October. The 9-4 favourite in a field of eight, David Loder having revealed beforehand that

Race record

2nd Somerville Tattersall Stakes (Group 3) (Newmarket, October 2) 2yo 7f Good to firm **111** (TS 94) 8 ran.

8th Weatherbys Superlative Stakes (Group 3) (Newmarket (July), July 10) 2yo 7f Good to firm **74** (TS 72) 9 ran.

1st Joe Mitford Faucets 'A Lifetime In Racing' EBF Maiden Stakes (Goodwood, May 21) 2yo 6f Good to firm **82** (TS 70) 13 ran.

Pedigree assessment

Sire Red Ransom (Roberto) Won both starts at 2 (5-6f) in minor company, placed sole start at 3. Highly promising, but career cut short by injury. Quite stoutly bred and likely to have stayed beyond 1m. Good sire of 2yos (Sri Pekan) and older horses over 8-12f (Casual Look, Ekraar, Intikhab). **Dam Elizabeth Bay** Gr3 winner at 2, later very smart miler. By outstanding sire out of a top-class US dirt performer at around 1m. Her two earlier foals (both by Danzig) have won over 1m. **Conclusion** Has the pedigree of a miler.

he felt the problem had been rectified, Bayeux got the better of a good tussle with the once-raced outsider Bachelor Duke, only to be headed near the finish by Milk It Mick.

While the Somerville Tattersall clearly represented useful form, it looked unexceptional at the time. But that was then. When Milk It Mick won the Dewhurst a fortnight later, with Bachelor Duke fourth, it looked rather stronger. Bayeux will be an interesting proposition when he returns for Godolphin after a winter in Dubai and steps up to a mile or more. *GD*

Boogie Street   104

b c Compton Place - Tart And A Half (Distant Relative) March 13
Owner Hippodrome Racing **Trainer** R Hannon **Breeder** Raffin Bloodstock
5 starts: won 2, second 0, third 1, £16,723 win and place

GOING into 2003, Richard Hannon trained a useful and unbeaten colt by Compton Place called Captain Saif. As a three-year-old Captain Saif proved something of a disaster, failing to win again, and that's one of the few cautionary notes – not a substantial one – attached to the year-younger Compton Place colt Boogie Street, who could easily make up into a smart sprinter.

Hannon had a lucrative success with another Compton Place juvenile in 2003, thanks to If Paradise in the Weatherbys Super Sprint, but Boogie Street looks the potential star. In a maiden at Sandown in August at just the second time of asking Boogie Street showed that he was a useful performer, his eight-length win prompting Richard Hughes to remark: "He's decent and he'll be even better when he gets some company. I had a look two out expecting something to be coming, but there was nothing there. He'll stay six furlongs, but why go further just

Boogie Street: potentially a top-notch sprinter

Race record

1st Christine Sadler Designer Harry Rosebery Stakes (Listed) (Ayr, September 18) 2yo 5f Good **104** (TS 92) 9 ran.

4th Polypipe Flying Childers Stakes (Group 2) (Doncaster, September 13) 2yo 5f Good **94** (TS 73) 13 ran.

3rd EBF Bobby Lorenz 60th Birthday Novice Median Auction Stakes (Windsor, August 23) 2yo 6f Good to firm **83** (TS 78) 9 ran.

1st Platinum Security Median Auction Maiden Stakes (Sandown, August 13) 2yo 5f Good to firm **89** (TS 82) 7 ran.

5th EBF Crocker Bulteel Maiden Stakes (Ascot, July 26) 2yo 6f Good **68** (TS 44) 7 ran.

Pedigree assessment

Sire Compton Place (Indian Ridge) Smart sprint 2yo, later won July Cup. Oldest progeny 3, capable of siring smart performers at up to 1m (If Paradise, Pleasure Place). **Dam Tart And A Half** Won over 5f at 2, later hardy, fair sprinter, from tough but modest family. Two previous foals made no impact. **Conclusion** Speedily bred on both sides of his pedigree and will be a sprinter.

now when he has that sort of speed?"

Surprisingly, Boogie Street was tried over six furlongs and beaten, but he was back on track in two subsequent appearances back at five, with fourth place in the Flying Childers at Doncaster, where he was hampered at halfway, and a smooth victory in a Listed race at Ayr. He wore a tongue tie for both those starts and comfortably reversed placings with the Flying Childers third Nights Cross on good ground at Ayr, making all to break the track record in a line-up that also contained If Paradise.

Flying Childers winner Howick Falls and Cornwallis victor Majestic Missile were better sprinters at two, but Boogie Street is a strapping colt who is open to further improvement and will surely be placed to win more good races. *RA*

Byron

108

b c Green Desert (USA) - Gay Gallanta (USA) (Woodman (USA)) April 5
Owner Sheikh Mohammed **Trainer** D R Loder **Breeder** Cheveley Park Stud
4 starts: won 2, second 0, third 1, £52,113 win and place

IT IS a mystery how Byron could be allowed to go off at 9-1 to beat old rival Grand Reward in Newbury's Mill Reef Stakes, and trainer David Loder was as surprised as anyone. Byron had finished a neck in front of Grand Reward when the pair were third and fourth respectively behind Balmont in the Gimcrack at York, before the placings were reversed, yet Grand Reward was a 4-9 chance at Newbury. It is true that Byron had checked Grand Reward just as the Aidan O'Brien colt was starting his move at York, but he had not had things his own way entirely, having been none too well away, and the pair's starting prices were completely at odds with their theoretical chances.

In the Mill Reef, which lacked strength in depth but was run at a strong gallop thanks to the O'Brien pacemaker Born In America, Byron led

---

Race record
1st Dubai Duty Free Mill Reef Stakes (Group 2) (Newbury, September 19) 2yo 6f Good to firm **106** (TS 97) 10 ran.
4th Scottish Equitable Gimcrack Stakes (Group 2) (York, August 20) 2yo 6f Good to firm **108** (TS 75) 9 ran.
3rd TNT July Stakes (Group 2) (Newmarket (July), July 9) 2yo 6f Good to firm **106** (TS 72) 8 ran.
1st NGK Spark Plugs Maiden Stakes (Newmarket (July), June 20) 2yo 6f Good to firm **89** (TS 57) 7 ran.

Pedigree assessment
Sire Green Desert (Danzig) High-class sprint 2yo, top-class sprinter-miler at 3, won July Cup and 2nd 2,000 Guineas. Excellent sire, excels with 2yos (Bint Allayl, Oasis Dream) and older horses at up to 1m (Cape Cross, Desert Prince, Owington, Sheikh Albadou, Tamarisk). **Dam Gay Gallanta** Won Queen Mary and Cheveley Park Stakes at 2, and showed smart placed form over 1m at 3. From superb family. Her four earlier foals include useful 2yo and sprinter Gallivant (by Danehill, thus very closely related to Byron). **Conclusion** Possibilities that he will stay 1m at 3 but probably will be suited by shorter and may be a sprinter. Dam best at 2 but many family members train on well.

---

approaching the furlong marker but then wandered left and right before holding on by three-quarters of a length. Grand Reward took second from Tahreeb close home.

The Mill Reef was Byron's fourth and last race of the season. An all-the-way winner from Balmont on his debut at Newmarket, he was then pitched straight into Group 2 company in the July Stakes on the same course, where he showed a lot of speed before finishing third to Nevisian Lad.

Loder said after the Mill Reef that he thought Byron would get a mile at three. However, both his pedigree and style of racing suggest that is doubtful. He joined Godolphin at the end of the year. *GD*

Cairns (UAE)   104+

b f Cadeaux Genereux - Tanami (Green Desert (USA)) April 5
Owner Sheikh Mohammed **Trainer** M R Channon **Breeder** Darley Dubai
2 starts: won **2, £38,557** win and place

CAIRNS has been switched to Godolphin to winter in Dubai, where she will presumably appear in one of the trials to determine her suitability for a Guineas challenge. She already carries the United Arab Emirates suffix, having been born there, and an unbeaten two-race career as a juvenile suggests strongly that she will continue to prove a fine advert.

This is one Classic hopeful that Sheikh Mohammed owned already, but she was trained in 2003 by Mick Channon, who also had charge of two more UAE-bred two-year-olds in Cedarberg and Holborn, both of them, like Cairns, Group-race performers.

Cairns's appearance in a Group event came in the Rockfel Stakes at

Race record

1st Owen Brown Rockfel Stakes (Group 2) (Newmarket, October 18) 2yo 7f Good to firm **104** (TS 94) 10 ran.
1st Sydenhams Maiden Stakes (Salisbury, September 16) 2yo 6f Good to firm **80** (TS 67) 11 ran.

Pedigree assessment

Sire Cadeaux Genereux (Young Generation) Unraced as a 2yo, top-class sprinter at three and four, also showed smart form over 7f and 1m. Very good sire, excels with 2yos (Bahamian Bounty, Embassy, Hoh Magic) but also gets progressive progeny, mostly at up to 1m (Touch Of The Blues). **Dam Tanami** Very smart 2yo over 5-6f, showed just fair form over 6-7f at three. Speedily bred on both sides of her pedigree. Her three earlier foals include a 5f 2yo winner and a successful sprinter. **Conclusion** Has proved effective at 7f but there has to be a doubt over 1m for her. In addition, she is precociously bred and there is no guarantee she will maintain her form at three on pedigree.

Newmarket on Champions Day, one month after winning a maiden over six furlongs at Salisbury, where she led inside the final furlong to score by a length at 10-1, amazing odds in hindsight given the performance she was about to put up at Newmarket.

A 12-1 chance against vastly stronger opposition in the seven-furlong Rockfel, Cairns was held up travelling smoothly but had to wait for a run and be switched to the outside to get it. Once in the clear, she cut down front-running favourite Snow Goose to win by one and a half lengths. Barry Hills's fancied duo Bay Tree and Tarot Card were disappointing, but the useful Snow Goose was on a four-timer, third-placed Kelucia had been third in the Oh So Sharp Stakes over course and distance two weeks earlier and fourth-placed Gracefully was a Group 3 winner.

Cairns needs to progress little to be regarded a bona fide Guineas candidate and she shapes as if she'll get a mile, although it's not guaranteed. *RA*

Carry On Katie 109

See entry in the top 100 horses, page 68

Charming Prince (Ire) 105

b c Barathea (Ire) - Most Charming (Fr) (Darshaan) January 20
Owner Maktoum Al Maktoum **Trainer** A Fabre **Breeder** Gainsborough Stud
Management 4 starts: won **2**, second **2**, **£82,279** win and place

TWO comprehensive defeats in his first campaign suggest that Charming Prince will be hard pressed to gain Classic victory in the Poulains or the Guineas, but he was still among the top two-year-old colts trained in France. He is also in the expert hands of André Fabre. Commencing 2004 without a Group-winning penalty, he looks sure to be placed to advantage as a three-year-old.

Charming Prince won his first two races, a minor event at Maisons-Laffitte in July and a Listed race at Vichy in August. At 1-2 in a

Race record
2nd Prix Jean Luc Lagardere (Grand Criterium) (Group 1) (Longchamp, October 5) 2yo 7f Holding **105** (TS 70) 6 ran.
2nd Prix la Rochette (Group 3) (Longchamp, September 11) 2yo 7f Soft **100** (TS 93) 7 ran.
1st Prix des Jouvenceaux et des Jouvencelles (Listed) (Vichy, August 6) 2yo 7f Good to soft **98** 5 ran.
1st Prix Dictaway (Maisons-Laffitte, July 18) 2yo 7f Good to soft **88** 9 ran.

Pedigree assessment
Sire **Barathea** (Sadler's Wells) Useful 7f winner at 2yo, progressed into top-class miler, won Irish 2,000 Guineas and Breeders' Cup Mile. Also showed useful form over 6f and 12f. Good record as a sire, especially with 2yos (Barathea Guest, Toboggg) and older performers over 1m+ (Enrique, Shield). Dam **Most Charming** Won over 1m at 2, later showed useful form over same distance. Grand-daughter of top-class 2yo and 1,000 Guineas winner Ma Biche. Her two earlier foals include a 6f 2yo winner by Marju. **Conclusion** Should be a miler.

five-runner race, the Listed contest went his way only in a bunched finish after overcoming trouble in running. In the Prix la Rochette at Longchamp five weeks later, Charming Prince again ran on late and to some effect, but it was good enough only for second behind his much better-fancied stable companion, the odds-on Diamond Green, who was never threatened.

Charming Prince might have been set too much to do in trying to come from the back of the field in the Rochette, grabbing second place in the final strides, and virtually the opposite tactics were adopted on him in the Prix Jean Luc Lagardere at the same track over three weeks later. In the late absence of Diamond Green because of the soft going, Charming

Charming Prince: looks to have a future as a miler

Prince started 14-10 favourite on the Pari-Mutuel in a six-runner renewal of the Group 1 but, after making the running, he had no answer to American Post and again had to settle for second.

All of Charming Prince's races as a two-year-old were over seven furlongs on an easy surface. One of two classy juveniles by Barathea in the care of Fabre in 2003, the other being Apsis, he comes from the family of Maktoum Al Maktoum's 1983 1,000 Guineas winner Ma Biche and should have no difficulty staying a mile himself. *RA*

Denebola   108

See entry in the top 100 horses, page 96

Diamond Green (Fr)   111+

br c Green Desert (USA) - Diamonaka (Fr) (Akarad (Fr)) April 7
Owner Lagardere Family **Trainer** A Fabre **Breeder** Jean-Luc Lagardere
3 starts: won 3, £36,364 win and place

THE decision to withdraw Diamond Green from the Prix Jean Luc Lagardere on the day of the race can only have been taken with great reluctance. The colt is owned by the Lagardere family and was expected to go off favourite for the first running of France's most prestigious two-year-old race under its new title, the Grand Criterium having been renamed in honour of France-Galop's late president, who had died in the spring.

The holding ground was given as the reason for the colt's withdrawal and, as things turned out, it was probably a shrewd move, for it would have taken another much-improved effort from him to have beaten American Post, who won in brilliant style by four lengths from Diamond Green's stablemate Charming Prince, and went on to confirm himself an outstanding prospect.

Diamond Green was not seen again and was put away for the winter

Race record
1st Prix la Rochette (Group 3) (Longchamp, September 11) 2yo 7f Soft **111** (TS 101) 7 ran.
1st Prix des Roches Noires (Deauville, August 19) 2yo 7f Good to soft **95** (TS 84) 5 ran.
1st Prix de Marolles (Unraced Colts & Geldings) (Deauville, July 6) 2yo 7f Good to soft 10 ran.

Pedigree assessment
Sire Green Desert (Danzig) High-class sprint 2yo, top-class sprinter-miler at 3, won July Cup and 2nd 2,000 Guineas. Excellent sire, excels with 2yos (Bint Allayl, Oasis Dream) and older horses at up to 1m (Cape Cross, Desert Prince, Owington, Sheikh Albadou, Tamarisk). **Dam Diamonaka** Smart filly over 12f in France. Half-sister to 10f+ Group winners Diamond Mix and Diasilixa. Her 6 earlier foals include 10f+ Group winners Diamilina and Diamonixa (both by Linamix). **Conclusion** Should stay 1m, may struggle to last 10f.

unbeaten in three races in which he improved each time and signed off with a two-and-a-half-length defeat of Charming Prince in the seven-furlong Prix la Rochette, also at Longchamp, in September. The ground was officially soft that day and he coped with it well, quickening up to win readily. He had won twice over seven furlongs at Deauville previously, bolting up by five lengths from subsequent Group 1 winner Voix du Nord when hot favourite for a newcomers race in July and following up with a smooth odds-on two-and-a-half-length defeat of Xapoteco in August. The obvious first target for Diamond Green is the Poule d'Essai des Poulains, where he could at last meet American Post. *GD*

Duke Of Venice (USA) 103

b c Theatrical - Rihan (USA) (Dayjur (USA)) March 25
Owner Sheikh Mohammed **Trainer** M Johnston **Breeder** Forenaghts Stud
3 starts: won **1**, second **0**, third **1**, **£5,035** win and place

"ANOTHER striking big horse who seems to cope effortlessly with all that we have thrown at him so far," was how Mark Johnston described Duke Of Venice in April. Those words would have been just about as appropriate when describing how the colt coped with a one-mile maiden race at Sandown in September, for while none of his ten rivals did anything noteworthy before or after the race, he did something remarkable for a maiden winner. He scorched home 13 lengths clear in a very good time.

If explanation was needed for the decision to supplement Duke Of Venice for the Dewhurst, Johnston provided it. He said: "I was asked if I thought Duke Of Venice was a Group 1 horse or a Group 3 horse. I thought he was a Group 1 horse and Sheikh Mohammed would prefer to have a

Race record
10th Darley Dewhurst Stakes (Group 1) (Newmarket, October 18) 2yo 7f Good to firm **103** (TS 94) 12 ran.
1st Ford Magic EBF Maiden Stakes (Sandown, September 17) 2yo 1m Good **100** (TS 98) 11 ran.
3rd EBF Maiden Stakes (Haydock, June 6) 2yo 6f Good to firm **72** (TS 75) 12 ran.

Pedigree assessment
Sire **Theatrical** (Nureyev) Smart middle-distance colt in Ireland, developed into top-class US performer, won Breeders' Cup Turf. Very good sire, particularly of turf performers over 10f+ (Broadway Flyer, Royal Anthem, Zagreb). Does get smart 2yos but progeny tend to progress well with age. Dam **Rihan** Fair 6f 2yo winner, daughter of Breeders' Cup Juvenile Fillies runner-up Sweet Roberta. Her only previous foal was unplaced in one start. **Conclusion** Has every chance of progressing well from two to three. Should stay 10f but not certain to last 12f.

shot at a Group 1 rather than go through the ranks at this time of year. He's an unknown quantity and it's a huge jump from winning a maiden . . . but he is a spectacular horse on the gallops. He is one of the few horses that has the speed to even lay upsides Attraction in her work."

In the Dewhurst, 13-2 shot Duke Of Venice, on his toes beforehand, lay up with the pace only until coming down the hill one and a half furlongs out and Frankie Dettori did not persevere with him in the final furlong. Johnston is sure that he has a great future and a return to further than seven furlongs will help.

Duke Of Venice is a tall colt and the type to improve significantly in his second season, as he did during the three-month absence that followed a debut third when he got upset in the stalls. He remains a colt to look forward to in 2004, when he will be with Godolphin. *RA*

Elshadi (Ire)   92

b c Cape Cross (Ire) - Rispoto (Mtoto) March 26
Owner Sheikh Ahmed Al Maktoum **Trainer** M P Tregoning **Breeder** Abbeville and Meadow Court Studs **3 starts: won 2**, second 0, third 0, **£15,812** win and place

IT WAS edge-of-the-seat stuff when Elshadi raced as a juvenile. Blinkered first time up over the stiff extended mile at Beverley, Elshadi showed plenty of pace to hold a good position before wandering somewhat under pressure close home. However, his wayward tendencies did not stop his forward momentum and he battled on well to beat the ill-fated Sun Of Speed. The half-brother to Highdown was stepped up significantly in grade at Newbury for his next start, the Haynes, Hanson and Clark Conditions Stakes, a race with a rich tradition as a source of high-class middle-distance three-year-olds. He produced a remarkable performance. Leading straight from the start, the son of Cape Cross appeared to be running far too freely early on under Martin Dwyer but had his opponents

- -

Race record

4th Tom McGee Autumn Stakes (Group 3) (Ascot, October 11) 2yo 1m Good to firm **74** (TS 50) 5 ran.

1st Haynes, Hanson And Clark Conditions Stakes (Newbury, September 19) 2yo 1m Good to firm **92** (TS 87) 5 ran.

1st EBF Beverley Lions Median Auction Maiden Stakes (Beverley, August 24) 2yo 8½f Good to firm **72** (TS 42) 12 ran.

Pedigree assessment

Sire Cape Cross (Green Desert) 1m winner at two, later high-class miler. Fair amount of speed in pedigree. Good start with first 2yos, mainly over 5-7f, sire of Gwaihir, Mokabra, Nights Cross, Privy Seal. **Dam Rispoto** Won over 12f at 3. Bred for middle distances, half-sister to 10f+ stakes performers Jahafil and Mondschein. Her 5 earlier foals feature high-class 10f performer Highdown (by Selkirk). **Conclusion** Plenty of stamina on the dam's side, rather less on the sire's. May last 10f but no further.

- -

in trouble a long way out and maintained a strong gallop to the line to leave them breathless. Newmarket maiden winner Let The Lion Roar, a half-brother to Millenary, finished a clear runner-up to help give the form a solid look.

Elshadi was a disappointing fourth on his only subsequent start when trying to repeat his front-running tactics in an Ascot conditions event won by Racing Post Trophy runner-up Fantastic View, but there were mitigating circumstances. Trainer Marcus Tregoning was unhappy with the heavily watered ground, Frankie Dettori did not force such a strong pace, and Elshadi reportedly returned home with a minor injury.

Forget Ascot. There was enough promise in his Newbury win to believe that Elshadi could be capable of winning some good races at three. *ST*

Fantastic View (USA) 110

ch c Distant View (USA) - Promptly (Ire) (Lead On Time (USA)) April 15
Owner Malih L Al Basti **Trainer** R Hannon **Breeder** George Strawbridge and London Thoroughbred Services 5 starts: won 3, second 2, £100,356 win & place

SUBSEQUENT Group-winning performances from recent winners Presenting, Beauchamp King, Dr Fong, Daliapour, Nayef, Fight Your Corner and Big Bad Bob, to say nothing of the 1988 victor Nashwan, helped make a decent case for the 2003 promotion of Ascot's Autumn Stakes from Listed to Group 3 status. The eyes are now fixed on Fantastic View.

Fantastic View: three wins and a Group 1 second

Race record

2nd Racing Post Trophy (Group 1) (Doncaster, October 25) 2yo 1m Good to firm **110** (TS 72) 4 ran.

1st Tom McGee Autumn Stakes (Group 3) (Ascot, October 11) 2yo 1m Good to firm **105** (TS 91) 5 ran.

1st Renault Van Range Stardom Stakes (Listed) (Goodwood, September 12) 2yo 1m Good **101** (TS 78) 8 ran.

2nd Butler & Co Equine Tax Planning EBF Novice Stakes (Salisbury, September 4) 2yo 1m Good to firm **96** (TS 74) 7 ran.

1st EBF Maiden Stakes (Ascot, July 25) 2yo 7f Good **85** (TS 94) 7 ran.

Pedigree assessment

Sire Distant View (Mr Prospector) Unraced at two, top-class miler at three, won Sussex Stakes. Very good US-based sire, does well with 2yos (Distant Music) and also with older progeny, generally around 1m, on both turf and dirt (Observatory, Sightseek). **Dam Promptly** Placed over 6f on only 2yo start and minor 6f winner at three, later won turf stakes event over an extended 1m in US. Her two earlier foals include 6-7f 2yo winner To The Rescue. **Conclusion** There is a fair amount of speed on the dam's side of his pedigree and 1m should prove to be his limit at three.

Steady improvement in five starts to date augurs well. Ridden by Pat Dobbs in all five, Fantastic View turned up for the Autumn Stakes with two wins under his belt already, in a seven-furlong maiden at Ascot in July and a Listed race over one mile at Goodwood in September. Starting 13-8 favourite against only four rivals, none more than twice raced, and with the Haynes, Hanson and Clark Stakes winner Elshadi reportedly unsuited by ground conditions amid allegations that the Ascot executive had overwatered, Fantastic View was not required to do anything remarkable to register win number three, but he did so smoothly by four lengths.

The Racing Post Trophy two weeks later was a much sterner test.

Fantastic View was supplemented into a very small field, but so was Prix Jean Luc Lagardere winner American Post, and the French colt was simply too good for him. After a steady early pace, however, Fantastic View was able to quicken past Magritte for second. Another improved show. "Our horse will win a Group 1 eventually," said Richard Hannon junior.

Ascot's mile can present a stiff test of stamina for a two-year-old and principals from the Racing Post Trophy usually figure more prominently in ante-post lists for the Derby, but the Guineas, or some version of it, is surely the more likely Classic assignment for Fantastic View judged on his pedigree. *RA*

Fokine (USA) 112

b c Royal Academy (USA) - Polar Bird (Thatching) April 18
Owner R E Sangster **Trainer** B W Hills **Breeder** Swettenham Stud
4 starts: won **1**, second **1**, third **0**, **£36,837** win and place

A CHOICE word spoken in the Manton dialect, or the Russian-born dancer and choreographer? The former might have seemed an apt inspiration for Fokine the racehorse judged by the post-race comments of his owner, Robert Sangster, after Fokine's winning debut at 12-1 in a novice stakes at the Newmarket July meeting. "We didn't fancy him at all and I went and backed Hannon's [Psychiatrist, who finished second]," said Sangster, adding that, "I'm lucky I wasn't playing on the exchanges, or I would have laid the winner as well."

Fokine didn't just win, he dashed clear in style, and the form was boosted by those behind him. In the Group 2 Richmond Stakes at

Race record
8th Shadwell Stud Middle Park Stakes (Group 1) (Newmarket, October 3) 2yo 6f Good to firm **105** (TS 90) 12 ran.
2nd Scottish Equitable Gimcrack Stakes (Group 2) (York, August 20) 2yo 6f Good to firm **112** (TS 99) 9 ran.
6th Four Star Sales Richmond Stakes (Group 2) (Goodwood, July 29) 2yo 6f Good 99 (TS 93) 7 ran.
1st Capannelle Racecourse EBF Novice Stakes (Newmarket (July), July 9) 2yo 6f Good to firm **94** (TS 65) 9 ran.

Pedigree assessment
Sire Royal Academy (Nijinsky) 6f winner at 2yo, progressed into top-class sprinter-miler at 3yo, won July Cup and Breeders' Cup Mile. Good sire, does get high-class sprint 2yos (Lavery) but does better with older horses, mostly at up to 1m (Ali-Royal, Carmine Lake, Sleepytime, Val Royal, Zalaiyka). **Dam Polar Bird** Smart 2yo over 5-6f, later showed useful form over 6f. Her six earlier foals include 6f 3yo winner Arctic Burst (also by Royal Academy) and high-class sprint 2yo and miling 3yo Ocean Ridge (by Storm Bird). **Conclusion** Speedily bred on both sides and should continue to appreciate 6f, though has possibilities of staying slightly further.

Goodwood three weeks later, therefore, Fokine started a well-backed 2-1 favourite. Sixth of seven might have prompted further mispronunciation for that renowned man of dance (1880-1942).

The Gimcrack Stakes at York in August showed Fokine in a vastly better light. He very nearly won it. Starting at 9-1 in a field of nine and racing close to the pacesetter Balmont from the word go, Fokine kept up the fight all the way and went down by just a head. "He is still a little bit weak and immature," reflected trainer Barry Hills, "and Michael [Hills, his jockey] feels he'll get further. He'll probably have just one more race this season, in the Middle Park."

On a line through Balmont, Fokine should have been in the thick of things in the Middle Park but, whereas Balmont finished runner-up, Fokine trailed about three lengths behind him in eighth, held up in rear and never able to challenge. Perhaps more forcing tactics would have suited him, but it is too early to make a confident judgement. His ideal trip is also open to debate. Confined to six furlongs so far, he may well have trouble getting a mile judged on his pedigree. *RA*

Fort Dignity (USA)   90+

b c Seeking The Gold (USA) - Kitza (Ire) (Danehill (USA)) February 6
Owner Britton House Stud **Trainer** Sir Michael Stoute **Breeder** Britton House Stud
1 start: won 1, £3,701 win and place

AS THE first foal of Irish 1,000 Guineas and Irish Oaks runner-up Kitza, Fort Dignity is bred to go a bit. Happily, he appears likely to make up into a smart performer.

Sir Michael Stoute's colt looked sure to benefit from the exercise when making his debut at Yarmouth in a warm novice event early in August but was still made an odds-on favourite on the strength of some promising home work. Green and looking far from the finished article during the early stages of the seven-furlong contest, Fort Dignity looked to be in

Race record
1st Constitution Motors Hyundai Novice Stakes (Yarmouth, August 6) 2yo 7f Good to firm **90** (TS 56) 6 ran.

Pedigree assessment
Sire Seeking The Gold (Mr Prospector) Top-class US dirt performer over 8-10f at three and four, won two Grade 1 events and 2nd Breeders' Cup Classic. Very effective sire, has had greatest overall impact with US dirt performers but notable in Europe as sire of Dubai Millennium and top-class 2yo Lujain. Rarely gets top-class performers over 10f+. **Dam Kitza** Quite useful 6f 2yo winner, improved at three to be smart from 8-12f, 2nd in Irish 1,000 Guineas/Oaks. Fairly speedy pedigree. This is her first foal. **Conclusion** Despite dam's Irish Oaks 2nd, this one is far from certain to stay much beyond 1m.

trouble before his rider momentarily got serious to get him racing. But once the penny dropped he came home in great style, leading well over a furlong out before comfortably getting the better of the decent yardstick Sew'N'So Character, who subsequently acquitted himself well off marks in the 90s in nurseries.

The manner of Fort Dignity's success strongly suggests he will be one of his powerful stable's premier league three-year-olds in 2004. He has shown enough pace to suggest the 2,000 Guineas could be an option, while there is enough stamina in his pedigree to offer a glimmer of hope that he might stay the Derby distance too. Whatever the future holds, Fort Dignity looks a most exciting young horse. *ST*

Grand Reward (USA) 112

b c Storm Cat (USA) - Serena's Song (USA) (Rahy (USA)) February 10
Owner M Tabor, Mrs J Magnier & Mrs B Lewis **Trainer** A P O'Brien **Breeder** Mr and Mrs R Lewis **4** starts: won **1**, second **1**, third **1**, £36,832 win and place

GRAND REWARD was one of the many of Aidan O'Brien's better two-year-olds who began their racing careers in Britain, winning a hot six-furlong Newbury maiden in May. Very strong in the market beforehand, the full-brother to top-class miler Sophisticat showed an impressive finishing burst to master subsequent July Stakes also-ran Farewell Gift.

Racegoers had to wait until York's Ebor meeting to see Grand Reward again, in the Gimcrack. Once again strong in the market, Grand Reward was ridden with plenty of confidence but met with interference over a furlong out which deprived him of a winning chance. Past the post in fourth, he was moved up a place following the demotion of Byron.

Most observers felt that without the trouble in running Grand Reward

Race record
6th Shadwell Stud Middle Park Stakes (Group 1) (Newmarket, October 3) 2yo 6f Good to firm **110** (TS 96) 12 ran.
2nd Dubai Duty Free Mill Reef Stakes (Group 2) (Newbury, September 19) 2yo 6f Good to firm **104** (TS 94) 10 ran.
3rd Scottish Equitable Gimcrack Stakes (Group 2) (York, August 20) 2yo 6f Good to firm **112** (TS 94) 9 ran.
1st Cantor Sport Maiden Stakes (Newbury, May 17) 2yo 6f Good **93** (TS 92) 14 ran.

Pedigree assessment
Sire Storm Cat (Storm Bird) Top-class US 2yo over 1m. Both sire and dam top-class 2yos. Outstanding US-based sire, European progeny generally excel at around 1m, best include Aljabr, Black Minnaloushe, Catrail, Giant's Causeway, Sophisticat. **Dam Serena's Song** Top class in US from 2 to 4, effective 8-9f on dirt. Her three earlier foals, all winners, feature top-class 2yo/miler Sophisticat. **Conclusion** Full-brother to a top-class miler and likely to follow suit distance wise. Serena's Song was progressive, as have been her foals, so should do well from 2 to 3.

Grand Reward: crying out for a mile

would have pushed narrow winner Balmont close in the Gimcrack and he was made a hot favourite for Newbury's Mill Reef Stakes, in which he was reopposed by Byron. A tardy start did not help, however, and he failed by three-quarters of a length to gain revenge on Byron.

Although O'Brien did not seem dissatisfied, Grand Reward had a question mark over him when he tried to redeem himself in a hot renewal of the Middle Park at Newmarket. Two pacemakers were employed to aid his cause, but to no avail. Once again he failed to deliver what work-watchers believe he is capable of. Yet to be tried beyond six furlongs, Grand Reward would seem to be crying out for a try over a mile and it is far too early to write him off. *ST*

Green Noon (Fr) 108

ch f Green Tune (USA) - Terring (Fr) (Bering) January 30
Owner Mme J-F Gerles **Trainer** C Lerner **Breeder** Gaetan Gilles & Ecurie Ouaki
Jules **4 starts:** won **3**, second **1**, **£73,474** win and place

GREEN NOON'S connections will be praying that Denebola runs in the 1,000 Guineas at Newmarket, rather than take the easier route and stay at home for the French equivalent, the Poule d'Essai des Pouliches. Denebola beat Green Noon fair and square in the Prix Marcel Boussac but Green Noon was another two lengths and more clear of a strong field, and in Denebola's absence she would be the one to beat back at Longchamp in May 2004.

There was no fluke whatsoever about Green Noon's fine effort in a race run at a fierce pace. Ridden by apprentice Yann Lerner, son of the filly's trainer, as she had been when winning all of her three previous races, she went to post third favourite in a field of 16, chiefly on the strength of her length-and-a-half defeat of Leila in the Group 3 Prix d'Aumale over the same course and distance the previous month, where she took it up inside the final furlong and won readily.

Race record

2nd Prix Marcel Boussac Royal Barriere de Deauville (Group 1) (Longchamp, October 5) 2yo 1m Holding **108** (TS 96) 16 ran.
1st Prix d'Aumale Casino Barriere de Biarritz (Group 3) (Longchamp, September 14) 2yo 1m Good to soft **101** (TS 68) 8 ran.
1st Prix Tanit (Deauville, August 19) 2yo 7f Good to soft **89** 4 ran.
1st Prix de Firfol (Unraced Fillies) (Deauville, July 6) 2yo 7f Good to soft **80** 13 ran.

Pedigree assessment

Sire Green Tune (Green Dancer) Useful 2yo winner, improved into top-class miler at 3 and 4, won Poulains and 9f Prix d'Ispahan. Half-brother to top-class 2yo/sprinter Pas de Reponse. Fair French sire, has decent record with 2yos, most progeny effective in 8-10f range. **Dam Terring** Unraced daughter of a Prix du Jockey-Club winner and a very useful sprint 2yo. This is her first foal. **Conclusion** Fair amount of pace close up on the distaff side of her pedigree, so though she is already proven at 1m she is far from certain to get the Prix de Diane distance of 10.5f.

That had been Green Noon's first appearance in Group company, following two seven-furlong wins at Deauville, but it will be Group races all the way from now on. Green Noon should be a force to reckon with at three. The Pouliches is likely to offer her best chance of Classic success, as she is by a miler out of a sprinter. She remains an unknown quantity on anything quicker than good to soft. *GD*

Grey Swallow   119+

See entry in the top 100 horses, page 154

Haafhd   114

ch c Alhaarth (Ire) - Al Bahathri (USA) (Blushing Groom (Fr)) February 18
Owner Hamdan Al Maktoum **Trainer** B W Hills **Breeder** Shadwell Estate Company
4 starts: won 2, second 0, third 2, £61,414 win and place

DESPITE renewals of fluctuating quality, the Washington Singer Stakes at Newbury in August boasts such a renowned list of former participants that the winner is always going to attract plenty of attention. Win it as

Race record

3rd Darley Dewhurst Stakes (Group 1) (Newmarket, October 18) 2yo 7f Good to firm **114** (TS 104) 12 ran.
3rd Champagne Stakes (Group 2) (Doncaster, September 12) 2yo 7f Good **107** (TS 77) 6 ran.
1st Stan James Online Stakes (Registered As The Washington Singer Stakes) (Listed) (Newbury, August 15) 2yo 7f Good to firm **109** (TS 106) 8 ran.
1st Hugo And The Huguenotes EBF Maiden Stakes (Newmarket (July), August 1) 2yo 6f Good to soft **89** (TS 75) 10 ran.

Pedigree assessment

Sire **Alhaarth** (Unfuwain) Unbeaten in five 7f races at 2, notably Dewhurst Stakes. Later showed high-class form over 8-10f. Good sire, does quite well with 2yos but better record with older horses at wide variety of trips, ranging from sprinter Dominica to 1m4f+ horses Bandari and Phoenix Reach, depending on dam. Dam **Al Bahathri** High-class 2yo over 6f, later top-class miler, won Irish 1,000 Guineas. Excellent broodmare, has produced several talented performers at up to 1m (Hasbah, Munir, Za-Im). **Conclusion** Likely to be suited by 1m and has pedigree to progress on 2yo form.

easily as Haafhd did, by five lengths, and a prominent position in the Classics lists is assured. This Listed race used to be for two-year-olds whose sires had won over at least a mile and a half. In 2003, it was for two-year-olds whose sires had won over 'one mile, about two furlongs or over' and, after some discussion, the BHB decreed that that included Haafhd's sire Alhaarth, who won the Prix Dollar over one mile, one furlong and 165 yards. With this sort of precision thinking, Haafhd might as well be described as 'just about the Dewhurst winner'.

The winner of a Newmarket maiden two weeks before the Washington Singer, Haafhd ran in two Group races after it, with the Dewhurst clearly his better effort. The Champagne at Doncaster had been a disappointment, with the 10-11 shot having to settle for third to Lucky Story and trainer Barry Hills reporting that Haafhd "could have been fitter". But he kept on stoutly to finish in the money in the Dewhurst, beaten about a length and a half by Milk It Mick, whom he had seen off with little fuss in the Washington Singer.

Haafhd is one of a stack of colts all within a few pounds of each other behind the top three or four in the two-year-old ratings and it is to be hoped that the Classic trials will help sort them out. *RA*

Holborn (UAE) 113

b c Green Desert (USA) - Court Lane (USA) (Machiavellian (USA)) February 26
Owner Sheikh Mohammed **Trainer** M R Channon **Breeder** Darley Dubai
7 starts: won **2**, second **0**, third **1**, **£55,694** win and place

THE Windsor Castle Stakes winner Holborn had yet to see a racecourse when Mick Channon singled him out as Royal Ascot material in one of the Racing Post's Pick 6 features, so all credit to the former England striker, whose reputation for having a very good eye for a two-year-old is well justified.

While the Windsor Castle is admittedly one of the Royal meeting's weakest events and Holborn had the advantage of being drawn right on the rail, it was still a good effort from the colt to overcome a slow start and win readily by a length and three-quarters from Vienna's Boy, with the subsequent Flying Childers winner, Howick Falls, another length and a quarter back in third.

Success at Royal Ascot, the first at the meeting for a horse bred in the United Arab Emirates, followed a debut win in a small field at Kempton. Surprisingly, however, it was Holborn's last win of the season. According to connections, he "went lazy" in the summer, so much so

Race record

3rd Shadwell Stud Middle Park Stakes (Group 1) (Newmarket, October 3) 2yo 6f Good to firm **113** (TS 98) 12 ran.
4th Dubai Duty Free Mill Reef Stakes (Group 2) (Newbury, September 19) 2yo 6f Good to firm **100** (TS 90) 10 ran.
4th Coral Sirenia Stakes (Group 3) (Kempton, September 6) 2yo 6f Good **98** (TS 72) 9 ran.
5th TNT July Stakes (Group 2) (Newmarket (July), July 9) 2yo 6f Good to firm **97** (TS 60) 8 ran.
1st Windsor Castle Stakes (Conditions Race) (Ascot, June 21) 2yo 5f Firm **98** (TS 101) 17 ran.
4th Isabel Morris Memorial Marble Hill Stakes (Listed) (Curragh, May 24) 2yo 5f Soft **91** (TS 89) 7 ran.
1st EBF Mike Ellis Maiden Stakes (Kempton, April 19) 2yo 5f Good to firm **88** (TS 84) 4 ran.

Pedigree assessment

Sire Green Desert (Danzig) High-class sprint 2yo, top-class sprinter-miler at three, won July Cup and 2nd 2,000 Guineas. Excellent sire, excels with 2yos (Bint Allayl, Oasis Dream) and older horses at up to 1m (Cape Cross, Desert Prince, Owington, Sheikh Albadou, Tamarisk). **Dam Court Lane** Won over 6f as a 2yo, later won over 1m, out of smart 2yo and sprinter Chicarica. This is her first foal. **Conclusion** Bred for speed and likely to continue to excel at sprint distances.

that he was tried, unsuccessfully, in a visor in Kempton's Sirenia Stakes. But there was more encouragement in his fourth to Byron in the Mill Reef Stakes at Newbury, and in the Middle Park Stakes at Newmarket on the final start he put up a performance that put all of his previous form in the shade and propelled him up the juvenile ranks to a position comfortably in the top 20.

Holborn was among the outsiders at 50-1 in what by common consent was a strong renewal of the Middle Park, but he was in the thick of the main action throughout and finished a very good third behind Three Valleys and Balmont, beaten little more than a length by the winner, with enough decent horses behind him to suggest that there was no fluke about it.

If he can reproduce the form at three he ought to have no trouble winning a Group 3 or possibly something a little better over six or seven furlongs. *GD*

Howick Falls: one of the season's fastest juveniles

Howick Falls (USA)   109

b c Stormin Fever (USA) - Hollins (USA) (Roanoke (USA)) February 1
Owner Sheikh Mohammed **Trainer** D R Loder **Breeder** Brereton C Jones
5 starts: won **3**, second **0**, third **1**, **£61,957** win and place

DAVID LODER toyed with running Howick Falls in the Prix de l'Abbaye
after the colt had overcome an awkward start to beat China Eyes by
three-quarters of a length in the Flying Childers Stakes at Doncaster.
One can only speculate upon how he might have fared at Longchamp,
for after consulting owner Sheikh Mohammed's team Loder eventually
rejected the idea and put Howick Falls away for the season. However,
two-year-olds enjoy such a hefty weight-for-age allowance in the Abbaye
that a well-developed colt like Howick Falls might well have made his
presence felt there with luck in running, as it turned out to be a far
from vintage renewal.

Howick Falls wore a visor in the Flying Childers, having been equipped
with one for the first time when trouncing the Super Sprint winner If
Paradise in the Roses Stakes at York. The application of headgear,
which Loder is prepared to use on unexposed two-year-olds probably
more than anyone, clearly helped, but the furlong-shorter trip was also
a factor, for speed is clearly Howick Falls' forte.

An early-season win at Newcastle and a subsequent third in Royal
Ascot's Windsor Castle Stakes had encouraged Loder to believe that Howick

Falls would be suited by six furlongs, but when tried at the trip in the July Stakes at Newmarket the colt shaped like a non-stayer. There is no question he looked much more at home back at five at York and Doncaster.

It will be interesting to see whether Howick Falls progresses sufficiently with Godolphin at three to pick up a major sprint prize, but with the exception of Cornwallis winner Majestic Missile there would be few better candidates among the juveniles of 2003. *GD*

Race record
1st Polypipe Flying Childers Stakes (Group 2) (Doncaster, September 13) 2yo 5f Good **109** (TS 90) 13 ran.
1st Costcutter Roses Stakes (Listed) (York, August 20) 2yo 5f Good to firm **106** (TS 90) 9 ran.
7th TNT July Stakes (Group 2) (Newmarket (July), July 9) 2yo 6f Good to firm **94** (TS 57) 8 ran.
3rd Windsor Castle Stakes (Conditions Race) (Ascot, June 21) 2yo 5f Firm **88** (TS 89) 17 ran.
1st Montana Wines Novice Stakes (Newcastle, May 22) 2yo 5f Good to soft **78** (TS 52) 7 ran.

Pedigree assessment
Sire Stormin Fever (Storm Cat) Minor 2yo winner in US, later progressed into very high-class dirt performer over 7-9f, won eight of 21 starts. First 2yos in 2003. **Dam Hollins** unraced half-sister to high-class 7-8f filly Laura's Pistolette. Her two earlier foals include a 3yo winner in US. **Conclusion** Fair amount of speed in his background and the signs are that Howick Falls has inherited it, though there is encouragement on pedigree that he will stay 7f.

Imperial Stride 112+

b c Indian Ridge - Place de l'Opera (Sadler's Wells (USA)) March 11
Owner Saeed Suhail **Trainer** Sir Michael Stoute **Breeder** Cliveden Stud
3 starts: won **2**, second **0**, third **0**, £16,162 win and place

IMPERIAL STRIDE is a close relation to the 2003 Irish 2,000 Guineas winner Indian Haven and the similarity does not end there, as he too may well have the class to earn his place in a Classic line-up. It would be much too bold to state here that he can win one, but his staying-on sixth in the Dewhurst suggests he deserves another crack at Group 1 glory.

The Dewhurst, jam-packed with some of the most promising colts around, was a radically different task to those that faced Imperial Stride when he easily saw off a total of eight opponents in a novice stakes at Yarmouth in May and a conditions stakes at Doncaster in July. A setback denied him any opportunity for further experience and he was slow to find his feet in the Dewhurst, fighting for his head when he saw daylight in the opening stages and hanging right, off the rails, when he was asked to improve from the rear. But he was beaten little more than two lengths behind the winner, Milk It Mick.

Race record
6th Darley Dewhurst Stakes (Group 1) (Newmarket, October 18) 2yo 7f Good to firm **112** (TS 102) 12 ran.
1st skybet.com Conditions Stakes (Doncaster, July 10) 2yo 7f Good to firm **91** (TS 77) 4 ran.
1st EBF Novice Stakes (Yarmouth, May 28) 2yo 6f Good to firm **75** (TS 56) 6 ran.

Pedigree assessment
Sire Indian Ridge (Ahonoora) Won at two, progressed into high-class performer over 5-7f at three and four. Excellent sire, does well with 2yos (Definite Article, Snow Ridge) and older progeny, mainly at up to 1m (Domedriver, Indian Haven, Namid, Ridgewood Pearl) but occasionally further (Indian Creek). **Dam Place de l'Opera** quite useful 12f winner. Stoutly bred, out of high-class 9-15f winner Madame Dubois. Her first two foals include Imperial Stride's brother High Pitched, a very smart 12f performer. **Conclusion** His brother stayed 12f but his very close relative Indian Haven won the Irish 2,000 Guineas. Imperial Stride will certainly appreciate step up to 1m and should stay 10f but there is a major doubt about him staying much further.

Plenty of other colts will resume in 2004 with similar form credentials – most of the Dewhurst field for a start – but Imperial Stride is a good-looking colt who could hardly be in better hands, so he has to be respected. He will be very well suited by the step up to a mile and by a good deal further if his brother, the St Simon Stakes winner High Pitched, is anything to go by. Indian Haven (whose dam is Imperial Stride's grandam) is more typical, though, of Indian Ridge's offspring in appearing to be a miler. *RA*

Kheleyf (USA)   103

b c Green Desert (USA) - Society Lady (USA) (Mr Prospector (USA)) January 11
Owner Sheikh Ahmed Al Maktoum **Trainer** D R Loder **Breeder** Darley
4 starts: won 2, second 1, third 0, £27,697 win and place

PLEASURE in the mornings and pain in the afternoons. This, seemingly, is what Kheleyf has so far given his connections – to say nothing of the Racing Post's Newmarket correspondent. Reports in the paper related how "his work has been of the highest order", that he had been "lapping, rather than just catching, the pigeons on the home gallops", and that "those privileged to witness his home work since have been in raptures". It looks safe to say that, from four actual races, wins in a maiden at York and a conditions stakes at Doncaster were not the anticipated haul and, with starting prices of 4-7 and 1-2, that nobody got rich backing him.

It wasn't just the work-watchers who were impressed, of course. What really sealed Kheleyf's talking-horse reputation was the talk from his jockey, Frankie Dettori. "I can safely say that only jockey error will get this horse beaten," said Dettori, rashly, before Royal Ascot. He also reportedly stated that Kheleyf was the best two-year-old he had ever sat on. Up against this, the efforts by Kheleyf's trainer, David Loder, to sound a much more cautionary note went in vain.

Dettori's two racecourse rides on Kheleyf would, therefore, have made unhappy viewing for him during the 'What happened next?' round in his role as team captain on A Question Of Sport. Jamie Spencer rode Kheleyf for his two wins, Dettori did so in two Group races and Kheleyf failed to make the grade. When push first came to shove, at 8-13 no less in the Norfolk Stakes at Royal Ascot, Kheleyf could not get to grips with Russian Valour. Dettori said that the colt was too green, Loder that

Race record

10th Shadwell Stud Middle Park Stakes (Group 1) (Newmarket, October 3) 2yo 6f Good to firm **101** (TS 85) 12 ran.
1st GNER Conditions Stakes (Doncaster, September 13) 2yo 6f Good **103** (TS 95) 6 ran.
2nd Norfolk Stakes (Group 3) (Ascot, June 19) 2yo 5f Good to firm **103** (TS 88) 8 ran.
1st ripleycollection.com Racing Jewellery Maiden Stakes (York, May 13) 2yo 5f Good to firm **101** (TS 69) 5 ran.

Pedigree assessment

Sire **Green Desert** (Danzig) High-class sprint 2yo, top-class sprinter-miler at three, won July Cup and 2nd 2,000 Guineas. Excellent sire, excels with 2yos (Bint Allayl, Oasis Dream) and older horses at up to 1m (Cape Cross, Desert Prince, Owington, Sheikh Albadou, Tamarisk). **Dam Society Lady** Placed over 7f at two. Her six earlier foals feature top-class sprint 2yo Bint Allayl (by Green Desert) and useful 2yo/sprinter Nasmatt (by Danehill) **Conclusion** Brother to Bint Allayl and very closely related to Nasmatt. There has to be a major doubt over his stamina for 1m and he could well be a sprinter.

he was a big horse who had gone "a bit weak" in the build-up. The Doncaster win followed a three-month break. Three weeks after that, Kheleyf was third favourite for the Middle Park and looked about to launch a challenge two furlongs out, but that hope had expired a furlong later. He finished tenth.

He is a brother to the ill-fated Bint Allayl, the top two-year-old filly of 1998, and his name reportedly means 'heir'. It's hard to be that bullish about his prospects, but his physical scope would usually mark him down as a good three-year-old prospect. He's no certainty to stay a mile. *RA*

Kinnaird (Ire)   108

ch f Dr Devious (Ire) - Ribot's Guest (Ire) (Be My Guest (USA)) February 27
Owner S A B Dinsmore **Trainer** P C Haslam **Breeder** Victor Stud
6 starts: won **5**, second **0**, third **0**, £69,371 win and place

FEW better bargains have been secured at the breeze-up sales than Kinnaird, who cost just 8,000 guineas at Doncaster in the spring but won her fifth race from only six starts when landing the Group 2 May Hill Stakes just over the road five months later. Her length-and-three-

Kheleyf: more than just a talking horse?

quarters defeat of Hathrah in ground much softer than the official description of "good" earned her long-odds quotes for the 1,000 Guineas. She is fully entitled to be trained for that race, especially as she is possibly a bit better than the bare form suggests, having been in front

Race record
1st Betdaq May Hill Stakes (Group 2) (Doncaster, September 11) 2yo 1m Good **108** (TS 107) 10 ran.
1st NSPCC Shergar Cup Juvenile (Auction Race) (Ascot, August 9) 2yo 7f Good to firm **96** (TS 89) 10 ran.
1st Lewis Geipel Challenge Cup Conditions Stakes (Thirsk, July 25) 2yo 7f Soft **91** (TS 95) 6 ran.
5th Dianne Nursery (Pontefract, July 8) 2yo 6f Good **79** (TS 43) 14 ran.
1st Scottish Daily Mail Novice Auction Stakes (Hamilton, June 26) 2yo 6f Firm **82** (TS 36) 6 ran.
1st Ben Raceday Maiden Auction Fillies' Stakes (Hamilton, June 12) 2yo 6f Good to soft **71** 14 ran.

Pedigree assessment
Sire **Dr Devious** (Ahonoora) Top-class 2yo, won Dewhurst Stakes. At three, unplaced in Kentucky Derby, then won Epsom Derby and Irish Champion Stakes. Retired to stud in Japan, later stood in Ireland. Overall stud record modest but is capable of getting very smart performers, generally over 1m+. Dam **Ribot's Guest** Unraced as a 2yo and unplaced in Italy as a 3yo. From fair middle-distance family. Her only previous foal has been placed over 6-7f. **Conclusion** Should continue to be effective at 1m and has a fair chance of staying 12f.

plenty soon enough according to Kevin Darley, who was riding her for the first time and was clearly taken with her.

Kinnaird was a 33-1 chance when making her debut in a humble maiden at Hamilton in June, but she belied her odds with a clear-cut win there and followed up when returned to the same track for a novice race a fortnight later. She raced prominently and was in front too soon in a race in which the leaders went too fast when meeting defeat for the only time so far in a nursery at Pontefract, but she had wasted little time putting that run behind her, bouncing back to win a conditions race at Thirsk and then beating colts in the Shergar Cup Juvenile at Ascot.

The step up to seven furlongs at Thirsk and Ascot clearly suited Kinnaird and she improved again when tackling a mile at Doncaster, so one has to wonder if she will have the speed to be effective at a mile at three, particularly at the top level. It is dangerous to be dogmatic with a filly who has already exceeded expectations, and connections are entitled to dream. However, she might need further. *GD*

Lucky Story   117

See entry in the top 100 horses, page 234

Magritte (Ire)   107

b c Sadler's Wells (USA) - Ionian Sea (Slip Anchor) March 9
Owner Mrs John Magnier **Trainer** A P O'Brien **Breeder** Orpendale
2 starts: won 1, second 0, third 1, £36,654 win and place

WHEN final declarations were made for the Racing Post Trophy in late October, Magritte was favourite at 6-4, American Post 7-4; on the morning of the race, Magritte still shaded favouritism in nearly all the major bookmakers' lists. That's Magritte, the Tipperary maiden winner, and American Post, the Group 1 Prix Jean Luc Lagardere winner.

It was not hard to spot the madness even without hindsight and raceday brought a major revision in the betting as American Post was

Race record
3rd Racing Post Trophy (Group 1) (Doncaster, October 25) 2yo 1m Good to firm **107** (TS 68) 4 ran.
1st Irish Stallion Farms EBF Maiden (Tipperary, July 20) 2yo 7½f Heavy **95** 12 ran.

Pedigree assessment
Sire Sadler's Wells (Northern Dancer) Smart 7-8f winner at two, improved into top-class colt over 8-12f at three, won Irish 2,000 Guineas, Eclipse and Irish Champion Stakes. Outstanding sire, particularly of 3yos+ over 8-12f, also has good record with autumn 2yos. **Dam Ionian Sea** Won 12f Listed race in France at 3. Half-sister to Derby 2nd Blue Stag and Prix du Jockey-Club 2nd Oscar (both by Sadler's Wells). Her five earlier foals have won, notably Derby 2nd The Great Gatsby (by Sadler's Wells). **Conclusion** Certain to stay 12f, may well relish further and has the pedigree to make considerable improvement from 2 to 3.

sent off at 5-6 and Magritte at 11-4. Magritte is, however, trained by Aidan O'Brien, whose four Racing Post Trophy wins in the previous six years were no doubt a factor in his odds, especially as Magritte was the trainer's choice from nine five-day entries. However, he had a lot to prove compared to American Post and was beaten by three lengths into third place.

As things turned out, Magritte almost certainly played against himself by setting a steady pace, the non-participation of the vastly longer-priced O'Brien colt Mikado possibly having upset the plans. Either way, American Post quickened past without difficulty and Fantastic View did so as well, before Magritte seemed to get going again in the final furlong. A brother to the 2003 Derby runner-up The Great Gatsby, Magritte's maiden win had come on heavy going and he looks much more of a stayer than the two that beat him on fast ground at Doncaster. A mile and a half at three years should see him in a much better light. *RA*

Majestic Desert 109

b f Fraam - Calcutta Queen (Night Shift (USA)) March 24
Owner Jaber Abdullah **Trainer** M R Channon **Breeder** Bloodhorse International
5 starts: won 2, second 2, third 1, £145,980 win and place

IT WAS by only the narrowest of margins that Majestic Desert failed to end Carry On Katie's unbeaten run in the Cheveley Park Stakes, and plenty will be fancying her to reverse the placings if they meet again in the 1,000 Guineas. In a finish dominated by the pair, Majestic Desert belied her odds of 16-1 by giving the winner's supporters a real fright, finishing strongly under a typically persuasive ride from Kieren Fallon. She looked much the more likely of the pair to benefit from the Guineas' extra two furlongs and, although connections had previously expressed a doubt about her staying beyond six furlongs, Fallon told them she would get a mile standing on her head.

If the Cheveley Park form is to be believed, and there is no obvious reason it should not be, Majestic Desert improved by more than 20lb there, earning a Racing Post Rating that places her firmly among the very best juveniles of her sex. However, while many will have been surprised at how well she ran, trainer Mick Channon was not, as he had maintained all season that she was not only his best, but also one of the best he had ever had.

The Cheveley Park was Majestic Desert's fifth race, every one of them on fastish ground, in a season that started back in April, when she landed odds of 8-11 in a lowly maiden auction at Warwick. Defeats at York and Royal Ascot, on the latter course outpaced by Attraction and hammered eight lengths into third, appeared to confirm her limitations. Returning from a break, she picked up a valuable prize when overcoming an unfavourably high draw in a huge field to score a narrow win over Totally Yours in the Tattersalls Breeders Stakes at The Curragh. The form did not amount to a great deal, but her win, the eighth in succession by a British-trained runner in the race, could not have been more timely, for it came just days after the death on the operating table of her dam, Calcutta Queen. *GD*

Race record
2nd Sky Bet Cheveley Park Stakes (Group 1) (Newmarket, October 2) 2yo 6f Good to firm **109** (TS 68) 10 ran.
1st Tattersalls Breeders Stakes (Curragh, August 23) 2yo 6f Good to firm **82** (TS 70) 24 ran.
3rd Queen Mary Stakes (Group 3) (Ascot, June 18) 2yo 5f Good to firm **84** (TS 79) 14 ran.
2nd EBF Novice Fillies' Stakes (York, May 13) 2yo 6f Good to firm **86** (TS 43) 8 ran.
1st Sunrise Median Auction Maiden Fillies' Stakes (Warwick, April 21) 2yo 5f Good to firm **64** (TS 35) 8 ran.

Pedigree assessment
Sire Fraam (Lead On Time) Unraced at two, later smart performer over 7-8f. Fair record as sire, hitherto from limited chances, has good record with 2yos at up to 7f, older progeny generally sprinters or milers. **Dam Calcutta Queen** Unraced at two, placed over 1m at three. From family that has good record with 2yos. Her three earlier foals have done little. **Conclusion** Quite an emphasis on juvenile speed on both sides of her pedigree, and not certain to be quite so effective at three. Has only a fair chance of staying 1m and may prove best at slightly shorter.

Majestic Missile (Ire) 118

b c Royal Applause - Tshusick (Dancing Brave (USA)) April 23
Owner Flying Tiger Partnership **Trainer** W J Haggas **Breeder** Victor Stud, B Cummins and O O'Connor **6** starts: won **4**, second **1**, third **0**, £63,804 win and place

MAJESTIC MISSILE was undoubtedly the top two-year-old colt over five furlongs. A clash with the filly Attraction would have been fascinating, but impressive victories in the Molecomb and Cornwallis Stakes put him well clear of his fellow colts and the latter race confirmed him among the best two-year-olds of 2003 over any distance.

Majestic Missile ran three times before turning up at Glorious Goodwood for the Molecomb, following up a short-head defeat on his debut by looking every inch the odds-on shot in a maiden at Kempton and a conditions stakes at Chester. The Chester runner-up, Nights Cross, filled the same position when Majestic Missile justified favouritism in very similar style in the Molecomb, travelling with ease while waiting for a gap and quickening in the final furlong, despite racing very freely for a long way.

While Majestic Missile looked a fine prospect, it was not at all clear if he could maintain the effort over six furlongs. The answer was

Majestic Missile: the best juvenile colt over five furlongs

Race record

1st Willmott Dixon Cornwallis Stakes (Group 3) (Ascot, October 11) 2yo 5f Good to firm **118** (TS 94) 11 ran.

6th Scottish Equitable Gimcrack Stakes (Group 2) (York, August 20) 2yo 6f Good to firm **108** (TS 94) 9 ran.

1st Betfair Molecomb Stakes (Group 3) (Goodwood, July 31) 2yo 5f Good **106** (TS 100) 9 ran.

1st Tessuti Conditions Stakes (Chester, July 11) 2yo 5f Good to firm **95** (TS 93) 6 ran.

1st Stan James Maiden Stakes (Kempton, July 2) 2yo 5f Good to firm **90** (TS 77) 5 ran.

2nd RBI Promotions Ltd - The Sports Promoters EBF Maiden Stakes (Windsor, June 16) 2yo 5f Good to firm **80** (TS 73) 12 ran.

Pedigree assessment

Sire **Royal Applause** (Waajib) Top-class 2yo and sprinter, won six Group races, notably Middle Park Stakes and Haydock Sprint Cup. Very good sprint sire, excels with 2yos (Auditorium, Mister Cosmi, Nevisian Lad, Peak To Creek), also sire of Acclamation. Dam **Tshusick** Unraced at 2, 7f winner at 3 but effective at 6f, from speedy family. Her four earlier foals include useful sprint 2yo Parisian Elegance. **Conclusion** Undoubtedly a sprinter and should continue to be effective at 5f.

emphatically in the negative in the Gimcrack Stakes at York, but the fact that he was beaten only about two and a half lengths, in much stronger company than at Goodwood, augured well for his return to the minimum trip. A late setback ruled him out of the Flying Childers before confirmation arrived with a runaway triumph in the Cornwallis at Ascot. Nights Cross was second best again, receiving 3lb and beaten three and a half lengths, as opposed to the two and three-quarters by which he had gone down to Howick Falls at levels in the Flying Childers.

Majestic Missile impresses in physique and should be a major force over five furlongs as a three-year-old, when a strong pace should help him to save his energies for racing, rather than running freely, which he got away with against his contemporaries as a juvenile. Connections decided against an early opportunity to take on his elders in the 2003 Prix de l'Abbaye because of the soft ground. *RA*

Milk It Mick   118

See entry in the top 100 horses, page 250

Mikado   98+

b c Sadler's Wells (USA) - Free At Last (Shirley Heights) February 12
Owner Mrs John Magnier **Trainer** A P O'Brien **Breeder** Gerald W Leigh
3 starts: won 2, second 1, £31,311 win and place

MIKADO is already assured a small place in the history books as the final winner for Mick Kinane as stable jockey at Ballydoyle. He has the potential, though, to be remembered for much more. As a 450,000 guineas son of Sadler's Wells, Mikado is bred to go a bit and showed enough as a juvenile to suggest he could make up into a smart colt in 2004.

Aidan O'Brien's colt made his debut in September, finishing runner-up to fellow smart prospect Opera Comique over nine furlongs at Tipperary. Like many of his stablemates, Mikado improved significantly for his debut exercise, scoring readily in a mile Listowel maiden under just hand riding a week later. That effort entitled Mikado to a crack at a bigger prize but he was unable to take up overnight engagements in the Beresford Stakes and Racing Post Trophy, being a late withdrawal from both

---

Race record
1st Eyrefield Stakes (Listed) (Leopardstown, November 8) 2yo 9f Good **98** 11 ran.
1st Irish Stallion Farms EBF Maiden (Listowel, September 18) 2yo 1m Good **85** 6 ran.
2nd Irish Stallion Farms EBF Maiden (Tipperary, September 11) 2yo 9f Good **71** 5 ran.

Pedigree assessment
Sire Sadler's Wells (Northern Dancer) Smart 7-8f winner at two, improved into top-class colt over 8-12f at three, won Irish 2,000 Guineas, Eclipse and Irish Champion Stakes. Outstanding sire, particularly of 3yos+ over 8-12f, also has good record with autumn 2yos. **Dam Free At Last** Smart 2yo and miler in Britain, later high-class US turf filly around 10f. Half-sister to Barathea and Gossamer (both by Sadler's Wells). Her five earlier foals include useful 10-12f filly Rosa Parks (by Sadler's Wells) and high-class 10f turf filly Coretta (by Caerleon). **Conclusion** Bred to a successful formula. Should stay 10f, has only fair chance of staying 12f.

events on raceday. Eventually reappearing on the final day of the season in the nine-furlong Listed Eyrefield Stakes at Leopardstown, Mikado showed what he was capable of, easily disposing of his rivals to earn a Racing Post Rating of 95+.

Likely to be suited by 12 furlongs-plus at three, Mikado has the potential to be competitive against the very best in 2004. *ST*

Moscow Ballet (Ire)   108

b c Sadler's Wells (USA) - Fire The Groom (USA) (Blushing Groom (Fr))
March 24 **Owner** Michael Tabor **Trainer** A P O'Brien **Breeder** R D Hubbard and Constance Sczesny **3 starts: won 1, second 1, third 0, £32,129** win and place

A THREE-PARTS brother to Stravinsky in the care of Aidan O'Brien, Moscow Ballet certainly looks the part on paper and did enough in his brief juvenile campaign to suggest he could be one of his powerful stable's better three-year-olds.

The son of Sadler's Wells made a successful racecourse debut over Tipperary's extended seven furlongs in August, getting the better of a tight battle with Favourite Nation, who went on to frank the form by taking a warm maiden before finishing runner-up in the Levy Stakes at The Curragh.

Moscow Ballet appeared next in Ascot's Royal Lodge Stakes and stepped up markedly on his maiden-race form, running on strongly inside the final furlong to hit the front, only to be deprived of success by Snow Ridge's telling finishing burst.

Despite his close links with the speedy Stravinsky, everything Moscow Ballet has done in public so far suggests he will not be seen to full advantage until tackling ten furlongs or more as a three-year-old. That was certainly the impression he created on his third and final start,

- -

Race record
5th Gran Criterium (Group 1) (San Siro, October 19) 2yo 1m Good **108** 11 ran.
2nd Hackney Empire Royal Lodge Stakes (Group 2) (Ascot, September 27) 2yo 1m Good to firm **108** (TS 104) 10 ran.
1st Irish Stallion Farms EBF Race (Tipperary, August 7) 2yo 7½f Good **92** 4 ran.

Pedigree assessment
Sire Sadler's Wells (Northern Dancer) Smart 7-8f winner at two, improved into top-class colt over 8-12f at 3, won Irish 2,000 Guineas, Eclipse and Irish Champion S. Outstanding sire, particularly of 3yos+ over 8-12f, also has good record with autumn 2yos. **Dam Fire The Groom** Unplaced sole start at 2 and useful miler at 3 in Britain. Later top-class turf filly over 8-9f in US. Half-sister to top-class sprinter Dowsing. Her four earlier foals feature top-class sprinter Stravinsky (by Nureyev). **Conclusion** Very closely related to Stravinsky but will stay further than him. Likely to make one of his sire's milers. Every chance he will progress well from 2 to 3, like both his parents and their best offspring.

- -

when finishing three and a quarter lengths behind Pearl Of Love in the Group 1 Gran Criterium at the San Siro, where, despite missing the break, he managed to run right up to his Ascot form, doing his best work in the last quarter-mile. A late-maturing sort who was not rushed in his first year, Moscow Ballet is likely to repay that patience in some of the better middle-distance three-year-old races. *ST*

Much Faster (Ire)   108

b f Fasliyev (USA) - Interruption (Zafonic (USA)) February 13
Owner Ecurie Jean-Louis Bouchard **Trainer** P Bary **Breeder** Sicea des Bissons
6 starts: won 4, second 1, third 0, £112,532 win and place

IN JUNE and July, the name was not so inappropriate. Horses with names like hers are more often than not destined for long-distance races on the all-weather or a prolonged spell pulling milk carts, but Much Faster kicked off her career with an unbeaten four-race spree. For a while she looked the top two-year-old in France.

She was not stretched to make all on the first two occasions, but had to work a lot harder in the Prix du Bois when Leila's effort in running

- -

Race record
9th Sky Bet Cheveley Park Stakes (Group 1) (Newmarket, October 2) 2yo 6f Good to firm **83** (TS 35) 10 ran.
2nd Prix Morny Casinos Barriere (Group 1) (Deauville, August 31) 2yo 6f Soft **106** (TS 90) 8 ran.
1st Prix Robert Papin (Group 2) (Maisons-Laffitte, July 27) 2yo 5½f Very soft **108** (TS 98) 8 ran.
1st Prix du Bois (Group 3) (Deauville, July 5) 2yo 5f Soft **96** (TS 89) 8 ran.
1st Prix la Fleche (Listed) (Maisons-Laffitte, June 17) 2yo 5½f Good **92** (TS 91) 9 ran.
1st Prix de la Verrerie (Unraced Fillies) (Chantilly, May 23) 2yo 5f Good to soft 6 ran.

Pedigree assessment
Sire **Fasliyev** (Nureyev) Top-class 2yo over 5-6f, won Phoenix S and Prix Morny, then suffered career-ending injury. First 2yos in 2003, has made excellent start with lots of precocious, generally fast offspring (Carry On Katie, Kings Point, Russian Valour). **Dam Interruption** Unraced. By top-class 2yo/miler, half-sister to high-class fillies Interval (6-8f; grand-dam of smart sprinters Continent and Dream Chief) and Interruption (10-12f) out of a smart miler. This is her first foal. **Conclusion** Speed on both sides of her pedigree and she is not certain to last 1m. May prove best over 6-7f.

- -

the winner to half a length so impressed Much Faster's owner, Jean-Louis Bouchard, that he bought a half-share in her. Three weeks later, the two of them started coupled second favourites at 23-10 for the Prix Robert Papin. André Fabre had the favourite, Marching West, and Aidan O'Brien was double-handed with Colossus and Haydn. Much Faster, however, won by three lengths.

In Britain, Thierry Thulliez may find it hard to live down his 1,000

Much Faster: impressive in the Prix Robert Papin

Guineas ride on Six Perfections, but the scale of Much Faster's triumph in the Robert Papin seemed to owe something to an astute move on his part in racing alone on the stands rail. The result of the following month's Prix Morny suggested that Much Faster had not been greatly flattered, but she met with her first defeat. She went like the winner for a long way but, having quickened a couple of lengths clear, she was mastered late on by Whipper.

The six-furlong Morny was over half a furlong further than the Robert Papin, but connections also believed that the ground was softer and that this helped to explain Much Faster's eclipse. When she encountered fast ground for the first time, however, in the Cheveley Park Stakes, Much Faster was second favourite and finished second last. Whatever her favoured ground turns out to be, Much Faster has so far looked a sprinter. *RA*

Mukafeh (USA) 95

b c Danzig (USA) - Bint Salsabil (USA) (Nashwan (USA)) February 10
Owner Hamdan Al Maktoum **Trainer** J L Dunlop **Breeder** Shadwell Farm
2 starts: won **1**, second **0**, third **1**, **£8,550** win and place

MUKAFEH looked a young colt with a big future when scoring narrowly on his debut at Newbury in August, where he and the talented and highly touted Akimbo finished clear of a decent field of maidens.

Ridden prominently throughout, Mukafeh showed the right attitude and plenty of natural ability as he quickened up with the Henry Cecil-trained runner-up before narrowly holding on in a driving finish. The pair pulled fully three and a half lengths clear of a field that contained plenty of talent – three of the next four home quickly claimed their maidens – and had more in hand over their rivals than the official distances suggest.

Made a short-priced favourite for Doncaster's McKeever St Lawrence Stakes on the strength of that performance, the son of Danzig came unstuck as he finished a well-beaten third behind the highly talented but inconsistent Sabbeeh and the Chesham Stakes fourth and Silver Tankard Stakes winner New Mexican.

Running green when put under pressure that day, Mukafeh gave the impression he was the type to do considerably better at three, when he should have filled some of his undoubted physical scope. Expect him to prove best around a mile. *ST*

Race record

3rd McKeever St Lawrence Conditions Stakes (Doncaster, September 10) 2yo 7f Good **89** (TS 62) 11 ran.

1st Stan James Online EBF Maiden Stakes (Newbury, August 16) 2yo 7f Good to firm **95** (TS 64) 11 ran.

Pedigree assessment

Sire Danzig (Northern Dancer) Unbeaten winner of three minor races at 2yo and 3yo at up to 7f in US. Outstanding sire, excels with 2yos, sprinters and milers, very rarely gets high-class horses over 10f+. **Dam Bint Salsabil** Smart 2yo winner over 6-7f (won Rockfel S-Gr3), later showed smart form at 7-10f. Superbly bred daughter of Salsabil. Her two earlier foals include a 1m 3yo winner. **Conclusion** Should be a miler and unlikely to stay 10f. Every chance he will make progress from two to three.

Necklace   109

See entry in the top 100 horses, page 296

Nevisian Lad   109

b c Royal Applause - Corndavon (USA) (Sheikh Albadou) February 3
Owner Sheikh Rashid Bin Mohammed **Trainer** M L W Bell **Breeder** Glebe Stud
5 starts: won 2, second 0, third 1, £53,158 win and place

CAPE FEAR, Byron, Milk It Mick, Holborn, Parkview Love and Howick Falls were a fine bunch of two-year-olds to go head to head with in July 2003, for by the end of the season the six colts had garnered victories in the St Leger Yearling Stakes, the Mill Reef Stakes, the Somerville

Tattersall Stakes and the Dewhurst, a close third place in the Middle Park, and further wins in the Woodcote Stakes, the Roses Stakes and the Flying Childers. Beating them all in clear-cut style in the July Stakes at Newmarket was some achievement by Nevisian Lad. It could not get much better than this. Unfortunately it got a good deal worse.

The July Stakes was Nevisian Lad's third run, following an odds-on maiden victory at the Craven meeting and third in the Norfolk Stakes at Royal Ascot. He put up an eye-catching display in the Norfolk and was subsequently sold to Sheikh Rashid Bin Mohammed, son of Sheikh

Race record

11th Shadwell Stud Middle Park Stakes (Group 1) (Newmarket, October 3) 2yo 6f Good to firm **98** (TS 81) 12 ran.
9th Veuve Clicquot Vintage Stakes (Group 2) (Goodwood, July 30) 2yo 7f Good to soft **81** (TS 66) 9 ran.
1st TNT July Stakes (Group 2) (Newmarket (July), July 9) 2yo 6f Good to firm **109** (TS 76) 8 ran.
3rd Norfolk Stakes (Group 3) (Ascot, June 19) 2yo 5f Good to firm **99** (TS 85) 8 ran.
1st Creature Comforts EBF Maiden Stakes (Newmarket, April 17) 2yo 5f Good to firm **87** (TS 63) 4 ran.

Pedigree assessment

Sire Royal Applause (Waajib) top-class 2yo and sprinter, won six Group races, notably Middle Park Stakes and Haydock Sprint Cup. Very good sprint sire, excels with 2yos (Auditorium, Majestic Missile, Mister Cosmi, Peak To Creek), also sire of Acclamation. **Dam Corndavon** Placed over 5f at 2yo, later won three races over 6f, related to several speedy and precocious sorts. This is her first foal. **Conclusion** Will continue to be suited by sprint trips. Precociously bred and not certain to make progress from 2 to 3.

Mohammed. There was no fluke about the way he won the July Stakes in the new colours, starting second favourite and bursting through late to score by a length, going away, but it was followed by last of nine in the Vintage Stakes at Goodwood and 11th of 12 in the Middle Park.

The extra furlong and, more importantly, the easier ground might help to explain what happened in the Vintage Stakes, but Nevisian Lad was back to six furlongs on fast ground when always behind in the Middle Park. After two such disappointing performances it is anybody's guess what he will be capable of as a three-year-old. *RA*

North Light (Ire) 88+

b c Danehill (USA) - Sought Out (Ire) (Rainbow Quest (USA)) March 1
Owner Exors of the late Lord Weinstock **Trainer** Sir Michael Stoute
Breeder Ballymacoll Stud Farm **2** starts: won **1**, second **1**, **£4,900** win & place

SIR MICHAEL STOUTE has a colt of considerable potential in the shape of North Light, who became the first foal of high-class mare Sought Out to win as a juvenile when scoring at the prohibitive odds of 1-5 in a one-mile maiden at Goodwood in September. A full-brother to Researched,

---

Race record
1st Uniq Foodservice Gold Cup EBF Maiden Stakes (Goodwood, September 24) 2yo 1m Good to firm **74** (TS 56) 5 ran.
2nd Pacemaker EBF Maiden Stakes (Sandown, August 29) 2yo 7f Soft **88** (TS 67) 14 ran.

Pedigree assessment
Sire Danehill (Danzig) Useful 6f 2yo winner, improved at three into top-class sprinter, won Haydock Sprint Cup, but also smart over 1m. Excellent sire, does well with 2yos and older progeny up to 1m but can get top-class 12f horses and also has a classy stayer now in Westerner. Best progeny include Aquarelliste, Banks Hill, Clodovil, Desert King, Mozart, Rock Of Gibraltar. **Dam Sought Out** Placed at two, later top-class stayer in France. Her five earlier foals feature smart 10-12f gelding Researched (by Danehill) and smart stayer Cover Up (by Machiavellian). **Conclusion** Should follow the pattern of his full-brother Researched in distance terms, with 12f within his compass. Likely to progress well from two to three.

North Light took up the running over a furlong out before readily seeing off the challenges of Take A Bow and subsequent Pontefract maiden winner Dumfries.

North Light started such a hot favourite at Goodwood on the strength of an excellent debut in a really competitive maiden at Sandown, where the son of Danehill narrowly lost out to equally exciting prospect Post And Rail under an educational ride, pulling three lengths and more clear of some talented opponents. The third, fourth, fifth, eighth and 12th home that day were all next-time-out winners, the majority displaying significantly improved form in the process.

North Light looks a sure-fire big improver at three and the strong form he already has in the book, coupled with his profile, strongly suggests he will be able to uphold the family tradition and land a big prize or two for the Stoute team in 2004. *ST*

Nyramba   102

---

b f Night Shift (USA) - Maramba (Rainbow Quest (USA)) March 18
Owner Salem Suhail **Trainer** J H M Gosden **Breeder** Five Horses Ltd
5 starts: won 3, second 1, third 0, £160,996 win and place

THE Watership Down Stud Sales Stakes and Tote Trifecta Handicap at Ascot on September 26 and 27 featured an aggregate of 55 runners chasing massive first prize-money of £174,000. But how many had a chance of winning it? The first four in the former race were drawn 30, 24, 27 and 22; in the latter they were 30, 29, 26 and 13. Later races at the meeting saw some frantic scrambling for position on the hugely favoured far rail.

The chief beneficiary among 30 fillies chasing the £133,400 top prize in the sales race was the John Gosden-trained Nyramba, drawn highest of all. She was a useful two-year-old, though, already successful at Salisbury in a maiden in May and a Listed race in September, and she started favourite in the six-and-a-half-furlong event.

North Light: likely to progress well as a three-year-old

"John is very pleased with her but not with her draw – I think you're 7lb better off to be on the stands side," said Joe Mercer, racing manager to Nyramba's owner, Salem Suhail, before the race. It didn't work out like that as Nyramba caught the front-running lightweight Dubaian Duel.

Nyramba's only subsequent start was in the Cheveley Park and, as 5-1 third favourite, she finished last of ten. The mere six-day break since her Ascot win was a plausible explanation, but she was well below form. Raced only on fast ground and not beyond six and a half furlongs, she is not guaranteed to stay a mile. *RA*

Race record

10th Sky Bet Cheveley Park Stakes (Group 1) (Newmarket, October 2) 2yo 6f Good to firm **81** (TS 32) 10 ran.

1st Watership Down Stud Sales Stakes (Ascot, September 26) 2yo 6½f Good to firm **102** (TS 86) 30 ran.

1st EBF Dick Poole Fillies' Stakes (Listed) (Salisbury, September 4) 2yo 6f Good to firm **93** (TS 54) 11 ran.

2nd Stan James St Hugh's Stakes (Listed) (Newbury, August 16) 2yo 5f Good to firm **86** (TS 76) 10 ran.

1st Knights & Co Maiden Stakes (Salisbury, May 15) 2yo 5f Good to firm **86** (TS 77) 12 ran.

Pedigree assessment

Sire **Night Shift** (Northern Dancer) minor winner over 6f at three. Very effective sire, generally an influence for speed, has good record with 2yos, sprinters and milers (Baron's Pit, Deportivo, Eveningperformance, Lochangel, Nicolotte), occasionally gets top-class performers over further (Daryaba, In The Groove). Dam **Maramba** Unraced at two, fair 1m winner at three. Daughter of smart 6-7f filly Gayane. This is her first foal. **Conclusion** Far from certain to stay 1m on pedigree and it is more likely this one will continue to be effective over 6f and 7f.

Offenbach (USA) 93+

b c Danzig (USA) - Aquilegia (USA) (Alydar (USA)) May 12
Owner Mrs John Magnier **Trainer** A P O'Brien **Breeder** H Alexander, H Groves and D Alexander **1** start: won **1**, **£8,441** win and place

THE final day of the Irish Flat season was a good one for Aidan O'Brien as he saddled a significant juvenile double, initiated by the exciting Offenbach. The majority of Ballydoyle two-year-olds improved significantly for a spin in 2003, with few posting a 90+ Racing Post Rating first time out. However, Offenbach bucked that trend, comprehensively beating 17 rivals in his seven-furlong maiden at Leopardstown.

Offenbach was weak in the market and somewhat green in the race itself, and there is every reason to expect him to improve massively on the bare form of his maiden win. The son of Danzig looks to have a big future and could develop into a live contender for the French or Irish 2,000 Guineas. *ST*

Race record
1st Irish Stallion Farms EBF Maiden (Leopardstown, November 8) 2yo 7f Good **93** (TS 72) 18 ran.

Pedigree assessment
Sire Danzig (Northern Dancer) unbeaten winner of three minor races at 2 and 3 at up to 7f in US. Outstanding sire, excels with 2yos, sprinters and milers, very rarely gets high-class horses over 10f+. **Dam Aquilegia** Grade 2 winner on turf in US, stayed beyond 1m. Daughter of outstanding broodmare Courtly Dee (also grand-dam of Green Desert). Her earlier foals include high-class 2yo/sprinter Bertolini (by Danzig). **Conclusion** Bred along very similar lines to top-class sprinter Green Desert. Has already won over 7f, which suggests he may stay a little better than his brother, but unlikely to want further than 1m.

Old Deuteronomy (USA) 113

br c Storm Cat (USA) - Jewel In The Crown (USA) (Seeking The Gold (USA)) February 11 **Owner** Mrs John Magnier **Trainer** A P O'Brien **Breeder** Pacelco SA and Chelston Ireland Ltd **6** starts: won **1**, second **2**, third **0**, **£70,528** win & place

OLD DEUTERONOMY made such a big impression on his debut in a six-furlong maiden at Newmarket in May that it seemed almost inconceivable that he would run another five times without winning. He showed breathtaking acceleration to sprint home five lengths clear of Divine Gift in what looked an above-average maiden and seemed obvious Coventry Stakes material, with the promise of even better things later on.

Instead, Old Deuteronomy was dropped back a furlong for the Norfolk Stakes, in which he never got a look in behind Russian Valour and Kheleyf after becoming unsettled during an uncomfortably long wait in the stalls. Strictly speaking, his fourth place represented an improvement on the level of form he had shown at Newmarket, but it was still disappointing.

It was back up to six furlongs every time for the remainder of the season, and up again in class too, Old Deuteronomy first tackling Group 2 company at Goodwood and then Group 1 opposition at The Curragh, Deauville and Newmarket.

He came closest to winning when running Carrizo Creek to half a length in the Richmond Stakes at Goodwood, where he could have done without

Race record
7th Shadwell Stud Middle Park Stakes (Group 1) (Newmarket, October 3) 2yo 6f Good to firm **107** (TS 92) 12 ran.
4th Prix Morny Casinos Barriere (Group 1) (Deauville, August 31) 2yo 6f Soft **94** (TS 73) 8 ran.
2nd Independent Waterford Wedgwood Phoenix Stakes (Group 1) (Curragh, August 10) 2yo 6f Good **113** (TS 108) 7 ran.
2nd Four Star Sales Richmond Stakes (Group 2) (Goodwood, July 29) 2yo 6f Good **105** (TS 99) 7 ran.
4th Norfolk Stakes (Group 3) (Ascot, June 19) 2yo 5f Good to firm **95** (TS 81) 8 ran.
1st EBF Maiden Stakes (Newmarket, May 31) 2yo 6f Good to firm **88** (TS 45) 9 ran.

Pedigree assessment
Sire Storm Cat (Storm Bird) Top-class US 2yo over 1m. Both sire and dam top-class 2yos. Outstanding US-based sire, European progeny generally excel at around 1m, best include Aljabr, Black Minnaloushe, Catrail, Giant's Causeway, Sophisticat. **Dam Jewel In The Crown** Unraced at 2, won over 1m in Ireland at 3, also placed 6-7f. By top-class 8-10f performer and sire of Dubai Millennium out of half-sister to I Will Follow (dam of Rainbow Quest) and Slightly Dangerous (dam of Commander In Chief, Warning). This is her first foal. **Conclusion** The pedigree of a miler. The family is not known for its precocious members, so Old Deuteronomy has a fair chance of progressing well from 2 to 3.

the rain that was just starting to get into the ground, but there is no question that his best form was his length second behind stablemate One Cool Cat in the Phoenix Stakes at The Curragh, where he looked dangerous at the furlong marker and put up a cracking performance.

It is easy to forgive a moderate effort in the Prix Morny at Deauville, where the ground was soft, but there was no such excuse when he was only seventh behind Three Valleys in the Middle Park and his starting price of 14-1 suggested that was just about where he was expected to finish. It's hard to say where he will fit in among the Ballydoyle colts in 2004, but the chances are that he is a sprinter and that he will probably continue to be best served by fast ground. *GD*

One Cool Cat   121+

See entry in the top 100 horses, page 310

Opera Comique (Fr) 102+

b f Singspiel (Ire) - Grace Note (Fr) (Top Ville) March 16
Owner Sheikh Mohammed **Trainer** John M Oxx **Breeder** Sheikh Mohammed
2 starts: won 1, second 0, third 1, £12,000 win and place

IT WOULD not be the end of the world if Opera Comique never won another race, for as a winning half-sister to the King George winner Belmez she is already a hot property as a potential broodmare. However, there was no disgrace at all in her third to Venturi in a Group 3 at The Curragh in September and there is every likelihood she will be more than capable of winning at that sort of level and probably better at three.

A maiden winner over nine furlongs at Tipperary in September on her debut, it was odds-on that she would not be seen to full advantage over

Race record
3rd CL Weld Park Stakes (Group 3) (Curragh, September 21) 2yo 7f Good to firm **102** (TS 79) 10 ran.
1st Irish Stallion Farms EBF Maiden (Tipperary, September 11) 2yo 9f Good **69** 5 ran.

Pedigree assessment
Sire Singspiel (In The Wings) Useful 2yo, later progressed with age into top-class 10-12f performer. Good sire, capable of getting useful 2yos (Bourbonnais, Via Milano) but better record with older horses over 10f+ (Moon Ballad). **Dam Grace Note** Won over 10f. Her earlier foals feature top-class 12f colt Belmez and several fair stayers. **Conclusion** Guaranteed to stay 12f and highly likely to improve considerably from 2 to 3.

the two-furlong shorter distance of the CL Weld Park Stakes just ten days later, and so it proved. But she confirmed herself a smart prospect by finishing little more than a length behind the winner and she is open to considerable improvement when she steps up to ten or 12 furlongs.

Her pedigree has middle-distance three-year-old written all over it, so bear her in mind for a decent prize. Indeed, she is arguably one of the likelier long-range types for the Oaks or its Irish equivalent. *GD*

Oriental Warrior 93+

b c Alhaarth (Ire) - Oriental Fashion (Ire) (Marju (Ire)) March 18
Owner Hadi Al Tajir **Trainer** M P Tregoning **Breeder** Hadi Al Tajir
2 starts: won 2, £13,569 win and place

IT'S very much a case of so far so good for Oriental Warrior, who headed off into winter quarters with his unbeaten record intact after two highly satisfactory wins towards the end of the season

Six furlongs was thought to be on the short side for the Alhaarth colt's

Oriental Warrior: bright prospect for Marcus Tregoning

Newbury debut, but his impressive home work filtered through to the track to ensure his odds were cramped. His supporters never had too much to worry about as Oriental Warrior scored readily in what turned out to be a fairly strong maiden after tracking the leaders until the final furlong.

Stepped up in class and trip at Ascot on his next start, Oriental Warrior overcame an unsuitably slow early pace to run out a smooth winner over the extra furlong, seeing off Newmarket maiden winner Primus Inter Pares by a fairly comfortable length and a quarter. With decent yardsticks like Ballykeating and Soonest well held in a dead-heat for third, the bare form of the Ascot race reads very well.

All the evidence suggests Oriental Warrior will do far better when upped to a mile in 2004. If finding the anticipated improvement he should be competitive in one of the 2,000 Guineas trials. *ST*

Race record

1st Mitsubishi Electric Hyperion Conditions Stakes (Ascot, October 11) 2yo 7f Good to firm **93** (TS 79) 6 ran.

1st EBF Dubai Tennis Championships Maiden Stakes (Newbury, September 19) 2yo 6f Good to firm **85** (TS 75) 16 ran.

Pedigree assessment

Sire Alhaarth (Unfuwain) Unbeaten in five 7f races at 2, notably Dewhurst S-Gr1. Later showed high-class form over 8-10f. Good sire, does quite well with 2yos but better record with older horses at wide variety of trips, ranging from sprinter Dominica to 12f+ horses Bandari and Phoenix Reach, depending on dam. **Dam Oriental Fashion** Won over 1m at 2, later won Gr2 event in Italy over 1m and Listed placed over 10f. Out of half-sister to Nashwan, Nayef and Unfuwain. This is her first foal. **Conclusion** Will stay at least 1m, has quite good chance of staying 10f.

Pastoral Pursuits 110

b c Bahamian Bounty - Star (Most Welcome) April 3
Owner The Pursuits Partnership **Trainer** H Morrison **Breeder** Red House Stud
4 starts: won 3, second 1, £31,468 win and place

PASTORAL PURSUITS was on course for a crack at either the Mill Reef or the Middle Park Stakes when his two-year-old campaign was brought to an abrupt end by an injury sustained in Kempton's six-furlong Sirenia Stakes.

The colt won that race, and won it well, beating the highly progressive dual nursery winner Diosypros Blue by two clear lengths after taking charge with more than two furlongs still to run. However, Hughie Morrison was concerned at the frequency with which Pastoral Pursuits changed his legs, and after finding him "hopping lame" the following morning he discovered a chipped bone in his off fore.

Morrison is clearly a talented trainer, but precocious two-year-olds are not his speciality and Pastoral Pursuits was allowed to go off a

- -

Race record

1st Coral Sirenia Stakes (Group 3) (Kempton, September 6) 2yo 6f Good **106** (TS 82) 9 ran.
1st Ian Hutchinson Memorial Conditions Stakes (Windsor, August 10) 2yo 6f Good to firm **110** (TS 84) 5 ran.
1st Averti Maiden Auction Stakes (Chepstow, July 25) 2yo 6f Good **90** (TS 73) 11 ran.
2nd Clio Renault Sport V6 EBF Median Auction Maiden Stakes (Windsor, June 9) 2yo 6f Good to firm **70** (TS 53) 20 ran.

Pedigree assessment

Sire Bahamian Bounty (Cadeaux Genereux) Top-class 2yo, won Prix Morny and Middle Park Stakes. Useful sprint form in two starts at 3. Fair sire of 2yos and sprinters (Berk The Jerk, Dubaian Gift, Lady Links). **Dam Star** 5f winner at 2, only season to race. Her two earlier foals are very modest. **Conclusion** Sire and dam both precocious, so Pastoral Pursuits is not certain to progress from 2 to 3. Has the pedigree of a sprinter.

- -

33-1 chance when beaten only by the subsequent Listed winner Privy Seal from an indifferent draw in a 20-runner field over six furlongs at Windsor first time out. Though unconsidered that day, he was a short-priced favourite for all three subsequent appearances and on his way to the Sirenia he was a runaway eight-length winner both at Chepstow and back at Windsor again, arguably putting up his best performance of all when trouncing the smart Ascot nursery winner King Carnival on the latter track.

Pastoral Pursuits' injury was operated upon immediately and Morrison is hopeful that he will make a full recovery. The 2,000 Guineas is said to be his target, but he will need to improve considerably to figure at Newmarket and he is far from certain to appreciate a mile. Sprinting is more likely to be his game. *GD*

Peak To Creek   110

b c Royal Applause - Rivers Rhapsody (Dominion) April 28
Owner C Fox & J Wright **Trainer** J Noseda **Breeder** Compton Down Stud
12 starts: won **7**, second **2**, third **2**, **£178,095** win and place

IN HIS second start in eight days, his 11th in all, and his umpteenth
tight finish, Peak The Creek dug deep again and landed the Listed Rockingham Stakes at York in October. It was his sixth victory in a two-year-old
season that began in April. Just 13 days later, he was upgraded to the
Group 3 Horris Hill Stakes at Newbury for win number seven. This time
he did it easily.

This was a very tough and game two-year-old and, in the end, a
markedly improved one. Profitable too for his owners, who paid 50,000

Race record
1st Vodafone Horris Hill Stakes (Group 3) (Newbury, October 24) 2yo 7f Good to firm **110** (TS 97)
9 ran.
1st Newton Fund Managers Rockingham Stakes (Listed) (York, October 11) 2yo 6f Good to firm **104**
(TS 87) 8 ran.
1st Redcar Two-Year-Old Trophy (Redcar, October 4) 2yo 6f Good to firm **101** (TS 91) 23 ran.
1st betfair.com Conditions Stakes (Yarmouth, September 18) 2yo 6f Good to firm **100** (TS 65) 6 ran.
3rd Prix d'Arenberg (Group 3) (Maisons-Laffitte, September 10) 2yo 5½f Soft **99** (TS 70) 4 ran.
2nd Ripon Champion Two Yrs Old Trophy (Listed) (Ripon, August 25) 2yo 6f Good to firm **94** (TS 72)
4 ran.
2nd Ripon Horn Blower Conditions Stakes (Ripon, August 16) 2yo 6f Good **96** (TS 73) 7 ran.
1st Halliwell Jones BMW Nursery (Handicap) (Chester, August 3) 2yo 6f Good to firm **94** (TS 77) 9 ran.
1st Hertel Services Nursery Stakes (Handicap) (Redcar, July 26) 2yo 6f Good to firm **94** (TS 95) 9 ran.
1st Manchesteronline EBF Maiden Stakes (Haydock, July 13) 2yo 6f Good to firm **89** (TS 77) 9 ran.
9th Windsor Castle Stakes (Conditions Race) (Ascot, June 21) 2yo 5f Firm **60** (TS 58) 17 ran.
3rd Brooklands Racing First For Horse Sponsorship Median Auction Maiden Stakes (Leicester, April 26)
2yo 5f Good to firm **76** (TS 55) 14 ran.

Pedigree assessment
Sire Royal Applause (Waajib) Top-class 2yo and sprinter, won six Group races notably Middle
Park Stakes and Haydock Sprint Cup. Very good sprint sire, excels with 2yos (Auditorium, Majestic
Missile, Mister Cosmi, Nevisian Lad), also sire of Acclamation. **Dam Rivers Rhapsody** 5f
winner at 2, later very useful miler. Her six earlier foals include useful miler For Your Eyes Only (by
Pursuit Of Love) and useful sprinter See You Later (by Emarati). **Conclusion** Speedily bred on
dam's side and very unlikely to be suited by further than 6f. Members of his family tend to make
good progress from 2 to 3.

guineas for him as a yearling, tried and failed to sell him in the summer,
and ended the year with prize-money of almost £180,000.

A maiden at Haydock and nurseries at Redcar and Chester quickly
established Peak To Creek as a useful performer, but it was not until
the autumn that he really came to prominence. A conditions stakes at
Yarmouth and the Rockingham at York gave extra cause for applause
for Pat Eddery on his farewell tour. In between came easily his biggest

payday when, in the hands of Shane Kelly, he took home £109,852 from the Redcar Two-Year-Old Trophy.

For each of those victories, Peak To Creek was produced with a late run to score by a head and waiting tactics were said to be instrumental in his success. That does not explain what happened in the seven-furlong Horris Hill. Both his parentage and the way he had been campaigned prompted doubts over whether he would stay, but by the end of the day he was a live outsider for the 2,000 Guineas. Sabbeeh's flop at 11-10 diminished what was required, but it was hard not to be impressed by the way Peak To Creek cruised up to win by three and a half lengths. *RA*

Pearl Of Love   115

See entry in the top 100 horses, page 320

Phantom Wind (USA)   91+

b f Storm Cat (USA) - Ryafan (USA) (Lear Fan (USA)) April 12
Owner K Abdullah **Trainer** J H M Gosden **Breeder** Juddmonte Farms
2 starts: won 1, second 0, third 0, £4,774 win and place

JOHN GOSDEN has an exciting filly on his hands in the shape of Phantom Wind. A daughter of Prix Marcel Boussac winner Ryafan, Phantom Wind made an inauspicious start to her racing career at Nottingham in late September. Strongly fancied in the market and fitted with a tongue-tie, she fluffed the start very badly, effectively ending her chance.

Plenty of work had clearly been done at home before she reappeared in mid-October at Newmarket over six furlongs, where she once again attracted strong market interest. This time her supporters collected with ease as she thrashed subsequent Redcar maiden winner Great Fox

---

Race record
1st National Stud EBF Maiden Stakes (Newmarket, October 16) 2yo 6f Good to firm **91** (TS 88) 12 ran.
15th Come Racing At Nottingham Maiden Fillies' Stakes (Nottingham, September 30) 2yo 6f Good to firm **32** 15 ran.

Pedigree assessment
Sire Storm Cat (Storm Bird) Top-class US 2yo over 1m. Both sire and dam top-class 2yos. Outstanding US-based sire, European progeny generally excel at around 1m, best include Aljabr, Black Minnaloushe, Catrail, Giant's Causeway, Sophisticat. **Dam Ryafan** Top-class 2yo, won Prix Marcel Boussac, later top class over 8-10f in Britain and US. Daughter of half-sister to dam of Tillerman. Her two earlier foals include modest placed gelding Volcanic. **Conclusion** Likely to be best at around 1m at three.

Phantom Wind: impeccably bred and a Classic possible

by a stylish eight lengths, racing just behind the leaders before readily outspeeding her field over a furlong out.

Those in behind may only turn out to be fair handicappers but the manner of Phantom Wind's success strongly suggests she will be able to make her mark in 2004. Her pedigree suggests she will be best at around a mile, and if progressing along the right lines she could yet develop into a genuine contender for the 1,000 Guineas. *ST*

Post And Rail (USA) 88+

b c Silver Hawk (USA) - Past The Post (USA) (Danzig (USA)) April 1
Owner Hesmonds Stud **Trainer** E A L Dunlop **Breeder** Martyn P Burke
1 start: won **1**, **£6,370** win and place

POST AND RAIL could hardly have made a more promising start to his career than when winning a hot seven-furlong maiden at Sandown in late August.

The corresponding race in 2002 featured Oasis Dream, Rimrod and Let Me Try Again, and it will be something of a surprise if Post And Rail fails to acquit himself well at a similarly high level. On unseasonably soft ground, the son of Silver Hawk travelled kindly in a prominent position before staying on in taking fashion under just hand riding to defeat subsequent Goodwood maiden winner North Light by the minimum margin. The front two pulled three lengths clear, which was quite an achievement given the subsequent exploits of those behind.

The form looked strong enough on the day, but it was franked again and again over the next month or two. The four who finished closest to Post And Rail – North Light, Ifraaj, Maraahel and Menokee – all went on to win their maidens next time, while the eighth home, Jazz Scene, won the valuable St Leger Yearling Stakes on his next start and 12th-placed Swagger Stick was a next-time-out nursery winner.

The manner of Post And Rail's victory strongly suggested there was plenty of improvement to come and it will be fascinating to see how he progresses in 2004. *ST*

Race record
1st Pacemaker EBF Maiden Stakes (Sandown, August 29) 2yo 7f Soft **88** (TS 67) 14 ran.

Pedigree assessment

Sire Silver Hawk (Roberto) High-class 2yo over 7-8f, later showed high-class form over 1m and 12f (placed in two Derbys). Very effective sire, occasionally sires smart 2yos but has much better record with older horses, mainly over 10-12f. Best runners include Benny The Dip, Mubtaker, Mutafaweq. **Dam Past The Post** 3yo winner in US. Sister to high-class miler Emperor Jones and two smart 2yos, half-sister to top-class 2yo/middle-distance horse Bakharoff. This is her first foal. **Conclusion** Fair amount of speed on dam's side, but sire is an influence for stamina and this colt should be effective at 10f, though he is not certain to stay 12f.

Punctilious   107

b f Danehill (USA) - Robertet (USA) (Roberto (USA)) May 7
Owner Sheikh Mohammed **Trainer** M A Jarvis **Breeder** B Neilsen
3 starts: won **2**, second **0**, third **1**, **£31,743** win and place

THIS filly's first two starts were sufficiently promising for her owner to receive the call from Sheikh Mohammed, but that is no guarantee of future success. Punctilious duly met with defeat on her first spin for her new owner, but all is not lost. Physically, she looks the type to improve as a three-year-old and that is probably why Sheikh Mohammed reached for his wallet, rather than because she was given a favourite's chance on that first engagement for him, the Fillies' Mile at Ascot.

Carrying the colours of the soon-to-be-rather-better-off Bjorn Neilsen, Punctilious was sent off at evens for her debut in a six-runner maiden at Yarmouth in July; she comfortably saw off the Sheikh Mohammed-owned Cherubim despite looking very green. Already quoted ante-post for the 1,000 Guineas, Punctilious was forced into an absence of two months because of a viral infection but returned for a second clear-cut success in a novice stakes at Salisbury, the form of which was franked repeatedly by runner-up Fantastic View.

"I've never really had such strength in depth in the two-year-old department," reflected her trainer Michael Jarvis afterwards. "We have a strong team of fillies and Punctilious is right up there with the best

---

Race record

3rd Meon Valley Stud Fillies' Mile (Group 1) (Ascot, September 27) 2yo 1m Good to firm **107** (TS 107) 7 ran.
1st Butler & Co Equine Tax Planning EBF Novice Stakes (Salisbury, September 4) 2yo 1m Good to firm **95** (TS 74) 7 ran.
1st EBF Maiden Fillies' Stakes (Yarmouth, July 3) 2yo 7f Good **75** (TS 71) 6 ran.

Pedigree assessment

Sire **Danehill** (Danzig) Useful 6f 2yo winner, improved at 3 into top-class sprinter, won Haydock Sprint Cup, but also smart over 1m. Excellent sire, does well with 2yos and older progeny up to 1m but can get top-class middle-distance horses and now has a high-class stayer in Westerner. Best progeny include Aquarelliste, Banks Hill, Clodovil, Desert King, Mozart, Rock Of Gibraltar. Dam **Robertet** High class over 12f+ in France. Her seven earlier foals include high-class French stayer Risk Seeker (by Elmaamul) and useful 10f winner Redwood Falls (by Dancing Brave). **Conclusion** Has pedigree to progress from 2 to 3, when she should stay 10f and may last 12f.

---

of them, but we are excited with them all."

Dunloskin, Dallaah and Qasirah showed useful form, with Dunloskin impressing in particular when third in the Lowther Stakes. Punctilious, however, became the clear pick among the Jarvis fillies in form terms when she took third in the Fillies' Mile at Ascot. Starting 13-8, she made most and kept on gamely in going down by one and a quarter lengths to Red Bloom. She failed by a short head to beat Sheikh Mohammed's second string, Sundrop. It was a smart effort, but do not be surprised if she turns out more of an Oaks than a Guineas filly when she reappears for Godolphin. *RA*

Red Bloom   110

See entry in the top 100 horses, page 346

Relaxed Gesture (Ire)   108

ch c Indian Ridge - Token Gesture (Ire) (Alzao (USA)) March 12
Owner Moyglare Stud Farm **Trainer** D K Weld **Breeder** Moyglare Stud Farm
4 starts: won **1**, second **1**, third **1**, **£25,649** win and place

---

NOTHING went right for Relaxed Gesture on his racecourse debut, as he fell out of the stalls and struggled to make an impact in a decent seven-furlong maiden at The Curragh. Clearly expecting better, connections again sent him to one of the bigger tracks and he did not disappoint, leading well over a furlong out in just an ordinary Leopardstown maiden to get the better of Asanine and Rock Of Cashel.

Dermot Weld next stepped Relaxed Gesture up into the Group 2 Beresford Stakes over an extra furlong at The Curragh and he acquitted himself with much credit in defeat, battling on strongly after forcing the pace to lose out narrowly to the exciting Azamour. If the Beresford was a jump in class, Relaxed Gesture's next start was something of a trip into the unknown, as he headed for Santa Anita and the Breeders' Cup Juvenile. Unfortunately he found things happening far too quickly Stateside and, rather like on his debut, failed to land any sort of blow after a tardy start.

It would be no surprise to see Relaxed Gesture make full use of his passport and head back to America, but wherever he goes the colt has already shown enough to suggest that he will be competitive in Group company. He should stay further and could do well. *ST*

Race record

8th Bessemer Trust Breeders' Cup Juvenile (Grade 1) (Santa Anita, October 25) 2yo 8½f Fast **79** 12 ran.

2nd Juddmonte Beresford Stakes (Group 2) (Curragh, October 12) 2yo 1m Good to yielding **108** (TS 66) 6 ran.

1st Irish Stallion Farms EBF Maiden (Leopardstown, August 17) 2yo 7f Good to firm **85** (TS 39) 14 ran.

3rd Jumeirah International EBF Maiden (Curragh, July 13) 2yo 7f Good **77** (TS 72) 8 ran.

Pedigree assessment

Sire Indian Ridge (Ahonoora) Won at 2, progressed into high-class performer from 5-7f at three and four. Excellent sire, does well with 2yos (Definite Article, Snow Ridge) and older progeny, mainly at up to 1m (Domedriver, Indian Haven, Namid, Ridgewood Pearl) but occasionally further (Indian Creek). **Dam Token Gesture** Smart 7f winner at 2 and very useful over 10-12f at 3. Her two earlier foals are 9.5f turf Grade 2 winner Evolving Tactics (by Machiavellian) and 8-12f winner Turn Of Phrase (by Cadeaux Genereux). **Conclusion** Indian Ridge does get horses who stay reasonably well out of stout mares, and Token Gesture is one. As a result, Relaxed Gesture should be effective over 8-10f.

Rule Of Law (USA)   108

b c Kingmambo (USA) - Crystal Crossing (Ire) (Royal Academy (USA)) March 6 **Owner** Sheikh Mohammed **Trainer** D R Loder **Breeder** R E Sangster and Ben Sangster **4** starts: won **2**, second **0**, third **2**, £**41,729** win and place

RULE OF LAW is one of the highest-rated two-year-olds in the latest batch handed over by David Loder to Saeed Bin Suroor. Byron and Howick Falls won a Group race apiece, while Catstar, Sundrop and Bayeux finished runner-up in one and Rule Of Law managed a third place.

Rule Of Law's Group appearance came in the Royal Lodge Stakes at Ascot in September. The shortest-priced of Sheikh Mohammed's three runners in the race, but carrying his second colours, second favourite Rule Of Law nearly made all the running; he appeared to have the rest in trouble early in the straight but the Ballydoyle colt Moscow Ballet got to him by fractions and favourite Snow Ridge surged past them both

Rule Of Law: dual York winner over seven furlongs

in the final strides. Jamie Spencer also had the ride for all of Rule Of Law's three starts before Ascot, hanging on in the Listed Acomb Stakes just under six weeks earlier and storming home by seven lengths in a maiden race just under six weeks before that, both races over seven furlongs at York. Rule Of Law's debut had not gone so well and he was subsequently equipped with a visor.

After the Acomb, Loder observed: "He is a tough, game, genuine type of horse but he is not straightforward. Jamie rode him again because he has ridden him the last two times and knows him well." After the Royal Lodge, Loder said that "a mile to a mile and a quarter will be the trip next year," though the latter distance might just be stretching things on pedigree. *RA*

Race record

3rd Hackney Empire Royal Lodge Stakes (Group 2) (Ascot, September 27) 2yo 1m Good to firm **108** (TS 104) 10 ran.
1st Acomb Stakes (Listed) (York, August 19) 2yo 7f Good to firm **104** (TS 93) 7 ran.
1st Ramesys Maiden Stakes (York, July 11) 2yo 7f Good to firm **89** (TS 96) 11 ran.
3rd Palletline Maiden Stakes (Sandown, June 14) 2yo 7f Good to firm **72** 8 ran.

Pedigree assessment

Sire Kingmambo (Mr Prospector) High-class 2yo, progressed into top-class miler at three, won three Group 1 races including Poulains and St James's Palace Stakes. Superbly bred, out of Miesque. Excellent US-based sire, has good record with 2yos but does best with older progeny at up to 1m (Dubai Destination, King's Best, Malhub, Russian Rhythm), occasionally gets top-class 10f+ horse. **Dam Crystal Crossing** Useful 6f winner at two. Sister to smart 6-7f 2yo winner Circle Of Gold. Her two earlier foals include a placed 2yo in Britain. **Conclusion** Plenty of high-class 2yos, sprinters and milers in the dam's family, so although this colt already has form over 1m, he is unlikely on pedigree to stay much further.

Russian Valour (Ire)   108

b c Fasliyev (USA) - Vert Val (USA) (Septieme Ciel (USA)) April 1
Owner A Latter & Partners **Trainer** M Johnston **Breeder** Gestut Sohrenhof
5 starts: won **3**, second **1**, third **1**, £62,863 win and place

PERUSING the runners before the 2003 Norfolk Stakes, one horse made it seem more like Ascot in December than Royal Ascot in June. The 8-13 favourite Kheleyf was a big colt, but Russian Valour was a giant, one who, as Rodney Masters reported in the Racing Post, "wouldn't look out of place alongside the likes of Best Mate and Florida Pearl". Russian Valour is a very different size and shape to those that racegoers have become accustomed to seeing in an early-season two-year-old contest – "I watched him during the winter going up the road and thought he was too big to gallop," reflected Mark Johnston, his trainer – but the Norfolk was his fifth race and third win.

Russian Valour was 4-1 in the Norfolk, splitting the David Loder-trained Kheleyf and Aidan O'Brien's Old Deuteronomy in the betting,

Race record
1st Norfolk Stakes (Group 3) (Ascot, June 19) 2yo 5f Good to firm **108** (TS 95) 8 ran.
1st betfair.com National Stakes (Listed) (Sandown, May 27) 2yo 5f Good to firm **101** (TS 95) 7 ran.
2nd windsor-racecourse.co.uk Conditions Stakes (Windsor, May 19) 2yo 5f Good to soft **96** (TS 86) 8 ran.
1st EBF Thorne Maiden Stakes (Pontefract, April 30) 2yo 5f Good to firm **82** (TS 80) 7 ran.
3rd Racecourse Video Services Maiden Stakes (Newcastle, April 22) 2yo 5f Good to firm **74** (TS 49) 7 ran.

Pedigree assessment
Sire Fasliyev (Nureyev) Top-class 2yo over 5-6f, won Phoenix Stakes and Prix Morny, then suffered career-ending injury. First 2yos in 2003, has made excellent start with lots of precocious, generally fast offspring (Carry On Katie, Kings Point, Much Faster). **Dam Vert Val** Won five races at two and three in France, effective over 7f. Her two earlier foals include Come Away With Me, a 7f 3yo winner by Machiavellian. **Conclusion** Fasliyev is an unknown quantity, both as a racehorse and as a sire, beyond the 2yo stage, but he was unlikely to last beyond 1m and indications are that he is passing on a fair amount of speed. Russian Valour has every chance of remaining a sprinter and is unlikely to stay beyond 7f.

and he joined Attraction and Pearl Of Love in helping Johnston to well and truly put one over the big-money players at the Royal meeting with his two-year-olds.

Cutting across from a wide draw to make the running against the rails, Russian Valour set a stern pace under Kevin Darley and saw off all challengers to beat Kheleyf by a length and three-quarters. Although he picked up a maiden at Pontefract and a Listed race at Sandown on his way to Ascot, Russian Valour had also hung badly to his left and right and was beaten twice. "This is the first time he has run straight," reported Darley after the Norfolk. "Mentally, perhaps he has been a bit behind himself physically."

An unspecified problem kept Russian Valour off the track after Royal Ascot. However, Johnston reported in November that "Russian Valour will be aimed for the 2,000 Guineas and I am surprised that he is omitted from all lists." Unraced beyond five furlongs and by a high-class juvenile who never had his chance to race at three, Russian Valour is not sure to stay the Guineas trip, but the dam's side gives plenty of hope. Connections are considering one of the Guineas trials.

Weighing in at 560 kilos, "Russian Valour is the heaviest successful horse that I have trained," said Johnston. "Others, like Desert Deer, reached 530 kilos at times but, at their best, raced off less. I would not expect Russian Valour to be any heavier at three. Many two-year-olds are heavier than they will be later in their careers. They tend to carry more condition and we probably train them a bit harder at three." *RA*

Salford City (Ire)　　　91+

b c Desert Sun - Summer Fashion (Moorestyle) April 20
Owner A J Thompson **Trainer** D R C Elsworth **Breeder** Dr D Davis
1 start: won 1, **£6,240** win and place

SALFORD CITY created quite an impression when winning his maiden at Newbury in late October. Paddock inspection suggested the half-brother to 1999 Dante winner Salford Express was in need of both the exercise and the experience but that did not prevent him from annihilating his opponents. Despite missing the break badly and taking a while to

Race record
1st CiSTM EBF Maiden Stakes (Div II) (Newbury, October 25) 2yo 1m Good to firm **91** (TS 89)17 ran.
Pedigree assessment
Sire **Desert Sun** (Green Desert) 7f winner at 2, later very useful 7-8f winner. Plenty of speed in pedigree. First European 2yos this year, previously sire of outstanding 7f+ racemare Sunline. **Dam Summer Fashion** Unraced at 2, later fair 8-10f winner. By sprinter out of half-sister to high-class 10-12f performer Candy Cane. Her 7 earlier foals feature top-class 2yo and 10-12f colt Definite Article (by Indian Ridge) and smart 10-12f colt Salford Express (by Be My Guest). **Conclusion** Has already won over 1m and, given the record of his half-brothers, should stay 10f. Not sure to get 12f.

get into an early rhythm, Salford City was soon back in touch with the leaders without Dane O'Neill having to work too hard.

As the race developed it became apparent that he was running all over his rivals from some way out, but O'Neill waited until just over a furlong out before letting the son of Desert Sun go. He quickly put daylight between himself and his rivals and strode home fully seven lengths clear, a margin that could easily have been increased. Within a week the form had been franked by sixth-placed Border Music's impressive Polytrack win at Lingfield.

The evidence on offer suggests Salford City is a young horse of immense ability. He has the potential and scope to be highly competitive in one of the recognised Derby trials before heading to Epsom. *ST*

Secret Charm (Ire)   96+

b f Green Desert (USA) - Viz (USA) (Kris S (USA)) April 18
Owner Maktoum Al Maktoum **Trainer** B W Hills **Breeder** Gainsborough Stud Management **2** starts: won **2**, **£17,577** win and place

---

TWO runs, two wins. Secret Charm has made an unblemished start to her racing career and promises to make an impact in Group races as a three-year-old. There is substance behind the strike-rate. First she won a 23-runner Newmarket maiden at the start of October, a race that promised quality as well as quantity judged by the pedigrees and which presented further difficulties for 11-2 chance Secret Charm, who did not have the best of the draw and was asked to come from off a modest pace. Getting home by a neck was enough to see her sent off 2-1 favourite

Race record
1st Punter Southall Radley Stakes (Listed) (Newbury, October 25) 2yo 7f Good to firm **96** (TS 81) 12 ran.
1st Beech House Stud EBF Maiden Stakes (Newmarket, October 3) 2yo 7f Good to firm **83** (TS 70) 23 ran.

Pedigree assessment
Sire Green Desert (Danzig) High-class sprint 2yo, top-class sprinter-miler at three, won July Cup and 2nd 2,000 Guineas. Excellent sire, excels with 2yos (Bint Allayl, Oasis Dream) and older horses at up to 1m (Cape Cross, Desert Prince, Owington, Sheikh Albadou, Tamarisk). **Dam Viz** Won over 1m in US. Closely related to Breeders' Cup Juvenile winner Brocco. Her three earlier foals include Oaks third Relish The Thought (by Sadler's Wells). **Conclusion** Her sire will prevent her from staying as far as Relish The Thought. She has only a fair chance of staying 10f and should be effective over 1m.

at Newbury three weeks later, despite the step up to Listed class against 11 rivals for the Radley Stakes.

Barry Hills, Secret Charm's trainer, had won two of the previous five renewals of the Radley, most recently in 2000 with Secret Charm's half-sister Relish The Thought. With the 2003 edition underway, there was never much doubt that the family and stable records would be improved. Market rival Hathrah, the May Hill runner-up, duly emerged as the biggest danger, but never a serious one, as Secret Charm was the only one still on the bridle two furlongs out and raced on to victory by a length and three-quarters.

Secret Charm: Listed winner and unbeaten in two starts

Relish The Thought (by Sadler's Wells) was placed in the Musidora and Oaks on her first two starts as a three-year-old before things went awry in two outings in midsummer, possibly because of an unsatisfactory temperament. Secret Charm is by Green Desert, so the Guineas would be her likely Classic destination if she comes up to scratch in the spring. Her two races at two years were over seven furlongs. Hills thinks she will get a mile and a quarter, but not much further. *RA*

Snow Goose   100

b f Polar Falcon (USA) - Bronzewing (Beldale Flutter (USA)) February 7
Owner Sir Thomas Pilkington **Trainer** J L Dunlop **Breeder** Sir Thomas Pilkington
5 starts: won **3**, second **1**, third **0**, **£44,195** win and place

SNOW GOOSE may well fall short of the standard required to win one of the domestic Classics, but it's possible to see her winning one of the trials and a decent prize abroad. She improved with every one of her five races at two, rattling off a hat-trick of wins at Leicester, Redcar and Newmarket before signing off with a more than respectable length-and-a-half second to Cairns in the Rockfel Stakes, back at Newmarket.

The level of form she showed when accounting for a huge field in a Newmarket nursery was always going to leave her vulnerable in as significant a Group 2 as the Rockfel, but having made the running again it was only inside the final furlong that she succumbed to the unexposed

Cairns, who has more speed and a bit more class.

What makes Snow Goose's achievements all the more creditable is that her family are seldom seen to full advantage until tackling longer distances in their second season, so further improvement is very much on the cards. She could do well. *GD*

Race record

2nd Owen Brown Rockfel Stakes (Group 2) (Newmarket, October 18) 2yo 7f Good to firm **100** (TS 89) 10 ran.

1st EBF Jersey Lily Fillies' Nursery (Newmarket, October 4) 2yo 7f Good to firm **96** (TS 90) 18 ran.

1st skybet.com Novice Median Auction Stakes (Redcar, August 23) 2yo 7f Good to firm **80** (TS 60) 4 ran.

1st EBF bmibaby Median Auction Maiden Fillies' Stakes (Leicester, July 30) 2yo 6f Good **79** (TS 69) 14 ran.

4th Little Ditton Maiden Fillies' Stakes (Newmarket (July), July 10) 2yo 6f Good to firm **69** 12 ran.

Pedigree assessment

Sire Polar Falcon (Nureyev) Unraced at 2, later very high-class form over 6-8f, won Lockinge and Haydock Sprint Cup. By outstanding miler out of high-class middle-distance filly. Very good sire, known for tough, progressive offspring, mainly over 7-10f but also sire of high-class sprinter Pivotal. **Dam Bronzewing** Fair 6f 2yo and 1m 3yo winner. Her nine earlier foals include 10f Listed winner Merry Merlin (by Polar Falcon) and smart 12f+ gelding Dusky Warbler (by Ezzoud). **Conclusion** Dam has tended to get middle-distance offspring, even out of quite speedy stallions. This one is certain to appreciate at least 1m and should stay 10f. Both sire and dam's progeny tend to be progressive, so there could be better to come from Snow Goose.

Snow Ridge (Ire)   112+

b c Indian Ridge - Snow Princess (Ire) (Ela-Mana-Mou) April 9
Owner Exors of the late Lord Weinstock **Trainer** M P Tregoning **Breeder** Ballymacoll Stud **3** starts: won **2**, second **0**, third **0**, **£63,930** win and place

THERE are two sides to the coin with Snow Ridge. Heads, Marcus Tregoning said he is the best two-year-old he has trained after a startling win in the Royal Lodge Stakes. Tails, Tregoning had trained only 31 individual two-year-old winners going into the latest season, and Snow Ridge finished only ninth of 12 in the Dewhurst. But don't forget the first half of that summary too quickly.

Snow Ridge lined up a 15-8 favourite for Ascot's Royal Lodge in September, having turned over the promising maiden winner Iqte Saab in striking fashion in a conditions stakes on his debut at Kempton three weeks earlier, but punters' confidence in him initially looked badly misplaced. The pace was not strong, which theoretically put the held-up-in-rear Snow Ridge at a disadvantage, and he was at an even bigger disadvantage when he showed his inexperience and floundered once asked to quicken on the home turn. Two furlongs out he had seven horses to pass, and a furlong later he still had four in front of him and about three lengths to make up. But he was only just putting his head down and when he found his stride he did so to such effect that he looked a comfortable winner as he passed the post.

Beating Moscow Ballet and Rule Of Law by three-quarters of a length does not put Snow Ridge anywhere near top of the pile, and being beaten by eight rivals in the Dewhurst, having raced closer to the pace, a bit freely early on, was clearly a big disappointment, even allowing

Race record

9th Darley Dewhurst Stakes (Group 1) (Newmarket, October 18) 2yo 7f Good to firm **107** (TS 99) 12 ran.

1st Hackney Empire Royal Lodge Stakes (Group 2) (Ascot, September 27) 2yo 1m Good to firm **112** (TS 106) 10 ran.

1st Coral Fantasy 4-4-2 Conditions Stakes (Kempton, September 6) 2yo 7f Good **92** (TS 65) 7 ran.

Pedigree assessment

Sire **Indian Ridge** (Ahonoora) Won at two, progressed into high-class performer from 5-7f at three and four. Excellent sire, does well with 2yos (Definite Article, Snow Ridge) and older progeny, mainly at up to 1m (Domedriver, Indian Haven, Namid, Ridgewood Pearl) but occasionally further (Indian Creek). Dam **Snow Princess** Won November Handicap (12f) at three, progressed into smart stayer at four, 2nd Gr1 Prix Royal-Oak (15f). Her two earlier foals include dual 12f Irish winner White Queen (by Spectrum). **Conclusion** Stoutly bred on dam's side and should appreciate step up to 10f, though 12f not certain to suit.

for the shorter distance. However, he must be given another chance, as he started his career only on September 6, has considerable physical scope and there is no denying the promise of his Ascot win.

He could still develop into a Classic contender, but which Classic is a matter of debate, with two starkly contrasting sides of the coin as far as his pedigree is concerned, too. Snow Ridge is still one to consider for the Guineas and is due to run in a Guineas trial. But while he should stay further than a mile, Indian Ridge's influence raises a significant doubt over his getting the Derby distance. *RA*

Spotlight   101

ch f Dr Fong (USA) - Dust Dancer (Suave Dancer (USA)) April 23
Owner Hesmonds Stud **Trainer** J L Dunlop **Breeder** Hesmonds Stud
4 starts: won **2**, second **1**, third **1**, **£20,879** win and place

THERE has to be a suspicion that Spotlight was flattered by her four-length defeat of St Francis Wood and Ouija Board in the Listed Montrose Fillies' Stakes on Newmarket's final day of the season. Pat Eddery, having his penultimate ride at the track, rode his rivals to sleep in a race in which he was allowed a soft lead at a moderate pace, and when he gradually wound things up from the front he was never going to be caught. Nevertheless, the wide margin by which Spotlight scored from a decent field suggests she would have won anyway and she is undoubtedly promising.

Spotlight had earlier won an above-average maiden at Warwick and had met her only defeats in races won by top prospects of Sir Michael Stoute's, finishing third to the subsequent Fillies' Mile winner Red

Race record

1st EBF Montrose Fillies' Stakes (Listed) (Newmarket, November 1) 2yo 1m Good to soft **101** (TS 88) 12 ran.

2nd Finnforest Oh So Sharp Stakes (Listed) (Newmarket, October 4) 2yo 7f Good to firm **101** (TS 83) 9 ran.

1st EBF Maiden Fillies' Stakes (Warwick, September 8) 2yo 7f Good to firm **84** (TS 77) 15 ran.

3rd Hoofbeats Maiden Fillies' Stakes (Newmarket (July), August 16) 2yo 7f Good to firm **82** (TS 74) 12 ran.

Pedigree assessment

Sire Dr Fong (Kris S) Smart 1m 2yo winner, progressed into top-class miler at three and also showed smart form over 10f, less successful thereafter in US. Full-brother to high-class 2yo Lucky Story. Has a fair record with first 2yos in 2003 (also sire of 6f Listed winner Miss Childrey) and should do at least as well with 3yos. **Dam Dust Dancer** Placed at 2 and very useful performer over 10-12f at 3 after breaking maiden over 7f. Half-sister to smart pair Bulaxie (7-10f) and Zimzalabim (10-12f). Her two earlier foals are 7f 2yo winner and useful miler Dusty Answer (by Zafonic) and fair 7f 3yo winner Tyranny (by Machiavellian). **Conclusion** Family members usually progressive, so there is every chance Spotlight can enhance her record at 3. Already proven at 1m and, though sire is an unknown quantity with his 3yos, there is a reasonable chance Spotlight will stay 10f.

Bloom on her debut at Newmarket, where she was doing all of her best work at the finish, and running the unbeaten Top Romance to a neck in the Oh So Sharp Stakes on the same course. She was again going on well at the finish in the latter race and Eddery, who had not ridden her before, said afterwards that he should have made more use of her.

There is a lot to like in Spotlight's profile and she looks sure to train on and get at least a mile and a quarter at three. *GD*

Sundrop (Jpn)   108

b f Sunday Silence (USA) - Oenothera (Ire) (Night Shift (USA)) March 16
Owner Sheikh Mohammed **Trainer** D R Loder **Breeder** Y Hosakawa
2 starts: won **1**, second **1**, **£47,406** win and place

THERE'S a wind of change on the all-weather, and not just the one that demands a thick overcoat with the onset of a grim winter. A few years back, for instance, you really knew your luck was out if you ran a horse on the sand and one of Sheikh Mohammed's turned up to beat you. But the standard of all-weather racing is on the rise all the time – it has been transformed at Lingfield by the introduction of the Polytrack

Sundrop (nearside): should improve at middle distances

surface – and the Sheikh's colours at Lingfield, Wolverhampton and, if you were really sharp-eyed, at Southwell in 2003 were no mirage. A maiden-race winner good enough to come second in a Group 1 next time is one indication of just how far things have come.

Horses trained by David Loder were regularly in action on the all-weather in the spring of 2003, with quality performers Parasol, With Reason and

Race record
2nd Meon Valley Stud Fillies' Mile (Group 1) (Ascot, September 27) 2yo 1m Good to firm **108** (TS 107) 7 ran.
1st EBF Maiden Fillies' Stakes (Div II) (Lingfield (AW), September 9) 2yo 7f Standard **82** (TS 73) 10 ran.

Pedigree assessment
Sire Sunday Silence (Halo) Top-class US dirt performer over 9f+, won six Grade 1 events, notably Preakness Stakes, Kentucky Derby and Breeders' Cup Classic. Outstanding sire in Japan, has decent record with 2yos but far better with older horses, mainly over 10f+. European Pattern winners include Silent Honor (6f at two) and Sunday Picnic (11f). **Dam Oenothera** Unraced at two, later very useful over 10f. Shares her dam with several high-class 12f+ performers, including Great Marquess and Northern Spur. **Conclusion** Strong encouragement on both sides of her pedigree that Sundrop will stay 12f, and every chance she will make substantial progress from two to three.

Etesaal among them. A series of two-year-olds got their chance later on, the most notable of whom was Sundrop who, carrying the maroon and white at 10-11, won a seven-furlong maiden at Lingfield in September by a head from Grandalea.

Eighteen days after that debut success, Sundrop was at Ascot for the Fillies' Mile and went down by just a length and a quarter. Starting at 10-1 and with her owner's new acquisition Punctilious sporting the first colours, Sundrop was hemmed in behind Punctilious and inside Red Bloom from entering the straight until approaching the final furlong, but although she got out to beat Punctilious by a short head, Red Bloom was going away at the finish. There is plenty of stamina in her pedigree and Sundrop will be suited by middle distances when she reappears with Godolphin. *RA*

The Mighty Tiger (USA) 110+

ch c Storm Cat (USA) - Clear Mandate (USA) (Deputy Minister (Can)) February 27 **Owner** M Tabor & Mrs John Magnier **Trainer** A P O'Brien **Breeder** G W Humphrey **4** starts: won **1**, second **1**, third **2**, **£32,662** win and place

A SALES-TOPPER at Keeneland, The Mighty Tiger created plenty of interest on his British debut at Newmarket in May but was eclipsed by his highly talented stablemate Old Deuteronomy, who produced a telling change of gear to sprint past his more expensive stablemate. Despite his defeat, the $2.5m yearling showed plenty of promise for the future and fulfilled some of it when easily getting the better of the consistent

- -

Race record

3rd Galileo EBF Futurity Stakes (Group 2) (Curragh, August 23) 2yo 7f Good to firm **103** (TS 96) 8 ran.

2nd Veuve Clicquot Vintage Stakes (Group 2) (Goodwood, July 30) 2yo 7f Good to soft **110** (TS 102) 9 ran.

1st U.A.E. Equestrian/Racing Federation Maiden (Curragh, June 28) 2yo 6f Good to yielding **94** (TS 35) 9 ran.

3rd EBF Maiden Stakes (Newmarket, May 31) 2yo 6f Good to firm **72** 9 ran.

Pedigree assessment

Sire Storm Cat (Storm Bird) top-class US 2yo over 1m. Both sire and dam top-class 2yos. Outstanding US-based sire, European progeny generally excel at around 1m, best include Aljabr, Black Minnaloushe, Catrail, Giant's Causeway, Sophisticat. **Dam Clear Mandate** Grade 1 winner at 2 in US, later top-class filly over 8-9f on dirt. Out of Grade 1-winning half-sister to Belmont S winner Creme Fraiche. Her 2 earlier foals are fair 6f 2yo winner Newfoundland (by Storm Cat) and US 9f stakes winner Full Mandate (by AP Indy). **Conclusion** Every chance he will make good progress from 2 to 3, as family members tend to be better at 3 or older. Should be suited by 1m and may stay slightly further.

- -

Clock Tower in a six-furlong Curragh maiden four weeks later, staying on strongly after leading just after halfway.

Stepped up in grade into Goodwood's Vintage Stakes on the back of that effort, the son of Storm Cat showed much-improved form in defeat, chasing subsequent good Doncaster winner Lucky Story hard and putting up a performance of real merit to run him to a length and a quarter. However, he failed to reproduce that form on his next and final start in the seven-furlong Futurity Stakes, in which Chesham Stakes winner Pearl Of Love, another classy colt from Mark Johnston's stable, proved far too sharp for him and had him nearly four lengths back in third.

With National Stakes runner-up Wathab filling fourth place, the Futurity form is solid enough, but The Mighty Tiger will have to make considerable progress over the winter if he is to move to the head of the Ballydoyle pecking order. *ST*

Three Valleys   117

See entry in the top 100 horses, page 402

Top Romance (Ire)   102+

ch f Entrepreneur - Heart's Harmony (Blushing Groom (Fr)) March 15
Owner Mrs Denis Haynes **Trainer** Sir Michael Stoute **Breeder** Wretham Stud
2 starts: won **2**, **£15,721** win and place

TOP ROMANCE was inevitably overshadowed by Fillies' Mile winner Red Bloom among her stable's juvenile fillies, but she could do no more than win her only two races, including the Listed Oh So Sharp Stakes at Newmarket. What's more, one could argue that everything she achieved at two was a bonus in any case, as her pedigree promises plenty of improvement as a three-year-old, particularly when she steps up in distance to a mile, or a mile and a quarter.

Not much appeared to be expected of Top Romance when she made her debut in a two-year-old maiden at Yarmouth in September, as she

Race record
1st Finnforest Oh So Sharp Stakes (Listed) (Newmarket, October 4) 2yo 7f Good to firm **102** (TS 83) 9 ran.
1st betfair.com Maiden Stakes (Yarmouth, September 2) 2yo 7f Good to firm **72** (TS 64) 12 ran.

Pedigree assessment
Sire **Entrepreneur** (Sadler's Wells) Won 2,000 Guineas and fourth in Derby. Quite modest record overall at stud, though generally an influence for late-developing horses who stay at least 1m. Sire of Irish Oaks winner Vintage Tipple and Scottish Classic winner Princely Venture. **Dam Heart's Harmony** Placed over 1m in France. Previous foals include smart middle-distance performer National Anthem. **Conclusion** Has the pedigree to improve from two to three and should stay at least 10f.

was a 13-2 chance in what looked an ordinary race. However, she won so well that day, given just one tap to cut down the favourite Golden Empire inside the final furlong and win easing down, that she deserved her chance in better company at Newmarket the following month. Allowed to dictate from the front this time in a race in which the pace was only steady, she put up another taking performance and held on well, by a neck from Spotlight.

While, at the time, Top Romance did not impress the odds compilers as a Classic prospect, the form worked out tremendously well, with Spotlight and fourth-placed Dowager going on to win Listed races on the same course and third-placed Kelucia occupying the same position in the Rockfel. She ought to improve sufficiently to win a Group race or two and already has a head start on her later-developing half-brother National Anthem, who was Group class by the time of his export to America as a four-year-old but had only one chance in that grade. *GD*

Troubadour (Ire) 112

b c Danehill (USA) - Taking Liberties (Ire) (Royal Academy (USA)) May 3
Owner R E Sangster **Trainer** A P O'Brien **Breeder** Swettenham Stud
3 starts: won 1, second 0, third 1, £18,073 win and place

ONE of the 2003 juvenile season's more remarkable statistics was Aidan O'Brien's failure to train a Group or Listed winner in Britain, but it would be dangerous to assume the Ballydoyle team will have a weak three-year-old team as a result.

Indeed, statistics tell us that O'Brien is now having fewer runners in British Pattern events than he was a few years back, his total runners in 2003 having been almost a third down on levels of 2000 and 2001, which suggests a slightly more patient policy with his young horses.

One who was tried at the highest level at two was Troubadour, who made the perfect start to his career when easily upsetting subsequent maiden winner Ulfah over six furlongs at The Curragh. Subsequently beaten comprehensively at 4-7 in the Round Tower Stakes by Wathab,

Race record
5th Darley Dewhurst Stakes (Group 1) (Newmarket, October 18) 2yo 7f Good to firm **112** (TS 102) 12 ran.
3rd Go And Go Round Tower Stakes (Listed) (Curragh, August 31) 2yo 6f Good to firm **97** (TS 73) 5 ran.
1st Waterford Crystal EBF Maiden (Curragh, August 10) 2yo 6f Good **97** (TS 64) 10 ran.

Pedigree assessment
Sire Danehill (Danzig) Useful 6f 2yo winner, improved at 3 into top-class sprinter, won Haydock Sprint Cup, but also smart over 1m. Excellent sire, does well with 2yos and older progeny up to 1m but can get top-class 12f horses and now has a classy stayer in Westerner. Best progeny include Aquarelliste, Banks Hill, Clodovil, Desert King, Mozart, Rock Of Gibraltar. **Dam Taking Liberties** Unplaced over 7f at 3 on only start. Sister to 1m 2yo Group 3 winner Equal Rights out of a middle-distance Australasian Group 1 winner. Her three earlier foals, all winners, have struck at up to 1m. **Conclusion** Dam's winners are by Indian Ridge and Spectrum, and Danehill is another who imparts quite a lot of speed. Troubadour should be effective at 1m.

Troubadour: has the makings of a smart miler

who went on to finish runner-up in the National Stakes, and Simple Exchange, a subsequent Listed winner, he was put away until the Dewhurst, where he went off at 40-1 but ran a cracking race in defeat, finishing only two lengths behind surprise winner Milk It Mick after forcing the pace for much of the journey.

There should be much better to come from Troubadour and he could make up into one of his stable's best three-year-old milers. *ST*

Venturi   112

b f Danehill Dancer (Ire) - Zagreb Flyer (Old Vic) February 7
Owner Mrs Paul Shanahan **Trainer** David Wachman **Breeder** Lloyd Farm Stud
3 starts: won **2**, second **0**, third **0**, £40,097 win and place

VENTURI stamped herself one of the best two-year-old fillies trained in Ireland when stepping up in class and distance to beat the Moyglare Stud Stakes fourth Misty Heights by three-quarters of a length in the Group 3 CL Weld Park Stakes at The Curragh in September. It has to be said that Ireland's leading juvenile fillies were an unexceptional bunch and the Moyglare form wasn't as strong as usual, but that is hardly Venturi's fault.

She could do no more than was asked of her and improved markedly with each of her three races, emerging from the long break that followed her debut sixth at Navan in early May to account for a big field in a similar race at The Curragh at the end of August and then returning to the same course for the CL Weld Stakes. Misty Heights was odds-on in a field of 10 for the latter race, but Venturi's maiden win was already starting to work out well and she won on merit, coming with a strong run from off the pace and quickening up inside the final furlong to give trainer David Wachman a career-first Group-race success.

Venturi has the size and scope to train on and there is no reason why she should not go on improving. How far she will progress is impossible to say, but Wachman is prepared to take her to the continent for the right opportunities and she ought to be placed to advantage. *GD*

- -

Race record

1st CL Weld Park Stakes (Group 3) (Curragh, September 21) 2yo 7f Good to firm **105** (TS 83) 10 ran.
1st Bloodstock Underwriting EBF Maiden (Curragh, August 31) 2yo 6f Good to firm **77** (TS 72) 15 ran.
6th Coolmore King Charlemagne EBF Maiden (Navan, May 4) 2yo 5f Soft **53** 10 ran.

Pedigree assessment

Sire Danehill Dancer (Danehill) Top-class 2yo, won Phoenix and National S and 2nd Dewhurst S. At 3, won 7f Greenham S but later showed useful sprint form. Good sire of 2yos and older horses at up to 1m (Barbajuan, Choisir, Lady Dominatrix, Where Or When, Ziria). **Dam Zagreb Flyer** Unraced. By top-class 12f performer and influence for stamina, half-sister to Italian Oaks runner-up Flying Girl out of a half-sister to top-class 2yo/miler To-Agori-Mou. Her three earlier foals have made very little impact. **Conclusion** Dam quite stoutly bred, so Venturi is sure to appreciate at least 1m and has every chance of lasting 10f.

- -

Voix du Nord   114

See entry in the top 100 horses, page 426

Wathab (Ire)   115

b c Cadeaux Genereux - Bally Souza (Ire) (Alzao (USA)) February 2
Owner Haif Mohammed Al-Ghatani **Trainer** Kevin Prendergast **Breeder** Haif Al-Qhantani **10 starts: won 2, second 4, third 1, £90,551** win and place

FROM runner-up in an early-season maiden to runner-up in one of the best juvenile Group 1s of the season, Wathab was certainly one of the success stories of the 2003 Irish juvenile season.

Starting off in a hot five-furlong maiden in April, Kevin Prendergast's colt shaped with stacks of promise behind subsequent nursery winner Steel Light before getting off the mark on his third start, when relishing the step up to six furlongs and showing Mick Channon's useful Cedarberg a clean pair of heels after making the running.

Having tried and failed to make a serious impact in some of the best juvenile company on his next starts, perhaps doing best when chasing home Royal Lodge fifth Privy Seal in the Listed Tyros Stakes at Leopardstown, Wathab seemed well exposed and little more than a useful form marker for some of the better Irish juvenile races.

But all that changed when he got the better of Dermot Weld's subsequent Listed winner Simple Exchange in the Round Tower Stakes, stepping up on his earlier form to record a Racing Post Rating of 107, and even better was to come when he lined up for the National Stakes on his final

Race record

2nd Dunnes Stores National Stakes (Group 1) (Curragh, September 14) 2yo 7f Good to firm **115** (TS 89) 8 ran.

1st Go And Go Round Tower Stakes (Listed) (Curragh, August 31) 2yo 6f Good to firm **107** (TS 87) 5 ran.

4th Galileo EBF Futurity Stakes (Group 2) (Curragh, August 23) 2yo 7f Good to firm **101** (TS 94) 8 ran.

6th Independent Waterford Wedgwood Phoenix Stakes (Group 1) (Curragh, August 10) 2yo 6f Good **95** (TS 85) 7 ran.

2nd Tyros Stakes (Listed) (Leopardstown, July 26) 2yo 7f Good to firm **102** (TS 53) 5 ran.

7th Anheuser Busch Railway Stakes (Group 2) (Curragh, June 29) 2yo 6f Good **64** 7 ran.

3rd Rochestown Stakes (Listed) (Leopardstown, June 11) 2yo 6f Yielding **85** (TS 86) 6 ran.

1st Sara Lee EBF Maiden (Curragh, May 25) 2yo 6f Soft **88** (TS 59) 9 ran.

2nd Limerick Junction EBF Race (Tipperary, May 8) 2yo 5f Soft **76** 4 ran.

2nd Mull Of Kintyre EBF Maiden (Curragh, April 27) 2yo 5f Good to yielding **81** (TS 67) 10 ran.

Pedigree assessment

Sire Cadeaux Genereux (Young Generation) Unraced at 2, top-class sprinter at 3 and 4, also showed smart form over 7-8f. Very good sire, excels with 2yos (Bahamian Bounty, Embassy, Hoh Magic) but also gets progressive progeny, mostly at up to 1m (Touch Of The Blues). **Dam Bally Souza** Placed over 7f at 2 and 11-12f winner at 3. Half-sister to useful miler A La Carte, from good US family. Her only previous foal is very modest. **Conclusion** Some stamina on dam's side, so Wathab should be able to stay 1m but unlikely to get further.

start. With more restrained tactics employed for the first time, Wathab made significant ground over one and a half furlongs out and stayed on determinedly to chase home Racing Post champion two-year-old One Cool Cat, depriving Pearl Of Love of second place and earning a Racing Post Rating of 115. Wathab's pedigree, attitude and style of racing all strongly suggest he will have no problem with a mile. *ST*

Well Known   81+

b f Sadler's Wells (USA) - Danefair (Danehill (USA)) January 25
Owner K Abdullah **Trainer** R Charlton **Breeder** Juddmonte Farms
1 start: won 0, second 1, £1,834 win and place

WELL KNOWN has no place in this company judged purely on racecourse achievement, yet one can see why she figures in ante-post lists for the 1,000 Guineas. There was considerable promise in her debut second to Park Accord in a conditions race over seven furlongs at Kempton in September and she is a Sadler's Wells half-sister to her stable's talented seven-furlong specialist Trade Fair.

Having been keen early on, she quickened to the front at the two-furlong

---

Race record
2nd Simon Weston Fillies' Conditions Stakes (Kempton, September 5) 2yo 7f Good to firm **81** (TS 57) 7 ran.

Pedigree assessment
Sire Sadler's Wells (Northern Dancer) Smart 7-8f winner at two, improved into top-class colt over 1m to 12f at three, won Irish 2,000 Guineas, Eclipse and Irish Champion Stakes. Outstanding sire, particularly of 3yos+ over 1m to 12f, also has good record with autumn 2yos. **Dam Danefair** Smart French 3yo over 10-12f. Sister to smart 9-10f filly Prove. Danefair's three earlier foals include high-class 7f performer Trade Fair (by Zafonic). **Conclusion** Guaranteed to have more stamina than Trade Fair. Highly likely to stay 10f and should get further.

---

marker but had to give best when Park Accord arrived on the scene and was not punished unduly. There was no disgrace in going down by a length to Carry On Katie's much-hyped stablemate, who even before her debut was among the market leaders for the Guineas. Park Accord was tragically put down shortly afterwards following an injury at exercise, but third-placed Spring Goddess and sixth-placed Unavailable gave the form a solid look by winning next time. Well Known was not seen out again, but she is a filly who looks certain to go places at three, when she is unlikely to suffer from her half-brother's stamina limitations. *GD*

Whipper   115

See entry in the top 100 horses, page 438

Wolfe Tone (Ire)   81+

b c Sadler's Wells (USA) - Angelic Song (Can) (Halo (USA)) May 24
Owner Mrs John Magnier **Trainer** A P O'Brien **Breeder** Linley Bloodstock
1 start: won 1, £8,737 win and place

THE maiden that Wolfe Tone won at Galway in August could hardly have worked out worse, since his six rivals that day were all still maidens at the end of the season, but that is no reason to condemn him. He won readily, by four and a half lengths from German Malt after taking a while to hit top gear, and it is probably no coincidence that Aidan O'Brien had won the same race a year earlier with Derby runner-up The Great Gatsby.

Wolfe Tone was not seen out again, but he was spoken of as being among the stable's better prospects and appeared among the five-day

Wolfe Tone: dark horse bred on impeccable lines

acceptors for some of the top races, including the Racing Post Trophy. While he needs to improve enormously on what he achieved at Galway to make his presence felt in Group company, there is every likelihood he will. His pedigree suggests he will do much better over middle distances, being a brother to the Hollywood Turf Cup winner Sligo Bay and bred on similar lines to Singspiel, and he could be anything. *GD*

Race record
1st Dawn Hi And Lo EBF Maiden (Galway, August 2) 2yo 8½f Yielding **81** 7 ran.

Pedigree assessment
Sire Sadler's Wells (Northern Dancer) Smart 7-8f winner at 2, improved into top-class colt over 8-12f at 3, won Irish 2,000 Guineas, Eclipse and Irish Champion S. Outstanding sire, particularly of 3yos+ over 8-12f, also has good record with autumn 2yos. **Dam Angelic Song** Unraced. Full-sister to top-class pair Devil's Bag and Glorious Song (dam of Rahy, Singspiel; grand-dam of Mezzo Soprano). Her 9 earlier foals feature smart 8-10f 2yo Sligo Bay (by Sadler's Wells), later a 12f Grade 1 winner. **Conclusion** Bred along very similar lines to Singspiel. There is no doubt Wolfe Tone will stay 12f and he will need at least 10f. Has background to be top class.

Yeats (Ire)   91+

b c Sadler's Wells (USA) - Lyndonville (Ire) (Top Ville) April 23
Owner Mrs John Magnier **Trainer** A P O'Brien **Breeder** Barronstown Stud and Orpendale **1** start: won **1**, **£8,441** win and place

"THIS colt is a beauty. He's been a proper horse all the way at home. It was always going to be the same as Galileo with this fellow – one run and then put him away until next season. If we get him through the winter okay then we'll go the Galileo route with him early next season, starting off in the Ballysax and then taking in the Derrinstown Stud Derby Trial."

So said Aidan O'Brien after Yeats' impressive four-length maiden win at The Curragh in September, and in doing so he unwittingly burdened the colt with ante-post favouritism for the Derby, a post-race quote of 16-1 mirroring that offered immediately after Galileo's 14-length debut romp at Leopardstown three years earlier.

By the end of the turf season some of the pressure had been taken

---

Race record

1st Korean Racing Association EBF Maiden (Curragh, September 21) 2yo 1m Good to firm **91** (TS 66) 15 ran.

Pedigree assessment

Sire Sadler's Wells (Northern Dancer) Smart 7-8f winner at 2, improved into top-class colt over 8-12f at 3, won Irish 2,000 Guineas, Eclipse and Irish Champion S. Outstanding sire, particularly of 3yos+ over 8-12f, also has good record with autumn 2yos. **Dam Lyndonville** Won over 14f and placed over 12f at 3. By top-class 12f performer and stamina influence, half-sister to Fillies' Mile winner Ivanka (by Dancing Brave) and to dam of both high-class stayer Alcazar and top-class 1m 2yo Lady Of Chad. Her 6 earlier foals feature high-class Japanese 1m+ colt Tsukuba Symphony (by Danehill). **Conclusion** Bred on the same cross (Sadler's Wells-Top Ville) as Montjeu. Guaranteed to stay 10f and should stay 12f.

---

off Yeats's shoulders by American Post, who was made Epsom favourite in most lists following his win in the Racing Post Trophy.

Nevertheless, the expectations of him at three are totally disproportionate to his achievement at two and there is a danger that he might be one of those unfortunates who unfairly ends up being labelled an under-achiever, despite improving two stone or more. Let's hope not.

Galileo did not put a foot wrong at three until he was dropped back in distance in the autumn, winning the Ballysax, the Derrinstown, two Derbys and the King George before he was touched off by Fantastic Light in an epic battle for the Irish Champion Stakes.

There could hardly be a harder act to follow, but O'Brien has clearly seen something very special in Yeats and the colt is undeniably an exciting prospect. Whatever the merit of his Curragh form – and he was an easy-to-back 6-4 chance for what turned out to be a fairly ordinary maiden – he could do no more than win easily and he will be open to any amount of improvement when he steps up to middle distances. One can only wish him well. *GD*

Racing Post Classification

The Racing Post Classification lists the Racing Post Ratings for the world's leading racehorses. The classification takes into account performances in Group 1 and Grade 1 races worldwide, Group racing as a whole throughout Europe and all racing in Britain and Ireland. They provide a fascinating insight into the relative merits of the best horses that represented each of the major racing nations in 2003. Racing Post Ratings are compiled by our team of independent handicappers who rely primarily on collateral form as the basis of the figures. The ratings incorporate weight-for-age allowances to facilitate direct comparison of the merit of horses of different ages. The 'distance(s)' column in the table indicates the distance, or distances, at which the horse achieved the rating

Note that the classification for dirt horses includes three-year-olds and upwards

Two-year-olds

Rating	Name & sex	Trainer	Country	Distance(s)
121	One Cool Cat (USA) C	A P O'Brien	Ireland	7f
119	Grey Swallow (Ire) C	D K Weld	Ireland	7f
118	Bago (Fr) C	J E Pease	France	8f
	Majestic Missile (Ire) C	W J Haggas	UK	5f
	Milk It Mick C	J A Osborne	UK	7f
117	American Post C	Mme C Head-Maarek	France	7f
	Attraction F	M Johnston	UK	6f
	Lucky Story (USA) C	M Johnston	UK	7f
	Three Valleys (USA) C	R Charlton	UK	6f, 7f
115	Balmont (USA) C	J Noseda	UK	6f
	Pearl Of Love (Ire) C	M Johnston	UK	7f, 8f
	Wathab (Ire) C	Kevin Prendergast	Ireland	7f
	Whipper (USA) C	Robert Collet	France	6f
114	Bachelor Duke (USA) C	J A R Toller	UK	7f
	Haafhd C	B W Hills	UK	7f
	Spirit Of Desert (Ire) C	L Brogi	Italy	8f
	Voix du Nord (Fr) C	D Smaga	France	10f
113	Holborn (UAE) C	M R Channon	UK	6f
	Old Deuteronomy (USA) C	A P O'Brien	Ireland	6f
112	Auditorium C	Sir Michael Stoute	UK	6f, 7f
	Barbajuan (Ire) C	N A Callaghan	UK	8f
	Colossus (Ire) C	A P O'Brien	Ireland	6f
	Fokine (USA) C	B W Hills	UK	6f
	Grand Reward (USA) C	A P O'Brien	Ireland	6f
	Imperial Stride C	Sir Michael Stoute	UK	7f
	Snow Ridge (Ire) C	M P Tregoning	UK	8f
	Troubadour (Ire) C	A P O'Brien	Ireland	7f
111	Bayeux (USA) C	D R Loder	UK	7f
	Diamond Green (Fr) C	A Fabre	France	7f
	Simplex (Fr) C	C Laffon-Parias	France	10f
110	Fantastic View (USA) C	R Hannon	UK	8f
	Pastoral Pursuits C	H Morrison	UK	6f
	Peak To Creek C	J Noseda	UK	7f
	Red Bloom F	Sir Michael Stoute	UK	8f

Rating	Name & sex	Trainer	Country	Distance(s)
	The Mighty Tiger (USA) C	A P O'Brien	Ireland	7f
	Whilly (Ire) C	B Grizzetti	Italy	8f

Three-year-olds

Rating	Name & sex	Trainer	Country	Distance(s)
134	Dalakhani (Ire) C	A de Royer-Dupre	France	12f
133	Alamshar (Ire) C	John M Oxx	Ireland	12f
131	Oasis Dream C	J H M Gosden	UK	5f
126	Kalaman (Ire) C	Sir Michael Stoute	UK	8f
	Refuse To Bend (Ire) C	D K Weld	Ireland	8f
	Trade Fair C	R Charlton	UK	7f
125	Brian Boru C	A P O'Brien	Ireland	15f
	Ikhtyar (Ire) C	J H M Gosden	UK	10f
	Kris Kin (USA) C	Sir Michael Stoute	UK	12f
	Magistretti (USA) C	N A Callaghan	UK	10f
123	Airwave F	H Candy	UK	5f
	High Accolade C	M P Tregoning	UK	12f
	Russian Rhythm (USA) F	Sir Michael Stoute	UK	8f
	Six Perfections (Fr) F	P Bary	France	8f
	Somnus G	T D Easterby	UK	6f
	Vespone (Ire) C	Saeed Bin Suroor	UK	10f
	Zafeen (Fr) C	Saeed Bin Suroor	UK	8f
122	Doyen (Ire) C	A Fabre	France	12f
121	Big Bad Bob (Ire) C	J L Dunlop	UK	10f, 11f
	Dai Jin C	A Schutz	Germany	12f
	L'Ancresse (Ire) F	A P O'Brien	Ireland	10f
	Powerscourt C	A P O'Brien	Ireland	12f, 14f
	Super Celebre (Fr) C	E Lellouche	France	12f
	The Great Gatsby (Ire) C	A P O'Brien	Ireland	12f
120	Avonbridge C	R Charlton	UK	6f
	Baron's Pit C	R Hannon	UK	6f
	Nebraska Tornado (USA) F	A Fabre	France	8f

Three-year-olds continued

Rating	Name & sex	Trainer	Country	Distance(s)
	Phoenix Reach (Ire) C	A M Balding	UK	15f
	Roosevelt (Ire) C	A P O'Brien	Ireland	12f
119	Arakan (USA) C	Sir Michael Stoute	UK	7f
	Leporello (Ire) C	P W Harris	UK	10f
	Mingun (USA) C	A P O'Brien	Ireland	10f
	Norse Dancer (Ire) C	D R C Elsworth	UK	12f
	Sabre d'Argent (USA) C	D R Loder	UK	11f
	Striking Ambition C	G C Bravery	UK	6f
118	Balestrini (Ire) C	A P O'Brien	Ireland	12f
	Casual Pass (Aus) G	M Ellerton	Australia	10f
	Checkit (Ire) C	M R Channon	UK	9f
	Deportivo C	R Charlton	UK	5f
	Etoile Montante (USA) F	Mme C Head-Maarek	France	7f
	Indian Haven C	P W d'Arcy	UK	8f
	Le Vie Dei Colori C	R Brogi	Italy	8f
	Maharib (Ire) C	D K Weld	Ireland	15f
	Martillo (Ger) C	R Suerland	Germany	8f
	Mezzo Soprano (USA) F	Saeed Bin Suroor	UK	12f
	Rhythm Mad (Fr) C	A Fabre	France	12f
	Soviet Song (Ire) F	J R Fanshawe	UK	8f
	Statue Of Liberty (USA) C	A P O'Brien	Ireland	8f
	Weightless G	P Bary	France	10f
	Westmoreland Road (USA) C	Mrs A J Perrett	UK	12f
	Yesterday (Ire) F	A P O'Brien	Ireland	12f
117	Clodovil (Ire) C	A Fabre	France	8f
	Hawk Flyer (USA) C	Sir Michael Stoute	UK	12f
	Look Honey (Ire) C	C Lerner	France	10f
	Muqbil (USA) C	J L Dunlop	UK	10f
	Neo Universe (Jpn) C	T Setoguchi	Japan	11f
	Ocean Silk (USA) F	J H M Gosden	UK	12f
	Tantina (USA) F	B W Hills	UK	7f
	Wando (Can) C	M Keogh	Canada	8f
116	Alberto Giacometti (Ire) C	A P O'Brien	Ireland	11f
	Ascetic Silver (Fr) C	D Prod'Homme	France	8f

Rating	Name & sex	Trainer	Country	Distance(s)
	Coroner (Ire) C	J-C Rouget	France	12f
	Dubai Success C	B W Hills	UK	12f
	Exceed And Excel (Aus) C	T Martin	Australia	7f
	France C	A P O'Brien	Ireland	8f
	Kalabar C	P Bary	France	12f
	Lateen Sails C	Saeed Bin Suroor	UK	9f
	Miss Emma (Ire) F	M Halford	Ireland	6f
	Policy Maker (Ire) C	E Lellouche	France	12f, 13f
	Ransom O'War (USA) C	Frau E Mader	Germany	10f
	Vintage Tipple (Ire) F	P Mullins	Ireland	12f

Four-year-olds-plus

Rating	Name & sex	Trainer	Country	Distance(s)
134	Hawk Wing (USA) C	A P O'Brien	Ireland	8f
132	Falbrav (Ire) H	L M Cumani	UK	10f
	Mubtaker (USA) H	M P Tregoning	UK	12f
129	Nayef (USA) H	M P Tregoning	UK	10f
128	Choisir (Aus) C	Paul Perry	Australia	5f
	High Chaparral (Ire) C	A P O'Brien	Ireland	12f
	Johar (USA) C	Richard E Mandella	USA	12f
	Sulamani (Ire) C	Saeed Bin Suroor	UK	12f
126	Domedriver (Ire) H	P Bary	France	8f
	Dubai Destination (USA) C	Saeed Bin Suroor	UK	8f
	Leadership C	Saeed Bin Suroor	UK	12f
	Rakti C	M A Jarvis	UK	10f
124	Bollin Eric C	T D Easterby	UK	12f
	Mamool (Ire) C	Saeed Bin Suroor	UK	12f
	Storming Home H	N Drysdale	USA	10f, 12f
	Warrsan (Ire) H	C E Brittain	UK	14f
123	Ange Gabriel (Fr) H	E Libaud	France	12f
	Black Sam Bellamy (Ire) C	A P O'Brien	Ireland	11f, 12f
	Denon (USA) H	R J Frankel	USA	10f
	Islington (Ire) F	Sir Michael Stoute	UK	10f

Four-year-olds-plus continued

Rating	Name & sex	Trainer	Country	Distance(s)
	Moon Ballad (Ire) C	Saeed Bin Suroor	UK	10f
	Mr Dinos (Ire) C	P F I Cole	UK	16f
	Nayyir G	G A Butler	UK	7f
	Telegnosis (Jpn) C	H Sugiura	Japan	8f
	Touch Of The Blues (Fr) H	N Drysdale	USA	8f
122	Cape Of Good Hope G	D Oughton	Hong Kong	6f
	Carnival Dancer H	Mrs A J Perrett	UK	10f
	Century City (Ire) C	C B Greely	USA	8f
	Good Journey (USA) H	W Dollase	USA	8f
	Grand Delight (Aus) G	J Size	Hong Kong	5f, 6f
	Highest (Ire) C	Saeed Bin Suroor	UK	12f
	Lohengrin (Jpn) C	M Ito	Japan	8f
	Lonhro (Aus) H	J Hawkes	Australia	8f
	Redattore (Brz) H	Richard E Mandella	USA	8f
	Vinnie Roe (Ire) H	D K Weld	Ireland	14f
	Westerner C	E Lellouche	France	20f
121	Asian Heights H	G Wragg	UK	13f
	Ekraar (USA) H	M P Tregoning	UK	12f
	Fair Mix (Ire) H	M Rolland	France	11f
	Gamut (Ire) C	Sir Michael Stoute	UK	14f
	Imperial Dancer H	M R Channon	UK	12f
	In Time's Eye C	D K Weld	Ireland	10f
	Kaieteur (USA) C	B J Meehan	UK	10f
	Millenary H	J L Dunlop	UK	12f
	Olden Times H	J L Dunlop	UK	10f
	Parasol (Ire) C	D R Loder	UK	10f
	Patavellian (Ire) G	R Charlton	UK	5f
	Special Kaldoun (Ire) C	D Smaga	France	8f
	Special Ring (USA) G	J Canani	USA	8f, 9f
	Symboli Kris S (USA) C	Kazuo Fujisawa	Japan	10f
	Tillerman H	Mrs A J Perrett	UK	8f
120	Bright Sky (Ire) F	E Lellouche	France	9f
	Dano-Mast H	F Poulsen	Denmark	12f
	Electronic Unicorn (USA) G	J Size	Hong Kong	8f

Rating	Name & sex	Trainer	Country	Distance(s)
	Firebolt (Ire) G	I W Allan	Hong Kong	5f
	Ipi Tombe (Zim) F	M F De Kock	South Africa	9f
	Next Desert (Ire) C	A Schutz	Germany	12f
	Paolini (Ger) H	A Wohler	Germany	10f
	Perfect Soul (Ire) H	R L Attfield	Canada	8f
	Soaring Free (Can) G	M Frostad	Canada	7f, 8f
119	Acclamation C	L G Cottrell	UK	5f
	Bandari (Ire) C	M Johnston	UK	12f
	Burning Sun (USA) C	H R A Cecil	UK	10f
	Clangalang (Aus) C	G Ryan	Australia	8f, 12f
	Darasim (Ire) G	M Johnston	UK	16f
	Desert Deer H	M Johnston	UK	8f
	Fayr Jag (Ire) G	T D Easterby	UK	6f
	Half Hennessy (Aus) C	E B Murray	Australia	12f
	Honor In War (USA) C	P McGee	USA	8f
	Indian Creek H	D R C Elsworth	UK	10f, 12f
	Irish Warrior (USA) H	W Dollase	USA	8f, 10f
	Jardines Lookout (Ire) G	A P Jarvis	UK	16f
	Just James C	J Noseda	UK	7f
	Persian Punch (Ire) G	D R C Elsworth	UK	16f, 18f
	Razkalla (USA) G	D R Loder	UK	12f
	The Tatling (Ire) G	J M Bradley	UK	5f, 6f
	The Tin Man (USA) G	Richard E Mandella	USA	11f, 12f
118	All Thrills Too (Aus) G	D Hayes	Hong Kong	5f
	Ashdown Express (Ire) G	C F Wall	UK	6f
	Bush Padre (Aus) G	Lee Freedman	Australia	11f
	Danger Over H	J A Osborne	UK	7f
	Dash For Cash (Aus) H	R Hore-Lacy	Australia	8f
	Designed For Luck (USA) H	V Cerin	USA	8f
	Eishin Preston (USA) H	S Kitahashi	Japan	10f
	Far Lane (USA) C	B W Hills	UK	10f, 11f
	Grand Armee (Aus) G	Mrs Gai Waterhouse	Australia	8f
	Hishi Miracle (Jpn) C	M Sayama	Japan	11f
	Island House (Ire) H	G Wragg	UK	10f, 11f

Four-year-olds-plus continued

Rating	Name & sex	Trainer	Country	Distance(s)
	Maktub (Ity) C	B Grizzetti	Italy	12f
	Northerly (Aus) G	F Kersley	Australia	10f
	Nysaean (Ire) C	R Hannon	UK	10f
	Passing Glance C	A M Balding	UK	8f
	Pentastic (Aus) G	D Hall	Australia	10f
	Polish Summer H	A Fabre	France	12f
	Priors Lodge (Ire) H	M P Tregoning	UK	8f
	Reel Buddy (USA) H	R Hannon	UK	8f
	Researched (Ire) G	Sir Michael Stoute	UK	12f
	Systematic C	M Johnston	UK	13f
	The Trader (Ire) H	M Blanshard	UK	5f
	Tsurumaru Boy (Jpn) H	K Hashiguchi	Japan	10f, 11f
	Twilight Blues (Ire) C	B J Meehan	UK	6f
	Where Or When (Ire) C	T G Mills	UK	8f
	Whitmore's Conn (USA) H	R Schulhofer	USA	12f
	With Anticipation (USA) G	J E Sheppard	USA	9f
	With Reason (USA) G	D R Loder	UK	7f
	Yell (Aus) G	J Hawkes	Australia	6f
117	Alcazar (Ire) G	H Morrison	UK	16f
	Arlington Road (Aus) G	Mrs Gai Waterhouse	Australia	8f
	Azevedo (Aus) C	R Laing	Australia	5f
	Bel Esprit (Aus) C	J Symons	Australia	7f
	Blatant C	Saeed Bin Suroor	UK	8f
	Capricho (Ire) G	J Akehurst	UK	6f
	Comfy (USA) C	Sir Michael Stoute	UK	10f
	Compton Bolter (Ire) G	G A Butler	UK	12f, 13f
	Dandoun H	J L Dunlop	UK	8f
	Deeliteful Irving (USA) H	M Dickinson	USA	12f
	Execute (Fr) H	J E Hammond	France	11f
	Freefourinternet (USA) H	Joan Scott	USA	8f
	Freemason (Aus) G	J Hawkes	Australia	10f, 11f, 12f
	Gateman G	M Johnston	UK	8f, 9f
	Heat Haze F	R J Frankel	USA	10f
	Loxias (Fr) C	C Laffon-Parias	France	12f

Rating	Name & sex	Trainer	Country	Distance(s)
	Macaw (Ire) G	B Tagg	USA	12f
	Maguire (NZ) G	J Collins	Ireland	11f
	Millstreet C	Saeed Bin Suroor	UK	12f
	Needwood Blade H	B A McMahon	UK	5f
	Royal Millennium (Ire) G	M R Channon	UK	6f, 7f
	Sarafan (USA) G	N Drysdale	USA	8f
	Shogun Lodge (Aus) G	Bob Thomsen	Australia	8f
	Strasbourg (Aus) G	Bart Cummings	Australia	12f
	Victory Moon (SAF) C	M F De Kock	South Africa	10f
	Zipping (Ire) C	Robert Collet	France	6f
116	Admire Max (Jpn) C	M Hashida	Japan	8f
	Agnes Digital (USA) H	T Shirai	Japan	8f
	Ana Marie (Fr) F	P Demercastel	France	10f
	Attache G	M A Jarvis	UK	7f
	Bahamian Pirate (USA) G	D Nicholls	UK	6f
	Balto Star (USA) G	T Pletcher	USA	11f, 12f
	Beauchamp Pilot G	G A Butler	UK	8f
	Bernebeau (Fr) C	A Fabre	France	9f
	Colonel Cotton (Ire) G	N A Callaghan	UK	6f
	Cover Up (Ire) G	Sir Michael Stoute	UK	16f
	D'Anjou G	John M Oxx	Ireland	7f
	Defier (Aus) G	G Walter	Australia	8f
	Delago Brom (Aus) C	T Hughes	Australia	8f
	Dress Circle (NZ) G	Mrs Gai Waterhouse	Australia	8f
	Epalo (Ger) C	A Schutz	Germany	10f
	Fields Of Omagh (Aus) G	T McEvoy	Australia	7f, 8f, 10f
	Germinis (Fr) G	P Chevillard	France	20f
	Helenus (Aus) C	Bart Cummings	Australia	10f
	Highdown (Ire) C	Saeed Bin Suroor	UK	10f
	Ho Choi G	I W Allan	Hong Kong	7f
	King Of Boxmeer (Ger) G	W Baltromei	Germany	12f
	Martaline C	A Fabre	France	12f
	Megahertz F	R J Frankel	USA	10f
	Morozov (USA) C	A Fabre	France	16f

Four-year-olds-plus continued

Rating	Name & sex	Trainer	Country	Distance(s)
	Mummify (Aus) G	Lee Freedman	Australia	10f, 12f, 13f
	Pawn Broker G	D R C Elsworth	UK	9f
	Polar Ben G	J R Fanshawe	UK	7f
	Polar Way G	Mrs A J Perrett	UK	6f
	Porlezza (Fr) F	Y De Nicolay	France	5f
	Princely Venture (Ire) C	Sir Michael Stoute	UK	10f
	Ratio G	J E Hammond	France	5f, 6f
	Repertory G	M S Saunders	UK	5f
	Requete C	R J Frankel	USA	9f, 10f
	Royal Tryst (USA) H	J D Sadler	United Arab Emirates	9f
	Sabiango (Ger) H	A Wohler	Germany	12f
	Sights On Gold (Ire) C	Saeed Bin Suroor	UK	10f
	Vangelis (USA) C	A De Royer-Dupre	France	10f
	Voodoo Dancer (USA) M	Christophe Clement	USA	9f
	Well Made (Ger) H	H Blume	Germany	12f
	Zee Zee Top F	Sir Michael Stoute	UK	10f
	Zindabad (Fr) H	M Johnston	UK	12f, 16f

Dirt

Rating	Name & sex	Trainer	Country	Distance(s)
131	Candy Ride (Arg) C	R McAnally	USA	10f
	Mineshaft (USA) C	N J Howard	USA	9f, 10f
	Moon Ballad (Ire) C	Saeed Bin Suroor	UK	10f
129	Congaree (USA) H	B Baffert	USA	9f
128	Aldebaran (USA) H	R J Frankel	USA	7f
	Pleasantly Perfect (USA) H	Richard E Mandella	USA	10f
127	Volponi (USA) H	Philip Johnson	USA	10f
126	Perfect Drift (USA) G	Murray W Johnson	USA	9f
125	Azeri (USA) M	Laura De Seroux	USA	9f
	Empire Maker (USA) C	R J Frankel	USA	9f, 12f
	Funny Cide (USA) G	B Tagg	USA	10f
	Ghostzapper (USA) C	R J Frankel	USA	7f

Rating	Name & sex	Trainer	Country	Distance(s)
	Medaglia D'Oro (USA) C	R J Frankel	USA	9f, 10f
	Shake You Down (USA) G	S Lake	USA	6f
	Valid Video (USA) G	D Manning	USA	6f, 7f
124	Dynever (USA) C	Christophe Clement	USA	10f
	Ten Most Wanted (USA) C	W Dollase	USA	10f
123	Cajun Beat (USA) G	S Margolis	USA	6f
	Starrer (USA) M	J Shirreffs	USA	9f
	Wild Spirit (Chi) F	R J Frankel	USA	9f, 10f
122	Harlan's Holiday (USA) C	T Pletcher	USA	9f, 10f
	Joey Franco (USA) C	Darrell Vienna	USA	7f
	Milwaukee Brew (USA) H	R J Frankel	USA	9f, 10f
121	During (USA) C	B Baffert	USA	7f
	Quest (USA) C	N Zito	USA	10f
	State City (USA) C	P Rudkin	United Arab Emirates	6f
120	Adoration (USA) F	D Hofmans	USA	9f
	Atswhatimtalknbout (USA) C	Ronald W Ellis	USA	10f
	Biwa Shinseiki (Jpn) H	H Matsuda	Japan	9f
	Composure (USA) F	B Baffert	USA	9f
	Got Koko (USA) F	B Headley	USA	9f
	Grandera (Ire) H	Saeed Bin Suroor	UK	10f
	Great Notion (USA) C	Darrin Miller	USA	7f
	Nayef (USA) H	M P Tregoning	UK	10f
	Peace Rules (USA) C	R J Frankel	USA	9f, 10f
	Zavata (USA) C	P L Biancone	USA	6f

The directory

Every horse who ran in Britain to the end of the 2003 turf season, plus top overseas performers. Each entry includes the horse's full form figures, with distance and going (in raised figures) for each run, seasonal wins-places-runs statistics and seasonal total prize-money. Each horse is given a definitive Racing Post Rating, and an all-weather rating (a) where appropriate

A Beetoo (Ire) *J R Best*   a66
3 b f Bahhare (USA) - Sonya's Pearl (Ire)
2⁷ˢᵈ 4¹⁰ˢᵈ 6¹⁰ˢᵈ 2⁸ˢᵈ 6⁸ˢᵈ **0-2-5 £2,420**

A Bid In Time (Ire) *D Shaw*   55 a36
2 b f Danetime (Ire) - Bidni (Ire)
7⁵ˢᵈ 6⁵ᵍᶠ 4⁵ᵍ 9⁵ˢᵈ 1⁵ᵍˢ 5⁵ᵍᶠ 7⁵ᵍᶠ 11⁶ᵍ
12⁷ˢᵈ 11⁵ᵍ 9⁵ᵍᶠ 7⁵ˢ **1-0-12 £3,108**

A Bit Of Fun *T D Barron*   24
2 ch g Unfuwain (USA) - Horseshoe Reef
7⁶ᶠ 12⁶ᵍ 19⁶ᵍᶠ **0-0-3**

A C Azure (Ire) *W A Murphy*   48 a34
5 br g Dolphin Street (Fr) - Kelvedon
10⁷ˢᵈ 12¹⁰ᶠ 3⁷ᶠ 4⁸ᵍᶠ 8⁶ʸ 3⁹ᶠ 4⁶ᵍᶠ 17⁸ᵍʸ
13¹⁴ᵍ 9⁸ᵍᶠ **0-3-10 £1,370**

A Little Bit Yarie *K R Burke*   81
2 b c Paris House - Slipperose
3⁵ᵍ 1⁵ᵍˢ 2⁵ᵍᶠ 3⁵ᵍᶠ **1-2-4 £7,382**

A Monk Swimming (Ire) *John Berry*   29
2 br g Among Men (USA) - Sea Magic (Ire)
9⁵ᵍᶠ 6⁶ᶠ 12⁶ᵍˢ **0-0-3**

A One (Ire) *B Palling*   62
4 b g Alzao (USA) - Anita's Contessa (Ire)
3⁸ᵍ 15⁷ᵍˢ 12⁷ᵍᶠ 9⁸ᶠ 8⁷ᵍᶠ **0-1-5 £612**

A Teen *P Howling*   72 a58
5 ch h Presidium - Very Good
12⁵ˢᵈ 2⁶ˢᵈ 4⁶ᵍᶠ 7⁷ˢᵈ 9⁵ᵍᶠ 4⁵ᵍᶠ 7⁶ᵍᶠ 2⁶ᵍᶠ
8⁶ᵍᶠ 1⁶ᵍ 3⁶ᵍᶠ 7⁶ᵍˢ 5⁶ᵍᶠ 12⁵ᵍᶠ 5⁶ᵍᶠ 7⁵ˢ 6⁶ᶠ
5⁶ᵍᶠ **2-3-21 £10,440**

A Two (Ire) *B Palling*   38
4 ch f Ali-Royal (Ire) - Rainelle
11¹⁵ˢᵈ 15¹²ᵍ **0-0-2**

A Vendre (Fr) *M C Pipe*
4 b/br g Kendor (Fr) - Waaria
20¹⁰ᶠ **0-0-1**

A Very Good Year (Ire) *T G Mills*   101 a94
3 b c Indian Ridge - Ma N'leme Biche (USA)
3⁷ˢᵈ 1⁷ᵍᶠ 9⁷ᵍᶠ 2⁶ˢᵈ 1⁶ᵍ 2⁶ᵍᶠ **2-3-6**
£24,605

A Woman In Love *Miss B Sanders*   65 a57
4 gr f Muhtarram (USA) - Ma Lumiere (Fr)
12⁷ˢᵈ 14⁷ˢᵈ 4⁶ᵍᶠ 7⁵ᶠ 7⁷ᵍᶠ 8⁷ᵍᶠ 4⁹ᶠ 1⁷ᵍᶠ
7⁶ᶠ 10⁷ᵍᶠ 3⁷ᶠ 5⁷ᵍ 4⁶ᵍᶠ 2⁸ᶠ 5⁶ˢᵈ **1-3-15**
£5,552

Aahgowangowan (Ire) *M Dods*   68
4 b f Tagula (Ire) - Cabcharge Princess (Ire)
7⁶ᵍ 8⁵ᵍᶠ 3⁵ᵍˢ 13⁵ᵍˢ 3⁵ᵍˢ 10⁵ᵍ 1⁵ᵍ 9⁵ᵍˢ
2⁵ᵍᶠ 3⁶ᵍ 7⁵ᵍ **1-4-11 £11,603**

Abaco Sunset *C G Cox*   47
2 ch f Bahamian Bounty - Thicket
8⁵ᵍᶠ **0-0-1**

Abajany *R J Baker*   43
9 b g Akarad (Fr) - Miss Ivory Coast (USA)
6¹⁰ᵍᶠ 7¹⁰ᵍ 16¹⁰ᵍ **0-0-3**

Abaninetoes (Ire) *P D Evans*   33 a42
3 b f General Monash (USA) - Gilly-G (Ire)
8⁵ˢᵈ 12⁶ˢᵈ 8⁵ˢᵈ 8⁶ᶠ 11⁷ᶠ **0-0-5**

Abbajabba *C W Fairhurst*   96
7 b g Barrys Gamble - Bo' Babbity
4⁶ᶠ 14⁶ᵍᶠ 17⁶ᶠ 7⁶ᵍᶠ 17⁶ᵍ 10⁶ᵍᶠ 9⁶ᵍˢ 6⁶ᵍ
0-0-8 £751

Abbaleva *C W Fairhurst*   a40
4 b f Shaddad (USA) - Bo' Babbity
7⁷ˢᵈ 8⁹ˢʷ **0-0-2**

Abbey's Valentine *M Mullineaux*
3 b c My Best Valentine - My Abbey

11⁵ᵍ **0-0-1**

Abbeygate *T Keddy*   53
2 b c Unfuwain (USA) - Ayunli
9⁸ˢ 11¹⁰ᵍˢ **0-0-2**

Abbiejo (Ire) *G Fierro*   30
6 b m Blues Traveller (Ire) - Chesham Lady (Ire)
8⁸ᵍˢ **0-0-1**

Abelard (Ire) *R A Fahey*   63
2 b g Fasliyev (USA) - Half-Hitch (USA)
3⁵ᵍᶠ 3⁵ᵍᶠ 3⁵ᵍᶠ **0-1-3 £2,264**

Abellabrig *A Berry*
3 b f Puissance - Rare Indigo
13⁶ᵍᶠ 6⁶ᵍᶠ 12⁶ˢᵈ **0-0-3**

Abercorn (Ire) *J L Spearing*   a12
4 b g Woodborough (USA) - Ravensdale Rose (Ire)
9⁵ˢᵈ 12⁷ˢᵈ **0-0-2**

Aberkeen *Jedd O'Keeffe*   49 a50
8 ch g Keen - Miss Aboyne
5⁸ˢʷ 6¹¹ˢᵈ 7¹¹ˢᵈ 6⁸ˢ 10¹²ᵍ 8¹¹ˢᵈ **0-0-6**

Ability *C E Brittain*   52 a44
4 b g Afflora (Ire) - Beatle Song
15⁷ˢᵈ 7¹⁰ᵍ 14¹⁰ᵍᶠ **0-0-3**

Abington Angel *B J Meehan*   80 a50
2 ch f Machiavellian (USA) - Band (USA)
3⁶ᵍᶠ 2⁷ᵍᶠ 6⁷ᵍᶠ 6⁷ˢᵈ **0-2-4 £3,659**

Ablaj (Ire) *E A L Dunlop*   63
2 ch c Horse Chestnut (SAF) - Passe Passe (USA)
4⁶ᵍ 12⁷ᵍᶠ 13⁷ᵍˢ **0-0-3 £263**

Able Baker Charlie (Ire) *J R Fanshawe*   95
4 b g Sri Pekan (USA) - Lavezzola (Ire)
7¹⁰ᵍˢ 12¹⁰ˢ 2¹⁰ᵍᶠ 5¹⁰ᵍˢ 1⁹ᵍᶠ 10⁹ᵍᶠ 1⁸ᵍᶠ
2-1-7 £14,809

Able Mind *A C Whillans*   78 a66
3 b g Mind Games - Chlo-Jo
2⁶ᵍ 2⁷ᵍˢ 3⁷ᶠ 2⁸ᵍ 3⁸ˢᵈ 3⁷ᵍᶠ **0-5-6**
£5,391

Abnoba (USA) *W Jarvis*   36
3 b f Celtic Swing - Zakousky (USA)
9⁸ʰʸ 17⁷ᵍᶠ **0-0-2**

Abou Zulu *H A McWilliams*   32
3 ch g Abou Zouz (USA) - Mary From Dunlow
10¹⁰ᵍˢ 9⁷ᶠ 15⁸ᵍᶠ 10⁹ᵍᶠ 11⁷ᵍᶠ 6⁹ᶠ 14⁷ᵍᶠ
0-0-7

Aboustar *M Brittain*   28
3 b g Abou Zouz (USA) - Three Star Rated (Ire)
7⁷ˢ 13⁷ᵍᶠ **0-0-2**

Above Board *R F Marvin*   a39
8 b g Night Shift (USA) - Bundled Up (USA)
11⁶ˢᵈ 8⁵ˢʷ 5⁵ˢᵈ 14⁶ˢᵈ **0-0-4**

Above The Cut (USA) *C P Morlock*   16
11 ch g Topsider (USA) - Placer Queen
14¹⁶ᵍᶠ **0-0-1**

Abracadabjar *Miss Z C Davison*   a38
5 b g Royal Abjar (USA) - Celt Song (Ire)
8¹²ˢᵈ 14¹²ˢᵈ 12¹⁶ˢᵈ 8¹¹ˢᵈ 11¹³ˢᵈ 13¹²ᵍᶠ
0-0-6

Abraxas *J Akehurst*   45 a40
5 b g Emperor Jones (USA) - Snipe Hall
10⁶ᵍ 8⁵ˢᵈ 8⁵ᵍᶠ 10⁵ᵍᶠ 14⁵ᵍ 9⁵ᵍᶠ 12⁵ᵍ
0-0-7

Abrogate (Ire) *P C Haslam*   55
2 b g Revoque (Ire) - Czarina's Sister
7⁶ˢᵈ 5⁶ˢ 8⁷ᵍˢ 3⁷ᵍᶠ 7⁸ᵍᶠ 10¹⁰ᵍᶠ **0-1-6**
£502

Absent Friends *J Balding*   103

6 b g Rock City - Green Supreme
11^{5f} 15^{5gf} 4^{5hy} 4^{5gf} 17^{5gf} 12^{6f} 15^{gf}
5^{5gf} 4^{5gf} 1^{5gf} 6^{5g} 2^{5gs} 5^{5gf} 8^{5gf} 10^{5gf} **2-3-15**
£29,086

Absinther *M R Bosley*   56 a47
6 b g Presidium - Heavenly Queen
13^{12sd} 11^{12sd} 7^{12d} 4^{10gf} 5^{12f} 9^{12g} 1^{12gf}
4^{12gf} 4^{12gf} 7^{10gf} 7^{12f} 16^{10f} **1-0-12 £4,251**

Absolute Pleasure *G C Bravery*   50 a46
2 br f Polar Falcon (USA) - Soluce
11^{7gf} 4^{8sd} 8^{10gf} **0-0-3**

Absolute Utopia (USA) *J L Spearing*   64 a69
10 b g Mr Prospector (USA) - Magic Gleam (USA)
1^{10sd} 6^{10sd} 3^{10sd} 2^{10sd} 1^{10f} 1^{10gf} 7^{10f}
8^{10sd} 1^{10sd} 9^{10sd} 2^{10gf} 3^{10g} 2^{11gf} 1^{10sd} 16^{11gf}
5-5-15 £19,525

Absolutely Fab (Ire) *Mrs C A Dunnett*   27 a17
2 ch f Entrepreneur - Hamama (USA)
9^{5sd} 9^{5f} 8^{6gf} 13^{7gf} 8^{6gf} **0-0-5**

Absolutely Soaked (Ire) *Dr J D Scargill*   54
2 b f Alhaarth (Ire) - Vasilopoula (Ire)
3^{7g} 9^{8gf} **0-1-2 £602**

Absolutelythebest (Ire) *Sir Michael Stoute*   54
2 b c Anabaa (USA) - Recherchee
9^{7gf} 11^{8gf} **0-0-2**

Abuelos *S Dow*   46 a55
4 b g Sabrehill (USA) - Miss Oasis
15^{7sd} 11^{7sd} 11^{7sd} 10^{7g} 15^{8gf} 9^{7gf} 11^{6sd}
5^{7f} 9^{7gf} 10^{8f} **0-0-10**

Abundant *J R Fanshawe*   84
3 b f Zafonic (USA) - Glorious
4^{7gf} **0-0-1 £1,500**

Academy (Ire) *Andrew Turnell*   68
8 ch g Archway (Ire) - Dream Academy
3^{14g} 7^{14gf} 18^{16gf} 5^{16g} 2^{16gf} 5^{16gf} 2^{17gf}
2^{16g} 9^{16gf} 2^{17f} 4^{18gf} **0-5-11 £5,543**

Academy Brief (Ire) *J W Mullins*   64 a58
3 b g Brief Truce (USA) - Stylish Academy (Ire)
9^{10sd} 3^{11sd} 12^{12sd} 9^{8sw} 3^{10gf} 2^{10gf} 11^{12gf}
6^{10f} 6^{10g} 11^{10gf} 6^{8f} **0-3-11 £1,931**

Acca Larentia (Ire) *R M Whitaker*   54
2 gr f Titus Livius (Fr) - Daisy Grey
17^{5sd} 7^{7gf} 6^{7gf} 2^{7f} **0-1-4 £820**

Acceleration (Ire) *Sir Mark Prescott*   66 a50
3 b g Groom Dancer (USA) - Overdrive
2^{14gf} 3^{14f} 3^{12sd} 1^{17gf} 6^{16sd} 10^{16gf} 4^{16g}
9^{18gf} **1-3-8 £5,346**

Accentor (Ire) *M J P O'Brien*   39 a33
3 ch f Bluebird (USA) - Law Review (Ire)
11^{6sd} 9^{8gy} 12^{12ys} 4^{12f} 13^{12gy} 7^{10gf} **0-0-6**
£438

Accepting *J Mackie*   62
6 b g Mtoto - D'Azy
8^{16sd} 11^{14g} 1^{17f} 8^{18gf} **1-0-4 £3,708**

Acclamation *L G Cottrell*   119
4 b c Royal Applause - Princess Athena
3^{5gf} 2^{5gf} 11^{6gf} 3^{5gf} 1^{6g} 1^{6gf} 1^{6gf} 4^{5ho}
3-2-8 £156,161

Ace Club *W J Haggas*   68
2 ch g Indian Rocket - Presently
2^{5gf} 1^{5g} **1-1-2 £4,654**

Ace Coming *D Eddy*   58
2 b g First Trump - Tarry
2^{5g} 4^{5f} 2^{6gs} 3^{7gf} 4^{6gs} 2^{7gf} 8^{8gf} 7^{8g}
12^{8gf} **0-3-9 £4,320**

Ace In The Hole *F Jordan*   27
3 br f So Factual (USA) - Timely Raise (USA)
15^{8gf} 11^{8gs} **0-0-2**

Ace Maite *S R Bowring*   49 a31
2 b f Komaite (USA) - Asmarina
8^{6gf} 9^{6gf} 4^{6sd} 13^{6sd} 8^{8sd} 14^{7g} **0-0-6**

Ace Of Hearts *C F Wall*   92
4 b g Magic Ring (Ire) - Lonely Heart
7^{8f} 3^{8g} 2^{8gs} 12^{9g} 8^{9gf} 2^{8gf} 5^{9g} 3^{8s}
6^{10gf} 2^{10s} **0-5-10 £10,129**

Ace Of Trumps *Miss L A Perratt*   68
7 ch g First Trump - Elle Reef
4^{9gf} 14^{8gf} 4^{10gf} 3^{8gs} 12^{10gf} 5^{8gs} 3^{10gs}
10^{9gs} 3^{10gf} 6^{9gf} **0-4-10 £3,709**

Aces Dancing (Ger) *M R Channon*   77
2 b f Big Shuffle (USA) - Auenglocke (Ger)
5^{5gf} 3^{5gs} 1^{5gf} 5^{6gf} 5^{5gf} 5^{5g} 4^{5gf} 8^{5gf}
5^{5gf} 9^{5gf} **1-1-10 £5,529**

Achilles Rainbow *K R Burke*   44
4 ch g Deploy - Naughty Pistol (USA)
11^{10g} 4^{9g} **0-0-3**

Achilles Thunder *K R Burke*   31 a51
4 b/br g Deploy - Aegean Sound
7^{12sd} 8^{13sd} 8^{12sd} 9^{12gf} 10^{12gf} **0-0-5**

Achilles Wings (USA) *Miss K M George*   a56
7 b g Irish River (Fr) - Shirley Valentine
2^{15sd} 13^{16sd} 5^{12sd} 7^{16sd} **0-1-4 £886**

Acid Test *M A Buckley*   40 a47
8 ch g Sharpo - Clunk Click
15^{6sd} 12^{6sw} 7^{7sd} 15^{8f} 11^{7g} 10^{7gf} 6^{6f}
0-0-7

Acomb *M W Easterby*   72
3 b g Shaamit (Ire) - Aurora Bay (Ire)
12^{5gf} 4^{8gf} 1^{7f} 3^{9f} 4^{7gf} 3^{7gs} 1^{8gf} 4^{10gf}
1^{8gs} 5^{8f} 9^{7f} **3-2-11 £14,047**

Acorazado (Ire) *G L Moore*   67 a65
4 b g Petorius - Jaldi (Ire)
2^{5sw} 6^{5sd} 6^{6sw} 6^{5sd} 9^{5gs} 14^{7g} 19^{6g} 12^{5gf}
4^{6sd} 7^{6gf} 5^{5s} **0-1-11 £1,251**

Across The Water *G H Jones*   33
9 b m Slip Anchor - Stara
7^{16g} **0-0-1**

Act Of Duty (USA) *D R Loder*   93
3 ch c Mr Prospector (USA) - Nuryette (USA)
2^{8gf} 6^{8gf} **0-1-2 £1,880**

Act Of Honor (Fr) *Mrs A J Perrett*   60 a33
3 ch f Alhaarth (Ire) - First Served (Fr)
7^{10gf} 3^{12gf} 9^{13sd} 14^{15ho} **0-0-4 £322**

Act Of The Pace (Ire) *M Johnston*   60
3 b f King's Theatre (Ire) - Lady In Pace
5^{10gf} **0-0-1**

Action Fighter (Ger) *N P Littmoden*   88
3 ch c Big Shuffle (USA) - Action Art (Ire)
7^{6g} 11^{7g} 14^{6g} 2^{8g} 1^{6s} 5^{8g} 17^{s} **2-0-7**
£12,532

Active Account (USA) *Mrs H Dalton*   77 a74
6 b/br g Unaccounted For (USA) - Ameritop (USA)
2^{11sd} 6^{11sd} 2^{8g} 3^{8g} 3^{10gf} **0-3-5 £3,554**

Activist *G M Moore*   65
5 ch g Diesis - Shicklah (USA)
11^{14gf} 3^{14gf} **0-0-2 £1,105**

Activity (Ire) *D R Loder*   89
4 gr c Pennekamp (USA) - Actoris (USA)
1^{7gf} 4^{7g} 9^{7gf} **1-0-3 £4,789**

Adaikali (Ire) *Sir Michael Stoute*   a60

2 b c Green Desert (USA) - Adaiyka (Ire)
7^{7sd} **0-0-1**

Adalpour (Ire) *Miss J Feilden*   a58
5 b g Kahyasi - Adalya (Ire)
1^{12sd} 6^{12sd} 1^{16sd} 3^{16sd} 3^{16sw} 9^{15sd} **2-2-6**
£6,821

Adamant James (Ire) *T D McCarthy*   50
4 b g Sri Pekan (USA) - Classic Romance
6^{9g} 6^{7g} 20^{7gf} **0-0-3**

Adamas (Ire) *Andrew Turnell*   a15
6 b m Fairy King (USA) - Corynida (USA)
6^{8sd} **0-0-1**

Adantino *B R Millman*   64 a55
4 b g Glory Of Dancer - Sweet Whisper
7^{7gf} 7^{6gf} 3^{6g} 16^{7gf} 7^{6gf} 5^{8gf} 6^{6sd} **0-1-7**
£484

Adaptable *H Candy*   66
2 b f Groom Dancer (USA) - Adeptation (USA)
8^{6gf} 3^{7gf} **0-1-2 £661**

Adayout *G C Bravery*   49
2 ch g Pursuit Of Love - Fanciful (Fr)
8^{6gf} **0-0-1**

Adecco (Ire) *R C Guest*
4 b g Eagle Eyed (USA) - Kharaliya (Fr)
11^{10gf} **0-0-1**

Adeeba (Ire) *E A L Dunlop*   54
2 b f Alhaarth (Ire) - Nedaarah
9^{7gf} 11^{8s} 9^{7g} **0-0-3**

Adees Dancer *B Smart*   61
2 b f Danehill Dancer (Ire) - Note (Ger)
4^{7g} **0-0-1**

Adekshan (Ire) *Sir Michael Stoute*   100
3 ch c Mark Of Esteem (Ire) - Adaiyka (Ire)
2^{8gf} 8^{8gf} 12^{8g} 6^{7gf} 4^{7gf} **0-0-5 £4,295**

Adelphi Boy (Ire) *M Todhunter*   45
7 ch g Ballad Rock - Toda
12^{12g} **0-0-1**

Adelphi Theatre (USA) *R Rowe*   a77
6 b g Sadler's Wells (USA) - Truly Bound (USA)
8^{12sd} 12^{12sd} 3^{16sd} **0-1-3 £736**

Adept *C W Fairhurst*   54 a51
4 b f Efisio - Prancing
4^{6sd} 11^{6sw} 9^{6sd} 5^{5gf} 14^{5gs} 5^{6f} 16^{6gf} 4^{6f}
6^{7sf} 11^{7sf} 5^{8gf} **0-0-11 £541**

Adiemus *J Noseda*   103 a113
5 b g Green Desert (USA) - Anodyne
7^{8g} 3^{10sd} 2^{10sd} 2^{10sd} 7^{10gf} 20^{10gf} 2^{9gf}
6^{10g} 10^{10gf} **0-4-9 £45,514**

Adios Amigo *A C Whillans*
4 ch g Efisio - Los Alamos
9^{12gf} 8^{13f} **0-0-2**

Adjawar (Ire) *J J Quinn*   91 a83
5 b g Ashkalani (Ire) - Adjriyna
7^{12sd} 7^{12sd} 2^{12g} 11^{12gf} 18^{12g} 2^{12gf} 12^{10gf}
1^{12gf} 4^{12gf} 4^{12f} 7^{12g} 6^{11gf} 1^{10gf} 13^{12gf} **2-2-14**
£21,270

Admiral (Ire) *Sir Michael Stoute*   74
2 b c Alhaarth (Ire) - Coast Is Clear (Ire)
6^{8gf} 4^{8gs} **0-0-2**

Admiral Collins (Ire) *J H M Gosden*   68
3 b g Sadler's Wells (USA) - Kanmary (Fr)
4^{11gf} **0-0-1 £420**

Admiral Compton *A C Stewart*   52
2 ch c Compton Place - Sunfleet
7^{6gf} **0-0-1**

Admiral Fitzroy (USA) *D Nicholls*   a40
3 ch c Hennessy (USA) - Dorothy Dear (USA)
5^{7sd} 7^{7sd} **0-0-2**

Adobe *W M Brisbourne*   80
8 b g Green Desert (USA) - Shamshir
4^{8g} 1^{8g} 6^{8gs} 4^{8gf} 4^{8gf} 9^{8gf} 4^{8gf} 3^{8f} 5^{8f}
1^{8hd} 4^{8gf} 5^{8gf} 4^{8f} 3^{8gf} 7^{8f} 7^{8gf} 8^{8gf} 2^{8f} 2^{8f} **2-3-22**
£15,765

Adopted Hero (Ire) *J H M Gosden*   103 a84
3 b g Sadler's Wells (USA) - Lady Liberty (NZ)
1^{10sd} 3^{11gf} 1^{12gs} 1^{15gs} 4^{15s} 4^{15ho} **3-0-6**
£32,831

Adriatic Adventure (Ire) *J L Spearing*   38
2 ch f Foxhound (USA) - Theda
8^{5g} 8^{6gf} **0-0-2**

Adronikus (Ire) *D J Wintle*
6 ch g Monsun (Ger) - Arionette
13^{12gf} **0-0-1**

Adventurist *J R Fanshawe*   84 a56
3 ch g Entrepreneur - Alik (Fr)
7^{8sd} 4^{10gf} 4^{10gf} 3^{12gf} 2^{8g} 1^{10g} 2^{10g} **1-2-7**
£8,000

Adventurous Girl *J G Portman*   58
2 b f Danzero (Aus) - Birthday Venture
27^{7gf} 6^{5g} 6^{6gf} 5^{7f} 7^{8gf} **0-0-5**

Advocatus (Ger) *A G Hobbs*   18 a24
5 b g Law Society (USA) - Aguilas
4^{12sd} 13^{12g} 8^{15sd} 10^{16sd} **0-0-4 £182**

Adweb *J Cullinan*   63
5 b m Muhtarram (USA) - What A Present
12^{5s} RR^{6g} **0-0-2**

Aegean Line *R Hannon*   64
3 b f Bijou D'Inde - Load Line
10^{8gf} 6^{8gf} 5^{7gf} 5^{8gf} 5^{7g} 6^{7f} **0-0-6 £215**

Aegean Magic *R Hannon*   80 a56
3 b f Wolfhound (USA) - Sayulita
6^{5sd} 7^{6sd} 5^{6gf} 13^{6gf} 5^{6gf} 1^{6gf} 1^{6g} 15^{6gf}
5^{6gf} 9^{7g} 10^{7gf} **2-0-11 £9,135**

Aegean Mist *P Howling*   43 a41
3 ch f Prince Sabo - Dizzydaisy
4^{8sd} 5^{9sd} 5^{8sd} 4^{7gf} 7^{8gf} 15^{7gf} 10^{8gf} 5^{8sd}
9^{12gf} **0-0-9**

Aesculus (USA) *L M Cumani*   63
2 b/br f Horse Chestnut (SAF) - Crafty Buzz (USA)
7^{7g} 5^{6gs} **0-0-2**

Afaan (Ire) *R F Marvin*   66 a41
10 ch h Cadeaux Genereux - Rawaabe (USA)
12^{5sw} 11^{5gf} 13^{5gs} 13^{5gs} 11^{5gf} 9^{5gf}
13^{5gf} 2^{5gf} 10^{5gf} 16^{5f} **0-1-10 £2,120**

Afadan (Ire) *J R Jenkins*   83 a86
5 br g Royal Academy (USA) - Afasara (Ire)
10^{12sd} 4^{12sd} 3^{12sd} 13^{12sd} 11^{12gf} 8^{14gf}
10^{14gf} **0-1-7 £1,673**

Afeef (USA) *R T Phillips*   58
4 b/br g Dayjur (USA) - Jah (USA)
10^{9gf} 13^{10gf} **0-0-2**

African Dawn *N P Littmoden*   14 a70
5 b g Spectrum (Ire) - Lamu Lady (Ire)
4^{11sw} 11^{14g} 2^{13sd} 2^{12sd} **0-2-4 £2,068**

African Sahara (Ire) *Miss D Mountain*   90 a82
4 br c El Gran Senor (USA) - Able Money (USA)
4^{8sd} 2^{8sd} 1^{9sd} 3^{10sd} 5^{8gf} 5^{8gs} 6^{9gs} 2^{8gf}
1^{9gf} 8^{8g} 4^{9gf} 10^{8gs} 5^{8gf} 1^{9gf} 2^{8gf} 1^{8s} 15^{9g}
7^{8gf} **4-6-21 £40,380**

African Spur (Ire) *P A Blockley*   86 a67

3 b g Flying Spur (Aus) - African Bloom
5^{5f} 2^{5gf} 12^{6gf} 1^{5gs} 8^{6gf} 8^{6gf} 3^{6gf} 7^{6gf}
4^{5f} 2^{7f} 7^{8gf} 13^{7sd} 9^{5gf} **1-3-13 £9,552**

African Star *Mrs A J Perrett* — 42
2 b c Mtoto - Pass The Rose (Ire)
10^{7g} **0-0-1**

After All (Ire) *G A Butler* — 52 a43
2 gr f Desert Story (Ire) - All Ashore
13^{6sd} 2^{5gf} 3^{5g} **0-2-3 £1,416**

After Shock (Ire) *E J O'Neill* — 59 a30
5 ch g Grand Lodge (USA) - Fancy Boots (Ire)
15^{6y} 10^{10gf} 10^{5y} 13^{7gs} 9^{5sw} 10^{6sd} **0-0-6**

After The Show *J R Jenkins* — 69 a60
2 b c Royal Applause - Tango Teaser
6^{6gs} 10^{6gs} 4^{6gf} 8^{6gf} 5^{6sd} 1^{5s} **1-0-6**
£4,267

Aggi Mac *N Bycroft* — 45 a40
2 b f Defacto (USA) - Giffoine
6^{5sd} 6^{5f} 7^{6gf} 2^{6gf} 9^{15g} 9^{7gf} 3^{6gf}
8^{6s} 8^{6gf} 5^{6gf} **0-3-11 £2,257**

Agilis (Ire) *Jamie Poulton* — 54 a89
3 b g Titus Livius (Fr) - Green Life
4^{7sd} 7^{10sd} 5^{8sd} 10^{8gf} **0-0-4 £1,686**

Agincourt Warrior *J M P Eustace* — 53 a64
4 b c Distant Relative - Careful (Ire)
9^{6sd} 12^{8sd} 14^{7sd} 5^{8gf} 11^{7gf} 13^{7g} 18^{6g}
11^{7gf} **0-0-8**

Aguila Loco (Ire) *E J Alston* — 39
4 ch g Eagle Eyed (USA) - Go Likecrazy
18^{5gf} 17^{5gf} 9^{5gs} 11^{5g} 11^{5gf} 14^{5gf} **0-0-6**

Aguilera *M Dods* — 25
2 ch f Wolfhound (USA) - Mockingbird
9^{7gf} 10^{8g} **0-0-2**

Ailincala (Ire) *C F Wall* — 93
5 b m Pursuit Of Love - Diabaig
3^{8gf} 2^{8g} 1^{8f} 8^{8gf} 1^{8f} 1^{8f} 1^{8f} 4^{10f} 12^{8gf}
4-2-9 £29,063

Aimee's Delight *J G Given* — 84
3 b f Robellino (USA) - Lloc
9^{7gf} 8^{7f} 1^{7g} 15^{6gs} 3^{7g} 1^{8gf} 9^{8gf} **2-1-7**
£15,352

Aiming *R Hannon* — 74
3 b f Highest Honor (Fr) - Sweeping
3^{8g} 12^{7g} 6^{7gf} 2^{8gf} 10^{8gf} 2^{8gf} 16^{8gf}
0-3-7 £2,533

Aintnecessarilyso *J M Bradley* — 48
5 ch g So Factual (USA) - Ovideo
11^{5gf} 5^{5gf} 6^{5gf} 5^{5gf} 11^{5gf} 9^{5gf} 12^{5f}
3^{5gf} 7^{6gf} 13^{5f} **0-1-10 £446**

Air Adair (USA) *J H M Gosden* — 63
3 b f Storm Cat (USA) - Beyrouth (USA)
5^{7gf} RO^{8vs} **0-0-2 £364**

Air Mail *Mrs N Macauley* — a98
6 b g Night Shift (USA) - Wizardry
2^{8sw} 8^{8sd} 7^{7sd} 12^{6sd} 7^{7sd} 6^{8sw} 8^{8sd} **0-1-7**
£2,508

Air Of Esteem *Ian Emmerson* — 57 a67
7 b g Forzando - Shadow Bird
3^{8sd} 7^{8sd} 4^{8sd} 1^{7sd} 3^{8sd} 1^{8sd} 2^{7gf} 7^{8sd}
8^{7g} 2^{8gf} 13^{8sw} 7^{8sd} 4^{8sd} **2-3-13 £8,534**

Airedale Lad (Ire) *J R Norton*
2 b g Charnwood Forest (Ire) - Tamarsiya (USA)
11^{6f} **0-0-1**

Airgusta (Ire) *C R Egerton* — 34 a59
2 b c Danehill Dancer (Ire) - Ministerial Model (Ire)
16^{6gf} 16^{6g} 9^{7sd} **0-0-3**

Airwave *H Candy* — 123
3 b f Air Express (Ire) - Kangra Valley
1^{5gf} 2^{6f} 3^{6gf} 3^{6gs} 6^{6gf} 11^{5ho} **1-3-6**
£166,750

Aisle *L R James* — 16 a30
6 b g Arazi (USA) - Chancel (USA)
6^{12sd} 6^{16sw} 9^{16gs} **0-0-3**

Aitana *S C Williams* — 60
3 b f Slip Anchor - Tsungani
14^{10gf} 7^{8gf} 6^{7gs} 10^{10g} **0-0-4**

Ajwaa (Ire) *J G M O'Shea* — 72
5 ch g Mujtahid (USA) - Nouvelle Star (Aus)
1^{8gf} 1^{7f} 6^{7gf} 7^{7g} 15^{8gf} 20^{8gf} 15^{8gf}
2-0-7 £8,789

Akebono (Ire) *Mrs S A Liddiard* — 46 a19
7 ch g Case Law - Elanmatina (Ire)
5^{8gf} 5^{8f} 10^{12sd} BD^{8gf} **0-0-4**

Akeydah (Ire) *D R Loder* — 71
3 ch f Selkirk (USA) - Abeyr
3^{8gf} 5^{7gf} **0-1-2 £776**

Akimbo (USA) *H R A Cecil* — 94
2 b c Kingmambo (USA) - All At Sea (USA)
2^{7gf} **0-1-1 £2,264**

Akritas *P F I Cole* — 72
2 b c Polish Precedent (USA) - Dazzling Heights
1^{8gf} 13^{10gs} PU^{9gs} **1-0-3 £3,549**

Akrmina *M A Jarvis* — 73
3 ch f Zafonic (USA) - Pastorale
2^{7gf} 11^{10gf} 3^{8g} 3^{8gf} 1^{7gf} 6^{7gf} 10^{6gf}
1-2-7 £6,398

Akshar (Ire) *Sir Michael Stoute* — 113
4 b c Danehill - Akilara (Ire)
1^{8gf} 1^{10g} 3^{10f} 1^{10gf} 26^{9gf} 3^{9gf} **3-1-6**
£65,869

Al Aali *A G Newcombe* — 91
5 b h Lahib (USA) - Maraatib (Ire)
14^{7g} 3^{7g} 5^{7g} 2^{6gf} PU^{6gs} **0-2-5 £3,960**

Al Awwam *J W Unett* — 47 a17
4 b g Machiavellian (USA) - Just A Mirage
13^{14gs} 13^{10gs} 5^{7gf} 7^{8gf} 7^{8gf} 6^{9sd} **0-0-6**

Al Azhar *M Dods* — 79
9 b g Alzao (USA) - Upend
4^{12g} 5^{12g} 3^{11gs} **0-1-3 £869**

Al Beedaa (USA) *J L Dunlop* — 70
2 ch f Swain (Ire) - Histoire (Fr)
11^{7gf} 3^{8gf} **0-1-2 £493**

Al Ihtithar (Ire) *B W Hills* — 102
3 b f Barathea (Ire) - Azyaa
5^{10gf} 7^{8gf} 1^{10gf} 1^{10g} **2-0-4 £38,630**

Al Jadeed (USA) *J H M Gosden* — 109
3 b c Coronado's Quest (USA) - Aljawza (USA)
3^{8gf} 2^{9gf} 9^{9gf} **0-1-3 £4,886**

Al Joudha (Fr) *M R Channon* — 40
2 b f Green Desert (USA) - Palacegate Episode (Ire)
5^{5gf} 9^{6gf} **0-0-2**

Al Muallim (USA) *Andrew Reid* — 46 a63
9 b g Theatrical - Gerri N Jo Go (USA)
2^{6sd} 4^{9sd} 9^{6sd} 10^{7sd} 1^{7sd} 13^{7f}
14^{7gf} 14^{7gs} 8^{7gf} 8^{7f} 12^{6gf} **1-1-12 £3,917**

Al Rajiba (USA) *C E Brittain* — 67
3 ch f Diesis - Nymphea (USA)
5^{10gf} 6^{10gs} 6^{7gf} 9^{10g} 2^{7gf} 18^{9f} 8^{9g} **1-1-7**

£5,416

Al Shuua *C E Brittain* 68
2 b f Lomitas - Sephala (USA)
3⁷ᵍᶠ 6⁷ᵍᶠ **0-1-2 £810**

Al Sifaat *Saeed Bin Suroor* 81
2 ch f Unfuwain (USA) - Almurooj
2⁶ᵍᶠ 1⁶ᵍᶠ **1-1-2 £6,203**

Al Turf (Ire) *R Hannon* 106 a92
3 ch c Alhaarth (Ire) - Petomi
6⁷ˢᵈ 5⁸ˢᵈ 2⁷ᵍ 6⁸ᵍ 8⁸ᵍ 2⁸ᵍ 9⁸ˢ **0-2-7**
£27,650

Al's Alibi *W R Muir* 35 a49
10 b g Alzao (USA) - Lady Kris (Ire)
3¹²ˢᵈ 4¹³ˢᵈ 2¹²ˢᵈ 8¹²ᵍᶠ 6¹⁵ˢᵈ 3¹²ˢʷ 9¹⁰ᵍᶠ
4¹²ˢᵈ 14¹²ᵍᶠ 8¹²ˢᵈ **0-3-10 £1,680**

Alaared (USA) *J L Dunlop* 86
3 b c King Of Kings (Ire) - Celtic Loot (USA)
6⁸ᵍᶠ 4¹⁰ᵍᶠ 2¹⁰ᶠ 2¹²ᵍᶠ 1¹²ᵍᶠ 4¹⁴ᶠ **1-2-6**
£9,735

Alabastrine *Sir Mark Prescott* 56 a38
3 gr f Green Desert (USA) - Alruccaba
2⁷ᶠ 4⁸ᵍ 6⁷ˢʷ 12⁸ᶠ **0-1-4 £1,145**

Alafdal (USA) *J L Dunlop* 72
3 b c Gone West (USA) - Aqaarid (USA)
6⁸ᵍᶠ 2¹⁰ᵍᶠ 7¹⁰ᵍ 12¹⁰ᶠ 11¹⁰ᵍᶠ **0-1-5**
£1,257

Alafzar (Ire) *P D Evans* 70
5 b g Green Desert (USA) - Alasana (Ire)
15⁷ᶠ 13⁸ᶠ 18⁷ᶠ 7⁸ᵍ 8⁷ᵍ 11⁷ᵍᶠ 15⁷ᶠ
14⁸ᶠ 8⁸ᶠ 4⁷ᵍᶠ 10⁷ᵍᶠ 7⁷ᵍᶠ 11⁸ᶠ 4⁷ᵍᶠ 13⁸ᵍ
0-1-15 £541

Alaloof (USA) *J L Dunlop* 62
2 b f Swain (Ire) - Alattrah (USA)
6⁸ᵍᶠ 12⁸ᶠ 5⁸ᵍᶠ **0-0-3**

Alam (USA) *P Monteith* 71
4 b g Silver Hawk (USA) - Ghashtah (USA)
9¹³ᵍˢ **0-0-1**

Alamouna (Ire) *Sir Michael Stoute* 82
3 ch f Indian Ridge - Alasana (Ire)
7¹⁰ᵍᶠ 5¹⁰ᵍ 3⁹ᵍᶠ 1¹⁰ᵍᶠ 6¹⁰ᵍᶠ 7¹⁰ᵍᶠ **1-0-6**
£4,546

Alamshar (Ire) *John M Oxx* 133
3 b c Key Of Luck (USA) - Alaiyda (USA)
3¹²ᵍ 12¹⁰ᵍᶠ 1¹⁰ᵍʸ 1¹²ᵍ 1¹²ᵍ 6¹⁰ᵍᶠ 4¹⁰ᵍᶠ
3-2-7 £1,172,764

Alasil (USA) *J L Dunlop* 92
3 b/br c Swain (Ire) - Asl (USA)
7¹⁰ᵍᶠ 6¹⁰ᵍᶠ 6¹²ᵍᶠ 4¹²ᵍᶠ 7¹²ᵍᶠ **0-0-5**
£1,530

Alastair Smellie *S L Keightley* 54 a25
7 ch g Sabrehill (USA) - Reel Foyle (USA)
12⁶ˢᵈ 12⁵ˢᵈ 3⁵ᵍᶠ 15⁶ᵍ **0-1-4 £636**

Alba Stella *Sir Mark Prescott* 95
3 gr f Nashwan (USA) - Alouette
1¹²ᵍᶠ 1¹²ᵍᶠ 3¹²ᵍᶠ 8¹²ᵍᶠ 12¹⁴ˢ **2-1-5**
£8,872

Albadi *C E Brittain*
2 b c Green Desert (USA) - Lyrist
13⁷ˢ **0-0-1**

Albanov (Ire) *J L Dunlop* 93
3 b c Sadler's Wells (USA) - Love For Ever (Ire)
3¹²ᵍˢ 2¹²ᵍˢ 1¹²ᵍˢ 3¹⁴ᵍ 5¹⁴ᵍ 5¹⁵ˢ 2¹⁶ˢ **1-3-7**
£15,595

Albanova *Sir Mark Prescott* 114
4 gr f Alzao (USA) - Alouette

7¹²ᵍ 1¹²ʰʸ 2¹²ˢ 6¹⁶ʰᵒ **1-1-4 £56,917**

Albany (Ire) *Mrs J R Ramsden* 92
3 ch g Alhaarth (Ire) - Tochar Ban (USA)
7⁸ᵍᶠ 5¹⁰ᵍᶠ 4¹⁰ᵍˢ 4¹²ᵍᶠ 3¹²ᶠ 1¹²ᵍᶠ 4¹²ᵍᶠ
1¹⁴ᵍᶠ **2-1-8 £16,182**

Albashoosh *J S Goldie* 81
5 b g Cadeaux Genereux - Annona (USA)
24⁸ᵍ 8⁶ᵍ 18⁶ᵍˢ 13⁷ᵍ 7⁷ᵍ 8⁶ᵍᶠ 28ᵍᶠ 6⁷ᵍˢ
6⁷ᵍᶠ 4⁷ᵍ 4⁸ᵍᶠ 3⁷ᶠ 12⁸ᵍᶠ 9⁸ᵍ 7⁸ᵍ 6⁷ᵍᶠ **0-1-16**
£4,721

Albavilla *P W Harris* 73
3 b f Spectrum (Ire) - Lydia Maria
5⁸ᵍᶠ 5¹⁰ᵍᶠ 6¹⁰ᵍᶠ **0-0-3**

Alberich (Ire) *A G Newcombe* a81
8 b g Night Shift (USA) - Tetradonna (Ire)
6¹⁶ˢᵈ **0-0-1**

Albertine *C F Wall* a16
3 b f Bahhare (USA) - Rosa Royale
10⁸ˢᵈ **0-0-1**

Alberto Giacometti (Ire) *A P O'Brien* 116
3 b c Sadler's Wells (USA) - Sweeten Up
12¹²ᵍ 3¹⁰ᵍᶠ 3¹¹ᵍˢ 6¹⁰ᵍˢ **0-0-4 £15,223**

Albinus *A M Balding* 36
2 gr c Selkirk (USA) - Alouette
12⁸ᵍˢ **0-0-1**

Albuhera (Ire) *P F Nicholls* 106
5 b g Desert Style (Ire) - Morning Welcome (Ire)
23⁸ᵍ 4¹⁰ᵍᶠ 3⁹ᵍ 19¹⁰ᵍᶠ 8¹⁰ᶠ 5¹⁰ᵍ 16⁸ᵍ
12¹⁰ᵍ 9¹¹ᵍᶠ **0-1-9 £5,087**

Alburack *G G Margarson* 25
5 b g Rock City - Suzannah's Song
11⁷ᵍᶠ **0-0-1**

Albury Heath *T M Jones* 35 a42
3 b g Mistertopogigo (Ire) - Walsham Witch
11⁸ˢᵈ 5⁶ˢᵈ 8⁶ˢᵈ 10⁶ᵍᶠ 16⁸ᵍᶠ **0-0-5**

Alcazar (Ire) *H Morrison* 117
8 b g Alzao (USA) - Sahara Breeze
1¹⁴ᵍ 12²⁰ᵍᶠ 1¹⁶ᵍ 4¹²ᵍ 2¹⁶ʰᵒ **2-1-5**
£70,826

Alchemist Master *R M Whitaker* 50 a88
4 b g Machiavellian (USA) - Gussy Marlowe
4⁸ˢᵈ 4⁸ˢᵈ 1⁸ˢᵈ 18⁸ᵍᶠ 16⁸ᵍᶠ 11⁷ᵍˢ 11⁶ᵍˢ
1-0-7 £3,876

Alchemystic (Ire) *Mrs A J Perrett* 73 a77
3 b g In The Wings - Kama Tashoof
7¹⁰ˢᵈ 11⁰ˢᵈ 3¹⁰ˢᵈ 7¹²ᵍ 9¹²ᵍˢ 3¹⁰ᵍᶠ 3¹²ᵍ
9¹⁴ᵍᶠ **1-1-8 £5,584**

Alchera *R F Johnson Houghton* 75
2 b c Mind Games - Kind Of Shy
6⁵ᵍᶠ 6⁵ᵍᶠ 17⁶ᵍᶠ 5⁶ᶠ 7⁷ᵍᶠ 2⁵ᵍᶠ 16⁹ᵍ **1-1-7**
£4,807

Alder Park *J G Given* 58
3 b g Alderbrook - Melody Park
6¹²ᶠ 13¹²ᵍᶠ 7⁸ᵍᶠ 17¹⁰ᶠ 7⁷ᵍᶠ 11⁶ᶠ **0-0-6**

Alderney Race (USA) *R Charlton* 83
2 ch c Seeking The Gold (USA) - Oyster Catcher (Ire)
4⁶ᵍᶠ **0-0-1 £373**

Aldora *M J Ryan* 108 a99
4 b f Magic Ring (Ire) - Sharp Top
1⁸ᵍ 2⁷ˢᵈ 1⁹ᵍˢ 3¹⁰ᵍᶠ 1⁸ᵍᶠ 1⁹ᵍ **4-1-6**
£87,906

Alejandro Barreras *B Hanbury* 13
3 b g Royal Applause - Andbell
13¹⁰ᵍ **0-0-1**

Alekhine (Ire) *P W Harris* 82

2 b c Soviet Star (USA) - Alriyaah
1^{7gf} 6^{8g} **1-0-2 £4,099**

Aleron (Ire) *J J Quinn* 87 a67
5 b h Sadler's Wells (USA) - High Hawk
5^{16sw} 1^{12sw} 6^{11sw} 4^{11sd} 2^{14gf} 1^{14gf} 2^{12gf}
3^{12gf} 3^{13gs} 10^{12gs} 11^{12f} 12^{12gf} 13^{12gf} 3^{13g}
3^{12s} 4^{15sd} 3^{14gs} 4^{17g} **2-7-18 £16,781**

Alessandro Severo *N P Littmoden* 77 a85
4 gr g Brief Truce (USA) - Altaia (Fr)
1^{12sd} 8^{12sd} 8^{10sd} 4^{10g} 7^{12g} 8^{10gf} 9^{10g}
10^{10g} 11^{10g} **1-0-9 £5,242**

Alethea Gee *John Berry* 32
5 b m Sure Blade (USA) - Star Flower
14^{8gf} **0-0-1**

Alexander Ballet *T D Easterby* 54
4 b f Mind Games - Dayville (USA)
14^{5g} 12^{8gs} 13^{6gf} **0-0-3**

Alexander Charlotte (Ire) *B W Hills* 75
2 b f Titus Livius (Fr) - Sabaniya (Fr)
5^{6gf} 7^{7gf} 3^{6gf} 2^{6f} 3^{6gs} **0-3-5 £1,813**

Alexander Prince (Ire) *Lady Herries* 73
3 b g Desert Prince (Ire) - National Ballet
6^{10gf} 8^{10gf} 9^{8g} **0-0-3**

Alexander Star (Ire) *P J McBride* 56
5 b/br m Inzar (USA) - Business Centre (Ire)
7^{6gf} 12^{6g} 5^{5f} 2^{5gf} 11^{5gf} 1^{5f} 8^{5g} **1-1-7**
£6,348

Alfano (Ire) *E L James* 68 a66
5 b g Priolo (USA) - Sartigila
11^{10gs} 1^{12sd} 4^{12s} **1-1-3 £3,526**

Alfelma (Ire) *P R Wood* 47
3 gr f Case Law - Billie Grey
3^{5gf} 7^{6f} 14^{5gf} 7^{6ft} **0-0-4 £572**

Alfie Lee (Ire) *D A Nolan* 48
6 ch g Case Law - Nordic Living (Ire)
16^{5gf} 12^{5gf} 7^{5g} 9^{5g} 10^{5gf} 12^{5gf} 4^{5f}
17^{6gs} 14^{5gf} **0-1-9 £324**

Alfonso *B W Hills* 73
2 ch c Efisio - Winnebago
4^{6g} 13^{6gf} **0-0-2 £321**

Alfred Sisley *S J Mahon* 67
3 b g Royal Applause - Dalu (Ire)
8^{8g} 1^{7gf} 13^{7g} 10^{7gs} 4^{6gf} 6^{7gf} 4^{6f} 18^{8s}
18^{7y} 11^{7g} 16^{6gf} **1-0-11 £3,743**

Alhaurin *Miss J A Camacho*
4 ch g Classic Cliche (Ire) - Fairey Firefly
20^{10gf} **0-0-1**

Alhesn (USA) *C N Allen* a20
8 b/br g Woodman (USA) - Deceit Princess (Can)
9^{16sd} **0-0-1**

Ali Can (Ire) *A P Jarvis* a61
4 b g Ali-Royal (Ire) - Desert Native
5^{10sd} 3^{9sd} 4^{12sd} 5^{12sd} **0-1-4 £430**

Ali D *Mrs N Macauley* 64 a74
5 b g Alhijaz - Doppio
2^{7sw} 5^{7sd} 5^{6sd} 11^{8sd} 2^{9sd} 9^{8gf} 4^{8gf} 12^{8gs}
11^{11gf} 4^{10gf} 8^{10g} 10^{10gf} **1-3-12 £6,272**

Ali Deo *W J Haggas* 76
2 ch c Ali-Royal (Ire) - Lady In Colour (Ire)
12^{6gf} 8^{7gf} **0-0-2**

Ali Pasha *M D I Usher* 48 a50
4 b g Ali-Royal (Ire) - Edge Of Darkness
10^{9sd} 4^{12gf} 3^{10g} 8^{12f} 19^{8gf} 12^{12gf} 13^{10f}
0-1-7 £701

Ali Zandra *Julian Poulton* 14 a5

2 b f Prince Sabo - Priceless Fantasy
11^{5g} 8^{5sd} **0-0-2**

Ali's Oasis *B Smart* 60
2 b g Ali-Royal (Ire) - Miss Walsh
1^{5gf} 5^{5gf} 4^{5s} 6^{6gf} 7^{5f} 11^{5gf} 10^{6gf} 11^{7gf}
1-0-8 £4,386

Aliabad (Ire) *J G M O'Shea* 36 a12
8 b/br g Doyoun - Alannya (Fr)
8^{16g} 8^{10g} 9^{12sd} 11^{16gf} **0-0-4**

Aliba (Ire) *B Smart* 62
2 ch g Ali-Royal (Ire) - Kiba (Ire)
3^{6g} 5^{5f} 4^{6s} **0-0-3 £1,162**

Alibongo (Cze) *R Bastiman* 35
2 ch c Dara Monarch - Alvilde
6^{5gf} 9^{6s} 6^{6gf} 6^{5sd} 8^{5gf} 10^{7gf} **0-0-6**

Alice Blackthorn *B Smart* 70
2 b f Forzando - Owdbetts (Ire)
11^{6gf} 11^{6gs} 4^{6gf} 4^{6gf} 5^{6f} 7^{6gs} 1^{6gf} **1-0-7**
£4,342

Alice Brand (Ire) *G M Moore* 54
5 b m Nucleon (USA) - Tormented (USA)
4^{8g} 16^{6gf} 3^{7s} **0-1-3 £980**

Aligatou *Mrs L Stubbs*
4 b g Distant Relative - Follow The Stars
12^{7sd} **0-0-1**

Alinda (Ire) *P W Harris* 54 a67
2 b f Revoque (Ire) - Gratclo
7^{6g} 1^{6sd} **1-0-2 £2,282**

Alizar (Ire) *M J Polglase* 50 a45
2 b f Rahy (USA) - Capua (USA)
10^{5g} 6^{5gf} 7^{5f} 7^{5gf} 9^{5sd} 4^{7gf} 4^{7gf} 12^{8gf}
6^{6g} 3^{5sd} 6^{6sd} **0-1-11 £1,141**

Alizarin (Ire) *A C Wilson*
4 b f Tagula (Ire) - Persian Empress (Ire)
17^{6gf} **0-0-1**

Aljard (USA) *Mrs S J Smith* 5
5 ch g Gilded Time (USA) - Diaspora (USA)
14^{8sd} 19^{8sd} 17^{8sd} **0-0-3**

Aljazeera (USA) *B Hanbury* 92
3 b f Swain (Ire) - Matiya (Ire)
15^{7g} 5^{7gf} 2^{7g} 4^{8g} 6^{10gf} 6^{10gf} 8^{7g}
0-1-8 £4,153

Aljomar *R E Barr* 43 a47
4 b g College Chapel - Running For You (Fr)
13^{8sw} 4^{9sd} 9^{7gf} 5^{7sd} 7^{7sd} 6^{8gf} 4^{7f}
12^{8g} 9^{7gf} 11^{8gs} 13^{8gf} 4^{6f} 8^{7f} **0-0-14 £735**

Alkaadhem *M P Tregoning* 102
3 b c Green Desert (USA) - Balalaika
2^{7gf} 1^{7g} 18^{8gf} **2-1-3 £20,511**

Alkaased (USA) *Sir Michael Stoute* 98
3 b c Kingmambo (USA) - Chesa Plana
2^{11g} 1^{12gf} 2^{14gf} 2^{12gf} **1-3-4 £9,980**

All Business *Jedd O'Keeffe* 70
4 b f Entrepreneur - Belle Esprit
11^{12gs} 8^{12gf} 5^{12gf} **0-0-3**

All Diamonds (Ire) *J G Given* 55
2 ch c Priolo (USA) - Afisiak
5^{8gs} 6^{8gf} **0-0-2**

All Embracing (Ire) *G C Bravery* 81
3 b f Night Shift (USA) - Rispoto
8^{7gf} 1^{7f} 9^{8gf} 4^{6gf} 5^{7g} 10^{7gf} 4^{7g} 13^{7gf}
15^{6gf} **1-0-9 £5,635**

All On My Own (USA) *I W McInnes* 45 a45
8 ch g Unbridled (USA) - Someforall (USA)
5^{8sw} 10^{12sd} 7^{8sd} 11^{8sd} 5^{9g} 5^{12gf} 10^{10gf}

8^{12gs} **0-0-8**

All Quiet *R Hannon*   64
2 b f Piccolo - War Shanty
9^{6gf} 8^{7gf} 8^{7gf} **0-0-3**

All The More (Ire) *Mrs P N Dutfield*   77
2 b f Ali-Royal (Ire) - Koukla Mou
8^{5gf} 4^{5gs} 8^{5gf} 7^{6f} 3^{5g} 2^{6gf} 5^{6gf} 3^{5s} 3^{5gf} 3^{5gf} 12^{6gf} **0-2-11 £3,925**

All's Not Lost *Don Enrico Incisa*   26
4 b f Binary Star (USA) - Flo's Choice (Ire)
8^{7gs} 14^{8gf} **0-0-2**

Alla Cappella (Ire) *C F Wall*   61
3 ch f College Chapel - Keiko
10^{6gf} 5^{6gs} 12^{6gf} 18^{6g} 9^{8gf} **0-0-5**

Allegedly (Ire) *P C Haslam*   70
2 b f Alhaarth (Ire) - Society Ball
5^{5g} 2^{6gf} 2^{7gf} 1^{7f} **1-2-4 £7,546**

Allegrina (Ire) *K A Ryan*   68
3 b f Barathea (Ire) - Pianola (USA)
1^{7gf} 4^{10gf} 7^{8g} 5^{8g} **1-0-4 £5,892**

Allenwood *D J S Cosgrove*   55 a57
3 b g Inchinor - Bumpkin
2^{5sd} 2^{5sd} 6^{6gf} 6^{5gf} 5^{6gf} 18^{6gf} 4^{7gf} 7^{7gf} 11^{5sd} **0-2-9 £1,644**

Allergy *R Charlton*   101
3 b f Alzao (USA) - Rash Gift
6^{11gf} 6^{14g} 6^{12gf} 10^{14s} **0-0-4 £1,275**

Allerton Boy *R J Hodges*   42
4 ch g Beveled (USA) - Darakah
7^{6f} 4^{5gf} 13^{5gf} 13^{5gf} 10^{5gf} 7^{6gf} 7^{8gf} 12^{5gf} **0-0-8 £319**

Allez Mousson *A Bailey*   66
5 b g Hernando (Fr) - Rynechra
6^{18g} 9^{16gf} 3^{17g} 8^{16gf} **0-0-4 £957**

Allied Victory (USA) *E J Alston*   81
3 b c Red Ransom (USA) - Coral Dance (Fr)
5^{10g} 3^{10s} 2^{9ys} 7^{8sh} 10^{10y} 2^{10gy} 3^{8g} 8^{11s} 3^{8f} 2^{10gs} 4^{10gs} **0-7-11 £7,108**

Allinjim (Ire) *J A Glover*   90
4 b g Turtle Island (Ire) - Bounayya (USA)
9^{12gf} 10^{14gf} 1^{14gf} 9^{12gf} 9^{15g} 6^{13g} 13^{14s} **1-0-7 £5,668**

Allodarlin (Ire) *P F I Cole*   60 a42
2 b f Cape Cross (Ire) - Sharp Circle (Ire)
5^{8gf} 7^{6gf} 8^{6gf} 6^{7sd} **0-0-4**

Ally Makbul *J R Best*   54
3 b f Makbul - Clarice Orsini
5^{10gf} 3^{10gf} 7^{10gf} **0-0-4 £434**

Ally McBeal (Ire) *J G Given*   55 a45
4 b f Ali-Royal (Ire) - Vian (USA)
4^{6f} 14^{8f} 11^{7gf} 5^{8sd} 16^{10gf} 8^{8sw} **0-0-6 £291**

Almanac (Ire) *B P J Baugh*
2 b c Desert Style (Ire) - Share The Vision
14^{6gs} **0-0-1**

Almara *Miss K B Boutflower*   25
3 b f Wolfhound (USA) - Alacrity
14^{5gf} 14^{6g} 14^{8f} 11^{6f} **0-0-4**

Almaviva (Ire) *J Noseda*   93
3 b f Grand Lodge (USA) - Kafayef (USA)
6^{8gf} 5^{12gf} **0-0-2 £1,280**

Almaydan *R Lee*   77
5 b g Marju (Ire) - Cunning
9^{16gf} 6^{14hy} 6^{14gs} 10^{14gs} **0-0-4**

Almeida (Ire) *John Berry*   46

5 b m Sadler's Wells (USA) - Benning (USA)
5^{14gf} 12^{16gf} **0-0-2**

Almizan (Ire) *M R Channon*   95
3 b c Darshaan - Bint Albaadiya (USA)
4^{11gf} 1^{12g} 4^{12g} 2^{14g} 11^{14gf} 1^{15g} 5^{14gf} 6^{16g} 4^{16gf} **2-1-9 £19,236**

Almond Beach *B J Meehan*   70 a30
3 ch g Hector Protector (USA) - Dancing Spirit (Ire)
5^{8f} 13^{9gf} 11^{7gf} 16^{7sd} **0-0-4**

Almond Mousse (Fr) *Robert Collet*   111
4 b f Exit To Nowhere (USA) - Missy Dancer
3^{10sd} 9^{13g} 3^{8gs} 2^{8g} 7^{8g} 4^{8g} 9^{8gs} 3^{10s} 5^{8gs} 7^{10gs} 3^{8gf} 4^{10s} 4^{10ho} 4^{10g} 10^{8g} 7^{8vs} **0-5-16 £51,885**

Almond Willow (Ire) *J Noseda*   64
2 b f Alhaarth (Ire) - Miss Willow Bend (USA)
12^{6gf} 6^{6gf} 8^{8gf} 3^{8gf} 6^{8gs} **0-1-5 £788**

Almost Famous (Ire) *J S Bolger*   101
4 ch g Grand Lodge (USA) - Smouldering (Ire)
5^{10g} 5^{9gf} 8^{8g} 33^{9gf} 2^{10gf} 8^{8gf} **0-1-6 £8,019**

Almost Royal (Ire) *R M Beckett*   41
2 b f Princely Heir (Ire) - A Little While
8^{6gf} 12^{8g} 7^{6g} 10^{5sd} **0-0-4**

Almost Welcome *S Dow*   23
2 b c First Trump - Choral Sundown
13^{6gf} 11^{5gf} 8^{7gf} **0-0-3**

Almotawag *Mrs L Stubbs*   a41
3 ch g Abou Zouz (USA) - As Mustard
6^{6sw} 9^{5sd} **0-0-2**

Almuraad (Ire) *Sir Michael Stoute*   99
2 b c Machiavellian (USA) - Wellspring (Ire)
6^{8gf} 1^{7gf} **1-0-2 £6,024**

Almutasader *J L Dunlop*   94
3 b c Sadler's Wells (USA) - Dreamawhile
1^{12g} 1^{12g} 1^{14gf} 4^{15g} **3-1-4 £18,526**

Alnaja (USA) *W J Haggas*   76
4 b g Woodman (USA) - Cursory Look (USA)
6^{10gf} 9^{10gf} 3^{10gf} 2^{12gs} 3^{14gf} 1^{14s} **1-2-6 £7,924**

Alnasreya (Ire) *Sir Michael Stoute*   81
3 b f Machiavellian (USA) - Littlewick (Ire)
1^{8gf} 5^{8gf} 8^{8g} **1-0-3 £5,525**

Alpen Wolf (Ire) *W R Muir*   78
8 ch g Wolfhound (USA) - Oatfield
16^{6gf} 12^{6gf} 7^{5gf} 5^{6gf} 2^{5f} 2^{5gf} 9^{6gf} 12^{6g} 2^{5f} 2^{5f} 2^{5f} 4^{5f} 2^{5gf} 3^{5gf} 2^{5f} 5^{6f} 16^{5g} **0-8-17 £9,731**

Alpha Apache (Ire) *M W Easterby*   a3
3 b g Primo Dominie - Apache Squaw
14^{8sd} 9^{7sd} **0-0-2**

Alpha Noble (Ger) *Miss Venetia Williams*   34
6 b g Lando (Ger) - Alpha (Ger)
10^{12g} **0-0-1**

Alpha Zeta *C W Thornton*
2 b c Primo Dominie - Preening
16^{6gs} **0-0-1**

Alphabar (Ire) *T D Easterby*   48
3 ch g Bahhare (USA) - Happy Flower
7^{8hy} 14^{7gf} 4^{12gf} 7^{7f} 11^{11gf} **0-0-5 £278**

Alphecca (USA) *Sir Michael Stoute*   29
2 b c Kingmambo (USA) - Limbo (USA)
13^{7gf} **0-0-1**

Alpine Hideaway (Ire) *J S Wainwright*   52
10 b g Tirol - Arbour (USA)

13^{7gf} 6^{8s} 1^{8gf} 4^{8gf} 15^{9gf} **1-0-5 £3,757**

Alpine Racer (Ire) *R E Barr*   11
4 b g Lake Coniston (Ire) - Cut No Ice
12^{12sd} 13^{12gf} 7^{14gf} **0-0-3**

Alpine Special (Ire) *P C Haslam*   72
2 gr g Orpen (USA) - Halomix
7^{5gf} 2^{6g} 7^{6gf} 3^{7g} 2^{8gf} 1^{8gf} 8^{8gf} **1-3-7**
£9,486

Alqaayid *M P Tregoning*   64
2 b c Machiavellian (USA) - One So Wonderful
8^{6gf} 6^{7gf} 10^{8gf} 11^{8gf} **0-0-4**

Alrabab *M P Tregoning*   109
3 ch f Nashwan (USA) - Jamrat Jumairah (Ire)
1^{10gf} 3^{8gf} 1^{10g} 1^{12gf} 1^{12f} 4^{10g} **4-1-6**
£33,317

Alrafid (Ire) *G L Moore*   92 a58
4 ch c Halling (USA) - Ginger Tree (USA)
12^{10sd} 10^{8gf} 15^{8gf} 1^{9g} 8^{8s} 6^{9g} 2^{10gf}
2^{9gf} **1-2-8 £14,777**

Alrida (Ire) *W Jarvis*   87
4 b g Ali-Royal (Ire) - Ride Bold (USA)
6^{16gf} 5^{16f} 6^{16gs} 8^{15gf} 9^{16gf} 5^{14g} 9^{11gf}
0-0-7 £317

Alsafi (USA) *J Noseda*   70
4 b g Red Ransom (USA) - Altair (USA)
7^{7gf} 17^{8g} 12^{6gs} **0-0-3**

Alshawameq (Ire) *J L Dunlop*   75
2 b c Green Desert (USA) - Azdihaar (USA)
6^{7f} 1^{8gf} 5^{8gf} **1-0-3 £3,926**

Alsyati *C E Brittain*   55 a54
5 ch g Salse (USA) - Rubbiyati
5^{10sd} 3^{9sw} 5^{8sd} 10^{10g} 10^{10gf} 13^{10gf}
9^{10gf} 4^{11gf} 12^{12sd} **0-2-10 £421**

Altares *P Howling*   49
2 b c Alhaarth (Ire) - Reach The Wind (USA)
12^{7g} 12^{7gf} 11^{7gs} **0-0-3**

Altay *R A Fahey*   a83
6 b g Erin's Isle - Aliuska (Ire)
1^{13sd} 1^{12sd} 6^{12sd} **2-0-3 £10,846**

Altitude Dancer (Ire) *B Ellison*   72 a44
3 b g Sadler's Wells (USA) - Height Of Passion
7^{12sw} 5^{12sd} 9^{14gf} 1^{14gf} 3^{16gf} 1^{16gs}
7^{14g} 5^{17g} 3^{16g} **2-3-10 £9,478**

Alumni News (USA) *J H M Gosden*   81
3 b c Belong To Me - Private Status (USA)
1^{8f} 9^{11gf} 14^{10s} **1-0-3 £5,746**

Alumnus *C A Horgan*   62
3 ch g Primo Dominie - Katyushka (Ire)
5^{6gf} 5^{7gf} 12^{6g} 10^{6gf} **0-0-4**

Alvaro (Ire) *D J Wintle*   29
6 ch g Priolo (USA) - Gezalle
7^{19gf} **0-0-1**

Always Believe (USA) *Mrs P Ford*   42 a57
7 b g Carr De Naskra (USA) - Wonder Mar (USA)
9^{6sd} 10^{8sd} 10^{6sd} 3^{8sd} 9^{10sd} 6^{8sd} 11^{8gf}
15^{8gf} **0-1-8 £429**

Always Daring *C J Teague*
4 b f Atraf - Steamy Windows
13^{7gs} **0-0-1**

Always Esteemed (Ire) *G Wragg*   102
3 b c Mark Of Esteem (Ire) - Always Far (USA)
1^{8f} 2^{8gf} 3^{8gf} 4^{10gf} 7^{10g} 10^{8g} 8^{8gf} 7^{10gf}
1-2-8 £14,409

Always First *Sir Michael Stoute*   88
2 b c Barathea (Ire) - Pink Cristal

1^{7gf} **1-0-1 £7,255**

Always Flying (USA) *M Johnston*   67 a51
2 ch f Fly So Free (USA) - Dubiously (USA)
3^{5gf} UR^{6sd} 6^{5f} 2^{7gf} 9^{7g} 3^{8gf} 5^{8gs}
5^{8sd} **0-3-9 £2,697**

Alyousufeya (Ire) *J L Dunlop*   68
2 ch f Kingmambo (USA) - Musicale (USA)
10^{6gf} 4^{7gs} **0-0-2 £323**

Amalfi Coast *W S Cunningham*   58
4 b g Emperor Jones (USA) - Legend's Daughter (USA)
5^{14f} 4^{9gf} 4^{10gf} 16^{12f} UR^{10g} **0-0-5 £328**

Amalianburg *H R A Cecil*   71
3 b f Hector Protector (USA) - Ayodhya (Ire)
4^{10gf} 2^{12gf} 1^{12gf} 7^{14gf} **1-0-4 £5,684**

Amamus *M A Jarvis*   65
3 b f Zafonic (USA) - Princess Sadie
3^{8hy} 3^{8gf} 5^{7gs} 13^{10gf} 12^{8sw} **0-2-5**
£1,861

Amanda's Lad (Ire) *M C Chapman*   57 a48
3 b g Danetime (Ire) - Art Duo
11^{6sw} 6^{5sd} 5^{5sd} 7^{5sd} 6^{5sd} 4^{5sd} 6^{5gf} 8^{5gf}
5^{5gf} 5^{5gf} 8^{7f} 9^{6gf} 5^{6g} 8^{5f} 16^{6gf} 8^{5gf} 8^{6g}
15^{5f} 9^{5gf} 3^{6f} **0-1-20 £767**

Amandus (USA) *D R Loder*   98 a87
3 b g Danehill (USA) - Affection Affirmed (USA)
2^{10sd} 7^{8ft} 1^{9sd} 4^{9f} **1-1-4 £5,840**

Amanpuri (Ger) *Miss Gay Kelleway*   48
5 b g Fairy King (USA) - Aratika (Fr)
20^{8sh} 3^{8gy} 13^{12sd} **0-0-3**

Amar (Cze) *R Bastiman*
2 ch c Beccari (USA) - Autumn (Fr)
4^{7gf} 6^{7s} 11^{7g} **0-0-3 £871**

Amaraku *A L Forbes*   42
4 b g Kylian (USA) - Shernborne
11^{11gf} **0-0-1**

Amaranth (Ire) *D Carroll*   66 a75
7 b g Mujadil (USA) - Zoes Delight (Ire)
13^{7sd} 4^{8sd} 10^{8sd} 3^{7g} 10^{7gf} 11^{7gf}
13^{7gf} 8^{6gf} 4^{7f} 5^{7gf} 9^{7gf} 14^{6gf} **0-0-13 £753**

Amaretto Express (Ire) *R E Barr*   31
4 b g Blues Traveller (Ire) - Cappuchino (USA)
18^{8gf} 18^{6gf} 9^{6f} 10^{6gf} **0-0-4**

Amber Fox (Ire) *A Berry*   52
2 b f Foxhound (USA) - Paradable (Ire)
4^{5gf} 5^{5gs} 6^{5gf} 16^{6gf} 9^{6gs} 4^{6gf} **0-0-6**
£572

Amber Legend *J G Given*   49 a52
2 b f Fraam - Abstone Queen
1^{5sd} 6^{5gf} 2^{6gf} 2^{5gs} 6^{6g} 10^{5sd} 2^{5f} 8^{6gf}
1-3-8 £6,581

Amber Nectar Two *Daniel Mark Loughnane*   16
3 b g Bluegrass Prince (Ire) - Another Batchworth
10^{5s} 17^{6gf} 12^{7f} **0-0-3**

Amber's Bluff *T D Easterby*   69
4 b f Mind Games - Amber Mill
10^{5gs} 12^{6g} 13^{5gf} **0-0-3**

Ambersong *A W Carroll*   49 a55
5 ch g Hernando (Fr) - Stygian (USA)
8^{8sd} 8^{12sd} 17^{8gf} 10^{10gf} 7^{10gf} 1^{12sw} 4^{14gf}
2^{15sd} **1-2-8 £2,362**

Ambitious Annie *R Hollinshead*   34 a43
4 b f Most Welcome - Pasja (Ire)
5^{16sd} 7^{10gf} 1^{15sd} **1-0-3 £2,996**

Ambonnay *Mrs A J Perrett*   89
3 ch f Ashkalani (Ire) - Babycham Sparkle

5^{6gf} 8^{6gf} 7^{7gf} 3^{6gf} 13^{6gf} **0-0-5 £2,211**

Ambrosine *Mrs A J Perrett* 79
3 ch f Nashwan (USA) - Tularosa
6^{10gf} 6^{13g} 4^{10gf} 3^{10gf} 1^{10g} 1^{12gf} 3^{12gf}
2-1-7 £9,535

Ambushed (Ire) *P Monteith* 71
7 b g Indian Ridge - Surprise Move (Ire)
4^{8gs} 2^{10gs} 7^{10gf} 3^{11g} 12^{12gf} **0-1-5**
£3,918

Amelia (Ire) *Andrew Reid* 55 a56
5 b m General Monash (USA) - Rose Tint (Ire)
3^{6sd} 3^{6sd} 6^{7sd} 12^{6sd} 5^{6gf} 1^{6f} 11^{6gf} 4^{6gf}
1-3-8 £4,644

Ameras (Ire) *Miss S E Forster* 22
5 b m Hamas (Ire) - Amerindian
12^{7s} **0-0-1**

America America (USA) *Franck Mourier* 93
2 ch f Mister Baileys - Gal Of Mine (USA)
2^{3ft} 1^{3ft} 8^{5gf} 5^{6gf} 3^{5gf} 2^{6gf} 2^{7gf} 2^{5s}
2^{8gf} **1-2-9 £45,877**

American Cousin *D Nicholls* 68
8 b g Distant Relative - Zelda (USA)
12^{6gf} 15^{5gs} 11^{5gf} 4^{5gf} 15^{6g} 11^{6gf} 5^{5gf}
9^{5gf} 4^{5f} 15^{6g} 4^{6f} 1^{5gf} 4^{5gf} 17^{5g} **2-1-14**
£7,673

American Duke (USA) *B J Meehan* 72
2 b c Cryptoclearance - Prologue (USA)
4^{6g} 4^{7gf} 9^{5s} 13^{6gf} **0-0-4 £374**

American Embassy (USA) *P W D'Arcy* 45
3 b c Quiet American (USA) - Foreign Courier (USA)
17^{8gf} 7^{8gs} 13^{10f} 7^{10g} **0-0-4**

American Post *Mme C Head-Maarek* 117
2 br c Bering - Wells Fargo
1^{8gf} 2^{6s} 1^{7gs} 1^{7ho} **3-1-4 £292,987**

Amethyst Rock *P L Gilligan* 39
5 b g Rock Hopper - Kind Lady
14^{10gf} 17^{10gf} 8^{10gf} 6^{10gf} 12^{14gf} **0-0-5**

Ameyrah (Ire) *M R Channon* 52
2 b f In The Wings - Alfaaselah (Ger)
11^{8gf} **0-0-1**

Amid The Chaos (Ire) *D K Weld* 94
3 ch c Nashwan (USA) - Celebrity Style (USA)
6^{10g} 4^{9ys} 8^{16f} 1^{10g} **1-0-4 £4,818**

Amie *Mrs A J Perrett* a52
3 b f Northern Amethyst - Break Point
8^{10sd} 8^{10sd} **0-0-2**

Amigo (Ire) *P Mitchell* 74 a88
5 b g Spectrum (Ire) - Eleanor Antoinette (Ire)
4^{16sd} 4^{12sd} 12^{13sd} 6^{12gf} **0-0-4 £1,018**

Amir Zaman *J R Jenkins* 68 a83
5 ch g Salse (USA) - Colorvista
11^{6sd} 6^{16sd} 8^{14g} 3^{16gf} 16^{6sd} 14^{13gf} 6^{14gf}
6^{16sd} 11^{2sd} 11^{2sd} 3^{12sd} **3-2-11 £8,525**

Ammenayr (Ire) *T G Mills* 83 a47
3 b c Entrepreneur - Katiyfa
6^{8sd} 1^{7gf} 8^{8gf} 5^{7gf} **1-0-4 £5,421**

Amnesty *H Candy* 74
4 ch g Salse (USA) - Amaranthus
5^{8gs} 3^{7gf} 2^{8g} 7^{7gf} 11^{8gf} 11^{8gf} 3^{8gf} **0-3-7**
£2,337

Among Dreams *J A Osborne* 54
2 ch f Among Men (USA) - Russell Creek
1^{6gs} 5^{5gs} **1-0-2 £3,388**

Among Friends (Ire) *B Palling* 72
3 b g Among Men (USA) - Anita's Contessa (Ire)

10^{6g} 3^{5gf} 6^{6gf} **0-1-3 £777**

Amongst Amigos (Ire) *G C Bravery* 33
2 b c Imperial Ballet (Ire) - Red Lory
5^{9gf} 13^{6gf} 7^{6g} **0-0-3**

Amoras (Ire) *J W Hills* 80
6 b m Hamas (Ire) - Red Lory
2^{9g} 1^{8gs} 7^{8g} 5^{9gf} 2^{9gf} 8^{8gf} 9^{8gf} **1-2-7**
£16,065

Ampoule *C E Brittain* 75 a74
4 b g Zamindar (USA) - Diamond Park (Ire)
2^{10sd} 2^{12sd} 1^{12sd} 10^{12sw} 1^{12sd} 5^{12gf} 6^{14gf}
7^{14gf} 5^{14gf} 3^{12gf} 6^{12gf} 3^{11gf} 11^{2f} 15^{12gf} 4^{12gf}
2^{14gf} 2^{11gf} **3-7-17 £27,785**

Amritsar *K G Wingrove*
6 ch g Indian Ridge - Trying For Gold (USA)
10^{9sd} **0-0-1**

Amundsen (USA) *J Jay* 60 a49
3 b g Gone West (USA) - Aunt Anne (USA)
9^{12gf} 5^{12s} 6^{16gf} 3^{12sd} 13^{16gf} **0-1-5 £415**

Amused *R A Fahey* 76
4 ch f Prince Sabo - Indigo
8^{5gs} 5^{6g} 2^{7gf} 1^{6gs} 5^{6g} 6^{6gf} **1-1-6**
£15,130

Amwell Brave *J R Jenkins* 63 a50
2 b c Pyramus (USA) - Passage Creeping (Ire)
19^{6gf} 5^{6gf} 7^{6gf} 7^{6sd} 3^{8s} **0-1-5 £506**

Ana Marie (Fr) *P Demercastel* 116
4 b f Anabaa (USA) - Marie De Ken (Fr)
1^{10g} 5^{11vs} 4^{12g} 2^{10g} 5^{12g} 5^{10ho} **1-1-6**
£96,016

Ana Winta (Fr) *J W Payne* 66
3 b g Anabaa (USA) - Steeple
5^{7gf} 10^{7gf} 4^{6gf} 5^{6gf} **0-0-4 £411**

Anacapri *W S Cunningham* 6
3 b f Barathea (Ire) - Dancerette
8^{10gf} **0-0-1**

Anak Pekan *M A Jarvis* 91
3 ch g In The Wings - Trefoil (Fr)
12^{10gf} 8^{11gf} 2^{12gs} 2^{14gf} 1^{14gf} 2^{14g} 2^{16gf}
2^{17g} **1-5-8 £14,371**

Analogy (Ire) *C J Mann* 70
3 ch g Bahhare (USA) - Anna Comnena (Ire)
7^{7gf} 11^{7gf} 5^{9gf} 2^{12f} 1^{13gf} 2^{12gf} 2^{12gf}
7^{16g} **1-3-8 £7,177**

Analyze (Fr) *B G Powell* 82 a68
5 b g Anabaa (USA) - Bramosia
6^{10sd} 6^{10sd} 2^{10g} 8^{10gf} 1^{10gf} 2^{10gf} 2^{10gf}
7^{10gf} 6^{10gf} 4^{10gf} 3^{10g} 7^{10f} 4^{10g} 3^{10gf} 3^{10f}
3^{10gf} 1^{10f} 5^{10g} 11^{10g} **2-7-20 £16,955**

Anani (USA) *E A L Dunlop* 107
3 ch c Miswaki (USA) - Mystery Rays (USA)
1^{8gf} 4^{12g} 2^{9g} 3^{10g} 5^{10gf} 1^{10gs} 8^{10g} 2^{11s}
2-3-8 £59,325

Anatom *M Quinn* 41 a9
2 ch f Komaite (USA) - Zamarra
7^{5f} 10^{6gf} 13^{5sd} 6^{5gf} **0-0-4**

Anchorsholme *J L Dunlop* 67
3 b g Fleetwood (Ire) - Loch Clair (Ire)
6^{10gf} 12^{12gf} 10^{10gf} 12^{12s} **0-0-4**

And Toto Too *P D Evans* 73 a70
3 br f Averti (Ire) - Divina Mia
10^{8sd} 2^{7sd} 2^{8sd} 2^{8sd} 2^{7sd} 5^{7sd} 3^{9sw} 12^{8sd}
8^{7gf} 1^{7sd} 4^{8sd} 5^{7gf} 1^{6gs} 3^{6gf} 8^{6gf} 1^{6gf} 3^{6gs}
3^{7gf} **5-12-30 £31,968**

Andean *D R Loder* 75

2 b c Singspiel (Ire) - Anna Matrushka
6^{7g} 0-0-1

Andreyev (Ire) J S Goldie — 59
9 ch g Presidium - Missish
19^{6gf} 8^{6s} 9^{7g} 13^{8gf} 20^{7g} 12^{7gs} 9^{8gf}
7^{8g} 5^{7g} 5^{7g} 12^{7gf} 10^{9g} 11^{8g} 0-0-13

Andromache G B Balding — 63
4 ch f Hector Protector (USA) - South Sea Bubble (Ire)
4^{10gf} 4^{10gf} 4^{12g} 4^{13gf} 6^{12g} 0-0-5 £953

Anduril J M P Eustace — 41 a66
2 c c Kris - Attribute
9^{6gf} 5^{8sd} 4^{7sd} 0-0-3

Andy's Elective J R Jenkins — 42 a24
6 b g Democratic (USA) - English Mint
13^{7sd} 8^{10f} 16^{7gs} 10^{8f} 6^{7g} 5^{7gf} 5^{7gf}
12^{7gf} 0-0-8 £229

Anecdote P D Evans
3 ch f Zamindar (USA) - Rainy Sky
5^{12gf} 11^{8sd} 0-0-2

Anemos (Ire) P W D'Arcy — 57 a65
8 ch g Be My Guest (USA) - Frendly Persuasion
3^{9sd} 1^{8sd} 3^{8sd} 3^{8sd} 5^{10gf} 3^{11gf} 3^{10gf} 3^{10f}
6^{7gs} 6^{9gf} 11^{8gf} 2^{8sd} 9^{9gf} 5^{8gf} 5^{9sd} 6^{8f} 1-7-16
£6,793

Ange Gabriel (Fr) E Libaud — 123
5 gr h Kaldounevees (Fr) - Mount Gable
2^{12g} 1^{12g} 1^{12g} 1^{12gs} 9^{12ho} 3-1-5
£455,740

Angel Annie J A Gilbert — 68 a50
3 b f Alzao (USA) - Pure
5^{6sd} 11^{6sd} 10^{8sd} 5^{7gf} 5^{10gf} 7^{7gs} 12^{8gf}
18^{6f} 12^{6sd} 17^{gf} 9^{7f} 9^{8gf} 14^{7gf} 5^{10f} 8^{5f} 7^{6gf}
7^{8f} 1-0-17 £3,692

Angel Isa (Ire) R A Fahey — 57 a47
3 b f Fayruz - Isa
7^{6sd} 6^{6sd} 14^{5sd} 1^{7f} 7^{7gf} 6^{7gs} 14^{7gf} 1-0-7
£4,212

Angel Maid G B Balding — 40
2 b f Forzando - Esilam
14^{6gf} 14^{6gf} 17^{6gf} 0-0-3

Angelica Garnett T E Powell — 45
3 ch f Desert Story (Ire) - Vanessa Bell (Ire)
13^{7gf} 10^{6gs} 12^{8f} 0-0-3

Angelo's Pride J A Osborne — a51
2 ch c Young Ern - Considerable Charm
7^{6sd} 0-0-1

Angels Venture J R Jenkins — 57 a54
7 ch g Unfuwain (USA) - City Of Angels
9^{11gf} 8^{12g} 6^{12sd} 0-0-3

Angelus Domini (Ire) B A McMahon — 25 a23
4 b f Blues Traveller (Ire) - Lyphards Goddess (Ire)
9^{6sd} 12^{11gf} 18^{10f} 12^{7g} 0-0-4

Angie's Double D J S Ffrench Davis — 44
3 ch f Double Trigger (Ire) - Arch Angel (Ire)
8^{10f} 0-0-1

Anglo Saxon (USA) D R Loder — 87
3 b c Seeking The Gold (USA) - Anna Palariva (Ire)
1^{7gs} 8^{8gf} 18^{gf} 2-0-3 £9,209

Anicaflash M Dods — 40
2 b f Cayman Kai (Ire) - Sharp Top
7^{8g} 10^{8gs} 0-0-2

Animal Cracker J Balding — 30 a41
5 gr m Primo Dominie - Child Star (Fr)
10^{7gf} 5^{6sd} 13^{6g} 0-0-3

Ann Summers Two (USA) B J Meehan — 83

2 ch f Elusive Quality (USA) - Lakeland (USA)
6^{5gf} 4^{5gf} 6^{5g} 2^{5gf} 3^{5gf} 2^{6gf} 5^{7g} 2^{7gf}
2^{6gf} 0-5-9 £11,113

Ann's Flyer P A Blockley
3 b f Cool Jazz - Spice And Sugar
15^{7gf} 0-0-1

Anna Almost T Wall
5 b m Tragic Role (USA) - Princess Hotpot (Ire)
10^{12sd} 0-0-1

Anna Walhaan (Ire) Ian Williams — 90 a7
4 b g Green Desert (USA) - Queens Music (USA)
13^{8sd} 12^{8g} 4^{8g} 8^{9g} 7^{8gf} 6^{8f} 4^{9g}
2^{8f} 12^{9g} 5^{8gf} 0-3-11 £12,025

Annabel Lee (UAE) M Johnston — 62
2 ch f Halling (USA) - Sheet Music (Ire)
1^{6g} 5^{6gf} 13^{7g} 1-0-3 £5,845

Annakita W J Musson — 62 a47
3 b f Unfuwain (USA) - Cuban Reef
15^{10g} 9^{10g} 14^{8gf} 11^{12sd} 6^{12sd} 0-0-5

Annambo D R Loder — 91
3 ch c In The Wings - Anna Matrushka
1^{12f} 2^{12s} 12^{16f} 1^{12hd} 13^{14g} 7^{14gf} 2-1-6
£18,105

Anneka C W Thornton — 22
3 b f Among Men (USA) - Treasure Hunt
10^{9s} 12^{7gf} 15^{8gf} 0-0-3

Annie Harvey B Smart — 75
2 ch f Fleetwood (Ire) - Resemblance
3^{6gf} 5^{6gs} 1^{7gs} DSQ^{8gf} 9^{7g} 1-1-5 £9,572

Annie Miller (Ire) M J Wallace — 67 a29
2 b f Night Shift (USA) - Lost Dream
5^{5gf} 3^{5f} 5^{6sd} 8^{7sd} 0-0-4 £669

Annijaz J M Bradley — 61
6 b m Alhijaz - Figment
2^{6gf} 1^{6gf} 4^{6f} 1^{8f} 9^{8gf} 1^{7gf} 8^{6gf} 8^{8f} 6^{8gf}
14^{7gf} 3-2-10 £13,393

Annishirani G A Butler — 68 a83
3 b f Shaamit (Ire) - Silent Miracle (Ire)
3^{8g} 2^{9f} 1^{10sd} 2^{8sd} 1^{7sd} 2-2-5 £7,754

Anniversary Guest (Ire) Mrs Lucinda Featherstone
51
4 b/br f Desert King (Ire) - Polynesian Goddess (Ire)
7^{15gf} 4^{16gf} 5^{16g} 14^{17gf} 6^{14gf} 8^{13gf} 3^{17f}
9^{17f} 5^{18gf} 0-0-9 £681

Another Aspect (Ire) Donal Kinsella — 33 a37
4 b g Inzar (USA) - The Aspecto Girl (Ire)
8^{14gf} 9^{16sd} 0-0-2

Another Bottle (Ire) T P Tate — 69
2 b c Cape Cross (Ire) - Aster Aweke (Ire)
13^{6gf} 3^{7g} 3^{8g} 0-1-3 £1,465

Another Choice (Ire) N P Littmoden — 65
2 ch c Be My Guest (USA) - Gipsy Rose Lee (Ire)
8^{7f} 6^{8gf} 8^{8gf} 7^{6gf} 7^{7g} 0-0-5

Another Con (Ire) Mrs P N Dutfield — a60
2 b f Lake Coniston (Ire) - Sweet Unison (USA)
6^{8sd} 0-0-1

Another Deal (Fr) R J Hodges — 69
4 ch g Barathea (Ire) - Mill Rainbow (Fr)
12^{7gf} 6^{8gs} 3^{12f} 13^{7g} 4^{12gf} 8^{12f} 0-0-6
£991

Another Expletive J White — 64 a38
2 b f Wizard King - French Project (Ire)
7^{7sd} 7^{6gf} 8^{5gf} 7^{5gf} 4^{7sd} 0-0-5

Another Faux Pas (Ire) R Hannon — 36
2 b f Slip Anchor - Pirie (USA)

7^{7gf} 0-0-1

Another Glimpse *Miss B Sanders*   73 a79
5 b g Rudimentary (USA) - Running Glimpse (Ire)
6^{6sd} 2^{6sd} 2^{6sd} 3^{7sd} 5^{5sd} 5^{7sd} 8^{6gf} 6^{5gf}
5^{7gf} 13^{5gf} 0-3-10 £2,987

Another Secret *G L Moore*   57
5 b m Efisio - Secrets Of Honour
9^{8gf} 16^{10gf} 11^{8gf} 12^{8g} 15^{8g} 6^{8gs} BD^{8gs}
0-0-7

Another Victim *M R Bosley*   54
9 ch g Beveled (USA) - Ragtime Rose
8^{5gf} 15^{5gf} 0-0-2

Anousa (Ire) *P Howling*   80
2 b c Intikhab (USA) - Annaletta
2^{7gf} 5^{7gf} 18^{7gf} 1^{8g} 1-1-4 £3,981

Anqood (Ire) *B Hanbury*   71
3 ch f Elmaamul (USA) - Mayaasa (USA)
7^{6gf} 1^{8gf} 12^{9gf} 1-0-3 £5,573

Answered Promise (Fr) *A W Carroll*   64
4 ro g Highest Honor (Fr) - Answered Prayer
8^{9gf} 17^{10gf} 8^{8f} 15^{8gf} 1^{9gf} 7^{8gf} 1^{8gf} 8^{8gf}
2-0-8 £7,120

Antediluvian *J G Given*   78
2 b f Air Express (Ire) - Divina Mia
1^{7gf} 1-0-1 £3,542

Anthemion (Ire) *Mrs J C McGregor*   69
6 ch g Night Shift (USA) - New Sensitive
4^{8gf} 13^{8gs} 6^{8gf} 6^{9g} 5^{8gf} 2^{8gf} 7^{9s} 8^{9gf}
8^{8gf} 2^{8gf} 5^{8gf} 0-2-11 £2,879

Anthony Royle *A Berry*   a13
5 ch g King's Signet (USA) - La Thuile
10^{6sd} 0-0-1

Anthos (Ger) *J R Fanshawe*   85
2 b f Big Shuffle (USA) - Anemoni (Ger)
2^{6g} 6^{6gs} 1^{6f} 4^{6gf} 1-1-4 £6,171

Anticipating *A M Balding*   95
3 b g Polish Precedent (USA) - D'Azy
3^{12f} 1^{12gf} 2^{15g} 14^{16gf} 2^{12gf} 1^{12gf} 4^{12gs}
6^{14gf} 7^{13gf} 2-2-9 £22,139

Anton De Looka (Ire) *R F Fisher*   41
3 b g Sesaro (USA) - Regal Fanfare (Ire)
6^{10g} 11^{12gf} 0-0-2

Antonio Canova *Bob Jones*   57
7 ch g Komaite (USA) - Joan's Venture
20^{7gs} 0-0-1

Antonius Pius (USA) *A P O'Brien*   104
2 b c Danzig (USA) - Catchascatchcan
1^{7ys} 1^{6g} 11^{7gf} 2-0-3 £58,818

Antony Ebeneezer *C R Dore*   51 a48
4 ch g Hurricane Sky (Aus) - Captivating (Ire)
1^{12sd} 4^{11sd} 2^{12sd} 2^{16sw} 2^{11gf} 11^{14gf} 7^{15sd}
10^{11gf} 17^{12g} 4^{13gf} 11^{12gf} 7^{14gf} 1-3-12 £5,683

Anuvasteel *N A Callaghan*   81
2 gr c Vettori (Ire) - Mrs Gray
10^{6gf} 8^{6gf} 5^{6gf} 1^{7g} 5^{8gf} 10^{8gf} 7^{6g} 1-0-7
£4,244

Anyaas (Ire) *Saeed Bin Suroor*   99 a77
3 b g Green Desert (USA) - Anwaar (Ire)
1^{8ft} 4^{8ft} 8^{8gs} 9^{8sd} 1-0-4 £7,262

Anyhow (Ire) *Miss K M George*   62 a74
6 b m Distant Relative - Fast Chick
8^{10sd} 8^{8sd} 3^{9sd} 14^{10sd} 8^{9gf} 9^{10g} 9^{10sd}
4^{10gf} 4^{12gf} 3^{8gf} 7^{10gf} 1^{12g} 11^{12sd} 2^{10sd} 10^{12gf}
8^{10gf} 11^{1gf} 6^{11gf} 8^{10gs} 4-5-22
£15,719

Aoninch *Mrs P N Dutfield*   68
3 ch f Inchinor - Willowbank
12^{7g} 10^{7gf} 3^{10g} 7^{10gf} 1^{12gf} 1^{13gf} 3^{10g}
2-2-7 £7,161

Apache Point (Ire) *N Tinkler*   73
6 ch g Indian Ridge - Ausherra (USA)
3^{7gf} 4^{8gf} 1^{9gf} 4^{9gs} 3^{8gf} 2^{8gs} 1^{8gf} 3^{8gf}
11^{9gf} 13^{8gf} 7^{10gf} 16^{8g} 2^{9f} 4^{8gs} 2-8-14
£13,367

Apache Queen *A M Balding*   49
3 b f Pennekamp (USA) - Croeso Cynnes
7^{6gs} 0-0-1

Apadi (USA) *R C Guest*   28 a22
7 ch g Diesis - Ixtapa (USA)
15^{11sd} 10^{7sd} 10^{10gf} 0-0-3

Aperitif *W J Haggas*   57
2 ch c Pivotal - Art Deco Lady
6^{6gf} 6^{5gf} 0-0-2

Apex *E A L Dunlop*   78
2 ch c Efisio - Royal Loft
8^{6gf} 4^{6gf} 4^{6gf} 3^{6g} 3^{6g} 3^{6gf} 8^{7g}
0-3-8 £4,924

Apex Star (USA) *H R A Cecil*   67
3 ch c Diesis - Imroz (USA)
6^{9gf} 15^{10gf} 7^{7gf} 5^{8gf} 9^{9g} 0-0-5 £480

Aphra Benn (Ire) *G Wragg*   63 a45
4 b f In The Wings - Aigue
12^{10gf} 3^{12gf} 10^{12g} 6^{12g} 0-1-4 £602

Apollo Gee (Ire) *B J Meehan*   59
2 b g Spectrum (Ire) - Suspiria (Ire)
7^{6gf} 3^{6gf} 9^{6gf} 0-1-3 £335

Apollo Victoria (Fr) *B G Powell*
6 b g Sadler's Wells (USA) - Dame Solitaire (Can)
14^{10sd} 0-0-1

Apollonius (Ire) *G M Moore*   a13
6 ch h Nucleon (USA) - Warthill Whispers
12^{7sd} 0-0-1

Appalachian Trail (Ire) *J H M Gosden*   67
2 b c Indian Ridge - Karinski (USA)
7^{7gf} 5^{7gf} 0-0-2

Appetina *J G Given*   74
2 b f Perugino (USA) - Tina Heights
10^{7gf} 2^{6gf} 3^{7g} 3^{8gs} 0-3-4 £9,519

Appleacre *B R Johnson*   a92
4 b f Polar Falcon (USA) - Absaloute Service
11^{2sd} 5^{12sd} 4^{12sd} 7^{15gf} 1-0-4 £5,135

Approach *Sir Mark Prescott*   103
3 gr f Darshaan - Last Second (Ire)
1^{10gf} 4^{12g} 2^{10f} 1-1-4 £85,378

Approval *R Hannon*   97
4 b c Royal Applause - Gentle Persuasion
4^{7gf} 8^{7gf} 0-0-2 £1,130

April Miss (Fr) *Mrs L Wadham*   36
3 bl f Averti (Ire) - Lady Of Jakarta (USA)
8^{7gf} 10^{8g} 8^{8g} 9^{7sd} 0-0-4

April Stock *G A Butler*   96 a85
8 ch m Beveled (USA) - Stockline
8^{13sd} 1^{12g} 2^{10g} 9^{14g} 16^{10gf} 6^{10f} 1-1-6
£27,169

Apsis *A Fabre*   104
2 b c Barathea (Ire) - Apogee
1^{8g} 1^{8gs} 2-0-2 £30,844

Aqribaa (Ire) *A J Lockwood*   60
5 b g Pennekamp (USA) - Karayb (Ire)
10^{9gf} 1^{8gf} 13^{9gf} 15^{8gf} 10^{10gs} 1-0-5

£3,666

Aqua Pura (Ger) *B J Curley* — a18
4 b c Acatenango (Ger) - Actraphane
5¹⁵sd **0-0-1**

Aqualung *B W Hills* — 67
2 b c Desert King (Ire) - Aquarelle
4⁷ᵍᶠ **0-0-1 £555**

Aquiform *K A Morgan* — 11
3 ch f Cadeaux Genereux - Aquarelle
11⁷ᵍᶠ **0-0-1**

Arabian Knight (Ire) *R J Hodges* — 65 a65
3 ch f Fayruz - Cheerful Knight (Ire)
7⁵sd 2⁵sd 3⁵sd 1⁵sd 2⁵sd 4⁵sw 3⁵sd 3⁵ᵍᶠ 4⁵sd 4⁶ᵍᶠ 1⁶ᵍᶠ 9⁶ᶠ 17⁷ᵍᶠ 6⁵ᵍᶠ **2-4-14 £11,528**

Arabian Moon (Ire) *S Dow* — 61 a71
7 ch h Barathea (Ire) - Excellent Alibi (USA)
12¹²sd 20²⁰ᵍᶠ 6¹⁰ᵍᶠ 7¹³ᵍᶠ **0-0-4 £308**

Arabie *M Johnston* — 100
5 b g Polish Precedent (USA) - Always Friendly
14¹²ᵍᶠ 5¹⁰ᵍᶠ **0-0-2**

Arabin *J M P Eustace* — a36
4 b g Bin Ajwaad (Ire) - Just Julia
12⁷sd 10⁵sw 12⁷sd **0-0-3**

Araf *N Wilson* — 40
4 b g Millkom - Euphyllia
7¹²sd 8⁸ᵍᶠ 10⁷ᵍᶠ 11¹⁰ᶠ 17⁸ᵍᶠ **0-0-5**

Araglin *Miss S J Wilton*
4 b g Sadler's Wells (USA) - River Caro (USA)
9¹⁶sd **0-0-1**

Aragon Dancer *T M Jones* — 14
2 b g Aragon - Jambo
15⁶ᵍ 16⁶ᵍᶠ 6⁹ᵍ **0-0-3**

Aragon's Boy *H Candy* — 72
3 ch g Aragon - Fancier Bit
10⁶ᵍᶠ 5⁷ᵍᶠ 4⁸ᵍᶠ **0-0-3 £429**

Arakan (USA) *Sir Michael Stoute* — 119
3 br c Nureyev (USA) - Far Across
1⁸ᵍᶠ 2⁸ᵍᶠ 1⁷ᵍᶠ 2⁷ᵍᶠ 6⁸ᵍᶠ 2⁷ᵍ 3⁷ᵍᶠ **2-4-7 £79,931**

Aramus (Chi) *F Castro* — 112
6 b h Royal Danzig (USA) - Anysha (Chi)
4⁵ᵍ 1⁶ᶠ DSQ⁶ˢ 6⁷ᵍ 1⁶ᵍ **2-0-5 £48,995**

Arbie (Can) *Mrs L C Jewell*
4 b g Mountain Cat (USA) - Empress Of Love (USA)
11¹⁰sd 12¹⁰ᵍᶠ 14¹⁰ᵍᶠ **0-0-3**

Arc El Ciel (Arg) *Mrs S A Liddiard* — 8 a76
5 b h Fitzcarraldo (Arg) - Ardoise (USA)
1⁷sd 1⁷sw 1⁷sd 3⁷sd 2⁸sd 3⁸sd 15⁸ᵍ 10⁸sd **3-3-8 £11,406**

Arcalis *Mrs J R Ramsden* — 94
3 gr g Lear Fan (USA) - Aristocratique
8⁸ᵍᶠ 4¹²ᵍᶠ 5¹²ᵍˢ 1¹⁰ᵍᶠ 3¹⁰ᵍᶠ 2¹⁰ᵍᶠ 4¹⁰ᵍ 1¹⁰ᵍᶠ 2¹⁰ᵍ **3-3-10 £42,477**

Archduke Ferdinand (Fr) *P F I Cole* — 102
5 ch g Dernier Empereur (USA) - Lady Norcliffe (USA)
5¹⁶ᵍᶠ 8¹⁹ᵍᶠ 29¹⁸ᵍᶠ 2¹⁴ᵍᶠ 4¹⁶ᵍᶠ 9¹⁶ᵍᶠ **0-1-6 £7,494**

Archerfield (Ire) *J W Hills* — 60 a44
2 ch f Docksider (USA) - Willow River (Can)
7⁷sd 7⁷ᵍᶠ 5⁷ᵍᶠ 5⁶ᵍᶠ **0-0-4**

Archie Babe (Ire) *J J Quinn* — 75 a50
7 ch g Archway (Ire) - Frensham Manor
8¹⁴sd 1¹²ᵍ 4¹⁰ᵍˢ 7¹²ᵍ 4¹²ᵍᶠ 1¹²ᵍ 13¹²sd
4¹¹ᵍˢ 11¹³ᵍˢ 14¹⁰ᵍᶠ 7¹⁰ᵍˢ **2-1-11 £10,000**

Archirondel *John Berry* — 71
5 b g Bin Ajwaad (Ire) - Penang Rose (NZ)
4⁸ᶠ 8⁸ᵍ 8⁸ᶠ 10¹⁰ᵍᶠ 9¹⁰ᵍᶠ 5¹⁰ᵍᶠ 5¹⁰ᶠ 6¹⁰ᶠ
7¹¹ᵍᶠ 3¹¹ᵍᶠ 7¹²ᶠ **0-2-11 £370**

Archmail (USA) *J H M Gosden* — 67
3 br c Arch (USA) - Crafty Nan (USA)
5¹⁰ᵍᶠ 8¹⁰ᵍᶠ 4¹⁰ᵍᶠ **0-0-3 £414**

Archon (Ire) *Mrs P N Dutfield* — 49 a63
6 ch g Archway (Ire) - Lindas Delight
2⁸sd 4⁸sd 6⁷sd 6⁸sd 6¹¹ᵍᶠ 7⁸sd 7⁸ᵍᶠ **0-1-7 £854**

Arctic Blue *J S Moore* — 64
3 b g Polar Prince (Ire) - Miss Sarajane
14⁸ᵍ 7¹⁴ᶠ 10¹²ᵍ 13¹⁴ᵍᶠ **0-0-4**

Arctic Burst (USA) *D Shaw* — 84
3 b/br g Royal Academy (USA) - Polar Bird
1⁶ᵍ 8⁷ᵍ **1-0-2 £5,590**

Arctic Desert *A M Balding* — 95 a82
3 b g Desert Prince (Ire) - Thamud (Ire)
1⁷sd 5⁸ᶠ 11⁷ᵍᶠ 13⁷ᵍ 4⁷ᵍ 3⁷ᵍᶠ 5⁶ᵍᶠ 2⁷ᵍᶠ
1-3-8 £10,560

Arctic Falcon (Ire) *S L Keightley* — a46
4 b f Polar Falcon (USA) - Chandni (Ire)
11⁶sd 7⁶sd **0-0-2**

Ardent Lady *E A L Dunlop* — 81
3 b f Alhaarth (Ire) - Arvika (Fr)
5⁸ᵍᶠ 7⁷ᵍ 1⁹ᶠ 2⁹ᵍᶠ 6⁹ᵍᶠ **1-1-5 £4,893**

Ardgowan *I Semple*
6 b g Ardkinglass - Final Fling
10¹¹ˢʷ 10¹⁵ˢʷ **0-0-2**

Ardkeel Lass (Ire) *D K Ivory* — 71
2 ch f Fumo Di Londra (Ire) - Wot-A-Noise (Ire)
1⁵ᵍᶠ 2⁵ᵍ 3⁵ᵍ 9⁶ᵍᶠ 6⁵ᵍ **1-0-5 £4,865**

Ardwelshin (Fr) *Mrs P Townsley* — 54 a58
5 b g Ajdayt (USA) - Reem Dubai (Ire)
12¹⁰sd 6¹²sd 4¹⁰ᶠ 20¹¹ᵍᶠ 15¹⁰ᵍᶠ 15¹⁰ᶠ
11⁹ᵍᶠ 11⁸ᶠ 13⁸ᵍᶠ 21⁷ᵍ **0-0-10 £298**

Are You There *T D Barron* — 67 a62
2 b f Presidium - Scoffera
3⁵ᵍᶠ 1⁵sd 1⁵ᵍᶠ 7⁵ᶠ 7⁶ᵍᶠ 11⁸ᵍᶠ **2-0-6 £6,856**

Areeb (Ire) *J D Czerpak* — 30
3 b f Emarati - Racing Brenda
12⁵ᵍᶠ 4⁵ᶠ 8⁵ᵍᶠ 12⁵ᶠ 9⁵ᵍᶠ **0-0-5 £418**

Arfabeat *J S Moore* — a20
3 ch f Abou Zouz (USA) - Sans Egale (Fr)
8⁸sd **0-0-1**

Arfinnit (Ire) *M R Channon* — 81
2 b g College Chapel - Tidal Reach (USA)
22⁶ᵍ 7⁵ᶠ 3⁵ʰʸ 6⁵ᵍˢ 5⁶ᵍᶠ 1⁶ᵍ 6⁷ᵍˢ 3⁶ᵍᶠ
9⁶ᶠ 9⁸ᵍᶠ **1-1-10 £6,339**

Argamia (Ger) *P J McBride* — 58
7 br m Orfano (Ger) - Arkona (Ger)
3¹⁴ᵍᶠ 15¹²ᵍᶠ 7¹⁵ᵍᶠ **0-1-3 £622**

Argent *D Carroll* — 50 a47
2 b c Barathea (USA) - Red Tiara (USA)
3⁵ᵍˢ 5⁶ᵍˢ 5⁷sd 9⁷sd **0-1-4 £856**

Argent Facile (Ire) *H J Collingridge* — 40
6 b g Midhish - Rosinish (Ire)
12⁶ᵍᶠ 12⁵ᵍ 9⁶ᵍᶠ **0-0-3**

Argentum *Lady Herries* — 61
2 b g Sillery (USA) - Frustration
16⁸ᵍᶠ 8⁸ᶠ **0-0-2**

Argonaut *Sir Michael Stoute* — 77
3 ch g Rainbow Quest (USA) - Chief Bee

3¹⁰ᵍᶠ 1¹⁰ᵍᶠ **1-1-2 £6,666**

Aricovair (Ire) *Mrs A J Bowlby* — 27 a17
3 ch g Desert Prince (Ire) - Linoise (Fr)
14⁸ᵍᶠ 13¹⁰ᵍᶠ 12¹⁰ˢᵈ **0-0-3**

Aries (Ger) *M J Wallace* — 80 a27
3 ch f Big Shuffle (USA) - Auenlust (Ger)
3⁸ᵍᶠ 2⁶ᵍᶠ 7⁷ᵍᶠ 10⁷ˢʷ 7⁶ᵍᶠ **0-2-5 £2,450**

Arizona (Ire) *B S Rothwell*
5 b g Sadler's Wells (USA) - Marie De Beaujeu (Fr)
17¹²ᵍᶠ **0-0-1**

Arjay *Andrew Turnell* — 64
5 b g Shaamit (Ire) - Jenny's Call
7⁸ᵍ 2¹⁰ᵍᶠ 4¹⁰ᵍᶠ 16¹²ᵍᶠ 13¹⁰ᵍ 9⁸ᵍ 13⁸ᵍᶠ
0-0-7 £1,513

Ark Admiral *B J Meehan* — 75
4 b g Inchinor - Kelimutu
6¹⁰ᵍ 7¹⁰ᵍ 18¹⁰ᵍᶠ 14¹⁰ᵍᶠ 11¹⁰ᵍᶠ **0-0-5
£140**

Arkholme *W J Haggas* — 78
2 b g Robellino (USA) - Free Spirit (Ire)
4⁷ᵍᶠ 1⁸ˢ **1-0-2 £5,047**

Armada Grove *A P Jarvis* — a68
3 ch f Fleetwood (Ire) - Wannaplantatree
11⁷ˢᵈ 8⁸ˢᵈ 6⁷ˢʷ **0-0-3**

Armagnac *M A Buckley* — 93
5 b g Young Ern - Arianna Aldini
17⁶ᵍ 14⁶ᵍ 8⁵ᵍ 7⁶ᵍ 1⁶ᵍᶠ 7⁶ᵍᶠ 4⁶ᵍˢ 6⁶ᵍ
9⁶ᵍᶠ **1-1-9 £7,889**

Armentieres *J L Spearing* — 62 a52
2 b f Robellino (USA) - Perfect Poppy
6⁶ᵍ 3⁷ᶠᵗ 8⁶ˢᵈ 6⁷ᵍᶠ 3⁸ᵍᶠ 9⁸ᵍᶠ 9¹⁰ᵍᶠ 1⁸ᵍᶠ
4⁸ᵍˢ **1-2-9 £2,939**

Arms Acrossthesea *F P Murtagh* — 49
4 b g Namaqualand (USA) - Zolica
19¹⁰ᵍᶠ 12⁹ᵍᶠ 13⁸ᶠ 11⁷ᶠ 6¹²ᵍᶠ 18¹⁰ᵍ
11⁷ᵍᶠ 14⁸ᵍᶠ **0-0-8**

Arnbi Dancer *P C Haslam* — 16 a67
4 b g Presidium - Travel Myth
2⁶ˢʷ 4⁷ˢᵈ 3⁶ˢᵈ 8⁶ˢᵈ 17⁶ᵍˢ 17⁶ᶠ 2⁷ˢʷ **0-3-7
£1,892**

Arogant Prince *I Semple* — 72 a69
6 ch g Aragon - Versaillesprincess
8⁶ˢᵈ 5⁵ˢᵈ 3⁵ᵍᶠ 3⁵ᵍᶠ 6⁶ᵍᶠ 5⁶ᵍˢ 4⁶ᶠ 15⁵ᵍᶠ
12⁷ˢᵈ 5⁶ᵍᶠ 6⁵ᵍᶠ 12⁶ˢʷ 2⁶ˢᵈ 19⁶ᵍᶠ 11⁵ᵍˢ **0-3-15
£2,517**

Arousha (USA) *E A L Dunlop* — 41 a53
3 ch g King Of Kings (Ire) - Hushi (USA)
17⁸ᵍ 6¹⁰ˢᵈ **0-0-2**

Arpeggio *D Nicholls* — 78 a86
8 b g Polar Falcon (USA) - Hilly
1⁸ˢᵈ 8⁷ˢᵈ 2⁹ˢᵈ 3¹⁰ˢᵈ 2⁸ˢᵈ 12¹⁰ˢᵈ 2⁸ˢᵈ 3⁹ᵍ
2⁸ᵍˢ 9⁸ᵍᶠ 2¹⁰ᵍᶠ 3⁸ᵍ 4⁹ᵍᶠ 3⁹ᵍᶠ **1-8-14
£15,655**

Arran *H J Collingridge* — a37
3 ch c Selkirk (USA) - Humble Pie
UR⁸ᵍᶠ 10⁸ˢᵈ 15⁷ˢᵈ **0-0-3**

Arran Scout (Ire) *Mrs L Stubbs* — 68
2 b g Piccolo - Evie Hone (Ire)
10⁸ᵍ 4⁸ᵍ **0-0-2 £303**

Arresting *J R Fanshawe* — 82
3 b g Hector Protector (USA) - Misbelief
3⁹ˢ 2¹⁰ᵍˢ 2¹²ᵍ 2¹¹ᵍ **0-4-4 £5,772**

Arrgatt (Ire) *M A Jarvis* — 49
2 gr c Intikhab (USA) - Nuit Chaud (USA)
17⁷ᵍᶠ **0-0-1**

Arrow *R A Fahey* — 37
4 b g Pivotal - Cremets
12⁸ᵍˢ 18⁸ᵍᶠ **0-0-2**

Arry Dash *M R Channon* — 91 a89
3 b g Fraam - Miletrian Cares (Ire)
2¹⁰ˢᵈ 1⁸ˢᵈ 7⁷ᵍ 1⁸ᵍᶠ 5⁸ᵍᶠ **2-1-5 £13,378**

Art Expert (Fr) *Mrs N Macauley* — a27
5 b g Pursuit Of Love - Celtic Wing
5¹⁶ˢʷ 5¹⁶ˢᵈ 16²²ᵍᶠ **0-0-3**

Art Trader (USA) *Mrs A J Perrett* — 85
2 b c Arch (USA) - Math (USA)
1⁸ᵍᶠ 4⁸ᵍ **1-0-2 £6,041**

Arte Et Labore (Ire) *K A Ryan* — 47
3 b f Raphane (USA) - Bouffant
13⁷ᵍᶠ 10⁸ᵍˢ 6⁸ᵍˢ 2⁷ᵍᶠ 10⁷ᵍᶠ 11⁸ᵍᶠ 13⁸ᵍᶠ
4¹⁰ᵍᶠ **0-1-8 £1,263**

Arthur Pendragon *B W Hills* — a57
3 b g Botanic (USA) - Blue Room
4⁸ˢᵈ UR⁸ᶠ **0-0-2**

Arthurs Kingdom (Ire) *Miss Kate Milligan*
7 b g Roi Danzig (USA) - Merrie Moment (Ire)
8¹⁶ˢᵈ **0-0-1**

Artic Reason (Ire) *E McNamara* — a24
4 b g Perugino (USA) - Vendetta Valentino (USA)
12¹⁰ˢᵈ **0-0-1**

Artie *T D Easterby* — 89
4 b g Whittingham (Ire) - Calamanco
9⁵ᵍᶠ 11⁵ᵍᶠ 12⁵ʰʸ 5⁶ᵍᶠ 3⁵ᵍᶠ 10⁵ᵍᶠ 2⁶ᵍᶠ
15⁶ᵍ 5³ᵍˢ 17⁵ᵍ **0-3-11 £9,197**

Artifact *J A Pickering*
5 b m So Factual (USA) - Ancient Secret
14⁸ˢᵈ **0-0-1**

Artisia (Ire) *W R Muir* — 68
3 ch f Peintre Celebre (USA) - Almaaseh (Ire)
2⁸ᵍᶠ 7⁷ᶠᵗ **0-0-2 £1,640**

Artistic Lad *Sir Michael Stoute* — 88
3 ch c Peintre Celebre (USA) - Maid For The Hills
11¹⁰ᵍ **0-0-1**

Artistic Style *B Ellison* — 71
3 b c Anabaa (USA) - Fine Detail (Ire)
3⁸ˢ 7⁸ᵍ 2⁶ˢ 2⁸ᵍᶠ 3¹⁰ᵍˢ **0-4-5 £6,451**

Artisticimpression (Ire) *E A L Dunlop* — 62
2 b c Rainbow Quest (USA) - Entice (Fr)
14⁷ᵍᶠ 6⁷ᵍᶠ **0-0-2**

Artistry *P Howling* — 67
3 b f Night Shift (USA) - Arriving
3¹⁰ᵍᶠ 3¹⁰ᶠ 3¹⁰ᵍᶠ 5¹⁰ᵍ 5¹⁰ᵍ 3⁹ᵍᶠ 4⁹ᵍᶠ 5¹⁰ᵍᶠ
4¹⁰ᵍᶠ 17⁸ᵍ **0-3-10 £4,210**

Artists Licence *R Charlton* — 19 a51
2 gr c Linamix (Fr) - Once Upon A Time
10⁷ˢᵈ 16⁸ᵍᶠ **0-0-2**

Artzola (Ire) *C A Horgan* — 54 a20
3 b f Alzao (USA) - Polistatic
16⁸ᵍᶠ 5⁸ᵍᶠ 14⁷ˢᵈ **0-0-3**

Arzoo (Ire) *L M Cumani* — 100
3 b c Bahhare (USA) - Ishtiyak
4⁶ᵍᶠ 3⁶ᵍᶠ 10⁶ᵍ 4⁸ᵍᶠ 5⁸ᵍ 4¹⁰ᵍᶠ 3⁸ᵍᶠ
1⁷ᵍᶠ 1⁸ᵍᶠ 11⁸ˢ PU⁷ᵍᶠ **3-1-12 £24,275**

Asaleeb *A C Stewart* — 77
2 b f Alhaarth (Ire) - Gharam (USA)
3⁷ᵍˢ 2⁸ᵍᶠ **0-1-2 £2,253**

Asbo *Dr J D Scargill* — 56
3 b f Abou Zouz (USA) - Star
11⁶ᵍᶠ 7⁵ˢ **0-0-2**

Ascari *A L Forbes* — 43

7 br g Presidium - Ping Pong
10^13gf 6^10gf **0-0-2**

Ascertain (Ire) *N P Littmoden* 23
2 ch g Intikhab (USA) - Self Assured (Ire)
15^7g **0-0-1**

Ash Laddie (Ire) *E J Alston* 66
3 ch g Ashkalani (Ire) - Lady Ellen
9^6f 5^8gf 8^7f **0-0-3**

Ash Moon (Ire) *W J Musson* 70 a60
5 ch m General Monash (USA) - Jarmar Moon
10^8g 8^10sd 2^10g 7^12gf 4^10gf 9^12gf **0-1-6**
£1,532

Ashdown Express (Ire) *C F Wall* 118
4 ch g Ashkalani (Ire) - Indian Express
11^6gf 3^6gf 2^6gf 2^6gf 4^6gs 2^6gf 1^6gf 3^7gf
4^6gf 5^7g 1^6gf 8^6g **2-4-12 £70,680**

Ashfield *J M P Eustace* 70
2 ch f Zilzal (USA) - Ninaki (USA)
2^7gf 4^7gf **0-1-2 £1,538**

Ashleigh Baker (Ire) *A Bailey* 37
8 b/br m Don't Forget Me - Gayla Orchestra
8^13gs **0-0-1**

Ashstanza *M A Jarvis* 35 a54
2 gr g Ashkalani (Ire) - Poetry In Motion (Ire)
13^6gf 4^7sd **0-0-2 £286**

Ashtaroute (USA) *M C Chapman* 61 a22
3 b f Holy Bull (USA) - Beating The Buzz (Ire)
4^10gf 4^10gf 3^11gf 4^11g 6^9g 8^12sw 9^12gf
5^12gs **0-0-8 £1,845**

Ashtoreth (Ire) *D McCain*
4 ch f Ashkalani (Ire) - Sally Chase
10^8sd **0-0-1**

Ashtree Belle *D Haydn Jones* 76 a78
4 b f Up And At 'Em - Paris Babe
13^6g 10^6sd 6^7sd 1^7sd 5^7gf 1^7g 5^7sd 2^7sd
2^7sd 4^7sd 11^6sd **2-2-11 £10,669**

Ashville Lad *B A McMahon* a55
6 b h Bigstone (Ire) - Hooray Lady
2^8sd **0-1-1 £952**

Ashwaaq (USA) *J L Dunlop* 76
2 b f Gone West (USA) - Wasnah (USA)
4^7gs **0-0-1 £323**

Asia Winds (Ire) *B W Hills* 92
2 ch f Machiavellian (USA) - Ascot Cyclone (USA)
7^6gf 1^5f 4^5gf 1^7gf 1^7g 5^7g 5^7gf **3-0-7**
£22,797

Asian Heights *G Wragg* 121
5 b h Hernando (Fr) - Miss Rinjani
2^12gf 1^13gf **1-1-2 £54,500**

Asian Persuasion (Ire) *B A Pearce*
4 gr g Danehill Dancer (Ire) - Kaitlin (Ire)
7^12sd 11^15sd **0-0-2**

Asiatic *M Johnston* 78
2 ch c Lomitas - Potri Pe (Arg)
2^8s 4^7gs 1^8gf **1-1-3 £6,034**

Ask The Driver *D J S Ffrench Davis* 45 a42
2 b g Ashkalani (Ire) - Tithcar
12^6gf 5^8sw 7^6s **0-0-3**

Askariyah (USA) *T Hogan* 48 a42
3 b f Kris S (USA) - Awaamir
11^8sd 8^8sd 8^8sd 13^11g 12^13gy 7^12gy
7^12f 4^13gf 7^12f **0-1-10 £688**

Askham (USA) *J G Given* 97
5 b h El Gran Senor (USA) - Konvincha (USA)
5^10gf 4^8g 10^8gf **0-0-3 £1,562**

Assignation *B R Millman* 51
3 b g Compton Place - Hug Me
15^7gf 20^6gf 9^7gf 12^7g 8^10gf 7^10gf 7^8gf
0-0-7

Assoon *G L Moore* 65
4 b c Ezzoud (Ire) - Handy Dancer
2^18f 3^14gf **0-1-2 £2,827**

Assraar *A C Stewart* 52
3 b f Cadeaux Genereux - Possessive Dancer
13^8s **0-0-1**

Astafort (Fr) *A C Whillans* 18
4 ch g Kendor (Fr) - Tres Chic (USA)
11^16gs **0-0-1**

Astaramongstthem (Ire) *P D Evans* 56
2 b g Among Men (USA) - Asturiana
5^6g **0-0-1**

Astle (Ire) *Mrs N Macauley* a11
5 ch g Spectrum (Ire) - Very Sophisticated (USA)
12^9sd **0-0-1**

Astormydayiscoming *G F Bridgwater* 17
5 b g Alhaarmi - Valentine Song
8^13gf 11^17gf **0-0-2**

Astrac (Ire) *Mrs A L M King* 57 a55
12 b g Nordico (USA) - Shirleen
12^7sd 10^7gs 14^7g 5^7s 3^7f 16^6f 17^f 1^6f
5^7gf **2-1-9 £6,319**

Astral Prince *Mrs K Walton* 51 a48
5 ch g Efisio - Val D'Erica
16^12gf 6^8gf 8^8g **0-0-3**

Astrocharm (Ire) *M H Tompkins* 87
4 b f Charnwood Forest (Ire) - Charm The Stars
12^8gf 12^8g 6^9gf 3^8f 14^8g 2^8gf 13^10gf
3^8gf 7^10gf 9^10gf 4^10gf 11^12g **0-1-12 £4,458**

Astromancer (USA) *M H Tompkins* 59 a59
3 b/br f Silver Hawk (USA) - Colour Dance
7^12gf 9^14g PU^11g 5^12gf 11^11sw **0-0-5**

Astronaut *M C Pipe* 44 a45
6 b g Sri Pekan (USA) - Wild Abandon (USA)
8^12sd 6^8sd 6^9sd 7^10f 7^12sw **0-0-5**

Astyanax (Ire) *Sir Mark Prescott* 76 a79
3 b c Hector Protector (USA) - Craigmill
1^12sd 3^13g 2^14gf 4^16gf 1^14gf **2-2-5**
£8,632

Aswan (Ire) *S R Bowring* 74 a73
5 ch g Ashkalani (Ire) - Ghariba
4^7sd 5^8sd 9^7sd 3^10gf 4^8gf 4^10f 10^10gf
0-2-7 £2,456

Atahuelpa *M F Harris* 88
3 b g Hernando (Fr) - Certain Story
4^8f 3^8g 1^9gf 7^10gf **1-0-4 £12,272**

Atavus *G G Margarson* 111
6 b h Distant Relative - Elysian
4^8g 5^7gy 2^8g 10^9g 5^7gf 11^7g 3^7gf 11^7gs
9^7g 1^6gf 9^6gf 4^7gf **1-2-12 £16,827**

Athboy *D Mullarkey* a50
2 ch c Entrepreneur - Glorious
6^7sd 10^8sd **0-0-2**

Atheer (USA) *E A L Dunlop* 75
3 b f Lear Fan (USA) - Rhumba Rage (USA)
10^8sd 5^8gf 1^8f 4^8gf 7^8gs 6^7gf 10^7f **1-0-7**
£5,266

Athenian *D Morris* 97
4 b g Distant Relative - Confection
2^10gf 2^10g 16^10gf 7^9gf 1^10gf 5^10g PU^11gf
1-2-7 £18,092

Athollbrose (USA) *T D Easterby*   50 a53
2 b g Mister Baileys - Knightly Cut Up (USA)
4^{5sd} 16^{5g} 8^{7gf} 0-0-3

Atlantic Ace *B Smart*   90
6 b g First Trump - Risalah
10^{8g} 6^{8gf} 12^{8g} 8^{8gf} 5^{8gs} 32^{8gf} 11^{8f}
5^{10gf} 9^{9gf} 1^{8gf} 8^{8g} 5^{8gf} 1-0-12 £4,961

Atlantic Breeze *Mrs N Macauley*   a53
2 br f Deploy - Atlantic Air
4^{6sd} 0-0-1

Atlantic City *W J Haggas*   72
2 ch g First Trump - Pleasuring
6^{7gf} 2^{8gf} 2^{8f} 0-1-3 £2,026

Atlantic Quest (USA) *G A Harker*   91 a86
4 b g Woodman (USA) - Pleasant Pat (USA)
5^{10sd} 13^{8gf} 13^{8g} 14^{10s} 18^{8g} 2^{8gf} 11^{8gf}
19^{8gf} 4^{11g} 2^{8gf} 13^{10g} 6^{8gf} 7^{9gf} 10^{10g} 4^{8g} 1^{8gf}
9^{8gf} 3-2-17 £24,266

Atlantic Sky *H Morrison*   60
3 b f Bishop Of Cashel - Naval Dispatch
8^{10gf} 10^{10gf} 5^{10gf} 12^{10g} 4^{10f} 0-0-5

Atlantic Tern *N M Babbage*   36
2 b c Atraf - Great Tern
14^{8gs} 0-0-1

Atlantic Viking (Ire) *D Nicholls*   107
8 b g Danehill (USA) - Hi Bettina
6^{5f} 2^{5gf} 25^{6f} 14^{5gf} 15^{g} 5^{5gf} 14^{5gs} 6^{5gf}
22^{6g} 1-1-9 £62,836

Atractive Girl *R Ingram*
4 ch f Atraf - Harold's Girl (Fr)
9^{9sd} 0-0-1

Attacca *J R Weymes*   72
2 b c Piccolo - Jubilee Place (Ire)
11^{7gf} 9^{6g} 2^{6g} 16^{gf} 1-1-4 £4,239

Attache *M A Jarvis*   116
5 ch g Wolfhound (USA) - Royal Passion
1^{7gf} 5^{6gf} 5^{7gf} 1^{7f} 8^{7g} 5^{7gf} 1^{7gf} 18^{7gf}
3^{8gs} 3-0-9 £55,681

Attack *P J Hobbs*   59 a66
7 gr g Sabrehill (USA) - Butsova
10^{16sd} 4^{12sd} 5^{13sd} 7^{12g} 8^{15gf} 13^{14gf} 0-0-6
£316

Attack Minded *L R James*
2 ch g Timeless Times (USA) - French Ginger
10^{6gf} 0-0-1

Attila The Hun *F Watson*   54
4 b g Piccolo - Katya (Ire)
18^{7gf} 15^{6gf} 8^{8g} 7^{7f} 14^{5gf} 0-0-5

Attorney *D Shaw*   60 a61
5 ch g Wolfhound (USA) - Princess Sadie
6^{6sw} 8^{5sd} 7^{6sd} 4^{5sd} 3^{5sw} 2^{6sw} 1^{5sw} 8^{5sd}
9^{6sd} 8^{5sw} 7^{5sd} 8^{6sd} 13^{5gf} 5^{6sd} 12^{5gf} 7^{5gs} 8^{5gs}
6^{5sd} 10^{6gf} 1-5-31 £7,906

Attorney General (Ire) *J A B Old*   74
4 b g Sadler's Wells (USA) - Her Ladyship
10^{12gf} 0-0-1

Attraction *M Johnston*   117
2 b f Efisio - Flirtation
1^{5g} 1^{5g} 1^{5gf} 1^{5gf} 1^{6g} 5-0-5 £101,450

Attune *B J Meehan*   56
2 br f Singspiel - Arriving
4^{7f} 0-0-1 £417

Audacious Prince (Ire) *Sir Mark Prescott*   101
3 b c Desert Prince (Ire) - Sheer Audacity
2^{8gs} 1^{10g} 1-1-2 £16,416

Audience *W J Haggas*   107
3 b c Zilzal (USA) - Only Yours
15^{8g} 7^{9g} 2^{7gf} 8^{8gs} 2^{8g} 6^{7gf} 0-2-6
£6,389

Auditorium *Sir Michael Stoute*   112
2 b c Royal Applause - Degree
8^{6gf} 2^{7g} 4^{6gf} 1^{6gf} 1^{6gf} 2-1-5 £61,153

Augustine *D R Loder*   72
2 b c Machiavellian (USA) - Crown Of Light
5^{6gf} 0-0-1

Aunt Hilda *M F Harris*   48
4 b f Distant Relative - Aloha Jane (USA)
10^{11gf} 10^{8gf} 7^{9gf} 5^{10gf} 16^{7gf} 0-0-5

Aunt Rita (Ire) *M L W Bell*   80
3 ch f Grand Lodge (USA) - Dance Alone (USA)
8^{8gf} 5^{6gf} 4^{7g} 3^{7g} 8^{8g} 5^{10g} 8^{12gf} 0-1-7
£2,992

Aunty Lil (USA) *P R Chamings*   46 a25
3 b/br f Swain (Ire) - Singular Broad (USA)
11^{10sd} 17^{10gf} 8^{9gf} 8^{9sd} 0-0-4

Aunty Nina (Ire) *J S Moore*
3 b f Mujadil (USA) - Nobodys Child (Ire)
PU^{6sd} 0-0-1

Aurelia (Ire) *Sir Mark Prescott*   73
2 b f Rainbow Quest (USA) - Fern
6^{8gf} 3^{8f} 11^{10f} 4^{10gf} 1-0-4 £4,025

Auroville *M L W Bell*   58
2 b c Cadeaux Genereux - Silent Tribute (Ire)
12^{7gf} 5^{7gf} 10^{7gf} 0-0-3

Authority (Ire) *W J Haggas*   74
3 b c Bluebird (USA) - Persian Tapestry
2^{7gf} 4^{7gf} 0-1-2 £2,955

Autumn Fantasy (USA) *B Ellison*   68 a47
4 b c Lear Fan (USA) - Autumn Glory (USA)
8^{16sd} 9^{12g} 10^{12gf} 12^{14gf} 12^{12gf} 10^{15gf}
0-0-6

Autumn Flyer (Ire) *C G Cox*   60 a59
2 ch g Salse (USA) - Autumn Fall (USA)
11^{7gf} 8^{7gf} 9^{7sd} 0-0-3

Autumn Glory (Ire) *G Wragg*   86
3 b c Charnwood Forest (Ire) - Archipova (Ire)
18^{8gf} 4^{7g} 7^{7gf} 1-0-3 £5,984

Autumn Pearl *M A Jarvis*   79 a79
2 b f Orpen (USA) - Cyclone Flyer
1^{5gf} 5^{6g} 1^{5sd} 2-0-3 £7,884

Aveiro (Ire) *B G Powell*   47 a44
7 b g Darshaan - Avila
4^{15sd} 3^{12f} 11^{11gf} 11^{12f} 6^{16gf} 7^{12gf} 3^{10f}
0-2-7 £773

Avening *R Hannon*   86
3 br c Averti (Ire) - Dependable
7^{5gf} 10^{6g} 13^{7gf} 14^{6gf} 0-0-4

Avenlea *R Hannon*
2 b c Averti (Ire) - Cloudslea (USA)
7^{5gf} 0-0-1

Aventura (Ire) *M J Polglase*   94 a85
3 b c Sri Pekan (USA) - La Belle Katherine (USA)
3^{6sd} 1^{8sd} 8^{7gf} 5^{7gf} 2^{7gf} 9^{7gf} 3^{6gs} 5^{6gs}
5^{7g} 6^{7g} 3^{7gf} 5^{8gs} 4^{9gf} 3^{8s} 16^{7sd} 1-4-15
£15,413

Averami *A M Balding*   36
2 b f Averti (Ire) - Friend For Life
10^{6gs} 0-0-1

Averlline *B De Haan*   71
2 b f Averti (Ire) - Spring Sunrise

9⁵ᵍ 9⁶ᵍᶠ 3⁶ᵍᶠ 7⁶ᵍ 3⁶ᵍᶠ 3⁶ᵍᶠ 7⁷ᵍᶠ 2⁶ᵍᶠ 2⁷ᶠ
1⁶ᵍˢ 16⁵ᵍˢ **1-3-11 £6,404**

Aversham R Hannon — 98
3 b c Averti (Ire) - Vavona
4⁶ᵍᶠ 5⁵ᵍᶠ 3⁷ᵍᶠ 4⁷ᵍᶠ 7⁶ʰʸ 4⁶ᵍᶠ 20⁷ᶠ 4⁷ᵍᶠ
4⁷ᵍᶠ 2⁷ᶠ 3⁶ᵍ **0-2-11 £11,716**

Avesa D A Nolan — 26
3 br f Averti (Ire) - Andalish
14⁵ᵍˢ 8⁸ᵍᶠ 6⁹ᵍᶠ 10¹¹ᵍ 10⁷ᶠ 10⁹ᵍˢ **0-0-6 £273**

Avesomeofthat (Ire) Mrs P N Dutfield — 70
2 b g Lahib (USA) - Lacinia
4⁸ᵍᶠ 5⁸ᵍᶠ 2⁸ᶠ 17⁸ᵍᶠ **0-1-4 £754**

Avessia R Charlton — 47
2 b f Averti (Ire) - Alessia
7⁶ᵍ **0-0-1**

Avid Spell (USA) R Charlton — 79
2 b c Expelled (USA) - Deep Magic (USA)
2⁵ᵍ 2⁶ᵍᶠ 1⁶ᵍˢ 4⁵ᵍᶠ **1-2-4 £6,401**

Avit (Ire) P L Gilligan — 52 a34
3 ch f General Monash (USA) - Breakfast Boogie
10⁶ˢᵈ 5⁶ᶠ 8⁵ᵍ 10⁶ᵍᶠ 18⁵ᵈ 8⁷ᵍᶠ **0-0-6**

Avonbridge R Charlton — 120
3 b c Averti (Ire) - Alessia
2⁶ᵍ 2⁶ᵍᶠ 1⁶ᵍᶠ 3⁷ᵍˢ 4⁶ˢ 3⁶ᵍ **1-4-6 £53,309**

Avondale Lad (Ire) M Dods — 54 a66
3 ch g Titus Livius (Fr) - Skinity
12⁶ᵍᶠ 15⁶ᵍ 7⁶ᵍᶠ 14⁶ᵍˢ 9⁶ˢᵈ 2⁶ᶠ 3⁶ˢᵈ 4⁷ᵍᶠ
4⁷ᵍ 6⁶ᵍᶠ 12⁷ˢᵈ **0-2-11 £2,137**

Avonloch R Hannon — 63
2 b g Averti (Ire) - Loch Fyne
8⁵ᵍ 3⁵ᵍᶠ **0-1-2 £542**

Awake D Nicholls — 87
6 ch g First Trump - Pluvial
5⁵ᵍ 6⁵ᵍᶠ 5⁵ᵍ 9⁵ᵍᶠ 19⁵ᵍˢ **0-0-5 £394**

Awarding R F Johnson Houghton — 84
3 ch g Mark Of Esteem (Ire) - Monaiya
2⁵ᵍᶠ 4⁶ᵍ 10⁶ᵍᶠ 4⁵ᵍᶠ 5⁵ᶠ 6⁶ᵍᶠ 5⁵ᵍᶠ **0-2-7 £10,154**

Aweigh Sir Mark Prescott — a37
3 b f Polar Falcon (USA) - Shore Line
5⁸ˢᵈ **0-0-1**

Awesome Love (USA) M Johnston — 75
2 br c Awesome Again (Can) - Circus Toons (USA)
2⁶ᵍᶠ **0-1-1 £1,702**

Axis T D Barron — 99
2 b c Pivotal - Bollin Victoria
3⁶ᵍ 11⁶ˢ 7⁵ˢ 1⁵ᵍᶠ 2⁶ᵍᶠ **1-2-5 £37,521**

Ayun (USA) J L Dunlop — 94
3 ch f Swain (USA) - Oumaldaaya (USA)
1⁸ᶠ 4⁸ᵍᶠ 4¹⁰ᵍᶠ 2¹²ᶠ 1¹⁰ᵍ 1¹⁰ᵍᶠ **3-1-6 £21,143**

Azamour (Ire) John M Oxx — 109
2 b c Night Shift (USA) - Asmara (USA)
1⁷ᵍᶠ 1⁸ᵍʸ **2-0-2 £63,311**

Azarole (Ire) J R Fanshawe — 107
2 b c Alzao (USA) - Cashew
2⁶ᵍᶠ 1⁶ᵍˢ 4⁷ᵍ 1⁶ᵍᶠ 4⁷ᵍᶠ **2-1-5 £20,102**

Azolla L M Cumani — 74
2 b f Cadeaux Genereux - Frond
4⁶ᵍᶠ 2⁷ᵍ 3⁷ᶠ 5⁶ᵍᶠ 2⁶ᵍˢ **0-3-5 £6,905**

Azreme P W D'Arcy — 74 a69
3 ch c Unfuwain (USA) - Mariette
2⁶ˢᵈ 6⁸ᵍ 1⁷ᵍˢ 11⁷ˢᵈ 11⁷ᵍˢ **1-1-5 £7,038**

Azur (Ire) Mrs A L M King — 76
6 b m Brief Truce (USA) - Bayadere (USA)
3¹⁰ᵍᶠ 3¹³ᵍ 4¹²ᵍᶠ 5¹²ᵍᶠ 2¹²ᵍᶠ 2¹¹ᵍᶠ 2¹²ᵍᶠ
1¹³ᵍᶠ 10¹²ᵍᶠ 2¹⁷ᶠ 4¹⁷ᶠ 3¹⁴ᶠ 4¹⁵ᵍᶠ **1-7-13 £11,589**

B A Highflyer M R Channon — 76 a68
3 b g Compton Place - Primulette
15⁶ᵍᶠ 8⁶ᵍˢ 6⁶ʰʸ 10⁶ᵍᶠ 5⁷ᵍ 3⁶ᵍ 3⁶ᵍᶠ 4⁶ᵍᶠ
2⁶ᵍᶠ 4⁶ᵍᶠ 8⁸ᵍᶠ 7⁷ᵍᶠ 5⁶ᵍᶠ 12⁷ᵍ 7⁷ᵍᶠ 11⁶ᵍᶠ 2⁶ˢᵈ
2⁷ᵍᶠ 1⁶ᵍˢ 6⁷ᵍˢ **1-4-20 £8,596**

Baawrah M R Channon — 35
2 ch c Cadeaux Genereux - Kronengold (USA)
14⁶ᵍᶠ 6⁸ᵍᶠ **0-0-2**

Baba Mia P T Midgley — 11
3 b f Gothenberg (Ire) - Kagram Queen
11¹⁰ᵍᶠ 18⁸ᵍᶠ 12¹¹ᵍᶠ 9¹⁶ᵍᶠ 9⁸ᵍˢ **0-0-5**

Babodana M H Tompkins — 114
3 ch c Bahamian Bounty - Daanat Nawal
4⁶ʰʸ 9⁷ᵍ 14⁷ᵍ 4⁸ᵍ 2⁸ᵍˢ 1⁸ᵍˢ **1-1-6 £20,023**

Baboosh (Ire) J R Fanshawe — 72
2 b f Marju (Ire) - Slipper
2⁷ᵍᶠ **0-1-1 £1,163**

Baboushka (Ire) C G Cox — 54
2 b f Soviet Star (USA) - Kabayil
9⁷ᵍ 4⁷ᵍˢ **0-0-2**

Baby Barry Mrs G S Rees — 63 a70
6 b g Komaite (USA) - Malcesine (Ire)
22⁶ᵍ 19⁶ᵍᶠ 15⁶ᵍᶠ 17⁶ᵍᶠ 5⁶ᵍ 6⁶ᵍᶠ 3⁶ˢᵈ
14⁶ᵍᶠ 9⁶ᵍᶠ 4⁶ˢᵈ 2⁶ˢᵈ 3⁶ˢᵈ **0-3-12 £1,380**

Bachelor Duke (USA) J A R Toller — 114
2 b c Miswaki (USA) - Gossamer (USA)
4⁷ᵍᶠ 3⁷ᵍᶠ 3⁷ᵍᶠ **0-2-3 £18,969**

Bachelor Of Arts D R Loder — 83
2 b c Stravinsky (USA) - Wannabe Grand (Ire)
2⁵ᵍᶠ 1⁵ᵍᶠ 4⁵ᵍ 2⁵ᵍ 6⁵ᵍᶠ **1-1-6 £11,324**

Bachelors Pad Miss S J Wilton — 14
9 b g Pursuit Of Love - Note Book
10¹²ᵍ **0-0-1**

Back At De Front (Ire) R Hannon — 70
2 b f Cape Cross (Ire) - Bold Fashion (Fr)
10⁵ᵍᶠ 1⁶ᵍᶠ 1⁶ᵍ **2-0-3 £10,933**

Back In Action M A Magnusson — 46 a49
3 b c Hector Protector (USA) - Lucca
5⁸ˢᵈ 9⁸ᵍᶠ **0-0-2**

Back In Fashion J Mackie —
2 b f Puissance - Spring Collection
14⁸ˢᵈ PU⁸ᵍᶠ **0-0-2**

Back In Spirit B A McMahon — a78
3 ch g Primo Dominie - Pusey Street Girl
8⁶ˢᵈ 17⁸ˢ **0-0-2**

Backofthenet K R Burke — 60
2 b c Timeless Times (USA) - Nuthatch (Ire)
8⁵ᵍᶠ 2⁵ᵍᶠ 2⁵ᵍᶠ 5⁶ᵍᶠ 3⁵ᶠ **0-2-5 £2,668**

Backwell (USA) M A Jarvis — 88 a57
3 b g Allied Forces (USA) - Shehazahome (USA)
13⁸ᵍᶠ 10⁸ᵍᶠ 18ˢᵈ 5⁸ᵍᶠ 6⁷ᵍᶠ 10⁹ᵍˢ 2¹⁰ˢ
6¹¹ˢ **2-1-8 £9,731**

Bad Intentions (Ire) G A Harker — 86
3 b f Victory Note (USA) - Fallacy
5⁷ᵍᶠ 3⁶ᵍᶠ 7⁶ᵍᶠ 12⁵ᵍᶠ 5⁶ᵍᶠ 6⁵ᵍ 5⁷ᶠ 12⁶ᵍᶠ
18⁸ˢ **0-1-9 £2,319**

Badhbh (Ire) G C Bravery — 58 a52
2 ch f Deploy - Painted Desert

13^6g 6^6g 3^7f 5^7sd 4^8gf 8^8gf 6^10f 8^8gf
0-0-8 £618

Badminton *C E Brittain* 103
2 b f Zieten (USA) - Badawi (USA)
1^6gf 2^6gf 3^6gf 1-2-3 £42,125

Badou *L Montague Hall* 57 a68
3 b g Averti (Ire) - Bint Albadou (Ire)
1^6sd 10^5sd 9^6sd 6^6sd 5^7sd 15^7gf 12^8g
12^6g 2^8gf 4^8f 1-1-10 £3,813

Badr (USA) *M Johnston* 69
2 b c Theatrical - Bejat (USA)
2^8gf 10^8g 0-1-2 £2,091

Badrinath (Ire) *H J Collingridge* 24
9 b g Imperial Frontier (USA) - Badedra
13^11gf 8^9g 9^11g 0-0-3

Baffle *J L Dunlop* 74
2 b f Selkirk (USA) - Elude
7^7gf 2^7gf 6^7gf 0-1-3 £1,688

Bag 'O' Nails (Ire) *H J Cyzer* 35
2 b c Desert Prince (Ire) - Dulcinea
12^7gf 0-0-1

Bagan (Fr) *H R A Cecil* 92
4 b/br c Rainbow Quest (USA) - Maid Of Erin (USA)
2^10gf 7^10gf 15^10g 1^12gf 5^12g 1-1-5
£24,220

Bago (Fr) *J E Pease* 118
2 b/br c Nashwan (USA) - Moonlight's Box (USA)
1^8gs 1^8s 1^8g 1^8vs 4-0-4 £129,123

Bahama Belle *H S Howe* 64
2 b f Bahamian Bounty - Barque Bleue (USA)
7^5gf 9^5gf 7^6gf 11^6gf 0-0-4

Bahama Reef (Ire) *B Gubby* 72
2 b g Sri Pekan (USA) - Caribbean Dancer
4^5gf 2^5f 10^6g 2^6gf 9^5gf 6^7g 4^8gf 10^7gf
7^8g 0-2-9 £3,117

Bahamian Belle *J Balding* 63 a51
3 b f Bahamian Bounty - Marjorie's Memory (Ire)
6^5sd 6^5gf 4^5g 5^5f 5^5g 6^5sd 2^5f 3^5g
4^5g 8^5gs 0-2-11 £2,493

Bahamian Breeze *J Noseda* 81
2 b c Piccolo - Norgabie
2^5f 1^5f 6^6gf 1-1-3 £7,339

Bahamian Heir (Ire) *N Wilson* a47
4 b c Lake Coniston (Ire) - Bally Souza (Ire)
4^12sw 5^11sd 14^11sd 16^12sw 0-1-4

Bahamian Pirate (USA) *D Nicholls* 116
8 ch g Housebuster (USA) - Shining Through (USA)
8^6gf 2^5g 8^5gf 5^6gf 2^6g 7^5gf 4^5g 4^5g 6^5g
6^5ho 0-2-10 £23,886

Bahiano (Ire) *C E Brittain* 53
2 ch c Barathea (Ire) - Trystero
6^7g 0-0-1

Bahita (Ire) *E J Alston* a39
3 b f Bahhare (USA) - Bolshoi Star
5^7sd 5^7sd 6^5sd 0-0-3

Bahlino (Ire) *W Jarvis* 83 a88
3 gr c Bahhare (USA) - Azulino (Ire)
7^7gf 2^9gf 2^10gs 1^11gf 1^12gf 3^12gf 2^12sd
3^12gs 4^12g 2^12gf 4^12gf 2-6-11 £17,091

Bahrqueen (USA) *D R C Elsworth* 82
4 b f Bahri (USA) - April In Kentucky (USA)
2^7gf 2^12gf 1^9gf 4^9gf 3^11gf 6^12gf 1-4-6
£11,433

Bailaora (Ire) *B W Duke* 78
2 b c Shinko Forest (Ire) - Tart (Fr)

4^7gf 4^7g 4^7gf 3^7gs 15^8g 2^7gf 0-2-6
£3,085

Baileys Dancer *M Johnston* 83
2 b f Groom Dancer (USA) - Darshay (Fr)
5^5gf 1^8gf 1^8gf 4^8g 11^8gs 2-0-5 £25,699

Baileys Imperial (USA) *M Johnston* 53
3 b g Imperial Ballet (Ire) - Ms Deborah Ann (USA)
6^7gf 10^7gf 9^8f 7^8g 15^8f 0-0-5

Bailieborough (Ire) *D Nicholls* 79
4 b g Charnwood Forest (Ire) - Sherannda (USA)
7^7f 7^7gf 5^7gf 8^7f 2^7gf 5^7gf 2^8gf 10^8f
1^7gf 8^7gf 7^7gf 11^7g 9^7g 1-2-13 £5,563

Bainesse *C W Thornton* 9
4 b f Hernando (Fr) - Aeolina (Fr)
12^9gs 12^10gs 11^14f 0-0-3

Bajan Desert *M Blanshard* a43
4 ch g Zamindar (USA) - Bajan Rose
12^7sd 8^7sd 12^7sw 0-0-3

Bajan Storm *M Blanshard* 50 a62
2 ch c First Trump - Bajan Rose
3^5gf 14^6gf 5^8gf 4^6f 2^7sd 6^7sd 13^7gf
3^7sd 2^6sd 8^6sd 0-2-11 £3,061

Baker Of Oz *R Hannon* 77
2 b c Pursuit Of Love - Moorish Idol
2^7gf 2^8gf 4^9g 6^8gf 0-2-4 £3,110

Bakers Dozen *T R George* a27
3 ch g Whittingham (Ire) - Blue Empress
11^8sd 8^9sw 0-0-2

Bakhtyar *R Charlton* 56 a41
2 gr c Daylami (Ire) - Gentilesse
12^8sd 7^8f 5^7gs 0-0-3

Balakheri (Ire) *Sir Michael Stoute* 109
4 b c Theatrical - Balanka
7^14gf 6^12gs 8^12f 3^12g 0-0-4 £7,977

Balakiref *M Dods* 66 a23
4 b g Royal Applause - Pluck
15^6g 10^6gf 11^6gf 2^7g 7^7gs 8^6gf 13^6gs
7^7g 14^7g 10^6sd 0-1-10 £3,148

Balalaika Tune (Ire) *W Storey* 59
4 b f Lure (USA) - Bohemienne (USA)
11^8gf 5^8gf 5^12g 0-0-3

Baldour (Ire) *E A L Dunlop* 90
4 b g Green Desert (USA) - Baldemara (Fr)
3^7gf 3^7gf 3^7gf 1^8gf 9^8g 2^7f 6^8gf 10^7g
2^7gf 10^7gf 1-5-10 £14,568

Balearic Star (Ire) *B R Millman* 71
2 b c Night Shift (USA) - La Menorquina (USA)
6^7f 8^6gf 7^6g 10^7f 8^8gf 0-0-5 £1,350

Balerno *R Ingram* 52 a67
4 b g Machiavellian (USA) - Balabina (USA)
4^10sd 16^12g 12^11gf 10^10sd 4^8sd 5^8sd
11^10gf 12^7g 10^7gf 5^8sd 3^10g 0-1-11 £938

Balestrini (Ire) *A P O'Brien* 118
3 b c Danehill (USA) - Welsh Love
5^12g 1^10gf 10^10gf 4^11gs 1-0-4 £71,857

Bali Royal *M S Saunders* 111
5 b m King's Signet (USA) - Baligay
7^5g 3^5gf 5^5f 3^5gf 10^5hy 5^5gf 2^5gf
4^5gf 2^5g 2^5g 1^5gf 2^5gf 4^5gf 1-7-14 £51,111

Bali-Star *R J Hodges* 61 a49
8 b g Alnasr Alwasheek - Baligay
2^6g 10^6sd 5^5gf 12^6gf 11^6g 4^5gf 7^5f 5^5gf
11^5s 11^5gf 0-1-10 £1,964

Balin's Sword (Ire) *B J Meehan* 106
3 b c Spectrum (Ire) - Green Delight (Ire)

1^{8gf} 2^{8g} 5^{8gf} 3^{8g} **1-1-4 £23,254**

Balkan Knight *D R Loder* 87
3 b c Selkirk (USA) - Crown Of Light
1^{10g} **1-0-1 £4,387**

Ball Games *James Moffatt* 36
5 b g Mind Games - Deb's Ball
9^{9g} 15^{8gf} **0-0-2**

Ball King (Ire) *P J Makin* 58 a67
5 ch g Ball Park (NZ) - Firey Encounter (Ire)
7^{7sd} 3^{8gf} 2^{7f} **0-2-3 £1,298**

Ballare (Ire) *Bob Jones* 56
4 b g Barathea (Ire) - Raindancing (Ire)
4^{10g} 9^{10gf} 2^{8gf} 9^{8gf} **0-2-4 £1,750**

Ballasilla *B Palling*
8 b m Puissance - Darussalam
20^{8gf} 15^{5gf} **0-0-2**

Ballerina Belle (Ire) *J R Fanshawe* a67
3 b f Zafonic (USA) - Bayadere (USA)
3^{8sd} 3^{8sd} **0-2-2 £1,258**

Ballet Ruse *Sir Mark Prescott* 28
2 ch f Rainbow Quest (USA) - El Opera (Ire)
15^{7g} 9^{7s} 18^{7g} **0-0-3**

Ballin Rouge *T J Fitzgerald*
2 ch f Dr Fong (USA) - Bogus John (Can)
11^{5gf} 13^{7g} **0-0-2**

Ballinger Ridge *A M Balding* 79
4 b g Sabrehill (USA) - Branston Ridge
2^{8gf} 14^{8gs} 9^{10gf} 11^{8gf} 6^{8gf} 3^{8gf} **0-2-6 £1,486**

Bally Hall (Ire) *G A Butler* 79 a45
3 b c Saddlers' Hall (Ire) - Sally Rose
5^{8sd} 1^{10gf} 7^{10gs} 1^{10f} 1^{10g} 3^{11gf} 5^{12gf} 4^{10g} **3-0-8 £17,492**

Ballyboro (Ire) *M J Wallace* 53
2 b f Entrepreneur - Tathkara (USA)
5^{8gf} **0-0-1**

Ballybunion (Ire) *D Nicholls* 76
4 ch g Entrepreneur - Clarentia
6^{6gf} 11^{7f} 11^{5gf} 12^{6gf} 15^{6gf} 1^{6gf} 5^{6gf} 9^{6gf} 2^{5gf} 11^{6gf} 1^{5gf} 6^{9g} 3^{5gf} 2^{6f} 6^{6g} 1^{6f} 13^{5gs} 12^{5gf} **3-3-18 £15,946**

Ballygriffin Kid *T P McGovern* 53
3 gr g Komaite (USA) - Ballygriffin Belle
13^{6gf} 8^{8gs} 5^{8f} 6^{6f} 3^{6f} **0-1-5 £428**

Ballyhurry (USA) *J S Goldie* 81
6 b g Rubiano (USA) - Balakhna (Fr)
1^{8gf} 6^{8gf} 8^{8gs} 2^{7gf} 1^{7gs} 2^{7gf} 1^{7gf} 5^{7g} 1^{7gf} 3^{7gf} 9^{7gf} 1^{7g} 5^{7g} 4^{7gf} **5-3-14 £37,548**

Ballykeating *N A Callaghan* 89
2 b c Danzero (Aus) - Pearly River
9^{6g} 9^{6gf} 9^{6gf} 1^{5gf} 2^{5gs} 3^{7gf} **1-1-6 £12,692**

Balmacara *Miss K B Boutflower* 54 a54
4 b f Lake Coniston (Ire) - Diabaig
2^{8sd} 9^{7sd} 10^{8sd} 9^{7gf} 5^{8gf} 7^{8f} 2^{7gf} 10^{7gf} 7^{7gf} 8^{6g} 7^{6f} 5^{7f} **0-2-12 £1,705**

Balmont (USA) *J Noseda* 115
2 b c Stravinsky (USA) - Aldebaran Light (USA)
2^{6gf} 1^{6gf} 1^{6gf} 1^{6g} 2^{6gf} 7^{7gf} **3-2-6 £123,719**

Baltic Blazer (Ire) *P W Harris* 74
3 b g Polish Precedent (USA) - Pine Needle
2^{8s} 1^{8gf} **1-1-2 £3,301**

Baltic Breeze (USA) *William Durkan* 53 a56
3 b f Labeeb - Blue Grass Baby (USA)

8^{7sd} 12^{8sd} 17^{10s} 6^{7f} 11^{7g} 20^{7gf} **0-0-6**

Baltic King *H Morrison* 111
3 b c Danetime (Ire) - Lindfield Belle (Ire)
1^{6g} 2^{5gf} 11^{5gs} 2^{6g} 4^{5gf} 3^{6g} 1^{5f} 17^{5gf} 13^{6gf} **2-3-9 £51,247**

Baltic Wave *T D Barron* 89
2 b g Polish Precedent (USA) - Flourish
1^{5gf} 2^{5gf} 1^{6gf} 4^{6gs} 4^{6gf} **2-1-5 £19,341**

Balwearie (Ire) *Miss L A Perratt* 65
2 b g Sesaro (USA) - Eight Mile Rock
8^{6gs} 4^{6gf} 4^{5gf} 2^{7gf} 5^{8gf} 4^{6g} **0-1-6 £2,682**

Band *B A McMahon* 84
3 b g Band On The Run - Little Tich
6^{7g} 2^{7gf} 6^{7g} 3^{8hy} 8^{8gf} 3^{8gf} 6^{10gf} 8^{8s} **0-3-8 £11,490**

Band Of Love *R Ingram* 40
4 b f Pursuit Of Love - Dixie Favor (USA)
16^{8sd} 8^{8f} 9^{8f} **0-0-3**

Bandanna *R J Hodges* 94
6 gr m Bandmaster (USA) - Gratclo
7^{6g} 17^{6gf} 6^{6gf} 5^{5g} 3^{6hd} 4^{6f} 9^{6g} **0-0-7 £2,312**

Bandari (Ire) *M Johnston* 119
4 b c Alhaarth (Ire) - Miss Audimar (USA)
4^{12g} 4^{12gs} 4^{12f} 2^{12g} **0-1-4 £49,500**

Bandbox (Ire) *I A Wood* 43 a42
8 ch g Imperial Frontier (USA) - Dublah (USA)
13^{6gf} 10^{7gf} 9^{7f} 6^{10sd} 17^{11gf} 11^{10f} **0-0-6**

Bandit Queen *M A Jarvis* 91 a16
3 b f Desert Prince (Ire) - Wildwood Flower
5^{6gf} 9^{5gf} 1^{6gf} 6^{6gf} 5^{6gf} 22^{6g} 14^{6sd} **1-0-8 £5,992**

Bandolina *I Semple* 31
3 b f Most Welcome - Choral Sundown
7^{10gf} 7^{9gs} **0-0-2**

Bandos *I Semple* 82
3 ch g Cayman Kai (Ire) - Lekuti
1^{7gf} 1^{7gf} 9^{6g} 2^{7gf} 2^{8f} 7^{7g} **2-2-6 £10,911**

Bang In Tune *J O'Reilly* 29 a54
3 b f Victory Note (USA) - Canlubang
2^{7sd} 3^{6sd} 2^{5sw} 3^{7sd} 5^{5sd} 11^{6sd} 3^{6sd} 11^{6gf} 3^{6sd} 14^{7gf} 4^{6sd} 7^{5sw} 6^{5sd} 8^{8ft} 7^{7sd} 10^{7sd} **0-6-16 £3,877**

Bangalore *Mrs A J Perrett* 108
7 ch g Sanglamore (USA) - Ajuga (USA)
9^{16gf} 2^{12gf} 7^{13g} **0-1-3 £4,532**

Banjaxed *Mrs S A Liddiard* a42
4 b f Prince Sabo - Classic Fan (USA)
8^{7sd} 10^{5sd} 9^{8sd} **0-0-3**

Banjo Bay (Ire) *J G Given* 97
5 b g Common Grounds - Thirlmere
10^{7gf} UR^{7g} 16^{gf} 27^{6f} 16^{6g} 15^{8gf} 14^{7g} **1-0-7 £10,634**

Bank On Him *C Weedon* 21 a67
8 b g Elmaamul (USA) - Feather Flower
4^{10sd} 2^{10sd} 2^{10sd} 1^{8sd} 1^{8sd} 3^{8sd} 7^{10sd} 9^{10sd} 9^{8gf} **2-3-9 £8,122**

Banners Flying (Ire) *B W Hills* 82
3 ch c Zafonic (USA) - Banafsajee (USA)
2^{8g} 4^{10gf} 5^{10gf} **0-1-3 £1,677**

Banningham Blaze *C R Dore* 67 a69
3 b f Averti (Ire) - Ma Pavlova (USA)

10^{8sd} 9^{7sd} 9^{7sd} 11^{8sw} 14^{7sd} 5^{12sd} 4^{8sw}
4^{12gf} 5^{10gf} 1^{12f} 2^{11gf} 2^{12gf} 10^{14gf} 4^{12gs} 2^{12gf}
7^{12g} 2^{11gf} 11^{12sd} 7^{12gf} **2-4-22**
£13,317

Bannister *D Nicholls* 68 a51
5 ch g Inchinor - Shall We Run
7^{6gf} 8^{5sd} 10^{6gf} 4^{5gf} 2^{6gf} 3^{6gf} 4^{5gs}
8^{5gf} 2^{5gf} 9^{6s} 11^{6gf} 1^{5f} 7^{7gf} 9^{6f} **1-4-15**
£7,719

Banutan (Ire) *K R Burke* 74
3 b f Charnwood Forest (Ire) - Banariya (USA)
8^{7ys} 7^{6s} 7^{7g} 4^{7gy} 2^{7f} 3^{7gf} 11^{7g} 6^{7g}
13^{7gf} 7^{8gf} **0-2-10** £3,084

Bar Of Silver (Ire) *R Brotherton* 64 a58
3 ch g Bahhare (USA) - Shaping Up (USA)
4^{7sd} 3^{7sd} 4^{8sw} 2^{7gf} 10^{7sw} 2^{8f} 5^{11gf}
10^{10gf} 5^{10f} **0-2-9** £2,202

Barabella (Ire) *R J Hodges* 66
2 gr f Barathea (Ire) - Thatchabella (Ire)
4^{6gf} 4^{7gf} 4^{7gf} 10^{8gf} **0-0-4** £698

Baralinka (Ire) *P F I Cole* 91
4 b f Barathea (Ire) - Kalinka (Ire)
19^{6gf} 8^{6g} 4^{6s} 5^{6g} 11^{6g} 12^{6g} 11^{6gf} 9^{6gf}
13^{6gf} **0-0-9** £2,198

Baraloti (Ire) *J H M Gosden* 71 a61
3 b f Barathea (Ire) - Charlotte Corday
2^{8gf} 3^{8g} 8^{8g} 4^{8sd} **0-2-4** £2,350

Barathea Blazer *P W Harris* 106
4 b c Barathea (Ire) - Empty Purse
4^{14g} 7^{12gf} 3^{12gf} 9^{13g} 18^{16gs} 3^{12gf} 1^{15g}
4^{13gf} 8^{13gs} 14^{15g} **1-0-10** £22,698

Barbajuan (Ire) *N A Callaghan* 112
2 b c Danehill Dancer (Ire) - Courtier
1^{5g} 15^{6gf} 4^{6gf} 5^{7gf} 1^{7gs} 4^{7gf} 3^{8g} **3-1-7**
£82,232

Barbilyrifle (Ire) *H Morrison* 74
2 b c Indian Rocket - Age Of Elegance
19^{5gf} 12^{5gs} 3^{5g} 1^{5f} 15^{5f} 15^{6gf} 16^{7gf}
1-1-7 £4,953

Barg *M R Channon* 44
2 b c Perugino (USA) - Dramatic Mood
7^{6gf} **0-0-1**

Bargain Hunt (Ire) *W Storey* 51
2 b g Foxhound (USA) - Atisayin (USA)
8^{5gs} 14^{6s} 8^{6f} 7^{5gf} 5^{7f} 4^{5gf} 8^{6gf} 6^{6gf}
8^{7gf} 6^{8gf} 4^{7gs} 7^{6g} 3^{7gf} **0-1-13** £706

Baritone *J Balding* a32
9 b g Midyan (USA) - Zinzi
10^{6sw} 12^{5sd} **0-0-2**

Barking Mad (USA) *M L W Bell* 92
5 b/br g Dayjur (USA) - Avian Assembly (USA)
9^{7g} 8^{7g} 2^{10gf} 1^{10gf} 16^{10gf} 1^{10g} 7^{10gf}
3^{10gf} 5^{10g} 18^{8gf} **2-2-10** £24,194

Barman (USA) *P F I Cole* 86
4 ch g Atticus (USA) - Blue Tip (Fr)
9^{10g} 4^{10g} 13^{13gs} 19^{12g} 7^{11g} 7^{11gf} 1^{12g}
6^{12gf} 3^{12f} 4^{12gf} 2^{12gf} 2^{12gf} 5^{12gf} 1^{12gf} **2-3-14**
£22,089

Barney McAll (Ire) *Mrs A J Perrett* 92
3 b g Grand Lodge (USA) - Persian Song
5^{10g} 3^{11gf} 1^{10g} 1^{10gf} 15^{10g} 14^{10g} **2-0-6**
£17,080

Barneys Lyric *N A Twiston-Davies* 70
3 ch g Hector Protector (USA) - Anchorage (Ire)
5^{12gs} 6^{12gs} 9^{12g} **0-0-3**

Barolo *P W Harris* 102

4 b g Danehill (USA) - Lydia Maria
4^{8gf} 14^{10gf} 1^{10gs} 3^{12g} 1^{12gf} 1^{14gf} 4^{14gf}
3-2-7 £36,349

Baron Rhodes *J S Wainwright* 68 a36
2 b f Presidium - Superstream
7^{5f} 3^{5s} 4^{5gf} 3^{5gf} 1^{5gs} 6^{5gf} 10^{5sw} 4^{5gs}
2^{5gf} **1-2-9** £7,765

Baron's Pit *R Hannon* 120
3 b c Night Shift (USA) - Incendio
2^{7gf} 3^{6f} 3^{6g} 12^{7g} 7^{6gf} 8^{7gf} **0-3-6**
£38,060

Barons Spy (Ire) *A W Carroll* 60
2 b c Danzero (Aus) - Princess Accord (USA)
8^{6gf} 7^{7g} **0-0-2**

Barouche *E A L Dunlop* 7
2 b g Danehill (USA) - Barbarella
13^{7s} **0-0-1**

Barrantes *Miss Sheena West* 90
6 b m Distant Relative - Try The Duchess
2^{7g} 4^{6g} 2^{5gf} 2^{6g} 2^{6gf} 1^{5gf} 4^{5gf} 16^{6f} 7^{7gf}
3^{5gf} 9^{5gf} 4^{5gs} 2^{6gf} 3^{6gf} 6^{5gf} 11^{6g} 15^{5f}
2-8-18 £29,146

Barras (Ire) *R F Fisher* 50 a44
2 b g Raphane (USA) - Lady Fleetsin (Ire)
9^{5gf} 17^{5gf} 4^{5f} 4^{6s} 5^{6f} 3^{5gs} 2^{7sd} 1^{5gf}
1-2-8 £4,948

Barresbo *A C Whillans*
9 b g Barrys Gamble - Bo' Babbity
10^{22gf} **0-0-1**

Barrissimo (Ire) *W J Musson* 104
3 b c Night Shift (USA) - Belle De Cadix (Ire)
3^{10gf} 5^{12gf} **0-0-2** £1,988

Barrosa *Miss K M George* 24
4 b f Sabrehill (USA) - Shehana (USA)
11^{10g} 12^{8gf} **0-0-2**

Barry Island *D R C Elsworth* 87
4 b g Turtle Island (Ire) - Pine Ridge
15^{12g} 6^{12gf} 3^{10gf} 6^{10f} 12^{10gs} 4^{12gf} **0-0-6**
£1,830

Barton Flower *M W Easterby* 48
2 br f Danzero (Aus) - Iota
11^{8gf} 7^{7gf} **0-0-2**

Barton Sands (Ire) *M C Pipe* 70
6 b g Tenby - Hetty Green
11^{10gf} 4^{12gf} 7^{12gf} 1^{11gf} 15^{11gf} 14^{10g}
1-1-7 £3,654

Barzak (Ire) *S R Bowring* 74 a58
3 b c Barathea (Ire) - Zakuska
6^{8g} 9^{8g} 8^{7sd} 15^{7g} 13^{7gs} 12^{7g} **0-0-6**
£253

Basbousate Nadia *W R Muir* 59
4 b f Wolfhound (USA) - Sarabah (Ire)
15^{6gf} 6^{7gf} 14^{7gs} 13^{6g} **0-0-4**

Basheera *E J Alston* 23
3 ch f Bahhare (USA) - Samheh (USA)
15^{10gf} 13^{7gf} **0-0-2**

Basinet *J J Quinn* 71 a68
5 b g Alzao (USA) - Valiancy
4^{9sw} 4^{8sd} 12^{8sd} 6^{8sd} 6^{8f} 3^{8g} 7^{8gf} 7^{9gf}
18^{8f} 5^{8f} 4^{8gs} 6^{8g} 5^{9g} 11^{10gf} 6^{8gs} **1-2-15**
£5,090

Batailley *Mrs H Dalton* 48
3 ch f First Trump - Phantom Ring
9^{6gf} 8^{6f} 2^{7gf} 12^{8gf} **0-1-4** £882

Batchworth Breeze *E A Wheeler* 35

5 ch m Beveled (USA) - Batchworth Dancer
8⁶ᵍ 16⁶ᶠ 13⁵ᵍᶠ 0-0-3

Batchworth Lock E A Wheeler   8
5 b g Beveled (USA) - Treasurebound
10⁷ᵍ 11⁶ᵍᶠ 0-0-2

Batchworth Park E A Wheeler   34 a31
3 b f Young Ern - Treasurebound
8⁷ˢᵈ 10⁷ˢᵈ 11⁶ˢᵈ 8⁸ᵍᶠ 8⁵ᵍˢ 16⁶ᵍᶠ 0-0-6

Bathwick Bill (USA) B R Millman   81
2 ch c Stravinsky (USA) - Special Park (USA)
19⁶ᵍ 6⁵ᵍᶠ 4⁵ᵍᶠ 1⁵ᶠ 1⁶ᵍᶠ 5⁷ᵍˢ 3⁶ᵍᶠ 2-1-7
£9,480

Bathwick Bruce (Ire) B R Millman   81 a85
5 b g College Chapel - Naivity (Ire)
9¹⁰ˢᵈ 3¹⁰ᵍ 7¹⁰ᵍᶠ 3¹⁰ᵍᶠ 6¹⁰ᵍᶠ 8⁸ᵍᶠ 10⁸ᵍᶠ
13⁸ᵍˢ 10⁸ˢᵈ 4⁸ˢᵈ 0-1-10 £1,938

Batiste P W Harris   57 a46
3 b c Barathea (Ire) - Mill Line
12⁸ᵍᶠ 5¹¹ʰʸ 9¹⁰ᵍ 11¹²ᵍˢ 8¹⁶ˢᵈ 0-0-5

Batool (USA) D Nicholls   29
4 b f Bahri (USA) - Mrs Paddy (USA)
13⁸ᵍᶠ 0-0-1

Batswing B Ellison   a58
8 b g Batshoof - Magic Milly
7¹¹ˢᵈ 0-0-1

Battle Back (Bel) S C Williams   21
2 b f Pursuit Of Love - Batalya (Bel)
18⁷ᵍˢ 0-0-1

Battle Chant (USA) E A L Dunlop   110
3 b c Coronado's Quest (USA) - Appointed One (USA)
7¹⁰ᵍᶠ 5⁸ᵍᶠ 4⁹ᵍ 10⁷ᵍᶠ 3⁸ᵍ 10⁸ᵍˢ 0-1-6
£7,570

Battle Warning P Bowen   76
8 b g Warning - Royal Ballet (Ire)
8¹⁶ᵍᶠ 2¹⁷ᵍᶠ 3¹⁷ᵍᶠ 8¹⁸ᵍᶠ 0-2-4 £2,931

Batto W J Haggas   57
3 b g Slip Anchor - Frog
7¹⁰ᵍᶠ 15¹⁴ᵍᶠ 9¹²ᵍˢ 4¹²ᵍᶠ 8¹⁴ᵍᶠ 0-0-5

Batushka (Ire) T Stack   56
3 b f Spectrum (Ire) - Ustka
11⁸ˢ 5¹²ᶠ 13¹²ᵍ 0-0-3

Bay Of Islands D Morris   96
11 b g Jupiter Island - Lawyer's Wave (USA)
8¹⁶ᵍᶠ 13¹⁹ᵍᶠ 1¹⁶ᵍᶠ 1-0-3 £9,750

Bay Solitaire T D Easterby   45
2 b g Charnwood Forest (Ire) - Golden Wings (USA)
18⁸ᵍᶠ 9⁷ᵍᶠ 10⁸ᵍ 0-0-3

Bay Tree (Ire) B W Hills   95
2 b f Daylami (Ire) - My Branch
1⁶ᵍᶠ 1⁷ᵍᶠ 7⁷ᵍᶠ 9⁸ʰᵒ 2-0-4 £20,402

Bayadere (Ger) Sir Michael Stoute   91
3 br f Lavirco (Ger) - Brangane (Ire)
3¹⁰ᵍ 8¹⁰ᵍᶠ 0-0-2 £1,719

Baychevelle (Ire) Mrs H Dalton   54
2 ch f Bahamian Bounty - Phantom Ring
9⁶ᵍᶠ 0-0-1

Bayeux (USA) D R Loder   111
2 b c Red Ransom (USA) - Elizabeth Bay (USA)
1⁶ᵍᶠ 8⁷ᵍᶠ 2⁷ᵍᶠ 1-1-3 £17,001

Bayhirr M A Jarvis   46
2 b c Selkirk (USA) - Pass The Peace
7⁷ᵍˢ 0-0-1

Baylaw Star J Balding   74
2 b c Case Law - Caisson
2⁵ᵍᶠ 1⁵ᵍᶠ 6⁵ᵍᶠ 2⁵ᵍᶠ 1⁵ᵍˢ 6⁶ᵍ 1⁵ᵍᶠ 4⁵ᶠ

3⁶ᵍᶠ 11⁶ᵍˢ 10⁶ᵍᶠ 3⁵ˢ 3-4-12 £20,311

Bayonet Jane Southcombe   45
7 b m Then Again - Lambay
17⁷ᵍᶠ 13⁷ᵍ 9⁷ᵍᶠ 8⁷ᵍᶠ 9⁷ᵍᶠ 7⁶ᶠ 0-0-6

Baytown Flyer J Balding   51 a51
3 ch f Whittingham (Ire) - The Fernhill Flyer (Ire)
6⁶ᵍ 10⁷ˢᵈ 11⁸ᵍᶠ 13⁷ᵍᶠ 6⁸ᵍˢ 13⁶ᵍᶠ 9⁸ᵍᶠ
13⁷ᵍᶠ 19⁸ᵍᶠ 20⁷ᵍᶠ 0-0-10

Baytown Shamrock (Ire) P S McEntee   59 a48
2 b f First Trump - Siana Springs (Ire)
7⁵ˢᵈ 3⁵ᶠ 9⁵ˢᵈ 2⁵ᶠ 5⁵ᵍᶠ 9⁵ᵍᶠ 6⁵ᵍ 2⁵ᵍˢ 3⁵ᵍ
2⁵ˢᵈ 8⁵ᵍᶠ 3⁵ᶠ 6⁵ᵍᶠ 6⁵ᵍᶠ 5⁵ᵍᶠ 10⁵ᵍᶠ 4⁶ᶠ
7⁵ᵍᶠ 13⁵ˢᵈ 0-3-20 £5,022

Be My Alibi (Ire) J S Moore   51 a46
2 ch f Daggers Drawn (USA) - Join The Party
5⁵ᵍᶠ 3⁵ᵍˢ 4⁶ˢᵈ 11⁶ᵍᶠ 5⁷ᶠ 18⁵ᵍˢ 0-1-6
£988

Be My Tinker M A Buckley   48
5 ch m Be My Chief (USA) - Tinkerbird
19⁵ᵍᶠ 14⁶ᵍˢ 12⁵ᵍᶠ 9⁶ᵍᶠ 11⁷ᵍᶠ 6⁶ᵍᶠ 12⁵ᵍᶠ
10⁶ᵍᶠ 0-0-8

Be Swift A J Chamberlain   a46
4 ch g Millkom - Conwy
6¹³ˢᵈ 9¹⁸ᵍᶠ 11¹³ᵍᶠ 0-0-3

Be Wise Girl J G Given   41 a41
2 ch f Fleetwood (Ire) - Zabelina (USA)
14⁷ᵍᶠ 3⁸ˢᵈ 0-1-2 £311

Beach Party (Ire) M L W Bell   55
2 b f Danzero (Aus) - Shore Lark (USA)
9⁶ᵍᶠ 5⁶ᶠ 0-0-2

Beacon Blue (Ire) M Johnston   66
2 ch f Peintre Celebre (USA) - Catch The Blues (Ire)
5⁶ᵍᶠ 9⁶ᶠ 5⁸ᵍˢ 5⁸ᵍˢ 0-0-4

Beacon Of Light (Ire) Ferdy Murphy   21
5 b m Lake Coniston (Ire) - Deydarika (Ire)
7¹²ᵍˢ 0-0-1

Beady (Ire) B Smart   46 a70
4 b g Eagle Eyed (USA) - Tales Of Wisdom
5¹¹ˢʷ 1¹²ˢᵈ 2¹²ˢᵈ 1¹²ˢᵈ 4¹⁴ˢʷ 9¹⁴ᵍᶠ 5¹²ˢᵈ
12¹²ᵍᶠ 2-1-8 £7,090

Beamish Prince M Johnston   67
4 ch g Bijou D'Inde - Unconditional Love (Ire)
16⁹ᶠᵗ 12¹²ᵍᶠ 11¹²ᶠ 12¹²ᵍᶠ 3⁸ᵍᶠ 8⁸ᵍᶠ 8⁸ᶠ
3⁹ᵍᶠ 3⁹ᵍ 0-3-9 £2,367

Beamsley Beacon G M Moore   43 a53
2 ch g Wolfhound (USA) - Petindia
5⁵ᵍˢ 6⁶ˢᵈ 2⁶ˢᵈ 8⁸ᵍᶠ 18⁶ᵍˢ 0-1-5 £864

Beat The Heat (Ire) Jedd O'Keeffe   82 a88
5 b g Salse (USA) - Summer Trysting (USA)
2¹¹ˢʷ 8¹²ˢᵈ 8¹²ᵍᶠ 11¹²ᵍᶠ 0-1-4 £1,344

Beat Time M W Easterby   51
4 ro f Lion Cavern (USA) - Brilliant Timing (USA)
12⁸ᶠ 16⁶ᶠ 11⁵ᵍᶠ 0-0-3

Beau Artiste Jedd O'Keeffe   78 a65
3 ch g Peintre Celebre (USA) - Belle Esprit
3⁸ᵍᶠ 12⁹ᵍᶠ 3¹⁰ᵍᶠ 2¹⁰ᵍᶠ 8¹⁰ᵍ 3⁹ᵍᶠ 2¹²ᵍ 6¹²ᵍᶠ
11¹²ˢᵈ 0-5-9 £7,659

Beau Jazz W De Best-Turner   64 a63
2 br c Merdon Melody - Ichor
12⁶ᵍᶠ 10⁶ᵍᶠ 9⁷ᵍᶠ 8⁶ᵍᶠ 12⁶ᵍᶠ
5⁵ˢᵈ 6⁵ᵍˢ 0-0-9 £1,434

Beau Sauvage M W Easterby   37 a38
5 b g Wolfhound (USA) - Maestrale
7⁸ˢᵈ 11⁷ᵍᶠ 6⁸ˢᵈ 10⁷ᶠ 6⁸ᵍˢ 16⁷ᵍᶠ 0-0-6

Beau West S Kirk   52

2 b f The West (USA) - Total Truth
5^{8gs} 0-0-1

Beaucette (USA) *Sir Michael Stoute*   73
3 br f Mr Prospector (USA) - Mackie (USA)
3^{8g} 2^{7f} 3^{8gf} 2^{10gf} 6^{9gs} 0-3-5 £4,358

Beauchamp Magic *K G Wingrove*   a51
8 b g Northern Park (USA) - Beauchamp Buzz
7^{15sd} 2^{16sd} 8^{16sd} 0-1-3 £838

Beauchamp Pilot *G A Butler*   116 a116
5 ch g Inchinor - Beauchamp Image
3^{10f} 9^{8gf} 2^{8gf} 12^{10g} 0-1-4 £18,042

Beauchamp Ribbon *G A Butler*   72 a64
3 b f Vettori (Ire) - Beauchamp Kate
5^{7gf} 2^{10gf} 2^{8gf} 11^{10s} 5^{8gf} 1^{12f} 1^{10f} 1^{10gf}
3^{11gf} 9^{10gf} 3^{10f} 7^{8sd} 3-3-12 £11,614

Beauchamp Rose *G A Butler*   79
3 ch f Pharly (Fr) - Beauchamp Cactus
3^{8g} 2^{10gf} 2^{10gf} PU^{12sd} 0-3-4 £2,884

Beauchamp Sun *G A Butler*   32
2 b f Pharly (Fr) - Beauchamp Jade
16^{6gf} 0-0-1

Beauchamp Surprise *G A Butler*   32
2 ch f Pharly (Fr) - Beauchamp Image
14^{7gs} 12^{6g} 0-0-2

Beausejour (USA) *B G Powell*   44 a44
5 ch m Diesis - Libeccio (NZ)
5^{8sd} 11^{8sd} 5^{9g} 0-0-3

Beauteous (Ire) *A Berry*   76 a37
4 ch g Tagula (Ire) - Beauty Appeal (USA)
12^{6sd} 8^{7sd} 1^{7gs} 7^{6gf} 6^{7gf} 10^{7f} 4^{7gf} 1^{7gf}
5^{7gf} 6^{7gf} 7^{7f} 2^{7g} 8^{7gf} 4^{7g} 14^{7g} 8^{7gf} 2-1-16
£15,124

Beautiful Noise *D Morris*   58
2 b f Piccolo - Mrs Moonlight
8^{7gf} 5^{8gf} 15^{8gf} 6^{8s} 0-0-4

Beautifultommorrow *K R Burke*
4 ch f Pursuit Of Love - Bella Domani
14^{8sd} 0-0-1

Beauty Of Dreams *M R Channon*   71
2 b f Russian Revival (USA) - Giggleswick Girl
2^{6gf} 2^{6gf} 4^{6gf} 1^{5s} 5^{5gf} 17^{7g} 1-2-6
£9,271

Beauvrai *J J Quinn*   78
3 b g Bahamian Bounty - Lets Be Fair
7^{6gf} 14^{5gf} 7^{5gf} 26^{5gf} 16^{5gs} 0-0-5

Beaver Diva *W M Brisbourne*
2 b f Bishop Of Cashel - Beaver Skin Hunter
10^{5s} 0-0-1

Bebopskiddly *B G Powell*   61 a5
2 b c Robellino (USA) - Adarama (Ire)
11^{8gf} 12^{7sd} 7^{8gf} 0-0-3

Beckon *P A Blockley*   34
7 m Beveled (USA) - Carolynchristensen
7^{8f} 7^{10f} 7^{12gf} 0-0-3

Bedazzled *J A Glover*   29
3 b f Wolfhound (USA) - Glowing Jade
15^{5gf} 0-0-1

Bee Dees Legacy *C Weedon*
2 b c Atraf - Bee Dee Dancer
14^{8gf} 0-0-1

Bee Health Boy *R A Fahey*   58
10 b g Superpower - Rekindle
3^{8f} 2^{8gf} 1^{7g} 10^{7g} 10^{8gf} 5^{11gf} 11^{8gf}
10^{8gf} 13^{9gs} 8^{8g} 1-2-10 £4,668

Bee J Gee *Mrs Lydia Pearce*   13 a35

5 b g Dilum (USA) - Sound Check
7^{8sd} 11^{10f} 12^{10gf} 9^{12sd} 0-0-4

Bee Minor *R Hannon*   69
2 b f Barathea (Ire) - Bee Off (Ire)
22^{7gf} 4^{5gf} 2^{6g} 6^{5gf} 5^{6gf} 3^{6gf} 5^{7gs} 17^{7g}
0-2-8 £2,910

Beeches Star (Ire) *R Brotherton*   30 a23
3 b f Lake Coniston (Ire) - Eleonora D'Arborea
16^{7sd} 11^{6sd} 18^{8g} 15^{6gs} 7^{7f} 8^{6gf} 15^{5gf}
0-0-7

Beechy Bank (Ire) *Mrs Mary Hambro*   76
5 b m Shareef Dancer (USA) - Neptunalia
4^{12gs} 3^{12g} 1^{14f} 1-1-3 £4,837

Beejay *P F I Cole*   57 a68
2 b f Piccolo - Letluce
3^{5g} 1^{5sd} 1-0-2 £4,495

Beenaboutabit *Mrs L C Jewell*   30
5 b m Komaite (USA) - Tassagh Bridge (Ire)
14^{7gf} 8^{7f} 14^{10gf} 0-0-3

Beersheba *G L Moore*   a46
3 b f Thowra (Fr) - Hymn Book (Ire)
10^{8sd} 18^{10g} 0-0-2

Beetle Bug *J G Portman*   60 a11
3 br f Robellino (USA) - Special Beat
5^{10g} 8^{10gf} 10^{12sd} 10^{12gs} 11^{16gf} 7^{16gf}
0-0-6

Before Dawn (Ire) *J D Czerpak*   a37
3 gr g Mujadil (USA) - Nirvavita (Fr)
6^{6sd} 10^{7sd} 19^{8g} 0-0-3

Begin The Beguine (Ire) *W Jarvis*   77
3 b/br f Peintre Celebre (USA) - Beguine (USA)
6^{8gf} 8^{10gf} 1^{10gf} 9^{10gf} 18^{11s} 1-0-5
£6,938

Behan *A Crook*   44 a22
4 ch g Rainbows For Life (Can) - With Finesse
9^{12sd} 11^{8sd} 8^{8sd} 4^{10gf} 10^{12gf} 3^{12gf} 15^{17gf}
9^{12gf} 6^{12gf} 0-2-9 £425

Belinda *K Bell*   19 a63
6 ch m Mizoram (USA) - Mountain Dew
6^{12sw} 12^{12sd} 12^{12sw} 8^{12sd} 6^{12sd} 11^{5sd}
11^{12g} 2-1-8 £7,263

Belisco (USA) *Mrs A J Perrett*   66
2 b c Royal Academy (USA) - A Mean Fit (USA)
5^{7gf} 10^{8s} 0-0-2

Bell Bottom Blues *C G Cox*   52
3 b f Whittingham (Ire) - Bella Coola
10^{7gf} 6^{7gf} 6^{8f} 12^{8gf} 0-0-4

Bella Bambina *M C Pipe*   51 a51
3 b f Turtle Island (Ire) - Lady Eurolink
15^{7gf} 12^{8g} 4^{10sd} 8^{12sd} 0-0-4

Bella Beguine *A Bailey*   65 a74
4 b f Komaite (USA) - On The Record
8^{7sd} 5^{5gf} 18^{6gf} 12^{6g} 4^{6gf} 3^{6gf} 5^{6gf} 8^{5g}
3^{6f} 2^{6gf} 2^{5gf} 5^{5gf} 3^{6sw} 9^{6g} 16^{sd} 7^{6gs} 14^{6gf}
2^{7sd} 1-6-18 £6,933

Bella Bianca (Ire) *R Hannon*   13
3 b f Barathea (Ire) - Alarme Belle
11^{6gs} 0-0-1

Bella Boy Zee (Ire) *R Wilman*   62 a38
2 b f Anita's Prince - Waikiki (Ger)
15^{5g} 3^{5sd} 1^{5gf} 2^{5gf} 1^{5f} 2^{6s} 1^{5g} 3^{5gf}
3^{5gf} 9^{5gf} 9^{6gf} 14^{6g} 8^{5gs} 3-2-13 £15,361

Bella Castana *A Charlton*   48 a19
3 ch f Efisio - Simple Logic
11^{7gf} 11^{8g} 11^{7sd} 0-0-3

Bella Tutrice (Ire) *John A Harris* 78 a43
2 b f Woodborough (USA) - Institutrice (Ire)
3^{5g} 2^{5g} 3^{5gf} 3^{5gf} 10^{6gf} 2^{5g}
8^{5gs} 8^{5sd} **1-6-10 £13,238**

Bellagio Princess *A M Balding* 57 a25
2 ch f Kris - Forest Call
8^{5gf} 3^{6gf} 9^{7sd} 9^{8gf} **0-0-4 £678**

Belle Bleu *M R Bosley* 13 a20
3 b f Bluegrass Prince (Ire) - Hello Lady
7^{10gf} 8^{12sd} **0-0-2**

Belle Du Jour (Aus) *D K Weld* 105 a105
6 b m Dehere (USA) - Delightful Belle (NZ)
1^{6g} 4^{6ft} 2^{6gs} 15^{6f} 4^{6s} 2^{5gf} **1-1-6**
£313,531

Bellesoeur *P Howling* 47
3 ch f Whittingham (Ire) - Trina's Pet
6^{10g} 5^{10gf} 8^{11gf} 11^{12sw} 6^{12gf} 3^{14s} **0-1-6**
£291

Bells Beach (Ire) *A G Newcombe* 55 a42
5 b m General Monash (USA) - Clifton Beach
6^{6sw} 5^{6sd} 10^{6sd} 3^{6gf} 9^{5gf} 7^{6f} 4^{5gf} 7^{5gf}
0-2-8 £911

Bells Boy's *K A Ryan* 39
4 b g Mind Games - Millie's Lady (Ire)
9^{6f} 5^{6gf} **0-0-2**

Belt And Braces *C Smith*
2 b g Merdon Melody - Dutyful
8^{5gf} 14^{6gf} 11^{6gf} **0-0-3**

Beltane *W De Best-Turner*
5 b g Magic Ring (Ire) - Sally's Trust (Ire)
PU^{10gs} **0-0-1**

Beluga Bay *J R Fanshawe* 90
4 b g Millkom - Bellyphax
3^{8gs} 2^{7gf} 4^{8s} 10^{8s} 1^{7gf} 1^{8gf} **2-2-6**
£21,130

Ben Hur *W M Brisbourne* 72 a73
4 b g Zafonic (USA) - Gayane
2^{9gf} 6^{9gf} 3^{10gf} 4^{10gf} 4^{9gf} 2^{8gf} 3^{8gf} 2^{8gf}
1^{8sw} 10^{8gs} 16^{8gf} 5^{8sd} 15^{8g} **1-5-13 £9,564**

Ben Kenobi *Mrs P Ford* 53
5 ch g Accondy (Ire) - Nour El Sahar (USA)
12^{9sd} 7^{9sw} 4^{13gf} 1^{13gf} 10^{12g} 17^{12f} **1-0-6**
£4,016

Ben Lomand *B W Duke* 83
3 ch g Inchinor - Benjarong
7^{7g} 9^{8gf} 12^{8g} 1^{6gf} 4^{6gf} 1^{6g} 2^{6gf} 9^{6gf}
11^{6gf} 16^{7gs} **2-1-10 £11,279**

Benbaun (Ire) *M J Wallace* 82
2 b c Stravinsky (USA) - Escape To Victory
7^{7f} 4^{7s} 7^{7gf} 15^{6f} 6^{6gf} 1^{5f} 2^{5g} 9^{5gf} **2-1-8**
£10,058

Bendarshaan *E A L Dunlop* 81
3 b c Darshaan - Calypso Run
2^{8gf} 2^{10gf} 3^{11gf} 2^{12gs} 3^{12gf} **0-4-5**
£6,046

Benefactor (Ire) *M W Easterby*
3 b c Hector Protector (USA) - Beneficiary
11^{9s} 9^{7gs} **0-0-2**

Beneking *J Gallagher* 74 a69
3 b/br g Wizard King - Gagajulu
4^{7sd} 5^{7gf} 8^{6gf} 2^{7gf} 3^{7gf} 5^{8gf} 5^{6gf} 2^{7gf}
6^{7gf} 10^{7sd} 4^{7gf} 10^{7sd} **0-3-12 £4,943**

Beneventa *J L Dunlop* 105
3 b f Most Welcome - Dara Dee
2^{8gf} 1^{10gf} 1^{10g} 1^{10gf} 1^{10gf} 3^{10gf} 12^{10gf}
4^{12s} **4-2-8 £37,162**

Benjamin (Ire) *Jane Southcombe* 55 a24
5 b g Night Shift (USA) - Best Academy (USA)
3^{8f} 7^{8sd} 14^{8g} 6^{8f} 7^{8gf} 8^{8gf} 3^{8gf} 6^{13f}
4^{8g} 2^{10g} **0-2-10 £1,599**

Benny The Ball (USA) *N P Littmoden* 82 a74
2 b/br c Benny The Dip (USA) - Heloise (USA)
4^{6gf} 2^{7sd} 6^{10gs} **0-1-3 £1,438**

Benny The Vice (USA) *Mrs A Duffield*
4 ch g Benny The Dip (USA) - Vice On Ice (USA)
5^{16sw} **0-0-1**

Bentley's Ball (USA) *R Hannon* 94
2 b/br c Stravinsky (USA) - Slide By
6^{6gf} 3^{5gf} 1^{6gs} 4^{6gf} 3^{7f} 2^{6gf} **2-2-7**
£27,737

Benvolio *P L Clinton* 17 a9
6 br g Cidrax (Fr) - Miss Capulet
9^{12gf} 10^{12sd} **0-0-2**

Beresford Boy *D K Ivory* 37
2 b c Easycall - Devils Dirge
12^{5gf} **0-0-1**

Bergamo *B Ellison* a57
7 b g Robellino (USA) - Pretty Thing
11^{6sd} 4^{14sd} 2^{16sw} 2^{16sd} 11^{16sd} **1-1-5**
£5,418

Bergerac Pie *R Hollinshead* 32
4 b f Cyrano De Bergerac - Foxtrot Pie
16^{10g} **0-0-1**

Berkeley Hall *R Lee* 56
6 b m Saddlers' Hall (Ire) - Serious Affair
7^{7gf} 5^{7f} 2^{8gf} 6^{8gf} 15^{8gf} **0-1-5 £988**

Berkeley Heights *B Smart* 57
3 b f Hector Protector (USA) - Dancing Heights (Ire)
5^{8gf} 11^{8gf} 8^{10g} **0-0-3**

Bernard *R Charlton* 69
3 b g Nashwan - Tabyan (USA)
13^{8f} 17^{10g} 4^{11hy} 4^{14gf} 2^{14g} 3^{14gf} **0-1-6**
£2,597

Bernini (Ire) *M L W Bell* 54 a73
3 b g Grand Lodge (USA) - Alsahah (Ire)
1^{12sd} 8^{12gf} 11^{12gf} 9^{12g} **1-0-4 £3,477**

Berry Racer *R J Smith* 48
2 ch f Titus Livius (Fr) - Opening Day
7^{5gf} 7^{6gf} 3^{6f} 8^{5f} 5^{6gf} **0-0-5 £458**

Bertie Bucks *J Hetherton* 49
3 br g Charmer - Dolly Mixture
8^{8gf} 8^{7gf} 7^{10gf} **0-0-3**

Bertocelli *G G Margarson* 74
2 ch c Vettori (Ire) - Dame Jude
5^{5g} 5^{5gf} 7^{7gf} 6^{8gf} 1^{7f} 22^{7g} **1-0-6**
£3,360

Bessemer (Jpn) *M Johnston* 84
2 b c Carnegie (Ire) - Chalna (Ire)
3^{5gf} 1^{6g} 3^{1gf} **1-1-3 £6,363**

Best Be Going (Ire) *P W Harris* 87
3 b g Danehill (USA) - Bye Bold Aileen (Ire)
3^{8gf} 4^{8gf} 1^{8gf} 5^{8s} **1-0-4 £4,897**

Best Before (Ire) *J A Osborne* 77 a30
3 b c Mujadil (USA) - Miss Margate (Ire)
2^{6f} 5^{5g} 2^{5g} 2^{6gf} 4^{6sd} 2^{6f} 7^{7g} 6^{6gf} **0-4-8**
£5,614

Best Bond *N P Littmoden* 55 a44
6 ch g Cadeaux Genereux - My Darlingdaughter
11^{6sd} 3^{6g} 11^{6gf} **0-1-3 £842**

Best Desert (Ire) *J R Best* 68
2 b g Desert Style (Ire) - La Alla Wa Asa (Ire)

3^{5gf} 5^{5gf} 6^{5gf} 12^{7f} 2^{7gf} **0-2-5 £1,255**

Best Flight *B W Hills* 61 a78
3 gr g Sheikh Albadou - Bustling Nelly
9^{7sd} 3^{7sd} 4^{7gs} 1^{8sd} **1-1-4 £2,796**

Best Force *G A Butler* 52
2 b f Compton Place - Bestemor
5^{6gf} 10^{6gf} 11^{6gs} **0-0-3**

Best Lead *Ian Emmerson* 64 a25
4 b g Distant Relative - Bestemor
13^{6sd} 15^{5gf} 19^{5g} 17^{6gf} 12^{6f} **0-0-5**

Best Port (Ire) *J Parkes* 71
7 b g Be My Guest (USA) - Portree
11^{12g} 4^{16g} 3^{12gf} 4^{16gf} 4^{16gf} 3^{14gf} 3^{14f} 10^{16g} 5^{14gf} 4^{14f} **0-2-10 £2,929**

Bestseller *E A L Dunlop* 31
3 ch f Selkirk (USA) - Top Shop
11^{10g} **0-0-1**

Bestwillintheworld *T T Clement*
3 c Winning Gallery - Earthly Pleasure
7^{11g} 7^{12g} 8^{12gf} 11^{10gf} **0-0-4**

Bethanys Boy (Ire) *B Ellison* 75
2 ch g Docksider (USA) - Daymoon (USA)
23^{8gf} 4^{5gs} 4^{6gs} 6^{6gf} 4^{6gs} 11^{6gf} 4^{7g} 2^{8gs} **0-1-8 £2,143**

Bettalatethannever (Ire) *S Dow* a52
2 ch g Titus Livius (Fr) - Shambodia (Ire)
11^{6sd} **0-0-1**

Better Gamble *R M Flower*
4 b g Bluegrass Prince (Ire) - Come To Good
12^{12sd} **0-0-1**

Better Off *Mrs N Macauley* a80
5 ch g Bettergeton - Miami Pride
9^{7sd} 5^{7sd} 1^{7sw} 17^{sd} 15^{7sd} 15^{8sd} 9^{7sd} **2-0-7 £7,339**

Better Pal *P R Wood* 66
4 ch g Prince Sabo - Rattle Along
6^{7g} 17^{7g} 14^{7gf} 9^{10gf} 8^{12f} **0-0-5**

Bettergetgone *W Clay*
4 b f Bettergeton - Impromptu Melody (Ire)
12^{7g} **0-0-1**

Betterware Boy *Mrs A J Perrett* 71
3 ch g Barathea (Ire) - Crystal Drop
5^{10gf} 4^{10g} **0-0-2 £436**

Betty Stogs (Ire) *N A Gaselee* 78
2 b f Perugino (USA) - Marabela (Ire)
15^{7gf} 6^{7gf} 7^{7gf} 1^{7gf} **1-0-4 £4,299**

Bettys Pride *M Dods* 58
4 b f Lion Cavern (USA) - Final Verdict (Ire)
17^{5gf} 20^{5gf} 6^{5f} 11^{5gf} 11^{5f} **0-0-5**

Bettys Tribute *C A Dwyer* 63 a63
2 ch f Daggers Drawn (USA) - Cavatina
7^{5gf} 1^{7sd} 4^{7sd} 2^{7sd} 4^{7gf} 4^{8gf} **1-1-6 £4,682**

Beveller *W M Brisbourne* 59 a52
4 ch g Beveled (USA) - Klairover
13^{11gs} 3^{8gf} 9^{7s} 4^{8gf} 2^{7gf} 10^{7gf} 4^{7sw} **0-2-7 £2,416**

Beverley Macca *A Berry* a57
5 ch m Piccolo - Kangra Valley
5^{5sd} **0-0-1**

Bevier *T Wall* 48 a52
9 b g Nashwan (USA) - Bevel (USA)
7^{16sw} 19^{sw} 9^{9sd} 7^{12g} 4^{13gf} 11^{13gf} **1-0-6 £2,940**

Beyond Calculation (USA) *J M Bradley* 8b

9 ch g Geiger Counter (USA) - Placer Queen
16^{5gf} 5^{6f} 2^{5gf} 3^{5f} 4^{5f} 14^{5gf} 8^{5f} 6^{5gf} 14^{5gf} 6^{5gf} 12^{6f} 10^{5gf} 18^{6gf} **0-2-13 £3,446**

Beyond The Clouds (Ire) *J S Wainwright* 97
7 b g Midhish - Tongabezi (Ire)
4^{5g} 5^{5gf} 10^{6g} 6^{5gs} 2^{5gf} 6^{5gf} 2^{5gf} 6^{5gf} 2^{5gs} 9^{5gs} 12^{5gf} 20^{6g} 7^{5s} 20^{6g} 3^{5gs} 13^{6gf} 10^{5gf} 14^{5gf} **0-5-19 £36,636**

Beyond The Pole (USA) *B R Johnson* 56 a72
5 b g Ghazi (USA) - North Of Sunset (USA)
13^{12sd} 2^{13sd} 4^{16sd} 7^{14g} 2^{12sd} 8^{16sd} 10^{12sd} **0-2-7 £1,704**

Bezant (Ire) *C B B Booth* 52
3 ch f Zamindar (USA) - Foresta Verde (USA)
5^{7gf} 3^{8gf} **0-1-2 £496**

Bhanoyi (Ire) *Mrs C A Dunnett* a16
4 ch g Perugino (USA) - Bourgeonette
13^{12sd} 15^{14gf} 12^{10g} 8^{14s} **0-0-4**

Bhutan (Ire) *G L Moore* a74
8 b g Polish Patriot (USA) - Bustinetta
2^{12sd} 2^{12sd} 1^{12sw} 2^{11sd} 4^{11sd} 1^{12sd} 1^{12sd} 3^{11sd} 5^{16sw} 9^{12sd} **3-4-10 £12,576**

Bi Polar *D R C Elsworth* 87 a66
3 b c Polar Falcon (USA) - Doctor Bid (USA)
5^{6sd} 1^{7gf} 8^{7gs} 10^{8gf} 12^{7gf} 6^{7gf} 7^{7sd} 2^{7gs} 10^{7g} **1-1-9 £7,087**

Bible Box (Ire) *Mrs Lydia Pearce* 91
5 b m Bin Ajwaad (Ire) - Addie Pray (Ire)
1^{8g} 4^{8gf} 8^{8gf} **1-0-3 £9,082**

Bid For Fame (USA) *N J Henderson* 92
6 b/br g Quest For Fame - Shroud (USA)
2^{16gf} 11^{20gf} 11^{16gf} 6^{16gf} **0-1-4 £4,676**

Bid Spotter (Ire) *Mrs Lucinda Featherstone*
4 b g Eagle Eyed (USA) - Bebe Auction (Ire)
12^{12sd} **0-0-1**

Bien Good *D Nicholls*
2 b f Bien Bien (USA) - Southern Sky
15^{7gs} **0-0-1**

Bienheureux *W J Musson* 44
2 b c Bien Bien (USA) - Rochea
9^{7gf} 13^{5gf} **0-0-2**

Big Bad Bob (Ire) *J L Dunlop* 121
3 br c Bob Back (USA) - Fantasy Girl (Ire)
8^{12gf} 2^{10gf} 11^{1gf} 1^{10gs} 11^{0g} 11^{10s} **3-0-6 £62,181**

Big Bad Burt *M J Wallace* 22 a60
2 ch c Efisio - Mountain Bluebird (USA)
6^{6sd} 8^{7g} **0-0-2**

Big Bertha *John Berry* 61 a74
5 ch m Dancing Spree (USA) - Bertrade
5^{8g} 16^{10g} 4^{9f} 11^{12sd} 6^{14g} 6^{12sd} 2^{12sd} **1-1-7 £4,769**

Big Bradford *E L James* 87 a84
2 b g Tamure (Ire) - Heather Honey
2^{5gf} 4^{6gf} 2^{6gs} 1^{5f} 6^{7gf} 4^{5gf} 3^{6gf} 2^{6gf} 2^{6sd} **1-4-9 £22,175**

Big Cheese (Ire) *D J S Cosgrove* 33
3 b c Danetime (Ire) - Pat Said No (Ire)
10^{8g} 8^{8gf} 11^{12gf} **0-0-3**

Big Luciano (USA) *M Johnston* a80
3 b c Pleasant Colony (USA) - Fast Tipper (USA)
2^{8sd} 5^{7sd} **0-1-2 £1,324**

Big Moment *Mrs A J Perrett* 103
5 ch g Be My Guest (USA) - Petralona (USA)
4^{12gf} 2^{19gf} 9^{16gs} 4^{14g} 4^{19gf} 15^{18gf} **0-1-6**

£30,972

Big Pee Tee *K A Ryan* 25
3 gr g Petong - Duchess Of Ferrara (Ire)
13^{8sd} 8^{5gf} **0-0-2**

Big Smoke (Ire) *B J Meehan* 81
3 gr g Perugino (USA) - Lightning Bug
7^{9gf} 8^{10gf} 3^{10gf} 2^{8gf} 7^{8g} 3^{8f} 8^{8g} 15^{10gf}
0-2-8 £4,295

Big Tom (Ire) *D Carroll* 71
2 ch c Cadeaux Genereux - Zilayah (USA)
4^{5gf} 2^{6s} 5^{6gf} 8^{5gf} 4^{5g} **0-1-5 £1,798**

Bigalothegigalo (Ire) *J J Quinn* 93
3 b g Desert Story (Ire) - Noble Clare (Ire)
2^{7g} 8^{7gf} 2^{7gf} **0-2-3 £8,768**

Bijan (Ire) *R Hollinshead* 37 a46
5 b m Mukaddamah (USA) - Alkariyh (USA)
8^{6sw} 8^{7sw} 10^{7sd} 3^{7sd} 6^{6sw} 11^{6gf} 4^{5gf}
10^{6gf} **0-1-8 £858**

Bijou Dancer *R Hannon* 58
3 ch g Bijou D'Inde - Dancing Diana
9^{6gs} 9^{6gf} 5^{5f} 6^{7gf} 9^{7gf} **0-0-5**

Bijoux (USA) *R Hannon* 78
3 ch f King Of Kings (Ire) - Golden Wreath (USA)
4^{10gf} 3^{12gf} 4^{10f} 6^{10gf} 5^{8gs} 4^{8gf} 2^{10g} **0-1-7**
£2,666

Bill Bennett (Fr) *J Jay* 67
2 b g Bishop Of Cashel - Concert
6^{7gf} 12^{7gf} 3^{8f} 3^{10gs} **0-1-4 £667**

Bill Middleton (USA) *D Shaw* 45 a51
3 b/br g K O Punch (USA) - Coin (USA)
6^{10sd} 6^{11sd} 8^{8sd} 7^{7sd} 9^{7gf} 10^{12sd} **0-0-6**

Billiard *R Charlton* 67
2 ch f Kirkwall - Ivorine (USA)
12^{7gf} 1^{8f} 13^{8gs} **1-0-3 £3,255**

Billy Allen (Ire) *R Hannon* 86
2 b c Night Shift (USA) - Daintree (Ire)
5^{5g} 4^{5gf} 2^{7gf} 1^{7gf} 2^{7f} 4^{7g} 2^{8gf} 4^{8gf} 4^{7g}
4^{7gf} 6^{6gf} **1-2-11 £10,841**

Billy Bathwick (Ire) *I A Wood* 69 a28
6 ch g Fayruz - Cut It Fine (USA)
8^{12sw} 11^{9sd} 4^{11gf} 2^{12gf} 3^{11gf} 1^{10gf} 1^{12gf}
7^{12gf} 4^{12gf} 4^{12gf} 6^{12gf} 5^{11gf} 5^{12g} 3^{12f} **2-3-14**
£14,126

Billy Whip Top (Ire) *T D Easterby* 64 a73
2 ch g Titus Livius (Fr) - Poker Dice
3^{5f} 11^{5gf} 3^{5sd} 5^{5gf} 6^{5gf} 9^{5gf} 11^{5gf}
8^{5f} 18^{6f} **0-3-10 £2,301**

Billy Whistler *J Balding*
2 ch c Dancing Spree (USA) - Polar Refrain
17^{5g} **0-0-1**

Binanti *P R Chamings* 97
3 b g Bin Ajwaad (Ire) - Princess Rosananti (Ire)
7^{7gf} 8^{7g} 8^{8gf} 4^{8gf} 2^{7g} 1^{7gf} 4^{8g}
10^{7gf} **1-1-9 £14,862**

Binary File (USA) *J H M Gosden* 114
5 b h Nureyev (USA) - Binary
2^{8gf} 6^{10f} 4^{10gf} 4^{8gs} 7^{8gf} 5^{8s} **0-0-6**
£8,901

Binnion Bay (Ire) *R Hannon* 79
2 b c Fasliyev (USA) - Literary
3^{5g} 1^{5g} 8^{6g} **1-0-3 £5,397**

Bint Alhaarth (Ire) *B W Hills* 76
3 b f Alhaarth (Ire) - Idle Fancy
6^{8gf} 11^{8gf} 6^{10gs} 1^{8s} **1-0-4 £3,523**

Bint Makbul *R Hannon* 61

4 b f Makbul - Victoria Sioux
6^{8ft} 3^{6g} 7^{7ft} 4^{9ft} 2^{7gf} 3^{6g} **0-3-6**
£2,617

Bint Royal (Ire) *Miss V Haigh* 68 a74
5 ch m Royal Abjar (USA) - Living Legend (USA)
11^{7sd} 10^{7gf} 3^{7sd} 4^{7gf} 2^{6gf} 2^{6sd} 2^{7sd} 6^{6g}
15^{7sd} 4^{7gf} 6^{6gs} 1^{7g} 6^{8gf} 7^{7g} 6^{8g} 2^{7gf} 10^{7gf}
9^{6gf} 1^{7sw} 9^{6sd} **2-6-20 £13,812**

Birchwood Sun *M Dods* 45
13 b g Bluebird (USA) - Shapely Test (USA)
8^{6gs} 17^{7gf} **0-0-2**

Birikina *A Berry* 70
2 b f Atraf - Fizzy Fiona
15^{6gf} 15^{5g} 3^{5gs} 6^{6gs} 2^{5gf} 6^{6f} 15^{7gf} 7^{6g}
6^{5f} 7^{5gf} 9^{5gf} 16^{6gs} 8^{5gf} **2-1-13 £10,787**

Birth Of The Blues *A Charlton* 46 a47
7 ch g Efisio - Great Steps
7^{10sd} 4^{10f} 12^{12f} 6^{12gf} 1^{12gf} 4^{12gf} 7^{12gf}
2^{12gf} 5^{12g} 6^{12gf} 7^{12f} **1-1-11 £5,029**

Birthday Suit (Ire) *T D Easterby* 96
2 ch f Daylami (Ire) - Wanton
1^{5gf} 1^{5gf} 3^{6g} **2-1-3 £21,545**

Biscar Two (Ire) *R M Whitaker* 39
2 b c Daggers Drawn (USA) - Thoughtful Kate
9^{8gf} 8^{8g} **0-0-2**

Bish Bash Bosh (Ire) *M F Harris* 35 a32
2 b f Bien Bien - Eurolink Virago
8^{5sd} 13^{5g} 6^{5sd} 7^{7gf} 4^{5gf} 7^{6gf} **0-0-6**

Bishop To Actress *M J Polglase* 45 a41
2 ch f Paris House - Chess Mistress (USA)
4^{7gf} 3^{5g} 6^{6gf} 5^{6sd} 6^{7gf} 9^{6sd} **0-1-6 £990**

Bishop's Lake *M G Quinlan* 49
3 b f Lake Coniston (Ire) - Clincher Club
10^{5gf} 8^{6f} 12^{6gf} **0-0-3**

Bishopric *H Candy* 78
3 b g Bishop Of Cashel - Nisha
4^{8gf} 1^{8gs} **1-0-2 £4,648**

Bishops Bounce *G M Moore* 64 a50
2 b c Bishop Of Cashel - Heights Of Love
2^{9g} 6^{6sd} 6^{6s} 7^{7gf} 7^{6gf} 14^{6gf} 2^{6gs} 8^{6sd}
13^{6g} **0-1-9 £848**

Bishops Court *Mrs J R Ramsden* 113
9 ch g Clantime - Indigo
4^{6gf} 6^{5gf} 4^{5g} 1^{5gf} 5^{5g} 3^{5g} **1-1-6**
£33,050

Bishops Finger *Jamie Poulton* 53 a62
3 b g Bishop Of Cashel - Bit Of A Tart
8^{10sd} 4^{10sd} 3^{8sd} 5^{8sd} 12^{8sd} 3^{8sd} 9^{12gf}
8^{10gf} 1^{10sd} 10^{12gs} 13^{12sd} **1-2-12 £4,431**

Bishopstone Man *H Candy* 80
6 b g Piccolo - Auntie Gladys
5^{8gf} 11^{7s} 5^{7gf} 1^{7gf} 3^{7g} 4^{8gf} 2^{8gf} 2^{8gf}
4^{8gf} 1^{8gf} **1-4-10 £9,334**

Bithnah *C R Dore*
4 b f Halling (USA) - Najmat Alshemaal (Ire)
17^{10gs} **0-0-1**

Bitter Sweet *J L Spearing* 60
7 gr m Deploy - Julia Flyte
11^{10gf} 7^{9gf} 6^{8gf} 1^{10gf} 3^{9g} 1^{10gs} 6^{10gf}
13^{10gf} 8^{10gf} 11^{10gf} **2-1-10 £8,185**

Black Falcon (Ire) *M R Channon* 95
3 ch c In The Wings - Muwasim (USA)
3^{10g} 1^{10gf} 4^{12g} 1^{10gf} 11^{10gf} 9^{10g} 5^{12g}
12^{12gf} **2-0-8 £21,775**

Black Legend (Ire) *R Lee* 44

4 b g Marju (Ire) - Lamping
13^{12gf} **0-0-1**

Black Oval *M R Channon*   79
2 b f Royal Applause - Corniche Quest (Ire)
26^{7gf} 1^{5gf} 3^{5gf} 8^{6g} 15^{7gf} 6^{6gs} 7^{6gf} 6^{6gs}
1-0-8 £5,431

Black Pagoda (Ire) *P Monteith*   34
4 b g Spectrum (Ire) - Melodrama
14^{11gs} 13^{7gs} 6^{9f} 10^{11gf} 12^{9gf} 8^{8g} 12^{7g}
0-0-7

Black Rainbow (Ire) *T J Etherington*   a13
5 br m Definite Article - Inonder
12^{13sd} **0-0-1**

Black Sam Bellamy (Ire) *A P O'Brien*   123
4 b c Sadler's Wells (USA) - Urban Sea (USA)
3^{12g} 1^{10g} 8^{20gf} 9^{11ys} 1^{11ys} 5^{10g} 2^{12g} 6^{12ho}
4^{12g} **2-2-9 £268,365**

Black Stripe Gem *M Todhunter*
2 ch f Precious Metal - Just Like You
UR^{5gf} **0-0-1**

Black Swan (Ire) *G A Ham*   43
3 b g Nashwan (USA) - Sea Spray (Ire)
5^{12gf} 10^{10gf} **0-0-2**

Blackheath (Ire) *D Nicholls*   91
7 ch g Common Grounds - Queen Caroline (USA)
8^{6g} 1^{5gf} 2^{6gf} 6^{5gf} 2^{6g} 5^{6g} 2^{6gf} 4^{5gf} 6^{6gf}
6^{5gf} 1^{5f} 2^{6g} 14^{6g} 5^{6g} 10^{6gf} 15^{gs} 9^{6gf} 2^{6g}
3^{5s} **3-6-19 £30,187**

Blackmail (USA) *Miss B Sanders*   66 a90
5 b g Twining (USA) - Black Penny (USA)
11^{8sd} 6^{10sd} 1^{10sd} 4^{10sd} 5^{10sd} 2^{10sd} 12^{10g}
5^{10gf} 8^{12f} 8^{12g} 16^{8g} **1-1-11 £5,854**

Blackmoll (Ire) *P D Evans*   37
2 b f Desert Story (Ire) - Sanctuary Cove
4^{5g} 7^{5f} 5^{5gf} 4^{6gs} 8^{7f} 5^{6gf} 14^{7f} **0-0-7**
£267

Blackpool Beau *K A Ryan*   57
3 b g Danetime (Ire) - Blackpool Belle
4^{5gf} 5^{6gf} **0-0-2**

Blackthorn *R A Fahey*   74
4 ch g Deploy - Balliasta (USA)
6^{10gs} 3^{10f} 9^{11gf} 9^{12gf} 3^{10g} 7^{12gs} 1^{12gf}
5^{12gf} 2^{12gf} 11^{12gf} 7^{13g} 2^{12gf} **1-4-12 £6,402**

Blackwater Angel (USA) *J L Dunlop*   65
3 b f Kingmambo (USA) - Zephyr (Can)
8^{10gf} 5^{10g} **0-0-2**

Blackwater Fever (USA) *T J O'Mara*   67
3 b c Irish River (Fr) - Crafty Buzz (USA)
3^{10gf} 8^{11s} 6^{10gf} 12^{12g} 1^{10g} **1-0-5**
£4,098

Blade's Dancer *D Shaw*
3 b g Komaite (USA) - Banningham Blade
15^{6sw} **0-0-1**

Blade's Daughter *K A Ryan*   26
2 gr f Paris House - Banningham Blade
12^{5gf} 13^{6gf} 10^{5gf} **0-0-3**

Blade's Edge *A Bailey*   64
2 b c Daggers Drawn (USA) - Hayhurst
3^{6gf} 4^{6f} 9^{7gs} **0-1-3 £1,171**

Blaeberry *P L Gilligan*   54
2 b f Kirkwall - Top Berry
14^{7gs} 8^{8g} **0-0-2**

Blaina *D R C Elsworth*   83
3 ch f Compton Place - Miss Silca Key
7^{8gf} 3^{7gf} 2^{8gs} 2^{7gf} 6^{8gs} **0-3-5 £4,292**

Blaise Castle (USA) *G A Butler*   96
3 b f Irish River (Fr) - Castellina (USA)
7^{8gf} 14^{10gf} 3^{6gs} 9^{7vs} 4^{8vs} **0-1-5 £4,785**

Blaise Wood (USA) *R Hannon*   53
2 b g Woodman (USA) - Castellina (USA)
6^{7g} **0-0-1**

Blakeset *T D Barron*   71 a72
8 ch g Midyan (USA) - Penset
6^{7sd} 2^{6sd} 1^{7sd} 1^{6sd} 1^{6gs} 15^{6g} **3-1-6**
£11,206

Blakeseven *W J Musson*   55 a59
3 b g Forzando - Up And Going (Fr)
10^{7sd} 3^{6sd} 9^{6g} 15^{6gf} 9^{6gf} 15^{5gf} 7^{6g} 4^{8gf}
0-2-8 £465

Blakeshall Boy *R Lee*   61 a61
5 b g Piccolo - Giggleswick Girl
6^{5gf} 9^{5gf} 12^{5gf} 19^{6gs} 8^{6g} 4^{6sd} **0-0-6**

Blakeshall Girl *J L Spearing*   57
3 ch f Piccolo - Giggleswick Girl
3^{6gf} 7^{6gf} 12^{6f} 15^{6gs} 14^{6gf} **0-0-5 £442**

Blakeshall Quest *R Brotherton*   62 a79
3 b f Piccolo - Corniche Quest (Ire)
2^{6sd} 1^{6sd} 2^{7sd} 6^{6gf} 1^{6sd} 7^{6gs} 15^{7sd} 10^{7sd}
2-2-8 £9,488

Blanco (Ire) *M J Wallace*   61 a58
3 ch g First Trump - Balance The Books
4^{8sw} 5^{8sd} 6^{10g} 1^{10gf} 1^{8gf} 3^{8g} 6^{8gf} 3^{8sd}
5^{8gf} 3^{9f} 5^{8f} 6^{7gf} **2-2-12 £8,159**

Blandys (Ire) *J White*   35 a55
3 b f Dolphin Street (Fr) - Bodfaridistinction (Ire)
3^{7sd} 4^{7sd} 3^{5sw} 1^{6sd} 10^{6sd} 7^{5f} 15^{6gs} 3^{5sd}
8^{7sd} **1-3-9 £4,412**

Blatant *Saeed Bin Suroor*   117
4 ch c Machiavellian (USA) - Negligent
6^{8gf} 3^{8g} 7^{8gs} 5^{9g} 4^{8gf} 12^{8gs} 2^{8gf} **0-2-7**
£67,859

Blau Grau (Ger) *K A Morgan*   40 a53
6 gr g Neshad (Ger) - Belle Orfana (Ger)
1^{8sd} 5^{9sd} 12^{8sd} 8^{9gf} 13^{12gf} **1-0-5**
£2,968

Blaze Of Colour *Sir Michael Stoute*   55
2 ch f Rainbow Quest (USA) - Hawait Al Barr
12^{8gf} **0-0-1**

Blazeaway (USA) *R S Brookhouse*   69
3 b/br g Hansel (USA) - Alessia's Song (USA)
5^{8ft} 5^{8gf} 7^{9gs} 3^{10gf} 11^{12gf} 9^{9g} **0-0-6**
£1,134

Blazing Moment *R Bastiman*   37 a26
3 ch c Timeless Times (USA) - Kabella
10^{5gs} 11^{5f} 11^{6sd} 9^{7gf} 4^{8gf} 8^{12gf} **0-0-6**
£744

Blazing Saddles (Ire) *P R Hedger*   47
4 b g Sadler's Wells (USA) - Dalawara (Ire)
11^{13g} 12^{12sd} **0-0-2**

Blazing The Trail (Ire) *J W Hills*   70
3 ch g Indian Ridge - Divine Pursuit
14^{7gf} 7^{10g} 3^{12gf} 7^{12gs} **0-0-4 £830**

Blazing Thunder *J H M Gosden*   108
3 b c Zafonic (USA) - Bright Spells (USA)
1^{7gf} 12^{7gf} 12^{8g} 3^{9gf} 3^{8gs} **1-0-5**
£12,893

Blenheim Terrace *W H Tinning*   51
10 b g Rambo Dancer (Can) - Roulevaud Girl
8^{16gf} 5^{16gs} 1^{14f} 3^{14t} **1-1-4 £4,426**

Bless Her *Mrs P N Dutfield*   45 a16

3 b f Piccolo - Bliss (Ire)
11^{6sd} 8^{5gf} 17^{7gf} 7^{5f} **0-0-4**

Blessed Place *Jean-Rene Auvray* 66 a64
3 ch g Compton Place - Cathedra
3^{5sd} 2^{6sd} 5^{6sd} 3^{5sd} 2^{5sd} 1^{5sd} 2^{5f} 2^{5f} 3^{5f}
5^{5s} 13^{5gf} 8^{5gf} 5^{5g} 8^{5gf} **1-6-14 £11,049**

Blessingindisguise *M W Easterby* 61
10 b g Kala Shikari - Blowing Bubbles
2^{6f} 10^{5gs} 3^{6gf} 8^{5gf} 5^{5f} 4^{5gf} 6^{5f}
6^{5gf} 8^{5gf} 2^{5gf} 2^{5f} 2^{5gf} 4^{5gf} **0-6-14 £8,922**

Bloemfontain (Ire) *M Johnston* 74
2 b f Cape Cross (Ire) - Carotene (Can)
4^{6gf} 2^{6g} 1^{6gs} **1-1-3 £4,195**

Blofeld *W Jarvis* 50 a54
2 b g Royal Applause - Bliss (Ire)
11^{5g} 6^{5gf} 9^{6gf} 8^{6gf} 5^{6sd} **0-0-5**

Blonde En Blonde (Ire) *N P Littmoden* 61 a77
3 ch f Hamas (Ire) - Hulm (Ire)
10^{5sd} 1^{6sd} 1^{6sd} 1^{6sd} 2^{7sw} 8^{5sd} 4^{7sw} 3^{7sd}
11^{8sd} 8^{7g} 1^{7gf} 6^{8f} 2^{7sw} 2^{7sd} 7^{7sd} 3^{7sd} **4-5-16**
£16,935

Blonde Streak (USA) *T D Barron* 87
3 ch f Dumaani (USA) - Katiba (USA)
1^{8g} 17^{8gf} 1^{8gs} 3^{8gf} 2^{8gf} 8^{8s} 4^{10gf} **2-2-7**
£12,803

Blooming Lucky (Ire) *J A Osborne* a24
4 b f Lucky Guest - Persian Flower
10^{7sd} 9^{9sd} 11^{8sd} **0-0-3**

Blossom Whispers *N G Ayliffe* 12
6 b m Ezzoud (Ire) - Springs Welcome
12^{16gs} **0-0-1**

Blowing Away (Ire) *Julian Poulton*
9 b/br m Last Tycoon - Taken By Force
11^{22gf} **0-0-1**

Blue A Fuse (Ire) *M Brittain*
3 b f Bluebird (USA) - Gleaming Heather (USA)
16^{7gs} **0-0-1**

Blue Bijou *T T Clement*
3 b g Bijou D'Inde - Jucea
11^{6gf} **0-0-1**

Blue Bounty (Ire) *J Akehurst* 34
3 b f Blues Traveller (Ire) - Cwm Deri (Ire)
14^{6g} 12^{8g} **0-0-2**

Blue Circle *M Mullineaux* 35 a54
3 b c Whittingham (Ire) - Reshift
7^{6sd} 8^{5sd} 5^{6sd} 13^{6sd} 2^{6sd} 6^{6s} 11^{5gs}
18^{5gf} 11^{7gf} 6^{8sd} 17^{5gs} 11^{6sd} **0-1-12 £1,022**

Blue Daze *R Hannon* 67
2 b f Danzero (Aus) - Sparkling
7^{5g} 1^{6gf} **1-0-2 £4,485**

Blue Emperor (Ire) *P A Blockley* 67 a31
2 b c Groom Dancer (USA) - Bague Bleue (Ire)
3^{5g} 4^{5sd} 6^{5gf} **0-1-3 £637**

Blue Empire (Ire) *P C Haslam* 57 a59
2 b g Second Empire (Ire) - Paleria (USA)
9^{6g} 18^{sd} 9^{8gs} **1-0-3 £2,042**

Blue Gallery (Ire) *P A Blockley* 27 a59
2 b f Bluebird (USA) - Lovely Deise (Ire)
4^{5sd} 1^{6sd} 3^{6sd} 8^{7gf} 8^{6gf} **1-0-5 £3,639**

Blue Hills *M Johnston* 73
2 br g Vettori (Fr) - Slow Jazz (USA)
10^{7gf} 5^{8gf} 2^{8g} **0-1-3 £1,335**

Blue Java *H Morrison* 50
2 ch c Bluegrass Prince (Ire) - Java Bay
15^{8gf} **0-0-1**

Blue Knight (Ire) *A P Jarvis* 81
4 ch g Bluebird (USA) - Fer De Lance (Ire)
10^{6gf} 14^{6gf} 14^{6gf} 2^{6gf} 6^{6gf} 12^{6gf} 10^{6gf}
0-1-7 £1,720

Blue Leader (Ire) *G Brown* 78
4 b g Cadeaux Genereux - Blue Duster (USA)
7^{7g} 14^{10gf} **0-0-2**

Blue Maeve (Ire) *J Hetherton* a21
3 b g Blue Ocean (USA) - Louisville Belle (Ire)
9^{7sw} 13^{10gs} **0-0-2**

Blue Monday *R Charlton* 96
2 b c Darshaan - Lunda (Ire)
8^{8gf} 1^{8gf} 1^{8g} **2-0-3 £10,694**

Blue Moon Hitman (Ire) *A Berry* 54
2 c c Blue Ocean (USA) - Miss Kookaburra (Ire)
8^{6gs} 5^{5f} 5^{5gs} 2^{5gf} 3^{5gf} 2^{5gf} 2^{5gf}
3^{5gf} 4^{5f} 5^{5gf} 4^{5gs} **0-5-12 £3,767**

Blue Muemonic *J S Moore* a15
3 b g Bluegrass Prince (Ire) - Forget To Remindme
9^{8sd} **0-0-1**

Blue Myst *G A Swinbank* 62 a45
3 b f Blue Ocean (USA) - Broom Isle
8^{10gf} 7^{12g} 3^{10s} 12^{12gf} 10^{10gs} 6^{11sw} 10^{11gs}
0-1-7 £576

Blue Mystique *M Mullineaux* 38 a59
4 b f Whittingham (Ire) - Gold And Blue (Ire)
9^{7sw} 11^{7sd} 3^{8sd} 4^{6sd} 6^{8sd} 7^{7gf} 10^{8gf}
0-1-7 £467

Blue Patrick *J M P Eustace* 92
3 gr g Wizard King - Great Intent
4^{8gf} 25^{8gf} 1^{8gf} 6^{8g} **1-0-4 £11,357**

Blue Planet (Ire) *P G Murphy* 60 a63
5 b g Bluebird (USA) - Millie Musique
12^{12sd} 8^{14gf} **0-0-2**

Blue Power (Ire) *K R Burke* 35 a59
2 b c Zieten (USA) - La Miserable (USA)
8^{6gs} 14^{7g} 4^{6sd} **0-0-3**

Blue Quiver (Ire) *C A Horgan* 42 a51
3 b c Bluebird (USA) - Paradise Forum
8^{8gf} 8^{7sd} **0-0-2**

Blue Reigns *J W Unett* a48
5 b g Whittingham (Ire) - Gold And Blue (Ire)
14^{7sd} **0-0-1**

Blue Rondo (Ire) *R Charlton* 30 a67
3 b g Hernando (Fr) - Blueberry Walk
4^{8sd} 10^{10sd} 9^{13g} **0-0-3 £265**

Blue Savanna *J G Portman* 58
3 ch g Bluegrass Prince (Ire) - Dusk In Daytona
12^{12sd} 10^{14gf} 7^{12g} 4^{11gf} 7^{10f} 11^{10gf} 2^{10gf}
6^{10gf} 6^{11gf} **0-2-9 £1,023**

Blue Sky Thinking (Ire) *K R Burke* 97
4 b g Danehill Dancer (USA) - Lauretta Blue (Ire)
9^{8gf} 1^{8gf} 6^{9gf} 3^{7g} 3^{8gs} **1-1-5 £10,228**

Blue Spinnaker (Ire) *M W Easterby* 97
4 b g Bluebird (USA) - Suedoise
2^{6gf} 3^{6f} 1^{5g} 3^{6gf} 2^{7gf} 4^{7g} 1^{8gf} 4^{8gf}
11^{10gf} 23^{9gf} 4^{8gf} **2-4-11 £27,469**

Blue Star *M Mullineaux* 82
7 b g Whittingham (Ire) - Gold And Blue (Ire)
UR^{7g} 12^{8gf} 5^{6gf} 3^{8g} 2^{11gf} 3^{11gf} 4^{11gf}
9^{12gf} 5^{16gf} 5^{12gf} PU^{16gf} **0-2-11 £12,366**

Blue Streak (Ire) *G L Moore* 57 a50
6 ch g Bluebird (USA) - Fleet Amour (USA)
7^{12sd} 8^{11gf} 5^{10gf} 6^{12gf} 5^{10g} 2^{12f} 2^{12f} 8^{12g}
0-1-8 £1,752

Blue Symphony *E A L Dunlop*   69 a68
3 b f Darshaan - Blue Duster (USA)
2^{10gf} 2^{10sd} 3^{10gf} 2^{10f} 13^{10gf} 16^{11gf} 1^{10f}
5^{10gf} **1-4-8 £6,759**

Blue Tomato *P F I Cole*   101
2 b c Orpen (USA) - Ocean Grove (Ire)
4^{5g} 1^{6gf} 1^{6g} 5^{6gf} 1^{6gf} 3^{6gf} 8^{6g} **3-1-7**
£35,920

Blue Trojan (Ire) *S Kirk*   85 a79
3 b g Inzar (USA) - Roman Heights (Ire)
7^{7sd} 5^{8sd} 13^{7gf} 8^{10gf} 2^{7g} 1^{8g} 8^{7sd} 3^{8f}
7^{9sd} 1^{8f} 5^{8g} **2-2-11 £14,112**

Blue Venture (Ire) *P C Haslam*   62 a63
3 ch g Alhaarth (Ire) - September Tide (Ire)
3^{7sd} 4^{8sd} 3^{7sw} 10^{7gf} 16^{8gf} **0-1-5**
£1,170

Blue Viking (Ire) *J R Weymes*
2 b c Danetime (Ire) - Jenny Spinner (Ire)
4^{7f} **0-0-1**

Blue Water *M Mullineaux*   45 a45
3 b f Shaamit (Ire) - November Song
10^{8sd} 8^{11sd} 5^{12sw} 6^{12sd} 9^{12sd} 2^{12sd} 3^{12sd}
12^{12gf} 6^{15sd} 3^{14gf} 7^{12sd} 6^{14g} 9^{16gf} **0-2-13**
£2,074

Blueberry Jim *T H Caldwell*   40
2 ch g First Trump - Short And Sharp
8^{5g} 6^{6gf} 12^{6gs} 7^{6gf} 13^{6s} **0-0-5**

Blueberry Rhyme *P J Makin*   a72
4 b g Alhijaz - Irenic
3^{5sd} **0-1-1 £442**

Bluebird Spirit *P W Harris*   69
3 ch f Bluebird (USA) - My Lewicia (Ire)
5^{8gf} 2^{10gf} 9^{12gf} **0-1-3 £1,160**

Bluebok *D R Loder*   61
2 b c Indian Ridge - Blue Sirocco
5^{6gs} **0-0-1**

Bluefield (Ire) *R F Johnson Houghton*   70
2 b c Second Empire (Ire) - Imco Reverie (Ire)
13^{7gf} 3^{8gf} **0-1-2 £960**

Bluegrass Beau *B G Powell*   65 a31
3 ch g Bluegrass Prince (Ire) - Blushing Belle
10^{10gf} 16^{8gf} 6^{12g} 10^{8f} 3^{8gf} 6^{11gf} 7^{12sd}
5^{10gf} 7^{12gf} 18^{11gf} 11^{15sd} **0-1-11 £630**

Bluegrass Boy *G B Balding*   70
3 b g Bluegrass Prince (Ire) - Honey Mill
10^{10gf} 2^{10gf} 5^{10gf} **0-1-3 £1,127**

Bluegrass Stampede *J D Czerpak*
2 ch c Bluegrass Prince (Ire) - Sylvaner (Ire)
6^{5g} **0-0-1**

Blues Princess *R A Fahey*   62
3 b f Bluebird (USA) - Queen Shirley (Ire)
10^{5gf} 7^{5gs} 13^{6gf} 20^{6gf} **0-0-4**

Bluestone *G Wragg*   28
4 ch c Bluebird (USA) - Romoosh
9^{7gf} **0-0-1**

Bluetoria *J A Glover*
2 b f Vettori (Ire) - Blue Birds Fly
10^{6f} **0-0-1**

Blunham *M C Chapman*   62
3 b g Danzig Connection (USA) - Relatively Sharp
9^{7g} 9^{7gf} 4^{6gf} 6^{6gf} 1^{7gf} 10^{6f} 7^{7f} **1-0-7**
£2,763

Blushing Grenadier (Ire) *S R Bowring*   a15
11 ch g Salt Dome (USA) - La Duse
13^{7sw} 13^{6sd} 8^{6sd} **0-0-3**

Blushing Prince (Ire) *Mrs L Stubbs*   51 a70
5 b g Priolo (USA) - Eliade (Ire)
9^{9sd} 1^{9sd} 7^{9sd} 1^{9sd} 3^{9sd} 5^{11gf} 6^{9gf} 3^{9sd}
3^{8sd} 6^{11gf} 7^{9sd} **2-3-11 £6,313**

Blushing Spur *A Charlton*   68 a69
5 b g Flying Spur (Aus) - Bogus John (Can)
2^{6sd} 1^{6sw} 4^{6sd} 2^{6sw} 3^{7sd} 7^{6sd} 4^{6g} 7^{7sd}
9^{7gf} 20^{5gf} 8^{6sd} 14^{7gf} **1-3-12 £6,670**

Blythe Knight (Ire) *E A L Dunlop*   108
3 ch c Selkirk (USA) - Blushing Barada (USA)
1^{10g} 5^{10gf} 1^{10gf} 5^{12gf} 12^{10gf} 4^{11gf} 3^{10gf}
9^{10gf} **2-1-8 £26,199**

Blythe Spirit *R A Fahey*   88
4 b g Bahamian Bounty - Lithe Spirit (Ire)
9^{6g} 6^{7g} 9^{7gf} 1^{8gf} 23^{7f} 8^{7gf} 8^{7gf} 5^{7g}
9^{7g} 4^{6gf} 5^{7gf} **1-0-12 £6,849**

Bo McGinty (Ire) *R A Fahey*   75
2 ch g Fayruz - Georges Park Lady (Ire)
3^{5gf} 11^{5f} 1^{5gf} **1-1-3 £5,926**

Boanerges (Ire) *J M Bradley*   75
6 br g Caerleon (USA) - Sea Siren
7^{5gf} 16^{5g} 14^{5gs} 15^{5gf} 7^{5gf} 9^{5gf} 9^{5gf} 5^{5g}
0-0-8

Boater *R J Baker*
9 b g Batshoof - Velvet Beret (Ire)
10^{10f} **0-0-1**

Boavista (Ire) *T D Easterby*   63 a46
3 b f Fayruz - Florissa (Fr)
6^{5g} 4^{6sd} 4^{5gs} 3^{6gf} 10^{6gf} 3^{5g} 2^{5gf} 2^{6gf}
4^{6f} 3^{6f} **0-5-10 £5,583**

Bob's Buzz *S C Williams*   74
3 ch g Zilzal (USA) - Aethra (USA)
3^{7gf} 1^{5gs} 1^{7gf} 14^{7gf} **2-0-4 £8,819**

Bob's Gone (Ire) *R J Smith*   a24
5 ch g Eurobus - Bob's Girl (Ire)
10^{12sd} **0-0-1**

Bob's Sherie *W M Brisbourne*
4 b f Bob's Return (Ire) - Sheraton Girl
12^{12sd} 7^{15sw} **0-0-2**

Bobanvi *J S Wainwright*   27
5 b m Timeless Times (USA) - Bobanlyn (Ire)
11^{14sd} 6^{14f} 4^{17gf} 5^{16gf} 12^{16gf} **0-0-5**

Bobby Kennard *J A Osborne*   a86
4 b g Bobinski - Midnight Break
1^{16sw} 7^{16sd} 2^{16sw} **1-1-3 £4,615**

Bobering *B P J Baugh*
3 b g Bob's Return (Ire) - Ring The Rafters
12^{8gf} **0-0-1**

Bobsleigh *Mrs A J Perrett*   85
4 b g Robellino (USA) - Do Run Run
4^{14gs} 2^{16gf} 8^{20gf} 3^{16gf} 11^{21gs} 3^{16gf} 21^{18gf}
11^{16gf} 4^{16gf} **0-4-9 £5,296**

Bocaccio (Ire) *R Ingram*   47 a77
5 b g Brief Truce (USA) - Idara
6^{10sd} 6^{8sd} 16^{8gf} 18^{8gf} **0-0-4**

Bodfari Pride (Ire) *A Bailey*   68 a56
8 b g Pips Pride - Renata's Ring (Ire)
6^{7sd} 7^{7sd} 2^{6gf} 1^{7gf} 10^{7sd} 3^{6gs} 5^{7g} 3^{7gs}
2^{6gs} 5^{6gf} 5^{7gf} 8^{6gs} 9^{8gf} 11^{6gf} PU^{7f} **1-4-15**
£7,280

Bodfari Rose *A Bailey*
4 ch f Indian Ridge - Royale Rose (Fr)
4^{16sd} 12^{14gf} **0 0-2**

Bodilla (Ire) *T D Easterby*   17
3 b f Mujadil (USA) - Shambodia (Ire)

11^{6f} **0-0-1**

Bogus Ballet *D Burchell*   41 a44
4 ch f Halling (USA) - Classic Ballet (Fr)
9^{7sd} 9^{9sw} 10^{7sd} 6^{7f} 9^{7sd} 14^{6gf} **0-0-6**

Bohola Flyer (Ire) *R Hannon*   71
2 b f Barathea (Ire) - Sharp Catch (Ire)
20^{7gf} 11^{7f} 2^{6g} **0-1-3 £1,090**

Boing Boing (Ire) *Miss S J Wilton*   66 a66
3 b g King's Theatre (Ire) - Limerick Princess (Ire)
6^{8sd} 11^{10g} 3^{8f} 10^{8gs} 9^{8gf} 5^{7gf} 10^{8gf}
7^{8sw} 1^{7gf} **1-0-9 £3,239**

Boisdale (Ire) *D Nicholls*   66 a72
5 b g Common Grounds - Alstomeria
5^{6gf} 16^{6sd} 5^{6gf} 2^{7gf} 11^{6sd} 6^{5gf} 6^{6gf} 16^{6sd}
11^{7sd} 7^{6sw} 6^{7sw} 12^{6sd} **2-1-12 £6,979**

Bojangles (Ire) *R Brotherton*   57 a35
4 b g Danehill (USA) - Itching (Ire)
9^{11gf} 7^{11gf} 4^{15g} 5^{10gf} 10^{9sd} 9^{11gf} **0-0-6**
£523

Bold Amusement *W S Cunningham*   53
13 ch g Never So Bold - Hysterical
6^{10gf} 2^{9g} 7^{10gf} **0-1-3 £1,275**

Bold Blade *B Smart*   45 a18
2 b g Sure Blade (USA) - Golden Ciel (USA)
6^{5f} 13^{6gf} 9^{7sd} **0-0-3**

Bold Effort (Fr) *K O Cunningham-Brown*   42 a12
11 b g Bold Arrangement - Malham Tarn
19^{6g} 12^{6sd} 15^{6g} 13^{5sd} 6^{6f} 12^{6f} 15^{6gf}
7^{6gf} **0-0-8**

Bold Ewar (Ire) *C E Brittain*   77 a71
6 ch g Persian Bold - Hot Curry (USA)
6^{13sd} 5^{13sd} 8^{16sw} 1^{14g} 2^{17gf} 6^{16gf} 11^{15sd}
4^{16sd} 4^{17gf} 11^{16g} 2^{14gf} 5^{16sd} **2-2-12 £10,413**

Bold Joe (Ire) *P Mitchell*   67
2 b c Singspiel (Ire) - Wavy Up (Ire)
7^{6gf} 10^{8gf} 9^{8g} 9^{8gf} 7^{8gf} 2^{10gs} **0-1-6**
£676

Bold Shout (Ire) *R F Johnson Houghton*   44 a22
2 b c Alzao (USA) - Bye Bold Aileen (Ire)
10^{8gf} 11^{7sd} 10^{8gf} **0-0-3**

Bold Trump *Jean-Rene Auvray*   44
2 b g First Trump - Blue Nile (Ire)
15^{7g} **0-0-1**

Bold Wolf *P W Harris*   47
2 b c Wolfhound (USA) - Rambold
7^{6gf} 11^{6g} 14^{6gf} 10^{6gf} 2^{5f} 12^{5gf} **0-1-6**
£846

Boleyn Castle (USA) *T G Mills*   107
6 ch g River Special (USA) - Dance Skirt (Can)
19^{5gf} 3^{5gf} 12^{5gs} 10^{5g} 8^{5gf} 13^{5f} 11^{5g}
0-1-7 £3,520

Bolham Lady *J Balding*   a27
5 b m Timeless Times (USA) - Stratford Lady
10^{6sd} 8^{5sw} **0-0-2**

Bollin Annabel *T D Easterby*   45
2 b f King's Theatre (Ire) - Bollin Magdalene
9^{8s} **0-0-1**

Bollin Edward *T D Easterby*   80
4 b g Timeless Times (USA) - Bollin Harriet
2^{6g} 9^{6gs} 18^{6g} 4^{6g} 3^{6g} 4^{6gs} 13^{6gf} 14^{6gf}
7^{7gs} 12^{6gs} 8^{6gf} **0-3-11 £4,702**

Bollin Eric *T D Easterby*   124
4 b c Shaamit (Ire) - Bollin Zola
3^{14gf} 4^{12gf} 2^{12f} 4^{12g} 4^{12g} 1^{16gf} 4^{14gf}
8^{12ho} **1-2-8 £157,633**

Bollin Janet *T D Easterby*   81
3 b f Sheikh Albadou - Bollin Emily
8^{6gf} 8^{5gs} 4^{5gf} 1^{6g} 5^{6gf} 12^{5gf} 16^{5gs} **1-0-7**
£11,106

Bollin Jeannie *T D Easterby*   66
3 b f Royal Applause - Bollin Joanne
UR^{6s} 9^{6hy} 4^{5gf} 5^{6gf} 8^{8gf} 4^{6gf} 18^{6g} **0-1-7**
£612

Bollin Thomas *T D Easterby*   88
5 b g Alhijaz - Bollin Magdalene
7^{13gs} 10^{14hy} 6^{14gf} 1^{15gf} 10^{16gf} 3^{15gf} **1-0-6**
£6,684

Bolshevik (Ire) *T D Easterby*   39
2 b g Fasliyev (USA) - Cheviot Amble (Ire)
13^{5gf} 6^{6gf} **0-0-2**

Bolshoi Ballet *J Mackie*   48 a74
5 b g Dancing Spree (USA) - Broom Isle
13^{14g} 4^{12sd} 10^{15sd} **0-1-3 £277**

Bomb Alaska *G B Balding*   86
8 br g Polar Falcon (USA) - So True
4^{7s} **0-1-1 £742**

Bon Ami (Ire) *A Berry*   82 a82
7 b g Paris House - Felin Special
7^{6sd} 6^{7sd} 4^{7sd} 2^{7gf} 10^{6gf} PU^{7gf} **0-1-6**
£2,308

Bond Becks (Ire) *B Smart*   102
3 ch g Tagula (Ire) - At Amal (Ire)
8^{8g} 3^{6gf} 4^{5gf} 15^{6g} 4^{6g} 6^{5gf} 5^{5f} 9^{5gs}
0-1-8 £6,470

Bond Boy *B Smart*   106
6 b g Piccolo - Arabellajill
3^{6gf} 6^{6g} 2^{6gs} 9^{5gf} 14^{6g} **0-2-5 £6,882**

Bond Brooklyn *B Smart*   65 a63
2 b c Mind Games - Crystal Sand (Ger)
7^{6gf} 5^{6g} 5^{5gf} 2^{6gs} 5^{6g} 3^{6sd} **0-2-6**
£1,531

Bond Diamond *P R Webber*   86
6 gr g Prince Sabo - Alsiba
1^{8gf} 16^{8g} 4^{8g} 11^{8gf} 8^{8gf} 11^{7f} 8^{8g} 3^{8f}
4^{8g} **1-2-9 £7,938**

Bond Domingo *B Smart*   38 a50
4 b g Mind Games - Antonia's Folly
9^{8sw} 8^{6sd} 6^{8sd} 7^{6sd} 17^{6gs} 20^{5gf} 12^{6f}
0-0-7

Bond Jovi (Ire) *B Smart*   77
4 b g Danehill Dancer (Ire) - Vieux Carre
12^{8sw} **0-0-1**

Bond May Day *B Smart*   77 a63
3 b f Among Men (USA) - State Romance
6^{7sw} 3^{8sd} 2^{10gf} 2^{10gf} 1^{12f} 2^{12f} 4^{12sd}
10^{11gf} 10^{11gf} 1^{10gf} 6^{12gf} 7^{10gf} **2-4-12 £14,467**

Bond Millennium *B Smart*   70
5 ch g Piccolo - Farmer's Pet
5^{8g} 6^{10gf} 14^{8gs} 1^{8f} 3^{8gf} 5^{8gf} 2^{8gf} 5^{7gf}
4^{9gf} 6^{8gf} 8^{8gf} 2^{10gf} 4^{10g} **1-3-13 £7,771**

Bond Mirage *B Smart*   11 a58
5 b g Primo Dominie - Arabellajill
3^{8sd} 15^{8gf} 11^{8sd} **0-1-3 £424**

Bond Moonlight *B Smart*   43 a57
2 ch g Danehill Dancer (Ire) - Interregnum
13^{8s} 4^{8sw} 4^{8gf} **0-0-3**

Bond Playboy *B Smart*   61 a91
3 b g Piccolo - Highest Ever (Fr)
6^{6sd} 2^{6sd} 13^{6gf} 15^{5g} 16^{6gs} 14^{6gs} **0-1-6**
£1,532

Bond Romeo (Ire) *B Smart*   60
2 ch g Titus Livius (Fr) - At Amal (Ire)
18⁵ᵍ 5⁵ᶠ 5⁵ᵍˢ 5⁵ᶠ 8⁵ᵍᶠ 2⁵ᵍ **0-1-6 £766**

Bond Royale *B Smart*   85 a89
3 ch f Piccolo - Passiflora
5⁶ˢᵈ 7⁶ᵍᶠ 13⁶ᵍᶠ 11⁶ᵍᶠ 14⁶ᵍˢ **0-0-5**

Bond Shakira *B Smart*   42
2 ch f Daggers Drawn (USA) - Cinnamon Lady
5⁵ᵍᶠ **0-0-1**

Bond Solitaire *B Smart*   44
3 ch f Atraf - Laena
9⁸ᵍᶠ 11⁷ᵍ 7⁶ᶠ 12⁶ᵍ 11⁷ˢᵈ **0-0-5**

Bond Stasia (Ire) *B Smart*   35
3 b f Mukaddamah (USA) - Idrak
11⁵ᵍ **0-0-1**

Bondi (Fr) *A M Balding*   39 a32
3 b f Sillery (USA) - Biscay
7⁹ᵍ 13⁶ᵍᶠ 5⁸ᵍ 10⁷ˢᵈ **0-0-4**

Bonecrusher *D R Loder*   109
4 b g Revoque (Ire) - Eurolink Mischief
4¹⁰ᶠᵗ 6¹⁰ᶠᵗ 4¹⁰ᵍᶠ 1¹⁰ᵍᶠ 14⁹ᵍᶠ 4¹⁰ᵍ **1-0-6
£15,057**

Bonella (Ire) *W J Musson*   31
5 gr m Eagle Eyed (USA) - Mettlesome
10¹²ᵍ 10¹⁰ᵍᶠ **0-0-2**

Bonito *P C Haslam*   61 a63
5 ch g Pivotal - Bonita
11⁷ˢᵈ 2⁷ᵍᶠ 6⁶ˢᵈ 6⁷ᵍᶠ 6⁶ᵍˢ 14⁷ˢᵈ 2⁷ˢ 4⁷ᵍᶠ
6⁷ᵍᶠ **0-2-9 £1,960**

Bonjour Bond (Ire) *B Smart*   58
2 ro c Portrait Gallery (Ire) - Musical Essence
4⁸ᵍᶠ 12⁸ˢ 7⁸ᵍˢ **0-0-3 £330**

Bonkers *T D Easterby*   56 a44
3 ch f Efisio - Flourishing (Ire)
9⁵ˢᵈ 10⁸ᵍˢ 6⁶ᵍˢ 8⁵ᵍᶠ 5⁶ˢᵈ **0-0-5**

Bonne De Fleur *B Smart*   80
2 b f Whittingham (Ire) - L'Estable Fleurie (Ire)
3⁵ᵍᶠ 1⁵ᵍᶠ 1⁶ᵍᶠ 2⁶ᵍᶠ 3⁶ᵍᶠ 2⁶ᵍᶠ **2-4-6
£10,415**

Bonnie Lad (Ire) *A Berry*   24
4 b g Tagula (Ire) - Sabonis (USA)
11⁵ᵍᶠ 8⁵ᵍ 10⁵ᵍˢ **0-0-3**

Bonny Ruan *D Haydn Jones*   67 a58
4 b f So Factual (USA) - Sans Diablo (Ire)
18⁵ᵍᶠ 5⁶ᵍᶠ 17⁶ᵍ 15⁶ᶠ 3⁶ᶠ 2⁵ˢʷ 3⁶ˢᵈ 8⁶ˢᵈ
12⁵ᵍᶠ 1⁵ˢʷ 12⁵ᵍᶠ **1-3-11 £3,759**

Bonsai (Ire) *R T Phillips*   19
2 b f Woodman (USA) - Karakia (Ire)
13⁶ᵍᶠ **0-0-1**

Bontadini *D Morris*   44 a70
4 b g Emarati (USA) - Kintail
11⁸ˢᵈ 2¹⁰ˢᵈ 9¹⁰ᶠ 10¹⁰ᵍᶠ 15⁸ˢᵈ 16⁸ˢᵈ 9¹⁴ˢ
0-1-7 £966

Bonus (Ire) *R Hannon*   114
3 b c Cadeaux Genereux - Khamseh
3⁶ᵍ 2⁶ᵍᶠ 1⁶ᵍᶠ 1⁶ᵍˢ 1⁶ᵍ 2⁶ᶠ 5⁶ᵍᶠ 1⁶ᵍ 5⁵ᵍᶠ
4-3-9 £90,837

Boogie Magic *C N Allen*   70
3 b f Wizard King - Dalby Dancer
7⁸ᵍ 13⁸ᵍᶠ 4⁸ˢ 8⁸ᵍˢ **0-0-4 £343**

Boogie Street *R Hannon*   104
2 b c Compton Place - Tart And A Half
5⁶ᵍ 1⁵ᵍᶠ 3⁶ᵍᶠ 4⁵ᵍ 1⁵ᵍ **2-1-5 £16,723**

Book Matched *B Smart*   51
2 b g Efisio - Princess Latifa

11⁷ᵍˢ 9⁶ᵍ **0-0-2**

Bookiesindexdotcom *J R Jenkins*   57 a62
2 b f Great Dane (Ire) - Fifth Emerald
7⁵ᵍᶠ 5⁶ᵍ 3⁷ᶠ 4⁷ᵍ 8⁷ᵍᶠ 4⁶ᶠ 6⁷ˢᵈ 2⁶ˢᵈ
2⁶ˢᵈ **0-4-10 £3,020**

Boom Or Bust (Ire) *Miss K M George*   55 a55
4 ch g Entrepreneur - Classic Affair (USA)
3¹²ˢʷ 9¹²ˢᵈ 7⁹ˢᵈ 5⁸ᵍᶠ 3¹²ᵍᶠ 2¹²ᶠ 8¹¹ᵍᶠ
10¹⁶ᵍᶠ **0-3-8 £1,710**

Boon Companion *John Berry*   11 a41
4 b g Sure Blade (USA) - Pea Green
9⁵ˢᵈ 17⁶ᵍˢ 18¹²ᵍᶠ 10¹²ˢᵈ **0-0-4**

Boozy Douz *H S Howe*
3 ch f Abou Zouz (USA) - Ackcontent (USA)
12⁸ˢᵈ **0-0-1**

Boppys Babe *J S Wainwright*   34
2 ch f Clan Of Roses - Joara (Fr)
10⁵ᵍˢ 9⁶ᵍᶠ 8⁵ᵍˢ 10⁵ᵍᶠ 13⁷ᵍ **0-0-5**

Boppys Princess *J S Wainwright*   31
2 b f Wizard King - Laurel Queen (Ire)
20⁶ᵍᶠ 14⁵ᵍᶠ 5⁶ᵍᶠ 10⁶ᵍᶠ 6⁷ᵍˢ 10⁸ᵍᶠ 9⁷ᵍ
12⁷ᵍᶠ **0-0-8**

Border Arrow *A M Balding*   106
8 ch g Selkirk (USA) - Nibbs Point (Ire)
3¹⁰ᵛˢ 8¹⁰ᵍ 5¹⁰ᵍ **0-0-3 £6,949**

Border Artist *D Nicholls*   71 a56
4 ch g Selkirk (USA) - Aunt Tate
4⁶ᵍᶠ 4⁷ˢᵈ 2⁸ᵍᶠ 8⁶ᶠ 1⁷ᵍᶠ 1⁷ᵍˢ 6⁷ᵍˢ 7⁶ᶠ
4⁷ᶠ 12⁶ᵍᶠ 3⁷ᵍᶠ 1⁶ᵍᶠ 1⁷ᵍᶠ 6⁷ᵍᶠ 14⁸ᵍ 11⁷ᵍᶠ
9⁸ᶠ 14⁸ᵍˢ **4-2-18 £26,850**

Border Castle *Sir Michael Stoute*   76
2 b c Grand Lodge (USA) - Tempting Prospect
4⁷ᵍ 4⁸ᵍᶠ 1⁸ᵍᶠ **1-0-3 £5,117**

Border Edge *J J Bridger*   95 a67
5 b g Beveled (USA) - Seymour Ann
1⁷ˢᵈ 4⁷ˢᵈ 7⁷ˢᵈ 3⁷ˢᵈ 5⁸ˢᵈ 9⁸ˢᵈ 13⁸ᵍ
1⁸ᵍᶠ 4⁸ᵍ 1⁸ᵍᶠ 4⁸ᵍᶠ 2⁷ᵍᶠ 2⁹ᵍᶠ 13⁸ᵍ 3⁸ᶠ 2⁸ᵍᶠ
12⁷ᵍᶠ 2⁶ᶠ 10⁸ᵍˢ **6-8-23 £41,613**

Border Music *A M Balding*   67 a77
2 b g Selkirk (USA) - Mara River
3⁸ᵍᶠ 1⁸ˢᵈ 6⁸ᵍᶠ **1-1-3 £4,092**

Border Run *M Mullineaux*
6 b g Missed Flight - Edraianthus
11¹²ˢᵈ **0-0-1**

Border Subject *R Charlton*   115
6 b g Selkirk (USA) - Topicality (USA)
6⁷ᵍᶠ 4⁶ᵍᶠ 1⁶ᵍᶠ 18⁶ᶠ 9⁶ᵍ **1-1-5 £17,378**

Border Tale *C Weedon*   85
3 b g Selkirk (USA) - Likely Story (Ire)
2¹²ᵍᶠ 2¹²ᵍᶠ 3¹²ᵍᶠ 11²ᵍ 4¹²ᵍˢ 2¹²ᵍ 3¹²ᵍˢ
6¹²ᵍᶠ 1¹²ᵍ 2¹¹ᵍᶠ 5¹⁰ᵍᶠ 4¹⁰ᵍ **2-6-12 £26,223**

Border Terrier (Ire) *M D Hammond*   62
5 b g Balnibarbi - Ring Side (Ire)
11⁷ˢʷ 2¹⁰ᵍᶠ 15¹⁰ᵍᶠ 5¹⁰ᵍ 13¹⁰ᵍˢ 1¹⁰ᵍ
15¹²ᵍᶠ **1-1-7 £3,587**

Boreas *L M Cumani*   112
8 b g In The Wings - Reamur
5¹²ᵍˢ 5¹⁶ᵍᶠ 4¹⁶ᵍ 6¹⁶ᵍᶠ **0-0-4 £11,500**

Bori Mirov (Ire) *Alex Fracas*   a49
5 ch h Carroll House - Borj Kadija (Fr)
9¹⁰ˢᵈ 11⁰ᵍˢ 6⁹ˢ 0¹⁰ʰᵒ **1-0-4 £5,195**

Boris The Spider *M D Hammond*   66
2 b g Makbul - Iry Vickers (USA)
8⁰ᵍᶠ 15⁶ˢᵈ 7⁶ᶠ 10⁶ᵍ **0-0-4**

Born In America (USA) *A P O'Brien*   78

2 b c Danzig (USA) - Flying Fairy
4⁶ᵍ 1⁵ᵍᶠ 12⁶ᵍᶠ 10⁶ᵍᶠ 7⁶ᵍ 6⁵ᵍ **1-0-6**
£8,396

Born Special P C Haslam   34 a23
4 b g Bluebird (USA) - Dixie Eyes Blazing (USA)
7⁸ˢᵈ 13⁷ᵍ **0-0-2**

Borodin G A Butler   a62
2 gr c Linamix (Fr) - Lady Of Jakarta (USA)
9⁸ˢᵈ **0-0-1**

Borodinsky A Berry   6
2 b c Magic Ring (Ire) - Valldemosa
14⁶ᵍ 14⁵ᵍ 13⁶ᵍ **0-0-3**

Boroughset Boy (Ire) J R Weymes   55
3 b/br g Woodborough (USA) - Alpine Sunset
8⁶ᵍᶠ 6⁷ᵍᶠ 6⁶ᵍᶠ 5⁵ᵍᶠ 9⁷ᵗ **0-0-5**

Borrego (Ire) C E Brittain   79
3 b c Green Desert (USA) - Pripet (USA)
11¹⁰ᵍᶠ 9⁷ᵍᶠ 7⁷ᵍᶠ 4¹⁰ᵍᶠ 13¹⁰ᵍᶠ 2⁸ᵍᶠ 1⁸ᵍᶠ
1⁸ᵍᶠ 2⁷ᵍᶠ **2-2-9 £12,213**

Boru Boru (Ire) P D Evans   56
4 b g Bluebird (USA) - Tudor Loom
13⁷ᵍᶠ 13⁸ᵍᶠ 11⁸ˢᵈ 11⁸ᵍᶠ **0-0-4**

Borzoi Maestro J L Spearing   79 a78
2 ch g Wolfhound (USA) - Ashkernazy (Ire)
10⁶ᵍᶠ 5⁵ᵍᶠ 6⁵ᵍᶠ 3⁵ᵍᶠ 7⁵ᵍᶠ 2⁵ˢᵈ 1⁵ˢᵈ 1⁵ᵍᶠ
1⁶ᶠᵗ 4⁶ᵍᶠ 4⁵ᵍᶠ 3⁵ᵍᶠ 10⁵ᵍᶠ 4⁵ᵍᶠ 9⁶ˢᵈ **3-2-15**
£14,369

Bosco (Ire) R Hannon   61
2 br c Petardia - Classic Goddess (Ire)
6⁶ᵍᶠ 7⁸ᵍᶠ 5⁸ᶠ **0-0-3**

Bosham Mill Jonjo O'Neill   97
5 ch g Nashwan (USA) - Mill On The Floss
7¹⁶ᵍᶠ **0-0-1**

Bosphorus D G Bridgwater   53 a51
4 b g Polish Precedent (USA) - Ancara
3¹²ˢᵈ 9¹²ˢᵈ 13¹⁰ᵍᶠ 12¹¹ᵍᶠ 4¹³ᶠ 3¹⁶ᶠᵗ 2¹⁵ˢᵈ
3¹⁶ˢᵈ 2¹³ᵍᶠ 5¹²ˢᵈ **0-4-10 £3,017**

Boss Man (Ire) T D Easterby   41
3 b g Entrepreneur - Triste Oeil (USA)
6¹⁰ᵍᶠ 12¹²ᵍᶠ 15¹⁷ᵍᶠ 8¹⁰ᵍᶠ **0-0-4**

Boston Lodge P F I Cole   96
3 ch g Grand Lodge (USA) - Ffestiniog (Ire)
3⁹ᵍᶠ 2⁸ᵍᶠ 4⁸ᵍ 7⁹ᵍ 12⁸ᵍᶠ 2⁸ᵍᶠ 3⁸ᵍᶠ 2⁸ᵍ
4⁸ᶠ 1⁸ᶠ **1-3-10 £22,974**

Bosworth Dixie (Ire) Miss J S Davis
3 b f Turtle Island (Ire) - Alice En Ballade
6⁶ᵍᶠ **0-0-1**

Botanical (USA) D R Loder   91
2 b c Seeking The Gold (USA) - Satin Flower (USA)
1⁶ᵍᶠ 2⁶ᵍᶠ 7⁷ᵍᶠ 4⁶ᵍᶠ **1-1-4 £22,995**

Bottom Drawer D J S Ffrench Davis
3 b g My Best Valentine - Little Egret
8⁹ᵍᶠ 10¹²ˢʷ **0-0-2**

Boudica (Ire) D W P Arbuthnot   a14
4 b f Alhaarth (Ire) - Supportive (Ire)
9⁶ˢᵈ **0-0-1**

Boule D'Or (Ire) R Ingram   75
2 b c Croco Rouge (Fr) - Saffron Crocus
1⁷ᵍᶠ 3⁷ᵍ 10⁸ᵍᶠ 9⁸ᵍᶠ **1-0-4 £6,948**

Boulton B N Doran   1
3 b c Syrtos - Penny Dip
15⁷ᵍᶠ 13¹⁰ᵍ 16⁸ᵍᶠ **0-0-3**

Boumahou (Ire) A P Jarvis   60 a70
3 b c Desert Story (Ire) - Kilbride Lass (Ire)
6⁹ᵍᶠ 4¹²ᵍ 4¹³ˢᵈ 12¹⁰ᵍᶠ **0-0-4 £274**

Bouncer W R Muir   26
2 ch g Night Shift (USA) - Blugem (Fr)
6⁵ᵍᶠ 12⁶ᵍᶠ 6⁶ᶠ **0-0-3**

Bouncing Bowdler S J Mahon   93
5 b g Mujadil (USA) - Prima Volta
7⁷ᵗ 6⁸ᶠᵗ 12⁹ᶠᵗ 5⁷ᵍ 7⁷ᵍᶠ 11⁷ᵍˢ 3⁸ᵍᶠ 4⁷ᵍ
2⁹ᵍᶠ 14⁸ᵍᶠ 10⁵ᵍ **0-2-11 £4,707**

Bound Mrs L Wadham   10
5 b g Kris - Tender Moment (Ire)
11¹²ᵍᶠ **0-0-1**

Boundless Prospect (USA) J W Hills   82
4 b g Boundary (USA) - Cape (USA)
15⁸ᵍ 16⁸ᵍ 5⁸ᵍᶠ 5⁸ᵍᶠ 7⁹ᵍᶠ 12⁹ᵍ **0-0-6**
£396

Bourgainville A M Balding   114 a107
5 b g Pivotal - Petonica (Ire)
5⁸ᵍ 4¹⁰ˢᵈ 3¹⁰ᵍᶠ 2¹⁰ᵍ 4¹²ᵍᶠ 5¹⁰ᵍᶠ 7¹⁰ᵍᶠ 5¹⁰ᶠ
2¹⁰ᵍᶠ 6⁹ᵍᶠ **0-2-10 £32,692**

Bourgeois T D Easterby   109
6 ch g Sanglamore (USA) - Bourbon Girl
1¹⁴ᵍᶠ 5¹⁹ᵍᶠ 2¹²ᵍˢ 19¹⁶ᵍˢ 3¹⁴ᵍᶠ 14¹⁴ᵍᶠ 3¹³ᵍᶠ
5¹⁵ᵍ 7¹³ᵍˢ **1-3-9 £34,220**

Bow River Gold J G Given   45
3 b f Rainbow Quest (USA) - Lady Blackfoot
7⁸ᵍᶠ 4⁸ᵍᶠ 12⁶ᵍᶠ **0-0-3 £285**

Bowing J H M Gosden   87
3 b g Desert Prince (Ire) - Introducing
3⁹ᵍᶠ 2¹¹ᵍ 13¹²ᵍᶠ 4¹²ᵍ 2¹⁰ᵍᶠ 3¹⁰ᵍᶠ **0-3-6**
£5,262

Bowlegs Billy J Balding   62 a24
3 gr g Raphane (USA) - Swallow Bay
2⁵ᵍˢ 5⁷ˢᵈ 8⁷ˢᵈ 17⁶ᵍᶠ 18⁵ᵍˢ **0-1-5**
£1,700

Bowling Along M E Sowersby   59
2 b f The West (USA) - Bystrouska
9⁶ᵍᶠ 10⁵ᶠ 8⁶ˢ 1⁶ᶠ 4⁶ᵍᶠ 4⁵ᵍ 3⁵ᵍᶠ 2⁷ᵍˢ
5⁶ᵍᶠ 3⁷ᵍᶠ 8⁶ᵍˢ **1-3-11 £7,019**

Bowman (USA) Saeed Bin Suroor   111
4 b c Irish River (Fr) - Cherokee Rose (Ire)
1⁸ᵍᶠ 9⁸ᵍᶠ **1-0-2 £18,560**

Bowsprit M R Channon   63 a58
3 ch g Fleetwood (Ire) - Longwood Lady
6⁸ˢᵈ 9¹⁰ˢᵈ 3⁸ᵍᶠ 18⁶ᵍᶠ 13⁸ᵍᶠ **0-0-5 £854**

Bowstring (Ire) J H M Gosden   44
2 b f Sadler's Wells (USA) - Cantanta
10⁸ˢ **0-0-1**

Bradley My Boy (Ire) Mrs A M Naughton   56
7 ch g Treasure Hunter - Clonaslee Baby
7¹⁴ᵍᶠ 7¹⁶ᶠ 3¹²ᵍᶠ 12¹²ᵍᶠ 4¹²ᶠ 8¹⁶ᵍᶠ 10¹²ᵍᶠ
0-1-7 £530

Brady Boys (USA) J G M O'Shea   a44
6 b g Cozzene (USA) - Elvia (USA)
3¹²ˢᵈ 6¹²ˢᵈ **0-1-2 £368**

Brain Box (Ire) T D Easterby   60
3 ch g Entrepreneur - Alcadia (Ire)
7¹²ᵍᶠ 9¹¹ᵍᶠ 10¹⁰ᵍᶠ **0-0-3**

Brain Teaser B J Meehan   44 a10
3 b f Mind Games - Salacious
5⁶ᵍᶠ 8⁷ᵍᶠ 11⁶ᵍᶠ 8⁶ˢᵈ 16⁸ᶠ **0-0-5**

Bramantino (Ire) R A Fahey   34
3 b g Perugino (USA) - Headrest
17⁷ᵍᶠ 12⁸ᵍᶠ 13¹⁰ᵍᶠ **0-0-3**

Bramley Dancer Miss B Sanders   38
4 b g Suave Dancer (USA) - Hailgaf
17¹⁰ᵍᶠ 11¹⁰ᵍᶠ 7¹⁶ᵍᶠ **0-0-3**

Brandy Cove *B Smart*   36 a71
6 b g Lugana Beach - Tender Moment (Ire)
3^{8sd} 1^{8sd} 3^{8sd} 2^{8sd} 1^{8sd} 17^{8g} **2-3-6**
£9,032

Brandywine Bay (Ire) *A P Jones*   50 a46
3 b f Mujadil (USA) - Ned's Contessa (Ire)
3^{7sd} 8^{7sd} 10^{8sd} 13^{7sd} 5^{6sd} 7^{5sd} 5^{6gf} 4^{6gf}
3^{6gf} 5^{7gf} 3^{8f} 5^{8gf} 8^{8gf} **0-4-13 £1,682**

Branston Melody *J G Given*   50 a50
2 b f Sri Pekan (USA) - Food Of Love
10^{5gf} 2^{5g} 6^{5sd} 8^{5gf} 3^{5gf} 5^{5gf} 7^{7gf} **0-2-7**
£1,654

Branston Nell *I A Wood*   48 a61
4 b f Classic Cliche (Ire) - Indefinite Article (Ire)
9^{16sd} 2^{16sd} 1^{16gf} 11^{17gf} 17^{11gf} **1-1-5**
£3,741

Branston Tiger *J G Given*   91 a77
4 b c Mark Of Esteem (Ire) - Tuxford Hideaway
4^{7sd} 6^{6g} 1^{6gs} 11^{6g} 5^{5gs} 17^{6g} 4^{6sd} **1-0-7**
£10,705

Brantwood (Ire) *B A McMahon*   89 a54
3 b c Lake Coniston (Ire) - Angelic Sounds (Ire)
13^{5gf} 5^{8g} 6^{6gs} 3^{6hy} 19^{6gf} 5^{6gf} 8^{5gs} 7^{8gf}
5^{8gf} 10^{6gf} 10^{6sd} 12^{5gf} **0-1-12 £4,498**

Brave Burt (Ire) *D Nicholls*   92
6 ch g Pips Pride - Friendly Song
12^{5g} 4^{5gf} 14^{5hy} 9^{5gf} 11^{5gf} 1^{5g} 3^{5g} **1-2-7**
£5,144

Brave Call (USA) *J W Hills*   92
3 ch c Theatrical - Darya (USA)
4^{8gf} 7^{8gf} 3^{10gf} 1^{10gf} **1-0-4 £7,586**

Brave Chief *J A Pickering*
2 ch c Komaite (USA) - Victoria Sioux
15^{6gf} **0-0-1**

Brave Dane (Ire) *A W Carroll*   64
5 b g Danehill (USA) - Nuriva (USA)
5^{11gf} 3^{11gf} 5^{12gf} 8^{10gf} 14^{8g} **0-1-5 £582**

Brave Dominie *C R Dore*   12 a40
3 b f Primo Dominie - Red Embers
6^{10sd} 4^{7sd} 11^{6sd} 7^{7sd} 12^{7sd} 6^{5f} 9^{6sd}
9^{10gf} 11^{8gf} **0-0-9**

Brave Knight *N Bycroft*   44
6 b g Presidium - Agnes Jane
9^{12gf} 7^{12gf} 6^{12gf} 6^{10gf} **0-0-4**

Brave Protector *A P Jones*
3 ch g Hector Protector (USA) - Brave Revival
17^{12gf} 10^{8sd} **0-0-2**

Bravo Dancer *M R Channon*   82
3 ch f Acatenango (Ger) - Nijoodh
3^{10f} 1^{8gs} 8^{8f} 2^{8gf} 6^{8gf} 7^{9gf} 1^{10gf} 11^{14s}
2-1-8 £13,456

Bravo Maestro (USA) *D W P Arbuthnot*   48 a85
2 b c Stravinsky (USA) - Amaranthus (USA)
13^{6gf} 1^{7sd} **1-0-2 £3,718**

Bravura *G L Moore*   43 a69
5 ch g Never So Bold - Sylvan Song
9^{10sd} 8^{10sd} 3^{10sd} 3^{8sd} 7^{8sd} 1^{10sd} 2^{8sd}
3^{10sd} 5^{10gf} **1-4-9 £5,294**

Brazilian Terrace *M L W Bell*   84
3 ch f Zilzal (USA) - Elaine's Honor (USA)
6^{8gf} 7^{7gf} 1^{8gf} 5^{8g} 2^{8gf} 8^{8gf} 2^{8gf} 5^{8gf}
3^{8g} 6^{8gf} 1^{8gf} 5^{8g} 17^{9gf} **2-2-13 £15,673**

Bread Of Heaven *Mrs A J Perrett*   81
2 b f Machiavellian (USA) - Khubza
3^{6g} 2^{6gf} 2^{6gf} 1^{6f} **1-2-4 £7,894**

Breathing Sun (Ire) *W J Musson*   75 a49
2 b c Bahhare (USA) - Zapata (Ire)
9^{5sd} 3^{6g} 10^{7gf} 1^{8gf} 1^{8g} **2-0-5 £19,974**

Breathtaking View (USA) *G Prodromou*   a66
7 b g Country Pine (USA) - Lituya Bay (USA)
8^{12sd} **0-0-1**

Brecongill Lad *D Nicholls*   65
11 b g Clantime - Chikala
7^{6f} 12^{5gf} 18^{6gf} 10^{6f} 1^{6f} 7^{5gf} 2^{6gf} 1^{5gf}
17^{5gf} 3^{5f} 2^{7gf} 10^{6f} 4^{6g} 8^{6gf} **2-4-14 £13,086**

Breezer *G B Balding*   62
3 b g Forzando - Lady Lacey
5^{8g} 5^{8gs} 10^{9gf} 9^{8g} **0-0-4**

Breezit (USA) *S R Bowring*   61
2 b f Stravinsky (USA) - Sharka
4^{5gf} 4^{5f} 7^{5g} 6^{7gf} 1^{6f} 12^{6gf} 6^{8gf} 13^{7gf}
3^{5f} 15^{5g} 9^{6f} **1-1-11 £4,328**

Bressbee (USA) *J W Unett*   59 a83
5 ch g Twining (USA) - Bressay (USA)
4^{9sd} 1^{9sw} 1^{10g} 7^{10f} 13^{8sd} 19^{10gf} 3^{8gs}
2-1-7 £28,535

Bretton *R Hollinshead*   40
2 b g Polar Prince (Ire) - Understudy
12^{6s} 6^{7g} 5^{8gf} 14^{10gf} **0-0-4**

Breuddwyd Lyn *D Burchell*   a45
5 br g Awesome - Royal Resort
9^{9sd} 4^{12sd} 7^{12sd} **0-1-3**

Brevity *J M Bradley*   72 a34
8 b g Tenby - Rive (USA)
12^{6sd} 19^{6g} 8^{6gf} 5^{6gf} 8^{6gs} 17^{6gf} 11^{6gf}
11^{6gf} 7^{6f} 5^{8f} 6^{6gf} 9^{6gf} 6^{5f} 11^{6f} 4^{6f} 17^{8gf}
11^{7gf} **0-0-17 £290**

Brian Boru *A P O'Brien*   125
3 b c Sadler's Wells (USA) - Eva Luna (USA)
16^{12g} 3^{10gy} 2^{12gf} 1^{15g} 4^{12g} 3^{12y} **1-2-6**
£374,321

Brian Potter *A Berry*   39
2 b g Pursuit Of Love - Elora Gorge (Ire)
6^{6g} 7^{5gf} 6^{6gs} 5^{7s} 7^{6g} **0-0-5 £868**

Briareus *A M Balding*   85
3 ch g Halling (USA) - Lower The Tone (Ire)
4^{8gf} 1^{10gf} 5^{10gs} 12^{10g} 3^{10gf} 2^{12gf} 4^{14g}
1-1-7 £9,300

Bridal White *M Wigham*   a12
7 b m Robellino (USA) - Alwatar (USA)
11^{7sd} 9^{5g} **0-0-2**

Bridewell (USA) *F Watson*   46
4 b g Woodman (USA) - La Alleged (USA)
11^{12gf} 9^{12g} 15^{12f} 12^{12gs} **0-0-4**

Bridge Pal *W Jarvis*   66 a58
3 ch f First Trump - White Domino
13^{6sd} 8^{7sd} 2^{8sw} 4^{8gf} 2^{10gf} 3^{10gf} 4^{12gf}
2^{12g} 7^{14gf} 9^{12gf} **0-4-10 £3,536**

Bridgewater Boys *K A Ryan*   56 a64
2 b g Atraf - Dunloe (Ire)
4^{5gf} 11^{5sd} 5^{5gf} 4^{6gs} 2^{6f} 3^{5gf} 9^{5gf} 2^{6gf}
5^{5gf} 6^{5g} **0-2-10 £3,977**

Brief Contact (Ire) *Jamie Poulton*   10 a41
5 b g Brief Truce (USA) - Incommunicado (Ire)
10^{12sd} 15^{16gf} **0-0-2**

Brief Goodbye *John Berry*   79
3 b g Slip Anchor - Queen Of Silk (Ire)
10^{6f} 4^{8gf} 8^{9gs} 1^{8gf} 6^{8f} 6^{10gf} 3^{8gf} **1-2-7**
£4,617

Briery Mec *H J Collingridge*   19 a43

8 b g Ron's Victory (USA) - Briery Fille
7¹²sd 13¹²sd 13¹³gf 18¹⁰gf **0-0-4**

Brigadore *J R Weymes*   82
4 b g Magic Ring (Ire) - Music Mistress (Ire)
20⁶gf 12⁵g 10⁵gf 11⁵gf 8⁵gs 5⁵gf 4⁵f
5⁵gf 4⁵gf 1⁵gf 3⁵g 8⁶gf 3⁶gf 13⁶gf 7⁵f 8⁵gf
8⁵g **1-2-17 £16,975**

Bright Eagle (Ire) *C F Wall*   61 a56
3 ch g Eagle Eyed (USA) - Lumiere (USA)
15⁷sd 7¹⁰gf 10¹⁰g 5¹⁰sd 3¹¹gf 2¹¹gf 3¹⁰gf
6¹²gf 5¹⁴gf 5¹⁶sd 9¹³gf **0-2-11 £2,397**

Bright Fire (Ire) *W J Musson*   58
2 b f Daggers Drawn (USA) - Jarmar Moon
13⁶g 6⁵gf **0-0-2**

Bright Green *J A B Old*
4 b g Green Desert (USA) - Shining High
10¹⁰g **0-0-1**

Bright Sky (Ire) *E Lellouche*   120
4 ch f Wolfhound (USA) - Bright Moon (USA)
2⁹s 18gs 3⁸gs 3¹⁰ho 6¹²f **1-3-5**
£100,100

Bright Spangle (Ire) *B Palling*   a46
4 ch f General Monash (USA) - No Shame
9¹⁵sd 12¹¹sd 5¹²sd 7¹²sw **0-0-4**

Bright Spark (Ire) *S Dow*   35
6 b g Sri Pekan (USA) - Exciting
8¹⁰gf 15⁷gs **0-0-2**

Bright Sun (Ire) *W Jarvis*   86
2 b c Desert Sun - Kealbra Lady
5⁶gf 2⁶gs 1⁶gf 8⁶g 8⁶gf **1-1-5 £5,602**

Brilliant Red *Jamie Poulton*   93 a100
10 b g Royal Academy - Red Comes Up (USA)
2¹⁰sd 3¹²sd 5¹⁰sd 7¹⁰sd 6¹⁰gf 15¹⁰g 3¹²gf
13¹⁰g 4¹²gf 3¹⁰gf 2¹⁰g 4¹⁰gs 4¹⁰gf **0-4-13**
£16,674

Brilliant Waters *D W P Arbuthnot*   58 a51
3 ch g Mark Of Esteem (Ire) - Faraway Waters
18⁷gs 6⁶sd 8⁶g 12⁶gf **0-0-4**

Brilliantrio *M C Chapman*   67 a37
5 ch m Selkirk (USA) - Loucoum (Fr)
3⁷gf 5⁸sd 15⁷gf 5⁸f 13¹⁰gf 1⁸f UR⁸gf
11¹⁰gf 6⁹f **1-1-9 £4,299**

Brillyant Dancer *Mrs A Duffield*   45
5 b m Environment Friend - Brillyant Glen (Ire)
14⁷gf 7¹⁰gf 8⁸g 12⁸f 9⁹gf 4⁹gf **0-0-6**
£294

Brimstone (Ire) *P L Gilligan*   14
8 ch g Ballad Rock - Blazing Glory (Ire)
15⁶gf **0-0-1**

Brindisi *B W Hills*   80
2 b f Dr Fong (USA) - Genoa
2⁷gf **0-1-1 £1,026**

Brios Boy *G A Harker*   43
3 ch g My Best Valentine - Rose Elegance
11⁶gf 6⁷f 9⁷f **0-0-3**

Brioso (Ire) *J M P Eustace*   24 a69
3 b c Victory Note (USA) - Presently
16⁶g 7⁷g 2⁶sd 1⁵sd 15⁵g 1⁶sd 7⁶sd 13⁵sd
14⁶sd **2-1-9 £8,222**

Brisscola *C B B Booth*   32
3 ch f First Trump - Princess Dancer
8¹⁰gf 8⁸sd 9⁸gf 14⁷gf 12⁸gf **0-0-5**

Broadway Blues *J W Hills*   59 a32
3 b f Broadway Flyer (USA) - Nashville Blues (Ire)
5¹⁰gf 6¹⁰gf 14¹²sd 10¹⁶sd **0-0-4**

Broadway Score (USA) *J W Hills*   107
5 b h Theatrical - Brocaro (USA)
21⁸g 2¹⁰gf 11⁹gf 7¹⁰g 14¹⁰g 10¹³gf
11¹⁰gf **1-1-8 £27,798**

Bronx Bomber *Dr J D Scargill*   40 a22
5 ch g Prince Sabo - Super Yankee (Ire)
6¹²gf 11¹²sd 11¹⁰gf **0-0-3**

Brooklands Lodge (USA) *John A Harris*   65
2 ch f Grand Lodge (USA) - Princess Dixieland (USA)
4⁶g 9⁸gf 5⁷gf **0-0-3 £360**

Brooklands Time (Ire) *I A Wood*   69 a61
2 b f Danetime (Ire) - Lute And Lyre (Ire)
4⁵gf 3⁵sd 3⁵sd **0-2-3 £1,375**

Brooklyn's Gold (USA) *Ian Williams*   83
8 b g Seeking The Gold (USA) - Brooklyn's Dance (Fr)
4¹⁰gf 7¹⁰gf **0-1-2 £556**

Brother Cadfael *John A Harris*   26 a40
2 ch g So Factual (USA) - High Habit
5⁵gf 3⁷sd 7⁶g 8⁶ft 13⁷f **0-0-5 £419**

Brother Kit *Dr J D Scargill*   a27
3 b g Bishop Of Cashel - Fabulous Night (Fr)
10⁸sd 16⁷sd **0-0-2**

Brough Supreme *H Morrison*   51
2 b g Sayaarr (USA) - Loriner's Lady
9⁸gs **0-0-1**

Broughton Bounty *W J Musson*   64
2 b f Bahamian Bounty - Sleave Silk (Ire)
15⁶g 6⁶gf 3⁷gf 5⁷gf **0-1-4 £685**

Broughton Knows *W J Musson*   26 a45
6 b g Most Welcome - Broughtons Pet (Ire)
12¹¹sd 8⁸sd 4¹⁶sd 1¹⁶sw 13¹²g 4¹⁴sd 3¹⁶sd
1-1-7 £3,364

Broughton Spirit *W J Musson*   56 a50
3 b f Bishop Of Cashel - Rainy Day Song
1⁸sw 1¹⁰gf 9¹⁰sd 7¹⁰gf 6¹⁰g 8¹²gs
8¹⁰gf **3-0-8 £9,044**

Broughton Zest *J R Best*   69 a67
4 b f Colonel Collins (USA) - Broughtons Relish
4¹⁰sd 7¹⁰sd 6¹²sd 2¹²g 1¹⁶gf 2¹²gf
13¹⁷gf 14¹⁰gf **1-2-9 £7,560**

Broughtons Mill *J A Supple*   16
8 gr g Ron's Victory (USA) - Sandra's Desire
12¹²gf 17¹⁰gf **0-0-2**

Brown Dragon *D Haydn Jones*   24
2 ch g Primo Dominie - Cole Slaw
14⁶gf 9⁶s **0-0-2**

Brown Holly *H E Haynes*
5 br g So Factual (USA) - Scarlett Holly
11¹⁵sd **0-0-1**

Brunel (Ire) *W J Haggas*   102
2 b c Marju (Ire) - Castlerahan (Ire)
2⁶g 2⁷gf 1⁷gf 5⁷gf **1-2-4 £8,871**

Brunston Castle *B R Millman*   58
3 b g Hector Protector (USA) - Villella
8¹⁰g 13¹⁰gf 16¹⁰gf 10¹²gf 1¹²gf 5¹²gf
1-0-6 £4,462

Bryano De Bergerac *J J Quinn*   66
4 b c Cyrano De Bergerac - Cow Pastures
15⁷gf 9⁶gf 7⁶f 10⁶gf 9⁵gf 3⁵g 7⁵gf
13⁵s 13⁶g **0-1-9 £668**

Bualadhbos (Ire) *F Jordan*   11 a48
4 b g Royal Applause - Goodnight Girl (Ire)
14¹¹sd 11¹⁰sd 11¹²sd 17¹²gf 18¹¹gf **0-0-5**

Bubble Up (Ire) *J G Portman*   46

4 b f Nicolotte - Mousseux (Ire)
14^{7gf} 0-0-1

Bubbling Fun *E A L Dunlop*   46
2 b f Marju (Ire) - Blushing Barada (USA)
10^{8gf} 2^{7gf} 0-0-2

Buchanan Street (Ire) *N A Callaghan*   30
2 b c Barathea (Ire) - Please Believe Me
13^{7g} 2^{6g} 16^{6g} 0-0-3 £1,448

Buckenham Stone *Mrs Lydia Pearce*   a18
4 ch f Wing Park - Walk That Walk
12^{7sd} 0-0-1

Buckeye Wonder (USA) *M A Jarvis*   84
2 b c Silver Hawk (USA) - Ameriflora (USA)
2^{8gf} 4^{8gf} 0-1-2 £2,121

Buckle In Baby (USA) *Mrs A M Naughton*   44
4 ch f Buckhar (USA) - Alzabella (USA)
5^{5gf} 14^{5f} 8^{6g} 0-0-3 £360

Bucks *D K Ivory*   69
6 b g Slip Anchor - Alligram (USA)
3^{12gf} 5^{16gf} 0-1-2 £316

Bud The Wiser *Miss D Mountain*   51 a5
3 ch g Forzando - Short And Sharp
10^{8sd} 9^{7gf} 12^{8sd} 7^{10f} 6^{10gf} 8^{10g} 2^{11gf}
18^{12gs} 9^{11gf} 4^{11gf} 11^{11gf} 5^{11gf} 0-1-12 £908

Bude *S A Brookshaw*   32
4 gr g Environment Friend - Gay Da Cheen (Ire)
7^{13gf} 0-0-1

Budelli (Ire) *M R Channon*   100
6 b g Elbio - Eves Temptation (Ire)
7^{6gf} 12^{6g} 4^{6gf} 3^{6gf} 19^{6f} 7^{6gf} 11^{6g} 6^{6gs}
3^{6gf} 4^{6gf} 3^{6g} 1^{6gf} 8^{6gf} 4^{6g} 16^{6gf} 2^{6gf} 9^{6g}
5^{6gf} 1-6-24
£27,613

Bugaloo Band (USA) *J R Jenkins*   50
6 b m Dixieland Band - Bugaloo (USA)
5^{5gf} 17^{6gf} 4^{6gf} 14^{6f} 20^{6g} 0-1-5

Buginarug *H A McWilliams*   31
3 b g Paris House - Sweeten Gale
12^{9s} 12^{6gf} 14^{6gf} 8^{5f} 6^{5gs} 5^{5gf} 16^{5gf}
10^{5g} 0-0-8

Bugle Call *K O Cunningham-Brown*   59 a18
3 b g Zamindar (USA) - Petillante
12^{6gs} 6^{8g} 12^{10gf} 7^{9sw} 9^{8g} 5^{8g} 9^{7g} 11^{7sw}
14^{7sd} 0-0-9

Bukit Fraser (Ire) *P F I Cole*   74
2 b c Sri Pekan (USA) - London Pride (USA)
3^{7g} 4^{8gf} 0-1-2 £1,476

Bulawayo *B A McMahon*   69 a63
6 b g Prince Sabo - Ra Ra Girl
3^{7sw} 4^{7sd} 3^{6sd} 3^{7sd} 5^{7sd} 5^{7sw} 7^{7sd} 1^{6gf}
7^{6gf} 3^{7gf} 6^{7gf} 3^{7sd} 1-5-12 £5,589

Bulgaria Moon *C Grant*   30
3 ch g Groom Dancer (USA) - Gai Bulga
9^{10gf} 10^{12f} 0-0-2

Bullfighter *N P Littmoden*   a64
4 b g Makbul - Bollin Victoria
6^{6sd} 1^{6sd} 13^{6sd} 8^{6sw} 3^{6sd} 12^{6sd} 7^{6sd}
1-1-7 £3,374

Bumblefly *Jamie Poulton*   a10
3 b g Petong - Doppio
9^{6sd} 0-0-1

Bumptious *M H Tompkins*   67
2 b c Mister Baileys - Gleam Of Light (Ire)
3^{8gf} 4^{8gf} 6^{8g} 0-0-3 £968

Bundaberg *P W Hiatt*   32

3 b c Komaite (USA) - Lizzy Cantle
12^{7sd} 5^{7gf} 0-0-2

Bundy *M Dods*   73
7 b g Ezzoud (Ire) - Sanctuary Cove
14^{6gs} 10^{6gf} 1^{6gs} 12^{7g} 10^{6gs} 4^{6g} 7^{6gs}
6^{7gf} 1^{6g} 4^{7g} 5^{7gf} 17^{6g} 2-1-12 £7,395

Bunino Ven *S C Williams*
2 gr c Silver Patriarch (Ire) - Plaything
17^{8gf} 13^{8gf} 16^{6gf} 0-0-3

Bunny Hug Bride *J G Given*   45
3 b f Groom Dancer (USA) - Tender Moment (Ire)
15^{7gf} 10^{10gf} 16^{14gf} 12^{9sw} 0-0-4

Bunyah (Ire) *E A L Dunlop*   53
2 ch f Distant View (USA) - Miss Mistletoes (Ire)
10^{7g} 0-0-1

Buon Amici *K R Burke*   22
2 b f Pivotal - Supreme Rose
9^{6s} 0-0-1

Burderop *R M Beckett*   45 a45
3 b f Sheikh Albadou - Grace Browning
11^{7sd} 9^{6gf} 9^{6gf} 12^{6gf} 6^{7f} 0-0-5

Burghmuir (Ire) *I Semple*   28
3 ch f Cadeaux Genereux - Luana
9^{8f} 7^{9gs} 12^{10gs} 0-0-3

Burgundy *P Mitchell*   78 a78
6 b g Lycius (USA) - Decant
9^{10sd} 11^{10sd} 11^{10sd} 13^{10gf} 11^{10g} 12^{12gf}
13^{10gf} 3^{10gf} 7^{10gf} 3^{12f} 8^{10g} 18^{sd} 5^{12sd} 1-1-13
£3,297

Burkees Graw (Ire) *D Nicholls*   64 a39
2 ch g Fayruz - Dancing Willma (Ire)
4^{5gf} 7^{5gf} 6^{5sd} 2^{5gf} 1^{5gf} 12^{6g} 7^{5gf} 5^{5gf}
3^{5gf} 1-1-9 £6,458

Burley Firebrand *J G Given*   65 a65
3 b c Bahamian Bounty - Vallauris
16^{7gf} 3^{8g} 1^{9g} 2^{9f} 10^{10gf} 2^{12sd} 7^{11sw}
1-3-7 £6,604

Burley Flame *J G Given*   46
2 b c Marju (Ire) - Tarsa
9^{8s} 0-0-1

Burlington Place *S Kirk*   59
2 b g Compton Place - Wandering Stranger
7^{6gf} 4^{6gf} 0-0-2

Burma *E A L Dunlop*   67
3 b f Sri Pekan (USA) - Bunting
11^{10gf} 3^{10gs} 5^{10gf} 5^{8gf} 9^{9gf} 0-1-5 £870

Burning Moon *J Noseda*   70
2 b c Bering - Triple Green
5^{7gf} 7^{8gf} 0-0-2

Burning Sun (USA) *H R A Cecil*   119
4 b c Danzig (USA) - Media Nox
3^{10g} 5^{11ys} 5^{10g} 0-0-3 £6,338

Burnt Copper (Ire) *J R Best*   62 a68
3 b g College Chapel - Try My Rosie
6^{7sd} 3^{8sd} 9^{10sd} 7^{10sd} 9^{6gf} 6^{7gf} 4^{10sd} 7^{10sd}
5^{7gf} 8^{10sd} 4^{8g} 2^{12gf} 5^{16gf} 10^{12g} 0-2-14
£1,987

Burry Brave *J S Goldie*   29
4 b g Presidium - Keep Mum
12^{5gs} 5^{6gf} 16^{5g} 9^{6gf} 0-0-4

Burton Gold *H Morrison*   33
3 b f Master Willie - Misowni
14^{10gf} 0-0-1

Bury St Edmunds (USA) *J R Fanshawe*   99
3 b c Swain (Ire) - Vibrant

4^{10g} 1^{9gf} 3^{10gf} 6^{8g} **1-0-4** £8,429

Buscador (USA) *W M Brisbourne* 59 a74
4 ch g Crafty Prospector (USA) - Fairway Flag (USA)
17^{7g} 3^{10gf} 8^{9gf} 3^{10gs} 6^{11g} 1^{9sd} 1^{9ft} 9^{8gf}
6^{9sd} **2-2-9** £7,846

Bush Cat (USA) *C E Brittain* 92
3 b f Kingmambo (USA) - Arbusha (USA)
14^{8gf} 6^{7gf} 4^{11gf} 5^{10gf} 10^{10gs} 5^{10gs} 5^{12gf}
6^{10gf} **0-0-8** £5,137

Bushie Bill *P R Hedger* a56
5 ch g Captain Webster - Mistress Royal
6^{12sd} **0-0-1**

Business *G A Ham* a18
4 br c Bluegrass Prince (Ire) - Dancing Doll (USA)
8^{9sw} 8^{8sd} **0-0-2**

Business Matters (Ire) *J C Fox* 62
3 b f Desert Style (Ire) - Hear Me
4^{6gf} 9^{9g} 18^{10f} 5^{6gf} 8^{9gf} 3^{8gf} 9^{6g} 7^{8gf}
8^{8gf} **0-1-9** £587

Business Mind *M W Easterby* 25
2 b g Mind Games - Business Woman
13^{5s} 4^{5gf} 14^{7gf} **0-0-3**

Business Traveller (Ire) *G A Swinbank* 45
3 ch g Titus Livius (Fr) - Dancing Venus
5^{10gf} 9^{11gs} 5^{14g} 4^{16gf} 8^{16gf} **0-0-5**

Bustan (Ire) *M P Tregoning* 112
4 c Darshaan - Dazzlingly Radiant
4^{10g} 4^{11g} 2^{10g} **0-1-3** £8,250

Busted Flush (Ire) *Andre Hermans* 59 a50
2 b g Desert Sun - Gold Stamp
5^{5g} 5^{5gf} 3^{5sd} 5^{9g} 6^{6sd} 2^{7f} 1^{6f} 1^{6gf} 2^{6f}
8^{5vs} **2-3-11** £8,678

Bustling Rio (Ire) *P C Haslam* 73 a73
7 b g Up And At 'Em - Une Venitienne (Fr)
2^{16sw} 11^{18g} 11^{17gf} 3^{17gf} 1^{17gf} 5^{18gf} 6^{16gf}
7^{17gf} **1-2-8** £10,082

Bustyerbubble *C N Kellett*
3 b f Sri Pekan (USA) - South Sea Bubble (Ire)
10^{10gf} **0-0-1**

Buthaina (Ire) *J L Dunlop* 72
3 b f Bahhare (USA) - Haddeyah (USA)
3^{7gf} 1^{8gf} **1-1-2** £2,983

Butrinto *B R Johnson* 45 a59
9 ch g Anshan - Bay Bay
9^{10sd} 1^{10sd} 8^{8sd} 8^{8sd} 9^{10f} 16^{10gs} 6^{8f}
5^{10gf} 7^{10sd} 7^{10sd} 14^{7g} 8^{10gf} **1-0-12** £2,961

Buy On The Red *W R Muir* 63 a63
2 b c Komaite (USA) - Red Rosein
4^{6sd} 2^{5gf} 4^{6g} **0-1-3** £1,155

Buy The Sport (USA) *Robert Barbara* 103 a108
3 b f Devil's Bag (USA) - Final Accord (USA)
1^{8sd} 5^{10gf} 6^{8g} 5^{8gf} 1^{9ft} 3^{9ft} 5^{9ft} **2-0-7**
£209,563

Buz Kiri (USA) *A W Carroll* 50 a52
5 b g Gulch (USA) - Whitecorners (USA)
10^{16sd} 6^{12sd} 6^{15gf} 11^{16gf} 6^{12gf} 8^{14f} 3^{12g}
7^{10gf} 8^{13gf} 4^{12gs} 6^{12gf} **0-1-11** £503

Buzz Buzz *C E Brittain* 67
2 b f Mtoto - Abuzz
7^{6gf} 2^{6gf} 10^{7gf} 4^{8gf} 10^{8g} **0-1-5** £2,340

By All Men (Ire) *N A Graham* a59
3 b g Among Men (USA) - Bellinzona
7^{8sd} **0-0-1**

By Definition (Ire) *J M Bradley* 18
5 gr m Definite Article - Miss Goodbody

12^{8sd} 12^{10g} 13^{8gf} **0-0-3**

By Far (Fr) *J E Hammond* 100
5 b h Machiavellian (USA) - Makri
18^{7gf} 3^{8gs} 9^{8gs} **0-0-3** £2,435

By Hec *M Dods* 43 a26
3 ch g Hector Protector (USA) - Dancing Wolf (Ire)
8^{10gf} 11^{8gs} 8^{12sd} 14^{14g} 5^{11g} **0-0-5**

Bygone Days *W J Haggas* 74
2 ch g Desert King (Ire) - May Light
9^{6g} 2^{5gf} **0-1-2** £902

Byinchka *S L Keightley* 49 a47
3 br g Inchinor - Bystrouska
10^{7sd} 9^{7gf} 8^{9sw} 6^{8gf} 7^{10gf} 4^{12gf} **0-0-6**

Byo (Ire) *M Quinn* 76 a76
5 gr g Paris House - Navan Royal (Ire)
2^{5sd} 4^{5sd} 6^{5sd} 4^{5sd} 1^{6f} 3^{5f} 2^{5gf} 3^{5g} 9^{6g}
6^{5gf} 2^{6f} 4^{6hd} 4^{5gf} 3^{6gf} 7^{5gf} 1^{6gf} 2^{6gf} 2^{5gf}
4^{5f} 8^{6f} **2-8-20** £17,488

Byron *D R Loder* 108
2 b c Green Desert (USA) - Gay Gallanta (USA)
1^{6gf} 4^{6gf} 3^{6gf} 1^{6gf} **2-1-4** £52,113

Ca Ne Fait Rien (Ire) *N M Babbage*
7 gr g Denel (Fr) - Fairytale-Ending
12^{12sw} **0-0-1**

Cabaret Quest *R C Guest* 23
7 ch g Pursuit Of Love - Cabaret Artiste
13^{10gf} **0-0-1**

Cabeza De Vaca *M Johnston* 76
3 ch g Lahib (USA) - Norbella
3^{7gf} 2^{8f} 2^{7f} **0-3-3** £3,426

Cache Creek (Ire) *P Hughes* 99
5 b m Marju (Ire) - Tongue River (USA)
11^{6gy} 1^{8s} 1^{10ys} 2^{8g} 4^{8s} 5^{7y} UR^{9gf} 7^{8gf}
5^{10gf} 3^{9gf} 5^{8gf} 13^{8g} **2-3-12** £34,149

Cadeau Speciale *R Guest* 29 a55
3 b f Cadeaux Genereux - Pat Or Else
6^{6sd} 3^{6sd} 7^{6sd} 10^{7gs} 9^{8sd} **0-0-5** £554

Cadeaux Des Mages *J G Given* 91
3 b g Cadeaux Genereux - On Tiptoes
1^{7gf} 6^{8gf} 2^{8s} **1-1-3** £6,941

Cadeaux Rouge (Ire) *Mrs P N Dutfield* 66
2 ch f Croco Rouge (Ire) - Gift Of Glory (Fr)
5^{7gf} 5^{7g} 6^{7g} 7^{8gf} **0-0-4**

Cadravel *J Gallagher* 42 a30
4 b g Cadeaux Genereux - Space Travel
13^{7sd} 11^{7gf} **0-0-2**

Cadwallader (USA) *M Johnston* 56 a6
3 ch g Kingmambo (USA) - Light On Your Feet (USA)
7^{12sd} 3^{12gf} 5^{12f} 12^{13g} **0-0-4** £830

Caernomore *W G M Turner* a39
5 b g Caerleon (USA) - Nuryana
12^{12sd} 5^{8sd} 7^{9sd} 10^{12sd} **0-0-4**

Caerphilly Gal *P L Gilligan* 60 a45
3 b f Averti (Ire) - Noble Lustre (USA)
10^{7sd} 8^{5sd} 7^{6sd} 16^{6gs} 11^{5gf} 3^{7gf} 5^{8g}
1^{7gf} 3^{7gf} 8^{7f} 4^{7gf} 8^{7gf} **1-2-12** £4,760

Caesarean Hunter (USA) *S Kirk* 67 a84
4 ch g Jade Hunter (USA) - Grey Fay (USA)
3^{13sd} 3^{12sd} 1^{11sd} 16^{12g} 9^{12gf} 2^{14f} 15^{16gf}
8^{12gf} 11^{6sd} 5^{14gf} **2-3-10** £8,096

Cafe Americano *D W P Arbuthnot* 59 a49
3 b g Labeeb - Coffee Ice
9^{8gf} 6^{8sd} 8^{7gf} 5^{6gf} 8^{8f} 7^{10gf} 16^{7f} **0-0-7**

Cafe Concerto (USA) *M L W Bell* 34

3 b f Trempolino (USA) - Charmie Carmie (USA)
5¹²gf 4¹²gf 11¹⁸t 0-0-3 £321

Cahan (Ire) S L Keightley 24
4 b f Up And At 'Em - Global Princess (USA)
9¹⁰gf 12¹⁰f 0-0-2

Cairns (UAE) M R Channon 104
2 b f Cadeaux Genereux - Tanami
1⁶gf 11⁷gf 2-0-2 £38,557

Caitland R Allan 41
4 b f Puissance - Lorlanne
6⁹gf 9¹⁴gf 7¹¹gf 8⁹gf 7¹⁶g 11¹²gf 6⁹gf
0-0-7

Cake It Easy (Ire) M Johnston 71
3 ch f Kendor (Fr) - Diese Memory (USA)
2¹²gs 1¹²hy 1-1-2 £6,706

Cal Mac H Morrison 91
4 b g Botanic (USA) - Shifting Mist
1⁸g 16⁸gf 6⁸gf 3⁸gf 6⁸gf 22⁷g 11⁸f 3⁸g
4⁸gf 1-2-9 £5,959

Cala (Fr) C E Brittain 98 a78
3 b f Desert Prince (Ire) - Badawi (USA)
3⁷sd 1⁷sd 1⁶gf 2⁷gf 4⁸g 5⁸f 10⁷gf 11⁶gf
2-2-8 £36,660

Calamint K C Bailey
4 gr g Kaldoun (Fr) - Coigach
14¹⁰gs 0-0-1

Calamintha R M Beckett 66
3 b f Mtoto - Calendula
5⁸g 7⁸f 3¹²gf 5¹⁴gf 8¹⁴gf 1¹⁴s 1-1-6
£2,676

Calara Hills W M Brisbourne 31 a43
2 ch f Bluegrass Prince (Ire) - Atlantic Line
14⁶gs 12⁸s 6⁸sd 0-0-3

Calbrae (Ire) D R C Elsworth a83
3 b f Indian Ridge - Willow Dale (Ire)
2⁵sd 2⁵sd PU⁵gf 0-2-3 £2,808

Calcar (Ire) Mrs S Lamyman 56 a50
3 b g Flying Spur (Aus) - Poscimur (Ire)
7¹⁰gf 8¹⁰sd 2¹³gs 7¹²sd 5¹⁶gs 12¹⁰gf 7¹²gs
0-1-7 £1,076

Calculus (Ire) J Nicol 48
3 b c Barathea (Ire) - Mood Swings (Ire)
8⁸gf 0-0-1

Calcutta B W Hills 110 a94
7 b h Indian Ridge - Echoing
6⁷gf 3⁸ft 6⁸ft 11⁸ft 5⁸gf 3⁸gf 9⁸gf 14⁸g
6⁸gf 5⁸gf 5⁸gf 4⁷g 5⁸g 3⁸gf 1⁸f 3⁷gf 1⁸gf 4⁸gf
2-3-18 £33,636

Caldy Dancer (Ire) M R Channon 102
2 ch f Soviet Star (USA) - Smile Awhile (USA)
1⁵gf 1⁵g 7⁵gf 12⁵gf 5⁶g 5⁷gf 2⁷gf 2-1-7
£26,971

Caledonian (Ire) D R C Elsworth 41
2 b c Soviet Star (USA) - Supercal
8⁷gs 0-0-1

Calendar Girl (Ire) P J Makin 53 a9
3 b f Revoque (Ire) - March Fourteenth (USA)
3⁵gf 5⁶gf 10⁶sd 0-1-3 £826

Caliban (Ire) Ian Williams 58 a63
5 ch g Rainbows For Life (Can) - Amour Toujours (Ire)
5¹⁶sd 11¹⁶sd 4¹²sd 5¹⁵sd 5¹⁵gf 8¹⁵sd 1-0-6
£2,926

Calibre (USA) J H M Gosden 98
3 b c Lear Fan (USA) - Carya (USA)
5¹⁰gf 2¹²g 0-0-2 £3,507

Californian Kristin Mulhall 108 a90
3 c c Zafonic (USA) - Asterita
1¹⁰sd 1¹⁰sd 3¹⁰sd 2¹⁰g 8¹⁰g 2-2-5
£48,183

Caliwag (Ire) Jamie Poulton 51 a54
7 b g Lahib (USA) - Mitsubishi Style
4¹⁰sd 6¹⁰sd 6¹²sd 10¹²gf 0-0-4 £296

Call Me Sunshine P C Haslam 69 a64
3 b f Robellino (USA) - Kirana
5⁸sd 4⁹gs 8⁸gs 2¹⁰g 0-1-4 £1,390

Call Of The Wild R A Fahey 65
3 ch g Wolfhound (USA) - Biba (Ire)
16⁷g 3⁸gf 5⁹gs 6⁸gf 8⁸f 3⁹g 4⁹f 6¹¹g
0-2-8 £1,813

Call The Mark (Ire) C N Kellett 15 a51
4 b g Goldmark (USA) - Shalerina (USA)
10⁷sd 3⁶sd 5⁷sd 12⁸sd 9⁷sd 18⁷gf 0-1-6
£427

Calligraphy W J Haggas 74
3 ch f Kris - Ink Pot (USA)
3⁷gf 8⁸gf 1⁷f 9⁸gf 1-1-4 £4,705

Calomeria R M Beckett 30 a29
2 b f Groom Dancer (USA) - Calendula
14⁷sd 16⁷gs 0-0-2

Calonnog (Ire) H R A Cecil 67
3 ch f Peintre Celebre (USA) - Meadow Spirit (USA)
5¹⁰sd 0-0-1

Calusa Lady (Ire) G B Balding 67
3 ch f Titus Livius (Fr) - Solas Abu (Ire)
4⁶gs 4⁶gf 6⁶gf 9⁶gf 0-1-4 £720

Camaderry (Ire) Mrs A M Naughton 44
5 ch g Dr Devious (Ire) - Rathvindon
11¹⁰g 10¹⁰g 0-0-2

Camaraderie A G Juckes a30
7 b g Most Welcome - Secret Valentine
7¹²sw 0-0-1

Camberley (Ire) P F I Cole 96
6 b g Sri Pekan (USA) - Nsx
1⁷gf 8⁷f 2⁷gs 16⁷g 1⁷gf 3⁷gf 2⁷g 2-3-7
£26,291

Camelot L M Cumani 98
4 br g Machiavellian (USA) - Bombazine (Ire)
7⁸gf 2⁸gf 1⁸gf 1⁸gf 6⁸gf 2-1-5 £33,686

Cameo Cooler Miss L A Perratt
4 ch g Inchinor - Mystique Smile
13⁷f 0-0-1

Cameo Role (Ger) C F Wall 73
3 b f Acatenango (Ger) - Coyaima (Ger)
1⁸gf 9⁸gf 13⁹gs 12⁷gf 1-0-4 £4,186

Camerosa A D Smith a33
7 b g Risk Me (Fr) - High Heather
7¹²sd 4¹⁶sd 8¹⁶sd 0-0-3

Camille Pissarro (USA) P F I Cole 98 a95
3 b g Red Ransom (USA) - Serenity
1⁸sd 3⁸gf 6⁸gf 2¹⁰gf 6¹⁰gf 2¹⁰g 5⁹gf 5¹¹gs
15⁸s 5⁸gf 3⁸gf 1-3-11 £17,000

Camlet L M Cumani 92
3 b f Green Desert (USA) - Brocade
10⁶gf 2⁶gf 10⁵gf 1⁶gf 10⁶gf 7⁶gf 1-1-6
£18,865

Camp Commander (Ire) C E Brittain 108
4 gr c Pennekamp (USA) - Khalatara (Ire)
7⁷gf 1⁷g 3⁸gf 2⁸gf 10⁷g 7⁸g 12⁷gf 12⁸gf
8⁷gf 1-2-9 £51,650

Campanini M R Channon 63

3 ch g Singspiel (Ire) - Fiddle-Dee-Dee (Ire)
7⁸ᵍᶠ 8¹¹ᵍᶠ 5¹¹ᵍ 8⁸ᵍᶠ 15⁸ᵍ **0-0-5**

Campbells Lad *A Berry*   43
2 b c Mind Games - T O O Mamma'S (Ire)
8⁶ᵍᶠ 5⁶ᵍ 4⁶ᵍˢ 15⁶ᵍᶠ **0-0-4**

Camrose *J L Dunlop*   75
2 c c Zafonic (USA) - Tularosa
4⁷ᵍ 3⁷ᵍ 2⁸ᵍᶠ 1⁹ᵍ **1-1-4 £6,275**

Camzo (USA) *P W Harris*   75 a76
5 ch g Diesis - Cary Grove (USA)
14¹²ᵍᶠ 4¹⁴ᶠ 10¹⁴ᵍᶠ 6¹²ᵍᶠ 5¹⁴ᵍᶠ 8¹⁴ᵍᶠ 3¹⁴ᵍᶠ
1¹⁶ˢᵈ **1-1-8 £3,108**

Can Can Flyer (Ire) *M Johnston*   56
2 ch c In The Wings - Can Can Lady
10⁸ᵍ **0-0-1**

Can't Buy Me Love *L Young*   65 a35
4 ch f Bijou D'Inde - Addicted To Love
12¹²ˢʷ 9¹⁰ˢᵈ 13⁸ʸ 1⁸ᵍ 3⁹ᶠ 8⁷ᵍ 11⁸ᶠ
16¹⁰ᶠ 9⁷ᵍᶠ **1-1-9 £5,207**

Canada *M C Pipe*   98
5 b g Ezzoud (Ire) - Chancel (USA)
15¹⁹ᵍᶠ 8¹⁴ᵍᶠ 4¹²ᵍᶠ 6¹²ᵍ 17¹⁴ᵍᶠ 2¹²ᵍᶠ 11¹²ᵍ
0-2-7 £7,451

Canadian Storm *M H Tompkins*   73 a43
2 gr c With Approval (Can) - Sheer Gold (USA)
13⁶ᵍᶠ 5⁷ᵍ 9⁷ˢᵈ **0-0-3**

Canatrice (Ire) *T D McCarthy*   51 a45
3 gr f Brief Truce (USA) - Cantata (Ire)
5¹⁰ᵍᶠ 4¹¹ᵍᶠ 3¹²ᶠ 4¹²ˢᵈ 7¹²ᵍᶠ 9¹⁴ᵍᶠ 1¹¹ᵍ
12¹²ˢᵈ 11¹⁰ᵍˢ **1-2-9 £4,666**

Candelabra *Sir Michael Stoute*   94
3 br f Grand Lodge (USA) - Chatterberry
1⁷ᵍᶠ 6⁷ᵍ 19⁷ᵍᶠ 9⁷ᶠ 17⁷ᵍᶠ **2-0-5 £8,115**

Candleriggs (Ire) *D Nicholls*   83
7 ch g Indian Ridge - Ridge Pool (Ire)
5⁵ᶠ 18⁶ᵍᶠ 6⁶ᵍᶠ 5⁵ᵍᶠ 13⁶ᶠ **0-0-5 £1,584**

Candy Anchor (Fr) *Andrew Reid*   38 a36
4 b f Slip Anchor - Kandavu
11¹²ˢᵈ 13¹²ᵍᶠ 3¹⁰ᶠ 9¹²ˢᵈ 6¹²ᵍᶠ **0-1-5
£428**

Canlis *K A Ryan*   42
4 b c Halling (USA) - Fajjoura (Ire)
10⁸ᵍᶠ 10⁸ᵍ 9⁸ᵍᶠ 14⁹ᵍˢ **0-0-4**

Canni Thinkaar (Ire) *P W Harris*   67
2 b g Alhaarth (Ire) - Cannikin (Ire)
8⁷ᵍ 4⁸ᵍᶠ 14⁸ᵍᶠ 6¹⁰ᵍᶠ **0-0-4 £389**

Cannon Fire (Fr) *M R Channon*   76
2 ch c Grand Lodge (USA) - Muirfield (Fr)
5⁷ᵍ 4⁸ᵍᶠ 2⁸ᵍᶠ 3⁸ᵍᶠ 3¹⁰ᶠ 3⁸ᶠ **0-1-6
£3,484**

Canosa (Ire) *E J Alston*   54
3 gr f Catrail (USA) - Abergwrle
11⁶ᵍ 6⁶ᵍᶠ 15⁶ᵍˢ 8⁷ᵍᶠ 10⁵ᵍ 7⁵ᵍᶠ
2⁵ᵍ 6⁵ᵍᶠ 4⁵ᵍᶠ **0-1-10 £1,468**

Canovas Kingdom *Bob Jones*   46
5 ch g Aragon - Joan's Venture
11⁸ᵍˢ 14⁸ᵍᶠ 15⁹ᵍᶠ 11⁶ᵍᶠ 9⁶ᵍᶠ 8⁷ᵍᶠ **0-0-6**

Cantemerle (Ire) *W M Brisbourne*   71
3 b f Bluebird (USA) - Legally Delicious
3¹¹ˢ 2¹²ʰʸ 7¹⁰ᵍˢ 9¹²ᵍᶠ 14¹¹ˢ 10¹⁰ᵍˢ 3¹²ᵍˢ
0-3-7 £2,904

Canterloupe (Ire) *P J Makin*   84 a82
5 b m Wolfhound (USA) - Missed Again
12⁶ˢ 8⁶ᵍᶠ 6⁶ᵍ 5⁶ᵍᶠ 3⁶ᵍ 3⁶ᵍᶠ 10⁶ᵍᶠ 5⁶ˢᵈ

0-2-8 **£6,201**

Cantoris *M Johnston*   70
3 b g Unfuwain (USA) - Choir Mistress
2¹⁰ᵍᶠ 7¹²ᶠ 4¹²ᵍ 6¹²ᵍˢ 19¹²ˢ 5¹²ᵍᶠ **0-1-6
£1,702**

Cantrip *R M Beckett*   70 a45
3 b f Celtic Swing - Circe
7¹⁰ˢᵈ 8¹⁰ᵍᶠ 9¹²ᵍ 1²¹⁴ᶠ 4¹²ᵍ 2¹²ᵍᶠ
6¹⁴ᵍᶠ 6¹⁴ᵍᶠ **1-2-9 £7,544**

Cap Ferrat *R Hannon*   88
3 b c Robellino (USA) - Trick (Ire)
4⁸ᵍᶠ 14⁸ᵍᶠ 6⁸ᵍᶠ 1¹¹ᵍ 10⁸ᵍᶠ 8¹²ᵍᶠ 2¹²ᵍᶠ
7¹⁰ᵍᶠ 1¹²ᵍᶠ 5¹²ᵍᶠ **2-0-10 £14,702**

Capal Garmon (Ire) *J H M Gosden*   91
5 b g Caerleon (USA) - Elevate
9¹⁰ᵍ 10¹³ᵍ **0-0-2**

Cape Coast (Ire) *P D Evans*   46 a20
6 b g Common Grounds - Strike It Rich (Fr)
11⁶ˢᵈ 4⁶ᵍ 11⁶ᵍᶠ 11⁶ᶠ 15⁷ᵍᶠ 11⁶ᵍᶠ **0-0-6
£296**

Cape Fear *B J Meehan*   108
2 b c Cape Cross (Ire) - Only In Dreams
1⁶ᵍ 1⁵ᵍᶠ 3⁶ᵍ 5⁶ᵍᶠ 2⁶ᵍᶠ 8⁷ᵍᶠ **2-2-6
£170,609**

Cape Fizz *Mrs G Harvey*   13
2 b f Efisio - Cape Siren
10⁶ᵍᶠ **0-0-1**

Cape Royal *Mrs J R Ramsden*   87
3 b g Prince Sabo - Indigo
2⁶ᵍ 1⁵ᵍᶠ 11⁵ᵍᶠ 2⁵ᵍᶠ 2⁵ᵍ 8⁵ᵍᶠ **1-3-6
£12,151**

Cape St Vincent *H Morrison*   75 a79
3 gr c Paris House - Cape Merino
4⁶ᵍᶠ 2⁶ˢᵈ 1⁶ᶠ 2⁶ᵍᶠ 8⁵ᵍᶠ 2⁶ˢᵈ 4⁷ˢᵈ **1-3-7
£7,406**

Cape Town (Ire) *R Hannon*   104
6 gr h Desert Style (Ire) - Rossaldene
20⁸ᵍ 5⁸ᵍ 3¹⁰ᵍ 1¹⁰ᵍ **1-1-4 £15,612**

Cape Trafalgar (Ire) *J A Osborne*   85 a55
2 b f Cape Cross (Ire) - West Escape
4⁵ᵍ 13⁶ᵍᶠ 2⁵ˢᵈ 5⁶ᵍᶠ 3⁶ᵍᶠ 1⁶ᵍᶠ 3⁶ᵍᶠ 1⁵ᵍᶠ
1⁵ᵍᶠ 1⁵ᶠ 4⁵ᵍ 7⁵ᵍᶠ 3⁶ᵍᶠ 10⁶ᵍᶠ 5⁶ᵍᶠ 9⁶ᵍᶠ 10⁵ˢ
4-3-17 £28,973

Cape Vincent *J H M Gosden*   80
2 b c Cape Cross (Ire) - Samhat Mtoto
9⁷ˢ 3⁸ᵍ **0-1-2 £1,120**

Caper *W M Brisbourne*   54
3 b g Salse (USA) - Spinning Mouse
10¹¹ᵍᶠ 6¹⁴ᵍᶠ 15¹⁴ᵍ **0-0-3**

Capetown Girl *K R Burke*   69 a49
2 b f Danzero (Aus) - Cavernista
3⁶ᵍᶠ 8⁶ᶠ 2⁶ᵍˢ 13⁷ᵍ 2⁷ᵍ 5⁷ˢᵈ **0-3-6
£3,481**

Capital Access *B J Meehan*   51 a36
4 b g Efisio - Thilda
11⁵ᵍ 13⁵ˢᵈ 5⁵ˢᵈ 8⁶ˢᵈ 15⁶ᵍ **0-0-5**

Capitano Corelli (Ire) *P F I Cole*   101
4 b c Sadler's Wells (USA) - Ahead
5¹²ᵍᶠ 11²ᵍᶠ 8¹⁴ᵍ 2¹¹ᵍ 18¹²ᵍ **1-1-5
£32,497**

Caplaw Song *A Berry*   38 a17
2 ch f Opening Verse (USA) - Mary From Dunlow
5⁶ˢ 4⁶ᶠ 7⁶ᵍᶠ 7⁷ᶠ 8⁷ʰᵗ 9⁵ˢᵈ 12⁷ᵍᶠ **0-0-7**

Capped For Victory (USA) *Sir Michael Stoute* 100
2 b c Red Ransom (USA) - Nazoo (Ire)

2^{7g} 3^{7gf} 2^{8gf} **0-2-3 £6,385**

Capriccio (Ire) *Mrs S C Bradburne*   54
6 gr g Robellino (USA) - Yamamah
10^{12g} 4^{13gf} 4^{16gf} **0-0-3 £663**

Capricho (Ire) *J Akehurst*   117
6 gr g Lake Coniston (Ire) - Star Spectacle
9^{7gf} 1^{6gf} 4^{6f} 4^{7g} 1^{6s} 10^{7vs} **2-2-6 £68,861**

Capricious *Lady Herries*   74
4 ch f Primo Dominie - Megan's Flight
1^{12gf} **1-0-1 £3,545**

Captain Becker (Ire) *M Johnston*   33
2 b c Cape Cross (Ire) - Zifta (USA)
10^{7gf} **0-0-1**

Captain Clipper *D Nicholls*   77
3 b g Royal Applause - Collide
6^{8g} 3^{8f} 3^{12s} 5^{10gf} 5^{8gf} 1^{10gf} 7^{10g} **1-1-7 £7,353**

Captain Cloudy *M Madgwick*   73 a63
3 b g Whittingham (Ire) - Money Supply
3^{5s} 9^{6g} 10^{6gf} 8^{7sd} 4^{6gf} 12^{5gf} 14^{6gs} **0-1-7 £1,072**

Captain Darling (Ire) *R M H Cowell*   71 a73
3 b g Pennekamp (USA) - Gale Warning (Ire)
5^{7gs} 3^{6gf} 4^{7f} 1^{7gf} 5^{8g} 4^{7gf} 5^{7gf} 14^{10gf} 4^{10sd} **1-1-9 £4,945**

Captain Ginger *A M Balding*   75
3 ch g Muhtarram (USA) - Brand
10^{7gf} 9^{6gf} 3^{7g} 4^{8gf} 8^{7gf} **0-0-5 £1,465**

Captain Hardy (Ire) *S Kirk*   82 a77
3 b g Victory Note (USA) - Airey Fairy (Ire)
2^{6sd} 9^{7sd} 1^{6sd} 5^{6sd} 6^{7gf} 6^{6gf} 6^{6gf} 2^{7gf} 8^{7g} 1^{8gf} 4^{8g} 4^{10s} 3^{8gf} 6^{9g} 4^{10gf} **2-4-16 £14,236**

Captain Marryat *P W Harris*   38
2 ch c Inchinor - Finlaggan
14^{8g} **0-0-1**

Captain Rio *D Nicholls*   110
4 ch c Pivotal - Beloved Visitor (USA)
7^{5gf} 2^{6s} 4^{5g} **0-1-3 £13,571**

Captain Saif *R Hannon*   98
3 b c Compton Place - Bahawir Pour (USA)
5^{8gf} 6^{8gf} 6^{8gf} 3^{7g} 5^{6gf} **0-0-5 £3,846**

Captain Sensible *D Nicholls*   45
3 ch g Pivotal - Il Doria (Ire)
8^{6g} 12^{8gf} 7^{5gs} 9^{6gf} 13^{5gf} **0-0-5**

Captain Venti *J J Quinn*   85
4 br g Ventiquattrofogli - Lady Liza
23^{8g} 11^{8gf} 10^{8gf} 7^{8hy} 2^{8gs} 12^{9gf} **0-1-6 £1,756**

Capulette (Ire) *W Jarvis*   82
3 b f Grand Lodge (USA) - Malabarista (Fr)
5^{11gf} 10^{12gf} 7^{10gf} 2^{8gf} 1^{8gf} 6^{8gf} 3^{8g} 2^{7gf} 3^{7gf} 1^{8gf} 6^{8g} **2-4-11 £14,543**

Caqui D'Or (Ire) *J L Dunlop*   72
5 b g Danehill (USA) - Ghaiya (USA)
10^{14g} 10^{16g} 9^{14s} 8^{16g} **0-0-4**

Cara Bella *D R Loder*   76
2 ch f Seeking The Gold (USA) - Cherokee Rose (Ire)
4^{6gf} **0-0-1 £547**

Cara Fantasy (Ire) *J L Dunlop*   84
3 b f Sadler's Wells (USA) - Gay Fantasy
1^{12gf} 6^{12gf} 6^{12gf} 1^{12g} **2-0-4 £13,819**

Caracal (Ire) *P J Makin*   23
2 b c Desert Style (Ire) - Telemania (Ire)

14^{6gf} **0-0-1**

Caracara (Ire) *M Johnston*   80
2 ch f Nashwan (USA) - Vividimagination (USA)
2^{7g} 1^{7gf} 9^{8g} **1-1-3 £7,130**

Card Table *J R Weymes*   20
2 ch f First Trump - Murray Grey
5^{7gf} 10^{7f} 8^{7g} **0-0-3**

Cardinal Venture (Ire) *K A Ryan*   94
5 b g Bishop Of Cashel - Phoenix Venture (Ire)
12^{6g} 1^{7g} 9^{7g} 10^{7gf} 3^{8gf} 5^{7g} 3^{7g} 2^{8f} 2^{7g} 8^{8g} 9^{8gs} **1-3-11 £17,611**

Carenage (Ire) *J L Dunlop*   83
3 b f Alzao (USA) - Key Change (Ire)
3^{10gf} 1^{12gf} 8^{12gf} **1-1-3 £6,591**

Carens Hero (Ire) *R Brotherton*
6 ch g Petardia - Clearglade
15^{8sw} **0-0-1**

Cargo *H J Collingridge*   57 a56
4 b g Emarati (USA) - Portvasco
8^{5sd} 5^{6sd} 10^{6sd} 9^{5sd} 5^{6sd} 10^{6f} 11^{6gf} 7^{5gf} 12^{5gf} **0-0-9**

Caribbean Blue *R M Whitaker*   61
2 b f First Trump - Something Blue
6^{6gf} 16^{6gf} 8^{6gf} **0-0-3**

Caribbean Coral *C F Wall*   97
4 ch g Brief Truce (USA) - Caribbean Star
18^{6gf} 1^{5gf} 8^{5gs} 6^{5g} 7^{5gf} 9^{5s} 9^{5g} 1^{5g} 2^{5gf} **2-1-9 £12,773**

Caribbean Man *B J Llewellyn*   69
3 b g Hector Protector (USA) - Caribbean Star
7^{8gf} 12^{7gf} 12^{7gf} 13^{8gf} **0-0-4**

Caribbean Sun (Ire) *B Palling*   46
3 b c Grand Lodge (USA) - Carranita (Ire)
8^{8hy} 17^{10gf} **0-0-2**

Carini *H Candy*   91
2 b f Vettori (Ire) - Secret Waters
1^{7gf} 18^{8gf} **2-0-2 £7,178**

Carino Amoure *C G Cox*   59
2 ch f Pursuit Of Love - Pretty Pollyanna
7^{7gf} 8^{7gf} **0-0-2**

Cark *J Balding*   56 a60
5 b g Farfelu - Precious Girl
5^{5sw} 9^{5sd} 15^{5gf} 4^{5hy} 4^{5gs} 1^{5gf} 9^{5f} 9^{5f} 3^{5f} 4^{5gf} 14^{5sw} 13^{5gf} 7^{5gf} **1-2-13 £5,618**

Carla Moon *C F Wall*   66
2 b f Desert Prince (Ire) - Khambani (Ire)
6^{6gf} 9^{6gs} 10^{6s} **0-0-3**

Carlburg (Ire) *C E Brittain*   68
2 b c Barathea (Ire) - Ichnusa
9^{6gf} 10^{6gf} 2^{7g} 12^{7g} 9^{7gf} **0-1-5 £2,004**

Carlton (Ire) *J J Quinn*   81 a72
9 ch g Thatching - Hooray Lady
5^{7sd} 5^{7sd} 16^{6sd} 3^{7sw} 16^{6s} 16^{9g} 10^{6gs} 5^{5gf} 5^{8sd} 7^{6g} 11^{6g} 11^{7gf} **3-1-13 £10,535**

Carmen Jones *J Hetherton*   47
3 b f Zamindar (USA) - Sipsi Fach
7^{10gf} 7^{9gf} 9^{12f} 11^{12gf} **0-0-4**

Carmine Silk (Ire) *J L Dunlop*   63
2 b c Barathea (Ire) - Scarlet Plume
9^{7g} PU^{12gf} **0-0-2**

Carnage (Ire) *P Bowen*   a48
6 b g Catrail (USA) - Caranina (USA)
6^{12sd} 7^{14sd} **0-0-2**

Carnival Dancer *Mrs A J Perrett*   122
5 b h Sadler's Wells (USA) - Red Carnival (USA)

5^{10g} 1^{10g} 3^{9s} 1^{10gs} 2^{10gf} 2^{10gf} 1^{10gs}
11^{10ho} **3-3-8 £163,941**

Carnt Spell *Ms Deborah J Evans*
2 b g Wizard King - Forever Shineing
PU^{8s} 9^{8sd} 7^{7g} **0-0-3**

Carolina Morning (Ire) *H J Collingridge*
3 gr f Entrepreneur - Caroline Lady (Jpn)
17^{8gf} **0-0-1**

Carollan (Ire) *R Guest*   a36
4 b f Marju (Ire) - Caroline Lady (Jpn)
13^{7sd} 13^{7sd} **0-0-2**

Carolou's Court *A P Jarvis*   63
2 b f Vettori (Ire) - Glascoed
9^{6gf} 5^{6g} 8^{6gf} 6^{7gf} 5^{6gf} 9^{5gf} **0-0-6**

Carols Choice *A Sadik*   a63
6 ch m Emarati (USA) - Lucky Song
6^{5sd} 11^{5sw} 5^{5sd} 4^{5sw} 6^{5sd} 2^{5sd} 4^{5sd} 7^{6sd}
5^{5sd} 9^{5sd} **0-1-10 £672**

Caronte (Ire) *S R Bowring*   44 a54
3 b g Sesaro (USA) - Go Likecrazy
6^{6sd} 8^{5sd} 7^{6sd} 2^{8sw} 5^{7sw} 10^{8sd} 9^{6sd} 9^{5gf}
4^{7gf} 6^{7f} 8^{8gf} 13^{6gf} 9^{8gs} 6^{6sd} 13^{5gf} 14^{7gf}
0-1-16 £1,096

Caroubier (Ire) *Ian Williams*   74 a86
3 ch g Woodborough (USA) - Patsy Grimes
1^{8sd} 1^{8sd} 2^{9sw} 8^{10sd} 3^{8sw} 2^{8sd} 1^{8sd} 1^{8sd}
12^{8sf} 8^{8f} 1^{8f} 5^{8gf} 8^{8g} 2^{10gs} **5-3-14 £20,703**

Carpet Lover (Ire) *Mrs P N Dutfield*   39
3 b f Fayruz - Bold As Love
8^{5gf} **0-0-1**

Carriacou *P W D'Arcy*   76
2 b f Mark Of Esteem (Ire) - Cockatoo Island
5^{6gf} 2^{8gs} 2^{8s} 8^{10gs} **0-2-4 £2,628**

Carrizo Creek (Ire) *B J Meehan*   106
2 b c Charnwood Forest (Ire) - Violet Spring (Ire)
3^{6gf} 1^{6gf} 1^{6y} 1^{6g} 5^{6s} **3-1-5 £99,897**

Carrowdore (Ire) *R Hannon*   82 a82
3 b c Danehill (USA) - Euromill
3^{10g} 3^{10sd} 5^{12g} 7^{10gf} 6^{10gf} 6^{8gf} 2^{10f} 3^{9gf}
3^{9gf} 4^{9g} 5^{10sd} 2^{8sd} 2^{10sd} **0-5-13 £7,568**

Carry On Doc *J W Hills*   71
2 b c Dr Devious (Ire) - Florentynna Bay
5^{7f} 3^{7gf} 5^{7gf} 5^{7gf} **0-1-4 £638**

Carry On Katie (USA) *J Noseda*   109
2 br f Fasliyev (USA) - Dinka Raja (USA)
1^{6gf} 1^{6g} 1^{6gf} **3-0-3 £153,308**

Carry The Fire (USA) *M J Roberts*   a32
3 ch c Smoke Glacken (USA) - Vibrant Future (USA)
9^{7sd} 10^{10sd} 11^{10sd} **0-0-3**

Carte Noire *J G Portman*   67
2 b f Revoque (Ire) - Coffee Cream
6^{6gf} 10^{7gf} 3^{8gf} 12^{8gs} **0-1-4 £784**

Carte Sauvage (USA) *M Johnston*   96
2 gr/ro c Kris S (USA) - See You (USA)
4^{7gf} 1^{7g} 2^{8g} 3^{8gf} 3^{10gs} **1-3-5 £13,394**

Cartography (Ire) *M A Jarvis*   104
2 b c Zafonic (USA) - Sans Escale (USA)
1^{6gf} 3^{6g} 1^{5gs} 7^{5gf} **2-1-4 £11,339**

Cartronageeraghlad (Ire) *J A Osborne*   78 a55
2 b c Mujadil (USA) - Night Scent (Ire)
17^{6gf} 7^{6gf} 1^{6sd} 6^{7sd} 4^{8gs} 1^{7g} **2-1-6
£8,185**

Casantella *M G Quinlan*   43
2 b f Atraf - Ramajana (USA)
6^{6gf} 10^{7gf} 10^{6gf} 13^{7gf} **0-0-4**

Casarabonela *T E Powell*   18 a29
3 b f Magic Ring (Ire) - Carmenoura (Ire)
12^{6sd} 10^{8gf} **0-0-2**

Case History *J J Bridger*
3 br g Case Law - Brigadore Gold
8^{8gf} **0-0-1**

Cash *Paul Johnson*   a86
5 b g Bishop Of Cashel - Ballad Island
8^{5sw} 7^{5sd} 7^{5sd} 3^{5sd} 14^{5sd} 13^{5sd} 20^{5gs}
11^{8sd} **0-1-8 £474**

Cashel Mead *J L Spearing*   44
3 b f Bishop Of Cashel - Island Mead
16^{7g} 16^{7g} 14^{8s} **0-0-3**

Cashema (Ire) *Mrs P N Dutfield*   47
2 b f Cape Cross (Ire) - Miss Shema (USA)
9^{7gf} 9^{7f} 13^{8gf} **0-0-3**

Cashneem (Ire) *W M Brisbourne*   68
5 b g Case Law - Haanem
18^{6gs} 14^{7f} 13^{6gf} 7^{6gf} 4^{7gf} 1^{8gf} 4^{8gf}
1^{7gf} 10^{7gs} 13^{8gf} **2-0-10 £9,257**

Caspian Dusk *W G M Turner*   50
2 b g Up And At 'Em - Caspian Morn
4^{5gf} 14^{6gf} 6^{7gf} **0-0-3 £334**

Cassanos (Ire) *Miss Gay Kelleway*   57 a46
2 b c Ali-Royal (Ire) - I'm Your Girl
10^{6gf} 19^{8gf} 7^{7sd} **0-0-3**

Casse-Noisette (Ire) *Miss Z C Davison*   7
5 b m Brief Truce (USA) - Highdrive
15^{12g} 9^{7f} 13^{10f} **0-0-3**

Cassiodorus *E A L Dunlop*   12
2 ch g Efisio - Chicodove
8^{7f} 17^{8s} **0-0-2**

Cassis (USA) *Kathy Walsh*   109
3 b f Red Ransom (USA) - Minstress (USA)
9^{7gf} 4^{8gf} 1^{10gf} 5^{11g} 6^{10g} 4^{9f} 7^{10f} **1-0-7
£71,836**

Cast Iron *J R Boyle*   a22
4 b g Efisio - Misellina (Fr)
11^{10sd} 12^{8sd} 8^{9sw} **0-0-3**

Castagna (USA) *H R A Cecil*   49
2 ch f Horse Chestnut (SAF) - Thrilling Day
8^{8s} **0-0-1**

Castaigne (Fr) *B W Duke*   72
4 ch f Pivotal - Storm Warning
8^{7gf} 10^{7g} 5^{6gs} 4^{7gf} 8^{7gf} 4^{8f} 4^{7g} 6^{8g}
2^{8gf} 5^{8gf} 8^{10gf} 6^{8gf} 7^{8g} 2^{8gf} 4^{8f} 15^{8sd} **0-2-17
£3,951**

Castaway Queen (Ire) *W R Muir*   69 a52
4 ch f Selkirk (USA) - Surfing
10^{9g} 12^{10sd} 5^{8gf} 3^{10gf} 3^{10g} 5^{9gf} 2^{10g}
15^{9g} 5^{10gf} 6^{10f} 2^{10gf} 10^{10gf} **0-4-12 £3,372**

Castle Frome (Ire) *Miss K B Boutflower*   58 a37
4 b g Spectrum (Ire) - Vendimia
7^{8gs} 7^{10gf} 5^{10f} 9^{8gf} 6^{7g} 14^{8gf} **0-0-7**

Castle Ring *R Hollinshead*   61 a49
4 b g Sri Pekan (USA) - Understudy
8^{12sd} 5^{9sw} 14^{10g} 7^{10g} 7^{12sd} 12^{10gf} 1^{10gf}
16^{11gf} 8^{10gf} 14^{12f} **1-0-10 £3,360**

Castle River (USA) *B G Powell*   60
4 b g Irish River (Fr) - Castellina (USA)
12^{8f} 19^{8gf} 12^{8gf} 11^{10g} 7^{10f} 2^{10gf} 10^{10gf}
0-1-7 £610

Castlebridge *K R Burke*   8
6 b g Batshoof - Super Sisters (Aus)

16¹²ᵍᶠ **0-0-1**

Castleshane (Ire) *S Gollings*   100
6 b g Kris - Ahbab (Ire)
10¹⁰ᵍ 8¹²ᵍᶠ 4¹⁰ᵍᶠ 7¹⁰ᵍᶠ 1¹⁰ᵍᶠ 1¹⁰ᶠ 2¹¹ᵍᶠ
1¹⁰ᵍᶠ 12¹¹ᵍᶠ 11¹²ᵍ 11¹⁰ᵍ 8¹⁰ᵍᶠ 15¹⁰ᵍᶠ **3-1-13**
£33,283

Castleton *H J Cyzer*   100
2 b c Cape Cross (Ire) - Craigmill
3⁶ᵍᶠ 4⁷ᵍˢ **0-1-2 £4,932**

Casual Fame (USA) *M Quinn*   a20
5 b h Quest For Fame - Never A Care (USA)
7¹²ᵍ 12¹⁰ˢᵈ 15¹²ᵍᶠ 9¹⁶ᵍ **0-0-4**

Casual Look (USA) *N J Howard*   114
3 b f Red Ransom (USA) - Style Setter (USA)
6⁸ᵍᶠ 1¹²ᵍ 7¹²ᵍᶠ 3¹²ᵍ 8¹²ᵍˢ 3¹ᵍᶠ **1-2-6**
£300,905

Cat Ona High (USA) *Mrs A J Perrett*   106
3 ch g Tabasco Cat (USA) - Uforia (USA)
10¹⁰ᵍᶠ 4⁸ᵍ 6⁸ᵍᶠ 2⁸ᵍᶠ 4⁹ᵍ **0-1-5 £5,467**

Cat's Whiskers *M W Easterby*   101
4 b g Catrail (USA) - Haut Volee
10⁸ᵍ 5⁸ᵍᶠ 2⁸ᵍ 2¹⁰ᵍᶠ 11⁹ᵍᶠ 14¹⁰ᵍᶠ 14⁸ᵍᶠ
18¹⁰ᵍ **0-2-8 £16,361**

Catalini *M R Channon*   80
2 ch c Seeking The Gold (USA) - Calando (USA)
5⁷ᵍ 5⁷ᵍᶠ 3⁷ᵍᶠ 6⁷ᵍˢ 3⁷ᵍ **0-2-5 £1,428**

Catch The Cat (Ire) *J S Wainwright*   74 a53
4 b g Catrail (USA) - Tongabezi (Ire)
12⁶ᵍᶠ 16⁵ᵍᶠ 8⁷ˢᵈ 3⁵ᵍᶠ 3⁵ᵍᶠ 2⁵ᵍ 1⁵ᵍᶠ 6⁵ᵍᶠ
4⁵ᵍᶠ 11⁵ᵍᶠ 5⁵ˢʷ 1⁵ᵍ 7⁵ᵍᶠ 16⁵ᵍ 5⁵ᵍᶠ 6⁵ᵍˢ 9⁵ᵍ
2-3-17 £13,715

Catch The Fox *J J Bridger*   47
3 b g Fraam - Versaillesprincess
16⁹ᵍᶠ 16⁸ᵍᶠ 15⁷ᵍᶠ 5⁸ᶠ 16⁹ᵍ **0-0-5**

Catch The Wind *I A Wood*   77
2 b f Bahamian Bounty - Tinkerbird
3⁵ᵍˢ 4⁶ᵍᶠ 1⁵ᵍᶠ 9⁶ᵍ **1-1-4 £8,008**

Catchthebatch *M J Wallace*   56 a58
7 b g Beveled (USA) - Batchworth Dancer
6⁵ᵍᶠ 7⁵ᵍᶠ 5⁶ᵍᶠ 15⁵ˢʷ 2⁵ᵍᶠ 9⁵ᵍᶠ **0-1-6**
£664

Cateel Bay *H Alexander*   5
5 ch m Most Welcome - Calachuchi
12¹⁴ᵍᶠ **0-0-1**

Caterham Common *D W Chapman*   34 a7
4 b g Common Grounds - Pennine Pink (Ire)
11⁸ˢᵈ 15⁸ˢᵈ 6⁷ˢʷ 16⁸ˢᵈ 14⁷ᶠ 11¹²ᵍᶠ 13⁶ˢ
8⁶ᶠ **0-0-8**

Catherine Howard *M R Channon*   68
2 b f Kingmambo (USA) - Darling Flame (USA)
1⁶ᵍ **1-0-1 £5,213**

Cathy Pee *J Hetherton*   24
2 ch f Groom Dancer (USA) - Stormswept (USA)
12⁵ᵍᶠ 13⁶ᵍᶠ 5⁶ᵍᶠ **0-0-3**

Cathy Ruan *D Haydn Jones*
3 bl f Robellino (USA) - Q Factor
10⁶ˢᵈ **0-0-1**

Catie Dash *R M Beckett*   79
2 ch f Daggers Drawn (USA) - Papita (Ire)
2⁵ᵍᶠ 2⁵ᵍᶠ 1⁵ᵍᶠ 5⁵ᵍ 1⁵ᶠ **2-2-5 £7,779**

Catmint *Mrs P N Dutfield*   88
3 b f Piccolo - Kitty Kitty Cancan
4⁵ᵍ 8⁶ᵍ 12⁵ᵍᶠ 8⁶ᵍᶠ **0-0-4 £438**

Catstar (USA) *D R Loder*   102
2 b f Storm Cat (USA) - Advancing Star (USA)

1⁵ᵍ 2⁵ᵍᶠ **1-1-2 £19,084**

Caught In The Dark *J L Dunlop*   86
3 b f Night Shift (USA) - Captive Heart
5⁶ᵍᶠ 3⁶ᵍᶠ 2⁶ᵍˢ 7⁶ᵍᶠ 2⁶ᵍᶠ 9⁶ᵍᶠ 1⁶ᵍᶠ 5⁵ᶠ
18⁶ᶠ **1-2-9 £11,281**

Caught Out *A Berry*   64
3 b g Ordway (USA) - Catch (USA)
7⁸ᵍˢ 3⁷ᵍᶠ 7⁸ᵍᶠ 8⁶ᵍᶠ 8⁷ᶠ 5⁷ᶠ 8⁷ᵍ 6⁶ᵍᶠ 7⁶ᵍᶠ
7⁸ᶠ 5⁸ᵍᶠ 9⁷ᶠ 5⁷ᶠ 7⁸ᵍᶠ 10⁸ᵍ 6⁶ᵍᶠ 14⁸ᵍᶠ 6⁸ᵍˢ
0-0-18 £2,519

Cause Celebre (Ire) *B W Hills*   75
2 gr f Peintre Celebre (USA) - Madame Belga (USA)
7⁷ᵍᶠ 3⁸ᶠ 4⁸ᵍᶠ 2⁸ᵍᶠ **0-2-4 £2,082**

Caustic Wit (Ire) *M S Saunders*   50 a56
5 b g Cadeaux Genereux - Baldemosa (Fr)
18⁶ᵍᶠ 12⁵ᵍ 17⁵ᵍᶠ 3⁵ˢʷ 11⁵ˢᵈ **0-1-5 £422**

Cautious *R M Beckett*   46
3 gr g Petong - Kind Of Shy
15⁶ᵍᶠ 5⁷ᵍᶠ 9⁷ᵍᶠ **0-0-3**

Caveral *R Hannon*   85
2 ch f Ashkalani (Ire) - Melting Gold (USA)
1⁶ᵍ 3⁶ᵍᶠ **1-1-2 £4,925**

Caversfield *J M Bradley*   a51
8 ch g Tina's Pet - Canoodle
7⁷ˢᵈ 10⁷ˢᵈ 4⁷ˢᵈ 14⁷ˢᵈ **0-0-4**

Cayenne *M R Channon*   37
2 b f Fraam - Katya (Ire)
7⁶ʰᵈ 7⁶ᵍᶠ 11⁷ᵍᶠ 11⁵ᵍᶠ **0-0-4**

Cayman Breeze *E A L Dunlop*   76 a16
3 b g Danzig (USA) - Lady Thynn (Fr)
3⁶ᵍᶠ 8⁶ᵍ 5⁶ᵍᶠ 2⁶ᵍᶠ 2⁶ᵍᶠ 1⁶ᶠ 12⁸ᶠ 13⁶ˢᵈ
7⁷ˢ **1-3-9 £7,927**

Cayman Mischief *James Moffatt*   7
3 b f Cayman Kai (Ire) - Tribal Mischief
15⁷ˢᵈ 12⁵ᵍˢ **0-0-2**

Cayman Sunrise (Ire) *E A L Dunlop*   70
3 gr f Peintre Celebre (USA) - Sum (USA)
3⁷ᵍᶠ 4⁸ᵍˢ 4¹⁰ᵍ 2⁸ᵍᶠ **0-2-4 £2,192**

Cazisa Star (USA) *P W Harris*   57
2 ch f Mister Baileys - Placer Queen
7⁸ᵍᶠ 3⁸ᵍᶠ 6⁷ᵍᶠ **0-0-3 £330**

Cd Europe (Ire) *K A Ryan*   100 a65
5 ch g Royal Academy (USA) - Woodland Orchid (Ire)
8⁵ˢʷ 13⁶ᵍᶠ 1⁶ᵍᶠ 4⁵ᵍᶠ 10⁶ᵍˢ 8⁵ᵍᶠ 2⁶ᵍᶠ 7⁶ᵍˢ
2⁶ᵍᶠ 8⁶ᵍ 2⁶ᵍᶠ 1⁶ᵍˢ **2-4-12 £25,127**

Cd Flyer (Ire) *M R Channon*   92 a79
6 ch g Grand Lodge (USA) - Pretext
4⁶ˢᵈ 5⁶ᵍᶠ 2⁶ᵍᶠ 3⁶ᵍ 5⁶ᵍˢ 14⁶ᵍˢ 3⁶ᵍᶠ 4⁶ᶠ
1⁶ᵍˢ 1⁶ᵍ 20⁶ᵍ **2-3-11 £34,211**

Cead Mile Failte *B J Llewellyn*
8 ch g Most Welcome - Avionne
12¹⁶ˢᵈ 9¹²ˢᵈ 12¹²ˢʷ **0-0-3**

Ceasar (Ire) *P C Haslam*   67
2 b g Orpen (USA) - Fen Princess (Ire)
6⁶ᵍᶠ 2⁶ᵍ 10⁶ᵍᶠ 6⁷ᵍᶠ 16⁸ᵍˢ **0-1-5 £1,702**

Cedar Grove *John A Harris*   42 a42
6 b g Shirley Heights - Trojan Desert
6¹⁶ˢᵈ 7¹²ˢʷ 3¹⁴ˢᵈ 4¹⁶ˢᵈ 2¹⁶ᵍˢ 9¹⁵ˢᵈ 4¹³ᵍᶠ
9¹⁴ᵍᶠ 2¹⁴ᵍᶠ 12¹⁶ᵍˢ **0-3-10 £2,803**

Cedar Master (Ire) *J R Boyle*   78
6 b g Soviet Lad (USA) - Samriah (Ire)
2¹⁵ᵍᶠ 10¹⁶ᵍᶠ 22²⁰ᵍᶠ 5¹⁶ᵍᶠ 8¹⁵ᵍᶠ **0-1-5**
£1,115

Cedar Rangers (USA) *G F Edwards*   a60
5 b g Anabaa (USA) - Chelsea (USA)

4^{7sd} 8^{10sd} 10^{8sd} 9^{8sd} 8^{7sd} **0-0-5**

Cedarberg (UAE) *M R Channon* — 104
2 b c Cape Cross (Ire) - Crinolette (Ire)
2^{6g} 2^{6s} 1^{6gf} 3^{6g} **1-2-4 £23,020**

Ceepio (Ire) *T G Mills* — 108
5 b g Pennekamp (USA) - Boranwood (Ire)
1^{7g} 10^{6gf} 2^{7g} 20^{7gf} 2^{7gf} **1-2-5 £17,060**

Cefira (USA) *M H Tompkins* — 58
2 b f Distant View (USA) - Bold Jessie
11^{6gf} **0-0-1**

Celadon (Ire) *N P Littmoden* — 71
2 b c Fasliyev (USA) - Dancing Drop
4^{5g} 3^{5gf} 5^{5gf} **0-1-3 £944**

Celestia *J L Dunlop* — 67
3 b f Anabaa (USA) - Divine Quest
12^{7gf} 9^{8gf} **0-0-2**

Cellarmaster (Ire) *A C Stewart* — 58 a65
2 c c Alhaarth (Ire) - Cheeky Weeky
3^{7gf} 5^{8gf} 2^{8sd} **0-1-3 £1,694**

Cellino *Andrew Turnell* — 54
2 b f Robellino (USA) - Celandine
8^{5gf} 11^{6f} 5^{5gf} 12^{5gf} **0-0-4**

Cello *R Hannon* — 71 a52
2 gr c Pivotal - Raffelina (USA)
6^{6gf} 3^{6gf} 5^{7gf} 5^{7sd} **0-1-4 £425**

Celtic Blaze (Ire) *B S Rothwell* — 65 a58
4 b f Charente River (Ire) - Firdaunt
2^{12sd} 6^{12sd} 1^{14gf} 3^{14gf} 8^{14g} 6^{16gf} 8^{12gf} **1-2-7 £7,775**

Celtic Cat (Ire) *A P O'Brien* — 104
2 b c Danehill (USA) - Golden Cat (USA)
1^{5g} 2^{7gf} 6^{7gf} **1-1-3 £17,649**

Celtic Charmer *R Craggs* — a35
4 b g Celtic Swing - Hamsah (Ire)
13^{12sw} 8^{8sd} **0-0-2**

Celtic Heroine (Ire) *M A Jarvis* — 72 a67
2 ch f Hernando (Fr) - Celtic Fling
5^{7gf} 1^{7sd} 5^{7gf} **1-0-3 £3,484**

Celtic Legend *Paul Johnson*
5 b m Celtic Swing - No Reprieve (NZ)
14^{6sd} **0-0-1**

Celtic Mill *D W Barker* — 94
5 b g Celtic Swing - Madam Millie
4^{7gf} 1^{6g} 1^{6gf} 2^{7g} 4^{6gf} 13^{6gf} 3^{7g} 11^{6gs} 1^{6gf} 4^{7gf} 12^{7gf} **3-2-11 £44,890**

Celtic Romance *D Nicholls* — 61
4 b f Celtic Swing - Southern Sky
13^{6g} 12^{7f} 20^{8f} 9^{10gs} **0-0-4**

Celtic Rover *C R Dore* — 11 a45
5 b g Celtic Swing - Lady Sabo
5^{6sw} 11^{7sd} 17^{6g} 15^{6gf} **0-0-4**

Celtic Sapphire (Fr) *T D Easterby* — 65
3 b f Celtic Swing - Smart 'n Noble (USA)
13^{10gf} 7^{12gf} 5^{8gf} 3^{8gf} 4^{9gf} 2^{12gf} 3^{10gf} 3^{14gf} 14^{12gf} 7^{10g} **0-1-11 £4,747**

Celtic Solitude (Ire) *M Johnston* — 34
2 b f Celtic Swing - Smart 'n Noble (USA)
6^{8gf} **0-0-1**

Celtic Star (Ire) *Nick Williams* — 70
5 b g Celtic Swing - Recherchee
1^{12g} 1^{12g} 6^{12g} **2-0-3 £7,280**

Celtic Style *M Johnston* — 85
4 b g Celtic Swing - Stylish Rose (Ire)
9^{12g} 7^{12gf} 2^{12f} 4^{15gf} 3^{16gf} 6^{15gf} 4^{14gf}

3^{14f} **0-1-8 £4,010**

Celtic Ted *P Butler* — 36 a30
5 b g Celtic Swing - Careful Dancer
12^{12g} 7^{9sd} **0-0-2**

Celtic Thatcher *N P Littmoden* — a42
5 b g Celtic Swing - Native Thatch (Ire)
16^{7sd} **0-0-1**

Celtic Thunder *T J Etherington* — 85
2 b g Mind Games - Lake Mistassiu
4^{5g} 3^{5gf} 1^{5gf} 2^{5gf} 4^{5gf} 6^{6gf} **1-1-6 £9,247**

Celtic Truth (USA) *R Charlton* — 90
3 b/br f Known Fact (USA) - Caithness (USA)
9^{8gf} 1^{10gf} 1^{10f} 4^{11gs} 5^{12gf} 5^{12gf} **2-0-6 £10,762**

Central Command *D J Daly* — 48
3 b g Cadeaux Genereux - Possessive Artiste
4^{8gf} 8^{8g} 8^{11gf} 7^{7gf} **0-0-4 £327**

Ceol Na Sraide (Ire) *B S Rothwell* — 83
4 b f King's Theatre (Ire) - My Lady's Key (USA)
8^{14g} 7^{10g} 6^{12gf} 6^{10sh} 11^{12ys} 5^{10gf} 12^{12gs} 9^{10gf} 19^{11s} 15^{10gs} **0-0-10**

Cerezo (USA) *S L Keightley* — 44 a52
2 b g Cherokee Run (USA) - Dahshah
6^{5g} 10^{5gs} 8^{7sd} 3^{8sd} 5^{8sd} 11^{8sd} **0-1-6 £291**

Certa Cito *T D Easterby* — 64
3 b f Mind Games - Bollin Dorothy
1^{6gf} 3^{6g} 15^{6sd} **1-1-3 £4,347**

Certain Justice (USA) *P F I Cole* — 96
5 gr g Lit De Justice (USA) - Pure Misk
13^{8g} 5^{7gf} 9^{8gf} 6^{8g} 13^{8gs} **0-0-5 £321**

Cerulean Rose *A W Carroll* — 77
4 ch f Bluegrass Prince (Ire) - Elegant Rose
8^{8g} 3^{6f} 14^{5gf} 1^{5gf} 1^{5g} 5^{5gs} 1^{5gf} 1^{5gf} 3^{6gf} 5^{6g} **5-2-10 £29,037**

Cesare Borgia (Ire) *R Johnson* — 45 a45
3 ch c Dr Devious (Ire) - Prospering
4^{7sd} 8^{8sd} 10^{7sd} 12^{7sd} 14^{10gf} 8^{8gs} 6^{7g} 5^{8gs} 7^{8gf} 9^{7gf} 6^{8gf} 5^{9gf} 4^{11gf} 6^{10g} 14^{8gf} **0-0-15 £1,775**

Cezzaro (Ire) *S R Bowring* — 53
5 ch g Ashkalani (Ire) - Sept Roses (USA)
11^{12sw} 8^{7gf} 5^{12gf} 8^{10gf} 14^{8g} 2^{8f} 2^{13gf} 6^{12gf} 1^{9g} 13^{8gf} 4^{10gf} 7^{10f} **1-2-12 £6,629**

Chaayid (Ire) *J L Dunlop* — 46
2 br c Grand Lodge (USA) - Shiny Waters (USA)
17^{7gf} 21^{7gf} 20^{8gf} **0-0-3**

Chabibi *T H Caldwell* — a31
4 br f Mark Of Esteem (Ire) - Nunsharpa
10^{7sd} **0-0-1**

Chaffinch (USA) *R Charlton* — 86
3 b f Lear Fan (USA) - Chain Fern (USA)
6^{10gf} 7^{11g} 1^{12f} 6^{12gf} 9^{10g} **1-0-5 £5,759**

Chai Walla *H R A Cecil* — 98
4 ch g In The Wings - Carmita
1^{12gf} 10^{14gf} **1-0-2 £9,685**

Chain Of Hope (Ire) *D E Cantillon* — 52
2 ch g Shinko Forest (Ire) - Fleeting Smile (Ire)
8^{6gs} 10^{6gf} 6^{6g} **0-0-3**

Chairman Bobby *D W Barker* — 77
5 ch g Clantime - Formidable Liz
3^{6gf} 9^{6gf} 1^{5gs} 1^{6gf} 2^{6f} 2^{6gs} 3^{7gf} 2^{5gf} 2^{5f} 3^{5gf} 3^{6gf} 11^{5g} 6^{5gf} 2^{5gf} **2-9-14 £22,909**

Chaka Zulu *A C Whillans* — 62

6 b g Muhtarram (USA) - African Dance (USA)
3¹²ᵍᶠ 3¹⁶ᵍᶠ PU¹⁶ᵍᶠ 2¹²ᵍ 7¹¹ᵍ 2¹⁴ᵍᶠ 2¹²ᵍᶠ
0-5-7 £3,998

Chalom (Ire) *O Sherwood* 3
5 b g Mujadil (USA) - The Poachers Lady (Ire)
26⁸ᵍ **0-0-1**

Chambray (Ire) *A M Balding* 50
2 b f Barathea (Ire) - Spurned (USA)
5⁸ᵍᶠ **0-0-1**

Champagne Cracker *Miss L A Perratt* 60
2 ch f Up And At 'Em - Kiveton Komet
3⁵ᵍᶠ 5⁶ᵍᶠ 2⁵ᶠ 6⁵ᶠ 2⁵ᵍ 2⁵ᵍᶠ **0-2-6**
£3,782

Champagne Rider *D Shaw* 33 a72
7 b g Presidium - Petitesse
3⁷ˢᵈ 10⁷ˢᵈ 8⁷ˢᵈ 12⁶ˢᵈ 9⁷ˢᵈ 13⁹ˢᵈ 11⁷ˢᵈ
12⁷ˢᵈ 5⁸ˢᵈ 11⁸ᵍˢ **0-1-10 £427**

Champain Sands (Ire) *J R Boyle* 73 a51
4 b g Green Desert (USA) - Grecian Bride (Ire)
3¹⁰ᶠ 19¹⁰ᵍᶠ 2⁸ᵍ 11⁹ᵍᶠ 8¹⁰ᵍᶠ 16⁸ᵍᶠ 15⁸ᶠ
6⁸ˢᵈ 2¹¹ᵍᶠ **0-3-9 £2,368**

Champion Lion (Ire) *M R Channon* 92
4 b c Sadler's Wells (USA) - Honey Bun
11¹²ᵍ 12¹²ᵍ 3¹⁴ᵍᶠ 11¹²ᵍ 7¹²ᵍᶠ 5¹⁶ᵍᶠ 12¹²ᵍ
0-0-7 £887

Chance For Romance *W R Muir* 90
2 ch f Entrepreneur - My First Romance
21⁷ᵍᶠ 10⁵ᶠ 2⁵ᵍᶠ 1⁶ʰᵈ 6⁶ᵍᶠ 8⁵ᵍ 5⁶ᵍᶠ 7⁶ᵍ
1-1-8 £6,092

Chandelier *M S Saunders* 54 a62
3 ch g Sabrehill (USA) - La Noisette
1⁸ˢᵈ 3⁸ˢᵈ 3⁸ˢᵈ 8⁸ˢᵈ 5⁸ˢᵈ 11¹²ᵍᶠ 9⁸ᵍ 6⁷ᵍᶠ
10⁸ᶠ **1-2-9 £4,297**

Chanfron *B R Millman* 65
2 ch g Double Trigger (Ire) - Mhargaidh Nua
14⁷ᵍᶠ 3⁸ᵍᶠ 6⁸ᵍᶠ 13¹⁰ᵍᶠ **0-1-4 £490**

Changari (USA) *R Charlton* 80
2 b f Gulch (USA) - Danzari
1⁵ᵍᶠ 2⁶ᵍᶠ 5⁶ᵍᶠ 5⁶ᵍᶠ **1-0-4 £5,946**

Change Of Heart (Ire) *T D Easterby* 39
3 b f Revoque (Ire) - Heart Of India (Ire)
12⁷ˢ **0-0-1**

Change Of Image *J R Weymes* 40
5 b m Spectrum (Ire) - Reveuse Du Soir
8¹²ᵍᶠ 5¹²ᵍᶠ 4¹²ᵍ 9¹²ᵍᶠ 8¹⁶ᵍᶠ **0-0-5 £259**

Change Partners (Ire) *R Charlton* 75 a69
3 ch f Hernando (Fr) - Favorable Exchange (USA)
3⁸ᵍᶠ 3¹²ˢᵈ 2¹⁰ᵍᶠ 2¹⁰ᵍᶠ 1¹²ᵍˢ **1-2-5**
£5,147

Chanterelle (Ire) *J L Dunlop* 77
2 ch f Indian Ridge - Chantereine (USA)
4⁶ᵍᶠ 4⁶ᵍᶠ 1⁶ˢ **1-0-3 £4,524**

Chanteuse *J A Glover* 61
3 b f Rudimentary (USA) - Enchanting Melody
6⁷ᵍˢ 4⁷ᵍᶠ 2⁸ᵍᶠ 9⁸ᵍ 10⁷ᵍᶠ 16⁸ᵍ **0-1-6**
£2,085

Chantilly Gold (USA) *J M Bradley* 34
4 ch f Mutakddim (USA) - Bouffant (USA)
18⁶ᵍᶠ 8⁸ᶠ 11⁸ᶠ 9⁸ᶠ 14⁷ᵍᶠ 16⁸ᵍᶠ **0-0-6**

Chantilly Sunset (Ire) *A Berry*
2 b f General Monash (USA) - Alpine Sunset
7⁵ᵍ **0-0-1**

Chantress *M Johnston* 98
3 b f Peintre Celebre (USA) - Up Anchor (Ire)
2⁸ᵍᶠ 1⁹ᵍᶠ 4¹²ᵍᶠ 1¹⁰ᵍ 3¹⁰ᵍ **2-2-5 £24,617**

Chantry Falls (Ire) *J R Weymes* 49
3 br g Mukaddamah (USA) - Woodie Dancer (USA)
2⁷ᶠ 3⁷ᶠ 14⁸ˢ 2⁷ᵍᶠ 5⁶ᶠ 9⁷ᵍᶠ 4⁸ᵍᶠ 6⁸ᶠ 3⁷ᵍᶠ
0-2-9 £4,709

Chapel Royale (Ire) *Evan Williams* 66
6 gr g College Chapel - Merci Royale
15⁸ᵍˢ 11⁸ʰʸ 7⁸ᵍᶠ 14⁸ᵍˢ 6⁸ᵍᶠ 6⁹ᵍ **0-0-6**

Chaplin *B W Hills* 48
2 b c Groom Dancer (USA) - Princess Borghese (USA)
11⁷ᵍᶠ **0-0-1**

Chapter House (USA) *D Nicholls* 57
4 b g Pulpit (USA) - Lilian Bayliss (Ire)
15⁶ᵍ **0-0-1**

Chara *J R Jenkins* 60
2 ch f Deploy - Subtle One (Ire)
4⁶ᵍᶠ 10⁷ᵍˢ **0-0-2 £265**

Charge *Mrs L Stubbs* a10
7 gr g Petong - Madam Petoski
13⁶ˢᵈ **0-0-1**

Chariot (Ire) *B W Hills* 57 a50
2 ch c Titus Livius (Fr) - Battle Queen
9⁵ᵍ 6⁶ᵍᶠ 4⁷ˢᵈ 7⁷ᵍᶠ 3⁸ᵍᶠ **0-1-5 £664**

Chariots Of Blue *W G M Turner* 7
2 ch g Bluebird (USA) - Boadicea's Chariot
15⁶ᵍᶠ 13⁸ᵍᶠ **0-0-2**

Charles Spencelayh (Ire) *J G M O'Shea* a30
7 b g Tenby - Legit (Ire)
5¹⁵ˢᵈ **0-0-1**

Charley Farley *E A Wheeler* a31
4 ch g Bluegrass Prince (Ire) - Miss Copyforce
12⁷ˢᵈ **0-0-1**

Charlie Bear *E A L Dunlop* 64
2 ch c Bahamian Bounty - Abi
5⁷ᵍᶠ 7⁶ᵍᶠ 10⁶ᵍᶠ **0-0-3**

Charlie Golf (Ire) *J W Hills* a61
3 b g Cadeaux Genereux - Keepers Dawn (Ire)
3¹⁰ˢᵈ 9⁹ˢᵈ 5¹²ˢᵈ PU¹²ᵍᶠ **0-1-4 £420**

Charlie Parkes *E J Alston* 94
5 ch g Pursuit Of Love - Lucky Parkes
1⁵ᶠ 4⁵ᵍᶠ 5⁵ᵍᶠ 9⁵ᵍᶠ 11⁵ᵍᶠ 14⁵ᵍᶠ 16⁵ᵍ
11⁵ᵍᶠ **1-1-8 £7,302**

Charlie Tango (Ire) *M R Channon* 68
2 b g Desert Prince (Ire) - Precedence (Ire)
5⁷ᵍ 9⁶ᵍᶠ 3⁸ᵍᶠ 14⁸ᵍ **0-0-4 £1,045**

Charlieismydarling *J A Osborne* a54
2 b g Mind Games - Blessed Lass (Hol)
4⁶ˢᵈ **0-0-1**

Charlies Bride (Ire) *M A Barnes* 10
8 b/br m Rich Charlie - Nordic Bride (Ire)
17⁸ᵍ 13⁸ᵍ **0-0-2**

Charlotte Vale *M D Hammond* 63
2 ch f Pivotal - Drying Grass Moon
2⁶ᵍˢ 4⁵ᵍᶠ 4⁷ᵍ 6⁶ᵍᶠ **0-1-4 £1,645**

Charlottebutterfly *T T Clement* 68 a58
3 b f Millkom - Tee Gee Jay
5⁵ᵍᶠ 3⁶ᵍᶠ 4⁷ᶠ 3⁶ᵍᶠ 12⁶ˢᵈ 3⁵ᵍᶠ 5⁶ᵍᶠ 3⁶ˢʷ
0-3-8 £2,367

Charmatic (Ire) *J A Glover* 52
2 br f Charnwood Forest (Ire) - Instamatic
13⁶ᵍ 7⁷ᵍˢ **0-0-2**

Charmaway *C E Brittain* a51
5 b g Charmer - Dismiss
8⁸ˢᵈ 9⁷ˢᵈ **0-0-2**

Charming Admiral (Ire) *Mrs A Duffield* 26
10 b g Shareef Dancer (USA) - Lilac Charm

11^16gs **0-0-1**

Charming Prince (Ire) *A Fabre* 105
2 b c Barathea (Ire) - Most Charming (Fr)
1^7gs 2^7s 2^7ho 1^7gs **2-2-4 £82,279**

Charnock Bates One (Ire) *T D Easterby* 64
2 b f Desert Sun - Fleetwood Fancy
4^6hy 5^6gf 3^7gf 3^7f 5^8gf 4^8gf **0-2-6**
£2,015

Charnwood Street (Ire) *D Shaw* a54
4 b g Charnwood Forest (Ire) - La Vigie
6^16sw 4^16sd 4^16sw 9^16sd 5^15sd **0-0-5**

Chase The Blues (Ire) *R Wilman*
6 b g Blues Traveller (Ire) - Highdrive
10^12sd 9^15sw **0-0-2**

Chase The Rainbow *M Johnston* 57
2 gr f Danzig Connection (USA) - Delta Tempo (Ire)
5^5gf 1^7gf 9^6g **1-0-3 £3,172**

Chateau Nicol *B G Powell* 69 a64
4 b g Distant Relative - Glensara
9^8g 6^8g 5^7g 11^7gf 6^7g 3^8sd 9^8gf 11^7sd
9^7sd **0-1-9 £458**

Chatifa (Ire) *M P Tregoning* 82
3 ch f Titus Livius (Fr) - Lagrion (USA)
2^8gf 4^7gf 1^8gf 11^7gf **1-1-4 £6,615**

Chauvinism (Ire) *N P Littmoden* 92
2 b g Danetime (Ire) - Ceannanas (Ire)
1^6g 2^6gf **1-1-2 £5,449**

Checkit (Ire) *M R Channon* 118
3 br c Mukaddamah (USA) - Collected (Ire)
16^8g 3^9s 4^7gf 3^9gf 4^8gs 1^8g 3^9gf 4^8s
2^8gs **1-4-9 £37,646**

Cheeky Girl *T D Easterby* 70 a27
3 b f College Chapel - Merry Rous
8^8sd 12^7gf 1^12gf 4^14gf 7^12gs 2^12g 2^12gf
1^12f 3^12g 5^12gf 4^12gf 4^12gf 5^14f 1^12gf **3-2-14**
£14,777

Cheeky Lad *R C Harper* 31
3 b g Bering - Cheeky Charm (USA)
15^16gs **0-0-1**

Cheese 'n Biscuits *G L Moore* 69 a91
3 b f Spectrum (Ire) - Bint Shihama (USA)
9^7sd 1^7sd 7^8sd 7^7sd 6^8sd 14^7gs 5^7gf 5^7sd
4^6sd 10^9g 3^7sd 3^7sd 1^7sd 3^7sd **2-3-14**
£11,853

Chelsea Blue (Ity) *J W Payne* 52
5 ch m Barathea (Ire) - Indigo Blue (Ire)
4^5gf 16^6gf **0-1-2**

Chemicalreaction *R A Fahey* 43 a41
3 b g Definite Article - Ewar Snowflake
9^7sd 8^8sd 12^8sd 7^13gf 8^12f 4^8gf 4^10gf
6^10gf **0-1-8 £431**

Cherine (Ire) *N P Littmoden* a48
4 b f Robellino (USA) - Escrime (USA)
5^8sd 7^12sw 1^7sw 8^8sd 4^9sd 5^10sd **1-0-6**
£3,454

Cherished Number *I Semple* 89
4 b g King's Signet (USA) - Pretty Average
7^8gf 5^8g 1^8gs 3^8hy 4^10gs 1^8gf 6^8gf 3^9gf
4^8gf 12^8g 10^8gf **2-2-11 £15,299**

Cherokee Bay *J A Osborne* 64 a64
3 b f Primo Dominie - Me Cherokee
6^10sd 9^9gf 8^8g 7^7sd 7^8g 9^8sd 3^10gf **0-1-7**
£294

Cherokee Nation *P W D'Arcy* 39 a43
2 br c Emperor Jones (USA) - Me Cherokee

10^6g 12^5sd 6^6sd **0-0-3**

Cherubim (Jpn) *D R Loder* 70
2 ch f Sunday Silence (USA) - Curly Angel (Jpn)
3^6gf 2^7g **0-0-2 £2,404**

Chesnut Cracker *P C Haslam* 30 a44
3 ch f Compton Place - Triple Tricks (Ire)
4^5sw 6^7s 9^5gf **0-0-3 £260**

Chesnut Ripple *R M Whitaker* 67
4 ch f Cosmonaut - Shaft Of Sunlight
2^10s 6^10g 9^10gf 4^10gf 8^10gs 6^10gf 6^12gf
0-1-7 £2,648

Chester Le Street (USA) *M Johnston* 103
2 b c Horse Chestnut (SAF) - Evening Primrose (USA)
4^6s 1^7gf 2^7gf **1-1-3 £14,833**

Chester Park *K Bishop* 4
5 ch g King's Signet (USA) - Good Skills
13^7g **0-0-1**

Chetak (Ire) *B W Hills* 88 a92
3 ch f Halling (USA) - Tithcar
1^8t 8^8gf 3^8g 4^9gs 3^8g 2^7sd **1-2-6**
£11,915

Cheverak Forest (Ire) *Don Enrico Incisa* 68 a61
2 ch g Shinko Forest (Ire) - Meranie Girl (Ire)
3^5f 3^5gf 4^5gf 1^6gs 4^5gf 5^7gf 8^6gf 6^7gf
5^7gf 16^7gf 11^7gf 5^7gf 5^6gf 3^6sd 1^6gf 5^7gf 15^7g
3-1-17 £11,088

Chevin *R A Fahey* 55
4 ch f Danzig Connection (USA) - Starr Danias (USA)
9^12gf 8^12g 11^4gf 11^1gf 5^12gf 4^12f 5^12g
7^16gs **2-0-8 £10,771**

Chevronne *L G Cottrell* 70 a75
3 b g Compton Place - Maria Isabella (Fr)
3^8g 3^8gf 17^8g 5^12sd 3^8sd **0-2-5 £2,140**

Cheyenne Chief *G M Moore*
4 b g Be My Chief (USA) - Cartuccia (Ire)
14^16gs **0-0-1**

Cheyenne Dawn *W G M Turner* 28 a27
3 ch f The West (USA) - Miss Lear
9^5sd 8^7t 13^7g **0-0-3**

Chiasso (USA) *H Morrison* 59
3 ch f Woodman (USA) - Qirmazi (USA)
4^8gf 0^8gs 10^10g 4^8g **0-0-4 £714**

Chic *Sir Michael Stoute* 107
3 ch f Machiavellian (USA) - Exclusive
1^7gf 1^8gf 3^8f 6^7gf 2^7g 1^7gf **3-2-6**
£46,433

Chica (Ire) *J A Osborne* 39
2 gr f Spectrum (Ire) - Wild Rose Of York
12^6gf 7^7gf 10^7gf **0-0-3**

Chicago Bond (USA) *B Smart* 58
2 b f Real Quiet (USA) - Shariyfa (Fr)
5^6g 4^5gf 3^6f 14^8gf **0-0-5 £1,028**

Chickado (Ire) *D Haydn Jones* 53 a65
2 b f Mujadil (USA) - Arcevia (Ire)
8^5f 8^6gs 6^5gf 16^sd **1-0-4 £2,296**

Chickasaw Trail *R Hollinshead* 42
5 ch m Be My Chief (USA) - Maraschino
7^12gf 9^10gf 7^11gf 7^7gf **0-0-4**

Chico Guapo (Ire) *J A Glover* 82 a62
3 b g Sesaro (USA) - Summer Queen
5^5sd 1^5sd 7^5gs 12^6gf 1^5gf 2^5g 2^5g 11^5gf
4^5gf 4^5gf 1^5gf 11^5g 1^5gs 5^5g **4-2-14**
£30,268

Chief Yeoman *Miss Venetia Williams* 91
3 br g Machiavellian (USA) - Step Aloft

3^{8g} 1^{7g} 7^{10g} 19^{12gf} 2^{10gf} **1-2-5 £8,555**

Chiffon *B J Meehan*   72
3 b f Polish Precedent (USA) - Photo Call
1^{7gf} 5^{10g} 18^{8gf} **1-0-3 £5,941**

Chigorin *J M P Eustace*   65
2 b g Pivotal - Belle Vue
8^{7gf} 3^{6gf} **0-1-2 £531**

Chili Pepper *P R Wood*   14
6 gr m Chilibang - Game Germaine
13^{8sd} 10^{11sd} 19^{10gf} 14^{7gf} **0-0-4**

Chimali (Ire) *J Nicol*   57
2 b g Foxhound (USA) - Mari-Ela (Ire)
4^{6gf} **0-0-1**

Chimichanga (Ire) *M J Polglase*   a10
3 b g Fayruz - Lindas Delight
13^{5sd} 17^{5gf} **0-0-2**

China Beauty *Mme M Bollack-Badel*   48
3 b f Slip Anchor - Tasseled (USA)
5^{8g} 2^{9gf} 10^{8gs} **0-1-3 £666**

China Eyes (Ire) *B W Hills*   103
2 b f Fasliyev (USA) - Limpopo
5^{5g} 2^{5gf} 1^{5gf} 6^{6gf} 2^{5g} **1-2-5 £21,793**

Chinkara *B J Meehan*   94 a81
3 ch g Desert Prince (Ire) - You Make Me Real (USA)
4^{10g} 1^{10sd} 4^{10gf} 1^{9gf} 1^{9g} 9^{8sd} **3-0-6**
£51,217

Chinsola (Ire) *R Hannon*   101 a83
2 ch c Inchinor - Skerray
4^{5f} 2^{6g} 1^{5sd} 1^{7gf} 2^{7gf} 1^{7gs} 4^{7gs} 4^{6g} 7^{7gf}
3-2-9 £37,139

Chiqitita (Ire) *M G Quinlan*   58
2 b f Saddlers' Hall (Ire) - Funny Cut (Ire)
6^{5sd} 13^{6gf} 4^{6gf} 6^{7f} 6^{6gs} 7^{7gf} 15^{10gf}
0-0-8 £380

Chispa *K R Burke*   80 a59
5 b m Imperial Frontier (USA) - Digamist Girl (Ire)
3^{6gs} 5^{6sd} 3^{5sd} 13^{6g} 2^{6gs} 1^{6gs} 7^{5hy} 10^{5gs}
15^{5g} 5^{5g} 3^{6gs} 7^{5gf} **1-4-12 £6,102**

Chivalry *J Howard Johnson*   99
4 b g Mark Of Esteem (Ire) - Gai Bulga
1^{9gf} **1-0-1 £63,800**

Chivite (Ire) *P J Hobbs*   a69
4 b g Alhaarth (Ire) - Laura Margaret
7^{13sd} **0-0-1**

Choisir (Aus) *Paul Perry*   128
4 ch c Danehill Dancer (Ire) - Great Selection (Aus)
1^{5g} 3^{6gs} 7^{7g} 6^{6g} 1^{6f} 1^{5gf} 2^{6gf} **3-2-7**
£384,545

Chookie Heiton (Ire) *I Semple*   113
5 br g Fumo Di Londra (Ire) - Royal Wolff
7^{6gf} 10^{6gs} 7^{6gf} 1^{6g} 11^{7gf} **1-0-5 £6,120**

Choral Chimes (Jpn) *D R Loder*   84
3 b f Sunday Silence (USA) - Polent
1^{12g} 5^{12gf} 6^{12gf} **1-0-3 £4,640**

Chorist *W J Haggas*   114
4 ch f Pivotal - Choir Mistress
2^{10gf} 1^{10gs} 8^{12gf} 1^{10g} 1^{10g} 3^{12gf} **3-2-6**
£111,318

Chorister *W R Muir*   56
2 ch c Inchinor - Star Tulip
7^{5gf} 6^{7gf} 13^{6gf} **0-0-3**

Chorus *B R Millman*   63 a66
6 b m Bandmaster (USA) - Name That Tune
3^{6sd} 10^{6sd} 3^{6sw} 2^{6sw} 4^{6sw} 2^{6gf} 1^{6gs} 9^{6g}
11^{6f} 1^{6sw} 2^{6sd} 6^{6sd} 4^{6sd} 16^{6g} 6^{6sw} **1-5-15**

£7,230

Choto Mate (Ire) *S Kirk*   41 a86
7 ch g Brief Truce (USA) - Greatest Pleasure
6^{8sd} 2^{8sd} 10^{7sd} 11^{7gf} **0-1-4 £1,280**

Christina Sanchez (USA) *Sir Mark Prescott*   35 a60
3 gr f El Prado (USA) - Cope's Light (USA)
10^{8sd} 3^{6sd} 3^{7sw} 9^{6sd} 10^{8s} **0-2-5 £1,005**

Christina's Dream *P W Harris*   78
2 b f Spectrum (Ire) - Christine Daae
3^{6gf} 3^{6gf} 4^{6gf} **0-1-3 £1,967**

Christmas Truce (Ire) *Ian Williams*   79 a73
4 b g Brief Truce (USA) - Superflash
6^{14sw} 7^{12g} 3^{12gs} 13^{12gs} 2^{12sd} 10^{13gf}
12^{17gf} 12^{12gf} 14^{12g} 20^{12s} 7^{12sd} **0-2-12 £3,000**

Chubbes *M C Pipe*   71
2 b c Kris - St Radegund
8^{6gf} 5^{6gf} 8^{6gf} 10^{7gf} 6^{7gf} 18^{6gf} 4^{7g} **1-1-7**
£2,478

Ciacole *Mrs A J Perrett*   63
2 b f Primo Dominie - Dance On A Cloud (USA)
6^{6gf} 5^{6gf} 4^{7gf} **0-0-3 £307**

Ciel *M L W Bell*   83
3 b f Rainbow Quest (USA) - River Caro (USA)
7^{12gf} 6^{9gf} 4^{10gf} 2^{12gf} 7^{12gf} **0-1-5**
£2,170

Cill Droichead (Ire) *E J O'Neill*   89 a91
3 b c Entrepreneur - Havinia
5^{10sd} 1^{10sd} 5^{8sd} 6^{10sd} 1^{10sd} 4^{10gf} 8^{10s}
2^{12gf} 16^{12gf} 9^{12gf} 5^{10gf} 5^{10g} 2^{12sd} 7^{12f} 6^{10g}
6^{12gf} 11^{12gf} **2-2-17 £14,788**

Cimyla (Ire) *C F Wall*   66 a81
2 b c Lomitas - Coyaima (Ger)
4^{7gf} 1^{8sd} **1-0-2 £3,540**

Cinnamon Ridge (Ire) *B J Meehan*   44
2 b g Indian Ridge - Savoury
15^{6gf} 9^{6g} **0-0-2**

Circassian (Ire) *Sir Mark Prescott*   52 a20
2 b c Groom Dancer (USA) - Daraliya (Ire)
9^{8sw} 10^{7gf} 14^{7gf} 7^{8gf} **0-0-4**

Circuit Dancer (Ire) *A Berry*   95
3 b g Mujadil (USA) - Trysinger (USA)
6^{6gf} 5^{6gf} 5^{6gs} 14^{6gf} 2^{6gf} 7^{6g} 1^{6gf} 2^{6g}
2^{6gf} 3^{6gf} 1^{6gf} 6^{7gf} **2-3-12 £29,962**

Circus Maximus (USA) *Ian Williams*   63 a61
6 b g Pleasant Colony (USA) - Crockadore (USA)
5^{12sd} 9^{16sd} 21^{4gf} 11^{16g} **0-1-4 £1,008**

Cita Verda (Fr) *P Monteith*   82
5 b m Take Risks (Fr) - Mossita (Fr)
1^{10gs} 4^{12gf} 8^{10gs} **1-0-3 £7,367**

Citrine (Ire) *C F Wall*   32
5 ch m Selkirk (USA) - Classic Coral (USA)
12^{16gf} **0-0-1**

Citrine Spirit (Ire) *J H M Gosden*   40
2 gr f Soviet Star (USA) - Casessa (USA)
12^{7gs} **0-0-1**

Citrus Magic *K Bell*   a51
6 b g Cosmonaut - Up All Night
7^{14sd} 5^{13sd} 4^{12sd} 7^{16sd} 6^{14sd} **0-0-5**

City Affair *Mrs L C Jewell*   65
2 b g Inchinor - Aldevonie
3^{6g} 10^{6s} 5^{5gf} 10^{8gf} 11^{7gf} 3^{7f} **0-2-6**
£902

City Flite *P Monteith*   24
3 b f Magic Ring (Ire) - Lady Mabel
7^{5gf} 8^{5f} 8^{5gf} **0-0-3**

City Flyer *Miss J Feilden* a44
6 br g Night Shift (USA) - Al Guswa
14^{8sd} 13^{8sd} 5^{9sd} 10^{9sd} 10^{9sd} **0-0-5**

City General (Ire) *J S Moore* 57 a54
2 ch g General Monash (USA) - Astra (Ire)
11^{5gf} 3^{6gs} 2^{7f} 1^{7f} 3^{7gf} 3^{7g} 4^{7gf} 14^{7g}
6^{8gf} 2^{7sd} **1-3-10 £6,534**

City Palace *B W Hills* 67
2 ch c Grand Lodge (USA) - Ajuga (USA)
6^{6gf} **0-0-1**

Clann A Cougar *I A Wood* 77
3 ch g Bahamian Bounty - Move Darling
6^{8g} 3^{7gs} 8^{8gf} 7^{8gf} 6^{7gf} 4^{7g} 4^{7gf} 9^{7gf}
4^{7f} **0-1-9 £2,469**

Claptrap *J A Osborne* 53 a70
3 b c Royal Applause - Stardyn
3^{9sd} 2^{12sd} 3^{11f} 2^{12sd} 3^{9sw} 3^{13f} 4^{16sd} 6^{13f}
7^{12sd} **0-6-9 £4,343**

Claradotnet *H R A Cecil* 83
3 b f Sri Pekan (USA) - Lypharitissima (Fr)
2^{10gf} 1^{12gf} 7^{11s} **1-0-3 £3,589**

Clarice Starling *C A Cyzer* a48
5 b m Saddlers' Hall (Ire) - Uncharted Waters
9^{16sd} 10^{13sd} **0-0-2**

Clarinch Claymore *J M Jefferson* 80
7 b g Sabrehill (USA) - Salu
3^{16g} 5^{14hv} 8^{12g} 1^{16gf} 7^{16gf} 16^{14gf} 14^{14s}
4^{13gs} 6^{16gf} **1-2-9 £11,338**

Clarisse *H Candy* 82
4 b f Salse (USA) - Celia Brady
1^{12f} 3^{12gs} 4^{10gf} 11^{12gs} 3^{12gs} 3^{10g} 5^{12gf}
4^{12gf} 2^{10gf} 10^{12g} **1-3-10 £10,278**

Classic Event (Ire) *T D Easterby* 58
2 ch c Croco Rouge (Ire) - Delta Town (USA)
9^{7gf} 3^{7g} 5^{7gf} 8^{8gs} **0-1-4 £486**

Classic Example *Miss S J Wilton* 66
4 ch c Mark Of Esteem (Ire) - Classic Form (Ire)
19^{12g} 6^{10g} 10^{11gf} 11^{12gf} **0-0-4**

Classic Millennium *W J Musson* 65
5 b m Midyan (USA) - Classic Colleen (Ire)
11^{12gf} 11^{3g} 4^{14gf} 9^{14gf} 11^{4gf} 1^{12gf} 2^{14gf}
5^{12gf} 4^{12gf} 8^{12gf} 1^{12gf} 5^{15gf} **4-0-12 £29,075**

Classic Quartet *Mrs L Williamson* 56
3 b f Classic Cliche (Ire) - Carolside
4^{12f} 9^{10gf} PU^{12gs} 14^{2hy} 10^{12gf} 5^{12g} **0-0-6**
£857

Classic Role *R Ingram* 79
4 b g Tragic Role (USA) - Clare Island
5^{14g} 7^{12gf} 13^{12gf} 2^{12g} 9^{13gf} 4^{12gf} 1^{10gf}
7^{10gf} 14^{10g} 9^{10gs} **1-1-10 £5,969**

Classic Vision *W J Haggas* 56 a32
3 b f Classic Cliche (Ire) - Orient
5^{8g} 3^{8sd} **0-0-2 £553**

Classical Dancer *H Candy* 79
2 ch f Dr Fong (USA) - Gorgeous Dancer (Ire)
3^{6gf} **0-1-1 £908**

Classical Song (Ire) *P W Harris* 56
3 b f Fayruz - Dieci Anno (Ire)
11^{7f} 8^{8g} 9^{8gf} 3^{6f} 11^{6gf} 12^{7gf} 16^{7gs}
6^{7gf} 8^{8gf} 9^{8g} **0-1-10 £463**

Classical Waltz (Ire) *J J Sheehan* a20
5 ch m In The Wings - Fascination Waltz
12^{12sd} **0-0-1**

Classy Lassie (Ire) *G A Swinbank* 67
3 ch f Goldmark (USA) - Okay Baby (Ire)

1^{6gf} 15^{6gs} 14^{6gf} 10^{7gf} 5^{6gf} **1-0-5**
£5,798

Classy Times *J S Wainwright*
2 b g Mind Games - Gay Ming
7^{5gf} 10^{7f} **0-0-2**

Claudia's Pearl *P W Harris* 60
3 ch f Deploy - Triple Zee (USA)
13^{10gf} 12^{10gf} 6^{10gf} 3^{12gs} **0-1-4 £732**

Clearing Sky (Ire) *Miss Z C Davison*
2 gr f Exploit (USA) - Litchfield Hills (USA)
14^{6sd} **0-0-1**

Clearly Tough (Ire) *I Semple* 53
2 b g Indian Rocket - Pharmacy
5^{5gf} 6^{5f} 8^{5f} 6^{6gf} 17^{6gs} 5^{6gf} 10^{7gf} **0-0-7**

Cleaver *W Jarvis* 33
2 ch c Kris - Much Too Risky
8^{7s} **0-0-1**

Cleveland Way *D Carroll* 54
3 b g Forzando - Fallal (Ire)
5^{5gf} 14^{8gf} 7^{7gf} 5^{5gs} 2^{6f} 9^{6gf} 4^{5f} 16^{5gf}
0-1-8 £1,494

Clever Clogs *E A L Dunlop* 95
3 ch f Nashwan - High Standard
3^{9gf} 2^{12gf} 1^{12gf} 7^{15gf} 3^{12gf} 1^{12gf} 3^{12gf}
6^{12g} 23^{12g} **2-3-9 £17,352**

Clifden (Ire) *M J Wallace* 84
2 ch c Gold Away (Ire) - Romora (Fr)
1^{5gf} 3^{5gs} 2^{6gs} 1^{6gs} 1^{6f} 6^{6gs} **3-1-6**
£41,739

Climate (Ire) *J R Boyle* 93
4 ch g Catrail (USA) - Burishki
19^{8gf} 9^{8g} 3^{8g} 4^{7gf} 4^{8gf} 10^{8gf} 16^{8g} 8^{8gf}
5^{8g} 11^{7gf} SU^{8f} 3^{10gf} **0-2-12 £4,812**

Clipperton *A M Balding* 85
4 b g Mister Baileys - Theresita (Ger)
4^{10gf} 5^{10gf} 7^{10g} **0-1-3 £1,474**

Clodovil (Ire) *A Fabre* 117
3 gr c Danehill (USA) - Clodora (Fr)
5^{8gf} 1^{8gs} 1^{8gs} 1^{8gs} 8^{8gs} 5^{8gs} **3-0-6**
£173,029

Clog Dance (USA) *J H M Gosden* 66 a67
2 b f Woodman (USA) - Royal Fandango (USA)
9^{7gf} 7^{7gf} 7^{8gs} 2^{7sd} **0-1-4 £1,120**

Close Fisted *B A McMahon* 57 a26
2 b c Forzando - Not So Generous (Ire)
9^{5g} 12^{5gf} 8^{5sd} 9^{5f} **0-0-4**

Cloud Catcher (Ire) *P S McEntee*
2 br f Charnwood Forest (Ire) - Notley Park
14^{5g} **0-0-1**

Cloud Dancer *D J Coakley* 85
4 b/br f Bishop Of Cashel - Summer Pageant
7^{8gs} 3^{8gf} 11^{8gf} 6^{8gf} 2^{7gf} 19^{7gf} 3^{7gf}
0-3-7 £3,180

Cloudingswell *I A Wood* 64 a62
2 b f Cloudings (Ire) - L'Ancressaan
8^{6gf} 4^{7gf} 3^{7sd} 13^{8gf} 16^{8gf} 6^{7f} **0-1-6**
£942

Cloudless (USA) *J W Unett* 28 a66
3 b/br f Lord Avie (USA) - Summer Retreat (USA)
0^{6g} 5^{7g} 10^{7s} 4^{7sw} 7^{8sd} 3^{6sd} 9^{5gs} **0-1-7**
£320

Club Oasis *M E Sowersby* 20
2 b f Forzando - Tatouma (USA)
5^{7gf} 3^{7gf} **0-0-2 £552**

Coat Of Honour (USA) *Sir Mark Prescott* 97
3 gr g Mark Of Esteem (Ire) - Ballymac Girl
2^{8g} 5^{8gf} 1^{10gf} 1^{10f} 3^{12g} 2^{11s} **2-3-6**
£16,674

Cobalt Blue (Ire) *W J Haggas* 51
2 b c Bluebird (USA) - Amy Hunter (USA)
11^{6gf} 11^{6gf} 14^{6gf} 10^{6gs} **0-0-4**

Cockney Boss (Ire) *B R Millman* 15 a33
4 b g General Monash (USA) - Cockney Ground (Ire)
11^{7sd} 17^{7gf} **0-0-2**

Coco Loco *Mrs Lydia Pearce* 72 a73
6 b m Bin Ajwaad (Ire) - Mainly Me
3^{16sw} 8^{16sd} 7^{16sw} 4^{18g} 11^{14gs} 3^{16gs} 7^{17gf}
0-1-7 £2,155

Coco Reef *B Palling* 20 a47
2 b f Kingsinger (Ire) - Highland Blue
7^{5gf} 3^{5sd} 3^{6sd} 7^{5sw} **0-2-4 £866**

Coconut Cookie *R Hannon* 67
2 ch f Bahamian Bounty - Spicy Manner (USA)
29^{7gf} 2^{6gf} 10^{7gf} **0-1-3 £1,448**

Coconut Penang (Ire) *B R Millman* 103
3 b c Night Shift (USA) - Play With Fire (Fr)
6^{6g} 2^{6hy} 3^{5gf} 6^{6g} 3^{6gf} 7^{6gf} 5^{6s} **0-3-7**
£20,665

Coctail Lady (Ire) *B W Duke* 38 a52
3 ch f Piccolo - Last Ambition (Ire)
7^{5sd} 7^{7sd} 6^{7sd} 7^{7sd} 13^{7gf} 13^{6gf} 13^{7f}
8^{10f} **0-0-8**

Cody *G A Ham* 55
4 ch g Zilzal (USA) - Ibtihaj (USA)
9^{10f} 4^{14gs} 15^{12f} **0-0-3 £355**

Coffee Time (Ire) *D J S Ffrench Davis* 64 a69
4 b f Efisio - Petula
2^{7sd} 6^{6sd} 3^{6sd} 8^{6sd} 4^{8sd} 6^{6gf} 14^{5gs} 6^{5gf}
5^{5gf} 6^{5gf} 10^{5gf} 8^{6gf} 13^{6gf} 4^{5gf} 8^{5gf} **0-2-15**
£1,969

Cohn Blue (Ire) *Mrs A J Perrett* 97
2 b c Bluebird (USA) - Kates Choice (Ire)
2^{7gf} 1^{8gf} 1^{10gf} 2^{10gs} 10^{10gs} **2-2-5**
£15,745

Cold Climate *Bob Jones* 62
8 ch g Pursuit Of Love - Sharpthorne (USA)
7^{7gf} 10^{7g} 6^{7gf} 3^{6g} 7^{6gf} 7^{6g} 4^{6gf} 10^{6gf}
5^{7f} 16^{9f} 5^{7s} **1-0-11 £4,687**

Cold Turkey *G L Moore* 81 a84
3 b/br g Polar Falcon (USA) - South Rock
6^{8sd} 5^{8sd} 9^{10f} 1^{10g} 4^{12gf} 2^{12gf} 2^{12gf} 7^{12gf}
12^{12sd} 1^{11gf} 1^{12sd} **3-1-11 £11,082**

Colemanstown *B Ellison* 83
3 b g Charnwood Forest (Ire) - Arme Fatale (Ire)
1^{7ys} 4^{7gf} 14^{8s} 12^{8y} 12^{7g} 5^{6gf} 6^{7gf} **1-1-7**
£6,087

Coleorton Prince (Ire) *K A Ryan* 32
2 b g Paris House - Tayovullin (Ire)
8^{5sd} 11^{5f} 8^{7gf} 12^{6gf} **0-0-4**

Colisay *A C Stewart* 110
4 b g Entrepreneur - La Sorrela (Ire)
4^{8g} 2^{8g} 1^{8gf} 10^{8gf} **1-2-4 £24,990**

College City (Ire) *R C Guest* 31
4 b g College Chapel - Polish Crack (Ire)
8^{16gs} **0-0-1**

College Delinquent (Ire) *K Bell* 64 a74
4 br g College Chapel - St Cyr Aty (Ire)
1^{8sd} 6^{8sd} 11^{10sd} 4^{8sd} 5^{8g} 8^{10gf} 9^{8sd} 3^{8sd}
1-1-8 £4,015

College Fund Girl (Ire) *G A Butler* 55 a73
3 b f Kahyasi - Pearl Kite (USA)
10^{10sd} 1^{12sd} 12^{12g} **1-0-3 £2,016**

College Hippie *J F Coupland* 66
4 b f Cosmonaut - Eccentric Dancer
15^{5gf} 8^{5gs} 13^{5gs} 2^{6gf} 7^{5f} 4^{5gf} 9^{5gf}
12^{5gf} 13^{6sd} 7^{6gf} 4^{5g} 9^{5gf} **0-2-12 £1,462**

College Maid (Ire) *J S Goldie* 69
6 b m College Chapel - Maid Of Mourne
7^{5gf} 4^{5gf} 4^{5gf} 11^{6gf} 7^{6gf} 8^{5gf} 7^{6gs} 5^{5gs}
1^{5gs} 3^{6gs} 7^{5gf} 12^{5gs} 1^{5gf} 16^{6gs} 4^{5g} 12^{5g} 8^{5gf}
7^{6g} **2-5-27 £10,380**

College Queen *S Gollings* 78
5 b m Lugana Beach - Eccentric Dancer
16^{6g} 3^{6gf} 12^{6g} 7^{6gf} 10^{5gf} 13^{6gs} 3^{6gf}
7^{6gf} 1^{6gf} 3^{5gf} 9^{5gf} 5^{6gf} 5^{5g} 4^{5gf} 13^{6gf}
11^{5g} **2-2-17 £11,263**

College Rock *A G Newcombe* 78
6 ch g Rock Hopper - Sea Aura
4^{7gf} 3^{7gf} 8^{8gf} 3^{7f} **0-2-4 £1,588**

College Song *G A Butler* a23
3 b g College Chapel - Celt Song (Ire)
9^{5sw} 13^{5f} **0-0-2**

College Star *J F Coupland* 28 a38
5 b g Lugana Beach - Alis Princess
8^{8sd} 4^{7sd} 7^{8sd} 6^{5sw} 5^{8sw} 10^{10gf} 7^{8gf} 12^{8f}
13^{7f} 11^{8gf} 9^{10gf} **0-0-11**

College Time (Ire) *P A Blockley* 31 a76
2 b g Danetime (Ire) - Respectful (Ire)
7^{8gf} 5^{6sd} 2^{6sd} **0-1-3 £934**

Collier Hill *G A Swinbank* 101
5 ch g Dr Devious (Ire) - Polar Queen
1^{13gs} 1^{12g} 6^{12gf} 11^{12g} 3^{13gs} 14^{13gs} 3^{16gf}
2-1-7 £49,913

Colloseum *T J Etherington* 54
2 b g Piccolo - Trig Point
5^{6g} 6^{7gf} **0-0-2**

Colne Valley Amy *G L Moore* 41 a38
6 b m Mizoram (USA) - Panchellita (USA)
8^{8sd} 6^{8f} 14^{10gs} **0-0-3**

Colonel Cotton (Ire) *N A Callaghan* 116
4 b g Royal Applause - Cutpurse Moll
15^{5gf} 11^{6g} 2^{5gf} 6^{6gf} 10^{5gf} 3^{6g} 7^{5gf} 5^{5gs}
2^{5g} 4^{5gf} 5^{6g} 8^{5f} 1^{5gf} 3^{6gf} 12^{6g} **1-4-15**
£41,944

Colonel Telford *M E Sowersby* 34
3 br g Emperor Fountain - Petaz
6^{12gf} 13^{10g} 10^{7gf} 12^{5gf} 8^{5gf} 9^{6gf} **0-0-6**

Colonnade *C Grant* 56 a55
4 b f Blushing Flame (USA) - White Palace
3^{11sw} 6^{16sd} 9^{12sd} 8^{14gf} 8^{14gf} **0-1-5 £417**

Colophony (USA) *H R A Cecil* 82
3 ch c Distant View (USA) - Private Line (USA)
3^{8gf} 2^{8s} 11^{11gf} 6^{10gf} **1-1-4 £8,612**

Colossus (Ire) *A P O'Brien* 112
2 b c Danehill (USA) - Mira Adonde (USA)
1^{5ys} 9^{6gf} 2^{6vs} 7^{6s} 1^{6gf} 6^{6g} 16^{gf} **3-1-7**
£77,685

Colour Sergeant (USA) *N Tinkler* 44
5 ch g Candy Stripes (USA) - Princess Afleet (USA)
15^{8f} 7^{7g} 9^{8gf} 5^{7f} 13^{7sw} **0-1-6**
£757

Colour Wheel *R Charlton* 88
2 ch c Spectrum (Ire) - Risanda

12^{6gf} 1^{7gf} 2^{7g} 2^{7gf} **1-1-4 £5,288**

Colourful Lady (USA) *P W Harris*   70
3 b f Quest For Fame - Special Park (USA)
17^{8gf} 4^{8g} 2^{10gf} 8^{10gf} 3^{10gs} 6^{10gf} 2^{12g}
17^{12s} 8^{12gf} 13^{16gf} **0-3-10 £3,277**

Colourful Life (Ire) *Mrs M Reveley*   78 a64
7 ch g Rainbows For Life (Can) - Rasmara
4^{12sd} 2^{12g} 9^{17g} **0-1-3 £1,013**

Columbine (Ire) *A Berry*   66 a53
5 b m Pivotal - Heart Of India (Ire)
3^{5sd} 1^{5gf} 2^{5gf} 6^{5gf} 4^{6gf} 12^{5gs} 9^{5gf} 3^{5gf}
9^{6g} 3^{5gf} 2^{5gf} 5^{5f} 10^{6gs} 3^{5gf} 6^{6gs} 2^{5gf} 3^{5f}
3^{5gf} 21^{6gs} 13^{5gf} **2-10-23**
£16,005

Colway Ritz *W Storey*   70
9 b g Rudimentary (USA) - Million Heiress
2^{12gf} 3^{12g} 9^{10s} 5^{14f} 7^{12s} 6^{12f} 15^{12gf}
8^{10gf} 4^{14gf} 2^{10g} 2^{10g} **0-4-11 £3,495**

Comanche Queen *J S Wainwright*   21
6 ch m Totem (USA) - Chess Mistress (USA)
7^{10gf} **0-0-1**

Comanche Woman *K O Cunningham-Brown*   35
3 b f Distinctly North (USA) - Possibility
9^{10f} 13^{11sd} 4^{12f} **0-0-3 £289**

Come Away With Me (Ire) *M A Buckley*   45 a59
3 b f Machiavellian (USA) - Vert Val (USA)
9^{8gf} 1^{7f} 2^{6sd} **1-1-3 £6,897**

Come On Patsy *J S Moore*   42
2 ch f Compton Place - Royal Roulette
6^{5g} 5^{5gf} 11^{6gf} 8^{6g} 8^{5sd} **0-0-5**

Come What July (Ire) *R Guest*   61
2 b c Indian Rocket - Persian Sally (Ire)
5^{6gf} 5^{6gf} 11^{5gf} 2^{7gf} 17^{6gf} **0-1-5**
£2,132

Comeraincomeshine (Ire) *T G Mills*   9
2 ch f Night Shift (USA) - Future Past (USA)
10^{7gf} **0-0-1**

Comfortable Call *H Alexander*
5 ch g Nashwan (USA) - High Standard
12^{16gf} **0-0-1**

Comfy (USA) *Sir Michael Stoute*   117
4 b c Lear Fan (USA) - Souplesse (USA)
7^{10gf} 1^{7g} 3^{9gf} **1-0-3 £10,394**

Comic Genius *D Haydn Jones*   a32
2 b f Comic Strip (USA) - Itsy Bitsy Betsy (USA)
4^{6sd} 7^{8sd} 6^{8sw} **0-0-3 £283**

Comic Tales *M Mullineaux*   6
2 b g Mind Games - Glorious Aragon
13^{6gs} **0-0-1**

Comic Times *M Mullineaux*   18
3 b f Puissance - Glorious Aragon
16^{6f} 17^{5g} **0-0-2**

Coming Again (Ire) *B W Hills*   86
2 b c Rainbow Quest (USA) - Hagwah (USA)
2^{6gf} **0-1-1 £1,492**

Coming Home *Sir Michael Stoute*   50
2 ch f Vettori (Ire) - Bonne Etoile
7^{7f} **0-0-1**

Commanche Wind (Ire) *E W Tuer*
8 b g Commanche Run - Delko
9^{16g} **0-0-1**

Commander Bond *B Smart*   67
2 b g Piccolo - Lonesome
11^{6g} 7^{7gf} 4^{6g} **0-0-3**

Commander Flip (Ire) *R Hollinshead*   61

Commanding (Ire)
3 ch g In Command (Ire) - Boldabsa
8^{7gs} 2^{12gf} 3^{10gf} 7^{10gf} **0-1-4 £1,771**

Commanding *Mrs A J Perrett*   91
4 ch g Pennekamp (USA) - Lady Joyce (Fr)
26^{8gf} 5^{8gf} 7^{8gf} 6^{8gf} 8^{7gf} **0-0-5 £355**

Commando Scott (Ire) *A Berry*   76
2 b g Danetime (Ire) - Faye
14^{6gf} 4^{5gf} 3^{6gf} 4^{6g} **0-1-4 £4,094**

Commemoration Day (Ire) *J G Given*   63
2 b c Daylami (Ire) - Bequeath (USA)
6^{8gf} 11^{7gf} **0-0-2**

Commissar (Ire) *J J Bridger*   a65
4 b g Common Grounds - Trescalini (Ire)
14^{12sd} **0-0-1**

Commission (USA) *G A Butler*   102
3 ch c Gulch (USA) - Accountable Lady (USA)
3^{8gf} 3^{10gf} UR^{8gs} 4^{7gf} 6^{8g} 6^{10gf} **0-1-6**
£8,434

Commitment Lecture *M Dods*   60 a19
3 b f Komaite (USA) - Hurtleberry (Ire)
12^{6f} 8^{7sd} 12^{6g} 2^{7gf} 18^{gs} 6^{8gf} 4^{8gf} 2^{8g}
10^{8gf} 9^{11gs} **1-2-10 £7,976**

Common Thought (Ire) *J J Quinn*   54
4 b g Common Grounds - Zuhal
12^{7gf} 15^{7f} 15^{8gf} 11^{9gf} 7^{7gf} 15^{7gf} 16^{8gf}
12^{7gf} **0-0-8**

Common World (USA) *G A Butler*   108 a81
4 ch c Spinning World (USA) - Spenderella (Fr)
7^{8ft} 3^{7g} 6^{9g} **0-0-3 £3,163**

Commondini (Ire) *P W Harris*   50
4 b f Common Grounds - Windini
16^{11gf} 8^{10gf} **0-0-2**

Companion *Miss Gay Kelleway*   34 a63
5 b m Most Welcome - Benazir
8^{12sd} 4^{8sd} 1^{10sd} 5^{10sd} 3^{10sd} 16^{10gf} 10^{10sd}
1-1-7 £3,535

Compassion (Ire) *Miss L A Perratt*   64
2 b f Alhaarth (Ire) - Titania
13^{5g} 4^{5g} 11^{5gf} 2^{6gf} 5^{6gf} 4^{6gs} 4^{5gf} 5^{6gs}
0-3-8 £1,724

Competitor *Mrs A J Perrett*   73
2 b c Danzero (Aus) - Ceanothus (Ire)
1^{8f} **1-0-1 £3,500**

Complete Circle *P W D'Arcy*   76 a87
3 ch f Vettori (Ire) - Cockatoo Island
1^{9sw} 6^{11g} 8^{12gf} 9^{12gs} 7^{12gf} 4^{8g} 5^{8sd} 5^{10gs}
1-1-8 £4,686

Complication *J A R Toller*   77
3 b f Compton Place - Hard Task
14^{7gs} 11^{7gf} 3^{6gf} 3^{5gf} 1^{6gf} 2^{6f} 17^{6gf}
12^{6gf} 18^{6gf} **1-1-9 £6,553**

Compos Mentis *D Morris*   56 a52
3 b g Bijou D'Inde - Red Cloud (Ire)
20^{8gf} 9^{8f} 12^{12sd} **0-0-3**

Compton Alice *N P Littmoden*   24 a47
3 ch f Compton Place - Secret Circle
5^{5sd} 16^{6g} 12^{6sd} **0-0-3**

Compton Arrow (Ire) *D Nicholls*   69
7 b g Petardia - Impressive Lady
13^{7gf} 5^{8gf} 8^{7gf} 2^{7gf} 6^{6gf} 4^{6gf} 8^{7gf}
17^{7gf} 15^{6g} **1-1-10 £4,833**

Compton Aviator *A W Carroll*   64 a67
7 ch g First Trump - Rifada
11^{12sd} 5^{10sd} 2^{12sd} 6^{12sd} 5^{10gf} 14^{8g} 7^{11gf}
7^{10gf} 5^{12gf} 1^{12f} 3^{12gf} 5^{12gf} 3^{12gf} 11^{12gf} 2^{12g}

4^{12gf} 4^{12sd} **1-5-17 £4,978**

Compton Banker (Ire) *G A Butler*   79 a88
6 br g Distinctly North (USA) - Mary Hinge
3^{6sd} 10^{7sd} 7^{5sd} 11^{7sd} 3^{5sd} 12^{5gf} 8^{5gf}
8^{5g} 11^{5gs} 5^{6f} 8^{5gf} 10^{6gf} 4^{7sd} **0-2-13**
£1,625

Compton Bay *M Brittain*   a26
3 b g Compton Place - Silver Sun
9^{7sd} **0-0-1**

Compton Bolter (Ire) *G A Butler*   117 a106
6 b g Red Sunset - Milk And Honey
6^{10sd} 10^{12sd} 5^{10sd} 2^{10gf} 3^{12gf} 6^{16gf} 4^{12gf}
9^{12f} 2^{13gf} 1^{12gs} 5^{12g} 1^{13gf} 1^{11gf} 2^{12f} 2^{12gf}
7^{12gf} **3-5-16 £112,186**

Compton Chick (Ire) *J W Mullins*   22
5 b m Dolphin Street (Fr) - Cecina
13^{16gf} **0-0-1**

Compton Commander *Ian Williams*   48 a95
5 ch g Barathea (Ire) - Triode (USA)
1^{12sd} 10^{12sd} 14^{12sd} 14^{10g} **1-0-4**
£12,238

Compton Dictator *G A Butler*   45 a50
4 b g Shareef Dancer (USA) - Princess Pati
6^{7sd} 11^{11gf} 14^{11gf} 11^{10gf} 16^{7f} **0-0-5**

Compton Dragon (USA) *D Nicholls*   85
4 ch g Woodman (USA) - Vilikaia (USA)
4^{8ft} 8^{9f} 9^{9g} 5^{8gf} 21^{6g} 7^{7g} 14^{6g} 21^{7gf}
8^{7gf} **0-0-9 £3,783**

Compton Drake *G A Butler*   66 a50
4 b g Mark Of Esteem (Ire) - Reprocolor
2^{7sd} 5^{10f} 4^{14gf} 7^{9gf} 5^{10gf} 9^{8gf} 2^{10gf} 1^{12gf}
1-3-8 £5,094

Compton Dynamo *W J Musson*   93 a78
4 b g Wolfhound (USA) - Asteroid Field (USA)
10^{6gf} 21^{6g} 9^{6gf} 12^{5gf} 1^{6gf} 5^{6gf} 8^{6g}
17^{6g} 7^{6gf} 3^{6gf} 4^{6g} 14^{6g} 5^{6gf} 6^{6gf} 8^{6sd} **1-2-15**
£11,289

Compton Eagle *G A Butler*   62
3 b g Zafonic (USA) - Gayane
8^{7gf} **0-0-1**

Compton Earl *G A Butler*   65
3 ch c Efisio - Bay Bay
11^{6gf} 9^{8gf} 5^{6gf} 1^{6f} 9^{7gf} **1-0-5 £3,575**

Compton Eclaire (Ire) *G A Butler*   66 a62
3 ch f Lycius (USA) - Baylands Sunshine (Ire)
7^{5sd} 10^{5gf} 9^{6g} 5^{8gf} 6^{9gf} 2^{12sd} 1^{14gf} 2^{12f}
6^{16sd} 4^{12gf} 9^{12sd} **1-2-11 £6,196**

Compton Eclipse *G A Butler*   81
3 ch c Singspiel (Ire) - Fatah Flare (USA)
8^{8sd} 6^{7gf} 2^{8gs} 1^{7f} 5^{8g} 1^{8f} 4^{10gf} 7^{8f} 3^{8f}
10^{10g} 2^{8f} 1^{7gf} 12^{7g} 13^{7gf} **3-2-14 £18,181**

Compton Emerald (Ire) *G A Butler*   71
3 ch f Bluebird (USA) - Cheviot Amble (Ire)
8^{7gf} 12^{8g} 3^{10gf} 4^{11gf} 6^{11g} **0-0-5 £453**

Compton Emperor *G A Butler*   90 a65
3 b c Bijou D'Inde - Princess Tara
13^{7sd} 5^{7gs} 1^{8g} 15^{7g} 6^{8gf} 18^{8gf} 6^{7g}
18^{9gf} 16^{7g} **1-0-9 £11,299**

Compton Expert (Ire) *G A Butler*   54 a60
3 b g Cadeaux Genereux - Samira
5^{7sd} 6^{12sd} 6^{8s} **0-0-3**

Compton Fair *J D Bethell*   18
3 b f Compton Place - Fair Dominion
14^{8f} 11^{10gs} 10^{8g} 8^{12gf} **0-0-4**

Compton Micky *J Balding*   23

2 ch c Compton Place - Nunthorpe
13^{6g} **0-0-1**

Compton Plume *W H Tinning*   65 a31
3 ch g Compton Place - Brockton Flame
6^{6sd} 9^{9sd} 5^{7gf} 8^{6gf} 3^{5g} 11^{6f} 10^{7f} 3^{5gf}
4^{5gf} 4^{6gf} 4^{6gf} 2^{6f} 2^{5gf} 8^{5gf} 6^{5gs} **0-7-16**
£5,484

Compton Princess *Mrs A Duffield*   55
3 b f Compton Place - Curlew Calling (Ire)
10^{6sd} 3^{7gf} 7^{7f} 3^{6f} 4^{7f} 11^{7gf} 8^{6gf} 12^{7f}
16^{5gf} 8^{8gf} **0-3-10 £1,290**

Compton Star *R J Hodges*   48
3 ch g Compton Place - Darakah
9^{7gf} 9^{6gf} 13^{5f} 12^{8f} **0-0-4**

Compton's Eleven *M R Channon*   92
2 gr g Compton Place - Princess Tara
16^{6gf} 8^{6gf} 5^{6g} 1^{5gf} 1^{6gf} 3^{5gf} 3^{6gf} **2-1-7**
£9,199

Comtake Dot Com (Ire) *S A Brookshaw*   16
2 b f Tagula (Ire) - Be Prepared (Ire)
5^{5g} 4^{6gf} 9^{7gf} 8^{5gf} **0-0-4**

Comtesse Noire (Can) *A M Balding*   60 a57
4 b f Woodman (USA) - Faux Pas (Ire)
3^{9sw} 3^{12sd} 3^{9sd} 2^{12g} 5^{12g} 4^{12sd} 4^{16sd} 3^{10gf}
7^{12gf} 3^{12gf} **0-6-10 £4,260**

Concer Eto *S C Williams*   81
4 ch g Sabrehill (USA) - Drudwen
14^{8gf} 3^{8gf} 12^{7gf} 1^{8gf} 2^{7gf} 7^{7f} 14^{8g}
1-2-7 £6,085

Concert Hall (USA) *Mrs A J Perrett*   66
2 b f Stravinsky (USA) - Proflare (USA)
3^{7gf} 3^{8f} 3^{8gs} **0-1-3 £1,345**

Conchonita *B Palling*   44 a41
3 b f Bishop Of Cashel - Cactus Road (Fr)
3^{8sd} 6^{8sd} 7^{10f} 6^{10f} 6^{12gf} **0-1-5 £525**

Concubine (Ire) *J R Boyle*   75
4 b f Danehill (USA) - Bye Bold Aileen (Ire)
14^{7gf} 2^{7f} 2^{7gf} 4^{7g} 7^{7f} 3^{6gf} 12^{7f} 7^{7g}
0-3-8 £4,052

Condoleezza (USA) *J L Dunlop*   72
3 gr f Cozzene (USA) - Rosabella
10^{10gf} 6^{12gs} 13^{14gs} 2^{12gf} 1^{14gf} PU^{16g}
1-1-6 £3,690

Confuzed *Andrew Reid*
3 b g Pivotal - Times Of Times (Ire)
9^{6gf} **0-0-1**

Confuzion (Ire) *A P Jones*   31 a32
2 b f Inzar (USA) - Fernlea (USA)
9^{8f} 13^{7sd} **0-0-2**

Coniston Bay (Ire) *E J Alston*   46
3 b f Lake Coniston (Ire) - Mary Ellen Best (Ire)
8^{9f} 16^{6gf} **0-0-2**

Connect *M H Tompkins*   96 a81
6 b g Petong - Natchez Trace
3^{5sd} 4^{5sd} 1^{6sd} 3^{6sd} 6^{5g} 11^{6gf} 4^{5g} 7^{5g}
7^{5gf} 1^{5gf} 2^{5g} 4^{5g} 2^{5gf} 3^{5gf} 19^{6g} 6^{5gf} 10^{5f}
16^{5gf} **2-5-19 £29,042**

Conquering Love (Ire) *B Ellison*   89
5 b g Pursuit Of Love - Susquehanna Days (USA)
2^{14gf} 1^{12g} 2^{12gf} 4^{12f} 1^{12gf} 1^{12f} 17^{12gf}
3-2-7 £30,499

Consensus (Ire) *M Brittain*   91
4 b f Common Grounds - Kilbride Lass (Ire)
5^{6g} 8^{6gf} 1^{5gf} 13^{5gf} 9^{6s} 18^{6g} 12^{5gf} 6^{6gs}
1-0-8 £6,877

Considine (USA) *J M P Eustace*   59 a59
2 b c Romanov (Ire) - Libeccio (NZ)
7^{6gf} 4^{6sd} 5^{6sd} **0-0-3**

Consignia (Ire) *D Haydn Jones*   53 a66
4 ch f Definite Article - Coppelia (Ire)
16^{6sw} 13^{6gf} 13^{6g} 11^{7sd} 11^{6gf} 14^{6f} 3^{7f}
3^{7gf} 8^{6f} 3^{7f} 18^{6f} 10^{7f} 11^{8gs} **1-3-13 £3,214**

Constable Burton *Mrs A Duffield*   46
2 b g Foxhound (USA) - Actress
9^{7g} 7^{6g} 10^{6g} **0-0-3**

Constantine *J S Goldie*   84
3 gr g Linamix (Fr) - Speremm (Ire)
7^{8g} 12^{10gf} 6^{8gs} 5^{10gf} 11^{11gf} 8^{10g} 2^{14gf}
1^{14gf} 7^{14gf} 7^{16gf} **1-1-10 £7,770**

Contact Dancer (Ire) *J L Dunlop*   77
4 b g Sadler's Wells (USA) - Rain Queen
5^{14gs} **0-0-1**

Contagious *W J Haggas*   71 a63
2 ch f Polar Falcon (USA) - Rash
2^{6gf} 2^{6sd} **0-2-2 £2,214**

Continent *D Nicholls*   113
6 ch h Lake Coniston (Ire) - Krisia
16^{6f} 15^{5gf} 6^{6gf} 8^{5gf} 10^{6gs} **0-0-5 £3,750**

Contraband *M C Pipe*   98
5 b g Red Ransom (USA) - Shortfall
5^{14gf} 3^{12gf} **0-1-2 £1,727**

Contract *Mrs A J Perrett*   88
4 b g Entrepreneur - Ispahan
12^{8g} 16^{7g} 5^{7gf} 7^{8gf} **0-0-4 £384**

Contractor *T G Mills*   96
3 gr c Spectrum (Ire) - Karsiyaka (Ire)
2^{7gf} 12^{8gf} 11^{8gf} 1^{7g} 2^{7g} 2^{7gf} 2^{8gf} 4^{7gf}
1-5-8 £23,704

Contrary Mary *J Akehurst*   81
8 b m Mujadil (USA) - Love Street
1^{6g} 3^{7gf} 11^{7g} 5^{6g} 8^{7g} 16^{7s} 8^{7g} **1-0-7 £6,033**

Conundrum (Ire) *A C Wilson*   37
5 ch g Dr Devious (Ire) - Wasabi (Ire)
9^{7gf} **0-0-1**

Convent Girl (Ire) *Mrs P N Dutfield*   104
3 b f Bishop Of Cashel - Right To The Top
10^{8gf} 9^{10gs} 10^{9g} 3^{10gf} 18^{8f} 8^{8gf} 18^{9g}
2^{8gf} 3^{9gf} 6^{9gf} 18^{9g} 2^{8gf} **3-4-13 £33,847**

Convex (USA) *R Guest*   78
3 b c Nureyev (USA) - Conical
11^{8g} 7^{8gf} 6^{7gf} 9^{7g} 4^{7gf} 5^{7gf} 5^{7gf} 6^{6f}
1^{7gf} **1-0-9 £3,909**

Convince (USA) *Sir Michael Stoute*   90
2 ch c Mt. Livermore (USA) - Conical
3^{6gf} 2^{6gf} 1^{6gf} 8^{5gf} **1-2-5 £7,408**

Cooden Beach (Ire) *M L W Bell*   54
3 b f Peintre Celebre (USA) - Joyful (Ire)
4^{8gf} 11^{8gf} 17^{7gf} 9^{10gf} 3^{8gf} 2^{8f} **0-3-6 £1,031**

Cool Alibi *J F Coupland*
3 b f Distinctly North (USA) - Alis Princess
15^{6gf} **0-0-1**

Cool Ballerina (Ire) *D G McArdle*   55 a33
4 b f Danehill Dancer (Ire) - Arctic Ford (Fr)
10^{5sd} 18^{6g} 10^{8sd} 9^{7gf} 12^{6gf} 9^{8f} RO^{6gf} **0-0-7**

Cool Bart *B P J Baugh*
3 ch g Cool Jazz - Margaretrose Anna

11^{7sd} 13^{6gf} **0-0-2**

Cool Bathwick (Ire) *B R Millman*   39 a54
4 b g Entrepreneur - Tarafa
8^{11sd} 7^{13gf} **0-0-2**

Cool Silk (Ire) *T D Easterby*   53
2 ch c Polar Falcon (USA) - Lady Barrister
7^{5f} 7^{5gf} 7^{7f} UR^{7gs} 4^{7f} 10^{7gf} 8^{8gf} **0-0-7**

Cool Singer *Jedd O'Keeffe*   a49
5 b g Sea Raven (Ire) - Clean Singer
4^{11sd} 5^{12sd} 10^{7sd} 9^{9sw} **0-0-4**

Cool Spice *P J Hobbs*   86
6 b m Karinga Bay - Cool Run
8^{12gf} 11^{2gf} 8^{13gf} 6^{12g} **1-0-4 £3,643**

Cool Temper *P F I Cole*   77
7 b g Magic Ring (Ire) - Ovideo
18^{9f} 18^{8f} 12^{8gf} 18^{9g} 4^{8s} 18^{8g} **3-0-6 £13,296**

Coolbythepool *M Johnston*   89 a58
3 b c Bijou D'Inde - Alchi (USA)
19^{5sd} 19^{9sw} 5^{10sd} 5^{12gf} 2^{11gs} 1^{12gf} 3^{12gf}
11^{2gf} 13^{12gf} 9^{11gf} 11^{13gf} 11^{13gf} 14^{14g} 2^{12gf}
10^{14gf} 3^{12gf} 5^{13g} **6-3-17 £39,997**

Coolfore Jade (Ire) *M J Wallace*   72
3 ch f Mukaddamah (USA) - Cashel Princess (Ire)
15^{6y} 1^{10f} 4^{8f} 7^{12gf} **1-0-4 £4,802**

Cooling Off (Ire) *J R Jenkins*   9 a18
6 b m Brief Truce (USA) - Lovers' Parlour
14^{12g} 13^{12sd} **0-0-2**

Coozinha (Ire) *J A Glover*   32 a32
3 b f Lake Coniston (Ire) - Desert Palace
9^{5sd} 6^{6gf} 9^{6gf} 10^{5gf} 7^{5gf} 6^{5gf} **0-0-6**

Cop Hill Lad *B R Millman*   99
2 ch c Atraf - Crofters Ceilidh
8^{6g} 2^{5gf} 1^{5g} 2^{5g} 5^{6gf} 1^{6g} 5^{6g} 5^{6g} 6^{6gf}
2-1-9 £65,643

Copperfields Lass *W G M Turner*   41 a5
4 b f Millkom - Salvezza (Ire)
13^{6gs} 11^{8sd} 6^{7f} 9^{7f} 7^{8f} **0-0-5**

Coppington Flyer (Ire) *B W Duke*   69 a68
3 ch f Eagle Eyed (USA) - Miss Flite (Ire)
1^{7sd} 3^{7sd} 4^{6sd} 2^{7sd} 5^{7sd} 2^{7sd} 12^{7gf} 11^{8g}
1^{7gf} 10^{7g} 3^{7gf} 4^{7gf} 11^{7gf} 12^{7gf} 5^{7gf} 6^{7gs}
10^{8gf} 15^{7g} 13^{7sd} **2-5-19 £10,650**

Copplestone (Ire) *W Storey*   45
7 b g Second Set (Ire) - Queen Of The Brush
2^{14f} 6^{12gf} 5^{14s} 6^{12gf} 5^{16gf} **0-1-5 £1,064**

Coqueteria (USA) *G Wragg*   78
2 b f Cozzene (USA) - Miss Waikiki (USA)
7^{6gf} 4^{6gf} 4^{7gf} 1^{7gf} **1-0-4 £8,574**

Coquetry (USA) *Sir Michael Stoute*   44
3 ch f Distant View (USA) - Souplesse (USA)
11^{6gf} **0-0-1**

Cora (Ire) *L M Cumani*   33
2 b f Machiavellian (USA) - Mythical Creek (USA)
11^{8s} **0-0-1**

Coracle King *C Boutin*   77
3 b g Compton Place - Dicentra
8^{5gs} 4^{5f} 3^{5gf} 1^{6g} 13^{6gf} 5^{6gf} 5^{6gf} 9^{5gs}
0^{6g} 7^{7hy} **1-1-10 £5,028**

Coranglais *T D Easterby*   83
3 ch g Piccolo - Antonia's Folly
8^{6f} 5^{5gf} 1^{6gf} 6^{6g} 2^{7gf} 7^{7g} 5^{7gf} 7^{7gf}
1-1-8 £8,836

Corbel (USA) *Sir Michael Stoute*   70

3 b f Diesis - Corsini
3^{7f} 0-0-1 £587

Cordial (Ire) *Sir Mark Prescott*   77
3 gr g Charnwood Forest (Ire) - Moon Festival
1^{10f} 3^{10gf} 7^{12gf} 1-1-3 £4,580

Corisa (Ire) *B R Millman*
3 ch f Be My Guest (USA) - Unalaska (Ire)
11^{10sd} 0-0-1

Cork Harbour (Fr) *P Bowen*   68
7 ch g Grand Lodge (USA) - Irish Sea
16^{8gf} 8^{9g} 4^{12gf} 4^{11gf} 7^{12gf} 8^{15gf} 2^{13f}
6^{12g} 7^{13gf} 0-3-9 £848

Cormorant Wharf (Ire) *P J Makin*   66
3 b c Alzao (USA) - Mercy Bien (Ire)
7^{6gf} 0-0-1

Cornelius *P F I Cole*   104
6 b g Barathea (Ire) - Rainbow Mountain
18^{8g} 3^{8gf} 7^{8gf} 16^{8g} 1^{8gs} 4^{8vs} 1-0-6
£8,700

Cornish Gold *D Haydn Jones*   57 a34
2 b f Slip Anchor - Sans Diablo (Ire)
9^{6gf} 11^{7sd} 5^{6g} 0-0-3

Coronado Forest (USA) *M R Hoad*   4 a75
4 b g Spinning World (USA) - Desert Jewel (USA)
2^{8sd} 8^{8sd} 3^{8sd} 12^{9g} 8^{8sd} 7^{8sd} 10^{7sd} 2^{8sw}
2^{8sd} 7^{8sd} 6^{8sd} 0-4-11 £2,540

Corps De Ballet (Ire) *J L Dunlop*   75
2 b f Fasliyev - Dwell (USA)
5^{6gf} 4^{6gf} 3^{6gf} 1^{5gf} 1-1-4 £3,812

Corridor Creeper (Fr) *J M Bradley*   99
6 ch g Polish Precedent (USA) - Sonia Rose (USA)
2^{5g} 2^{5gf} 2^{5gf} 3^{5gs} 7^{5gf} 5^{5gf} 3^{5gf}
1^{5gf} 8^{6g} 2^{6g} 2^{5gf} 12^{5f} 9^{5gf} 1-7-14 £55,240

Corryong *B Mactaggart*
2 ch f Wolfhound (USA) - Easy Risk
7^{5gs} 0-0-1

Corsican Native (USA) *Mrs A J Perrett*   66
2 b c Lear Fan (USA) - Corsini
3^{7s} 0-1-1 £529

Corton (Ire) *P F I Cole*   88
4 gr g Definite Article - Limpopo
14^{10gf} 2^{12gf} 9^{14gf} 2^{12gf} 5^{12gf} 9^{13gf} 0-2-6
£7,172

Corylus (USA) *Sir Mark Prescott*   50
2 b f Kingmambo (USA) - Pennygown
7^{8gf} 11^{7gf} 9^{7gf} 10^{8gs} 0-0-4

Cosabawn (Ire) *L M Cumani*   57
3 b f Barathea (Ire) - Riyda
11^{8g} 6^{8g} 5^{10gf} 6^{12g} 0-0-4

Cosmic Case *J S Goldie*   55
8 b m Casteddu - La Fontainova (Ire)
8^{14gf} 9^{13gs} 3^{12gf} 5^{16gf} 1^{14f} 5^{12f} 5^{16gf}
3^{14gf} 10^{14gf} 11^{12gf} 1-0-10 £5,077

Cosmic Royale (Ire) *T P McGovern*   55 a37
3 ch f Pennekamp (USA) - Windmill Princess
9^{6sd} 6^{7gf} 8^{8g} 9^{6g} 0-0-4

Cosmic Song *R M Whitaker*   a31
6 b m Cosmonaut - Hotaria
4^{8sd} 8^{8sd} 0-0-2

Cosmocrat *R M Stronge*   63
5 b g Cosmonaut - Bella Coola
7^{10g} 0-0-1

Costa Del Sol (Ire) *J J Bridger*   55 a51
2 ch g General Monash (USA) - L'Harmonie (USA)
6^{5g} 6^{5sd} 4^{6sd} 4^{6gf} 5^{7f} 3^{5sd} 3^{5g} 2^{6f} 3^{6g}

4^{6gf} 4^{6gf} 2^{5gf} 11^{6gf} 6^{6gs} 0-2-14 £2,656

Cote Soleil *C R Egerton*   59 a56
6 ch g Inchinor - Sunshine Coast
6^{8sd} 6^{9gf} 8^{8g} 9^{9sd} 0-0-4

Cotebrook *J M Jefferson*   a42
4 ch g First Trump - Chantelys
4^{11sw} 8^{12sw} 0-0-2

Cotosol *B A McMahon*   73 a73
2 b g Forzando - Emerald Dream (Ire)
13^{5g} 5^{5gf} 2^{5gf} 1^{5sd} 4^{6gs} 5^{5gf} 4^{6gs} 14^{6g}
6^{6ft} 3^{6gf} 2^{6gf} 3^{7gf} 10^{7g} 2^{7gf} 6^{7g} 1-5-15
£10,387

Cottam Grange *M W Easterby*   45
3 b c River Falls - Karminski
6^{12gf} 7^{10gf} 11^{12gf} 9^{8gf} 6^{10gf} 5^{14gf} 0-0-6

Cottingham (Ire) *M C Chapman*   67
2 b c Perugino (USA) - Stately Princess
5^{5g} 5^{6f} 4^{5gf} 2^{7f} 4^{7gf} 8^{6gf} 11^{8gf} 0-1-7
£2,094

Cotton Eyed Joe (Ire) *A Berry*   42
2 b c Indian Rocket - Cwm Deri (Ire)
10^{5gf} 5^{5gs} 6^{5gf} 11^{7f} 9^{7gs} 0-0-5

Cotton House (Ire) *M R Channon*   97
6 b m Mujadil - Romanovna
5^{5gf} 6^{6gs} 7^{6gf} 8^{6gs} 8^{5g} 0-0-5 £3,100

Could She Be Magic (Ire) *T D Easterby*   42 a42
2 b f Titus Livius (Fr) - Ponteilla (Fr)
10^{5gf} 8^{5g} 5^{6gs} 3^{6sd} 8^{7gs} 0-1-5 £432

Coulters Candy *A C Whillans*   21
5 ch g Clantime - Heldigvis
9^{7f} 0-0-1

Counsel's Opinion (Ire) *C F Wall*   108
6 ch g Rudimentary (USA) - Fairy Fortune
11^{10gf} 3^{10g} 11^{2g} 12^{12gf} 3^{12g} 7^{12g} 9^{12g}
1^{10gf} 11^{0gf} 7^{10g} 3-2-10 £50,782

Count Cougar (USA) *T D Barron*   69 a69
3 b g Sir Cat (USA) - Gold Script (USA)
4^{5g} 3^{5gf} UR^{5f} 8^{5gs} 6^{5gf} 14^{5f} 10^{5sw} 1^{5sd}
1-0-8 £3,078

Count Davanti *M Mullineaux*   7
4 b g Puissance - I'm Playing
7^{5gf} 17^{5g} 7^{11gf} 0-0-3

Count Dracula *A M Balding*   55 a67
2 b c Dracula (Aus) - Chipaya
10^{6gf} 2^{7sd} 8^{7sd} 0-1-3 £1,072

Count On Us *Miss E C Lavelle*   6 a41
3 ch g Danehill Dancer (Ire) - Capricious Lady (Ire)
12^{7sd} 6^{8gf} 0-0-2

Count Walewski *J L Dunlop*   76
3 b g Polish Precedent (USA) - Classic Beauty (Ire)
7^{8f} 2^{8g} 2^{8gf} 1^{8gf} 12^{8f} 1-2-5 £4,963

Countess Elton (Ire) *R E Barr*   37
3 ch f Mukadamah (USA) - Be Prepared (Ire)
13^{6gf} 9^{8gf} 11^{7gf} 16^{8g} 13^{11g} 0-0-5

Countess Kiri *P Bowen*   38
5 b m Opera Ghost - Ballagh Countess
8^{18f} 0-0-1

Countess Miletrian (Ire) *M R Channon*   73
4 b f Barathea (Ire) - Sweet Alma
17^{10gf} 6^{9g} 0-0-2

Country Reel (USA) *Saeed Bin Suroor*   115
3 b c Danzig (USA) - Country Belle (USA)
2^{6gs} 8^{6gf} 5^{6gf} 0-1-3 £12,000

Countrywide Dancer (Ire) *A Derry*   53

3 b f Danehill Dancer (Ire) - Meadow Grass (Ire)
4[6gf] 6[8gf] 0-0-2 £610

Countrywide Flyer (Ire) *A Berry*　　　61 a89
2 b g Revoque (Ire) - Unbidden Melody (USA)
9[5gf] 4[7sd] 12[5gf] 4[7gs] 2[7f] 2[8gf] 2[8sw] 3[8gf]
1[8sd] 4[7f] 2[8sd] 1-5-11 £5,926

Countrywide Girl (Ire) *A Berry*　　　38
4 ch f Catrail (USA) - Polish Saga
15[7sd] 9[6gf] 13[6f] UR[6gf] 0-0-4

Countrywide Star (Ire) *C N Kellett*　　　a26
5 ch g Common Grounds - Silver Slipper
15[8sd] 8[8sd] 13[12sd] 0-0-3

Countykat (Ire) *K R Burke*　　　84
3 b g Woodborough (USA) - Kitty Kildare (USA)
5[9gf] 5[8gf] 3[10gf] 6[9gf] 0-0-4 £658

Coup De Chance (Ire) *P A Blockley*　　　93
3 ch f Ashkalani (Ire) - Tout A Coup (Ire)
4[10g] 3[10sh] 6[9ys] 2[12hy] 1[12gf] 4[11gy] 1[11f] 8[10g]
10[12g] 1[12g] 4[12gs] 1[12f] 1[12f] 5-2-13 £21,413

Couplet *H R A Cecil*　　　58
2 b f Trempolino (USA) - Coigach
3[8gf] 10[7gf] 0-0-2 £652

Courageous Duke (USA) *J Noseda*　　　104 a66
4 b c Spinning World (USA) - Araadh (USA)
12[10sd] 14[8g] 17[8gf] 4[10gf] 1[10gf] 2[10g] 6[12gf]
7[10g] 15[9gf] 1-2-9 £25,794

Courant D'Air (Ire) *P C Haslam*　　　47
2 b g Indian Rocket - Red River Rose (Ire)
4[5gs] 7[5gs] 12[6sd] 8[6gf] 0-0-4 £428

Court Alliance *R J Price*　　　50
4 ch g Alhijaz - Fairfields Cone
14[16gf] 5[14gs] 1[13g] 11[16gf] 6[16gf] 1-0-5
£4,257

Court Chancellor *P Mitchell*　　　40
2 b c Primo Dominie - Welcome Home
7[6gf] 11[8g] 10[7gf] 0-0-3

Court Masterpiece *E A L Dunlop*　　　113
3 b c Polish Precedent (USA) - Easy Option (Ire)
4[6gf] 2[7g] 3[8gf] 13[7gf] 1[8g] 1-2-5 £37,300

Court Music (Ire) *R E Barr*　　　38
4 b/br f Revoque (Ire) - Lute And Lyre (Ire)
12[6gs] 8[7s] 12[7gf] 13[8g] 0-0-4

Court Of Appeal *B Ellison*　　　79 a83
6 ch g Bering - Hiawatha's Song (USA)
2[12sd] 11[10g] 1[12gf] 10[12gf] 6[10gf] 4[12gf]
8[12gf] 2[14gs] 1-2-9 £11,449

Court One *R J Price*　　　45 a27
5 b g Shareef Dancer (USA) - Fairfields Cone
7[15sd] 9[12sd] 11[13gf] 4[16gs] 2[16gf] 6[16gf]
7[14g] 7[17gf] 10[16gf] 0-1-10 £1,631

Court Shareef *R J Price*　　　96
8 b g Shareef Dancer (USA) - Fairfields Cone
3[12g] 5[14g] 9[14gf] 13[18gf] 6[13gf] 0-0-5
£3,664

Courtelimorr *B S Rothwell*　　　35
3 b f Defacto (USA) - Auntie Fay (Ire)
15[10g] 10[7gf] 5[8gf] 10[10s] 0-0-4

Courtyard *J H M Gosden*　　　62
2 b f Halling (USA) - Jubilee Trail
6[8gf] 0-0-1

Coustou (Ire) *M A Jarvis*　　　74
3 b g In Command (Ire) - Carranza (Ire)
7[8sd] 9[7gs] 7[8sd] 5[8gf] 0-0-4

Coventina (Ire) *J L Dunlop*　　　84
2 gr f Daylami (USA) - Lady Of The Lake

5[7gf] 3[7gf] 1[8gf] 12[8gf] 1-1-4 £4,905

Cover Up (Ire) *Sir Michael Stoute*　　　116
6 b g Machiavellian (USA) - Sought Out (Ire)
6[19gf] 1[22f] 2[16gf] 2[16gf] 1-2-4 £54,040

Cowboy (Ire) *G C Bravery*　　　51
3 b c Unfuwain (USA) - Wynona (Ire)
10[10gf] 10[10gf] 4[10gf] 7[14gf] 8[14f] 0-0-5
£312

Cowboys And Angels *Mrs Lydia Pearce*　　　34 a56
6 b g Bin Ajwaad (Ire) - Halimah
8[7sd] 15[7sd] 11[7sd] 8[7gf] 9[8sd] 7[7sd] 6[8sd]
0-0-7

Coxmoore (Ire) *J J Quinn*　　　83
2 b g Among Men (USA) - Esh Sham (USA)
1[6gs] 1[7gf] 2-0-2 £7,231

Coy (Ire) *Sir Michael Stoute*　　　88
2 b f Danehill (USA) - Demure
7[6gf] 1[6g] 1-0-2 £2,597

Cracka Shakoon *R Hollinshead*　　　8
2 ch f First Trump - Natural Key
14[5gf] 15[6gs] 0-0-2

Cracking Blade *J White*
6 b g Sure Blade (USA) - Norstock
10[11g] 0-0-1

Cracking Rosie (Ire) *J Noseda*　　　53 a70
2 b f Alzao (USA) - Crystal Land
5[6g] 1[8sd] 1-0-2 £2,341

Crafty Calling (USA) *P F I Cole*　　　103
3 b c Crafty Prospector - Glorious Calling (USA)
3[6gf] 7[7g] 13[7g] 1[7gf] 5[7gf] 4[8gf] 1-1-6
£21,609

Crafty Fancy (Ire) *D J S Ffrench Davis*　　　92
2 ch f Intikhab (USA) - Idle Fancy
3[5gf] 1[5g] 1[5gs] 11[5gf] 6[6g] 5[5gf] 6[6gf] 5[5gf]
5[6g] 2-1-9 £18,588

Crafty Politician (USA) *G L Moore*　　　51
6 ch h Supremo (USA) - Sauve Qui Peut (Can)
1[7s] 4[6gf] 3[7g] 1[6gf] 2[6g] 2[7g] 9[7g] 7[6g] 10[8g]
7[7gf] 11[7g] 2[6g] 2-0-12 £13,099

Craic Sa Ceili (Ire) *M S Saunders*　　　80 a38
3 b f Danehill Dancer (Ire) - Fay's Song (Ire)
5[8gf] 7[7g] 4[7g] 5[8g] 9[7sd] 0-1-5 £2,250

Crail *C F Wall*　　　70 a35
3 b g Vettori (Ire) - Tendency
11[8sd] 18[10g] 18[8gf] 7[8gf] 1-0-4 £5,652

Craiova (Ire) *B W Hills*　　　96 a65
4 b c Turtle Island (Ire) - Velvet Appeal (Ire)
3[7sd] 1[7gs] 11[7g] 1[7g] 2[8gs] 5[7g] 16[8gs]
3-2-8 £22,325

Cranachan *J H M Gosden*　　　72
2 b f Selkirk (USA) - Baked Alaska
4[7gf] 14[7gf] 14[8s] 0-0-3 £424

Crathorne (Ire) *J D Bethell*　　　93
3 b c Alzao (USA) - Shirley Blue (Ire)
7[10g] 5[12gf] 2[12gf] 16[10g] 2[12g] 9[14g] 4[12gf]
5[12gf] 10[10gf] 3[12gf] 9[12gf] 0-3-11 £8,727

Credenza Moment *M Madgwick*　　　a16
5 b g Pyramus (USA) - Mystoski
15[12sd] 0-0-1

Creed (Ire) *F P Murtagh*　　　58
3 ch g Entrepreneur - Ardent Range (Ire)
4[10gf] 6[12g] 4[14gf] 10[14gf] 5[12gf] 6[17gf] 0-0-6
£573

Creg Ny Shee *W A Murphy*　　　20 a54
4 b g Anabaa (USA) - Cos I Do (Ire)

8⁸ˢᵈ 10¹⁰ˢᵈ 16⁹ᵍ **0-0-3**

Creskeld (Ire) *B Smart*   79 a94
4 b g Sri Pekan (USA) - Pizzazz
1⁸ˢᵈ 2⁸ˢᵈ 14⁸ᵍ 12⁸ᵍˢ 8⁷ᵍᶠ 8⁶ˢ 4⁷ᵍᶠ 5⁸ᵍᶠ
3⁸ᵍᶠ 1⁷ᵍˢ 13⁷ᵍ 8⁷ᵍˢ **2-2-12 £16,287**

Cressex Katie *J Cullinan*   79 a61
4 b f Komaite (USA) - Kakisa
2⁶ˢᵈ 11⁶ˢᵈ 7⁵ˢᵈ 9⁷ˢᵈ 16⁹ᶠ 16⁹ 8⁶ᵍ
6⁶ᵍᶠ 4⁶ᶠ 10⁶ˢʷ **3-1-11 £11,741**

Cresta Dance *Mrs Lydia Pearce*   54
3 c f Hector Protector (USA) - Red Hot Dancer (USA)
5¹²ᵍᶠ 4¹²ᵍ 5¹⁸ᶠ **0-0-3 £430**

Cretan Gift *N P Littmoden*   80
12 ch g Cadeaux Genereux - Caro's Niece (USA)
7⁶ᵍˢ **0-0-1**

Crewes Miss Isle *A G Newcombe*   72 a64
2 b f Makbul - Riviere Rouge
4⁵ˢᵈ 3⁵ᶠ 2⁵ᵍᶠ 16⁶ᶠ 5⁶ᶠ 6⁷ᵍᶠ 4⁶ᵍᶠ 2⁶ᵍᶠ
1-3-8 £7,040

Crimson Dancer *W J Haggas*   77 a76
3 b f Groom Dancer (USA) - Crimson Rosella
8⁸ᵍᶠ 1⁸ˢᵈ 18⁸ᵈ 4¹⁰ᵍᶠ 5¹⁰ᵍ 2⁹ᶠ 2¹²ˢᵈ 1¹⁰ᵍᶠ
6¹⁰ᵍ 1¹⁰ᵍᶠ 3¹⁰ᵍᶠ **4-4-11 £19,505**

Crimson Silk *D Haydn Jones*   102
3 ch g Forzando - Sylhall
3⁶ᵍ 11⁶ᵍᶠ 6⁶ᵍʸ 3⁶ᵍ **0-2-4 £3,842**

Crimson Topaz *M L W Bell*   71
3 b f Hernando (Fr) - Bronzewing
6¹⁰ᵍᶠ 1¹¹ᵍˢ **1-0-2 £3,786**

Cripsey Brook *Don Enrico Incisa*   95
5 ch g Lycius (USA) - Duwon (Ire)
1¹⁰ᵍᶠ 2¹⁰ᵍᶠ 1¹⁰ᶠ 1¹⁰ᵍᶠ 1¹¹ᵍᶠ 6¹⁰ᵍ 5¹⁰ᵍ
1¹¹ᵍᶠ 3¹⁰ᵍᶠ 1¹⁰ᵍᶠ 3¹⁰ᵍ 10¹⁰ᵍᶠ **6-3-12 £53,362**

Crispin Girl (Ire) *J L Spearing*   55 a8
2 c f General Monash (USA) - Penultimate Cress (Ire)
7⁶ᵍˢ 11⁶ᵍᶠ 4⁶ᵍᶠ 5⁶ᵍ 8⁷ˢᵈ 12⁶ᵍᶠ 9⁵ᵍ 12⁵ᵍˢ
0-0-8 £278

Crispin House *R J Price*   24
3 b f Inchinor - Ayr Classic
16⁸ᵍ 7¹²ˢᵈ 13⁶ᵍᶠ 16⁶ᵍᶠ 12¹¹ᵍᶠ **0-0-5**

Critical Stage (Ire) *John Berry*   68 a70
4 b g King's Theatre (Ire) - Zandaka (Fr)
13¹⁰ˢᵈ 1¹¹ˢᵈ 2¹²ˢʷ 3¹¹ˢʷ 1¹¹ˢᵈ 3¹²ˢᵈ 5¹⁴ᵍᶠ
8¹³ᵍˢ 12¹⁶ᵍᶠ 13¹⁰ᵍ 3⁹ᵍᶠ **2-4-12 £9,797**

Crociera (Ire) *M H Tompkins*   63
2 b c Croco Rouge (Ire) - Ombry Girl (Ire)
14⁸ᵍᶠ 8⁷ᵍˢ **0-0-2**

Crocodile Dundee (Ire) *Jamie Poulton*   88 a77
2 b c Croco Rouge (Ire) - Miss Salsa Dancer
1⁷ˢᵈ 9⁷ᵍᶠ **1-0-2 £3,066**

Croeso Croeso *J L Spearing*   104
5 b m Most Welcome - Croeso-I-Cymru
1⁵ᶠ 6⁵ᵍᶠ 4⁶ᵍˢ 11⁶ᵍᶠ 4⁶ᵍᶠ 7⁵ᵍᶠ 8⁵ᵍᶠ
1-0-8 £26,840

Croix De Guerre (Ire) *Sir Mark Prescott*   55 a36
3 gr c Highest Honor (Fr) - Esclava (USA)
10⁷ᵍ 9⁸ᶠ 10¹⁰ˢᵈ 1¹⁰ᵍᶠ 5¹⁰ᶠ 5¹²ᵍᶠ 3¹²ᶠ
2¹⁰ᵍᶠ **1-1-8 £4,923**

Crosby Donjohn *J R Weymes*   56 a24
6 ch g Magic Ring (Ire) - Ovideo
9⁸ˢᵈ 11⁸ᵍᶠ 5¹⁰ᵍᶠ 18⁹ᵍˢ 8⁹ᶠ 7⁸ᶠ 7⁹ᵍ 9⁸ᵍ
7⁹ᵍᶠ 5⁹ᵍᶠ 4¹⁰ᵍᶠ **0-0-11**

Crosby Jubilee (Ire) *J R Weymes*
2 b g Shinko Forest (Ire) - Quicksand (Ire)
15⁶ᵍ **0-0-1**

Crosby Rocker *John A Harris*
5 b m Rock Hopper - Mary Macblain
6¹²ᵍᶠ 17⁸ᵍ 11⁸ᵍᶠ 12¹¹ᵍᶠ 15⁷ᵍᶠ **0-0-5**
£480

Cross Ash (Ire) *R Hollinshead*   78
3 ch g Ashkalani (Ire) - Priorite (Ire)
7⁶ᶠ 5⁷ᵍᶠ 1⁷ᶠ 11⁷ᵍᶠ 18⁷ᵍ **1-0-5 £3,465**

Crossed Wire *Miss J Feilden*   56 a53
5 ch m Lycius (USA) - Maze Garden (USA)
11¹²ᵍ 10¹⁶ˢᵈ 12¹⁶ᵍ **0-0-3**

Crow Wood *J G Given*   96
4 b g Halling (USA) - Play With Me (Ire)
1¹⁰ᵍ 3¹⁰ᵍᶠ 1¹¹ᵍᶠ 1⁹ᵍᶠ 1⁹ᵍ 12¹⁰ᵍᶠ 3¹⁰ᵍ
5¹⁰ᵍᶠ **3-2-8 £33,019**

Crown Agent (Ire) *A M Balding*   76
3 b g Mukaddamah (USA) - Supreme Crown (USA)
7¹⁰ᵍ 18¹²ᵍᶠ 2¹³ᵍ 2¹²ᵍˢ UR¹²ᵍ **0-2-5**
£3,183

Crown City (USA) *B P J Baugh*   53 a8
3 b f Coronado's Quest (USA) - Trisha Brown (USA)
10⁷ᵍᶠ 6⁷ᵍ 11⁶ᵍ 6⁸ᵍᶠ 9⁸ˢᵈ 12⁸ᵍᶠ **0-0-6**

Crown Counsel *Mrs A J Perrett*   86
3 b c Machiavellian (USA) - Confidante (USA)
1⁷ᵍᶠ 4⁷ᵍᶠ **1-0-2 £4,791**

Crownfield *Mrs M Reveley*   76
4 b g Blushing Flame (USA) - Chief Island
1¹⁴ᵍᶠ **1-0-1 £3,900**

Crozon *J H M Gosden*   70
3 ch f Peintre Celebre (USA) - Armorique (Ire)
1¹⁰ᶠ 9¹⁰ᵍ **1-0-2 £2,632**

Cruise Director *W J Musson*   86 a74
3 b g Zilzal (USA) - Briggsmaid
5⁷ˢᵈ 3⁸ˢᵈ 8⁸ˢᵈ 2¹⁰ˢᵈ 2¹⁰ᵍ 1¹²ᵍ **2-2-6**
£12,697

Crunchy (Ire) *B Ellison*   17 a76
5 ch g Common Grounds - Credit Crunch (Ire)
11¹ˢᵈ 11¹ˢᵈ 3¹¹ˢᵈ 5¹²ˢᵈ 14¹¹ᵍᶠ **2-1-5**
£6,918

Crusoe (Ire) *A Sadik*   27 a73
6 b g Turtle Island (Ire) - Self Reliance
1⁷ˢᵈ 2⁸ˢᵈ 6⁷ˢᵈ 7⁸ˢᵈ 5⁷ˢʷ 3⁷ˢᵈ 1⁸ˢᵈ 9⁷ˢʷ
3⁷ˢᵈ 1⁸ˢᵈ 7⁸ˢᵈ 4⁹ˢᵈ 8⁸ˢᵈ 2⁹ˢᵈ 1⁸ˢᵈ 8⁷ˢᵈ 3⁸ˢᵈ
12⁸ˢᵈ 3⁹ᶠᵗ **5-6-22 £19,411**

Crusty Lily *P D Evans*   42
7 gr m Whittingham (Ire) - Miss Crusty
12⁵ˢʷ 9⁶ˢᵈ 8⁵ᵍᶠ 13⁵ᵍᶠ 16⁶ᵍᶠ 14⁶ᵍᶠ **0-0-6**

Cruzspiel *John M Oxx*   103
3 br c Singspiel (USA) - Allespagne (USA)
9¹⁰ᵍ 1¹⁰ᵍᶠ 4¹²ᵍ 1¹²ᵍᶠ 4¹²ᵍʸ 3¹⁴ᵍ 1¹⁴ᵍᶠ 6¹⁵ʰᵒ
2-2-8 £46,789

Cryfield *N Tinkler*   73 a62
6 b g Efisio - Ciboure
14⁸ᵍ 4⁸ᵍᶠ 5⁸ᵍᶠ 1⁸ᵍᶠ 6⁷ᵍᶠ 6⁷ᵍ 3⁸ᵍᶠ 8⁷ᵍᶠ
6⁷ᵍᶠ 8⁷ᵍˢ 5⁸ˢᵈ **1-1-11 £4,704**

Cryptogam *M E Sowersby*   59
3 b f Zamindar (USA) - Moss
9⁸ᵍ 2⁸ᵍ 10⁸ᵍᶠ 8⁷ᵍᶠ 13¹²ᵍᶠ 4¹⁰ᵍᶠ 4¹⁰ᵍᶠ
12⁸ᵍᶠ **0-1-8 £1,150**

Crystal (Ire) *B J Meehan*   83
2 b f Danehill (USA) - Solar Crystal (Ire)
8⁸ᵍˢ **0-0-1**

Crystal Castle (USA) *J E Hammond*   103 a104
5 b g Gilded Time (USA) - Wayage (USA)
4⁶ᶠᵗ 7⁶ᶠᵗ 10⁶ᵍᶠ 3⁶ˢ /ᵇʰᵒ **0-1-5 £9,400**

Crystal Choir *R Charlton* 27
3 b f Singspiel (Ire) - Crystal Ring (Ire)
10¹⁰ᵍˢ **0-0-1**

Crystal Colleen (Ire) *R Guest* 43 a46
3 gr f Desert King (Ire) - Silver Kristal
3⁸ˢᵈ 5⁸ˢʷ 5⁷ᵍᶠ 4⁸ᶠ 6⁹ᵍ 7⁸ˢ 9⁸ᵍᶠ **0-1-7**
£410

Crystal Curling (Ire) *B W Hills* 77
2 b f Peintre Celebre (USA) - State Crystal (Ire)
2⁶ᵍᶠ 1⁷ˢ **1-1-2 £4,320**

Crystal Seas *M W Easterby* 47 a26
3 ch f Zamindar (USA) - Abi
7⁷ᵍˢ 4⁸ᵍᶠ 6⁷ˢᵈ 5¹⁰ᵍᶠ 8⁷ᶠ **0-0-5 £457**

Crystal Star *Sir Michael Stoute* 103
3 ch f Mark Of Esteem (Ire) - Crystal Cavern (USA)
2⁷ᵍᶠ 9⁸ᵍˢ 10⁷ᵍ 10⁷ᵍ **0-1-4 £11,000**

Crystal Theatre (Ire) *H R A Cecil* 76 a38
3 b f King's Theatre (Ire) - Solar Crystal (Ire)
2¹⁰ᵍ 4¹⁰ᶠ 2¹²ᵍ 7¹²ˢᵈ **0-2-4 £3,773**

Ctesiphon (USA) *J G Given* 47
2 b f Arch (USA) - Beautiful Bedouin (USA)
7⁷ᵍˢ **0-0-1**

Cubapesky *E J O'Neill*
3 b f Fleetwood (Ire) - Robert's Daughter
8⁸ˢᵈ **0-0-1**

Cuchi *K O Cunningham-Brown* 20 a9
3 b f Danzig Connection (USA) - Classic Faster (Ire)
7⁵ˢᵈ 9⁵ᵍᶠ 10⁵ᶠ 14⁵ᵍᶠ 18⁶ᶠ 14⁸ᶠ **0-0-6**

Cuddles (Fr) *C E Brittain* 76 a87
4 b f Anabaa (USA) - Palomelle (Fr)
8⁸ˢᵈ 10¹²ˢᵈ 6⁹ᵍᶠ 13¹⁰ᵍᶠ 3⁹ᵍᶠ 5¹⁰ˢᵈ 4¹⁰ᵍ
3⁹ᵍˢ 3¹⁰ᶠ 4⁸ᵍᶠ 5¹⁰ᵍᶠ 13¹⁰ᵍˢ **0-2-12 £7,081**

Culcabock (Ire) *P Monteith* 67
3 b g Unfuwain (USA) - Evidently (Ire)
7¹¹ᶠ 12⁷ᶠ 6¹²ᵍ 2¹¹ʸ 5¹²ᵍᶠ 6⁹ᵍᶠ 7¹¹ᵍˢ **0-1-7**
£1,142

Culminate *J E Long* 30
6 ch g Afzal - Straw Blade
12¹⁰ᵍᶠ 6⁷ᵍ 8¹⁰ᵍ 16⁸ᵍ 10⁷ᵍᶠ **0-0-5**

Cumbrian Crystal *T D Easterby* 51
4 b f Mind Games - Crystal Sand (Ger)
17⁶ᵍ 11⁶ᶠ 14⁶ᵍᶠ 15⁷ᶠ **0-0-4**

Cumbrian Princess *M Blanshard* 46 a48
6 gr m Mtoto - Cumbrian Melody
9⁶ˢʷ 8⁹ˢᵈ 14⁷ᵍ 10⁸ᵍ 8⁷ᵍᶠ **0-0-5**

Cumwhitton *R A Fahey*
4 b f Jumbo Hirt (USA) - Dominance
6¹⁶ᵍᶠ 10¹⁸ᵍᶠ **0-0-2**

Cupola *P W D'Arcy* 85
2 b c Fasliyev (USA) - Spring Mood (Fr)
4⁵ᵍ 3⁶ᵍᶠ 2⁵ᵍᶠ 4⁵ᶠ **0-1-4 £5,129**

Curate (USA) *J Parkes* 51 a23
4 ch g Unfuwain (USA) - Carniola
14¹⁶ˢᵈ 10¹²ˢʷ 7¹²ˢᵈ 9⁸ˢᵈ 4¹²ᵍᶠ 7¹²ᵍᶠ 4¹⁰ᵍᶠ
9¹⁰ᵍᶠ **0-0-8 £527**

Curfew *J R Fanshawe* 102
4 b f Marju (Ire) - Twilight Patrol
5⁷ᵍ 9⁶ᶠ 5⁵ᵍᶠ **0-0-3 £1,330**

Curlew River (Ire) *D R C Elsworth* 86
3 b g Alhaarth (Ire) - Sudden Interest (Fr)
6¹⁰ᵍᶠ 2¹⁰ᵍᶠ 2⁹ᵍᶠ 7¹²ᵍ 1¹²ᵍᶠ 5¹²ᵍˢ PU¹²ᵍᶠ
1-2-7 £8,447

Curragh Gold (Ire) *Mrs P N Dutfield* 48 a56
3 b f Flying Spur (Aus) - Go Indigo (Ire)
9¹⁰ˢᵈ 6⁷ˢᵈ 1⁷ˢʷ 3⁷ˢᵈ 8⁸ᵍᶠ 8¹¹ˢʷ **1-1-6**

£3,350

Currency *J M Bradley* 89 a78
6 b g Sri Pekan (USA) - On Tiptoes
1⁵ᵍᶠ 9⁶ᵍˢ 7⁶ᵍ 14⁶ᵍᶠ 7⁶ᵍ 5⁶ᵍᶠ 10⁶ᵍᶠ 3⁶ᵍ
6⁶ᵍ 14⁶ᵍᶠ 6⁵ᵍᶠ 6⁶ˢᵈ 15⁵ᵍ **1-1-13 £9,448**

Curzon Lodge (Ire) *A J Lidderdale* 18
3 ch g Grand Lodge (USA) - Curzon Street
8⁷ᵍ **0-0-1**

Cusco (Ire) *R Hannon* 85
2 ch f Titus Livius (Fr) - John's Ballad (Ire)
3⁷ᵍ 1⁸ᵍᶠ 3⁷ᵍᶠ 8⁷ᵍᶠ 5⁸ᵍˢ **1-2-5 £8,091**

Cusin *M E Sowersby*
7 ch g Arazi (USA) - Fairy Tern
9¹⁰ᵍᶠ **0-0-1**

Cusp *C W Thornton* 38
3 b f Pivotal - Bambolona
11⁹ˢ 10¹²ᵍ 3¹²ᵍˢ 11¹⁶ᵍ **0-0-4 £589**

Cut And Dried *W Jarvis* 61 a59
2 ch g Daggers Drawn (USA) - Apple Sauce
4⁵ᵍᶠ 6⁵ˢᵈ 6⁵ᵍˢ 7⁶ᵍᶠ 17⁵ᵍ **0-0-5 £379**

Cut Rate *K Bell* 62 a76
5 ch g Diesis - Itsamazing (USA)
13¹⁰ˢᵈ 2⁸ˢᵈ 10⁸ˢᵈ 3⁸ᵍ 4⁸ˢᵈ 8⁸ˢᵈ 9⁸ˢᵈ
0-2-7 £2,481

Cut Ridge *J S Wainwright* 56
4 b f Indian Ridge - Cutting Ground (Ire)
11⁶ᵍᶠ 15⁶ᵍᶠ 12⁶ᵍ 11⁵ᵍˢ 4⁵ᵍˢ 3⁵ᵍˢ 4⁶ᵍᶠ
16ᵍᶠ 5⁵ᵍᶠ 19⁵ᵍᶠ 2⁷ᵍˢ 11⁶ᵍᶠ **1-2-12 £6,482**

Cute Cait *Mrs L Stubbs* 48
2 b f Atraf - Clunk Click
6⁵ˢ 2⁵ᵍ 16⁶ᶠ 3⁷ᵍᶠ 5⁷ᵍˢ 7⁶ᵍᶠ 9⁷ᵍᶠ 11⁸ᵍᶠ
1-1-8 £5,536

Cutting Crew (USA) *P W Harris* 82 a78
2 ch c Diesis - Poppy Carew (Ire)
4⁷ᵍᶠ 7⁸ˢ 2⁸ˢᵈ **0-1-3 £1,543**

Cyber Cinders *Miss L A Perratt*
3 ch f Cayman Kai (Ire) - Petticoat Rule
21⁵ᵍˢ RR⁵ᵍ RR⁵ᵍᶠ **0-0-3**

Cyclone Connie *C A Cyzer* 67
5 ch m Dr Devious (Ire) - Cutpurse Moll
12⁶ᵍᶠ 7⁵ᶠ **0-0-2**

Cyclonic Storm *R A Fahey* 78
4 b f Catrail (USA) - Wheeler's Wonder (Ire)
2⁸ᵍˢ 8⁹ᵍᶠ 1⁹ᵍˢ 2⁹ᶠ 3⁹ᵍ 8¹⁰ᵍᶠ 13¹⁰ᵍ 20¹¹ˢ
11¹⁰ᵍ **1-2-9 £12,861**

Cyfrwys (Ire) *B Palling* 78 a66
2 b f Foxhound (USA) - Divine Elegance (Ire)
4⁶ᵍᶠ 2⁶ᵍ 5⁶ᵍᶠ 2⁶ᵍᶠ 4⁷ˢᵈ **0-2-5 £2,661**

Czar Wars *J Balding* 65 a73
8 b g Warrshan (USA) - Dutch Czarina
3⁶ˢᵈ 1⁶ˢᵈ 6⁶ˢʷ 3⁵ˢᵈ 2⁷ˢᵈ 3⁷ˢᵈ 5⁶ˢʷ 1⁶ˢᵈ
3⁶ˢᵈ 12⁷ᵍᶠ 7⁶ˢᵈ 3⁶ᵍˢ 15⁶ˢʷ 17⁶ᵍˢ 5⁶ˢᵈ 16⁶ˢᵈ 2⁶ˢʷ
1⁶ˢʷ 3⁶ˢᵈ 12⁶ˢᵈ **5-7-20 £17,833**

Czarina Waltz *C F Wall* 87 a92
4 b f Emperor Jones (USA) - Ballerina Bay
2¹⁰ᵍˢ 3¹⁰ˢ 1¹⁰ᵍᶠ 3⁹ᵍᶠ 5¹⁰ᵍᶠ 1¹⁰ˢᵈ 3¹⁹ᵍᶠ
4¹⁰ˢ **2-2-8 £17,505**

Czars Princess (Ire) *G L Moore* 62
2 b f Soviet Star (USA) - Pearl Shell (USA)
8⁶ᶠ 7⁵ᵍᶠ 15⁷ᵍᶠ **0-0-3**

D'Accord *S Kirk* 77 a74
6 ch g Beveled (USA) - National Time (USA)
11⁶ˢʷ 3⁶ˢᵈ 16⁵ᵍᶠ 16⁶ᶠ 7⁶ᵍ 16⁶ᶠ **2-1-6**
£9,828

Da Wolf (Ire) *D Nicholls* 37 a43

5 ch g Wolfhound (USA) - Lady Joyce (Fr)
8⁶ˢʷ 4⁵ˢᵈ 10⁷ˢᵈ 12⁶ᵍᶠ 16⁶ᵍ **0-0-5**

Dabus *M C Chapman*   37
8 b g Kris - Licorne
10¹²ᵍᶠ 7¹²ᵍᶠ 6¹⁰ᵍˢ 18¹²ᵍᶠ 6¹²ᵍᶠ 12¹⁰ᵍᶠ
0-0-6

Daffodil Girl *B Palling*   a4
4 ch f Vettori (Ire) - Top Treat (USA)
9⁸ˢᵈ **0-0-1**

Daffodilly *M A Jarvis*   62
2 ch f Dr Fong (USA) - Daffodil Fields
6⁵ᵍˢ 7⁶ᵍᶠ 9⁶ᵍᶠ 5⁷ᵍᶠ **0-0-4**

Daggers Canyon *Julian Poulton*   45
2 ch g Daggers Drawn (USA) - Chipewyas (Fr)
9⁷ᵍ **0-0-1**

Dagola (Ire) *C G Cox*   50
2 b g Daggers Drawn (USA) - Diabola (USA)
9⁵ᵍˢ 11⁶ᵍᶠ 9⁶ᵍᶠ 17⁷ᵍᶠ **0-0-4**

Dahlidya *R Wilman*   a44
8 b m Midyan (USA) - Dahlawise (Ire)
3⁶ˢᵈ 6⁷ˢᵈ 10⁸ˢᵈ 5⁶ˢʷ 9⁷ˢʷ **0-1-5 £518**

Dai Jin *A Schutz*   121
3 b c Peintre Celebre (USA) - Dawlah
11¹ᵍ 11²ˢ 11²ᵍ 7¹²ʰᵒ 2¹¹ᵍ 2⁹ˢ **3-0-6**
£347,012

Daimajin (Ire) *D W P Arbuthnot*   73 a53
4 b g Dr Devious (Ire) - Arrow Field (USA)
12¹⁰ˢᵈ 9⁷ᵍᶠ 7⁷ᵍᶠ 10⁸ˢᵈ 7⁸ᵍ 11⁸ᶠ 10¹⁰ᵍᶠ
0-0-7

Daintree Affair (Ire) *K R Burke*   7 a66
3 b g Charnwood Forest (Ire) - Madam Loving
7⁵ˢᵈ 3⁵ˢᵈ 3⁵ˢᵈ 1⁵ˢᵈ 19⁵ᵍᶠ **1-2-5 £4,790**

Daisycutter *G Wragg*   56
3 ch f Zafonic (USA) - Ingozi
5⁸ᶠ 5¹⁰ᵍᶠ **0-0-2**

Dakhira *D R C Elsworth*   a24
5 b m Emperor Jones (USA) - Fakhira (Ire)
11¹⁰ˢᵈ 17¹⁰ᶠ **0-0-2**

Dakota Blackhills *J G Given*   84
2 b c Singspiel (Ire) - Lady Blackfoot
2⁷ᵍ **0-1-1 £1,123**

Dalakhani (Ire) *A De Royer-Dupre*   134
3 gr c Darshaan - Daltawa (Ire)
1¹¹ᵍˢ 1¹¹ᵍˢ 1¹²ᵍ 2¹²ᵍ 1¹²ᵍˢ 1¹²ʰᵒ **5-1-6**
£1,296,388

Dalaram (Ire) *Sir Michael Stoute*   111
3 b c Sadler's Wells (USA) - Dalara (Ire)
11¹⁰ᵍᶠ 11²ᵍˢ 11²ᵍᶠ 7¹⁶ᶠ 5¹⁵ᵍᶠ 1¹⁴ᵍᶠ 5¹⁴ᵍᶠ
3-0-7 £31,941

Dalblair (Ire) *M Todhunter*   74
4 b g Lake Coniston (Ire) - Cartagena Lady (Ire)
17¹⁰ᵍᶠ 4¹²ᵍ 8¹²ᵍᶠ 10¹²ᵍ 15¹⁰ᵍˢ 4¹²ᵍᶠ 8¹⁶ᵍᶠ
9¹²ˢ **0-0-8 £844**

Dalida *P C Haslam*   45
2 ch f Pursuit Of Love - Debutante Days
8⁷ᵍ **0-0-1**

Dalisay (Ire) *Sir Michael Stoute*   42
2 b f Sadler's Wells (USA) - Dabiliya
20⁷ᵍᶠ **0-0-1**

Dallaah *M A Jarvis*   91
2 b f Green Desert (USA) - Saeedah
1⁶ᵍ 3⁵ᵍ 10⁵ᵍᶠ 6⁶ᵍ **1-1-4 £9,003**

Dalyan (Ire) *A J Lockwood*   29
6 b g Turtle Island (Ire) - Salette
14¹⁰ᵍᶠ 13¹⁶ᵍᶠ **0-0-2**

Damachida (Ire) *T Langvad*   85
4 ch c Mukaddamah (USA) - Lady Loire
7⁷ᵍ 6⁹ᵍ 7⁷ᵍᶠ 14⁶ᵍᶠ 12⁶ˢ 1⁷ᵍ **1-0-6**
£3,577

Damalis (Ire) *E J Alston*   102
7 b m Mukaddamah (USA) - Art Age
1⁵ᵍᶠ 2⁵ᵍ 8⁵ᵍ **1-1-3 £37,242**

Damask Dancer (Ire) *J A Supple*   a51
4 b g Barathea (Ire) - Polish Rhythm (Ire)
5⁷ˢᵈ 5⁷ˢᵈ 14¹⁰ᵍᶠ 8¹⁰ˢᵈ 10¹²ˢᵈ **0-0-5**

Dame Blanche (Ire) *C F Wall*   65
3 ch f Be My Guest (USA) - Streetcar (Ire)
10⁸ˢ 6¹⁰ᵍᶠ 6¹⁰ᵍᶠ 3⁸ᵍᶠ **0-0-4 £952**

Dame De Noche *J G Given*   99
3 b f Lion Cavern (USA) - Goodnight Kiss
1⁸ᵍ 12⁷ᵍᶠ 3⁸ᵍᶠ 3⁸ᵍᶠ 10⁸ᵍᶠ 1⁷ᵍ 1⁷ᵍ 8⁷ᵍᶠ
3⁷ᵍᶠ 7⁷ᵍᶠ 9⁷ᵍᶠ **3-3-11 £46,294**

Dame Edna (Fr) *Miss Sheena West*   35
3 b f Octagonal (NZ) - Mohave Desert (USA)
9⁸ᵍᶠ 15⁸ᵍᶠ **0-0-2**

Dame Margaret *M L W Bell*   49
3 ch f Elmaamul (USA) - Pomorie (Ire)
4¹⁰ᵍᶠ 17¹²ᵍˢ 2¹⁰ᵍᶠ 10¹⁰ᵍᶠ 6¹²ᵍᶠ **0-1-5**
£1,142

Dame Nova (Ire) *P C Haslam*   49
2 b f Definite Article - Red Note
15⁶ᵍᶠ 10⁸ᵍᶠ 11⁷ᵍᶠ **0-0-3**

Dami (USA) *C E Brittain*   61
2 b f Dynaformer (USA) - Trampoli (USA)
4⁷ᵍ 4⁷ᵍᶠ 12⁷ᵍᶠ 13⁷ᵍᶠ **0-0-4 £798**

Damsel *J H M Gosden*   87
2 b f Danzero (Aus) - Rensaler (USA)
5⁸ᶠ 3⁷ᵍᶠ 1⁷ᵍˢ **1-1-3 £4,575**

Danaan Prince (Ire) *R Hannon*   70
3 ch c Danehill Dancer (Ire) - Classic Queen (Ire)
6⁷ᵍᶠ 6⁷ᵍᶠ 7⁷ᵍᶠ 13⁷ᵍ 4¹⁰ᵍᶠ 10¹⁰ᵍᶠ
0-0-7 £340

Danakil *S Dow*   86 a84
8 b g Warning - Danilova (USA)
14¹²ˢᵈ 6¹²ˢᵈ 8¹²ˢᵈ 4¹²ᵍ 5¹²ᵍᶠ 7¹²ᵍ 9¹⁴ᵍᶠ
4¹²ᵍᶠ 3¹²ᵍᶠ **0-2-9 £3,521**

Danakim *J R Weymes*   42
6 b g Emarati (USA) - Kangra Valley
15⁵ᵍᶠ 14⁶ᵍᶠ 12⁵ᵍᶠ 9⁵ᵍᶠ 8⁶ᶠ 8⁵ᵍᶠ 7⁶ᵍᶠ
10⁶ᶠ 13⁵ᶠ 5⁵ᵍᶠ 10⁶ᵍᶠ 6⁵ᵍᶠ 10⁶ᵍᶠ **0-0-13**

Dance Class (Ire) *P Hughes*   48
3 b f Desert Prince (Ire) - Dance Ahead
11⁷ᵍᶠ 8⁶ᶠ 12⁶ᵍᶠ 6⁸ᶠ 6⁶ᵍᶠ SU⁶ᵍ 13⁷ᶠ
0-0-7

Dance In The Day (Ire) *E J Alston*   70
5 b g Caerleon (USA) - One To One
10¹⁶ᵍᶠ 6¹⁶ᵍᶠ 11¹⁴ʰʸ **0-0-3**

Dance In The Sun *Mrs A J Perrett*   81 a88
3 ch f Halling (USA) - Sunny Davis (USA)
2⁸ˢᵈ 1¹⁰ᵍ 5¹⁰ᵍᶠ 2⁹ᵍᶠ 4¹²ˢᵈ **1-2-5 £6,481**

Dance Light (Ire) *T T Clement*   24
4 b f Lycius (USA) - Embracing
13¹⁴ᶠ 6¹⁶ᵍᶠ **0-0-2 £525**

Dance Of Life *S Gollings*   12
4 b f Shareef Dancer (USA) - Regan (USA)
11¹¹ᵍ **0-0-1**

Dance On The Top *J R Boyle*   83 a88
5 ch g Caerleon (USA) - Fern
1⁸ˢᵈ 7¹⁰ᵍ 16⁸ᵍ 9⁸ᵍᶠ 4⁸ᵍᶠ 3⁸ᵍᶠ 2⁸ᵍ 9⁸ᶠ
1-2-8 £8,080

Dance Party (Ire) *A M Balding*   67 a26
3 b f Charnwood Forest (Ire) - Society Ball
9^{7gf} 4^{8gf} 3^{8gf} 4^{9gf} 7^{8g} 11^{9sd} **0-1-6**
£1,654

Dance Solo *Sir Michael Stoute*   65
2 b f Sadler's Wells (USA) - Obsessive (USA)
8^{7gf} 3^{7gf} 4^{8f} **0-0-3 £850**

Dance To My Tune *M E Sowersby*   63
2 b f Halling (USA) - Stolen Melody
3^{5gf} 3^{6gf} 4^{7gf} 9^{6gf} 6^{6f} 7^{6gf} 6^{6gf} **0-2-7**
£1,658

Dancehall Darcy *A Charlton*   49 a29
4 ch f Bahamian Bounty - Dancing Chimes
7^{5sd} 4^{6g} 6^{5gf} 8^{5gf} **0-0-4 £419**

Dancer Polish (Pol) *A Sadik*
5 b g Professional (Ire) - Doloreska (Pol)
12^{12sd} **0-0-1**

Dances With Angels (Ire) *Mrs A L M King*   48 a29
3 b f Mukaddamah (USA) - Lady Of Leisure (USA)
12^{10sd} 11^{8sd} 5^{12gf} 8^{11gf} 4^{10f} 4^{10s} 4^{12f}
7^{12gf} 9^{10gf} **0-0-9 £883**

Dances With Rivers *R A Fahey*   47
4 b f River Falls - Make Merry (Ire)
6^{11gf} **0-0-1**

Dancing Bear *Julian Poulton*   19
2 b c Groom Dancer (USA) - Sickle Moon
12^{10gs} **0-0-1**

Dancing Forest (Ire) *D K Ivory*   68 a74
3 br g Charnwood Forest (Ire) - Fauna (Ire)
3^{5sd} 5^{6sd} 11^{7sd} 1^{7sd} 3^{7sd} 1^{8sd} 7^{7g} 5^{8gf}
5^{9gf} 7^{8g} 7^{7gf} 7^{8gf} 13^{7sd} 2^{10g} 9^{8f} 14^{10gf} 8^{7sd}
2-3-17 £8,569

Dancing Key *B W Hills*   34 a49
3 ch f Halling (USA) - Fleet Key
5^{8sd} 9^{10gf} 5^{8gf} **0-0-3**

Dancing King (Ire) *P W Hiatt*   58
7 b g Fairy King (USA) - Zariysha (Ire)
7^{8g} 10^{7gs} 4^{8gf} 1^{8gf} 5^{8gf} 11^{8gf} 4^{8gs}
11^{8gf} 8^{9g} 18^{8gf} **1-0-10 £4,224**

Dancing Lily *J J Bridger*   35
6 ch m Clantime - Sun Follower
7^{8f} 9^{9g} 7^{7f} 7^{8g} 10^{10gf} 7^{8gf} **0-0-6**

Dancing Lyra *J W Hills*   84
2 b c Alzao (USA) - Badaayer (USA)
9^{6g} 3^{6gf} 7^{7gf} 7^{7gf} **0-1-4 £556**

Dancing Mo (Ire) *J L Spearing*   50 a5
2 b f Danehill Dancer (Ire) - Honey Bee
9^{5gf} 9^{5gf} 3^{5f} 3^{5gf} 6^{5gf} 10^{5gf} 9^{5sd} **0-1-7**
£1,002

Dancing Mystery *E A Wheeler*   94
9 b g Beveled (USA) - Batchworth Dancer
5^{5g} 6^{5gf} 5^{6gf} 21^{6f} 10^{6gf} 7^{5f} 12^{5gf} 3^{5gf}
5^{6f} 8^{5g} 2^{5f} 5^{5gf} 10^{5gf} 9^{5gs} 1^{5g} **1-2-15**
£9,878

Dancing Nelly *B W Hills*   49
3 b f Shareef Dancer (USA) - Silent Witness
10^{9sw} 3^{6gf} 7^{7f} 9^{6g} **0-1-4 £839**

Dancing Nugget (USA) *J W Hills*   70
3 b f Seeking The Gold (USA) - Shalimar Garden (Ire)
4^{7gf} 5^{7gf} 9^{7g} 4^{10gf} 3^{12gf} 3^{12gf} 3^{10f} 6^{10gf}
4^{10f} **0-1-9 £2,731**

Dancing Pearl *C J Price*   a30
5 ch m Dancing Spree (USA) - Elegant Rose
5^{12sd} **0-0-1**

Dancing Phantom *James Moffatt*   84 a33

---

8 b g Darshaan - Dancing Prize (Ire)
10^{12gf} 6^{12sd} 5^{12f} 2^{13gs} 1^{11g} **1-1-5**
£4,650

Dancing Prince (Ire) *A P Jarvis*   47 a12
2 b c Imperial Ballet (Ire) - Eastern Aura (Ire)
14^{6sd} 11^{6gf} 5^{9gf} **0-0-3**

Dancing Ridge (Ire) *A Senior*
6 b g Ridgewood Ben - May We Dance (Ire)
13^{5g} **0-0-1**

Dancing Tassel *D Morris*   a44
4 b f Most Welcome - Delicious
14^{12sd} 8^{10sd} **0-0-2**

Dancing Tilly *R A Fahey*   41
5 b m Dancing Spree (USA) - L'Ancressaan
8^{10gf} 10^{11gf} 12^{14f} 6^{10gf} 5^{8gf} 3^{8gf} 13^{8gf}
6^{10f} **0-1-8 £481**

Dancing-Alone *D Mullarkey*
11 ch g Adbass (USA) - Lady Alone
8^{12sw} **0-0-1**

Dancinginthestreet *J G Given*   90
3 b g Groom Dancer (USA) - Usk The Way
14^{8gf} 4^{11hy} 3^{12gf} 4^{14gf} 2^{16gf} 8^{14gf} 2^{16gf}
1^{16gf} 3^{16gf} **1-4-9 £12,216**

Danclare (USA) *J H M Gosden*   77
2 ch f Stravinsky (USA) - Beyond Temptation (USA)
4^{6gf} 2^{6gf} 17^{gf} 15^{8ho} **1-1-4 £5,100**

Dandouce *S L Keightley*   50
2 b f Danzero (Aus) - Douce Maison (Ire)
4^{5gf} **0-0-1**

Dandoun *J L Dunlop*   117
5 b h Halling (USA) - Moneefa
1^{8g} 1^{8g} 7^{9s} 10^{8gs} 8^{8ho} **2-0-5 £57,813**

Danebank (Ire) *J W Hills*   60
3 b g Danehill (USA) - Snow Bank (Ire)
11^{12g} 5^{10f} 6^{10gf} 7^{8gf} 6^{10f} 4^{12g} 6^{13gf}
10^{12gf} 9^{7f} **0-1-9**

Danecare (Ire) *J G Burns*   101
3 b c Danetime (Ire) - Nordic Flavour (Ire)
11^{7gf} 6^{6s} 6^{6hy} 1^{6sh} 1^{6gf} 11^{6g} 8^{6gf} **2-0-7**
£21,583

Danefonique (Ire) *D Carroll*   51
2 b f Danetime (Ire) - Umlaut
5^{5gf} 5^{5gf} 7^{6gf} 3^{7gf} 11^{8sd} 19^{8gf} 5^{7gf}
0-0-7 £619

Danehill Lad (Ire) *T Keddy*   66 a75
3 b g Danehill (USA) - River Missy (USA)
5^{10sd} 2^{10sd} 9^{12g} 14^{9gf} 4^{10g} 11^{10f} 11^{10gf}
18^{10g} 2^{12sd} 2^{12sd} **0-4-11 £3,293**

Danehill Miss (Ire) *Joseph Crowley*   13
3 b f Danehill Dancer (Ire) - Persian Flower
15^{6f} 11^{6g} 14^{6f} 14^{14f} **0-0-4**

Danehill Stroller (Ire) *R M Beckett*   95
3 b g Danetime (Ire) - Tuft Hill
5^{6gf} 6^{6g} 2^{6g} 2^{6gf} 1^{6gf} 8^{6gf} 1^{6gf} 2^{6gf}
4^{6gf} 3^{6gf} **2-4-10 £20,720**

Danehurst *Sir Mark Prescott*   101
5 b m Danehill (USA) - Miswaki Belle (USA)
10^{6g} 1^{6g} 13^{5ho} 8^{6ho} **1-0-4 £18,560**

Danelor (Ire) *R A Fahey*   95
5 b g Danehill (USA) - Formulate
4^{8gf} 2^{10g} 2^{10g} 18^{10gf} **0-3-4 £19,600**

Danesmead (Ire) *T D Easterby*   94
2 b c Danehill Dancer (Ire) - Indian Honey
3^{5gf} 2^{5gf} 4^{5gf} 2^{5gs} 1^{6g} 2^{6y} 3^{6gf} 3^{6g}
1-4-8 £41,155

Danestat *B Palling*
4 b f Danehill Dancer (Ire) - Statuette
11⁵ˢᵈ **0-0-1**

Daneswood *K F Clutterbuck*
4 b g Be My Chief (USA) - Floria Tosca
13⁹ˢᵈ **0-0-1**

Danetime Lady (Ire) *John A Quinn*   65 a43
3 b f Danetime (Ire) - Hawattef (Ire)
12⁸ˢᵈ 9⁵ˢᵈ 5⁹ᵍʸ 19⁹ᵍᶠ **0-0-4**

Danger Bird (Ire) *R Hollinshead*   41 a51
3 ch f Eagle Eyed (USA) - Danger Ahead
3⁷ˢᵈ 2⁸ˢᵈ 8⁸ˢᵈ 8⁵ᵍᶠ 5⁷ᵍᶠ **0-2-5 £1,542**

Danger Over *J A Osborne*   118
6 b h Warning - Danilova (USA)
1⁶ᵍᶠ 4⁵ᵍᶠ 3⁶ᵍˢ 3⁷ᵍ 8⁷ᵍ 4⁷ᵍ 5⁶ᵍˢ 3⁷ᵍᶠ 7⁸ᵍˢ
2⁸ᵍˢ **1-3-10 £36,455**

Dangerous Beans *S Kirk*   61 a52
3 b g Bluegrass Prince (Ire) - A Little Hot
5¹⁰ˢᵈ 6¹²ˢᵈ 8¹²ˢᵈ 13¹¹ᵍᶠ 11¹⁶ᵍᶠ 2⁸ᶠ 1¹⁰ᵍˢ
1-1-7 £3,114

Dangerous Dave *Jamie Poulton*   a35
4 b g Superpower - Lovely Lilly
10⁷ˢᵈ 9⁸ˢᵈ 12⁶ˢᵈ **0-0-3**

Dangerously Good *R C Guest*   73
5 b g Shareef Dancer (USA) - Ecologically Kind
6¹²ᵍᶠ 5¹⁴ᵍ 9¹²ᵍᶠ **0-0-3**

Dani Ridge (Ire) *E J Alston*   92 a88
5 b m Indian Ridge - Daniella Drive (USA)
4⁶ᵍᶠ 1⁶ˢ 7⁷ᵍᶠ 11⁶ᵍᶠ 7⁷ᵍ 10⁶ᵍ 3⁶ˢᵈ 10⁶ᵍ
1-2-8 £12,360

Danielle's Lad *B Palling*   83 a86
7 b g Emarati (USA) - Cactus Road (Fr)
3⁷ˢᵈ 11⁶ˢᵈ 7⁸ˢᵈ 2⁸ˢᵈ 2⁷ˢᵈ 7⁷ᵍ 2⁷ˢᵈ 3⁸ˢᵈ
11⁷ᵍ 7⁷ˢᵈ 10⁶ˢᵈ **0-5-11 £4,875**

Danifah (Ire) *P D Evans*   69
2 b f Perugino (USA) - Afifah
5⁵ᵍ 3⁵ᵍᶠ 3⁵ᵍᶠ 7⁵ᶠ 8⁶ᵍᶠ 2⁵ᵍᶠ 2⁵ᶠ 1⁵ᵍᶠ 7⁵ᵍ
8⁵ᵍᶠ 5⁵ᵍᶠ 1⁵ᵍ UR⁵ᵍᶠ 8⁶ᵍᶠ 9⁵ᵍ 8⁵ᵍᶠ 13⁵ᵍᶠ 9⁵ᶠ
2-4-18 £11,643

Danish Decorum (Ire) *Evan Williams*   85
4 ch g Danehill Dancer (Ire) - Dignified Air (Fr)
2¹⁰ᵍᶠ 8¹¹ᵍᶠ 15¹⁰ᵍᶠ 7¹²ᵍᶠ **0-1-4 £1,720**

Danish Monarch *J L Dunlop*   76
2 b c Great Dane (Ire) - Moly
2⁶ᵍᶠ 6⁶ᵍᶠ 2⁷ᵍᶠ 2⁷ᵍᶠ 4⁷ᵍᶠ **0-3-5 £2,886**

Danny Leahy (Fr) *J G Given*   74 a63
3 b c Danehill (USA) - Paloma Bay (Ire)
3⁷ᵍ 6⁹ˢ 4¹⁰ᵍᶠ 11¹⁰ᵍᶠ 5¹²ˢʷ 3⁸ˢᵈ **0-2-6**
£1,498

Dano-Mast *F Poulsen*   120
7 b h Unfuwain (USA) - Camera Girl
10¹²ᵍ 10¹⁰ᵍᶠ 1¹²ᵍˢ 3¹²ᵍ **1-1-4 £70,573**

Dante's Devine (Ire) *A Bailey*   56
2 b g Ashkalani (Ire) - Basilea (Fr)
8⁷ᵍ 7⁷ᵍˢ 5⁸ᵍᶠ **0-0-3**

Danum *R Hollinshead*   68
3 b c Perpendicular - Maid Of Essex
4¹⁰ᵍᶠ 6⁸ʰʸ 5⁸ᵍᶠ 6¹⁰ᵍᶠ **0-0-4 £619**

Danzig Prince *K A Morgan*   30 a33
4 b g Danzig Connection (USA) - Lovely Greek Lady
6¹²ˢᵈ 8¹²ˢʷ 9¹²ᵍᶠ 10¹⁴ᵍˢ 11¹⁶ᶠ **0-0-5**

Danzig River (Ire) *B W Hills*   92
2 b c Green Desert (USA) - Sahara Breeze
7⁷ᵍ 4⁷ᵍ 6⁶ᵍ 1⁶ᶠ 1⁶ᵍᶠ 5⁶ᵍᶠ **2-0-6**
£11,482

Danzig Twister *C J Teague*
3 b f Danzig Connection (USA) - Early Gales
17⁸ᶠ 12⁷ˢʷ **0-0-2**

Danzig's Heiress *J G Given*   51
2 b f Danzig Connection (USA) - Zielana Gora
17⁸ᵍᶠ 9⁷ᵍᶠ **0-0-2**

Daphne's Doll (Ire) *Dr J R J Naylor*   42 a39
8 b m Polish Patriot (USA) - Helietta
7⁷ˢᵈ 3¹⁰ᶠ 6¹²ᶠ 17⁹ᵍᶠ 10¹⁰ᵍᶠ 11⁸ᵍᶠ 7¹⁰ᵍᶠ
8¹²ᵍᶠ 15⁸ᵍᶠ 9¹⁰ᵍᶠ UR¹⁶ᵍᶠ 7¹⁶ᵍᶠ **0-1-12 £434**

Dara Mac *N Bycroft*   57
4 b c Presidium - Nishara
13⁸ᵍᶠ 8⁹ᵍᶠ 7⁸ᵍᶠ 6⁸ᶠ 4⁷ˢ BD⁷ᵍᶠ 2⁸ᵍˢ
8⁸ᶠ 10⁸ᵍᶠ 5⁸ᵍᶠ **0-2-11 £1,568**

Darasim (Ire) *M Johnston*   119
5 b g Kahyasi - Dararita (Ire)
4¹²ᵍ 2¹⁴ᵍ 7¹⁶ᵍᶠ 4¹⁶ᵛˢ 4¹²ᵍᶠ 4¹²ᵍᶠ 1¹⁴ᵍ 3¹²ᵍ
1¹⁵ᵍˢ 1¹⁶ᵍˢ 3²⁰ʰᵒ 14¹⁶ʰᵒ **3-3-12 £121,490**

Darcie Mia *J R Weymes*   42 a29
2 ch f Polar Falcon (USA) - Marie La Rose (Fr)
7⁷ᵍ 9⁶ᵍᶠ 13⁸ˢᵈ 9⁷ᵍˢ **0-0-4**

Dare *R Lee*   a35
8 b g Beveled (USA) - Run Amber Run
10¹⁴ˢᵈ **0-0-1**

Dare To Run *J O'Reilly*
3 b f Presidium - Kabs Twist
9⁸ˢᵈ **0-0-1**

Daring Affair *K R Burke*   59 a57
2 b f Bien Bien (USA) - Daring Destiny
9⁶ᵍˢ 4⁷ᵍᶠ 4⁶ᵍˢ 5⁷ˢᵈ **0-0-4 £807**

Daring Aim *Sir Michael Stoute*   75
2 b f Daylami (Ire) - Phantom Gold
4⁷ᵍᶠ **0-0-1 £417**

Daring Connection *K R Burke*   18
3 b f Danzig Connection (USA) - Daring Destiny
7⁷ᶠ 16⁸ᵍᶠ **0-0-2**

Daring News *O O'Neill*
8 b g Risk Me (Fr) - Hot Sunday Sport
10¹²ˢʷ **0-0-1**

Dark Champion *Jedd O'Keeffe*   67
3 b g Abou Zouz (USA) - Hazy Kay (Ire)
15⁷ᵍᶠ 5⁶ᵍᶠ 2⁵ᵍˢ 3⁵ᵍᶠ 3⁶ᶠ 2⁵ᵍ 3⁵ᵍˢ 4⁶ᵍ
0-5-8 £3,577

Dark Charm (Fr) *A M Balding*   100
4 b g Anabaa (USA) - Wardara
5⁷ᵍ 2⁷ᵍᶠ 7⁷ᵍᶠ 9⁷ᵍᶠ 4⁷ᵍᶠ **0-1-6**
£4,478

Dark Cut (Ire) *A Charlton*   60
3 b g Ali-Royal (Ire) - Prima Nox
2⁹ᵍˢ 1⁹ᵍˢ 9⁸ᵍᶠ 15⁸ᵍᶠ **1-1-4 £5,832**

Dark Day Blues (Ire) *R Hannon*   74
2 ch c Night Shift (USA) - Tavildara (Ire)
3⁶ᵍᶠ 2⁶ᵍᶠ 10⁶ᵍᶠ 6⁶ᵍ 2⁶ˢ 3⁷ᵍᶠ 13⁷ᵍᶠ **0-3-7**
£3,459

Dark Dolores *J R Boyle*   50 a37
5 b/br m Inchinor - Pingin
8⁸ˢʷ 6⁸ˢᵈ 5⁷ᵍᶠ 9⁸ᵍ 9⁸ᵍᶠ 6⁹ᵍ 2¹⁰ᶠ 11¹²ˢʷ
9¹²ᶠ 5¹⁰ᶠ **0-1-10 £834**

Dark Empress (Ire) *R M Beckett*   92
2 br f Second Empire (Ire) - Good Reference (Ire)
18⁹ᵍᶠ 2⁶ᵍᶠ 1⁷ᵍᶠ 5⁷ᵍᶠ 5⁷ᵍᶠ 3⁸ᵍᶠ 5⁶ᵍᶠ **1-1-7**
£6,948

Dark Raider (Ire) *A P Jones*   68
2 br/gr f Definite Article - Lady Shikari
8⁷ᵍᶠ 8⁷ᵍᶠ **0-0-2**

Dark Shadows *W Storey*   41
8 b g Machiavellian (USA) - Instant Desire (USA)
8^{12g} 13^{13gs} **0-0-2**

Dark Shah (Ire) *A M Balding*   75
3 b g Night Shift (USA) - Shanjah
6^{6gf} 6^{7gs} 4^{8gf} 7^{8f} 7^{8g} 11^{7gf} **0-0-6 £339**

Dark Skye (Ire) *D Shaw*   47
2 b f Idris (Ire) - Bobby's Dream
5^{6g} 2^{7gf} 6^{7gf} 5^{7gf} **0-1-4 £1,562**

Dark Victor (Ire) *D Shaw*   a19
7 b g Cadeaux Genereux - Dimmer
10^{8sd} **0-0-1**

Darkwood Beach (Ire) *S Kirk*   94
4 b g Darkwood Bay - Call Of The Night (Ire)
10^{12sd} **0-0-1**

Darla (Ire) *J W Payne*   72 a57
2 b f Night Shift (USA) - Darbela (Ire)
13^{7gf} 4^{5gf} 2^{5gf} 3^{5gf} 6^{5sd} **0-1-5 £2,086**

Darmagi (Ire) *Mrs A J Perrett*   94
3 b f Desert King (Ire) - Safe Care (Ire)
2^{9gf} 3^{10gf} 2^{11gf} 3^{10g} 7^{12gs} 7^{12gs} **0-3-6
£4,828**

Darn Good *R Hannon*   72
2 b c Bien Bien (USA) - Thimbalina
8^{6gf} 4^{7gf} 5^{7f} 3^{7gf} 6^{8gf} 4^{10f} 5^{8gf} **0-0-7
£1,657**

Darsalam (Ire) *M Johnston*   3
2 b c Desert King (Ire) - Moonsilk
9^{10f} 7^{10gf} **0-0-2**

Darting (USA) *G A Butler*   73
2 b f Sahm (USA) - Mur Taasha (USA)
3^{6gf} 3^{7g} **0-1-2 £1,403**

Darzao (Ire) *E J O'Neill*
3 b f Alzao (USA) - Arctic Maid (Ire)
5^{12f} 6^{10gf} **0-0-2**

Dasar *M Brittain*   61
3 ch f Catrail (USA) - Rising Of The Moon (Ire)
16^{8g} 6^{6g} 9^{7gf} 8^{7g} 9^{6gf} 10^{7gf} 9^{7gf} **0-0-7**

Dash For Cover (Ire) *R Hannon*   76
3 b g Sesaro (USA) - Raindancing (Ire)
3^{7gf} 3^{8gs} 14^{8gf} 8^{7g} 1^{7gf} **1-2-5 £7,077**

Dash For Glory *M Blanshard*   55
4 ch g Bluegrass Prince (Ire) - Rekindled Flame (Ire)
12^{8g} 14^{10gf} 8^{10gf} 12^{10gf} 10^{9g} 10^{13gf}
10^{14g} **0-0-7**

Dash Of Ginger (Ire) *J G Given*   42
2 ch f General Monash (USA) - Kingdom Pearl
7^{6gf} 11^{7gf} 13^{8sd} **0-0-3**

Dash Of Magic *J Hetherton*   50 a53
5 b m Magic Ring (Ire) - Praglia (Ire)
2^{11sd} 1^{12sd} 4^{12g} 14^{12sd} 1^{10gf} 4^{12gf} 1^{12s}
8^{12g} 4^{12gf} 13^{12sd} **3-1-10 £11,691**

Dashing Dane *D W Chapman*   a60
3 b c Danehill (USA) - Baldemara (Fr)
4^{8sd} **0-0-1**

Dashing Gent *M S Saunders*   37
3 ch g Prince Sabo - Sistabelle
9^{10gf} 9^{8gs} 11^{7gf} **0-0-3**

Dashing Steve *Mrs A M Thorpe*   8 a42
4 b g Danzig Connection (USA) - Blazing Sunset
11^{8sd} 4^{8sd} 7^{6sd} 14^{6f} 14^{7f} 11^{9sd} **0-0-6**

Dave (Ire) *J R Best*   63
2 b g Danzero (Aus) - Paradise News
7^{5g} 12^{5gf} 5^{5gf} 13^{5gf} **0-0-4**

Dave Best (Ire) *A Berry*
3 b c Marju (Ire) - Tajanama (Ire)
14^{6gf} 8^{5gf} **0-0-2**

David's Girl *D Morris*   57
2 b f Royal Applause - Cheer
5^{6g} 4^{7gf} 11^{8f} 6^{8gf} **0-0-4 £329**

Davids Mark *J R Jenkins*   70 a66
3 b g Polar Prince (Ire) - Star Of Flanders
8^{6sd} 9^{7sd} 1^{6sd} 6^{6sd} 1^{6g} 7^{6gf} 3^{5gf} 3^{5f} 5^{5f}
5^{6gf} 5^{6sd} 9^{6g} 8^{6gf} 3^{6gf} 5^{6gf} 12^{5f} 3^{6sd} 7^{7sd}
2-4-18 £8,510

Davos *N P Littmoden*   a58
3 gr g Wolfhound (USA) - Misty Goddess (Ire)
4^{6sd} 5^{7sd} 4^{7sw} 4^{7sd} 4^{6sd} 14^{6gf} 20^{7gs}
10^{6sd} 13^{7sd} **0-0-9**

Davy Leese *W Storey*   9
3 b g Overbury (Ire) - Mac's Type (Ire)
20^{6g} 13^{8gs} 14^{8s} 15^{8s} 13^{6gf} **0-0-5**

Dawaarr (Ire) *M A Jarvis*   82 a82
3 ch c Indian Ridge - Zarawa (Ire)
8^{8gf} 4^{8gf} 2^{10g} 1^{12sd} **1-1-4 £4,786**

Dawari (Ire) *P Haley*   59
5 b g In The Wings - Dawala (Ire)
26^{18gf} 7^{14g} 2^{12ft} 7^{12ft} 5^{11sd} 6^{12sd} 4^{15gs}
0-0-7 £740

Dawn Air (USA) *D J Daly*   31
2 b f Diesis - Midnight Air (USA)
15^{7gs} **0-0-1**

Dawn Duel (Ire) *B Smart*   44
2 b f Daggers Drawn (USA) - Dawn's Folly (Ire)
13^{6gs} **0-0-1**

Dawn Invasion (Ire) *Mrs A J Perrett*   109
4 b c Common Grounds - Princess Of Zurich (Ire)
10^{12g} 4^{14gf} 1^{12gf} **1-0-3 £10,706**

Dawn Piper (USA) *D R Loder*   85
3 b g Desert Prince - June Moon (USA)
3^{8gf} 2^{7g} **0-2-2 £2,650**

Dawn Surprise (USA) *Saeed Bin Suroor*   76
2 b f Theatrical - Lignify (Arg)
3^{8gf} **0-1-1 £727**

Dawnus (Ire) *H R A Cecil*   102
3 b f Night Shift (USA) - Dame's Violet (Ire)
2^{7gf} 2^{8g} 2^{8f} 1^{8gf} 1^{10g} 4^{12gf} 1^{10f} 7^{10gf}
3-3-8 £35,447

Day Diesis (USA) *M R Channon*   55
3 ch f Diesis - Bird Of Time (Ire)
10^{8gf} 5^{11s} 9^{10gf} 6^{9gs} **0-0-4**

Day Fort (Ire) *M P Tregoning*   96
3 b c Tagula (Ire) - Young Affair (Ire)
5^{7gf} 1^{8g} 1^{9gf} 3^{10gf} **2-1-4 £18,742**

Day To Remember *A C Stewart*   74
2 gr c Daylami (Ire) - Miss Universe (Ire)
4^{7gf} 3^{7gf} **0-1-2 £884**

Daydream Dancer *C G Cox*   44
2 gr f Daylami (Ire) - Dancing Wolf (Ire)
15^{6gf} 9^{8gf} 12^{6gf} **0-0-3**

Dayglow Dancer *M R Channon*   84
5 b g Fraam - Fading
14^{8g} 13^{8gf} 8^{8gf} 10^{8hy} 1^{7gf} 3^{7gf} 8^{7gf} 3^{7g}
12^{7gf} 12^{8g} 12^{8gf} **1-3-12 £9,805**

Days Of Grace *L Montague Hall*   a61
8 gr m Wolfhound (USA) - Inshirah (USA)
13^{7sd} 5^{6sd} 5^{6sw} 10^{6sd} 12^{7sd} **0-0-5**

Daytime Girl (Ire) *B W Hills*   71
2 gr f Daylami (Ire) - Snoozeandyoulose (Ire)

5^{7f} 1^{8s} 1-0-2 £4,436

Dazzling Bay *T D Easterby*   112
3 b g Mind Games - Adorable Cherub (USA)
12^{5gs} 2^{6gf} 1^{6gf} 1^{6gf} 1^{6gf} 9^{6g} 2^{6cf} 13^{6g}
6^{6gs} 3-2-9 £101,430

Dazzling Rio (Ire) *Miss Kate Milligan*   a15
4 b g Ashkalani (Ire) - Dazzling Fire (Ire)
6^{16sd} 16^{10g} 0-0-2

Dbest (Ire) *Ms Joanna Morgan*   68
3 b g Woodborough (USA) - Leopard Lily (Ire)
14^{6f} 23^{7ys} 2^{9gy} 1^{10f} 1^{8s} 4^{8y} 12^{10gf}
13^{10gf} 7^{8gy} 2-2-9 £12,733

Dear Sir (Ire) *Mrs P N Dutfield*   56 a30
3 ch g Among Men (USA) - Deerussa (Ire)
8^{10gf} 5^{14f} 11^{12sd} 2^{12gf} 6^{13gf} 0-1-5
£1,285

Debandy Boy *J S Wainwright*
3 b g Timeless Times (USA) - Judys Girl (Ire)
15^{10gf} 0-0-1

Debbie *I A Wood*   65 a46
4 b f Deploy - Elita
3^{12sd} 6^{10sd} 7^{10g} 13^{12gf} 3^{10g} 1^{10gf} 1^{10gf}
3^{10gf} 3^{10gf} 2-3-9 £10,142

Decelerate *I A Wood*   a63
3 ch c Polar Falcon (USA) - Speed To Lead (Ire)
1^{10sd} 3^{10sd} 3^{10sd} 3^{10sd} 3^{10sd} 1-4-5
£4,897

Decisive *P R Webber*   80 a72
4 b g Alhaarth (Ire) - Alys
1^{16sd} 1^{16gf} 2^{18gf} 10^{20gf} 7^{16g} 1^{16gf} 3-1-6
£19,742

Deco Lady *P D Evans*   61
3 ch f Wolfhound (USA) - Art Deco Lady
17^{6gf} 5^{6g} 10^{6gf} 9^{8gf} 9^{9sd} 0-0-5

Deco Star (Ire) *I A Wood*   a62
4 b g Dolphin Street (Fr) - Ecco Mi (Ire)
4^{12sd} 5^{12sw} 3^{12sd} 1^{12sd} 1-1-4 £3,349

Dee Dee Girl (Ire) *R Hannon*   54
2 b f Primo Dominie - Chapel Lawn
14^{6g} 11^{7gf} 14^{6gf} 1^{7f} 1-0-4 £2,870

Deekazz (Ire) *F Watson*   a42
4 b f Definite Article - Lyric Junction (Ire)
11^{8sd} 7^{9sw} 4^{8sd} 6^{9sd} 0-0-4

Deeper In Debt *J Akehurst*   77 a84
5 ch g Piccolo - Harold's Girl (Fr)
3^{8sd} 11^{8gf} 16^{8gf} 11^{8gf} 12^{9gf} 9^{10gf} 3^{8g}
1^{8f} 1^{8f} 2-1-9 £7,074

Deewaar (Ire) *J S Moore*   57 a53
3 b g Ashkalani (Ire) - Chandni (Ire)
7^{9sd} 2^{10sd} 8^{12sd} 8^{10sd} 5^{10f} 3^{11gf} 2^{10gf}
9^{10gf} 10^{12f} 10^{10gf} 0-3-10 £2,897

Defana *M Dods*   46
2 b g Defacto (USA) - Thalya
9^{5gf} 6^{6gs} 5^{7f} 3^{7gs} 0-1-4 £451

Defiance *A P James*   23
8 b g Warning - Princess Athena
10^{5g} 10^{6f} 0-0-2

Defining *J R Fanshawe*   101
4 b g Definite Article - Gooseberry Pie
7^{13gf} 12^{14gf} 10^{14g} 3^{12gf} 0-0-4 £5,722

Definite Flash (Ire) *M Wellings*
5 b m Definite Article - Superflash
11^{14sd} 0-0-1

Definite Guest (Ire) *R A Fahey*   90 a75
5 gr g Definite Article - Nicea (Ire)

5^{7g} 12^{8gf} 5^{8gf} 3^{8sd} 2^{8gf} 1^{8gf} 1^{8gf} 3^{10g}
5^{8gf} 6^{10gf} 5^{8f} 2-3-11 £48,343

Definite Return (Ire) *D J Wintle*
5 ch m Definite Article - Keen Note
11^{9sd} 0-0-1

Definitely Special (Ire) *J M Bradley*   47 a52
5 b m Definite Article - Legit (Ire)
8^{7sd} 4^{7sd} 9^{7sd} 4^{7sd} 13^{8f} 3^{8f} 12^{8gf} 6^{7g}
8^{6gf} 14^{8gf} 11^{8gf} 0-1-11 £1,032

Deign To Dance (Ire) *J G Portman*   75
2 b f Danetime (Ire) - Lady Montekin
7^{5gs} 7^{6gf} 2^{6gf} 6^{6gf} 2^{6gf} 17^{7gf} 0-2-6
£3,963

Del Mar Sunset *W J Haggas*   76 a97
4 b g Unfuwain (USA) - City Of Angels
2^{8sd} 5^{8g} 9^{8sd} 9^{9gf} 20^{8gs} 4^{8gf} 3^{10gf} 2^{8gf}
2^{10f} 12^{8g} 1-3-10 £13,206

Delaware Trail *J S Wainwright*   46
4 b g Catrail (USA) - Dilwara (Ire)
6^{8gf} 13^{12gf} 15^{10gf} 7^{7gf} 6^{8g} 0-0-5

Delcienne *G G Margarson*   44
2 b f Golden Heights - Delciana (Ire)
9^{7gf} 4^{6gf} 7^{6gf} 9^{8gf} 0-0-4

Delegate *N A Callaghan*   75
10 ch g Polish Precedent (USA) - Dangora (USA)
7^{5gf} 7^{5gf} 10^{5gf} 11^{5gf} 1^{5f} 5^{5f} 2^{5gf} 3^{5gf}
3^{5gf} 11^{5gf} 1-2-10 £9,112

Delham (Ire) *J D Czerpak*   59 a50
3 ch c Machiavellian (USA) - Matila (Ire)
4^{8sd} 3^{12sd} 5^{12gf} 8^{14sd} 4^{11gf} 5^{12sd} 3^{14gf}
7^{10f} 3^{12gs} 6^{12gf} 6^{12sd} 7^{14g} 4^{12gf} 2^{16gf} 5^{14gf}
5^{12gf} 4^{16gs} 0-4-17 £3,883

Delichon (Ire) *G L Moore*   34 a48
3 b f Bluebird (USA) - Summer Style (Ire)
10^{6sd} 6^{7sd} 10^{6sd} 7^{8sd} 7^{6sd} 5^{7gf} 10^{6gf}
0-0-7

Delightful Gift *M Brittain*   43
3 b f Cadeaux Genereux - Delightful Chime (Ire)
9^{6gf} 17^{6g} 6^{6gf} 4^{7s} 14^{7gs} 0-0-5 £428

Delightfully *B W Hills*   64
2 b f Definite Article - Kingpin Delight
8^{6gf} 0-0-1

Dellagio (Ire) *R Hannon*   82
2 b c Fasliyev (USA) - Lady Ounavarra (Ire)
12^{6gf} 15^{9f} 13^{6gf} 1-0-3 £5,193

Delsarte (USA) *M Johnston*   114
3 b c Theatrical - Delauncy
1^{10gf} 1^{10gs} 2^{12gf} 13^{10gf} 4^{12gf} 3^{10g} 2-2-6
£80,296

Delta Flyer (Ire) *W R Muir*   57 a54
4 b g Zafonic (USA) - Pacy (USA)
8^{8gf} 9^{7g} 4^{7sw} 12^{8sd} 0-0-4

Delta Force *P A Blockley*   45 a49
4 b g High Kicker (USA) - Maedaley
5^{7sw} 7^{5sw} 7^{6sd} 3^{5sd} 9^{6gs} 19^{5gf} 6^{6gf} 3^{7gf}
5^{5gs} 6^{7sd} 10^{6sd} 0-2-11 £908

Delta Lady *C W Fairhurst*   43 a37
2 b f River Falls - Compton Lady (USA)
9^{5g} 3^{7f} 4^{7f} 7^{5gf} 2^{7gs} 6^{7f} 18^{6gf} 13^{7f}
0-2-8 £1,341

Delusion *T D Easterby*   66
2 b f Hennessy (USA) - Another Fantasy (Ire)
3^{6gf} 2^{6f} 8^{6gs} 4^{5gf} 15^{7g} 4^{6f} 17^{6f} 0-1-7
£2,535

Demi Bouteille *Mrs J R Ramsden*   42

2 b f Wolfhound (USA) - Tattinger
9^{5gf} 12^{5g} 4^{5gs} 10^{6f} 0-0-4

Demolition Molly *R F Marvin*   71
2 b f Rudimentary (USA) - Persian Fortune
7^{5gf} 5^{6gf} 1^{5g} 5^{5gf} 8^{5gf} 5^{5f} 1-0-6
£4,644

Demonstrate (USA) *J H M Gosden*   114
5 ch h Storm Bird (Can) - Substance (USA)
3^{8g} 1^{6gf} 4^{7gs} 1-0-3 **£26,879**

Den'S-Joy *Miss D A McHale*   71 a85
7 b m Archway (Ire) - Bonvin
7^{8sw} 8^{9sd} 3^{8gf} 12^{8g} 14^{8gf} 9^{10gf}
11^{8g} 8^{9gf} 4^{8gf} 7^{10gf} 9^{10g} 10^{8gf} 12^{10g} 10^{9sd}
9^{10gf} 5^{9f} 1-1-17 **£5,270**

Denebola (USA) *P Bary*   108
2 br f Storm Cat (USA) - Coup De Genie (USA)
4^{6gs} 1^{6gs} 3^{6s} 1^{8ho} 2-1-4 **£134,627**

Denise Best (Ire) *M Johnston*   59 a37
5 ch m Goldmark (USA) - Titchwell Lass
8^{8sd} 5^{12gs} 7^{7gf} 1^{10gf} 1-0-4 **£3,786**

Denmark (Ire) *P G Murphy*   64 a8
4 b c Danehill (USA) - Shamarra (Fr)
9^{8f} 18^{10gs} 12^{10f} 11^{8sd} 0-0-4

Dennis Our Menace *S Dow*   68 a82
5 b g Piccolo - Free On Board
12^{8sd} 5^{8sd} 3^{8sd} 12^{8sd} 12^{8g} 5^{8gs} 6^{8gf}
13^{8gf} 0-1-8 **£804**

Deportivo *R Charlton*   118
3 b c Night Shift (USA) - Valencia
6^{5gf} 1^{5gf} 8^{5gf} 1^{5g} 1^{5gf} 3-0-5 **£122,337**

Deraasaat *E A L Dunlop*   87
2 ch f Nashwan (USA) - Nafhaat (USA)
7^{7gf} 18^{8f} 1-0-2 **£3,454**

Derriche (Ire) *I A Wood*   55 a50
2 ch f Ali-Royal (Ire) - Royal Daughter
7^{7gf} 5^{7f} 4^{7ft} 4^{7ft} 16^{8gf} 10^{8sd} 0-0-6
£316

Derwent (USA) *J D Bethell*   43
4 b/br g Distant View (USA) - Nothing Sweeter (USA)
17^{10gf} 3^{10gf} 0-0-2 **£1,702**

Des *J J Quinn*   59
3 b g Timeless Times (USA) - Song's Best
14^{5gf} 3^{6gf} 12^{6f} 10^{6f} 0-1-4 **£445**

Desert Arc (Ire) *A M Balding*   61
5 b g Spectrum (Ire) - Bint Albadou (Ire)
4^{9g} 6^{6gs} 6^{6gf} 7^{6gf} 16^{6g} 0-0-5 **£423**

Desert Battle (Ire) *M Blanshard*   65
2 ch g Desert Sun - Papal
3^{6gf} 4^{6gf} 9^{7gf} 9^{7g} 9^{7gf} 0-1-5 **£889**

Desert Beau (Ire) *Mrs P N Dutfield*   55
2 b g Desert Style (Ire) - Miss Siham (Ire)
8^{6gf} 5^{6gf} 12^{6gf} 0-0-3

Desert Cristal (Ire) *J R Boyle*   83
2 ch f Desert King (Ire) - Damiana (Ire)
2^{6g} 5^{7gf} 0-1-2 **£1,496**

Desert Daisy (Ire) *I A Wood*   68
2 gr f Desert Prince (Ire) - Pomponette (USA)
2^{7gs} 2^{6gf} 12^{6g} 6^{7gf} 0-2-4 **£3,813**

Desert Dance (Ire) *G Wragg*   73
3 b c Desert Story (Ire) - Cindy's Star (Ire)
4^{8gf} 3^{8gf} 14^{8f} 12^{8gf} 0-0-4 **£1,078**

Desert Deer *M Johnston*   119
5 ch h Cadeaux Genereux - Tuxford Hideaway
2^{9gf} 1^{8g} 10^{8gf} 1-1-3 **£69,000**

Desert Destiny *D R Loder*   109

3 b g Desert Prince (Ire) - High Savannah
1^{7gf} 5^{8gs} 10^{8s} 5^{7gf} 4^{7gf} 1-0-5 **£19,354**

Desert Diplomat (Ire) *Sir Michael Stoute*   67
2 br c Machiavellian (USA) - Desert Beauty (Ire)
23^{7gf} 4^{7gf} 11^{7s} 0-0-3 **£348**

Desert Dreamer (Ire) *B W Hills*   93
2 b g Green Desert (USA) - Follow That Dream
4^{6g} 1^{7g} 5^{7gf} 4^{6g} 2^{6gf} 8^{7g} 1-0-6
£12,449

Desert Flame *A M Balding*   60 a23
3 b g Desert Prince (Ire) - Paradise Soul (USA)
10^{9g} 2^{8f} 11^{12g} 10^{8gf} 19^{11gf} 12^{10sd} 0-1-6
£1,157

Desert Fortune (Ire) *M J Wallace*   65
3 ch g Desert Prince (Ire) - Fairy Fortune
13^{10g} 16^{8gs} 6^{8gf} 3^{10gf} 11^{10gf} 10^{10f} 9^{8f}
0-1-7 **£425**

Desert Fury *R Bastiman*   55 a55
6 b g Warning - Number One Spot
2^{7sd} 5^{7sd} 6^{7sw} 6^{7sd} 7^{7gf} 3^{7gf} 11^{8gs} 10^{10s}
10^{8gf} 7^{8sd} 5^{8sd} 12^{7g} 7^{6gf} 10^{7s} 0-2-14
£1,540

Desert Glow (Ire) *S Seemar*   10 a93
3 b f Machiavellian (USA) - Alumisiyah (USA)
3^{8ft} 7^{8ft} 5^{8ft} 4^{8ft} 2^{9ft} 11^{10gf} 0-1-6
£36,170

Desert Heat *H R A Cecil*   64 a45
5 b h Green Desert (USA) - Lypharitissima (Fr)
6^{10gf} 4^{8gf} 10^{7sd} 0-0-3

Desert Image (Ire) *A J Lidderdale*   53 a61
2 b c Desert King (Ire) - Identical (Ire)
7^{6g} 3^{8sd} 3^{8sw} 0-1-3 **£845**

Desert Island Disc *J J Bridger*   84 a51
6 b m Turtle Island (Ire) - Distant Music
2^{10f} 9^{10gf} 4^{12f} 10^{12f} 7^{10gf} 3^{10gf} 6^{12gf}
8^{12gf} 2^{9gf} 2^{10gf} 4^{10gf} 1^{12g} 1^{12gf} 3^{12gf} 3^{10gs}
6^{10g} 6^{13gf} 8^{12gf} 3^{12f} 7^{12sd} 2-7-20 **£23,812**

Desert Light (Ire) *D Shaw*   a6
2 b c Desert Sun - Nacote (Ire)
10^{5sd} 9^{6sd} 15^{6sd} 0-0-3

Desert Loch (Ire) *N Tinkler*   40
3 b f Desert King (Ire) - Kinlochewe
13^{12sd} 11^{10gf} 11^{12gs} 8^{12gf} 9^{12gf} 4^{10g} 4^{12gf}
7^{10gf} 9^{10gf} 0-0-9 **£266**

Desert Opal *J H M Gosden*   99
3 ch c Cadeaux Genereux - Nullarbor
7^{7gf} 4^{7gf} 1^{6gs} 2^{8gf} 1^{8g} 1^{8s} 14^{8gs} 3-1-7
£28,686

Desert Quest (Ire) *Sir Michael Stoute*   94
3 b c Rainbow Quest (USA) - Jumilla (USA)
1^{10g} 4^{12gs} 6^{12gf} 1^{10gf} 2-0-4 **£12,446**

Desert Quill (Ire) *D R C Elsworth*   55 a42
3 ch f In The Wings - Aljood
9^{10sd} 5^{8g} 14^{8gf} 15^{10gf} 10^{12gf} 3^{12gf} 8^{11gf}
0-0-7 **£520**

Desert Reign *A P Jarvis*   66
2 ch c Desert King (Ire) - Moondance
7^{6gf} 13^{7gf} 19^{8gf} 0-0-3

Desert Rock (Ire) *N Tinkler*   29
3 b g Desert Style (Ire) - Olympic Rock (Ire)
18^{7gs} 15^{8gf} 0-0-2

Desert Royal (Ire) *A Bailey*   45 a28
4 ch g Ali-Royal (Ire) - Hajat
12^{7sd} 6^{7gf} 10^{8f} 9^{5hy} 13^{6f} 20^{6gf} 0-0-6

Desert Royalty (Ire) *E A L Dunlop*   86

3 b f Alhaarth (Ire) - Buraida
1⁸ᵍ 6⁹ᵍᶠ 2¹⁰ᶠ 5⁹ᶠ 1¹¹⁰ᶠ 3¹⁰ᵍᶠ 1¹¹²ᵍ 2¹⁰ᵍ
3¹²ᵍᶠ **3-3-9 £17,119**

Desert Spa (USA) *G E Jones*   a43
8 b g Sheikh Albadou - Healing Waters (USA)
8¹²ˢʷ 8¹³ˢᵈ 7¹²ˢᵈ 6⁸ˢᵈ 12¹²ˢᵈ 8¹²ˢᵈ 8¹²ˢᵈ
0-0-7

Desert Spirit (Ire) *J R Best*   a94
3 b g Desert Style (Ire) - Lady Bennington
1⁷ˢᵈ 4⁶ˢᵈ 1⁶ˢᵈ 1¹⁰ˢᵈ **3-0-4 £25,886**

Desert Tommy *T G Mills*   24
2 b c Desert King (Ire) - Flambera (Fr)
14⁷ᵍᶠ **0-0-1**

Desert Valentine *L G Cottrell*   43 a12
8 b g Midyan (USA) - Mo Ceri
17¹²ᵍᶠ 8¹²ᵍ 9¹²ˢᵈ **0-0-3**

Design Perfection (USA) *J H M Gosden*   100
3 b f Diesis - Bella Ballerina
1¹⁰ᵍᶠ 3¹⁰ˢ **1-1-2 £9,688**

Designer City (Ire) *A Berry*   61 a61
2 b f Mujadil (USA) - Carnickian (Ire)
PU⁵ᵍˢ 5⁵ᵍᶠ 5⁵ˢᵈ 36ˢᵈ 7⁶ˢᵈ 6⁵ᵍ 4⁵ˢᵈ 4⁵ᵍᶠ
6⁶ˢᶠ 6⁶ˢᵈ **0-1-10 £569**

Desires Destiny *M Brittain*   50
5 b m Grey Desire - Tanoda
6¹⁰ᵍˢ 6¹⁰ᵍˢ 7⁷ᵍᶠ **0-0-3**

Desperate Dan *J A Osborne*   87 a86
2 b c Danzero (Aus) - Alzianah
16⁶ᵍ 1⁶ˢᵈ 2⁶ᵍ **1-1-3 £5,274**

Desraya (Ire) *K A Ryan*   73
6 b g Desert Style (Ire) - Madaraya (USA)
8⁶ᵍᶠ 3⁶ᶠ 3⁵ᵍᶠ 9⁶ᵍᶠ 16⁶ᵍˢ 9⁶ᵍᶠ 9⁶ᵍᶠ 9⁷ᵍᶠ
0-2-8 £2,039

Destination Dubai (USA) *D R Loder*   85
2 b/br c Kingmambo (USA) - Mysterial (USA)
2⁸ᵍ 2⁸ᵍᶠ **0-2-2 £3,816**

Destiny Star *Miss V Haigh*   7
2 b f Forzando - Troia (Ire)
15⁶ᵍᶠ 7⁶ᶠ **0-0-2**

Destructive (USA) *J Mackie*
5 b/br g Dehere (USA) - Respectability (USA)
8¹⁶ˢʷ **0-0-1**

Detailed (Ire) *R Hannon*   74
2 b c Alhaarth (Ire) - Arab Scimetar (Ire)
4⁷ᵍᶠ 2⁷ᵍᶠ 4⁷ᵍ 4⁸ᵍᶠ **0-1-4 £2,141**

Detonateur (Fr) *Ian Williams*   a58
5 b g Pistolet Bleu (Ire) - Soviet Princess (Ire)
6¹²ˢᵈ **0-0-1**

Devant (NZ) *M A Jarvis*   98
3 b f Zabeel (NZ) - Frenetic (NZ)
1⁸ᵍᶠ 6⁸ᵍᶠ 14¹⁰ᵍ 1⁷ᵍ 8⁷ᵍ 6⁸ᵍᶠ 7⁸ᵍᶠ 5¹⁰ˢ
2-0-8 £17,630

Devil Moon (Ire) *A P O'Brien*   102
2 b c Danehill (USA) - Moon Drop
2⁵ʸ 1⁵ʸ 6⁶ᵍ 3⁷ᵍˢ 4⁶ᵍ **1-2-5 £24,414**

Devil's Bite *B W Hills*   76
2 ch c Dracula (Aus) - Niggle
6⁶ᵍᶠ 5⁶ᵍᶠ 6⁶ᵍᶠ 2⁷ᵍˢ 7⁸ᵍᶠ **0-1-5 £1,120**

Devil's Teardrop *D J S Cosgrove*   59
3 ch g Hernando (Fr) - River Divine (USA)
18⁸ᵍᶠ 5⁸ᵍᶠ **0-0-2**

Devine Light (Ire) *B Mactaggart*   67 a61
3 b f Spectrum (Ire) - Siskin (Ire)
4⁷ˢᵈ 11¹⁰ˢᵈ 14⁸ᵍ 16⁸ᵍ 10⁸ᵍᶠ 8⁸ˢᵈ 5⁸ᶠ
13⁷ᵍᶠ 1⁹ᵍᶠ **1-1-9 £4,888**

Devious Boy *P C Haslam*   a98
3 br g Dr Devious (Ire) - Oh Hebe (Ire)
3⁷ˢᵈ 3¹⁰ˢᵈ **0-1-2 £3,646**

Devise (Ire) *M S Saunders*   81 a33
4 b g Hamas (Ire) - Soreze (Ire)
15⁵ˢᵈ 11⁵ᵍ 1⁵ᵍᶠ 11⁶ᵍᶠ 3⁵ᵍᶠ 6⁵ᵍᶠ 11⁵ᵍᶠ
11⁶ᵍ **1-1-8 £4,439**

Devito (Fr) *M F Harris*
2 ch c Trempolino (USA) - Snowy (Fr)
9⁸ˢʷ **0-0-1**

Devolution (Ire) *J M P Eustace*   82 a35
5 b g Distinctly North (USA) - Election Special
9⁹ˢᵈ 7¹⁰ᵍˢ 1¹⁰ᵍ **1-0-3 £5,681**

Devon Flame *R J Hodges*   77
4 b g Whittingham (Ire) - Uaeflame (Ire)
4⁸ᵍˢ 1⁶ᵍᶠ 1⁶ᵍᶠ 1⁶ᵍᶠ **3-0-4 £14,242**

Dexileos (Ire) *A D W Pinder*   76 a37
4 b g Danehill (USA) - Theano (Ire)
13⁸ᵍᶠ 4⁸ᵍˢ 18⁷ᵍ 14⁸ˢᵈ 11⁸ᵍˢ **0-1-5**

Dhabyan (USA) *B Hanbury*   101
3 ch c Silver Hawk (USA) - Fleur De Nuit (USA)
5⁸ᵍ 6¹⁰ᵍᶠ **0-0-2 £784**

Dhakhirah (Ire) *A C Stewart*   75
3 b f Sadler's Wells (USA) - Good Luck Charm (USA)
9¹⁰ᵍᶠ 7¹¹ˢ 2⁸ᵍᶠ 3⁸ᵍ 2¹⁰ᵍᶠ **0-3-5 £4,344**

Dhehdaah *N A Graham*   55
2 b c Alhaarth (Ire) - Carina Clare
6⁸ᵍᶠ 7⁸ᵍ 14⁷ᵍ **0-0-3**

Di Young *J W Hills*   57 a64
3 b f Hernando (Fr) - Mo Chos Chle
7⁸ˢᵈ 5¹⁰ˢᵈ 7¹⁰ˢᵈ 7¹¹ᶠ 7¹²ᶠ 5¹²ᶠ **0-0-6**

Diacada (Ger) *H Blume*   110
3 b f Cadeaux Genereux - Diasprina (Ger)
8⁸ᵍᶠ 1⁸ᵍ 9⁸ᵍˢ 3⁸ˢ **1-1-5 £79,545**

Diagon Alley (Ire) *K W Hogg*   30
3 ro g Petong - Mubadara (Ire)
9⁸ᶠ 19⁷ᵍˢ 10⁸ᵍᶠ 12⁸ᵍᶠ **0-0-4**

Dial Square *P Howling*   31
2 b g Bluegrass Prince (Ire) - Honey Mill
11⁷ˢ **0-0-1**

Dialing Tone (USA) *Sir Michael Stoute*   88
3 b f Distant View (USA) - Call Account (USA)
8⁷ᵍᶠ 8⁸ᶠ **0-0-2**

Diamond Darren (Ire) *Miss Victoria Roberts* 41
4 ch g Dolphin Street (Fr) - Deerussa (Ire)
9¹²ˢᵈ 14¹²ᵍᶠ **0-0-2**

Diamond Decorum (Ire) *J Hetherton*   48
7 ch g Fayruz - Astra Adastra
9⁶ᵍᶠ 5⁶ᵍᶠ 8⁷ᵍˢ **0-0-3**

Diamond Dreamer *M G Quinlan*   57
2 b f Loup Solitaire (USA) - Wakeful Night (Fr)
12⁸ᵍᶠ 6⁷ᵍ 6⁸ᵍᶠ **0-0-3**

Diamond George (Ire) *John Berry*   54
2 b g Sri Pekan (USA) - Golden Choice
2⁶ᵍᶠ 6⁷ᵍᶠ 6⁶ᵍᶠ **0-1-3 £1,217**

Diamond Girl *T D Easterby*   25
3 b f Mind Games - Its All Relative
18⁵ˢᵈ 12⁶ᶠ **0-0-2**

Diamond Green (Arg) *B R Millman*   32 a98
5 ch g Roy (USA) - Diamond Ring (Arg)
5⁹ˢᵈ 6⁸ˢᵈ 1⁸ˢᵈ 1⁸ˢᵈ 17⁸ˢᵈ **3-0-6**
£10,277

Diamond Green (Fr) *A Fabre*   111
2 br c Green Desert (USA) - Diamonaka (Fr)

1⁷ᵍˢ 1⁷ᵍˢ 1⁷ˢ **3-0-3 £36,364**

Diamond Holly (Ire) *P D Evans* 23
2 b f Imperial Ballet (Ire) - Common Bond (Ire)
12⁵ᵍᶠ 14⁶ᵍˢ 8⁵ᵍᶠ **0-0-3**

Diamond Jobe (Ire) *J Hetherton* a10
4 ch g College Chapel - Dazzling Maid (Ire)
10⁸ˢᵈ 12⁹ˢᵈ 18⁸ᵍ **0-0-3**

Diamond Joshua (Ire) *M E Sowersby*
5 b g Mujadil (USA) - Elminya (Ire)
15¹⁷ᵍᶠ **0-0-1**

Diamond Max (Ire) *P D Evans* 97 a90
5 b g Nicolotte - Kawther
15⁸ᵍ 3⁸ˢᵈ 4⁸ˢʷ 11⁸ˢᵈ 15⁶ᵍᶠ 6⁶ᵍᶠ 2⁹ᵍᶠ
18ᵍˢ 7⁸ᵈ 1⁶ᵍ 10⁸ᶠ 8⁸ᵍᶠ 5⁷ᵍ **2-2-13 £14,162**

Diamond Maxine (Ire) *John Berry*
3 b f Turtle Island (Ire) - Kawther
14⁸ᵍᶠ **0-0-1**

Diamond Mick *G G Margarson* 68
3 ch g Pivotal - Miss Poll Flinders
9⁸ᵍ 15¹²ᵍ 5⁸ᵍᶠ 3⁸ᶠ 2¹⁰ᵍᶠ 4¹²ᵍᶠ 9¹⁰ᵍᶠ
13¹⁰ᵍ **0-2-8 £2,960**

Diamond Orchid (Ire) *P D Evans* 59 a39
3 gr f Victory Note (USA) - Olivia's Pride (Ire)
12⁸ᵍ 17⁶ᵍᶠ 10⁷ˢᵈ 8⁸ˢᵈ 7¹²ᵍˢ 11⁶ᵍᶠ 6¹⁰ᵍᶠ
2⁹ᵍˢ **0-1-8 £711**

Diamond Racket *D W Chapman* 44 a42
3 b g Cyrano De Bergerac - Reina
8⁶ˢᵈ 9⁸ˢᵈ 8⁵ˢᵈ 6⁶ˢᵈ 6⁶ˢᵈ 9⁵ᵍ 11⁶ᵍ 10⁶ᵍᶠ
12⁵ˢᵈ 16⁵ᵍᶠ 14⁶ᶠ **0-0-11**

Diamond Ribby (Ire) *P D Evans* 11
2 br f Desert Sun - Kathleen's Dream (USA)
19⁷ᵍᶠ **0-0-1**

Diamond Right *M Wigham*
3 b f Robellino (USA) - Petrikov (Ire)
11¹²ˢᵈ **0-0-1**

Diamond Ring *Mrs J Candlish* 59 a55
4 b f Magic Ring (Ire) - Reticent Bride (Ire)
7⁶ˢᵈ 14⁶ˢᵈ 12¹²ˢᵈ 20⁶ᵍ 7⁵ᵍᶠ 9⁵ᵍᶠ 3⁶ᵍᶠ
6⁵ᵍᶠ 16⁵ᵍᶠ 5⁵ᵍ 3⁵ᵍᶠ 6⁵ᵍ 9⁶ᵍᶠ **0-2-13 £895**

Diamond Shannon (Ire) *D Carroll* 44
2 b f Petorius - Balgren (Ire)
2⁶ᵍᶠ **0-1-1 £614**

Diamond Way (USA) *D R Loder* 57 a38
2 ch c Boundary (USA) - Discover Silver (USA)
8⁷ᵍᶠ 13⁶ᵍᶠ 9⁶ˢᵈ **0-0-3**

Diamonds Red Ruby *J S Wainwright* 13
2 b f Factual (USA) - Dispol Diamond
14⁵ᵍˢ 15⁵ᵍᶠ **0-0-2**

Diamonds Will Do (Ire) *Miss Venetia Williams* 64
6 b m Bigstone (Ire) - Clear Ability (Ire)
2¹²ᵍᶠ 12¹⁶ᵍᶠ **0-1-2 £1,732**

Diaphanous *E A Wheeler* 47 a46
5 b m Beveled (USA) - Sharp Venita
12⁶ˢᵈ 5⁵ˢʷ 4⁵ˢᵈ 17⁶ᵍˢ 3⁵ᵍ 2⁵ᶠ 13⁵ᵍᶠ 3⁵ᵍᶠ
13⁵ᶠ 7⁵ᵍᶠ 6⁵ᵍᶠ 4⁵ᵍᶠ **0-2-12 £2,705**

Dibble's Barn *R J Hodges*
3 b f Thowra (Fr) - Colette's Choice (Ire)
16¹¹ᵍᶠ **0-0-1**

Dicharachera *H R A Cecil* 88
3 b f Mark Of Esteem (Ire) - Al Persian (Ire)
4⁹ᵍᶠ 3⁸ᵍᶠ 3¹⁰ᵍᶠ 1⁸ᵍˢ 2⁸ᵍ 9⁸ᵍᶠ 3⁸ᵍᶠ **1-3-7**
£10,793

Dick The Taxi *R J Smith* 75 a84
9 b g Karlinsky (USA) - Another Galaxy (USA)
5¹²ˢᵈ 2¹²ˢᵈ 1¹²ˢᵈ 3¹²ˢᵈ 2¹⁰ᵍˢ **1-3-5**

£4,890

Dickie Deadeye *G B Balding* 56
6 b g Distant Relative - Accuracy
15¹⁰ᵍ 15⁹ᵍᶠ **0-0-2**

Didifon *N P McCormack* 61
8 b g Zafonic (USA) - Didicoy (USA)
8¹²ᵍᶠ 9¹⁷ᵍᶠ **0-0-2**

Didnt Tell My Wife *C F Wall* 73 a72
4 ch g Aragon - Bee Dee Dancer
8⁸ˢᵈ 11⁸ˢᵈ 8⁷ˢᵈ 12⁷ᵍᶠ 1⁷ᵍ 2⁷ᵍ 8⁷ᵍᶠ 4⁸ᵍᶠ
1⁸ˢ 17⁸ᵍ 2⁸ᵍˢ **2-3-11 £10,410**

Didoe *P W Hiatt* 57 a56
4 br f Son Pardo - My Diamond Ring
7⁷ˢᵈ 6⁸ˢᵈ 10⁷ˢᵈ 11⁷ˢᵈ 11⁸ˢᵈ 5⁶ˢᵈ 4⁷ˢʷ
12⁷ˢʷ 3⁷ᶠ 8¹⁰ᶠ 3⁸ᵍᶠ 3⁸ᶠ 3¹⁰ᶠ 9⁷ᵍᶠ **0-2-14**
£1,914

Diequest (USA) *Jamie Poulton* 20
2 ch c Diesis - Nuance (Ire)
16⁶ᵍᶠ **0-0-1**

Differential (USA) *B Smart* 79 a76
6 b/br g Known Fact (USA) - Talk About Home (USA)
11⁸ˢᵈ 17ˢᵈ 7⁷ᵍᶠ 1⁷ˢᵈ 1⁷ᶠ 11⁷ᵍᶠ 6⁸ᵍᶠ 11⁷ᵍ
1⁷ᵍᶠ **4-0-9 £18,514**

Digdaga (USA) *Mrs S Lamyman* a28
4 b/br f Machiavellian (USA) - Baaderah (Ire)
7¹¹ˢᵈ 9⁸ˢᵈ 9¹²ˢʷ **0-0-3**

Digger (Ire) *Miss Gay Kelleway* 71 a76
4 ch g Danzig Connection (USA) - Baliana
9⁷ˢᵈ 7⁷ˢᵈ 4⁷ˢᵈ 3⁸ˢᵈ 3⁷ˢᵈ 4⁸ˢᵈ 11⁷ᵍ 2⁹ˢᵈ
8¹⁰ᵍˢ 3¹²ˢᵈ 1¹²ᵍᶠ 3¹³ᵍᶠ 2¹⁶ˢᵈ 11¹⁶ᵍ 8¹⁴ᵍᶠ **1-6-15**
£7,992

Digital *M R Channon* 109
6 ch g Safawan - Heavenly Goddess
11⁷ᵍ 5⁷ᵍ 1⁸ᵍ 2⁷ᵍ 6⁷ᵍᶠ 25⁷ᶠ 2⁷ᵍ 14⁷ᵍᶠ
2⁷ᵍ 9⁸ᵍᶠ 4⁷ᵍᶠ 2⁸ᵍᶠ 15⁷ᵍᶠ 1⁷ᵍᶠ 6⁷ᵍᶠ 10⁷ᵍᶠ 2⁷ᵍᶠ
2-5-17 £37,406

Dignified *Mrs C A Dunnett* 37 a21
3 b f Entrepreneur - Awtaar (USA)
9⁸ᵍ 19¹⁰ᵍ 12¹²ˢᵈ 9¹⁴ᶠ 13¹²ˢᵈ 16⁷ᵍᶠ 5¹⁰ᵍᶠ
0-0-7

Dil *Mrs N Macauley* 30 a69
8 b g Primo Dominie - Swellegant
5⁶ˢʷ 9⁶ˢᵈ 9⁶ˢᵈ 16⁶ˢᵈ 7⁶ˢʷ 6⁶ˢʷ 7⁷ˢᵈ 6⁶ˢᵈ
8⁷ˢᵈ 3⁶ˢᵈ 13⁶ᵍᶠ 15⁷ᵍᶠ 6⁶ˢʷ **1-1-13 £3,345**

Dileer (Ire) *L M Cumani* 95
4 b g Barathea (Ire) - Stay Sharpe (USA)
6¹⁰ᵍᶠ 1¹⁰ᵍˢ 20¹²ᵍᶠ 8¹¹ᵍᶠ 5¹⁰ᵍᶠ 2¹²ᵍᶠ 12¹²ᵍᶠ
1-0-7 £8,343

Diligent Lad *D W Barker*
3 b g Secret Appeal - Mohibbah (USA)
7¹²ᶠ **0-0-1**

Diliza *G B Balding* 61
4 b f Dilum (USA) - Little White Lies
10⁸ᵍᶠ 9⁸ᵍᶠ 13⁸ᵍᶠ 4⁸ᵍᶠ 5⁸ᵍᶠ 3⁸ᵍᶠ 2⁸ᵍᶠ 7⁹ᵍ
5⁸ᵍ 13⁸ᵍᶠ **0-3-10 £3,074**

Dilsaa *K A Ryan* 36
6 ch g Night Shift (USA) - Llia
5¹¹ᵍᶠ **0-0-1**

Dilys *W S Kittow* 59
4 b f Efisio - Ramajana (USA)
10⁶ᵍ 8⁸ᵍ 17⁷ᵍᶠ 9⁷ᵍ 11⁶ˢᵈ **0-0-5**

Dimple Chad *L M Cumani* 81
4 b g Sadler's Wells (USA) - Fern
8¹⁴ᵍᶠ **0-0-1**

Dingley Lass *H Morrison* 56 a21

3 ch f Fleetwood (Ire) - Riverine
7^{10gf} 13^{12sd} 0-0-2

Dinofelis *W M Brisbourne*   44
5 b g Rainbow Quest (USA) - Revonda (Ire)
6^{12gf} 2^{11gf} 7^{12g} 6^{12gf} 7^{12gf} 7^{12gf} 0-1-6
£1,255

Diorama (Ger) *L A Dace*
8 b m Bakharoff (USA) - Dosha (Fr)
8^{16sd} 0-0-1

Diosypros Blue (Ire) *J A Osborne*   100
2 b c Bluebird (USA) - Calamander (Ire)
6^{6gf} 7^{7gf} 5^{6gf} 1^{6g} 1^{6gf} 1^{6gf} 2^{6g} 3-1-7
£32,818

Direct Bearing (Ire) *D K Weld*   97
6 b g Polish Precedent (USA) - Uncertain Affair (Ire)
7^{19gf} 4^{12g} 4^{18gf} 3^{16gf} 3^{16g} 0-3-5
£14,100

Direct Reaction (Ire) *Miss Gay Kelleway*   a36
6 b g College Chapel - Mary's Way (Gr)
9^{9sd} 12^{7sd} 5^{16sd} 0-0-3

Disabuse *S C Williams*   54
3 ch g Fleetwood (Ire) - Agony Aunt
11^{10g} 13^{12gf} 9^{12g} 2^{7gf} 6^{8gf} 0-1-5 £994

Disco Diva *M Blanshard*   69
2 ch f Spectrum (Ire) - Compact Disc (Ire)
6^{6g} 4^{5gf} 3^{5gf} 6^{6gf} 7^{5gf} 1^{6gf} 5^{6gf} 2^{7f}
1-1-8 £5,501

Discoed *M J Polglase*   a23
3 b f Distinctly North (USA) - Lunar Music
6^{7sd} 12^{6sd} 8^{11sd} 0-0-3

Discreet Brief (Ire) *J L Dunlop*   111
3 b f Darshaan - Quiet Counsel (Ire)
1^{10gf} 3^{11g} 2^{15gf} 2^{12f} 2^{14g} 1^{15g} 4^{14s} 2-4-7
£64,163

Discreet Girl *Mrs S Lamyman*   6
4 b f Mistertopogigo (USA) - Pillow Talk (Ire)
16^{6sd} 9^{10gs} 16^{8f} 0-0-3

Disengage (USA) *G A Butler*   73 a65
2 gr/ro c Runaway Groom (Can) - Teeming Shore (USA)
4^{7sd} 3^{7f} 1^{7gf} 1-0-3 £3,880

Disgrace *Mrs S J Smith*   6
3 b g Distinctly North (USA) - Ace Girl
10^{7f} 11^{9gf} 0-0-2

Disko Bay (Ire) *A M Balding*   53 a38
3 b f Charnwood Forest (Ire) - Mermaid Beach
7^{10sd} 8^{10sd} 4^{7gf} 8^{8gf} 15^{8gf} 0-0-5 £279

Dispol Evita *Jamie Poulton*   57 a45
4 ch f Presidium - She's A Breeze
13^{10sd} 7^{8sd} 12^{10f} 14^{9gf} 1^{10f} 1^{10gf} 13^{10gf}
4^{10gf} 4^{10f} 7^{10gf} 6^{10gf} 5^{10gf} 3^{10f} 5^{10f} 13^{10sd}
2-0-15 £7,241

Dispol Katie *T D Barron*   88
2 ch f Komaite (USA) - Twilight Time
2^{6gf} 3^{5f} 2^{5g} 1^{5f} 3^{5f} 1^{5gf} 14^{7g} 2^{5g} 2-5-8
£31,618

Dispol Peto *Ian Emmerson*   67 a72
3 gr g Petong - Plie
9^{5sd} 4^{8sw} 1^{7sw} 5^{7gf} 8^{8g} 10^{7gf} 1-0-6
£3,211

Dispol Veleta *T D Barron*   17
2 b f Makbul - Foxtrot Pie
7^{5gf} 0-0-1

Distant Connection (Ire) *A P Jarvis*   73
2 b c Cadeaux Genereux - Night Owl
16^{8gf} 4^{8gf} 5^{8gf} 9^{8gf} 3^{7gf} 0-1-5 £1,590

Distant Country (USA) *Mrs J R Ramsden*   81
4 b g Distant View (USA) - Memsahb (USA)
0^{8g} 3^{7gf} 4^{7f} 1^{7f} 9^{8sd} 7^{8g} 3^{8sd} 10^{8gf}
1^{7gf} 4^{7g} 2-2-10 £9,365

Distant Cousin *M A Buckley*   69
6 b g Distant Relative - Tinaca (USA)
13^{10gf} 17^{12g} 9^{12gf} 3^{12g} 3^{15gf} 2^{14f} 2^{12gf}
2^{12gf} 2^{12gf} 5^{12gf} 6^{15gf} 0-6-11 £8,758

Distant Diva *D Nicholls*   54
4 b f Distant Relative - Miss Poll Flinders
14^{5gf} 5^{5gf} 15^{6g} 6^{5gf} 14^{5gf} 0-0-5

Distant King *G P Kelly*   53
10 b g Distant Relative - Lindfield Belle (Ire)
6^{6gf} 5^{5gf} 7^{6gf} 0-0-3

Distant Light *M S Saunders*   28 a44
3 b f Groom Dancer (USA) - Warning Star
9^{8f} 7^{7gf} 6^{6sd} 7^{7sd} 0-0-4

Distant Prospect (Ire) *A M Balding*   100
6 b g Namaqualand (USA) - Ukraine's Affair (USA)
7^{16g} 7^{16gs} 7^{18gf} 3^{15g} 3^{17g} 0-2-5 £4,959

Distant Scene (USA) *T D McCarthy*   50 a61
5 b g Distant View (USA) - Dangora (USA)
2^{6sd} 4^{6sd} 7^{6g} 8^{7f} 0-1-4 £1,172

Distant Sky (USA) *Miss J S Davis*   a29
6 ch g Distant View (USA) - Nijinsky Star (USA)
8^{16sd} 0-0-1

Distant Storm *B J Llewellyn*   3
10 ch g Pharly (Fr) - Candle In The Wind
9^{22gf} 0-0-1

Distant Times *T D Easterby*   76
2 b c Orpen (USA) - Simply Times (USA)
4^{6gf} 3^{6gs} 2^{6gf} 2^{6gf} 3^{6g} 0-4-5 £4,368

Distinction (Ire) *Sir Michael Stoute*   114
4 b g Danehill (USA) - Ivy Leaf (Ire)
3^{14gf} 4^{16gf} 7^{14gf} 5^{12f} 1^{14gf} 1-1-5
£17,052

Distinctive Dancer (Ire) *I A Wood*   a34
5 b/br h Distinctly North (USA) - Resiusa (Ity)
10^{10sd} 12^{14sw} 15^{12g} 0-0-3

Distinctive Dream (Ire) *A Bailey*   a51
9 b g Distinctly North (USA) - Green Side (USA)
3^{6sd} 6^{7sw} 6^{6sd} 2^{6sw} 0-2-4 £1,355

Distinctlysplendid *I A Wood*   46 a55
3 b g Distinctly North (USA) - Shelley Marie
8^{8sd} 10^{10gf} 7^{11gf} 8^{8gf} 11^{7gf} 6^{10sd} 4^{10gf}
9^{11g} 0-0-8

Distinctlythebest *F Watson*
3 b c Distinctly North (USA) - Euphyllia
16^{6gf} 0-0-1

Dium Mac *N Bycroft*   76
2 b g Presidium - Efipetite
4^{6gf} 2^{7gf} 0-1-2 £2,903

Diva Dancer *J Hetherton*   35
3 ch f Dr Devious (Ire) - Catina
7^{10gf} 11^{8gf} 0-0-2

Diva Maria *R F Johnson Houghton*   52
4 b f Kris - May Light
10^{7g} 11^{7sd} 12^{7gf} 0-0-3

Diversification *P D Evans*   18
2 ch f Piccolo - Atan's Gem (USA)
11^{6gs} 5^{5gf} 0-0-2

Divine Gift *M A Jarvis*   85
2 b c Groom Dancer (USA) - Child's Play (USA)
2^{6gf} 10^{7gf} 1^{7g} 2^{7gs} 1-2-4 £6,366

Divine Spirit *M Dods*   83

2 b g Foxhound (USA) - Vocation (Ire)
4^{5gf} 5^{6gf} 4^{5gf} 3^{5f} 10^{6g} 4^{5f} 4^{6gf} 4^{6gf}
2^{5f} 1^{5f} 6^{6g} 1^{5gf} **2-1-12 £17,030**

Divorce Action (Ire) *S R Bowring*
7 b g Common Grounds - Overdue Reaction
18^{10gs} **0-0-1**

Divulge (USA) *A Crook*
6 b g Diesis - Avira
12^{12gf} **0-0-1**

Dixie Dancing *C A Cyzer*   a70
4 ch f Greensmith - Daylight Dreams
5^{7gf} 15^{7sd} 3^{7sd} 12^{7sd} **0-1-4 £310**

Dizzy In The Head *J O'Reilly*   81
4 b g Mind Games - Giddy
5^{5gf} 1^{6gs} 5^{6gf} 6^{6gf} 7^{6gf} 12^{5g} 19^{6g} **1-0-7**
£3,851

Dmitri *M L W Bell*   88
3 b c Emperor Jones (USA) - Shining Cloud
12^{7gf} 2^{8gf} 10^{8g} 4^{8f} 8^{8gf} 4^{7gf} 5^{10gf}
15^{9gf} 2^{8f} **0-2-9 £5,018**

Do Buy Me (Ire) *W J Haggas*   32 a23
3 b f First Trump - Reticent Bride (Ire)
4^{7sd} 6^{6gf} 13^{8gf} **0-0-3**

Doberman (Ire) *P D Evans*   45 a49
8 br g Dilum (USA) - Switch Blade (Ire)
6^{8sd} 6^{12sd} 3^{9sd} 9^{10f} 4^{10gf} 7^{8gf} **0-1-6**
£419

Doc Watson (Fr) *R Hannon*   88 a83
3 ch c Dr Devious (Ire) - Blinding (Ire)
5^{8gf} 2^{9gf} 1^{8sd} **1-1-3 £4,769**

Docduckout *J M P Eustace*   a63
3 b g Bluegrass Prince (Ire) - Fayre Holly (Ire)
9^{7sd} 1^{7sd} 6^{9sw} 10^{7sd} **1-0-4 £2,933**

Docklands Babygirl *N P Littmoden*   61
2 b f Polar Falcon (USA) - Anytime Baby
3^{6gf} 4^{6g} 6^{6gf} **0-1-3 £1,115**

Docklands Brian *P S McEntee*   57
2 ch g First Trump - Mystique
7^{6gf} 12^{6gf} 5^{7gf} 10^{6gs} 5^{7gf} 7^{7gf} 12^{8gf}
12^{7sd} **0-0-8**

Docklands Maximus (Ire) *N P Littmoden*   87
3 ch g Danehill Dancer (Ire) - Thats Luck (Ire)
6^{8gf} 5^{8hy} 4^{7g} 6^{8gf} 4^{7gf} **0-1-5 £3,924**

Docklands Prince (USA) *N P Littmoden*   a6
3 ch g Distant View (USA) - Texas Trophy (USA)
7^{7gf} 13^{10sd} **0-0-2**

Docklands Princess (Ire) *M H Tompkins*   45 a18
3 ch f Desert Prince (Ire) - Alamiya (Ire)
14^{10sd} 12^{12g} **0-0-2**

Dockside Story (Ire) *A Berry*   32
2 b g Docksider (USA) - Fiction
7^{5gf} 15^{6gs} 6^{5f} 12^{7f} **0-0-4**

Doctor Dennis (Ire) *Mrs Lydia Pearce*   51 a61
6 b g Last Tycoon - Noble Lustre (USA)
5^{6sd} 9^{6sw} 15^{7sd} 19^{7gf} 9^{6sd} 4^{6gs} 7^{6sd} 3^{7sd}
6^{6sd} 5^{6gf} 15^{6f} 4^{6gf} 7^{6gf} 7^{6gf} 4^{7s} **0-2-15**
£1,523

Doctor One *M Dods*   75
2 ch g Dr Fong (USA) - City Of Angels
18^{7f} **1-0-1 £6,513**

Doctor Price *K A Ryan*   48
2 ch g Wolfhound (USA) - Water Pixie (Ire)
3^{5gf} **0-1-1 £424**

Doctor Spin (Ire) *D Nicholls*   65
7 b g Namaqualand (USA) - Madam Loving

12^{6gs} 2^{7f} 3^{6gf} **0-2-3 £1,504**

Doctorate *E A L Dunlop*   72
2 b c Dr Fong (USA) - Aunt Tate
4^{6gf} **0-0-1 £400**

Doctored *B J Meehan*   58 a52
2 ch g Dr Devious (Ire) - Polygueza (Fr)
5^{7sd} 2^{7sd} 5^{7gf} 6^{8gs} 13^{7sd} 2^{7f} 11^{7gf} 2^{8gf}
3^{8sd} **0-4-9 £2,690**

Doctrine *J H M Gosden*   88
2 b f Barathea (Ire) - Auspicious
6^{6gf} 2^{8gf} 1^{8gf} 1^{7gf} 6^{8g} **2-1-5 £10,436**

Dodger (Ire) *Jamie Poulton*   37 a42
3 b g Among Men (USA) - Hazy Image
13^{6sd} 9^{10sd} 6^{10gf} 4^{7gf} 8^{6gf} 12^{5gf} 4^{12gf}
0-0-7 £697

Dodona *T D McCarthy*   70
5 b/br m Lahib (USA) - Dukrame
3^{10gf} 3^{10f} 2^{10gf} 2^{10gf} 6^{8f} 1^{10gf} 1^{11gf}
2-4-7 £7,716

Dolce Piccata *B J Meehan*   86 a60
2 ch f Piccolo - Highland Rhapsody (Ire)
12^{5gf} 4^{5sd} 2^{5gf} 2^{5gf} 2^{5gf} 4^{5g} 2^{5sd} 3^{5gf}
1^{5gf} 3^{5gf} 2^{6gf} **1-7-11 £18,033**

Dollar King (Ire) *B J Llewellyn*   62
5 b g Ela-Mana-Mou - Summerhill
9^{10gf} **0-0-1**

Dollar Law *R J Price*   a37
7 ch g Selkirk (USA) - Western Heights
9^{11sd} **0-0-1**

Dolly Wotnot (Ire) *N P Littmoden*   63
2 b f Desert King (Ire) - Riding School (Ire)
9^{7gf} 4^{8gf} 4^{8gf} **0-0-3 £583**

Dolphinelle (Ire) *Jamie Poulton*   a56
7 b g Dolphin Street (Fr) - Mamie's Joy
7^{8sd} 11^{10sd} 9^{10sd} 5^{7sd} 8^{8sd} 7^{8sd} **0-0-6**

Dolzago *P W Harris*   53 a49
3 b g Pursuit Of Love - Doctor's Glory (USA)
11^{8gf} 12^{8f} 14^{10gf} 5^{12g} 5^{12sd} **0-0-5**

Dom Shadeed *R J Baker*   14 a40
8 b g Shadeed (USA) - Fair Dominion
4^{13sd} 8^{13sd} 3^{13sd} 7^{15sd} 15^{12sd} 13^{12f} **0-1-6**
£421

Dombeya (Ire) *J H M Gosden*   66
3 b f Danehill (USA) - The Faraway Tree
4^{8gf} 3^{12g} 11^{10gs} **0-0-3 £1,466**

Domedriver (Ire) *P Bary*   126
5 b h Indian Ridge - Napoli
4^{8g} 2^{8g} 5^{8gs} 2^{8gs} 7^{8gs} **0-2-5 £100,650**

Domenico (Ire) *J R Jenkins*   83
5 b g Sadler's Wells (USA) - Russian Ballet (USA)
6^{16gf} 7^{15gf} 11^{22f} 2^{16gf} **0-1-4 £3,070**

Domestica (Ire) *A M Balding*   12
2 b f Robellino - Pictina
16^{7g} **0-0-1**

Dominaite *G P Kelly*
5 b g Komaite (USA) - Fairy Kingdom
16^{6g} **0-0-1**

Dominica *M P Tregoning*   107
4 ch f Alhaarth (Ire) - Dominio (Ire)
4^{5gf} 4^{5gf} 2^{5gf} 18^{5ho} **0-1-4 £25,360**

Dominion Prince *D Mullarkey*
5 b g First Trump - Lammastide
12^{16sd} 11^{12sw} **0-0-2**

Dominion Rose (USA) *W R Muir*   46 a57
4 b/br f Spinning World (USA) - Louju (USA)

1^{7sd} 6^{7gf} 17^{7gf} **1-0-3 £3,255**

Domirati *R Charlton*   85 a79
3 b g Emarati (USA) - Julia Domna
1^{5sd} 3^{5f} 2^{6gf} 3^{5gf} 13^{5g} 2^{5gf} 2^{5gf} 3^{6gf}
4^{6gf} **1-6-9 £16,828**

Domquista D'Or *G A Ham*   a37
6 b g Superpower - Gild The Lily
8^{12sd} 6^{12sw} 6^{12sw} 9^{12sd} **0-0-4**

Don Argento *Mrs A J Bowlby*   41
2 gr c Sri Pekan (USA) - Grey Galava
18^{6gf} 9^{6gf} 18^{7gf} **0-0-3**

Don Fayruz (Ire) *Mrs A J Bowlby*   47
11 b g Fayruz - Gobolino
14^{8gf} 9^{8gf} 8^{8gf} **0-0-3**

Don Fernando *M C Pipe*   88
4 b c Zilzal (USA) - Teulada (USA)
11^{16gs} 7^{20gf} 9^{16g} 33^{18gf} **0-0-4**

Don't Matter *B Palling*   14
3 b f Petong - Cool Run
12^{8g} 13^{8sd} **0-0-2**

Don't Sioux Me (Ire) *C R Dore*   85
5 b g Sadler's Wells (USA) - Commanche Belle
4^{14gf} **0-0-1 £1,028**

Don't Tell Rosey *M Blanshard*   76
3 b c Barathea (Ire) - Patsy Western
8^{6gf} 7^{6g} 6^{5s} 2^{5gf} 2^{5gf} 1^{5gf} 7^{5gf} **1-2-7**
£6,266

Don't Worry Mike *G F Bridgwater*
9 ch g Forzando - Hat Hill
12^{9sd} **0-0-1**

Dona Maria *A Berry*   5
3 b f Titus Livius (Fr) - Distant Isle (Ire)
5^{8sd} 13^{6sd} 9^{6gf} **0-0-3**

Donatello Primo (Ire) *G L Moore*   71 a41
4 ch g Entrepreneur - Mystical River (USA)
18^{7g} 9^{7gf} 5^{7f} 11^{7gf} 8^{8sd} 11^{7gf} **0-0-6**

Donegal Dancer (Ire) *B W Hills*   80
3 ch g Spectrum (Ire) - Unfuwaanah
1^{8f} 6^{9gf} 5^{8f} 11^{8g} 3^{8gf} 9^{7gf} 6^{8gf} 6^{8f}
1-1-8 £6,663

Donegal Shore (Ire) *Mrs J Candlish*   44 a81
4 b c Mujadil (USA) - Distant Shore (Ire)
15^{12sd} 7^{8sd} 6^{12gf} 14^{8gf} 12^{15sd} **0-0-5**
£233

Donizetti (Ire) *R Charlton*   77
3 b c Deputy Minister (Can) - Festival Song (USA)
12^{7g} 10^{7gf} 15^{6g} 7^{7gf} 18^{6gf} **0-0-5**

Donna Anna *C F Wall*   a17
4 b f Be My Chief (USA) - Countess Olivia
13^{12sd} 11^{12sd} **0-0-2**

Donna Vita *G A Butler*   79 a76
2 b f Vettori (Ire) - Soolaimon (Ire)
1^{7sd} 14^{8ho} **1-0-2 £3,406**

Donna's Double *D Eddy*   71
8 ch g Weldnaas (USA) - Shadha
8^{10gs} 19^{8gf} 15^{10s} 6^{10gf} 8^{10f} 3^{10gf} 16^{8gf}
3^{9s} 18^{10g} 5^{9g} 38^{9s} 4^{10gf} 9^{10gf} 5^{10gf} 5^{10g}
5^{12gf} **0-2-16 £2,764**

Donny Bowling *M E Sowersby*   51
3 b f Sesaro (USA) - Breakfast Creek
UR^{5gf} 15^{5gf} 3^{7gf} 6^{8s} 14^{8gf} 7^{7gf} 16^{8gf}
3^{14gs} 13^{12gf} **0-1-9 £867**

Dont Call Me Derek *S C Williams*   49
2 b g Sri Pekan (USA) - Cultural Role
7^{5gf} **0-0-1**

Dont Talk Shop (Ire) *N P Littmoden*   a50
4 b g Desert Style (Ire) - Madam Loving
3^{6sd} 6^{6sd} 8^{6sd} **0-1-3 £461**

Dontstopthemusic (Ire) *M R Channon*   75
2 b f Night Shift (USA) - Sevi's Choice (USA)
5^{6gf} 2^{5gf} 3^{5gf} 1^{5gf} 9^{6gf} 2^{5gf} 8^{6gf} 18^{7g}
1-3-8 £8,124

Doohulla (USA) *G A Butler*   85 a79
2 ch f Stravinsky (USA) - Viva Zapata (USA)
3^{6gf} 5^{6gf} 1^{6sd} 3^{6g} **1-1-4 £6,976**

Dora Corbino *R Hollinshead*   47
3 b f Superpower - Smartie Lee
5^{8gf} 6^{12g} 8^{10gf} **0-0-3**

Dorchester *W J Musson*   84
6 b g Primo Dominie - Penthouse Lady
11^{6gf} 4^{6g} 4^{6gf} 7^{6gf} 1^{6g} 3^{6gf} 9^{6gf} 5^{7gs}
1-3-8 £11,759

Doringo *J L Spearing*   37
2 b c Prince Sabo - Mistral's Dancer
11^{6g} **0-0-1**

Doris Souter (Ire) *R Hannon*   78 a67
3 b/br f Desert Story (Ire) - Hope And Glory (USA)
4^{7sd} 4^{9gf} 2^{8sd} 6^{12gf} 1^{10gf} 2^{10g} 3^{10gf} 1^{10gf}
5^{10gf} 3^{10gf} **2-4-10 £15,444**

Dorisima (Fr) *D Nicholls*   22
2 ch f Mark Of Esteem (Ire) - Suhaad
11^{7g} **0-0-1**

Dormy Two (Ire) *Mrs P N Dutfield*   55
3 b f Eagle Eyed (USA) - Tartan Lady (Ire)
3^{10gf} 4^{12gf} 7^{10gf} **0-0-3 £662**

Dorothy's Friend *R Charlton*   87
3 b g Grand Lodge (USA) - Isle Of Flame
5^{10gf} 11^{2f} 1^{14g} 11^{6g} **3-0-4 £8,546**

Dorothys Swift (Ire) *Miss D Mountain*   40 a41
3 b f Petardia - Verica (USA)
4^{5sd} 13^{7sd} 7^{6gf} 8^{6gf} 12^{8gf} 13^{10gf} **0-0-6**

Dottie Digger (Ire) *Miss Lucinda V Russell*
4 b f Catrail (USA) - Hint-Of-Romance (Ire)
9^{9gf} **0-0-1**

Double Assembly *J R Best*   53 a63
3 ch f Presidium - Zamarra
4^{6sd} 8^{5sd} 12^{6sd} 10^{6gf} 9^{6gf} 10^{6gf} **0-0-6**
£259

Double Blade *N Wilson*   53
8 b g Kris - Sesame
4^{12gf} 15^{12gf} 6^{12f} 4^{16f} 14^{14f} 4^{14gf} **0-1-6**
£594

Double Brew *J L Spearing*   a65
5 ch g Primo Dominie - Boozy
2^{5sd} 7^{5sd} 8^{6sw} 2^{6sd} 5^{6sd} 10^{6sd} 9^{7sd} 9^{6sd}
0-2-8 £1,704

Double Demon *B R Millman*   a32
3 ch c Double Eclipse (Ire) - Stately Favour
7^{10sd} UR^{10sd} 7^{9sw} **0-0-3**

Double Helix *M E Sowersby*   47
4 b g Marju (Ire) - Totham
5^{8gf} 8^{10gf} 12^{8gf} **0-0-3**

Double Honour (Fr) *P J Hobbs*   107
5 gr g Highest Honor (Fr) - Silver Cobra (USA)
3^{22f} 13^{16gf} **0-1-2 £4,400**

Double M *Mrs L Richards*   55 a63
6 ch h First Trump - Girton Degree
12^{6sd} 4^{6sd} 5^{6sd} 3^{6sd} 6^{7sd} 5^{6sd} 5^{7sd} 11^{6sd}
4^{5gf} 6^{5gf} 8^{5gf} 2^{5gf} 4^{5gf} 4^{6hd} 2^{6g} 6^{5gf} DSQ^{5gf}

4^{6f} 8^{5f} **0-4-22 £4,010**

Double Mystery (Fr) *Jamie Poulton*   45 a71
3 ch g Starborough - Chene De Coeur (Fr)
5^{10sd} 3^{12sd} 7^{8gf} 17^{10f} 8^{12gf} 5^{10gf} 7^{8gf}
9^{8sd} 6^{12sd} 14^{8gf} 9^{11gf} **0-1-11 £927**

Double Obsession *M Johnston*   104
3 b c Sadler's Wells (USA) - Obsessive (USA)
5^{12gf} 5^{11g} 5^{12gf} 6^{12gf} 1^{12gf} 1^{12g} 14^{12gs}
2^{12gf} 7^{13gf} 9^{12f} 11^{12gf} **2-1-11 £25,186**

Double Oscar (Ire) *D Nicholls*   a58
10 ch g Royal Academy (USA) - Broadway Rosie
8^{6sd} 6^{6sd} 13^{6sd} 14^{6sd} **0-0-4**

Double Ransom *Mrs L Stubbs*   62
4 b g Bahamian Bounty - Secrets Of Honour
11^{10gs} 16^{10g} 11^{9gs} 12^{10g} 3^{8gs} **0-1-5**
£326

Double Spey *P C Haslam*   48 a28
4 b g Atraf - Yankee Special
8^{8sw} 19^{10gs} 6^{9gf} 7^{14gf} 8^{17gf} **0-0-5**

Double Turn *J G Given*   33
3 ch g Double Trigger (Ire) - Its My Turn
5^{12gf} **0-0-1**

Double Vodka (Ire) *M Dods*   64
2 b/br c Russian Revival (USA) - Silius
6^{6gs} 8^{7gf} 3^{7gf} 5^{8g} **0-0-4 £701**

Douglas (Ire) *R Hannon*   75
2 b c Marju (Ire) - Keylock (USA)
10^{6gf} 1^{7gf} 4^{7gf} 10^{8gf} 4^{7gf} 12^{8gf} BD^{7f}
1-1-7 £4,917

Dove Tree (Fr) *H Candy*   94
3 b f Charnwood Forest (Ire) - Quaver (USA)
1^{8gs} 1^{7gf} 9^{7g} **2-0-3 £19,747**

Dovedon Hero *P J McBride*   85
3 ch g Millkom - Hot Topic (Ire)
2^{8g} 1^{10f} 4^{10gf} 8^{10gf} 3^{12gf} 3^{12g} 8^{14gf} 1^{12gf}
6^{12gf} **2-3-9 £13,633**

Dowager *R Hannon*   98
2 b f Groom Dancer (USA) - Rose Noble (USA)
7^{6gf} 1^{7gf} 6^{7gf} 2^{6gf} 4^{7gf} 6^{7gf} 1^{6g} **2-1-7**
£28,051

Dower House *Andrew Turnell*   85 a86
8 ch g Groom Dancer (USA) - Rose Noble (USA)
5^{8sd} 7^{10sd} 6^{10sd} 2^{10g} 12^{10g} 3^{10gs} **0-2-6**
£2,729

Dowhatjen *M R Channon*   86
4 b f Desert Style (Ire) - Cupid Miss
3^{7gf} 4^{7gf} 7^{8gf} 9^{7gf} 2^{7g} 3^{9gf} 5^{7gf} 2^{8gf}
2^{7g} 2^{7gf} 7^{7g} 13^{7g} 5^{7g} 16^{7gf} **0-6-14**
£13,669

Down Memory Lane *B W Hills*   84 a83
3 b c Pursuit Of Love - Sirene Bleu Marine (USA)
2^{8sd} 1^{8sd} 4^{10gf} 9^{10gf} 3^{11hy} 6^{12gf} 6^{10g} 1^{9gf}
2-1-8 £12,554

Down To The Woods (USA) *M J Polglase*   62 a67
5 ch g Woodman (USA) - Riviera Wonder (USA)
13^{10sd} 3^{9sw} 8^{10sd} 7^{8sd} 5^{12sd} 13^{10g} 9^{8f}
16^{9gf} 6^{8gf} 7^{8sd} 7^{8f} 4^{14f} 7^{16g} **0-1-13 £942**

Downing Street (Ire) *A M Balding*   59
2 b c Sadler's Wells (USA) - Photographie (USA)
5^{8g} 4^{8g} 8^{8gf} **0-0-3**

Downland (Ire) *N Tinkler*   64
7 b g Common Grounds - Boldabsa
8^{6gs} 6^{6gs} 9^{6gf} 14^{5gf} 9^{7s} **0-0-5**

Downtherefordancin (Ire) *M C Pipe*   69 a57
3 b g Groom Dancer (USA) - Merlin's Fancy

4^{7sd} 9^{7sd} 6^{6sd} 2^{7sd} 2^{7sd} 2^{12sd} 11^{1gf} 4^{12f}
1^{12g} **2-3-9 £10,522**

Downtime (Ire) *J R Fanshawe*   69
3 ch g Perugino (USA) - Razana (Ire)
3^{7gf} 9^{8gf} 1^{10gf} 2^{10gf} 13^{12gf} **1-1-5**
£8,930

Doyen (Ire) *A Fabre*   122
3 b c Sadler's Wells (USA) - Moon Cactus
1^{12g} 1^{12gs} 2^{12gs} 4^{12ho} 1^{12s} **3-1-5**
£115,949

Dr Cerullo *A J Lidderdale*   66 a70
2 b c Dr Fong (USA) - Precocious Miss (USA)
2^{5gf} 6^{6f} 3^{8sd} **0-2-3 £1,935**

Dr Fox (Ire) *N P Littmoden*   60
2 b g Foxhound - Eleonora D'Arborea
5^{5gf} 7^{5g} 8^{6gs} 9^{7f} 5^{6gf} 8^{8gf} 5^{6f} **0-0-7**

Dr Julian (Ire) *Miss A Stokell*   53 a53
3 b g Sesaro (USA) - Toda
8^{7sd} 3^{8sd} 3^{8sd} 6^{8sd} 3^{12gf} 5^{11gf} 3^{9gf} 10^{7sd}
4^{8sd} 3^{10gf} 4^{12f} 2^{14gf} 7^{16gs} 10^{16g} 12^{14gf} 5^{12gf}
8^{12gf} 9^{12gs} **0-4-18 £6,229**

Dr Raj *B A McMahon*   39
4 ch g In The Wings - Tawaaded (Ire)
11^{10gf} **0-0-1**

Dr Sharp (Ire) *T P Tate*   76
3 ch g Dr Devious (Ire) - Stoned Imaculate (Ire)
9^{12gf} 1^{12s} 11^{11gs} 4^{12g} **2-0-4 £11,043**

Dr Synn *J Akehurst*   61
2 b c Danzero (Aus) - Our Shirley
6^{6g} **0-0-1**

Dr Thong *P F I Cole*   66
2 ch g Dr Fong (USA) - Always On My Mind
5^{7gf} **0-0-1**

Dragon Flyer (Ire) *M Quinn*   110 a75
4 b f Tagula (Ire) - Noble Rocket
8^{5sd} 5^{5gf} 2^{5f} 3^{5gf} 2^{5gf} 2^{5gf} 2^{5g} 7^{5g}
3^{5gf} 13^{6gf} 10^{5ho} **0-6-12 £42,955**

Drama King *B J Llewellyn*
11 b g Tragic Role (USA) - Consistent Queen
14^{22gf} **0-0-1**

Dramatic Quest *Ian Williams*   78 a71
6 b g Zafonic (USA) - Ultra Finesse (USA)
7^{16sd} 2^{12sd} 2^{12sd} 4^{12g} **0-3-4 £2,230**

Dramraire Mist *B J Meehan*   a23
4 gr f Darshaan - Marie Dora (Fr)
7^{12sd} **0-0-1**

Dream Falcon *R J Hodges*   53
3 b g Polar Falcon (USA) - Pip's Dream
9^{13gf} 13^{8f} **0-0-2**

Dream King (Ire) *M J Polglase*   48
3 b g Petardia - Barinia
6^{12gf} 7^{10f} 7^{13gf} 8^{12sd} 14^{8g} 5^{7g} 12^{8gf} 8^{8f}
5^{9g} 8^{8gf} 6^{7gf} **0-0-11 £218**

Dream Magic *M J Ryan*   93 a91
5 b g Magic Ring (Ire) - Pip's Dream
3^{10sd} 2^{10sd} 3^{12sd} 10^{5sd} 6^{11sd} 1^{10g} 12^{10gf}
5^{10gf} 3^{9gf} 9^{10gs} 11^{10gf} 4^{9gf} 4^{8gs} **1-4-13**
£16,978

Dream Of Dubai (Ire) *P Mitchell*   a61
2 b f Vettori (Ire) - Immortelle
8^{6sd} 5^{7sd} **0-0-2**

Dream Scene (Ire) *J H M Gosden*   71
2 b f Sadler's Wells (USA) - Highest Accolade
4^{7gf} **0-0-1 £580**

Dream Valley (Ire) *B W Hills*   45

2 b f Sadler's Wells (USA) - Vallee Des Reves (USA)
12⁷ᵍˢ 9⁶ᵍ **0-0-2**

Dream With Me (Fr) *M C Pipe*   50
6 b g Johann Quatz (Fr) - Midnight Ride (Fr)
13¹²ᵍᶠ **0-0-1**

Dreamie Battle *R Hollinshead*
5 br m Makbul - Highland Rossie
9¹²ˢᵈ **0-0-1**

Dreaming Diva *J C Fox*   a51
4 ch f Whittingham (Ire) - Any Dream (Ire)
10¹⁰ˢᵈ 12⁸ˢᵈ 18¹⁰ᵍ 10¹⁰ˢᵈ **0-0-4**

Dreaming Of You (Ire) *Sir Michael Stoute*   44
2 b f Spectrum (Ire) - Gay Hellene
12⁷ᵍᶠ **0-0-1**

Dreaming Waters *R F Johnson Houghton*   53
2 ch f Groom Dancer (USA) - Faraway Waters
6⁷ᵍ 8⁶ᵍᶠ 10⁶ᵍᶠ **0-0-3**

Dreams Forgotten (Ire) *S Kirk*   66
3 b f Victory Note (USA) - Sevens Are Wild
37ᵍᶠ 2⁸ᵍ 8⁸ᵍᶠ 19⁷ᵍᶠ **0-2-4 £1,640**

Dreams United *A G Newcombe*   35
2 br f Dancing Spree (USA) - Kaliala (Fr)
18⁶ᵍ 57ᵍᶠ 118ᵍᶠ **0-0-3**

Dress Pearl *A Berry*   67 a28
2 b f Atraf - Dress Design (Ire)
75ᵍᶠ 25ˢ 65ᵍᶠ 2⁶ʰʸ 8⁶ᵍᶠ 66ᵍᶠ 75ˢᵈ 67ᵍᶠ
7⁷ᵍ 13⁶ˢ **0-2-10 £3,098**

Drizzle *Mrs A J Perrett*   68
2 ch c Hector Protector (USA) - Rainy Sky
3⁸ᶠ **0-0-1 £500**

Druid *P C Haslam*   34 a22
2 b g Magic Ring (Ire) - Country Spirit
8⁶ˢᵈ 6⁶ᵍ **0-0-2**

Drury Lane (Ire) *B W Hills*   84 a71
3 b/br c Royal Applause - Ghost Tree (Ire)
13⁸ᵍᶠ 97ᵍˢ 10⁶ᵍᶠ 16ᵍᶠ 55ᵍᶠ 96ˢᵈ 36ᵍᶠ 96ᵍˢ
97ᵍᶠ 97ᵍᶠ **1-0-10 £7,536**

Dry Wit (Ire) *R M Beckett*   64
2 b f Desert Prince (Ire) - Nawasib (Ire)
2⁷ᶠ 47ᵍˢ 27ᵍᶠ 6⁸ᵍᶠ 87ᵍᶠ **0-2-5 £3,371**

Du Pre *Mrs A J Perrett*   63
2 b f Singspiel (Ire) - Child Prodigy (Ire)
3⁶ᵍᶠ 10⁶ᵍᶠ **0-0-2 £732**

Dubai Destination (USA) *Saeed Bin Suroor*   126
4 b c Kingmambo (USA) - Mysterial (USA)
18ᵍᶠ 18ᵍᶠ 8⁸ᵍᶠ 58ᵍˢ **2-0-4 £163,790**

Dubai Dreams *M J Polglase*   77 a71
3 b g Marju (Ire) - Arndilly
11¹ˢᵈ 41⁰ˢᵈ 91⁰ᵍ 4⁸ᵍ 2⁷ᶠ 21⁰ᵍᶠ 11⁸ᵍᶠ 5⁸ᵍᶠ
51⁰ᵍᶠ 41²ᵍᶠ 61⁶ᵍᶠ 71⁰ᵍᶠ 181⁰ᵍᶠ 8⁸ᵍˢ **1-3-14**
£7,206

Dubai Prince (Ire) *M J Wallace*   59
4 b g Anita's Prince - Balqis (USA)
71²ᵍᶠ 71²ᵍᶠ 7⁸ᵍᶠ 41⁰ᵍᶠ **0-0-4**

Dubai Seven Stars *M C Pipe*   79
5 ch m Suave Dancer (USA) - Her Honour
111⁶ᵍᶠ 182⁰ᵍᶠ 81⁶ᵍᶠ 11⁸ᶠ 51⁶ᵍᶠ 361⁸ᵍᶠ
21⁶ᵍᶠ 61⁶ᵍᶠ 141⁶ᵍᶠ 111⁶ᵍᶠ **1-1-10 £8,397**

Dubai Success *B W Hills*   116
3 b c Sadler's Wells (USA) - Crystal Spray
11⁰ᵍˢ 51²ᵍᶠ 71²ᵍ 11²ᵍ 31²ᵍᶠ **2-1-5**
£25,705

Dubai Tower (USA) *M Johnston*   76 a73
3 b c Imperial Ballet (Ire) - Multimara (USA)
47ˢᵈ 96ˢᵈ 37ˢᵈ 18ˢʷ 49ˢᵈ 41⁰ᵍᶠ 29ᵍˢ 11⁰ᵍᶠ

2-2-8 **£10,587**

Dubaian Duel *A M Balding*   91
2 b f Daggers Drawn (USA) - River's Rising (Fr)
27ᵍᶠ 8⁶ᵍᶠ 17ᵍᶠ 27ᵍ 37ᵍᶠ **1-2-5 £65,965**

Dubaian Gift *A M Balding*   109
4 b g Bahamian Bounty - Hot Lavender (Can)
85ᶠ 85ᵍᶠ 15ᵍ 15ᵍᶠ 75ᵍ 95ᵍ 25ᵍᶠ 25ᵍᶠ 15ᵍ
65ᵍᶠ **3-2-10 £58,557**

Dubaian Mist *A M Balding*   53
2 b f Docksider (USA) - Robellino Miss (USA)
85ᵍ **0-0-1**

Dubois *D R Loder*   75
2 b c Sadler's Wells (USA) - Dazzle
27ᵍᶠ 5⁸ᵍᶠ **0-1-2 £1,338**

Dubonai (Ire) *Andrew Turnell*   60
3 ch c Peintre Celebre (USA) - Web Of Intrigue
4⁸ᵍᶠ 111⁰ᵍᶠ 91⁰ᵍᶠ 31²ᵍᶠ 21²ᵍᶠ 31⁰ᵍᶠ 111⁰ᵍˢ
0-2-7 £3,218

Dubrovsky *J R Fanshawe*   88
3 ch c Hector Protector (USA) - Reuval
11⁸ᵍᶠ 3⁸ᵍˢ 9⁸ᵍᶠ **0-1-3 £1,488**

Duc's Dream *D Morris*   68 a69
5 b g Bay Tern (USA) - Kala's Image
311ˢᵈ 611ˢᵈ 711ˢᵈ 51⁰ᵍᶠ 31⁰ᵍᶠ 21²ˢᵈ 61⁰ˢᵈ
21²ᵍ 21²ᵍ 31⁴ᵍᶠ 111ᵍᶠ 61²ˢ 31²ᶠ 91⁶ᵍᶠ **1-7-14**
£12,703

Duck Egg Blue (Ire) *Edward Butler*   a57
4 b g Flying Spur (Aus) - Trojan Treasure
8⁸ˢᵈ 10⁷ˢᵈ 137ˢᵈ **0-0-3**

Duck Row (USA) *J A R Toller*   113
8 ch g Diesis - Sunny Moment (USA)
4⁸ᵍᶠ 1⁸ᵍˢ 47ᵍᶠ 4⁹ᵍᶠ 4⁸ʰᵒ 8⁸ᵍˢ **1-0-6**
£24,367

Dudie *Mrs C A Dunnett*
4 b f Pebble Powder - Valise
7⁶ᵍᶠ **0-0-1**

Due Diligence (Ire) *C W Fairhurst*   69 a12
4 ch g Entrepreneur - Kerry Project (Ire)
117ᵍ 4⁸ᵍᶠ 14⁸ˢʰ 4⁸ᵍ 13⁸ᵍᶠ 137ᵍᶠ 10⁸ᶠ
151⁰ᵍᶠ 13⁸ˢᵈ **0-0-9 £636**

Due Respect (Ire) *R Hannon*   82
3 b c Danehill (USA) - Stylish
12⁸ᵍᶠ 57ᵍ 61⁰ᵍᶠ 10⁸ᵍᶠ **0-0-4**

Due To Me *G L Moore*   40
3 gr f Compton Place - Always Lucky
45ᶠ 17⁶ᵍᶠ 7⁶ᵍ **0-0-3**

Duelling Banjos *J Akehurst*   74 a71
4 ch g Most Welcome - Khadino
1⁸ˢᵈ 18⁸ᵍ 4⁸ᵍˢ 6⁸ˢᵈ 7⁸ᵍᶠ 10⁸ᵍ 9⁹ᵍᶠ 14⁸ᵍ
18ᵍˢ **2-0-9 £5,734**

Duescals (USA) *J H M Gosden*   69 a21
3 b f Danzig (USA) - Vue (USA)
2⁸ᵍᶠ 21⁰ᶠ 121⁰ˢᵈ **0-1-3 £2,180**

Dugdale *Sir Mark Prescott*   60 a8
3 b g Vettori (Ire) - Coigach
41⁴ᵍᶠ 71²ᵍ 41¹ᵍᶠ 91⁶ᵍˢ 141²ˢᵈ **0-0-5 £325**

Duggan's Dilemma (Ire) *Ian Emmerson*   47
2 b g Lake Coniston (Ire) - Miss Ironwood
75ᵍᶠ 55ᶠ 11⁶ᶠ 11⁶ˢᵈ **0-0-4**

Duke Of Earl (Ire) *S Kirk*   89
4 ch g Ali-Royal (Ire) - Faye
132¹ᵍˢ 91⁴ᵍᶠ 21⁴ˢ **0-1-3 £1,435**

Duke Of Modena *G B Balding*   101
6 ch g Salse (USA) - Palace Street (USA)
20⁸ᵍᶠ 1⁸ᵍ 3⁸ᵍᶠ 2⁸ᵍᶠ 11⁸ᵍᶠ 4⁸ᵍᶠ 11⁸ᵍᶠ

15^{8gs} 1-2-8 £23,317

Duke Of Venice (USA) *M Johnston*　　103
2 b c Theatrical - Rihan (USA)
3^{6gf} 10^{7gf} 1^{8g} 1-1-3 £5,035

Duke's View (Ire) *Mrs A J Perrett*　　63
2 b c Sadler's Wells (USA) - Igreja (Arg)
10^{7gf} 7^{7gf} 6^{7g} 0-0-3

Dulce De Leche *S C Williams*　　45
2 b g Cayman Kai (Ire) - Give Us A Treat
8^{7f} 10^{5gf} 0-0-2

Dumaran (Ire) *A M Balding*　　102
5 b g Be My Chief (USA) - Pine Needle
6^{8g} 8^{10g} 5^{8gs} 9^{7gf} 32^{9gf} 4^{10gf} 3^{10gf}
0-1-8 £3,635

Dumfries *J H M Gosden*　　79
2 ch g Selkirk (USA) - Pat Or Else
14^{6g} 3^{8gf} 1^{10f} 1-0-3 £4,719

Dumnoni *Julian Poulton*　　60 a67
2 b f Titus Livius (Fr) - Lamees (USA)
6^{7gf} 3^{7sd} 3^{7sd} 0-2-3 £1,084

Dunaskin (Ire) *D Eddy*　　94
3 b g Bahhare (USA) - Mirwara (Ire)
6^{10g} 1^{10gf} 2^{12f} 1^{10gf} 14^{10gf} 1^{8gs} 17^{10g}
5^{10gf} 8^{9gf} 5^{12gf} 3^{10g} 3-2-11 £21,998

Duncan Dock (USA) *W J Haggas*　　76
4 ch g Rakeen (USA) - Smailer (USA)
15^{10g} 6^{10g} 10^{10gs} 14^{9gf} 0-0-4

Duncanbil (Ire) *R F Fisher*　　54
2 b f Turtle Island (Ire) - Saintly Guest
6^{6gf} 10^{6gs} 5^{7gf} 9^{7gf} 9^{6gs} 6^{7gs} 0-0-6

Dundonald *M Appleby*　　49 a42
4 ch g Magic Ring (Ire) - Cal Norma's Lady (Ire)
9^{6sd} 2^{8sd} 8^{7sd} 8^{7gf} 12^{7f} 11^{10gf} 7^{8gf}
10^{8sd} 4^{7f} 8^{7gf} 0-2-10 £828

Dundry *R Hannon*　　61
2 b g Bin Ajwaad (Ire) - China's Pearl
12^{7g} 0-0-1

Dune Safari (Ire) *M A Allen*　　10
4 br f Key Of Luck (USA) - Zafaaf
14^{10gf} 19^{7g} 11^{8ft} 0-0-3

Dunedin Rascal *E A Wheeler*　　59 a81
6 b g Piccolo - Thorner Lane
10^{7sd} 1^{6sd} 4^{6sd} 9^{6sd} 10^{6sd} 14^{6gs} 12^{5gf}
11^{6gf} 9^{5gf} 7^{5gf} 1-0-0 £3,630

Dunhill Star (Ire) *B W Hills*　　109
3 b c Danehill (USA) - Sueboog (Ire)
15^{12g} 1^{9g} 3^{10gf} 2^{9gf} 5^{10gf} 1-2-5
£29,276

Dunlea Dancer *M Johnston*　　54
2 b g Groom Dancer (USA) - Be My Lass (Ire)
5^{5gs} 12^{6gf} 5^{6f} 7^{6gf} 16^{8gf} 0-0-5

Dunloskin *M A Jarvis*　　100
2 b f Selkirk (USA) - Dalinda (USA)
5^{7gf} 3^{6gf} 2^{6gs} 0-2-3 £19,170

Dunmidoe *C Drew*　　44 a35
3 b f Case Law - Rion River (Ire)
18^{6gf} 7^{10sd} 7^{12gf} 7^{8gf} 5^{10gf} 8^{8gf} 9^{7gf}
0-0-7

Dunn Almu (Ire) *R J Osborne*　　a47
6 br g Hamas (Ire) - Art Age
7^{7sd} 14^{12sd} 16^{16ys} 0-0-3

Dunn Deal (Ire) *W M Brisbourne*　　66
3 b c Revoque (Ire) - Buddy And Soda (Ire)
6^{5f} 5^{5gf} 4^{6gf} 12^{5hy} 6^{5gf} 6^{5gf} 9^{5gf} 0-0-7

Dunnett Again (Ire) *Mrs C A Dunnett*　　55 a41
2 b c Petardia - Pat Said No (Ire)
8^{5g} 4^{5g} 8^{5gf} 11^{6gf} 15^{6gs} 14^{6gf} 8^{6sd} 8^{6sd}
14^{6sd} 13^{6sd} 0-0-10 £335

Duo Leoni *R M Beckett*　　70
3 ch f Vettori (Ire) - La Dolce Vita
6^{8gf} 2^{7gf} 3^{7gf} 3^{7f} 7^{8f} 2^{7gf} 1^{7gs} 5^{8gf}
1-2-8 £4,975

Dupont *W J Haggas*　　104
4 b c Zafonic (USA) - June Moon (Ire)
7^{8g} 7^{9g} 5^{8gf} 3^{8g} 5^{8gf} 0-1-5 £5,127

Duraid (Ire) *C Grant*　　26
11 ch g Irish River (Fr) - Fateful Princess (USA)
18^{8gf} 10^{8gs} 8^{8gf} 16^{8gf} 0-0-4

Durkar Star (Ire) *M C Chapman*
5 b g Bin Ajwaad (Ire) - Faith Alone
20^{6g} 0-0-1

Dusk Dancer (Fr) *B J Meehan*　　74
3 b g Groom Dancer (USA) - Nightitude
4^{8g} 8^{8gf} 0-0-2 £431

Dusky Warbler *M L W Bell*　　109
4 br g Ezzoud (USA) - Bronzewing
3^{14g} 3^{12gs} 5^{13s} 3^{18gf} 3^{16gf} 2^{18g} 5^{15g} 0-3-7
£31,608

Dust Cover *P J Makin*　　106
3 b c Desert Story (Ire) - Convenience (Ire)
38^{8gf} 4^{10gf} 5^{10gf} 0-0-3 £6,370

Dust Goddess *E A L Dunlop*　　72
3 ch f Hector Protector (USA) - Galaxie Dust (USA)
2^{7gf} 6^{8s} 4^{8g} 9^{10g} 0-1-4 £1,969

Dusty Dazzler (Ire) *W G M Turner*　　92 a98
3 ch f Titus Livius (Fr) - Satinette
1^{5sd} 5^{5sd} 3^{5gf} 7^{5g} 13^{6s} 23^{5gf} 4^{5gf} 2^{6gf}
14^{6g} 1-2-9 £13,802

Dusty Wugg (Ire) *A Dickman*　　53 a61
4 b f General Monash (USA) - Welsh Berry (USA)
8^{7sd} 2^{7sd} 15^{7sw} 9^{7sd} 4^{6f} 7^{7gs} 0-2-6
£1,208

Dutch Gold (USA) *C E Brittain*　　114 a77
3 ch c Lahib (USA) - Crimson Conquest (USA)
6^{12g} 10^{5sd} 3^{10gf} 2^{10gf} 11^{10gf} 1^{12g} 7^{12gf}
6^{13s} 2-2-8 £76,915

Duty Paid (Ire) *D R C Elsworth*　　100 a90
3 b f Barathea (Ire) - Local Custom (Ire)
10^{8gf} 6^{8gf} 3^{7g} 8^{8gf} 6^{7g} 9^{6gf} 2^{7gf} 10^{6gf}
4^{8sd} 0-2-9 £15,067

Dvinsky (USA) *G A Butler*　　85
2 b c Stravinsky (USA) - Festive Season (USA)
6^{6gf} 16^{6gf} 1-0-2 £2,975

Dynamo Minsk (Ire) *John A Harris*
4 b f Polish Precedent (USA) - Blazing Glory (Ire)
15^{8sd} 0-0-1

E C Too *J L Spearing*　　60 a13
3 b f Sheikh Albadou - Scarlett Holly
6^{6gf} 9^{7sd} 4^{5f} 4^{5gs} 6^{6f} 12^{6gf} 11^{6gf} 0-0-7
£611

E Minor (Ire) *T Wall*　　63
4 b f Blushing Flame (USA) - Watch The Clock
3^{15gf} 9^{14g} 8^{14hy} 4^{16gf} 5^{15gf} 9^{15gf} 4^{16gf}
4^{16gf} 7^{16gf} 7^{16gf} 0-2-10 £1,223

Eachy Peachy (Ire) *J R Best*　　40 a51
4 ch f Perugino (USA) - Miss Big John (Ire)
3^{13sd} 13^{13sd} 5^{13sd} 8^{12f} 7^{12sd} 2^{16gf} 5^{12gf}
3^{14gf} 6^{14f} 0-3-9 £1,758

Eager Angel (Ire) *R F Marvin*　　35 a45
5 b m Up And At 'Em - Seanee Squaw

3⁵ˢᵈ 9⁶ˢᵈ 9⁶ˢᵈ 2⁵ˢʷ 7⁵ˢʷ 8⁶ˢʷ 6⁵ᵍᶠ 8⁵ˢʷ
7⁵ᵍˢ **0-2-9 £1,247**

Eagle's Landing *D K Ivory*　　　　46 a52
5 b m Eagle Eyed (USA) - Anchorage (Ire)
14¹⁰ˢᵈ 9⁸ˢᵈ 5¹²ˢʷ 11¹²ˢᵈ 5¹¹ˢᵈ 11⁴ˢᵈ 6¹⁴ᵍᶠ
6¹²ˢᵈ 3¹⁵ˢᵈ 11¹⁶ˢᵈ 11¹⁵ˢᵈ 3¹⁴ᶠ **2-2-12 £7,302**

Eagles In The Wind (Ire) *A Berry*　　　42
3 ch f Eagle Eyed (USA) - Quiver Tree
13⁷ᵍᶠ 6⁸ᵍᶠ 8¹²ᵍ 4⁸ᵍᶠ **0-0-4 £922**

Eagles View (Ire) *Mrs P N Dutfield*　　　61
3 b f Eagle Eyed (USA) - Rock On (Ire)
9⁸ᵍᶠ 4⁷ᵍᶠ 11⁶ᵍᶠ 13⁸ᵍᶠ 6⁸ᵍᶠ 4⁸ᶠ 2⁷ᵍᶠ 9⁷ᵍᶠ
8⁸ᵍᶠ 15⁶ᵍᶠ 7⁶ᵍᶠ 2⁷ᵍᶠ 6⁷ᵍᶠ 11⁸ᶠ 16⁷ᵍᶠ **0-2-15**
£2,800

Eaglet (Ire) *Miss V Scott*　　　41
5 b g Eagle Eyed (USA) - Justice System (USA)
13⁷ᵍˢ 11⁸ᶠ 8¹²ᵍᶠ 5¹⁴ᵍᶠ **0-0-4**

Earlsfield Raider *G L Moore*　　　65 a36
3 ch g Double Trigger (Ire) - Harlequin Walk (Ire)
6¹⁰ᵍ 8¹⁰ᵍᶠ 9¹⁰ᵍᶠ 4¹⁰ᵍ 7¹²ᶠ 15¹²ˢᵈ **0-0-6**
£284

Earlston *J S Goldie*　　　73
3 ch g Fleetwood (Ire) - Mystique Smile
4⁷ᵍᶠ 3⁹ᵍˢ 8⁸ᵍˢ 6⁸ᵍᶠ 6⁸ᵍᶠ 2⁷ᵍᶠ 2⁷ᵍᶠ 4⁶ᵍᶠ
9⁷ᵍ 7⁸ᵍˢ 9⁷ᵍᶠ **0-3-11 £5,517**

Easibet Dot Net *J Semple*　　　63
3 gr g Atraf - Silverly
7⁸ᵍᶠ 7⁷ᵍ 4⁹ᵍˢ 4¹²ᵍᶠ 3¹¹ᵍᶠ 2¹¹ᵍ 3¹²ᵍᶠ **0-3-7**
£3,082

Easily Averted (Ire) *J A Osborne*　　69 a66
2 b c Averti (Ire) - Altishaan
6⁷ᵍ 12⁸ᵍᶠ 2⁶ᵍ 4⁵ᵍᶠ 1⁸ᵍᶠ 3⁶ˢᵈ 11⁵ˢ **1-2-7**
£4,362

East Cape *Don Enrico Incisa*　　54 a54
6 b g Bering - Reine De Danse (USA)
8¹²ᵍᶠ 8¹¹ᵍᶠ 6¹²ᵍ 7¹⁰ᵍᶠ 6¹²ˢ 6¹¹ᵍᶠ 3¹⁰ᵍᶠ
4¹⁰ᶠ 4¹²ˢᵈ **0-1-9 £880**

East Flares *J W Unett*　　　65
3 gr g Environment Friend - Ijada Bianca
6⁸ᵍᶠ 1¹⁰ᵍᶠ 8¹²ᵍᶠ **1-0-3 £3,038**

East Riding *Miss A Stokell*　　　58
3 b f Gothenberg (Ire) - Bettynouche
14⁶ᵍ 7⁹ᵍˢ 11⁶ᵍˢ 6⁶ᶠ 14⁷ˢᵈ 2⁷ᵍᶠ 11⁷ᵍᶠ
9⁶ᶠ 5⁷ᶠ **0-1-9 £1,514**

East Tycoon (Ire) *Jonjo O'Neill*　　　79
4 ch g Bigstone (Ire) - Princesse Sharpo (USA)
14¹⁰ᵍ **0-0-1**

Easter Ogil (Ire) *Jane Southcombe*　　66 a75
8 ch g Pips Pride - Piney Pass
1⁷ˢᵈ 3⁷ˢᵈ 1⁸ˢᵈ 1⁷ˢᵈ 1⁸ˢᵈ 8⁸ˢᵈ 10⁸ˢᵈ
9¹⁰ˢᵈ 4¹⁰ᵍᶠ 1⁸ᵍ 4¹²ᵍ 3¹²ᵍᶠ 8⁸ᵍᶠ **6-3-14**
£18,005

Easter Parade *R Charlton*　　　82
3 b f Entrepreneur - Starlet
7⁸ᵍᶠ 1¹²ᵍˢ 1¹⁴ᶠ 8¹⁴ᵍᶠ 4¹³ᵍᶠ **2-0-5**
£12,829

Eastern Blue (Ire) *Mrs L Stubbs*　　60 a45
4 ch f Be My Guest (USA) - Stifen
5⁶ᵍˢ 6⁷ˢᵈ 1⁶ᵍ 9⁶ᵍᶠ 12⁶ᵍˢ 8⁶ᵍ 10⁷ᵍᶠ 4⁶ᵍˢ
5⁶ᶠ 10⁶ᵍᶠ 8⁶ᶠ 6⁶ᵍᶠ **1-0-12 £4,203**

Eastern Breeze (Ire) *P W D'Arcy*　110 a99
5 b g Sri Pekan (USA) - Elegant Bloom (Ire)
4¹⁰ˢᵈ 4¹⁰ˢᵈ 3⁸ˢᵈ 3¹²ᵍˢ 7¹⁰ᵍᶠ 3¹²ᵍᶠ 3¹⁰ᵍᶠ
1¹²ᵍᶠ 6¹²ᵍᶠ 6¹²ᵍ **1-3-10 £19,226**

Eastern Dagger *R Wilman*　　75 a75
3 b c Kris - Shehana (USA)

4⁸ˢᵈ 1⁷ˢᵈ 9⁷ᵍ 1⁸ᵍ 5⁷ᵍᶠ 7⁸ᵍ 4⁷ᵍᶠ 7⁸ᵍ 6⁸ˢᵈ
18⁸ᵍ **2-0-10 £7,284**

Eastern Faith *Mrs L Stubbs*　　62 a45
2 ch g Perugino (USA) - Bright Fountain (Ire)
9⁵ᵍᶠ 4⁶ᵍ 7⁷ᵍˢ 10⁷ᵍᶠ 5⁷ˢᵈ **0-0-5 £283**

Eastern Gate *Miss A Stokell*　　　14
3 b g Elmaamul (USA) - Redgrave Design
14⁷ᵍᶠ **0-0-1**

Eastern Hope (Ire) *Mrs L Stubbs*　　　78
4 b g Danehill Dancer (Ire) - Hope And Glory (USA)
8⁸ᵍˢ 5⁸ˢ 9⁸ᵍˢ 6⁷ᵍ 13⁷ᵍˢ **0-0-5**

Eastern Magenta (Ire) *Mrs L Stubbs*　　71
3 b g Turtle Island (Ire) - Blue Heights (Ire)
10⁶ˢ 10⁶ʰʸ 7⁷ᵍᶠ 21⁷ᵍ **0-0-4**

Eastern Pearl *Mrs L Stubbs*　　　73
2 ch f Wolfhound (USA) - Wild Humour (Ire)
6⁵ᵍᶠ 10⁵ᵍᶠ 7⁵ᵍᶠ 25⁶ᶠ 2⁵ᶠ 1⁵ˢ 9⁵ᵍ 11⁵ᵍᶠ
1-2-8 £6,811

Eastern Royal *Mrs L Stubbs*　　　17
4 b g Royal Applause - Kentfield
11⁸ˢᵈ 16⁷ᵍᶠ 15⁷ᵍ **0-0-3**

Eastern Scarlet (Ire) *Mrs L Stubbs*　　52
3 b g Woodborough (USA) - Cuddles (Ire)
8⁷ᵍᶠ 18⁶ᵍᶠ 12⁷ᵍᶠ 3⁹ᵍᶠ 5¹²ᵍˢ 5¹⁰ᵍ 5¹⁰ᵍᶠ
0-1-7 £483

Eastern Trumpeter *H J Cyzer*　　59 a38
7 b h First Trump - Oriental Air (Ire)
7⁵ᵍ 14⁵ᵍᶠ 9⁵ᵍ 11⁵ᵍˢ 13⁵ᵍᶠ 15⁵ᵍᶠ 7⁵ᵍᶠ
6⁵ᵍˢ 5⁵ᵍᶠ 6⁵ᵍᶠ 10⁵ᶠ 12⁵ˢᵈ 4⁵ᶠ 9⁶ˢʷ 9⁶ᵍᶠ 20⁵ᵍᶠ
7⁵ᶠ **0-0-17 £307**

Easternking *J S Wainwright*
4 ch f Sabrehill (USA) - Kshessinskaya
12¹²ᵍˢ **0-0-1**

Eastwell Violet *R T Phillips*　　32 a52
3 b f Danzig Connection (USA) - Kinchenjunga
9⁸ˢᵈ 4¹⁰ˢᵈ 4¹²ˢᵈ 10¹²ᵍ 6¹²ᵍᶠ **0-0-5 £598**

Easy Rider (Ire) *E L James*　　52 a63
3 b g Blues Traveller (Ire) - Curie Express (Ire)
2⁸ˢᵈ 2⁷ˢᵈ 6⁸ˢᵈ 9⁷ˢᵈ 3⁶ᶠ 4⁶ᶠ 8⁸ᵍᶠ 2⁷ᶠ 4⁷ᵍᶠ
0-4-9 £3,347

Eau Pure (Fr) *B A Pearce*
6 b m Epervier Bleu - Eau De Nuit
11⁸ˢᵈ **0-0-1**

Eboracum (Ire) *T D Easterby*　　　64
2 b f Alzao (USA) - Fire Of London
4⁶ᵍᶠ 5⁶ᵍ 2⁸ᵍ 7⁸ᵍˢ **0-1-4 £1,347**

Eboracum Lady (USA) *J D Bethell*　　57
3 b f Lure (USA) - Konvincha (USA)
10¹⁰ᵍˢ 3⁹ᵍᶠ 4⁸ᶠ 6¹²ᵍ **0-0-4 £915**

Eccentric *Andrew Reid*　　　11
2 ch g Most Welcome - Sure Care
15⁷ᵍᶠ **0-0-1**

Echoes In Eternity (Ire) *Saeed Bin Suroor*　112
3 b f Spinning World (USA) - Magnificent Style (USA)
8¹⁰ᵍᶠ 3¹⁰ᵍᶠ 8⁸ᵍˢ 1¹⁰ᵍᶠ 1⁸ᵍᶠ **2-0-5**
£64,350

Ecuador (Ire) *J G M O'Shea*　　　33
3 ch g Among Men (USA) - Christle Mill
8⁸ᶠ 6¹⁰ᵍᶠ 14¹³ᵍᶠ **0-0-3**

Eddies Jewel *J S Wainwright*　　　38
3 b g Presidium - Superstream
12⁵ᵍˢ 10⁵ᵍ 11⁸ᵍ 3⁷ᵍˢ 10⁸ᶠ **0-0-5 £325**

Eddu *W M Brisbourne*　　　a72
5 ch g Casteddu - Cabra
2¹⁰ˢᵈ 2¹³ˢᵈ 13¹⁰ˢᵈ **0-2-3 £1,957**

Ede's *W G M Turner* 43
3 ch g Bijou D'Inde - Ballagarrow Girl
6^{7gf} 5^{12gf} **0-0-2**

Eden Rock (Ire) *Sir Michael Stoute* 77
2 b c Danehill (USA) - Marlene-D
6^{7gf} 1^{7gf} **1-0-2 £4,348**

Edgehill (Ire) *C R Egerton* 52 a46
2 b c Ali-Royal (Ire) - Elfin Queen (Ire)
7^{7sd} 7^{6g} **0-0-2**

Edifice (Jpn) *B Ellison* 44
7 ch g Carroll House - Moon Tosho (Jpn)
16^{10gf} 11^{11gf} 9^{14gf} 8^{12f} 8^{8gf} 11^{10gf} **0-0-6**

Educating Rita *M A Buckley* 68
3 b f Emarati (USA) - Charnwood Queen
1^{5g} 12^{5gf} **1-0-2 £4,192**

Edward's Brother *M Wigham* 55 a62
3 b g Wolfhound (USA) - Dolly Bevan
3^{6sd} 9^{8sd} 19^{7gf} 4^{6f} 10^{6f} 3^{7gf} 9^{8f} 18^{7gf}
10^{8f} **0-2-9 £855**

Eezaa Geezer (Ire) *R Hannon* 70
2 b/br c Lahib (USA) - Baylands Sunshine (Ire)
13^{6gf} 4^{5gf} 5^{5gf} 5^{6gf} 1^{7gf} 4^{7gs} 5^{7g} **1-0-7**
£4,616

Effective *A P Jarvis* 69 a73
3 ch g Bahamian Bounty - Efficacy
8^{7sd} 2^{6sd} 2^{6sd} 1^{6sd} 4^{6sd} 8^{6gf} 11^{6gf} 2^{6g}
7^{7gs} 14^{7sd} **1-3-10 £7,478**

Effervesce (Ire) *M A Buckley* 86 a76
5 b m Sri Pekan (USA) - Arctic Winter (Can)
3^{7sd} 8^{8sd} 12^{7gf} 3^{6f} 1^{6gf} 7^{6g} 3^{7gf} 7^{6g}
8^{6gs} 9^{6g} 1^{6gf} 5^{6gf} 5^{6gf} $F7^{6g}$ **2-3-14 £15,039**

Effie Gray *P Monteith* 51
4 b f Sri Pekan (USA) - Rose Bouquet
5^{13gf} 6^{12g} **0-0-2**

Efidium *N Bycroft* 76
5 b g Presidium - Efipetite
7^{5gf} 1^{8gf} 1^{7gf} 9^{6gf} 1^{7g} 4^{7f} 8^{6gf} 2^{7f} 6^{7gf}
5^{8gf} 1^{7f} 4^{8s} 6^{8f} 10^{8gf} 10^{7gf} 7^{7gf} 4^{7gf} 6^{7gf}
4-2-18 £18,018

Efimac *N Bycroft* a49
3 b f Presidium - Efipetite
5^{6sd} 7^{7sd} 5^{8sd} 11^{7sd} 8^{7sd} **0-0-5**

Efinew (Ire) *M G Quinlan* 62
2 b c Efisio - Silly Mid-On
8^{7g} 4^{7g} 10^{6gf} **0-0-3 £301**

Efrhina (Ire) *A C Stewart* 66
3 ch f Woodman (USA) - Eshq Albahr (USA)
10^{7gf} 8^{8gs} 2^{10f} **0-1-3 £884**

Ego *G Wragg* 97
3 b f Green Desert (USA) - Myself
5^{7gf} 3^{6gf} 6^{5g} 3^{5gf} 5^{5gf} 12^{6g} **0-2-6**
£10,600

Ego Trip *M W Easterby* 57
2 b c Deploy - Boulevard Rouge (USA)
9^{5gf} 3^{6f} 6^{6gf} 7^{8gf} 8^{7g} 13^{6f} 17^{8gf} **0-0-7**
£575

Ehab (Ire) *P J Makin* 62 a73
4 b g Cadeaux Genereux - Dernier Cri
1^{9sw} 2^{8sd} 9^{7g} 16^{7gf} 4^{9sd} 14^{7g} 12^{8g} 7^{7sw}
1-1-8 £4,521

Ei Ei *M C Chapman* 19
8 b g North Briton - Branitska
8^{12f} **0-0-1**

Eight (Ire) *C G Cox* 56 a46
7 ch g Thatching - Up To You
9^{11sd} 2^{12sd} 2^{12g} 12^{11gf} 10^{11g} **0-2-5**
£1,626

Eight Ellington (Ire) *R F Johnson Houghton* 65 a34
2 b c Ali-Royal (Ire) - Where's Charlotte
3^{6gf} 4^{6gf} 7^{6g} 11^{5sw} 10^{6sd} 15^{7gf} **0-1-6**
£902

Eight Trumps *P R Wood* 48 a29
3 ch g First Trump - Misty Silks
7^{10gs} 5^{12sd} 9^{9gf} 14^{11sw} **0-0-4**

Eight Woods (Ire) *T D Barron* a69
5 ch g Woods Of Windsor (USA) - Cd Super Targeting (Ire)
6^{12sd} 6^{9sd} 3^{9sd} **0-1-3 £634**

Ejay *Julian Poulton* a39
4 b/br f Emperor Jones (USA) - Lough Erne
11^{8sd} 12^{7sd} **0-0-2**

Ekraar (USA) *M P Tregoning* 121
6 b h Red Ransom (USA) - Sacahuista (USA)
3^{12g} 1^{10g} 10^{10gf} 1^{12gf} 1^{12g} **3-1-5**
£281,029

El Coto *B A McMahon* 100
3 b c Forzando - Thatcherella
1^{7g} 2^{8gf} 20^{8gf} 3^{8gf} 6^{8gf} 1^{7gf} 7^{8gf} 3^{11gs}
10^{8g} 4^{10gf} **2-2-10 £28,064**

El Gran Hombre (USA) *Miss Kariana Key* a32
7 ch g El Gran Senor (USA) - Conquistress (USA)
9^{7sd} **0-0-1**

El Hamra (Ire) *M J Haynes*
5 gr g Royal Abjar (USA) - Cherlinoa (Fr)
12^{8sd} **0-0-1**

El Laoob (USA) *J H M Gosden* 94
3 b f Red Ransom (USA) - Ajfan (USA)
3^{7gs} 6^{8g} 1^{10gf} 4^{10gs} 2^{12gf} 6^{13g} **1-2-6**
£17,352

El Magnifico *P D Cundell* 36 a55
2 b g Forzando - Princess Poquito
17^{7gf} 7^{6sd} 6^{6sd} **0-0-3**

El Misti *K R Burke* a37
4 b f Elmaamul (USA) - Sherrington
16^{6sd} 6^{5sw} 6^{5sw} **0-0-3**

El Palmar *T D Barron* 63
2 b g Case Law - Aybeegirl
6^{5g} 2^{5gf} **0-1-2 £1,144**

El Pedro *N E Berry* 59 a66
4 b g Piccolo - Standard Rose
5^{8sd} 5^{12gf} 8^{12g} 2^{11gf} 3^{12gf} 10^{7f} 13^{10gs}
12^{10gf} 3^{10gf} 7^{10gf} 3^{10gf} 14^{8gf} 1^{12gf} 8^{10gf} 5^{12g}
4^{10g} 5^{10gf} 5^{12f} 4^{10f} 11^{9sd}
1-5-23 £5,378

El Raymondo *M Blanshard* 44 a59
4 b g Night Shift (USA) - Alaraby (Ire)
9^{7sd} 2^{8sd} 10^{7sd} 7^{8sd} 6^{7sd} 12^{8gf} **0-1-6**
£850

Ela Agori Mou (Ire) *D Eddy* 44
6 ch g Ela-Mana-Mou - La Courant (USA)
13^{12gf} 9^{12g} 10^{16gs} 14^{16gs} 8^{16g} 9^{14gf} 7^{14f}
0-0-7

Ela D'Argent (Ire) *Miss K Marks* 71
4 b f Ela-Mana-Mou - Petite-D-Argent
2^{12f} 19^{12gf} 5^{13g} **0-1-3 £1,772**

Ela Figura *A W Carroll* 67

3 ch f The West (USA) - Chili Bouchier (USA)
7⁵ᶠ 12⁶ᵍᶠ 4⁵ᵍᶠ 7⁶ᵍᶠ 8⁵ᵍᶠ 4⁵ᵍᶠ 9⁵ᵍ 3⁵ᵍᶠ
3⁵ᵍ 3⁵ˢ 2⁶ᵍᶠ 8⁵ᵍᶠ 18⁶ᵍᶠ 2⁶ᶠ 11⁶ᵍˢ **0-4-15**
£4,330

Ela Jay *H Morrison*   58
4 b f Double Eclipse (Ire) - Papirusa (Ire)
2¹⁴ᵍ 6¹⁶ᵍˢ 9¹⁶ᵍᶠ 6¹⁶ᵍᶠ 8¹⁶ᵍᶠ **0-1-5**
£1,186

Ela Paparouna *H Candy*   73
2 b f Vettori (Ire) - Pretty Poppy
5⁶ᵍᶠ 4⁶ᵍᶠ 3⁶ᶠ **0-1-3 £783**

Ela Re *C R Dore*   a22
4 ch g Sabrehill (USA) - Lucia Tarditi (Fr)
13¹²ˢᵈ **0-0-1**

Electrique (Ire) *J A Osborne*   81
3 b g Elmaamul (USA) - Majmu (USA)
3¹⁰ᶠ 3¹⁰ᵍᶠ 2¹⁰ᵍᶠ 2⁸ᵍᶠ 1¹⁰ᵍᶠ **1-1-5**
£10,172

Elegant Shadow *R Charlton*   71
3 ch f Grand Lodge (USA) - White Shadow (Ire)
2⁷ᵍᶠ 3⁸ᵍᶠ 9⁸ᵍᶠ **0-1-3 £2,625**

Eleonor Sympson *R M H Cowell*   22
4 b f Cadeaux Genereux - Anne Bonny
13⁸ᵍ 16⁷ᵍᶠ **0-0-2**

Elfhelm (Ire) *Edward Butler*   a82
3 b c Perugino (USA) - Symphony (Ire)
2⁸ˢᵈ **0-1-1 £932**

Elheba (Ire) *M Wigham*   a71
4 b/br g Elbio - Fireheba (Ity)
10⁹ˢᵈ 4⁹ˢᵈ 4⁸ˢᵈ 11¹²ˢᵈ 13⁹ˢᵈ 10¹²ˢᵈ **0-0-6**
£630

Elidore *B Palling*   85 a56
3 b f Danetime (Ire) - Beveled Edge
3⁷ᵍᶠ 8⁷ᵍ 11⁸ᵍ 10⁷ˢᵈ **0-0-4 £1,601**

Eliipop *R J Price*   a65
5 b g First Trump - Hasty Key (USA)
2¹²ˢᵈ 5¹⁴ˢʷ 6¹⁵ˢᵈ **0-1-3 £830**

Elitista (Fr) *E J O'Neill*   32 a48
2 gr f Linamix (Fr) - Elacata (Ger)
17⁶ᵍᶠ 5⁷ᵍ 5⁸ˢᵈ **0-0-3**

Ella Carisa *A Charlton*   37 a32
4 b f Elmaamul (USA) - Salty Girl (Ire)
7¹⁶ˢᵈ 9¹⁶ˢʷ 8¹³ˢᵈ 8¹⁷ᶠ 5¹⁶ᵍ 15¹⁶ᵍᶠ **0-0-6**

Ella Falls (Ire) *Mrs H Dalton*   48
8 b m Dancing Dissident (USA) - Over Swing (Fr)
4¹⁴ᵍᶠ 5¹⁴ᶠ 5¹⁷ᵍᶠ **0-0-3 £311**

Ella's Wish (Ire) *J H M Gosden*   58 a61
3 ch f Bluebird (USA) - Red Rita (Ire)
9⁸ᵍᶠ 4¹⁰ˢᵈ 10⁸ᵍᶠ 14¹⁰ˢᵈ **0-0-4 £303**

Ellamyte *D G Bridgwater*   62 a47
3 b f Elmaamul (USA) - Deanta In Eirinn
13⁶ᵍᶠ 9⁵ᵍᶠ 14⁶ᵍᶠ 10⁶ᵍ 5⁵ᵍᶠ 3⁶ᵍᶠ 11⁶ᵍᶠ
3⁶ᶠ 10⁶ˢᵈ **0-2-9 £755**

Elle Royal (Ire) *T P McGovern*   26
4 br f Ali-Royal (Ire) - Silvretta (Ire)
13¹²ᶠ **0-0-1**

Ellen Mooney *B Smart*   77 a76
4 ch f Efisio - Budby
7⁸ᵍ 7⁸ᵍᶠ 14⁸ᵍ 10⁸ᵍˢ 7⁸ᵍ 2⁸ᵍˢ 1⁸ˢᵈ 5⁸ᵍ
10⁸ᵍ **1-1-9 £3,864**

Ellen's Rock *Paul Johnson*
5 b m Rock Hopper - Hellene
12⁶ˢᵈ **0-0-1**

Ellens Academy (Ire) *E J Alston*   87
8 b g Royal Academy (USA) - Lady Ellen

5⁶ˢ 7⁶ᵍᶠ 8⁵ʰʸ 9⁶ᵍᶠ 12⁶ᵍˢ 6⁵ᵍᶠ 8⁷ᵍ 7⁶ᵍᶠ
6⁶ᵍᶠ 1⁶ᶠ 3⁵ᵍᶠ 1⁶ᵍ **2-1-12 £10,296**

Ellens Lad (Ire) *W J Musson*   47
9 b g Polish Patriot (USA) - Lady Ellen
20⁵ˢ **0-0-1**

Ellina *Mrs Lydia Pearce*   48
2 b f Robellino (USA) - Native Flair
15⁷ᵍᶠ 11⁸ᵍ **0-0-2**

Elliot's Choice (Ire) *D Carroll*   70
2 b c Foxhound (USA) - Indian City
11⁵ᵍ 3⁵ᵍᶠ 8⁵ᵍᶠ 2⁵ᵍᶠ 8⁵ᵍᶠ **0-2-5 £2,245**

Ellovamul *W M Brisbourne*   56 a58
3 b f Elmaamul (USA) - Multi-Soffit
4⁹ᶠ 10¹⁰ᶠ 9¹⁰ˢ 6¹²ˢᵈ 1¹⁰ᵍᶠ 1¹¹ᵍᶠ 5¹⁰ᵍᶠ
4¹¹ˢʷ 5¹²ᶠ **2-1-9 £5,655**

Ellway Heights *W M Brisbourne*   58
6 b g Shirley Heights - Amina
11¹⁴ˢ 11²ᵍᶠ 11²ᵍᶠ 11²ᵍ 13¹²ᵍᶠ 2¹²ᶠ 16¹²ᵍᶠ
3-1-7 £10,112

Eloquent Silence *B W Hills*   63
3 ch f Nashwan (USA) - Flower Girl
8¹⁰ᵍᶠ 5¹⁰ᵍᶠ 7¹²ᵍᶠ **0-0-3**

Elshadi (Ire) *M P Tregoning*   92
2 b c Cape Cross (Ire) - Rispoto
1⁸ᵍᶠ 1⁸ᵍᶠ 4⁸ᵍᶠ **2-0-3 £15,812**

Elsie B *P Howling*   a5
3 gr f First Trump - Evening Falls
7⁷ˢᵈ 11⁸ˢᵈ **0-0-2**

Elsinora *H Morrison*   64
2 b f Great Dane (Ire) - Deanta In Eirinn
13⁶ᵍᶠ 3⁶ᵍᶠ 13⁶ᵍᶠ 25⁶ᵍᶠ **0-1-4 £587**

Elucidate *C R Dore*   43 a47
4 ch f Elmaamul (USA) - Speed To Lead (Ire)
10⁸ˢᵈ 12⁷ˢᵈ 10⁹ˢᵈ 9⁸ᵈ 11¹¹ᵍᶠ 6⁷ᵍᶠ 8¹⁰ᵍ
13⁸ᵍᶠ **0-0-8**

Elusive City (USA) *G A Butler*   103
3 b c Elusive Quality (USA) - Star Of Paris (USA)
5⁷ᵍᶠ 9⁸ᵍˢ 6⁵ᵍᶠ **0-0-3 £3,350**

Elusive Dream *Sir Mark Prescott*   48
2 b c Rainbow Quest (USA) - Dance A Dream
10⁷ᵍˢ 12⁸ᵍˢ **0-0-2**

Elusive Kitty (USA) *G A Butler*   65 a67
2 b f Elusive Quality (USA) - Al Fahda
5⁶ᵍᶠ 2⁸ˢᵈ **0-1-2 £669**

Elvington Boy *M W Easterby*   76
6 ch g Emarati (USA) - Catherines Well
6⁵ᶠ 17⁷ᵍ 13⁵ᵍᶠ 12⁵ᵍ **0-0-4**

Emaradia *P D Evans*   52 a57
2 ch f Emarati (USA) - Rewardia (Ire)
11⁵ᵍ 3⁵ˢᵈ 7⁵ˢᵈ 2⁵ˢᵈ 4⁵ᵍᶠ 5⁵ᵍᶠ 2⁵ᶠ 1⁵ᵍᶠ
4⁵ᵍᶠ 2⁵ˢᵈ 10⁵ᵍᶠ 5⁶ᵍᶠ 6⁵ᵍᶠ 2⁵ˢᵈ **1-5-14**
£7,131

Emarati's Image *R M Stronge*   47 a48
5 b g Emarati (USA) - Choir's Image
3⁶ˢʷ 8⁵ᵍ 4⁵ˢᵈ 8⁵ᵍˢ 15⁷ᶠ 9⁶ˢᵈ **0-2-6 £783**

Embassy Lord *J O'Reilly*   62 a60
2 b g Mind Games - Keen Melody (USA)
9⁶ᵍˢ 6⁶ᵍᶠ 5⁶ˢᵈ 4⁶ᶠ 6⁷ᶠ 2⁶ᵍ 2⁶ˢᵈ 5⁶ᵍᶠ 5⁷ᵍᶠ
14⁶ˢᵈ **1-2-10 £4,881**

Ember Days *J L Spearing*   35
4 gr f Reprimand - Evening Falls
15⁸ᵍ **0-0-1**

Emerald Fire *A M Balding*   82 a86
4 b f Pivotal - Four-Legged Friend
1⁶ˢᵈ 9⁷ˢᵈ 6⁶ᵍ 10⁷ᵍ 3⁶ᵍ 12⁶ᵍˢ 12⁶ˢᵈ **1-1-7**

£4,331

Emerald Mist (Ire) *G B Balding* 7
4 b f Sacrament - Jade's Gem
13¹²ᵍᶠ 10¹⁶ᵍᶠ **0-0-2**

Emerald Spirit (Ire) *M R Channon* 23
2 br f Key Of Luck (USA) - Watch Me (Ire)
12⁵ᵍᶠ **0-0-1**

Emerging Star (Ire) *G M Moore* 75
3 b g Desert Style (Ire) - Feather Star
10¹⁰ᵍ 3¹⁰ᵍᶠ 7¹²ᵍᶠ 5¹⁰ᵍˢ 14¹⁰ᵍᶠ 1¹⁰ᵍᶠ 12¹⁰ᵍ
14¹⁰ᵍᶠ **1-1-8 £4,328**

Emhala (Ire) *P A Blockley*
2 ch f Docksider (USA) - Adarika
10⁶ˢᵈ **0-0-1**

Emigrate *P J Makin* 16 a49
4 b f Emarati (USA) - Fly South
3⁷ˢᵈ 8⁶ˢᵈ 4⁵ˢʷ 4⁵ˢᵈ 8⁵ᵍᶠ **0-1-5 £427**

Emily Dee *J M Bradley* 44
4 b f Classic Cliche (Ire) - Alpi Dora
12⁶ᵍᶠ 11⁶ᵍᶠ 2¹⁰ᵍ 3¹²ᵍᶠ 12¹⁰ᵍᶠ **0-1-5**
£1,328

Emilys Dawn *D K Ivory* a33
2 b f Komaite (USA) - Spice And Sugar
13⁶ˢᵈ 8⁸ˢᵈ **0-0-2**

Eminent Aura (USA) *A Dickman*
2 ch f Charismatic (USA) - Perfectly Clear (USA)
9⁵ᶠ 10⁵ᵍᶠ **0-0-2**

Emmeffaich (Ire) *J G Portman* 50
2 ch f Foxhound (USA) - Shalstayholy (Ire)
7⁷ᵍᶠ 4⁷ᵍᶠ 5⁷ᶠ 4⁷ᵍᶠ 13⁸ˢᵈ 16⁸ᵍᶠ **0-0-6**

Emmervale *R M H Cowell* 57 a34
4 b f Emarati (USA) - Raintree Venture
17⁷ᵍᶠ 10⁷ˢᵈ 5⁵ᶠ 1⁶ᶠ 9⁶ᶠ 3⁶ᵍᶠ 6⁷ᶠ
1⁷ᵍˢ 13⁶ᵍᶠ 16⁸ˢᵈ **2-1-11 £6,237**

Emperor Cat (Ire) *P A Blockley* 60 a59
2 b g Desert Story (Ire) - Catfoot Lane
11⁵ᵍᶠ 4⁵ᶠ 6⁷ᶠ 3⁶ᶠ 9⁶ᶠ 3⁶ᵍᶠ 3⁵ᵍᶠ
6⁶ᵍᶠ 1⁵ᶠ 6⁶ᵍᶠ 9⁶ᵍᶠ 1⁵ˢᵈ 7⁵ᶠ 5⁷ᵍᶠ **2-1-15**
£7,613

Emperor Star *T G Mills* 22 a59
3 b f Emperor Jones (USA) - Blu Tamantara (USA)
7⁸ˢᵈ 14¹⁰ˢᵈ 2⁷ˢᵈ 5⁸ˢᵈ 16⁷ᵍᶠ **0-1-5**
£1,121

Emperor's Well *M W Easterby* 63 a59
4 ch g First Trump - Catherines Well
10⁶ᵍᶠ 16⁷ᵍᶠ 10⁸ᵍˢ 2⁸ᵍᶠ 11⁸ᵍᶠ 4¹⁰ᶠ 1⁸ᵍᶠ
4¹⁰ᵍˢ 6⁸ˢᵈ **1-2-9 £4,390**

Emperors Lot *M Wellings* 56
3 b f Emperor Jones (USA) - Westering
8⁸ᵍ 8⁸ᶠ 19⁸ᵍᶠ 10⁸ˢᵈ **0-0-4**

Empire Maker (USA) *R J Frankel* a125
3 br c Unbridled (USA) - Toussaud (USA)
2⁹ᶠᵗ 1⁹ᶠᵗ 1⁹ᵐʸ 2¹⁰ᶠᵗ 1¹²ˢʸ 2⁹ᶠᵗ **3-2-6**
£1,210,125

Empire Park *C R Egerton* 45
8 b g Tragic Role (USA) - Millaine
8²²ᵍᶠ **0-0-1**

Empress Josephine *J R Jenkins* 50 a62
3 b f Emperor Jones (USA) - Valmaranda (USA)
10⁷ˢᵈ 4⁵ˢᵈ 7⁵ᵍᶠ 17⁵ᵍᶠ 15⁶ᵍᶠ 1⁵ˢᵈ 2⁵ˢʷ
4⁵ˢᵈ **1-2-8 £3,639**

Emran (USA) *E A L Dunlop* 98
3 br c Silver Hawk (USA) - Indihash (USA)
6¹¹ᵍ 1⁸ᵍᶠ 15⁸ᵍᶠ 10¹⁰ᵍᶠ **1-0-4 £10,035**

Emtee *J L Dunlop* 49

Emteyaz *Allan Smith* 89
5 b h Mark Of Esteem (Ire) - Najmat Alshemaal (Ire)
1¹⁰ᶠᵗ 3¹⁰ᶠᵗ 4⁸ᶠᵗ 1¹⁰ᶠᵗ 12¹⁶ᵍ 14⁸ᵍᶠ 11¹¹ᵍᶠ
2-1-7 £35,443

Emtilaak *B Hanbury* 72
2 b c Marju (Ire) - Just A Mirage
9⁷ᵍᶠ 2⁶ᵍᶠ 3⁶ᵍᶠ **0-2-3 £1,784**

Enchanted *G G Margarson* 99
4 b f Magic Ring (Ire) - Snugfit Annie
3⁷ᵍ 6⁶ᵍᶠ 7⁶ᶠ 17⁷ᵍᶠ 19⁷ᵍ 6⁶ᵍᶠ 8⁸ᵍᶠ 4⁷ᵍᶠ
6⁶ᵍᶠ 3⁷ᶠ **0-0-10 £7,254**

Enchanted Princess *J H M Gosden* 67
3 b f Royal Applause - Hawayah (Ire)
7⁷ᵍᶠ 1⁸ᵍᶠ **1-0-2 £4,329**

Enchantment *I A Wood* 80
2 b f Compton Place - Tharwa (Ire)
7⁵ᵍᶠ 1⁵ᵍᶠ 6⁵ᵍ 11⁷ᵍᶠ 1⁶ᵍᶠ **2-0-5 £24,114**

Encore Royale *P W Harris* 61
3 b f Royal Applause - Verbena (Ire)
5⁷ᵍ 10⁷ᵍᶠ 13⁷ᵍᶠ 2⁸ᶠ 5⁸ᵍ 12¹⁰ᵍᶠ 9¹⁰ᵍᶠ
14⁸ᵍᶠ **0-1-8 £1,178**

Encounter *J Hetherton* 59
7 br g Primo Dominie - Dancing Spirit (Ire)
4⁷ᵍᶠ 5⁸ᵍᶠ 8⁷ᵍˢ 1⁸ᵍᶠ 6⁷ᵍᶠ 7⁸ᵍˢ 12⁸ᵍˢ 3⁸ᵍᶠ
5⁷ᵍᶠ 16⁷ᵍᶠ 2⁹ᵍ 4⁹ᵍˢ 2⁸ᵍᶠ 4¹⁰ᵍᶠ 13¹⁰ᵍᶠ
6⁸ᵍᶠ 5⁸ᵍᶠ 10¹⁰ᵍᶠ 9⁸ᵈ **1-4-20 £11,178**

Endless Hall *L M Cumani* 110
7 b h Saddlers' Hall (Ire) - Endless Joy
8¹⁰ᵍ 3¹⁰ᵍᶠ **0-0-2 £3,850**

Endless Summer *K A Ryan* 97
5 b g Zafonic (USA) - Well Away (Ire)
5⁶ᵍ 2⁷⁶ᵍ 10⁶ᵍ 4⁶ᵍᶠ 15⁶ᵍ 15⁶ᵍᶠ 4⁵ᵍˢ
0-0-7 £740

Enford Princess *R Hannon* 85
2 b f Pivotal - Expectation (Ire)
1⁶ᵍ 1⁶ᵍᶠ 7⁶ᵍᶠ 19⁷ᵍᶠ **2-0-4 £13,751**

English Rocket (Ire) *D J S Ffrench Davis* 70 a64
2 b c Indian Rocket - Golden Charm (Ire)
14⁶ᵍᶠ 2⁶ˢᵈ 5⁷ᵍ 3⁶ˢᵈ 2⁷ᵍᶠ 3⁷ᵍ **0-4-6**
£4,557

Engulfed (USA) *W Jarvis* a44
3 b f Gulch (USA) - Storm Dove (USA)
10⁸ˢᵈ **0-0-1**

Enjoy The Buzz *J M Bradley* 39 a29
4 b c Prince Of Birds (USA) - Abaklea (Ire)
10⁶ˢᵈ 9⁶ˢᵈ 2⁶ᶠ **0-1-3 £908**

Enrapture (USA) *Mrs A J Perrett* 72
2 b f Lear Fan (USA) - Cheviot Hills (USA)
5⁷ᵍᶠ **0-0-1**

Ensemble *M W Easterby* 9
3 b g Polish Precedent (USA) - Full Orchestra
14¹²ᵍᶠ 11¹²ᵍᶠ **0-0-2**

Entrap (USA) *W J Haggas* 98
4 b f Phone Trick (USA) - Mystic Lure
2⁷ᵍ 3⁶ᵍᶠ 7⁶ᵍᶠ **0-2-3 £10,615**

Environment Audit *J R Jenkins* a55
4 ch g Kris - Bold And Beautiful
15¹²ˢᵈ **0-0-1**

Environmentalist *M A Jarvis* 12
4 b c Danehill (USA) - Way O'Gold (USA)
2⁹⁸ᵍ 18⁸ᵍᶠ 6⁸ᵍᶠ **0-0-3**

Eoz (Ire) *M A Jarvis* 75 a85
3 b f Sadler's Wells (USA) - Greek Moon (Ire)

2^{9s} 4^{12sd} 2^{12sd} 1^{12sd} 1^{11s} 2^{12sd} 10^{12sd}
1-3-7 £7,589

Epaminondas (USA) *R Hannon* 73
2 ch c Miswaki (USA) - Nora Nova (USA)
8^{6gf} 5^{6gf} 3^{7gs} **0-1-3 £639**

Ephesus *Miss Gay Kelleway* 87 a89
3 b c Efisio - Composition
5^{7sd} 1^{8sd} 1^{10sd} 3^{10sd} 2^{8sw} 2^{9sd} 10^{10gs}
1^{7sd} 3^{8g} 3^{7g} 8^{7sw} **3-4-11 £23,019**

Equus (Ire) *R Hannon* 63 a29
2 b c Desert Style (Ire) - Iolanta (Ire)
5^{8gf} 15^{8gf} 11^{8sd} **0-0-3**

Ermine Grey *D Haydn Jones* 66 a68
2 gr g Wolfhound (USA) - Impulsive Decision (Ire)
7^{6sd} 6^{6gf} 5^{7gf} 1^{8sw} 11^{6g} **1-0-5 £2,912**

Erracht *K R Burke* 75 a61
5 gr m Emarati (USA) - Port Na Blath
11^{5sd} 3^{5sd} 1^{5sw} 9^{5sw} 1^{5sd} 7^{5sd} 1^{5gf} 9^{5gf}
15^{5gf} 3^{5f} 4^{5gf} 3^{6f} 5^{5f} 3^{5gf} 1^{5gf} 3^{5gf} 6^{5f} 2^{5f}
9^{5f} **4-6-19 £16,996**

Errol *J F Coupland* 37 a42
4 ch g Dancing Spree (USA) - Primo Panache
4^{9sw} 7^{8sd} 7^{11sd} 8^{8sd} 7^{10gf} 11^{12f} 7^{12gf}
8^{14gf} 8^{16gf} **0-0-9**

Ersaal (USA) *J Jay* 51 a39
3 ch g Gulch (USA) - Madame Secretary (USA)
12^{10gf} 6^{12sw} 5^{12sd} 17^{16gf} **0-0-4**

Erte *M R Channon* 71
2 ch g Vettori (Ire) - Cragreen
4^{7gf} 9^{8gf} 3^{7f} 4^{7gf} 12^{6gf} 6^{7gf} **0-1-6**
£1,321

Erupt *M Brittain* 59
10 b g Beveled (USA) - Sparklingsovereign
3^{10gs} 9^{10gf} 16^{8gf} 8^{10gf} 13^{12gs} 6^{9gs} 8^{11g}
0-1-7 £1,054

Esatto *P A Blockley* 85
4 b g Puissance - Stoneydale
7^{5f} 13^{7gs} 14^{6gs} 6^{7gf} 9^{6f} 11^{7gf} 1^{5f} 2^{5g}
13^{5s} 5^{6gf} 12^{5gf} 6^{5f} 3^{6f} **1-2-13 £6,503**

Escalade *W M Brisbourne* 66 a60
6 b g Green Desert (USA) - Sans Escale (USA)
3^{11sd} 7^{11sd} 5^{10g} 2^{10gf} 7^{10g} 3^{9gs} 6^{10f}
10^{9gf} 4^{10f} 2^{10f} 4^{10gf} 10^{10gf} 4^{9gf} 5^{9sd} **0-4-14**
£3,418

Escayola (Ire) *W J Haggas* 89 a43
3 b g Revoque (Ire) - First Fling (Ire)
5^{8sd} 7^{12gs} 1^{16gf} 1^{14gf} 1^{17g} 2^{16g} 1^{16gf}
1^{16gf} **5-1-8 £31,287**

Esenin *D G Bridgwater* 39 a45
4 b g Danehill (USA) - Boojum
12^{7sd} 13^{6gf} 11^{7sd} 14^{12f} 15^{10g} **0-0-5**

Espada (Ire) *J A Osborne* 90 a76
7 b g Mukaddamah (USA) - Folk Song (Can)
6^{7sd} 1^{8gf} 24^{7g} 12^{8gf} **1-0-4 £5,638**

Esperance (Ire) *J Akehurst* 65 a67
3 ch g Bluebird (USA) - Dioscorea (Ire)
9^{7gf} 20^{7gs} 14^{12g} 2^{11gs} 7^{10g} 4^{10sd} **0-1-6**
£1,280

Esplanade *Sir Michael Stoute* 78
3 b f Danehill (USA) - Atropa (USA)
3^{8gf} 2^{10gf} 3^{10gf} 1^{10f} 14^{9gf} **1-2-5**
£5,502

Espresso Time (Ire) *S L Keightley* 72 a59
3 b g Danetime (Ire) - Cappuchino (Ire)
3^{6g} 2^{7gf} 3^{6gf} 6^{7gf} 5^{7gf} 4^{6sw} 14^{7sd} 3^{7sw}
5^{6sd} **0-4-9 £2,830**

Essay Baby (Fr) *P D Cundell* 58 a23
3 b f Saumarez - Easter Baby
8^{12sd} 4^{8g} 7^{8gf} 8^{10g} 14^{12sd} 5^{8gf} 11^{8g}
0-1-7 £295

Essequibo (Ire) *M J Polglase* a60
3 b g Spectrum (Ire) - Far From Home
1^{7sd} 5^{7sd} 11^{7sd} 13^{7sd} 21^{7g} 16^{11sw} **1-0-6**
£2,968

Essex (Ire) *Sir Michael Stoute* 77
3 b c Sadler's Wells (USA) - Knight's Baroness
4^{10gf} 2^{12g} 6^{12g} 8^{10gs} **0-1-4 £2,147**

Essex Star (Ire) *Miss J Feilden* 62
2 b f Revoque (Ire) - Touch Of White
12^{6gs} 8^{6gf} 11^{6gf} 10^{6f} **0-0-4**

Essex Street (Ire) *D Shaw* a37
6 b g Dolphin Street (Fr) - Filet Mignon (USA)
6^{6sw} 9^{7sd} 5^{6sd} 8^{6sd} **0-0-4**

Essnaad (USA) *B W Hills* 86
3 b c Swain (Ire) - Shfoug (USA)
3^{12gf} 4^{12gs} 1^{13gf} 11^{14g} 4^{13gf} 6^{16gf} 11^{13gf}
1-0-7 £6,780

Estabella (Ire) *M Wellings*
6 ch m Mujtahid (USA) - Lady In Green
14^{12sw} 12^{12sd} **0-0-2**

Established *J R Best* a11
6 b g Not In Doubt (USA) - Copper Trader
7^{16sd} 11^{16sd} 9^{16sw} **0-0-3**

Establishment *C A Cyzer* 88
6 b g Muhtarram (USA) - Uncharted Waters
2^{16gf} 12^{16gf} 5^{14gf} 4^{20gf} 5^{22f} 12^{16gf} 2^{16gf}
8^{18gf} 1^{16g} 5^{17g} **1-3-10 £13,826**

Esteban *J J Quinn* 62
3 b g Groom Dancer (USA) - Ellie Ardensky
8^{8gf} 14^{8gs} 4^{10f} 5^{11g} 8^{12gf} **0-0-5 £296**

Esteemed Lady (Ire) *Sir Michael Stoute* 89
2 b f Mark Of Esteem (Ire) - Bareilly (USA)
3^{6gf} 4^{7gf} **0-1-2 £14,015**

Esti Ab (Ire) *M P Tregoning* 80
2 b c Danehill (USA) - Bintalshaati
7^{7gf} 11^{8gf} 2^{8g} 3^{8gf} 17^{7sd} **0-2-5 £2,174**

Estihlal *E A L Dunlop* 44
2 b f Green Desert (USA) - Ta Rib (USA)
6^{7g} 14^{6gs} **0-0-2**

Estilhaam (USA) *Sir Michael Stoute* 62
2 b f Gulch (USA) - Mamlakah (Ire)
5^{7gf} **0-0-1 £401**

Estilo *R M Flower* a40
3 b g Deploy - Vilcabamba (USA)
10^{12sd} 10^{11sd} 11^{12sd} 10^{12sd} **0-0-4**

Estimada *H R A Cecil* 45
3 ch f Mark Of Esteem (Ire) - Gisarne (USA)
2^{11gf} **0-0-1 £1,164**

Estimate *C E Brittain* 74
3 b f Mark Of Esteem (Ire) - Mistle Thrush (USA)
6^{8gf} 3^{9g} 3^{10gf} 8^{7g} 7^{8f} 2^{10f} 6^{12gf} 2^{10gf}
6^{10g} **0-3-9 £3,912**

Estimation *R M H Cowell* 75 a75
3 b f Mark Of Esteem (Ire) - Mohican Girl
3^{8sd} 3^{8g} 8^{10gf} 7^{8sd} 9^{9gf} 9^{7gf} 13^{6gf} 2^{8sd}
4^{8sd} 4^{8gf} 2^{8gf} 1^{8sd} 1^{8g} **2-4-13 £8,614**

Estrella Levante *G L Moore* 71 a50
3 ch g Abou Zouz (USA) - Star Of Modena (Ire)
11^{7gf} 5^{8sd} 8^{8sd} 4^{7gf} UR^{7gf} 7^{9g} 5^{6sd} **0-0-7**
£318

Etching (USA) *J R Fanshawe* 68 a35

3 b f Groom Dancer (USA) - Eternity
6⁸ˢᵈ 10⁸ˢᵈ 6¹⁰ᵍᶠ 2¹²ᶠ 3¹²ᵍ 3¹⁶ᵍᶠ 2¹⁶ᵍᶠ
2¹⁶ᵍᶠ 2¹⁶ᵍᶠ 1¹⁶ᵍᶠ 8¹⁷ᶠ **1-5-11 £7,248**

Eternal Beauty (USA) *M J Wallace*   74
3 b f Zafonic (USA) - Strawberry Roan (Ire)
7⁸ˢ 6⁶ᵍ 8⁶ᵍᶠ **0-0-3**

Eternal Bloom *M Brittain*   24 a29
5 b m Reprimand - Forever Roses
7⁸ˢᵈ 8⁷ˢʷ 16⁵ᵍˢ **0-0-3**

Eternal Dancer (USA) *M Johnston*   28
2 b c Royal Academy (USA) - Tara Roma (USA)
13⁷ᵍᶠ 11⁸ᵍᶠ **0-0-2**

Etesaal (USA) *D R Loder*   115 a93
3 br c Danzig (USA) - Electric Society (Ire)
1⁸ˢᵈ 1¹⁰ᵍᶠ 4¹²ᵍᶠ 2¹⁰ᵍᶠ **2-2-4 £49,463**

Ethos *B R Millman*   40
3 b g Emarati (USA) - Leprechaun Lady
12¹⁰ᶠ 14⁸ᵍᶠ 12¹⁰ᵍᶠ 13⁸ᵍˢ **0-0-4**

Etmaam *M Johnston*   61
2 b c Intikhab (USA) - Sudeley
4⁶ᵍᶠ **0-0-1 £327**

Etoile Montante (USA) *Mme C Head-Maarek*   118
3 ch f Miswaki (USA) - Willstar (USA)
4⁸ᵍˢ 3⁸ᵍˢ 1⁸ᵛˢ 2⁷ᵍˢ 1⁷ᵍ 1⁷ᵛˢ **3-2-6
£126,822**

Etoile Solitaire (USA) *M A Jarvis*   69 a76
3 gr g Lit De Justice (USA) - Cydalia (USA)
6⁶ˢᵈ 4⁶ᵍ 1⁶ᶠ 4⁷ᵍᶠ 13⁷ᵍᶠ 2⁷ᵍᶠ 14⁸ᵍ 2⁷ˢᵈ
1-2-8 £6,742

Eton (Ger) *D Nicholls*   79
7 ch g Suave Dancer (USA) - Ermione
12¹²ᵍ 12¹⁰ᵍ 19¹⁰ᵍˢ 4¹¹ᵍˢ 6¹⁰ᵍᶠ 6¹⁰ᵍᶠ 2¹⁰ᵍᶠ
5¹⁰ᵍᶠ 9¹⁰ᵍˢ 2¹²ᶠ 9¹⁰ᵍ 5¹⁰ᵍᶠ 3¹²ᵍᶠ 1¹²ᵍ
18¹²ᵍᶠ **1-4-16 £16,426**

Ettrick Water *L M Cumani*   92
4 ch g Selkirk (USA) - Sadly Sober (Ire)
17¹⁰ᵍˢ 5¹⁰ᵍᶠ 1⁷ᵍᶠ 4⁸ᵍᶠ 2⁷ᶠ 1⁸ᶠ 1⁸ᵍᶠ 3⁸ᶠ
3-2-8 £30,646

Eucalyptus (Ire) *S Dow*   a55
6 ch g Mujtahid (USA) - Imprecise
9⁸ˢᵈ 6⁷ˢᵈ 10⁸ˢᵈ **0-0-3**

Eugenie *R Hannon*
2 ch f Primo Dominie - Misty Goddess (Ire)
11⁶ˢ **0-0-1**

Euippe *J G Given*   66
2 b f Air Express (Ire) - Myth
4⁷ᵍᶠ 5⁷ᵍᶠ 6⁸ᵍᶠ **0-0-3 £343**

Eujane (Ire) *M L W Bell*   60
3 b f Alzao (USA) - Tribal Rite
5⁸ᵍᶠ 5⁷ᵍᶠ 10⁷ᵍ 19¹⁰ᵍ 5¹¹ᶠ 6⁸ᵍ **0-0-6**

Eunice Choice *M J Haynes*   a9
2 b g College Chapel - Aquiletta
7⁶ᵍᶠ 15⁷ˢᵈ **0-0-2**

Euro Import *P D Niven*
5 ch g Imp Society (USA) - Upper Club (Ire)
12¹²ᵍˢ **0-0-1**

Euro Route (Ire) *Edgar Byrne*   82
2 b g Desert Style (Ire) - Fresh Look (Ire)
8⁷ˢʰ 5⁶ʸ 5⁵ᵍʸ 10⁷ᵍᶠ 1⁶ᵍᶠ 4⁶ᵍᶠ 4⁶ᵍᶠ **1-1-7
£9,266**

Euro Venture *P A Blockley*   42 a53
8 b g Prince Sabo - Brave Advance (USA)
11⁷ˢᵈ 2⁶ˢᵈ 5⁷ˢʷ 13⁶ˢʷ 10⁷ᶠ **0-1-5 £844**

Eurolink Artemis *Miss Gay Kelleway*   62 a64
6 b m Common Grounds - Taiga

9⁸ˢᵈ 2⁹ˢᵈ 2⁸ˢᵈ 4⁸ˢᵈ 4⁹ˢʷ 8⁸ˢᵈ 3¹²ˢᵈ 7⁸ˢᵈ
6⁸ˢᵈ 2¹⁰ᵍᶠ 10⁹ˢᵈ 14¹⁰ᵍ 13⁹ˢᵈ **0-4-13 £3,427**

Eurolink Zante (Ire) *T D McCarthy*   64 a53
7 b g Turtle Island (Ire) - Lady Eurolink
9⁸ˢᵈ 8⁹ᵍ 8⁷ᵍᶠ 7⁷ᵍᶠ 8⁷ᵍˢ 8⁸ᵍˢ **0-0-7**

Eurolis (Fr) *T T Clement*
4 gr f Highest Honor (Fr) - Eidothea (Ger)
10¹⁴ᵍ **0-0-1**

Eva Jean *H Morrison*   54
2 b f Singspiel (Ire) - Go For Red (Ire)
11⁸ᵍᶠ **0-0-1**

Eva Peron (Ire) *H Morrison*   71 a62
3 b f Alzao (USA) - High Flying Adored (Ire)
9¹²ᵍᶠ 10⁸ᵍˢ 7⁸ᵍ 10⁷ᵍᶠ 8⁹ᵍᶠ 6⁹ᵍᶠ 16⁸ˢʷ
7¹⁰ᵍᶠ 12⁹ᵍᶠ **0-0-9**

Evaluator (Ire) *T G Mills*   a64
2 b c Ela-Mana-Mou - Summerhill
3⁷ˢᵈ **0-1-1 £572**

Evangelist (Ire) *A Berry*   59 a42
3 b f Namaqualand (USA) - Errazuriz (Ire)
8⁵ˢᵈ 12⁵ˢᵈ 7⁶ˢᵈ 2⁵ᵍˢ 5⁶ᶠ 8⁶ᵍᶠ 6⁵ˢᵈ 8⁷ᵍᶠ
4⁶ˢᵈ 4⁶ᵍᶠ 7⁶ᵍᶠ 10⁶ᵍᶠ 12⁶ᵍᶠ 8⁶ᵍᶠ 16⁶ᶠ **0-1-15
£1,578**

Even Easier *G L Moore*   57 a38
2 gr f Petong - Comme Ca
15⁵ᵍ 7⁵ᵍᶠ 4⁵ˢᵈ 1⁶ᶠ 2⁷ᵍᶠ **1-1-6
£4,053**

Even Hotter *D W P Arbuthnot*   30
2 b f Desert Style (Ire) - Level Pegging (Ire)
14⁶ᵍ **0-0-1**

Evening Encore *H Candy*   69
3 b f Kris - Eveningperformance
5⁸ᵍᶠ 1⁷ᵍ 14⁶ᵍ 11⁷ᶠ **1-0-4 £4,221**

Evening Post *J R Boyle*   38 a44
3 b g Petong - Nevis
5⁷ˢᵈ 12⁷ˢᵈ 15⁶ᵍ 11⁷ᵍᶠ 12⁶ᵍᶠ 7⁷ᵍᶠ 9⁸ˢᵈ
14⁸ᶠ 8¹⁰ᵍᶠ 10¹²ᶠ 10¹²ᵍᶠ **0-0-11**

Evening Press *T J Etherington*   29
4 b f River Falls - Shiny Kay
9⁷ᵍᶠ 13¹⁰ᵍ 8⁷ᵍᶠ 13⁸ˢ **0-0-4**

Eventuail (Arg) *W J Haggas*   115
5 b g Candy Stripes (USA) - Evidenciable (Arg)
5¹⁰ᵍ 4⁹ᵍ 6⁸ᵍˢ 8⁸ᵍˢ 2⁹ᵍᶠ 6⁹ᵍᶠ **0-1-6
£73,817**

Ever Cheerful *W G M Turner*   75 a70
2 b g Atraf - Big Story
4⁵ᵍ 2⁵ᵍᶠ 2⁵ᵍᶠ 2⁵ᵍᶠ 2⁵ˢᵈ 13⁷ᵍᶠ 3⁵ᶠ 4⁵ˢᵈ
3⁶ˢᵈ **0-5-9 £7,142**

Everest (Ire) *B Ellison*   96 a71
6 ch g Indian Ridge - Reine D'Beaute
5⁸ˢᵈ 5⁸ᵍᶠ 1⁸ᵍ 1⁸ᵍ 13⁹ᵍ 2⁸ᵍ 3⁸ᵍᶠ 7⁸ᵍᶠ
11⁸ᵍ 7⁹ᵍᶠ **2-2-10 £23,225**

Every Note Counts *W Jarvis*   85 a81
3 b c Bluegrass Prince (Ire) - Miss Mirror
4⁶ˢᵈ 4⁷ˢᵈ 9⁸ᵍᶠ 2¹⁰ˢᵈ 2¹⁰ᵍᶠ 4¹²ᵍᶠ 2¹¹ᵍ 4¹²ᵍᶠ
5¹⁰ˢ 2¹⁰ᵍ 12¹⁰ᵍᶠ **0-4-11 £9,753**

Eves Wood *J G Portman*   40
2 ch f Fleetwood (Ire) - Maesteg
8⁶ᵍᶠ 12⁸ˢᵈ 17⁸ᵍᶠ **0-0-3**

Evezio Rufo *N P Littmoden*   a42
11 b g Blakeney - Empress Corina
10¹¹ˢᵈ 9¹²ˢᵈ 2¹⁶ˢᵈ 7¹⁶ˢᵈ 9¹⁶ˢᵈ **0-1-5 £828**

Evolution Baby (Ire) *John A Quinn*   63 a86
3 b g Inzar (USA) - Go Flightline (Ire)
3⁸ˢᵈ 6⁷ˢᵈ 3⁶ˢʷ 3⁶ˢᵈ 4⁷ˢᵈ 6⁷ᶠ 10⁶ᵍʸ **0-2-7**

£2,553

Evolving Tactics (Ire) *D K Weld* 105
3 b g Machiavellian (USA) - Token Gesture (Ire)
3^{8g} 1^{8f} 9^{8s} 3^{10gf} 1^{10g} 6^{10g} **2-2-6**
£112,925

Exalted (Ire) *T A K Cuthbert* 66
10 b g High Estate - Heavenward (USA)
12^{13gs} 4^{13gs} 1^{13gs} 4^{13f} 2^{15g} 2^{14s} 7^{14f}
9^{16g} **1-2-8 £6,566**

Excalinor *P F I Cole* 91 a77
3 br c Inchinor - Noble Story
4^{5sd} 1^{5gf} 1^{6gf} 5^{7gf} 5^{7g} 8^{7sd} **2-0-6**
£9,923

Excellento (USA) *D R Loder* 107
3 ch c Rahy (USA) - Golden Opinion (USA)
1^{8gf} 1^{7gf} 1^{8gs} 3^{8gf} **3-1-4 £43,058**

Excelsius (Ire) *J L Dunlop* 103
3 ch c Dr Devious (Ire) - Folgore (USA)
3^{9gf} 7^{11g} 3^{8g} 3^{8vs} 11^{8gs} **0-2-5 £11,364**

Exclusive Air (USA) *T D Barron* 43 a72
4 ch g Affirmed (USA) - Lac Dessert (USA)
4^{8sw} 6^{8sd} 5^{11sd} 6^{11sd} 1^{12sd} 11^{13sd} 4^{12sd}
11^{10gf} 9^{9gf} 9^{12sd} 9^{8sd} 6^{12sd} 12^{12gf} **1-0-13**
£3,849

Exclusive Danielle *B W Hills* 70
2 ch f Thunder Gulch (USA) - Hasta (USA)
3^{7g} **0-1-1 £378**

Executive Choice (Ire) *J R Weymes*
9 b g Don't Forget Me - Shadia (USA)
12^{14gf} **0-0-1**

Exit To Heaven *J L Dunlop* 68 a46
3 ch f Exit To Nowhere (USA) - Shona (USA)
3^{8f} 12^{10f} 13^{10sd} 6^{12g} 13^{16gf} 8^{12sd} 9^{8sd}
0-0-7 £587

Exodous (Arg) *J A B Old* 44
7 ch g Equalize (USA) - Empire Glory (Arg)
7^{12gf} **0-0-1**

Expected Bonus (USA) *S C Williams* 30 a69
4 b/br g Kris S (USA) - Nidd (USA)
15^{12sd} 13^{12sd} 13^{12sd} 8^{16g} 14^{16gf} 11^{12gf}
11^{10gf} **0-0-7**

Expertise *E A L Dunlop* 63
3 ch g Selkirk (USA) - Bacinella (USA)
7^{12g} 7^{10gf} 14^{8f} 7^{10s} **0-0-4**

Explode *Miss L C Siddall* 73
6 b g Zafonic (USA) - Didicoy (USA)
12^{8hy} 7^{11gf} 5^{10gf} 3^{8gf} 5^{9s} 12^{9gf} 11^{10g}
12^{8s} 8^{8g} 13^{8gf} 15^{8gs} **0-0-11 £550**

Exploring (Ire) *John A Quinn* 44 a66
4 br g Charnwood Forest (Ire) - Caribbean Quest
5^{8sd} 8^{7sd} 8^{8sd} 8^{10g} 4^{8sd} **0-0-5**

Expressionist *R Guest* 46
3 b c Peintre Celebre (USA) - Pato
12^{12g} **0-0-1**

Exquisite Affair *J L Dunlop* 74
3 b f Alzao (USA) - Excellent Alibi (USA)
8^{8gf} 8^{10gf} 3^{12gf} 8^{12gs} 6^{12g} 1^{17f} 8^{16gf}
1-1-7 £3,623

Extemporise (Ire) *P J McBride* 42 a38
3 ch c Indian Ridge - No Rehearsal (Fr)
8^{6sd} 5^{8gf} 10^{5gf} **0-0-3**

Exterior (USA) *Mrs A J Perrett* 66
2 ch c Distant View (USA) - Alvernia (USA)
3^{7gf} **0-1-1 £297**

Extinguisher *D Nicholls* 80

4 ch g Zamindar (USA) - Xaymara (USA)
15^{5g} 10^{6gf} 16^{6gs} 8^{6g} 18^{6g} 21^{7g} **0-0-6**

Extra Cover (Ire) *R Charlton* 68
2 b g Danehill Dancer (Ire) - Ballycurrane (Ire)
5^{8g} **0-0-1**

Extra Gear (USA) *G A Butler* a72
3 ch c Diesis - Petiteness (USA)
3^{10sd} **0-1-1 £628**

Exzilarating *R F Johnson Houghton* 72 a66
3 ch c Zilzal (USA) - Personal Best (Ire)
9^{7gf} 9^{8gf} 5^{7gf} 12^{8gf} 4^{8f} 7^{10gf} 3^{8gf} 2^{8gf}
2^{7gf} **0-4-10 £2,898**

Eyecatcher *J R Fanshawe* a100
6 b g Green Desert (USA) - Reuval
2^{7sd} **0-1-1 £4,631**

Eyes Dont Lie (Ire) *D A Nolan* 41
5 b g Namaqualand (USA) - Avidal Park
6^{16gf} 6^{14gf} 10^{16gs} 11^{11gs} 13^{9gs} 8^{8gf} 5^{16gf}
6^{16g} 2^{12gf} 10^{12gf} **0-1-10 £850**

Eyes To The Right (Ire) *A J Chamberlain* a42
4 ch g Eagle Eyed (USA) - Capable Kate (Ire)
12^{11sd} 7^{10sd} 5^{12sd} 9^{9sd} **0-0-4**

Eyes Wide Open *P F I Cole* 25 a41
5 b m Fraam - Dreamtime Quest
4^{8sd} 10^{7sd} 11^{16sd} 6^{8sd} 7^{7sd} 10^{8f} **0-0-6**

Eyre O Plain Jane *P C Haslam* a36
3 ch f Wolfhound (USA) - Pushkinia (Fr)
9^{7sd} 7^{7sd} **0-0-2**

Ezz Elkheil *J W Payne* 85
4 b g Bering - Numidie (Fr)
17^{8g} 16^{10gs} 10^{10gf} 2^{10gf} 1^{12gs} 7^{12gf}
11^{14gf} 5^{11gf} 8^{12gf} **1-1-9 £7,557**

Faayej (Ire) *Sir Michael Stoute* 71
3 b c Sadler's Wells (USA) - Russian Ballet (USA)
5^{10gf} 2^{12gs} 1^{10gf} **1-1-3 £6,719**

Fabranese *P Howling* 24
3 b f Dr Devious (Ire) - Babsy Babe
5^{11gf} 4^{12gf} **0-0-2 £418**

Fabrian *D W P Arbuthnot* 64 a74
5 b g Danehill (USA) - Dockage (Can)
9^{7sd} 10^{6sd} 11^{7gf} 17^{6g} 3^{6gf} 16^{6gf} 9^{7sd}
5^{8gs} **0-1-8 £892**

Fabuco (Ire) *S L Keightley* 66 a52
2 b f Mujadil (USA) - Beechwood (USA)
3^{5gf} 5^{5g} 5^{5gf} 4^{5gf} 7^{5gf} 1^{5f} 6^{5sw} 10^{5gf}
5^{5f} 8^{6gf} **1-1-10 £5,208**

Fabuloso *S L Keightley* 48 a44
2 b f Dr Fong (USA) - Shafir (Ire)
5^{5sd} 13^{5gs} 9^{6gf} 12^{6gf} 11^{7sd} 7^{8sd} **0-0-6**

Fabulous Jet (Fr) *M R Channon* 101
3 ch g Starborough - Jetty (Fr)
2^{8gf} 2^{9gf} 1^{10gs} 7^{12gf} 8^{12gf} 1^{10g} 5^{10gf}
1^{11gs} 19^{10gf} 1^{11s} **4-2-10 £30,395**

Face The Limelight (Ire) *H Morrison* 76
4 b g Quest For Fame - Miss Boniface
1^{10gf} 5^{10gf} 5^{10gf} 11^{13gf} 5^{10gf} 17^{10gf} **1-0-6**
£3,965

Facing The Facts *C A Dwyer*
2 ch g Defacto (USA) - Sassy Lady (Ire)
10^{6sd} **0-0-1**

Fact O' The Matter *M Blanshard* 26 a66
4 b g So Factual (USA) - Edgeaway
7^{7sd} 4^{7sd} 6^{7sd} 5^{7sd} 16^{8g} 5^{7sd} **0-0-6**

Factor Fifteen *E A L Dunlop* 88
4 gr g Hector Protector (USA) - Catch The Sun

4^{16g} 6^{14gs} 1^{10gf} 2^{10gf} 2^{10f} 3^{12gf} 2^{10gf}
4^{10gs} 6^{10gf} 6^{10gf} **1-4-10 £18,758**

Factorsforvalue *Ronald Thompson* 6
3 b f Entrepreneur - Jeanne Avril
8^{9s} 18^{8gf} **0-0-2**

Factual Lad *B R Millman* 75 a64
5 b g So Factual (USA) - Surprise Surprise
3^{8sd} 2^{10sd} 4^{8sd} 5^{10gf} 1^{10gf} 1^{10f} 8^{10gf}
2-2-7 £8,562

Fadeela (Ire) *P W D'Arcy* 53 a61
2 ch f Desert King (Ire) - Gift Box (Ire)
4^{8sd} 9^{8sd} 2^{7sd} 5^{7gs} **0-1-4 £640**

Fahlawi (Ire) *B W Hills* 74
2 gr c Daylami (Ire) - Dancing Sea (USA)
4^{7gf} 2^{8g} **0-1-2 £1,838**

Failed To Hit *N P Littmoden* a59
10 b g Warrshan (USA) - Missed Again
1^{15sd} 4^{12sd} 5^{12sw} **1-0-3 £2,898**

Failte (Ire) *L A Dace* 30
5 b g Most Welcome - Esh Sham (USA)
14^{11gf} 9^{8gf} 7^{12f} **0-0-3**

Fair Compton *R Hannon* 63
2 b f Compton Place - Fair Eleanor
12^{5gf} 4^{6gf} **0-0-2 £345**

Fair Mix (Ire) *M Rolland* 121
5 gr h Linamix (Fr) - Fairlee Wild (USA)
5^{10vs} 2^{10g} 1^{11vs} 6^{12gs} **1-1-4 £71,370**

Fair Shake (Ire) *D Eddy* 75 a65
3 b g Sheikh Albadou - Shamrock Fair (Ire)
4^{5sd} 9^{5sd} 1^{5gs} 5^{5f} 10^{6gf} 10^{6g} 1^{6gs} 9^{6gs}
6^{6gs} 17^{7gf} 9^{7gs} **2-0-11 £16,756**

Fair Spin *M D Hammond* 79
3 ch g Pivotal - Frankie Fair (Ire)
7^{6f} 8^{5gf} 8^{5gf} 7^{5hy} 9^{6gf} 4^{6gf} 7^{6gs} 12^{6gs}
11^{8s} **0-0-9 £781**

Fairfax Flicker (Ire) *C R Egerton* a9
3 b f Sri Pekan (USA) - Charwelton
11^{8sd} 12^{12g} **0-0-2**

Fairgame Man *A Berry* 47 a27
5 ch g Clantime - Thalya
11^{6gf} 15^{5gf} 10^{5gf} 3^{6gs} 5^{5gf} 2^{6f} 4^{5g}
10^{6g} 17^{5g} 11^{5gf} 3^{5gf} 11^{6sd} 15^{5gf} 11^{5gf} 15^{6f}
13^{7gf} **0-3-16 £3,602**

Fairlie *Mrs J R Ramsden* 66
2 b f Halling (USA) - Fairy Flax (Ire)
4^{6gf} 1^{6gf} 11^{6g} 4^{7f} 6^{7gf} **1-0-5 £6,293**

Fairly High (Ire) *P G Murphy* 57 a48
3 b f Sri Pekan (USA) - Ecco Mi (Ire)
5^{8sd} 7^{8sw} 6^{10sd} 7^{13g} 5^{12g} 5^{12sd} **0-0-6**

Fairly Wild (USA) *M J Wallace* 57 a57
2 ch f Forest Wildcat (USA) - Markham Fair (Can)
5^{5f} 3^{5gf} 7^{6gf} 4^{5sw} 12^{6gf} 8^{6gf} **0-0-6**
£548

Fairmorning (Ire) *J W Unett* a35
4 b g Ridgewood Ben - The Bratpack (Ire)
6^{9sd} 5^{12sd} 5^{12sd} 4^{15sd} **0-0-4**

Fairy Monarch (Ire) *P T Midgley* 62
4 b g Ali-Royal (Ire) - Cookawara (Ire)
8^{10f} 14^{10gf} 6^{10gf} 10^{10gf} 8^{10gf} 5^{8gf} 19^{8gf}
7^{8gf} 9^{9gf} 13^{8gf} **0-0-10**

Fairy Wind (Ger) *B J Curley* 69 a56
6 b h Dashing Blade - Fairy Bluebird
13^{10sd} 8^{9sd} 6^{12sw} 9^{13sd} 7^{14g} 18^{14g} 9^{14gf}
2^{12sd} **0-1-8 £471**

Faites Vos Jeux *C N Kellett* 53 a53
2 b f Foxhound (USA) - Desert Bloom (Fr)
6^{5gf} 6^{5gf} 4^{5gf} 4^{6gf} 3^{6sd} **0-2-5 £328**

Faithful Warrior (USA) *B W Hills* 100
5 ch g Diesis - Dabaweyaa (Ire)
2^{8gf} 10^{10g} 4^{8gf} 14^{8gf} 9^{8gf} 1^{8gf} 13^{8gf}
2^{8g} 11^{8gf} **1-3-9 £44,239**

Falbrav (Ire) *L M Cumani* 132
5 b h Fairy King (USA) - Gift Of The Night (USA)
3^{11vs} 1^{9s} 5^{10gf} 1^{10gf} 5^{12g} 1^{10gf} 2^{10gf} 1^{8gf}
3^{12f} **4-3-9 £1,032,666**

Falcon Georgie *Miss B Sanders*
4 b f Sri Pekan (USA) - Georgia Stephens (USA)
15^{12sd} **0-0-1**

Falcon Hill *M Johnston* 50
4 b g Polar Falcon (USA) - Branston Jewel (Ire)
13^{7ft} 14^{6ft} 5^{6ft} 15^{8ft} 8^{6ft} 6^{7ft} 14^{6ft}
13^{7g} 12^{7gf} **0-0-9 £483**

Falcon On The Hill (USA) *M Johnston* 56
3 b g Southern Halo (USA) - Inca Empress (USA)
4^{10gf} 16^{11gf} **0-0-2 £526**

Fall In Line *Sir Mark Prescott* 61 a57
3 gr g Linamix (Fr) - Shortfall
3^{9sd} 4^{8gf} 3^{12sw} **0-2-3 £1,183**

Fame *Mrs A J Perrett* 79
3 ch c Northern Amethyst - First Sapphire
4^{10gf} 3^{12g} 2^{10gf} **0-2-3 £1,895**

Familiar Affair *B Smart* 81
2 b c Intikhab (USA) - Familiar (USA)
1^{7gf} 4^{7g} **1-0-2 £4,121**

Family Folly *J Nicol* 30
3 b g Green Horizon - Dry Land
12^{7gf} 14^{7gf} **0-0-2**

Famous Grouse *R Charlton* 104
3 b c Selkirk (USA) - Shoot Clear
2^{10gf} 11^{12gf} 2^{10g} 19^{9gf} **0-1-4 £14,112**

Fancy Affair *H R A Cecil* 72
3 b f Kris - Mafatin (Ire)
5^{10gf} 3^{12gf} **0-0-2 £319**

Fancy Foxtrot *B J Meehan* 87 a64
2 b c Danehill Dancer (Ire) - Smooth Princess (Ire)
11^{6g} 2^{6gf} 5^{6gf} 2^{7gf} 3^{7gf} 2^{8gf} 6^{8sd} **0-3-7**
£8,549

Fancy Lady *B W Hills* 95
3 ch f Cadeaux Genereux - Ascot Cyclone (USA)
6^{7gf} 7^{6gs} 4^{6gf} 16^{5gf} 8^{6g} 7^{6g} 10^{6gf} 12^{6gf}
0-0-8 £2,375

Fanling Lady *A P Jarvis* 72
2 gr f Highest Honor (Fr) - Pain Perdu (Ire)
6^{6gs} 3^{7gf} 8^{7gf} 3^{8gf} 8^{8g} 3^{8gf} 2^{10f} **0-3-7**
£5,486

Fanny's Fancy *C F Wall* 97 a97
3 b f Groom Dancer (USA) - Fanny's Choice (Ire)
1^{6sd} 1^{6sd} 4^{6g} 3^{6gf} **2-1-4 £15,945**

Fantasize *Sir Michael Stoute* 106
3 ch f Groom Dancer (USA) - Belle Et Deluree (USA)
1^{8g} 3^{8gf} 5^{8gf} 5^{10gf} **1-0-4 £30,765**

Fantasmic River (Ire) *B Smart* 46
3 ch f Magic Ring (Ire) - River Maiden (USA)
9^{8g} 6^{8gf} **0-0-2**

Fantastic Love (USA) *M Johnston* 108
3 b c Peintre Celebre (USA) - Moon Flower (Ire)
2^{8gf} 2^{8gf} 1^{11gf} 2^{12gf} 1^{12gf} **2-2-5**
£46,111

Fantastic View (USA) *R Hannon* 110
2 ch c Distant View (USA) - Promptly (Ire)

1⁷ᵍ 2⁸ᵍᶠ 1⁸ᵍ 1⁸ᵍᶠ 2⁸ᵍᶠ **3-1-5 £100,356**

Fantastic World (Fr) *P Laloum*   25 a74
4 b c Spinning World (USA) - Fanjica (Ire)
15¹⁰ᵍᶠ 1⁶ˢᵈ 9⁷ˢᵈ 0⁵ᵍ **1-0-4 £3,604**

Fantastico (Ire) *Mrs K Walton*   72 a58
3 b f Bahhare (USA) - Minatina (Ire)
10¹²ᵍˢ 4¹²ᵍˢ 6¹⁴ᵍᶠ 6¹²ᵍ 3¹²ˢᵈ 5¹⁶ᵍᶠ 6¹⁶ᵍᶠ
1¹²ᵍᶠ 4¹⁴ᵍᶠ 3¹²ᶠ 14¹²ᵍᶠ **1-1-11 £4,685**

Fantasy Believer *J J Quinn*   101
5 b g Sure Blade (USA) - Delicious
15⁶ᵍᶠ 29⁶ᵍ 15⁶ᵍᶠ 1⁶ᵍˢ 2⁶ᵍᶠ 2⁶ᵍ 1⁶ᵍ 13⁶ᵍ
2⁶ᵍ 11⁶ᵍ 4⁰ᵍ 1⁷ᵍ **3-4-12 £40,757**

Fantasy Crusader *J A Gilbert*   57 a13
4 ch g Beveled (USA) - Cranfield Charger
11⁸ˢᵈ 13¹⁰ᵍˢ 9⁸ᵍˢ 2⁸ᶠ 13⁷ᵍᶠ 2¹⁰ᵍᶠ 6¹⁰ᶠ
7¹¹ᵍᶠ 3¹⁰ᵍᶠ 1¹⁰ᵍᶠ 7¹²ᵍᶠ 11¹⁰ᵍᶠ 8¹¹ᵍᶠ 16¹⁰ᵍˢ
1-3-14 £5,530

Far For Lulu *W R Muir*   37 a27
2 ch f Farfelu - Shady Habitat
8⁵ˢᵈ 5⁶ˢᵈ 4⁵ᵍᶠ 5⁶ᶠ 9⁷ᶠᵗ 10⁷ᵍᶠ **0-0-6**

Far Lane (USA) *B W Hills*   118
4 b c Lear Fan (USA) - Pattimech (USA)
3¹⁰ᵍᶠ 1¹⁰ᵍᶠ 2¹¹ᵍᶠ 3¹⁰ᵍ 3¹⁰ᵍᶠ 5⁹ᵍᶠ 1⁹ᵍᶠ 1¹⁰ᵍ
3-2-8 £149,931

Far Note (USA) *S R Bowring*   73
5 ch g Distant View (USA) - Descant (USA)
2⁶ᵍᶠ 6⁵ᵍᶠ 6⁵ᵍᶠ 4⁶ᵍᶠ 1⁵ᵍ 13⁶ᵍᶠ 4⁶ᵍᶠ 2⁶ᵍ
1-2-8 £7,727

Far Storm (USA) *A M Balding*   60 a44
3 ch g Smart Strike (Can) - Kadeena
10¹²ˢᵈ 3¹²ᵍᶠ 19¹²ᵍᶠ **0-0-3 £622**

Faraway Echo *M L W Bell*   60
2 gr f Second Empire (USA) - Salalah
5⁶ᵍᶠ 12⁶ᵍᶠ 14⁶ᵍᶠ **0-0-3**

Faraway John (Ire) *G P Enright*   21
5 b g Farhaan - Indiana Dancer
16¹¹ˢᵈ 11¹²ᵍ **0-0-2**

Faraway Lady *L M Cumani*   84
3 b f Alzao (USA) - Eurolinka (Ire)
7⁸ᵍᶠ 13⁸ᵍ 11⁸ᵍᶠ 15⁸ᶠ 7¹¹ᵍᶠ 1¹⁶ᵍᶠ 1¹⁶ᵍ
1¹⁷ᵍᶠ 2¹⁶ᵍᶠ 1¹⁶ᵍᶠ 2¹⁶ᵍᶠ 2¹⁶ᵍᶠ 6¹⁴ᵍᶠ **4-3-13**
£17,485

Faraway Look (USA) *J G M O'Shea*   71 a74
6 br g Distant View (USA) - Summer Trip (USA)
5⁸ˢʷ 4¹¹ˢᵈ 4¹¹ˢᵈ 2⁹ˢᵈ 4⁸ˢᵈ 6¹⁰ᵍᶠ 3¹⁰ᵍ 5⁸ˢᵈ
5¹²ᵍᶠ 3¹¹ˢᵈ **0-3-10 £2,595**

Fareham *Mrs N Macauley*
5 b m Komaite (USA) - Lizzy Cantle
6¹²ˢᵈ **0-0-1**

Farewell Gift *R Hannon*   93
2 b c Cadeaux Genereux - Daring Ditty
2⁶ᵍ 8⁶ᵍᶠ 9⁶ᵍ **0-1-3 £2,370**

Farewell To Arms *B W Hills*   81
2 ch f Efisio - Blow Me A Kiss
2⁵ᵍ 1⁵ᵍᶠ 2⁵ᵍ 8⁶ᵍᶠ **1-2-4 £11,679**

Farmers Market *M C Pipe*
2 ch c Mark Of Esteem (Ire) - La Fazenda
12⁸ᵍᶠ **0-0-1**

Farqad (USA) *M P Tregoning*   108
4 b c Danzig (USA) - Futuh (USA)
7⁶ᶠᵗ 3⁸ᵍᶠ UR⁷ᵍᶠ 9⁷ᵍ 8⁷ᵍᶠ 5⁶ᵍᶠ **0-0-6**
£4,395

Farriers Charm *D J Coakley*   59
2 b f In Command (Ire) - Carn Maire
6⁶ᵍᶠ 4⁶ᶠ 4⁷ᶠᵗ **0-0-3**

Fast And Neat (Ire) *R Guest*   58
7 ch g Soviet Lad (USA) - Stop The Cavalry
5¹²ᵍᶠ 5¹²ᶠ 1¹⁶ᵍ 3¹⁴ᵍᶠ 8¹⁷ᵍᶠ 3¹⁴ᵍᶠ 11¹⁶ᵍˢ
1-2-7 £4,040

Fast Cindy (USA) *J W Unett*   71
4 b f Fastness (Ire) - Forever Cindy (Arg)
2¹⁵ᵍᶠ 8¹⁶ᵍᶠ **0-1-2 £1,744**

Fast Foil (Ire) *M R Channon*   85 a78
5 b m Lahib (USA) - Fast Chick
5¹¹ˢᵈ 5¹²ᵍᶠ 11¹²ᵍ 7¹²ᶠ 4¹²ʰʸ 2¹⁰ᵍᶠ 4¹¹ᵍᶠ
4¹²ᵍᶠ 1¹⁰ᶠ 2¹⁰ᵍᶠ 3¹⁰ᵍᶠ 3¹⁰ᵍᶠ 6¹⁰ᵍᶠ 3¹⁰ᵍ 4¹²ᵍᶠ
1-4-15 £17,406

Fast Forward Fred *L Montague Hall*   50
12 gr g Sharrood (USA) - Sun Street
7¹⁶ᵍᶠ **0-0-1**

Fast Heart *B J Meehan*   97
2 b c Fasliyev (USA) - Heart Of India (Ire)
12⁶ᵍᶠ 6⁵ᵍᶠ 1⁵ᵍᶠ 3⁵ᵍᶠ 1⁵ᵍᶠ 8⁵ᵍ 9⁶ᵍᶠ 3⁵ᵍᶠ
2-2-8 £18,348

Fatal Flaw (USA) *A Ennis*   a61
6 b g Hansel (USA) - Fateful (USA)
5¹¹ˢᵈ 9¹⁰ˢᵈ 7¹²ˢʷ 5¹⁶ˢᵈ 1¹²ˢʷ 15¹²ˢᵈ 6¹³ˢᵈ
1-0-7 £2,940

Fatayaat (Ire) *B W Hills*   57
2 b f Machiavellian (USA) - Maraatib (Ire)
8⁶ᵍᶠ **0-0-1**

Fatehalkhair (Ire) *B Ellison*   56
11 ch g Kris - Midway Lady (USA)
6¹⁶ˢʷ 8¹⁴ᵍᶠ **0-0-2**

Fatik (USA) *M P Tregoning*   93
3 br c Gone West (USA) - Muhbubh (USA)
2⁸ᵍᶠ 2⁷ᵍᶠ 4⁷ᵍˢ **0-1-3 £4,244**

Fattaan (Ire) *J G M O'Shea*   62
3 b c Danehill (USA) - Bintalshaati
10⁸ᵍ 5¹⁰ᵍᶠ UR⁸ᶠ 6⁸ᵍᶠ 13⁹ˢᵈ **0-0-5**

Favia *W J Haggas*   a65
4 b f Mujadil (USA) - Gustavia (Ire)
4⁷ˢᵈ 8⁸ˢᵈ 6⁷ˢᵈ 10⁸ˢᵈ **0-0-4 £275**

Favorisio *Miss J A Camacho*   a52
6 br g Efisio - Dixie Favor (USA)
1¹⁵ˢʷ 5¹²ˢʷ 2¹⁴ˢᵈ 1¹²ˢᵈ 3¹⁵ˢᵈ 3¹²ˢᵈ 5¹⁵ˢᵈ
3¹⁵ˢᵈ 7¹⁵ˢᵈ 2¹⁶ˢᵈ **2-5-10 £8,280**

Favour *Mrs J R Ramsden*   80
3 b f Gothenberg (Ire) - Prejudice
6⁶ᵍᶠ 5⁶ᵍᶠ 13⁷ᵍᶠ 6¹ᶠ 10⁵ᵍᶠ 2⁶ᵍᶠ 2⁶ᵍ
3⁷ᵍˢ **1-3-9 £6,385**

Favourable Terms *Sir Michael Stoute*   108
3 b f Selkirk (USA) - Fatefully (USA)
1⁷ᵍ 1⁸ᵍᶠ 2¹⁰ᵍ 1⁸ᵍᶠ 5⁸ᵍᶠ **3-0-5 £92,492**

Fax To Sooty *M R Bosley*
4 b g Factual (USA) - Saltina
16⁷ᵍ **0-0-1**

Fayr Firenze (Ire) *M F Harris*   29 a52
2 b c Fayruz - Shillay
7⁶ˢᵈ 10⁷ᵍᶠ 7⁶ˢᵈ 7⁶ᵍᶠ 6⁶ˢᵈ **0-0-5**

Fayr Jag (Ire) *T D Easterby*   119
4 b g Fayruz - Lominda (Ire)
2⁵ᶠ 3⁸ᵍᶠ 1⁶ᵍᶠ 1⁶ᵍᶠ 1⁶ᶠ 8⁶ᵍ 1⁶ᵍᶠ 5⁶ᵍˢ 1⁶ᵍ
12⁶ᵍᶠ UR⁶ᵍᶠ **5-2-11 £124,424**

Fayrway Rhythm (Ire) *Ian Emmerson*   44 a14
6 b g Fayruz - The Way She Moves
8¹²ˢᵈ 12¹²ˢᵈ 7¹²ᶠ 8¹⁶ᶠ 5¹⁴ᵍᶠ **0-0-5**

Fayrz Please (Ire) *M C Chapman*
2 ch g Fayruz - Castlelue (Ire)
16⁶ᵍ **0-0-1**

Fearby Cross (Ire) *W J Musson* — 75
7 b g Unblest - Two Magpies
15^{6gs} 12^{6g} 6^{6gf} 1^{7gf} 5^{7gf} 1^{6gs} 4^{6gf} 4^{6gf}
11^{6gf} **2-0-9 £15,854**

Feast Of Romance *P Howling* — 22 a65
6 b g Pursuit Of Love - June Fayre
4^{6sd} 8^{7sd} 6^{8sd} 7^{6sw} 5^{7sd} 14^{6sd} 8^{7sd} 2^{7sd}
14^{7sd} 13^{7gf} 4^{7sd} DSQ^{7sd} 10^{7sd} 2^{7sw} 8^{6sd} 10^{6g}
2^{6sd} 15^{7f} 3^{7sw} **0-4-19 £2,809**

Feather Boa (Ire) *M Blanshard* — 77 a73
3 b f Sri Pekan (USA) - Dancing Feather
19^{6gf} 7^{6s} 7^{7gf} 8^{7gf} 5^{7gf} 2^{8g} 4^{8gf} 8^{9gf}
5^{8gf} 3^{9gf} 9^{10gf} 7^{8s} 9^{8gf} 8^{10sd} **0-2-14 £3,297**

Feed The Meter (Ire) *Miss D Mountain* — 35
3 b f Desert King (Ire) - Watch The Clock
14^{8gf} **0-0-1**

Feel Good Factor *L M Cumani* — 74
3 b g Singspiel (Ire) - Colorspin (Fr)
4^{10g} 4^{10gf} 3^{12g} 11^{10gf} **0-0-4 £1,283**

Feel The Pride (Ire) *Jonjo O'Neill* — 50
5 b m Persian Bold - Nordic Pride
7^{12gf} **0-0-1**

Feeling Blue *B N Pollock* — 52
4 b f Missed Flight - Blues Indigo
6^{5gf} 17^{5gf} **0-0-2**

Feet So Fast *Saeed Bin Suroor* — 105
4 ch g Pivotal - Splice
3^{6g} 1^{7gf} 1^{6ft} 7^{6gf} **2-1-4 £62,596**

Feisty Flora (Ire) *A M Balding* — 36 a17
2 b f Petardia - Highland Crumpet
11^{5gf} 4^{6f} 14^{6gf} 9^{7gf} 7^{5sd} 10^{6gf} **0-0-6 £283**

Feizor (Ire) *R F Fisher* — 42
3 ch f Titus Livius (Fr) - Blues Queen
9^{5gf} 8^{6gf} 8^{9gf} 9^{9gf} 3^{10g} 11^{12sd} 8^{11gf}
11^{11gs} **0-1-8 £533**

Felicity (Ire) *J H M Gosden* — 101
3 b f Selkirk (USA) - Las Flores (Ire)
3^{10gf} 3^{10g} 2^{10gf} 3^{10gf} 1^{10gf} 3^{10gs} 5^{12s}
3^{10g} **1-5-8 £23,145**

Felidae (USA) *M Brittain* — 46
3 ch c Storm Cat (USA) - Colcon (USA)
7^{8f} 7^{10gs} **0-0-2**

Felix Holt (Ire) *J R Best* — 29
3 b g Woodborough (USA) - In The Mind (Ire)
4^{14s} **0-0-1**

Fellow Ship *P Butler* — 83 a84
3 b g Elmaamul (USA) - Genoa
1^{7gf} 8^{8g} 5^{7gf} 3^{6sd} 4^{7gf} 11^{7sd} 3^{8gf} 5^{11gf}
1-2-8 £6,969

Felony (Ire) *L P Grassick*
8 ch g Pharly (Fr) - Scales Of Justice
13^{16sd} **0-0-1**

Fen Gypsy *P D Evans* — 75
5 b g Nashwan (USA) - Didicoy (USA)
3^{6gs} 1^{8gs} 2^{7g} 2^{8gf} 14^{8gf} 1^{8gs} 6^{10gf} 10^{7g}
14^{8gf} 12^{10gs} **2-3-10 £12,036**

Fenwicks Pride (Ire) *R A Fahey* — 42
5 b g Imperial Frontier (USA) - Stunt Girl (Ire)
14^{6gs} **0-0-1**

Fernery *L M Cumani* — 81
3 b f Danehill (USA) - Fern
9^{8gf} 3^{8s} 1^{10gs} **1-1-3 £6,224**

Fernworthy *Jamie Poulton* — 23 a21
3 ch g Sheikh Albadou - Daring Damsel

14^{7gf} 12^{8sd} 9^{6g} **0-0-3**

Festive Affair *B Smart* — 42 a65
5 b g Mujadil (USA) - Christmas Kiss
1^{6sd} 6^{6sd} 4^{6sd} 3^{6sd} 11^{6f} **1-1-5 £3,382**

Festor *A Berry* — 24
3 ch g Paris House - Miami Dolphin
11^{5gs} 8^{8gf} 7^{7gs} **0-0-3**

Feu Duty (Ire) *T J Etherington* — 55 a30
2 b f Fayruz - Fire Reply (Ire)
12^{5sd} 9^{5gf} 1^{5gf} 16^{5gf} **1-0-4 £3,357**

Ffynnon Gold *B J Llewellyn* — 61
6 b m Beveled (USA) - Sparklingsovereign
9^{7gf} 4^{7gf} 4^{6g} 9^{7gf} 7^{7gf} 4^{6gf} 3^{7gf} **0-2-7 £1,327**

Fiamma Royale (Ire) *M S Saunders* — 62 a69
5 b m Fumo Di Londra (Ire) - Ariadne
2^{6sd} 3^{6sd} 2^{6sw} 10^{5sd} 5^{6sd} 12^{6gf} 5^{6sw} 2^{5gf}
17^{5gs} 5^{5gf} 13^{5gf} 12^{6sd} **0-4-12 £3,509**

Fictional *B A McMahon* — 81
2 b c Fraam - Manon Lescaut
2^{6gf} 7^{6s} 3^{6g} 1^{6gf} 2^{6gf} **1-4-6 £7,754**

Fiddle Me Blue *H Morrison* — 67
2 ch f Bluebird (USA) - Fiddle-Dee-Dee (Ire)
3^{6s} 1^{6gf} **1-1-2 £4,009**

Fiddlers Creek (Ire) *R Allan* — 71 a84
4 b g Danehill (USA) - Mythical Creek (USA)
2^{12sd} 4^{12sd} 12^{12gs} 3^{9gf} 6^{12gf} 8^{16gf} **0-2-6 £6,562**

Fiddlers Ford (Ire) *J Noseda* — 47
2 b g Sadler's Wells (USA) - Old Domesday Book
13^{7gf} **0-0-1**

Fiddlers Reach (Can) *B J Meehan* — 103 a101
3 ch g Kingmambo (USA) - Tiny Decision (USA)
3^{7sd} 6^{7gf} 4^{6g} 5^{6gf} 7^{7g} **0-1-5 £11,400**

Fiddles Music *M R Channon* — 24
2 b f Fraam - Fiddles Delight
8^{6gf} **0-0-1**

Fidelis Semper (Ire) *T J Etherington* — 45 a31
3 b f College Chapel - Reflection Time (Ire)
4^{5gf} 7^{5sd} 7^{5gs} 18^{5g} 9^{5gf} 11^{5gf} 12^{7gf}
13^{8f} **0-0-8**

Fidelite (Ire) *Mme C Head-Maarek* — 113
3 ch f In The Wings - Onereuse
1^{10g} 4^{9vs} 1^{10s} 8^{11g} 3^{12gs} 7^{12gs} **2-1-6 £87,913**

Field Spark *J A Glover* — 71
3 b g Sillery (USA) - On The Top
1^{12gf} 1^{12gf} 5^{12gf} 5^{14gf} 2^{12gs} 4^{11gf} 3^{12gf}
5^{12gf} 7^{13gf} 4^{16gf} 6^{12gf} 6^{16gf} 1^{12gf} 6^{14gf} **2-3-14 £9,681**

Fiennes (USA) *Mrs N Macauley* — 34 a59
5 b/br g Dayjur (USA) - Artic Strech (USA)
11^{6sw} 12^{6gf} **0-0-2**

Fife And Drum (USA) *Miss J Feilden* — 62 a66
6 b/br g Rahy (USA) - Fife (Ire)
6^{10gf} 12^{10gf} 8^{10sd} 1^{10f} 3^{12gf} 4^{11gf} 2^{10sd}
2^{8gf} 2^{8sd} **1-4-9 £5,386**

Fifth Column (USA) *J R Fanshawe* — 32
2 b g Allied Forces (USA) - Miff (USA)
13^{8gf} **0-0-1**

Fifth Edition *R Guest* — 58
7 b m Rock Hopper - Glossary
1^{12gs} 5^{12g} 2^{16gf} **1-1-3 £4,762**

Fig Leaf (Fr) *P W D'Arcy* — a55

4 b f Distant Relative - Shady Leaf (Ire)
7^{7sd} 5^{8sd} **0-0-2**

Fight The Feeling *J W Unett*　　59 a68
5 ch g Beveled (USA) - Alvecote Lady
1^{12sd} 4^{12sd} 8^{12sd} 4^{9sd} 8^{12sd} 1^{12s} 3^{13gf}
5^{12g} 3^{15sd} 10^{12sd} **2-0-10 £8,876**

Fight Your Corner *Saeed Bin Suroor*　　113
4 b c Muhtarram (USA) - Dame Ashfield
5^{12f} 2^{13g} 11^{20gf} **0-1-3 £8,823**

Figura *R Ingram*　　64 a77
5 b m Rudimentary (USA) - Dream Baby
1^{10sd} 10^{10sd} 1^{10sd} 4^{12sd} 5^{10sd} 2^{10sd} 2^{12sd}
1^{10sd} 11^{10g} 3^{12f} 18^{10gs} 10^{9gf} 3^{10f} 14^{12sd} 3^{10gf}
12^{10gf} 13^{10gf} 10^{9s} **3-5-18 £14,821**

Fille De Roi *Jedd O'Keeffe*　　47
3 b f Desert King (Ire) - Western Heights
8^{7gf} 15^{8gf} 11^{8gf} **0-0-3**

Filliemou (Ire) *A W Carroll*　　67
2 gr f Goldmark (USA) - St Louis Lady
9^{5g} 4^{5gs} 4^{6g} 7^{8gf} 4^{8gf} 7^{7gf} 18^{7gf} **0-0-7**
£1,021

Final Dividend (Ire) *J M P Eustace*　　59 a54
7 b g Second Set (Ire) - Prime Interest (Ire)
12^{10g} 10^{12sd} 1^{12f} 6^{12gf} 5^{11g} 5^{12sd} 9^{12sd}
6^{10gs} **1-0-8 £3,656**

Final Faze *D J Coakley*　　4 a40
4 ch f Chaddleworth (Ire) - Fine Fettle
13^{10sd} 16^{8gs} **0-0-2**

Final Lap *S T Lewis*　　a9
7 b g Batshoof - Lap Of Honour
13^{17f} 7^{12sw} **0-0-2**

Final View (Fr) *N P Littmoden*
4 b g Distant View (USA) - Unafurtivalagrima (USA)
11^{12sd} 5^{14gf} **0-0-2**

Financial Future *M Johnston*　　99
3 b g Barathea (Ire) - In Perpetuity
2^{9g} 3^{10gf} 2^{10gf} 2^{11gf} 1^{12gf} 1^{12g} 8^{12gs}
2-4-7 £32,726

Finders Keepers *E A L Dunlop*　　80
2 b c Selkirk (USA) - La Nuit Rose (Fr)
3^{6gf} 2^{6gs} 9^{6gf} **0-2-3 £4,365**

Fine Frenzy (Ire) *Miss S J Wilton*　　48 a55
3 b f Great Commotion (USA) - Fine Project (Ire)
5^{7sd} 6^{8sd} 5^{7sd} 8^{7sd} 5^{6f} 2^{7gf} 9^{7gf}
3^{7gf} 6^{7gf} 4^{7gf} 16^{7gf} **0-2-12 £1,292**

Fine Palette *H R A Cecil*　　78
3 ch c Peintre Celebre (USA) - Filly Mignonne (Ire)
2^{10gs} **0-1-1 £940**

Fine Silver (Ire) *P F I Cole*　　82
2 gr c Intikhab (USA) - Petula
2^{5gf} 2^{5gf} 1^{6f} 4^{7f} 6^{8gf} **1-1-5 £9,503**

Fingal Nights (Ire) *E J O'Neill*　　81 a74
4 ch f Night Shift (USA) - Advantageous
5^{7gf} 4^{6gs} 4^{10sd} 6^{9s} 3^{8gf} 3^{8gf} 13^{7gf} 4^{8gf}
14^{8gf} 14^{8gf} **0-2-10 £3,414**

Finger Of Fate *I Semple*　　74
3 b r c Machiavellian (USA) - La Nuit Rose (Fr)
6^{8g} 11^{8gf} 14^{8g} 7^{7gf} 6^{6gf} 15^{6gs} **0-0-6**
£455

Finians Gold *J G M O'Shea*　　49
2 b c Fasliyev (USA) - Belle Esprit
5^{5gs} 4^{5gf} 7^{5gf} 7^{5gf} **0-0-4 £291**

Finished Article (Ire) *D R C Elsworth*　　99
6 b g Indian Ridge - Summer Fashion
19^{8g} 18^{8gf} 6^{10g} 5^{8g} 11^{8gf} 5^{8gf} 2^{8gf} 1^{8g}

5^{8gf} 2^{9g} 2^{8f} 13^{8gf} 4^{8gs} **1-4-13 £30,820**

Finmar *Miss L A Perratt*　　66
5 b g Efisio - Patiala (Ire)
6^{9gf} 9^{8gf} 10^{8gf} 1^{9gf} 14^{8gf} 4^{8f} 3^{9f} 2^{9gf}
2^{8f} 5^{9g} 4^{8g} 6^{9g} 12^{8gf} **1-4-13 £7,171**

Finnforest (Ire) *Mrs A J Bowlby*　　59
3 ch g Eagle Eyed (USA) - Stockrose
12^{8gf} 9^{7gf} 17^{6gf} 11^{7gf} 4^{8gf} 8^{8gf} 2^{10f}
5^{10gf} **0-1-8 £1,269**

Finningley Connor *Ronald Thompson*　　22
3 b g Cosmonaut - Arroganza
19^{6g} 13^{8gs} **0-0-2**

Fiore Di Bosco (Ire) *T D Barron*　　78 a75
2 b f Charnwood Forest (Ire) - Carabine (USA)
1^{5sd} 2^{5gf} 2^{5g} 8^{5gf} 16^{gf} 3^{6g} 11^{6gf} 18^{6g}
2^{7gf} **2-3-9 £14,274**

Fire Dome (Ire) *Andrew Reid*　　69
11 ch g Salt Dome (USA) - Penny Habit
3^{6gs} 4^{6g} **0-1-2 £776**

Fire In Ice *B P J Baugh*
4 b f Missed Flight - Boulabas (Ire)
PU^{8sd} 9^{8sd} 11^{10gf} **0-0-3**

Fire Me (Cze) *A G Newcombe*　　28 a1
3 ch f Beccari (USA) - Fantasy Friend (USA)
9^{8gf} 15^{10f} 6^{12sd} **0-0-3**

Fire Moon (Ire) *S R Bowring*　　a24
4 b g Royal Applause - Welwyn
10^{12sd} 12^{6sd} **0-0-2**

Fire Up The Band *D Nicholls*　　114
4 b c Prince Sabo - Green Supreme
3^{6g} 1^{6gf} 1^{6g} 2^{6g} 11^{6g} 2^{5g} 3^{6g} **2-4-7**
£76,339

Firebelly *M J Wallace*　　85
2 b f Nicolotte - Desert Delight (Ire)
1^{6gf} 3^{6gf} 1^{6gf} 1^{8gf} **3-1-4 £32,698**

Firebird Rising (USA) *T D Barron*　　70
2 b f Stravinsky - Capable (USA)
3^{5gf} **0-0-1 £1,090**

Firebolt (Ire) *I W Allan*　　120
5 b g Flying Spur (Aus) - Musianica
2^{5gf} 2^{5g} 3^{6gf} 9^{5gf} **0-3-4 £325,800**

Firebreak *Saeed Bin Suroor*　　98 a117
4 b c Charnwood Forest (Ire) - Breakaway
2^{6ft} 1^{8ft} 11^{6f} 10^{7g} **1-1-4 £388,084**

Fireburst *T J Naughton*　　a32
4 ch f Spectrum (USA) - Explosiva (USA)
9^{12sd} 6^{8sd} **0-0-2**

Firecat *A P Jones*　　54 a53
4 ch g Beveled (USA) - Noble Soul
2^{7gf} 2^{7sw} 5^{6g} 8^{7sd} **0-2-4 £1,250**

Firestone (Ger) *A W Carroll*　　a64
6 b g Dictator's Song (USA) - Fatinizza (Ire)
3^{10sd} **0-1-1 £425**

Firewire *Miss B Sanders*　　72
5 b g Blushing Flame (USA) - Bay Risk
5^{8gf} 2^{9gf} 1^{8g} 2^{8gf} 12^{8s} 9^{9g} 8^{8gf} **1-2-7**
£6,655

Firework *J Akehurst*　　72 a64
5 b g Primo Dominie - Prancing
1^{6sd} 3^{6sw} 11^{6sd} 4^{7f} 9^{6gf} 9^{6sd} 16^{6gf} 1^{6f}
3^{6g} 16^{6gf} 3^{5f} 4^{6gf} 2^{6f} 14^{6gf} **4-4-14**
£16,188

Fireworks (Fr) *K O Cunningham-Brown*　　42
3 gr g Kendor (Fr) - Little Emily
5^{7g} 6^{7sd} 7^{7hy} 8^{9gf} 12^{7gf} 6^{9gf} **0-0-6**

£649

Firozi *R A Fahey*   55
4 b f Forzando - Lambast
12^{8f} 13^{7f} 4^{7f} 5^{8s} 9^{8gf} 2^{10gf} 2^{8f} 3^{10f}
0-3-8 £2,879

First Acorn *G M Moore*   45 a30
2 b f Petong - Mimining
7^{5gf} 5^{5gf} 10^{6gf} 11^{6gs} 13^{6s} 4^{8gf} 9^{6gf}
11^{5f} 6^{8sd} **0-0-9 £319**

First Ballot (Ire) *D R C Elsworth*   108
7 br g Perugino (USA) - Election Special
4^{16gf} 4^{16g} 6^{13g} 4^{22f} 3^{14gf} 3^{12gf} 11^{12g}
5^{14gf} 5^{12gf} **0-0-9 £10,729**

First Base *R E Barr*   24
4 ch g First Trump - Rose Music
10^{14f} 10^{12gf} 15^{8gf} **0-0-3**

First Candlelight *J G Given*   79
2 b f First Trump - No Candles Tonight
2^{6s} 1^{7g} **1-1-2 £3,762**

First Celebration *B W Hills*   80
3 ch f Cadeaux Genereux - Loving Claim (USA)
7^{8ft} 6^{8ft} 5^{7gf} 1^{10gf} **1-0-4 £4,124**

First Centurion *J W Hills*   a60
2 b c Peintre Celebre (USA) - Valley Of Hope (USA)
6^{7sd} **0-0-1**

First Charter *Sir Michael Stoute*   115
4 b c Polish Precedent (USA) - By Charter
3^{12gf} 1^{12gf} 1^{14gf} 2^{12g} 12^{12ho} **2-1-5**
£39,200

First Class Lady *P Mitchell*   48 a43
3 ch f Lion Cavern (USA) - Tino-Ella
9^{10sd} 6^{10sd} 7^{8sd} 12^{11gf} 4^{10gf} 6^{11gf} **0-0-6**

First Dawn *M R Channon*   65
2 ch f Dr Fong (USA) - Delight Of Dawn
7^{7gf} 6^{7gf} **0-0-2**

First Eagle *Mrs N Macauley*   a55
4 b g Hector Protector (USA) - Merlin's Fancy
7^{12sd} 12^{12sd} 3^{12sd} 2^{9sd} **0-2-4 £1,149**

First Eclipse (Ire) *J Balding*   55
2 b f Fayruz - Naked Poser (Ire)
8^{6g} 1^{5gf} 5^{5g} 4^{5gf} 6^{5f} 11^{5gf} 17^{5gs} **1-0-7**
£4,385

First Footing *M L W Bell*   45
3 ch g Inchinor - Laleston
17^{6gf} 5^{6s} 10^{8f} 10^{8sd} PU^{7gf} **0-0-5**

First Fortune *P W Harris*   49
3 br g Primo Dominie - Jeewan
9^{8gf} 9^{11gf} **0-0-2**

First Maite *S R Bowring*   70 a81
10 b g Komaite (USA) - Marina Plata
8^{7sd} 7^{7sd} 4^{7sd} 8^{7gf} 11^{8g} 9^{6gs} 3^{8g} 5^{9gf}
2^{8sd} 4^{8gf} 3^{8sd} 2^{8sd} 3^{8s} 14^{8gf} 4^{9g} 6^{6gf} 4^{7gf}
4^{10gf} 7^{10gf} 6^{10g} **0-7-23 £7,107**

First Note (USA) *B J Meehan*   69 a59
2 ch c Pioneering (USA) - Angelic Note (USA)
7^{6sd} 5^{7g} 2^{8gf} **0-1-3 £1,092**

First Of May *M A Jarvis*   52
2 b f Halling (USA) - Finger Of Light
9^{7gs} **0-0-1**

First Ordained (Ire) *A D W Pinder*   44 a57
4 b g Mujadil (USA) - Ordinate
8^{8sd} 15^{8gf} 11^{10gf} 11^{9sd} 10^{10g} 10^{12gf}
11^{12sd} 9^{10sd} **0-0-8**

First Order *Sir Mark Prescott*   96

2 b c Primo Dominie - Unconditional Love (Ire)
3^{6f} 1^{5gf} 2^{5s} 1^{5gf} 1^{5gf} 3^{5g} **3-1-6**
£20,165

First Pressure *D R C Elsworth*   60 a58
3 b g Double Trigger (Ire) - Princesse Lyphard
10^{12gf} 8^{14gf} 4^{12gf} 11^{12sd} **0-0-4 £285**

First Tarf *G L Moore*   11
2 ch f Primo Dominie - Tarf (USA)
6^{5gf} **0-0-1**

Fisby *S Kirk*   14
2 ch c Efisio - Trilby
16^{6gf} **0-0-1**

Fisher's Dream *J R Norton*   37 a40
2 b g Groom Dancer (USA) - Cremets
9^{5f} 10^{6s} 13^{7f} 13^{7gs} 6^{6sd} 4^{5sd} **0-0-6**

Fishlake Flyer (Ire) *J G Given*   73
2 b f Desert Style (Ire) - Millitrix
2^{5s} 2^{5gf} 2^{5gs} 18^{5gf} 4^{5gf} 3^{5gf} 2^{5f} **0-5-7**
£5,528

Fisio Therapy *M Johnston*   91
3 b g Efisio - Corn Lily
6^{8f} 1^{8hy} 4^{7gf} 3^{10f} 3^{10g} 5^{11gf} **1-2-6**
£9,569

Fission *Sir Mark Prescott*   67 a73
2 ch f Efisio - Area Girl
4^{5f} 4^{5sd} 1^{6sd} 4^{6gf} 5^{5gf} 1^{6sd} **2-0-6**
£6,706

Fit To Fly (Ire) *S Kirk*   69
2 b c Lahib (USA) - Maid Of Mourne
9^{6gf} 5^{6f} 17^{6s} **0-0-3**

Fitting Guest (Ire) *G G Margarson*   57
2 ch c Grand Lodge (USA) - Sarah-Clare
4^{8gf} 8^{8gs} **0-0-2 £333**

Fittleworth (Ire) *W G M Turner*   47
3 gr f Bijou D'Inde - Remany
6^{11gf} 10^{10f} 3^{11gf} 5^{12gf} **0-1-4 £446**

Fitz The Bill (Ire) *N B King*   41
3 b f Mon Tresor - In The Sky (Ire)
7^{7gf} 6^{6gf} 7^{8gf} 15^{7gf} **0-0-4**

Fitzwarren *N Bycroft*   68
2 b g Presidium - Coney Hills
2^{5f} 9^{5gf} 2^{5gf} 3^{5gf} 1^{5f} 6^{5gf} 11^{6gf} 7^{5gf}
4^{5gf} 4^{6gf} 7^{6f} 2^{6g} **1-4-12 £8,465**

Five Gold (Ire) *B R Millman*   70 a71
2 b c Desert Prince (Ire) - Ceide Dancer (Ire)
10^{6gf} 6^{6gf} 2^{8sw} 4^{8gf} 1^{8sd} 12^{7gf} **1-1-6**
£3,011

Five Years On (Ire) *W J Haggas*   46
2 b g Desert Sun - Snowspin
9^{5gf} **0-0-1**

Fiveoclock Express (Ire) *C A Dwyer*   90 a97
3 gr g Woodborough (USA) - Brooks Masquerade
3^{7g} 12^{7gs} 3^{8gf} 9^{8gf} 7^{5sd} 7^{5gf} 1^{7sw}
3^{8gf} 10^{7g} 9^{8gf} **1-5-11 £8,048**

Fizzy Lady *B W Hills*   65
2 b f Efisio - The Frog Lady (Ire)
5^{6gf} 4^{6gs} **0-0-2**

Fizzy Lizzy *Jedd O'Keeffe*   52
3 b f Cool Jazz - Formidable Liz
10^{6g} 6^{2gf} 4^{6g} 13^{5gs} 10^{5gf} 5^{6g}
13^{6gf} 9^{6gf} 17^{6gf} 9^{6gf} **0-1-11 £597**

Flak Jacket *D Nicholls*   75
8 b g Magic Ring (Ire) - Vaula
20^{6g} 16^{5gs} 4^{5gf} 13^{5gs} 5^{6g} 12^{6gf} 13^{6gf}
0-0-7 £1,622

Flake *Mrs S J Smith* 44
3 ch g Zilzal (USA) - Impatiente (USA)
10^{9gs} 9^{7gf} 7^{11gf} **0-0-3**

Flambe *P C Haslam* 46
5 b g Whittingham (Ire) - Uaeflame (Ire)
14^{8f} 13^{8gf} **0-0-2**

Flamboyant Lad *B W Hills* 75
2 ch c Nashwan (USA) - Cheeky Charm (USA)
2^{7s} **0-1-1 £1,058**

Flame Of Zara *Mrs M Reveley* 58
4 ch f Blushing Flame (USA) - Sierra Madrona (USA)
11^{12g} 4^{12gs} 6^{12gf} 13^{14gf} **0-0-4 £293**

Flame Phoenix (USA) *P R Webber* 71
4 b/br g Quest For Fame - Kingscote
3^{10gf} 3^{11g} **0-1-2 £1,255**

Flame Princess *J R Boyle* 44 a49
3 ch f Bluegrass Prince (Ire) - Rekindled Flame (Ire)
9^{6sd} 7^{7sd} 13^{7sw} 11^{8sd} 11^{7gf} 5^{8gf} 5^{7gf}
11^{7f} 11^{7gf} **0-0-9**

Flame Queen *Miss K B Boutflower* 69
2 b f The West (USA) - Red Cloud (Ire)
8^{7g} 9^{6gf} 2^{6f} **0-1-3 £888**

Flame Royale (Ire) *C A Horgan* 61
4 ch f Ali-Royal (Ire) - Paradise Forum
7^{10gf} 7^{8s} 6^{9gf} 15^{12sd} 8^{12gf} 10^{8g} 14^{14gf}
0-0-7

Flamenca (USA) *R Allan* a30
4 b f Diesis - Highland Ceilidh (Ire)
5^{12sd} **0-0-1**

Flamenco Bride *D R C Elsworth* 77
3 b f Hernando (Fr) - Premier Night
7^{10gf} 1^{14f} 2^{14gf} 3^{14gf} 4^{12g} 5^{12gf} 16^{16gf}
10^{17g} **1-1-8 £8,329**

Flaming Spirt *J S Moore* a8
4 b f Blushing Flame (USA) - Fair Test
9^{11sd} **0-0-1**

Flamjica (USA) *J A R Toller* 71
2 ch f Real Quiet (USA) - Fiamma (Ire)
3^{8gf} 5^{8gf} **0-1-2 £1,421**

Flapdoodle *A W Carroll* 63 a35
5 b m Superpower - My Concordia
9^{6sd} 12^{6f} 1^{5f} 8^{5f} 7^{5gf} 2^{5gf} 7^{5f} 6^{5gf}
3^{5gf} 16^{5gf} 5^{5gf} 8^{5g} **1-2-12 £4,664**

Flaran *A C Stewart* 69
3 b c Emarati (USA) - Fragrance
8^{7f} 7^{8gf} 1^{6gf} 5^{5gf} 17^{6gf} 4^{6gs} **1-0-6**
£4,251

Flash Of Gold *Sir Michael Stoute* 79 a63
3 b f Darshaan - Trying For Gold (USA)
6^{10gf} 2^{12gf} 4^{12g} 2^{12gf} 5^{13sd} **0-2-5**
£3,360

Flash Ram *T D Easterby* 62
2 b c Mind Games - Just A Gem
3^{5f} 3^{5gf} 3^{5gs} **0-2-3 £1,943**

Flashing Blade *B A McMahon* 93
3 b f Inchinor - Finlaggan
9^{7gf} 8^{7gf} 5^{6g} **0-0-3 £308**

Flat Stanley *R Bastiman* 43 a53
4 b g Celtic Swing - Cool Grey
4^{12sd} 6^{16sw} 2^{12sd} 14^{14g} 9^{14sd} 4^{10gf} 17^{10gf}
0-2-7 £1,156

Fleet Anchor *J M Bradley* 61
2 b c Fleetwood (Ire) - Upping The Tempo
5^{6gf} 9^{6gf} **0-0-2**

Fleet Of Light *J R Fanshawe* 89

4 b f Spectrum (Ire) - Fleet Amour (USA)
8^{8s} 2^{7gf} 1^{7gf} 2^{8gf} 5^{8g} 1^{10gf} **2-2-6**
£19,747

Fleetfoot Mac *P D Evans* 52 a28
2 b g Fleetwood (Ire) - Desert Flower
11^{6gf} 14^{7gf} 8^{7sd} 6^{10gf} **0-0-4**

Fleeting Moon *A M Balding* a40
3 ch f Fleetwood (Ire) - Aunt Judy
9^{8sd} **0-0-1**

Fleetwood Bay *B R Millman* 80
3 b g Fleetwood (Ire) - Caviar And Candy
11^{7gf} 13^{6g} 7^{6gs} 2^{6f} 7^{6g} **0-1-6**
£1,281

Fletcher *H Morrison* 51
9 b g Salse (USA) - Ballet Classique (USA)
8^{12gf} 8^{12gf} 6^{12g} 2^{12gf} 12^{12gf} 4^{12f} **0-1-6**
£1,166

Flight Commander (Ire) *I Semple* 62
3 b g In The Wings - Lucrezia (Ire)
5^{12gf} 5^{12g} **0-0-2**

Flight Of Eagles (Ire) *A Berry* 49
4 gr g Paris House - Wisdom To Know
13^{5gf} 5^{6f} 6^{5gf} 9^{6f} **0-0-4**

Flight Of Esteem *P W Harris* 97 a77
3 b g Mark Of Esteem (Ire) - Miss Up N Go
2^{10sd} 1^{10sd} 5^{10gf} 7^{12gf} 2^{10gf} 2^{10f} 1^{10gf}
2^{10gf} 3^{10gf} 1^{12gf} 4^{12gf} 3^{12f} 8^{12gf} **3-5-13**
£39,109

Flight Times *N Bycroft* a21
5 b g Timeless Times (USA) - Petite Elite
12^{7sw} 13^{7sd} **0-0-2**

Flight To Tuscany *J M Bradley* 43
5 b m Bonny Scot (Ire) - Tuscan Butterfly
3^{8g} 8^{10f} 8^{g} 11^{8gf} 13^{10gf} 14^{11gf} **0-1-6**
£427

Flighty Fellow (Ire) *T D Easterby* 99
3 ch g Flying Spur (Aus) - Al Theraab (USA)
8^{7gf} 10^{8g} 6^{8g} 2^{8g} 7^{8f} 1^{8gs} 3^{8gf} 10^{10g}
1^{8gf} 4^{10g} 3^{8g} 2^{8s} 2^{8gf} **2-5-13 £33,081**

Flighty Mac *N Bycroft* 36
3 gr f Paris House - Stilvella
11^{6sd} 8^{5gf} 14^{5gf} 11^{6gf} 10^{7gf} 12^{10gf}
0-0-6

Flint River *H Morrison* 82 a83
5 b g Red Ransom (USA) - She's All Class (USA)
2^{7sd} 6^{7sd} 1^{8sd} 1^{8sd} 1^{8sd} 1^{9sg} 1^{7gf} 2^{7gf}
24^{7f} 13^{6gf} 2^{6sd} **4-3-11 £20,770**

Flip Flop And Fly (Ire) *S Kirk* 94
2 b c Woodborough (USA) - Angelus Chimes
9^{6gf} 1^{6gs} 3^{6gf} 10^{6gf} 21^{6g} **1-0-5 £9,588**

Flipando (Ire) *T D Barron* 83
2 b g Sri Pekan (USA) - Magic Touch
3^{5f} 1^{6g} 22^{6gf} **1-1-3 £4,371**

Floppie Disk *J A Pickering* 76
3 b f Magic Ring (Ire) - Floppie (Fr)
13^{5g} 11^{5gs} 3^{5gf} 7^{5gf} 6^{5f} 11^{5f} 6^{6f} 7^{5g}
3^{5g} 13^{5g} 9^{5gf} 18^{5gf} **0-0-12 £2,238**

Floreeda *H R A Cecil* 102
3 gr f Linamix (Fr) - La Sky (Ire)
3^{10gf} 2^{10g} 6^{10gf} 1^{11g} 1^{12gf} 4^{13g} 2^{15g} 5^{12gf}
6^{14s} **2-3-9 £40,178**

Florenzar (Ire) *P D Evans* 60
5 b m Inzar (USA) - Nurse Tyra (USA)
8^{10gf} 2^{10gf} 6^{10f} 2^{11g} 16^{14gf} **0-2-5**
£2,000

Florette *D Morris*
3 ch f Fleetwood (Ire) - Antum
16^{7g} 18^{7gf} **0-0-2**

Florian *T G Mills*   71 a71
5 b g Young Ern - Murmuring
7^{8sd} 2^{7sd} 4^{7sd} 1^{8sd} 1^{8gf} 3^{8sd} 3^{7sd} **2-3-7**
£9,206

Florida (Ire) *I A Wood*   33 a38
5 b m Sri Pekan (USA) - Florinda (Can)
10^{16sd} 3^{15sd} 8^{14f} 9^{17f} 3^{15sd} 5^{16sd} 4^{16gf}
8^{16gf} 6^{14sw} **0-1-9 £860**

Florida Heart *A M Balding*   73
2 ch f First Trump - Miami Dancer (USA)
4^{6gf} 8^{6gf} 5^{7g} 4^{7gf} 2^{8gf} 2^{8gf} 1^{8g} **1-2-7**
£10,590

Flotta *M R Channon*   90 a86
4 ch g Elmaamul - Heavenly Goddess
3^{13sd} 3^{12gf} 2^{14gs} 6^{12sd} 3^{12gf} 3^{12gf} 4^{10g}
10^{10g} 1^{12g} 2^{14gf} 1^{15gf} 8^{12g} **2-5-12 £22,977**

Flow Beau *J O'Reilly*   46
6 b m Mtoto - Radiance (Fr)
9^{11gf} 16^{10gf} 18^{11gf} 8^{10gf} 11^{9gf} **0-0-5**

Flower Breeze (USA) *M W Easterby*   61 a14
3 ch f Rahy (USA) - Now Showing (USA)
20^{7g} 15^{7f} 4^{8gs} 8^{12gf} 7^{8f} 5^{10gf} 7^{8sd} **0-0-7**
£266

Flowerdrum (USA) *W J Haggas*   81 a86
3 b f Mister Baileys - Norelands (USA)
1^{8g} 1^{8g} 6^{7sd} 1^{7sd} **3-0-4 £13,351**

Flownaway *W Jarvis*   104 a92
4 b g Polar Falcon (USA) - No More Rosies
1^{16sd} 2^{13sd} 1^{16gf} 10^{19gf} 1^{14gf} 11^{14g} 5^{12gf}
11^{14gf} 3^{16f} 20^{18gf} **3-1-10 £37,879**

Flur Na H Alba *I Semple*   90
4 b g Atraf - Tyrian Belle
4^{6g} 3^{6g} 3^{6gs} 1^{7gf} 6^{7g} 2^{8gf} 8^{7g} 8^{7g} 14^{7g}
1-3-9 £15,937

Fly Kicker *W Storey*   40
6 ch g High Kicker (USA) - Double Birthday
7^{17gf} 6^{15g} 4^{14gf} **0-0-3 £301**

Fly More *J M Bradley*   87
6 ch g Lycius (USA) - Double River (USA)
11^{5gf} 3^{5gs} 1^{5gf} 4^{5gf} 2^{5gf} 6^{5gf} 2^{6gf} 1^{5gs}
4^{6g} 8^{5gf} 2^{6f} 4^{5gf} 15^{5gs} 1^{5gf} 3^{5gf} 11^{6gf} 13^{6g}
9^{6g} **3-5-21 £25,160**

Flying Adored *J L Dunlop*   76
2 b f Polar Falcon (USA) - Shining High
7^{6gf} 4^{6gf} 7^{7gf} **0-0-3 £376**

Flying Bantam (Ire) *R A Fahey*   72
2 b g Fayruz - Natural Pearl
2^{5f} 2^{5s} 5^{6gf} 9^{6g} 3^{5g} **0-3-5 £4,554**

Flying Edge (Ire) *E J Alston*   69
3 b g Flying Spur (Aus) - Day Is Dawning (Ire)
14^{7gf} 11^{5gf} 8^{5gs} 2^{6gf} 1^{6gf} 5^{6gf}
1^{7f} 6^{7gf} 12^{7f} **2-1-11 £14,271**

Flying Express *B W Hills*   95
3 ch c Air Express (Ire) - Royal Loft
6^{6gf} 19^{6gf} 6^{7gf} 4^{7gf} 4^{7g} **0-1-5 £1,106**

Flying Faisal (USA) *J M Bradley*   62 a55
5 b h Alydeed (Can) - Peaceful Silence (USA)
2^{6sw} 5^{7sd} 8^{7sd} 7^{5sw} 4^{6gw} 7^{6sd} 9^{6sd} 7^{6gf}
8^{6gf} 10^{6gf} 5^{7gf} 6^{6gf} 14^{6g} 7^{6g} 9^{6gf} **1-1-15**
£4,366

Flying Patriarch *G L Moore*   35
2 gr c Silver Patriarch (Ire) - Flying Wind
10^{8g} 7^{10gs} **0-0-2**

Flying Phin (Ire) *B Hanbury*   a17
6 ch g Dolphin Street (Fr) - Robin Red Breast
7^{11sw} 8^{12sd} **0-0-2**

Flying Ribot (USA) *B W Hills*   58
3 b c Exclusive Ribot (USA) - Flying Starlet (USA)
6^{8f} 14^{10f} 9^{8sd} 6^{8f} 16^{9gf} **0-0-5**

Flying Romance (Ire) *P D Evans*   a39
5 b m Flying Spur (Aus) - State Romance
6^{12sd} 8^{12sd} **0-0-2**

Flying Spirit (Ire) *G L Moore*   67 a62
4 b g Flying Spur (Aus) - All Laughter
12^{10sd} 10^{12gf} 12^{12f} 1^{12gf} 2^{12f} 3^{12gf}
1^{12gf} 7^{10f} 2^{12f} **3-4-10 £17,041**

Flying Spud *J L Spearing*   a32
2 ch g Fraam - Lorcanjo
9^{6sd} 7^{6sd} **0-0-2**

Flying Tackle *M Dods*   59
5 ch g First Trump - Frighten The Life
10^{5gf} 16^{5gs} 17^{5sd} 3^{5gf} 2^{6gf} 5^{6gf} 9^{6f}
16^{9g} 3^{5g} **0-3-9 £3,713**

Flying Treaty (USA) *Miss A Stokell*   84 a98
6 br h You And I (USA) - Cherie's Hope (USA)
1^{8sw} 2^{8sd} 1^{8sd} 1^{7sd} 8^{8sw} 16^{12sd} 10^{8sd} 7^{8g}
4^{7gf} 10^{7gf} 3^{7gf} 9^{8f} 8^{7gf} 4^{8gf} 9^{8gf} **3-3-15**
£28,806

Flying Wanda *J Noseda*   107
3 b f Alzao - Royal York
8^{12gf} 2^{10gf} 2^{12g} 4^{14g} 4^{12gf} 3^{12gf} 4^{14gf}
9^{14s} **0-3-8 £28,810**

Flyoff (Ire) *K A Morgan*   55
6 b g Mtoto - Flyleaf (Fr)
13^{12sd} 1^{12gf} 1^{11f} 6^{14gf} 4^{12gf} **2-0-5**
£7,734

Flyover *J C Fox*   7
6 b m Presidium - Flash-By
9^{12gf} 14^{12gf} **0-0-2**

Foggieloan *C G Cox*   51
3 b f Cyrano De Bergerac - Sea Mist (Ire)
7^{8gf} 8^{8g} 12^{8gf} **0-0-3**

Fokine (USA) *B W Hills*   112
2 b c Royal Academy (USA) - Polar Bird
1^{6gf} 6^{8g} 2^{6gf} 8^{6gf} **1-1-4 £36,837**

Foley Millennium (Ire) *M Quinn*   a54
5 ch g Tagula (Ire) - Inshirah (USA)
6^{5sd} PU^{5sw} **0-0-2**

Foley Prince *D Flood*   65 a38
2 b g Makbul - Princess Foley (Ire)
10^{6f} 5^{6f} 7^{6f} 3^{6sd} 10^{7gf} 3^{7gf} 0^{7ho} 5^{7gf}
1^{8gf} 4^{8gf} 6^{7f} **1-2-11 £6,709**

Folio (Ire) *W J Musson*   97
3 b g Perugino (USA) - Bayleaf
8^{6g} 3^{6g} 18^{6gf} 11^{6g} 7^{7g} 10^{8s} **0-0-6**
£1,775

Follow Me *F P Murtagh*   7
7 ch g Keen - Fairlead
15^{22gf} **0-0-1**

Fonthill Road (Ire) *R A Fahey*   73 a77
3 ch g Royal Abjar (USA) - Hannah Huxtable (Ire)
1^{6sd} 1^{5gf} 6^{6gf} 1^{6g} 2^{7sd} **3-1-5 £14,794**

Foodbroker Founder *D R C Elsworth*   107
3 ch g Groom Dancer (USA) - Nemea (USA)
1^{9gf} 5^{12gf} 9^{10g} 2^{10gf} 12^{10g} 13^{10g} **1-1-6**
£18,103

Fool On The Hill *L G Cottrell*   89

6 b g Reprimand - Stock Hill Lass
10^{12g} 1^{12gf} 5^{12gf} 6^{10g} 8^{12g} 4^{10gf} 8^{10gs} 10^{13gf} 10^{12gf} **1-0-9 £6,937**

Foolish Gift (Fr) *W R Muir* 52 a52
3 b f Barathea (Ire) - Fancy Wrap
12^{12gs} 2^{13gf} 6^{12gf} 3^{12sd} 7^{12g} 12^{12sw} **0-2-6 £1,763**

Foolish Thought (Ire) *R A Fahey* 13 a63
3 b g Green Desert (USA) - Trusted Partner (USA)
10^{6sd} 13^{6g} 11^{6sd} 4^{7sd} **0-0-4**

Fools Entire *M R Channon* 68
2 ch g Fraam - Poly Blue (Ire)
2^{7gf} 3^{7gf} 7^{7gs} 2^{7gf} 4^{7gf} 3^{8gf} 8^{7gf} 19^{6gf} 7^{7f} **0-3-9 £3,252**

Foot Fault (Ire) *N A Callaghan* 50
2 b f Danehill (USA) - Mockery
14^{7gf} 10^{7gf} **0-0-2**

Football Crazy (Ire) *S Gollings* 99
4 b g Mujadil (USA) - Schonbein (Ire)
8^{10gf} 5^{10g} 3^{8gs} 1^{10gs} 16^{10f} 3^{11g} 1^{10gf} 3^{12g} 3^{9gf} 2^{9g} 10^{10gf} 12^{10s} **2-4-12 £21,091**

For Freedom (Ire) *Alex Vanderhaeghen* 61
3 b f King Of Kings (Ire) - Louju (USA)
5^{7gf} 4^{7gf} 0^{8s} **0-0-3 £428**

For Your Eyes Only *C E Brittain* 32
9 b g Pursuit Of Love - Rivers Rhapsody
9^{7f} 7^{7gf} **0-0-2**

Forbearing (Ire) *M C Pipe* 86
6 b g Bering - For Example (USA)
12^{12gf} 12^{10g} 1^{10gf} 7^{10g} 1^{12f} 6^{12gs} 1^{12gf} 7^{10gf} **3-0-8 £13,658**

Force Of Nature (USA) *H R A Cecil* 86
3 b f Sadler's Wells (USA) - Yashmak (USA)
2^{10gf} **0-1-1 £1,728**

Forceful *J G Portman* a26
3 b f Forzando - Instinction
11^{6sd} **0-0-1**

Foreign Affairs *Sir Mark Prescott* 107
5 ch h Hernando (Fr) - Entente Cordiale (USA)
4^{12s} 10^{10f} 4^{12g} 2^{12gf} 8^{14gf} 1^{13g} 5^{12ho} **1-0-7 £32,801**

Foreign Editor *J J Quinn* 43 a71
7 ch g Magic Ring (Ire) - True Precision
5^{7sd} 13^{7sd} 8^{6sw} 8^{6sw} UR^{7gf} 11^{7f} **0-0-6**

Forest Air (Ire) *Miss L A Perratt* 62
3 br f Charnwood Forest (Ire) - Auriga
5^{7f} 5^{8g} 7^{7gf} 3^{9f} 7^{10g} 11^{8gf} **0-1-6 £616**

Forest Dane *J Cullinan* 61
3 b g Danetime (Ire) - Forest Maid
19^{6g} 7^{5g} 6^{6gf} 4^{5gf} **0-0-4 £267**

Forest Heath (Ire) *H J Collingridge* a44
6 gr g Common Grounds - Caroline Lady (Jpn)
11^{10sd} **0-0-1**

Forest Prize *T D Easterby* 65
4 b f Charnwood Forest (Ire) - Midnight's Reward
14^{10g} 7^{8g} 20^{7gf} 5^{7f} 18^{8f} **0-0-5**

Forest Queen *A Berry* 9
6 b m Risk Me (Fr) - Grey Cree
9^{9sd} 11^{8gf} **0-0-2**

Forest Rail (Ire) *Mrs N Macauley* a40
3 b f Catrail (USA) - Forest Heights
6^{5sd} 4^{7sw} **0-0-2**

Forest Tune (Ire) *B Hanbury* 69 a76
5 b g Charnwood Forest (Ire) - Swift Chorus
9^{12sd} 6^{11gf} 1^{10gs} 8^{10g} 6^{12sd} **1-0-5 £3,486**

Foretold (Ire) *J Noseda* 59 a77
3 b g Darshaan - For Example (USA)
3^{10sd} 6^{8gf} 4^{9gs} 2^{12sd} **0-1-4 £2,032**

Forever Fantasy (Ire) *J L Dunlop* 50
2 b c Daylami (Ire) - Gay Fantasy
9^{7gf} 7^{8gf} 3^{8gf} 6^{8gs} **0-0-4 £510**

Forever Loved *D Haydn Jones* 87 a83
4 ch f Deploy - Truly Madly Deeply
7^{12sd} 2^{14g} 4^{14gs} 3^{13gf} 1^{14gs} 7^{19gf} **1-2-6 £8,351**

Forever My Lord *J R Best* 63 a57
5 b g Be My Chief (USA) - In Love Again (Ire)
3^{12sd} 1^{10gf} 4^{16gf} 2^{16sd} 4^{14g} 4^{15gf} 4^{12g} 2^{14gf} 1^{14f} 2^{12gf} 8^{16gf} 11^{14gf} **2-4-12 £11,868**

Forever Phoenix *J R Fanshawe* 79
3 b f Shareef Dancer (USA) - With Care
4^{8g} 2^{7gf} 7^{7gf} **0-1-3 £1,335**

Forever Times *T D Easterby* 95
5 b m So Factual (USA) - Simply Times (USA)
7^{6gf} 11^{6gs} 3^{6gf} 1^{6gf} 3^{6gf} 8^{6g} 5^{7g} 7^{6gf} 19^{6g} 5^{6gf} 5^{7gf} **1-2-11 £15,107**

Forge Valley Lady *D Carroll* 66 a51
4 ch f Hamas (Ire) - Salul
10^{7sd} 16^{7sd} 7^{7sw} 7^{7sd} 2^{6gf} 9^{7gf} 4^{7f} 5^{8gf} 12^{7gf} 4^{7gs} 3^{8gs} 2^{8gs} **0-4-12 £5,139**

Formalise *G B Balding* 84
3 b g Forzando - Esilam
9^{6gf} 14^{6gf} 4^{5gf} 12^{6g} 5^{6gf} 8^{6gf} 6^{5gf} 11^{5gf} **0-0-8 £544**

Formeric *Miss L C Siddall* 38
7 ch g Formidable (USA) - Irish Limerick
14^{6gf} 15^{6f} 14^{6gf} 11^{6gs} 18^{6gf} **0-0-5**

Formidable Stella *Miss Z C Davison*
7 b m Formidable (USA) - Stellajoe
12^{10sd} **0-0-1**

Forrest Gump *C J Teague*
3 ch g Zilzal (USA) - Mish Mish
13^{7sw} 16^{8f} **0-0-2**

Forsythia *Mrs K Walton* 71
3 b f Most Welcome - No More Rosies
8^{10gf} 2^{12gf} 7^{11g} 12^{14gs} **0-1-4 £644**

Fort *M Johnston* 87
2 ch c Dr Fong (USA) - Chief's Quest (USA)
1^{7gf} 3^{7g} **1-0-2 £5,481**

Fort Churchill (Ire) *M H Tompkins* 39
2 b c Barathea (Ire) - Brisighella (Ire)
10^{7s} 10^{7gs} **0-0-2**

Fort Dignity (USA) *Sir Michael Stoute* 90
2 b c Seeking The Gold (USA) - Kitza (Ire)
1^{7gf} **1-0-1 £3,701**

Fort McHenry (Ire) *N A Callaghan* 82
3 b g Danehill Dancer (Ire) - Griqualand
13^{7gs} 12^{7gf} 6^{7gf} 7^{8gf} 4^{7g} 1^{7gf} 1^{5s} 8^{5gf} 16^{6gf} **2-0-9 £9,093**

Fort Saumarez *Mrs L Richards* 29
4 b g Magic Ring (Ire) - Rocquaine Bay
13^{10gf} 16^{10gf} **0-0-2**

Forthright *C E Brittain* 86
2 b c Cadeaux Genereux - Forthwith
2^{6gf} 1^{7gf} 6^{7gf} 7^{7gs} 6^{8gf} 9^{10gs} **1-1-6 £7,272**

Fortino *M D Hammond* 22
2 ch c Abou Zouz (USA) - Blazing Sunset
11^{5gf} 14^{5gf} 8^{5gs} 7^{5gf} **0-0-4**

Fortuna Mea *W M Brisbourne*   43
3 b f Mon Tresor - Veni Vici (Ire)
9^{9f} 6^{12g} 10^{10gf} 8^{10gs} 7^{10gf} 8^{9gs} **0-0-6**

Fortunate Dave (USA) *Ian Williams*   a60
4 b g Lear Fan (USA) - Lady Ameriflora (USA)
5^{12sw} 9^{15sd} **0-0-2**

Fortunately *P D Evans*   92 a78
2 b f Forzando - Lucky Dip
4^{5sd} 2^{5f} 1^{5gf} 1^{5gf} 2^{5g} 3^{5gf} 1^{5g} 8^{6g}
5^{5g} 5^{6gf} **4-2-11 £29,392**

Fortunately Mine *A G Newcombe*   a4
2 b f Dancing Spree (USA) - Fortuitious (Ire)
5^{5sd} 9^{5f} 9^{6sd} **0-0-3**

Fortune Island (Ire) *M C Pipe*   94
4 b g Turtle Island (Ire) - Blue Kestrel (Ire)
1^{16gf} 16^{19gf} 21^{20gf} **1-0-3 £12,267**

Fortune Point (Ire) *A W Carroll*   76
5 ch g Cadeaux Genereux - Mountains Of Mist (Ire)
6^{8gf} 2^{8gf} 2^{10f} 12^{11gf} 6^{7g} 4^{8g} 8^{8g} **0-3-7**
£2,296

Fortunes Favourite *G M Moore*   39
3 ch f Barathea (Ire) - Golden Fortune
8^{12gs} **0-0-1**

Forty Forte *Miss S J Wilton*   52 a77
7 b g Pursuit Of Love - Cominna
11^{11sd} 18^{sd} 9^{8sd} 4^{10sd} 7^{10g} 11^{8sd} 8^{9sd}
16^{11gf} 17^{8gf} **1-0-9 £2,933**

Forza Glory *Miss B Sanders*   20
4 ch f Forzando - Glory Isle
9^{14g} **0-0-1**

Forzacurity *J L Spearing*   58 a28
4 ch g Forzando - Nice Lady
14^{8gf} 8^{8gf} 12^{7sd} 14^{8g} **0-0-4**

Forzenuff *J R Boyle*   69 a45
2 b c Mujadil (USA) - Sada
10^{5sd} 5^{5gf} 4^{5gf} 5^{5gf} 1^{6f} 6^{5f} **1-0-6**
£3,520

Fosforito (Fr) *G L Moore*   70
5 b g Zieten (USA) - Bardouine (USA)
10^{8sd} 5^{8sd} 3^{8sd} 6^{10g} 6^{10gf} **0-0-5 £351**

Fossgate *J D Bethell*   70
2 ch g Halling (USA) - Peryllys
8^{7gf} 5^{7gs} **0-0-2**

Fou Doux (Fr) *P W Hiatt*   a5
7 b g Le Grillon Ii (Fr) - Folie Douce (Fr)
10^{16sd} **0-0-1**

Four Amigos (USA) *J G Given*   76 a55
2 b c Southern Halo (USA) - Larentia
5^{5f} 8^{5gs} 5^{20gf} 5^{6g} 7^{6s} 1^{5g} 15^{5gf}
2^{5g} **2-1-9 £7,444**

Four Corona *W M Brisbourne*   25
3 b f Perpendicular - Pixel (Ire)
7^{11gs} 13^{12gf} 6^{10g} **0-0-3**

Four Jays (Ire) *N P Littmoden*   92 a85
3 b g Alzao (USA) - Paparazzi (Ire)
2^{8g} 9^{8g} 2^{7gf} 11^{7g} 2^{7gf} 13^{8gf} 5^{6gf}
3^{7gf} 7^{7f} 12^{7sd} 2^{8f} 6^{8gf} **0-5-13 £13,712**

Four Pence (Ire) *B W Hills*   66
2 b c Rainbow Quest (USA) - American Queen (Fr)
4^{8g} 7^{7gs} **0-0-2 £274**

Fourali *A C Stewart*
3 b c Lion Cavern (USA) - Zobaida (Ire)
10^{7gs} **0-0-1**

Foursquare (Ire) *J Mackie*   84
2 b c Fayruz - Waroonga (Ire)
5^{6gf} 1^{5gf} 10^{5gf} 2^{5s} **1-1-4 £4,560**

Fourswainby (Ire) *B Ellison*   39
2 b g Foxhound (USA) - Arena
8^{5gf} 7^{6gs} **0-0-2**

Fourth Dimension (Ire) *A C Stewart*   97
4 b c Entrepreneur - Isle Of Spice (USA)
6^{12gf} 3^{14gf} 1^{14g} 3^{13gf} 8^{15g} 12^{16gf} 19^{18gf}
1-2-7 £7,896

Fovant *M P Tregoning*   66
3 ch f Night Shift (USA) - Sheppard's Cross
9^{6gs} 9^{7gf} 19^{16g} **0-0-3**

Fox Covert (Ire) *D W Barker*   72
2 b g Foxhound (USA) - Serious Contender (Ire)
7^{6gs} 3^{6gf} 3^{6gf} 6^{6g} 5^{6g} 3^{7gf} 2^{6gf} 3^{7g} 2^{6gf}
3^{6gs} 11^{6gs} **0-6-11 £8,708**

Fox Hollow (Ire) *M J Haynes*   30
2 b c Foxhound (USA) - Soignee
6^{6gf} 6^{7g} 5^{5gf} 10^{6gf} **0-0-4**

Fox Wood (Ire) *B A McMahon*   38 a39
2 ch c Woodborough (USA) - Fastnet
8^{5g} 3^{5sd} 10^{7gf} **0-0-3 £432**

Foxdale Lady *J R Weymes*   17
2 b f First Trump - Nordesta (Ire)
11^{6s} 9^{7f} **0-0-2**

Foxey Loxey (Ire) *W Storey*   14
2 b c Foxhound (USA) - Lamp Of Phoebus (USA)
15^{5gf} **0-0-1**

Foxglove *J R Fanshawe*   65 a16
3 b f Hernando (Fr) - Rynechra
4^{10gf} 2^{12gf} 9^{12sd} **0-0-3 £1,965**

Foxies Future (Ire) *J R Weymes*   47 a64
2 b f General Monash (USA) - Indescent Blue
7^{6gs} 5^{6sd} 6^{7gf} 1^{6sd} 15^{6g} **1-0-5 £3,276**

Foxilla (Ire) *D R C Elsworth*   51
2 ch f Foxhound (USA) - Lilissa (Ire)
7^{7g} 14^{7gf} 15^{8gf} **0-0-3**

Foxtrot Too (Ire) *M H Tompkins*   73
2 b c Foxhound (USA) - Dance Desire (Ire)
4^{6gf} 1^{5gf} 7^{6g} 5^{7gf} 8^{6gf} 17^{6gs} **1-0-6**
£5,932

Foxtrotromeoyankee *L A Dace*   31 a57
3 b g Tragic Role (USA) - Hope Chest
4^{10sd} 10^{8sd} 7^{10sd} 4^{10sd} 9^{11gf} 2^{10sd} 7^{11f}
0-1-7 £1,461

Foxy Diva (Ire) *Miss V Haigh*   37 a20
2 b f Foxhound (USA) - Quest For Best (USA)
11^{6s} 10^{5sd} 3^{6gf} 3^{6g} 4^{6gf} **0-1-5 £1,114**

Fraamtastic *B A Pearce*   a42
6 b m Fraam - Fading
5^{7sd} 10^{8sd} 4^{11sd} 9^{8sd} **0-0-4**

Fragrant Star *C E Brittain*   75
2 gr f Soviet Star (USA) - Norfolk Lavender (Can)
9^{5s} 4^{6gf} 12^{6gf} 1^{6g} 7^{7gf} 5^{6gs} **1-0-6**
£9,498

Frambo (Ire) *J G Portman*   54 a49
2 b f Fraam - Wings Awarded
11^{5sd} 14^{5g} 2^{7gf} 2^{8sd} **0-1-4 £583**

Fran's Future *A G Newcombe*   10
3 ch f Danzig Connection (USA) - Revoke (USA)
7^{8gf} 12^{8gf} **0-0-2**

France *A P O'Brien*   116
3 b c Desert Prince (Ire) - Hyperspectra
4^{8gf} 1^{7g} 4^{8gs} 2^{8s} 9^{8gf} 3^{8g} 4^{10g} 6^{10gf}
1-1-8 £124,243

Frances Canty (USA) *E J O'Neill*   25 a44

2 b f Lear Fan (USA) - Beyond The Realm (USA)
4⁷gs 6⁸gf 10⁷sd **0-0-3 £397**

Francis Flute *B Mactaggart*   63
5 b g Polar Falcon (USA) - Darshay (Fr)
11⁶gs 4⁹gf 6⁷f 8⁶gs 13⁶gs 10⁸gf **0-0-6**
£296

Francken (Ity) *Don Enrico Incisa*
4 ro g Petit Loup (USA) - Filicaia
10¹⁰gf **0-0-1**

Francport *K A Ryan*   a64
7 b g Efisio - Elkie Brooks
4⁶sw 7⁶sd 1⁶sd 2⁷sw 4⁶sw **1-2-5 £4,067**

Frangipani (Ire) *P F I Cole*   60
2 b f Sri Pekan (USA) - Sharkashka (Ire)
3⁶gf 3⁷g 4⁸g **0-1-3 £5,017**

Frank Sonata *M G Quinlan*   85
2 b c Opening Verse (USA) - Megdale (Ire)
7⁷g 1⁷g 4⁷g 9⁸gf 7¹⁰gs **1-0-5 £3,944**

Frank's Quest (Ire) *John A Harris*   63 a61
3 b g Mujadil (USA) - Questuary (Ire)
11⁸sd 9⁷sd 2⁷sw 2⁸sd 4⁸sd 10⁸gf 1⁸gs 4⁷gf
2⁸gf 7⁸g 14⁸gf 4⁸g 9¹⁰gf **1-4-13 £7,590**

Frankincense (Ire) *A J Lockwood*   29
7 gr g Paris House - Mistral Wood (USA)
9¹⁶gs **0-0-1**

Franklins Gardens *M H Tompkins*   111
3 b c Halling (USA) - Woodbeck
1¹⁰g 1¹²gf 14¹²g **2-0-3 £50,997**

Franksalot (Ire) *Miss B Sanders*   70
3 ch g Desert Story (Ire) - Rosie's Guest (Ire)
11⁷gs 5⁷gf 5⁵gf 3⁶g 4⁶gf 3⁶gf 2⁶g 1⁷f
2⁷g 2⁷gf 2⁸gf **1-5-11 £9,007**

Frankskips *Miss B Sanders*   19 a74
4 b g Bishop Of Cashel - Kevins Lady
1⁸sd 8⁸sd 5⁸sd 10⁸g **1-0-4 £3,269**

Frantic Annie (Ire) *D W P Arbuthnot*   32 a50
3 b f Among Men (USA) - Queen Sigi (Ire)
14⁷sd 3⁵sd 9⁶sd 5⁵sd 5⁶sd 9⁷sd 10⁶g
9⁶g **0-1-9 £411**

Frascati *A Berry*   76
3 b f Emarati (USA) - Fizzy Fiona
5⁵gs 3⁵gf 6⁵gf 2⁵gf 6⁵f 2⁵g 6⁵gf 17⁵g
10⁵gf 4⁵gs **0-3-10 £4,683**

Fraternity *J A Pickering*   a38
6 b g Grand Lodge (USA) - Catawba
15⁷f 5¹⁰f 16¹²gf 6¹⁵sd 4¹⁵sd **0-0-5**
£153

Frazers Fortune *G Brown*   10
3 ch g Environment Friend - Safidar
11¹²sd 15⁸g 15⁸g **0-0-3**

Frazzled *C A Cyzer*   73 a88
4 b g Greensmith - Time For Tea (Ire)
4⁸sd 9⁸sd 9⁸sd 14⁷sd 4⁸sd 3⁸sd 3⁸sd 8⁸gf
6⁷f 10⁸f **0-2-10 £1,789**

Freak Occurence (Ire) *Miss E C Lavelle*   75
2 b c Stravinsky (USA) - Date Mate (USA)
11⁷g 8⁷gf 7⁶gf 7⁸gf 4⁸gf 1⁸gs **1-1-6**
£3,165

Freddie Freccles *J G Given*   a66
2 ch c Komaite (USA) - Leprechaun Lady
1⁷sd **1-0-1 £2,240**

Free Flying *L M Cumani*   56
3 ch f Groom Dancer (USA) - Free Guest
7¹⁰gf 8⁸gf **0-0-2**

Free Option (Ire) *B Hanbury*   78 a82

8 ch g Indian Ridge - Saneena
1¹⁰sd 7¹⁰sd 5⁸sd 10¹⁰g 7⁸gf 5¹⁰f 3¹⁰gf
11¹⁰g 12⁸gf 3⁸sd **1-2-10 £5,316**

Free Trip *J H M Gosden*   78
2 ch c Cadeaux Genereux - Well Away (Ire)
11⁶gf 1⁶gs 1⁶gf 2⁶gf 9⁷gf **2-1-5**
£10,153

Free Wheelin (Ire) *W Jarvis*   92
3 b c Polar Falcon (USA) - Farhana
8⁶gf 10⁶gf 2⁶hy 16⁶gf 14⁶g 14⁵s 9⁶g
0-1-7 £1,846

Freecom Net (Ire) *A Crook*   60
5 b g Zieten (USA) - Radiance (Ire)
9¹⁶sw **0-0-1**

Freedom Bay *Mrs P N Dutfield*   60
3 b g Slip Anchor - Bobbie Dee
7¹²gs 11¹²gf 8¹⁰gf 11¹⁴g 9¹⁴gf **0-0-5**

Freedom Now (Ire) *J W Hills*   87
5 b g Sadler's Wells (USA) - Free At Last
3¹²gf 6¹⁰gs 6¹²gf 9¹²gf **0-0-4 £1,791**

Freeholder *A G Newcombe*   a36
3 ch f Zamindar (USA) - Wild Humour (Ire)
9⁸sd 5¹⁰sd 8⁸sd **0-0-3**

Freeloader (Ire) *J W Hills*   83 a66
3 b c Revoque (Ire) - Indian Sand
7⁸gf 1¹⁰sd 3⁸gf 3⁸g 3⁸gf 3⁸gs 1¹⁰gf 1¹⁰gf
2¹⁰gf 6¹⁰g 9¹⁰gf **3-4-11 £16,872**

Fremen (USA) *Sir Michael Stoute*   99
3 ch c Rahy (USA) - Northern Trick (USA)
2⁸gf 3⁸gf 1⁸gf 1⁸gf 10⁷gf **2-2-5**
£15,634

French Cat (USA) *G Fierro*
5 b/br g Storm Cat (USA) - Shannkara (Ire)
10⁵sd 12¹³gf **0-0-2**

French Connection *B D Leavy*
8 b g Tirol - Heaven-Liegh-Grey
12¹²sw **0-0-1**

French Gigolo *C N Allen*   56
3 ch g Pursuit Of Love - French Mist
10⁸g 9¹⁰f 8⁸gf **0-0-3**

French Horn *M J Ryan*   72 a44
6 b g Fraam - Runcina
14¹⁰sd 12¹⁰sd 6⁸sd 3⁸gf 7⁸gs 9⁸g 11⁸g
14⁷s **0-1-8 £902**

French Risk (Ire) *N A Graham*   55 a51
3 b c Entrepreneur - Troyes
10⁸sd 4⁹sw 2¹⁰sd 7¹⁰gf 3¹⁰gf 5¹²gf 5¹²sd
0-2-7 £1,650

French Tune (Fr) *Miss S E Hall*   54
5 ch g Green Tune (USA) - Guerre De Troie
10¹²gf **0-0-1**

Frenchmans Bay (Fr) *R Charlton*   109 a113
5 br h Polar Falcon (USA) - River Fantasy (USA)
1⁷sd 5⁸g 7⁷vs **1-0-3 £14,564**

Frenchmans Lodge *D J S Ffrench Davis*   35 a60
3 b g Piccolo - St Helena
3⁵sd 5⁵sd 16⁶gf 16⁶gf 13⁶g 17⁸gf **0-0-6**
£622

Freya Alex *Mrs S J Smith*   39
4 b f Makbul - Crissem (Ire)
16¹⁰gf 4¹⁶gs **0-0-2 £311**

Freya's Dream (Ire) *T D Easterby*   92
4 b f Danehill Dancer (Ire) - Ruwy
3⁷g 4⁷g 8⁷gf 1⁸f 4⁸gf 7⁸gf 19⁸g 7⁸gf
9⁸gf 14⁸g **1-2-10 £12,947**

Friar Tuck *Miss L A Perratt* 71
8 ch g Inchinor - Jay Gee Ell
8⁵gf 11⁶gs 16⁵gf 16⁶gf 5⁶gs 11⁶gf 7⁶f
7⁶g 8⁵g 7⁶gf 5⁶gs 8⁶gf 16⁶gf 3⁶f 2⁶f
24⁶gs 13⁵g **0-2-18 £1,504**

Friday's Takings *B Smart* 61 a78
4 ch g Beveled (USA) - Pretty Pollyanna
1⁸sd 2⁸sd 2⁸gf 19⁸gf 17⁸g **1-2-5 £5,738**

Frieda Kahlo (Ire) *G Wragg* 79
3 ch f Indian Ridge - Devil's Bones (USA)
3⁷gf 4⁸gs 10⁸gf 10⁸g 5¹⁰gf 4⁸gf 9¹⁰gf 4⁷gf
0-1-8 £1,627

Friendly Alliance *R M Flower* 48 a52
7 b g Shareef Dancer (USA) - Snow Huntress
13¹⁶gf 13¹³g 12²²f 7¹²gf 11¹⁶gf 3¹⁶sd
5¹⁵gf **0-1-7 £559**

Frimley's Matterry *A P Jarvis* 44 a57
3 b c Bluegrass Prince (Ire) - Lonely Street
5⁷sd 6⁶sd 3⁶sd 10⁶sd 14⁶gf **0-1-5 £421**

Fritillary *Sir Mark Prescott* 72
2 b f Vettori (Ire) - Fetlar
9⁷gf 8⁷g 1⁷gf 5⁸gf **1-0-4 £5,408**

Frixos (Ire) *M Scudamore* 54 a77
3 ch g Barathea (Ire) - Local Lass
5⁸gf 1⁹sd 2¹²sd 6¹⁰g 8¹⁰f PU¹⁰g 11¹⁰gf
1-1-7 £3,970

Frizzante *J R Fanshawe* 108
4 b f Efisio - Juliet Bravo
1⁶g 1⁶g 4⁶g 6⁶g 1⁶gf 1⁶gf **4-1-6**
£44,085

From The North (Ire) *A Dickman* 16
2 ch f Foxhound (USA) - Best Swinger (Ire)
PU⁶gs 13⁶g **0-0-2**

Fromsong (Ire) *B R Millman* 101
5 b g Fayruz - Lindas Delight
8⁵g 3⁵g 7⁵gf 10⁵gf 1⁶gf 24⁶f 8⁵gf 15⁶gf
1-1-8 £11,595

Front Rank (Ire) *Sir Michael Stoute* 5 a72
3 b c Sadler's Wells (USA) - Alignment (Ire)
12¹⁰g 9¹²sd 2⁹sd 2¹²sw **0-2-4 £1,754**

Frontier *B J Llewellyn* 84
6 b g Indian Ridge - Adatiya (Ire)
4¹²gf 2¹⁰g 1¹⁰gf 2¹⁰gf 6¹⁰g 8⁹gf 11¹⁰g
8¹²gf 9¹⁰gs **1-2-9 £10,019**

Fruit Of Glory *J R Jenkins* 98
4 b f Glory Of Dancer - Fresh Fruit Daily
1⁷gf 2⁸gf 18⁷g 1⁶gf 1⁷gf 6⁶gf 3⁵gf
3⁶gf 3⁵gf 5⁶gf **4-4-11 £45,794**

Fu Fighter *J A Osborne* a72
2 b g Unfuwain (USA) - Runelia
5⁷sd 4⁸sd **0-0-2**

Fubos *Julian Poulton* 65 a52
2 b g Atraf - Homebeforemidnight
12⁷sd 12⁷sd 7⁸g **0-0-3**

Fujisawa *M R Channon* 70
2 b f Green Desert (USA) - Fursa (USA)
3⁵g 3⁶gf 2⁶f 3⁵gf **0-3-4 £3,050**

Full Egalite *B A Pearce* a19
7 gr g Ezzoud (Ire) - Milva
14¹⁶sd **0-0-1**

Full House (Ire) *P R Webber* 71
4 br g King's Theatre (Ire) - Nirvavita (Fr)
2¹³gf 4¹⁴gf **0-1-2 £1,900**

Full Kwai Ma (Ire) *Miss L A Perratt* 59
3 b c Night Shift (USA) - So Kind

3⁵gf 4⁵gs **0-0-2 £1,997**

Full Spate *J M Bradley* 84
8 ch g Unfuwain (USA) - Double River (USA)
6⁶g 2⁶gf 16⁶gf 14⁶gf 5⁶gf 19⁶gf 5⁶gf
9⁶gf 10⁶gf 3⁶gf 2⁶gf 10⁶g 10⁶gf 6⁶g 9⁶gf 6⁶gf
11⁷g 6⁶gf 1⁶gf **1-3-20 £8,483**

Full Time (Ire) *G A Swinbank* 42
4 b g Bigstone (Ire) - Oiche Mhaith
5¹¹gf 12¹⁵sd **0-0-2**

Fully Fledged *G B Balding* 57
3 b f Fraam - Alarming Motown
10⁸gf 3¹²gf **0-0-3 £844**

Fulvio (USA) *Jamie Poulton* 72 a76
3 b g Sword Dance - One Tuff Gal (USA)
3⁷sd 3⁸sd 1⁶sd 3⁷sd 4⁸sd 1⁷sd 1⁷sd
4⁷sd 3⁸gf 10⁷gf 14⁷gf 3⁶gf 6⁶gf 6⁶sd 5⁶g
9⁷gf **3-6-18 £13,621**

Fun And Games (Ire) *M R Channon* 94
2 ch f Rahy (USA) - Sharpwitted
1⁵gf 4⁵gf 4⁷gf 3⁸gf 1¹⁰gs **2-0-6**
£22,428

Fun To Ride *B W Hills* 79
2 ch f Desert Prince (Ire) - Zafaaf
2⁶g 2⁶g **0-2-2 £2,029**

Funfair *Sir Michael Stoute* 111
4 b g Singspiel (Ire) - Red Carnival (USA)
1⁸gf 8⁸gf 2⁸gf 11⁷g **1-1-4 £42,300**

Funfair Wane *D Nicholls* 97
4 b g Unfuwain (USA) - Ivory Bride
12⁶g 8⁶f 1⁵gf 8⁵gf 7⁶g 18⁶g 19⁶g 7⁷gf
25⁶g **1-0-9 £12,110**

Funny Cide (Ire) *B Tagg* a125
3 ch g Distorted Humor - Belle's Good Cide (USA)
5⁹ft 2⁹ft 2⁹my 1¹⁰ft 1¹⁰g 3¹²sy 3⁹ft 9¹⁰ft
2-1-8 £1,227,000

Funny Valentine (Ire) *T G Mills* 82
5 ch g Cadeaux Genereux - Aunt Hester (Ire)
23⁶g 13⁵gf **0-0-2**

Furaat (Ire) *J H M Gosden* 83
3 b f Danehill (Ire) - Istibshar (USA)
6⁸ft 3⁸ft 2⁸gf 1⁷f 7⁸f **1-2-5 £8,745**

Furniture Factors (Ire) *Ronald Thompson*
3 b g Magic Ring (Ire) - Make Hay
15⁸gf 7¹⁰gf **0-0-2**

Further Outlook (USA) *D K Ivory* 81 a70
9 gr g Zilzal (USA) - Future Bright (USA)
9⁶sd 13⁷sd 13¹⁰sd 7⁶g 2⁶gs 7⁵gf 8⁶g **0-1-7**
£922

Fusillade (Ire) *M A Jarvis* 36
3 ch g Grand Lodge (USA) - Lili Cup (Fr)
8¹⁰gf 10¹¹gf **0-0-2**

Futoo (Ire) *G M Moore* 69
2 b g Foxhound (USA) - Nicola Wynn
3⁵gf 6⁵gf 3⁶gs 4⁶gs 9⁷gf 1⁶gf 7⁶gf 6⁷gf
11⁸g 19⁷gs 9⁸gs 6⁷g **2-1-12 £8,989**

Future Coup (USA) *J R Norton* 51
7 b g Lord At War (Arg) - Holymoly (USA)
12¹¹gf 6¹²gf 15¹²g 2¹²gf 5¹³gf 14¹²gf 4¹²f
5¹²gf 4¹²gf 11¹⁴gf 8¹²gs **0-1-11 £1,185**

Futuristic *J G Given* 38 a68
3 b g Magic Ring (Ire) - Corn Futures
10⁷gf 7⁷sd 7²sw 6⁸sd 17⁷gs 11⁹sd 6⁸sd
1-1-7 £4,161

Futuro Vencedor *M W Easterby* 38
3 b g Komaite (USA) - Takeall

16⁸ᵍᶠ 9¹⁰ᵍᶠ UR⁸ᵍᶠ 10¹⁰ᵍᶠ 16⁸ᵍᶠ **0-0-5**

Fyodor (Ire) *W J Haggas*   85
2 b c Fasliyev (USA) - Royale Figurine (Ire)
2⁶ᵍˢ 3⁶ᵍˢ 1⁵ᵍᶠ 2⁵ᵍᶠ **1-3-4 £13,984**

Gabana (Ire) *C F Wall*   65 a57
2 br f Polish Precedent (USA) - Out West (USA)
7⁷ᵍᶠ 7⁷ˢᵈ 3⁸ᵍ **0-1-3 £606**

Gabor *G L Moore*   69
4 b g Danzig Connection (USA) - Kiomi
14¹⁰ᵍᶠ 4¹⁰ᵍᶠ 10¹⁰ᵍᶠ 3¹²ᵍᶠ 8¹²ᵍᶠ 3¹¹ᵍᶠ 2¹⁰ᶠ
1¹⁰ᶠ 7¹⁰ᶠ 4¹⁰ᵍᶠ 5¹²ᶠ **1-1-11 £5,600**

Gaelic Princess *A G Newcombe*   95 a85
3 b f Cois Na Tine (Ire) - Berenice (Ity)
1⁵ˢᵈ 3⁵ᵍᶠ 14⁵ᵍᶠ 8⁵ᵍ 5⁶ᵍ 2⁶ᵍᶠ 4⁶ᵍᶠ 12⁷ᵍᶠ
3⁶ᵍᶠ 10⁶ᵍᶠ **1-3-10 £18,930**

Gaelic Probe (Ire) *R M H Cowell*   a26
9 b g Roi Danzig (USA) - Scottish Gaelic (USA)
6¹⁵ˢᵈ **0-0-1**

Gaelic Roulette (Ire) *P W Harris*   78 a46
3 b f Turtle Island (Ire) - Money Spinner (USA)
5⁸ᵍᶠ 6⁸ᵍᶠ 9⁸ᵍ 7¹⁰ᵍᶠ 10¹²ˢᵈ 3¹²ᵍᶠ 1¹²ᵍᶠ
1¹²ᵍᶠ 6¹²ᵍᶠ 5¹¹ᵍᶠ 7¹⁴ᵍᶠ **2-1-11 £10,358**

Gaiety Girl (USA) *T D Easterby*   68
2 b f Swain (Ire) - Knoosh (USA)
4⁷ᵍᶠ 4⁷ᵍᶠ 3⁷ᵍᶠ 7⁸ᵍᶠ **0-1-4 £1,077**

Gala Affair *C A Cyzer*   44
4 ch f Zilzal (USA) - Sally Slade
13⁶ᵍᶠ 8⁵ᵍ 13⁶ᶠ 7⁹ᵍ **0-0-4**

Gala Sunday (USA) *B W Hills*   104
3 b c Lear Fan (USA) - Sunday Bazaar (USA)
1¹⁰ᵍ 2¹⁰ᵍ 5¹⁰ʸˢ 1⁹ᵍᶠ 16¹⁰ᵍ 11¹⁰ᵍᶠ **2-0-6**
£20,452

Galandora *Dr J R J Naylor*   57 a35
3 b f Bijou D'Inde - Jelabna
11¹⁰ᶠ 4¹²ᵍ 5¹²ᶠ 5¹²ᵍ 6¹²ˢᵈ 3¹⁶ᵍᶠ 5¹⁶ᵍᶠ
9¹⁶ᵍᶠ 6¹⁶ᵍᶠ 3¹³ᵍᶠ 7¹⁴ᵍᶠ 8¹⁵ˢᵈ **0-2-12 £1,317**

Galapagos Girl (Ire) *J G M O'Shea*
5 b m Turtle Island (Ire) - Shabby Doll
13⁷ᵍ 15⁸ᵍᶠ **0-0-2**

Galaxy Thunderbird *S Dow*   a60
4 ch g Bahamian Bounty - Milva
8¹⁰ˢᵈ 6⁸ˢᵈ 9⁸ˢᵈ 7⁸ˢᵈ 7⁷ˢᵈ **0-0-5**

Galey River (USA) *J J Sheehan*   59
4 ch g Irish River (Fr) - Carefree Kate (USA)
21⁸ᵍ 8⁸ᵍˢ 12¹⁰ᶠ 8⁸ᵍ 10⁸ᵍᶠ 12⁸ˢᵈ 11⁸ᵍ
0-0-7

Galfan *B Palling*   a34
3 ch g Atraf - Clunk Click
4¹²ˢᵈ 11¹⁵ˢᵈ **0-0-2**

Gallant Boy (Ire) *P D Evans*   93 a91
4 ch g Grand Lodge (USA) - Damerela (Ire)
2⁸ˢᵈ 5¹⁰ˢᵈ 11⁰ˢᵈ 8¹²ˢᵈ 21⁸ᵍ 10¹⁰ᵍᶠ 7¹⁰ᵍ
5¹⁰ᵍ 11¹²ᵍ 8⁸ᵍᶠ 10¹⁰ᵍ 8⁹ᵍᶠ 1¹⁰ᵍᶠ 2¹⁰ᵍᶠ 8¹⁰ᵍ
15¹⁰ᵍᶠ 3¹¹ᵍᶠ 7¹⁰ᵍᶠ 8¹⁰ᵍᶠ 9¹²ᵍ **3-3-26 £30,831**

Gallant Hero *P J Hobbs*   108
4 b g Rainbow Quest (USA) - Gay Gallanta (USA)
6¹⁰ᵍ 4¹²ᵍᶠ 5¹²ᵍᶠ 2¹⁰ᵍᶠ 4¹⁰ᵍ **0-0-5 £6,882**

Gallas (Ire) *J S Wainwright*   64
2 b c Charnwood Forest (Ire) - Nellie's Away (Ire)
9⁶ᵍᶠ 5⁸ᵍᶠ 5⁶ᵍᶠ 12⁵ᵍᶠ 9⁷ᵍᶠ 8⁷ᵍˢ **0-0-6**

Galleon Beach *W M Brisbourne*   41
6 b g Shirley Heights - Music In My Life (Ire)
13¹⁶ᵍᶠ 6¹⁷ᶠ **0-0-2**

Gallery Breeze *J L Spearing*   60 a68
4 b f Zamindar (USA) - Wantage Park

12⁸ᵍᶠ 15⁶ᵍᶠ 4⁶ᵍᶠ 1⁶ᵍ 1⁷ˢᵈ **2-1-5 £5,236**

Gallery God (Fr) *S Dow*   109
7 ch g In The Wings - El Fabulous (Fr)
11³ᵍ 6¹³ᵍ 11²ᵍ 15¹²ᵍᶠ 7¹³ᵍˢ 4¹²ᵍ 12¹⁰ᵍᶠ
2-0-7 £36,494

Galley Law *R Craggs*   16
3 ch g Most Welcome - Miss Blitz
11¹⁰ᵍ 12¹¹ᵍ **0-0-2**

Gallivant *Sir Michael Stoute*   97
3 b f Danehill (USA) - Gay Gallanta (USA)
3⁶ᵍᶠ 4⁶ᵍᶠ 5⁶ᵍ 17⁷ᵍᶠ 3⁷ᵍᶠ **0-1-5 £5,430**

Galore (Ire) *J M Bradley*   21
3 b f Desert Style (Ire) - Rend Rover (Fr)
16⁷ᵍᶠ 20⁶ᵍᶠ **0-0-2**

Galvanise (USA) *B W Hills*   71
2 b c Run Softly (USA) - Shining Bright
7⁷ᵍ **0-0-1**

Game Dame *B W Hills*   76
2 ch f Nashwan (USA) - Gentle Dame
3⁷ᵍᶠ 3⁷ᵍᶠ **0-2-2 £2,351**

Game Flora *M E Sowersby*   51
2 b f Mind Games - Breakfast Creek
4⁵ᶠ 4⁵ᵍᶠ 5⁵ᵍᶠ 9⁶ᶠ 13⁶ᵍᶠ **0-0-5 £279**

Game Guru *T D Barron*   a76
4 b g First Trump - Scarlett Holly
11⁷ˢᵈ 3⁶ˢʷ 3⁶ˢᵈ 6⁶ˢʷ 6⁷ˢᵈ 14⁷ˢᵈ 9⁷ˢᵈ
0-2-7 £930

Game Time *A G Newcombe*   29 a41
4 b f Atraf - Real Popcorn (Ire)
9⁹ˢᵈ 15⁸ˢᵈ 4⁷ˢᵈ 8⁷ᶠ 10¹⁰ᵍᶠ **0-1-5**

Gameset'N'Match *W G M Turner*   69
2 b g Hector Protector (USA) - Tanasie
17⁵ᵍ 2⁵ᵍᶠ 7⁵ᵍ 6⁶ᵍ 5⁵ᵍᶠ **0-1-5 £1,652**

Gamut (Ire) *Sir Michael Stoute*   121
4 b c Spectrum (Ire) - Greektown
1¹³ᵍ 3¹²ᵍ 1¹²ᵍᶠ 2¹⁴ᵍᶠ 3¹²ᵍ **2-1-5**
£78,387

Gandon *P G Murphy*   a52
6 ch g Hernando (Fr) - Severine (USA)
7⁹ˢᵈ 12¹⁶ˢᵈ **0-0-2**

Ganesha *J Balding*   1
4 b f Magic Ring (Ire) - Breed Reference
11⁸ˢʷ 15⁶ᵍᶠ **0-0-2**

Ganymede *M L W Bell*   68
2 gr c Daylami (Ire) - Germane
6⁷ᵍᶠ 3⁷ᵍᶠ **0-1-2 £697**

Gardor (Fr) *T J Fitzgerald*   26
5 b g Kendor (Fr) - Garboesque
14¹¹ᵍᶠ **0-0-1**

Gargoyle Girl *J S Goldie*   69
6 b m Be My Chief (USA) - May Hills Legacy (Ire)
7¹²ᵍᶠ 6¹²ᵍᶠ 13¹²ᵍˢ 9⁹ᵍᶠ 2¹²ᵍᶠ 3¹²ᵍˢ 1¹²ᵍ
4¹²ᵍᶠ 2¹³ᵍᶠ 12¹²ᵍᶠ 8¹²ᵍᶠ 6¹⁴ᵍᶠ 4¹¹ᵍ 19¹²ᵍᶠ
1-4-14 £9,135

Garmoucheh (USA) *R Hannon*   90
3 b f Silver Hawk (USA) - Flowing (USA)
7⁷ᵍᶠ 7¹⁰ᵍᶠ 1¹⁰ᵍ 3¹⁰ᵍᶠ 7¹⁰ᵍ **1-0-5**
£10,732

Garnock Belle (Ire) *A Berry*   43
2 b f Marju (Ire) - Trojan Relation
5⁶ᵍᶠ 8⁵ᶠ 7⁵ᵍᶠ **0-0-3**

Garnock Venture (Ire) *A Berry*   58
2 b c Mujadil (USA) - Stay Sharpe (USA)
6⁵ᵍᶠ 6⁷ᶠ 5⁷ᵍᶠ 16⁷ᶠ **0-0-4**

Garrigon *N P Littmoden*   69 a49

2 b c Hector Protector (USA) - Queen Of The Keys
16⁶ᵍᶠ 2⁷ᵍ 6⁷ᵍᶠ 9⁷ˢᵈ 6⁷ᵍ 2⁶ᶠ 12⁶ᵍᶠ **0-2-7**
£2,453

Garros (USA) *M Johnston*　　　　　92
3 b c Grand Slam (USA) - Affirmatively (USA)
5¹⁰ᵍᶠ 2¹⁰ᵍᶠ **0-0-2 £3,405**

Garryurra *Sir Michael Stoute*　　　70
2 gr f Daylami (Ire) - Tropical
2⁷ᵍᶠ 6⁸ᵍᶠ **0-1-2 £1,084**

Garston Star *J S Moore*　　　56 a16
2 ch g Fleetwood (Ire) - Conquista
8⁶ᵍᶠ 6⁷ᵍᶠ 5⁸ᵍᶠ 7⁸ˢᵈ 7⁸ᵍᶠ 12⁸ᵍᶠ 6¹⁰ᵍˢ **0-0-7**

Garw Valley *Miss J Feilden*　　　45
4 b f Mtoto - Morgannwg (Ire)
12⁸ˢᵈ 12⁸ᵍˢ 9¹⁰ᶠ 9¹⁴ᵍᶠ **0-0-4**

Gasparini (Ire) *T D Easterby*　　52
2 ch c Docksider (USA) - Tarjou
2⁶ˢ **0-1-1 £1,512**

Gate Expectations *R J Price*
5 b m Alflora (Ire) - Dorazine
10¹²ˢᵈ **0-0-1**

Gateman *M Johnston*　　　　117
6 b g Owington - Scandalette
2⁷ᵍᶠ 3⁸ᵍᶠ 1⁹ᵍ 5⁸ᵍᶠ 1⁸ᵍˢ 3⁸ʰᵒ 5⁸ᵍᶠ **2-2-7**
£116,944

Gatwick (Ire) *M R Channon*　　70
2 b c Ali-Royal (Ire) - Airport
3⁶ᵍᶠ **0-1-1 £635**

Gavroche (Ire) *M J Wallace*　　63 a31
2 b c Docksider (USA) - Regal Revolution
4⁷ᵍᶠ 9⁷ᵍᶠ 8⁶ˢᵈ **0-0-3**

Gay Breeze *P S Felgate*
10 b g Dominion - Judy's Dowry
PU⁶ˢᵈ **0-0-1**

Gayle Storm (Ire) *A J Lidderdale*　60 a40
2 b f Mujadil (USA) - Mercy Bien (Ire)
6⁵ˢᵈ 5⁶ˢᵈ 3⁶ᵍᶠ 6⁶ᵍᶠ **0-0-4 £517**

Gazing (USA) *M R Channon*　　a61
3 b f Gulch (USA) - Hidden Dreams
2⁸ˢᵈ **0-1-1 £1,275**

Gdansk (Ire) *A Berry*　　　84
6 b g Pips Pride - Merry Twinkle
19⁵ᵍ 14⁶ᵍᶠ 11⁵ᵍᶠ 5⁵ʰʸ 10⁶ᵍᶠ 2⁶ᵍˢ 7⁶ᵍ
9⁶ᵍ 23⁶ᵍ **0-1-9 £2,036**

Gee Bee Boy *G F Bridgwater*
9 ch g Beveled (USA) - Blue And White
10⁹ˢᵈ 10¹⁶ˢᵈ **0-0-2**

Geespot *D J S Ffrench Davis*　45 a51
4 b f Pursuit Of Love - My Discovery (Ire)
8⁷ˢᵈ 11⁷ˢᵈ 5⁷ˢᵈ 9⁷ᶠ 11⁸ᶠ **0-0-5**

Gekkoaccountdotcom (Ire) *R M Flower*　47
4 b g Grand Lodge (USA) - House Music (Ire)
2⁷ᵍᶠ 8⁷ᵍᶠ 10⁷ᵍᶠ 13⁶ᵍᶠ 13⁷ᵍᶠ 14⁷ᵍᶠ **0-1-6**
£1,142

Geller *R Hannon*　　　76
2 b g Mind Games - Time To Tango
2⁸ᵍᶠ 2⁶ᵍᶠ 14⁶ᵍ 4⁸ᵍᶠ **0-2-4 £3,072**

Gem Bien (USA) *Andrew Turnell*　88
5 b g Bien Bien (USA) - Eastern Gem (USA)
13⁷ᵍᶠ 1⁸ᵍ 6⁸ᵍᶠ 4⁸ᵍᶠ **1-0-4 £6,009**

Gemeister *B P J Baugh*　　11
3 b g Superlative - Enfant Du Paradis (Ire)
5¹⁰ᵍᶠ 16¹⁰ᵍᶠ **0-0-2**

Gemi Bed (Fr) *G L Moore*　54 a51

8 b g Double Bed (Fr) - Gemia (Fr)
6¹¹ˢᵈ 6¹²ˢᵈ 5¹²ˢᵈ 1¹²ˢᵈ 1¹²ᵍ 5¹²ᵍ **2-0-6**
£6,069

Gemini Future (Ire) *A C Stewart*　77
3 b c Flying Spur (Aus) - Bianca Cappello (Ire)
11⁷ᵍᶠ 4⁷ᵍᶠ 4⁷ᶠ 4⁹ᵍᶠ **1-0-5 £6,750**

Gemini Girl (Ire) *M D Hammond*　57
2 b f Petardia - Miss Sabre
14⁵ᵍ 8⁵ᵍᶠ 5⁵ᵍᶠ 3⁵ᵍ 6⁵ᵍᶠ 6⁵ᵍᶠ **0-0-6 £722**

Gemini Lady *Mrs G S Rees*　　54
3 b f Emperor Fountain - Raunchy Rita
5⁸ᵍᶠ 8¹⁰ᶠ 3⁹ᶠ 3⁸ᵍᶠ 3⁸ˢ 11⁸ᵍᶠ 4⁸ᶠ 2¹⁰ᵍᶠ
7¹²ᵍᶠ **0-3-9 £2,634**

Geminiani (Ire) *B W Hills*　　106
3 b f King Of Kings (Ire) - Tadkiyra (Ire)
2¹⁰ᵍᶠ 9¹²ᵍ 8¹⁰ᵍ **0-1-3 £13,200**

Gemma *P J Makin*　　48 a4
3 b f Petong - Gem
8⁷ᵍᶠ 10⁷ᵍᶠ 6⁸ᵍᶠ 12⁹ᵍ 12⁸ᵍ 9⁸ˢʷ 12¹⁰ᵍᶠ
0-0-7

Gems Bond *R Hannon*　　89
3 b g Magic Ring (Ire) - Jucinda
14⁷ᵍᶠ 6⁸ᵍᶠ 9⁷ᵍᶠ 2⁸ᵍᶠ 2⁷ᵍᶠ 1⁸ᵍ 4⁸ᵍᶠ 16⁷ᵍᶠ
1⁸ᵍᶠ 15⁹ᵍᶠ **2-2-10 £13,687**

Gemtastic *R Hollinshead*　　a39
5 b m Tagula (Ire) - It's So Easy
4⁵ˢʷ 9⁵ˢᵈ **0-0-2**

General (Ksa) *C F Wall*　52 a65
2 b c Wiorno - Cloette
10⁷ᵍᶠ 7⁷ˢᵈ **0-0-2**

General Feeling (Ire) *S Kirk*　63
2 b c General Monash (USA) - Kamadara (Ire)
3⁶ᵍᶠ **0-1-1 £337**

General Flumpa *C F Wall*　　a65
2 b g Vettori (Ire) - Macca Luna (Ire)
7⁸ˢᵈ **0-0-1**

General Hawk (Ire) *R A Fahey*　55
5 b g Distinctly North (USA) - Sabev (USA)
8⁸ᵍ 13⁷ᵍᶠ **0-0-2**

General Jackson *Jane Southcombe*
6 ch g Cadeaux Genereux - Moidart
10¹⁵ᵍᶠ **0-0-1**

General Smith *J M Bradley*　67
4 b g Greensmith - Second Call
6⁵ᶠ 2⁵ᵍᶠ 10⁵ᵍᶠ 7⁵ᵍᶠ 8⁵ᵍ 10⁵ᵍᶠ 8⁵ᵍᶠ 5⁵ᵍᶠ
3⁵ᵍᶠ 1⁵ᵍᶠ 11⁵ᵍ 3⁵ᶠ 8⁵ᵍ 3⁵ᵍᶠ 6⁵ᶠ 3⁶ᶠ 2⁶ᵍᶠ 4⁵ᵍᶠ **1-6-21**
£9,600

Generous Gesture (Ire) *M L W Bell*　69
2 b f Fasliyev (USA) - Royal Bounty (Ire)
6⁶ᵍᶠ 10⁶ᵍᶠ 4⁶ᵍᶠ **0-0-3 £269**

Generous Share *M S Saunders*　21 a47
3 ch f Cadeaux Genereux - Marl
12⁶ᵍᶠ 9⁷ˢʷ 5⁷ˢᵈ 8⁷ˢᵈ **0-0-4**

Generous Ways *R Lee*　　27
8 ch g Generous (Ire) - Clara Bow (USA)
7¹⁶ᵍᶠ **0-0-1**

Genghis (Ire) *P R Webber*　74
4 br g Persian Bold - Cindys Baby
3¹⁰ᵍᶠ **0-1-1 £904**

Genial Genie *R Hollinshead*　64 a47
7 b g Sizzling Melody - Needwood Sprite
10⁸ᶠ 4⁷ᵍ 12⁷ᶠ 12⁷ᵍᶠ 10⁷ˢᵈ 9⁷ˢᵈ **0-1-6**
£340

Genteel (Ire) *P D Evans*　34
3 b f Titus Livius (Fr) - Danseuse Davis (Fr)

12⁷ᵍ 15⁶ᶠ **0-0-2**

Gentle Response *C A Dwyer*   61
3 b f Puissance - Sweet Whisper
11⁵ᵍᶠ 4⁵ᶠ 15⁵ᵍᶠ 11⁶ᵍˢ 2⁵ᵍᶠ 11⁶ᵍᶠ 8⁶ᵍᶠ
6⁵ᵍᶠ 5⁶ʰᵈ 2⁵ᵍᶠ 11⁶ᵍᶠ 9⁵ᵍᶠ 13⁵ᶠ 15⁸ᶠ **0-2-14**
£2,386

Gentleman George *D K Ivory*   10 a47
2 b g Kingsinger (Ire) - Miss Bigwig
14⁵ᵍᶠ 5⁵ˢᵈ 8⁶ˢᵈ **0-0-3**

Gentleman Venture *J Akehurst*   86
7 b g Polar Falcon (USA) - Our Shirley
4¹⁰ᵍˢ 5¹²ᵍ 13¹⁰ᵍ 17¹²ᵍ **0-1-4 £1,580**

Genuine Jay Gee (Ire) *G G Margarson*   10
2 b c Fasliyev (USA) - Jay Gee (Ire)
12⁷ᵍᶠ **0-0-1**

Genuinely (Ire) *W J Musson*   34
2 b f Entrepreneur - Fearless
11⁶ᵍᶠ 16⁷ᵍˢ **0-0-2**

Geoffstar *T G Mills*   45 a67
3 b c Groom Dancer (USA) - Skuld
4¹⁰ˢᵈ 7⁹ˢʷ 3¹⁰ᵍᶠ 15⁸ᵍᶠ **0-0-4 £726**

Geography (Ire) *P Butler*   60 a53
3 ch g Definite Article - Classic Ring (Ire)
6¹²ᵍᶠ 16¹²ᵍᶠ 3⁸ˢᵈ 7⁸ᵍ 7¹²ᵍᶠ 11⁸ᵍᶠ 8¹¹ᵍᶠ
5¹²ᵍᶠ **0-1-8 £548**

George Romney (USA) *H J Cyzer*   a53
4 b g Distant View (USA) - Polish Socialite (USA)
10⁸ˢᵈ 4⁸ˢᵈ 4⁸ˢᵈ **0-0-3**

George Stubbs (USA) *N P Littmoden*   81
5 b/br g Affirmed (USA) - Mia Duchessa (USA)
3⁷ᵍ 13⁸ᵍᶠ 6⁷ᵍᶠ 7⁷ᶠ 3⁷ᵍᶠ 2⁷ᵍ 3⁶ᵍᶠ 9⁵ᵍᶠ
0-4-8 £4,359

George The Best (Ire) *M D Hammond*   77
2 b g Imperial Ballet (Ire) - En Retard (Ire)
2⁵ᵍˢ 5⁵ᵍᶠ 3⁵ᵍᶠ 1⁵ᵍˢ 1⁶ᵍ 8⁵ᶠ 20⁶ᵍ 15⁶ᵍˢ
2-1-8 £13,223

Georgic Blaze *G A Ham*
9 b g Petoski - Pooka
PU¹⁴ᵍˢ **0-0-1**

Geri Roulette *E J Alston*   62 a54
5 b m Perpendicular - Clashfern
6¹⁴ˢᵈ 7¹²ˢᵈ 2¹²ˢʷ 2¹²ᵍᶠ 1¹²ᵍᶠ 3¹⁰ᵍ 1¹³ᵍˢ
6¹²ᵍˢ 6¹²ᵍᶠ 8¹⁴ˢ 15¹⁰ᵍ **2-3-11 £10,025**

Geronimo *Miss Gay Kelleway*   a71
6 b g Efisio - Apache Squaw
4⁶ˢᵈ 2⁶ˢᵈ 3⁶ˢᵈ 7⁵ˢᵈ 1⁶ˢʷ 7⁶ˢᵈ 8⁷ˢᵈ 11⁶ˢᵈ
5⁶ˢᵈ 3⁷ˢᵈ 4⁶ˢᵈ 2⁶ˢᵈ 5⁶ˢᵈ 6⁷ˢᵈ 6⁶ˢᵈ 11⁷ˢᵈ 6⁵ˢᵈ
1-4-17 £7,113

Get Stuck In (Ire) *Miss L A Perratt*   30
7 b g Up And At 'Em - Shoka (Fr)
18⁵ᵍ **0-0-1**

Get To The Point *P W D'Arcy*   73 a58
2 ch c Daggers Drawn - Penny Mint
5⁵ˢᵈ 4⁵ᶠ 7⁶ᵍᶠ 8⁶ᵍᶠ 7⁵ᵍˢ **0-0-5 £2,016**

Getatem (Ire) *Miss L A Perratt*   41
4 b g Up And At 'Em - Fiaba
14⁵ᵍᶠ 8⁶ᵍᶠ 9⁷ᵍˢ 18⁶ᵍᶠ 16⁶ᵍˢ 14⁵ᵍˢ 4⁶ᶠ
11⁵ᵍᶠ 5⁶ᵍᶠ 7⁶ᵍᶠ 9⁶ᵍᶠ 7⁶ᵍᶠ 12⁵ᶠ **0-0-13 £337**

Ghutah *Mrs A M Thorpe*   25
9 ch g Lycius (USA) - Barada (USA)
8¹⁹ᵍᶠ **0-0-1**

Gift Horse *J R Fanshawe*   82
3 ch g Cadeaux Genereux - Careful Dancer
2⁸ᵍᶠ 1⁸ᵍᶠ 6⁸ᵍᶠ **1-1-3 £6,892**

Gifted Flame *I Semple*   77

4 b g Revoque (Ire) - Littleladyleah (USA)
3⁸ᵍᶠ 15⁸ᵍᶠ 4⁸ᵍ 5¹⁰ᵍᶠ 2⁸ᵍᶠ 1⁸ᵍᶠ 6⁸ᵍᶠ 7⁷ᵍᶠ
4⁹ˢ 7⁹ᵍᶠ 10⁹ᵍᶠ 6⁸ᶠ **1-2-12 £10,218**

Gig Harbor *Miss E C Lavelle*   84 a94
4 b c Efisio - Petonica (Ire)
1¹²ˢᵈ 11²ˢᵈ 2¹⁰ˢᵈ 3¹²ˢᵈ 7¹⁰ˢᵈ 7¹⁰ᵍᶠ 12¹²ᵍ
15¹⁰ᵍˢ 34¹⁸ᵍᶠ 6¹⁰ᵍᶠ **2-2-10 £15,112**

Giko *Jane Southcombe*   48 a46
9 b g Arazi (USA) - Gayane
12¹⁴ᵍ 7¹²ˢᵈ 1¹²ᶠ 1¹²ᵍ 9¹²ᶠ 4¹²ᵍᶠ 1¹³ᵍᶠ
6¹²ᶠ 3¹²ᵍ 7¹²ᵍᶠ 2¹³ᶠ 9¹²ᵍ 12¹⁴ᵍᶠ **3-2-13 £8,343**

Gilded Cove *R Hollinshead*   a75
3 b c Polar Prince (Ire) - Cloudy Reef
4⁶ˢʷ 6⁵ˢᵈ 2⁵ˢᵈ 2⁶ˢᵈ 13⁶ˢᵈ 1⁵ˢᵈ 3⁵ˢᵈ 1⁵ˢᵈ
2⁵ˢᵈ 1⁵ˢᵈ 3⁶ˢᵈ 1⁶ˢᵈ **4-5-12 £16,494**

Gilded Dancer *W R Muir*   96
5 b g Bishop Of Cashel - La Piaf (Fr)
16⁸ᵍᶠ 22⁸ᵍ 1⁷ᵍᶠ 1⁸ᵍᶠ 1⁸ᵍ 1⁸ᵍˢ **4-0-6 £30,648**

Gilden Magic *P W Hiatt*   49 a58
5 b g Magic Ring (Ire) - Have Form
11⁹ˢᵈ 1⁸ˢʷ 2⁸ˢᵈ 11⁷ˢᵈ 8⁸ˢᵈ 11¹⁰ᶠ 4⁸ᵍᶠ
11⁸ˢᵈ BD⁸ᵍᶠ 10⁸ᵍᶠ 8⁸ᵍᶠ **1-1-11 £4,153**

Gilly's General (Ire) *J W Unett*   46 a53
3 ch g General Monash (USA) - Good Aim (Ire)
11⁷ᵍᶠ 9⁸ˢᵈ 2⁶ˢᵈ 7⁶ˢᵈ 5⁷ᵍᶠ 8⁷ᶠ **0-1-6 £884**

Gin 'N' Fonic (Ire) *H J Cyzer*   72 a67
3 ch g Zafonic (USA) - Crepe Ginger (Ire)
11¹⁰ᵍᶠ 5¹¹ᵍᶠ 6¹⁰ᵍᶠ 4¹²ᶠ 1¹²ˢᵈ 7¹¹ᵍ 14¹⁶ˢᵈ
1-0-7 £3,216

Gin Palace (Ire) *G L Moore*   92
5 gr g King's Theatre (Ire) - Ikala
3¹⁴ᵍᶠ **0-1-1 £862**

Ginger Ice *G G Margarson*   40
3 ch g Bahamian Bounty - Sharp Top
15¹⁰ᵍ 17⁸ᵍ 9⁷ᵍᶠ 13⁸ˢᵈ **0-0-4**

Ginger Jack *S P Griffiths*
3 ch g Case Law - Miss Realm
7⁵ᶠ F⁵ᵍ **0-0-2**

Gingko *P R Webber*   70 a77
6 b g Pursuit Of Love - Arboretum (Ire)
2¹²ˢᵈ 3¹¹ˢᵈ 11¹¹ˢʷ 9¹¹ˢᵈ 7¹⁰ᵍ 6¹⁰ᵍ 13¹⁰ᵍᶠ
7¹²ˢᵈ **1-2-8 £5,880**

Ginner Morris *J Hetherton*   22
8 b g Emarati (USA) - Just Run (Ire)
11⁹ˢᵈ 12⁸ᵍᶠ 10⁸ˢ **0-0-3**

Ginolin (Ire) *D Carroll*
2 b c Perugino (USA) - Nahlin
13⁶ˢ **0-0-1**

Giocomo (Ire) *P Monteith*   23
5 ch g Indian Ridge - Karri Valley (USA)
14¹³ᵍˢ **0-0-1**

Giocoso (USA) *B Palling*   93
3 b c Bahri (USA) - Wing My Chimes (USA)
2⁸ᵍᶠ 1⁸ᵍˢ 2⁹ᵍᶠ 7⁸ᵍ 6⁸ᵍ 20⁷ᵍ **1-2-6 £8,903**

Girl Friday *D Shaw*
5 ch m Ajraas (USA) - Miss Nonnie
16⁷ˢᵈ 9⁶ˢᵈ **0-0-2**

Girl Warrior (USA) *P F I Cole*   69
2 ch f Elusive Quality (USA) - Qhazeenah
3⁷ᵍˢ **0-1-1 £646**

Girls Night Out *J W Hills*   a11

2 b f Docksider (USA) - Beaucatcher (Ire)
11^8sd **0-0-1**

Gironde *Sir Michael Stoute* 53
2 b c Sadler's Wells (USA) - Sarah Georgina
5^8gs **0-0-1**

Giuliani *L M Cumani* 79
3 b c Sadler's Wells (USA) - Anka Germania
1^12gs 2^12g 5^12g **1-1-3 £6,949**

Giunchiglio *P J Makin* 76
4 ch g Millkom - Daffodil Fields
2^10gf 9^10gf 3^10f 6^8gf 5^8gf 6^12gf 8^11gf
12^8gf **0-1-8 £2,035**

Giust In Temp (Ire) *P W Hiatt* 47 a59
4 b c Polish Precedent (USA) - Blue Stricks
5^8sd 2^9sd 2^9sw 6^9sd 6^8sw 6^9sd 12^10gf
16^11gf 14^9gf 5^8f 10^8g 9^10gf **0-2-12 £1,768**

Give Back Calais (Ire) *P J Makin* 56 a13
5 b g Brief Truce (USA) - Nichodoula
13^10sd 18^7gf 7^7gf **0-0-3**

Give Him Credit (USA) *Mrs A Duffield* 77
3 b g Quiet American (USA) - Meniatarra (USA)
1^7gf 4^6hy 11^7f 7^7gf 4^7gf 7^6sf 11^7gf **1-0-7**
£4,714

Givemethemoonlight *L G Cottrell* 25 a62
4 ch f Woodborough (USA) - Rockin' Rosie
4^8sd 8^9sw 5^7sd 6^8sd 18^7gf **0-0-5**

Given A Chance *J G Given* 34
2 b g Defacto (USA) - Milly Molly Mango
10^6gs 11^7gf 6^7gf **0-0-3**

Giverand *Miss Jacqueline S Doyle* 39
4 b f Royal Applause - Petersford Girl (Ire)
8^8f 12^7g 3^6gf **0-1-3 £320**

Givimaninch *D R C Elsworth* 54
3 ch g Inchinor - Tea And Scandals (USA)
6^5f 4^6gf 6^6gf 11^6gf 7^5gf 9^6gf 10^6f **0-0-7**
£298

Gjovic *B J Meehan* 75
2 br c Singspiel (Ire) - Photo Call
3^7gf 4^7gf 2^8gf **0-1-3 £2,683**

Gladys Aylward *A Crook* 63 a38
3 b f Polar Falcon (USA) - Versami (USA)
11^7g 7^7f 3^8g 1^7gf 13^7gf 9^7g 13^8gs 4^7sd
1-1-8 £4,367

Glamorous Girl (Ire) *M P Tregoning* 83
3 b/br f Darshaan - Masharik (Ire)
2^8gf 2^10gf 1^8gf **1-2-3 £8,534**

Glanbehy (Ire) *J A Glover* a44
3 b f General Monash (USA) - Ron's Secret
10^6sd 12^7sd **0-0-2**

Glandore (Ire) *E J O'Neill* 52
4 ch f Persian Bold - Sheen Falls (Ire)
UR^12hy 8^10gf 9^12g **0-0-3**

Glanmire *N A Callaghan* 25
2 b c Inchinor - Bella Helena
4^6g 8^8gs 13^7gf **0-0-3 £362**

Glaramara *A Bailey* 89
2 b c Nicolotte - Digamist Girl (Ire)
9^6gf 1^6gf 3^7g **1-0-3 £18,683**

Glass Note (Ire) *S T Lewis* 9 a48
5 b m Spectrum (Ire) - Alice En Ballade
11^7sw 17^11gf 9^13f **0-0-3**

Glebe Garden *M L W Bell* 85
2 b f Soviet Star (USA) - Trounce
3^6gs 1^6g 8^6g **1-1-3 £5,501**

Glen Vale Walk (Ire) *Mrs G S Rees* 55
6 ch g Balla Cove - Winter Harvest
9^10gf 5^11gf 15^12g 4^11gf 7^10gs 4^10gf 4^11gf
0-2-7 £1,114

Glencairn Star *J S Goldie* 52
2 b c Selkirk (USA) - Bianca Nera
7^7g 5^7gs **0-0-2**

Glencoe Solas (Ire) *S Kirk* 76
3 ch f Night Shift (USA) - Boranwood (Ire)
1^6g 5^7gf 5^6gf 9^6g 1^6gf 3^6gf 4^5gf 2^5gf 6^5g
2^6gf 5^5s 6^6gf 11^6gf 12^6gf **2-3-14 £14,123**

Glencoyle (Ire) *A C Stewart* 82
3 b c In The Wings - Lucky State
3^10gf 5^12gf 3^10gf 8^11gf 1^12gf 4^16gf 5^12gf
1-2-7 £4,329

Glendale *C A Dwyer* 71
2 ch g Opening Verse (USA) - Kayartis
11^7gf 9^8gf 8^8gf 15^8gs **0-0-4**

Glenhurich (Ire) *J S Goldie* 56
6 b m Sri Pekan (USA) - Forli's Treat (USA)
3^9gf 6^8gs 3^7gf 7^6gf 3^8gf 2^8s 1^8gf 12^8gf
3^8gf 11^8f 8^10g 8^8gf **1-4-12 £9,671**

Glenrock *A Berry* 63 a52
6 ch g Muhtarram (USA) - Elkie Brooks
9^7sd 9^7gf 15^6gf 1^8gf 11^7gf 12^7gf **1-0-6**
£4,355

Glenshian (Ire) *R A Fahey* 20
2 ch g Ali-Royal (Ire) - Goodnight Girl (Ire)
11^6g 10^7gf **0-0-2**

Glenviews Polly (Ire) *Ian Emmerson* 41 a39
3 b f Poliglote - Fun Board (Fr)
15^7sd 8^6sd 14^7f 6^8sd 13^6gf 10^7gf **0-0-6**

Glenviews Purchase (Ire) *Miss I T Oakes* 72
3 b f Desert Story (Ire) - Whitethroat
10^6hy 9^6gf 4^8f 7^8gs 6^7g 7^11f 3^10g 9^12gf
9^9gf 19^10g **0-1-10 £1,761**

Glide *R Charlton* 61
2 ch g In The Wings - Ash Glade
7^8gf 4^8g 5^8gf **0-0-3 £318**

Gliding By *P R Chamings* a28
2 ch f Halling (USA) - Waft (USA)
8^8sd **0-0-1**

Glimmer Of Light (Ire) *P W Harris* 77
3 b g Marju (Ire) - Church Light
4^8gf 1^8gf 5^9gf 14^10g **1-0-4 £6,047**

Glimpse Of Glory *C W Thornton* 28
3 b g Makbul - Bright-One
11^7gs 10^8gf 12^7gf 10^14f 9^11g **0-0-5**

Glistening Silver *J Gallagher* 62
3 b f Puissance - Silver Blessings
1^7gf 14^6g 20^7gf 15^8sd 14^7f **1-0-5**
£3,402

Glitter And Glory *C A Cyzer* a62
4 b g Classic Cliche (Ire) - Veuve
3^16sd 3^12sd 13^16sd 7^14sd 8^10sd 4^12sd 2^15sd
5^15sd **0-3-8 £1,895**

Gloaming *J Gallagher* 56 a44
5 b m Celtic Swing - Kandavu
4^8sd 9^8sd 16^6g 18^11gf 11^7gf 7^6g 12^6gs
12^6gf **0-0-8**

Global Challenge (Ire) *Sir Michael Stoute* 101
4 b g Sadler's Wells (USA) - Middle Prospect (USA)
1^12g 13^12g 10^15g **1-0-3 £9,178**

Glory Ayr *B Ellison*
4 b f Cool Jazz - Sea-Ayr (Ire)

9^{5sd} **0-0-1**

Glory Girl *M Brittain* 44 a21
3 ch f Factual (USA) - Glory Gold
6^{6ft} 3^{5gs} 8^{5g} **0-1-3 £435**

Glory Quest (USA) *Miss Gay Kelleway* 77 a81
6 b g Quest For Fame - Sonseri
3^{14sd} 1^{12sd} 5^{12sd} 3^{11sw} 2^{12sw} 3^{12sw} 4^{16sw}
2^{12ts} 1^{12sd} 9^{14gs} 6^{13gs} 5^{12s} 4^{12sd} **2-5-13**
£13,945

Go Bananas *B J Meehan* 87
2 b g Primo Dominie - Amsicora
3^{5g} 6^{5g} 1^{6gf} 3^{7gf} 5^{6gf} 1^{7g} 6^{7f} **2-1-7**
£14,369

Go Between *E A L Dunlop* 81
2 b f Daggers Drawn (USA) - Pizzicato
5^{6gf} 4^{6gs} 3^{5gf} 2^{7gf} 1^{6gf} 8^{6gf} **1-2-6**
£7,146

Go Classic *J Cullinan* 69
3 b f Classic Cliche (Ire) - Edraianthus
11^{10g} 7^{10gf} 4^{10gf} 13^{12g} **0-0-4 £440**

Go For Success (USA) *E A L Dunlop* 78
3 b g Royal Academy (USA) - Barad
5^{7g} 6^{10gf} 2^{8gs} 3^{10gf} 7^{10gf} 2^{10f} **0-3-6**
£3,788

Go Free *J Cullinan* 25 a53
2 b g Easycall - Miss Traxdata
10^{6sd} 8^{8g} **0-0-2**

Go Go Girl *L G Cottrell* 69
3 ch f Pivotal - Addicted To Love
6^{5g} 5^{5gf} 6^{6gf} 5^{5gf} 3^{5gf} 3^{6g} **0-2-6 £852**

Go In Gently *P C Ritchens* 46
2 b f Piccolo - Careful (Ire)
9^{5gf} 8^{7f} **0-0-2**

Go Padero (Ire) *M Johnston* 79
2 ch c Night Shift (USA) - Watch The Clock
6^{7gf} 5^{7gf} 1^{7gs} **1-0-3 £3,262**

Go Polar *J Cullinan* 87
3 b f Polar Falcon (USA) - Twilight Patrol
9^{6gf} 2^{6g} 1^{5gf} 9^{5gf} 5^{5g} 6^{6gf} 4^{6g} **1-1-7**
£8,267

Go Sheek (Ire) *J J Quinn* 50
3 b f Kahyasi - Terrama Sioux
9^{8sd} 4^{10gf} 5^{12f} 8^{14gf} 2^{12gf} 5^{12f} 6^{16gf}
7^{11gf} **0-1-8 £1,340**

Go Solo *B W Hills* 78
2 b c Primo Dominie - Taza
10^{6gf} 2^{6gf} 1^{7gf} 5^{8g} 1^{7g} 6^{8gf} **2-1-6**
£14,139

Go Tech *T D Easterby* 91
3 b g Gothenberg (Ire) - Bollin Sophie
5^{9g} 14^{7gf} 8^{8gf} 7^{8hy} 5^{10gf} **0-0-5 £1,040**

Go Thunder (Ire) *D A Nolan* 10
9 b g Nordico (USA) - Moving Off
4^{9gf} **0-0-1 £433**

Go To Shul *M W Easterby*
4 b g Runnett - Kopjes
12^{12sd} **0-0-1**

Go Yellow *P D Evans* 70
2 b g Overbury (Ire) - Great Lyth Lass (Ire)
7^{7f} 6^{7gf} 2^{6gf} 6^{7gf} **0-1-4 £1,078**

Goblet Of Fire (USA) *P F Nicholls* 108 a107
4 b g Green Desert (USA) - Laurentine (USA)
3^{10sd} 2^{10gf} 2^{10gf} 9^{10f} 9^{8gf} 5^{10g} 6^{10g}
11^{9gf} **0-3-8 £20,753**

Goblin *R Hannon* 75

Gojo (Ire) *B Palling* 72
2 b f Danetime (Ire) - Pretonic
7^{6g} 6^{6gf} 7^{6gs} **0-0-3**

Golano *C F Wall* 84 a81
3 gr g Linamix (Fr) - Dimakya (USA)
3^{10sd} 3^{12g} 3^{11g} 4^{11gs} 3^{11s} 1^{10sd} 1^{12sd}
2-3-7 £9,601

Gold Bar (Ire) *M P Tregoning* 77
3 b f Barathea (Ire) - Sun Princess
8^{10g} 7^{10gf} 3^{10gs} 4^{12gf} 2^{10gf} 4^{11g} 2^{10gf}
0-3-7 £4,292

Gold Bond (Ire) *P Mitchell* a45
4 b g Goldmark (USA) - Mujadil Princess (Ire)
10^{7sd} **0-0-1**

Gold Card *J R Weymes* 68
2 b c First Trump - Fleuve D'Or (Ire)
6^{7g} 3^{8gf} 4^{8gf} **0-1-3 £1,091**

Gold Dust Woman *J Balding* 54
2 b f Hector Protector (USA) - Hannalou (Fr)
7^{5gf} 13^{6gs} 5^{6g} 12^{7g} 8^{7gf} 6^{7sd} **0-0-6**

Gold Fervour (Ire) *W M Brisbourne* 45
4 b g Mon Tresor - Fervent Fan (Ire)
13^{8gf} 5^{6gf} 10^{7gf} 9^{6gf} 5^{6f} **0-0-5**

Gold Guest *P D Evans* 70 a85
4 ch g Vettori (Ire) - Cassilis (Ire)
11^{7sd} 13^{6sw} 6^{8sd} 1^{9gf} 3^{9gf} 5^{7gf} 13^{8gf}
10^{8sd} 4^{7g} 6^{8gf} 15^{8gf} 7^{8g} **1-1-12 £5,075**

Gold History (USA) *M Johnston* 92
2 b c Seeking The Gold (USA) - Battle Hymn (USA)
1^{7f} 1^{7g} 7^{7gf} **2-0-3 £10,486**

Gold Mask (USA) *J H M Gosden* 68
2 b/br c Seeking The Gold (USA) - Leo's Gypsy Dancer (USA)
7^{6gf} **0-0-1**

Gold Medallist *D R C Elsworth* 108
3 ch g Zilzal (USA) - Spot Prize (USA)
2^{10gf} 2^{11gf} 1^{12gs} 8^{11g} 1^{12gf} 5^{16f} 1^{15gf}
6^{12g} 8^{15g} 3^{14gf} **3-2-10 £38,052**

Gold Millenium (Ire) *C A Horgan* a48
9 gr g Kenmare (Fr) - Gold Necklace
6^{16sd} **0-0-1**

Gold Ring *G B Balding* 97
3 ch g Groom Dancer (USA) - Indubitable
5^{9g} 3^{10gs} 7^{11g} 3^{12gs} 7^{12gf} 6^{12g} 2^{12gs} 2^{13gf}
4^{12gf} 1^{12g} 3^{12g} **1-5-11 £15,981**

Gold Riviera (USA) *M C Pipe*
3 ch c Irish River (Fr) - Raj Dancer (USA)
10^{10gf} 13^{7gf} 15^{8gf} **0-0-3**

Goldbricker *C A Cyzer* 64 a13
3 b g Muhtarram (USA) - Sally Slade
11^{8sd} 10^{9sw} 5^{10gf} 3^{10f} 3^{10gf} 11^{16gf}
2^{11gf} **0-2-8 £1,553**

Golden Aruba *B Ellison*
4 ch g Golden Lahab (USA) - Clover Girl
19^{10gf} 8^{6f} **0-0-2**

Golden Biff (Ire) *J J Matthias* a26
7 ch g Shalford (Ire) - Capable Kate (Ire)
5^{6sd} 12^{8sd} **0-0-2**

Golden Boot *A Bailey* 81 a29
4 ch g Unfuwain (USA) - Sports Delight
6^{11sw} 7^{8gf} 5^{10f} 5^{12gf} 3^{8gs} 13^{12g} 2^{11gs}
2^{13f} 11^{14gs} 6^{16gf} 7^{13gf} 8^{12gf} 2^{12gf} 3^{12gf} 4^{13g}
3^{16g} **0-6-16 £7,567**

Golden Bounty *R Hannon* — 97
4 b c Bahamian Bounty - Cumbrian Melody
10^{5gf} 6^{6gf} 7^{5gf} 18^{5gf} 2^{5gf} 10^{5g} 5^{6gf} 9^{5g} 10^{5gs} 15^{6gf} **0-1-10 £3,767**

Golden Brief (Ire) *K R Burke* — 73 a92
5 ch g Brief Truce (USA) - Tiffany's Case (Ire)
1^{7sd} 15^{7sd} 3^{7sd} 2^{7sd} 4^{7sd} 1^{7f} 3^{7gf} 3^{7gf} 13^{7f} 14^{7f} 11^{7f} PU^{7gf} **2-4-13 £13,354**

Golden Chalice (Ire) *A M Balding* — 100
4 ch g Selkirk (USA) - Special Oasis
3^{8gf} 7^{7g} 16^{8gf} 7^{8g} 5^{8gs} 2^{7g} **0-2-6 £6,067**

Golden Chance (Ire) *M W Easterby* — 53
6 b g Unfuwain (USA) - Golden Digger (USA)
11^{8gf} 3^{11gf} 3^{10gf} 11^{12g} 2^{14f} 4^{16gf} 2^{17gf} **0-4-7 £3,746**

Golden Dixie (USA) *A M Balding* — 94
4 ch g Dixieland Band (USA) - Beyrouth (USA)
9^{6g} 2^{6gf} 4^{6g} 17^{6g} 12^{6g} 14^{7gf} 7^{7gf} **0-1-7 £4,052**

Golden Dual *B W Hills* — 69 a72
3 b c Danehill (USA) - Golden Digger (USA)
4^{7sd} 3^{10gf} 7^{10g} 4^{10f} 3^{12gf} 6^{8gf} **0-1-6 £2,302**

Golden Empire (USA) *E A L Dunlop* — 69
2 br c Red Ransom (USA) - Golden Gorse (USA)
3^{6gf} 2^{7gf} **0-1-2 £1,608**

Golden Fact (USA) *B A McMahon* — 60 a39
9 b g Known Fact (USA) - Cosmic Sea Queen (USA)
8^{12sd} 9^{8sd} 1^{8gf} **1-0-3 £3,601**

Golden Fields (Ire) *A P Jones* — 55 a47
3 b f Definite Article - Quickstep Queen (Fr)
11^{8sd} 10^{10sd} 4^{10gf} 14^{12g} 4^{11gs} 9^{12sd} 1^{11gf} 15^{12gf} 14^{12f} 2^{14s} **1-1-10 £4,024**

Golden Goose *N A Callaghan* — 29
2 ch c Pivotal - Desert Ditty
10^{6gs} 10^{7g} **0-0-2**

Golden Grace *E A L Dunlop* — 87
2 b c Green Desert (USA) - Chief Bee
6^{8gf} 3^{7gf} 1^{7gs} **1-1-3 £4,797**

Golden Heart *D R C Elsworth* — 78
3 ch f Salse (USA) - Lonely Heart
5^{8gf} 1^{7gf} 5^{8f} 7^{9gf} 11^{7gf} 2^{11gf} 9^{8gs} **1-1-7 £6,598**

Golden Island (Ire) *J W Hills* — 52
2 ch f Selkirk (USA) - Daftiyna (Ire)
10^{7gs} **0-0-1**

Golden Lariat (USA) *Sir Michael Stoute* — 93
4 ch c Mr Prospector (USA) - Larrocha (Ire)
9^{12g} 14^{12gf} 1^{12gf} 8^{12gf} 5^{12gf} 11^{12gf} **1-0-6 £10,645**

Golden Nun *T D Easterby* — 103 a87
3 b f Bishop Of Cashel - Amber Mill
9^{7sd} 2^{6gf} 4^{6gs} 5^{6hy} 6^{6gf} 9^{6gs} 2^{6gf} 8^{6gf} 10^{6g} 2^{6g} 3^{6gy} 10^{6ho} 5^{6g} **0-4-14 £28,539**

Golden Quest *M Johnston* — 54
2 ch c Rainbow Quest (USA) - Souk (Ire)
8^{8gf} **0-0-1**

Golden Remedy *D W Barker* — 58
2 b f Dr Fong (USA) - Golden Daring (Ire)
7^{5gf} 3^{5gf} 3^{6g} 15^{6s} 20^{6gf} 6^{7gf} **0-0-6 £1,346**

Golden Sahara (Ire) *Saeed Bin Suroor* — 94
2 b c Green Desert (USA) - Golden Digger (USA)
1^{6gf} 2^{6g} 2^{7gf} **1-1-3 £9,924**

Golden Silca *M R Channon* — 98
7 ch m Inchinor - Silca-Cisa
3^{9gs} 5^{10gf} **0-1-2 £4,395**

Golden Skiis (Ire) *J L Dunlop* — 71
3 ch f Hector Protector (USA) - Ski For Gold
17^{10g} 4^{11f} 2^{16gf} 2^{14f} **0-1-4 £2,657**

Golden Spectrum (Ire) *R Hannon* — 69 a66
4 ch g Spectrum (Ire) - Plessaya (USA)
9^{8sd} 8^{6g} 11^{8f} 16^{7g} 14^{8gf} 12^{10gf} **0-0-6**

Golden Wells (Ire) *M Johnston* — 103
5 b g Sadler's Wells (USA) - Golden Bloom
6^{12g} **0-0-1 £750**

Goldeva *R Hollinshead* — 98
4 gr f Makbul - Gold Belt (Ire)
8^{6g} 5^{7gf} 8^{6gs} 9^{6gf} 6^{6gf} 5^{6gf} 6^{6g} 2^{6gf} 11^{6g} **0-1-9 £11,620**

Golfagent *Miss K Marks* — a6
5 b g Kris - Alusha
7^{15sd} **0-0-1**

Golly Gosh (Ire) *M Halford* — 99
4 b f Danehill (USA) - Miss Declared (USA)
1^{12gf} 4^{12gy} 10^{12f} 14^{12g} 6^{14g} 5^{12gf} 2^{14gf} 8^{16gs} 6^{12gf} **1-1-9 £19,191**

Gondolin (Ire) *G A Butler* — 91 a54
3 b g Marju (Ire) - Galletina (Ire)
6^{7sd} 1^{10g} 2^{11hy} 20^{12gf} 3^{12hd} 4^{10gf} 5^{10gf} **1-0-7 £9,074**

Gone Loco *H S Howe* — 46
2 b f Piccolo - Missed Again
8^{8gf} 6^{5gf} 18^{6gf} **0-0-3**

Gone To Ground *R E Barr* — 55 a37
2 ch g Foxhound (USA) - Charlie Girl
4^{5gf} 6^{5gf} 3^{6f} 7^{6gf} 3^{6gs} 3^{5sd} 6^{6gf} 1^{7f} 7^{6f} 13^{7gf} **1-3-10 £4,835**

Gone Too Far *M C Pipe* — 53
5 b g Reprimand - Blue Nile (Ire)
4^{14gf} 7^{16gf} 3^{16gs} 3^{16g} **0-2-4 £1,548**

Gone'N'Dunnett (Ire) *Mrs C A Dunnett* — 69 a79
4 b g Petardia - Skerries Bell
5^{6sd} 5^{5sd} 15^{6sd} 11^{6sd} 19^{5gf} 3^{6f} 15^{5gf} 12^{5gf} 7^{6sf} 5^{6gf} 8^{5gf} 2^{5gf} 2^{5f} 11^{6gf} 11^{6sd} 4^{6sd} **0-3-16 £3,276**

Gonfilia (Ger) *Saeed Bin Suroor* — 104
3 b f Big Shuffle (USA) - Gonfalon
2^{8ft} 12^{8gf} 2^{7g} 2^{8gs} 5^{7g} 1^{7g} **1-3-6 £34,165**

Good Article (Ire) *A P Jones* — 37
2 b c Definite Article - Good News (Ire)
11^{8gf} 16^{8gf} **0-0-2**

Good Form (Ire) *Miss K M George* — 49 a49
3 b g Danetime (Ire) - Faapette
9^{8sd} 9^{7sd} 2^{7s} 6^{9sd} 6^{8gf} 5^{8gs} 11^{5f} 3^{8f} 18^{8s} 11^{7gf} 13^{8f} **0-2-11 £1,495**

Good Girl (Ire) *T D Easterby* — 95
4 b f College Chapel - Indian Honey
8^{6s} 14^{5gf} 8^{6g} 15^{6f} 5^{6gs} 10^{6g} 17^{5gf} 8^{5s} 8^{5gs} 10^{5s} 15^{5gf} **1-0-11 £9,509**

Good Health *W J Haggas* — 73 a49
3 b f Magic Ring (Ire) - Fiddling
9^{5f} 6^{6gf} 5^{5gs} 8^{5s} 11^{6sd} **0-0-5**

Good Loser (Ire) *C R Dore* — 68
3 b g Mujadil (USA) - Cockney Star (Ire)
7^{7sw} 12^{8g} 4^{10gf} 4^{12f} 10^{12gf} 2^{10gf} 8^{12gs} 2^{10g} 4^{12gf} 4^{14f} **0-2-10 £2,683**

Good Penny (Ire) *T P Tate* — 76

2 b g Pennekamp (USA) - The Good Life (Ire)
2⁵ᵍᶠ 2⁶ᵍˢ **0-2-2 £3,268**

Good Shot *M W Easterby*
2 b f Mind Games - Penny Hasset
12⁶ˢ 8⁶ᵍᶠ **0-0-2**

Good Timing *J Hetherton*
5 bl g Timeless Times (USA) - Fort Vally
10⁸ˢᵈ **0-0-1**

Good To Go *P C Haslam*   69
2 ch g Deploy - Lets Fall In Love (USA)
11⁵ᵍᶠ 2⁶ᵍᶠ 9⁷ᵍ 4⁷ᵍᶠ 18ᵍᶠ 8⁸ᵍᶠ **1-1-6**
£5,430

Good Vibrations *P F I Cole*   28 a27
2 b f Bijou D'Inde - Showcase
7⁵ˢᵈ 7⁷ᶠᵗ 13⁶ᵍᶠ **0-0-3**

Goodbye Goldstone *B Ellison*   40
7 b g Mtoto - Shareehan
12¹²ᶠ 15¹²ᵍᶠ 8¹²ᵍ 16¹⁰ᵍ **0-0-4**

Goodbye Mr Bond *E J Alston*   65 a65
3 b g Elmaamul - Fifth Emerald
1⁹ᵍˢ 16¹⁰ᵍᶠ 8¹⁰ᵍᶠ 5⁸ᵍᶠ 3⁸ˢᵈ 4⁹ˢᵈ **1-1-6**
£4,498

Goodenough Mover *J S King*   83
7 ch g Beveled (USA) - Rekindled Flame (Ire)
16⁷ᵍᶠ 8⁷ᵍᶠ 6⁷ᵍᶠ 7⁷ᵍᶠ 3⁶ᵍᶠ 11⁷ᵍᶠ 7⁶ᵍᶠ 9⁶ᵍᶠ
0-1-8 £600

Goodenough Star *J S King*   38
3 b f Stronz (Ire) - Goodenough Girl
8⁷ᵍ 6⁸ᶠ 10⁷ᵍᶠ 15⁶ᶠ **0-0-4**

Goodly News (Ire) *A W Carroll*   22
7 b g Project Manager - Nordic Relation (Ire)
13¹¹ᵍᶠ **0-0-1**

Goodness Gracious (Ire) *J L Dunlop*   95
3 b f Green Desert (USA) - Trois Graces (USA)
4⁷ᵍᶠ 7¹⁰ᵍᶠ 8⁹ᵍ 9⁸ᶠ **0-0-4 £2,500**

Goodwood Finesse (Ire) *J L Dunlop*   63
2 b f Revoque (Ire) - Key To Paris (Arg)
5⁸ᵍᶠ 5⁸ᵍᶠ **0-0-2**

Goodwood Prince *J L Dunlop*   85
3 b g Emperor Jones (USA) - Scarlet Lake
7⁷ᵍᶠ 17⁶ᵍᶠ 5⁷ᵍᶠ 14⁶ᵍᶠ 2⁶ᵍᶠ 2⁶ᵍᶠ 2⁷ᵍ 7⁶ᶠ
8⁶ᵍᶠ 9⁷ᵍ 6⁷ᵍᶠ 9⁸ᵍᶠ **0-3-12 £5,176**

Goodwood Promise *N E Berry*   35 a22
4 b g Primo Dominie - Noble Destiny
13⁷ᵍˢ 16⁶ᶠ 11⁵ˢʷ 7⁶ᵍᶠ 7⁶ᵍ **0-0-5**

Gordons Friend *B S Rothwell*   35
5 ch g Clantime - Auntie Fay (Ire)
16⁸ᵍ 10⁷ᵍᶠ 13⁸ᶠ **0-0-3**

Gordy's Joy *G A Ham*   41
3 b f Cloudings (Ire) - Beatle Song
11¹⁰ᵍᶠ 5¹⁰ᵍᶠ 4¹²ᵍᶠ **0-0-3**

Got One Too (Fr) *N J Henderson*   78
6 ch g Green Tune (USA) - Gloria Mundi (Fr)
1¹⁴ᵍᶠ 1¹⁴ᵍᶠ 3¹⁶ᵍᶠ **2-1-3 £9,987**

Got To Be Cash *W M Brisbourne*   59
4 ch f Lake Coniston (Ire) - Rasayel (USA)
3¹²ᵍᶠ 10¹²ᵍ 7¹³ᵍ 5¹²ᵍ 9¹²ᵍᶠ 2¹⁰ᵍᶠ 5¹⁰ᵍᶠ
6¹¹ᵍᶠ 10¹¹ᵍᶠ 2¹⁰ᵍᶠ 6¹²ᶠ 11¹⁰ᵍᶠ **0-3-12 £2,601**

Gotarapofahames (Ire) *N F Glynn*   88 a73
5 b Midhish - Quench The Lamp (Ire)
11⁶ˢᵈ 5⁷ᵍᶠ 9⁶ʸˢ 7⁵ᵍ 13⁶ᵍ 7⁵ᵍ 12⁵ᵍ
16⁸ᵍʸ 10⁶ˢ **0-0-9**

Gothic Bay *M W Easterby*
3 b g Gothenberg (Ire) - Greyhill Lady
14⁸ᵍᶠ **0-0-1**

Gotya *T D Easterby*   5
3 b f Gothenberg (Ire) - Water Well
6⁸ᵍᶠ **0-0-1**

Grace Bankes *W G M Turner*   37 a43
2 ch f Efisio - Amaranthus
6⁵ˢᵈ 4⁵ᵍᶠ 17⁶ˢ **0-0-3**

Grace Darling *Miss E C Lavelle*
2 b f Botanic (USA) - Light On The Waves
7⁷ˢᵈ **0-0-1**

Graceful Air (Ire) *J R Weymes*   61
2 b f Danzero (Aus) - Samsung Spirit
3⁵ᵍ 4⁵ᵍᶠ 2⁶ᵍ 5⁶ᵍ 8⁷ᵍˢ 3⁶ᶠ 12⁷ᶠ 3⁷ᵍᶠ
0-3-9 £5,402

Gracefully (Ire) *S Kirk*   97
2 b f Orpen (USA) - Lady Taufan (Ire)
1⁶ᵍᶠ 1⁶ᶠ 1⁷ᵍᶠ 4⁷ᵍᶠ **3-0-4 £34,516**

Gracia *S C Williams*   76
4 gr f Linamix (Fr) - Francia
3¹⁰ᵍᶠ 5⁹ᵍˢ 8¹⁰ᵍᶠ 3¹²ʰʸ 3⁸ᵍᶠ 3⁸ᵍ 7⁸ᵍᶠ 1⁹ᵍᶠ
12¹⁰ᵍˢ 13⁸ᵍᶠ 3⁸ᵍ **1-4-11 £12,634**

Gracious Air (USA) *J R Weymes*   47
5 b m Bahri (USA) - Simply Bell (USA)
11¹²ᵍᶠ 16¹⁰ᵍᶠ 8⁸ᵍᶠ 9¹⁰ᵍᶠ 6¹⁰ᵍᶠ **0-0-5**

Gracious Dancer *J A Osborne*   20 a74
3 b g Mark Of Esteem (Ire) - Gracious Beauty (USA)
6⁸ˢᵈ 2⁹ˢᵈ 3⁸ᵈ 14⁹ᵍᶠ 12¹⁰ᵍᶠ **1-1-5**
£4,437

Graduation Day *P W Harris*   64 a63
3 b f College Chapel - Golden Ciel (USA)
8⁷ᵍᶠ 3⁷ᵍ 9⁷ᵍ 16⁸ᵍᶠ 6⁷ˢʷ 8⁸ᵍ 9⁷ᵍ 8⁷ᵍᶠ 5⁸ᶠ
10⁸ˢᵈ **0-1-10 £587**

Grady *Miss Jacqueline S Doyle*   43
4 ch g Bluegrass Prince (Ire) - Lady Sabina
10¹²ᵍᶠ 12¹²ᵍᶠ 13¹¹ᵍᶠ 6¹⁰ᵍ 8¹²ᵍᶠ 8¹⁰ᵍᶠ
0-0-6

Graffiti Girl (Ire) *D Haydn Jones*   37 a30
4 b f Sadler's Wells (USA) - Maharani (USA)
6¹²ˢᵈ 11¹¹ˢᵈ 17¹²ᵍᶠ 8¹⁰ᵍᶠ **0-0-4**

Graft *M W Easterby*   77
4 b g Entrepreneur - Mariakova (USA)
9¹⁰ᶠ 16⁸ᵍ 13¹⁰ˢ 4¹²ᶠ 12¹⁰ᵍᶠ 16¹⁰ᵍᶠ
14¹⁰ᵍˢ **0-0-7 £416**

Graham Island *G Wragg*   66
2 b c Acatenango (Ger) - Gryada
12⁷ᵍᶠ 5⁷ᵍᶠ **0-0-2**

Graikos *Saeed Bin Suroor*   106
3 b c Rainbow Quest (USA) - Grecian Slipper
5¹⁰ᵍᶠ 8¹²ᵍ **0-0-2 £3,625**

Gralmano (Ire) *K A Ryan*   90 a87
8 b g Scenic - Llangollen (Ire)
8¹⁰ˢᵈ 3¹⁶ˢᵈ 3¹⁸ᵍ 1¹⁶ᶠ 8¹⁶ᵍᶠ 3¹⁵ᵍᶠ 1¹⁶ᵍᶠ
13¹⁵ᵍ 2¹⁵ᵍᶠ **2-3-9 £29,200**

Gran Clicquot *G P Enright*   53
8 gr m Gran Alba (USA) - Tina's Beauty
14⁸ᵍᶠ 1¹⁰ᵍᶠ 4¹⁰ᵍᶠ 4¹⁰ᶠ 5¹¹ᵍᶠ 9¹¹ᵍᶠ 8¹⁰ᶠ
1-0-7 £2,982

Granato (Ger) *A C Stewart*   78
2 b c Cadeaux Genereux - Genevra (Ire)
2⁶ᵍᶠ 2⁶ᵍᶠ 1⁶ᵍᶠ **1-2-3 £7,351**

Grand Apollo *J H M Gosden*   65
2 ch f Grand Lodge (USA) - Narva
6⁷ᵍᶠ **0-0-1**

Grand Cross *W Jarvis*   64
3 ch c Zafonic (USA) - La Papagena
6⁸ᵍᶠ 11⁸ᵍᶠ 8⁸ᵍᶠ 13¹⁰ᶠ **0-0-4**

Grand Folly (Fr) *J Cullinan* 73
3 ch f Grand Lodge (USA) - Folmanie (USA)
5⁸ᵍᵗ 2⁹ᵍᵗ 12¹⁰ᵍᵗ 7¹²ᵍ 3¹⁰ᵍ 10¹⁰ᵍᵗ **0-1-6**
£2,146

Grand Gift *M A Jarvis* 58
3 br f Grand Lodge (USA) - Black Velvet Band
9⁸ˢ 7¹⁰ᵍᵗ 15¹⁰ᵍ 10¹⁰ᵍᵗ **0-0-4**

Grand Halo (Ire) *J J Sheehan* 59 a60
3 b g Grand Lodge (USA) - Band Of Angels (Ire)
9⁷ˢᵈ 10¹⁰ᵍᵗ 7⁸ˢᵈ 2¹¹ᵍᵗ 13¹⁰ᵍᵗ 4¹²ᵍᵗ 2¹¹ˢʷ
5¹²ˢᵈ **0-2-8 £2,050**

Grand Lass (Ire) *T D Barron* 51
4 b f Grand Lodge (USA) - Siskin (Ire)
12¹⁰ᵍᵗ 2¹¹ᵍᵗ 6¹²ᵍ 4¹²ᵍˢ 7¹²ᵍ 19¹²ᵍᵗ 2¹²ᵍˢ
9¹²ᵍ 4¹¹ᵍ **0-2-9 £2,043**

Grand Passion (Ire) *G Wragg* 110
3 b g Grand Lodge (USA) - Lovers' Parlour
3⁷ᵍᵗ 1⁸ᵍᵗ 8¹⁰ᵍᵗ 4⁸ᵍᵗ 1⁸ᵍᵗ 2⁸ᵍˢ 8⁹ᵍᵗ 3⁸ᵍˢ
2-4-8 £40,850

Grand Prairie (Swe) *R C Guest* 59
7 b g Prairie - Platonica (Ity)
12¹²ᵍᵗ 17¹²ᵍ **0-0-2**

Grand Prompt *B R Johnson* 59 a33
4 ch g Grand Lodge (USA) - Prompting
12¹⁶ˢᵈ 12¹²ᵍ 9¹²ˢᵈ **0-0-3**

Grand Reward (USA) *A P O'Brien* 112
2 b c Storm Cat (USA) - Serena's Song (USA)
1⁶ᵍ 3⁶ᵍᵗ 2⁶ᵍᵗ 6⁶ᵍᵗ **1-2-4 £36,832**

Grand Rich King (Ire) *B J Meehan* 91
2 b c Grand Lodge (USA) - Richly Deserved (Ire)
6⁵ᵍᵗ 2⁶ᵍˢ 1⁷ᵍᵗ 7⁷ᵍᵗ 2⁷ᵍᵗ 3⁸ˢ **1-2-6**
£9,290

Grand View *T D Barron* 43
7 ch g Grand Lodge (USA) - Hemline
5⁵ᵍᵗ 10⁵ᵍ 5⁵ᵍ 16⁵ᵍᵗ 8⁶ᵍᵗ 9⁵ᵗ 16⁶ᵗ **0-0-7**

Grand Wizard *W Jarvis* 47 a53
3 b c Grand Lodge (USA) - Shouk
10¹⁰ᵍ 7¹²ˢᵈ **0-0-2**

Grandalea *Sir Michael Stoute* 72 a82
2 b f Grand Lodge (USA) - Red Azalea
7⁷ᵍᵗ 2⁷ˢᵈ 3⁸ᵍᵗ 6⁷ˢᵈ **0-2-4 £1,541**

Grande Terre (Ire) *J G Given* 68
2 b f Grand Lodge (USA) - Savage (Ire)
9⁷ᵍᵗ 7⁷ᵍᵗ 16⁷ᵍᵗ **0-0-3**

Grandera (Ire) *Saeed Bin Suroor* 115 a120
5 ch h Grand Lodge (USA) - Bordighera (USA)
1¹⁰ᶠᵗ 4¹⁰ᵗ 7¹⁰ᵍᵗ 8¹⁰ᵍᵗ 11¹²ᵍ **1-0-5**
£223,154

Grandissimo (Ire) *N P Littmoden*
2 b c Grand Lodge (USA) - Tuscaloosa
8⁸ᵍᵗ **0-0-1**

Grandma Lily (Ire) *M C Chapman* 81 a73
5 b m Bigstone (Ire) - Mrs Fisher (Ire)
10⁶ˢᵈ 3⁵ˢᵈ 4⁶ˢʷ 16ᵍᵗ 12⁶ᵍ 1⁵ᵍˢ 4⁵ᵍᵗ 8⁵ᵍᵗ
8⁵ᵗ 10⁵ᵍᵗ 10⁵ᵗ 13⁶ᵍᵗ 8⁶ᵗ **2-1-13 £11,138**

Granny's Pet *P F I Cole* 110 a97
9 ch g Selkirk (USA) - Patsy Western
3⁷ˢᵈ 12⁷ˢᵈ 2⁷ᵍᵗ 5⁷ˢ **0-1-4 £6,868**

Granston (Ire) *J D Bethell* 71
2 gr c Revoque (Ire) - Gracious Gretclo
4⁵ᵍᵗ 3⁵ᵍᵗ 2⁵ᵍᵗ 7⁶ᵍ 5⁶ᵍᵗ 5⁶ᵍᵗ 4⁷ᵍᵗ 8⁷ᵍ
1⁷ᵍᵗ **1-2-9 £6,061**

Granuaile O'Malley (Ire) *P W D'Arcy* 53 a44
3 b f Mark Of Esteem (Ire) - Dame Laura (Ire)

7⁶ˢᵈ 10⁷ᵍᵗ 6⁸ᵍᵗ 12⁵ᵍᵗ 19⁷ᵍᵗ 3⁶ᵍᵗ **0-1-6**
£473

Grasslandik *Miss A Stokell* 58 a33
7 b g Ardkinglass - Sophisticated Baby
14⁵ˢᵈ 6⁵ˢʷ 5⁵ˢᵈ 5⁵ᵍᵗ 9⁵ᵍᵗ 9⁵ᵍᵗ 7⁵ᵍᵗ 10⁵ᵍᵗ
15⁵ᵍ 7⁵ᵍᵗ 6⁵ᵗ 7⁵ᵍᵗ 5⁵ᵍᵗ 14⁵ᵍᵗ 7⁵ᵗ 6⁶ᵗ 14⁵ᵍ
9⁶ᵍˢ 11⁵ᵍᵗ **0-1-22 £931**

Gravardlax *B J Meehan* 87
2 ch c Salse (USA) - Rubbiyati
4⁷ᵍᵗ 2⁷ᵍᵗ **0-1-2 £2,680**

Gravia (Ire) *G Wragg* 65 a65
3 b f Grape Tree Road - Anafi
5⁸ᵍᵗ 5⁸ᵍᵗ 11¹⁰ᵍᵗ 9¹⁰ˢᵈ **0-0-4**

Great As Gold (Ire) *B Ellison* 67 a64
4 b g Goldmark (USA) - Great Land (USA)
2¹⁴ˢᵈ 4¹⁶ˢᵈ 3¹⁶ˢᵈ 5¹⁸ᵍ 6¹⁷ᵍᵗ 2²²ᵍᵗ
7¹⁶ᵗ **0-4-8 £3,791**

Great Blasket (Ire) *E J O'Neill* 58 a37
2 b f Petardia - Alexander Goddess (Ire)
8⁵ᵍˢ 1⁷ᵗ 7⁷ᵍᵗ 3⁷ᵗ 10⁷ᵍᵗ 8⁷ˢᵈ 11⁸ᵍᵗ 4⁸ᵍᵗ
1-0-8 £3,473

Great Exhibition (USA) *D R Loder* 84
2 b c Gone West (USA) - Touch Of Greatness (USA)
3⁶ᵍᵗ 2⁷ᵗ **0-1-2 £4,072**

Great Fox (Ire) *P L Gilligan* 73
2 b c Foxhound - Good Enough (Ire)
3⁶ᵍᵗ 2⁶ᵍᵗ 1⁵ᵍ **1-2-3 £4,674**

Great Game *B S Rothwell* 36
3 b g Indian Ridge - Russian Grace
6⁶ᵗ 16⁷ᵍᵗ 16⁶ᵗ 15⁶ˢᵈ **0-0-4**

Great Lass *M W Easterby* 34
2 b f Great Dane (Ire) - Impala Lass
6⁶ˢ 13⁵ᵍᵗ 12⁷ᵍˢ 8⁵ᵍᵗ 14⁷ᵍᵗ 7⁸ᵍ **0-0-6**

Great News *N Tinkler* 60
8 b g Elmaamul (USA) - Amina
7⁸ᵍˢ 8¹⁰ᵍᵗ 8¹⁰ᵍᵗ 10⁸ᵍ **0-0-4**

Great Ovation (Fr) *R T Phillips* 57
4 ch f Boston Two Step - Baldiloa
15⁸ᵍ 9¹⁰ᵍᵗ **0-0-2**

Great Pyramid (Ire) *A P O'Brien* 110
3 b c Danehill (USA) - Offshore Boom
5⁸ˢ 5⁷ʸ 9¹⁰ᵍᵗ 7⁸ᵍ 4⁸ᵍ **0-0-5 £6,461**

Great Scott *M Johnston* 86
2 b g Fasliyev (USA) - Arabis
2⁵ᵍᵗ 1⁵ʸ 1⁵ᵍ 5⁷ᵍ 8⁵ᵍᵗ 5⁸ᵍᵗ **2-1-7**
£17,178

Great View (Ire) *Mrs A L M King* 63 a52
4 b g Great Commotion (USA) - Tara View (Ire)
10¹⁰ˢᵈ 12¹⁰ˢᵈ 9⁸ᵗ 4⁷ᵍˢ 9⁷ᵍ 2¹²ᵍᵗ 4⁸ˢᵈ
3¹⁰ᵍ 9¹⁰ᵍᵗ 11⁰ᵍᵗ 5¹⁰ᵗ 5¹¹ᵍᵗ 4¹¹ᵍᵗ 3¹²ᵍ 2¹⁰ᵍᵗ
1-5-15 £8,332

Greek Revival (USA) *B W Hills* 89
3 b c Royal Academy (USA) - Las Meninas (Ire)
6⁷ᵍᵗ 15⁷ᵍᵗ 10⁷ᵍᵗ 17⁷ᵍ **0-0-4 £480**

Greek Star *Sir Michael Stoute* 25
2 b c Soviet Star (USA) - Graecia Magna (USA)
15⁷ᵍᵗ **0-0-1**

Green 'N' Gold *M D Hammond* 56 a52
3 b f Cloudings (Ire) - Fishki
3⁷ˢʷ 9⁸ˢᵈ 4¹²ᵍᵗ 7¹²ᵗ 10¹⁰ᵍᵗ 12¹⁰ᵍᵗ 4¹²ᵍᵗ
9¹⁴ᵗ 10¹⁷ᵍᵗ **0-1-9 £1,091**

Green Casket (Ire) *J A Glover* 21 a23
6 b g Green Desert (USA) - Grecian Urn
14¹²ˢᵈ 10¹⁰ᵗ 13¹²ᵍᵗ 9¹²ᵍᵗ 12¹⁰ᵍᵗ **0-0-5**

Green Ginger *W M Brisbourne* 54

7 ch g Ardkinglass - Bella Maggio
8^{8gf} 5^{10gf} 3^{11gf} 10^{11gf} 5^{10gf} 5^{11gf} 18^{10gf}
0-1-7 £474

Green Go (Ger) *A Sadik*
5 ch g Secret 'n Classy (Can) - Green Fee (Ger)
7^{12sd} 0-0-1

Green Ideal *Ferdy Murphy*   78 a91
5 b g Mark Of Esteem (Ire) - Emerald (USA)
8^{12sd} 8^{12gf} 14^{12g} 0-0-3

Green In Blue (Ire) *W J Haggas*   79
3 b c Kahyasi - Sea Mistress
3^{10gf} 3^{10g} 1^{10gf} 1-2-3 £5,145

Green Line *Sir Michael Stoute*   100
4 b g Green Desert (USA) - Marl
1^{8gf} 12^{7f} PU^{8gf} 2^{8gf} 2^{8f} 1-1-5
£26,559

Green Manalishi *D W P Arbuthnot*   78
2 b c Green Desert (USA) - Silca-Cisa
7^{5gf} 5^{5g} 2^{5gf} 2^{5gf} 5^{5gf} 5^{5gf} 1^{5gf} 1-2-7
£5,729

Green Noon (Fr) *C Lerner*   108
2 ch f Green Tune (USA) - Terring (Fr)
1^{7gs} 1^{7gs} 1^{8gs} 2^{8ho} 3-1-4 £73,474

Green Ocean *J W Unett*   53
3 gr f Environment Friend - Northern Swinger
5^{8gf} 5^{8gf} 6^{10gf} 0-0-3

Green Ridge *P W D'Arcy*   64
2 b f Muhtarram (USA) - Top Of The Morning
2^{5gf} 5^{5gf} 7^{7gs} 0-1-3 £922

Greenaway Bay (USA) *J J Quinn*   59 a59
9 ch g Green Dancer (USA) - Raise 'n Dance (USA)
4^{8sd} 2^{10g} 6^{8sd} 5^{8gs} 4^{9gf} 1^{12sw} 9^{8sd} 5^{10gs}
3^{12sd} 13^{10gs} 5^{9gs} 1-2-11 £4,949

Greenborough (Ire) *Mrs P Ford*   a15
5 b g Dr Devious (Ire) - Port Isaac (USA)
10^{12sd} 10^{9sd} 0-0-2

Greenfire (Fr) *Mrs Dianne Sayer*
5 ch g Ashkalani (Ire) - Greenvera (USA)
7^{12gf} 0-0-1

Greenhill Scene (Ire) *Takashi Kodama*   50 a43
3 gr f Victory Note (USA) - Saratoga Scene (USA)
5^{5sd} 20^{7ys} 10^{7s} 5^{7g} 5^{7y} 5^{8f} 8^{10gf} 0-0-7

Greenslades *P J Makin*   96
4 ch c Perugino (USA) - Woodfield Rose
8^{6gf} 1^{6gf} 10^{6gf} 5^{7gf} 1-0-4 £12,934

Greenwich Meantime *H R A Cecil*   87
3 b c Royal Academy (USA) - Shirley Valentine
3^{10gf} 2^{10gf} 2^{12g} 1^{12g} 1-3-4 £6,297

Greenwood *P G Murphy*   96 a89
5 ch g Emarati (USA) - Charnwood Queen
3^{5sw} 5^{5sd} 11^{5sd} 6^{6g} 6^{6gf} 1^{6gf} 15^{6gf} 10^{5g}
2^{6gf} 9^{5gf} 8^{6gs} 11^{6g} 6^{6gs} 2^{5gf} 9^{6gf} 8^{6gf}
1-4-17 £13,717

Greenwood Tree *C W Thornton*   58
3 b f Keen - Sublime
12^{8gs} 8^{8g} 7^{8g} 7^{8gf} 9^{10gf} 4^{9f} 15^{10f} 0-0-7
£308

Gregorian (Ire) *J G M O'Shea*   55 a54
6 b g Foxhound (USA) - East River (Fr)
4^{12sw} 1^{16g} 5^{15sd} 1-0-3 £3,997

Grele (USA) *R Hollinshead*   31
2 gr f Loup Sauvage (USA) - Fiveblushingroses (USA)
10^{5gf} 0-0-1

Greta D'Argent (Ire) *M Johnston*   102 a36

3 b f Great Commotion (USA) - Petite-D-Argent
10^{10sd} 3^{12gf} 1^{10gf} 15^{10gf} 8^{10g} 1^{10gf} 5^{12gs}
6^{10g} 5^{10gf} 5^{10f} 1^{12g} 15^{10gf} 10^{8gf} 3-1-13
£38,399

Gretna *J L Dunlop*   64
2 ch f Groom Dancer (USA) - Llia
6^{7gf} 0-0-1

Grey Admiral (USA) *A M Balding*   67 a58
2 gr c Cozzene - Remarkable Style (USA)
9^{8gf} 9^{8gf} 7^{8sd} 0-0-3

Grey Boy (Ger) *G C Bravery*   a55
2 gr c Medaaly - Grey Perri
8^{6sd} 0-0-1

Grey Clouds *T D Easterby*   73
3 gr f Cloudings (Ire) - Khalsheva
6^{11gf} 6^{10f} 3^{13gf} 10^{14g} 2^{10gf} 1^{10gs} 1^{10gf}
4^{10g} 3^{10g} 9^{11s} 2-2-10 £11,827

Grey Cossack *P T Midgley*   88
6 gr g Kasakov - Royal Rebeka
20^{6g} 7^{7gf} 9^{6gf} 10^{6gf} 13^{6g} 1^{5gf} 1^{6g}
11^{6gf} 10^{6gf} 15^{7gf} 13^{7g} 2-0-11 £14,673

Grey Medallion *M Brittain*   a25
3 gr g Medaaly - Thevetia
12^{5sd} 0-0-1

Grey Orchid *T J Etherington*   43
2 gr f Opening Verse (USA) - Marjorie's Orchid
13^{7g} 7^{7gf} 0-0-2

Grey Pearl *Miss Gay Kelleway*   56
4 gr f Ali-Royal (Ire) - River's Rising (Fr)
8^{7gf} 7^{6gf} 4^{8g} 9^{8g} 0-0-4 £706

Grey Swallow (Ire) *D K Weld*   119
2 gr c Daylami (Ire) - Style Of Life (USA)
1^{7s} 1^{7g} 2-0-2 £38,282

Grigoriev *J W Hills*   50
2 br c Petardia - Danz Danz
17^{6g} 3^{7g} 5^{7gf} 11^{8gf} 17^{8gf} 0-0-5
£1,078

Grist Mist (Ire) *Mrs P N Dutfield*   48 a47
2 gr f Imperial Ballet (Ire) - Ard Dauphine (Ire)
9^{8sd} 7^{8gs} 0-0-2

Grizedale (Ire) *J Akehurst*   101
4 ch g Lake Coniston (Ire) - Zabeta
25^{7g} 1^{7gf} 9^{7gf} 16^{6g} 2^{7gf} 20^{8gs} 1-1-6
£25,923

Groomer *M R Channon*   55
2 b g Fraam - Canadian Capers
8^{6gf} 12^{6gf} 9^{7gf} 5^{8g} 16^{10gf} 0-0-5

Grooms Affection *P W Harris*   79
3 b c Groom Dancer (USA) - Love And Affection (USA)
7^{10g} 1^{10gs} 1-0-2 £3,290

Ground Command (USA) *C R Egerton*   53
2 b c Kingmambo (USA) - Cymbala (Fr)
6^{6gs} 6^{8g} 0-0-2

Ground Zero (Ire) *T D Easterby*   83
3 b/br g Marju (Ire) - Zifta (USA)
3^{7g} 3^{7gs} 1^{6gf} 6^{8g} 1^{6g} 3^{6gf} 6^{7f}
14^{6gf} 14^{6gf} 2-2-10 £16,478

Groundswell (Ire) *Ferdy Murphy*   45 a34
7 b g Common Grounds - Fuchsia Belle
11^{16sd} 1^{12sd} 3^{16f} 0-1-3 £458

Grove Lodge *P R Hedger*   15 a33
6 b g Donna's Red - Shanuke (Ire)
4^{7sw} 10^{9sw} 8^{8sd} 14^{10g} 0-0-4

Growler *J L Dunlop*   66
2 ch c Foxhound (USA) - Femme Femme (USA)

8^{6gf} 8^{7gf} 10^{6s} 20^{7g} **0-0-4**

Gruff *P T Midgley* 27
4 ch g Presidium - Kagram Queen
11^{5gf} 15^{5gf} 15^{6sd} 20^{6g} 12^{5gf} 12^{6gf}
20^{5gf} **0-0-7**

Grumpyintmorning *Mrs P Townsley* 59
4 b g Magic Ring (Ire) - Grecian Belle
16^{8f} 12^{8gf} 4^{8g} 2^{7f} 8^{7f} 5^{8gf} 4^{8f} **0-1-7**
£1,224

Gryffindor *B J Meehan* 100
5 b g Marju (Ire) - Hard Task
9^{8gf} 6^{8g} 18^{8g} 31^{8gf} **0-0-4 £312**

Gryngolette *G A Butler* 80 a80
3 b/br f Linamix (Fr) - Imperial Scholar (Ire)
8^{8g} 2^{10gf} 4^{10gs} 4^{12f} 4^{10gf} 1^{9g} 5^{8s} 5^{7sd}
4^{8sd} 10^{7sd} **1-1-10 £5,299**

Guard *N P Littmoden* 5 a62
3 b c Night Shift (USA) - Gaijin
8^{8sd} 8^{7sd} 19^{7gf} 13^{8f} **0-0-4**

Guarded Secret *J Mackie* 69 a54
6 gr g Mystiko (USA) - Fen Dance (Ire)
8^{12gf} 7^{14hy} 7^{12sd} **0-0-3**

Guardian Spirit *H J Collingridge*
4 b f Hector Protector (USA) - Amongst The Stars (USA)
11^{8gf} **0-0-1**

Guild's Delight (Ire) *W S Kittow* 16
4 b g College Chapel - Tamburello (Ire)
18^{9gf} 16^{7g} **0-0-2**

Guilded Flyer *W S Kittow* 93
4 b g Emarati (USA) - Mo Ceri
1^{10g} 2^{9g} 1^{10gf} 6^{9g} 5^{10gs} 14^{10gf} 10^{12sd}
2-1-7 £9,821

Guilsborough *D Haydn Jones* 58
8 br g Northern Score (USA) - Super Sisters (Aus)
10^{10gf} 7^{11gf} 9^{8g} 14^{8gf} **0-0-4**

Gulf (Ire) *D R C Elsworth* 113
4 ch g Persian Bold - Broken Romance (Ire)
3^{16gf} 5^{14gf} 8^{12g} 1^{14gf} 3^{16gf} 6^{16g} 8^{15gs}
6^{15g} 13^{18gf} 6^{15g} **1-2-10 £28,001**

Gun Salute *G L Moore* 55 a55
3 b g Mark Of Esteem (Ire) - Affair Of State (Ire)
12^{7sd} 13^{7gf} 2^{7g} 11^{7gf} 16^{8gf} 14^{6gf} 7^{6gf}
18^{7gf} 5^{7sd} **0-1-9 £1,172**

Gunnhildr (Ire) *P J Makin* 62 a59
3 ch f In Command (Ire) - Queen Canute (Ire)
5^{7gf} 9^{7gf} 4^{8gf} 8^{10sd} 10^{10sd} **0-0-5 £333**

Guns At Dawn (Ire) *K R Burke*
2 b c Daggers Drawn (USA) - Princess Tycoon (Ire)
PU^{6gf} **0-0-1**

Guns Blazing *Miss V Haigh* 70 a35
4 b g Puissance - Queen Of Aragon
9^{5sd} 7^{6gf} 14^{5gf} 6^{5gf} 10^{5sw} 7^{5gf} 1^{5gf} 1^{5gf}
6^{5f} 1^{5gf} 6^{5gf} 5^{5gs} 9^{5gf} 10^{5gf} 2^{5gf} 12^{5gf}
3^{5gf} **4-2-24**
£21,806

Gwaihir (Ire) *J H M Gosden* 102
2 b c Cape Cross (Ire) - Twilight Tango
2^{6gf} 1^{6gf} 6^{6y} 3^{7gf} 1^{8gs} 2^{8gs} **2-2-6**
£59,546

Gwazi *Miss D A McHale* 35
3 b g Pennekamp (USA) - Made Of Pearl (USA)
9^{7g} **0-0-1**

Gwen John (USA) *H Morrison* 67
2 ch f Peintre Celebre (USA) - River Jig (USA)
5^{7gf} **0-0-1**

Gwungy *W Jenks* 33
3 b g Mind Games - Kinlet Vision (Ire)
9^{8gf} 9^{11s} **0-0-2**

H Harrison (Ire) *I W McInnes* 93
3 b g Eagle Eyed (USA) - Penrose (Ire)
13^{5gs} 10^{5hy} 6^{5gs} 5^{5gf} 5^{5f} 4^{5gf} 5^{5f} 4^{5gf}
5^{5gf} 2^{6gf} 5^{5gf} 1^{7gf} 1^{7gf} 1^{7g} 10^{7gf} 3^{7gf} **3-4-16**
£13,623

Haafel (USA) *G L Moore* 72 a71
6 ch g Diesis - Dish Dash
2^{16sd} 13^{13sd} 2^{16sd} 5^{16sd} 3^{16sd} 2^{14g} 3^{16sd}
9^{14g} 11^{16sd} **0-5-9 £4,235**

Haafhd *B W Hills* 114
2 ch c Alhaarth (Ire) - Al Bahathri (USA)
1^{6gs} 1^{7gf} 3^{7g} 3^{7gf} **2-1-4 £61,414**

Habanero *R Hannon* 73 a45
2 b c Cadeaux Genereux - Queen Of Dance (Ire)
14^{7g} 6^{6gs} 7^{7sd} 2^{8gf} 2^{8gf} 1^{8gf} **1-2-6**
£5,326

Habibti Sara *J D Czerpak* 32
3 ch f Bijou D'Inde - Cut Velvet (USA)
8^{6gf} 10^{8g} 7^{10gs} **0-0-3**

Habitual (Ire) *Sir Mark Prescott* a35
2 b g Kahyasi - Kick The Habit
11^{6sd} 14^{7sd} **0-0-2**

Habitual Dancer *Jedd O'Keeffe* 51
2 b c Groom Dancer (USA) - Pomorie (Ire)
7^{6gf} 11^{7g} 9^{7gf} **0-0-3**

Habshan (USA) *M A Jarvis* 74
3 ch c Swain (Ire) - Cambara
5^{10gf} 2^{8s} **0-1-2 £1,084**

Hadath (Ire) *B G Powell* 79 a71
6 br g Mujtahid (USA) - Al Sylah
2^{7g} 12^{7g} 5^{7y} 9^{7ys} 4^{7y} 2^{8g} 16^{7s} 7^{7y} 2^{7gf}
6^{8s} 9^{7gf} 8^{8sd} **0-3-12 £8,214**

Hagel *Ian Emmerson* 31
2 b g Mtoto - Loving Legacy
11^{7gf} 5^{6gs} 13^{7gf} **0-0-3**

Hagley Park *M Quinn* a64
4 b f Petong - Gi La High
3^{5sd} 9^{5sd} 11^{6sd} 2^{5sw} 8^{5sd} 1^{5sd} 6^{5sd} 4^{5sd}
1-2-8 £4,193

Haikal *R H Buckler* 29 a15
6 b g Owington - Magic Milly
8^{12sd} 9^{16gf} 7^{16gs} **0-0-3**

Hail The Chief *D Nicholls* 43
6 b h Be My Chief (USA) - Jade Pet
6^{9h} 5^{9h} 17^{7g} **0-0-3 £287**

Hail The King (USA) *R M Beckett* 55 a1
3 gr g Allied Forces (USA) - Hail Kris (USA)
10^{7gf} 10^{8gf} 6^{10gf} 6^{10gf} 8^{8sw} **0-0-5**

Haile Selassie *B W Hills* 64 a58
3 b g Awesome - Lady Of The Realm
6^{8g} 9^{8s} 8^{10gf} 1^{12g} 6^{10gf} 3^{12sd} 7^{10gf}
11^{10g} 15^{10gf} **1-1-9 £4,185**

Haithem (Ire) *D Shaw* 31 a47
6 b g Mtoto - Wukk (Ire)
10^{8sd} 9^{8sd} 6^{8sd} 7^{7sd} 8^{8sd} 11^{9sw} 8^{8sd}
6^{7sd} 5^{6gf} 10^{7gf} 10^{8gf} 11^{8gf} **0-0-13**

Hajeer (Ire) *P W Hiatt* a62
5 b g Darshaan - Simouna
3^{16sd} 3^{16sd} 4^{15sd} 2^{15sd} 3^{16sd} 2^{16sd} 1^{16sd}
2^{16sw} 3^{16sw} **1-6-9 £7,637**

Hakam (USA) *John Berry* 49
4 ch g Woodman (USA) - Haniya (Ire)

9^{7gf} 9^{9gf} 5^{14gf} 5^{12gf} 3^{14f} 7^{14gf} 7^{14gf}
3^{10gf} 5^{12f} 10^{12f} **0-1-10 £1,301**

Halawanda (Ire) *Sir Michael Stoute* 98
3 b f Ashkalani (Ire) - Haladiya (Ire)
1^{10gf} 2^{11gf} 14^{12g} **1-1-3 £16,902**

Halawellfin Hala *C E Brittain* 99
4 ch g Kris - Tegwen (USA)
8^{10gf} 8^{8g} 3^{8gf} 23^{8gf} 3^{7gf} 10^{10gs} 2^{7gf}
2^{8gf} 4^{8gf} **0-3-9 £12,789**

Halcyon Magic *Miss J Feilden* 60
5 b g Magic Ring (Ire) - Consistent Queen
8^{7g} 18^{7gf} 12^{8gf} 5^{8gs} 13^{8gf} 6^{7s} **0-0-6**

Half Hunter (USA) *T D Barron* a39
3 ch g Halory Hunter (USA) - Elegant Wish (USA)
4^{7sd} 8^{7sd} **0-0-2**

Half Inch *B I Case* 70 a40
3 b f Inchinor - Anhaar
9^{8sd} 1^{8g} 3^{8gf} 10^{8gf} 4^{8gf} 8^{10gf} 8^{9gf} 7^{8gf}
2^{10gf} 4^{10gf} **1-2-10 £5,209**

Halicardia *P W Harris* 93
2 br f Halling (USA) - Pericardia
3^{7gf} 1^{7gf} 1^{7gf} **2-1-3 £16,062**

Halland *N P Littmoden* 51
5 ch g Halling (USA) - Northshiel
24^{8g} 17^{12gf} **0-0-2**

Halland Park Lad (Ire) *S Kirk* a31
4 ch g Danehill Dancer (Ire) - Lassalia
16^{12sd} **0-0-1**

Hallion (Ire) *J G Given* 96
4 b g Halling (USA) - Elisa War
1^{8g} 25^{8gf} 15^{8g} 3^{8g} **1-1-4 £17,675**

Halmahera (Ire) *K A Ryan* 110
8 b g Petardia - Champagne Girl
3^{6f} 2^{5gf} 9^{6g} 15^{6f} 7^{6g} 2^{7gf} 8^{6gf} 19^{6g}
6^{6g} 1^{6g} 7^{5gf} 8^{5gf} 1^{5gf} 12^{6gf} 4^{6g} **2-3-15**
£57,941

Hamaasy *J L Dunlop* 67
2 b c Machiavellian (USA) - Sakha
7^{6gf} 6^{7gf} 7^{7gf} 19^{7gf} **0-0-4**

Hambleden *M A Jarvis* 107
6 b g Vettori (Ire) - Dalu (Ire)
15^{14gf} 2^{14gf} 1^{12gf} 3^{12gf} 2^{12gf} 5^{14g} 3^{12gf}
1^{12gf} 2^{12f} **2-5-9 £48,998**

Hamlyn (Ire) *N Nelson* 49 a59
6 gr g Lure (USA) - Passamaquoddy (USA)
1^{5sw} 4^{6sd} 5^{5sd} 7^{6sd} 9^{6sd} 4^{6sd} 10^{5sd} 7^{6gf}
4^{5s} 5^{7f} 9^{6gy} 9^{8f} 10^{6gf} 4^{6g} 15^{10gf} 6^{5gy} 2^{6f}
1-2-17 £4,666

Hammer And Sickle (Ire) *J R Boyle* 50
6 b g Soviet Lad (USA) - Preponderance (Ire)
8^{6gf} 8^{5gf} 8^{5gf} 10^{5gf} 9^{5gf} 12^{7f} 11^{6gf}
0-0-7

Hammiya (Ire) *M P Tregoning* 101
3 b f Darshaan - Albacora (Ire)
1^{8gf} 1^{11gf} 11^{12g} 11^{12g} 5^{9gf} **2-0-5**
£35,753

Hammock (Ire) *M J Gingell*
5 b/br g Hamas (Ire) - Sure Victory (Ire)
15^{12sd} **0-0-1**

Hampton Lucy (Ire) *M A Buckley* a63
4 b f Anabaa (USA) - Riveryev (USA)
6^{6sw} 19^{6f} 5^{7sd} 5^{6sd} 9^{6sd} **0-0-5**

Hamunaptra *M Wigham* a40
4 ch g Alhijaz - Princess Dancer
10^{10sd} 12^{8sd} **0-0-2**

Hana Dee *M R Channon* 61
2 b f Cadeaux Genereux - Jumairah Sun (Ire)
7^{7gf} 3^{7gf} 8^{7g} **0-1-3 £506**

Hanabad (Ire) *John M Oxx* 115
3 c c Cadeaux Genereux - Handaza (Ire)
2^{7g} 2^{8g} 4^{8gf} 5^{7gf} 1^{8f} 2^{6g} 2^{5f} 1^{6gy} **2-4-8**
£61,801

Hanami *J A R Toller* 108
3 b f Hernando (Fr) - Russian Rose (Ire)
5^{8gf} 6^{12g} 1^{10g} 11^{12g} 10^{8gf} **1-0-5**
£64,874

Hancora (Fr) *Sir Mark Prescott* 76
3 ch f Septieme Ciel (USA) - Minaudeuse (USA)
15^{6gf} 9^{7gs} **0-0-2**

Hand Chime *W J Haggas* 90 a98
6 ch g Clantime - Warning Bell
3^{7sd} 4^{6sw} 6^{6gf} 15^{7g} 9^{7g} 12^{7gs} **0-1-6**
£2,362

Handshake *W McKeown* 49
3 ch g Most Welcome - Lady Day (Fr)
10^{5gf} 17^{8gs} 5^{8gs} 10^{12gf} **0-0-4**

Handsome Cross (Ire) *I A Wood* 88
2 b c Cape Cross (Ire) - Snap Crackle Pop (Ire)
4^{5gf} 7^{6gf} 3^{6g} 1^{5gf} 2^{5gf} 3^{5g} 2^{5gf}
1-5-8 £7,934

Hannamie (Ire) *R Hannon* 61 a53
3 ch g Alhaarth (Ire) - Bold Timing
8^{8sd} 2^{6g} 10^{7gf} 5^{7gf} 15^{7gf} 9^{7gf} 7^{8f} **0-1-7**
£1,106

Hannibal Two *P D Evans*
6 b g Rock City - Appealing
12^{9sd} **0-0-1**

Hans Christian (Ire) *Paul Johnson* 76
3 b c Danehill (USA) - Mira Adonde (USA)
1^{7f} 19^{8g} 8^{8g} 9^{7gf} 11^{6gf} **1-0-5 £3,861**

Hansard (USA) *D R Loder* 72
3 b g Deputy Minister (Can) - Astoria (Arg)
2^{7gf} **0-1-1 £1,169**

Hanton (Ire) *M J Wallace* 48
2 b f Orpen (USA) - Yafford
1^{6f} 5^{6g} 7^{6gf} **1-0-3 £2,877**

Happy Crusader (Ire) *P F I Cole* 100
2 b c Cape Cross (Ire) - Les Hurlants (Ire)
3^{5gf} 3^{6g} 3^{5gf} 1^{7g} 1^{8gf} 3^{8g} 6^{10gs} **2-2-7**
£36,796

Happy Holiday (Ire) *M R Channon* 72
2 b c Fasliyev (USA) - Ms Calera (USA)
14^{6gf} 4^{6gf} 1^{6gf} 8^{6gf} 4^{6gf} 2^{6g} 8^{7gf} **1-1-7**
£6,930

Happy Union *K R Burke* 31
4 b g First Trump - Heights Of Love
11^{7gf} **0-0-1**

Harare *R M Whitaker* 64
2 b g Bahhare (USA) - Springs Eternal
10^{6s} 6^{6gf} 3^{7gf} **0-1-3 £640**

Harb (Ire) *J L Dunlop* 99
3 b c Green Desert (USA) - Ajayib (USA)
13^{6g} 10^{7g} 4^{8gf} 2^{8g} 8^{10g} 17^{8gf} **0-1-6**
£2,881

Harbour Bell *J White* a48
4 b g Bal Harbour - Bellara
4^{16sd} 5^{16sd} **0-0-2**

Harbour House *J J Bridger* 62 a51
4 b g Distant Relative - Double Flutter
5^{5sd} 16^{5g} 5^{5gf} 12^{6gf} 3^{6gf} 14^{6gf} 19^{5gs}

18⁸ᵍᶠ 17¹⁰ᶠ 13⁸ᵍˢ **0-1-10 £902**

Harbridge *J A R Toller* 49 a75
4 ch g Muhtarram (USA) - Beacon
4¹¹ᵍᶠ 2¹²ˢᵈ 6¹³ˢᵈ **0-1-3 £867**

Harcourt (USA) *P F I Cole* 86
3 b c Cozzene (USA) - Ballinamallard (USA)
3⁸ᵍᶠ 1¹⁰ᵍᶠ 24¹²ᵍ **1-1-3 £10,598**

Hard Nose (Ire) *J H M Gosden* 93
3 b c Entrepreneur - Cutlers Corner
6⁷ᵍᶠ 2⁷ᵍˢ 12⁸ᵍᶠ **0-1-3 £4,290**

Hard To Catch (Ire) *D K Ivory* 78
5 b g Namaqualand (USA) - Brook's Dilemma
16⁸ᵍᶠ 7⁵ᵍ 13⁸ᵍ 5⁷ᵍᶠ 3⁵ᵍᶠ 7⁵ᵍᶠ 12⁵ᵍˢ
5⁵ᶠ 5⁵ᵍᶠ 5⁵ᶠ **1-2-11 £5,464**

Harelda *H Morrison* 84
3 ch f Hector Protector (USA) - Hen Harrier
4¹⁰ᵍᶠ 2¹²ᵍ **0-1-2 £2,108**

Harewood End *A Crook* 34
5 b g Bin Ajwaad (Ire) - Tasseled (USA)
11¹²ᵍᶠ 15⁷ᵍᶠ 10⁶ᵍᶠ 11⁸ˢ 3⁹ᵍᶠ 14¹⁰ᶠ **0-0-6 £577**

Haribini *J A R Toller* 60 a52
3 b/br f Groom Dancer (USA) - Mory Kante (USA)
10⁸ᵍ 5⁷ᶠ 11⁷ᵍᶠ 4¹⁰ˢᵈ 3¹⁰ᵍᶠ 10¹⁴ᵍᶠ 3¹²ᵍᶠ
8¹¹ᵍᶠ **0-0-8 £1,006**

Harik *G L Moore* 49 a85
9 ch g Persian Bold - Yaqut (USA)
10¹²ˢᵈ 4¹²ˢᵈ 2¹⁶ˢᵈ 10¹⁶ˢᵈ 6¹⁷ᶠ **0-1-5 £1,812**

Haripur *Andrew Reid* 73 a106
4 b c Rainbow Quest (USA) - Jamrat Jumairah (Ire)
3¹⁰ˢᵈ 5¹⁰ˢᵈ 5¹⁰ᵍˢ 4⁹ᵍᶠ 18ˢᵈ 2⁸ᵍ 7⁷ˢᵈ
7⁷ˢᵈ 7⁷ˢᵈ **5-3-10 £30,933**

Harlequin Dancer *B Mactaggart* 43
7 b g Distant Relative - Proudfoot (Ire)
14⁶ᵍˢ 15⁸ᵍᶠ 7⁸ᵍᶠ 10⁸ᶠ PU⁷ᵍ **0-0-5**

Harlestone Bay *J L Dunlop* 46
4 b g Shaamit (Ire) - Harlestone Lake
15¹⁴ᵍ 12¹⁴ᵍᶠ 8¹⁷ᶠ **0-0-3**

Harlestone Grey *J L Dunlop* 111
5 gr g Shaamit (Ire) - Harlestone Lake
3¹²ᵍᶠ 3¹⁵ᵍᶠ 2¹⁹ᵍᶠ 5¹⁴ᵍᶠ 2¹⁸ᵍᶠ **0-3-5 £16,661**

Harleybrook *J G Given* 38 a11
2 b c Bijou D'Inde - Tous Les Jours (USA)
10⁷ᶠ 12⁶ˢᵈ 6⁸ᵍ **0-0-3**

Harlot *John Berry* 44 a65
3 b f Bal Harbour - Queen Of The Quorn
4⁶ˢᵈ 4⁸ˢᵈ 14⁷ᵍᶠ 8⁸ᶠ 11¹⁰ˢᵈ **0-0-5 £579**

Harmonic (USA) *H J Collingridge* a42
6 b m Shadeed (USA) - Running Melody
8⁸ˢᵈ 4⁸ˢʷ 10⁸ˢᵈ **0-0-3**

Harmony Hall *J M Bradley* 51
9 ch g Music Boy - Fleeting Affair
9⁸ᵍᶠ 5⁸ᵍᶠ 4⁸ᵍᶠ 6⁸ᵍᶠ **0-1-4**

Harmony Row *G L Moore* 66 a40
5 ch h Barathea (Ire) - Little Change
7¹¹ˢᵈ 3¹¹ˢᵈ 10⁸ᵍˢ 13⁷ᵍᶠ 14⁸ᵍᶠ 11¹⁰ᵍ
11¹⁰ˢᵈ **0-0-7 £519**

Harriet's Touch (USA) *M R Channon* 58
2 b f Touch Gold (USA) - I'm Harriet (USA)
8⁶ᵍᶠ 5⁷ᵍ **0-0-2**

Harrison Point (USA) *J H M Gosden* 81
3 br c Nureyev (USA) - Maid's Broom (USA)
6⁸ᵍᶠ 1⁸ᵍᶠ 8⁸ᵍᶠ 2⁷ᵍᶠ 3⁸ᶠ 10⁸ᶠ **1-2-6**

£6,622

Harrison's Flyer (Ire) *R A Fahey* 61
2 b g Imperial Ballet (Ire) - Smart Pet
4⁶ᵍᶠ **0-0-1 £565**

Harry Anchor *J R Jenkins* 22
3 b g Slip Anchor - Subtle One (Ire)
5⁸ᵍᶠ 6¹⁰ᵍᶠ 16¹²ᵍᶠ 10⁷ᵍᶠ 7¹⁰ᵍˢ 6¹⁰ᵍᶠ 14¹⁰ᵍᶠ
0-0-7

Harry The Hoover (Ire) *M J Gingell* 65
3 b g Fayruz - Mitsubishi Style
9⁶ᵍˢ **0-0-1**

Harry Up *J G Given* 94
2 ch c Piccolo - Faraway Lass
3⁵ᵍ 2⁵ᵍᶠ 1⁶ˢᶠ 1⁵ᵍᶠ 2⁵ᵍᶠ 4⁵ᵍ 6⁵ᵍᶠ 1⁵ᵍᶠ
11⁵ᵍ 4⁵ᵍ 8⁵ᵍᶠ **3-2-12 £25,443**

Harry's Game *A P Jones*
6 gr g Emperor Jones (USA) - Lady Shikari
17⁸ᵍᶠ **0-0-1**

Hartshead *G A Swinbank* 68
4 b g Machiavellian (USA) - Zalitzine (USA)
3¹¹ᵍᶠ 10¹²ᵍ 4⁸ᶠ 4⁸ᵍᶠ 6⁹ᵍᶠ **0-0-5 £1,617**

Hasanpour (Ire) *Sir Michael Stoute* 101
3 b c Dr Devious (Ire) - Hasainiya (Ire)
3¹¹ᵍᶠ 11¹¹ᵍˢ 7¹²ᵍᶠ 1¹³ᵍˢ **2-0-4 £18,814**

Hasayis *J L Dunlop* 55
2 b f Danehill (USA) - Intizaa (USA)
8⁶ᵍᶠ 11⁶ᵍᶠ **0-0-2**

Hashid (Ire) *M P Tregoning* 83
3 b g Darshaan - Alkaffeyeh (Ire)
5¹²ᵍ 3¹²ᵍ **0-0-2 £838**

Hasina (Ire) *B W Duke* a60
4 b f King's Theatre (Ire) - Smaointeach (Ire)
8¹⁰ˢᵈ 4¹⁰ˢᵈ 11⁹ˢʷ **0-0-3**

Hasty Hannah *M R Hoad* a7
2 ch f Pursuit Of Love - Tenderetta
16⁶ᵍᶠ 13⁶ˢᵈ 12⁸ˢᵈ **0-0-3**

Hasty Prince *Jonjo O'Neill* 91
5 ch g Halling (USA) - Sister Sophie (USA)
8¹²ᵍ **0-0-1**

Hat Trick Man *J Akehurst* 53 a51
2 gr c Daylami (Ire) - Silver Kristal
10⁷ᵍᶠ 7⁷ˢᵈ **0-0-2**

Hatch *R Charlton* 76
2 ch c Cadeaux Genereux - Footlight Fantasy (USA)
5⁷ᵍᶠ 4⁸ᵍᶠ 7⁷ᵍᶠ 8⁷ᶠ **0-1-4 £1,450**

Hatch A Plan (Ire) *R M Beckett* 61
2 b g Vettori (Ire) - Fast Chick
9⁶ᵍᶠ 12⁶ᵍᶠ 9⁶ᵍᶠ **0-0-3**

Hathlen (Ire) *M R Channon* 72
2 b c Singspiel (Ire) - Kameez (Ire)
15⁷ᵍᶠ 2⁸ᵍᶠ 2⁹ᶠ 3¹⁰ᶠ 7⁸ᵍˢ 2⁸ᶠ 2⁸ᵍᶠ **0-5-7 £5,990**

Hathrah (Ire) *J L Dunlop* 105
2 gr f Linamix (Fr) - Zivania (Ire)
4⁷ᵍᶠ 1⁷ᵍˢ 2⁸ᵍ 2⁷ᵍᶠ **1-2-4 £21,026**

Hattington *M Todhunter* 69
5 b g Polish Precedent (USA) - Ruffle (Fr)
6¹²ᵍᶠ 5¹²ᵍᶠ 11¹⁴ᶠ 3¹²ᵍᶠ 6¹⁴ᵍᶠ **0-1-5 £1,060**

Haulage Man *D Eddy* 74
5 ch g Komaite (USA) - Texita
15⁸ᵍᶠ 2⁶ᵍᶠ 15⁸ᵍᶠ 7⁸ᵍᶠ 8⁸ᶠ 14⁷ᵍᶠ 10⁸ᵍ
4⁸ᵍᶠ 12⁶ᵍᶠ **0-1-9 £1,706**

Haunt The Zoo *John A Harris* a68
8 b m Komaite (USA) - Merryhill Maid (Ire)

9[8sd] 8[8sd] 9[8sd] 11[8sd] 10[8sd] 3[8sd] 3[8sd] 2[8ft]
5[8sd] 1[9sd] 3[8sw] **1-4-11 £5,032**

Havantadoubt (Ire) *J G Portman*   79
3 ch f Desert King (Ire) - Batiba (USA)
9[9g] 13[8gf] 8[10f] 7[7gf] 9[8gf] 1[11gf] 5[10s] 3[12gf]
3[12f] 13[12gf] 7[11gf] 7[11gf] **1-0-12 £7,079**

Have Faith (Ire) *B W Hills*   79
2 b f Machiavellian (USA) - Fatefully (USA)
6[7gf] 2[7g] 1[7gf] 7[7g] **1-1-4 £6,870**

Havetoavit (USA) *J D Bethell*   58 a56
2 b g Theatrical - Summer Crush (USA)
5[7gf] 5[7gs] 4[8sw] 7[8gf] 8[8gf] **0-0-5**

Havoc *N Wilson*   a24
4 b g Hurricane Sky (Aus) - Padelia
12[12sw] 7[8sd] **0-0-2**

Havva Danz *J G Given*   33
2 b f Danzero (Aus) - Possessive Lady
13[7g] **0-0-1**

Hawk *P R Chamings*   82 a78
5 b g A P Jet (USA) - Miss Enjoleur (USA)
2[5sd] 19[5gf] 3[5sd] 8[5sd] 15[5gs] 2[5gf] 7[5gf]
13[6gf] 9[5gf] 8[5g] 11[5gs] 1[5gf] 3[5gf] 14[5gf] 5[7sd]
1-4-15 £8,819

Hawk Flyer (USA) *Sir Michael Stoute*   117
3 b c Silver Hawk (USA) - Dawn's Curtsey (USA)
2[8gf] 1[10gf] 1[12gf] 3[12g] 3[12gf] **2-3-5**
£44,715

Hawk Wing (USA) *A P O'Brien*   134
4 b c Woodman (USA) - La Lorgnette (Can)
1[8g] 7[8gf] **1-0-2 £116,000**

Hawkit (USA) *J A Osborne*   81 a65
2 b g Silver Hawk (USA) - Hey Ghaz (USA)
2[8g] 3[7sd] 2[8sd] **0-3-3 £2,130**

Hawkley *P W D'Arcy*   a24
4 ch g Arctic Tern (USA) - Last Ambition (Ire)
8[8sd] **0-0-1**

Hawksbill (USA) *J H M Gosden*   110
3 ch c Silver Hawk (USA) - Binary
1[9g] 2[10gs] 3[12gf] 5[10gf] 4[10gf] 10[10g] **1-1-6**
£13,922

Hawridge Prince *L G Cottrell*   77
3 b g Polar Falcon (USA) - Zahwa
7[7gf] 3[8gf] 1[8g] 2[10gf] **1-2-4 £5,714**

Hayhaat (USA) *B W Hills*   73
3 ch f Irish River (Fr) - Ball Gown (USA)
3[7gf] 6[10gf] 5[11g] 3[12g] 1[12gs] **1-2-5 £3,285**

Haystacks (Ire) *James Moffatt*   56
7 b g Contract Law (USA) - Florissa (Fr)
13[16gs] 14[12g] 6[14gf] 8[14f] 6[16gs] 13[17gf] **0-0-6**

Haze Babybear *R A Fahey*   60 a60
3 b f Mujadil (USA) - River's Rising (Fr)
11[7gf] 17[6gf] 7[6gs] 3[5sd] 3[6sw] 1[5gs] 7[5g] **1-2-7**
£6,604

Hazewind *E A L Dunlop*   41
2 gr c Daylami (Ire) - Fragrant Oasis (USA)
12[7gf] 14[7gf] **0-0-2**

Hazim *Sir Michael Stoute*   110
4 b c Darshaan - Souk (Ire)
1[10gf] 10[12gf] 11[10gf] **1-0-3 £37,050**

Hazy *R M H Cowell*   a30
3 b f Vettori (Ire) - Shifting Mist
6[7sd] 8[7gf] PU[6sd] 5[6ft] 14[6gf] 14[7sw] **0-0-6**

Hazy Morn *R J Hodges*   34
4 gr f Cyrano De Bergerac - Hazy Kay (Ire)

6[5f] 6[8gf] **0-0-2**

Hazyview *N A Callaghan*   68
2 b c Cape Cross (Ire) - Euridice (Ire)
11[7g] 16[7gf] 7[8gf] 3[8gf] 1[8gs] **1-1-5 £3,118**

He Who Dares (Ire) *A W Carroll*   67
5 b g Distinctly North (USA) - Sea Clover (Ire)
4[7gf] 8[6gf] 1[7gf] 17[9gf] 18[9s] **2-0-5 £4,861**

He's A Rocket (Ire) *Mrs C A Dunnett*   53 a42
2 b c Indian Rocket - Dellua (Ire)
12[5g] 4[5gf] 4[5f] 5[7gs] 6[7gf] 13[6gf] 10[7sd] 8[6sd]
0-0-8 £280

Head Boy *S Dow*   61
2 ch g Forzando - Don't Jump (Ire)
12[6g] 11[6gf] 14[6g] 5[6g] 1[7gf] 10[7f] **1-0-6**
£2,441

Head Of College (Ire) *M C Chapman*   43 a6
3 ch c Ashkalani (Ire) - Ceide Dancer (Ire)
13[6sd] 10[6gf] **0-0-2**

Head Of State *R M Beckett*   31 a25
2 br g Primo Dominie - Lets Be Fair
8[5gf] 12[5gf] 6[5sd] **0-0-3**

Head To Kerry (Ire) *D J S Ffrench Davis*   72 a56
3 b g Eagle Eyed (USA) - The Poachers Lady (Ire)
8[12gf] 5[10gf] 3[12g] 6[12f] 2[12sd] 1[12gf] 3[14g] 5[12g]
1[16gf] 3[16gf] **2-4-10 £9,948**

Headland (USA) *D W Chapman*   64 a86
5 b/br g Distant View (USA) - Fijar Echo (USA)
14[7sd] 11[7sd] 7[7sd] 2[7sd] RR[7gf] 19[6g] 15[8g]
4[7f] 14[7gf] 13[7sd] 8[7sd] 8[6sd] **1-1-12 £4,992**

Heads Your Gray *D Morris*   48
2 gr g Atraf - Port Hedland
4[6gf] 8[6gf] 7[8gs] **0-0-3 £338**

Healey (Ire) *P R Wood*   53 a36
5 ch g Dr Devious (Ire) - Bean Siamsa
4[11sd] 8[9sd] 3[10gf] 2[10s] **0-2-4 £2,020**

Heart Springs *Dr J R J Naylor*   37 a52
3 b f Parthian Springs - Metannee
7[12sd] 7[10gf] **0-0-2**

Heart's Desire (Ire) *B W Hills*   69
2 b f Royal Applause - Touch And Love (Ire)
5[6gf] 2[7s] **0-1-2 £1,056**

Heartbeat *M A Jarvis*   31 a35
2 b f Pursuit Of Love - Lyrical Bid (USA)
12[6gf] 6[7sd] **0-0-2**

Heartbreaker (Ire) *M W Easterby*   5
3 b g In Command (Ire) - No Hard Feelings (Ire)
11[7gf] 9[16gf] **0-0-2**

Hearthstead Dream *M Johnston*   67
2 ch c Dr Fong (USA) - Robin Lane
7[6g] 3[6gf] 2[7gf] 14[8gs] **0-0-4 £2,289**

Hearthstead Pride *M Johnston*   72
4 ch g Dr Devious (Ire) - Western Heights
6[12g] 7[16gf] **0-0-2**

Hearts 'n Minds *C A Cyzer*   97 a77
3 ch f Mark Of Esteem (Ire) - Magical Retreat (USA)
9[7sd] 5[10gf] 3[10gf] 10[12g] 3[12gf] 1[12sd]
1-1-7 £9,146

Heathyards Joy *R Hollinshead*   20
2 ch f Komaite (USA) - Heathyards Lady (USA)
7[6gf] **0-0-1**

Heathyards Mate *R J Baker*   a9
6 b g Timeless Times (USA) - Quenlyn
10[8sw] 13[9sd] **0-0-2**

Heathyards Swing *R Hollinshead*   43 a55
5 b g Celtic Swing - Butsova

12^{12gf} 16^{12g} 13^{10gs} 5^{9sd} 17^{10g} 16^{12sd}
2^{12sw} 7^{11sd} 5^{12sw} 2^{12sd} **0-2-10 £1,690**

Heathyardsblessing (Ire) *R Hollinshead*   43 a36
6 b g Unblest - Noble Nadia
13^{6sw} 12^{5gf} 10^{5sd} 10^{5g} **0-0-4**

Heavenly Bay (USA) *C E Brittain*   93
3 b f Rahy (USA) - Bevel (USA)
3^{10g} 3^{6gf} 2^{8g} 3^{12gf} 8^{10gf} 2^{12g} 1^{12gf} 7^{15g}
7^{12gf} **1-5-9 £21,725**

Hebenus *T A K Cuthbert*   49 a36
4 b g Hamas (Ire) - Stinging Nettle
7^{7gs} 9^{6gs} 5^{6gf} 13^{6sd} 13^{8g} 5^{9g} 2^{8gf}
5^{8gf} 8^{8gf} **0-1-10 £868**

Hectic Tina *Jedd O'Keeffe*
4 ch f Hector Protector (USA) - Tinashaan (Ire)
10^{9gs} **0-0-1**

Hector's Girl *Sir Michael Stoute*   98
3 ch f Hector Protector (USA) - Present Imperfect
3^{7gf} 18^{8gf} 6^{8f} **0-1-3 £5,995**

Hecuba *B W Hills*   96
3 ch f Hector Protector (USA) - Ajuga (USA)
1^{10gf} 5^{11gf} 3^{10gf} 8^{14g} 7^{14s} **1-0-5 £8,534**

Hefin *I A Wood*   68 a66
6 ch g Red Rainbow - Summer Impressions (USA)
2^{13g} 7^{14gf} 2^{16gf} 1^{16sd} 3^{15gf} 10^{15sd} 3^{16sd}
3^{16gf} 1^{14gf} 3^{16sd} **2-6-10 £11,483**

Heidelburg (Ire) *S Kirk*   63 a71
3 b f Night Shift (USA) - Solar Attraction (Ire)
10^{6sd} 7^{5g} 4^{7sd} 7^{7gf} 6^{7sd} 13^{9gf} **0-1-6**
£438

Heir To Be *J L Dunlop*   83
4 b g Elmaamul (USA) - Princess Genista
11^{16gf} 7^{14gs} 1^{16gs} 14^{20gf} 15^{16gf} 6^{21gs}
1-0-6 £6,411

Heir To The Throne (Ire) *Mrs A J Perrett*   73
2 b c Desert Prince (Ire) - Scandisk (Ire)
3^{8gf} 2^{10gf} **0-2-2 £1,740**

Heir Today (Ire) *R M Beckett*   69
2 b f Princely Heir (Ire) - Ransomed (Ire)
10^{5f} 8^{5g} 2^{5f} 1^{6gf} 7^{6sf} 10^{6gf} 7^{5gf} **1-1-7**
£4,496

Heisse *D R Loder*   96
3 b c Darshaan - Hedera (USA)
1^{12gf} 2^{10gf} 7^{12gf} **1-1-3 £7,809**

Hektikos *S Dow*
3 ch g Hector Protector (USA) - Green Danube (USA)
14^{13sd} **0-0-1**

Helderberg (USA) *C E Brittain*   80
3 b f Diesis - Banissa (USA)
7^{10gf} 7^{10gf} 3^{11gf} 5^{11f} 7^{10g} 8^{10g} 8^{12g} 2^{9gs}
2^{8f} 1^{7f} 13^{10g} **1-3-11 £7,840**

Helen Bradley (Ire) *N P Littmoden*   a64
4 ch f Indian Ridge - Touraya
10^{8sd} 9^{8sd} 11^{7sd} 12^{7sd} 7^{6sd} 7^{8sd} **0-0-6**

Helensburgh (Ire) *M Johnston*   65
2 ch c Mark Of Esteem (Ire) - Port Helene
4^{9f} 7^{8gs} 9^{10gf} **0-0-3**

Helibel (Ire) *Mrs A J Perrett*   73
2 gr f Pivotal - Boughtbyphone
4^{6gf} 4^{6gf} 2^{6gs} **0-1-3 £976**

Hello Holly *Mrs A L M King*   44
6 b m Lake Coniston (Ire) - Amandine (Ire)
10^{12f} **0-0-1**

Hello It's Me *H J Collingridge*   79
2 ch g Deploy - Evening Charm (Ire)

3^{8s} 3^{8gf} 1^{8g} **1-1-3 £5,541**

Hello Roberto *M J Polglase*   62 a72
2 b f Up And At 'Em - Hello Hobson'S (Ire)
11^{6gf} 1^{5gf} 15^{6gf} 3^{5sd} 11^{6gf} 4^{6g} 3^{5gs}
1-2-7 £4,053

Helm Bank *M Johnston*   111
3 b c Wild Again (USA) - Imperial Bailiwick (Ire)
9^{10gf} 11^{8hy} 5^{12gf} 2^{8gf} **0-1-4 £13,735**

Heneseys Leg *John Berry*   66 a66
3 b f Sure Blade - Away's Halo (USA)
9^{7gf} 4^{10gf} 1^{10f} 2^{10gf} 2^{12f} 6^{12g} 4^{12f} 5^{10sd}
1-2-8 £5,474

Hengrove *M S Saunders*   30 a42
3 b/br f Fraam - Java Rupiah (Ire)
6^{7sd} 6^{6sd} 9^{5f} 15^{6f} **0-0-4**

Henndey (Ire) *M A Jarvis*   17
2 b c Indian Ridge - Del Deya (Ire)
19^{6gf} **0-0-1**

Henry Hall (Ire) *N Tinkler*   101
7 b h Common Grounds - Sovereign Grace (Ire)
7^{5f} 1^{5g} 15^{6gf} 3^{5gf} 5^{5gs} 1^{5g} 3^{5gf} **2-5-14 £31,737**
3^{5gf} 3^{5gf} 6^{5gs} 5^{5gs} 1^{5g} 3^{5gf}

Henry Island (Ire) *Mrs A J Bowlby*   78
10 ch g Sharp Victor (USA) - Monterana
15^{14gf} 12^{12gf} 7^{12f} 4^{17f} 2^{17f} 11^{9gf} 1^{15gf}
4^{16gf} 7^{21gs} 1^{16gf} 4^{16gf} 4^{16gf} 4^{17f} 3^{18gf} **3-2-14**
£15,368

Henry Tun *J Balding*   37 a69
5 b g Chaddleworth (Ire) - B Grade
11^{5sd} 14^{5sd} 6^{5sd} 10^{5sd} 2^{5sd} 1^{5sd} 2^{5sd} 9^{5gf}
13^{5g} 5^{5gf} 9^{5sd} 13^{5sw} 12^{5sd} **2-2-13 £8,940**

Henry Windsor *N Tinkler*   57
3 b g Forzando - Ski Baby
13^{5gs} 9^{6gf} 11^{6gf} 9^{5g} 1^{6f} 6^{7gf} 8^{7gf} 8^{6gf}
1^{6gf} **2-0-9 £6,656**

Heraclea *L M Cumani*   45
3 ch f Groom Dancer (USA) - Tamassos
5^{8g} 6^{7gf} 3^{8gf} 10^{10g} **0-0-4 £637**

Here Comes Tom *Jamie Poulton*   a32
5 b g Puissance - Young Holly
11^{7sd} **0-0-1**

Here To Me *R Hannon*   69
2 ch f Muhtarram (USA) - Away To Me
3^{6g} 2^{5gf} 24^{7gf} 3^{6gf} 5^{8gf} 7^{7gf} 2^{6gs}
0-4-8 £4,209

Heretic *J R Fanshawe*   109
5 b g Bishop Of Cashel - Barford Lady
4^{8g} 1^{8gf} 10^{8g} 12^{8gs} 7^{8gs} **1-0-5**
£14,226

Herminoe *W R Muir*   81
3 b f Rainbow Quest (USA) - Hamasaat (Ire)
5^{11vs} 2^{12g} 3^{13g} 4^{12g} 1^{10gs} 6^{11gf} 8^{14s} **1-1-7**
£11,053

Hermione O Really *W Storey*   22
3 b f Overbury (Ire) - Sallyoreally (Ire)
11^{9gs} 7^{9s} 11^{9gf} 9^{5gf} 12^{6gf} 13^{7g} 12^{6s}
18^{5gf} **0-0-8**

Hernando's Boy *Mrs M Reveley*   54
2 b g Hernando (Fr) - Leave At Dawn
12^{7g} 7^{7gf} 7^{7gs} **0-0-3**

Herne Bay (Ire) *A Bailey*   64 a64
3 b g Hernando (Fr) - Charita (Ire)
11^{11sd} 9^{10sd} 5^{11sd} 3^{12sd} 5^{12gf} 4^{12sd} 5^{16gf}
8^{13f} 13^{14gf} 1^{16gf} 4^{16gf} 13^{16g} **2-1-12 £7,665**

Herodotus *C E Brittain*   87 a106

5 b g Zafonic (USA) - Thalestria (Fr)
5¹²ˢᵈ 6¹⁰ˢᵈ 10¹⁰ˢᵈ 9¹²ˢᵈ 7¹²ˢᵈ 5¹²ᵍ 12¹⁶ᵍᶠ
0-0-7 £1,361

Heselrig (Ire) *T D Easterby* 49
2 b g Entrepreneur - Castara Beach (Ire)
5⁷ᵍᶠ 7⁸ᵍᶠ 10⁸ˢ UR¹⁰ᶠ **0-0-4**

Hestherelad (Ire) *C J Teague*
4 b g Definite Article - Unbidden Melody (USA)
7⁹ᵍᶠ 13¹²ˢʷ 10¹²ᵍ **0-0-3**

Hey Presto *C G Cox* 86
3 b g Piccolo - Upping The Tempo
3⁶ᵍᶠ 14⁶ᵍᶠ 1⁶ᵍᶠ 2⁶ᵍᶠ 8⁶ᵍᶠ 6⁶ᵍ 7⁶ᵍᶠ 8⁶ᵍˢ
4⁶ᵍᶠ 9⁵ᵍᶠ **1-2-10 £13,776**

Hezaam (USA) *J L Dunlop* 75
2 b c Red Ransom (USA) - Ashraakat (USA)
9⁶ᵍᶠ 1⁷ᵍˢ **1-0-2 £4,153**

Hi Darl *J G Given* 45 a40
2 ch f Wolfhound (USA) - Sugar Token
6⁵ᵍᶠ 4⁵ˢᵈ 1⁶ᵍᶠ **1-0-3 £2,905**

Hi Dubai *Saeed Bin Suroor* 111
3 ch f Rahy (USA) - Jood (USA)
1¹⁰ᵍᶠ 2¹⁰ˢ 5¹²ᵍ 4¹⁰ᵍ 3¹⁰ˢ **1-2-5 £94,070**

Hiawatha (Ire) *I Semple* 79
4 b g Danehill (USA) - Hi Bettina
1⁸ᵇʸˢ 3⁸ᵍᶠ 7⁷ᵍ 9⁹ˢ 5U⁹ʸˢ 7⁸ʸ 2⁸ᵍ 14⁸ʸ
8⁸ᵍᶠ 4⁸ᵍ 11⁸ʸˢ 7⁷ᵍᶠ 2¹²ᵍ 11⁸ᵍˢ 2¹⁰ᵍˢ **0-5-15
£4,565**

Hiccups *Mrs J R Ramsden* 89
3 b g Polar Prince (Ire) - Simmie's Special
6⁶ᶠ 2⁵ᵍᶠ 3⁵ᵍᶠ 2⁵ᵍ 7⁶ᵍᶠ 1⁵ᶠ 7⁵ᵍᶠ 1⁵ᵍᶠ
19⁵ᵍᶠ 6⁶ᵍᶠ 3⁵ᵍ 17⁵ˢ **2-4-12 £21,917**

Hickleton Dream *G A Swinbank* 35
6 b m Rambo Dancer (Can) - Elegant Approach
4¹²ᵍᶠ 8¹⁴ᵍᶠ **0-0-2**

Hidden Dragon (USA) *P A Blockley* 107 a92
4 b g Danzig (USA) - Summer Home (USA)
5⁷ˢᵈ 1⁶ᶠ 4⁶ᵍᶠ 6⁵ᵍᶠ 20⁶ᶠ 3⁶ᵍᶠ 3⁶ᵍᶠ 1⁶ᵍ
4⁵ᵍᶠ 7⁶ᵍ 11⁵ᶠ 9⁶ᵍᶠ **2-1-12 £46,037**

Hidden Hope *G Wragg* 55 a58
2 ch f Daylami (Ire) - Nuryana
8⁶ᵍᶠ 8⁷ˢᵈ **0-0-2**

Hidden Smile (USA) *F Jordan* a38
6 b m Twilight Agenda (USA) - Smooth Edge (USA)
8¹¹ˢᵈ 6⁹ˢᵈ 5⁸ˢᵈ **0-0-3**

Hidden Surprise *W A O'Gorman* a93
4 b g Bin Ajwaad (Ire) - Dawawin (USA)
3⁸ˢᵈ 2¹⁰ˢᵈ **0-2-2 £2,944**

High Accolade *M P Tregoning* 123
3 b c Mark Of Esteem (Ire) - Generous Lady
1¹⁰ᵍᶠ 1¹¹ᵍ 1¹²ᵍᶠ 6¹²ᵍ 2¹²ᵍ 6¹²ᵍᶠ 2¹⁵ᵍ 1¹²ᶠ
2¹²ᵍᶠ **4-3-9 £281,385**

High Action (USA) *Sir Michael Stoute* 107
3 ch c Theatrical - Secret Imperatrice (USA)
2⁹ᵍᶠ 2⁹ᵍᶠ 1⁸ᵍᶠ 4¹⁰ᵍᶠ 1¹²ᵍᶠ 1¹²ᵍᶠ 8¹²ᵍᶠ
6¹²ᵍˢ **3-2-8 £29,200**

High And Mighty *G Barnett* 81
8 b g Shirley Heights - Air Distingue (USA)
9¹⁸ᵍ 13¹⁶ᵍᶠ 8¹⁹ᵍᶠ 5¹⁷ᵍᶠ **0-0-4**

High Cane (USA) *J Noseda* 65
3 ch f Diesis - Aerleon Jane
6⁸ᵍᶠ 10⁸ᵍᶠ 3⁸ˢ 6⁸ᵍᶠ **0-1-4 £542**

High Chaparral (Ire) *A P O'Brien* 128
4 b c Sadler's Wells (USA) - Kasora (Ire)
1¹⁰ᵍᶠ 1¹⁰ᵍᶠ 3¹²ʰᵒ 1¹²ᶠ **3-1-4
£1,028,932**

High Diva *B R Johnson* 51 a68
4 b f Piccolo - Gifted
5¹⁰ˢᵈ 5¹³ˢᵈ 4¹³ˢᵈ 10¹⁰ˢᵈ 2⁸ᵍᶠ 7¹⁰ᶠ 7¹⁰ᶠ
0-1-7 £868

High Diving *G T Lynch* 77
3 b c Barathea (Ire) - High And Low
2¹²ᶠ 3¹²ᵍˢ 3¹²ᵍ 7¹⁰ᵍ **0-2-4 £2,750**

High Drama *P Bowen* 45
6 b/br g In The Wings - Maestrale
5¹⁵ᵍᶠ 2¹⁶ᵍˢ 7¹⁶ᵍᶠ **0-1-3 £1,400**

High Esteem *M A Buckley* 54 a68
7 b g Common Grounds - Whittle Woods Girl
6⁵ᵍˢ 1⁶ˢᵈ 9⁶ˢᵈ 10⁵ᵍ 11⁶ˢᵈ **1-0-5 £3,199**

High Finale *D K Ivory* 70
4 b f Sure Blade (USA) - High Velocity
7⁵ᵍᶠ **0-0-1**

High Finance (Ire) *J W Hills* 85 a64
3 b/br f Entrepreneur - Phylella
1⁸ˢᵈ 4⁷ˢᵈ 1⁷ᵍᶠ 5⁷ᵍ 1⁷ᵍᶠ 10⁷ᵍ 4⁷ᵍᶠ 5⁷ᵍᶠ
5⁸ᵍ **3-0-9 £15,571**

High Hope (Fr) *G L Moore* 69 a90
5 b h Lomitas - Highness Lady (Ger)
2¹²ˢᵈ 5¹²ˢᵈ 10¹²ᵍᶠ 14¹²ᵍ 9¹²ᵍᶠ **0-1-5
£4,953**

High Point (Ire) *G P Enright* 84 a78
5 b g Ela-Mana-Mou - Top Lady (Ire)
1¹²ˢᵈ 2¹⁴ᵍ 5¹⁶ᵍᶠ 2¹⁴ᵍᶠ 1¹⁴ᵍᶠ 5¹⁶ᵍᶠ 12¹⁶ᵍ
11¹²ᵍᶠ 17¹⁸ᵍᶠ **2-2-9 £12,581**

High Policy (Ire) *R Hollinshead* 61 a86
7 ch g Machiavellian (USA) - Road To The Top
6¹⁶ˢᵈ 9¹⁴ˢʷ 2¹⁶ᵍᶠ 9¹⁶ᵍˢ 6¹⁶ᵍ 1¹⁵ˢᵈ 3¹⁴ˢʷ
7¹⁶ᵍ 1¹⁵ˢᵈ **2-2-9 £7,033**

High Powered (Ger) *D W Thompson* 15
4 br f So Factual (USA) - High Habit
1⁷⁸ᵍᶠ 1⁶⁷ᶠ **0-0-2**

High Praise (USA) *J H M Gosden* 108
3 b f Quest For Fame - Stellaria (USA)
12¹²ᵍ 1¹²ᵍ **1-0-2 £35,162**

High Reach *T G Mills* 95 a93
3 b c Royal Applause - Lady Of Limerick (Ire)
3⁶ˢᵈ 3⁷ˢᵈ 1⁷ˢᵈ 2⁸ˢᵈ 2⁷ᵍᶠ 4⁶ᵍᶠ 3⁶ᵍᶠ 1⁶ᵍᶠ
4⁷ˢᵈ 4⁶ᵍᶠ **2-5-10 £19,121**

High Reserve *J R Fanshawe* 71
2 b f Dr Fong (USA) - Hyabella
3⁷ᵍᶠ 5⁷ᵍᶠ **0-1-2 £542**

High Resolve *J R Fanshawe* 66 a69
3 ch c Unfuwain (USA) - Asteroid Field (USA)
15¹⁰ᵍ 3¹¹ʰʸ 5¹²ᵍᶠ 4¹²ˢᵈ 4¹⁰ᵍ **0-1-5
£1,225**

High Ridge *J M Bradley* 69
4 ch g Indian Ridge - Change For A Buck (USA)
5⁸ᵍᶠ 15⁸ᵍᶠ 7⁸ᵍᶠ 17⁷ᵍᶠ 8⁷ᵍᶠ 36⁶ᶠ 5⁶ᶠ
3⁶ᵍᶠ 6⁶ᵍᶠ 8⁶ᵍᶠ **0-3-11 £2,050**

High Sirocco *D W Barker* 24
3 ch g First Trump - Amid The Stars
20⁸ᵍˢ 14⁷ᵍᶠ **0-0-2**

High Swainston *R Craggs* 65
2 ch g The West (USA) - Reamzafonic
9⁵ᵍᶠ 5⁷ᵍᶠ 5⁵ᵍ 3⁵ᵍᶠ 16⁵ᵍ **0-0-5 £513**

High Voltage *K R Burke* 86
2 ch c Wolfhound (USA) - Real Emotion (USA)
11⁵ᵍᶠ 2⁵ᵍᶠ 2⁶ᵍˢ 1⁵ᵍᶠ 2⁵ᵍᶠ 2⁶ᵍᶠ 7⁵ᵍᶠ 2⁵ᵍᶠ
8⁵ᵍ **1-4-9 £12,884**

High-Street *Mrs Lydia Pearce* 30
3 b g Mark Of Esteem (Ire) - Kentmere (Fr)

13^{11gf} 12^{8gf} **0-0-2**

Highcal *Ronald Thompson* — 6
6 gr g King's Signet (USA) - Guarded Expression
10^{12gf} **0-0-1**

Highclere Memory (USA) *J L Dunlop* — 58
3 b f Cryptoclearance (USA) - Regal State (USA)
12^{8g} 5^{10f} 5^{10f} 7^{12f} **0-0-4**

Highdown (Ire) *Saeed Bin Suroor* — 116
4 b c Selkirk (USA) - Rispoto
6^{9f} 2^{11ys} 2^{10g} 5^{10gf} 2^{10g} **0-3-5 £60,618**

Highest (Ire) *Saeed Bin Suroor* — 122
4 b c Selkirk (USA) - Pearl Kite (USA)
1^{12f} 7^{12g} 3^{12gs} 2^{12g} 5^{12f} **1-1-5 £116,404**

Highest Honour (Ire) *A M Balding* — 29
3 b g Polish Precedent (USA) - Victoria Cross (USA)
7^{8f} 18^{6f} **0-0-2**

Highfield Jen *C W Fairhurst* — 26
4 ch f Presidium - Jendorcet
8^{10gf} 12^{16f} **0-0-2**

Highgate Hill *M H Tompkins* — 67 a56
3 b g Revoque (Ire) - Long View
6^{7gf} 4^{8gf} 10^{8gf} PU^{8gs} 6^{8g} 4^{10gf} 4^{12sd} **0-0-7 £298**

Highland Gait *T D Easterby* — 58
4 ch f Most Welcome - Miller's Gait
2^{7gf} 8^{8gs} 12^{8gf} 3^{8gf} 1^{7gf} 11^{8gf} **1-2-6 £7,272**

Highland Games (Ire) *Sir Michael Stoute* — 90
3 b c Singspiel (Ire) - Highland Gift (Ire)
5^{10gf} 11^{11gf} 1^{12gf} 8^{12gf} 6^{12gs} 11^{10gf} **2-0-6 £13,523**

Highland Gold (Ire) *Miss L A Perratt* — 42
6 ch g Indian Ridge - Anjuli
12^{12gf} 8^{12g} **0-0-2**

Highland Reel *D R C Elsworth* — 96
6 ch g Selkirk (USA) - Taj Victory
16^{8g} 12^{8gf} 3^{10g} 3^{10gf} 6^{9g} 1^{8gf} 11^{10g}
16^{8gf} 9^{10gf} 12^{10gf} **1-2-10 £12,320**

Highland Shot *A M Balding* — 95 a82
5 b m Selkirk (USA) - Optaria
2^{7gf} 1^{8sd} 1^{9g} 8^{8g} 1^{7gf} 2^{9g} 18^{7f} 2^{6gf}
7^{6gf} 5^{7gf} 13^{7g} **3-3-11 £34,589**

Highland Toffee (Ire) *M L W Bell* — 47 a49
3 ch g Miswaki (USA) - Natural Forest (USA)
10^{7sd} 10^{7gf} 7^{7gf} 7^{11f} 13^{9sw} 14^{7gf} **0-0-6**

Highland Warrior *J S Goldie* — 70
4 b c Makbul - Highland Rowena
11^{8gs} 9^{9gs} 5^{9gf} 9^{8gs} 2^{8g} 8^{9g} 13^{9gf} 14^{8g}
1^{6gs} 3^{6g} 9^{6g} **1-3-11 £6,516**

Highly Liquid *W Jarvis* — 72 a27
3 b f Entrepreneur - Premiere Cuvee
2^{8gf} 4^{8g} 14^{8gs} 11^{8sd} **0-1-4 £1,576**

Highly Pleased (USA) *S L Keightley* — a46
8 b g Hansel (USA) - Bint Alfalla (USA)
15^{7sd} 6^{8sd} **0-0-2**

Hilarious (Ire) *B R Millman* — 62
3 b f Petorius - Heronwater (Ire)
8^{8gf} 3^{8gf} 8^{7gf} 5^{8gf} 8^{7gf} 3^{8gf} 4^{8gf} 4^{8f}
9^{10gf} **0-2-9 £1,586**

Hilbre Island *B J Meehan* — 113
3 b c Halling (USA) - Faribole (Ire)
2^{10gf} 4^{10gs} 6^{10gf} 6^{11g} 8^{13gf} 3^{11gf} 1^{14gf}
8^{12gf} **1-1-8 £26,423**

Hilites (Ire) *J S Moore* — 81
2 ch f Desert King (Ire) - Slayjay (Ire)
4^{5gf} 5^{5g} 7^{6gf} 5^{5gf} 3^{5gf} 7^{6gf} 4^{6y} 2^{7gf}
11^{7gf} 1^{6s} 1^{6gf} 7^{6gf} 1^{6f} 9^{6gf} 16^{7g} 4^{6gf} **3-2-16**
£17,862

Hill Farm Classic *M Wellings*
3 ch g Meqdaam (USA) - Wing Of Freedom
10^{8gf} 14^{12gf} **0-0-2**

Hill Magic *W S Kittow* — 74 a45
8 br g Magic Ring (Ire) - Stock Hill Lass
3^{8gf} 8^{8g} 11^{7gf} 5^{7gf} 6^{8gf} 1^{8gf} 6^{8gf} 6^{8sd}
1-1-8 £2,806

Hills Of Gold *M W Easterby* — 76
4 b g Danehill (USA) - Valley Of Gold (Fr)
9^{10gf} 17^{8g} 17^{10s} 14^{8gf} 5^{8gf} 10^{8s} 17^{gf}
17^{gf} 4^{8gf} 9^{7gf} 12^{8g} **2-0-11 £11,925**

Hills Spitfire (Ire) *P W Harris* — 93
2 b/br c Kahyasi - Questina (Fr)
2^{8gf} 4^{10gs} **0-1-2 £2,574**

Hillside Girl (Ire) *A Berry* — 67
2 b f Tagula (Ire) - Kunucu (Ire)
4^{5gf} 1^{5g} 3^{5g} 4^{5gf} PU^{5gf} **1-0-5 £5,804**

Hilltime (Ire) *J J Quinn* — 45
3 b g Danetime (Ire) - Ceannanas (Ire)
9^{8s} **0-0-1**

Hilltop Warning *D J Daly* — 97
6 b g Reprimand - Just Irene
12^{7gf} 1^{7gf} 16^{7gf} **1-0-3 £8,541**

Hilly Be *J R Jenkins*
2 b f Silver Patriarch (Ire) - Lolita (Fr)
17^{8s} **0-0-1**

Hilton Park (Ire) *J Balding* — 23
4 b f Dolphin Street (Fr) - Test Case
8^{6f} 12^{7gf} 14^{7sd} **0-0-3**

Hip Hop Harry *E A L Dunlop* — 67
3 b c First Trump - Rechanit (Ire)
3^{8g} 1^{10gf} 14^{10gs} **1-1-3 £4,646**

Hirvine (Fr) *T P Tate* — 54
5 ch g Snurge - Guadanella (Fr)
5^{12gf} 4^{14s} 5^{16gf} 3^{16gf} 10^{16gf} **0-0-5 £515**

Hit's Only Money (Ire) *P A Blockley* — 110
3 br g Hamas (Ire) - Toordillon (Ire)
4^{6g} 1^{6gf} 1^{6gf} 3^{6g} 22^{6s} **3-1-6**
£24,853

Hitman (Ire) *M Pitman* — 49
8 b g Contract Law (USA) - Loveville (USA)
14^{14gs} **0-0-1**

Ho Leng (Ire) *Miss L A Perratt* — 80
8 ch g Statoblest - Indigo Blue (Ire)
11^{7gf} 6^{8gf} 10^{8gf} 9^{7gf} 3^{7gf} 12^{8gf} 7^{8gf}
4^{7f} 4^{8gf} 17^{8g} **0-1-10 £2,223**

Ho Pang Yau *Miss L A Perratt* — 30
5 b/br g Pivotal - La Cabrilla
9^{6g} 12^{7gf} 15^{6gf} 14^{6f} **0-0-4**

Hoh Bleu Dee *S Kirk* — 87
2 b c Desert Style (Ire) - Ermine (Ire)
1^{6gf} 1^{6gf} 6^{7gf} 6^{6gf} 6^{7gf} **2-0-5 £8,932**

Hoh Buzzard (Ire) *M L W Bell* — 101
3 b f Alhaarth (Ire) - Indian Express
3^{9gf} 4^{9gf} 3^{8gf} 1^{8gf} 1^{9gs} 1^{10gf} 2^{10gs} 4^{9f}
3-4-8 £62,994

Hoh Invader (Ire) *Mrs A Duffield* — 49
11 b g Accordion - Newgate Fairy
10^{12gf} 3^{10gf} **0-1-2 £443**

Hoh Investor (Ire) *A M Balding* — 82 a97

3 b g Charnwood Forest (Ire) - Uffizi (Ire)
14^{7sd} 1^{7sd} 4^{8sd} 8^{7sd} 9^{8gf} 7^{8gf} 15^{7gf} 3^{7gf}
5^{7gf} 3^{7gf} 5^{8g} 9^{8gf} 5^{8gf} **1-2-13 £9,512**

Hoh Nelson *H Morrison* 63
2 b c Halling (USA) - Birsay
11^{8gf} 9^{8gf} 7^{8gf} **0-0-3**

Hoh Viss *S Kirk* 78
3 b g Rudimentary (USA) - Now And Forever (Ire)
4^{10gf} 4^{10gf} 5^{10gf} 2^{11gf} 2^{12gf} 5^{11gf} **0-2-6**
£3,677

Hoh's Back *Paul Johnson* 73 a78
4 b g Royal Applause - Paris Joelle (Ire)
3^{9sd} 2^{8sd} 5^{9sd} 6^{7sd} 9^{8sd} 3^{8sd} 4^{10gf} 10^{9gf}
5^{9gs} 6^{11sd} 8^{10gf} 1^{8gf} 1^{8sd} 4^{8y} 1^{8sd} 5^{9gf} 8^{8sd}
1^{8gf} 2^{8sd} 19^{7gs} **4-6-23**
£16,930

Holborn (UAE) *M R Channon* 113
2 b c Green Desert (USA) - Court Lane (USA)
1^{5gf} 4^{5s} 1^{5f} 5^{6gf} 4^{6g} 4^{6gf} 3^{6gf} **2-1-7**
£55,694

Hold That Tiger (USA) *A P O'Brien* 114 a118
3 ch c Storm Cat (USA) - Beware Of The Cat (USA)
17^{8g} 4^{8gf} 9^{10gf} 2^{9ft} 5^{10ft} **0-1-5**
£151,000

Hold The Line *W G M Turner* 57 a68
2 b g Titus Livius (Fr) - Multi-Sofft
7^{7gf} 6^{7gf} 2^{8sd} **0-1-3 £622**

Hold To Ransom (USA) *E A L Dunlop* 114
3 b f Red Ransom (USA) - Wassifa
4^{7gf} 2^{10gf} 6^{10gf} 1^{8f} 7^{8gf} 5^{9f} 7^{8gf} **1-1-7**
£48,575

Hold Up *E A L Dunlop* 42
2 ch f Daggers Drawn (USA) - Select Sale
10^{8gf} **0-0-1**

Holle Berry *G C H Chung* 12
3 b f Petoski - Plectrum
7^{10gf} 8^{11g} 7^{11gf} 7^{10gf} **0-0-4**

Hollow Jo *J R Jenkins* 77
3 b g Most Welcome - Sir Hollow (USA)
2^{6gf} 1^{6f} 1^{7gf} 1^{6gf} 1^{6g} 2^{5g} 11^{7gf} **4-2-7**
£16,326

Holly Hayes (Ire) *H Candy* 47
3 b f Alzao (USA) - Crystal Land
4^{10gf} 6^{10gf} **0-0-2 £438**

Holly Rose *D E Cantillon* 66
4 b f Charnwood Forest (Ire) - Divina Luna
14^{8f} 3^{8f} 5^{9gf} 6^{10gf} 2^{8gf} 1^{10gf} 11^{8gf}
3^{10gf} 4^{10f} 1^{10gf} 13^{10gf} 8^{10gf} **2-4-12 £7,941**

Holly Ryder (USA) *P F I Cole* 28 a2
3 ch f Spinning World (USA) - Ethyl Mae (USA)
11^{6gf} 8^{6sd} 7^{6gf} 18^{8gf} **0-0-4**

Holly Walk *R Hannon* 57
2 ch f Dr Fong (USA) - Holly Blue
11^{7gf} 9^{7gf} 9^{8gf} 4^{8gf} **0-0-4**

Hollybell *J Gallagher* 38 a60
4 b f Beveled (USA) - Fayre Holly (Ire)
13^{6sd} 12^{6sd} 19^{6gf} **0-0-3**

Hollywood Henry (Ire) *J Akehurst* 66
3 b g Bahhare (USA) - Takeshi (Ire)
8^{8gf} 11^{9gf} 9^{8f} 14^{8g} 16^{8g} 14^{9g} **0-0-6**

Holy Orders (Ire) *W P Mullins* 114
6 b h Unblest - Shadowglow
2^{10g} 1^{13s} 3^{12gy} 1^{14ys} 6^{14gf} UR^{12gy} 17^{16g}
2-2-7 £55,519

Home Coming *P S Felgate* 36 a24

5 br g Primo Dominie - Carolside
6^{8sd} 17^{6f} 16^{7gf} 12^{6gf} 8^{6f} 12^{7sw} **0-0-6**

Home Fleet (USA) *H R A Cecil* 77
3 ch c Gone West (USA) - All At Sea (USA)
1^{7g} 4^{8gf} **1-0-2 £6,192**

Homelife (Ire) *P W D'Arcy* 66
5 b g Persian Bold - Share The Vision
13^{16gf} 5^{15gf} 5^{15g} 6^{12gf} **0-0-4**

Homeric Trojan *M Brittain* 55
3 ch c Hector Protector (USA) - Housefull
10^{8gf} 7^{10gf} 9^{8gf} **0-0-3**

Homeward (Ire) *G A Butler* 22
2 ch f Kris - Home Truth
14^{6gf} **0-0-1**

Honest Injun *B W Hills* 74
2 b c Efisio - Sioux
14^{6gf} 2^{7gs} **0-1-2 £932**

Honey's Gift *G G Margarson* 45
4 b f Terimon - Honeycroft
14^{12sd} 8^{12g} **0-0-2**

Honeybourne *Mrs Mary Hambro* 52
4 b f Sri Pekan - Peetsie (Ire)
15^{10g} 8^{10gf} 11^{8gf} 2^{7gf} **0-1-4 £966**

Honeystreet (Ire) *J S Moore* 60 a33
3 b f Woodborough (USA) - Ring Of Kerry (Ire)
10^{8sd} 13^{6gf} 14^{7gf} 3^{7gf} 7^{7gf} 10^{8gf} 1^{8f}
5^{10f} 1^{8g} 6^{8f} 12^{8gf} 8^{8f} **2-1-12 £7,454**

Honor Rouge (Ire) *P W Harris* 93
4 ch f Highest Honor (Fr) - Ayers Rock (Ire)
15^{10gf} 11^{12gf} 6^{12gf} 10^{10gf} 8^{12gf} 13^{11gf}
1-0-6 £9,579

Honor's Lad *Mrs L C Jewell* a45
4 ch g Sabrehill (USA) - Ackcontent (USA)
13^{12sd} 8^{7sd} 9^{11sd} **0-0-3**

Honorine (Ire) *J W Payne* 90
3 b f Mark Of Esteem (Ire) - Blue Water (USA)
2^{8f} 1^{8gf} 2^{8f} 1^{8g} 2^{8gf} 4^{8g} 3^{8g} **2-4-7**
£16,812

Hoopz *Mrs A J Perrett* 46
3 gr f Linamix (Fr) - Pearl Venture
12^{7gf} 4^{8gf} **0-0-2 £282**

Hope Diamond (Ire) *Mrs J Candlish* 33
5 ch g Bigstone (Ire) - Mujtahida (Ire)
4^{12y} 7^{7sd} 10^{12f} **0-0-3 £259**

Hope Sound (Ire) *J Noseda* 65
3 b g Turtle Island (Ire) - Lucky Pick
2^{10gs} 7^{10gf} 7^{10gf} **0-1-3 £1,154**

Horizon Hill (USA) *Mrs J R Ramsden* 62
3 b g Distant View (USA) - Accadia Rocket (USA)
10^{7y} 5^{7gf} 7^{7gf} 9^{8g} 6^{8g} 8^{7gf} 4^{6gf} 3^{6gf}
8^{5gf} 6^{6gf} 13^{7gs} 14^{8gf} 4^{7gf} **0-1-13 £932**

Horizontal (USA) *H R A Cecil* 62
3 ch c Distant View (USA) - Proud Lou (USA)
5^{8gf} **0-0-1**

Hormuz (Ire) *Paul Johnson* 56 a57
7 b g Hamas (Ire) - Balqis (USA)
8^{7sw} 15^{7gf} 9^{8sd} 5^{8f} 16^{8gf} 4^{6gs} 13^{6gs}
8^{10gf} 14^{9gf} 4^{9f} 7^{8sd} 12^{8gf} 9^{7y} 6^{8gf} 14^{7gf} 4^{8sw}
15^{10gf} **0-2-17 £686**

Horner (USA) *P F I Cole* 83
2 b c Rahy (USA) - Dynashore (Can)
4^{6gf} 4^{8gf} 6^{7gf} **0-0-3 £1,878**

Horton Dancer *I W McInnes* a27
6 b g Rambo Dancer (Can) - Horton Lady
6^{16sd} 6^{16sd} **0-0-2**

Hot Lips Page (Fr) *R Hannon* 65
2 b f Hamas (Ire) - Salt Peanuts (Ire)
7⁶ᵍᶠ 7⁷ᵍᶠ 5⁶ᵍᶠ **0-0-3**

Hot Love *John J Walsh* 28 a55
4 b Blushing Flame (USA) - Tiama (Ire)
2¹²ˢᵈ 3¹²ˢʷ 4¹⁶ˢᵈ 10¹²ˢᵈ 14⁸ᵍᶠ 13¹¹ˢ **0-2-6**
£1,419

Hoteliers' Dream *W S Kittow* 31
5 b m Reprimand - Pride Of Britain (Can)
15¹⁰ᵍᶠ 8¹²ᵍ 8¹²ˢʷ 10¹⁴ᵍᶠ **0-0-4**

House Of Blues *J A Osborne* 38 a58
2 b c Grand Lodge (USA) - Sartigila
10⁸ˢᵈ 9⁸ˢᵈ 13⁸ᵍˢ **0-0-3**

House Of York (USA) *M R Channon* 62
2 b c Seeking The Gold (USA) - Housa Dancer (Fr)
6⁷ᵍᶠ 5⁷ᵍ 12⁶ᵍᶠ **0-0-3**

Houseparty (Ire) *J A B Old* 75
5 b/br g Grand Lodge (USA) - Special Display
10¹⁰ᵍᶠ 15¹²ᵍ **0-0-2**

Hout Bay *Jedd O'Keeffe* 70 a54
6 ch g Komaite (USA) - Maiden Pool
7⁶ˢʷ 6⁶ˢᵈ 3⁵ᵍ 6⁵ᵍᶠ 13⁶ᵍᶠ 5⁶ᶠ 3⁵ᵍˢ 9⁵ᵍᶠ
7⁵ᵍˢ 6⁵ᵍ 5⁵ᵍᶠ 13⁶ᵍᶠ 10⁶ᵍˢ **0-2-13 £1,426**

Hov *J J Quinn* 82 a92
3 gr g Petong - Harifa
3⁷ᵍ 3⁷ᵍᶠ 8⁶ᵍᶠ 4⁶ᵍ 1⁷ˢᵈ 1⁸ˢᵈ 2⁸ᵍˢ 5¹⁰ᵍ 4⁸ˢ
13⁷ˢᵈ **2-4-10 £11,929**

How's Things *D Haydn Jones* 48 a74
3 b g Danzig Connection (USA) - Dim Ots
4⁷ˢᵈ 6⁷ˢʷ 6⁹ˢᵈ 4⁷ᵍᶠ 14⁸ᵍ 3⁹ˢᵈ 1⁷ˢᵈ 1⁹ˢᵈ
2-0-8 £4,932

Howaboys Quest (USA) *Ferdy Murphy* 27 a29
6 b g Quest For Fame - Doctor Black (USA)
5¹²ˢʷ 9¹⁷ᵍᶠ **0-0-2**

Howards Dream (Ire) *D A Nolan* 54
5 b g King's Theatre (Ire) - Keiko
10¹¹ᵍˢ 6¹²ᵍˢ 3¹⁰ᵍˢ 12¹³ᵍˢ 3¹⁴ᶠ 8¹²ᵍᶠ 8¹⁶ᵍᶠ
1¹²ᵍᶠ 5¹¹ᵍᶠ 4¹³ᵍᶠ 11¹²ᵍ 5¹³ᵍᶠ 5¹⁴ᶠ 11¹²ᵍᶠ 9¹⁴ᵍᶠ
6¹¹ᵍ 11¹³ᵍˢ **1-1-17 £6,249**

Howards Hero (Ire) *Paul Johnson* a60
4 gr g Paris House - Gold Braisim (Ire)
10⁵ˢʷ 4⁵ˢᵈ 8⁵ˢᵈ **0-0-3**

Howick Falls (USA) *D R Loder* 109
2 b c Stormin Fever (USA) - Hollins (USA)
1⁵ᵍˢ 3⁵ᶠ 7⁶ᵍ 1⁵ᵍᶠ 1⁵ᵍ **3-1-5 £61,957**

Howle Hill (Ire) *A King* 109
3 b g Ali-Royal (Ire) - Grandeur And Grace (USA)
9¹⁰ᵍᶠ 3⁸ᵍᶠ 3⁸ᵍᶠ 21⁸ᵍᶠ 1¹⁰ᵍˢ 2¹⁰ᵍᶠ 7¹²ᵍᶠ
1-3-7 £22,484

Hoxne Star (Ire) *M R Channon* 66
2 b g Soviet Star (USA) - Shakanda (Ire)
1⁷ᵍ 4⁸ᵍᶠ **1-0-2 £3,916**

Hsi Wang Mu (Ire) *G C Bravery* 46 a29
2 ch f Dr Fong (USA) - Oh Hebe (Ire)
4⁶ᵍ 5⁵ˢᵈ 8⁶ᵍ 3⁷ᵍᶠ 10⁸ᵍᶠ 9⁸ᵍᶠ **0-0-6 £370**

Hub Hub *W R Muir* a53
5 b g Polish Precedent (USA) - Ghassanah
6⁸ˢᵈ 5⁷ˢʷ 5⁷ˢʷ 7¹²ˢᵈ **0-0-4**

Hufflepuff (Ire) *J L Dunlop* 93
4 b f Desert King (USA) - Circle Of Chalk (Fr)
6⁵ᵍ 6⁵ᶠ 11⁵ᵍ 5⁵ᵍᶠ 4⁵ᵍᶠ 9⁶ᵍ 9⁵ˢ
0-0-8 £2,019

Huge Heart (NZ) *W M Brisbourne* 40
7 b g T V Heart Throb (USA) - Christmas Lady (NZ)
8⁹ᵍ **0-0-1**

Hugh The Man (Ire) *N P Littmoden* 55 a76
4 b g Hamas (Ire) - Run To Jenny
1⁷ˢᵈ 8⁷ˢᵈ 9⁷ˢᵈ 2⁷ˢʷ 1⁸ˢᵈ 2⁸ˢᵈ 5⁹ᶠᵗ 7⁸ᵍˢ
9⁸ᵍ 13⁸ᵍˢ **2-2-10 £8,625**

Hugs Dancer (Fr) *J G Given* 109
6 b g Cadeaux Genereux - Embracing
1¹⁹ᵍᶠ 8¹⁶ᵍᶠ 8¹⁶ᵍˢ 1¹⁴ᵍᶠ 22¹⁴ᵍᶠ 3¹⁸ᵍ 7¹²ᵍ
9¹⁶ᵍ **2-0-8 £130,790**

Hugwity *G C Bravery* 42
11 ch g Cadeaux Genereux - Nuit D'Ete (USA)
12⁸ᵍᶠ 4⁸ᵍᶠ 10¹⁰ˢᵈ 10¹²ᵍᶠ 4¹⁰ᵍᶠ **0-0-5**

Huja (Ire) *Sir Michael Stoute* 92
3 b f Alzao (USA) - Nasanice (Ire)
6⁷ᵍ **0-0-1 £480**

Hula Ballew *M Dods* 65
3 ch f Weldnaas (USA) - Ballon
3¹⁰ᵍᶠ 13¹⁴ᵍᶠ 14¹⁰ᶠ 4⁹ᵍᶠ 2⁹ᵍ 1¹⁸ˢ 3⁸ᵍᶠ 3⁸ᶠ
6⁸ᶠ 6⁸ᵍ **1-2-10 £7,386**

Hum (Ire) *A C Stewart* 66
2 ch f Cadeaux Genereux - Ensorceleuse (Fr)
6⁶ᵍᶠ 8⁷ᵍᶠ 9⁷ᵍᶠ **0-0-3**

Humdinger (Ire) *D J Daly* 67 a66
3 b f Charnwood Forest (Ire) - High Finish
9⁸ˢᵈ 9⁸ᵍᶠ 11¹⁰ᵍᶠ 2¹¹ᵍᶠ 2¹²ᵍᶠ 12¹²ᵍᶠ 3¹²ᶠ
6¹⁵ᵍᶠ 1¹⁴ˢʷ **2-3-9 £8,403**

Humid Climate *Mrs A J Perrett* 85
3 ch c Desert King (Ire) - Pontoon
1¹⁰ᵍᶠ 3¹²ᵍᶠ 12¹⁰ᵍ **1-0-3 £5,401**

Humility *C A Cyzer* 38
2 b f Polar Falcon (USA) - Rich In Love (Ire)
11⁶ᵍᶠ **0-0-1**

Humouresque *Sir Mark Prescott* 108 a87
3 b f Pivotal - Miswaki Belle (USA)
1⁸ˢᵈ 1⁰ˢᵈ 4¹⁰ˢᵈ 1¹¹ᵍ 1¹¹ᵍ 1¹¹ᵍ 6¹⁰ˢ 8¹²ᵍᶠ
5-0-8 £55,482

Hunter's Mark (USA) *J W Hills* 46 a25
3 b f Titus Livius (Fr) - Manfath (Ire)
5⁷ˢᵈ 14⁸ᵍ 7⁸ᵍᶠ **0-0-3**

Hunter's Valley *R Hannon* 74
2 b f Nicolotte - Down The Valley
8⁶ᵍᶠ 5⁷ᵍᶠ 3⁷ᵍᶠ **0-1-4 £2,972**

Hunting Lodge (Ire) *D R Loder* 97
2 ch c Grand Lodge (USA) - Vijaya (USA)
1⁵ᵍᶠ 1⁸ᵍᶠ 7⁸ᵍ **2-0-3 £11,782**

Hunting Pink *H Morrison* 55
2 b f Foxhound (USA) - Dancing Bluebell (Ire)
8⁶ᵍᶠ 4⁷ᵍᶠ 4⁶ʰᵈ 6⁴ᵍᶠ 3⁷ᶠ 7¹⁰ᵍᶠ 11⁸ᵍᶠ **0-1-7**
£340

Hurricane Alan (Ire) *R Hannon* 111
3 b c Mukaddamah (USA) - Bint Al Balad (Ire)
1⁸ᵍᶠ 7⁸ᵍ 6⁸ᵍᶠ 5⁷ᵍ 2⁸ᵍ 9⁷ᵍᶠ 5⁸ᵍᶠ **1-1-7**
£45,750

Hurricane Coast *P A Blockley* 64
4 b g Hurricane Sky (Aus) - Tread Carefully
12⁷ᵍᶠ 5⁷ᶠ 8⁸ᵍᶠ 6¹¹ᵍᶠ 5⁸ᵍᶠ 8⁸ᵍᶠ 3⁷ᵍᶠ 11⁷ᵍᶠ
2⁸ᵍˢ 17⁸ᵍ **0-2-10 £949**

Hurricane Floyd (Ire) *M C Pipe* 96
5 ch g Pennekamp (USA) - Mood Swings (Ire)
3⁸ᵍ 8⁸ᵍ 7⁷ᵍ 2⁸ᵍˢ 2⁷ᶠ 16⁸ᵍ 7⁷ᵍ 3⁷ᵍᶠ
4⁷ᵍᶠ 13⁷ᵍᶠ 27⁹ᵍᶠ **0-4-13 £17,029**

Hurricane Lily (Ire) *B J Meehan* 56
2 b f Ali-Royal (Ire) - Bint Al Balad (Ire)
4⁶ᵍᶠ 3⁶ᵍᶠ 13⁶ᵍᶠ 4⁶ᶠ **0-1-4 £980**

Hurricane Love (USA) *B W Hills* 78
3 b f Quiet American (USA) - Outlasting (USA)

9^{11gf} 6^{7gf} **0-0-2**

Husky (Pol) *R M H Cowell*   55 a52
5 b g Special Power - Hallo Bambina (Pol)
13^{6sw} 37^{7sd} 7^{8f} 2^{10gf} 10^{10f} 15^{10gf} 12^{8gf}
9^{8gf} 9^{10f} **0-2-9 £1,439**

Huwaidah *G A Butler*   52
3 b f Shareef Dancer (USA) - Romoosh
7^{10gf} 4^{8gf} **0-0-2 £300**

Hymns And Arias *Ronald Thompson*   43
2 b f Mtoto - Ewenny
13^{7gf} 9^{7gf} 13^{6gf} 1^{7gf} 9^{7f} **1-0-5 £2,268**

I Am Trouble (Ire) *J S Moore*   a8
3 b f Darnay - Secret Combe (Ire)
7^{8sd} 13^{7sd} **0-0-2**

I Cried For You (Ire) *J G Given*   a81
8 b g Statoblest - Fall Of The Hammer (Ire)
13^{10sd} **0-0-1**

I Got Rhythm *Mrs M Reveley*   43
5 gr m Lycius (USA) - Eurythmic
6^{16gf} 7^{16gf} **0-0-2**

I See No Ships *M Mullineaux*   31 a15
3 b f Danzig Connection (USA) - Killick
8^{7sd} 7^{7gf} 8^{6g} **0-0-3**

I T Consultant *Miss L A Perratt*   61 a49
5 b g Rock City - Game Germaine
8^{9sd} 13^{6gs} 6^{5gf} 8^{5g} 13^{6gf} 8^{5gf} **0-0-6**

I Tina *A G Juckes*   7 b m Lycius (USA) - Tintomara (Ire)
12^{10gf} **0-0-1**

I Wish *M Madgwick*   70 a76
5 b m Beveled (USA) - Ballystate
2^{7sd} 8^{6gf} 2^{6g} 7^{7gf} 7^{7gf} 16^{6g} 8^{7gf} 7^{6gf}
6^{7sd} **0-2-9 £2,963**

I Wish I Knew *P J Makin*   a33
2 br c Petong - Hoh Dancer
10^{5sd} **0-0-1**

I Won't Dance (Ire) *R Hannon*   78
2 b c Marju (Ire) - Carnelly (Ire)
10^{6gf} 1^{6gf} 2^{7gf} **1-0-3 £5,512**

I'm Dancing *T D Easterby*   59
2 b f Polish Precedent (USA) - Dancing Heights (Ire)
9^{6gf} 5^{7gf} 3^{7gs} 6^{7g} 7^{8gf} **0-1-5 £802**

I'm Magic *R Hannon*   71
3 ch f First Trump - Crystal Magic
13^{7gf} 4^{7gf} 10^{5gf} 2^{8g} 1^{8f} 10^{8gf} 19^{7gs}
1-2-7 £5,108

I'm No Time Waster *Mrs H Dalton*   29
4 ch f Timeless Times (USA) - Forbidden Monkey
9^{8g} 12^{9sw} **0-0-2**

Iamback *M G Quinlan*   41 a25
3 b f Perugino (USA) - Smouldering (Ire)
8^{10gf} 6^{7gf} 7^{6sd} **0-0-3**

Iberus (Ger) *M C Pipe*   104
5 b g Monsun (Ger) - Iberica (Ger)
6^{13gf} 7^{8g} 5^{12gf} 17^{12gf} 5^{10g} **0-0-5**
£1,646

Icannshift (Ire) *P W Harris*   84
3 b c Night Shift (USA) - Cannikin (Ire)
7^{7g} 11^{8g} 10^{7g} 8^{7gf} 7^{7gf} 14^{7gf} 4^{7g} 7^{7gs}
6^{7gf} **0-0-9 £756**

Ice And Fire *B D Leavy*   65
4 b g Cadeaux Genereux - Tanz (Ire)
10^{10gf} 6^{8gs} 13^{7g} 6^{8gf} 11^{8gs} 10^{7g} 5^{10g}
0-0-7

Ice Cracker *Mrs A J Bowlby*   71 a47

4 b f Polar Falcon (USA) - Blessed Honour
8^{10gf} 10^{8gf} 10^{10sd} 2^{8f} 10^{7gf} 3^{8gf} 6^{9gf}
2^{8gf} 2^{8gf} 1^{8g} 10^{9gf} **1-4-11 £8,205**

Ice Dragon *M H Tompkins*   57 a67
2 b f Polar Falcon (USA) - Qilin (Ire)
6^{7gf} 2^{7sd} **0-1-2 £1,048**

Ice Dynasty *J S Wainwright*   3 b f Polar Prince (Ire) - Yankee Special
14^{9gf} 5^{8f} **0-0-2 £513**

Ice Palace *J R Fanshawe*   99
3 ch f Polar Falcon (USA) - White Palace
3^{8gf} 1^{8gf} 1^{8g} 4^{8gf} 8^{10gf} **2-1-5 £12,638**

Icecap *P Butler*   65 a60
3 b f Polar Falcon (USA) - Warning Light
4^{8sd} 2^{8sd} 9^{8sd} 4^{7gf} 4^{7f} 5^{7g} 6^{8gf} 6^{8gf}
0-1-8 £1,392

Iced Diamond (Ire) *W M Brisbourne*   61
4 b g Petardia - Prime Site (Ire)
8^{7gf} 16^{6gf} 7^{7g} 10^{6gf} 9^{7gf} 2^{6g} 5^{6gf} 6^{6f}
2^{6gf} 2^{7g} 7^{6gf} **0-2-11 £2,868**

Icenaslice (Ire) *J J Quinn*   63
2 b f Fayruz - Come Dancing
3^{7g} 4^{6gf} 6^{7gs} **0-1-3 £587**

Icey Run *D G Bridgwater*   25
3 b g Runnett - Polar Storm
15^{7g} 8^{8f} 15^{12sw} **0-0-3**

Icklingham (Ire) *John M Oxx*   100
3 b c Sadler's Wells (USA) - Braiswick
11^{10g} 2^{10s} 11^{10ys} 6^{16f} 4^{14ys} **1-1-6**
£14,617

Idle Chatter *M L W Bell*   24
3 b f Spectrum (Ire) - Elfin Laughter
12^{8gs} **0-0-1**

Idle Power (Ire) *J R Boyle*   87 a86
5 b g Common Grounds - Idle Fancy
2^{6gf} 1^{6g} 5^{6gf} 13^{6gf} 17^{6g} 3^{6gf} 8^{7gf} 9^{6g}
9^{7gf} 13^{6g} 4^{7sd} 16^{7gf} 10^{6f} 7^{7sd} **0-1-14**
£3,917

If *B R Millman*   29
4 b f Emperor Jones (USA) - Mighty Flash
9^{8gf} 17^{7f} **0-0-2**

If By Chance *R Craggs*   73 a75
5 ch g Risk Me (Fr) - Out Of Harmony
4^{6sd} 1^{6sd} 3^{7gf} 4^{6gs} 15^{6sd} 1^{6sd} 5^{6gf} 11^{6sw}
7^{6sd} 1^{6g} 11^{6gf} **4-0-11 £12,586**

If I Can Dream (Ire) *B J Meehan*   a49
3 ch f Brief Truce (USA) - Only In Dreams
11^{6sd} 4^{8sd} 3^{7sd} 18^{6sd} **1-1-4 £3,359**

If Paradise *R Hannon*   98
2 b c Compton Place - Sunley Stars
3^{5gf} 1^{5g} 4^{6f} 1^{5gf} 6^{5g} 2^{5gf} 15^{6g} 5^{5g}
2-2-8 £90,620

Iffraaj *M A Jarvis*   82
2 b c Zafonic (USA) - Pastorale
3^{7s} 1^{7gf} **1-1-2 £4,242**

Iffy *P D Cundell*   52 a46
2 b g Orpen (USA) - Hopesay
9^{7gf} 5^{6sd} 8^{5gf} **0-0-3**

Iftikhar (USA) *W M Brisbourne*   65
4 b g Storm Cat (USA) - Muhubh (USA)
10^{8gf} 2^{8gf} 2^{12gf} 4^{12gf} **0-2-4 £3,294**

Ijtihad *M P Tregoning*   78
3 b/br c Darshaan - Asfurah (USA)
6^{7gf} 2^{7gf} 2^{9gf} 2^{8gf} 2^{10g} 2^{8gf} 1^{10f} **1-3-7**
£8,904

Ikan (Ire) *N P Littmoden* 100
3 br f Sri Pekan (USA) - Iktidar
4⁶ˢ 10⁶ᵍˢ 8⁶ʰʸ 12⁶ᵍᶠ 6⁶ᵍᶠ 4⁵ᶠ 1⁵ᵍᶠ 3⁵ᵍ
1⁵ᵍᶠ 2⁵ᵍᶠ 4⁵ᵍᶠ 18⁶ᵍ 11⁵ᵍᶠ **2-2-13 £22,612**

Ikhtyar (Ire) *J H M Gosden* 125
3 b c Unfuwain (USA) - Sabria (USA)
3⁸ᵍᶠ 1⁸ᵍᶠ 2⁸ᵍᶠ 1¹⁰ᵍ 9¹⁰ʰᵒ **2-2-5 £36,071**

Il Cavaliere *Mrs M Reveley* 68
8 b g Mtoto - Kalmia
4¹⁶ᵍ **0-0-1 £799**

Ile Michel *M C Pipe* 94
6 b g Machiavellian (USA) - Circe's Isle
1⁷ᵍᶠ 1⁷ᵍᶠ 1⁸ᵍ 6⁷ᵍᶠ 6⁷ᵍᶠ 3⁷ᵍᶠ 2⁸ᵍ 1⁹ᵍᶠ
24⁷ᵍᶠ **4-1-9 £22,011**

Illeana (Ger) *W R Muir* 52
2 ch f Lomitas - Illyria (Ire)
9⁷ᵍᶠ 8⁸ᵍᶠ **0-0-2**

Illusionist *Mrs N Macauley* 44 a53
5 b g Mujtahid (USA) - Merlin's Fancy
3⁷ˢʷ 4⁷ˢᵈ 8⁸ˢᵈ 11⁸ˢᵈ 8⁷ˢʷ 12⁷ˢʷ 13⁸ˢᵈ
5⁸ᶠ 8¹⁰ᶠ **0-2-9 £427**

Illusive (Ire) *M Wigham* a74
6 b g Night Shift (USA) - Mirage
9⁵ˢᵈ 5⁶ˢᵈ 3⁶ˢᵈ 7⁶ˢᵈ 4⁶ˢᵈ 3⁶ˢᵈ 2⁶ˢᵈ **0-2-7**
£2,060

Illusive Gait *T D Easterby* 45
3 b g Cloudings (Ire) - Miller's Gait
8¹⁰ᵍˢ 11¹²ᵍᶠ 5¹²ᵍᶠ **0-0-3**

Illustrator *H-A Pantall* 110
3 b c Sadler's Wells (USA) - Illusory
2¹⁰ᵍᶠ 1¹⁰ᵍᶠ 8¹⁰ᵍˢ 6¹²ʰᵒ **1-0-4 £12,068**

Illustria *M R Channon* 94
3 b f Seeking The Gold (USA) - Noble Rose (Ire)
5⁷ᵍᶠ 8¹¹ᵍᶠ 4⁷ᵍᶠ 8⁸ᵍᶠ **0-0-4 £2,850**

Illustrious Duke *M Mullineaux* 7 a60
5 b g Dancing Spree (USA) - Killick
8⁷ˢᵈ 7⁸ˢᵈ 8⁸ˢᵈ 8⁸ˢʷ 6⁸ˢᵈ 7⁷ˢᵈ 7⁷ˢᵈ 10⁸ˢᵈ
4⁸ˢᵈ 12¹¹ˢᵈ 1⁷ˢᵈ 2⁸ˢᵈ 12⁸ˢᵈ 9⁹ˢᵈ **1-1-14**
£4,352

Iloveturtle (Ire) *M C Chapman* 73 a63
3 b g Turtle Island (Ire) - Gan Ainm (Ire)
9⁸ˢᵈ 2⁸ˢʷ 12¹⁰ˢᵈ 6⁸ˢᵈ 3¹²ᵍᶠ 6¹²ˢᵈ 7¹²ˢᵈ
4¹⁰ᵍ 2¹²ᵍˢ 7¹⁴ᵍᶠ 9¹²ᵍᶠ 9¹¹ˢʷ 7¹⁶ᵍᶠ **0-2-13**
£2,502

Ilwadod *M R Channon* 36
2 b c Cadeaux Genereux - Wedoudah (Ire)
15⁶ᵍᶠ 13⁸ᵍ **0-0-2**

Imnotalady *P R Hedger* a56
5 ch m Shalford (Ire) - Lissahane Lass
7¹⁰ˢᵈ 5¹²ˢᵈ 4¹²ˢʷ **0-0-3 £257**

Imoya (Ire) *B J Meehan* 102
4 b f Desert King (Ire) - Urgent Liaison (Ire)
5¹²ᵍᶠ 9¹⁰ᵍ 5¹⁴ᵍ **0-0-3 £1,675**

Impeller (Ire) *W R Muir* 94
4 ch g Polish Precedent (USA) - Almaaseh (Ire)
14⁸ᵍᶠ 4⁸ᵍ 3⁸ᵍ 6⁸ᵍᶠ 16⁷ᶠ 2⁸ᵍᶠ 4⁸ᵍᶠ 5⁸ᶠ
1⁹ᵍᶠ 11¹⁰ᵍ 1⁹ᵍ 13¹⁰ᵍᶠ 21⁹ᵍᶠ 2⁸ᵍᶠ 2⁸ᵍᶠ **2-5-15**
£20,012

Imperative (USA) *J W Unett* 58 a70
3 ch c Woodman (USA) - Wandesta
5¹²ᵍˢ 5⁸ᵛˢ 0⁸ᵍˢ 7⁷ˢʷ **0-0-5 £2,978**

Imperial Dancer *M R Channon* 121
5 b h Primo Dominie - Gorgeous Dancer (Ire)
4¹⁰ᵛˢ 7¹⁰ᵍ 5¹²ᵍᶠ 3¹⁰ᵍ 5¹³ᵍᶠ 7¹¹ʸˢ 5¹⁰ᵍ 1¹⁰ᵍ
2¹⁰ᵍᶠ 3¹²ᵍˢ 1¹¹ᵍ 6¹⁰ʰᵒ 4¹⁰ᵍᶠ 1¹²ᵍᶠ **3-2-14**
£116,949

Imperial Echo (USA) *T D Barron* 81
2 b g Labeeb - Regal Baby (USA)
2⁵ᵍᶠ 4⁶ᵍ 2⁶ᵍᶠ 1⁷ᶠ 4⁶ᵍ 3⁵ᵍˢ 3⁶ᵍᶠ **1-4-7**
£28,936

Imperial Princess (Ire) *D Haydn Jones* 51 a27
2 b f Imperial Ballet (Ire) - Rose Tint (Ire)
7⁶ᶠ 10⁶ᵍ 16⁵ˢᵈ 11⁶ˢᵈ 11⁸ˢᵈ **0-0-5**

Imperial Royale (Ire) *P L Clinton* 64
2 ch g Ali-Royal (Ire) - God Speed Her
11⁷ᵍᶠ 6⁷ᵍᶠ 3⁹ᵍ 8⁷ᵍᶠ 14⁸ᵍᶠ 5⁷ᵍᶠ 2⁸ᵍᶠ **0-1-7**
£1,117

Imperial Stride *Sir Michael Stoute* 112
2 b c Indian Ridge - Place De L'Opera
1⁶ᵍᶠ 1⁷ᵍᶠ 6⁷ᵍᶠ **2-0-3 £16,162**

Imperialistic (Ire) *K R Burke* 86 a81
2 b f Imperial Ballet (Ire) - Shefoog
5⁶ᵍᶠ 1⁶ʰʸ 9⁶ᵍᶠ 4⁶ᵍ 3⁷ˢᵈ 4⁸ˢʷ 2⁷ᵍ 3⁶ᵍˢ
1-3-8 £8,448

Imperium *B J Meehan* 79
2 b c Imperial Ballet (Ire) - Partenza (USA)
11⁵ᵍᶠ 3⁶ᵍˢ 4⁶ᶠ 6⁵ᵍ 2⁶ᵍ 8⁶ᵍᶠ 11⁶ᵍᶠ **0-1-7**
£2,126

Impero *W Clay* 5
5 b g Emperor Jones - Fight Right (Fr)
18⁸ᵍᶠ **0-0-1**

Impersonator *J L Dunlop* 87
3 b g Zafonic (USA) - Conspiracy
12⁸ᵍᶠ 11⁸ᵍᶠ 12⁹ᵍ 8¹⁰ᵍ 7¹⁰ᵍˢ 4⁸ˢ 17⁷ᵍˢ
0-0-7 £1,074

Impinda (Ire) *P Monteith* 51
4 b f Idris (Ire) - Last Finale (USA)
3¹⁰ᵍᶠ 4¹¹ᵍᶠ 6¹¹ᵍˢ 5¹³ᵍˢ 9¹²ᵍᶠ 11¹³ᵍˢ **0-0-6**
£1,001

Impressive Flight (Ire) *T D Barron* 94
4 b f Flying Spur (Aus) - Certain Impression (USA)
5⁶ᵍˢ 3⁶ᵍᶠ 6⁶ᵍᶠ **0-0-3 £3,339**

Imprint (UAE) *M R Channon* 60
2 b c Mark Of Esteem (Ire) - Temora (Ire)
2⁵ᵍᶠ 10⁷ᵍᶠ **0-1-2 £1,166**

Impulsive Air (Ire) *J R Weymes* 37
11 b g Try My Best (USA) - Tracy's Sundown
14¹⁰ᵍᶠ 11¹⁰ᵍᶠ 11¹⁰ᵍᶠ 8¹⁰ᵍᶠ 10¹⁰ᵍᶠ **0-0-5**

Impulsive Bid (Ire) *Jedd O'Keeffe* 60
2 b f Orpen (USA) - Tamburello (Ire)
4⁵ᵍᶠ 13⁶ᵍˢ 4⁶ᵍ **0-0-3 £581**

Impulsivo *Simon Earle* 31 a29
3 ch g Millkom - Joytime
10⁸ᵍᶠ 13¹³ˢᵈ **0-0-2**

Imshy (Ire) *R Pritchard-Gordon* 80
2 ch f Daggers Drawn (USA) - Paganina (Fr)
4⁶ᵍ 1⁷ʰᵒ 16ᵍˢ 6⁷ᵍᶠ **2-0-4 £23,683**

Imtihan (Ire) *S C Burrough* 46
4 ch c Unfuwain (USA) - Azyaa
23²⁰ᵍᶠ 13¹²ᵍ 9¹²ᶠ 9¹²ᵍ 12¹⁶ᵍᶠ **0-0-5**

Imtiyaz (USA) *Saeed Bin Suroor* 113 a115
4 ro c Woodman (USA) - Shadayid (USA)
1⁸ᵗ 8⁹ᵍ 6⁹ˢ 3¹⁰ᵍᶠ 1¹⁰ᵍᶠ **2-0-5 £59,998**

In A Silent Way (Ire) *M A Jarvis* 96
3 b f Desert Prince (Ire) - Pray (Ire)
10⁶ᵍᶠ 2⁸ᵍ 1⁹ᵍᶠ 1¹⁰ᵍᶠ 8¹⁰ᵍᶠ 2¹⁰ᶠ 2¹⁰ᵍᶠ
11¹⁰ᵍᶠ **2-3-8 £27,014**

In Deep *Mrs P N Dutfield* 89
2 b f Deploy - Bobbie Dee
5⁷ᵍ 5⁷ᵍᶠ 6⁸ᵍ 2⁸ᵍᶠ **0-1-4 £1,208**

In For The Craic (Ire) *P Butler* 27 a59

4 b g Our Emblem (USA) - Lucky State (USA)
3^{10sd} 2^{12sd} 3^{10sd} 4^{12sd} 6^{12sd} 17^{11gf} 16^{14gs}
0-3-7 £1,999

In Love *E A L Dunlop*   96
3 b f Unfuwain (USA) - Nemesia
3^{10gf} 1^{10gf} 3^{12g} 12^{12gs} 19^{13gs} 2^{12g} **1-3-6**
£10,589

In Luck *C E Brittain*   73
5 b m In The Wings - Lucca
7^{12sd} 6^{11gf} 4^{9gs} 4^{12gf} 8^{12gf} 4^{12g} 5^{12gf}
11^{11s} 6^{10gf} 7^{12g} 3^{12gs} **0-1-11 £3,341**

In Spirit (Ire) *D J S Cosgrove*   67
5 b g Distinctly North (USA) - June Goddess
9^{8sd} 5^{10gf} 5^{10g} 3^{12g} **0-1-4 £634**

In The Gloaming (Ire) *James Moffatt*   33
3 b f Avarice - Katherine Kath
7^{5gf} 12^{5gs} 14^{5gf} **0-0-3**

In The Green *J J Quinn*   47
4 b g Greensmith - Carn Maire
8^{5f} 7^{5gf} 18^{5gf} **0-0-3**

In The Leather (Ire) *Mrs J R Ramsden*
2 ch f Dr Devious (Ire) - Bodfari Quarry
10^{8gf} **0-0-1**

In The Pink (Ire) *M R Channon*   70
3 gr f Indian Ridge - Norfolk Lavender (Can)
5^{7gf} 8^{7gf} 4^{8gf} 3^{7f} 5^{5g} 1^{7gf} **1-0-6**
£3,864

In The Stars (Ire) *P R Webber*   58 a65
5 ch g Definite Article - Astronomer Lady (Ire)
8^{12sd} 4^{12sd} 13^{14g} 8^{12g} 14^{12sd} **0-0-5 £321**

In Time's Eye *D K Weld*   121
4 b c Singspiel (Ire) - Irish Edition (USA)
4^{11ys} 1^{10f} 3^{10gf} 3^{10gf} 10^{12g} **1-0-5**
£45,753

In Tune *P Mitchell*   a61
3 b g Distinctly North (USA) - Lingering
5^{7sd} 5^{10sd} **0-0-2**

In Xanadu (Ire) *J L Dunlop*   70
4 b g Persian Bold - Dromoland
4^{10g} 10^{10gf} 9^{8gf} 3^{8g} 5^{8g} **0-1-5 £884**

Inca Moon *R Brotherton*   55 a52
3 b f Sheikh Albadou - Incatinka
5^{8sd} 2^{7sd} 5^{8sd} 5^{8gf} 11^{7gf} 6^{7sd} 14^{8f}
13^{10gf} 12^{7gf} **0-1-9 £848**

Inch Again *M H Tompkins*   105
3 ch c Inchinor - Spoilt Again
1^{9gf} 2^{10gf} 5^{11g} 4^{10g} **1-1-4 £27,131**

Inch By Inch *P J Makin*   65 a40
4 b f Inchinor - Maid Welcome
14^{7sd} 10^{6sw} 11^{6sd} 10^{6gf} 4^{6f} 12^{5gf} 4^{5f}
1^{6f} 8^{6g} 6^{6gf} 2^{6gf} 11^{6g} 8^{6gf} 36^{gf} 11^{5f} 9^{6f}
1-2-16 £5,019

Inch High *J S Goldie*   50
5 ch g Inchinor - Harrken Heights (Ire)
12^{6gf} 6^{6f} 11^{7g} 2^{7g} 8^{6gf} 13^{8gf} **0-1-6**
£1,136

Inch Island (Ire) *J J Quinn*   73
3 b g Turtle Island (Ire) - Persian Light (Ire)
2^{7gs} 10^{8g} 1^{8gf} 3^{9gs} 6^{7gf} 12^{7gf} 10^{9sd}
1-2-7 £5,909

Inch Perfect *R A Fahey*   a89
8 b g Inchinor - Scarlet Veil
11^{1sd} 1^{14sd} 3^{12sd} **2-1-3 £7,390**

Inchberry *G A Butler*   110
3 b f Barathea (Ire) - Inchyre

2^{12gf} 4^{12g} 6^{12gf} 3^{9gf} **0-1-4 £26,810**

Inchconnel *Bob Jones*   60
2 b g Inchinor - Sharanella
9^{7g} 3^{7gf} 17^{8gs} **0-1-3 £362**

Inchcoonan *K R Burke*   a70
5 b m Emperor Jones (USA) - Miss Ivory Coast (USA)
6^{7sd} 4^{8sd} 5^{8sd} 4^{7sw} 4^{8sd} 2^{8sd} 4^{8sd} **0-1-7**
£1,583

Inchdura *N Tinkler*   79
5 ch g Inchinor - Sunshine Coast
13^{7gf} 15^{8gs} 11^{8gf} 12^{7g} 9^{8gf} 10^{8gf} 10^{7gf}
0-0-7

Incheni (Ire) *G Wragg*   68 a68
2 b f Nashwan (USA) - Inchmurrin
6^{6gf} 1^{7sd} **1-0-2 £3,640**

Inching *R M H Cowell*   68 a70
3 b f Inchinor - Tshusick
3^{5sd} 2^{5sd} 3^{5gf} 7^{6g} 3^{5f} 6^{5gf} 7^{5gf} 4^{6gf}
12^{6gf} 12^{6sd} **0-4-10 £3,423**

Inchinnan *C Weedon*   68 a66
6 b m Inchinor - Westering
4^{10sd} 6^{10sd} 5^{8g} 10^{10gf} 7^{8sd} **0-0-5 £525**

Inchnadamph *T J Fitzgerald*   50
3 b g Inchinor - Pelf (USA)
13^{8gs} 8^{8gf} 12^{11sw} **0-0-3**

Inchpast *M H Tompkins*   43
2 ch c Inchinor - Victor Ludorum
14^{7g} **0-0-1**

Incise *B J Meehan*   89
2 ch f Dr Fong (USA) - Pretty Sharp
3^{5gf} 2^{5gf} 9^{5gf} 1^{5gf} **1-1-4 £10,653**

Incisor *S Kirk*   53
2 b c Dracula (Aus) - Last Night's Fun (Ire)
7^{8sd} 5^{8gf} 6^{7gf} **0-0-3**

Incline (Ire) *T G Mills*   75
4 b g Danehill (USA) - Shalwar Kameez (Ire)
15^{8g} 15^{8gs} 7^{9gs} **0-0-3**

Incroyable *Sir Mark Prescott*   45
2 br f Linamix (Fr) - Crodelle (Ire)
17^{7gf} 10^{8f} 9^{7gf} 6^{8gf} **0-0-4**

Incursion *A King*   71
2 b c Inchinor - Morgannwg (Ire)
7^{7gf} 6^{8gf} 3^{8gf} **0-1-3 £964**

Indeco (Ire) *Mrs P N Dutfield*   43 a43
2 b g Indian Rocket - Canary Bird (Ire)
11^{6f} 14^{8gf} 4^{8sd} 10^{6sd} **0-0-4**

Indelible *J Hetherton*   a15
4 br f Polar Falcon (USA) - Ink Pot (USA)
12^{8sd} 12^{7sd} 17^{8gf} **0-0-3**

Indian Bazaar (Ire) *J M Bradley*   57
7 ch g Indian Ridge - Bazaar Promise
2^{5gf} 7^{5gf} 5^{5gf} 4^{5gf} 3^{5gf} 3^{5f} 6^{5gf} 15^{5gf}
3^{5g} 13^{5gf} 6^{5gf} 10^{5gf} 3^{5s} 1^{5gf} 4^{6f} 5^{5gf}
1-5-16 £6,378

Indian Beat *C L Popham*   28
6 ch g Indian Ridge - Rappa Tap Tap (Fr)
10^{10f} 10^{17f} 8^{18gf} **0-0-3**

Indian Beau *N P Littmoden*   59
2 b c Indian Rocket - Girl Next Door
4^{5gf} 12^{7gf} 12^{6gs} 19^{6gf} 26^{6gf} **0-0-5**
£416

Indian Blaze *Andrew Reid*   65 a73
9 ch g Indian Ridge - Odile
1^{10sd} 1^{10sd} 1^{10sd} 5^{10sd} 3^{10sd} 6^{10sd} 10^{10sd}
4^{10sd} 12^{10gf} 15^{10gs} 3^{8g} 4^{8gf} 7^{8gf} BD^{8gs} **3-3-14**

£10,373

Indian Call *B A McMahon* 64
2 ch c Classic Cliche (Ire) - Crees Sqaw
12^{5gf} 7^{6gs} 4^{6s} 15^{6gf} 14^{6gf} 0-0-5

Indian Creek *D R C Elsworth* 119 a105
5 br h Indian Ridge - Blue Water (USA)
4^{10sd} 1^{10g} 3^{10gf} 1^{12f} 5^{10gf} 3^{12g} 3^{12f} 3^{10gf}
2-2-8 £187,661

Indian Dream (Ire) *H R A Cecil* 48 a31
3 ch f Indian Ridge - Karri Valley (USA)
5^{8gf} 6^{9sd} 3^{10gf} 14^{10g} 0-1-4 £434

Indian Edge *B Palling* 61 a47
2 ch g Indian Rocket - Beveled Edge
6^{5g} 6^{6gf} 6^{7sd} 0-0-3

Indian Haven *P W D'Arcy* 118
3 ch c Indian Ridge - Madame Dubois
1^{7gf} 14^{8g} 1^{8s} 11^{8gf} 11^{10gf} 2-0-5
£164,793

Indian Maiden (Ire) *M S Saunders* 76 a73
3 br f Indian Ridge - Jinsiyah (USA)
7^{6sd} 1^{6sd} 1^{6sd} 1^{6g} 8^{6gf} 6^{6gs} 9^{6sd} 3-0-7
£10,386

Indian Music *A Berry* 41 a50
6 b g Indian Ridge - Dagny Juel (USA)
7^{6sw} 7^{7sd} 8^{8sd} 2^{9sw} 7^{8sd} 5^{7gs} 3^{8sd} 8^{7f}
14^{8f} 9^{8sd} 12^{8g} 0-2-11 £1,271

Indian Oak (Ire) *M P Muggeridge*
2 b f Indian Rocket - Marathon Maid
5^{5gf} 10^{6gf} 0-0-2

Indian Rum *M W Easterby* 39 a34
2 b c Spectrum (Ire) - Apache Squaw
5^{6f} 8^{6s} 10^{6sd} 0-0-3

Indian Sapphire *A Berry* 32
2 ch f Bijou D'Inde - Capriati (USA)
10^{7gf} 4^{7g} 10^{7gf} 12^{7sd} 0-0-4 £478

Indian Shores *M Mullineaux* 66
4 b f Forzando - Cottonwood
1^{6f} 14^{6gf} 20^{6g} 6^{7gf} 8^{8gs} 1-0-5 £3,977

Indian Solitaire (Ire) *R A Fahey* 82
4 b g Bigstone - Terrama Sioux
5^{11gf} 14^{12gf} 6^{12gf} 8^{12gf} 7^{12g} 12^{16gf} 2^{12gf}
11^{12gf} 15^{14gf} 0-1-9 £2,960

Indian Spark *J S Goldie* 113
9 ch g Indian Ridge - Annes Gift
2^{5g} 4^{5g} 2^{6f} 14^{6gf} 1^{5hy} 14^{5gf} 7^{6g} 10^{6gf}
6^{6g} 10^{6g} 4^{5gf} 9^{6g} 12^{6g} 5^{6gf} 8^{5gf} 13^{6g}
1-2-16 £25,409

Indian Steppes (Fr) *Julian Poulton* 82 a82
4 b f Indian Ridge - Ukraine Venture
1^{6sd} 2^{7sd} 5^{6sd} 5^{6sd} 2^{6gf} 2^{6gf} 8^{7f} 8^{6gf}
3^{7sd} 1-4-9 £10,642

Indian Trail *D R C Elsworth* 87
3 ch c Indian Ridge - Take Heart
3^{6gs} 1^{7gf} 1^{6gf} 8^{7gf} 12^{5s} 2-1-5 £11,760

Indian Warrior *J Jay* 52 a49
7 b g Be My Chief (USA) - Wanton
8^{7sd} 12^{6sw} 5^{7sd} 10^{6sw} 10^{7gf} 7^{6sd} 1^{7f}
11^{7g} 14^{8gf} 2^{6f} 5^{6gf} 1-1-11 £4,349

Indian Welcome *H Morrison* 70 a84
4 ch g Most Welcome - Qualitair Ridge
13^{10gf} 6^{12gf} 12^{9ft} 1^{8sd} 5^{8gs} 7^{8sd} 1^{8sd}
7^{10gs} 2-0-8 £4,250

Indiana Blues *A M Balding* 89
2 ch f Indian Ridge - Blue Siren
11^{6gf} 4^{6gf} 8^{6gf} 0-0-3 £468

Indigo Bay (Ire) *R Bastiman* 41 a22
7 b g Royal Academy (USA) - Cape Heights
12^{12sd} 9^{11sd} 9^{12sw} 12^{12sw} 13^{10gf} 9^{10gf}
7^{12gf} 2^{10gf} 10^{12gf} 2^{12gf} 4^{11gf} 10^{12gf} 8^{12f} 7^{12f}
11^{12gs} 0-2-15 £2,418

Individual Talents (USA) *S C Williams* 76
3 ch f Distant View (USA) - Indigenous (USA)
7^{10g} 9^{10gf} 9^{8gf} 2^{10gf} 2^{10g} 5^{12gs} 1^{12g} 3^{12g}
1-3-8 £6,711

Indrani *John A Harris* 51
2 b f Bijou D'Inde - Tea And Scandals (USA)
9^{5gf} 6^{5f} 6^{5gf} 4^{5gs} 5^{5f} 6^{6gf} 18^{6gf} 0-0-7
£368

Indrapura Star (USA) *Miss J Feilden* 32
3 b g Foxhound (USA) - Royal Recall (USA)
19^{8f} 12^{6gf} 0-0-2

Indulene (Ire) *D Carroll* 12 a62
3 b c Alhaarth (Ire) - Don't Care (Ire)
8^{6sd} 4^{8sd} 5^{9sd} 4^{15sd} 15^{11sw} 19^{7gf}
0-0-7 £292

Infidelity (Ire) *A Bailey* 71
2 b f Bluebird (USA) - Madaniyya (USA)
3^{6gs} 4^{7f} 3^{7f} 5^{7gs} 4^{8gf} 5^{7g} 5^{8s} 1^{10gf} 2^{8gf}
11^{8gs} 1-2-10 £4,461

Inglewood *C W Thornton* 42
3 ch g Fleetwood (Ire) - Preening
7^{9sd} 11^{12sd} 4^{12gf} 8^{16gf} 0-0-4 £283

Inglis Drever *J Howard Johnson* 105 a91
4 b g In The Wings - Cormorant Creek
1^{12sd} 2^{12gs} 1^{12gf} 1^{15gf} 11^{18gf} 3-1-5
£23,708

Inistrahull Island (Ire) *M H Tompkins* 60 a49
3 b g Flying Spur (Aus) - Dolcezza (Fr)
11^{7sd} 6^{8sd} 10^{9g} 2^{8f} 9^{10f} 5^{8s} 7^{8f} 2^{7gf}
6^{7f} 0-2-9 £2,112

Initiative *J Hetherton* 15
7 ch g Arazi (USA) - Dance Quest (Fr)
8^{12gf} 0-0-1

Injaaz *J L Dunlop* 92
5 ch m Sheikh Albadou - Ferber's Follies (USA)
8^{5gf} 13^{6g} 10^{6s} 16^{6g} 10^{6gf} 4^{6gf} 11^{6gf}
0-0-7 £741

Inmom (Ire) *S R Bowring* 45
2 b f Barathea (Ire) - Zakuska
5^{7sf} 13^{8f} 0-0-2

Innclassic (Ire) *B J Meehan* 55 a68
2 b f Stravinsky (USA) - Kyka (USA)
7^{6sf} 3^{5sd} 0-1-2 £522

Innovation *R Charlton* 79
3 b f Salse (USA) - I Will Lead (USA)
7^{10gf} 3^{10gf} 2^{12f} 1^{12gf} 10^{12gf} 1-2-5
£5,603

Innstyle *B J Meehan* 71
2 b f Daggers Drawn (USA) - Tarneem (USA)
3^{5gf} 3^{6g} 5^{5gf} 2^{6gf} 6^{6gf} 5^{6g} 6^{7gf} 15^{7gf}
3^{6gf} 4^{5gf} 4^{6gf} 10^{5gs} 0-3-12 £3,716

Inspector Blue *Miss J Feilden* 50
5 ch g Royal Academy (USA) - Blue Siren
7^{11gf} 10^{8hd} 11^{10g} 0-0-3

Inspector General (Ire) *T D Barron* a64
5 b g Dilum (USA) - New Generation
5^{8sd} 3^{8sd} 2^{8sd} 4^{8sd} 0-2-4 £1,317

Inspector Hector (Ire) *M Blanshard* 30
3 b g Hector Protector (USA) - Sombre Lady
20^{10g} 14^{10sd} 11^{8s} 13^{7gf} 5^{9sd} 0-0-5

Instant Hit *R P Burns* 72 a71
4 b g Indian Ridge - Pick Of The Pops
10⁷ˢᵈ 7⁷ˢᵈ 5⁸ˢᵈ 9⁹ˢᵈ 1⁸ᵍᶠ 11⁹ʸ 6⁷ᵍᶠ **1-0-7**
£6,272

Instinct *R Hannon* 64
2 b c Zafonic (USA) - Gracious Gift
8⁶ᵍᶠ **0-0-1**

Instructor *R Hannon* 71 a72
2 ch c Groom Dancer (USA) - Doctor's Glory (USA)
8⁶ᵍᶠ 4⁷ᵍᶠ 2⁷ˢᵈ **0-1-3 £1,253**

Insubordinate *J S Goldie* 66 a45
2 ch c Subordination (USA) - Manila Selection (USA)
8⁷ᶠ 6⁶ˢᵈ 4⁶ᶠ 1⁶ᵍᶠ 11⁶ᵍᶠ 12⁶ᵍˢ 6⁶ᵍ **1-0-7**
£3,350

Integration *P W Harris* 54
3 b c Piccolo - Discrimination
16⁸ᵍ 12⁸ᵍᶠ 5⁸ᶠ 2¹⁰ᶠ 12¹⁰ᵍᶠ 5¹⁰ᶠ 3¹²ᵍᶠ
0-2-7 £1,495

Intellibet One *P D Evans* 74 a54
3 b f Compton Place - Safe House
8⁶ˢᵈ 9⁵ˢᵈ 8⁵ˢᵈ 4⁵ᵍᶠ 10⁵ᵍᶠ 8⁶ᵍᶠ 9⁶ᵍˢ 8⁵ᶠ
4⁵ᵍᶠ 11⁶ᶠ 12⁵ᵍᶠ 1⁶ᵍᶠ 1⁵ᵍᶠ 2⁵ᵍᶠ 4⁵ᵍᶠ 6⁶ᵍᶠ 2⁵ᵍᶠ
9⁶ᶠ **2-5-24**
£12,340

Inter Vision (USA) *A Dickman* 99
3 b c Cryptoclearance (USA) - Fateful (USA)
9⁸ᵍ 13⁶ᵍᶠ 16⁵ᵍᶠ 6⁵ᵍᶠ 4⁶ᵍᶠ 6⁶ᵍᶠ 9⁶ᵍᶠ 1⁶ᵍᶠ
2⁶ᵍᶠ 11⁷ʸ 5⁷ᵍᶠ 4⁵ᵍᶠ **1-1-12 £11,128**

Interceptor *J W Hills* 94
3 ch c Hector Protector (USA) - Moorish Idol
2⁸ᵍᶠ 8⁹ᵍ 3¹⁰ᵍᶠ 9¹²ᵍᶠ **0-1-4 £6,369**

Intercession *P W Harris* 92
3 ch f Bluebird (USA) - Intercede
5⁸ᵍᶠ 5⁸ᵍ 13⁸ᵍᶠ 5¹⁰ᵍᶠ 4⁸ᵍᶠ 8¹⁰ᵍᶠ 5¹⁰ᵍ
PU¹⁴ᵍᶠ **0-0-8 £2,382**

Intercontinental *A Fabre* 112
3 b f Danehill (USA) - Hasili (Ire)
1⁶ᵍ 3⁸ᵍᶠ 3⁸ᵍ 1⁷ᵍˢ 2⁷ˢ 4⁷ᵛˢ **2-2-6**
£75,632

Internationalguest (Ire) *G G Margarson* 91
4 b g Petardia - Banco Solo
13¹⁰ᵍ 8⁸ʰʸ 28⁸ᵍᶠ 3¹⁰ᵍᶠ 6¹⁰ˢ 7¹²ᵍ **0-1-6**
£540

Interstice *A G Newcombe* 55 a71
6 b h Never So Bold - Mainmast
1¹²ˢʷ 1¹¹ˢᵈ 4¹¹ˢᵈ 2¹²ˢᵈ 7¹⁴ˢʷ 9¹²ˢᵈ 3¹⁰ᵍ
7¹²ᵍ 14¹¹ᵍ **2-2-9 £7,753**

Intikraft (Ire) *Mrs S A Liddiard* 70 a50
2 ch c Intikhab (USA) - Mysistra (Fr)
8⁵ˢᵈ 6⁶ᵍᶠ 3⁶ᵍ 8⁷ᵍᶠ 11⁷ᵍᶠ 8⁶ᵍᶠ 11⁶ᶠ 6⁷ˢᵈ
2⁶ᶠ 10⁶ᵍˢ **0-2-10 £2,119**

Intimate Friend (USA) *B W Hills* 78
2 b f Expelled (USA) - Intimate (USA)
4⁶ᵍᶠ 2⁷ᶠ 6⁵ᵍᶠ **0-1-3 £1,690**

Intitnice (Ire) *A Berry* 54 a26
2 b c Danehill Dancer (Ire) - Gathering Place (USA)
11⁵ᵍᶠ 7⁶ˢ 5⁶ᵍᶠ 6⁶ᵍᶠ 4⁶ᶠ 5⁵ˢᵈ 2⁶ᵍᶠ 8⁶ᵍᶠ
2⁶ᵍᶠ 5⁷ᵍᶠ 2⁶ᵍᶠ 7⁵ᵍᶠ 4⁵ᶠ 8⁶ᶠ 11⁶ᵍᶠ **0-3-15**
£3,201

Into The Blue (Ire) *T M Jones*
4 b g Blues Traveller (Ire) - Lux Aeterna
12⁹ˢᵈ **0-0-1**

Into The Breeze (Ire) *J W Hills* 101
3 b g Alzao (USA) - Catalane (USA)
7⁷ᵍˢ 2⁷ᵍᶠ 6⁷ᵍ 5⁷ᵍᶠ 1⁷ᵍᶠ 2⁷ᵍᶠ 5⁸ᵍᶠ **1-2-7**
£26,227

Intricat *A P Jones* 43 a42
3 ch g Bluegrass Prince (Ire) - Noble Soul
6⁸ˢᵈ 7⁸ˢʷ 14¹⁰ᶠ 5⁷ᶠ 2¹⁰ᶠ 10⁸ᵍᶠ 6⁸ᵍᶠ
11⁸ᵍᶠ **0-1-8 £1,190**

Intricate Web (Ire) *E J Alston* 83 a79
7 b g Warning - In Anticipation (Ire)
5⁸ˢʷ 4⁸ˢʷ 11¹⁰ᵍ 2¹⁰ᶠ 4¹²ᵍᶠ 4¹⁰ˢ 5¹¹ᵍᶠ
10¹²ᵍᶠ 4¹⁰ˢ **0-3-9 £4,027**

Intriguing Glimpse *Miss B Sanders* 55
2 b/br f Piccolo - Running Glimpse (Ire)
6⁶ᵍᶠ 18⁶ᵍᶠ **0-0-2**

Introducing (USA) *B W Hills* 89
3 b f Deputy Minister (Can) - Interim
2⁷ᵍᶠ 3¹⁰ᵍ 1⁹ᵍᶠ 4¹²ᵍ **1-2-4 £7,647**

Invader *C E Brittain* 92 a97
7 b h Danehill (USA) - Donya
13⁷ˢᵈ 3¹⁰ˢᵈ 4¹⁰ˢᵈ 7⁸ˢᵈ 8⁸ᵍᶠ 6¹¹ᵍᶠ 8⁸ᵍᶠ
2⁸ᵍᶠ 9⁸ᵍᶠ 1⁸ᵍᶠ **1-2-10 £14,148**

Invasian (Ire) *H R A Cecil* 58
2 ch c Desert Prince (Ire) - Jarrayan
8⁸ᵍᶠ **0-0-1**

Inver Gold *Jane Southcombe* 62 a79
6 ch h Arazi (USA) - Mary Martin
5¹¹ˢʷ 2¹²ˢᵈ 6⁹ˢᵈ 10¹²ᵍᶠ 1¹⁵ˢᵈ **1-1-5**
£4,446

Inverness *J R Fanshawe* 97
3 ch g Inchinor - Inimitable
5⁸ᵍᶠ 1⁸ᵍᶠ 1⁸ᵍᶠ 2⁸ᵍᶠ **2-1-4 £17,089**

Investment Affair (Ire) *M Johnston* 73
3 b g Sesaro (USA) - Superb Investment (Ire)
4⁷ᵍˢ 7⁸ᵍᶠ 1⁸ᵍˢ 6⁷ᶠ 1⁸ᵍᶠ 3⁸ᵍᶠ 6⁸ᵍᶠ 7⁸ᵍᶠ
15⁷ᵍᶠ 12⁷ᵍᶠ **2-1-10 £10,388**

Investment Force (Ire) *C J Mann* 55
5 b g Imperial Frontier (USA) - Superb Investment (Ire)
11⁷ˢᵈ 11⁸ˢᵈ 11⁷ˢᵈ 9⁹ᵍᶠ 6⁶ᵍᶠ 15⁹ᵍᶠ 3⁸ᵍᶠ
11⁷ᵍᶠ 11⁸ᵍᶠ 13⁸ᵍᶠ 6⁷ˢ 4⁸ᵍᶠ 1⁸ᵍᶠ 8⁷ᵍᶠ **1-2-14**
£5,544

Invicta *T J O'Mara* 64 a76
4 b f Distant Relative - Blue Zulu (Ire)
4¹⁰ˢᵈ 10¹⁰ᵍᶠ 9⁹ᵍᶠ 4¹⁰ˢ 11⁹ᵍʸ **0-1-5 £389**

Invitado (Ire) *T J Fitzgerald* 23
4 ch g Be My Guest (USA) - Lady Dulcinea (Arg)
10¹²ᵍᶠ 18¹⁰ᵍᶠ 11¹⁴ᵍᶠ **0-0-3**

Invitation *A Charlton* 84
5 b g Bin Ajwaad (Ire) - On Request (Ire)
5¹⁰ᵍ 12¹⁰ᵍˢ 4⁸ᵍˢ 5¹⁰ᵍ 5¹⁰ᵍ 9¹¹ᵍᶠ 10¹⁰ᵍ
0-0-7 £1,698

Inzabar (Ire) *R M Beckett* 62
2 b g Inzar (USA) - Faypool (Ire)
5⁵ᶠ 2⁶ᵍ 6⁶ᵍᶠ 8⁶ᵍᶠ 2⁷ᵍᶠ 10⁷ᶠ 7⁷ᵍᶠ 8⁷ᵍᶠ
0-2-8 £1,844

Inzarmood (Ire) *K R Burke*
5 b m Inzar (USA) - Pepilin
9¹²ˢᵈ 7¹¹ˢᵈ **0-0-2**

Io Callisto *R A Fahey* 44
2 br f Hector Protector (USA) - Queen Shirley (Ire)
6⁶ᶠ 8⁶ᵍᶠ **0-0-2**

Ionian Spring (Ire) *C G Cox* 92 a94
8 b g Ela-Mana-Mou - Well Head (Ire)
5¹⁰ᵍˢ 1¹⁰ᵍᶠ 11¹⁰ᵍ 8¹⁰ᵍᶠ 15¹⁰ᵍᶠ 6¹⁰ᵍ 5¹⁰ᵍᶠ
3¹²ˢᵈ 10¹⁰ᵍᶠ **1-1-9 £9,130**

Iphigenia (Ire) *P W Hiatt* 57 a48
2 b/br f Orpen (USA) - Silver Explosive
8⁵ˢᵈ 2⁶ᵍᶠ 3⁵ˢᵈ 11⁶ˢᵈ **0-2-4 £1,653**

Ipledgeallegiance (USA) *D W Chapman* 71 a52

7 b g Alleged (USA) - Yafill (USA)
7⁷ˢᵈ 8⁷ᶠ 9⁹ᵍᶠ 5⁸ˢᵈ 3⁸ᵍˢ 2¹²ᶠ 1¹¹ᵍᶠ 7¹²ᶠ
3¹¹ᵍ 6¹³ᵍᶠ 4¹⁰ᵍ 6¹²ᵍᶠ 7¹²ᵍᶠ 5¹⁰ᶠ 8¹⁰ᵍᶠ 13¹²ᶠ
4¹²ˢᵈ **1-4-17 £7,261**

Ipsa Loquitur S C Williams   a63
3 b f Unfuwain (USA) - Plaything
5⁸ˢᵈ **0-0-1**

Iqte Saab (USA) J L Dunlop   87
2 b c Bahri (USA) - Shuhrah (USA)
1⁶ᵍᶠ 2⁷ᵍ **1-1-2 £7,501**

Ireland's Eye (Ire) J R Norton
8 b g Shareef Dancer (USA) - So Romantic (Ire)
13²²ᵍᶠ **0-0-1**

Irie Rasta (Ire) S Kirk   73
4 ch g Desert King (Ire) - Seeds Of Doubt (Ire)
6¹⁵ᵍᶠ 3¹⁴ᵍ 6¹⁴ᵍˢ 3¹⁰ᵍˢ 4¹²ᵍᶠ 2¹³ᵍᶠ **0-3-6**
£2,916

Irish Blessing (USA) F Jordan   47
6 b g Ghazi (USA) - Win For Leah (USA)
6¹⁴ᵍ 10¹⁴ᵍᶠ **0-0-2**

Irish Tycoon (Ire) M A Magnusson   74 a71
3 ch g Entrepreneur - Aoife (Ire)
4⁷ˢᵈ 2⁷ˢᵈ 8⁸ˢᵈ 4⁸ᵍ 10⁸ᵍᶠ 2⁷ᶠ 14⁶ᵍᶠ 8⁷ᵍˢ
4⁷ᵍᶠ **0-3-9 £3,338**

Irma La Douce (Ire) M Halford   57
4 b f Elbio - Eves Temptation (Ire)
12⁷ᵍᶠ 11⁶ᵍᶠ 7⁶ᵍ 5⁶ᶠ 7⁸ᵍᶠ 8⁷ᵍᶠ 9⁶ᵍᶠ 3⁶ᶠ
5⁷ᵍᶠ 2⁶ᵍᶠ 3⁶ᵍᶠ 8⁶ᵍᶠ 1⁷ᵍᶠ 8⁶ᵍᶠ 13⁸ᵍᶠ **1-3-15**
£4,236

Iron Temptress (Ire) G M Moore   69 a42
2 ch f Piccolo - River Divine (USA)
5⁵ˢᵈ 1⁵ᶠ 2⁵ᵍ 8⁶ᵍᶠ 4⁶ᵍᶠ 4⁵ᵍᶠ 3⁶ᶠ 5⁷ᶠ 2⁷ᵍᶠ
20⁷ᵍ 13⁶ᵍˢ 17⁶ᵍᶠ **1-1-12 £7,327**

Iron Warrior (Ire) G M Moore   16 a64
3 b c Lear Fan (USA) - Robalana (USA)
2¹¹ˢᵈ 6¹¹ˢᵈ 2¹²ˢᵈ 11¹²ˢᵈ 8¹²ᵍᶠ **0-2-5**
£2,174

Irony (Ire) A M Balding   96
4 gr g Mujadil (USA) - Cidaris (Ire)
14⁷ᵍᶠ 9⁶ᵍᶠ 13⁶ᵍᶠ 5⁷ᵍᶠ 3⁸ᵍᶠ 6⁸ᵍ 6⁸ᵍ 7⁷ᵍᶠ
18ᵍᶠ 6⁸ᵍᶠ 3⁸ˢ **1-2-11 £14,296**

Iroquois Chief (USA) C N Kellett   45 a31
4 b g Known Fact (USA) - Celtic Shade
9⁷ᶠ 18⁷ᵍᶠ 9⁷ˢʷ **0-0-3**

Irresistible M L W Bell   97
3 b f Cadeaux Genereux - Polish Romance (USA)
16ᵍˢ 2⁷ᵍʸ 11⁶ˢ **1-1-3 £33,687**

Irtahal (USA) M P Tregoning   100
3 b f Swain (Ire) - Elhasna (USA)
2⁷ᵍˢ 3¹⁰ᵍᶠ 4⁸ᵍᶠ 1⁸ᵍᶠ 6⁸ᵍ 9¹⁰ᵍᶠ **1-2-6**
£16,685

Isa'Af (Ire) P W Hiatt   59 a59
4 b g Darshaan - Shauna's Honey (Ire)
9¹²ˢʷ 3¹²ˢᵈ 5¹²ˢᵈ 1¹²ᵍᶠ 1¹⁵ᵍᶠ 13¹⁶ᵍᶠ 14¹⁴ᵍˢ
8¹⁴ᵍᶠ 6¹⁴ᵍᶠ 6¹⁴ᵍᶠ 8¹⁶ˢᵈ 2¹²ᶠ **2-2-12 £9,122**

Isaz H Candy   47
3 b c Elmaamul (USA) - Pretty Poppy
4⁷ˢᵈ **0-0-1 £283**

Isengard (USA) B J Meehan   80 a43
3 b/br f Cobra King (USA) - January Moon (USA)
5⁷ᵍ 6⁵ᵍˢ 1⁵ᵍᶠ 2⁶ᵍᶠ 3⁵ᵍᶠ 14⁶ˢᵈ **1-2-6**
£5,506

Ishela (Ire) A Berry
4 gr f Barathea (Ire) - Lalandria (Fr)
15¹¹ᵍˢ 14¹²ᵍᶠ **0-0-2**

Isidore Bonheur (Ire) B W Hills   90
2 b c Mtoto - Way O'Gold (USA)
1⁷ᵍᶠ 4⁸ᵍᶠ **1-0-2 £6,427**

Iskander K A Ryan   91
2 b g Danzero (Aus) - Amber Mill
5⁵ʰʸ 2⁵ᶠ 3⁶ᶠ 6⁵ᵍᶠ 1⁶ᵍᶠ 5⁶ᵍ 4⁷ᶠ **1-2-7**
£16,103

Isla Azul (Ire) G Wragg   72
3 ch f Machiavellian (USA) - Nuryana
4⁷ᵍᶠ 5⁸ᵍᶠ 6¹⁰ᵍᶠ 6¹⁰ᵍᶠ 9⁸ᵍᶠ **0-0-5 £416**

Island House (Ire) G Wragg   118
7 ch h Grand Lodge (USA) - Fortitude (Ire)
5¹⁰ᵍᶠ 10⁴ᵍ 4¹⁰ᵍ 4¹¹ᵍᶠ 3¹⁰ᵍᶠ 2¹¹ᵍ **1-1-6**
£36,125

Island Lady (Ire) J W Hills   60 a53
3 b f Hernando (Fr) - Prosperous Lady
2¹⁰ᵍᶠ 6¹¹ᵍˢ 3¹⁰ᶠ 8¹²ˢᵈ **0-1-4 £1,479**

Island Light A C Stewart   104
5 b g Inchinor - Miss Prism
11⁸ᵍ 2⁸ᵍᶠ 3¹⁰ᵍᶠ 1⁸ᵍᶠ 4⁸ᵍᶠ 2⁸ᵍ 25⁹ᵍᶠ **1-2-7**
£25,447

Island Light (USA) E A L Dunlop   96
3 ch c Woodman (USA) - Isla Del Rey (USA)
7⁸ᵍˢ 1¹⁰ᵍᶠ 3¹²ᵍᶠ 5¹⁰ᵍᶠ 8¹⁰ᵍ **1-0-5**
£11,869

Island Rapture Mrs A J Perrett   87 a69
3 b f Royal Applause - Gersey
1¹⁰ˢᵈ 8⁹ᵍᶠ 2¹⁰ᵍᶠ 2¹⁰ᵍᶠ 3¹⁰ᵍᶠ 8⁹ᵍˢ 5¹⁰ᵍᶠ
5¹⁰ᵍᶠ **1-3-8 £9,368**

Island Saint J L Dunlop   56
3 b g Efisio - Kembla
5⁸ᵍ 13⁸ᵍ **0-0-2**

Island Sound D R C Elsworth   109
6 b g Turtle Island (Ire) - Ballet
6¹⁰ᵍᶠ 1¹⁰ᵍᶠ 10¹⁰ᵍ 2¹⁰ᵍ 4¹⁰ᵍᶠ 6¹⁰ᵍ **1-1-6**
£18,190

Island Spell C Grant   73
2 b f Singspiel (Ire) - Shifty Mouse
9⁶ᵍˢ 8⁶ᵍᶠ 3⁵ᵍᶠ 9⁷ᵍᶠ 6⁶ᵍᶠ 3⁵ᵍᶠ **0-2-6**
£8,200

Island Star (Ire) P W Harris   67
3 b g Turtle Island (Ire) - Orthorising
4⁸ᶠ 6⁸ᵍ 4⁸ᵍᶠ 12⁷ˢʷ 14⁸ᵍᶠ 13⁷ˢʷ **0-0-6**
£613

Island Stream (Ire) J R Jenkins   31
4 b g Turtle Island (Ire) - Tilbrook (Ire)
8¹⁴ᵍ **0-0-1**

Islands Farewell Mrs M Reveley   56
3 b g Emarati (USA) - Chief Island
8⁸ˢ 12⁶ᵍᶠ 7⁶ᶠ **0-0-3**

Islington (Ire) Sir Michael Stoute   123
4 b f Sadler's Wells (USA) - Hellenic
3¹⁰ᵍᶠ 6¹⁰ᵍᶠ 1¹²ᵍᶠ 3¹⁰ᵍᶠ 1¹⁰ᶠ **2-1-5**
£591,342

Isobel Scarlett T D McCarthy   a59
4 b f Emperor Jones (USA) - Key West (Fr)
5⁷ˢᵈ 7⁷ˢᵈ PU⁷ˢᵈ **0-0-3**

Isolde's Idol C F Wall   59
3 ch f Night Shift (USA) - Atmospheric Blues (Ire)
12⁷ᵍᶠ 10⁸ᵍᶠ 12⁸ᵍ **0-0-3**

It Must Be Speech S L Keightley   54
2 b c Advise (Fr) - Maiden Speech
10⁷ᵍ 7⁸ᵍᶠ 12⁷ᵍᶠ **0-0-3**

It's A Blessing N P Littmoden
2 b f Inchinor - Benedicite

24⁸ᵍ **0-0-1**

It's A Wizard *M A Barnes*   19
3 b g Wizard King - Axed Again
14⁶ᶠ 12⁹ᵍᶠ **0-0-2**

It's An Omen *R A Fahey*   17
2 br c Efisio - Another Nightmare (Ire)
13⁶ᵍˢ **0-0-1**

It's Definite (Ire) *P Bowen*   81 a78
4 b g Definite Article - Taoveret (Ire)
8⁸ˢᵈ 7¹⁰ˢᵈ 10¹⁰ˢᵈ 11¹⁶ˢᵈ 9¹⁶ᵍᶠ 11¹⁷ᵍᶠ 7¹⁷ᵍᶠ
3²⁰ᵍᶠ 2¹⁵ᵍᶠ 9²¹ᵍˢ 28¹⁸ᵍᶠ **2-2-11 £16,199**

It's Our Secret (Ire) *M H Tompkins*   86
7 ch g Be My Guest (USA) - Lady Dulcinea (Arg)
3⁸ᶠ 1⁸ᵍᶠ 10⁸ᵍᶠ 5⁷ᵍᶠ 6⁸ᵍᶠ 4⁷ᵍˢ **1-2-6**
£6,652

It's Rumoured *Jean-Rene Auvray*   67 a45
3 ch g Fleetwood (Ire) - Etourdie (USA)
6¹²ˢᵈ 9¹²ˢᵈ 10¹²ᵍˢ 9¹²ˢᵈ 2¹²ᵍ 5¹²ᵍᶠ **0-1-6**
£1,112

It's The Limit (USA) *Mrs A J Perrett*   96
4 b g Boundary (USA) - Beside (USA)
4¹²ᵍᶠ 2¹²ᵍ **0-2-2 £3,576**

Italian Affair *A Bailey*   50 a49
5 ch m Fumo Di Londra (Ire) - Sergentti (Ire)
13⁷ˢʷ 5⁶ˢᵈ 4⁷ˢᵈ 3⁶ˢᵈ 4⁶ˢᵈ 7⁷ˢʷ 4⁸ˢᵈ 3⁸ˢᵈ
13⁷ᵍᶠ 10⁸ᵍᶠ 4⁶ᵍˢ 6⁵ᵍᶠ 18⁶ᵍᶠ **0-2-13 £1,129**

Italian Mist (Fr) *Julian Poulton*   46
4 b g Forzando - Digamist Girl (Ire)
12⁶ᶠ 9⁵ᵍᶠ 7⁶ᵍᶠ 6⁷ᶠ 2⁶ᶠ 7⁵ᶠ 9⁶ᵍᶠ 5⁷ᵍᶠ
7⁶ᵍᶠ **0-1-9 £1,026**

Itcanbedone Again (Ire) *Ian Williams*   58 a50
4 b g Sri Pekan (USA) - Maradata (Ire)
13⁸ᵍᶠ 6¹⁰ᵍᶠ 4¹²ˢᵈ **0-0-3**

Itch *R Bastiman*   a11
8 b g Puissance - Panienka (Pol)
12⁸ˢʷ **0-0-1**

Itchington (Ire) *M P Tregoning*   73
5 b h Royal Academy (USA) - Itching (Ire)
7¹⁰ᵍ 3¹²ᵍᶠ 4¹⁰ᵍᶠ 1¹⁰ᵍᶠ 7¹⁰ᵍᶠ **1-0-5**
£3,709

Itemise (USA) *M Johnston*   109
3 ch f Kris S (USA) - Company Binness (USA)
2¹²ᵍ 3¹⁰ᶠ 3¹²ᵍᶠ 2¹⁵ᵍ 4¹⁴ˢ **0-4-5 £16,858**

Ithaca (USA) *H R A Cecil*   98
2 ch f Distant View (USA) - Reams Of Verse (USA)
1⁷ᵍ 2⁷ᵍᶠ 7⁸ᵍᶠ **1-1-3 £19,525**

Itnab *B Hanbury*   115
3 b f Green Desert (USA) - Midway Lady (USA)
1⁹ᵍᶠ 5⁸ᵍᶠ 1¹⁰ᵍ 1¹²ᵍᶠ **3-0-4 £52,764**

Its A Mystery (Ire) *R T Phillips*   34
4 b f Idris (Ire) - Blue Infanta
13⁸ˢ 9⁷ᵍᶠ 11⁹ˢʷ 7¹⁰ᵍˢ **0-0-4**

Its A Nightmare (Ire) *P R Hedger*
3 ch g Shahrastani (USA) - Suntan City (Ire)
9¹¹ᵍᶠ **0-0-1**

Its All Eurs (Ire) *R Hannon*   a43
3 b f Barathea (Ire) - Brief Sentiment (Ire)
5⁷ˢᵈ **0-0-1**

Its All Pink (Ire) *D G Bridgwater*   a16
3 gr f Victory Note (USA) - Chickamauga (USA)
12⁶ˢᵈ 12⁵ˢᵈ **0-0-2**

Its Ecco Boy *P Howling*   72 a62
5 ch g Clantime - Laena
7⁷ˢᵈ 3⁷ˢᵈ 2⁷ˢᵈ 7⁷ˢᵈ 3⁷ˢᵈ 5⁶ᵍᶠ 10⁶ᵍᶠ 6⁷ᵍᶠ
3⁷ᵍ 3⁷ᶠ 10⁷ᵍᶠ 1⁶ᶠ 2⁶ᶠ 4⁵ᶠ 2⁶ˢ 4⁶ᵍᶠ 3⁶ᵍᶠ 2⁷ᶠ 10⁶ᵍᶠ **2-**

11-25
£13,080

Its Wallace Jnr *Miss Sheena West*   a40
4 b g Bedford (USA) - Built In Heaven
9¹²ˢᵈ **0-0-1**

Its Your Bid *S Woodman*   58 a55
5 b m Dilum (USA) - By Arrangement (Ire)
5¹⁶ˢᵈ 9¹⁵ᵍᶠ 7¹⁶ˢᵈ 3¹⁷ᶠ 3¹⁷ᶠ 2¹⁷ʰᵈ 2¹⁵ᵍᶠ
3¹⁶ᵍᶠ 4¹⁶ˢᵈ 3¹⁶ᵍᶠ 6¹⁶ᵍᶠ 5¹⁷ᶠ 10¹⁶ᵍᶠ **0-4-13**
£5,013

Itsaboy *J R Boyle*   22
3 b g Wizard King - French Project (Ire)
17⁸ᵍᶠ 14⁸ᵍᶠ **0-0-2**

Itsanothergirl *M W Easterby*   a5
7 b m Reprimand - Tasmim
10¹²ˢʷ **0-0-1**

Itsdedfast (Ire) *L Lungo*   21
7 ch g Lashkari - Amazing Silks
14⁷ᵍˢ 8⁹ᵍᶠ 12¹¹ᵍˢ 8¹⁴ᶠ 13¹⁷ᵍᶠ **0-0-5**

Itsonlyagame *R Ingram*   66 a37
3 b c Ali-Royal (Ire) - Mena
5¹⁰ᵍᶠ 4¹²ᵍ 11¹⁰ˢᵈ 6¹²ᵍᶠ **0-0-4 £433**

Ivania *T D Easterby*   81
3 ch f First Trump - Antonia's Choice
12⁵ᵍ 9⁵ᵍᶠ 10⁵ᶠ 2⁶ᵍˢ 13⁶ᵍᶠ **0-1-5**
£1,810

Ivory Bay *J Hetherton*   52 a30
4 b g Piccolo - Fantasy Racing (Ire)
9⁸ˢᵈ 13⁸ˢᵈ 11⁸ᵍᶠ 14⁷ᵍ 19¹⁰ᵍᶠ 5⁸ᶠ 8⁸ˢᵈ
1⁷ᵍᶠ 9⁸ᵍᶠ 13⁷ᵍᶠ 11⁷ˢ 9⁷ᶠ 16⁸ᵍᶠ 17⁸ᵍᶠ **1-0-14**
£4,342

Ivory Coast (Ire) *W R Muir*   a57
2 b f Cape Cross (Ire) - Ivory League
8⁷ˢᵈ **0-0-1**

Ivory Lace *D K Ivory*   63 a49
2 b f Atraf - Miriam
7⁵ˢᵈ 3⁵ᵍᶠ 3⁵ᵍᶠ 6⁵ᵍᶠ 1⁵ᵍᶠ 5⁵ᵍᶠ 7⁵ᵍᶠ **1-1-7**
£4,469

Ivory Prince (USA) *D Shaw*   41
2 b g King Of Kings (Ire) - Ivory Lane (USA)
UR⁷ᵍᶠ 12⁷ᵍᶠ 6⁷ᵍˢ 8⁶ᵍᶠ 10⁶ˢᵈ 13⁷ˢᵈ 11⁸ᵍᶠ
0-0-7

Ivory Venture *D K Ivory*   25 a57
3 b f Reprimand - Julietta Mia (USA)
5⁵ᶠ 4⁵ˢᵈ **0-0-2 £272**

Ivy League Star (Ire) *B W Hills*   50
2 b f Sadler's Wells (USA) - Ivy (USA)
13⁷ᵍˢ 6⁶ᵍ **0-0-2**

Ivy Moon *M Blanshard*   71 a34
3 b f Emperor Jones (USA) - Bajan Rose
3⁸ᵍᶠ 11⁸ˢ RO⁸ˢ 6⁷ᵍᶠ 10⁷ᵍᶠ 15⁷ᵍᶠ 6⁶ᵍᶠ
1⁷ᵍᶠ 12⁷ᶠ 3⁷ᵍᶠ 8⁸ˢᵈ 3⁷ᶠ **1-3-12 £5,048**

Iwo Jima (Ire) *N P Littmoden*   66 a74
3 b c Desert King (Ire) - Allegheny River (USA)
3⁷ˢᵈ 2¹⁰ˢᵈ 6¹⁰ˢᵈ 4¹¹ᵍᶠ 3¹⁰ᵍ 6¹²ᵍ 8⁹ˢᵈ 2¹¹ᵍᶠ
0-3-8 £4,686

Izdiham (Ire) *M P Tregoning*   112
4 ch c Nashwan (USA) - Harayir (USA)
4¹⁰ᵍ 4¹⁰ᵍᶠ 14¹⁰ᵍᶠ 9¹²ᵍ 3¹¹ᵍᶠ 8¹⁰ᵍᶠ 2⁸ᶠ
0-0-7 £13,289

Izmail (Ire) *D Nicholls*   77
4 b g Bluebird (USA) - My-Lorraine (Ire)
18⁵ᵍ 11⁵ᵍᶠ 7⁵ᶠ 2⁵ᵍᶠ 13⁵ᵍᶠ 12⁵ᵍ 20⁶ᵍ
1⁵ᶠ 5⁵ᶠ **1-1-9 £7,392**

Izza *W Storey*   25

2 br f Wizard King - Nicholas Mistress
9^{7gf} 7^{7f} 11^{6gf} 14^{7gf} 9^{6g} 0-0-5

J M W Turner *N P Littmoden* 71 a109
4 b c Forzando - Noor El Houdah (Ire)
4^{6sd} 2^{6sd} 4^{6sd} 5^{6sw} 1^{5sd} 6^{7sd} 9^{6g} 5^{5gf}
1^{6g} 13^{6g} 2-1-10 £17,636

J R Stevenson (USA) *M Wigham* 92 a84
7 ch g Lyphard (USA) - While It Lasts (USA)
2^{8g} 15^{8gf} 8^{8g} 10^{9g} 12^{8gf} 4^{8gs} 2^{8sd} 6^{8g}
0-3-8 £6,769

Jabaar (USA) *D Nicholls* 96
5 gr g Silver Hawk (USA) - Sierra Madre (Fr)
15^{10gf} 5^{10gf} 15^{10f} 10^{10gf} 4^{12gf} 2^{12f}
17^{10g} 0-1-7 £5,842

Jabulani (Ire) *G M Moore* 54
4 b g Marju (Ire) - Houwara (Ire)
7^{8sd} 5^{9gf} 0-0-2

Jacaranda (Ire) *B J Meehan* 84 a66
3 ch g Bahhare (USA) - Near Miracle
15^{8gf} 11^{7g} 13^{7gs} 10^{7gf} 1^{7gf} 4^{7gf} 2^{8gf}
DSQ^{7g} 8^{7gf} 4^{7f} 10^{7g} 2^{7gf} 4^{7sd} 1-3-13 £8,592

Jacinto *R A Fahey* 38
3 b g Komaite (USA) - Times Zando
10^{7gf} 10^{11s} 15^{8gs} 11^{11gf} 0-0-4

Jack Dawson (Ire) *John Berry* 82
6 b g Persian Bold - Dream Of Jenny
2^{10g} 4^{12gs} 3^{16gf} 5^{15gf} 4^{16gf} 12^{14gf} 0-2-6
£4,013

Jack Durrance (Ire) *M Johnston* 78
3 b g Polish Precedent (USA) - Atlantic Desire (Ire)
5^{8g} 9^{7g} 1^{10g} 17^{10g} 16^{8gs} 1-0-5 £3,770

Jack Of Trumps (Ire) *G Wragg* 65
3 b c King's Theatre (Ire) - Queen Caroline (USA)
3^{10gf} 0-1-1 £347

Jack Point *J J Bridger*
2 b g Fraam - Queen's Hat
9^{5gf} 19^{6gf} 0-0-2

Jack Sullivan (USA) *B J Meehan* 93 a90
2 ch c Belong To Me (USA) - Provisions (USA)
5^{6gs} 3^{6gf} 2^{7sd} 8^{6g} 1^{7sd} 5^{7gf} 1-1-6
£6,826

Jackie Kiely *T G Mills* 45
2 ch c Vettori (Ire) - Fudge
7^{7g} 0-0-1

Jackie's Baby *W G M Turner* 53 a35
7 b g Then Again - Guarded Expression
9^{5sd} 10^{5gf} 6^{6f} 9^{5gf} 10^{5gf} 3^{5f} 0-0-6
£302

Jacks Delight *Mrs A L M King*
3 b g Bettergeton - Impromptu Melody (Ire)
12^{8gf} 10^{7gf} 0-0-2

Jacob (Ire) *P A Blockley* 54
2 b g Victory Note (USA) - Persian Mistress (Ire)
3^{5f} 5^{5gf} 5^{6gs} 0-1-3 £560

Jacqui Evans *Ronald Thompson* 41
2 b f Komaite (USA) - Rudda Flash
9^{5gf} 5^{5f} 4^{6f} 0-0-3

Jadan (Ire) *E J Alston* 70
2 b g Imperial Ballet - Sports Post Lady (Ire)
4^{6g} 4^{6gf} 5^{6s} 1^{6g} 1-0-5 £3,372

Jade *Mrs A J Perrett* 37 a59
3 ch g Efisio - Nagnagnag (Ire)
4^{7sd} 15^{8gf} 0-0-2 £309

Jade Forest (Ire) *B Smart* 45
3 gr f Charnwood Forest (Ire) - Jade Vine (Ire)

7^{10gf} 5^{12gs} 14^{14gf} 10^{12sd} 9^{12gf} 6^{12f} 0-0-6

Jade Star (USA) *Miss Gay Kelleway* 56 a49
3 b f Jade Hunter (USA) - Danzig's Girl (USA)
18^{8sd} 7^{8sd} 7^{7sd} 2^{10gf} 6^{8gf} 11^{7f} 3^{10g}
2^{10gf} 5^{9gf} 1-3-10 £5,182

Jade's Promise *J R Best* a65
4 b g Definite Article - Zacinta (USA)
11^{13sd} 5^{10sd} 6^{12sd} 9^{12sd} 0-0-4

Jadeeron *Miss D A McHale* 66 a61
4 b g Green Desert (USA) - Rain And Shine (Fr)
12^{10sd} 6^{8sd} 5^{9sd} 2^{12sd} 4^{12sd} 5^{11gf}
4^{12f} 3^{11gf} 8^{11gf} 12^{12gf} 6^{13gf} 7^{13gf} 3^{16sd} 2^{11f}
1^{14gf} 4^{14gf} 4^{16gf} 15^{16gf} 7^{16sd} 1-4-20 £8,993

Jagged (Ire) *K R Burke* 65 a69
3 b g Sesaro (USA) - Latin Mass
6^{6sd} 2^{5sd} 5^{6g} 5^{6g} 12^{6gf} 3^{6gs} 7^{7sw} 5^{6gf}
15^{6g} 4^{6g} 12^{6gf} 2^{7sd} 0-4-12 £2,562

Jagger *G A Butler* 102 a89
3 gr c Linamix (Fr) - Sweetness Herself
3^{5sd} 2^{5f} 4^{9gs} 1^{10sd} 6^{11gf} 1^{14g} 1^{14gf} 1^{12f}
4-2-8 £73,004

Jahangir *B R Johnson* 48 a49
4 b g Zamindar (USA) - Imperial Jade
5^{6sd} 10^{8sd} 7^{6sd} 4^{7sd} 7^{7sd} 5^{6g} 7^{5gf} 9^{6gf}
15^{7f} 3^{7gf} 8^{6gf} 0-1-11 £303

Jailbird *R M Beckett* 52
2 b f Nicolotte - Grace Browning
5^{6gf} 11^{6gf} 5^{6f} 0-0-3

Jaipur Gait *T D Easterby* 12
2 b f Thowra (Fr) - Dawn Gait
6^{6hy} 6^{7gf} 0-0-2

Jair Ohmsford (Ire) *W J Musson* 61 a63
4 b g Hamas (Ire) - Harry's Irish Rose (USA)
7^{7sw} 5^{8sd} 4^{8sd} 10^{10gs} 0-0-4 £316

Jakarmi *B Palling* 40
2 b g Merdon Melody - Lady Ploy
11^{6gs} 0-0-1

Jake Black (Ire) *J J Quinn* 51 a18
3 b g Definite Article - Tirhala (Ire)
9^{5gf} 6^{8gf} 5^{10gf} 12^{12gf} 8^{12sd} 0-0-5

Jakeal (Ire) *R M Whitaker* 56
4 b g Eagle Eyed (USA) - Karoi (Ire)
13^{6gf} 12^{7gf} 3^{7gf} 12^{7sw} 0-1-4 £499

Jakester *M Halford* 89
3 b c Lion Cavern (USA) - Torrid Tango (USA)
4^{7f} 1^{7gv} 14^{8gf} 2^{8g} 1-1-4 £9,324

Jalouhar *B P J Baugh* 66 a71
3 b g Victory Note (USA) - Orient Way (Ire)
2^{6sd} 3^{6g} 7^{6gf} 7^{6gs} 10^{8gs} 11^{7f} 3^{6sd} 2^{6ft}
2^{7sd} 5^{7sw} 14^{7gf} 6^{7sd} 0-5-12 £4,014

Jam Today *J M Bradley* 50
3 b f Elmaamul (USA) - Sonic Sapphire
6^{8gf} 4^{8g} 14^{7f} 0-0-3 £320

Jamaican Flight (USA) *Mrs S Lamyman* 64 a59
10 b h Sunshine Forever (USA) - Kalamona (USA)
4^{16sd} 5^{16sd} 1^{16sd} 4^{16sw} 1^{16sd} 2^{16sd} 8^{16sd}
3^{17gf} 1^{22gf} 5^{16gf} 4^{16gf} 16^{8sd} 8^{17gf} 1^{18gf} 1^{16gf}
3^{16gf} 6^{16g} 4^{18gf} 5^{16g} 7^{17f} 5-3-20 £30,526

James Caird (Ire) *M H Tompkins* 87 a77
3 ch g Catrail (USA) - Polish Saga
9^{7g} 5^{7sd} 2^{8sd} 7^{9gs} 7^{8gf} 6^{7gf} 5^{7gf} 5^{12gf}
1^{10gf} 1^{10gf} 6^{10gf} 2^{10gf} 2-2-12 £8,300

James Dee (Ire) *Mrs P Ford* 36 a32
7 b g Shalford (Ire) - Glendale Joy (Ire)

7^{8sd} 7^{8sd} 7^{7gf} 13^{6f} **0-0-4**

James Drummond *B Mactaggart*   13
4 b g Shaddad (USA) - Miss Drummond
15^{9gs} 5^{8gf} 10^{16gf} **0-0-3**

James Stark (Ire) *N P Littmoden*   78 a96
6 b g Up And At 'Em - June Maid
6^{6sd} 6^{6sd} 12^{5sd} 8^{6sd} 3^{5sd} 11^{6sw} 7^{6g} 1^{5sd}
10^{5f} 5^{6gf} **1-1-10 £5,723**

Jamestown *C Smith*   65
6 b g Merdon Melody - Thabeh
11^{11sd} 13^{8sd} 3^{7gf} 8^{8f} 9^{8gf} 5^{10gf} 1^{8g} 5^{8gf}
4^{9gf} 3^{8gf} 5^{8g} 4^{8g} 11^{8gs} **1-3-13 £5,169**

Jan Brueghel (USA) *T D Barron*   45 a73
4 ch g Phone Trick (USA) - Sunk (USA)
3^{7sw} 3^{6sd} 11^{6sw} 1^{7sd} 14^{7gf} 2^{6sd} **2-3-6**
£7,752

Janayen (USA) *M P Tregoning*   93
3 b f Zafonic (USA) - Saafeya (Ire)
6^{9gf} 1^{8gf} 1^{8gf} **2-0-3 £7,423**

Janes Gem (Ire) *A Bailey*   46 a52
3 b f Among Men (USA) - Kingdom Queen (Ire)
3^{8sd} 2^{8sd} 6^{12gs} 4^{11gf} 5^{8s} **0-2-5 £1,240**

Janes Valentine *J R Boyle*   59 a60
3 b f My Best Valentine - Jane Herring
5^{6sd} 3^{6sd} 7^{6sd} 2^{6sd} 7^{6f} 2^{7f} 7^{7gf} 7^{7gf} 8^{6f}
14^{7gf} 14^{7sd} **0-3-11 £3,048**

Jango Malfoy (Ire) *B W Duke*   19
2 ch c Russian Revival (USA) - Sialia (Ire)
13^{7g} 8^{10gs} **0-0-2**

Jannadav (Ire) *J A Osborne* 67 a60
3 b f Barathea (Ire) - Sweet Alma
4^{7sd} 4^{7f} 14^{8g} **0-1-3 £605**

Janoueix (Ire) *C R Egerton* 51 a43
4 b g Desert King (Ire) - Miniver (Ire)
6^{7gs} 9^{8gf} 5^{10sd} **0-0-3**

Jaolins *R Hannon*   36 a44
2 b f Groom Dancer (USA) - On The Top
16^{6gf} 7^{5sd} **0-0-2**

Jardines Lookout (Ire) *A P Jarvis* 119
6 b g Fourstars Allstar (USA) - Foolish Flight (Ire)
6^{14gf} 4^{20gf} 2^{16g} 5^{16gf} 3^{16g} **0-2-5**
£157,058

Jarjoor *M A Jarvis*   93
3 b c Alhaarth (Ire) - Neptunalia
1^{8g} 1^{8g} 2^{7gf} 10^{8gf} 3^{8gf} **2-2-5 £12,310**

Jarraaf *J W Unett*   63 a71
3 ch c Desert Story (Ire) - Bee Off (Ire)
7^{6gf} 15^{5g} 13^{7gf} 2^{6sd} 6^{7gf} 5^{10gf} 2^{8sd} 4^{8gf}
2^{8sd} **0-4-9 £2,885**

Jarvo *N P Littmoden*   65
2 b g Pursuit Of Love - Pinkie Rose (Fr)
12^{6gf} 2^{6gf} 2^{7gf} 3^{8gs} 16^{6gf} **0-2-5**
£3,171

Jaseur (USA) *S T Lewis*   56
10 b g Lear Fan (USA) - Spur Wing (USA)
8^{16gs} **0-0-1**

Jasmick (Ire) *H Morrison*   91
5 ch m Definite Article - Glass Minnow (Ire)
4^{16gf} 11^{14gs} UR^{20gf} 13^{12g} 7^{15gf} 5^{14gf}
9^{13gf} 2^{12gf} 6^{16gf} 8^{12g} **0-1-10 £4,041**

Jasmine Pearl (Ire) *B J Meehan*   71
2 b f King Of Kings (Ire) - Tumbleweed Pearl
5^{6g} 2^{6gf} 7^{6gf} 5^{6gf} **0-1-4 £1,688**

Jath *Julian Poulton*   81
2 b f Bishop Of Cashel - Night Trader (USA)

1^{8gf} **1-0-1 £4,730**

Java Dawn (Ire) *Miss D A McHale*   39
3 b f Fleetwood (Ire) - Krakatoa
15^{7gf} 11^{8gf} 9^{7f} **0-0-3**

Javelin *Ian Williams*   56
7 ch g Generous (Ire) - Moss
4^{10f} 9^{14gf} 4^{14g} 5^{13gf} **0-0-4 £762**

Jawhari *T G Mills* 78 a83
9 b g Lahib (USA) - Lady Of The Land
1^{6sd} 11^{6gf} 13^{6gf} 6^{5gf} **1-0-4 £5,083**

Jawleyford Court *C Smith*   a23
4 b f Moshaajir (USA) - Mrs Jawleyford (USA)
3^{8sw} **0-1-1 £420**

Jawwala (USA) *J R Jenkins*   67
4 b f Green Dancer (USA) - Fetch N Carry (USA)
8^{14gf} 11^{16gf} **0-0-2**

Jay Gee's Choice *M R Channon* 104
3 b g Barathea (Ire) - Llia
9^{8g} 6^{7gf} 12^{8hy} 4^{7g} 22^{8gf} 2^{8gf} 6^{8gf} 18^{8gs}
9^{8gs} **0-2-9 £7,090**

Jay Jay Lass *R Williams*   a1
3 b f Bold Fort - Suelizelle
12^{9sd} 9^{7sd} 12^{12sd} **0-0-3**

Jayanjay *Miss B Sanders* 87 a73
4 b g Piccolo - Morica
13^{6sd} 1^{5f} 10^{5gf} 16^{6gf} 13^{6g} 1^{6g} 5^{6gf}
10^{6g} 4^{5gf} 2^{5gf} 16^{5gf} 7^{6g} 6^{5g} 6^{6f} 7^{6sd} **2-1-15**
£20,157

Jayceer *P W Harris*   a69
4 b g Green Desert (USA) - Centaine
3^{8sd} 4^{8sd} 7^{7sd} **0-1-3 £851**

Jazz Messenger (Fr) *G A Butler* 104
3 b g Acatenango (Ger) - In The Saltmine (Fr)
1^{7gf} 3^{7gf} 1^{8hy} 1^{10g} 8^{10gf} 17^{9gf} 6^{8gs} **3-1-7**
£95,022

Jazz Scene (Ire) *M R Channon*   91
2 b c Danehill Dancer (Ire) - Dixie Jazz
8^{7s} 1^{6g} 8^{6g} 2^{6gf} **1-1-4 £30,419**

Jazzaam *M D I Usher*   50
4 ch f Fraam - Aldwick Colonnade
6^{12g} 5^{9gf} 6^{8gf} **0-0-3**

Jazzy Millennium *B R Millman* 65 a59
6 ch g Lion Cavern (USA) - Woodcrest
10^{6sd} 12^{6sd} 4^{6sd} 3^{5sd} 1^{7f} 15^{6gf} 11^{6sd}
1^{7gf} 5^{6f} 13^{7gf} 15^{6gf} **2-1-11 £7,942**

Jeanette Romee *A Charlton*   61
3 b f Victory Note (USA) - Latest Flame (Ire)
12^{7gf} 8^{7gs} 14^{7gf} 8^{6g} 4^{6f} 16^{7gf} **0-0-6**
£128

Jeannie Wiz *A Bailey* 17 a38
3 b f Wizard King - One For Jeannie
10^{7sd} 10^{6sd} 4^{6sd} 6^{5sd} 7^{5sd} 16^{5gf} **0-0-6**

Jebal Suraaj (USA) *M Johnston*   97
3 b g Gone West (USA) - Trishyde (USA)
2^{8gf} 1^{9gf} 1^{10gf} 24^{8gf} 8^{10gf} **2-1-5**
£17,257

Jedburgh *J L Dunlop*   90
2 b c Selkirk (USA) - Conspiracy
3^{7gf} 2^{7f} 12^{7g} 1^{7gf} 1^{7gf} 1^{7gf} **3-2-6**
£20,801

Jedeydd *M Dods*   69
6 b g Shareef Dancer (USA) - Bilad (USA)
10^{6g} 13^{6sd} 8^{6gf} 11^{8g} 16^{7gf} 15^{7gf} 7^{8g}
7^{6gf} **0-0-8**

Jeepstar *T D Easterby*   85

3 b g Muhtarram (USA) - Jungle Rose
3^{7gf} 11^{7gf} 3^{8g} 5^{8gf} 1^{10gf} 2^{12gf} 1^{12gf} 2^{10g}
5^{10gf} 3^{12gf} **2-5-10 £24,019**

Jelba *N P Littmoden*   a95
5 b m Pursuit Of Love - Gold Bracelet
6^{8sd} 4^{7sd} 1^{8sd} 11^{10sd} 8^{10sd} **1-0-5**
£8,378

Jellyhead *Mrs S A Liddiard*   11
3 b c Distinctly North (USA) - Homebeforemidnight
15^{7gf} 7^{6gf} 12^{7gf} **0-0-3**

Jenavive *T D Easterby*   63
3 b f Danzig Connection (USA) - Promise Fulfilled (USA)
6^{10gf} 11^{7gf} 13^{7gf} 6^{9f} 3^{7gf} 10^{8gf} 8^{10s}
13^{8s} 2^{14gf} 2^{14gf} 12^{16gf} 3^{14gf} **0-4-12 £3,083**

Jerome *T D Easterby*   70
2 b c Nicolotte - Mim
4^{5gf} 4^{5gf} 2^{6f} 10^{5s} 4^{6gf} 9^{6s} 3^{7gf} 4^{8gf}
0-2-8 £3,639

Jervaulx Flicka *C W Fairhurst*   14
4 b f Magic Ring (Ire) - Tirolina (Ire)
13^{6f} 17^{8gf} **0-0-2**

Jesmund *Mrs L C Jewell*
3 b f Bishop Of Cashel - Foretell
11^{7sd} 11^{11sd} **0-0-2**

Jesse Samuel *J R Jenkins*   52 a29
2 ch c First Trump - Miss Kellybell
5^{5g} 6^{6gf} 6^{6f} 13^{5gf} 10^{5gf} 8^{6gf} 10^{6sd}
0-0-7

Jessie *Don Enrico Incisa*   52
4 ch f Pivotal - Bold Gem
15^{7g} 13^{8g} 4^{7s} **0-0-3 £316**

Jessie Macdougall *P D Evans*   60
3 br f Overbury (Ire) - Miss Crusty
3^{8f} 8^{16gf} 14^{11gf} 4^{10gf} 4^{10gf} **0-2-5 £527**

Jessinca *A P Jones*   53 a54
7 b m Minshaanshu Amad (USA) - Noble Soul
12^{8sd} 8^{7sd} 6^{12f} 12^{10gf} 4^{10f} 10^{6f} 1^{8sd}
6^{8sd} 9^{9gf} 9^{8hd} 2^{9sd} 4^{10gf} 6^{10f} **1-2-13 £4,954**

Jewel Of India *P J Hobbs*   86 a94
4 ch g Bijou D'Inde - Low Hill
3^{10sd} 5^{10sd} 8^{8g} **0-1-3 £686**

Jezadil (Ire) *Mrs L Stubbs*   53
5 b m Mujadil (USA) - Tender Time
11^{2gf} 15^{11gf} 2^{10gf} 9^{10g} 11^{4gf} 3^{12f} 12^{14f}
6^{12gf} 12^{12gf} 4^{12gf} 3^{14gf} 9^{16gf} **2-1-12 £8,733**

Jiffies Flyer (Ire) *D Carroll*   53 a46
2 ch f Desert Story (Ire) - Moon Dust
4^{5gf} 3^{6sd} 5^{6gf} 6^{7f} 7^{5gf} 7^{8gf} 6^{7gf}
14^{6gf} 4^{7f} **0-1-10 £1,137**

Jilly Why (Ire) *Ms Deborah J Evans*   67 a39
2 b f Mujadil (USA) - Ruwy
6^{6sd} 3^{6gf} 4^{5gf} 7^{7g} **0-1-4 £1,029**

Jim Lad *Dr J R J Naylor*   39
3 b g Young Ern - Anne's Bank (Ire)
7^{9g} 10^{10gf} 11^{16gf} 12^{16gf} **0-0-4**

Jimmy Byrne (Ire) *M R Channon*   76
3 ch g Red Sunset - Persian Sally (Ire)
9^{7gf} 1^{7gf} 5^{7gf} 2^{8gf} 3^{10g} 7^{10gf} 11^{8f} **1-1-7**
£11,415

Jimmy Gee (Ire) *D Nicholls*   54
2 b g Efisio - Stica (Ire)
2^{8g} 11^{10f} 11^{7f} **0-1-3 £1,000**

Jimmy Ryan (Ire) *T D McCarthy*   85
2 b c Orpen (USA) - Kaysama (Fr)
3^{6gf} 1^{6gf} 4^{6gf} **1-1-3 £4,547**

Jinksonthehouse *M D I Usher*   72 a7
2 b f Whittingham (Ire) - Aldwick Colonnade
3^{5g} 5^{6gf} 5^{5f} 8^{6gf} 9^{7g} 10^{6sd} 16^{8gf} **0-1-7**
£445

Job Rage (Ire) *A Bailey*   a37
9 b/br g Yashgan - Snatchingly
8^{16sd} 6^{16sd} 7^{12sw} **0-0-3**

Jocks Boy *P R Wood*   45
2 b g Defacto (USA) - Lady Khadija
11^{6sd} 9^{6gs} **0-0-2**

Jodeeka *J A Glover*   86 a84
6 ch m Fraam - Gold And Blue (Ire)
1^{5sd} 1^{5sd} 8^{5sd} 4^{6sd} 9^{5gf} 6^{5g} 1^{5gf} 1^{5gf}
4-0-8 £24,174

Jodonstay *D Shaw*   22 a26
3 b f Komaite (USA) - Cliburnel News (Ire)
13^{5gf} 8^{5sd} 7^{8sd} **0-0-3**

Joe Bear (Ire) *P Mitchell*   106
3 ch c Peintre Celebre (USA) - Maharani (USA)
6^{10gf} 1^{10gf} 1^{10gf} 2^{10g} 3^{9f} **2-1-5**
£81,625

Joe Charlie *K A Ryan*   54
2 ch c Daggers Drawn (USA) - La Ballerine
8^{6g} 12^{7g} 8^{7gs} **0-0-3**

Joe Lieberman *G B Balding*   43
2 b g Polish Precedent (USA) - Inchkeith
9^{6g} **0-0-1**

Joely Green *N P Littmoden*   58 a76
6 b g Binary Star (USA) - Comedy Lady
3^{16sd} 5^{12sd} 5^{12sd} 1^{12sw} 12^{12sd} 2^{12sd} 5^{16sd}
4^{12f} 8^{11gf} 2^{14gf} 1^{16f} 5^{19gf} 10^{14gf} 3^{16gf}
13^{16g} 4^{14gf} 3^{16gf} 5^{16gf} **2-6-19 £10,845**

Joey Perhaps *J R Best*   68
2 b g Danzig Connection (USA) - Realms Of Gold (USA)
7^{5gf} 4^{6gf} 5^{5gf} 13^{7gf} **0-0-4**

Johannian *I A Wood*   77
5 b h Hernando (Fr) - Photo Call
7^{10gf} 11^{10g} 5^{10gf} **0-0-3 £567**

Johar (USA) *Richard E Mandella*   128
4 b c Gone West (USA) - Windsharp (USA)
1^{10f} 3^{9f} 2^{10f} 1^{12f} **2-0-4 £570,239**

John O'Groats (Ire) *M Dods*   87
5 b g Distinctly North (USA) - Bannons Dream (Ire)
17^{5g} 4^{5f} 26^{5g} 12^{6gs} 12^{6gf} 19^{5gf} **0-0-6**
£722

John's Champ (Ire) *A P Jarvis*   12 a57
3 b g Mujadil (USA) - Big Buyer (USA)
4^{10sd} 8^{7sd} 4^{12gf} **0-1-5 £826**

Johnny Alljays (Ire) *J S Moore*   47
2 b g Victory Note (USA) - It's Academic
14^{5g} 11^{5gf} 13^{7gf} 8^{8gf} **0-0-4**

Johnny From Donny *Ronald Thompson*   46
2 ch g Young Ern - Polish Lady (Ire)
5^{5sd} 7^{5sd} 14^{5gf} 5^{5gs} 7^{6gf} 8^{7gs} 8^{7f} **0-0-7**

Johnny Parkes *Mrs J R Ramsden*   76
2 b g Wolfhound (USA) - Lucky Parkes
2^{5gf} 2^{5g} 2^{5gf} 2^{5gf} 1^{5f} 5^{6gf} **1-3-6**
£8,122

Johnny Reb *Mrs S J Smith*
5 b g Danehill (USA) - Dixie Eyes Blazing (USA)
18^{8gf} **0-0-1**

Johnson's Point *M W Easterby*   70
5 ch m Sabrehill (USA) - Watership (USA)
10^{10gf} 3^{12gf} 5^{14gf} 6^{12g} 14^{12s} **0-1-5 £579**

Johnston's Diamond (Ire) *E J Alston*   93 a67
5 b g Tagula (Ire) - Toshair Flyer
1⁶ˢʷ 8⁶ˢᵈ 2⁶ˢʷ 1⁶ᵍ 2⁶ᵍᶠ 4⁶ᵍᶠ 4⁶ᵍˢ 1⁶ᵍˢ
18⁶ᵍ 1⁵ᵍ **4-4-10 £20,961**

Joint Destiny (Ire) *G L Moore*   67
2 b f Desert Prince (Ire) - Brogan's Well (Ire)
5⁵ᵍᶠ 2⁶ᵍᶠ 2⁶ᵍ 5⁶ᵍᶠ 8⁶ᵍ 2⁶ᵍᶠ 3⁶ᵍ 4⁶ᵍᶠ
0-2-8 £4,391

Joint Statement *M R Channon*   90
4 b g Barathea (Ire) - Gena Ivor (USA)
10⁸ᵍᶠ 5⁸ᵍ 6⁸ᵍᶠ 11⁹ᵍ 2⁸ᵍᶠ 3⁸ᵍᶠ 10⁸ᵍᶠ 1⁸ᶠ
1-2-8 £15,436

Joking Apart *B W Hills*   22
2 b f Rainbow Quest (USA) - Jood (USA)
17⁷ᵍ **0-0-1**

Joli Ernest *R J Hodges*   28
2 ch g Young Ern - Pip's Dream
13⁵ᵍᶠ 10⁷ᵍᶠ 8⁵ᵍᶠ 11⁶ᵍᶠ **0-0-4**

Jolizero *G G Margarson*   45
2 br c Danzero (Aus) - Jolis Absent
9⁸ᵍᶠ 12⁸ᵍ **0-0-2**

Jomus *L Montague Hall*   68
2 b g Soviet Star (USA) - Oatey
8⁶ᵍˢ 4⁶ᵍᶠ 7⁵ᶠ 7⁶ᵍᶠ 2⁶ᵍᶠ 13⁷ᵍ **0-1-6**
£1,089

Jonalton (Ire) *C R Dore*   52
4 b g Perugino (USA) - Vago Pequeno (Ire)
7¹⁰ᵍᶠ 9¹⁵ᵍᶠ 7¹⁶ᵍˢ 15¹⁶ᵍᶠ **0-0-4**

Jonjo *B P J Baugh*   a7
5 b g Charnwood Forest (Ire) - Katy-Q (Ire)
10⁸ˢᵈ **0-0-1**

Jonny Ebeneezer *R M H Cowell*   82 a72
4 b g Hurricane Sky (Aus) - Leap Of Faith (Ire)
9⁶ᵍᶠ 14⁶ᵍ 4⁸ˢᵈ 2⁶ᵍᶠ 2⁶ᵍᶠ 4⁷ᵍ 6⁶ˢᵈ 4⁷ᵍˢ
0-2-8 £2,821

Jools *D K Ivory*   84 a77
5 b g Cadeaux Genereux - Madame Crecy (USA)
8⁶ˢᵈ 5⁷ˢᵈ 22⁸ᵍ 6⁶ᶠ 4⁷ᵍᶠ 3⁸ᵍˢ 8⁷ᵍᶠ 16ᵍᶠ
1⁹ᵍ 2⁸ˢᵈ 1¹⁰ᵍ 4⁷ᵍᶠ 1⁸ᵍᶠ 15¹⁰ᵍ 16⁹ᵍᶠ **4-2-15**
£18,290

Jordans Elect *I Semple*   77
3 ch g Fleetwood (Ire) - Cal Norma's Lady (Ire)
2⁸ᵍ 3⁸ᵍᶠ 12⁸ᵍᶠ 4⁹ᵍᶠ 1⁹ᵍᶠ 10¹²ᵍᶠ 5¹⁰ᵍᶠ
7¹⁰ᵍˢ 13⁸ᵍ **1-2-9 £4,999**

Josephus (Ire) *R Charlton*   101
2 ch c King Of Kings (Ire) - Khulasah (USA)
4⁶ᵍᶠ 1⁷ᵍ 2⁷ᵍᶠ **1-1-3 £15,436**

Joshua's Bay *J R Jenkins*
5 b g Karinga Bay - Bonita Blakeney
13²²ᶠ **0-0-1**

Joshua's Gold (Ire) *D Carroll*   55
2 b c Sesaro (USA) - Lady Of The Night (Ire)
13⁵ᵍᶠ 6⁶ᵍᶠ 11⁵ˢ 3⁷ᵍᶠ 5⁷ᵍᶠ 5⁸ᵍᶠ 5⁷ᵍˢ **0-1-7**
£648

Joshuas Boy (Ire) *K A Ryan*   7
3 ch c Bahhare (USA) - Broadway Rosie
15⁵ᵍᶠ **0-0-1**

Jouvert *R Hannon*   52
3 ch c Grand Lodge (USA) - Polygueza (Fr)
10⁶ᵍˢ 15⁸ᵍ 9⁶ᵍᶠ 18⁸ᵍᶠ **0-0-5**

Joyce's Choice *A Berry*   60 a32
4 b g Mind Games - Madrina
13⁵ˢʷ 9⁶ˢᵈ 3⁵ᵍᶠ 5⁵ᵍᶠ 14⁵ᵍᶠ 2⁵ᶠ 7⁵ᵍᶠ 5⁵ᵍᶠ
18⁵ᵍᶠ 11⁵ᵍᶠ 5⁵ᵍᶠ 10⁵ᵍᶠ **0-2-12 £1,439**

Juan Carlos (Ire) *B Gubby*   8 a38

---

4 ch g Ashkalani (Ire) - Mimansa (USA)
9¹⁰ˢᵈ 11¹²ᵍᶠ **0-0-2**

Jubilee *B J Meehan*   73
3 ch f Selkirk (USA) - Royal Passion
7¹⁰ᵍ 9¹⁰ᵍᶠ 12¹²ᵍ 10¹⁰ᵍᶠ 6¹¹ᵍᶠ **0-0-5**

Jubilee Street (Ire) *D Nicholls*   65
4 b g Dr Devious (Ire) - My Firebird
9⁷ᵍᶠ 18⁸ᵍᶠ 8⁸ᵍᶠ 11¹⁰ᵍ 1⁷ᵍᶠ 6⁶ᵍˢ 8⁸ˢ 9⁷ᵍᶠ
10⁶ᵍ 5⁶ᶠ **1-0-10 £3,283**

Jubilee Time *L M Cumani*   78
3 b c Mark Of Esteem (Ire) - Bella Colora
12⁸ᶠ 3¹⁰ᵍᶠ **0-1-2 £449**

Jubilee Treat (USA) *G Wragg*   85
3 b f Seeking The Gold (USA) - Dance Treat (USA)
8⁷ᵍᶠ 4⁸ᵍ 5⁸ˢ 5¹⁰ᵍᶠ 1¹⁰ᵍ 2¹⁰ᵍ 11¹⁰ᵍᶠ **1-1-7**
£10,607

Judes Law *S C Burrough*   30
5 gr m Contract Law (USA) - Linen Thread
9¹⁰ᵍ **0-0-1**

Judhoor *B W Hills*   98
3 b f Alhaarth (Ire) - Almurooj
1⁶ᵍᶠ 17⁵ᵍᶠ 7⁶ᵍ 5⁶ᵍ 11⁶ᵍᶠ **1-0-5**
£19,360

Jufiscea *J L Spearing*   11 a48
4 b g Efisio - Jucea
18⁶ᶠ 7⁸ᶠᵗ 12⁹ˢᵈ **0-0-3**

Julian Ronjoyles *I A Wood*   44
3 b c Danzig Connection (USA) - Pearl Dawn (Ire)
9⁷ᵍᶠ 9⁶ᵍᶠ 10⁷ᵍᶠ 10⁸ᵍ LFT⁹ˢᵈ 18⁸ᵍᶠ **0-0-6**

Juliette (Ire) *John M Oxx*   107
3 b f Sadler's Wells (USA) - Arutua (USA)
7⁷ᵍ 6¹⁰ʸˢ 2¹²ᶠ 5¹²ᵍ 1¹²ᵍᶠ 6¹⁵ᵍ 3¹²ᵍʸ **1-2-7**
£47,370

Jumhoor (Ire) *E A L Dunlop*   77
3 b c Bahhare (USA) - West Of Eden
2⁷ᵍᶠ 15⁷ᵍˢ 3⁸ᶠ 1⁷ᶠ 4⁷ᵍᶠ **1-2-5 £8,103**

Jummana (Fr) *G A Butler*   a80
3 ch f Cadeaux Genereux - Forty Belles (USA)
8⁸ˢᵈ **0-0-1**

Jungle Lion *J O'Reilly*   a45
5 ch g Lion Cavern (USA) - Star Ridge (USA)
6⁹ˢᵈ 15¹²ˢʷ 6⁸ˢᵈ **0-0-3**

Junikay (Ire) *R Ingram*   52 a62
9 b g Treasure Kay - Junijo
9¹⁰ˢᵈ 9¹⁶ˢᵈ 6¹³ˢᵈ 5¹²ˢᵈ 7¹⁰ᵍᶠ **0-0-5**

Juniper Banks *Miss A Stokell*   62
2 ch c Night Shift (USA) - Beryl
7⁶ᵍᶠ 6⁷ᵍᶠ 8⁷ᵍᶠ 4⁵ᵍᶠ 2⁶ᵍᶠ 9⁶ᵍ **0-1-6**
£2,224

Junkanoo *Mrs M Reveley*
7 ch g Generous (Ire) - Lupescu
14¹⁸ᵍ **0-0-1**

Junowot *M D I Usher*   28
3 b f Cyrano De Bergerac - Aldwick Colonnade
15⁸ᵍ 12⁸ˢ 18⁷ᵍᶠ **0-0-3**

Juristicia (Ire) *M Johnston*   64 a13
3 ch f Nashwan (USA) - Jural
5¹⁰ᵍ 2¹⁰ᵍᶠ 2¹²ᵍᶠ 5¹²ˢᵈ **0-0-4 £3,390**

Just A Fluke (Ire) *M Johnston*   71
2 b c Darshaan - Star Profile (Ire)
2⁷ᵍᶠ 2⁷ᵍ **0-2-2 £3,210**

Just A Gigolo *N Tinkler*   14 a10
3 b g Inchinor - Courtisane
13⁶ˢᵈ 16⁶ᵍ 12⁸ᵍˢ **0-0-3**

Just A Glimmer *L G Cottrell*   a83
3 b f Bishop Of Cashel - Rockin' Rosie
7^8sd **0-0-1**

Just A Martian (Fr) *W R Muir*   87 a77
3 b c Marju (Ire) - Stamatina
2^7sd 13^8gf 2^8f 1^8f 4^8gf 2^8g 5^8g 4^10gf
1-3-8 £11,139

Just A Promise (Fr) *M Johnston*   37
2 ch f Grand Lodge (USA) - Jural
7^8gf **0-0-1**

Just Dance Me (Fr) *W J Haggas*   48
2 gr f Linamix (Fr) - Reine De La Ciel (USA)
10^7gf **0-0-1**

Just Ern *P C Haslam*   45 a21
4 ch g Young Ern - Just Run (Ire)
7^8sd 8^6gf 10^5sd 10^7g **0-0-4**

Just Fly *S Kirk*   84 a82
3 b g Efisio - Chrysalis
5^7sd 14^8gf 7^7g 1^7gf 14^7g **1-0-5 £6,340**

Just James *J Noseda*   119
4 b c Spectrum (Ire) - Fairy Flight (Ire)
2^6gf 5^6f 2^7gf 12^6gf 1^7gf **1-2-5 £85,650**

Just Jennifer *P W D'Arcy*   41 a58
3 b f Emperor Jones (USA) - Highest Bid (Fr)
5^7sd 2^7sd 6^6sd 12^10gf **0-1-5 £908**

Just One Look *M Blanshard*   80
2 b f Barathea (Ire) - Western Sal
4^6gf 2^6gf 1^6g 4^6g 2^6gf 6^6gf 5^6gf 7^7g
14^7gf **1-2-9 £8,413**

Just One Smile (Ire) *T D Easterby*   66
3 b f Desert Prince (Ire) - Smile Awhile (USA)
12^8g 3^8g 3^7f 2^7f 1^6f 4^6gf **1-2-6**
£5,647

Just Red *R Hollinshead*   45
5 ch h Meqdaam (USA) - Orchard Bay
5^10gf 10^9sd **0-0-2**

Just Serenade *M J Ryan*   26 a58
4 ch f Factual (USA) - Thimbalina
2^8sd 10^8sd 2^7sd 11^8g 4^8sd **0-2-5 £1,812**

Just Tim (Ire) *R Hannon*   73 a73
2 ch c Inchinor - Simply Sooty
9^7g 6^7g 7^8gf 2^8sd **0-1-4 £944**

Just Wiz *N P Littmoden*   47 a85
7 b g Efisio - Jade Pet
1^9sd 1^9sd 10^10sd 4^8sd 5^8sd 9^9sd 5^10gf
2-0-7 £6,346

Justafancy *Miss J Feilden*   29 a62
5 b g Green Desert (USA) - Justsayno (USA)
9^7sw 10^6sd 4^7sd 8^7sd 8^12f 15^11gf
11^9sd **0-1-8**

Justalord *J Balding*   73 a92
5 b g King's Signet (USA) - Just Lady
5^5sd 4^5sd 1^5sd 3^5sd 5^5sd 7^5gs 3^5gs
1^5g 5^5f 2^5gf 1^5gf 5^5gf 2^5g 7^5gf **3-5-15**
£26,135

Justastrop (Ire) *J S Moore*   30
2 ch f Daggers Drawn (Ire) - Just Blink (Ire)
5^5f 7^5sd 6^6f **0-0-3**

Juste Pour L'Amour *J R Fanshawe*   87
3 ch g Pharly (Fr) - Fontaine Lady
11^8gf 4^8g 2^7gf 4^8gf 5^8gf 8^8g 8^8gf **0-1-7**
£3,390

Juwwi *J M Bradley*   79 a83
9 ch g Mujtahid (USA) - Nouvelle Star (Aus)
7^5sw 8^6sd 10^6sd 9^6sd 12^6sw 4^6sd 8^6g
14^6gf 2^6gf 6^6gf 1^6g 8^6g 3^6gf 6^6gf 13^6gf 6^6gf
10^6gs 6^6gf **1-3-27 £9,560**

Juyush (USA) *P Bowen*   65
11 b g Silver Hawk (USA) - Silken Doll (USA)
3^22gf **0-1-1 £1,052**

Kabis Booie (Ire) *H R A Cecil*   66 a59
2 ch c Night Shift (USA) - Perfect Welcome
2^8f 4^8sd **0-1-2 £912**

Kabreet *E A L Dunlop*   68
2 b c Night Shift (USA) - Red Rabbit
5^6gf 5^6gs 3^6g **0-1-3 £545**

Kafil (USA) *J J Bridger*   13 a44
9 b/br g Housebuster (USA) - Alchaasibiyeh (USA)
5^9sd 8^7sd 7^6gf **0-0-3**

Kafuwain *J Noseda*   76 a75
2 b c Mark Of Esteem (Ire) - Anneli Rose
3^5g 8^5g 8^5gf 1^6gf 11^6g 5^6sd **1-0-6**
£6,574

Kagoshima (Ire) *J R Norton*   44
8 b g Shirley Heights - Kashteh (Ire)
9^16gf 10^16g **0-0-2**

Kahyasi Princess (Ire) *M Johnston*   92
3 b f Kahyasi - Dungeon Princess (Ire)
3^12gf 2^12gf 3^11gs 5^11gs 4^12s 11^12f 11^12sd
1^16gs 3^16gf 1^16gf 1^16g **4-3-11 £26,251**

Kaieteur (USA) *B J Meehan*   121
4 b c Marlin (USA) - Strong Embrace (USA)
8^11vs 6^10gf 3^10gf 2^10g 3^10gf 7^10gf **0-2-6**
£148,800

Kairos (Ire) *J M Bradley*   29
3 b g Kadeed (Ire) - Oriental Air (Ire)
10^8gs 16^7gf 7^6gf 11^7g **0-0-4**

Kaiser (Ire) *J R Fanshawe*   64
3 b g Barathea (Ire) - Emerald Waters
19^10g 8^10gf 4^12gf 14^14gf **0-0-4 £319**

Kalaman (Ire) *Sir Michael Stoute*   126
3 b c Desert Prince (Ire) - Kalamba (Ire)
1^8gf 1^8gf 2^8gf 7^10gf 2^8gf **2-1-5 £92,870**

Kalani Girl (Ire) *Mrs P N Dutfield*   75
2 b f Ashkalani (Ire) - Sopran Marida (Ire)
5^6g 4^5gf 3^6y 4^6f 9^7gf 2^7gf 19^7g 3^7gf
14^7gf **0-2-9 £11,614**

Kalanisha (Ire) *N A Graham*   39
3 ch c Ashkalani (Ire) - Camisha (Ire)
11^10gf 14^12g 9^11g **0-0-3**

Kalarram *T Wall*
6 ch m Muhtarram (USA) - Kalandariya
11^7sd **0-0-1**

Kalishka (Ire) *Andrew Turnell*   59
2 b c Fasliyev (USA) - Andromaque (USA)
8^5gf 14^6gs 9^7gf **0-0-3**

Kallista's Pride *J A Osborne*   a33
3 b f Puissance - Clan Scotia
7^6sd **0-0-1**

Kalou (Ger) *B J Curley*   a50
5 br g Law Society (USA) - Kompetenz (Ire)
6^12sd 5^8sd 7^15sd **0-0-3**

Kaluana Court *R J Price*   70
7 b m Batshoof - Fairfields Cone
3^18gf 11^14gf 2^15gf 1^15gf 4^16g 1^15g 7^16gf
2-1-7 £16,338

Kalush *Ronald Thompson*   64
2 b g Makbul - The Lady Vanishes
13^5g 7^5f 10^5g 3^6s 9^6g 2^7f 6^7gf 3^8gf
3^7gf 6^7gs **0-4-10 £2,740**

Kama's Wheel *John A Harris*   50 a35
4 ch f Magic Ring (Ire) - Tea And Scandals (USA)
14^{8sd} 5^{9sd} 7^{9sw} 8^{8sd} 10^{8sw} 6^{5sw} 6^{8gf}
11^{8f} 5^{8gf} 4^{7f} 8^{7gf} DSQ^{7gs} 6^{8f} 12^{10f} **0-1-14**

Kamala *R Brotherton*
4 b f Priolo (USA) - Fleeting Vision (Ire)
10^{16sw} **0-0-1**

Kamanda Laugh *W Jarvis*   69
2 ch g Most Welcome - Kamada (USA)
6^{7gf} 10^{6gf} **0-0-2**

Kamenka *R A Fahey*   71 a52
2 ch f Wolfhound (USA) - Aliuska (Ire)
6^{5f} 3^{5gf} 14^{7gf} 4^{6gf} 4^{6sd} **0-0-5 £6,672**

Kanga *N P Littmoden*   48 a48
4 b f Primo Dominie - Princess Zara
6^{7sd} 5^{7gf} 11^{8sd} 6^{6gf} 5^{6gf} 7^{5gs} 7^{6sw} 6^{8sd}
0-0-8

Kangarilla Road *Mrs J R Ramsden*   78
4 b g Magic Ring (Ire) - Kangra Valley
6^{5gf} 11^{5gf} 14^{5gf} **0-0-3 £239**

Kanz Wood (USA) *A W Carroll*   57 a72
7 ch g Woodman (USA) - Kanz (USA)
1^{8sd} 3^{8sd} 4^{8sw} 5^{7sw} 3^{7g} 7^{7gf} 15^{7gf} **1-2-7**
£4,479

Kapalua (USA) *B W Hills*   46
3 b f King Of Kings (Ire) - Numero Privee (USA)
4^{12gf} **0-0-1 £425**

Kaparolo (USA) *Mrs A J Perrett*   81
4 ch g El Prado (Ire) - Parliament House (USA)
5^{14gs} 3^{14hy} 9^{12g} 6^{14gs} 5^{13gf} 15^{21gs} **0-1-6**
£1,291

Karakum *A J Chamberlain*
4 b g Mtoto - Magongo
17^{12g} **0-0-1**

Karamea (Swi) *J L Dunlop*   74
2 gr f Rainbow Quest (USA) - Karapucha (Ire)
7^{7gf} 3^{8gf} **0-1-2 £787**

Karaoke (Ire) *S Kirk*   76
3 b g Mujadil (USA) - Kayoko (Ire)
3^{10gf} 1^{8g} 8^{8g} 2^{10g} 3^{9gf} 3^{8gf} 1^{10f} **2-4-7**
£10,926

Karaoke King *J E Long*   70 a70
5 ch h King's Signet (USA) - Brampton Grace
9^{7sd} 7^{6sd} 3^{7sd} 2^{7sd} 10^{7sd} 2^{6gs} 4^{6g} 2^{7g}
3^{6gf} 7^{5gf} 13^{6gf} 11^{6g} 4^{6g} 6^{7g} 1^{6gf} 6^{7gf} 13^{7sd}
9^{7sd} **1-5-18 £10,127**

Karathaena (Ire) *J W Hills*   78
3 b f Barathea (Ire) - Dabtara (Ire)
5^{8g} 10^{9gf} 3^{8g} **0-1-3 £1,658**

Kareeb (Fr) *W J Musson*   91
6 b g Green Desert (USA) - Braari (USA)
4^{6gf} 13^{6gf} 4^{7gf} 4^{7gf} 13^{7f} 1^{7gf} 20^{7g} 1^{7gf}
3^{7gf} 12^{7gf} 9^{7gf} 8^{7gs} 16^{7g} **2-3-13 £33,762**

Karju (Ire) *M Todhunter*   60
4 b g Marju (Ire) - Karmisymixa (Fr)
3^{8gs} **0-0-1 £898**

Karli *D W Barker*   35
3 b f Superpower - Saraswati
11^{7gf} 13^{7gf} 6^{6gf} 7^{7gf} 12^{8gf} **0-0-5**

Karlinight (Ire) *T J Naughton*   38 a47
3 b f Night Shift (USA) - Karlinaxa
3^{8sd} 7^{7sd} 7^{8f} 8^{6sd} **0-0-4 £522**

Karma Chamelian (USA) *J W Hills*   26
2 b f Diesis - Wild Rumour (Ire)
10^{6gf} **0-0-1**

Karminskey Park *T J Etherington*   77 a67
4 b f Sabrehill (USA) - Housefull
1^{5sd} 6^{5sd} 4^{5sw} 2^{5sd} 4^{5gf} 4^{6g} 1^{5gs} 5^{5g}
2^{5gs} 3^{5gf} 7^{5gf} 13^{5gf} 4^{5g} 4^{6gs} 11^{5gf}
2-7-16 £16,880

Kartuzy (Jpn) *M A Jarvis*   86
3 b f Polish Precedent (USA) - Marienbad (Fr)
2^{12gs} 11^{1f} 3^{12gf} 3^{10gf} **1-1-4 £7,441**

Karyon (Ire) *P C Haslam*   35 a21
3 b f Presidium - Stealthy
6^{7sd} 10^{8sw} 13^{8gf} 15^{8gf} 3^{10gf} **0-1-5 £338**

Kasamba *Miss J A Camacho*   50 a23
4 b f Salse - Kabayil
9^{10g} 9^{8gs} 7^{8sd} 8^{12sw} **0-0-4**

Kaseh (USA) *Saeed Bin Suroor*   65
2 b/br c Storm Cat (USA) - Magical Allure (USA)
4^{6gf} **0-0-1**

Kashmir Sapphire (Ire) *J A Osborne*   61 a51
3 b g Bluebird (USA) - Tudor Loom
9^{8sd} 14^{10g} 6^{11s} 5^{12sd} 4^{12sd} 16^{12gf} 4^{11gf}
6^{8gf} 3^{12f} 8^{12sw} **0-1-10 £417**

Kasthari (Ire) *Sir Michael Stoute*   113
4 gr g Vettori (Ire) - Karliyka (Ire)
3^{16gf} 2^{16gf} 3^{16gf} **0-1-3 £15,400**

Kataholic *G A Ham*   a25
4 b c Bluegrass Prince (Ire) - Langton Herring
12^{7sd} **0-0-1**

Katano *J W Payne*   71
2 ch g Kris - Flagship
5^{7gf} **0-0-1**

Kate Maher (Ire) *M A Jarvis*   a27
4 b f Rainbow Quest (USA) - Melodist (USA)
9^{12sd} 10^{8sd} **0-0-2**

Kathology (Ire) *D R C Elsworth*   96 a64
6 b g College Chapel - Wicken Wonder (Ire)
10^{5sd} 15^{9f} 7^{5gf} 17^{5gf} 6^{5g} 28^{6f} 11^{5g} 5^{5g}
3^{5gf} **1-1-9 £11,656**

Katie Savage *J Mackie*   24
3 b f Emperor Jones (USA) - Coax Me Molly (USA)
9^{10gf} **0-0-1**

Katie's Bath Time *Ian Emmerson*   28
2 b f Lugana Beach - Eucharis
7^{5gs} 7^{5g} 10^{5gf} **0-0-3**

Katie's Role *Ian Emmerson*   50
2 b f Tragic Role (USA) - Mirkan Honey
6^{6g} 3^{6gs} 8^{7g} 12^{6f} 4^{7gs} **0-0-5 £424**

Katies Tight Jeans *R E Peacock*
9 b m Green Adventure (USA) - Haraka Sasa
15^{6sw} 9^{8sd} 10^{9sw} 11^{8sd} 15^{7g} 19^{8g} **0-0-6**

Katiypour (Ire) *Miss B Sanders*   79 a79
6 ch g Be My Guest (USA) - Katiyfa
13^{12sd} 2^{11sw} 6^{10sd} 3^{9sd} 6^{8sd} 7^{10gf} 2^{9gf}
8^{8gf} 1^{11sd} 11^{2sd} 3^{10gf} 8^{12g} 6^{12gf} 1^{10g} 3^{10g} 4^{10g}
6^{12g} **3-4-17 £23,180**

Katmandu *L M Cumani*   83
4 b g Sadler's Wells (USA) - Kithanga (Ire)
2^{14gf} 4^{14gf} 4^{16g} **0-1-3 £1,244**

Katy O'Hara *Miss S E Hall*   59 a56
4 b f Komaite (USA) - Amy Leigh (USA)
7^{6sw} 8^{6gf} 6^{7f} 11^{7f} 11^{6g} 13^{6sd} 9^{6gs}
13^{6gf} **0-0-9**

Katz Pyjamas (Ire) *Mrs A Duffield*   46
2 b f Fasliyev (USA) - Allepolina (USA)
7^{5f} 8^{5gf} 6^{5gf} 6^{6gf} 7^{5gf} 7^{5f} 15^{5sd} 7^{5gf}

14^{5gf} **0-0-9**

Kavi (Ire) *P C Haslam*   53 a61
3 ch g Perugino (USA) - Premier Leap (Ire)
4^{8sd} 3^{8sd} 6^{9gs} 6^{10g} 6^{10gf} **0-1-5 £450**

Kawader (USA) *A C Stewart*   51
3 ch c Kingmambo (USA) - Tajannub (USA)
6^{7gf} **0-0-1**

Kawagino (Ire) *Mrs P N Dutfield*   81
3 b g Perugino (USA) - Sharakawa (Ire)
4^{7gf} 2^{8g} 10^{7g} 16^{8gf} 5^{8g} 6^{6gf} **0-1-6 £2,364**

Kawakib (Ire) *J L Dunlop*   75
2 b f Intikhab (USA) - Haddeyah (USA)
3^{7gf} 4^{7g} 6^{7gf} 2^{8gf} 2^{10f} **0-2-5 £2,977**

Kayo Nobile (USA) *T Keddy*   14
3 b/br g Torrential (USA) - Nobile Decretum (USA)
9^{12sd} 9^{8gs} **0-0-2**

Kayseri (Ire) *Allan Smith*   102
4 b c Alzao (USA) - Ms Calera (USA)
5^{10g} 1^{16g} 5^{14gf} 8^{16g} **1-0-4 £37,165**

Kaysglory *C A Dwyer*
4 b g Glory Of Dancer - Kayartis
8^{12gf} 15^{12sd} **0-0-2**

Kebreya (USA) *R Ford*   24
4 ch g Affirmed (USA) - Minifah (USA)
16^{12s} **0-0-1**

Kedross (Ire) *R P Elliott*   65 a41
2 ch f King Of Kings (Ire) - Nom De Plume (USA)
4^{5f} 3^{5s} 6^{6gf} 4^{6g} 3^{6g} 7^{6ft} 8^{6gs} 13^{8s} **0-1-8 £2,314**

Keelung (USA) *M A Jarvis*   a63
2 b c Lear Fan (USA) - Miss Universal (Ire)
7^{8sd} **0-0-1**

Keen Hands *Mrs N Macauley*
7 ch g Keen - Broken Vow (Ire)
15^{7sd} **0-0-1**

Keep On Movin' (Ire) *T G Mills*   57 a71
2 b f Danehill Dancer (Ire) - Tormented (USA)
9^{8gf} 6^{7gf} 5^{8sd} **0-0-3**

Keep The Peace (Ire) *D J Wintle*
5 br g Petardia - Eiras Mood
13^{9sd} **0-0-1**

Keeper's Lodge (Ire) *B A McMahon*   75
2 ch f Grand Lodge (USA) - Gembira (USA)
4^{5gf} 8^{6gf} 5^{6gf} 20^{7g} 4^{6s} **0-0-5 £1,071**

Keepers Knight (Ire) *P F I Cole*   53
2 b c Sri Pekan (USA) - Keepers Dawn (Ire)
11^{7gf} 5^{7gf} 5^{7g} **0-0-3**

Kelbrook *A Bailey*   55
4 b g Unfuwain (USA) - Pidona
2^{11gf} **0-1-1 £1,762**

Kells (Ire) *D G Bridgwater*   36 a39
5 b g Dilum (USA) - Elizabethan Air
13^{10sd} 11^{9g} **0-0-2**

Kelly's Tune *A P Jarvis*   a36
4 b f Alhaarth (Ire) - Roxy Music (Ire)
5^{6sd} **0-0-1**

Kelpie (Ire) *A M Balding*   75 a85
4 b f Kahyasi - Darrouzett
2^{12sd} 2^{10sd} 9^{12sd} 8^{12sd} 12^{10sd} 1^{10sd} 10^{10sd} 2^{10g} 4^{10gf} 2^{12g} 5^{10gf} 2^{10g} 2^{10gf} 3^{11gf} 1^{11gf} **3-7-16 £27,656**

Kelseas Kolby (Ire) *J A Glover*   60
3 b g Perugino (USA) - Notre Dame (Ire)
10^{6gf} 11^{6s} 4^{8g} 11^{8sd} 15^{8s} 13^{8gf} 2^{7gf}

1^{7gf} 2^{7f} 15^{8g} **1-2-10 £4,613**

Kelsey Rose *P D Evans*   a83
4 b f Most Welcome - Duxyana (Ire)
10^{6sd} 5^{8sd} **0-0-2**

Keltic Rainbow (Ire) *D Haydn Jones*   28 a50
2 b f Spectrum (Ire) - Secrets Of Honour
7^{6s} 8^{7sd} 3^{8sd} **0-1-3 £319**

Kelucia (Ire) *J S Goldie*   99
2 ch f Grand Lodge (USA) - Karachi (Spa)
6^{7g} 2^{7gf} 1^{8gf} 2^{8gf} 1^{8g} 3^{7gf} 3^{7gf} 4^{8gs} **2-4-8 £24,341**

Kenley Lass (Ire) *M D I Usher*   58 a54
3 b f Danetime (Ire) - Big Fandango
4^{6sd} 7^{7sd} 3^{7sd} 3^{7sd} 4^{6gf} 5^{5gf} 6^{6gf} 7^{6gf} 10^{6gf} 2^{7gf} 6^{6gf} 10^{6g} 11^{6f} 10^{7f} 12^{6gf} 6^{6g} 7^{5gf} 5^{7gf} **1-3-21 £4,494**

Kennet *P D Cundell*   a40
8 b g Kylian (USA) - Marwell Mitzi
11^{13sd} **0-0-1**

Kenny The Truth (Ire) *Mrs J Candlish*   14 a52
4 b g Robellino (USA) - Just Blink (Ire)
7^{8sd} 8^{7sd} 2^{8sw} 4^{8sd} 5^{8sd} 16^{11gf} 15^{8g} 16^{10g} **0-1-8 £840**

Kensington (Ire) *D K Weld*   70
2 b c Cape Cross (Ire) - March Star (Ire)
3^{5y} 3^{6s} 13^{5f} 6^{6gy} 4^{5g} **0-1-5 £2,331**

Kent *P D Cundell*   54 a87
8 b g Kylian (USA) - Precious Caroline (Ire)
12^{13sd} 2^{16sd} 1^{16sw} 1^{16sw} 1^{16sd} 8^{18g} 8^{16gf} 5^{12sd} 13^{16gf} **3-1-9 £12,878**

Kentmere (Ire) *M Johnston*   73 a54
2 b c Efisio - Addaya (Ire)
2^{7t} 2^{7gf} 5^{6g} 8^{9g} 9^{8sd} **0-2-5 £2,548**

Kentucky Blue (Ire) *T D Easterby*   92
3 b g Revoque (Ire) - Delta Town (USA)
9^{8gf} 11^{11hy} 6^{10gf} 3^{12gf} 8^{10gf} 5^{10g} 5^{11s} 22^{12g} **1-0-8 £12,321**

Kentucky Bullet (USA) *A G Newcombe*   42 a56
7 b g Housebuster (USA) - Exactly So
8^{11sd} 3^{12sd} 1^{12sd} 14^{11gf} 6^{12sd} 1^{12sd} 7^{12gf} 4^{10gf} **3-1-9 £9,274**

Kentucky King (USA) *M Johnston*   91
3 b g Tale Of The Cat (USA) - Anna's Honor (USA)
4^{8gs} **0-0-1 £705**

Kepler (USA) *P F I Cole*   98 a103
4 ch c Spinning World (USA) - Perfect Arc (USA)
8^{10sd} 1^{12sd} 4^{12g} 5^{12s} **1-0-4 £14,055**

Kerala (Ire) *Don Enrico Incisa*
4 b f Mujadil (USA) - Kalisz (Ire)
14^{6gs} 16^{6f} 12^{6gf} **0-0-3**

Kerensans Prince *A D Smith*
4 b g Rislan (USA) - Skippy
13^{9sd} 19^{10f} **0-0-2**

Kernel Dowery (Ire) *P W Harris*   71 a64
3 b g Sri Pekan (USA) - Lady Dowery (USA)
4^{8f} 5^{10f} 9^{10sd} 3^{10gf} 12^{10f} 18^{10g} 9^{10gf} 4^{10gf} 3^{10gs} **0-3-10 £2,538**

Kerrs Pink *Mrs L Stubbs*   51 a3
2 b f Averti (Ire) - Julietta Mia (USA)
5^{5gf} 10^{5g} 6^{7gf} 12^{7gf} 6^{5gf} 8^{5sd} **0-0-6**

Keshena Falls (Ire) *R Guest*   54
3 b f Desert Prince (Ire) - Menominee
6^{7gf} 3^{8gf} 7^{8g} 15^{8gf} 5^{8gf} **0-0-5 £654**

Keshya *D J Coakley*   63
2 b f Mtoto - Liberatrice (Fr)

7^{6gf} 11^{6gf} 6^{6gf} 2^{8gs} **0-1-4 £722**

Ketan *P A Blockley* 90
3 ch g Zilzal (USA) - Vividimagination (USA)
8^{8gf} 11^{7gs} 14^{7gf} 2^{6f} 6^{6g} **0-1-5 £1,768**

Kew *C L Popham* 21 a33
4 b g Royal Applause - Cutleaf
9^{12sd} 8^{12sd} 15^{12f} 10^{12gf} **0-0-4**

Kew The Music *M R Channon* 69 a70
3 b g Botanic (USA) - Harmonia
4^{7sd} 12^{5gf} 4^{6gs} 15^{gf} 11^{6f} 7^{6gf} 12^{7gf}
8^{6gf} **1-0-8 £4,067**

Key Of Gold (Ire) *D Carroll* 59 a80
2 b c Key Of Luck (USA) - Damaslin
3^{5gf} 8^{5gf} 1^{6sd} 2^{7sd} 7^{6gs} **1-1-5 £5,424**

Key Oneothree (Ire) *M Johnston* 55 a11
3 b f Entrepreneur - Wallflower
8^{8gf} 10^{10gf} 3^{9gs} 2^{8gs} 7^{12sd} 10^{11gf} 11^{12f}
0-2-7 £1,594

Key Partners (Ire) *P A Blockley* 65
2 b g Key Of Luck (USA) - Teacher Preacher (Ire)
5^{6gf} 2^{6gf} **0-1-2 £1,682**

Khabfair *Mrs A J Perrett* 80 a86
2 b c Intikhab (USA) - Ruby Affair (Ire)
3^{6gf} 1^{6sd} 2^{6sd} **1-2-3 £5,176**

Khabir (USA) *B Hanbury* 79
3 b c Gulch (USA) - Jafn
2^{7gf} 10^{7gs} 5^{7gf} **0-1-3 £1,716**

Khaizarana *E A L Dunlop* 86
3 b f Alhaarth (Ire) - Ta Rib (USA)
1^{7gf} 3^{8g} 7^{10gf} 16^{11s} **1-0-4 £8,928**

Khalidia (USA) *M A Magnusson* 49
2 b c Boundary (USA) - Maniches Slew (USA)
8^{6g} **0-0-1**

Khalkissa (USA) *Saeed Bin Suroor* 96
3 b f Diesis - Khamsin (USA)
1^{8ft} 18^{gf} 6^{8vs} **2-0-3 £11,222**

Khalyanee (Ire) *L A Dace*
2 b f Prospector J (USA) - Dead End (USA)
13^{6g} 15^{7sd} **0-0-2**

Khanjar (USA) *D R Loder* 61
3 ch g Kris S (USA) - Alyssum (USA)
2^{8ft} 2^{8gs} **0-2-2 £3,504**

Kharak (Fr) *Mrs S C Bradburne* 51
4 gr g Danehill (USA) - Khariyda (Fr)
11^{13g} **0-0-1**

Khayyam (USA) *S Gollings* 54
5 b g Affirmed (USA) - True Celebrity (USA)
11^{8gf} 13^{8gf} 6^{11gf} 13^{11gf} 7^{11g} **0-0-5**

Kheleyf (USA) *D R Loder* 103
2 b c Green Desert (USA) - Society Lady (USA)
1^{5gf} 2^{5gf} 1^{6g} 10^{6gf} **2-1-4 £27,697**

Khuchn (Ire) *M Brittain* 39
7 b h Unfuwain (USA) - Stay Sharpe (USA)
18^{10gs} 6^{12gf} 19^{10gf} **0-0-3**

Khulood (USA) *J L Dunlop* 104
3 ch f Storm Cat (USA) - Elle Seule (USA)
1^{7gf} 19^{8gf} 9^{6f} 2^{6gf} 6^{7g} 5^{6gf} **1-1-6**
£38,050

Khuzdar (Ire) *M R Channon* 58 a59
4 ch g Definite Article - Mariyda (Ire)
15^{12sd} 11^{9sd} 8^{16sd} 6^{16gf} 7^{12gf} 6^{11gf} 2^{14gf}
4^{13gf} 7^{12s} 4^{14f} 3^{12gf} 4^{12g} 3^{16gf} 4^{12f} 14^{16gf}
11^{12gf} 9^{11gf} 3^{12gs} 9^{10gs} 6^{12gf}
1-4-23 £6,935

Kibryaa (USA) *M A Jarvis* 73

2 c c Silver Hawk (USA) - Fleur De Nuit (USA)
8^{7gf} 27^{7gf} 17^{7gf} **1-1-3 £6,516**

Kickback *B A Pearce* a46
3 b g High Kicker (USA) - Moniques Venture
9^{11sd} 6^{10sd} 6^{7sd} 9^{8f} 11^{10sd} **0-0-5**

Kid'Z'Play (Ire) *J S Goldie* 71 a23
7 b g Rudimentary (USA) - Saka Saka
11^{12sd} 4^{10g} 13^{12gf} 16^{12gf} 1^{12gf} 3^{13gs}
2^{11gs} 3^{12gf} 5^{12gs} 6^{13f} 4^{12g} **1-4-11 £14,736**

Kier Park (Ire) *M A Jarvis* 92 a101
6 b h Foxhound (USA) - Merlannah (Ire)
2^{5sd} 7^{5g} **0-1-2 £6,600**

Kikoi (Ire) *D R C Elsworth*
3 b f Alzao (USA) - Kimono (Ire)
19^{7gf} **0-0-1**

Kilbride King (Ire) *I A Wood* 66 a66
8 ch g Shalford (Ire) - Marj
12^{9sd} 9^{10sd} 14^{10sd} 9^{7sd} 4^{8sd} 10^{10gf} **0-0-6**

Kilcullen Lass (Ire) *P D Evans* 37 a44
2 ch f Fayruz - Foretell
10^{7sd} 11^{7gf} 6^{7sd} **0-0-3**

Kilkenny Castle (Ire) *S Dow* 78
7 b g Grand Lodge (Ire) - Shahaamh (Ire)
7^{10g} 9^{10g} 5^{12g} 8^{10g} **0-0-4**

Killala (Ire) *M H Tompkins* 73
3 b g Among Men (USA) - Hat And Gloves
6^{7gs} 5^{9gf} 1^{7f} 7^{7gf} 4^{7gf} 7^{7gf} 4^{7gf}
3^{7gf} 6^{7gf} **1-1-10 £5,878**

Killer Bee (Ire) *R A Fahey* 25
3 b g Lake Coniston (Ire) - So Far Away
9^{5gs} 9^{5g} 7^{9gf} **0-0-3**

Killerby Nicko *T D Easterby* 53
2 ch g Pivotal - Bit Of A Tart
8^{5gf} 18^{6gs} **0-0-2**

Killinallan *H Morrison* a65
2 b f Vettori (Ire) - Babycham Sparkle
5^{7sd} **0-0-1**

Killing Joke *J G Given* 63 a68
3 b c Double Trigger (USA) - Fleeting Vision (Ire)
8^{11g} 6^{16sd} 8^{14gs} **0-0-3**

Killoch Place (Ire) *J A Glover* 52
2 b c Compton Place - Hibernica (Ire)
8^{5g} 5^{6gf} 13^{6g} 21^{7g} **0-0-4**

Kilmeena Rose *J C Fox* 24
3 ch f Compton Place - Kilmeena Glen
16^{6gs} 13^{7gf} 9^{6gf} **0-0-3**

Kilmeena Star *J C Fox* 42 a42
5 b h So Factual (USA) - Kilmeena Glen
3^{7sd} 15^{6gs} 9^{6gf} 3^{6gf} 9^{5f} 3^{6sd} 7^{6f} **0-2-7**
£1,677

Kilmory *J Cullinan* 35
4 b f Puissance - Lizzy Cantle
8^{9g} 13^{13g} 11^{10gf} **0-0-3**

Kimoe Warrior *M Mullineaux* a19
5 g Royal Abjar (USA) - Thewaari (USA)
8^{12sd} **0-0-1**

Kinabalu (Ire) *J S Moore* 58 a55
3 b g Danetime (Ire) - Highly Fashionable (Ire)
5^{8sd} 12^{10sd} 3^{9sd} 6^{8sw} 4^{7sd} 1^{8gf} 8^{8gf} **1-1-7**
£3,451

Kinbrace *M P Tregoning* 56
2 b f Kirkwall - Cache
7^{7gf} 5^{6gs} 11^{6gf} **0-0-3**

Kincob (USA) *J Nicol* 51

3 b f Kingmambo (USA) - Gossamer (USA)
2⁸ᶠ 16¹⁰ᵍˢ **0-1-2 £1,304**

Kind (Ire) *R Charlton* 76
2 b f Danehill (USA) - Rainbow Lake
3⁶ᵍᶠ 4⁶ᵍᶠ **0-1-2 £1,025**

Kind Emperor *P L Gilligan* 73
6 br g Emperor Jones (USA) - Kind Lady
1⁷ᵍᶠ 1¹⁰ᵍᶠ 5⁷ᵍ 1¹⁰ᵍᶠ 5⁸ᵍᶠ 8¹⁰ᵍᶠ **3-0-6**
£8,900

Kinda Cute *M Quinn* 42
2 b f Bahamian Bounty - Feiticeira (USA)
18⁶ᵍᶠ 11⁷ᵍᶠ 8⁷ᵍᶠ 17⁶ᵍᶠ **0-0-4**

Kindlelight Debut *D K Ivory* 87 a72
3 b f Groom Dancer (USA) - Dancing Debut
4⁸ᵍ 2⁷ᵍᶠ 2⁸ᵍᶠ 1⁷ᵍᶠ 6⁷ᶠ 2⁷ᵍˢ 3⁸ᵍᶠ 1⁷ᵍᶠ
11⁷ᵍᶠ 9⁷ˢᵈ **2-5-10 £19,096**

Kindness *A D W Pinder* 62 a56
3 ch f Indian Ridge - Kissing Gate (USA)
8¹⁰ᵍᶠ 6¹⁰ᵍᶠ 13⁸ᵍᶠ 5⁷ᵍᶠ 14⁷ᵍ 5⁷ᵍᶠ 6⁸ᵍ
12⁸ᶠ 7⁸ˢᵈ 3⁸ᶠ **0-1-10 £311**

King Carnival (USA) *R Hannon* 88
2 ch c King Of Kings (Ire) - Miss Waki Club (USA)
7⁶ᵍ 5⁶ᵍᶠ 1⁶ᵍᶠ 1⁶ᵍᶠ 2⁶ᵍᶠ **2-1-5 £14,710**

King Creole *Ian Williams* 54
4 b g Slip Anchor - Myrrh
15¹²ᵍᶠ 7¹²ᵍ SU¹³ᵍᶠ 12¹²ᵍ 14¹⁶ᵍᶠ 8¹²ᵍᶠ
0-0-6

King Darshaan *P R Hedger* 64 a76
3 b g Darshaan - Urchin (Ire)
3¹⁰ˢᵈ 12¹⁰ᵍ 11¹¹ᵍᶠ 8¹²ˢᵈ **0-1-4 £630**

King David *D Burchell* 59 a71
4 b g Distant Relative - Fleur Rouge
4⁷ˢʷ 10⁷ˢʷ 3⁸ˢᵈ 6⁸ᵍ 3⁸ᵍᶠ 7⁸ᵍᶠ 11⁸ˢᵈ 3⁷ˢᵈ
0-3-8 £1,522

King Egbert (Fr) *J L Dunlop* 49
2 b c Fasliyev (USA) - Exocet (USA)
3⁶ᵍᶠ 7⁶ᵍ 18⁶ᵍ 11⁶ᵍᶠ **0-1-4 £760**

King Eider *J L Dunlop* 96
4 b/br g Mtoto - Hen Harrier
5¹²ᵍᶠ 6¹⁴ᵍᶠ 8¹⁶ᵍᶠ 3¹⁶ᵍᶠ **0-1-4 £1,416**

King Flyer (Ire) *Miss J Feilden* 85
7 b g Ezzoud (Ire) - Al Guswa
2¹⁶ᵍ 5¹⁶ᵍᶠ 4¹⁶ᵍᶠ 7¹⁶ᵍᶠ 8¹⁴ᵍᶠ 4¹⁸ᵍᶠ 1¹⁶ᵍᶠ
4¹⁶ᵍᶠ 6¹⁵ᵍᶠ 9¹⁴ᵍᶠ 3¹⁶ᵍᶠ 6¹⁶ᵍᶠ **1-1-12 £15,915**

King Harson *J D Bethell* 87
4 b g Greensmith - Safari Park
7⁶ᵍᶠ 11⁷ᵍ 7⁷ᵍᶠ 5⁶ᵍᶠ 8⁶ᵍᶠ 10⁶ᵍᶠ 1⁷ᵍᶠ
16⁶ᵍᶠ 1⁷ᵍᶠ 6⁷ᵍ 3⁷ᵍᶠ 3⁷ᵍ 1⁷ˢ **3-2-13 £18,997**

King Hesperus (USA) *A P O'Brien* 102
2 b c Kingmambo (USA) - Victorica (USA)
2⁷ᵍʸ 1⁶ʸ 3⁷ᵍᶠ **1-2-3 £27,270**

King Maximus (USA) *Mrs A J Perrett* 65 a76
2 b g King Of Kings (USA) - Excedent (USA)
8⁸ᶠ 1⁸ˢᵈ **1-0-2 £3,304**

King Nicholas (USA) *J Parkes* 30 a66
4 b g Nicholas (USA) - Lifetime Honour (USA)
1⁷ˢᵈ 9⁷ˢᵈ 13⁷ˢ 16⁸ᵍᶠ 9⁸ˢʷ **1-0-5 £2,954**

King Of Adoc *P R Hedger* 37
4 ch g Dr Devious (Ire) - Urchin (Ire)
14⁶ᵍˢ 12⁷ᵍˢ **0-0-2**

King Of Cashel (Ire) *R Hannon* 86
2 b c King Of Kings (Ire) - Jaya (USA)
5⁷ᵍ 3⁷ᵍᶠ 4⁸ᵍ 1⁷ᵍ **1-1-4 £5,614**

King Of Dreams (Ire) *M Johnston* 81
2 b c Sadler's Wells (USA) - Koniya (USA)

4⁸ᵍᶠ 2⁸ᵍᶠ **0-1-2 £2,167**

King Of Happiness (USA) *Sir Michael Stoute* 112
4 ch c Spinning World (USA) - Mystery Rays (USA)
9⁹ᵍ 3⁹ᵍ 3⁷ᵍᶠ 7⁸ᵍˢ 10⁸ᵍᶠ **0-2-5 £16,500**

King Of Knight (Ire) *G Prodromou* 57
2 gr c Orpen (USA) - Peace Melody (Ire)
11⁷ᵍᶠ 7⁸ᵍᶠ 12⁸ˢ **0-0-3**

King Of Mommur (Ire) *B G Powell* a39
8 b g Fairy King (USA) - Monoglow
5¹²ˢᵈ **0-0-1**

King Of Music (USA) *G Prodromou* 65
2 ch c Jade Hunter (USA) - Hail Roberta (USA)
3⁷ᵍᶠ 5⁸ᵍᶠ **0-1-2 £423**

King Of Peru *D Nicholls*
10 b g Inca Chief (USA) - Julie's Star (Ire)
18⁶ᵍᶠ 20⁵ᵍᶠ **0-0-2**

King Of The Tweed (Ire) *J J Sheehan* 38 a43
4 b g Robellino (USA) - River Tweed
10⁶ˢᵈ 6⁵ˢᵈ 9⁵ˢ **0-0-3**

King Priam (Ire) *M J Polglase* 50 a46
8 b g Priolo (USA) - Barinia
1¹⁶ˢᵈ 5¹⁴ˢᵈ 3¹¹ˢᵈ 5¹²ˢᵈ 6¹⁴ˢʷ 6¹²ˢʷ 2¹²ˢʷ
6¹²ˢʷ 13¹²ᵍ 10¹⁴ᵍ 12¹⁴ˢᵈ 9¹⁰ᵍᶠ 7¹²ᵍᶠ 17⁸ᵍ
11¹⁴ᵍᶠ 5¹²ˢᵈ 5¹¹ˢᵈ 4¹⁵ˢᵈ 12¹²ᵍᶠ 9¹⁰ᶠ **1-2-20**
£4,256

King Revo (Ire) *P C Haslam* 88 a81
3 b g Revoque (Ire) - Tycoon Aly (Ire)
2¹⁰ˢᵈ 3¹⁰ˢᵈ 5⁸ᵍᶠ 10¹⁰ᵍˢ 11¹¹ᵍᶠ 6¹²ᵍᶠ 12¹²ᵍᶠ
1-2-7 £5,890

King Tara (Ire) *J J Quinn* 64 a37
2 b g Foxhound (USA) - Bradwell (Ire)
6⁵ᶠ 5⁵ᶠ 6⁵ᵍˢ 2⁷ᶠ 4⁶ᵍ 5⁶ᶠᵗ 5⁶ᵍᶠ 5⁶ᵍᶠ **0-1-8**
£1,216

King's Ballet (USA) *P R Chamings* 75
5 b g Imperial Ballet (Ire) - Multimara (USA)
10⁵ᵍᶠ 7⁶ᵍᶠ 1⁵ʰʸ 6⁵ᵍˢ 10⁵ᵍˢ 11⁵ᵍ
9⁵ᵍᶠ 8⁶ᵍ 12⁵ᵍᶠ 15⁵ᵍˢ 7⁵ᵍ 3⁵ᵍ **1-1-13 £4,302**

King's Caprice *G B Balding* 87
2 ch c Pursuit Of Love - Palace Street (USA)
5⁶ᵍᶠ 2⁶ᵍᶠ 3⁶ᵍᶠ **0-1-3 £3,057**

King's Consul (USA) *D R Loder* 109
4 b c Kingmambo (USA) - Battle Creek Girl (USA)
5¹²ᵍᶠ 6¹⁰ᵍ 2¹²ᵍᶠ 6¹²ᵍᶠ 2¹⁴ᵍᶠ 4¹⁰ᵍᶠ **0-1-6**
£9,834

King's County (Ire) *L M Cumani* 104
5 b g Fairy King (USA) - Kardelle
5¹⁰ᵍ 5¹⁰ᵍᶠ 1⁸ᵍᶠ 2⁸ᵍˢ **1-1-4 £15,599**

King's Crest *R A Fahey* 59 a48
5 b g Deploy - Classic Beauty (Ire)
15¹²ˢᵈ 9¹²ᵍᶠ 6¹²ᵍᶠ 12¹²ᵍᶠ **0-0-4**

King's Envoy (USA) *Mrs J C McGregor* 32
4 b g Royal Academy (USA) - Island Of Silver (USA)
17¹¹ᵍ **0-0-1**

King's Ironbridge (Ire) *S Kirk* 102 a92
5 b h King's Theatre (Ire) - Dream Chaser
6⁷ˢᵈ 5⁷ᵍᶠ 10⁷ᵍ 4⁸ᵍ 5¹⁰ᵍᶠ 13⁸ᵍᶠ 10⁸ᵍᶠ
6⁷ᵍᶠ **0-0-8 £3,550**

King's Mill (Ire) *N A Graham* 77
6 b g Doyoun - Adarika
11¹⁰ᵍ 7¹²ᵍ **0-0-2**

King's Mountain (USA) *Mrs A L M King* 56
3 b g King Of Kings (Ire) - Statistic (USA)
10¹²ᵍᶠ 6¹²ˢ 10⁸ᵍᶠ 15¹¹ᵍᶠ **0-0-4**

King's Protector *T D Easterby* 66
3 b c Hector Protector (USA) - Doliouchka

12^{10gf} 12^{8gf} **0-0-2**

King's Thought *S Gollings* 99 a90
4 b c King's Theatre (Ire) - Lora's Guest
1^{8sd} 1^{8sd} 11^{8gf} 3^{10s} 1^{10s} 4^{10g} 17^{10gf}
3^{10g} 1^{10gs} 9^{13gf} **4-2-10 £30,129**

Kingdom Come (Ire) *S Kirk* 93
2 b c Foxhound (USA) - Garter Royale (Ire)
6^{5gf} 1^{6gf} 12^{5f} 5^{7gf} 10^{6gf} 2^{8gf} 10^{8gf} 2^{8g}
1-2-8 £9,632

Kingfisher Eve (Ire) *C Grant* 38
5 b m Hamas (Ire) - Houwara (Ire)
8^{8f} 9^{12gs} 8^{16gf} **0-0-3**

Kingham *Mrs Mary Hambro* 81
3 ch g Desert Prince (Ire) - Marie De Flandre (Fr)
7^{10gs} 8^{8gf} **0-0-2**

Kingkohler (Ire) *K A Morgan* 76 a69
4 b g King's Theatre (Ire) - Legit (Ire)
1^{12sd} 1^{11gs} **2-0-2 £7,150**

Kings College Boy *R A Fahey* 67
3 b g College Chapel - The Kings Daughter
6^{5gf} 7^{6g} 2^{5gs} 5^{6hy} 13^{6gs} 2^{5gs} 7^{7gf} 2^{6gf}
3^{5gf} 15^{gf} 10^{5gf} 4^{5s} 2^{5g} 6^{5g} 19^{5gs} **1-5-15**
£10,044

Kings Empire *D Carroll* 77 a77
2 b g Second Empire (Ire) - Dancing Feather
3^{8g} 1^{8sd} **1-1-2 £2,762**

Kings Of Albion (USA) *R Hannon* 45
3 b c King Of Kings (Ire) - Akadya (Fr)
11^{8gf} 15^{12gf} **0-0-2**

Kings Point (Ire) *R Hannon* 103
2 b c Fasliyev (USA) - Rahika Rose
2^{5gf} 4^{6g} 1^{6gf} 1^{7gf} 6^{7gs} **2-1-5 £33,306**

Kings Rock *K A Ryan* 68 a59
2 ch c Kris - Both Sides Now (USA)
5^{7gf} 3^{8gf} 5^{7gf} 3^{8sw} 10^{8gs} **0-1-5 £1,461**

Kings Square *M W Easterby* 31
3 b g Bal Harbour - Prime Property (USA)
10^{8gf} 8^{12gf} 15^{8f} 12^{12gf} **0-0-4**

Kings Topic (USA) *G Wragg* 43
3 ch g Kingmambo (USA) - Topicount (USA)
9^{12gs} **0-0-1**

Kingscross *M Blanshard* 82
5 ch g King's Signet (USA) - Calamanco
11^{6g} 18^{6g} 7^{6gf} 4^{6gf} 3^{6g} 7^{6g} 10^{7g} 9^{7gs}
0-1-8 £2,472

Kingsdon (Ire) *T J Fitzgerald* 59
6 b g Brief Truce (USA) - Richly Deserved (Ire)
13^{10gf} 4^{10gf} 11^{10g} 4^{10g} 9^{10gf} 8^{10g} 11^{11g}
0-0-7 £586

Kingsmaite *S R Bowring* 51
2 b g Komaite (USA) - Antonias Melody
6^{6gf} 12^{6gs} 3^{5gf} 6^{6g} 4^{5g} **0-0-5 £1,341**

Kingston Game *Miss K M George* a23
4 b g Mind Games - Valmaranda (USA)
10^{8sd} 11^{8sd} **0-0-2**

Kingston Town (USA) *N P Littmoden* 60
3 ch g King Of Kings (Ire) - Lady Ferial (Fr)
4^{8f} 15^{7gf} **0-0-2 £337**

Kingston Wish (Ire) *Ian Emmerson* 40
4 b g Mujadil (USA) - Well Wisher (USA)
16^{11sd} 9^{6f} 15^{7gf} 13^{8g} 7^{8g} 13^{10f} **0-0-6**

Kingsword (USA) *Sir Michael Stoute* 88
2 bl c Dynaformer (USA) - Western Curtsey (USA)
4^{7gf} 1^{7gf} **1-0-2 £3,936**

Kiniska *B Palling* 55 a63

2 b f Merdon Melody - Young Whip
4^{7sd} 8^{7g} **0-0-2 £280**

Kinkozan *N P Littmoden* 47
2 ch c Peintre Celebre (USA) - Classic Design
18^{8gf} 6^{7gs} **0-0-2**

Kinnaird (Ire) *P C Haslam* 108
2 ch f Dr Devious (Ire) - Ribot's Guest (Ire)
1^{6gs} 1^{6f} 5^{6g} 1^{7s} 1^{7gf} 1^{8g} **5-0-6**
£69,371

Kinnescash (Ire) *P Bowen* 30
10 ch g Persian Heights - Gayla Orchestra
14^{12g} **0-0-1**

Kinsman (Ire) *T D McCarthy* 56 a67
6 b g Distant Relative - Besito
14^{10gf} 4^{7sd} 7^{7sd} 2^{7sd} 6^{7sd} 7^{7gf} 5^{7gf} 5^{8sd}
5^{8sd} 10^{7f} **0-1-10 £952**

Kintore *J S Goldie* 42
2 ch c Inchinor - Souadah (USA)
16^{6gf} 9^{7gf} 10^{7g} **0-0-3**

Kirk Wynd *Sir Michael Stoute* 82
3 b f Selkirk (USA) - Abbey Strand (USA)
1^{10gf} 7^{10gf} 3^{10gf} 10^{11s} **1-0-4 £5,195**

Kirkby's Treasure *A Berry* 64
5 ro g Mind Games - Gem Of Gold
10^{7gf} 12^{7gf} 9^{8gs} 10^{9gf} 11^{7gs} 3^{7s} 7^{8g}
9^{7g} 1^{6s} 2^{7f} 2^{7f} 6^{7gf} 13^{7gs} 9^{8gf} **1-3-14**
£6,322

Kirkham Abbey *M A Jarvis* 69 a64
3 b g Selkirk (USA) - Totham
1^{12sd} 6^{12sd} 9^{12gs} 1^{9sw} 5^{9g} 3^{8sd} 1^{10gf}
16^{10f} 1^{10gf} 1^{9f} **5-1-10 £15,421**

Kirkstone (Ire) *M Johnston* 76
2 b g Alzao (USA) - Night Mirage (USA)
6^{6g} 2^{7gf} 2^{7gf} 2^{7gf} 7^{7gf} 9^{7f} **0-2-6**
£4,059

Kirovski (Ire) *P W Harris* 9 a116
6 b g Common Grounds - Nordic Doll (Ire)
1^{10sd} 10^{10sd} 14^{10gf} **1-0-3 £12,354**

Kismet Queen (Ire) *C W Thornton* 34 a51
3 b f Desert King (Ire) - Kiya (USA)
4^{11sd} 8^{9sd} 5^{11gs} 10^{11sd} 7^{8g} 4^{9sd} **0-0-6**
£282

Kiss The Rain *R Brotherton* 62
3 b f Forzando - Devils Dirge
15^{7gf} 11^{7sw} 2^{7g} 6^{6g} 5^{7gf} 1^{6f} 8^{6gs} **1-1-7**
£3,473

Kiteflyer (Ire) *John M Oxx* 100
3 ch f In The Wings - Afraah (Ire)
4^{12y} 1^{12g} 2^{12gf} 8^{12gf} 7^{12gf} 3^{12f} **1-1-6**
£21,720

Kitley *B G Powell* 63 a51
2 b c Muhtarram (USA) - Salsita
10^{6gf} 16^{6gf} 7^{5gf} 4^{7gf} 8^{7gf} 6^{7sd} 4^{7gf} 3^{8gf}
0-1-8 £726

Kituhwa (USA) *J H M Gosden* 65
3 br c Cherokee Run (USA) - Ruhnke (USA)
3^{8gf} 7^{8gf} 12^{8gf} 10^{8gf} **0-1-4 £862**

Knavesmire Omen *M Johnston* 107
4 b g Robellino (USA) - Signs
6^{14gf} 3^{16gf} 3^{19gf} 11^{14gf} 12^{20gf} 1^{16s} 9^{16gf}
12^{1gs} 3^{19gf} 8^{16gf} **2-3-10 £55,348**

Knickyknackienoo *T T Clement* 52 a30
2 b g Bin Ajwaad (Ire) - Ring Fence
8^{5sd} 6^{6gf} 6^{5gf} 9^{5gf} 4^{7gs} 8^{8gf} 7^{7gs} 6^{6g}
0-0-8 £1,103

Knight Onthe Tiles (Ire) *J R Best* 75
2 ch g Primo Dominie - Blissful Night
8⁵ᵍ 5⁵ᵍ 15⁵ᵍ 6⁶ᵍᶠ 8⁷ᵍᶠ 3⁶ᶠ 16ᶠ 11⁶ᵍᶠ
5⁶ᶠ 16ᵍᶠ 4⁵ˢ 16ᵍˢ **3-0-12 £9,914**

Knight To Remember (Ire) *K A Ryan* 42
2 ch g Fayruz - Cheerful Knight (Ire)
8⁷ᵍ 10⁷ᵍᶠ 6⁸ˢʷ **0-0-3**

Knockdoo (Ire) *J S Goldie* 47
10 ch g Be My Native (USA) - Ashken
3¹⁶ᵍˢ 12¹⁷ᵍᶠ 7²²ᵍᶠ 8¹⁶ᵍˢ 6¹³ᵍᶠ 2¹⁶ᵍ 7¹⁵ᵍ
3¹⁶ᵍᶠ **0-3-8 £2,329**

Knockemback Nellie *J M Bradley* a30
7 b m Forzando - Sea Clover (Ire)
7⁶ˢᵈ 10⁵ˢᵈ **0-0-2**

Knot In Doubt (Ire) *J A Glover* 50
2 b c Woodborough (USA) - In The Mind (Ire)
7⁶ᵍ 12⁶ᵍ **0-0-2**

Knotty Ash Girl (Ire) *B A McMahon* 52
4 ch f Ashkalani (Ire) - Camisha (Ire)
16¹⁰ᵍ 15¹⁰ᵍᶠ 17¹⁰ᵍᶠ 8¹²ᵍˢ 9¹²ᵍᶠ 5¹⁶ᵍᶠ
10¹²ᵍˢ 3¹³ᵍᶠ 11¹²ᵍᶠ 1¹⁴ᵍᶠ **1-1-10 £3,519**

Knowle Park (Ire) *M S Saunders*
4 br f Woodborough (USA) - Nagida
12⁵ˢᵈ **0-0-1**

Known Maneuver (USA) *M C Chapman* 15
5 b g Known Fact (USA) - Northernmaneuver (USA)
15¹⁰ᵍ **0-0-1**

Kodiac *J L Dunlop* 77
2 b c Danehill (USA) - Rafha
3⁶ᵍᶠ **0-1-1 £760**

Kohima (Ire) *G C Bravery* 41 a51
3 ch f Barathea (Ire) - Albenita (Ire)
9⁸ˢᵈ 12⁸ˢᵈ 8⁸ᵍ 6¹¹ᵍᶠ **0-0-4**

Komash *A Berry* 37
2 b f Komaite (USA) - Phoenix Princess
6⁵ᵍˢ 15⁶ˢ 6⁷ᶠ 9⁷ᵍᶠ 8⁶ᵍᶠ 6⁵ᶠ 7⁶ᵍᶠ 2¹⁶ᵍᶠ
0-0-8

Komati River *J Akehurst* 58 a57
4 b g Wesaam (USA) - Christening (Ire)
6¹⁰ˢᵈ 2¹²ᵍᶠ 5¹²ᵍᶠ **0-1-3 £942**

Komena *J W Payne* 58 a49
5 b m Komaite (USA) - Mena
9⁷ˢᵈ 3⁶ᵍᶠ 7⁶ᵍᶠ 2⁶ᶠ 7⁶ᵍ 2⁶ᵍᶠ 3⁶ᵍᶠ 13⁷ᶠ
5⁶ᵍᶠ **0-4-9 £3,050**

Konfuzius (Ger) *P Monteith* 41
5 b g Motley (USA) - Katrina (Ger)
11¹⁴ᵍᶠ 7⁹ᵍᶠ 12¹¹ᵍᶠ 8¹²ᵍᶠ **0-0-4**

Konica *Mrs A L M King* 10 a35
4 b f Desert King (Ire) - Haboobti
12⁸ˢᵈ 10¹²ˢᵈ 15¹²ᵍ **0-0-3**

Konker *Mrs M Reveley* 71
8 ch g Selkirk (USA) - Helens Dreamgirl
6¹⁰ᵍˢ **0-0-1**

Koodoo *A Crook* 49
2 gr c Fasliyev (USA) - Karsiyaka (Ire)
11⁶ᵍᶠ 7⁸ᵍᶠ 7⁸ᵍᶠ **0-0-3**

Kosmic Lady *P W Hiatt* 32 a42
6 b m Cosmonaut - Ktolo
6⁸ˢᵈ 13¹⁰ᵍ 13¹¹ᵍᶠ **0-0-3**

Kotori (Ire) *M S Saunders* 31 a49
4 gr g Charnwood Forest (Ire) - La Kermesse (USA)
8⁵ˢᵈ 11⁶ˢʷ 10⁶ᶠ 9⁸ᶠ 2⁵ˢᵈ 16⁶ᵍᶠ 9⁶ˢᵈ
0-1-7 £830

Koyaanisqatsi *Jamie Poulton* 47
3 ch g Selkirk (USA) - Bogus John (Can)

9⁸ᵍᶠ **0-0-1**

Kozando *Mrs G S Rees* 74
2 ch g Komaite (USA) - Times Zando
4⁶ᵍᶠ 4⁵ᶠ 14⁶ᵍˢ 3⁶ᵍᶠ 1⁶ᵍ 2⁶ᵍᶠ 1⁶ᵍᶠ 6⁷ᵍ
4⁶ᵍˢ 12⁶ᵍᶠ **2-3-10 £12,097**

Kris Kin (USA) *Sir Michael Stoute* 125
3 ch c Kris (USA) - Angel In My Heart (Fr)
1¹⁰ᵍᶠ 1¹²ᵍ 3¹²ᵍ 3¹²ᵍˢ 11¹²ʰᵒ **2-1-5**
£986,000

Kristal Dancer (Ire) *J L Dunlop* 86
3 b f Charnwood Forest (Ire) - Kristal's Paradise (Ire)
7⁷ᵍᶠ 3⁸ᵍ 4¹⁰ᵍᶠ 2¹⁰ˢ 6¹⁰ᵍ 1¹¹ᵍ 5¹²ᵍ **1-2-7**
£6,639

Kristal Forest (Ire) *Mrs S Lamyman* 37 a62
4 b g Charnwood Forest (Ire) - Kristal's Paradise (Ire)
2¹²ˢᵈ 8¹⁴ˢʷ 7¹²ˢʷ 20¹²ᵍ 8¹²ˢᵈ 18¹⁰ᵍᶠ
18¹²ᵍ **0-2-8 £1,458**

Kristal's Dream (Ire) *J L Dunlop* 75
2 b f Night Shift (USA) - Kristal's Paradise (Ire)
5⁶ᶠ 6⁶ᵍᶠ 9⁶ᵍᶠ 3⁷ᵍᶠ 1⁸ᵍᶠ **1-1-5 £4,193**

Kristensen *D Eddy* 87 a84
4 ch g Kris (USA) - Papaha (Fr)
7¹²ˢᵈ 2¹⁶ˢᵈ 4¹⁴ᵍᶠ 8¹⁰ᵍᶠ 2¹⁶ᵍ 2¹⁶ᵍᶠ 2¹⁶ᵍᶠ
5²⁰ᵍᶠ 5²¹ᵍˢ 6¹⁶ᵍᶠ 2¹⁶ᵍ 3¹⁸ᵍᶠ 3¹⁶ᵍᶠ **0-7-13**
£33,875

Kristiansand *M R Channon* 72
3 b c Halling (USA) - Zonda
9¹⁰ᵍ 4⁹ᵍᶠ 2¹⁰ᵍᶠ 6⁹ᵍᶠ 10⁷ᵍ 1¹⁰ᵍᶠ 9⁸ᶠ 5¹⁰ᶠ
8⁹ᵍ 5⁸ᶠ **1-1-10 £4,646**

Kristoffersen *R M Stronge* 81 a81
3 ch c Kris - Towaahi (Ire)
2⁸ˢᵈ 4⁹ˢᵈ 1⁸ᶠ 10⁸ᵍᶠ 3¹⁰ᵍᶠ 5¹²ᵍᶠ 4¹⁰ᵍ 3¹²ˢᵈ
1-3-8 £8,452

Krugerrand (USA) *W J Musson* 91
4 ch g Gulch (USA) - Nasers Pride (USA)
17⁶ᵍᶠ 20⁷ᵍ 6⁸ᵍᶠ 1⁹ᵍᶠ 9¹⁰ᵍ 10⁸ᵍ 5⁸ᵍˢ 4⁸ᵍᶠ
7⁹ᵍ 4⁸ᶠ 8⁸ᵍᶠ **1-0-11 £22,989**

Krypton *P D Cundell* a24
3 b g Kylian (USA) - Tiama (Ire)
13¹⁰ˢᵈ 7¹¹ˢᵈ **0-0-2**

Kschessinka (USA) *W J Haggas* 54
2 br f Nureyev (USA) - Gran Dama (USA)
9⁶ᵍᶠ **0-0-1**

Kufoof (USA) *A C Stewart* 69
3 b f Silver Hawk (USA) - Barakat
5¹⁰ᵍᶠ **0-0-1**

Kuka *R Hollinshead* 57
2 b c Polar Prince (Ire) - Crissem (Ire)
11⁷ᵍ **0-0-1**

Kukini *B S Rothwell* a20
2 ch g Presidium - Auntie Fay (Ire)
10⁵ˢᵈ **0-0-1**

Kumakawa *E A Wheeler* a57
5 ch g Dancing Spree (USA) - Maria Cappuccini
5⁸ˢʷ 7⁷ˢᵈ 2⁸ˢᵈ 1⁸ˢᵈ 5⁸ˢᵈ 12⁸ˢʷ 9¹⁰ˢᵈ **1-1-7**
£3,808

Kumari (Ire) *W M Brisbourne* 42 a51
2 b f Desert Story (Ire) - Glow Tina (Ire)
6⁵ˢᵈ 5⁵ᵍᶠ 10⁶ᵍᶠ 7⁶ᶠ **0-0-4 £333**

Kunda (Ire) *R Hannon* 94
2 b f Intikhab (USA) - Ustka
2⁶ᵍᶠ 3⁶ᵍˢ 1⁵ᵍᶠ 5⁷ᵍᶠ 2⁶ᵍ **1-2-5 £17,065**

Kuringai *B W Duke* 74 a65
2 b c Royal Applause - Talighta (USA)
4⁵ˢᵈ 7⁵ᵍ 3⁵ˢᵈ 4⁵ᵍᶠ 3⁵ᵍᶠ 2⁵ᵍᶠ 2⁶ᵍᶠ 1⁵ᶠ

3⁶ᵍᶠ 16⁵ᵍᶠ 3⁶ᵍ 3⁵ᵍᶠ 3⁶ᵍᶠ 9⁶ᵍᶠ 2⁵ᵍᶠ **1-7-15**
£12,162

Kuster *L M Cumani*   97
7 b g Indian Ridge - Ustka
9¹⁰ᵍ 9¹⁰ᵍᶠ 3¹²ᵍᶠ 1¹²ᵍ 9¹²ᵍ 1¹²ᶠ 1¹²ᵍᶠ 5¹²ᵍᶠ
3-1-8 £36,494

Kustom Kit For Her *S R Bowring*   43 a43
3 b f Overbury (Ire) - Antonias Melody
7¹¹ˢᵈ 9⁷ˢᵈ 5⁸ˢʷ 9⁶ˢᵈ 5¹⁰ᵍᶠ 4⁷ˢᵈ 10⁷ᵍᶠ 2⁷ˢᵈ
0-1-8 £872

Kuwait Thunder *D Carroll*   a16
7 ch g Mac's Imp (USA) - Romangoddess (Ire)
8¹⁴ˢᵈ 7¹²ˢᵈ 13¹²ᵍᶠ **0-0-3**

Kwai Baby (USA) *J J Bridger*   30
2 gr f Charnwood Forest (Ire) - Roses In The Snow (Ire)
9⁵ᵍˢ 7⁶ᵍᶠ 14⁷ᵍᶠ **0-0-3**

Kyle Of Lochalsh *G G Margarson*   62
3 gr g Vettori (Ire) - Shaieef (Ire)
8¹⁰ᵍᶠ 11⁸ᵍᶠ 5⁹ᵍᶠ 1⁹ᵍᶠ 13¹⁰ᵍᶠ 3¹⁰ᵍ 16¹⁰ᵍᶠ
1-1-7 £7,124

Kylkenny *H Morrison*   97 a98
8 b g Kylian (USA) - Fashion Flow
2¹¹ˢᵈ 1¹¹ˢʷ 1¹¹ˢᵈ 3¹²ˢᵈ 1¹¹ˢᵈ 6¹⁰ᵍᶠ 4¹⁰ᵍᶠ
14¹²ᵍᶠ 2¹²ᵍᶠ 4¹¹ᵍᶠ 9¹²ᵍᶠ 5¹²ᶠ 12¹²ᵍ 17¹²ᵍ **3-4-14**
£26,956

Kyo Bid *M Brittain*   32
3 b g Endoli - Hebe (Ire)
13⁸ᵍᶠ 8¹⁰ᵍᶠ 6¹⁰ᵍᶠ **0-0-3**

Kythia (Ire) *H Morrison*   70
2 b f Kahyasi - Another Rainbow (Ire)
3⁷ᵍᶠ 1⁷ᵍᶠ 5⁸ᵍᶠ **1-1-3 £3,125**

L'Ancresse (Ire) *A P O'Brien*   121
3 b f Darshaan - Solo De Lune (Ire)
2⁷ᵍᶠ 15⁸ᵍᶠ 4⁸ˢ PU²¹²ᵍ 2¹²ᵍ 5¹²ᵍᶠ 4¹⁵ᵍ
1¹²ᵍʸ 2¹⁰ᶠ **1-3-9 £229,034**

L'Oiseau D'Argent (USA) *Sir Michael Stoute*   104
4 ch g Silver Hawk (USA) - Isla Del Rey (USA)
4⁷ᵍ 3⁶ᵍ **0-1-2 £2,439**

La Corujera *T D Barron*   72
3 b f Case Law - Aybeegirl
2⁷ᵍᶠ 7⁷ᵍᶠ 5⁷ᶠ 5⁶ᵍᶠ 17⁶ᵍᶠ 6⁶ᵍᶠ **0-1-6**
£2,250

La Coruna *R Charlton*   91
2 b f Deploy - Valencia
1⁸ᵍᶠ 1⁷ᵍ **2-0-2 £6,771**

La Cucaracha *B W Hills*   93
2 b f Piccolo - Peggy Spencer
1⁵ᵍᶠ 1⁵ᵍᶠ **2-0-2 £12,098**

La Danseuse *G C Bravery*   47 a34
2 b f Groom Dancer (USA) - Alik (Fr)
10⁶ᵍᶠ 6⁷ᵍᶠ 3⁸ˢᵈ **0-1-3 £310**

La Dolfina *H Morrison*   93
3 b f Pennekamp (USA) - Icecapped
2¹⁰ᶠ 4¹⁰ᶠ 1¹⁰ᵍᶠ 1⁹ᶠ 4¹⁰ᵍᶠ 8¹⁰ᵍ 5⁸ˢ 1⁹ᵍ
10¹⁰ᵍᶠ **3-2-9 £19,029**

La Fonteyne *C B B Booth*   25
2 b f Imperial Ballet (Ire) - Baliana
10⁵ᵍ **0-0-1**

La Grace *R Hannon*   64
2 b f Lahib (USA) - Prima Sinfonia
2⁶ᵍᶠ 5⁷ᵍᶠ 4⁷ᵍᶠ 4⁷ᶠ 1⁸ᵍ **1-1-5 £5,447**

La Landonne *P M Phelan*   a62
2 b f Fraam - Le Pin
3⁶ˢᵈ **0-1-1 £453**

La Luna (Ire) *Noel T Chance*   60

6 b m Gothland (Fr) - Diane's Glen
3¹⁸ᶠ **0-1-1 £1,120**

La Mouline (Ire) *G A Butler*   92
3 ch f Nashwan (USA) - Lamarque (Ire)
1¹¹ᵍᶠ 5¹²ᵍᶠ **1-0-2 £10,935**

La Muette (Ire) *Mrs A J Perrett*   87
3 b f Charnwood Forest (Ire) - Elton Grove (Ire)
5¹⁰ᵍᶠ 3¹⁰ᵍᶠ 7¹⁰ᵍᶠ 14¹²ᵍ **0-0-4 £1,888**

La Persiana *W Jarvis*   64
2 gr f Daylami (Ire) - La Papagena
4⁷ᵍᶠ 8⁷ᵍᶠ **0-0-2 £271**

La Petite Chinoise *R Guest*   67
2 ch f Dr Fong (USA) - Susi Wong (Ire)
3⁵ᵍᶠ 4⁵ᵍˢ 8⁶ᵍᶠ 6⁶ᵍᶠ **0-0-4 £1,024**

La Professoressa (Ire) *Mrs P N Dutfield*   66
2 b f Cadeaux Genereux - Fellwah (Ire)
10⁶ᵍᶠ 3⁷ᵍ 12⁶ᵍᶠ 8⁸ᵍ 5⁸ᵍᶠ **0-0-5 £1,002**

La Puce *Miss Gay Kelleway*   57 a57
2 b f Danzero (Aus) - Verbena (Ire)
3⁵ᵍ 1⁵ˢᵈ 5⁵ᵍˢ 4⁵ᵍ 2⁶ᶠ 3⁷ᵍᶠ 10⁷ᵍᶠ 12⁶ᵍᶠ
1-2-8 £4,981

La Rose *J W Unett*   41 a35
3 b f Among Men (USA) - Marie La Rose (Fr)
10⁷ᵍᶠ 5¹²ˢᵈ 6¹²ˢᵈ 6¹⁰ˢ 2¹²ᵍᶠ 8¹⁰ᵍᶠ **0-1-6**
£900

La Scala (USA) *H R A Cecil*   81
3 b f Theatrical - Estala
2¹⁰ᵍ 5¹⁰ᵍᶠ 1⁸ᵍ 11⁸ᵍᶠ 10¹¹ˢ **1-1-5**
£7,293

La Stellina (Ire) *C A Dwyer*   a64
5 b m Marju (Ire) - Supportive (Ire)
8⁷ˢᵈ **0-0-1**

La Sylphide *G M Moore*   83
6 ch m Rudimentary (USA) - Primitive Gift
8¹⁰ˢ 2⁹ᵍˢ 1⁹ᵍ 1⁹ᵍ 6⁹ᵍᶠ 1¹¹ˢ 20¹²ᵍ **3-1-7**
£26,445

La Vie Est Belle *B R Millman*   75
2 b f Makbul - La Belle Vie
6⁵ᵍᶠ 4⁵ᵍᶠ 3⁵ᶠ 2⁵ᵍᶠ 7⁵ᵍᶠ 16ᵍᶠ 6⁵ᵍᶠ 3⁷ᵍ
2⁶ᵍᶠ 9⁶ᵍᶠ **1-4-10 £12,105**

La Vigna (Ire) *Mrs Lucinda Featherstone*   24 a25
2 ch g Woodborough (USA) - Bona Fide
7⁶ᵍ 14⁶ᵍ 12⁸ᵍᶠ 12⁶ˢᵈ **0-0-4**

Laabbij (USA) *M P Tregoning*   64
2 ch c Shuailaan (USA) - United Kingdom (USA)
7⁸ᵍᶠ **0-0-1**

Laawaris (USA) *J A Osborne*   73
2 b c Souvenir Copy (USA) - Seattle Kat (USA)
1⁷ᶠ **1-0-1 £3,835**

Labelled With Love *W G M Turner*   24
3 ch g Zilzal (USA) - Dream Baby
11¹⁰ᵍᶠ **0-0-1**

Labrett *Miss Gay Kelleway*   89 a83
6 b g Tragic Role (USA) - Play The Game
6⁷ᵍ 5⁸ᵍᶠ 1⁷ 10⁷ᶠ 4⁸ᵍᶠ 1⁹ᵍᶠ 2⁷ᵍ 3⁸ᶠ 4¹⁰ᵍ
3⁷ᵍ 6⁸ᵍᶠ 5⁹ᵍᶠ **2-3-12 £19,316**

Laconia (Ire) *J S Moore*   55
2 b f Orpen (USA) - Mislead (Ire)
12⁵ˢᵈ 15⁶ᵍᶠ 3⁵ᵍᶠ **0-1-3 £442**

Ladies Day *T G Mills*   74 a31
3 b f Robellino (USA) - Fighting Run
5¹⁰ᵍ 9¹²ᵍᶠ 5¹⁰ᵍᶠ 7⁹ˢᵈ **0-0-4**

Ladies Knight *D Shaw*   54 a66
3 b g Among Men (USA) - Lady Silk
4⁵ˢᵈ 2⁵ˢᵈ 4⁵ˢᵈ 2⁵ˢᵈ 1⁵ˢᵈ 5⁵ˢᵈ 9⁵ᵍˢ 4⁵ᵍᶠ

14⁶ˢʷ 14⁵ᵍˢ 11⁶ˢᵈ **1-2-11 £6,931**

Lady Alruna (Ire) *P T Midgley*   51 a61
4 ch f Alhaarth (Ire) - In Tranquility (Ire)
8⁶ˢᵈ 9⁶ˢᵈ 11⁶ˢʷ 14⁶ᵍᶠ 5⁷ᵍˢ 17⁷ᵍᶠ 19⁸ᵍ
0-0-7

Lady Arnica *A W Carroll*   14
4 b f Ezzoud (Ire) - Brand
12¹⁴ᵍˢ **0-0-1**

Lady At Leisure (Ire) *W G M Turner*   a40
3 ch f Dolphin Street (Fr) - In A Hurry (Fr)
5¹⁰ˢᵈ **0-0-1**

Lady Bahia (Ire) *R P Elliott*   61
2 b f Orpen (USA) - Do The Right Thing
8⁶ˢᵈ 7⁵ᵍᶠ 2⁸ᵍᶠ 4⁷ᵍ 8⁶ᵍᶠ **0-1-5 £1,094**

Lady Bear (Ire) *R A Fahey*   107
5 b m Grand Lodge (USA) - Boristova (Ire)
3¹⁰ᵍᶠ 4¹⁰ᵍᶠ 2⁹ᵍˢ 1⁸ᵍˢ 6⁹ᵍ 6⁸ᵍᶠ 3⁸ᶠ 6⁸ᵍᶠ
1⁸ᵍ 6⁸ᵍᶠ 1⁸ᵍˢ 4⁹ᵍᶠ **3-3-12 £107,981**

Lady Betambeau (Ire) *L M Cumani*   52
3 b f Grand Lodge (USA) - Boristova (Ire)
9⁷ᵍˢ 15⁸ᵍ 7¹⁰ᵍᶠ **0-0-3**

Lady Birgitta *K R Burke*   a65
5 b m Emperor Jones (USA) - Badiane (USA)
2⁸ˢᵈ 4⁷ˢʷ 6⁸ˢᵈ 3⁸ˢᵈ 12⁸ˢᵈ **0-2-5 £1,523**

Lady Blade (Ire) *B Hanbury*   63
2 b f Daggers Drawn (USA) - Singhana (Ire)
6⁶ᵍᶠ 3⁷ᶠ 8⁷ᵍ 13⁸ᵍᶠ **0-0-4 £325**

Lady Boxer *M Mullineaux*   81
7 b m Komaite (USA) - Lady Broker
10⁵ˢᵈ 7⁶ˢ 11⁶ᵍˢ 5⁶ˢ 12⁷ˢᵈ 11⁶ᵍ 2⁶ᵍᶠ
0-1-7 £1,100

Lady Broughton (Ire) *W J Musson*   25
2 ch f Grand Lodge (USA) - Veronica
17⁷ᵍˢ **0-0-1**

Lady Connie *K A Ryan*
2 ch f Atraf - Paris Mist
9⁵ᵍᶠ **0-0-1**

Lady Dominatrix (Ire) *Mrs P N Dutfield*   104
4 b f Danehill Dancer (Ire) - Spout House (Ire)
8⁵ᵍ 12⁶ᵍᶠ 5⁵ᵍ 20⁵ᵍᶠ **0-0-4 £2,159**

Lady Drue (Ire) *A P Jarvis*   40
4 b f Darnay - Sharkiyah (USA)
12¹¹ᵍᶠ 9¹²ᵍ 14¹³ᵍˢ **0-0-3**

Lady Dulcet *D Burchell*   41
3 b f Thowra (Fr) - Freedom Weekend (USA)
8⁸ˢᵈ 10¹²ᵍˢ 4⁸ᵍᶠ **0-0-3 £318**

Lady Dunkirk (Ire) *Mrs Lydia Pearce*   53 a40
2 b f Daggers Drawn (USA) - La Soeur D'Albert
6⁶ʰᵈ 3⁵ᶠ 11⁶ˢᵈ 7⁷ˢᵈ 8⁷ᵍᶠ 7⁶ᶠ **0-0-6 £451**

Lady Ellendune *D J S Ffrench Davis*   43 a25
2 b f Piccolo - Eileen's Lady
9⁶ᵍᶠ 13⁶ᵍᶠ 7⁶ᵍᶠ 15⁸ᵍᶠ 27⁶ᵍᶠ 9⁸ˢᵈ **0-0-6**

Lady Ern *W G M Turner*   41 a49
2 b f Young Ern - Just Lady
5⁵ˢᵈ 2⁶ˢᵈ 3⁵ˢᵈ 6⁵ᵍᶠ 5⁵ˢᵈ 5⁵ᵍᶠ 3⁶ᵍᶠ 11⁶ᵍᶠ
0-3-8 £1,550

Lady Franpalm (Ire) *M J Haynes*   59 a52
3 b f Danehill Dancer (Ire) - Be Nimble
5⁵ˢᵈ 4⁶ᵍ 4⁵ᵍᶠ 10⁶ᵍᶠ **0-0-4 £553**

Lady Georgina *J R Fanshawe*   80
2 br f Linamix (Fr) - Georgia Venture
3⁷ᵍᶠ 4⁷ᵍᶠ 3⁷ᵍᶠ 12⁸ᵍˢ 10⁷ᵍ **0-2-5 £1,831**

Lady Glyde *A D Smith*   36
3 b f Inchinor - Happy And Blessed (Ire)

12⁷ᵍ 8⁷ᵍᶠ 12⁹ˢᵈ 6⁸ᵍᶠ 8¹¹ᵍᶠ 5¹⁰ᶠ 10¹²ˢᵈ
4¹⁰ᶠ 11¹²ᶠ **0-0-9**

Lady Hamilton *M E Sowersby*
3 ch f Double Trigger (Ire) - Crown Flight
5¹²ᵍᶠ **0-0-1**

Lady Hibernia *J Noseda*   57 a47
3 b f Anabaa (USA) - Taj Victory
9⁶ˢᵈ 11¹⁰ᵍᶠ 9¹¹ᵍᶠ 12⁸ˢᵈ **0-0-4**

Lady In Command (Ire) *Mrs J Candlish*   7 a26
3 b f In Command (Ire) - Harmer (Ire)
8⁸ˢᵈ 11⁸ᵍᶠ 16⁷ᵍᶠ 12⁷ᵍᶠ 15⁷ᵍ **0-0-5**

Lady Justice *W Jarvis*   66
3 b f Compton Place - Zinzi
5⁵ᵍ 7⁵ᵍ **0-0-2**

Lady Killer (Ire) *W G M Turner*   73 a10
2 b/br f Daggers Drawn (USA) - Dee-Lady
3⁵ᵍ 1⁵ᶠ 1⁵ᶠ 6⁵ᵍˢ DSQ⁵ˢᵈ 9⁵ᵍᶠ **2-0-6
£7,417**

Lady Korrianda *M J Wallace*   30 a32
2 ch f Dr Fong (USA) - Prima Verde
10⁶ˢᵈ 8⁷ᵍˢ **0-0-2**

Lady Lakshmi *R Guest*   51
3 ch f Bahhare (USA) - Polish Honour (USA)
14⁸ᵍ 11⁸ᵍᶠ 3¹²ᵍᶠ 5¹²ᶠ 7¹⁴ˢ 3¹²ᵍᶠ 12¹⁶ᵍᶠ
0-1-7 £1,063

Lady Laureate *G C Bravery*   71
5 b m Sir Harry Lewis (USA) - Cyrillic
9¹⁴ᵍᶠ 8¹⁶ᵍᶠ 9¹⁷ᶠ 3¹⁶ᵍᶠ 4¹⁶ᵍ 2¹⁶ᵍᶠ 8¹⁷ᵍ
0-1-7 £1,342

Lady Lenor *Mrs G S Rees*   52
5 b m Presidium - Sparkling Roberta
14⁶ᶠ 2⁷ᵍᶠ 10⁸ᶠ 4⁸ᶠ 5⁷ᵍᶠ 10⁸ᵍ 5⁸ᵍᶠ 10⁸ᵍᶠ
13⁶ᵍᶠ **0-2-9 £1,386**

Lady Liesel *J J Bridger*   55 a57
3 b f Bin Ajwaad (Ire) - Griddle Cake (Ire)
3⁷ˢᵈ 10⁶ˢᵈ 4⁷ᵍᶠ 14⁶ᵍᶠ 10⁷ᵍᶠ 7⁸ᵍᶠ 6⁷ᵍᶠ
11⁷ᵍᶠ 6⁶ᵍ 4⁷ᵍᶠ 5⁷ᶠ 8⁸ᶠ 9⁷ᵍᶠ 13⁷ᵍᶠ **0-2-14
£422**

Lady Lindsay (Ire) *R Guest*   101
4 ch f Danehill Dancer (Ire) - Jungle Jezebel
5⁸ᵍᶠ 7⁷ᵍʸ 2⁶ᵍᶠ 9⁶ᵍ 12⁶ˢ **0-1-5 £11,875**

Lady Llanover *S C Williams*   59
3 ch f Halling (USA) - Francia
12⁶ᵍ 11⁷ᵍ 8⁹ˢʷ 15¹⁰ˢ 7¹⁰ᵍᶠ **0-0-5**

Lady Lucia (Ire) *N A Callaghan*   49
2 b f Royal Applause - Inventive
7⁶ᵍᶠ 4⁵ᵍˢ 7⁷ᵍᶠ 4⁷ᶠ 8⁷ᵍᶠ **0-1-5 £288**

Lady Lucinda *John A Harris*   35
2 b f Muhtarram (USA) - Lady Phyl
13⁸ᵍ **0-0-1**

Lady McNair *P D Cundell*   80
3 b f Sheikh Albadou - Bonita Bee
15⁸ᵍᶠ 8⁸ᵍᶠ 4⁸ᵍ 4¹²ᵍᶠ 4¹⁰ᵍᶠ 6¹²ᵍᶠ **0-1-6
£540**

Lady Midnight *W G M Turner*   6 a3
2 ch f Young Ern - Amathus Glory
6⁵ˢᵈ 8⁶ᶠ **0-0-2**

Lady Mo *Andrew Reid*   55
2 b f Young Ern - Just Run (Ire)
3⁵ᵍˢ 5⁵ᵍᶠ 3⁵ᵍᶠ 7⁶ˢ 6⁵ᵍˢ 3⁶ᶠ 5⁵ᵍᶠ 1⁶ᵍᶠ
4⁶ᵍᶠ 3⁶ᵍᶠ 6⁶ᵍᶠ 15⁸ᵍᶠ 5⁷ᶠ **1-3-13 £5,228**

Lady Mytton *A Bailey*   74
3 ch f Lake Coniston (Ire) - The In-Laws (Ire)
4⁷ᵍᶠ **0-0-1 £728**

Lady Natilda *D Haydn Jones*   62 a62

3 ch f First Trump - Ramajana (USA)
6^{6sd} 9^{6sd} 11^{5f} 8^{6gs} 3^{6f} 8^{5sd} 4^{6sw} 5^{6sd}
12^{8gs} 0-1-9 £911

Lady Netbetsports (Ire) *B S Rothwell*   73
4 b f In The Wings - Auntie Maureen (Ire)
15^{10g} 4^{14g} 4^{14g} 9^{16gf} 12^{16gs} 13^{17gf} 0-1-6
£638

Lady Oasis (Ire) *A Berry*   26
2 ch f Desert King (Ire) - Olivia Jane (Ire)
7^{5gf} 8^{6gf} 16^{6gf} 0-0-3

Lady Of Eminence *Miss J Feilden*   35
3 b/br f Bishop Of Cashel - Astrid Gilberto
13^{8gf} 10^{8gf} 0-0-2

Lady Of Gdansk (Ire) *H J Collingridge*   56 a48
4 ch f Danehill Dancer (Ire) - Rebecca's Girl (Ire)
9^{6sd} 15^{7sd} 9^{7sd} 15^{6g} 10^{8gf} 8^{9gf} 4^{7g}
10^{6gf} 19^{7s} 0-0-9 £432

Lady Of The Links (Ire) *N Tinkler*   54
2 b f Desert Style (Ire) - Itkan (Ire)
5^{5gf} 4^{5gf} 7^{6gf} 11^{6g} 0-0-4

Lady Oriande *A M Balding*   62
2 b f Makbul - Lady Roxanne
9^{5gf} 0-0-1

Lady P *A Berry*   a17
4 b f Makbul - Octavia
8^{6sd} 8^{6sw} UR7^{7gf} 0-0-3

Lady Pahia (Ire) *A P Jarvis*   56 a73
5 ch m Pivotal - Appledorn
5^{7sd} 5^{8sd} 2^{10sd} 10^{10sd} 9^{10sd} 9^{7gf} 12^{7g}
0-1-7 £950

Lady Past Times *E J Alston*   55
3 b f Tragic Role (USA) - Just A Gem
10^{8hy} 20^{6f} 8^{7gf} 7^{11gf} 10^{7gf} 2^{8gf} 2^{9f}
2^{9gf} 12^{11gs} 0-3-9 £2,989

Lady Peaches *D Mullarkey*
2 ch f Bien Bien (USA) - Upper Club (Ire)
9^{6sd} 0-0-1

Lady Pekan *P S McEntee*   71 a41
4 b f Sri Pekan (USA) - Cloudberry
13^{5gs} 10^{5gf} 2^{5gf} 9^{5gf} 18^{5g} 7^{5gf} 4^{5gf}
2^{5gf} 9^{6f} 5^{6gf} 11^{5gf} 12^{6g} 18^{6gf} 13^{6sd} 0-2-14
£3,747

Lady Percy *B R Millman*   53
3 ch f Double Trigger (Ire) - Dundeelin
6^{8f} 7^{11gf} 13^{14gf} 8^{10gf} 4^{7gf} 7^{8f} 2^{11gf} 2^{8gf}
6^{10g} 5^{10gf} 6^{12f} 0-2-11 £1,754

Lady Piste (Ire) *P D Evans*   74
2 b f Ali-Royal (Ire) - Alpine Lady (Ire)
3^{5g} 1^{5gf} 4^{5gf} 5^{6f} 5^{5g} 3^{6gf} 1-2-6
£9,607

Lady Predominant *M R Channon*   71 a20
2 b f Primo Dominie - Enlisted (Ire)
4^{5g} 9^{5gf} 4^{5f} 9^{6gf} 15^{6f} 5^{8sd} 8^{6f} 0-0-7
£619

Lady Protector *S R Bowring*   58 a38
4 b f Sri Pekan (USA) - Scared
7^{5sd} 9^{5sw} 4^{6f} 2^{5gf} 2^{5gs} 14^{6g} 18^{7gf} 7^{5gf}
16^{5sw} 6^{5g} 0-2-10 £2,534

Lady Redera (Ire) *H S Howe*   51
2 b f Inzar (USA) - Era
5^{7g} 4^{8gf} 9^{7f} 10^{8gf} 0-0-4 £377

Lady Shopper *S Dow*   18 a49
3 b f Merdon Melody - Young Whip
8^{7sd} 12^{7gf} 8^{10sd} 14^{9g} 0-0-4

Lady Stripes *D Mullarkey*   53

2 gr f Alzao (USA) - Shamaya (Ire)
12^{6gf} 6^{6gf} 12^{6gf} 0-0-3

Lady Sunrize *Mrs A L M King*   29
4 ch f Whittingham (Ire) - Scenic Air
12^{5f} 14^{5gf} 7^{5gf} 8^{6gf} 11^{7f} 0-0-5

Lady Sunset (Ire) *K A Ryan*   63
2 b f Entrepreneur - Sunset Reigns (Ire)
7^{5gf} 5^{5gf} 2^{5gf} 8^{6gf} 17^{5gf} 0-1-5 £1,236

Lady Tearaway *J E Long*   22
4 b f Arrasas (USA) - Manageress
12^{7g} 14^{8s} 9^{10gf} 0-0-3

Lady Tilly *B Mactaggart*
6 b m Puissance - Lady Of Itatiba (Bel)
14^{7gf} 0-0-1

Lady Trace (Ire) *S Dow*   4
2 b f Piccolo - Zelda (USA)
13^{7gf} 10^{7g} 0-0-2

Lady West *Dr J R J Naylor*   19 a16
3 b f The West (USA) - Just Run (Ire)
9^{5sd} 13^{5gf} 19^{7gf} 0-0-3

Lady Wurzel *W S Kittow*
4 b f Dilum (USA) - Fly The Wind
4^{10f} 0-0-1

Lady Xanthia *I A Wood*   47 a27
2 ch f Bien Bien (USA) - Carmosa (USA)
9^{5g} 8^{5gf} 6^{5sd} 6^{6gf} 0-0-4

Ladystgeorge *M Mullineaux*   31
4 b f Mind Games - Indiahra
10^{5sd} 8^{8gs} 7^{7gf} 9^{7gf} 4^{6f} 0-0-5

Ladywell Blaise (Ire) *J J Bridger*   54
6 b m Turtle Island (Ire) - Duly Elected
13^{10f} 8^{7gf} 10^{6g} 4^{7gf} 3^{7gf} 12^{8gf} 8^{7gf}
13^{8g} 13^{7gf} 0-1-9 £1,415

Laffah (USA) *G L Moore*   62
8 b g Silver Hawk (USA) - Sakiyah (USA)
5^{14f} 0-0-1

Lafi (Ire) *A C Stewart*   98
4 ch c Indian Ridge - Petal Girl
1^{7gf} 4^{8gf} 3^{7g} 1^{7gf} 17^{7gf} 2-2-5 £29,400

Laggan Bay (Ire) *R Hannon*   78 a80
3 b c Alzao (USA) - Green Lucia
2^{8sd} 7^{10sd} 3^{10gf} 10^{10f} 5^{12gf} 2^{12gf} 1^{12f}
2^{12gf} 1-4-8 £9,508

Laggan Minstrel (Ire) *P W D'Arcy*   61
5 b g Mark Of Esteem (Ire) - Next Episode (USA)
18^{8g} 12^{8gs} 9^{8gf} 12^{7g} 7^{8f} 11^{7gs} 0-0-6

Lago D'Orta (Ire) *C G Cox*   113
3 ch c Bahhare (USA) - Maelalong (Ire)
1^{7gf} 7^{8gf} 1^{8g} 4^{8hy} 1^{8gf} 1^{8g} 20^{8g} 1^{8gf}
2^{7gf} 1^{9s} 6-1-10 £85,005

Lagosta (SAF) *G M Moore*   54
3 ch g Fort Wood (USA) - Rose Wine
10^{8gf} 11^{10gf} 8^{8g} 9^{10f} 5^{11gf} 0-0-5

Lahob *P Howling*   68
3 ch c First Trump - Mystical Song
10^{10gf} 3^{12gf} 6^{14gf} 2^{11gf} 3^{12gf} 2^{12gf} 6^{12gf}
0-1-7 £4,644

Laidlow (USA) *Sir Michael Stoute*   105
3 ch c Mt. Livermore (USA) - Cato Lady (USA)
18^{8f} 4^{7gf} 5^{8g} 3^{8gf} 1-0-4 £12,431

Laird Dara Mac *N Bycroft*   37
3 b c Presidium - Nishara
7^{10gf} 6^{8f} 10^{8s} 0-0-3

Laird Of The Glen *P S McEntee*   11
2 ch g Muhtarram (USA) - Strath Kitten

8⁵ᵍˢ 20⁶ᵍᶠ 15⁷ᵍᶠ 15⁷ᵍᶠ **0-0-4**

Lais *G C H Chung*
3 ch f Inchinor - Night Transaction
12⁷ᵍᶠ 13⁷ᵍᶠ **0-0-2**

Lakatoi *J W Payne*   a60
4 b f Saddlers' Hall (Ire) - Bireme
8¹²ˢᵈ 3¹⁰ˢᵈ 4¹²ˢᵈ **0-1-3 £853**

Lake 'O' Gold *D W Thompson*   55 a2
4 ch f Karinga Bay - Ginka
6¹⁵ˢᵈ 5¹²ᵍᶠ 10¹⁶ᵍᶠ 5¹²ᶠ 8¹²ᵍᶠ 10¹⁶ᵍᶠ **0-0-6**

Lake Diva *M J Wallace*   31 a41
2 ch f Docksider (USA) - Cutpurse Moll
11⁷ˢᵈ 10⁷ᵍˢ **0-0-2**

Lake Eyre (Ire) *J Balding*   48 a26
4 b f Bluebird (USA) - Pooh Wee
7⁶ᵍˢ 5⁷ˢᵈ 4⁷ᵍᶠ 6⁶ᵍᶠ **0-0-4**

Lake Garda *B A McMahon*   81
2 b c Komaite (USA) - Malcesine (Ire)
2⁵ᵍ 2⁶ᵍᶠ 14⁵ᵍᶠ 10⁶ᵍ 1⁶ᶠ **1-2-5 £12,920**

Lake Verdi (Ire) *B Hanbury*   72
4 ch g Lake Coniston (Ire) - Shore Lark (USA)
9⁶ᵍ 15⁶ᵍᶠ 14⁶ᵍᶠ 8⁶ᵍᶠ 6⁶ᵍᶠ **0-0-5**

Lakehaven Lady *M G Quinlan*   a26
2 b f Abou Zouz (USA) - Sans Egale (Fr)
9⁸ˢᵈ **0-0-1**

Lakelands Lady (Ire) *S R Bowring*   73 a73
3 ch f Woodborough (USA) - Beautyofthepeace (Ire)
3⁷ˢᵈ 8⁸ˢᵈ 9⁷ᵍ 11⁷ˢ 15⁷ˢᵈ 10⁷ᵍˢ 18⁷ᵍ
0-0-7 £672

Lakota Brave *Mrs S A Liddiard*   72 a99
9 ch g Anshan - Pushkinia (Fr)
6⁸ˢᵈ 10⁷ˢᵈ 2⁷ᵍᶠ 2⁹ᵍ 18ᵍᶠ 8¹⁰ᵍᶠ 4¹⁰ᵍᶠ 3⁸ᵍᶠ
3⁷ˢᵈ **1-4-9 £6,224**

Lalapaanzi (Ire) *R M Beckett*   60
3 b f Night Shift (USA) - Sharp Deposit
5⁵ᵍᶠ 10⁶ᵍ 5⁶ᶠ 6⁶ᵍᶠ 6⁶ᵍᶠ 11⁵ᵍᶠ **0-0-6**

Lampos (USA) *Miss J A Camacho*   63 a50
3 b/br g Southern Halo (USA) - Gone Private (USA)
4⁸ˢᵈ 6⁸ˢʷ 8⁸ᵍᶠ 11¹⁰ᵍᶠ 4⁹ˢ 12¹²ᵍˢ 8¹²ᵍᶠ
3¹²ˢʷ 8¹⁶ᵍ **0-1-9 £534**

Lamzig *M Todhunter*   24
4 b g Danzig Connection (USA) - Lamsonetti
12¹⁰ᵍ **0-0-1**

Lana *J G Given*   57
3 gr f Linamix (Fr) - Beaming
3⁸ᵍ **0-1-1 £862**

Land 'n Stars *C A Cyzer*   77
3 b g Mtoto - Uncharted Waters
4¹⁰ᵍᶠ 2¹⁴ᵍᶠ 2¹⁴ᵍᶠ **0-2-3 £2,284**

Land Of Fantasy *D K Ivory*   53 a69
4 ch g Hernando (Fr) - Height Of Folly
9⁸ˢᵈ 11¹⁰ˢᵈ 7¹²ˢᵈ 10¹⁰ˢᵈ 7¹²ˢᵈ 7⁸ˢᵈ 12⁸ᵍᶠ
13⁸ˢᵈ BD⁸ᵍᶠ 5⁸ˢᵈ 10⁸ᵍ 8⁸ᵍᶠ **0-0-12**

Land Of Nod (Ire) *G A Butler*   59
2 b f Barathea (Ire) - Rafif (USA)
10⁸ᵍᶠ **0-0-1**

Land Sun's Legacy (Ire) *J S Wainwright* 50
2 b g Red Sunset - Almost A Lady (Ire)
5⁶ᵍ 7⁸ᵍˢ 11⁸ᵍᶠ 9⁷ᵍ 4⁷ˢ 6⁷ᵍᶠ **0-0-7
£2,137**

Landescent (Ire) *M Quinn*   58 a61
3 b g Grand Lodge (USA) - Traumerei (Ger)
4¹⁰ˢᵈ 6¹⁰ˢᵈ 5⁹ˢᵈ 17⁸ᵍ 6⁸ᶠ 8¹⁰ᵍᶠ 14⁷ᵍᶠ 5⁸ᵍ
5⁷ᵍ 4⁹ᵍᶠ 11¹⁸ᶠ 7⁸ˢᵈ 4¹²ˢᵈ **0-0-13 £1,448**

Landing Light (Ire) *N J Henderson*   110
8 b g In The Wings - Gay Hellene
1¹⁴ᵍᶠ 2²⁰ᵍᶠ 10¹⁶ᵍˢ 1¹⁸ᵍᶠ **2-1-4 £93,130**

Landing Strip (Ire) *J M P Eustace*   85 a84
3 b g Dolphin Street (Fr) - Funny Cut (Ire)
3⁵ˢᵈ 4⁶ˢᵈ 8⁷ˢᵈ 9⁶ᵍᶠ 3⁵ᵍˢ 5⁵ᵍᶠ 1⁵ᵍᶠ 2⁵ᵍᶠ
10⁶ᵍ 9⁶ᶠ 13⁵ᵍᶠ 11⁷ᵍᶠ 1⁶ˢᵈ 1⁵ᶠ 4⁶ᶠ 4⁶ˢᵈ **3-3-16
£11,635**

Landinium (Ity) *C F Wall*   100
4 b f Lando (Ger) - Hollywood Girl
2¹¹ᵍ 2¹⁰ᵍ 4¹⁰ᵍ 9¹²ᵍ 5¹²ᵍᶠ 4¹²ᵍᶠ 4¹¹ˢ 8¹⁰ᵍ
0-0-8 £28,613

Landofheartsdesire (Ire) *J S Wainwright* 61 a54
4 b f Up And At 'Em - Ahonita
5⁶ᵍ 13⁶ᵍᶠ 8⁷ˢᵈ 9⁷ᶠ 8⁷ˢᵈ 6⁸ᵍᶠ 8⁷ᵍᶠ 6⁸ᵍ
7⁸ᵍᶠ 11⁷ˢ **0-0-10**

Landucci *J W Hills*   68
2 b c Averti (Ire) - Divina Luna
9⁷ᵍᶠ 11⁷ᵍᶠ **0-0-2**

Langford *M H Tompkins*   84
3 ch g Compton Place - Sharpening
2¹⁰ᵍᶠ 2¹⁰ᵍᶠ 4¹⁰ᵍ 4¹⁰ᵍ 2¹⁰ᵍᶠ 2¹⁰ᵍᶠ 3¹⁰ᵍᶠ
1¹⁰ᵍᶠ 3¹¹ᵍᶠ 6⁸ᶠ **1-7-10 £17,427**

Lanos (Pol) *R Ford*   68 a69
5 ch g Special Power - Lubeka (Pol)
2¹³ˢᵈ 3¹²ˢᵈ 6¹²ˢᵈ 1¹³ˢᵈ 6¹²ˢᵈ 6¹⁴ᵍᶠ 5¹⁴ᵍᶠ
4¹⁵ᵍᶠ **1-2-8 £4,652**

Lapadar (Ire) *J R Weymes*   a83
4 b/br f Woodborough (USA) - Indescent Blue
7¹⁴ˢʷ 9¹²ˢᵈ 6¹³ᵍˢ 14¹²ˢᵈ 5¹⁶ᵍᶠ **0-0-5 £875**

Lapdancing *Miss L A Perratt*   28
2 ch f Pursuit Of Love - Petrikov (Ire)
10⁷ᵍˢ 12⁸ᵍᶠ **0-0-2**

Lara Bay *A M Balding*   60
3 b f Polish Precedent (USA) - Way O'Gold (USA)
11⁸ᵍᶠ 5⁹ᶠ **0-0-2**

Lara Falana *Miss B Sanders*   81 a66
5 b m Tagula (Ire) - Victoria Mill
3¹⁰ˢᵈ 5¹⁰ˢᵈ 1¹⁰ᵍ 3¹⁰ᵍᶠ 4⁹ᵍ 1¹⁰ᵍᶠ 8¹⁰ᵍᶠ
8¹⁰ᵍᶠ 5¹⁰ᵍᶠ 7⁹ᵍᶠ 10¹⁰ᵍ **2-2-11 £14,894**

Larad (Ire) *J S Moore*   55
2 br g Desert Sun - Glenstal Priory
9⁵ᵍ 5⁵ᵍ 17⁶ᵍᶠ 4⁶ᶠ **0-0-4**

Largo (Ire) *J L Dunlop*   (96)
3 ch f Selkirk (USA) - Lady Of The Lake
12¹¹ᵍ 1¹²ᵍᶠ 1¹²ᵍᶠ 15¹²ᵍˢ 9¹²ᵍᶠ 5¹⁵ˢ **2-0-6
£13,813**

Largs *J Balding*   62 a52
3 ch f Sheikh Albadou - Madam Zando
14⁵ᵍᶠ 5⁶ᵍᶠ 9⁶ᵍᶠ 6⁶ᵍᶠ 7⁷ˢʷ 13⁶ᵍ 4⁶ᶠᵗ 5⁶ᵍᶠ
5⁵ᵍᶠ 5⁵ᵍᶠ 2⁵ᵍ 9⁶ᶠ 3⁶ᵍᶠ 4⁶ˢᵈ 5⁶ᵍˢ **0-2-15 £881**

Lark In The Park (Ire) *W M Brisbourne*   52
3 ch f Grand Lodge (USA) - Jarrayan
16⁸ᵍᶠ 17⁶ᵍˢ 9⁹ᵍᶠ 4⁸ᵍᶠ 8⁸ˢ 3⁸ᵍᶠ 1⁸ᶠ 10⁸ᶠ
7⁸ᶠ 6⁸ᵍˢ **1-1-10 £4,467**

Larking About (USA) *H R A Cecil*   63 a69
3 ch f Silver Hawk (USA) - Milly Ha Ha
5¹²ᵍ 4¹²ᵍᶠ 2¹³ˢᵈ 10¹⁴ᵍˢ **0-1-4 £593**

Larkwing (Ire) *G Wragg*   56
2 b c Ela-Mana-Mou - The Dawn Trader (USA)
4⁷ˢ **0-0-1 £264**

Larky's Lob *Paul Johnson*   52 a64
4 b g Lugana Beach - Eucharis
3⁷ˢᵈ 2⁶ˢᵈ 2⁶ˢʷ 2⁶ˢᵈ 2⁶ˢᵈ 3⁶ˢᵈ 4⁷ˢᵈ 3⁷ˢᵈ
11⁷ˢᵈ 5⁶ˢᵈ 10⁷ᵍᶠ 10⁶ᵍᶠ 9⁷ˢᵈ 4⁷ˢʷ 11⁶ˢᵈ 7⁶ᶠ

9^{8ft} 11^{8gf} **0-8-18 £5,292**

Las Ramblas (Ire) *D A Nolan* 57
6 b g Thatching - Raise A Warning
12^{8gs} 19^{6gs} 10^{8gf} 8^{6gf} 5^{6f} 13^{6g} 9^{6gf}
7^{10g} 8^{5gf} 6^{5f} 4^{6f} 16^{6gs} **0-1-12 £302**

Lasanga *Lady Herries* 73
4 ch g Zamindar (USA) - Shall We Run
3^{8gf} 2^{8gf} **0-2-2 £2,154**

Lasser Light (Ire) *D G Bridgwater* 14
3 b g Inchinor - Light Ray
7^{7gf} **0-0-1**

Lassitude *C W Thornton* 49
3 ch f Efisio - Lassoo
14^{9gs} 9^{10gs} 7^{12g} 7^{8s} 2^{7gf} 12^{8gs} **0-1-6**
£919

Last Appointment (USA) *J M P Eustace* 81 a78
3 b c Elusive Quality (USA) - Motion In Limine (USA)
4^{6sd} 2^{7gf} 1^{7gf} 20^{7g} **1-1-4 £7,712**

Last Exhibit *R Guest* a66
5 b m Royal Academy (USA) - Noirmant
4^{6sd} 7^{6sd} 13^{6gf} **0-0-3**

Last Question *A Berry*
4 b f Tragic Role (USA) - Question Ali
16^{8sd} **0-0-1**

Last Ring *P W Hiatt*
5 br m Charmer - Bells Of Longwick
16^{8gf} **0-0-1**

Lasting Delight *Sir Mark Prescott* 39 a49
2 b f Robellino (USA) - Last Result
13^{6gf} 5^{6sd} **0-0-2**

Latalomne (USA) *B Ellison* 71
9 ch g Zilzal (USA) - Sanctuary
8^{8g} **0-0-1**

Late Arrival *M D Hammond* a41
6 b g Emperor Jones (USA) - Try Vickers (USA)
5^{8sd} **0-0-1**

Late Claim (USA) *B W Hills* 92
3 ch g King Of Kings (Ire) - Irish Flare (USA)
9^{8g} 5^{10gf} 1^{12gf} 5^{12gf} 1^{13g} 9^{13gs} **2-0-6**
£18,485

Late Opposition *E A L Dunlop* 56
2 b c Unfuwain (USA) - Hawa (USA)
9^{8g} 9^{7gf} 6^{7gs} **0-0-3**

Lateen Sails *Saeed Bin Suroor* 116
3 ch c Elmaamul (USA) - Felucca
20^{8g} 1^{10gf} 4^{10gs} 1^{9vs} **2-0-4 £61,635**

Latest Edition *Mrs A J Perrett* 70
3 b f Charnwood Forest (Ire) - Star Of The Future (USA)
6^{6gf} 7^{7gf} **0-0-2 £217**

Latice (Ire) *J-M Beguigne* 105
2 ch f Inchinor - Laramie (USA)
1^{9gs} **1-0-1 £21,429**

Latif (USA) *J H M Gosden* 68
2 b c Red Ransom (USA) - Awaamir
4^{7gf} **0-0-1 £428**

Latin Review (Ire) *A P Jarvis* 92
2 ch f Titus Livius (Fr) - Law Review (Ire)
4^{5gs} 1^{5gf} 4^{5gf} 1^{6gf} 9^{6g} **2-0-5 £16,899**

Laud Karelia *A C Stewart* 44
4 b c Royal Applause - Finlandaise (Fr)
13^{10gs} 12^{14s} 13^{11gf} **0-0-3**

Laurel Dawn *I W McInnes* 64 a73
5 gr g Paris House - Madrina
7^{5sd} 10^{5sd} 7^{5sw} 10^{5sd} 14^{5gf} 8^{5gf} 4^{5gs}
5^{5gs} 5^{5gf} 10^{5gf} 2^{5gf} 5^{5gs} 2^{5gf} 7^{5f} 6^{5gf} 5^{6gf}

10^{5f} 11^{5gf} 2^{5sd} 9^{6sd} **0-4-20 £4,522**

Lauro *Miss J A Camacho* 79 a79
3 b f Mukaddamah (USA) - Lapu-Lapu
3^{7sd} 2^{8gf} 1^{8gf} 2^{8sd} 1^{8f} 4^{10g} **2-3-6**
£13,750

Lautrec (Swi) *J L Dunlop* 71
3 ch c Peintre Celebre (USA) - La Venta (USA)
10^{10gf} 7^{11gf} 1^{9f} 3^{10f} 8^{11gf} 11^{12gf} **1-1-6**
£4,412

Lavish Times *A Berry* 58 a43
2 ch c Timeless Times (USA) - Lavernock Lady
8^{5g} 5^{5gf} 16^{5sd} 5^{5gf} 10^{5gf} 1^{5gf} 5^{5gf} 5^{5gf}
8^{5f} 8^{5sd} 3^{5f} 12^{6gf} **1-1-12 £3,286**

Law Breaker (Ire) *J A Gilbert* 95 a97
5 ch g Case Law - Revelette
5^{5sw} 10^{6sd} 7^{6sd} 10^{6sd} 9^{6sw} 1^{6g} 17^{6gf}
16^{6g} **1-0-8 £9,973**

Law Commission *J M Bradley* 37
13 ch g Ela-Mana-Mou - Adjala
13^{8gf} **0-0-1**

Law Maker *C W Fairhurst* 51
3 b g Case Law - Bo' Babbity
9^{6gf} 9^{7gf} 8^{6gf} 9^{6gs} 11^{6gf} 11^{6gf} 16^{8s}
0-0-7

Lawaaheb (Ire) *J L Dunlop* 65
2 b c Alhaarth (Ire) - Ajayib (USA)
9^{8gf} 5^{8g} 6^{8gf} **0-0-3**

Lawgiver (Ire) *T J Fitzgerald* 11
2 b c Definite Article - Marylou Whitney (USA)
12^{7gf} 11^{8g} 14^{7gs} **0-0-3**

Lawless *James Moffatt* 25
3 ch g Case Law - Oh My Oh My
15^{5gf} 18^{5gs} 8^{5f} 13^{5sd} **0-0-4**

Lawood (Ire) *Francis Ennis* 86 a73
3 gr g Charnwood Forest (Ire) - La Susiane
2^{7sd} 2^{7sd} 5^{8g} 7^{6sh} 4^{5s} 5^{7gy} 3^{7gf} 8^{6gy}
0-4-8 £3,757

Lay Down Sally (Ire) *J White* 55 a60
5 ch m General Monash (USA) - Sally Fay (Ire)
5^{8sd} 2^{6sd} 11^{7sd} 8^{6sd} 3^{6sd} 9^{5f} 3^{6f} 7^{6f}
0-3-8 £1,742

Layan *Miss L C Siddall* 32
6 b m Puissance - Most Uppitty
11^{5gf} 7^{6gf} 14^{7g} 6^{6s} 7^{5g} 19^{6gf} **0-0-6**

Lazer Lass (Ire) *N P Littmoden* a45
3 b f Ali-Royal (Ire) - Lingdale Lass
10^{6sd} 6^{5sd} **0-0-2**

Lazzaz *P W Hiatt* 58 a74
5 b g Muhtarram (USA) - Astern (USA)
8^{10sd} 6^{9sd} 8^{11sd} 4^{9sw} 2^{8sd} 1^{9sd} 6^{12sd} 3^{9sd}
1^{9sd} 2^{8sd} 2^{10gf} 7^{10gs} 3^{10f} 3^{11gf} 3^{10gf} 2^{11g}
3^{11gf} 3^{12g}
3^{14gf} **3-13-25 £18,267**

Le Grand Vizier *J R Jenkins* a30
4 br g Doyoun - Just Visiting
12^{12sd} **0-0-1**

Le Meridien (Ire) *J S Wainwright* 68
5 ch m Magical Wonder (USA) - Dutch Queen
7^{5gf} 5^{5gs} 4^{6g} 1^{5gf} 4^{5gf} 7^{5gs} 12^{5gf} 16^{5gf}
15^{5g} 19^{5gf} **1-0-10 £4,668**

Le Ruban Bleu (Ire) *H J Collingridge* 21
4 ch g Bluebird (USA) - Minervitta
15^{11gf} 8^{12gf} 12^{14gf} 19^{10gf} **0-0-4**

Le Tiss (Ire) *M R Channon* 80
2 b c Croco Rouge (Ire) - Manarah

7⁸ᵍᶠ 8⁸ᵍᶠ 6⁸ᵍᶠ 1⁸ᵍᶠ 9⁸ᵍᶠ 1⁸ᵍ 6⁸ᵍᶠ 2⁸ᵍᶠ
2-1-8 £9,414

Leadership *Saeed Bin Suroor* 126
4 b c Selkirk (USA) - Louella (USA)
1¹²ᵍᶠ 1¹²ᶠ 12¹²ᵍ **2-0-3 £177,222**

Leahstar *Miss L C Siddall* 29
4 ch f In The Wings - Moondance
12¹²ᵍᶠ 14¹⁷ᵍᶠ 6¹⁴ᶠ 11¹⁶ᵍ 5¹⁶ᵍˢ **0-0-5**

Leap Year Lass *D Morris* 36
3 ch f Fleetwood (Ire) - Lady Phyl
9⁷ᵍᶠ 11⁸ᵍ 5⁹ᵍᶠ 9⁶ᵍᶠ 15⁶ᵍ **0-0-5**

Leaping Brave (Ire) *B R Millman* 74 a71
2 b c Indian Rocket - Island Heather (Ire)
11⁶ᵍ 5⁹ᵍ 3⁵ᵍ 8⁶ᵍ 16ᵍᶠ 3⁶ˢᵈ 14⁶ᵍᶠ **1-1-7 £5,130**

Learned Lad (Fr) *Jamie Poulton* 67 a78
5 ch g Royal Academy (USA) - Blushing Storm (USA)
7¹⁰ˢᵈ 2⁸ˢᵈ 7¹⁰ˢᵈ 1¹⁰ˢᵈ 3¹⁰ᵍ 14⁸ᵍ 3⁸ᵍᶠ 4⁹ᵍᶠ 8⁹ᵍᶠ 2¹⁰ᵍᶠ 9¹⁰ᵍᶠ 8¹⁰ᵍᶠ 14⁸ᵍ **1-4-13 £7,693**

Leatherback (Ire) *N A Callaghan* 77
5 b g Turtle Island (Ire) - Phyllode
7¹⁰ᵍᶠ 15¹²ᵍ 16⁹ᵍˢ 7¹²ᵍᶠ 2¹⁰ᵍᶠ 7¹⁰ᵍ **0-1-6 £1,190**

Leave To Appeal (Ire) *L M Cumani* 85
3 b f Victory Note (USA) - Justice System (USA)
1⁸ᵍᶠ 5⁸ᵍˢ 6⁸ᵍᶠ 6⁷ᵍ 7⁹ᵍˢ 3⁹ᵍᶠ 2¹⁰ᵍᶠ 5¹¹ˢ **1-2-8 £9,652**

Legal Set (Ire) *K R Burke* 78 a76
7 gr g Second Set (Ire) - Tiffany's Case (Ire)
7⁶ˢᵈ 5⁶ˢᵈ 2⁶ˢᵈ 6⁶ˢᵈ 1⁷ˢᵈ 2⁶ᵍˢ 13⁶ˢᵈ 9⁶ᵍ 3⁶ˢᵈ 10⁶ᵍᶠ 3⁶ᶠ 9⁶ᵍᶠ 9⁶ᵍᶠ 10⁸ᵍᶠ 6⁷ˢᵈ **1-4-15 £6,071**

Legalis (USA) *K A Ryan* 23
5 ch g Gone West (USA) - Loyalize (USA)
17⁶ᵍᶠ 16⁶ᵍˢ 17⁶ᵍᶠ **0-0-3**

Legality *P Mitchell* 65 a65
3 b f Polar Falcon (USA) - Lady Barrister
9¹⁰ˢᵈ 9⁸ˢᵈ 5⁸ᵍ 7⁸ˢᵈ 8⁷ᵍᶠ 14⁷ᵍᶠ 14⁸ˢᵈ **0-0-7**

Legion Of Honour (Ire) *Miss S J Wilton* 31
4 b c Danehill (USA) - Total Chic (USA)
18¹⁰ᵍᶠ 13¹⁰ᵍᶠ 14¹⁰ᵍᶠ **0-0-3**

Leicester Square (Ire) *M Johnston* 105
2 ch c Gone West (USA) - Stage Manner
1⁶ᵍᶠ 2⁶ᵍ 7⁶ᵍᶠ 4⁸ᵍᶠ **1-1-4 £19,369**

Leighton (Ire) *J D Bethell* 88
3 b g Desert Story (Ire) - Lady Fern
9⁸ᵍᶠ 4⁸ᵍᶠ 3¹⁰ᵍᶠ 4¹⁰ᵍᶠ 10¹⁰ᵍ 3¹⁰ᵍᶠ **0-1-6 £5,124**

Leisurely Way *P R Chamings* 74
4 b f Kris - Arietta's Way (Ire)
1⁸ˢ 13¹²ᵍ **1-0-2 £4,459**

Leitrim House *B J Meehan* 89
2 c c Cadeaux Genereux - Lonely Heart
1⁶ᵍᶠ 6⁷ᵍ **1-0-2 £5,122**

Leitrim Rock (Ire) *D W P Arbuthnot* 58 a58
3 b g Barathea (Ire) - Kilshanny
10⁷ˢᵈ 5⁹ˢᵈ 2⁸ˢᵈ 4⁹ˢʷ 2⁷ˢᵈ 2⁸ᵍᶠ 7⁷ᵍᶠ 3⁸ᵍᶠ 15⁸ᵍ 16⁸ᵍᶠ 10¹⁰ᵍᶠ **0-4-11 £3,328**

Lemagurut *W M Brisbourne* 64
3 b f Mukaddamah (USA) - Fervent Fan (Ire)
7⁸ᵍᶠ 8⁸ᵍᶠ 3⁶ᵍ 5⁹ᶠ 7⁷ᵍᶠ 11⁶ᵍᶠ 11⁷ᵍᶠ **0-1-7 £786**

Lemarate (USA) *D W Chapman* 35 a35
6 b g Gulch (USA) - Sayyedati

13⁸ˢᵈ 15⁷ˢᵈ 9⁷ˢʷ 5⁷ᵍᶠ 3⁶ˢᵈ 10⁷ˢᵈ 6⁶ᶠ 12⁶ᵍᶠ 11⁶ˢ 15¹⁶ᵍᶠ 13⁶ᶠ **0-1-11 £560**

Lennel *A Bailey* 76
5 b g Presidium - Ladykirk
7⁹ᵍᶠ 4¹⁰ᵍ 17⁸ᵍˢ 1¹¹ᵍ 6⁸ᵍ 7¹⁰ᵍᶠ 1¹¹ᵍᶠ 1¹⁰ᵍᶠ 4¹²ᵍᶠ **3-0-9 £18,136**

Lenwade *G G Margarson* 59
2 gr f Environment Friend - Branitska
15⁶ᵍᶠ 6⁷ᵍᶠ 7⁷ᵍᶠ 8⁸ᵍᶠ 8¹⁰ᵍᶠ **0-0-5**

Leo Boy (USA) *J L Dunlop* 84
3 b c Danehill (USA) - Leo Girl (USA)
3⁷ᵍᶠ 10⁸ᵍᶠ 5⁷ᵍˢ 2¹⁰ᵍᶠ 1¹⁰ᵍᶠ 6⁸ᶠ 5¹⁰ᵍᶠ 10¹⁰ᵍᶠ **1-2-8 £7,746**

Leo's Luckyman (USA) *M Johnston* 110
4 b g Woodman (USA) - Leo's Lucky Lady (USA)
2¹⁰ᵍ 2¹⁰ᵍ 13¹⁰ᶠ 1¹⁰ᵍᶠ 7¹⁰ᵍ **1-1-5 £24,049**

Leoballero *H J Collingridge* 77 a67
3 ch g Lion Cavern (USA) - Ball Gown
3⁸ᵍᶠ 5⁸ᵍᶠ 2⁸ᵍ 2⁸ᵍᶠ 3⁸ᵍᶠ 1⁷ˢᵈ **1-4-6 £5,932**

Leonardo De Vinci (Ire) *K A Ryan* 47 a38
3 b c Sadler's Wells (USA) - Andromaque (USA)
6⁹ˢᵈ 17⁷ᵍ 11¹⁰ᵍᶠ **0-0-3**

Leonor De Soto *M R Channon* 64
3 b f Fraam - Wings Awarded
11¹⁰ᵍᶠ 6⁸ᵍ 1⁸ᶠ 18ᵍᶠ 4⁸ᵍᶠ 6¹⁰ᶠ 6⁹ᵍᶠ 12⁸ᵍᶠ **2-1-8 £6,995**

Leonora Truce (Ire) *Mrs J L Le Brocq* a57
4 b f Brief Truce (USA) - Eleonora D'Arborea
5⁸ˢᵈ 3⁸ˢᵈ 3⁹ˢᵈ 2⁹ˢᵈ 2⁸ᵍ 2¹⁰ᵍ 2⁸ᶠ 3⁷ᶠ 2⁸ᵍ **0-3-9 £4,209**

Leopard Creek *Mrs J R Ramsden* 59
2 ch f Weldnaas (USA) - Indigo
4⁵ᵍᶠ 8⁵ᵍᶠ 13⁵ᵍ **0-0-3**

Leopard Hunt (USA) *J H M Gosden* 87
2 ch f Diesis - Alcando
1⁷ᵍᶠ 3⁷ᵍᶠ 8⁸ᵍ **1-1-3 £7,521**

Leophin Dancer (USA) *P W Hiatt* 53 a44
5 b g Green Dancer (USA) - Happy Gal (Fr)
6¹²ˢᵈ 3¹²ˢᵈ 3¹²ˢᵈ 3¹⁵ˢʷ 8¹²ˢᵈ 5¹³ᵍᶠ 5¹³ᶠ 7¹⁴ᵍᶠ 2¹⁶ᵍᶠ 3¹⁶ᵍᶠ 8¹⁶ᵍᶠ 5¹³ᵍᶠ 8¹⁶ᵍˢ **0-5-13 £2,460**

Leporello (Ire) *P W Harris* 119
3 b c Danehill (USA) - Why So Silent
1⁷ᵍˢ 1⁸ᵍᶠ 3⁸ᵍᶠ 1¹⁰ᵍᶠ 1¹¹ᵍᶠ 1¹⁰ᵍᶠ 1¹⁰ᵍᶠ **6-0-7 £139,271**

Les Arcs (USA) *J H M Gosden* 87
3 br c Arch (USA) - La Sarto (USA)
2¹⁰ᶠ 1¹⁰ᵍᶠ 13¹⁰ᵍ **1-1-3 £4,916**

Lesath (USA) *J R Fanshawe* 89
3 b g Mister Baileys - Green Moon (Fr)
1¹⁰ᵍᶠ 3¹²ᵍᶠ 3¹²ᶠ 6¹²ᵍᶠ 9¹²ᵍᶠ **1-1-5 £5,436**

Less Of A Mystery (USA) *M Johnston* 76
2 b c Red Ransom (USA) - State Secret
4⁵ᵍˢ 2⁶ᵍᶠ 4⁶ᵍᶠ 3⁸ᵍ 11⁸ᵍˢ **0-1-5 £4,760**

Let It Be *Mrs M Reveley* 34
2 ch f Entrepreneur - Noble Dane (Ire)
11⁷ᵍ 8⁷ᵍᶠ 10⁷ᵍ **0-0-3**

Let Me Try Again (Ire) *T G Mills* 111 a81
3 b c Sadler's Wells (USA) - Dathiyna (Ire)
2¹⁰ˢᵈ 1¹²ˢᵈ 1¹²ᵍᶠ 2¹²ᵍᶠ 7¹²ᵍ 5¹²ᵍ 4¹³ᵍᶠ 7¹⁵ᵍ **2-2-8 £28,180**

Let The Lion Roar *J L Dunlop* 92

2 b c Sadler's Wells (USA) - Ballerina (Ire)
1⁸ᵍᶠ 2⁸ᵍᶠ **1-1-2 £8,410**

Let's Celebrate *F Jordan* 30 a18
3 b g Groom Dancer (USA) - Shimmer
10⁷ˢᵈ 17⁶ᵍᶠ 10⁷ᵍᶠ 10⁸ᵍᶠ 10¹²ᶠ **0-0-5**

Let's Dance Again *T D Easterby* 53
2 b f Forzando - Dancing Em
4⁶ᶠ 9⁵ᵍ 8⁷ᵍ **0-0-3 £283**

Let's Party (Ire) *P L Clinton* 71
3 b f Victory Note (USA) - Mashoura
6⁶ᵍˢ 4⁶ᵍᶠ 14⁶ᵍˢ 15⁷ᵍᶠ 6⁸ᵍ 4⁸ᵍˢ 9⁷ᵍˢ
13⁸ˢᵈ 4¹⁰ᵍᶠ 10⁷ᵍᶠ 18⁸ᵍˢ **0-0-11 £1,342**

Lets Get It On (Ire) *J J Quinn* 77
2 b f Perugino (USA) - Lets Clic Together (Ire)
1⁵ᵍᶠ 3⁶ᵍᶠ 5⁶ᵍᶠ 10⁷ᵍ 2⁶ᵍˢ **1-1-5 £7,217**

Lets Roll *C W Thornton* 73
2 b g Tamure (Ire) - Miss Petronella
9⁶ᵍ 2⁷ᵍ 2⁶ᵍ 5⁸ᵍᶠ 1⁷ᵍ **1-2-5 £4,724**

Letsimpress (Ire) *J A Osborne* 81
2 b f General Monash (USA) - Vezelay (USA)
4⁵ˢ 1⁶ʸˢ 3⁶ᵍ 6⁶ᵍᶠ 2⁶ᶠ 3⁶ᵍᶠ 5⁵ᵍᶠ 2⁵ˢ 7⁷ᵍ
10⁶ᵍˢ **1-3-10 £14,460**

Levantine (Ire) *A G Newcombe* 54
6 b g Sadler's Wells (USA) - Spain Lane (USA)
3⁷ᵍ 8¹⁰ᵍᶠ 6⁸ᵍᶠ **0-1-3 £580**

Levelled *D W Chapman* 31
9 b g Beveled - Baino Charm (USA)
12⁶ˢᵈ 10⁶ᵍᶠ **0-0-2**

Levitator *Sir Michael Stoute* 60
2 b c Sadler's Wells (USA) - Cantilever
18⁸ᵍᶠ **0-0-1**

Leyaaly *B A Pearce*
4 ch f Night Shift (USA) - Lower The Tone (Ire)
10⁸ᵍ 11⁹ᵍ **0-0-2**

Lezara *M A Buckley*
2 b f Aragon - Lezayre
13⁶ˢᵈ **0-0-1**

Li Galli (USA) *D K Weld* 38 a36
3 b f Nureyev (USA) - Redwood Falls (Ire)
6⁵ˢᵈ 12⁶ᵍ **0-0-2**

Li'l Lees (Ire) *I Semple* 33
2 ch g Lake Coniston (Ire) - Kayrava
4⁷ᶠ 9⁸ᵍ 13⁸ᵍᶠ **0-0-3 £340**

Liam's Story (Ire) *K A Ryan* 45
3 gr g Desert Story (Ire) - Sweet Class
14⁸ᵍ 9¹⁰ᵍˢ **0-0-2**

Liberty *Sir Michael Stoute* 74
2 b f Singspiel (Ire) - Virtuous
2⁶ᵍᶠ 1⁶ᵍᶠ **1-1-2 £6,160**

Liberty Royal *P J Makin* 81
4 b g Ali-Royal (Ire) - Hope Chest
15⁸ᵍᶠ 4⁸ᵍᶠ 12⁹ᵍᶠ **0-0-3 £433**

Liberty Seeker (Fr) *G A Swinbank* 75
4 ch g Machiavellian (USA) - Samara (Ire)
16¹⁰ᵍˢ 14⁸ᵍˢ 7¹⁰ᵍ 17⁸ˢ **0-0-4**

Libre *F Jordan* 78
3 b g Bahamian Bounty - Premier Blues (Fr)
12⁷ᵍ 15¹²ᵍᶠ 16⁸ᵍᶠ 2⁸ᵍ 3⁷ᵍᶠ 1⁹ᵍˢ 9¹⁰ᵍᶠ
4¹⁰ᶠ 14⁸ᵍᶠ 1⁸ᶠ 4⁸ᵍᶠ 7⁸ᵍˢ **2-2-12 £9,525**

Lieuday *W M Brisbourne* 57 a36
4 b g Atraf - Figment
14⁷ᵍᶠ 6⁸ᶠ 8⁸ˢᵈ 2⁸ᵍᶠ 12⁸ˢ DSQ⁷ᵍᶠ 5⁷ᵍᶠ
8⁷ᵍ 5⁷ᵍᶠ 3⁷ᵍᶠ **0-2-10 £1,671**

Life Estates *T J Fitzgerald* 42
3 b g Mark Of Esteem (Ire) - Chepstow Vale (USA)

9⁷ᵍᶠ 8⁶ᶠ **0-0-2**

Life Is Beautiful (Ire) *W H Tinning* 50 a24
4 b f Septieme Ciel (USA) - Palombella (Fr)
8¹²ᵍᶠ 7¹²ᵍᶠ 12¹²ˢᵈ 11¹²ᵍᶠ 6¹⁰ᵍᶠ 2¹¹ᵍᶠ 9¹⁴ᵍᶠ
1¹²ᵍˢ 12¹²ᶠ **1-1-9 £3,306**

Liffey (Ire) *P F I Cole* 73
3 b c Desert Prince (Ire) - Toujours Irish (USA)
2⁷ᵍ **0-1-1 £1,720**

Lifted Way *P R Chamings* 82 a68
4 b c In The Wings - Stack Rock
5¹⁰ᵍᶠ 6¹⁰ᵍᶠ 10⁸ᵍᶠ 1⁸ᵍᶠ 3⁸ᵍᶠ 5⁷ᵍᶠ 4⁷ᵍᶠ 9⁷ˢᵈ
9⁸ᵍᶠ **1-1-9 £5,444**

Light Brigade *J M P Eustace* a59
4 b g Kris - Mafatin (Ire)
9¹¹ˢᵈ 3¹²ˢᵈ **0-1-2 £302**

Light Scent (USA) *J Akehurst* 87
4 ch g Silver Hawk (USA) - Music Lane (USA)
13¹⁰ᵍ 8¹²ᵍᶠ 15¹⁰ᵍᶠ 2¹²ᵍᶠ 2¹²ᵍᶠ 6¹⁴ᵍ **0-2-6
£4,738**

Light The Dawn (Ire) *J H M Gosden* a44
3 ch f Indian Ridge - Flaming June (USA)
7⁸ˢᵈ **0-0-1**

Lightsabre *Sir Mark Prescott* 16 a62
3 ch f Polar Falcon - Heavenly Ray (USA)
2⁶ˢᵈ 2⁶ˢᵈ 5⁶ˢᵈ 6⁸ˢᵈ 14⁷ᵍ **0-2-5 £1,905**

Ligne D'Eau *P D Evans* 65
2 b c Cadeaux Genereux - Miss Waterline
11⁶ᵍᶠ 8⁷ᵍᶠ 8⁶ᵍ **0-0-3**

Likely Lady (Ire) *D Burchell* 13 a37
4 b f Revoque (Ire) - Harmer (Ire)
9⁸ˢʷ 11⁸ˢᵈ 12⁶ˢᵈ 7⁹ˢᵈ 3⁸ˢᵈ 12⁸ˢᵈ 16⁸ᵍᶠ
0-1-7 £423

Lilac *R J Price* 34
4 ch f Alhijaz - Fairfield's Breeze
9¹³ᵍᶠ 3¹²ᵍᶠ **0-0-2 £469**

Lilardo *B Palling* a34
6 b/br m Son Pardo - Jimlil
9¹⁶ˢᵈ 5¹²ˢʷ 11¹⁴ˢᵈ **0-0-3**

Lilian *A M Balding* 49 a47
3 b f First Trump - Lillibella
8⁷ˢᵈ 7⁷ˢᵈ 13¹⁰ᶠ 10⁷ᵍᶠ 2⁸ᶠ 4⁹ᵍ 6⁸ᵍᶠ 14⁸ᶠ
2¹⁰ᵍᶠ 2¹⁰ᵍᶠ **0-4-10 £2,422**

Lill's Star Lad *P R Wood* 18
5 ch g Kasakov - Lady Khadija
12¹¹ˢᵈ 11⁷ᵍᶠ 13⁷ᵍᶠ 15¹⁴ᵍᶠ **0-0-4**

Lillebror (Ger) *B J Curley* 62
5 b h Top Waltz (Fr) - Lady Soliciti (Ger)
10¹⁰ᵍ 5¹²ᵍ 4¹²ᵍᶠ 7¹⁰ᵍ 8¹⁰ᵍᶠ 16¹²ᵍᶠ 16¹⁶ᵍ
0-0-7 £783

Lilli Marlane *G G Margarson* 83
3 b f Sri Pekan (USA) - Fiveofive (Ire)
5⁷ᵍˢ 8⁷ᵍˢ 2⁸ᵍ 2¹⁰ᶠ 3¹⁰ᵍᶠ 3⁸ᵍᶠ 5⁸ᵍᶠ
12⁹ᵍᶠ **1-4-9 £7,926**

Lillies Bordello (Ire) *K A Ryan* a55
4 b f Danehill Dancer (Ire) - Lunulae
11⁶ˢᵈ 4⁶ˢʷ 5⁶ˢᵈ 9⁶ˢʷ **0-0-4 £317**

Lily Of The Guild (Ire) *W S Kittow* 62 a43
4 ch f Lycius (USA) - Secreto Bold
9⁷ˢᵈ 11⁸ᵍᶠ 4⁷ᵍ 4⁷ᵍ 4⁶ᵍ 6⁷ᵍᶠ **0-2-6 £987**

Limit Down (Ire) *M J Wallace* 14 a56
2 b g Desert Story (Ire) - Princess Raisa
10⁶ˢᵈ 7⁶ᵍˢ **0-0-2**

Limited Magician *C Smith*
2 b f Wizard King - Pretty Scarce
14⁸ᵍ 9⁶ᵍᶠ **0-0-2**

Lin In Gold (Ire) *P A Blockley* 77
2 b g Second Empire (Ire) - Wasmette (Ire)
1⁸ᶠ 8⁸ᵍ **1-0-2 £2,303**

Linby Lad (Ire) *J J Quinn* 43
3 ch g Dolphin Street (Fr) - Classic Look (Ire)
12⁸ᵍᶠ 11⁸ᵍ **0-0-2**

Lincoln Dancer (Ire) *D Nicholls* 100
6 b g Turtle Island (Ire) - Double Grange (Ire)
11⁵ᵍ 6⁶ᵍᶠ 17⁷ᵍ 18⁶ᵍ 11⁶ᵍˢ **0-0-5 £240**

Linda Green *R Bastiman* 60 a53
2 b f Victory Note (USA) - Edge Of Darkness
6⁵ˢᵈ 4⁵ᵍᶠ 4⁵ᵍ 2⁵ᵍᶠ 10⁵ᵍᶠ 3⁵ˢʷ 9⁵ˢᵈ **0-2-7 £1,926**

Linden's Lady *J R Weymes* 83
3 b f Compton Place - Jubilee Place (Ire)
11⁷ᵍᶠ 3⁶ᵍ 2⁶ᵍᶠ 3⁶ᶠ 13⁶ᵍᶠ 4⁷ᶠ
6⁶ᶠ 4⁶ᵍᶠ 4⁶ᵍᶠ 12⁶ᵍᶠ 5⁶ᶠ **0-4-13 £8,476**

Lindop *J A R Toller* 82
3 ch c Nashwan (USA) - Footlight Fantasy (USA)
1⁸ᵍ **1-0-1 £6,526**

Linens Flame *B G Powell* 43 a55
4 ch g Blushing Flame (USA) - Atlantic Air
13¹⁰ˢᵈ 13¹⁰ˢᵈ 10¹⁰ᵍ **0-0-3**

Lingo (Ire) *Jonjo O'Neill* 105
4 b g Poliglote - Sea Ring (Fr)
14⁸ᵍ 1¹⁰ᵍᶠ 1¹⁰ᵍ **2-0-3 £29,522**

Linning Wine (Ire) *B G Powell* 93 a103
7 b g Scenic - Zallaka (Ire)
4¹²ˢᵈ 9¹⁰ˢᵈ 9¹⁰ˢᵈ 3¹⁰ᵍᶠ 12¹⁰ᵍᶠ 2¹⁰ᵍ 15¹²ᵍᶠ
14¹⁰ᵍˢ 8¹¹ᵍᶠ **0-3-9 £6,493**

Lion Guest (Ire) *Mrs S C Bradburne* 37
6 ch g Lion Cavern (USA) - Decrescendo (Ire)
8¹⁵ᵍ 9¹²ᵍᶠ **0-0-2**

Lion's Domane *A Berry* 74 a17
6 b g Lion Cavern (USA) - Vilany
11⁷ˢᵈ 2⁷ᵍᶠ 16⁷ᵍᶠ 1⁷ᶠ 1⁷ᶠ 16⁷ᵍ 17⁷ᵍᶠ 7⁷ᶠ
2-1-8 £8,501

Lionel Andros *K A Ryan* 47 a30
5 b g Lion Cavern (USA) - Guyum
10⁵ˢᵈ 6⁶ᵍ 17⁶ᵍᶠ 14⁶ᵍᶠ 12⁷ˢᵈ 11⁵ᵍˢ **0-0-6**

Lips Lion (Ire) *Andreas Lowe* 108
4 ch c Lion Cavern (USA) - Glamour Model
3⁸ᵍ 5⁸ᵍᶠ **0-0-2 £1,667**

Liquid Form (Ire) *B Hanbury* 92
3 br g Bahhare (USA) - Brogan's Well (Ire)
5⁸ᵍᶠ 4⁸ᵍ 6¹¹ᶠ 1¹⁰ᵍᶠ 4¹⁰ᵍᶠ 7¹⁰ᵍ 1¹¹ᵍᶠ 3¹⁰ᵍᶠ
2-1-8 £9,027

Liquidate *J W Hills* 52
2 b g Hector Protector (USA) - Cut And Run
12⁷ᵍᶠ 11⁷ᵍᶠ 6⁸ᵍᶠ **0-0-3**

Lisa's Looney *Mrs C A Dunnett* 52
4 b f Bahamian Bounty - Starfida
19⁶ᵍ 8⁶ᵍᶠ 10⁶ᵍ 5⁶ᵍᶠ 8⁶ᵍ 8⁶ᵍᶠ 19⁶ᶠ 9⁷ᵍᶠ
8⁶ᵍᶠ **0-0-9**

Liscombe Park *D J Daly*
2 b f Young Ern - Little Park
10⁸ˢʷ **0-0-1**

Listen Kid (USA) *Mrs A J Bowlby* 32
4 b g Royal Academy (USA) - Prosper (USA)
8¹⁴ᵍˢ 19¹²ᵍᶠ 18¹²ᵍᶠ PU¹¹ⁿᵍ 11¹¹ᵍ **0-0-5**

Listen To Reason (Ire) *J G Given* 60
2 b c Mukaddamah (USA) - Tenalist (Ire)
5⁶ᵍ 13⁶ᵍ **0-0-2**

Litany *John A Harris* 46

4 b f Colonel Collins (USA) - Hymn Book (Ire)
10¹²ᵍ 10¹⁴ᵍᶠ PU¹⁶ᵍᶠ **0-0-3**

Literacy (USA) *C E Brittain* 74
3 b f Diesis - Tuviah (USA)
6¹⁰ᵍᶠ 6¹²ᵍ 5¹²ᵍ 1¹¹ᵍᶠ 4¹⁰ᶠ 14¹⁰ᵍ 1¹⁰ᵍᶠ
2-0-7 £8,337

Litewska (Ire) *R Hannon* 83
3 b f Mujadil (USA) - Old Tradition (Ire)
18⁶ᶠ 12⁶ᵍˢ 4⁶ᵍᶠ 1⁵ᵍᶠ 8⁵ᵍᶠ 1⁶ᵍᶠ 7⁶ᵍᶠ
12⁶ᵍᶠ 10⁷ᵍᶠ **2-0-9 £11,013**

Lithuanian (Aus) *W J Haggas* 28 a64
5 br h Nureyev (USA) - Doe (USA)
1⁶ˢᵈ 10⁸ᵍᶠ **1-0-2 £3,809**

Litigious *A Senior* a19
6 b m Mtoto - Kiomi
10⁸ˢᵈ 10¹⁵ˢᵈ 12⁹ˢᵈ **0-0-3**

Little Amin *J D Czerpak* 79
7 b g Unfuwain (USA) - Ghassanah
7⁸ᵍ 5¹⁰ᵍᶠ 5⁸ᵍˢ 8⁸ᵍˢ **0-0-4 £296**

Little Bob *J D Bethell* 38
2 ch c Zilzal (USA) - Hunters Of Brora (Ire)
12⁷ᵍ **0-0-1**

Little Daisy *K A Ryan* 26
5 ch m Factual (USA) - Twice In Bundoran (Ire)
9¹⁴ᶠ 10¹²ˢʷ **0-0-2**

Little Edward *B G Powell* 104
5 gr g King's Signet (USA) - Cedar Lady
3⁶ᵍᶠ 2⁵ᵍᶠ 1¹ᵍᶠ 13⁶ᵍᶠ 1⁶ᵍ 9⁵ᵍ 1⁶ʰᵈ 9⁵ᵍᶠ
2⁵ˢ 2⁵ᵍ 5⁵ᶠ **2-4-11 £35,486**

Little Englander *H Candy* 56
3 b g Piccolo - Anna Karietta
6¹⁰ᵍᶠ 2¹⁰ᵍᶠ 10⁸ᵍᶠ 8¹²ᵍᶠ **0-1-4 £1,324**

Little Eye (Ire) *J R Best* 70
2 b g Groom Dancer (USA) - Beaming
8⁵ᵍᶠ 6⁵ᵍᶠ 4⁵ᵍᶠ 7⁶ᵍˢ 15⁷ᵍ 14⁸ᵍᶠ **0-0-6 £278**

Little Flute *C G Cox* 51 a53
2 b c Piccolo - Nordic Victory (USA)
4⁵ᵍᶠ 7⁵ˢᵈ 16⁷ᵍᶠ 10⁶ᵍᶠ 7⁷ᵍᶠ 12⁶ᵍᶠ **0-0-6 £276**

Little Good Bay *J H M Gosden* 105
3 b c Danehill (USA) - Brave Kris (Ire)
2⁸ᵍᶠ 5⁸ᵍᶠ 4⁸ᵍ 3⁷ᵍᶠ 1⁷ᵍ 3⁷ᵍᶠ 1⁷ᵍ 6⁷ᵍᶠ
2-2-8 £33,227

Little Jimbob *R A Fahey* 64
2 b g Desert Story (Ire) - Artistic Licence
4⁵ᵍᶠ 3⁵ᵍᶠ 6⁵ᵍˢ 4⁵ᵍᶠ 3⁸ᵍᶠ 2⁷ᵍᶠ 3⁸ᵍᶠ 4⁷ᵍᶠ
2⁸ᵍᶠ **0-5-9 £7,671**

Little John *Miss L A Perratt* 24
7 b g Warrshan (USA) - Silver Venture (USA)
12¹⁶ᵍˢ 9¹⁴ᵍᶠ 9¹²ᶠ **0-0-3**

Little Laura *K W Hogg* 34
7 ch m Casteddu - At First Sight
4¹²ᵍˢ 7¹²ᵍᶠ **0-0-2 £294**

Little London *J L Dunlop* 75
2 b g Bahhare (USA) - North Kildare (USA)
9⁷ᵍ 3⁷ᵍ 5⁸ᵍᶠ 2⁸ᶠ **0-2-4 £1,295**

Little Louis *P D Evans* a56
3 b g Defacto (USA) - Naufrage
2⁷ˢᵈ 13⁶ˢᵈ 6⁷ˢᵈ 7⁸ˢᵈ 7⁶ˢᵈ 8⁷ˢᵈ **0-1-6 £840**

Little Miss Cody *T D Easterby* 38
2 b f Mind Games - Madam Cody
8⁵ᶠ 8⁵ᵍˢ **0-0-2**

Little Miss Tricky *P Mitchell* a34

4 br f Magic Ring (Ire) - Mistook (USA)
13⁷ˢᵈ 7⁸ˢᵈ 9¹²ˢᵈ 11¹⁰ˢᵈ **0-0-4**

Little Nobby *R Hollinshead*
4 b g Makbul - Simply Style
9¹¹ˢʷ **0-0-1**

Little Richard (Ire) *M Wellings*   10 a61
4 b g Alhaarth (Ire) - Intricacy
8¹⁶ˢᵈ 2¹²ˢᵈ 2¹⁵ˢʷ 2¹²ˢʷ 3¹²ˢʷ 9¹²ˢʷ 10¹²ˢʷ
13¹⁶ᵍᶠ **0-4-8 £2,752**

Little Ridge (Ire) *H Morrison*   81
2 b g Charnwood Forest (Ire) - Princess Natalie
3⁶ᵍᶠ 6⁵ᵍᶠ 18⁶ᵍ 1⁵ᵍᶠ 1⁵ᵍˢ **2-1-5 £6,452**

Little Robs' Girl *M Mullineaux*   35
4 ch f Cosmonaut - David James' Girl
11¹⁰ᵍ 4¹¹ᵍᶠ 10¹²ᵍᶠ 6¹¹ᵍᶠ 11¹²ᵍ **0-1-5**

Little Sky *D Mullarkey*   58 a32
6 gr m Terimon - Brown Coast
2¹⁴ᵍᶠ 14¹²ˢʷ 10¹³ˢᵈ **0-1-3 £1,175**

Little Task *J S Wainwright*   27
5 b g Environment Friend - Lucky Thing
5¹⁴ᶠ **0-0-1**

Little Tiger Livi (Ire) *Mrs P N Dutfield*
3 b f Namaqualand (USA) - Shahroza (USA)
8⁸ˢᵈ 5¹¹ˢʷ **0-0-2**

Little Tobias (Ire) *Andrew Turnell*   57
4 ch g Millkom - Barbara Frietchie (Ire)
1¹⁵ᵍ 10¹⁶ᵍˢ 1¹⁶ᵍˢ 14¹⁶ᵍᶠ **2-0-4 £6,092**

Little Tumbler (Ire) *S Woodman*   47
8 b m Cyrano De Bergerac - Glass Minnow (Ire)
16¹⁰ᶠ 12⁹ᵍᶠ 7⁹ᵍᶠ 12¹⁰ᶠ **0-0-4**

Little Venice (Ire) *C F Wall*   86
3 b f Fumo Di Londra (Ire) - Petrine (Ire)
14⁷ᵍ 3⁶ᵍˢ 3⁷ᵍᶠ 1⁷ᵍᶠ 3⁷ᵍ 1⁷ᵍᶠ 6⁸ᵍ 3⁷ᵍᶠ
2⁷ᵍᶠ 4⁷ᵍᶠ 8⁷ᵍᶠ **2-5-11 £17,070**

Littlemissattitude *K R Burke*   a75
4 ch f Common Grounds - Last Look
1⁸ˢᵈ 1⁸ˢᵈ 6⁹ˢᵈ 1⁹ˢᵈ 5⁸ˢᵈ 10⁸ˢᵈ **3-0-6
£9,289**

Littlestar (Fr) *J L Dunlop*   61
2 b c Robellino (USA) - Green Charter
16⁷ᵍᶠ 7⁷ᵍᶠ 14⁸ᵍᶠ **0-0-3**

Littleton Amethyst (Ire) *Mrs P Ford*   33 a48
4 ch f Revoque (Ire) - Sept Roses (USA)
4¹²ˢᵈ 2¹²ˢᵈ 3¹²ˢᵈ 12¹⁶ˢᵈ 7¹⁶ˢʷ 8¹²ᵍᶠ 8¹²ˢᵈ
7¹²ˢᵈ 12¹⁶ˢᵈ **0-3-9 £2,474**

Littleton Arwen (USA) *T G Mills*   98 a76
3 b f Bahri (USA) - Jathibiyah (USA)
12⁷ˢᵈ 11⁷ᵍᶠ 5⁶ᵍˢ 4⁷ᵍ 2⁷ᵍᶠ 8⁷ᵍ **0-1-6
£9,568**

Littleton Liberty *T J Naughton*   25
2 b f Royal Applause - Lammastide
4⁵ᶠ 17⁵ᵍ **0-0-2 £334**

Littleton Valar (Ire) *J R Weymes*   50 a49
3 ch g Definite Article - Fresh Look (Ire)
10⁷ˢᵈ 4⁸ˢᵈ 9⁸ᵍᶠ 9⁷ˢᵈ 7¹⁰ᵍᶠ 2¹⁰ᵍᶠ 11¹⁴ᵍᶠ
13¹¹ˢʷ 6¹⁰ᵍᶠ **0-1-9 £1,174**

Littleton Zephir (USA) *Mrs P Townsley*   31 a59
4 b f Sandpit (Brz) - Miss Gorgeous (USA)
5⁹ˢᵈ 4⁸ˢᵈ 1⁸ˢᵈ 2⁹ˢᵈ 3⁸ˢᵈ 3⁸ˢᵈ 9⁸ˢᵈ 6¹²ᶠ
1-3-8 £5,273

Littleton Zeus (Ire) *W S Cunningham*   15
4 ch g Woodborough (USA) - La Fandango (Ire)
14⁷ˢᵈ 7¹⁰ˢᵈ **0-0-2**

Litza *M W Easterby*   2
2 b f Paris House - Strelitza (Ire)

13⁷ᵍᶠ 15⁸ˢᵈ **0-0-2**

Litzinsky *C B B Booth*   62
5 b g Muhtarram (USA) - Boulevard Girl
13¹⁸ᵍ 5¹⁶ᵍ 16¹⁴ᵍ 11¹⁶ᵍˢ **0-0-4**

Lively Felix *D W P Arbuthnot*   28 a51
6 b g Presidium - Full Of Life
5⁹ˢᵈ 2⁸ˢᵈ 3⁸ˢᵈ 8⁷ˢᵈ 6¹¹ˢᵈ 13⁸ˢᵈ 16⁶ᵍˢ
12¹²ᵍᶠ 14¹⁰ᶠ 8¹⁰ᵍᶠ **0-2-10 £1,220**

Lively Lady *J R Jenkins*   60
7 b m Beveled (USA) - In The Papers
7⁶ᵍˢ 13⁵ᵍᶠ 8⁵ᵍᶠ 11⁵ᵍᶠ **0-0-4**

Living Daylights (Ire) *J L Dunlop*   73
4 b f Night Shift (USA) - Shesadelight
1¹²ᵍᶠ 11¹⁴ᵍ 1¹²ᵍ **2-0-3 £8,060**

Livius (Ire) *C A Dwyer*   a56
9 b g Alzao (USA) - Marie De Beaujeu (Fr)
7¹⁰ˢᵈ **0-0-1**

Livy (Ire) *S Kirk*   a58
3 ch g Titus Livius (Fr) - Shalerina (USA)
11⁵ˢᵈ 9⁵ᵍ 12⁷ᵍᶠ 8⁶ᶠ 10⁶ˢᵈ 11⁷ˢᵈ 12⁶ˢᵈ
0-0-7

Lizhar (Ire) *M J Polglase*   53 a74
2 b f Danetime (Ire) - Amelesa (Ire)
3⁵ˢᵈ 6⁵ᵍᶠ 7⁶ʰʸ 5⁵ᵍᶠ 2⁵ᵍᶠ 9⁶ᶠ 3⁶ᶠᵗ 5⁵ᶠ
21⁷ᵍ 2⁵ˢᵈ 2⁶ˢᵈ 3⁶ˢᵈ 1⁶ˢᵈ 4⁶ᵍˢ **1-5-14 £6,239**

Llan Elli Wellie *B J Llewellyn*   16
2 ch g Binary Star (USA) - Runabay
5⁵ᶠ 13⁷ᵍᶠ **0-0-2**

Loaded Gun *Miss J Feilden*   34 a54
3 ch g Highest Honor (Fr) - Woodwardia (USA)
12⁸ᵍᶠ 13¹⁰ˢᵈ **0-0-2**

Lobos (Swi) *G L Moore*   65 a69
4 ch g Rainbow Quest (USA) - Lady Of Silver (Ire)
4⁷ˢᵈ 3¹⁰ˢᵈ 4⁷ˢᵈ 9⁸ˢᵈ 4⁷ˢᵈ 16⁸ᵍ 15⁷ᵍ 12⁸ᵍ
9⁷ᶠ 14⁷ᵍᶠ 10⁶ᵍᶠ 1⁸ᶠ 9⁸ᵍˢ **1-1-13 £3,543**

Local Poet *B A McMahon*   95
2 b c Robellino (USA) - Laugharne
6⁶ᵍᶠ 2⁵ᵍᶠ 2⁶ᵍᶠ 4⁶ᵍᶠ **0-2-4 £45,100**

Loch Inch *J M Bradley*   65
6 ch g Inchinor - Carrie Kool
9⁶ᶠ 8⁵ᵍᶠ 7⁶ʰᵈ 4⁵ᵍᶠ 8⁵ᵍ 1⁶ᶠ 1⁵ᵍᶠ 10⁵ᶠ
1⁵ᵍᶠ 10⁵ᵍᶠ 10⁵ᵍᶠ 10⁵ᵍᶠ **3-0-12 £15,563**

Loch Laird *M Madgwick*   61 a49
8 b g Beveled (USA) - Daisy Loch
8⁶ˢᵈ 2⁶ᵍᶠ 7⁷ᵍᶠ 1⁷ᵍᶠ 9⁸ᵍᶠ 10⁸ᵍᶠ 8⁶ᶠ **1-1-7
£4,759**

Loch Maree *M W Easterby*   a31
4 b f Primo Dominie - Aurora Bay (Ire)
11⁶ˢᵈ **0-0-1**

Lochbuie (Ire) *G Wragg*   68
2 b c Definite Article - Uncertain Affair (Ire)
6⁶ᵍᶠ 14⁷ᵍᶠ **0-0-3 £308**

Lochridge *A M Balding*   112
4 ch f Indian Ridge - Lochsong
4⁶ᵍᶠ 7⁶ᵍ 9⁶ᵍᶠ 16⁶ᶠ 6⁷ᵍ 16⁶ᵍᶠ 16⁶ᵍᶠ 3⁶ᵍᶠ
8⁵ʰᵒ **3-2-9 £69,948**

Lock Inn *Miss Z C Davison*   a42
4 b g Dolphin Street (Fr) - Highest Bid (Fr)
11¹²ˢᵈ 5¹⁴ˢᵈ 6¹⁴ˢᵈ 6¹⁶ˢᵈ 12¹³ˢᵈ 12¹⁴ˢᵈ
10¹⁵ˢᵈ **0-0-7**

Lockstock (Ire) *M S Saunders*   67 a74
5 b g Inchinor - Risalah
27⁸ᵍ 9⁸ᵍᶠ 7⁷ˢᵈ 12⁷ˢᵈ **0-0-4**

Locombe Hill (Ire) *D Nicholls*   78
7 b g Barathea (Ire) - Roberts Pride

6^7f 14^8gf 8^7gf 6^8g 13^8gf 11^8gf 9^7gs 1^8g **1-0-8 £3,220**

Lodger (Fr) *J Noseda* 100
3 ch c Grand Lodge (USA) - Light River (USA)
3^10gf 2^10gf 3^12gf 2^12gf 1^12gs 4^14gf **1-3-6 £16,616**

Logique (Ire) *C F Wall* a51
4 b g Revoque (Ire) - Logstown (Ire)
5^12sd 11^12sd **0-0-2**

Logistical *A D W Pinder* 79
3 b c Grand Lodge (USA) - Magic Milly
5^6gf 6^7gf 1^7g 8^7gf 9^8f 5^7gf 4^7gf 5^7gf 6^7gf 14^7gs **1-0-10 £5,141**

Logsdail *P J Hobbs* 88
3 b g Polish Precedent (USA) - Logic
9^7gf 16^7g 5^8gf 12^10g 7^7g 7^8g **0-0-6**

Lola Lola (Ire) *J L Dunlop* 36
2 b f Piccolo - French Gift
9^5gf 9^6gf 12^6gs **0-0-3**

Lola's Destiny *A M Balding* 44
2 b f Mark Of Esteem (Ire) - Kristiana
10^6g 10^7gf 7^7f **0-0-3**

Lolanita *B Palling* a50
5 b m Anita's Prince - Jimlil
2^8sd 9^9sd 15^7sd **0-1-3 £832**

Lolita's Gold (USA) *J Noseda* a56
4 b f Royal Academy (USA) - Shamisen
11^10sd 8^10sd **0-0-2**

Lomapamar *Mrs A J Perrett* 72
2 b f Nashwan (USA) - Morina (USA)
13^7gf 3^8gf 8^8gf **0-1-3 £555**

Lommel (UAE) *D R Loder* 77 a60
2 b c Lomitas - Idrica
1^6f 5^7sd **1-0-2 £3,770**

Londolozi Lad (Ire) *P C Haslam* 30
4 b g Ali-Royal (Ire) - Ashdown
11^8sd 10^8f **0-0-2**

London By Night (USA) *T G Mills* 29 a43
3 b g Mt. Livermore (USA) - Sheenasgold (USA)
6^9sd 10^8sd 13^8g **0-0-3**

London Mixture *J D Bethell*
3 b g Mind Games - Surrealist (Ity)
7^7f 10^7f **0-0-2**

Londoner (USA) *S Dow* 76
5 ch g Sky Classic (Can) - Love And Affection (USA)
16^7g 22^8gf 13^8gf 17^8g 10^8gf 14^9g 10^8gf 13^9g 10^10g 9^12gf **0-0-10**

Londonnetdotcom (Ire) *M R Channon* 102
3 ch f Night Shift (USA) - Hopeful Sign
0^8gs 5^10gf 2^9g 10^8f 3^8gf 7^8g 4^7g 1^8f 6^8gs 7^7g 6^8gf 6^8gf 9^8g **1-2-13 £36,095**

Lone Pine *M E Sowersby* 12
2 b f Sesaro (USA) - North Pine
16^6s 9^5gf 9^8gf 9^6gf **0-0-4**

Lone Piper *J M Bradley* 49 a44
8 b g Warning - Shamisen
12^5gf 12^5sd 14^5gf 7^5f 9^6gf 10^6f 5^5f **0-0-7**

Loner *M Wigham* 61
5 b g Magic Ring (Ire) - Jolis Absent
4^8gf 1^8gf 14^7gf 2^7gf 7^7gf 5^7gf 12^8gf 7^7f **1-3-8 £5,236**

Long Roads (Ire) *B R Millman* 46
2 ch c Fayruz - Mystique Air (Ire)
12^8gf **0-0-1**

Long Tall Sally (Ire) *D W P Arbuthnot* 73 a67
4 b f Danehill Dancer (Ire) - Miss Galwegian
6^6sd 7^5sd 11^6sd 4^6sd 3^6sd 13^7sd 16^9gf 9^6f 7^5gf 8^6gf 4^6gf 7^6gf 5^6g 4^6gf 4^6gf 11^6f **1-1-16 £5,199**

Long Weekend (Ire) *D Shaw* 55 a48
5 b h Flying Spur (Aus) - Friday Night (USA)
8^8sd 4^6sd 11^8sd 5^6sw 8^6sd 10^6gs 7^6gf 10^5gf 8^6gf 9^5gs 1^6gf 4^6gf 6^6g 10^6gs **1-0-14 £4,324**

Longmeadows Boy (Ire) *A Berry* 60
3 b g Victory Note (USA) - Karoi (Ire)
4^7gf 12^9gf 14^8gf 5^8gf 5^9gf 4^12gf 3^12f 1^11gf 4^12gf **1-0-9 £5,110**

Look East *Mrs C A Dunnett* 52
4 b g Ezzoud (Ire) - College Night (Ire)
7^8sd 6^7g 10^8gf 13^7f 17^7s **0-0-5**

Look First (Ire) *I A Wood* 85 a87
5 b g Namaqualand (USA) - Be Prepared (Ire)
1^16sd 4^12sd 2^16sd 11^13sd 4^16gf 5^16gf 6^16gf 5^18gf PU^16sd **1-0-10 £4,997**

Look Here Now *B A McMahon* 77 a83
6 gr g Ardkinglass - Where's Carol
1^6sd 6^7gf 13^7gf 10^6sd 16^7g 3^7gf 2^7g 5^6g 4^6gf 4^8gf 16^8f **1-3-11 £6,688**

Look Here's Carol (Ire) *B A McMahon* 97
3 ch f Safawan - Where's Carol
2^6gf 3^6gf 11^8gf 2^6gs 6^7gf 2^7gs 8^6gf 1^7s 7^6gf 10^6gf 9^7g 4^6gf **1-4-12 £24,159**

Look No Hands *Mrs S A Liddiard*
2 ch f Timeless Times (USA) - Belltina
18^5g **0-0-1**

Look No More *W G M Turner* 46 a36
2 ch g First Trump - Jadebelle
8^5f 4^7sd 5^8sd 6^8gf **0-0-4**

Looking Down *R Hannon* 87
3 ch f Compton Place - High Stepping (Ire)
5^7g 4^7gf 3^8gf 4^7gf 12^8g 14^7g 4^8g 16^7gf **0-1-8 £3,775**

Looking For Love (Ire) *J G Portman* 74
5 b m Tagula (Ire) - Mousseux (Ire)
3^7gf 4^7g 5^7g 11^7g 3^7g 2^7s **0-4-6 £4,130**

Looks Like Trouble (Ire) *Noel T Chance* 44
11 b g Zaffaran (USA) - Lavengaddy
9^22f **0-0-1**

Looks The Business (Ire) *W G M Turner* 67 a56
2 b c Marju (Ire) - Business Centre (Ire)
4^7sd 4^8gf 5^10f **0-0-3 £335**

Loop The Loup *Mrs M Reveley* 85
7 b g Petit Loup (USA) - Mithi Al Gamar (USA)
17^20gf 2^15gf 7^17g **0-1-3 £1,739**

Lord Arthur *M W Easterby* 49 a6
2 b g Mind Games - Flower O'Cannie (Ire)
8^6sd 13^7g **0-0-2**

Lord Baskerville *M G Quinlan* 62
2 b c Wolfhound (USA) - My Dear Watson
4^6g 10^6g 3^6gf 17^6gs **0-0-4 £974**

Lord Brex (Fr) *J G M O'Shea* 51 a39
7 gr g Saint Estephe (Fr) - Light Moon (Fr)
7^13sd 7^16sd 13^8gf 3^16g **0-1-4 £465**

Lord Chamberlain *J M Bradley* 62
10 b g Be My Chief (USA) - Metaphysique (Fr)
11^8gs 4^8f 8^10f 3^8gf 10^10f 3^7g 2^8gf 3^8g 2^8f 8^8gf 5^7g 3^8gf 5^7gf 4^8gf 5^8gf 7^9f **0-7-16**

£6,572

Lord Crispin J H M Gosden 74
3 ch c Kris - Lamu Lady (Ire)
16¹⁰g 4¹⁰g 2¹¹hy PU¹²gf **0-1-4 £2,054**

Lord Eurolink (Ire) M H Tompkins 79
9 b g Danehill (USA) - Lady Eurolink
8¹⁰gf 7¹⁰gf 6¹⁰gf 3¹⁰gs 6¹⁰g 3¹⁰gf 2¹⁰gf
1¹¹g **1-3-8 £5,627**

Lord Gizzmo J Cullinan 51
6 ch g Democratic (USA) - Figrant (USA)
14¹³g 1¹³gf 3¹²gf 5¹²f 5¹³f **1-1-5**
£4,707

Lord Greystoke (Ire) C P Morlock 67 a54
2 b c Petardia - Jungle Story (Ire)
10⁶g 10⁷gf 5⁷gf 8⁸gf 4⁷sd **0-0-5**

Lord Invincible M Mullineaux
5 b g Dancing Spree (USA) - Lady Broker
10⁶sd 10¹²sw 14⁸sd **0-0-3**

Lord Kintyre B R Millman 92 a92
8 b g Makbul - Highland Rowena
6⁵sd 13⁵gf 3⁵g 6⁶f 1⁵f 13⁵gf 3⁵f 13⁵gf
1-1-8 £8,934

Lord Lahar M R Channon a39
4 b g Fraam - Brigadiers Bird (Ire)
12¹⁰sd 9⁸sd **0-0-2**

Lord Lamb Mrs M Reveley 73
11 gr g Dunbeath (USA) - Caroline Lamb
8¹⁶g 1¹⁴gf 4¹⁴gf **1-0-3 £3,971**

Lord Links (Ire) R Hannon 80
2 ch c Daggers Drawn (USA) - Lady From Limerick (Ire)
1⁵g 3⁶gf 7⁷gf 4⁷gs 13⁶g **1-0-5 £8,822**

Lord Mayor Sir Michael Stoute 72 a79
2 b c Machiavellian - Misleading Lady
6⁷gf 3⁷f 7⁷sd **1-1-3 £4,184**

Lord Melbourne (Ire) J A Osborne 50 a23
4 b g Lycius (USA) - Adana (Ire)
13⁷sd 8⁷sd 6⁸sd 16⁷sd 3⁷f 5⁷f **0-1-6**
£420

Lord Of Methley R M Whitaker 57 a33
4 gr g Zilzal (USA) - Paradise Waters
6¹²sd 1¹⁰gf 5⁸g 5¹⁰gs 8¹⁰gs 5⁷gf 9¹⁰g 8⁸gf
1⁸gs 3⁸gf 4⁸gf 14¹⁰gs 14¹⁰gf 3⁹f **2-2-14**
£8,310

Lord Of The East D Nicholls 74 a28
4 b g Emarati (USA) - Fairy Free
12⁶sd 12⁶sd 9⁶gf 14⁶g 4⁵gf 5⁶f 9⁵gf
11⁵gf 10⁵gf 1⁷gf 9⁷gf 16⁶f 10⁷g 13⁵g 5⁵gf
10⁷gf 2⁷gf **2-1-17 £9,750**

Lord Of The Sea (Ire) R F Johnson Houghton 46 a66
2 b c Perugino (USA) - Sea Mistress
13⁶gf 6⁶s 5⁷sd **0-0-3**

Lord Protector (Ire) E J Creighton 89
5 b g Nicolotte - Scared
1⁸sd 7⁸g **1-0-2 £2,338**

Lord Temuchin (Ire) M J Wallace 74 a66
3 ch g Desert Prince (Ire) - Lady Nash
5⁸sw 2¹⁰sd 4⁷sd 4¹⁰gf 2¹²gf 4¹¹gs
8¹²f **0-3-8 £2,087**

Lord Wishingwell (Ire) J S Wainwright 36
2 b g Lake Coniston (Ire) - Spirito Libro (USA)
12⁶gf 16⁶gf 13⁷gs **0-0-3**

Lordofenchantment (Ire) N Tinkler 58
6 ch g Soviet Lad (USA) - Sauvignon (Ire)
7⁸f 16⁷gf 6⁷f 4⁷gs 9⁷gf 7⁷s **0-1-6 £495**

Loreto Rose G A Butler a74
4 b f Lahib (USA) - Pinkie Rose (Fr)
4⁷sd 3¹⁰sd 5⁸sd **0-2-3 £834**

Lorien Hill (Ire) B W Hills 72 a60
2 b f Danehill (USA) - Lothlorien (USA)
7⁶gf 3⁷g 4⁷sd **0-1-3 £912**

Lost Spirit P W Hiatt 58 a36
7 b g Strolling Along (USA) - Shoag (USA)
6¹²sd 2¹²g 8¹²gf 9¹²g 11¹²g 7¹³gf 11¹²sd
10¹²g 4¹²gf 1¹²gf 4¹²gf 2¹²gf 5¹²gs 8¹²gf **1-2-14**
£5,647

Lots Of Love (USA) M Johnston 49
5 b g Woodman (USA) - Accountable Lady (USA)
5⁸ft 15⁹ft 15⁷g 14⁸gf 9⁸gs 16⁷gs 15⁸gs
0-0-7 £432

Lotto P J Makin 69
2 b f Nicolotte - Hope Chest
3⁵f 7⁶gf 1⁶f 3⁶f 8⁷gf 1⁵gf 13⁶gf **2-0-7**
£6,801

Lotus Eater S C Williams 9
4 gr f Linamix (Fr) - La Adrada
11¹²gf **0-0-1**

Lou's Wish R E Barr 22
6 b g Thatching - Shamaka
6¹¹gs **0-0-1**

Lough Bow (Ire) M W Easterby 47
5 b g Nicolotte - Gale Force Seven
11¹²gf 5¹²s 15¹²sd **0-0-3**

Loughlorien (Ire) K A Ryan 66 a49
4 b g Lake Coniston (Ire) - Fey Lady (Ire)
9⁵gf 10⁵gf 15⁶gf 19⁵gf 8⁶sd 4⁶gf 1⁵gf
14⁵gf 9⁵g 18⁵gf 4⁵f 5⁶s 15⁵gf 7⁶gf 7⁵gf 6⁶gs
1-0-16 £7,557

Louis Napoleon Mrs A J Perrett 79
3 b c Indian Ridge - Napoleon's Sister (Ire)
9⁸gf 11⁹g 11¹⁰s 19¹²g **0-0-4**

Louis Prima Miss L A Perratt 27
2 gr c Paris House - Chanson D'Amour (Ire)
6⁶g 7⁶gf 7⁵gf 12⁵f 7⁵g 14⁶gs **0-0-6**

Louisiade (Ire) T D Easterby 73
2 b c Tagula (Ire) - Titchwell Lass
6⁵hy 15⁵gf 2⁵gf 7⁶gf 10⁵g 7⁶gf 11⁶g **1-1-7**
£7,801

Love (Ire) R J Osborne 52
5 b g Royal Academy (USA) - Kentmere (Fr)
13¹⁰sd 1⁶sd 13⁵gf 21⁷g 9⁶g 15⁸g **1-0-6**
£4,032

Love Affairs (Ger) H Hiller a38
9 b h Konigsstuhl (Ger) - Lilac Dance
10⁸sd **0-0-1**

Love Connection (Ire) S J Mahon 68
3 b g Entrepreneur - Soha (USA)
14¹⁰g 8¹²ys 4¹⁰g 5¹⁰gf 4¹⁶gf 23¹⁶gy **0-0-6**
£662

Love Excelling (Fr) H R A Cecil a38
4 b f Polish Precedent (USA) - La Sky (Ire)
15¹⁰gs **0-0-1**

Love Games T D Easterby
2 b f Mind Games - Gymcrak Lovebird
10⁶gf 11⁷f 9⁷gs **0-0-3**

Love In Seattle (Ire) M Johnston 82
3 b c Seattle Slew (USA) - Tamise (USA)
4¹⁰g 2¹⁰gf 2¹²gf **0-1-3 £3,730**

Love In The Mist N P Littmoden a37
4 gr f Pursuit Of Love - Misty Goddess (Ire)
4⁹sd **0-0-1**

Love In The Mist (USA) *E A L Dunlop*　62
2 b f Silver Hawk (USA) - Fast Nellie (USA)
4^{6gf} 6^{7gf} 5^{6gf} 13^{7f} **0-0-4 £575**

Love On Request *T G McCourt*　44 a28
3 b f Revoque (Ire) - Search For Love (Fr)
10^{7gf} 9^{10gf} 4^{12sd} 6^{12sw} 5^{7y} 2^{13gy} 14^{9gf}
11^{12g} **0-1-8 £935**

Love Regardless (USA) *M Johnston*　106 a89
4 b c Storm Bird (Can) - Circus Toons (USA)
12^{8ft} 6^{8g} 6^{7s} **0-0-3 £1,980**

Love That Benny (USA) *J H M Gosden*　91
3 ch c Benny The Dip (USA) - Marie Loves Emma (USA)
3^{10gf} 1^{10gf} 10^{12gf} 11^{12gf} 15^{13gs} 12^{17g}
2-1-6 £8,077

Love Triangle (Ire) *D R C Elsworth*　81
2 ch g Titus Livius (Fr) - Kirsova
2^{5g} 3^{5gf} 5^{6gf} 3^{6gf} 2^{7gf} 1^{7ys} 4^{7gf} 6^{7gs}
7^{8gf} 9^{7gf} **1-3-10 £11,721**

Love's Design (Ire) *Miss S J Wilton*　a65
6 b/br g Pursuit Of Love - Cephista
8^{10sd} 6^{10sd} 4^{8sd} 9^{8sd} 3^{8sd} 3^{8sd} 5^{9sd}
8^{8sd} **1-2-9 £3,783**

Loved Up *W Jarvis*　a55
3 b f Bin Ajwaad (Ire) - To Love With Love
7^{6sd} 5^{6sd} **0-0-2**

Loveisdangerous *Don Enrico Incisa*　55
2 b f Pursuit Of Love - Brookhead Lady
5^{5gf} 5^{6gs} 4^{5gf} 2^{5g} 1^{5gf} 2^{5gf} 3^{6gf} 5^{5gf}
2^{5gf} 7^{6gf} 6^{6gf} **1-3-11 £6,182**

Lovellian *B R Millman*　51 a33
3 b f Machiavellian (USA) - Baby Loves
12^{8gf} 8^{10gf} 5^{10f} 4^{12sd} **0-0-4 £269**

Lovely You (Ire) *Miss D A McHale*　a55
3 b g Fayruz - Lovely Me (Ire)
14^{7sd} 13^{7gf} **0-0-2**

Lover's Mission (Fr) *Takashi Kodama*　69 a50
4 ch f Jeune Homme (USA) - Tokyo Girl (Fr)
11^{7sd} 8^{8g} 16^{7g} 8^{9gy} 15^{7ys} 3^{7g} 10^{7g} 2^{7gf}
11^{8f} **0-2-9 £2,038**

Loves Reward *T D Easterby*　28
3 ch c Pursuit Of Love - Love Returned
13^{7gf} 11^{6gf} 15^{6f} **0-0-3**

Loves Travelling (Ire) *L M Cumani*　78 a63
3 b g Blues Traveller (Ire) - Fast Love (Ire)
4^{8sd} 5^{8sd} 3^{10sd} 5^{9gf} 7^{10gf} 9^{10sd} 1^{12f}
1^{12gf} 2^{12gf} 3^{12f} **2-3-11 £9,405**

Low Cloud *A C Stewart*　85
3 b c Danehill (USA) - Raincloud
12^{7gf} 1^{8gf} 6^{8gs} 6^{10gf} 5^{8gf} 9^{10gf} **1-0-6
£6,201**

Lowe Go *J G Portman*　71 a52
3 b g First Trump - Hotel California (Ire)
8^{10g} 12^{12gf} 5^{13g} 8^{14g} PU^{12sd} 2^{12g} 7^{14sw}
0-1-7 £1,696

Loweswater (USA) *J H M Gosden*　102
4 b c Nureyev (USA) - River Empress (USA)
25^{8gf} 2^{10g} 11^{10gf} 2^{10gf} 1^{10gf} 4^{10g} **1-1-6
£19,077**

Loyal (Ger) *P Hughes*　70
3 b g Bluebird (USA) - La Luganese
4^{12gf} 11^{14gf} 3^{14gf} 6^{18gf} 14^{12y} 8^{12g}
7^{12gf} **0-1-8 £2,060**

Loyal Tycoon (Ire) *D Nicholls*　101 a98
5 br g Royal Abjar (USA) - Rosy Lydgate
1^{6sd} 1^{6sd} 3^{6sd} 2^{7sd} 1^{6sd} 14^{7sd} 5^{6sd} 21^{6g}

2^{6gf} 17^{6gf} 16^{7g} 6^{6gs} 26^{6gf} 3^{6gf} 1^{6g} 11^{6f} 5^{6gs}
8^{7gf} 11^{6g} 23^{7gf} **4-5-23
£63,919**

Lualua *T D Barron*　73
2 ch g Presidium - Tawny
1^{5g} 7^{5gf} 5^{5gf} **1-0-3 £4,046**

Lubinas (Ire) *F Jordan*　48
4 b g Grand Lodge (USA) - Liebesgirl
8^{12g} **0-0-1**

Lucayan Beauty (Ire) *M J Wallace*　80
2 b f Marju (Ire) - Koumiss
8^{5g} 2^{6gf} 5^{6gf} 2^{8g} 7^{6gf} 4^{7gf} 7^{8g} 3^{7gf}
1^{8gf} 4^{8gf} **1-4-12 £12,331**

Lucayan Dancer *J S Goldie*　72
3 b g Zieten (USA) - Tittle Tattle (Ire)
7^{8g} 9^{2gf} 11^{gf} 7^{10gf} 8^{8hy} 6^{10g} 7^{10gf} 7^{11gf}
7^{10g} 2^{11gf} 6^{9gf} 6^{10f} 4^{9gf} 9^{12gf} 3^{10gf} 3^{11gs} 4^{7gf}
0-4-17 £8,877

Lucayan Legacy (Ire) *D Nicholls*　43
4 b g Persian Bold - Catherinofaragon (USA)
17^{8gf} **0-0-1**

Lucayan Melody (Ire) *M Johnston*　58
3 b g Fayruz - Magic Melody
8^{6gf} 3^{7gf} 5^{6g} **0-1-3 £584**

Lucayan Monarch *P A Blockley*　80 a69
5 ch g Cadeaux Genereux - Flight Soundly (Ire)
3^{6gf} 1^{6sd} 8^{6gf} 3^{6gf} 3^{6gf} 6^{6gf} 13^{7gf} 9^{6gf}
11^{7sd} **1-3-9 £6,444**

Luceball (Ire) *K J Condon*　50
3 b f Bluebird (USA) - Mysterious Plans (Ire)
18^{6gs} 6^{6gf} 5^{6gf} 5^{5g} 6^{6g} 9^{6gf} 4^{6f} 8^{5gy}
7^{5f} 10^{8gy} **0-1-10 £285**

Lucefer (Ire) *G C H Chung*　52
5 b g Lycius (USA) - Maharani (USA)
11^{7f} 10^{7f} 5^{7gf} 10^{8gf} 4^{7gf} 3^{7gf} 4^{7g} 1^{8f}
2^{8gf} **1-4-9 £5,343**

Lucid Dreams (Ire) *M Wigham*　58 a62
4 b g Sri Pekan (USA) - Scenaria (Ire)
1^{7sd} 3^{7sd} 3^{7sd} 7^{7g} 6^{6sd} 8^{7sd} 2^{7gf} 5^{8gf}
8^{7f} 1^{7g} 2^{7gf} 4^{7gf} 9^{7gf} **2-5-13 £10,443**

Lucindi *C W Thornton*　72
3 b f Tamure (Ire) - Miss Petronella
5^{10gs} 2^{12gf} 4^{12gf} 3^{15g} 9^{16g} **0-1-5 £2,419**

Lucius Verrus (USA) *D Shaw*　47
3 b c Danzig (USA) - Magic Of Life (USA)
10^{9sd} 4^{5g} **0-0-2**

Lucky Archer *Ian Williams*　70
10 b g North Briton - Preobrajenska
7^{8g} 2^{9gf} 6^{8hd} 7^{10gf} 10^{10g} 12^{8gf} **0-1-6
£2,145**

Lucky Break (Ire) *C A Horgan*　a45
5 ch g Brief Truce (USA) - Paradise Forum
8^{10sd} **0-0-1**

Lucky Date (Ire) *M A Magnusson*　94
3 ch f Halling (USA) - Hesperia
2^{8gf} 7^{11gf} 7^{10gs} 5^{8g} 6^{12gf} 8^{9gf} **0-1-6
£8,320**

Lucky Heather (Ire) *R J Baker*　
6 b m Soviet Lad (USA) - Idrak
10^{15sd} **0-0-1**

Lucky Largo (Ire) *S Gollings*　74
3 b/br g Key Of Luck (USA) - Lingering Melody (Ire)
2^{7ys} 2^{8y} 2^{9ys} 7^{9ys} 2^{8s} 7^{8gf} **0-4-6
£5,844**

Lucky Leo *Ian Williams*　72

3 b g Muhtarram (USA) - Wrong Bride
3⁸ᵍ 10⁸ˢ 12¹⁰ᵍᶠ **0-1-3 £557**

Lucky Pipit *B W Hills* 101
2 b f Key Of Luck (USA) - Meadow Pipit (Can)
9⁷ᵍᶠ 1⁷ᵍᶠ 1⁷ᵍᶠ 12⁷ᵍᶠ 3⁸ᵍ **2-1-5 £25,177**

Lucky Romance *B J Meehan* 35 a32
4 b f Key Of Luck (USA) - In Love Again (Ire)
10⁶ˢᵈ 9⁶ᶠ **0-0-2**

Lucky Star *J Balding* 39 a42
6 b m Emarati (USA) - Child Star (Fr)
6⁶ˢᵈ 4⁵ˢᵈ 12⁶ˢᵈ 9⁷ˢᵈ 9⁶ˢᵈ 8⁶ᵍᶠ 8⁵ᵍᶠ 8⁵ᵍᶠ
2⁶ˢʷ 12⁵ᵍᶠ 9⁶ᶠ 5⁵ᵍᶠ **0-1-12 £1,085**

Lucky Story (USA) *M Johnston* 117
2 br c Kris S (USA) - Spring Flight (USA)
4⁶ᵍˢ 1⁶ᵍᶠ 1⁶ᵍˢ 1⁷ᵍˢ 1⁷ᵍ **4-0-5 £132,593**

Lucky Valentine *G L Moore* 50 a54
3 b f My Best Valentine - Vera's First (Ire)
9⁶ˢᵈ 3⁶ˢᵈ 3⁵ˢᵈ 10⁷ˢᵈ 3⁵ᶠ 8⁵ᶠ 7⁶ᵍᶠ 1⁶ᵍᶠ
10⁶ᵍᶠ 7⁶ᵍˢ **1-3-10 £3,957**

Lucretius *D K Ivory* 47 a50
4 b g Mind Games - Eastern Ember
9⁵ˢᵈ 6⁶ᵍ 9⁸ˢᵈ 18⁶ᵍᶠ **0-0-4**

Luferton Lane (Ire) *Don Enrico Incisa* 45
6 b m Ela-Mana-Mou - Saddle 'Er Up (Ire)
16¹⁶ᵍᶠ 7¹⁶ᵍˢ 9¹⁶ᶠ 12¹²ᶠ 5¹²ᶠ 11¹²ᵍᶠ 6¹⁴ᵍᶠ
8¹²ᵍᶠ 7¹⁶ᵍ 9¹⁶ᵍᶠ **0-0-10**

Luftikus (Ger) *A G Hobbs* a34
6 ch g Formidable (USA) - La Paz (Ger)
18¹²ᵍ 7¹²ˢᵈ **0-0-2**

Lugton (Ire) *J S Goldie* a38
3 b g Mujadil (USA) - Titchwell Lass
4⁷ˢᵈ 8⁶ˢᵈ **0-0-2 £256**

Luke After Me (Ire) *N Waggott* 67 a50
3 b g Victory Note (USA) - Summit Talk
6⁸ˢᵈ 4⁷ᵍᶠ 11⁶ᵍᶠ 7⁷ᵍᶠ 7⁷ᵍᶠ **0-1-5 £339**

Luke Sharp *K A Ryan* 18
2 gr g Muhtarram (USA) - Heaven-Liegh-Grey
16⁸ᵍ 11⁷ᵍ 12⁷ᵍᶠ **0-0-3**

Luna Tacumana (Ire) *R J Osborne* a29
3 b f Bahhare (USA) - Orange And Blue
6⁵ˢᵈ **0-0-1**

Lunar Colony (USA) *J H M Gosden* 74
3 b/br f A.P. Indy (USA) - Solar Colony (USA)
2¹⁰ᵍᶠ 1¹⁰ᵍᶠ 14¹⁴ˢ **1-1-3 £4,026**

Lunar Exit (Ire) *Lady Herries* 93
2 gr g Exit To Nowhere (USA) - Moon Magic
3⁸ᵍ 1⁸ᵍᶠ 5¹⁰ᵍˢ **1-1-3 £6,163**

Lunar Leader (Ire) *Mrs L Stubbs* 81 a63
3 b f Mujadil (USA) - Moon River (Fr)
7⁷ˢᵈ 6⁷ˢᵈ 4⁷ᵍᶠ 4⁷ᵍᶠ 15⁷ᵍᶠ 18⁸ᵍ 5⁸ˢᵈ 5¹⁰ˢᵈ
2⁸ᵍ 1⁸ᵍᶠ 4⁸ᵍᶠ 1⁹ᶠ 2⁸ᶠ 1⁹ˢ 2¹⁰ᵍᶠ 9⁹ᵍᶠ 9¹⁰ᵍ 7⁹ᵍ
3-4-18 £16,361

Lunar Leo *S C Williams* 99 a94
5 b g Muhtarram (USA) - Moon Mistress
7⁷ˢᵈ 3⁷ᵍᶠ 19⁷ᵍ 6⁷ᵍ 15⁷ᶠ 5⁷ᵍᶠ 4⁷ᶠ 10⁸ᵍᶠ
7⁶ᵍ 2⁶ᵍᶠ 6⁷ᵍ 6⁷ᵍᶠ **0-2-12 £9,502**

Lunar Lord *D Burchell* a50
7 b g Elmaamul (USA) - Cache
5¹²ˢᵈ **0-0-1**

Lunar Rainbow (Ire) *Sir Mark Prescott* a56
4 b f Spectrum (Ire) - Brilleaux
2⁸ˢᵈ 8⁹ˢᵈ **0-1-2 £1,054**

Lunar Wind *M G Quinlan* 78
2 gr g Piccolo - Faraway Moon
4⁵ᵍᶠ 1⁶ᵍᶠ 8⁶ᵍᶠ 4⁶ᶠ 2⁵ᵍᶠ 6⁵ᵍᶠ 8⁶ᵍᶠ 6⁵ᵍˢ

10⁶ᵍᶠ **1-1-9 £6,840**

Lundy's Lane (Ire) *C E Brittain* 110 a91
3 b c Darshaan - Lunda (Ire)
1⁸ˢᵈ 1¹⁰ˢᵈ 7¹⁰ᶠ 2⁸ᵍᶠ 19⁸ᵍ 3¹²ᵍᶠ 19¹²ᵍ
8¹⁰ᵍ 2¹¹ᵍᶠ 1⁹ᵍᶠ 3⁸ᵍᶠ 4⁹ᵍᶠ 6⁹ᵍᶠ **3-4-13**
£159,107

Lupine Howl *B A McMahon* 63 a21
2 b c Wolfhound (USA) - Classic Fan (USA)
7⁷ᵍᶠ 15⁶ᵍ 6⁶ᵍ 3⁶ˢ 7⁶ˢᵈ 6⁷ᵍᶠ 12⁶ᵍˢ **0-1-7**
£643

Luxi River (USA) *M Halford* 62
3 b g Diesis - Mariella (USA)
6⁸ᶠ 4¹²ᵍ **0-1-2 £259**

Luxor *W M Brisbourne* 50
6 ch g Grand Lodge (USA) - Escrime (USA)
12¹⁰ᵍˢ 11¹⁰ᵍᶠ 6¹⁰ᶠ 8¹⁰ᵍᶠ 9¹¹ᵍᶠ 6¹⁰ᵍᶠ
14¹⁰ᵍᶠ 7¹⁰ᵍᶠ 9⁹ᵍᶠ 13¹⁰ᵍᶠ **0-0-10**

Luxury Launch (USA) *B W Hills* 54
2 b f Seeking The Gold (USA) - Ocean Ridge (USA)
4⁷ᵍˢ **0-0-1 £399**

Ly's West *W G M Turner*
3 ch g The West (USA) - Lysithea
10⁶ᵍᶠ 8⁶ᵍᶠ **0-0-2**

Lyca Ballerina *B W Hills* 75
2 b f Marju (Ire) - Lovely Lyca
8⁵ᵍˢ 4⁶ᵍ 5⁶ᵍᶠ 6⁷ᵍ 4⁷ᵍ 6⁸ᵍᶠ 3⁸ᵍᶠ 4⁷ᵍᶠ
0-3-8 £2,673

Lycian (Ire) *Mrs Edwina Finn* 52 a61
8 b g Lycius (USA) - Perfect Time (Ire)
8¹⁰ˢᵈ 7¹⁰ˢᵈ 8¹²ˢᵈ 4¹²ˢʷ 6¹²ˢᵈ 4¹²ˢᵈ 9¹²ᵍᶠ
14¹²ᶠ 10¹¹ʸ 8¹⁴ᶠ **0-0-10**

Lyciat Sparkle (Ire) *R Ford* 39
5 b g Lycius (USA) - Benguiat (Fr)
12¹⁰ᵍᶠ 15¹⁰ᶠ 6⁸ᵍ 13¹¹ᵍᶠ 13⁷ᵍ 11⁸ᵍ 15⁸ᵍᶠ
0-0-7

Lydia's Look (Ire) *T J Etherington* 61 a37
6 b m Distant View (USA) - Mrs Croesus (USA)
10⁶ˢᵈ 4⁵ᵍᶠ 20⁵ᵍᶠ 7⁵ᵍᶠ 7⁵ᵍᶠ 5⁶ᵍˢ 7⁵ᵍᶠ 8⁶ᵍˢ
9⁵ᵍᶠ **0-0-9 £438**

Lygeton Lad *Miss Gay Kelleway* 84 a100
5 b g Shaamit (Ire) - Smartie Lee
4⁷ˢᵈ 1⁸ˢᵈ 5¹⁰ˢᵈ 1⁷ˢᵈ 4⁸ˢᵈ 4⁸ˢᵈ 1⁷ˢᵈ 3⁷ᵍ
4⁷ˢᵈ 9⁹ᵍ 9⁷ᵍᶠ 5⁸ᵍᶠ 5⁷ᵍ 2⁸ᵍᶠ 7⁸ᵍᶠ **3-2-15**
£31,545

Lyric Maestro *S Dow* 41
4 b g Merdon Melody - Dubitable
13¹¹ᵍᶠ 18¹²ᵍᶠ 13¹⁴ᵍˢ **0-0-3**

Lyric Soprano (Ire) *M Johnston* 54
3 ch f Entrepreneur - Lyric Theatre (USA)
8⁸ᵍᶠ **0-0-1**

Lyrical Girl (USA) *S Kirk* 68
2 b f Orpen (USA) - Lyric Theatre (USA)
9⁶ᵍ 2⁶ʰᵈ 22⁵ᵍᶠ 2⁵ᵍᶠ 3⁶ᶠ 10⁷ᵍᶠ 13⁶ᵍᶠ
0-2-7 £2,079

Lyrical Lady *Mrs A J Bowlby* 55
2 b f Merdon Melody - Gracious Imp (USA)
15⁶ᶠ 5⁶ᵍᶠ **0-0-2**

Lyrical Way *P R Chamings* 62 a61
4 b g Vettori (Ire) - Fortunate
8¹⁰ˢᵈ 6¹⁰ᶠ 7¹⁰ᵍᶠ 7¹⁰ᵍᶠ 8¹⁰ᵍ 14¹⁰ᵍᶠ
2¹⁰ᶠ **1-1-8 £5,018**

Lyringo *B J Llewellyn*
9 b m Rustingo - Lyricist
13¹⁶ˢᵈ **0-0-1**

Lysander's Quest (Ire) *L Montague Hall* 54 a51

5 br g King's Theatre (Ire) - Haramayda (Fr)
4¹³sd 5¹⁴g 6¹²gf 8¹⁶sd 5¹³g 10¹³gf 10¹²g
8¹²g 11¹²gf **0-0-9**

M For Magic *C W Fairhurst*   51
4 ch g First Trump - Celestine
19⁷gf 3⁶gf 14⁷gf 9⁷gf 5¹⁰gf 12¹⁰gf 4¹¹gf
5⁹gf **0-1-8 £770**

Ma Cherie *P W D'Arcy*   57 a45
3 b f Hernando (Fr) - Chere Amie (USA)
4¹⁰gf 8¹²gf 3¹²gf 16¹⁴g 4¹⁰g 6⁹sd **0-0-6**
£851

Ma Yahab *L M Cumani*   65
2 ch c Dr Fong (USA) - Bay Shade (USA)
13⁸gf 2⁸gf 10⁸gs **0-1-3 £1,332**

Ma'Soola *M R Channon*   80
2 b f Green Desert (USA) - First Waltz (Fr)
2⁵gf 5⁵gf **0-1-2 £3,555**

Maaloof *J L Dunlop*   77
2 b c A.P. Indy (USA) - Alabaq (USA)
3⁷gf 9⁷gf 2⁷gf **0-2-3 £2,335**

Mabel Riley (Ire) *M A Buckley*   65 a67
3 b f Revoque (Ire) - Mystic Dispute (Ire)
1⁷sd 2⁸sd 2⁸sd 9⁷sd 3⁸g 8⁸sd 8⁸gf 5⁷gf
5⁸f 6⁸f 11⁸gf 3⁷g 5⁹f 7⁵g 16⁷sd **1-4-15**
£6,189

Mac *M P Tregoning*   96
3 ch g Fleetwood (Ire) - Midnight Break
7⁸gf 6¹⁰gf 9¹²gf 1¹³gf 1¹³gf 5¹⁴gf 18¹⁴gf
2-0-7 £17,170

Mac Love *M R Channon*   100
2 b g Cape Cross (Ire) - My Lass
6⁵g 2⁵g 3⁵gf 1⁵gf 3⁵gs 6⁵gf 1⁵gf 1⁵gf
3⁶gf 3⁵gf 6⁵g 3⁵hy 2⁶gf 3⁶gf 2⁶gf **3-5-16**
£34,018

Mac The Knife (Ire) *R Hannon*   78
2 b c Daggers Drawn (USA) - Icefern
1⁵g 2⁵gf 4⁵g 3⁵g 4⁶gf 2⁶gs 15⁵gf **1-2-7**
£10,412

Mac's Elan *W A O'Gorman*
3 b c Darshaan - Elabella
9⁸g **0-0-1**

Mac's Talisman (Ire) *W A O'Gorman*   75 a80
3 ch c Hector Protector (USA) - Inherent Magic (Ire)
3⁶sw 8⁷sd 1⁷sd 2⁷sd 4⁶gf 10⁷gf 4⁷gf
3⁷gs 2⁶gf 8⁶gf 11⁷sd 3⁶sd **1-6-13 £8,930**

Macadamia (Ire) *J R Fanshawe*   113
4 b f Classic Cliche (Ire) - Cashew
2⁸gf 1⁸gf 1⁸gf 5¹⁰g 2⁸gf 11⁹gf **3-2-7**
£176,530

Macanillo (Ger) *Ian Williams*   a33
5 gr g Acatenango (Ger) - Midday Girl (Ger)
4⁷sw 13⁹sw 10⁸sd **0-0-3**

Macaroni Gold (Ire) *W Jarvis*   69 a63
3 b g Rock Hopper - Strike It Rich (Fr)
5¹⁰gf 7¹²gf 3¹⁰gs 11¹²sd **0-1-4 £577**

Macchiato *R F Johnson Houghton*   54
2 br f Inchinor - Tereyna
7⁹gs 14⁶gf 6⁸gf 7⁸gf 2¹⁰gf **0-1-5 £651**

Maceo (Ger) *Mrs M Reveley*   70
9 ch g Acatenango (Ger) - Metropolitan Star (USA)
6¹⁴gf **0-0-1**

Machinist (Ire) *Sir Michael Stoute*   87
3 br c Machiavellian (USA) - Athene (Ire)
7¹⁰gf 4⁷g 8⁸gf **0-1-3 £789**

Machiventa *M G Quinlan*   76

2 b f First Trump - Jomel Amou (Ire)
1⁷gf 2⁸gf 1⁷gf 12⁷gf 10⁸gf **2-0-5**
£6,942

Machrihanish *Miss L A Perratt*   46
3 b g Groom Dancer (USA) - Goodwood Lass (Ire)
6⁸gf 11⁹g 10⁹g LFT⁹gf **0-0-4**

Maclean *Sir Michael Stoute*   71
2 b c Machiavellian (USA) - Celtic Cross
2⁷gf **0-1-1 £1,792**

Macmillan *C J Mann*   67 a66
3 b g Machiavellian (USA) - Mill On The Floss
3¹⁰g 2¹²gf 3¹²gf 5¹⁶sd 7¹²sd **0-2-5**
£3,132

Macondo (Ire) *D Nicholls*
3 b c Dr Devious (Ire) - Dreaming Spires
16⁸f **0-0-1**

Mad Carew (USA) *G L Moore*   78 a78
4 ch g Rahy (USA) - Poppy Carew (Ire)
4¹⁰sd 1¹⁰sd 0¹⁰sd 11¹⁰sd 1⁸sd 6⁸sd 4⁹g
9¹⁰g 2⁸sd 8⁸gf 10¹⁰gf 12¹⁰f 4¹⁰g 3⁸f
2¹⁰gs **3-4-16 £13,837**

Mad Maurice *J Noseda*   54
2 ch c Grand Lodge (USA) - Amarella (Fr)
13⁶g **0-0-1**

Mad Mick Meeson *G B Balding*   64
3 b g Whittingham (Ire) - Meeson Times
4⁶gs 5⁷gs 8⁵g 5⁵gf 7⁶gf 4⁶gf **0-0-6 £434**

Madaar (USA) *P D Evans*   57 a49
4 b c Spinning World (USA) - Mur Taasha (USA)
10¹⁰sd 5⁷gf 12⁸gf 13⁸g 11¹⁰sd 6⁷gf 3⁸gf
3¹⁰gf 10⁸gf 8⁸gf 3⁸gf 7⁸f 3⁹gs 7¹¹gf **0-4-14**
£1,806

Madaeh (USA) *J L Dunlop*   95
2 b/br f Swain (Ire) - Tamgeed (USA)
3⁷g 1⁷gf 1⁷gf 5⁷gf **2-0-4 £13,530**

Madalyar (Ire) *Jonjo O'Neill*   79
4 b g Darshaan - Madaniyya (USA)
9¹⁰gf 13¹²gf 9¹²gf **0-0-3**

Madame Komet *Mrs S A Liddiard*
2 b f Komaite (USA) - Sky Fighter
13⁵gf **0-0-1**

Madame Marie (Ire) *S Dow*   58
3 b f Desert King (Ire) - Les Trois Lamas (Ire)
4¹⁰g 11⁸g 13⁷gf 10¹⁰gf 4¹¹gf **0-0-5 £703**

Madame Marjou (Ire) *M R Channon*   73
3 b f Marju (Ire) - Sudeley
4¹⁰gf 5¹⁰gf 9¹⁰gf 6⁸gs 6¹⁰gf 6¹¹gf **0-0-6**
£585

Madame Maxi *H S Howe*   70
9 ch m Ron's Victory (USA) - New Pastures
10⁷gf 2⁸gf 4⁸g 13⁸gf 16⁸gf 6⁷g 3⁸gf 8⁷gf
11⁸s **0-1-9 £1,245**

Madame Monica *Mrs K Walton*   22
3 ch f Paris House - Merry Molly
7⁶gf 11⁷sd 7⁷gf 13¹⁰gf **0-0-4**

Madame Roux *C Drew*   28
5 b m Rudimentary (USA) - Foreign Mistress
11⁵f 18⁶g 14⁵gf 12⁵gf **0-0-4**

Madamoiselle Jones *H S Howe*   72 a51
3 b f Emperor Jones (USA) - Tiriana
12⁶g 3⁸gf 16⁸gf 11⁹gf 3⁷gf 18⁸gf 3⁸gf
4⁸gf 18⁸g 9⁸gf **2-3-11 £10,965**

Maddie's A Jem *J R Jenkins*   78 a73
3 b f Emperor Jones (USA) - Royal Orchid (Ire)
10⁶gf 2⁵gf 2⁵g 16⁶gf 13⁶gf 2⁵s 13⁶gf 3⁶sd
4⁶sd 6⁶sd **1-4-10 £7,923**

Made In Japan (Jpn) *M A Magnusson*   87 a84
3 b g Barathea (Ire) - Darrery
8^{9g} 3^{10f} 15^{11gf} 3^{12f} 6^{12f} 5^{14s} 2^{12sd} 2^{12f}
6^{12sd} **0-4-9 £4,041**

Madeline Bassett (Ire) *G A Butler*   a66
5 b m Kahyasi - Impressive Lady
16^{12sd} **0-0-1**

Madhahir (Ire) *C A Dwyer*   67
3 b c Barathea (Ire) - Gharam (USA)
9^{8gf} 6^{10gf} 10^{12g} 15^{12gs} 4^{14gf} 15^{11gf} 6^{16g}
0-0-7 £305

Madiba *P Howling*   68 a68
4 b g Emperor Jones (USA) - Priluki
5^{16sd} 14^{14g} 10^{16gf} 8^{13g} 7^{13gf} 5^{12gf} 14^{12g}
4^{12sw} 7^{13sd} **0-0-9 £210**

Madies Pride (Ire) *J J Quinn*   56
5 b m Fayruz - June Lady
7^{5gs} 11^{5gf} **0-0-2**

Madison Avenue (Ger) *T M Jones*   52 a48
6 b g Mondrian (Ger) - Madly Noble (Ger)
12^{14g} 10^{16sd} **0-0-2**

Madrasee *L Montague Hall*   86 a75
5 b m Beveled (USA) - Pendona
2^{6sd} 2^{5sd} 9^{5sd} 7^{5sd} 8^{6sd} 3^{5gf} 9^{6gf} 11^{5gf}
5^{6gf} 11^{6gf} 2^{5gs} 3^{5gf} 1^{5f} 12^{6gf} 2^{5g} 1^{6f} **2-6-16**
£25,161

Maedance *G B Balding*   76
3 br f Groom Dancer (USA) - Maestrale
4^{8f} 8^{11g} 3^{12gf} 3^{12gf} 4^{12g} **0-2-5 £2,313**

Mafruz *R A Fahey*   77
4 ch g Hamas (Ire) - Braari (USA)
3^{8gf} 6^{8gs} 8^{8gs} 3^{7f} 6^{7f} 17^{8gf} **0-1-6**
£1,084

Maganda (Ire) *M A Jarvis*   82
2 b f Sadler's Wells (USA) - Minnie Habit
2^{8gf} 9^{8gs} **0-1-2 £1,030**

Magari *J G Given*   57
2 b f Royal Applause - Thatcher's Era (Ire)
3^{7g} **0-1-1 £316**

Magelta *R M H Cowell*   a52
6 b g Magic Ring (Ire) - Pounelta
12^{9sd} 4^{8sd} **0-0-2**

Magenta Rising (Ire) *D Burchell*   66 a83
3 ch f College Chapel - Fashion Queen
3^{8sd} 1^{8sd} 9^{10sd} 6^{9sd} 8^{7sd} 5^{8gf} 13^{7g} 10^{6gs}
13^{7gf} 2^{6gf} 11^{7sd} 11^{9sd} **1-0-12 £9,491**

Maggie's Pet *K Bell*   40 a58
6 b m Minshaanshu Amad (USA) - Run Fast For Gold
4^{11gf} 9^{11g} 8^{8sd} 8^{8sd} **0-1-4**

Maggies Choice (Ire) *N P Littmoden*   47 a55
2 b f Mujadil (USA) - Big Buyer (USA)
6^{5gf} 4^{7gf} 8^{7gf} 1^{7ft} 12^{7gf} 12^{7gf} 17^{7f}
1-0-7 £2,919

Maghanim *J L Dunlop*   95
3 b c Nashwan (USA) - Azdihaar (USA)
7^{8gf} **0-0-1**

Maghas (Ire) *J M Bradley*   a22
9 ch g Lahib (USA) - Rawaabe (USA)
11^{6sd} **0-0-1**

Magic Amigo *J R Jenkins*   66
2 ch g Zilzal (USA) - Emaline (Fr)
13^{6gf} 5^{7gf} 4^{6gf} 2^{6gf} 11^{7g} **0-1-5 £1,856**

Magic Amour *Ian Williams*   66
5 ch g Sanglamore (USA) - Rakli
3^{7gf} 12^{7gf} 2^{7gf} 7^{7gf} 1^{7gf} 18^{7gf} 2^{7f} 13^{8gf}

2^{8gf} 12^{8gs} **2-4-10 £17,716**

Magic Arrow (USA) *Ian Emmerson*   a26
7 b g Defensive Play (USA) - Magic Blue (USA)
7^{16sd} 8^{16sd} **0-0-2**

Magic Charm *A G Newcombe*   47 a37
5 b m Magic Ring (Ire) - Loch Clair (USA)
3^{9sd} 4^{9sw} 7^{9sd} 6^{12sw} 5^{12gf} 6^{10gf} 1^{12f} 1^{12f}
8^{12g} 5^{10gs} **2-1-10 £6,990**

Magic Flight *J G Given*
3 b f Lear Fan (USA) - Carpet Of Leaves (USA)
16^{10gf} **0-0-1**

Magic Hanne *G C H Chung*   a30
4 ch f Magic Ring (Ire) - Sunfleet
6^{7sd} 10^{9sw} **0-0-2**

Magic Mamma's Too *T D Barron*   63 a66
3 b g Magic Ring (Ire) - Valona Valley (Ire)
2^{7sd} 4^{7sw} 2^{6sd} 3^{8sw} 7^{6sd} 4^{6sd} 2^{8gf} 3^{8g}
7^{8gf} 2^{8gf} 16^{7gf} 6^{8gf} 4^{8gf} 11^{7gs} 3^{7f} 4^{8sd}
0-9-16 £6,837

Magic Mistress *S C Williams*   88
4 b f Magic Ring (Ire) - Sight'n Sound
7^{8gs} 4^{8gf} 1^{9gf} 4^{9gf} 1^{10gf} 5^{10gf} 5^{13gf} 2^{11s}
4^{12gf} **2-1-9 £25,804**

Magic Music (Ire) *Mrs H Dalton*   84
4 b f Magic Ring (Ire) - Chiming Melody
4^{6g} 2^{6g} 11^{6gs} 1^{6gf} 1^{6gf} 4^{6g} 9^{6gf} 2^{6gf}
2-3-8 £14,157

Magic Myth (Ire) *T D Easterby*   81
3 b f Revoque (Ire) - Family At War (USA)
4^{5gs} 8^{6s} 9^{5gs} 9^{6gf} 10^{6g} 5^{7gf} 5^{6g} 15^{7g}
0-1-8 £448

Magic Rainbow *M L W Bell*   57 a76
8 b g Magic Ring (Ire) - Blues Indigo
2^{7sd} 7^{6sw} 2^{6sd} 4^{7sd} 3^{6f} **0-2-5 £3,017**

Magic Red *M J Ryan*   41 a35
3 ch g Magic Ring (Ire) - Jacquelina (USA)
12^{10sd} 17^{12g} 11^{8g} 7^{8g} 8^{10gf} **0-0-5**

Magic Sting *M L W Bell*   55
2 ch c Magic Ring (Ire) - Ground Game
5^{7s} **0-0-1**

Magic Stone *A Charlton*   a43
3 br g Magic Ring (Ire) - Ridgewood Ruby (Ire)
8^{6sd} **0-0-1**

Magic Trick *Mrs P N Dutfield*   52
4 b g Magic Ring (Ire) - Les Amis
12^{7gf} 17^{7g} 13^{6gf} **0-0-3**

Magic Warrior *J C Fox*   61 a67
3 b g Magic Ring (Ire) - Clarista (USA)
5^{6g} 13^{8g} 9^{6sd} 5^{7sd} **0-0-4**

Magical Day *W G M Turner*   a35
4 ch f Halling (USA) - Ahla
8^{12sd} **0-0-1**

Magical Field *Mrs M Reveley*   56
5 ch m Deploy - Ash Glade
4^{14gf} 3^{16gf} **0-1-2 £925**

Magical Fool *N Wilson*   29 a31
4 b g Magic Ring (Ire) - Vera's First (Ire)
15^{8sw} 8^{6sd} 10^{7sd} 13^{5gf} 9^{7gf} 17^{8sd} 14^{10gf}
15^{7gf} **0-0-8**

Magical Mimi *N P Littmoden*   75
2 b f Magic Ring (Ire) - Naval Dispatch
5^{6f} 16^{6f} 3^{6gf} 10^{7gf} **1-1-4 £13,167**

Magical River *I A Wood*   26
6 ch m Lahib (USA) - Awtaar (USA)
6^{6hd} 11^{7g} 9^{6gf} **0-0-3**

Magically *C J Teague*
3 ch f Ali-Royal (Ire) - Meadmore Magic
10⁵ᵍᶠ 15⁵ᶠ 11⁵ᵍᶠ **0-0-3**

Magico *A M Balding* 59
2 ch c Magic Ring (Ire) - Silken Dalliance
9⁶ᵍᶠ 7⁵ᵍᶠ 21¹⁶ᵍᶠ **0-0-3**

Magistretti (USA) *N A Callaghan* 125
3 b c Diesis - Ms Strike Zone (USA)
1⁹ᵍᶠ 1¹⁰ᵍᶠ 9¹²ᵍ 2¹⁰ᵍˢ 2¹⁰ᵍᶠ **2-2-5**
£278,081

Magnetic Pole *Sir Michael Stoute* 74
2 b c Machiavellian (USA) - Clear Attraction (USA)
3⁸ᵍᶠ **0-1-1 £715**

Magnifico *Sir Michael Stoute* 58
4 b g Mark Of Esteem (Ire) - Blush Rambler (Ire)
17¹⁰ᶠ 7¹⁰ᵍᶠ **0-0-2**

Magritte (Ire) *A P O'Brien* 107
2 b c Sadler's Wells (USA) - Ionian Sea
1⁷ʰʸ 3⁸ᵍᶠ **1-0-2 £36,654**

Maharib (Ire) *D K Weld* 118
3 b c Alhaarth (Ire) - Diali (USA)
2⁷ʸˢ 2¹⁰ᵍ 1¹⁰ˢ 1¹²ᵍʸ 1¹⁴ᵍ 4¹⁵ᵍ 5¹²ᵍʸ **3-2-7**
£82,448

Mahasi (USA) *H R A Cecil* 89
3 ch c Woodman (USA) - Lingerie
4¹⁰ᵍᶠ 1¹⁰ᵍᶠ 4¹¹ᵍ **1-0-3 £6,783**

Mahmoom *M R Channon* 86
2 b c Dr Fong (USA) - Rohita (Ire)
2⁶ᵍᶠ 1⁶ᵍᶠ 1⁷ᵍᶠ **2-1-3 £14,493**

Mai Scene *G M Moore*
3 ch f Among Men (USA) - Scenicris (Ire)
16⁷ᵍᶠ **0-0-1**

Mai Tai (Ire) *R Hollinshead* 56 a65
8 b m Scenic - Oystons Propweekly
4⁸ˢʷ 3¹¹ˢᵈ 1¹¹ˢᵈ 4¹²ˢᵈ 3¹¹ˢᵈ 8¹²ˢʷ 1¹²ᵍᶠ
3¹⁴ᵍᶠ 3¹²ᵍᶠ 4¹⁶ᵍᶠ **2-4-10 £8,215**

Maid For A Monarch *J G Given* 32 a28
3 b f King's Signet (USA) - Regan (USA)
6¹²ˢᵈ 12¹⁰ᶠ 10¹²ᵍˢ **0-0-3**

Maid For Life (Ire) *M J Wallace* 63
3 b f Entrepreneur - Arandora Star (USA)
12¹⁰ᵍ 4⁸ᵍᶠ 6⁸ᵍᶠ **0-0-3**

Maid For The Aisle *J G Given* 57 a34
3 ch f College Chapel - Debutante Days
7⁸ᵍᶠ 6⁸ᵍ 10¹⁰ˢᵈ 6¹⁰ᵍᶠ **0-0-4**

Maid The Cut *A D Smith* 8
2 ch f Silver Wizard (USA) - Third Dam
16⁸ᵍˢ **0-0-1**

Maid To Treasure (Ire) *J L Dunlop* 70
2 b f Rainbow Quest (USA) - Maid For The Hills
2⁷ᵍˢ **0-1-1 £1,293**

Mail The Desert (Ire) *M R Channon* 111
3 b f Desert Prince (Ire) - Mail Boat
3⁸ᵍᶠ 2⁸ᵍ 10⁷ᵍˢ **0-2-3 £43,986**

Mainpower (Ire) *R M Flower* a55
3 b g Lake Coniston (Ire) - Chipewyas (Fr)
7⁸ˢᵈ **0-0-1**

Majestic (Ire) *Ian Williams* 60
8 b g Belmez (USA) - Noble Lily (USA)
7¹²ᵍᶠ **0-0-1**

Majestic Bay (Ire) *J A B Old* 46
7 b g Unfuwain (USA) - That'Ll Be The Day (Ire)
10¹⁶ᵍᶠ **0-0-1**

Majestic Desert *M R Channon* 109
2 b f Fraam - Calcutta Queen

1⁵ᵍᶠ 2⁶ᵍᶠ 3⁵ᵍᶠ 1⁶ᵍᶠ 2⁶ᵍᶠ **2-3-5**
£145,980

Majestic Horizon *Saeed Bin Suroor* 91
3 b c Marju (Ire) - Jumairah Sunset
1⁸ᵍᶠ 5⁸ᵍˢ **1-0-2 £5,837**

Majestic Missile (Ire) *W J Haggas* 118
2 b c Royal Applause - Tshusick
2⁵ᵍᶠ 1⁵ᵍᶠ 1⁵ᵍ 6⁶ᵍᶠ 1⁵ᵍᶠ **4-1-6**
£63,804

Majestic Swing *Miss L A Perratt* 31
3 ch g Wolfhound (USA) - Royal Girl
5⁷ᵍᶠ 4⁵ᵍᶠ 11⁶ᵍᶠ **0-0-3 £312**

Majestic Times (Ire) *T D Easterby* 88 a57
3 b g Bluebird (USA) - Simply Times (USA)
3⁶ᵍᶠ 9⁸ᵍᶠ 1⁶ᵍ 4⁶ᵍˢ 5⁶ᵍ 9⁶ᵍᶠ 7⁷ˢᵈ 7⁶ᵍᶠ
11⁶ᵍᶠ 6⁷ˢᵈ 8⁷ᵍ **1-2-11 £5,452**

Majestic Vision *P W Harris* 62
2 ch c Desert King (Ire) - Triste Oeil (USA)
3¹⁰ᵍᶠ **0-1-1 £438**

Majhool *G L Moore* 53 a82
4 b g Mark Of Esteem (Ire) - Be Peace (USA)
14⁵ᵍˢ 13⁷ˢᵈ 1⁷ˢᵈ **1-0-3 £2,171**

Majhud (Ire) *J L Dunlop* 93
3 b f Machiavellian (USA) - Winsa (USA)
4¹⁰ᵍᶠ 2¹²ᵍᶠ 1¹²ᵍˢ 10¹²ᵍᶠ 3¹²ᵍ 9¹¹ˢ **1-1-6**
£10,547

Majic Dust *J A Supple* a44
3 b g Wizard King - Fuchu
13⁷ˢᵈ 9⁷ˢᵈ **0-0-2**

Majik *D J S Ffrench Davis* 33 a67
4 ch g Pivotal - Revoke (USA)
16⁶ᵍᶠ 3⁶ˢᵈ 15⁶ᵍᶠ 12⁶ˢᵈ 7⁶ˢʷ 4⁷ˢʷ 2⁶ˢᵈ
0-2-7 £1,042

Majlis (Ire) *R M H Cowell* 73
6 b g Caerleon (USA) - Ploy
9¹²ᵍ 5¹²ᵍᶠ 7¹²ᵍᶠ 8¹²ᵍᶠ **0-0-4**

Major Attraction *W M Brisbourne* 62
8 gr g Major Jacko - My Friend Melody
4¹¹ᵍᶠ 3¹¹ᵍᶠ 2¹²ᶠ 1¹¹ᵍᶠ 2¹¹ᵍᶠ 6¹²ᵍᶠ 5¹³ᵍᶠ
5¹²ᵍᶠ 9¹²ᵍᶠ 5¹²ᵍ 11¹¹ᵍᶠ 9¹²ᶠ **1-3-12 £6,836**

Major Blade (Ger) *B G Powell* 65 a65
5 b g Dashing Blade - Misniniski
13¹⁰ˢᵈ 12¹⁰ˢᵈ 6¹⁰ᵍᶠ **0-0-3**

Major Danger *Sir Mark Prescott* 75 a51
2 b g Marju (Ire) - Threatening
8⁶ᵍᶠ 5⁷ᵍᶠ 3⁷ˢᵈ 2⁷ᵍᶠ 1⁷ᵍᶠ 2⁷ᵍᶠ 10⁸ᵍᶠ **1-3-7**
£7,128

Major Effort (USA) *Sir Michael Stoute* 82
2 b c Rahy (USA) - Tethkar
11⁷ᵍᶠ 5⁷ᵍᶠ 2⁷ᵍ **0-1-3 £1,288**

Major Project (Ire) *P C Haslam* a14
2 ch g General Monash (USA) - Mini Project (Ire)
11⁵ᵍᶠ 9⁸ˢᵈ 10⁸ˢᵈ **0-0-3**

Major Smile *M R Channon* 26
2 ch c Wolfhound (USA) - Session
9⁶ᶠ 14⁵ᵍᶠ **0-0-2**

Major Speculation (Ire) *G A Butler* 75 a68
3 b g Spectrum (Ire) - Pacific Grove
6⁷ᵍᶠ 6¹⁰ᵍ 12⁷ˢᵈ 13⁸ᵍᶠ **0-0-4**

Majorca *J H M Gosden* 66
2 b c Green Desert (USA) - Majmu (USA)
7⁶ᵍᶠ **0-0-1**

Majors Mistress *J C Fox* 39
4 b f Superpower - Polola
16¹⁰ᵍᶠ 15¹²ˢᵈ 11⁶ᵍ **0-0-3**

Makarim (Ire) *M R Bosley*   51 a67
7 ch g Generous (Ire) - Emmaline (USA)
3^{12sd} 3^{12sd} 6^{12sd} 14^{14gf} 4^{13f} 12^{14gf}
10^{12sd} **0-1-7 £1,205**

Make My Hay *J White*   49
4 b g Bluegrass Prince (Ire) - Shashi (Ire)
6^{12f} 4^{10gs} 3^{10gf} 3^{12gf} 3^{12g} 4^{11gf} 7^{13gf}
7^{12gf} **0-4-8 £2,146**

Makfool (Fr) *M R Channon*   98
2 b c Spectrum (Ire) - Abeyr
4^{7gf} 3^{7gf} 2^{7g} 3^{7g} 1^{7gs} 2^{8gf} 4^{7gf} 3^{8g}
1-4-8 £16,005

Makhlab (USA) *B W Hills*   108
3 b c Dixieland Band (USA) - Avasand (USA)
8^{7gf} 8^{8s} 1^{8gs} **1-0-3 £6,509**

Makila King *A M Balding*   87
2 b g Wizard King - Roonah Quay (Ire)
1^{5gf} 9^{6g} 7^{6g} 11^{6gf} **1-0-4 £11,874**

Making Waves (Ire) *Mrs G S Rees*   19
4 b f Danehill (USA) - Wavey
12^{7gs} 12^{11gf} **0-0-2**

Maktavish *I Semple*   85 a93
4 b c Makbul - La Belle Vie
1^{5sd} 10^{5sd} 14^{5g} 16^{5gf} 5^{5gs} 5^{5g} 9^{5g} 1^{5gs}
2-0-8 £8,923

Makulu (Ire) *B J Meehan*   82 a82
3 b g Alzao (USA) - Karinski (USA)
7^{10sd} 1^{10sd} 2^{10sd} 5^{10sd} 1^{10sd} 2^{10sd} 1^{10sd}
8^{10gf} 2^{12gf} 3^{12g} 5^{12gf} 16^{14g} **3-3-12 £16,300**

Malaah (Ire) *Julian Poulton*   17
7 gr g Pips Pride - Lingdale Lass
15^{7gf} 14^{6gf} 12^{6gf} **0-0-3**

Malahide Express (Ire) *M J Polglase*   67 a55
3 gr g Compton Place - Gracious Gretclo
14^{5g} 4^{6gf} 6^{6sd} 16^{5gf} 10^{5g} 11^{5g} 7^{7sd}
5^{5gs} **0-0-8 £280**

Malaica (Fr) *R Pritchard-Gordon*   98
2 gr f Roi Gironde (Ire) - Carmel (Fr)
1^{5s} 1^{6ho} 3^{6gf} 7^{6gs} 2^{8s} 11^{8ho} 4^{7g} 2^{7ho}
2-2-8 £31,932

Malak Al Moulouk (USA) *J M P Eustace*   65 a65
3 ch g King Of Kings (Ire) - Honor To Her (USA)
4^{8f} 2^{7sw} 5^{8sd} **0-1-3 £1,086**

Malapropism *M R Channon*   98
3 ch g Compton Place - Mrs Malaprop
9^{6gf} 14^{6gf} 9^{7gf} 6^{6gf} 1^{6f} 4^{5gf} 3^{6g} 3^{6g}
3^{5gf} 2^{5gf} 4^{5g} 3^{6f} 1^{5g} 11^{5s} 10^{6gf} 3^{5g} 14^{5gf}
11^{5gf} 1^{5gf} **3-6-19 £22,405**

Male-Ana-Mou (Ire) *Jamie Poulton*
10 ch g Ela-Mana-Mou - Glasson Lady (Ger)
13^{16sd} **0-0-1**

Maleyna *R F Johnson Houghton*   59
3 ch f Elmaamul (USA) - Tereyna
5^{8g} 6^{8g} 9^{7gf} 3^{10g} 4^{12gf} 9^{12f} **0-0-6**
£292

Malhub (USA) *J H M Gosden*   112
5 b/br h Kingmambo (USA) - Arjuzah (Ire)
7^{6f} **0-0-1**

Malin (Ire) *J L Dunlop*   96
2 b c Cape Cross (USA) - Just Lock (USA)
6^{7gf} 1^{8gf} 1^{8gf} **2-0-3 £8,666**

Mallard (Ire) *J G Given*   67 a81
5 b g Tagula (Ire) - Frill
6^{11sd} 6^{10sd} 2^{7sd} 2^{8sd} 8^{8sd} 6^{12sd} 1^{8sd} 17^{7g}
7^{7sd} 1^{7sd} 1^{7g} 14^{8gs} 1^{8sd} **5-2-13 £17,314**

Mallia *T D Barron*   52 a52
10 b g Statoblest - Pronetta (USA)
7^{6gf} 4^{6sd} 6^{27sd} 2^{7sd} 9^{7sd} 2^{6gf} 1^{6gf}
4^{6s} 14^{6gf} 6^{6gf} **1-3-11 £7,716**

Malling *R F Johnson Houghton*   41
2 ch c Halling (USA) - Queens Way (Fr)
11^{8gf} **0-0-1**

Malmand (USA) *R Brotherton*   35 a59
4 ch g Distant View (USA) - Bidski (USA)
6^{7sd} 9^{8sd} 3^{9sd} 1^{8sd} 6^{8sd} 5^{8sd} 17^{8gf} 8^{8sd}
5^{7sd} 11^{8gf} 10^{10g} 16^{7f} **1-1-12 £3,253**

Maltese Falcon *P F I Cole*   106
3 b c Mark Of Esteem (Ire) - Crime Ofthecentury
2^{6g} 3^{5g} 2^{5s} 5^{5gf} **0-3-4 £11,002**

Maluti *R Guest*   49
2 ch c Piccolo - Persian Blue
10^{6gf} 18^{7gf} 23^{6gf} 6^{5gf} **0-0-4**

Malvern Light *W J Haggas*   84
2 b f Zieten (USA) - Michelle Hicks
4^{6gf} 1^{6gs} **1-0-2 £3,227**

Mama Jaffa (Ire) *K R Burke*   59 a33
3 ch f In The Wings - Harir
3^{12hy} 3^{12gf} 12^{14g} 9^{14s} 5^{12sd} 5^{11gf} 1^{14gs}
2^{16gf} 4^{12gf} **1-2-9 £3,993**

Mambina (USA) *M R Channon*   70
2 ch f Kingmambo (USA) - Sonata
5^{7gs} **0-0-1**

Mamcazma *D Morris*   103
5 gr g Terimon - Merryhill Maid (Ire)
2^{12gf} 3^{14gf} 2^{14gf} 14^{16gs} 2^{14gf} 7^{12gf} 10^{14gf}
8^{12gf} 7^{12gf} 2^{15g} **0-5-10 £18,220**

Mameyuki *C E Brittain*   94
4 ch f Zafonic (USA) - Musetta (Ire)
6^{9gs} 4^{7g} 7^{8gf} 8^{8gf} 4^{7g} 3^{8g} **0-0-6**
£4,399

Mammas F-C (Ire) *J M Bradley*   50 a6
7 ch m Case Law - Wasaif (Ire)
15^{6gf} 12^{5gf} 14^{5sd} 15^{6gf} 17^{6gf} 8^{6f} 2^{5gf}
10^{5gf} 9^{6gf} 9^{6hd} 9^{5gf} **0-1-11 £928**

Mamool (Ire) *Saeed Bin Suroor*   124
4 b c In The Wings - Genovefa (USA)
1^{14g} 1^{14gf} 5^{20gf} 3^{13gf} 1^{12g} 1^{12s} 23^{16g}
4-0-7 £541,598

Mamore Gap (Ire) *R Hannon*   87
5 b h General Monash (USA) - Ravensdale Rose (Ire)
5^{8gf} 1^{7gf} 1^{9g} 8^{9g} 5^{9gf} 13^{10g} **2-0-6**
£7,462

Man At Arms (Ire) *R Hannon*   69
2 b c Daggers Drawn (USA) - Punta Gorda (Ire)
13^{6gf} 8^{7g} 11^{7gf} 3^{8gf} **0-1-4 £1,144**

Man Crazy (Ire) *R M Beckett*   73
2 b f Foxhound (USA) - Schonbein (Ire)
3^{5gf} 3^{6g} 4^{6gs} 2^{6gf} 2^{6gf} 3^{7gf} 3^{6gf} 2^{7f} 3^{6f}
11^{7g} **0-4-10 £7,266**

Man Eater *Thomas Cooper*   45 a38
3 gr f Mark Of Esteem (Ire) - Desert Delight (Ire)
6^{5sd} 9^{5gf} 7^{5gf} 15^{7g} 9^{6s} 19^{5gf} **0-0-6**

Man Of Letters (UAE) *M Johnston*   61
2 b c Belong To Me (USA) - Personal Business (USA)
5^{8gf} **0-0-1**

Man The Gate *P D Cundell*   72 a69
4 b g Elmaamul (USA) - Girl At The Gate
5^{12sd} 10^{8sd} 5^{10gf} 2^{12sd} 4^{10sd} 1^{12gf}
9^{12gf} 9^{12gf} DSQ^{12sd} 5^{9gf} **1-1-11 £5,563**

Mana D'Argent (Ire) *M Johnston*   98

6 b g Ela-Mana-Mou - Petite-D-Argent
10^{16gf} 6^{12gf} 9^{14gf} 6^{16gf} 6^{20gf} 15^{16gs} 1^{16gf}
4^{21gs} 3^{16gf} 3^{12gf} **1-2-10 £45,171**

Mana Pools (Ire) *J A Glover*   75 a73
4 b f Brief Truce (USA) - Pipers Pool (Ire)
7^{10sd} 1^{10sd} 6^{10sd} 3^{10gf} 2^{9gf} 9^{12f} 2^{12gs}
9^{12sd} 4^{10g} **1-3-9 £7,763**

Mana-Mou Bay (Ire) *B Ellison*   65
6 b g Ela-Mana-Mou - Summerhill
13^{10gs} **0-0-1**

Manaar (Ire) *J Noseda*   100 a82
3 b g Titus Livius (Fr) - Zurarah
3^{5sd} 1^{5gf} 2^{6gf} 2^{5f} 2^{6gf} 12^{5gf} **1-4-6**
£10,055

Manama Rose (Ire) *G A Butler*   102
3 ch f Kris - Top Table
11^{7gf} 3^{10gf} 6^{10gs} 2^{9gf} 2^{10gf} 1^{12g} 6^{12gf}
2^{16f} 7^{12gf} **1-2-9 £21,911**

Mananiyya (Ire) *Sir Michael Stoute*   97
3 ch f Ashkalani (Ire) - Madiriya
1^{8gf} 4^{10gf} **1-0-2 £7,186**

Manashin *B Smart*   25
3 b f Whittingham (Ire) - Montagne
9^{7gs} 10^{8gf} **0-0-2**

Manchester (Ire) *Miss A M Newton-Smith*
4 b g Danehill Dancer (Ire) - Lils Fairy
13^{10sd} **0-0-1**

Mandarin Spirit (Ire) *G C H Chung*   84 a68
3 b g Primo Dominie - Lithe Spirit (Ire)
5^{6sw} 6^{8sw} 4^{8f} 2^{7gf} 1^{7gf} 1^{8sd} 8^{7gf} 4^{7gf}
1^{7gf} 1^{7g} 9^{7gf} 7^{7g} 8^{7sd} **4-1-13 £15,389**

Mandinka *J F Coupland*   39
3 b g Distinctly North (USA) - Primo Panache
10^{10gs} 9^{9gf} 7^{10gf} 7^{10g} 5^{8gf} 7^{8gf} 7^{10gf}
0-0-7

Mandobi (Ire) *A C Stewart*   88
2 ch c Mark Of Esteem (Ire) - Miss Queen (USA)
3^{6gf} 2^{6gs} 1^{7gf} 2^{7gf} 8^{7gf} **1-3-5 £9,744**

Mandoob *B R Johnson*   a72
6 b g Zafonic (USA) - Thaidah (Can)
5^{13sd} 6^{12sd} 3^{12sd} **0-1-3 £323**

Mandown *J S Moore*   a47
4 b g Danehill Dancer (Ire) - Golden Decoy
6^{12sd} 5^{9sw} 7^{9sd} **0-0-3**

Mandy's Collection *A G Newcombe*   a28
4 ch f Forzando - Instinction
8^{6sd} 11^{7sw} **0-0-2**

Mane Frame *H Morrison*   a65
8 b g Unfuwain (USA) - Moviegoer
8^{16sd} 5^{16sd} **0-0-2**

Mango Mischief (Ire) *J L Dunlop*   82
2 ch f Desert King (Ire) - Eurolink Mischief
1^{7f} 10^{8gs} **1-0-2 £5,427**

Mangus (Ire) *K O Cunningham-Brown*   33 a48
9 b g Mac's Imp (USA) - Holly Bird
11^{5sd} 3^{5sw} 6^{5sw} 11^{5sd} 7^{5gf} 10^{5sd} 6^{5gf}
11^{5sd} 12^{6gf} **0-1-9 £418**

Manicani (Ire) *A M Balding*   a71
5 ch g Tagula (Ire) - Pluvia (USA)
10^{7sd} 4^{6sd} 7^{6sd} 6^{6sd} **0-0-4 £320**

Manikato (USA) *R Curtis*   45
9 b g Clever Trick (USA) - Pasampsi (USA)
5^{12f} 7^{10gf} 2^{10f} 16^{10f} 12^{8gf} 6^{10gf} 6^{12f}
10^{10f} **0-1-8 £952**

Manipulator (Ire) *Sir Mark Prescott*   83 a98

6 b c Danehill (USA) - Misallah (Ire)
5^{6gs} 1^{6gf} 1^{7sd} 5^{8gf} 3^{8g} 8^{8gf} **2-0-6**
£10,369

Mannora *P Howling*   62
3 b f Prince Sabo - Miss Bussell
5^{6gf} 4^{6gf} 1^{6gf} 17^{7gf} 7^{6gf} 4^{6gf} 3^{6gf} 15^{6gf}
1-1-8 £4,328

Manntab (USA) *D R Loder*   98 a78
2 b c Kingmambo (USA) - Saafeya (Ire)
2^{6gf} 1^{7sd} 4^{7gf} 6^{7gs} **1-1-4 £8,493**

Mannyman (Ire) *W Jarvis*
2 b/br f Dr Devious (Ire) - Lithe Spirit (Ire)
11^{6g} **0-0-1**

Manor From Heaven *P T Dalton*
5 ch m Most Welcome - Manor Adventure
13^{11sd} **0-0-1**

Manoubi *Sir Michael Stoute*   98
4 b g Doyoun - Manuetti (Ire)
3^{12gf} 3^{14gf} 1^{12gs} 4^{12g} 9^{12g} **1-3-5**
£17,926

Mansfield Park *D R Loder*   82
2 b f Green Desert (USA) - Park Appeal
2^{7gf} 1^{7gf} **1-1-2 £5,975**

Mantilla *Ian Williams*
6 b m Son Pardo - Well Tried (Ire)
11^{9sd} **0-0-1**

Mantles Pride *M Dods*   62
8 br g Petong - State Romance
14^{8gs} 16^{8gs} 6^{7gf} 6^{7g} 5^{7g} 7^{7gf} 4^{9gf} 7^{8gf}
6^{8gf} 4^{8gf} 5^{12f} 9^{9gs} **0-1-12 £288**

Manx Fizz *J Hetherton*   59
3 b f Efisio - Stica (Ire)
3^{8gf} 10^{7f} 16^{8gf} 5^{9gs} 12^{8gf} 1^{8gf} 3^{8gs}
5^{10f} 3^{9gf} 5^{8gf} 8^{9f} 5^{10gf} 7^{10gf} 5^{9gf} 15^{8gf} 6^{10gf}
1-3-16 £5,227

Manx Mini *A Berry*   32
3 b f Distinctly North (USA) - Octavia
8^{6f} 11^{9gf} 10^{11gf} **0-0-3**

Many Thanks *E A L Dunlop*   75
3 b f Octagonal (NZ) - Answered Prayer
2^{8gf} 4^{8g} 4^{10gf} 4^{8gf} **0-1-4 £2,298**

Manyana (Ire) *M P Tregoning*   84
2 b c Alzao (USA) - Sometime (Ire)
1^{7g} **1-0-1 £5,213**

Maraahel (Ire) *Sir Michael Stoute*   87
2 b c Alzao (USA) - Nasanice (Ire)
4^{7s} 1^{8gf} 4^{8gf} **1-0-3 £7,362**

Maraakeb (Fr) *J H M Gosden*   83
2 br c Linamix (Fr) - Raheefa (USA)
3^{7gs} **0-1-1 £637**

Marabar *D W Chapman*   88
5 b m Sri Pekan (USA) - Erbaya (Ire)
3^{6gf} 15^{6g} 12^{6gf} 2^{6g} 5^{6g} 5^{6gf} 10^{6g} 14^{7gf}
0-2-8 £2,587

Marabello *A M Balding*   61 a66
3 b g Robellino (USA) - Mara River
6^{7sd} 12^{9gf} 5^{8g} 4^{10sd} 10^{10g} 4^{12f} 11^{14g}
3^{12gf} **0-0-8 £883**

Marain (Ire) *Mrs P N Dutfield*
3 b f Marju (Ire) - Rainstone
13^{12g} **0-0-1**

Marakabei *R Guest*   102
5 ch m Hernando (Fr) - Kirsten
1^{14g} 6^{12gs} 3^{14gs} 12^{21gs} 8^{16g} 1^{14s} **2-1-6**
£17,133

Marakash (Ire) *M R Bosley*   50
4 b g Ashkalani (Ire) - Marilaya (Ire)
8^{8gf} 10^{8gf} **0-0-2**

Maravedi (Ire) *S L Keightley*   44 a47
3 ch f Hector Protector (USA) - Manuetti (Ire)
17^{8gf} 7^{10sd} 8^{12gf} 13^{12sd} **0-0-4**

Marble Arch *H Morrison*   93 a69
7 b g Rock Hopper - Mayfair Minx
1^{12sd} 8^{12gf} 9^{12gf} 3^{12gf} 9^{20gf} 4^{16gf} **1-1-6**
£6,377

Marble Garden (USA) *J R Fanshawe*   75
2 b/br g Royal Academy - Maria De La Luz
11^{7gf} 2^{7gf} 2^{7gf} 11^{7gf} **0-1-4 £2,649**

Marble Lodge (Ire) *H Morrison*   43 a23
3 ch f Grand Lodge (USA) - Marble Halls (Ire)
9^{8gf} 11^{10gf} 13^{12gf} 6^{9sw} **0-0-4**

March Alone *Mrs A J Perrett*   58 a64
4 b f Alzao (USA) - I Will Lead (USA)
3^{12sd} 3^{12sd} 2^{16sd} 6^{10g} 6^{13g} 7^{12gf} 11^{12gf}
9^{16gf} **0-3-8 £2,017**

March For Liberty *C A Dwyer*   53 a33
2 ch f Wolfhound (USA) - Badger Bay (Ire)
8^{5sd} 6^{5gf} 7^{5sd} 11^{7gf} 16^{gf} **1-0-5 £2,065**

Marching Band (USA) *J H M Gosden*   102
3 b c Dixieland Band (USA) - More Silver (USA)
2^{8gf} 4^{7gf} 8^{8vs} **0-1-3 £8,275**

Marcus Aurelius (Ire) *T D Barron*   74
4 b g Alzao (USA) - Kaguyahime
4^{5gf} 11^{5g} 13^{6f} 4^{5gs} **0-1-4 £846**

Marcus Eile (Ire) *K R Burke*   84
2 b c Daggers Drawn (USA) - Sherannda (USA)
2^{5gs} 1^{5f} 1^{5gf} 8^{6g} 4^{6f} 4^{7gf} 2^{7gf} 6^{8gf}
2-1-8 £11,592

Mardoof *M R Channon*   76
3 gr c Piccolo - Cumbrian Melody
5^{5gs} 5^{6gf} 12^{5gs} 8^{5gf} 10^{6gf} **0-0-5**

Mare Of Wetwang *J D Bethell*
5 b m River Falls - Kudos Blue
13^{12sw} **0-0-1**

Maren (USA) *A C Stewart*   80
2 b c Gulch (USA) - Fatina
3^{7gf} 1^{7gf} **1-1-2 £4,454**

Marengo *Paul Johnson*   53 a79
9 b g Never So Bold - Born To Dance
6^{8sw} 6^{8sd} 8^{7sw} 9^{8sw} 11^{12sw} 4^{8sd} 10^{8sd}
15^{8sd} 7^{8g} 11^{8f} 12^{8sd} 8^{8sd} 16^{7sd} 5^{10g} 11^{11gf}
8^{10g} 4^{10gf} 11^{9gf} 6^{11g} 10^{12sd} **0-1-20 £286**

Marfooq (USA) *E A L Dunlop*   83
3 ch c Diesis - Fabulous Fairy (USA)
7^{8g} 6^{7gf} 3^{8gf} 2^{8gf} 2^{10gf} **0-2-5 £3,995**

Margarets Wish *T Wall*   43
3 gr f Cloudings (Ire) - Gentle Gain
11^{7gf} 10^{11gf} 7^{8gf} 11^{10gf} 2^{10gf} 10^{11gf}
0-1-6 £593

Margarita Time (Ire) *R A Fahey*   35
3 ch f Grand Lodge (USA) - Brillantina (Fr)
8^{10gf} **0-0-1**

Margery Daw (Ire) *M P Tregoning*   58
3 b f Sri Pekan (USA) - Suyayeb (USA)
2^{8gf} **0-1-1 £633**

Marghub (Ire) *Miss D A McHale*   50 a38
4 b g Darshaan - Arctique Royale
4^{12sd} 5^{12g} 10^{12gf} 10^{16sd} **0-0-4 £286**

Margold (Ire) *R Hollinshead*   60
3 ch f Goldmark (USA) - Arcevia (Ire)

6^{10gf} 7^{10f} 3^{14gf} 3^{14f} 3^{12gf} 10^{14gf} **0-0-6**
£1,653

Margooba (Ire) *B Hanbury*   73
3 ch f Selkirk (USA) - Particular Friend
4^{7gf} 7^{7gf} 2^{6gf} 8^{7gf} **0-1-4 £1,767**

Maria Bonita (Ire) *R M Beckett*   62
2 b f Octagonal (NZ) - Nightitude
11^{7gf} 3^{8gf} **0-1-2 £640**

Maria Vetsera *Sir Mark Prescott*   43
2 ch f Selkirk (USA) - Scandalette
11^{6gf} **0-0-1**

Marie Laurencin *R Charlton*   70
3 b f Peintre Celebre (USA) - Glatisant
8^{10gf} 2^{12gf} **0-1-2 £1,692**

Marinas Charm *M Johnston*   95
3 b f Zafonic (USA) - Marina Park
4^{8ft} 4^{6ft} 9^{7ft} 2^{7g} 11^{7g} 1^{9gf} 1^{8g} 6^{9gf}
1^{10g} **3-1-10 £33,876**

Marine City (Jpn) *M A Jarvis*   27
2 b f Carnegie (Ire) - Marienbad (Fr)
17^{7gs} **0-0-1**

Marino Wood (Ire) *C N Kellett*   a20
4 ch f Woodpas (USA) - Forgren (Ire)
7^{8sd} **0-0-1**

Marita *J G Given*   22 a55
2 ch f Dancing Spree (USA) - Maria Cappuccini
4^{6sd} 10^{7gf} 2^{7ft} 11^{7gf} 5^{7sd} 8^{8sd} **0-1-6**
£1,122

Maritime Blues *J G Given*   78 a72
3 b g Fleetwood (Ire) - Dixie D'Oats
7^{10g} 6^{10sd} 1^{8sd} 2^{9sw} 5^{8gf} 1^{10f} 1^{10gf} 3^{10gf}
5^{12gf} 6^{10gf} 16^{10gf} **3-2-11 £12,551**

Marjurita (Ire) *N P Littmoden*   61 a83
4 b f Marju (Ire) - Unfuwaanah
1^{9sd} 1^{9sd} 4^{10sd} 14^{10sd} 12^{8gf} 8^{8gs} **2-0-6**
£8,201

Mark Of Zorro (Ire) *R Hannon*   88
3 b g Mark Of Esteem (Ire) - Sifaara (Ire)
10^{8gf} 10^{10gf} 8^{8g} 5^{8gf} 6^{8g} 3^{8gf} 6^{8g} 1^{10gf}
6^{10s} 1^{10gf} 6^{10gf} 8^{10gf} **2-0-12 £11,441**

Mark Your Way *P R Chamings*   55
3 b g Spectrum (Ire) - Titania's Way
6^{8gf} 8^{10gf} 10^{10gf} **0-0-3**

Mark-Antony (Ire) *A D Smith*   38 a16
9 ch g Phardante (Fr) - Judysway
6^{13gf} 6^{12f} 7^{15sd} 19^{12gf} **0-0-4**

Marker *G B Balding*   96
3 ch f Pivotal - Palace Street (USA)
11^{6gf} 4^{6gs} 14^{6g} 6^{6g} 16^{gf} 6^{5s} 10^{6g}
21^{7gf} **1-0-9 £11,546**

Market Avenue *R A Fahey*   77
4 b f Factual (USA) - The Lady Vanishes
9^{8g} 12^{8gf} 1^{10gf} 10^{9gs} 4^{10gf} 1^{9f} 5^{10g} 1^{10gf}
2^{10gf} 1^{10gf} $1^{9^{10g}}$ 3^{11gf} 6^{8gf} 10^{8gf} 15^{8f} 15^{11s}
13^{10gf} 6^{8g} **4-2-18 £24,974**

Market Hill (Ire) *S Kirk*   73
3 b f Danehill (USA) - Well Bought (Ire)
6^{8g} 4^{8gf} 3^{8g} 16^{gf} 18^{7gf} 12^{7gf} **1-1-6**
£6,674

Market Leader *Mrs A J Perrett*   66
2 b f Marju (Ire) - I Will Lead (USA)
5^{7gf} 11^{8gf} 2^{8g} **0-1-3 £1,213**

Marking Time (Ire) *K R Burke*   52 a53
5 b g Goldmark (USA) - Tamarsiya (USA)
6^{12sd} 3^{12sd} 11^{11sd} 6^{12sd} 3^{12gf} **1-2-5**

£3,856

Marksgold (Ire) *K Bell*   41
2 b c Goldmark (USA) - Lady Of Shalott
10⁶ᵍ 7⁸ˢʷ **0-0-2**

Marlo *B W Hills*   93 a93
4 b c Hector Protector (USA) - Tender Moment (Ire)
2⁸ˢᵈ 2⁷ᵍ 21⁷ᵍ 15⁸ᵍ 5⁸ʰʸ 9⁷ᵍ 21⁸ᵍˢ **0-2-7**
£4,356

Marnie *J Akehurst*   63 a51
6 ch m First Trump - Miss Aboyne
8⁷ˢᵈ 6⁷ˢᵈ 13⁸ᶠ 2⁸ᶠ 7⁸ᵍ 2⁸ʰᵈ 10⁸ᶠ 4⁸ᵍᶠ
7⁸ᶠ 11⁹ᵍ 15⁸ᵍᶠ **0-2-11 £3,594**

Maroma *A G Newcombe*   30
5 b m First Trump - Madurai
20¹²ᵍᶠ 9¹⁰ᵍᶠ 13⁸ᵍᶠ 9¹⁰ᵍᶠ **0-0-4**

Maromito (Ire) *C R Dore*   61 a39
6 b g Up And At 'Em - Amtico
14⁵ᵍᶠ 17⁶ᶠ 8⁵ᵍᶠ 8⁵ᵍᶠ 8⁵ˢᵈ **0-0-5**

Maron *A Berry*   a33
6 b g Puissance - Will Be Bold
11⁶ˢᵈ 12⁶ˢᵈ 12⁶ˢᵈ 11⁷ᵍᶠ **0-0-4**

Marooned (Ire) *J G Given*   1
3 ch f Definite Article - No Islands
17¹⁰ᵍᶠ **0-0-1**

Marrel *D Burchell*   a46
5 b g Shareef Dancer (USA) - Upper Caen
3¹⁵ˢᵈ 3¹²ˢᵈ 3¹⁶ˢᵈ **0-3-3 £1,263**

Marsad (Ire) *J Akehurst*   101
9 ch g Fayruz - Broad Haven (Ire)
17⁷ᵍ 4⁶ᵍᶠ 5⁶ᵍ 11⁶ᵍᶠ 5⁶ᵍᶠ 2⁶ᵍᶠ 7⁶ᵍᶠ 3⁷ᵍᶠ
0-3-8 £8,412

Marshal Bond *B Smart*   40 a62
5 b g Celtic Swing - Arminda
5¹²ˢᵈ 5¹¹ˢᵈ 14¹¹ˢᵈ 14¹⁰ᵍˢ 13¹²ᵍᶠ 11¹⁰ᵍᶠ
15¹⁰ᶠ 9¹¹ᵍ **0-0-8**

Marshall Warning *B De Haan*   47
3 b g Averti (Ire) - Spring Sunrise
8⁸ʰᵈ 10¹⁰ᶠ **0-0-2**

Marshallspark (Ire) *R A Fahey*   78
4 b g Fayruz - Lindas Delight
15⁷ᵍᶠ 13⁷ᶠ 2⁶ᵍᶠ 10⁶ᵍˢ 4⁷ᵍᶠ 1⁷ᶠ 3⁶ᵍᶠ 1⁷ᵍᶠ
6⁷ᵍ 7⁷ᵍᶠ 11⁷ᵍ **2-2-11 £9,025**

Marshman (Ire) *M H Tompkins*   96 a98
4 ch g College Chapel - Gold Fly (Ire)
2⁷ˢᵈ 6⁷ˢᵈ 8⁷ᵍ 4⁷ᵍ 8⁷ᵍ 1⁷ᵍᶠ 5⁷ᵍ 3⁷ᵍ
1-3-9 £14,875

Martaline *A Fabre*   116
4 gr c Linamix (Fr) - Coraline
1¹²ᵍ 3¹²ˢ 2¹²ᵍ 1¹⁴ᵍˢ 2¹²ᵍˢ 4¹²ᶠ **2-1-6**
£94,853

Martillo (Ger) *R Suerland*   118
3 b c Anabaa (USA) - Maltage (USA)
1⁸ˢ 1⁸ᵍ 3⁸ᵍᶠ 1⁸ᵍ 7⁸ᵍˢ **3-1-5 £156,323**

Martin House (Ire) *J D Bethell*   52
4 b g Mujadil (USA) - Dolcezza (Fr)
4¹¹ᵍᶠ 16¹⁰ᵍ 9¹⁰ᵍᶠ 17¹²ᵍᶠ 14¹⁰ᵍ 17¹⁰ᵍᶠ
0-0-6 £807

Martin's Sunset *W R Muir*   51 a42
5 ch g Royal Academy (USA) - Mainly Sunset
10¹²ˢᵈ 7¹⁴ᵍᶠ 9¹²ᵍᶠ 5¹²ᵍᶠ 8¹²ˢᵈ 7¹²ᵍ 1¹⁰ᶠ
3¹⁰ᶠ 6¹⁰ᵍ 4¹⁰ᵍᶠ 8¹¹ᵍᶠ 9⁸ᶠ **1-0-12 £4,027**

Marton Mere *A J Lockwood*   44
7 ch g Cadeaux Genereux - Hyatti
4¹⁰ᵍᶠ 10⁸ᵍᶠ **0-0-2 £270**

Marwell's Kris (Ire) *Andre Hermans*   a48

7 b g Kris - Marwell
6⁶ˢᵈ 8⁵ᵍ **0-0-2**

Mary Jane *N Tinkler*   67
8 br m Tina's Pet - Fair Attempt (Ire)
14⁶ᵍ 17⁵ᵍᶠ 9⁵ᵍᶠ 14⁵ᵍᶠ 4⁵ᵍˢ 2⁵ᵍᶠ 11⁵ᵍᶠ
3⁵ᵍᶠ 12⁵ᵍ 2⁵ᶠ 4⁵ᵍ 4⁵ᵍᶠ 1⁵ᵍᶠ **1-4-13 £10,992**

Mary Sea (Fr) *Mrs K Walton*   21
3 ch f Selkirk (USA) - Mary Astor (Fr)
5¹¹ᵍ 7¹²ᵍ 6⁹ᵍᶠ 9⁹ᵛˢ 10⁸ᵍ 11⁷ᶠ **0-0-6**
£584

Mary's Baby *Mrs A J Perrett*   76
3 b f Magic Ring (Ire) - Everdene
4⁷ᵍᶠ 13⁶ᵍᶠ 18⁹ᶠ 7⁸ᵍᶠ 2⁸ᵍᶠ 6⁸ᵍᶠ **1-1-6**
£6,253

Marysienka *R Hannon*   77
2 b f Primo Dominie - Polish Romance (USA)
4⁵ᵍ 3⁵ᵍˢ 6⁵ᶠ 2⁵ᵍᶠ 9⁶ᵍ 2⁵ᵍ 6⁵ᵍᶠ 4⁵ᵍ **0-2-8**
£3,843

Masaader (USA) *E A L Dunlop*   93
3 gr f Wild Again (USA) - Futuh (USA)
2⁶ᵍᶠ 6⁶ᵍᶠ 10⁵ᵍᶠ 3⁷ᵍ 1⁶ᵍ **1-2-5 £11,767**

Masafi (Ire) *Sir Mark Prescott*   a44
2 b c Desert King (Ire) - Mrs Fisher (Ire)
7⁶ˢᵈ 9⁶ˢᵈ **0-0-2**

Masjoor *N A Graham*   66
3 ch g Unfuwain (USA) - Mihnah (Ire)
10¹²ᵍᶠ 3¹⁰ᵍᶠ 14¹¹ᵍ **0-0-3 £1,067**

Masonry (Ire) *P F I Cole*   50
3 b g Grand Lodge (USA) - Tumble
5⁸ᵍᶠ 4⁷ᵍᶠ 7¹⁰ˢ 8⁷ᵍᶠ **0-0-4 £295**

Massey *T D Barron*   36 a104
7 br g Machiavellian (USA) - Massaraat (USA)
1⁶ˢᵈ 1⁶ˢʷ 2⁶ˢᵈ 13⁶ᵍᶠ **2-1-4 £20,950**

Massomah (USA) *D R Loder*   84
3 b f Seeking The Gold (USA) - Kerenza
2¹⁰ᵍᶠ 1⁸ᵍ **1-1-2 £5,453**

Master Corbin *P T Dalton*
4 b g Mind Games - Cafe Solo
13⁶ᵍᶠ **0-0-1**

Master David (USA) *B J Meehan*   87
2 ch c Grand Slam (USA) - Nadra (Ire)
2⁶ᵍᶠ 2⁷ᵍᶠ 1⁷ᶠ **1-2-3 £7,488**

Master Gatemaker *F P Murtagh*   24
5 b g Tragic Role (USA) - Girl At The Gate
12¹²ᵍᶠ **0-0-1**

Master Nimbus *J J Quinn*   55
3 b g Cloudings (Ire) - Miss Charlie
17⁶ᵍˢ 11⁷ᶠ 7⁶ᵍᶠ 9⁶ᵍᶠ 14⁶ᵍᶠ 15⁷ᵍˢ **0-0-6**

Master Papa (Ire) *N A Twiston-Davies*   68
4 br g Key Of Luck (USA) - Beguine (USA)
4¹²ᵍ **0-0-1 £509**

Master Peewee *J Cullinan*   42
2 ch c Cigar - Divine Miss-P
5⁵ᵍ 14⁷ˢᵈ 6⁶ᵍᶠ **0-0-3**

Master Rattle *Jane Southcombe*   41 a67
4 b g Sabrehill (USA) - Miss Primula
5⁵ˢᵈ 6⁶ˢᵈ 6⁶ˢᵈ 1⁷ˢᵈ 13⁷ˢᵈ 5⁷ˢᵈ 11⁸ˢᵈ
13⁷ˢᵈ 10⁷ᵍᶠ **1-0-9 £4,095**

Master Robbie *M R Channon*   99
4 b g Piccolo - Victoria's Secret (Ire)
15⁵ᵍ 2⁷ᵍᶠ 5⁷ᶠ 11⁹ᵍ 14⁷ᵍ 1⁷ᵍᶠ 2⁷ᵍᶠ 1⁷ᵍ
5⁷ᵍᶠ 2⁷ᵍᶠ 1⁷ᵍᶠ 22⁷ᶠ 5⁷ᵍ 1⁷ᵍᶠ 4⁷ᵍ 9⁷ᵍ 2⁷ᵍᶠ
2⁷ᵍᶠ 6⁷ᵍᶠ 14⁷ᵍᶠ
7-5-26 £99,064

Master T (USA) *G L Moore* 45 a70
4 b g Trempolino (USA) - Our Little C (USA)
4¹⁰sd 8¹²sd 14¹⁰sd 11¹¹gf **0-0-4**

Master Theo (USA) *H J Collingridge* 73 a75
2 b c Southern Halo (USA) - Lilian Bayliss (Ire)
3⁷gf 3⁸sd **0-2-2 £1,228**

Master Tommy (Ire) *B W Hills* a42
3 b c Entrepreneur - Dame Rose (Ire)
9⁷sd 8⁷sd 11⁷sd 12⁸sd **0-0-4**

Master Webb *Dr J R J Naylor* a37
3 b c Whittingham (Ire) - Jackies Webb
10⁶sd **0-0-1**

Masterman Ready *P W Harris* a53
2 b c Unfuwain (USA) - Maria Isabella (Fr)
6⁸sd **0-0-1**

Masterpoint *R T Phillips* 91
3 ch g Mark Of Esteem (Ire) - Baize
6⁸gs 2⁸g 11⁸gf 27⁸gf 12⁹gf 4¹⁰g 9¹⁰gf
1⁷gf 1⁸gf **2-1-9 £12,718**

Matabele *W J Musson* 32
3 ch g Muhtarram - Newala
13¹⁰gf 6⁹sd 10¹¹gf **0-0-3**

Material Witness (Ire) *W R Muir* 97
6 b g Barathea (Ire) - Dial Dream
2⁶g 14⁶gf 9⁷f 2⁶g 1⁶gf 22⁶g 8⁷gf **1-2-7
£13,892**

Mathmagician *R F Marvin* a42
4 ch g Hector Protector (USA) - Inherent Magic (Ire)
3¹¹sd 7⁸sd 7¹²sd 12¹²sd 4¹⁶sd 8¹⁵sw **0-1-6
£519**

Matloob *M A Jarvis* 105
2 b c Halling (USA) - Belle Argentine (Fr)
1⁶gf 1⁷gf 3⁷gs **2-1-3 £16,404**

Matriarchal *Don Enrico Incisa* 47
3 ch f Presidium - Mayor
10⁶g 8⁷gf 5⁵gf 12⁶gf 8⁶gf 12⁷gf 4⁶f
0-0-7 £275

Matt Blanc (Ire) *R Hannon* 92
2 b c Night Shift (USA) - New Tycoon (Ire)
4⁶g 8⁶y 1⁶gf 2⁶g 2⁶gf 1⁶g 5⁷g 4⁶gf **2-2-8
£17,480**

Matthew My Son (Ire) *F P Murtagh* 17
3 ch g Lake Coniston (Ire) - Mary Hinge
11⁶gf 15⁹gs **0-0-2**

Matty Tun *J Balding* 94 a75
4 b g Lugana Beach - B Grade
6⁵sw 5⁵g 3⁵g 1⁵gf 1⁵gf 12⁶gs 17⁶g **2-1-7
£48,093**

Maugwenna *J Noseda* 83
3 b f Danehill (USA) - River Abouali
4⁵gf 14⁶gf 15⁶gf 10⁵gf **0-0-4 £1,057**

Mauira (Ire) *G C Bravery* 62
2 b f Docksider (USA) - Easy Romance (USA)
9⁶gf 11⁷g 15⁶gf **0-0-3**

Maunby Raver *P C Haslam* 46
2 ch g Pivotal - Colleen Liath
11⁵gs 6⁷g 6⁵gf 4⁶f **0-1-4 £286**

Maunby Rocker *P C Haslam* 12 a63
3 ch g Sheikh Albadou - Bullion
7¹⁰sd 1¹⁰sw 2¹¹sw **1-1-4 £4,056**

Maunby Roller (Ire) *K A Morgan* 22 a59
4 b g Flying Spur (Aus) - Brown Foam
2⁸sw 1⁸sd 4⁹sd 8⁸sd 3⁸sd 11¹²gf 11⁹gf
1-2-7 £4,168

Maureen Ann *Miss B Sanders* 64

3 b f Elmaamul (USA) - Running Glimpse (Ire)
10¹⁰gf 5⁹g 12⁷gf 1⁷g 7⁹gf 12⁸sd 10⁸gs
1-0-7 £5,499

Mawaani *A C Stewart* 68
3 b f Indian Ridge - Ginger Tree (USA)
2⁸gf 5⁷gf 5⁸gf **0-1-3 £1,275**

Mawdsley *A Senior*
6 b m Piccolo - Legendary Dancer
9¹²sw 8¹²sd **0-0-2**

Mawhoob (USA) *Mrs N Macauley* 35 a43
5 gr g Dayjur (USA) - Asl (USA)
1¹²sd 8¹⁰g 8¹²sd 10⁸gf 16¹²sd **1-0-5
£2,905**

Max Scal (Ire) *Mrs A M O'Shea* 71
2 b c Danehill Dancer (Ire) - Slightly Latin
6⁶gf 2⁹g 6⁸f **0-1-3 £1,766**

Maxi's Princess (Ire) *P J Makin* 51 a42
2 b f Revoque (Ire) - Harmer (Ire)
8⁵gf 4⁶sd 9⁶gf 9⁵gs **0-0-4**

Maxilla (Ire) *L M Cumani* 74
3 b/br f Lahib - Lacinia
2⁸gf **0-1-1 £1,718**

Maxim (Ire) *W A O'Gorman* 57 a63
4 b g Zamindar (USA) - Lavanda
5⁵sd 14⁵gf **0-0-2**

Maximinus *M Madgwick* 8
3 b g The West (USA) - Candarela
11¹⁰gf **0-0-1**

Maybach *J Noseda* 67
2 gr c Machiavellian (USA) - Capote Line (USA)
4⁷gf 3⁷gf **0-0-2 £674**

Maybe A Lady *G C H Chung* 15 a29
2 b f Woodborough (USA) - Danseuse Davis (Fr)
8⁶g 12⁷gf 7⁷sd **0-0-3**

Maybe Baby (Ire) *D Carroll* a38
4 b g Lake Coniston (Ire) - Nadedge (Ire)
10⁶sw 8⁵sd 11⁶sd **0-0-3**

Maybe Someday *I A Wood* 57 a78
2 ch c Dr Fong (USA) - Shicklah (USA)
6⁵gf 7⁷f 2⁸sd 1⁷sd 3⁸gs **1-2-5 £3,078**

Maysie (Ire) *B G Powell* 41 a44
2 b f Imperial Ballet (Ire) - Mysticism
7⁶gf 11⁶gf 9⁷sd 5⁶gf 12⁷f **0-0-5**

Maystock *G A Butler* 66 a72
3 ch f Magic Ring (Ire) - Stockline
9⁸g 3¹⁰gf 5⁸gf 7¹⁰gf 3¹²sd 6¹²sd 8¹²s 4¹⁶sd
0-2-8 £1,021

Mayzin (Ire) *R M Flower* 45
3 b g Fayruz - Peep Of Day (USA)
6⁸sd 15⁸sd 19⁶gs 7⁷gf 10⁸f 12¹⁰gs **0-0-6**

Mazepa (Ire) *N A Callaghan* 102
3 b c Indian Ridge - Please Believe Me
10⁶gf 12⁶gf 9⁶gf 1⁶gf 13⁵gf 7⁶gf **1-0-6
£17,400**

Mazram *G P Kelly*
4 b f Muhtarram (USA) - Royal Mazi
16⁸f **0-0-1**

Mazuna (Ire) *C E Brittain* 60 a53
2 b f Cape Cross (Ire) - Keswa
9⁶gf 4⁷g 4⁷f 10⁷g 6⁶sd **0-0-5 £647**

Mbosi (USA) *M Johnston* 77
2 b c Kingmambo (USA) - April Starlight (USA)
1⁸gf 5⁸gf **1-0-2 £6,176**

Mcbain (USA) *R F Johnson Houghton* 91

4 br c Lear Fan (USA) - River City Moon (USA)
13^{12g} 12^{10g} 3^{10gf} 3^{10gf} 2^{10g} 2^{10gs} 2^{10gs}
8^{10g} 17^{10gf} **0-4-9 £11,995**

Mcgillycuddy Reeks (Ire) *Don Enrico Incisa*   63
12 b m Kefaah (USA) - Kilvarnet
10^{10s} 5^{10gf} 3^{12g} 4^{10g} 1^{12gf} 5^{12f} 8^{12gf}
7^{12gf} 7^{12gf} 5^{12gf} 6^{11gf} 10^{10g} 5^{12f} **1-2-13**
£4,889

Mcqueen (Ire) *Mrs H Dalton*   58 a73
3 ch g Barathea (Ire) - Bibliotheque (USA)
3^{10sd} 3^{10sd} 2^{12gf} 9^{12sd} 3^{10sd} **0-4-5**
£2,827

Meadaaf (Ire) *A C Stewart*   68
2 b c Swain (Ire) - Virgin Hawk (USA)
7^{7f} 4^{8gs} 5^{7gf} **0-0-3 £315**

Meadow *R Hannon*   69
2 b f Green Desert (USA) - Marl
6^{5gf} 4^{6gf} 4^{6f} **0-0-3**

Meadows Boy *R Lee*   35 a33
11 gr g Derrylin - What A Coup
4^{12sd} 6^{8f} 5^{12sd} 6^{16sd} **0-0-4 £269**

Measure Up *J M Bradley*   72
4 ch g Inchinor - Victoria Blue
13^{7gf} 7^{6gf} 9^{7gf} 6^{6g} 7^{6gf} **0-0-5**

Mecca's Mate *D W Barker*   13
2 gr f Paris House - Clancassie
9^{5gf} **0-0-1**

Medallist *B Ellison*   85 a75
4 b g Danehill (USA) - Obsessive (USA)
7^{8sd} 8^{11sd} 5^{10g} 3^{11gf} 19^{12g} 3^{10gf} 3^{10g}
12^{8f} **0-1-8 £3,577**

Medeena (Ire) *J L Dunlop*   101
3 b f Green Desert (USA) - Tanouma (USA)
1^{6gf} 6^{6gf} 13^{6gs} 9^{6gf} 10^{6gf} 9^{6gf} **1-0-6**
£8,971

Medkhan (Ire) *F Jordan*   42
6 ch g Lahib (USA) - Safayn (USA)
6^{16gf} 6^{15gf} 4^{17hd} 7^{13f} **0-0-4 £315**

Medusa *D Morris*   76
3 b f Emperor Jones (USA) - Diebiedale
2^{6gf} 3^{6gf} 11^{7g} 7^{6gf} **0-2-4 £2,748**

Meelup (Ire) *A G Newcombe*   69
3 ch g Night Shift (USA) - Centella (Ire)
12^{8gf} 12^{7g} 8^{6gf} 12^{7gf} 9^{8gf} 6^{8gf} 12^{7gs}
1^{7gf} 14^{7sd} **1-0-9 £4,182**

Megabond *B Smart*   66
2 b g Danehill Dancer (Ire) - Apple Peeler (Ire)
13^{5gf} 5^{6gf} 2^{5gf} 3^{6gf} 12^{7g} **0-2-5 £1,136**

Megan's Bay *R Charlton*   65
2 b f Muhtarram (USA) - Beacon
3^{6gf} **0-0-1 £828**

Megan's Magic *W Storey*   65
3 b f Blue Ocean (USA) - Hot Sunday Sport
6^{10g} 5^{9s} 5^{7f} 4^{7gf} 7^{12f} 2^{10gs} 3^{10gf} 4^{12gf}
8^{10gf} 1^{8f} 5^{10gf} 4^{7f} 2^{8g} **1-3-13 £10,669**

Megarole *B P J Baugh*   18
4 b g Tragic Role (USA) - Our Megan
14^{8gf} 15^{8gf} **0-0-2**

Mehmaas *R E Barr*   73
7 b g Distant Relative - Guest List
5^{8gf} 2^{8g} 13^{8gs} 14^{7gf} 5^{8gf} 15^{8gf} 9^{7f} 9^{7gf}
12^{8gf} 2^{8gf} 11^{8gf} 12^{7gf} 13^{7gf} 4^{8gf} 5^{7gf} 10^{8gf}
10^{8gf} 5^{7gs} 9^{8gs} **0-3-22 £3,918**

Meissen *C E Brittain*   67
2 ch f Amfortas (Ire) - Musetta (Ire)

6^{8f} 9^{7gf} **0-0-2**

Mejhar (Ire) *E J Creighton*   86
3 b c Desert Prince (Ire) - Factice (USA)
2^{9sd} 2^{8sd} 8^{7g} 4^{8sd} 6^{8sd} 1^{8sd} 11^{12sd} 3^{10g}
2-1-8 £12,792

Mekuria (Jpn) *M Johnston*   78
2 b f Carnegie (Ire) - Noble Air (Ire)
2^{8gf} 4^{8s} 1^{8gs} **1-0-3 £5,781**

Melaina *M S Saunders*   62
2 b f Whittingham (Ire) - Oh I Say
8^{5gf} 5^{5g} 4^{6gf} 6^{5f} 7^{5gf} 11^{7sd} **0-0-6 £321**

Melford Red (Ire) *R F Marvin*   28 a6
3 b g Sri Pekan - Sunflower (Ire)
7^{7sd} 15^{12gf} 5^{7sd} **0-0-3**

Melinda's Girl *A P Jarvis*   48
2 b f Intikhab (USA) - Polish Honour (USA)
8^{5gf} 6^{5g} 5^{7gf} 20^{7gf} **0-0-4**

Mellino *T D Easterby*   67
3 b f Robellino (USA) - Krista
3^{12f} 8^{12gf} 6^{10gs} 6^{8gs} 8^{7f} 2^{8g} 2^{8gf} 6^{8gf}
6^{8gf} 9^{8gs} **0-2-10 £3,223**

Melmott *C A Cyzer*   40 a54
3 ch g Piccolo - Time For Tea (Ire)
8^{8sd} 6^{10sd} 7^{7gf} 9^{8gf} 7^{6f} 10^{8f} 10^{7f} **0-0-7**

Melodian *M Brittain*   68
8 b h Grey Desire - Mere Melody
11^{8gf} 6^{10gs} 1^{10gs} 5^{10gs} 6^{10g} **1-0-5**
£2,713

Melody King *P D Evans*   65
2 b g Merdon Melody - Retaliator
6^{5gf} 2^{6gf} 7^{6gf} 3^{5gf} 1^{6gf} 4^{6gf} 7^{7g}
1-2-8 £6,232

Melody Master (Ire) *M J Ryan*   62 a70
3 b c Woodborough (USA) - Tabasco Jazz
7^{8sd} 1^{8sd} 9^{8sd} 7^{8sd} 4^{8sd} 14^{8g} 10^{7gf} 2^{8sd}
8^{8g} 3^{8gf} **1-2-10 £4,883**

Melody's Lass *J M Bradley*   33
3 b f Danzig Connection (USA) - Keen Melody (USA)
15^{6sd} 7^{8gf} 11^{6gf} 17^{6f} 17^{6gf} **0-0-5**

Melograno (Ire) *R M Beckett*   62 a51
3 ch g Hector Protector (USA) - Just A Treat (Ire)
5^{8sd} 7^{10gf} 8^{12g} 14^{11gf} 6^{10gf} 10^{12g} 3^{11g}
0-1-7 £392

Melusina (Ire) *Mrs A J Perrett*   48
3 b f Barathea (Ire) - Moon Masquerade (Ire)
8^{12g} 12^{14gf} 9^{19gf} 6^{14f} **0-0-4**

Membership (USA) *C E Brittain*   115 a104
3 ch c Belong To Me (USA) - Shamisen
1^{7sd} 2^{8sd} 3^{7g} 7^{7s} 6^{6gf} 2^{7gf} 1^{7gf} 13^{6gf}
7^{7g} 10^{7gf} 3^{7gf} 1^{7gf} 4^{7sd} **3-2-13 £126,730**

Menacing Rio *P C Haslam*   34
2 b g Timeless Times (USA) - Marfen
13^{5sd} 9^{6gs} 5^{7f} 8^{6gf} **0-0-4**

Menai Straights *R F Fisher*   64
2 ch g Alhaarth (Ire) - Kind Of Light
9^{7g} 5^{7g} 5^{8gf} 3^{8gf} **0-1-4 £666**

Meneef (USA) *M P Tregoning*   80
2 b c Kingmambo (USA) - Black Penny (USA)
4^{7gf} **0-0-1 £549**

Menfee (Ire) *E A L Dunlop*   88
2 gr c Linamix (Fr) - Wildwood Flower
8^{6gf} 3^{6gf} 1^{6gf} 5^{7g} 7^{7gf} 3^{7gf} 6^{8g} **1-1-7**
£6,948

Menhoubah (USA) *C E Brittain*   104

2 b f Dixieland Band (USA) - Private Seductress (USA)
1^{6gf} 4^{6gf} 4^{6g} 4^{7gf} 3^{7gf} 4^{8gf} **1-1-6**
£38,725

Menokee (USA) *Sir Michael Stoute*   93
2 b c Cherokee Run (USA) - Meniatarra (USA)
5^{7s} 1^{8g} 2^{8gf} **1-1-3 £11,262**

Mephisto (Ire) *L M Cumani*   89
4 b g Machiavellian (USA) - Cunning
3^{10gf} 2^{10gf} 1^{12g} 6^{13gs} **1-2-4 £8,304**

Mercenary (Ire) *A Berry*   a11
4 b g General Monash (USA) - Battle Rage (Ire)
14^{6sd} 8^{5sd} **0-0-2**

Mercurious (Ire) *J Mackie*   40 a45
3 ch f Grand Lodge (USA) - Rousinette
12^{10g} 6^{10gs} 3^{11sw} **0-1-3 £296**

Merdiff *W M Brisbourne*   68 a73
4 b g Machiavellian (USA) - Balwa (USA)
4^{11gf} 9^{12g} 7^{11gf} 10^{8f} 3^{9gf} 2^{8sd} 7^{8gs} **0-2-7**
£2,946

Merely A Monarch *I A Wood*   43 a59
4 b g Reprimand - Ruby Princess (Ire)
11^{7sw} 3^{8sd} 14^{8sd} 11^{7sw} 13^{8gf} 13^{8sd} 12^{8f}
0-1-7 £423

Merengue *T J Etherington*   3
3 b f Salse (USA) - Swing And Brave (Ire)
9^{8gf} 8^{9gs} 15^{12gf} **0-0-3**

Merlin's Dancer *W R Muir*   86
3 b g Magic Ring (Ire) - La Piaf (Fr)
4^{7g} 5^{6gf} 6^{6g} 2^{6gf} 9^{6gf} 1^{6gf} 8^{6g}
10^{6gf} 11^{6gf} 4^{5g} 12^{6gf} 18^{5gf} **2-1-13 £16,271**

Merlin's Gift *Bob Jones*   25
3 b g Wizard King - Formosanta (USA)
9^{5gf} 14^{7g} **0-0-2**

Merlins Pride *P D Evans*   34 a52
2 b f Wizard King - Longden Pride
2^{5sd} 5^{5sd} 5^{5f} 7^{5sd} 9^{5sd} 8^{6gf} **0-1-6 £672**

Merlins Profit *M Todhunter*   48
3 b g Wizard King - Quick Profit
15^{10gf} 9^{14gf} 12^{12gf} 3^{9gf} **0-0-4 £333**

Merrymaker *Sir Michael Stoute*   65
3 b g Machiavellian (USA) - Wild Pavane
9^{8g} 6^{10gf} 10^{10gf} 14^{10gf} 3^{12gf} 4^{14gf} 3^{14gf}
3^{12gf} **0-3-8 £1,955**

Merryvale Man *R Bastiman*   a35
6 b g Rudimentary (USA) - Salu
15^{12sw} 8^{11sd} 8^{11sd} 10^{16sd} **0-0-4**

Mersey Mirage *S J Magnier*   44
6 b g King's Signet (USA) - Kirriemuir
9^{7gf} **0-0-1**

Mersey Sound (Ire) *S Kirk*   75 a71
5 b g Ela-Mana-Mou - Coral Sound (Ire)
4^{10sd} 10^{12sd} 9^{13g} 7^{14gf} 1^{13gf} 3^{15gf} 2^{14gf}
2^{13gf} 4^{14gf} 7^{13gf} 3^{16gf} 2^{16gf} 1^{16gf} 10^{16gf} **2-5-14**
£22,702

Meshaheer (USA) *Saeed Bin Suroor*   110
4 b c Nureyev (USA) - Race The Wild Wind (USA)
7^{8ft} 2^{7vs} 4^{7gf} 1^{7gf} **1-1-4 £24,179**

Mesmeric (Ire) *E A L Dunlop*   106
5 b g Sadler's Wells (USA) - Mesmerize
2^{12g} 7^{14g} 2^{12gf} 6^{12g} 8^{12g} **0-2-5 £9,865**

Mesmerised *A Berry*   51 a57
3 b f Merdon Melody - Gracious Imp (USA)
12^{7sd} 12^{7sd} 8^{7sd} 13^{6gf} 4^{7gf} 2^{6sd} 14^{7gf}
9^{7gf} 7^{7gf} 13^{7s} 3^{7gf} 15^{6gf} 8^{7gf} 8^{7gf} 9^{7sd}
0-2-15 £1,347

Mesmerizing (Ire) *L M Cumani*   58
3 ch g Dr Devious (Ire) - Mesenzana (Ire)
7^{7gf} 10^{7gf} 5^{10gf} 16^{10f} 5^{8gf} **0-0-5**

Messe De Minuit (Ire) *R Charlton*   60
2 ch c Grand Lodge (USA) - Scrimshaw
3^{7gs} **0-1-1 £466**

Meticulous *M C Chapman*   6
5 gr g Eagle Eyed (USA) - Careful (Ire)
10^{5gf} **0-0-1**

Meticulous (USA) *Mrs A M Thorpe*   a43
5 b g Theatrical - Sha Tha (USA)
6^{11sd} **0-0-1**

Mexican (USA) *M D Hammond*   58
4 b c Pine Bluff (USA) - Cuando Quiere (USA)
17^{10g} 13^{8gf} 12^{10gf} 12^{8gf} 7^{9f} 5^{8gs} 16^{11gf}
9^{7gf} **0-0-8**

Mexican Pete *P W Hiatt*   84
3 b g Atraf - Eskimo Nel (Ire)
6^{10gf} 11^{11gf} 2^{12gf} 2^{11f} 4^{12gs} 2^{10f} 1^{11gf}
1^{12g} 8^{12gf} 3^{12gs} **3-5-10 £17,342**

Mezereon (USA) *D Carroll*   61 a61
3 b f Alzao (USA) - Blown-Over
5^{9gf} 19^{sd} 5^{12sd} 9^{10gs} 1^{9f} 8^{10gf} **2-0-6**
£7,066

Mezuzah *G Wragg*   92
3 b c Barathea (Ire) - Mezzogiorno
6^{8gf} 3^{8gf} 9^{12gf} 4^{10g} 11^{10g} 6^{10gf} **0-1-6**
£4,592

Mezzo Soprano (USA) *Saeed Bin Suroor*   118
3 b f Darshaan - Morn Of Song (USA)
1^{8ft} 14^{8gf} 2^{10gf} 3^{12gf} 3^{10gs} 1^{12gf} 1^{12gs}
10^{10f} **3-3-8 £173,755**

Mi Amor (Ire) *W J Haggas*   52
3 b f Alzao (USA) - Splicing
8^{7gf} 3^{7g} 15^{8s} 9^{8sd} **0-1-4 £586**

Mi Castano (Ire) *N P Littmoden*   43
4 ch g Fayruz - Tadasna (Ire)
10^{8sw} 10^{7gf} 13^{7gf} 17^{7gf} **0-0-4**

Mi Odds *Mrs N Macauley*   61 a83
7 b g Sure Blade (USA) - Vado Via
1^{12sw} 1^{12sw} 6^{12sd} 7^{12sd} 5^{11sd} 5^{10g} 7^{11gf}
12^{12sd} 2^{11sd} 4^{12sd} 1^{11g} 9^{17gf} 6^{10gf} 5^{11f} 8^{10gf}
1^{9sd} 2^{12sd} **5-2-17 £15,775**

Mi Sombrero *D K Ivory*   a50
4 ch f Factual (USA) - Rose Elegance
7^{8sw} 2^{7sw} 4^{7sd} 5^{7sd} 7^{7sd} 14^{7sw} **0-1-6**
£854

Mia Fool *G G Margarson*
4 ch f Cosmonaut - Young Annabel (USA)
16^{12sd} **0-0-1**

Mia's Reform *Ronald Thompson*   25 a60
4 b g Lugana Beach - Lady Caroline Lamb (Ire)
9^{6sw} 1^{5sd} 11^{5sd} 10^{5sw} 15^{5sd} 9^{6gf} 12^{5sd}
17^{5gf} 13^{5gf} **1-0-9 £2,891**

Miami Explorer *H Morrison*   44
3 b f Pennekamp (USA) - Elaine Tully (Ire)
6^{12f} 7^{9f} 8^{12f} **0-0-3**

Michabo (Ire) *D R C Elsworth*   19
2 b g Robellino (USA) - Mole Creek
7^{6g} **0-0-1**

Michaels Dream (Ire) *J Hetherton*   52 a63
4 b g Spectrum (Ire) - Stormswept (USA)
4^{12sd} 2^{11sd} 14^{12sd} 5^{12sd} 18^{12g} 14^{12gf}
14^{12gf} 7^{12gf} 10^{14gf} 7^{14gf} 3^{12f} 7^{14gf} 11^{14gf} **0-2-13**
£1,659

Michelle Ma Belle (Ire) *S Kirk* 86
3 b f Shareef Dancer (USA) - April Magic
6⁶ᵍˢ 11⁷ᵍ 7⁶ᵍᶠ 7⁶ᵍᶠ 3⁶ᵍᶠ 3⁷ᵍᶠ 3⁶ᵍᶠ 3⁷ᵍ
6⁶ᵍᶠ 5⁹ᵍ 5⁸ᵍᶠ **0-4-11 £3,784**

Mickledor (Fr) *M Dods* 53
3 ch f Lake Coniston (Ire) - Shamasiya (Fr)
11⁶ᵍᶠ 13⁸ᵍᶠ 6⁶ᵍᶠ 10⁸ˢ 11⁷ᵍᶠ 3⁶ᶠ 4⁷ᵍᶠ
0-1-7 £580

Micklegate *J D Bethell* 63
2 b f Dracula (Aus) - Primulette
10⁵ᵍᶠ 6⁶ᵍᶠ 4⁶ᵍ 4⁷ᵍᶠ 3⁷ᵍˢ **0-1-5 £1,151**

Mickleham Magic *Michael Hourigan*
3 b f Shareef Dancer (USA) - Princess Lily
11¹⁰ˢᵈ **0-0-1**

Mickley (Ire) *P R Hedger* a75
6 b g Ezzoud (Ire) - Dawsha (Ire)
6¹²ˢᵈ 7¹²ˢᵈ **0-0-2**

Micklow Magic *C Grant* 15
5 b m Farfelu - Scotto's Regret
12⁷ᵍᶠ **0-0-1**

Micky Thin *R Hannon* 63
2 br c Prince Sabo - Walsham Witch
4⁵ᵍᶠ 1⁵ᶠ 6⁶ᵍˢ 4⁷ᵍᶠ 6⁷ᵍ 5⁷ᵍᶠ 13⁸ᵍᶠ **1-0-7
£4,948**

Midas Way *R Charlton* 103
3 ch g Halling (USA) - Arietta's Way (Ire)
6¹²ᵍᶠ 1¹²ᵍᶠ 6¹⁵ᵍᶠ 4¹⁴ᵍ 2¹⁴ᵍᶠ 11¹⁵ᵍ **1-2-6
£25,149**

Middleham Park (Ire) *P C Haslam* 66
3 b g Revoque (Ire) - Snap Crackle Pop (Ire)
3⁸ᵍᶠ 2⁷ᵍᶠ 7⁶ᵍᶠ 14⁸ᵍᶠ **0-2-4 £1,972**

Middleham Rose *P C Haslam* 33
2 b f Dr Fong (USA) - Shallop
8⁷ᵍᶠ 15⁸ᵍᶠ 8⁷ᶠ **0-0-3**

Middlemarch (Ire) *J S Goldie* 113
3 ch c Grand Lodge (USA) - Blanche Dubois
1⁸ᵍ 3²ᵍᶠ 3⁸ᵍᶠ 2¹⁰ᵍᶠ 5¹⁰ʰᵒ 9¹⁰ᵍᶠ 1⁸ᵍ 6¹²ᵍ
2-2-8 £35,730

Middlemiss (Ire) *J W Mullins* 35
3 b f Midhish - Teresa Deevey
5⁸ᶠ 5¹⁰ᵍᶠ 5¹²ᵍᶠ 4¹⁰ᶠ **0-0-4 £337**

Middlethorpe *M W Easterby* 73
6 b g Noble Patriarch - Prime Property (Ire)
3¹²ᵍᶠ 3¹²ᵍᶠ 7¹⁴ᵍᶠ 10¹²ˢ 5¹³ᵍˢ 5¹⁴ᵍˢ **0-2-6
£1,216**

Middleton Grey *A G Newcombe* 74 a99
5 gr g Ashkalani (Ire) - Petula
1⁷ˢᵈ 2⁶ˢᵈ 4⁷ˢᵈ 7⁸ˢʷ 3⁶ˢᵈ 2⁷ˢᵈ 5⁸ˢʷ 2⁷ˢᵈ
13⁷ˢᵈ 3⁷ᵍ 6⁷ᵍᶠ 10⁷ᵍ **1-6-12 £16,334**

Midges Pride *Mrs A Duffield* 51 a51
3 b g Puissance - It's All Academic (Ire)
12⁶ˢʷ 3⁵ˢᵈ 4⁶ˢᵈ 4⁸ˢᵈ 4⁶ᵍᶠ 10⁷ᵍᶠ 11⁶ᵍᶠ
7⁷ˢʷ **0-1-8 £969**

Midnight Ballard (USA) *R F Johnson Houghton* 80
2 b/br c Mister Baileys - Shadow Music (USA)
5⁶ᵍᶠ 3⁷ᵍᶠ 6⁷ᵍˢ **0-1-3 £968**

Midnight Chief *A P Jarvis* 57 a59
3 b g Bluegrass Prince (Ire) - Midnight Romance
5⁹ˢᵈ 4⁸ˢᵈ 7⁷ˢᵈ 10⁸ˢᵈ 11⁷ˢᵈ 7¹⁰ᶠ 5⁷ᵍ 16⁸ᵍ
0-0-8 £260

Midnight Coup *B G Powell* 20 a30
7 br g First Trump - Anhaar
14¹⁶ˢᵈ 7¹⁶ˢᵈ 8¹⁵ˢᵈ 8¹²ᵍᶠ 9¹⁶ᵍᶠ **0-0-5**

Midnight Creek *Miss V Scott* 54
5 br g Tragic Role (USA) - Greek Night Out (Ire)

10¹⁷ᵍᶠ **0-0-1**

Midnight Parkes *E J Alston* 80
4 br g Polar Falcon (USA) - Summerhill Spruce
5⁶ᵍᶠ 17⁶ᵍ 10⁵ᵍˢ 3⁵ᵍᶠ 12⁶ᵍᶠ 4⁶ᵍᶠ 5⁵ᵍ
10⁵ᵍᶠ 18⁷ᵍᶠ **0-2-9 £2,070**

Midnight Prince *M W Easterby* 64
2 b c Dracula (Aus) - Phylian
12⁵ᵍᶠ 4⁵ᵍᶠ 12⁶ᵍᶠ 9⁷ᵍ 14⁶ᶠ 6⁷ᵍᶠ **0-0-6
£293**

Midnight Song (USA) *E A L Dunlop* 78
3 ch g Hennessy (USA) - Gratify (USA)
11⁷ᵍ 2¹⁰ᵍᶠ 2¹⁰ᵍᶠ 5¹²ᶠ 3¹⁰ᵍ **0-2-5 £5,702**

Midnight Special (Ire) *D Carroll* 78 a51
3 b f Danetime (Ire) - Daffodil Dale (Ire)
8⁵ˢᵈ 1⁵ᶠ 12⁵ᵍᶠ 10⁵ᵍᶠ 10⁵ᵍ 10⁵ᵍˢ 8⁵ᵍᶠ
11⁵ᵍᶠ **1-0-8 £10,036**

Midshipman *M J Wallace* a93
5 b h Executive Man - Midler
11⁸ˢᵈ **0-0-1**

Midshipman Easy (USA) *P W Harris* 45
2 ch g Irish River (Fr) - Winger
8⁸ᵍᶠ **0-0-1**

Midsummer *H R A Cecil* 101
3 ch f Kingmambo (USA) - Modena (USA)
1¹¹ᵍᶠ 2¹²ᵍᶠ 4¹⁰ᵍᶠ **1-1-3 £18,210**

Midy's Risk (Fr) *Mrs N Smith* a33
6 gr g Take Risks (Fr) - Martine Midy (Fr)
9¹³ˢᵈ **0-0-1**

Mighty Pip (Ire) *M R Bosley* 56
7 b g Pips Pride - Hard To Stop
9¹⁰ᵍᶠ 8¹⁰ᶠ 2¹⁰ᵍᶠ 7¹²ᵍᶠ 11⁰ᶠ 8¹⁰ᶠ 2¹¹ᵍᶠ
7¹¹ᵍᶠ 12¹⁰ᵍᶠ **1-2-9 £4,784**

Migration *M Pitman* a44
7 b g Rainbow Quest (USA) - Armeria (USA)
4¹²ˢʷ **0-0-1**

Mikasa (Ire) *R F Fisher* 51
3 b g Victory Note (USA) - Resiusa (Ity)
15⁷ᵍˢ 12⁷ᵍᶠ 6⁶ᵍᶠ 9⁷ᵍᶠ 8⁶ᵍᶠ 16⁵ˢᵈ **0-0-6**

Mikati Maid *A P Jarvis* 45
2 ch f Piccolo - Dame Helene (USA)
8⁶ᵍᶠ 2⁶ᵍᶠ **0-1-2 £670**

Militaire (Fr) *M D Hammond* 55
5 ch g Bering - Moon Review (USA)
13¹⁰ᵍᶠ 20⁸ᵍᶠ **0-0-2**

Military Two Step (Ire) *K R Burke* 66 a42
2 b c General Monash (USA) - Con Dancer
4⁵ᵍˢ 2⁶ᵍˢ 3⁶ᵍᶠ 5⁸ˢʷ 12⁶ᵍ 7⁶ᵍˢ 2⁷ᵍˢ **0-2-7
£3,193**

Milk And Sultana *W M Brisbourne* 67 a73
3 b f Millkom - Premier Princess
1⁷ˢᵈ 3⁸ˢᵈ 8¹⁰ᵍᶠ 13⁸ᵍᶠ 9⁷ˢʷ 8⁸ᵍᶠ **1-0-6
£4,152**

Milk It Mick *J A Osborne* 118
2 b c Millkom - Lunar Music
5⁵ᵍᶠ 1⁵ᵍᶠ 16⁶ᶠ 3⁷ᵍᶠ 1⁶ᶠ 4⁶ᵍᶠ 3⁷ᵍᶠ
2⁷ᵍˢ 5⁷ᵍ 17ᵍᶠ 1⁷ᵍᶠ **5-3-12 £214,565**

Mill Byre (Ire) *T G Mills* 75
3 b c Definite Article - Mummys Best
4¹⁰ᵍ 5¹⁰ᵍ 10⁸ᵍᶠ **0-0-3 £347**

Mill End Teaser *M W Easterby* 39 a25
2 b f Mind Games - Mill End Quest
8⁵ᵍᶠ 9⁵ᶠ 7⁵ᵍ 6⁵ᵍ 7⁵ᵍᶠ 8⁵ˢʷ 8⁵ᵍᶠ **0-0-7**

Millafonic *L M Cumani* 97
3 b c Zafonic (USA) - Milligram
3⁸ᵍᶠ 1⁸ᵍᶠ 1⁸ᵍˢ 5⁸ᵍ 22⁹ᵍᶠ **2-1-5 £14,852**

Millagros (Ire) *I Semple* 87
3 b f Pennekamp (USA) - Grey Galava
2⁹ᵍᶠ 8¹¹ᵍˢ 2⁹ᵍˢ 5⁹ᵍˢ 7⁸ᵍᶠ 1⁹ᶠ 4⁸ᵍ 3⁹ᵍᶠ
5⁹ᵍᶠ 1⁸ᶠ 9⁸ᵍᶠ 6⁸ᵍ 4⁸ᵍˢ 1⁸ᵍᶠ 9¹⁰ᵍ **3-2-15**
£22,617

Millbag (Ire) *M R Channon* 96
2 b/br c Cape Cross (Ire) - Play With Fire (Fr)
3⁶ᵍᶠ 1⁵ᵍᶠ 3⁶ᵍ 1⁶ᵍᶠ 3⁷ᵍᶠ **2-1-5 £15,663**

Millenary *J L Dunlop* 121
6 b h Rainbow Quest (USA) - Ballerina (Ire)
2¹²ᵍˢ 2¹²ˢ 1¹²ᵍ 8¹²ᵍ 4¹³ˢ 2¹⁶ᵍᶠ **1-3-6**
£108,280

Millennium Force *M R Channon* 113
5 b g Bin Ajwaad (Ire) - Jumairah Sun (Ire)
1⁷ᵍʸ 3⁷ᵍᶠ 4⁷ˢ 4⁷ᵍᶠ 2⁷ᵍˢ 3⁷ᵍ 20⁷ᵍ **1-1-7**
£51,516

Millennium Hall *P Monteith* 71
4 b g Saddlers' Hall (Ire) - Millazure (USA)
7¹⁰ᶠ 6⁸ᵍ 5¹¹ᵍˢ 5¹¹ᵍˢ 1⁹ᵍᶠ 11⁹ᵍ 12⁹ᵍᶠ 6¹⁰ᵍ
13¹²ˢ **1-0-9 £5,421**

Millennium King *Mrs N S Sharpe* 49
4 b g Piccolo - Zabelina (USA)
16⁶ᵍᶠ 16⁵ˢᵈ 9⁶ᵍᶠ 3⁶ᵍᶠ 11⁷ᵍᶠ 14⁵ᵍᶠ 14⁶ᶠ
18⁶ᵍᶠ **0-1-8 £596**

Millfields Dreams *R Brotherton* 54
4 b g Dreams End - Millfields Lady
11⁸ᵍᶠ 4¹¹ᵍᶠ 11¹⁰ᵍᶠ 4⁷ᵍ 6⁶ᶠ 8⁷ᵍᶠ 4⁷ᵍᶠ
0-0-7 £1,066

Millietom (Ire) *K A Ryan* a27
2 b g General Monash (USA) - June Lady
10⁶ˢᵈ **0-0-1**

Milligan (Fr) *R A Fahey* 13
8 b g Exit To Nowhere (USA) - Madigan Mill
21¹²ᵍ **0-0-1**

Million Percent *K R Burke* 91
4 b g Ashkalani (Ire) - Royal Jade
13⁵ᶠ 18⁶ᵍ 9⁶ᶠ 6⁶ᵍ 5⁶ᵍˢ 1⁶ᵍᶠ 3⁶ᵍ 1⁶ᵍ 2⁶ᵍ
16⁶ᶠ 5⁶ᵍᶠ 4⁶ᵍ 3⁶ᵍˢ **3-4-13 £21,781**

Millkom Elegance *K A Ryan* 51
4 b f Millkom - Premier Princess
16⁸ᶠ 5⁸ᵍˢ 11¹⁰ᵍᶠ 1¹⁰ᶠ **1-0-4 £2,744**

Millstreet *Saeed Bin Suroor* 117
4 ch c Polish Precedent (USA) - Mill Path
4¹⁴ᵍ 2¹²ᵍᶠ 5¹²ᵍ 21¹⁶ᵍ **0-1-5 £6,755**

Milly Fleur *R Guest* 71
3 ch f Primo Dominie - My Cadeaux
2⁶ᵍᶠ 1⁶ᵍ 4⁶ᵍᶠ 9⁶ᵍᶠ 15⁷ˢ 15⁷ᵍˢ **1-1-6**
£7,683

Milly Hatch *W S Kittow* 43
3 b f Atraf - Pie Hatch (Ire)
10¹⁰ᶠ 3¹²ᵍᶠ 12¹⁰ᵍᶠ **0-0-3 £637**

Milly Lahib (Ire) *D J Coakley* 52 a52
3 b f Lahib (USA) - Treadmill (Ire)
7⁷ˢᵈ 7⁸ˢᵈ 17⁸ᵍ 7⁷ᵍᶠ 9⁷ᵍᶠ 7⁸ᵍᶠ 13⁸ᵍ 11⁶ᵍ
2⁸ᶠ 7⁷ᵍᶠ 5⁸ᶠ 9⁸ᶠ **0-1-12 £626**

Milly Waters *W M Brisbourne* 87 a67
2 b f Danzero (Aus) - Chilly Waters
2⁵ᵍ 2⁵ˢᵈ 4⁵ᵍᶠ 1⁵ᵍ 11⁶ᵍᶠ 12⁷ᵍ 17⁷ᵍᶠ 1⁶ᵍᶠ
1⁶ᵍᶠ **3-2-9 £61,987**

Milly's Lass *J M Bradley* 26 a40
5 b m Mind Games - Millie's Lady (Ire)
4⁵ˢʷ 8⁵ˢᵈ 4⁵ˢᵈ 13⁵ᵍᶠ 11⁶ᵍᶠ 11⁶ᵍᶠ **0-0-6**

Millybaa (USA) *R Guest* 104
3 b f Anabaa (USA) - Millyant
1⁶ᵍ 3⁶ᵍˢ 9⁶ᵍ 2⁶ᵍʸ 13⁶ʰᵒ **1-2-5 £14,936**

Mimas Girl *S R Bowring* 41 a41
4 b f Samim (USA) - Cocked Hat Girl
12⁸ˢᵈ 13⁸ˢᵈ 10⁶ˢᵈ 3⁸ˢᵈ 7⁸ˢʷ 5⁸ˢᵈ 12⁷ᵍᶠ
4⁷ᵍᶠ 6⁷ˢᵈ **0-1-9 £469**

Mimic *R Guest* 76
3 b f Royal Applause - Stripanoora
6⁷ᵍᶠ 9⁶ᵍᶠ 4⁶ᵍᶠ 1⁶ᵍᶠ 3⁵ᵍᶠ 3⁶ᵍᶠ 2⁵ᵍᶠ 2⁶ᵍ
5⁵ᵍ 16ᵍᶠ 1⁶ᵍᶠ 4⁵ᵍᶠ 16⁶ᵍᶠ **3-5-13 £13,974**

Mind Alert *T D Easterby* 70
2 b g Mind Games - Bombay Sapphire
4⁵ᵍ 4⁵ᵍ 5⁵ᵍᶠ 2⁶ᵍᶠ 1⁶ᵍᶠ 10⁶ᵍᶠ 17⁶ᵍ 6⁶ᵍˢ
1-1-8 £7,770

Mind Bobby *J Gallagher* 28
3 b g Mind Games - Young Holly
16⁵ᵍ 14⁷ᵍᶠ **0-0-2**

Mind Play *M E Sowersby* 32
2 b f Mind Games - Diplomatist
14⁷ᵍᶠ 15⁷ᵍᶠ 13⁸ᵍᶠ 6⁸ˢᵈ **0-0-4**

Mindanao *L Lungo* a11
7 b m Most Welcome - Salala
11¹²ˢᵈ **0-0-1**

Minderoo *Jamie Poulton* 44 a61
5 b g Efisio - Mindomica
7⁶ˢᵈ 7⁶ˢᵈ 2⁶ˢᵈ 5⁶ˢᵈ 1⁶ˢᵈ 6⁶ˢᵈ 15⁶ᵍ 14⁶ᵍ
9⁶ᵍᶠ 9⁵ᵍᶠ 17⁶ᵍ **1-1-11 £3,839**

Mindset (Ire) *L M Cumani* 71
2 b f Vettori (Ire) - Eden (Ire)
2⁷ᵍᶠ 3⁷ᵍᶠ **0-2-2 £1,538**

Mine (Ire) *J D Bethell* 107
5 b h Primo Dominie - Ellebanna
15⁸ᵍᶠ 1⁷ᵍ 3⁷ᶠ 2⁷ᵍᶠ 18⁷ᵍ 3⁷ᵍᶠ 4⁷ᵍᶠ 7⁷ᵍᶠ
6⁸ᵍˢ **1-4-9 £37,031**

Mine Behind *J R Best* 78 a80
3 b c Sheikh Albadou - Arapi (Ire)
10⁷ᵍˢ 1⁶ᵍᶠ 6⁶ᵍ 13⁶ᵍ 10⁵ᵍ 3⁷ˢᵈ 2⁷ˢᵈ 2⁷ˢᵈ
6⁸ᵍ 3⁸ᵍᶠ **1-4-10 £9,918**

Minelly *M E Sowersby* 12
3 b f Defacto (USA) - Lady Liza
11¹⁰ᵍ **0-0-1**

Mineshaft (USA) *N J Howard* a131
4 b/br c A.P. Indy (USA) - Prospectors Delite (USA)
1⁹ᶠᵗ 2⁹ᶠᵗ 1⁹ᶠᵗ 1⁹ᶠᵗ 1¹⁰ˢʸ 2⁹ᶠᵗ 1¹⁰ᶠᵗ 1⁹ᶠᵗ
1¹⁰ᶠᵗ **7-1-9 £1,381,054**

Ming The Merciless *J G Given* 57 a20
3 b g Hector Protector (USA) - Sundae Girl (USA)
6¹⁰ᵍᶠ 13⁸ᵍˢ 10¹²ᵍ 10¹²ˢᵈ **0-0-4**

Mingun (USA) *A P O'Brien* 119
3 b/br c A.P. Indy (USA) - Miesque (USA)
1⁸ˢʰ 1⁸ᵍ 1¹⁰ᵍᶠ 4¹⁰ᵍᶠ **3-0-4 £101,922**

Minimum Bid *Miss B Sanders* 49
2 b f First Trump - La Noisette
8⁶ᵍᶠ 6⁶ᵍᶠ 3⁵ᵍᶠ **0-0-3 £464**

Minirina *C Smith* 55 a62
3 b f Mistertopogigo (Ire) - Fabulous Rina (Fr)
7⁵ˢᵈ 7⁵ˢʷ 9⁵ˢᵈ 2⁵ᵍᶠ 3⁵ᵍˢ 8⁵ᵍᶠ 5⁵ᵍᶠ 4⁵ᵍᶠ
10⁵ᵍᶠ **0-2-9 £1,506**

Minivet *T D Easterby* 63
8 b g Midyan (USA) - Bronzewing
6¹⁰ᵍᶠ 11¹⁰ᵍᶠ 9¹⁰ᵍᶠ 5¹⁶ᵍ 4¹⁶ᵍˢ **0-0-5**

Minnina (Ire) *B Hanbury* 30
3 ch f In The Wings - Cheyenne Spirit
8¹⁰ᵍˢ **0-0-1**

Mirant *M C Pipe* 42
4 b c Danzig Connection (USA) - Ingerence (Fr)
25²⁰ᵍ **0-0-1**

Mirasol Princess *D K Ivory*   81
2 ch f Ali-Royal (Ire) - Yanomami (USA)
1^{5gf} 2^{5g} 1^{5gf} 14^{5gf} 11^{5gf} 4^{5gf} 1^{5gf} 1^{5gf}
8^{6gf} 9^{6gf} **4-1-10 £15,907**

Mis Chicaf (Ire) *J S Wainwright*   69 a21
2 b f Prince Sabo - Champagne Season (USA)
9^{5sd} 5^{5gf} 3^{5gf} 5^{5gf} 9^{6gf} 1^{5gf} **1-1-6**
£4,280

Misaaayef (USA) *Sir Michael Stoute*   86
3 b f Swain (Ire) - Zakiyya (USA)
3^{10gf} 1^{11gf} 8^{10gf} **1-1-3 £6,342**

Misaro (Ger) *P A Blockley*   76
2 b g Acambaro (Ger) - Misniniski
3^{7gf} 5^{10gs} 1^{6gs} **1-0-3 £3,596**

Misbehaviour *P Butler*
4 b g Tragic Role (USA) - Exotic Forest
12^{16sd} **0-0-1**

Mischief *K Bell*   43
7 ch g Generous (Ire) - Knight's Baroness
6^{10gf} 10^{12gf} 7^{13f} 14^{17gf} 1^{14f} **1-0-5**
£3,650

Misconduct *J G Portman*   7
9 gr m Risk Me (Fr) - Grey Cree
17^{14gf} **0-0-1**

Mishall (USA) *M P Tregoning*   81
2 ch c Distant View (USA) - Virgin Stanza (USA)
2^{7gf} 5^{7g} **0-1-2 £1,528**

Mishead *M C Chapman*
5 ch g Unfuwain (USA) - Green Jannat (USA)
8^{16sd} **0-0-1**

Mishka *Julian Poulton*   a34
5 b g Mistertopogigo (Ire) - Walsham Witch
14^{6sd} **0-0-1**

Miskina *M R Channon*   53
2 b f Mark Of Esteem (Ire) - Najmat Alshemaal (Ire)
9^{7gf} 2^{7gf} 4^{6gs} **0-1-3 £906**

Miss Adelaide (Ire) *B W Hills*   79
2 b f Alzao (USA) - Sweet Adelaide (USA)
4^{7gf} 3^{6gf} **0-1-2 £1,548**

Miss Amazer *I A Wood*   38
4 b f Shaamit (Ire) - Kiss On Time
7^{8gf} 6^{8f} 13^{8gf} **0-0-3**

Miss Assertive *N P Littmoden*   82 a71
3 b f Zafonic (USA) - Self Assured (Ire)
14^{7sd} 12^{6gf} 8^{7gf} 6^{9gs} **0-0-4 £421**

Miss Brookie *W G M Turner*   67 a65
2 br f The West (USA) - Galacia (Ire)
4^{5g} 3^{5sd} 1^{5f} 3^{5gf} 2^{5f} 5^{6gs} 3^{5gf} 3^{5gf}
10^{5gf} 9^{5gf} **1-2-10 £9,403**

Miss Cap Ferrat *G Wragg*   55
3 b f Darshaan - Miss Beaulieu
6^{8gf} 5^{9gf} **0-0-2**

Miss Celerity *M J Haynes*   27
3 b f Compton Place - Film Buff
20^{10g} 6^{7gf} 10^{6gf} **0-0-3**

Miss Ceylon *Miss A Stokell*   51 a7
3 b f Brief Truce (USA) - Five Islands
10^{5gf} 14^{6s} 6^{5gf} 14^{5gf} 10^{5sd} 18^{5gf} 6^{7f}
14^{7f} 10^{6g} 12^{12gf} 12^{5gf} 7^{6gf} 12^{7gs} **0-0-13**
£212

Miss Champers (Ire) *P D Evans*   50 a84
3 b/br f Grand Lodge (USA) - Katherine Gorge (USA)
6^{8sd} 4^{6sd} 5^{7gf} 6^{8g} 9^{8gf} 13^{6gf} 8^{8gf} 6^{7sw}
7^{8gf} 3^{9sd} 8^{7sd} **0-1-11 £552**

Miss Childrey (Ire) *Francis Ennis*   97

2 ch f Dr Fong (Ire) - Blazing Glory (Ire)
3^{5ys} 1^{5g} 1^{6g} 5^{5gf} 8^{7gf} 7^{7gf} 4^{8g} **2-1-7**
£48,258

Miss Combustible (Ire) *A Berry*   13
3 b f Titus Livius (Fr) - Highly Motivated
F^{7gf} 9^{6f} 13^{9gf} **0-0-3**

Miss Concept (Ire) *F Jordan*   33 a24
4 b f Frimaire - Hard Sweet
5^{11sd} 4^{15sw} 10^{12sw} 7^{12gf} **0-0-4**

Miss Coranche *T D Easterby*   40
2 b f Piccolo - Sunny Davis (USA)
6^{5g} 8^{6gs} 4^{6gf} 7^{7f} **0-0-4 £288**

Miss Corniche *G Wragg*   108
4 b f Hernando (Fr) - Miss Beaulieu
6^{12gf} 3^{12gf} 9^{12gf} 9^{10s} 2^{10gf} 3^{10gf} 7^{11s}
0-2-7 £14,389

Miss Croisette *Mrs H Dalton*
4 ch f Hernando (Fr) - Miss Riviera
6^{16sw} **0-0-1**

Miss Eloise *T D Easterby*   53
2 b f Efisio - Zaima (Ire)
5^{6gf} 14^{6gf} 7^{7gf} 5^{6gf} 2^{7gs} **0-1-5 £644**

Miss Fara (Fr) *M C Pipe*   90
8 ch m Galetto (Fr) - Faracha (Fr)
12^{14gf} 15^{20gf} 10^{18gf} **0-0-3**

Miss Faye *J M Bradley*   34
3 b/br f Puissance - Bingo Bongo
4^{7gf} 6^{6gf} 6^{6gf} **0-0-3 £320**

Miss George *D K Ivory*   91 a94
5 b m Pivotal - Brightside (Ire)
4^{6sd} 2^{7sd} 6^{6sd} 2^{7sd} 1^{7sd} 1^{7sd} 1^{7sd} 13^{6gf}
1^{6gf} 20^{6g} 5^{8g} 6^{6g} 1^{5gf} 10^{5gf} 14^{5gs} 5^{5gf} 1^{6gf}
3^{6gf} 12^{6gf} **5-3-19 £28,655**

Miss Glory Be *Miss Gay Kelleway*   52 a67
5 b m Glory Of Dancer - Miss Blondie (USA)
6^{10sd} 2^{8sd} 2^{9sd} 6^{10sd} 2^{7sw} 5^{8sd} 12^{10gf}
1^{7sd} 9^{7sd} 17^{7gf} 5^{7g} 8^{8sd} 6^{10gf} 3^{8gf} 2^{8sw}
1-5-15 £6,992

Miss Grace *J J Sheehan*   64 a69
3 ch f Atticus (USA) - Jetbeeah (Ire)
3^{8sd} 2^{10sd} 1^{10sd} 3^{10gf} 3^{10g} 6^{10f} 13^{8g}
1-2-7 £7,456

Miss Holly *M Johnston*   a79
4 b f Makbul - Seraphim (Fr)
1^{11sd} **1-0-1 £3,376**

Miss Hoofbeats *Miss J Feilden*   43
2 b f Unfuwain (USA) - Oiselina (Fr)
11^{7gf} 3^{7gs} 12^{7gf} **0-0-3 £794**

Miss Inquisitive *Mrs C A Dunnett*   30 a18
3 b f Bijou D'Inde - Forget Me (Ire)
15^{7sd} 9^{7sd} 6^{10gf} 13^{7gf} 9^{8g} 9^{8g} **0-0-6**

Miss Issy (Ire) *J Gallagher*   68 a63
3 b f Victory Note - Shane's Girl (Ire)
3^{8sd} 7^{12sd} 2^{7gf} 7^{8g} 6^{7gf} 2^{7gf} 3^{7gf} 4^{7gf}
13^{8g} **0-4-9 £3,299**

Miss Ivanhoe (Ire) *G Wragg*   107
3 b f Selkirk (USA) - Robellino Miss (USA)
1^{8g} 6^{10gf} 4^{10gf} 2^{8g} 6^{7gf} 1^{7s} 2^{7g}
2-3-8 £39,746

Miss Jingles *J A Gilbert*   73 a71
4 b f Muhtarram (USA) - Flamingo Times
9^{6sw} 7^{7sd} 12^{8gf} 12^{7gf} 4^{7g} 7^{7g} 8^{9gf} 10^{8gf}
4^{8sd} 5^{12sd} **0-1-10 £1,626**

Miss Judged *A P Jones*   33
2 b f Case Law - Marie's Crusader (Ire)

6⁶ᵍˢ 14⁶ᵍᶠ 12⁵ˢᵈ **0-0-3**

Miss Judgement (Ire) *W R Muir* 40 a2
2 b f Revoque (Ire) - Mugello
7⁵ᵍᶠ 13⁶ˢᵈ 11⁵ᵍᶠ **0-0-3**

Miss Julie Jay (Ire) *Noel T Chance* 50
2 b f Bahhare (USA) - Gentle Papoose
9⁶ᵍᶠ 14⁶ᵍᶠ 13⁷ᶠ **0-0-3**

Miss Koen (Ire) *D L Williams* 65
4 b f Barathea (USA) - Fanny Blankers (Ire)
6⁸ᵍᶠ 9⁸ᶠ 6¹⁰ᶠ 11¹³ᵍ **0-0-4**

Miss La Napoule *G Wragg* 42
2 b f Nashwan (USA) - Miss Riviera
5⁵ᵍˢ **0-0-1**

Miss Lady Ash (Ire) *J S Moore* 18
2 b f General Monash (USA) - La Fandango (Ire)
5⁵ᵍ 10⁵ᵍᶠ 12⁸ˢᵈ **0-0-3**

Miss Ladybird (USA) *J G Given* 66 a53
2 b/br f Labeeb - Bird Dance (Can)
2⁷ᵍˢ 1⁷ᵍᶠ 3⁸ˢʷ 3⁸ᵍ 6⁸ᵍᶠ **1-1-5 £6,780**

Miss Langkawi *G Wragg* 65
2 gr f Daylami (Ire) - Miss Amanpuri
3⁶ᶠ 1⁶ᵍ **1-0-2 £4,202**

Miss Lehman *Mrs M Reveley* 33
5 m Beveled (USA) - Lehmans Lot
10⁹ᵍˢ 6¹⁰ᵍᶠ 10¹²ᵍˢ **0-0-3**

Miss Lyvennet *M Todhunter* 49
2 ch f Then Again - Precious Girl
5⁵ᵍˢ 6⁵ᶠ 11⁵ᵍᶠ **0-0-3**

Miss Madame (Ire) *T P McGovern* 59
2 b f Cape Cross (Ire) - Cosmic Countess (Ire)
11⁶ᵍᶠ 6⁶ᵍᶠ 30⁷ᵍᶠ **0-0-3**

Miss Millietant *L Montague Hall* 8
2 b f Up And At 'Em - Annie Hall
10⁶ᵍ **0-0-1**

Miss Mirage (Ire) *B W Hills* 67
3 b f Alhaarth (Ire) - Mahrah (USA)
6⁷ᵍᶠ 4⁷ᵍᶠ 1⁶ᵍᶠ 2⁷ᵍᶠ **1-1-4 £7,670**

Miss Mirasol *K A Ryan* 89
3 b f Sheikh Albadou - Play The Game
9⁶ᵍᶠ 7⁷ᵍᶠ 10⁷ᵍᶠ 22⁶ᵍ **0-0-4**

Miss Mytton (USA) *A Bailey* 70 a39
2 ch f Mt. Livermore (USA) - Sisterella (USA)
6⁵ᵍᶠ 3⁶ˢ 6⁶ˢᵈ 10⁵ᵍᶠ 3⁵ᵍ 5⁵ᵍᶠ 2⁶ᵍ 2⁶ᵍᶠ
9⁶ᵍᶠ 4⁷ᵍ 7⁶ᵍ **0-3-11 £6,300**

Miss Noteriety *C J Teague*
3 b f Victory Note (USA) - Mystic Maid (Ire)
13⁵ᵍ **0-0-1**

Miss Ocean Monarch *D W Chapman* 50
3 ch f Blue Ocean (USA) - Faraway Grey
8⁹ˢᵈ 7¹⁰ᵍᶠ 6⁸ᵍᶠ 7⁷ᵍᶠ 3⁸ᵍˢ 3¹¹ᵍˢ 3⁸ᵍᶠ 2⁸ᵍᶠ
4⁸ᶠ 4⁹ᵍ 5¹⁰ᶠ 3⁸ˢ 12⁸ˢ 4¹⁰ᵍˢ 4⁸ᵍᶠ 10¹⁰ᵍᶠ
0-5-16 £4,926

Miss Opulence (Ire) *B Ellison* 88
4 b f Kylian (USA) - Oriental Splendour
13⁸ᵍ 11¹¹ᵍᶠ 8¹⁰ᵍ 4⁸ʰʸ 6¹¹ᵍᶠ 7¹⁰ᵍᶠ **1-0-6**
£11,280

Miss Peaches *G G Margarson* a42
5 b m Emperor Jones (USA) - Dear Person
10⁸ˢᵈ 7⁷ˢᵈ **0-0-2**

Miss Pebbles (Ire) *B R Johnson* 75 a79
3 ch f Lake Coniston (Ire) - Sea Of Stone (USA)
2⁸ᵍᶠ 3⁸ᵍˢ 2⁸ᵍᶠ 1⁸ˢᵈ 9⁷ˢᵈ **1-2-5 £5,961**

Miss Poppets *D R C Elsworth* 62 a78
3 ch f Polar Falcon (USA) - Alifandango (Ire)
10⁸ᵍᶠ 5⁷ᵍᶠ 7⁷ᵍᶠ 3⁶ᵍᶠ 9⁸ᵍˢ 4⁸ᵍᶠ 2⁶ᵍ 1⁶ˢᵈ

1-2-8 £4,021

Miss Porcia *M G Quinlan* 57 a20
2 ch f Inchinor - Krista
8⁷ᵍˢ 8⁷ᵍᶠ 6⁸ᵍ 7⁶ˢᵈ **0-0-4**

Miss Procurer (Ire) *P F I Cole* 74
2 b f Entrepreneur - Kariyh (USA)
6⁶ᵍᶠ 5⁷ᵍᶠ **0-0-2**

Miss Samantha *K R Burke* 42 a36
5 b m Emarati (USA) - Puella Bona
10⁶ˢᵈ 6⁶ˢᵈ 9⁶ˢᵈ 5⁷ᵍᶠ 12⁷ˢᵈ **0-0-5**

Miss Sandy Claws (Ire) *Eamon Tyrrell* 45 a31
5 b m Catrail (USA) - Arabian Princess
6⁸ˢᵈ 3¹⁰ᵍ 4⁸ᵍᶠ 13¹⁰ˢ 7¹⁰ˢ **0-1-5 £642**

Miss Tilly *G B Balding* 28
2 b f Nicolotte - Little White Lies
19⁵ᵍ 14⁵ᵍˢ 19⁶ᵍᶠ **0-0-3**

Miss Trigger *W R Muir* 30
3 ch f Double Trigger (Ire) - Saint Navarro
6¹²ᵍᶠ **0-0-1**

Miss Trinity *C N Allen* 63
3 b f Catrail (USA) - Rosy Sunset (Ire)
12⁵ᵍᶠ 5⁶ᵍᶠ 8⁶ᵍᶠ **0-0-3**

Miss Twti *B Smart* 32
3 b f Ali-Royal (Ire) - Gargren (Ire)
8⁶ᵍ 12⁶ᵍ 7⁵ᶠ 11⁵ᵍᶠ **0-0-4**

Miss Vettori *G L Moore* a28
4 b f Vettori (Ire) - Dahlawise (Ire)
11¹²ˢᵈ **0-0-1**

Miss Wizz *W Storey* 48
3 b f Wizard King - Fyas
7⁶ᵍᶠ 13⁵ᵍᶠ 19⁵ᵍᶠ 8⁶ᶠ 8⁸ˢ 4⁷ᵍᶠ 6⁷ᵍᶠ 8⁸ᶠ
0-0-8

Miss Woodpigeon *J D Frost* 47 a3
7 b m Landyap (USA) - Pigeon Loft (Ire)
10⁸ᵍᶠ 9⁸ᵍᶠ 10⁷ˢᵈ **0-0-3**

Miss You *N A Callaghan* a69
3 ch f Grand Lodge (USA) - Miss Queen (USA)
2⁷ˢᵈ 8¹⁰ˢᵈ 10⁸ˢᵈ **0-1-3 £1,081**

Misscostalot *W Jarvis*
3 b f Hernando (Fr) - Glamour Game
6¹¹ᵍ **0-0-1**

Missie *G A Swinbank* 51
3 ch f Compton Place - About Face
5⁷ᵍ 9⁷ᵍᶠ 4⁷ᵍˢ 5⁶ᵍᶠ **0-0-4**

Missile Toe (Ire) *D Morris* 65
10 b g Exactly Sharp (USA) - Debach Dust
12¹⁰ᵍᶠ 3¹⁰ᵍ 3¹¹ᵍᶠ 10¹⁰ᵍᶠ **0-2-4 £1,263**

Mission Affirmed (USA) *T P Tate* 57
2 ch c Stravinsky (USA) - Affirmed Legacy (USA)
5⁶ᵍ 5⁷ᵍ **0-0-2**

Mission Man *R Hannon* 77
2 b c Revoque (Ire) - Opopmil (Ire)
12⁷ᵍᶠ 2⁸ᵍᶠ 4⁷ᵍˢ **0-1-3 £2,246**

Mission To Mars *P R Hedger* 69 a69
4 b g Muhtarram (USA) - Ideal Candidate
4¹²ˢᵈ 1¹²ˢᵈ 10¹⁵ˢᵈ 7¹⁰ᵍᶠ 9¹¹ᵍᶠ 2¹²ˢʷ 1¹²ˢᵈ
1¹²ᵍᶠ 1¹²ˢᵈ 1¹²ˢᵈ **5-1-10 £13,476**

Mister Arjay (USA) *B Ellison* 85
3 b c Mister Baileys - Crystal Stepper (USA)
4⁶ᵍᶠ 2⁷ᵍᶠ 1⁸ᵍᶠ 7⁸ᵍᶠ 3⁸ᵍᶠ 5⁸ᵍᶠ
2¹⁰ᵍᶠ 16⁸ᵍ **1-2-10 £15,073**

Mister Benji *B P J Baugh* 39 a64
4 b g Catrail (USA) - Katy-Q (Ire)
14⁵ʰʸ 16⁵ᵍᶠ 18⁶ᵍᶠ 3⁶ˢᵈ 5⁶ˢᵈ 4⁷ˢᵈ 10⁶ˢʷ

14[5gf] 11[5sd] **0-1-9 £758**

Mister Clinton (Ire) *D K Ivory*   65
6 ch g Lion Cavern (USA) - Thewaari (USA)
5[7gf] 3[7gf] 4[8f] 10[7gf] 6[6f] 16[6g] 5[7gf] 11[8gf]
4[7f] 16[6g] 2[7g] 6[8gf] 4[7gf] 2[8f] 15[8gf] 4[7g] 1[10f]
9[10f] 13[8g] **1-4-19 £6,096**

Mister Completely (Ire) *J R Best*   48 a44
2 b g Princely Heir (Ire) - Blue Goose
9[6gf] 3[6f] 6[6g] 4[7sd] 14[7gf] **0-0-5 £854**

Mister Links (Ire) *Saeed Bin Suroor*   107
3 b c Flying Spur (Aus) - Lady Anna Livia
3[7gf] 11[8g] **0-1-2 £5,500**

Mister Mal (Ire) *R A Fahey*   67 a67
7 b g Scenic - Fashion Parade
5[6sd] 6[6gf] 6[7gs] 16[7g] 6[7sd] 2[7sd] 6[6sd] 2[7sd]
4[8ft] 16[8gf] 8[8sd] **0-2-11 £2,036**

Mister Man *J S Wainwright*
3 b g Mistertopogigo (Ire) - Louisa Anne
7[8gf] 6[11gf] **0-0-2**

Mister Merlin (Ire) *M C Chapman*   35
2 ch g Titus Livius (Fr) - Official Secret
3[5g] 5[6gf] 11[5gf] **0-0-3 £581**

Mister Monet (Ire) *M Johnston*   82
2 b c Peintre Celebre (USA) - Breyani
3[6gf] 1[7g] **1-0-2 £7,633**

Mister Putt (USA) *Mrs N Smith*   66
5 b/br g Mister Baileys - Theresita (Ger)
6[12g] 7[12gf] **0-0-2 £405**

Mister Rambo *D Nicholls*   71 a53
8 b g Rambo Dancer (Can) - Ozra
3[7gf] 10[7sd] 14[7gs] 12[7g] 2[7f] 3[7gf] 12[7gf]
3[8gf] 2[8gf] 12[11gf] **0-5-10 £5,274**

Mister Right (Ire) *K Bell*   56
2 ch g Barathea (Ire) - Broken Spirit (Ire)
12[6gf] 13[6gf] **0-0-2**

Mister Rushby *D W Chapman*   28
3 b g Hamas (Ire) - Final Rush
11[6gf] 9[5f] 16[8s] 9[7gs] 14[6gf] 11[7f] **0-0-6**

Mister Saif (USA) *R Hannon*   85
2 ch c Miswaki (USA) - Shawgatny (USA)
3[6gs] 3[8gf] 1[6gf] 9[6gf] 6[6gf] **1-0-5 £5,135**

Mister Sweets *M C Chapman*   88 a76
4 ch g Nashwan (USA) - Keyboogie (USA)
2[6sw] 5[6sd] 3[8sd] 2[7sd] 4[12sd] 1[7sd] 2[6g] 1[7gf]
3[6g] 14[7g] 4[8s] 3[7gf] 5[8gf] 3[8gf] 12[7g] 8[8gs]
11[6gf] 9[8gf] **2-7-19 £17,956**

Mister Trickster (Ire) *R Dickin*   61
2 b c Woodborough (USA) - Tinos Island (Ire)
10[7gf] 4[7gf] 6[7f] 6[6gf] 5[8gf] 13[8g] **0-0-6**
£290

Mister Twister *R Hannon*   39
2 gr c Mind Games - Its All Relative
11[6gf] 8[6gf] 3[6f] **0-0-3 £411**

Mister Waterline (Ire) *P D Evans*   29
4 b g Mujadil (USA) - Cree's Figurine
14[6gf] **0-0-1**

Misternando *M R Channon*   103
3 b c Hernando (Fr) - Mistinguett (Ire)
8[12gs] 7[14gs] 9[12gs] 11[14f] 1[14gf] 11[6gf] UR[16g]
11[6gf] 11[6gf] 11[6gf] 11[6gf] 11[6gf] 2[17g] 2[16gf] 6[18gf]
11[6gf] 11[6gf] **10-2-17 £67,594**

Mistral Sky *Mrs S A Liddiard*   66 a77
4 b g Hurricane Sky (Aus) - Dusk In Daytona
11[7sw] 7[6sd] 3[7sd] 2[8sd] 4[7g] 8[8sd] 6[7gf] 15[8gf]
6[7gf] 1[7gf] 2[6gf] 3[7f] 7[8gf] 4[8sd] 1[7f] 1[7sd] **3-4-16**

£11,581

Mistress Ellie *J Nicol*   a56
4 b f Royal Applause - Ellie Ardensky
7[10sd] **0-0-1**

Mistress Hollie (Ire) *Mrs P N Dutfield*   9 a21
2 b f Titus Livius (Fr) - Soden (Ire)
9[8gf] 10[8sd] **0-0-2**

Mistress Page *E A Wheeler*
5 b m Beveled (USA) - Pallomere
14[7sd] **0-0-1**

Mistress Twister *T D Barron*   73
2 b f Pivotal - Foreign Mistress
7[6gf] 3[6f] **0-1-2 £474**

Misty Dancer *Miss Venetia Williams*   82
4 gr g Vettori (Ire) - Light Fantastic
1[10gf] 8[10gf] 3[10gs] 17[10g] **1-1-4 £7,675**

Misty Man (USA) *Miss J Feilden*   31 a24
5 ch g El Gran Senor (USA) - Miasma (USA)
17[8gf] 10[8gf] 9[10g] 11[12gf] 11[14gf] 4[12sw]
0-0-6

Mitcham (Ire) *T G Mills*   100 a88
7 br g Hamas (Ire) - Arab Scimetar (Ire)
5[5sd] 6[6gf] 6[6g] 1[6g] 9[6gf] 12[6f] **1-0-6**
£11,103

Mitrash *B Hanbury*   64
3 b c Darshaan - L'Ideale (USA)
6[10gf] **0-0-1**

Mitsuki *J D Bethell*   83
4 b f Puissance - Surrealist (Ity)
3[5f] 19[6g] 10[5gf] 12[5gs] 1[5gf] 9[5f] 4[5gf] 7[5gf]
4[6gf] 8[6gf] 5[6gf] 10[6gf] 9[5g] 4[5gf] 15[5gf] 13[5gf]
1-1-16 £8,415

Mix It Up *R M Beckett*   a40
2 gr f Linamix (Fr) - Hawayah (Ire)
11[8sd] **0-0-1**

Mixed Marriage (Ire) *G L Moore*   a45
5 ch g Indian Ridge - Marie De Flandre (Fr)
6[12sd] 10[13sd] **0-0-2**

Mizhar (USA) *J J Quinn*   68 a57
7 b/br g Dayjur (USA) - Futuh (USA)
8[6sw] 11[5sd] 6[6gf] 1[6gf] 3[6gf] 2[6gf] 9[6f] 3[6gf]
11[6gs] 17[6gf] **1-3-10 £6,318**

Moarban (Ire) *M R Channon*   83
3 b c Bahhare (USA) - Suave Star
8[8g] 6[8gf] 8[13gf] 2[8g] 5[8gs] 3[9gf] 2[8gf]
2[8gf] **0-4-9 £6,275**

Moayed *N P Littmoden*   70 a91
4 b g Selkirk (USA) - Song Of Years (Ire)
1[8sd] 7[7sd] 1[8sd] 5[7sd] 11[8gf] 15[7sd] **3-0-6**
£10,152

Mobil-One Dot Com *J S Goldie*
5 b g Magic Ring (Ire) - Not So Generous (Ire)
11[5gs] **0-0-1**

Mobo-Baco *R J Hodges*   71
6 ch g Bandmaster (USA) - Darakah
1[7gf] 1[8gf] 4[11gf] 4[8gf] 1[8f] 12[8g] 4[8f] 14[8s]
7[7gf] 3[8f] 7[8f] **3-1-11 £13,482**

Mocca (Ire) *D J Coakley*   72
2 b f Sri Pekan (USA) - Ewan (Ire)
3[7gf] 4[7gf] 1[8gf] 5[8gf] 2[10gf] **1-2-5 £6,395**

Mochras *R F Johnson Houghton*   65
3 b f Mtoto - Natchez Trace
8[7gs] 15[8gf] 11[8gf] 2[6gf] 3[6gf] 9[6g] 5[8gf] 9[8f]
16[6gf] **0-2-9 £1,978**

Model Figure (USA) *B W Hills*   70

2 b f Distant View (USA) - Sylph (USA)
4^{6g} 13^{6gf} 1^{6f} **1-0-3 £3,447**

Modem (Ire) *D Shaw*   a49
6 b g Midhish - Holy Water
7^{8sd} 3^{7sd} 7^{7sd} 5^{6sw} 7^{6sd} **0-1-5 £419**

Modesty Blaise (Swe) *J G Given*   57
3 br f Mango Express - Singoalla (Ire)
7^{7gf} 7^{8g} **0-0-2**

Mofeyda (Ire) *A C Stewart*   74
3 b f Mtoto - Princess Haifa (USA)
5^{10gs} 4^{10gf} **0-0-2**

Mokabra (Ire) *M R Channon*   104
2 b c Cape Cross (Ire) - Pacific Grove
3^{5gf} 1^{6gf} 3^{6g} 3^{6g} 1^{6g} 1^{6g} 6^{7gf} 5^{6ho} **3-1-8 £57,860**

Molcon (Ire) *N A Callaghan*   73
2 b c Danetime (Ire) - Wicken Wonder (Ire)
6^{5f} 1^{5gf} 1^{5gf} 5^{5gf} 7^{6gf} **2-0-5 £11,088**

Molinia *R M Beckett*   51
2 b f Nicolotte - Themeda
5^{6gf} 5^{7gf} 11^{6g} **0-0-3**

Molly Be *W J Musson*   43 a45
3 ch f First Trump - Broughton Singer (Ire)
6^{8sd} 6^{8sd} 10^{9sd} 7^{12sd} 12^{12gs} 3^{10gf} **0-1-6 £450**

Molly Malone *J C Tuck*   a30
6 gr m Formidable (USA) - Pharland (Fr)
7^{5sw} 7^{8sd} 11^{5sd} **0-0-3**

Molly Moon (Ire) *M Blanshard*   77
2 br f Primo Dominie - Snowing
2^{5g} 2^{5g} 3^{5gf} 1^{5gf} 3^{5gf} 1^{5gf} 6^{5gf} 4^{5gf} **2-3-8 £13,400**

Molly's Dream (Ire) *C W Thornton*   58
2 b f Night Shift (USA) - Shirley Blue (Ire)
8^{5gf} 8^{5s} 3^{6gs} 5^{7gf} PU^{7gf} **0-1-5 £468**

Molly's Secret *C G Cox*   56 a61
5 b m Minshaanshu Amad (USA) - Secret Miss
4^{10sd} 6^{9sd} 5^{12sd} 3^{12sd} 8^{12sd} 9^{10gf} 1^{10f} 5^{10f} 2^{11gf} 7^{10gf} 5^{12gf} 9^{10gf} 5^{10gf} 2^{10gf} 3^{11gf} 11^{11gf} 12^{12f} **1-4-17 £6,388**

Mollys Rainbow (Ire) *K A Ryan*   11
2 b f Desert Style (Ire) - Rainbow Reliance
10^{5gf} **0-0-1**

Molotov *I W McInnes*   54 a46
3 b g Efisio - Mindomica
5^{6sd} 5^{6sd} 3^{6sd} 5^{7sd} 6^{6sd} 10^{6gf} 13^{6sd} 7^{7gf} 16^{6gf} 3^{6sd} 8^{6sd} 8^{5sd} 19^{6f} 12^{7gf} 19^{6gf} **0-1-15 £910**

Momentous Jones *M Madgwick*   11
6 b g Emperor Jones (USA) - Ivory Moment (USA)
11^{17f} 10^{12gf} **0-0-2**

Moments I Treasure (USA) *Sir Michael Stoute*   66 a53
2 ch f Mt. Livermore (USA) - Munnaya (USA)
7^{8gf} 8^{8sd} **0-0-2**

Moments Of Joy *R Guest*   113
3 b f Darshaan - My Emma
1^{12gf} 1^{14g} 5^{15g} **2-0-3 £25,812**

Mommkin *M R Channon*   72
2 b f Royal Academy - Walimu (Ire)
4^{8gf} 2^{8gs} 5^{8gf} **0-1-3 £1,360**

Momtic (Ire) *W Jarvis*   72
2 ch c Shinko Forest (Ire) - Uffizi (Ire)
10^{6g} 3^{5gf} 2^{6f} 16^{6f} **1-1-4 £5,127**

Mon Petit Diamant *M G Quinlan*   48 a36

3 b f Hector Protector (USA) - Desert Girl
11^{7sd} 13^{7gs} 17^{10f} 5^{13gf} 5^{12gf} 6^{10f} **0-0-6**

Mon Secret (Ire) *B Smart*   63 a64
5 b g General Monash (USA) - Ron's Secret
1^{7sd} 3^{7sd} 15^{7gf} 8^{7f} 7^{8gf} 1^{7gf} **2-0-6 £7,520**

Monash Freeway (Ire) *Miss Jacqueline S Doyle*   16
5 ch h General Monash (USA) - Pennine Pearl (Ire)
15^{13g} 12^{17f} 8^{16gf} **0-0-3**

Monash Girl (Ire) *B R Johnson*   28
2 b f General Monash (USA) - Maricica
8^{7gf} 12^{8gf} **0-0-2**

Monash Lady (Ire) *J S Moore*   a49
5 ch m General Monash (USA) - Don't Be That Way (Ire)
10^{10sd} **0-0-1**

Monduru *G L Moore*   26 a44
6 b g Lion Cavern (USA) - Bint Albadou (Ire)
5^{7sw} 15^{8gf} 13^{12gf} 7^{10f} **0-0-4**

Moneybags (Ire) *B Palling*   69
3 b g Petorius - Creggan Vale Lass
6^{8g} 6^{8g} 11^{8gf} 6^{8g} 10^{8gf} **0-0-5**

Monica Geller *Ian Williams*   61
5 b m Komaite (USA) - Rion River (Ire)
5^{10g} 18^{gf} **1-0-2 £5,655**

Monksford *B J Llewellyn*   71 a27
4 b g Minster Son - Mortify
13^{11sd} 1^{10gs} 11^{10g} 11^{10gf} 5^{10gf} 8^{10gf} **1-0-6 £4,192**

Monkston Point (Ire) *D W P Arbuthnot*   98
7 b g Fayruz - Doon Belle
15^{6gf} 7^{7gf} 10^{6s} 6^{7gf} 5^{5s} **0-0-5 £865**

Monroe Gold *M L W Bell*   41
3 ch g Pivotal - Golden Daring (Ire)
9^{8g} 8^{8gf} 11^{7gf} 10^{14f} 7^{10gf} 2^{8s} **0-1-6 £1,090**

Monsal Dale (Ire) *B J Llewellyn*   62 a65
4 ch g Desert King (Ire) - Zanella (Ire)
1^{12sd} 4^{12sd} 4^{12sd} 4^{12sd} 7^{12gf} 2^{16gf} 4^{15sd} 6^{16sd} 4^{18gf} 2^{16gf} 3^{15sd} 5^{16gf} **1-3-12 £5,772**

Monsieur Bond (Ire) *B Smart*   113
3 ch c Danehill Dancer (USA) - Musical Essence
3^{8f} 6^{8g} 10^{8gf} 1^{7gf} 6^{7g} 2^{7gf} 1^{7g} 2^{7gf} 5^{6ho} **2-2-9 £58,968**

Mont Rocher (Fr) *J E Hammond*   105
8 gr g Caerleon (USA) - Cuixmala (Fr)
6^{10sd} 7^{10gs} 2^{12vs} 2^{13g} 3^{11gs} 8^{10g} **0-1-6 £14,870**

Montana *R Hannon*   76
3 b c Puissance - Mistral's Dancer
2^{6gf} 2^{6gf} 3^{6gf} 8^{6gf} **0-3-4 £3,549**

Monte Bianco (Ire) *L M Cumani*   76
2 b c King Of Kings (Ire) - Creme Caramel (USA)
9^{6gf} 9^{6gs} 2^{6gf} 1^{7gf} 5^{7f} 4^{8gf} 9^{7gf} **1-2-7 £4,576**

Monte Mayor Lad (Ire) *D Haydn Jones*   a69
3 b g Sesaro (USA) - Alcalali (USA)
4^{7sd} 3^{6sd} 3^{7sd} 8^{6sd} **0-2-4 £1,376**

Monte Verde (Ire) *B Palling*   62 a53
3 b f Whittingham (Ire) - Anita's Love (Ire)
2^{6sd} 11^{7sd} 16^{6g} 5^{5gs} 1^{5f} 6^{5gf} 9^{5gf} 4^{6gf} **1-1-8 £4,398**

Montecassino Abbey (Ire) *P W Harris*   84 a92
4 b g Danehill (USA) - Battle Mountain (Ire)
3^{8sd} 9^{7sd} 5^{7gf} 7^{8g} 5^{7gf} 17^{7sd} **0-1-6**

£744

Montecristo *R Guest* 82
10 br g Warning - Sutosky
3^{12g} 5^{12g} 3^{12gf} 2^{12gf} 3^{14gf} **0-3-5 £7,443**

Montessori Mio (Fr) *R Ford* 55
4 b g Robellino (USA) - Child's Play (USA)
6^{13gf} 11^{17f} **0-0-2**

Montez (USA) *W M Brisbourne* 66
4 ch g Royal Academy (USA) - Omara (USA)
11^{7g} 13^{8gs} 3^{6f} 6^{5g} 5^{6gf} 13^{6gf} 7^{5gf} **0-1-7**
£565

Montmartre (Ire) *N A Callaghan* 98
3 b f Grand Lodge (USA) - French Quarter
10^{10gf} 12^{9gf} 2^{9gs} 6^{8g} 5^{10g} 5^{12f} 2^{10gs}
1^{10g} 4^{10g} 2^{9gf} 2^{10gf} 3^{10s} 1^{10gf} 1^{12gf} 14^{12gf}
3-4-15 £33,805

Montosari *P Mitchell* 52
4 ch g Persian Bold - Sartigila
8^{11gf} 8^{12f} 4^{13gf} 6^{14f} 8^{12gf} 8^{12gf} **0-0-6**
£315

Montoya (Ire) *P D Cundell* a45
4 b g Kylian (USA) - Saborinie
7^{12sd} **0-0-1**

Monturani (Ire) *G Wragg* 109
4 b f Indian Ridge - Mezzogiorno
6^{8gf} 2^{8gf} 2^{10gs} 3^{10g} 4^{8gf} 2^{8g} **0-3-6**
£42,249

Moon At Night *Mrs P Ford*
8 gr g Pursuit Of Love - La Nureyeva (USA)
12^{7sd} **0-0-1**

Moon Ballad (Ire) *Saeed Bin Suroor* 123 a131
4 ch c Singspiel (Ire) - Velvet Moon (Ire)
1^{9ft} 1^{10ft} 9^{10gf} 5^{8gs} 5^{10gf} 5^{10ft} **2-0-6**
£2,323,866

Moon Edge *M P Tregoning* 55 a58
4 gr f Beveled (USA) - Zamoon
9^{10sd} 6^{8sd} 5^{6sd} 7^{7g} 9^{8f} BD^{8gf} **0-0-6**

Moon Emperor *J R Jenkins* 102 a101
6 b g Emperor Jones (USA) - Sir Hollow (USA)
1^{13sd} 8^{14g} 6^{14gf} 5^{14gf} 5^{16gf} 10^{21gs} 7^{16gf}
1-0-7 £14,246

Moon Jaguar (Ire) *J G Given* a52
3 b c Bahhare - Top Of The Form (Ire)
5^{11sd} 4^{9sd} **0-0-2**

Moon Legend (USA) *W Jarvis* 60
2 ch f Gulch (USA) - Highland Legend (USA)
10^{6gf} 6^{6gf} **0-0-2**

Moon Royale *Mrs N Macauley* 48 a38
5 ch m Royal Abjar (USA) - Ragged Moon
5^{8sd} 5^{9sd} 8^{8sd} 4^{8sd} 8^{8sd} 14^{8sd} 6^{8f} 2^{7g}
5^{8gf} 17^{8gf} 9^{8gf} **0-1-11 £936**

Moonglade (USA) *Miss J Feilden* 24
3 ch f Carson City (USA) - Moonshine Girl (USA)
12^{8ft} 12^{8ft} 9^{8gf} **0-0-3**

Moonlight Man *R Hannon* 99
2 ch c Night Shift (USA) - Fleeting Rainbow
3^{6g} 4^{6gf} 1^{6gf} 1^{6gf} 1^{7gf} 3^{6gf} **3-1-6**
£21,146

Moonlight Song (Ire) *John A Harris* 46 a7
6 b m Mujadil (USA) - Model Show (Ire)
13^{6sd} 16^{6gs} 9^{7gs} 11^{7sd} 7^{7gf} 12^{7gf} 7^{7g}
6^{7g} 15^{7gf} **0-0-9**

Moonlight Tango (USA) *J H M Gosden* 64
2 br f Benny The Dip (USA) - Summer Dance
8^{7gf} 4^{8gf} **0-0-2 £480**

Moonshine Beach *P W Hiatt* 71
5 b g Lugana Beach - Monongelia
6^{12gf} 1^{18gf} 7^{15gf} 5^{17gf} **1-0-4 £3,887**

Moonshine Bill *P W Hiatt* 60
4 ch g Master Willie - Monongelia
10^{12sd} 13^{10gf} 9^{14gs} 1^{10g} 5^{12gf} 2^{10gf} 8^{12f}
1-1-7 £5,913

Moonsprite *E A L Dunlop* 87
3 b f Seeking The Gold (USA) - Moonshell (Ire)
1^{10gs} 1^{10gf} 7^{12gf} 9^{10gf} **2-0-4 £10,832**

Moonstone Myth (Ire) *D W P Arbuthnot* 41
2 ch f Night Shift (USA) - Marble Halls (Ire)
11^{5gf} 11^{6gf} 4^{5f} 6^{6gf} 12^{7f} **0-0-5**

Moorlaw (Ire) *J A Osborne* 32
2 b c Mtoto - Belle Etoile (Fr)
17^{8g} **0-0-1**

Moors Myth *B W Hills* 55
2 b c Anabaa (USA) - West Devon (USA)
12^{7g} **0-0-1**

Moqui Marble (Ger) *B J Curley* a49
7 b g Petit Loup - Margo's New Hope (USA)
5^{12sd} 3^{8sd} **0-1-2 £421**

Morag *I A Wood* 70
2 b f Aragon - Minnehaha
5^{7gf} 4^{7gf} 9^{7g} 1^{7gf} 1^{7gf} 8^{7gf} 18^{7gf} 5^{6gf}
21^{7g} **2-0-9 £16,116**

Morahib *M P Tregoning* 95
5 ch h Nashwan (USA) - Irish Valley (USA)
1^{8g} 5^{8gf} **1-0-2 £13,785**

Morefinesse *T D Easterby* 52
3 ch g Efisio - With Finesse
10^{7gf} 4^{7t} 5^{7f} 2^{7gs} 2^{7f} 10^{8gf} **0-2-6**
£2,733

Morgan Lewis (Ire) *G B Balding* 61
2 b g Orpen (USA) - Party Piece
4^{5g} 11^{5gf} 8^{5gf} **0-0-3 £320**

Morgan The Red *T D Easterby* 22
3 ch g Presidium - Warning Bell
15^{10f} 9^{11gf} **0-0-2**

Morgans Orchard (Ire) *A G Newcombe*
7 ch g Forest Wind (USA) - Regina St Cyr (Ire)
10^{12sd} **0-0-1**

Moritat (Ire) *P S McEntee* 67
3 b c Night Shift (USA) - Aunty Eileen
10^{6gf} 2^{5gf} 10^{5g} 6^{6gf} **0-1-4 £1,106**

Morluc (USA) *Randy L Morse* 31
7 b h Housebuster (USA) - Flashing Eyes (USA)
2^{5f} 7^{5s} 17^{6f} **0-0-3 £14,413**

Mornin Reserves *I Semple* 111
4 b g Atraf - Pusey Street Girl
9^{5hy} 1^{5gs} 1^{5gf} 3^{5g} 10^{5gf} 1^{5s} 2^{5gf} **3-2-7**
£52,930

Morning After *J R Fanshawe* 79
3 b f Emperor Jones (USA) - Oneforditch (USA)
4^{7gf} 3^{8gf} **0-0-2 £1,301**

Morning Echo *M Dods* 17
3 ch f Pivotal - Crofters Ceilidh
12^{10g} **0-0-1**

Morning Hawk (USA) *J S Moore* 58
2 b f Silver Hawk (USA) - Dawn Aurora (USA)
9^{6gf} 5^{6gf} 8^{7gf} 7^{7gf} 7^{8gs} **0-0-5**

Morning Light *L R James*
3 b g Danehill Dancer (Ire) - Edge Of Darkness
5^{14gs} **0-0-1**

Morning Sun *K O Cunningham-Brown* 48 a38

3 b f Starborough - Malham Tarn
12^{8sd} 11^{8sd} 6^{10g} 6^{10gf} 5^{10gf} 11^{8sd} 13^{9gf}
10^{10g} **0-0-8**

Morning Warning (Ire) *J G Given*   42
2 b f Inzar (USA) - Morning Stroll
16^{5gf} 9^{5gf} 11^{6gf} 10^{5gf} 13^{6gf} **0-0-5**

Morris Dancing (USA) *B P J Baugh*
4 b g Rahy (USA) - Summer Dance
12^{8sd} 15^{11sd} 19^{8gf} **0-0-3**

Morse (Ire) *J A Osborne*   78 a68
2 b c Shinko Forest (Ire) - Auriga
9^{5gf} 1^{6gs} 1^{6gf} 10^{6g} 5^{7f} 7^{7gf} 3^{7sd} 3^{6g}
6^{6gf} **2-2-9 £13,878**

Morson Boy (USA) *M Johnston*   104
3 b c Lear Fan (USA) - Esprit D'Escalier (USA)
1^{12gf} 1^{15g} 5^{14gf} 1^{12gf} **3-0-4 £23,800**

Morvern (Ire) *J G Given*   65 a22
3 ch g Titus Livius (Fr) - Scotia Rose
11^{8g} 12^{10sd} 3^{10f} 6^{10f} 10^{11gf} 13^{10sd} 10^{8g}
4^{10gf} **0-1-8 £558**

Moscow (Ire) *P D Evans*   41
4 ch g Cadeaux Genereux - Madame Nureyev (USA)
6^{8gs} 9^{10gf} 14^{8gf} 14^{8g} 14^{8gf} 13^{8gf} 14^{8f}
0-0-7

Moscow Ballet (Ire) *A P O'Brien*   108
2 b c Sadler's Wells (USA) - Fire The Groom (USA)
1^{8g} 2^{8gf} 5^{8g} **1-1-3 £32,129**

Moscow Blue *J H M Gosden*   55
2 ch c Soviet Star (USA) - Aquamarine
11^{7gf} **0-0-1**

Moscow Express (Ire) *Miss F M Crowley*   74
11 ch g Moscow Society (USA) - Corrielek
6^{22f} 9^{16gf} 4^{16f} **0-0-3 £872**

Moscow Mary *A G Newcombe*   60
2 b f Imperial Ballet (Ire) - Baileys Firecat
6^{5gf} 11^{5g} 2^{6gs} 2^{6gf} 4^{6f} 1^{6gf} 2^{5gf} 7^{7gs}
3^{5gf} 2^{6gf} 4^{7gf} **1-5-11 £8,104**

Moscow Times *D R C Elsworth*   72
2 b c Soviet Star (USA) - Bargouzine
6^{5g} 10^{7gf} **0-0-2**

Moss Vale (Ire) *B W Hills*   96
2 b c Shinko Forest (Ire) - Wolf Cleugh (Ire)
5^{6gs} 1^{6g} 6^{6g} 3^{5g} **1-1-4 £7,072**

Most Definitely (Ire) *T D Easterby*   70 a8
3 b g Definite Article - Unbidden Melody (USA)
4^{12gf} 8^{12sd} 9^{12gf} 3^{14gf} 2^{17gf} 2^{16gs} 2^{16gf}
2^{14gf} 2^{14f} **0-6-9 £6,922**

Most-Saucy *I A Wood*   79 a75
7 br m Most Welcome - So Saucy
7^{10sd} 3^{8sd} 1^{10sd} 3^{9sd} 7^{10sd} 6^{12sd} 1^{11gf}
3^{12f} 5^{10sd} 13^{11gf} 3^{12gf} 1^{12gf} 7^{10gf} 5^{12gf} 2^{10sd}
8^{12g} 2^{12gf} 1^{12g}
3^{12gf} **4-8-25 £23,672**

Mostarsil (USA) *G L Moore*   77 a55
5 ch g Kingmambo (USA) - Naazeq
1^{12sd} 3^{12sd} 5^{12gf} 2^{12f} 5^{22gf} 7^{12gf} 1^{12f}
2^{12gf} 1^{12g} 4^{12g} 1^{12gf} 5^{12g} 2^{16gf} 7^{16gf} 6^{16gf}
4-4-15 £30,130

Moten Swing *R Hannon*   68 a77
4 b g Kris - Lady Bankes (Ire)
15^{7g} 1^{8sd} 11^{7gf} 5^{7g} **1-0-4 £3,614**

Mother Corrigan (Ire) *M Brittain*   a45
7 gr m Paris House - Missed Opportunity (Ire)
3^{6sd} 13^{7sw} **0-1-2 £418**

Motivus (USA) *Christophe Clement*   69 a91

2 b c Cherokee Run (USA) - Noble Cause (Can)
2^{6gf} 4^{6gs} 1^{7sd} **1-1-3 £6,688**

Motu (Ire) *J L Dunlop*   79
2 b c Desert Style (Ire) - Pink Cashmere (Ire)
4^{6gs} 1^{6gf} 14^{6gf} **1-0-3 £4,918**

Mouftari (USA) *B W Hills*   56
2 b c Miswaki (USA) - Nature's Magic (USA)
8^{7gf} **0-0-1**

Moulin De Mougins (Ire) *P C Haslam*   86
2 b c Night Shift (USA) - Sama Veda (Ire)
7^{5gf} 6^{6s} 1^{7gf} 2^{7gs} 1^{7gf} 1^{7gs} 2^{7gf} 7^{8gf}
3-2-8 £19,766

Mount Benger *R M Beckett*   65 a30
3 ch g Selkirk (USA) - Vice Vixen (Can)
14^{6sd} 9^{10g} 9^{9sd} **0-0-3**

Mount Heaton (Ire) *E J O'Neill*
3 b f Among Men (USA) - Dollar Magic
9^{8sd} **0-0-1**

Mount Hesse (Fr) *G Wragg*   78
4 ch g Midyan (USA) - Minaudeuse (USA)
15^{7gf} 6^{8gf} **0-0-2 £132**

Mount Hillaby (Ire) *M W Easterby*   66 a46
3 b f Mujadil (USA) - Tetradonna (Ire)
9^{7gf} 10^{8gf} 8^{10gs} 6^{8gf} 12^{7gf} 13^{6gf} 8^{5sd}
0-0-7

Mount Pekan (Ire) *J S Goldie*   66
3 b c Sri Pekan (USA) - The Highlands (Fr)
14^{7g} 11^{7gf} 5^{8g} 9^{8g} 4^{8gs} 14^{7f} 5^{9gf} 7^{9g}
9^{9g} 7^{8f} **0-0-10 £286**

Mount Royale (Ire) *J A Osborne*   60 a73
5 ch g Wolfhound (USA) - Mahabba (USA)
2^{7sd} 2^{7sd} 2^{7sd} 1^{7sw} 1^{7sd} 4^{7sw} 12^{7sd} 5^{7sd}
2^{6sd} 3^{6gf} 3^{7gf} 4^{7sd} 7^{6sd} 1^{7f} 5^{6f} **3-6-15**
£13,195

Mount Superior (USA) *P W D'Arcy*   40 a40
7 b g Conquistador Cielo (USA) - Zum Solitair (USA)
6^{7sw} 6^{7f} **0-0-2**

Mount Vettore *Mrs J R Ramsden*   54
2 br g Vettori (Ire) - Honeyspike (Ire)
5^{5gf} **0-0-1**

Mountain Meadow *Mrs A J Perrett*   76
2 ch g Deploy - Woodwardia (USA)
2^{8gf} **0-1-1 £1,920**

Mountcharge (Ire) *C N Allen*   75
2 b g Intikhab (USA) - Zorilla
11^{6gf} 6^{6gs} 1^{8gf} **1-0-3 £3,770**

Mountrath Rock *Miss B Sanders*   44 a32
6 b m Rock Hopper - Point Of Law
3^{15gf} 5^{17f} 4^{12f} 5^{16gf} 8^{16sd} **0-1-5 £838**

Mountsorrel (Ire) *T Wall*   a36
4 b g Charnwood Forest (Ire) - Play The Queen (Ire)
9^{15sd} 9^{8sd} 8^{9sd} 17^{11gf} **0-0-4**

Mouseman *C N Kellett*   57 a27
2 b c Young Ern - Scottish Royal (Ire)
6^{6f} 6^{7sd} 3^{7f} 9^{6gf} 3^{7gf} 1^{6gf} 10^{6gf} **1-2-7**
£3,013

Move It *R Charlton*   108
3 ch c Cadeaux Genereux - Midnight Shift (Ire)
1^{5f} 1^{6gf} 1^{5gf} 2^{6g} 8^{5gf} 1^{6g} 1^{6gf} 3^{6gf}
5-1-8 £106,096

Movie King (Ire) *S Gollings*   86 a90
4 ch g Catrail (USA) - Marilyn (Ire)
9^{10sd} 1^{10sd} 6^{10sd} 13^{10gf} 4^{10g} 8^{12gf} 7^{10gf}
4^{9gf} 5^{10g} 15^{10g} **1-1-10 £17,293**

Mowelga *Lady Herries*   85

9 ch g Most Welcome - Galactic Miss
PU12sd 1512gf 612gf 412gf **0-0-4 £420**

Moyanna (Ire) *T D Barron* 78
3 b f Sri Pekan (USA) - Certain Impression (USA)
36f 26gf 146g 148gs 28gf 57gf 27f 16gf
1-4-8 £7,131

Moyeala (Ire) *Eamon Tyrrell* 69 a18
5 b m Royal Academy (USA) - Khalsheva
108sd 28gf 38y 28g UR10f **0-3-5 £3,668**

Moyne Pleasure (Ire) *Paul Johnson* 59 a60
5 b g Exit To Nowhere (USA) - Ilanga (Ire)
711sw 68sd 1410gs 1113gs 216sd 814gf 216gs
412gf 413gs 513gf **0-2-10 £3,336**

Mozzarella *Don Enrico Incisa*
3 ch f King's Signet (USA) - Martine
135gs 145g **0-0-2**

Mr Belvedere *R Hannon* 69
2 b c Royal Applause - Alarming Motown
65f 46gs 26gf 117gf 57gf 97gf 37f 197g
0-2-8 £1,922

Mr Bill *Mrs N Macauley*
3 ch g Cosmonaut - Latch On (Ire)
810gf 118g 1411sd 98g **0-0-4**

Mr Bountiful (Ire) *M Dods* 65 a64
5 b g Mukaddamah (USA) - Nawadder
97sd 17sw 17sd 137sd 47gf 37gs 107sf 107f
77sd 37f 77gf 37gf 87gf 26gf 76g 67gf 47gf
2-5-17 £9,109

Mr Chestnut Tree *Mrs A M Naughton* 39 a11
4 ch f Forzando - Sure Flyer (Ire)
75sd 99sd 77gs 116gf 128gf 148gf 811gf
812gf 912gf 1111gf **0-0-10**

Mr Dave *M A Jarvis* 9
3 b g General Monash (USA) - Cavatina
157gs **0-0-1**

Mr Dinos (Ire) *P F I Cole* 123
4 b c Desert King (Ire) - Spear Dance
116gf 120gf 620ho **2-0-3 £203,000**

Mr Dip *A W Carroll* 65
3 b g Reprimand - Scottish Lady
1410g 58hy 97gf **0-0-3**

Mr Dumby (Ire) *R Hannon* 62
3 b c Sri Pekan (USA) - Lady Windermere (Ire)
26g 118gf 96gf **0-1-3 £1,676**

Mr Ed (Ire) *P Bowen* 85
5 ch g In The Wings - Center Moriches (Ire)
716gf 912g 114gs 114gs 1920gf 214g 614g
816gf 912gf 1414gf **2-1-10 £20,881**

Mr Fleming *Dr J D Scargill* 39 a55
4 b/br g Bin Ajwaad (Ire) - Fabulous Night (Fr)
88sd 167sd 1212sd 410sd 411gf **0-0-5**

Mr Fortywinks (Ire) *B Ellison* 69
9 ch g Fool's Holme (USA) - Dream On
716gf 713gs 516gs 317gf 415g 116gf 417gf
816g 616g **1-1-9 £4,644**

Mr Gisby (USA) *Mrs L Wadham* a77
5 b g Chief's Crown (USA) - Double Lock
716sd DSQ14sd 214sw 316sw 112sw 812sd **1-2-6
£5,163**

Mr Hawkeye (USA) *Ms A E Embiricos* 18
4 ch g Royal Academy (USA) - Port Plaisance (USA)
912f 1316gf **0-0-2**

Mr Independent (Ire) *E A L Dunlop* 59
2 b c Cadeaux Genereux - Iris May
87g 38g 106gf **0-1-3 £358**

Mr Jack Daniells (Ire) *W R Muir* 69
2 b c Mujadil (USA) - Neat Shilling (Ire)
76g 17gf 187g 197gf **1-0-4 £3,542**

Mr Lear (USA) *T D Barron* 80 a73
4 b g Lear Fan (USA) - Majestic Mae (USA)
48sd 38gf 310gf 1010gs 410gs 112gf 512g
612f 213gf 110gf 212gf 112gf 912gf 412gf 1010f
3-3-15 £20,143

Mr Lewin *R A Fahey* 49
2 ch g Primo Dominie - Fighting Run
86f 77g 57gf **0-0-3**

Mr Loverman (Ire) *Miss V Haigh* 61
3 ch g Spectrum (Ire) - Soviet Artic (Fr)
88g 138gf 118gf 810gf 198gf 147sw **0-0-6**

Mr Malarkey (Ire) *Mrs C A Dunnett* 87
3 b g Pivotal - Girl Next Door
76g 16f 16gf 56g 46gf 26g 16gf 36gf 75gf
46gf 156gf 95gf 86gf **3-2-13 £27,070**

Mr Midasman (Ire) *R Hollinshead* 68
2 b c Entrepreneur - Sifaara (Ire)
96g 46g 17gs **1-0-3 £2,554**

Mr Mischief *P C Haslam* 72
3 b g Millkom - Snow Huntress
810gf 88gf 510gf 1811g 211gs **0-1-5 £892**

Mr Mischievous *N P Littmoden* 26
2 b c Magic Ring (Ire) - Inya Lake
95g **0-0-1**

Mr Moon *M D Hammond* 21 a6
2 b c Pursuit Of Love - Sound Of Sleat
136gf 106sd 126sd **0-0-3**

Mr Pertemps *R A Fahey* 44 a62
5 b g Primo Dominie - Amber Mill
16sw 36sw 16sw 15sd 96gf **3-1-5 £10,491**

Mr Piano Man (Ire) *Mrs A M Naughton* 5
5 gr g Paris House - Winter March
196gf 166gf **0-0-2**

Mr Sandancer *P Mitchell* a66
4 b g Zafonic (USA) - Um Lardaff
1310sd 1012sd 512sd **0-0-3**

Mr Smithers Jones *S C Williams* a26
3 br g Emperor Jones (USA) - Phylian
56sd **0-0-1**

Mr Spliffy (Ire) *K R Burke* 69 a45
4 b g Fayruz - Johns Conquerer (Ire)
85gf 85gf 146gf 85gf 25gf 135gf 55gf 45g
135f 25gf 55f 75gf 135gf 85gf 75sd 25gf 75gs
0-4-17 £3,964

Mr Stylish *J S Moore* 47 a67
7 b g Mazilier (USA) - Moore Stylish
137sd 76sd 27sw 47sd 67sd 26sd 66gf 67sd
146gf **0-2-9 £1,690**

Mr Tambourine Man (Ire) *P F I Cole* 78
2 b c Rainbow Quest (USA) - Girl From Ipanema
27gf 67gf 18gf **1-1-3 £5,568**

Mr Tangerine (Ire) *M J Wallace* 28
2 b c Fayruz - Mildred Anne (Ire)
85gf 166gf **0-0-2**

Mr Tango (Arg) *C Von Der Recke* 104
5 b h Numerous (USA) - Milonguera Fitz (Arg)
810sd 110sd 138g 188gf 188g 610gf 88sd
610gs **2-0-9 £13,238**

Mr Uppity (Ire) *Julian Poulton* 35 a50
4 b g Shareef Dancer (USA) - Queenfisher
97sd 35sw 25sw 56sd 125sd 126gf 117sd

12⁷ˢᵈ **0-2-8 £1,453**

Mr Velocity (Ire) *A C Stewart*   75 a69
3 b c Tagula (Ire) - Miss Rusty (Ire)
6⁷ᵍᶠ 3⁷ᵍᶠ 3⁸ᵍᶠ 3⁸ˢᵈ 3⁸ᵍ 8⁸ᵍ **0-4-6**
£2,023

Mr Whizz *A P Jones*   53
6 ch g Manhal - Panienka (Pol)
5⁷ᶠ 7¹⁰ᵍᶠ 5¹⁰ᶠ 14¹²ᵍ 7⁹ᵍ 7⁷ᶠ 11¹¹ᵍᶠ 9¹⁰ᶠ
0-0-8

Mr Wolf *D W Barker*   61
2 b c Wolfhound (USA) - Madam Millie
12⁶ᵍ 4⁵ᶠ 5⁵ᵍᶠ 14⁶ᵍᶠ 13⁶ᵍˢ **0-0-5 £476**

Mrs Boz *A W Carroll*   30
3 b f Superpower - Bar None
11⁷ᵍᶠ 6⁸ᵍᶠ **0-0-2**

Mrs Cee (Ire) *M G Quinlan*   72
2 b f Orpen (USA) - Cutleaf
1⁷ᵍ 10⁷ᵍᶠ 4⁶ᵍᶠ 4⁹ᵍ 6¹⁰ᵍᶠ **1-0-5 £7,785**

Mrs Cube *J M Bradley*   45
4 ch f Missed Flight - Norska
12⁸ᵍˢ 7⁷ᵍᶠ 6⁶ᵍᶠ 13⁸ᵍᶠ 6⁷ᵍᶠ 8⁸ᵍᶠ **0-0-6**

Mrs Gee (Ire) *R Hollinshead*   61
2 b f Desert Story (Ire) - My Gloria (Ire)
5⁸ᵍᶠ 5⁸ᵍᶠ 4⁸ᵍ **0-0-3 £293**

Mrs Moh (Ire) *T D Easterby*   80 a59
2 b f Orpen (USA) - My Gray (Fr)
1⁵ˢᵈ 4⁵ᵍ 8⁵ᵍᶠ 4⁶ᵍᶠ 2⁷ᵍ 2⁶ᵍ 9⁷ᵍᶠ 3⁷ᵍᶠ 2⁷ᵍ
1-4-9 £25,420

Mrs Pankhurst *B W Hills*   76
2 b f Selkirk (USA) - Melodist (USA)
7⁷ᵍᶠ 1⁸ᵍ 10¹⁰ᵍˢ **1-0-3 £3,811**

Mrs Plum *I A Wood*
4 b f Emarati (USA) - Aubade
16⁸ˢᵈ **0-0-1**

Mrs Pooters (Ire) *D W P Arbuthnot*   a31
4 b f Petardia - Mrs Hooters
11¹⁰ˢᵈ 12¹²ˢᵈ **0-0-2**

Mrs Shilling *J R Fanshawe*   54
2 b f Dr Fong (USA) - Papaha (Fr)
6⁶ᵍᶠ **0-0-1**

Mrs Spence *M W Easterby*   56
2 b f Mind Games - Maid O'Cannie
12⁵ˢ 2⁶ᶠ 5⁷ᵍᶠ **0-1-3 £1,151**

Mualafah *M P Tregoning*   74
3 b f Indian Ridge - Dalayil (Ire)
3¹⁰ᶠ 3⁹ᵍᶠ 5⁸ᶠ **0-1-3 £1,788**

Mubeen (Ire) *E A L Dunlop*   102
3 ch c Barathea (Ire) - Fernanda
2⁹ᵍᶠ 3⁸ᵍˢ 3¹⁰ᵍᶠ 2⁸ᵍᶠ 1⁸ᵍᶠ 3¹⁰ᵍᶠ 21⁸ᵍ **1-3-7**
£28,379

Mubtaker (USA) *M P Tregoning*   132
6 ch h Silver Hawk (USA) - Gazayil (USA)
1¹⁰ᵍᶠ 1¹³ᵍᶠ 1¹²ᵍ 2¹²ʰᵒ **3-1-4 £336,391**

Much Faster (Ire) *P Bary*   108
2 b f Fasliyev (USA) - Interruption
1⁵ᵍˢ 1⁶ᵍ 1⁵ˢ 1⁶ᵛˢ 2⁶ˢ 9⁶ᵍᶠ **4-1-6**
£112,532

Muchachodelcastill (Ire) *P C Haslam*   37
2 b g Spectrum (Ire) - Nationalartgallery (Ire)
10⁵ᵈˢ 12⁶ᵍᶠ 17⁶ᵍᶠ **0-0-3**

Muchea *M R Channon*   100
9 ch h Shalford - Bargouzine
13⁸ᵍ 4⁹ᵍᶠ 5⁸ᵍᶠ 5⁸ᵍ 7⁸ᵍᶠ 4⁸ᵍᶠ 13⁸ˢ 2⁹ᵍᶠ
1⁸ᵍ 7⁸ᵍ 1⁸ᵍᶠ 5⁸ᵍᶠ 6⁸ᵍᶠ 11¹⁰ᵍᶠ 8⁸ᵍˢ 5⁸ᵍˢ
2-1-16 £35,338

Mucho Gusto *R F Marvin*   38 a31
5 b g Casteddu - Heather Honey
10⁷ᵍᶠ 10¹²ᵍᶠ 9¹⁰ᵍᶠ 13⁷ᵍᶠ 6⁹ˢʷ 8¹¹ᵍ 5¹²ᵍᶠ
0-0-7

Muckabell (Ire) *A M Balding*   47
2 ch c Mukaddamah (USA) - Mystic Belle (Ire)
7⁷ᵍᶠ **0-0-1**

Mucky Business *T G Mills*   a61
3 b g Lahib (USA) - Berliese (Ire)
8¹⁰ˢᵈ 3¹¹ˢᵈ 11¹⁰ˢᵈ 11¹³ᵍ **0-1-4 £465**

Mudawin (Ire) *M P Tregoning*   68
2 b g Intikhab (USA) - Fida (Ire)
5⁷ᵍ **0-0-1**

Muffit (Ire) *Paul Johnson*
4 b f Alhaarth (Ire) - Calash
12⁶ˢᵈ **0-0-1**

Mufreh (USA) *A G Newcombe*   37 a85
5 br g Dayjur (USA) - Mathkurh (USA)
2⁶ˢᵈ 2⁶ˢʷ 3⁷ˢʷ 1⁷ˢᵈ 1⁷ˢᵈ 8⁸ˢᵈ 2⁶ˢᵈ 12⁶ᵍˢ
1⁶ˢᵈ **3-4-9 £13,899**

Muhareb (USA) *C E Brittain*   106
4 ch c Thunder Gulch (USA) - Queen Of Spirit (USA)
15¹⁰ᵍᶠ 6¹⁰ᵍ 1¹²ᵍᶠ 3¹²ᵍ 11¹²ᵍᶠ 3¹²ᵍᶠ 13¹⁴ᵍᶠ
10¹²ᶠ 4¹²ᵍᶠ **1-2-9 £20,857**

Muhaymin (USA) *J L Dunlop*   79
2 ch c A.P. Indy (USA) - Shadayid (USA)
9⁷ᵍᶠ 3⁷ᵍᶠ 1⁸ᵍᶠ **1-1-3 £4,995**

Mujalia (Ire) *P S McEntee*   11
5 b g Mujtahid (USA) - Danalia (Ire)
8¹²ᶠ 9¹²ᵍᶠ 1⁸ᵍᶠ 12¹⁰ˢᵈ 13⁸ᵍᶠ **0-0-5**

Mujarad (USA) *S J Mahon*   81
3 b/br g King Of Kings (Ire) - Happy Result (USA)
11⁷ᵍˢ 1⁷ᵍᶠ 23⁸ᵍᶠ **1-0-3 £5,570**

Mujkari (Ire) *J M Bradley*   54 a58
7 ch g Mujtahid (USA) - Hot Curry (USA)
4⁸ˢᵈ 5¹⁰ˢᵈ 13¹²ˢᵈ 7¹⁰ˢᵈ 15⁷ˢᵈ 5¹⁰ᶠ
10¹⁰ᶠ 5¹⁰ᵍᶠ 2⁸ᵍ 2⁷ᶠ 4⁷ᵍᶠ 1⁷ᵍ 4⁸ᵍᶠ **1-3-14**
£6,556

Mukafeh (USA) *J L Dunlop*   95
2 b c Danzig (USA) - Bint Salsabil (USA)
1⁷ᵍᶠ 3⁷ᵍ **1-1-2 £8,550**

Muktasb (USA) *M P Tregoning*   58
2 b c Bahri (USA) - Maghaarb
7⁶ᵍᶠ 7⁶ᵍˢ **0-0-2**

Mulabee (USA) *R T Phillips*   26 a58
4 br g Gulch (USA) - Shir Dar (Fr)
9⁸ˢᵈ 11⁹ˢᵈ 12⁷ˢᵈ 11¹⁰ˢᵈ 11¹⁰ᶠ 12⁷ᵍᶠ
10⁷ˢᵈ **0-0-7**

Mulan Princess (Ire) *S C Burrough*   56 a66
3 b f Mukaddamah (USA) - Notley Park
1⁷ˢᵈ 3⁷ˢᵈ 10⁷ˢʷ 4⁷ᵍᶠ 6⁸ᵍ 7⁷ᶠ 7⁷ᵍᶠ
14⁸ᵍᶠ **1-1-9 £6,279**

Muller (Ire) *J S Haldane*
3 gr g Bigstone (Ire) - Missie Madam (Ire)
10⁹ᵍˢ 12¹²ᶠ **0-0-2**

Mullion *A M Balding*   76
3 b g Reprimand - Royal Jade
6⁷ᵍᶠ 10⁶ᵍˢ 10⁷ᵍᶠ 5⁸ᵍᶠ 8⁸ᶠ **0-0-5 £218**

Mulsanne *P A Pritchard*   17
5 b g Clantime - Prim Lass
9⁶ᵍᶠ 13⁸ᵍᶠ **0-0-2**

Multahab *Miss D A McHale*   50 a58
4 b/br c Zafonic (USA) - Alumisiyah (USA)
2⁵ˢᵈ 8⁵ˢᵈ 5⁶ᵍ 5⁶ᶠ **0-1-4 £1,130**

Multaka (USA) *J L Dunlop*   16

3 b f Gone West (USA) - Wasnah (USA)
13[8gf] 0-0-1

Multicolour *R Hannon*   59
3 ch f Rainbow Quest (USA) - Raymouna (Ire)
8[10g] 6[12gf] 10[12g] 12[12g] 0-0-4

Multiple Choice (Ire) *N P Littmoden*   79 a78
2 ch c Woodborough (USA) - Cosmona
10[6gf] 8[5gf] 4[5gf] 3[5f] 6[5gf] 1[5sd] 3[6gs] 3[5gf]
2[5gf] 7[5g] 7[5g] 4[5sd] 1-3-12 £11,301

Multistore *R Charlton*   74
3 ch f Elmaamul (USA) - Superstore (USA)
2[8gs] 3[7gf] 7[6gf] 4[8gf] 0-2-4 £2,232

Mumbling (Ire) *B G Powell*   86
5 ch g Dr Devious (Ire) - Valley Lights (Ire)
11[12gf] 10[14gf] 1[12f] 8[12f] 2[12gf] 9[12gf] 8[12gf]
6[12gf] 6[11gf] 7[12gf] 3[12gf] 3[15gf] 1-2-12 £8,596

Munaafis (USA) *J L Dunlop*   44
3 b/br c Storm Cat (USA) - Firdous
16[8gf] 11[7gf] 10[8s] 0-0-3

Munaahej (Ire) *B W Hills*   53
2 b c Soviet Star (USA) - Azyaa
10[5g] 5[6gs] 0-0-2

Munaawashat (Ire) *M Johnston*   65
2 b f Marju (Ire) - Simaat (USA)
2[6gf] 6[6gs] 1[6g] 1-1-3 £5,384

Munaawesh (USA) *M P Tregoning*   73
2 b c Bahri (USA) - Istikbal (USA)
7[7s] 5[8gf] 0-0-2

Mundo Raro *R M Stronge*   a30
8 b g Zafonic (USA) - Star Spectacle
6[16sd] 0-0-1

Mungo Duff (Ire) *J Jay*
8 b g Priolo (USA) - Noble Dust (USA)
16[9gf] 0-0-1

Mungo Jerry (Ger) *J G Given*   40
2 b c Tannenkonig (Ire) - Mostly Sure (Ire)
14[7gf] 0-0-1

Muqarrar (Ire) *T J Fitzgerald*   59
4 c c Alhaarth (Ire) - Narjis (USA)
8[7gf] 6[8gf] 5[8gf] 14[7gf] 7[7gf] 19[8g] 0-0-6

Muqbil (USA) *J L Dunlop*   117
3 ch c Swain (Ire) - Istiqlal (USA)
1[7gf] 12[8g] 2[10gf] 3[8gf] 4[9gf] 1-1-5
£46,400

Muqtadi (Ire) *C R Dore*   59 a60
5 b g Marju (Ire) - Kadwah (USA)
6[6sd] 9[6sd] 1[6sd] 9[6sd] 5[6sd] 3[5sd] 8[6sd] 10[5g]
8[5f] 16[5gf] 15[5gf] 8[6gf] 4[6gf] 9[6gf] 6[5gf] 19[6f] 4[6gf]
16[5gf] 12[8gf] 2-5-34
£10,683

Muraqeb *J H M Gosden*   57
3 ch g Grand Lodge (USA) - Oh So Well (Ire)
5[10gf] 5[12g] 0-0-2

Murashah (USA) *Saeed Bin Suroor*   81
3 ch c Storm Cat (USA) - Shadayid (USA)
1[8gf] 1-0-1 £3,984

Murdinga *A M Hales*   63
4 br g Emperor Jones (USA) - Tintinara
4[10gs] 0-0-1 £320

Murtakez *S Dow*   30 a23
3 b g Alhaarth (Ire) - Raaqiyya (USA)
11[8sd] 15[7gf] 9[10gf] 0-0-3

Murzim *J Gallagher*   77 a69
4 b g Salse (USA) - Guilty Secret (Ire)
10[16sd] 1[14g] 4[15gf] 8[14gf] 5[14gf] 8[16gs] 12[13g]

6[15gf] 3[13f] 11[12g] 1-1-10 £4,522

Musaayer (USA) *E A L Dunlop*   71
2 br g Erhaab (USA) - Hachiyah (Ire)
2[6gf] 6[7gf] 12[8gf] 0-1-4 £1,764

Musanid (USA) *Sir Michael Stoute*   77
3 ch c Swain (Ire) - Siyadah (USA)
1[9s] 1-0-1 £5,707

Musawah (USA) *J L Dunlop*   73
3 b f Gulch (USA) - Haniya (Ire)
2[7gf] 5[8g] 10[7gf] 3[7f] 2[8f] 1[7f] 1-3-6
£6,536

Muscida (USA) *H R A Cecil*   80
2 b f Woodman (USA) - Space Time (Fr)
3[7f] 1[8gf] 1-1-2 £4,289

Mush (Ire) *N P Littmoden*   51 a68
6 b g Thatching - Petite Jameel (Ire)
2[7sd] 3[8sd] 1[8sd] 2[7sd] 4[7sd] 9[8sd] 12[8gf] 11[9gf]
15[8g] 7[8gf] PU[8g] 1-3-11 £5,397

Music Maid (Ire) *H S Howe*   69
5 b m Inzar (USA) - Richardstown Lass (Ire)
9[9g] 8[7gf] 1[7g] 5[7gf] 2[8gf] 1[7gf] 1[8gf]
4[8gf] 5[7g] 1[8gf] 1[7gf] 5[7gf] 4-2-13 £33,234

Musical Chimes (USA) *N Drysdale*   115
3 b f In Excess - Note Musicale
4[8g] 1[8gs] 3[8g] 3[11g] 10[8gs] 2[10f] 11[10f] 2-2-7
£239,279

Musical Fair *J A Glover*   84
3 b f Piccolo - Guarded Expression
6[6g] 3[6gf] 9[6gf] 8[6gf] 1[5gf] 2[6gf] 1[5f]
2[6gf] 12[5g] 1[5gf] 3[5gf] 4[6gf] 7[5gf] 4-5-14
£23,271

Musical Gift *C N Allen*   a73
3 ch c Cadeaux Genereux - Kazoo
2[8sd] 2[9sw] 4[10sd] 0-2-3 £2,864

Musical Heath (Ire) *T D Barron*   a48
6 b g Common Grounds - Song Of The Glens
14[7sw] 3[8sd] 18[8gf] 0-1-3 £416

Musical Key *J G Given*   44 a32
3 b f Key Of Luck (USA) - Musianica
9[5f] 8[6sd] 10[6gf] 0-0-3

Musical Lyrics (USA) *M Johnston*   66
2 b f Quiet American (USA) - Foreign Courier (USA)
4[5gf] 9[6gf] 3[6f] 9[7gf] 0-0-4 £734

Musical Sleuth *G C Bravery*   47
4 ch g Piccolo - My Dear Watson
16[6sd] 12[7gf] 14[5gf] 6[6gf] 12[7gs] 16[8gf] 18[6f]
0-0-7

Musical Stage (USA) *P R Webber*   73
4 b g Theatrical - Changed Tune (USA)
9[16g] 0-0-1

Musiotal *J S Goldie*   47
2 ch c Pivotal - Bemuse
5[6g] 7[6g] 0-0-2

Muskatsturm (Ger) *B J Curley*   74
4 b g Lecroix (Ger) - Myrthe (Ger)
10[14g] 18[12gf] 13[17g] 0-0-3

Must Be Magic *H J Collingridge*   70 a68
6 b g Magic Ring (Ire) - Sequin Lady
2[10sd] 2[10sd] 1[10sd] 11[10sd] 2[8gf] 17[8g] 4[8sd]
3[8gf] 1[9gf] 2[8g] 11[9gf] 2-5-11 £13,596

Must Be So *D R C Elsworth*   62
2 b f So Factual (USA) - Ovideo
12[6gf] 4[6gf] 8[6gf] 14[5gs] 0-0-4 £289

Mustajed *M P Tregoning*   84
2 b c Alhaarth (Ire) - Jasarah (Ire)

1⁵ᵍ **1-0-1 £7,247**

Mustaneer (USA) *Sir Michael Stoute*   107
3 b c Gone West (USA) - Market Booster (USA)
3⁷ᵍᶠ 4⁸ᵍ **0-0-2 £6,052**

Mustang Ali (Ire) *S Kirk*   65 a30
2 ch c Ali-Royal (Ire) - Classic Queen (Ire)
6⁶ᵍᶠ 5⁶ˢᵈ 2⁷ᵍᶠ 2⁷ᶠ 11⁸ᵍᶠ 8⁷ᶠ **0-2-6 £1,740**

Mustawa (USA) *Miss D Mountain*   66 a27
4 b g Wild Again (USA) - Tatwij (USA)
5⁸ᵍᶠ 5⁹ᵍᶠ 6¹²ᵍᶠ 8¹⁰ˢᵈ 8⁷ᵍᶠ 7¹⁰ᵍᶠ 6¹⁰ᵍᶠ **0-0-7**

Mutabari (USA) *J L Spearing*   54 a56
9 ch g Seeking The Gold (USA) - Cagey Exuberance (USA)
1⁷ˢᵈ 16⁷ˢᵈ 6⁷ˢᵈ 14⁷ᵍᶠ 5⁷ᵍᶠ 5⁷ˢᵈ 11⁸ʰᵈ
11⁸ˢᵈ 7⁹ˢᵈ 10⁸ᶠᵗ **1-0-10 £3,122**

Mutabassir (Ire) *Andrew Reid*   63 a55
9 ch g Soviet Star (USA) - Anghaam (USA)
5⁷ˢᵈ 6⁷ˢᵈ 6⁶ˢᵈ 13⁷ˢᵈ 8⁶ᵍᶠ 2⁷ᵍᶠ 4⁷ᵍᶠ 8⁷ᶠ
2⁷ᵍᶠ 6⁹ᵍᶠ 7⁷ᵍᶠ 1⁶ᶠ 18⁶ᵍᶠ **1-2-13 £5,903**

Mutafanen *E A L Dunlop*   82
2 gr c Linamix (Fr) - Doomna (Ire)
7⁷ᵍᶠ 4⁷ᵍᶠ 3⁸ᵍᶠ 3⁸ᵍᶠ 1⁸ᵍˢ **1-2-5 £5,563**

Mutahayya (Ire) *J L Dunlop*   100
2 b c Peintre Celebre (USA) - Winsa (USA)
1⁷ᶠ 4⁷ᵍᶠ 2⁷ᵍᶠ 1⁸ᵍᶠ 2⁸ᵍ **2-2-5 £20,514**

Mutajjeb (Ire) *E A L Dunlop*   94
3 b c Darshaan - Nightlark (Ire)
1¹⁰ᵍᶠ 4¹¹ᵍ 9¹⁶ᶠ 5¹²ᵍˢ **1-0-4 £5,920**

Mutamared (USA) *Saeed Bin Suroor*   60
3 ch c Nureyev (USA) - Alydariel (USA)
2⁸ᶠᵗ 2⁷ᵍᶠ 6⁷ᵍᶠ **0-1-3 £3,422**

Mutarafaa (USA) *D Shaw*   a51
4 b g Red Ransom (USA) - Mashaarif (USA)
10⁷ˢᵈ 6⁶ˢᵈ 6⁷ˢʷ 3⁷ˢʷ 7⁷ˢᵈ 10⁶ˢᵈ 8⁷ˢᵈ 6⁸ˢᵈ
0-1-8 £431

Mutared (Ire) *N P Littmoden*   72 a83
5 b g Marju (Ire) - Shahaada (USA)
3⁷ˢᵈ 5⁷ˢᵈ 12⁸ˢᵈ 3⁹ᵍᶠ 8⁸ᵍᶠ 15⁷ᵍ 15⁸ᵍᶠ
16¹¹ᵍ 22⁸ᵍ **0-2-9 £1,093**

Mutasawwar *J M Bradley*   64 a47
9 ch g Clantime - Keen Melody (USA)
4⁵ᵍ 16⁵ˢᵈ 2⁵ᶠ 1⁵ᵍᶠ 2⁵ᵍᶠ 8⁵ˢᵈ 2⁵ᵍˢ 5⁵ʰʸ
10⁵ᵍᶠ 1⁵ᵍᶠ 16⁵ᵍ 5⁵ᵍᶠ 8⁵ᶠ 5⁶ᵍᶠ 4⁵ˢ
12⁵ᵍᶠ 14⁵ᵍᶠ **2-4-19 £12,889**

Mutassem (Fr) *E A L Dunlop*   69
2 b c Fasliyev (USA) - Fee Eria (Fr)
6⁷ᵍᶠ **0-0-1**

Mutawaffer *B W Hills*   100
2 b c Marju (Ire) - Absaar (USA)
1⁶ᵍ 5⁷ᵍᶠ 1⁸ᵍ 8⁷ᵍᶠ **2-0-4 £13,733**

Mutawaqed (Ire) *M A Magnusson*   97 a91
5 ch g Zafonic (USA) - Waqood (USA)
1⁶ˢᵈ 6⁷ˢᵈ 10⁶ᵍ 2⁶ᵍᶠ 3⁶ᵍ 1⁶ᵍˢ 7⁶ᵍ 3⁶ᵍ
6⁶ᵍᶠ 3⁶ᵍᶠ 16⁶ʸ **2-4-11 £42,226**

Mutawassel (USA) *B W Hills*   85
2 b c Kingmambo (USA) - Danzig Darling (Can)
7⁷ᵍᶠ 1⁸ᵍ **1-0-2 £7,280**

Mutayam *D A Nolan*   45
3 b g Compton Place - Final Shot
4⁵ᵍᶠ 6⁵ᵍˢ 13⁵ᵍˢ 5⁵ᵍᶠ 2⁵ᵍᶠ 8⁵ᶠ 7⁵ᵍᶠ 11⁵ᶠ
10⁵ˢ **0-1-9 £2,033**

Muwajaha *B W Hills*   76
3 b f Night Shift (USA) - Maraatib (Ire)
1⁶ᵍᶠ **1-0-1 £5,421**

Muy Bien *J R Jenkins*   57 a79
2 ch c Daggers Drawn (USA) - Primula Bairn
4⁵ˢᵈ 5⁵ᵍᶠ 2⁵ˢᵈ 1⁵ˢᵈ 5⁵ˢᵈ 28⁶ᵍᶠ 15⁵ᵍˢ
1-1-7 £4,506

Muyassir (Ire) *Miss B Sanders*   78 a65
8 b g Brief Truce (USA) - Twine
5⁸ˢᵈ 10⁷ˢᵈ 16⁸ᵍᶠ 2⁸ᵍᶠ 5⁹ᵍᶠ 8⁹ᵍᶠ 14⁹ᵍ 3⁸ᶠ
8⁸ᶠ 11⁸ᵍ 1⁸ᵍᶠ 10⁸ᶠ **1-2-12 £6,210**

My American Beauty *T D Easterby*   91
5 ch m Wolfhound (USA) - Hooray Lady
10⁵ᶠ 3⁵ᵍᶠ 7⁶ˢ 14⁶ᵍ 9⁶ᶠ 1⁵ᶠ 1⁵ᵍ 9⁵ᵍᶠ
13¹⁶ᵍ 12⁵ᵍᶠ 7⁵ᵍᶠ 3⁵ᶠ 14⁶ᵍ 6⁵ᶠ 4⁵ᵍᶠ 12⁵ᵍᶠ
2-2-16 £20,416

My Bayard *J O'Reilly*   57 a77
4 ch g Efisio - Bay Bay
4⁸ˢᵈ 2¹¹ˢᵈ 2⁹ˢᵈ 2⁸ˢᵈ 2⁸ˢᵈ 2⁸ˢʷ 1⁸ˢᵈ 2⁸ˢᵈ
2⁸ˢᵈ 8⁷ᵍᶠ 2⁸ˢᵈ 14⁸ᵍᶠ **1-8-12 £10,751**

My Brother *Dr J R J Naylor*   47
9 b g Lugana Beach - Lucky Love
15⁶ᵍ 10⁵ᵍᶠ 7⁶ᵍᶠ 4⁶ᵍᶠ 10⁶ᶠ 7⁵ᵍᶠ 6⁵ˢ
15⁵ᵍᶠ 13⁶ᵍᶠ 17⁸ᵍᶠ **0-0-10 £290**

My Chickawicka *S Kirk*   19
2 b f Chickawicka (Ire) - Jimlil
9⁷ᵍᶠ 16⁸ᵍᶠ **0-0-2**

My Daisychain *M Johnston*   78
3 ch f Hector Protector (USA) - Dayville (USA)
7⁸ᵍ 6⁶ᶠ 15⁷ᵍᶠ 11⁰ˢ 5¹²ᵍᶠ 5¹²ᵍᶠ 2¹⁰ᵍᶠ 1¹²ᵍᶠ
2¹⁰ᵍᶠ 3¹²ᵍᶠ 4¹¹ˢ **2-4-11 £12,498**

My Fas (USA) *M A Jarvis*   65
3 b/br g King Of Kings (Ire) - Granny Kelly (USA)
4⁸ᵍᶠ 4⁷ᵍᶠ 8⁷ᵍᶠ **0-0-3 £750**

My Galliano (Ire) *B G Powell*   72 a67
7 b g Muharib (USA) - Hogan Stand
2¹⁰ˢᵈ 2¹²ˢᵈ 2¹²ˢᵈ 6¹⁰ˢᵈ 6¹⁰ᵍᶠ 8¹⁰ᵍᶠ 2¹⁰ᵍᶠ
1¹⁰ᵍᶠ 6¹⁰ᵍ **1-4-9 £8,531**

My Girl Georgie *M W Easterby*   36
2 b f Bin Ajwaad (Ire) - At My Command (Ire)
6⁵ᵍᶠ 10⁵ᶠ 12⁶ᵍᶠ **0-0-3**

My Girl Pearl (Ire) *J M Bradley*   56 a8
3 b f Sri Pekan (USA) - Desert Bloom (Fr)
4⁶ᵍ 10⁶ˢᵈ 3⁶ᵍᶠ 13⁶ᵍˢ 8⁷ᵍᶠ 9⁶ᶠ 4⁷ᵍ 11⁸ᵍᶠ
0-1-8 £1,131

My Hope (Ire) *R Charlton*   60 a43
2 b f Danehill (USA) - Lady Elgar (Ire)
10⁷ˢᵈ 8⁷ᵍˢ **0-0-2**

My Jodie *M G Quinlan*   53
3 b f Bluegrass Prince (Ire) - Sally Green (Ire)
6⁷ᵍᶠ 13⁸ᵍˢ 9¹⁰ᵍᶠ **0-0-3**

My Last Bean (Ire) *B Smart*   60 a71
6 gr g Soviet Lad (USA) - Meanz Beanz
5¹²ˢᵈ 5¹¹ˢʷ 4¹⁴ˢʷ 3¹²ᵍᶠ 6¹⁴ᵍˢ **0-1-5 £751**

My Legal Eagle (Ire) *R J Price*   a34
9 b g Law Society (USA) - Majestic Nurse
5¹⁶ˢᵈ **0-0-1**

My Lilli (Ire) *P Mitchell*   32 a60
3 b f Marju (Ire) - Tamburello (Ire)
4¹⁰ˢᵈ 3⁹ᵍᶠ 8¹⁰ˢᵈ 14¹⁰ᵍᶠ 8¹²ˢᵈ 10¹⁰ˢᵈ **0-0-6 £1,880**

My Line *Mrs M Reveley*   69
6 b g Perpendicular - My Desire
6¹⁶ᵍˢ 2¹²ˢ **0-1-2 £941**

My Lovely *D J S Cosgrove*   62
5 b m Dolphin Street (Fr) - My Bonus
5⁵ᵍ **0-0-1**

My Maite (Ire) *R Ingram*   64 a74

4 b g Komaite (USA) - Mena
3^{10sd} 4^{10sd} 5^{10g} 7^{8g} 9^{10gs} 11^{10gf} 3^{12g}
6^{13gf} 14^{12gf} 10^{12gf} 5^{12g} 8^{10gf} 8^{12sd} **0-2-13**
£1,522

My Man Friday *P W Hiatt*   43
7 b g Lugana Beach - My Ruby Ring
15^{8f} 11^{7gs} 7^{6f} 15^{7gf} 5^{6f} 5^{7f} 5^{7f} 6^{7gf}
8^{8f} 13^{7g} 7^{7f} **0-0-11**

My Mary Lou (Ire) *J A Glover*   28
3 ch f Septieme Ciel (USA) - Kutaisi (Ire)
12^{10gf} 15^{7gf} **0-0-2**

My Mate Henry *T T Clement*   36
4 ch g Pursuit Of Love - Gopi
8^{10gf} 6^{9gf} 7^{12g} **0-0-3**

My Mellors (USA) *H R A Cecil*   82
3 ch c Woodman (USA) - Breath Taking (Fr)
2^{7gf} 2^{8gf} 3^{9gf} 2^{7s} **0-4-4 £6,020**

My Michelle *B Palling*   73
2 b f Ali-Royal (Ire) - April Magic
5^{5gf} 5^{6gf} 3^{6g} **0-1-3 £543**

My Penny (USA) *E J O'Neill*   a24
4 b f Gulch (USA) - My Special Song (USA)
11^{8sd} 10^{12sd} **0-0-2**

My Personal Space (USA) *G A Butler*   78
2 ch f Rahy (USA) - Pattimech (USA)
1^{6gf} 11^{7gf} **1-0-2 £4,745**

My Philosophy *L A Dace*   22
4 gr g Green Desert (USA) - Anneli Rose
13^{7gf} 15^{7gf} 13^{8gf} **0-0-3**

My Pledge (Ire) *C A Horgan*   57 a61
8 b g Waajib - Pollys Glow (Ire)
7^{13sd} 11^{12gf} 3^{12gf} 12^{16gf} 4^{12gf} 7^{14gf} **0-2-6**
£471

My Raggedy Man *D Nicholls*   79
4 b g Forzando - Ragged Moon
14^{7f} 16^{8f} 10^{9gf} 24^{8d} 18^{8gs} 10^{9gf} 9^{9g}
0-0-7

My Renee (USA) *M J Grassick*   107
3 b/br f Kris S (USA) - Mayenne (USA)
3^{10gy} 1^{12g} 5^{10gf} 1^{12gf} **2-1-4 £27,728**

My Retreat (USA) *G L Moore*   5 a65
6 b g Hermitage - My Jessica Ann (USA)
2^{8sw} 3^{8sd} 6^{8sd} 16^{7gf} 7^{7sd} 6^{8sd} 4^{8sd} 2^{9sd}
4^{9ft} 8^{9sd} 14^{10sd} **0-3-11 £2,399**

My Sharp Grey *J Gallagher*   62 a53
4 gr f Tragic Role (USA) - Sharp Anne
8^{8sd} 6^{10gf} 5^{8f} 7^{7sd} 6^{7gf} 7^{8gf} 2^{8gf} 9^{8gf}
13^{8g} 2^{8gf} **0-2-10 £1,614**

My Sunshine (Ire) *B W Hills*   63
2 b f Alzao (USA) - Sunlit Ride
10^{7gf} 8^{7g} **0-0-2**

My Valentine *P R Chamings*   42 a61
4 gr g Samim (USA) - Sea Farer Lake
11^{11sd} 3^{9sw} 2^{9sd} 3^{9sw} 4^{8sd} 5^{8sd} 11^{8gf}
5^{8sd} **0-3-8 £1,934**

My Wild Rover *P A Blockley*   26
3 b g Puissance - June Fayre
11^{7gf} PU^{7sd} **0-0-2**

My Yorkshire Rose *T J Etherington*   41
3 b f Bishop Of Cashel - Gloriana
13^{8g} 9^{10gs} 12^{8s} 10^{9gf} 8^{14gf} **0-0-6**

Myannabanana (Ire) *P Howling*   45 a50
2 ch c Woodborough (USA) - Raging Storm
8^{7f} 6^{6gf} 9^{7gf} 10^{7gf} 8^{8sw} 6^{8sd} 15^{8gf} **0-0-7**

Mynd *R M Whitaker*   65 a65
3 b g Atraf - Prim Lass
9^{6gf} 5^{6g} 9^{6sd} 7^{6sd} 3^{5gs} **0-1-5 £324**

Myriad *P Howling*
2 ch f Amfortas (Ire) - Spriolo
20^{8gf} **0-0-1**

Myrtus *Mrs M Reveley*   43
4 ch g Double Eclipse (Ire) - My Desire
9^{12gs} **0-0-1**

Mysteri Dancer *P J Hobbs*   a57
5 b g Rudimentary (USA) - Mystery Ship
9^{10sd} **0-0-1**

Mysterinch *N P Littmoden*   a97
3 b c Inchinor - Hakone (Ire)
3^{8sd} **0-1-1 £2,821**

Mysterium *N P Littmoden*   51
9 gr g Mystiko (USA) - Way To Go
5^{16gf} 8^{16gf} 5^{16gf} 9^{16g} 10^{17f} **0-0-5**

Mysterlover (Ire) *N P Littmoden*   a50
3 b g Night Shift (USA) - Jacaranda City (Ire)
4^{12sd} PU^{12sd} **0-0-2 £312**

Mystery Mountain *Mrs J R Ramsden*   45 a59
3 b g Mistertopogigo (Ire) - Don't Jump (Ire)
6^{5sd} 4^{6sd} 3^{5sw} 11^{8g} 12^{7f} **0-1-5 £780**

Mystery Pips *N Tinkler*   57 a29
3 b f Bin Ajwaad (Ire) - Le Shuttle
10^{7sd} 8^{5sw} 7^{5sw} 18^{6g} 6^{5gf} 10^{5g} 7^{5gf} 7^{5sd}
3^{5gf} 1^{5gf} 4^{5f} 3^{5gf} 4^{6gf} 1^{5gf} 5^{5gs} **2-2-15**
£7,344

Mystic Forest *C J Mann*   64 a84
4 b g Charnwood Forest (Ire) - Mystic Beauty (Ire)
5^{16sd} 7^{16sd} 1^{14sw} 11^{16sd} 3^{14sw} 9^{14gs} **1-1-6**
£5,011

Mystic Man (Fr) *K A Ryan*   98 a81
5 b g Cadeaux Genereux - Shawanni
3^{7sd} 17^{7gf} 18^{gf} 4^{7g} 7^{10gf} 9^{9g} **2-2-6**
£32,542

Mystic Mayhem *R Bastiman*
4 b f Danzig Connection (USA) - Mrs Meyrick
13^{8gf} **0-0-1**

Mystic Mile (Ire) *M A Jarvis*   97
4 gr f Sadler's Wells (USA) - Delage
3^{12gf} 4^{13gs} 2^{14s} 4^{15g} **0-2-4 £7,642**

Mystic Promise (Ire) *Mrs N Macauley*   12
2 gr g Among Men (USA) - Ivory's Promise
8^{6sd} 16^{7gf} 9^{8gf} 11^{7sd} **0-0-4**

Mystic Venture (Ire) *K A Ryan*   a44
4 b g Woodborough (USA) - Paganina (Fr)
5^{7sw} 7^{7sw} 13^{7sd} 16^{7gf} **0-0-4**

Mystic Witch *G A Swinbank*   47
4 b f Mistertopogigo (Ire) - Walsham Witch
9^{5gf} 3^{5gs} 12^{5gf} 11^{5gf} UR^{5gf} **0-1-5 £567**

Mystical Charm (Ire) *D Nicholls*   49 a36
4 ch f Indian Ridge - Manazil (Ire)
6^{8sd} 11^{7sw} 7^{6f} 5^{5gf} 16^{gf} 10^{6gf} 16^{5gf}
1-0-7 £3,770

Mystical Girl (USA) *M Johnston*   66
2 ch f Rahy (USA) - Miss Twinkletoes (Ire)
2^{7gf} 3^{7gs} 8^{8gf} **0-2-3 £1,569**

Mystical Star (Fr) *J J Sheehan*   a56
6 b g Nicolotte - Addaya (USA)
1^{7sw} **1-0-1 £2,251**

Mythic *J R Fanshawe*   79
4 ch f Zafonic (USA) - Fetlar
4^{10g} 9^{8gf} **0-0-2 £1,032**

Mythical Air (Ire) *J R Weymes*   36
2 b f Magic Ring (Ire) - Legendary Dancer
6^{5gf} 7^{6g} 17^{6gf} **0-0-3**

Mythical Charm *J J Bridger*   63 a57
4 b f Charnwood Forest (Ire) - Triple Tricks (Ire)
10^{13sd} 2^{10sd} 1^{10sd} 9^{8g} 6^{10sd} 13^{8gf} 16^{9gf}
12^{12g} 8^{8gf} 6^{7gf} 5^{8g} 14^{8gf} 1^{8g} **2-1-13 £7,510**

Mythical King (Ire) *R Lee*   62
6 b g Fairy King (USA) - Whatcombe (USA)
3^{12g} 5^{10gf} 12^{11gf} **0-1-3 £572**

Mytton's Magic (Ire) *A Bailey*   17
3 br g Danetime (Ire) - Maldinion
6^{8gf} 9^{8gf} 11^{9g} **0-0-3**

Mytton's Quest (Ire) *Mrs L Williamson*   a18
3 ch g Grand Lodge (USA) - Fleeting Quest
7^{8sd} 12^{7sd} 17^{7gf} 12^{7gf} **0-0-4**

Myttons Mistake *R J Baker*
10 b g Rambo Dancer (Can) - Hi-Hunsley
12^{8sd} **0-0-1**

Naaddey *M R Channon*   93
2 b c Seeking The Gold (USA) - Bahr
2^{7f} 1^{7gs} 2^{7gf} 5^{7gf} 4^{8s} 3^{8g} 5^{9g} 3^{7gf} **1-2-8**
£11,640

Naahy *M R Channon*   109 a81
3 ch c Bahamian Bounty - Daffodil Fields
13^{7sd} 1^{7gf} 1^{7gf} 2^{7g} 13^{7gf} 5^{7gf} 7^{7g} 21^{6g}
19^{7gf} 1^{7gf} **3-1-10 £63,593**

Nabokov *Sir Mark Prescott*
4 b g Nashwan (USA) - Ninotchka (USA)
9^{16sd} **0-0-1**

Nabtat Saif *R Hannon*   66
2 b f Compton Place - Bahawir Pour (USA)
7^{6gf} 2^{7g} 4^{5gf} 8^{7gf} **0-1-4 £3,300**

Nadayem (USA) *B Hanbury*   69
2 ch f Gulch (USA) - Tajannub (USA)
5^{6gf} 4^{7g} **0-0-2 £330**

Nadeszhda *Sir Mark Prescott*   84 a71
3 ch f Nashwan (USA) - Ninotchka (USA)
1^{12f} 1^{12f} 2^{16ft} **2-0-3 £8,744**

Nadir *P Howling*   69
2 b c Pivotal - Amid The Stars
3^{7g} **0-1-1 £560**

Nadour Al Bahr (Ire) *T G Mills*   111
8 b g Be My Guest (USA) - Nona (Ger)
8^{10gf} 4^{10g} 1^{10gf} 8^{10g} 1^{10g} 5^{12f} 5^{12f} **2-0-7**
£24,658

Nafferton Girl (Ire) *J A Osborne*   39
2 b f Orpen (USA) - Petomi
12^{5gf} 3^{7gf} **0-1-2 £781**

Nafferton Heights (Ire) *M W Easterby*   39
2 b c Peintre Celebre (USA) - Gold Mist
10^{6gf} 15^{6gf} 7^{6g} **0-0-3**

Nafsika (USA) *N J Henderson*   44 a14
3 b f Sky Classic (Can) - Exotic Beauty (USA)
8^{6g} 9^{6sd} 9^{8gf} 13^{8gf} 10^{6gf} 11^{10gf} 6^{9f}
5^{8gf} 9^{8s} **0-0-9**

Nahane (Ire) *Sir Michael Stoute*   78
2 b c Rainbow Quest (USA) - Winona (Ire)
7^{7gf} 2^{7g} 2^{7gf} 3^{8gf} 9^{8gf} **0-2-5 £4,251**

Naheef (Ire) *Saeed Bin Suroor*   115
4 b c Marju (Ire) - Golden Digger (USA)
1^{10f} 7^{9f} 7^{9g} 2^{10gs} 3^{10g} 1^{9gf} 2^{10s} 5^{9gf}
2-3-8 £89,041

Nailbiter *Mrs A Duffield*   52
4 b g Night Shift (USA) - Scylla

5^{12gf} **0-0-1**

Naj-De *S Dow*   32 a45
5 ch g Zafonic (USA) - River Jig (USA)
7^{8sd} 10^{7sd} 19^{11gf} 9^{7g} 17^{6gf} 9^{10f} 8^{8f}
0-0-7

Najaaba (USA) *Miss J Feilden*   29
3 b f Bahhare (USA) - Ashbilya (USA)
11^{8gf} **0-0-1**

Najeebon (Fr) *M R Channon*   96
4 c c Cadeaux Genereux - Jumairah Sun (Ire)
1^{6gf} 4^{6g} 2^{7g} 5^{6gf} 6^{7f} 5^{7gs} 13^{6gf} 16^{8gs}
2^{6gf} 3^{6gf} 6^{6g} 16^{gf} 19^{g} 9^{6gf} 16^{gf} 4^{6gf} 5^{6gs}
7^{7g} **3-4-18 £59,091**

Nakota *J Gallagher*   14
3 ch f Emarati (USA) - Naulakha
11^{8g} 7^{8g} 7^{5f} 13^{7gf} **0-0-4**

Nakwa (Ire) *E J Alston*   57 a50
5 b g Namaqualand - Cajo (Ire)
3^{12sw} 5^{12sd} 4^{12sd} 7^{11gf} 1^{12g} 11^{12f} 4^{10gf}
1-2-7 £4,975

Namaste *H R A Cecil*   68
3 b f Alzao (USA) - Bahamian
3^{10gf} 2^{12gs} **0-2-2 £1,356**

Named At Dinner *B J Meehan*   72
2 c c Halling (USA) - Salanka (Ire)
8^{7g} 4^{8gf} 2^{6gf} 2^{7gf} 4^{8gf} **0-2-5 £2,296**

Namroud (USA) *Sir Michael Stoute*   99
4 b g Irish River (Fr) - Top Line (Fr)
3^{9gf} 1^{8gf} 2^{8g} 1^{7gf} 29^{6f} **2-2-5 £19,447**

Nandoo *A G Juckes*   41
4 b f Forzando - Ascend (Ire)
10^{16gs} 7^{12gf} 18^{10gf} 13^{14f} 6^{12gf} 9^{12gf}
8^{12gf} **0-0-7**

Nanna (Ire) *R Hollinshead*   a40
2 b f Danetime (Ire) - Pre Catelan
7^{5sd} **0-0-1**

Nantucket Sound (USA) *M C Pipe*   61
2 b c Quiet American (USA) - Anna
6^{7gf} 3^{8gf} **0-1-2 £666**

Naomi (Ire) *J Nicol*   72
2 br f Polar Falcon (USA) - Duck Over
6^{6gf} 2^{6g} **0-1-2 £1,087**

Naomi Wildman (USA) *W R Muir*   45 a25
3 b f Kingmambo (USA) - Divinite (USA)
9^{10g} 10^{11gf} 5^{12gf} 9^{15sd} **0-0-4**

Narooma *Lady Herries*   37
3 b f Emperor Jones (USA) - Cassilis (Ire)
4^{7g} 8^{7gf} **0-0-2 £293**

Narrative (Ire) *Saeed Bin Suroor*   110
5 b h Sadler's Wells (USA) - Barger (USA)
4^{12f} 3^{11ys} 15^{10gf} 8^{12gs} **0-1-4 £18,165**

Nashaab (USA) *P D Evans*   100
6 b g Zafonic (USA) - Tajannub (USA)
2^{7g} 7^{7g} 2^{7gf} 22^{8gf} 5^{8gf} 11^{8g} 10^{7gf} 3^{8g}
5^{8gf} 13^{8gf} 4^{8gf} 2^{8g} 12^{9gf} 7^{8gf} 7^{8gf} 3^{8gs}
0-4-16 £26,170

Nashwan Star (Ire) *B W Hills*   73
3 ch f Nashwan (USA) - Ibtisamm (USA)
3^{7gf} 3^{10gf} 4^{7gf} 4^{7gf} 3^{12f} 3^{12f} 3^{10f} 8^{10gs}
11^{12gs} **0-1-9 £4,697**

Nasij (USA) *E A L Dunlop*   103
3 ch f Elusive Quality (USA) - Hachiyah (Ire)
1^{8gf} 4^{10gf} 6^{8f} 4^{8gf} 9^{7g} 7^{8gs} **1-0-6**
£26,060

Nassau Street *D J S Ffrench Davis*   12 a43

3 gr g Bahamian Bounty - Milva
10^{8gf} 4^{9sd} **0-0-2**

Nasty Nick *Julian Poulton* 32
4 gr g Petong - Silver Spell
9^{7f} 11^{10gf} 4^{10f} 13^{6gf} **0-0-4**

Nataliya *J L Dunlop* 92
2 b f Green Desert (USA) - Ninotchka (USA)
1^{6gf} 3^{7gf} **1-1-2 £10,095**

Nathan Brittles (USA) *T D Barron* 76
3 ch g Cat's Career (USA) - Doc's Answer (USA)
1^{5f} 2^{5gf} 1^{5gf} 7^{5gf} 20^{5g} 18^{5g} **2-0-6 £14,562**

Nathan Detroit *P J Makin* a61
3 b c Entrepreneur - Mainly Sunset
10^{7sw} 7^{7sd} **0-0-2**

National Pride *J Nicol* 66
3 b c Vettori (Ire) - Branston Express
2^{9gf} 1^{8g} 1^{10f} **2-1-3 £21,048**

Native Title *D Nicholls* 88
5 b g Pivotal - Bermuda Lily
8^{5g} 1^{6g} 25^{7gf} **1-0-3 £10,660**

Native Turk (USA) *J A R Toller* 58
2 b c Miswaki (USA) - Churn Dat Butter (USA)
8^{7gf} **0-0-1**

Natmsky (Ire) *K A Ryan*
4 b g Shadeed (USA) - Cockney Lass
11^{8sd} 14^{12sd} 16^{7sw} **0-0-3**

Natural Dancer *C N Allen* 45
4 b f Shareef Dancer (USA) - Naturally Fresh
12^{8sd} 12^{12sd} 8^{10g} 13^{10sd} **0-0-4**

Naughty Girl (Ire) *M L W Bell* 82
3 b f Dr Devious (Ire) - Mary Magdalene
21^{5gf} 1^{6gf} 2^{6gf} 6^{6gf} 5^{5g} 6^{6gf} **1-1-7 £7,531**

Nautical *M C Pipe* 44
5 gr g Lion Cavern (USA) - Russian Royal (USA)
11^{10g} **0-0-1**

Navado (USA) *Sir Michael Stoute* 106
4 b g Rainbow Quest (USA) - Miznah (Ire)
4^{10gf} 18^{12gf} 1^{10gf} 2^{10gf} **1-1-4 £62,968**

Naviasky (Ire) *Miss E C Lavelle* 45
8 b/br g Scenic - Black Molly (Ire)
9^{7gs} 20^{7gf} **0-0-2**

Nawadi *B W Hills* 88
3 ch f Machiavellian (USA) - Nawaiet (USA)
3^{7gf} 7^{8gs} 1^{10g} 9^{12g} 12^{10g} **1-0-5 £3,765**

Nawamees (Ire) *G L Moore* 76 a87
5 b h Darshaan - Truly Generous (Ire)
5^{12sd} 2^{12sd} 3^{12sd} 6^{14gf} **0-2-4 £7,206**

Nawow *P D Cundell* 88 a85
3 b g Blushing Flame (USA) - Fair Test
3^{10sd} 2^{10sd} UR^{10gs} 3^{11g} 6^{12gf} 5^{11gf} 9^{10gs} 3^{12gf} 12^{12sd} **0-5-9 £7,162**

Nayef (USA) *M P Tregoning* 129 a120
5 b h Gulch (USA) - Height Of Fashion (Fr)
3^{10ft} 1^{10gf} 2^{10gf} 7^{12g} 3^{10gf} 8^{10gf} **1-3-6 £710,000**

Nayyir *G A Butler* 123
5 ch g Indian Ridge - Pearl Kite (USA)
6^{6gs} 1^{7g} 8^{7gs} 2^{7gf} **1-1-4 £76,350**

Nayzak (USA) *Sir Michael Stoute* 95
3 b f Silver Hawk (USA) - Mamlakah (Ire)
7^{9g} **0-0-1**

Nazimabad (Ire) *Mrs A Duffield* 49 a76
4 b g Unfuwain (USA) - Naziriya (Fr)

7^{12sd} 11^{8sd} 11^{12sd} 17^{12gf} 5^{12gf} 15^{10gf} 17^{10gs} **0-0-7**

Neap Tide *J H M Gosden* 64
2 br c Zafonic (USA) - Love The Rain
13^{7g} 6^{8g} 4^{7gs} **0-0-3 £278**

Near Dunleer (Ire) *Michael Hourigan* 55 a28
8 b m Soviet Lad (USA) - Clipper Queen
9^{12sd} 12^{13sd} 6^{10s} 7^{13gf} 3^{12f} 12^{12g} 6^{11sh} 5^{12g} 12^{12f} 2^{12f} 2^{12g} 5^{14gf} 1^{13gf} **1-3-13 £7,409**

Nearly A Fool *G G Margarson* 74 a67
5 b g Komaite (USA) - Greenway Lady
1^{7sd} 7^{7sd} 7^{7sd} 7^{6sd} 7^{10sd} 1^{7sd} 6^{6sd} 8^{8sw} 3^{7gf} 5^{7gf} 3^{8gf} **2-2-11 £7,351**

Nearly Before Time (Ire) *A Berry* 48 a58
2 b c Orpen (USA) - First Encounter (Ire)
14^{5g} 6^{5gf} 7^{5gs} 1^{6sd} 10^{6ft} 7^{5f} **1-0-6 £2,912**

Nebraska City *B Gubby* 66
2 b g Piccolo - Scarlet Veil
5^{5g} 5^{5gf} 12^{6gf} 5^{5gf} 13^{6gf} **0-0-5**

Nebraska Tornado (USA) *A Fabre* 120
3 br f Storm Cat (USA) - Media Nox
1^{8s} 1^{10vs} 1^{11g} 6^{8gs} 1^{8gs} **4-0-5 £315,662**

Neckar Valley (Ire) *R A Fahey* 85
4 b g Desert King (Ire) - Solar Attraction (Ire)
2^{12gf} 17^{10s} 13^{13s} 4^{10gs} 11^{11gf} 2^{9gf} 8^{10g} 5^{11gf} 5^{12gf} 3^{12g} 12^{12gf} **1-3-11 £11,123**

Necklace *A P O'Brien* 109
2 b f Darshaan - Spinning The Yarn
2^{6gy} 1^{7gf} 1^{7gf} 10^{8ho} **2-1-4 £141,493**

Needles And Pins (Ire) *M L W Bell* 99
2 b f Fasliyev (USA) - Fairy Contessa (Ire)
8^{5f} 1^{5s} 2^{5gf} 6^{6g} 1^{5gf} 2^{6s} 5^{5gf} **2-1-7 £30,836**

Needwood Blade *B A McMahon* 117
5 ch h Pivotal - Finlaggan
4^{6g} 1^{6gf} 1^{5g} 13^{6gf} 13^{6f} 7^{6gf} 9^{6gf} **2-0-7 £49,160**

Needwood Brave *T J Fitzgerald* 42
5 b g Lion Cavern (USA) - Woodcrest
2^{11gf} 5^{12gf} 11^{17gf} **0-1-3 £914**

Needwood Merlin *K W Hogg*
7 b g Sizzling Melody - Enchanting Kate
11^{13gf} **0-0-1**

Needwood Mystic *Mrs A J Perrett* 74
8 b m Rolfe (USA) - Enchanting Kate
3^{12f} 1^{13f} 1^{17gf} 7^{14gf} 2^{14f} **2-2-5 £9,823**

Needwood Spirit *Mrs A M Naughton* 42 a8
8 b g Rolfe (USA) - Needwood Nymph
10^{14sd} 7^{16gs} 9^{17gf} 4^{16gs} **0-0-4 £469**

Needwood Trickster (Ire) *R Brotherton* a14
6 gr g Fayruz - Istaraka (Ire)
10^{8sd} 9^{8sd} 8^{6sd} **0-0-3**

Negwa (Ire) *M R Channon* 70
2 b f Bering - Ballet
4^{6g} 3^{7gf} 3^{10gf} **0-1-3 £2,048**

Nellie Melba *Miss I E Craig* 80
4 b f Hurricane Sky (Aus) - Persuasion
11^{8gf} 10^{10g} 4^{8gf} 10^{8gf} 2^{7gf} 1^{7gf} 1^{7s} 2^{7gf} 7^{7gf} 6^{7gf} **2-3-12 £16,445**

Neminos (Ire) *Ms Joanna Morgan* 43
4 b g Lake Coniston (Ire) - Bandit Girl
15^{8gf} 7^{10s} 12^{10g} 17^{10gy} **0-0-4**

Nemo Fugat (Ire) *D Nicholls* 79
4 b g Danehill Dancer (Ire) - Do The Right Thing
9[5f] 5[5gf] 14[6g] 14[6gf] 4[6gf] 13[6g] 15[5gs]
0-0-7 £1,069

Neon Blue *R M Whitaker* 75
2 b/br c Atraf - Desert Lynx (Ire)
3[5gf] 3[5gs] 2[5f] 2[5gs] 10[6g] 4[5g] 8[6gf] 4[6gf]
8[6g] 0-4-9 £7,393

Nephetriti Way (Ire) *P R Chamings* 84
2 b f Docksider (USA) - Velvet Appeal (Ire)
2[6gf] 1[6gf] 2[7gf] 1-1-3 £6,973

Neptune's Gift *I W McInnes*
4 b f Lugana Beach - Not So Generous (Ire)
15[6sw] 15[6sd] 0-0-2

Neqaawi *B Hanbury* 56
2 br f Alhaarth (Ire) - Jinsiyah (USA)
7[6gf] 9[6gf] 0-0-2

Nero's Return (Ire) *M Johnston* 100
2 b c Mujadil - Snappy Dresser
1[6gf] 1[6gf] 2-0-2 £15,216

Nesnaas (USA) *B Hanbury* 76
2 ch c Gulch (USA) - Sedrah (USA)
3[7gf] 9[7gf] 7[7gf] 0-0-3 £569

Nessen Dorma (Ire) *J G Given* 46 a67
2 b g Entrepreneur - Goldilocks (Ire)
2[6sd] 2[6sd] 5[7g] 7[7sd] 0-2-4 £2,433

Neutral Night (Ire) *R Brotherton* 56 a46
3 b f Night Shift (USA) - Neutrality (Ire)
9[6sd] 11[6sd] 12[6sd] 8[6gf] 2[7gf] 4[6gf] 7[6f] 5[7gf]
11[8f] 8[8f] 6[6gf] 8[7gf] 6[7sd] 0-2-13 £1,040

Nevada Desert (Ire) *R M Whitaker* 75
3 b g Desert King (Ire) - Kayanga
13[10gf] 2[8gf] 3[8g] 1[8gf] 3[8gf] 3[11gf] 4[10gf] 2[8gf]
5[9gf] 1-5-9 £17,893

Neven *T D Barron* 69 a69
4 b g Casteddu - Rose Burton
1[7sd] 3[7sw] 9[8sd] 5[8gf] 1-1-4 £3,848

Never Promise (Fr) *Daniel Mark Loughnane* 42
5 b m Cadeaux Genereux - Yazeanhaa (USA)
6[10gf] 12[10gf] 10[7f] 0-0-3

Never Will *M Johnston* 52
2 b c Cadeaux Genereux - Answered Prayer
5[6gf] 0-0-1

Never Without Me *P J McBride* 41 a46
3 ch g Mark Of Esteem (Ire) - Festival Sister
5[7sw] 8[8sd] 10[8gf] 0-0-3

Neverending Magic *Jean-Rene Auvray* 30
2 ch g Timeless Times (USA) - Lady Magician
13[5gf] 7[6gs] 9[7gf] 7[7f] 0-0-4

Nevica *C Smith*
2 ch f Prince Sabo - Snow Eagle (Ire)
9[5g] 10[6gf] 6[6gf] 0-0-3

Nevinstown (Ire) *Niall Moran* 30 a13
3 b c Lahib (USA) - Moon Tango (Ire)
10[10sd] 16[9ys] 12[9gy] 0-0-3

Nevisian Lad *M L W Bell* 109
2 b c Royal Applause - Corndavon (USA)
1[5gf] 3[5gf] 1[6gf] 9[7gs] 11[6gf] 2-1-5
£53,158

New Day Dawning *C Smith* 60
2 ch f First Trump - Tintinara
16[5gf] 4[6f] 6[6gf] 10[5gf] 10[7g] 0-0-5 £348

New Design (Ire) *M J Wallace* 62
3 ch f Bluebird (USA) - Ashirah (USA)
12[6g] 0-0-1

New Diamond *Mrs P Ford* 31 a66
4 ch g Bijou D'Inde - Nannie Annie
10[8sd] 11[12gf] 14[8sd] 9[12sd] 0-0-4

New Foundation (Ire) *Mrs S A Liddiard* 81 a61
3 b f College Chapel - Island Desert (Ire)
8[6gf] 5[6g] 4[6gf] 4[5gf] 6[6gf] 8[6gf] 13[6sd] 6[6gf]
4[6f] 9[7g] 2[6gf] 5[5gf] 4[6gf] 9[6gf] 5[6gf] 8[6sd] 8[7sd]
0-1-17 £4,751

New Mexican *Mrs J R Ramsden* 99
2 ch c Dr Fong (USA) - Apache Star
2[6g] 4[7gf] 1[6gf] 2[7g] 1[8gf] 2-2-5 £32,267

New Morning (Ire) *M A Jarvis* 67
2 b f Sadler's Wells (USA) - Hellenic
4[8gs] 0-0-1 £340

New Options *W J Musson* 62 a75
6 b g Formidable (USA) - No Comebacks
4[6sd] 2[7sd] 2[6sd] 3[6sd] 11[5gs] 14[5gf] 0-3-6
£2,626

New Orchid (USA) *B W Hills* 105
3 b f Quest For Fame - Musicanti (USA)
6[7gf] 1[10g] 3[12g] 2[12gf] 10[12gf] 1-2-5
£17,507

New Prospective *G L Moore* 51 a48
5 b g Cadeaux Genereux - Amazing Bay
5[8g] 8[6sd] 10[8gs] 10[10gf] 15[9gf] 6[10sd] 3[10sd]
8[10gf] 3[11g] 7[10sd] 0-2-10 £852

New Seeker *C G Cox* 108
3 b c Green Desert (USA) - Ahbab (Ire)
3[7gs] 2[8gf] 1[7gs] 3[7gf] 1[8gf] 1[7g] 3-3-6
£141,056

New South Wales *Saeed Bin Suroor* 106
3 b c In The Wings - Temora (Ire)
6[11gs] 4[16f] 20[12s] 1[15g] 1-0-4 £9,467

New Wish (Ire) *M W Easterby* 76
3 b g Ali-Royal (Ire) - False Spring (Ire)
5[8gf] 3[8gf] 7[10gs] 5[9g] 13[10g] 17[8gf] 7[7gf] 9[8f]
7[8gf] 12[9gf] 13[8f] 13[10g] 11[10gf] 0-1-13 £4,694

New York (Ire) *W J Haggas* 67 a65
2 b f Danzero (Aus) - Council Rock
3[7sd] 2[7gf] 0-2-2 £1,659

Newclose *N Tinkler* 60 a30
3 b c Barathea (Ire) - Wedgewood (USA)
8[8g] 7[9sd] 5[8g] 15[8g] 0-0-4

Newcorp Lad *Mrs G S Rees* 77
3 b g Komaite (USA) - Gleam Of Gold
10[8g] 5[8gf] 1[8gf] 1[8g] 2[8f] 6[10gf] 2-1-6
£9,071

Newton (Ire) *A P O'Brien* 101
2 b c Danehill (USA) - Elite Guest (Ire)
2[5y] 1[6g] 1[5s] 9[6gf] 5[7gf] 4[7ho] 2[7g] 2-1-7
£56,217

Newtonian (USA) *J Parkes* a68
4 ch g Distant View (USA) - Polly Adler (USA)
2[12sd] 0-1-1 £1,145

Next Flight (Ire) *A P Jarvis* 54 a46
4 b g Woodborough (USA) - Sans Ceriph (Ire)
11[10sd] 9[12sw] 10[11gf] 13[12g] 14[10gf] 0-0-5

Niagara (Ire) *M H Tompkins* 65 a65
6 b g Rainbows For Life (Can) - Highbrook (USA)
8[13sd] 6[12gf] 0-0-2

Nice Balance (USA) *M C Chapman* 9 a31
8 b g Shadeed (USA) - Fellwaati (USA)
11[8sd] 8[8sd] 10[8sd] 8[6sd] 10[7sd] 7[6sd] 7[8sw]
11[14gf] 0-0-8

Nice Cote D'Azur *G Wragg* 67

2 ch c Hernando (Fr) - Miss Beaulieu
7⁷ᵍ 12⁷ᵍᶠ **0-0-2**

Nichol Fifty *N Wilson*　　　　35 a46
9 b g Old Vic - Jawaher (Ire)
4¹⁶ˢᵈ 11¹²ˢᵈ 4¹⁶ˢᵈ 15¹⁶ᵍᶠ 7¹⁴ᵍᶠ 5¹⁴ᵍᶠ 2¹²ᶠ
9¹²ᵍᶠ 7¹⁶ᵍᶠ 6¹²ᶠ 7¹⁶ᵍᶠ 5¹⁶ᵍᶠ 7¹²ᵍᶠ **0-1-13 £966**

Nick The Silver *G B Balding*　　　63
2 gr c Nicolotte - Brillante (Fr)
11⁶ᵍᶠ 3⁸ᵍᶠ 14⁸ᵍᶠ **0-1-3 £604**

Nick's Grey (Ire) *R Hannon*　　70 a48
2 gr c Midyan (USA) - Grey Goddess
8⁵ᶠ 4⁶ᵍᶠ 4⁶ᵍ 2⁶ᵍᶠ 8⁶ᵍᶠ 5⁶ˢᵈ 2⁷ᶠ **0-2-7
£2,549**

Nickel Sungirl (Ire) *R Hollinshead*　55 a45
3 b f Petorius - Sharp Hint
10⁵ˢʷ 8⁷ᵍᶠ 2⁸ᵍˢ 8⁸ᵍᶠ 15⁷ᶠ **0-1-5 £1,064**

Nicklette *C N Allen*　　　　　a40
4 b f Nicolotte - Cayla
6⁵ˢᵈ 11⁶ˢᵈ **0-0-2**

Niembro *Mrs Lydia Pearce*　　　56
3 b g Victory Note (USA) - Diabaig
4¹⁰ᵍᶠ 11¹⁰ᵍᶠ 7¹²ᵍᶠ 11¹¹ᵍᶠ 8⁹ᵍ 6¹⁰ᶠ **0-0-6**

Nieve Lady *C R Dore*　　　60 a49
4 b f Komaite (USA) - Nikoola Eve
10⁷ˢᵈ 11⁸ˢᵈ 7⁶ˢʷ 8⁶ˢᵈ 6⁷ᵍᶠ 4⁷ᵍᶠ 8⁶ᵍ 7⁶ᵍˢ
10⁷ᵍᶠ 4⁷ᵍˢ 9⁷ᵍᶠ 9⁸ᵍᶠ **0-2-12 £306**

Nifty Dan *J M Bradley*
4 b g Suave Dancer (USA) - Nifty Fifty (Ire)
10⁷ˢᵈ **0-0-1**

Nifty Major *Miss K M George*　　17 a42
6 b g Be My Chief (USA) - Nifty Fifty (Ire)
15⁶ˢʷ 7⁵ˢᵈ 7⁶ˢᵈ 13⁵ˢᵈ 9⁵ˢʷ 8⁵ˢᵈ 6⁵ˢᵈ
17⁶ᵍˢ 19⁷ᵍᶠ 12⁶ᶠ **0-0-10**

Night Arrangement *S Woodman*　　52
3 ch f Night Shift (USA) - By Arrangement (Ire)
10¹⁰ᵍᶠ 11¹⁴ᵍᶠ 6¹¹ᵍᶠ 8¹⁰ᵍᶠ 13¹¹ᵍᶠ **0-0-5**

Night Beauty *E A L Dunlop*　　74
3 b f King Of Kings (Ire) - Kymin (Ire)
6⁸ᵍ 9¹²ᵍˢ 4¹⁰ᵍˢ **0-0-3 £426**

Night Cap (Ire) *T D McCarthy*　53 a53
4 ch g Night Shift (USA) - Classic Design
8⁷ˢᵈ 10⁶ˢᵈ 5⁶ᵍᶠ 12⁶ᵍᶠ 10⁶ᵍ **0-0-5**

Night Driver (Ire) *P J Hobbs*　　29
4 b g Night Shift (USA) - Highshaan
12⁸ᵍᶠ **0-0-1**

Night Frolic *J W Hills*　　　42
2 b f Night Shift (USA) - Miss D'Ouilly (Fr)
15⁷ᵍᶠ 12⁶ᵍ **0-0-2**

Night Kiss (Fr) *R Hannon*　　71 a67
3 ch f Night Shift (USA) - Roxy
6⁷ˢᵈ 1⁷ᵍ 3⁷ᵍ 8⁸ᵍ 3⁷ᵍᶠ 9⁷ᵍᶠ 15⁷ᵍᶠ 2⁸ᵍᶠ
2⁷ˢᵈ **1-4-9 £10,687**

Night Mail *M W Easterby*　　45 a42
3 b g Shaamit (Ire) - Penlanfeigan
6⁷ˢᵈ 15⁸ˢᵈ 7¹⁰ᶠ 9¹⁰ᵍᶠ 4¹²ᶠ 4¹⁴ᵍᶠ UR¹⁶ᵍᶠ
10¹²ᵍᶠ **0-0-8**

Night Market *N Wilson*　　65 a58
5 ch g Inchinor - Night Transaction
3⁸ˢᵈ 9⁸ˢᵈ 5⁷ˢᵈ 3⁸ˢʷ 3⁸ᶠ 18ᶠ 1¹⁰ᵍᶠ
3⁹ᵍᶠ 3⁹ᵍᶠ 9⁸ᶠ 4¹⁰ᵍᶠ 8¹⁰ᵍˢ 9⁸ᵍᶠ 16¹⁰ᵍᶠ 12⁸ᵍᶠ
12¹⁰ᵍˢ 6¹⁰ᵍᶠ 9⁹ᶠ 12⁹ˢᵈ **2-5-20 £10,621**

Night Mist (Ire) *M Johnston*　　83
3 b f Alzao (USA) - Night Mirage (USA)
2⁸ᶠ **0-1-1 £4,521**

Night Pearl (Ire) *G A Butler*　　74 a64
2 b f Night Shift (USA) - Miss Pickpocket (Ire)
3⁵ᶠ 9⁷ᵍᶠ 4⁶ˢᵈ 5⁶ˢ 15⁶ᵍᶠ **0-0-5 £914**

Night Prospector *J W Payne*　　98
3 b c Night Shift (USA) - Pride Of My Heart
2⁶ᵍᶠ 1⁵ᵍᶠ 2⁵ᵍᶠ 5⁵ᵍᶠ 1⁵ᵍ 9⁵ᵍ 9⁵ᵍᶠ **2-2-7
£15,525**

Night Runner *T D Easterby*　　63
4 b c Polar Falcon (USA) - Christmas Kiss
15⁵ᵍ 16⁵ᵍˢ 9⁶ᵍˢ 14⁶ᵍᶠ 10⁷ᵍᶠ 20⁷ᵍᶠ 16⁷ᵍˢ
0-0-7

Night Shift Blue'S (Ire) *M J Polglase*　30 a70
4 b g Night Shift (USA) - Tommelise (USA)
14⁶ˢʷ 3⁵ˢᵈ 7⁶ˢᵈ 2⁶ˢᵈ 7⁶ˢᵈ 14⁷ˢᵈ 3⁵ˢᵈ
11⁶ᵍ **0-3-8 £1,974**

Night Sight (USA) *M C Chapman*　80 a77
6 b g Eagle Eyed (USA) - El Hamo (USA)
7⁸ˢᵈ 7¹¹ˢᵈ 5¹²ˢᵈ 7¹²ᵍ 4¹²ᵍᶠ 9¹⁰ᵍ 6¹²ᵍᶠ 2¹²ᵍ
3¹⁰ᵍᶠ 5¹²ᵍᶠ 6¹²ᵍ 5¹²ᵍᶠ 8¹²ᵍᶠ 7¹²ᵍᶠ 7¹²ᵍ 4¹²ᵍᶠ
0-2-16 £6,430

Night Spot *R Charlton*　　74 a69
2 ch c Night Shift (USA) - Rash Gift
5⁶ᵍᶠ 5⁶ᵍᶠ 1⁶ᵍᶠ 5⁶ˢᵈ **1-0-4 £3,503**

Night Storm *S Dow*　　　67
2 b f Night Shift (USA) - Monte Calvo
12⁶ᵍ 2⁶ᵍᶠ 5⁷ᵍˢ **0-1-3 £1,136**

Night Warrior (Ire) *D Flood*　　81 a73
3 b g Alhaarth (Ire) - Miniver (Ire)
4⁶ˢᵈ 6⁷ˢᵈ 7¹²ᵍᶠ 6¹⁰ᶠ 1¹²ˢᵈ 9¹⁶ˢᵈ 15¹⁰ᵍ
5¹²ᵍᶠ 2¹¹ᵍᶠ 1¹¹ˢʷ 2¹⁰ᵍᶠ 11¹²ˢᵈ 9¹⁰ᵍᶠ **2-2-13
£6,735**

Night Wolf (Ire) *M R Channon*　78 a49
3 gr g Indian Ridge - Nicer (Ire)
3⁸ˢᵈ 3⁷ᵍᶠ 4⁶ᵍᶠ 4⁸ᵍ 1⁸ᵍᶠ 5⁸ᵍᶠ **1-4-6
£4,776**

Night Worker *R Hannon*　　74
2 b c Dracula (Aus) - Crystal Magic
4⁶ᵍᶠ 3⁶ᵍ 7⁷ᵍᶠ 4⁶ᵍᶠ 11⁶ᵍᶠ **0-1-5 £1,057**

Nights Cross (Ire) *M R Channon*　108
2 b c Cape Cross (Ire) - Cathy Garcia (Ire)
5⁵ᵍᶠ 3⁵ᵍ 1⁶ᶠ 6⁶ᵍ 6⁵ᵍᶠ 6⁶ᶠ 1⁵ˢ 2⁵ᵍᶠ 5⁶ᵍᶠ
2⁵ᵍ 3⁵ᵍˢ 11⁶ᵍ 3⁵ᵍ 2⁵ᵍ 1⁵ᵍᶠ 2⁵ᵍᶠ **3-6-16
£73,590**

Nightwatchman (Ire) *W R Muir*　60 a76
4 b g Hector Protector (USA) - Nightlark (Ire)
9¹²ᵍᶠ 4¹⁴ᵍᶠ 5¹⁶ˢᵈ 6¹³ᵍ 6¹⁴ᵍᶠ 4¹⁴ᵍᶠ 3¹⁶ᵍˢ
2¹⁵ˢᵈ 1¹⁶ᶠᵗ 4¹⁶ᵍᶠ 3¹⁵ˢᵈ **1-3-11 £6,052**

Nijmah *Miss D Mountain*　　50
3 ch f Halling (USA) - Star Ridge (USA)
15⁸ᵍᶠ 13¹¹ᵍᶠ 11¹⁰ᶠ 6¹¹ᵍˢ **0-0-4**

Nikaia *R Hannon*　　　37
2 b f Nicolotte - Noble Haven
15⁷ᵍᶠ **0-0-1**

Nimbus Twothousand *P R Wood*　48 a45
3 b f Cloudings (Ire) - Blueberry Parkes
4⁷ᶠ 5⁸ᵍ 10⁹ᵍᶠ 9¹²ᵍᶠ 5¹¹ˢʷ 7¹¹ᵍ **0-0-6**

Nimello (USA) *A G Newcombe*　55 a87
7 b g Kingmambo (USA) - Zakota (Ire)
4⁶ˢᵈ 4⁷ˢᵈ 3⁸ˢʷ 11⁹ᵍᶠ 4⁹ᵍᶠ 1⁷ˢᵈ 1⁸ˢᵈ 13⁷ᵍᶠ
6⁸ᵍᶠ 1⁷ˢʷ **3-1-10 £10,524**

Nina Fontenail (Fr) *N J Hawke*　　18
2 gr f Kaldounevees (Fr) - Ninon Fontenail (Fr)
14⁷ˢ 6⁶ᵍᶠ **0-0-2**

Ninah *J M Bradley*　　71 a60
2 b f First Trump - Alwal

2^{5sd} 5^{5gf} 4^{5sd} 5^{6hy} 13^{6g} 3^{5gf} 3^{8gf} 12^{7gf}
2^{7gf} 2^{7gf} 4^{8gf} 11^{8sd} **0-5-12 £3,404**

Nine Red B W Hills   60
2 b f Royal Applause - Sarcita
5^{6gf} 5^{6gf} 5^{5f} 16^{6gs} **0-0-4**

Nineacres J M Bradley   45 a60
12 b g Sayf El Arab (USA) - Mayor
4^{5sd} 3^{6sd} 8^{6sd} 11^{6sd} 3^{5sw} 10^{6sw} 2^{5sw} 5^{5sw}
9^{6sd} 3^{5sd} 10^{6sd} 7^{5sd} 11^{5gf} 8^{6f} 10^{5gf} 11^{6f}
0-4-16 £2,008

Nite-Owl Fizz J O'Reilly   a75
5 b g Efisio - Nite-Owl Dancer
10^{8sd} 10^{8sd} 1^{8sd} 9^{8sd} 13^{8sd} 5^{9sd} 6^{8sw}
11^{8sd} 12^{8sd} **1-0-9 £2,947**

Niteowl Dream J O'Reilly   38 a15
3 ch f Colonel Collins (USA) - Nite-Owl Dancer
11^{7sd} 13^{10g} **0-0-2**

Niteowl Express (Ire) J O'Reilly   32
2 b f Royal Applause - Nordan Raider
8^{6f} **0-0-1**

Nivernais H Candy   88
4 b g Forzando - Funny Wave
1^{6gf} 3^{6gf} 3^{5gf} 6^{6gf} **1-2-4 £13,570**

No Argument C C Bealby
4 b g Young Ern - As Sharp As
9^{6sd} 10^{9f} **0-0-2**

No Bitz (Ire) J S Moore   51 a46
2 ch f Woodborough (USA) - Riskie Things
5^{5sd} 4^{5g} **0-0-2 £655**

No Chance To Dance (Ire) H J Collingridge   61
3 b c Revoque (Ire) - Song Of The Glens
10^{8gf} 5^{10g} 10^{11g} **0-0-3**

No Dilemma (USA) E A L Dunlop   51
2 ch g Rahy (USA) - Cascassi (USA)
9^{7gs} 8^{8gs} **0-0-2**

No Disruption (Ire) T D Barron   51 a17
3 b g Lahib (USA) - Angela's Venture (Ger)
12^{5gf} 8^{7gf} 7^{6gf} 10^{6sd} 17^{5gf} **0-0-5**

No Grouse E J Alston   82 a68
3 b g Pursuit Of Love - Lady Joyce (Fr)
3^{8sd} 2^{9sw} 5^{7g} 1^{7gf} 16^{gf} 10^{8gf} 14^{7f} 10^{7g}
7^{6g} **2-2-9 £18,197**

No Illusions R Ingram   a44
4 b g Bluegrass Prince (Ire) - Dancing Years (USA)
9^{12sd} 5^{16sd} **0-0-2**

No Looking Back (Ire) T D Easterby   47
3 b g Revoque (Ire) - Chloe (Ire)
6^{12gf} 10^{8gf} 9^{10gf} 5^{10gf} 6^{9gf} 7^{12gs} 10^{10g}
17^{8s} **0-0-8**

No Mercy B A Pearce   a39
7 ch g Faustus (USA) - Nashville Blues (Ire)
4^{7sw} 14^{10sd} 7^{8sd} 7^{2sd} 12^{6sd} 9^{8sd} 9^{7sd}
6^{8sd} 7^{7sd} **0-1-9 £840**

No Refuge (Ire) Sir Mark Prescott   109 a94
3 ch c Hernando (Fr) - Shamarra (Fr)
1^{12sd} 3^{12gf} 11^{2sd} 1^{12g} 2^{12g} 1^{12gs} 3^{12g}
2^{13gs} **4-4-8 £77,004**

No Time (Ire) M J Polglase   105 a100
3 b c Danetime (Ire) - Muckross Park
5^{6sd} 11^{6sd} 4^{5sd} 2^{5sd} 6^{6g} 16^{6gf} 15^{gf}
26^{sd} 3^{5gf} 8^{7gf} 13^{6gf} 18^{6g} **2-3-13 £64,251**

Nobigsuprise (Ire) W G M Turner
4 b f Courtship - Pennine Sue (Ire)
11^{8sd} **0-0-1**

Noble Calling (Fr) R J Hodges   63

6 b h Caller I.D. (USA) - Specificity (USA)
3^{10gf} 4^{12f} 1^{10f} 1^{10gf} 5^{9gf} 6^{10f} 7^{10gf} 9^{8g}
7^{8gf} 6^{10gf} **2-1-10 £7,312**

Noble Cyrano Jedd O'Keeffe   46 a50
8 ch g Generous (Ire) - Miss Bergerac
3^{12sd} 1^{12sd} 12^{10gs} 5^{12gf} 10^{10gf} 5^{10gf}
13^{14gf} 10^{12sd} 6^{11gf} 10^{12gf} 14^{10gf} **1-1-11**
£3,308

Noble Lady Sir Mark Prescott   64 a79
3 ch f Primo Dominie - Noble Destiny
2^{5sd} 1^{6sd} 2^{5gf} 7^{7sd} 1^{6sw} 4^{6sw} **2-2-6**
£7,849

Noble Locks (Ire) J W Unett   19 a74
5 ch g Night Shift (USA) - Imperial Graf (USA)
5^{7sd} 6^{7sd} 2^{7sw} 3^{7sd} 2^{7sd} 2^{7sd} 4^{7sd} 1^{6sd}
4^{6sd} 11^{8sw} 16^{7sd} 17^{6g} 14^{6sd} **2-4-13 £8,897**

Noble Nick M J Wallace   79
4 gr g Primo Dominie - Pericardia
4^{6gf} 18^{6gs} 21^{6g} 9^{7gf} 12^{7gf} **0-1-5 £351**

Noble Pasao (Ire) Andrew Turnell   82
6 b g Alzao (USA) - Belle Passe
11^{10gf} 6^{10f} 7^{10gf} 13^{10gf} 2^{10g} **0-1-5**
£1,200

Noble Penny Mrs K Walton   67 a8
4 b f Pennekamp (USA) - Noble Form
3^{7g} 6^{8gs} 14^{7gf} 18^{8g} 8^{8sd} 9^{10g} **0-1-6**
£681

Noble Philosopher R M Beckett   30 a41
3 ch g Faustus (USA) - Princess Lucy
7^{10gs} 6^{10sd} 10^{12sd} **0-0-3**

Noble Profile C A Cyzer
3 b g Fleetwood (Ire) - Springs Welcome
7^{10f} **0-0-1**

Noble Pursuit R Bastiman   77 a81
6 b g Pursuit Of Love - Noble Peregrine
3^{8sd} 5^{8sd} 6^{8sd} 8^{8gf} 6^{10gf} 11^{10gf} 10^{8gf}
8^{8gf} 6^{8gf} 15^{8gs} 11^{8gf} **0-1-11 £640**

Noble View (USA) R Guest   61
4 ch f Distant View (USA) - Proud Lou (USA)
13^{8f} 5^{9gf} 9^{8gs} 14^{10gf} **0-0-4**

Nobratinetta (Fr) Mrs M Reveley   73
4 b f Celtic Swing - Bustinetta
4^{11gs} 1^{12gs} 8^{16gf} **1-0-3 £4,262**

Nocatee (Ire) P C Haslam   54
2 b g Vettori (Ire) - Rosy Sunset (Ire)
11^{7gf} 7^{8sf} 10^{10f} 4^{7gf} **0-0-4**

Nod's Nephew D E Cantillon   68 a56
6 b g Efisio - Nordan Raider
8^{8sw} 10^{8sd} 9^{6sd} 5^{6gf} 4^{8gf} 8^{9sd} 7^{6sd} 4^{7gf}
12^{8gf} 4^{8sd} 13^{10sd} 3^{8gf} 1^{10sd} 1^{10g} 8^{9sd} **2-3-15**
£6,734

Noels Ganador (USA) E J Creighton   90
4 b c Our Emblem (USA) - Carolita (USA)
7^{8s} 6^{8sd} 2^{11sd} 6^{8g} **0-0-4 £740**

Nofa's Magic (Ire) J L Dunlop   79
3 b f Rainbow Quest (USA) - Garah
2^{10gf} 10^{10gf} **0-1-2 £1,816**

Nofan (Ire) J D Czerpak   46
3 br c Marju (Ire) - Auntie Maureen (Ire)
7^{8sd} 11^{10g} 4^{12gf} 5^{10gf} **0-0-4 £415**

Nominate (Ger) S T Lewis   61
3 b g Desert King (Ire) - Northern Goddess
8^{8g} 3^{11gf} 5^{10g} 9^{12f} 15^{12sd} 14^{8gf} **0-1-6**
£632

Non Ultra (USA) B J Meehan   58 a60

3 ch f Peintre Celebre (USA) - Susun Kelapa (USA)
2^{8sd} 7^{8sd} 4^{8sd} 13^{10sd} 7^{12sd} 6^{10gf} 7^{9sd}
1^{8gs} 7^{8gs} 6^{8sd} 4^{10g} **1-1-11 £4,289**

Noora (Ire) *M P Tregoning*   50
2 ch f Bahhare (USA) - Esteraad (Ire)
8^{6g} **0-0-1**

Noosa Court (USA) *Miss V Scott*   40
4 b f Hansel (USA) - Mahmoud Dancer (USA)
11^{8f} 13^{11gf} 7^{12f} **0-0-3**

Nopekan (Ire) *P Mullins*   103
3 b g Sri Pekan (USA) - Giadamar (Ire)
6^{8g} 5^{9g} 1^{10g} 3^{10ys} 1^{9gy} 8^{10gf} 13^{8s} 10^{10gf}
6^{12gy} 11^{10gf} 6^{10s} **2-1-11 £28,068**

Nordic Dancer (Ire) *R M H Cowell*   a60
2 b f Danehill Dancer (Ire) - Nordic Abu (Ire)
8^{7sd} 7^{7sd} 11^{7gs} **0-0-3**

Noreen *E L James*   32
2 b f Komaite (USA) - Fair Minded
14^{5gf} 9^{6g} 8^{5gf} 5^{8f} 13^{7gf} **0-0-5**

Norse Dancer (Ire) *D R C Elsworth*   119
3 b c Halling (USA) - River Patrol
3^{8g} 4^{12g} 12^{10gf} 3^{8gs} 6^{10gf} 7^{8gf} **0-2-6**
£146,950

North By Northeast (Ire) *J W Payne*   73 a63
5 ch g Polish Precedent (USA) - Catalonda
7^{7g} 12^{7f} 1^{8gf} 6^{7gf} 6^{7f} 5^{8sd} 2^{8g} 12^{8gs}
1-1-8 £5,783

North Landing (Ire) *H A McWilliams*   61
3 b g Storm Bird (Can) - Tirol Hope (Ire)
6^{8gf} 11^{10gs} 2^{8gf} 9^{8gf} 11^{8g} 10^{10gf} 14^{11g}
0-1-7 £1,193

North Light (Ire) *Sir Michael Stoute*   88
2 b c Danehill (USA) - Sought Out (Ire)
2^{7s} 1^{8gf} **1-1-2 £4,900**

North Of Kala (Ire) *G L Moore*   47
10 b g Distinctly North (USA) - Hi Kala
4^{12f} **0-0-1 £285**

North Point (Ire) *R Curtis*   63
5 b g Definite Article - Friendly Song
10^{14gs} 6^{17f} 6^{16gf} 6^{16gf} **0-0-4**

North Sea (Ire) *M R Channon*   59
2 b f Selkirk (USA) - Sea Spray (Ire)
12^{7gf} **0-0-1**

Northern Danzig *G A Swinbank*
4 b f Danzig Connection (USA) - Kristiana
13^{6gf} 10^{6f} **0-0-2**

Northern Desert (Ire) *P W Hiatt*   91
4 b g Desert Style (Ire) - Rosie's Guest (Ire)
9^{8g} **0-0-1**

Northern Friend *J A Glover*   55
3 b g Distinctly North (USA) - Pharaoh's Joy
9^{10gf} 13^{8gs} 9^{10f} 5^{10gf} 8^{11gf} 3^{8gf} 8^{8gf}
0-1-7 £431

Northern Games *K A Ryan*   72 a49
4 b g Mind Games - Northern Sal
9^{5gf} 6^{6gs} 4^{7f} 6^{7f} 4^{7gf} 14^{8f} 2^{6gf}
16^{6gf} 4^{7sd} **0-2-10 £1,778**

Northern Mill (Ire) *Eoin Doyle*   32 a47
6 b m Distinctly North (USA) - Aladja
5^{12sd} 12^{13g} 11^{16gy} 7^{14f} **0-0-4**

Northern Spirit *K A Ryan*   51
2 b g Kadeed (Ire) - Elegant Spirit
8^{7gf} 5^{7gf} 5^{8gf} 12^{10gf} **0-0-4**

Northern Summit (Ire) *J R Norton*   28
2 b g Danehill Dancer (Ire) - Book Choice

6^{7gf} 12^{7g} 10^{7gf} **0-0-3**

Northern Svengali (Ire) *D A Nolan*   44
7 b g Distinctly North (USA) - Trilby's Dream (Ire)
11^{5gf} 7^{5gs} 13^{5gf} 10^{5g} 13^{5g} 12^{5f} 5^{10g}
45^{6f} 13^{5f} 17^{6f} 15^{6gs} **0-0-11 £270**

Northside Lodge (Ire) *P W Harris*   92
5 b g Grand Lodge (USA) - Alongside
5^{10g} 3^{10g} 9^{10gf} 2^{10gf} 2^{12gf} 7^{12gf} 15^{10g}
2^{10gf} 2^{10gf} 8^{10g} 4^{10gf} 8^{10gf} **0-6-12 £15,376**

Norton (Ire) *T G Mills*   113 a106
6 ch g Barathea (Ire) - Primrose Valley
6^{10sd} 3^{8gf} 7^{8f} 11^{8g} 10^{8gf} 9^{8g} **0-2-7**
£17,500

Nosey Native *Mrs Lydia Pearce*   42
10 b g Cyrano De Bergerac - Native Flair
4^{12g} 13^{12g} 8^{14gf} 6^{12gf} 4^{14f} 8^{14gf} **0-1-6**

Not Amused (UAE) *B W Hills*   84
3 ch g Indian Ridge - Amusing Time (Ire)
1^{8g} 7^{8gf} 2^{10gf} 2^{10g} 4^{11gf} 6^{14gf} **1-2-6**
£11,995

Not Proven *T J Fitzgerald*
4 br g Mark Of Esteem (Ire) - Free City (USA)
9^{12gf} **0-0-1**

Not So Dusty *P J Makin*   93 a89
3 b c Primo Dominie - Ann's Pearl (Ire)
2^{5sd} 1^{5sd} 15^{g} 9^{5gf} 10^{5s} 18^{5s} **2-1-6**
£18,435

Notable Guest (USA) *Sir Michael Stoute*   93
2 b c Kingmambo (USA) - Yenda
2^{7g} 2^{8gf} **0-2-2 £2,903**

Notable Lady (Ire) *N A Callaghan*   98
2 b f Victory Note (USA) - Griqualand
8^{6gf} 1^{5f} 5^{6g} 7^{7gf} 5^{5g} **1-0-5 £7,442**

Notanother *M Halford*   79 a70
3 b f Inchinor - Select Sale
2^{7sd} 3^{7sd} 2^{6sw} 7^{6sd} 3^{6sd} 7^{7ys} 12^{6gy} 10^{7y}
1^{7g} 3^{6gf} 14^{6gf} 6^{6f} 3^{7gf} 15^{8f} **1-6-14**
£9,317

Nothing Daunted *T A K Cuthbert*   58 a48
6 ch g Selkirk (USA) - Khubza
12^{7sd} 6^{8sd} 6^{7g} 10^{7gs} 14^{8gf} **0-0-5**

Nothing Matters *P R Chamings*   45
2 b f Foxhound (USA) - Dawn Alarm
11^{6g} 5^{6g} 4^{6f} 9^{7f} 12^{8gs} **0-0-5 £315**

Notty Bitz (Ire) *J S Moore*   55
3 b/br g Darnay - Riskie Things
12^{8gf} 2^{7gf} 9^{8sd} 3^{8gs} **0-2-4 £936**

Noul (USA) *K A Ryan*   75 a81
4 ch g Miswaki (USA) - Water Course (USA)
10^{8sd} 1^{7sw} 9^{10sd} 10^{7gf} 6^{8gf} 10^{7gf} 3^{7g}
6^{7sd} 13^{8g} 4^{7sd} **1-1-10 £3,751**

Now Look Here *B A McMahon*   93
7 b g Reprimand - Where's Carol
7^{5g} 9^{5gf} 14^{6g} 9^{5gf} 2^{5hy} 10^{6gf} 4^{5gf} 10^{6g}
5^{5gf} 14^{6g} 4^{5gs} 17^{6g} 3^{5g} **0-2-13 £6,780**

Now Then Sophie *D Shaw*   26 a54
3 ch f Keen - Rachels Eden
2^{8sd} 6^{8sd} 7^{8sd} 5^{7sw} 11^{6gf} 5^{6sd} 10^{8gf}
0-1-7 £832

Nowell House *M W Easterby*   89
7 ch g Polar Falcon (USA) - Langtry Lady
5^{13gs} 1^{13gs} 4^{14hy} 1^{13gs} **2-0-4 £13,587**

Noyac (Ire) *R Hannon*   83
2 b f Bluebird (USA) - Jolly Dame (USA)
2^{7g} 1^{6gf} 7^{6g} 6^{6gf} 9^{7gf} **1-1-5 £9,860**

Nuclear Prospect (Ire) *G M Moore*   34
3 ch g Nucleon (USA) - Carraigbyrne (Ire)
10⁸ᵍ 5¹²ᵍˢ **0-0-2**

Nugget (Ire) *P Mitchell*   34 a30
5 b g Goldmark (USA) - Folly Vision (Ire)
10¹²ˢᵈ 9¹²ᵍ 8¹⁵ᵍᶠ **0-0-3**

Nuit Sombre (Ire) *M Johnston*   99
3 b g Night Shift (USA) - Belair Princess (USA)
2⁸ᵍᶠ 4⁸ᵍᶠ 6⁹ᵍ 8⁷ᵍ 2¹⁰ᵍᶠ 1⁸ᵍᶠ 1¹⁰ᵍ 2⁸ᵍᶠ
8⁸ᵍᶠ 15¹⁰ᵍ 10¹¹ᵍᶠ 9¹⁰ᵍᶠ 5⁸ᵍᶠ 4⁸ᵍ 10⁸ᵍ 5¹⁰ᵍᶠ
6⁸ᵍˢ 13¹²ᵍ **2-4-18 £48,962**

Nukhbah (USA) *B W Hills*   71
2 b f Bahri (USA) - El Nafis (USA)
4⁷ᵍᶠ 3⁹ᶠ **0-0-2 £910**

Null And Void *D W Chapman*   34 a34
4 b g Zamindar (USA) - Nullarbor
14⁶ˢʷ 10⁸ˢᵈ 6⁶ˢʷ 6⁸ˢʷ 7⁷ˢᵈ 15⁷ᵍᶠ 11⁹ᵍᶠ
12⁷ᵍᶠ 15⁶ᵍᶠ **0-0-9**

Numitas (Ger) *Sir Mark Prescott*   98
3 b c Lomitas - Narola (Ger)
3¹⁴ᵍᶠ 11¹²ᵍᶠ 3¹⁴ᵍ 8¹⁴ᵍᶠ 1¹⁸ᵍᶠ 18¹⁸ᵍᶠ **1-1-6**
£9,443

Numpty (Ire) *N Tinkler*   34
2 b g Intikhab (USA) - Atsuko (Ire)
9⁶ᵍᶠ 14⁸ᵍ 9⁸ᵍᶠ **0-0-3**

Nuts For You (Ire) *R Charlton*   43
2 b f Sri Pekan (USA) - Moon Festival
11⁷ᵍˢ **0-0-1**

Nutty (Ire) *Mrs P N Dutfield*
3 b f Sri Pekan (USA) - Mitra (Ire)
18¹⁰ᵍ 7⁹ᵍᶠ **0-0-2**

Nuzooa (USA) *M P Tregoning*   78
2 b/br f A.P. Indy (USA) - Min Alhawa (USA)
2⁷ᵍᶠ **0-1-1 £3,470**

Nuzzle *M Quinn*   70 a69
3 b f Salse (USA) - Lena (USA)
4⁸ˢᵈ 3⁸ˢʷ 5¹⁰ˢᵈ 7⁸ˢᵈ 2⁸ᶠ 10¹⁰ᶠ 13⁸ᵍ 3⁸ᵍᶠ
8⁸ᶠ 6⁸ᵍᶠ 7⁸ᵍᶠ 5⁸ᶠ 5⁸ᵍ 9⁸ᶠ 2¹⁰ᶠ 3¹⁰ᶠ 3¹⁰ˢᵈ
6¹⁰ᵍᶠ 12¹⁰ˢᵈ **0-4-19 £4,818**

Nyramba *J H M Gosden*   102
2 b f Night Shift (USA) - Maramba
1⁵ᵍᶠ 2⁵ᵍᶠ 1⁶ᵍᶠ 1⁷ᵍᶠ 10⁶ᵍᶠ **3-1-5**
£160,996

Nysaean (Ire) *R Hannon*   118
4 b c Sadler's Wells (USA) - Irish Arms (Fr)
6¹²ᵍᶠ 2¹⁰ᵍᶠ 1¹⁰ᵍ 1¹⁰ʸˢ 7¹⁰ʰᵒ **2-1-5**
£75,322

O'l Lucy Broon *J S Goldie*   50
2 b f Royal Applause - Jay Gee Ell
6⁶ᵍᶠ 2⁶ᵍ 6⁶ᵍᶠ 9⁵ᵍᶠ 10⁵ᶠ **0-1-5 £1,696**

Oakley Blue *M Madgwick*   17
3 ch g Bluegrass Prince (Ire) - Westminster Waltz
13⁸ᵍ 11⁷ᵍᶠ 8⁸ᵍ **0-0-3**

Oakley Prince *M Madgwick*   19
2 ch g Bluegrass Prince (Ire) - Susie Oakley Vii
15⁶ᵍᶠ 8⁵ᵍᶠ 18⁸ᵍᶠ **0-0-3**

Oakley Rambo *R Hannon*   86 a78
4 br c Muhtarram (USA) - Westminster Waltz
9⁸ˢᵈ 9⁸ᵍ 8⁷ᵍ 19⁸ᵍ 13⁸ᵍᶠ **0-0-5**

Oases *D Shaw*   73 a77
4 ch g Zilzal (USA) - Markievicz (Ire)
5⁷ˢᵈ 10⁷ˢᵈ 6⁸ˢᵈ 7⁸ˢᵈ 1⁶ᵍˢ 2⁶ᵍˢ 6⁶ᵍ 10⁶ᵍ
14⁶ᵍ 17⁶ᵍˢ 8⁶ˢᵈ 4⁷ˢᵈ **1-1-12 £6,537**

Oasis Dream *J H M Gosden*   131
3 b c Green Desert (USA) - Hope (Ire)
3⁵ᵍᶠ 1⁶ᵍᶠ 1⁵ᵍᶠ 2⁶ᵍˢ 10⁸ᶠ **2-2-5**
£325,900

Oasis Star (Ire) *P W Harris*   70
2 b f Desert King (Ire) - Sound Tap (USA)
1⁶ᶠ **1-0-1 £3,108**

Obay *E A L Dunlop*   78
2 ch c Kingmambo (USA) - Parade Queen (USA)
7⁷ᵍᶠ **0-0-1**

Obe Bold (Ire) *A Berry*   71
2 b f Orpen (USA) - Capable Kate (Ire)
2⁵ᶠ 1⁵ᵍᶠ 3⁵ᵍᶠ 8⁵ᵍᶠ 3⁵ˢ 7⁵ᵍᶠ 5⁵ᵍᶠ 3⁶ᵍᶠ 3⁵ᶠ
5⁵ᵍᶠ 3⁵ᵍᶠ 3⁵ᵍᶠ 12⁶ᵍᶠ 9⁵ᵍ 7⁶ᵍ **1-4-15**
£10,331

Obe One *A Berry*   84
3 b g Puissance - Plum Bold
7⁵ᶠ 3⁵ᵍᶠ 4⁵ᵍ 3⁵ᵍᶠ 6⁵ᵍᶠ 3⁵ᶠ 8⁵ᵍᶠ 1⁵ᵍ 9⁵ᵍᶠ
7⁵ˢ 10⁵ᵍᶠ 10⁵ᵍˢ **1-3-12 £13,395**

Oblige *A M Balding*   95
3 b f Robellino (USA) - Acquiesce
3⁸ᵍᶠ 3¹⁰ᵍᶠ 6¹⁰ᵍᶠ 8⁸ᶠ **0-2-4 £7,565**

Obrigado (USA) *W J Haggas*   86
3 b g Bahri (USA) - Glorious Diamond (USA)
4⁸ᵍᶠ 2⁸ᵍᶠ 1⁸ᵍᶠ 6⁸ˢ **1-1-4 £11,421**

Obscure *J H M Gosden*   55
3 gr f Salse - Oscura (USA)
11¹⁰ᵍᶠ **0-0-1**

Ocarina *P G Murphy*   25 a43
3 ch g Piccolo - Nanny Dove
7⁸ˢᵈ 10⁷ᵍ 18⁷ᵍᶠ **0-0-3**

Occam (Ire) *A Bailey*   a47
9 ch g Sharp Victor (USA) - Monterana
6¹¹ˢᵈ 11¹²ˢᵈ 7¹²ˢᵈ 8¹²ˢʷ **1-0-4 £2,926**

Ocean Avenue (Ire) *C A Horgan*   82
4 b g Dolphin Street (Fr) - Trinity Hall
2¹⁴ᵍᶠ 4¹⁴ᵍᶠ 3¹⁴ᵍᶠ 1¹⁴ᵍᶠ **1-2-4 £10,284**

Ocean Dream (Ire) *A G Newcombe*   18 a24
2 b f Mujadil (USA) - Women In Love (Ire)
6⁵ˢᵈ 11⁶ᵍᶠ 8⁷ˢᵈ 10¹⁰ᵍˢ **0-0-4**

Ocean Rock *C A Horgan*   38
2 b c Perugino (USA) - Polistatic
11⁷ᵍˢ **0-0-1**

Ocean Silk (USA) *J H M Gosden*   117
3 b f Dynaformer (USA) - Mambo Jambo (USA)
1¹⁰ᵍᶠ 11¹²ᵍ 2¹²ᵍᶠ 2¹²ᵍᶠ 7¹²ᵍˢ 3¹³ʰᵒ
2-3-7 £171,409

Ocean Tide *R Ford*   a71
6 b g Deploy - Dancing Tide
9¹⁶ˢᵈ **0-0-1**

Ocean Victory *J Noseda*   98
3 ch g Cattrail (USA) - Persian Victory (Ire)
5⁸ᵍ 2¹⁰ᵍˢ 1⁸ᵍ 1⁹ᵍᶠ 2⁸ᵍᶠ 1⁸ᵍᶠ 2⁸ᵍᶠ **3-3-7**
£31,103

Ocotillo *D R Loder*   a66
3 b c Mark Of Esteem (Ire) - Boojum
5⁸ˢᵈ **0-0-1**

Octane (USA) *W M Brisbourne*   82 a76
7 b g Cryptoclearance (USA) - Something True (USA)
9¹³ˢᵈ 8¹⁶ᵍᶠ 11⁴ᵍᶠ 6¹³ᵍˢ 5¹²ᵍᶠ 7¹⁶ᵍᶠ 6¹²ᵍ
12¹²ᵍ 1¹²ᵍᶠ 2¹⁴ᵍᶠ **1-2-10 £8,413**

Octennial *P A Blockley*   57 a57
4 gr g Octagonal (NZ) - Laune (Aus)
2⁷ᵍᶠ 6⁶ˢᵈ 5⁶ˢᵈ 7⁷ᵍᶠ **0-1-4 £888**

October Mist (Ire) *Mrs M Reveley*   66
9 gr g Roselier (Fr) - Bonny Joe
2¹²ᵍˢ **0-1-1 £642**

October Moon *W Jarvis*   65
3 b f Octagonal (NZ) - Moon Carnival
3⁷ᵍˢ 9⁷ᵍᶠ 3⁶ᵍᶠ 4⁷ᶠ **0-1-4 £1,196**

Odabella (Ire) *J H M Gosden*   74 a79
3 b f Selkirk (USA) - Circe's Isle
2⁸ᵍ 3⁸ᶠ 2¹⁰ᵍ 3¹⁰ˢᵈ 4¹⁰ᵍᶠ 8¹⁰ᵍᶠ **0-4-6**
£5,983

Odabella's Charm *Sir Michael Stoute*   77
3 b f Cadeaux Genereux - One Life (USA)
1⁸ᵍ 8⁸ᵍᶠ **1-0-2 £4,251**

Oddsmaker (Ire) *P D Evans*   71
2 b g Barathea (Ire) - Archipova (USA)
7⁵ᵍᶠ 3⁶ᵍᶠ 10⁶ᵍ 7⁷ᵍᶠ 4⁸ᵍᶠ 7⁶ᵍᶠ 22⁷ᵍ 7⁸ᵍᶠ
7⁸ᵍᶠ 1⁸ᵍᶠ 5⁷ᶠ **1-0-11 £4,597**

Odiham *H Morrison*   66 a74
2 b g Deploy - Hug Me
11⁷ˢᵈ 7⁸ᵍᶠ 2⁸ˢᵈ **0-1-3 £944**

Oeuf A La Neige *E A L Dunlop*   77
3 b c Danehill (USA) - Reine De Neige
5⁸ᵍ 17⁸ᵍᶠ 5⁸ᵍᶠ 3⁸ᵍᶠ 10⁸ᵍ **0-1-5 £661**

Ofaraby *M A Jarvis*   50 a88
3 b g Sheikh Albadou - Maristax
7⁸ᵍ 1¹⁰ˢᵈ 7⁹ᶠᵗ 2⁹ˢᵈ 1⁹ˢᵈ **2-1-5 £5,822**

Off Air *C N Allen*   47
2 b f Robellino (USA) - Sprite
8⁶ᵍᶠ **0-0-1**

Off Beat (USA) *R F Johnson Houghton*   79
2 ch g Mister Baileys - Off Off (USA)
12⁶ᵍᶠ 8⁷ᵍᶠ 3⁷ᵍᶠ 4⁶ᵍᶠ 4⁷ᵍᶠ 7⁶ᵍᶠ 8⁷ᵍᶠ 6⁷ᵍᶠ
1⁶ᶠ 9⁶ᵍᶠ 6⁶ᵍᶠ **1-1-11 £4,139**

Off Hire *C Smith*   60 a46
7 b g Clantime - Lady Pennington
10⁵ˢʷ 13⁵ˢᵈ 17⁵ᵍᶠ 11⁵ᵍᶠ 5⁵ˢᵈ 4⁵ᵍᶠ 10⁶ᵍᶠ
9⁵ˢʷ **0-1-8 £403**

Officer's Pink *P F I Cole*   76 a58
3 ch f Grand Lodge (USA) - Arethusa
13⁷ᵍᶠ 6⁷ˢᵈ 6⁶ᵍᶠ 2⁶ᵍᶠ 4⁶ᶠ 1⁵ᵍ 3⁶ᵍᶠ 5⁵ᵍᶠ
1-2-8 £7,413

Offtoworkwego *P Monteith*   31
3 b g Fraam - Hi Hoh (Ire)
13⁵ᵍᶠ 16⁶ᵍᶠ 8⁵ᵍˢ 9⁸ᶠ 13⁸ᵍˢ 12⁶ᵍᶠ 7⁵ᵍᶠ
0-0-7

Offwiththefairies *W R Muir*   25
3 b f Farfelu - My Ruby Ring
7⁶ᵍᶠ 19⁶ᵍᶠ **0-0-2**

Oh Boy (Ire) *R Hannon*   68
3 b c Tagula (Ire) - Pretty Sally (Ire)
10⁶ᵍˢ 4⁶ᵍᶠ 14⁷ᵍ **0-0-3 £310**

Oh Frigate *H Candy*   a27
2 b g Muhtarram (USA) - Sole Control
10⁷ˢᵈ **0-0-1**

Oh Golly Gosh *N P Littmoden*   a68
2 ch g Exit To Nowhere (USA) - Guerre De Troie
3⁶ˢᵈ 8⁸ˢᵈ **0-1-2 £453**

Oh So Dusty *N P Littmoden*   a43
5 b m Piccolo - Dark Eyed Lady (Ire)
12¹⁰ˢᵈ **0-0-1**

Oh So Rosie (Ire) *J S Moore*   67
3 b f Danehill Dancer (Ire) - Shinkoh Rose (Fr)
13⁷ᵍ 11⁶ᵍ 10⁷ᵍᶠ 5⁸ᵍᶠ 9⁸ᵍᶠ 2⁹ᵍᶠ
7⁸ᶠ 6⁸ᶠ 4¹⁰ᵍˢ 10⁸ᵍˢ 2⁸ᵍ **0-3-13 £3,608**

Oh Sunny Boy (Ire) *J S Moore*   44
2 b g Desert Sun - Naivement (Ire)
4⁶ᵍᶠ 12⁶ᵍ 6⁶ᶠ 14⁶ᵍᶠ 3⁶ᵍᶠ 15⁷ᵍ **0-1-6**
£295

Ok Pal *T G Mills*   94
3 b c Primo Dominie - Sheila's Secret (Ire)
10⁶ᵍᶠ 4⁵ˢ **0-0-2 £1,053**

Okoboji (Ire) *M P Tregoning*   67
2 ch c Indian Ridge - Pool Party (USA)
4⁷ᵍ **0-0-1 £280**

Old Bailey (USA) *T D Barron*   51 a6
3 gr g Lit De Justice (USA) - Olden Lek (USA)
11⁹ˢᵈ 16⁷ᵍᶠ 13⁷ᶠ 10⁷ᶠ 9⁷ᶠ 11⁸ˢ 5⁷ᵍˢ
2⁶ᵍᶠ 6⁶ᵍᶠ 2⁶ᵍᶠ 6⁷ᶠ **0-2-11 £1,864**

Old Blue Eyes *P W Harris*   91
4 b c Whittingham (Ire) - Special One
20⁶ᵍᶠ 27⁶ᵍ 4⁶ᵍᶠ 3⁶ᵍᶠ 17⁶ᵍˢ **0-2-5**
£2,635

Old Deuteronomy (USA) *A P O'Brien*   113
2 br c Storm Cat (USA) - Jewel In The Crown (USA)
1⁶ᵍᶠ 4⁵ᵍᶠ 2⁶ᵍ 2⁶ˢ 4⁶ˢ 7⁶ᵍᶠ **1-2-6**
£70,528

Old Harry *L G Cottrell*   67
3 b g Case Law - Supreme Thought
8⁶ᵍᶠ 5⁶ᵍ 4⁶ᵍᶠ 18⁷ᵍᶠ 7⁶ᵍᶠ 8⁶ᵍ **0-0-6 £418**

Old Irish *O O'Neill*
10 gr g Old Vic - Dunoof
10¹⁵ˢᵈ 14¹⁰ᵍᶠ **0-0-2**

Old Malt (Ire) *R Hannon*   85
2 ch c Ashkalani (Ire) - Dona Royale (Ire)
7⁶ᵍ 3⁷ᵍᶠ 1⁷ᶠ 2⁸ᵍᶠ 1⁷ᵍᶠ 2⁹ᵍ **2-3-6**
£12,588

Old Tom (Ire) *R M H Cowell*   44 a31
3 ch g Bering - Lovely Lyca
5⁹ˢᵈ 5¹⁰ᵍᶠ 4⁸ᶠ 5⁷ᵍᶠ 7⁷ᶠ **0-1-5**

Olden Times *J L Dunlop*   121
5 b h Darshaan - Garah
1⁹ᵍᶠ 3⁸ᵍ 4¹⁰ᵍᶠ 4¹⁰ᵍᶠ 13¹⁰ᵍ **1-0-5**
£87,000

Oldenway *R A Fahey*   83
4 b g Most Welcome - Sickle Moon
13¹⁰ᵍ 11⁰ᵍ 2¹²ᵍᶠ 5¹²ᵍᶠ 9⁹ᵍᶠ 2¹⁰ᵍᶠ 7¹⁰ᵍᶠ
1-2-7 £8,929

Olihider (USA) *M L W Bell*   81
2 gr c Woodman (USA) - Ingot's Dance Away (USA)
4⁶ᵍᶠ 5⁷ᵍᶠ 6⁶ᵍᶠ 1⁷ᶠ **1-0-4 £11,487**

Olivander *G A Butler*   73 a65
2 b c Danzero (Aus) - Mystic Goddess (USA)
5⁵ᵍᶠ 2⁶ᵍᶠ UR⁷ᵍᶠ 6⁷ˢᵈ **0-1-4 £2,864**

Olivia Grace *L M Cumani*   102
5 ch m Pivotal - Sheila's Secret (Ire)
1⁵ᵍ 3⁵ᵍᶠ 10⁵ᵍᶠ 7⁵ᵍᶠ 11⁶ᵍᶠ **1-0-5**
£12,643

Olivia Rose (Ire) *Mrs Lydia Pearce*   68 a14
4 b f Mujadil (USA) - Santana Lady (Ire)
9⁷ˢʷ 13⁸ᵍ 7¹⁰ᵍ 6¹⁰ᵍᶠ 5¹¹ᵍᶠ 3¹⁰ᵍ 3¹²ᵍ
13¹²ᵍᶠ 2⁹ᵍᶠ 2¹⁰ᵍᶠ 8¹⁰ᵍ 5¹⁰ᵍᶠ 2⁹ᵍᶠ 18⁸ᵍᶠ 8¹⁰ᵍᶠ
15¹⁰ᵍᶠ 4⁹ᶠ 5¹¹ᵍ 2⁸ᵍˢ **0-6-19 £5,217**

Omaha City (Ire) *B Gubby*   93
9 b g Night Shift (USA) - Be Discreet
9⁸ᵍ 7⁸ᵍ 4⁸ᵍᶠ 21⁷ᶠ 14⁸ᵍᶠ 5⁸ᵍ 6⁷ᵍᶠ 7⁹ᵍᶠ
10⁸ᵍ **0-0-9 £1,034**

Omaimah *M R Channon*   a67
4 b f Mark Of Esteem (Ire) - Gracious Beauty (USA)
10⁷ˢᵈ 2⁶ˢᵈ 4⁶ˢʷ 7⁶ˢᵈ **0-1-4 £854**

Oman Gulf (USA) *B W Hills*   79
2 b c Diesis - Dabaweyaa (Ire)
1⁶ᵍᶠ **1-0-1 £4,940**

Oman Sea (USA) *B W Hills*   84

2 b f Rahy (USA) - Ras Shaikh (USA)
2⁵ᵍᶠ 1⁶ᵍᶠ **1-1-2 £8,581**

Omega Bay (Ire) *J Balding*   37
2 b g Imperial Ballet (Ire) - Autumn Affair
6⁶ᶠ 9⁷ᶠ 9⁸ᵍᶠ 6⁸ᵍˢ **0-0-4**

Omey Strand (Ire) *J G M O'Shea*   53 a9
4 b g Desert Style (Ire) - Ex-Imager
19⁷ᵍᶠ 14⁶ˢᵈ 6⁸ᶠ 5⁸ᵍᶠ 12¹²ˢʷ 78ᵍᶠ **0-0-6**

Omniscient (Ire) *T T Clement*   37
4 b f Distinctly North (USA) - Mystic Shadow (Ire)
10⁷ᵍᶠ 12⁸ᵍ **0-0-2**

On Every Street *H J Cyzer*   65
2 b c Singspiel (Ire) - Nekhbet
5⁸ᵍᶠ **0-0-1**

On Guard *P G Murphy*   67 a48
5 b g Sabrehill (USA) - With Care
10⁹ˢᵈ 6¹²ˢᵈ 11¹ᵍᶠ 11⁰ᵍᶠ 18¹⁰ᵍ 9¹⁰ᵍ 11¹⁰ᵍᶠ
7⁸ˢᵈ 8¹⁰ᵍ 6¹²ˢᵈ 5¹⁰ᵍᶠ 8⁹ᵍᶠ **2-0-12 £7,893**

On Point *Sir Mark Prescott*   a75
3 b f Kris - Odette
1⁵ˢᵈ 10⁵ˢᵈ 1⁵ˢᵈ 5⁵ˢᵈ 9⁵ˢᵈ **2-0-5 £6,174**

On Porpoise *P W D'Arcy*   24 a49
7 b g Dolphin Street (Fr) - Floppie (Fr)
5⁸ˢᵈ 10¹¹ᵍ **0-0-2**

On The Brink *T D Easterby*   89
3 b f Mind Games - Ocean Grove (Ire)
4⁶ᵍᶠ 6⁵ᵍᶠ 9⁶ᵍ 4⁶ᵍˢ 13⁵ᵍᶠ 2⁶ᵍˢ 5⁶ᵍᶠ 9⁶ᵍᶠ
5⁶ᵍᶠ 4⁶ᵍᶠ 7⁶ᵍᶠ **0-1-11 £9,565**

On The Fairway (Ire) *J J Bridger*   36 a27
4 b f Danehill Dancer (Ire) - Asta Madera (Ire)
12⁶ˢᵈ 17⁷ᶠ 6⁵ᵍ 15⁶ᵍᶠ **0-0-4**

On The Level *Mrs N Macauley*   48
4 ch f Beveled (USA) - Join The Clan
11⁷ᵍᶠ 4⁵ᵍᶠ 11⁵ᵍᶠ 7⁵ᵍᶠ 4⁵ᵍᶠ 3⁵ᵍᶠ 5⁶ᵍᶠ
5⁶ᶠ **0-2-9 £1,687**

On The Trail *D W Chapman*   a67
6 ch g Catrail (USA) - From The Rooftops (Ire)
3⁶ˢʷ 1⁶ˢᵈ 13⁶ˢᵈ 12⁶ˢᵈ 9⁶ˢʷ 7⁶ˢʷ 2⁶ˢᵈ
13⁶ᵍᶠ 3⁶ˢᵈ 3⁶ˢᵈ 2⁶ˢᵈ 3⁶ˢᵈ 15⁶ˢᵈ **1-6-13
£6,913**

On The Wing *A P Jarvis*   78 a58
2 b f Pivotal - Come Fly With Me
5⁷ˢᵈ 5⁷ᵍᶠ 5⁶ᵍᶠ 1⁷ᵍᶠ 5⁸ᵍᶠ **1-0-5 £2,534**

Once (Fr) *M L W Bell*   79
3 gr g Hector Protector (USA) - Moon Magic
2¹⁰ᵍᶠ 3¹⁰ᵍᶠ 7¹²ᵍᶠ 12¹³ᵍᶠ **0-1-4 £3,568**

Once Seen *R M Beckett*   77 a65
3 b g Celtic Swing - Brief Glimpse (Ire)
15⁸ᵍᶠ 2⁸ᵍ 9⁸ˢᵈ 12⁸ᵍ 1⁸ᵍᶠ **1-1-5 £4,856**

One 'N' Only (Ire) *Miss L A Perratt*   59
2 b f Desert Story (Ire) - Alpina (USA)
11⁶ᵍᶠ 4⁷ᵍᶠ 5⁷ᶠ 4⁶ᵍ 5⁷ᵍᶠ 7⁷ᵍᶠ **0-0-6 £297**

One Alone *J G Given*   28 a53
2 b f Atraf - Songsheet
10⁶ᵍᶠ 7⁶ˢᵈ 8⁷ˢᵈ **0-0-3**

One Cool Cat (USA) *A P O'Brien*   121
2 b c Storm Cat (USA) - Tacha (USA)
4⁵ᵍʸ 1⁶ᵍᶠ 1⁶ᵍ 1⁶ᵍ 1⁷ᵍᶠ **4-0-5 £265,786**

One For Me *Jean-Rene Auvray*   43 a39
5 br m Tragic Role (USA) - Chantallee's Pride
11¹⁶ˢᵈ 11¹²ᵍᶠ **0-0-2**

One Last Time *R Hannon*   81 a61
3 b g Primo Dominie - Leap Of Faith (Ire)
7⁶ᵍᶠ 11⁶ᵍˢ 8⁸ᵍᶠ 6⁸ᵍᶠ 12⁸ˢᵈ **0-0-6**

One More Hymn (Ire) *S L Keightley*   a44

3 b g General Monash (USA) - Maz (Ire)
9⁶ˢᵈ 6⁵ˢᵈ 8⁶ˢᵈ **0-0-3**

One More Round (USA) *D K Weld*   115 a95
5 b g Ghazi (USA) - Life Of The Party (USA)
2⁶ᶠᵗ 10⁸ᶠᵗ 2⁷ᵍʸ 3⁸ʸˢ 2⁷ʸ 5⁶ᵍ 2⁷ᵍ 4⁷ʸ
2⁷ᵍᶠ 7⁶ᵍ 7⁷ᵍ **0-7-11 £69,982**

One Off *Sir Mark Prescott*   93 a66
3 b g Barathea (Ire) - On Call
9¹²ᵍᶠ 1¹²ᵍᶠ 1¹²ˢᵈ 1¹⁴ᵍ 1¹⁵ᵍᶠ 1¹⁴ᵍᶠ 1¹⁴ᵍᶠ
2¹⁶ᵍᶠ **6-1-8 £27,461**

One Upmanship *J G Portman*   73
2 ch g Bahamian Bounty - Magnolia
8⁵ᵍˢ 6⁵ᵍᶠ 7⁵ᵍᶠ 5⁶ᵍᶠ 21⁵ᵍᶠ 2⁷ᵍᶠ 4⁶ᵍᶠ 3⁶ᵍᶠ
14⁶ᵍᶠ **0-2-9 £1,323**

One Way Ticket *J M Bradley*   77 a51
3 ch c Pursuit Of Love - Prima Cominna
2⁷ᵍᶠ 2⁷ᵍᶠ 5⁷ᶠ 3⁶ᵍᶠ 2⁶ᵍᶠ 3⁷ᵍᶠ 4⁷ˢᵈ 1⁷ᵍᶠ
13⁷ᵍᶠ 2⁷ᵍᶠ 12⁷ˢᵈ **1-6-11 £9,524**

Onefortheboys (Ire) *D Flood*   36 a25
4 b g Distinctly North (USA) - Joyful Prospect
12⁹ˢᵈ 9⁷ˢᵈ 9⁸ˢʷ 6⁶ᵍᶠ 9⁶ᵍ **0-0-5**

Onefourseven *P C Haslam*   44
10 b g Jumbo Hirt (USA) - Dominance
6²²ᵍᶠ 7¹⁴ᶠ 3¹⁷ᵍᶠ **0-1-3 £790**

Oniz Tiptoes (Ire) *W R Muir*
2 ch c Russian Revival - Edionda (Ire)
7⁸ᶠ 15⁷ˢᵈ **0-0-2**

Online Investor *C G Cox*   84
4 b g Puissance - Anytime Baby
9⁶ᵍᶠ 4⁶ᵍ 10⁶ᵍᶠ 4⁶ᵍ 8⁵ᵍᶠ 7⁶ᵍ 6⁵ᵍᶠ 13⁶ᵍᶠ
7⁶ᵍᶠ 15⁵ᵍᶠ **0-1-10 £3,372**

Only For Gold *Dr P Pritchard*   55 a37
8 b g Presidium - Calvanne Miss
7⁹ˢᵈ PU⁹ˢᵈ 5⁷ᵍᶠ 14⁸ᵍᶠ 8⁷ˢᵈ 5⁷ᵍˢ 8⁸ᵍᶠ 5⁸ᵍᶠ
11⁸ᵍ 11⁸ᵍᶠ 6¹¹ᵍ 11¹⁰ᵍ 9⁶ᵍᶠ **0-0-13**

Only For Sue *W S Kittow*   44
4 ch g Pivotal - Barbary Court
10⁸ˢᵈ 6¹²ᵍᶠ **0-0-2**

Only If I Laugh *B J Meehan*   78 a61
2 ch g Piccolo - Agony Aunt
4⁵ˢᵈ 2⁵ᶠ 6⁵ᵍᶠ 13⁵ᵍᶠ 3⁵ᵍᶠ 1⁵ˢᵈ 1⁵ᶠ
4⁵ᵍᶠ 7⁵ᵍᶠ 2⁵ᶠ 5⁶ᵍᶠ 1⁵ᵍᶠ 6⁵ᵍᶠ 5⁵ᵍ 16⁶ᵍᶠ **3-3-16
£11,380**

Only Just In Time *D K Ivory*
3 ch f Bahamian Bounty - Badger Bay (Ire)
9⁵ˢᵈ 10⁷ˢᵈ **0-0-2**

Only One Legend (Ire) *K A Ryan*   72 a82
5 b g Eagle Eyed (USA) - Afifah
7⁶ˢʷ 2⁶ˢᵈ 6⁶ˢᵈ 1⁶ˢᵈ 6⁶ˢʷ 1⁶ˢᵈ 2⁶ᵍ 7⁶ˢᵈ
7⁶ᵍᶠ 9⁶ᵍᶠ 8⁶ᵍᶠ 5⁶ᵍᶠ 2⁶ᵍᶠ 4⁵ᵍᶠ 6⁶ᵍᶠ 6⁵ᶠ **2-3-16
£13,800**

Only Penang (Ire) *G A Butler*   85 a66
4 b f Perugino (USA) - Unalaska (Ire)
17⁸ᵍ 2⁸ᵍᶠ 8⁷ᵍ 17⁸ᵍᶠ 3⁹ᵍᶠ 10⁹ᵍᶠ 10⁷ˢᵈ
17¹⁰ᵍˢ **0-2-8 £3,259**

Onlytime Will Tell *D Nicholls*   109
5 ch g Efisio - Prejudice
4⁶ᵍᶠ 18⁷ᵍ 11⁶ᵍᶠ 2⁶ᵍ 14⁶ᶠ 11⁷ᵍᶠ 2⁶ᵍ 5⁶ᵍ
9⁶ᵍ 20⁶ᵍ **0-3-10 £17,596**

Onya *J W Hills*   53 a27
3 ch f Unfuwain (USA) - Reel Foyle (USA)
12⁸ᵍ 12¹⁰ᵍᶠ 9⁹ˢʷ 11¹²ˢᵈ **0-0-4**

Oops (Ire) *J F Coupland*   48
4 b g In The Wings - Atsuko (Ire)
11¹⁶ᵍᶠ 9¹⁶ᵍˢ 4¹⁴ᵍᶠ 2¹⁶ᶠ **0-1-4 £916**

Oopsie Daisy *J R Fanshawe* — 82
4 b f Singspiel (Ire) - Oops Pettie
6[10gf] 10[8g] 18[9f] 7[8gf] 6[8gf] 8[10gf] 1-0-6
£6,952

Oos And Ahs *C W Fairhurst* — 27
3 b f Silver Wizard (USA) - Hot Feet
8[8f] 0-0-1

Opal's Helmsman (USA) *B Mactaggart* — 37
4 b g Helmsman (USA) - Opal's Notebook (USA)
7[12f] 8[9g] 9[15g] 0-0-3

Open Ground (Ire) *Ian Williams* — a38
6 ch g Common Grounds - Poplina (USA)
12[16sd] 7[16sd] 0-0-2

Open Handed (Ire) *B Ellison* — 68 a34
3 b g Cadeaux Genereux - Peralta (Ire)
18[7ys] 21[8g] 1[8y] 13[9ys] 7[9sh] 6[7ys] 12[8gf]
12[7gs] 10[7sw] 1-0-9 £4,480

Open Mind *E J Alston* — 57
2 b f Mind Games - Primum Tempus
2[5gf] 4[5s] 7[5gf] 4[5f] 11[6gf] 0-1-5 £1,609

Opening Ceremony (USA) *R A Fahey* — 77
4 br f Quest For Fame - Gleam Of Light (Ire)
5[7gf] 6[10gs] 6[12f] 6[9gf] 9[12gf] 8[10gf] 1[10gf]
3[10gf] 15[10gf] 5[10g] 3[10gf] 1[10g] 2-2-12 £7,705

Opening Hymn *M P Tregoning* — 70
3 b f Alderbrook - Hymne D'Amour (USA)
5[10g] 5[10gf] 0-0-2

Opera Babe (Ire) *H S Howe* — 74
2 b f Kahyasi - Fairybird (Fr)
4[6gf] 8[7gf] 10[8gf] 5[8s] 0-0-4 £731

Opera Comique (Fr) *John M Oxx* — 102
2 b f Singspiel (Ire) - Grace Note (Fr)
1[9g] 3[7gf] 1-1-2 £12,000

Opera Glass *A M Balding* — 91
3 b f Barathea (Ire) - Optaria
2[8gf] 6[10gf] 18[8gf] 8[8gf] 2[9gs] 5[8g] 7[9gf] 1-2-7
£9,390

Opera Knight *M L W Bell* — a58
3 ch g In The Wings - Sans Escale (USA)
2[12sd] 5[12sd] 0-1-2 £1,248

Operashaan (Ire) *T T Clement* — 44 a30
3 b g Darshaan - Comic Opera (Ire)
6[12sd] 8[7gf] 9[9s] 0-0-3

Opportune (Ger) *W M Brisbourne* — 65
8 br g Shirley Heights - On The Tiles
12[12g] 6[17gf] 1[16gf] 2[18gf] 1[16gf] 6[13gf] 5[16g]
2[16g] 3[16gf] 2[16gf] 1[16gf] 3-3-11 £21,000

Optimaite *B R Millman* — 79
6 b g Komaite (USA) - Leprechaun Lady
10[14gs] 8[12g] 9[10g] 7[10gf] 8[11gf] 5[12gf] 7[11gf]
0-0-7

Optimal (Ire) *Sir Mark Prescott* — 50 a48
2 gr f Green Desert (USA) - On Call
4[8gf] 8[7sd] 11[7gf] 0-0-3 £443

Optimum Night *P D Niven* — 46
4 b g Superlative - Black Bess
9[7gs] 8[10gf] 13[8gf] 0-0-3

Orange Touch (Ger) *Mrs A J Perrett* — 100
3 b c Lando (Ger) - Orange Bowl
5[10gf] 4[10gf] 0-0-2 £3,250

Orangino *J S Haldane* — 53
5 b g Primo Dominie - Sweet Jaffa
10[6gs] 8[6gf] 2[8gf] 10[10g] 11[7g] 15[11g] 11[8gf]
0-1-7 £876

Orapa *Julian Poulton* — a53

4 b g Spectrum (Ire) - African Dance (USA)
8[10sd] 0-0-1

Orcadian *J M P Eustace* — 99
2 b g Kirkwall - Rosy Outlook (USA)
3[6gf] 1[6gf] 2[7gf] 2[6gf] 7[6gf] 1-3-5 £12,645

Orchestra Stall *J L Dunlop* — 101
11 b g Old Vic - Blue Brocade
6[16s] 9[16g] 0-0-2

Orchestration (Ire) *R Charlton* — 76
2 ch c Stravinsky (USA) - Mora (Ire)
2[5gf] 6[6gf] 0-1-2 £1,702

Oriel Lady *A Berry* — 41
2 b f Cyrano De Bergerac - Hicklam Millie
8[5gf] 14[5sd] 6[5gf] 10[6gs] 6[5gf] 6[7f] 0-0-6

Oriental Mist (Ire) *P Monteith* — 33
5 gr g Balla Cove - Donna Katrina
13[9gs] 8[13gf] 10[8gf] 0-0-3

Oriental Moon (Ire) *G C H Chung* — 54 a57
4 ch f Spectrum (Ire) - La Grande Cascade (USA)
12[9sw] 12[10gf] 20[10gf] 10[10gf] 10[8gf] 0-0-5

Oriental Warrior *M P Tregoning* — 93
2 b c Alhaarth (Ire) - Oriental Fashion (Ire)
1[6gf] 1[7gf] 2-0-2 £13,569

Orientor *J S Goldie* — 115
5 b h Inchinor - Orient
2[6g] 2[6s] 9[6gf] 12[6f] 1[6gs] 9[6gf] 7[6g] 5[5gf]
8[6gs] 2[6g] 13[6gf] 6[6gf] 1-2-12 £44,025

Original Sin (Ire) *J R Fanshawe* — 51
3 b g Bluebird - Majakerta (Ire)
10[7gf] 5[6gf] 6[7g] 13[8sd] 0-0-4

Orinocovsky (Ire) *C R Egerton* — 68
4 ch c Grand Lodge (USA) - Brillantina (Fr)
12[10gf] 7[12g] 4[14s] 0-0-3 £358

Orion Express *M W Easterby* — 49
2 b c Bahhare (USA) - Kaprisky (Ire)
9[6f] 8[5s] 10[6gf] 0-0-3

Orion's Belt *G B Balding*
3 ch g Compton Place - Follow The Stars
10[6g] 0-0-1

Ormolu (Ire) *G A Butler* — 48
3 ch f Perugino (USA) - Gloire
4[6gf] 10[5gf] 7[5gf] 12[8gf] 6[6gf] 7[5gs] 0-0-6
£419

Ornellaia (Ire) *P M Phelan* — 51 a51
3 b f Mujadil (USA) - Almost A Lady (Ire)
8[7gf] 5[7sd] 5[10sd] 5[10g] 12[12sd] 0-0-5

Oro Puro (Ire) *M G Quinlan* — 60
2 b c Goldmark (USA) - Mount Soufriere (USA)
6[6gf] 1[7gs] 8[7gf] 5[8gf] 10[8gf] 1-0-5 £3,160

Oro Verde *R Hannon* — 88 a79
2 ch c Compton Place - Kastaway
6[6gf] 5[7gf] 2[5gf] 2[8g] 7[7g] 3[6gf] 3[6g] 4[6sd]
1-1-8 £7,858

Orpenberry (Ire) *J Balding* — 70
2 b f Orpen (USA) - Forest Berries (Ire)
3[5gf] 15[6g] 10[6gf] 1-0-4 £5,314

Orthodox *G L Moore* — 83 a91
4 gr g Baryshnikov (Aus) - Sancta
11[13sd] 11[12sd] 6[13sd] 12[12g] 8[12gf] 2[12g] 8[12gf]
2-1-7 £11,999

Oscar Madison (Ire) *B Mactaggart* — 41
2 b g Petorius - She's Our Lady (Ire)
6[5gs] 7[6gf] 6[7gf] 7[6gf] 0-0-4

Oscar Pepper (USA) *T D Barron* — 80 a99
6 b g Brunswick (USA) - Princess Baja (USA)

2^{8sd} 11^{10sd} 3^{8sw} 2^{8sw} 5^{8sd} 7^{8gf} 2^{8gf} 3^{8g}
11^{8gf} 1^{7f} 11^{8gf} 6^{8gf} 3^{7gf} 9^{8gf} 5^{8gf} 12^{10gf} 4^{10g}
7^{8gf} 4^{8g} **1-7-19 £14,297**

Osorno *C F Wall* — a22
3 ch g Inchinor - Pacifica
13^{7sd} **0-0-1**

Other Business *P L Gilligan* — 27
2 b f Muhtarram (USA) - Carnbrea Belle (Ire)
6^{8gf} 14^{8f} **0-0-2**

Other Routes *G L Moore* — 65 a67
4 ch g Efisio - Rainbow Fleet
2^{10sd} 5^{10f} 7^{10f} 6^{9gf} 2^{8hd} 4^{8gf} 7^{8gf}
5^{8f} 2^{8gf} 5^{8gf} 6^{8gf} 9^{9gf} **0-4-13 £3,679**

Otototm *A C Stewart* — 68
3 b c Mtoto - Najmat Alshemaal (Ire)
6^{10gf} 11^{2f} 12^{12g} 12^{14g} 4^{12gf} **1-1-5**
£5,461

Otylia *A Berry* — 58 a29
3 ch f Wolfhound (USA) - Soba
10^{6gf} 14^{5g} 10^{6f} 12^{7gf} 3^{6f} 10^{6sd} 3^{6gf}
12^{6gf} 6^{5g} 4^{5gf} 2^{6f} 3^{6gf} 5^{5g} 4^{6gf} 4^{6f} **0-2-15**
£3,655

Ouija Board *E A L Dunlop* — 92
2 b f Cape Cross (Ire) - Selection Board
3^{7gf} 1^{7gf} 3^{8gs} **1-2-3 £7,038**

Oundle Scoundrel (Fr) *Y-M Porzier* — 61 a65
4 b g Spinning World (USA) - Tidal Treasure (USA)
7^{8sd} 5^{9sd} 9^{8sd} 7^{8sd} 2^{8sd} 11^{8sd} 5^{7gf} 1^{9ho}
3^{8sd} 3^{10ho} **1-3-10 £9,010**

Our Chelsea Blue (USA) *A W Carroll* — 62 a67
5 ch m Distant View (USA) - Eastern Connection (USA)
4^{6sd} 1^{7sd} 13^{6sd} 14^{7sd} 5^{6sd} 5^{6sd} 6^{5g}
15^{7gf} 10^{7sd} 10^{6gf} **3-0-11 £8,918**

Our Destiny *D Burchell* — 31 a55
5 b g Mujadil (USA) - Superspring
1^{9sd} 4^{8sd} 4^{9sd} 1^{8sd} 8^{10sd} 7^{9sd} 10^{10f} 8^{12sd}
2-0-8 £6,062

Our Emmy Lou *Sir Mark Prescott* — 55
2 ch f Mark Of Esteem (Ire) - Regent's Folly (Ire)
10^{7gf} 6^{6f} 6^{8gf} **0-0-3**

Our Fred *T G Mills* — 65 a76
6 ch g Prince Sabo - Sheila's Secret (Ire)
7^{5sd} 13^{5g} 13^{5gf} 3^{5gf} 11^{5gf} 6^{5gf} **0-1-6**
£581

Our Gamble (Ire) *R Hannon* — 82
2 b f Entrepreneur - Manilia (Fr)
12^{5g} 4^{5gf} 1^{5gf} 7^{6g} **1-0-4 £5,362**

Our Glenard *S L Keightley* — 62 a58
4 b g Royal Applause - Loucoum (Fr)
12^{10sd} 4^{10sd} 1^{13sd} 1^{10gf} 10^{11gf} 14^{10g} 5^{8gf}
9^{12sd} 13^{12sd} **2-0-9 £6,652**

Our Imperial Bay (USA) *R M Stronge* — 46
4 b g Smart Strike (Can) - Heat Lightning (USA)
14^{12g} 6^{13gf} **0-0-2**

Our Kid *T D Easterby* — 58
2 ch g Pursuit Of Love - Flower Princess
6^{6f} 6^{7gf} 4^{7gf} 7^{7gf} **0-0-4 £320**

Our Lady *G G Margarson* — 69
3 b f Primo Dominie - Polytess (Ire)
12^{7gf} 18^{6g} 18^{8gf} 4^{10gf} 16^{8gf} 3^{7gf} 6^{8gf}
8^{8gf} 2^{8g} 4^{7f} **1-2-10 £4,007**

Our Lodge *B J Meehan* — 50
2 br c Grand Lodge (USA) - Hakkaniyah
7^{7g} 14^{6gf} 5^{8f} **0-0-3**

Our Monogram *R M Beckett* — 69

7 b g Deploy - Darling Splodge
10^{14gf} 11^{16gs} 11^{17f} 5^{17f} 6^{16g} 2^{16gf} 4^{16gf}
1^{16gf} **3-1-8 £15,633**

Our Paddy (Ire) *Mrs L C Jewell* — 64 a43
4 b g Ali-Royal (Ire) - Lilting Air (Ire)
7^{12sd} 9^{7sd} 11^{8sd} 9^{9sd} 5^{7g} 5^{9f} 17^{6gf} 3^{7gy}
8^{7f} 18^{7gf} **0-1-10 £659**

Our Teddy (Ire) *G G Margarson* — 103 a100
3 ch g Grand Lodge (USA) - Lady Windley
2^{7sd} 6^{8gf} 1^{8g} 8^{10gf} 8^{9g} 9^{8g} 10^{10gf} 7^{8g}
1-1-8 £27,058

Our Wol *G G Margarson* — 23
4 b g Distant Relative - Lady Highfield
11^{7gf} **0-0-1**

Out After Dark *C G Cox* — 74
2 b c Cadeaux Genereux - Midnight Shift (Ire)
10^{6gf} 4^{6gf} 2^{6gs} **0-1-3 £1,217**

Out For A Stroll *S C Williams* — 82
4 b g Zamindar (USA) - The Jotter
17^{8gf} 24^{8g} 1^{7f} 1^{8gf} 17^{8gs} **2-0-5**
£5,791

Out Of Mind *B A McMahon* — 78
2 b c Mind Games - Distant Isle (Ire)
15^{5f} 3^{5gf} 7^{5hy} 3^{5gs} 9^{5gs} 3^{5gf} 5^{5gf} 1^{5gf}
1^{5g} **2-2-9 £11,020**

Out Of My Way *T M Jones* — 21
2 ch f Fraam - Ming Blue
14^{7gf} 4^{9gf} 9^{6gf} **0-0-3**

Out Of Tune *C Weedon* — 44
3 ch g Elmaamul (USA) - Strawberry Song
5^{8gf} 9^{8f} 12^{8f} **0-0-3**

Outeast (Ire) *G A Harker* — 40
3 b f Mujadil (USA) - Stifen
14^{5f} 13^{5gf} 10^{5f} 13^{6gs} 11^{5g} 11^{6gf} 12^{6f}
16^{5gf} **0-0-8**

Outer Hebrides *D R Loder* — 79 a63
2 b g Efisio - Reuval
2^{7gf} 2^{7gf} 1^{6sd} **1-2-3 £5,659**

Outward (USA) *J H M Gosden* — 65
3 b c Gone West (USA) - Seebe (USA)
5^{8gf} 4^{9gf} **0-0-2 £376**

Over Rating *J H M Gosden* — 73
3 ch f Desert King (Ire) - Well Beyond (Ire)
4^{8f} 2^{9g} 3^{10gf} 4^{8gf} **0-1-4 £2,070**

Over The Rainbow (Ire) *B W Hills* — 85
2 b c Rainbow Quest (USA) - Dimakya (USA)
2^{7g} 3^{8gf} 10^{8gf} **0-2-3 £3,892**

Over The Years (USA) *T P Tate* — 26
2 b g Silver Hawk (USA) - Sporting Green (USA)
14^{8gs} **0-0-1**

Over To You Bert *Mrs P N Dutfield* — 44 a61
4 b g Overbury (Ire) - Silvers Era
5^{8sd} 7^{8sd} 4^{10sd} 15^{11gf} 5^{9gf} 9^{6sd} 10^{6gf}
0-0-7 £288

Overdrawn (Ire) *J A Osborne* — 93 a73
2 b g Daggers Drawn (USA) - In Denial (Ire)
4^{5gf} 2^{5gf} 1^{6sd} 4^{6f} 1^{7gf} 2^{8g} 3^{7g} 8^{4hy}
1^{7gf} 5^{8g} **3-3-10 £30,704**

Override (Ire) *J M P Eustace* — 85
3 b c Peintre Celebre (USA) - Catalonda
2^{6gf} 2^{6gf} 11^{7gf} 7^{7gf} **0-2-4 £3,484**

Overstrand (Ire) *Mrs M Reveley* — 77
4 b g In The Wings - Vaison La Romaine
12^{13gs} 2^{16gf} **0-1-2 £4,590**

Ovigo (Ger) *P A Blockley* — 76

4 b g Monsagem (USA) - Ouvea (Ger)
1⁸ˢ 5⁹ᵍᶠ 7⁵ᵍˢ 12⁶ᵍˢ 11¹⁰ᵍˢ **1-0-5**
£1,331

Own Line *J Hetherton* 52
4 b g Classic Cliche (Ire) - Cold Line
4²²ᵍᶠ 8¹⁶ᵍᶠ 10¹⁶ᵍˢ 4¹⁴ᶠ 9¹⁷ᵍᶠ 8¹¹ᵍᶠ 1¹²ᵍᶠ
3¹²ᵍᶠ 8¹²ᵍᶠ **1-2-9 £4,945**

Oysterbed (Ire) *J Nicol* 55
3 b f Night Shift (USA) - Pearl Shell (USA)
11⁵ᵍ 8⁶ᵍᶠ 3⁶ᵍᶠ 17⁶ᶠ 1⁶ᶠ **1-1-5 £3,485**

Pablo *B W Hills* 112
4 b c Efisio - Winnebago
1⁸ᵍ 4⁹ᵍᶠ 5¹⁰ᵍ 5⁸ᵍˢ **1-0-4 £69,000**

Paciano (Ire) *C G Cox* 80
3 b g Perugino (USA) - Saucy Maid (Ire)
2⁶ᵍᶠ 10⁷ᵍᶠ 3⁶ᵍᶠ 3⁵ᵍ 7⁶ᵍ 6⁶ᵍᶠ 2⁶ᵍᶠ 3⁷ᵍᶠ
4⁷ᵍᶠ 2⁷ᵍᶠ **0-6-10 £6,685**

Pacific Alliance (Ire) *Michael Butler* 39
7 b g Fayruz - La Gravotte (Fr)
9¹²ᵍᶠ 17¹²ᵍᶠ **0-0-2**

Pacific Ocean (Arg) *Mrs S A Liddiard* 43 a52
4 b c Fitzcarraldo (Arg) - Play Hard (Arg)
5⁷ᵍ 6⁸ᵍ 6⁷ᵍᶠ 6⁸ˢʷ 5⁷ˢʷ **0-0-5**

Packin Em In *J R Boyle* a28
5 b h Young Ern - Wendy's Way
7⁷ˢᵈ 12⁷ˢᵈ 15⁶ˢᵈ 13⁷ˢᵈ **0-0-4**

Pacwan (Ire) *D Carroll*
2 b g Woodborough (USA) - Solway Lass (Ire)
11⁶ᵍᶠ 8⁵ᵍᶠ **0-0-2**

Paddy Mul *W Storey* 48
6 ch h Democratic (USA) - My Pretty Niece
4¹⁶ᵍ 6¹⁶ᵍᶠ 2¹²ᵍᶠ 6¹⁶ᵍᶠ **0-1-4 £1,155**

Paddy Winalot (Ire) *D Nicholls* 50
3 ch g College Chapel - Six Penny Express
10⁷ᵍ 9⁹ᵍˢ 8⁹ᵍᶠ 4⁸ᵍᶠ **0-0-4 £298**

Paddywack (Ire) *D W Chapman* 87 a88
6 b g Bigstone (Ire) - Millie's Return (Ire)
13⁵ˢᵈ 16⁸ˢᵈ 2⁵ˢᵈ 8⁵ˢᵈ 7⁵ˢᵈ 15⁵ᶠ 10⁵ᶠ
8⁵ᵍ 13⁵ᵍᶠ 12⁵ᵍᶠ 13⁶ᵍᶠ 8⁶ᶠ 4⁵ᵍˢ 12⁶ᵍ 8⁵ᵍᶠ
2⁵ᵍ 15⁶ᶠ 7⁶ᵍᶠ
6⁷ᵍ **1-4-25 £10,467**

Pagan Ceremony (USA) *Mrs A J Perrett* 12
2 ch g Rahy (USA) - Delightful Linda (USA)
7⁸ᵍᶠ **0-0-1**

Pagan Dance (Ire) *Mrs A J Perrett* 101
4 b g Revoque (Ire) - Ballade D'Ainhoa (Fr)
5¹⁰ᵍˢ 12⁹ᵍᶠ 1¹⁰ᵍᶠ 3¹⁰ᵍ 5¹²ᵍᶠ 7¹⁰ᵍ 1¹²ᵍˢ
4¹⁵ᵍᶠ 4¹³ᵍᶠ 12¹²ᵍᶠ **2-2-10 £26,625**

Pagan Magic (USA) *J A R Toller* 60
2 b c Diesis - Great Lady Slew (USA)
14⁷ᵍᶠ 5⁸ˢ **0-0-2**

Pagan Prince *J A R Toller* 83
6 br g Primo Dominie - Mory Kante (USA)
6⁸ᵍᶠ 8⁸ᵍᶠ 7⁸ˢ 2⁹ᵍ 1⁸ᶠ 1⁹ᵍᶠ 15⁸ᵍᶠ **2-1-7**
£42,569

Pagan River *G M Moore* 29
2 b g River Falls - Pagan Star
10⁶ᵍᶠ 10⁶ᶠ **0-0-2**

Pagan Sky (Ire) *J A R Toller* 91
4 ch g Inchinor - Rosy Sunset (Ire)
2⁸ᵍᶠ 7⁷ᵍ 5¹⁰ᶠ 6¹¹ᵍᶠ 1¹⁰ᵍᶠ 6¹⁰ᵍᶠ 1¹⁰ᵍᶠ **2-1-7**
£21,868

Pagan Storm (USA) *Mrs A J Perrett* 83
3 ch g Tabasco Cat (USA) - Melodeon (USA)
4⁷ᵍᶠ 15⁷ᵍᶠ 3⁷ᶠ 6⁷ᵍᶠ 1⁶ᵍᶠ 4⁷ᵍᶠ 1⁶ᵍᶠ **1-1-7**

£6,744

Pagan Wolf *W Jarvis* 39 a49
3 b g Wolfhound (USA) - Sharp Girl (Fr)
5⁷ˢᵈ 10¹⁰ᶠ 16¹²ᵍˢ **0-0-3**

Page Nouvelle (Fr) *W M Brisbourne* 70 a46
5 b m Spectrum (Ire) - Page Bleue
9¹⁰ˢᵈ 4¹⁰ᵍᶠ 1¹⁰ᵍ 11¹²ᵍᶠ 9¹⁰ᵍᶠ 7¹¹ᵍᶠ 8¹⁰ᵍᶠ
1-1-7 £6,188

Pageant *J M Bradley* 55
6 br m Inchinor - Positive Attitude
12¹⁰ᵍᶠ 15⁸ᵍᶠ 8⁸ᵍᶠ 7⁸ᵍᶠ 2⁸ᵍᶠ 10⁸ᵍᶠ 4⁸ᵍᶠ
5⁸ᵍᶠ 3⁷ᵍᶠ 9⁸ᵍᶠ 14⁸ᵍˢ **0-3-11 £1,532**

Pailitas (Ger) *G A Swinbank* 50
6 b g Lomitas - Pradera (Ger)
12⁸ᵍᶠ 4¹⁰ᵍᶠ **0-0-2 £299**

Paintbrush *Mrs L Stubbs* 44
3 b f Groom Dancer (USA) - Bristle
3⁷ˢ 5⁷ᶠ 6⁷ᵍᶠ **0-1-3 £856**

Painted Moon (USA) *D R Loder* 54
2 ch f Gone West (USA) - Crimson Conquest (USA)
8⁷ᵍᶠ **0-0-1**

Palace Theatre (Ire) *T D Barron* 71
2 b g Imperial Ballet (Ire) - Luminary
1⁶ᵍᶠ **1-0-1 £5,512**

Palacegate Touch *A Berry* 25 a44
13 gr g Petong - Dancing Chimes
4⁶ˢᵈ 5⁶ˢᵈ 10⁷ˢʷ 15⁷ˢᵈ **0-0-4**

Palamedes *P W Harris* 88
4 b g Sadler's Wells (USA) - Kristal Bridge
1¹²ᵍᶠ 3¹⁴ᵍᶠ 12¹²ᵍᶠ 7¹²ᵍ 10¹²ᵍ 2¹²ᵍᶠ 5¹²ᵍ
1-2-7 £8,565

Palanzo (Ire) *D Nicholls* 66
5 b g Green Desert (USA) - Karpacka (Ire)
14⁶ᵍᶠ 10⁶ᵍᶠ 20⁵ᵍᶠ 17⁶ᵍᶠ 11⁵ᵍᶠ 25⁶ᵍ
15⁷ᵍ **0-0-7**

Palawan *A M Balding* 92 a77
7 br g Polar Falcon (USA) - Krameria
1⁵ˢᵈ 4⁵ˢᵈ 13⁵ᵍ 9⁵ˢᵈ 6⁵ˢᵈ 9⁵ᵍᶠ 8⁵ᵍᶠ 10⁵ᵍᶠ
1⁵ᵍᶠ 1⁵ᵍᶠ 14⁵ᵍ 1⁵ᵍᶠ 9⁵ᶠ **4-0-13 £21,847**

Palvic Moon *C Smith* 54
2 ch f Cotation - Palvic Grey
15⁵ˢᵈ 11⁵ˢᵈ 6⁵ˢ 7⁵ᵍᶠ 6⁶ᵍᶠ 6⁶ᶠ **0-0-6**

Panama (Ire) *M L W Bell* 59 a30
3 b c Peintre Celebre (USA) - Bay Queen
5⁹ᵍˢ 4¹⁰ᵍᶠ 15¹⁰ᵍᶠ 11¹⁰ˢᵈ **0-0-4 £336**

Pancake Role *D Haydn Jones* a25
3 b g Tragic Role (USA) - My Foxy Lady
5⁹ˢʷ 12⁹ˢᵈ **0-0-2**

Pancakehill *D K Ivory* 34 a69
4 ch f Sabrehill (USA) - Sawlah
10¹⁰ˢᵈ 2⁸ˢᵈ 3⁸ˢᵈ 2⁸ˢᵈ 3⁸ˢʷ 2⁷ˢᵈ 2⁷ˢᵈ
13⁷ᵍᶠ 2⁷ˢᵈ 3⁹ˢᵈ 6⁸ˢᵈ 5⁷ᵍᶠ **0-8-12 £6,091**

Pangloss (Ire) *G L Moore* 75 a50
2 ch g Croco Rouge (Ire) - Kafayef (USA)
13⁷ᵍ 3⁸ᵍᶠ 12⁸ᵍᶠ 11⁸ˢᵈ **0-1-4 £542**

Panglossian (Ire) *M Johnston* 71
3 b f Barathea (Ire) - Overcall
11⁹ᶠ 15⁸ᶠᵗ 5¹⁰ᵍᶠ 11⁸ᵍᶠ 3¹²ˢ 12¹²ᶠ 5¹⁰ᵍᶠ
3¹¹ᵍᶠ **0-0-8 £1,420**

Pango *H Morrison* 81
4 ch g Bluegrass Prince (Ire) - Riverine
6⁸ᵍˢ 2⁹ᵍᶠ 4⁹ᵍ 5¹⁰ᵍᶠ 2¹⁰ᵍᶠ 1⁹ᵍ 7¹⁰ᵍ 5⁹ᵍᶠ
7⁹ᵍᶠ **1-2-9 £6,303**

Panjandrum *N E Berry* 55 a70
5 b g Polar Falcon (USA) - Rengaine (Fr)

3^{6sd} 12^{8gf} 7^{6sd} **0-1-3 £622**

Panshir (Fr) *C F Wall* 27
2 ch c Unfuwain (USA) - Jalcamin (Ire)
12^{7s} **0-0-1**

Pantita *B R Millman* 72
3 b f Polish Precedent (USA) - Dedara
2^{8gf} 3^{10gf} 2^{10gf} 4^{12g} 4^{10f} **0-2-5 £4,110**

Pantone *M Johnston* 92
3 b f Spectrum (Ire) - Tinashaan (Ire)
1^{7g} 2^{7gf} 1^{8gf} 5^{8gf} 7^{7g} 2^{12gf} 1^{12gf} 3^{10g}
12^{10gf} 7^{10f} **3-3-10 £34,297**

Pants *Andrew Reid* 56 a60
4 b f Pivotal - Queenbird
2^{7sd} 3^{7sd} 6^{7sw} 11^{7sw} 2^{7g} 7^{7gf} 4^{6g} 7^{6gf}
10^{7gf} 3^{7sd} **0-5-10 £3,333**

Paolini (Ger) *A Wohler* 120
6 ch h Lando (Ger) - Prairie Darling
2^{9g} 3^{10gf} 8^{10gf} 2^{10g} **0-3-4 £467,350**

Papeete (Ger) *W J Haggas* 71
2 b f Alzao (USA) - Prairie Vela
3^{6gf} 3^{7gf} 1^{7gf} 7^{8gf} 14^{8gf} **1-1-5 £5,476**

Pappy (Ire) *J G Given* 45
2 b f Petardia - Impressive Lady
13^{6gf} 10^{6f} 3^{6gf} 5^{5gf} 10^{6gf} 9^{6gf} **0-1-6 £768**

Parachute *Sir Mark Prescott* 87 a84
4 ch g Hector Protector (USA) - Shortfall
4^{12sd} 1^{12sd} 1^{12sd} 1^{13sd} 3^{12sw} 3^{16gf} 7^{14gs}
3-1-7 £12,481

Paradise Breeze *C A Horgan* 34
2 b f Perugino (USA) - Paradise Forum
8^{6gf} **0-0-1**

Paradise Eve *T D Barron* 87 a66
3 b f Bahamian Bounty - Twilight Time
2^{5sw} 1^{5sw} 1^{5gs} **3-1-4 £18,683**

Paradise Garden (USA) *P L Clinton* 38
6 b g Septieme Ciel (USA) - Water Course (USA)
14^{10gf} 7^{12g} 12^{10gf} 7^{14gf} 5^{12gf} 10^{11gf}
0-0-6

Paradise Isle *C F Wall* 88
2 b f Bahamian Bounty - Merry Rous
2^{6gf} 2^{6gs} 2^{6gf} 1^{5gf} 1^{6gf} **2-3-5 £11,592**

Paradise Valley *Mrs S A Liddiard* 59 a68
3 b g Groom Dancer (USA) - Rose De Reve (Ire)
2^{9sd} 5^{9sw} 3^{8sd} 5^{8sd} 9^{10gf} 6^{10g} 3^{10f} 15^{10g}
2^{10f} 5^{11gf} 1^{10gf} **1-2-11 £5,191**

Paragon Of Virtue *P Mitchell* a83
6 ch g Cadeaux Genereux - Madame Dubois
1^{10sd} 6^{12sd} 3^{10sd} 3^{12sd} **1-2-4 £6,459**

Parallel Lines (Ire) *R F Johnson Houghton* 61
2 ch c Polish Precedent (USA) - Phone Booth (USA)
8^{6g} 11^{6gf} 6^{7gf} 2^{5f} 2^{6f} 9^{5gf} 7^{6f} 8^{6gf}
0-1-8 £2,567

Parasol (Ire) *D R Loder* 121 a111
4 br c Halling (USA) - Bunting
1^{10sd} 1^{10sd} 1^{10gf} 1^{10g} 2^{10gf} 6^{12f} 2^{10gf}
4-2-7 £109,166

Parc Aux Boules *R Charlton* 25
2 gr c Royal Applause - Aristocratique
15^{6gf} **0-0-1**

Pardon Moi *Mrs C A Dunnett* 47 a40
2 ch f First Trump - Mystical Song
10^{5sd} 7^{5gf} 14^{6gf} 3^{6sd} 4^{7f} 16^{9g} 5^{6g}
3^{6gf} 8^{6gf} 2^{6gf} 6^{7f} 7^{6sd} 6^{6gf} **1-2-14 £4,364**

Paris Dreamer *M W Easterby* 38

2 b f Paris House - Stoproveritate
8^{6g} 8^{8gf} 11^{5g} 11^{7g} **0-0-4**

Paris Piper (Ire) *D Carroll* a10
4 gr g Paris House - Winter March
11^{7sd} **0-0-1**

Parisian Playboy *Jedd O'Keeffe* 53
3 gr g Paris House - Exordium
10^{6f} 9^{6gf} 7^{6gf} 3^{7s} **0-1-4 £611**

Parisien Star (Ire) *J R Boyle* 88
7 ch g Paris House - Auction Maid (Ire)
11^{10gf} 6^{10g} 7^{10gf} 8^{10g} 1^{9gf} 2^{10f} 3^{9g} 5^{10gf}
6^{10gf} 8^{9g} 7^{12gf} **1-2-11 £13,739**

Parisienne (USA) *C Ligerot* 86
2 b/br f Good And Tough (USA) - Genuine Concern (Can)
13^{ft} 11^{6gf} 7^{5s} 10^{8g} 7^{9gf} **1-0-5 £12,000**

Park Accord (Ire) *J Noseda* 83
2 b/br f Desert Prince (Ire) - Tiavanita (USA)
1^{7gf} **1-0-1 £4,837**

Park Ave Princess (Ire) *N P Littmoden* 63 a15
2 b f Titus Livius (Fr) - Satinette
12^{6gf} 3^{6gf} 1^{7gf} 4^{7f} 1^{7gf} 8^{7sd} 9^{7g} 11^{7gf}
4^{7f} **2-1-9 £10,113**

Park Hill (Ire) *G A Swinbank* 52
3 b g Mujadil (USA) - Modest (USA)
7^{8gf} 7^{9gs} 11^{8gs} 8^{7gf} 6^{7f} **0-0-5**

Park Star *D Shaw* 72 a66
3 b f Gothenberg (Ire) - Miriam
2^{5sd} 1^{5sd} 1^{5sd} 7^{6sd} 4^{5sd} 2^{5sd} 5^{5sd} 1^{5gs}
1^{5s} 10^{5g} 8^{6sd} 14^{5gs} **4-2-12 £20,762**

Park Street (USA) *G A Butler* a77
3 b c Mr Prospector (USA) - Sunlit Silence (USA)
2^{7sd} **0-1-1 £1,169**

Parker *B Palling* 70 a77
6 b g Magic Ring (Ire) - Miss Loving
8^{8sd} 2^{7sd} 8^{7sd} 10^{8sd} 9^{7gf} 3^{7gs} 15^{7gf}
11^{7f} 4^{7gf} 4^{6gf} 13^{7gf} 6^{7sd} 2^{6sd} 1^{6gf} 5^{7gf}
1-5-15 £6,886

Parkland (USA) *R Charlton* 93
3 ch c Distant View (USA) - Victorian Style
2^{7gf} **0-1-1 £3,205**

Parknasilla *M W Easterby* 76 a76
3 b g Marju (Ire) - Top Berry
13^{10gs} 4^{10gf} 3^{10f} 5^{12sd} 3^{10gf} 3^{10g} 1^{12sw}
13^{12gf} **1-3-8 £4,254**

Parkside Pursuit *J M Bradley* 78
5 b g Pursuit Of Love - Ivory Bride
10^{5g} 16^{6gs} 15^{8gs} 6^{6gf} 5^{6gf} 4^{6gf} 1^{6f}
12^{6g} 2^{6g} 4^{6gf} 10^{6gf} 6^{7gf} 11^{7gf} 2^{5s} 14^{6gf}
17^{6gf} **1-2-17 £8,923**

Parkview Love (USA) *M Johnston* 99
2 b c Mister Baileys - Jerre Jo Glanville (USA)
1^{5gs} 2^{6g} 1^{6g} 6^{6gf} 5^{7gs} **2-1-5 £35,207**

Parlight *Mrs Lucinda Featherstone* 25 a44
4 b f Woodborough (USA) - Skedaddle
13^{8sd} 3^{11sd} 5^{16sd} 11^{6sd} 16^{8sd} 8^{14sd} 14^{17gf}
2^{16sd} 6^{16gs} 10^{16sd} 4^{15sd} 5^{15sd} 10^{17gf} 10^{16g}
1-2-14 £4,063

Parnassian *G B Balding* 67
3 ch g Sabrehill (USA) - Delphic Way
4^{7g} 4^{8gf} 8^{7g} 4^{7gs} 3^{8gf} 3^{8f} 4^{8g} 2^{9g} 5^{9gf}
8^{8gf} 8^{8gs} **0-5-11 £4,072**

Parndon Belle *J S Wainwright*
4 ch f Clan Of Roses - Joara (Fr)
11^{7gf} 10^{5gs} **0-0-2**

Parting Shot *T D Easterby*   73
5 b g Young Ern - Tribal Lady
7⁸ᵍˢ 17⁸ᵍᶠ 11⁸ˢ 5⁸ᵍᶠ 9⁸ˢ 13⁹ᵍᶠ 11⁸ᵍ
0-0-7

Partners In Jazz (USA) *T D Barron*   90
2 ro c Jambalaya Jazz (USA) - Just About Enough (USA)
2⁶ᵍˢ 2⁵ᵍᶠ 2⁵ᵍᶠ 1⁶ᵍˢ **1-3-4 £17,012**

Party Ploy *K R Burke*   76
5 b g Deploy - Party Treat (Ire)
17¹²ᵍᶠ 10¹⁶ᵍᶠ 3¹⁶ᵍˢ 5¹⁴ᵍᶠ 11¹²ᵍᶠ 3¹⁴ᶠ 1¹²ᶠ
1¹²ᶠ 3¹²ᵍᶠ 7¹²ᵍᶠ 9¹²ᵍ 4¹¹ᵍᶠ 2¹⁴ᵍᶠ 6¹⁴ᶠ 7¹²ᵍᶠ
2-4-15 £12,443

Party Princess (Ire) *J A Glover*   59 a45
2 b f Orpen (USA) - Summer Queen
2⁵ᵍᶠ 5⁵ˢᵈ 3⁵ᵍᶠ **0-2-3 £1,538**

Party Turn *C E Brittain*   52 a59
3 gr f Pivotal - Third Party
2⁶ˢᵈ 1⁷ˢᵈ 13⁷ᵍ 9⁷ᵍᶠ 6⁸ᵍᶠ **1-1-5 £5,274**

Pas De Surprise *P D Evans*   67 a51
5 b g Dancing Spree (USA) - Supreme Rose
8⁶ˢᵈ 6⁷ᵍᶠ 2⁷ᵍˢ 2⁷ᵍᶠ 11⁷ᵍᶠ 1⁹ᵍᶠ 8⁸ᵍᶠ 3⁸ᵍᶠ
8¹⁰ᵍᶠ 15⁸ᵍ 1⁷ᵍ 14⁷ᶠ 10⁷ᵍᶠ 3⁸ᵍᶠ 6⁸ᵍᶠ 4⁸ᶠ
2-4-16 £11,165

Pascali *H Morrison*   58
3 b f Compton Place - Pass The Rose (Ire)
9⁸ᵍᶠ 1⁶ᵍᶠ 4⁶ᵍᶠ **1-1-3 £2,251**

Paso Doble *B R Millman*   70 a73
5 b g Dancing Spree (USA) - Delta Tempo (Ire)
3⁸ˢᵈ 9⁷ˢᵈ 3⁹ˢᵈ 5⁹ˢʷ 11⁸ᵍ 16¹²ᵍᶠ 1⁹ˢᵈ
12¹⁰ᵍ 4¹⁰ᶠ 2¹⁰ᵍᶠ 4¹⁰ᶠ 7¹²ᶠ 7¹⁰ᵍ **1-4-13 £5,576**

Passando *A M Balding*   61
3 b f Kris - Iota
4⁸ᵍ **0-0-1 £323**

Passerine *J R Weymes*   35
5 b m Distant Relative - Oare Sparrow
11⁶ᵍ 10⁶ᵍᶠ 3⁷ᵍᶠ 5⁷ᵍᶠ 14⁶ᵍᶠ 7⁷ᵍᶠ **0-1-6 £863**

Passing Glance *A M Balding*   118
4 br c Polar Falcon (USA) - Spurned (USA)
8⁸ᵍᶠ 12⁸ᵍ 19⁸ᵍᶠ 18⁸ᶠ 2⁸ᵍᶠ 18⁹ᵍ 6⁸ᵍᶠ
3-2-8 £119,508

Passion For Life *J Akehurst*   64
10 br g Charmer - Party Game
13⁵ᵍ 8⁶ᵍ 14⁷ᵍᶠ 13⁶ᵍ 17⁶ᵍ 18⁷ˢ **0-0-6**

Passion Fruit *C W Fairhurst*   54
2 b f Pursuit Of Love - Reine De Thebes (Fr)
6⁵ᵍᶠ 7⁶ᶠ 7⁶ᵍˢ 6⁷ᵍᶠ 3⁷ᵍᶠ 10⁷ᶠ **0-1-6 £552**

Pastoral Pursuits *H Morrison*   110
2 b c Bahamian Bounty - Star
2⁶ᵍᶠ 1⁶ᵍ 1⁶ᵍᶠ 1⁶ᵍ **3-1-4 £31,468**

Pat's Miracle (Ire) *John Berry*
3 ch f College Chapel - Exemplaire (Fr)
18⁸ᵍ **0-0-1**

Patandon Girl (Ire) *M R Channon*   70
3 b f Night Shift (USA) - Petite Jameel (Ire)
10⁶ᵍ 2⁶ᵍᶠ 4⁶ᵍᶠ UR⁵ᶠ 1⁶ᵍᶠ 3⁶ᵍᶠ 12⁷ᵍᶠ 7⁶ᵍᶠ
13⁸ᵍᶠ 12⁷ᵍᶠ 11⁶ᵍᶠ 3⁷ᶠ 6⁶ᵍᶠ 8⁶ᶠ 5⁶ᶠ 37ᵍᶠ 14⁶ˢᵈ
10⁶ᵍˢ **1-3-18 £6,390**

Patavellian (Ire) *R Charlton*   121
5 b g Machiavellian (USA) - Alessia
1⁶ᵍ 5⁶ᶠ 1⁷ᵍᶠ 1⁶ᵍ 15ʰᵒ **4-0-5 £187,293**

Patientes Virtis *Miss Gay Kelleway*   39 a64
4 ch f Lion Cavern (USA) - Alzianah
11⁷ˢᵈ 11⁷ˢᵈ 10⁷ˢʷ 4⁵ˢᵈ 5⁵ˢʷ 16ˢᵈ 1⁵ˢᵈ
8⁵ˢ 6⁵ˢʷ 9⁵ˢᵈ **2-0-10 £6,069**

Patricia Philomena (Ire) *T D Barron*   60
5 br m Prince Of Birds (USA) - Jeewan
10¹⁴ᶠ 5¹³ᵍˢ 11¹⁴ᶠ 6¹²ᶠ 9¹⁶ᵍᶠ 1¹⁴ˢ 2¹⁴ᵍᶠ
2-1-7 £8,814

Patricks Day *J Balding*
3 b c Wizard King - Honour And Glory
17⁶ᶠ **0-0-1**

Patrixprial *M H Tompkins*   42
2 gr c Linamix (Fr) - Magnificent Star (USA)
9⁷ˢ **0-0-1**

Patrixtoo (Fr) *M H Tompkins*   52
2 gr c Linamix (Fr) - Maradadi (USA)
7⁷ᵍᶠ 9⁸ˢ **0-0-2**

Patsy's Double *M Blanshard*   109 a100
5 b g Emarati (USA) - Jungle Rose
3⁷ˢᵈ 1⁷ˢ 6⁸ᵍ 2⁷ᵍᶠ 11⁷ᵍᶠ 4⁷ᵍᶠ 7⁷ᵍᶠ 8⁷ᵍᶠ
11⁷ᵍᶠ **1-2-9 £29,080**

Patterdale *M Johnston*   80
2 b c Octagonal (NZ) - Baize
5⁵ᵍ 2⁶ᶠ 8⁷ᵍᶠ 7⁶ᵍᶠ **0-1-4 £1,220**

Pattern Man *J R Norton*   37 a13
2 b c Wizard King - Quick Profit
9⁸ᵍ 10⁸ˢᵈ **0-0-2**

Paula Lane *R Curtis*   64 a71
3 b f Factual (USA) - Colfax Classic
6¹⁰ˢᵈ 5⁸ˢᵈ 1⁹ˢʷ 2¹¹ˢᵈ 4¹²ˢᵈ 8¹³ᵍ 5¹²ᵍˢ
3¹²ˢᵈ 2¹²ˢᵈ **1-3-9 £6,291**

Paulas Pride *J R Best*   71 a74
5 ch m Pivotal - Sharp Top
4¹³ˢᵈ 11¹²ˢᵈ 7¹²ˢᵈ 13¹⁰ˢᵈ 6¹²ᵍ 2¹⁰ᵍᶠ 9¹⁰ᵍᶠ
7¹⁰ᵍᶠ 3¹⁰ᵍᶠ **0-2-9 £1,722**

Paulines Gem (Ire) *P J Makin*   55
3 b/br f Petorius - Clifton Lass (Ire)
7⁶ᵍᶠ **0-0-1**

Paulinski *F Jordan*   27
2 b f Suluk (USA) - Tsu Hsi
13⁷ᵍᶠ 18⁷ᵍᶠ **0-0-2**

Pauls Pride *M Dods*   51
2 b g Desert Sun - E Sharp (USA)
13⁶ᵍ 7⁷ᵍᶠ 6⁸ᵍᶠ 10⁷ᵍ 13⁷ᵍᶠ **0-0-5**

Pauluke *N J Hawke*   54
4 b f Bishop Of Cashel - Beacon Blaze
8¹¹ᵍᶠ 6¹²ᶠ 15¹⁴ᵍᶠ **0-0-3**

Pavement Gates *W M Brisbourne*   76
3 b f Bishop Of Cashel - Very Bold
5¹²ᶠ 6¹²ᵍᶠ 5¹²ᵍᶠ 2¹¹ᵍᶠ 4¹¹ᵍᶠ 4¹²ᵍ 2¹²ᵍᶠ
1¹²ᵍᶠ 3¹²ᵍᶠ 2¹²ᵍᶠ 3¹²ᵍᶠ **1-5-11 £12,209**

Pavla (USA) *N Wilson*   34
6 ch m St Jovite (USA) - Big E Dream (USA)
6¹²ᵍˢ **0-0-1**

Pawan (Ire) *N Tinkler*   58
3 ch g Cadeaux Genereux - Born To Glamour
2⁷ᵍ 11⁸ᶠ 2⁶ᶠ **0-2-3 £2,079**

Pawn Broker *D R C Elsworth*   116 a105
6 ch g Selkirk (USA) - Dime Bag
3¹⁰ˢᵈ 7¹⁰ˢᵈ 1¹⁰ᵍᶠ 10¹²ᵍᶠ 4¹⁰ᵍ 8¹²ᵍ 6¹⁰ᵍ
6¹⁰ᵍᶠ 13⁹ᵍᶠ 2⁹ᵍᶠ 5¹⁰ᵍ **1-2-11 £26,374**

Pawn In Life (Ire) *T D Barron*   a68
5 b g Midhish - Lady-Mumtaz
2⁸ˢᵈ 4⁸ˢᵈ 2⁸ˢᵈ 2⁷ˢʷ 5⁸ˢʷ 14⁷ˢᵈ **0-3-6 £2,843**

Pax *D Nicholls*   90
6 ch g Brief Truce (USA) - Child's Play (USA)
14⁶ᵍ 12⁶ᵍᶠ 16ᵍᶠ 5⁶ᵍᶠ 8⁶ᵍ 3⁵ᵍᶠ 18⁶ᵍ 1⁵ᶠ
6⁵ᵍᶠ 4⁵ᵍ 11⁶ᵍ **2-2-11 £12,724**

Pay Attention *T D Easterby*   53
2 b f Revoque (Ire) - Catch Me
7⁶ᵍᶠ 6⁶ᵍᶠ 5⁷ᵍᶠ 3⁷ᶠ 9⁸ᵍᶠ 12⁸ᵍᶠ **0-0-6**
£478

Pay The Bill (Ire) *Mrs P N Dutfield*   36 a18
2 b f Lahib (USA) - Jack-N-Jilly (Ire)
16⁵ᵍ 7⁵ᵍˢ 7⁵ˢᵈ 9⁵ᶠ 7⁶ᵍᶠ **0-0-5**

Pay The Silver *I A Wood*   80 a57
5 gr g Petong - Marjorie's Memory (Ire)
8⁷ᵍᶠ 14¹⁰ᵍᶠ 10⁸ᵍᶠ 5¹²ᶠ 2¹⁰ᵍˢ 2¹⁰ᵍᶠ 7⁹ᵍᶠ
1¹⁰ᵍᶠ 8¹⁰ᵍᶠ 2¹⁰ᵍᶠ 6⁹ᵍᶠ 4¹²ᵍ 9¹⁰ᵍ 2¹²ᵍ 3¹²ˢᵈ
12¹²ˢᵈ **1-5-16 £10,528**

Pay Time *M Brittain*   40
4 ch f Timeless Times (USA) - Payvashooz
6⁶ᵍᶠ 19⁷ᵍ 10⁶ᵍᶠ 17⁵ᵍᶠ **0-0-4**

Paylander *G L Moore*   a47
7 ch g Karinga Bay - Bichette
7¹³ˢᵈ 8¹²ˢᵈ **0-0-2**

Payola (USA) *C E Brittain*   64
2 b f Red Ransom (USA) - Bevel (USA)
8⁷ᵍᶠ **0-0-1**

Pays D'Amour (Ire) *D Nicholls*   72 a17
6 b g Pursuit Of Love - Lady Of The Land
5⁷ᵍᶠ 7⁸ˢᵈ 1⁶ᵍᶠ 1⁶ᵍᶠ 4⁷ᵍᶠ 6⁶ᵍᶠ 8⁷ᵍˢ 15⁶ᵍᶠ
2-0-8 £9,621

Peace *J R Fanshawe*   78
3 b f Sadler's Wells (USA) - Virtuous
2¹⁰ᵍᶠ 1¹⁰ᵍᶠ 6¹⁰ᵍᶠ 13¹⁰ˢ **1-1-4 £6,016**

Peace Flag (USA) *J H M Gosden*   79
3 ch f Gold Fever (USA) - Foldtheflag (USA)
12⁷ᵍᶠ 2⁶ᵍᶠ 1⁶ᵍᶠ 6⁷ᵍᶠ 6⁶ᵍᶠ **1-1-5 £5,270**

Peace Offering (Ire) *T G Mills*   111
3 b c Victory Note (USA) - Amnesty Bay
7⁷ᵍᶠ 5⁵ᵍ 7⁵ᵍᶠ 13⁵ᵍᶠ 6⁶ᵍᶠ 4⁵ᵍᶠ 11⁵ᵍᶠ **0-0-7**
£2,477

Peace Treaty (Ire) *S R Bowring*   44
2 b f Turtle Island (Ire) - Beautyofthepeace (Ire)
7⁵ᵍᶠ 5⁸ᵍᶠ 15⁶ᵍᶠ 9⁸ˢᵈ **0-0-4**

Peak Of Perfection (Ire) *M A Jarvis*   38 a51
2 b c Deploy - Nsx
13⁷ᵍᶠ 10⁸ˢᵈ **0-0-2**

Peak Park (USA) *J A R Toller*   57 a26
3 br c Dynaformer (USA) - Play Po (USA)
7⁸ᵍᶠ 10⁷ᵍᶠ 7¹²ᶠ 13¹²ᵍˢ 3¹⁶ᵍᶠ 6¹⁴ᵍᶠ 11¹⁶ˢᵈ
0-0-7 £441

Peak Practice *D Burchell*   6
5 b m Saddlers' Hall (Ire) - High Habit
9⁸ᶠ **0-0-1**

Peak To Creek *J Noseda*   110
2 b c Royal Applause - Rivers Rhapsody
3⁵ᵍᶠ 9⁵ᶠ 1⁶ᵍᶠ 1⁶ᵍᶠ 2⁶ᵍ 2⁶ᵍᶠ 3⁶ˢ 1⁶ᵍᶠ
1⁶ᵍᶠ 1⁶ᵍᶠ 1⁷ᵍᶠ **7-2-12 £178,095**

Pearl Dance (USA) *J H M Gosden*   79
3 b f Nureyev (USA) - Ocean Jewel (USA)
9⁸ᵍᶠ 0⁸ᵍˢ **0-0-2**

Pearl Grey *D R Loder*   99
2 gr f Gone West (USA) - Zelanda (Ire)
3⁶ᵍᶠ 1⁵ᵍᶠ 1⁶ᵍᶠ 2⁶ᵍ **2-2-4 £35,306**

Pearl Island (USA) *D R Loder*   30
2 b c Kingmambo (USA) - Mother Of Pearl (Ire)
7⁷ᵍᶠ **0-0-1**

Pearl Of Love (Ire) *M Johnston*   115
2 b c Peintre Celebre (USA) - Aunt Pearl (USA)
2⁶ᵍᶠ 1⁶ᵍ 1⁷ᵍᶠ 1⁷ᵍᶠ 3⁷ᵍᶠ 1⁸ᵍ **4-2-6**
£227,117

Pearl Of York (Den) *R Guest*   45 a43
2 b f Richard Of York - Laser Show (Ire)
10⁷ᵍᶠ 8⁷ᵍᶠ 9⁷ˢᵈ **0-0-3**

Pearl Pride (USA) *M Johnston*   67
2 ch f Theatrical - Spotlight Dance (USA)
6⁶ᵍᶠ 4⁶ᵍᶠ 2⁷ᵍᶠ 9⁸ᵍᶠ **0-1-4 £2,090**

Pearl Queen (Ger) *Andreas Lowe*   98
5 b m Lando (Ger) - Prime Lady (Ger)
1⁸ᵍ 3⁹ᵍ 3⁸ᵍ **1-2-3 £20,907**

Pearly Brooks *T J Naughton*   a44
5 b m Efisio - Elkie Brooks
11⁷ˢᵈ 11⁶ˢᵈ **0-0-2**

Pearson Glen (Ire) *G A Swinbank*   62
4 ch g Dolphin Street (Fr) - Glendora
15⁸ᵍ 7¹⁰ᵍᶠ 5¹⁰ᵍ 4¹²ᵍᶠ **0-0-4**

Peartree House (Ire) *D W Chapman*   67 a41
9 b g Simply Majestic (USA) - Fashion Front
10⁹ˢᵈ 7⁸ˢᵈ 5⁸ᶠ 8⁸ᵍᶠ 1⁷ᵍᶠ 2⁸ᵍᶠ 6⁸ʰʸ 4⁸ᵍˢ
3⁷ᵍᶠ 2⁹ᶠ 7⁸ᶠ 9⁹ᵍᶠ 7⁸ᵍᶠ 9⁸ˢ 14⁸ᵍ **1-3-15**
£7,089

Pedrillo *Sir Mark Prescott*   83
2 b g Singspiel (Ire) - Patria (USA)
3⁶ᵍˢ 2⁶ᵍᶠ 1⁷ᵍᶠ **1-2-3 £4,807**

Pedro Jack (Ire) *B J Meehan*   87 a92
6 b g Mujadil (USA) - Festival Of Light
8⁶ˢᵈ 6⁷ˢᵈ 5⁶ˢᵈ 7⁶ˢʷ 1⁶ˢᵈ 13⁶ᵍ 3⁶ᵍᶠ 8⁶ᵍᶠ
3⁶ᵍᶠ 10⁶ᵍᶠ 7⁶ᵍ **1-2-11 £7,083**

Peeress *Sir Michael Stoute*   81
2 ch f Pivotal - Noble One
3⁷ᵍˢ **0-1-1 £646**

Peggy Lou *B J Llewellyn*   55
3 b f Washington State (USA) - Rosemary Nalden
4⁸ᵍˢ 5¹¹ᵍᶠ 4¹⁰ᵍ 1¹²ᵍˢ 4¹²ᵍᶠ 3¹²ᵍᶠ 3¹⁶ᵍᶠ
6¹⁴ᵍᶠ **1-3-8 £5,014**

Peggy Naylor *James Moffatt*   33
2 ch f Presidium - Bitch
6⁵ᵍˢ **0-0-1**

Peka Bou (Ire) *Andrew Reid*   56
2 b c Sri Pekan (USA) - Chambolle Musigny (USA)
6⁶ᵍ 3⁸ᵍᶠ **0-1-2 £297**

Pekan Lady (Ire) *R A Fahey*   50
3 b f Sri Pekan (USA) - Lady Dulcinea (Arg)
6⁷ᵍˢ 7⁸ᶠ 7⁹ᵍᶠ 12¹⁰ˢ 7¹²ᵍᶠ 11¹²ᵍᶠ **0-0-6**

Penalta *W M Brisbourne*   37 a42
7 ch g Cosmonaut - Targuette
5¹⁵ˢᵈ 3¹⁶ˢᵈ 4¹⁶ˢᵈ 5¹⁶ˢᵈ 7¹⁷ᵍᶠ 7¹⁶ˢᵈ **0-1-6**
£414

Penalty Clause (Ire) *K A Morgan*   52 a11
3 b g Namaqualand (USA) - Lady Be Lucky (Ire)
13⁶ˢᵈ 8⁷ᵍᶠ 7¹⁰ᵍᶠ 18⁸ᵍᶠ 15¹⁴ᵍᶠ 6¹¹ᶠ 4¹²ᵍˢ
0-0-7 £267

Pending (Ire) *J R Fanshawe*   73
2 b c Pennekamp (USA) - Dolcezza (Fr)
7⁷ᵍᶠ 5⁸ᵍᶠ **0-0-2**

Penel (Ire) *B R Millman*   55
2 b g Orpen (USA) - Jayess Elle
6⁵ᵍ 5⁵ᵍᶠ 4⁶ᵍᶠ 7⁵ᶠ **0-0-4 £294**

Penelewey *H Candy*   95
3 b f Groom Dancer (USA) - Peryllys
2⁷ᵍᶠ 1⁵ᵍˢ 2⁷ᵍ 9⁷ᵍᶠ 1⁷ᵍ 1⁷ᵍˢ **3-2-6**
£18,931

Penniless Dancer *M E Sowersby*   44
4 b g Pennekamp (USA) - Villella
11⁸ᵍᶠ 10⁸ᵍᶠ 9¹²ᶠ 16¹⁰ᵍᶠ 13⁸ᵍᶠ **0-0-5**

Penny Cross *M Johnston*   95

3 b f Efisio - Addaya (Ire)
2^{7g} 3^{7gf} 3^{6f} 1^{7gf} 1^{7gf} 2^{8gf} 2^{8gf} 1^{8gf} 3^{8g}
3^{8gf} 3^{8gf} **3-7-11 £34,591**

Penny Ha'Penny *D W Barker* 72
4 b f Bishop Of Cashel - Madam Millie
2^{5g} 5^{5gf} 13^{5gf} 10^{5gf} 6^{5gf} 15^{6gs} 7^{5gs}
12^{6gf} 4^{5g} 3^{5g} 22^{6gs} 15^{5g} **0-3-12 £3,048**

Penny Pie (Ire) *P W Harris* 69
3 b f Spectrum (Ire) - Island Lover (Ire)
3^{8g} 5^{8gs} 3^{8gf} 8^{10gf} 10^{10g} **0-1-5 £1,348**

Penny Stall *J L Dunlop* 56
2 b f Silver Patriarch (Ire) - Madiyla
10^{7f} 4^{8gf} 4^{10gf} **0-0-3 £273**

Penny Valentine *J Cullinan* 33 a42
3 ch f My Best Valentine - Precision Finish
6^{7sd} 8^{7sd} 9^{10gf} 8^{8f} 5^{10gf} **0-0-5**

Pennyghael (UAE) *M R Channon* 78
3 ch f Pennekamp (USA) - Kerrera
2^{7gf} 2^{7f} 1^{7gf} 5^{9gs} 6^{8gf} **1-2-5 £6,664**

Penric *C G Cox* 54
3 b g Marju (Ire) - Nafhaat (USA)
6^{10f} 9^{10f} 4^{14gf} 4^{12g} 17^{14g} 5^{16gf} 9^{16gf}
5^{16gf} **0-1-8 £287**

Penrith (Fr) *M Johnston* 81
2 b c Singspiel - Queen Mat (Ire)
1^{7gf} **1-0-1 £4,533**

Pension Fund *M W Easterby* 69
9 b g Emperor Fountain - Navarino Bay
8^{8gs} 5^{10gf} 7^{8s} 4^{8gf} 3^{10gf} 9^{10gf} 12^{11g}
8^{10gs} 12^{9gs} **0-2-9 £1,011**

Pentecost *A M Balding* 107
4 ch g Tagula (Ire) - Boughtbyphone
12^{7g} 4^{8gf} 5^{8gf} 15^{8gf} 1^{8gf} 3^{8gf} 2^{8gs} 4^{9gf}
30^{9gf} **1-3-9 £42,575**

Penthesilea (USA) *Sir Mark Prescott* a31
2 b f Sadler's Wells (USA) - Grazia
8^{6sd} **0-0-1**

Penwell Hill (USA) *T D Barron* a80
4 b g Distant View (USA) - Avie's Jill (USA)
2^{11sd} 1^{8sd} 1^{8sd} 1^{8sd} 3^{7sd} 4^{7sw} **3-1-6**
£11,923

Penzance *J R Fanshawe* 73
2 ch c Pennekamp (USA) - Kalinka (Ire)
1^{8gf} 3^{9g} **1-0-2 £2,932**

Pepe (Ire) *R Hollinshead* 52
2 b f Bahhare (USA) - Orange And Blue
9^{6gs} 6^{7gs} **0-0-2**

Pepe Galvez (Swe) *Mrs L C Taylor* 76
6 br g Mango Express - Mango Sampaquita (Swe)
9^{19gf} **0-0-1**

Pepper Road *R Bastiman* 61
4 ch g Elmaamul (USA) - Floral Spark
6^{7gf} 9^{7gs} 12^{7gf} 3^{8gf} 5^{8gf} 8^{9gf} 3^{7gf} 3^{8gf}
2^{7gf} 1^{8f} 11^{8gf} 6^{8gf} 21^{8g} **1-4-13 £8,143**

Peppershot *G P Enright* 68 a34
3 b g Vettori (Ire) - No Chili
5^{12gs} 4^{12gf} 9^{10sd} 10^{16gf} 6^{14gf} **0-0-5 £470**

Peppiatt *N Bycroft* 24
9 ch g Efisio - Fleur Du Val
13^{6gs} 18^{7g} 18^{6gs} 13^{6gs} **0-0-5**

Pequenita *G L Moore* 66 a57
3 b f Rudimentary (USA) - Sierra Madrona (USA)
2^{7gs} 8^{7f} 15^{7gf} 9^{9gf} 9^{10g} 4^{12sd} 2^{12sw} 1^{11gs}
1-2-8 £4,792

Per Amore (Ire) *P J Hobbs* 74

5 ch g General Monash (USA) - Danny's Miracle
8^{15gf} **0-0-1**

Perchance To Win *R Guest* a55
6 b m Pelder (Ire) - French Plait
13^{7sd} 4^{8sw} 4^{10sd} **0-0-3**

Perchancer (Ire) *P C Haslam* 28
7 ch g Perugino (USA) - Irish Hope
10^{9g} **0-0-1**

Percussionist (Ire) *J H M Gosden* 69
2 b c Sadler's Wells (USA) - Magnificent Style (USA)
3^{8g} 2^{8s} **0-2-2 £1,648**

Percy Douglas *Miss A Stokell* 75 a68
3 b c Elmaamul (USA) - Qualitair Dream
3^{6sd} 12^{5sd} 8^{5f} 10^{5gf} 11^{5g} 7^{5gs} 12^{6g}
6^{5gf} 6^{5gf} 9^{6gf} 8^{6gf} 7^{5g} 10^{5g} 13^{5gf} 3^{6gf} 9^{6sd}
6^{5g} **0-1-17 £1,549**

Peregian (Ire) *J Akehurst* 60 a58
5 b g Eagle Eyed (USA) - Mo Pheata
3^{10sd} 6^{10sd} 3^{8sd} 2^{8sd} 7^{7sd} 4^{8gf} 7^{7f} 2^{8f}
1^{7gf} 9^{8gf} 10^{9gf} 13^{8gf} 11^{10gf} 5^{8gs} **1-4-14**
£6,271

Perelandra (USA) *J Noseda* 69 a59
3 ch f Cadeaux Genereux - Larentia
6^{10gf} 6^{10g} 6^{12sd} 14^{12sd} **1-0-5**
£2,114

Pererin *I A Wood* 48
2 b c Whittingham (Ire) - Antithesis (Ire)
11^{6gf} 15^{6gf} 7^{8sw} **0-0-3**

Perfect Balance (Ire) *N Tinkler* 52
2 b/br g Shinko Forest (Ire) - Tumble
3^{6gs} 12^{8g} 14^{8s} **0-1-3 £672**

Perfect Distance (USA) *B J Meehan* 68 a61
2 b f Distant View - Theycallmecharlie (USA)
3^{5f} 5^{6gf} 5^{5sd} 10^{5gf} 11^{5sd} 1^{5f} 6^{5gf} 4^{5f}
2-1-8 £10,249

Perfect Echo *M P Tregoning* a76
4 ch f Lycius (USA) - Perfect Timing
1^{8sd} 2^{7sd} **1-1-2 £5,592**

Perfect Hindsight (Ire) *C G Cox* 66
2 b g Spectrum (Ire) - Vinicky (USA)
14^{5gf} 7^{6gf} 5^{5gf} **0-0-3**

Perfect Love *G A Butler* a84
3 b f Pursuit of Love - Free Spirit (Ire)
1^{6sd} 2^{7sd} 12^{7gs} **1-1-3 £5,358**

Perfect Night *R Charlton* 76 a73
3 b f Danzig Connection (USA) - Blissful Night
8^{8gf} 15^{8gf} 2^{8g} 2^{8f} 7^{8gf} 2^{8gf} 2^{7sd} **0-4-7**
£4,069

Perfect Picture *M Johnston* 43
4 b g Octagonal (NZ) - Greenvera (USA)
8^{10gf} **0-0-1**

Perfect Portrait *D R Loder* 55
3 ch g Selkirk (USA) - Flawless Image (USA)
1^{7gf} **1-0-1 £3,688**

Perfect Punch *C F Wall* 68 a71
4 b g Reprimand - Aliuska (Ire)
4^{10sd} 11^{2sd} 7^{12sd} 2^{12g} 5^{12g} 4^{12sd} 18^{12s}
1-1-7 £4,620

Perfect Setting *P J Makin* 75
3 b g Polish Precedent (USA) - Diamond Park (Ire)
4^{5g} 10^{5gs} 7^{5g} 13^{5s} **0-0-4 £430**

Perfect Storm *M Blanshard* 103
4 b c Vettori (Ire) - Gorgeous Dancer (Ire)
13^{8gf} 6^{8g} 4^{10gf} 6^{10gf} 21^{8gf} 16^{10g} 1^{10s}
2^{12g} **1-1-8 £15,987**

Perfect Touch (USA) *D K Weld*   104
4 b f Miswaki (USA) - Glen Kate
4⁶ᵍʸ 2⁶ᵍ 2⁷ᵍ 1⁷ᵍʸ 5⁷ᵍ 2⁷ᵍ 2⁸ᵍᶠ 3⁷ᵍᶠ 6⁸ᵍᶠ
1-6-9 £86,389

Perfidious (USA) *J R Boyle*   76 a79
5 b g Lear Fan (USA) - Perfolia (USA)
2¹⁰ˢᵈ 6⁹ˢᵈ 2¹⁰ˢᵈ 2¹⁰ˢᵈ 1¹⁰ᵍᶠ 2¹⁰ᵍᶠ 8¹⁰ᵍᶠ
9¹⁰ᵍᶠ 6¹⁰ᵍᶠ 2¹⁰ᵍ 5¹⁰ᵍ 2¹⁰ᵍᶠ 16¹⁰ᵍᶠ 1¹⁰ᶠ **2-6-14
£18,066**

Pergolacha (Ire) *L M Cumani*   67
2 b f Sadler's Wells (USA) - Posta Vecchia (USA)
14⁸ᵍᶠ 3⁷ᵍˢ **0-1-2 £466**

Perle D'Or (Ire) *W J Haggas*   62
2 b f Entrepreneur - Rose Society
4⁶ᵍᶠ 5⁷ᵍᶠ 10⁷ᵍᶠ **0-0-3 £716**

Persario *J R Fanshawe*   83
4 b f Bishop Of Cashel - Barford Lady
6⁷ᵍ 2⁷ᵍᶠ 6⁷ᵍ 2⁷ᵍ 7⁷ᵍˢ **0-2-5 £3,237**

Persephone Heights *D J Coakley*   74 a53
3 br f Golden Heights - Jalland
6⁸ˢᵈ 4¹⁰ˢᵈ 4¹⁰ˢᵈ 8¹²ˢᵈ 2¹²ᶠ 1¹²ᵍˢ 11¹²ᵍᶠ
9¹¹ᵍᶠ 6¹²ᶠ **1-1-9 £6,224**

Pershaan (Ire) *J L Dunlop*   92
3 br f Darshaan - Persian Fantasy
4¹⁰ᵍᶠ 2¹²ᵍ 7¹²ˢ 5¹²ᵍˢ 1¹²ᵍᶠ 2¹⁶ᵍ 9¹⁶ᵍᶠ
1-2-7 £5,746

Persian Bandit (Ire) *J R Jenkins*   20
5 b g Idris (Ire) - Ce Soir
8⁸ᵍᶠ **0-0-1**

Persian Brook *M W Easterby*   16 a16
3 b g Atraf - Persian Role
17⁶ᶠ 7⁷ˢᵈ 6⁸ᵍᶠ **0-0-3**

Persian Dagger (Ire) *J L Dunlop*   7
2 b c Daylami (Ire) - Persian Fantasy
17⁸ᵍᶠ **0-0-1**

Persian Fact *K R Burke*
4 b g Greensmith - Forest Song
13⁸ˢʷ 11⁸ˢᵈ **0-0-2**

Persian Genie (Ire) *G B Balding*   20
2 br f Grand Lodge (USA) - Persia (Ire)
17⁶ᵍᶠ **0-0-1**

Persian King (Ire) *J A B Old*   88
6 ch g Persian Bold - Queen's Share
14¹⁰ᵍ 5¹²ᵍ 7¹⁰ᵍᶠ **0-0-3 £1,250**

Persian Lass (Ire) *P W Harris*   103
4 ch f Grand Lodge (USA) - Noble Tiara (USA)
4¹⁰ᵍ 4¹⁰ᵍᶠ 3¹²ʰʸ 7¹⁰ᶠ 3¹⁰ᵍˢ 3¹⁰ᵍ 5¹⁰ᵍ **0-1-7
£14,030**

Persian Lightning (Ire) *J L Dunlop*   110
4 b g Sri Pekan (USA) - Persian Fantasy
5¹⁰ᵍᶠ 1¹⁰ᵍ 4¹⁰ᵍᶠ 2¹⁰ᶠ 3¹⁰ᵍᶠ 10¹⁰ᵍ 6¹⁰ᵍᶠ
2⁹ᵍᶠ 16⁹ᵍᶠ 11¹⁰ᵍ **1-4-10 £43,783**

Persian Majesty (Ire) *P W Harris*   107
3 b c Grand Lodge (USA) - Spa
1¹⁰ᵍᶠ **1-0-1 £29,000**

Persian Pearl *H J Collingridge*   71
4 b f Hurricane Sky (Aus) - Persian Fountain (Ire)
20⁷ᵍᶠ 2⁷ᵍᶠ 18ᵍᶠ 1⁷ᵍᶠ 18ᵍᶠ 3⁷ᵍᶠ 3⁷ᵍᶠ 5⁸ᵍᶠ
14⁸ᵍᶠ 8¹⁰ᵍᶠ 5¹⁰ᵍᶠ 11⁹ᵍᶠ **3-2-12 £17,850**

Persian Punch (Ire) *D R C Elsworth*   119
10 ch g Persian Heights - Rum Cay (USA)
4¹³ᵍ 4¹⁶ᵍᶠ 2²⁰ᵍᶠ 1¹⁶ᵍᶠ 1¹⁶ᵍ 4¹⁶ᵍᶠ 1¹⁸ᵍ
8²⁰ʰᵒ 1¹⁶ᵍᶠ **4-1-9 £214,840**

Persian Waters (Ire) *J R Fanshawe*   78
7 b g Persian Bold - Emerald Waters

4¹⁶ᵍᶠ **0-0-1 £428**

Pertemps Bianca *A D Smith*   14 a45
3 b f Dancing Spree (USA) - Bay Bianca (Ire)
5⁸ˢᵈ 4⁸ˢᵈ 8⁸ˢᵈ 13¹⁰ᵍᶠ **0-0-4**

Pertemps Conection *A D Smith*   26
3 b f Danzig Connection (USA) - Royal Celerity (USA)
10⁸ᵍˢ **0-0-1**

Pertemps Machine *A D Smith*
4 b g Danzig Connection (USA) - Shamrock Dancer (Ire)
7¹²ᵍᶠ **0-0-1**

Pertemps Magus *R A Fahey*   69
3 b f Silver Wizard (USA) - Brilliant Future
6⁷ᵍ PU⁸ᵍᶠ 5⁶ᵍᶠ 13⁶ᶠ 12⁶ᵍᶠ 8⁶ᵍ 7⁶ᵍ **0-0-7**

Pertemps Red *A D Smith*
2 ch c Dancing Spree (USA) - Lady Lullaby (Ire)
11⁷ᶠ **0-0-1**

Pertemps Sia *A D Smith*   51 a27
3 b c Distinctly North (USA) - Shamrock Dancer (Ire)
7¹²ˢᵈ 5¹⁰ᵍ 14¹²ᵍᶠ 6¹⁴ᵍᶠ 6¹⁴ᶠ 13¹⁴ᵍ 6¹⁶ᵍᶠ
0-0-7

Pertemps Silenus *A D Smith*   a37
5 b g Silca Blanka (Ire) - Silvie
10¹³ˢᵈ 11⁹ˢᵈ 9¹²ˢᵈ **0-0-3**

Pertemps Wizard *F Jordan*   a14
3 br c Silver Wizard (USA) - Peristyle
8⁸ˢʷ **0-0-1**

Peruvia (Ire) *H Morrison*   82 a62
3 b f Perugino (USA) - Dane's Lane (Ire)
4⁸ᵍˢ 4¹²ˢᵈ 1⁹ᵍˢ 2¹⁰ᵍˢ **1-1-4 £7,457**

Peruvian Breeze (Ire) *N P Littmoden*   53
2 b g Foxhound (USA) - Quietly Impressive (Ire)
14⁷ᵍᶠ 6⁸ᵍᶠ 6⁸ᵍᶠ **0-0-3**

Peruvian Chief (Ire) *N P Littmoden*   115 a114
6 b g Foxhound (USA) - John's Ballad (Ire)
9⁶ˢᵈ 5⁵ˢᵈ 2⁶ˢᵈ 2⁶ˢʷ 4⁵ˢᵈ 1⁶ˢᵈ 1⁵ˢᵈ
10⁶ᵍ 1⁵ᵍᶠ 8⁶ᵍᶠ 2⁵ᵍᶠ 1⁵ᵍᶠ 4⁶ᵍᶠ 16⁵ᵍᶠ 22⁶ᶠ 7⁵ᵍ
9⁶ᵍᶠ 5⁵ᵍᶠ
6⁵ᵍᶠ **4-4-26 £74,551**

Peruvian Style (Ire) *N P Littmoden*   77
2 b g Desert Style (Ire) - Lady's Vision (Ire)
2⁵ᶠ 4⁵ᵍᶠ 13⁶ʸ 1⁵ᵍ **1-1-4 £5,115**

Pessoa (Ger) *Mario Hofer*   a89
4 ch c Platini (Ger) - Prairie Lila (Ger)
1¹⁰ˢᵈ 2¹⁰ˢᵈ 4¹⁰ᵍ 12¹⁰ˢᵈ **1-0-4 £11,122**

Petana *M Dods*   47
3 br f Petong - Duxyana (Ire)
10⁶ᵍᶠ 12⁷ᵍᶠ 10⁵ᵍᶠ 13⁵ᵍ 7⁵ᶠ 4⁶ᶠ 6⁵ᶠ 6⁵ᵍˢ
2⁵ᵍᶠ 5⁶ᵍᶠ 9⁶ᵍᶠ 2⁵ᵍᶠ 12⁵ᵍᶠ **0-2-13 £3,550**

Petardias Magic (Ire) *E J O'Neill*   80 a76
2 ch c Petardia - Alexander Confranc (Ire)
6⁵ᵍˢ 1⁵ᵍᶠ 2⁶ᵍ 3⁶ˢᵈ 10⁶ʰᵒ **1-1-5 £5,063**

Peter The Great (Ire) *R M Beckett*   46
4 b g Hector Protector (USA) - Perfect Alibi
15¹²ᵍ 12⁸ᵍᶠ 4⁸ᶠ 19⁸ᵍᶠ **0-0-4 £287**

Peter's Imp (Ire) *A Berry*   38 a8
8 b g Imp Society - Catherine Clare
11¹²ˢʷ 9¹¹ᵍᶠ 7¹⁴ᵍᶠ **0-0-3**

Peter's Puzzle *R A Fahey*   39
2 gr f Mind Games - Maytong
3⁵ᵍᶠ 9⁶ᵍᶠ 7⁵ᵍᶠ **0-1-3 £425**

Peters Choice *I Semple*   69
2 ch g Wolfhound (USA) - Dance Of The Swans (Ire)
4⁵ᵍᶠ 2⁵ᵍᶠ 8⁶ᵍ **0-1-3 £1,298**

Petit Calva (Fr) *R Gibson*   95

2 b/br f Desert King (Ire) - Jimkana (Fr)
1^{5g} 6^{6g} 4^{5g} 1^{6f} 5^{6g} 7^{6g} **2-0-6 £24,582**

Petite Colleen (Ire) *D Haydn Jones*   64 a67
2 b f Desert Sun - Nishiki (USA)
10^{7gf} 2^{8gf} 3^{8sd} **0-2-3 £1,370**

Petite Futee *D Haydn Jones*   61 a52
4 b f Efisio - Q Factor
7^{10sd} 3^{11gf} 10^{12f} 8^{12gf} 8^{10gf} 4^{10gf} 12^{11gf}
0-1-7 £1,192

Petite Mac *N Bycroft*   57 a55
3 b f Timeless Times (USA) - Petite Elite
9^{6sd} 4^{6sd} 7^{5sd} 7^{6sd} 17^{5gs} 7^{5g} 3^{5f} 6^{6gf}
4^{6gf} 9^{5gf} 5^{5gs} 1^{5gf} 8^{5gf} 7^{6f} **1-1-14 £4,675**

Petongski *B Ellison*   55 a24
5 b g Petong - Madam Petoski
16^{6gf} 12^{6gf} 15^{6gf} 13^{5gf} 14^{6sd} 2^{5gs}
12^{5gs} 5^{6gs} 6^{6gf} 4^{6gf} 9^{5gf} **0-2-11 £1,610**

Petrolero (Arg) *Mrs S A Liddiard*   29 a41
4 gr g Perfect Parade (USA) - Louise (Arg)
15^{7g} 17^{10g} 7^{7gf} 7^{7sw} **0-0-4**

Petrosa (Ire) *D R C Elsworth*   71
3 ch f Grand Lodge (USA) - Top Brex (Fr)
3^{10gf} 4^{10gf} 10^{8g} 3^{10gf} 2^{8f} 3^{10f} **0-2-6**
£4,415

Petrula *K A Ryan*   86
4 ch g Tagula (Ire) - Bouffant
14^{8gf} 25^{8g} 1^{10g} 4^{12gf} 12^{10gf} 2^{10gf} 14^{12g}
4^{10gf} 16^{10g} 3^{12g} 4^{10g} **1-3-11 £16,767**

Petrus (Ire) *C E Brittain*   66 a81
7 b g Perugino (USA) - Love With Honey (USA)
4^{8sd} 8^{7sd} 9^{8sd} 4^{7sd} 8^{8sd} 1^{7gf} 20^{8g} 6^{8sd}
9^{8sd} 11^{10sd} **1-0-10 £2,507**

Peyto Princess *M A Buckley*   72
5 b/br m Bold Arrangement - Bo' Babbity
3^{5gf} 11^{5gf} 10^{6f} 6^{6s} 8^{5gf} 3^{6g} 4^{6gf} 4^{6f}
9^{6gs} 16^{6gf} 7^{6g} **0-3-11 £2,795**

Phamedic (Ire) *T D Easterby*   81
3 b f Imperial Ballet (Ire) - Beeper The Great (USA)
6^{10gf} 6^{10gf} 2^{10f} 4^{10gf} 4^{12gf} 2^{12f} 2^{10gf}
1^{11gf} 3^{10gf} 6^{10gf} 6^{12gf} **1-4-11 £8,994**

Phantom Flame (USA) *M Johnston*   52 a76
3 b g Mt. Livermore (USA) - Phantom Creek
2^{7sd} 11^{6sd} 2^{7gf} 5^{6gf} 14^{6f} 9^{9sd} 8^{7f} 10^{8gs}
13^{7gf} 14^{8gs} **0-2-10 £2,419**

Phantom Wind (USA) *J H M Gosden*   91
2 b f Storm Cat (USA) - Ryafan (USA)
15^{6gf} 1^{6gf} **1-0-2 £4,774**

Pharly Reef *D Burchell*
11 b g Pharly (Fr) - Hay Reef
10^{12sd} **0-0-1**

Pharoah's Gold (Ire) *D Shaw*   37 a70
5 b g Namaqualand (USA) - Queen Nefertiti (Ire)
3^{6sw} 1^{7sd} 10^{7sd} 1^{7sw} 5^{8sd} 7^{8sd} 7^{7sd} 8^{7sd}
4^{7sd} 14^{7g} 9^{7sw} 3^{8sd} 4^{8sd} 2^{8sd} 8^{7sd} **2-4-15**
£7,696

Pheckless *R F Johnson Houghton*   66 a79
4 ch g Be My Guest (USA) - Phlirty
1^{7sd} 12^{7sd} 9^{8sd} 5^{7gs} **1-0-4 £3,513**

Phi Beta Kappa (USA) *D Morris*   86
3 ch f Diesis - Thrilling Day
6^{7gf} 2^{8g} 8^{10gf} 2^{10gs} 5^{12gf} 7^{8s} **0-2-6**
£2,996

Philharmonic *R A Fahey*   95
2 b g Victory Note (USA) - Lambast
2^{5gf} 1^{6gf} 1^{6g} 4^{6gf} **2-1-4 £13,778**

Philly Dee *J Jay*   48 a26
2 b f Bishop Of Cashel - Marbella Beach (Ire)
2^{6gf} 8^{6gs} 5^{6f} 2^{5gf} 6^{6g} 6^{5sd} 10^{6gf} 4^{5gf}
0-2-8 £1,658

Philly's Folly *G C H Chung*   29 a27
3 b f Catrail (USA) - Lucie Edward
13^{7sd} 4^{10gf} 13^{10sd} **0-0-3**

Phinda Forest (Ire) *W Storey*   30
4 br f Charnwood Forest (Ire) - Shatalia (USA)
14^{12gf} **0-0-1**

Phluke *R F Johnson Houghton*   77
2 b g Most Welcome - Phlirty
6^{5gf} 2^{6gf} 2^{5g} 4^{5s} **0-2-4 £2,456**

Phnom Penh (Ire) *Miss J Feilden*   a2
4 b g Alhaarth (Ire) - Crystal City
13^{7sd} **0-0-1**

Phoebe Buffay (Ire) *J W Payne*   54 a60
6 b m Petardia - Art Duo
8^{8sd} 2^{8sd} 7^{7sw} 2^{9sw} 8^{10sd} 11^{10sd} 3^{8sd} 1^{9sd}
5^{8sd} 4^{8gf} 3^{9f} 3^{9f} 11^{12g} **1-5-13 £7,508**

Phoenix Eye *M Mullineaux*   12
2 b c Tragic Role (USA) - Eye Sight
15^{8gs} **0-0-1**

Phoenix Nights (Ire) *A Berry*   52 a32
3 b g General Monash (USA) - Beauty Appeal (USA)
4^{6sd} 10^{6sd} 1^{7gf} 7^{7g} 3^{8f} 11^{7f} **1-1-6**
£4,722

Phoenix Reach (Ire) *A M Balding*   120
3 b c Alhaarth (Ire) - Carroll's Canyon (Ire)
1^{12g} 1^{12g} 3^{15g} 1^{12y} **3-1-4 £442,446**

Photofit *J L Dunlop*   70
3 b c Polish Precedent (USA) - Photogenic
6^{7gs} 2^{8gf} **0-1-2 £1,332**

Phred *R F Johnson Houghton*   75 a61
3 ch g Safawan - Phlirty
6^{8gf} 2^{8g} 6^{10sd} 1^{8gf} 11^{8g} 6^{8g} 11^{8gf} 1^{8gf}
8^{8f} 10^{10sd} **2-1-10 £7,424**

Phrenologist *J R Fanshawe*   47 a66
3 gr g Mind Games - Leading Princess (Ire)
5^{6gf} 6^{7sd} **0-0-2**

Physical Force *D W Chapman*   a33
5 b g Casteddu - Kaiserlinde (Ger)
3^{14sd} 11^{16sd} 7^{16sd} 7^{16sw} 6^{16sd} 9^{12gf} 14^{12gf}
0-1-7 £424

Piano Star *Sir Michael Stoute*   103
3 b g Darshaan - De Stael (USA)
2^{10gf} 4^{11g} 1^{10gf} 9^{12gf} 3^{12gf} **1-0-5**
£14,598

Pic N Mix (Ire) *C W Thornton*   44
3 b f Piccolo - Kingdom Princess
17^{8gf} 9^{8gf} 10^{9f} 5^{7gf} 6^{7gf} **0-0-5**

Pic Up Sticks *M R Channon*   106
4 gr g Piccolo - Between The Sticks
1^{5f} 10^{5g} 7^{5gf} 8^{5gf} 13^{6g} 23^{6g} PU^{6g}
1-0-8 £9,392

Piccled *E J Alston*   92 a107
5 b g Piccolo - Creme De Menthe (Ire)
1^{5sw} 1^{5sd} 1^{5g} 3^{5f} 7^{5gf} 6^{5gf} 10^{5gf} 6^{5gs}
14^{5s} 7^{5gf} 8^{5gs} **3-1-11 £35,712**

Piccleyes *R Hannon*   66
2 b g Piccolo - Dark Eyed Lady (Ire)
9^{6f} 5^{6gf} 2^{6g} 6^{6gf} 13^{6gf} 3^{6gs} **0-1-6**
£2,192

Piccolezza *D E Cantillon*   a34
4 b f Piccolo - Sound Check

11^{6sd} **0-0-1**

Piccolo Lady M Wigham 27
4 b f Piccolo - Tonic Chord
11^{5gf} 8^{6gf} 9^{8gf} 8^{6gf} **0-0-4**

Piccolo Prince B W Hills 58
2 ch c Piccolo - Aegean Flame
9^{5gf} 10^{6gs} 3^{5gf} 5^{5gf} 7^{7gf} 8^{7f} **0-1-6 £812**

Pick Of The Crop J R Jenkins 71 a70
2 ch c Fraam - Fresh Fruit Daily
4^{7gf} 9^{7gf} 5^{7sd} 2^{6sd} **0-1-4 £936**

Pickpocket H A McWilliams 15
3 ch g Paris House - Sabo Song
15^{6gf} 19^{6f} 15^{7gf} 12^{9gf} **0-0-4**

Pickwick Ayr I A Wood a2
4 b g Bijou D'Inde - Ayr Classic
13^{8sd} 8^{12sw} **0-0-2**

Pie High M Johnston 94
4 ch f Salse (USA) - Humble Pie
3^{8gs} 2^{9gf} 5^{8gf} 19^{7f} 4^{8s} 4^{8g} 9^{9gs} 8^{10f}
0-2-8 £8,375

Pierpoint (Ire) Mrs A M Thorpe 44
8 ch g Archway (Ire) - Lavinia
3^{8f} 9^{7gf} 10^{8gf} **0-1-3 £430**

Pierre Precieuse J S Goldie 28
4 ch f Bijou D'Inde - Time Or Never (Fr)
5^{10gs} 10^{10gf} 4^{8gf} **0-0-3 £438**

Pieter Brueghel (USA) D Nicholls 100
4 b g Citidancer (USA) - Smart Tally (USA)
16^{7gf} 8^{6gf} 3^{7gf} 6^{6gf} 8^{6f} 3^{6gs} 21^{7g} 20^{6g}
12^{6g} 11^{7g} 11^{8gf} **0-2-11 £5,797**

Pigeon Point (Ire) R Hannon 46
3 b f Victory Note (USA) - Mevlana (Ire)
19^{7g} 11^{6gf} 13^{6gf} 16^{7gf} 14^{6gf} **0-0-5**

Pikestaff (USA) M A Barnes 38
5 ch g Diesis - Navarene (USA)
8^{12gf} **0-0-1**

Pilgrim Goose (Ire) Jedd O'Keeffe
5 ch g Rainbows For Life (Can) - Across The Ring (Ire)
7^{12sd} 8^{11sd} **0-0-2**

Pilgrim Princess (Ire) E J Alston 57 a59
5 b m Flying Spur (Aus) - Hasaid Lady (Ire)
3^{6sd} 2^{6sd} 2^{7sd} 7^{7sw} 4^{6gf} 16^{7gf} 3^{6gf} 5^{6gs}
6^{7s} 5^{6gf} 46^{6gf} **0-6-11 £4,252**

Pilgrim Spirit (USA) J H M Gosden 67
3 b/br f Saint Ballado (Can) - Oshima (USA)
5^{10gf} 5^{12gf} 17^{10g} 2^{14f} PU^{14gf} **0-1-5**
£1,684

Piliberto C N Kellett a9
3 br g Man Of May - Briska (Ire)
9^{6sd} 11^{7sd} 9^{12sd} **0-0-3**

Pinchbeck M A Jarvis 82
4 b g Petong - Veuve Hoornaert (Ire)
11^{6gf} 16^{6g} 5^{6f} 3^{6gf} 4^{6gf} 1^{6g} 8^{7g} 3^{6gf}
3^{6gf} **1-3-9 £5,802**

Pinchincha (Fr) D Morris 86
9 b g Priolo (USA) - Western Heights
8^{10gs} 4^{10gf} 3^{10gf} 2^{12gf} 4^{12gf} 1^{10g} 9^{10gf}
5^{10gf} **1-3-8 £26,261**

Pines Of Rome G G Margarson a49
3 b c Charnwood Forest (Ire) - Ninfa Of Cisterna
7^{8sd} 2^{7sd} 5^{8sd} **0-1-3 £848**

Pinini Mrs C A Dunnett 53 a41
4 b f Pivotal - Forget Me (Ire)
6^{10sd} 12^{10sd} 8^{8gf} 7^{7g} 12^{6gf} 3^{7gs} 12^{6gf}

0-1-7 **£438**

Pink Fizz J G Portman 30
3 b f Efisio - Pennine Pink (Ire)
10^{8g} 9^{11sd} 12^{8gf} **0-0-3**

Pink Sapphire (Ire) D R C Elsworth 64
2 ch f Bluebird (USA) - Highbrook (USA)
5^{6g} 1^{6gf} 15^{6g} **1-0-3 £5,226**

Pink Supreme I A Wood 74
2 ch f Night Shift (USA) - Bright Spells
2^{5gs} **0-1-1 £1,396**

Pinkerton R Hannon 92
3 b c Alzao (USA) - Dina Line (USA)
2^{9gf} 3^{8gs} 3^{8gf} 18^{8gf} **0-0-4 £4,629**

Pinot Noir G J Smith 2
5 b g Saddlers' Hall (Ire) - Go For Red (Ire)
15^{10gf} **0-0-1**

Pintle J L Spearing 73
3 b f Pivotal - Boozy
2^{5gf} 1^{5gf} 5^{5gf} **1-1-3 £6,438**

Piper D W Barker 41
3 ch g Atraf - Lady-H
7^{5g} 18^{6f} 15^{6gf} 14^{8gf} 8^{10gf} **0-0-5**

Pips Magic (Ire) J S Goldie 68
7 b g Pips Pride - Kentucky Starlet (USA)
10^{5gf} 2^{9g} 7^{6gs} 11^{6gs} 1^{6gf} 13^{6gs} 4^{6g}
4^{6gs} 4^{6gf} 11^{6gf} 5^{6f} 6^{6f} 13^{5g} **1-1-13**
£9,727

Pips Song (Ire) P W Hiatt 65 a77
8 ch g Pips Pride - Friendly Song
4^{7sd} 9^{6sd} 11^{6sd} 12^{6sd} 8^{6gs} 11^{6g} 2^{5sd}
6^{7sw} 11^{6sd} 8^{6sd} 3^{6sd} **0-2-11 £1,634**

Pipssalio (Spa) Jamie Poulton 36 a45
6 b g Pips Pride - Tesalia (Spa)
12^{10sd} 9^{12sd} 7^{9sd} 10^{12g} 4^{11sd} **0-0-5**

Piquet J J Bridger 54 a43
5 br m Mind Games - Petonellajill
9^{8sd} 12^{10sd} 14^{8gf} 5^{8f} 10^{9gf} 4^{6f}
6^{6gf} 12^{6gf} 8^{6f} 7^{10f} 5^{10f} 18^{10f} **0-0-13**

Piri Piri (Ire) P J McBride 73 a64
3 b/br f Priolo (USA) - Hot Curry (USA)
6^{7gf} 5^{7gf} 13^{7gf} 9^{8g} 4^{10gf} 3^{10g} 5^{8gf} 1^{10gf}
3^{12gf} 6^{10gf} 6^{10gf} 7^{12sd} **1-1-12 £7,438**

Pirlie Hill Miss L A Perratt 63
3 b f Sea Raven (USA) - Panayr
4^{6f} 4^{6gf} 4^{5gf} 6^{6f} 8^{5g} 9^{5gs} 10^{5gf} **0-0-7**
£730

Pirouettes (Ire) J H M Gosden 56 a48
3 b f Royal Applause - Dance Serenade (Ire)
4^{6gf} 3^{7sw} 10^{6g} **0-1-3 £655**

Piste Bleu (Fr) R Ford 62 a54
3 b f Pistolet Bleu (Ire) - Thamissia (Fr)
8^{7sd} 11^{10gf} 8^{12g} 3^{10g} 9^{10gf} 3^{11gf} 1^{12f}
6^{14gf} 5^{13gf} **1-2-9 £4,429**

Pivotal Guest M R Channon 85
2 b c Pivotal - Keep Quiet
3^{5gf} 1^{5gf} 3^{7g} 2^{7s} 2^{7gs} 5^{7gf} 4^{7g} 7^{7g} 5^{6g}
7^{7f} 5^{7gf} 4^{7gf} 8^{7gf} 16^{7g} **1-2-14 £15,239**

Pivotal Point P J Makin 97
3 b g Pivotal - True Precision
2^{6gs} 1^{5gf} 2^{6g} **1-3-5 £10,915**

Pizazz B J Meehan 71
2 b c Pivotal - Clare Celeste
7^{6gf} **0-0-1**

Place Cowboy (Ire) J A Osborne a71
2 b c Compton Place - Paris Joelle (Ire)

2^{6sd} **0-1-1 £864**

Place Rouge (Ire) *J H M Gosden*   114
4 b f Desert King (Ire) - Palmeraie (USA)
1^{12g} 7^{10g} 2^{10gf} 7^{13ho} 4^{12gf} **1-1-5**
£49,871

Planters Punch (Ire) *R Hannon*   58
2 b c Cape Cross (Ire) - Jamaican Punch (Ire)
12^{8gf} 10^{8gf} **0-0-2**

Plateau *D Nicholls*   90
4 b g Zamindar (USA) - Painted Desert
14^{6gf} 12^{5gf} 26^{6f} 8^{5gf} 25^{6g} 7^{6g} **0-0-6**

Platinum Boy (Ire) *M Wellings*   8 a63
3 b g Goldmark (USA) - Brown Foam
2^{8sd} 3^{9sd} 3^{8sd} 1^{9sd} 5^{8sd} 8^{9sd} 9^{10gf} **1-2-7**
£4,673

Platinum Charmer (Ire) *K A Ryan*   63 a78
3 b g Kahyasi - Mystic Charm
5^{10sd} 4^{8sd} 3^{11sw} 11^{7sw} 10^{12gf} 7^{16g} 9^{14gs}
0-0-7 £750

Platinum Chief *A Berry*   54
2 b g Puissance - Miss Beverley
7^{5gf} 10^{5gf} 3^{6gf} 6^{6g} 12^{7gf} 2^{7gf} 8^{8g} 4^{7gf}
14^{8gf} **0-1-9 £1,442**

Platinum Pirate *K R Burke*   58 a16
2 b g Merdon Melody - Woodland Steps
7^{6gs} 11^{6sd} 7^{6g} 6^{8g} 7^{8sd} **0-0-5**

Plausabelle *T D Easterby*   49
2 b f Royal Applause - Sipsi Fach
8^{6g} 18^{6sd} 6^{6gf} **0-0-3**

Play Misty (Ire) *B R Johnson*   a28
4 b f Dr Devious (Ire) - Mystic Step (Ire)
10^{8sd} **0-0-1**

Play That Tune *H R A Cecil*   101
3 ch f Zilzal (USA) - Military Tune (Ire)
1^{7gs} 2^{7gf} 11^{7g} 3^{8gs} 3^{7g} **1-3-5 £16,096**

Play The Flute *M Blanshard*   a30
3 ch f Piccolo - Son Et Lumiere
9^{12sd} 7^{9sd} **0-0-2**

Playful Dane (Ire) *W S Cunningham*   63 a48
6 b g Dolphin Street (Fr) - Omicida (Ire)
4^{6sw} 4^{5sd} 7^{6gs} 1^{6gf} 9^{6g} 4^{7g} 3^{6gf} 1^{6gf}
12^{6f} 17^{5g} **2-1-10 £7,586**

Playful Spirit *S R Bowring*   58 a59
4 b f Mind Games - Kalimat
3^{8sw} 3^{7sd} 11^{6sd} 5^{8sd} 11^{6gf} 8^{5gf} 12^{7gf}
3^{5gf} 9^{6gf} 11^{6sw} 14^{7gs} **0-3-11 £1,652**

Playtime Blue *K R Burke*   68 a69
3 b g Komaite (USA) - Miss Calculate
17^{7g} 8^{5s} 4^{5sd} 7^{5gf} 1^{5gf} 7^{5g} 1^{5gf} 4^{5gf}
4^{5g} 10^{5s} **2-0-10 £8,527**

Please The Prince (Ire) *C F Wall*   a66
3 br g Desert Prince (Ire) - Inner Door (Ire)
2^{8sd} **0-1-1 £1,169**

Pleasure Seeker *M D I Usher*   47
2 b f First Trump - Purse
12^{6gf} 20^{6gf} **0-0-2**

Pleasure Time *C Smith*   56 a56
10 ch g Clantime - First Experience
4^{5sw} 8^{5sw} 12^{5sd} 13^{5gf} 10^{5gf} 11^{5sd} 5^{5f}
5^{5gf} **0-0-8**

Pleinmont Point (Ire) *P D Evans*   a65
5 b g Tagula (Ire) - Cree's Figurine
4^{7sd} 7^{7sd} 3^{7sd} 11^{7sd} 4^{8sd} 12^{8sd} **0-1-6**
£630

Plough Boy *M J Gingell*   a3

5 br g Komaite (USA) - Plough Hill
10^{12sw} **0-0-1**

Plovers Lane (Ire) *M P Tregoning*   43 a24
2 b c Dushyantor (USA) - Sweet Alma
8^{8gf} 15^{7sd} **0-0-2**

Plum *A C Stewart*   66
3 br f Pivotal - Rose Chime (Ire)
4^{6gf} 4^{7gf} 3^{8g} **0-1-3 £1,312**

Plume Of Feathers (Ire) *L G Cottrell*   14
3 b f Ali-Royal (Ire) - Feather-In-Her-Cap
8^{6gf} 11^{8gf} **0-0-2**

Plumpie Mac (Ire) *N Bycroft*   40
2 b c Key Of Luck (USA) - Petrine (Ire)
7^{5g} 6^{5g} 9^{6gf} **0-0-3**

Pluralist (Ire) *A P Jones*   41
7 b g Mujadil (USA) - Encore Une Fois (Ire)
16^{9gf} 8^{12f} 6^{16g} 5^{14gf} **0-0-4**

Plutocrat (USA) *Mrs L Stubbs*   69 a63
6 ch g Silver Hawk (USA) - Satin Velvet (USA)
6^{7sw} 8^{7gf} 11^{7gf} 3^{7f} 8^{7gf} 5^{7f} 7^{7gf} 5^{8g}
1^{7gf} 5^{7f} 5^{7gf} **1-1-11 £4,357**

Poacher's Paradise *M W Easterby*   41 a37
2 ch g Inchinor - Transylvania
7^{5gf} 8^{5gf} 8^{5sd} **0-0-3**

Point Calimere (Ire) *C R Egerton*   75 a41
2 b c Fasliyev (USA) - Mountain Ash
7^{6sd} 3^{6gs} 3^{5gf} 8^{6gf} **0-1-4 £1,329**

Point Man (Ire) *J W Payne*   31
3 b g Pivotal - Pursuit Of Truth (USA)
10^{7g} 16^{7gs} 7^{6g} 5^{10gf} 8^{10gf} **0-0-5**

Point Of Dispute *P J Makin*   95 a83
8 b g Cyrano De Bergerac - Opuntia
8^{7gf} 13^{7gs} 5^{7g} 6^{6gf} 3^{7gf} 13^{7g} 2^{7sd} **0-2-7**
£3,081

Poise (Ire) *Sir Michael Stoute*   87
2 b f Rainbow Quest (USA) - Crepe Ginger (Ire)
2^{7gf} **0-1-1 £3,528**

Poker *W J Haggas*   44 a17
2 ch g Hector Protector (USA) - Clunie
10^{6sd} 6^{6gf} 14^{6sd} **0-0-3**

Polanski Mill *C A Horgan*   77
4 b g Polish Precedent (USA) - Mill On The Floss
7^{10gf} 8^{13gf} 8^{12gf} 8^{16gf} **0-0-4**

Polar Bear *W J Haggas*   94
3 ch g Polar Falcon (USA) - Aim For The Top (USA)
1^{7gs} 1^{8g} **2-0-2 £26,026**

Polar Ben *J R Fanshawe*   116
4 b g Polar Falcon (USA) - Woodbeck
2^{7s} 5^{7gf} 5^{7g} 3^{8gs} 1^{7g} 8^{7vs} 9^{8gs} **1-1-7**
£37,819

Polar Dance (USA) *J W Unett*   5 gr g Nureyev (USA) - Arctic Swing (USA)
15^{8sd} 12^{7sd} **0-0-2**

Polar Dancer *Mrs A J Perrett*   a46
2 b f Polar Falcon (USA) - Petonica (Ire)
10^{8sd} **0-0-1**

Polar Force *M R Channon*   81 a69
3 ch g Polar Falcon (USA) - Irish Light (USA)
4^{8g} 6^{6gf} 6^{7gf} 18^{5gf} 10^{6g} 6^{7g} 5^{6gf} 8^{7gf}
6^{7sd} 5^{5gf} 9^{6gf} 9^{6gs} **0-0-14 £957**

Polar Galaxy *C W Fairhurst*   54
2 br f Polar Falcon (USA) - June Brilly (Ire)
5^{5f} 9^{5gf} 5^{5gf} 4^{7gf} 10^{6gf} 12^{6s} **0-0-6**
£421

Polar Haze *Mrs Lydia Pearce*   44 a58

6 ch g Polar Falcon (USA) - Sky Music
2^{5sd} 9^{6sd} 11^{5gf} 13^{6f} 14^{7gf} 10^{7gf} 8^{7s}
9^{7g} 4^{6sd} **0-1-9 £826**

Polar Impact A Berry   83
4 br c Polar Falcon (USA) - Boozy
7^{7g} 12^{5gf} 13^{7g} 4^{6gf} 2^{5g} 3^{5g} 6^{6g} 7^{5g}
7^{5gf} 13^{5g} 14^{5g} 1^{5g} 12^{6gf} **1-2-13 £6,481**

Polar Jem G G Margarson   75
3 b f Polar Falcon (USA) - Top Jem
6^{8gf} 3^{10gf} 2^{10gf} 1^{10gf} **1-2-4 £4,250**

Polar Kingdom T D Barron   77
5 b g Pivotal - Scarlet Lake
2^{7g} **0-1-1 £1,386**

Polar Rock Jean-Rene Auvray   21
5 ch m Polar Falcon (USA) - South Rock
9^{12g} **0-0-1**

Polar Tryst Lady Herries   67
4 ch f Polar Falcon (USA) - Lovers Tryst
7^{14g} 2^{13gf} 2^{13gf} **0-2-3 £2,273**

Polar Way Mrs A J Perrett   116
4 ch g Polar Falcon (USA) - Fetish
3^{6gf} 6^{6f} 14^{6gf} 2^{6gf} 8^{6gf} 1^{7gf} **1-2-6**
£44,252

Polden Chief J W Mullins   64
3 br g Atraf - Maid Of Mischief
1^{7gf} 7^{7g} 6^{7g} 9^{8g} **1-0-4 £3,750**

Pole Star J R Fanshawe   114
5 b g Polar Falcon (USA) - Ellie Ardensky
3^{16g} 2^{16gf} 3^{20gf} 7^{15gs} 6^{18g} **0-2-5**
£55,000

Policastro Miss K M George   a36
5 b g Anabaa (USA) - Belle Arrivee
14^{13sd} 12^{10sd} 8^{12sw} **0-0-3**

Polish Corridor M Dods   92
4 b g Danzig Connection (USA) - Possibility
9^{10gs} 3^{10gf} 2^{11gf} 2^{10gf} 2^{11gf} 3^{10gf} 3^{11gf}
4^{10gf} 1^{10g} 6^{10g} 2^{10gf} **1-6-11 £19,656**

Polish Emperor (USA) P W Harris   81 a72
3 ch g Polish Precedent (USA) - Empress Jackie (USA)
4^{6f} 4^{6gf} 11^{6g} 8^{6gf} 13^{7g} 12^{6gf} 7^{7sd} 6^{6sd}
4^{5g} **0-1-9 £1,507**

Polish Flame Mrs M Reveley   75
5 b g Blushing Flame (USA) - Lady Emm
2^{13gs} 2^{13gs} 6^{14s} 6^{13gs} **0-2-4 £4,796**

Polish Legend B R Millman   42 a47
4 b g Polish Precedent (USA) - Chita Rivera
5^{10sd} 14^{11gf} **0-0-2**

Polish Monarch B R Millman   8
3 b g Mon Tresor - Gentle Star
15^{10gf} 18^{10gf} **0-0-2**

Polish Rhapsody (Ire) J A Supple   a52
2 b f Charnwood Forest (Ire) - Polish Rhythm (Ire)
10^{7sd} **0-0-1**

Polish Spirit B R Millman   69
8 b g Emarati (USA) - Gentle Star
5^{10g} **0-0-1**

Polish Summer A Fabre   118
6 b h Polish Precedent (USA) - Hunt The Sun
4^{12g} 6^{12g} 2^{12g} 2^{13s} 5^{12f} **0-2-5**
£151,589

Polish Trick (USA) B G Powell   79
2 b c Clever Trick (USA) - Sunk (USA)
5^{7gf} 2^{8gf} 2^{7gf} **0-2-3 £1,512**

Polka Princess M Wellings   54 a51
3 b f Makbul - Liberatrice (Fr)

5^{7sd} 12^{7sd} 6^{8gf} 7^{11gf} 9^{8gf} 10^{8gf} 8^{11gf}
0-0-7

Polly Plunkett W M Brisbourne   82
3 b f Puissance - Expectation (Ire)
2^{8g} 3^{8f} 4^{10gf} 1^{8g} 2^{8g} 5^{10gf} 2^{8f} 1^{8g} 2^{8g}
2^{8g} 7^{8gf} **2-5-11 £20,415**

Polonius H Candy   91
2 b g Great Dane (Ire) - Bridge Pool
1^{7gf} 3^{7gf} 1^{6gf} **2-1-3 £5,376**

Polyvia H R A Cecil   26
3 b f Polish Precedent (USA) - Epagris
10^{8g} **0-0-1**

Pomfret Lad P J Makin   107
5 b g Cyrano De Bergerac - Lucky Flinders
6^{6gf} 5^{6gf} 12^{5g} 5^{6hd} 1^{7gf} 8^{7gf} 5^{7g} 2^{7gf}
1-1-8 £15,148

Pompeii (Ire) A J Lockwood   45 a9
6 b g Salse (USA) - Before Dawn (USA)
13^{8sd} 13^{11sd} 7^{12sw} 7^{11gf} 5^{12g} 10^{10gf}
14^{9gf} **0-0-7**

Pompey Blue P J McBride   69
2 b f Abou Zouz (USA) - Habla Me (Ire)
2^{5gf} 3^{6gf} 5^{6gf} 5^{5s} **0-2-4 £5,756**

Pompey Chimes G B Balding   42
3 b g Forzando - Silver Purse
5^{6g} **0-0-1**

Ponderon R F Johnson Houghton   99 a81
3 ch c Hector Protector (USA) - Blush Rambler (Ire)
4^{10gf} 3^{10g} 3^{10f} 8^{12gf} 1^{13sd} 3^{13gs} 1^{17g}
2-3-7 £15,271

Pongee L M Cumani   90 a83
3 b f Barathea (Ire) - Puce
1^{10gf} 1^{10sd} 1^{10gf} 1^{12gf} 7^{12gf} **4-0-5**
£16,337

Pont Allaire (Ire) H Candy   69
2 b f Rahy (USA) - Leonila (Ire)
4^{7gf} **0-0-1 £867**

Pont Neuf (Ire) J W Hills   69 a67
3 b f Revoque (Ire) - Petite Maxine
7^{10sd} 2^{9gs} 13^{10gf} 13^{12sd} **0-1-4 £1,288**

Pooka's Daughter (Ire) J M Bradley   38 a67
3 b f Eagle Eyed (USA) - Gaelic's Fantasy (Ire)
1^{7sd} 2^{7sd} 1^{8sd} 7^{7sw} 4^{8sd} 2^{8sd} 12^{8sd} 12^{7gf}
2-2-8 £7,073

Pop Gun Miss K Marks   70
4 ch g Pharly (Fr) - Angel Fire
1^{10f} 2^{12gf} 4^{12g} 1^{14gf} 3^{16gf} 16^{12g} 14^{16g}
2-3-7 £9,836

Pop Play Again G A Swinbank   26
2 ch c Vettori (Ire) - Bellair
10^{7gf} 17^{8gf} **0-0-2**

Pop Up Again G A Swinbank   87
3 ch f Bahamian Bounty - Bellair
2^{7f} 9^{7s} 3^{7f} 2^{7gf} 11^{7g} 5^{7gf} 1^{7gf} 3^{7f}
1-4-8 £8,622

Poppyline W R Muir   71 a63
3 b f Averti (Ire) - Shalverton (Ire)
2^{8gf} 7^{7gf} 2^{8gf} 8^{10gf} 11^{10g} 2^{8gf} 5^{9g} 5^{9gf}
4^{8f} 4^{8sd} 4^{8gf} 14^{8sd} **0-3-12 £3,924**

Poppys Footprint (Ire) K A Ryan   83
2 ch f Titus Livius (Fr) - Mica Male (Ity)
7^{6gf} 1^{6gf} 14^{7g} 1^{6gf} 6^{6g} 2^{8g} 7^{8gf} **2-1-7**
£20,487

Popular Deb Peter McCreery   54
3 b f Abou Zouz (USA) - Pharling

128y 95s 96g 187gf 0-0-4

Porak (Ire) *G L Moore*   70 a65
6 ch g Perugino (USA) - Gayla Orchestra
313sd 412sd 612gf 0-1-3 £736

Porlezza (Fr) *Y De Nicolay*   116
4 ch f Sicyos (USA) - Pupsi (Fr)
75gs 15g DSQ6gs 17gs 55ho 2-0-5
£94,532

Porsa System (Den) *F Poulsen*   80
4 b/br c Richard Of York - Natalja (Den)
29s 39g 69f 512g 512g 112g 616gf 1-0-7
£13,871

Port Moreno (Ire) *J G M O'Shea*   58 a51
3 b c Turtle Island (Ire) - Infra Blue (Ire)
49sd 39sw 411sd 212sd 112gf 412sd 911gf
913gf 611f 1-2-9 £5,800

Port St Charles (Ire) *P R Chamings*   82 a82
6 b/b g Night Shift (USA) - Safe Haven
47sd 16sd 25sd 26sw 46sw 116sd 97g 26g
36gf 96g 1-4-10 £10,978

Portacasa *R A Fahey*   69
4 b f Robellino (USA) - Autumn Affair
310g 510gf 0-1-2 £908

Porthcawl *M L W Bell*   50
2 b f Singspiel (Ire) - Dodo (Ire)
106gf 0-0-1

Portichol Princess *R M Stronge*   a36
3 b f Bluegrass Prince (Ire) - Barbrallen
910sd 1110sd 0-0-2

Portmanteau *Sir Michael Stoute*   54
2 b f Barathea (Ire) - Dayanata
97gf 0-0-1

Portrait Of A Lady (Ire) *H R A Cecil*   67
2 ch f Peintre Celebre (USA) - Starlight Smile (USA)
58gf 47gf 188gf 0-0-3 £330

Positive Profile (Ire) *P C Haslam*   84 a89
5 b g Definite Article - Leyete Gulf (Ire)
116sd 416sd 218g 116gf 416gs 1620gf 716gf
816g 221gs 114gf 918gf 2-2-11 £21,535

Post And Rail (USA) *E A L Dunlop*   88
2 b c Silver Hawk (USA) - Past The Post (USA)
17s 1-0-1 £6,370

Pot Of Gold (Fr) *T J Fitzgerald*   13 a19
5 gr g Kendor (Fr) - Golden Rainbow (Fr)
611sw 1312gf 0-0-2

Potemkin (Ire) *R Hannon*   111
5 ch h Ashkalani (Ire) - Ploy
59gf 710g 212gf 0-1-3 £8,290

Potsdam *Niall Moran*   54
5 ch g Rainbow Quest (USA) - Danilova (USA)
1512sd 28y 47g 0-1-3 £1,714

Potwash *Andre Hermans*   a59
3 b f Piccolo - Silankka
16sd 106hy 28g 28g 66g 38s 57vs 38gs
08gs 78g 07ho 1-4-11 £13,417

Poule De Luxe (Ire) *J L Dunlop*   61
2 b f Cadeaux Genereux - Likely Story (Ire)
126gf 46gf 0-0-2 £402

Power Nap *N Tinkler*   33
2 b f Acatenango (Ger) - Dreams Are Free (Ire)
98gs 168g 0-0-2

Power Strike (USA) *R Charlton*   34
2 b c Coronado's Quest (USA) - Galega
127gs 0-0-1

Power To Burn *K Bell*   53 a53

2 b g Superpower - Into The Fire
45g 75g 66sd 96gs 0-0-4 £313

Powerful Parrish (USA) *P F I Cole*   86
2 b f Quiet American (USA) - Parish Business (USA)
25gs 58gf 0-1-2 £2,807

Powerscourt *A P O'Brien*   121
3 b c Sadler's Wells (USA) - Rainbow Lake
612gf 110g 112gf 314gf 2-0-4 £126,577

Poyle Heather *J G Portman*   52
3 b f Air Express (Ire) - Hithermoor Lass
57gf 128gf 47gf 86gf 47gf 36g 56gf 67gf
0-3-8 £757

Poyle Jenny *G Barnett*   23
4 b f Piccolo - Poyle Amber
78g 128gf 0-0-2

Prado *L M Cumani*   81
4 b g Hernando (Fr) - Harefoot
210gf 0-1-1 £1,253

Praetorian Force *J M Bradley*   53 a44
4 b g Atraf - Zaima (Ire)
118sd 117sd 67sd 96g 147gf 166gf 36gf
166f 156gf 0-1-9 £596

Prairie Falcon (Ire) *B W Hills*   95
9 b g Alzao (USA) - Sea Harrier
216gf 116gf 414gf 516gf 616gs 412gf 1314g
2114gf 814gf 114f 1116gf 2-1-11 £23,406

Prairie Sun (Ger) *Mrs A Duffield*   56
2 b f Law Society (USA) - Prairie Flame (Ire)
96gf 710f 168gf 0-0-3

Prairie Wolf *M L W Bell*   93
7 ch g Wolfhound (USA) - Bay Queen
1610gf 1010gf 1110g 310gf 210gf 39g
210gf 910s 0-4-9 £7,512

Prayerful *B N Doran*   33
4 b f Syrtos - Pure Formality
1010g 0-0-1

Pre Eminance (Ire) *C R Egerton*   69
2 b c Peintre Celebre (USA) - Sorb Apple (Ire)
47gs 0-0-1 £319

Precious Days (USA) *Sir Michael Stoute*   36
3 ch f Deputy Minister (Can) - Pricket (USA)
1010gf 0-0-1

Precious Freedom *J Balding*   60 a36
3 b g Ashkalani (Ire) - Prayers'n Promises (USA)
196gf 66g 46gs 106gf 87sw 116g 96sd
0-1-7 £330

Precious Mystery (Ire) *J Nicol*   63 a54
3 ch f Titus Livius (Fr) - Ascoli
68g 28gf 78gs 18gf 68sd 1-1-5 £3,673

Pregnant Pause (Ire) *S Kirk*   61
2 b c General Monash (USA) - Dissidentia (Ire)
96g 57f 45gf 56gf 36f 166f 87f 0-1-7
£794

Prelotte (Ire) *C Roberts*   27
4 b g Nicolotte - Prepare (Ire)
108gs 813gf 1212gf 0-0-3

Premier Cheval (USA) *R Rowe*   57 a58
4 ch g Irish River (Fr) - Restikarada (Fr)
812sd 712sd 48sd 1310gf 117sd 0-0-5 £318

Premier Grand *P C Haslam*   70 a76
3 ch g Case Law - Seamill (Ire)
26sd 26f 46gf 86gs 36f 0-3-5 £3,614

Premiere's Pride *D Morris*   15 a7
3 ch f Young Ern - Premiere Moon
97sd 96gf 0-0-2

Prenup (Ire) *L M Cumani*   40
2 ch f Diesis - Mutual Consent (Ire)
5⁶ᶠ 9⁶ᵍˢ **0-0-2**

Present 'n Correct *J M Bradley*   46 a1
10 ch g Cadeaux Genereux - Emerald Eagle
10⁶ˢᵈ 10⁵ˢʷ 11⁷ˢᵈ 15⁷ᶠ 6⁶ᶠ 10⁵ᶠ 3⁶ᶠ
12⁶ᶠ 7⁶ᶠ 6⁶ᵍᶠ **0-1-10 £461**

Present Oriented (USA) *H R A Cecil*   76
2 ch c Southern Halo (USA) - Shy Beauty (Can)
5⁸ᵍ 6⁸ᵍᶠ **0-0-2**

Presenter (Ire) *J H M Gosden*   79
3 ch c Cadeaux Genereux - Moviegoer
3⁸ᵍᶠ **0-1-1 £888**

Presto Shinko (Ire) *R Hannon*   69
2 b c Shinko Forest (Ire) - Swift Chorus
9⁶ᵍᶠ 3⁶ᵍᶠ 3⁶ᵍᶠ **0-2-3 £1,070**

Presto Tempo (Ire) *P W Harris*   63
3 b g College Chapel - Dance Suite (Ire)
4⁸ᵍᶠ 7⁸ᶠ 9⁸ˢ **0-0-3 £426**

Presto Vento *R Hannon*   103 a96
3 b f Air Express (Ire) - Placement
7⁷ᵍᶠ 9⁸ᵍᶠ 1⁷ᵍ 5⁶ᵍᶠ 11⁷ᵍᶠ 12⁷ᵍ 5⁶ᵍᶠ 8⁷ᵍ
5⁷ᵍᶠ 8⁶ᵍᶠ 7⁶ᵍᶠ 3⁸ˢᵈ 9⁶ᵍ **1-1-13 £24,322**

Presumptive (Ire) *J Noseda*   87
3 b c Danehill (USA) - Demure
3⁷ᵍˢ **0-1-1 £896**

Pretence (Ire) *J Noseda*   99 a99
3 b c Danehill (USA) - Narva
1⁸ˢᵈ 1⁸ˢᵈ 1⁸ˢᵈ 4⁸ᵍᶠ 11⁸ᵍᶠ 9⁸ᵍᶠ **3-1-6**
£26,652

Pretty Kool *S C Williams*   48
3 b f Inchinor - Carrie Kool
8⁸ᵍᶠ 12¹⁰ᵍ **0-0-2**

Pretty Pekan (Ire) *G G Margarson*   46
3 b f Sri Pekan (USA) - Pretty Precedent
4⁷ᵍᶠ 11¹⁰ᶠ 7⁸ᵍ 3¹¹ᵍᶠ 7¹¹ᵍˢ 12⁸ᵍᶠ 9¹²ᵍˢ
0-1-7 £584

Preveza *J White*   a8
4 br f Presidium - Ping Pong
13⁸ᵍ 16⁷ˢᵈ **0-0-2**

Preview *J H M Gosden*   22
2 b c Green Desert (USA) - Well Warned
7⁷ᵍ **0-0-1**

Prickly Poppy *T T Clement*   29 a22
5 b m Lear Fan (USA) - Prickwillow (USA)
7⁹ˢᵈ 9⁹ᵍˢ 15⁶ᵍᶠ **0-0-3**

Pride (Fr) *G A Butler*   91 a67
3 b f Peintre Celebre (USA) - Specificity (USA)
2⁸ˢᵈ 1¹⁰ᵍᶠ 7¹⁰ᵍ **1-1-3 £5,219**

Pride Of Kinloch *J Hetherton*   78 a37
3 ch f Dr Devious (Ire) - Stormswept (USA)
6⁸ˢᵈ 3⁷ᵍ 4⁷ᵍ 17⁶ᵍˢ 5⁸ᵍˢ 7⁸ᵍᶠ **0-2-6**
£1,885

Pride Of Peru (Ire) *M Brittain*   a15
6 b m Perugino (USA) - Nation's Game
7⁶ˢᵈ **0-0-1**

Prideway (Ire) *W M Brisbourne*   52 a76
7 b m Pips Pride - Up The Gates
1⁹ˢᵈ 3⁸ˢᵈ 4⁹ˢᵈ 7¹⁰ˢᵈ 1⁹ˢʷ 1⁹ˢʷ 5⁹ˢᵈ 6¹⁰ᵍ
3-1-8 £9,620

Prideyev (USA) *Mrs A J Perrett*   66
3 ch c Nureyev (USA) - Pride Of Baino (USA)
DSQ¹⁰ᵍᶠ 3¹⁴ᶠ 4¹²ᵍᶠ **0-0-3 £1,146**

Prima Cielo *E J Alston*   40 a26
2 b f Primo Dominie - Song Of Skye

12⁵ᵍ 5⁶ᶠ 11⁵ᵍᶠ 7⁷ᵍᶠ 5⁵ᵍᶠ 5⁵ˢᵈ **0-0-6**

Prima Falcon *G G Margarson*   45 a9
3 b f Polar Falcon (USA) - Prima Silk
7⁵ᵍᶠ 13⁶ᵍ 9⁵ᶠ 20⁶ᵍᶠ 7⁶ˢᵈ **0-0-5**

Prima Stella *N P Littmoden*   43 a82
4 gr f Primo Dominie - Raffelina (USA)
1⁶ˢᵈ 1⁶ˢᵈ 3⁶ˢᵈ 2⁶ˢᵈ 4⁶ᶠ 1⁵ˢᵈ **3-2-6**
£10,431

Primary Classic *Miss V Haigh*   16
3 b g Classic Cliche (Ire) - Zarzi (Ire)
12⁸ᵍ **0-0-1**

Prime Attraction *W M Brisbourne*   57
6 gr m Primitive Rising (USA) - My Friend Melody
6¹⁰ᵍᶠ 9¹³ᵍ 2¹²ᵍˢ 2¹²ᵍ 6¹³ᵍˢ 5¹³ᵍᶠ 6¹²ᵍ
10¹²ᵍᶠ 4¹²ᶠ 6¹²ᵍᶠ 3¹⁶ᵍᶠ **0-3-11 £3,994**

Prime Powered (Ire) *G L Moore*   85
2 b g Barathea (Ire) - Caribbean Quest
11⁶ᵍ 2⁹ᵍ 1⁹ᵍ **1-1-3 £5,112**

Prime Recreation *P S Felgate*   86 a60
6 b g Primo Dominie - Night Transaction
11⁵ˢʷ 1⁵ᵍ 11⁵ˢᵈ 12⁵ᵍᶠ 16⁵ᵍᶠ 13⁵ᵍᶠ 8⁵ᵍᶠ
2⁵ᵍᶠ 4⁵ᵍᶠ 7⁵ᵍ **1-1-10 £8,828**

Primo Dawn *N P Littmoden*   a49
4 b g Primo Dominie - Sara Sprint
12⁸ˢᵈ 5⁶ˢᵈ 4⁶ˢᵈ **0-0-3**

Primo Rose *R Guest*   38
3 b f Primo Dominie - My Dear Watson
15⁶ᵍ 6⁵ᶠ 19⁶ᵍᶠ 14⁵ᵍᶠ 14⁶ˢ 8⁷ᵍᶠ
0-0-7 £452

Primo Way *B W Hills*   75
2 b c Primo Dominie - Waypoint
4⁵ᵍᶠ 3⁶ᵍᶠ 5⁶ᵍ **0-1-3 £2,316**

Primrose And Rose *J J Bridger*   44 a29
4 b f Primo Dominie - Cointosser (Ire)
10⁶ˢᵈ 8⁵ˢᵈ 11⁸ˢᵈ 9⁶ᵍᶠ 16⁵ᵍᶠ 4⁵ᵍ 8⁵ᵍᶠ
3⁵ᵍᶠ 10⁵ᵍᶠ 5⁵ᵍᶠ 16⁶ᵍᶠ 12⁵ᵍᶠ 10⁶ᵍ 9⁵ᵍᶠ **0-1-14**
£938

Primus Inter Pares (Ire) *J R Fanshawe*   90 a63
2 b c Sadler's Wells (USA) - Life At The Top
3⁷ˢᵈ 1⁷ᵍᶠ 2⁷ᵍᶠ **1-2-3 £7,759**

Prince Aaron (Ire) *C N Allen*   44
3 b g Marju (Ire) - Spirito Libro (USA)
6⁸ᵍᶠ 12⁷ᵍˢ PU¹⁰ˢᵈ 9¹⁰ᵍᶠ 12⁷ᵍᶠ 6⁷ᵍᶠ **0-0-6**

Prince Adjal (Ire) *G M Moore*   9
3 b g Desert Prince (Ire) - Adjalisa (Ire)
12⁸ᵍ 15⁶ᶠ **0-0-2**

Prince Albert *J R Jenkins*   a45
5 ch g Rock City - Russell Creek
7¹¹ˢᵈ 5¹⁰ˢᵈ **0-0-2**

Prince Atraf *B R Millman*   a64
4 b g Atraf - Forest Fantasy
10¹³ˢᵈ 11¹¹ˢᵈ 9¹³ˢᵈ **0-0-3**

Prince Cyrano *W J Musson*   99
4 b g Cyrano De Bergerac - Odilese
9⁶ᵍ 4⁵ᵍᶠ 7⁵ᵍᶠ 5⁸ᵍᶠ 2⁶ᵍᶠ 11⁶ᵍᶠ 29⁶ᵍ
0-1-7 £4,102

Prince Darkhan (Ire) *G A Harker*
7 br g Doyoun - Sovereign Dona
15¹⁴ᶠ **0-0-1**

Prince Dayjur (USA) *M J Wallace*   81
4 b/br g Dayjur (USA) - Distinct Beauty (USA)
12⁵ᵍᶠ 13⁶ᵍˢ 15⁶ᵍᶠ 10⁷ᵍˢ **0-0-4**

Prince Dimitri *M C Pipe*   38
4 ch g Desert King (Ire) - Pinta (Ire)

8^{8gf} 12^{13gf} **0-0-2**

Prince Domino *G L Moore*   70 a46
4 b g Primo Dominie - Danzig Harbour (USA)
10^{8sd} 13^{7gf} 18^{7g} 1^{7gs} 6^{7gf} 2^{9g} 10^{7gf}
14^{7f} 48^{gs} **1-1-9 £4,187**

Prince Du Soleil (Fr) *J R Jenkins*   46
7 b g Cardoun (Fr) - Revelry (Fr)
9^{8gf} 10^{8gf} 8^{8gf} 11^{8gf} **0-0-4**

Prince Hector *W J Haggas*   89
4 ch g Hector Protector (USA) - Ceanothus (Ire)
6^{8gs} 7^{8gf} 6^{7gf} 8^{7gf} 3^{7gf} 8^{8gf} 15^{8s} 1^{8gf}
7^{8f} **1-1-9 £6,902**

Prince Holing *J H M Gosden*   91
3 ch g Halling (USA) - Ella Mon Amour
4^{10gf} 1^{10f} 2^{12hd} 2^{12gf} **1-1-4 £13,762**

Prince Ivor *R Hannon*   46 a49
3 b g Polar Falcon (USA) - Mistook (USA)
8^{10sd} 10^{9sd} 15^{10gf} 14^{10gf} 5^{10g} 8^{12g} 11^{8gf}
0-0-7

Prince Millennium *R A Fahey*   49
5 b g First Trump - Petit Point (Ire)
15^{10gf} 4^{10gf} 5^{10gf} 9^{12gf} 8^{12gf} 12^{10gs} **0-1-6**
£285

Prince Minata (Ire) *P W Hiatt*   a63
8 b g Machiavellian (USA) - Aminata
8^{8sw} 2^{10sd} 6^{10sd} 6^{8sd} 7^{9sw} 1^{8sd} 5^{9sd} 11^{8sd}
8^{8sd} 7^{8sd} 6^{10sd} **1-1-11 £3,772**

Prince Nasseem (Ger) *A G Juckes*   a8
6 b h Neshad (USA) - Penola (Ger)
10^{12sw} **0-0-1**

Prince Nureyev (Ire) *B R Millman*   103
3 b c Desert King (Ire) - Annaletta
6^{10gf} 1^{11g} 20^{12g} 2^{12gf} 4^{10gs} 4^{14gf} 11^{12f}
1-0-7 £15,658

Prince Of Blues (Ire) *M Mullineaux*   81 a83
5 b g Prince Of Birds (USA) - Reshift
8^{6sd} 7^{5sd} 15^{6gf} UR^{6g} 12^{5gf} 6^{5g} 11^{5gf}
18^{5gf} 17^{6gf} 17^{5gs} **0-0-10**

Prince Of Denmark (Ire) *R Hannon*   91 a91
2 b c Danetime (Ire) - Villa Nova (Ire)
1^{5g} 1^{5sd} 1^{5g} 4^{5gf} 5^{5gf} 2^{5g} 4^{5gf} **3-1-7**
£25,631

Prince Of Gold *R Hollinshead*   78 a76
3 b c Polar Prince (Ire) - Gold Belt (Ire)
3^{8sd} 4^{10gf} 7^{8g} 1^{8gf} 18^{8gs} 15^{8gs} 4^{10gf} 5^{8gf}
4^{8gs} 2^{7gf} 8^{10gf} 4^{8gf} 1^{8sw} 3^{7sw} 10^{10g} 7^{8f} 9^{7sd}
3-3-17 £17,561

Prince Of Perles *A Berry*   38
2 b c Mind Games - Pearls
8^{5gf} 9^{6f} 9^{6gf} 7^{5gs} 8^{6gf} **0-0-5**

Prince Of Persia *R Hannon*   44
3 b g Turtle Island (Ire) - Sianiski
13^{8f} 8^{8gs} **0-0-2**

Prince Of The Wood (Ire) *A Bailey*   57 a57
3 ch g Woodborough (USA) - Ard Dauphine (Ire)
11^{6sd} 3^{8gf} 5^{10sd} 7^{12sd} 2^{12g} 8^{14gf} 9^{14gf}
10^{12gs} 6^{10gs} **0-1-9 £1,157**

Prince Of Thebes (Ire) *A M Balding*   80
2 b c Desert Prince (Ire) - Persian Walk (Fr)
11^{6gf} 3^{7g} 1^{7gf} **1-1-3 £6,703**

Prince Prospect *Mrs L Stubbs*   a56
7 b g Lycius (USA) - Princess Dechtra (Ire)
4^{12sd} 6^{12sd} 4^{9sd} **0-0-3**

Prince Pyramus *C Grant*   52
5 b g Pyramus (USA) - Rekindled Flame (Ire)

17^{8gf} 14^{8gf} 9^{7f} 19^{8g} 10^{5gs} 15^{6gs} 10^{5gf}
0-0-7

Prince Restate *T T Clement*   46
4 ch g Prince Of Birds (USA) - Restate (Ire)
14^{13sd} 6^{7gf} 8^{7g} 16^{7gf} 9^{6g} 11^{6gs} 6^{5gf}
14^{5gf} **0-0-8**

Prince Tara (Ire) *J J Quinn*   80
2 ch g Docksider (USA) - Bird In My Hand (Ire)
8^{5gf} 9^{5gf} 1^{5gf} 3^{6g} 9^{6gf} 1^{5gf} **2-1-6**
£10,645

Prince Tulum (USA) *N P Littmoden*   75 a93
4 ch g Bien Bien (USA) - Eastsider (USA)
1^{8sd} 3^{8sd} 12^{8sd} 7^{8sd} 5^{7sd} 12^{8sd} 11^{8gf}
3^{9g} **1-1-8 £5,274**

Prince Tum Tum (USA) *J L Dunlop*   110
3 b c Capote (USA) - La Grande Epoque (USA)
1^{8gf} **1-0-1 £18,560**

Prince Zar (Ire) *A M Hales*   a48
3 b g Inzar (USA) - Salonniere (Fr)
3^{7sd} 5^{8sd} 9^{8gf} 11^{12sd} **0-1-5 £534**

Prince's Passion *D J Coakley*   72 a76
4 b f Brief Truce (USA) - Green Bonnet (Ire)
12^{10sd} 8^{8sd} 5^{10sd} 2^{8sd} 4^{8f} 4^{8hd} 10^{9gf}
6^{8gf} **0-1-8 £1,777**

Princely Venture (Ire) *Sir Michael Stoute*   116
4 ch c Entrepreneur - Sun Princess
1^{12gf} 1^{10g} 7^{13s} **2-0-3 £70,093**

Princes Grant *R A Fahey*   64
2 b c Compton Place - Penny Dip
4^{5gf} 9^{7gf} **0-0-2**

Princes Theatre *M W Easterby*   73
5 b g Prince Sabo - Frisson
3^{8g} 1^{9gf} 1^{8gf} 12^{10gf} **2-1-4 £8,276**

Princess Alina (Ire) *A M Balding*   30 a67
2 b f Sadler's Wells (USA) - Eilanden (Ire)
5^{9g} 2^{7sd} **0-1-2 £1,120**

Princess Anabaa (Fr) *M R Channon*   69
3 b f Anabaa (USA) - Valley Road (Fr)
10^{7g} 3^{7gf} 10^{8gs} 1^{8f} 11^{8f} **1-0-5 £4,975**

Princess Claudia (Ire) *M F Harris*   39
5 b m Kahyasi - Shamarra (Fr)
7^{18f} **0-0-1**

Princess Erica *T D Easterby*   64 a60
3 b f Perpendicular - Birichino
18^{7g} 3^{6g} 8^{6gf} 3^{6sd} 12^{7gf} 5^{6gf} **0-2-6**
£1,129

Princess Faith *A J Chamberlain*   a19
3 b f Polar Prince (Ire) - Crissem (Ire)
9^{8sd} 8^{8sw} 14^{12gf} **0-0-3**

Princess Galadriel *J R Best*   49 a25
2 b f Magic Ring (Ire) - Prim Lass
11^{5sd} 10^{6gf} 4^{5gf} 14^{7f} **0-0-4**

Princess Grace *M L W Bell*   a43
4 b f Inchinor - Hardiprincess
8^{12sd} 2^{9sw} **0-1-2 £840**

Princess Ismene *J Jay*   60 a37
2 b f Sri Pekan (USA) - Be Practical
12^{6gf} 5^{6sd} 4^{7gf} 2^{7gf} 5^{7f} 2^{7gf} 7^{7gf} 1^{7f}
7^{8gf} 4^{7f} 9^{7f} 5^{8gs} **1-3-12 £5,554**

Princess Kai (Ire) *R Ingram*   53 a60
2 b f Cayman Kai (Ire) - City Princess
9^{6gf} 4^{5f} 4^{5sd} 6^{6g} 4^{5gf} 3^{5g} 7^{6sd}
0-0-8 £1,093

Princess Kiotto *T D Easterby*   43
2 b f Desert King (Ire) - Ferghana Ma

8^{7gf} 7^{8g} 8^{8sd} **0-0-3**

Princess Magdalena *L G Cottrell* 66
3 ch f Pennekamp (USA) - Reason To Dance
18^{8g} 10^{7gf} 8^{8gf} 12^{8gf} 11^{11gf} 1^{10gf}
12^{11gf} **1-0-7 £2,059**

Princess Perfect (Ire) *A Berry* 35
2 b f Danehill Dancer (Ire) - Resiusa (Ity)
10^{6gf} 8^{6gf} **0-0-2**

Princess Renesis (Ire) *J A Glover* 25
2 gr f Perugino (USA) - Tajarib (Ire)
9^{5gf} 12^{6gs} **0-0-2**

Princess Royale (Ire) *G A Butler* 62 a55
4 b f Royal Applause - On The Bank (Ire)
8^{8gf} 6^{9gf} 10^{12sd} **0-0-3**

Princess Shoka (Ire) *R Hannon* 70 a58
3 b f Definite Article - Shoka (Fr)
6^{8sd} 2^{7sd} 4^{10f} 10^{10sd} 5^{10g} 6^{10sd} 1^{8gf} 5^{10g}
3^{8gf} 12^{10gf} 7^{8gf} 1^{8f} 15^{9gf} **2-1-13 £7,283**

Princess Speedfit (Fr) *G G Margarson* 77
3 b f Desert Prince (Ire) - Perfect Sister (USA)
4^{8gf} 1^{7gf} 18^{7gs} 2^{8g} 4^{8f} 13^{9g} 1^{8gf} 4^{9gf}
9^{8gf} 6^{8f} **1-1-10 £6,186**

Princess Valentina *J White* 19 a25
3 b f My Best Valentine - Sandkatoon (Ire)
9^{5sw} 8^{7sd} 12^{6gf} 9^{5sd} 12^{6f} 6^{5gf} **0-0-6**

Principessa *B Palling* 54
2 b f Machiavellian (USA) - Party Doll
3^{8gs} **0-1-1 £430**

Pringipessa's Way *P R Chamings* 44 a60
5 b m Machiavellian (USA) - Miss Fancy That (USA)
7^{8sd} 8^{7sd} 11^{10sd} 8^{9sd} 8^{8sd} 5^{7f} 17^{6g} **0-0-7**

Prins Willem (Ire) *J R Fanshawe* 93
4 b g Alzao (USA) - American Gardens (USA)
7^{12gf} 1^{12g} 16^{12g} 5^{12g} 2^{12gf} 6^{12g} 1^{13gf}
11^{16g} **2-1-8 £17,959**

Printsmith (Ire) *J R Norton* 38 a36
6 br m Petardia - Black And Blaze
7^{8sd} 16^{8sd} 9^{8sd} 16^{7g} 5^{7s} **0-0-5**

Priors Dale *K Bell* 70
3 b c Lahib (USA) - Mathaayl (USA)
10^{8gf} 4^{8g} 9^{10gf} **0-0-3 £502**

Priors Lodge (Ire) *M P Tregoning* 118
5 br h Grand Lodge (USA) - Addaya (Ire)
3^{9gf} 2^{8gf} 1^{8gf} 4^{10gf} **1-1-4 £77,000**

Prissy (Ire) *C J Teague*
3 b f Desert Story (Ire) - Practical
11^{5gf} 16^{5f} **0-0-2**

Private Benjamin *Jamie Poulton* 65
3 gr g Ridgewood Ben - Jilly Woo
7^{7g} 18^{7gf} 7^{7gf} 3^{8gf} 8^{8gs} 6^{8f} 4^{8f} 3^{10gf}
6^{10g} 6^{12f} 4^{11gf} **0-1-11 £1,810**

Private Charter *B W Hills* 114 a80
3 b c Singspiel (Ire) - By Charter
1^{10sd} 3^{10gf} 2^{12gf} 6^{12gf} 4^{10g} 5^{10gf} **1-1-6**
£226,847

Private Seal *Julian Poulton* 48 a53
8 b g King's Signet (USA) - Slender
5^{10sd} 5^{10sd} 7^{11gf} 7^{12gf} 3^{12sd} 5^{8gf} 4^{10sd}
6^{12gf} 4^{10f} 7^{10sd} 3^{8f} 18^{8gf} 8^{7gf} 10^{10f} **0-2-14**
£878

Privy Seal (Ire) *J H M Gosden* 104
2 b c Cape Cross (Ire) - Lady Joshua (Ire)
6^{6g} 1^{6gf} 3^{6gf} 1^{7gf} 5^{8g} 5^{8gf} **2-1-6**
£35,009

Prix Star *C W Fairhurst* 70
8 ch g Superpower - Celestine
9^{6gs} 7^{6gs} 8^{7f} 8^{6gf} 7^{6gs} 4^{6gf} 5^{7gf} 7^{6gf}
8^{7gf} 18^{6g} 7^{6gf} 3^{7gf} **0-1-12 £1,040**

Prize Ring *G M Moore* 63 a44
4 ch g Bering - Spot Prize (USA)
6^{9sw} 9^{12sw} 7^{12sd} 15^{10gs} 3^{12gf} 8^{10gf} 6^{12g}
11^{10s} 3^{12gf} 6^{12f} 4^{10g} 1^{10gf} 10^{14f} **1-3-13**
£5,044

Procreate (Ire) *J A Osborne* 46 a30
3 b g Among Men (USA) - Woodbury Princess
5^{7sd} 14^{6sd} 7^{7gf} **0-0-3**

Profiler (USA) *Ferdy Murphy* 47 a49
8 b g Capote (USA) - Magnificent Star (USA)
3^{12sw} 8^{12gf} 5^{13f} 12^{12g} 4^{16gf} 8^{14f} **0-1-6**
£691

Profiteer (Ire) *D R Loder* 67
4 b g Entrepreneur - Champagne Girl
2^{5g} 1^{5gf} 10^{7gf} **1-1-3 £5,742**

Promenade *M L W Bell* 79
2 b f Primo Dominie - Hamsah (Ire)
1^{5gf} 1^{5gf} 6^{5gf} 1^{5gf} **3-0-4 £12,114**

Promised (Ire) *N P Littmoden* a56
5 b m Petardia - Where's The Money
4^{8sd} 1^{7sw} 11^{8sd} 4^{7sd} 13^{10sd} **1-0-5**
£3,614

Promising (Fr) *M C Chapman* 56 a35
5 ch m Ashkalani (Ire) - Sea Thunder
7^{10sd} 8^{11gf} 2^{10gs} 3^{12gf} 7^{10gf} **0-1-5**
£1,873

Promising King (Ire) *G A Butler* a67
3 ch c Desert King (Ire) - Bazaar Promise
1^{8sd} 2^{8sd} **1-1-2 £3,911**

Promote *Ms A E Embiricos* 30
7 gr g Linamix (Fr) - Rive (USA)
14^{11gf} **0-0-1**

Promoter *J Noseda* 98 a64
3 ch c Selkirk (USA) - Poplina (USA)
5^{10sd} 2^{10gf} 1^{10gf} 4^{12g} 7^{13gs} 4^{16gf} **1-2-6**
£8,941

Promotion *Sir Michael Stoute* 88
3 b c Sadler's Wells (USA) - Tempting Prospect
1^{10gf} 3^{12gf} 2^{12f} **1-0-3 £9,192**

Prompt Payment (Ire) *J R Fanshawe* 105
5 b/br m In The Wings - Lady Lucre (Ire)
2^{12hy} 2^{12gf} 10^{12g} 3^{14g} 4^{16gs} 5^{14s} 3^{15g}
0-3-7 £25,655

Proprius *B Smart* a16
3 b g Perpendicular - Pretty Pollyanna
6^{8sw} **0-0-1**

Prospector's Cove *J M Bradley* a29
10 b g Dowsing (USA) - Pearl Cove
6^{11sd} 7^{9sd} 7^{8sd} 8^{7sd} 12^{9sw} **0-0-5**

Prospects Of Glory (USA) *E J O'Neill* 87
7 b h Mr Prospector (USA) - Hatoof (USA)
3^{12gf} 6^{16f} 8^{15gf} **0-0-3 £1,592**

Protection Money *Mrs M Reveley* 21
3 ch g Hector Protector (USA) - Three Piece
14^{12gf} **0-0-1**

Protectorate *Miss Gay Kelleway* 63 a74
4 ch f Hector Protector (USA) - Possessive Lady
5^{8sd} 9^{8g} **0-0-2**

Protocol (Ire) *Mrs S Lamyman* 33
9 b g Taufan (USA) - Ukraine's Affair (USA)
13^{12gf} 8^{10gf} 9^{14gf} 10^{16gf} 4^{11gf} 11^{10gf}

0-0-6

Proud Boast *Mrs G S Rees* 104
5 b m Komaite (USA) - Red Rosein
14^{6gs} 4^{5gf} 8^{6gf} 5^{6gf} 6^{5gf} 9^{5gs} 3^{6gf} 8^{5gf}
9^{6gf} 3^{5gf} 2^{6gf} 4^{5g} 8^{5gf} 3^{6g} 6^{5gf} 8^{6gf} **0-3-16**
£18,076

Proud Native (Ire) *D Nicholls* 96
9 b g Imp Society (USA) - Karamana
8^{6gf} 5^{6g} 4^{5gf} 1^{5gf} 7^{5g} 1^{5gf} 8^{5gf} 1^{6gf}
1^{5gf} 11^{5s} 5^{5gf} **4-0-11 £22,950**

Proud Tradition (USA) *J H M Gosden* 68
2 b f Seeking The Gold (USA) - Family Tradition (Ire)
1^{8gf} **1-0-1 £4,163**

Proud Victor (Ire) *D Shaw* 37 a61
3 b g Victory Note (USA) - Alberjas (Ire)
8^{6sd} 11^{7sd} 6^{8sd} 4^{8sw} 5^{6sd} 4^{7sw} 4^{7sd} 14^{7sd}
12^{6sd} 9^{6sd} 18^{7gf} 7^{5sd} 7^{7gs} 7^{6sd} 6^{9sd} 12^{8g}
0-0-16 £568

Proud Western (USA) *B Ellison* 56 a15
5 b/br g Gone West (USA) - Proud Lou (USA)
8^{8sd} 19^{10gf} 4^{7gf} 3^{7gf} 2^{5gf} 8^{5gs} 7^{6gf} 9^{6gf}
1^{5g} 4^{5gf} 16^{5g} **1-2-11 £5,263**

Provender (Ire) *S Dow* 42 a61
4 b g Ashkalani (Ire) - Quiche
12^{7sd} 12^{10sd} 13^{10g} 13^{8g} **0-0-4**

Prowse (USA) *A M Balding* 62
3 b f King Of Kings (Ire) - Chelsey Dancer (USA)
6^{8gf} 4^{10f} 12^{9gf} **0-0-3 £295**

Proxima (Ire) *G Wragg* 80
3 b f Cadeaux Genereux - Alusha
5^{7gf} 1^{8gf} 9^{8gf} **1-0-3 £5,044**

Psalter (Ire) *H Candy* 90
3 b g College Chapel - Rebecca's Girl (Ire)
3^{8gf} **0-1-1 £1,087**

Psychiatrist *R Hannon* 105
2 ch g Dr Devious (Ire) - Zahwa
2^{6gf} 2^{6gf} 1^{7g} 4^{7gf} 1^{8s} 2^{6g} **2-3-6**
£80,140

Ptarmigan *T T Clement*
6 ch g Rock Hopper - Tee Gee Jay
PU^{18f} **0-0-1**

Ptarmigan Ridge *Miss L A Perratt* 90
7 b h Sea Raven (Ire) - Panayr
16^{5g} 9^{5gf} 5^{5gf} 11^{5g} 15^{5gf} 1^{5s} **1-0-6**
£14,901

Pugin (Ire) *Saeed Bin Suroor* 109
5 b h Darshaan - Gothic Dream (Ire)
2^{14g} 9^{12g} 8^{14gf} 10^{20gf} 6^{16gs} 9^{16ho} **0-1-6**
£13,084

Pukka (Ire) *L M Cumani* 70
2 b c Sadler's Wells (USA) - Puce
10^{7gf} 4^{7gs} **0-0-2**

Pulau Tioman *M A Jarvis* 108
7 b g Robellino (USA) - Ella Mon Amour
8^{8g} 7^{8gf} 1^{8gs} 6^{10g} 6^{10gs} 6^{8gs} 19^{8gs} **1-0-7**
£9,957

Pulse *J M Bradley* 69 a63
5 b g Salse (USA) - French Gift
6^{6sd} 3^{5sd} 6^{6sd} 2^{5sw} 3^{6sw} 12^{5sd} 1^{5sw} 9^{5sd}
6^{5sd} 4^{5sd} 4^{6gf} 4^{6gf} 2^{6gf} 1^{7gf} 1^{5f} 1^{5f}
2^{5gf} 5^{5f} 6^{6gf} **3-7-20 £13,998**

Pulverize (Ire) *J Noseda* a24
2 b c Cape Cross (Ire) - Grade A Star (Ire)
17^{6gf} 14^{6gf} 14^{7sd} **0-0-3**

Punctilious *M A Jarvis* 107
2 b f Danehill (USA) - Robertet (USA)
1^{7g} 18^{8gf} 3^{8gf} **2-0-3 £31,743**

Pup's Pride *Mrs N Macauley* a71
6 b g Efisio - Moogie
4^{8sd} 5^{8sd} 6^{6sd} 6^{7sw} 3^{7sd} 4^{7sd} 1^{7sw} 3^{8sd}
5^{7sd} 1^{8sd} 6^{6sd} 10^{7sd} 8^{7sw} **2-2-13 £7,245**

Pupillage (USA) *M A Jarvis* 65
3 ch f Spinning World (USA) - Shadowlawn
13^{7g} 12^{7sd} **0-0-2**

Puppet King *A C Whillans*
4 b g Mistertopogigo (Ire) - Bold Gift
15^{12gf} **0-0-2**

Puppet Play (Ire) *E J Alston* 57 a55
8 ch m Broken Hearted - Fantoccini
14^{8sd} 7^{7sd} 3^{7f} 10^{7gf} 8^{8gf} 6^{6gf} 11^{8gf}
0-0-7 £572

Purdey *H Morrison* 54 a38
3 ch f Double Trigger (Ire) - Euphorie (Ger)
6^{10gf} 13^{10gf} 8^{10gf} 4^{16ft} **0-0-4**

Pure Coincidence *B Smart* a51
8 b g Lugana Beach - Esilam
7^{5sd} 5^{6sd} 7^{6sd} 4^{5sw} 11^{5sd} 13^{5sd} 13^{6gf}
0-0-7

Pure Elegancia *G A Butler* a50
7 b m Lugana Beach - Esilam
10^{5sd} **0-0-1**

Pure Folly (Ire) *Sir Mark Prescott* a50
2 b f Machiavellian (USA) - Spirit Willing (Ire)
4^{6sd} **0-0-1**

Pure Speculation *M L W Bell* 79
3 b f Salse (USA) - Just Speculation (Ire)
3^{9g} 14^{8gf} 11^{8g} 13^{11s} **0-1-4 £844**

Puri *J G Given* 25
4 b g Mujadil (USA) - Prosperous Lady
12^{7g} **0-0-1**

Purr *J L Dunlop* 38
2 b c Pursuit Of Love - Catawba
15^{8g} **0-0-1**

Putra Ku (Ire) *P F I Cole* a42
3 b c Sri Pekan (USA) - London Pride (USA)
10^{10sd} 5^{8sw} **0-0-2**

Putra Kuantan *M A Jarvis* 100
3 b c Grand Lodge (USA) - Fade
1^{10gf} 6^{10g} 10^{12gs} 1^{10gf} 2^{10gf} 10^{10gf} 8^{10gf}
2-0-7 £17,494

Putra Pekan *M A Jarvis* 112
5 b h Grand Lodge (USA) - Mazarine Blue
1^{8gf} 6^{8gf} 1^{8gf} 13^{8g} 7^{7g} 1^{9gf} 7^{9gf} **3-0-7**
£84,761

Putra Sandhurst (Ire) *M A Jarvis* 109
5 b h Royal Academy (USA) - Kharimata (Ire)
7^{10g} 7^{12gs} 3^{12gf} 1^{12gf} 2^{12gf} 16^{14gf} 3^{12g}
5^{12g} **0-0-8 £15,732**

Putra Sas (Ire) *P F I Cole* 82
2 b c Sri Pekan (USA) - Puteri Wentworth
2^{7gf} 1^{8gf} **1-1-2 £9,073**

Pyrrhic *R M Flower* 47
4 b g Salse (USA) - Bint Lariaaf (USA)
15^{7sd} 4^{7gf} 6^{7gf} 6^{7gf} 10^{7gf} 13^{8f} 20^{7gf}
10^{10gf} 4^{14gf} 5^{11g} 11^{8gf} **0-0-11 £579**

Qaadimm *M P Tregoning*   46
2 b c Rahy (USA) - Zahrat Dubai
13⁷ˢ 4⁸ᶠ **0-0-2**

Qabas (USA) *A C Stewart*   77
3 b c Swain (Ire) - Classical Dance (Can)
2⁸ᵍᶠ 5⁷ᵍᶠ 4¹⁰ᵍᶠ 6⁸ᵍᶠ 2¹²ᶠ 2¹⁰ᵍᶠ 2¹⁰ᵍᶠ 2⁹ᵍᶠ
0-4-8 £6,595

Qandil (USA) *Miss J Feilden*   22 a43
7 ch g Riverman (USA) - Confirmed Affair (USA)
11⁹ˢᵈ 3⁶ˢᵈ 10⁷ˢᵈ 16⁷ˢᵈ 8⁶ᵍᶠ **0-1-5 £415**

Qasirah (Ire) *M A Jarvis*   92
2 b f Machiavellian (USA) - Altaweelah (Ire)
1⁷ᵍᶠ 2⁷ᵍᶠ 7⁸ᵍ **1-1-3 £13,040**

Qobtaan (USA) *M R Bosley*   42 a55
4 b g Capote (USA) - Queen's Gallery (USA)
4⁸ˢʷ 5⁸ˢᵈ 10⁸ˢᵈ 11⁸ᵍᶠ 2⁹ˢᵈ 4⁸ˢᵈ 6⁷ˢᵈ
10⁷ˢʷ **0-1-8 £744**

Qualitair Wings *J Hetherton*   79
4 b g Colonel Collins (USA) - Semperflorens
16⁸ᵍᶠ 2⁷ᶠ 15⁷ᵍ 12⁸ᵍᶠ 8⁸ˢ 10⁷ᵍᶠ 10⁸ᶠ
6⁸ᵍᶠ 9⁸ᶠ 2⁷ᵍˢ 1⁸ᵍˢ 8⁸ᵍᶠ 2⁷ᵍˢ **1-3-13 £10,224**

Quantica (Ire) *N Tinkler*   74
4 b g Sri Pekan (USA) - Touche-A-Tout (Ire)
18⁶ᵍᶠ 12⁵ᵍᶠ 14⁶ᵍᶠ 14⁶ᵍˢ 10⁵ᵍᶠ 2⁵ᵍ **0-1-6
£700**

Quantum Leap *S Dow*   75 a65
6 b g Efisio - Prejudice
13⁷ᵍ 13⁸ᵍᶠ 11⁸ᵍ 4⁸ᵍᶠ 9⁸ᵍᶠ 2⁹ᵍᶠ 12⁸ᵍ
7⁸ᵍᶠ 4⁸ᵍ 10⁸ᵍᶠ 9⁸ˢᵈ **0-3-11 £3,686**

Quarry Island (Ire) *P D Evans*   34 a27
2 b f Turtle Island (Ire) - Last Quarry
6⁵ᵍᶠ 6⁶ˢᵈ 13⁶ᵍᶠ **0-0-3**

Quarrymount *Sir Mark Prescott*   54
2 b g Polar Falcon (USA) - Quilt
10⁷ᵍᶠ 10⁷ᵍᶠ 7⁷ᵍᶠ **0-0-3**

Quartino *J H M Gosden*   85
2 b c Dynaformer (USA) - Qirmazi (USA)
5⁷ᵍᶠ 2⁸ᵍᶠ 1⁸ᵍᶠ **1-1-3 £4,734**

Quay Walloper *J R Norton*   31
2 b g In Command (Ire) - Myrrh
UR⁷ᵍᶠ 7⁷ᵍ 8⁸ᵍᶠ 12⁸ᵍ **0-0-4**

Quedex *R J Price*   61
7 b g Deploy - Alwal
12¹⁸ᵍ 6¹⁶ᵍ **0-0-2**

Queen Charlotte (Ire) *Mrs K Walton*   74
4 ch f Tagula (Ire) - Tisima (Fr)
18ᵍᶠ 14⁸ˢ **1-0-2 £6,714**

Queen Chief (Ire) *J H M Gosden*   53 a64
3 ch f Grand Lodge (USA) - Granza (Fr)
10⁷ᵍˢ 3⁷ᵍᶠ 4⁷ˢᵈ **0-0-3 £590**

Queen Excalibur *J M Bradley*   50
4 ch f Sabrehill (USA) - Blue Room
15⁷ᵍᶠ 2⁸ᵍ 6⁸ᵍˢ 7⁷ᵍᶠ 12⁷ᵍᶠ 9⁷ᵍ 12⁸ᵍᶠ 9⁸ᵍᶠ
9⁸ᵍᶠ 9⁸ᵍᶠ 4⁷ᵍᶠ 7⁸ᵍˢ **0-2-12 £1,155**

Queen G (USA) *K R Burke*   a56
4 b/br f Matty G (USA) - Neieb (USA)
1¹¹ˢʷ 3¹²ˢᵈ 4¹²ˢᵈ 10¹¹ˢᵈ **1-1-4 £3,703**

Queen Louisa *F Watson*
3 b f Piccolo - Queen Of Scotland (Ire)
11⁶ˢᵈ **0-0-1**

Queen Nefertari (USA) *J A Osborne*   a50
3 b f King Of Kings (Ire) - Lyric Fantasy (Ire)
7⁶ˢᵈ 8⁵ˢᵈ 8⁶ˢᵈ **0-0-3**

Queen Of Arabia (USA) *M R Channon*   57
3 b f Wild Again (USA) - Inca Princess (USA)

6¹⁰ᶠ 3⁸ᵍᶠ **0-0-2 £820**

Queen Of Bulgaria (Ire) *Mrs Lydia Pearce*   60 a51
2 b f Imperial Ballet (Ire) - Sofia Aurora (USA)
7⁵ᵍ 4⁵ˢᵈ 6⁵ᵍᶠ 1⁶ᵍ 6⁶ᵍᶠ 2⁶ᵍᶠ 8⁶ᵍᶠ 2⁶ᵍᶠ
1-2-8 £4,710

Queen Of Night *T D Barron*   77 a84
3 b f Piccolo - Cardinal Press
10⁶ᵍᶠ 3⁶ᵍᶠ 8⁶ᵍ 8⁶ᶠ 1⁶ˢᵈ 5⁷ᵍᶠ **1-1-6
£2,976**

Queen Of Scots (Ire) *Sir Michael Stoute*   72
2 b f Dr Fong (USA) - Mary Stuart (Ire)
3⁸ᵍᶠ 4⁸ᵍᶠ **0-0-2 £878**

Queen's Echo *M Dods*   46
2 b f Wizard King - Sunday News'N'Echo (USA)
5⁶ˢ **0-0-1**

Queen's Fantasy *D Haydn Jones*   28
2 ch f Grand Lodge (USA) - Alcalali (USA)
13⁸ᵍˢ **0-0-1**

Queen's Pageant *J L Spearing*   52
9 ch m Risk Me (Fr) - Mistral's Dancer
12¹⁴ᵍˢ **0-0-1**

Queens Jubilee *P Howling*   36 a59
3 ch f Cayman Kai (Ire) - Miss Mercy (Ire)
6⁷ˢᵈ 2⁶ˢᵈ 13⁶ˢᵈ 17⁷ᵍᶠ 11⁵ᵍᶠ 15⁷ᵍᶠ **0-1-6
£842**

Queens Rhapsody *A Bailey*   83 a95
3 b/br g Baryshnikov (Aus) - Digamist Girl (Ire)
1⁷ˢʷ 1⁷ˢʷ 5⁷ˢᵈ 8⁶ᵍˢ **2-0-4 £9,168**

Queens Square *N Tinkler*   49
2 b f Forzando - Queens Check
12⁵ᵍ 3⁵ᵍᶠ 3⁵ᵍˢ 3⁶ᵍᶠ 4⁵ᵍᶠ 4⁵ᵍᶠ 2⁶ᵍˢ 9⁵ᵍᶠ
8⁶ᵍᶠ **0-4-9 £2,444**

Queensberry *J O'Reilly*   a72
4 b g Up And At 'Em - Princess Poquito
15⁷ˢᵈ 2⁶ˢᵈ 1⁸ˢᵈ 1⁸ˢᵈ 6⁸ˢᵈ 2⁸ˢᵈ 10⁸ˢᵈ 3⁸ᶠᵗ
7⁹ˢᵈ 3⁷ˢʷ 3⁹ˢᵈ 9⁸ˢᵈ 2¹²ˢᵈ **2-6-13 £8,811**

Queensland (Ire) *J R Jenkins*   a7
5 ch m Dr Devious (Ire) - Fairy Fortune
10⁹ˢᵈ **0-0-1**

Queenslander (Ire) *J G Given*
2 b f Inchinor - Royal Subject (USA)
PU⁶ᵍᶠ **0-0-1**

Queenstown (Ire) *B J Meehan*   88
2 b g Desert Style (Ire) - Fanciful (Ire)
4⁷ᵍ 2⁷ᵍᶠ 6⁷ᵍᶠ 2⁷ᵍˢ 4⁸ᵍ 4⁹ᵍ 1⁷ᶠ **1-3-7
£8,851**

Quel Fontenailles (Fr) *L A Dace*   77
5 b g Tel Quel (Fr) - Sissi Fontenailles (Fr)
6¹⁰ᵍ 4¹⁰ᵍˢ 6⁷ᵍ 2¹⁰ᶠ 4¹²ᵍᶠ 7²²ᶠ 6¹⁷ᵍᶠ **0-2-7
£2,612**

Querida Rose (Ire) *B S Rothwell*   52
3 b f Desert Story (Ire) - Sanctuary Cove
7⁵ᵍᶠ 6⁵ᵍ 7⁵ᵍ 5⁶ᶠ 4⁵ᵍᶠ 2⁵ᵍᶠ 7⁵ᵍᶠ
4⁵ᵍᶠ 11⁵ᵍᶠ 16⁵ᶠ **0-2-12 £1,411**

Quest On Air *J R Jenkins*   50 a41
4 b g Star Quest - Stormy Heights
9¹⁰ˢᵈ 11¹³ˢᵈ 4¹⁰ᵍᶠ 2¹¹ᵍᶠ 1¹¹ᵍᶠ 9¹²ᵍᶠ 3¹¹ᶠ
1-1-7 £6,137

Quick *M C Pipe*   a45
3 b g Kahyasi - Prompt
8¹⁰ˢᵈ **0-0-1**

Quick Flight *J R Weymes*   72
3 ch f Polar Falcon (USA) - Constant Delight
4⁷ᵍᶠ 6⁸ᵍ 8⁸ᵍˢ 4⁷ᵍᶠ 10⁸ᵍᶠ 10⁷ᵍᶠ 15⁷ᵍᶠ
0-0-7 £710

Quick To Move (Ire) *C N Kellett*   a43
3 b g Night Shift (USA) - Corynida (USA)
8^{7sd} 6^{7sd} 6^{9sd} 7^{8sw} 7^{12gf} **0-0-5**

Quicks The Word *C W Thornton*   82
3 b g Sri Pekan (USA) - Fast Tempo (Ire)
2^{5gs} 8^{6gf} 2^{6s} 14^{6gs} 5^{5gs} 6^{6g} 11^{6g} 1^{5gf}
6^{5s} 15^{5g} 17^{6gf} **1-2-11 £7,355**

Quidditch *P Bowen*   7
3 b f Wizard King - Celtic Chimes
13^{8gf} 14^{12sd} **0-0-2**

Quidnet *Paul Johnson*   46 a44
2 ch f Primo Dominie - Youdontsay
5^{5gf} 3^{6sd} 4^{5sd} 12^{5sw} 17^{6gf} **0-1-5 £566**

Quiet Assassin *K J Burke*   a22
3 b g Dashing Blade - High Habit
14^{12sd} **0-0-1**

Quiet Reading (USA) *M R Bosley*   a80
6 b g Northern Flagship (USA) - Forlis Key (USA)
3^{8sd} 7^{8sd} 3^{8sd} 3^{8sd} 3^{8sw} 1^{8sd} 9^{8sd} 6^{8sd}
1^{8sd} 3^{8sd} 4^{7sd} 6^{9ft} **2-5-12 £10,436**

Quiet Storm (Ire) *G Wragg*   98 a91
3 b f Desert Prince (Ire) - Hertford Castle
1^{7sd} 7^{8gf} 2^{8gs} 1^{10gf} 3^{12gf} 2^{10gf} 4^{10gf}
2-3-7 £29,381

Quiet Times (Ire) *K A Ryan*   73 a82
4 ch g Dolphin Street (Fr) - Super Times
4^{6sw} 2^{6sd} 10^{7sd} 7^{5sw} 1^{6sw} 1^{5sd} 3^{6g} 4^{5gf}
19^{6gf} LFT^{6f} 6^{5g} 5^{5gf} 6^{6g} 5^{6gs} 13^{6sd} 1^{6sd}
3-4-16 £10,518

Quiff *Sir Michael Stoute*   67
2 b f Sadler's Wells (USA) - Wince
5^{7gf} **0-0-1**

Quincannon (USA) *T D Barron*   a40
2 b g Kayrawan (USA) - Sulalat
7^{6sd} **0-0-1**

Quinn *C W Fairhurst*   42
3 ch g First Trump - Celestine
15^{8gs} 7^{12gf} 5^{17gf} 18^{14g} 5^{14gf} 12^{16gf} **0-0-6**

Quinta Special (Ire) *G G Margarson*   a42
4 b f Spectrum (Ire) - Al Galop (USA)
11^{11sd} **0-0-1**

Quintillion *T J Etherington*   33
2 gr g Petong - Lady Quinta (Ire)
10^{6gf} 10^{7gs} **0-0-2**

Quintoto *R A Fahey*   83
3 b g Mtoto - Ballet
1^{10f} 6^{9gf} 17^{9g} 17^{8t} 13^{7g} 17^{7gf} 16^{8g}
1-0-7 £3,744

Quite Remarkable *Ian Williams*   73 a25
4 b g Danzig Connection (USA) - Kathy Fair (Ire)
9^{8sd} 21^{12g} 8^{8gf} 3^{10gs} 10^{10g} **0-1-5 £645**

Quito (Ire) *D W Chapman*   104 a97
6 b r Machiavellian (USA) - Qirmazi (USA)
11^{6sd} 7^{5sd} 1^{6sd} 2^{6sw} 7^{6sd} 6^{7gf} 3^{6gf} 1^{7gf}
5^{7g} 3^{6gs} 2^{6g} 1^{7gf} 17^{6gf} 8^{7g} 11^{6g} 4^{6gf}
1^{7g} 5^{7gf} **5-6-28 £113,802**

Quizzical Lady *T J Naughton*   a32
5 b m Mind Games - Salacious
13^{6sd} 14^{6sd} **0-0-2**

Rabitatit (Ire) *J G M O'Shea*   64
2 b f Robellino (USA) - Coupled
7^{6gf} 7^{6gf} 9^{7gf} 3^{7gf} 2^{7gf} 1^{7gf} 1^{8gf} 5^{8gf}
8^{7gf} **2-2-9 £8,330**

Raccoon (Ire) *T D Barron*   85

3 b g Raphane (USA) - Kunucu (Ire)
8^{6gf} 2^{6gf} 8^{5gs} 1^{5gf} 1^{5gf} **2-1-5 £9,067**

Rachel *Mrs A J Perrett*   92
3 ch f Spectrum (Ire) - Agnus (Ire)
3^{10gf} 11^{10gf} 7^{10gf} PU^{10g} **1-1-4 £5,075**

Racing Night (USA) *E A L Dunlop*   83
3 b g Lear Fan (USA) - Broom Dance (USA)
4^{8gf} 4^{8g} 1^{9gf} 4^{9gf} 5^{10gf} 9^{12gf} **1-0-6**
£5,476

Racingformclub Boy *Miss Gay Kelleway*   44
4 ch g Blushing Flame (USA) - Sonoco
8^{7gf} 13^{8f} 17^{7f} **0-0-3**

Radiant Bride *D W P Arbuthnot*   43 a65
3 ch f Groom Dancer (USA) - Radiancy (Ire)
4^{8sd} 5^{8sd} 7^{10gf} 10^{13g} 12^{12g} 5^{12sd} 7^{14s}
0-0-7 £312

Radiant Dawn *M Johnston*   58
2 b f Danzero (Aus) - Indigo Dawn
4^{8gf} **0-0-1 £357**

Radiant Energy (Ire) *J H M Gosden*   75
3 b f Spectrum (Ire) - Blaine
2^{8s} 2^{8gf} 6^{8gs} 2^{8gs} 1^{8s} **1-3-5 £8,430**

Radish (Ire) *A C Stewart*   58
2 b f Alhaarth (Ire) - Nichodoula
9^{7gs} **0-0-1**

Radley Park (Ire) *E W Tuer*
4 b g Vettori (Ire) - Livry (USA)
11^{11sd} **0-0-1**

Rafferty (Ire) *C E Brittain*   98 a101
4 ch c Lion Cavern (USA) - Badawi (USA)
1^{7sd} 3^{7sd} 9^{8g} 3^{8gf} 6^{8g} 4^{9g} 4^{10gf} 6^{10g}
5^{8gf} 8^{8g} 29^{9gf} 19^{7gf} **1-3-12 £15,894**

Rafters Music (Ire) *Julian Poulton*   74 a78
8 b g Thatching - Princess Dixieland (USA)
8^{6sd} 1^{6sd} 6^{6sd} 9^{7sd} 11^{6gs} 3^{6sd} 5^{6g} 5^{6gs}
2^{6sd} 2^{6sw} 5^{7sd} **1-3-11 £6,407**

Rag Top (Ire) *R Hannon*   99
3 ch f Barathea (Ire) - Petite Epaulette
3^{7gf} 10^{8g} 12^{6gs} 13^{7g} **0-1-4 £5,500**

Ragamuffin *T D Easterby*   85
5 ch g Prince Sabo - Valldemosa
2^{5gf} 11^{6gs} 15^{6gf} **0-1-3 £2,116**

Ragasah *Miss Gay Kelleway*
5 b m Glory Of Dancer - Slight Risk
9^{16sd} **0-0-1**

Ragged Jack (Ire) *G A Butler*   63
2 b g Cape Cross (Ire) - Isticanna (USA)
5^{7gf} 14^{8gf} **0-0-2**

Raging Mind *T D Easterby*   28
2 b f Mind Games - Naufrage
5^{5s} 6^{7f} 14^{7gf} **0-0-3**

Rahaf (USA) *M Johnston*   92 a76
3 b g Theatrical - Gozo Baba (USA)
2^{10sd} 3^{9ft} 12^{10ft} 2^{14gs} 1^{12gf} 4^{12gf} 15^{12gf}
1-3-7 £20,011

Rahbar *L M Cumani*   71
3 b g Mtoto - Arruhan (Ire)
10^{10g} 2^{11gs} 3^{12gs} **0-1-3 £1,752**

Raheed (Ire) *E A L Dunlop*   61
2 b g Daggers Drawn (USA) - In Due Course (USA)
4^{7f} 6^{8gf} **0-0-2 £300**

Raheel (Ire) *P Mitchell*   68 a65
3 ch g Barathea (Ire) - Tajawuz
5^{11gf} 8^{8gf} 7^{9gf} 10^{10gf} 4^{10gf} 6^{10gf} 3^{12sd}
12^{10gf} 8^{13sd} 9^{12sd} **0-1-10 £1,477**

Rahjel Sultan *B A McMahon*   46 a22
5 b g Puissance - Dalby Dancer
7^{6sd} 4^{7gf} 8^{7g} 13^{7g} 5^{7gf} 4^{7f} 14^{7gf} **0-0-7**
£308

Rahlex (Ire) *Ronald Thompson*
5 ch g Rahy (USA) - Lady Express (Ire)
17^{8gf} **0-0-1**

Rahwaan (Ire) *C W Fairhurst*   94
4 b g Darshaan - Fawaakeh (USA)
9^{16gf} 4^{19gf} 2^{16gf} 5^{16gs} 5^{16gf} 5^{19gf} 10^{16gf}
3^{14s} 4^{14gf} **0-3-9 £15,217**

Rainbow Chase (Ire) *R A Fahey*   17 a47
5 b g Rainbow Quest (USA) - Fayrooz (USA)
4^{12sd} 10^{12gf} 7^{12sd} **0-0-3**

Rainbow City (Ire) *Sir Michael Stoute*   70
3 b f Rainbow Quest (USA) - Greektown
1^{10gf} **1-0-1 £6,155**

Rainbow Colours (Ire) *J R Fanshawe*   32
2 gr f Linamix (Fr) - Mill Rainbow (Fr)
6^{7s} **0-0-1**

Rainbow End *D R C Elsworth*   95
4 ch f Botanic (USA) - High Finish
6^{10gf} 8^{10gf} 9^{10gf} 13^{8gs} 14^{10g} **0-0-5 £525**

Rainbow River (Ire) *M C Chapman*   a44
5 ch g Rainbows For Life (Can) - Shrewd Girl (USA)
11^{12sw} 5^{11sd} **0-0-2**

Rainbow Spectrum (Fr) *P W Harris*   55
4 b f Spectrum (Ire) - Iguassu (Fr)
8^{7gf} 4^{8gs} 6^{8gf} 11^{10g} 10^{10g} **0-0-5 £449**

Rainhill (Ire) *R Hannon*   61
2 b c Fasliyev (USA) - Sweet Emotion (Ire)
10^{5gf} 7^{5gf} 10^{6gf} 6^{6gf} 8^{7gf} **0-0-5**

Rainsborough Hill *A King*   38 a37
2 b c Groom Dancer (USA) - Ellebanna
8^{6f} 11^{6sd} 10^{7sd} **0-0-3**

Rainstorm *W M Brisbourne*   53
8 b g Rainbow Quest (USA) - Katsina (USA)
11^{10gf} 8^{10gf} 11^{10f} 6^{8gf} 13^{9gf} 2^{8gf} 1^{10gf}
1^{8gf} 4^{8g} 10^{11g} 13^{10gf} **2-2-11 £9,511**

Rainwashed Gold *Mrs A J Perrett*   106
3 b c Rainbow Quest (USA) - Welsh Autumn
1^{9gf} 6^{12gf} 3^{12f} **1-0-3 £11,217**

Raise Your Glass (Ire) *Miss V Scott*   32
4 b/br g Namaqualand (USA) - Toast And Honey (Ire)
12^{8g} 10^{12f} **0-0-2**

Rajam *D Nicholls*   84
5 b g Sadler's Wells (USA) - Rafif (USA)
8^{10gf} 12^{10f} 2^{12g} 3^{12gf} 2^{14gf} 7^{12gf}
7^{16gf} 7^{17g} **0-2-9 £3,769**

Rajayoga *M H Tompkins*   61
2 ch c Kris - Optimistic
4^{6g} 4^{7gf} 12^{6gf} **0-0-3 £779**

Rakti *M A Jarvis*   126
4 b c Polish Precedent (USA) - Ragera (Ire)
1^{10g} 2^{10gf} 1^{10gf} **2-1-3 £503,968**

Rambler *J H M Gosden*   69 a76
3 b f Selkirk (USA) - Rahaam (USA)
1^{7sd} 5^{8f} **1-0-2 £4,007**

Rampant (Ire) *C J Teague*   24
5 b g Pursuit Of Love - Flourishing (Ire)
18^{10s} 17^{7gf} 19^{8gf} **0-0-3**

Random Quest *P F I Cole*   98
5 b g Rainbow Quest (USA) - Anne Bonny
7^{16gf} 13^{16gf} 2^{16gf} 3^{21gs} 2^{16gf} 5^{14gf} 30^{18gf}
0-3-7 £14,576

Rangoon (USA) *Mrs A J Perrett*   78
2 ch c Distant View (USA) - Rustic (Ire)
3^{6g} **0-1-1 £643**

Rani Two *W M Brisbourne*   78 a60
4 b f Wolfhound (USA) - Donya
5^{10g} 7^{10sd} 5^{10g} 1^{10gf} 2^{10f} 1^{9gf} 1^{10g} 9^{12gs}
6^{9gs} 7^{10g} 4^{10gf} 1^{10g} 17^{11s} **4-1-13 £21,980**

Ranny *Dr J D Scargill*   56 a29
3 b f Emperor Jones (USA) - Defined Feature (Ire)
7^{7f} 5^{9sw} 7^{8gf} 4^{8f} 1^{8f} 10^{8gf} 7^{8g} **1-0-7**
£2,487

Raoul Dufy (USA) *P F I Cole*   69 a73
3 gr g El Prado (Ire) - Parrish Empress (USA)
2^{9sd} 3^{8sd} 8^{8sd} 12^{10gf} 2^{8sd} 3^{8gs} 12^{10gf}
2^{9sw} **0-4-8 £4,837**

Raphael (Ire) *T D Easterby*   82
4 b f Perugino (USA) - Danny's Miracle
2^{7gf} 7^{7f} 4^{7g} 5^{7gf} 1^{7gf} 2^{7gf} 1^{8gf} 4^{7gs}
4^{7gf} 2^{7g} 7^{7g} 6^{8gf} 6^{7gf} 5^{8f} 2^{7g} 2^{7gf} 3^{7gs}
2-8-17 £21,672

Raphoola (Ire) *Andre Hermans*   76 a67
2 b f Raphane (USA) - Acicula (Ire)
9^{5g} 2^{5gf} 3^{5f} 1^{6gs} 1^{5sd} 3^{5g} 5^{5s} 4^{7gs} 2^{6s}
5^{6gs} 11^{5vs} **2-4-11 £15,667**

Rapid Liner *B G Powell*   a13
10 b g Skyliner - Stellaris
9^{8sd} **0-0-1**

Rapscallion (Ger) *J M P Eustace*   86
4 b g Robellino (USA) - Rosy Outlook (USA)
9^{8gf} 7^{8gf} 30^{8gf} 12^{8g} **0-0-4**

Rapt (Ire) *M A Barnes*   46
5 b g Septieme Ciel (USA) - Dream Play (USA)
11^{10gf} 18^{8gf} 14^{6gs} 7^{14f} 7^{16gf} 13^{12gf}
0-0-6

Rare Coincidence *R F Fisher*   58
2 ch g Atraf - Green Seed (Ire)
10^{5gf} 4^{5gf} 7^{6g} 8^{6s} 6^{7g} 5^{8g} 7^{7gf} 5^{8gf}
0-0-8 £271

Rare Destiny (Ire) *A Berry*   58 a41
3 b g Mujadil (USA) - Jamaican Law (Ire)
5^{6g} 11^{6f} 18^{7gf} 5^{6f} 6^{6sd} 3^{5gf} 11^{6gf} 3^{5gs}
1^{5gf} 11^{5gf} 16^{5gs} 5^{5gf} **1-2-12 £4,301**

Rare Presence (Ire) *C P Morlock*   43
4 b g Sadler's Wells (USA) - Celebrity Style (USA)
12^{16gf} 14^{12gf} 14^{12sd} **0-0-3**

Rarefied (Ire) *R Charlton*   66
2 b c Danehill (USA) - Tenuous
6^{8gf} 2^{8gs} **0-1-2 £860**

Rasid (USA) *C A Dwyer*   88 a10
5 b g Bahri (USA) - Makadir (USA)
13^{10gf} 4^{10gf} 7^{10g} 9^{12sd} 15^{10s} **0-0-5 £729**

Rathmullan *E A Wheeler*   32 a5
4 ch g Bluegrass Prince (Ire) - National Time (USA)
12^{8sd} 13^{6gf} 16^{7g} 8^{6f} **0-0-4**

Ratified *M C Chapman*
6 b g Not In Doubt (USA) - Festival Of Magic (USA)
10^{12sd} 10^{8sd} **0-0-2**

Ratio *J E Hammond*   116
5 ch g Pivotal - Owdbetts (Ire)
11^{8vs} 1^{6gs} 1^{6f} 15^{7g} 1^{5gf} 14^{6gf} **3-0-6**
£71,642

Rave Reviews (Ire) *J L Dunlop*   69
2 b f Sadler's Wells (USA) - Pieds De Plume (Fr)
6^{8gf} 1^{8gf} **1-0-2 £6,266**

Ravel (Ire) *M L W Bell*   35

2 b c Fasliyev (USA) - Lili Cup (Fr)
7^7s 15^7g **0-0-2**

Ravenglass (USA) *J G M O'Shea* 91
4 b c Miswaki (USA) - Urus (USA)
3^10gf 2^10gf 5^10gf 1^12f 4^10f 3^13gf 2^12g
6^14gf 1^16gf 27^18gf 7^16gf **2-3-11 £22,465**

Rawalpindi *J A R Toller* 48
2 ch c Intikhab (USA) - Just A Treat (Ire)
12^7gs **0-0-1**

Rawwaah (Ire) *J L Dunlop* 64
3 ch c Nashwan (USA) - Muhaba (USA)
4^10g 4^12gf **0-0-2 £621**

Rawyaan *J H M Gosden* 115
4 b c Machiavellian (USA) - Raheefa (USA)
4^10gf 2^10gf 7^12f 2^10gf 12^12g 1^10g **1-2-6**
£25,421

Raybaan (Ire) *S Dow* 72 a9
4 b g Flying Spur (Aus) - Genetta
9^8gf 7^12gf 9^12gf 2^12gf 2^12f 2^12gf 7^11gf
13^12g 14^12sd 14^10f **0-3-10 £3,162**

Rayik *G L Moore* a47
8 br g Marju (Ire) - Matila (Ire)
3^16sd **0-1-1 £419**

Raymond's Pride *K A Ryan* 77 a58
3 b g Mind Games - Northern Sal
11^6gf 4^5gs 5^5sd 8^6gf 1^5gs F^5g **1-0-6**
£3,976

Raysoot (Ire) *A C Stewart* 47
2 b c Cape Cross (Ire) - Mashkorah (USA)
14^7gf 7^6gf 12^6gf **0-0-3**

Rayware Boy (Ire) *D Shaw* a27
7 b g Scenic - Amata (USA)
6^11sd 8^11sd 12^12sw **0-0-3**

Razkalla (USA) *D R Loder* 119 a100
5 b g Caerleon (USA) - Larrocha (USA)
1^8sw 1^12g 3^13gf 4^14gf 1^12gf 1^12gf 2^12g
4^10gf **4-1-8 £88,055**

Razotti (Ire) *N Tinkler* 58 a18
3 b f Raphane (USA) - Zalotti (Ire)
12^6sd 14^7gf 15^8gf 8^5gs 2^6g 3^7gf 7^6gf
0-1-7 £2,152

Realism (Fr) *P W Hiatt* 37
3 b g Machiavellian (USA) - Kissing Cousin (Ire)
10^8gf **0-0-1**

Reap *Mrs Lydia Pearce* 75 a49
5 b g Emperor Jones (USA) - Corn Futures
11^8sd 4^10g 17^8gf 17^8gf 1^8g 9^9ft 1^8gs 1^8g
1^8gf 2^8g **4-1-10 £16,452**

Reason (Ire) *D W Chapman*
5 b g Sadler's Wells (USA) - Marseillaise
12^12sd **0-0-1**

Rebanna *J Balding*
3 ch f Rock City - Fuwala
8^7sd **0-0-1**

Rebate *R Hannon* 80
3 b g Pursuit Of Love - Aigua Blava (USA)
3^8gf 11^10gs 9^9g 8^9gf 12^7g 3^8gf 1^10gf 4^10g
7^9g 10^9gf 12^8g **1-2-11 £12,630**

Rebel Rouser *W R Muir* 29 a36
2 b c Kris - Nanouche
14^7gf 12^7sd 11^7sd **0-0-3**

Rebel Star *John Berry*
2 b g Sure Blade (USA) - Tamara
10^6g 6^6f 11^7g 7^7g **0-0-4**

Rebel Times *D W Barker* 20

2 ch f Timeless Times (USA) - Skiddaw Bird
11^5f 7^5gf **0-0-2**

Rebelle *I A Wood* a69
4 b/br g Reprimand - Blushing Belle
1^16sd 2^16sd **1-1-2 £3,807**

Recall (Ire) *J G Given* 48
3 b f Revoque (Ire) - Toffee
7^8gf **0-0-1**

Reckless Moment *W G M Turner* a38
2 b f Victory Note (USA) - Blue Indigo (Fr)
5^5sd 10^5sd 7^5sd **0-0-3**

Recollecting *A M Balding* 52
2 b f Polish Precedent (USA) - Introducing
9^8g **0-0-1**

Recording Session (USA) *P J McBride*
5 ch h Colonial Affair (USA) - Cynthia Dean (USA)
3^10gf **0-0-1 £578**

Recount (Fr) *J R Best* 81 a60
3 b g Sillery (USA) - Dear Countess (Fr)
6^7sd 7^12gf 7^10gf 1^12gf 4^12gf 5^11g 8^12gf
2-0-7 £13,808

Rectangle (Ire) *D Nicholls* 88
3 ch g Fayruz - Moona (USA)
10^5gs 2^6gf 6^5gf 3^5gs 20^5gf **0-2-5**
£12,885

Recycling Rita *P R Hedger*
4 ch f Karinga Bay - Gaynor Goodman (Ire)
10^6gf **0-0-1**

Red Acer (Ire) *P S McEntee* 35
2 ch g Shinko Forest (Ire) - Another Baileys
12^5gf 10^6g 9^6gf **0-0-3**

Red Beaufighter *N P Littmoden* 21 a51
3 b g Sheikh Albadou - Tart And A Half
4^8sd 7^7sd 8^8sd 16^8g **0-0-4 £261**

Red Birr (Ire) *A M Balding* 69
2 b g Bahhare (USA) - Cappella (USA)
10^7g 4^6gf 3^6gf **0-1-3 £1,036**

Red Blooded (Ire) *Mrs L C Jewell* 13 a31
6 b g River Falls - Volkova
11^12sd 9^10f **0-0-2**

Red Bloom *Sir Michael Stoute* 110
2 b f Selkirk (USA) - Red Camellia
3^6gf 1^7gf 1^8gf **2-1-3 £122,642**

Red Carpet *D Nicholls* 114
5 ch h Pivotal - Fleur Rouge
1^6g 6^7gf 5^6gf 3^6s 13^6gf **1-0-5 £28,433**

Red Chief (Ire) *M L W Bell* 79
3 b g Lahib (USA) - Karayb (Ire)
4^8gf 8^10g 12^8g 6^8g 5^8gf 14^10gf **0-1-7**
£666

Red China *M Blanshard* a49
4 ch g Inchinor - Little Tramp
7^5sd 5^8sd 8^8sd 13^6sd **0-0-4**

Red Crepe *Mrs A J Perrett* 73
3 b f Polish Precedent (USA) - Red Tulle (USA)
7^8g 2^10gf 5^10gf 2^12f 3^12gf 2^12gf 3^12f **0-3-7**
£3,696

Red Damson (Ire) *Sir Mark Prescott* 78
2 b g Croco Rouge (Ire) - Damascene (Ire)
15^6gf 4^7f 9^7sd 2^8gf 2^8gf 2^8gs **0-3-6**
£7,162

Red Delirium *R Brotherton* 34 a69
7 b g Robellino (USA) - Made Of Pearl (USA)
1^7sw 1^8sd 3^8sd 5^8sd 5^7sd 5^8sd 4^8sd 14^7gf
11^8sd **2-1-9 £6,372**

Red Flame (Ire) *E A L Dunlop*   70
3 ch f Selkirk (USA) - Branston Jewel (Ire)
6^{7gf} 4^{7gs} 4^{8gs} 9^{6g} **0-0-4 £843**

Red Flyer (Ire) *P C Haslam*   a42
4 br g Catrail (USA) - Marostica (Ity)
4^{11sd} 11^{8sw} **0-1-2**

Red Forest (Ire) *J Mackie*   60
4 b g Charnwood Forest (Ire) - High Atlas
16^{8gf} 10^{8gf} 5^{11gf} 4^{11gf} 5^{11gf} 6^{11gf} 7^{12sd} **0-0-7 £290**

Red Fort (Ire) *M A Jarvis*   93
3 b g Green Desert (USA) - Red Bouquet
7^{10g} 11^{12g} 4^{12g} 9^{12gf} **1-0-4 £6,176**

Red Fred *P D Evans*   34
3 ch g Case Law - Mississipi Maid
8^{6f} 9^{8gf} 6^{10gf} **0-0-3**

Red Galaxy (Ire) *D W P Arbuthnot*   85
3 b f Tagula (Ire) - Dancing Season
7^{6g} 13^{7gf} 9^{7gf} **0-0-3**

Red Halo *S Kirk*   56
4 b g Be My Guest (USA) - Pray (Ire)
12^{13gf} 6^{10gf} 6^{12gf} **0-0-3**

Red Hot Polka (Ire) *P Mitchell*   60 a68
3 b g Marju (Ire) - Mochara
13^{6g} 3^{7sd} 7^{9gf} 3^{10sd} 6^{8f} 15^{9g} 11^{10sd} 11^{7sd} **0-2-8 £998**

Red Lancer *R J Price*   51 a52
2 ch g Deploy - Miss Bussell
6^{6gf} 5^{7gs} 5^{6gf} 7^{7f} 1^{7sd} 9^{7sd} **1-0-6 £2,325**

Red Leicester *J A Glover*   57
3 b f Magic Ring (Ire) - Tonic Chord
4^{5gf} 6^{5gf} 12^{5g} 8^{6gf} 13^{5gs} **0-0-5**

Red Lion (Fr) *N J Henderson*   51
6 ch g Lion Cavern (USA) - Mahogany River
9^{12g} 7^{12g} **0-0-2**

Red Moor (Ire) *R Hollinshead*   54
3 gr g Eagle Eyed (USA) - Faakirah
6^{7gf} 5^{8f} 7^{8gf} 16^{8g} **0-0-4**

Red Morocco (USA) *Mrs P Townsley*   a12
9 gr g Seattle Dancer (USA) - Lady's Slipper (Aus)
14^{13sd} **0-0-1**

Red Mountain *D W Barker*   32
2 b c Unfuwain (USA) - Red Cascade (Ire)
15^{8g} **0-0-1**

Red Power (Ire) *P A Blockley*   89
2 b c Intikhab (USA) - Sabayik (Ire)
1^{5g} 1^{5gf} 3^{5g} 4^{6gf} **2-0-4 £16,518**

Red Rackham (Ire) *J Nicol*   a69
3 b g Groom Dancer (USA) - Manarah
5^{8sd} **0-0-1**

Red Rag (USA) *J A Osborne*   71
2 ch c Gold Fever (USA) - Host Of Angels
6^{8gf} 6^{8f} 6^{8gf} 4^{10f} 10^{10gf} **0-0-5 £330**

Red Renegade (Ire) *B R Millman*   34
2 ch c Raphane (USA) - Our Duchess (Ire)
14^{6gf} 6^{5f} 7^{6f} **0-0-3**

Red River Rebel *J R Norton*   67
5 b g Inchinor - Bidweaya (USA)
5^{12gf} 15^{14g} 6^{12g} 5^{12gf} 4^{12gf} 1^{12gf} 2^{12gf} 6^{12gf} 3^{13gf} 4^{12f} 7^{14gf} **1-3-11 £5,971**

Red Rocky *J Gallagher*   48
2 b f Danzero (Aus) - Post Mistress (Ire)
5^{6gf} **0-0-1**

Red Romeo *G A Swinbank*   71

---

2 ch g Case Law - Enchanting Eve
2^{6gf} 7^{7gf} 1^{7gf} 6^{8g} **1-0-4 £6,144**

Red Sahara (Ire) *W J Haggas*   55 a75
2 ch f Desert Sun - Red Reema (Ire)
9^{7gf} 1^{6sd} **1-0-2 £2,262**

Red Scorpion (USA) *W M Brisbourne*   77 a77
4 ch g Nureyev (USA) - Pricket (USA)
7^{8g} 6^{12gf} 4^{12g} 5^{15gf} 12^{14gs} 8^{12gf} 13^{12gf} 5^{16gf} 2^{16sd} 7^{16g} **0-1-10 £1,715**

Red Skelton (Ire) *W J Haggas*   44 a69
2 ch c Croco Rouge (Ire) - Newala
10^{8gf} 1^{7sd} **1-0-2 £2,240**

Red Sovereign *I A Wood*   78 a70
2 b f Danzig Connection (USA) - Ruby Princess (Ire)
2^{6g} 1^{6gf} 3^{6g} 6^{6sd} 6^{5s} **1-2-5 £6,049**

Red Storm *J R Boyle*   38 a60
4 ch f Dancing Spree (USA) - Dam Certain (Ire)
7^{9sw} 11^{10sd} 2^{11sd} 1^{9sd} 14^{11gf} 5^{9sd} **1-1-6 £3,973**

Red Sun *J Mackie*   52
6 b g Foxhound (USA) - Superetta
2^{17gf} 4^{15gf} 4^{16gf} **0-1-3 £3,903**

Red To Violet *J A Glover*   85 a71
4 b f Spectrum (Ire) - Khalsheva
7^{8sd} 2^{10gs} 18^{10gf} 12^{10g} 3^{8g} 6^{10gf} 10^{8gf} 16^{8s} 6^{8sd} 13^{10gs} **0-2-10 £3,236**

Red Top (Ire) *R Hannon*   79
2 b f Fasliyev (USA) - Petite Epaulette
3^{6gf} **0-1-1 £1,095**

Red Trance (Ire) *A M Balding*   78
2 b f Soviet Star (USA) - Truly Bewitched (USA)
7^{5gf} 2^{5g} 2^{5gf} 5^{5gf} 4^{5gf} 3^{5gf} 9^{5g} 2^{5gf} 1^{5f} 3^{5gf} 10^{5vs} **1-3-12 £10,721**

Red Wine *J A Osborne*   101
4 b g Hamas (Ire) - Red Bouquet
5^{12gs} 3^{12g} 9^{12gf} 4^{16gs} 10^{16gf} **0-1-5 £11,162**

Red Wizard *Jonjo O'Neill*   72
3 b g Wizard King - Drudwen
10^{7gf} 7^{7gf} 9^{6g} 9^{11f} 12^{7gf} **0-0-5**

Redbank (Ire) *N A Callaghan*   65
2 b c Night Shift (USA) - Bush Rose
6^{6gf} 6^{7gf} 8^{7gf} 9^{8g} 4^{10gs} **0-0-5**

Redi (Ity) *L M Cumani*   63
2 b c Danehill Dancer (Ire) - Rossella
4^{8gf} 11^{8s} 5^{8gf} 4^{8f} **0-0-4 £779**

Redmarley (Ire) *J G Given*   53
2 b g Croco Rouge (Ire) - Dazzling Fire (Ire)
8^{8s} 10^{8gs} **0-0-2**

Redouble *E L James*   16 a34
7 b g First Trump - Sunflower Seed
10^{12sd} 5^{17hd} **0-0-2**

Redoubtable (USA) *D W Chapman*   49 a36
12 b h Grey Dawn Ii - Seattle Rockette (USA)
11^{7sd} 11^{6sd} 8^{7sd} 16^{6sd} 10^{7sw} 15^{8f} 5^{7gs} 13^{6gs} 9^{5gf} 13^{5gf} 12^{7gf} 6^{6gf} 6^{6gf} 11^{6gf} 11^{6f} **0-0-15**

Redspin (Ire) *J S Moore*   82
3 ch c Spectrum (Ire) - Trendy Indian (Ire)
11^{8gf} 4^{10gf} 2^{10gf} 5^{10gf} 7^{11gf} 2^{10gf} **0-2-6 £3,397**

Redvic *Mrs N Macauley*
3 b g Alhaatmi - Sweet Fortune
8^{8sw} 7^{9sw} 10^{8g} 11^{8sd} **0-0-4**

Redwood Rocks (Ire) *B Smart*   84

2 b c Blush Rambler (USA) - Crisp And Cool (USA)
8⁶ᶠ 4⁶ᵍ 3⁶ᵍᶠ 3⁶ᵍᶠ 2⁷ᵍ 1⁷ᵍ 7⁸ᵍᶠ 7⁷ᵍᶠ **1-3-8**
£6,037

Redwood Star *P L Gilligan*   63 a41
3 b f Piccolo - Thewaari (USA)
6⁵ˢᵈ 14⁶ᵍᶠ 8⁵ᵍᶠ 17⁷ᵍᶠ 8⁵ᵍᶠ 2⁵ᵍᶠ 1⁵ᵍᶠ
11⁵ᵍ 3⁵ᶠ 15⁶ᵍˢ **1-2-10 £4,211**

Reeds Rains *D A Nolan*   18
5 b m Mind Games - Me Spede
19⁵ᵍˢ 7⁵ᶠ 11⁵ᵍ **0-0-3**

Reedsman (Ire) *M H Tompkins*   48
2 ch c Fayruz - The Way She Moves
8⁷ᶠ 12⁷ᵍᶠ 7⁸ᵍᶠ 12⁷ᵍᶠ **0-0-4**

Reel Buddy (USA) *R Hannon*   118
5 ch h Mr Greeley (USA) - Rosebud
8⁸ᵍ 11⁶ᵍ 3⁸ᵍ 5⁸ᵍ 2⁹ᵍ 1⁸ᵍˢ 14⁸ᵍˢ **1-2-7**
£203,300

Reem Al Barari (USA) *J L Dunlop*   64
3 b/br f Storm Cat (USA) - Histoire (Fr)
4⁶ᵍᶠ **0-0-1 £444**

Reemaal Alsahra (Ksa) *C F Wall*   46
2 b f Thoughtless (USA) - Nayasha
15⁷ᵍᶠ 7¹⁰ᵍᶠ **0-0-2**

Reflectance *Saeed Bin Suroor*   53
2 b c Sadler's Wells (USA) - Spain Lane (USA)
5⁷ᵍ **0-0-1**

Refuse To Bend (Ire) *D K Weld*   126
3 b c Sadler's Wells (USA) - Market Slide (USA)
1⁸ᵍᶠ 1⁸ᵍ 13¹²ᵍ 1⁸ᵍᶠ 11⁸ᵍˢ 11⁸ᶠ **3-0-6**
£236,249

Regal Agenda (Ire) *H R A Cecil*   99
3 b c Ali-Royal (Ire) - Hidden Agenda (Fr)
1⁹ᵍᶠ 2¹⁰ᵍᶠ 9¹⁰ᵍ **1-1-3 £7,817**

Regal Ali (Ire) *Mrs A Malzard*   a3
4 ch g Ali-Royal (Ire) - Depeche (Fr)
12¹¹ˢᵈ 11¹²ˢᵈ 10¹²ˢᵈ **0-0-3**

Regal Flight (Ire) *I A Wood*   55
2 b c King's Theatre (Ire) - Green Belt (Fr)
5⁶ᶠ 7⁷ᵍ 5⁷ᵍᶠ **0-0-3**

Regal Performer (Ire) *S Kirk*   57
2 b c Ali-Royal (Ire) - Khatiynza
9⁷ᵍᶠ 13⁸ᵍᶠ **0-0-2**

Regal Ransom (Ire) *B S Rothwell*   a18
4 b f Anabaa (USA) - Queen's Ransom (Ire)
13⁸ˢᵈ 8⁵ˢʷ **0-0-2**

Regal Repose *A J Chamberlain*   50 a50
3 b f Classic Cliche (Ire) - Ideal Candidate
7¹²ˢᵈ 6¹⁰ᶠ 11²ᵍ 12¹²ˢᵈ 2¹⁶ᵍ 7¹⁶ᵍᶠ
11¹²ˢᵈ **1-1-8 £3,961**

Regal Setting (Ire) *Sir Mark Prescott*   a67
2 br g King's Theatre (Ire) - Cartier Bijoux
2⁸ˢʷ 1⁸ˢᵈ **1-1-2 £3,835**

Regal Song (Ire) *T J Etherington*   79
7 b g Anita's Prince - Song Beam
20⁵ᵍ 13⁵ᵍᶠ 2⁵ᵍˢ 11⁵ʰʸ 13⁵ᵍˢ 6⁵ᵍ 1⁵ᵍˢ
10⁵ᵍ 21⁵ᵍ 5⁵ᵍˢ **1-1-10 £15,724**

Regal Vintage (USA) *C Grant*   74
3 ch g Kingmambo (USA) - Grapevine (Ire)
6⁷ᵍᶠ 7⁸ᵍᶠ 11¹¹ᵍ **0-0-3**

Regency Malaya *M F Harris*   54
2 b f Sri Pekan (USA) - Paola (Fr)
9⁶ˢᵈ 7⁷ᵍᶠ 10⁶ᵍˢ 6⁷ᵍᶠ 7⁷ᵍˢ 9⁸ᵍˢ **0-0-6**

Regent's Secret (USA) *J S Goldie*   83
3 br c Cryptoclearance (USA) - Misty Regent (Can)
3⁷ᵍᶠ 13⁸ᵍ 3⁹ᵍ 9⁸ᵍˢ 3⁷ᵍᶠ 16⁸ᵍᶠ 7⁸ᵍᶠ 8¹²ᵍᶠ

4¹²ᵍ 16¹⁰ᵍˢ **0-2-10 £9,739**

Regimental Dance *C Grant*   60 a12
3 b f Groom Dancer (USA) - Enlisted (Ire)
8⁷ˢᵈ 8⁸ˢʷ 5⁷ᵍᶠ 6⁷ᵍᶠ 2⁷ᵍᶠ 6⁷ᶠ 4⁷ᵍᶠ 16⁸ᵍ
7⁷ᵍᶠ 8¹²ᵍ 7¹²ᵍᶠ 8¹⁰ᶠ 8⁷ᵍˢ **0-1-13 £1,108**

Regulated (Ire) *J A Osborne*   71
2 b g Alzao (USA) - Royal Hostess (Ire)
5⁷ᵍᶠ 2⁷ᵍᶠ 10⁷ᵍ 4⁸ᵍᶠ 5⁸ᵍ 11⁷ᶠ **0-1-6**
£1,371

Rehia *J W Hills*   60
2 b f Desert Style (USA) - Goes A Treat (Ire)
9⁶ᵍᶠ 1⁵ᵍ 3⁵ᵍᶠ 5⁵ᵍᶠ 5⁵ˢ 7⁵ᵍᶠ **1-1-6**
£3,427

Reidies Choice *J G Given*   86
2 b c Royal Applause - Fairy Ring (Ire)
1⁵ᵍᶠ 2⁵ᵍᶠ 8⁶ᵍᶠ 7⁵ᵍˢ 15⁶ᵍˢ 8⁵ˢ **1-1-6**
£5,606

Reign Of Fire (Ire) *J W Hills*   60 a61
2 b f Perugino (USA) - White Heat
4⁸ᵍᶠ 6⁷ˢᵈ **0-0-2 £549**

Reine Cleopatre (Ire) *L M Cumani*
3 b f Danehill (USA) - Nomothetis (Ire)
PU⁸ᵍᶠ **0-0-1**

Reine Marie *Don Enrico Incisa*   1
4 b f Tragic Role (USA) - Regal Salute
10⁷ᶠ **0-0-1**

Rejess (Ire) *J D Czerpak*   72
3 b c Septieme Ciel (USA) - Vallee Dansante (USA)
4¹⁰ᵍ 10¹⁰ᵍᶠ 7¹¹ᵍᶠ 6¹²ᵍᶠ 12¹⁴ᶠ **0-0-5**
£1,306

Rejuvenate (Ire) *Mrs A J Perrett*   95
3 ch c Grand Lodge (USA) - Nawara
1⁸ᵍᶠ 3⁹ᵍᶠ **1-1-2 £3,862**

Relative Hero (Ire) *Miss S J Wilton*   66 a66
3 ch g Entrepreneur - Aunty (Fr)
5⁸ˢᵈ 5⁷ˢᵈ 3⁷ᶠ 4⁹ˢᵈ 10⁸ᵍᶠ 13⁸ᵍᶠ 1⁷ᵍᶠ 1⁷ᵍ
6⁷ᵍᶠ 5⁷ᶠ **2-1-10 £7,233**

Relaxed (USA) *Sir Michael Stoute*   77
2 b f Royal Academy (USA) - Sleep Easy (USA)
2⁷ᵍᶠ **0-1-1 £1,323**

Relaxed Gesture (Ire) *D K Weld*   108 a79
2 ch c Indian Ridge - Token Gesture (Ire)
3⁷ᵍ 1⁷ᵍᶠ 2⁸ᵍʸ 8⁹ᶠᵗ **1-2-4 £25,649**

Rellim *R Wilman*   56 a67
4 b f Rudimentary (USA) - Tycoon Girl (Ire)
7⁵ˢᵈ 11⁵ˢʷ 2⁵ˢᵈ 3⁵ˢᵈ 6⁵ᵍᶠ 6⁵ᵍᶠ 7⁵ᵍᶠ 4⁵ˢᵈ
9⁵ˢᵈ 6⁵ᵍᶠ 4⁵ˢᵈ 4⁵ᵍᶠ **0-3-12 £1,962**

Remedy *Sir Mark Prescott*   a55
4 gr f Pivotal - Doctor Bid (USA)
5⁸ˢᵈ 10¹⁰ˢᵈ **0-0-2**

Remembrance *J M P Eustace*   73 a73
3 b g Sabrehill (USA) - Perfect Poppy
4⁸ᵍᶠ 13¹¹ᵍᶠ 5⁸ᵍᶠ 9¹⁰ᵍ 2¹⁰ˢᵈ 7¹⁰ˢᵈ **0-1-6**
£1,281

Reminiscent (Ire) *R F Johnson Houghton*   60 a77
4 b g Kahyasi - Eliza Orzeszkowa (Ire)
2¹⁴ˢʷ 9¹⁴ᵍ 11¹⁶ˢᵈ 5¹⁵ᵍᶠ 9¹⁶ˢᵈ 3¹⁰ᵍᶠ 4¹³ᵍᶠ
5¹²ˢᵈ **0-2-8 £2,320**

Ren's Magic *J R Jenkins*   40 a55
5 gr g Petong - Bath
2¹²ˢᵈ 9¹³ˢᵈ 12¹²ˢᵈ 7¹²ᶠ 8¹⁰ᶠ 8¹³ᵍᶠ 4¹¹ᵍ
10¹²ᵍᶠ 4¹⁴ᵍᶠ **0-1-9 £1,362**

Rendoro (USA) *R Hannon*   a69
2 c c Crafty Prospector (USA) - Renge (Ire)
6⁸ˢᵈ 3⁸ˢᵈ **0-1-2 £334**

Reno *C W Thornton* — 56
3 ch f Efisio - Los Alamos
10^{8g} 6^{9gs} 4^{10gs} 18^{8g} 9^{12sd} **0-0-5 £435**

Reno's Magic *W G M Turner* — a35
2 b f Hello Mister - Mountain Magic
9^{6gf} 8^{6sd} **0-0-2**

Renzo (Ire) *John A Harris* — 47 a53
10 b g Alzao (USA) - Watership (USA)
3^{16sd} 10^{18g} **0-1-2 £421**

Repeat (Ire) *K A Ryan* — 55 a56
3 ch g Night Shift (USA) - Identical (Ire)
8^{6sd} 3^{7sd} 5^{7sw} 3^{6sd} 13^{6gf} 7^{6gf} 15^{7gf} 3^{7sd}
0-3-8 £1,159

Repertory *M S Saunders* — 116
10 b g Anshan - Susie's Baby
2^{5g} 2^{5gf} 1^{5gf} 6^{5g} 2^{5gf} 3^{5g} 6^{5g} 4^{5g} 7^{5gf}
1^{5gs} 14^{5ho} **2-4-11 £86,866**

Repetoire (Fr) *K O Cunningham-Brown* — 67
3 ch f Zafonic (USA) - Lady Kate (USA)
4^{12gf} 9^{10gf} BD^{8gf} **0-0-3 £315**

Replacement Pet (Ire) *H S Howe* — 52
6 b m Petardia - Richardstown Lass (Ire)
10^{12g} 6^{11gf} 8^{10f} 5^{10gf} 1^{10gf} 5^{10gf} 12^{10gf}
7^{10gf} 7^{10gf} **1-0-9 £4,114**

Reprise *J H M Gosden* — 69
3 b f Darshaan - Rapid Repeat (Ire)
13^{7gf} 4^{10gf} **0-0-2 £429**

Repulse Bay (Ire) *J S Goldie* — 69 a51
5 b g Barathea (Ire) - Bourbon Topsy
6^{8sd} 6^{8sd} 5^{12sd} 8^{8gf} 12^{10gf} 7^{8gs} 16^{6g}
8^{8gf} 1^{12g} 7^{12gf} 4^{12f} 2^{12gf} 1^{10gf} 4^{12gf} 2^{12g}
10^{10gf} 3^{11gf} 5^{12gf} 13^{11g} 7^{10gf} **2-2-20 £16,316**

Repute *G A Swinbank* — 48
5 b g Unfuwain (USA) - Someone Special
4^{12gf} 9^{10gf} **0-0-2**

Requestor *T J Fitzgerald* — 32 a26
8 br g Distinctly North (USA) - Bebe Altesse (Ger)
13^{11sd} 13^{8sd} 12^{8gf} **0-0-3**

Requite (USA) *Kathy Walsh* — 95 a87
3 b c Red Ransom (USA) - Rhetorical Lass (USA)
2^{8sd} 1^{8sd} 6^{9g} 4^{8sd} 5^{10gf} **1-1-5 £7,158**

Rescind (Ire) *Jedd O'Keeffe* — 34
3 b f Revoque (Ire) - Sunlit Ride
10^{8gf} 15^{7f} 12^{7gs} **0-0-3**

Researched (Ire) *Sir Michael Stoute* — 118
4 b g Danehill (USA) - Sought Out (Ire)
1^{10gf} 2^{12gf} 13^{10gf} 1^{12g} 8^{14gf} 2^{11gf} 5^{12f}
2-2-7 £64,008

Reservoir (Ire) *W J Haggas* — 71
2 b c Green Desert (USA) - Spout
7^{7gf} 4^{7s} 3^{8gf} **0-0-3 £1,136**

Residential *Mrs A J Perrett* — 68
2 ch c Zilzal (USA) - House Hunting
5^{8gf} **0-0-1**

Resilience *B Mactaggart* — 48
3 b f Most Welcome - Abstone Queen
8^{5gs} 10^{5f} 7^{7gf} 7^{7gf} 5^{7gf} 16^{6gf} 8^{10f} 7^{9gf}
0-0-8

Resonance *Mrs A J Perrett* — a56
2 b f Slip Anchor - Music In My Life (Ire)
9^{7sd} **0-0-1**

Resonate (Ire) *A G Newcombe* — 80 a65
5 b h Erin's Isle - Petronelli (USA)
6^{8sd} 6^{7sd} 7^{7sw} 8^{7sd} 11^{7gf} 7^{8gf} 12^{7sw} 3^{9gf}
1^{7g} 5^{8f} 2^{7gf} 11^{7s} **1-2-12 £12,552**

Resourceful (Ire) *T D Easterby* — 17
3 b f Entrepreneur - No Reservations (Ire)
16^{7gf} **0-0-1**

Resplendent Cee (Ire) *P W Harris* — 109
4 ch c Polar Falcon (USA) - Western Friend (USA)
2^{6gf} 1^{6s} 8^{6gf} 3^{6gf} 7^{6gs} 1^{6gf} 8^{7gf} 5^{6g}
3^{7gf} 10^{6gf} 15^{6g} **2-1-11 £42,762**

Resplendent King (USA) *T G Mills* — 78
2 b g King Of Kings (Ire) - Sister Fromseattle (USA)
8^{7f} 3^{7g} 11^{7g} 4^{8gf} 16^{7gf} **0-0-5 £1,137**

Resplendent One (Ire) *T G Mills* — 78
2 b c Marju (Ire) - Licentious
13^{7sd} 18^{9f} **1-0-2 £3,783**

Resplendent Star (Ire) *Mrs L Wadham* — 69 a90
6 b g Northern Baby (Can) - Whitethroat
6^{12sd} 5^{13sd} 4^{12gf} 9^{16gf} **0-0-4 £1,022**

Resplendently *P W Harris* — 16 a54
3 b c Piccolo - Llyn Gwynant
11^{8sd} 11^{8g} 16^{8gf} **0-0-3**

Ressource (Fr) *G L Moore* — a2
4 b c Broadway Flyer (USA) - Rayonne
12^{16sd} **0-0-1**

Restart (Ire) *P C Haslam* — 42 a63
2 b g Revoque (Ire) - Stargard
6^{5gf} 17^{6gf} 3^{7sd} **0-1-3 £320**

Retail Therapy (Ire) *M A Buckley* — 36 a10
3 b f Bahhare (USA) - Elect (USA)
15^{7g} 10^{12g} 9^{8gf} 8^{9sd} **0-0-4**

Retirement *M H Tompkins* — 82
4 b g Zilzal (USA) - Adeptation (USA)
7^{8gs} 7^{8gs} 2^{9gf} 4^{8gf} 2^{9s} 1^{9g} **1-2-6**
£6,580

Return To Due'S *Mrs J R Ramsden* — 36
3 b g Revoque (Ire) - High Matinee
8^{6gf} **0-0-1**

Returnofthefairy *S Woodman* — 25
3 b f Bluegrass Prince (Ire) - Brown Fairy (USA)
12^{7g} 14^{9gf} 15^{10gf} 7^{8gf} **0-0-4**

Reveillez *J R Fanshawe* — 99
4 gr g First Trump - Amalancher (USA)
4^{12gf} 2^{14gf} 2^{14gf} 1^{12gf} 2^{12gf} 4^{12gf} 3^{15gf}
6^{12gf} 1^{12g} 3^{12gf} **2-4-10 £24,666**

Revenue (Ire) *M L W Bell* — 102
3 ch c Cadeaux Genereux - Bareilly (USA)
4^{6g} 4^{6gf} 8^{5g} 11^{6gf} **0-0-4 £2,365**

Reversionary *M W Easterby* — 50
2 b c Poyle George - Harold's Girl (Fr)
8^{5f} 5^{5g} 6^{6gs} 13^{6g} **0-0-4**

Reverso (Fr) *N J Hawke*
3 b c Kaldounevees (Fr) - Sweet Racine (Fr)
8^{14gf} **0-0-1**

Revolve *H Morrison* — 72
3 b g Pivotal - Alpine Time (Ire)
5^{8g} 5^{8gf} 8^{10gf} 2^{7gf} 16^{7gf} 2^{7g} **0-2-6**
£1,574

Rewayaat *B Hanbury* — 78
2 b f Bahhare (USA) - Alumisiyah (USA)
5^{5gf} 2^{5g} 1^{5f} 7^{5gf} 14^{5g} **1-0-5 £5,203**

Reyadi (Ire) *B Hanbury* — 88
3 b c Peintre Celebre (USA) - Valley Of Hope (USA)
2^{10g} 4^{12g} 18^{9f} 28^{9f} **1-2-4 £10,271**

Rheinpark *J R Best* — a1
4 ch g Cadeaux Genereux - Marina Park
11^{8sd} 15^{6sd} 8^{6sd} **0-0-3**

Rhetoric (Ire) *D G Bridgwater* — a28

4 b g Desert King (Ire) - Squaw Talk (USA)
12¹⁶ˢᵈ 9¹⁶ˢᵈ 5¹⁵ˢʷ **0-0-3**

Rhetorical *Sir Mark Prescott*   43 a46
2 b g Unfuwain (USA) - Miswaki Belle (USA)
7⁸ˢʷ 6⁷ᵍ 9⁶ᵍ 9⁷ᵍˢ **0-0-4**

Rhinefield Boy *J S Goldie*   46
2 ch g Wolfhound (USA) - Rhinefield Beauty (Ire)
12⁶ᵍᶠ 7⁷ᶠ 9⁶ᵍ **0-0-3**

Rhinefield Lass *J S Goldie*   40
3 ch f Bijou D'Inde - Rhinefield Beauty (Ire)
11⁸ᵍᶠ 13⁶ᶠ 10⁷ᵍᶠ 8⁵ᵍᶠ 3⁵ᵍᶠ 20⁵ᵍᶠ 15⁵ᶠ
0-1-7 £417

Rhossili (Ire) *John Allen*   18
3 b g Perugino (USA) - Velinowski
10¹⁰ᵍᶠ **0-0-1**

Rianatta (Ire) *P Butler*
4 b f Nicolotte - Asturiana
20⁷ᵍᶠ **0-0-1**

Ribbons And Bows (Ire) *C A Cyzer*   88 a71
3 gr f Dr Devious (Ire) - Nichodoula
7⁸ᵍ 5¹⁰ᵍ 6¹⁰ᵍᶠ 10¹²ᵍᶠ 11⁸ˢᵈ **0-0-5**

Rich Affair *Sir Michael Stoute*   99
3 br f Machiavellian (USA) - Much Too Risky
4¹²ᵍᶠ 2¹²ᵍᶠ 7¹²ᵍ 1¹¹ᵍᶠ 7¹²ᵍᶠ 3¹⁴ˢ **1-2-6**
£9,746

Rich Dancer *J D Bethell*   54
3 b f Halling (USA) - Fairy Flight (Ire)
8⁸ᵍ 3¹⁰ᵍᶠ 13¹⁰ˢ 11⁷ᵍᶠ **0-0-4 £567**

Richard *P Mitchell*   57 a6
3 b/br c Distinctly North (USA) - Murmuring
5⁶ᵍᶠ 9⁵ˢ 10⁵ᵍᶠ 10⁵ᶠ 16⁷ˢᵈ **0-0-5**

Richemaur (Ire) *M H Tompkins*   89 a71
3 b f Alhaarth (Ire) - Lady President (USA)
7¹⁰ᵍᶠ 8¹⁰ᵍᶠ 10⁸ˢᵈ 16¹²ᵍ **0-0-4**

Richie Boy *M A Jarvis*   46
2 b c Dr Fong (USA) - Alathezal (USA)
9⁶ᵍ **0-0-1**

Richtee (Ire) *R A Fahey*   52
2 ch f Desert Sun - Santarene (Ire)
8⁵ᵍᶠ 6⁵ᵍᶠ 9⁶ᵍᶠ **0-0-3**

Ricky Martan *G C Bravery*   62
2 ch c Foxhound (USA) - Cyrillic
12⁵ᵍᶠ 6⁵ᵍᶠ 4⁶ᵍᶠ **0-0-3 £315**

Ridapour (Ire) *D J Wintle*   a8
4 b g Kahyasi - Ridiyara (Ire)
9¹²ˢᵈ **0-0-1**

Ride The Tiger (Ire) *R Wilman*   a56
6 ch g Imp Society (USA) - Krisdaline (USA)
2¹²ˢʷ **0-1-1 £846**

Ridgeback *B W Hills*   76
3 ch c Indian Ridge - Valbra
6⁶ᵍ 3⁶ᵍ 1⁶ᶠ **1-1-3 £5,872**

Ridgeway (Ire) *M W Easterby*   30
8 b g Indian Ridge - Regal Promise
15¹²ᵍᶠ **0-0-1**

Ridicule *J G Portman*   77
4 b g Piccolo - Mockingbird
18⁶ᵍᶠ 9⁶ᵍᶠ 4⁶ᵍᶠ 6⁶ᵍᶠ 3⁶ᵍˢ 8⁷ᵍ 5⁶ᵍᶠ 4⁵ᵍᶠ
0-2-8 £1,030

Rifleman (Ire) *Mrs A Duffield*   89 a76
3 ch g Starborough - En Garde (USA)
6⁸ˢᵈ 3¹⁰ᵍᶠ 7⁸ˢᵈ 1⁸ᵍᶠ 4⁸ᵍᶠ 7⁸ᵍᶠ 4⁷ᵍᶠ 9⁷ᵍ
19⁸ᵍᶠ 3⁷ᵍᶠ 3⁸ᵍᶠ 5⁸ᵍᶠ 3⁸ᵍᶠ 4⁸ᵍᶠ 12¹⁰ᵍ **1-5-15**
£18,780

Rigadoon (Ire) *M W Easterby*   43

7 b g Be My Chief (USA) - Loucoum (Fr)
14¹⁶ᵍᶠ 6¹⁶ᵍˢ 8¹⁷ᵍᶠ **0-0-3**

Right Approach *Sir Michael Stoute*   115
4 b c Machiavellian (USA) - Abbey Strand (USA)
1⁸ᵍ 3⁸ᵍᶠ 3⁸ᵍᶠ 5¹¹ᵍᶠ 8⁹ᵍᶠ **1-1-5 £55,850**

Righty Ho *W H Tinning*   51
9 b g Reprimand - Challanging
3¹²ᵍᶠ 2¹⁴ᵍᶠ 12¹²ᵍᶠ 7¹²ᵍˢ **0-2-4 £1,324**

Rigonza *T D Easterby*   68
2 ch g Vettori (Ire) - Desert Nomad
5⁶ᵍˢ 4⁶ᵍˢ 3⁷ᶠ 4⁶ᵍ 6⁷ᵍˢ **0-1-5 £1,552**

Riley Boys (Ire) *J G Given*   63 a63
2 ch c Most Welcome - Scarlett Holly
11⁶ᵍˢ 3⁶ᵍ 3⁶ˢᵈ 9⁶ᵍᶠ 9⁶ᶠᵗ 10⁸ᵍˢ **0-2-6**
£1,102

Rileys Dream *B J Llewellyn*   68
4 b f Rudimentary (USA) - Dorazine
12⁶ᵍ 14⁶ᵍᶠ 9⁷ᵍᶠ 13⁸ᵍ 1⁷ᵍˢ 15⁷ᶠ 14⁷ᵍᶠ
3⁷ᵍᶠ 16⁷ᵍᶠ 10⁷ˢ 12⁷ᵍᶠ 14⁸ᵍˢ **1-1-12 £4,578**

Rileys Rocket *R Hollinshead*   46 a50
4 b f Makbul - Star Of Flanders
9⁷ˢᵈ 3⁹ˢʷ 6⁹ˢʷ 13⁹ˢᵈ 9⁸ᵍᶠ 9¹⁰ᶠ 5¹²ᵍˢ **0-1-7**
£465

Rimrod (USA) *A M Balding*   113
3 b c Danzig (USA) - Annie Edge
4⁸ᵍᶠ 3⁸ᵍᶠ 1⁷ᵍ 3⁷ᵍᶠ 7⁷ᵛˢ 6⁷ᵍᶠ **1-1-6**
£37,770

Ring Of Destiny *P W Harris*   99
4 b g Magic Ring (Ire) - Canna
7¹²ᵍᶠ 16¹²ᵍᶠ 3¹²ᵍ 14¹²ᵍᶠ 1¹²ᵍᶠ 8¹³ᵍᶠ **1-1-6**
£8,360

Ringing Hill *H Candy*   56
4 b f Charnwood Forest (Ire) - Not Before Time (Ire)
15¹⁰ᵍˢ **0-0-1**

Ringmoor Down *D W P Arbuthnot*   101
4 b f Pivotal - Floppie (Fr)
12⁶ᵍ 16⁶ᶠ 3⁶ᵍ 6⁶ᵍ 1⁶ᵍ 6⁷ᵍᶠ 5⁶ᵍᶠ 15⁶ᵍᶠ
9⁶ᵍ 2⁶ᵍᶠ 4⁶ᵍᶠ 3⁶ᵍᶠ **2-3-12 £31,107**

Ringside Jack *C W Fairhurst*   57
7 b g Batshoof - Celestine
10¹³ᵍˢ 8¹³ᵍˢ 9¹⁴ʰʸ 6¹⁴ᵍᶠ 7¹³ᵍˢ 9¹³ᵍᶠ 3¹⁶ᵍ
4¹⁶ᵍᶠ 4¹⁶ᵍᶠ **0-1-9 £1,815**

Ringsider (Ire) *G A Butler*   75
2 ch g Docksider (USA) - Red Comes Up (USA)
10⁵ᵍᶠ 1⁷ᵍᶠ **1-0-2 £6,938**

Rinjani (USA) *D R Loder*   83
2 b c Gone West (USA) - Ringshaan (Fr)
4⁷ᵍᶠ 1⁸ᵍᶠ **1-0-2 £4,597**

Rinneen (Ire) *R Hannon*   69 a47
2 b f Bien Bien (USA) - Sparky's Song
8⁵ᵍᶠ 3⁶ᵍᶠ 8⁶ᵍᶠ 10⁷ˢᵈ 12⁸ᵍ **0-0-5 £844**

Rio Branco *B W Hills*   53
2 b f Efisio - Los Alamos
7⁶ᵍ **0-0-1**

Rio De Jumeirah *C E Brittain*   69
2 b f Seeking The Gold (USA) - Tegwen (USA)
3⁵ᵍ 11⁷ᵍᶠ 3⁷ᵍᶠ 5⁶ᵍᶠ **0-1-4 £1,422**

Rio's Diamond *M J Ryan*   a52
6 b m Formidable (USA) - Rio Piedras
4¹⁰ˢᵈ 11⁸ˢᵈ **0-0-2**

Ripcord (Ire) *Lady Herries*   21
5 b g Diesis - Native Twine
14¹¹ᵍᶠ **0-0-1**

Ripple Effect *C A Dwyer*   77 a76
3 ch f Elmaamul (USA) - Sharp Chief

2^6sd 6^7sd 3^7gf 4^6gf 1^6f 5^5gf 3^5gf **1-3-7**
£6,988

Riquewihr *J A R Toller* — 64
3 ch f Compton Place - Juvenilia (Ire)
1^6gf 14^8gs **1-0-2 £3,311**

Rise *Andrew Reid* — 70 a81
2 b f Polar Falcon (USA) - Splice
4^5f 3^6gf 5^6f 2^6ft 3^7sd 1^7sd **1-3-6**
£6,109

Rising Shadow (Ire) *R A Fahey* — 73 a81
2 b g Efisio - Jouet
10^6gf 1^6g 3^6sd 5^7g **1-0-4 £2,946**

Risk Free *P D Evans* — 71 a79
6 ch g Risk Me (Fr) - Princess Lily
10^5sd 12^8sd 9^7sd 2^7sd 6^7sd 16sd 1^7f
10^6gf 5^7gf 3^7gf 9^7gf 7^8gf 1^8ft 8^11gf 5^8gf 3^7gf
5^7sw **3-4-18 £14,342**

Risk Of Lightning *Miss Z C Davison* — 12
7 ch m Risk Me (Fr) - Lightning Legend
16^8s 11^8gs **0-0-2**

Risk Taker *B W Hills* — 103
3 ch c Rainbow Quest (USA) - Post Modern (USA)
1^12gf 3^12g 10^12gf 13^10gf 13^12gs 13^10gs
1-0-6 £12,834

Riska King *R A Fahey* — 81
3 b g Forzando - Artistic Licence
4^7gf 4^7gf 4^7gs 4^8g 8^7gf 13^8gf 1^7gf 7^7gf
1-0-8 £11,314

Risque Sermon *Miss B Sanders* — 39 a61
5 b g Risk Me (Fr) - Sunday Sport Star
6^6sd 11^6gf 9^7g 2^6sd 8^5gf **0-1-5 £898**

Risucchio *A W Carroll*
4 ch g Thatching - Skip To Somerfield
16^6sd **0-0-1**

Rita's Rock Ape *R Brotherton* — a65
8 b m Mon Tresor - Failand
8^5sd 8^6sw 4^5sw 5^5sd **0-0-4**

Riva Royale *I A Wood* — 90 a71
3 b f Royal Applause - Regatta
3^5gf 11^6sd 2^6gf 7^5gf 3^7gf 5^7gf 10^6gf
12^7gf 1^7s **1-2-9 £11,321**

Rival (Ire) *S T Lewis*
4 b g Desert Style (Ire) - Arab Scimetar (Ire)
14^7g 11^12f 15^11gf 16^8gf 15^8gf **0-0-5**

Rivelli (Ire) *P R Webber* — 60
4 b f Lure (USA) - Kama Tashoof
7^8f 7^10gf 19^7gf **0-0-3**

Rivendell *M Wigham* — 9
7 b m Saddlers' Hall (Ire) - Fairy Kingdom
12^9sd 8^10f **0-0-2**

River Belle *A P Jarvis* — 99
2 ch f Lahib (USA) - Dixie Favor (USA)
1^6gf 1^6g 5^7gf 6^8gf **2-0-4 £38,871**

River Canyon (Ire) *W Storey* — 54
7 b g College Chapel - Na-Ammah (Ire)
7^8gs 18^8gf **0-0-2**

River Days (Ire) *Miss Gay Kelleway* — 53 a78
5 b m Tagula (Ire) - Straw Boater
1^5sd 4^5sd 1^5sw 6^6sd 12^5sd 1^5sd 4^6sd 4^5gf
3-0-8 £10,225

River Ensign *W M Brisbourne* — a38
10 br m River God (USA) - Ensigns Kit
4^9sd **0-0-1**

River Falcon *J S Goldie* — 85
3 b g Pivotal - Pearly River

6^5gs 4^6gf 3^6s 12^6gs 1^5gf 4^6gf 2^5gf 12^6gf
7^5gf 11^6gf 24^6g **1-4-11 £19,003**

River Gypsy *D R C Elsworth* — a69
2 b c In The Wings - River Erne (USA)
4^8sd **0-0-1**

River Lark (USA) *M A Buckley* — 51
4 b f Miswaki (USA) - Gold Blossom (USA)
5^6gf 14^6f 7^7g 16^6gf 13^5gf **1-0-5 £5,388**

River Line (USA) *C W Fairhurst* — 51
2 b g Keos (USA) - Portio (USA)
11^6g 9^6gf 9^8g **0-0-3**

River Nurey (Ire) *B W Hills* — 70
2 b c Fasliyev (USA) - Dundel (Ire)
6^6g 9^6gf 12^6g 5^6gf 2^7gf **0-1-5 £2,246**

River Of Babylon *M L W Bell* — 60
2 b f Marju (Ire) - Isle Of Flame
5^8gf 7^8s **0-0-2**

River Of Fire *C N Kellett* — 46 a50
5 ch g Dilum (USA) - Bracey Brook
3^12sd 8^16sd 8^12sd 8^15sd 7^14sd 5U^12gf 4^14gf
1^16gf 8^16g 3^14gf 6^14f 13^16sd **1-1-12 £4,319**

River Tern *J M Bradley* — 32
10 b g Puissance - Millaine
11^5gf 13^5gf 9^5gf **0-0-3**

River Treat (Fr) *G Wragg* — 77
2 ch c Irish River (Fr) - Dance Treat (USA)
5^6gf 2^6gf 4^6gf **0-1-3 £1,728**

Riverboat Dancer *S Dow* — 70 a60
3 b f Muhtarram (USA) - South Wind
14^6sd 8^7sd 11^8gf 8^7gf 9^10gf 3^10gf 5^9gf
7^10gf **0-1-8 £1,591**

Riyadh *J R Fanshawe* — 95
5 ch g Caerleon (USA) - Ausherra (USA)
11^19gf 4^14gf 17^16gs 6^16gf 14^21gs **0-0-5**
£1,373

Ro Eridani *T J Etherington* — 51
3 b f Binary Star (USA) - Hat Hill
6^7gf 8^7g 2^9f 15^10f 10^9g 13^12gf 6^8g **0-1-6**
£1,144

Roaming Vagabond (Ire) *G G Margarson* — 42
2 ch c Spectrum (Ire) - Fiveofive (Ire)
8^7gf 8^7s **0-0-2**

Roan Raider (USA) *M J Polglase* — 47 a42
3 gr/ro g El Prado (Ire) - Flirtacious Wonder (USA)
10^8sd 4^10gf 15^10gf 5^7f 4^8gf 3^7gf 15^8gf
14^16gf 8^10gf 12^9gf 3^8f 6^7sw 2^9gf 4^6g 6^6gs **0-2-15**
£2,337

Roanokee *R Guest* — a37
3 gr g College Chapel - Grey Again
12^6sd 11^8sd **0-0-2**

Robbie Can Can *A W Carroll* — 56 a51
4 b g Robellino (USA) - Can Can Lady
5^12sd 3^16sd 5^12gf 3^18gf 7^16gf 2^12g 6^14gf
1^12gf **1-3-8 £4,229**

Robe Chinoise *J L Dunlop* — 89
4 b f Robellino (USA) - Kiliniski
6^14g 4^12g 7^14gf 4^12gf 6^12gf **0-0-5 £5,389**

Robespierre *H Morrison* — 56
3 b g Polar Falcon (USA) - Go For Red (Ire)
3^7gf 8^6s 8^7gs 14^8gf 6^5gf 3^6s 5^6f 17^6gf
12^6f **0-2-9 £1,097**

Robin Sharp *J Akehurst* — a65
5 ch h First Trump - Mo Stopher
4^7sd 2^7sd 1^7sw 16^7g PU^7sd 12^7sd **1-1-6**
£4,077

Robocop *S Kirk* 85
2 b g Robellino (USA) - Seattle Ribbon (USA)
8⁵ᵍᶠ 3⁶ᶠ 4⁶ᵍᶠ 1⁶ᵍ 8⁷ᵍᶠ 6⁷ᵍ 10⁶ᵍᶠ **1-1-7**
£5,755

Robshaw *T P Tate* 63
3 b g Robellino (USA) - Panorama
14⁶ᵍᶠ 6⁷ᵍᶠ 7⁷ᵍˢ 11⁸ᵍ **0-0-4**

Robwillcall *A Berry* 70 a53
3 b f Timeless Times (USA) - Lavernock Lady
11⁵ᵍˢ 7⁶ᵍ 11⁶ʰʸ 6⁵ᶠ 1⁵ᵍᶠ 4⁵ˢᵈ 11⁵ᵍᶠ 6⁵ᶠ
4⁵ᵍˢ 17⁵ᵍ 13⁵ᵍˢ 11⁵ᵍ 8⁵ᵍˢ **1-0-13 £4,437**

Roches Fleuries (Ire) *Andrew Turnell* 37
3 b f Barathea (Ire) - Princess Caraboo (Ire)
14¹⁰ˢ 5¹⁰ᵍᶠ **0-0-2**

Rocinante (Ire) *J J Quinn* 63 a63
3 b g Desert Story (Ire) - Antapoura (Ire)
10⁵ᶠ 2⁶ᵍᶠ 6⁶ᵍˢ 3⁸ᵍᶠ 5⁹ˢʷ 5⁸ᵍᶠ 4⁷ᵍˢ 4⁶ᵍᶠ
3⁷ᵍᶠ 19⁶ᵍ 18⁵ᵈ 9⁹ˢᵈ **1-5-12 £4,093**

Rock Concert *I W McInnes* 60 a66
5 b m Bishop Of Cashel - Summer Pageant
8⁸ˢʷ 12⁸ˢᵈ 11¹⁰ᵍᶠ 9¹⁰ᵍᶠ 1⁸ᶠ 6⁸ᶠ 8⁸ᵍᶠ 4⁸ᶠ
17⁸ᵍᶠ 10⁸ˢʷ 7⁷ᶠ 5¹⁰ᵍˢ 3⁸ᵍᶠ 3⁸ᵍᶠ 2⁹ˢᵈ **1-3-15**
£5,069

Rock Forest *M Mullineaux* 28
4 b g Superlative - Rockefillee
14¹⁰ᵍˢ 10¹³ᵍᶠ 11⁸ᵍ 10⁸ᵍᶠ 18¹⁰ᵍˢ 17⁷ᵍᶠ
0-0-6

Rock Lobster *J G Given* 64 a63
2 b c Desert Sun - Distant Music
1⁸ˢʷ 4⁸ᵍ **1-0-2 £3,238**

Rock Of Cashel (Ire) *A P O'Brien* 89
2 b c Danehill (USA) - Offshore Boom
2⁷ᵍ 2⁷ˢ 3⁷ᵍᶠ 2⁷ᵍ 8⁸ᵍᶠ **0-4-5 £8,129**

Rock'n Cold (Ire) *J G Given* a56
5 b g Bigstone (Ire) - Unalaska (Ire)
3¹²ˢᵈ 13¹²ˢᵈ 7¹³ˢᵈ 5¹³ˢᵈ 5¹²ˢᵈ 6¹²ˢᵈ **0-1-6**
£533

Rockabelle *J White* 29
3 b f Bigstone (Ire) - Belle De Nuit (Ire)
11⁵ˢʷ 10⁷ᵍᶠ 9⁶ᶠ 15⁶ᵍᶠ **0-0-4**

Rockerfella Lad (Ire) *M Todhunter* 70
3 b g Danetime (Ire) - Soucaro
7⁸ᵍᶠ 14⁸ᵍᶠ 14⁸ᵍᶠ 11⁷ᵍᶠ 1⁸ˢ 2⁸ˢ 4⁸ᵍˢ
5¹⁰ᵍᶠ 3⁹ᵍ 7¹⁰ᵍ **1-2-10 £5,638**

Rocket Force (USA) *E A L Dunlop* 104
3 ch c Spinning World (USA) - Pat Us (USA)
3¹⁰ᵍᶠ 2¹⁰ᵍᶠ 7¹²ᵍᶠ **0-1-3 £10,890**

Rocket Ship *R Charlton* 92
3 b c Pennekamp (USA) - Rock The Boat
4⁹ᵍ 1¹⁰ᵍˢ 9¹¹ᵍ 2¹⁰ᵍᶠ 11¹²ᵍˢ 4¹¹ˢ **1-0-6**
£13,644

Rockets 'n Rollers (Ire) *R Hannon* 106
3 b c Victory Note (USA) - Holly Bird
4⁷ᵍᶠ 13⁸ᵍ 7⁸ᵍᶠ **0-0-3 £2,500**

Rockley Bay (Ire) *P J Makin* 56
2 b c Mujadil (USA) - Kilkee Bay (Ire)
11⁶ᵍᶠ 5⁶ᵍˢ **0-0-2**

Rockspur (Ire) *Mrs P N Dutfield* a47
3 b f Flying Spur (Aus) - Over The Rocks
8⁶ˢᵈ 4⁷ˢᵈ 10⁷ˢᵈ **0-0-3**

Rockwelda *M P Muggeridge*
8 b m Weld - Hill's Rocket
6¹⁴ᵍᶠ **0-0-1**

Rocky Rambo *R D E Woodhouse*
2 b g Sayaarr (USA) - Kingston Girl

12¹⁰ᵍᶠ **0-0-1**

Rocky Reppin *J Balding* 67
3 b g Rock City - Tino Reppin
5⁸ᵍᶠ 6⁸ᵍ 4¹⁰ᵍᶠ 8⁸ᵍᶠ **0-0-4 £533**

Roehampton *Sir Michael Stoute* 73
2 b c Machiavellian (USA) - Come On Rosi
10⁸ᵍᶠ 1⁸ˢ **1-0-2 £3,542**

Rojabaa *W G M Turner* 59
4 b g Anabaa (USA) - Slava (USA)
2¹⁰ᶠ 11¹²ᶠ 4¹⁰ᶠ 3¹⁰ᶠ 9¹⁰ᶠ 4¹²ᶠ 5⁸ᵍᶠ 3¹⁰ᵍᶠ
4¹²ᵍᶠ 11¹ᵍᶠ 1¹⁰ᶠ **2-2-11 £6,212**

Rolex Free (Arg) *Mrs L C Taylor* a82
5 ch g Friul (Arg) - Karolera (Arg)
4⁸ˢᵈ 9¹⁶ˢᵈ **0-0-2 £631**

Roller *J M Bradley* a53
7 b g Bluebird (USA) - Tight Spin
3⁸ˢʷ 6⁸ˢᵈ 4⁸ˢᵈ 6⁹ˢᵈ 3⁸ˢᵈ 4⁷ˢʷ 10⁸ˢᵈ 4⁸ˢᵈ
4⁹ˢᵈ 2⁸ˢᵈ **0-3-10 £1,688**

Roman Empire *T J Etherington* 13 a62
3 b g Lycius (USA) - Maze Garden (USA)
1⁷ˢᵈ 5⁷ˢᵈ 14⁶ᵍᶠ 16⁸ᵍˢ **1-0-4 £2,982**

Roman Maze *W M Brisbourne* a68
3 ch g Lycius (USA) - Maze Garden (USA)
9¹⁰ʰᵒ 5⁷ˢᵈ 5⁹ˢᵈ **0-0-3**

Roman Mistress (Ire) *T D Easterby* 80
3 ch f Titus Livius (Fr) - Repique (USA)
4⁶ᵍᶠ 3⁵ᵍ 4⁵ᵍᶠ 1⁵ᵍᶠ 7⁵ᵍᶠ 7⁵ᵍᶠ 10⁵ᵍᶠ 2⁵ᵍˢ
11⁵ᵍᶠ 15⁶ᵍᶠ 14⁵ᵍᶠ 10⁵ᵍ **1-1-12 £10,999**

Roman Quintet (Ire) *D W P Arbuthnot* 68 a74
3 ch c Titus Livius (Fr) - Quintellina
1⁵ˢᵈ 10⁶ᶠ 6⁵ᵍᶠ 4⁶ᵍ 7⁶ˢᵈ 3⁵ᵍᶠ 4⁶ˢᵈ **1-1-7**
£4,716

Roman The Park (Ire) *T D Easterby* 32
2 b f Titus Livius (Fr) - Missfortuna
6⁷ᵍ 8⁶ᵍᶠ 9⁷ᵍˢ **0-0-3**

Romancero (Ire) *M J Wallace* 91 a80
2 b c Princely Heir (Ire) - Batilde (Ire)
5⁵ᵍ 1⁵ˢᵈ 2⁶ᶠ 1⁷ᵍᶠ 2⁶ᶠ 1⁸ᵍᶠ 1⁸ᵍ **4-2-7**
£59,245

Romantic Drama (Ire) *B J Meehan* 61 a58
2 b f Primo Dominie - Antonia's Choice
11⁶ᵍᶠ 15⁶ᵍᶠ 4⁷ˢᵈ 6⁸ᵍᶠ **0-0-4 £262**

Romantic Liason *Saeed Bin Suroor* 83
3 b f Primo Dominie - My First Romance
11⁵ᵍᶠ PU⁵ᵍ **0-0-2**

Romany Nights (Ire) *R Wilman* 86 a69
3 b g Night Shift (USA) - Gipsy Moth
10⁷ˢᵈ 5⁷ᵍˢ 5⁸ᵍ 4⁶ᵍᶠ 1⁶ᵍᶠ 12⁶ᵍᶠ 5⁶ᵍᶠ
16⁶ᵍᶠ 7⁶ᵍᶠ 5⁶ᵍ 15⁶ᵍ 6⁶ᵍᶠ 10⁷ᵍ 10⁶ˢᵈ 11⁷ᵍ
1-2-17 £12,050

Romany Prince *D R C Elsworth* 108
4 b g Robellino (USA) - Vicki Romara
3¹⁶ᵍᶠ 14¹⁹ᵍᶠ 11¹⁴ᵍᶠ 2¹⁴ᵍ 3¹⁴ᵍᶠ 3¹⁴ᵍᶠ
24¹⁸ᵍᶠ **0-2-7 £17,818**

Romaric (USA) *D R Loder* 80 a70
2 b c Red Ransom (USA) - Eternal Reve (USA)
1⁶ˢᵈ 9⁷ᵍᶠ 3⁷ᵍᶠ **1-0-3 £4,451**

Rome (Ire) *G P Enright* 40 a74
4 br g Singspiel (Ire) - Ela Romara
6¹⁰ᵍᶠ 4¹²ˢᵈ 5¹²ˢᵈ 3¹³ˢᵈ **0-1-4 £603**

Romeo Tias (Ire) *A Berry* 9
2 ch g General Monash (USA) - Victim Of Love
11⁵ᶠ 17⁵ᵍᶠ 8⁵ᵍᶠ 8⁵ᶠ 12⁶ˢᵈ **0-0-5**

Romeo's Day *M R Channon* 45
2 ch g Pursuit Of Love - Daarat Alayaam (Ire)

7^{7g} 14^{7gf} 7^{8gf} 7^{8f} **0-0-4**

Romil Star (Ger) *G M Moore* ~~~~~~~~~~ 67 a77
6 b g Chief's Crown - Romelia (USA)
4^{12sd} 1^{14sw} 7^{16sd} 17^{12g} 12^{12f} 5^{13gf} 5^{14gf}
6^{14gf} 11^{14s} **1-0-9 £4,356**

Rondelet (Ire) *R M Beckett* ~~~~~~~~~~ 77
2 b g Bering - Triomphale (USA)
17^{6g} 6^{7s} 4^{7g} **0-0-3 £322**

Rondinay (Fr) *M Halford* ~~~~~~~~~~ 73
3 ch f Cadeaux Genereux - Topline (Ger)
10^{9gf} 13^{8gy} 18^{8g} 12^{8g} **0-0-4**

Ronnie From Donny (Ire) *B Ellison* ~~~~~~~~~~ 87 a88
3 b c Eagle Eyed (USA) - New Rochelle (Ire)
1^{6sd} 7^{6sd} 9^{6sd} 3^{5gs} 3^{6gf} 9^{6gf} 5^{5gf} 8^{6g}
15^{5gf} 16^{6gf} 12^{5g} **1-2-11 £14,958**

Rood Boy (Ire) *J S King* ~~~~~~~~~~ a51
2 b c Great Commotion (USA) - Cnocma (Ire)
20^{6gf} 7^{8sd} **0-0-2**

Rookwith (Ire) *J D Bethell* ~~~~~~~~~~ 66 a62
3 b g Revoque - Resume (Ire)
2^{8sd} 5^{7f} 8^{8gf} 12^{8gs} 4^{10f} 4^{12gf} 1^{9gf} 5^{8gs}
4^{8gf} 6^{8f} **1-2-10 £6,130**

Room Enough *R M Beckett* ~~~~~~~~~~ 44
3 b g Muhtarram (USA) - Salsita
11^{8g} 8^{8f} 3^{12gf} 7^{16gf} 7^{16gf} 5^{16gf} 13^{13gf}
0-0-7 £571

Rooster Jupaga *I A Wood* ~~~~~~~~~~ 39
2 b c Young Ern - So Bold
11^{7gf} 11^{7gf} 10^{8gf} 10^{8gf} **0-0-4**

Roppongi Dancer *Mrs N Macauley* ~~~~~~~~~~ 43 a31
4 b f Mtoto - Ice Chocolate (USA)
10^{16f} 6^{12sd} 4^{10gf} **0-0-3**

Rosacara *Sir Michael Stoute* ~~~~~~~~~~ 68
2 b f Green Desert (USA) - Rambling Rose
5^{6gf} 7^{7gf} 4^{7gf} **0-0-3**

Rose Of America *Miss L A Perratt* ~~~~~~~~~~ 70
5 ch m Brief Truce (USA) - Kilcoy (USA)
10^{7gf} 9^{7g} 9^{7gf} 4^{7gf} 6^{8gf} **0-0-5 £441**

Rose Of York (Ire) *J G Portman* ~~~~~~~~~~ 42
3 b f Emarati (USA) - True Ring
11^{12gs} 18^{10gf} **0-0-2**

Rose Tea (Ire) *N A Graham* ~~~~~~~~~~ 55
4 ro f Alhaarth (Ire) - Shakamiyn
15^{10g} 12^{11gf} 9^{14gf} 7^{12gf} 9^{14sw} **0-0-5**

Rose Tinted *M E Sowersby* ~~~~~~~~~~ 56
4 b f Spectrum (Ire) - Marie La Rose (Fr)
5^{8f} 8^{10gf} 15^{8gf} 2^{8gf} 6^{10gf} 10^{10f} 6^{10gs}
9^{16gf} 5^{12gs} **0-1-9 £2,717**

Rosehearty (USA) *D R Loder* ~~~~~~~~~~ 95
2 ch f Rahy (USA) - Rosebrook (USA)
2^{5gf} 2^{5gf} 1^{6gf} 7^{6g} 2^{6g} 4^{6g} 21^{6gf} **1-3-7**
£18,430

Roses Of Spring *R M H Cowell* ~~~~~~~~~~ 93 a89
5 gr m Shareef Dancer (USA) - Couleur De Rose
1^{6sd} 1^{5sd} 12^{6sd} 6^{5sd} 6^{5sd} 1^{5sd} 6^{5sd} 8^{5sd}
4^{5f} 1^{5gf} 2^{5g} 1^{5g} 15^{5gf} 10^{6g} 2^{6f} 6^{5g} 11^{5gf}
2^{6hd} **6-3-24**
£36,990

Rosetta Roebuck *D Shaw* ~~~~~~~~~~ a21
3 b f Fleetwood (Ire) - Alwal
7^{6sw} 8^{10sd} 11^{12sd} 16^{8sd} **0-0-4**

Rosewings *M H Tompkins* ~~~~~~~~~~ 65
3 b f In The Wings - Calvia Rose
12^{10gf} 1^{14gf} 5^{14f} 2^{14f} 5^{14gf} **1-1-5**
£4,487

Rosey Glow *Mrs G S Rees* ~~~~~~~~~~ 56 a38
3 b f Elmaamul (USA) - Red Rosein
12^{6g} 6^{6sd} 12^{8gf} 7^{7f} 5^{6gf} 6^{6gf} 6^{6sd} 3^{6gf}
16^{6gf} 3^{6f} 13^{7f} **0-2-11 £985**

Rosie Maloney (Ire) *N P Littmoden* ~~~~~~~~~~ a23
2 b f Docksider (USA) - Magic Lady (Ire)
13^{7sd} **0-0-1**

Rosie's Result *M Todhunter* ~~~~~~~~~~ 65
3 ch g Case Law - Precious Girl
14^{5gs} 2^{5f} 7^{5gf} 5^{5gs} 6^{5gf} 10^{5f} 15^{6gf} 8^{5f}
8^{6f} 13^{5gf} **0-1-10 £3,088**

Rosina May (Ire) *Mrs P N Dutfield* ~~~~~~~~~~ 80
2 b f Danehill Dancer (Ire) - Gay Paris (Ire)
1^{5gf} 1^{5gf} 1^{5g} **3-0-3 £11,652**

Roskilde (Ire) *M R Channon* ~~~~~~~~~~ 102
3 b c Danehill (USA) - Melisendra (Fr)
3^{10gf} 9^{10gf} 3^{10gf} 10^{10gf} 10^{10g} 2^{9gf} **0-1-6**
£9,156

Rosselli (USA) *A Berry* ~~~~~~~~~~ 53
7 b g Puissance - Miss Rossi
5^{6f} 11^{6gf} 6^{6s} 3^{6gs} 6^{6gs} 15^{6gs} 11^{6gf}
13^{6gs} 15^{6gf} 11^{6g} 3^{6gf} 8^{6gf} 7^{6f} 9^{6gf} 11^{5gf} 3^{6gf}
6^{8gf} 10^{5gs} **0-2-21 £4,228**

Rossellini (USA) *Sir Michael Stoute* ~~~~~~~~~~ 81
3 b f Spinning World (USA) - Camilla B (USA)
9^{8g} 3^{8gf} 2^{8gf} 1^{8gf} 3^{8g} 5^{8gf} **1-2-6**
£9,186

Rossiya (Fr) *M P Tregoning* ~~~~~~~~~~ 76
3 gr f Machiavellian - Russian Royal (USA)
8^{8gf} 1^{8gf} 7^{10gf} 7^{8gf} **1-0-4 £5,473**

Rosti *P C Haslam* ~~~~~~~~~~ 56 a44
3 b g Whittingham (Ire) - Uaeflame (Ire)
8^{7sd} 5^{5sw} 8^{7g} 12^{6gf} 9^{6f} **0-0-5**

Rotheram (USA) *P F I Cole* ~~~~~~~~~~ 78 a76
3 b g Dynaformer (USA) - Out Of Taxes (USA)
1^{12sd} 3^{12gf} 2^{14gf} 3^{15gs} 7^{14g} 9^{14g} **1-1-6**
£13,600

Rotuma (Ire) *M Dods* ~~~~~~~~~~ 73
4 b g Tagula (Ire) - Cross Question (USA)
1^{8gs} 9^{10gs} 4^{10gf} 4^{13gf} 5^{12gf} 6^{12gf} 3^{10gf}
2^{10gf} 2^{10f} 2^{11gf} 4^{8gs} 1^{10gs} 8^{10gs} 4^{10gs} **2-5-14**
£13,614

Rouge Blanc (USA) *G A Harker* ~~~~~~~~~~ 61 a44
3 b f King Of Kings (Ire) - Style N' Elegance (USA)
10^{10gf} 9^{10gf} 5^{12sd} 3^{16gf} 4^{16gf} 2^{14gf} 4^{14gf}
2^{16gf} 3^{17f} 1^{18gf} **1-4-10 £7,150**

Rousing Thunder *W Storey* ~~~~~~~~~~ 54
6 b g Theatrical - Moss (USA)
11^{14f} 5^{9gf} 2^{12gf} 6^{12f} 11^{12gf} 6^{16gf} 7^{12gf}
5^{14gf} 4^{14gf} 4^{12f} 6^{16gs} 3^{12gf} **1-2-12 £4,602**

Route Barree (Fr) *S Dow* ~~~~~~~~~~ 61 a60
5 ch g Exit To Nowhere (USA) - Star Des Evees (Fr)
11^{12g} 9^{12gf} 2^{12f} 1^{12g} 3^{12sd} 4^{12sd} 2^{12sd}
7^{15sd} 7^{12g} 6^{12sd} **0-3-10 £2,218**

Route Sixty Six (Ire) *Jedd O'Keeffe* ~~~~~~~~~~ 49
7 b m Brief Truce (USA) - Lyphards Goddess (Ire)
18^{9gf} 11^{8gf} 7^{10gf} 3^{9g} 5^{10g} 7^{10f} **0-1-6**
£592

Rovella *Mrs H Dalton* ~~~~~~~~~~ 41
2 b f Robellino (USA) - Spring Flyer (Ire)
9^{6f} 7^{6gf} 16^{8gf} **0-0-3**

Rowan Applause *W J Haggas* ~~~~~~~~~~ 52
2 b f Royal Applause - Chatterberry
4^{5gf} 2^{6f} **0-1-2 £1,210**

Rowan Express *M H Tompkins* ~~~~~~~~~~ 53 a68
3 b f Air Express (Ire) - Nordico Princess

5⁶ˢᵈ 7⁶ᵍ **0-0-2**

Rowan Lake (Ire) *Andrew Reid*   39 a38
3 b f Lake Coniston (Ire) - Kind Of Cute
13⁶ˢᵈ 6⁷ˢʷ 18⁶ᵍᶠ 6⁶ᵍᶠ 12⁷ᵍᶠ 8⁵ᵍᶠ **0-0-6**

Rowan Pursuit *M H Tompkins*   58
2 b f Pursuit Of Love - Golden Seattle (Ire)
6⁶ᶠ 4⁶ᵍᶠ PU⁸ᵍᶠ 4⁷ᵍᶠ 16⁸ᵍᶠ 12⁸ˢᵈ 1⁷ᵍᶠ
1-0-7 £3,333

Roxanne Mill *J M Bradley*   87 a57
5 b m Cyrano De Bergerac - It Must Be Millie
8⁵ˢᶠ 3⁵ᵍᶠ 6⁵ᶠ 9⁵ᵍ 7⁵ᶠ 16⁵ᵍˢ 2⁵ᵍᶠ 9⁵ᵍᶠ
4⁵ᶠ 7⁵ˢ 9⁵ᵍᶠ 2⁵ᵍᶠ **0-3-12 £5,786**

Roy McAvoy (Ire) *C A Cyzer*   68 a79
5 b g Danehill (USA) - Decadence
2⁷ˢᵈ 1⁶ˢᵈ 1⁷ˢᵈ 6⁶ˢᵈ 5⁷ˢᵈ 10⁸ˢᵈ 9⁷ᵍ 6⁸ᵍ
15⁷ᵍᶠ 12⁷ˢᵈ 11⁷ˢᵈ 11⁸ˢᵈ **2-1-12 £7,192**

Royal Advocate *J W Hills*   60
3 b g Royal Applause - Kept Waiting
9⁸ᵍᶠ 13⁷ᵍˢ 6⁶ᵍᶠ 5⁶ᵍᶠ 4⁸ᵍᶠ **0-0-5 £434**

Royal Approach *M Blanshard*   62
2 b f Royal Applause - Passionelle
6⁸ᵍᶠ 15⁸ᶠ **0-0-2**

Royal Approval *J L Dunlop*   73
4 b c Royal Applause - Inimitable
5¹⁰ᵍᶠ 4¹⁰ᵍ 8¹⁰ᶠ 6¹⁰ᵍᶠ 4¹⁰ᶠ 3¹²ᵍᶠ 10¹²ᶠ
0-0-7 £1,160

Royal Awakening (Ire) *A P Jarvis*   50
2 b c Ali-Royal (Ire) - Morning Surprise
3⁵ᶠ **0-0-1 £465**

Royal Axminster *Mrs P N Dutfield*   48 a49
8 b g Alzao (USA) - Number One Spot
3¹⁶ˢᵈ 2¹²ˢᵈ 14¹⁰ᶠ 3¹²ᵍᶠ 1¹²ᶠ 6¹²ᵍ 7¹²ᵍᶠ
1-3-7 £5,360

Royal Bathwick (Ire) *B R Millman*   87
3 b f King's Theatre (Ire) - Ring Of Light
5⁸ᶠ 1⁸ᵍ 8¹⁰ᵍᶠ 4⁹ᵍᶠ 7⁸ᵗ 1¹¹ᶠ 9¹²ᶠ 6¹⁰ᵍᶠ
2-0-8 £9,931

Royal Beacon *M Johnston*   107
3 b c Royal Applause - Tenderetta
5⁵ᵍᶠ 9⁷ᵍᶠ 7⁶ᵍᶠ 2⁶ᵍᶠ 1⁶ᵍᶠ 5⁶ᵍᶠ 8⁶ᵍᶠ 12⁶ᵍᶠ
1-1-8 £27,516

Royal Blazer (Ire) *C Grant*   41
3 b g Barathea (Ire) - Royale (Ire)
7⁷ˢᵈ 7¹²ᵍ 8¹²ᵍ **0-0-3**

Royal Cascade (Ire) *B A McMahon*   a51
9 b g River Falls - Relative Stranger
8⁸ˢᵈ 5⁸ˢᵈ 7⁸ˢᵈ 5⁸ˢᵈ 4⁸ˢᵈ **0-0-5**

Royal Castle (Ire) *Mrs K Walton*   61 a58
9 b g Caerleon (USA) - Sun Princess
7¹⁶ˢᵈ 1¹⁶ᵍ 4¹⁵ˢᵈ 1¹¹⁷ᵍᶠ 10¹⁶ᵍᶠ 3¹⁶ᵍˢ
11¹⁶ᵍᶠ **1-1-7 £6,087**

Royal Cavalier *R Hollinshead*   104
6 b g Prince Of Birds (USA) - Gold Belt (Ire)
5¹⁴ᵍᶠ 12¹⁹ᵍᶠ 4¹²ᵍᶠ 4¹⁴ᵍᶠ 2¹²ᵍ 7¹²ᵍᶠ 2¹²ᵍᶠ
10¹²ᵍ **0-3-8 £12,130**

Royal Challenge *G A Butler*   50
2 b c Royal Applause - Anotheranniversary
10⁶ᵍ **0-0-1**

Royal Dignitary (USA) *D R Loder*   108
3 br g Saint Ballado (Can) - Star Actress (USA)
1⁸ᶠ 3⁸ᵍ 4⁸ᵍᶠ 5⁷ᵍ 16⁸ᵍᶠ 11⁸ᵍ **1-1-6
£52,127**

Royal Distant (USA) *J H M Gosden*   78
2 ch f Distant View (USA) - Encorenous (USA)
6⁶ᵍᶠ 3⁸ᵍᶠ 1⁸ᵍᶠ 2⁸ᵍᶠ 4⁸ᵍˢ **1-3-5 £5,205**

Royal Enclosure (Ire) *Mrs S M Johnson*   a23
5 b g Royal Academy (USA) - Hi Bettina
9¹²ˢᵈ 9⁹ˢᵈ **0-0-2**

Royal Fashion (Ire) *Miss Sheena West*   68
3 b f Ali-Royal (Ire) - Fun Fashion (Ire)
3⁶ᵍᶠ 16⁶ᵍᶠ **0-1-2 £1,090**

Royal Flight *D J Daly*   49
2 b c Royal Applause - Duende
5⁷ᵍˢ **0-0-1**

Royal Grand *T D Barron*   78 a72
3 ch c Prince Sabo - Hemline
4⁶ˢᵈ 3⁶ˢᵈ 5⁷ˢʷ 3⁶ˢᵈ 1⁶ˢᵈ 2⁶ᵍᶠ **1-2-6
£6,445**

Royal Hector (Ger) *A G Hobbs*
4 b g Hector Protector (USA) - Rudolfina (Can)
15¹²ˢᵈ **0-0-1**

Royal Indulgence *M Dods*   53
3 b g Royal Applause - Silent Indulgence (USA)
15⁵ᵍˢ 11⁷ᵍᶠ 19⁶ᵍ 19⁸ᵍᶠ 8⁷ᵍᶠ 9⁷ᵗ 6⁷ᵍᶠ
6⁷ᵍᶠ 13⁸ˢ 5⁷ᵍᶠ 10⁷ᵍᶠ 8⁷ᵍᶠ **0-0-12**

Royal Melbourne (Ire) *Miss J A Camacho*   50 a25
3 ch g Among Men (USA) - Calachuchi
7⁷ˢᵈ 10⁷ᵍᶠ 7⁷ᵍˢ 8¹²ˢᵈ **0-0-4**

Royal Millennium (Ire) *M R Channon*   117
5 b g Royal Academy (USA) - Galatrix
4⁷ᵍᶠ 3⁶ᵍᶠ 4⁶ᵍᶠ 16⁶ᶠ 22⁷ᵍ 8⁷ᵍ 5⁶ᵍ 7⁷ᵍᶠ
2⁷ᵛˢ 2⁶ᵍᶠ 1⁶ᵍᶠ 4⁶ʰᵒ 2⁶ᵍ **1-5-13 £54,243**

Royal Nite Owl *J O'Reilly*   42
2 b g Royal Applause - Nite-Owl Dancer
10⁸ᵍᶠ 9⁷ᵍˢ **0-0-2**

Royal Partnership (Ire) *D L Williams*   a41
7 b g Royal Academy (USA) - Go Honey Go
14¹²ˢᵈ 7¹¹ˢᵈ 9¹²ˢᵈ **0-0-3**

Royal Pavillion (Ire) *W J Musson*   56
2 b c Cape Cross (Ire) - Regal Scintilla
8⁶ᵍᶠ **0-0-1**

Royal Portrait *J L Dunlop*   63
3 b f Perugino (USA) - Kaguyahime
10⁸ᵍᶠ 6¹⁰ᵍᶠ 16⁷¹⁰ᵍ 1¹⁰ᶠ 2¹⁰ᶠ 4¹⁰ᶠ 2¹³ᵍᶠ
3¹⁰ᵍᶠ **1-3-8 £5,895**

Royal Prince *J R Fanshawe*   71 a70
2 b c Royal Applause - Onefortheditch (USA)
3⁶ˢᵈ 4⁷ᵍᶠ **0-1-2 £916**

Royal Prodigy (USA) *R J Hodges*   47 a77
4 ch g Royal Academy (USA) - Prospector's Queen (USA)
5⁸ˢᵈ 1¹²ˢʷ 3¹²ˢᵈ 12¹²ᵍᶠ 1¹²ˢʷ 3¹²ˢᵈ **2-2-6
£6,971**

Royal Racer (Fr) *J R Best*   a13
5 b g Danehill (USA) - Green Rosy (USA)
13¹²ˢᵈ **0-0-1**

Royal Robe (Ire) *B J Meehan*   a82
3 gr g King Of Kings (Ire) - Sallanches (USA)
1⁷ˢᵈ 4⁷ˢᵈ 3⁷ˢʷ 2⁶ˢᵈ **1-1-4 £5,965**

Royal Romeo *I Semple*   25
6 ch g Timeless Times (USA) - Farinara
10¹⁰ᵍᶠ 11¹²ᵍᶠ **0-0-2**

Royal Satin (Ire) *B Mactaggart*   62
5 b g Royal Academy (USA) - Satinette
7¹⁶ᵍᶠ 6¹²ᵍ 9¹²ᵍ **0-0-3**

Royal Spin *J A Osborne*   a72
4 b g Prince Sabo - Cabaret Artiste
2⁹ˢʷ 1⁷ˢᵈ 8⁷ˢᵈ 2⁸ˢᵈ **1-2-4 £5,272**

Royal Stamp (USA) *J H M Gosden*   113
4 br c With Approval (Can) - Louis D'Or (USA)
2¹⁰ᵍ 6¹⁰ᵍ **0-1-2 £8,540**

Royal Starlet *Mrs A J Perrett*   46
2 b f Royal Applause - Legend
9⁷ᵍ 9⁶ᵍᶠ 17⁶ᵍᶠ **0-0-3**

Royal Storm (Ire) *Mrs A J Perrett*   103 a87
4 b c Royal Applause - Wakayi
3⁷ˢᵈ 3⁷ˢᵈ 6⁷ᵍ 21⁸ᵍᶠ 2⁷ᵍ 1⁷ᵍ 5⁷ᵍᶠ 5⁷ᵍᶠ
2⁷ᵍᶠ 7⁷ᶠ 7⁷ᵍ 5⁷ᵍᶠ 2⁷ᵍᶠ 2⁷ᵍᶠ 7⁷ˢᵈ 5⁷ᵍᶠ 3⁷ᵍᶠ
2⁷ᵍᶠ **2-8-21 £43,813**

Royal Supremacy (Ire) *C G Cox*   57
2 ch f Desert Prince (Ire) - Saucy Maid (Ire)
5⁵ᶠ 9⁶ᶠ 3⁵ᵍᶠ 9⁵ᵍᶠ UR⁵ᵍᶠ 3⁵ᵍᶠ **0-1-6**
£1,101

Royal Time *T D Barron*   a40
3 b f Emperor Jones (USA) - Anytime Baby
11⁵ˢᵈ 6⁵ˢᵈ **0-0-2**

Royal Trigger *B W Hills*   75 a80
3 b c Double Trigger (Ire) - Jeronime (USA)
1¹⁰ˢᵈ 6¹⁰ᵍˢ 11¹¹ᵍ 2¹²ᵍᶠ 9¹²ᵍᶠ **1-1-5**
£6,037

Royal Twist (USA) *J S Wainwright*   64
3 ch g Royal Academy (USA) - Musical Twist (USA)
3⁷ᵍᶠ 5⁸ᵍ 5⁶ᵍˢ 5⁷ᵍᶠ 3⁸ᵍᶠ 12¹⁰ᵍᶠ 17⁶ᵍᶠ 8⁶ᵍᶠ
14⁷ᵍᶠ **0-2-9 £1,144**

Royal Upstart *W M Brisbourne*   52 a13
2 b g Up And At 'Em - Tycoon Tina
7⁶ˢᵈ 3⁶ᵍᶠ 5⁶ᵍ 10⁷ᵍᶠ 13⁸ᵍᶠ 10⁸ᵍᶠ **0-1-6**
£580

Royal Warrant *A M Balding*   80
2 b c Royal Applause - Brand
4⁶ᵍ 3⁶ᵍᶠ 1⁶ᵍᶠ 9⁷ᵍᶠ **1-1-4 £8,282**

Royal Windmill (Ire) *M D Hammond*   56 a53
4 b g Ali-Royal (Ire) - Salarya (Fr)
7⁸ˢᵈ 3⁷ˢᵈ 9⁷ˢᵈ 4⁷ˢʷ 3⁷ᵍᶠ 5⁶ᵍᶠ 6⁷ᵍˢ 8⁷ˢʷ
6⁷ᶠ 3⁸ᶠ 1⁸ᵍ 2⁷ᶠ 3⁸ˢ 2⁸ᵍᶠ 8⁸ᶠ 6⁸ᵍᶠ **1-6-16**
£7,028

Royal Zephyr (USA) *Sir Mark Prescott*   51
2 b f Royal Academy (USA) - Cassation (USA)
3⁶ᵍ 6⁶ᵍᶠ 8⁷ᵍᶠ **0-0-3 £520**

Royale Pearl *R Ingram*   58
3 gr f Cloudings (Ire) - Ivy Edith
16⁶ᵍᶠ 11⁸ᵍᶠ 12⁸ᵍᶠ 3¹⁰ᶠ 4¹²ᵍᶠ 8⁸ᵍᶠ **0-0-6**
£1,096

Rozanee *J W Payne*   68
3 ch f Nashwan (USA) - Belle Genius (USA)
3⁹ᵍˢ 3¹⁰ᵍᶠ **0-2-2 £1,265**

Rubaiyat (Ire) *G Wragg*   45
2 b c Desert Story (Ire) - Lovers' Parlour
7⁶ᵍᶠ 6⁷ˢ **0-0-2**

Ruby Anniversary *J Balding*   47
3 b f Catrail (USA) - River Of Fortune (Ire)
9⁸ᵍᶠ 4⁷ᶠ 7⁸ᵍᶠ 7⁷ᵍᶠ **0-0-4**

Ruby Legend *Mrs M Reveley*   78
5 b g Perpendicular - Singing High
10⁸ᵍᶠ 4⁸ᵍᶠ 2¹¹ᵍᶠ 4¹⁰ᵍᶠ 2⁹ᵍᶠ 1¹⁰ᵍ 2⁸ᵍ
14¹⁰ᵍᶠ 1¹⁰ᵍᶠ 12¹⁰ᵍˢ **2-4-10 £9,202**

Ruby Rocket (Ire) *H Morrison*   100
2 b f Indian Rocket - Geht Schnell
1⁶ᵍᶠ 1⁶ᵍᶠ 3⁶ᵍᶠ 1⁶ᵍ 4⁶ᵍᶠ **3-1-5 £31,895**

Ruddington Grange *J Balding*
3 gr f Bahamian Bounty - Rain Splash
14⁶ᵍᶠ 8⁷ˢᵈ **0-0-2**

Rudetski *M Dods*   47 a51
6 b g Rudimentary (USA) - Butosky
2¹¹ˢᵈ 7¹¹ˢᵈ 9⁹ˢʷ 3¹²ˢʷ 4¹¹ˢᵈ 4¹⁶ᵍˢ 3¹²ᶠ
0-3-7 £2,133

Rudi's Pet (Ire) *D Nicholls*   103
9 ch g Don't Forget Me - Pink Fondant
5⁵ᵍ 10⁶ᵍᶠ 10⁵ᵍ 7⁵ᵍᶠ 4⁵ᵍᶠ 9⁶ᵍᶠ 3⁵ˢ 12⁶ᵍ
1⁵ᵍᶠ 4⁵ᵍˢ 10⁵ᵍ **1-1-11 £6,655**

Rudik (USA) *K G Wingrove*   a76
6 b/br g Nureyev (USA) - Nervous Baba (USA)
7⁶ˢᵈ 3⁷ˢᵈ 2⁶ˢᵈ 4⁶ˢᵈ 2⁷ˢʷ 5⁷ˢᵈ 2⁶ˢᵈ **0-4-7**
£3,057

Rudood (USA) *A C Stewart*   82
3 b c Theatrical - Kardashina (Fr)
4⁸ᵍᶠ 1¹⁰ᶠ 10¹¹ᵍᶠ **1-0-3 £4,637**

Rue De Paris *N Bycroft*   57
3 br g Paris House - Innocent Abroad (Den)
9⁵ᵍᶠ 4⁶ᵍᶠ 16⁶ᵍᶠ 3⁶ᵍᶠ 7⁵ᶠ 10⁶ᵍᶠ 15⁶ᵍᶠ
12⁷ᵍᶠ 11⁵ᵍᶠ 8⁷ᵍᶠ **0-1-10 £848**

Rue De Vertbois (USA) *J C Fox*   53
2 ch f King Of Kings (Ire) - Tea Cozzy (Ire)
12⁶ᵍᶠ 10⁶ᵍ 15⁶ᵍ 11⁸ᵍᶠ **0-0-4**

Rule Britannia *J R Fanshawe*   88
4 b f Night Shift (USA) - Broken Wave
11¹⁰ᵍᶠ 11²ᵍᶠ 6¹²ᵍᶠ 7¹²ᵍ 5¹³ᵍᶠ 2¹⁰ᵍ 10¹⁰ᵍᶠ
1-1-7 £7,578

Rule Of Law (USA) *D R Loder*   108
2 b c Kingmambo (USA) - Crystal Crossing (Ire)
3⁷ᵍᶠ 1⁷ᵍᶠ 1⁷ᵍᶠ 3⁸ᵍᶠ **2-2-4 £41,729**

Rules For Jokers (Ire) *J A Osborne*   82 a48
2 b g Mujadil (USA) - Exciting
4⁶ᵍᶠ 3⁸ᵍᶠ 5⁵ˢᵈ 8⁷ᵍˢ 3⁷ᵍᶠ 3⁶ᵍᶠ 1⁶ˢ 1⁶ᶠ
9⁶ᶠ **2-3-9 £8,858**

Rum Destiny (Ire) *J S Wainwright*   64
4 b g Mujadil (USA) - Ruby River
18⁵ᵍᶠ 16⁵ᵍᶠ 4⁵ᵍᶠ 10⁵ᵍᶠ 1⁵ᵍᶠ 8⁵ᵍᶠ 9⁵ᶠ
14⁵ᵍᶠ 13⁵ᵍᶠ 16⁵ᵍᶠ 10⁵ᵍˢ **1-1-11 £4,385**

Rum Shot *H Candy*   100
2 b c Efisio - Glass
6⁶ᵍᶠ 1⁶ᵍᶠ 1⁶ᵍᶠ **2-0-3 £7,652**

Rumbling Bridge *J L Dunlop*   55
2 ch g Air Express (Ire) - Rushing River (USA)
5⁷ᵍᶠ 4⁷ᵍᶠ 6⁷ᵍᶠ **0-0-3 £272**

Rumour *J R Fanshawe*   68
3 b f Lion Cavern (USA) - Thea (USA)
3⁸ᵍᶠ **0-1-1 £494**

Rumour Mill (Ire) *Sir Mark Prescott*   a60
2 b c Entrepreneur - Pursuit Of Truth (USA)
9⁵ˢᵈ 12⁶ˢᵈ 8⁷ˢᵈ **0-0-3**

Run On *D G Bridgwater*   60
5 b h Runnett - Polar Storm (Ire)
4⁵ᶠ 17⁶ᶠ 2⁵ᵍᶠ 7⁶ᶠ 4⁵ᵍᶠ 6⁵ᵍᶠ 3⁵ᵍᶠ
4⁵ᶠ 6⁵ᶠ 6⁵ᵍᶠ **0-2-11 £2,292**

Runaway Star *W J Musson*   59 a59
6 ch m Superlative - My Greatest Star
10¹⁰ˢᵈ 1¹²ᵍ 2¹²ˢᵈ 4¹²ᵍᶠ 5¹²ᵍ 4¹⁵ᵍᶠ 5¹²ᵍᶠ
4¹⁴ᶠ 6¹⁶ᵍᶠ **1-1-9 £6,456**

Running Times (USA) *H J Manners*   18
6 b g Brocco (USA) - Concert Peace (USA)
16¹²ᵍ **0-0-1**

Rupert Brooke *P W Harris*   59
4 b g Polar Falcon (USA) - Vayavaig
4⁸ᵍᶠ 8¹⁰ᵍ **0-0-2**

Rupesh (Ire) *D W P Arbuthnot*   3
3 ch f Fayruz - Maricica
11⁹ˢᵈ 10⁹ᵍ **0-0-2**

Rushcutter Bay *P L Gilligan*   86
10 br g Mon Tresor - Llwy Bren
7⁵ᵍ 5⁵ᵍ 7⁶ᵍᶠ 14⁵ᵍᶠ **0-0-4 £368**

Russalka *Julian Poulton*   58
2 b f Opening Verse (USA) - Philarmonique (Fr)
4^{8gf} 6^{8f} 7^{7g} 0-0-3 £302

Russian Comrade (Ire) *J C Tuck*   69
7 b g Polish Patriot (USA) - Tikarna (Fr)
9^{12gf} 1^{10vs} 13^{8gf} 1-0-3 £4,928

Russian Dance (USA) *Sir Michael Stoute*   97
2 b f Nureyev (USA) - Population
2^{6gf} 1^{6gf} 4^{7gf} 10^{8g} 1-1-4 £7,624

Russian Doll (Cze) *R Bastiman*
2 b f Beccari (USA) - Russian Olive
11^{5gf} 0-0-1

Russian Icon *L A Dace*
2 b f Wace (USA) - Lady Millennium (Ire)
16^{7sd} 11^{10gs} 0-0-2

Russian Princess (Ire) *P W Harris*   73
3 b f Mujadil (USA) - Romanovna
4^{7gf} 4^{7g} 8^{7gf} 5^{7gf} 10^{8g} 11^{9g} 0-0-6
£758

Russian Rhythm (USA) *Sir Michael Stoute*   123
3 ch f Kingmambo (USA) - Balistroika (USA)
1^{8gf} 1^{8gf} 1^{10g} 2^{8gf} 5^{10gf} 3-1-5
£539,700

Russian Ruby (Fr) *N A Callaghan*   84
2 b f Vettori (Ire) - Pink Soviestaia (Fr)
8^{5gf} 2^{6g} 9^{6gf} 1^{6f} 8^{6gf} 16^{7g} 4^{6gf} 5^{7gf}
1^{6gf} 1^{7f} 6^{6g} 3-1-11 £15,823

Russian Society *Saeed Bin Suroor*   98
3 b f Darshaan - Russian Snows (Ire)
1^{10gf} 2^{10g} 1-1-2 £9,716

Russian Symphony (USA) *C R Egerton*   67
2 ch c Stravinsky (USA) - Backwoods Teacher (USA)
13^{6gf} 5^{6gf} 0-0-2

Russian Valour (Ire) *M Johnston*   108
2 b c Fasliyev (USA) - Vert Val (USA)
3^{5gf} 1^{5gf} 2^{5gs} 1^{5gf} 1^{5gf} 3-1-5 £62,863

Rust En Vrede *D Carroll*   53 a48
4 b g Royal Applause - Souveniers
14^{10sd} 10^{7sd} 19^{10g} 14^{9gf} 12^{10g} 3^{8f} 6^{7gf}
19^{6g} 15^{7f} 0-1-9 £541

Rustic Charm (Ire) *C G Cox*   73
3 b f Charnwood Forest (Ire) - Kabayil
3^{8g} 3^{8gs} 4^{8s} 11^{10gs} 0-2-4 £1,764

Rustle In The Wind *Joseph Quinn*   55
3 b f Barathea (Ire) - Night Owl
12^{8gf} 10^{8gf} 10^{7g} 12^{7gf} 0-0-4

Rusty Boy *A Crook*   17
2 b g Defacto (USA) - Berl's Gift
6^{9f} 10^{7gs} 0-0-2

Ruthie *T D Easterby*   69
2 ch f Pursuit Of Love - Moogie
3^{7gf} 1^{7gf} 9^{7gf} 1-1-3 £6,357

Rutland Chantry (USA) *S Gollings*   50
9 b g Dixieland Band (USA) - Christchurch (Fr)
16^{10gf} 7^{12g} 12^{12gf} 8^{10g} 0-0-4

Rutters Rebel (Ire) *G A Swinbank*   73
2 b g Entrepreneur - No Quest (Ire)
4^{6gf} 7^{7gf} 13^{7gf} 1^{8gf} 2^{8g} 6^{8gs} 1-0-6
£5,589

Ryan's Academy (Ire) *G T Lynch*   93
3 b c Ali-Royal (Ire) - Bradwell (Ire)
3^{8y} 5^{7gf} 6^{6ys} 5^{5gf} 9^{8g} 3^{8g} 16^{7y} 0-1-7
£2,922

Ryan's Bliss (Ire) *T D McCarthy*   40
3 b f Danetime (Ire) - Raja Moulana

9^{6gf} 11^{6gf} 11^{6gf} 15^{8g} 0-0-4

Ryan's Future (Ire) *J Akehurst*   83
3 b c Danetime (Ire) - Era
7^{6gf} 1^{6gf} 3^{6gf} 4^{7gs} 9^{8s} 5^{7gf} 1^{8gf} 2-0-7
£7,115

Ryan's Gold (Ire) *B Mactaggart*   38
5 b g Distant View (USA) - Kathleen's Dream (USA)
9^{6g} 8^{6gf} 11^{9g} 0-0-3

Ryan's Quest (Ire) *T D McCarthy*   55 a49
4 b f Mukaddamah (USA) - Preponderance (Ire)
12^{6sd} 3^{5sd} 7^{5sd} 9^{5f} 12^{5gf} 4^{5gf} 4^{5gf}
16^{5gf} 5^{5gf} 0-0-9 £565

Ryans Mistake (Ire) *G A Swinbank*   67
3 ch g Dr Devious (Ire) - Jane Heller (USA)
9^{8gf} 7^{11gs} 6^{9gf} 2^{12g} 3^{14gf} PU^{11gs} 0-2-6
£1,676

Rydal (USA) *G A Butler*   84 a75
2 ch c Gilded Time (USA) - Tennis Partner (USA)
4^{6gs} 2^{6gf} 2^{7sd} 2^{7gf} 1^{8gf} 1-3-5 £9,341

Rye (Ire) *J A Osborne*   63
2 b f Charnwood Forest (Ire) - Silver Hut (USA)
5^{7gf} 0-0-1

Rye N Dry (Ire) *A Berry*
3 ch f Timeless Times (USA) - Inonder
9^{7sd} 0-0-1

Ryefield *Miss L A Perratt*   64
8 b g Petong - Octavia
9^{7gf} 8^{6gf} 12^{7gf} 15^{7gs} 18^{7g} 9^{7gf} 10^{7g}
1^{7g} 7^{7g} 1-0-9 £3,276

Ryeland *Mrs P Sly*
7 b m Presidium - Ewe Lamb
15^{8sd} 0-0-1

Ryme Intrinseca *M R Channon*   92
4 ch f Hector Protector (USA) - Star And Garter
7^{7gf} 3^{8gf} 27^{8gf} 1^{8f} 15^{8gf} 1-1-5
£16,077

Rymer's Rascal *E J Alston*   55
11 b g Rymer - City Sound
6^{8f} 6^{8gf} 4^{8g} 17^{9gs} 14^{8g} 3^{8gs} 9^{8gf} 2^{8gf}
0-2-8 £1,761

Saada One (Ire) *L M Cumani*   63
3 b/br f Polish Precedent (USA) - Donya
4^{8gf} 3^{8gf} 0-1-2 £442

Saafend Rocket (Ire) *H D Daly*   a32
5 b g Distinctly North (USA) - Simple Annie
11^{9sd} 0-0-1

Saameq (USA) *E A L Dunlop*   33
2 b c Bahhare (USA) - Tajawuz
10^{8gf} 0-0-1

Sabalara (Ire) *P W Harris*   66
3 b f Mujadil (USA) - Sabaniya (Fr)
5^{6gf} 6^{6gf} 2^{6g} 16^{6g} 0-1-4 £1,708

Sabana (Ire) *J M Bradley*   59
5 b g Sri Pekan (USA) - Atyaaf (USA)
16^{6gs} 13^{6gf} 3^{6f} 7^{6gf} 17^{7gf} 0-1-5 £593

Sabbeeh (USA) *M A Jarvis*   107
2 b c Red Ransom (USA) - Capistrano Day (USA)
1^{6s} 7^{6gf} 1^{7g} 6^{7gf} 2-0-4 £11,651

Sabiyah *N A Graham*   81
3 b f Machiavellian (USA) - Waqood (USA)
4^{8g} 2^{8hy} 2^{8g} 1^{8g} 12^{7g} 11^{10g} 1-2-6
£9,394

Sabre D'Argent (USA) *D R Loder*   119
3 br c Kris S (USA) - Sterling Pound (USA)
1^{10gf} 3^{12g} 1^{10gf} 1^{11gf} 3-0-4 £61,224

Sabre's Edge (Ire) *J H M Gosden*   69
2 b c Sadler's Wells (USA) - Brave Kris (Ire)
10⁷ˢ 2⁷ᵍ 0-1-2 £1,120

Sabreline *D W P Arbuthnot*   54 a46
4 ch f Sabrehill (USA) - Story Line
4¹²ˢᵈ 4⁹ˢʷ 9⁸ᵍᶠ 9¹⁰ᵍᶠ 3¹⁰ᵍᶠ 11¹¹⁰ᶠ 0-1-6
£582

Sabrina Brown *G B Balding*   44
2 br f Polar Falcon (USA) - So True
8⁶ᵍˢ 0-0-1

Saccharine *N P Littmoden*   32
2 b f Whittingham (Ire) - Sweet And Lucky
7⁶ᶠ 13⁶ᵍᶠ 0-0-2

Sachin *G A Butler*   71 a49
2 b c Bijou D'Inde - Dark Kristal (Ire)
15⁶ᵍᶠ 4⁶ˢᵈ 3⁶ᵍᶠ 4⁷ᵍˢ 0-1-4 £540

Sacred Love (Ire) *E A L Dunlop*   61
3 ch f Barathea (Ire) - Abstraction
4⁸ᵍ 9¹⁰ᵍᶠ 15¹²ᵍ 0-0-3 £327

Sacsayhuaman *D W Thompson*   33 a51
4 b f Halling (USA) - La Dolce Vita
11¹⁰ˢᵈ 13¹⁰ᵍ 17⁸ᶠ 0-0-3

Saddad (USA) *Doug Watson*   112
4 ch c Gone West (USA) - Lite Light (USA)
4⁵ᵍᶠ 12⁵ᵍᶠ 5⁶ᵍˢ 4⁶ᵍᶠ 5⁵ᶠᵗ 0-0-5 £7,850

Saddler's Quest *J White*   80 a40
6 b g Saddlers' Hall (Ire) - Seren Quest
1¹²ᵍᶠ 18¹²ᵍᶠ 6¹⁵ˢᵈ 5¹²ᵍᶠ 9¹²ᵍᶠ 1-0-5
£3,171

Sadie Jane *J M Bradley*   41
3 b f Zahran (Ire) - So We Know
5⁶ᶠ 16⁷ᵍᶠ 0-0-2

Sadika (Ire) *A M Balding*   45
3 b f Bahhare (USA) - Nordica
8⁸ᵍ 10⁸ᵍ 12⁸ᵍᶠ 0-0-3

Sadler's Cove (Fr) *Mrs L C Jewell*   66 a57
5 b g King's Theatre (Ire) - Mine D'Or (Fr)
4¹²ᵍᶠ 1¹²ˢᵈ 8¹⁶ᵍᶠ 1¹⁴ᵍ 8¹²ᵍ 6¹²ᵍᶠ 7¹⁶ˢᵈ
2-0-7 £6,836

Sadler's Pride (Ire) *Andrew Turnell*   62
3 b c Sadler's Wells (USA) - Gentle Thoughts
3¹²ᵍᶠ 13¹¹ᵍ 0-0-2 £578

Sadlers Swing (USA) *J J Sheehan*   25 a42
7 b g Red Ransom (USA) - Noblissima (Ire)
6⁸ˢᵈ 8¹⁰ᵍ 5⁹ˢᵈ 0-0-3

Sadlers Wings (Ire) *W P Mullins*   103
5 b g In The Wings - Anna Comnena (Ire)
4¹⁴ᵍ 3¹⁴ʸˢ 15¹⁴ᵍᶠ 8¹⁶ᵍᶠ 0-1-4 £4,480

Saffron Fox *J G Portman*   85
2 ch f Safawan - Fox Oa (Fr)
4⁷ᵍᶠ 9⁷ᵍᶠ 1⁸ᵍˢ 2⁸ˢ 7⁸ᵍˢ 1-1-5 £7,197

Saffron River *R Hollinshead*   a59
2 b c Polar Prince (Ire) - Cloudy Reef
4⁵ˢᵈ 3⁵ˢᵈ 0-1-2 £884

Safranine (Ire) *Miss A Stokell*   84 a47
6 b m Dolphin Street (Fr) - Webbiana
13⁵ˢᵈ 3⁵ˢʷ 8⁶ˢᵈ 3⁵ˢᵈ 5⁵ˢᵈ 6⁵ᵍᶠ 8⁵ᵍᶠ 2⁵ᵍᶠ
7⁵ᵍˢ 15⁵ᵍˢ 6⁵ᵍᶠ 3⁵ᶠ 1⁶ᵍᶠ 5⁵ᶠ 1⁶ᶠ 12⁵ᵍᶠ 9⁵ᵍᶠ
16⁶ᶠ 13⁵ᵍˢ
3-3-25 £19,704

Sages End (Ire) *T D Easterby*
3 b c College Chapel - Celtic Guest (Ire)
15⁶ᶠ 0-0-1

Sagittate *D R Loder*   60 a50
3 ch c Grand Lodge (USA) - Pretty Sharp

57ᵍᶠ 56ˢᵈ 0-0-2

Sahaat *J A Osborne*   100 a102
5 b/br g Machiavellian (USA) - Tawaaded (Ire)
10¹⁰ˢᵈ 2⁸ˢʷ 17⁸ᵍ 5⁸ᵍᶠ 6⁸ᵍ 4⁸ᵍᶠ 5¹⁰ᵍᶠ 7¹⁰ᵍ
20⁸ᵍᶠ 8¹⁰ˢ 0-1-10 £6,039

Sahara Scirocco (Ire) *I A Wood*   53
2 b c Spectrum (Ire) - St Bride's Bay
7⁵ᵍ 5⁵ᵍᶠ 12⁶ᵍ 4⁸ᶠ 13⁸ᵍᶠ 0-0-5

Sahara Shade (USA) *S L Keightley*   29
3 ch f Shadeed (USA) - Tadwin
13⁶ᵍ 0-0-1

Sahara Silk (Ire) *D Shaw*   59 a67
2 b f Desert Style (Ire) - Buddy And Soda (USA)
7⁵ˢᵈ 7⁵ᵍᶠ 2⁵ᵍᶠ 1⁵ˢᵈ 7⁵ᵍˢ 2⁵ᵍᶠ 1⁵ˢʷ 13⁵ᵍ
5⁶ᵍᶠ 7⁵ᵍ 9⁵ˢᵈ 2-2-11 £9,465

Sahara Spirit (Ire) *R J Baker*   19
6 b g College Chapel - Desert Palace
14¹⁰ˢᵈ 16⁸ᵍᶠ 0-0-2

Sahara Storm (Ire) *L M Cumani*   71
2 b f Desert Prince (Ire) - Deluge
3⁶ᵍᶠ 17⁸ᵍ 4⁸ᶠ 11⁷ᶠ 0-2-4 £2,320

Saharan Song (Ire) *B W Hills*   a57
2 ch f Singspiel (Ire) - Sahara Baladee (USA)
4⁷ˢᵈ 0-0-1 £268

Sahem (Ire) *D Eddy*   90
6 b g Sadler's Wells (USA) - Sumava (Ire)
2¹²ᵍᶠ 3¹⁰ᵍ 1⁹ᵍˢ 3¹²ᵍᶠ 3¹⁴ᵍᶠ 16¹⁶ᵍˢ 1-2-6
£10,549

Sahnour *M R Channon*   61
3 ch c Singspiel (Ire) - Carmita
5¹⁰ᵍᶠ 2¹¹ᵍᶠ 10¹⁰ᵍᶠ 16¹²ᵍ 5¹⁴ᵍᶠ 4¹²ᵍᶠ 1¹⁶ᵍᶠ
3¹⁷ʰᵈ 4¹⁴ᵍᶠ 5¹⁴ᵍᶠ 12¹⁷ᵍᶠ 6¹⁶ᵍᶠ 5¹²ᵍ 6¹⁴ᵍ 6¹⁷ᶠ
8¹²ᶠ 1-1-16 £7,095

Sahool *M P Tregoning*   74
2 b f Unfuwain (USA) - Mathaayl (USA)
6⁷ᵍ 1⁸ᵍˢ 1-0-2 £3,012

Saida Lenasera (Fr) *M R Channon*   74
2 b f Fasliyev (USA) - Lanasara
4⁷ᵍᶠ 3⁷ᵍᶠ 1⁷ᵍᶠ 4⁸ᵍᶠ 8⁸ᵍ 1-1-5 £5,845

Sailing Through *T G Mills*   101 a76
3 b g Bahhare (USA) - Hopesay
2¹⁰ˢᵈ 3¹⁰ᵍᶠ 3¹⁰ˢᵈ 8¹²ᵍ 5¹⁰ᵍᶠ 1⁹ᵍ 1¹⁰ᵍᶠ
1¹⁰ᵍᶠ 1¹⁰ᵍᶠ 4¹⁰ᵍ 7¹⁰ᵍᶠ 4-2-11 £21,692

Sailmaker (Ire) *R Charlton*   56
2 ch c Peintre Celebre (USA) - Princess Amalie (USA)
6⁸ᵍˢ 0-0-1

Saint Alebe *D R C Elsworth*   100
4 b g Bishop Of Cashel - Soba Up
1¹²ᵍᶠ 12²ᵍ 2¹²ᵍᶠ 5¹⁴ᵍ 6¹⁶ᵍᶠ 1¹⁴ᵍᶠ 2-1-6
£136,573

Saint Johann (Ire) *L G Cottrell*   28
4 b g Ali-Royal (Ire) - Up To You
19⁷ᵍᶠ 11⁵ᵍᶠ 10⁶ʰᵈ 0-0-3

Saint Lazare (Ire) *J G Given*   59
2 b c Peintre Celebre (USA) - Height Of Passion
6⁸ˢ 15⁸ˢ 0-0-2

Saintly Place *M R Channon*   53
2 ch g Compton Place - Always On A Sunday
9⁵ᵍᶠ 6⁷ᵍᶠ 14⁶ᵍ 0-0-3

Saintly Thoughts (USA) *B J Llewellyn*   67 a62
8 b/br g St Jovite (USA) - Free Thinker (USA)
1¹⁶ᵍ 3¹⁵ˢᵈ 2¹⁶ᵍᶠ 3¹⁶ᵍᶠ 2¹⁵ˢᵈ 14¹⁶ᵍᶠ 16¹⁶ᵍᶠ
1-3-7 £5,547

Saipan (Fr) *R Hannon*   59
2 b c Alhaarth (Ire) - Ishtiyak

9^{7gf} 9^{7gf} 7^{7gf} 15^{8gf} **0-0-4**

Sakhya (Ire) *M R Channon*   55
2 b f Barathea (Ire) - Um Lardaff
9^{8gf} **0-0-1**

Sal's Gal *D G Bridgwater*   54 a59
5 b m Efisio - Ann's Pearl (Ire)
6^{6sd} 6^{7sd} 6^{6sw} 2^{8sd} 8^{7sd} 3^{7sd} 2^{7g} 4^{7sd}
5^{7sd} **0-3-9 £2,144**

Salagama (Ire) *P F I Cole*   80
3 br f Alzao (USA) - Waffle On
1^{7gf} **1-0-1 £5,746**

Salamba *M H Tompkins*   73
2 ch c Indian Ridge - Towaahi (Ire)
5^{7gf} 3^{7gs} **0-1-2 £560**

Salcombe *B W Hills*   105
3 ch c Elmaamul (USA) - West Devon (USA)
2^{8f} 3^{7g} 2^{8gf} 8^{11gf} 4^{10gf} **0-1-5 £13,134**

Salerno *Miss Gay Kelleway*   28 a71
4 ch g Mark Of Esteem (Ire) - Shamwari (USA)
1^{5sd} 7^{6sd} 9^{5sd} 8^{5sd} 11^{6gf} 4^{5sd} 8^{5sd} **1-1-7**
£3,425

Salford City (Ire) *D R C Elsworth*   91
2 b c Desert Sun - Summer Fashion
1^{8gf} **1-0-1 £6,240**

Salford Lass *Mrs Lydia Pearce*
4 b f Mtoto - Heresheis
8^{12sd} **0-0-1**

Salford Rocket *G C H Chung*
3 b g Slip Anchor - Mysterious Maid (USA)
10^{10gf} **0-0-1**

Salieri *S Dow*   a45
3 b f Silver Wizard (USA) - Queen Of Tides (Ire)
6^{8sd} 14^{7sd} 11^{10sd} **0-0-3**

Salim *Miss J S Davis*   47 a55
6 b g Salse (USA) - Moviegoer
1^{9sd} 6^{9sd} 14^{10gf} 6^{10gf} 6^{10f} **1-0-5**
£4,124

Salim Toto *H Morrison*   106
5 b m Mtoto - Villasanta
4^{12g} 14^{10f} 8^{12g} **0-0-3 £2,500**

Salinor *A C Stewart*   87 a47
3 ch c Inchinor - Salanka (Ire)
3^{8g} 4^{9sw} 1^{8gf} 3^{8g} 2^{8gf} 3^{8gf} **1-4-6**
£6,806

Salisbury Plain *D R Loder*   70
2 b c Mark Of Esteem (Ire) - Wild Pavane
4^{6gf} 1^{7gf} **1-0-2 £5,027**

Sally Traffic *R M Whitaker*   43
4 b f River Falls - Yankeedoodledancer
12^{5gf} 9^{5gf} 7^{5gf} 13^{5gf} 13^{5gf} 7^{8gs} 14^{6gf}
0-0-7

Salon Prive *C A Cyzer*   59 a72
3 b g Green Desert (USA) - Shot At Love (Ire)
8^{7gf} 2^{6g} 3^{7sd} **0-2-3 £1,177**

Salonika Sky *C W Thornton*   36
2 ch f Pursuit Of Love - Willisa
11^{5g} 5^{5gf} 9^{6gf} 11^{5sd} 7^{6gf} **0-0-5**

Salsalino *A King*   113 a86
3 ch c Salse (USA) - Alicedale (USA)
10^{7sd} 4^{9gf} 2^{10gs} 4^{10gf} 3^{12gf} 2^{12gf} 4^{12g}
3^{14gf} **0-3-8 £42,532**

Salt Lake City (USA) *A P O'Brien*   89
3 b/br c Danzig (USA) - Good Example (Fr)
15^{8s} 9^{7gf} **0-0-2**

Saltrio *W M Brisbourne*   105

5 b g Slip Anchor - Hills' Presidium
5^{13gs} 25^{18gf} **0-0-2 £525**

Salut Saint Cloud *Miss V Haigh*   64 a39
2 b c Primo Dominie - Tiriana
6^{6gf} 4^{6gf} 6^{6gf} 7^{7g} 11^{6gf} 6^{6g} 9^{6sd} 19^{6gf}
7^{8gf} 12^{7gs} **0-0-10 £370**

Salute (Ire) *J M P Eustace*   102
4 b g Muhtarram (USA) - Alasib
3^{10gf} 2^{10gf} 6^{10gf} 12^{10f} 6^{12gs} 7^{12gf} **0-2-6**
£9,363

Salviati (USA) *J M Bradley*   100
6 b g Lahib (USA) - Mother Courage
13^{5hy} 2^{5gf} 4^{5gf} 10^{6f} 3^{5gf} 8^{5gf} 1^{5f} 1^{5gs}
18^{5gf} 12^{6gf} 12^{5gs} 4^{6gf} 2^{5f} 18^{5gf} 5^{5gf} **2-4-15**
£63,261

Sam The Sorcerer *J R Norton*   28 a32
2 b c Wizard King - Awham (USA)
10^{6g} 15^{7gf} 9^{6sd} **0-0-3**

Samar Qand *Julian Poulton*   44 a60
4 b f Selkirk (USA) - Sit Alkul (USA)
7^{10gf} 3^{9sd} 7^{8sw} 7^{12sd} 8^{12sd} 3^{9sd} **0-2-6**
£787

Samara Sound *A G Newcombe*   43
2 b c Savahra Sound - Hosting
11^{6gf} 10^{6gf} 16^{8s} **0-0-3**

Samba Beat *R F Marvin*   a42
4 ch f Efisio - Special Beat
14^{8sw} 5^{11sd} 10^{12sd} **0-0-3**

Sambaman *W R Muir*   10 a64
3 b g Groom Dancer (USA) - Guest Of Anchor
7^{12gf} 14^{14gf} 2^{12sd} 1^{12sd} 4^{12sd} 1^{16sd} **2-1-6**
£7,321

Sambucan Daze (Ire) *J D Bethell*   38 a27
3 b c Mujadil (USA) - Non Dimenticar Me (Ire)
2^{8sd} 5^{7s} 10^{8gf} 13^{8gf} 12^{8sd} **0-1-5**
£2,597

Samhari (USA) *D R Loder*   109
4 ch c Indian Ridge - Cambara
4^{10f} 4^{10g} 7^{11gf} 4^{10gf} **0-1-4 £6,094**

Sammie Durose (Ire) *Ronald Thompson*   46
6 b g Forest Wind (USA) - La Calera
8^{10g} 5^{12gf} 5^{12gf} 9^{13gs} 6^{11gf} 5^{12gf} 7^{12f}
0-0-7

Sammy's Sister *Jamie Poulton*   a16
4 gr f Touch Of Grey - Northwold Star (USA)
11^{8sd} 12^{7sd} **0-0-2**

Samolis (Ire) *R Curtis*   7
2 b g College Chapel - Joyful Music (Ire)
10^{6gf} 13^{6sd} 23^{8g} **0-0-3**

Samuel Charles *Mrs A L M King*   56
5 b g Green Desert (USA) - Hejraan (USA)
4^{8gf} 4^{7f} 8^{8gf} 11^{8gf} 13^{10gf} **0-0-5 £746**

San Antonio *B W Hills*   91 a32
3 b g Efisio - Winnebago
13^{7g} 13^{7sd} 1^{7g} 1^{8g} 2^{8gs} 2^{7g} 19^{7g} 12^{8s}
14^{7g} **2-2-9 £27,178**

San Hernando *E A L Dunlop*   79
3 b g Hernando (Fr) - Sandrella (Ire)
5^{10gf} 2^{11f} 1^{12gf} 6^{12gf} 8^{13g} 6^{16gf} 12^{16gf}
1-1-7 £6,966

San Juan Matia *Dr J R J Naylor*
3 br f Makbul - The Lady Vanishes
7^{14f} 13^{14g} **0-0-2**

San Marco (Ire) *Mrs P Sly*   55 a58
5 b g Brief Truce (USA) - Nuit Des Temps

1^{12sd} 9^{12sd} 9^{13sd} 15^{11gf} 4^{12gf} 8^{12gf} 4^{16gf}
1-0-7 £3,729

San Remy (Ire) *J Noseda* — 68
2 b c Danehill (USA) - Gazette
7^{6gf} 1^{6f} 3^{7gf} **1-0-3 £4,508**

Sanbonah (USA) *N A Callaghan* — 73
2 b f King Of Kings (Ire) - Oh Nellie (USA)
10^{7gf} 7^{6gf} 12^{6gf} 1^{7gf} 2^{8gf} 5^{8gf} **1-1-6 £5,920**

Sand And Stars (Ire) *M H Tompkins* — 59
2 ch f Dr Devious (Ire) - Charm The Stars
5^{7gf} 4^{8gf} 8^{8gs} **0-0-3 £320**

Sandabar *G A Swinbank*
10 b g Green Desert (USA) - Children's Corner (Fr)
14^{14gf} **0-0-1**

Sandenista *L M Cumani* — 72
3 b f Diesis - Santi Sana
4^{8g} 1^{8gf} 3^{8f} **1-1-3 £4,815**

Sanderstead *K G Wingrove*
4 b g So Factual (USA) - Charnwood Queen
13^{8sd} **0-0-1**

Sandgate Cygnet *I Semple* — 66
3 ch f Fleetwood (Ire) - Dance Of The Swans (Ire)
5^{6g} 13^{6gs} 9^{5g} 12^{5gf} 2^{5gs} **0-1-5 £912**

Sandles *Miss K M George* — a43
5 b g Komaite (USA) - Miss Calculate
13^{12g} 6^{12sw} **0-0-2**

Sandorra *M Brittain* — 38
5 b m Emperor Jones (USA) - Oribi
5^{7gs} 15^{10gf} 17^{8gf} 10^{7s} **0-0-4**

Sandrone (Ire) *P M Phelan* — 31
3 b f In Command (Ire) - Florinda (Can)
10^{6gf} 10^{10gf} **0-0-2**

Sands Island (Ire) *G A Swinbank* — 55
3 b g Spectrum (Ire) - Dazzling Fire (Ire)
10^{9gf} 5^{8gs} 10^{10g} **0-0-3**

Sandy Bay (Ire) *M W Easterby* — 43
4 b g Spectrum (Ire) - Karinski (USA)
16^{10s} 14^{7f} 7^{10f} 14^{10gf} 13^{10g} **0-0-5**

Sandy Lady (Ire) *R Hannon* — 88
4 b f Desert King (Ire) - Mamma's Too
2^{8gf} 10^{8g} 2^{8g} 6^{7gf} 7^{8gf} 7^{8g} 3^{7gf} 7^{7g} 10^{7gf} **0-3-9 £4,309**

Sangiovese *H Morrison* — a71
4 b g Piccolo - Kaprisky (Ire)
3^{8sd} 14^{7sd} **0-1-2 £317**

Santa Catalina (Ire) *J J Matthias* — 38 a32
4 br f Tagula (Ire) - Bui-Doi (Ire)
15^{7sd} 7^{10gf} 6^{10g} 15^{10gf} **0-0-4**

Santa Caterina (Ire) *J L Dunlop* — 60
2 b f Daylami (Ire) - Samara (Ire)
17^{7gf} 7^{8gf} 10^{8gf} **0-0-3**

Santa Sophia (Ire) *J L Dunlop* — 106
3 gr f Linamix (Fr) - Samara (Ire)
1^{10gf} 1^{12gf} 7^{12g} 5^{12g} 14^{10gf} **2-0-5 £34,777**

Santando *C E Brittain* — 108 a71
3 b c Hernando (Fr) - Santarem (USA)
6^{8sd} 4^{10sd} 2^{12sw} 1^{12sd} 1^{10g} 3^{10gf} 1^{12gf} 2^{11g} 11^{16f} 4^{15gf} 2^{12gs} 5^{13gf} 11^{12gf} 6^{15g} **3-4-14 £48,110**

Santiburi Lad (Ire) *N Wilson* — 61
6 b g Namaqualand (USA) - Suggia
8^{8f} 1^{10gf} 3^{9gf} 11^{10gf} 4^{8gf} 6^{9gf} 11^{10gf} **1-1-7 £4,277**

Santisima Trinidad (Ire) *T D Easterby* — 95
5 b m Definite Article - Brazilia
15^{7g} 2^{8gf} 9^{7gf} 26^{7f} 6^{7g} 4^{8gf} 5^{7g} 1^{8gf} 3^{8gf} 6^{7g} 16^{7g} 7^{7gf} 9^{7gf} **1-2-13 £18,302**

Saphila (Ire) *L M Cumani* — 69
3 b f Sadler's Wells (USA) - Fanny Cerrito (USA)
8^{8gf} 6^{11hy} 12^{10gf} 2^{12gf} 12^{12gf} 3^{14gf} 7^{14gf} 5^{14gf} **0-0-8 £2,090**

Saponi (Ire) *W J Haggas* — 75 a84
5 b g Indian Ridge - Taking Liberties (Ire)
3^{7sd} 1^{8sd} 1^{8sw} 6^{10g} **2-1-4 £7,481**

Sapperdot *F Watson*
6 b g St Ninian - Beau Gem
7^{12gf} 10^{10g} 11^{15sd} **0-0-3**

Sapphire Allise *D K Ivory* — a28
3 b f Royal Applause - Paradise News
10^{6sd} 13^{5sd} **0-0-2**

Saratoga Splendour (USA) *Jedd O'Keeffe* — 42
2 b f Diesis - Saratoga One (USA)
12^{7g} 8^{7gs} **0-0-2**

Saree *M G Quinlan* — 69
2 b f Barathea (Ire) - Shouk
1^{7gf} **1-0-1 £4,459**

Sarena Pride (Ire) *J D Frost* — a54
6 b m Persian Bold - Avidal Park
7^{9sd} **0-0-1**

Sarena Special *J D Frost*
6 b g Lucky Guest - Lariston Gale
12^{8sd} **0-0-1**

Sariba *A Charlton* — 48 a42
4 b f Persian Bold - En Vacances (Ire)
8^{12sd} 4^{13g} 4^{18gf} 1^{17hd} 13^{16sd} **1-0-5 £4,693**

Sarin *L M Cumani* — 84
5 b g Deploy - Secretilla (USA)
8^{10gs} 10^{12gf} 4^{12gf} **0-0-3 £790**

Saristar *P F I Cole* — 89 a77
2 b f Starborough - Sari
5^{5gf} 1^{5gf} 7^{6gf} 1^{5sd} 7^{5gf} **2-0-5 £6,630**

Sarn *A Bailey* — 63
4 b g Atraf - Covent Garden Girl
5^{8gf} 2^{8gs} 8^{7gs} 15^{8gf} 1^{7g} 1^{7g} 4^{9g} 8^{10g} 15^{8gs} 13^{8gf} **2-1-10 £9,159**

Saros (Ire) *B Smart* — 47 a23
2 b/br c Desert Sun - Fight Right (Fr)
10^{5f} 9^{7gf} 6^{8gf} 9^{8gf} 6^{8sd} **0-0-5**

Sarraaf (Ire) *I Semple* — 85 a83
7 ch g Perugino (USA) - Blue Vista (Ire)
4^{8sd} 3^{7sw} 1^{7sd} 22^{8g} 10^{8g} 4^{7gf} 9^{8gs} 3^{8gf} 4^{8gs} 3^{9gf} 9^{8gf} 1^{9gf} 8^{8gf} 3^{9gf} 7^{6s} 7^{7gf} 3^{8gf} 2^{9gf} **3-5-25 £21,744**

Sarrego *R Hollinshead* — 65
4 b g Makbul - Simmie's Special
7^{6gf} 6^{5hy} 8^{6gf} **0-0-3**

Sartorial (Ire) *P J Makin* — 101
7 b g Elbio - Madam Slaney
4^{6g} 12^{6gf} 10^{6gs} 12^{6gf} **0-0-4 £837**

Sashay *R Hollinshead* — 57 a71
5 b m Bishop Of Cashel - St James's Antigua (Ire)
11^{6sd} 4^{16sd} 12^{16sd} 9^{16sw} 16^{16sd} 7^{17f} 4^{17f} 7^{16gf} 6^{16sd} 1^{15sd} **2-0-10 £6,923**

Satelcom (USA) *Noel T Chance* — 83 a84
3 b c Alhaarth (Ire) - Tommelise (USA)
1^{8sd} 2^{7sd} 3^{7sd} 4^{8sd} 3^{6gf} 2^{8gf} 8^{8g} 10^{7sd}

1-3-8 £12,939

Satsu (Ire) *J G Given*   55
2 ch f Shinko Forest (Ire) - Cap And Gown (Ire)
10^{6gf} 8^{7gf} 5^{6g} **0-0-3**

Sattam *M P Tregoning*   86
4 b c Danehill (USA) - Mayaasa (USA)
2^{9g} 4^{7gf} 5^{8gf} 5^{9g} 3^{7gf} 2^{7gf} 1^{7gf} 8^{7gf}
1-4-8 £8,713

Saturn (Ire) *M L W Bell*   111
3 b g Marju (Ire) - Delphinus
4^{8gf} 5^{8g} 4^{8s} 7^{7gf} 2^{10gs} **0-1-5 £32,642**

Saturnalia *B J Meehan*   58
3 ch f Cadeaux Genereux - Treasure Trove (USA)
14^{7gf} 5^{7gf} 9^{7gs} 12^{6gf} 6^{7f} **0-0-5**

Satyr *W J Musson*   70
5 b g Pursuit Of Love - Sardonic
16^{8g} 6^{8g} 5^{8gf} 11^{8gf} 9^{10gf} 10^{10gf} 1^{10g}
2^{10gf} 2^{10gf} **1-2-9 £6,525**

Saucy *B J Meehan*   56
2 b f Saucy Kit - So Saucy
11^{6gf} **0-0-1**

Saucy Ship (Ire) *D J Daly*   41
2 b c Blue Ocean (USA) - Cyrano's Song (Ire)
13^{6gs} 9^{6gf} **0-0-2**

Savannah Bay *B J Meehan*   114
4 ch c In The Wings - High Savannah
2^{16g} 6^{20gf} 3^{16g} 5^{18g} 5^{16gf} **0-2-5**
£26,750

Savannah River (Ire) *C W Thornton*   46
2 b f Desert King (Ire) - Hayward
16^{6gf} 8^{7gf} 8^{6gs} **0-0-3**

Savannah Sue *J R Norton*
2 b f Emarati (USA) - Bidweaya (USA)
8^{5gs} **0-0-1**

Savernake Brave (Ire) *K R Burke*   64
2 b c Charnwood Forest (Ire) - Jordinda (Ire)
7^{6f} 9^{6gf} 2^{5f} 6^{5gf} 6^{5gf} 5^{6f} 15^{7f} **0-1-7**
£906

Savile's Delight (Ire) *R Brotherton*   71 a36
4 b g Cadeaux Genereux - Across The Ice (USA)
12^{6gf} 7^{5gf} 8^{6g} 4^{6f} 1^{6f} 7^{7g} 2^{7gf} 12^{7gf}
3^{7gf} 8^{6sd} 2^{6gf} 10^{7sd} **1-3-12 £5,424**

Saviours Spirit *T G Mills*   71
2 ch c Komaite (USA) - Greenway Lady
8^{6g} 7^{6gf} 5^{6g} **0-0-3**

Savitsky (USA) *N A Callaghan*   80
2 ch c Stravinsky (USA) - Odori (USA)
3^{5gf} 2^{5g} 5^{6gf} 5^{5s} 1^{6g} 3^{6gf} 4^{5gf} 4^{6s} **1-2-8**
£11,118

Sawwaah (Ire) *D Nicholls*   92
6 b g Marju (Ire) - Just A Mirage
6^{8g} 4^{10g} 3^{8gf} 8^{8gf} 1^{9gf} 8^{8g} 2^{8g} 8^{10gf} 5^{9g}
11^{10f} 1^{8gf} 10^{8gs} 3^{8g} 16^{9g} **2-3-14 £22,365**

Saxe-Coburg (Ire) *G A Ham*   63 a58
6 b g Warning - Saxon Maid
10^{10sd} 8^{9sd} 4^{10g} 3^{7sw} 7^{7sd} 5^{8sd} 10^{8gf}
1^{12gf} 7^{12gf} 2^{12gf} 2^{10g} 6^{13gf} 3^{10gf} 5^{12gf} 4^{12f}
11^{12sd} **1-4-16 £6,045**

Say What You See (Ire) *J W Hills*   82
3 b c Charnwood Forest (Ire) - Aster Aweke (Ire)
7^{8gf} 10^{8g} 1^{10f} 4^{10gf} 6^{9gf} 3^{10gs} 2^{10gf} 8^{9gf}
13^{10gf} **1-1-9 £6,252**

Sayadaw (Fr) *H R A Cecil*   85
3 b c Darshaan - Vingt Et Une (Fr)
2^{12gs} 1^{12gf} **1-1-2 £7,354**

Scalado (USA) *R J Osborne*   68 a71
4 ch c Mister Baileys - Lady Di Pomadora (USA)
8^{10sd} 11^{8sd} 8^{12s} 13^{10g} 9^{10gf} 6^{16gf} **0-0-6**

Scalloway (Ire) *D J Wintle*   73
3 b g Marju (Ire) - Zany
11^{10f} 4^{12gf} 4^{11f} **1-0-3 £4,618**

Scarlet Empress *R Hannon*   68 a74
2 b f Second Empire (Ire) - Daltak
7^{6gf} 4^{6gf} 12^{7gf} 7^{6gf} 7^{6gf} 6^{6gf} 12^{7gf} 1^{6sd}
4^{6sd} **1-0-9 £3,093**

Scarlet Fantasy *E A Wheeler*   47 a47
3 b g Rudimentary (USA) - Katie Scarlett
12^{8sd} 7^{6sd} 9^{6gs} 9^{5g} 9^{6sd} 5^{6g} 9^{8gf} 14^{6f}
0-0-8

Scarlet Secret *C A Cyzer*   70 a66
3 ch f Piccolo - Rise 'n Shine
12^{7sd} 8^{7sd} 1^{6sd} 3^{6sd} 3^{6sd} 7^{5sd} 3^{6g} 5^{6sd}
3^{5gf} 1^{6sd} 2^{6gf} 7^{6gf} 1^{6sd} 5^{7sw} 8^{6sd} **3-5-15**
£12,185

Scarlett Breeze *J W Hills*   47 a49
2 b f Shinko Forest (Ire) - La Suquet
4^{5gf} 7^{5gf} 12^{6gf} 6^{6sd} 5^{5gs} **0-0-5 £381**

Scarlett Rose *Dr J D Scargill*   62
2 b f Royal Applause - Billie Blue
3^{6gf} 6^{7gs} **0-1-2 £525**

Scarletti (Ger) *I Semple*   75
6 ch g Master Willie - Solidago (USA)
3^{12g} 5^{12gf} 10^{13g} 8^{9gs} 15^{10gs} **0-1-5 £632**

Scarpia *E L James*   20
3 ch g Rudimentary (USA) - Floria Tosca
9^{5gf} 7^{5gf} 7^{5gf} 13^{8gf} **0-0-4**

Scarrabus (Ire) *B G Powell*   59
2 b c Charnwood Forest (Ire) - Errazuriz (Ire)
5^{8gf} 6^{7g} 13^{7gf} **0-0-3 £153**

Scarrottoo *S C Williams*   61
5 ch g Zilzal (USA) - Bold And Beautiful
12^{7gf} 10^{6gf} 28^{8g} 13^{8gf} 6^{6gf} 6^{7gf} 4^{7gf}
5^{7f} 3^{7gf} 4^{7gf} 7^{7g} **0-2-11 £2,356**

Scarto *G M Moore*   22
2 b g First Trump - Lawn Order
7^{5gf} 10^{7f} 10^{5gf} **0-0-3**

Scary Night (Ire) *J Balding*   a79
3 b g Night Shift (USA) - Private Bucks (USA)
1^{6sd} 2^{5sd} 2^{6sd} 2^{5sd} 9^{6s} 10^{6sd} **1-3-6**
£6,265

Scenic Flight *Mrs A J Perrett*   59
2 b f Distant View (USA) - Bird Of Time (Ire)
8^{5f} 4^{6gf} 7^{7gf} 9^{6gf} 12^{7gf} **0-0-5 £362**

Scenic Lady (Ire) *L A Dace*   68
7 b m Scenic - Tu Tu Maori (Ire)
13^{10gf} 1^{11gf} 10^{12gf} 11^{11gf} 5^{10gf}
6^{12gf} 5^{8gf} 5^{10f} 2^{12f} **1-1-10 £5,025**

Scent Ahead (USA) *Mrs G S Rees*   a39
4 b g Foxhound (USA) - Sonseri
7^{5sd} 5^{5sd} **0-0-2**

Scent Of Victory (Ire) *P F I Cole*   91
4 b/br g Polish Precedent (USA) - Dayanata
16^{12g} 6^{10gf} 3^{10gf} 3^{12g} 2^{10g} 7^{10gf} 2^{12gf}
0-3-7 £9,998

Scented Air *J D Czerpak*   63 a62
6 b m Lion Cavern (USA) - Jungle Rose
1^{9sd} 1^{9sd} 6^{9sw} 5^{9sd} 7^{9sd} 11^{9gf} 7^{9gs} 8^{10g}
13^{12g} **3-0-9 £11,747**

Schapiro (USA) *J H M Gosden*   70

2 b c Nureyev (USA) - Konvincha (USA)
8⁷ᵍ 4⁷ᶠ 5⁷ᵍˢ **0-0-3 £350**

Schinken Otto (Ire) *J M Jefferson*   50
2 ch c Shinko Forest (Ire) - Athassel Rose (Ire)
10⁶ᵍˢ 6⁵ᵍᶠ 10⁶ᵍᶠ **0-0-3**

Scholarship (Ire) *B J Meehan*   69 a58
2 b g College Chapel - Royal Bracelet (Ire)
3⁶ᵍ 3⁶ᵍᶠ 4⁶ˢᵈ 8⁶ᵍ 4⁶ᵍ 5⁸ˢ 8⁷ᵍᶠ **0-2-7**
£2,364

School Days *P A Blockley*
4 b f Slip Anchor - Cradle Of Love (USA)
PU⁹ˢᵈ **0-0-1**

Schooner (Ger) *Lady Herries*   a60
3 b g Slip Anchor - Sweet Enough
6¹²ˢᵈ **0-0-1**

Science Academy (USA) *P F I Cole*   56 a46
2 ch f Silver Hawk (USA) - Dance Design (Ire)
5⁷ᵍ 8⁷ˢᵈ **0-0-2**

Scientist *J H M Gosden*   77
2 ch c Dr Fong (USA) - Green Bonnet (Ire)
6⁶ᵍ 5⁶ᵍᶠ **0-0-2**

Scippit *N Waggott*
4 ch g Unfuwain (USA) - Scierpan (USA)
14⁶ˢᵈ 19⁶ᵍᶠ **0-0-2**

Sconced (USA) *M J Polglase*   49 a40
8 ch g Affirmed (USA) - Quaff (USA)
8¹⁶ˢʷ 9¹⁴ˢᵈ 1¹⁶ᵍˢ 12¹⁵ˢᵈ 8¹⁷ᵍᶠ 1¹⁶ᵍˢ 12¹⁴ᵍˢ
8¹⁴ᵍᶠ 7¹⁶ᵍˢ 4¹⁴ᵍᶠ 3¹⁹ᵍᶠ 5¹⁶ᵍ 10¹⁶ᵍᶠ **2-1-13**
£8,924

Scooby Dooby Do *R M Whitaker*   55
2 b f Atraf - Redgrave Design
6⁶ᵍ 15⁵ᵍ **0-0-2**

Scorch *M R Channon*   57
2 b c Mark Of Esteem (Ire) - Red Hot Dancer (USA)
5⁶ᵍᶠ 6⁵ᵍᶠ **0-0-2**

Scorching *R F Johnson Houghton*   67
2 b c Efisio - Catch The Flame (USA)
4⁵ᵍᶠ 4⁵ᵍ 8⁶ᵍᶠ 10⁶ᵍᶠ 7⁷ᵍ **0-0-5 £685**

Scorchio (Ire) *M F Harris*   48 a20
2 b c Desert Sun - White-Wash
6⁷ᵍᶠ 7⁷ᵍᶠ 9⁶ˢᵈ 12⁸ˢᵈ 6⁶ᵍᶠ **0-0-5**

Scotch N' Dry *M R Channon*   83
2 ch g Piccolo - Magical Dancer (Ire)
3⁵ᵍᶠ 3⁶ᵍᶠ 2⁷ᵍᶠ 1⁷ᵍᶠ 4⁶ᵍᶠ 2⁶ᵍˢ 2⁶ᵍᶠ 6⁷ᵍᶠ
3⁶ᵍᶠ 7⁶ᵍᶠ 24⁶ᵍᶠ 5⁶ᵍᶠ **1-4-12 £15,376**

Scotish Law (Ire) *P R Chamings*   64
5 ch g Case Law - Scotia Rose
2¹⁰ᶠ 3¹⁰ᵍᶠ **0-2-2 £1,650**

Scotland The Brave *J D Bethell*   76
3 ch f Zilzal (USA) - Hunters Of Brora (Ire)
1⁷ᵍᶠ 4⁷ᵍᶠ 15⁷ᵍ 5⁸ᵍᶠ 10⁸ᵍ **1-0-5 £4,644**

Scots Guard (Ire) *J G Given*   33
2 b c Selkirk (USA) - Island Race
11⁷ᵍˢ **0-0-1**

Scott's View *M Johnston*   113
4 b g Selkirk (USA) - Milly Of The Vally
4¹²ᵍᶠ 2¹⁴ᵍᶠ 2¹⁴ᵍᶠ 3¹¹ᵍ 4¹²ᶠ 2¹²ᵍʸ 9¹²ᵍᶠ
2¹⁶ᵍᶠ 1¹²ᵍ **1-4-9 £44,280**

Scottish Exile (Ire) *K R Burke*   59
2 b f Ashkalani (Ire) - Royal Jade
4⁵ᵍˢ 8⁵ᵍᶠ 4⁶ᵍᶠ 4⁵ᵍᶠ 18⁶ᵍᶠ **0-0-5 £620**

Scottish River (USA) *M D I Usher*   81 a68
4 b g Thunder Gulch (USA) - Overbrook
6⁷ᶠ 13⁶ᶠᵗ 9⁷ᵍᶠ 5⁹ᵍᶠ 5¹⁰ᵍᶠ 8⁸ˢᵈ 7¹²ᶠ **0-0-7**

Scottish Song *Mrs M Reveley*   17
10 b g Niniski (USA) - Miss Saint-Cloud
9¹⁶ᵍˢ **0-0-1**

Scotty's Future (Ire) *D Nicholls*   95
5 b g Namaqualand - Persian Empress (Ire)
11⁸ᵍ 22⁷ᵍ 7⁸ᵍ 5¹⁰ᵍᶠ 14¹⁰ᵍᶠ 16¹²ᵍᶠ 11¹⁰ᶠ
13⁸ᵍ **0-0-8 £564**

Scraggles *J J Quinn*   37
2 b f Young Ern - Georgia Stephens (USA)
7⁵ᵍᶠ 10⁵ᵍᶠ **0-0-2**

Scramble (USA) *B Ellison*   58 a47
5 ch g Gulch (USA) - Syzygy (Arg)
6⁸ˢᵈ 16⁸ᵍᶠ 13⁷ᵍ 12⁸ᶠ 10¹⁰ᵍᶠ 2⁸ᵍ 6⁸ᵍᶠ
6⁸ᵍᶠ 4⁸ᵍᶠ 4⁸ᶠ 1⁸ᵍ **1-2-11 £4,287**

Scrappy Doo *Miss V Haigh*   3 b g Petong - Maziere
14¹⁰ˢᵈ PU¹⁰ᵍᶠ 13⁹ˢᵈ 19⁷ᵍᶠ **0-0-4**

Scraps *T D Easterby*   59
3 b g Wolfhound (USA) - Jamarj
11⁸ᵍᶠ 18⁶ᵍˢ 3⁷ᵍᶠ 3⁷ᶠ 3⁷ᵍᶠ 2⁷ᶠ 14⁸ˢ
17⁸ᵍᶠ 5⁷ᵍᶠ **0-4-9 £2,521**

Screaming Shamal (USA) *R Hannon*   43
2 gr f Tabasco Cat (USA) - Carefree Cheetah (USA)
12⁷ᶠ 10⁷ᵍᶠ **0-0-2**

Screenplay *Sir Michael Stoute*   73
2 ch c In The Wings - Erudite
10⁷ᵍᶠ 4⁸ᵍᶠ 4⁷ᵍᶠ **0-0-3 £737**

Scriptorium *L M Cumani*   44
2 b c Singspiel (Ire) - Annie Albright (USA)
7⁷ˢ **0-0-1**

Scurra *A C Whillans*   53
4 b g Spectrum (Ire) - Tamnia
11⁹ᵍᶠ 14⁶ᵍᶠ 4¹¹ᵍᶠ 13¹⁰ᵍᶠ 3⁹ᵍ 2¹¹ᵍ **0-1-6**
£1,930

Scythian *R Hannon*   73
3 b g Selkirk (USA) - Sarmatia (USA)
12⁶ᵍᶠ 5⁶ᵍᶠ 6⁶ᵍᶠ 8⁶ᵍ 11⁶ᵍ 7⁷ᵍᶠ 10⁶ᵍᶠ
0-0-7

Sea Cove *J M Jefferson*   30
3 b f Terimon - Regal Pursuit (Ire)
6¹²ᵍˢ 5¹⁰ᵍᶠ 9¹⁰ᵍᶠ 7¹⁰ᵍᶠ **0-0-4**

Sea Fern *D Eddy*   48
2 b g Petong - Duxyana (Ire)
7⁵ᵍˢ 9⁵ˢ 16⁶ᵍˢ **0-0-3**

Sea Holly (Ire) *G G Margarson*   81
3 b g Barathea (Ire) - Mountain Holly
2¹⁰ᵍ 3¹⁰ᵍᶠ 13¹¹ᵍ 6¹¹ᵍᶠ 7¹⁰ᵍᶠ **0-2-5**
£3,097

Sea Jade (Ire) *J W Payne*   51
4 b f Mujadil (USA) - Mirabiliary (USA)
13⁹ᵍᶠ 11⁷ᵍˢ 2⁷ᵍᶠ 6⁷ᵍᶠ 4⁸ᶠ 6⁷ᶠ 11⁷ᵍˢ
0-1-7 £1,175

Sea Of Happiness *C Grant*   46
3 b g Pivotal - Ella Lamees
7¹⁰ᵍᶠ 4⁸ᵍᶠ 12⁸ᵍᶠ 4¹⁴ᵍˢ **0-0-4 £288**

Sea Plume *Lady Herries*   82
4 b f Slip Anchor - Fine Quill
4¹⁰ᵍ 3¹³ᵍ 9¹⁴ᵍˢ 2¹⁶ᵍ **0-3-4 £3,881**

Sea Ridge *J L Dunlop*   66
3 b f Slip Anchor - Beveridge (USA)
2¹⁰ᵍ 5¹²ᵍᶠ 6¹²ᵍᶠ **0-1-3 £1,091**

Sea Skate (USA) *R Donohoe*   76 a57
3 b f Gilded Time (USA) - Sea Of Serenity (USA)
4⁸ˢᵈ 7⁸ᵈ 4⁹ˢᵈ 4⁸ᵍ 5⁷ᶠ 2⁸ˢ 2⁸ʸ 2¹⁰ᶠ 4¹⁰ᵍᶠ
2¹⁰ᵍ 3¹¹ᶠ 10¹⁰ᵍᶠ 8¹⁰ˢ **0-5-13 £11,027**

Sea Storm (Ire) *R F Fisher*   96 a90
5 b g Dolphin Street (Fr) - Prime Interest (Ire)
10⁸ˢᵈ 9⁷ᵍ 3⁷ᵍᶠ 5⁷ᵍᶠ 7⁷ᵍᶠ 1⁷ᵍˢ 4⁷ᵍ 11⁷ᵍᶠ
1⁷ᶠ 6⁸ᵍᶠ 8⁷ᵍᶠ 10⁷ᵍ 2⁸ᵍᶠ 8⁷ᵍ 5⁷ᵍ **2-2-15**
£28,206

Sea Swallow *J S Wainwright*
4 b f Sea Raven (Ire) - Denby Wood
9¹⁰ᵍᶠ **0-0-1**

Sea Tern *N M Babbage*   6
3 b f Emarati (USA) - Great Tern
12⁷ᵍᶠ 15⁶ᵍ **0-0-2**

Sea The World (Ire) *D Shaw*   46 a72
3 b g Inzar (USA) - Annie's Travels (Ire)
4⁵ˢᵈ 1⁵ˢʷ 18⁵ᵍˢ 8⁵ˢᵈ 4⁶ˢ 18⁸ᵍˢ 13⁶ˢᵈ
1-0-7 £4,143

Sea Victor *John A Harris*
11 b g Slip Anchor - Victoriana (USA)
15¹⁴ᵍˢ **0-0-1**

Sea Ya Maite *S R Bowring*   37 a39
9 b g Komaite (USA) - Marina Plata
9⁸ˢᵈ 13⁸ˢᵈ 13⁸ˢʷ 7⁸ˢᵈ 6⁹ˢᵈ 8⁹ˢᵈ 14⁸ˢᵈ
3¹⁰ᵍᶠ 15¹¹ˢᵈ 11⁸ᶠ 9⁸ᵍᶠ **0-1-11 £596**

Seafield Towers *Miss L A Perratt*   85
3 ch g Compton Place - Midnight Spell
20⁸ᵍᶠ 8⁵ᵍ 11⁶ᵍˢ 10⁶ᵍˢ 2⁵ᶠ 9⁶ᵍˢ 3⁵ᵍᶠ 2⁵ᶠ
2⁶ᵍ 16⁹ᵍ 1⁵ᵍᶠ 6⁶ᵍᶠ 10⁶ᵍ **2-5-14 £39,700**

Seagold *C F Wall*   15
2 b f Shahrastani (USA) - Raeleen
12⁷ˢ **0-0-1**

Seahorse Boy (Ire) *Mrs A C Tate*
6 b g Petardia - Million At Dawn (Ire)
15⁸ˢᵈ 9¹²ˢᵈ **0-0-2**

Seal Of Office *J Cullinan*   78 a84
4 ch g Mark Of Esteem (Ire) - Minskip (USA)
10⁸ˢᵈ 6⁸ˢᵈ 3¹⁰ˢᵈ 6¹⁰ᵍᶠ 11⁸ᵍ 6¹⁰ᵍᶠ 7¹⁰ᶠ
19¹⁰ᵍ **0-1-8 £951**

Sealily (Ire) *Mrs A Duffield*   61
2 gr f Docksider (USA) - Hariyana (Ire)
8⁶ᵍᶠ 3⁶ᵍˢ 5⁶ᵍˢ **0-1-3 £994**

Search Mission (USA) *Mrs A J Perrett*   78
2 b f Red Ransom (USA) - Skimble (USA)
5⁶ᵍᶠ 1⁷ᵍᶠ 2⁷ᵍᶠ **1-1-3 £6,057**

Seattle Express *M A Buckley*   74 a76
3 b g Salse (USA) - Seattle Ribbon (USA)
1⁷ˢᵈ 8⁸ᵍᶠ 5⁸ᵍᶠ 10¹¹ᵍ 5¹⁰ᵍᶠ 4⁸ᵍᶠ 3¹⁰ᵍ 1¹⁰ᵍᶠ
3¹¹ᵍᶠ 4¹⁰ᵍᶠ 8¹⁰ᵍᶠ **2-2-11 £10,777**

Seattle Prince (USA) *S Gollings*   58
5 gr g Cozzene (USA) - Chicken Slew (USA)
13¹⁴ᵍ 7¹²ᵍᶠ 4¹⁶ᵍᶠ **0-0-3**

Sebring *A J Martin*   73
4 ch g Hurricane Sky (Aus) - Carmenoura (Ire)
14⁸ᵍᶠ 6¹⁰ᵍᶠ 1¹²ᵍᶠ 7¹⁰ᵍᶠ 8⁸ʸˢ 7¹²ᵍ 10⁹ᵍᶠ
6¹²ᵍ 17¹²ᵍ **1-0-9 £3,656**

Secluded *A C Stewart*   71 a71
3 b c Compton Place - Secret Dance
4⁸ˢᵈ 3⁹ˢʷ 5¹²ˢᵈ 5⁸ᵍ **0-1-4 £841**

Second Minister *D Flood*   33 a34
4 ch g Lion Cavern (USA) - Crime Of Passion
8⁸ˢᵈ 12⁵ˢᵈ 12⁶ᵍᶠ **0-0-3**

Second Of May *P R Chamings*   70 a63
3 ch f Lion Cavern (USA) - Giant Nipper
6⁸ᵍᶠ 8⁸ᵍᶠ 2⁸ᵍᶠ 1⁸ᵍᶠ 5⁸ᶠ 4⁷ˢᵈ **1-1-6
£2,899**

Second Paige (Ire) *N A Graham*   52 a53
6 b g Nicolotte - My First Paige (Ire)

1¹⁶ˢᵈ 6¹⁶ˢᵈ 10¹⁶ˢᵈ 4¹⁴ᵍ 5¹⁷ᵍᶠ 10¹⁴ᵍᶠ **1-0-6
£3,214**

Second To Go (USA) *E A L Dunlop*   78 a58
3 b/br f El Prado (Ire) - Sharp Tradition (USA)
8¹⁰ˢᵈ 10⁷ᵍ 3⁷ᵍᶠ 5⁷ᵍᶠ **1-1-5 £4,308**

Second Venture (Ire) *J R Weymes*   57 a49
5 b g Petardia - Hilton Gateway
14⁷ˢᵈ 9⁶ˢ 4⁷ᵍ 5⁸ᵍ 14⁷ᵍ 10⁶ˢ 8⁷ᵍ 7⁸ᵍᶠ
5⁸ᶠ 10⁷ᵍᶠ **0-0-10**

Second Warning *D J Daly*   49 a49
2 ch c Piccolo - St Helena
10⁶ᵍᶠ 7⁶ᵍˢ 8⁷ˢᵈ **0-0-3**

Second Wind *D A Nolan*   50
8 ch g Kris - Rimosa's Pet
8⁷ᵍᶠ 9⁶ᵍᶠ 11⁷ᵍˢ 6⁶ᵍˢ 11⁸ᵍˢ 9⁸ᵍᶠ 14⁹ᵍˢ
8⁶ᶠ 8⁷ᵍᶠ 11⁶ᵍ 7¹¹ᵍ **0-0-11**

Secret Bloom *J R Norton*   a37
2 b g My Best Valentine - Rose Elegance
17⁷ᵍᶠ 11⁸ˢᵈ 5⁷ˢᵈ **0-0-3**

Secret Charm (Ire) *B W Hills*   96
2 b f Green Desert (USA) - Viz (USA)
1⁷ᵍᶠ 1⁷ᵍᶠ **2-0-2 £17,577**

Secret Conquest *A Crook*   48
6 b m Secret Appeal - Mohibbah (USA)
10⁸ˢᵈ 12⁸ᵍᶠ 5⁸ᵍᶠ 19⁸ᶠ 14⁸ᵍ 11⁷ᶠ
10⁷ᵍ **0-0-8**

Secret Flame *W J Haggas*   63
2 b f Machiavellian (USA) - Secret Obsession (USA)
5⁷ᵍˢ **0-0-1**

Secret Formula *S Kirk*   89
3 b f So Factual (USA) - Ancient Secret
3⁶ᵍˢ 2⁷ᵍ 4⁸ᶠ 13⁷ᵍ 15⁷ᵍᶠ 3⁸ᵍᶠ 16⁹ᵍᶠ **0-3-7
£8,648**

Secret Jewel (Fr) *Lady Herries*   68
3 b f Hernando (Fr) - Opalette
7¹⁰ᵍᶠ **0-0-1**

Secret Pride *B W Hills*   87
3 b f Green Desert (USA) - Talented
24⁵ᵍᶠ 7⁶ᵍᶠ 3⁶ᵍᶠ 5⁶ᵍᶠ 17⁷ᵍᶠ 13⁶ᵍˢ **0-1-6
£2,145**

Secret Spell *J W Unett*   33
3 b f Wizard King - Clonavon Girl (Ire)
9⁸ᵍ 8¹⁰ᵍˢ **0-0-2**

Secret Spoof *T D Easterby*   72
4 b g Mind Games - Silver Blessings
9⁶ᵍᶠ 10⁶ᵍ 15⁶ᵍˢ 11⁵ʰʸ 15⁵ᵍᶠ 13⁵ᶠ 7⁶ᵍᶠ
6⁷ᵍᶠ 10⁷ᶠ **0-0-9**

Secret Vision (USA) *Mrs A J Perrett*   70
2 ch f Distant View (USA) - Secret Angel
2⁷ᶠ **0-1-1 £1,670**

Secretary General (Ire) *P F I Cole*   84
2 b c Fasliyev (USA) - Katie McLain (USA)
2⁷ᵍ 4⁷ᵍ 1⁷ᵍᶠ **1-1-3 £9,475**

See You Harry *R Hollinshead*   26
3 b g Polar Prince (Ire) - Etma Rose (Ire)
14⁸ᵍᶠ **0-0-1**

Seejay *M A Allen*
3 b f Bahamian Bounty - Grand Splendour
6⁸ᵍᶠ **0-0-1**

Seeking A Way (USA) *J H M Gosden*   81
2 b f Seeking The Gold (USA) - Seattle Way (USA)
2⁸ᵍᶠ 1⁷ᵍᶠ **1-1-2 £987**

Seeking Answers (Ire) *A C Stewart*   82
2 b c Shinko Forest (Ire) - Lady At War
3⁶ᵍᶠ 1⁶ᵍᶠ 13⁶ᵍ 6⁸ᵍᶠ 13⁸ᵍᶠ 6⁷ᵍᶠ **1-1-6**

£4,911

Seeking The Sun (Ire) C F Wall   75
4 b/br g Petardia - Femme Savante
14^{8gf} 15^{8g} 5^{7g} 147^{7gf} 5^{7g} PU^{7g} **0-0-6**

Seel Of Approval R Charlton   110
4 b g Polar Falcon (USA) - Petit Point (Ire)
7^{6gf} 1^{6gf} 5^{6gf} 2^{6g} 4^{7gf} 1^{6gf} 6^{6gf} 1^{6gf}
1^{6gf} 2^{6g} **4-2-10 £67,230**

Seems So Easy (USA) J Jay   a19
4 b f Palmister (USA) - I'm An Issue (USA)
11^{8sd} **0-0-1**

Seeyaaj A C Stewart   89
3 b g Darshaan - Subya
14^{8gf} 1^{10g} 3^{12f} 15^{10gf} 7^{10g} **1-0-5**
£6,486

Sefton Blake R D Wylie
9 b g Roscoe Blake - Rainbow Lady
9^{12sd} **0-0-1**

Sefton Lodge M A Barnes   27 a54
4 b g Barathea (Ire) - Pine Needle
4^{7sd} 2^{6sd} 12^{6sd} 11^{6g} 6^{6sd} 14^{8gf} **0-1-6**
£1,116

Segretezza (Ire) D Haydn Jones   52 a47
3 b f Perugino (USA) - Secrets Of Honour
10^{7sd} 14^{6gf} 3^{7sd} 5^{8gf} 8^{7gf} 10^{7sw} 7^{7sd}
0-1-7 £435

Seguidilla (Ire) G C Bravery   75
2 b f Mujadil (USA) - Alzeam (Ire)
2^{5f} 7^{5gf} 4^{5g} **0-1-3 £1,305**

Seifi B Ellison   53 a3
4 b g Hector Protector (USA) - Garconniere
9^{13gs} 7^{12gf} 6^{12gf} 5^{14gs} 8^{15sd} **0-0-5**

Selebela L M Cumani   53
2 ch f Grand Lodge (USA) - Risarshana (Fr)
3^{8gf} 6^{8s} 19^{8gf} 5^{7gs} **0-1-4 £1,558**

Selective A C Stewart   112
4 b g Selkirk (USA) - Portelet
2^{8g} 2^{7gf} 2^{7g} 3^{7gf} 9^{8gf} **0-3-5 £35,967**

Self Belief D E Cantillon   67
2 b f Easycall - Princess Of Spain
4^{5f} 3^{5gf} 4^{5gf} 8^{6gf} **0-1-4 £1,226**

Self Evident (USA) Mrs A J Perrett   102
3 b/br c Known Fact (USA) - Palisade (USA)
8^{8gf} 1^{7gf} 1^{8gf} 29^{8gf} 3^{8g} 2^{8gf} 12^{8gf} **2-0-7**
£28,351

Semah's Parc Mrs A M Naughton   12
5 b g Pure Melody (USA) - Semah's Dream
14^{14gd} **0-0-1**

Semelle De Vent (USA) J H M Gosden   45 a62
2 b f Sadler's Wells (USA) - Heeremandi (Ire)
8^{8gf} 5^{7sd} **0-0-2**

Semenovskii P W D'Arcy   91
3 b g Fraam - Country Spirit
11^{6gf} 7^{6gf} 9^{6gf} 1^{6gf} 2^{6g} 2^{5gf} 4^{6gf} 1^{6f}
6^{6gf} 21^{6g} 11^{7g} 12^{6f} 6^{6g} 18^{5g} **2-2-14**
£17,135

Semper Paratus (USA) H J Collingridge   47 a66
4 b g Foxhound (USA) - Bletcha Lass (Aus)
9^{6sw} 17^{6g} 5^{5sd} 6^{6sd} 18^{6gf} 5^{6sd} 11^{6sd}
18^{6g} 16^{7gf} 15^{7sd} **0-0-10**

Sempergreen J L Dunlop   12
3 ch f Hector Protector (USA) - Star Tulip
12^{7gf} **0-0-1**

Sempre Sorriso A Charlton   64
3 b f Fleetwood (Ire) - Ever Genial

10^{8g} 9^{7g} 6^{7gf} 8^{8gf} 10^{8gf} 13^{8f} **0-0-6**

Sendintank S C Williams   45 a53
3 ch g Halling (USA) - Colleville
6^{8gs} 7^{8sd} 8^{8g} **0-0-3**

Seneschal M R Channon   83
2 b c Polar Falcon (USA) - Broughton Singer (Ire)
2^{5gf} 1^{5gf} **1-0-2 £5,352**

Senior Minister P W Hiatt   71
5 b g Lion Cavern (USA) - Crime Ofthecentury
5^{6gs} 13^{6gf} 11^{5gf} 3^{6gf} 19^{7g} 8^{6gf} 8^{5gf}
0-1-7 £687

Senna (Ire) P D Cundell   40 a61
3 b g Petardia - Saborinie
8^{8sd} 8^{8sd} 9^{8sd} 9^{10gf} **0-0-4**

Sennen Cove R Bastiman   45 a51
4 ch g Bering - Dame Laura (Ire)
14^{7sd} 6^{7sd} 2^{9gf} 5^{9gf} 15^{8f} 13^{10gf} 6^{8gf}
8^{7gf} 9^{8f} 4^{8gf} 5^{7f} 9^{7gf} 10^{8gf} **0-1-13 £1,278**

Senor Bond (USA) B Smart   82
2 ch c Hennessy (USA) - Troppa Freska (USA)
7^{5gf} 7^{7gf} 4^{6gf} 7^{6gf} 1^{6gf} 16^{6g} 18^{6gf} 4^{7gf}
10^{7gf} 18^{7g} **1-0-10 £3,172**

Senor Eduardo S Gollings   60 a37
6 gr g Terimon - Jasmin Path
11^{7gf} 7^{10gf} 7^{12g} 4^{10gf} 3^{7gf} 15^{7f} 5^{8sd}
0-1-7 £1,008

Senor Manx Touch B D Leavy
4 b g Magic Ring (Ire) - Inveraven
11^{7sd} **0-0-1**

Senor Miro J Akehurst   56 a36
5 b g Be My Guest (USA) - Classic Moonlight (Ire)
8^{7sd} 10^{7gf} 4^{7gs} **0-0-3**

Senor Pedro Miss Gay Kelleway   31 a61
3 b g Piccolo - Stride Home
2^{10sd} 1^{8sd} 7^{8sd} 7^{9sd} 3^{8sd} 11^{8sd} 10^{12gf}
8^{8sd} **1-1-8 £4,143**

Senor Sol (USA) P F I Cole   81
3 b c El Prado (Ire) - One Moment In Time (USA)
4^{11gf} 10^{11g} 3^{11f} 5^{12g} 18^{10gf} **0-0-5**
£1,629

Senor Toran (USA) P F I Cole   a42
3 b g Barathea (Ire) - Applaud (USA)
5^{9sd} 5^{12sd} 9^{12sd} **0-0-3**

Senorita (Ire) T D Easterby   38
3 b f Spectrum (Ire) - Princess Natalie
10^{7gf} 12^{7g} 17^{5gs} **0-0-3**

Sensational Mover (USA) P F I Cole   a65
3 ch f Theatrical - Blushing Heiress (USA)
2^{12sd} 3^{12sd} 4^{8sd} **0-2-3 £1,905**

Sensible (Fr) P Bary   109
5 b h Sadler's Wells (USA) - Raisonnable
7^{10gs} 2^{10g} 3^{11gs} 1^{10s} 6^{10s} **1-2-5**
£15,550

Sentinel G A Butler   106
4 ch c Hector Protector (USA) - Soolaimon (Ire)
7^{12g} 2^{16gs} 7^{16g} 12^{14gf} 12^{15g} **0-1-5**
£38,500

Sentry (Ire) J H M Gosden   86
3 b c In Command (Ire) - Keep Bobbin Up (Ire)
2^{11gf} 3^{10gs} **0-2-2 £2,190**

Senza Scrupoli L M Cumani   70
3 ch g Inchinor - Gravette
12^{8gf} 12^{7gf} 5^{8g} **0-0-3**

Sequential S Gollings
4 b g Rainbow Quest (USA) - Dance Sequence (USA)

18^{12gf} 12^{12g} **0-0-2**

Sequin Slippers (Ire) *K A Ryan* a29
3 b f Revoque (Ire) - Strutting (Ire)
4^{7sd} **0-0-1 £267**

Seraph *John A Harris* 52
3 ch g Vettori (Ire) - Dahlawise (Ire)
5^{8gf} 8^{10gf} 10^{8f} 3^{8gf} 19^{7gf} 12^{7gf} 17^{7gf}
7^{8f} **0-1-8 £527**

Serbelloni *P W Harris* 75
3 b g Spectrum (Ire) - Rose Vibert
4^{8gf} 6^{8g} 6^{10gf} 7^{10g} **0-0-4 £545**

Sergeant Cecil *B R Millman* 95
4 ch g King's Signet (USA) - Jadidh
2^{12gf} 10^{12gf} 1^{14gf} 2^{14gf} 1^{14g} 8^{16gf} 2^{12gf}
17^{14gf} **2-3-8 £26,142**

Sergeant Slipper *C Smith* 40 a53
6 ch g Never So Bold - Pretty Scarce
4^{6sd} 6^{6sd} 5^{6sd} 2^{5sw} 5^{5sd} 1^{5sd} 10^{5sd} 12^{5sw}
7^{6f} 9^{6gf} **1-1-10 £3,951**

Serieux *Mrs A J Perrett* 106
4 b c Cadeaux Genereux - Seranda (Ire)
3^{7gf} 1^{8g} 5^{8g} 19^{8gf} 4^{8gf} 3^{10gs} 8^{10gf} 7^{10g}
1-0-8 £18,251

Serrafina *B De Haan* 63
3 ch f Bluegrass Prince (Ire) - Josifina
7^{8g} 6^{8f} 9^{10gf} 4^{8gf} 6^{10gf} 8^{11gf} 9^{8g} **0-0-7**
£312

Serramanna *H R A Cecil* 80
2 ch f Grand Lodge (USA) - Spry
6^{7g} 2^{8gf} **0-1-2 £1,257**

Service *J Akehurst* a50
3 ch f College Chapel - Centre Court
6^{5sd} 5^{5sd} 6^{5sd} 4^{6sd} 5^{5sd} **0-0-5**

Sessay *D Nicholls* 65
2 b g Cyrano De Bergerac - Green Supreme
3^{5gf} 2^{5gs} 20^{6gf} **0-1-3 £2,438**

Sestina (Fr) *S Dow* a5
3 ch f Bering - Secrecy (USA)
3^{8g} 4^{7g} 11^{6s} 11^{6g} 15^{7sd} **0-1-5 £3,961**

Set The Style (Ire) *R Ingram* 82
4 b f Desert Style (Ire) - Penka (Ire)
7^{8gf} 12^{7g} 11^{6s} 11^{7ys} 9^{7gy} 9^{7y} 4^{8g} 9^{9gf}
5^{8gf} 15^{8gf} 16^{12sd} **0-0-11 £438**

Settlement Craic (Ire) *T G Mills* 73
2 b c Ela-Mana-Mou - Medway (Ire)
2^{7gf} **0-1-1 £1,232**

Seven No Trumps *B W Hills* 91
6 ch g Pips Pride - Classic Ring (Ire)
10^{5g} 11^{7gf} 11^{7g} 3^{5hy} 12^{6g} 8^{6g} 15^{5s}
0-1-7 £2,232

Seven Shirt *M R Channon* 61
2 b g Great Dane (Ire) - Bride's Answer
8^{6gf} 5^{7gf} 4^{6g} 8^{8gf} 8^{8gf} **0-0-5 £260**

Seven Springs (Ire) *R Hollinshead* 35 a32
7 b g Unblest - Zaydeen
6^{7sd} 8^{8sd} 13^{5sd} 9^{7f} 10^{6gf} 4^{5f} 12^{5gf} 8^{6gf}
0-0-8

Seviche (Ire) *F Jordan* a44
5 ch m College Chapel - Smeraldina (USA)
9^{12sw} 6^{8sd} 5^{8sd} **0-0-3**

Sevillano *P D Cundell* 87 a79
2 b g Nicolotte - Nashville Blues (Ire)
2^{5sd} 1^{6gf} 3^{7gs} 2^{6gf} **1-3-4 £8,030**

Sew'N'So Character (Ire) *M Blanshard* 100
2 b c Imperial Ballet (Ire) - Hope And Glory (USA)

4^{6gf} 2^{6g} 1^{6g} 3^{7gf} 2^{7gf} 6^{7gf} 2^{7g} 2^{8g} 5^{8gf}
1-4-9 £14,868

Sewmore Character *M Blanshard* 75
3 b c Hector Protector (USA) - Kyle Rhea
4^{8g} 10^{7g} 4^{8hy} 6^{8s} **0-0-4 £806**

Sewmuch Character *M Blanshard* 79
4 b g Magic Ring (Ire) - Diplomatist
2^{7gf} 17^{7g} 1^{6gf} 4^{8gf} 6^{6g} 8^{6gf} 5^{6gs} 8^{5gf}
3^{6gf} 7^{6gf} 4^{6gf} **1-3-11 £7,662**

Sforzando *J A R Toller* 59
2 b f Robellino (USA) - Mory Kante (USA)
6^{6gf} 5^{6gf} 9^{6gf} 12^{7gf} **0-0-4**

Sgt Pepper (Ire) *R Hannon* 102
2 b c Fasliyev (USA) - Amandine (Ire)
3^{6gf} 1^{7f} 1^{8gf} 4^{7gf} 9^{10gs} **2-0-5 £26,092**

Shaamit's All Over *B A Pearce*
4 b f Shaamit (Ire) - First Time Over
13^{13sd} **0-0-1**

Shaandar (Ire) *D W Chapman*
5 br h Darshaan - Moon Parade
PU^{18gf} **0-0-1**

Shabernak (Ire) *M L W Bell* 115
4 gr g Akarad (Fr) - Salinova (Fr)
8^{14gs} 2^{12g} 7^{12gf} 5^{12g} 3^{14g} 1^{16gf} 1^{15g}
16^{18gf} **2-2-8 £55,206**

Shades Of The West *G A Ham*
3 b f The West (USA) - Spanish Luck
20^{7gf} **0-0-1**

Shadow Captain *E J Alston* 49
3 gr g Compton Place - Magnolia
6^{5f} 5^{6gf} 6^{7gs} 10^{6gf} 13^{7gf} 13^{7gf} 20^{5gs}
0-0-7

Shadowland (USA) *A M Balding* 72
2 ch c Distant View (USA) - Fire And Shade (USA)
1^{6f} **1-0-1 £3,679**

Shadowy *R F Johnson Houghton* 55
2 b f Unfuwain (USA) - Shady Leaf (Ire)
6^{6s} 6^{8gs} 11^{10gf} **0-0-3**

Shady Deal *J M Bradley* 60
7 b g No Big Deal - Taskalady
4^{5gf} 7^{5gf} 5^{6f} 2^{5gf} 4^{6g} 6^{5gf} 6^{5f} 2^{5g} 3^{5gf}
5^{5gf} **0-4-10 £2,893**

Shady Lites (Fr) *C G Cox* 53 a50
3 ch f Definite Article - Shade
15^{8g} 13^{7gf} 3^{8sd} 9^{12gf} 3^{9g} 14^{9gf} **0-1-6**
£975

Shady Reflection (USA) *J H M Gosden* 73
2 b f Sultry Song (USA) - Woodland Melody (USA)
5^{7f} 5^{8gf} 1^{8gs} **1-0-3 £4,338**

Shahm (Ire) *B J Curley* a44
4 b g Marju (Ire) - Istibshar (USA)
5^{8sd} **0-0-1**

Shahzan House (Ire) *M A Jarvis* 97
4 b c Sri Pekan (USA) - Nsx
6^{12g} 9^{10gf} 4^{10g} 1^{10g} 13^{10gf} **1-0-5**
£8,091

Shalamak *B R Millman* 41
2 b f Makbul - Shalateeno
5^{5gf} 6^{6f} 10^{6gf} **0-0-3**

Shalaya (Ire) *Sir Michael Stoute* 85
2 b f Marju (Ire) - Shalama (Ire)
1^{8f} 6^{8gs} **1-0-2 £4,541**

Shalbeblue (Ire) *B Ellison* 55 a50
6 b g Shalford (Fr) - Alberjas (Ire)
7^{11sd} 4^{12sd} 4^{11sd} 2^{12gf} 1^{12gf} 4^{12gf} 2^{10g}

5^{10g} 7^{10gf} 3^{12gf} 2^{12gf} 5^{11g} **1-4-12 £7,616**

Shaman *G L Moore* 56 a62
6 b g Fraam - Magic Maggie
1^{10sd} 8^{10sd} 6^{10gf} 6^{10f} 10^{10gs} 11^{9gf} **1-0-6**
£2,968

Shamara (Ire) *C F Wall* 86
3 b f Spectrum (Ire) - Hamara (Fr)
4^{10g} 3^{10gf} 1^{10g} 3^{11s} 1^{12g} **2-2-5 £13,761**

Shami *D R Loder* 103 a104
4 ch c Rainbow Quest (USA) - Bosra Sham (USA)
5^{10sd} 11^{12sd} 7^{8sw} 1^{10sd} 11^{10sd} 2^{12gf} 12^{10g}
1-1-7 £15,694

Shamone *H A McWilliams* 24
2 ch c Case Law - Seek The Jade (USA)
18^{6s} 12^{5gf} PU^{5gf} 16^{5g} **0-0-4**

Shamrock City (Ire) *P Howling* 102
6 b g Rock City - Actualite
9^{10g} 2^{8gs} 4^{10gf} 15^{8gf} 11^{8g} **0-1-5**
£5,282

Shamrock Tea *M E Sowersby* 69
2 b c Imperial Ballet (Ire) - Yellow Ribbon (Ire)
10^{5gf} 5^{5gf} 1^{6s} 5^{6gs} 5^{5gf} 7^{5gf} 14^{6s} **1-0-7**
£3,954

Shams Wa Matar *B Hanbury* a24
2 ch f Polish Precedent (USA) - Rain And Shine (Fr)
5^{5sd} **0-0-1**

Shamwari Fire (Ire) *I W McInnes* 62 a57
3 ch g Idris (Ire) - Bobby's Dream
3^{7gf} 4^{9gf} 12^{8gf} 10^{7gf} 7^{8gf} 5^{8sd} 2^{8gf} 4^{8gf}
0-3-8 £1,291

Shanghai Surprise *I A Wood* 50 a2
2 b c Komaite (USA) - Shanghai Lil
4^{7g} 6^{8sd} 10^{8gf} 8^{8gf} 11^{7sd} **0-0-5 £539**

Shank *Sir Mark Prescott* a52
4 b c Lahib (USA) - Mixwayda (Fr)
10^{11sd} 4^{12sw} 6^{16sd} **0-0-3**

Shank On Fourteen (Ire) *K R Burke* 90 a89
2 b c Fayruz - Hever Rosina
2^{5gf} 1^{5gf} 1^{5g} 5^{5gs} 7^{5f} 4^{5gf} 3^{5gf} 4^{5f} 4^{5gf}
9^{5gf} 2^{5sd} 6^{5gf} **2-2-12 £16,720**

Shanook *M Johnston* 89
4 ch g Rainbow Quest (USA) - Twafeaj (USA)
1^{7gf} 2^{67g} 10^{7gf} **1-0-3 £6,532**

Shanty Star (Ire) *M Johnston* 105
3 gr c Hector Protector (USA) - Shawanni
1^{12gf} 3^{12gf} 1^{16f} **2-0-3 £52,759**

Shape Up (Ire) *T Keddy* 71 a70
3 b g Octagonal (NZ) - Bint Kaldoun (Ire)
2^{12sd} 4^{12sd} 5^{11gf} 4^{12gf} 9^{12gf} 5^{11gf} 6^{11gf}
7^{12g} 3^{12sd} 4^{12gf} 2^{12g} 6^{12gs} 4^{12gf} 9^{14gf} **0-3-14**
£5,033

Sharaab (USA) *B Hanbury* 75
2 b/br c Erhaab (USA) - Ghashtah (USA)
3^{8gf} 7^{8s} **0-1-2 £738**

Sharakka (Ire) *E A L Dunlop* 68
2 b f Daylami (Ire) - Mafaatin (Ire)
3^{7gf} 11^{7gf} **0-1-2 £542**

Shararah *S C Williams* 29
4 br f Machiavellian (USA) - Raknah (Ire)
14^{5gf} **0-0-1**

Shardda *F Watson* 73
3 b f Barathea (Ire) - Kronengold (USA)
4^{8gf} 3^{9f} 9^{9gs} **0-0-3 £1,517**

Shares (Ire) *G A Butler* 63 a50
3 b g Turtle Island (Ire) - Glendora

16^{7gf} 3^{8f} 3^{11gf} 7^{10sd} **0-2-4 £1,018**

Sharma *J L Spearing* 58
3 b f Bijou D'Inde - Star Of Jupiter
7^{8t} 10^{6gf} 6^{5gf} 3^{7gf} 14^{7gf} 10^{7gf} 19^{8gf}
0-1-7 £241

Sharmy (Ire) *Ian Williams* a111
7 b g Caerleon (USA) - Petticoat Lane
1^{12sd} 1^{12sd} 10^{10sd} 8^{10sd} **2-0-4 £27,442**

Sharoura *R A Fahey* 70 a43
7 ch m Inchinor - Kinkajoo
12^{6sd} 9^{5sd} 10^{6sd} 10^{6sw} 10^{5sw} 4^{7f} 2^{7gf}
1^{6gf} 3^{7f} 1^{6gs} 2^{6gs} 3^{6gf} 3^{6f} 5^{6gf} 8^{6gf} **2-5-15**
£16,791

Sharp As Croesus *J R Best* 34
3 b f Sesaro (USA) - Chushan Venture
10^{14gf} 14^{8g} **0-0-2**

Sharp Breeze (USA) *D R Loder* a88
3 b g Mr Prospector (USA) - Windy Mindy (USA)
3^{9sw} 1^{8sd} 3^{9sd} 7^{8sd} 1^{8sd} 18^{8gf} **2-0-6**
£9,140

Sharp Gossip (Ire) *J R Weymes* 62 a59
7 b g College Chapel - Idle Gossip
8^{7sw} 6^{8sd} 1^{7sd} 5^{7sd} 9^{8sd} 8^{7sd} 3^{7sd} 9^{7sw}
9^{7sd} 14^{7gf} 16^{8sd} 3^{6gf} 9^{7gf} 7^{7g} 9^{7f} 11^{7sd}
1-2-16 £3,993

Sharp Hat *D W Chapman* 82 a75
9 b g Shavian - Madam Trilby
8^{5sd} 9^{6sw} 5^{5sw} 7^{5gf} 5^{5sd} 16^{sd} 7^{5sd} 12^{6gs}
1^{5gf} 1^{6gf} 12^{6gs} 1^{7sw} 6^{5f} 3^{5gs} 2^{5g} 4^{5gf} 2^{5f}
2^{6gf} 1^{5gs}
5-4-25 £23,710

Sharp Rigging (Ire) *E A L Dunlop* 71
3 b g Son Of Sharp Shot (Ire) - In The Rigging (USA)
4^{8gf} 3^{10gf} 4^{9g} 10^{8gf} **0-0-4 £475**

Sharp Secret (Ire) *J A R Toller* 66
5 b m College Chapel - State Treasure (USA)
10^{8g} 9^{7g} 2^{8gf} 3^{7gf} 4^{8g} 1^{8f} 3^{8gf} 4^{8gf}
2^{8gf} 6^{8g} 5^{8gs} **1-5-11 £10,039**

Sharp Spice *D L Williams* 41 a52
7 b m Lugana Beach - Ewar Empress (Ire)
5^{10sd} 3^{11sd} 5^{12sd} 7^{12sd} 5^{12sd} 9^{12g} 6^{10gf}
6^{11g} 11^{12f} **0-1-9 £467**

Sharp Steel *Miss S J Wilton* a23
8 ch g Beveled (USA) - Shift Over (USA)
12^{8sd} **0-0-1**

Sharpinch *P R Chamings* a82
5 b g Beveled (USA) - Giant Nipper
4^{7sd} 10^{7sd} 13^{6sd} **0-0-3 £311**

Sharplaw Destiny (Ire) *W J Haggas* 42 a45
2 br f Petardia - Coolrain Lady (Ire)
12^{6sd} 11^{7gf} 4^{6sd} **0-0-3**

Sharplaw Venture *W J Haggas* 97
3 b f Polar Falcon (USA) - Breakaway
5^{7gf} 2^{8f} 3^{8gf} 9^{8g} **0-1-4 £16,545**

Sharpsport (Fr) *I Semple* a41
4 b g Charnwood Forest (Ire) - Wild Sable (Ire)
9^{9sd} 4^{9sd} **0-0-2**

Shasta *R M Beckett* 70
4 b f Shareef Dancer (USA) - Themeda
8^{13g} 7^{12gf} 7^{12g} 5^{10gf} 2^{10gf} 1^{10g} 5^{10gf}
1^{10gf} **2-1-8 £7,007**

Shatin Hero *G C H Chung* 67
3 ch c Lion Cavern (USA) - Moogie
11^{7gf} 7^{5gs} 4^{8gf} 9^{8gs} 7^{9gs} 5^{8gf} 9^{10g} 6^{9g}
8^{11g} 5^{8f} 3^{8gf} 4^{9gs} 1^{9gs} 4^{10g} 4^{8gs} **1-2-15**
£3,844

Shatin Special *Miss L A Perratt* — 57
3 ch f Titus Livius (Fr) - Lawn Order
10^{8gf} 9^{9gs} 2^{8gs} 5^{7gf} 12^{9g} 5^{8gf} 8^{9gs} 4^{9gs}
11^{8g} 4^{12gs} **0-1-10 £1,144**

Shava *W J Haggas* — 58
3 b g Atraf - Anita Marie (Ire)
1^{7gf} 8^{8gs} 6^{7gf} 12^{6g} 5^{6gf} **1-0-5 £4,407**

Shawnee Warrior (Ire) *M Mullineaux* — 36
2 b c So Factual (USA) - It's So Easy
13^{5gf} 9^{6g} 11^{6gf} 11^{5sd} **0-0-4**

Shayadi (Ire) *M Johnston* — 86 a67
6 b g Kahyasi - Shayrdia (Ire)
14^{12sd} 6^{16gf} 7^{12g} 4^{12gs} 6^{10gf} 10^{12f} 1^{10g}
7^{10gf} **1-0-8 £4,965**

Shaydeylaydeh (Ire) *Miss J Feilden* — a33
4 b f Shaddad (USA) - Spirito Libro (USA)
12^{17gf} 10^{12sd} **0-0-2**

She Legged It (Ire) *R Hannon* — 54
2 b f Cape Cross (Ire) - Mrs Siddons (Ire)
11^{6g} 7^{6gf} 9^{5gf} 4^{8gf} **0-0-4**

She Who Dares Wins *L R James* — 43 a44
3 b f Atraf - Mirani (Ire)
4^{5f} 8^{5sd} 10^{6gs} 18^{5gf} **0-0-4 £433**

She's A Diamond *T T Clement* — 15
6 b m Mystiko (USA) - Fairy Kingdom
16^{6gs} 9^{6gf} 7^{6f} **0-0-3**

She's A Fox *S T Lewis*
2 b f Wizard King - Foxie Lady
9^{6f} **0-0-1**

She's A Gem *T T Clement*
8 b m Robellino (USA) - Rose Gem (Ire)
13^{14sd} **0-0-1**

She's Flash (Ire) *J A Supple* — 16 a10
4 b f Woodborough (USA) - Beechwood Quest (Ire)
9^{7sd} 15^{7gf} 8^{10gf} **0-0-3**

She's My Valentine *B R Millman* — 56
3 b f My Best Valentine - Hong Kong Girl
3^{7gf} 7^{6g} 16^{7gf} 3^{7gf} 3^{6gf} 9^{7gf} **0-1-6**
£1,621

She's Our Lass (Ire) *D Carroll* — 50 a58
2 b f Orpen (USA) - Sharadja (Ire)
2^{5gf} 6^{5sd} 5^{8sd} 4^{8sd} 2^{7sd} **0-2-5 £1,597**

Sheapys Lass *A Crook* — 56
2 b f Perugino (USA) - Nilu (Ire)
6^{5gf} 5^{5g} 2^{5gf} 6^{5f} **0-0-4 £1,695**

Shebaan *P S McEntee* — 55
2 b f Compton Place - Chairmans Daughter
14^{6gs} 2^{7gf} UR^{7gf} 8^{8gf} 5^{8gf} 18^{7gf} **0-1-6**
£1,317

Shebeen *H Candy* — 83
3 ch f Aragon - Sheesha (USA)
2^{6gf} 2^{6f} 2^{6gf} 1^{7gf} **1-3-4 £7,647**

Sheer Focus (Ire) *E J Alston* — 57 a56
5 b g Eagle Eyed (USA) - Persian Danser (Ire)
7^{8gf} 11^{9gf} 12^{9gf} 5^{9f} 6^{8gs} 15^{8gf} 4^{8gf}
3^{9gf} 10^{8f} 3^{9sd} **0-3-10 £1,306**

Sheer Guts (Ire) *John A Harris* — 29
4 b g Hamas (Ire) - Balakera (Fr)
5^{10gf} 18^{10gf} 8^{12sd} 6^{14s} **0-0-4**

Sheik'n Swing *W G M Turner* — 68
4 b f Celtic Swing - Elegantissima
4^{7gf} 8^{7f} 15^{7gf} 9^{8f} 7^{8gf} 14^{8gf} **0-0-6**
£278

Sheliak *B S Rothwell* — 22
2 b f Binary Star (USA) - Flo's Choice (Ire)

5^{8g} 14^{7gs} **0-0-2**

Shelini *M A Jarvis* — 79
3 b f Robellino (USA) - Agama (USA)
8^{8g} 4^{9gf} 11^{8g} **0-0-3 £426**

Shell Garland (USA) *Sir Michael Stoute* — 78
3 b f Sadler's Wells (USA) - Shell Ginger (Ire)
3^{10gs} 6^{10g} **0-1-2 £647**

Shenley Charm *H Morrison* — 86 a79
3 b c First Trump - Glimpse
3^{8gf} 4^{8gf} 17^{8gs} 6^{7sd} 2^{8f} 7^{10gf} **0-2-6**
£4,820

Sheppard's Watch *G Wragg* — 103
5 b m Night Shift (USA) - Sheppard's Cross
5^{8f} 7^{7g} 2^{8f} 4^{7g} 5^{7gf} 1^{7gf} **1-1-6**
£41,415

Sherazade *C N Kellett*
4 ch f Beveled (USA) - Miss Ritz
11^{5sd} **0-0-1**

Sheriff's Deputy *J W Unett* — 78 a83
3 b g Atraf - Forest Fantasy
2^{7g} 5^{7gf} 2^{8gf} 2^{8gf} 2^{8gs} 1^{8gf} 10^{8gf}
4^{10gf} 2^{9sd} **1-6-10 £11,360**

Sherwood Forest *Miss L A Perratt* — 58
3 ch g Fleetwood (Ire) - Jay Gee Ell
8^{9gs} 5^{9gs} 7^{8gf} 3^{8gf} 3^{8gf} 4^{11g} 11^{1g} 4^{12gf}
12^{12gf} 6^{12gf} 8^{11g} 5^{11g} 12^{12gf} 8^{11gs} **1-0-14**
£6,394

Sherzabad (Ire) *H J Collingridge* — 49 a47
6 b/br g Doyoun - Sheriya (USA)
7^{12sd} 6^{11g} 4^{17gf} 6^{14gf} 1^{11gf} 9^{12gf} 15^{11gf}
9^{12g} **1-0-8 £3,987**

Shibumi *H Morrison* — 44
2 ch f Cigar - Hurricane Rose
8^{7gf} **0-0-1**

Shielaligh *H Candy* — 82
2 ch f Aragon - Sheesha (USA)
1^{6g} 2^{6f} 4^{6gf} 3^{6gf} **1-2-4 £5,885**

Shield *G A Butler* — 108
3 b c Barathea (Ire) - Shesadelight
1^{10gf} 10^{12g} **1-0-2 £34,800**

Shifty *D Nicholls* — 70
4 b g Night Shift (USA) - Crodelle (Ire)
11^{6f} 13^{9gf} 9^{7g} 15^{7gf} 1^{7f} 8^{7gf} 13^{7gf} 7^{7f}
9^{8gf} 4^{7gf} 9^{8gf} 6^{8f} 5^{8gf} 10^{9f} **1-1-14 £5,074**

Shifty Night (Ire) *Mrs C A Dunnett* — 56
2 b f Night Shift (USA) - Bean Island (USA)
9^{6gf} 12^{7gf} **0-0-2**

Shin Paradise *T D Easterby* — 56 a56
3 b g Night Shift (USA) - Silent Love (USA)
9^{7sd} 4^{8sd} 6^{7sd} 18^{gf} 17^{8g} 9^{8s} 13^{10gf}
12^{8gs} 13^{8f} **1-0-9 £4,026**

Shingalana *Miss D A McHale*
6 ch m Lion Cavern (USA) - Zealous Kitten (USA)
13^{12sd} **0-0-1**

Shingles (Ire) *N P Littmoden* — 82 a88
3 ch c Desert Prince (Ire) - Nibbs Point (Ire)
5^{10sd} 7^{12sd} 1^{11sw} 1^{9sd} 1^{12sd} 7^{12gf} **3-0-6**
£10,553

Shining White *J M P Eustace* — 70 a78
4 b f Zafonic (USA) - White Shadow (Ire)
5^{5sd} 6^{5sd} 16^{6gf} 13^{6gf} **0-0-4**

Shinko Femme (Ire) *N Tinkler* — 57
2 b f Shinko Forest (Ire) - Kilshanny
6^{6gf} 11^{6gf} 6^{6g} 2^{6f} 4^{6f} 6^{7f} 3^{6gf} 11^{6gs}
0-2-8 £2,067

Shiny *C E Brittain*   98 a81
4 b f Shambo - Abuzz
5^{6g} 7^{7sd} 4^{7gf} 4^{9g} 9^{7gf} 8^{7gf} 3^{7f} 6^{7g} 0-0-8
£4,923

Shirazi *D R Gandolfo*   52 a81
5 b g Mtoto - Al Shadeedah (USA)
5^{10sd} 1^{10sd} 3^{10sd} 6^{12g} 1-1-4 £4,934

Shirley Collins *Lady Herries*   72
4 b f Robellino (USA) - Kisumu
6^{10g} 15^{8gs} 4^{9gf} 15^{8gf} 4^{8gf} 0-0-5 £727

Shirley Not *D Nicholls*   59 a31
7 gr g Paris House - Hollia
10^{7gf} 18^{7g} 9^{5f} 11^{5sw} 18^{5gf} 9^{5gf} 0-0-6

Shirley Oaks (Ire) *Miss Z C Davison*   40 a17
5 b m Sri Pekan (USA) - Duly Elected
9^{6sd} 11^{7gf} 4^{8f} 13^{7gf} 4^{7f} 11^{8f} 12^{7f} 8^{8f}
0-0-8

Shirleys Quest *G C H Chung*   48
4 b f Bin Ajwaad (Ire) - Mainly Me
8^{10g} 11^{12g} 11^{14gf} 13^{9f} 18^{7f} 0-0-5

Shock And Awe *K A Ryan*   45
2 b f Danzig Connection (USA) - No Comebacks
7^{6gs} 7^{7gf} 0-0-2

Shoeshine Boy (Ire) *B J Meehan*   83
5 b/br g Prince Sabo - Susie Sunshine (Ire)
8^{5g} 12^{5gf} 10^{6f} 10^{5gs} 3^{5gf} 3^{5f} 14^{5gf}
8^{5gf} 4^{5g} 0-0-9 £2,000

Sholay (Ire) *E Danel*   45 a78
4 b g Bluebird (USA) - Splicing
10^{10sd} 5^{10sd} 11^{8sd} 6^{7gf} 4^{12g} 9^{11gs} 9^{11vs}
0-0-7 £909

Sholokhov (Ire) *M A Jarvis*   84
4 b c Sadler's Wells (USA) - La Meilleure
8^{10g} 0-0-1

Sholto *J O'Reilly*   78
5 b g Tragic Role (USA) - Rose Mill
1^{5gf} 4^{6gf} 9^{5g} 1^{5gf} 13^{5gf} 6^{5gf} 6^{5gf} 7^{5gf}
10^{5gf} 18^{5g} 2-0-10 £8,801

Shoot *J H M Gosden*   78
3 b f Barathea (Ire) - Prophecy
2^{7gf} 1^{7gf} 3^{7gf} 1-1-3 £8,881

Shooting Lodge (Ire) *Sir Michael Stoute*   49
2 b f Grand Lodge (USA) - Sidama (Fr)
13^{7gf} 0-0-1

Shore Vision *P W Harris*   72 a76
5 b g Efisio - South Shore
4^{8sd} 4^{8sd} 2^{8sd} 2^{8sd} 4^{8sd} 4^{8g} 7^{10gs} 8^{8gf}
4^{8gf} 2^{8gf} 7^{8f} 4^{10gf} 17^{8g} 0-9-13 £3,758

Shoreline Suite (Ire) *M E Sowersby*   34
2 ch f Woodborough (USA) - Hyannis (Fr)
8^{5f} 12^{5gf} 6^{5f} 9^{5gs} 0-0-4

Short Change (Ire) *A W Carroll*   63
4 b g Revoque (Ire) - Maafi Esm
20^{12gf} 12^{10gs} 10^{10gf} 9^{10f} 2^{10gf} 3^{10gf}
3^{12gf} 1^{12gf} 4^{10g} 8^{12gf} 3^{11gf} 2^{10gs} 2^{12f} 2^{12f}
1-7-14 £9,293

Short Chorus *J Balding*   57 a29
2 ch f Inchinor - Strawberry Song
5^{5gf} 1^{5gf} 9^{5sw} 10^{6gf} 28^{7gf} 1-0-5
£3,087

Short Respite *K A Ryan*   58
4 b f Brief Truce (USA) - Kingdom Princess
8^{10g} 13^{10g} 7^{10g} 8^{9gs} 8^{11g} 2^{11g} 4^{9g} 16^{8gf}
7^{9gs} 0-1-9 £1,394

Shot To Fame (USA) *P W Harris*   105

4 b g Quest For Fame - Exocet (USA)
6^{8gf} 16^{8gf} 12^{10g} 5^{8gf} 6^{10g} 3^{8gf} 2^{8gf}
10^{8gs} 0-1-8 £3,447

Shotacross The Bow (Ire) *M Blanshard*   51 a84
6 b g Warning - Nordica
7^{8sd} 14^{12gf} 5^{10gs} 6^{10f} 6^{8gf} 4^{10gf} 7^{8hd}
11^{10f} 2^{10gf} 6^{10gf} 8^{10gf} 16^{8gf} 4^{9sd} 1^{8sd} 1-1-14
£3,583

Shotley Dancer *N Bycroft*   55
4 ch f Danehill Dancer (Ire) - Hayhurst
5^{10gs} 6^{7gf} 7^{11gf} 15^{8g} 3^{8gf} 2^{8gf} 5^{8f} 7^{10gf}
6^{7f} 8^{10gf} 0-2-10 £2,176

Shotstoppa (Ire) *M Dods*   a20
5 ch g Beveled (Ire) - From The Rooftops (Ire)
10^{7sd} 0-0-1

Shouette (Ire) *B W Hills*   73
3 b f Sadler's Wells (USA) - Sumava (Ire)
2^{11s} 3^{9gs} 11^{0gs} 1-2-3 £6,732

Shouting The Odds (Ire) *J G Given*   94
3 br f Victory Note (USA) - Spout House (Ire)
8^{6gf} 2^{5gs} 12^{5gf} 10^{5gf} 9^{5g} 8^{5s} 11^{5gs}
0-1-7 £3,136

Show Me The Lolly (Fr) *P J McBride*   58
3 b f Sri Pekan (USA) - Sugar Lolly (USA)
7^{8gf} 5^{8gf} 0-0-2

Show Me The Roses (USA) *A P O'Brien*   93
2 b f Storm Cat (USA) - Myth (USA)
3^{5gf} 13^{5gf} 2^{6g} 6^{7gf} 9^{6gy} 0-1-5 £3,230

Show No Fear *H J Cyzer*   66 a52
2 c Groom Dancer (USA) - La Piaf (Fr)
3^{6gf} 10^{6gf} 9^{8g} 5^{8sw} 5^{10gf} 2^{8gf} 0-1-6
£2,009

Showtime Annie *A Bailey*   65
2 b f Wizard King - Rebel County (Ire)
7^{5s} 8^{5gf} 5^{6gs} 4^{6gf} 17^{7gf} 7^{7gf} 3^{8g} 3^{8s} 8^{7gf}
13^{8gs} 0-2-10 £2,067

Shredded (USA) *J H M Gosden*   71
3 b c Diesis - Shiitake (USA)
5^{9gf} 4^{10gs} 0-0-2 £315

Shriek *J A Osborne*   34 a52
3 gr f Sheikh Albadou - Normanby Lass
7^{6sd} 4^{5sd} 10^{5sd} 13^{6gf} 0-0-4 £311

Shrink *M L W Bell*   77
2 b f Mind Games - Miss Mercy (Ire)
2^{5gf} 2^{5gf} 0-2-2 £2,099

Shudder *R J Hodges*   62 a26
8 b g Distant Relative - Oublier L'Ennui (Fr)
15^{6g} 5^{6gs} 8^{6sd} 14^{6gf} 0-0-4

Shuhood (USA) *E A L Dunlop*   90
3 b g Kingmambo (USA) - Nifty (USA)
3^{10gf} 2^{10gf} 5^{10gf} 0-1-3 £4,998

Shush *C E Brittain*   66 a65
5 b g Shambo - Abuzz
6^{10sd} 2^{12sd} 2^{13sd} 1^{12sd} 8^{12g} 7^{14gs}
4^{12g} 4^{11f} 1^{10gf} 2^{11gf} 8^{10gf} 2-3-12 £11,227

Si Si Amiga (Ire) *B W Hills*   72
2 b f Desert Style (Ire) - No Hard Feelings (Ire)
1^{7gs} 1-0-1 £4,202

Sicily (USA) *J H M Gosden*   71
3 b f Kris S (USA) - Najecam (USA)
10^{10gf} 2^{10gf} 3^{12gf} 1^{14gf} 5^{12gf} 1-2-5
£6,755

Siegfrieds Night (Ire) *M C Chapman*   61
2 ch g Night Shift (USA) - Shelbiana (USA)
8^{6gf} 4^{7f} 7^{6gf} 6^{7f} 5^{7gf} 5^{7gf} 4^{5gf} 10^{5gf}

9⁵ᵍᶠ 13⁵ᵍˢ 0-0-10 £751

Siena Star (Ire) P F I Cole   84 a85
5 b g Brief Truce (USA) - Gooseberry Pie
2¹⁰ˢᵈ 2¹²ˢᵈ 4¹⁰ˢᵈ 1⁰¹⁰ˢᵈ 2¹⁰ᵍᶠ 3¹⁰ᶠ 5¹⁰ᵍ
6¹⁰ᵍ 1¹⁰ᵍᶠ 13¹⁰ᵍ 2¹⁰ᵍᶠ 5¹²ᵍᶠ 1-5-12 £13,649

Sienna Sunset (Ire) Mrs H Dalton   69
4 ch f Spectrum (Ire) - Wasabi (Ire)
4¹⁰ᶠ 2¹⁰ᵍᶠ 15¹²ᵍ 2⁸ᶠ 8⁸ᵍᶠ 1⁰¹⁰ᵍᶠ 0-2-6
£2,838

Sierra C E Brittain   38
2 ch f Dr Fong (USA) - Warning Belle
11⁸ᵍᶠ 0-0-1

Sierra Vista D W Barker   90
3 ch f Atraf - Park Vista
4⁶ᵍᶠ 5⁵ᵍ 3⁶ᵍˢ 5⁵ᵍᶠ 10⁶ᵍᶠ 15⁵ᵍˢ 3⁵ᵍᶠ 4⁵ᵍ
5⁵ᵍᶠ 8⁶ᵍᶠ 3⁵ᵍˢ 6⁵ˢ 13⁵ᵍᶠ 4⁵ᵍᶠ 0-3-14 £7,593

Sight Screen B W Hills   52
3 b f Eagle Eyed (USA) - Krisia
6¹⁰ᵍ 7⁸ᵍᶠ 0-0-2

Sights On Gold (Ire) Saeed Bin Suroor   117
4 ch c Indian Ridge - Summer Trysting (USA)
2⁹ᶠ 6⁹ᵍ 1¹⁰ᵍᶠ 2¹⁰ᵍ 1-2-4 £87,885

Signor Panettiere R Hannon   80
2 b c Night Shift (USA) - Christmas Kiss
1⁵ᵍ 4⁵ᵍᶠ 4⁵ᵍ 4⁶ᵍ 7⁵ᵍᶠ 7⁵ᵍᶠ 19⁶ᵍ 11⁵ᵍᶠ
5⁶ᵍᶠ 1-0-9 £7,714

Signora Panettiera (Fr) M R Channon   53
2 ch f Lord Of Men - Karaferya (USA)
6⁷ᶠ 4⁸ᵍᶠ 9⁸ᶠ 0-0-3 £314

Sigwells Club Boy W G M Turner   39
3 b g Fayruz - Run With Pride
8⁶ˢᵈ 14⁷ᶠ 10⁶ᵍᶠ 8⁶ᵍᶠ 11⁷ᵍᶠ 0-0-5

Silca Boo M R Channon   73
3 b f Efisio - Bunty Boo
7⁶ᵍᶠ 9⁶ʰᵛ 13⁷ᵍ 16⁵ᵍᶠ 12⁶ᵍ 18⁷ᵍᶠ 8⁶ᵍᶠ
11⁷ᵍˢ 8⁵ᵍ 0-0-9

Silca's Gift M R Channon   103
2 b f Cadeaux Genereux - Odette
1⁵ᵍˢ 1⁶ᵍᶠ 9⁶ᵍᶠ 7⁷ᵍᶠ 12⁶ᵍᶠ 2-0-5
£34,407

Silence Is Golden B J Meehan   101
4 ch f Danehill Dancer (Ire) - Silent Girl
3¹⁰ᵍ 2¹²ᵍᶠ 4¹⁰ᵍ 13¹²ᵍᶠ 2¹⁰ᵍ 2¹¹ᵍᶠ 3¹⁰ᵍᶠ
2¹⁰ᵍᶠ 5¹⁰ᵍᶠ 0-5-9 £38,302

Silent Angel Mrs Lucinda Featherstone   18
3 b f Petong - Valls D'Andorra
11⁸ᵍᶠ 11⁸ᵍᶠ 7⁸ᶠ 0-0-3

Silent Comfort B W Hills   51 a65
3 b f Cadeaux Genereux - Siwaayib
3⁷ˢᵈ 7⁷ˢᵈ 5¹⁰ᶠ 9¹⁰ᵍˢ 0-1-4 £551

Silent Hawk (Ire) Saeed Bin Suroor   86
2 b c Halling (USA) - Nightbird (Ire)
2⁷ᵍˢ 0-1-1 £1,295

Silent Heir (Aus) J Noseda   73
4 br f Sunday Silence (USA) - Park Heiress (Ire)
1¹⁰ᵍᶠ 6¹⁰ᵍᶠ 13¹⁰ᵍᶠ 1-0-3 £4,127

Silent Memory (Ire) G M Moore   57
4 b f Danehill (USA) - All Hush (Ire)
11²ᶠ 5¹²ᵍᶠ 7¹²ᵍᶠ 9¹⁰ᶠ 4¹²ᵍᶠ 5¹⁶ᵍᶠ 1⁰¹⁴ᵍᶠ
3¹²ᶠ 3¹⁰ᶠ 11¹²ˢᵈ 12¹⁴ᶠ 1-1-11 £4,465

Silent Revenge (Ire) R Hannon   56 a64
2 b f Daggers Drawn (USA) - Tread Softly (Ire)
6⁵ᵍᶠ 6⁵ᵍᶠ 1⁵ˢᵈ 8⁷ᵍᶠ 5⁷ˢᵈ 3⁷ᵍᶠ 3⁷ᶠ 1-2-7
£4,240

Silent Thunder J Noseda   69

3 ch c Cadeaux Genereux - Silent Tribute (Ire)
4⁸ˢ 5¹⁰ᵍˢ 0-0-2 £271

Silent Waters A P Jarvis   63
3 gr f Polish Precedent (USA) - Gleaming Water
9⁹ᵍᶠ 14¹⁰ᵍᶠ 5¹¹ᵍᶠ 0-0-3

Silente Tribute (USA) D Carroll
3 gr g Distant View (USA) - Homestead West (USA)
PU⁷ᵍᶠ 0-0-1

Silistra Mrs L C Jewell
4 gr g Sadler's Wells (USA) - Dundel (Ire)
10¹²ˢᵈ 0-0-1

Silk Cravat (Ire) G Wragg   32
2 ch c Dr Devious (Ire) - Dances With Dreams
13⁷ᵍᶠ 0-0-1

Silk Fan (Ire) P W Harris   92
2 b f Unfuwain (USA) - Alikhlas
2⁶ᵍᶠ 2⁷ᵍᶠ 1⁷ᵍᶠ 1⁷ᵍᶠ 2-2-4 £23,575

Silk On Song (USA) W M Brisbourne   a21
5 b g Hazaam (USA) - Wazeerah (USA)
7¹²ˢᵈ 13¹⁴ᵍᶠ 0-0-2

Silk Screen (Ire) W P Mullins   83
3 b c Barathea (Ire) - Sun Screen
18¹²ᵍᶠ 6¹²ᵍ 11¹⁰ˢ 0-0-3

Silk St Bridget W M Brisbourne   42 a1
6 b m Rock Hopper - Silk St James
2¹⁰ᵍᶠ 7⁸ᵍ 13⁷ˢᵈ 4⁷ᵍᶠ 10⁸ᵍ 13⁶ᵍ 0-0-6
£1,457

Silk St John W M Brisbourne   49
9 b g Damister (USA) - Silk St James
11⁸ᵍ 9¹⁰ᵍᶠ 0-0-2

Silken Brief (Ire) Sir Michael Stoute   81
4 b f Ali-Royal (Ire) - Tiffany's Case (Ire)
10⁷ᵍᶠ 4⁹ᵍᶠ 0-0-2 £721

Silvaline T Keddy   82 a71
4 gr g Linamix (Fr) - Upend
3¹²ˢᵈ 2¹²ˢᵈ 8¹²ˢᵈ 3¹²ᵍᶠ 5¹²ᵍ 6¹²ᵍᶠ 5¹⁰ᵍᶠ
2¹⁰ᵍ 3⁹ᵍᶠ 9⁸ˢ 7⁸ᵍᶠ 3⁸ᵍᶠ 1¹⁰ᵍᶠ 1¹⁰ᵍˢ 2¹²⁰ᵍ 3¹⁰ᵍᶠ
3¹²ˢᵈ 2-8-17 £24,557

Silver Calling (USA) P F I Cole   78
2 b f Silver Deputy (Can) - Glorious Calling (USA)
4⁶ᵍᶠ 1⁶ᵍᶠ 1-0-2 £5,890

Silver Charter (USA) H S Howe   a60
4 b g Silver Hawk (USA) - Pride Of Darby (USA)
11¹⁰ˢᵈ 16¹²ˢᵈ 0-0-2

Silver Chevalier D Burchell   37 a37
5 gr g Petong - Princess Eurolink
5¹²ᶠ 5¹²ˢᵈ 0-0-2

Silver Chime J M P Eustace   79 a70
3 gr f Robellino (USA) - Silver Charm
2⁶ᵍᶠ 3⁶ᵍᶠ 1⁶ᵍ 11⁶ᵍᶠ 5⁶ˢᵈ 12⁷ˢᵈ 1-2-6
£7,237

Silver City Mrs A J Perrett   83
3 ro c Unfuwain (USA) - Madiyla
3¹¹ᵍᶠ 2¹²ᵍ 6¹¹ᵍ 1¹²ᵍᶠ 16¹⁰ᵍᶠ 1-2-5
£6,198

Silver Coin (Ire) T D Easterby   65 a49
3 gr g Night Shift (USA) - Eurythmic
11⁸ˢᵈ 5⁷ˢᵈ 14¹⁰ᵍᶠ 17⁶ᵍ 8⁸ᵍᶠ 3¹²ˢᵈ 7¹²ˢᵈ
5¹²ᵍᶠ 9¹⁶ᵍˢ 3¹²ᵍᶠ 15¹⁰ᵍᶠ 2¹²ᶠ 11⁴ᵍᶠ 4¹⁴ᵍᶠ 2¹⁴ᶠ
1-3-15 £5,674

Silver Crystal (Ire) Mrs N Macauley   51 a53
3 b f Among Men (USA) - Silver Moon
6⁸ˢᵈ 5⁸ᶠ 12⁸ᵍᶠ 12⁸ᵍᶠ 9⁸ᵍ 3⁸ᵍᶠ 10⁸ᶠ 6⁸ᵍᶠ
0-1-8 £474

Silver Elite Miss Gay Kelleway   59 a70

4 gr f Forzando - Final Call
5^{6gs} 7^{5g} 1^{6sd} 8^{6sw} 4^{6sd} 1^{5sd} 7^{6gf} 12^{6sw}
8^{6sd} 2-0-9 £6,737

Silver Gilt *J H M Gosden*   103
3 b c Silver Hawk (USA) - Memory's Gold (USA)
3^{10g} 4^{12s} 0-0-2 £7,191

Silver Island *G A Butler*   28
2 ch c Silver Patriarch (Ire) - Island Maid
16^{7g} 0-0-1

Silver Kris (USA) *M Johnston*   23 a8
3 gr f Diesis - P J's Affair (USA)
7^{8sd} 9^{8sw} 11^{10gf} 0-0-3

Silver Louie (Ire) *G B Balding*   67
3 gr f Titus Livius (Fr) - Shakamiyn
5^{8g} 11^{12g} 13^{7gf} 14^{10g} 12^{10gf} 9^{10gf}
LFT^{8g} LFT^{8gf} 0-0-8

Silver Mascot *R Hollinshead*   43 a65
4 gr g Mukaddamah (USA) - Always Lucky
10^{6sd} 6^{6gf} 8^{5sw} 0-0-3

Silver Mode (USA) *G L Moore*   48 a62
4 ch g Silver Deputy (Can) - A La Mode (USA)
4^{8sd} 10^{6sd} 7^{8sd} 4^{10sd} 13^{10gf} 11^{8gf} 0-0-6
£263

Silver Prelude *D K Ivory*   88
2 b c Prince Sabo - Silver Blessings
7^{5g} 2^{5gf} 2^{5gf} 1^{5gf} 5^{5gf} 2^{5f} 5^{5gf} 10^{5g}
1-3-8 £12,271

Silver Prophet (Ire) *M R Bosley*   85 a74
4 gr g Idris (Ire) - Silver Heart
10^{11sd} 9^{10gf} 4^{11gf} 3^{10g} 13^{10g} 0-1-5
£1,320

Silver Rhythm *K R Burke*   35
2 ch f Silver Patriarch (Ire) - Party Treat (Ire)
10^{7gf} 0-0-1

Silver Seeker (USA) *D R Loder*   77
3 gr c Seeking The Gold (USA) - Zelanda (Ire)
8^{6gf} 0-0-1

Silver Shoes *J Parkes*   37 a9
4 b f Woodborough (USA) - Emerald Dream (Ire)
8^{11sw} 11^{16sd} 6^{15sw} 13^{8sd} 5^{12gf} 5^{10gf} 0-0-6

Silver Wood *J C Fox*   37
3 b f Silver Wizard (USA) - Eastwood Heiress
11^{6gs} 0-0-1

Silverdale Lady (Ire) *B A McMahon*   19
4 b f Great Commotion (USA) - Holme Sound
14^{7g} 9^{8gs} 10^{7gf} 8^{9sd} 0-0-4

Silverhay *T D Barron*   76
2 b g Inchinor - Moon Spin
5^{5gf} 2^{7g} 3^{7gs} 0-2-3 £956

Silverine (USA) *L M Cumani*   34
2 br f Silver Deputy (Can) - Special Broad (USA)
15^{6gf} 0-0-1

Silvertown *L Lungo*   79
8 b g Danehill (USA) - Docklands (USA)
1^{12gf} 1^{12f} 2-0-2 £21,008

Simianna *A Berry*   99 a86
4 b f Bluegrass Prince (Ire) - Lowrianna (Ire)
4^{5sd} 8^{5f} 3^{6s} 3^{6s} 4^{6gf} 11^{6g} 4^{6gf} 5^{6f} 1^{6gf}
5^{6gf} 6^{6gf} 6^{6g} 8^{6gf} 4^{6gf} 3^{6gf} 6^{6g} 3^{6g} 7^{6g} 8^{7gf}
1-5-19 £26,193

Simiola *S T Lewis*
4 b f Shaamit (Ire) - Brave Vanessa (USA)
10^{12sd} 0-0-1

Simlet *E W Tuer*   47

8 b g Forzando - Besito
5^{16gs} 7^{16gf} 0-0-2

Simon The Poacher *L P Grassick*   43
4 br g Chaddleworth (Ire) - Lady Crusty
15^{10gf} 7^{8gs} 7^{10gf} 13^{12gf} 12^{8gs} 0-0-5

Simon's Seat (USA) *J A R Toller*   74
4 ch g Woodman (USA) - Spire (USA)
13^{10gf} 11^{10gf} 6^{12g} 5^{16gf} 9^{15gf} 3^{16gf}
14^{16gf} 0-1-7 £1,740

Simonovski (USA) *J A Osborne*   a66
2 b c Miswaki (USA) - Eartha (USA)
5^{7sd} 5^{8sd} 0-0-2

Simons Wood *G M Moore*   46
2 b g Up And At 'Em - Roleover Mania
6^{5gs} 7^{5gf} 9^{7gf} 3^{5gf} 3^{6gf} 13^{7gf} 3^{7gf} 0-1-7
£1,387

Simple Ideals (USA) *Don Enrico Incisa*   48
9 b/br g Woodman (USA) - Comfort And Style
8^{12gf} 8^{14gs} 10^{14gf} 8^{14gs} 5^{14f} 5^{15g} 6^{14s}
5^{14gf} 8^{14gf} 8^{14f} 0-0-10

Simple Song *T D Easterby*
3 ch f Simply Great (Fr) - Cumbrian Rhapsody
12^{12gs} 0-0-1

Simply Red *R Brotherton*   14
2 ch g Vettori (Ire) - Amidst
9^{7f} 9^{5gf} 4^{6f} 0-0-3 £288

Simply Remy *John Berry*   15
5 ch g Chaddleworth (Ire) - Exemplaire (Fr)
10^{12gf} 0-0-1

Simply Sid *W H Tinning*   40
2 b g Presidium - Chadwick's Ginger
8^{6gf} 11^{6gf} 10^{7gs} 0-0-3

Simply The Guest (Ire) *Don Enrico Incisa*   a46
4 b g Mujadil (USA) - Ned's Contessa (Ire)
13^{6sd} 8^{7sd} 7^{7sw} 7^{8sd} 7^{8sd} 15^{6sd} 15^{6s}
0-0-7

Simpsons Supreme *R M Flower*   29 a47
3 ch f Abou Zouz (USA) - Conwy
9^{7g} 17^{7gs} 5^{10sd} 14^{12gs} 0-0-4

Sinamatella *C G Cox*   50
4 ch f Lion Cavern (USA) - Regent's Folly (Ire)
8^{8g} 17^{8gs} 19^{7g} 10^{7gf} 11^{7gf} 0-0-5

Sindapour (Ire) *M C Pipe*   89
5 b g Priolo (USA) - Sinntara (Ire)
4^{8f} 6^{10gf} 12^{8gs} 3^{8gs} 13^{10f} 11^{14gf} 1^{20gf}
2^{16g} 22^{18gf} 2-2-9 £36,176

Sindy (USA) *P F I Cole*   91
3 b f A.P. Indy (USA) - Dance Design (Ire)
7^{10gf} 11^{12f} 7^{13g} 9^{12gf} 1-0-4 £4,026

Singing Poet (Ire) *Saeed Bin Suroor*   75
2 b c Singspiel (Ire) - Bright Finish (USA)
1^{7s} 1-0-1 £3,432

Single Track Mind *J R Boyle*   35
5 b g Mind Games - Compact Disc (Ire)
10^{6gf} 13^{6gf} 0-0-2

Single Trigger (Ire) *H E Haynes*   49 a30
5 ch m Ela-Mana-Mou - Tycoon Aly (Ire)
5^{11gf} 8^{12sd} 5^{10gf} 10^{13gf} 0-0-4

Singlet *H J Collingridge*   59
2 ch c Singspiel (Ire) - Ball Gown
9^{7gs} 0-0-1

Singleton *H R A Cecil*   105
3 b f Singspiel (Ire) - Rive (USA)
2^{10gf} 1^{12gf} 2^{16f} 3^{12gf} 3^{15g} 2^{14gf} 5^{12gf}
1-5-7 £37,257

Singularity *W R Muir*   61 a24
3 b g Rudimentary (USA) - Lyrical Bid (USA)
12^{6sd} 9^{5sd} 4^{6gf} 3^{7f} 6^{6f} 3^{5gf} 7^{6g} 8^{5gf}
3^{10f} 14^{7gf} 5^{10gf} 5^{8f} **0-3-12 £1,438**

Sinjaree *Mrs S Lamyman*   67 a65
5 b g Mark Of Esteem (Ire) - Forthwith
10^{11sd} 4^{8sd} 5^{8sd} 3^{8sd} 10^{8sd} 9^{10gf} 4^{10gf}
2^{10gs} 12^{12g} 11^{10gf} 13^{8g} 13^{8gf} 14^{10gf} 14^{8sd}
7^{8gs} **0-2-15 £2,361**

Sinora Wood (Ire) *Mrs P N Dutfield*   68
2 b f Shinko Forest (Ire) - Moira My Girl
6^{5gf} 8^{6gf} 2^{5f} 4^{5gf} 5^{6g} 9^{6gf} 4^{6gf} 6^{6gf}
2^{7gf} 7^{7gf} 7^{7f} **0-2-11 £3,164**

Sion Hill (Ire) *Sir Michael Stoute*   70
2 b g Desert Prince (Ire) - Mobilia
2^{5gf} 8^{6gf} 2^{6gf} **0-2-3 £2,542**

Sioux River *B J Meehan*   74
2 ch f Indian Ridge - Washm (USA)
10^{6gf} 5^{7gf} 1^{7g} 5^{8gf} 4^{7gf} 16^{7gf} **1-0-6**
£5,398

Sioux Ryder (Ire) *R A Fahey*   73
2 gr f Intikhab (USA) - Street Lina (Fr)
2^{5gf} **0-1-1 £2,180**

Sipowitz *J Mackie*
9 b g Warrshan (USA) - Springs Welcome
16^{14gf} **0-0-1**

Sir Alfred *A King*   71
4 b g Royal Academy (USA) - Magnificent Star (USA)
8^{10g} 6^{10gs} 2^{10f} 9^{10gf} 8^{10g} 6^{14g} 3^{13f} 7^{16gf}
0-2-8 £1,954

Sir Bond (Ire) *B Smart*
2 ch g Desert Sun - In Tranquility (Ire)
11^{8g} **0-0-1**

Sir Brastias *S Dow*   88 a86
4 b g Shaamit (Ire) - Premier Night
7^{13sd} 3^{12g} 7^{14gf} 7^{14gf} 5^{12gf} **0-1-5**
£2,972

Sir Desmond *R Guest*   88 a88
5 gr g Petong - I'm Your Lady
10^{5sw} 6^{6sd} 16^{6g} 4^{6gs} 15^{6g} 1^{5g} 4^{6g} 9^{5s}
1-2-8 £10,688

Sir Don (Ire) *D Nicholls*   73 a62
4 b g Lake Coniston (Ire) - New Sensitive
8^{6sw} 5^{8sd} 7^{6sd} 5^{7sd} 4^{6gf} 1^{8f} 3^{8gf} 8^{7gf}
12^{6f} 7^{7f} 2^{7f} 7^{7gf} 2^{7gf} 1^{6gf} 5^{6gf} 3^{6g} 11^{6gf}
2-4-17 £21,706

Sir Edwin Landseer (USA) *P F I Cole*   89
3 gr c Lit De Justice (USA) - Wildcat Blue (USA)
4^{7gf} 7^{6gf} 3^{7gf} 5^{7gf} 5^{6g} 5^{6gf} 6^{7gf} 11^{7gf}
11^{6f} **0-0-9 £5,585**

Sir Ernest (Ire) *M J Polglase*   80 a66
2 b g Daggers Drawn (USA) - Kyra Crown (Ire)
3^{5sd} 2^{5sd} 6^{5f} 1^{5gf} 16^{5f} 1^{5g} 13^{5gf} 4^{5g}
9^{5gf} 9^{6gf} 8^{5gf} **2-2-11 £16,066**

Sir Francis (Ire) *J Noseda*   79 a85
5 b g Common Grounds - Red Note
10^{6sd} 5^{7sd} 5^{7sd} 25^{6g} 4^{7g} 9^{7f} 6^{7g} 11^{7sd}
0-1-8 £674

Sir Frank Gibson *M Johnston*   57
2 b c Primo Dominie - Serotina (Ire)
14^{6gf} 7^{6gf} 3^{6gf} 8^{6gf} 4^{8g} **0-1-5 £1,036**

Sir Galahad *T D Easterby*   55
2 ch g Hector Protector (USA) - Sharpening
6^{7gf} **0-0-1**

Sir Haydn *N P Littmoden*   75
3 ch c Definite Article - Snowscape

9^{4gf} 11^{12gs} 6^{10gf} 8^{12gf} 3^{8gf} 3^{10f} **0-1-6**
£3,091

Sir Jasper (Ire) *T D Barron*   a49
2 b g Sri Pekan (USA) - Ashover Amber
5^{6sd} 5^{6sd} **0-0-2**

Sir Laughalot *Miss E C Lavelle*   71
3 b c Alzao (USA) - Funny Hilarious (USA)
9^{8gf} 9^{9gf} 9^{7gs} **0-0-3**

Sir Loin *N Tinkler*   68
2 ch c Compton Place - Charnwood Queen
2^{5g} 7^{5gf} 6^{5gf} 7^{5gf} 8^{5g} **0-1-5 £970**

Sir Night (Ire) *J D Bethell*   65 a57
3 b c Night Shift (USA) - Highly Respected (Ire)
4^{8sd} 6^{7sd} 2^{7sd} 6^{7sw} 1^{7sd} 9^{8g} 2^{8gf} 1^{10gf}
3^{10gs} 2^{10gf} 2^{10g} 4^{10gf} 3^{10gf} 4^{10gf} 15^{10gs} 14^{10gf}
13^{10g} **2-6-17 £17,078**

Sir Northerndancer (Ire) *B Ellison*   76 a84
4 b c Danehill Dancer (Ire) - Lady At War
2^{7sd} 12^{6sd} 1^{6sw} 6^{6sw} 6^{6sd} 8^{7gf} 6^{7gf} 8^{6gf}
6^{6gf} 2^{6gs} 7^{6gf} 9^{6gf} **1-2-12 £5,886**

Sir Sandrovitch (Ire) *R A Fahey*   75
7 b g Polish Patriot (USA) - Old Downie
18^{5gf} 11^{5gf} 5^{5gs} 2^{5gf} 2^{5gf} 1^{5gf} 1^{5f} 1^{5g}
10^{5gs} 4^{5gf} 13^{5gf} 9^{5g} 11^{5gf} 6^{5gf} 6^{5gf} 10^{5gf}
7^{5gf} 12^{5gf} **3-2-18 £27,564**

Sir Sidney *D Morris*   85 a68
3 b g Shareef Dancer (USA) - Hattaafeh (Ire)
3^{8sd} 2^{10gf} 2^{12gf} 4^{12gf} 2^{12gf} 3^{10gf} 2^{11gf}
4^{14gf} **0-6-8 £8,992**

Siraj *N A Graham*   73 a70
4 b g Piccolo - Masuri Kabisa (USA)
20^{6g} 4^{6sd} 1^{6gf} 14^{6gf} 11^{7sd} **1-0-5**
£4,901

Sirius Lady *E L James*   35
3 b f Sir Harry Lewis (USA) - Intrepida
8^{10gf} **0-0-1**

Sissy Slew (USA) *D K Weld*   93
3 b f Unbridled's Song (USA) - Missy Slew (USA)
1^{8y} 3^{7ys} 4^{8ys} 7^{8f} 6^{10g} 6^{7g} 1^{9gf} 7^{9gf}
2-1-8 £21,428

Sister Bluebird *B J Meehan*   91
3 b f Bluebird (USA) - Pain Perdu (Ire)
6^{7gf} 10^{7gs} 4^{6gf} 5^{8f} 12^{7g} **0-0-5 £2,974**

Sister In Law (Fr) *H Candy*   38
4 b f Distant Relative - Despina
17^{5gf} **0-0-1**

Sister Sophia (USA) *G Wragg*   75 a67
3 b/br f Deputy Commander (USA) - Sophiaschoice (USA)
3^{7gf} 2^{7gf} 8^{9gf} 14^{7gf} 6^{6gf} 7^{10sd} **0-2-6**
£3,298

Six Pack (Ire) *Andrew Turnell*   44 a30
5 ch g Royal Abjar (USA) - Regal Entrance
7^{7sd} 10^{10gf} 13^{8sd} 18^{8gf} 7^{8s} 6^{8gf} 9^{10gf}
0-0-7

Six Perfections (Fr) *P Bary*   123
3 bl f Celtic Swing - Yogya (USA)
1^{7g} 2^{8gf} 2^{8s} 2^{8gs} 1^{8gs} 1^{8f} **3-3-6**
£821,146

Six Star *B W Duke*   50
3 b f Desert Story (Ire) - Adriya
8^{6g} 15^{7gf} 11^{6gf} 11^{5gf} 12^{6g} **0-0-5**

Sixtilsix (Ire) *J C Fox*   50
2 ch c Night Shift (USA) - Assafiyah (Ire)
6^{5y} 17^{5s} 9^{5gf} 13^{6gf} 13^{5gf} **0-0-5**

Skara Brae *G G Margarson*

3 b f Inchinor - Tahilla
13^{7sd} 0-0-1

Skater Boy *Miss Sheena West*   38
2 b g Wizard King - Makalu
10^{6gf} 9^{8gf} 0-0-2

Skehana (Ire) *J Nicol*   67
3 b f Mukaddamah (USA) - Lominda (Ire)
14^{7gf} 6^{10gf} 14^{10gs} 0-0-3

Skelligs Rock (Ire) *B W Duke*   72
3 b c Key Of Luck (USA) - Drew (Ire)
2^{10gf} 8^{12g} 0-1-2 £1,775

Sketch (Ire) *R Charlton*   67
2 ch f Perugino (USA) - Skew
5^{6gf} 1^{7gf} 1-0-2 £3,157

Ski Jump (USA) *R Charlton*   87
3 gr c El Prado (Ire) - Skiable (Ire)
1^{10gf} 6^{12gf} 8^{12gs} 1^{10f} 2-0-4 £11,310

Skibereen (Ire) *J H M Gosden*   79 a76
3 b g Ashkalani (Ire) - Your Village (Ire)
2^{10g} 4^{12gs} 2^{10sd} 3^{12sd} 2^{12gf} 0-3-5
£3,921

Skiddaw Jones *Miss L A Perratt*   67
3 b g Emperor Jones (USA) - Woodrising
1^{9gf} 9^{9g} 2^{9g} 5^{11gf} 4^{8f} 8^{10g} 11^{10gf} 9^{10gs}
1-1-8 £5,869

Skiff *D J Coakley*   53
3 b f Fleetwood (Ire) - Dame Helene (USA)
10^{8gf} 2^{10f} 4^{10gs} 2^{12gf} 6^{12gf} 0-1-5
£2,744

Skirt Around *W J Musson*   a51
5 b/br m Deploy - Fairy Feet
5^{12sd} 12^{12sw} 0-0-2

Sky Cove *M W Easterby*   33 a23
2 b c Spectrum (Ire) - Aurora Bay (Ire)
10^{8gf} 8^{6sd} 0-0-2

Sky Dome (Ire) *M H Tompkins*   67 a71
10 ch g Bluebird (USA) - God Speed Her
6^{10sd} 3^{10sd} 2^{10g} 12^{9sd} 6^{9gf} 11^{8g} 10^{8gf}
18^{8g} 4^{8gf} 8^{7sw} 5^{8sd} 0-3-11 £1,599

Sky Galaxy (USA) *E A L Dunlop*   82
2 ch f Sky Classic (Can) - Fly To The Moon (USA)
2^{6gf} 1^{6f} 5^{7gf} 8^{7g} 8^{6g} 8^{6gs} 1-1-6
£6,568

Sky Quest (Ire) *P W Harris*   89 a74
5 b g Spectrum (Ire) - Rose Vibert
3^{12sd} 2^{10sd} 5^{10sd} 2^{12gf} 7^{11gf} 2^{10gf} 1^{10f}
2^{10gf} 2^{10g} 6^{11gf} PU^{10gf} 2^{10gf} 1^{10gf} 2-7-13
£18,630

Skye's Folly (USA) *Mrs A J Perrett*   85 a71
3 b g Kris S (USA) - Bittersweet Hour (USA)
4^{8sd} 5^{10gf} 9^{10g} 1^{12f} 5^{14g} 11^{16gf} 5^{16gf} 2-0-7
£7,785

Skyers A Kite *Ronald Thompson*
8 b m Deploy - Milady Jade (Ire)
11^{12sw} 9^{12sd} 0-0-2

Skyharbor *D Nicholls*   89
2 b g Cyrano De Bergerac - Pea Green
4^{5gf} 1^{6gs} 3^{6gs} 1^{5gf} 14^{5f} 17^{6g} 2-0-6
£9,681

Skylark *Don Enrico Incisa*   66
6 ch m Polar Falcon (USA) - Boozy
12^{6gf} 7^{6gf} 15^{7gf} 8^{7g} 14^{6gf} 3^{6gf} 6^{6g} 2^{6gf}
13^{6g} 4^{8gf} 0-2-10 £1,325

Skylarker (USA) *W S Kittow*   86 a82
5 b g Sky Classic (Can) - O My Darling (USA)

6^{10sd} 2^{9sw} 3^{8gf} 6^{10gf} 9^{12gf} 4^{10gf} 3^{12gf}
7^{14g} 0-2-8 £4,273

Skymaite *Mrs G S Rees*   21 a26
3 b f Komaite (USA) - Sky Fighter
9^{6sd} 15^{8gf} 9^{7gf} 12^{6sd} 0-0-4

Slalom (Ire) *Miss Gay Kelleway*   74
3 b g Royal Applause - Skisette
5^{8gf} 3^{8s} 0-1-2 £542

Slap Shot (Ire) *L Riccardi*   113
4 ch f Lycius (USA) - Katanning
1^{5g} 1^{5gf} 3^{5g} 7^{5gf} 2^{5g} 2-2-5 £60,367

Slavonic (USA) *J H M Gosden*   78
2 ch c Royal Academy (USA) - Cyrillic (USA)
5^{7gf} 5^{8gf} 4^{8s} 0-0-3

Slink Along (USA) *J H M Gosden*   57
3 b c Gone West (USA) - Kool Kat Katie (Ire)
9^{8gf} 8^{10gf} 6^{9gf} 10^{16gf} 0-0-4

Slip Killick *M Mullineaux*   26 a23
6 b m Cosmonaut - Killick
13^{10g} UR^{6gs} 17^{10g} 7^{11gf} 9^{12gf} 11^{8sd} 0-0-6

Slippy Hitherao *B R Johnson*   57 a51
3 b f First Trump - Child Star (Fr)
8^{7gf} 3^{12sd} 8^{10gf} 16^{8gf} 15^{12sd} 7^{12sd} 4^{10f}
5^{10gf} 6^{10f} 0-1-9 £416

Sloe Gin *J L Dunlop*   71
4 b f A.P. Indy (USA) - Rose Bourbon (USA)
8^{12f} 13^{10gf} 10^{10gf} 0-0-3

Smart Boy Prince (Ire) *John A Harris*   49
2 b g Princely Heir - Miss Mulaz (Fr)
8^{6g} 9^{8gf} 12^{6gf} 5^{10gf} 0-0-4 £238

Smart Danny *J J Quinn*   38
2 gr g Danzero (Aus) - She's Smart
5^{7gf} 12^{7gs} 0-0-2

Smart Hostess *J J Quinn*   102 a86
4 gr f Most Welcome - She's Smart
4^{6sd} 1^{6sw} 1^{6sw} 9^{7gf} 5^{6gf} 6^{6gf} 14^{7g} 5^{8gs}
1^{6g} 1^{5gf} 7^{5gf} 1^{5gf} 1^{5gf} 6-1-13 £28,794

Smart John *B P J Baugh*   67
3 b g Bin Ajwaad (Ire) - Katy-Q (Ire)
7^{8g} 3^{8gs} 8^{8gf} 5^{11gf} 7^{10gf} 0-1-5 £605

Smart Minister *J J Quinn*   61 a49
3 gr g Muhtarram (USA) - She's Smart
12^{7gf} 8^{8gs} 7^{7gf} 3^{8f} 6^{7gf} 4^{8sw} 2^{8gs} 15^{8sd}
0-2-8 £1,571

Smart Predator *J J Quinn*   104
7 gr g Polar Falcon (USA) - She's Smart
16^{6gf} 14^{6gf} 7^{5g} 12^{5gf} 9^{6g} 2^{7gf} 6^{7g} 1^{6f}
2^{6gs} 4^{6gf} 1^{6gf} 1^{6gf} 2^{6gf} 13^{6g} 1^{5gs}
7^{6gf} 1^{5gf} 2^{5gf} 5-5-20 £71,451

Smart Scot *B P J Baugh*   31 a24
4 ch g Selkirk (USA) - Amazing Bay
15^{10gf} 9^{11gf} 9^{8f} 11^{11gf} 14^{10gf} 6^{9sd} 7^{7gf}
0-0-7

Smart Squall (USA) *A J Lidderdale*   56
8 b h Summer Squall (USA) - Greek Wedding (USA)
13^{14gs} 0-0-1

Smart Starprincess (Ire) *P A Blockley*   57 a68
2 b f Soviet Star (USA) - Takeshi (Ire)
3^{5sd} 2^{5sd} 3^{5sd} 9^{6gf} 9^{5f} 5^{5sw} 3^{5sd} 3^{5gf}
5^{5gf} 0-4-9 £3,299

Smarter Charter *Mrs L Stubbs*   22
10 br g Master Willie - Irene's Charter
11^{17g} 11^{12gf} 10^{12gf} 12^{14gf} 0-0-4

Smashing Time (USA) *M C Chapman*   24

5 b m Smart Strike (Can) - Broken Peace (USA)
15^{11sd} 11^{12sd} 8^{8gs} 15^{10g} **0-0-4**

Smirfys Dance Hall (Ire) *W M Brisbourne*   49
3 b f Halling (USA) - Bigger Dances (USA)
9^{8g} 6^{12f} **0-0-2**

Smirfys Linclon *W M Brisbourne*   a28
4 b g Never So Bold - Party Scenes
12^{8sd} 13^{6gf} **0-0-2**

Smirfys Party *D Nicholls*   66
5 ch g Clantime - Party Scenes
13^{5g} 15^{8gf} 8^{6gs} 14^{7g} 13^{7f} 14^{7gf} 15^{7gf}
16^{gf} 9^{5gf} 6^{6gf} **1-0-10 £4,111**

Smirfys Systems *W M Brisbourne*   86
4 b g Safawan - Saint Systems
5^{7gf} 10^{7gf} 16^{7gf} 16^{gf} 2^{6gf} **1-1-5**
£11,987

Smirk *D R C Elsworth*   113
5 ch h Selkirk (USA) - Elfin Laughter
9^{8g} 3^{8g} 2^{8g} 8^{9g} 17^{8g} **0-2-5 £25,200**

Smith N Allan Oils *M Dods*   67
4 b g Bahamian Bounty - Grand Splendour
16^{6gf} 7^{7gs} 11^{6gf} 6^{7f} 10^{6gf} 4^{7f} 5^{7f} 8^{8gf}
2^{7gf} 2^{7gf} 2^{7gf} 12^{7gf} 9^{7gf} 7^{8f} 5^{7gf} 2^{7f} **0-4-16**
£4,716

Smithy *Mrs N Macauley*   a48
4 ch f Greensmith - Biscay
14^{7sd} 11^{7sd} 5^{7sd} 5^{6sd} 9^{8sw} **0-0-5**

Smockington Hollow *J A Pickering*
2 b f Makbul - Indian Flower
8^{6g} **0-0-1**

Smokin Beau *N P Littmoden*   114
6 b g Cigar - Beau Dada (Ire)
3^{6g} 7^{6gf} 3^{5g} 15^{6gf} 6^{5g} 8^{5g} 5^{5g} 4^{6gf}
23^{6g} 13^{5gf} **0-2-10 £10,670**

Smokin Joe *J R Best*   62 a42
2 b c Cigar - Beau Dada (Ire)
12^{5gf} 6^{6sd} 6^{6gs} **0-0-3**

Smoking Barrels *Patrick J Flynn*   58
3 ch c Desert Prince (Ire) - Scandalette
11^{9gf} 20^{10g} 13^{7gy} **0-0-3**

Smooth Passage *J Gallagher*   16 a18
4 b g Suave Dancer (USA) - Flagship
9^{10sd} 11^{10gf} 11^{10gf} 14^{10g} **0-0-4**

Smoothie (Ire) *Ian Williams*   69 a72
5 gr g Definite Article - Limpopo
4^{12sd} 11^{10sd} 10^{10sd} 4^{10sd} 7^{9gf} 7^{10gf}
14^{10gs} 1^{10g} 6^{15sd} 6^{10gs} **1-1-10 £3,365**

Smoothly Does It *Mrs A J Bowlby*   69 a26
2 b c Efisio - Exotic Forest
5^{5gs} 5^{6gf} 5^{6sd} 3^{6g} 11^{7gf} 7^{7gf} 2^{8gf} 15^{8gf}
0-2-8 £1,496

Smyslov *P R Webber*   69
5 b g Rainbow Quest (USA) - Vlaanderen (Ire)
8^{10gf} 5^{10f} 8^{14g} 5^{12g} **0-0-4**

Sninfia (Ire) *L M Cumani*   69
3 b f Hector Protector (USA) - Christmas Kiss
7^{10g} 11^{10g} 4^{8gf} 9^{8g} 2^{10gf} 7^{10gf} 9^{12f} **0-1-7**
£1,611

Snip Snap *L Montague Hall*   53
4 b f Revoque (Ire) - Snap Crackle Pop (Ire)
14^{6g} 14^{5g} 14^{5gf} 18^{6g} 11^{5gf} **0-0-5**

Snippets (Ire) *J S Bolger*   105
3 b f Be My Guest (USA) - Sniffle (Ire)
4^{10g} 3^{11gf} 1^{12f} 2^{10g} 8^{12g} 5^{8f} 11^{9gf} **1-2-7**
£53,227

Snooker At Ray'S *M W Easterby*   22
2 ch c Komaite (USA) - Hollia
14^{5gf} 17^{6gf} **0-0-2**

Snooty Romance (Ire) *M P Sunderland*   57
3 br f Grand Lodge (USA) - Easy Romance (USA)
6^{7f} 6^{7f} 13^{8gf} 8^{12sd} 19^{7gf} **0-0-5**

Snow Bunting *Jedd O'Keeffe*   68
5 ch g Polar Falcon (USA) - Marl
17^{6gf} 14^{6gf} 2^{7g} 4^{6gf} 11^{6f} 4^{7gf} 10^{6gf}
6^{6gf} 5^{6f} 6^{7f} 11^{7gf} **0-3-11 £2,890**

Snow Chance (Ire) *K R Burke*   39
2 ch f Compton Place - Snowscape
8^{6gf} 12^{7gf} 4^{8g} 10^{8sd} **0-0-4 £250**

Snow Goose *J L Dunlop*   100
2 b f Polar Falcon (USA) - Bronzewing
4^{6gf} 1^{6g} 1^{7gf} 1^{7gf} 2^{7gf} **3-1-5 £44,195**

Snow Joke (Ire) *Mrs P N Dutfield*   60
2 b f Desert Sun - Snowcap (Ire)
9^{5gf} 7^{6gf} 7^{6g} **0-0-3**

Snow Leopard (Ire) *J L Dunlop*   91
4 gr g Highest Honor (Fr) - Leopardess (Ire)
9^{10g} 13^{10gf} **0-0-2**

Snow Ridge (Ire) *M P Tregoning*   112
2 b c Indian Ridge - Snow Princess (Ire)
1^{7g} 1^{8gf} 9^{7gf} **2-0-3 £63,930**

Snow Wolf *M P Tregoning*   76
2 ch c Wolfhound (USA) - Christmas Rose
8^{6f} 2^{5gf} 3^{6g} **0-2-3 £1,328**

Snow's Ride *W R Muir*   81 a73
3 gr c Hernando (Fr) - Crodelle (Ire)
6^{11gf} 8^{9gf} 7^{12g} 2^{12gf} 5^{12g} 3^{14f} 6^{14gf} 5^{14gf}
2^{16sd} 1^{16g} 5^{16g} 10^{16g} **1-2-12 £6,900**

Snowdrop (Ire) *J W Hills*   a48
3 ch f Petardia - Richardstown Lass (Ire)
8^{6sd} 10^{6sd} 12^{6sd} **0-0-3**

Snowed Under *J D Bethell*   22
2 gr g Most Welcome - Snowy Mantle
19^{8g} **0-0-1**

Snuki *G L Moore*   41 a81
4 b c Pivotal - Kennedys Prima
10^{10sd} 6^{10sd} 2^{10sd} 9^{8sd} 12^{8gf} 12^{10sd} **0-1-6**
£963

So Determined (Ire) *G A Butler*   44 a51
2 b g Soviet Star (USA) - Memory Green (USA)
11^{7gf} 10^{8sd} **0-0-2**

So Precious (Ire) *D K Ivory*   a58
6 b m Batshoof - Golden Form
6^{12sd} 2^{12sd} 1^{11sd} 8^{12sd} 5^{11sd} 2^{12sw} 4^{12sw}
11^{12sd} 4^{14sd} **1-2-10 £4,598**

So Sober (Ire) *D Shaw*   38 a54
5 b g Common Grounds - Femme Savante
10^{6sd} 4^{5sd} 6^{5sw} 2^{5sd} 3^{5sw} 8^{5sw} 2^{5sd} 14^{5gf}
7^{5sd} 9^{5gf} **0-3-10 £2,292**

So Sure (Ire) *J G M O'Shea*   65 a46
3 b g Definite Article - Zorilla
5^{8sd} 1^{9gf} 17^{10g} 1^{10gf} **2-0-4 £5,457**

So Tempted *N Wilson*   31
4 br f So Factual (USA) - Bystrouska
9^{10gf} 6^{9gf} 5^{10gf} **0-0-3**

So Vital *Mrs Lydia Pearce*   69
3 b c Pivotal - Sumoto
6^{10gs} **0-0-1**

So Will I *M P Tregoning*   90
2 ch c Inchinor - Fur Will Fly
4^{6gf} 1^{6gf} **1-0-2 £5,486**

Soaked *D W Chapman* 72 a64
10 b g Dowsing (USA) - Water Well
6^{5sd} 6^{5sd} 4^{5sd} 7^{5sd} 9^{5d} 19^{5gf} 3^{5gf} 3^{5hy}
11^{5gs} 1^{5gf} 5^{5gf} 5^{5gs} 12^{5g} 2^{5sd} 6^{5gf} 4^{5gf} 2^{5gf}
5^{6g} 5^{5g} 1-6-22 £14,084

Soap Stone *Miss A M Newton-Smith*
8 b m Gunner B - Tzarina (USA)
10^{12f} 0-0-1

Soap Watcher (Ire) *R A Fahey* 62
2 b g Revoque (Ire) - Princess Of Zurich (Ire)
14^{6g} 4^{7gf} 8^{6gf} 12^{8gs} 0-0-4

Soba Jones *J Balding* 82 a82
6 b g Emperor Jones (USA) - Soba
7^{6sd} 1^{6sw} 5^{5sw} 4^{6sd} 4^{6g} 17^{5gf} 11^{6g} 5^{6g}
7^{6gf} 10^{6gs} 9^{5gf} 13^{5gf} 5^{6sd} 2^{5gs} 1-2-14
£5,788

Social Contract *S Dow* 70 a66
6 b g Emarati (USA) - Just Buy Baileys
6^{6sd} 12^{7sd} 5^{7sw} 1^{6sd} 3^{6sw} 2^{7gf} 11^{7gf}
11^{6gs} 3^{7gf} 5^{7f} 12^{6gf} 10^{7f} 15^{6g} 9^{6f} 2^{7gf} 6^{8gf}
6^{6gf} 10^{7f} 1-5-21 £8,404

Socialise *W J Haggas* 46
3 b f Groom Dancer (USA) - Society Rose
5^{7f} 0-0-1

Society Pet *D G Bridgwater*
4 b f Runnett - Polar Storm (Ire)
8^{9sw} 0-0-1

Solanza *Noel T Chance* 33
4 ch f Bahamian Bounty - Son Et Lumiere
10^{9sd} 5^{7g} 11^{8f} 0-0-3

Solar Power (Ire) *J R Fanshawe* 72
2 b f Marju (Ire) - Next Round (Ire)
1^{7gf} 1-0-1 £3,523

Solar Prince (Ire) *J C Fox* 58
2 b g Desert Prince (Ire) - Quiche
12^{5ys} 4^{5y} 15^{5s} 9^{5gf} 9^{6gf} 16^{7gf} 0-0-6
£415

Soldera (USA) *J R Fanshawe* 106
3 b f Polish Numbers (USA) - La Pepite (USA)
4^{8gf} 1^{8g} 4^{8gf} 8^{8gf} 1-0-4 £22,692

Soldier On (Ire) *M J Wallace* 37 a42
5 b g General Monash (USA) - Golden Form
23^{8g} 8^{6sd} 0-0-2

Soleil D'Hiver *P C Haslam* 39
2 b f Bahamian Bounty - Catriona
10^{5g} 4^{7gf} 13^{6gf} 4^{7gf} 7^{6gf} 0-0-5 £390

Soliniki *J A Osborne* 71
2 b g Danzero (Aus) - Pride Of My Heart
1^{6gf} 1-0-1 £4,966

Soller Bay *K R Burke* 86
6 b g Contract Law (USA) - Bichette
8^{8g} 1^{8g} 8^{8g} 1^{8hy} 8^{8gs} 12^{7g} 12^{8gs} 4^{8gf}
6^{8gf} 6^{8s} 2-0-10 £14,809

Solo Flight *B W Hills* 100
6 gr g Mtoto - Silver Singer
9^{10gf} 8^{10g} 13^{10gf} 8^{12gf} 6^{10gf} 9^{10g} 6^{11gf}
7^{12gf} 2^{10g} 7^{10gf} 6^{12gf} 0-1-11 £3,768

Solo Solero (Ire) *Bernard Lawlor* 55
4 b f Bigstone (Ire) - Dreaming Spires
10^{6s} 10^{6g} 4^{5f} 7^{5gy} 1^{5gf} 7^{5f} 5^{5f} 20^{5gf}
1-0-8 £4,714

Solomon's Mine (USA) *M J Polglase* 81 a66
4 b g Rahy (USA) - Shes A Sheba (USA)
7^{11sw} 5^{14sw} 5^{16sw} 1^{18g} 2^{16gf} 3^{16gf} 1-2-6
£12,333

Somayda (Ire) *Miss Jacqueline S Doyle* 58
8 b g Last Tycoon - Flame Of Tara
6^{8gf} 13^{10gf} 9^{9gf} 4^{8gf} 4^{10g} 2^{8g} 5^{8gf} 9^{7gf}
11^{8gf} 13^{8gf} 0-1-10 £1,886

Someone's Angel (USA) *E A L Dunlop* 54
2 gr f Runaway Groom (Can) - Yazeanhaa (USA)
12^{8gf} 15^{8gf} 0-0-2

Somerset West (Ire) *B R Millman* 73 a63
3 b g Catrail (USA) - Pizzazz
5^{5sd} 8^{6sd} 5^{5sd} 4^{5sd} 7^{8gf} 15^{6g} 16^{6f} 1-0-7
£2,958

Somethingabouther *P W Hiatt* 64 a20
3 b f Whittingham (Ire) - Paula's Joy
9^{5gf} 3^{5gf} 2^{5gs} 3^{5gf} 10^{5f} 5^{5gf} 10^{5gf} 2^{5gf}
8^{5gf} 14^{5sd} 0-4-10 £3,240

Somewhere My Love *T G Mills* 57
2 br f Pursuit Of Love - Grand Coronet
5^{7gf} 7^{7gf} 0-0-2

Somnus *T D Easterby* 123
3 b g Pivotal - Midnight's Reward
5^{6g} 8^{7gf} 1^{6g} 4^{6gf} 2^{6gf} 1^{6gs} 7^{5ho}
3-1-8 £170,365

Son Of A Gun *M J Polglase* a52
9 b g Gunner B - Sola Mia
5^{16sd} 9^{16sd} 9^{16g} 0-0-3

Son Of Flighty *R J Hodges* 13
5 b g Then Again - Record Flight
16^{10gf} PU^{15sd} 10^{10gf} 0-0-3

Son Of Greek Myth (USA) *J H M Gosden* 81
2 b c Silver Hawk (USA) - Greek Myth (Ire)
2^{8gf} 3^{8gf} 4^{8s} 0-1-3 £2,554

Son Of Halling *D J Daly* 75
3 ch c Halling (USA) - La Sorrela (Ire)
2^{7g} 3^{8gf} 1^{8f} 15^{8f} 1-1-4 £6,108

Son Of Rembrandt (Ire) *D K Ivory* 67
2 b g Titus Livius (Fr) - Avidal Park
6^{5gf} 7^{5g} 5^{6g} 7^{6gf} 5^{5gf} 3^{5gf} 0-0-6 £451

Son Of Thunder (Ire) *M Dods* 37
2 ch g Dr Fong (USA) - Sakura Queen (Ire)
7^{6gf} 8^{7gs} 0-0-2

Sonderborg *H Candy* 60
2 b f Great Dane (Ire) - Nordico Princess
6^{6g} 3^{7f} 8^{6gf} 15^{6gf} 0-1-4 £642

Song Koi *J G Given* 58
2 b f Sri Pekan (USA) - Eastern Lyric
4^{5gf} 4^{5g} 0-0-2 £750

Song Of The Sea *J W Hills* a52
2 ch f Bering - Calypso Run
7^{7sd} 0-0-1

Song Of Vala *R Charlton* 72
2 ch c Peintre Celebre (USA) - Yanka (USA)
11^{8g} 4^{8gf} 2^{8gs} 0-1-3 £1,342

Songino (Ire) *J Parkes* 2
7 ch g Perugino (USA) - Sonbere
12^{14gf} 15^{16g} 12^{12gf} 11^{14sw} 0-0-4

Songlark *Saeed Bin Suroor* 109 a115
3 br c Singspiel (Ire) - Negligent
2^{10ft} 10^{8g} 4^{10gf} 5^{12gf} 2^{10g} 0-2-5
£261,650

Sonne De Loup *Mrs S A Liddiard*
2 ch f Wolfhound (USA) - Son Et Lumiere
16^{6g} 0-0-1

Sono *P D Niven* 89
6 b g Robellino (USA) - Sweet Holland (USA)
7^{10s} 2^{12gf} 9^{12gs} 9^{12g} 9^{10gf} 16^{13gs} 0-1-6

£2,170

Sonoma (Ire) *M L W Bell*   75
3 ch f Dr Devious (Ire) - Mazarine Blue (USA)
6^11gf 14^12gf 1^14gf 2^14gf 2^16gf 5^16gf **1-2-6**
£5,981

Soonest (Ire) *R Hannon*   99
2 br c Intikhab (USA) - Oklahoma
2^5gf 1st 3^5gs 7^5gf 1^5gf 7^5g 1^6gf 3^7gf
3-1-8 £22,400

Sophie Em *D Shaw*   17
3 ch f High Kicker (USA) - Golden Target (USA)
13^7g 13^7gf **0-0-2**

Sophies Symphony *K R Burke*   57 a39
4 b f Merdon Melody - Gracious Imp (USA)
6^7sw 12^6sd 5^7gf 6^7gf 9^7gf 7^7f 5^5gf 4^7gf
3^6gs 3^6f 12^6gf 16^6gf **0-2-12 £1,896**

Sophomore *John A Harris*   38
9 b g Sanglamore (USA) - Livry (USA)
13^7gf **0-0-1**

Sophrano (Ire) *P W Harris*   71 a72
3 b g Spectrum (Ire) - Sophrana (Ire)
6^8gf 8^10gf 13^8g 6^10sd **0-0-4**

Sorbiesharry (Ire) *Mrs N Macauley*   a64
4 gr g Sorbie Tower (Ire) - Silver Moon
2^8sd 8^8sd 1^8sd 5^8sd 8^10sd 11^10sd 12^8sd
8^9ft 12^8sw 3^12sd 9^7sd **1-2-12 £4,218**

Sotonian (Hol) *P S Felgate*   46 a49
10 br g Statoblest - Visage
6^5sd 9^5sw 11^5sd 17^5gf 5^5gs 19^5gf 5^5gf
9^5gf 12^6gf 8^5gf **0-0-10**

Sou'Wester *B J Llewellyn*   48
3 b g Fleetwood (Ire) - Mayfair
10^9gf 15^10gs **0-0-2**

Soul Provider (Ire) *I A Wood*   69 a63
2 ch f Danehill Dancer (Ire) - Wing And A Prayer (Ire)
5^5gf 2^5sd 5^6gf **0-1-3 £870**

Soulacroix *Mrs A J Perrett*   78
2 b c Kylian (USA) - California Dreamin
3^7gf 2^7gf 2^8gf 1^10gs **1-3-4 £4,936**

Sound Blaster (Ire) *A M Balding*   70
2 ch g Zafonic (USA) - Blasted Heath
11^6gf 4^8gf 1^8f **1-0-3 £2,957**

Sound Leader (USA) *J W Hills*   46 a33
3 ch c Diesis - Colledge Leader (USA)
10^8gf 8^8g 8^10g 4^12gf 10^10sd 9^10gf 12^10gf
0-0-7

Sound Of Fleet (USA) *P F I Cole*   71
2 ch c Cozzene (USA) - Tempo (USA)
2^7gf **0-1-1 £2,220**

Sounds Lucky *N P Littmoden*   52 a75
7 b g Savahra Sound - Sweet And Lucky
1^6sd 1^6sd 4^6sd 10^7sd 10^5sd 12^6sd 10^6sd
10^6g 2^6sd 5^6gs 4^6sd 10^8sd **2-1-12 £7,520**

South Atlantic *Sir Michael Stoute*   99
3 b c Sadler's Wells (USA) - Shimmering Sea
2^6f 1^8gf 6^7gf 1^8gf 8^7gf **2-1-5 £22,833**

Southampton Joe (USA) *A M Balding*   54 a38
3 ch g Just A Cat (USA) - Maple Hill Jill (USA)
11^7sd 2^7g 18^6gf 7^6gf 14^8g 16^7gf 11^8sd
0-0-7

Southern Bazaar (USA) *B W Hills*   66
2 ch c Southern Halo (USA) - Sunday Bazaar (USA)
5^7gf **0-0-1**

Southern Bound (Ire) *J G Burns*   89
2 b f Fasliyev (USA) - Headrest

1^5s 6^6g 7^7gf 1^6gf 4^6gf 5^6g **2-0-6**
£15,558

Southern Haze (USA) *J S Moore*
2 ch c Southern Halo (USA) - Hollow Haze (USA)
7^8t **0-0-1**

Sovereign Dreamer (USA) *P F I Cole*   85
3 b c Kingmambo (USA) - Spend A Dream (USA)
1^12gf 3^12gf 3^15g 9^11g 3^12g 14^11gf 6^12gs
1^12g 1^12gf 9^12gf **3-1-10 £22,063**

Sovereign Seal *M Johnston*   a39
3 b f Royal Applause - Downeaster Alexa (USA)
12^7sd **0-0-1**

Soviet Sceptre (Ire) *G A Butler*   74
2 ch c Soviet Star (USA) - Princess Sceptre
5^7g **0-0-1**

Soviet Song (Ire) *J R Fanshawe*   118
3 b f Marju (Ire) - Kalinka (Ire)
4^8gf 2^8gf 4^8gs 5^8gf **0-1-4 £94,648**

Soyuz (Ire) *M A Jarvis*   92 a70
3 ch g Cadeaux Genereux - Welsh Mist
3^6gf 2^8hy 3^7g 9^7g 17^7g 15^7sd **0-3-6**
£23,742

Spa Lane *J F Coupland*   69 a56
10 ch g Presidium - Sleekit
7^16g 11^7gf 1^16gf 3^16gf 2^16gs 6^17gf 5^16f
5^16gf 5^16gf 4^14sw 5^18gf 5^17f 6^18gf 1^16gf **3-2-14**
£12,632

Space Cowboy (Ire) *Mrs A J Perrett*   81 a55
3 b c Anabaa (USA) - Lady Moranbon (USA)
3^10gf 4^12sd 1^10gf **1-0-3 £3,578**

Space Star *J G Given*   64
3 b g Cosmonaut - Sophiesue
6^8gf 4^10gf 8^12gf 8^10gf **0-0-4 £425**

Spainkris *A Crook*   45
4 b g Kris - Pennycairn
10^16gf **0-0-1**

Spaniola (Ire) *D Haydn Jones*   a32
3 ch f Desert King (Ire) - Baddi Baddi (USA)
8^7sd **0-0-1**

Spanish Ace *A M Balding*   103
2 b c First Trump - Spanish Heart
2^5gf 1^5g 6^6gf 2^6g 6^7gf 8^7gs **1-1-6**
£29,810

Spanish Don *D R C Elsworth*   95
5 b g Zafonic (USA) - Spanish Wells (Ire)
8^8g 8^12gf 6^10gf 1^8gf 4^9gf 1^9gf **2-1-6**
£8,251

Spanish Gold *P J Makin*   70 a85
3 b f Vettori (Ire) - Spanish Heart
2^8sd 1^8sd 6^8gf **1-1-3 £4,546**

Spanish John (USA) *P F I Cole*   107
4 b/br g Dynaformer (USA) - Esprit D'Escalier (USA)
5^16g 4^13gf 8^13g 6^14gf 18^14gf 6^12g 2^12f
0-0-7 £6,791

Spanish Star *Mrs N Macauley*   a58
6 b g Hernando (Fr) - Desert Girl
5^11sd 5^9sd 2^11sd 3^9sw 6^9sw 5^12sw 3^9sd
4^12sd 10^9sd 7^9sd **0-4-11 £2,718**

Spanish Sun (USA) *Sir Michael Stoute*   109
3 b f El Prado (Ire) - Shining Bright
1^12gf 6^12g **1-0-2 £84,576**

Spark Of Life *T D McCarthy*   a51
6 b m Rainbows For Life (Can) - Sparkly Girl (Ire)
2^12sd **0-1-1 £1,048**

Spark Up *J W Unett*   70 a72

3 b f Lahib (USA) - Catch The Flame (USA)
10⁶ᵍᶠ 8⁶ʰʸ 9⁶ᵍᶠ 4⁷ᵍᶠ 9⁶ᵍ 6⁷ˢʷ 1⁷ˢᵈ **1-0-7**
£3,862

Sparkling Clear *R M H Cowell*   a42
2 b f Efisio - Shoot Clear
5⁵ᶠ 13⁷ˢᵈ 6⁶ˢᵈ **0-0-3**

Sparkling Jewel *R Hannon*   73 a73
3 b f Bijou D'Inde - Jobiska
3⁶ˢᵈ 1⁵ᵍ **1-1-2 £6,180**

Sparkling Water (USA) *D L Williams*   63
4 b c Woodman - Shirley Valentine
8²²ᶠ 14¹⁰ᵍ 5¹⁰ᵍᶠ 10¹²ᵍᶠ **0-0-4 £513**

Sparky's Mate *M H Tompkins*   88 a73
3 b g Vettori (Ire) - Nikiya (Ire)
5⁷ˢᵈ 2⁸ˢᵈ 1¹⁰ᵍᶠ 3¹⁰ᵍᶠ **1-2-4 £8,179**

Spartacus (Ire) *A P O'Brien*   100
3 b c Danehill (USA) - Teslemi (USA)
11¹⁰ᵍˢ 9⁸ᵍˢ **0-0-2**

Spartan Odyssey *A Senior*
2 b g Overbury (Ire) - Spartan Native
10⁵ˢᵈ 8⁵ᵍᶠ **0-0-2**

Spartan Principle *R Guest*   31
3 b f Spartan Monarch - Altar Point
9¹⁰ᵍᶠ **0-0-1**

Spartan Spear *D Morris*   69
2 b g Sure Blade (USA) - Confection
18⁸ˢ 4⁷ᵍ **0-0-2 £280**

Spearious (Ire) *B R Millman*   72 a62
2 b c Tagula (Ire) - Gloria Crown (Ire)
15⁶ᵍᶠ 6⁶ᵍ 7⁶ᵍᶠ 2⁵ˢʷ 2⁵ᵍᶠ **0-2-5 £1,453**

Special Branch *Jedd O'Keeffe*   53 a43
3 ch g Woodborough (USA) - Sixslip (USA)
5¹²ˢᵈ 6¹²ᵍᶠ 10¹²ᵍˢ 2¹²ᵍᶠ 7¹⁴ᶠ 3¹²ᵍ 4¹²ˢᵈ
5¹⁵ˢᵈ **0-1-8 £1,516**

Special Ellie (Fr) *I A Wood*   44 a61
3 b f Celtic Swing - Recherchee
4¹⁰ˢᵈ 9¹⁰ᵍᶠ **0-0-2 £397**

Special Thread (Ire) *Mrs A Duffield*   30 a17
2 b c Ela-Mana-Mou - Treadmill (Ire)
5⁵ˢᵈ 6⁶ᶠ **0-0-2**

Speciali (Ire) *J H M Gosden*   50
4 b g Bluebird (USA) - Fille Dansante (Ire)
14⁷ᵍᶠ 3⁸ᵍ **0-1-2 £693**

Specialism *M J Gingell*   a36
5 ch g Spectrum (Ire) - Waft (USA)
7¹²ˢʷ 10¹⁶ˢᵈ **0-0-2**

Speciality (Ire) *R Charlton*   45
3 ch f Entrepreneur - Park Special
8¹⁰ᵍ **0-0-1**

Specotia *M C Pipe*   50
2 ch c Spectrum (Ire) - Clan Scotia
5⁶ᵍ 5⁶ᵍᶠ 9⁵ᵍᶠ **0-0-3**

Spectacular Hope *R M Beckett*   53
3 b f Marju (Ire) - Distant Music
16⁸ᵍ 5¹⁰ᵍᶠ 7¹²ᵍᶠ 5¹²ᵍᶠ 5¹⁰ᵍᶠ 2⁸ᵍᶠ 14⁸ᶠ
12⁷ᶠ **0-1-8 £766**

Spectested (Ire) *B J Meehan*   71 a59
2 ch g Spectrum (Ire) - Nisibis
5⁷ᵍᶠ 5⁸ˢᵈ 8⁸ˢᵈ **0-0-3 £196**

Spectrometer *M Johnston*   94
6 ch g Rainbow Quest (USA) - Selection Board
8¹⁴ᵍᶠ 3¹⁴ᵍᶠ 1¹³ᵍᶠ 11¹²ᵍᶠ 3¹⁴ᵍᶠ 16¹⁵ᵍ **1-1-6**
£11,143

Spectroscope (Ire) *Jonjo O'Neill*   65
4 b g Spectrum (USA) - Paloma Bay (Ire)

15¹²ᵍᶠ 7¹⁴ˢ 5¹⁴ᵍᶠ **0-0-3**

Spectrum Star *F P Murtagh*
3 b g Spectrum (Ire) - Persia (Ire)
10⁸ˢᵈ **0-0-1**

Speed Cop *A M Balding*   106
3 ch f Cadeaux Genereux - Blue Siren
4⁵ᶠ 6⁵ᵍᶠ 4⁵ᶠ 4⁵ᶠ 1⁵ᵍᶠ 7⁵ᵍᶠ **1-1-6**
£14,597

Speed On *H Candy*   49
10 b g Sharpo - Pretty Poppy
6⁶ᵍ 15⁵ᵍᶠ 6⁶ᵍᶠ **0-0-3**

Speed Racer *M R Channon*   61
2 b f Zieten (USA) - Sharenara (USA)
3⁶ᶠ 7⁷ᵍᶠ 5⁶ᶠ **0-1-3 £696**

Speedbird (USA) *G Wragg*   66
2 ch f Sky Classic (Can) - Egoli (USA)
2⁶ᵍᶠ 7⁷ᵍˢ **0-1-2 £1,062**

Speedfit Free (Ire) *I Semple*   67 a68
6 b g Night Shift (USA) - Dedicated Lady (Ire)
8⁶ˢᵈ 3⁵ˢᵈ 6⁶ˢᵈ 8⁷ˢʷ 9⁶ˢʷ 1⁶ˢʷ 6⁷ˢᵈ 6⁶ᵍˢ
7⁶ˢᵈ 12⁶ᵍˢ 4⁵ᵍᶠ 1⁶ᶠ 8⁶ᵍ 7⁷ᵍ 3⁷ᵍ 5⁶ˢᵈ 13⁵ᵍᶠ
1⁶ᶠ 15⁶ᵍˢ **3-2-19 £12,540**

Speedwell *P J Makin*   22 a57
4 b f Spectrum (Ire) - Missed Again
6¹⁰ˢᵈ 7¹⁰ˢᵈ 8⁸ᵍˢ 11¹²ˢʷ **0-0-4**

Speedy Gee (Ire) *D Nicholls*   a37
5 b g Petardia - Champagne Girl
16⁶ˢʷ 5⁵ˢᵈ 10⁶ˢᵈ 6⁵ˢʷ **0-0-4**

Speedy James (Ire) *D Nicholls*   a17
7 ch g Fayruz - Haraabah (USA)
12⁶ˢʷ **0-0-1**

Spencers Wood (Ire) *P J Makin*   89
6 b g Pips Pride - Ascoli
4⁷ᵍ 18⁷ᵍᶠ **0-0-2 £1,009**

Sphinx (Fr) *Jamie Poulton*   83 a85
5 b g Snurge - Egyptale
13¹²ᵍᶠ 9¹²ˢᵈ 8¹²ˢᵈ 24²⁰ᵍᶠ 4¹⁴ᵍ 3¹⁵ᵍ **0-0-6**
£1,813

Spider McCoy (USA) *Miss B Sanders*   49 a29
3 ch g Irish River (Fr) - Indy's Princess (USA)
14¹⁰ᵍ 7¹²ᶠ 5¹⁰ᵍᶠ 4¹⁵ᵍ 11¹⁴ᵍᶠ 6¹²ˢᵈ 8¹²ᵍˢ
6¹¹ᵍᶠ 11¹⁰ᶠ **0-0-9 £422**

Spin King (Ire) *M L W Bell*   76
2 b c Intikhab (USA) - Special Dissident
5⁶ᵍᶠ 6⁶ᵍᶠ 1⁷ᵍᶠ 3⁷ᵍˢ **1-0-4 £5,831**

Spindor (USA) *J A Osborne*   72 a70
4 ch g Spinning World (USA) - Doree (USA)
4⁷ˢᵈ 1⁶ˢᵈ 8⁸ˢᵈ 12⁷ᵍᶠ 9⁶ˢᵈ 10⁷ᵍᶠ 1⁶ᵍᶠ
11⁷ᵍᶠ 13⁶ᶠ 8⁶ᵍ 5⁷ˢᵈ **2-0-11 £6,667**

Spinetail Rufous (Ire) *D W P Arbuthnot*   a60
5 b g Prince Of Birds (USA) - Miss Kinabalu
7⁶ˢᵈ 8⁶ˢᵈ 9⁵ˢᵈ **0-0-3**

Spinnaker *G A Butler*   50
3 b f Nashwan (USA) - Throw Away Line (USA)
16¹⁰ᵍᶠ **0-0-1**

Spinning Dove *N A Graham*   68 a47
3 ch f Vettori (Ire) - Northern Bird
4⁸ˢᵈ 6⁸ᵍᶠ 4⁷ᵍᶠ 2⁷ᵍᶠ 3⁷ᵍᶠ **0-2-5 £2,297**

Spinning Jenni *S Dow*   51 a55
3 b f Mind Games - Giddy
8⁶ˢᵈ 13⁶ˢᵈ 11⁶ᵍ 18⁷ᵍᶠ 8⁹ᵍ **0-0-5**

Spinola (Fr) *P W Harris*   102
3 b f Spinning World (USA) - Exocet (USA)
13⁸ᵍᶠ 10⁷ᵛˢ 6⁸ᵍᶠ 8⁸ᵍˢ 15⁷ᵍ 4⁷ᵍᶠ **0-0-6**
£2,950

Spinsky (USA) *P F I Cole* 27
3 b f Spinning World (USA) - Walewskaia (Ire)
12¹²ᵍˢ 12¹⁰ᵍᶠ 14⁸ᵍᶠ **0-0-3**

Spirit Of Gold (USA) *E A L Dunlop* 6
3 ch c Silver Hawk (USA) - Gazayil (USA)
7¹¹ʰʸ **0-0-1**

Spirit's Awakening *J Akehurst* 67
4 b g Danzig Connection (USA) - Mo Stopher
10⁸ᵍ 6⁸ᵍᶠ 15⁸ᵍᶠ 4⁹ᵍ 2⁸ᵍᶠ 2⁹ᵍᶠ **0-2-6**
£2,328

Spiritual Air *J R Weymes* 90
3 b f Royal Applause - Samsung Spirit
4⁸ᶠ 2⁸ᵍˢ 3⁸ᵍˢ 6⁸ᵍᶠ 7¹⁰ᵍ 5⁸ᵍˢ 10⁹ʰᵒ **0-0-7**
£7,972

Spiritus *C N Kellett*
2 ch g Double Trigger (Ire) - Nafla (Fr)
PU⁸ᵍ 11⁷ᵍˢ **0-0-2**

Spitfire Bob (USA) *T D Barron* 68 a77
4 b g Mister Baileys - Gulf Cyclone (USA)
1⁹ˢᵈ 5¹²ˢᵈ 17¹⁰ᵍˢ 4⁹ˢᵈ 8⁸ᵍᶠ 16⁸ᶠ 2¹⁰ᵍᶠ
7¹²ᵍᶠ 2¹⁰ᵍᶠ 1¹⁰ᵍᶠ 7¹⁰ᵍ 7¹⁰ᵍᶠ **2-2-12 £10,621**

Spitting Image (Ire) *Mrs M Reveley* 70
3 ch f Spectrum (Ire) - Decrescendo (Ire)
2¹²ᵍᶠ 4¹²ᶠ 2¹²ᵍᶠ 11¹²ᵍᶠ 2¹²ᵍᶠ 4¹⁴ᵍˢ **0-3-6**
£3,696

Splash Out Again *H Morrison* 70
5 b g River Falls - Kajetana (Fr)
5¹¹ᵍᶠ 1¹²ᵍᶠ 4¹⁴ᵍᶠ 7¹⁷ᶠ 3¹⁴ᵍ 4¹⁶ᵍᶠ **1-0-6**
£4,800

Splendid Era (UAE) *B W Hills* 113
3 b c Green Desert (USA) - Valley Of Gold (Fr)
3⁸ᵍᶠ 3¹⁰ᵍˢ 3¹⁰ᵍ 1⁸ᵍᶠ **1-0-4 £35,534**

Spliff *H Candy* 88
2 b c Royal Applause - Snipe Hall
9⁵ᵍᶠ 2⁵ᵍᶠ 1⁵ᵍᶠ **1-1-3 £4,830**

Splodger Mac (Ire) *N Bycroft* 50
4 b g Lahib (USA) - Little Love
15⁵ᵍᶠ 4⁷ᵍᶠ 3⁸ᵍᶠ 10⁹ᵍᶠ 6⁷ᵍᶠ **0-1-5 £942**

Sporting Affair (Ire) *N P Littmoden* a43
3 ch f Ashkalani (Ire) - The Multiyorker (Ire)
13⁷ˢᵈ 11⁷ˢᵈ 11⁸ˢᵈ 8⁶ˢᵈ **0-0-4**

Sporting Gesture *M W Easterby* 84
6 ch g Safawan - Polly Packer
4¹⁰ᵍᶠ 1¹⁰ᵍᶠ 4¹¹ᵍᶠ 2¹²ᵍᶠ 2¹²ᵍᶠ 4¹²ᵍᶠ 1¹²ᵍᶠ
2¹²ᶠ 9¹⁶ᵍᶠ 6¹²ᵍᶠ 1¹²ᵍᶠ 2¹²ᵍᶠ 9¹²ᵍᶠ 8¹²ᵍᶠ 15¹²ᵍ
3-4-15 £38,446

Sporting Grand (USA) *J R Weymes* 26 a26
2 b g Southern Halo (USA) - Al Yazi (USA)
18⁵ᵍᶠ 7⁶ˢᵈ 7⁶ᶠ 11⁷ᵍˢ 10⁶ᵍᶠ **0-0-5**

Sports Express *G A Swinbank* 59 a59
5 ch m Then Again - Lady St Lawrence (USA)
2¹⁴ˢᵈ 4¹⁴ᵍˢ 3¹⁴ˢ **0-2-3 £1,882**

Sportsman (Ire) *M W Easterby* a49
4 b g Sri Pekan (USA) - Ardent Range (Ire)
3¹²ˢᵈ **0-1-1 £422**

Sportula *Mrs A J Perrett* 22
2 b f Silver Patriarch (Ire) - Portent
13⁷ᵍᶠ 14⁸ˢ **0-0-2**

Spotlight *J L Dunlop* 101
2 ch f Dr Fong (USA) - Dust Dancer
3⁷ᵍᶠ 1⁷ᵍᶠ 2⁷ᵍᶠ 18⁹ˢ **2-2-4 £20,879**

Spring Adieu *Mrs A J Perrett* 55
2 b f Green Desert (USA) - Nanda
13⁸ᵍᶠ 9⁷ᵍ **0-0-2**

Spring Breeze *M Dods* 50

2 ch g Dr Fong (USA) - Trading Aces
16⁶ᵍᶠ 4⁶ᵍ 10⁷ᶠ 3⁸ᵍᶠ 11¹⁰ᵍᶠ **0-1-5 £467**

Spring Dancer *A P Jarvis* 73
2 b f Imperial Ballet (Ire) - Roxy Music (Ire)
2⁶ᵍᶠ 1⁶ᵍᶠ 3⁶ᵍᶠ 2⁶ᵍᶠ 9⁶ᵍᶠ 6⁷ᵍᶠ 6⁷ᵍᶠ 12⁶ᶠ
13⁶ᵍᶠ **1-2-9 £7,483**

Spring Goddess (Ire) *A P Jarvis* 80
2 b f Daggers Drawn (USA) - Easter Girl
16⁶ᵍᶠ 3⁷ᵍᶠ 1⁷ᵍᶠ 6⁷ᵍᶠ 8⁸ᵍᶠ **1-0-5 £4,697**

Spring Jim *J R Fanshawe* 70
2 b g First Trump - Spring Sixpence
4⁶ᵍᶠ 5⁶ᵍᶠ 7⁶ᵍᶠ **0-0-3 £1,089**

Spring Pursuit *R J Price* 53
7 b g Rudimentary (USA) - Pursuit Of Truth (USA)
7¹⁰ᵍ 13¹²ᵍ **0-0-2**

Spring Surprise *B W Hills* 70
2 b f Hector Protector (USA) - Tender Moment (Ire)
10⁶ᵍᶠ 1⁷ᵍ **1-0-2 £3,640**

Spring Whisper (Ire) *E A L Dunlop* 9
2 b f Halling (USA) - Light Fresh Air (USA)
17⁷ᵍ **0-0-1**

Springalong (USA) *H R A Cecil* 77
3 ch c Gone West (USA) - Seven Springs (USA)
4⁸ᵍᶠ 3⁹ᵍᶠ 3⁷ᵍᶠ 7⁸ˢ **0-1-4 £1,732**

Spuradich (Ire) *L M Cumani* 99
3 b c Barathea (Ire) - Svanzega (USA)
3¹⁰ᵍᶠ 5¹⁰ᵍᶠ 1⁸ᵍ 12⁸ᵍᶠ 1⁹ᵍ 1¹⁰ᵍᶠ 18¹⁰ᵍᶠ
3-1-7 £34,019

Spy Gun (USA) *E A L Dunlop* 48
3 ch g Mt. Livermore (USA) - Takeover Target (USA)
7⁸ᵍᶠ 14¹⁰ᵍᶠ **0-0-2**

Spy Master *J Parkes* 34
5 b g Green Desert (USA) - Obsessive (USA)
14⁸ˢʷ 12⁸ˢᵈ 11⁶ᵍˢ 8⁶ˢ 10⁶ᵍᶠ **0-0-5**

Square Dancer *D A Nolan* 23
7 b g Then Again - Cubist (Ire)
10⁹ᵍᶠ 10⁷ᵍˢ 12⁷ᶠ **0-0-3**

Squeaky *Miss K M George* 71
6 ch m Infantry - Steady Saunter Vii
2¹⁰ᵍᶠ 2¹²ᵍ 9¹⁰ᵍᶠ 13¹⁴ᵍˢ **0-2-4 £2,890**

Squire Michael (USA) *P F I Cole* 63
3 b c Affirmed (USA) - Elle Meme (USA)
8¹⁰ᶠ 6¹¹ᵍᶠ 4¹⁰ᵍᶠ **0-0-3**

Squirtle Turtle *P F I Cole* 77
3 ch g Peintre Celebre (USA) - Hatton Gardens
7¹⁰ᵍ 13¹²ᵍ 3⁷ᵍ 5¹⁰ᵍᶠ 13⁸ᵍᶠ 3¹¹ᵍᶠ **0-2-6**
£1,075

Sri (Ire) *P Monteith* 6 a53
4 b f Sri Pekan (USA) - Verify (Ire)
14⁷ˢᵈ 15⁷ˢᵈ 11⁷ˢᵈ 11⁶ᵍ 7⁸ˢᵈ 17¹⁰ᵍ 12⁹ᵍ
16⁹ᵍˢ **0-0-8**

Sri Angkasa (Ire) *M A Jarvis* 88
3 ch c Night Shift (USA) - Miss Kelly
13⁸ᵍ 2⁸ᵍᶠ 3⁸ᵍᶠ **0-1-3 £2,040**

Sri Diamond *S Kirk* 82 a88
3 b c Sri Pekan (USA) - Hana Marie
9¹⁰ᵍ 3⁷ˢᵈ 7⁸ᵍᶠ **0-1-3 £640**

St Austell *J A R Toller* 76
3 b g Compton Place - Paris Joelle (Ire)
3⁵ᵍ 2⁵ᵍᶠ 15⁶ᵍᶠ 2⁵ᵍᶠ 1⁵ᵍᶠ **1-3-5 £6,157**

St Cassien (Ire) *T M Jones* 11
3 b g Goldmark (USA) - Moonlight Partner (Ire)
10⁷ᵍᶠ **0-0-1**

St Edith (Ire) *C F Wall* 52
3 ch f Desert King (Ire) - Carnelly (Ire)

6⁷ᵍᶠ 7¹⁰ᵍˢ 9¹⁰ᵍ **0-0-3**

St Francis Wood (USA) *J Noseda*   93
2 ch f Irish River (Fr) - Francisco Road (USA)
2⁸ᵍˢ **0-1-1 £4,400**

St George's Girl *J R Jenkins*   16
2 b f Muthahb (Ire) - Nickelodeon
14⁷ᵍᶠ 10⁶ᵍᶠ 15⁶ˢᵈ **0-0-3**

St Ivian *Mrs N Macauley*   73 a75
3 b g Inchinor - Lamarita
3⁶ˢᵈ 6⁶ˢᵈ 1⁶ˢᵈ 9⁷ᵍ UR⁵ˢᵈ 11⁶ᵍᶠ 5⁵ˢᵈ 2⁵ˢ
3⁶ᵍᶠ 5⁵ᵍᶠ 4⁶ᵍ 3⁵ᵍᶠ 6⁵ᵍ 11⁷ᵍᶠ 6⁵ᵍᶠ 14⁵ᵍᶠ 7⁶ˢᵈ
10⁶ˢᵈ **1-4-18 £9,623**

St Jerome *N P Littmoden*   67
3 ch g Danzig Connection (USA) - Indigo Dawn
3¹³ᵍᶠ 7¹⁸ᵍᶠ 1¹⁴ᶠ 12¹⁶ᵍᶠ 5¹⁴ᶠ **1-1-5**
£4,392

St Jude *K A Ryan*   33
3 b c Deploy - Little Nutmeg
11⁶ᵍᶠ 13⁸ᵍᶠ **0-0-2**

St Pancras (Ire) *N A Callaghan*   93
3 b c Danehill Dancer (Ire) - Lauretta Blue (Ire)
5⁷ᵍ 4⁹ᵍᶠ 5⁶ᵍᶠ 6⁷ᵍᶠ **0-0-4 £2,422**

St Petersburg *M H Tompkins*   90 a83
3 ch g Polar Falcon (USA) - First Law
12⁷ᵍˢ 7⁷ᵍ 1⁷ˢᵈ 8⁷ˢᵈ 11⁷ˢᵈ 3⁷ˢᵈ 1⁸ᵍ 5⁷ˢᵈ
2-1-8 £8,259

St Regs (Ire) *R Hannon*   78
2 b c Sri Pekan (USA) - Young Isabel (Ire)
4⁶ᵍ 2⁶ᵍᶠ 2⁵ᵍᶠ 6⁵ˢ 1⁶ᵍᶠ **1-2-5 £7,255**

St Savarin (Fr) *J R Best*   74 a62
2 ch g Highest Honor (Fr) - Sacara (Ger)
5⁵ᵍᶠ 10⁵ᵍᶠ 9⁵ᵍᶠ 7⁵ᵍᶠ 10⁶ᵍᶠ 2⁶ˢᵈ 6⁶ᵍᶠ
1⁷ᵍˢ **1-1-8 £4,153**

St Tropez (Ire) *B G Powell*   30 a24
2 b f Revoque (Ire) - Kaziranga (USA)
10⁷ˢᵈ 9⁸ᵍᶠ **0-0-2**

Staff Nurse (Ire) *N Tinkler*   51
3 b f Night Shift (USA) - Akebia (USA)
13⁸ᵍ 13⁷ᶠ 12⁸ᵍ 6⁹ᵍˢ 11¹⁰ᵍˢ 5¹²ᵍᶠ 3¹⁰ᵍᶠ
2¹⁴ᵍˢ 3¹⁰ᵍᶠ 5¹¹ᵍˢ 3¹¹ᵍᶠ **0-4-11 £1,539**

Stage By Stage (USA) *C R Egerton*   90
4 ch g In The Wings - Lady Thynn (Fr)
11¹⁰ᵍᶠ 19¹²ᵍᶠ 19¹⁴ᵍᶠ **0-0-3**

Stage Direction (USA) *B J Llewellyn*   27
6 b g Theatrical - Carya (USA)
12¹⁶ᵍᶠ **0-0-1**

Stage Shy (USA) *J H M Gosden*   94
3 ch f Theatrical - Garimpeiro (USA)
1¹⁰ᵍᶠ 7¹⁰ᵍ 7¹²ᵍᶠ **1-0-3 £5,681**

Stagecoach Revival (Ire) *M Johnston*   60
3 ch c Nashwan (USA) - Hill Of Snow
5¹¹ᵍˢ **0-0-1**

Stagecoach Ruby *J R Best*   55
2 b f Bijou D'Inde - Forum Girl (USA)
7⁵ᶠ 7⁵ᵍᶠ 8⁶ʰʸ 9⁶ᵍᶠ 1⁷ᶠ 1⁷ᵍᶠ 3⁶ᶠ 6⁶ᵍᶠ 7⁷ᵍᶠ
6⁷ᵍᶠ 5⁷ᵍᶠ 12⁸ᵍᶠ **2-1-12 £6,661**

Stagnite *K R Burke*   63 a61
3 ch g Compton Place - Superspring
8⁶ˢᵈ 7⁶ˢᵈ 5⁷ˢᵈ 4⁷ˢᵈ 4⁷ˢᵈ 8⁶ᶠ 13⁷ᵍᶠ 8⁷ᵍˢ
2⁶ᵍᶠ 2⁶ᶠ 2⁶ᵍᶠ 2⁶ᵍᶠ 8⁶ᶠ 10⁵ᵍᶠ 2⁶ᶠ 8⁶ᵍᶠ
9⁶ᶠ **0-6-18 £7,366**

Stakhanovite (Ire) *D R Loder*   80
3 b c Darshaan - Homage
3⁸ᵍᶠ **0-1-1 £617**

Stallone *N Wilson*   84 a46

6 ch g Brief Truce (USA) - Bering Honneur (USA)
7⁸ˢᵈ 2⁸ᶠ 3⁸ᵍᶠ 1¹⁰ᵍᶠ 1¹⁰ᵍᶠ 3¹⁰ᵍᶠ 3⁹ᵍᶠ 5⁰ˢᵈ
5¹⁰ᵍᶠ 2¹²ᵍᶠ 3¹⁰ᵍᶠ 1¹²ᶠ 18¹²ᵍᶠ **3-6-13 £15,747**

Stamford Blue *J S Moore*   58 a29
2 b c Bluegrass Prince (Ire) - Fayre Holly (Ire)
6⁵ᵍᶠ 1⁵ᵍᶠ 12⁵ᵍᶠ 11⁶ˢᵈ 11⁵ᵍˢ **1-0-5**
£3,045

Stance *R C Guest*   60
4 b g Salse (USA) - De Stael (USA)
9¹⁴ᵍᶠ 15¹³ᵍˢ **0-0-2**

Stand By *T D McCarthy*   38 a64
6 b m Missed Flight - Ma Rivale
2⁶ˢᵈ 8⁶ˢᵈ 2⁵ˢᵈ 4⁶ˢᵈ 9⁶ˢᵈ 6⁶ˢᵈ 2⁵ˢᵈ 2⁵ˢᵈ
5⁵ˢ 16⁷ᵍᶠ 10⁵ᵍᶠ 15⁵ˢᵈ **0-4-12 £3,432**

Standiford Girl (Ire) *L A Dace*   a27
6 b m Standiford (USA) - Pennine Girl (Ire)
13¹⁶ˢᵈ 6⁸ˢᵈ 12¹⁶ˢᵈ **0-0-3**

Stanhope Forbes (Ire) *N P Littmoden*   73
2 b c Danehill Dancer (Ire) - Hinari Disk Deck
7⁵ᵍˢ 6⁷ᵍᶠ 3⁷ᵍᶠ 5⁸ᶠ 16⁸ᵍˢ **0-0-5 £580**

Stanley Crane (USA) *B Hanbury*   70 a69
2 br c Bahri (USA) - Grey Starling
4⁶ᵍᶠ 3⁷ˢᵈ 5⁷ᵍᶠ **0-1-3 £798**

Star Applause *J Balding*   52 a52
3 b f Royal Applause - Cominna
1⁵ˢᵈ 5⁵ˢᵈ 2⁵ᵍᶠ 14⁵ᵍˢ 6⁵ᵍᶠ 10⁵ˢᵈ 17⁵ᵍᶠ
1-1-7 £3,825

Star Cross (Ire) *J L Dunlop*   87
4 b g Ashkalani (Ire) - Solar Star (USA)
10¹⁰ᵍ 13¹²ᵍ 7¹²ᵍᶠ 2¹⁵ᵍ 12¹⁴ˢ **0-1-5**
£2,092

Star Lad (Ire) *R Brotherton*   63 a63
3 ch g Lake Coniston (Ire) - Simply Special (Ire)
5⁵ˢᵈ 4⁵ˢᵈ 3⁶ˢᵈ 5⁶ˢᵈ 5⁵ᶠ 2⁶ᵍᶠ 11⁶ᶠ
6⁶ᶠ 7⁶ˢᵈ 11⁶ˢᵈ **0-3-11 £2,519**

Star Member (Ire) *A P Jarvis*   87 a57
4 b g Hernando (Fr) - Constellation (Ire)
8¹¹ˢᵈ 6¹⁴ᵍᶠ 3¹⁴ᵍᶠ 2¹⁴ᵍᶠ 15¹⁵ᵍ 5¹⁶ˢᵈ 8¹⁶ᵍᶠ
0-1-7 £11,055

Star Of Arabia (Ire) *N A Gaselee*   62 a52
4 b f Hamas (Ire) - Thank One's Stars
7⁵ᵍᶠ 10⁵ᵍᶠ 16⁵ᵍᶠ 4⁷ᶠ 1⁶ᵍ 7⁶ᶠ 8⁵ᵍᶠ 1⁶ᵍᶠ
9⁶ˢᵈ 13⁷ˢᵈ **2-0-10 £7,599**

Star Of Germany (Ire) *T P Tate*   a20
3 b g Germany (USA) - Twinkle Bright (USA)
5⁸ˢᵈ 4¹¹ˢʷ **0-0-2**

Star Of Light *B J Meehan*   42 a70
2 b g Mtoto - Star Entry
12⁷ᵍᶠ 6⁷ˢᵈ 2⁷ˢᵈ **0-1-3 £1,144**

Star Of Normandie (USA) *G G Margarson*   81 a87
4 b f Gulch (USA) - Depaze (USA)
4¹⁰ᵍᶠ 6⁸ᵍ 9⁸ˢ 11⁸ˢᵈ 3⁸ᵍ 1¹⁰ᵍˢ **1-1-6**
£3,253

Star Ovation (Ire) *Mrs A M Naughton*   62
6 ch g Fourstars Allstar (USA) - Standing Ovation
6⁹ᵍᶠ 14⁷ᵍᶠ 6⁶ᵍ 4⁸ᵍᶠ **0-0-4 £293**

Star Pete *M R Channon*   61
2 b g Fraam - Stride Home
5⁸ᵍᶠ **0-0-1**

Star Princess *J Gallagher*   25 a51
6 b m Up And At 'Em - Princess Sharpenup
13⁶ˢᵈ 13⁸ˢᵈ 4⁸ˢᵈ 7⁸ˢᵈ 6⁸ˢᵈ 9⁷ˢᵈ 8⁸ᵍᶠ
1-0-8 £3,290

Star Pupil *A M Balding*   75
2 ch c Selkirk (USA) - Lochangel

19⁷ᵍᶠ 2⁷ᵍˢ 0-1-2 £1,278

Star Sensation (Ire) *P W Harris*　　97
3 b/br f Sri Pekan (USA) - Dancing Sensation (USA)
6⁸ᵍᶠ 4⁸ᵍˢ 2⁸ᵍᶠ 6⁸ᶠ 1⁸ᵍᶠ 15⁸ᵍᶠ 4⁸ᵍᶠ 2⁸ᵍ
5⁸ˢ 4⁸ᵍᶠ 9⁸ˢ 8⁸ᵍᶠ 1-2-12 £15,765

Star Seventeen *T H Caldwell*　　a8
5 ch m Rock City - Westminster Waltz
7¹²ˢᵈ 0-0-1

Star Sound *T D Barron*　　a33
3 br g Millkom - Tarnside Rosal
7⁸ˢᵈ 8⁷ˢᵈ 0-0-2

Star Welcome *W J Musson*　　40
2 ch f Most Welcome - My Greatest Star
10⁶ᵍᶠ 0-0-1

Star Wonder *B N Doran*　　18
3 b f Syrtos - Galava (Can)
10¹⁰ᵍᶠ 11⁷ᵍ 4⁷ᵍᶠ 7⁷ᵍᶠ 0-0-4 £430

Starbeck (Ire) *P S McEntee*　　89 a54
5 b m Spectrum (Ire) - Tide Of Fortune
8⁸ˢᵈ 12⁷ᵍ 4⁷ᵍᶠ 8⁶ᵍᶠ 3⁶ᵍ 10⁷ᵍᶠ 6⁷ᵍᶠ 8⁶ᵍᶠ
5⁷ᵍᶠ 5⁷ᵍᶠ 2⁷ᵍᶠ 20⁷ᵍᶠ 0-2-12 £7,881

Starbright *Miss S E Hall*　　15
2 b g Polar Falcon (USA) - Treasure Hunt
7⁶ᵍᶠ 0-0-1

Stargem *Mrs Lydia Pearce*　　75
2 b f Compton Place - Holy Smoke
8⁶ᵍᶠ 2⁶ᵍᶠ 0-1-2 £1,712

Starlight Night (USA) *Mrs A J Perrett*　　a67
4 ch f Distant View (USA) - Diese (USA)
4¹⁰ˢᵈ 0-0-1

Starminda *Mrs C A Dunnett*　　31
3 b f Zamindar (USA) - Starfida
13⁷ᵍᶠ 0-0-1

Starry Lodge (Ire) *L M Cumani*　　99
3 b c Grand Lodge (USA) - Stara
11¹¹ᵍᶠ 11¹¹ᵍᶠ 3¹²ᵍᶠ 11¹¹ᵍˢ 6¹²ᵍᶠ 4¹¹ᵍᶠ 1¹²ᵍᶠ
2¹²ᵍᶠ 1¹³ᵍᶠ 5-3-9 £37,908

Starry Mary *E L James*　　64
5 b m Deploy - Darling Splodge
3¹²ᵍᶠ 5¹²ᶠ 2¹³ᵍ 7¹²ᵍˢ 10¹⁴ˢ 0-1-5
£1,705

Stars At Midnight *I A Wood*　　53
3 b f Magic Ring (Ire) - Boughtbyphone
4⁸ᵍᶠ 8⁶ᵍᶠ 8⁸ᵍᶠ 1⁸ᵍᶠ 8⁸ᵍ 16⁸ᵍᶠ 1-0-6
£4,636

Start Over (Ire) *E J O'Neill*　　84 a82
4 b c Barathea (Ire) - Carnelly (Ire)
3⁸ˢᵈ 20¹⁰ᵍˢ 2⁸ˢᵈ 5¹⁰ᵍˢ 5⁸ᵍᶠ 8⁸ᶠ 3⁸ᶠ 1⁹ᵍᶠ
1⁸ᵍᶠ 6¹⁰ᵍˢ 2⁹ᵍᶠ 10⁸ᵍᶠ 2⁸ᵍᶠ 2⁸ᵍ 11⁹ᵍᶠ 2-5-15
£17,121

Startled *J Jay*　　28
4 ch f Zilzal (USA) - Zelda (USA)
11⁸ˢᵈ 12⁸ᵍˢ 0-0-2

State Dilemma (Ire) *B W Hills*　　90
2 b c Green Desert (USA) - Nuriva (USA)
3⁷ᵍᶠ 3⁷ᵍᶠ 1⁷ᵍᶠ 4⁸ᵍᶠ 1-2-4 £8,928

State Of Balance *K Bell*　　a55
5 ch m Mizoram (USA) - Equilibrium
11⁷ˢʷ 8⁸ˢᵈ 0-0-2

Statement (Ire) *Sir Michael Stoute*　　95
3 b c Singspiel (Ire) - Last Spin
2¹²ᵍᶠ 4¹⁰ᵍᶠ 0-1-2 £2,517

Stateroom (USA) *J A R Toller*　　81 a76
5 ch g Affirmed (USA) - Sleet (USA)
18⁶ᵍᶠ 5⁷ᵍᶠ 5¹⁰ᶠ 10¹⁰ᵍ 7¹⁰ᵍᶠ 1⁸ᵍᶠ 5⁸ˢᵈ 4⁸ᶠ

1-0-8 £3,344

Statoyork *D Shaw*　　51 a53
10 b g Statoblest - Ultimate Dream
4⁵ˢᵈ 10⁵ˢʷ 5⁵ˢʷ 11⁵ᵍᶠ 4⁵ᵍᶠ 8⁵ᶠ 8⁵ᵍᶠ 9⁶ᶠ
0-1-8 £280

Statue Of Liberty (USA) *A P O'Brien*　　118
3 b/br c Storm Cat (USA) - Charming Lassie (USA)
8⁸ᵍᶠ 2⁸ᵍˢ 9⁸ᵍˢ 7⁸ʰᵒ 8⁹ᶠᵗ 0-1-5 £62,700

Stavros (Ire) *J S Wainwright*　　55
3 b c General Monash (USA) - Rivers Rainbow
12⁶ᵍ 13⁶ᶠ 13⁶ᵍ 7⁵ᵍᶠ 5⁶ᶠ 12⁷ᶠ 8⁵ᵍᶠ 3⁵ᶠ
11⁶ᵍᶠ 5⁵ᵍᶠ 9⁵ᵍᶠ 7⁵ᵍ 7⁶ᵍᶠ 6⁶ᶠ 0-1-14 £578

Stealing Beauty (Ire) *L M Cumani*　　74
3 b f Sadler's Wells (USA) - Imitation
9¹⁰ᵍᶠ 1¹²ᶠ 1-0-2 £2,184

Stealthelimelight (Ire) *N A Callaghan*　　83
2 b c Royal Applause - Scylla
3⁵ᵍᶠ 4⁵ᵍᶠ 1⁵ᵍᶠ 5⁶ᵍˢ 2⁵ᵍᶠ 4⁵ᵍᶠ 3⁵ᵍᶠ 5⁶ᵍᶠ
1⁶ᵍᶠ 1⁷ᵍ 10⁷ᵍ 11⁶ᵍᶠ 3-1-12 £20,531

Steel Blue *R M Whitaker*　　89
3 b c Atraf - Something Blue
5⁸ᶠᵗ 6⁶ᶠᵗ 9⁶ᵍ 4⁶ᵍ 24⁶ᵍ 5⁵ˢ 11⁶ᵍᶠ 8⁵ᵍᶠ
2⁶ᵍˢ 2⁵ᵍ 0-2-10 £5,161

Steel Cat (USA) *L M Cumani*　　91 a52
3 b/br c Sir Cat (USA) - Daisy Daisy (Ire)
3⁷ᵍᶠ 7⁷ˢᵈ 1¹⁰ᵍᶠ 6¹⁰ᵍᶠ 7¹²ᵍˢ 4⁹ᵍᶠ 2-1-6
£11,271

Steely Dan *J R Best*　　52 a55
4 b g Danzig Connection (USA) - No Comebacks
9⁷ˢᵈ 11⁸ˢᵈ 12¹⁰ᵍᶠ 9¹⁰ᵍᶠ 17⁸ˢ 5⁶ᵍᶠ 0-0-6

Steenberg (Ire) *M H Tompkins*　　112
4 ch g Flying Spur (Aus) - Kip's Sister
6⁶ᵍᶠ 5⁶ᵍᶠ 14⁶ᶠ 16⁶ᵍᶠ 4⁹ᵍᶠ 4⁸ᵍᶠ 3⁷ᵍᶠ 4⁶ᵍˢ
9⁶ᵍᶠ 1⁶ᵍ 1-1-10 £33,178

Stella Marais (Ire) *P R Chamings*　　56
2 b f Second Empire (Ire) - Karakapa (Fr)
4⁷ᵍᶠ 7⁶ᵍᶠ 8⁷ᵍˢ 0-0-3

Stellite *J S Goldie*　　43
3 ch g Pivotal - Donation
15⁶ᵍ 9⁸ᵍ 5⁹ᵍˢ 9¹⁰ᵍˢ 0-0-4

Stemagnum *H Morrison*　　31
4 ch c Beveled (USA) - Stemegna
15⁷ᵍ 19⁶ᵍ 8⁶ᵍ 0-0-3

Step Perfect (USA) *M Johnston*　　58
2 b c Royal Academy (USA) - Gossiping (USA)
6⁸ᵍᶠ 6¹⁰ᶠ 5⁸ᵍᶠ 0-0-3

Stepalong *Mrs P N Dutfield*
2 b f Piccolo - Saunders Lass
12⁵ᵍᶠ 6⁶ᵍˢ 0-0-2

Stepastray *R E Barr*　　52 a53
6 gr g Alhijaz - Wandering Stranger
2¹¹ˢʷ 6¹²ˢᵈ 5¹²ˢᵈ 6¹²ᵍᶠ 6⁸ᵍᶠ 4⁸ᵍᶠ 10⁸ˢᵈ
7¹⁰ᵍᵖ 8¹⁶ᵍᶠ 3⁸ᵍᶠ 1¹⁰ᵍᶠ 7¹¹ᵍᶠ 14¹⁰ᵍ 9¹⁰ᵍˢ 16¹⁰ᵍᶠ
1-2-15 £6,717

Stephano *B W Hills*　　77
2 ch g Efisio - Polo
5⁶ᵍᶠ 11⁷ᵍᶠ 0-0-2

Steppenwolf *W De Best-Turner*　　43
2 gr c Sesaro (USA) - Lozzie
8⁶ᵍᶠ 7⁶ᵍᶠ 17⁸ᵍᶠ 9¹⁰ᵍˢ 0-0-4

Sterling Guarantee (USA) *D Nicholls*　　76
5 b g Silver Hawk (USA) - Sterling Pound (USA)
11⁷ᵍᶠ 6⁸ᵍᶠ 3¹²ᵍ 14¹²ᵍ 0-1-4 £654

Stevedore (Ire) *B J Meehan*　　77

2 ch c Docksider (USA) - La Belle Katherine (USA)
10^{6gf} 2^{6gf} 1^{7gf} 4^{7gf} **1-1-4 £3,611**

Stila (Ire) *B W Duke*   a51
4 b f Desert Style (Ire) - Noorajo (Ire)
11^{7sd} 9^{10sd} **0-0-2**

Stiletto Lady (Ire) *J G Given*   59
2 b f Daggers Drawn (USA) - Nordic Pride
8^{7gf} 4^{7g} 8^{7gs} **0-0-3 £277**

Still Speedy (Ire) *Noel T Chance*   51
6 b g Toulon - Gorge
6^{18f} **0-0-1**

Sting Like A Bee (Ire) *J S Goldie*   57 a62
4 b c Ali-Royal (Ire) - Hidden Agenda (Fr)
2^{9sd} 8^{9sd} 5^{12g} 5^{10gf} 6^{12g} 9^{12gf} 6^{12f} 7^{10g}
0-1-8 £942

Stitch In Time *G C Bravery*   a38
7 ch g Inchinor - Late Matinee
10^{11sd} 11^{13sd} 6^{12sw} 13^{16sd} **0-0-4**

Stoic Leader (Ire) *R F Fisher*   78 a48
3 b g Danehill Dancer (Ire) - Starlust
5^{6sd} 3^{6gf} 3^{5g} 1^{6gf} 1^{5gs} 2^{5gf} 4^{6gf} 9^{5gs}
4^{6g} 8^{6sd} 6^{6gf} 8^{6gs} 7^{6gf} 9^{5f} 4^{6gf} 2^{6f} 17^{5gf}
11^{5gs} 9^{6g} 7^{6gf} **2-3-20 £12,157**

Stokesies Boy *J L Spearing*   48 a46
3 gr c Key Of Luck (USA) - Lesley's Fashion
8^{8gf} 5^{7sd} 6^{7gf} 4^{6gf} **0-0-4**

Stokesies Wish *J L Spearing*   68
3 ch f Fumo Di Londra (Ire) - Jess Rebec
12^{5gf} 16^{6gf} 8^{5gf} 3^{5gf} 8^{6f} 3^{6gf} 13^{5gf}
8^{5gf} 3^{5gf} 3^{6gf} 7^{5gf} 1^{6g} 15^{6gf} 2^{6gs} **1-5-14**
£5,531

Stolen Hours (USA) *E A L Dunlop*   76
3 b/br c Silver Deputy (Can) - Fasta (USA)
4^{10gf} 6^{11g} 4^{10gf} 3^{14gf} 4^{12g} **0-1-5 £759**

Stolen Song *M J Ryan*   65 a63
3 b g Sheikh Albadou - Sparky's Song
19^{7gs} 9^{7gf} 4^{7f} 7^{10gf} 3^{10gf} 3^{10sd} 5^{10gf}
2^{12sd} **0-3-8 £1,786**

Stonegrave *M W Easterby*   51
4 ch f Selkirk (USA) - Queen Midas
5^{12gf} 6^{17g} 11^{14gf} **0-0-3**

Stonor Lady (USA) *B J Meehan*   14
2 b/br f French Deputy (USA) - Blush With Love (USA)
18^{6gf} **0-0-1**

Stoop To Conquer *J L Dunlop*   77
3 b g Polar Falcon (USA) - Princess Genista
7^{10gf} 5^{10gs} 3^{12g} 5^{16gf} 6^{17g} **0-1-5 £860**

Stop The Nonsense (Ire) *E J O'Neill*   47
2 b c Orpen (USA) - Skip The Nonsense (Ire)
17^{8gf} 9^{8gf} 8^{8g} **0-0-3**

Stopwatch (Ire) *Mrs L C Jewell*
8 b g Lead On Time (USA) - Rose Bonbon (Fr)
11^{12f} **0-0-1**

Storm Clear (Ire) *R Hannon*   63
4 b c Mujadil (USA) - Escape Path
4^{8g} 6^{9g} 12^{8gf} 7^{7gf} 7^{8gf} 5^{8hd} 9^{8f} **0-1-7**
£306

Storm Clouds *T D Easterby*   47
2 gr c Cloudings (Ire) - Khalsheva
10^{7gf} 5^{9f} **0-0-2**

Storm Shower (Ire) *Mrs N Macauley*   a63
5 b g Catrail (USA) - Crimson Shower
6^{7sd} 7^{7sd} 2^{8sd} 5^{7sw} 10^{8sd} 6^{8sd} 9^{7sw} 3^{7sd}
0-2-8 £1,262

Storm Wizard (Ire) *D G Bridgwater*

6 b g Catrail (USA) - Society Ball
PU^{16sd} **0-0-1**

Storming Home *N Drysdale*   124
5 b h Machiavellian (USA) - Try To Catch Me (USA)
11^{2f} 11^{4g} 4^{10g} 1^{10f} 7^{12f} **3-0-5**
£406,250

Storming Star (Ity) *C F Wall*   69
3 b f Shantou (USA) - Somalia (Fr)
6^{10gf} 9^{10gs} **0-0-2 £220**

Stormont (Ire) *H J Collingridge*   112
3 gr c Marju (Ire) - Legal Steps (Ire)
8^{6gf} 8^{6gf} 2^{6gf} 6^{6gf} 3^{6gf} 1^{6g} 7^{6gf} **1-1-7**
£61,555

Stormville (Ire) *M Brittain*   46
6 b g Catrail (USA) - Haut Volee
13^{7gf} **0-0-1**

Stormy Day *M A Jarvis*   58
3 b f Rainbow Quest (USA) - Broken Peace (USA)
6^{8gf} 7^{8gs} **0-0-2**

Stormy Nature (Ire) *P W Harris*   72
2 b/br f Mujadil (USA) - Ossana (USA)
4^{6gf} 2^{5gs} 8^{6gs} **0-1-3 £2,053**

Stormy Rainbow *M Blanshard*   51 a54
6 b g Red Rainbow - Stormy Heights
11^{10sd} 9^{8g} 8^{10gs} 9^{10g} 16^{12gf} 12^{12sd} 8^{10gf}
19^{11gf} **0-0-8**

Stormy Skye (Ire) *G L Moore*   51
7 b g Bluebird (USA) - Canna
9^{16gf} **0-0-1**

Stracomer Thalia (Ire) *Ian Williams*   a19
5 b m Mujadil (USA) - Peach Melba
14^{8sd} 10^{7sw} 10^{12sd} **0-0-3**

Stracomer Urania (Ire) *Ian Williams*
5 gr m Paris House - Pheopotstown
14^{12sd} 9^{12sd} **0-0-2**

Straight Eight *T D Easterby*   29
4 b g Octagonal (NZ) - Kalymnia (Ger)
5^{12hy} 7^{10g} 0^{9s} 10^{7ho} 10^{12gs} **0-0-5 £487**

Straighten Up (Ire) *Sir Michael Stoute*   32
2 b f Nashwan (USA) - Alignment (Ire)
15^{7gs} **0-0-1**

Strange (Ire) *E J O'Neill*
5 b g Alzao (USA) - Partie De Dames (USA)
13^{12sd} **0-0-1**

Strangely Brown (Ire) *S C Williams*   44
2 b g Second Empire (Ire) - Damerela (Ire)
13^{6gf} 10^{5gf} **0-0-2**

Strategy *Sir Michael Stoute*   86
3 br f Machiavellian (USA) - Island Story
3^{10gf} 4^{12gf} 1^{11gf} 6^{10gf} 1^{10gf} 2^{10gf} 3^{10gf}
2-2-7 £14,457

Strath Fillan *H J Collingridge*   35
5 b m Dolphin Street (Fr) - Adarama (Ire)
9^{12f} 10^{19gf} 17^{9gf} **0-0-3**

Strathclyde (Ire) *J Cullinan*   92
4 b g Petong - It's Academic
2^{6gf} 12^{6gf} 3^{6gf} 9^{5gf} 11^{6gf} 1^{5gf} 11^{5gf}
5^{5gf} 8^{6g} 16^{6g} 8^{6gf} 7^{5f} 20^{5gf} **1-2-13**
£16,949

Strathspey *C F Wall*   76
4 ch f Dancing Spree (USA) - Diebiedale
5^{8g} 3^{9gf} 4^{9gf} 2^{10gf} 3^{10f} 4^{8gf} **0-3-b**
£2,952

Stravmour *R Hollinshead*   59 a43
7 ch h Seymour Hicks (Fr) - La Stravaganza

5^{10g} 7^{10gf} 7^{12sw} 6^{12sd} 12^{10g} **0-0-5**

Straw Bear (USA) *Sir Mark Prescott*   55 a76
2 ch c Diesis - Highland Ceilidh (Ire)
5^{6sd} 2^{6sd} 3^{7gf} 1^{8sw} **1-2-4 £3,930**

Straw Boss (Ire) *Mrs A J Perrett*   74 a73
3 b g Darshaan - Ezana
3^{12sd} 4^{14gf} **0-1-2 £302**

Straw Poll (USA) *M R Channon*   80
2 ch c Dixieland Band (USA) - Golden Opinion (USA)
1^{5gs} 3^{6gf} 2^{5g} 3^{5gf} **1-1-4 £7,698**

Strawberry Dawn *J R Boyle*   56 a59
5 gr m Fayruz - Alasib
2^{5sd} 5^{5sw} 1^{5sd} 11^{5sw} 1^{5sw} 10^{5sd} 2^{5g} 5^{5sd}
7^{5sd} 19^{6gf} **2-2-10 £10,180**

Strawberry Fair *D R Loder*   65
2 b f Kingmambo (USA) - Storm Song (USA)
2^{8gf} **0-1-1 £1,281**

Strawberry Patch (Ire) *Miss L A Perratt*   71
4 b g Woodborough - Okino (USA)
11^{6g} 17^{6gf} 6^{5gf} 16^{6gf} 9^{5g} **0-0-5**

Streaky (Ire) *Mrs P N Dutfield*   52
3 b f Danetime (Ire) - Solo Symphony (Ire)
12^{6g} 9^{6f} 12^{5gf} **0-0-3**

Street Games *J Gallagher*   31
4 b g Mind Games - Pusey Street
8^{7gf} 9^{8g} **0-0-2**

Street Life (Ire) *W J Musson*   70 a79
5 ch g Dolphin Street (Fr) - Wolf Cleugh (Ire)
6^{12sd} 3^{12sd} 12^{12sd} 8^{10sd} 8^{10g} 10^{10gf} **0-1-6**
£1,686

Strength 'n Honour *C A Cyzer*   106 a59
3 b g Hernando (Fr) - Seasonal Splendour (Ire)
1^{12sd} 1^{10gf} 3^{10gf} 17^{12g} 5^{12gf} 8^{15gf} **2-1-6**
£23,293

Strensall *R E Barr*   86 a49
6 b g Beveled (USA) - Payvashooz
6^{5sw} 14^{5sd} 2^{5gf} 2^{5f} 11^{5gf} 4^{5g} 12^{5gf} 3^{5gs}
3^{5gf} 3^{5gf} 2^{5f} 13^{5gf} 3^{5gf} 14^{5gf} 3^{5f} 1^{5g} 2^{5gf}
7^{5g} 1^{5gf} 4^{5gs} **2-10-23**
£27,215

Stretton (Ire) *J D Bethell*   88
5 br g Doyoun - Awayil (USA)
12^{10sd} 6^{9gf} 4^{10gf} 4^{8gf} 9^{10g} 3^{10gf} 3^{9gf}
1^{10gf} 9^{9gf} **1-2-9 £13,030**

Streyza (Ire) *J R Jenkins*   43
6 b m Shernazar - Millzao
9^{10g} 7^{8sd} 14^{10f} **0-0-3**

Strictly Speaking (Ire) *R Brotherton*   a62
6 b g Sri Pekan (USA) - Gaijin
10^{16sd} 3^{11sd} 3^{12sd} 8^{12sd} 2^{15sd} **0-3-5**
£1,690

Strident (USA) *G A Butler*   53
2 ch c Deputy Commander (USA) - Regrets Only (USA)
6^{5g} **0-0-1**

Strider *Sir Michael Stoute*   66
2 ch c Pivotal - Sahara Belle (USA)
16^{7gf} 7^{7gf} **0-0-2**

Strike Lucky *P J Makin*   55
3 ch g Millkom - Lucky Flinders
4^{7gf} 7^{9gf} **0-0-2 £631**

Striking Ambition *G C Bravery*   119 a90
3 br c Makbul - Lady Roxanne
3^{8sd} 1^{6g} 1^{6gf} 14^{6gf} 7^{6s} 16^{5ho} **2-0-6**
£40,620

Striptease *T D Easterby*   27

Strong Hand *M W Easterby*   83 a69
3 b f First Trump - Better Still (Ire)
13^{8gf} 5^{6sd} 3^{7gf} 1^{8gs} 3^{8gs} 3^{8gf} 5^{7sd} **1-2-7**
£8,653

Strong Will *C W Fairhurst*   54
3 b g Primo Dominie - Reine De Thebes (Fr)
5^{8gf} 15^{7gf} 13^{7f} 8^{10f} 3^{12gf} 7^{16gf} **0-1-6**
£450

Studmaster *P F I Cole*   70 a43
3 ch g Snurge - Danlu (USA)
9^{10g} 7^{12gs} 6^{12gf} 9^{12sd} 5^{18gf} 9^{16gf} **0-0-6**

Stunning Force (Ire) *M Johnston*   97
4 b c Ezzoud (Ire) - New Wind (Ger)
11^{12gf} 1^{12gf} 1^{12gf} 4^{12gs} 4^{12g} **2-0-5**
£21,819

Stunning Magic *Mrs Barbara Waring*   24 a11
3 b g Magic Ring (Ire) - Absolutelystunning
9^{8gf} 9^{7sw} **0-0-2**

Stutter *John G Carr*   29
5 ch h Polish Precedent (USA) - Bright Spells
11^{8gf} **0-0-1**

Style Dancer (Ire) *T D Easterby*   73
9 b g Dancing Dissident (USA) - Showing Style
6^{8gf} 13^{8gf} 8^{8gf} 11^{8gf} 11^{8g} 11^{9g} 4^{10gf}
4^{9gf} 6^{10gf} 9^{11g} 9^{10gf} **0-0-11 £1,076**

Stylish Prince *J G M O'Shea*   17
3 b g Polar Prince (Ire) - Simply Style
16^{8gf} 14^{12g} **0-0-2**

Stylish Sunrise (Ire) *M L W Bell*   66
2 b c Desert Style (Ire) - Anita At Dawn (Ire)
16^{8gf} 3^{8gf} 6^{8gs} **0-1-3 £1,098**

Sualda (Ire) *R A Fahey*   73
4 b g Idris (Ire) - Winning Heart
10^{8gf} 8^{9gf} 4^{9gf} 7^{10gf} 10^{10f} 11^{12gf} 5^{12gf}
7^{12f} 5^{12gf} 12^{12gf} 17^{12gf} **1-1-11 £7,206**

Suave Performer *S C Williams*   55
6 b g Suave Dancer (USA) - Francia
10^{10gf} 5^{10gf} 12^{9gf} 7^{10gf} 8^{9g} **0-0-5**

Suave Quartet (USA) *G A Butler*   58 a77
2 b c Slew City Slew (USA) - Leallah M (USA)
6^{7gf} 2^{8sd} **0-1-2 £669**

Subadar Major *Mrs G S Rees*   17
6 b g Komaite (USA) - Rather Gorgeous
10^{12gf} 9^{14f} 13^{12gf} 8^{12g} **0-0-4**

Sublimity (Fr) *Sir Michael Stoute*   108
3 b c Selkirk (USA) - Fig Tree Drive (USA)
4^{7gf} 1^{8gf} 1^{8gf} 4^{8gs} **2-0-5 £20,146**

Subtle Move (USA) *D Shaw*   65
3 b f Known Fact (USA) - Substance (USA)
4^{8g} 7^{7gf} 3^{6g} 16^{6g} 15^{7gf} 10^{6gf} 19^{8g}
0-1-7 £1,122

Suchwot (Ire) *F Jordan*   59
2 b g Intikhab (USA) - Fairy Water
6^{6g} 9^{6gf} 8^{7gf} **0-0-3**

Sudden Flight (Ire) *R Ingram*   76 a88
6 b g In The Wings - Ma Petite Cherie (USA)
11^{12sd} 1^{11sd} 3^{12sd} 8^{14sw} 10^{13sd} 7^{12gf}
6^{14gf} 6^{14gf} 11^{12g} 9^{12gf} 1^{12s} **2-2-12 £9,426**

Sudra *J O'Reilly*   39 a68
6 b g Indian Ridge - Bunting
1^{8sw} 8^{8sd} 9^{8sd} 3^{8sd} 5^{8sd} 7^{10sd} 6^{8sd} 2^{7sd}
2^{8sd} 4^{7sd} 4^{7sd} 1^{8sd} 2^{8sd} 9^{8sd} 5^{8sw} 14^{8gf} 8^{9sd}
10^{8sd} **2-5-18 £9,115**

Sue Allen (Ire) *R F Fisher*   43 a20
3 b f Pennekamp (USA) - Jambo Jambo (Ire)
11^6sd 11^6gs 5^5gf 10^5sd 12^5f 5^6gf **0-0-6**

Suerte *J G Given*   63
3 b f Halling (USA) - Play With Me (Ire)
7^10gs **0-0-1**

Sugar Snap *C Drew*   16
3 b f Sesaro (USA) - Cuddle Bunny (Ire)
11^7gf 17^6f 8^6gf **0-0-3**

Sugarbabe *M Blanshard*   50
2 b f Kirkwall - Lightning Legacy (USA)
7^6g 8^7gf 3^7gf 3^7gf 14^7f **0-2-5 £1,040**

Suggestive *W J Haggas*   112
5 b g Reprimand - Pleasuring
4^6gf 2^7g 4^7g 4^7g 18^gf 5^8ho **1-1-6**
£28,212

Suitcase Murphy (Ire) *Ms Deborah J Evans*   48 a33
2 b g Petardia - Noble Rocket
12^6gf 11^6s 7^5sd 8^5g **0-0-4**

Sujoise *J J Quinn*   46
2 b c Prince Sabo - Statuette
8^5gf 9^7gf 14^8g **0-0-3**

Sulamani (Ire) *Saeed Bin Suroor*   128
4 b c Hernando (Fr) - Soul Dream (USA)
1^12g 4^12g 2^12g 1^10g 1^12f 5^12f **3-1-6**
£1,623,977

Sullivan's Gold *L A Dace*   28
3 ch f Bedford (USA) - Lady Millennium (Ire)
8^8f 8^12gf 14^14gf **0-0-3**

Sullys Hope *Nick Williams*   a45
6 b g Rock Hopper - Super Sally
8^12sd **0-0-1**

Summer Bounty *F Jordan*   71 a45
7 b g Lugana Beach - Tender Moment (Ire)
6^12sw 4^9sd 2^12gf 2^11gf 4^12gf 5^10g
7^10g **0-3-8 £5,290**

Summer Cherry (USA) *Jamie Poulton*   a56
6 b g Summer Squall (USA) - Cherryrob (USA)
5^8sd 9^12sd 3^12sd **0-1-3 £427**

Summer Lightning (Ire) *R M Beckett*   80
3 b f Tamure (Ire) - Papita (Ire)
9^6gs 5^6gf 1^5gf 9^5gf 4^5gf 12^5g 14^5gs 8^5g
6^5g **1-0-9 £8,067**

Summer Magic (Ire) *T D Barron*   74
2 ch f Desert Sun - Cimeterre (Ire)
4^7gf 1^6gs 6^6gf 2^5gf 13^5f **1-1-5 £7,479**

Summer Recluse (USA) *B R Johnson*   85 a86
4 gr g Cozzene (USA) - Summer Retreat (USA)
4^7sd 2^7sd 1^7sd 10^7g 1^8sd 3^8gf **2-2-6**
£10,558

Summer Shades *W M Brisbourne*   76 a62
5 b m Green Desert (USA) - Sally Slade
3^8sd 2^7f 2^8f 2^8f 1^8gf 2^9gf 1^8gf 6^8gf
2^8gf 7^8gf **2-6-11 £20,208**

Summer Special *D W Barker*   73 a34
3 b g Mind Games - Summerhill Special (Ire)
2^6gf 5^6f 3^7gf 3^6g 2^6gs 7^6gf 9^7sd 10^6gf
7^6gf 3^6gf 20^6g 16^6gs **0-4-12 £7,119**

Summer Spice (Ire) *R Hannon*   81
3 b f Key Of Luck (USA) - Summer Fashion
8^8gf 4^8g 7^7gf 18^7gf **0-0-4 £1,600**

Summer Stock (USA) *J A Supple*   67 a58
5 b g Theatrical - Lake Placid (Ire)
9^10sd 9^10g 4^11gf 9^11gf 13^10f 11^10gs **0-1-6**

Summer View (USA) *R Charlton*   100
6 ch g Distant View (USA) - Miss Summer
11^8g 4^8gf 8^8gf 2^8gf 16^8g **0-1-5 £3,033**

Summer Wine *C F Wall*   71
4 b f Desert King (Ire) - Generous Lady
13^12gf 12^11s 13^14s **0-0-3**

Summerise *D W Barker*   59 a26
2 b f Atraf - Summerhill Special (Ire)
12^7gf 6^7gf 1^7gf 12^6sd **1-0-4 £3,514**

Summerland (Ire) *J H M Gosden*   111
3 b g Danehill (USA) - Summerosa (USA)
6^10gf 2^12g 11^12g 3^12gf 2^12gf **0-1-5**
£40,390

Summerson *M R Channon*   36
4 b g Whittingham (Ire) - Summer Sky
12^6gf 18^6gf 15^7g 23^6gs **0-0-4**

Summery (Ire) *B J Meehan*   a58
4 b f Indian Ridge - Please Believe Me
3^8sd 9^7sd 17^7gf **0-1-3 £452**

Summitville *J G Given*   113
3 b f Grand Lodge (USA) - Tina Heights
7^8gf 8^10s 3^12g 5^12gf 3^12gf 11^15g 2^12gf
0-3-7 £87,650

Sumut *G A Swinbank*   30
4 b g Hamas (Ire) - Simaat (USA)
10^7gs 10^12sd 8^8gf 12^10g 17^10gf **0-0-5**

Sun Bird (Ire) *R Allan*   107
5 ch g Prince Of Birds (USA) - Summer Fashion
5^12gf 11^6gf 11^5gf 12^16gs 8^12g 11^9gf 2^14gf
5^13gf 10^13gs 2^18gf **3-2-10 £104,993**

Sun Cat (Ire) *Mrs S J Smith*   65 a44
3 br g Catrail (USA) - Susie Sunshine (Ire)
6^7sd 5^5sw 3^6sd 9^8sd 10^6sd 3^12gf 4^12gf
11^12gf 11^12sd **0-1-9 £1,815**

Sun Hill *M Blanshard*   56
3 b g Robellino (USA) - Manhattan Sunset (USA)
10^8g 9^12g 17^8gs **0-0-3**

Sun King *Mrs M Reveley*   67
6 ch g Zilzal (USA) - Opus One
4^12gf 14^14f 4^9gf 2^16gs 16^6gp **0-1-5 £1,409**

Sun Of Speed (Ire) *Mrs A J Perrett*   72
2 b c Desert Sun - Spout House (Ire)
9^7g 2^8gf 2^8gf SU^8f **0-2-4 £3,516**

Sun On The Sea (Ire) *B J Meehan*   105
3 ch f Bering - Shimmer (Fr)
4^7gf 4^8gf 1^10gf 4^12gf 6^10g **1-0-5**
£27,602

Sun Slash (Ire) *Ms Joanna Morgan*   103
3 b f Entrepreneur - Charmed Lady
3^5g 6^5gf 4^6gf 2^6g 5^7g 6^5gf 8^6g 7^7gf
13^6gy **0-2-9 £17,288**

Sundari (Ire) *J H M Gosden*   97
4 b f Danehill (USA) - My Ballerina (USA)
6^8gf 9^10gs 7^10s 5^8gf **0-0-4 £1,280**

Sunday Gold *H S Howe*   35
3 b f Lion Cavern (USA) - Sunday Night (Ger)
11^8gs **0-0-1**

Sunday's Well (Ire) *N A Gaselee*   64
4 b f Sadler's Wells (USA) - Marie De Beaujeu (Fr)
9^12gf 7^10gs 11^10gs 11^12s **0-0-4**

Sundial *A E Jones*   16
4 ch f Cadeaux Genereux - Ruby Setting
13^6sd 13^7gf 13^6gf **0-0-3**

Sundried Tomato *P W Hiatt*   93 a100

4 b g Lugana Beach - Little Scarlett
4^{5sw} 5^{6sd} 6^{5sd} 3^{6sd} 2^{6sd} 1^{7sd} 6^{6sw} 3^{6sd}
9^{7sd} 1^{6gf} 7^{6g} 2^{6gs} 8^{6gf} 12^{6gs} 6^{5g} 12^{5s} 10^{6gs}
2-4-17 £29,138

Sundrop (Jpn) *D R Loder* 108 a82
2 b f Sunday Silence (USA) - Oenothera (Ire)
1^{7sd} 2^{8gf} **1-1-2 £47,406**

Sunisa (Ire) *B W Hills* 74
2 b f Daggers Drawn (USA) - Winged Victory (Ire)
6^{6gf} 2^{6gf} 4^{6gf} **0-1-3 £1,350**

Sunny Glenn *Mrs P N Dutfield* 87
5 ch h Rock Hopper - La Ballerine
2^{10s} 5^{12ho} 8^{12gs} 12^{10g} **0-0-4 £1,850**

Sunnyside Royale (Ire) *R Bastiman* 52
4 b g Ali-Royal (Ire) - Kuwah (Ire)
3^{14gf} 4^{14f} 6^{14f} **0-1-3 £866**

Sunridge Fairy (Ire) *Ronald Thompson* a10
4 b f Definite Article - Foxy Fairy (Ire)
9^{12sd} **0-0-1**

Sunset King (USA) *J C Fox* 62
3 b c King Of Kings (Ire) - Sunset River (USA)
13^{10gf} 12^{10gf} 9^{8gf} 7^{7gf} 2^{8f} 2^{7f} 8^{7gf}
15^{10gf} **0-2-8 £1,954**

Sunset Mirage (USA) *E A L Dunlop* 54
2 br f Swain (Ire) - Yafill (USA)
8^{8gf} **0-0-1**

Suntagonal (Aus) *W J Haggas* 82
4 b g Octagonal (NZ) - Urge To Merge (Aus)
8^{6gf} 12^{6gs} 7^{6gf} **0-0-3**

Super Cannes *G Wragg* 82
3 b c Alzao (USA) - Miss Riviera
3^{12gs} 3^{12gf} 2^{12gf} 4^{12gf} 1^{12gf} 12^{14g} 6^{12gs}
10^{10gf} **1-1-8 £9,805**

Super Canyon *P W Harris* 64 a74
5 ch g Gulch (USA) - Marina Park
16^{6gf} 3^{6g} 3^{6gf} 4^{6f} 1^{6sd} 5^{6sw} 5^{6gf} 3^{6sd}
2^{6sd} **1-4-9 £5,486**

Super Celebre (Fr) *E Lellouche* 121
3 b c Peintre Celebre (USA) - Supergirl (USA)
1^{11gs} 2^{11gs} 2^{12g} **1-2-3 £220,714**

Super Dolphin *T P Tate*
4 ch g Dolphin Street (Fr) - Supergreen
LFT^{12gf} **0-0-1**

Super Dominion *R Hollinshead* 57 a33
6 ch g Superpower - Smartie Lee
7^{8sd} 9^{8sd} 8^{9sd} 8^{8gf} 7^{8g} 3^{8gf} 11^{8g} **0-1-7**
£772

Super King *N Bycroft* 67
2 b g Kingsinger (Ire) - Super Sisters (Aus)
7^{8gf} 2^{7gf} **0-1-2 £724**

Super Song *Sir Michael Stoute* 75
3 b c Desert Prince (Ire) - Highland Rhapsody (Ire)
2^{7gf} 8^{7g} 1^{7gf} **1-1-3 £4,944**

Superapparos *S R Bowring* 44 a60
9 b g Superpower - Ayodessa
3^{6sd} 3^{6sd} 2^{6sd} 3^{6sw} 8^{6sd} 2^{6sd} 7^{6gf} 8^{6sd}
5^{5sd} 6^{6sd} 13^{6sd} **0-5-11 £3,229**

Superchief *Miss B Sanders* a76
8 b g Precocious - Rome Express
3^{7sd} 4^{7sd} 12^{7sd} 2^{7sd} 7^{8sd} 11^{10sd} 12^{8sd}
0-3-7 £1,902

Superclean *A W Carroll* 17
3 ch f Environment Friend - Star Mover
15^{8g} 5^{12hy} 5^{12gf} **0-0-3**

Superfrills *Miss L C Siddall* 11 a48

10 b m Superpower - Pod's Daughter (Ire)
10^{6sw} 14^{6sd} 5^{6sw} 9^{6sd} 4^{6sw} 5^{6sw} 11^{6gs}
10^{5gf} **0-0-8 £257**

Superpridetwo *P D Niven* 23
3 b g Superpower - Lindrake's Pride
16^{6f} 16^{7f} 10^{6gf} 5^{6f} 18^{8gf} 7^{7f} 5^{7gs}
0-0-7

Supremacy *Sir Michael Stoute* 110
4 ch g Vettori (Ire) - High Tern
20^{16gs} 9^{14gf} 2^{13gf} 11^{6f} **1-1-4 £28,640**

Supreme Salutation *D W Chapman* 81 a73
7 ch g Most Welcome - Cardinal Press
7^{8sd} 4^{9sd} 2^{9sd} 5^{8sd} 3^{8sd} 7^{6sd} 3^{8gf} 2^{7gs}
1^{9gf} 3^{8gs} 11^{7gf} 17^{gf} 6^{8f} 10^{10gf} 9^{7sd} 8^{8gs}
10^{8g} 5^{7gs} **2-5-18 £13,272**

Supreme Silence (Ire) *Jedd O'Keeffe* a32
6 b g Bluebird (USA) - Why So Silent
11^{16sd} 8^{16sw} 7^{16sd} 10^{14sd} 12^{22gf} **0-0-5**

Surdoue *P Howling* 73 a86
3 b g Bishop Of Cashel - Chatter's Princess
15^{7gf} 19^{8gf} 5^{8g} 8^{7sd} 14^{8g} **0-0-5**

Sure Quest *D W P Arbuthnot* a53
8 b m Sure Blade (USA) - Eagle's Quest
6^{12sd} **0-0-1**

Sure Sign *D Shaw* 66 a43
3 ch g Selkirk (USA) - Beyond Doubt
7^{8sd} 3^{8gf} 7^{8sd} 14^{8sw} 15^{10g} 10^{8sd} 17^{13gs}
0-1-7 £982

Surf The Net *R Hannon* 89
2 b f Cape Cross (Ire) - On The Tide
16^{6gf} 6^{7gf} **1-0-2 £5,658**

Surprise Encounter *E A L Dunlop* 110
7 ch g Cadeaux Genereux - Scandalette
3^{8gf} 7^{7gf} 18^{8gf} 3^{8gf} 3^{8gf} **0-2-5 £8,437**

Surval (Ire) *L M Cumani* 87
3 b f Sadler's Wells (USA) - Courtesane (USA)
6^{10gf} 11^{11hy} 9^{12gf} **1-0-3 £6,226**

Susan's Dowry *Andrew Turnell* a67
7 b m Efisio - Adjusting (Ire)
4^{11sd} 4^{10sd} **0-0-2 £259**

Susiedil (Ire) *P W Harris* 63
2 b f Mujadil (USA) - Don't Take Me (Ire)
8^{6g} 9^{7gf} 17^{f} 4^{7gf} 11^{8gf} **1-0-5 £2,561**

Sussex *D R Loder* 81
2 b c Danehill (USA) - Oh So Sharp
2^{7gf} **0-1-1 £1,736**

Sussex Lad *Mrs A J Perrett* 68 a62
6 b g Prince Sabo - Pea Green
5^{7sd} 7^{6sd} 9^{5sd} 9^{6sd} 5^{6g} 12^{6gf} 6^{7f} 5^{7gs}
2^{7gf} 4^{5f} 3^{6gf} 5^{6f} 5^{8gf} 4^{7f} 2^{6gf} 3^{7g} **0-4-16**
£4,259

Sutter's Fort (Ire) *D R Loder* 94
2 br c Seeking The Gold (USA) - Mayenne (USA)
2^{5gf} 1^{6gf} 1^{7gf} 3^{7gf} 1^{6g} 5^{6gf} **3-1-6**
£81,877

Suzuka (USA) *M Johnston* 82
3 b c A.P. Indy (USA) - Sha Tha (USA)
2^{10gf} 7^{10gs} 2^{12gf} 12^{11gf} 11^{12g} 14^{14g} 3^{12gf}
8^{16gf} 7^{16gf} 2^{15g} **1-0-10 £11,484**

Svenson *J J Matthias* 21
2 ch c Dancing Spree (USA) - Bella Bambola (Ire)
15^{7gf} **0-0-1**

Swagger Stick (USA) *J L Dunlop* 67
2 gr/ro c Cozzene (USA) - Regal State (USA)
8^{6g} 7^{6gf} 12^{7s} 18^{gf} 4^{10gf} **1-1-5 £2,681**

Swahili (Ire) *R Hannon* 78
2 br f Kendor (Fr) - Irish Celebrity (USA)
2⁶ᵍᶠ **0-1-1 £1,460**

Swain Davis *D J S Ffrench Davis* 59 a69
3 b f Swain (Ire) - Exclusive Davis (USA)
9¹⁰ᵍᶠ 9¹⁰ᵍᶠ 6¹⁰ᶠ 5¹²ᵍᶠ 9¹²ˢᵈ 1¹⁶ˢᵈ **1-0-6**
£3,087

Swanky Lad (Ire) *A Crook* 48
2 b g Atraf - Sweet As A Nut (Ire)
6⁵ᵍᶠ 5⁵ᵍᶠ 3⁵ᵍᶠ 7⁷ᶠ 10⁶ᵍᶠ 16⁶ᵍᶠ **0-0-6**
£542

Swedish Shave (Fr) *R Gibson* 113
5 ch h Midyan (USA) - Shavya
1⁶ʰᵒ 1⁶ᵍ 1⁶ᵍ 7⁵ᵍ 1⁶ᵍˢ 4⁷ᵍˢ 9⁶ᵍˢ 8⁶ᵍᶠ 6⁶ʰᵒ
4-0-9 £65,060

Sweep The Board (Ire) *A P Jarvis* 30
2 b c Fasliyev (USA) - Fun Board (Fr)
11⁶ᵍˢ **0-0-1**

Sweet Aroma *Mrs N Macauley* a5
4 b f Bedford (USA) - Tango Country
15⁵ˢᵈ 10⁷ˢʷ **0-0-2**

Sweet Az *S C Burrough* 45 a20
3 b f Averti (Ire) - Yen Haven (USA)
10¹⁰ˢᵈ 16¹⁰ᵍ 14⁷ᵍ 8⁸ᵍ 11⁹ᶠ 11⁸ᶠ 5⁷ᵍ
12⁸ᶠ 8⁷ᵍᶠ **0-0-9**

Sweet Briar *H Candy* a40
4 b f Common Grounds - Pervenche
8⁸ˢᵈ **0-0-1**

Sweet Broomstick *C Grant* 6
2 b f Wizard King - Sweet Compliance
11⁶ᵍˢ 6⁷ᵍᶠ 14⁸ᵍᶠ **0-0-3**

Sweet Cando (Ire) *Miss L A Perratt* 65
2 b/br f Royal Applause - Fizzygig
3⁵ᶠ 3⁶ᵍ 6⁵ᵍᶠ 1⁵ᵍᶠ 8⁵ᵍ 3⁶ᵍˢ 3⁶ᵍ **1-3-7**
£5,838

Sweet Coral (Fr) *B S Rothwell* 35
3 b f Pennekamp (USA) - Sweet Contralto
5⁸ᶠ 11⁸ᵍᶠ 9⁶ᵍᶠ **0-0-3**

Sweet Finesse (Ire) *Mrs P N Dutfield* 53
3 b f Revoque (Ire) - Moira My Girl
12¹³ᵍ 13¹²ᵍ 6¹⁰ᵍᶠ 7¹⁰ᵍ 6¹²ᶠ 4¹⁰ᵍᶠ 6¹⁰ᵍᶠ
5¹⁰ᵍᶠ 9¹⁰ᶠ **0-1-9 £291**

Sweet Fury (Ire) *E A L Dunlop* 59
2 b c Imperial Ballet (Ire) - Muneera (USA)
15⁷ᵍᶠ 11⁸ᵍᶠ 7⁸ᵍᶠ **0-0-3**

Sweet Harriet *M P Tregoning* 44 a23
3 ch f Hector Protector (USA) - Swame (USA)
9¹⁰ᵍ 12¹²ˢᵈ **0-0-2**

Sweet Indulgence (Ire) *B Hanbury* 81
2 ch c Inchinor - Silent Indulgence (USA)
1⁷ᵍᶠ 3⁷ᵍᶠ **1-0-2 £5,626**

Sweet Military Man (USA) *D Shaw* 58 a46
2 b c Allied Forces (USA) - Brown Sugar (Ven)
7⁵ᵍ 6⁵ᵍˢ 4⁶ˢᵈ **0-0-3**

Sweet Pickle *D J Coakley* 57
2 b f Piccolo - Sweet Wilhelmina
3⁶ʰᵈ 11⁶ᵍ 1⁶ᵍᶠ 17⁶ᵍᶠ **1-0-4 £2,827**

Sweet Portia (Ire) *R T Phillips* 60
3 ch f Pennekamp (USA) - My Mariam
UR⁷ᵍ UR⁶ᵍˢ 8⁶ᵍ 4⁸ᵍ 10⁸ˢʷ 11⁸ᵍˢ **0-0-6**
£295

Sweet Reflection (Ire) *W J Musson* 49
3 b f Victory Note (USA) - Shining Creek (Can)
11⁷ᵍˢ 12⁸ᵍ 11⁸ᵍᶠ 7¹⁰ᵍᶠ **0-0-4**

Sweet Reply *I A Wood* 80

---

2 ch f Opening Verse (USA) - Sweet Revival
9⁷ᵍᶠ 4⁶ᵍᶠ 5⁶ᵍᶠ 1⁶ᵍᶠ 11⁷ᵍᶠ 4⁶ᵍ **1-0-6**
£4,480

Sweet Repose (USA) *E A L Dunlop* 38
2 b f Gulch (USA) - Bint Baladee
5⁷ˢ **0-0-1**

Sweet Talking Girl *J M Bradley* 38
3 b f Bin Ajwaad (Ire) - Arabellajill
6⁶ᵍᶠ 5⁷ᵍᶠ **0-0-2**

Sweetest Revenge (Ire) *M D I Usher* 65 a80
2 ch f Daggers Drawn (USA) - Joza
7⁵ᵍᶠ 3⁵ᵍᶠ 2⁶ˢᵈ 12⁵ᵍ 1⁶ˢᵈ 16⁶ᵍᶠ 4⁵ˢᵈ **1-2-7**
£5,320

Sweetstock *Mrs G S Rees* 28
5 b m Anshan - Stockline
10¹³ᵍᶠ 9¹²ˢᵈ 7¹²ᵍ **0-0-3**

Swell (Ire) *P F I Cole* 58
3 b c Sadler's Wells (USA) - Lydara (USA)
4¹⁰ᵍᶠ 6¹¹ᵍᶠ 13¹⁰ᵍ **0-0-3 £324**

Swift Alchemist *K R Burke* 74 a80
3 b f Fleetwood (Ire) - Pure Gold
1⁸ᵍᶠ 2⁸ᵍᶠ 4⁸ᵍᶠ 9⁹ᵍᶠ 5⁸ᵍ 2⁷ˢᵈ 8⁷ˢᵈ 8⁷ˢᵈ
1-2-8 £5,683

Swift Appraisal *S C Williams* 41
4 gr g Slip Anchor - Minsden's Image
12¹⁴ᵍ 10¹¹ᵍᶠ **0-0-2**

Swift Sailing (USA) *B W Hills* 76
2 b c Storm Cat (USA) - Saytarra (USA)
15⁶ᵍᶠ 1⁶ᵍ 5⁷ᵍᶠ **1-0-3 £5,193**

Swift Tango (Ire) *E A L Dunlop* 94
3 b g Desert Prince (Ire) - Ballet Society (Fr)
13⁷ᵍᶠ 3⁸ᵍᶠ 1⁸ᵍᶠ 2⁸ᵍᶠ 3¹⁰ᵍᶠ 2⁹ᵍᶠ 2⁸ᵍ 2⁸ᵍᶠ
1⁹ᵍᶠ 2⁹ᵍ 3¹⁰ᵍᶠ **2-5-12 £25,571**

Swiftmix *P F I Cole* 70
3 gr f Linamix (Fr) - Swift Spring (Fr)
9¹⁰ᵍ 2¹²ᵍᶠ 10¹³ᵍ 14¹⁴ᵍᶠ 11¹²ᵍ 8¹²ˢᵈ **0-1-6**
£1,085

Swinbrook (USA) *J A R Toller* 88
2 ch g Stravinsky (USA) - Dance Diane (USA)
5⁶ᵍᶠ 2⁶ᵍᶠ **0-1-2 £1,889**

Swing Wing *P F I Cole* 112
4 b g In The Wings - Swift Spring (Fr)
3¹³ᵍ 1¹⁶ᵍ 5¹⁶ᵍ 3¹⁵ᵍˢ 3¹⁵ʰʸ **1-3-5**
£31,264

Sworn To Secrecy *S Kirk* 63
2 ch f Prince Sabo - Polly's Teahouse
10⁶ᵍᶠ 4⁶ᵍᶠ 3⁶ᵍᶠ 5⁵ᵍᶠ **0-1-4 £1,146**

Swynford Elegance *I A Wood* 45
6 ch m Charmer - Qualitairess
8⁷ᵍˢ 9⁹ᶠ 2⁸ᵍᶠ 8⁷ᵍᶠ 7⁸ᵍᶠ 3⁸ᶠ 7⁸ᵍ 10⁸ᵍᶠ
3¹⁰ᶠ **0-3-9 £2,332**

Swynford Pleasure *J Hetherton* 65
7 b m Reprimand - Pleasuring
4¹⁰ᵍᶠ 11¹²ᵍᶠ 10¹⁰ᵍ 2¹⁰ᵍᶠ 1¹²ᵍᶠ 8¹²ᵍ 3¹²ᶠ
9¹⁰ᶠ 4¹²ˢ 4¹²ᵍᶠ 4¹²ᶠ 1¹²ᵍᶠ 1¹²ᵍᶠ 8¹²ᵍˢ 10¹²ᵍᶠ
10¹²ᵍᶠ 5¹⁴ᶠ 10¹²ᵍᶠ **3-2-18 £22,565**

Swynford Welcome *I A Wood* 51
7 b m Most Welcome - Qualitair Dream
16⁷ᵍᶠ 18⁶ᶠ 9⁷ᵍˢ 9⁵ᵍᶠ 3⁷ᵍᶠ 8⁷ᵍᶠ 12⁸ᶠ
16⁷ᵍᶠ UR¹⁰ᵍ 1⁷ᵍ 7⁸ᵍᶠ 8⁶ᵍᶠ 7⁷ᶠ 11⁹ᵍᶠ 13⁷ᵍᶠ
11⁵ᵍᶠ 15⁷ᵍᶠ 8⁶ᵍᶠ 8¹⁰ᵍˢ **1-1-25 £7,433**

Sydney Star *B W Hills* 86
2 b f Machiavellian (USA) - Sena Desert
2⁷ᵍˢ **0-1-1 £1,293**

Sylva Bounty *B P J Baugh*

4 br g Bahamian Bounty - Spriolo
12^8sd 14^12sd 12^10gf **0-0-3**

Sylva Storm (USA) *C E Brittain*   65
5 ch g Miswaki (USA) - Sudden Storm Bird (USA)
6^9gf **0-0-1**

Sylvan Twister *P Mitchell*   a35
4 br c First Trump - Storm Party (Ire)
10^12sd 11^16sd **0-0-2**

Syrian Flutist *D E Cantillon*   a56
5 b m Shaamit (Ire) - Brave Vanessa (USA)
2^12sd **0-1-1 £1,069**

Systematic *M Johnston*   118
4 b c Rainbow Quest - Sensation
2^13gf 5^12g 5^11gf **0-1-3 £29,219**

T C Flyer *P D Evans*   43
3 b f Wizard King - Kaleidophone
18^7gf 6^7gf **0-0-2**

T K O Gym *D Nicholls*   49 a54
4 b g Atraf - Pearl Pet
5^7sd 9^11gf BD^7gf 3^10gf 6^10gf 2^10f **0-1-6 £1,468**

Taaqaah *M P Tregoning*   70
2 ch c Grand Lodge (USA) - Belle Ile (USA)
6^7g 2^8gf **0-1-2 £1,561**

Tabadul (Ire) *E A L Dunlop*   74
2 b c Cadeaux Genereux - Amaniy (USA)
1^7gs **1-0-1 £3,623**

Tabarka (Ger) *P A Blockley*   51
2 b f Big Shuffle (USA) - Tirana (Ger)
4^5f 5^5gf 3^5gf 8^6gf **0-0-4 £803**

Tabinda *N P Littmoden*   11 a22
3 b c Wizard King - Mouchez Le Nez (Ire)
12^10sd 17^8gf **0-0-2**

Tableau (USA) *B W Hills*   54
2 ch c Marquetry (USA) - Model Bride (USA)
5^7g **0-0-1**

Taboor (Ire) *J W Payne*   67 a78
5 b g Mujadil (USA) - Christoph's Girl
4^5sd 3^5sd 5^6sd 9^5sd 9^5g 4^5gf 1^5gf 11^5gf
8^5gf 14^5gf **1-2-10 £4,605**

Tacitus (Ire) *R Hannon*   105
3 ch c Titus Livius (Fr) - Idara
1^8g 8^10gf 4^8g 7^8vs **1-0-4 £9,158**

Tactile *Sir Michael Stoute*   45
2 b f Groom Dancer (USA) - Trinity Reef
8^8gf **0-0-1**

Tadeo *I A Wood*   7
10 ch g Primo Dominie - Royal Passion
19^6g **0-0-1**

Tadris (USA) *M P Tregoning*   100 a102
3 b f Red Ransom (USA) - Manwah (USA)
2^10gf 1^8gs 3^8f 4^8gs 1^8gf 2^10gf 1^8sd **3-3-7
£51,304**

Tadsbii *T D Easterby*   40
2 ch c Entrepreneur - Intervene
15^8s 9^8gf 15^7f **0-0-3**

Tafaahum (USA) *M Johnston*   85
2 b c Erhaab (USA) - Makadir (USA)
6^7gf 1^7g 9^8gf **1-0-3 £6,688**

Taffrail *J L Dunlop*   102
5 b g Slip Anchor - Tizona
9^16gf 6^16g 10^16gf 10^22sf 5^16gf 9^16gf 5^16gf
0-0-7 £1,550

Taffs Well *B Ellison*   18
10 b g Dowsing (USA) - Zahiah

20^8g **0-0-1**

Taffy Dancer *H Morrison*   60 a61
5 b g Emperor Jones (USA) - Ballerina Bay
16^13g 4^10gf 3^12gf 3^12f 4^12g 4^16sd 2^14sw
2^18gf **0-4-8 £3,331**

Tag Team (Ire) *A M Balding*   53
2 ch c Tagula (Ire) - Okay Baby (Ire)
8^6gf **0-0-1**

Taggerty (Ire) *M J Polglase*   51 a54
5 b m Definite Article - Kewaashi (USA)
7^7sw 6^7sd 3^7sd 13^7sd 12^7sd 5^6f 10^7gs
2^7gf 2^7gf 8^6gf 2^7gf 2^6gf 5^7gf 9^7g 2^5gf 3^5f 7^6f
5^6gf 6^6g **0-7-22 £8,478**

Tagula Blue (Ire) *J A Glover*   87
3 b g Tagula (Ire) - Palace Blue (Ire)
9^7gf 1^8g 4^8gf 6^9gf 2^8g 1^8gf 15^8g 7^8s
6^8gf **2-2-9 £12,470**

Tahirah *R Guest*   97
3 b f Green Desert (USA) - Kismah
2^7gf 1^8gf 7^8g 4^7gf 8^7gf 1^7gf 1^7g **3-1-7
£13,122**

Tahreeb (Fr) *M P Tregoning*   103
2 ch c Indian Ridge - Native Twine
2^6gf 2^6g 1^6gs 3^6gf 4^5gf 4^8gf **1-2-6
£36,336**

Tai Lass *P R Hedger*   49
3 b/br f Taipan (Ire) - Kerry's Oats
6^14gf **0-0-1**

Taili *D A Nolan*   15
2 b f Taipan (Ire) - Doubtfire
7^6gs 8^7gf 7^8gf **0-0-3**

Taipan Lad (Ire) *G M Moore*   3
3 b g Taipan (Ire) - Newgate Lady (Ire)
17^8gf 19^8s 11^12gs **0-0-3**

Taipo Prince (Ire) *Miss Kate Milligan*   61 a59
3 b g Entrepreneur - Dedicated Lady (Ire)
9^10g 8^8g 8^7gf 11^8gf 9^10g 2^9sd **0-1-6
£874**

Taiyo *J W Payne*   56
3 b f Tagula (Ire) - Tharwa (Ire)
5^6gf 11^6g 5^6gf **0-0-3**

Tajar (USA) *T Keddy*
11 b g Slew O'Gold (USA) - Mashaarif (USA)
12^12gf **0-0-1**

Take A Bow *P R Chamings*   71
2 b c Royal Applause - Giant Nipper
7^7gf 2^8gf **0-1-2 £840**

Take Good Time (Ire) *John Berry*   39
3 ch g Among Men (USA) - Bold Motion
6^6g **0-0-1**

Takes Tutu (USA) *M Johnston*   97
4 b g Afternoon Deelites (USA) - Lady Affirmed (USA)
9^8ft 8^7mh 1^8ft 3^8ft 8^7ft 7^8gf 16^9g
4^7f 12^8gf 15^7gf 11^10g 6^8g 5^9gf **1-2-14
£14,491**

Talbot Avenue *M Mullineaux*   98
5 b g Puissance - Dancing Daughter
4^5gf 16^5gf 18^5gf 3^5g 1^5gf 4^5gf 18^6gf
15^6g 14^5f 7^5g 9^6gf 13^5gf **1-1-12 £15,078**

Tale Of The Tiger *Julian Poulton*
2 ch c Bijou D'Inde - La Belle Dominique
13^5gf **0-0-1**

Talent Star *A W Carroll*
6 b g Mizoram (USA) - Bells Of Longwick
9^9sw 5^8f **0-0-2**

Talking Chalk *W R Muir* 46 a31
2 ch c Docksider (USA) - Zoom Lens (Ire)
7^{5f} 4^{5gf} 18^{6sd} 5^{6gf} 8^{7gf} 5^{7f} 12^{6sd} **0-0-7**

Tallassee *G A Butler* 65
3 ch f Indian Ridge - Red Rose Garden
10^{6g} 8^{9gs} 7^{7gf} 3^{11g} **0-1-4 £597**

Talldark'N'Andsome *N P Littmoden* 83 a73
4 b g Efisio - Fleur Du Val
12^{12sd} 13^{10sd} 7^{10g} 12^{10gf} 4^{10gf} 8^{10gf} 5^{11g}
2^{10g} 9^{10g} 6^{10g} 6^{10g} 1^{10gs} **1-1-12 £4,982**

Tally (Ire) *A Berry* 66 a72
3 ch g Tagula (Ire) - Sally Chase
9^{6sw} 3^{6sd} 3^{6sd} 1^{6sd} 1^{6sd} 4^{6sd} 14^{7gf} 7^{6gf}
2^{6gf} 1^{6gf} 12^{6g} 6^{6gf} 4^{7f} 6^{6gf} **3-3-14 £15,517**

Tamarella (Ire) *G G Margarson* 73 a8
3 b f Tamarisk (Ire) - Miss Siham (Ire)
11^{6g} 3^{6gf} 1^{5f} 3^{6gf} 11^{5s} 4^{6f} 9^{5sd} 4^{5gf}
5^{6f} 12^{6gf} 16^{5gf} 14^{6g} 5^{6gf} **1-2-13 £6,957**

Tamarillo *M L W Bell* 93
2 gr f Daylami (Ire) - Up And About
2^{7gf} 2^{7gf} 1^{8gf} 5^{8g} **1-2-4 £7,356**

Tamarina (Ire) *M P Tregoning* 53
2 ch f Foxhound (USA) - Tamasriya (Ire)
5^{8g} **0-0-1**

Tamesis (Ire) *T D Easterby* 61
2 b f Fasliyev (USA) - Cocktail Party (USA)
3^{5gf} 3^{5gf} 4^{6gf} 4^{5gf} 4^{5gf} 4^{6gf} 4^{5gf} 6^{5gf}
10^{5gf} **0-1-9 £1,757**

Tamiami Trail (Ire) *B J Meehan* 106
5 ch g Indian Ridge - Eurobird
6^{10gf} 2^{22f} 4^{16gf} 6^{19gf} **0-1-4 £11,278**

Taminoula (Ire) *Mrs A J Perrett* 78
2 b f Tagula (Ire) - Taormina (Ire)
8^{6g} 3^{7gf} 1^{7f} 1^{7gf} **2-1-4 £8,210**

Tamweel (USA) *A C Stewart* 86
3 ch f Gulch (USA) - Naazeq
7^{7gf} 2^{7gf} 2^{7gf} 1^{8gf} 1^{7gf} **2-2-5 £14,808**

Tanaffus *B W Hills* 55
3 ch c Cadeaux Genereux - El Rabab (USA)
5^{7gf} 6^{6gf} **0-0-2**

Tanaghum *J L Dunlop* 105
3 b f Darshaan - Mehthaaf (USA)
1^{10g} 4^{10gf} 2^{12gf} 4^{12gf} 10^{10g} **1-1-5 £19,960**

Tanaji *P R Webber* 70
4 b f Marju (Ire) - Hamsaat (Ire)
16^{12g} 6^{10gf} **0-0-2**

Tanara *R Brotherton* 49 a42
2 ch f Bianconi (USA) - Tryarra (Ire)
5^{5gf} 4^{5f} 4^{5gf} 6^{5sd} 10^{6gf} 6^{6g} 2^{5sd} 7^{5gf}
8^{5sd} **0-1-9 £1,111**

Tancred Arms *D W Barker* 51 a11
7 b m Clantime - Mischievous Miss
7^{7gf} 6^{6gf} 17^{7gf} 13^{7gf} 5^{6sf} 10^{7sd} 17^{7gf}
16^{8gf} 6^{7g} 7^{7s} **1-0-10 £3,861**

Tancred Imp *D W Barker* 45
2 b f Atraf - Tancred Mischief
13^{7gf} 7^{7gf} 3^{8g} **0-0-3 £500**

Tancred Miss *D W Barker* 30 a52
4 b f Presidium - Mischievous Miss
4^{6sd} 15^{7sd} 12^{7sw} 13^{6sd} 16^{7gf} 15^{7gf}
14^{7gf} 9^{7gs} **0-0-8 £258**

Tancred Times *D W Barker* 69 a28

8 ch m Clantime - Mischievous Miss
14^{5sd} 7^{5gf} 9^{6gf} 5^{5gf} 1^{6f} 9^{5gs} 2^{6gf} 12^{5gf}
2^{5f} 4^{5g} 7^{6gs} 3^{6gf} 1^{5gf} 9^{6gf} 10^{5gf} 12^{6g}
2-3-16 £16,319

Tancred Tyke *D W Barker* 19
3 b f Atraf - Tancred Mischief
11^{8gf} 11^{7gf} **0-0-2**

Tancred Walk *D W Barker*
5 b m Clantime - Mischievous Miss
11^{5sd} 15^{6sd} **0-0-2**

Tandava (Ire) *I Semple* 86
5 ch g Indian Ridge - Kashka (USA)
8^{12gs} 2^{15gf} 18^{12g} 2^{13gf} 7^{16gf} 4^{17g} 8^{13gs}
11^{17g} **0-2-8 £5,030**

Tanga Dancer *B Smart* 53
3 ch f Blue Ocean (USA) - Tangalooma
7^{8gf} 4^{8s} 6^{8s} 1^{8gf} **1-1-4 £4,725**

Tango Cat (USA) *W Jarvis* 82
3 b/br f Tale Of The Cat (USA) - Rutledge Place (USA)
4^{10gf} 2^{10g} 2^{10gf} 1^{12gf} 8^{12g} 10^{12gf} **1-2-6 £8,439**

Tango Tango *P A Blockley* 53 a35
2 ch f Rudimentary (USA) - Lady Mabel
4^{5g} 6^{5f} 6^{5gf} 4^{5f} 5^{5f} 9^{6sd} 19^{6gf} **0-0-7 £262**

Tannoor (USA) *M A Jarvis* 68
2 b c Miswaki (USA) - Iolani
8^{7gf} 3^{7gf} 3^{7s} **0-2-3 £1,638**

Tanshan *R Rowe* a34
8 ch g Anshan - Nafla (Fr)
11^{12sd} **0-0-1**

Tante Rose (Ire) *B W Hills* 111
3 b f Barathea (Ire) - My Branch
1^{7gf} 16^{8gf} 6^{7gf} 8^{6gf} 3^{7g} 7^{7gs} 4^{7g} 7^{7gf}
1-1-8 £43,325

Tantina (USA) *B W Hills* 117
3 ch f Distant View (USA) - Didina
1^{7gs} 1^{7f} 1^{7g} 1^{7g} 3^{7gf} **4-0-5 £55,620**

Tantric *J O'Reilly* 76 a59
4 br g Greensmith - Petunia (Ger)
8^{9sd} 6^{8sd} 13^{6sd} 6^{7sd} 11^{7sd} 12^{7sd} 11^{8gf}
7^{7f} 3^{7sd} 4^{8g} 10^{9ft} 1^{7gf} 1^{7f} 11^{7gf} 15^{7gs} 7^{7gf}
2-2-16 £8,012

Tap *D Nicholls* 65 a58
6 b g Emarati (USA) - Pubby
6^{5sd} 2^{8sd} 5^{8sd} 3^{8sd} 9^{7sw} 4^{7gf} 2^{7gs} 2^{7gs}
9^{8sd} 5^{8gf} 1^{7sd} 1^{7s} 4^{6gf} 2^{7g} 15^{8sw} **2-5-15 £12,097**

Tapau (Ire) *I A Wood* 80 a27
5 b m Nicolotte - Urtica (Ire)
4^{6gs} 9^{6sd} 3^{7f} 2^{6gf} 1^{7gf} 3^{6g} 8^{6gf} **1-3-7 £13,369**

Tapleon *C J Teague*
2 br f Danzig Connection (USA) - Reem El Fala (Fr)
12^{8g} 12^{7gf} 12^{7gs} **0-0-3**

Tappit (Ire) *J M Bradley* 73
4 b g Mujadil (USA) - Green Life
2^{7gs} 8^{7gf} 4^{7gf} 2^{6gf} 16^{6gf} 1^{6hd} 3^{6f} 18^{5gs}
10^{5gf} 9^{5gf} 10^{5gf} **1-3-11 £8,578**

Tara's Flame *Mrs M Reveley* 57
3 ch g Blushing Flame (USA) - Lady Emm
8^{7gf} 4^{9s} 11^{14f} 15^{12sd} 18^{13gs} **0-0-5 £439**

Tarafah *Ian Williams* 80 a33
4 ch g Machiavellian (USA) - Elfaslah (Ire)
5^{8gf} 3^{12gf} 6^{10gf} 12^{13sd} **0-0-4 £826**

Taranai (Ire) *B W Duke* — 57
2 ch f Russian Revival (USA) - Miss Flite (Ire)
7^{6gf} 6^{6gf} 9^{6gf} 13^{6gf} 8^{6f} **0-0-5**

Taranaki *P D Cundell* — 87 a74
5 b h Delta Dancer - Miss Ticklepenny
3^{7sd} 4^{7sd} 4^{7gf} 3^{7gf} 3^{6gf} 3^{7g} 3^{7g} 2^{7gf}
7^{7f} 17^{7f} 1^{7gf} 5^{7g} 9^{7gf} 6^{7gf} 1^{6gf} 15^{7gf}
2-5-16 £24,473

Tarandot (Ire) *G G Margarson* — 53
2 b f Singspiel (Ire) - Rifada
7^{8gf} **0-0-1**

Taras Emperor (Ire) *J J Quinn* — a16
5 b g Common Grounds - Strike It Rich (Fr)
8^{6sw} UR^{7gf} **0-0-2**

Tarashani (Ire) *B Ellison* — 36
5 ch g Primo Dominie - Tarakana (USA)
13^{8sd} 17^{9gs} 6^{12gf} 11^{11gf} **0-0-4**

Tarawan *A M Balding* — 79 a70
7 ch g Nashwan (USA) - Soluce
3^{10sd} 10^{16sd} 9^{12sd} 2^{10sd} 1^{10sd} 1^{10g} 1^{10gf}
5^{10sd} 8^{10gf} 4^{10sd} 9^{10gf} 3^{10g} 6^{10gf} 10^{12f} **3-2-14**
£14,953

Tarbiyah *Saeed Bin Suroor* — 81
3 b/br f Singspiel (Ire) - Amanah (USA)
1^{8gf} **1-0-1 £5,902**

Tardis *M L W Bell* — 60
2 ch f Vettori (Ire) - Time Lapse
5^{6gf} 6^{7gf} 6^{7gf} 1^{7gf} 5^{6gf} 2^{8gf} 4^{8gf} **1-1-7**
£5,301

Targa *J W Unett* — 73
3 b g Royal Applause - Tintinara
4^{12gf} 11^{12g} 9^{9sd} 14^{16gf} **0-0-4 £423**

Tarjman *A C Stewart* — 115
3 b c Cadeaux Genereux - Dodo (Ire)
1^{6gf} 1^{7g} 1^{7g} 2^{7gf} 3^{7g} 4^{8gf} **3-2-6**
£59,203

Tarkwa *R M H Cowell* — 53
4 gr f Doyoun - Shining Fire
4^{10gf} 8^{10gf} 5^{12f} 3^{10g} 2^{10gf} 6^{12f} **0-2-6**
£2,579

Tarnation (Ire) *J R Weymes* — 24
3 ch g Tagula (Ire) - Steal 'Em
12^{8g} 14^{12sd} **0-0-2**

Tarot Card *B W Hills* — 100
2 b f Fasliyev (USA) - Well Beyond (Ire)
1^{6gs} 5^{8gf} 8^{7gf} **1-0-3 £15,237**

Tarski *W S Kittow* — 44
9 ch g Polish Precedent (USA) - Illusory
13^{10f} 4^{16g} **0-0-2**

Tartiruga (Ire) *L G Cottrell* — 29
2 b g Turtle Island (Ire) - Palio Flyer
18^{6gf} 13^{6gf} **0-0-2**

Taruskin (Ire) *N A Callaghan* — 80
2 b g Danehill Dancer (Ire) - Jungle Jezebel
3^{7gf} 2^{7g} 3^{6gs} 1^{6f} **1-3-4 £6,703**

Tarwij (USA) *M P Tregoning* — 72
3 br f Diesis - Roseate Tern
3^{10gf} 9^{10gf} **0-1-2 £944**

Tashkil (Ire) *J H M Gosden* — 103
2 b c Royal Applause - Surprise Visitor (Ire)
4^{7f} 1^{7g} 1^{7g} 12^{7gf} **2-0-4 £10,902**

Task Trump *J A Osborne* — 15 a13
2 ch f First Trump - Taskone
7^{5f} 10^{7f} **0-0-2**

Tasneef (USA) *T D McCarthy* — 70
4 b g Gulch (USA) - Min Alhawa (USA)
14^{12gf} 11^{14gf} 5^{12gf} 7^{14gf} 2^{12gf} 6^{11gf} 1^{12gf}
4^{12gf} 8^{12f} **1-1-9 £4,416**

Tass Heel (Ire) *M R Channon* — 62 a72
4 b g Danehill (USA) - Mamouna (USA)
1^{14sd} 2^{14sd} 2^{15sd} 6^{16sd} 5^{14gf} 1^{16gf} 2^{14gf}
7^{16gf} 5^{14gf} 2^{16g} 13^{16gf} 9^{15gf} 8^{17gf} 1^{16gf} 1^{16gf}
9^{16gf} 9^{14f} 1^{14gf} **5-4-18 £20,767**

Tata Naka *Mrs C A Dunnett* — 49 a37
3 ch f Nashwan (USA) - Overcast (Ire)
9^{8sd} 6^{10gf} **0-0-2**

Tatweer (Ire) *D Shaw* — 20 a45
3 b g Among Men (USA) - Sandystones
9^{7sd} 21^{6g} **0-0-2**

Taw Park *R J Baker* — 29
9 b g Inca Chief (USA) - Parklands Belle
15^{11gf} **0-0-1**

Tawaddod (Ire) *P T Midgley* — 33
4 b f Alhaarth (Ire) - Gloire
10^{7gf} 11^{8g} 6^{6f} **0-0-3**

Tawny Way *W Jarvis* — 89
3 b f Polar Falcon (USA) - Ma Petite Anglaise
4^{7g} 9^{9gf} 4^{7gf} 9^{7gf} 1^{9gf} 2^{10gf} 2^{10g} 11^{10g}
1-2-8 £9,904

Tayash *A W Carroll* — 24 a33
3 b g Fleetwood (Ire) - Wassl's Sister
11^{11gf} 7^{12gs} 5^{12sd} SU^{16gf} **0-0-4**

Tayif *D Nicholls* — 70 a70
7 gr g Taufan (USA) - Rich Lass
9^{5sw} 10^{5sd} 7^{6sd} 12^{7sd} 6^{7sd} 4^{6sd} 7^{6gf} 3^{6g}
2^{6gf} 13^{6gs} 6^{6gf} 15^{5g} 10^{6g} 6^{5gs} **0-2-14**
£1,629

Tbm Can *W M Brisbourne* — 76
4 b g Rock City - Fire Sprite
5^{11gf} 1^{12f} 1^{13gf} 1^{12gf} 4^{13gf} 1^{13f}
3^{12g} 3^{12g} 1^{12gf} 5^{12gf} 7^{12gf} 6^{12gf} **5-3-13**
£20,006

Te Quiero *Miss Gay Kelleway* — 73 a100
5 gr g Bering - Ma Lumiere (Fr)
2^{9sd} 14^{10sd} 1^{8sd} 7^{10s} **1-1-4 £24,130**

Tea's Maid *J G Given* — 33
3 b f Wizard King - Come To Tea (Ire)
5^{9f} 6^{10gf} 5^{14s} **0-0-3**

Team-Mate (Ire) *Miss J Feilden* — 88
5 b g Nashwan (USA) - Ustka
9^{14gf} 6^{12gf} 10^{12gf} 7^{12gf} 6^{12gf} 1^{12gf} 5^{12gf}
4^{12gf} 7^{12gf} **1-0-9 £5,720**

Tease (Ire) *R Hannon* — 75 a74
3 b f Green Desert (USA) - Mockery
11^{7sd} 7^{7sd} 1^{7sd} UR^{8gf} 3^{7gf} 10^{7g} 11^{8gf}
3^{7g} 6^{8gf} 8^{6f} 11^{7g} 3^{8gf} **1-1-12 £7,574**

Technician (Ire) *E J Alston* — 59
8 ch g Archway (Ire) - How It Works
2^{7f} 5^{7gf} 15^{6f} 44^{8gf} 13^{8gf} 11^{8gf}
5^{8gf} 10^{7gf} **0-2-9 £1,819**

Tedburrow *E J Alston* — 104
11 b g Dowsing (USA) - Gwiffina
5^{6gf} 13^{6gf} 6^{7gf} 11^{6gs} 5^{6gf} **0-0-5**
£2,162

Tedeska (Ire) *M Johnston* — 70
3 b f Up And At 'Em - Tropicana (Ire)
6^{6f} 2^{7gf} 12^{7f} **1-2-5 £9,472**

Tedsdale Mac *N Bycroft* — 65
4 ch g Presidium - Stilvella
4^{6gf} 2^{5gf} 9^{7gf} 6^{5gf} 5^{6g} 12^{5f} 5^{7gf} 7^{8gf}
6^{8gf} 4^{8gf} 3^{7gf} 3^{8g} 7^{7f} 4^{8g} **0-6-14 £2,113**

Tedstale (USA) *T D Easterby* 94
5 ch g Irish River (Fr) - Carefree Kate (USA)
1⁸gf 4⁸gf 9⁸hy 2⁸gf 2⁹gf 6¹⁰gf 8⁸gf 4⁹gf
1-3-8 £17,150

Tedzar (Ire) *B R Johnson* 31 a9
3 b g Inzar (USA) - Chesham Lady (Ire)
12⁷gf 7¹⁰gf 12¹⁰sd 0-0-3

Tee Jay Kassidy *Julian Poulton* 43 a31
3 b g Petong - Priceless Fantasy
9⁷gf 11⁷gf 5¹⁰gf 10⁶sd 15⁷gf 4⁷f 0-0-6
£293

Teehee (Ire) *B Palling* a76
5 b g Anita's Prince - Regal Charmer
2⁷sw 8⁷sw 3⁷sd 2⁷sd 8⁷sd 3⁷sd 4⁷sd 5⁷sd
9⁶sw 2⁷sw 7⁶sd 1⁷sd 1-5-12 £6,023

Tees Components *Mrs M Reveley* 63
8 b g Risk Me (Fr) - Lady Warninglid
6¹²g 0-0-1 £308

Tefi *S R Bowring* a55
5 ch g Efisio - Masuri Kabisa (USA)
7⁶sw 3⁷sd 11⁶sd 8¹²sd 1⁸sw 13⁷sd 10⁸sd
2⁸sd 6⁷sd 11⁸sd 6⁷sd 1-2-11 £4,260

Teg *I A Wood*
5 b m Petong - Felinwen
11⁷g 14¹²gf 0-0-2

Telefonica (USA) *Sir Michael Stoute* 70
2 b f Distant View (USA) - Call Account (USA)
4⁷gf 2⁷g 0-1-2 £1,027

Telegram Girl *D Haydn Jones* a47
4 b f Magic Ring (Ire) - Lucky Message (USA)
6⁷sd 4⁹sd 0-0-2

Telemachus *J G Given* 98 a71
3 b c Bishop Of Cashel - Indian Imp
3⁸gf 1⁸sd 4¹⁰gf 14¹²gf 1¹⁰gf 4¹⁰gf 5¹⁰g
5¹⁰gf 3¹⁰s 14¹²g 2-2-10 £19,306

Telepathic (Ire) *A Berry* 81
3 b g Mind Games - Madrina
7⁵gf 8⁵g 6⁵gs 7⁶g 2⁵gf 5⁵gf 5⁵gf 6⁶f
7⁶gf 7⁵gf 15⁵gf 12⁵gf 0-1-13 £2,958

Telephone Sal (Ire) *Eoin Doyle* 64 a52
5 b m Namaqualand (USA) - Lyphard's Lady
7¹⁰sd 7¹²gf 6¹⁶g 6¹²g 6¹⁴f 0-0-5

Tell Her Off *Mrs C A Dunnett* 51 a21
3 b f Reprimand - My Valentina
8¹⁰sd 7⁸g 7⁸gf 12⁷gs 7⁷gf 11⁸sd 4¹⁰gf
0-0-7

Tell Nothing (Ire) *K R Burke* 49
7 b m Classic Secret (USA) - Derbouka (Fr)
5¹²f 6¹⁶f 3¹⁷gf 1¹⁶gf 7¹⁶sd 9¹⁶gf 1-1-6
£4,515

Tell The Trees *R M Beckett* 50
2 br f Tamure (Ire) - Bluebell Copse
15⁶gf 12⁷gf 14⁸gf 0-0-3

Telori *I A Wood* 61 a63
5 ch m Muhtarram (USA) - Elita
11⁶sd 3⁷sd 9⁷sd 7⁶sw 16⁷gf 15⁶gf 9⁶gf
6⁷f 13⁷gf 8⁶gf 10⁷f 4⁷gf 4⁷gs 5⁷sw 0-3-14
£432

Temper Tantrum *Andrew Reid* 68 a69
5 b g Pursuit Of Love - Queenbird
6⁸sd 2⁸sd 1⁷sd 14⁷sd 6⁷gf 17⁷gf 7⁸f 11⁸sd
14⁸gf 3⁷g 1⁷f 6⁷gf 1⁷f 6⁷g 3⁸f 7⁷sd 5⁷sd
5-3-18 £20,204

Temple Of Artemis *P A Blockley* 67 a36
4 b c Spinning World (USA) - Casessa (USA)

7¹⁶f 9⁸gs 12¹²gf 15¹²sd 8¹²sd 0-0-5

Temple Place (Ire) *M L W Bell* 88
2 b c Sadler's Wells (USA) - Puzzled Look (USA)
5⁸gf 1⁸gf 3⁸gf 1-0-3 £7,457

Templet (USA) *J H M Gosden* 70
3 b c Souvenir Copy - Two Step Trudy (USA)
4¹⁰gf 0-0-1 £357

Tempsford (USA) *Sir Mark Prescott* 93 a97
3 b c Bering - Nadra (Ire)
1¹²sd 1¹²sd 3¹⁴g 1¹⁴gf 5¹⁴gf 1¹²gs 1¹²sd
5-1-7 £20,544

Tempting Tilly (Ire) *C J Teague*
4 b f Namaqualand (USA) - Go Tally-Ho
12⁸sd 0-0-1

Ten Carat *Mrs A J Perrett* 97
3 ch c Grand Lodge (USA) - Emerald (USA)
4¹²gs 11⁴gs 1¹⁶gf 1¹⁴gf 31¹⁸gf 3-0-5
£18,689

Ten Past Six *H A McWilliams*
11 ch g Kris - Tashinsky (USA)
9¹²sw 14¹²sw 8¹²gf 16⁹gf 0-0-4

Tender (Ire) *D J Daly* 73 a67
3 b f Zieten (USA) - Jayess Elle
7⁵sd 12⁶gf 6⁵g 4⁵s 3⁶gf 6⁵gf 6⁵gf 4⁵gf
7⁵gf 13⁶gf 6⁷sd 0-0-11 £1,519

Tender Falcon *R J Hodges* 71
3 br g Polar Falcon (USA) - Tendresse (Ire)
7⁸g 5¹¹gf 1¹⁰gf 3¹⁰f 3¹²g 3¹⁰gf 2¹⁰g 1¹⁰gf
4¹⁰gf 2-2-9 £12,909

Tenny's Gold (Ire) *B W Hills* 67
2 b f Marju (Ire) - Itatinga (USA)
11⁶gf 2⁷gs 0-1-2 £932

Tentative (USA) *R Charlton* 88
2 ch f Distant View (USA) - Danzante (USA)
3⁵g 1⁵f 2⁵f 15⁵gf 15⁵gf 8⁵gf 3⁶g 3-1-7
£16,847

Teorban (Pol) *M Pitman* 40 a80
4 b g Don Corleone - Tabaka (Pol)
2¹⁵sd 11⁶sd 17¹⁴g 13¹⁶gs 2-1-5
£6,480

Teresa *J L Dunlop* 83
3 b f Darshaan - Morina (USA)
7⁸gf 11¹⁰gf 3¹²gf 3¹²g 1¹⁴gf 3¹²gf 3¹⁶g
1-3-7 £7,357

Terfel *M L W Bell* 103
4 ch g Lion Cavern (USA) - Montserrat
11⁸gf 2⁸gs 2⁷gf 11⁷g 5⁸gs 1⁸gf 14⁸g 3⁷gf
3⁸gf 12⁸gs 1-2-10 £40,006

Terimon's Dream *A W Carroll* a29
6 gr g Terimon - I Have A Dream (Swe)
10⁷sd 14⁷sd 0-0-2

Termonfeckin *P W Hiatt* 55 a6
5 b g Runnett - Crimson Sol
3¹⁴gs 4¹¹g 6¹²g 11¹⁵sd 0-1-4 £1,005

Tern Intern (Ire) *Miss J Feilden* a30
4 b/br g Dr Devious (Ire) - Arctic Bird (USA)
9⁷sd 11⁹sd 16¹²g 0-0-3

Terraquin (Ire) *J A R Toller* 83
3 b c Turtle Island (Ire) - Play The Queen (Ire)
1⁷gf 4⁷gf 6⁸gf 4⁸g 1⁷g 6⁷gf 2-0-6
£11,156

Tertullian (Ire) *S Dow* a73
4 b g Petorius - Fiddes (Ire)
13¹⁰sd 11¹⁰sd 0-0-2

Tesio *P J Hobbs* 95

5 b g Danehill (USA) - Pale Grey
9^{5g} 11^{5gf} 17^{7gf} 10^{7g} 8^{5gs} 13^{6gf} **1-0-6**
£3,526

Test The Water (Ire) *Dr J R J Naylor* — 34
9 ch g Maelstrom Lake - Baliana (Can)
11^{10gf} **0-0-1**

Tetou (Ire) *B J Meehan* — 60
3 ch f Peintre Celebre (USA) - Place Of Honour
3^{8gf} 7^{10gf} **0-1-2 £613**

Tetragon (Ire) *Miss Lucinda V Russell* — 69 a59
3 b g Octagonal (NZ) - Viva Verdi (Ire)
3^{8sw} 2^{8sd} 3^{9sd} 2^{12sd} 3^{12sd} 1^{9gs} 1^{11gs} **2-5-7**
£11,610

Teutonic (Ire) *R F Fisher* — 15
2 b f Revoque (Ire) - Classic Ring (Ire)
8^{5gs} 6^{5g} **0-0-2**

Texas Gold *W R Muir* — 94 a93
5 ch g Cadeaux Genereux - Star Tulip
2^{5sd} 5^{5gf} 5^{6gf} 14^{5gf} 1^{6f} 1^{6gf} 3^{6gf} 6^{6g}
6^{5gf} 1^{5gf} 2^{6g} 7^{6gf} 5^{5gf} 3^{5f} 6^{6gf} 15^{5gf} 1^{6sd}
4-3-17 £40,321

Text *J White* — 55 a65
2 b g Atraf - Idle Chat (USA)
6^{5gf} 3^{5sd} 2^{6f} 11^{7sd} **0-2-4 £1,679**

Teyaar *Mrs N Macauley* — a82
7 b g Polar Falcon (USA) - Music In My Life (Ire)
8^{6sd} 2^{5sd} 5^{6sd} 9^{5sd} 11^{6sd} 8^{6sd} 5^{7sd} 9^{5sd}
12^{8sd} 7^{6sd} 4^{5sw} 8^{6sw} 11^{7sw} 3^{6sd} 5^{5sd} 1^{6sd}
1-3-16 £3,571

Thaayer *I A Wood* — a64
8 b g Wolfhound (USA) - Hamaya (USA)
8^{6sd} 7^{7sd} 13^{6sd} 10^{7sw} 11^{8sd} 10^{8sd} **0-0-6**

Thadea (Ire) *J G Given* — 64
2 b/br f Grand Lodge (USA) - Kama Tashoof
3^{5gf} 9^{6gf} 3^{7gs} 19^{7g} 3^{8gf} **0-1-5 £1,854**

Thajja (Ire) *J L Dunlop* — 80
2 b c Daylami (Ire) - Jawlaat (USA)
1^{7gs} **1-0-1 £5,161**

Thaminah (USA) *M P Tregoning* — 79
2 b f Danzig (USA) - Bashayer (USA)
12^{8gf} 1^{6g} **1-0-2 £3,532**

Thanks Max (Ire) *Miss L A Perratt* — 49
5 b g Goldmark (USA) - Almost A Lady (Ire)
13^{8gf} 12^{7gf} 15^{6gs} 15^{9gs} 7^{9gf} 5^{8g} 7^{11gf}
0-0-7

That Man Again *S C Williams* — 36
11 ch g Prince Sabo - Milne's Way
8^{6gf} 12^{5gf} **0-0-2**

That's Racing *J Hetherton* — 53
3 ch g Classic Cliche (Ire) - All On
6^{12gf} 4^{11gs} 6^{10gs} 10^{12gf} 13^{12gf} 19^{14g}
7^{14gf} 10^{16gs} **0-0-8 £291**

Thats All Jazz *C R Dore* — 48 a51
5 b m Prince Sabo - Gate Of Heaven
10^{7sw} 10^{8sd} 8^{6sd} 8^{7sw} 8^{7sd} 10^{7sd} 8^{7gf}
10^{7f} 12^{10f} 6^{9g} 7^{8gf} 9^{7gf} 8^{8gf} 8^{8f} **0-0-14**

Thats Enough *S C Williams* — 62
3 b g Robellino (USA) - Sea Fairy
6^{6g} 5^{5gf} 12^{6gf} 12^{8f} **0-0-4**

Thaw *R Charlton* — 71
4 ch f Cadeaux Genereux - Ice House
4^{6gf} **0-1-1 £332**

The Angel Gabriel *D A Nolan*
8 ch g My Generation - Minsk

8^{5gf} 6^{6gf} **0-0-2**

The Baroness (Ire) *J R Best* — 66 a60
3 b f Blues Traveller (Ire) - Wicken Wonder (Ire)
1^{5sd} 2^{6sd} 4^{5sd} 4^{5sd} 1^{5gf} 10^{7sd} 2^{6gf} 15^{5gf}
5^{6gf} 4^{5gf} 5^{5f} **2-2-11 £8,383**

The Beduth Navi *D G Bridgwater* — 28
3 b c Forzando - Sweets (Ire)
12^{8gf} 8^{8gf} 7^{12gf} **0-0-3**

The Best Yet *A G Newcombe* — 77 a81
5 ch h King's Signet (USA) - Miss Klew
6^{6sw} 1^{6sd} 2^{6sd} 9^{6gf} 1^{6f} 2^{6hd} 4^{6gf} 6^{7sd}
3^{6f} 12^{7gf} 27^{sd} **2-4-11 £14,303**

The Bolter *James Moffatt* — 7
4 b g Puissance - Miami Dolphin
13^{9gf} 15^{8gs} **0-0-2**

The Bonus King *M Johnston* — 96
3 b g Royal Applause - Selvi
11^{5gf} 7^{6g} 6^{7gf} 9^{7gf} 6^{7g} 11^{7gf} **0-0-6**
£880

The Butterfly Boy *P F I Cole* — 64
2 ch c Inchinor - Crime Of Passion
6^{6gf} **0-0-1**

The Butterwick Kid *T P Tate* — 31
10 ch g Interrex (Can) - Ville Air
14^{12g} **0-0-1**

The Chocolatier (Ire) *Mrs Lydia Pearce* — 4
5 b m Inzar (USA) - Clover Honey
15^{10f} **0-0-1**

The Copt *Mrs S Lamyman* — a14
4 b g Charmer - Coptic Dancer
18^{8f} 9^{10f} 15^{7sd} **0-0-3**

The Cute Won (USA) *Patrick J Flynn* — 61
5 b g Defensive Play (USA) - Alzabella (USA)
10^{11gf} 6^{10gf} 16^{12g} 7^{10gf} 7^{7f} 6^{8gf} **0-0-6**

The Diddy Man (Ire) *A Berry*
3 b c Night Shift (USA) - March Star (Ire)
13^{6sw} 9^{8sd} **0-0-2**

The Fairy Flag (Ire) *A Bailey* — 64
5 ch m Inchinor - Good Reference (Ire)
5^{10g} 6^{14gf} 3^{9gf} 2^{11gf} 7^{12gf} 1^{12gs} 15^{10g}
3^{10g} 4^{9g} 7^{12gf} 2^{11gf} 2^{10gf} 6^{10gf} 1^{12g} 9^{11gf} 3^{11g}
4^{10g} 3^{10g} 6^{11s} **2-7-19 £17,797**

The Fisio *A M Balding* — 77 a65
3 b g Efisio - Misellina (Fr)
10^{5sd} 9^{5gs} 16^{5s} 12^{5gs} 14^{5g} **0-0-5**

The Footballresult *Mrs G Harvey* — 50
2 b f The West (USA) - Bunny Gee
8^{7gf} 6^{7f} 13^{7gf} **0-0-3**

The Fun Merchant *W Jarvis* — 57
2 b c Mind Games - Sinking
6^{6g} 7^{6gf} **0-0-2**

The Gaikwar (Ire) *N E Berry* — 73
4 b c Indian Ridge - Broadmara (Ire)
23^{8gf} 16^{8gf} 13^{9gf} **0-0-3**

The Gambler *Paul Johnson* — 71
3 ch g First Trump - Future Options
3^{6gf} 2^{6gf} 1^{6gf} 12^{6gs} 2^{6gf} 13^{5gf} 3^{7f} 6^{5gf}
2^{8gf} 7^{7f} 7^{7gf} 5^{7gf} 12^{7gf} **1-5-13 £8,021**

The Gay Fox *B G Powell* — 57 a57
9 gr g Never So Bold - School Concert
9^{6sd} 6^{6sd} 7^{7sd} 10^{6sw} 5^{8sd} 12^{7sd} 5^{6sd} 2^{7sd}
3^{7f} 2^{7f} 16^{7gf} 17^{7g} 7^{7gs} 10^{7gf} 6^{7gf} 2^{5g} 5^{7f}
3^{6gf} 5^{5gf} **0-3-19 £3,541**

The Glen *M H Tompkins* — 94 a87
5 gr g Mtoto - Silver Singer

7^{10sd} 13^{10sd} 18^{8g} 3^{10g} 9^{10g} 10^{10gf} 3^{10gf}
2^{10g} 1^{10gf} 3^{10g} 2^{10gf} 3^{9gf} 4^{10g} 14^{10gf} **1-4-14**
£18,548

The Great Gatsby (Ire) *A P O'Brien* 121
3 b c Sadler's Wells (USA) - Ionian Sea
2^{10gy} 2^{12g} 5^{12g} **0-2-3 £358,984**

The Guinea Stamp *C Grant* 19
4 b g Overbury (Ire) - Gagajulu
14^{8f} 11^{12sd} 14^{7f} **0-0-3**

The Job *A D Smith* 59
2 ch c Dancing Spree (USA) - Bay Bianca (Ire)
10^{5g} 4^{5gf} 9^{6gf} 8^{8gs} **0-0-4 £276**

The Jobber (Ire) *M Blanshard* 82
2 b g Foxhound (USA) - Clairification (Ire)
17^{6gf} 2^{6gf} 1^{6s} **1-1-3 £4,344**

The Judge *L Lungo* 95
5 b g Polish Precedent (USA) - Just Speculation (Ire)
4^{8gf} 7^{8g} 9^{8gf} 5^{8gs} 2^{10gf} 1^{10gf} 7^{10f} 1^{10g}
13^{10g} 1^{9gf} **3-1-10 £21,676**

The Kiddykid (Ire) *P D Evans* 111
3 b g Danetime (Ire) - Mezzanine
3^{7gf} 2^{6gs} 1^{6gs} 1^{6hy} 5^{6gf} 3^{6g} 6^{6gf} 5^{6gf}
2-2-8 £47,272

The King Of Rock *A G Newcombe* 58
2 b c Nicolotte - Lv Girl (Ire)
10^{5gf} 5^{5gf} 7^{5g} 4^{7gf} 2^{7g} 14^{8sd} **0-1-6**
£2,450

The Lady Would (Ire) *D G Bridgwater* 32 a39
4 ch f Woodborough (USA) - Kealbra Lady
5^{6sd} 13^{6sd} 16^{10f} 13^{6gf} 10^{6gf} **0-0-5**

The Last Mohican *P Howling* a42
4 b g Common Grounds - Arndilly
5^{16sd} 9^{15sd} **0-0-2**

The Laverton Lad *C W Thornton* 28
2 ch g Keen - Wyse Folly
15^{5gf} 7^{6gs} 12^{7f} **0-0-3**

The Leather Wedge (Ire) *A Berry* 46 a48
4 b c Hamas (Ire) - Wallflower
6^{5sd} 13^{5gf} 11^{5gf} 13^{5gf} 11^{5f} 3^{5sd} 11^{5f}
7^{5sd} 10^{5f} 4^{5f} 7^{5sw} **0-2-11 £415**

The Local *M Blanshard* 75 a33
3 b g Selkirk (USA) - Finger Of Light
4^{12gf} 3^{12gs} 5^{10gf} 9^{12gf} 12^{12sd} 3^{10g} 8^{14g}
9^{10gf} 9^{12sd} 8^{12sd} **0-3-10 £1,736**

The Loose Screw (Ire) *G M Moore* 57
5 b g Bigstone (Ire) - Princess Of Dance (Ire)
9^{7gf} 14^{5gf} 6^{10gf} 2^{10g} 10^{8gf} **0-1-5 £704**

The Lord *W G M Turner* 100
3 b c Averti (Ire) - Lady Longmead
18^{5g} 2^{5gf} 9^{6g} 6^{6g} 11^{5gf} 25^{5gf} 8^{5g} **0-1-7**
£7,940

The Mighty Tiger (USA) *A P O'Brien* 110
2 ch c Storm Cat (USA) - Clear Mandate (USA)
3^{6gf} 1^{6gy} 2^{7gs} 3^{7gf} **1-3-4 £32,662**

The Mog *S R Bowring* a54
4 b g Atraf - Safe Secret
14^{7sw} 10^{6sd} 6^{7sw} 3^{7sw} **0-1-4 £422**

The Names Bond *Andrew Turnell* 44
5 b g Tragic Role (USA) - Artistic Licence
10^{12gf} **0-0-1**

The Number *I Semple* 62
2 gr g Silver Wizard (USA) - Elite Number (USA)
5^{7g} 6^{7gf} **0-0-2**

The Old Soldier *A Dickman* 65
5 b g Magic Ring (Ire) - Grecian Belle

3^{5f} 1^{5gf} 3^{6gf} 9^{5gf} 5^{5f} 2^{6g} 9^{7gf} 9^{5g} **1-3-8**
£5,385

The Persuader (Ire) *M Johnston* 87 a55
3 b g Sadler's Wells (USA) - Sister Dot (USA)
6^{12sd} 1^{14gf} 1^{12gf} 1^{12gs} 2^{12gf} 1^{14gf} 10^{13gs}
4-1-7 £49,157

The Player *A M Balding* 52 a70
4 b g Octagonal (NZ) - Patria (USA)
4^{8gf} 1^{7sw} **1-0-2 £2,580**

The Prince *Ian Williams* 92 a95
9 b g Machiavellian (USA) - Mohican Girl
2^{8sd} 1^{8y} 9^{8gf} 3^{8gf} 1^{9gf} **2-2-5 £15,017**

The Privateer *R Hannon* 86
3 b g Bahamian Bounty - Petriece
1^{6g} 5^{7gf} 8^{6gf} 5^{6gf} 16^{7g} 8^{5gf} 11^{7gf} **1-0-7**
£5,512

The Recruiter *J G M O'Shea* 40 a37
3 gr g Danzig Connection (USA) - Tabeeba
7^{10sd} 5^{8sd} 14^{10gf} 9^{9sw} 8^{12f} 7^{11g} 8^{10gf}
0-0-7

The Ring (Ire) *Mrs M Reveley* 76
3 b g Definite Article - Renata's Ring (Ire)
5^{12gf} 6^{12gf} 7^{12gf} 3^{12g} 4^{14g} 4^{12gs} 4^{11g}
3^{12gf} 1^{16g} **1-3-9 £5,039**

The Rip *T D Easterby* 62
2 ch c Definite Article - Polgwynne
11^{6gf} 13^{7g} 4^{7gf} **0-0-3 £300**

The Risen Lark (Ire) *D W P Arbuthnot* 61
3 b f Celtic Swing - May Hills Legacy (Ire)
15^{10gf} 3^{12f} 8^{10gf} **0-1-4 £598**

The Risk Of Reform *E J Alston* 23
3 b f Petorius - Bedtime Model
10^{5gf} 15^{5gs} 18^{7gf} **0-0-3**

The Scaffolder *Mrs N Macauley* a24
5 b g Tachyon Park - Fallal (Ire)
10^{8sw} 10^{8sd} 12^{6sd} **0-0-3**

The Singing Butler *B Hanbury*
3 ch f Primo Dominie - Funny Choice (Ire)
F^{8gf} **0-0-1**

The Spook *J S Goldie* 47
3 b g Bin Ajwaad (Ire) - Rose Mill
14^{8gf} 7^{9gf} 5^{5g} 3^{5gs} 11^{6f} 12^{5gs} **0-1-6**
£555

The Stick *M R Channon* 58
2 b f Singspiel (Ire) - Fatah Flare (USA)
6^{7gf} 5^{8gf} 6^{8gf} **0-0-3 £240**

The Tatling (Ire) *J M Bradley* 119
6 b/br g Perugino (USA) - Aunty Eileen
2^{6gf} 2^{6gf} 2^{6gf} 4^{5gf} 3^{6f} 6^{5gf} 1^{5g} 3^{6gf} 1^{5g}
2^{5gf} 6^{6gs} 5^{5gf} 5^{6gf} 3^{5ho} 4^{6gf} **2-8-15**
£148,536

The Toff *P D Evans* a12
4 b f Overbury (Ire) - Fenian Court (Ire)
14^{10sd} **0-0-1**

The Trader (Ire) *M Blanshard* 118
5 ch h Selkirk (USA) - Snowing
3^{5g} 5^{5gf} 1^{5g} 6^{6gf} 6^{5gf} 1^{5f} 4^{5gf} 2^{5ho}
2-2-9 £60,272

The Varlet *M P Tregoning* 82 a35
3 b g Groom Dancer (USA) - Valagalore
3^{12gf} 4^{13g} 2^{14gf} 6^{16gf} 2^{12gf} 6^{12gf} 11^{13sd}
5^{12g} **0-3-8 £4,057**

The Violin Player (USA) *W Jarvis* 75
2 b c King Of Kings (Ire) - Silk Masque (USA)
7^{6gs} 3^{6gf} 1^{7gf} 3^{7gf} **1-1-4 £4,256**

The Warley Warrior *M W Easterby*   45
2 b g Primo Dominie - Brief Glimpse (Ire)
5^{6s} **0-0-1**

The Way We Were *T G Mills*   50   a72
2 ch c Vettori (Ire) - Pandrop
3^{7gf} 1^{8sd} **1-0-2 £2,886**

The Whistling Teal *G Wragg*   111
7 b g Rudimentary (USA) - Lonely Shore
4^{12gf} 4^{12gf} 5^{12gf} 2^{12g} **0-1-4 £7,800**

The Wizard Mul *W Storey*   70
3 br g Wizard King - Longden Pride
9^{8gf} 11^{8g} 1^{6gs} 7^{6gf} 1^{7gs} 10^{6g} 4^{8g} **2-1-7**
£7,790

Theatre (USA) *Jamie Poulton*   92   a88
4 b g Theatrical - Fasta (USA)
3^{12sd} 4^{12sd} 8^{16sd} 3^{14g} 1^{16gf} 2^{14gf} 4^{14gf}
11^{16gf} 12^{14g} 7^{16gf} 4^{16g} **1-3-11 £20,987**

Theatre Belle *T D Easterby*   52   a24
2 b f King's Theatre (Ire) - Cumbrian Rhapsody
8^{8sw} 7^{8s} **0-0-2**

Theatre Lady (Ire) *P D Evans*   56   a19
5 b m King's Theatre (Ire) - Littlepace
7^{8sd} 10^{8gf} 6^{8f} 4^{8gf} 11^{9gf} 3^{8gf} 5^{9gf}
6^{8gf} 4^{10gf} 3^{8g} 2^{8g} 2^{10f} 1^{8gf} 3^{8gf} 9^{8gf} 11^{9f}
1-6-17 £10,140

Theatre Time (USA) *B W Hills*   78
3 b c Theatrical - Kyka (USA)
1^{10gf} 10^{10gf} **1-0-2 £3,688**

Theatre Tinka (Ire) *R Hollinshead*   73
4 b g King's Theatre (Ire) - Orange Grouse (Ire)
12^{12gf} 8^{12g} 5^{10gf} 9^{10gf} 11^{10gs} 3^{12f} 2^{12gs}
11^{14gs} **0-2-8 £1,562**

Theme Park *H Morrison*   45   a56
3 b g Classic Cliche (Ire) - Arcady
7^{12sd} PU^{15g} 6^{12sd} 7^{12gf} **0-0-4**

Themesofgreen *M R Channon*   27
2 ch g Botanic (USA) - Harmonia
8^{7gf} **0-0-1**

Theorist *J L Spearing*   80
3 b g Machiavellian (USA) - Clerio
1^{9g} 4^{8gf} 8^{10g} 6^{10g} 5^{10gf} 13^{9g} 16^{10gf}
13^{10gf} **1-0-8 £5,930**

Thesaurus *A Crook*   80
4 gr g Most Welcome - Red Embers
17^{10gf} 13^{8gs} 12^{8gf} 7^{8gf} 1^{9gf} 4^{9gf} 7^{8g}
8^{8f} 3^{8gf} 5^{10gf} 12^{8f} 9^{10gf} 8^{12gf} **1-0-13**
£8,443

Thevenis *J S King*   58
2 ch c Dr Fong (USA) - Pigeon Hole
8^{5g} 5^{5f} 7^{6f} 8^{7gf} 9^{8gf} **0-0-5**

Thewhirlingdervish (Ire) *T D Easterby*   91
5 ch g Definite Article - Nomadic Dancer (Ire)
5^{16gf} 3^{16f} 4^{16gf} 13^{20gf} 2^{16gf} 10^{16gf}
13^{14gf} 13^{16gf} **0-1-8 £16,902**

Thihn (Ire) *J L Spearing*   98
8 ch g Machiavellian (USA) - Hasana (USA)
5^{8s} 14^{8gf} 14^{8g} 2^{8gf} 15^{9g} 6^{7g} 15^{10gf} 1^{7g}
18^{gs} **2-1-9 £25,354**

Thingmebob *M H Tompkins*   108
3 b f Bob Back (USA) - Kip's Sister
1^{8gs} 4^{10gf} 8^{12g} 1^{12gf} 3^{12gf} 2^{12gf} 8^{15g}
2-1-7 £18,894

Think Quick (Ire) *R Hollinshead*   48   a48
3 b f Goldmark (USA) - Crimson Ring
6^{6sd} 3^{12sd} 5^{8gs} 4^{12sd} 10^{10gf} 3^{12gs} 2^{10g}

11^{8s} 7^{10gf} 10^{10gf} 4^{10gf} **0-2-11 £2,034**

Think Tank *M Johnston*   91
2 b c Robellino (USA) - Lucca
3^{6gf} 1^{6gs} 1^{7f} 3^{7gf} **2-2-4 £10,931**

Third Empire *C Grant*   62
2 b g Second Empire (Ire) - Tahnee
4^{5gs} 8^{5gf} 5^{10f} 18^{8gf} **0-0-4 £334**

Thirn *D Carroll*   a35
4 b g Piccolo - Midnight Owl (Fr)
14^{7sd} 12^{7sd} 15^{7sw} **0-0-3**

Thirteen Tricks (USA) *Mrs A J Perrett*   73   a66
2 b f Grand Slam (USA) - Talltalelady (USA)
9^{7gf} 3^{7gf} 4^{8sd} **0-1-3 £661**

Tholjanah (Ire) *M P Tregoning*   112
4 b g Darshaan - Alkaffeyeh (Ire)
9^{20gf} 4^{11gf} 4^{16gf} **0-0-3 £3,450**

Thomas Lawrence (USA) *P F I Cole*   85
2 ch c Horse Chestnut (SAF) - Olatha (USA)
4^{5gf} 3^{7f} 2^{6gf} **0-1-3 £2,616**

Thomas Paine *P W D'Arcy*   36
4 b g Green Desert (USA) - Glorious
16^{10gf} 9^{10gf} 9^{8f} 6^{10f} **0-0-4**

Thornaby Green *T D Barron*   63
2 b c Whittingham (Ire) - Dona Filipa
5^{5gf} 4^{5gf} 1^{5gf} 5^{5gf} 6^{5gf} 12^{5g} 10^{6g} **1-0-7**
£5,684

Thorntoun Gold (Ire) *I A Wood*   59
7 ch m Lycius (USA) - Gold Braisim (Ire)
4^{11gf} 4^{13gs} 8^{12gf} 3^{12gf} 8^{8f} 6^{13gf} 5^{12g}
3^{10gf} 2^{12gf} 9^{12gf} 4^{12f} 3^{12gf} 13^{11gf} **0-4-13**
£3,166

Threat *J M Bradley*   57   a36
7 br g Zafonic (USA) - Prophecy (Ire)
9^{6g} 11^{6sd} 16^{7f} 10^{6g} 17^{7gf} 3^{5gf} 2^{6f} 4^{6f}
3^{5gf} 2^{5f} 8^{6f} 10^{5gf} 16^{5gf} **0-4-13 £3,162**

Three Days In May *M R Channon*   63   a68
4 b f Cadeaux Genereux - Corn Futures
6^{7sd} 2^{6sd} 9^{6g} 10^{6sd} 6^{5f} 11^{6g} 7^{6f} 7^{6g}
3^{7gf} 3^{7gf} 7^{6gf} 15^{6gf} 12^{7gf} **0-3-13 £2,036**

Three Dimensions (Ire) *L M Cumani*   76
3 b f Sadler's Wells (USA) - Bequest (USA)
10^{10gf} 3^{10gf} 3^{10gf} **0-1-3 £1,202**

Three Graces (Ger) *M P Tregoning*   107
3 ch c Peintre Celebre (USA) - Trefoil
1^{8gf} 7^{10g} 2^{8gf} 1^{8gf} 2^{9gf} 1^{8g} 5^{8gs} 1^{7gf}
2^{7gf} **4-3-9 £49,001**

Three Points *Saeed Bin Suroor*   99
6 b h Bering - Trazl (Ire)
10^{6f} 7^{6g} **0-0-2**

Three Secrets (Ire) *G G Margarson*   88
2 b f Danehill (USA) - Castilian Queen (USA)
2^{6g} 7^{6gf} **0-1-2 £1,664**

Three Ships *B W Hills*   63
2 ch c Dr Fong (USA) - River Lullaby (USA)
9^{7gf} **0-0-1**

Three Valleys (USA) *R Charlton*   117
2 ch c Diesis - Skiable (Ire)
1^{6gs} 1^{6gf} 3^{6g} 1^{6gf} 2^{7gf} **3-1-5 £219,716**

Three Welshmen *B R Millman*   51   a67
2 b c Muhtarram (USA) - Merch Rhyd-Y-Grug
2^{5sd} 2^{5sd} 7^{5gf} 13^{6gf} 10^{7gf} 5^{6gf} 9^{6g} **0-2-7**
£6,837

Through The Rye *G A Swinbank*   54
7 ch g Sabrehill (USA) - Baharlilys
7^{14gs} **0-0-1**

Thumamah (Ire) *B P J Baugh*   64 a42
4 b f Charnwood Forest (Ire) - Anam
8^6sd 12^7f 6^7gf 14^7gf 12^7f **0-0-5**

Thumper (Ire) *Jonjo O'Neill*   64
5 b g Grand Lodge (USA) - Parkeen Princess
6^12gf 5^11gf **0-0-2**

Thunder Canyon (USA) *P A Blockley*   57
4 b/br g Gulch (USA) - Naazeq
8^12gf 6^14gf **0-0-2**

Thunderclap *J W Hills*   68 a65
4 b/br c Royal Applause - Gloriana
8^10sd 9^10sd 3^8sd 6^8g 2^8g 14^8f 3^8f 2^8gf
9^8f 7^8f 4^8gf 4^8gf 8^9f 7^9gf **0-6-14 £4,648**

Thundered (USA) *G A Swinbank*   a50
5 gr g Thunder Gulch (USA) - Lady Lianga (USA)
3^8sd **0-1-1 £417**

Thundering Bah Bou *J R Jenkins*
3 ch f Bahamian Bounty - Thunder Bug (USA)
19^10g 11^11gf 10^10gf **0-0-3**

Thurlestone Rock *B J Meehan*   85 a75
3 ch g Sheikh Albadou - Don't Smile
6^6sd 7^6gf 4^5g 11^6gf 2^6gf 16^6gf 10^6gf
10^7gf 16^6f **2-1-9 £17,054**

Thyolo (Ire) *C G Cox*   91
2 ch c Bering - Topline (Ger)
4^7g 18^gf 18^gf **2-0-3 £11,383**

Tiber (Ire) *J H M Gosden*   110
3 b c Titus Livius (Fr) - Exciting
2^11gf 4^10gs 2^10gf 2^10g 2^10gf 1^10g **1-4-6**
£63,276

Tiber Tiger (Ire) *N P Littmoden*   84
3 b g Titus Livius (Fr) - Genetta
11^7gf 5^7g 4^8gs 1^7gf 2^7f 1^7gf 2^7gf 18^gs
6^8gf 9^8gf 5^7gf 8^8gf 12^8f **3-3-13 £25,950**

Ticero *C E Brittain*   74
2 ch c First Trump - Lucky Flinders
16^5g 4^7gf **0-0-2 £287**

Tick Tock *M Mullineaux*   55
6 ch m Timeless Times (USA) - Aquiletta
11^6s 17^5gs 9^5gf 7^5g 13^5gf 12^5g 14^6gf
18^5gs **0-0-8**

Ticker Tape *J A Osborne*   88
2 b f Royal Applause - Argent Du Bois (USA)
2^6g 1^7f 7^7g 1^7g 4^7gf 2^6gf 3^7gf **2-4-7**
£54,231

Tickle *P J Makin*   64 a32
5 b m Primo Dominie - Funny Choice (Ire)
2^5g 14^6gs 12^6sd 5^6gf 15^7sd **0-1-5**
£1,112

Ticklepenny Lock (Ire) *C Smith*   52
2 b c Mujadil (USA) - Barncogue
6^5gf 10^6gf 6^7gf 6^7gf 16^7f 14^5sd **0-0-6**
£301

Tictactoe *D J Daly*   64 a49
2 b f Komaite (USA) - White Valley (Ire)
7^5f 4^5gf 4^5sd 2^6f 5^7gf 7^6gf 4^6g 5^5gf
0-1-8 £1,923

Tidal *P Howling*   66 a18
4 br f Bin Ajwaad (Ire) - So Saucy
11^14g 16^10gf 14^10g 6^10g 12^10gf 6^12gs
12^10gf 9^8sd 11^10g **0-0-9**

Tidy (Ire) *J A Osborne*   84 a62
3 b c Mujadil (USA) - Neat Shilling (Ire)
1^6s 3^7gf 11^7gf 6^7sd 10^8g **1-1-5**
£11,519

Tiffany's Quest *D W P Arbuthnot*   32 a20
4 b f Atraf - Pleasure Quest
10^7sd 14^6gs 7^6f **0-0-3**

Tiger Baby *W S Kittow*   21
3 b c Averti (Ire) - Risky Baby
6^7gf 5^7gf **0-0-2**

Tiger Tiger (Fr) *Jamie Poulton*   a32
2 b c Tiger Hill (Ire) - Adorable Emilie (Fr)
12^8sd **0-0-1**

Tiger Tops *J A Supple*   74 a78
4 ch g Sabrehill (USA) - Rose Chime (Ire)
3^10sd 3^10sd 1^8sd 7^8sd 3^8g 7^8sd 7^8gf 2^8gf
5^8gf 9^8gs 3^9g 8^8g 8^9gf 6^9gf **1-5-14 £7,415**

Tigerette (USA) *R Guest*   a19
3 b f Swain (USA) - Hot Thong (Brz)
16^7sd 8^9sd **0-0-2**

Tigertail (Fr) *Rod Collet*   111
4 b f Priolo (USA) - Tiger Stripes
5^10g 2^10g 9^12g 4^12gf 2^10s **0-2-5**
£170,321

Tight Squeeze *P W Hiatt*   83 a77
6 br m Petoski - Snowline
2^11sd 6^11sd 6^9sw 1^10sd 2^9sd 2^10sd 1^10sd
4^10sd 5^10s 5^10gf 3^10gf 5^10gf 4^12g 4^10gf 6^10gf
17^10g 6^10f 1^10gf 1^10gf **4-4-22**
£24,683

Tigress (Ire) *J W Unett*   a71
4 b f Desert Style (Ire) - Ervedya (Ire)
6^6sd 1^5sd 1^5sw 3^5sd 2^5sd 6^5sd 6^5sd **2-2-7**
£6,974

Tikitano (Ire) *D K Ivory*   55
2 b f Dr Fong (USA) - Asterita
6^5g **0-0-1**

Tikkun (Ire) *R Charlton*   48
4 gr g Grand Lodge (USA) - Moon Festival
7^10gf 7^8g **0-0-2**

Tikram *G L Moore*   81
6 ch g Lycius (USA) - Black Fighter (USA)
12^18gf **0-0-1**

Tilla *H Morrison*   76 a42
3 b f Bin Ajwaad (Ire) - Tosca
8^10g 13^10gf 6^12sd 2^12gf 1^12f 3^16gf 1^14gs
2-2-7 £7,334

Tillerman *Mrs A J Perrett*   121
7 b h In The Wings - Autumn Tint (USA)
1^7gf 6^8g 2^8gf 1^8gf 13^7g 3^8gf 3^8gf 9^7gf
2-2-8 £166,475

Timber Ice (USA) *H R A Cecil*   68
3 b f Woodman (USA) - Salchow (USA)
4^11gf 3^12gf **0-1-2 £1,157**

Timbuktu *C W Thornton*
2 b c Efisio - Sirene Bleu Marine (USA)
15^6gs **0-0-1**

Time Ahead *J L Dunlop*   113
3 b f Spectrum (Ire) - Not Before Time (Ire)
2^8gf 1^10g 2^11g 6^12g 7^10gs **1-2-5 £82,873**

Time Bomb *Simon Earle*   35
6 b m Great Commotion (USA) - Play For Time
11^6gf 14^6g 12^6gf 10^6gf 9^7gf **0-0-5**

Time Can Tell *A G Juckes*   a20
9 ch g Sylvan Express - Stellaris
8^16sd 8^15sd **0-0-2**

Time Crystal (Ire) *H R A Cecil*   84
3 b f Sadler's Wells (USA) - State Crystal (Ire)
10^10g 4^12gf 1^12g 4^12gf **1-0-4 £6,765**

Time Flyer *W De Best-Turner*   39
3 b c My Best Valentine - Sally's Trust (Ire)
8⁵ᵍᶠ 12⁸ᵍᶠ 12⁶ᵍᶠ 16⁶ᵍᶠ **0-0-4**

Time For Fame (USA) *W J Musson*
6 b g Quest For Fame - Intimate (USA)
10⁹ˢᵈ **0-0-1**

Time For Music (Ire) *T G Mills*   a55
6 b g Mukaddamah (USA) - Shrewd Girl (USA)
7⁷ˢᵈ **0-0-1**

Time Marches On *Mrs M Reveley*   45
5 b g Timeless Times (USA) - Tees Gazette Girl
2¹²ᵍᶠ 12¹⁰ᶠ **0-1-2 £1,057**

Time N Time Again *E J Alston*   77 a71
5 b g Timeless Times (USA) - Primum Tempus
16⁵ᵍᶠ 11⁵ᵍˢ 3⁵ᵍ 3⁵ᵍ 12⁵ᵍᶠ 3⁵ᵍᶠ 6⁵ᵍᶠ 5⁵ᶠ
3⁶ᶠ 15ᵍᶠ 16⁵ᵍ 3⁵ᵍ 4⁵ᵍᶠ 16⁵ᵍᶠ 5⁶ˢᵈ **1-3-15
£11,127**

Time Spin *C Grant*   64
3 b g Robellino (USA) - Chiltern Court (USA)
3¹⁰ᵍᶠ 11¹²ᵍˢ **0-1-2 £424**

Time To Regret *J J Quinn*   57 a27
3 b g Presidium - Scoffera
10⁶ˢᵈ 6⁷ᵍᶠ 15⁸ᵍ 12⁶ᵍᶠ 2⁷ᵍᶠ 4⁸ᵍᶠ 2⁹ᵍᶠ
3⁸ᵍᶠ 5⁹ᶠ **0-3-9 £2,722**

Time To Relax (Ire) *J J Quinn*   63
2 b f Orpen (USA) - Lassalia
4⁶ᵍᶠ 3⁷ᵍᶠ 6⁸ᵍᶠ 11⁸ᵍᶠ 13⁷ᵍ **0-1-5 £1,049**

Time To Remember (Ire) *D Nicholls*   83
5 b g Pennekamp (USA) - Bequeath (USA)
11⁷ᵍᶠ 6⁸ᵍᶠ 14⁶ᵍ 16⁷ᵍᶠ 15⁶ᵍ 12⁶ᵍᶠ 10⁶ᵍ
10⁶ᵍ 13⁶ᵍᶠ LFT⁷ᵍᶠ **1-0-10 £9,983**

Time To Shine *B R Johnson*   73 a70
4 b f Pivotal - Sweet Jaffa
4¹⁶ˢᵈ 6¹³ˢᵈ 7¹²ˢᵈ 9¹²ˢᵈ 2¹³ˢᵈ 3¹²ᵍ 7¹²ᶠ
10¹⁴ᵍ **0-2-8 £1,302**

Time's The Master (Ire) *M F Harris*   45 a19
2 b g Danetime (Ire) - Travel Tricks (Ire)
8⁵ᵍᶠ 6⁵ᵍᶠ 8⁵ˢᵈ 4⁵ᵍᶠ 5⁶ᵍᶠ 11⁵ˢᵈ 11⁶ˢᵈ
0-0-7

Timely Twist *S Kirk*   56 a43
2 b f Kirkwall - Timely Raise (USA)
15⁷ᵍᶠ 4⁷ᶠ 6⁶ᶠ 9⁶ᵍᶠ 5⁸ᵍᶠ 3⁷ˢᵈ **0-1-6 £614**

Times Of Times (Ire) *Andrew Reid*
10 b m Distinctly North (USA) - Lady Fandet
20⁶ᵍᶠ 16⁶ᵍᶠ **0-0-2**

Times Review (USA) *T D Easterby*   83 a70
2 b c Crafty Prospector (USA) - Previewed (USA)
5⁵ᵍᶠ 2⁶ˢᵈ 1⁵ᵍᶠ 3⁶ᵍˢ 2⁵ᵍᶠ 5⁵ᶠ 9⁶ᵍᶠ 10⁸ᵍᶠ
1-2-8 £8,990

Timetobenice (Ire) *J L Spearing*
3 b f Danetime (Ire) - Woodenitbenice (USA)
18⁷ᵍᶠ 7⁷ᵍᶠ **0-0-2**

Timing *T D Easterby*   90
4 b f Alhaarth (Ire) - Pretty Davis (USA)
4¹⁴ᵍᶠ 6¹⁴ᵍᶠ 4¹⁶ᵍᶠ 4¹⁵ᵍᶠ 13¹⁶ᵍˢ 4¹⁶ᵍᶠ 15¹⁴ᵍ
0-0-7 £3,340

Tinas Prince (Ire) *J S Wainwright*   28
3 b c Desert Prince (Ire) - Bold Tina (Ire)
11⁷ᵍ 17⁶ᶠ **0-0-2**

Ting (Ire) *M J Polglase*
6 b g Magical Wonder (USA) - Rozmiyn
12⁸ˢᵈ **0-0-1**

Tink's Man *Mrs A Duffield*   a2
4 b g Puissance - Expectation (Ire)
12⁶ˢᵈ **0-0-1**

Tintawn Gold (Ire) *S Woodman*   64
3 b f Rudimentary (USA) - Clear Ahead
6⁷ᵍᶠ 7⁹ᵍᶠ 4⁸ᵍᶠ 4⁸ᵍᶠ 5¹⁰ᵍ 2¹⁰ᵍ 7¹⁰ᵍ 2¹⁰ᵍᶠ
5⁸ᶠ 8⁸ᶠ 10¹⁰ᵍˢ **0-4-11 £2,339**

Tioga Gold (Ire) *L R James*   a54
4 b g Goldmark (USA) - Coffee Bean
5¹⁴ˢʷ 4¹²ˢʷ 4¹²ˢᵈ 11¹⁵ˢᵈ 15¹²ˢᵈ **0-0-5
£257**

Tioman (Ire) *M A Jarvis*   84 a71
4 b/br g Dr Devious (Ire) - Tochar Ban (USA)
1¹²ˢᵈ 5¹⁶ᵍᶠ 16¹²ᵍᶠ **1-0-3 £3,721**

Tip The Dip (USA) *J H M Gosden*   91
3 ch c Benny The Dip (USA) - Senora Tippy (USA)
2⁸ᵍᶠ 1¹⁰ᵍᶠ 3¹²ᵍᶠ 1¹²ᵍᶠ **2-1-4 £8,847**

Tipu Sultan *E A L Dunlop*   61
3 ch c Kris - Eye Witness (Ire)
2⁸ᵍ 5⁸ˢ **0-1-2 £752**

Tirailleur (Ire) *J White*   66 a55
3 b f Eagle Eyed (USA) - Tiralle (Ire)
9⁷ˢᵈ 7⁶ˢᵈ 3⁵ˢᵈ 3⁵ᶠ 7⁵ᵍᶠ 5⁸ᵍ 3⁸ᶠ 9⁷ᵍᶠ 1⁸ᵍᶠ
7⁷ᵍ 1¹⁰ᵍᶠ 7⁸ᶠ 6¹¹ᵍᶠ **2-2-13 £7,659**

Tirana (Ire) *D Burchell*   a38
5 b g Brief Truce (USA) - Cloche Du Roi (Fr)
8⁹ˢᵈ 13⁸ˢᵈ **0-0-2**

Tirari (Ire) *C R Dore*   15 a45
4 b f Charnwood Forest (Ire) - Desert Victory
6⁸ˢʷ 5¹¹ˢᵈ 11¹⁶ˢᵈ 9¹²ᵍᶠ **0-0-4**

Tishomingo *Ronald Thompson*
4 ch g Alhijaz - Enchanted Guest (Ire)
8¹²ˢᵈ 9¹¹ˢᵈ **0-0-2**

Titian Flame (Ire) *Mrs P N Dutfield*   67
3 ch f Titus Livius (Fr) - Golden Choice
9¹⁰ᵍᶠ 4¹³ᵍ 3¹²ᵍ 6¹²ᵍ 4¹²ᵍ 7¹⁰ᵍ **0-1-6
£1,206**

Titian Lass *C E Brittain*   56 a56
4 ch f Bijou D'Inde - Liebsidelass (Ire)
13⁷ˢᵈ 5⁷ˢʷ 16⁸ᵍᶠ 2⁸ˢᵈ 15⁷ᵍ 7⁸ᶠ 7⁷ᵍ 9⁸ᵍᶠ
11⁸ᵍᶠ 2⁷ᵍᶠ 17⁷ᵍᶠ 2⁸ᵍᶠ **0-3-12 £2,446**

Titinius (Ire) *L M Cumani*   85
3 ch c Titus Livius (Fr) - Maiyria (Ire)
16ᵍᶠ 11⁶ᵍᶠ 2⁶ᵍᶠ **1-1-3 £6,962**

Titurel *C E Brittain*   101
3 b g Amfortas (Ire) - Musetta (Ire)
3⁸ᵍ 4¹⁰ᵍᶠ 4¹⁰ᵍᶠ 4¹²ᵍᶠ 9¹²ᵍ 12¹⁵ᵍ **0-1-6
£8,359**

Titus Salt (USA) *T D Barron*   64
2 ch g Gentlemen (Arg) - Farewell Partner (USA)
4⁵ᵍᶠ 4⁸ᶠ **0-0-2 £312**

Tiyoun (Ire) *Jedd O'Keeffe*   81 a17
5 b g Kahyasi - Taysala (Ire)
8¹¹ˢʷ 16¹²ᵍ 6¹⁰ᵍᶠ 3¹²ᵍᶠ 5¹²ᵍᶠ 3¹²ᵍᶠ 4¹²ᵍᶠ
2¹⁶ᵍᶠ 10¹⁴ᵍᶠ 2¹⁴ᶠ 5¹⁶ᵍ **0-3-11 £7,655**

Tiz Molly (Ire) *M R Channon*   45
2 ch f Definite Article - Almadaniyah
13⁸ᵍᶠ 11⁸ᵍˢ **0-0-2**

Tiz Wiz *W Storey*   36
2 b f Wizard King - Dannistar
11⁷ᵍᶠ 6⁵ᵍ 11⁷ᵍ **0-0-3**

Tizi Ouzou (Ire) *J L Dunlop*
2 ch f Desert Prince (Ire) - Tresor (USA)
UR⁷ᵍᶠ 22⁸ᵍᶠ **0-0-2**

Tizzy May (Fr) *R Hannon*   104
3 ch c Highest Honor (Fr) - Forentia
5⁷ᵍᶠ 18⁸ᵍ 4⁸ᵍˢ 8⁸ʰʸ 2⁷ᵍᶠ 4⁹ᵍᶠ 2⁹ᵍᶠ 2¹¹ᵍˢ
3¹⁰ᵍᶠ 2¹⁰ᵍᶠ 4¹⁰ᵍ **0-4-11 £23,680**

Tizzy's Law *M A Buckley*   45
2 b f Case Law - Bo' Babbity
10^{6gf} **0-0-1**

To The Woods (Ire) *N P Littmoden*   a57
4 ch f Woodborough (USA) - Iktidar
12^{7sd} **0-0-1**

To Wit To Woo *B W Hills*   56 a63
3 b g Efisio - Sioux
9^{6g} 4^{7gf} 11^{6gs} 10^{8sd} 1^{9sd} **1-0-5 £2,861**

Toberoe Commotion (Ire) *W R Muir*   59 a61
5 b g Great Commotion (USA) - Fionn Varragh (Ire)
3^{10sd} 7^{12sd} 4^{12gf} 8^{13gf} 7^{10gf} 7^{10f} 6^{12gf}
0-1-7 £545

Toccata Aria *J M Bradley*   49
5 b m Unfuwain (USA) - Distant Music
17^{10gf} 12^{10gf} 3^{8gs} 17^{10f} 9^{11gf} 6^{8gf} **0-1-6**
£631

Toddeano *G Fierro*
7 b g Perpendicular - Phisus
13^{10gf} 11^{7sw} **0-0-2**

Todlea (Ire) *J A Osborne*   82
3 b g Desert Prince (Ire) - Imelda (USA)
4^{7gf} 1^{8g} 11^{10g} 12^{12gf} **1-0-4 £5,833**

Toejam *R E Barr*   a34
10 ch g Move Off - Cheeky Pigeon
7^{8sw} 11^{8sd} **0-0-2**

Tojoneski *K A Morgan*   50 a50
4 b g Emperor Jones (USA) - Sampower Lady
9^{10sd} 11^{9sd} 8^{6sd} 8^{7gf} 8^{11gf} 9^{12sw} 3^{12gf}
5^{10f} 3^{12gf} 9^{12sw} **0-2-10 £836**

Tokewanna *C E Brittain*   62
3 b f Danehill (USA) - High Atlas
7^{5gf} 4^{6gf} 6^{6g} 4^{7gf} 8^{5g} 4^{6gf} 19^{6gf} **0-0-7**
£1,119

Toldya *A P Jarvis*   90 a73
6 b m Beveled (USA) - Run Amber Run
10^{6sw} 9^{6sd} 12^{6gf} 16^{5gf} 8^{5gf} 2^{6s} 16^{6g}
16^{6gf} 12^{6gf} 5^{6g} 10^{5gf} 5^{6g} 14^{6gf} 14^{6g} **0-1-14**
£4,561

Toledo Sun *H J Collingridge*   59 a62
3 b g Zamindar (USA) - Shafir (Ire)
7^{7sd} 8^{8g} 13^{8g} 8^{7g} 11^{7gf} 3^{10sd} 9^{12sd} 7^{12sd}
0-1-8 £453

Tolzey (USA) *M R Channon*   94
2 ch f Rahy (USA) - Legal Opinion (Ire)
2^{5g} 3^{6hy} 2^{5gf} 2^{6gf} 5^{6g} 1^{6gf} 6^{7gf} 5^{6gf}
1-4-8 £24,918

Tom Bell (Ire) *J G M O'Shea*   52 a22
3 b g King's Theatre (Ire) - Nordic Display (Ire)
14^{10f} 7^{12sd} 7^{10f} 5^{14gf} **0-0-4**

Tom From Bounty *B R Millman*   51
3 ch g Opera Ghost - Tempus Fugit
7^{6gs} 12^{7gf} 7^{8f} 9^{8gf} 11^{6gf} 7^{8gf} 13^{7f}
0-0-7

Tom Paddington *H Morrison*   93
8 b g Rock Hopper - Mayfair Minx
4^{12g} 2^{14gs} 3^{16g} 7^{15g} 5^{18gf} 5^{16g} **0-3-6**
£8,267

Tom Tun *J G Given*   94 a93
8 b g Bold Arrangement - B Grade
8^{7sd} 16^{6gf} 8^{6g} 26^{6g} 12^{7g} 1^{6gs} 20^{6g}
1-0-7 £11,194

Tom's Cruising *H J Cyzer*   85 a29
4 b g Fraam - Fading
11^{8g} 17^{7g} 6^{8g} 6^{8gf} 14^{7sd} **0-0-5**

Tomahawk (USA) *A P O'Brien*   111
3 b c Seattle Slew (USA) - Statuette (USA)
1^{7ys} 4^{8gs} 8^{8g} 11^{8s} 15^{6gf} **1-0-5**
£27,500

Tomasino *M Johnston*   88
5 br h Celtic Swing - Bustinetta
6^{12gs} 6^{12gf} **0-0-2 £600**

Tomillie *A Berry*   a22
4 ch g Ventiquattrofogli (Ire) - Royal Comedian
11^{5sd} **0-0-1**

Tomina *N A Graham*   80 a56
3 b g Deploy - Cavina
6^{8sd} 1^{13g} 4^{12gf} 3^{14gf} **1-1-4 £5,867**

Tommy Nutter (Ire) *R Brotherton*   53 a54
3 b g Desert Style (Ire) - Ahakista (Ire)
6^{6sd} 5^{6sd} 7^{5sd} 5^{5sd} 5^{6gf} 6^{5f} UR^{7gf} 17^{6gf}
0-0-8

Tommy Smith *J S Wainwright*   89
5 ch g Timeless Times (USA) - Superstream
20^{5g} 12^{5f} 6^{5g} 2^{5gf} 10^{5gf} 3^{5gf} 10^{5f} 8^{5gf}
6^{5gs} 5^{5gf} 2^{5gf} 6^{5gf} 3^{5f} 19^{5g} **0-4-14**
£10,247

Tommy Two Hairs (Ire) *P S McEntee*   29 a40
2 b f Mujadil (USA) - Grosvenor Miss (Ire)
7^{5g} 6^{5f} 6^{5sd} 8^{5gf} **0-0-4**

Tomokim (Ire) *M Quinn*   a7
2 b c Mujadil (USA) - Snowtop
12^{6s} 12^{6sd} **0-0-2**

Tomsk (Ire) *A Berry*   14
3 b g Definite Article - Merry Twinkle
8^{7gf} 4^{7gf} **0-0-2 £481**

Tomthevic *P R Chamings*   69 a31
5 ch g Emarati (USA) - Madame Bovary
13^{5sd} 12^{5g} 7^{5f} 13^{5gf} 2^{5gf} 5^{5gf} 3^{5gf} 1^{5gf}
5^{5gf} 5^{5gf} 7^{5gf} 2^{5gf} 2^{5gf} 9^{5gf} **1-4-14 £8,907**

Ton-Chee *K W Hogg*   45
4 b g Vettori (Ire) - Najariya
12^{17gf} 10^{14s} 4^{12gf} 3^{16gs} **0-1-4 £700**

Tong Ice *B A Pearce*
4 gr g Petong - Efficacious (Ire)
8^{5gf} **0-0-1**

Toni Alcala *R F Fisher*   73 a72
4 b g Ezzoud (Ire) - Etourdie (USA)
3^{12sd} 4^{12sd} 2^{12sd} 2^{16gs} 3^{16gf} 6^{14sd} 9^{15sd}
5^{17gf} 3^{13gf} 6^{18gf} 9^{16gf} 3^{13gf} 7^{13f} 3^{15g} 1^{14gf}
10^{17gf} 2^{14f} 11^{16gf} 4^{16g} **1-7-19 £10,744**

Toni's Pet *B N Pollock*   49 a24
3 b g Wizard King - Dannistar
6^{9sw} 7^{8sw} 5^{7gf} 13^{6f} 9^{11gf} **0-0-5**

Tonto (Fr) *P R Webber*   82
2 gr g Second Empire (Ire) - Malabarista (Fr)
2^{6f} 10^{5f} 3^{6f} 4^{7g} 3^{6gf} 7^{6gf} 2^{6f} **0-4-7**
£3,764

Tony Tie *J S Goldie*   84
7 b g Ardkinglass - Queen Of The Quorn
19^{8g} 9^{8gf} 17^{10gf} 9^{8g} 8^{10gs} 10^{8gs} 7^{8gf}
2^{9g} 5^{9gf} 7^{8gf} 4^{10gf} 3^{9gf} 9^{9gf} 7^{8gf} 6^{8g}
12^{10gs} **1-1-17 £11,057**

Tootin Mac *N Bycroft*   34
2 b f Piccolo - Bangles
6^{5gf} 13^{5gf} 10^{6gf} 8^{5gs} 6^{7gf} 11^{7gf} 7^{7f}
0-0-7

Top Achiever (Ire) *Mrs L Stubbs*   44
2 ch c Intikhab (USA) - Nancy Maloney (Ire)
5^{5gf} **0-0-1**

Top Dirham *M W Easterby* 84
5 ch g Night Shift (USA) - Miller's Melody
10^{7f} 10^{8gs} 18^{gf} 18^{gf} 5^{8gf} 11^{8gf} 8^{8s}
12^{8gf} 9^{9gf} 9^{8g} **2-0-10 £19,061**

Top Hat *M W Easterby* 45
2 b c Easycall - Whispering Sea
8^{5f} 8^{5gf} 7^{5f} 9^{6f} 9^{6gf} **0-0-5**

Top Line Dancer (Ire) *M Johnston* 72
2 b c Fasliyev (USA) - Twafeaj (USA)
5^{6gf} 4^{6gf} **0-0-2 £554**

Top Of The Class (Ire) *P D Evans* 63 a52
6 b m Rudimentary (USA) - School Mum
6^{8sd} 6^{9sd} 6^{9sd} 4^{9sd} 7^{9sw} 8^{9sw} 11^{9sd} 5^{9gf}
11^{1gf} 7^{9gf} 3^{10gf} 4^{9g} 7^{12gs} 6^{10sd} 6^{10gf} 1^{10gf}
13^{10gf} 7^{9gf} **3-4-27 £14,550**

Top Place *C A Dwyer* 45
2 b f Compton Place - Double Top (Ire)
7^{5gf} **0-0-1**

Top Romance (Ire) *Sir Michael Stoute* 102
2 ch f Entrepreneur - Heart's Harmony
1^{7gf} 1^{7gf} **2-0-2 £15,721**

Top Seed (Ire) *M R Channon* 106
2 b c Cadeaux Genereux - Midnight Heights
2^{7g} 3^{7f} 1^{7gf} 4^{7gf} 5^{7gs} 3^{8g} 7^{8gf} 3^{9gf} 6^{8g}
2^{8vs} 4^{10gs} **1-5-11 £61,524**

Top Son *A P Jones* a13
4 b c Komaite (USA) - Top Yard
18^{7gf} 15^{7sd} **0-0-2**

Top Spec (Ire) *R Hannon* 86
2 b c Spectrum (Ire) - Pearl Marine (Ire)
4^{5gf} 3^{5gf} 3^{7g} 2^{7g} 2^{7gf} 1^{8gf} 6^{8gf} 1^{8gf}
2-2-8 £19,518

Top Spot *C E Brittain* 60
3 b f Cadeaux Genereux - Number One Spot
8^{8gf} 2^{7t} 5^{8gf} 5^{7gf} **0-0-4 £1,175**

Top Tenor (Ire) *J L Dunlop* 78
3 b c Sadler's Wells (USA) - Posta Vecchia (USA)
18^{12g} 4^{14f} 1^{14gf} 2^{14gf} 3^{16gf} **1-1-5**
£5,614

Top Trees *W S Kittow* 52 a44
5 b g Charnwood Forest (Ire) - Low Line
5^{12sw} 11^{12sw} 7^{12g} 1^{13gf} **1-0-4 £2,681**

Top Tune *A Bailey* 38 a40
3 b f Victory Note (USA) - Topwinder (USA)
5^{9sw} 13^{8sd} 5^{12gf} 13^{12gs} **0-0-4**

Toparudi *M H Tompkins* 69
2 b c Rudimentary (USA) - Topatori (Ire)
7^{6gf} 5^{6g} 3^{6gf} 3^{7g} 3^{8gs} 17^{7g} **0-2-6**
£2,164

Topkamp *M L W Bell* 108
3 b f Pennekamp (USA) - Victoria Regia (Ire)
9^{5gf} 1^{6gf} 1^{6gf} 3^{7gf} 4^{6gf} 2^{7g} 3^{7g} 5^{7s}
2-3-8 £44,774

Toppling *J M Bradley* 70
5 b g Cadeaux Genereux - Topicality (USA)
16^{7gf} 4^{7gf} 2^{7gf} 1^{6g} 1^{6g} 5^{6gf} 2^{6gf} 8^{6hd}
9^{5f} 14^{6sd} 15^{6gf} **2-3-11 £10,444**

Topton (Ire) *P Howling* 87 a80
9 b g Royal Academy (USA) - Circo
7^{8sd} 10^{10sd} 4^{8sd} 11^{8sw} 10^{8sd} 6^{8gf} 10^{8g}
10^{8gf} 2^{8gf} 10^{7g} 1^{8gf} 13^{8gf} 4^{8g} 1^{8gf} 6^{8gs} 4^{8gf}
4^{9gf} 7^{8gf} 9^{7g} **2-2-22**
£15,855

Tora Bora *P W D'Arcy* 102
3 ch f Grand Lodge (USA) - Brilliance

4^{6g} 4^{8g} 1^{7gf} 1^{7gf} 3^{7g} 7^{7gf} 11^{7g} 8^{6gf}
2-1-8 £30,097

Torchlight (USA) *J H M Gosden* 68
3 b/br f Seeking The Gold (USA) - Cap Beino (USA)
5^{7gf} **0-0-1**

Torcross *M P Tregoning* 88
2 b f Vettori (Ire) - Sheppard's Cross
1^{7gf} 4^{7gf} **1-0-2 £5,199**

Torinmoor (USA) *Mrs A J Perrett* 86
2 ch c Intikhab (USA) - Tochar Ban (USA)
3^{7g} 1^{7gf} 6^{8g} **1-1-3 £7,672**

Toro Bravo (Ire) *R M Beckett* 70 a47
3 b g Alhaarth (Ire) - Set Trail (Ire)
7^{10gf} 12^{10gs} 8^{12sd} 8^{10gf} 9^{10sd} **0-0-5**

Toronto Heights (USA) *B W Hills* 84 a58
2 ch c King Of Kings (Ire) - Revoltosa (Ire)
2^{5gf} 3^{5gs} 10^{6g} 3^{7gf} 2^{6gf} 10^{6gf} 6^{5sd}
0-3-8 £4,448

Torosay Spring *J R Fanshawe* 115
5 ch m First Trump - Spring Sixpence
3^{6gf} 6^{6f} 1^{6gf} 9^{6gf} 2^{6gf} 11^{6gf} 4^{5gf} **1-2-7**
£41,021

Torquemada (Ire) *W Jarvis* 60
2 ch c Desert Sun - Gaelic's Fantasy (Ire)
6^{6gf} 7^{6gf} **0-0-2**

Torrent *D W Chapman* 67 a58
8 ch g Prince Sabo - Maiden Pool
5^{5sd} 10^{6sd} 5^{6sd} 7^{6sw} 5^{6sd} 7^{5sd} 5^{7sd} 4^{6sd}
7^{5sd} 4^{5gf} 5^{5gf} 8^{5gf} 3^{5gf} 11^{5gs} 5^{5gs} 7^{5gf}
6^{6f} **1-3-24**
£8,518

Torrid Kentavr (USA) *B Ellison* 75
6 b g Trempolino (USA) - Torrid Tango (USA)
7^{9gf} 3^{8gf} 4^{8gf} 2^{8s} 3^{10gf} 9^{9g} 5^{8gf} **0-3-7**
£6,063

Tortuette *Jean-Rene Auvray* 34 a20
2 b f Turtle Island (Ire) - Allmosa
16^{6gf} 3^{7gf} 10^{7sd} 8^{10f} 11^{8gs} **0-0-5 £726**

Tortuga Dream (Ire) *A Charlton* 61
4 b g Turtle Island (Ire) - Tycoon's Catch (USA)
5^{8gs} 10^{10gf} 10^{12sd} 10^{12sd} **0-0-4**

Torzal *R F Marvin* 36 a30
3 br g Hector Protector (USA) - Alathezal (USA)
8^{6sd} 10^{7gf} **0-0-2**

Total Devotion *H R A Cecil* 71
3 b f Desert Prince (Ire) - Totality
4^{10gf} 1^{10gf} 14^{10g} **1-0-3 £4,627**

Total Force (Ire) *R Hannon* 56
2 b c Night Shift (USA) - Capegulch (USA)
12^{7gf} 5^{7gf} **0-0-2**

Total Package *M S Saunders* 48 a48
3 b f Fraam - Sunley Solaire
7^{7sd} 6^{8sd} 6^{7sd} 5^{8f} 5^{7gf} 10^{8f} 9^{8f} **0-0-7**

Totally Scottish *Mrs M Reveley* 49
7 b g Mtoto - Glenfinlass
4^{17gf} 2^{13gs} **0-1-2 £1,459**

Totally Yours (Ire) *W R Muir* 90
2 b f Desert Sun - Total Aloof
9^{6gf} 2^{6gf} 2^{6gf} 1^{6g} 7^{6gf} **1-2-5 £42,000**

Touch Down (Ger) *D K Richardson* 102
5 b h Dashing Blade - Time To Run (Ger)
5^{8gs} 7^{8gs} 9^{7gf} 8^{8g} 6^{8g} **0-0-5**

Touch Of Ebony (Ire) *Daniel Mark Loughnane* 64
4 b h Darshaan - Cormorant Wood
4^{12gf} 7^{15gf} 15^{11gf} 9^{12g} 13^{14f} 2^{12y} **0-1-6**

£2,027

Touch Of Fairy (Ire) *J M Bradley*   58
7 b g Fairy King (USA) - Decadence
8^{6gf} 3^{6gf} 13^{6gf} 15^{6gf} **0-1-4 £514**

Touch Of Gold *R Hannon*   71 a17
3 b c Robellino (USA) - Nanouche
11^{8g} 10^{6g} 8^{6g} 6^{8gf} 3^{9g} 15^{8g} 7^{8g} 10^{8sd}
14^{6gf} **0-1-9 £577**

Tough Leader *M C Pipe*
9 b g Lead On Time (USA) - Al Guswa
PU^{10gf} **0-0-1**

Tough Love *T D Easterby*   101
4 ch g Pursuit Of Love - Food Of Love
1^{8gf} 3^{8g} 2^{8gs} 2^{8gf} 1^{8gf} 3^{8gf} 3^{7gf} 17^{7g}
2-5-8 £47,794

Tough Nut (Ire) *J A Osborne*   a64
3 b g Sri Pekan (USA) - Dancing At Lunasa (Ire)
7^{6sd} 1^{7sd} 5^{6sd} 8^{7sw} 5^{7sd} 6^{7sd} 3^{7sd} 5^{7sd}
1-1-8 £3,338

Toumai *Mrs A Duffield*   54
3 b f Mind Games - Flower Princess
9^{7gf} 8^{6f} 4^{7gs} 11^{7gf} 7^{8gf} 6^{12gf} 8^{12gf} **0-0-7**
£322

Tour De Force *W J Haggas*   88
4 b g Saddlers' Hall (Ire) - Rensaler (USA)
1^{8g} 6^{10g} 11^{10gf} 1^{8g} 14^{8gf} **2-0-5 £8,521**

Tourmalet *M R Channon*   80 a80
3 b f Night Shift (USA) - Robsart (Ire)
15^{8g} 10^{7gf} 7^{7gf} 4^{7g} 4^{8g} 2^{7gf} 2^{7gf} 3^{8gs}
5^{7sd} 15^{6gf} 6^{6sd} 2^{7sd} 8^{7s} **0-3-13 £6,464**

Tout Les Sous *Jean-Rene Auvray*
2 ch g Tout Ensemble - Suzie Sue (Ire)
16^{8gs} **0-0-1**

Tout Seul (Ire) *R F Johnson Houghton*   114
3 b c Ali-Royal (Ire) - Total Aloof
4^{8g} 3^{8s} 7^{8gf} 6^{8ho} **0-1-4 £40,155**

Town Called Malice (USA) *N P Littmoden*   a82
3 b g Mister Baileys - Dubiously (USA)
5^{10sd} 2^{8sd} 2^{12sd} **0-1-3 £828**

Toy Show (Ire) *R Hannon*   96
3 b f Danehill (USA) - March Hare
13^{9gf} 1^{10gf} 6^{10g} 5^{10gf} 2^{10gf} 1^{10g} 5^{10gf}
13^{9gf} **2-1-8 £9,711**

Trace Clip *W J Musson*   84
5 b g Zafonic (USA) - Illusory
10^{5gf} 28^{6g} 14^{6gf} 13^{5s} 14^{5gf} 19^{5g} **0-0-6**

Trade Fair *R Charlton*   126
3 b c Zafonic (USA) - Danefair
17^{gf} 17^{gf} 68^{gs} 17^{gf} 57^{gf} **3-0-5 £71,570**

Trained Bythe Best *M C Pipe*   85
5 b m Alderbrook - Princess Moodyshoe
2^{14g} 9^{16gf} 15^{16g} 35^{18gf} **0-1-4 £1,688**

Tranquil Sky *N A Callaghan*   85
2 b f Intikhab (USA) - Tranquillity
6^{6gf} 3^{6gs} 1^{6gf} 3^{6gf} 1^{7f} 10^{7g} **2-2-6**
£9,217

Transcendantale (Fr) *Mrs S Lamyman*   56 a35
5 b/br m Apple Tree (Fr) - Kataba (Fr)
9^{8sd} 10^{12sd} 7^{8sd} 5^{9sw} 6^{8sd} 8^{10gf} 2^{10gf}
9^{10g} 4^{8f} 5^{8gf} 7^{9gf} 8^{12gf} 8^{10g} 13^{10f} **0-1-14**
£1,877

Transit *B Ellison*   64 a50
4 b c Lion Cavern (USA) - Black Fighter (USA)
8^{8sd} 7^{9sd} 3^{12gf} 7^{9gf} **0-0-4 £583**

Travel Tardia (Ire) *I A Wood*   a32
5 br h Petardia - Annie's Travels (Ire)
15^{7gf} 13^{7sd} **0-0-2**

Traveller's Tale *P W Harris*   79
4 b g Selkirk (USA) - Chere Amie (USA)
4^{10gf} 3^{10gf} 12^{10g} 3^{10gs} **0-2-4 £1,751**

Travellers Joy *R J Hodges*   53
3 b f The West (USA) - Persian Fortune
3^{6gf} 7^{5gs} 2^{5f} 8^{6f} 13^{8f} 7^{6gf} 5^{5gf} 6^{5gf}
6^{6f} 11^{6gf} **0-2-10 £1,402**

Travelling Band (Ire) *A M Balding*   83 a38
5 b g Blues Traveller (Ire) - Kind Of Cute
9^{8sw} 20^{8g} 2^{10g} 4^{10g} **0-1-4 £2,107**

Travelling Times *J S Wainwright*   64 a55
4 ch g Timeless Times (USA) - Bollin Sophie
16^{6g} 16^{7f} 8^{6gs} 14^{5gf} 19^{7g} 14^{6gf} 20^{6gf}
4^{6gf} 2^{6gf} 14^{7gf} 5^{6sw} 11^{6g} 18^{6gs} **0-1-13**
£1,742

Trawlers *A J Chamberlain*   25
3 b f Polish Precedent (USA) - My Preference
6^{10gs} 13^{8gf} 9^{7gf} **0-0-3**

Traytonic *H J Cyzer*   101
2 b c Botanic (USA) - Lady Parker (Ire)
1^{5g} 3^{6f} 1^{5g} 2^{5gf} 4^{5gf} 7^{7gs} 4^{6gf} 1^{6gf} 7^{6gf}
3-1-9 £22,754

Tre Colline *C F Wall*   82
4 b g Efisio - Triple Joy
11^{6gf} 12^{7g} 1^{7g} 6^{7gf} 3^{7gf} 2^{6gf} 14^{6gs}
1-2-7 £9,820

Treason Trial *J R Fanshawe*   63
2 b c Peintre Celebre (USA) - Pampabella (Ire)
4^{7g} 13^{8s} **0-0-2 £439**

Treasure House (Ire) *B J Meehan*   95
2 b c Grand Lodge (USA) - Royal Wolff
4^{6g} 2^{6gf} 2^{6f} 7^{6gf} **1-1-5 £8,463**

Treasure Trail *S Kirk*   88
4 b g Millkom - Forever Shineing
13^{12gf} 3^{13gf} 2^{12g} 7^{14g} 6^{13gf} 8^{14gf} 8^{14s}
0-1-7 £5,029

Treaty Of Utrecht (Ire) *I Semple*   62
3 b g College Chapel - Next Round (Ire)
10^{6gs} 10^{8gs} 13^{7gf} 14^{5gf} 12^{6gf} **0-0-5**

Treble Heights (Ire) *J H M Gosden*   105
4 b f Unfuwain (USA) - Height Of Passion
4^{12g} 1^{12gf} 2^{14gs} 5^{15g} **1-1-4 £35,611**

Treble Trigger *W G M Turner*
3 ch f Double Trigger - Fresh Lady (Ire)
16^{8g} 18^{10g} 14^{12sd} **0-0-3**

Treculiar (USA) *G A Butler*   88
3 b c Trempolino (USA) - Lady Peculiar (Can)
9^{10gf} 4^{10gf} 2^{13gf} 15^{14g} 3^{10gf} 3^{13gf} 2^{12g}
1^{14gf} 11^{16g} 5^{12gf} **2-2-10 £18,974**

Tree Chopper (USA) *M P Tregoning*   68
2 ch f Woodman (USA) - Gazayil (USA)
1^{8f} **1-0-1 £3,192**

Tree Peony *R Charlton*   78
3 ch f Woodman (USA) - Pivoine (USA)
1^{7gf} 6^{8g} 6^{8gf} **1-0-3 £6,318**

Tree Roofer *N P Littmoden*   49 a58
4 b g King's Signet (USA) - Armaiti
4^{5sd} 8^{6sd} 2^{5sd} 10^{6sd} 5^{6sd} 3^{5sd} 5^{5sd} 10^{6f}
4^{6gf} 11^{5f} **0-3-10 £1,586**

Treetops Hotel (Ire) *B R Johnson*   64 a86
4 ch g Grand Lodge (USA) - Rousinette
8^{7sd} 7^{8sd} 12^{8sd} 10^{8gf} 12^{6gf} 17^{7g} 17^{8gf}

11¹²ᵍᶠ **0-0-8**

Tregarron *R Hannon*   66
2 br c Efisio - Language Of Love
12⁵ᵍ 4⁵ᵍᶠ 7⁵ᵍᶠ 2⁵ᵍᶠ 4⁶ᵍᶠ 2⁶ᵍˢ 6⁶ˢ 7⁵ᵍ
10⁶ᵍᶠ **0-2-9 £3,826**

Trench Coat (USA) *A M Balding*   53 a68
2 ch c Gulch (USA) - Glamor Queen (USA)
2⁶ᶠ 5⁶ˢ 3⁷ˢᵈ **0-1-3 £1,576**

Trevian *S C Williams*   60
2 ch g Atraf - Ascend (Ire)
11⁶ᵍˢ 5⁶ᵍᶠ 6⁶ᵍᶠ **0-0-3**

Trevors Spree *Mrs Lydia Pearce*   39 a4
4 ch g Dancing Spree (USA) - Trevorsninepoints
14⁶ᵍᶠ 16⁷ᵍˢ 10⁷ˢᵈ 12⁶ᵍᶠ 8⁸ᵍᶠ 11⁸ᵍᶠ **0-0-6**

Tribal Prince *P W Harris*   83
6 b g Prince Sabo - Tshusick
4⁷ᵍᶠ 9⁸ᵍᶠ 12⁷ᵍᶠ 14⁷ᵍ 5⁸ᵍᶠ 4⁷ᵍ 3⁷ᵍᶠ 3⁷ᵍᶠ
1⁷ᵍᶠ 5⁷ᵍᶠ 8⁷ᵍᶠ **1-2-11 £9,770**

Tribalinna (Ire) *I Semple*   29
2 b f Indian Rocket - Cappuchino (Ire)
7⁵ᵍᶠ 5⁵ᵍᶠ 12⁶ᵍ 12⁵ᵍ **0-0-4**

Tribute (Ire) *D R Loder*   85
2 b c Green Desert (USA) - Zooming (Ire)
6⁵ᵍᶠ 3⁶ᵍᶠ 2⁶ᵍ 6⁶ᵍˢ 1⁵ᵍᶠ **1-2-5 £6,180**

Trick Cyclist *A M Balding*   80 a50
2 b c Mind Games - Sabonis (USA)
3⁵ᶠ 2⁵ᵍᶠ 1⁵ᵍ UR⁵ᶠ 9⁵ᵍᶠ 12⁶ᵍ 2⁶ᵍ 11⁶ˢ
10⁶ˢᵈ **1-3-9 £7,876**

Tricky Lady (Ire) *Miss K M George*   33 a38
4 b f Persian Bold - Tropicana (Ire)
11¹⁰ˢᵈ 5⁸ˢᵈ 7⁷ˢᵈ 12⁷ᶠ 12⁸ˢᵈ **0-0-5**

Tricky Venture *P W Hiatt*   69 a60
3 gr g Linamix (Fr) - Ukraine Venture
5¹⁰ˢᵈ 4⁹ˢʷ 12⁷ᵍᶠ 4⁸ᵍᶠ 5⁸ˢᵈ 2¹⁰ᵍᶠ **0-1-6**
£1,987

Trigger Mead *M Johnston*   57
3 b f Double Trigger (Ire) - Normead Lass
9¹⁰ᵍᶠ 4¹⁴ᶠ 3¹¹ᵍᶠ 14¹⁰ᵍᶠ **0-0-4 £1,168**

Trilemma *Sir Mark Prescott*   47
2 b f Slip Anchor - Thracian
8⁸ˢʷ 8⁸ᵍᶠ 16⁷ᵍᶠ 6⁷ᵍˢ **0-0-4**

Trinaree (Ire) *S Gollings*
2 b g Revoque (Ire) - Ball Cat (Fr)
14⁷ˢ **0-0-1**

Trinculo (Ire) *N P Littmoden*   97
6 b g Anita's Prince - Fandangerina (USA)
13⁶ᵍᶠ 8⁶ᵍᶠ 11⁵ᵍ 7⁵ᵍᶠ 7⁵ᵍ 6⁶ᵍ 6⁶ᵍᶠ 3⁶ᵍᶠ
2⁵ˢ 9⁵ᵍ 16⁵ᵍᶠ 7⁵ᵍᶠ **0-2-12 £5,808**

Trinity (Ire) *M Brittain*   62
7 b h College Chapel - Kaskazi
13⁶ᵍᶠ 14⁶ᵍᶠ 9⁵ᵍˢ 4⁶ᵍˢ 8⁶ᵍˢ **0-1-5 £440**

Triple Act (USA) *D R Loder*   65
3 b f Theatrical - Multiply (USA)
7⁷ᵍᶠ **0-0-1**

Triple Jump *M P Tregoning*   31
2 ch g Inchinor - Meteoric
4⁷ᵍᶠ **0-0-1 £724**

Triple Play (Ire) *Don Enrico Incisa*   46
4 br g Tagula (Ire) - Shiyra
12⁸ᵍᶠ 11⁸ᵍ 8⁸ᶠ 9⁸ˢ 9⁸ᵍ 13⁷ᵍᶠ 10⁸ᵍᶠ 7⁸ᵍᶠ
9⁸ᶠ 6⁸ᵍᶠ **0-0-10**

Triplemoon (USA) *P W Harris*   66
4 ch f Trempolino (USA) - Placer Queen
4¹²ᵍᶠ 6¹⁴ᵍ 7¹⁴ᵍᶠ 5¹³ᵍᶠ 3¹⁶ᵍ 5¹⁴ᵍᶠ 6¹⁶ᵍ

4¹⁴ᵍᶠ 1¹⁴ᵍᶠ 1¹⁴ᵍᶠ 1¹⁴ᶠ 15¹⁶ᵍᶠ **3-0-12 £11,240**

Tripti (Ire) *D W P Arbuthnot*   69 a61
3 b f Sesaro (USA) - Chatelsong (USA)
6⁵ˢᵈ 3⁵ᶠ 1⁵ᶠ 6⁵ᵍˢ 5⁵ᵍᶠ 3⁵ᵍᶠ 11⁶ᵍ 8⁵ᵍᶠ
6⁵ᵍ 15⁵ᵍᶠ 6⁵ᵍᶠ 16⁶ᵍᶠ 4⁶ᶠ **1-1-13 £5,313**

Trishay *A P Jarvis*   58 a58
2 gr f Petong - Marjorie's Memory (Ire)
14⁶ᵍ 4⁶ᵍᶠ 2⁵ˢᵈ 6⁶ᵍᶠ 5⁵ᵍᶠ **0-1-5 £1,573**

Triumph Of Dubai (Ire) *J S Moore*   48 a59
3 b g Eagle Eyed (USA) - Jack-N-Jilly (Ire)
9⁷ˢᵈ 3⁷ᵍᶠ 16¹⁰ᶠ 10⁶ᶠ 17⁷ᵍᶠ 12⁸ᵍᶠ **0-1-6**
£426

Triwan *Sir Mark Prescott*   a58
3 b g Nashwan (USA) - Triple Joy
5⁷ˢᵈ **0-0-1**

Trois Etoiles (Ire) *J W Hills*   37 a36
2 ch f Grand Lodge (USA) - Stardance (USA)
12⁷ˢᵈ 13⁷ᵍˢ **0-0-2**

Trojan (Ire) *J G Given*   41
4 ch g Up And At 'Em - Fantasise (Fr)
11⁸ᵍˢ **0-0-1**

Trojan Flight *Mrs J R Ramsden*   62
2 ch g Hector Protector (USA) - Fairywings
7⁵ᵍˢ 9⁵ᵍᶠ 7⁶ᵍˢ **0-0-3**

Trojan Wolf *P Howling*   a58
8 ch g Wolfhound (USA) - Trojan Lady (USA)
11⁸ˢʷ 2¹¹ˢᵈ 8⁹ˢᵈ 4¹²ˢʷ 7¹²ˢʷ 16¹²ˢᵈ 11¹²ˢᵈ
11¹¹ˢᵈ **0-1-8 £826**

Trompe L'Oeil (Ire) *E A L Dunlop*   55
2 b f Distant View (USA) - Milly Ha Ha
4⁶ᵍᶠ 9⁶ᵍ 5⁷ᶠ 9⁸ᵍᶠ **0-0-4 £366**

Troodos Jet *A Berry*   69
2 b g Atraf - Costa Verde
2⁵ʰʸ 4⁵ᵍᶠ 6⁶ᵍᶠ 4⁶ᵍˢ **0-1-4 £2,143**

Tropical Coral (Ire) *A J Lidderdale*   82 a70
3 ch f Pennekamp (USA) - Tropical Dance (USA)
1⁹ˢᵈ 1⁸ᶠ 1⁸ᵍᶠ 16⁸ᵍ 5⁹ᵍᶠ 5¹⁰ᵍᶠ 7⁹ᵍᶠ 1⁹ᵍᶠ
4⁸ᵍᶠ 5¹⁰ᵍᶠ **4-0-10 £15,514**

Tropical Son *D Shaw*   37 a52
4 b g Distant Relative - Douce Maison (Ire)
12¹⁵ˢᵈ 14¹⁰ᵍ 12¹⁴ᵍᶠ 12⁹ᵍˢ 7¹²ˢᵈ 7⁸ᵍᶠ
2¹⁰ˢᵈ 9¹²ᵍ 3⁸ˢʷ 8⁸ᵍᶠ 8⁷ˢʷ 11¹⁰ᵍˢ **0-2-12**
£1,072

Tropical Storm (Ire) *J Noseda*   68
2 ch g Alhaarth (Ire) - Rainstone
2⁶ˢ 4⁶ᵍ **0-1-2 £911**

Trotters Bottom *Andrew Reid*   78 a78
2 b g Mind Games - Fleeting Affair
11⁵ᵍˢ 8⁷ᵍᶠ 3⁵ᶠ 1⁶ᵍᶠ 8⁶ᵍᶠ 2⁶ᵍᶠ 19⁶ᵍᶠ 6⁶ˢᵈ
3⁶ᵍᶠ 12⁶ˢᵈ **1-3-10 £6,805**

Troubadour (Ire) *A P O'Brien*   112
2 b c Danehill (USA) - Taking Liberties (Ire)
1⁶ᵍ 3⁶ᵍᶠ 5⁷ᵍᶠ **1-0-3 £18,073**

Trouble At Bay (Ire) *A King*   95
3 b g Slip Anchor - Fight Right (Fr)
2¹⁰ᵍᶠ 7¹⁰ᶠ 2¹²ᵍᶠ 1¹²ᵍᶠ 3¹²ᵍᶠ 8¹⁴ᵍ 1¹²ᵍᶠ
4¹²ᵍ **2-3-8 £24,365**

Trouble Mountain (USA) *M W Easterby*   81
6 br g Mt. Livermore (USA) - Trouble Free (USA)
7¹⁰ᵍˢ 1¹⁰ᶠ 2¹²ᵍ 7¹²ᵍᶠ 5¹²ᵍᶠ 7¹⁰ᵍˢ 12¹⁰ᵍᶠ
3¹⁰ᵍᶠ 7¹⁰ᵍ 8¹¹ᵍᶠ 14¹²ᵍᶠ 5¹⁰ᵍ 4¹⁰ᵍᶠ 4¹²ᵍᶠ **1-3-14**
£10,002

Troubleinparadise (Ire) *J G Given*   51
2 b f Pursuit Of Love - Sweet Holland (USA)
12⁶ᵍˢ 3⁷ᵍᶠ 5⁷ᵍᶠ **0-1-3 £722**

Trousers *Andrew Reid*   60 a77
4 b g Pivotal - Palo Blanco
7⁷ᵍᶠ 3⁸ˢᵈ 2⁹ᵍ 1⁸ˢᵈ **1-2-4 £5,947**

True (Ire) *Sir Michael Stoute*   63
2 ch f Barathea (Ire) - Bibliotheque (USA)
4⁶ᵍˢ 3⁷ᵍᶠ **0-0-2 £1,015**

True Companion *N P Littmoden*   71 a69
4 b g Brief Truce (USA) - Comanche Companion
5¹⁰ˢᵈ 5⁸ˢᵈ 9¹²ᵍᶠ 9¹⁰ᵍᶠ 4¹⁰ᵍᶠ 6¹²ᵍᶠ 1⁹ᵍᶠ
5¹⁰ᵍˢ **1-0-8 £4,013**

True Holly *J D Bethell*   39
3 b f Bishop Of Cashel - Polly's Teahouse
12⁶ᵍᶠ 9⁵ᵍᶠ 9⁷ᵍᶠ 8⁶ᵍᶠ **0-0-4**

True Magic *J D Bethell*   59
2 b f Magic Ring (Ire) - True Precision
3⁵ᵍᶠ 3⁶ᵍᶠ 23⁷ᵍᶠ 6⁵ᵍ **0-1-4 £908**

True Night *D Nicholls*   92
6 b g Night Shift (USA) - Dead Certain
28⁶ᵍ 17⁶ᵍˢ 16⁷ᵍ 9⁷ᶠ 8⁷ᵍ 11⁶ᵍᶠ 3⁶ᶠ 12⁸ᵍ
7⁷ᵍᶠ 6⁷ᵍ 3⁸ᵍˢ 4⁸ᵍ 2⁸ᵍᶠ 1⁸ᵍᶠ 5⁸ᵍ **1-4-15
£22,068**

True Patriot *E A L Dunlop*   41
2 b c Rainbow Quest (USA) - High Standard
17⁷ᵍᶠ 13⁷ᵍᶠ 8⁸ᵍᶠ **0-0-3**

True Thunder *Julian Poulton*   81 a77
6 b g Bigstone (Ire) - Puget Dancer (USA)
7¹⁰ˢᵈ 8⁸ˢʷ 9¹²ᵍᶠ 6¹⁰ᵍˢ 6¹⁰ˢ 8¹⁰ᵍᶠ 4¹⁰ᵍᶠ
12¹⁰ᵍᶠ 12¹⁰ᵍ 11¹⁰ᵍᶠ **0-0-10 £526**

True To Yourself (USA) *J G Given*   a26
2 b g Royal Academy (USA) - Romilly
13⁵ᵍˢ 13⁸ᵍ 10⁷ˢᵈ **0-0-3**

Trueno (Ire) *L M Cumani*   87
4 b g Desert King (Ire) - Stitching (Ire)
2¹²ᶠ 5¹²ᵍˢ 2¹⁵ᵍᶠ 4¹⁴ᵍᶠ **0-2-4 £5,192**

Trullitti (Ire) *J L Dunlop*   66
2 b f Bahri (USA) - Penza
6⁷ᵍᶠ 5⁷ᵍᶠ **0-0-2**

Truly Wonderful (Ire) *M R Channon*   72 a66
2 b f Highest Honor (Fr) - Ahliyat (USA)
6⁷ᵍᶠ 2⁵ᶠ 1⁵ᵍᶠ 11⁷ᵍ 5⁶ᵍᶠ 3⁶ᵍᶠ 4⁶ᵍᶠ 4⁶ᵍᶠ
2⁶ᶠ 2⁶ᵍᶠ 4⁶ᵍᶠ 5⁶ˢᵈ SU⁷ᵍᶠ **1-3-13 £7,548**

Truman *J A R Toller*   61
2 b c Entrepreneur - Sabria (USA)
5⁶ᵍᶠ **0-0-1 £222**

Trust Rule *B W Hills*   103 a68
3 b c Selkirk (USA) - Hagwah (USA)
2¹⁰ˢᵈ 2¹⁰ᵍ 3¹²ᵍᶠ 2¹²ᵍᶠ 1¹⁰ᵍᶠ 9¹⁰ᵍᶠ 3¹²ᵍˢ
2¹²ᶠ 1¹²ᵍᶠ 7¹²ᶠ 2¹²ᵍᶠ **2-7-11 £42,047**

Trusted Mole (Ire) *W M Brisbourne*   59
5 b g Eagle Eyed (USA) - Orient Air
1¹²ᵍᶠ 5¹⁰ᵍᶠ 5¹²ᵍᶠ 3¹⁴ᵍᶠ 5¹²ᶠ 3¹³ᵍᶠ **1-2-6
£5,360**

Try The Air (Ire) *A J Lidderdale*   56
2 ch f Foxhound (USA) - Try To Catch Me (USA)
8⁶ᵍᶠ 10⁷ᵍᶠ 9⁷ᵍᶠ **0-0-3**

Tryfan *A Bailey*
4 b g Distant Relative - Sister Sal
11⁸ˢᵈ 6⁷ˢʷ **0-0-2**

Tsarbuck *R M H Cowell*
2 b c Perugino (USA) - Form At Last
8⁷ᵍᶠ **0-0-1**

Tshukudu *T D McCarthy*   42 a27
2 ch f Fleetwood (USA) - Pab's Choice
19⁶ᵍᶠ 5⁶ᵍ 8⁸ᵍᶠ 10⁶ᵍᶠ 7⁶ˢᵈ **0-0-5**

Tuareg (Ire) *R M H Cowell*

---

2 b c Ashkalani (Ire) - Shining Fire
9⁷ᵍ 6⁸ᵍᶠ **0-0-2**

Tucker Fence *Ian Emmerson*   36
4 br g So Factual (USA) - Daisy Topper
10⁹ˢᵈ 11⁸ᶠ **0-0-2**

Tudor Bell (Ire) *J G M O'Shea*   59
2 b c Definite Article - Late Night Lady (Ire)
4⁷ᵍᶠ **0-0-1 £274**

Tug Of Love (Ire) *Sir Michael Stoute*   105
3 ch c Halling (USA) - Heart's Harmony
3⁷ᵍˢ 4⁹ᵍ 28⁸ᵍᶠ 4¹⁰ᵍᶠ 2¹⁰ᵍᶠ 1¹⁰ᵍ 18⁹ᵍᶠ
1-2-7 £32,445

Tumblebrutus (USA) *A P O'Brien*   104 a66
2 br c Storm Cat (USA) - Mariah's Storm (USA)
6⁷ᵍᶠ 2⁶ᵍʸ 1⁶ᵍʸ 2⁷ᵍᶠ 6⁸ᵗ **1-2-5 £27,019**

Tumbleweed Quartet (USA) *Jean-Rene Auvray*   a45
7 b g Manila (USA) - Peggysstring (USA)
10⁸ˢᵈ 9¹⁰ˢᵈ 11¹²ˢᵈ **0-0-3**

Tumbleweed Tenor (Ire) *J White*   57 a57
5 b g Mujadil (USA) - Princess Carmen (Ire)
8¹⁰ˢᵈ 13⁷ᵍᶠ 3¹²ᶠ 6¹⁰ᵍ 8¹⁵ˢᵈ 2¹²ˢᵈ 5¹²ˢᵈ
3¹⁰ˢᵈ PU¹²ᵍᶠ **0-3-9 £1,701**

Tumbling Sand (Ire) *T D Easterby*   50
3 b f Desert Prince (Ire) - Velvet Morning (Ire)
10⁸ᵍ 8¹²ᶠ 6¹⁰ᵍᶠ **0-0-3**

Tuneful *Mrs A J Perrett*   90
3 b f Pivotal - Music In My Life (Ire)
6⁸ᵍᶠ 9¹⁰ᵍᶠ 7⁸ᵍˢ **0-0-3 £480**

Tungsten Strike (USA) *Mrs A J Perrett*   64
2 ch c Smart Strike (Can) - Bathilde (Ire)
4⁸ᵍᶠ 13⁸ᵍᶠ 7⁸ᵍᶠ **0-0-3 £369**

Tuning Fork *H R A Cecil*   110
3 b c Alzao (USA) - Tuning
1¹¹ˢ 2¹⁰ᵍᶠ 6¹⁰ᵍᶠ 6¹⁰ᵍᶠ 5¹⁰ᵍ 10⁹ᵍᶠ **1-1-6
£39,356**

Tuppence Ha'Penny *G G Margarson*   a17
4 gr f Never So Bold - Mummy's Chick
10⁸ˢᵈ 15⁶ᵍ **0-0-2**

Tuppenny *J Noseda*   a57
4 b f Salse (USA) - Dazzling Heights
2¹²ˢᵈ 5¹²ˢᵈ **0-1-2 £1,030**

Tuppenny Blue *R Hannon*   53 a45
3 ch f Pennekamp (USA) - Seal Indigo (Ire)
4⁷ˢᵈ 8⁷ᵍᶠ **0-0-2 £292**

Turbo (Ire) *G B Balding*   104
4 b g Piccolo - By Arrangement (Ire)
6⁸ᵍᶠ 10¹⁰ᵍˢ 8¹⁰ᵍᶠ 24⁹ᵍᶠ 2¹⁰ᵍᶠ 1¹²ᵍ **1-1-6
£34,654**

Turf Princess *J R Best*   56 a60
2 b f Wizard King - Turf Moor (Ire)
7⁵ᵍᶠ 3⁵ᶠ 5⁵ᵍᶠ 1⁶ˢᵈ 11⁶ᵍᶠ 2⁷ᵍᶠ **1-1-6
£3,372**

Turftanzer (Ger) *Don Enrico Incisa*   34
4 b g Lomitas - Tower Bridge (Ger)
10¹²ᵍᶠ **0-0-1**

Turibius *T E Powell*   85 a72
4 b g Puissance - Compact Disc (Ire)
6⁵ˢᵈ 3⁶ˢᵈ 5⁵ˢᵈ 8⁶ˢᵈ 3⁵ᵍᶠ 3⁵ᵍᶠ 3⁵ᶠ
4⁵ᵍᶠ 1⁵ᵍᶠ 3⁵ᶠ 4⁶ᵍ 12⁵ˢ 2⁶ᵍᶠ 1⁵ᵍᶠ **2-5-15
£20,600**

Turkish Delight *D Morris*   70
2 b f Prince Sabo - Delicious
4⁶ᵍᶠ 4⁶ᵍ 4⁶ᶠ **0-0-3 £943**

Turks And Caicos (Ire) *P C Haslam*   9
2 b/br g Turtle Island (Ire) - Need You Badly

7^6gf 0-0-1

Turku D Shaw   63 a56
5 b g Polar Falcon (USA) - Princess Zepoli
7^8sd 8^7gf 9^8g 6^8ft 8^7sd 5^10sd 0-0-6

Turn 'n Burn C A Cyzer   a72
2 b c Unfuwain (USA) - Seasonal Splendour (Ire)
5^8sd 3^8sd 0-1-2 £334

Turn Around B W Hills   44
3 b g Pivotal - Bemuse
13^6g 21^5g 0-0-2

Turn Back Miss S E Hall   38 a29
4 b f Pivotal - Trachelium
13^11sd 18^10gf 11^12g 9^17gf 0-0-4

Turn Of Phrase (Ire) R A Fahey   64 a63
4 b g Cadeaux Genereux - Token Gesture (Ire)
5^8sd 2^10sd 1^12gf 3^13gs 1-2-4 £4,381

Turnberry (Ire) J W Hills   54 a53
2 b c Petardia - Sunrise (Ire)
11^6gf 10^7gf 7^7sd 9^7f 0-0-4

Turner J H M Gosden   67 a63
2 gr c El Prado (Ire) - Gaily Royal (Ire)
3^8gf 6^8gf 7^8sd 0-0-3 £778

Turning The Tide I A Wood   37 a11
4 b g Lugana Beach - Robert's Daughter
5^14gf 7^16sd 11^13gf 0-0-3

Turnstile R Hannon   59
2 gr c Linamix (Fr) - Kissing Gate (USA)
4^8gs 0-0-1

Turtle Love (Ire) Miss V Haigh   45
4 b f Turtle Island (Ire) - A Little Loving
13^17gf 2^12gf 4^14gf 0-2-3 £1,087

Turtle Patriarch (Ire) Mrs A J Perrett   66
2 b c Turtle Island (Ire) - La Doyenne (Ire)
6^6gf 14^6gf 0-0-2

Turtle Valley (Ire) S Dow   78 a63
7 b g Turtle Island (Ire) - Primrose Valley
11^12sd 13^16sd 6^14g 14^14g 3^14gs 1^14hy
15^14s 1-1-7 £6,827

Tuscan Dream A Berry   a49
8 b g Clantime - Excavator Lady
6^5sd 2^5sd 8^5sd 3^5sw 9^5sw 6^5sw 8^5sd 6^5sw
0-2-8 £1,243

Tuscan Flyer R Bastiman   71
5 b g Clantime - Excavator Lady
11^5f 8^6gs 18^5gf 11^6gf 2^5gf 4^5f 1^5f 7^5f
1^5f 4^6gf 2^6gf 2-2-11 £9,668

Tuscan Sky (USA) B W Hills   64
3 b g Gulch - Search Committee (USA)
11^8gf 9^7gf 14^7gf 0-0-3

Tuscan Treaty T T Clement   65 a46
3 b f Brief Truce (USA) - Fiorenz (USA)
3^8sd 8^12sd 5^7gf 1^7gf 2^7gf 8^7gf 7^7g 11^7gf
16^f 7^7gf 9^6gf 12^6gs 2-2-12 £7,738

Tuscarora (Ire) A W Carroll   72 a63
4 b f Revoque (Ire) - Fresh Look (Ire)
1^6sd 4^6sd 8^6sd 6^7sd 1^7sd 5^7sd 2^8gf 2^8g
1^8f 6^8f 4^8gf 6^8f 4^7gf 8^7g 6^7gs 3-2-15
£12,690

Tusk M R Channon   94
3 ch g Fleetwood (Ire) - Farmer's Pet
6^8gf 1^10f 8^10gf 12^12gf 5^11gf 2^8gf 1^8gf 4^8g
1^10gf 10^12gf 4^10gf 1^10gf 4-1-12 £28,264

Tutum (Ire) T P McGovern   43 a49
2 b c Revoque (Ire) - Dieci Anno (Ire)
5^6sd 5^5gf 12^7gf 0-0-3

Tweed B Ellison   53 a70
6 b g Barathea (Ire) - In Perpetuity
4^16sw 7^18g 11^16gf 12^16gs 2^15sd 0-1-5
£1,143

Tweedsmuir P W Harris   69 a44
4 b g Zilzal (USA) - Sakura Queen (Ire)
6^12sd 9^14g 4^12gf 14^11gf 9^12gf 11^12gf 0-1-6

Twentytwosilver (Ire) J A Osborne   73
3 ro g Emarati (USA) - St Louis Lady
10^6gf 5^6gf 15^7g 10^6gf 6^7gf 15^7g 8^7gf
16^6gf 0-0-8

Twice Upon A Time B Smart   80
4 ch f Primo Dominie - Opuntia
12^5f 7^5g 1^5f 8^5g 7^5gf 9^5gf 2^5gf 1^5gf
8^5gf 2-1-9 £14,536

Twilight Blues (Ire) B J Meehan   118
4 ch c Bluebird (USA) - Pretty Sharp
4^7gf 1^6gf 8^6f 10^6gf 7^6gs 10^7gf 1-0-6
£60,500

Twilight Haze Miss Gay Kelleway   30 a84
5 b g Darshaan - Hiwayati
3^15sd 3^14sw 6^16sd 1^12sd 2^11sd 10^14g 1-2-6
£7,033

Twilight Mistress D W P Arbuthnot   83
5 b m Bin Ajwaad (Ire) - By Candlelight (Ire)
3^5f 2^5gf 14^6gf 5^6gf 4^5gf 6^5gf 2^5gf 9^7gf
16^gf 1-2-9 £10,199

Two Jacks (Ire) W S Cunningham   a30
6 b g Fayruz - Kaya (Ger)
7^8sw 9^8sd 0-0-2

Two Of A Kind (Ire) J W Hills   66 a58
3 ch g Ashkalani (Ire) - Dulcinea
12^8sd 5^10gs 5^12sd 5^14gf 0-0-4

Two Of Clubs P C Haslam   69
2 b g First Trump - Sulaka
4^5s 3^6gs 4^6gf 5^6gs 0-1-4 £1,166

Two Step Kid (USA) J Noseda   a87
2 ch c Gone West (USA) - Marsha's Dancer (USA)
1^6sd 1-0-1 £3,080

Two Steps To Go (USA) Ian Emmerson   44 a51
4 b g Rhythm (USA) - Lyonushka (Can)
9^8sd 4^11sw 5^12sw 16^10gf 7^12sd 4^9sd 12^14gf
4^12f 0-0-8 £311

Tychy S C Williams   96
4 ch f Suave Dancer (USA) - Touch Of White
3^6g 5^6gf 1^5g 1^6g 7^6g 5^7f 2^7gf 1^7g 1^6gf
11^7gf 4-2-10 £28,585

Tycoon A P O'Brien   98
2 b c Sadler's Wells (USA) - Fleeting Glimpse
3^7gy 2^7gf 1^7gf 5^7ho 1-2-4 £27,724

Tycoon Hall (Ire) R Hannon   99
3 ch c Halling (USA) - Tycooness (Ire)
5^8gf 5^10gs 7^7gf 0-0-3 £1,082

Tykeyvor (Ire) Lady Herries
13 b g Last Tycoon - Ivoronica
16^12sd 0-0-1

Tyne T D Barron   87
2 b c Komaite (USA) - High Typha
2^5gf 1^5gf 6^5gf 1-1-3 £4,487

Tyneham G C Bravery
3 b c Robellino (USA) - Diamond Wedding (USA)
11^9ft 0-0-1

Type One (Ire) T G Mills   84 a80
5 b g Bigstone (Ire) - Isca

1^{6sd} 2^{5gf} 1^{5s} 4^{5gf} 3^{5gf} 2^{6gf} **2-4-6** **£10,001**

Typhonic (Ire) *R Charlton* 58 a70
2 c c Efisio - Blown-Over
2^{6sd} 7^{6gf} **0-1-2** **£906**

Typhoon Tilly *C R Egerton* 83
6 b g Hernando (Fr) - Meavy
1^{13f} 3^{14gf} 3^{13gf} 10^{16gf} 3^{14gf} **1-2-5** **£9,774**

Typhoon Todd (Ire) *P G Murphy* a67
4 ch g Entrepreneur - Petite Liqueurelle (Ire)
1^{12sd} PU^{12sd} **1-0-2** **£3,474**

Tyranny *J L Dunlop* 98
3 b f Machiavellian (USA) - Dust Dancer
4^{8gf} 1^{7g} 4^{6g} 1^{7gf} 5^{7g} 8^{8gs} 16^{7g} **2-0-7** **£11,117**

Tytheknot *Jedd O'Keeffe* 72
2 b c Pursuit Of Love - Bundled Up (USA)
7^{7gs} 2^{8gf} **0-1-2** **£1,311**

Tyup Pompey (Ire) *B Smart* 62
2 ch c Docksider (USA) - Cindys Baby
3^{7gf} **0-1-1** **£356**

Tyzack (Ire) *J G Given* 73
2 b c Fasliyev (USA) - Rabea (USA)
2^{7gf} 5^{6gf} 2^{8g} 4^{7gf} 7^{7gs} **0-2-5** **£2,456**

Tzar *J R Best* a48
4 b g Makbul - Tzarina (USA)
12^{10sd} 13^{6sd} 7^{8sd} F^{8gf} **0-0-4**

Ugie Girl *A C Whillans*
4 gr f Passing Point (Ire) - Nawtinookey
10^{9gf} **0-0-1**

Uhoomagoo *K A Ryan* 91 a81
5 b g Namaqualand (USA) - Point Of Law
7^{7sw} 6^{8sw} 12^{8g} 17^{8gf} 1^{7sd} 8^{8gf} 7^{7gf} 3^{7gf}
7^{7gs} 5^{7gf} 1^{7g} 3^{8gf} 4^{7gf} 4^{8gf} 12^{8gf} 3^{7g} 3^{7g}
4^{7gf} 3^{7gf} 12^{7g} **2-6-20** **£22,497**

Uhuru Dawn (Ire) *Andre Hermans* a54
3 b c Fayruz - Come Dancing
4^{5sd} 6^{6hy} 3^{6g} 8^{8vs} 4^{6g} 7^{6ho} **0-2-6** **£4,026**

Ulshaw *B J Llewellyn* 64 a58
6 ch g Salse (USA) - Kintail
2^{16sd} 3^{16sd} 1^{16sd} 3^{16sw} 9^{16sd} 3^{16sd} 1^{18gf}
2^{19gf} 2^{16gf} 8^{21gs} 8^{16sd} **2-6-11** **£16,099**

Ulster Prince *D Carroll* 3 a1
2 b g Prince Sabo - Tonic Chord
6^{5gf} 9^{5sd} 11^{5sd} **0-0-3**

Ultima *J R Fanshawe* 75
3 ch f Unfuwain (USA) - Last Look
1^{8g} **1-0-1** **£3,503**

Ultra Marine (Ire) *J S Wainwright* 57
3 b c Blues Traveller (Ire) - The Aspecto Girl (Ire)
8^{8gf} 11^{8gs} 12^{12sd} 5^{9gf} 8^{10gf} 4^{8gf} 5^{10gf}
6^{10gf} 7^{10gs} 13^{10gf} 12^{11g} 4^{12gs} **0-0-12** **£679**

Ulundi *P R Webber* 102
8 b g Rainbow Quest (USA) - Flit (USA)
7^{10gf} 9^{12g} 10^{10g} **0-0-3**

Umista (Ire) *M Quinn* a27
4 b f Tagula (Ire) - Nishiki (USA)
3^{7sw} 9^{8sd} 13^{6sd} 12^{8f} **0-0-4** **£530**

Umoja (Fr) *C F Wall* 73 a73
3 b/br f Anabaa (USA) - Frustration
5^{10gf} 3^{10sd} 6^{10g} 5^{12sd} **0-1-4** **£858**

Un Autre Espere *T Wall* 38
4 b g Golden Heights - Drummer's Dream (Ire)

3^{11gf} 9^{13f} 5^{11gf} 12^{10gf} 8^{13f} **0-0-5** **£881**

Unavailable (Ire) *M A Magnusson* 95
2 b f Alzao (USA) - Maid Of Killeen (Ire)
1^{6gf} 6^{7gf} 1^{8gf} **2-0-3** **£12,020**

Uncle Bernon *G B Balding* 73
4 ch g Pivotal - Magical Veil
8^{6g} 16^{7gf} **0-0-2**

Uncle Cent (Ire) *E J O'Neill* 83
2 ch c Peintre Celebre (USA) - Butter Knife (Ire)
5^{7gf} 3^{8gf} 3^{8gf} 1^{10gf} **1-2-4** **£4,648**

Uncle John *S Kirk* 51 a60
2 b c Atraf - Bit O' May
12^{8gf} 8^{8g} 1^{8sd} **1-0-3** **£2,233**

Uncle Max (Ire) *N A Twiston-Davies* 70 a77
3 b g Victory Note (USA) - Sunset Park (Ire)
3^{8sd} 2^{8sw} 3^{7sd} 3^{10sd} 13^{10f} 8^{8gf} 5^{10g} 4^{12f}
7^{12g} **0-3-9** **£2,983**

Uncomprehendable (USA) *B Hanbury*
3 ch f Loup Sauvage (USA) - Benguela (USA)
6^{9gf} **0-0-1**

Under My Spell *P D Evans* 77
2 b f Wizard King - Gagajulu
1^{5gf} 3^{5g} 4^{5gs} 3^{5gf} 9^{5gf} 3^{5gf} 3^{6f} 5^{6gs}
5^{6gf} **1-1-10** **£12,503**

Underwriter (USA) *J H M Gosden* 4
3 br c With Approval (Can) - Night Risk (USA)
9^{8gf} **0-0-1**

Undeterred *T D Barron* 88
7 ch g Zafonic (USA) - Mint Crisp (Ire)
3^{6g} 15^{6gs} 6^{6gf} 2^{6gf} 2^{6gf} 1^{6g} 2^{6g} 4^{6gf}
8^{6g} 16^{6g} 11^{6gf} **1-5-11** **£37,076**

Unholy Alliance (Ire) *R M Flower*
2 ch g General Monash (USA) - Holy Water
16^{7sd} 14^{7sd} **0-0-2**

Unicorn Reward (Ire) *R Hannon* 89
3 b c Turtle Island (Ire) - Kingdom Pearl
17^{8gf} 3^{7gf} 5^{8gf} 1^{8g} 1^{8g} 1^{8gf} 1^{8g} 5^{8g}
13^{8f} **4-0-9** **£23,926**

Unigold (USA) *E A L Dunlop* 111
3 ch c Silver Deputy (Can) - Desert Queen (USA)
1^{10g} 2^{11g} 18^{12g} 3^{11gf} 10^{12g} 3^{10g} 10^{12g}
1-1-7 **£18,614**

Unintentional *R Brotherton* 50
2 b f Dr Devious (Ire) - Tamnia
11^{6gf} 6^{6gs} **0-0-2**

United Spirit (Ire) *M A Magnusson* 61
2 b f Fasliyev (USA) - Atlantic Desire (USA)
5^{6gf} 11^{6g} **0-0-2**

United Union (Ire) *D Haydn Jones* 65 a53
2 b/br g Imperial Ballet (Ire) - Madagascar
9^{6sd} 3^{6g} 9^{6sd} **0-1-4** **£852**

Universal King (USA) *Mrs L Stubbs* 75
2 b c El Prado (Ire) - Arjunand (USA)
5^{5gf} 3^{5f} 2^{5gf} 2^{7g} **0-2-4** **£4,122**

Unleaded *J Akehurst* 22
3 ch f Danzig Connection (USA) - Mo Stopher
15^{7gf} 9^{10gf} 12^{12g} **0-0-3**

Unleash (USA) *P J Hobbs* 103
4 ch g Benny The Dip (USA) - Lemhi Go (USA)
1^{16gs} 4^{16gf} 4^{14gf} 32^{18gf} **1-1-4** **£113,500**

Uno Mente *Mrs P N Dutfield* 74 a60
4 b f Mind Games - One Half Silver (Can)
3^{8sd} 4^{8sd} 10^{8sd} 3^{10gf} 9^{10gf} 1^{8gf} 3^{8gf}
5^{8gf} 17^{8gf} **1-2-10** **£5,814**

Unperturbed *J Balding* 4

3 ch f Unfuwain (USA) - Mudflap
9⁸ˢᵈ 14⁷ᵍᶠ **0-0-2**

Unprecedented (Ire) *R Hannon*   51
2 br g Primo Dominie - Misellina (Fr)
6⁵ᵍ 13⁶ᵍ 9⁶ᵍᶠ **0-0-3**

Unrivalled *J H M Gosden*   80 a66
2 b c Unfuwain (USA) - No Sugar Baby (Fr)
2⁶ᵍᶠ 12⁷ᵍᶠ 3⁷ˢᵈ 1⁶ᶠ **1-2-4 £6,530**

Unscrupulous *J R Fanshawe*   88
4 ch g Machiavellian (USA) - Footlight Fantasy (USA)
8⁷ᵍ 3⁷ᵍ 2⁷ᵍᶠ 1⁸ᵍᶠ **1-2-4 £8,535**

Unshakable (Ire) *Bob Jones*   108
4 b c Eagle Eyed (USA) - Pepper And Salt (Ire)
7⁸ᵍᶠ 6⁸ᵍᶠ 2⁸ᵍᶠ 8⁸ᵍ 14⁸ᵍᶠ 22⁷ᵍᶠ 7⁸ᵍˢ **0-1-7 £10,675**

Unshaken *E J Alston*   66
9 b h Environment Friend - Reel Foyle (USA)
8⁸ᵍᶠ 4⁷ᶠ 3⁸ᵍᶠ 3⁸ᵍˢ 4⁸ᵍᶠ 3¹⁰ᵍᶠ 11⁹ᵍˢ **0-4-7 £2,578**

Unshooda *B W Hills*   91
2 ch f Machiavellian (USA) - Rawaabe (USA)
2⁶ᵍᶠ 1⁶ᵍᶠ 2⁶ᵍ 6⁷ᵍᶠ **1-2-4 £14,035**

Unsigned (USA) *R H Buckler*   a41
5 b/br g Cozzene (USA) - Striata (USA)
9¹⁶ˢᵈ **0-0-1**

Unsuited *J E Long*   52
4 b f Revoque (Ire) - Nagnagnag (Ire)
10⁶ᵍ 6⁵ᵍᶠ 5⁷ᵍᶠ **0-0-3**

Untidy Daughter *B Ellison*   36 a19
4 b f Sabrehill (USA) - Branitska
9⁸ˢᵈ 14¹⁰ᵍ **0-0-2**

Up Front (Ire) *A Berry*   a31
4 b f Up And At 'Em - Sable Lake
6⁸ˢʷ 9⁸ˢᵈ 5⁸ˢᵈ 5⁹ˢʷ 9⁹ˢᵈ 11⁸ˢᵈ 9¹⁰ᵍᶠ **0-0-7**

Up In Flames (Ire) *Mrs G S Rees*
12 b g Nashamaa - Bella Lucia
11¹²ˢᵈ **0-0-1**

Up Tempo (Ire) *T D Easterby*   75 a68
5 b g Flying Spur (Aus) - Musical Essence
9⁷ˢᵈ 4⁸ˢᵈ 14⁷ᵍᶠ 3⁶ᵍᶠ 4⁶ᵍˢ 8⁷ᵍ 11⁷ᵍ 2⁶ᵍᶠ
3⁶ᵍˢ 9⁷ᵍᶠ 8⁶ᵍ 7⁷ᵍᶠ 6⁷ᵍᶠ 4⁶ᶠ 9⁶ᵍ **0-4-15 £4,548**

Upthedale (Ire) *J R Weymes*   41 a36
2 b g General Monash (USA) - Pimpinella (Ire)
15⁵ᵍ 5⁵ᵍ 10⁶ˢᵈ 10⁷ᵍˢ **0-0-4**

Uraib (Ire) *B Hanbury*   93
3 b/br f Mark Of Esteem (Ire) - Hamsaat (Ire)
1¹⁰ᵍᶠ 8⁸ᵍ 4¹⁰ᵍᶠ 7⁸ᵍᶠ 3⁹ᵍ 2⁷ᵍᶠ 3⁸ᵍᶠ 10⁷ᵍˢ
1-3-8 £10,612

Urban Knight *J W Unett*   39
2 br g Dracula (Aus) - Anhaar
6⁵ᵍᶠ 9⁵ᵍᶠ 9⁷ᵍᶠ **0-0-3**

Urban Myth *J W Unett*   a73
5 b g Shaamit (Ire) - Nashville Blues (Ire)
4⁹ˢᵈ 3⁹ˢᵈ 1⁸ˢᵈ 2⁸ˢᵈ 8⁷ˢʷ 8⁸ˢᵈ 12⁸ᶠᵗ **1-2-7 £4,448**

Urban Rose *J W Unett*   68
2 b f Piccolo - Blue Lamp (USA)
7⁶ᵍᶠ 1⁶ᵍᶠ 11⁶ᵍᶠ 4⁶ᵍᶠ 4⁶ᵍᶠ **1-0-5 £2,359**

Urgent Swift *A P Jarvis*   a51
10 ch g Beveled (USA) - Good Natured
4¹⁶ˢᵈ 4¹²ˢʷ 5¹⁴ˢᵈ **0-0-3**

Urowells (Ire) *E A L Dunlop*   84
3 b g Sadler's Wells (USA) - Highest Accolade

4¹¹ˢ 1¹⁰ᵍᶠ **1-0-2 £6,576**

Uvani *J A R Toller*   33 a59
3 ch f Classic Cliche (Ire) - Spirit Of The Wind (USA)
4¹²ˢᵈ 9¹²ˢʷ 8¹⁰ᵍᶠ **0-0-3**

Va Pensiro *D Haydn Jones*
3 b g Lugana Beach - Hopperetta
13⁶ˢᵈ **0-0-1**

Vademecum *B Smart*   76
2 br c Shinko Forest (Ire) - Sunshine Coast
8⁷ᵍᶠ 4⁸ᵍˢ 1⁷ᵍᶠ 3⁸ᵍᶠ **1-1-4 £3,300**

Val De Fleurie (Ger) *J G M O'Shea*   62
8 b m Mondrian (Ger) - Valbonne
11¹²ᶠ 11¹⁰ᶠ 7¹⁰ᵍᶠ 3¹²ᶠ 7¹²ᵍ 1¹²ᵍᶠ 4¹³ᵍᶠ
1-0-7 £3,867

Val De Maal (Ire) *G C H Chung*   80 a76
3 ch c Eagle Eyed (USA) - Miss Bojangles
14⁶ᵍᶠ 10⁶ᵍᶠ 9⁸ᵍ 9⁷ᵍᶠ 1⁷ˢʷ 3⁷ᵍ 8⁷ˢᵈ 3⁷ˢᵈ
36ᵍᶠ 14ᵍᶠ 5⁵ᵍᶠ 2⁶ᵍᶠ 4⁶ᵍᶠ 11⁶ᵍᶠ **2-4-14 £12,596**

Valance (Ire) *C R Egerton*   83 a74
3 br g Bahhare (USA) - Glowlamp (Ire)
11⁸ᵍᶠ 4¹⁰ᵍᶠ 1¹²ˢᵈ 7¹²ᵍᶠ 3¹⁴ᵍᶠ **1-1-5 £3,663**

Valazar (USA) *T D Barron*   a72
4 b g Nicholas (USA) - Valor's Minion (USA)
5⁶ˢᵈ 2⁵ˢᵈ 4⁵ˢᵈ **0-1-3 £1,981**

Valdasho *J D Bethell*   35
4 b f Classic Cliche (Ire) - Ma Rivale
11⁶ᵍᶠ 15⁶ᵍᶠ **0-0-2**

Valentia (Ire) *M H Tompkins*   56
2 b f Perugino (USA) - Teide
10⁵ᵍ 5⁶ᵍᶠ **0-0-2**

Valentine's Dream *Bruce Hellier*   65
2 b f Mind Games - I'm Playing
4⁷ᵍ 4⁶ᵍ 3⁷ˢ 8⁶ˢ 6⁶ˢᵈ 8⁶ᵍᶠ **0-0-6 £1,869**

Valerie Ann Burton (Ire) *M R Hoad*
3 br f Charnwood Forest (Ire) - Ezilana (Ire)
9¹⁰ᵍᶠ 8¹²ˢᵈ **0-0-2**

Valeureux *J Hetherton*   64
5 ch g Cadeaux Genereux - La Strada
4⁸ᵍˢ 3¹²ᵍ 3¹³ᵍˢ 9⁸ᶠ 10¹⁰ᵍˢ 2¹¹ᵍ **0-2-6 £2,475**

Valiant Air (Ire) *J R Weymes*   58
2 b c Spectrum (Ire) - Shining Desert (Ire)
7⁷ᵍ 4⁸ᵍᶠ 13⁸ᵍ **0-0-3 £256**

Valiant Romeo *R Bastiman*   63
3 b c Primo Dominie - Desert Lynx (Ire)
9⁵ᵍ 13⁵ᵍˢ 10⁵ᵍᶠ 14⁵ᵍˢ 14⁵ᶠ 17⁵ᵍᶠ 17⁵ᵍᶠ
0-0-7

Valiantly *Andrew Lee*   104
4 b f Anabaa (USA) - Valbra
2⁶ᵍᶠ 4⁶ᵍᶠ 11⁶ᵍʸ **0-1-3 £7,872**

Valjarv (Ire) *N P Littmoden*   94
2 b f Bluebird (USA) - Iktidar
2⁵ᵍᶠ 2⁶ᵍᶠ 3⁸ᵍᶠ 4⁶ᵍᶠ 4⁶ᵍ 7⁶ᵍ 3⁷ᵍᶠ 1⁶ᵍᶠ
1-3-8 £57,207

Valuable (Ire) *R Johnson*   ✓
6 b m Jurado (USA) - Can't Afford It (Ire)
10⁹ˢᵈ **0-0-1**

Valuable Gift *R C Guest*   38 a66
6 ch g Cadeaux Genereux - Valbra
4⁶ˢʷ 6⁷ˢᵈ 3⁶ˢᵈ 2⁶ˢᵈ 13⁶ᶠ 13⁶ˢᵈ **0-2-6 £1,609**

Value Added *M A Jarvis*   53 a63
3 b f Petoski - Valiancy

6^{10sd} 4^{9sw} 6^{12sd} 4^{12gf} **0-0-4 £546**

Vamose (Ire) *Miss Gay Kelleway* 68
2 ro c Victory Note (USA) - Narrow Band (Ire)
7^{7g} 2^{7gs} 3^{8gs} 8^{7gf} **0-2-4 £2,219**

Vanbrugh (Fr) *Miss D A McHale* 69 a78
3 ch g Starborough - Renovate
1^{8sd} 2^{10sd} 8^{10g} 13^{7gs} 7^{10g} 9^{10gf} 7^{12sd}
6^{10sd} 6^{12sd} **1-1-9 £3,969**

Vandal *J A R Toller* 71 a79
3 b c Entrepreneur - Vax Star
6^{7gf} 2^{7gf} 3^{7gf} 14^{7gs} 1^{7sd} 7^{7sd} 10^{8gf}
1-2-7 £7,866

Vandenberghe *J A Osborne* 18 a50
4 b g Millkom - Child Star (Fr)
13^{14gf} 13^{12sd} 6^{9sd} **0-0-3**

Vanderlin *A M Balding* 111
4 ch g Halling (USA) - Massorah (Fr)
3^{6gf} 10^{6f} 7^{7g} 12^{6g} 1^{7gf} 2^{7g} 2^{7g} 24^{6g}
4^{7gf} 10^{6gf} **1-3-10 £39,990**

Vanilla Moon *J R Jenkins* 60 a56
3 b f Emperor Jones (USA) - Daarat Alayaam (Ire)
7^{7sd} 13^{12gf} 4^{10gf} 8^{10gf} 8^{12gf} 8^{12sd} 4^{12sd}
11^{8gf} 5^{11gf} **0-0-9 £280**

Vanished (Ire) *K A Ryan* 62 a67
3 b f Fayruz - Where's The Money
16^{5gs} 4^{6sd} 7^{6hy} 2^{5sd} 4^{6sd} 4^{5g} 10^{5sd} **0-1-7**
£1,752

Vanishing Dancer (Swi) *B Ellison* 64
6 ch g Llandaff (USA) - Vanishing Prairie (USA)
4^{16gf} 9^{14gf} 6^{14f} 3^{14f} **0-1-4 £971**

Vantage (Ire) *N P Littmoden* 78
2 b g Marju (Ire) - Anna Comnena (Ire)
10^{6gf} 3^{7gf} 3^{8gf} 16^{8g} **0-1-4 £1,413**

Variety Club *A M Balding* 63
2 b c Royal Applause - Starfida
10^{7gf} 7^{8gf} 8^{8gf} **0-0-3**

Varnay *D R Loder* 89
2 b f Machiavellian (USA) - Valleria
5^{6gf} 1^{5gf} 2^{6gf} 6^{7g} 3^{7gf} **1-2-5 £10,317**

Varuni (Ire) *J G Portman* 40
2 b f Ali-Royal (Ire) - Sauvignon (Ire)
12^{6gf} **0-0-1**

Vas Y Carla (USA) *J L Dunlop* 70
2 ch f Gone West (USA) - Lady Carla
6^{7gf} 2^{7gf} 6^{7gs} **0-1-3 £1,323**

Vaudevire *A Berry*
2 b c Dancing Spree (USA) - Approved Quality (Ire)
6^{5gf} **0-0-1**

Vaughan *Mrs A J Perrett* 76
2 b c Machiavellian (USA) - Labibeh (USA)
12^{8gf} 1^{8gs} **1-0-2 £3,012**

Veinte Siete (USA) *P R Webber* 54
3 ch g Trempolino (USA) - Satz (USA)
15^{7gf} 5^{7gf} 6^{8gf} 3^{8f} LFT 1^{14gf} 15^{10gf} **0-1-6**
£559

Velocitas *H J Collingridge* a30
2 b g Magic Ring (Ire) - Folly Finnesse
11^{7sd} **0-0-1**

Velocity Belle *M L W Bell* 57
2 b f Groom Dancer (USA) - Rapid Repeat (Ire)
5^{7gf} 8^{7gf} 4^{8gf} 3^{10gf} 14^{8gs} **0-1-5 £615**

Velocitys Image (Ire) *E J Alston* 33
3 b f Tagula (Ire) - Pike Creek (USA)
8^{8gf} 6^{6f} 15^{8f} **0-0-3**

Velvet Touch *J R Jenkins* 65

2 b f Danzig Connection (USA) - Soft Touch (Ger)
3^{6gs} **0-1-1 £423**

Velvet Waters *R F Johnson Houghton* 56
2 b f Unfuwain (USA) - Gleaming Water
6^{6gs} 8^{7gf} 8^{8f} **0-0-3**

Venables (USA) *R Hannon* 102
2 ch c Stravinsky (USA) - Hope For A Breeze (Can)
6^{6gf} 1^{6gf} 4^{6g} 8^{6gf} **2-0-5 £23,796**

Vendome (Ire) *J A Osborne* a26
5 b g General Monash (USA) - Kealbra Lady
7^{5sw} **0-0-1**

Vendors Mistake (Ire) *Andrew Reid* a54
2 b f Danehill (USA) - Sunspangled (Ire)
6^{7sd} 9^{6sd} **0-0-2**

Venerdi Tredici (Ire) *P A Blockley* 54 a19
2 b f Desert Style (Ire) - Stifen
7^{5sd} 8^{6gf} 3^{6f} 9^{6gf} **0-0-4 £716**

Venetian Pride (USA) *M Johnston* 87
2 b f Gone West (USA) - Via Borghese (USA)
1^{6gs} 6^{6gf} 3^{6g} 8^{6gf} 8^{6gs} **1-1-5 £9,149**

Venetian Romance (Ire) *A P Jones* 54
2 ch f Desert Story (Ire) - Cipriani
13^{5g} 7^{6gf} 11^{6gf} 3^{7gs} 7^{8g} 5^{8f} **0-1-6**
£555

Veneziana *P F I Cole* 50 a60
2 ch f Vettori (Ire) - Fairy Story (Ire)
8^{7gf} 3^{7sd} 9^{7sd} **0-1-3 £536**

Vengeance *Mrs A J Perrett* 96
3 b c Fleetwood (Ire) - Lady Isabell
2^{10gf} 1^{10gf} 1^{12gf} 2^{12gf} 1^{12gf} 9^{12gs} 5^{12gf}
3-2-7 £21,415

Vengerov *M L W Bell* 68
2 b c Piccolo - Shining Cloud
5^{6gs} 7^{6gf} 3^{7gf} 4^{7gf} 8^{8gf} **0-1-5 £297**

Venturi *David Wachman* 105
2 b f Danehill Dancer (Ire) - Zagreb Flyer
6^{5s} 1^{6gf} 1^{7gf} **2-0-3 £40,097**

Verasi *R Charlton* 50
2 b g Kahyasi - Fair Verona (USA)
15^{8gf} 9^{7gs} **0-0-2**

Verkhotina *R Charlton* 73
2 b f Barathea (Ire) - Alusha
5^{6gf} 5^{6gf} 7^{6gf} **0-0-3**

Vermilion Creek *R Hollinshead* 63 a53
4 b f Makbul - Cloudy Reef
2^{12sw} 4^{8sd} 3^{9sd} 6^{12sd} 7^{8gf} 18^{gf} 6^{10gf} 1^{10gf}
4^{8gf} 10^{9sd} 13^{8gs} **2-2-11 £8,695**

Vermilliann (Ire) *R Hannon* 89
2 b f Mujadil (USA) - Refined (Ire)
1^{5gf} 1^{5gs} 6^{5gf} **2-0-3 £12,683**

Vertedanz (Ire) *Miss I E Craig* 46 a60
3 b f Sesaro (USA) - Blade Of Grass
5^{8sd} 6^{10sd} 10^{8sd} 7^{8g} 11^{10gf} **0-0-5**

Vertical *P R Chamings* 58
3 ch g Ashkalani (Ire) - Waft (USA)
4^{7gf} 12^{10gf} 3^{10f} 13^{10gf} 3^{10gf} **0-1-5**
£1,202

Very Exclusive (USA) *G L Moore* 44
4 b g Royal Academy (USA) - Exclusive Davis (USA)
16^{11gf} 5^{11gf} 12^{10gf} 14^{11gf} 4^{10f} 3^{12g}
11^{12gf} **0-1-7 £427**

Vespone (Ire) *Saeed Bin Suroor* 123
3 ch c Llandaff (USA) - Vanishing Prairie (USA)
1^{8g} 2^{7g} 10^{5s} 1^{9g} 1^{10gs} 12^{10gf} **4-1-6**
£275,072

Vesta Flame M Johnston — 14
2 b f Vettori (Ire) - Ciel De Feu (USA)
20^8g 0-0-1

Veverka W S Kittow — 72
2 b f King's Theatre (Ire) - Once Smitten (Ire)
16^6g 2^7gf 6^7f 2^8f 3^8gf 7^7gf 0-3-6
£3,088

Vevina (USA) Sir Mark Prescott — 7 a27
2 b f Rahy (USA) - Lovely Keri (USA)
15^6gf 9^7sd 12^7gf 0-0-3

Vi Et Virtite R C Guest
4 b f Dancing Spree (USA) - Princess Scully
10^12sd 16^12sw 0-0-2

Viburnum M Wellings
9 b m Old Vic - Burning Desire
10^9sd 0-0-1

Vicario M L W Bell — 14
2 gr c Vettori (Ire) - Arantxa
19^8s 15^8gs 0-0-2

Vicars Destiny Mrs S Lamyman — 72
5 b m Sir Harry Lewis (USA) - Church Leap
6^12gf 5^12g 6^8gf 2^16gf 6^18gf 0-1-5 £1,844

Vicereine J H M Gosden — 93
3 b f Zamindar (USA) - Victoriana (USA)
5^9gf 1^8f 5^10gf 5^10gf 2^8gf 1-0-5 £6,973

Vicious Knight L M Cumani — 106
5 b g Night Shift (USA) - Myth
1^7gf 5^8gf 1-0-2 £13,423

Vicious Lady R M Whitaker — 28
3 b f Vettori (Ire) - Ling Lane
9^10gs 12^10g 10^12gs 8^10gf 0-0-4

Vicious Prince (Ire) R M Whitaker — 82
4 b c Sadler's Wells (USA) - Sunny Flower (Fr)
9^12ft 10^12gf 20^14gf 9^13g 8^13gs 13^13gs
0-0-6

Vicious Warrior R M Whitaker — 93
4 b g Elmaamul (USA) - Ling Lane
4^10ft 9^9ft 11^9ft 10^8ft 2^10gf 7^10g 7^10g
4^8g 11^10gf 2^8gf 0-2-10 £6,344

Victor Valentine (Ire) M D Hammond — 30
4 ch g Ridgewood Ben - Tarliya (Ire)
16^7f 14^6gs 0-0-2

Victoria Park (Ire) D Nicholls — 59 a15
3 b f Victory Note (USA) - Break For Tee (Ire)
8^7sw 10^6sd 6^6f 2^5gf 4^6gf 1^5f 2^5gf 5^5gf
10^5gf 14^6gs 15^5gf 1-2-11 £8,038

Victorian Dancer (Ire) K A Ryan — 58 a15
2 b f Groom Dancer (USA) - Victoria Regia (Ire)
8^6s 4^6f 9^6sd 8^7f 4^7gf 0-0-5 £305

Victory Flip (Ire) R Hollinshead — 21 a61
3 b f Victory Note (USA) - Two Magpies
2^7sd 5^7sw 8^6sd 6^7sd 2^6sd 16^6gs 2^8sd 7^8sd
16^8gf 7^8sd 0-3-10 £2,821

Victory Moon (SAF) M F De Kock — 117 a116
4 b c Al Mufti (USA) - Dancing Flower (SAF)
1^8ft 2^9ft 1^10ft 8^8gf 5^10gf 10^12g 2-1-6
£878,000

Victory Quest (Ire) Mrs S Lamyman — 68
3 b g Victory Note (USA) - Marade (USA)
13^8gf 13^10g 8^12gs 1^14gf 2^12gf 5^14gf 1-0-6
£6,252

Victory Roll Miss E C Lavelle — a55
7 b g In The Wings - Persian Victory (Ire)
6^16sd 0-0-1

Victory Sign (Ire) K R Burke — 64

3 b g Forzando - Mo Ceri
6^10gf 5^12gf 2^10gf 4^12g 3^12gf 6^12gf 5^12g
11^12gf 4^11g 1-2-9 £5,054

Victory Vee M Blanshard — 24 a65
3 ch g Vettori (Ire) - Aldevonie
9^7sw 2^6sd 4^6sd 6^6sd 2^6sd 13^6gf 12^6hy 2^8sd
7^6sd 4^8sd 1^7sd 3^7sd 12^7sd 7^7sd 1-4-14
£7,095

Victory Venture (Ire) M Johnston — 80
3 b g Victory Note (USA) - Shirley Venture
2^8g 1^12gf 7^12gf 12^11gf 3^10gf 11^10gs 1-2-6
£5,946

Vienna's Boy (Ire) R Hannon — 96
2 b c Victory Note (USA) - Shinkoh Rose (Fr)
1^5gf 6^5gf 2^5f 1^5g 3^5g 4^7gf 2^5gs 7^6g 2^7gf
10^6gf 2-3-10 £29,233

View The Facts P L Gilligan — a29
4 br f So Factual (USA) - Scenic View (Ire)
12^8sd 13^7sd 0-0-2

Viewforth I Semple — 91
5 b g Emarati (USA) - Miriam
20^5gf 10^6gf 13^6gs 2^6gs 2^5gs 2^5gs 10^5gf
5^5g 16^6f 15^6gf 2^5gs 5^6g 4^5s 6^5gf 13^7gf 15^6gs
2-5-16 £28,824

Vigorous (Ire) M R Channon — 80
3 b f Danetime (Ire) - Merrily
1^6gf 1^5gf 12^6g 12^6gf 17^5gf 4^5gf 4^5gf
7^5gf 2-1-8 £13,618

Vigoureux (Fr) S Gollings — 50
4 b g Villez (USA) - Rouge Folie (Fr)
6^12gs 0-0-1

Vikings Bay J H M Gosden — 94 a88
2 b c Intikhab (USA) - Night At Sea
5^6g 1^5sd 1^6gs 2-0-3 £5,967

Vilamoura W J Haggas — a76
2 b g Forzando - Alpi Dora
2^6sd 1^6sd 1-1-2 £4,175

Villa Del Sol B Smart — a44
4 br f Tagula (Ire) - Admonish
13^7sd 4^8sd 5^7sw 4^7sd 0-1-4

Vin Du Pays M Blanshard — 46 a79
3 b g Alzao (USA) - Royale Rose (Fr)
6^10sd 8^12g 14^8g 9^10gf 16^10gf 8^12gf 9^16sd
5^8sd 5^10g 1^12sd 1-0-10 £2,086

Vinando C R Egerton — 75
2 ch c Hernando (Fr) - Sirena (Ger)
5^7gs 0-0-1

Vincent John A Harris — 41 a41
8 b g Anshan - Top-Anna (Ire)
9^14sd 2^16sd 4^16sw 5^14gf 7^16gf 6^16gf
0-1-7 £862

Vincentia C Smith — 65 a55
5 ch m Komaite (USA) - Vatersay (USA)
6^6g 6^5gf 9^6gf 3^5sw 0-1-4 £290

Vindication J R Fanshawe — 101 a84
3 ch g Compton Place - Prince's Feather (Ire)
8^7gf 1^7gf 2^7gf 5^7gf 17^7g 6^7gf 5^7sd 1^7gf
1^7gf 11^7sd 3-1-10 £22,924

Vinnie Roe (Ire) D K Weld — 122
5 b/br h Definite Article - Kayu
1^12gf 1^14gf 4^16ho 2-0-4 £173,652

Vintage Premium R A Fahey — 113
6 b g Forzando - Julia Domna
6^10g 2^10g 4^10gf 3^10g 2^10gf 15^12g 0-1-6
£17,003

Vintage Style *H A McWilliams* — 66
4 ch g Piccolo - Gibaltarik (Ire)
19^{6gf} 3^{6g} 9^{6gf} 10^{6gs} 11^{6gf} 4^{6gf} 7^{7gf} 4^{6g}
7^{8g} 0-3-9 £660

Vintage Tipple (Ire) *P Mullins* — 116
3 b f Entrepreneur - Overruled (Ire)
2^{7g} 1^{12g} 7^{10gf} 6^{12gy} 1-1-4 £156,720

Viola Da Braccio (Ire) *D J Daly* — 55
2 ch f Vettori (Ire) - Push A Button
17^{8gf} 0-0-1

Violent *Miss A M Newton-Smith* — 6
5 b m Deploy - Gentle Irony
14^{10f} 16^{12f} 0-0-2

Violet Avenue *J G Given* — 64
2 ch f Muhtarram (USA) - Ivoronica
2^{6g} 8^{6g} 4^{6gf} 0-1-3 £1,135

Vipassana *D Sepulchre* — 76
3 b f Sadler's Wells (USA) - Reef Squaw
3^{10gf} 2^{12gf} 1^{14f} 4^{12gs} 6^{12s} 4^{12ho} 1-1-6
£14,752

Virgin Soldier (Ire) *G A Swinbank* — 87
7 ch g Waajib - Never Been Chaste
11^{14gf} 3^{16f} 6^{16gf} 0-0-3 £1,162

Virtuoso *B G Powell* — a22
9 ch g Suave Dancer (USA) - Creake
15^{12sd} 0-0-1

Virtus *J R Fanshawe* — 68
3 ch c Machiavellian (USA) - Exclusive Virtue (USA)
4^{8gf} 0-0-1 £460

Vision Of Dreams *B J Meehan* — 89
3 b f Efisio - Dark Eyed Lady (Ire)
5^{6gf} 6^{6gs} 9^{5gf} 14^{6gf} 19^{5s} 11^{5gf} 0-0-6
£682

Vision Of Night *J L Dunlop* — 108
7 b h Night Shift (USA) - Dreamawhile
6^{6gf} 10^{6gf} 2^{5gf} 1^{6f} 3^{5g} 11^{6gf} 2^{6gf} 1^{6gf}
3^{6gf} 10^{5gf} 6^{6gf} 2-3-11 £36,389

Vita Spericolata (Ire) *J S Wainwright* — 102
6 b m Prince Sabo - Ahonita
9^{5gf} 9^{5g} 5^{5g} 2^{6gf} 4^{6gf} 3^{6gf} 10^{5gf} 9^{5gf}
8^{6g} 19^{5gf} 0-2-10 £15,700

Vitelucy *Miss S J Wilton* — 43 a57
4 b f Vettori (Ire) - Classic Line
2^{13sd} 1^{13sd} 9^{12gf} 10^{15sd} 1-1-4 £3,817

Viva Atlas Espana *Miss B Sanders* — 39
3 b f Piccolo - Bay Risk
19^{6gf} 10^{7gf} 6^{9g} 8^{9gf} 0-0-4

Vizulize *B R Millman* — 67
4 b f Robellino (USA) - Euridice (Ire)
4^{12gf} 9^{12f} 3^{12gf} 5^{10gf} 4^{10gf} 12^{9gf} 5^{10gf}
5^{10gf} 4^{8gf} 10^{8gf} 0-1-10 £2,287

Vlasta Weiner *J M Bradley* — 47
3 b g Magic Ring (Ire) - Armaiti
7^{6g} 8^{5f} 14^{7gf} 8^{5gf} 18^{6gf} 10^{7gf} 6^{7gf}
0-0-7

Vodka Queen (Ire) *K R Burke* — a20
4 b f Ali-Royal (Ire) - Gentle Guest (Ire)
4^{12sd} 8^{11sd} 0-0-2

Voice Mail *A M Balding* — 80 a79
4 b g So Factual (USA) - Wizardry
3^{7sd} 3^{7sd} 8^{8sd} 6^{8sd} 4^{8sd} 4^{8sd} 5^{8g} 6^{8gf}
7^{8gf} 8^{8gf} 1^{8f} 2^{9gf} 3^{9gf} 8^{8f} 4^{9g} 4^{8f} 5^{8f} 5^{9g}
8^{8gf} 1-6-19 £12,813

Voile (Ire) *R Hannon* — 100
2 b f Barathea (Ire) - Samriah (Ire)
1^{6gf} 2^{6gf} 4^{6g} 3^{6g} 4^{7gf} 5^{6gf} 1-2-6
£24,610

Voix Du Nord (Fr) *D Smaga* — 114
2 b c Valanour (Ire) - Dame Edith (Fr)
2^{7gs} 1^{8gs} 2^{8gs} 4^{8g} 2^{9gs} 1^{10gs} 2-3-6
£95,007

Volaticus (Ire) *D Nicholls* — 43
2 b c Desert Story (Ire) - Haysel (Ire)
8^{6g} 0-0-1

Volcanic *P D Evans* — 40 a46
4 b g Zafonic (USA) - Ryafan (USA)
12^{7sd} 13^{10sd} 7^{7gf} 19^{6gf} 0-0-4

Voluptuous *T H Caldwell* — 28 a78
3 b f Polish Precedent (USA) - Alzianah
1^{6sw} 12^{7sd} 3^{7sw} 2^{7sd} 3^{7sd} 7^{6sd} 12^{7gf}
17^{8gf} 12^{6sd} 1-3-9 £5,563

Vonadaisy *W J Haggas* — 67
2 b f Averti (Ire) - Vavona
6^{6gs} 10^{8gf} 3^{6gf} 4^{7g} 4^{8g} 0-2-5 £2,980

Vortex *Miss Gay Kelleway* — 78 a83
4 b c Danehill (USA) - Roupala (USA)
2^{7gf} 6^{8gf} 2^{7g} 1^{8f} 1^{7sd} 6^{8gs} 7^{7gf} 2-2-7
£10,762

Voyager (Ire) *J L Dunlop* — 3
3 b c Green Desert (USA) - Rafha
18^{8g} 0-0-1

Vrisaki (Ire) *Miss D Mountain* — 45
2 b c Docksider (USA) - Kingdom Queen (Ire)
7^{6f} 0-0-1

Vrubel (Ire) *H J Collingridge* — 57 a57
4 ch g Entrepreneur - Renzola
9^{10sd} 12^{10sd} 3^{10gf} 10^{9gf} 8^{9gf} 0-1-5 £570

Waaedah (USA) *M R Channon* — 75
2 ch f Halling (USA) - Agama (USA)
11^{5f} 1^{7g} 6^{7gf} 7^{7gf} 14^{7gf} 1-1-5 £6,639

Wadud *J L Dunlop* — 60
3 b f Nashwan (USA) - The Perfect Life (Ire)
10^{10gf} 9^{12gf} 4^{12gf} 13^{16gf} 0-0-4 £443

Wafani *W J Musson*
4 b g Mtoto - Wafa (Ire)
11^{10gf} 0-0-1

Wages *P M Phelan* — 66 a76
3 b g Lake Coniston (Ire) - Green Divot
10^{7sd} 11^{6g} 17^{7gs} 16^{7sd} 12^{10gf} 16^{9gf}
0-0-6

Wahchi (Ire) *E A L Dunlop* — 74
4 ch c Nashwan (USA) - Nafhaat (USA)
4^{12gf} 13^{12g} 0-0-2 £721

Wahj (Ire) *C A Dwyer* — 68 a27
8 ch g Indian Ridge - Sabaah (USA)
12^{7g} 14^{7g} 3^{7gf} 7^{7gf} 8^{8sd} 0-1-5 £583

Wahoo Sam (USA) *T D Barron* — 68
3 ch g Sandpit (Brz) - Good Reputation (USA)
UR^{7sd} 9^{6gf} 9^{10gf} 8^{8gf} 8^{7gf} 0-0-5

Wahsheeq *E A L Dunlop* — 98
3 b c Green Desert (USA) - Moss (USA)
7^{6gf} 19^{7gf} 0-0-2

Wainak (USA) *Miss Lucinda V Russell* — 10
5 b g Silver Hawk (USA) - Cask
10^{14gf} 0-0-1

Wainwright (Ire) *P A Blockley* — 77 a68
3 b g Victory Note (USA) - Double Opus (Ire)
2^{6g} 2^{7gf} 4^{8g} 2^{7sw} 5^{6sd} 2^{6sd} 3^{6gs}
0-5-8 £4,806

Wait For The Will (USA) *G L Moore* — 96 a96

7 ch g Seeking The Gold (USA) - You'd Be Surprised (USA)
4^{13sd} 10^{12g} 3^{14gs} 5^{14gf} 1^{12gf} 5^{12gf} 9^{14g}
2^{12gs} 4^{12gf} 2^{12g} 6^{12f} **1-2-11 £19,818**

Wake Up Henry R Charlton 26
2 ch c Nashwan (USA) - River Saint (USA)
18^{8g} **0-0-1**

Waldmark (Ger) Sir Michael Stoute 108
3 ch f Mark Of Esteem (Ire) - Wurftaube (Ger)
2^{10gf} 13^{12g} 2^{8gf} 4^{8g} 9^{10gs} 11^{8gf} **0-2-6**
£30,640

Walker Bay (Ire) J C Fox 51
5 ch m Efisio - Lalandria (Fr)
8^{7ft} 2^{6gf} 4^{6g} **0-1-3 £643**

Wall Street Runner D R C Elsworth 60
2 ch f Kirkwall - Running Tycoon (Ire)
6^{6gf} 8^{6gf} 5^{5gf} **0-0-3 £234**

Walton Manor Boy (Ire) C N Kellett
2 b c Titus Livius (Fr) - Burren Breeze (Ire)
9^{5gf} 10^{5sd} 11^{6gf} **0-0-3**

Waltzing Wizard A Berry 66
4 b g Magic Ring (Ire) - Legendary Dancer
13^{8gf} 15^{7gf} 9^{8g} 6^{6g} 7^{8g} **0-0-5**

Walzerkoenigin (USA) P Schiergen 112
4 b f Kingmambo (USA) - Great Revival (Ire)
1^{8gf} 3^{8gf} 4^{10g} 2^{10f} 5^{10s} **1-2-5**
£187,651

Wanchai Lad A P Jarvis 84
2 b c Danzero (Aus) - Frisson
1^{5gf} 1^{5gf} 6^{6gf} 20^{6gf} **2-0-4 £6,190**

Wanna Shout R Dickin 47
5 b m Missed Flight - Lulu
6^{10gf} 18^{12g} 4^{10f} 9^{13gf} 10^{10gf} 8^{8gf} 4^{10gf}
0-0-7 £639

Wannabe Around D Nicholls 97 a77
5 b g Primo Dominie - Noble Peregrine
14^{7sd} 5^{8g} 15^{7gf} 27^{7f} 10^{7g} 9^{8g} 6^{8gf}
9^{10gf} 9^{9g} **0-0-9 £1,600**

Want (USA) J H M Gosden 62
2 ch c Miswaki (USA) - Substance (USA)
6^{6gf} **0-0-1**

War Owl (USA) Ian Williams 29
6 gr g Linamix (Fr) - Ganasheba (USA)
13^{8gs} **0-0-1**

War Valor (USA) J Nicol 73 a63
4 b g Royal Academy (USA) - Western Music (USA)
11^{8sd} 12^{7g} 4^{6gf} 4^{6gs} 2^{6gf} 9^{6gf} 1^{7ft}
1-2-8 £14,120

Waraqa (USA) J A Osborne 48
4 b f Red Ransom (USA) - Jafn
17^{6g} 16^{7sd} 13^{7f} 6^{6gf} **0-0-4**

Warden Complex J R Fanshawe 69
2 b c Compton Place - Miss Rimex (Ire)
3^{7gf} **0-1-1 £696**

Warden Warren Mrs C A Dunnett 81 a79
5 b g Petong - Silver Spell
1^{7sd} 5^{7sd} 4^{7sd} 6^{6g} 14^{7f} 18^{7gf} 8^{7gf} 1^{7gf}
3^{7f} 8^{7g} 9^{7gf} 1^{7gf} 9^{8gf} 16^{7gf} 10^{7gf} 7^{7gf} 12^{7s}
14^{7g} **3-1-18 £14,156**

Wared (USA) B W Hills
2 gr c El Prado (Ire) - My Shafy
14^{6g} **0-0-1**

Wareed (Ire) D R Loder 112
5 b h Sadler's Wells (USA) - Truly Special
2^{12g} 12^{16ho} **0-1-2 £4,000**

Wares Home (Ire) K R Burke 82

2 b c Indian Rocket - Pepilin
2^{5gs} 3^{5gf} 2^{6gf} 1^{6g} 9^{6gf} 14^{6gs} **1-3-6**
£8,262

Warif (USA) E J O'Neill 52
2 ch c Diesis - Alshoowg (USA)
11^{7gf} 9^{7gf} **0-0-2**

Warlingham (Ire) M Pitman a76
5 b g Catrail (USA) - Tadjnama (USA)
10^{7sd} **0-0-1**

Warm Hill A King 73
2 b c Great Dane (Ire) - Ballet Rambert
4^{6gf} 5^{6g} 3^{6g} 15^{7gf} PU^{6sd} **0-1-5 £1,121**

Warrad (USA) G A Butler 82
2 b c Kingmambo (USA) - Shalimar Garden (Ire)
1^{6gf} **1-0-1 £4,829**

Warren Place N Bycroft 51
3 ch g Presidium - Coney Hills
14^{6g} 9^{6g} 11^{7gf} 10^{6gf} 7^{6f} 12^{6gf} 9^{5gs}
8^{8gf} **0-0-8**

Warrsan (Ire) C E Brittain 124
5 b h Caerleon (USA) - Lucayan Princess
11^{2gf} 1^{12gs} 2^{14gf} 1^{12g} 2^{12f} 6^{12g} 3^{12g} 3^{12g}
3-2-8 £435,664

Waseyla (Ire) Julian Poulton a13
6 b m Sri Pekan (USA) - Lady Windley
9^{11sd} **0-0-1**

Washbrook Andrew Turnell 61
2 b c Royal Applause - Alacrity
11^{5gf} 9^{6g} 8^{5gf} 4^{7gf} 15^{8gs} **0-0-5 £350**

Washington Pink (Ire) C Grant 47
4 b g Tagula (Ire) - Little Red Rose
15^{11g} **0-0-1**

Wasted Talent (Ire) J G Portman 82 a69
3 b f Sesaro (USA) - Miss Garuda
3^{12sd} 2^{12f} 3^{12f} 4^{12gf} 2^{10gf} 6^{10gf} 2^{12gf}
2^{10gf} 4^{10gf} 4^{10gf} 2^{12gf} 6^{12gf} 2^{12f} **0-6-13**
£9,375

Watamu (Ire) P J Makin 77
2 b c Groom Dancer (USA) - Miss Golden Sands
10^{7gf} 1^{7g} **1-0-2 £3,601**

Watching D Nicholls 104 a76
6 ch g Indian Ridge - Sweeping
9^{5sd} 3^{5g} 12^{6gf} 14^{5gf} 6^{7g} 4^{6g} 9^{6gf} 21^{6g}
7^{6gs} 4^{6gs} 19^{7g} **0-2-11 £5,239**

Watchword Mrs C A Dunnett 21 a45
4 ch f Polish Precedent (USA) - Step Aloft
12^{7sd} 13^{8sd} 11^{7sd} 5^{6sw} 9^{7sw} 15^{12sd} 16^{6gf}
0-0-7

Water King (USA) G Brown 27
4 b g Irish River (Fr) - Brookshield Baby (Ire)
9^{9sw} 12^{10g} **0-0-2**

Water Melody (Ire) B R Johnson 38
2 gr f Lake Coniston (Ire) - Cantata (Ire)
18^{6gf} 5^{8gf} 6^{7gf} **0-0-3**

Water Nymph (Ire) B A McMahon 23
3 ch f Be My Guest (USA) - Justitia
8^{7gf} 8^{11hy} **0-0-2**

Water Of Life (Ire) J R Boyle 57 a57
4 b f Dr Devious (Ire) - Simulcast
1^{7sw} 2^{7sd} 11^{7gf} 7^{9g} 11^{7sd} 15^{8f} 12^{8g}
11^{6gf} 8^{8g} 9^{10gf} **1-1-10 £4,323**

Waterfall One R Charlton 19
3 ch f Nashwan (USA) - Spout
9^{12f} **0-0-1**

Waterford Spirit (Ire) G J Smith a8

7 ch g Shalford (Ire) - Rebecca's Girl (Ire)
9⁵ˢᵈ 0-0-1

Waterline Blue (Ire) P D Evans — 84
2 b g Mujadil (USA) - Blues Queen
5⁵ᵍᶠ 8⁶ᵍᶠ 1⁶ᵍᶠ 3⁶ᵍᶠ 2⁷ᵍˢ 6⁷ᵍᶠ 2⁶ᶠ 4⁶ᵍᶠ
6⁶ᵍ 6⁶ᵍᶠ 1-1-10 £10,855

Waterline Dancer (Ire) P D Evans — 57 a60
3 b/br f Danehill Dancer (Ire) - Thrill Seeker (Ire)
4⁸ˢᵈ 9⁸ˢᵈ 10⁷ˢᵈ 17⁶ᵍᶠ 7⁸ᵍᶠ 11⁶ˢᵈ 3⁶ᵍᶠ
7⁶ᵍᶠ 4⁶ᵍ 11⁷ᵍᶠ 13⁷ᵍᶠ 19⁶ᵍᶠ 0-2-12 £849

Waterline Queen P D Evans — 29
3 b f Wizard King - Miss Waterline
11⁸ᵍᶠ 13⁶ᵍˢ 12⁵ᶠ 19⁷ᵍᶠ 0-0-4

Waterline Spirit P D Evans — 30
3 b g Piccolo - Gina Of Hithermoor
14⁸ᵍˢ 9⁸ᵍ 0-0-2

Watermouse R Dickin — 26
3 b g Alhaarth (Ire) - Heavenly Waters
11¹¹ᵍᶠ 0-0-1

Waterpark R Craggs — 54 a46
5 b m Namaqualand (USA) - Willisa
8⁸ˢᵈ 1⁸ˢᵈ 3⁷ᵍˢ 1⁷ᵍᶠ 2-1-4 £10,922

Watership Crystal (Ire) J H M Gosden — 46
2 b f Sadler's Wells (USA) - Crystal Spray
11⁷ᵍˢ 0-0-1

Waterside (Ire) J W Hills — 76 a89
4 ch g Lake Coniston (Ire) - Classic Ring (Ire)
14⁷ᵍᶠ 10⁸ᵍᶠ 9⁷ᵍᶠ 2⁷ˢᵈ 6⁷ˢᵈ 3⁷ᵍˢ 1⁶ᵍᶠ 4⁷ˢᵈ
1-2-8 £5,288

Waterstone M Johnston — 79
2 b c Cape Cross (Ire) - Aquaba (USA)
2⁵ᵍˢ 1⁵ᵍˢ 8⁵ᶠ 1-1-3 £5,870

Wathab (Ire) Kevin Prendergast — 115
2 b c Cadeaux Genereux - Bally Souza (Ire)
2⁵ᵍʸ 2⁵ˢ 1⁶ˢ 3⁶ʸ 7⁶ᵍ 2⁷ᵍᶠ 6⁶ᵍ 4⁷ᵍᶠ 1⁶ᵍᶠ
2⁷ᵍᶠ 2-3-10 £90,551

Waverley (Ire) H Morrison — 105
4 b c Catrail (USA) - Marble Halls (Ire)
7¹⁰ᵍᶠ 5¹⁰ᵍᶠ 11²ᵍᶠ 2¹²ᵍ 1-1-4 £48,000

Waverley Road A P Jarvis — 53 a54
6 ch g Pelder (Ire) - Lillicara (Fr)
9¹³ˢᵈ 7¹²ˢᵈ 9¹⁴ᵍᶠ 6¹²ᵍ 10¹¹ᵍᶠ 5¹⁶ᵍᶠ 0-0-6

Wavertree Boy (Ire) D R C Elsworth — 108
3 ch g Hector Protector (USA) - Lust
5¹⁰ᵍᶠ 11¹²ᵍᶠ 1¹¹ᵍ 1¹⁴ᵍᶠ 10¹⁶ᶠ 3¹⁵ᵍᶠ 8¹²ᵍ
3¹⁴ᵍᶠ 9¹⁵ᵍ 4¹⁶ᶠ 2-2-10 £23,605

Wavertree Dream N P Littmoden — 88
2 b g Dushyantor (USA) - Dream On Deya (Ire)
7⁵ᵍᶠ 2⁵ᵍᶠ 8⁵ᵍᶠ 2⁷ᵍᶠ 1⁷ᵍ 6⁶ᵍᶠ 2⁸ᵍᶠ 7⁸ᵍ
1-3-8 £11,448

Wavertree Girl (Ire) N P Littmoden — 89
2 b f Marju (Ire) - Lust
3⁶ᵍᶠ 4⁶ᵍ 7⁶ᵍᶠ 4⁶ᵍᶠ 0-1-4 £4,433

Wavertree Spirit N P Littmoden — 59
2 ch c Hector Protector (USA) - Miss Clarinet
6⁷ᵍᶠ 0-0-1

Wavet Mrs Lydia Pearce — 56
3 b f Pursuit Of Love - Ballerina Bay
6¹²ᵍˢ 0-0-1

Waxwing A W Carroll — 51 a69
4 b f Efisio - Mountain Bluebird (USA)
9⁷ˢʷ 3⁶ˢʷ 2⁷ˢʷ 2⁷ˢᵈ 4⁵ˢᵈ 8⁷ᵍᶠ 11⁶ᵍ 12⁷ᵍ
3⁷ˢᵈ 1⁷ˢᵈ 12⁶ˢᵈ 11⁷ᶠ 8⁸ᵍᶠ 7⁶ᵍᶠ 4⁷ˢʷ 6⁶ˢᵈ 6⁸ˢᵈ
1-4-17 £6,283

Wayward Melody S Dow — 43 a32
3 b f Merdon Melody - Dubitable
10¹⁰ˢᵈ 7¹⁴ᵍᶠ 12¹⁴ᵍᶠ 8¹⁰ᶠ 0-0-4

Waziri (Ire) H Morrison — a74
2 b c Mtoto - Euphorie (Ger)
4⁸ˢᵈ 6⁸ˢᵈ 0-0-2

We'Ll Make It (Ire) G L Moore — 66
5 b g Spectrum (Ire) - Walliser
5¹⁴ᵍᶠ 3¹⁴ᵍᶠ 10¹⁴ᵍᶠ 0-1-3 £855

We're Not Joken P A Blockley
6 b m Foxhound (USA) - We're Joken
13⁷ˢᵈ 10⁵ˢʷ 0-0-2

We'll Meet Again M W Easterby — 61
3 ch g Bin Ajwaad (Ire) - Tantalizing Song (Can)
14¹²ˢᵈ 3⁸ᵍᶠ 1⁷ᶠ 7⁷ᵍ 6⁸ᵍˢ 5⁸ᵍˢ 1-1-6
£4,208

Weakest Link Miss S E Hall — 39
2 b g Mind Games - Sky Music
10⁶ᵍ 0-0-1

Weaver Of Dreams (Ire) G A Swinbank — 50
3 b g Victory Note (USA) - Daziyra (Ire)
11¹⁰ᵍᶠ 9⁹ᵍˢ 5¹⁰ᵍˢ 5⁹ᶠ 7¹⁴ᶠ 0-0-5

Weaver Spell J R Norton — 31 a2
2 b g Wizard King - Impy Fox (Ire)
9⁶ᵍˢ 8⁶ᵍᶠ 7⁷ˢᵈ 6⁶ᵍˢ 0-0-4

Weavers Pride (Fr) B W Hills — 104
3 ch c Barathea (Ire) - Creese (USA)
1⁷ᵍ 7¹⁰ᵍᶠ 3⁸ᵍ 10⁸ʰʸ 26⁸ᵍᶠ 5⁸ᵍᶠ 1-1-6
£8,683

Web Perceptions (USA) M F Harris — 92
3 ch c Distant View (USA) - Squaw Time (USA)
10⁸ᵍᶠ 15⁹ᵍᶠ 2¹⁰ᶠ 10¹²ᵍᶠ 3¹⁰ᵍᶠ 11¹¹ᵍᶠ 6¹⁴ᵍ
1¹²ᵍᶠ 9¹⁴ᵍᶠ 11⁰ˢ 11²ᵍᶠ 4-1-11 £41,763

Webbington Lass (Ire) Dr J R J Naylor — 46
2 b f Petardia - Richardstown Lass (Ire)
11⁶ᵍᶠ 7⁶ᶠ 11⁷ᵍᶠ 16⁶ᵍᶠ 0-0-4

Wedding J G Given — 62
3 ch f Groom Dancer (USA) - Champagne 'n Roses
5⁸ᵍᶠ 6¹⁰ᵍᶠ 6⁷ᵍᶠ 7⁸ᵍᶠ 0-0-4

Wedgewood Star R Hannon — 62
3 b f Bishop Of Cashel - Away To Me
16⁷ᵍ 8⁷ᵍ 13⁶ᵍ 0-0-3

Wee Dinns (Ire) S Kirk — 64
2 b f Marju (Ire) - Tir-An-Oir (Ire)
13⁷ᵍᶠ 10⁷ˢ 9⁸ᵍᶠ 0-0-3

Weecandoo (Ire) C N Allen — 95 a71
5 b m Turtle Island (Ire) - Romantic Air
1¹⁰ˢᵈ 3¹⁰ˢᵈ 3¹⁰ˢᵈ 4¹⁰ˢᵈ 2¹⁰ˢᵈ 9⁸ᵍˢ 1¹⁰ᵍᶠ
3¹⁰ᵍ 3¹⁰ᵍᶠ 1¹⁰ᵍᶠ 5¹⁰ᵍᶠ 4¹⁰ᵍᶠ 3-5-12 £33,897

Weet A Head (Ire) R Hollinshead — 88
2 b c Foxhound (USA) - Morale
1⁶ᵍᶠ 4⁶ᵍᶠ 3⁶ˢ 2⁸ᵍᶠ 6⁸ᵍᶠ 1-2-5 £6,869

Weet A Mo (Ire) R Hollinshead — 65
3 b g Sri Pekan (USA) - Ozwood (Ire)
3⁸ᵍ 3⁸ᵍᶠ 6⁸ᵍᶠ 2⁷ᵍˢ 11⁹ˢʷ 10⁸ᵍᶠ 8⁷ᵍᶠ 8⁸ᵍᶠ
4⁸ᵍᶠ 5⁷ᵍᶠ 3⁷ᵍᶠ F⁷ᵍᶠ 0-4-12 £3,133

Weet A Round P A Blockley — 74 a40
4 ch g Whittingham (Ire) - Hollia
5⁶ᵍ 9⁷ᶠ 14⁷ᵍᶠ 1⁶ᵍˢ 13⁶ᵍ 4⁶ᵍˢ 9⁷ˢᵈ 13⁶ˢʷ
1-0-8 £4,126

Weet An Haul J D Bethell — 30 a38
2 b g Danzero (Aus) - Island Ruler
12⁵ᵍˢ 6⁶ˢᵈ 11⁶ˢ 11⁸ᵍ 9⁷ˢᵈ 0-0-5

Weet An Store (Ire) R Hollinshead
2 gr c Spectrum (Ire) - Karnisymixa (Fr)

12^{sd} 0-0-1

Weet Watchers R Hollinshead   74 a72
3 b g Polar Prince (Ire) - Weet Ees Girl (Ire)
1^{7sd} 13^{8g} 3^{6hy} 8^{6gf} PU^{8sd} 1-1-5 £4,299

Weetman's Weigh (Ire) R Hollinshead   41 a58
10 b h Archway (Ire) - Indian Sand
1^{8sw} 6^{8sd} 2^{7sd} 4^{7sw} 14^{8sd} 10^{8gf} 11^{7g}
1-1-7 £3,785

Welcome Back K A Ryan   a40
6 ch g Most Welcome - Villavina
2^{12sd} 0-1-1 £848

Welcome On Line F Jordan
4 ch g Most Welcome - Pegs
9^{13gf} 0-0-1

Welcome Signal J R Fanshawe   71 a66
3 ch g Most Welcome - Glenfinlass
3^{8sd} 3^{7gf} 7^{8sd} 3^{10gf} 5^{10gf} 0-3-5 £1,589

Welcome Stranger J M P Eustace   84 a74
3 b g Most Welcome - Just Julia
1^{8sd} 8^{10sd} 1^{8gf} 1^{8gf} 7^{8gf} 3^{8gf} 4^{8f} 3-1-7
£15,490

Welcome Sun (Ire) J S Moore   24
2 ch g Desert Sun - Ever Welcome
8^{7gf} 11^{8gf} 0-0-2

Welcome To Unos M C Pipe   53
6 ch g Exit To Nowhere (USA) - Royal Loft
7^{14gf} 0-0-1

Well Chosen E A L Dunlop   89
4 b c Sadler's Wells (USA) - Hawajiss
2^{14hy} 4^{17gf} 3^{12gf} 0-2-3 £2,999

Well Connected (Ire) B Smart   56
3 b g Among Men (USA) - Wire To Wire
3^{8gf} 8^{9gf} 9^{8gs} 6^{7f} 11^{8gf} 3^{8gs} 13^{10gf}
0-2-7 £1,065

Well Known R Charlton   81
2 b f Sadler's Wells (USA) - Danefair
2^{7gf} 0-1-1 £1,834

Well Red (Ire) C G Cox   a56
3 ch c Prince Of Birds (USA) - Fairy Domino
7^{5sd} 7^{5sd} 11^{5sw} 0-0-3

Wellington Hall (Ger) A Charlton   57 a84
5 b g Halling (USA) - Wells Whisper (Fr)
11^{12sd} 14^{13sd} 17^{14gs} 26^{20gf} 5^{14g} 7^{12g}
0-0-6

Welsh And Wylde (Ire) B Palling   57 a57
3 b g Anita's Prince - Waikiki (Ger)
5^{7sd} 2^{8sd} 7^{7gf} 6^{8g} 13^{8sd} 7^{10gf} 0-1-6
£826

Welsh Diva Mrs A J Perrett   108
4 b f Selkirk (USA) - Khubza
9^{8g} 9^{9gs} 2^{8gf} 7^{8gf} 9^{8gf} 0-1-5 £7,700

Welsh Emperor (Ire) T P Tate   105 a89
4 b g Emperor Jones (USA) - Simply Times (USA)
8^{7sd} 3^{7s} 4^{5hy} 2^{6s} 4^{6gs} 2^{6ho} 0-2-6
£27,808

Welsh Empress P L Gilligan   47
2 b f Bahamian Bounty - Azola (Ire)
7^{6gf} 6^{7g} 9^{7gs} 6^{8gf} 6^{6gf} 22^{6gf} 3^{8gf} 0-1-7
£292

Welsh Holly (Ire) Miss Gay Kelleway   46
4 br f Idris (Ire) - Jane Avril (Ire)
8^{6gs} 12^{6gs} 19^{6gf} 0-0-3

Welsh Whisper S A Brookshaw
4 b f Overbury (Ire) - Grugiar
12^{9sd} 0-0-1

Welsh Wind (Ire) M Wigham   75 a70
7 b g Tenby - Bavaria
6^{7sd} 5^{8sd} 2^{8g} 7^{8gf} 2^{8gf} 3^{8gf} 4^{8g} 10^{8gf}
7^{8s} 3^{8g} 7^{8g} 0-3-11 £5,059

Wend's Day (Ire) A M Hales   a42
8 br g Brief Truce (USA) - Iswara (USA)
7^{11sd} 0-0-1

Wendy's Girl (Ire) R P Elliott   63 a55
2 b f Ashkalani (Ire) - Mrs Evans (Ire)
3^{5sd} 3^{5gf} 3^{5gf} 5^{6gf} 5^{5sd} 7^{6gs} 4^{5gf} 6^{5gf}
5^{7g} 3^{5gf} 3^{6gf} 12^{6gs} 0-5-12 £3,170

Wendylynne J G Given   15
3 b f Weldnaas (USA) - Dusty's Darling
13^{8gf} 9^{10gf} 0-0-2

Wensley Blue (Ire) P C Haslam   a46
4 b g Blues Traveller (Ire) - Almasa
3^{11sd} 5^{12sd} 16^{16sd} 0-1-3 £425

Wensleydale Lad (USA) T D Barron   1 a63
3 ch g Is It True (USA) - Miss Tarheel (USA)
5^{6sd} 4^{6sd} 4^{6sd} 3^{8sw} 1^{7sd} 4^{7sd} 18^{8g} 4^{8sd}
1-1-8 £3,738

Wentbridge Boy J O'Reilly
3 gr g Keen - Wentbridge Girl
18^{8gf} 12^{10gs} 0-0-2

Weqaar (USA) J L Dunlop   83
3 b f Red Ransom (USA) - Thawakib (Ire)
1^{10f} 2^{10gf} 7^{12g} 7^{10gf} 8^{11s} 5^{10gf} 1-1-6
£5,876

Wessex (USA) M Johnston   89
3 ch c Gone West (USA) - Satin Velvet (USA)
8^{10gs} 1^{8gf} 8^{8gf} 1-0-3 £7,085

West Country (UAE) M Johnston   81
2 br c Gone West (USA) - Crystal Gazing (USA)
2^{7f} 3^{7f} 2^{7gf} 0-2-3 £3,782

West Highland Way (Ire) I Semple   80
2 b g Foxhound (USA) - Gilding The Lily (Ire)
9^{6gs} 4^{7gf} 8^{7gf} 2^{6g} 2^{6g} 5^{6gs} 7^{6gf} 2^{7g}
0-3-8 £4,691

West Hill Dancer Mrs P N Dutfield   30
3 b f Man Among Men (Ire) - My Poppet
11^{5gf} 11^{7gf} 0-0-2

Westborough (Ire) N Tinkler   57
2 ch g Woodborough (USA) - Filey Brigg
7^{5gs} 9^{5gf} 7^{5gf} 4^{5gf} 9^{6gf} 2^{5f} 13^{5g} 5^{5g}
0-1-8 £1,210

Westbound Road (USA) D R Loder   58 a94
6 b g Gone West (USA) - Jood (USA)
6^{8sw} 2^{12sd} 13^{13sd} 10^{12gf} 0-1-4 £3,048

Westcourt Dream M W Easterby   49
3 ch f Bal Harbour - Katie's Kitty
11^{8gf} 3^{7f} 3^{7f} 3^{7gs} 0-2-4 £1,708

Westerly Air (USA) Sir Michael Stoute   53 a75
3 b f Gone West (USA) - Midnight Air (USA)
12^{10g} 3^{10sd} 1^{9sw} 10^{10gf} 1-1-4 £4,279

Western (Ire) J Akehurst   78 a76
3 ch g Gone West (USA) - Madame Est Sortie (Fr)
4^{10gf} 7^{12gf} 10^{10gf} 16^{10g} 5^{12gf} 6^{12f} 4^{12sd}
0-1-7 £329

Western Applause Jedd O'Keeffe   37
4 b f Royal Applause - Western Sal
UR^{7gf} 15^{7gf} 13^{9gf} 0-0-3

Western Belle Mrs Lucinda Featherstone
4 b f Magic Ring (Ire) - Western Horizon (USA)
11^{6sd} 0-0-1

Western Command (Ger) Mrs N Macauley   a37

7 b g Saddlers' Hall (Ire) - Western Friend (USA)
10¹¹sd 7⁹sd 5⁹sd 9¹¹sd 7⁹sd 6¹²sw 8⁹sd
7¹²sd 5¹⁴sd 5¹⁶sd 5¹⁵sd 10¹⁴sw **0-0-12**

Western Ridge (Fr) *B J Llewellyn*   51 a45
6 b g Darshaan - Helvellyn (USA)
9¹²sd 8¹²gf **0-0-2**

Western Roots *P F I Cole*   a74
2 ch g Dr Fong (USA) - Chrysalis
1⁵sd **1-0-1 £15,196**

Westerner *E Lellouche*   122
4 b c Danehill (USA) - Walensee
11⁸gs 1¹²s 5¹²g 2¹⁴gs 2¹⁵gs 2¹⁶gs 1²⁰ho
1¹⁶ho **3-3-8 £181,048**

Westfield Star (Ire) *Thomas Cooper*   93
6 b g Fourstars Allstar (USA) - Mokaite
19⁸ys 3¹⁰g 5⁷g 10¹⁰g 11⁸g 6⁷y 10⁸g 2⁷gf
6⁷y 1⁷gf 4⁷gf 8⁸s 7⁶f 11¹²gf 14⁸g **1-3-15**
£14,142

Westgate Run *R A Fahey*   50 a42
6 b m Emperor Jones (USA) - Glowing Reference
8¹²sd 6¹⁰g 7¹⁰g 10¹²gf **0-0-4**

Westmead Etoile *J R Jenkins*   51
3 b f Unfuwain (USA) - Glossary
6⁸gf 4¹⁰gf 8¹¹f 12¹⁰g 13⁸gf 3⁸g 8⁷gf 8⁷gf
0-1-8 £881

Westmead Tango *J R Jenkins*   54 a52
3 b f Pursuit Of Love - Tango Teaser
9⁵sd 1⁵sd 2⁶gf **1-1-3 £4,062**

Westmoreland Road (USA) *Mrs A J Perrett*   118
3 b c Diesis - Tia Gigi (USA)
1¹¹gf 1¹²g 3¹¹g 1¹²gf 10¹⁵g **3-0-5**
£32,771

Westwood Lady (Ire) *J S Moore*   29 a31
2 b f Fayruz - Payne's Grey
6⁵g 7⁵sd 5⁵f 5⁵gf 5⁵sd **0-0-5**

Wethaab (USA) *Miss A Stokell*   20 a43
6 b g Pleasant Colony (USA) - Binntastic (USA)
10¹²sd 3¹⁴sd 4¹²sd 9¹²sd 10¹⁴gf 10¹⁴gf
0-1-6 £450

Whaleef *P R Webber*   82
5 br g Darshaan - Wilayif (USA)
10¹⁰gf 5¹⁰gf 1⁸gf 2⁹gf **1-0-4 £5,029**

What-A-Dancer (Ire) *G A Swinbank*   86 a86
6 b g Dancing Dissident (USA) - Cool Gales
10⁷g 15⁷g 6⁷f 2⁷gf 3⁷gs 15⁸g 3⁷gf 2⁷gf
1⁷gf 5⁷sd 4⁷g **1-4-11 £13,198**

Where Or When (Ire) *T G Mills*   118
4 ch c Danehill Dancer (Ire) - Future Past (USA)
2⁸g 4⁸gf 4⁸gf 6⁸gs 6⁸gf **0-1-5 £66,375**

Which Witch (Ire) *P Monteith*
5 b m Alzao (USA) - First Fastnet
16⁹gs 9⁵gf 9⁵gf **0-0-3**

Whinhill House *D W Barker*   55 a61
3 ch g Paris House - Darussalam
13⁶sd 3⁵sd 1⁵sd 9⁵gs 6⁵g 3⁵gs 17⁵f **1-1-7**
£4,663

Whiplash (Ire) *R Hannon*   66
2 b c Orpen (USA) - La Colombari (Ity)
9⁵gf 2⁵gf 10⁷gf 13⁸gf 12⁸gf **0-1-5**
£1,339

Whippasnapper *J R Best*   67 a82
3 b g Cayman Kai (Ire) - Give Us A Treat
1⁷sd 3⁶sd 7⁶sd 14⁶gf 13⁸gf 7⁷gf 7⁶gf 6⁷gs
8⁷gf 9⁶gf **1-1-10 £4,880**

Whipper (USA) *Robert Collet*   115

---

2 b c Miesque's Son (USA) - Myth To Reality (Fr)
5⁵s 3⁵g 4⁶gs 1⁶s 1⁶s 5⁶gf 1⁶ho **3-1-7**
£184,324

Whisper To Me (Ire) *M R Channon*   16
3 b f Brief Truce (USA) - Watch Me (Ire)
8⁶gf **0-0-1**

Whispered Promises (USA) *M Johnston*   77
2 b c Real Quiet (USA) - Anna's Honor (USA)
4⁶gs 2⁷f 1⁷gf 1⁷gf **2-1-4 £10,762**

Whispering Valley *Mrs A J Perrett*   44
3 ch f The West - Taciturn (USA)
10¹⁰gf **0-0-1**

Whist Drive *Mrs N Smith*   65
3 ch g First Trump - Fine Quill
5¹⁰g 12¹⁴gf 7¹⁴gf **0-0-3**

Whistful (Ire) *C F Wall*   62
2 b f First Trump - Atmospheric Blues (Ire)
10⁶gf 5⁷gf 4⁷g 2⁶gf **0-1-4 £1,084**

Whistler *J M Bradley*   88
6 ch g Selkirk (USA) - French Gift
14⁵g 6⁵g 1⁵gs 2⁵hy 5⁵gf 4⁵gs 1⁵f 3⁵gf
8⁶f 2⁵gf 6⁵gs 2⁵gf 1⁵gf 4⁵gf 5⁵gf 10⁵gs 11⁵gf
3-4-17 £36,851

Whistling Dixie (Ire) *Mrs M Reveley*   66
7 ch g Forest Wind (USA) - Camden's Gift
5¹⁶gf **0-0-1**

Whitbarrow (Ire) *B R Millman*   93 a71
4 b g Royal Abjar (USA) - Danccini (USA)
10⁵sd 5⁷gf 6⁵f **0-0-3 £539**

White Emir *L G Cottrell*   63 a60
10 b g Emarati (USA) - White African
12¹⁰f 5⁸g 12⁷g 12⁸gf 2¹⁰sd 5¹⁰sd 4⁸sd
3¹⁰sd 15⁸gf 5⁸sd **0-2-10 £1,146**

White Hawk *D R Loder*   78 a100
2 b c Silver Hawk (USA) - Polska (USA)
1⁷gf 2⁷gf 1⁷sd 4⁷sd **2-0-4 £10,611**

White Ledger (Ire) *I A Wood*   51 a29
4 ch g Ali-Royal (Ire) - Boranwood (Ire)
12⁵f 15⁶gs 15⁵gf 10⁶gf 10⁷sd **0-0-5**

White Park Bay (Ire) *J Gallagher*   58 a72
3 b f Blues Traveller (Ire) - Valiant Friend (USA)
10¹⁰gf 4⁷g 3⁷gf 3⁸sd 2⁸sd 4⁸s 9⁸gf 3⁸sd
0-5-8 £3,007

White Plains (Ire) *A G Newcombe*   38 a61
10 b g Nordico (USA) - Flying Diva
2¹⁶sd 3¹¹sd 4¹⁵sd 3¹²sw 1¹²sw 4¹²sw 1¹⁴sd
10¹³sd 1¹²sd 6¹⁵sd 4¹²gf 2¹²sd 9¹²f 8¹⁴sw **3-4-14**
£11,815

White Rose (Ger) *M A Jarvis*   106
3 b f Platini (Ger) - Wild Romance (Ger)
2⁸g 2¹¹s 8¹¹g 5¹¹s 6¹⁰g **0-2-5 £76,610**

White Star Prince *J R Weymes*   33
2 b g Whittingham (Ire) - Logarithm
14⁷f 9⁷f 5⁶gf 7⁶gf 6⁷f **0-0-5**

Whitgift Rock *S Dow*   66
2 b c Piccolo - Fly South
5⁶gf 9⁵gf 4⁶gf 10⁶g 5⁶gf 6⁶gf 3⁷g **0-1-7**
£926

Whitkirk Star (Ire) *S P Griffiths*
2 b g Alhaarth (Ire) - Three Stars
15⁷g **0-0-1**

Whitsbury Cross *D R C Elsworth*   53
2 b c Cape Cross (Ire) - Vallauris
10⁷sd **0-0-1**

Whittinghamvillage *A Berry*   56 a38

2 b f Whittingham (Ire) - Shaa Spin
9^{6s} 4^{5gf} 3^{6gf} 6^{5sd} 5^{5gs} 3^{6gf} 3^{6s} 3^{5gf} 6^{6g}
4^{5f} 4^{5gf} 6^{6f} 7^{5g} **0-4-13 £2,737**

Whittle Warrior C W Fairhurst — 59
3 b g Averti (Ire) - Polish Descent (Ire)
10^{8gf} 8^{7g} 13^{8s} **0-0-3**

Whizz Kid J M Bradley — a39
9 b m Puissance - Panienka (Pol)
13^{6sd} 5^{5sd} 8^{5sw} **0-0-3**

Who Cares Wins J R Jenkins — a19
7 ch g Kris - Anne Bonny
12^{16sd} 13^{16sd} **0-0-2**

Who's Winning (Ire) C A Dwyer — 75
2 ch g Docksider (USA) - Quintellina
1^{5gf} 5^{5g} 6^{6gs} 4^{6gf} 7^{6g} 4^{5gf} 3^{6gf} 6^{6f}
1-1-8 £7,720

Whole Grain Sir Michael Stoute — 38
2 b f Polish Precedent (USA) - Mill Line
10^{7gf} **0-0-1**

Why Dubai (USA) R Hannon — 91
2 br f Kris S (USA) - Highest Goal (USA)
8^{6gf} 1^{7gf} 7^{6gf} 2^{7gf} **1-1-4 £12,336**

Wicked Uncle S Gollings — 87
4 b g Distant Relative - The Kings Daughter
17^{6g} 10^{5gf} 7^{5g} 8^{5g} 2^{5g} 3^{5gf} 2^{5gf} 13^{5g}
0-3-8 £3,252

Wiggy Smith H Candy — 86
4 ch g Master Willie - Monsoon
4^{12g} 1^{11gf} **1-0-2 £6,081**

Wigmo Princess A W Carroll — 48 a49
4 ch f Factual (USA) - Queen Of Shannon (Ire)
3^{7sw} 4^{8sd} 9^{8gf} 4^{10gf} 11^{7gf} 12^{7sd} 9^{10sd}
9^{10gf} 10^{8gf} **0-1-9 £467**

Wild Ovation R Hannon — 64
3 b c Royal Applause - Daring Ditty
5^{7gf} 11^{6gf} 12^{6f} **0-0-3**

Wild Pitch P Mitchell — 43
2 ch c Piccolo - Western Horizon (USA)
6^{6gf} **0-0-1 £187**

Wilderbrook Lahri B Smart — 58
4 b g Lahib (USA) - Wilsonic
4^{9gf} 2^{8f} 14^{8gf} 8^{9gf} 8^{8gf} 5^{8g} **0-2-6**
£1,083

Wilfram J M Bradley — a22
6 b g Fraam - Ming Blue
8^{8sd} 10^{8sd} **0-0-2**

Wilfred (Ire) Jonjo O'Neill — 67
2 b g Desert King (Ire) - Kharaliya (Fr)
9^{6gf} 6^{7gf} 3^{8gf} 15^{8gf} **0-1-4 £449**

Wilful Saeed Bin Suroor — 105
3 ch c Bering - Prickwillow (USA)
2^{10gs} 2^{10g} **0-1-2 £10,468**

Wilheheckaslike W Storey — 46
2 b g Wizard King - La Ciotat (Ire)
12^{6s} 9^{5gf} 8^{5gf} 2^{5gf} 8^{5gf} 17^{5gf} **0-1-6**
£818

Wilkie Miss L C Siddall
4 br g Mistertopogigo (Ire) - Titian Girl
14^{6sw} **0-0-1**

Will He Wish S Gollings — 101
7 b g Winning Gallery - More To Life
13^{8g} 7^{7gf} 1^{6f} 1^{6gf} 7^{7gf} 5^{7gf} 3^{6gs}
4^{7gf} 5^{6gf} 1^{7g} 2^{7g} 6^{7gf} 1^{7f} **5-2-14 £30,076**

Willheconquertoo Andrew Reid — 83 a83
3 ch g Primo Dominie - Sure Care

7^{6gf} 5^{6gf} 8^{5gf} 1^{7gf} 16^{7gs} 13^{8gf} 6^{7g} 2^{7g}
2^{7g} 8^{7gf} 9^{7g} 5^{7sd} 6^{7g} 5^{7gf} 14^{7sd} 10^{8sd}
1-1-16 £11,641

Willhefly C A Dwyer — 18 a51
2 b g Most Welcome - Leave It To Lib
7^{5g} 13^{6gs} 8^{6gf} 2^{6sd} 4^{5sd} **0-1-5 £832**

Willhego J R Best — 45
2 ch g Pivotal - Woodrising
11^{6gf} 13^{7gs} 8^{6gs} **0-0-3**

Willhewiz C A Dwyer — 97
3 b c Wizard King - Leave It To Lib
6^{6gf} 9^{5f} 2^{6gs} 4^{6gf} 19^{5gf} 5^{6g} 1^{6f} 13^{5gf}
1^{6gf} **2-2-9 £15,126**

William's Well M W Easterby — 70
9 ch g Superpower - Catherines Well
3^{7f} 1^{7gf} 5^{7gf} 8^{7f} 10^{7gf} 6^{7gf} 3^{6gs} 4^{7gf}
1^{6gf} 2^{6gf} 8^{7gf} 2^{6gs} 13^{6g} **2-4-13 £10,246**

Willjojo R A Fahey — 54 a49
2 b f Mind Games - Millie's Lady (Ire)
3^{6sd} 2^{6f} 3^{5gs} 5^{6gf} 10^{6s} 3^{6gf} **0-3-6**
£2,723

Willofcourse H Candy — 72
2 b g Aragon - Willyet
6^{6gf} 2^{6gf} **0-1-2 £1,247**

Willoughby's Boy (Ire) B Hanbury — 75 a72
6 b g Night Shift (USA) - Andbell
4^{10sd} 10^{10sd} 7^{10sd} 10^{10gs} 4^{10gf} 1^{10gf} 7^{10sd}
7^{8sd} 6^{11gf} 10^{7g} 2^{10f} 7^{10gf} 17^{10gf} 9^{10gf} **1-1-14**
£5,956

Wilom (Ger) M R Hoad — 43 a47
5 ch g Lomitas - Whispering Willows
12^{10sd} 9^{10sd} 11^{9g} 17^{7gs} 5^{10f} 3^{10gf} 4^{10sd}
8^{10t} **0-1-8 £461**

Wilson Bluebottle (Ire) M W Easterby — 53
4 ch g Priolo (USA) - Mauras Pride (Ire)
13^{7gf} 18^{9f} 4^{9gf} 8^{8gf} 9^{8gf} 10^{11gf} **1-0-6**
£3,483

Wimple (USA) C E Brittain — 93 a97
3 b f Kingmambo (USA) - Tunicle (USA)
2^{8sd} 10^{7gf} 17^{8gf} 8^{7gf} 10^{6gf} 5^{7gf} 8^{6gf}
11^{7g} 2^{7f} 8^{6gf} 6^{7gf} 9^{6g} 4^{7sd} **0-2-13 £10,509**

Win Alot M C Chapman — 50 a54
5 b g Aragon - Having Fun
9^{12sw} 4^{14sd} 3^{12sd} 8^{12sd} 7^{12sd} 4^{9sd} 4^{12sd}
1^{10gs} 7^{12gf} 10^{10gf} **1-1-10 £4,844**

Wind Chime (Ire) A G Newcombe — 76 a58
6 ch h Arazi (USA) - Shamisen
2^{8sd} 7^{10sd} 4^{10sd} 5^{8g} 1^{9gf} 18^{9f} 4^{8f} 8^{10f}
11^{7gf} 10^{8f} **2-1-10 £12,513**

Windermere (Ire) J H M Gosden — 113
4 b c Lear Fan (USA) - Madame L'Enjoleur (USA)
1^{12gf} 5^{13g} 2^{15g} **1-1-3 £18,073**

Windshift (Ire) S R Bowring — 53 a63
7 b g Forest Wind (USA) - Beautyofthepeace (Ire)
8^{8sd} 8^{11sd} 3^{8sd} 10^{8sd} 5^{11sd} 3^{12sw} 1^{9sd}
3^{12sd} 2^{12sd} 1^{15sd} 8^{14gf} 5^{16gs} 8^{16gs} **2-4-13**
£8,115

Windy Breeze (Ire) M R Channon — a50
3 b f Mujadil (USA) - Bosa
8^{5sd} 12^{6sd} **0-0-2**

Windy Britain L M Cumani — 89 a67
4 b f Mark Of Esteem (Ire) - For My Love
2^{10sd} 10^{10gf} 1^{12gf} 1^{10g} 3^{11gs} 3^{10gf} 1^{10f}
3^{10gf} 1^{10gf} **5-2-9 £21,662**

Wing Collar T D Easterby — 57
2 b c In The Wings - Riyoom (USA)

4^{7gs} 4^{7gf} 4^{8gf} 13^{8gf} 0-0-4 £1,121

Wing Commander M L W Bell ... 98
4 b g Royal Applause - Southern Psychic (USA)
5^{8gf} 4^{8gf} 15^{8gf} 2^{10g} 3^{12g} 3^{10gf} 0-2-6
£7,404

Wing West J Gallagher ... 31
3 ch g The West (USA) - Ballet On Ice (Fr)
14^{7gf} 6^{8g} 0-0-2

Wings Of Love J R Fanshawe ... 62
3 b f Groom Dancer (USA) - Dance To The Top
8^{10g} 4^{9gf} 0-0-2 £297

Wings To Soar (USA) R Hannon ... 71
3 b f Woodman (USA) - Only Royale (Ire)
7^{8gf} 7^{10gf} 4^{10gf} 0-0-3 £284

Winners Delight A P Jarvis ... 77
2 ch c First Trump - Real Popcorn (Ire)
6^{6gf} 1^{7gf} 6^{7gf} 5^{7g} 1-0-4 £3,662

Winning Note (Ire) J L Dunlop ... 66
3 b f Victory Note (USA) - Ruby Affair (Ire)
2^{7gf} 12^{7gf} 0-1-2 £918

Winning Pleasure (Ire) J Balding ... 67 a91
5 b g Ashkalani (Ire) - Karamana
8^{5sd} 6^{6sd} 16^{6g} 10^{6g} 8^{6gf} 19^{6gf} 0-0-6
£197

Winning Venture D Nicholls ... 97
6 b g Owington - Push A Button
4^{8gs} 4^{7gf} 29^{8gf} 4^{8gf} 4^{8g} 6^{7gf} 3^{7gf} 13^{6g}
5^{7g} 0-2-9 £10,202

Winslow Boy (USA) C F Wall ... 46
2 b/br c Expelled (USA) - Acusteal (USA)
12^{6gf} 8^{8s} 0-0-2

Winthorpe (Ire) J J Quinn ... 88 a68
3 b g Tagula (Ire) - Zazu
3^{6sd} 11^{6sd} 4^{6f} 18^{6g} 2^{6gs} 5^{6gf} 2^{6gf} 2^{6gf}
1^{5gf} 1^{5gf} 1^{5g} 12^{5gf} 10^{5s} 3-4-13 £19,670

Wisdom Penang (Ire) G A Butler
3 b f Hamas (Ire) - Firey Encounter (Ire)
RR^{6g} 12^{5gf} 0-0-2

Wise Petorius (Ire) Mrs N Macauley ... 47
3 b g Petorius - Wise Wish
9^{5sd} 12^{7gf} 13^{8gf} 7^{8gs} 16^{10g} 0-0-5

Wise Tale P D Niven ... 71
4 b g Nashwan (USA) - Wilayif (USA)
2^{14gf} 7^{18gf} 5^{16gf} 4^{14gf} 0-1-4 £2,503

Wiseguy (Ire) M P Tregoning ... 86
4 b g Darshaan - Bibliotheque (USA)
8^{12g} 5^{9g} 2^{9gf} 3^{10g} 10^{9gf} 0-2-5 £4,459

With Distinction J L Dunlop ... 63
3 br f Zafonic (USA) - Air Of Distinction (Ire)
9^{7gf} 14^{8g} 10^{10gf} 5^{11gf} 3^{12gf} 5^{12f} 6^{10gf}
0-0-7 £443

With Reason (USA) D R Loder ... 118 a95
5 ch g Nashwan (USA) - Just Cause
1^{9sw} 5^{10sd} 2^{8g} 7^{9gf} 2^{8g} 2^{8gf} 1^{7gf} 6^{7g}
1^{7gf} 2^{7g} 1^{7gf} 4-4-11 £110,904

Withorwithoutyou (Ire) B A McMahon ... 89
2 b f Danehill (USA) - Morningsurprice (USA)
2^{5gf} 2^{5f} 9^{7gf} 1^{7gf} 7^{7gf} 5^{7gf} 4^{6g} 1-2-7
£9,471

Without Words W M Brisbourne ... 41 a50
5 ch m Lion Cavern (USA) - Sans Escale (USA)
2^{9sd} 6^{8sd} 10^{9gf} 10^{9gf} 0-1-4 £840

Witness B W Hills ... a66
4 b f Efisio - Actualite
4^{7sd} 4^{6sd} 1^{7sd} 1-0-3 £3,224

Witticism N Clement ... 76 a68
3 b f Barathea (Ire) - Applecross
14^{10gf} 3^{12g} 2^{12sd} 3^{11g} 7^{12sd} 0-2-5
£2,133

Wittily A Berry ... 52 a35
3 ch f Whittingham (Ire) - Lucky Dip
14^{5sd} 9^{6sd} 4^{5gs} 6^{5gs} 4^{5f} 9^{5f} 9^{5gf} 9^{6f}
7^{5gf} 12^{5gf} 5^{6f} 2^{5gf} 10^{5gf} 0-1-13 £1,392

Wizard Looking R Hannon ... 72
2 b c Wizard King - High Stepping (Ire)
6^{7g} 8^{7f} 5^{7gf} 2^{6gf} 0-1-4 £1,081

Wizard Of Edge G B Balding ... 69
3 b g Wizard King - Forever Shineing
3^{8f} 0-1-1 £884

Wizard Of Noz J Noseda ... 107
3 b c Inchinor - Winning Girl
4^{7gf} 12^{7g} 0-0-2 £3,750

Wizard Of The West Miss Sheena West ... 29 a63
3 b g Wizard King - Rose Burton
9^{10sd} 3^{9sd} 6^{9sw} 12^{10g} 17^{12gf} 0-0-5 £525

Wizard Of Us B Smart ... 12
3 b g Wizard King - Sian's Girl
16^{8g} 0-0-1

Wodhill Folly D Morris ... 49 a55
6 ch m Faustus (USA) - Muarij
6^{8sd} 5^{10sd} 4^{8sd} 3^{8sd} 4^{9sd} 1^{10g} 5^{10gf} 8^{10f}
16^{10gf} 1-1-9 £4,536

Wolfe Tone (Ire) A P O'Brien ... 81
2 b c Sadler's Wells (USA) - Angelic Song (Can)
1^{8y} 1-0-1 £8,737

Wolverene K A Ryan ... 27
2 b g Wolfhound (USA) - Blushing Victoria
14^{5s} 14^{5gf} 0-0-2

Wonder Wolf R A Fahey ... 28
2 b f Wolfhound (USA) - Wrangbrook
14^{6gf} 0-0-1

Wonderful Man R D E Woodhouse ... 3 a57
7 ch g Magical Wonder (USA) - Gleeful
3^{8sd} 7^{7sw} 10^{8sw} 10^{12f} 0-1-4 £525

Wondrous Joy E A L Dunlop ... 97
3 b f Machiavellian (USA) - Girl From Ipanema
1^{8f} 6^{8gf} 1^{10gf} 5^{10gf} 1^{10gf} 6^{10gf} 15^{10g}
3-0-7 £15,942

Wondrous Story (USA) J H M Gosden ... 95
3 ch f Royal Academy (USA) - Gossiping (USA)
5^{9g} 11^{8f} 0-0-2 £1,000

Wonky Donkey S C Williams
2 b g Piccolo - Salinas
10^{5g} 0-0-1

Wood Be King A P James
4 c Prince Sabo - Sylvan Dancer (Ire)
18^{10gf} 0-0-1

Wood Dalling (USA) C A Dwyer ... 63 a81
5 b g Woodman (USA) - Cloelia (USA)
6^{7sd} 14^{10sd} 4^{7sd} 12^{8gf} 4^{8f} 3^{7gf} 14^{8gf}
5^{8ft} 0-1-8 £1,032

Wood Fern (UAE) M R Channon ... 81
3 b c Green Desert (USA) - Woodsia
3^{8gf} 3^{8gf} 0-1-2 £1,910

Wood Street (Ire) R J Baker ... 51 a62
4 b g Eagle Eyed (USA) - San-Catrinia (Ire)
8^{10sd} 13^{8g} 13^{8gf} 0-0-3

Woodboro Kat (Ire) M Blanshard ... 32 a56
4 b g Woodborough (USA) - Kitty Kildare (USA)
6^{11sd} 18^{10gf} 14^{12g} 11^{11gf} 0-0-4

Woodbury *K R Burke*   71 a60
4 b f Woodborough (USA) - Jeewan
11^{6sd} 14^{6sd} 18^{6g} 2^{6f} 7^{6gf} 7^{6gf} 7^{6g} 6^{6f}
3^{6gf} 10^{6g} 5^{6gf} 2^{6f} 2^{6f} 5^{6gf} DSQ^{6gf} 2^{6g} 6^{6gf}
0-5-17 £5,183

Woodcracker *M L W Bell*   66
2 ch g Docksider (USA) - Hen Harrier
11^{8gf} **0-0-1**

Woodie (Ire) *D Nicholls*   a32
3 ch g Woodborough (USA) - Better Goods (Ire)
7^{6sd} 6^{6sd} 10^{5sd} **0-0-3**

Woodland Blaze (Ire) *P R Chamings*   66 a81
4 b g Woodborough (USA) - Alpine Sunset
1^{5sd} 8^{5g} 8^{6sd} 2^{5sd} 1^{5sd} 13^{5hy} 7^{5gf} **2-1-7**
£8,096

Woodland River (USA) *M W Easterby*   35
6 ch g Irish River (Fr) - Wiener Wald (USA)
10^{7gf} 17^{8gf} **0-0-2**

Woodland Spirit *B Ellison*   78 a76
4 b g Charnwood Forest (Ire) - Fantastic Charm (USA)
5^{8sd} 1^{8sd} 3^{8sd} 11^{10g} 2^{8gf} 5^{8gf} 7^{9gf}
4^{8gf} 9^{8gf} 9^{8g} **1-2-11 £6,826**

Woodsmoke (Ire) *J S Moore*   22
4 b g Woodborough (USA) - Ma Bella Luna
14^{6gf} **0-0-1**

Woodstock Express *P Bowen*
3 b g Alflora (Ire) - Young Tess
9^{8f} 6^{12gf} 7^{14gf} **0-0-3**

Woody Valentine (USA) *M Johnston*   78
2 ch g Woodman (USA) - Mudslinger (USA)
3^{7gf} 2^{8gf} 1^{8gf} 4^{8g} 11^{8gf} 9^{8gf} **1-2-6**
£7,728

Woodyates *W J Musson*   64
6 b m Naheez (USA) - Night Mission (Ire)
10^{12gf} 3^{14gf} 17^{16gf} 2^{14gs} 10^{13g} 10^{17gf}
2^{14gf} 6^{14gf} 2^{14gf} **0-4-9 £4,900**

Woodybetheone *O Sherwood*   46
3 b g Wolfhound (USA) - Princesse Zelda (Fr)
15^{8gf} 13^{14gf} **0-0-2**

Woolfe *D A Nolan*   21
6 ch m Wolfhound (USA) - Brosna (USA)
10^{7gf} 16^{11gs} 10^{8gs} **0-0-3**

Woolloomooloo Bay *Mrs G S Rees*   44
3 br f Bin Ajwaad (Ire) - Marton Maid
3^{9f} 10^{8f} 7^{9f} 6^{8gf} 10^{10gf} **0-1-5 £572**

Worcester Lodge *R Charlton*   53 a62
2 ch c Grand Lodge (USA) - Borgia
8^{8sd} 4^{8gf} 11^{8gs} **0-0-3 £333**

Words And Deeds (USA) *R A Fahey*   56
4 ch g Shadeed (USA) - Millfit (USA)
15^{8gf} 7^{10gf} 4^{12g} 9^{10gf} **0-1-4 £327**

Worlaby Dale *Mrs S Lamyman*   52
7 b g Terimon - Restandbethankful
9^{12g} 6^{14gs} 4^{12gf} 7^{12f} 2^{16g} 3^{16gf} 3^{16g} 3^{18gf}
4^{16gf} **0-4-9 £3,283**

Wotan (Fr) *Miss I E Craig*
4 ch g Beaudelaire (USA) - Woglinde (USA)
11^{11g} 15^{12gf} **0-0-2**

Wotan (Ire) *R Curtis*   a48
5 ch g Wolfhound (USA) - Triple Tricks (Ire)
6^{15sd} 6^{13sd} 4^{12sd} **0-1-3**

Wou Oodd *M R Channon*   25
2 ch f Barathea (Ire) - Abyaan (Ire)
11^{7gf} **0-0-1**

Wozzeck *J R Fanshawe*   71 a42

3 b g Groom Dancer (USA) - Opera Lover (Ire)
6^{10g} 6^{10gf} 6^{12g} 4^{10gs} 11^{16sd} **0-0-5 £310**

Wrenlane *R A Fahey*   69
2 ch g Fraam - Hi Hoh (Ire)
3^{5gf} 9^{6gf} **0-0-2 £562**

Wroot Danielle (Ire) *Ronald Thompson*   64
3 b g Fayruz - Pounding Beat
15^{7sd} 9^{7t} 15^{6gf} 17^{6g} 14^{7s} 17^{gf} 8^{7gs}
15^{8gf} 2^{7gf} 13^{8gf} **1-1-10 £4,950**

Wub Cub *A Dickman*   51 a23
3 b f Averti (Ire) - Ray Of Hope
13^{6gf} 12^{6sd} 4^{7f} 14^{5t} 7^{5gf} **0-0-5 £440**

Wun Chai (Ire) *F Jordan*   a40
4 b g King's Theatre (Ire) - Flower From Heaven
10^{10sd} 12^{11sd} **0-0-2**

Wunders Dream (Ire) *J G Given*   97
3 b f Averti (Ire) - Pizzicato
9^{5g} 9^{6gs} 17^{5gf} 9^{5g} 10^{5gf} **0-0-5**

Wunderwood (USA) *Lady Herries*   101 a74
4 b g Faltaat (USA) - Jasoorah (Ire)
1^{10sd} 1^{10gf} 2^{10gf} 2^{12gf} 8^{12f} 1^{12gf}
4^{12g} **3-4-8 £32,598**

Wuxi Venture *R A Fahey*   72
8 b g Wolfhound (USA) - Push A Button
2^{9gf} 1^{9gf} 6^{9gf} 9^{8gs} **1-1-4 £13,733**

Wyatt Earp (Ire) *J A R Toller*   71
2 b c Piccolo - Tribal Lady
9^{6gf} 4^{6gf} 6^{6g} **0-0-3 £367**

Wychbury (USA) *M J Wallace*   76
2 ch c Swain (Ire) - Garden Rose (Ire)
5^{8gs} 3^{6gf} 2^{5gf} **0-2-3 £2,290**

Wyoming *J A R Toller*   40 a2
2 ch f Inchinor - Shoshone
22^{7gf} 13^{7sd} **0-0-2**

Xaloc Bay (Ire) *K R Burke*   60 a65
5 br g Charnwood Forest (Ire) - Royal Jade
8^{7gf} 12^{6ft} 4^{6sd} 10^{7sd} 2^{6sd} 9^{6sd} 5^{6g} 14^{6f}
7^{6sd} 4^{8gf} 3^{8gf} 2^{8gf} 3^{8sd} 6^{8gf} **0-4-14 £2,650**

Xanadu *Miss L A Perratt*   61
7 ch g Casteddu - Bellatrix
11^{5gf} 15^{6gf} 11^{5gf} 12^{6gf} 12^{6gf} 14^{5g} 5^{6gf}
18^{6gf} 16^{gf} 2^{5f} 7^{6f} 14^{6g} 7^{6f} 14^{5g} **1-1-14**
£6,024

Xcess Baggage *W J Haggas*   35 a52
3 b g Air Express (Ire) - Abundance
13^{8gf} 10^{7sd} 7^{7gf} 10^{7gf} **0-0-4**

Xibalba *Mrs M Reveley*   a29
6 b g Zafonic (USA) - Satanic Dance (Fr)
7^{9sd} **0-0-1**

Xixita *Dr J D Scargill*   a44
3 ch f Fleetwood (Ire) - Conquista
4^{7sd} 7^{9sw} 4^{9sd} 5^{12sw} 10^{11sw} **0-0-5 £275**

Xpres Digital *S R Bowring*   74 a65
2 b c Komaite (USA) - Kustom Kit Xpres
6^{5gs} 1^{6sd} 4^{5gf} 8^{6g} 2^{6gf} 3^{6g} 4^{5gf} 5^{7gf} 6^{6f}
1^{6g} 11^{7g} **2-1-11 £11,595**

Xpressions *R A Fahey*   54
2 b g Turtle Island (Ire) - Make Ready
4^{7gf} 10^{7gf} 1^{8g} 5^{10gf} **1-0-4 £3,250**

Xsynna *P S McEntee*   55 a58
7 b g Cyrano De Bergerac - Rose Ciel (Ire)
16^{7sd} 11^{5sd} 7^{7gf} 8^{7sd} 7^{7g} 12^{6f} 3^{7gf}
12^{8gf} 13^{7gf} **0-1-9 £842**

Yafoul (USA) *B W Hills*   92
3 b f Torrential (USA) - My Shafy

10⁸ᵍᶠ 4⁶ᵍ 2⁸ᵍ 11⁷ᵍᶠ 13⁷ᵍᶠ **0-0-5**
£3,901

Yaheska (Ire) *I A Wood* 45
6 b m Prince Of Birds (USA) - How Ya Been (Ire)
6¹⁴ᶠ 11⁷ᶠ 4¹⁹ᵍᶠ 10¹⁶ᵍᶠ 3¹⁶ᵍ 6¹⁷ᵍᶠ **1-1-6**
£4,802

Yakimov (USA) *P F I Cole* 98 a97
4 ch g Affirmed (USA) - Ballet Troupe (USA)
4⁸ᵍ 11⁸ᵍᶠ 1⁸ˢᵈ 13⁸ᵍ 2⁸ʰʸ 3⁸ᵍᶠ 1⁸ˢ 3⁸ᵍ
1⁸ᵍᶠ 7⁸ᵍᶠ 2⁸ᵍᶠ 3⁹ᵍᶠ **3-6-12 £28,956**

Yalla (Ire) *W J Haggas* 62 a70
3 b g Groom Dancer (USA) - Creeking
1⁸ˢʷ 1⁸ˢᵈ 6⁹ᵍˢ 6¹⁰ᶠ 5⁸ˢᵈ 4¹⁰ᵍᶠ 10⁸ˢᵈ **2-0-7**
£5,706

Yalla Lara *A M Balding* 74 a83
4 b f Marju (Ire) - Versami (USA)
1⁷ˢᵈ 11⁸ˢᵈ 16⁷ˢᵈ 5⁷ˢᵈ 5⁸ˢᵈ 3⁷ˢᵈ 8¹⁰ᵍ
1-1-7 £4,977

Yamato Pink *K R Burke* 48
2 ch f Bijou D'Inde - Time Or Never (Fr)
5⁵ᶠ 8⁶ᵍᶠ 4⁵ᶠ 6⁶ᶠ **0-0-4 £283**

Yankeedoodledandy (Ire) *P C Haslam* 39
2 b g Orpen (USA) - Laura Margaret
13⁵ᵍ 4⁶ᵍˢ 10⁶ˢᵈ 11⁸ᵍᶠ **0-0-4 £336**

Yarn Spinner (Ire) *Mrs J R Ramsden* 58 a50
2 b g Turtle Island (Ire) - Pam Story
9⁵ᶠ 4⁶ᵍᶠ 10⁵ᵍᶠ 5⁷ᵍᶠ 1⁷ᵍᶠ 11⁸ᵍᶠ 11⁷ᶠ
2⁷ˢᵈ 9⁶ᵍᶠ **1-1-10 £3,836**

Yarrita *K A Ryan* 42 a47
3 b f Tragic Role (USA) - Yanomami (USA)
5⁸ˢʷ 14⁸ˢᵈ 16⁷ᶠ 12⁷ˢᵈ 10¹⁰ᵍᶠ 15⁷ᵍˢ
11⁸ᵍˢ **0-0-7**

Yashin (Ire) *M H Tompkins* 53
2 b c Soviet Star (USA) - My Mariam
7⁶ᵍᶠ 5⁷ᵍ 16⁷ᵍᶠ **0-0-3**

Yavari (Ire) *B J Meehan* a75
4 b f Alzao (USA) - Twin Island (Ire)
2⁸ˢᵈ 1⁸ˢᵈ 1⁸ˢᵈ 11¹⁰ˢᵈ 8¹⁰ˢᵈ **2-1-5**
£7,615

Yawmi *B W Hills* 108
3 ch c Zafonic (USA) - Reine Wells (Ire)
1¹⁰ᵍ 1¹²ᵍᶠ 8¹²ᵍᶠ **2-0-3 £27,381**

Yeats (Ire) *A P O'Brien* 91
2 b c Sadler's Wells (USA) - Lyndonville (Ire)
1⁸ᵍᶠ **1-0-1 £8,441**

Yellow River (Ire) *R Curtis* 28 a70
3 b g Sesaro (USA) - Amtico
7⁷ˢᵈ 2⁷ˢᵈ 2⁷ˢʷ 6⁷ˢᵈ 17⁷ᵍᶠ 17⁶ᵍᶠ 14⁶ᵍ
10¹⁰ᵍᶠ **0-1-8 £2,280**

Yenaled *I Semple* 71 a83
6 gr g Rambo Dancer (Can) - Fancy Flight (Fr)
3⁸ˢʷ 6⁹ˢᵈ 5⁸ˢᵈ 5⁹ˢʷ 8⁸ˢᵈ 3⁹ᵍᶠ 5⁷ᵍᶠ 4⁸ᵍᶠ
2¹⁰ᵍᶠ 5⁸ᵍᶠ 4⁹ᵍᶠ **0-4-11 £4,202**

Yeoman Lad *A M Balding* 87
3 b g Groom Dancer (USA) - First Amendment (Ire)
6⁷ᵍᶠ 4⁸ᵍᶠ 3⁸ᵍˢ 13⁸ᵍᶠ 7¹⁰ᵍᶠ 7⁸ᵍ 7⁹ᵍᶠ **0-0-7**
£2,675

Yertle (Ire) *J A R Toller* 69 a67
6 b g Turtle Island (Ire) - Minatina (Ire)
2¹⁶ˢᵈ 2¹⁷ᶠ 3¹⁸ᵍᶠ **0-3-3 £3,544**

Yesterday (Ire) *A P O'Brien* 118
3 b f Sadler's Wells (USA) - Jude
8⁸ᵍᶠ 1⁸ˢ 2¹²ᵍ 4¹²ᵍ 2¹²ᵍˢ 2¹⁰ʰᵒ 3¹⁰ᶠ **1-4-7**
£398,427

Ymlaen (Ire) *B Palling* 79 a72

3 b f Desert Prince (Ire) - Dathuil (Ire)
10⁷ᵍᶠ 6⁶ᵍᶠ 6⁷ᵍ 9⁷ˢᵈ 12⁷ˢᵈ **0-0-5 £162**

Ynys *B Palling* 12 a29
2 b c Turtle Island (Ire) - Kiss Me Goodknight
8⁶ˢᵈ 5⁶ᵍˢ 5⁶ˢᵈ 8⁸ˢᵈ **0-0-4**

Ynysmon *S R Bowring* 57 a39
5 b g Mind Games - Florentynna Bay
8⁶ˢʷ 10⁵ˢᵈ 10⁷ˢᵈ 8⁶ᵍᶠ 9⁶ˢᵈ 2⁶ᵍ 2⁶ᵍᶠ 6⁷ᵍᶠ
F⁷ˢᵈ **0-2-9 £2,075**

Yob (Ire) *P D Evans* 33 a25
4 b c Common Grounds - First Veil
11⁷ˢᵈ 10⁶ˢᵈ 10⁵ᵍᶠ 11⁵ᶠ **0-0-4**

Yockleton *N P Littmoden* a22
3 b g Wizard King - Awham (USA)
6⁸ˢᵈ 7⁷ˢʷ **0-0-2**

Yomalo (Ire) *R Guest* 75 a55
3 ch f Woodborough (USA) - Alkariyh (USA)
6⁶ᵍᶠ 7⁶ᶠ 2⁷ˢᵈ 4⁶ᵍᶠ 1⁵ᵍᶠ 1⁶ᵍᶠ 2⁶ᵍᶠ 2⁶ᵍᶠ
11⁶ᵍ **2-3-9 £11,662**

York Cliff *J H M Gosden* 88
5 b g Marju (Ire) - Azm
2⁸ᵍᶠ 19⁸ᵍˢ 2⁸ˢ 15⁸ᵍ 10¹⁰ᵍᶠ **0-2-5**
£7,186

Yorke's Folly (USA) *C W Fairhurst* 27 a35
2 b f Stravinsky (USA) - Tommelise (USA)
5⁵ᵍᶠ 7⁷ˢᵈ **0-0-2**

Yorker (USA) *Ms Deborah J Evans* 73 a77
5 b g Boundary (USA) - Shallows (USA)
2⁹ˢᵈ 2⁸ˢᵈ 6⁸ˢᵈ 3⁸ˢᵈ 1⁸ˢᵈ 5⁸ᵍᶠ 4⁸ᵍᶠ 11⁸ᵍˢ
6⁸ᵍᶠ 5⁸ᵍᶠ 3⁸ᵍᶠ 7⁸ᵍᶠ 7⁷ˢᵈ 1⁸ᵍˢ **2-5-14 £9,119**

Yorkie *D Carroll* 69
4 b g Aragon - Light The Way
9⁵ᵍ 15⁶ᵍ 7⁵ᵍᶠ 5⁶ᵍˢ 8⁵ʰʸ 7⁵ᵍᶠ 11⁷ᶠ 4⁷ᵍᶠ
11⁸ᵍᶠ 6⁷ᵍᶠ 2⁸ᵍᶠ 9⁷ᵍᶠ 13⁷ᵍᶠ **0-2-13 £1,872**

Yorkies Boy *J M Bradley* 62
8 gr g Clantime - Slipperose
9⁶ᵍᶠ 5⁵ᵍ 11⁶ᵍᶠ 7⁵ᵍᶠ 5⁶ᵍᶠ 3⁵ᵍᶠ 5⁵ᵍᶠ 6⁶ᵍᶠ
10⁶ᵍ 9⁵ᵍ 4⁶ᵍᶠ 13⁷ᵍᶠ 10⁷ᵍ **0-1-13 £938**

Yorkshire Blue *R M Whitaker* 64 a54
4 b g Atraf - Something Blue
13⁸ᶠ 1⁷ᵍᶠ 11⁸ᵍᶠ 4⁷ᵍᶠ 6⁸ᵍᶠ 9⁸ᵍᶠ 7⁸ᵍᶠ
15⁸ᵍᶠ 10⁹ᵍˢ 7⁸ˢᵈ **1-0-10 £3,974**

Yorkshire Spirit *N Tinkler*
2 b g Imperial Ballet (Ire) - Barnacla (Ire)
18⁶ᵍᶠ **0-0-1**

Yoshka *M Johnston* 73
2 ch c Grand Lodge (USA) - Greenvera (USA)
1⁹ᶠ **1-0-1 £3,080**

You Just Know *P C Haslam* a41
3 b g Forzando - Petindia
7⁷ˢᵈ **0-0-0**

You Never No (Ire) *E J O'Neill* 72
3 b c Eagle Eyed (USA) - Nordic Doll (Ire)
3¹¹ᵍˢ 3¹¹ᵍˢ 4⁸ᵍᶠ 6⁷ᵍ 4⁷ᵍᶠ **0-0-5 £2,141**

Young Alex (Ire) *K R Burke* 83 a51
5 ch g Midhish - Snipe Hunt (Ire)
12⁷ˢᵈ 6⁶ᵍˢ 4⁷ᵍ 4⁷ᵍᶠ 2⁷ᵍᶠ 6⁷ᵍᶠ 4⁷ᵍᶠ 5⁷ᵍᶠ
6⁷ᵍᶠ 3⁷ᵍᶠ 4⁷ᵍᶠ 3⁸ᵍᶠ **0-2-12 £4,031**

Young Butt *L A Dace*
10 ch g Bold Owl - Cymbal
9⁸ˢᵈ **0-0-1**

Young Collier *Sir Mark Prescott* a72
4 b g Vettori (Ire) - Cockatoo Island
2¹²ˢᵈ 1¹⁶ˢᵈ 1¹⁵ˢᵈ 2¹⁶ˢᵈ 11⁶ˢʷ 3¹⁶ˢᵈ **3-2-6**
£12,037

Young Jackart *J W Mullins* 31
2 b g Compton Place - Princesse Lyphard
10⁷ᶠ **0-0-1**

Young Love *Miss E C Lavelle* a51
2 ch f Pursuit Of Love - Polar Fair
10⁷ˢᵈ 7⁷ˢᵈ **0-0-2**

Young Mr Grace (Ire) *T D Easterby* 85 a51
3 b c Danetime (Ire) - Maid Of Mourne
2⁶ᵍᶠ 8⁷ᵍᶠ 4⁷ᵍᶠ 6⁸ᵍᶠ 11⁷ˢᵈ **0-1-5 £4,258**

Young Mystery *C Grant*
2 gr g Young Ern - Court Mystery
6⁶ᵍᶠ **0-0-1**

Young Owen *Mrs L B Normile* 68
5 b g Balnibarbi - Polly Potter
5⁹ᵍᶠ 4⁹ᵍᶠ 2¹¹ᵍˢ 10¹³ᵍˢ 13¹²ᶠ **0-1-5**
£2,194

Young Patriarch *J L Dunlop* 62
2 b c Silver Patriarch (Ire) - Mortify
4⁷ᵍᶠ 4⁸ᵍᶠ **0-0-2 £319**

Young Rooney *M Mullineaux* 71 a70
3 b c Danzig Connection (USA) - Lady Broker
4⁸ˢᵈ 2⁸ˢᵈ 2⁹ˢᵈ 12⁸ᵍ 4¹⁰ᵍ 3⁹ᵍˢ 2⁹ᵍᶠ 4¹⁰ᵍ
0-3-8 £5,359

Young Safawan *P W Harris* 73
3 ch g Safawan - Madame Bovary
6⁸ᵍ 4⁸ᶠ 7⁸ᵍ 6¹⁰ᵍᶠ 1¹⁰ᵍᶠ 10¹⁰ᵍᶠ 5¹⁰ᵍᶠ
13¹⁰ᵍᶠ 17¹⁰ᵍᶠ 15¹⁰ᵍᶠ **1-0-10 £4,805**

Young Tern *B J Llewellyn* a37
5 b g Young Ern - Turnaway
14¹¹ˢᵈ 5⁹ˢᵈ 6⁹ˢᵈ **0-0-3**

Youngs Forth *A W Carroll* 51 a38
3 b f Most Welcome - Pegs
11⁵ˢʷ 5⁶ᵍ 5⁶ˢᵈ 8⁶ᵍᶠ 14⁸ᵍᶠ **0-0-5**

Your Just Lovely (Ire) *A M Balding* 55 a38
2 b f Second Empire (Ire) - Nawaji (USA)
7⁶ˢᵈ 6⁶ᵍᶠ **0-0-2**

Zabadou *C B B Booth* 13
2 b g Abou Zouz (USA) - Strapped
17⁸ᵍ 21⁸ᵍ **0-0-2**

Zabaglione *R Charlton* 108
3 ch g Zilzal (USA) - Satin Bell
4⁸ᵍᶠ 4⁷ᵍᶠ 9⁸ʰʸ 9⁸ᵍᶠ 5¹⁰ᵍᶠ 3¹⁰ᵍ 1⁹ᵍᶠ 2¹⁰ᵍᶠ
9⁹ᵍᶠ **1-2-9 £42,947**

Zadok The Priest (Ire) *J W Hills* 60 a43
3 b/br g Zafonic (USA) - Valencay (Ire)
15¹⁰ᶠ 11¹⁴ᵍˢ 5¹²ᵍᶠ 7¹²ᶠ 6¹²ˢᵈ 2¹⁸ᵍᶠ 4¹⁸ᶠ
4¹⁶ᵍᶠ 3¹⁴ᵍᶠ 10¹³ᵍᶠ 3¹⁶ᵍᶠ 12¹⁷ᶠ 7¹⁸ᵍᶠ **0-2-13**
£2,518

Zafarshah (Ire) *P D Evans* 72 a69
4 b g Danehill (USA) - Zafarana (Fr)
1⁸ˢᵈ 9⁸ˢᵈ 7¹⁰ˢᵈ 3⁷ˢᵈ 9⁹ˢᵈ 7¹⁰ˢᵈ 10¹⁰ᵍ 2⁸ᶠ
9⁸ᵍ 3⁸ᵍᶠ 1⁸ᵍᶠ 5⁷ᵍᶠ 5⁸ᵍᶠ 3⁸ᵍᶠ 9⁸ᵍᶠ 9⁸ᶠ 8⁸ᵍᶠ
3⁸ᵍ 20⁸ᵍ **2-5-22 £13,375**

Zafeen (Fr) *Saeed Bin Suroor* 123
3 b c Zafonic (USA) - Shy Lady (Fr)
2⁷ᵍᶠ 2⁸ᵍ 14⁸ˢ 18⁸ᶠ 4⁸ᵍˢ **1-2-5**
£252,250

Zaffrani (Ire) *David Wachman*
4 b/br f Danehill (USA) - Zariysha (Ire)
11⁸ᵍ **0-0-1**

Zagala *S L Keightley* a60
3 b f Polar Falcon (USA) - Whittle Woods Girl
6⁶ˢᵈ 3⁸ˢᵈ 8⁶ˢʷ 8⁷ˢʷ **0-1-4 £466**

Zahunda (Ire) *W M Brisbourne* 44 a59
4 b f Spectrum (Ire) - Gift Of Glory (Fr)

14¹²ᵍ 8⁹ᵍᶠ 9¹¹ᵍᶠ 10¹⁵ᵍᶠ 1⁸ˢᵈ 13⁸ˢᵈ 7⁸ˢᵈ
7⁸ˢᵈ **1-0-8 £3,080**

Zaibas (USA) *A Dickman* 18
3 b g Tabasco Cat (USA) - Sudden Sun (USA)
6⁷ᶠ 12⁸ᵍ 8⁷ˢ **0-0-3**

Zak Facta (Ire) *Miss D A McHale* 71 a73
3 b g Danetime (Ire) - Alexander Goddess (Ire)
9⁵ˢ 3⁶ᵍᶠ 11⁶ᵍ 5⁶ᵍᶠ 6⁵ᵍᶠ 3⁶ᶠ 2⁶ᶠ 9⁵ᵍ
8⁸ᵍˢ 4⁸ˢᵈ 2⁷ˢᵈ **0-3-11 £2,837**

Zakfree (Ire) *N P Littmoden* 67
2 b g Danetime (Ire) - Clipper Queen
16⁶ᵍᶠ 3⁸ᵍᶠ 8⁸ᵍᶠ 4⁸ᵍᶠ 10⁸ᵍᶠ 3⁸ᵍˢ 14⁷ᵍ
0-2-7 £1,297

Zaktoo (Ire) *N P Littmoden* 54
2 b c Sri Pekan (USA) - Alpine Symphony
8⁷ᵍᶠ 16⁸ˢ **0-0-2**

Zalda *R Charlton* 56 a46
2 ch f Zilzal (USA) - Gold Luck (USA)
9⁸ᵍᶠ 9⁷ˢᵈ 6⁸ᶠ **0-0-3**

Zalkani (Ire) *B G Powell* 46
3 ch g Cadeaux Genereux - Zallaka (Ire)
6⁹ᵍᶠ 9¹⁰ᵍᶠ 11⁸ᵍ **0-0-3**

Zamat *P Monteith* 65
7 b g Slip Anchor - Khandjar
4¹³ᵍˢ 15¹²ˢ **0-0-2 £664**

Zameel (Ire) *Jedd O'Keeffe* 40
2 b c Marju (Ire) - Impatiente (USA)
10⁸ᵍᶠ 22⁸ᵍ **0-0-2**

Zamir *A Crook*
4 ch g Zamindar (USA) - Fairy Flax (Ire)
PU¹²ˢʷ 10¹²ˢᵈ **0-0-2**

Zamorin *Mrs Jane Galpin*
4 b g Zafonic (USA) - Armeria (USA)
12¹⁶ˢᵈ 11¹²ˢᵈ **0-0-2**

Zamyatina (Ire) *P L Clinton* 65
4 br f Danehill Dancer (Ire) - Miss Pickpocket (Ire)
11⁶ᵍᶠ 10⁶ᵍᶠ 16⁸ᵍ 7¹²ᵍᶠ 12⁸ᵍᶠ 6⁷ᵍᶠ 4⁸ᵍᶠ
9⁷ᵍᶠ 11⁷ᵍᶠ 13⁷ᵍᶠ **1-0-10 £4,408**

Zanay *Miss Jacqueline S Doyle* 40
7 b g Forzando - Nineteenth Of May
7⁸ᵍᶠ 14¹⁰ᵍ 8⁸ᵍᶠ 10⁸ᵍᶠ **0-0-4**

Zanjeer *D Nicholls* 41
3 b g Averti (Ire) - Cloudslea (USA)
4¹⁰ᵍˢ 9⁷ᶠ **0-0-2 £445**

Zanog *Miss Jacqueline S Doyle* 28 a34
4 b g Forzando - Logarithm
10⁶ˢᵈ 15⁷ᵍᶠ 11⁵ᵍᶠ **0-0-3**

Zap Attack *J Parkes* 75 a47
3 b g Zafonic (USA) - Rappa Tap Tap (Fr)
9⁸ᵍᶠ 11¹⁰ˢᵈ 9⁹ᵍᶠ 3⁷ᵍᶠ 3⁷ᵍᶠ 16⁶ᶠ 8⁷ᵍᶠ 2⁶ᵍᶠ
19⁷ᵍᶠ 14⁷ᵍˢ **1-2-10 £7,294**

Zaqrah (USA) *J L Dunlop* 78
2 b f Silver Hawk (USA) - Istiqlal (USA)
4⁷ᵍ **0-0-1 £634**

Zara Louise *R P Elliott* 52
3 b f Mistertopogigo (Ire) - Petonica (Ire)
10⁶ˢᵈ 2⁶ᵍ 7⁷ᵍᶠ 3⁸ᵍˢ 10⁸ᵍᶠ 7⁶ᵍᶠ 10⁶ᵍᶠ
11⁸ᵍᶠ 6⁷ᵍᶠ **0-2-9 £1,620**

Zargus *W R Muir* 80
4 b g Zamindar (USA) - My First Romance
22⁶ᵍ 12⁷ᵍᶠ 7⁵ᵍᶠ 7⁵ᵍᶠ 19⁶ᵍ 4⁵ᶠ 18⁵ᵍ
0-0-7 £431

Zariano *S L Keightley* 102 a85
3 b c Emperor Jones (USA) - Douce Maison (Ire)
11⁷ˢᵈ 2⁸ᵍ 5⁹ᵍᶠ 1⁸ᵍᶠ 6⁶ᵍᶠ 8⁸ᵍ **1-1-6**

£9,965

Zarin (Ire) *D W Chapman*   76 a92
5 b g Inzar (USA) - Non Dimenticar Me (Ire)
5^{8sd} 2^{8sd} 16^{8g} 3^{7f} 7^{7g} 12^{8gf} 6^{7sd} **0-2-7**
£3,824

Zarneeta *I A Wood*   58
2 b f Tragic Role (USA) - Compton Amber
3^{6gf} 5^{7f} 5^{6f} 9^{7gf} 7^{7gf} 7^{8sd} **0-1-6 £882**

Zarza Bay (Ire) *R M Stronge*   59 a63
4 b g Hamas (Ire) - Frill
7^{12sd} 4^{13sd} 3^{13sd} 7^{16sd} 5^{16gs} 3^{14gf} 7^{14gf}
16^{14gf} 5^{12sd} **0-2-9 £1,382**

Zarzu *K R Burke*   85 a92
4 b g Magic Ring (Ire) - Rivers Rhapsody
2^{5sw} 3^{6sd} 9^{5sd} 5^{6sd} 3^{5sd} 8^{6sw} 5^{6sd} 5^{7sd}
5^{7f} 7^{7gf} 9^{6g} 11^{8gf} 3^{5gf} 5^{7f} 9^{7gf} 1^{5f} 8^{7g}
3^{5gf} 2^{5gs} **2-8-25**
£14,829

Zawrak (Ire) *I W McInnes*   66
4 ch g Zafonic (USA) - Gharam (USA)
24^{8g} 7^{10gf} 6^{11gf} 13^{10g} 9^{10gf} 10^{12gf}
10^{11gf} 12^{16g} **0-0-8**

Zaynaat *M R Channon*   64
3 b f Unfuwain (USA) - Walesiana (Ger)
12^{10g} 9^{10gf} 5^{8g} 7^{8gf} 12^{8gf} **0-0-5**

Zazous *A King*   67
2 b c Zafonic (USA) - Confidentiality (USA)
7^{6gf} 3^{6gf} **0-1-2 £790**

Zee Zee Top *Sir Michael Stoute*   116
4 b f Zafonic (USA) - Colorspin (Fr)
1^{10gf} 3^{10g} 3^{10g} 6^{12gf} 1^{10ho} **2-2-5**
£146,407

Zeis (Ire) *H Morrison*   61
3 ch c Bahhare (USA) - Zoom Lens (Ire)
10^{10s} 8^{8gs} **0-0-2**

Zeitgeist (Ire) *L M Cumani*   74
2 b c Singspiel (Ire) - Diamond Quest
15^{7gf} 1^{7gs} **1-0-2 £3,262**

Zeitlos *R M Flower*   50 a50
4 b g Timeless Times (USA) - Petitesse
5^{7sd} 8^{6sd} 5^{6sw} 4^{6sd} 3^{5sw} 9^{5sw} 7^{6g} 11^{5sd}
10^{6gf} 12^{5gf} 10^{6gf} 8^{5gf} 19^{5gf} 14^{5gf} **0-2-14**
£418

Zerlina (USA) *R Hannon*   67 a82
2 b f Singspiel (Ire) - Tass
2^{7f} 25^{7gf} 1^{7sd} **1-1-3 £5,041**

Zero Gravity *M Madgwick*   24
6 b g Cosmonaut - Comfort
12^{12gf} **0-0-1**

Zero Tolerance (Ire) *T D Barron*   93 a80
3 ch g Nashwan (USA) - Place De L'Opera
2^{8sd} 1^{8sw} 9^{10gs} 1^{10gs} 3^{10gf} 17^{12gf} 4^{10gf}
2-2-7 £11,740

Zeryaab (Ire) *M A Jarvis*   76
3 b c Barathea (Ire) - Safa
3^{10g} **0-1-1 £694**

Zeuss *B W Hills*   83 a81
3 b c Zamindar (USA) - Shallop
1^{7sd} 8^{8g} 2^{8gf} 9^{7sd} 12^{8gf} **1-1-5 £5,487**

Zhitomir *M Dods*   68 a6
5 ch g Lion Cavern (USA) - Treasure Trove (USA)
6^{7gf} 13^{8gf} 10^{6gs} 10^{6gs} 11^{7gf} 11^{8sd} **0-0-6**

Zibeline (Ire) *B Ellison*   99
6 b g Cadeaux Genereux - Zia (USA)

17^{12g} 2^{12g} 3^{16gs} 7^{16gf} 19^{14gf} 2^{13g} 23^{18gf}
0-3-7 £32,448

Ziet D'Alsace (Fr) *A W Carroll*   60 a53
3 b f Zieten (USA) - Providenc Mill (Fr)
6^{8sd} 6^{8sw} 4^{6sd} 6^{5sd} 6^{5sd} 6^{6g} 7^{6gf} 7^{7sd}
1^{7gf} 3^{7gf} 2^{8gf} 3^{7gf} 8^{8f} 10^{7gf} 1^{7gf} 11^{8gf} 8^{8sd}
5^{8f} 4^{7gf} **2-3-19 £8,638**

Zietory *P F I Cole*   104 a99
3 b f Zieten (USA) - Fairy Story (Ire)
1^{7g} 6^{7g} 2^{7g} 1^{8gs} 2^{8g} 4^{8g} 2^{8sd} **2-3-7**
£39,665

Zietzig (Ire) *H A McWilliams*   62
6 b g Zieten (USA) - Missing You
11^{8sw} 1^{7gf} 12^{7g} 12^{6gf} 4^{6gf} 2^{7gf} 3^{8gf}
7^{7gf} 6^{7gf} **1-3-9 £5,807**

Zigali *John A Harris*   46
4 b g Zilzal (USA) - Alilisa (USA)
5^{12gf} 10^{16gf} **0-0-2**

Ziggy Dan *Ms Deborah J Evans*
3 b g Slip Anchor - Nikatino
11^{9sd} **0-0-1**

Ziggy Zen *C A Cyzer*   74 a70
4 b g Muhtarram (USA) - Springs Welcome
9^{10sd} 7^{13sd} 2^{16sd} 1^{15gf} 5^{16gf} **1-1-5**
£7,232

Zilch *M L W Bell*   73
5 ch g Zilzal (USA) - Bunty Boo
24^{6g} 9^{7g} **0-0-2**

Zilmaid Dancer *P W Harris*   68 a55
4 b f Zilzal (USA) - Briggsmaid
14^{7sd} 3^{7g} 15^{7gf} 13^{7gf} 15^{10gf} **0-0-5**
£946

Zilzalaha (Ire) *C B B Booth*   57
2 b f Zilzal (USA) - Fear Not (Ire)
7^{7gf} 21^{8gf} 5^{6g} **0-0-3**

Zindabad (Fr) *M Johnston*   116
7 b h Shirley Heights - Miznah (Ire)
14^{12g} 4^{14gf} 5^{12g} 3^{12f} 5^{12g} 4^{14gs} 3^{16gf}
4^{18g} **0-1-8 £53,218**

Zingari *Sir Mark Prescott*   89
3 ch f Groom Dancer (USA) - Antigua
1^{8gf} 2^{8gf} 13^{8s} 7^{7g} **1-1-4 £12,354**

Zinging *J J Bridger*   47 a56
4 b g Fraam - Hi Hoh (Ire)
10^{7sd} 2^{8sd} 3^{10sd} 1^{7sd} 9^{6sd} 20^{7g} 11^{7gf}
8^{9gf} 9^{8gf} 15^{10gf} 15^{7f} 10^{7gf} 10^{8gf} **1-2-13**
£5,184

Zipping (Ire) *Robert Collet*   117
4 b c Zafonic (USA) - Zelda (Ire)
2^{5gs} 2^{5g} 4^{6f} 4^{6gf} F^{7gs} **0-2-5 £47,142**

Zither *R Hannon*   91 a87
3 b f Zafonic (USA) - Rose Noble (USA)
13^{8g} 1^{7gf} 2^{8gf} 5^{7g} 3^{7f} 9^{8gs} 5^{7gf} 6^{8sd}
1-0-8 £15,008

Zoeanna (Ire) *R Guest*   61 a42
3 b f Danetime (Ire) - Age Of Elegance
7^{8sd} 9^{7gf} 7^{8g} 5^{14gf} 13^{12sd} 6^{12g} **0-0-6**

Zolube (Ire) *John Berry*   57 a27
3 b f Titus Livius (Fr) - Seattle Siren (USA)
5^{5f} 10^{6gf} 6^{5g} 9^{5sd} **0-0-4**

Zolushka (Ire) *B W Duke*   42
2 ch f Russian Revival (USA) - Persian Myth
12^{7gf} 16^{7gf} 16^{7gf} **0-0-3**

Zonergem *Lady Herries*   103
5 ch g Zafonic (USA) - Anasazi (Ire)

6^{8gf} 4^{8gf} 10^{8g} 13^{8gf} 3^{8gf} 6^{10gf} 11^{8gs}
0-1-7 £3,729

Zonic Boom (Fr) *J R Fanshawe*   60
3 b/br c Zafonic (USA) - Rosi Zambotti (Ire)
8^{8gf} 7^{8gf} **0-0-2**

Zonnebeke *K R Burke*   48 a30
2 b f Orpen (USA) - Canlubang
4^{7gf} 7^{8sd} **0-0-2**

Zonus *B W Hills*   79
2 b c Pivotal - Jade Mistress
2^{6gf} **0-1-1 £1,486**

Zoot *Mrs A J Perrett*
3 br g Zafonic (USA) - Bint Zamayem (Ire)
16^{8gf} **0-0-1**

Zorn *P Howling*   a52
4 br c Dilum (USA) - Very Good
5^{12sd} 9^{12sd} 8^{13sd} 12^{12sd} 8^{10sd} **0-0-5**

Zoroaster *J H M Gosden*   79
3 gr c Linamix (Fr) - Persian Walk (Fr)
4^{8gf} **0-0-1 £470**

Zota (Ire) *J G Given*
4 b f Barathea (Ire) - Afisiak
18^{6g} **0-0-1**

Zouave (Ire) *B J Meehan*   86
2 b c Spectrum (Ire) - Lady Windley
1^{8gf} 8^{8g} 3^{8gf} **1-0-3 £6,707**

Zouche *W M Brisbourne*   51 a65
3 b g Zamindar (USA) - Al Corniche (Ire)
12^{6g} 6^{7sd} 7^{8sd} 3^{7gf} 14^{6gf} 6^{7gf} 13^{6g} 6^{8sd}
5^{9sd} **0-1-9 £577**

Zucchero *D W P Arbuthnot*   97
7 br g Dilum (USA) - Legal Sound
23^{7g} 12^{8gf} 12^{8gf} 13^{8g} 20^{9gf} 17^{8gs} **0-0-6**

Zuhair *D Nicholls*   83
10 ch g Mujtahid (USA) - Ghzaalh (USA)
3^{5gf} 9^{5gs} 8^{5gf} 9^{6gf} 6^{6f} 4^{6gf} 11^{5f} 8^{5gs}
2^{6g} 2^{5gf} 16^{6g} 7^{6g} **0-3-12 £9,590**

Zuleta *M Blanshard*   44 a49
2 ch f Vettori (Ire) - Victoria
17^{6g} 7^{7g} 7^{7gf} 8^{8gf} 4^{7sd} 4^{8sd} **0-0-6**

Zuma (Ire) *R Hannon*   59
2 b c Grand Lodge (USA) - Paradise Waters
11^{7s} 8^{7gf} **0-0-2**

Zurs (Ire) *H J Collingridge*   45 a39
10 b g Tirol - Needy
10^{16sd} 8^{12sd} 5^{12g} 13^{12f} **0-0-4**

Zwadi (Ire) *B W Hills*   73 a62
2 b f Docksider (USA) - Local Custom (Ire)
3^{6sd} 4^{6gf} 3^{6gf} 2^{7gf} 4^{7sd} **0-3-5 £3,737**

Zweibrucken (Ire) *S Kirk*   83
2 b f Alhaarth (Ire) - Solar Attraction (Ire)
7^{6g} 3^{6gf} 2^{7gf} 1^{7gs} 2^{7f} 9^{7gf} **1-3-6**
£11,894

Zygomatic *R F Fisher*   8
5 ch g Risk Me (Fr) - Give Me A Day
11^{16gs} **0-0-1**

Zyzania *H Morrison*   98 a76
4 br f Zafonic (USA) - Moneefa
3^{8sd} 1^{9sd} 2^{7s} 1^{8gf} 4^{8f} 2^{8gs} 14^{7g} **2-3-7**
£18,095